THE SUPER HEROES NIrV BIBLE

TO:

_____

FROM:

_____

DATE:

_____

I can do everything by the power of Christ.
He gives me strength.

PHILIPPIANS 4:13

The LORD will march out like a mighty warrior.
He will stir up his anger like a soldier getting ready to fight.
He will shout the battle cry.
And he will win the battle over his enemies.

[The LORD says],
"I will lead them along paths they had not known before.
I will guide them on roads they are not familiar with.
I will turn the darkness into light as they travel.
I will make the rough places smooth.
Those are the things I will do.
I will not desert my people."

ISAIAH 42:13, 16

THE SUPER HEROES NIrV BIBLE

Features Written By:
Jean E. Syswerda

New International Reader's Version

ADVENTURE BIBLE

Features Written By
Jean E. Syswerda

New International Reading Version

zonderkidz

*Dedicated to my grandson, **Elijah Monroe Grate**. May you live and learn and grow up to be a super hero for God. I love you!*

—Grandma

Holy Bible, New International Reader's Version®
Copyright ©1995, 1996, 1998 by Biblica, Inc.™
All rights reserved

The NIrV Super Heroes Bible
©2001 by Zondervan
All rights reserved

Published by Zonderkidz
5300 Patterson Ave SE, Grand Rapids, Michigan 49530, U.S.A.

www.zonderkidz.com

Library of Congress Catalog Card Number 2001096613

You will be pleased to know that a portion of the purchase price of your new NIrV Bible has been provided to Biblica, Inc.™ to help spread the gospel of Jesus Christ around the world!

TABLE OF
CONTENTS

Ordinary people in the Bible were zapped by God and became

SUPER HEROES!!

Are you ready? Do you want to be a super hero for God? You can, you know.

The super heroes of the Bible were regular people, just like you are, but they followed a super God. He worked in them so they became heroes for him. And so can you!

The NIrV Super Heroes Bible cracks the code of how to live for God. The "Super Heroes Decoder" will show you all the traits of a hero. You'll find it on the back cover of your Bible. It will reveal the "code of honor" for each Bible character you read about.

Check out the features of this Bible:

▶ **THE NEW INTERNATIONAL READER'S VERSION:**
The Bible text itself is the most important part of this Bible, because it's God's Word, written for you. The NIrV is easy to read and understand. That's why it's known as the "NIV for kids."

▶ **BOOK INTRODUCTIONS:**
At the beginning of each book of the Bible, you'll find an introduction that tells you all about the super-hero impact of that book.

▶ **PROFILES:** There are over 200 of these. You can use your Super Heroes Decoder to discover each person's super-hero traits. For example, turn to page 18 and use your decoder to reveal Abraham's code of honor. You might be surprised to find that these sketches are not always about the good guys but also include some bad guys, like Pharaoh, Ahab and Jezebel, and Herod. After their names it says "(Not!)" to show you right away that they are *not* super heroes. Instead of a code of honor, these people have a code of *dishonor*. Each of the traits has a slash through it. To see an example, turn to Pharaoh's profile on page 82.

▶ **POWER SURGE:** True super heroes get their power from God himself. You can plug into that power by looking at these Bible verses. Each one highlights code of honor traits.

▶ **GREAT COLOR PICTURES:**
Best-selling artist Dennis Jones painted 40 amazing, colorful, action-packed pictures of super heroes. Turn to page 1480 for a list of where they are located throughout your Bible.

▶ **INDEX:** Turn to page 1481 to find the traits of a hero index in this Bible.

▶ **DICTIONARY:** It's on page 1485 and will help you discover the meanings of hard words in this Bible.

▶ **QUIZ:** Turn to page 1473 to take the Super Heroes Bible Quiz..

If you have any questions or comments about this Bible, please write and tell us:

The Bible Editors, Zonderkidz, 5300 Patterson SE, Grand Rapids, MI 49530

the **OLD** TESTAMENT

GENESIS

*G*enesis tells the story of the beginning of the world—when God created the earth, plants, animals and people. It tells about the first people God created, Adam and Eve. Genesis also records the stories of the first people to follow God faithfully. Some of the Bible's most famous heroes appear in Genesis. Read Genesis to understand how the world begins, how sin comes into the world, and how God shows his love for his people.

HEROES IN THIS BOOK . . .

The Beginning

1 In the beginning, God created the heavens and the earth. **2**The earth didn't have any shape. And it was empty. Darkness was over the surface of the ocean. At that time, the ocean covered the earth. The Spirit of God was hovering over the waters.

3God said, "Let there be light." And there was light. **4**God saw that the light was good. He separated the light from the darkness. **5**God called the light "day." He called the darkness "night." There was evening, and there was morning. It was day one.

6God said, "Let there be a huge space between the waters. Let it separate water from water." **7**And that's exactly what happened. God made the huge space between the waters. He separated the water that was under the space from the water that was above it. **8**God called the huge space "sky." There was evening, and there was morning. It was day two.

9God said, "Let the water under the sky be gathered into one place. Let dry ground appear." And that's exactly what happened. **10**God called the dry ground "land." He called the waters that were gathered together "oceans." And God saw that it was good.

11Then God said, "Let the land produce plants. Let them bear their own seeds. And let there be trees on the land that bear fruit with seeds in it. Let each kind of plant or tree have its own kind of seeds." And that's exactly what happened.

12The land produced plants. Each kind of plant had its own kind of seeds. The land produced trees that bore fruit with seeds in it. Each kind of tree had its own kind of seeds. God saw that it was good. **13**And there was evening, and there was morning. It was day three.

14God said, "Let there be lights in the huge space of the sky. Let them separate the day from the night. Let them serve as signs to mark off the seasons and the days and the years. **15**Let them serve as lights in the huge space of the sky to give light on the earth." And that's exactly what happened.

16God made two great lights. He made the larger light to rule over the day. He made the smaller light to rule over the night. He also made the stars.

17God put the lights in the huge space of the sky to give light on the earth. **18**He put them there to rule over the day and the night. He put them there to separate light from darkness.

God saw that it was good. **19**And there was evening, and there was morning. It was day four.

20God said, "Let the waters be filled with living things. Let birds fly above the earth across the huge space of the sky." **21**So God created the great creatures of the ocean. He created every living and moving thing that fills the waters. He created all kinds of them. He created every kind of bird that flies. And God saw that it was good.

22God blessed them. He said, "Have little ones and increase your numbers. Fill the water in the oceans. Let there be more and more birds on the earth."

23There was evening, and there was morning. It was day five.

24God said, "Let the land produce all kinds of living creatures. Let there be livestock, and creatures that move along the ground, and wild animals. Let there be all kinds of them." And that's exactly what happened.

25God made all kinds of wild animals. He made all kinds of livestock. He made all kinds of creatures that move along the ground. And God saw that it was good.

26Then God said, "Let us make man in our likeness. Let them rule over the fish in the waters and the birds of the air. Let them rule over the livestock and over the whole earth. Let them rule over all of the creatures that move along the ground."

27So God created man in his own likeness.
He created him in the likeness of God.
He created them as male and female.

28God blessed them. He said to them, "Have children and increase your numbers. Fill the earth and bring it under your control. Rule over the fish in the waters and the birds of the air. Rule over every living creature that moves on the ground."

29Then God said, "I am giving you every plant on the face of the whole earth that bears its own seeds. I am giving you every tree that has fruit with seeds in it. All of them will be given to you for food.

³⁰"I am giving every green plant to all of the land animals and the birds of the air for food. I am also giving the plants to all of the creatures that move on the ground. I am giving them to every living thing that breathes." And that's exactly what happened.

³¹God saw everything he had made. And it was very good. There was evening, and there was morning. It was day six.

2 So the heavens and the earth and everything in them were completed.

²By the seventh day God had finished the work he had been doing. So on the seventh day he rested from all of his work. ³God blessed the seventh day and made it holy. He rested on it. After he had created everything, he rested from all of the work he had done.

Adam and Eve

⁴Here is the story of the heavens and the earth when they were created.

The Lord God made the earth and the heavens. ⁵At that time, bushes had not appeared on the earth. Plants had not come up in the fields. The Lord God had not sent rain on the earth. And there wasn't any man to work the ground. ⁶But streams came up from the earth. They watered the whole surface of the ground.

⁷Then the Lord God formed a man. He made him out of the dust of the ground. He breathed the breath of life into him. And the man became a living person.

⁸The Lord God had planted a garden in the east. It was in Eden. There he put the man he had formed. ⁹The Lord God made all kinds of trees grow out of the ground. Their fruit was pleasing to look at and good to eat.

The tree that gives life forever was in the middle of the garden. The tree that gives the ability to tell the difference between good and evil was also there.

¹⁰A river watered the garden. It flowed from Eden. From there it separated into four other rivers.

¹¹The name of the first river is the Pishon. It winds through the whole land of Havilah. Gold is found there. ¹²The gold of that land is good. Onyx and sweet-smelling resin are also found there.

¹³The name of the second river is the Gihon. It winds through the whole land of Cush. ¹⁴The name of the third river is the Tigris. It runs along the east side of Asshur. And the fourth river is the Euphrates.

¹⁵The Lord God put the man in the Garden of Eden. He put him there to work its ground and to take care of it.

¹⁶The Lord God gave the man a command. He said, "You can eat the fruit of any tree that is in the garden. ¹⁷But you must not eat the fruit of the tree of the knowledge of good and evil. If you do, you can be sure that you will die."

¹⁸The Lord God said, "It is not good for the man to be alone. I will make a helper who is just right for him."

¹⁹The Lord God had formed all of the wild animals. He had also formed all of the birds of the air. He had made all of them out of the ground. He brought them to the man to see what names he would give them. And the name the man gave each living creature became its name.

²⁰So the man gave names to all of the livestock. He gave names to all of the birds of the air. And he gave names to all of the wild animals.

But Adam didn't find a helper that was right for him. ²¹So the Lord God caused him to fall into a deep sleep. While the man was sleeping, the Lord God took out one of his ribs. He closed up the opening that was in his side. ²²Then the Lord God made a woman. He made her from the rib he had taken out of the man. And he brought her to him.

²³The man said,

"Her bones have come from my bones.
    Her body has come from my body.
She will be named 'woman,'
    because she was taken out of a
        man."

²⁴That's why a man will leave his father and mother and be joined to his wife. The two of them will become one.

²⁵The man and his wife were both naked. They didn't feel any shame.

Adam and Eve Fall Into Sin

3 The serpent was more clever than any of the wild animals the Lord God had made. The serpent said to the woman, "Did God really say, 'You must not eat the fruit of any tree that is in the garden'?"

²The woman said to the serpent, "We can eat the fruit of the trees that are in the

garden. **3**But God did say, 'You must not eat the fruit of the tree that is in the middle of the garden. Do not even touch it. If you do, you will die.' "

4"You can be sure that you won't die," the serpent said to the woman. **5**"God knows that when you eat the fruit of that tree, you will know things you have never known before. You will be able to tell the difference between good and evil. You will be like God."

6The woman saw that the fruit of the tree was good to eat. It was also pleasing to look at. And it would make a person wise. So she took some of the fruit and ate it. She also gave some to her husband, who was with her. And he ate it.

7Then both of them knew things they had never known before. They realized they were naked. So they sewed fig leaves together and made clothes for themselves.

8Then the man and his wife heard the Lord God walking in the garden. It was the coolest time of the day. They hid from the Lord God among the trees of the garden.

9But the Lord God called out to the man. "Where are you?" he asked.

10"I heard you in the garden," the man answered. "I was afraid. I was naked, so I hid."

11The Lord God said, "Who told you that you were naked? Have you eaten the fruit of the tree I commanded you not to eat?"

12The man said, "It was the woman you put here with me. She gave me some fruit from the tree. And I ate it."

13Then the Lord God said to the woman, "What have you done?"

The woman said, "The serpent tricked me. That's why I ate the fruit."

14So the Lord God spoke to the serpent. He said, "Because you have done this,

"I am putting a curse on you.
  You are cursed more than all of the
    livestock
  and all of the wild animals.
You will crawl on the ground.
  You will eat dust
  all of the days of your life.
15I will put hatred
  between you and the woman.
  Your children and her chil[d]
    be enemies.
Her son will crush your hea[d]
  And you will crush his [

16The Lord God said to [

"I will greatly increase your pain when
    you give birth.
  You will be in pain when you have
    children.
You will long for your husband.
  And he will rule over you."

17The Lord God said to Adam, "You listened to your wife. You ate the fruit of the tree that I commanded you about. I said, 'You must not eat its fruit.'

"So I am putting a curse on the ground
    because of what you did.
  All the days of your life you will have
    to work hard
  to get food from the ground.
18You will eat the plants of the field,
  even though the ground produces
    thorns and thistles.
19You will have to work hard and sweat a
    lot
  to produce the food you eat.
You were made out of the ground.
  And you will return to it.
You are dust.
  So you will return to it."

20Adam named his wife Eve. She would become the mother of every living person.

21The Lord God made clothes out of animal skins for Adam and his wife to wear. **22**The Lord God said, "The man has become like one of us. He can now tell the difference between good and evil. He must not be allowed to reach out his hand and pick fruit from the tree of life and eat it. If he does, he will live forever."

23So the Lord God drove the man out of the Garden of Eden to work the ground he had been made out of. **24**The Lord God drove him out and then placed cherubim on the east side of the Garden of Eden. He also placed a flaming sword there. It flashed back and forth. The cherubim and the sword guarded the way to the tree of life.

Cain and Abel

4 Adam made lov[e] [. . .] She [. . .] [L]ord's help [. . .] irth to [. . .] [she] gave [. . .] became [. . .] eep. Cain worked [. . .]me time, Cain gath-[. . .] Cain. S[. . .] ings he had grown. He [. . .] an offering to the Lord. He [. . .] brought the fattest parts of [. . .] lambs from his flock. The[y]

ADAM AND EVE

(Not!)

GENESIS 3:6-7

> So [Eve] took some of the fruit and ate it. She also gave some to her husband, who was with her. And he ate it. Then both of them knew things they had never known before. They realized they were naked.

A dam grabbed Eve's hand and ran with her through the Garden of Eden. They ran barefoot through cool grass toward the river and went swimming. Eve took a shower under a waterfall. How happy they were!

Later Eve sat by herself under a tree. The serpent she had talked to earlier found her again. He wanted her to eat from a tree that God had said they should not eat from. Eve was sitting next to that tree. SHE GOT UP TO WALK AWAY, BUT A SINGLE PIECE OF THE FORBIDDEN FRUIT HUNG RIGHT IN FRONT OF HER EYES.

What if the serpent is right? Eve thought. *What if I eat this fruit and nothing happens? Or I eat it and I know things I've never known before?* Quickly—before she could change her mind again—Eve picked the fruit and took a bite. A feeling of sadness rushed through her. Her ears rang with clashing sounds. When Adam arrived, Eve dropped the fruit into his hand, like it was burning hers.

Adam turned the fruit over and over in his hand. He knew it was from the forbidden tree. But if Eve dared to eat it, why shouldn't he? He took a bite. Instantly everything was different. Pulling Eve along with him, Adam ran deep into the garden. They tried to hide from God behind a bush.

ADAM AND EVE

Satan, in the form of a serpent, tempted Adam and Eve to eat what God had told them not to. When they ate, they committed the first sin in the world God had created. From that day on, sin has been in every person born. Adam and Eve sinned, and so do people today. But God sent Jesus to die on the cross to forgive your sins. If you trust him, he will set you free from your sins.

ADAM AND EVE ATE THE FRUIT FORBIDDEN BY GOD.

THE WHOLE STORY: GENESIS 2:4–3:8

next Super Hero

were the male animals that were born first to their mothers.

The LORD was pleased with Abel and his offering. **5**But he wasn't pleased with Cain and his offering. So Cain became very angry. His face was sad.

6Then the LORD said to Cain, "Why are you angry? Why are you looking so sad? **7**Do what is right. Then you will be accepted. If you don't do what is right, sin is waiting at your door to grab you. It longs to have you. But you must rule over it."

8Cain said to his brother Abel, "Let's go out to the field." So they went out. There Cain attacked his brother Abel and killed him.

9Then the LORD said to Cain, "Where is your brother Abel?"

"I don't know," he replied. "Am I supposed to look after my brother?"

10The LORD said, "What have you done? Listen! Your brother's blood is crying out to me from the ground.

11"So I am putting a curse on you. I am driving you away from the ground. It has opened its mouth to receive your brother's blood from your hand. **12**When you work the ground, it will not produce its crops for you anymore. You will be a restless person who wanders around on the earth."

13Cain said to the LORD, "You are punishing me more than I can take. **14**Today you are driving me away from the land. I will be hidden from you. I'll be a restless person who wanders around on the earth. Anyone who finds me will kill me."

15But the LORD said to him, "No. Anyone who kills you will be paid back seven times." The LORD put a mark on Cain. Then anyone who found him wouldn't kill him.

16So Cain went away from the LORD. He lived in the land of Nod. It was east of Eden.

17Cain made love to his wife. She became pregnant and gave birth to Enoch. At that time Cain was building a city. He named it after his son Enoch.

18Enoch had a son named Mehujael was the father of Mehujael the father of Methush shael was the father of

19Lamech married was named Adah named Zillah. **20** He was the fa tents and ra name was everyone

22Zillah also had a son. His name was Tubal-Cain. He made all kinds of tools out of bronze and iron. Tubal-Cain's sister was Naamah.

23Lamech said to his wives,

"Adah and Zillah, listen to me.
    You wives of Lamech, hear my
        words.
I have killed a man because he
        wounded me.
    I have killed a young man because
        he hurt me.
24Anyone who would have killed Cain
        would have been paid back
        seven times.
    But anyone who hurts me will be
        paid back 77 times."

25Adam made love to his wife again. She gave birth to a son and named him Seth. She said, "God has given me another child. The child will take the place of Abel, because Cain killed him."

26Seth also had a son. He named him Enosh.

At that time people began to worship the LORD.

The Family Line of Adam

5 Here is the written story of Adam's family line.

When God created man, he made him in his own likeness. **2**He created them as male and female. He blessed them. And he called them "man" when they were created.

3When Adam was 130 years old, he had a son in his own likeness. He named him Seth. **4**Adam lived 800 years after Seth was born. He also had other sons and daughters. **5**Adam lived a total of 930 years. Then he died.

6Seth lived 105 years. Then he became the father of Enosh. **7**Seth lived 807 years after Enosh was born. He also had other sons and daughters. **8**Seth lived a total of 912 years. Then he died.

9Enosh
ahalalel. Then he
al of 910 years. Then he born.
el lived 65 years. Then he
e father of Jared. **16**Mahalalel

had
lived a
13Kenan
sons and daughters.
was born.

lived 830 years after Jared was born. He also had other sons and daughters. ¹⁷Mahalalel lived a total of 895 years. Then he died.

¹⁸Jared lived 162 years. Then he became the father of Enoch. ¹⁹Jared lived 800 years after Enoch was born. He also had other sons and daughters. ²⁰Jared lived a total of 962 years. Then he died.

²¹Enoch lived 65 years. Then he became the father of Methuselah. ²²Enoch walked with God 300 years after Methuselah was born. He also had other sons and daughters. ²³Enoch lived a total of 365 years.

²⁴Enoch walked with God. Then he couldn't be found, because God took him from this life.

²⁵Methuselah lived 187 years. Then he became the father of Lamech. ²⁶Methuselah lived 782 years after Lamech was born. He also had other sons and daughters. ²⁷Methuselah lived a total of 969 years. Then he died.

²⁸Lamech lived 182 years. Then he had a son. ²⁹He named him Noah. Lamech said, "He will comfort us when we are working. He'll comfort us when our hands work so hard they hurt. We have to work hard. That's because the LORD has put a curse on the ground."

³⁰Lamech lived 595 years after Noah was born. He also had other sons and daughters. ³¹Lamech lived a total of 777 years. Then he died.

³²After Noah was 500 years old, he became the father of Shem, Ham and Japheth.

The Flood

6 Men began to increase their numbers on the earth, and daughters were born to them. ²The sons of God saw that the daughters of men were beautiful. So they married any of them they chose.

³Then the LORD said, "My Spirit will not struggle with man forever. He will die. He will have only 120 years to live until I ___ him."

___philim were on the earth in men ___ at was when the sons of er on. ___ The ___ughters of men and had bec___ ⁸Nephilim were thoughts i___ ___ere famous only toward tha___ ___th lat- very sad tha___

earth. His heart was filled with pain. ⁷So the LORD said, "I created man on the earth. But I will wipe them out. I will destroy people and animals alike. I will also destroy the creatures that move along the ground and the birds of the air. I am very sad that I have made man."

⁸But the LORD was pleased with Noah.

⁹Here is the story of Noah.

Noah was a godly man. He was without blame among the people of his time. He walked with God. ¹⁰Noah had three sons. Their names were Shem, Ham and Japheth.

¹¹The earth was very sinful in God's eyes. It was full of mean and harmful acts. ¹²God saw how sinful the earth had become. All of the people on earth were leading very sinful lives.

¹³So God said to Noah, "I am going to put an end to all people. They have filled the earth with their harmful acts. You can be sure that I am going to destroy both them and the earth.

¹⁴"So make yourself an ark out of cypress wood. Make rooms in it. Cover it with tar inside and out. ¹⁵Here is how I want you to build it. The ark has to be 450 feet long. It has to be 75 feet wide and 45 feet high. ¹⁶Make a roof for it. Leave the sides of the ark open a foot and a half from the top. Put a door in one side of the ark. Make lower, middle and upper decks.

¹⁷"I am going to bring a flood on the earth. It will destroy all life under the sky. It will destroy every living creature that breathes. Everything on earth will die.

¹⁸"But I will make my covenant with you. You will enter the ark. Your sons and your wife and your sons' wives will enter it with you.

¹⁹"Bring two of every living thing into the ark. Bring male and female of them into it. They will be kept alive with you. ²⁰Two of every kind of bird will come to you. Two of every kind of animal will come to you. And two of every kind of creature that moves along the ground will come to you. All of them will be kept alive with you.

²¹"Take every kind of food that you will need. Store it away. It will be food for you and for them."

²²Noah did everything exactly as God commanded him.

7 Then the LORD said to Noah, "Go into the ark with your whole family. I ___ you are a godly man among ___ day.

___very kind of 'clean'

NOAH

GENESIS 6:22

Noah did everything exactly as God commanded him.

Noah tossed his hammer down. His back was killing him. His hands were sore, his arms were sore—and he had a headache. Day after long day he and his sons worked on the gigantic boat. He looked way up to the top. The boat was almost finished. Just a few more pegs to hammer and a bit more pitch to make it leak-proof. Then the rain could come.

Noah knew he looked silly, even stupid, to the people around him. After all, there wasn't any water for miles. But God had said to build a boat. The rain would come and wouldn't stop for days and days. There was going to be a huge flood. God said the people had become so wicked that he decided to start over again with his creation. Only the people and the animals on Noah's boat would survive.

The flood came, just as God had said it would. The water rose until the boat started to float, until all the trees were under water, until the mountains were, too. Higher and higher the water went. Their long boat ride had begun . . .

One year later, Noah stepped off his boat onto dry ground. How wonderful to feel solid ground beneath his feet again! As he hugged his wife and his family close, Noah gazed at the arch of colors in the sky. **THE FIRST RAINBOW!** It was God's promise that he would never destroy the people and animals with a flood again. Noah lifted his hands and jumped up and down. He grabbed the hands of his wife and sons. They danced in a circle, praising God for keeping them safe, for keeping his promise.

BE A NOAH

Obeying God isn't always easy. Sometimes what he wants you to do is hard. But it's worth it. Noah and his family were blessed because he obeyed God. You will be, too!

NOAH OBEYED G
THE WHOLE

animal with you. Take male and female of them. Take two of every kind of animal that is not 'clean.' Take male and female of them. ³Also take seven of every kind of bird. Take male and female of them. That will keep every kind alive. Then they can spread out again over the whole earth.

⁴"Seven days from now I will send rain on the earth. It will rain for 40 days and 40 nights. I will destroy from the face of the earth every living thing I have made."

⁵Noah did everything the LORD commanded him to do.

⁶Noah was 600 years old when the flood came on the earth. ⁷He and his sons entered the ark. His wife and his sons' wives went with them. They entered the ark to escape the waters of the flood.

⁸Pairs of "clean" animals and pairs of animals that were not "clean" came to Noah. So did pairs of birds and pairs of all of the creatures that move along the ground. ⁹Male and female of all of them came to Noah and entered the ark.

Everything happened exactly as God had commanded Noah. ¹⁰After seven days the flood came on the earth.

¹¹Noah was 600 years old. It was the 17th day of the second month of the year. On that day all of the springs at the bottom of the oceans burst open. God opened the windows of the skies. ¹²Rain fell on the earth for 40 days and 40 nights.

¹³On that same day Noah entered the ark together with Shem, Ham and Japheth. Noah's wife and the wives of his three sons also entered it.

¹⁴They had every kind of wild animal with them. They had every kind of livestock. They had every kind of creature that moves along the ground. And they had every kind of bird that flies. ¹⁵Pairs of all living creatures that breathe came to Noah and entered the ark. ¹⁶The animals going in were male and female of every living thing.

Everything happened exactly as God had commanded Noah. Then the LORD ⁿ him in.

ᵉ days the flood kept coming on
of waters rose higher, they
sky ris' ove the earth. ¹⁸The
to m higher on the
by 21Ev disigher on the
earth dis he water.
til all

the wild animals died. All of the creatures that fill the earth also died. And so did every human being. ²²Everything on dry land that had the breath of life in it died. ²³Every living thing on the earth was wiped out. People and animals were destroyed. The creatures that move along the ground and the birds of the air were wiped out.

Everything was destroyed from the earth. Only Noah and those who were with him in the ark were left.

²⁴The waters flooded the earth for 150 days.

8 But God showed concern for Noah. He also showed concern for all of the wild animals and livestock that were with Noah in the ark.

So God sent a wind over the earth. And the waters began to go down. ²The springs at the bottom of the oceans had been closed. The windows of the skies had been closed. And the rain had stopped falling from the sky.

³The water continued to go down from the earth. At the end of the 150 days the water had gone down. ⁴On the 17th day of the seventh month, the ark came to rest on the mountains of Ararat. ⁵The waters continued to go down until the tenth month. On the first day of the month, the tops of the mountains could be seen.

⁶After 40 days Noah opened the window he had made in the ark. ⁷He sent a raven out. It kept flying back and forth until the water had dried up from the earth.

⁸Then Noah sent a dove out. He wanted to see if the water had gone down from the surface of the ground. ⁹But the dove couldn't find any place to put its feet down. There was still water over the whole surface of the earth. So the dove returned to Noah in the ark. Noah reached out his hand and took the dove in. He brought it back to himself in the ark.

¹⁰He waited seven more days. Then he sent the dove out from the ark again. ¹¹In the evening the dove returned to him. There in its beak was a freshly picked olive leaf! So Noah knew that the water on the earth had gone down.

¹²He waited seven more days. Then he sent the dove out again. But that time it didn't return to him.

was the first day of the first month
¹st year. The water had dried
h. Then Noah removed
ark. He saw that the

surface of the ground was dry. **14**By the 27th day of the second month the earth was completely dry.

15Then God said to Noah, **16**"Come out of the ark. Bring your wife and your sons and their wives with you.

17"Bring out every kind of living thing that is with you. Bring the birds, the animals, and all of the creatures that move along the ground. Then they can multiply on the earth. They can have little ones and increase their numbers."

18So Noah came out of the ark. His sons and his wife and his sons' wives were with

NOAH'S WIFE

GENESIS 7:7

[Noah] and his sons entered the ark. His wife and his sons' wives went with them. They entered the ark to escape the waters of the flood.

Mrs. Noah wiped the dirt from her hands as she walked to the pigpen. Lots of squeaks and squeals came from inside. She smiled as the newborn baby pigs squirmed next to their big mother.

They had been together on the ark for six months now. She and Noah, their sons and their wives, and hundreds of animals. SIX MONTHS OF LOOKING AT WOODEN WALLS AND WALKING ON TILTING FLOORS AND LISTENING TO ANIMALS GRUNT AND SCREECH AND SQUAWK. Six months of feeding and cleaning and cooking and feeding and cleaning and cooking again. Noah's wife tucked some of her hair behind her ear. She wondered if she would ever see dry ground again.

She had agreed to go with Noah on to the ark. But now everyone was getting tired and cranky. Including Mrs. Noah. But she reminded herself that they were safe for now on the ark when everyone else in the world had died from the flood.

BE LIKE NOAH'S WIFE

Life can be hard sometimes. Although the Bible doesn't tell us much about Noah's wife, we do know that she was willing to go along with Noah on the ark. She must have been afraid at times, but she bravely got through those long days until the flood was over. When you have something hard to do, remember Mrs. Noah and try hard to be willing and brave, too!

NOAH'S WIFE WAS WILLING AND BRAVE EVEN THOUGH LIFE ON THE ARK WAS HARD.

Go to page 16 for the next person

him. **19**All of the animals came out of the ark. The creatures that move along the ground also came out. So did all of the birds. Everything that moves on the earth came out of the ark. One kind after another came out.

20Then Noah built an altar to honor the LORD. He took some of all of the "clean" animals and birds. He sacrificed burnt offerings to the LORD on the altar.

21Their smell was pleasant to the LORD. He said to himself, "I will never put a curse on the ground again because of man. I will not do it even though his heart is always directed toward what is evil. His thoughts are evil from the time he is young. I will never destroy all living things again, as I have just done.

22 "As long as the earth lasts,
　　there will always be a time to plant
　　and a time to gather the crops.
As long as the earth lasts,
　　there will always be cold and heat.
There will always be summer and
　　winter,
　　day and night."

God Makes a Covenant With Noah

9 Then God gave his blessing to Noah and his sons. He said to them, "Have children and increase your numbers. Fill the earth.

2"All of the land animals will be afraid of you. All of the birds of the air will fear you. Every creature that moves along the ground will fear you. Every fish in the oceans will also be afraid of you. Every living thing is put under your control.

3"Everything that lives and moves will be food for you. I have already given you the green plants for food. Now I am giving you everything.

4"But you must not eat meat that still has blood in it. **5**You can be sure that I will hold someone accountable if you are murdered. I will even hold animals accountable if they kill you. I will also hold anyone accountable who murders another person.

6 "Anyone who murders man
　　will be killed by man.
That is because I have made man
　　in my own likeness.

7"Have children and increase your numbers. Multiply on the earth and increase your numbers on it."

8Then God spoke to Noah and to his sons who were with him. He said, **9**"I am now making my covenant with you and with all of your children who will be born after you. **10**I am making it also with every living thing that was with you in the ark. I am making my covenant with the birds, the livestock and all of the wild animals. I am making it with all of the creatures that came out of the ark with you. I am making it with every living thing on earth.

11"Here is my covenant that I am making with you. The waters of a flood will never destroy all life again. A flood will never destroy the earth again."

12God continued, "My covenant is between me and you and every living thing with you. It is a covenant for all time to come.

"Here is the sign of the covenant I am making. **13**I have put my rainbow in the clouds. It will be the sign of the covenant between me and the earth. **14**Sometimes when I bring clouds over the earth, a rainbow will appear in them. **15**Then I will remember my covenant between me and you and every kind of living thing. The waters will never become a flood to destroy all life again.

16"When the rainbow appears in the clouds, I will see it. I will remember that my covenant will last forever. It is a covenant between me and every kind of living thing on earth."

17So God said to Noah, "The rainbow is the sign of my covenant. I have made my covenant between me and all life on earth."

The Sons of Noah

18The sons of Noah who came out of the ark were Shem, Ham and Japheth. Ham was the father of Canaan. **19**The people who were scattered over the earth came from Noah's three sons.

20Noah was a man who worked the ground. He decided to plant a vineyard. **21**He drank some of its wine. It made him drunk. Then he lay down inside his tent without any clothes on. **22**Ham saw his father's naked body. Ham was the father of Canaan. Ham went outside and told his two brothers.

23But Shem and Japheth took a piece of clothing. They laid it across their shoulders. Then they walked backward into the tent. They covered their father's body. They turned their faces away. They didn't want to see their father's naked body.

24Then Noah woke up from his sleep that was caused by the wine. He found out what his youngest son had done to him. **25**He said,

"May a curse be put on Canaan.
  He will be the lowest of slaves to his
    brothers."

26 Noah also said,

"May the LORD, the God of Shem, be
  blessed.
  May Canaan be the slave of Shem.
27 May God add land to Japheth's
    territory.
  May Japheth live in the tents of
    Shem.
  And may Canaan be their slave."

28 After the flood Noah lived 350 years.
29 Noah lived a total of 950 years. Then he
died.

A List of Nations

10 Here is the story of Shem, Ham
     and Japheth. They were Noah's
sons. After the flood, they too had sons.

The Sons of Japheth

2 The sons of Japheth were
    Gomer, Magog, Madai, Javan,
    Tubal, Meshech and Tiras.
3 The sons of Gomer were
    Ashkenaz, Riphath and Togarmah.
4 The sons of Javan were
    Elishah, Tarshish, the Kittim and
    the Rodanites. 5 The people who
    lived by the sea came from all of
    them. Their tribes and nations
    spread out into their own territo-
    ries. Each tribe and nation had its
    own language.

The Sons of Ham

6 The sons of Ham were
    Cush, Egypt, Put and Canaan.
7 The sons of Cush were
    Seba, Havilah, Sabtah, Raamah
    and Sabteca.
  The sons of Raamah were
    Sheba and Dedan.

8 Cush was the father of Nimrod. Nimrod grew up to be a mighty hero on the
earth. 9 He was a mighty hunter in the
LORD's eyes. That's why people sometimes
compare others with Nimrod. They say,
"They are like Nimrod, who is a mighty
hunter in the LORD's eyes."
  10 At first Nimrod's kingdom was made
up of Babylon, Erech, Akkad and Calneh.
Those cities were in the land of Babylonia.
  11 From that land he went to Assyria.
There he built Nineveh, Rehoboth Ir and
Calah. 12 He also built Resen. It is betwe—
Nineveh and Calah. Nineveh is the g—
city.

13 Egypt was the father of
    the Ludites, Anamites, Lehabites
    and Naphtuhites. 14 He was also
    the father of the Pathrusites, Cas-
    luhites and Caphtorites. The Phi-
    listines came from the Casluhites.
15 Canaan was the father of
    Sidon. Sidon was his oldest son.
    Canaan was also the father of the
    Hittites, 16 Jebusites, Amorites and
    Girgashites. 17 And he was the
    father of the Hivites, Arkites,
    Sinites, 18 Arvadites, Zemarites and
    Hamathites.

Later the Canaanite tribes scattered.
19 The borders of Canaan went from Sidon
toward Gerar all the way to Gaza. Then
they went toward Sodom, Gomorrah,
Admah and Zeboiim all the way to Lasha.
  20 Those are the sons of Ham. They are
listed by their tribes and languages in
their territories and nations.

The Sons of Shem

21 Sons were also born to Shem. Shem
was Japheth's younger brother. All of the
sons of Eber came from Shem.

22 The sons of Shem were
    Elam, Asshur, Arphaxad, Lud and
    Aram.
23 The sons of Aram were
    Uz, Hul, Gether and Meshech.
24 Arphaxad was the father of Shelah.
    Shelah was the father of Eber.
25 Eber was the father of two sons.
    One was named Peleg. That's
    because the earth was divided up
    in his time. His brother was named
    Joktan.
26 Joktan was the father of
    Almodad, Sheleph, Hazarmaveth
    and Jerah. 27 He was also the father
    of Hadoram, Uzal, Diklah, 28 Obal,
    Abimael, Sheba, 29 Ophir, Havilah

POWER-SURGE

STRONG...
NIMROD GR—ER IN
BE A ...EYES.
...10:8-9 —

and Jobab. All of them were sons of Joktan.

30The area where they lived stretched from Mesha toward Sephar. It was in the eastern hill country.

31Those are the sons of Shem. They are listed by their tribes and languages in their territories and nations.

32Those are the tribes of Noah's sons. They are listed by their family lines within their nations. From them the nations spread out over the earth after the flood.

The Tower of Babel

11 The whole world had only one language. All people spoke it. 2They moved to the east and found a broad valley in Babylonia. There they settled down.

3They said to each other, "Come. Let's make bricks and bake them well." They used bricks instead of stones. They used tar to hold the bricks together.

4Then they said, "Come. Let's build a city for ourselves. Let's build a tower that reaches to the sky. We'll make a name for ourselves. Then we won't be scattered over the face of the whole earth."

5But the LORD came down to see the city and the tower the people were building. 6The LORD said, "They are one people. And all of them speak the same language. That is why they can do this. Now they will be able to do anything they plan to. 7Come. Let us go down and mix up their language. Then they will not understand each other."

8So the LORD scattered them from there over the whole earth. And they stopped building the city. 9The LORD mixed up the language of the whole world there. That's why the city was named Babel. From there the LORD scattered them over the face of the whole earth.

The Family Line of Shem

10Here is the story of Shem.

It was two years after the flood. When Shem was 100 years old, he became the father of Arphaxad. 11After Arphaxad was born, Shem lived 500 years. And he had other sons and daughters.

12When Arphaxad had lived 35 years, he became the father of Shelah. 13After Arphaxad lived 403 years, he became the father of other sons and daugh-

ters, he

was born, Shelah lived 403 years. And he had other sons and daughters.

16When Eber had lived 34 years, he became the father of Peleg. 17After Peleg was born, Eber lived 430 years. And he had other sons and daughters.

18When Peleg had lived 30 years, he became the father of Reu. 19After Reu was born, Peleg lived 209 years. And he had other sons and daughters.

20When Reu had lived 32 years, he became the father of Serug. 21After Serug was born, Reu lived 207 years. And he had other sons and daughters.

22When Serug had lived 30 years, he became the father of Nahor. 23After Nahor was born, Serug lived 200 years. And he had other sons and daughters.

24When Nahor had lived 29 years, he became the father of Terah. 25After Terah was born, Nahor lived 119 years. And he had other sons and daughters.

26Terah lived for 70 years. Then he became the father of Abram, Nahor and Haran.

27Here is the story of Terah.

Terah became the father of Abram, Nahor and Haran. And Haran became the father of Lot. 28Haran died in Ur in Babylonia. That was the land where he had been born. Haran died while his father Terah was still alive.

29Abram and Nahor both got married. The name of Abram's wife was Sarai. The name of Nahor's wife was Milcah. She was the daughter of Haran. Haran was the father of Milcah and Iscah. 30But Sarai wasn't able to have children.

31Terah started out from Ur in Babylonia. He took his son Abram with him. He also took his grandson Lot. Lot was the son of Haran. And Terah took his daughter-in-law Sarai. She was the wife of his son Abram.

All of them left together to go to Canaan. But when they came to Haran, they settled down.

32Terah lived for 205 years. He died in Haran.

God Chooses Abram

12 The LORD had said to Abram, "Leave your country and your people. Leave your father's family. Go to the land I will show you.

2 "I will make you into a great nation.
   I will bless you.
I will make your name great.
   You will be a blessing to others.

3 I will bless those who bless you.
I will put a curse on anyone who
calls down a curse on you.
All nations on earth
will be blessed because of you."

4 So Abram left, just as the LORD had told him. Lot went with him. Abram was 75 years old when he left Haran. **5** He took his wife Sarai and his nephew Lot. They took all of the things they had gotten in Haran. They also took the workers they had gotten there.

They set out for the land of Canaan. And they arrived there.

6 Abram traveled through the land. He went as far as the large tree of Moreh at Shechem. At that time the people of Canaan were living in the land. **7** The LORD appeared to Abram at Shechem. He said, "I will give this land to your children after you." So Abram built an altar there to honor the LORD, who had appeared to him.

8 From there, Abram went on toward the hills east of Bethel. He set up his tent there. Bethel was to the west, and Ai was to the east.

Abram built an altar there and worshiped the LORD. **9** Then Abram left and continued toward the Negev Desert.

Abram Goes to Egypt

10 At that time there wasn't enough food in the land. So Abram went down to Egypt to live there for a while.

11 As he was about to enter Egypt, he spoke to his wife Sarai. He said, "I know what a beautiful woman you are. **12** The people of Egypt will see you. They will say, 'This is his wife.' And they will kill me. But they will let you live. **13** Say you are my sister. Then I'll be treated well because of you. My life will be spared because of you."

14 Abram arrived in Egypt. The people of Egypt saw that Sarai was a very beautiful woman. **15** When Pharaoh's officials saw her, they bragged to Pharaoh about her. Sarai was taken into his palace. **16** Pharaoh treated Abram well because of her. So Abram gained more sheep and cattle. He also got more male and female donkeys. And he gained more male and female servants and some camels.

17 But the LORD sent terrible sicknesses on Pharaoh and everyone in his palace. He did it because of Abram's wife Sarai. **18** So Pharaoh sent for Abram. "W have you done to me?" he said. " didn't you tell me she was your **19** Why did you say, 'She's my

That's why I took her to be my wife. Now then, here's your wife. Take her and go!"

20 Then Pharaoh gave orders about Abram to his men. They sent him on his way. He left with his wife and everything he had.

Abram and Lot Separate

13 Abram went up from Egypt to the Negev Desert. He took his wife and everything he had. Lot went with him. **2** Abram had become very rich. He had a lot of livestock and silver and gold.

3 From the Negev Desert, he went from place to place until he came to Bethel. He came to a place between Bethel and Ai. That's where his tent had been earlier. **4** He had also built an altar there. He worshiped the LORD there.

5 Lot was moving around with Abram. Lot also had flocks and herds and tents.

6 But the land didn't have enough food for both of them. They had large herds and many servants. So they weren't able to stay together. **7** The people who took care of Abram's herds and those who took care of Lot's herds began to argue.

The Canaanites and Perizzites were also living in the land at that time.

8 So Abram said to Lot, "Let's not argue with each other. The people who take care of your herds and those who take care of mine shouldn't argue with one another. After all, we're part of the same family. **9** "Isn't the whole land in front of you? Let's separate. If you go to the left, I'll go to the right. If you go to the right, I'll go to the left."

10 Lot looked up. He saw that the whole Jordan River valley had plenty of water. It was like the garden of the LORD. It was like the land of Egypt near Zoar. That was before the LORD destroyed Sodom and Gomorrah.

11 So Lot chose the whole Jordan River valley for himself. Then he started out toward the east.

The two men separated. **12** Abram lived in the land of Canaan. Lot lived among the cities of the Jordan River valley. He set up his tents near Sodom.

13 The men of Sodom were evil
were sinning greatly against
14 The LORD spok
had left hi
where

it can, then your children can be counted. **17**Go. Walk through the land. See how long and wide it is. I am giving it to you."

18So Abram moved his tents. He went to live near the large trees of Mamre at Hebron. There he built an altar to honor the Lord.

Abram Saves Lot

14 At that time Amraphel was the king of Babylonia. Arioch was the king of Ellasar. Kedorlaomer was the king of Elam. And Tidal was the king of Goiim. **2**They went to war against five kings. The kings were Bera king of Sodom, Birsha

LOT

(Not!)

GENESIS 13:11-13

Lot chose the whole Jordan River valley for himself...Lot lived among the cities of the Jordan River valley. He set up his tents near Sodom. The men of Sodom were evil. They were sinning greatly.

L ot stood on the hill with his uncle, Abraham. The cool breeze felt wonderful and refreshing on their hot faces. Lot and Abraham were both very rich men. They both had large herds of camels and cows and flocks of sheep and goats. And they both had servants who were fighting. Abraham's servants fought Lot's servants over the land and the water for the animals.

Abraham and Lot were from the same family. They didn't want to fight. So Abraham gave Lot first choice. As they stood on the hill together, LOT LOOKED OVER THE VALLEY BELOW. The water of the Jordan River sparkled in the sunshine. Tall green grasses and trees grew along the river as far as they could see into the distance. That was certainly the best land around. So Lot chose it for himself.

Lot and his family went to live in their new land. The land was close to two very wicked cities. Lot lived near those cities. Instead of staying away from the evil people there, Lot lived close to them. He didn't join in the evil, but he and his family were influenced by it.

LOT

Lot was sort of a fence sitter. With good on one side and evil on the other, he just sat on the fence and didn't choose one or the other. He looked at sin and didn't want to choose that. But he looked at living for God and didn't quite choose that either. Don't be like him! Eventually, sin will grab you if you sit on the fence. Choose instead to live for God.

LOT CHOSE THE BEST FOR HIMSELF AND LIVED WITH ╵VIL ON EVERY SIDE.

╵WHOLE STORY: GENESIS 13:1-12

for the next Super Hero

king of Gomorrah, Shinab king of Admah, Shemeber king of Zeboiim, and the king of Bela. Bela was also called Zoar.

³Those five kings all gathered their armies together in the Valley of Siddim. It was the valley of the Dead Sea. ⁴For 12 years they had been under the rule of Kedorlaomer. But in the 13th year they opposed him.

⁵In the 14th year, Kedorlaomer and the kings who helped him went to war. They won the battle against the Rephaites in Ashteroth Karnaim. They also won the battle against the Zuzites in Ham and the Emites in Shaveh Kiriathaim. ⁶They did the same thing to the Horites in the hill country of Seir. They marched all the way to El Paran near the desert.

⁷Then they turned back. They went to En Mishpat. En Mishpat was also called Kadesh. They took over the whole territory of the Amalekites. They also won the battle against the Amorites who were living in Hazazon Tamar.

⁸Then the king of Sodom and the king of Gomorrah marched out. The kings of Admah, Zeboiim and Bela went with them. Bela was also called Zoar.

They lined up their armies for battle in the Valley of Siddim. ⁹They got ready to fight against Kedorlaomer king of Elam, Tidal king of Goiim, Amraphel king of Babylonia, and Arioch king of Ellasar. There were four kings against five.

¹⁰The Valley of Siddim was full of tar pits. The kings of Sodom and Gomorrah ran away from the battle. Some of their men fell into the pits. The rest escaped to the hills.

¹¹The four kings took all of the things that belonged to Sodom and Gomorrah. They also took all of their food. Then they went away.

¹²They carried away Lot, Abram's nephew, and the things he owned. Lot was living in Sodom at that time.

¹³One man escaped. He came and reported everything to Abram. Abram was a Hebrew. He was living near the large trees of Mamre the Amorite. Mamre was a brother of Eshcol and Aner. All of them helped Abram.

¹⁴Abram heard that Lot had been captured. So he called out his 318 trained men. All of them were sons of his servants. They chased the enemy as far as Dan. ¹⁵During the night Abram separated his men into groups. They attacked the enemy and drove them away. They chased them north of Damascus as far as Hobah.

¹⁶Abram took back all of the things the kings had taken. He brought back his nephew Lot and the things Lot owned. He also brought back the women and the other people.

¹⁷After Abram won the battle over Kedorlaomer and the kings who helped him, he returned. The king of Sodom came out to meet him in the Valley of Shaveh. The Valley of Shaveh was also called the King's Valley.

¹⁸Melchizedek was the king of Jerusalem. He brought out bread and wine. He was the priest of God Most High. ¹⁹He gave a blessing to Abram. He said,

"May God Most High bless Abram.
　May the Creator of heaven and
　　earth bless him.
²⁰Give praise to God Most High.
　He gave your enemies into your
　　hand."

Then Abram gave Melchizedek a tenth of everything.

²¹The king of Sodom said to Abram, "Give me the people. Keep everything else for yourself."

²²But Abram said to the king of Sodom, "I have raised my hand to the LORD. He is God Most High. He is the Creator of heaven and earth. I have taken an oath. ²³I have said that I won't accept anything that belongs to you. I won't take even a thread or the strap of a sandal. You will never be able to say, 'I made Abram rich.'

²⁴"I'll accept only what my men have eaten and what belongs to Aner, Eshcol and Mamre. Those three men went with me. Let them have their share."

God Makes a Covenant With Abram

15 Some time later, Abram had a vision. The LORD said to him,

"Abram, do not be afraid.
　I am like a shield to you.
　I am your very great reward."

²But Abram said, "LORD and King, what

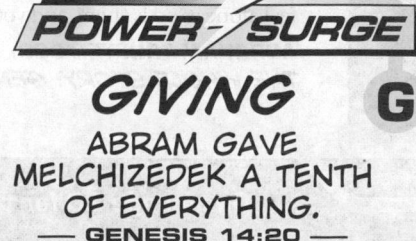

POWER-SURGE

GIVING　G

ABRAM GAVE
MELCHIZEDEK A TENTH
OF EVERYTHING.
— GENESIS 14:20 —

can you give me? I still don't have any children. My servant Eliezer comes from Damascus. When I die, he will get everything I own." ³Abram continued, "You haven't given me any children. So a servant in my house will get everything I own."

⁴Then a message came to Abram from the Lord. He said, "This man will not get what belongs to you. A son will come from your own body. He will get everything you own."

⁵The Lord took Abram outside and said, "Look up at the sky. Count the stars,

ABRAHAM

GENESIS 15:6

> **[Abraham] believed the Lord. The Lord accepted [Abraham] because he believed. So his faith made him right with the Lord.**

Abraham was confused. He ran his fingers through his gray hair and rubbed his wrinkled cheek. Could what God's messenger was telling him really be true? Behind him, he heard his wife Sarah giggle. So she had heard, too. They both laughed to think they would have a son. They were old enough to be a grandpa and a grandma, not a dad and a mom!

Abraham and Sarah had both wanted children, more than anything else. But they never had any. Sarah would cry herself to sleep because she had no children. Abraham would cry, too. But now they were so happy about the news!

They were old, way past the time when people had babies. But a messenger had come to tell them that God was going to give them a son. God promised that the son of Abraham and Sarah would grow up and have children. And those children would have children and those children would have children until there were millions—a whole nation of people!

Late that night Abraham sat next to Sarah by the fire outside their tent. **A SON!** They looked up at the millions of stars in the sky. And they remembered that the messenger had said they would have that many children! They sat in comfort and quiet joy. What wonderful news they had had today!

BE AN ABRAHAM

Even when you are sad or bad things happen, even when you feel alone, God is there, and you can trust him.

ABRAHAM TRUSTED GOD.
THE WHOLE STORY: GENESIS 18:1-15; 21:1-7

Go to page 20 for the next Super Hero

if you can." Then he said to him, "That is how many children you will have."

⁶Abram believed the LORD. The LORD accepted Abram because he believed. So his faith made him right with the LORD.

⁷He also said to Abram, "I am the LORD. I brought you out of Ur in Babylonia. I wanted to give you this land to take as your very own."

⁸But Abram said, "LORD and King, how can I know I will take this land as my own?"

⁹So the LORD said to him, "Bring me a young cow. Also bring a goat and a ram. All of them must be three years old. Bring a dove and a young pigeon along with them."

¹⁰Abram brought all of them to the LORD. Abram cut them in two. He placed the halves opposite each other. But he didn't cut the birds in half. ¹¹Then large birds came down to eat the dead bodies of the animals and birds. But Abram chased the large birds away.

¹²As the sun was going down, Abram fell into a deep sleep. A thick and terrible darkness covered him.

¹³Then the LORD said to him, "You can be sure of what I am about to tell you. Your children who live after you will be strangers in a country that does not belong to them. They will become slaves. They will be treated badly for 400 years. ¹⁴But I will punish the nation that makes them slaves. After that, they will leave with all kinds of valuable things.

¹⁵"But you will die in peace. You will join the members of your family who have already died. You will be buried when you are very old.

¹⁶"Your children's grandchildren will come back here. That is because the sin of the Amorites has not yet reached the point where I must judge them."

¹⁷The sun set and darkness fell. Then a burning torch and a fire pot filled with smoke appeared. They passed between the pieces of the animals.

¹⁸On that day the LORD made a covenant with Abram. He said, "I am giving this land to your children after you. It reaches from the river of Egypt to the great river Euphrates. ¹⁹It includes the land of the Kenites, Kenizzites, Kadmonites, ²⁰Hittites, Perizzites and Rephaites. ²¹The Amorites, Canaanites, Girgashites and Jebusites also live there."

Hagar and Ishmael

16 Abram's wife Sarai had never had any children by him. But she had a female servant from Egypt named Hagar. ²So she said to Abram, "The LORD has kept me from having children. Go and make love to my servant. Maybe I can have a family through her."

Abram agreed to what Sarai had said. ³After he had been living in Canaan for ten years, his wife Sarai gave him her servant Hagar to be his wife. ⁴He made love to Hagar. And she became pregnant.

When Hagar knew she was pregnant, she began to look down on the woman who owned her.

⁵Then Sarai said to Abram, "It's your fault that I'm suffering like this. I put my servant in your arms. Now that she knows she's pregnant, she looks down on me. May the LORD judge between you and me. May he decide which of us is right."

⁶"Your servant belongs to you," Abram said. "Do with her what you think is best." Then Sarai treated Hagar badly. So Hagar ran away from her.

⁷The angel of the LORD found Hagar near a spring of water in the desert. The spring was beside the road to Shur. ⁸He said, "Hagar, you are the servant of Sarai. Where have you come from? Where are you going?"

"I'm running away from my owner Sarai," she answered.

⁹Then the angel of the LORD told her, "Go back to the woman who owns you. Obey her." ¹⁰The angel continued, "I will greatly increase the number of your children after you. You will have more of them than anyone can count."

¹¹The angel of the LORD also said to her,

"You are now pregnant.
    You will have a son.
You will name him Ishmael.
    That is because the LORD has heard
        about your suffering.
¹² He will be like a wild donkey.
    He will use his power against
        everyone.
    And everyone will be against him.
He will not be friendly
    toward any of his relatives."

¹³She gave a name to the LORD who spoke to her. She called him "You are the God who sees me." That's because she said, "I have now seen the One who sees me."

¹⁴That's why the well was named Beer Lahai Roi. It's still there, between Kadesh and Bered.

¹⁵So Hagar had a son by Abram. And Abram gave the name Ishmael to the son

she had by him. **16**Abram was 86 years old when Hagar had Ishmael by him.

The Covenant of Circumcision

17 When Abram was 99 years old, the LORD appeared to him. He said, "I am the Mighty God. Walk with me and live without any blame. **2**I will now put into practice my covenant between me and you. I will greatly increase your numbers."

3Abram fell with his face to the ground. God said to him, **4**"As for me, this is my covenant with you. You will be the father of many nations. **5**"You will not be called Abram anymore. Your name will be Abraham, because I have made you a father of many nations. **6**I will give you many children. Nations will come from you. And kings will come from you.

7"I will make my covenant with you. It will last forever. It will be between me and you and your children after you for all time to come. I will be your God. And I will be the God of all of your family after you.

8"You are now living in Canaan as an outsider. But I will give you the whole land of Canaan. You will own it forever. So will your children after you. And I will be their God."

9Then God said to Abraham, "As for you, you must keep my covenant. You and your children after you for all time to come must keep it.

HAGAR

GENESIS 16:9

B

✔

T

The angel of the LORD told her, "Go back to the woman who owns you. Obey her."

Hagar slumped against a rock. She had been so thirsty from running in the hot desert air. But she had found a spring and gotten fresh water. Hagar put her hands against the mound of her belly. Her baby grew there. Her mistress, Sarah, had given Hagar to Abraham. But now Hagar was pregnant, and Sarah was angry. Sarah had been so mean that Hagar ran away.

As Hagar rested, an angel from God came and told her to return to Sarah and to obey her. God promised to then bless Hagar and give her a large family through her son.

Hagar obeyed God and returned to Sarah. Before leaving the spring, she gave the place a beautiful name: *Beer Lahai Roi*, which means **"THE GOD WHO SEES ME."** God had seen Hagar and had taken care of her.

BE A HAGAR

God asked Hagar to do something hard—to go back to her mean mistress, Sarah. Hagar obeyed, and God blessed her. Be like Hagar! Even when it's hard, obey God. He'll be sure to bless you, too!

HAGAR OBEYED GOD AND HER MISTRESS SARAH.

Go to page 25 for the next Super Hero

10"Here is my covenant that you and your children after you must keep. Every male among you must be circumcised. **11**You must be circumcised. That will be the sign of the covenant between me and you. **12**It must be done for all time to come.

"Every male among you who is eight days old must be circumcised. That includes those who are born in your house. It also includes those who are bought with money from a stranger. Even those who are not your own children must be included. **13**Any male who is born in your house or bought with your money must be circumcised.

"My covenant will last forever. Your body will have the mark of my covenant on it.

14"Any male who has not been circumcised will be cut off from his people. He has broken my covenant."

15God also said to Abraham, "As for Sarai your wife, do not call her Sarai anymore. Her name will be Sarah. **16**I will give her my blessing. You can be sure that I will give you a son by her. I will bless her so that she will be the mother of nations. Kings of nations will come from her."

17Abraham fell with his face to the ground. He laughed and said to himself, "Will a son be born to a man who is 100 years old? Will Sarah have a child at the age of 90?"

18Abraham said to God, "I wish Ishmael could receive your blessing!"

19Then God said, "I will bless Ishmael. But your wife Sarah will have a son by you. And you will name him Isaac. I will establish my covenant with him. It will be a covenant that lasts forever. It will be for Isaac and for his family after him.

20"As for Ishmael, I have heard you. You can be sure that I will bless him. I will give him children. I will greatly increase his numbers. He will be the father of 12 rulers. And I will make him into a great nation.

21"But I will establish my covenant with Isaac. By this time next year, Sarah will have a son by you."

22When he had finished speaking with Abraham, God left him.

23On that very day Abraham circumcised his son Ishmael. He also circumcised every male who was born in his house or bought with his money. He did exactly as God had told him. **24**Abraham was 99 years old when he was circumcised. **25**His son Ishmael was 13.

26Abraham and his son Ishmael were both circumcised on that same day. **27**And every male in Abraham's house was circumcised along with him. That included those who were born in his house or bought from a stranger.

Three Men Visit Abraham

18 The LORD appeared to Abraham near the large trees of Mamre. Abraham was sitting at the entrance to his tent. It was the hottest time of the day.

2Abraham looked up and saw three men standing nearby. He quickly left the entrance to his tent to meet them. He bowed low to the ground.

3He said, "My lord, if you are pleased with me, don't pass me by. **4**Let a little water be brought. All of you can wash your feet and rest under this tree.

5"Let me get you something to eat to give you strength. Then you can go on your way. I want to do this for you now that you have come to me."

"All right," they answered. "Go ahead and do it."

6So Abraham hurried into the tent to Sarah. "Quick!" he said. "Get about half a bushel of fine flour. Mix it and bake some bread."

7Then he ran to the herd. He picked out a choice, tender calf. He gave it to a servant, who hurried to prepare it. **8**Then he brought some butter and milk and the calf that had been prepared. He served them to the three men.

While they ate, he stood near them under a tree.

9"Where is your wife Sarah?" they asked him.

"Over there, in the tent," he said.

10Then the LORD said, "You can be sure that I will return to you about this time next year. Your wife Sarah will have a son."

Sarah was listening at the entrance to the tent behind him. **11**Abraham and Sarah were already very old. Sarah was too old to have a baby. **12**So she laughed to herself. She thought, "I'm worn out, and my husband is old. Can I really know the joy of having a baby?"

13Then the LORD said to Abraham, "Why did Sarah laugh? Why did she say, 'Will I really have a baby, now that I am old?' **14**Is anything too hard for me? I will return to you at the appointed time next year. Sarah will have a son."

15Sarah was afraid. So she lied and said, "I didn't laugh."

But the LORD said, "Yes, you did."

Abraham Makes an Appeal for Sodom

16The men got up to leave. They looked down toward Sodom. Abraham walked along with them to see them on their way.

17Then the LORD said, "Should I hide from Abraham what I am about to do? **18**He will certainly become a great and powerful nation. All nations on earth will be blessed because of him.

19"I have chosen him. He must direct his children. He must see that the members of his family after him live the way I want them to. So he must direct them to do what is right and fair. Then I, the LORD, will do for Abraham what I have promised him."

20The LORD said, "The cries against Sodom and Gomorrah are very great. Their sin is so bad **21**that I will go down and see for myself. I want to see if what they have done is as bad as the cries that have reached me. If it is not, then I will know."

22The men turned away. They went toward Sodom. But Abraham remained standing in front of the LORD.

23Then Abraham came up to him. He said, "Will you sweep away godly people along with those who are evil? **24**What if there are 50 godly people in the city? Will you really sweep it away? Won't you spare the place because of the 50 godly people in it?

25"You would never kill godly people along with those who are evil, would you? You wouldn't treat godly and evil people alike. You would never do anything like that! Won't the Judge of the whole earth do what is right?"

26The LORD said, "If I find 50 godly people in the city of Sodom, I will save it. I will spare the whole place because of them."

27Then Abraham spoke up again. He said, "I have been very bold to speak to the Lord. After all, I'm only dust and ashes. **28**What if the number of godly people is five less than 50? Will you destroy the whole city because of five people?"

"If I find 45 there," he said, "I will not destroy it."

29Once again Abraham spoke to him. He asked, "What if only 40 are found there?"

He said, "If there are 40, I will not do it."

30Then Abraham said, "Lord, don't let your anger burn against me. Let me speak. What if only 30 can be found there?"

He answered, "If there are 30, I will not do it."

31Abraham said, "I have been very bold to speak to the Lord. What if only 20 are found there?"

He said, "If there are 20, I will not destroy it."

32Then he said, "Lord, don't let your anger burn against me. Let me speak just one more time. What if only ten are found there?"

He answered, "If there are ten, I will not destroy it."

33When the LORD had finished speaking with Abraham, he left. And Abraham returned home.

The LORD Destroys Sodom and Gomorrah

19 The two angels arrived at Sodom in the evening. Lot was sitting near the gate of the city.

When Lot saw them, he got up to meet them. He bowed down with his face to the ground. **2**"My lords," he said, "please come to my house. You can wash your feet and spend the night here. Then you can go on your way early in the morning."

"No," they answered. "We'll spend the night in the street."

3But Lot wouldn't give up. So they went with him and entered his house. He prepared a meal for them. He baked bread without using yeast. And they ate.

4Before Lot and his guests had gone to bed, all of the men came from every part of the city of Sodom. Young and old men alike surrounded the house. **5**They called out to Lot. They said, "Where are the men who came to you tonight? Bring them out to us. We want to have sex with them."

6Lot went outside to meet them. He shut the door behind him. **7**He said, "No, my friends. Don't do such an evil thing. **8**Look, I have two daughters. No man has ever made love to them. I'll bring them out to you now. Then do to them what you want to. But don't do anything to these men. I've brought them inside so they can be safe."

9"Get out of our way!" the men of Sodom replied. They said, "This fellow came here as an outsider. Now he wants to act like a judge! We'll treat you worse than them." They kept trying to force Lot to open the door. Then they moved forward to break it down.

10But the men inside reached out and pulled Lot back into the house. They shut the door. **11**Then they made the men who were at the door of the house blind. They blinded young and old men alike. So the men couldn't find the door.

12The two men said to Lot, "Do you

have anyone else here? Do you have sons-in-law, sons or daughters? Does anyone else in the city belong to you? Get them out of here. ¹³We are going to destroy this place. There has been a great cry to the LORD against the people of this city. So he has sent us to destroy it."

¹⁴Then Lot went out and spoke to his sons-in-law. They had promised to get married to his daughters. He said, "Hurry up! Get out of this place! The LORD is about to destroy the city!" But his sons-in-law thought he was joking.

¹⁵The sun was coming up. So the angels tried to get Lot to leave. They said, "Hurry up! Take your wife and your two daughters who are here. Get out! If you don't, you will be swept away when the city is punished."

¹⁶Lot didn't move right away. So the men grabbed him by the hand. They also took hold of the hands of his wife and two daughters. They led all of them safely out of the city. The LORD had mercy on them.

¹⁷As soon as the angels had brought them out, one of them spoke. He said, "Run for your lives! Don't look back! Don't stop anywhere in the valley! Run to the mountains! If you don't, you will be swept away!"

¹⁸But Lot said to them, "No, my lords! Please! ¹⁹You have done me a big favor. You have been very kind to me by sparing my life. But I can't run to the mountains. This horrible thing that's going to happen will catch up with me. And then I'll die. ²⁰"Look, here's a town near enough to run to. It's small. Let me run to it. It's very small, isn't it? Then my life will be spared."

²¹The LORD said to Lot, "All right. I will also give you what you are asking for. I will not destroy the town you are talking about. ²²But run there quickly. I can't do anything until you reach it."

The town was named Zoar. Zoar means "small."

²³By the time Lot reached Zoar, the sun had risen over the land. ²⁴Then the LORD sent down burning sulfur. It came down like rain on Sodom and Gomorrah. It came from the LORD out of the sky. ²⁵He destroyed those cities and the whole valley. All of the people who were living in the cities were wiped out. So were the plants in the land.

²⁶But Lot's wife looked back. When she did, she became a pillar made out of salt.

²⁷Early the next morning Abraham got up. He returned to the place where he had stood in front of the LORD. ²⁸He looked down toward Sodom and Gomorrah and the whole valley. He saw thick smoke rising from the land. It looked like smoke from a furnace.

²⁹So when God destroyed the cities of the valley, he showed concern for Abraham. He brought Lot out safely when he destroyed the cities where Lot had lived.

Lot and His Daughters

³⁰Lot and his two daughters left Zoar. They went to settle down in the mountains. Lot was afraid to stay in Zoar. So he and his daughters lived in a cave.

³¹One day the older daughter spoke to the younger one. She said, "Our father is old. There aren't any other men around here to make love to us, as people all over the earth do. ³²So let's get our father to drink wine. Then we can make love to him. We can use our father to continue our family line."

³³That night they got their father to drink wine. Then the older daughter went in and made love to him. He didn't know when she lay down or when she got up. ³⁴The next day the older daughter spoke to the younger one again. She said, "Last night I made love to my father. Let's get him to drink wine again tonight. Then you go in and make love to him. In that way, we can use our father to continue our family line."

³⁵So they got their father to drink wine that night also. Then the younger daughter went and made love to him. Again he didn't know when she lay down or when she got up.

³⁶So both of Lot's daughters became pregnant by their father. ³⁷The older daughter had a son. She named him Moab. He's the father of the Moabites of today. ³⁸The younger daughter also had a son. She named him Ben-Ammi. He's the father of the Ammonites of today.

POWER-SURGE

HELPFUL ★

YOU HAVE DONE ME A BIG FAVOR. YOU HAVE BEEN VERY KIND TO ME.
— GENESIS 19:19 —

K

KIND

Abraham and Abimelech

20 Abraham moved away from there into the Negev Desert. He lived between Kadesh and Shur. For a while he stayed in Gerar. ²There Abraham said about his wife Sarah, "She's my sister." Then Abimelech sent for Sarah and took her. He was the king of Gerar.

³God came to Abimelech in a dream one night. He said to him, "You are as good as dead because of the woman you have taken. She is already married."

⁴But Abimelech hadn't gone near her. So he said, "Lord, will you destroy a nation that hasn't done anything wrong? ⁵Didn't Abraham say to me, 'She's my sister'? And didn't she also say, 'He's my brother'? I had no idea I was doing anything wrong. I'm not guilty."

⁶Then God spoke to him in the dream. He said, "Yes, I know you had no idea you were doing anything wrong. So I have kept you from sinning against me. That is why I did not let you touch her. ⁷"Now return the man's wife to him. He is a prophet. He will pray for you, and you will live. But what if you do not return her? Then you can be sure that you and all of your people will die."

⁸Early the next morning Abimelech sent for all of his officials. He told them everything that had happened. They were really afraid. ⁹Then Abimelech called Abraham in. He said, "What have you done to us? Have I done something wrong to you? Why have you brought so much guilt on me and my kingdom? You have done things to me that shouldn't be done."

¹⁰Abimelech also asked Abraham, "Why did you do this?"

¹¹Abraham replied, "I thought, 'There isn't any respect for God in this place at all. They will kill me because of my wife.' ¹²Besides, she really is my sister. She's the daughter of my father, but not the daughter of my mother. And she became my wife.

¹³"God had me wander away from my father's house. So I said to her, 'Here is how you can show your love to me. Everywhere we go, say about me, "He's my brother." ' "

¹⁴Then Abimelech gave Abraham sheep and cattle and male and female slaves. He also returned his wife Sarah to him. ¹⁵Abimelech said, "Here is my land. Live anywhere you want to."

¹⁶He said to Sarah, "I'm giving your brother 25 pounds of silver. It will take care of the problem we caused you. And all those who are with you will know that you aren't guilty of doing anything wrong."

¹⁷Then Abraham prayed to God. And God healed Abimelech. He also healed his wife and his female slaves so they could have children again. ¹⁸The LORD had kept the women in Abimelech's house from having children. He had done it because of Abraham's wife Sarah.

Isaac Is Born

21 The LORD was gracious to Sarah, just as he had said he would be. He did for Sarah what he had promised to do. ²Sarah became pregnant. She had a son by Abraham when he was old. He was born at the exact time God had promised him.

³Abraham gave the name Isaac to the son Sarah had by him. ⁴When his son Isaac was eight days old, Abraham circumcised him. He did it exactly as God had commanded him. ⁵Abraham was 100 years old when his son Isaac was born to him.

⁶Sarah said, "God has given laughter to me. Everyone who hears about this will laugh with me."

⁷She continued, "Who would have said to Abraham that Sarah would nurse children? But I've had a son by him when he is old."

Abraham Sends Hagar and Ishmael Away

⁸Isaac grew. The time came for his mother to stop nursing him. On that day Abraham had a big dinner prepared.

⁹But Sarah saw Ishmael making fun of Isaac. Ishmael was the son Hagar had by Abraham. Hagar was Sarah's servant from Egypt.

¹⁰Sarah said to Abraham, "Get rid of that slave woman. Get rid of her son. The slave woman's son will never have a share of the family's property with my son Isaac."

¹¹What Sarah said upset Abraham very much. After all, Ishmael was his son.

¹²But God said to him, "Do not be so upset about the boy and your servant Hagar. Listen to what Sarah tells you, because your family line will continue through Isaac. ¹³I will make the son of your servant into a nation also. I will do it because he is your child."

¹⁴Early the next morning Abraham got some food and a bottle of water. The bottle was made out of animal skin. He

gave the food and water to Hagar. He placed them on her shoulders. Then he sent her away with the boy. She went on her way and wandered in the desert of Beersheba.

¹⁵When the water in the bottle was gone, she put the boy under a bush. ¹⁶Then she went off and sat down nearby. She was about as far away as a person can shoot an arrow. She thought, "I can't stand to watch the boy die." As she sat nearby, she began to sob.

¹⁷God heard the boy crying. Then the angel of God called out to Hagar from heaven. He said to her, "What is the matter, Hagar? Do not be afraid. God has heard the boy crying as he lies there. ¹⁸Lift the boy up. Take him by the hand. I will make him into a great nation."

¹⁹Then God opened Hagar's eyes. She saw a well of water. So she went and filled the bottle with water. And she gave the boy a drink.

²⁰God was with the boy as he grew up. He lived in the desert and learned to shoot with a bow. ²¹While he was living in the Desert of Paran, his mother got him a wife from Egypt.

SARAH

GENESIS 21:1-2

The LORD was gracious to Sarah, just as he had said he would be. He did for Sarah what he had promised to do. Sarah became pregnant. She had a son by Abraham when he was old. He was born at the exact time God had promised him.

Sarah sat in her tent and watched little Isaac. Her baby boy lay in front of her on the blankets. He waved his arms and legs as hard as he could. Every time he looked at her, he smiled a big toothless smile. Sarah smiled back at Isaac, her heart full of love for him.

For many years Sarah had had no children. Then, when she was very old and way past the time when women have children, she had Isaac. God had made a promise to Sarah and her husband Abraham that he would give them a son. Sarah had laughed when she heard the promise. But then God's promise came true. **SARAH WAS STILL LAUGHING.** But now she was laughing with joy instead of unbelief.

BE A SARAH

Sarah saw firsthand that God keeps his promises. Be a Sarah. Believe that God loves you enough to keep every promise he makes. And thank him for it.

SARAH DISCOVERED THAT GOD'S KEEPS HIS PROMISES AND SHE WAS THANKFUL.

Go to page 27 for the next Super Hero

KIND   K

I'VE BEEN KIND TO YOU. NOW YOU BE KIND TO ME.
—— GENESIS 21:23 ——

The Peace Treaty at Beersheba

22 At that time Abimelech and Phicol spoke to Abraham. Phicol was the commander of Abimelech's army. They said, "God is with you in everything you do. **23** Now make a promise to me here while God is watching. Take an oath that you will treat me fairly. Promise that you will treat my children and their children the same way.

"I've been kind to you. Now you be kind to me. And be kind to the country where you are living as an outsider."

24 Abraham said, "I promise with an oath that I'll do it."

25 Then Abraham objected to Abimelech about what Abimelech's servants had done. They had taken over a well of water.

26 But Abimelech said, "I don't know who has done this. You didn't tell me. Today is the first time I heard about it."

27 So Abraham gave Abimelech sheep and cattle. The two men made a peace treaty. **28** Then Abraham took out seven female lambs from his flock.

29 Abimelech asked Abraham, "What's the meaning of these seven female lambs? Why have you taken them out and put them by themselves?"

30 Abraham replied, "Accept the seven lambs from me. They will be a witness that I dug this well."

31 That place was named Beersheba. That's because there the two men made a promise with an oath.

32 After the peace treaty had been made at Beersheba, Abimelech went back to the land of the Philistines. His army commander Phicol went with him.

33 Abraham planted a tamarisk tree in Beersheba. There he worshiped the LORD, the God who lives forever. **34** Abraham stayed in the land of the Philistines for a long time.

God Puts Abraham to the Test

22 Some time later God put Abraham to the test. He said to him, "Abraham!"

"Here I am," Abraham replied.

2 Then God said, "Take your son, your only son. He is the one you love. Take Isaac. Go to Moriah. Give him to me there as a burnt offering. Sacrifice him on one of the mountains I will tell you about."

3 Early the next morning Abraham got up. He put a saddle on his donkey. He took two of his servants and his son Isaac with him. He cut enough wood for the burnt offering. Then he started out for the place God had told him about.

4 On the third day Abraham looked up. He saw the place a long way off. **5** He said to his servants, "Stay here with the donkey. The boy and I will go over there and worship. Then we'll come back to you."

6 Abraham put the wood for the burnt offering on his son Isaac. He himself carried the fire and the knife. The two of them walked on together.

7 Then Isaac spoke up. He said to his father Abraham, "Father?"

"Yes, my son?" Abraham replied.

"The fire and wood are here," Isaac said. "But where is the lamb for the burnt offering?"

8 Abraham answered, "God himself will provide the lamb for the burnt offering, my son." The two of them walked on together.

9 They reached the place God had told Abraham about. There Abraham built an altar. He arranged the wood on it. He tied up his son Isaac. He placed him on the altar, on top of the wood. **10** Then he reached out his hand. He took the knife to kill his son.

11 But the angel of the LORD called out to him from heaven. He said, "Abraham! Abraham!"

"Here I am," Abraham replied.

12 "Do not lay a hand on the boy," he said. "Do not do anything to him. Now I know that you have respect for God. You have not held back from me your son, your only son."

13 Abraham looked up. There in a bush he saw a ram. It was caught by its horns. He went over and took the ram. He sacrificed it as a burnt offering instead of his son.

14 So Abraham named that place The LORD Will Provide. To this day people say, "It will be provided on the mountain of the LORD."

15 The angel of the LORD called out to

ISAAC

GENESIS 22:12

B

✔

⚡

"Now I know that you have respect for God. You have not held back from me your son, your only son."

Isaac looked up at his father, Abraham, as they walked along. Isaac knew they were going to make a sacrifice to God. He carried the wood, and his father carried a knife and the fire. But Abraham acted strange; he was very quiet and looked very concerned. Isaac noticed one thing that was missing.

"Father," Isaac asked, "where is the lamb for the sacrifice?"

Abraham's face twisted in pain at the question. "God himself will provide the lamb," he answered.

Isaac didn't understand what his father meant, but he trusted him and bravely followed him up the mountain. Little did Isaac know that he himself would be the sacrifice. God was testing Abraham to see whom Abraham loved more—his son or God. More than anything else, Abraham loved God. So now he was trudging up a mountain to sacrifice his own son.

Isaac was confused as he watched his father build an altar of stones and layer the wood on top. Then Abraham looked at Isaac. Only then did Isaac realize what was happening. His father took some rope, tied Isaac up and Isaac bravely climbed up on the altar. TEARS STREAMED DOWN BOTH OF THEIR FACES AS ABRAHAM PICKED UP THE KNIFE.

Just then they both heard a voice. "Abraham!" the voice called. "I know now that you love me more than anything. Don't hurt your son Isaac."

Cutting the ropes with his knife, Abraham grabbed Isaac and hugged him fiercely. That day they did make a sacrifice—a ram that was caught in some nearby bushes.

BE AN ISAAC

Both Isaac and Abraham obeyed God. Abraham was willing to sacrifice his only son, just because God asked him to. The Bible doesn't tell us anything about how Isaac felt that day. But it never says that Isaac fought or rebelled against his father. He was obedient. Remember Isaac and try to be obedient as he was.

ISAAC WAS OBEDIENT.
THE WHOLE STORY: GENESIS 22:1-14

Go to page 32 for the next Super Hero

POWER-SURGE

OBEYS ✔

ALL NATIONS ON EARTH WILL BE BLESSED BECAUSE...YOU HAVE OBEYED ME.
— GENESIS 22:18 —

Abraham from heaven a second time. **16**He said, "I am taking an oath in my own name. I will bless you because of what you have done," announces the LORD. "You have not held back your son, your only son.

17"So I will certainly bless you. I will make your children after you as many as the stars in the sky. I will make them as many as the grains of sand on the seashore. Your children will take over the cities of their enemies. **18**All nations on earth will be blessed because of your children. All of that will happen because you have obeyed me."

19Then Abraham returned to his servants. They started out together for Beersheba. And Abraham stayed in Beersheba.

Nahor's Sons

20Some time later Abraham was told, "Milcah has become a mother. She has had sons by your brother Nahor. **21**Uz was born first. Then came his brother Buz. Next came Kemuel, the father of Aram. **22**The other sons are Kesed, Hazo, Pildash, Jidlaph and Bethuel." **23**Bethuel became the father of Rebekah. Milcah had the eight sons by Abraham's brother Nahor. **24**Nahor had a concubine named Reumah. She also had sons. They were Tebah, Gaham, Tahash and Maacah.

Sarah Dies

23 Sarah lived to be 127 years old. **2**She died at Kiriath Arba. Kiriath Arba is also called Hebron. It's in the land of Canaan.

Sarah's death filled Abraham with sorrow. He went to the place where her body was lying. There he sobbed over her.

3Then Abraham got up from beside his dead wife. He spoke to the Hittites. He said, **4**"I'm an outsider. I'm a stranger among you. Sell me some property here as

a place for a family tomb. Then I can bury my wife's body."

5The Hittites replied to Abraham, **6**"Sir, listen to us. You are a mighty prince among us. Bury your dead wife in the best of our tombs. None of us will refuse to sell you his tomb for burying her."

7Then Abraham bowed down in front of the Hittites, the people of the land. **8**He said to them, "If you are willing to let me bury my dead wife, then listen to me. Speak to Zohar's son Ephron for me. **9**Ask him to sell me the cave of Machpelah. It belongs to him and is at the end of his field. Ask him to sell it to me for the full price. I want it as a place to bury my dead wife among you."

10Ephron the Hittite was sitting there among his people. He replied to Abraham. All of the Hittites who had come to the gate of his city heard him. **11**"No, sir," Ephron said. "Listen to me. I will sell you the field. I'll also sell you the cave that's in the field. I will sell it to you in front of my people. Bury your wife."

12Again Abraham bowed down in front of the people of the land. **13**He spoke to Ephron so they could hear him. He said, "Please listen to me. I'll pay the price of the field. Accept it from me. Then I can bury my dead wife there."

14Ephron answered Abraham, **15**"Sir, listen to me. The land is worth ten pounds of silver. But what is that between you and me? Bury your wife."

16Abraham agreed to Ephron's offer. He weighed out for him the price he had named. The Hittites there had heard it. The price was ten pounds of silver. Abraham measured it by the weights that were used by those who bought and sold.

17So Ephron sold his field in Machpelah near Mamre to Abraham. He bought the field and the cave that was in it. He also bought all of the trees that were inside the borders of the field. Everything was sold **18**to Abraham as his property. He bought it in front of all of the Hittites who had come to the gate of the city.

19Then Abraham buried the body of his wife Sarah. He buried her in the cave in the field of Machpelah near Mamre in the land of Canaan. Mamre is at Hebron. **20**So the field and the cave that was in it were sold to Abraham by the Hittites. The property became a place for his family tomb.

Abraham's Servant Finds a Wife for Isaac

24 By that time Abraham was very old. The LORD had blessed him in every way. ²The best servant in his house was in charge of everything he had.

Abraham said to him, "Put your hand under my thigh. ³The LORD is the God of heaven and the God of earth. I want you to make a promise with an oath in his name.

"I'm living among the people of Canaan. But I want you to promise me that you won't get a wife for my son from their daughters. ⁴Instead, promise me that you will go to my country and to my own relatives. Get a wife for my son Isaac from there."

⁵The servant asked him, "What if the woman doesn't want to come back with me to this land? Then should I take your son back to the country you came from?"

⁶"Make sure you don't take my son back there," Abraham said. ⁷"The LORD, the God of heaven, took me away from my father's family. He brought me out of my own land. And he made me a promise with an oath. He said, 'I will give this land to your family after you.' The LORD will send his angel ahead of you. So you will be able to get a wife for my son from there.

⁸"The woman may not want to come back with you. If she doesn't, you will be free from your oath. But don't take my son back there."

⁹So the servant put his hand under Abraham's thigh. He promised with an oath to do what his master wanted.

¹⁰The servant took ten of his master's camels and left. He took with him all kinds of good things from his master. He started out for Aram Naharaim. He made his way to the town of Nahor.

¹¹He stopped near the well outside the town. There he made the camels get down on their knees. It was almost evening. It was the time when women go out to get water.

¹²Then he prayed, "LORD, you are the God of my master Abraham. Give me success today. Be kind to my master Abraham. ¹³I'm standing beside this spring. The daughters of the people who live in the town are coming out here to get water. ¹⁴"I will speak to a young woman. I'll say, 'Please lower your jar so I can have a drink.' Suppose she says, 'Have a drink of water. And I'll get some for your camels too.' Then let her be the one you have chosen for your servant Isaac. That's how I'll know you have been kind to my master."

¹⁵Before he had finished praying, Rebekah came out. She had a jar on her shoulder. She was the daughter of Bethu-el, the son of Milcah. Milcah was the wife of Abraham's brother Nahor. ¹⁶The young woman was very beautiful. She was a virgin. No man had made love to her. She went down to the spring. She filled her jar and came up again.

¹⁷The servant hurried to meet her. He said, "Please give me a little water from your jar."

¹⁸"Have a drink, sir," she said. She quickly lowered the jar to her hands. And she gave him a drink.

¹⁹After she had given him a drink, she said, "I'll get water for your camels too. I'll keep doing it until they finish drinking." ²⁰So she quickly emptied her jar into the stone tub. Then she ran back to the well to get more water. She got enough for all of his camels.

²¹The man didn't say a word. He watched her closely. He wanted to learn whether the LORD had given him success on the journey he had made.

²²The camels finished drinking. Then the man took out a gold nose ring. It weighed a fifth of an ounce. He also took out two gold bracelets. They weighed four ounces.

²³Then he asked, "Whose daughter are you? And please tell me something else. Is there room in your father's house for us? Can we spend the night there?"

²⁴She answered, "I'm the daughter of Bethuel. He's the son Milcah had by Nahor." ²⁵She continued, "We have plenty of straw and feed for your camels. We also have room for you to spend the night."

²⁶Then the man bowed down and worshiped the LORD. ²⁷He said, "I praise the LORD, the God of my master Abraham. He hasn't stopped being kind and faithful to my master. The LORD has led me on this journey. He has brought me to the house of my master's relatives."

²⁸The young woman ran home. She told her mother's family what had happened.

²⁹Rebekah had a brother named Laban. He hurried out to the spring to meet the man. ³⁰Laban had seen the nose ring. He had seen the bracelets on his sister's arms. And he had heard Rebekah tell what the man had said to her. So he went out to the man. He found him standing by the camels near the spring. ³¹"The LORD has given you his blessing," he said. "So come. Why are you standing out here? I've prepared my house for you. I also have a place for the camels."

³²So the man went to the house. The

camels were unloaded. Straw and feed were brought for the camels. And water was brought for him and his men to wash their feet.

33 Then food was placed in front of him. But he said, "I won't eat until I've told you what I have to say."

"Then tell us," Laban said.

34 So he said, "I am Abraham's servant. **35** The LORD has blessed my master greatly. He has become wealthy. The LORD has given him sheep and cattle. He has given him silver and gold. He has also given him male and female servants, and camels and donkeys.

36 "My master's wife Sarah had a son by him when she was old. He has given that son everything he owns. **37** My master made me take an oath. He said, 'I'm living in the land of the people of Canaan. But promise me that you won't get a wife for my son from their daughters. **38** Instead, go to my father's family and to my own relatives. Get a wife for my son there.'

39 "Then I asked my master, 'What if the woman won't come back with me?'

40 "He replied, 'I have walked with the LORD. He will send his angel with you. He will give you success on your journey. So you will be able to get a wife for my son. You will get her from my own relatives and from my father's family.

41 'When you go to my relatives, suppose they refuse to give her to you. Then you will be free from your oath.'

42 "Today I came to the spring. I said, 'LORD, you are the God of my master Abraham. Please give me success on this journey I've made.

43 " 'I'm standing beside this spring. A young woman will come out to get water. I will speak to her. I'll say, "Please let me drink a little water from your jar." **44** Suppose she says, "Have a drink of water. And I'll get some for your camels too." Then let her be the one the LORD has chosen for my master's son.'

45 "Before I finished praying in my heart, Rebekah came out. She had a jar on her shoulder. She went down to the spring and got water. I said to her, 'Please give me a drink.'

46 "She quickly lowered her jar from her shoulder. She said, 'Have a drink. And I'll get water for your camels too.' So I drank. She also got water for the camels.

47 "I asked her, 'Whose daughter are you?'

"She said, 'The daughter of Bethuel. He's the son Milcah had by Nahor.'

"Then I put the ring in her nose. I put the bracelets on her arms. **48** And I bowed down and worshiped the LORD. I praised the LORD, the God of my master Abraham. He had led me on the right road. He had led me to get for my master's son the granddaughter of my master's brother.

49 "Now will you be kind and faithful to my master? If you will, tell me. And if you won't, tell me. Then I'll know which way to turn."

50 Laban and Bethuel answered, "The LORD has done all of this. We can't say anything to you one way or the other. **51** Here is Rebekah. Take her and go. Let her become the wife of your master's son, just as the LORD has said."

52 Abraham's servant heard what they said. So he bowed down to the LORD with his face to the ground. **53** He brought out gold and silver jewelry. He brought out articles of clothing. He gave all of it to Rebekah. He also gave expensive gifts to her brother and her mother.

54 Then Abraham's servant and the men who were with him ate and drank. They spent the night there.

They got up the next morning. Abraham's servant said, "Send me back to my master."

55 But her brother and her mother replied, "Let the young woman stay with us ten days or so. Then you can go."

56 But he said to them, "Don't make me wait. The LORD has given me success on my journey. Send me on my way so I can go to my master."

57 Then they said, "Let's get Rebekah. We'll ask her about it." **58** So they sent for her. They asked her, "Will you go with this man?"

"Yes," she said.

59 So they sent their sister Rebekah on her way with Abraham's servant and his men. They also sent Rebekah's attendant with her. **60** And they gave Rebekah their blessing. They said to her,

"Dear sister, may your family grow
　by thousands and thousands.
May your children after you take over
　the cities of their enemies."

61 Then Rebekah and her female servants got ready. They got on their camels to go with the man. So the servant took Rebekah and left.

62 By that time Isaac had come from Beer Lahai Roi. He was living in the Negev Desert.

63 One evening he went out to the field. He wanted to spend some time thinking.

When he looked up, he saw camels approaching. **64**Rebekah also looked up and saw Isaac. She got down from her camel. **65**She asked the servant, "Who is that man in the field coming to meet us?"

"He's my master," the servant answered. So she took her veil and covered her face.

66Then the servant told Isaac everything he had done.

67Isaac brought Rebekah into the tent that had belonged to his mother Sarah. And he married Rebekah. She became his wife, and he loved her. So Isaac was comforted after his mother died.

Abraham Dies

25 Abraham married another woman. Her name was Keturah. **2**She had Zimran, Jokshan, Medan, Midian, Ishbak and Shuah by Abraham. **3**Jokshan was the father of Sheba and Dedan. The children of Dedan were the Asshurites, the Letushites and the Leummites. **4**The sons of Midian were Ephah, Epher, Hanoch, Abida and Eldaah. All of them came from Keturah.

5Abraham left everything he owned to Isaac. **6**But while he was still living, he gave gifts to the sons of his concubines. Then he sent them away from his son Isaac. He sent them to the land of the east.

7Abraham lived a total of 175 years. **8**He took his last breath and died when he was very old. He had lived a very long time. Then he joined the members of his family who had already died.

9Abraham's sons Isaac and Ishmael buried his body. They put it in the cave of Machpelah near Mamre. It was in the field of Ephron, the son of Zohar the Hittite. **10**Abraham had bought it from the Hittites. He was buried there with his wife Sarah.

11After Abraham died, God blessed his son Isaac. At that time Isaac lived near Beer Lahai Roi.

The Sons of Ishmael

12Here is the story of Abraham's son Ishmael. Hagar had Ishmael by Abraham. She was Sarah's servant from Egypt.

13Here are the names of the sons of Ishmael. They are listed in the order they were born. Nebaioth was Ishmael's oldest son. Then came Kedar, Adbeel, Mibsam, **14**Mishma, Dumah, Massa, **15**Hadad, Tema, Jetur, Naphish and Kedemah. **16**All of them were Ishmael's sons. They were rulers of 12 tribes. They all lived in their own settlements and camps.

17Ishmael lived a total of 137 years. Then he took his last breath and died. He joined the members of his family who had already died. **18**His children settled in the area between Havilah and Shur. It was near the eastern border of Egypt, as you go toward Asshur.

Ishmael's children weren't friendly toward any of the tribes that were related to them.

Jacob and Esau

19Here is the story of Abraham's son Isaac.

Abraham was the father of Isaac. **20**Isaac was 40 years old when he married Rebekah. She was the daughter of Bethuel the Aramean from Paddan Aram. She was also the sister of Laban the Aramean.

21Rebekah couldn't have children. So Isaac prayed to the Lord for her. And the Lord answered his prayer. His wife Rebekah became pregnant.

22The babies struggled with each other inside her. She said, "Why is this happening to me?" So she went to ask the Lord what she should do.

23The Lord said to her,

"Two nations are in your body.
　Two tribes that are now inside you
　　will be separated.
One nation will be stronger than the
　　other.
　The older son will serve the younger
　　one."

24The time came for Rebekah to have her babies. There were twin boys in her body. **25**The first one to come out was red. His whole body was covered with hair. So they named him Esau. **26**Then his brother came out. His hand was holding onto Esau's heel. So he was named Jacob. Isaac was 60 years old when Rebekah had them.

27The boys grew up. Esau became a skillful hunter. He was a man who liked the open country. But Jacob was a quiet man. He stayed at home among the tents. **28**Isaac liked the meat of wild animals. So Esau was his favorite son. But Rebekah's favorite was Jacob.

29One day Jacob was cooking some stew. Esau came in from the open country. He was very hungry. **30**He said to Jacob, "Quick! Let me have some of that red stew! I'm very hungry!" That's why he was also named Edom.

REBEKAH

GENESIS 24:67

Isaac brought Rebekah into the tent that had belonged to his mother Sarah. And he married Rebekah. She became his wife, and he loved her. So Isaac was comforted after his mother died.

Rebekah carried a jar full of fresh water. She enjoyed this job every day—walking to the well when the sun began to go down. She whistled as she went along. A stranger greeted Rebekah at the well.

"PLEASE, MAY I HAVE A LITTLE WATER FROM YOUR JUG?" HE ASKED.

Rebekah smiled at the stranger, then put her jug down and gave him a drink. She offered to give his camels water, too. The stranger and his animals looked tired and thirsty.

Rebekah poured water from her jug into a nearby stone tub. As the camels began to drink, she went back to the well for more water. Without complaining, Rebekah again and again filled her jug at the well and poured it into the stone tub, until the camels had had enough.

The stranger watched her closely.

Rebekah didn't know it, but the stranger was looking for a wife for his master, Isaac. He presented her with a gold ring for her nose and two gold bracelets. She couldn't believe how quickly everything happened. Only a few days later Rebekah traveled on a camel to meet the man she would marry.

When Rebekah saw Isaac for the first time, she quickly got down from her camel and covered her face with a veil. First Isaac spoke to his servant. Then he turned to look at Rebekah and meet her. Soon after, Isaac married Rebekah. She loved Isaac almost from the beginning, and he loved her. They lived together in his tent. His mother had died only a short time before, and Isaac had been sad. But now his tent was filled with Rebekah's laughter and smiles. And Isaac felt much better.

BE A REBEKAH

Rebekah was helpful and kind. She made Isaac happy. You can be like Rebekah. Tell a joke, give a hug, give a compliment—do something to make others happy.

REBEKAH WAS A HELPFUL AND KIND PERSON.
THE WHOLE STORY: GENESIS 24:1-67

Go to page 37 for the next person

³¹Jacob replied, "First sell me the rights that belong to you as the oldest son in the family."

³²"Look, I'm dying of hunger," Esau said. "What good are those rights to me?"

³³But Jacob said, "First promise me with an oath that you are selling me your rights." So Esau promised to do it. He sold Jacob all of the rights that belonged to him as the oldest son.

³⁴Jacob gave Esau some bread and some lentil stew. Esau ate and drank. Then he got up and left.

So Esau didn't care anything at all about the rights that belonged to him as the oldest son.

Isaac and Abimelech

26 There was very little food in the land. The same thing had been true earlier, in Abraham's time. Isaac went to Abimelech in Gerar. Abimelech was the king of the Philistines.

²The LORD appeared to Isaac. He said, "Do not go down to Egypt. Live in the land where I tell you to live. ³Stay here for a while. I will be with you and give you my blessing. I will give all of these lands to you and your children after you. And I will keep the promise I made with an oath to your father Abraham. ⁴I will make your children after you as many as the stars in the sky. And I will give them all these lands. All nations on earth will be blessed because of your children.

⁵"I will do all of those things because Abraham obeyed me. He did what I required. He kept my commands, my rules and my laws." ⁶So Isaac stayed in Gerar.

⁷The men of that place asked him about his wife. He said, "She's my sister." He was afraid to say, "She's my wife." He thought, "The men of this place might kill me because of Rebekah. She's a beautiful woman."

⁸Isaac had been there a long time. One day Abimelech, the king of the Philistines, looked down from a window. He saw Isaac hugging and kissing his wife Rebekah.

⁹So Abimelech sent for Isaac. He said, "She's really your wife, isn't she? Why did you say, 'She's my sister'?"

Isaac answered him, "I thought I might lose my life because of her."

¹⁰Then Abimelech said, "What have you done to us? What if one of the men had sex with your wife? Then you would have made us guilty."

¹¹So Abimelech gave orders to all of the people. He said, "You can be sure that anyone who harms this man or his wife will be put to death."

¹²Isaac planted crops in that land. That same year he gathered 100 times more than he planted. That was because the LORD blessed him.

¹³Isaac became rich. His wealth continued to grow until he became very rich. ¹⁴He had many flocks and herds and servants.

Isaac had so much that the Philistines became jealous of him. ¹⁵So they stopped up all of the wells the servants of his father Abraham had dug. They filled them with dirt.

¹⁶Then Abimelech said to Isaac, "Move away from us. You have become too powerful for us."

¹⁷So Isaac moved away from there. He camped in the Valley of Gerar and settled there. ¹⁸Isaac opened up the wells again. They had been dug in the time of his father Abraham. The Philistines had stopped them up after Abraham died. Isaac gave the wells the same names his father had given them.

¹⁹Isaac's servants dug for wells in the valley. There they discovered a well of fresh water. ²⁰But the people of Gerar who took care of their herds argued with the people who took care of Isaac's herds. "The water is ours!" the people of Gerar said. So Isaac named the well Esek. That's because they argued with him.

²¹Then Isaac's servants dug another well. They argued about that one too. So he named it Sitnah.

²²He moved on from there and dug another well. But no one argued about that one. So he named it Rehoboth. He said, "Now the LORD has given us room. Now we will do well in the land."

²³From there Isaac went up to Beersheba. ²⁴That night the LORD appeared to him. He said, "I am the God of your father Abraham. Do not be afraid. I am with you. I will bless you. I will increase the number of your children because of my servant Abraham."

²⁵Isaac built an altar there and worshiped the LORD. There he set up his tent. And there his servants dug a well.

²⁶During that time, Abimelech had come to him from Gerar. Ahuzzath had come with him. So had Phicol, Abimelech's army commander. Ahuzzath was Abimelech's personal adviser.

²⁷Isaac asked them, "Why have you come to me? You were angry with me and sent me away."

28They answered, "We saw clearly that the LORD was with you. So we said, 'We should make an agreement by taking an oath.' The agreement should be between us and you. We want to make a peace treaty with you. **29**Promise that you won't harm us. We didn't harm you. We always treated you well. We sent you away in peace. Now the LORD has blessed you."

30Then Isaac had a big dinner prepared for them. They ate and drank. **31**Early the next morning the men made an agreement with an oath. Then Isaac sent the men of Gerar on their way. And they left in peace.

32That day Isaac's servants came to him. They told him about the well they had dug. They said, "We've found water!" **33**So he named it Shibah. To this day the name of the town has been Beersheba.

34When Esau was 40 years old, he got married to Judith. She was the daughter of Beeri the Hittite. He also married Basemath. She was the daughter of Elon the Hittite. **35**Isaac and Rebekah became very upset because Esau had married Hittite women.

Isaac Gives Jacob His Blessing

27 Isaac had become old. His eyes were so weak he couldn't see anymore. One day he called for his older son Esau. He said to him, "My son."

"Here I am," he answered.

2Isaac said, "I'm an old man now. And I don't know when I'll die. **3**Now then, get your weapons. Get your bow and arrows. Go out to the open country. Hunt some wild animals for me. **4**Prepare for me the kind of tasty food I like. Bring it to me to eat. Then I'll give you my blessing before I die."

5Rebekah was listening when Isaac spoke to his son Esau. Esau left for the open country. He went to hunt for a wild animal and bring it back.

6Then Rebekah said to her son Jacob, "Look, I heard your father speaking to your brother Esau. **7**He said, 'Bring me a wild animal. Prepare some tasty food for me to eat. Then I'll give you my blessing before I die. The LORD will be my witness.' "

8Rebekah continued, "My son, listen carefully. Do what I tell you. **9**Go out to the flock. Bring me two of the finest young goats. I will prepare tasty food for your father. I'll make it just the way he likes it. **10**I want you to take it to your father to eat. Then he'll give you his blessing before he dies."

11Jacob said to his mother Rebekah, "My brother Esau's body is covered with hair. But my skin is smooth. **12**What if my father touches me? He would know I was trying to trick him. That would bring a curse down on me instead of a blessing."

13His mother said to him, "My son, let the curse fall on me. Just do what I say. Go and get the goats for me."

14So he went and got the goats. He brought them to his mother. And she prepared some tasty food. She made it just the way his father liked it.

15The clothes of her older son Esau were in her house. She took the best of them and put them on her younger son Jacob. **16**She covered his hands with the skins of the goats. She also covered the smooth part of his neck with them.

17Then she handed to her son Jacob the tasty food and the bread she had made.

18He went to his father and said, "My father."

"Yes, my son," Isaac answered. "Who is it?"

19Jacob said to his father, "I'm your oldest son Esau. I've done as you told me. Please sit up. Eat some of my wild meat. Then give me your blessing."

20Isaac asked his son, "How did you find it so quickly, my son?"

"The LORD your God gave me success," he replied.

21Then Isaac said to Jacob, "Come near so I can touch you, my son. I want to know whether you really are my son Esau."

22Jacob went close to his father. Isaac touched him and said, "The voice is the voice of Jacob. But the hands are the hands of Esau."

23Isaac didn't recognize him. His hands were covered with hair like those of his brother Esau. So Isaac blessed him. **24**"Are you really my son Esau?" he asked.

"I am," Jacob replied.

25Isaac said, "My son, bring me some of your wild meat to eat. Then I'll give you my blessing."

Jacob brought it to him. So Isaac ate. Jacob also brought some wine. And Isaac drank. **26**Then Jacob's father Isaac said to him, "Come here, my son. Kiss me."

27So Jacob went to him and kissed him. When Isaac smelled the clothes, he gave Jacob his blessing. He said,

"It really is the smell of my son.
    It's like the smell of a field
    that the LORD has blessed.
28 May God give you dew from heaven.

May he give you the richness of the
earth.
May he give you plenty of grain and
fresh wine.
29 May nations serve you.
May they bow down to you.
Rule over your brothers.
May the sons of your mother bow
down to you.
May those who call down curses on
you be cursed.
And may those who bless you be
blessed."

30When Isaac finished blessing him,
Jacob left his father. Just then his brother
Esau came in from hunting. 31He too prepared some tasty food. He brought it to
his father. Then Esau said to him, "My
father, sit up. Eat some of my wild meat.
Then give me your blessing."
32His father Isaac asked him, "Who are
you?"
"I'm your son," he answered. "I'm your
oldest son. I'm Esau."
33Isaac was shaking all over. He said,
"Then who was it that hunted a wild animal and brought it to me? I ate it just
before you came. I gave him my blessing.
And he will certainly be blessed!"
34Esau heard his father's words. Then
he began crying loudly and bitterly. He
said to his father, "Bless me! Bless me too,
my father!"
35But Isaac said, "Your brother came
and tricked me. He took your blessing."
36Esau said, "Isn't Jacob just the right
name for him? He has cheated me two
times. First, he took my rights as the oldest son. And now he's taken my blessing!"
Then Esau asked, "Haven't you saved any
blessing for me?"
37Isaac answered Esau, "I've made him
ruler over you. I've made all of his relatives
serve him. And I've provided him with
grain and fresh wine. So what can I possibly do for you, my son?"
38Esau said to his father, "Do you have
only one blessing, my father? Bless me
too, my father!" Then Esau sobbed loudly.
39His father Isaac answered him,

"You will live far away from the
richness of the earth.
You will live far away from the dew
of heaven above.
40 You will live by the sword.
And you will serve your brother.
But you will grow restless.
Then you will throw off the heavy
load
he put on your shoulders."

Jacob Runs Away to Laban

41Esau was angry with Jacob. He was
angry because of the blessing his father
had given to Jacob. He said to himself,
"My father will soon die. The days of sorrow over him are near. Then I'll kill my
brother Jacob."
42Rebekah was told what her older son
Esau had said. So she sent for her younger
son Jacob. She said to him, "Your brother
Esau is comforting himself with the
thought of killing you.
43"Now then, my son, do what I say. Go
at once to my brother Laban in Haran.
44Stay with him until your brother's anger
calms down. 45Stay until your brother
isn't angry with you anymore. When he
forgets what you did to him, I'll let you
know. Then you can come back from
there. Why should I lose both of you in
one day?"
46Then Rebekah spoke to Isaac. She
said, "I'm sick of living because of Esau's
Hittite wives. Suppose Jacob also marries a
Hittite woman. If he does, my life won't
be worth living."

28 So Isaac called for Jacob and
blessed him. He commanded
him, "Don't get married to a woman from
Canaan. 2Go at once to Paddan Aram. Go
to the house of your mother's father
Bethuel. Find a wife for yourself there.
Take her from among the daughters of
your mother's brother Laban.
3"May the Mighty God bless you. May
he give you children. May he increase
your numbers until you become a community of nations. 4May he give you and
your children after you the blessing he
gave to Abraham. Then you can take over
the land where you now live as an outsider. It's the land God gave to Abraham."
5Isaac sent Jacob on his way. Jacob went
to Paddan Aram. He went to Laban, the
son of Bethuel the Aramean. Laban was
the brother of Rebekah. And Rebekah was
the mother of Jacob and Esau.
6Esau found out that Isaac had blessed
Jacob and had sent him to Paddan Aram.
Isaac wanted him to get a wife from there.
Esau heard that when Isaac blessed Jacob,
he commanded him, "Don't get married
to a woman from Canaan." 7Esau also
learned that Jacob had obeyed his father
and mother and had gone to Paddan
Aram.
8Then Esau realized how much his
father Isaac disliked the women of
Canaan. 9So he went to Ishmael and married Mahalath. She was the sister of Nebaioth and the daughter of Abraham's son

Ishmael. Esau added her to the wives he already had.

Jacob Has a Dream at Bethel

¹⁰Jacob left Beersheba and started out for Haran. ¹¹He reached a certain place and stopped for the night. The sun had already set. He took one of the stones there and placed it under his head. Then he lay down to sleep.

¹²In a dream he saw a stairway standing on the earth. Its top reached to heaven. The angels of God were going up and coming down on it.

¹³The LORD stood above the stairway. He said, "I am the LORD. I am the God of your grandfather Abraham and the God of Isaac. I will give you and your children after you the land on which you are lying. ¹⁴They will be like the dust of the earth that can't be counted. They will spread out to the west and to the east. They will spread out to the north and to the south. All nations on earth will be blessed because of you and your children after you.

¹⁵"I am with you. I will watch over you everywhere you go. And I will bring you back to this land. I will not leave you until I have done what I have promised you."

¹⁶Jacob woke up from his sleep. Then he thought, "The LORD is certainly in this place. And I didn't even know it."

¹⁷Jacob was afraid. He said, "How holy this place is! This must be the house of God. This is the gate of heaven."

¹⁸Early the next morning Jacob took the stone he had placed under his head. He set it up as a pillar. And he poured oil on top of it. ¹⁹He named that place Bethel. But the city used to be called Luz.

²⁰Then Jacob made a promise. He said, "May God be with me. May he watch over me on this journey I'm taking. May he give me food to eat and clothes to wear. ²¹May he do as he has promised so that I can return safely to my father's home. Then you, LORD, will be my God. ²²This stone I've set up as a pillar will be God's house. And I'll give you a tenth of everything you give me."

Jacob Arrives in Paddan Aram

29 Then Jacob continued on his journey. He came to the land where the eastern tribes lived. ²There he saw a well in the field. Three flocks of sheep were lying near it. The flocks were given water from the well. The stone over the opening of the well was large. ³All of the flocks would gather

there. The shepherds would roll the stone away from the well's opening. They would give water to the sheep. Then they would put the stone back in its place over the opening of the well.

⁴Jacob asked the shepherds, "My friends, where are you from?"

"We're from Haran," they replied.

⁵He said to them, "Do you know Nahor's grandson Laban?"

"Yes, we know him," they answered.

⁶Then Jacob asked them, "How is he?"

"He's fine," they said. "Here comes his daughter Rachel with the sheep now."

⁷"Look," he said, "the sun is still high in the sky. It's not time for the flocks to be brought together. Give water to the sheep and take them back to the grasslands."

⁸"We can't," they replied. "We have to wait until all of the flocks are brought together. The stone has to be rolled away from the opening of the well. Then we'll give water to the sheep."

⁹He was still talking with them when Rachel came with her father's sheep. It was her job to take care of the flock. ¹⁰Rachel was the daughter of Laban. He was the brother of Jacob's mother.

When Jacob saw Rachel with Laban's sheep, he went over to the well. He rolled the stone away from the opening. He gave water to his uncle's sheep.

¹¹Jacob kissed Rachel. Then he began to sob loudly. ¹²He had told Rachel he was a relative of her father. He had also said he was Rebekah's son. Rachel ran and told her father what Jacob had said.

¹³As soon as Laban heard the news about his sister's son Jacob, he hurried to meet him. Laban hugged Jacob and kissed him. Then he brought him to his home. There Jacob told him everything. ¹⁴Then Laban said to him, "You are my own flesh and blood."

Jacob Gets Married to Leah and Rachel

Jacob stayed with Laban for a whole month. ¹⁵Then Laban said to him, "You are one of my relatives. But is that any reason for you to work for me for nothing? Tell me what your pay should be."

¹⁶Laban had two daughters. The name of the older one was Leah. And the name of the younger one was Rachel. ¹⁷Leah had weak eyes. But Rachel was beautiful. She had a nice figure.

¹⁸Jacob was in love with Rachel. He said to Laban, "I'll work for you for seven years to get your younger daughter Rachel."

¹⁹Laban said, "It's better for me to give

RACHEL

GENESIS 29:17-18; 30:1

> **Rachel was beautiful. She had a nice figure. Jacob was in love with Rachel....[But] she couldn't have any children. So she became jealous of her sister.**

Rachel walked down the path to the well with her sheep. For once not even the smallest one tried to run away.

A stranger stepped in front of Rachel when she arrived at the well. There were other shepherds and their sheep at the well, but the stranger moved the stone from the opening so that Rachel could water her sheep.

Suddenly the stranger took Rachel by the shoulders and kissed her! He said, "Don't worry. I'm your father's relative, and I've come to visit him."

Each day, Rachel watched for Jacob as she went to take care of her sheep. Jacob watched for Rachel, too. He thought she was beautiful, and he was in love with her. He told Laban he wanted to marry her and would work seven years for free if Laban would let Rachel be his wife.

Seven years went by. **AND NOW THE BEST DAY OF RACHEL'S LIFE HAD TURNED INTO THE WORST DAY OF HER LIFE.** She sat in her tent and cried because her father was tricking Jacob into marrying her sister Leah instead of her. He wanted Jacob to work for him another seven years for Rachel. Jacob loved Rachel enough to do it. Shortly after the wedding, Laban allowed Jacob to marry Rachel. But Jacob still had to work for Laban another seven years.

Rachel and Jacob got married. Jacob worked for Laban another seven years. But they weren't a very happy family. Rachel and Leah fought for Jacob's attention and his love. Leah gave Jacob lots of children, which was important to Jacob. Rachel only gave him two. But Jacob loved Rachel more than Leah.

RACHEL

Rachel spent most of her years unhappy because she didn't have children and she had to share her husband with her sister. Though she was beautiful on the outside, Rachel doesn't seem to have been very beautiful on the inside. Don't be like her. You don't want to be just a good-looking *face*, like Rachel. You want to be a beautiful *person*.

RACHEL WAS A BEAUTIFUL WOMAN ON THE OUTSIDE, BUT NOT SO BEAUTIFUL ON THE INSIDE. THE WHOLE STORY: GENESIS 29:1-30

Go to page 39 for the next Super Hero

her to you than to some other man. Stay here with me."

²⁰So Jacob worked for seven years to get Rachel. But they seemed like only a few days to him because he loved her so much.

²¹Then Jacob said to Laban, "Give me my wife. I've completed my time. I want to make love to her."

²²So Laban brought all of the people of the place together and had a big dinner prepared. ²³But when evening came, he gave his daughter Leah to Jacob. And Jacob made love to her. ²⁴Laban gave his female servant Zilpah to his daughter as her servant.

²⁵When Jacob woke up the next morning, there was Leah next to him! So he said to Laban, "What have you done to me? I worked for you to get Rachel, didn't I? Why did you trick me?"

²⁶Laban replied, "It isn't our practice here to give the younger daughter to be married before the older one. ²⁷Complete this daughter's wedding week. Then we'll give you the younger one also. But you will have to work for another seven years."

²⁸So Jacob did it. He completed the week with Leah. Then Laban gave him his daughter Rachel to be his wife. ²⁹Laban gave his female servant Bilhah to his daughter Rachel as her servant. ³⁰Jacob made love to Rachel also. He loved Rachel more than he loved Leah. And he worked for Laban for another seven years.

Jacob Becomes the Father of Many Children

³¹The Lord saw that Jacob didn't love Leah as much as he loved Rachel. So he let Leah have children. But Rachel wasn't able to have children. ³²Leah became pregnant. She had a son. She named him Reuben. She said, "The Lord has seen me suffer. Certainly my husband will love me now."

³³She became pregnant again. She had a son. Then she said, "The Lord heard that Jacob doesn't love me very much. That's why the Lord gave me this one too." So she named him Simeon.

³⁴She became pregnant again. She had a son. Then she said, "Now at last my husband will want me. I have had three sons by him." So the boy was named Levi.

³⁵She became pregnant again. She had a son. Then she said, "This time I'll praise the Lord." So she named him Judah. Then she stopped having children.

30 Rachel saw that she couldn't have any children by Jacob. So she became jealous of her sister. She said to Jacob, "Give me children, or I'll die!"

²Jacob became angry with her. He said, "Do you think I'm God? He's the one who has kept you from having children."

³Then she said, "Here's my servant Bilhah. Make love to her so that she can have children for me. Then I too can have a family through her."

⁴So she gave him her servant Bilhah as a wife. Jacob made love to her. ⁵And Bilhah became pregnant. She had a son by him. ⁶Then Rachel said, "God has stood up for my rights. He has listened to my prayer and given me a son." So she named him Dan.

⁷Rachel's servant Bilhah became pregnant again. She had a second son by Jacob. ⁸Then Rachel said, "I've had a great struggle with my sister. Now I've won." So she named him Naphtali.

⁹Leah saw that she had stopped having children. So she gave her servant Zilpah to Jacob as a wife. ¹⁰Leah's servant Zilpah had a son by Jacob. ¹¹Then Leah said, "What good fortune!" So she named him Gad.

¹²Leah's servant Zilpah had a second son by Jacob. ¹³Then Leah said, "I'm so happy! The women will call me happy." So she named him Asher.

¹⁴While the wheat harvest was being gathered, Reuben went out into the fields. He found some mandrake plants. He brought them to his mother Leah. Rachel said to Leah, "Please give me some of your son's mandrakes."

¹⁵But Leah said to her, "Isn't it enough that you took my husband away? Are you going to take my son's mandrakes too?"

Rachel said, "All right. Jacob can make love to you tonight if you give me your son's mandrakes."

¹⁶Jacob came in from the fields that evening. Leah went out to meet him. "You have to sleep with me tonight," she said. "I've bought you with my son's mandrakes." So he made love to her that night.

POWER-SURGE

CHEERFUL ✳

LEAH SAID, "I'M SO HAPPY! THE WOMEN WILL CALL ME HAPPY."
— GENESIS 30:13 —

LEAH

GENESIS 29:17-18

Leah had weak eyes. But Rachel was beautiful. She had a nice figure. Jacob was in love with Rachel.

Leah squinted through her veil. It was dark outside the tent, but she wanted to see him. Jacob, that is. Today she had married him. She wasn't at all sure about this plan of her father's. Heavily veiled and covered, she had been married to Jacob instead of her sister Rachel. Leah knew that Jacob loved Rachel and that he thought he had married Rachel. But Leah's father had decided that instead of Rachel, Leah would be today's bride.

Leah wasn't sure why her father wanted to trick Jacob. But she obeyed him. She always obeyed her father. When she saw Jacob approaching the tent, Leah promised herself fiercely, *I'll make him love me. I will! It won't be long before he'll forget all about Rachel.*

As the sun came up the next morning, Jacob turned to smile at Rachel. But next to him in his bed was not beautiful Rachel, but her older sister Leah! **JACOB JUMPED UP AND RAN TO THEIR FATHER, SHOUTING THAT HE HAD BEEN TRICKED.**

Leah stayed back in the tent alone. Tears began to roll down her cheeks. Maybe her plan to make Jacob love her wouldn't work. But even if he didn't love her, she would love him. And she would be a good wife to him as long as she lived.

BE A LEAH

Leah is often remembered more because she was Jacob's unwelcome bride, rather than because she was a faithful wife to him until the day she died. Though she and her sister Rachel fought for Jacob's love, it was Leah who had seven of Jacob's children, and Leah who was eventually buried next to Jacob. She was faithful to him, even when it was difficult. So, be a Leah. Be a loving son or daughter, be a dependable friend—even when it's not easy.

LEAH WAS A FAITHFUL WIFE TO HER HUSBAND, JACOB.
THE WHOLE STORY: GENESIS 29:16-30

Go to page 44 for the next Super Hero

17God listened to Leah. She became pregnant and had a fifth son by Jacob. **18**Then Leah said, "God has rewarded me because I gave my female servant to my husband." So she named the boy Issachar.

19Leah became pregnant again. She had a sixth son by Jacob. **20**Then Leah said, "God has given me a priceless gift. This time my husband will treat me with honor. I've had six sons by him." So she named the boy Zebulun.

21Some time later she had a daughter. She named her Dinah.

22Then God listened to Rachel. He showed concern for her. He made it possible for her to have children. **23**She became pregnant. She had a son. She said, "God has taken my shame away." **24**She continued, "May the LORD give me another son." So she named him Joseph.

Jacob's Flocks Increase Their Numbers

25After Rachel had Joseph, Jacob spoke to Laban. He said, "Send me on my way. I want to go back to my own home and country. **26**Give me my wives and children. I worked for you to get them. So I'll be on my way. You know how much work I've done for you."

27But Laban said to him, "If you are pleased with me, stay here. I've discovered that the LORD has blessed me because of you." **28**He continued, "Name your pay. I'll give it to you."

29Jacob said to him, "You know how hard I've worked for you. You know that your livestock has done better under my care. **30**You had only a little before I came. But that little has become a lot. The LORD has blessed you everywhere I've been. But when can I do something for my own family?"

31"What should I give you?" Laban asked.

"Don't give me anything," Jacob replied. "Just do one thing for me. Then I'll go on taking care of your flocks and watching over them.

32"Let me go through all of your flocks today. Let me remove every sheep that has speckles or spots on it. Let me remove every dark-colored lamb. Let me remove every goat that has spots or speckles on it. They will be my pay.

33"My honesty will give witness about me in days to come. It will give witness every time you check on what you have paid me. Suppose I have a goat that doesn't have speckles or spots. Or suppose I have a lamb that isn't dark-colored. Then it will be considered stolen."

34"I agree," said Laban. "Let's do what you have said."

35That same day Laban removed all of the male goats that had stripes or spots. He removed all of the female goats that had speckles or spots. They were the ones that had white on them. He also removed all of the dark-colored lambs. He had his sons take care of them.

36Then he put a journey of three days between himself and Jacob. But Jacob continued to take care of the rest of Laban's flocks.

37Jacob took branches that were freshly cut from poplar, almond and plane trees. He made white stripes on them by peeling off the bark. He uncovered the white wood inside the branches.

38Then he placed the peeled branches in all of the stone tubs where the animals drank water. He placed them so they would be right in front of the flocks when they came to drink. The flocks were ready to mate when they came to drink. **39**So they mated in front of the branches. And they had little ones that were striped or speckled or spotted. **40**Jacob put the little ones of the flock to one side by themselves. But he made the older ones face the striped and dark-colored animals that belonged to Laban. In that way, he made separate flocks for himself. He didn't put them with Laban's animals.

41Every time the stronger females were ready to mate, Jacob would place the branches in the stone tubs. He would place them in front of the animals so they would mate near the branches.

42But if the animals were weak, he wouldn't place the branches there. So the weak animals went to Laban. And the strong ones went to Jacob.

43In this way, Jacob became very rich. He became the owner of large flocks. He also had many male and female servants. And he had many camels and donkeys.

Jacob Runs Away From Laban

31 Jacob heard what Laban's sons were saying. "Jacob has taken everything our father owned," they said. "He has gained all of this wealth from what belonged to our father."

2Jacob noticed that Laban's feelings toward him had changed.

3Then the LORD spoke to Jacob. He said, "Go back to your father's land and to your relatives. I will be with you."

4So Jacob sent word to Rachel and

Leah. He told them to come out to the fields where his flocks were.

⁵He said to them, "I see that your father's feelings toward me have changed. But the God of my father has been with me. ⁶You know that I've worked for your father with all of my strength.

⁷"But your father has cheated me. He has changed my pay ten times. In spite of everything that's happened, God hasn't let him harm me. ⁸Sometimes Laban would say, 'The speckled ones will be your pay.' Then all the flocks had little ones with speckles. At other times he would say, 'The striped ones will be your pay.' Then all the flocks had little ones with stripes. ⁹So God has taken away your father's livestock and given it to me.

¹⁰"Once during the mating season I had a dream. In my dream I looked up and saw male goats mating with the flock. The goats had stripes, speckles or spots. ¹¹"The angel of God said to me in the dream, 'Jacob.' I answered, 'Here I am.' ¹²He said, 'Look up. See the male goats mating with the flock. All of them have stripes, speckles or spots. That is because I have seen everything that Laban has been doing to you.

¹³" 'I am the God of Bethel. That is where you poured oil on a pillar. There you made a promise to me. Now leave this land. Go back to your own land.' "

¹⁴Rachel and Leah replied, "Do we still have any share in our father's property? ¹⁵Doesn't our father think of us as strangers? First he sold us. Now he has used up what he was paid for us. ¹⁶All of the wealth God took away from our father really belongs to us and our children. So do what God has told you to do."

¹⁷Then Jacob put his children and wives on camels. ¹⁸He drove all of his livestock ahead of him. He also took with him everything he had gotten in Paddan Aram. He left to go to his father Isaac in the land of Canaan.

¹⁹Laban had gone to clip the wool from his sheep. While he was gone, Rachel stole the statues of family gods that belonged to her father. ²⁰And that's not all. Jacob tricked Laban the Aramean. He didn't tell him he was running away.

²¹So Jacob ran off with everything he had. He crossed the Euphrates River. And he headed for the hill country of Gilead.

Laban Chases Jacob

²²On the third day Laban was told that Jacob had run away. ²³He took his relatives with him and went after Jacob. Sev-

en days later he caught up with him in the hill country of Gilead.

²⁴Then God came to Laban the Aramean in a dream at night. He said to him, "Be careful. Do not say anything to Jacob, whether it is good or bad."

²⁵Jacob had set up his tent in the hill country of Gilead. That's where Laban caught up with him. Laban and his relatives camped there too.

²⁶Laban said to Jacob, "What have you done? You have tricked me. You have taken my daughters away like prisoners of war. ²⁷Why did you run away in secret and trick me? Why didn't you tell me? Then I could have sent you away happily. We could have sung to the music of tambourines and harps. ²⁸You didn't even let me kiss my grandchildren and my daughters good-by. You have done a foolish thing.

²⁹"I have the power to harm you. But last night the God of your father spoke to me. He said, 'Be careful. Do not say anything to Jacob, whether it is good or bad.'

³⁰"Now you have run away. You longed to go back to your father's home? But why did you have to steal my gods?"

³¹Jacob answered Laban, "I was afraid. I thought you would take your daughters away from me by force. ³²But if you find anyone who has your gods, he will not remain alive. While our relatives are watching, look for yourself. See if there's anything of yours here with me. If you find anything belonging to you, take it." But Jacob didn't know that Rachel had stolen the gods.

³³So Laban went into Jacob's tent and Leah's tent. He went into the tent of their two female servants. But he didn't find anything.

After he came out of Leah's tent, he entered Rachel's tent. ³⁴Rachel was the one who had taken his family gods. She had put them inside her camel's saddle. She was sitting on them. Laban searched the whole tent. But he didn't find anything.

³⁵Rachel said to her father, "I'm sorry, sir. I can't get up for you right now. But don't be angry with me. I'm having my monthly period." So he searched everywhere but couldn't find his family gods.

³⁶Jacob was very angry with Laban. "What have I done wrong?" he asked. "What sin have I committed to make you hunt me down like this? ³⁷You have searched through all of my things. What have you found that belongs to your family? Put it here in front of your relatives

and mine. Let them decide between the two of us.

38"I've been with you for 20 years now. The little ones of your sheep and goats were not dead when they were born. I haven't eaten rams from your flocks. 39I didn't bring you animals that were torn apart by wild beasts. I made up for the loss myself. Also, you made me pay for anything that was stolen by day or night.

40"And what was my life like? The heat burned me in the daytime. And it was so cold at night that I froze. I couldn't sleep. 41That's what it was like for the 20 years I was living with you.

"I worked for 14 years to get your two daughters. I worked for six years to get my share of your flocks. You changed my pay ten times.

42"But the God of my father was with me. He is the God of Abraham and the God Isaac worshiped. If he hadn't been with me, you would certainly have sent me away without anything to show for all of my work. But God has seen my hard times. He has seen all of the work my hands have done. So last night he warned you."

43Laban answered Jacob, "The women are my daughters. The children are my children. The flocks are my flocks. Everything you see is mine. But what can I do today about these daughters of mine? What can I do about the children they've had?

44"Come now. Let's make a covenant, you and I. Let it be a witness between us."

45So Jacob took a stone. He set it up as a pillar. 46He said to his relatives, "Get some stones." So they took stones and put them in a pile. And they ate there by it.

47Laban named the pile of stones Jegar Sahadutha. Jacob named it Galeed.

48Laban said, "This pile of stones is a witness between you and me today." That's why it was named Galeed. 49It was also called Mizpah. That's because Laban said, "May the LORD keep watch between you and me when we are away from each other. 50Don't treat my daughters badly. Don't get married to any women besides my daughters. There isn't anyone here to see what we're doing. But remember that God is a witness between you and me."

51Laban also said to Jacob, "Here is this pile of stones. And here is this pillar. I've set them up between you and me. 52This pile is a witness. And this pillar is a witness. They give witness that I won't go past this pile to harm you. And they give

witness that you won't go past this pile and pillar to harm me.

53"The God of Abraham and Nahor is also the God of their father. May their God decide which of us is right."

So Jacob took an oath in the name of the God his father Isaac worshiped. 54He offered a sacrifice there in the hill country. And he invited his relatives to a meal. After they had eaten, they spent the night there.

55Early the next morning Laban kissed his grandchildren and his daughters. He gave them his blessing. Then he left and returned home.

Jacob Gets Ready to Meet Esau

32 Jacob also went on his way. The angels of God met him. 2Jacob saw them. He said, "This is the army of God!" So he named that place Mahanaim.

3Jacob sent messengers ahead of him to his brother Esau. Esau lived in the land of Seir. It was also called the country of Edom.

4Jacob told the messengers what to do. He said, "Here's what you must tell my master Esau. 'Your servant Jacob says, "I've been staying with Laban. I've remained there until now. 5I have cattle and donkeys and sheep and goats. I also have male and female servants. Now I'm sending this message to you. I hope I can please you." ' "

6The messengers came back to Jacob. They said, "We went to your brother Esau. He's coming now to meet you. He has 400 men with him."

7Jacob was very worried and afraid. So he separated the people who were with him into two groups. He also separated the flocks and herds and camels. 8He thought, "Esau may come and attack one group. If he does, the group that's left can escape."

9Then Jacob prayed, "You are the God of my grandfather Abraham. You are the God of my father Isaac.

"LORD, you are the one who said to me, 'Go back to your country and your relatives. Then I will give you success.' 10You have been very kind and faithful to me. But I'm not worthy of any of this. When I crossed this Jordan River, all I had was my walking stick. But now I've become two groups.

11"Please save me from the hand of my brother Esau. I'm afraid he'll come and attack me and the mothers with their children. 12But you have said, 'I will certainly give you success. I will make your children as many as the grains of sand on the seashore. People will not be able to count them.' "

¹³Jacob spent the night there. He chose a gift for his brother Esau from what he had with him. ¹⁴He chose 200 female goats and 20 male goats. He chose 200 female sheep and 20 male sheep. ¹⁵He chose 30 female camels with their little ones. He chose 40 cows and ten bulls. And he chose 20 female donkeys and ten male donkeys. ¹⁶He put each herd by itself.

Then he put his servants in charge of them. He said to his servants, "Go on ahead of me. Keep some space between the herds."

¹⁷Jacob spoke to his servant who was leading the way. He said, "My brother Esau will meet you. He'll ask, 'Who is your master? Where are you going? And who owns all of these animals in front of you?'

¹⁸"Then say to Esau, 'They belong to your servant Jacob. They are a gift to you from him. And he is coming behind us.' "

¹⁹He also spoke to the second and third servants. He told them and all of the others who followed the herds what to do. He said, "Say the same thing to Esau when you meet him. ²⁰Make sure you say, 'Your servant Jacob is coming behind us.' " Jacob was thinking, "I'll make peace with him with these gifts I'm sending on ahead. When I see him later, maybe he'll welcome me."

²¹So Jacob's gifts went on ahead of him. But he himself spent the night in the camp.

Jacob Struggles With God

²²That night Jacob got up. He took his two wives, his two female servants and his 11 sons and sent them across the Jabbok River. ²³After they had crossed the stream, he sent over everything he owned.

²⁴So Jacob was left alone. A man struggled with him until morning. ²⁵The man saw that he couldn't win. So he touched the inside of Jacob's hip. As Jacob struggled with the man, Jacob's hip was twisted. ²⁶Then the man said, "Let me go. It is morning."

But Jacob replied, "I won't let you go unless you bless me."

²⁷The man asked him, "What is your name?"

"Jacob," he answered.

²⁸Then the man said, "Your name will not be Jacob anymore. Instead, it will be Israel. You have struggled with God and with men. And you have won."

²⁹Jacob said, "Please tell me your name."

But he replied, "Why do you want to know my name?" Then he blessed Jacob there.

³⁰So Jacob named the place Peniel. He said, "I saw God face to face. But I'm still alive!"

³¹The sun rose above Jacob as he passed by Peniel. He was limping because of his hip. ³²That's why the people of Israel don't eat the meat attached to the inside of the hip. They don't eat it to this very day. It's because the inside of Jacob's hip was touched.

Jacob Meets Esau

33 Jacob looked up. And there was Esau, coming with his 400 men! So Jacob separated the children. He put them with Leah, Rachel and the two female servants. ²He put the servants and their children in front. He put Leah and her children next. And he put Rachel and Joseph last.

³He himself went on ahead. As he came near his brother, he bowed down to the ground seven times.

⁴But Esau ran to meet Jacob. He hugged him and threw his arms around his neck. He kissed him, and they cried. ⁵Then Esau looked up and saw the women and children. "Who are these people with you?" he asked.

Jacob answered, "They are the children God has so kindly given to me."

⁶Then the female servants and their children came near and bowed down. ⁷Next, Leah and her children came and bowed down. Last of all came Joseph and Rachel. They bowed down too.

⁸Esau asked, "Why did you send all of those herds I saw?"

"I hoped I could do something to please you," Jacob replied.

⁹But Esau said, "I already have plenty, my brother. Keep what you have for yourself."

¹⁰"No, please!" said Jacob. "If I've pleased you, accept this gift from me. Seeing your face is like seeing the face of God. You have welcomed me so kindly. ¹¹Please accept the present that was brought to you. God has been gracious to me. I have everything I need." Jacob wouldn't give in. So Esau accepted it.

¹²Then Esau said, "Let's be on our way. I'll go with you."

¹³But Jacob said to him, "You know that the children are young. You also know that I have to take care of the cows

JACOB

B

T

GENESIS 32:28

The man said, "Your name will not be Jacob anymore. Instead, it will be Israel. You have struggled with God and with men. And you have won."

Late at night Jacob watched in the moonlight as the last camel clumped across the river. Everything he owned was now on the other side—his wives, his eleven sons, his sheep and goats and cows and camels.

Jacob was returning to his homeland (which now belonged to his brother Esau). And he was frightened. He had run away years before because Esau was angry with him. Esau had even threatened to kill him. Jacob thought to himself, *After all these years will he still want to kill my family and me?*

Jacob got up to make his own way across the river. But a man stopped him. Jacob didn't know this man. The man wrestled down Jacob. But Jacob pushed him off. They fought all night long. Neither of them could win. But neither of them would give in. Then, without warning, the man touched Jacob's hip. PAIN STREAKED THROUGH JACOB'S LEG, AND HE FELL TO THE GROUND, TAKING THE MAN WITH HIM.

Jacob now understood that the person he was wrestling wasn't a normal man; it was God clothed in the body of a man. Still Jacob struggled with him. For the first time the man spoke: "Let me go. It is morning." But Jacob refused. He held onto the man. Gritting his teeth with the pain in his hip, Jacob told him, "I won't let you go until you give me a blessing."

Then the man surprised Jacob. He said, "Your name is no longer Jacob. You will now be called Israel." Jacob's new name meant, "he struggles with God." Jacob had struggled with God and hadn't given up the fight.

Limping because of his sore hip, Jacob crossed the river as the sun rose. He was still afraid of his brother Esau, but he was also certain that God was with him and would protect him.

BE A JACOB
Don't give up! Be like Jacob and don't quit. Keep trying. Keep on going. God will be with you and will make you strong.

JACOB STRUGGLED WITH GOD AND DIDN'T GIVE UP.
THE WHOLE STORY: GENESIS 32:22-32

Go to page 46 for the next Super Hero

and female sheep that are nursing their little ones. If the animals are driven hard for just one day, all of them will die.

14"So you go on ahead of me. I'll move along only as fast as the herds and the children can go. I'll go slowly until I come to you in Seir."

15Esau said, "Then let me leave some of my men with you."

"Why do that?" Jacob asked. "I just hope I've pleased you."

16So that day Esau started on his way back to Seir. 17But Jacob went to Succoth. There he built a place for himself. He also made shelters for his livestock. That's why the place is named Succoth.

18After Jacob came from Paddan Aram, he arrived safely at the city of Shechem in Canaan. He camped where he could see the city. 19For 100 pieces of silver he bought a piece of land. He got it from the sons of Hamor. Hamor was the father of Shechem. Jacob set up his tent on that piece of land. 20He also set up an altar there. He named it El Elohe Israel.

Simeon and Levi Kill the Men of Shechem

34 Dinah was the daughter Leah had by Jacob. Dinah went out to visit the women of the land.

2Hamor the Hivite was the ruler of that area. When his son Shechem saw Dinah, he took her and raped her. 3Then his heart longed for Jacob's daughter Dinah. He fell in love with her and spoke tenderly to her.

4Shechem said to his father Hamor, "Get me that woman. I want her to be my wife."

5Jacob heard that his daughter Dinah had been made "unclean." His sons were in the fields with his livestock. So he kept quiet about it until they came home.

6Then Shechem's father Hamor went out to talk with Jacob. 7Jacob's sons had come in from the fields. They came as soon as they heard what had happened. They were filled with sadness and anger. Shechem had done a very terrible thing. He had forced Jacob's daughter to have sex with him. He had done something that should never be done in Israel.

8But Hamor said to them, "My son Shechem wants your daughter. Please give her to him to be his wife. 9"Let your people and ours get married to each other. Give us your daughters as our wives. You can have our daughters as your wives. 10You can settle among us.

Here is the land. Live in it. Trade in it. Buy property in it."

11Then Shechem spoke to Dinah's father and brothers. He said, "I want to please you. I'll give you anything you ask. 12Make the price for the bride as high as you want to. I'll pay anything you ask me. Just give me the woman. I want to get married to her."

13Their sister Dinah had been made "unclean." So Jacob's sons lied to Shechem and his father Hamor. 14They said to them, "We can't do it. We can't give our sister to a man who isn't circumcised. That would bring shame on us. 15We'll agree, but only on one condition. You will have to become like us. You will have to circumcise all of your males.

16"Then we'll give you our daughters as your wives. And we'll take your daughters as our wives. We'll settle among you and become one people with you. 17But if you won't agree to it, then we'll take our sister and go."

18Their offer seemed good to Hamor and his son Shechem. 19The young man was the most honored of all of the men in his father's family. He didn't lose any time in doing what they said, because he was delighted with Jacob's daughter.

20Hamor and his son Shechem went to the city gate. They spoke to the other men in town. 21"These men are friendly toward us," they said. "Let them live in our land. Let them trade in it. The land has plenty of room for them. We can get married to their daughters. And they can marry ours.

22"But they will agree to live with us as one people only on one condition. All of our males must be circumcised, just as they are.

23"Won't their livestock and their property belong to us? Won't all of their animals become ours? So let's say yes to them. Then they'll settle among us."

24All of the men who went out through the city gate agreed with Hamor and his son Shechem. So every male in the city was circumcised.

25Three days later, all of them were still in pain. Then Simeon and Levi took their swords. They were Jacob's sons and Dinah's brothers. They attacked the city when the people didn't expect it. They killed every male. 26They also killed Hamor and his son Shechem with their swords. Then they took Dinah from Shechem's house and left.

27Jacob's other sons found the dead bodies. They robbed the city where their sister had been made "unclean." **28**They took the flocks and herds and donkeys. They took everything that was in the city and out in the fields. **29**They carried everything away. And they took all of the women and children. They took away everything that was in the houses.

30Then Jacob said to Simeon and Levi, "You have brought trouble on me. Now I'm like a very bad smell to the Canaanites and Perizzites who live in this land. There aren't many of us. They may join together against me and attack me. Then I and my family will be destroyed."

31But they replied, "Should he have treated our sister like a prostitute?"

Jacob Returns to Bethel

35 Then God said to Jacob, "Go up to Bethel and settle there. Build an altar there to honor me. That's where I appeared to you when you were running away from your brother Esau."

2So Jacob spoke to his family and to everyone who was with him. He said, "Get rid of the strange gods you have with you. Make yourselves pure, and change your clothes. **3**Come, let's go up to Bethel.

ESAU

GENESIS 33:4

F

K

♥

Esau ran to meet Jacob. He hugged him and threw his arms around his neck. He kissed him, and they cried.

Esau (EEE-saw) watched the dust from a huge group of people and animals billowing up on the horizon. When he and his soldiers met the group, a servant ran forward and stated, "All these animals are a gift to you from your brother, Jacob. He is coming behind us."

Soon Esau met another group with a servant who had the same message. And another. And another. All were gifts from Jacob, Esau's brother. Many years ago, Jacob tricked Esau and made him so angry Esau said he would kill Jacob. But that was so long ago. The past was forgiven.

Esau came to another large crowd of people and animals. Another person bounded out. **BUT THIS WAS NO SER-VANT.** This was Jacob! His very own brother. Jacob bowed down in front of Esau. But Esau would have none of it. He threw his arms around his brother and kissed him.

BE AN ESAU

Esau had been very angry when his brother Jacob tricked him, so angry he wanted to kill Jacob. But now, Esau had forgiven Jacob and was eager to see him. Be like Esau. Oh, don't get so angry you want to hurt someone. Instead, be forgiving and loving.

ESAU FORGAVE HIS BROTHER JACOB.

Go to page 64 for the next Super Hero

There I'll build an altar to honor God. He answered me when I was in trouble. He's been with me everywhere I've gone."

4So they gave Jacob all of the strange gods they had. They also gave him their earrings. Jacob buried them under the oak tree at Shechem.

5Then Jacob and everyone who was with him started out. The terror of God fell on the towns all around them. So no one chased them.

6Jacob and all of the people who were with him came to Luz. Luz is also called Bethel. It's in the land of Canaan. **7**Jacob built an altar at Luz. He named the place El Bethel. There God made himself known to Jacob when he was running away from his brother.

8Rebekah's attendant Deborah died. They buried her body under the oak tree below Bethel. So it was called Allon Bacuth.

9After Jacob returned from Paddan Aram, God appeared to him again. And God blessed him. **10**God said to him, "Your name is Jacob. But you will not be called Jacob anymore. Your name will be Israel." So he named him Israel.

11God said to him, "I am the Mighty God. Have children and increase your numbers. A nation and a community of nations will come from you. Kings will come from your body. **12**I am giving you the land I gave to Abraham and Isaac. I will also give it to your children after you."

13Then God left him at the place where he had talked with him.

14Jacob set up a stone pillar at the place where God had talked with him. He poured out a drink offering on it. He also poured oil on it. **15**Jacob named the place Bethel. That's where God had talked with him.

Rachel and Isaac Die

16They moved on from Bethel. Ephrath wasn't very far away when Rachel began to have a baby. She was having a very hard time of it.

17The woman who helped her saw that she was having problems. So she said to her, "Don't be afraid. You have another son."

18But Rachel was dying. As she took her last breath, she named her son Ben-Oni. But his father named him Benjamin.

19So Rachel died. Her body was buried beside the road to Ephrath. Ephrath was also called Bethlehem. **20**Jacob set up a

pillar over her tomb. The pillar marks the place of Rachel's tomb to this very day.

21Israel moved on again. He set up his tent beyond Migdal Eder.

22While Israel was living in that area, Reuben went in and made love to Bilhah. She was the concubine of Reuben's father. And Israel heard about it.

Here are the 12 sons Jacob had.
23Leah was the mother of
Reuben, Jacob's oldest son.
Her other sons were
Simeon, Levi, Judah, Issachar and Zebulun.
24The sons of Rachel were
Joseph and Benjamin.
25The sons of Rachel's female servant Bilhah were
Dan and Naphtali.
26The sons of Leah's female servant Zilpah were
Gad and Asher.
Those were Jacob's sons. They were born in Paddan Aram.

27Jacob came home to his father Isaac in Mamre. Mamre is near Kiriath Arba, where Abraham and Isaac had stayed. The place is also called Hebron. **28**Isaac lived 180 years. **29**Then he took his last breath and died. He was very old when he joined the members of his family who had already died. His sons Esau and Jacob buried his body.

The Family Line of Esau

36 Here is the story of Esau. Esau was also called Edom.

2Esau got his wives from among the women of Canaan. He married Adah, the daughter of Elon the Hittite. He also married Oholibamah, the daughter of Anah and the granddaughter of Zibeon the Hivite. **3**And he married Basemath, the daughter of Ishmael and the sister of Nebaioth.

4Adah had Eliphaz by Esau. Basemath had Reuel. **5**Oholibamah had Jeush, Jalam and Korah. All of them were Esau's sons. They were born in Canaan.

6Esau moved to a land far away from his brother Jacob. He took with him his wives, his sons and daughters, and all of the people who lived with him. He also took his livestock and all of his other animals. He took everything he had gotten in Canaan. **7**Jacob and Esau owned so much that they couldn't remain together. There wasn't enough land for both of them. They had too much livestock. **8**So Esau settled in the hill country of Seir. Esau was also called Edom.

9Here is the story of Esau. He's the father of the people of Edom. They live in the hill country of Seir.

10Here are the names of Esau's sons.
They are Eliphaz, the son of Esau's wife Adah, and Reuel, the son of Esau's wife Basemath.
11The sons of Eliphaz were
Teman, Omar, Zepho, Gatam and Kenaz.
12Esau's son Eliphaz also had a concubine named Timna. She had Amalek by Eliphaz. They were grandsons of Esau's wife Adah.
13The sons of Reuel were
Nahath, Zerah, Shammah and Mizzah. They were grandsons of Esau's wife Basemath.
14Esau's wife Oholibamah was the daughter of Anah and the granddaughter of Zibeon. She had Jeush, Jalam and Korah by Esau.

15Here are the chiefs who were among Esau's sons.
Eliphaz was Esau's oldest son. The sons of Eliphaz were
Chiefs Teman, Omar, Zepho, Kenaz, **16**Korah, Gatam and Amalek. They were the chiefs in Edom who were sons of Eliphaz. They were Adah's grandsons.
17The sons of Esau's son Reuel were
Chiefs Nahath, Zerah, Shammah and Mizzah. They were the chiefs in Edom who were sons of Reuel. They were grandsons of Esau's wife Basemath.
18The sons of Esau's wife Oholibamah were
Chiefs Jeush, Jalam and Korah. They were the chiefs who were sons of Esau's wife Oholibamah. She was Anah's daughter.
19That was the family line of Esau. And those were the chiefs. Esau was also called Edom.

20Seir the Horite had sons living in the same area.
They were Lotan, Shobal, Zibeon, Anah, **21**Dishon, Ezer and Dishan. The sons of Seir in Edom were Horite chiefs.
22The sons of Lotan were

Hori and Homam. Timna was Lotan's sister.
23The sons of Shobal were
Alvan, Manahath, Ebal, Shepho and Onam.
24The sons of Zibeon were
Aiah and Anah. He was the Anah who discovered the hot springs of water in the desert. He found them while he was taking care of the donkeys that belonged to his father Zibeon.
25The children of Anah were
Dishon and Oholibamah. Oholibamah was the daughter of Anah.
26The sons of Dishon were
Hemdan, Eshban, Ithran and Keran.
27The sons of Ezer were
Bilhan, Zaavan and Akan.
28The sons of Dishan were
Uz and Aran.
29The Horite chiefs were
Lotan, Shobal, Zibeon, Anah, **30**Dishon, Ezer and Dishan. They were the Horite chiefs in the land of Seir. They are listed tribe by tribe.

The Rulers of Edom

31Before Israel had a king, there were kings who ruled in Edom.

32Bela became the king of Edom. Bela was the son of Beor. Bela's city was called Dinhabah.
33When Bela died, Jobab became the next king. Jobab was the son of Zerah from Bozrah.
34When Jobab died, Husham became the next king. Husham was from the land of the Temanites.
35When Husham died, Hadad became the next king. Hadad was the son of Bedad. Hadad had won the battle over Midian in the country of Moab. Hadad's city was called Avith.
36When Hadad died, Samlah became the next king. Samlah was from Masrekah.
37When Samlah died, Shaul became the next king. Shaul was from Rehoboth on the river.
38When Shaul died, Baal-Hanan became the next king. Baal-Hanan was the son of Acbor.
39When Baal-Hanan died, Hadad became the next king. Hadad's city was called Pau. His wife's name was Mehetabel. She was the

daughter of Matred. Matred was the daughter of Me-Zahab.

40Here are the chiefs who were in the family line of Esau. They are listed by name as chiefs in charge of their tribes and territories. They are

Timna, Alvah, Jetheth, **41**Oholibamah, Elah, Pinon, **42**Kenaz, Teman, Mibzar, **43**Magdiel and Iram. They were the chiefs of Edom. They ruled over their settlements in the land where they lived.

That's the end of the story of Esau. He was the father of the people of Edom.

Joseph Has Two Dreams

37 Jacob lived in the land of Canaan. It's the land where his father had stayed.

2Here is the story of Jacob.

Joseph was a young man. He was 17 years old. He was taking care of the flocks with some of his brothers. They were the sons of Bilhah and the sons of Zilpah, his father's wives. Joseph brought their father a bad report about them.

3Israel loved Joseph more than any of his other sons. Joseph had been born to him when he was old. Israel made him a beautiful robe.

4Joseph's brothers saw that their father loved him more than any of them. So they hated Joseph. They couldn't even speak one kind word to him.

5Joseph had a dream. When he told it to his brothers, they hated him even more. **6**He said to them, "Listen to the dream I had. **7**We were tying up bundles of grain out in the field. Suddenly my bundle rose and stood up straight. Your bundles gathered around my bundle and bowed down to it."

8His brothers said to him, "Do you plan to be king over us? Will you really rule over us?" So they hated him even more because of his dream. They didn't like what he had said.

9Then Joseph had another dream. He told it to his brothers. "Listen," he said. "I had another dream. This time the sun and moon and 11 stars were bowing down to me."

10He told his father as well as his brothers. Then his father objected. He said, "What about this dream you had? Will your mother and I and your brothers really do that? Will we really come and bow down to the ground in front of you?"

11His brothers were jealous of him. But his father kept the matter in mind.

Joseph Is Sold by His Brothers

12Joseph's brothers had gone to take care of their father's flocks near Shechem. **13**Israel said to Joseph, "As you know, your brothers are taking care of the flocks near Shechem. Come. I'm going to send you to them."

"All right," Joseph replied.

14So Israel said to him, "Go to your brothers. See how they are doing. Also see how the flocks are doing. Then come back and tell me." So he sent him away from the Hebron Valley.

Joseph arrived at Shechem. **15**A man found him wandering around in the fields. He asked Joseph, "What are you looking for?"

16He replied, "I'm looking for my brothers. Can you tell me where they are taking care of their flocks?"

17"They've moved on from here," the man answered. "I heard them say, 'Let's go to Dothan.' "

So Joseph went to look for his brothers. He found them near Dothan. **18**But they saw him a long way off. Before he reached them, they made plans to kill him.

19"Here comes that dreamer!" they said to one another. **20**"Come. Let's kill him. Let's throw him into one of these empty wells. Let's say that a wild animal ate him up. Then we'll see whether his dreams will come true."

21Reuben heard them. He tried to save Joseph from them. "Let's not take his life," he said. **22**"Let's not spill any blood. Throw him into this empty well here in the desert. But don't harm him yourselves."

Reuben said that to save Joseph from them. He was hoping he could take him back to his father.

23When Joseph came to his brothers, he was wearing his beautiful robe. They took it away from him. **24**And they threw him into the well. The well was empty. There wasn't any water in it.

25Then they sat down to eat their meal. As they did, they saw some Ishmaelite traders coming from Gilead. Their camels were loaded with spices, lotion and myrrh. They were on their way to take them down to Egypt.

26Judah said to his brothers, "What will we gain if we kill our brother and try to cover up what we've done? **27**Come. Let's sell him to these traders. Let's not harm him ourselves. After all, he's our brother.

He's our own flesh and blood." Judah's brothers agreed with him.

28The traders from Midian came by. Joseph's brothers pulled him up out of the well. They sold him to the Ishmaelite traders for eight ounces of silver. Then the traders took him to Egypt.

29Later, Reuben came back to the empty well. He saw that Joseph wasn't there. He was so upset that he tore his clothes. **30**He went back to his brothers and said, "The boy isn't there! Now what should I do?"

31Then they got Joseph's beautiful robe. They killed a goat and dipped the robe in the blood. **32**They took it back to their father. They said, "We found this. Take a look at it. See if it's your son's robe."

33Jacob recognized it. He said, "It's my son's robe! A wild animal has eaten him up. Joseph must have been torn to pieces."

34Jacob tore his clothes. He put on black clothes. Then he sobbed over his son for many days.

35All of Jacob's other sons and daughters came to comfort him. But they weren't able to. He said, "I'll be full of sorrow when I go down into the grave to be with my son." So Joseph's father sobbed over him.

36But the traders from Midian sold Joseph to Potiphar in Egypt. Potiphar was one of Pharaoh's officials. He was the captain of the palace guard.

Judah and Tamar

38 At that time, Judah left his brothers. He went down to stay with a man named Hirah. Hirah was from the town of Adullam.

2There Judah met the daughter of a man from Canaan. His name was Shua. Judah married her and made love to her. **3**She became pregnant. She had a son. They named him Er. **4**She became pregnant again and had another son. She named him Onan. **5**She had still another son. She named him Shelah. He was born at Kezib.

6Judah got a wife for his oldest son Er. Her name was Tamar. **7**But Judah's oldest son Er was evil in the LORD's eyes. So the LORD put him to death.

8Then Judah said to Onan, "Make love to your brother's wife. After all, you are her brother-in-law. So carry out your duty to her. Produce children for your brother."

9But Onan knew that the children wouldn't belong to him. So every time he made love to his brother's wife, he spilled his semen on the ground. He did it so he wouldn't produce children for his brother.

10What he did was evil in the LORD's eyes. So the LORD put him to death also.

11Then Judah spoke to his daughter-in-law Tamar. He said, "Live as a widow in your father's home. Wait there until my son Shelah grows up."

Judah was thinking, "Shelah might die too, just like his brothers." So Tamar went to live in her father's home.

12After a long time Judah's wife died. She was the daughter of Shua. When Judah got over his sadness, he went up to Timnah. His friend Hirah from Adullam went with him. Men were clipping the wool from Judah's sheep at Timnah.

13Tamar was told, "Your father-in-law is on his way to Timnah to clip the wool from his sheep." **14**So she took off her widow's clothes. She covered her face with a veil so people wouldn't know who she was. Then she sat down at the entrance to Enaim. Enaim is on the road to Timnah. Tamar knew that Shelah had grown up. But she hadn't been given to him as his wife.

15Judah saw her. He thought she was a prostitute because she had covered her face with a veil. **16**He didn't realize that she was his daughter-in-law. He went over to her by the side of the road. He said, "Come. Let me make love to you."

"What will you give me to make love to you?" she asked.

17"I'll send you a young goat from my flock," he said.

"Will you give me something that belongs to you?" she asked. "I'll keep it until you send the goat."

18He said, "What should I give you?"

"Give me your seal and its string," she answered. "And give me your walking stick."

So he gave them to her. Then he had sex with her. And she became pregnant by him. **19**After she left, she took off her veil. She put on her widow's clothes again.

20Judah sent his friend Hirah with the young goat he had promised. He wanted to get back what he had given to the woman.

But his friend Hirah couldn't find her. **21**He asked the men who lived at Enaim, "Where's the temple prostitute? She used to sit beside the road here."

"There hasn't been any temple prostitute here," they said.

22So Hirah went back to Judah. He said,

STRONG

JOSEPH WAS STRONG AND HANDSOME.
—— GENESIS 39:6 ——

"I couldn't find her. Besides, the men who lived there didn't know anything about her. They said, 'There hasn't been any temple prostitute here.' "

23Then Judah said, "Let her keep what she has. I don't want people making fun of us. After all, I did send her this young goat. We can't help it if you couldn't find her."

24About three months later people brought word to Judah. They said, "Your daughter-in-law Tamar is guilty of being a prostitute. Now she's pregnant."

Judah said, "Bring her out! Have her burned to death!"

25As Tamar was being brought out, she sent a message to her father-in-law. She said, "I am pregnant by the man who owns these." She continued, "Do you recognize this seal and string and walking stick? Do you know who they belong to?"

26Judah recognized them. He said, "She's a better person than I am. I should have given her to my son Shelah, but I didn't." Judah never had sex with Tamar again.

27The time came for Tamar to have her baby. There were twin boys inside her.

28As the babies were being born, one of them stuck out his hand. So the woman who was helping Tamar took a bright red thread. The woman tied it on the baby's wrist. She said, "This one came out first."

29But he pulled his hand back, and his brother came out first instead. She said, "Just look at how you have broken out!" So he was called Perez.

30Then his brother, who had the red thread on his wrist, came out. So he was named Zerah.

Joseph and Potiphar's Wife

39 Joseph had been taken down to Egypt. An Egyptian named Potiphar had bought him from the Ishmaelite traders who had taken him there. Potiphar was one of Pharaoh's officials. He was the captain of the palace guard.

2The LORD was with Joseph. He gave him great success. Joseph lived in Potiphar's house.

3Joseph's master saw that the LORD was with him. He saw that the LORD gave Joseph success in everything he did. 4So Potiphar was pleased with Joseph. He made him his attendant. He put Joseph in charge of his house. He told Joseph to take good care of everything he owned.

5From that time on, the LORD blessed Potiphar's family and servants because of Joseph. He blessed everything Potiphar had in his house and field.

6So Potiphar told Joseph to take good care of everything he owned. With Joseph in charge, he didn't have to worry about anything except the food he ate.

Joseph was strong and handsome. 7After a while, his master's wife noticed Joseph. She said to him, "Make love to me!"

8But he said no. "My master has put me in charge," he told her. "Now he doesn't have to worry about anything in the house. He trusts me to take care of everything he owns.

9"No one in this house is in a higher position than I am. My master hasn't held anything back from me, except you. You are his wife. So how could I do an evil thing like that? How could I sin against God?"

10She spoke to Joseph day after day. But he told her he wouldn't make love to her. He didn't even want to be with her.

11One day Joseph went into the house to take care of his duties. None of the family servants was inside.

12Potiphar's wife grabbed hold of him by his coat. "Make love to me!" she said. But he left his coat in her hand. And he ran out of the house.

13She saw that he had left his coat in her hand and had run out of the house. 14So she called her servants. "Look," she said to them, "this Hebrew slave has been

TRUSTED

MY MASTER HAS PUT ME IN CHARGE...HE TRUSTS ME TO TAKE CARE OF EVERYTHING HE OWNS.
—— GENESIS 39:8 ——

brought here to make fun of us! He came in here to sleep with me. But I screamed for help. [15]He heard my scream. So he left his coat beside me and ran out of the house."

[16]She kept Joseph's coat with her until Potiphar came home. [17]Then she told him her story. She said, "That Hebrew slave you brought us came to me to make sport of me. [18]But I screamed for help. So he left his coat beside me and ran out of the house."

[19]Potiphar's wife told him, "That's how your slave treated me." When Joseph's master heard her story, he became very angry. [20]So he put Joseph in prison. It was the place where the king's prisoners were kept.

While Joseph was there in the prison, [21]the LORD was with him. He was kind to him.

So the man who was running the prison was pleased with Joseph. [22]He put Joseph in charge of all of the prisoners. He made him accountable for everything that was done there. [23]The man who ran the prison didn't pay attention to anything that was in Joseph's care.

The LORD was with Joseph. He gave Joseph success in everything he did.

The Wine Taster and the Baker

40 Some time later, the Egyptian king's baker and wine taster did something their master didn't like.

[2]So Pharaoh became angry with his two officials, the chief wine taster and the chief baker. [3]He put them in prison in the house of the captain of the palace guard. It was the same prison where Joseph was kept.

[4]The captain put Joseph in charge of those men. So Joseph took care of them.

Some time passed while they were in prison. [5]Then each of the two men had a dream. The men were the Egyptian king's baker and wine taster. They were being held in prison. Both of them had dreams the same night. Each of their dreams had its own meaning.

[6]Joseph came to them the next morning. He saw that they were sad. [7]They were Pharaoh's officials, and they were in prison with Joseph in his master's house. So he asked them, "Why do you look so sad today?"

[8]"We both had dreams," they answered. "But no one can tell us what they mean."

Then Joseph said to them, "Only God knows what dreams mean. Tell me your dreams."

[9]So the chief wine taster told Joseph his dream. He said to him, "In my dream I saw a vine in front of me. [10]There were three branches on the vine. As soon as it budded, it flowered. And bunches of ripe grapes grew on it.

[11]"Pharaoh's cup was in my hand. I took the grapes. I squeezed them into Pharaoh's cup. Then I put the cup in his hand."

[12]"Here's what your dream means," Joseph said to him. "The three branches are three days. [13]In three days Pharaoh will let you out of prison. He'll give your position back to you. And you will put Pharaoh's cup in his hand. That's what you used to do when you were his wine taster.

[14]"But when everything is going well with you, remember me. Do me a favor. Speak to Pharaoh about me. Get me out of this prison. [15]I was taken away from the land of the Hebrews by force. Even here I haven't done anything to be put in prison for."

[16]The chief baker saw that Joseph had given a positive meaning to the wine taster's dream. So he said to Joseph, "I had a dream too. There were three baskets of bread on my head. [17]All kinds of baked goods for Pharaoh were in the top basket. But the birds were eating them out of the basket that was on my head."

[18]"Here's what your dream means," Joseph said. "The three baskets are three days. [19]In three days Pharaoh will cut your head off. Then he will stick a pole through your body and set the pole up. The birds will eat up your body."

[20]The third day was Pharaoh's birthday. He had a big dinner prepared for all of his officials. He brought the chief wine taster and the chief baker out of prison. He did it in front of his officials. [21]He gave the chief wine taster's position back to him. Once again the wine taster put the cup into Pharaoh's hand.

[22]But Pharaoh had a pole stuck through the chief baker's body. Then he had the pole set up.

Everything happened exactly as Joseph had told them when he explained their dreams.

[23]But the chief wine taster didn't remember Joseph. In fact, he forgot all about him.

Pharaoh Has Two Dreams

41 When two full years had passed, Pharaoh had a dream. In his dream, he was standing by the Nile River. ²Seven cows came up out of the river. They looked healthy and fat. They were eating some of the tall grass that was growing along the river.

³After them, seven other cows came up out of the Nile. They looked ugly and skinny. They were standing beside the other cows on the riverbank.

⁴The ugly, skinny cows ate up the seven cows that looked healthy and fat. Then Pharaoh woke up.

⁵He fell asleep again and had a second dream. In that dream, seven heads of grain were growing on one stem. They were healthy and good.

⁶After them, seven other heads of grain came up. They were thin and dried up by the east wind.

⁷The thin heads of grain swallowed up the seven healthy, full heads. Then Pharaoh woke up. It had been a dream.

⁸In the morning he was worried. So he sent for all of the magicians and wise men of Egypt. Pharaoh told them his dreams. But no one could tell him what they meant.

⁹Then the chief wine taster spoke up. He said to Pharaoh, "Now I remember that I've done something wrong. ¹⁰Pharaoh was once angry with his servants. He put me and the chief baker in prison. We were in the house of the captain of the palace guard. ¹¹Each of us had a dream the same night. Each dream had its own meaning.

¹²"A young Hebrew servant was there with us. He was a servant of the captain of the guard. We told him our dreams. And he explained them to us. He told each of us the meaning of our dreams. ¹³Things turned out exactly as he said they would. I was given back my position. The other man had a pole stuck through his body."

¹⁴So Pharaoh sent for Joseph. He was quickly brought out of the prison. Joseph shaved himself and changed his clothes. Then he came to Pharaoh.

¹⁵Pharaoh said to Joseph, "I had a dream. No one can tell me what it means. But I've heard that when you hear a dream you can explain it."

¹⁶"I can't do it," Joseph replied to Pharaoh. "But God will give Pharaoh the answer he wants."

¹⁷Then Pharaoh told Joseph what he had dreamed. He said, "I was standing on the bank of the Nile River. ¹⁸Seven cows came up out of the river. They were fat and good-looking. They were eating the tall grass that was growing along the river.

¹⁹"After them, seven other cows came up. They were bony and very ugly and thin. I had never seen such ugly cows in the whole land of Egypt.

²⁰"The thin, ugly cows ate up the seven fat cows that came up first. ²¹But even after the thin cows ate up the fat ones, no one could tell that they had eaten them. They looked just as ugly as before. Then I woke up.

²²"In my dreams I also saw seven heads of grain. They were full and good. They were all growing on one stem.

²³"After them, seven other heads of grain came up. They were weak and thin and dried up by the east wind.

²⁴"The thin heads of grain swallowed up the seven good heads. I told my dreams to the magicians. But none of them could explain them to me."

²⁵Then Joseph said to Pharaoh, "Both of Pharaoh's dreams have the same meaning. God has shown Pharaoh what he is about to do. ²⁶The seven good cows are seven years. And the seven good heads of grain are seven years. Both dreams mean the same thing.

²⁷"The seven thin, ugly cows that came up later are seven years. So are the seven worthless heads of grain that were dried up by the east wind. They are seven years when there won't be enough food.

²⁸"It's exactly as I said to Pharaoh. God has shown Pharaoh what he's about to do. ²⁹Seven years with plenty of food are coming to the whole land of Egypt.

³⁰"But seven years when there won't be enough food will follow them. Then everyone will forget about all of the food Egypt had. Terrible hunger will destroy the land. ³¹There won't be anything left to remind people of the years when there was plenty of food in the land. That's how bad the hunger that follows will be.

³²"God gave the dream to Pharaoh in two forms. That's because the matter has been firmly decided by God. And it's because God will do it soon.

³³"So Pharaoh should look for a wise and understanding man. He should put him in charge of the land of Egypt. ³⁴"Pharaoh should appoint officials to be in charge of the land. They should take a fifth of the harvest in Egypt during the seven years when there's plenty of food. ³⁵They should collect all of the extra food of the good years that are coming. Pharaoh should give them authority to store

POWER / SURGE

WISE   W

THEN PHARAOH SAID TO JOSEPH, "GOD HAS MADE ALL OF THIS KNOWN TO YOU. NO ONE IS AS WISE AND UNDERSTANDING AS YOU ARE."
—— GENESIS 41:39 ——

up the grain. They should keep it in the cities for food.

36"The grain should be stored up for the country to use later. It will be needed during the seven years when there isn't enough food in Egypt. Then the country won't be destroyed just because it doesn't have enough food."

37The plan seemed good to Pharaoh and all of his officials. 38So Pharaoh said to them, "The spirit of God is in this man. We can't find anyone else like him, can we?"

39Then Pharaoh said to Joseph, "God has made all of this known to you. No one is as wise and understanding as you are. 40You will be in charge of my palace. All of my people must obey your orders. I will be greater than you only because I'm the one who sits on the throne."

Joseph Is Put in Charge of Egypt

41So Pharaoh said to Joseph, "I'm putting you in charge of the whole land of Egypt."

42Then Pharaoh took his ring off his finger. It was the ring he used to stamp all of the official papers. He put it on Joseph's finger. He dressed him in robes that were made out of fine linen. He put a gold chain around his neck.

43He also had him ride in a chariot. Joseph was now next in command after Pharaoh. People went in front of him and shouted, "Get down on your knees!"

By doing all of those things, Pharaoh put Joseph in charge of the whole land of Egypt.

44Then Pharaoh said to Joseph, "I am Pharaoh. But without your word, no one will do anything in the whole land of Egypt."

45Pharaoh gave Joseph the name Zaphenath-Paneah. He gave him a wife.

She was Asenath, the daughter of Potiphera. Potiphera was the priest of On.

Joseph traveled all over the land of Egypt.

46Joseph was 30 years old when he began serving Pharaoh, the king of Egypt. He left Pharaoh's palace and traveled all over Egypt.

47During the seven years when there was plenty of food, the land produced more than the people needed.

48Joseph collected all of the extra food produced in those seven years in Egypt. He stored it in the cities. In each city he stored up the food that was grown in the fields around it. 49Joseph stored up huge amounts of grain. It was like the sand of the sea. There was so much grain it couldn't be measured. So Joseph stopped keeping records of it.

50Before the years when there wasn't enough food, two sons were born to Joseph. He had them by Asenath, the daughter of Potiphera. Potiphera was the priest of On.

51Joseph named his first son Manasseh. That's because he said, "God has made me forget all of my trouble and my father's whole family."

52He named the second son Ephraim. That's because he said, "God has given me children in the land where I've suffered so much."

53The seven years when there was plenty of food in Egypt came to an end. 54Then the seven years when there wasn't enough food began. It happened exactly as Joseph had said it would. There wasn't enough food in any of the other lands. But in the whole land of Egypt there was food.

55When all of the people of Egypt began to get hungry, they cried out to Pharaoh for food. He told all of the Egyptians, "Go to Joseph. Do what he tells you."

56There wasn't enough food anywhere in the country. So Joseph opened the storerooms. He sold grain to the Egyptians because people were very hungry all over Egypt.

57People from all of the other countries came to Egypt. They came to buy grain from Joseph. That's because people were very hungry all over the world.

Joseph's Brothers Go Down to Egypt

42 Jacob found out that there was grain in Egypt. So he said to his sons, "Why do you just keep looking at each other?" **2**He continued, "I've heard there's grain in Egypt. Go down there. Buy some for us. Then we'll live and not die."

3So ten of Joseph's brothers went down to Egypt to buy grain there. **4**But Jacob didn't send Joseph's brother Benjamin with them. He was afraid Benjamin might be harmed.

5Israel's sons were among the people who went to buy grain. There wasn't enough food in the land of Canaan.

6Joseph was the governor of the land. He was the one who sold grain to all of its people. When Joseph's brothers arrived, they bowed down to him with their faces to the ground.

7As soon as Joseph saw his brothers, he recognized them. But he pretended to be a stranger. He spoke to them in a mean way. "Where do you come from?" he asked.

"From the land of Canaan," they replied. "We've come to buy food."

8Joseph recognized his brothers, but they didn't recognize him. **9**Then Joseph remembered his dreams about them. So he said to them, "You are spies! You have come to see the places where our land isn't guarded very well."

10"No, sir," they answered. "We've come to buy food. **11**All of us are the sons of one man. We're honest men. We aren't spies."

12"No!" he said to them. "You have come to see the places where our land isn't guarded very well."

13But they replied, "We were 12 brothers. All of us were the sons of one man. He lives in the land of Canaan. Our youngest brother is now with our father. And one brother is gone."

14Joseph said to them, "I still say you are spies! **15**So I'm going to put you to the test. You can be sure that Pharaoh lives. And you can be just as sure that you won't leave this place unless your youngest brother comes here. I promise with an oath that you won't leave here. **16**Send one of you back to get your brother. The rest of you will be kept in prison.

"I'll put your words to the test. Then we'll find out whether you are telling the truth. You can be sure that Pharaoh lives. And you can be just as sure that if you aren't telling the truth, we'll know that you are spies!"

17So Joseph kept all of them under guard for three days.

18On the third day, Joseph spoke to them again. He said, "Do what I say. Then you will live, because I have respect for God. **19**If you are honest men, let one of your brothers stay here in prison. The rest of you may go and take grain back to your hungry families.

20"But you must bring your youngest brother to me. That will prove that your words are true. Then you won't die." So they did what he said.

21They said to one another, "God is certainly punishing us because of our brother. We saw how troubled he was when he begged us to let him live. But we wouldn't listen. That's why all of this trouble has come to us."

22Reuben replied, "Didn't I tell you not to sin against the boy? But you wouldn't listen! Now we're being held accountable for killing him."

23They didn't realize that Joseph could understand what they were saying. He was using someone else to explain their words to him in the Egyptian language.

24Joseph turned away from them and began to sob. Then he turned around and spoke to them again. He had Simeon taken and tied up right there in front of them.

25Joseph gave orders to have their bags filled with grain. He had each man's money put back into his sack. He also made sure they were given food for their journey.

26Then the brothers loaded their grain on their donkeys and left.

27When night came, they stopped. One of them opened his sack to get feed for his donkey. He saw his money in the top of his sack. **28**"My money has been given back," he said to his brothers. "Here it is in my sack."

They had a sinking feeling in their

hearts. They began to tremble. They turned to each other and said, "What has God done to us?"

²⁹They came to their father Jacob in the land of Canaan. They told him everything that had happened to them.

They said, ³⁰"The man who is the governor of the land spoke to us in a mean way. He treated us as if we were spying on the land. ³¹But we said to him, 'We're honest men. We aren't spies. ³²We were 12 brothers. All of us were the sons of one father. But now one brother is gone. And our youngest brother is with our father in Canaan.'

³³"Then the man who is the governor of the land spoke to us. He said, 'Here's how I will know whether you are honest men. Leave one of your brothers here with me. Take food for your hungry families and go.

³⁴" 'But bring your youngest brother to me. Then I'll know that you are honest men and not spies. I'll give your brother back to you. And you will be free to trade in the land.' "

³⁵They began emptying their sacks. There in each man's sack was his bag of money! When they and their father saw the money bags, they were afraid.

³⁶Their father Jacob said to them, "You have taken my children away from me. Joseph is gone. Simeon is gone. Now you want to take Benjamin. Everything is going against me!"

³⁷Then Reuben spoke to his father. He said, "You can put both of my sons to death if I don't bring Benjamin back to you. Place him in my care. I'll bring him back."

³⁸But Jacob said, "My son will not go down there with you. His brother is dead. He's the only one left here with me. Suppose he's harmed on the journey you are taking. Then I would die as a sad old man. I would go down into the grave full of sorrow."

Joseph's Brothers Go Down to Egypt Again

43 There still wasn't enough food anywhere in the land. ²After a while Jacob's family had eaten all of the grain the brothers had brought from Egypt.

So their father said to them, "Go back. Buy us a little more food."

³But Judah said to him, "The man gave us a strong warning. He said, 'You won't see my face again unless your brother comes with you.' ⁴So send our brother along with us. Then we'll go down and buy food for you.

⁵"If you won't send him, we won't go down. The man said to us, 'You won't see my face again unless your brother comes with you.' "

⁶Israel asked, "Why did you bring this trouble to me? Why did you tell the man you had another brother?"

⁷They replied, "The man questioned us closely about ourselves and our family. 'Is your father still living?' he asked us. 'Do you have another brother?'

"We just answered his questions. How could we possibly know he would say, 'Bring your brother down here'?"

⁸Judah spoke to Israel his father. "Send the boy along with me," he said. "We'll go at once. Then we and you and our children will live and not die.

⁹"I myself promise to keep him safe. You can hold me accountable for him. I'll bring him back to you. I'll set him right here in front of you. If I don't, you can put the blame on me for the rest of my life.

¹⁰"As it is, we've already waited too long. We could have gone to Egypt and back twice by now."

¹¹Then their father Israel spoke to them. He said, "If that's the way it has to be, then do what I tell you. Put some of the best things from our land in your bags. Take them down to the man as a gift. Take some lotion and a little honey. Take some spices and myrrh. Take some pistachio nuts and almonds. ¹²Take twice the amount of money with you. You have to give back the money that was put in your sacks. Maybe it was a mistake.

¹³"Also take your brother. Go back to the man at once. ¹⁴May the Mighty God cause him to show you mercy. May the man let your other brother and Benjamin come back with you. And if I lose my sons, I lose them."

¹⁵So the men took the gifts. They took twice the amount of money. They also took Benjamin. They hurried down to Egypt and went to Joseph.

¹⁶When Joseph saw Benjamin with them, he spoke to the manager of his house. "Take these men to my house," he said. "Kill an animal and prepare dinner. I want them to eat with me at noon."

¹⁷The manager did what Joseph told him to do. He took the men to Joseph's house.

¹⁸They were afraid when they were taken to Joseph's house. They thought, "We were brought here because of the money that was put back in our sacks the first

time. He wants to attack us and overpower us. Then he can hold us as slaves and take our donkeys."

19So they went up to Joseph's manager. They spoke to him at the entrance to the house. 20"Please, sir," they said. "We came down here the first time to buy food. 21We opened our sacks at the place where we stopped for the night. Each of us found in our sacks the money we had paid. So we've brought it back with us. 22We've also brought more money with us to buy food. We don't know who put our money in our sacks."

23"It's all right," the manager said. "Don't be afraid. Your God, the God of your father, has given you riches in your sacks. I received your money." Then he brought Simeon out to them.

24The manager took the men into Joseph's house. He gave them water to wash their feet. He provided feed for their donkeys. 25They prepared their gifts for Joseph. He was planning to arrive at noon. They had heard that they were going to eat there.

26When Joseph came home, they gave him the gifts they had brought into the house. They bowed down to the ground in front of him.

27He asked them how they were. Then he said, "How is your old father you told me about? Is he still living?"

28They replied, "Your servant our father is still alive and well." And they bowed low to show him honor.

29Joseph looked around. Then he saw his brother Benjamin, his own mother's son. He asked, "Is this your youngest brother? Is he the one you told me about?" He continued, "May God be gracious to you, my son."

30It moved him deeply to see his brother. So Joseph hurried out and looked for a place to cry. He went into his own room and cried there.

31Then he washed his face and came

out. He calmed down and said, "Serve the food."

32They served Joseph by himself. They served the brothers by themselves. They also served the Egyptians who ate with him by themselves. Because of their beliefs, Egyptians couldn't eat with Hebrews.

33The brothers had been given places in front of Joseph. They had been seated in the order of their ages, from the oldest to the youngest. That made them look at each other in great surprise.

34While they were eating, some food was brought to them from Joseph's table. Benjamin was given five times as much as anyone else. So all of Joseph's brothers ate and drank a lot with him.

A Silver Cup in a Sack

44 Joseph told the manager of his house what to do. "Fill the men's sacks with as much food as they can carry," he said. "Put each man's money in his sack.

2"Then put my silver cup in the youngest one's sack. Put it there along with the money he paid for his grain." So the manager did what Joseph told him to do.

3When morning came, the men were sent on their way with their donkeys. 4They hadn't gone very far from the city when Joseph spoke to his manager. "Go after those men at once," he said. "Catch up with them. Say to them, 'My master was good to you. Why have you paid him back by doing evil? 5Isn't this the cup my master drinks from? Doesn't he also use it to figure things out? You have done an evil thing.' "

6When the manager caught up with them, he told them what Joseph had said. 7But they said to him, "Why do you say these things? We would never do anything like that! 8We even brought back to you from Canaan the money we found in our sacks. So why would we steal silver or gold from your master's house? 9"If you find out that any of us has the cup, he will die. And the rest of us will become your slaves."

10"All right, then," he said. "As you wish. The one who is found to have the cup will become my slave. But the rest of you will be free from blame."

11Each of them quickly put his sack down on the ground and opened it. 12Then the manager started to search. He began with the oldest and ended with

POWER-SURGE

GIVING Ⓖ

WHEN JOSEPH CAME HOME, THEY GAVE HIM THE GIFTS THEY HAD BROUGHT.
—— GENESIS 43:26 ——

the youngest. The cup was found in Benjamin's sack.

13When that happened, they were so upset they tore their clothes. Then all of them loaded their donkeys and went back to the city.

14Joseph was still in the house when Judah and his brothers came in. They threw themselves down on the ground in front of him.

15Joseph said to them, "What have you done? Don't you know that a man like me has ways to figure things out?"

16"What can we say to you?" Judah replied. "What can we say? How can we prove we haven't done anything wrong? God has shown you that we are guilty. We are now your slaves. All of us are, including the one who was found to have the cup."

17But Joseph said, "I would never do anything like that! Only the man who was found to have the cup will become my slave. The rest of you may go back to your father in peace."

18Then Judah went up to him. He said, "Please, sir. Let me speak a word to you. Don't be angry with me, even though you are equal to Pharaoh himself. **19**You asked us, 'Do you have a father or a brother?' **20**We answered, 'We have an old father. A young son was born to him when he was old. His brother is dead. He's the only one of his mother's sons left. And his father loves him.'

21"Then you said to us, 'Bring him down to me. I want to see him for myself.' **22**"We said to you, 'The boy can't leave his father. If he does, his father will die.' **23**"But you told us, 'Your youngest brother must come down here with you. If he doesn't, you won't see my face again.' **24**So we went back to my father. We told him what you had said.

25"Then our father said, 'Go back. Buy a little more food.'

26"But we said, 'We can't go down. We'll only go if our youngest brother goes there with us. We can't even see the man's face unless our youngest brother goes with us.'

27"Your servant my father said to us, 'You know that my wife had two sons by me. **28**One of them went away from me. And I said, "He must have been torn to pieces." I haven't seen him since. **29**What if you take this one from me too and he is harmed? Then you would cause me to die as a sad old man. I would go down into the grave full of pain and suffering.'

30"So now, what will happen if the boy isn't with us when I go back to my father? His life is closely tied up with the boy's life. **31**When he sees that the boy isn't with us, he'll die as a sad old man. Because of us, he'll go down into the grave full of sorrow.

32"I promised my father I would keep the boy safe. I said, 'Father, I'll bring him back to you. If I don't, you can put the blame on me for the rest of my life.'

33"Now then, please let me stay here. Let me be your slave in place of the boy. Let the boy return with his brothers. **34**How can I go back to my father if the boy isn't with me? Don't let me see the pain and suffering that would come to my father."

Joseph Tells His Brothers Who He Is

45 Joseph couldn't control himself anymore in front of all of his attendants. He cried out, "Have everyone leave me!"

So there wasn't anyone with Joseph when he told his brothers who he was. **2**He sobbed so loudly that the Egyptians heard him. Everyone in Pharaoh's house heard about it.

3Joseph said to his brothers, "I am Joseph! Is my father still alive?"

But his brothers weren't able to answer him. They were too afraid of him.

4Joseph said to his brothers, "Come close to me." So they did.

Then he said, "I am your brother Joseph. I'm the one you sold into Egypt. **5**But don't be upset. And don't be angry with yourselves because you sold me here. God sent me ahead of you to save many lives.

6"For two years now, there hasn't been enough food in the land. And for the next five years, people won't be plowing or gathering crops. **7**But God sent me ahead of you to keep some of you alive on earth. He sent me here to save your lives by an act of mighty power.

8"So then, it wasn't you who sent me here. It was God. He made me like a father to Pharaoh. He made me master of Pharaoh's whole house. He made me ruler of the whole land of Egypt.

9"Now hurry back to my father. Say to him, 'Your son Joseph says, "God has made me master of the whole land of Egypt. Come down to me. Don't waste any time. **10**You will live in the area of Goshen. You, your children and grandchildren, your flocks and herds, and everything you have will be near me.

11There I will provide everything you need.

" ' "Five years without enough food are still coming. If you don't come down here, you and your family and everyone who belongs to you will lose everything." ' "

12"Brothers, you can see for yourselves that it's really I, Joseph, speaking to you. My brother Benjamin can see it too.

13"Tell my father about all of the honor that has been given to me in Egypt. Tell him about everything you have seen. And bring my father down here quickly."

14Then Joseph threw his arms around his brother Benjamin and sobbed. Benjamin also hugged him and sobbed. **15**Joseph kissed all of his brothers and sobbed over them. After that, his brothers talked with him.

16The news reached Pharaoh's palace that Joseph's brothers had come. Pharaoh and all of his officials were pleased.

17Pharaoh said to Joseph, "Here's what I want you to tell your brothers. Say to them, 'Load your animals. Return to the land of Canaan. **18**Bring your father and your families back to me. I'll give you the best land in Egypt. You can enjoy all of the good things in the land.'

19"And here's something else I want you to tell them. Say to them, 'Take some carts from Egypt. Your children and your wives can use them. Get your father and come back. **20**Don't worry about the things you have back there. The best of everything in Egypt will belong to you.' "

21So the sons of Israel did it. Joseph gave them carts, as Pharaoh had commanded. He also gave them supplies for their journey. **22**He gave new clothes to each of them.

But he gave more than seven pounds of silver to Benjamin. He also gave him five sets of clothes.

23He sent his father ten donkeys loaded with the best things from Egypt. He also sent ten female donkeys loaded with grain and bread and other supplies for his journey.

24Then Joseph sent his brothers away. As they were leaving he said to them, "Don't argue on the way!"

25So they went up out of Egypt. They came to their father Jacob in the land of Canaan. **26**They told him, "Joseph is still alive! In fact, he is ruler of the whole land of Egypt."

Jacob was shocked. He didn't believe them. **27**So they told him everything Joseph had said to them.

Jacob saw the carts Joseph had sent to carry him back. That gave new life to their father Jacob. **28**Israel said, "I believe it now! My son Joseph is still alive. I'll go and see him before I die."

Jacob Goes Down to Egypt

46 So Israel started out with everything that belonged to him. When he reached Beersheba, he offered sacrifices to the God of his father Isaac.

2God spoke to Israel in a vision at night. "Jacob! Jacob!" he said.

"Here I am," Jacob replied.

3"I am God. I am the God of your father," he said. "Do not be afraid to go down to Egypt. There I will make you into a great nation. **4**I will go down to Egypt with you. You can be sure that I will bring you back again. And when you die, Joseph will close your eyes with his own hand."

5Then Jacob left Beersheba. Israel's sons put their father Jacob and their families in the carts that Pharaoh had sent to carry them.

6So Jacob and his whole family went to Egypt. They took their livestock with them. And they took everything they had gotten in Canaan. **7**Jacob took his sons and grandsons with him to Egypt. He also took his daughters and granddaughters. He took all of his children and grandchildren with him.

8Here are the names of Israel's children and grandchildren who went to Egypt. Jacob and all of his children and grandchildren are included.

Reuben was Jacob's oldest son.

9The sons of Reuben were
  Hanoch, Pallu, Hezron and Carmi.
10The sons of Simeon were
  Jemuel, Jamin, Ohad, Jakin, Zohar
  and Shaul. Shaul was the son of
  a woman from Canaan.
11The sons of Levi were
  Gershon, Kohath and Merari.
12The sons of Judah were
  Er, Onan, Shelah, Perez and Zerah.
  But Er and Onan had died in the
  land of Canaan. The sons of
  Perez were Hezron and Hamul.
13The sons of Issachar were
  Tola, Puah, Jashub and Shimron.
14The sons of Zebulun were
  Sered, Elon and Jahleel.

15Those were the sons and grandsons who were born to Jacob and Leah in Paddan Aram. Leah also had a daughter by Jacob. Her name was Dinah. The total number of people in the family line of Jacob and Leah was 33.

16 The sons of Gad were
Zephon, Haggi, Shuni, Ezbon, Eri, Arodi and Areli.

17 The sons of Asher were
Imnah, Ishvah, Ishvi and Beriah. Their sister was Serah. The sons of Beriah were Heber and Malkiel.

18 Those were the children and grandchildren who were born to Jacob and Zilpah. Laban had given Zilpah to his daughter Leah. The total number of people in the family line of Jacob and Zilpah was 16.

19 The sons of Jacob's wife Rachel were
Joseph and Benjamin. 20 In Egypt, Asenath had Manasseh and Ephraim by Joseph. Asenath was the daughter of Potiphera. Potiphera was the priest of On.

21 The sons of Benjamin were
Bela, Beker, Ashbel, Gera, Naaman, Ehi, Rosh, Muppim, Huppim and Ard.

22 Those were the sons and grandsons who were born to Jacob and Rachel. The total number of people in the family line of Jacob and Rachel was 14.

23 The son of Dan was
Hushim.

24 The sons of Naphtali were
Jahziel, Guni, Jezer and Shillem.

25 Those were the sons and grandsons who were born to Jacob and Bilhah. Laban had given Bilhah to his daughter Rachel. The total number of people in the family line of Jacob and Bilhah was seven.

26 The total number of those who went to Egypt with Jacob was 66. That number includes only his own children and grandchildren. It doesn't include his sons' wives or his grandsons' wives.

27 The total number of the members of Jacob's family who went to Egypt was 70. That includes the two sons who had been born to Joseph in Egypt.

28 Jacob sent Judah ahead of him to Joseph. He sent him to get directions to Goshen. And so they arrived in the area of Goshen.

29 Then Joseph had his servants get his chariot ready. He went to Goshen to meet his father Israel. As soon as he came to his father, Joseph threw his arms around him. Then Joseph sobbed for a long time.

30 Israel said to Joseph, "I have seen for myself that you are still alive. Now I'm ready to die."

31 Then Joseph spoke to his brothers and to the rest of his father's family. He said, "I will go up and speak to Pharaoh. I'll say to him, 'My brothers and the rest of my father's family have come to me. They were living in the land of Canaan. 32 The men are shepherds. They take care of livestock. They've brought along their flocks and herds and everything they own.'

33 "Pharaoh will send for you. He'll ask, 'What do you do for a living?' 34 You should answer, 'We've taken care of livestock from the time we were boys. We've done just as our fathers did.' It's the practice of the people of Egypt not to mix with shepherds.

"So Pharaoh will let you settle in the area of Goshen."

47 Joseph went to Pharaoh. He told him, "My father and brothers have come from the land of Canaan. They've brought along their flocks and herds and everything they own. They are now in Goshen."

2 Joseph had chosen five of his brothers to meet with Pharaoh.

3 Pharaoh asked the brothers, "What do you do for a living?"

"We're shepherds," they replied to Pharaoh. "And that's what our fathers were." 4 They also said to him, "We've come to live in Egypt for a while. There isn't enough food anywhere in Canaan. There isn't any grass for our flocks. So please let us settle in Goshen."

5 Pharaoh said to Joseph, "Your father and your brothers have come to you. 6 The land of Egypt is open to you. Settle your father and brothers in the best part of the land. Let them live in Goshen. Do any of them have special skills? If they do, put them in charge of my own livestock."

7 Then Joseph brought his father Jacob in. He brought him in to meet Pharaoh. Jacob gave Pharaoh his blessing. 8 Then Pharaoh asked him, "How old are you?"

9 Jacob said to Pharaoh, "The years of my journey through life are 130. My years have been few and hard. They aren't as many as the years of my fathers before me."

10 Jacob gave Pharaoh his blessing. Then he left him.

11 So Joseph settled his father and his brothers in Egypt. He gave them property in the best part of the land, just as Pharaoh had directed him to do. That part was known as the territory of Rameses.

12 Joseph also provided food for his

father and brothers. He provided for them and the rest of his father's family. He gave them enough for all of their children.

Joseph Saves Many Lives

13But there wasn't any food in the whole area. In fact, there wasn't enough food anywhere. Both Egypt and Canaan lost their strength because there wasn't enough food to go around.

14Joseph collected all of the money that was in Egypt and Canaan. People paid it to him for the grain they were buying. And Joseph brought it to Pharaoh's palace. 15When the money of the people of Egypt and Canaan was gone, all of the Egyptians came to Joseph. They said, "Give us food. Why should we die right in front of your eyes? Our money is all gone."

16"Then bring your livestock," said Joseph. "You say your money is gone. So I'll trade you food for your livestock."

17They brought their livestock to Joseph. He traded them food for their animals. They gave him their horses, sheep, goats, cattle and donkeys. He brought the people through that year by trading them food for all of their livestock.

18When that year was over, they came to him the next year. They said, "We can't hide the truth from you. Our money is gone. Our livestock belongs to you. We don't have anything left to give you except our bodies and our land. 19Why should we die right in front of your eyes? Why should our land be destroyed as well? Trade us food for ourselves and our land. Then we and our land will belong to Pharaoh. Give us some seeds so we can live and not die. We don't want the land to become a desert."

20So Joseph bought all of the land in Egypt for Pharaoh. All of the people of Egypt sold their fields. They did that because there wasn't enough food anywhere. In that way, the land became Pharaoh's. 21Joseph made the people slaves from one end of Egypt to the other.

22But he didn't buy the land that belonged to the priests. They received a regular share of food from Pharaoh. They had enough food from what Pharaoh gave them. That's why they didn't have to sell their land.

23Joseph said to the people, "I've bought you and your land today for Pharaoh. So here are some seeds for you to plant in the ground. 24But when the crop comes in, give a fifth of it to Pharaoh.

Keep the other four-fifths for yourselves. They will be seeds for the fields. And they will be food for yourselves, your children, and the other people who live with you."

25"You have saved our lives," they said. "If you are pleased with us, we will be slaves to Pharaoh."

26So Joseph made a law about land in Egypt. It's still the law today. A fifth of the produce belongs to Pharaoh. Only the land belonging to the priests didn't become Pharaoh's.

27The people of Israel settled in Egypt in the area of Goshen. They received property there. They had children and greatly increased their numbers.

28Jacob lived 17 years in Egypt. He lived a total of 147 years.

29The time came near for Israel to die. So he sent for his son Joseph. He said to him, "If you are pleased with me, put your hand under my thigh. Promise me that you will be kind and faithful to me. Don't bury me in Egypt. 30When I join the members of my family who have already died, carry me out of Egypt. Bury me where they are buried."

"I'll do exactly as you say," Joseph said.

31"Promise me with an oath that you will do it," Jacob said. So Joseph promised him. And Israel worshiped God as he leaned on the top of his wooden staff.

Ephraim and Manasseh

48 Some time later Joseph was told, "Your father is sick." So he took his two sons Manasseh and Ephraim along with him. 2Jacob was told, "Your son Joseph has come to you." So Israel became stronger and sat up in bed.

3Jacob said to Joseph, "The Mighty God appeared to me at Luz in the land of Canaan. He blessed me there. 4He said to me, 'I am going to give you children. I will increase your numbers. I will make you a community of nations. And I will give this land to your children after you. It will belong to them forever.'

5"Now then, two sons were born to you in Egypt. It happened before I came to you here. They will be counted as my own sons. Ephraim and Manasseh will belong to me, in the same way that Reuben and Simeon belong to me.

6"Any children who are born to you after them will belong to you. Any territory they receive will come from the land that is given to Ephraim and Manasseh.

7"As I was returning from Paddan, Rachel died. It made me very sad. She died in the land of Canaan while we were still on the way. We weren't very far away from Ephrath. So I buried her body there beside the road to Ephrath." Ephrath was also called Bethlehem.

8Israel saw Joseph's sons. He asked, "Who are they?"

9"They are the sons God has given me here," Joseph said to his father.

Then Israel said, "Bring them to me. I want to give them my blessing."

10Israel's eyes were weak because he was old. He couldn't see very well. So Joseph brought his sons close to him. His father kissed them and hugged them.

11Israel said to Joseph, "I never thought I'd see your face again. But now God has let me see your children too."

12Then Joseph took his sons away from Israel's knees. He bowed down with his face to the ground.

13Joseph placed Ephraim on his right, toward Israel's left hand. He placed Manasseh on his left, toward Israel's right hand. Then he brought them close to Jacob.

14But Israel reached out his right hand and put it on Ephraim's head. He did it even though Ephraim was the younger son. He crossed his arms and put his left hand on Manasseh's head. He did it even though Manasseh was the older son.

15Then Israel gave Joseph his blessing. He said,

"May God bless these boys.
　He is the God of my grandfather
　　Abraham and my father Isaac.
　They walked with him.
He is the God who has been my
　　shepherd
　all of my life to this very day.
16He is the Angel who has saved me from
　　all harm.
　May he bless these boys.
　May they be called by my name.
　May they also be called by the
　　names of my grandfather
　　Abraham and my father Isaac.
　And may they greatly increase their
　　numbers
　on the earth."

17Joseph saw his father putting his right hand on Ephraim's head. And Joseph didn't like it. So he took hold of his father's hand to move it over to Manasseh's head. **18**Joseph said to him, "No, my father. Here's my older son. Put your right hand on his head."

19But his father wouldn't do it. He said, "I know, my son. I know. He too will become a nation. He too will become

great. But his younger brother will be greater than he is. His children after him will become a group of nations."

20On that day, Jacob gave them his blessing. He said,

"In the land of Israel, people will bless
　　others in your names.
　They will say, 'May God make you
　　like Ephraim and Manasseh.' "

So he put Ephraim ahead of Manasseh.

21Then Israel said to Joseph, "I'm about to die. But God will be with all of you. He'll take you back to the land of your fathers. **22**But you, Joseph, are over your brothers. So I'm giving you the range of hills I took from the Amorites. I took it with my sword and bow."

Jacob Gives Blessings to His Sons

49 Then Jacob sent for his sons. He said, "Gather around me so I can tell you what will happen to you in days to come.

2 "Sons of Jacob, come together and
　　listen.
　Listen to your father Israel.

3 "Reuben, you are my oldest son.
　You were my first child. You were
　　the first sign of my strength.
　You were first in honor. You were
　　first in power.
4 But you are as unsteady as water. So
　　you won't be first anymore.
　You had sex with your father's
　　concubine in his bed.
　You lay on his couch and made it
　　'unclean.'

5 "Simeon and Levi are brothers.
　Their swords have killed a lot of
　　people.
6 I won't share in their plans.
　I won't have anything to do with
　　them.
　They became angry and killed people.
　They cut the legs of oxen just for the
　　fun of it.
7 May the LORD put a curse on them
　　because of their terrible anger.
　I will scatter them in Jacob's land.
　I will spread them around in Israel.

8 "Judah, your brothers will praise you.
　Your enemies will be brought under
　　your control.
　Your father's sons will bow down to
　　you.
9 Judah, you are like a lion's cub.
　You return from hunting, my son.
　Like a lion, you lie down and sleep.

You are like a mother lion. Who
    dares to wake you up?
10 The right to rule will not leave Judah.
    The ruler's rod will not be taken
        from between his feet.
    It will be his until the king it belongs to
        comes.
    It will be his until the nations obey
        him.
11 He will tie his donkey to a vine.
    He will tie his colt to the very best
        branch.
    He will wash his clothes in wine.
    He will wash his robes in the red
        juice of grapes.
12 His eyes will be darker than wine.
    His teeth will be whiter than milk.

13 "Zebulun will live by the seashore.
    He will become a safe harbor for
        ships.
    His border will go out toward Sidon.

14 "Issachar is like a donkey
    lying down between two
        saddlebags.
15 He sees how good his resting place is.
    He sees that his land is pleasant.
So he'll carry a heavy load on his back.
    He will obey when he's forced to
        work.

16 "Dan will do what is fair for his
        people.
    He will do it as one of the tribes of
        Israel.
17 Dan will be a serpent by the side of the
        road.
    He will be a poisonous snake along
        the path.
    It bites the horse's heels
        so that the rider falls off backward.

18 "LORD, I look to you to save me.

19 "Gad will be attacked by a group of
        robbers.
    But he'll attack them as they run
        away.

20 "Asher's food will be rich and sweet.
    He will provide food that even a king
        would enjoy.

21 "Naphtali is a female deer that is set
        free
    and gives birth to beautiful fawns.

22 "Joseph is a vine that grows a lot of
        fruit.
    It grows close by a spring.
    Its branches climb over a wall.
23 Mean people shot arrows at him.
    They shot at him because they were
        angry.

24 But his bow remained steady.
    His strong arms moved freely.
    The hand of the Mighty One of Jacob
        was with him.
    The Shepherd, the Rock of Israel,
        stood by him.
25 Your father's God helps you.
    The Mighty One blesses you.
    He gives you blessings from the
        highest heavens.
    He gives you blessings from the
        deepest oceans.
    He blesses you with children and
        with a mother's milk.
26 Your father's blessings are great.
    They are greater than the blessings
        from the age-old mountains.
    They are greater than the gifts from
        the ancient hills.
    Let all of those blessings rest on the
        head of Joseph.
    Let them rest on the head of the one
        who is prince among his
        brothers.

27 "Benjamin is a hungry wolf.
    In the morning he eats what he has
        killed.
    In the evening he shares what he has
        stolen."

28 All of those are the 12 tribes of Israel. That's what their father said to them when he blessed them. He gave each one the blessing that was just right for him.

Jacob Dies

29 Then Jacob gave directions to his sons. He said, "I'm about to join the members of my family who have already died. Bury me with them in the cave in the field of Ephron the Hittite.

30 "The cave is in the field of Machpelah near Mamre in Canaan. Abraham had bought it as a place where he could bury his wife's body. He had bought the cave from Ephron the Hittite, along with the field.

31 "The bodies of Abraham and his wife Sarah were buried there. So were the bodies of Isaac and his wife Rebekah. I also buried Leah's body there. 32 Abraham bought the field and the cave from the Hittites."

33 When Jacob had finished telling his sons what to do, he pulled his feet up into his bed. Then he took his last breath and joined the members of his family who had already died.

50 Joseph threw himself on his father's body. He sobbed over him and kissed him.

JOSEPH

GENESIS 50:19-20

F

⚡

◆

> **Joseph said to [his brothers], "Don't be afraid...You planned to harm me. But God planned it for good. He planned to do what is now being done. He wanted to save many lives."**

Joseph thought back to when he was in prison. What long, dreary days, months, even years those had been. His brothers had stripped off his beautiful, colorful coat and had sold him as a slave. His own brothers! Joseph wondered what they told their father when Joseph didn't return with them.

Little did Joseph know that his brothers had torn his coat and stained it with goat's blood. Then they had shown it to their father, telling him an animal had killed Joseph. They didn't want their father to know what a terrible thing they had done.

Now it was years later. Life had gotten better for Joseph. He was out of prison and no longer a slave. In fact, he was now a ruler in Egypt. God had used Joseph to save many people in Egypt from a famine, a time when there was no food to eat. When some men from another country came to Joseph to ask for food, Joseph realized they were his brothers. He was powerful now. He could get back at them for the terrible things they had done. HE COULD HAVE THEM KILLED! BUT DID HE?

No. Joseph didn't do any of those things. He knew that everything that had happened was part of God's plan. Even when he was in prison. Even when he had been sad and hungry. Joseph knew God was working. So instead of hurting his brothers, Joseph forgave them. He told them he loved them anyway, because God had used their awful deeds to save many people.

BE A JOSEPH

Joseph knew that God had brought good out of the bad things that had happened to him. You can forgive like Joseph. It will take God's help. But you can forgive those who hurt you.

JOSEPH FORGAVE HIS BROTHERS FOR THE TERRIBLE THINGS THEY HAD DONE TO HIM.

THE WHOLE STORY: GENESIS 37; 39-48; 50

Go to page 70 for the next Super Hero

POWER-SURGE

FORGIVING F

FORGIVE YOUR BROTHERS. FORGIVE THE TERRIBLE THINGS THEY DID TO YOU. FORGIVE THEM FOR TREATING YOU SO BADLY.
—— GENESIS 50:17 ——

2Then Joseph talked to the doctors who served him. He told them to prepare the body of his father Israel to be buried. So the doctors prepared it. 3They took 40 days to do it. They needed that much time to prepare a body in the right way. The Egyptians sobbed over Jacob for 70 days.

4After the days of sorrow had passed, Joseph went to Pharaoh's officials. He said to them, "If you are pleased with me, speak to Pharaoh for me. Tell him, 5'My father made me take an oath and make a promise to him. He said, 'I'm about to die. Bury me in the tomb I dug for myself in the land of Canaan.' So let me go up and bury my father. Then I'll come back.' "

6Pharaoh said, "Go up and bury your father. Do what he made you promise to do."

7So Joseph went up to bury his father. All of Pharaoh's officials went with him. They were the important people of his court and all of the leaders of Egypt.

8All of Joseph's family also went. His brothers and all of the rest of his father's family went too. Only their children and their flocks and herds were left in Goshen.

9Chariots and horsemen also went up with him. It was a very large group.

10They came to the threshing floor of Atad. It was near the Jordan River. There they sobbed loudly and bitterly. Joseph set apart seven days of sadness to honor his father's memory.

11The people of Canaan who were living there saw how sad all of them were at the threshing floor of Atad. They said, "The Egyptians are having a very special service for the dead." That's why that place near the Jordan River is called Abel of the Egyptians.

12So Jacob's sons did exactly as he had commanded them. 13They carried his body to the land of Canaan. They buried it in the cave in the field of Machpelah near Mamre. Abraham had bought the cave as a place where he could bury his wife's body. He had bought it from Ephron the Hittite, along with the field.

14After Joseph buried his father, he went back to Egypt. His brothers and all of the others who had gone to help him bury his father went back with him.

Joseph Sets His Brothers Free From Their Fears

15Now that their father was dead, Joseph's brothers were worried. They said, "Remember all of the bad things we did to Joseph? What if he decides to hold those things against us? What if he pays us back for them?"

16So they sent a message to Joseph. They said, "Your father gave us directions before he died. 17He said, 'Here's what you must say to Joseph. Tell him, "I'm asking you to forgive your brothers. Forgive the terrible things they did to you. Forgive them for treating you so badly." ' Now then, please forgive our sins. We serve the God of your father."

When their message came to Joseph, he sobbed.

18Then his brothers came and threw themselves down in front of him. "We are your slaves," they said.

19But Joseph said to them, "Don't be afraid. Do you think I'm God? 20You planned to harm me. But God planned it for good. He planned to do what is now being done. He wanted to save many lives.

21"So then, don't be afraid. I'll provide for you and your children." He set them free from their fears. And he spoke in a kind way to them.

Joseph Dies

22Joseph stayed in Egypt, along with all of his father's family. He lived 110 years.

POWER-SURGE

KIND K

[JOSEPH] SET [HIS BROTHERS] FREE FROM THEIR FEARS. AND HE SPOKE IN A KIND WAY TO THEM.
—— GENESIS 50:21 ——

23He lived long enough to see Ephraim's children and grandchildren. When the children of Makir were born, they were placed on Joseph's knees and counted as his own children. Makir was the son of Manasseh.

24Joseph said to his brothers, "I'm about to die. But I'm sure that God will come to help you. He'll take you up out of this land. He'll bring you to the land he promised with an oath to give to Abraham, Isaac and Jacob."

25Joseph made the sons of Israel take an oath and make a promise to him. He said, "I'm sure that God will come to help you. Then you must carry my bones up from this place."

26So Joseph died at the age of 110. They prepared his body to be buried. Then he was placed in a casket in Egypt.

EXODUS

At the beginning of the exciting book of Exodus, the Israelites are slaves in Egypt. The Pharaoh, Egypt's king, will not let them leave. The excitement begins when God uses Moses and ten plagues to convince Pharaoh to let the Israelites go. Then the Israelites cross the Red Sea, watch as Pharaoh's soldiers drown, and travel into the desert. The heroes of Exodus love God and trust in his faithfulness. Read Exodus for thrilling stories of God's miracles, miracles that show his amazing love for his people.

HEROES IN THIS BOOK . . .

SHIPHRAH AND PUAH
PAGE 70

JOCHEBED
PAGE 72

MOSES
PAGE 74

AARON
PAGE 76

The People of Israel Are Slaves in Egypt

1 Here are the names of Israel's children who went to Egypt with Jacob. Each one went with his family.

²Jacob's sons were Reuben, Simeon, Levi, Judah, ³Issachar, Zebulun, Benjamin, ⁴Dan, Naphtali, Gad and Asher. ⁵The total number of Jacob's children and grandchildren was 70. Joseph was already in Egypt.

⁶Joseph and all of his brothers died. So did all of their children.

⁷The people of Israel had many children. They greatly increased their numbers. There were so many of them that they filled the land.

⁸Then a new king came to power in Egypt. He didn't know anything about Joseph.

⁹"Look," he said to his people. "The Israelites are far too many for us. ¹⁰Come. We must deal with them carefully. If we don't, they will increase their numbers even more. Then if war breaks out, they'll join our enemies. They'll fight against us and leave the country."

¹¹So the Egyptians put slave drivers over the people of Israel. The slave drivers beat them down and made them work hard. The Israelites built the cities of Pithom and Rameses so Pharaoh could store things there.

¹²But the more the slave drivers beat them down, the more the Israelites increased their numbers and spread out. So the Egyptians became afraid of them. ¹³They made them work hard. They didn't show them any pity. ¹⁴They made them suffer with hard labor. They forced them to work with bricks and mud. And they made them do all kinds of work in the fields. The Egyptians didn't show them any pity at all. They made them work very hard.

¹⁵There were two Hebrew women named Shiphrah and Puah. They helped other women who were having babies. The king of Egypt spoke to them. He said, ¹⁶"You are the ones who help the other Hebrew women. Watch them when they get into a sitting position to have their babies. Kill the boys. Let the girls live."

¹⁷But Shiphrah and Puah had respect for God. They didn't do what the king of Egypt had told them to do. They let the boys live.

¹⁸Then the king of Egypt sent for the women. He asked them, "Why have you done this? Why have you let the boys live?"

¹⁹The women answered Pharaoh, "Hebrew women are not like the women of Egypt. They are strong. They have their babies before we get there."

²⁰So God was kind to Shiphrah and Puah. And the people of Israel increased their numbers more and more. ²¹Shiphrah and Puah had respect for God. So he gave them families of their own.

²²Then Pharaoh gave an order to all of his people. He said, "You must throw every baby boy into the Nile River. But let every baby girl live."

Moses Is Born

2 A man and a woman from the tribe of Levi got married. ²She became pregnant and had a son by him. She saw that her baby was a fine child. So she hid him for three months.

³After that, she couldn't hide him any longer. So she got a basket that was made out of the stems of tall grass. She coated it with tar. Then she placed the child in it. She put the basket in the tall grass that grew along the bank of the Nile River. ⁴The child's sister wasn't very far away. She wanted to see what would happen to him.

⁵Pharaoh's daughter went down to the Nile River to take a bath. Her attendants were walking along the bank of the river. She saw the basket in the tall grass. So she sent her female slave to get it. ⁶When she opened it, she saw the baby. He was crying. She felt sorry for him. "This is one of the Hebrew babies," she said.

⁷Then his sister spoke to Pharaoh's daughter. She asked, "Do you want me to go and get one of the Hebrew women? She could nurse the baby for you."

8"Yes. Go," she answered. So the girl went and got the baby's mother.

9Pharaoh's daughter said to her, "Take this baby. Nurse him for me. I'll pay you." So the woman took the baby and nursed him.

10When the child grew older, she took him to Pharaoh's daughter. And he became her son. She named him Moses. She said, "I pulled him out of the water."

Moses Escapes to Midian

11Moses grew up. One day, he went out to where his own people were. He watched them while they were hard at work. He saw an Egyptian hitting a Hebrew man. The man was one of Moses' own people. 12Moses looked around and didn't see anyone. So he killed the Egyptian. Then he hid his body in the sand.

SHIPHRAH AND PUAH

EXODUS 1:17

B
★
K

But Shiphrah and Puah had respect for God. They didn't do what the king of Egypt had told them to do. They let the boys live.

Shiphrah (SHIFF-ruh) and Puah (POO-uh) stood in the street, holding hands and crying. They lived as slaves in Egypt. Whenever a Hebrew slave woman had a baby, they would go to help. Pharaoh had just ordered them to kill all the boy babies as soon as they were born.

Shiphrah and Puah knew they could never do such a thing! So they didn't. Whenever a boy baby was born, they let him live.

Soon Pharaoh realized the boy babies weren't being killed. He asked Shiphrah and Puah why they let the boy babies live. **THEIR LEGS FELT WEAK WITH FEAR AS THEY KNELT BEFORE PHARAOH.** But they had an answer for him.

"These Hebrew women are so strong. Not like weak Egyptian women. Before we can even get there to help them, they have their babies."

God heard Shiphrah and Puah's brave answer to Pharaoh. He was pleased with their answer, and he blessed them because of it. He gave each of them many children of their own.

BE A SHIPHRAH AND PUAH

When someone asks you to do something you know is wrong, be like these two women. Don't do it! God is pleased when you do right instead of wrong.

SHIPHRAH AND PUAH OBEYED GOD INSTEAD OF PHARAOH.

Go to page 72 for the next Super Hero

13The next day Moses went out again. He saw two Hebrew men fighting. He asked the one who had started the fight a question. He said, "Why are you hitting another Hebrew man?"

14The man said, "Who made you ruler and judge over us? Are you thinking about killing me as you killed the Egyptian?" Then Moses became afraid. He thought, "People must have heard about what I did."

15When Pharaoh heard about what had happened, he tried to kill Moses. But Moses escaped from Pharaoh and went to live in Midian. There he sat down by a well.

16A priest of Midian had seven daughters. They came to fill the stone tubs with water. They wanted to give water to their father's flock. **17**Some shepherds came along and drove the women away. But Moses got up and helped them. Then he gave water to their flock.

18The young women returned to their father Reuel. He asked them, "Why have you returned so early today?"

19They answered, "An Egyptian saved us from the shepherds. He even got water for us and gave it to the flock."

20"Where is he?" he asked his daughters. "Why did you leave him? Invite him to have something to eat."

21Moses agreed to stay with the man. And the man gave his daughter Zipporah to Moses to be his wife. **22**Zipporah had a son by him. Moses named him Gershom. Moses said, "I'm an outsider in a strange land."

23After a long time, the king of Egypt died. The people of Israel groaned because they were slaves. They also cried out to God. Their cry for help went up to him. **24**God heard their groans. He remembered his covenant with Abraham, Isaac and Jacob. **25**So God looked on the Israelites with favor. He was concerned about them.

The LORD Sends Moses to Save His People

3 Moses was taking care of the flock of his father-in-law Jethro. Jethro was the priest of Midian. Moses led the flock to the western side of the desert. He came to Horeb. It was the mountain of God.

2There the angel of the LORD appeared to him from inside a burning bush. Moses saw that the bush was on fire. But it didn't burn up. **3**So Moses thought, "I'll go over and see this strange sight. Why doesn't the bush burn up?"

4The LORD saw that Moses had gone over to look. So God spoke to him from inside the bush. He called out, "Moses! Moses!"

"Here I am," Moses said.

5"Do not come any closer," God said. "Take off your sandals. The place you are standing on is holy ground." **6**He continued, "I am the God of your father. I am the God of Abraham. I am the God of Isaac. And I am the God of Jacob."

When Moses heard that, he turned his face away. He was afraid to look at God.

7The LORD said, "I have seen my people suffer in Egypt. I have heard them cry out because of their slave drivers. I am concerned about their suffering.

8"So I have come down to save them from the Egyptians. I will bring them up out of that land. I will bring them into a good land. It has a lot of room. It is a land that has plenty of milk and honey. It is the home of the Canaanites, Hittites, Amorites, Perizzites, Hivites and Jebusites.

9"And now Israel's cry for help has reached me. I have seen the way the Egyptians are beating them down. **10**So now, go. I am sending you to Pharaoh. I want you to bring the Israelites out of Egypt. They are my people."

11But Moses spoke to God. "Who am I that I should go to Pharaoh?" he said. "Who am I that I should bring the Israelites out of Egypt?"

12God said, "I will be with you. I will give you a miraculous sign. It will prove that I have sent you. When you have brought the people out of Egypt, all of you will worship me on this mountain."

13Moses said to God, "Suppose I go to the people of Israel. Suppose I say to them, 'The God of your fathers has sent me to you.' Suppose they ask me, 'What is his name?' Then what should I tell them?"

14God said to Moses, "I AM WHO I AM. Here is what you must say to the Israelites. Tell them, 'I AM has sent me to you.' "

15God also said to Moses, "Say to the Israelites, 'The LORD is the God of your fathers. He has sent me to you. He is the God of Abraham. He is the God of Isaac. And he is the God of Jacob.' My name will always be The LORD. Remember me by that name for all time to come.

16"Go. Gather the elders of Israel together. Say to them, 'The LORD, the God of your fathers, appeared to me. He is the God of Abraham, Isaac and Jacob.

" 'He said, "I have watched over you. I have seen what the Egyptians have done

JOCHEBED

EXODUS 2:2-3

She saw that her baby was a fine child. So she hid him for three months. After that, she couldn't hide him any longer. So she got a basket...[and] coated it with tar. Then she placed the child in it. She put the basket in the tall grass that grew along the bank of the Nile River.

Jochebed (JOCK-uh-bed) pressed against the wall, hiding her baby from the guards outside her window. She was a slave in Egypt. The king had told the guards to kill all the baby boys born to the slaves. But Jochebed wasn't about to let them hurt her baby boy. She had a plan. Jochebed made a basket. She fed baby Moses until he was full and sleepy. Trying not to cry, Jochebed placed him in the basket.

Jochebed could barely see because of the tears in her eyes. She prayed that her baby wouldn't cry as she walked past the guards. She pretended she was just going to the river to wash some clothes.

Jochebed put the basket into the river and watched it float away with her baby inside. She couldn't watch!

Her daughter Miriam followed as the basket floated away. **OH NO! IT WAS TANGLED IN SOME WEEDS ALONG THE RIVERBANK.** And Moses was crying. A young slave girl went into the river and brought the basket to her mistress. The mistress was the princess! The princess smiled and held Moses to comfort him.

Miriam told the princess she would find someone to care for the baby. Then she raced back to her house with a huge smile on her face. She gave her mom wonderful news! Little Moses was safe. And he didn't have to go away. He could stay with his family until he got older.

BE A JOCHEBED

Are you brave? Or mostly scared? Even people who look brave on the outside are often scared on the inside. Jochebed was definitely afraid. But she was also determined to save her son. When something frightens you, remember Jochebed. God gave her the strength to be brave. He'll help you be brave, too.

JOCHEBED BRAVELY SET OUT TO SAVE HER SON.
THE WHOLE STORY: EXODUS 2:1-10

Go to page 74 for the next Super Hero

to you. **17**I have promised to bring you up out of Egypt where you are suffering. I will bring you into the land of the Canaanites, Hittites, Amorites, Perizzites, Hivites and Jebusites. It is a land that has plenty of milk and honey." '

18"The elders of Israel will listen to you. Then you and the elders must go to the king of Egypt. You must say to him, 'The LORD has met with us. He is the God of the Hebrews. Let us take a journey that lasts about three days. We want to go into the desert to offer sacrifices to the LORD our God.'

19"But I know that the king of Egypt will not let you and your people go. Only a mighty hand could make him do that. **20**So I will reach my hand out. I will strike the Egyptians with all kinds of miracles. After that, he will let you go.

21"I will cause the Egyptians to treat you in a kind way. Then when you leave, you will not go out with your hands empty. **22**Every woman should ask her neighbor and any woman living in her house for articles made out of silver and gold. Ask them for clothes too. Put them on your children. In that way, you will take the wealth of Egypt along with you."

Miraculous Signs for Moses to Do

4 Moses answered, "What if the elders of Israel won't believe me? What if they won't listen to me? Suppose they say, 'The LORD didn't appear to you.' Then what should I do?"

2The LORD said to him, "What do you have in your hand?"

"A wooden staff," he said.

3The LORD said, "Throw it on the ground."

So Moses threw it on the ground. It turned into a snake. He ran away from it. **4**Then the LORD said to Moses, "Reach your hand out. Take the snake by the tail." So he reached out and grabbed hold of the snake. It turned back into a staff in his hand.

5The LORD said, "When they see this

POWER-SURGE

KIND   **K**

I WILL CAUSE THE EGYPTIANS TO TREAT YOU IN A KIND WAY.
— EXODUS 3:21 —

POWER-SURGE

BELIEVES †

THE LORD SAID, "WHEN THEY SEE THIS MIRACULOUS SIGN, THEY WILL BELIEVE THAT I APPEARED TO YOU. I AM THE GOD OF THEIR FATHERS. I AM THE GOD OF ABRAHAM. I AM THE GOD OF ISAAC. AND I AM THE GOD OF JACOB."
— EXODUS 4:5 —

miraculous sign, they will believe that I appeared to you. I am the God of their fathers. I am the God of Abraham. I am the God of Isaac. And I am the God of Jacob."

6Then the LORD said, "Put your hand inside your coat." So Moses put his hand inside his coat. When he took it out, it was as white as snow. It was covered with a skin disease.

7"Now put it back into your coat," the LORD said. So Moses put his hand back into his coat. When he took it out, the skin was healthy again. His hand was like the rest of his skin.

8Then the LORD said, "Suppose they do not believe you or pay attention to the first miracle. Then maybe they will believe the second one.

9"But suppose they do not believe either miracle. Suppose they will not listen to you. Then get some water from the Nile River. Pour it on the dry ground. The water you take from the river will turn to blood on the ground."

10Moses spoke to the LORD. He said, "Lord, I've never been a good speaker. And I haven't gotten any better since you spoke to me. I don't speak very well at all."

11The LORD said to him, "Who makes a man able to talk? Who makes him unable to hear or speak? Who makes him able to see? Who makes him blind? It is I, the LORD. **12**Now go. I will help you speak. I will teach you what to say."

MOSES

EXODUS 4:10-12

> *Moses spoke to the LORD. He said, "Lord, I've never been a good speaker...I don't speak very well at all." The LORD said to him, "Who makes a man able to talk?...It is I, the LORD. Now go. I will help you speak. I will teach you what to say."*

Thunder crashed and lightning flashed. Moses' eyes opened wide with wonder at what he saw there on top of the mountain. God's finger moved over two pieces of stone, carving Ten Commandments for the people of Israel to follow. Moses knew how much God loved him and the people of Israel. And Moses knew that God wanted the people to love and obey God.

Moses had been up on that mountain for many days. He talked with God there. They were just like two friends who get together for a visit. God showed Moses things he had never shown anyone else. And Moses told God about the people of Israel and asked God for wisdom in leading them.

MOSES STOOD UP AND LOOKED ALL AROUND. HE COULD SEE FOR MILES. He could see the dry, bare desert. He could see the people of Israel camped near the mountain.

Moses remembered when God had called him to lead the people. He told God he was too weak, that he wasn't a good speaker. But God insisted. God told Moses that he would give him strength and the right words to speak. And God had kept his promise. God helped him. And now the people of Israel were no longer slaves! They were free!

Moses still didn't feel like he was a good enough leader. But God was giving him the strength and the wisdom he needed.

BE A MOSES

Some people are strong because of their huge muscles. Some people are strong because they are smart. But the best way to be strong is rely on God's strength instead of your own. Next time you think you just can't do something, ask God for his help. He helped Moses. He will help you, too.

MOSES BECAME A GREAT LEADER THROUGH GOD'S STRENGTH.

THE WHOLE STORY: EXODUS 3:1—4:17; 19:1—20:21

Go to page 76 for the next Super Hero

13But Moses said, "Lord, please send someone else to do it."

14Then the LORD's anger burned against Moses. He said, "What about your brother, Aaron the Levite? I know he can speak well. He is already on his way to meet you. He will be glad to see you. **15**Speak to him. Put your words in his mouth. Tell him what to say. I will help both of you speak. I will teach you what to do. **16**He will speak to the people for you. He will be like your mouth. And you will be like God to him.

17"But take this wooden staff in your hand. You will be able to do miraculous signs with it."

Moses Returns to Egypt

18Then Moses went back to his father-in-law Jethro. He said to him, "Let me go back to my own people in Egypt. I want to see if any of them are still alive."

Jethro said, "Go. I hope everything goes well with you."

19The LORD had said to Moses in Midian, "Go back to Egypt. All of the men who wanted to kill you are dead."

20So Moses got his wife and sons. He put them on a donkey. Together they started back to Egypt. And he took the wooden staff in his hand. It was the staff God would use in a powerful way.

STRONG

THE LORD SPOKE TO MOSES. HE SAID, "WHEN YOU RETURN TO EGYPT, DO ALL OF THE MIRACLES I HAVE GIVEN YOU THE POWER TO DO."

— EXODUS 4:21 —

21The LORD spoke to Moses. He said, "When you return to Egypt, do all of the miracles I have given you the power to do. Do them in the sight of Pharaoh. But I will make his heart stubborn. He will not let the people go.

22"Then say to Pharaoh, 'The LORD says, "Israel is like an oldest son to me. **23**I told you, 'Let my son go. Then he will be able to worship me.' But you refused to let him go. So I will kill your oldest son." ' "

24On the way to Egypt, Moses stopped for the night. There the LORD met him and was about to kill him.

25But Zipporah got a knife that was made out of hard stone. She circumcised her son with it. Then she touched Moses' feet with the skin she had cut off. "You are a husband who has forced me to spill my son's blood," she said. **26**So the LORD didn't kill Moses. When she said "husband who has forced me to spill my son's blood," she was talking about circumcision.

27The LORD said to Aaron, "Go into the desert to see Moses." So he greeted Moses at the mountain of God and kissed him.

28Then Moses told Aaron everything the LORD had sent him to say. He also told him about all of the miraculous signs he had commanded him to do.

29Moses and Aaron gathered all of the elders of Israel together. **30**Aaron told them everything the LORD had said to Moses. He also did the miracles in the sight of the people.

31And they believed. They heard that the LORD was concerned about them. He had seen their suffering. So they bowed down and worshiped him.

Pharaoh Makes the Israelites Work Even Harder

5 Later on, Moses and Aaron went to Pharaoh. They said, "The LORD is the God of Israel. He says, 'Let my people go. Then they will be able to hold a feast in my honor in the desert.' "

2Pharaoh said, "Who is the LORD? Why should I obey him? Why should I let Israel go? I don't even know the LORD. And I won't let Israel go."

3Then Moses and Aaron said, "The God of the Hebrews has met with us. Now let us take a journey that lasts about three days. We want to go into the desert to offer sacrifices to the LORD our God. If we don't, he might strike us with plagues. Or he might let us be killed with swords."

4But the king of Egypt said, "Moses and Aaron, why are you taking the people away from their work? Get back to work!" **5**Pharaoh continued, "There are large numbers of your people in the land. But you are stopping them from working."

6That same day Pharaoh gave orders to the slave drivers and the others who were in charge of the people. **7**He said, "Don't give the people any more straw to make bricks. Let them go and get their own straw. **8**But require them to make the same number of bricks as before. Don't lower the number they have to make. They don't want to work. That's why they are crying out, 'Let us go. We want to offer sacrifices to our God.' 9Make them work harder. Then they will be too busy to pay attention to lies."

10The slave drivers and the others who were in charge left. They said to the people, "Pharaoh says, 'I won't give you any more straw. 11Go and get your own straw anywhere you can find it. But you still have to make the same number of bricks.' "

12So the people scattered all over Egypt. They went to gather any pieces of straw that were left in the fields.

13The slave drivers kept making the people work hard. They said, "Finish the work you are required to do each day. Make the same number of bricks you made when you had straw." 14They whipped the Israelites who were in charge of the people. Those Israelites had been appointed by Pharaoh's slave drivers. The slave drivers asked, "Why didn't you make

AARON

EXODUS 4:27-28

★

✔

T

The LORD said to Aaron, "Go into the desert to see Moses." So [Aaron] greeted Moses at the mountain of God and kissed him. Then Moses told Aaron everything.

Aaron walked as fast as he could along the dusty road. God had told him to go into the desert to see his brother Moses. Right away Aaron had packed up and left.

Aaron squinted his eyes against the bright desert sun, looking in the distance for his brother. Finally, he saw Moses up ahead and ran up to him.

Moses had a lot of news for Aaron. God had appeared to Moses and asked him to lead the people of Israel out of Egypt, where they were slaves. Moses didn't think he was good enough for the job. God said he would send Aaron to help him. Now Moses asked Aaron if he would help. HELP? OF COURSE!

Aaron shook his head in amazement at all that had happened to Moses. And at all that God was asking them to do. But he didn't hesitate. He willingly obeyed.

BE AN AARON

Aaron jumps right into action. First God tells him to go to Moses. And he does it. Then he agrees to help Moses. Be an Aaron. When you're told to do something, obey. Do it willingly and right away.

AARON WILLINGLY OBEYED GOD.

Go to page 82 for the next person

the same number of bricks yesterday or today, just as before?"

15Then the Israelites who were in charge of the people made their appeal to Pharaoh. They asked, "Why have you treated us like this? **16**You didn't give us any straw. But you told us, 'Make bricks!' We are being whipped. But it's the fault of your own people."

17Pharaoh said, "You just don't want to work! That's why you keep saying, 'Let us go. We want to offer sacrifices to the LORD.' **18**Now get to work. We won't give you any straw. But you still have to make the same number of bricks."

19The Israelites who were in charge of the people realized they were in trouble. They knew it when they were told, "Don't lower the number of bricks you are required to make each day."

20When they left Pharaoh, they found Moses and Aaron waiting to meet them. **21**They said to Moses and Aaron, "We want the LORD to look at what you have done! We want him to judge you for it! We are like a very bad smell to Pharaoh and his officials. You have given them an excuse to kill us with their swords."

The LORD Promises to Save the Israelites

22Moses returned to the LORD. He said to him, "Lord, why have you brought trouble on these people? Is this why you sent me? **23**I went to Pharaoh to speak to him in your name. Ever since then, he has brought nothing but trouble on these people. And you haven't saved your people at all."

6 Then the LORD spoke to Moses. He said, "Now you will see what I will do to Pharaoh. Because of my powerful hand, he will let the people of Israel go. Because of my mighty hand, he will drive them out of his country."

2God continued, "I am the LORD. **3**I appeared to Abraham, Isaac and Jacob as the Mighty God. But I did not show them the full meaning of my name, The LORD. **4**"I also made my covenant with them. I promised to give them the land of Canaan. That is where they lived as outsiders. **5**Also, I have heard the groans of the Israelites. The Egyptians are keeping them as slaves. But I have remembered my covenant.

6"So tell the people of Israel, 'I am the LORD. I will throw off the heavy load the Egyptians have put on your shoulders. I will set you free from being slaves to them.

I will reach out my arm and save you with mighty acts when I judge Egypt.

7" 'I will take you to be my own people. I will be your God. You will know that I am the LORD your God when I throw off the load the Egyptians have put on your shoulders.

8" 'I will bring you to the land I promised with an oath to give to Abraham, Isaac and Jacob. I lifted up my hand and promised it to them. The land will belong to you. I am the LORD.' "

9Moses reported those things to the Israelites. But they didn't listen to him. That's because they had lost all hope and had to work very hard.

10Then the LORD said to Moses, **11**"Go. Tell Pharaoh, the king of Egypt, to let the people of Israel leave his country."

12But Moses spoke to the LORD. "The people won't listen to me," he said. "So why would Pharaoh listen to me? After all, I don't speak very well."

The Family Line of Moses and Aaron

13The LORD had spoken to Moses and Aaron. He had talked with them about the Israelites and about Pharaoh, the king of Egypt. He had commanded Moses and Aaron to bring the people of Israel out of Egypt.

14Here were the leaders of the family groups of Reuben, Simeon and Levi.

Reuben was the oldest son of Israel. His sons were Hanoch, Pallu, Hezron and Carmi. Those were the family groups of Reuben.

15The sons of Simeon were Jemuel, Jamin, Ohad, Jakin, Zohar and Shaul. Shaul was the son of a woman from Canaan. Those were the family groups of Simeon.

16Here were the names of the sons of Levi that were recorded in their family history. They were Gershon, Kohath and Merari. Levi lived for 137 years.

17The sons of Gershon, by their family groups, were Libni and Shimei.

18The sons of Kohath were Amram, Izhar, Hebron and Uzziel. Kohath lived for 133 years.

19The sons of Merari were Mahli and Mushi.

Those were the family groups of Levi that were recorded in their family history.

20Amram got married to his father's sister Jochebed. Aaron and Moses were born in Amram's family line. Amram lived for 137 years.

21The sons of Izhar were Korah, Nepheg and Zicri.

22The sons of Uzziel were Mishael, Elzaphan and Sithri.

23Aaron married Elisheba. She was the daughter of Amminadab and the sister of Nahshon. She had Nadab, Abihu, Eleazar and Ithamar by Aaron.

24The sons of Korah were Assir, Elkanah and Abiasaph. Those were the family groups of Korah.

25Eleazar, the son of Aaron, married one of the daughters of Putiel. She had Phinehas by Eleazar.

Those were the leaders of the families of Levi that were recorded by their groups.

26The LORD had spoken to that same Aaron and Moses. He had told them, "Bring the Israelites out of Egypt like an army on the march." 27They spoke to Pharaoh, the king of Egypt, about bringing the people of Israel out of Egypt. They were that same Moses and Aaron.

Aaron Speaks for Moses

28The LORD had spoken to Moses in Egypt. 29He had told him, "I am the LORD. Tell Pharaoh, the king of Egypt, everything I tell you."

30But Moses said to the LORD, "I don't speak very well. So why would Pharaoh listen to me?"

7 Then the LORD said to Moses, "I have made you like God to Pharaoh. And your brother Aaron will be like a prophet to you. 2You must say everything I command you to say. Then your brother Aaron must tell Pharaoh to let the people of Israel leave his country.

3"But I will make Pharaoh's heart stubborn. I will multiply my miraculous signs and wonders in Egypt. 4In spite of that, he will not listen to you. So I will use my powerful hand against Egypt. When I judge them with mighty acts, I will bring my people Israel out like an army on the march.

5"Then the Egyptians will know that I am the LORD. I will reach out my powerful hand against Egypt. I will bring the people of Israel out of it."

6Moses and Aaron did exactly as the LORD had commanded them. 7Moses was 80 years old and Aaron was 83 when they spoke to Pharaoh.

Aaron's Wooden Staff Becomes a Snake

8The LORD spoke to Moses and Aaron. 9He said, "Pharaoh will say to you, 'Do a miracle.' When he does, speak to Aaron. Tell him, 'Take your wooden staff and throw it down in front of Pharaoh.' It will turn into a snake."

10So Moses and Aaron went to Pharaoh. They did exactly as the LORD had commanded them. Aaron threw his staff down in front of Pharaoh and his officials. It turned into a snake.

11Then Pharaoh sent for wise men and those who do evil magic. By doing their magic tricks, the Egyptian magicians did the same things Aaron had done. 12Each one threw his staff down. Each staff turned into a snake. But Aaron's staff swallowed theirs up.

13In spite of that, Pharaoh's heart became stubborn. He wouldn't listen to them, just as the LORD had said.

The Nile River Turns Into Blood

14Then the LORD said to Moses, "Pharaoh's heart is very stubborn. He refuses to let the people go. 15In the morning Pharaoh will go down to the water. Go and wait on the bank of the Nile River to meet him. Take in your hand the wooden staff that turned into a snake.

16"Say to Pharaoh, 'The LORD, the God of the Hebrews, has sent me to you. He says, "Let my people go. Then they will be able to worship me in the desert. But up to now you have not listened."

17" 'The LORD says, "Here is how you will know that I am the LORD. I will strike the water of the Nile River with the staff that is in my hand. The river will turn into blood. 18The fish in the river will die. The river will stink. The Egyptians will not be able to drink its water." ' "

19The LORD said to Moses, "Tell Aaron, 'Get your staff. Reach your hand out over the waters of Egypt. The streams, waterways, ponds and all of the lakes will turn into blood. There will be blood everywhere in Egypt. It will even be in the wooden buckets and stone jars.' "

20Moses and Aaron did exactly as the LORD had commanded them. Aaron held out his staff in front of Pharaoh and his officials. He struck the water of the Nile River. And all of the water turned into blood.

21The fish in the Nile died. The river smelled so bad the Egyptians couldn't drink its water. There was blood everywhere in Egypt.

22But the Egyptian magicians did the same things by doing their magic tricks. So Pharaoh's heart became stubborn. He wouldn't listen to Moses and Aaron, just as the LORD had said. 23Even that miracle didn't change Pharaoh's mind. In fact, he turned around and went into his palace. 24All of the Egyptians dug holes near the Nile River to get drinking water. They couldn't drink water from the river.

The Plague of Frogs

25Seven days passed after the LORD

8 struck the Nile River. 1Then the LORD said to Moses, "Go to Pharaoh. Tell him, 'The LORD says, "Let my people go. Then they will be able to worship me.

2" ' "If you refuse to let them go, I will plague your whole country with frogs. 3The Nile River will be full of frogs. They will come up into your palace. You will have frogs in your bedroom and on your bed. They will be in the homes of your officials and your people. They will be in your ovens and in your bread pans. 4The frogs will be on you, your people and all of your officials." ' "

5Then the LORD spoke to Moses. He said, "Tell Aaron, 'Reach your hand out. Hold your staff over the streams, waterways and ponds. Make frogs come up on the land of Egypt.' "

6So Aaron reached his hand out over the waters of Egypt. The frogs came up and covered the land. 7But the magicians did the same things by doing their magic tricks. They also made frogs come up on the land of Egypt.

8Pharaoh sent for Moses and Aaron. He said to them, "Pray to the LORD to take the frogs away from me and my people. Then I'll let your people go to offer sacrifices to the LORD."

9Moses said to Pharaoh, "You can have the honor of setting the time for me to pray. I will pray for you, your officials and your people. I'll pray that the frogs will leave you and your homes. The only frogs left will be the ones in the Nile River."

10"Tomorrow," Pharaoh said.

Moses replied, "It will happen just as you say. Then you will know that there is no one like the LORD our God. 11The frogs will leave you and your houses. They will leave your officials and your people. They will remain only in the Nile River."

12Moses and Aaron left Pharaoh. Then Moses cried out to the LORD about the frogs he had brought on Pharaoh. 13And the LORD did what Moses asked. The frogs died in the houses, courtyards and fields.

14The Egyptians piled them up. The land smelled very bad because of them.

15But when Pharaoh saw that the frogs were dead, his heart became stubborn. He wouldn't listen to Moses and Aaron, just as the LORD had said.

The Plague of Gnats

16Then the LORD spoke to Moses. He said, "Tell Aaron, 'Reach your wooden staff out. Strike the dust on the ground with it.' Then all over the land of Egypt the dust will turn into gnats."

17So they did it. Aaron reached out the staff that was in his hand. He struck the dust on the ground with it. The dust all over the land of Egypt turned into gnats. They landed on people and animals alike.

18The magicians tried to produce gnats by doing their magic tricks. But they couldn't. The gnats stayed on people and animals alike.

19The magicians said to Pharaoh, "God's powerful finger has done this." But Pharaoh's heart was stubborn. He wouldn't listen, just as the LORD had said.

The Plague of Flies

20Then the LORD spoke to Moses. He said, "Get up early in the morning. Talk to Pharaoh as he goes down to the river. Say to him, 'The LORD says, "Let my people go. Then they will be able to worship me. 21If you do not let my people go, I will send large numbers of flies. I will send them on you and your officials. I will send them on your people and into your homes. The houses of the Egyptians will be full of flies. Even the area where they live will be full of flies.

22" ' "But on that day I will treat the area of Goshen differently from yours. That is where my people live. There will not be large numbers of flies in Goshen. Then you will know that I, the LORD, am in this land. 23I will treat my people differently from yours. The miraculous sign will take place tomorrow." ' "

24So the LORD did it. Huge numbers of flies poured into Pharaoh's palace. They came into the homes of his officials. All over Egypt the flies destroyed the land.

25Then Pharaoh sent for Moses and Aaron. He said to them, "Go. Offer sacrifices to your God here in the land."

26But Moses said, "That wouldn't be right. The sacrifices we offer to the LORD our God wouldn't be accepted by the Egyptians because of their beliefs. Suppose we offered sacrifices they couldn't accept. Then they would throw stones at us and try to kill us. ²⁷We have to take a journey that lasts about three days. We want to go into the desert to offer sacrifices to the LORD our God, exactly as he commands us."

²⁸Pharaoh said, "I will let you and your people go to offer sacrifices. You can offer them to the LORD your God in the desert. But you must not go very far. And pray for me."

²⁹Moses replied, "As soon as I leave you, I will pray to the LORD. Tomorrow the flies will leave you. They will also leave your officials and your people. Just be sure you don't try to trick us again. Let the people go to offer sacrifices to the LORD."

³⁰Then Moses left Pharaoh and prayed to the LORD. ³¹And the LORD did what Moses asked. The flies left Pharaoh, his officials and his people. Not one fly remained. ³²But Pharaoh's heart became stubborn that time also. He wouldn't let the people go.

The Plague on Livestock

9 Then the LORD spoke to Moses. He said, "Go to Pharaoh. Tell him, 'The LORD, the God of the Hebrews, says, "Let my people go. Then they will be able to worship me. ²Do not refuse to let them go. Do not keep holding them back.

³" ' "If you refuse, my powerful hand will bring a terrible plague on you. I will strike your livestock in the fields. I will strike your horses, donkeys, camels, cattle, sheep and goats. ⁴But I will treat Israel's livestock differently from yours. No animal that belongs to the people of Israel will die." ' "

⁵The LORD set a time for the plague. He said, "Tomorrow I will send it on the land." ⁶So the next day the LORD sent it. All of the livestock of the Egyptians died. But not one animal that belonged to the Israelites died.

⁷Pharaoh sent people to find out what had happened. They discovered that not even one animal that belonged to the Israelites had died. But his heart was still very stubborn. He wouldn't let the people go.

The Plague of Boils

⁸Then the LORD spoke to Moses and Aaron. He said, "Take handfuls of ashes from a furnace. Have Moses toss them into the air in front of Pharaoh. ⁹The ashes will turn into fine dust all over the whole land of Egypt. Then boils will break out on people and animals all over the land. Their bodies will be covered with them."

¹⁰So Moses and Aaron took ashes from a furnace and stood in front of Pharaoh. Moses tossed them into the air. Then boils broke out on people and animals alike. ¹¹The bodies of all of the Egyptians were covered with boils. The magicians couldn't stand in front of Moses because of the boils that were all over them.

¹²But the LORD made Pharaoh's heart stubborn. Pharaoh wouldn't listen to Moses and Aaron, just as the LORD had said to Moses.

The Plague of Hail

¹³Then the LORD spoke to Moses. He said, "Get up early in the morning. Go to Pharaoh and say to him, 'The LORD, the God of the Hebrews, says, "Let my people go. Then they will be able to worship me.

¹⁴" ' "If you do not let them go, I will send the full force of my plagues against you this time. They will strike your officials and your people. Then you will know that there is no one like me in the whole earth.

¹⁵" ' "By now I could have reached out my hand. I could have struck you and your people with a plague that would have wiped you off the earth. ¹⁶But I had a special reason for making you king. I decided to show you my power. I wanted my name to become known everywhere on earth.

¹⁷" ' "But you are still against my people. You will not let them go. ¹⁸So at this time tomorrow I will send the worst hailstorm ever to fall on Egypt in its entire history.

¹⁹" ' "Give an order now to bring your livestock inside to a safe place. Bring in everything that is outside. The hail will fall on all of the people and animals that are left outside. They will die." ' "

²⁰The officials of Pharaoh who had respect for what the LORD had said obeyed him. They hurried to bring their slaves and their livestock inside.

²¹But others didn't pay attention to what the LORD had said. They left their slaves and livestock outside.

²²Then the LORD spoke to Moses. He said, "Reach your hand out toward the sky. Then hail will fall all over Egypt. It will beat down on people and animals alike. It will strike everything that is growing in the fields of Egypt."

²³Moses reached his wooden staff out toward the sky. Then the LORD sent thunder and hail. Lightning flashed down to

the ground. The LORD rained hail on the land of Egypt. **24**Hail fell and lightning flashed back and forth. It was the worst storm in Egypt's entire history.

25All over Egypt hail struck everything in the fields. It fell on people and animals alike. It beat down everything that was growing in the fields. It tore all of the leaves off the trees.

26The only place it didn't hail was in the area of Goshen. That's where the people of Israel were.

27Then Pharaoh sent for Moses and Aaron. "This time I've sinned," he said to them. "The LORD has done what is right. I and my people have done what is wrong. **28**Pray to the LORD, because we've had enough thunder and hail. I'll let you and your people go. You don't have to stay here any longer."

29Moses replied, "When I've left the city, I'll lift up my hands and pray to the LORD. The thunder will stop. There won't be any more hail. Then you will know that the earth belongs to the LORD. **30**But I know that you and your officials still don't have any respect for the LORD God."

31The barley was ripe. The flax was blooming. So they were both destroyed. **32**But the wheat and spelt weren't destroyed. That's because they ripen later.

33Then Moses left Pharaoh and went out of the city. He lifted up his hands and prayed to the LORD. The thunder and hail stopped. The rain didn't pour down on the land any longer.

34Pharaoh saw that the rain, hail and thunder had stopped. So he sinned again. He and his officials made their hearts stubborn. **35**So Pharaoh's heart was stubborn. He wouldn't let the people of Israel go, just as the LORD had said through Moses.

The Plague of Locusts

10 Then the LORD said to Moses, "Go to Pharaoh. I have made his heart stubborn. I have also made the hearts of his officials stubborn so I can do my miraculous signs among them. **2**Then you will be able to tell your children and grandchildren how hard I was on the Egyptians. You can tell them I did great miracles among the people of Egypt. And all of you will know that I am the LORD."

3So Moses and Aaron went to Pharaoh. They said to him, "The LORD, the God of the Hebrews, says, 'How long will you refuse to obey me? Let my people go. Then they will be able to worship me.

4" 'If you refuse to let them go, I will bring locusts into your country tomorrow. **5**They will cover the ground so that it can't be seen. They will eat what little you have left after the hail. That includes every tree that is growing in your fields. **6**They will fill your houses. They will be in the homes of all of your officials and your people. Your parents and your people before them have never seen anything like it as long as they have lived here.' " Then Moses turned around and left Pharaoh.

7Pharaoh's officials said to him, "How long will this man be a trap for us? Let the people go. Then they'll be able to worship the LORD their God. After everything that's happened, don't you realize that Egypt is destroyed?"

8Moses and Aaron were brought back to Pharaoh. "Go. Worship the LORD your God," he said. "But just who will be going?"

9Moses answered, "We'll go with our young people and old people. We'll go with our sons and daughters. We'll take our flocks and herds. We are supposed to hold a feast in the LORD's honor."

10Pharaoh said, "The LORD will really be with all of you if I ever let you go, along with your women and children! Clearly you are planning to do something bad. **11**No! I'll only allow the men to go. Then all of you can worship the LORD. After all, that's what you have been asking for."

Then Pharaoh drove Moses and Aaron out of his sight.

12The LORD said to Moses, "Reach out your hand over Egypt. Locusts will cover the land. They will eat up everything that is growing in the fields. They will eat up everything that was left by the hail."

13So Moses reached his wooden staff out over Egypt. Then the LORD made an east wind blow across the land. It blew all that day and all that night. By morning the wind had brought the locusts. **14**They came into every part of Egypt. They settled down in every area of the country in large numbers. There had never been a plague of locusts like it before. And there will never be one like it again.

15The locusts covered the ground until it was black. They ate up everything that was left after the hail. They ate up everything that was growing in the fields. They ate up the fruit on the trees. There was nothing green left on any tree or plant in the whole land of Egypt.

16Pharaoh quickly sent for Moses and Aaron. He said, "I have sinned against the

LORD your God. I've also sinned against you. **17**Now forgive my sin one more time. Pray to the LORD your God to take this deadly plague away from me."

18After Moses left Pharaoh, he prayed to the LORD. **19**The LORD changed the wind to a very strong west wind. The wind picked up the locusts. It blew them into the Red Sea. Not even one locust was left anywhere in Egypt.

20But the LORD made Pharaoh's heart stubborn. And Pharaoh wouldn't let the people of Israel go.

The Plague of Darkness

21The LORD spoke to Moses. He said,

PHARAOH (Not!)

EXODUS 5:2; 10:20

> Pharaoh said, "Who is the LORD? Why should I obey him? Why should I let Israel go? I don't even know the LORD."...The LORD made Pharaoh's heart stubborn. And Pharaoh wouldn't let the people of Israel go.

Pharaoh (FARE-oh), king of Egypt, jumped up from his throne. His hands made fists by his sides. His face turned dark red. He shook from head to foot. Then he raised his hand and pointed right at Moses and Aaron and bellowed, **"NO! I WILL NOT LET YOUR PEOPLE GO!"**

Moses and Aaron stood firm and brave in front of Pharaoh. They knew God was on their side. God sent plagues of flies and sickness and hail on Egypt to make Pharaoh let the people go. But Pharaoh was stubborn. He wouldn't do what God wanted. He just kept saying no. . .

Until God sent the worst plague of all. Only when an angel went through Egypt one night and killed the oldest son in each Egyptian house did Pharaoh listen and let the Israelites go free.

PHARAOH

Stubborn. That's what Pharaoh was. He wanted things his own way instead of God's way. He didn't know that God's way is always best. But you can know that. Don't be stubborn and difficult, like Pharaoh. Instead, be willing to let God have his way in your life.

PHARAOH WAS STUBBORN AND WOULDN'T LET THE ISRAELITES GO.

THE WHOLE STORY: EXODUS 5; 7–11

Go to page 89 for the next Super Hero

"Reach out your hand toward the sky. Darkness will spread over Egypt. It will be so dark that people can feel it."

22So Moses reached out his hand toward the sky. Then complete darkness covered Egypt for three days. 23No one could see anyone else or go anywhere for three days. But all of the people of Israel had light where they lived.

24Then Pharaoh sent for Moses. He said to him, "Go. Worship the LORD. Even your women and children can go with you. Just leave your flocks and herds behind."

25But Moses said, "You must allow us to take animals to offer as sacrifices and burnt offerings to the LORD our God. 26Our livestock must also go with us. We have to use some of them to worship the LORD our God. We can't leave even one animal behind. Until we get there, we won't know what we are supposed to use to worship the LORD."

27But the LORD made Pharaoh's heart stubborn. So he wouldn't let the people go.

28Pharaoh said to Moses, "Get out of my sight! Make sure you don't come to see me again! If you do, you will die."

29"I'll do just as you say," Moses replied. "I will never come to see you again."

The LORD Announces the Tenth Plague

11 The LORD had spoken to Moses. He had said, "I will bring one more plague on Pharaoh and on Egypt. After that, he will let you and your people go. When he does, he will drive you completely away. 2Tell the men and women alike to ask their neighbors for articles made out of silver and gold."

3The LORD caused the Egyptians to treat the Israelites in a kind way. Pharaoh's officials and the people had great respect for Moses.

4Moses said, "The LORD says, 'About midnight I will go through every part of Egypt. 5Every oldest son in Egypt will die. The oldest son of Pharaoh, who sits on the throne, will die. The oldest son of the female slave, who works at her hand mill, will die. All of the male animals that were born first to their mothers among the cattle will also die. 6There will be loud crying all over Egypt. It will be worse than it's ever been before. And nothing like it will ever be heard again.

7" 'But among the people of Israel not even one dog will bark at any man or animal.' Then you will know that the LORD treats Egypt differently from us.

8"All of your officials will come and bow down to me. They will say, 'Go, you and all of the people who follow you!' After that, I will leave."

Moses burned with anger when he left Pharaoh.

9The LORD had spoken to Moses. He had said, "Pharaoh will refuse to listen to you. So I will multiply my miracles in Egypt."

10Moses and Aaron did all of those miracles in the sight of Pharaoh. But the LORD made Pharaoh's heart stubborn. He wouldn't let the people of Israel go out of his country.

The First Passover Sacrifice

12 The LORD spoke to Moses and Aaron in Egypt. 2He said, "From now on, this month will be your first month. Each of your years will begin with it.

3"Speak to the whole community of Israel. Tell them that on the tenth day of this month each man must get a lamb from his flock. A lamb should be chosen for each family and home.

4"Suppose there are not enough people in your family to eat a whole lamb. Then you must share some of it with your nearest neighbor. You must add up the total number of people there are. You must decide how much lamb is needed for each person.

5"The animals you choose must be males that are a year old. They must not have any flaws. You may choose either sheep or goats. 6Take care of them until the 14th day of the month. Then the whole community of Israel must kill them when the sun goes down. 7Take some of the blood. Put it on the sides and tops of the doorframes of the houses where you eat the lambs.

8"That same night eat the meat cooked over the fire. Also eat bitter plants. And eat bread that is made without yeast. 9Do not eat the meat raw or boiled in water. Instead, cook it over the fire. Cook the head, legs and inside parts. 10Do not leave any of it until morning. If some is left over until morning, burn it.

11"Eat the meat while your coat is tucked into your belt. Put your sandals on your feet. Take your walking stick in your hand. Eat the food quickly. It is the LORD's Passover.

12"That same night I will pass through Egypt. I will strike down every oldest son. I will also kill all of the male animals that were born first to their mothers. And I will judge all of the gods of Egypt. I am the LORD.

13 "The blood on your houses will be a sign for you. When I see the blood, I will pass over you. No deadly plague will touch you when I strike Egypt.

14 "Always remember this day. For all time to come, you and your children after you must celebrate this day as a feast in honor of the LORD. It is a law that will last forever.

15 "Eat bread made without yeast for seven days. On the first day remove the yeast from your homes. For the next seven days, anyone who eats anything that has yeast in it must be cut off from Israel.

16 "On the first and seventh days, come together for a special service. Do not work at all on those days. All you are allowed to do is prepare food for everyone to eat.

17 "Celebrate the Feast of Unleavened Bread. I brought you out of Egypt on this very day like an army on the march. It is a law that will last for all time to come. 18 In the first month eat bread that is made without yeast. Eat it from the evening of the 14th day until the evening of the 21st day.

19 "For seven days do not let any yeast be found in your homes. Anyone who eats anything that has yeast in it must be cut off from the community of Israel. That applies to outsiders and Israelites alike. 20 Do not eat anything that is made with yeast. No matter where you live, eat bread that is made without yeast."

21 Then Moses sent for all of the elders of Israel. He said to them, "Go at once. Choose the animals for your families. Each family must kill a Passover lamb. 22 Get a branch of a hyssop plant. Dip it into the blood in the bowl. Put some of the blood on the top and on both sides of the doorframe. None of you can go out the door of your house until morning.

23 "The LORD will go through the land to strike the Egyptians down. He'll see the blood on the top and sides of the doorframe. He will pass over that house. He won't let the destroying angel enter your homes to kill you.

24 "Obey all of these directions. It's a law for you and your children after you for all time to come. 25 The LORD will give you the land, just as he promised. When you enter it, keep this holy day.

26 "Your children will ask you, 'What does this holy day mean to you?' 27 Tell them, 'It's the Passover sacrifice in honor of the LORD. He passed over the houses of the people of Israel in Egypt. He spared our homes when he struck the Egyptians down.' "

Then the people of Israel bowed down and worshiped. 28 They did just what the LORD commanded Moses and Aaron.

29 At midnight the LORD struck down every oldest son in Egypt. He killed the oldest son of Pharaoh, who sat on the throne. He killed all of the oldest sons of prisoners, who were in prison. He also killed all of the male animals that were born first to their mothers among the livestock.

30 Pharaoh and all of his officials got up during the night. So did all of the Egyptians. There was loud crying in Egypt because someone had died in every home.

The People of Israel Leave Egypt

31 During the night, Pharaoh sent for Moses and Aaron. He said to them, "Get out of here! You and the Israelites, leave my people! Go. Worship the LORD, just as you have asked. 32 Go. Take your flocks and herds, just as you have said. And also give me your blessing."

33 The Egyptians begged the people of Israel to hurry up and leave the country. "If you don't," they said, "we'll all die!"

34 So the people took their dough before the yeast was added to it. They carried it on their shoulders in bread pans that were wrapped in clothes.

35 They did just as Moses had directed them. They asked the Egyptians for articles that were made out of silver and gold. They also asked them for clothes. 36 The LORD had caused the Egyptians to treat the people of Israel in a kind way. So they gave them what they asked for. The people of Israel took many expensive things that belonged to the Egyptians.

37 The Israelites traveled from Rameses to Succoth. There were about 600,000 men who were old enough to go into battle. The women and children went with them. 38 So did many other people. The Israelites also took large flocks and herds with them.

39 They brought dough from Egypt. With it they baked bread without yeast. The dough didn't have any yeast in it. That's because the people had been driven out of Egypt before they had time to prepare their food.

40 The people of Israel lived in Egypt for 430 years. 41 At the end of the 430 years, to the very day, all of the LORD's people marched out of Egypt like an army.

42The LORD kept watch that night to bring them out of Egypt. So on that same night every year all of the Israelites must keep watch. They must do it to honor the LORD for all time to come.

Rules for the Passover

43The LORD spoke to Moses and Aaron. He said, "Here are the rules for the Passover.

"No one from another country is allowed to eat the Passover meal. **44**Any slave you have bought is allowed to eat it after you have circumcised him. **45**But a hired worker or someone who lives with you for a while is not allowed to eat it. **46**"It must be eaten inside a house. Do not take any of the meat outside. Do not break any of the bones. **47**The whole community of Israel must celebrate the Passover.

48"Suppose an outsider who is living among you wants to celebrate the LORD's Passover. Then all of the males in that home must be circumcised. After that, the person can take part, just like an Israelite. Only males who are circumcised can eat it.

49"The same law applies to Israelites and to outsiders who are living among you."

50All of the people of Israel did just what the LORD had commanded Moses and Aaron. **51**On that very day the LORD brought the Israelites out of Egypt like an army on the march.

POWER-SURGE

GIVING G

THE LORD HAD CAUSED THE EGYPTIANS TO TREAT THE PEOPLE OF ISRAEL IN A KIND WAY. SO THEY GAVE THEM WHAT THEY ASKED FOR. THE PEOPLE OF ISRAEL TOOK MANY EXPENSIVE THINGS THAT BELONGED TO THE EGYPTIANS.
—— EXODUS 12:36 ——

Setting Apart the Oldest Sons

13 The LORD said to Moses, **2**"Set apart for me the first boy born in every family. The oldest son of every Israelite mother belongs to me. Every male animal that is born first to its mother also belongs to me."

3Then Moses said to the people, "Remember this day. It's the day you came out of Egypt. That's the land where you were slaves. The LORD used his mighty hand to bring you out of Egypt. Don't eat anything that has yeast in it. **4**You are leaving today. It's the month of Abib.

5"The LORD will bring you into the land of the Canaanites, Hittites, Amorites, Hivites and Jebusites. He took an oath and promised your people of long ago that he would give that land to you. It's a land that has plenty of milk and honey. When you get there, keep this holy day in this month.

6"For seven days eat bread that is made without yeast. On the seventh day hold a feast in the LORD's honor. **7**Eat bread that is made without yeast during those seven days. Nothing that has yeast in it should be found among you. No yeast should be seen anywhere inside your borders.

8"On that day talk to your son. Tell him, 'I'm doing this because of what the LORD did for me when I came out of Egypt.'

9"When you celebrate this day, it will be like a mark on your hand. It will be like a reminder on your forehead. The law of the LORD must be on your lips. The LORD used his mighty hand to bring you out of Egypt. **10**Obey this law at the appointed time year after year.

11"The LORD will bring you into the land of Canaan. He will give it to you, just as he promised he would. He even took an oath when he made the promise to you and your people of long ago. **12**"After you arrive there, give to the LORD the oldest son of every mother. Every male animal that is born first to its mother among your livestock belongs to the LORD. **13**By sacrificing a lamb, buy back every male donkey that is born first to its mother. But if you don't buy the donkey back, break its neck. Buy back every oldest son.

14"In days to come, your son will ask you, 'What does this mean?'

"When he does, say to him, 'The LORD used his mighty hand to bring us out of Egypt. That's the land where we were slaves. **15**Pharaoh was stubborn. He refused to let us go. So the LORD killed every oldest son in Egypt. He also killed every male animal that was born first to its mother. That's why I sacrifice to the LORD every male animal that was born first. And that's why I buy back each oldest son for him.'

16"This day will be like a mark on your hand. It will be like a sign on your forehead. It will remind you that the LORD used his mighty hand to bring us out of Egypt."

Israel Goes Through the Red Sea

17Pharaoh let the people go. The shortest road from Goshen to Canaan went through the Philistine country. But God didn't lead them that way. God said, "If they have to go into battle, they might change their minds. They might return to Egypt."

18So God led the people toward the Red Sea by taking them on a road through the desert. The Israelites were prepared for battle when they went up out of Egypt.

19Moses took the bones of Joseph along with him. Joseph had made the sons of Israel take an oath and make a promise. He had said, "I'm sure that God will come to help you. When he does, you must carry my bones up from this place with you." *(Genesis 50:25)*

20The people left Succoth. They camped at Etham on the edge of the desert.

21By day the LORD went ahead of them in a pillar of cloud. It guided them on their way. At night he led them with a pillar of fire. It gave them light. So they could travel by day or at night. 22The pillar of cloud didn't leave its place in front of the people during the day. And the pillar of fire didn't leave its place at night.

14 Then the LORD spoke to Moses. 2He said, "Tell the people of Israel to turn back. Have them camp near Pi Hahiroth between Migdol and the Red Sea. They must camp by the sea, right across from Baal Zephon. 3Pharaoh will think, 'The people of Israel are wandering around the land. They don't know which way to go. The desert is all around them.' 4"I will make Pharaoh's heart stubborn. He will chase them. But I will gain glory for myself because of what will happen to Pharaoh and his whole army. And the Egyptians will know that I am the LORD." So the Israelites camped by the Red Sea.

5The king of Egypt was told that the people had gotten away. Then Pharaoh and his officials changed their minds about them. They said, "What have we done? We've let the people of Israel go! We've lost our slaves and all of the work they used to do for us!"

6So he had his chariot made ready. He took his army with him. 7He took 600 of the best chariots in Egypt. He also took along all of the other chariots. Officers were in charge of all of them.

8The LORD made the heart of Pharaoh, the king of Egypt, stubborn. So he chased the Israelites, who were marching out boldly. 9The Egyptians went after the Israelites. All of Pharaoh's horses and chariots and horsemen and troops went after them. They caught up with them as they camped by the sea. The Israelites were near Pi Hahiroth, across from Baal Zephon.

10As Pharaoh approached, the people of Israel looked up. There were the Egyptians marching after them! The Israelites were terrified. They cried out to the LORD.

11They said to Moses, "Why did you bring us to the desert to die? Weren't there any graves in Egypt? What have you done to us by bringing us out of Egypt? 12We told you in Egypt, 'Leave us alone. Let us serve the Egyptians.' It would have been better for us to serve the Egyptians than to die here in the desert!"

13Moses answered the people. He said, "Don't be afraid. Stand firm. You will see how the LORD will save you today. Do you see those Egyptians? You will never see them again. 14The LORD will fight for you. Just be still."

15Then the LORD spoke to Moses. He said, "Why are you crying out to me? Tell the people of Israel to move on. 16Hold your wooden staff out. Reach your hand out over the Red Sea to part the water. Then the people can go through the sea on dry ground.

17"I will make the hearts of the Egyptians stubborn. They will go in after the Israelites. I will gain glory for myself because of what will happen to Pharaoh, his whole army, his chariots and his horsemen.

18"The Egyptians will know that I am the LORD. I will gain glory because of what will happen to all of them."

19The angel of God had been traveling in front of Israel's army. Now he moved back and went behind them. The pillar of cloud also moved away from in front of them. Now it stood behind them. 20It came between the armies of Egypt and Israel. All through the night the cloud brought darkness to one side and light to

POWER-SURGE

TRUSTED ✦

**THE ISRAELITES SAW
THE GREAT POWER
THE LORD SHOWED
AGAINST THE
EGYPTIANS. SO THEY
HAD RESPECT FOR THE
LORD. THEY PUT THEIR
TRUST IN HIM AND IN
HIS SERVANT MOSES.**

— EXODUS 14:31 —

the other. Neither army went near the other all night long.

21Then Moses reached his hand out over the Red Sea. All that night the LORD pushed the sea back with a strong east wind. He turned the sea into dry land. The waters were parted. 22The people of Israel went through the sea on dry ground. There was a wall of water on their right side and on their left.

23The Egyptians chased them. All of Pharaoh's horses and chariots and horsemen followed them into the sea.

24Near the end of the night the LORD looked down from the pillar of fire and cloud. He saw the Egyptian army and threw it into a panic. 25He kept their chariot wheels from turning freely. That made the chariots hard to drive.

The Egyptians said, "Let's get away from the Israelites! The LORD is fighting for Israel against Egypt."

26Then the LORD spoke to Moses. He said, "Reach your hand out over the sea. The waters will flow back over the Egyptians and their chariots and horsemen." 27So Moses reached his hand out over the sea. At sunrise the sea went back to its place. The Egyptians tried to run away from the sea. But the LORD swept them into it. 28The water flowed back and covered the chariots and horsemen. It covered the entire army of Pharaoh that had followed the people of Israel into the sea. Not one of the Egyptians was left.

29But the Israelites went through the sea on dry ground. There was a wall of water on their right side and on their left. 30That day the LORD saved Israel from the power of Egypt. Israel saw the Egyptians lying dead on the shore. 31The Israelites

saw the great power the LORD showed against the Egyptians. So they had respect for the LORD. They put their trust in him and in his servant Moses.

The Song of Moses and Miriam

15 Here is the song that Moses and the people of Israel sang to the LORD. They said,

"I will sing to the LORD.
    He is greatly honored.
He has thrown Pharaoh's horses and
        their riders
    into the Red Sea.
2 The LORD gives me strength. I sing
        about him.
    He has saved me.
He is my God. I will praise him.
    He is my father's God. I will honor
        him.
3 The LORD goes into battle.
    The LORD is his name.
4 He has thrown Pharaoh's chariots and
        army
    into the Red Sea.
Pharaoh's best officers
    drowned in the sea.
5 The deep waters covered them.
    They sank to the bottom like a stone.

6 "LORD, your right hand
    was majestic and powerful.
LORD, your right hand
    destroyed your enemies.
7 Because of your great majesty,
    you threw down those who opposed
        you.
Your burning anger blazed out.
    It burned them up like straw.
8 The powerful blast from your nose
    piled up the waters.
The rushing waters stood firm like a
        wall.

POWER-SURGE

STRONG

**THE LORD GIVES ME
STRENGTH. I SING
ABOUT HIM.
HE HAS SAVED ME.
HE IS MY GOD. I WILL
PRAISE HIM.**

— EXODUS 15:2 —

The deep waters stood up in the
middle of the sea.
9 "Your enemies bragged,
'We will chase Israel. We will catch
them.
We'll divide up what we take from
them.
We'll eat them alive.
We'll pull our swords out.
Our powerful hands will destroy
them.'
10 But you blew with your breath.
The Red Sea covered your enemies.
They sank like lead
in the mighty waters.

11 "LORD, who among the gods is like
you?
Who is like you?
You are majestic and holy.
Your glory fills me with wonder.
You do wonderful miracles.
12 You reached out your right hand.
The earth swallowed up the
Egyptians.

13 "Because your love is faithful,
you will lead the people you have set
free.
Because you are so strong,
you will guide them to the holy
place where you live.
14 The nations will hear about it and
tremble.
Pain and suffering will take hold of
the Philistines.
15 The chiefs of Edom will be terrified.
The leaders of Moab will tremble
with fear.
The people of Canaan will melt away.
16   Fear and terror will fall on them.
Your powerful arm
will make them as still as a stone.
Then your people will pass by, LORD.
Then the people you created will
pass by.
17 You will bring them in.
You will plant them on the
mountain you gave them.
LORD, you have made that place your
home.
Lord, your hands have made your
holy place secure.

18 "The LORD will rule
for ever and ever."

19 Pharaoh's horses, chariots and horsemen went into the Red Sea. The LORD
brought the waters of the sea back over
them. But the people of Israel walked
through the sea on dry ground.

20 Aaron's sister Miriam was a prophet.
She took a tambourine in her hand. All
the women followed her. They played
tambourines and danced. 21 Miriam sang
to them,

"Sing to the LORD.
He is greatly honored.
He has thrown Pharaoh's horses and
their riders
into the Red Sea."

At the Waters of Marah and Elim

22 Then Moses led Israel away from the
Red Sea. They went into the Desert of
Shur. For three days they traveled in the
desert. They didn't find any water there.
23 When they came to Marah, they
couldn't drink its water. It was bitter.
That's why the place is named Marah.
24 The people told Moses they weren't
happy with him. They said, "What are
we supposed to drink?"
25 Then Moses cried out to the LORD.
The LORD showed him a stick. Moses
threw it into the water. The water became
sweet.

There the LORD made a rule and a law
for the people. And there he put them to
the test. 26 He said, "I am the LORD your
God. Listen carefully to my voice. Do
what is right in my eyes. Pay attention to
my commands. Obey all of my rules. If
you do, I will not send on you any of the
sicknesses I sent on the Egyptians. I am
the LORD who heals you."

27 The people came to Elim. It had 12
springs and 70 palm trees. They camped
there near the water.

The LORD Gives Israel Food
Every Day

16 The whole community of Israel
started out from Elim. They came
to the Desert of Sin. It was between Elim
and Sinai. They arrived there on the 15th
day of the second month after they had
come out of Egypt.

2 In the desert the whole community
told Moses and Aaron they weren't happy
with them. 3 The Israelites said to them,
"We wish the LORD had put us to death in
Egypt. There we sat around pots of meat.
We ate all of the food we wanted. But you
have brought us out into this desert. You
must want this entire community to die
of hunger."

4 Then the LORD spoke to Moses. He
said, "I will rain down bread from heaven
for you. The people must go out each day.
Have them gather enough bread for that

MIRIAM

EXODUS 15:20-21

**Aaron's sister Miriam...took a tambourine
in her hand. All the women followed her.
They played tambourines and danced.
Miriam sang to them.**

Miriam's robes flew in a whirl as she twirled in a dance. One of her sandals came loose, but she didn't even notice. She kept dancing with one foot bare. She lifted her hands high above her head and pounded on her tambourine. Then she began to sing a praise song:

> "LET'S ALL SING TO THE LORD!
> HE IS OUR AMAZING GOD.
> HE HAS THROWN PHARAOH'S HORSES
>   AND THEIR RIDERS
> INTO THE RED SEA."

Miriam was Moses' sister. She had watched as her mother put him into a basket on the river. She had watched as a princess picked him up . . . and as her mother cried when he went to live at the palace. Now she watched as Moses led their people out of Egypt to freedom.

As they followed God into the desert, they faced the Red Sea, with no way to cross it. Miriam watched as her brother had raised his staff over the sea and the water rushed apart. A path opened right through the water! All of the Israelites walked through the sea between two walls of water. They hurried as the Egyptians followed them. As soon as the last Israelite stepped out of the sea, the water came rushing back. All the Egyptian soldiers drowned that day. God protected Miriam and her people. Now they were truly free!

With a grin of relief and praise, Miriam began to sing and dance. Her feet moved wildly in the steps. All the other women followed her. Soon their dance snaked through the camp of the Israelites. And their song rang in the desert hills. God had freed them from slavery in Egypt. They wanted to praise him!

BE A MIRIAM

You can praise God in many ways. If you can't dance, sing. If you can't sing, play an instrument. If you can't play, just speak your words of praise. God is just as worthy of your praise today as when he saved the Israelites. So, be a Miriam and praise God!

**MIRIAM PRAISED GOD FOR HIS PROTECTION.
THE WHOLE STORY: EXODUS 14:19-31; 15:20-21**

Go to page 105 for the next Super Hero

day. Here is how I will put them to the test. I will see if they will follow my directions.

5"On the sixth day they must prepare what they bring in. On that day they must gather twice as much as on the other days."

6So Moses and Aaron spoke to all of the people of Israel. They said, "In the evening you will know that the LORD brought you out of Egypt. 7And in the morning you will see the glory of the LORD. He has heard you say you aren't happy with him. Who are we? Why are you telling us you aren't happy with us?"

8Moses also said, "You will know that the LORD has heard you speak against him. He will give you meat to eat in the evening. He'll give you all of the bread you want in the morning. But who are we? You aren't speaking against us. You are speaking against the LORD."

9Then Moses told Aaron, "Talk to the whole community of Israel. Say to them, 'Come to the LORD. He has heard you speak against him.' "

10While Aaron was talking to the whole community of Israel, they looked toward the desert. There was the glory of the LORD appearing in the cloud!

11The LORD said to Moses, 12"I have heard the people of Israel talking about how unhappy they are. Tell them, 'When the sun goes down, you will eat meat. In the morning you will be filled with bread. Then you will know that I am the LORD your God.' "

13That evening quail came and covered the camp. In the morning the ground around the camp was covered with dew. 14When the dew was gone, thin flakes appeared on the desert floor. They looked like frost on the ground. 15The people of Israel saw the flakes. They asked each other, "What's that?" They didn't know what it was.

Moses said to them, "It's the bread the LORD has given you to eat. 16Here is what the LORD has commanded. He has said, 'Each one of you should gather as much as you need. Take two quarts for each person who lives in your tent.' "

17The people of Israel did as they were told. Some gathered a lot, and some gathered a little. 18When they measured it out, those who gathered a lot didn't have too much. And those who gathered a little had enough. All of them gathered only what they needed.

19Then Moses said to them, "Don't keep any of it until morning."

20Some of them didn't pay any attention to Moses. They kept part of it until morning. But it was full of maggots and began to stink. So Moses became angry with them.

21Each morning all of them gathered as much as they needed. But by the hottest time of the day, the thin flakes had melted away.

22On the sixth day, the people gathered twice as much. It amounted to four quarts for each person. The leaders of the community came and reported that to Moses. 23He said to them, "Here is what the LORD commanded. He said, 'Tomorrow will be a day of rest. It will be a holy Sabbath day. It will be set apart for the LORD. So bake what you want to bake. Boil what you want to boil. Save what is left. Keep it until morning.' "

24So they saved it until morning, just as Moses commanded. It didn't stink or get maggots in it.

25"Eat it today," Moses said. "Today is a Sabbath day in the LORD's honor. You won't find any flakes on the ground today. 26Gather them for six days. But on the seventh day there won't be any. It's the Sabbath."

27In spite of what Moses said, some of the people went out on the seventh day to gather the flakes. But they didn't find any.

28Then the LORD spoke to Moses. He said, "How long will all of you refuse to obey my commands and my teachings? 29Keep in mind that I have given you the Sabbath day. That is why on the sixth day I give you bread for two days. All of you must stay where you are on the seventh day. No one can go out." 30So the people rested on the seventh day.

31The people of Israel called the bread manna. It was white like coriander seeds. It tasted like wafers that were made with honey.

32Moses said, "Here is what the LORD has commanded. He has said, 'Get two quarts of manna. Keep it for all time to come. Then those who live after you will see the bread I gave you to eat in the desert. I gave it to you when I brought you out of Egypt.' "

33So Moses said to Aaron, "Get a jar. Put two quarts of manna in it. Then place it in front of the LORD. Keep it there for all time to come."

34Aaron did exactly as the LORD had commanded Moses. He put the manna in front of the tablets of the covenant. He put it there so it would be kept for all time to come.

35The people of Israel ate manna for 40 years. They ate it until they came to a land that was settled. They ate it until they reached the border of Canaan.

36The jar had an omer of manna in it. An omer was two quarts.

The LORD Gives Israel Water Out of the Rock

17 The whole community of Israel started out from the Desert of Sin. They traveled from place to place, just as the LORD commanded.

They camped at Rephidim. But there wasn't any water for the people to drink. **2**So they argued with Moses. They said, "Give us water to drink."

Moses replied, "Why are you arguing with me? Why are you putting the LORD to the test?"

3But the people were thirsty for water there. So they told Moses they weren't happy with him. They said, "Why did you bring us up out of Egypt? Did you want us, our children and our livestock to die of thirst?"

4Then Moses cried out to the LORD. He said, "What am I going to do with these people? They are almost ready to kill me by throwing stones at me."

5The LORD answered Moses. He said, "Walk on ahead of the people. Take some of the elders of Israel along with you. Take in your hand the wooden staff you used when you struck the Nile River. Go. **6**I will stand there in front of you by the rock at Mount Horeb. Hit the rock. Then water will come out of it for the people to drink." So Moses hit the rock in the sight of the elders of Israel.

7Moses called the place Massah and Meribah. That's because the people of Israel argued with him there. They also put the LORD to the test. They asked, "Is the LORD among us or not?"

Joshua Wins the Battle Over the Amalekites

8The Amalekites came and attacked the Israelites at Rephidim. **9**Moses said to Joshua, "Choose some of our men. Then go out and fight against the Amalekites. Tomorrow I will stand on top of the hill. I'll stand there with the staff of God in my hands."

10So Joshua fought against the Amalekites, just as Moses had ordered. Moses, Aaron and Hur went to the top of the hill. **11**As long as Moses held his hands up, the Israelites were winning. But every time he lowered his hands, the Amalekites began to win.

12When Moses' arms got tired, Aaron and Hur got a stone and put it under him. Then he sat on it. Aaron and Hur held his hands up. Aaron was on one side, and Hur was on the other. Moses' hands remained steady until sunset.

13So Joshua destroyed the Amalekite army with swords.

14Then the LORD said to Moses, "That is something to be remembered. So write it on a scroll. Make sure Joshua knows you have done it. I will completely erase the memory of the Amalekites from the earth."

15Then Moses built an altar. He called it The LORD Is My Banner. **16**He said, "I raised my hands toward the throne of the LORD. The LORD will fight against the Amalekites for all time to come."

Jethro Visits Moses

18 Moses' father-in-law Jethro was the priest of Midian. He heard about everything God had done for Moses and for his people Israel. He heard how the LORD had brought Israel out of Egypt.

2Moses had sent his wife Zipporah to his father-in-law. So Jethro welcomed her **3**and her two sons. One son was named Gershom. That's because Moses had said, "I'm an outsider in a strange land." **4**The other was named Eliezer. That's because Moses had said, "My father's God helped me. He saved me from Pharaoh's sword."

5Moses' father-in-law Jethro came to Moses in the desert. Moses' sons and wife came with Jethro. Moses was camped near the mountain of God. **6**Jethro had sent a message to him. It said, "I, your father-in-law Jethro, am coming to you. I'm bringing your wife and her two sons."

7So Moses went out to meet his father-in-law. Moses bowed down and kissed him. They greeted each other. Then they went into the tent.

8Moses told his father-in-law about everything the LORD had done to Pharaoh and the Egyptians because of how much he loved Israel. He told him about all of their hard times along the way. He told him about how the LORD had saved them.

9Jethro was delighted to hear about all of the good things the LORD had done for Israel. He heard about how God had saved them from the power of Egypt. **10**He said, "I praise the LORD. He saved you and your people from the power of Pharaoh and Egypt. **11**Now I know that the LORD is greater than all other gods. See what he did to those who looked down on Israel."

¹²Then Moses' father-in-law Jethro brought a burnt offering and other sacrifices to God. Aaron came with all of the elders of Israel. They ate with Moses' father-in-law in the sight of God.

¹³The next day Moses took his seat to serve the people as their judge. They stood around him from morning until evening. ¹⁴His father-in-law saw everything Moses was doing for the people. So he said, "Aren't you trying to do too much for the people? You are the only judge. And all of these people are standing around you from morning until evening."

¹⁵Moses answered him. He said, "The people come to me to find out what God wants them to do. ¹⁶Anytime they don't agree, they come to me. I decide between them. I tell them about God's rules and laws."

¹⁷Moses' father-in-law replied, "What you are doing isn't good. ¹⁸You will just get worn out. And so will these people who come to you. There's too much work for you. You can't possibly handle it by yourself.

¹⁹"Listen to me. I'll give you some advice, and may God be with you. You must speak to God for the people. Take their problems to him. ²⁰Teach them the rules and laws. Show them how to live and what to do.

²¹"But choose men of ability from all of the people. They must have respect for God. You must be able to trust them. They must not try to get money by cheating others. Appoint them as officials over thousands, hundreds, fifties and tens. ²²Let them serve the people as judges. But have them bring every hard case to you.

POWER-SURGE

TRUSTED ◆

BUT CHOOSE MEN OF ABILITY FROM ALL OF THE PEOPLE. THEY MUST HAVE RESPECT FOR GOD. YOU MUST BE ABLE TO TRUST THEM.
— EXODUS 18:21 —

POWER-SURGE

OBEYS ✔

OBEY ME COMPLETELY.
— EXODUS 19:5 —

They can decide the easy ones themselves. That will make your load lighter. They will share it with you.

²³"If this is what God wants and if you do it, then you will be able to carry the load. And all of these people will go home satisfied."

²⁴Moses listened to his father-in-law. He did everything Jethro said. ²⁵He chose men of ability from the whole community of Israel. He made them leaders of the people. They became officials over thousands, hundreds, fifties and tens. ²⁶They judged the people at all times. They brought the hard cases to Moses. But they decided the easy ones themselves.

²⁷Moses sent his father-in-law on his way. So Jethro returned to his own country.

Israel Comes to Mount Sinai

19 Exactly three months after the people of Israel left Egypt, they came to the Desert of Sinai. ²After they started out from Rephidim, they entered the Desert of Sinai. They camped there in the desert in front of the mountain.

³Then Moses went up to God. The Lord called out to him from the mountain. He said, "Here is what I want you to say to my people, who came from Jacob's family. Tell the Israelites, ⁴'You have seen for yourselves what I did to Egypt. You saw how I carried you on the wings of eagles and brought you to myself.

⁵"'Now obey me completely. Keep my covenant. If you do, then out of all of the nations you will be my special treasure. The whole earth is mine. ⁶But you will be a kingdom of priests to serve me. You will be my holy nation.' That is what you must tell the Israelites."

⁷So Moses went back. He sent for the elders of the people. He explained to them everything the Lord had commanded him to say. ⁸All of the people answered together. They said, "We will do everything the Lord has said."

So Moses brought their answer back to the Lord.

⁹The Lord spoke to Moses. He said, "I am going to come to you in a thick cloud.

The people will hear me speaking with you. They will always put their trust in you." Then Moses told the LORD what the people had said.

10The LORD said to Moses, "Go to the people. Today and tomorrow set them apart for me. Have them wash their clothes. **11**Have the people ready by the third day. On that day I will come down on Mount Sinai. Everyone will see it.

12"Put limits for the people around the mountain. Tell them, 'Be careful that you do not go up the mountain. Do not even touch the foot of it. You can be sure that all who touch the mountain will be put to death. **13**Do not lay a hand on any of them. Kill them with stones or shoot them with arrows. Whether they are people or animals, do not let them live.' They may go up to the mountain only when the ram's horn gives out a long blast."

14Moses went down the mountain to the people. After he set them apart for the LORD, they washed their clothes. **15**Then he spoke to the people. He said, "Get ready for the third day. Don't make love."

16On the morning of the third day there was thunder and lightning. A thick cloud covered the mountain. A trumpet gave out a very loud blast. Everyone in the camp trembled with fear.

17Then Moses led the people out of the camp to meet with God. They stood at the foot of the mountain.

18Smoke covered Mount Sinai, because the LORD came down on it in fire. The smoke rose up from it like smoke from a furnace. The whole mountain trembled and shook. **19**The sound of the trumpet got louder and louder. Then Moses spoke. And the voice of God answered him.

20The LORD came down to the top of Mount Sinai. He told Moses to come to the top of the mountain. So Moses went up.

21The LORD said to him, "Go down and warn the people. They must not force their way through to see me. If they do, many of them will die. **22**The priests approach me when they serve me. But even they must set themselves apart for me. If they do not, my anger will break out against them."

23Moses said to the LORD, "The people can't come up Mount Sinai. You yourself warned us. You said, 'Put limits around the mountain. Set it apart as holy.' "

24The LORD replied, "Go down. Bring Aaron up with you. But the priests and the people must not force their way through. They must not come up to me. If

they do, my anger will break out against them."

25So Moses went down to the people and told them.

God Gives His People the Ten Commandments

20 Here are all of the words God spoke. He said,

2 "I am the LORD your God. I brought you out of Egypt. That is the land where you were slaves.

3 "Do not put any other gods in place of me.

4 "Do not make statues of gods that look like anything in the sky or on the earth or in the waters. **5**Do not bow down to them or worship them. I, the LORD your God, am a jealous God. I punish the children for the sin of their parents. I punish the grandchildren and great-grandchildren of those who hate me. **6**But for all time to come I show love to all those who love me and keep my commandments.

7 "Do not misuse the name of the LORD your God. The LORD will find guilty anyone who misuses his name.

8 "Remember to keep the Sabbath day holy. **9**Do all of your work in six days. **10**But the seventh day is a Sabbath in honor of the LORD your God. Do not do any work on that day. The same command applies to your sons and daughters, your male and female servants, and your animals. It also applies to any outsiders who live in your cities. **11**In six days I made the heavens and the earth. I made the oceans and everything in them. But I rested on the seventh day. So I blessed the Sabbath day and made it holy.

12 "Honor your father and mother. Then you will live a long time in the land the LORD your God is giving you.

13 "Do not commit murder.

14 "Do not commit adultery.

15 "Do not steal.

16 "Do not give false witness against your neighbor.

17 "Do not long for anything that belongs to your neighbor. Do

OBEYS ✔

HONOR YOUR FATHER AND MOTHER.
— **EXODUS 20:12** —

not long for your neighbor's house, wife, male or female servant, ox or donkey."

18The people saw the thunder and lightning. They heard the trumpet. They saw the mountain covered with smoke. They trembled with fear and stayed a long way off.

19They said to Moses, "Speak to us yourself. Then we'll listen. But don't let God speak to us. If he does, we'll die."

20Moses said to the people, "Don't be afraid. God has come to put you to the test. He wants you to have respect for him. That will keep you from sinning."

21Moses approached the thick darkness where God was. But the people remained a long way off.

Worshiping the LORD

22Then the LORD said to Moses, "Here is what you must tell the people of Israel. Say to them, 'You have seen for yourselves what I said to you from heaven. **23**Do not put any other gods in place of me. Do not make silver or gold statues of them for yourselves.

24" 'Make an altar out of dirt for me. Sacrifice your burnt offerings and friendship offerings on it. Sacrifice your sheep, goats and cattle on it. I will come to you and bless you everywhere I cause my name to be honored.

25" 'If you make an altar out of stones in honor of me, do not build it with blocks of stone. You will make it "unclean" if you use a tool on it.

26" 'Do not walk up steps to my altar. If you do, someone might see your naked body under your robes.'

21 "Here are the laws you must explain to the people of Israel.

Set Your Hebrew Servants Free

2"Suppose you buy a Hebrew servant. He must serve you for six years. But in the seventh year, you must set him free. He does not have to pay anything.

3"If he does not have a wife when he comes, he must go free alone. But if he has a wife when he comes, she must go with him. **4**Suppose his master gives him a wife. And suppose she has sons or daughters by him. Then only the man will go free. The woman and her children will belong to her master.

5"But suppose the servant says, 'I love my master and my wife and children. I don't want to go free.' **6**Then his master must take him to the judges. He must be taken to the door or doorpost of his master's house. His master must poke a hole through his ear lobe into the doorpost. Then he will become his servant for life.

7"Suppose a man sells his daughter as a servant. Then she can't go free as male servants do.

8"But what if the master who has chosen her does not like her? Then he must let the man buy her back. He has no right to sell her to strangers. He has broken his promise to her.

9"What if he chooses her to get married to his son? Then he must grant her the rights of a daughter.

10"What if he marries another woman? He must still give the first one her food and clothes and make love to her. **11**If he does not provide her with those three things, she can go free. She does not have to pay anything.

Laws About Harming Others

12"You can be sure that if anyone hits and kills someone else, he will be put to death. **13**Suppose he did not do it on purpose. Suppose I let it happen. Then he can escape to a place I will choose. **14**But suppose he kills someone on purpose. Then take him away from my altar and put him to death.

15"If anyone attacks his father or mother, he will be put to death.

16"If anyone kidnaps and sells another person, he will be put to death. If he still has the person with him when he is caught, he will be put to death.

17"If anyone calls down a curse on his father or mother, he will be put to death.

18"Suppose two men get into a fight and argue with each other. One hits the other with a stone or his fist. He does not die but has to stay in bed. **19**And later he gets up and walks around outside with his walking stick. Then the man who hit him will not be held accountable. But he must pay the one who was hurt for the time he spent in bed. He must be sure that the person is completely healed.

20"Suppose a man beats his male or

female slave to death with a club. Then he must be punished. ²¹But he will not be punished if the slave gets up after a day or two. After all, the slave is his property.

²²"Suppose some men are fighting and one of them hits a pregnant woman. And suppose she has her baby early but is not badly hurt. Then the man who hurt her must pay a fine. He must pay what the woman's husband asks for and the court allows.

²³"But if someone is badly hurt, a life must be taken for a life. ²⁴An eye must be put out for an eye. A tooth must be knocked out for a tooth. A hand must be cut off for a hand and a foot for a foot. ²⁵A burn must be given for a burn, a wound for a wound, and a bruise for a bruise.

²⁶"Suppose a man hits his male or female servant in the eye and destroys it. Then he must let the servant go free to pay for the eye.

²⁷"Suppose he knocks out the tooth of a male or female servant. Then he must let the servant go free to pay for the tooth.

²⁸"Suppose a bull kills a man or woman with its horns. Then you must kill the bull by throwing stones at it. Its meat must not be eaten. The owner of the bull will not be held accountable.

²⁹"But suppose the bull has had the habit of attacking people. And suppose the owner has been warned but has not kept it fenced in. Then if it kills a man or woman, you must kill it with stones. The owner must also be put to death.

³⁰"But suppose payment is required of him instead. Then he can save his life by paying what is required.

³¹"The same law applies if the bull wounds a son or daughter with its horns.

³²"Suppose the bull wounds a male or female slave. Then the owner must pay the slave's master 12 ounces of silver. You must kill the bull with stones.

³³"Suppose a man uncovers a pit or digs one and does not cover it. And suppose an ox or donkey falls into it. ³⁴Then the owner of the pit must pay the animal's owner for the loss. The dead animal will belong to the owner of the pit.

³⁵"Suppose a man's bull wounds a neighbor's bull and it dies. Then they must sell the live one. And they must share the money and the dead animal equally.

³⁶"But suppose people knew that the bull had the habit of attacking. And suppose the owner did not keep it fenced in. Then he must give another animal to pay

for the dead animal. The dead animal will belong to him.

Laws About Keeping Property Safe

22 "Suppose a man steals an ox or a sheep. And suppose he kills it or sells it. Then he must pay back five head of cattle for the ox. Or he must pay back four sheep or goats for the sheep.

²"Suppose you catch a thief breaking into your house. And suppose you hit the thief and kill him. Then you are not guilty of murder. ³But suppose it happens after the sun has come up. Then you are guilty of murder.

"A thief must pay for what he has stolen. But suppose he does not have anything. Then he must be sold to pay for what he has stolen.

⁴"What if the stolen ox, donkey or sheep is found alive with him? Then the thief must pay back twice as much as he stole.

⁵"Suppose a man lets his livestock eat grass in someone else's field or vineyard. Then he must pay that person back from the best crops of his own field or vineyard.

⁶"Suppose a fire breaks out and spreads into bushes. It burns grain that has been cut and stacked. Or it burns grain that is still growing. Or it burns the whole field. Then the one who started the fire must pay for the loss.

⁷"Suppose a man gives his neighbor silver or other things to keep safe. And suppose they are stolen from the neighbor's house. If the thief is caught, he must pay back twice as much as he stole.

⁸"But suppose the thief is not found. Then the neighbor must go to the judges. They will decide whether the neighbor has stolen the other person's property.

⁹"Suppose you have an ox, donkey, sheep or clothing that does not belong to you. Or you have other property that was lost by someone else. And suppose someone says, 'That belongs to me.' Then both people must bring their case to the judges. The one the judges decide is guilty must pay back twice as much to the other person.

¹⁰"Suppose a man asks his neighbor to take care of a donkey, ox, sheep or any other animal. And suppose the animal dies or gets hurt. Or suppose it is stolen while no one is looking. ¹¹Then the problem will be settled by taking an oath and promising the LORD to tell the truth.

"Suppose the neighbor takes an oath and says, 'I didn't steal your property.'

Then the owner must accept what the neighbor says. No payment is required.

12 "But suppose the animal really was stolen. Then the neighbor must pay the owner back.

13 "Or suppose it was torn to pieces by a wild animal. Then the neighbor must bring in what is left as proof. No payment is required.

14 "Suppose a man borrows an animal from his neighbor. And it gets hurt or dies while the owner is not there. Then the man must pay for it.

15 "But suppose the owner is with the animal. Then the man will not have to pay. If he hired the animal, the money he paid to hire it covers the loss.

Laws About Social Problems

16 "Suppose a man meets a virgin who is not engaged. And he talks her into having sex with him. Then he must pay her father the price for a bride. And he must get married to her.

17 "But suppose her father absolutely refuses to give her to him. Then he must still pay the price for getting married to a virgin.

18 "Do not let a woman who does evil magic stay alive. Put her to death.

19 "Anyone who has sex with an animal must be put to death.

20 "Anyone who sacrifices to any god other than me must be destroyed.

21 "Do not treat outsiders badly. Do not beat them down. Remember, you were outsiders in Egypt.

22 "Do not take advantage of widows. Do not take advantage of children whose fathers have died.

23 "If you do, they might cry out to me. Then I will certainly hear them. **24** And I will get angry. I will kill you with a sword. Your wives will become widows. Your children's fathers will die.

25 "Suppose you lend money to one of my people among you who is in need. Then do not be like those who lend money and charge interest. Do not charge any interest.

26 "Suppose your neighbor owes you money and gives you a coat as a promise to pay it back. Then return it to him by sunset. **27** That coat is the only thing he owns to wear or sleep in. When he cries out to me, I will listen, because I am loving and kind.

28 "Do not speak evil things against me. Do not call down a curse on the ruler of your people.

29 "Do not hold back your grain offerings or wine offerings.

"You must give me the oldest of your sons. **30** Do the same with your cattle and sheep. Let them stay with their mothers for seven days. But give them to me on the eighth day.

31 "I want you to be my holy people. So do not eat the meat of any animal that has been torn by wild animals. Throw it to the dogs.

Laws About Mercy and Fairness

23 "Do not spread reports that are false. Do not help an evil person by telling lies in court.

2 "Do not follow the crowd when they do what is wrong. When you are a witness in court, do not turn what is right into wrong. Do not go along with the crowd. **3** Do not show favor to a poor person in court.

4 "Suppose you come across your enemy's ox or donkey wandering away. Then be sure to take it back to him.

5 "Suppose you see that the donkey of someone who hates you has fallen down under its load. Then do not leave it there. Be sure you help him with it.

6 "Be fair to your poor people in their court cases. **7** Do not have anything to do with a charge that is false. Do not put to death those who are not guilty of doing anything wrong. I will not let those who are guilty go free.

8 "Do not take money from people who want special favors. It makes you blind to the truth. It twists the words of godly people.

9 "Do not beat an outsider down. You yourselves know how it feels to be outsiders. Remember, you were outsiders in Egypt.

Laws About Sabbaths

10 "For six years plant your fields and gather your crops. **11** But during the seventh year do not plow your land or use it. Then the poor people who are among you can get food from it. The wild animals can eat what is left over. Do the same thing with your vineyards and your groves of olive trees.

12 "Do all of your work in six days. But do not do any work on the seventh day. Then your oxen and donkeys can rest. The slaves who are born in your house can be renewed. And so can the outsiders.

13 "Be careful to do everything I have said to you. Do not use the names of other gods. Do not even let them be heard on your lips.

Laws About Celebrating the Main Feasts

14 "Three times a year you must celebrate a feast in my honor.

15 "Celebrate the Feast of Unleavened Bread. Eat bread that is made without yeast for seven days, just as I commanded you. Do it at the appointed time in the month of Abib. You came out of Egypt in that month.

"You must not come to worship me with your hands empty.

16 "Celebrate the Feast of Weeks. Bring the first share of your crops from your field.

"Celebrate the Feast of Booths. Hold it in the fall when you gather in your crops from the field.

17 "Three times a year all of your men must come to worship me. I am your LORD and King.

18 "Do not include anything that is made with yeast when you offer me the blood of a sacrifice.

"Suppose the fat from sacrifices is left over from my feasts. Then do not keep it until morning.

19 "Bring the best of the first share of your crops to my house. I am the LORD your God.

"Do not cook a young goat in its mother's milk.

God's Angel Will Prepare the Way

20 "I am sending an angel ahead of you. He will guard you along the way. He will bring you to the place I have prepared. **21** Pay attention to him. Listen to what he says. Do not refuse to obey him. He will not forgive you if you turn against him. My very Name is in him. **22** Listen carefully to what he says. Do everything I say. Then I will be an enemy to your enemies. I will fight against those who fight against you.

23 "My angel will go ahead of you. He will bring you into the land of the Amorites, Hittites, Perizzites, Canaanites, Hivites and Jebusites. I will wipe them out.

24 "Do not do what they do. Do not bow down to their gods or worship them. You must destroy the statues of their gods. You must break their sacred stones to pieces.

25 "I am the LORD your God. Worship me. Then I will bless your food and water. I will take away sickness from among you. **26** In your land no woman will give birth

to a dead baby. Every woman will be able to have children. I will give you a long life.

27 "I will send my terror ahead of you. I will throw every nation you meet into a panic. I will make all of your enemies turn their backs and run away. **28** I will send hornets ahead of you. They will drive the Hivites, Canaanites and Hittites out of your way.

29 "But I will not drive them out in just one year. If I did, the land would be deserted. There would be too many wild animals for you. **30** I will drive them out ahead of you little by little. I will do it until your numbers have increased enough for you to take control of the land.

31 "I will make your borders secure from the Red Sea to the Mediterranean Sea. They will go from the desert to the Euphrates River.

"I will hand over to you the people who live in the land. You will drive them out to make room for you. **32** Do not make a covenant with them or with their gods. **33** Do not let them live in your land. If you do, they will cause you to sin against me. If you worship their gods, that will certainly be a trap for you."

The Blood of the Covenant

24 The LORD said to Moses, "You and Aaron, Nadab and Abihu, and 70 of the elders of Israel must come up to me. Do not come close when you worship. **2** Only Moses can come close to me. The others must not come near. And the people may not go up with him."

3 Moses went and told the people all of the LORD's words and laws. They answered with one voice. They said, "We will do everything the LORD has told us to do." **4** Then Moses wrote down everything the LORD had said.

Moses got up early the next morning. He built an altar at the foot of the mountain. He set up 12 stone pillars. They stood for the 12 tribes of Israel.

5 Then he sent young Israelite men to offer burnt offerings. They also sacrificed young bulls as friendship offerings to the LORD. **6** Moses took half of the blood and put it in bowls. He sprinkled the other half on the altar.

7 Then he took the Scroll of the Covenant and read it to the people.

They answered, "We will do everything the LORD has told us to do. We will obey him."

8 Then Moses took the blood and sprinkled it on the people. He said, "This is the blood that puts the covenant into effect. The LORD has made this covenant with you in keeping with all of these words."

⁹Moses and Aaron, Nadab and Abihu, and the 70 elders of Israel went up. ¹⁰They saw the God of Israel. Under his feet was something like a street made out of sapphire. It was as clear as the sky itself. ¹¹But God didn't raise his hand against those leaders of the people of Israel. They saw God. And they ate and drank.

¹²The LORD said to Moses, "Come up to me on the mountain. Stay here. I will give you the stone tablets. They contain the law and commands I have written to teach the people."

¹³Then Moses and Joshua, his helper, started out. Moses went up on the mountain of God. ¹⁴He said to the elders, "Wait for us here until we come back to you. Aaron and Hur are with you. Anyone who has a problem can go to them."

¹⁵Moses went up on the mountain. Then the cloud covered it. ¹⁶The glory of the LORD settled on Mount Sinai. The cloud covered the mountain for six days. On the seventh day the LORD called out to Moses from inside the cloud. ¹⁷The people of Israel saw the glory of the LORD. It looked like a fire burning on top of the mountain. ¹⁸Moses entered the cloud as he went on up the mountain. He stayed on the mountain for 40 days and 40 nights.

Offerings for the Holy Tent

25 The LORD said to Moses, ²"Tell the people of Israel to bring me an offering. You must receive the offering for me from all whose hearts move them to give.

POWER-SURGE

GIVING Ⓖ

TELL THE PEOPLE OF ISRAEL TO BRING ME AN OFFERING. YOU MUST RECEIVE THE OFFERING FOR ME FROM ALL WHOSE HEARTS MOVE THEM TO GIVE.

—— EXODUS 25:2 ——

³"Here are the offerings you must receive from them.

"gold, silver and bronze
⁴blue, purple and bright red yarn
　　and fine linen
goat hair
⁵ram skins that are dyed red
the hides of sea cows
acacia wood
⁶olive oil for the lights
spices for the anointing oil and for
　　the sweet-smelling incense
⁷onyx stones and other jewels for
　　the linen apron and chest cloth

⁸"Have them make a sacred tent for me. I will live among them. ⁹Make the holy tent and everything that belongs to it. Make them exactly like the pattern I will show you.

The Ark of the Covenant

¹⁰"Have them make a chest out of acacia wood. Make it three feet nine inches long and two feet three inches wide and high. ¹¹Cover it inside and outside with pure gold. Put a strip of gold around it.

¹²"Make four gold rings for it. Join them to its four bottom corners. Put two rings on one side and two rings on the other.

¹³"Then make poles out of acacia wood. Cover them with gold. ¹⁴Put the poles through the rings on the sides of the chest to carry it. ¹⁵The poles must remain in the rings of the chest. Do not remove them. ¹⁶I will give you the tablets of the covenant. When I do, put them into the chest.

¹⁷"Make its cover out of pure gold. The cover is the place where sin will be paid for. Make it three feet nine inches long and two feet three inches wide.

¹⁸"Make two cherubim out of hammered gold at the ends of the cover. ¹⁹Put one cherub on each end of it. Make the cherubim as part of the cover itself. ²⁰The cherubim must have their wings spread up over the cover. The cherubim must face each other and look toward the cover.

²¹"Place the cover on top of the chest. I will give you the tablets of the covenant. Put them into the chest.

²²"The chest is the ark where the tablets of the covenant are kept. I will meet with you above the cover between the two cherubim that are over the ark. There I will give you all of my commands for the people of Israel.

The Table for the Holy Bread

23 "Make a table out of acacia wood. Make it three feet long, one foot six inches wide and two feet three inches high. 24 Cover it with pure gold. Put a strip of gold around it. 25 Also make a rim around it that is three inches wide. Put a strip of gold around the rim.

26 "Make four gold rings for the table. Join them to the four corners, where the four legs are. 27 The rings must be close to the rim. They must hold the poles that will be used to carry the table.

28 "Make the poles out of acacia wood. Cover them with gold. Use them to carry the table.

29 "Make its plates and dishes out of pure gold. Also make its pitchers and bowls out of pure gold. Use the pitchers and bowls to pour out drink offerings.

30 "Put the holy bread on the table. It must be near my holy throne on the ark of the covenant at all times.

The Gold Lampstand

31 "Make a lampstand out of pure gold. Hammer out its base and stem. Its buds, blooms and cups must branch out from it.

32 "Six branches must come out from the sides of the lampstand. Make three on one side and three on the other. 33 On one branch make three cups that are shaped like almond flowers with buds and blooms. Then put three on the next branch. Do the same with all six branches that come out from the lampstand.

34 "On the lampstand there must be four cups that are shaped like almond flowers with buds and blooms. 35 One bud must be under the first pair of branches that come out from the lampstand. Put a second bud under the second pair. And put a third bud under the third pair. Make a total of six branches. 36 The buds and branches must come out from the lampstand.

"The whole lampstand must be one piece that is hammered out of pure gold.

37 "Then make its seven lamps. Set them up on it so that they light the space in front of it. 38 The trays and wick cutters must be made out of pure gold. 39 Use 75 pounds of pure gold to make the lampstand and everything that is used with it.

40 "Be sure to make everything just like the pattern I showed you on the mountain.

The Holy Tent

26 "Make ten curtains out of finely twisted linen for the holy tent. Make them with blue, purple and bright red yarn. Have a skilled worker sew cherubim into the pattern. 2 Make all of the curtains the same size. They must be 42 feet long and six feet wide.

3 "Join five of the curtains together. Do the same thing with the other five. 4 Make loops out of blue strips of cloth along the edge of the end curtain in one set. Do the same thing with the end curtain in the other set. 5 Make 50 loops on the end curtain of the one set. Do the same thing on the end curtain of the other set. Put the loops across from each other. 6 Make 50 gold hooks. Use them to join the curtains together so that the holy tent is all one piece.

7 "Make a total of 11 curtains out of goat hair to put over the holy tent. 8 Make all 11 curtains the same size. They must be 45 feet long and six feet wide.

9 "Join five of the curtains together into one set. Do the same thing with the other six. Fold the sixth curtain in half at the front of the tent. 10 Make 50 loops along the edge of the end curtain in the one set. Do the same thing with the other set. 11 Then make 50 bronze hooks. Put them in the loops to join the tent together all in one piece.

12 "Let the extra half curtain hang down at the rear of the holy tent. 13 The tent curtains will be one foot six inches longer on both sides. What is left over will hang over the sides of the holy tent and cover it.

14 "Make a covering for the tent. Make it out of ram skins that are dyed red. Put a covering of the hides of sea cows over that.

15 "Make frames out of acacia wood for the holy tent. 16 Make each frame 15 feet long and two feet three inches wide. 17 Add two small wooden pins to each frame. Make the pins stick out so that they are even with each other. Make all of the frames for the holy tent in the same way.

18 "Make 20 frames for the south side of the holy tent. 19 And make 40 silver bases to go under them. Make two bases for each frame. Put one under each pin that sticks out.

20 "For the north side of the holy tent make 20 frames 21 and 40 silver bases. Put two bases under each frame.

22 "Make six frames for the west end of the holy tent. 23 Make two frames for the corners at the far end. 24 At those two corners the frames must be double from top to bottom. They must be fitted into a single ring. Make both of them the same.

²⁵There will be eight frames and 16 silver bases. There will be two bases under each frame.

²⁶"Also make crossbars out of acacia wood. Make five for the frames on one side of the holy tent. ²⁷Make five for the frames on the other side. And make five for the frames on the west, at the far end of the holy tent. ²⁸The center crossbar must reach from end to end at the middle of the frames.

²⁹"Cover the frames with gold. Make gold rings to hold the crossbars. Also cover the crossbars with gold.

³⁰"Set up the holy tent in keeping with the plan I showed you on the mountain.

³¹"Make a curtain out of blue, purple and bright red yarn and finely twisted linen. Have a skilled worker sew cherubim into the pattern. ³²Hang the curtain with gold hooks on four posts that are made out of acacia wood. Cover the posts with gold. Stand them on four silver bases. ³³Hang the curtain from the hooks.

"Place the ark of the covenant behind the curtain. The curtain will separate the Holy Room from the Most Holy Room. ³⁴Put the cover on the ark of the covenant in the Most Holy Room. The cover will be the place where sin is paid for.

³⁵"Place the table outside the curtain on the north side of the holy tent. And put the lampstand across from it on the south side.

³⁶"For the entrance to the tent make a curtain out of blue, purple and bright red yarn and finely twisted linen. Have a person who sews skillfully make it. ³⁷Make gold hooks for the curtain. Make five posts out of acacia wood. Cover them with gold. And make five bronze bases for them.

The Altar for Burnt Offerings

27 "Build an altar out of acacia wood. It must be four feet six inches high and seven feet six inches square. ²Make a horn stick out from each of its upper four corners. Cover the altar with bronze.

³"Make all of its tools out of bronze. Make its pots to remove the ashes. Make its shovels, sprinkling bowls, meat forks, and pans for carrying ashes.

⁴"Make a bronze grate for the altar. Make a bronze ring for each of the four corners of the grate. ⁵Put the grate halfway up the altar on the inside.

⁶"Make poles out of acacia wood for the altar. Cover them with bronze. ⁷Put the poles through the rings. They will be on two sides of the altar for carrying it.

⁸"Make the altar out of boards. Make it hollow. You must make it just as I showed you on the mountain.

The Courtyard

⁹"Make a courtyard for the holy tent. The south side must be 150 feet long. It must have curtains that are made out of finely twisted linen. ¹⁰The curtains must be hung on 20 posts and 20 bronze bases. The posts must have silver hooks and bands on them.

¹¹"The north side must also be 150 feet long. It must have curtains with 20 posts and 20 bronze bases. The posts must have silver hooks and bands on them.

¹²"The west end of the courtyard must be 75 feet wide. It must have curtains with ten posts and ten bases.

¹³"The east end of the courtyard, toward the sunrise, must also be 75 feet wide. ¹⁴On one side of the entrance you must put curtains that are 22 feet six inches long. Hang them on three posts. Each post must have a base. ¹⁵On the other side you must also put curtains that are 22 feet six inches long. Hang them on three posts. Each post must have a base.

¹⁶"For the entrance to the courtyard, provide a curtain that is 30 feet long. Make it out of blue, purple and bright red yarn and finely twisted linen. Have someone who sews skillfully make it. Hang it on four posts. Each post must have a base.

¹⁷"All of the posts that are around the courtyard must have silver bands and hooks. They must also have bronze bases. ¹⁸The courtyard must be 150 feet long and 75 feet wide. It must have curtains that are made out of finely twisted linen. They must be seven feet six inches high. The posts must have bronze bases.

¹⁹"Make all of the other articles used for any purpose in the holy tent out of bronze. That includes all of the tent stakes for the tent and the courtyard.

Oil for the Lampstand

²⁰"Command the people of Israel to bring you clear oil that is made from pressed olives. Use it to keep the lamps burning and giving light.

²¹"Aaron and his sons must keep the lamps burning in the Tent of Meeting. The lamps will be outside the curtain that is in front of the tablets of the covenant. The lamps must be kept burning in my sight from evening until morning. That is a law for the people of Israel that will last for all time to come.

Clothes for the Priests

28 "Have your brother Aaron brought to you from among the people of Israel. His sons Nadab, Abihu, Eleazar and Ithamar must also be brought. They will serve me as priests.

2 "Make sacred clothes for your brother Aaron. When he is wearing them, people will honor him. They will have respect for him.

3 "Speak to all of the skilled workers. I have given them the skill to do this kind of work. Tell them to make clothes for Aaron. He will wear them when he is set apart to serve me as priest. **4** They must make a chest cloth, a linen apron, an outer robe, an inner robe, a turban and a belt. They must make sacred clothes for your brother Aaron and his sons. Then they will serve me as priests. **5** Have them use fine gold wire, and blue, purple and bright red yarn, and fine linen.

The Linen Apron

6 "Make the linen apron out of fine gold wire, and out of blue, purple and bright red yarn, and out of finely twisted linen. Have a skilled worker make it. **7** It must have two shoulder straps joined to two of its corners.

8 "Its skillfully made waistband must be like it. The waistband must be part of the apron itself. Make the waistband out of fine gold wire, and out of blue, purple and bright red yarn, and out of finely twisted linen.

9 "Get two onyx stones. Carve the names of the sons of Israel on them. **10** Arrange them in the order of their birth. Carve six names on one stone and six on the other. **11** Carve the names of the sons of Israel on the two stones the way a jewel cutter carves a seal.

"Then put the stones in fancy gold settings. **12** Connect them to the shoulder straps of the linen apron. The stones will stand for the sons of Israel. Aaron must carry the names on his shoulders as a reminder while he is serving me. **13** Make fancy gold settings. **14** Make two braided chains out of pure gold. Make them like ropes. Join the chains to the settings.

The Chest Cloth

15 "Make a chest cloth that will be used for making decisions. Have a skilled worker make it. Make it like the linen apron. Use fine gold wire, and blue, purple and bright red yarn, and finely twisted linen. **16** Make it nine inches square. Fold it in half.

17 "Put four rows of valuable jewels on it. Put a ruby, a topaz and a beryl in the first row. **18** Put a turquoise, a sapphire and an emerald in the second row. **19** Put a jacinth, an agate and an amethyst in the third row. **20** And put a chrysolite, an onyx and a jasper in the fourth row. Put them in fancy gold settings.

21 "Use a total of 12 stones. Use one for each of the names of the sons of Israel. Each stone must be carved like a seal with the name of one of the 12 tribes.

22 "Make braided chains out of pure gold for the chest cloth. Make them like ropes. **23** Make two gold rings for the chest cloth. Connect them to two corners of it. **24** Join the two gold chains to the rings at the corners of the chest cloth. **25** Join the other ends of the chains to the two settings. Join them to the shoulder straps on the front of the linen apron.

26 "Make two gold rings. Connect them to the other two corners of the chest cloth. Put them on the inside edge next to the apron. **27** Make two more gold rings. Connect them to the bottom of the shoulder straps on the front of the apron. Put them close to the seam. Put them right above the waistband of the apron. **28** The rings of the chest cloth must be tied to the rings of the apron. Tie them to the waistband with blue cord. Then the chest cloth will not swing out from the linen apron.

29 "When Aaron enters the Holy Room, he will carry the names of the sons of Israel over his heart. Their names will be on the chest cloth of decision. They will be a continuing reminder while he is serving me.

30 "Also put the Urim and Thummim into the chest cloth. Then they will be over Aaron's heart when he comes to serve me. In that way, Aaron will always have what he needs to make decisions for the people of Israel. He will carry the Urim and Thummim over his heart while he is serving me.

More Clothes for the Priests

31 "Make the outer robe of the linen apron completely from blue cloth. **32** In the center of the robe, make an opening for the head of the priest. Make an edge like a collar around the opening. Then it will not tear.

33 "Make pomegranates out of blue, purple and bright red yarn. Sew them around the hem of the robe. Sew gold bells between them. **34** Sew a gold bell between every two pomegranates all around the hem of the robe.

³⁵"Aaron must wear the robe when he serves. The bells will jingle when he enters the Holy Room while he is serving me. And they will jingle when he goes out. Then he will not die.

³⁶"Make a plate out of pure gold. Carve words on it as if it were a seal. Carve the words SET APART FOR THE LORD. ³⁷Tie the plate to the front of the turban with a blue cord.

³⁸"Aaron must wear it on his forehead all the time. He will be held accountable for all of the sacred gifts the Israelites set apart. Then I will accept the gifts.

³⁹"Make the inner robe out of fine linen. And make the turban out of fine linen. Have the belt made by a person who sews skillfully.

⁴⁰"Make inner robes, belts and headbands for Aaron's sons. When they are wearing them, people will honor them. They will also have respect for them.

⁴¹"Put all of the clothes on your brother Aaron and his sons. Then pour olive oil on them and prepare them to serve me. Set them apart to serve me as priests.

⁴²"Make linen underwear that reaches from the waist to the thigh. ⁴³Aaron and the priests who are in his family line must wear it when they enter the Tent of Meeting. They must wear it when they approach the altar to serve in the Holy Room. Then they will not be found guilty and die.

"For all time to come, that will be a law for Aaron and the priests who are in his family line.

Directions for Setting the Priests Apart

29 "Here is what you must do to set Aaron and his sons apart to serve me as priests.

"Get a young bull and two rams. They must not have any flaws. ²Get fine wheat flour that does not have yeast in it. Use the flour to make bread, flat cakes that are mixed with olive oil, and wafers that are spread with oil. ³Put everything in a basket. Offer them along with the bull and the two rams.

⁴"Then bring Aaron and his sons to the entrance of the Tent of Meeting. Wash them with water.

⁵"Take the inner robe, the outer robe of the linen apron, the apron itself and the chest cloth. Dress Aaron in them. Take the skillfully made waistband and tie the apron on him with it. ⁶Put the turban on

his head. Connect the sacred crown to the turban. ⁷Take the anointing oil and pour it on his head.

⁸"Bring his sons and dress them in their inner robes. ⁹Put headbands on them. Tie belts on Aaron and his sons. The work of the priests belongs to them. This is my law that will last for all time to come.

"And that is how you must prepare Aaron and his sons to serve me.

¹⁰"Bring the bull to the front of the Tent of Meeting. Have Aaron and his sons place their hands on its head. ¹¹Kill it in my sight at the entrance to the Tent of Meeting.

¹²"Dip your finger into some of the bull's blood. Put it on the horns that stick out from the upper four corners of the altar. Pour the rest of it out at the base of the altar.

¹³"Then take all of the fat around the inside parts. Take the covering of the liver. Take both kidneys with the fat on them. And burn all of it on the altar.

¹⁴"But burn the bull's meat, hide and guts outside the camp. It is a sin offering.

¹⁵"Get one of the rams. Have Aaron and his sons place their hands on its head. ¹⁶Kill it. Take the blood and sprinkle it against every side of the altar.

¹⁷"Cut the ram into pieces. Wash the inside parts and the legs. Put them with the head and the other pieces. ¹⁸Then burn the whole ram on the altar. It is a burnt offering to me. It has a pleasant smell. It is an offering that is made to me with fire.

¹⁹"Get the other ram. Have Aaron and his sons place their hands on its head. ²⁰Kill it. Put some of its blood on the right ear lobes of Aaron and his sons. Put some on the thumbs of their right hands. Also put some on the big toes of their right feet. Then sprinkle blood against every side of the altar.

²¹"Get some of the blood from the altar. Also get some of the anointing oil. Sprinkle both of them on Aaron and his clothes and his sons and their clothes. Then he and his sons and their clothes will be set apart to serve me.

²²"Here is what you must take from the second ram. Take the fat, the fat tail, the fat around the inside parts, the covering of the liver, both kidneys with the fat on them, and the right thigh. It is the ram you must use when you prepare the priests to serve me. ²³Get a loaf, a flat cake that is made with oil, and a wafer. Take them from the basket of bread that was

made without yeast. It is the one that is in front of me.

24"Put everything in the hands of Aaron and his sons. Tell them to lift it up and wave it in front of me as a wave offering. 25Then take it from their hands. Burn it on the altar along with the burnt offering. It gives a smell that is pleasant to me. It is an offering that is made to me with fire.

26"Get the breast of the ram that is used when you prepare Aaron to serve me. Wave it in front of me as a wave offering. It will be your share of the meat.

27"Here are the parts of the second ram that belong to Aaron and his sons. You must set apart the breast that was waved and the thigh that was offered. 28It will always be the regular share from the people of Israel for Aaron and his sons. The people must give it to me from their friendship offerings.

29"Aaron's sacred clothes will belong to his sons who will come after him. Then they can wear them when you anoint them and prepare them to serve me. 30The son who comes after him as priest must wear them seven days. He will come and serve in the Holy Room in the Tent of Meeting.

31"Get the ram that is sacrificed when you prepare Aaron and his sons to serve me. Cook the meat in a sacred place. 32Aaron and his sons must eat the ram's meat. And they must eat the bread that is in the basket. They must eat all of it at the entrance to the Tent of Meeting. 33Those are the offerings to pay for their sins. They must eat them. The offerings must be made when Aaron and his sons are set apart and prepared to serve me. No one else can eat them. They are sacred.

34"And if any parts of the ram or bread that are sacrificed when you prepare Aaron and his sons to serve me are left until morning, burn them up. They must not be eaten. They are sacred.

35"Do everything I have commanded you to do for Aaron and his sons. Take seven days when you prepare them to serve me. 36Sacrifice a bull each day. It is a sin offering to pay for their sins.

"Make the altar pure. Pour olive oil on it to set it apart. 37Take seven days to make the altar pure. Set it apart. Then the altar will be a very holy place. Anything that touches it will be holy.

38"Every day offer on the altar two lambs that are a year old. 39Offer one in the morning. Offer the other one when the sun goes down. 40Along with the first lamb, offer eight cups of fine flour. Mix it

with a quart of oil that is made from pressed olives. Along with that, offer a quart of wine as a drink offering.

41"Sacrifice the other lamb when the sun goes down. Sacrifice it along with the same grain offering and its drink offering as you do in the morning. It has a pleasant smell. It is an offering that is made to me with fire.

42"For all time to come, the burnt offering must be sacrificed regularly. Sacrifice it at the entrance to the Tent of Meeting in my sight. There I will meet you and speak to you. 43There I will also meet with the people of Israel. My glory will make the place holy.

44"So I will set the Tent of Meeting and the altar apart. And I will set Aaron and his sons apart to serve me as priests.

45"Then I will live among the people of Israel. And I will be their God. 46They will know that I am the LORD their God. They will know that I brought them out of Egypt so I could live among them. I am the LORD their God.

The Altar for Burning Incense

30 "Make an altar for burning incense. Make it out of acacia wood. 2It must be one foot six inches square and three feet high. Make a horn stick out from each of its upper four corners. 3Cover the top, sides and horns with pure gold. Put a strip of gold around it.

4"Make two gold rings for the altar below the strip. Put the rings across from each other. They will hold the poles that are used to carry it. 5Make the poles out of acacia wood. Cover them with gold.

6"Put the altar in front of the curtain that hangs in front of the ark where the tablets of the covenant are kept. The ark will have a cover. It will be the place where sin is paid for. There I will meet with you.

7"Aaron must burn sweet-smelling incense on the altar. He must do it every morning when he takes care of the lamps. 8He must burn incense again when he lights the lamps at sunset. Incense must be burned regularly to me. Do it for all time to come.

9"Do not burn any other incense on the altar. Do not use the altar for burnt offerings or grain offerings. Do not pour drink offerings on it.

10"Once a year Aaron must put the blood of a sin offering on its horns to make it pure. He must do it on the day Israel's sin is paid for. Do it for all time to come. The altar is a very holy place to me."

Money to Pay for the People's Lives

11Then the LORD spoke to Moses. He said, **12**"When you make a list of the people of Israel and count them, they must pay me for their lives at the time they are counted. Then a plague will not come on them when you count them.

13"Each one who is counted must pay a fifth of an ounce of silver. It must be weighed out in keeping with the standard weights that are used in the sacred tent. The payment is an offering to me. **14**Each one who is counted must be 20 years old or more. He must give an offering to me.

15"When you make the offering, rich people must not give more than a fifth of an ounce of silver. And poor people must not give less. The offering you give to me will pay for your lives.

16"Receive the money from the people of Israel. Use it for any purpose in the Tent of Meeting. It will remind the people that they are paying me for their lives."

The Large Bowl for Washing

17Then the LORD spoke to Moses. He said, **18**"Make a large bronze bowl for washing. Make a bronze stand to put it on. Place the bowl between the Tent of Meeting and the altar. Put water in it.

19"Aaron and his sons must wash their hands and feet with water from it. **20**When they enter the Tent of Meeting, they must wash with water so that they will not die. They will come to the altar to serve me. They will bring an offering that is made to me with fire. **21**When they do, they must wash their hands and feet so that they will not die. For all time to come, that will be a law for Aaron and the priests who are in his family line."

Anointing Oil

22Then the LORD spoke to Moses. **23**He said, "Get some fine spices. Get 12 pounds eight ounces of liquid myrrh. Get six pounds four ounces of sweet-smelling cinnamon and the same amount of sweet-smelling cane. **24**Also get 12 pounds eight ounces of cassia. All of the spices must be weighed out in keeping with the standard weights that are used in the sacred tent. Get four quarts of olive oil.

25"Have a person who makes perfume mix everything into a sacred anointing oil. It will smell sweet.

26"Then anoint the Tent of Meeting and the ark where the tablets of the covenant are kept. **27**Anoint the table for the holy bread and all of its articles. Anoint the lampstand and the things that are used with it. Anoint the altar for burning incense. **28**Anoint the altar for burnt offerings and all of its tools. And anoint the large bowl together with its stand. **29**You must set them apart so that they will be very holy. Anything that touches them will be holy.

30"Anoint Aaron and his sons. Set them apart so that they can serve me as priests.

31"Say to the people of Israel, 'This will be my sacred anointing oil for all time to come. **32**Do not pour it on the bodies of any other men. Do not make any other oil in the same way. It is sacred. So you must think of it as sacred. **33**Anyone who makes perfume in the same way and puts it on someone who is not a priest must be cut off from his people.' "

Incense

34Then the LORD spoke to Moses. He said, "Get some sweet-smelling spices. Get some gum resin, onycha and galbanum. Also get some pure frankincense. Make sure everything is in equal amounts.

35"Have a person who makes perfume mix it all up into a sweet-smelling incense. It must have salt in it. It will be pure and sacred. **36**Grind some of it into powder. Place it in front of the tablets of the covenant in the Tent of Meeting. There I will meet with you. The incense will be very holy to you.

37"Do not make any incense for yourselves in the same way. Think of it as holy to me. **38**Anyone who makes incense in the same way to enjoy its sweet smell must be cut off from his people."

Bezalel and Oholiab

31 Then the LORD spoke to Moses. **2**He said, "I have chosen Bezalel, the son of Uri. Uri is the son of Hur. Bezalel is from the tribe of Judah. **3**I have filled him with the Spirit of God. I have filled him with skill, ability and knowledge in all kinds of crafts. **4**He can make beautiful patterns in gold, silver and bronze. **5**He can cut and set stones. He can work with wood. In fact, he can work in all kinds of crafts.

6"I have also appointed Oholiab, the son of Ahisamach, to help him. Oholiab is from the tribe of Dan.

"I have given ability to all of the skilled workers. They can make everything I have commanded you to make. Here is the complete list.

7 "the Tent of Meeting
the ark where the tablets of the
covenant are kept
the cover for the ark
8 the table for the holy bread and its
articles
the pure gold lampstand and
everything that is used with it
the altar for burning incense
9 the altar for burnt offerings and
all of its tools

the large bowl with its stand
10 the sacred clothes for Aaron the
priest
the clothes for his sons when they
serve as priests
11 the anointing oil
the sweet-smelling incense for the
Holy Room

"The skilled workers must make them
just as I commanded you."

BEZALEL AND OHOLIAB

EXODUS 31:4-5; 38:23

★ T

*[Bezalel] can make beautiful patterns in gold,
silver and bronze. He can cut and set stones.
He can work with wood. In fact, he can work
in all kinds of crafts...[Oholiab] could carve
things and make patterns. And he could sew
skillfully with blue, purple and bright red yarn
and on fine linen.*

B ezalel (BEE-zu-lel) stood back, tilting his head to examine
the two golden angels he had just finished. They glowed in
the sunshine. The angels would go on top of the ark of the covenant. Bezalel's eyes were drawn to the glitter of the golden
threads that Oholiab (oh-HO-lee-ub) used to sew designs on
heavy cloth curtains. FOLDS OF BEAUTIFUL PURPLE AND
RED CLOTH TUMBLED DOWN OFF OHOLIAB'S LAP. Both
Bezalel and Oholiab used their talents to help Moses build a Tent
of Meeting, a place for the Israelites to worship. When Moses
asked them to work on the Tent of Meeting, they left their other
jobs and willingly went to work for Moses and for God. They built
a beautiful Tent of Meeting and filled it with carvings and fine
fabrics and gold. God's people gathered there to worship him for
many years.

BE A BEZALEL AND OHOLIAB

You have talents. You are good at some things. As you grow up
and discover what your talents are, be sure to use them to hon-
or God. Be like Bezalel and Oholiab and use your gifts not just
for yourself, but for God and others.

BEZALEL AND OHOLIAB USED THEIR TALENTS FOR
GOD.

Go to page 170 for the next Super Hero

The Sabbath Day

¹²Then the LORD spoke to Moses. ¹³He said, "Tell the people of Israel, 'You must always keep my Sabbath days. That will be the sign of the covenant I have made between me and you for all time to come. Then you will know that I am the LORD. I make you holy.

¹⁴" 'Keep the Sabbath day. It is holy to you. Those who misuse it must be put to death. Those who do any work on that day must be cut off from their people. ¹⁵Do your work in six days. But the seventh day is a Sabbath. You must rest on it. It is set apart for me. Those who work on the Sabbath day must be put to death.

¹⁶" 'The people of Israel must keep the Sabbath. They must celebrate it for all time to come. It will be a covenant that lasts forever. ¹⁷It will be the sign of the covenant I have made between me and the people of Israel forever.

" 'I made the heavens and the earth in six days. But on the seventh day I did not work. I rested.' "

¹⁸The LORD finished speaking to Moses on Mount Sinai. Then he gave him the two tablets of the covenant. They were made out of stone. The words on them were written by the finger of God.

Israel Worships a Golden Calf

32 The people saw that Moses took a long time to come down from the mountain. So they gathered around Aaron. They said to him, "Come. Make us a god that will lead us. This fellow Moses brought us up out of Egypt. But we don't know what has happened to him."

²Aaron answered them, "Take the gold earrings off your wives, your sons and your daughters. Bring the earrings to me."

³So all of the people took off their earrings. They brought them to Aaron. ⁴He took what they gave him and made it into a metal statue of a god. It looked like a calf. He shaped it with a tool.

Then the people said, "Israel, here is your god who brought you up out of Egypt."

⁵When Aaron saw it, he built an altar in front of the calf. He said, "Tomorrow will be a feast day in the LORD's honor."

⁶So the next day the people got up early. They sacrificed burnt offerings and brought friendship offerings. They sat down to eat and drink. Then they got up to dance wildly in front of their god.

⁷The LORD spoke to Moses. He said, "Go down. Your people you brought up out of Egypt have become very sinful. ⁸They have quickly turned away from what I commanded them. They have made themselves a statue of a god that looks like a calf. They have bowed down and sacrificed to it. And they have said, 'Israel, here is your god who brought you up out of Egypt.'

⁹"I have seen those people," the LORD said to Moses. "They are stubborn. ¹⁰Now leave me alone. My anger will burn against them. I will destroy them. Then I will make you into a great nation."

¹¹But Moses asked the LORD his God to show favor to the people. "LORD," he said, "why should your anger burn against your people? You used your great power and mighty hand to bring them out of Egypt. ¹²Why should the Egyptians say, 'He brought them out to hurt them. He wanted to kill them in the mountains. He wanted to wipe them off the face of the earth'? Turn away from your burning anger. Please take pity on your people. Don't destroy them!

¹³"Remember your servants Abraham, Isaac and Israel. You made a promise. You took an oath in your name. You said, 'I will make your children after you as many as the stars in the sky. I will give them all of this land I promised them. It will belong to them forever.' "

¹⁴Then the LORD took pity on his people. He didn't destroy them as he had said he would.

¹⁵Moses turned and went down the mountain. He had the two tablets of the covenant in his hands. Words were written on both sides of the tablets, front and back. ¹⁶The tablets were the work of God. The words had been written by God. They had been carved on the tablets.

¹⁷Joshua heard the noise of the people shouting. So he said to Moses, "It sounds like war in the camp."

¹⁸Moses replied,

"It's not the sound of winning.
It's not the sound of losing.
It's the sound of singing that I hear."

¹⁹As Moses approached the camp, he saw the calf. He also saw the people dancing. So he burned with anger. He threw the tablets out of his hands. They broke into pieces at the foot of the mountain.

²⁰He took the calf the people had made. He burned it in the fire. Then he ground it into powder. He scattered it on the water. And he made the people of Israel drink it.

²¹He said to Aaron, "What did these

people do to you? How did they make you lead them into such terrible sin?"

22"Please don't be angry," Aaron answered. "You know how these people like to do what is evil. 23They said to me, 'Make us a god that will lead us. This fellow Moses brought us up out of Egypt. But we don't know what has happened to him.'

24"So I told them, 'Anyone who has any gold jewelry, take it off.' They gave me the gold. I threw it into the fire. And out came this calf!"

25Moses saw that the people were running wild. Aaron had let them get out of control. The people had become a joke to their enemies.

26Moses stood at the entrance to the camp. He said, "Anyone who is on the LORD's side, come to me." All of the Levites joined him.

27Then he spoke to them. He said, "The LORD, the God of Israel, says, 'Each man must put on his sword. Then he must go back and forth through the camp from one end to the other. Each man must kill his brother, friend and neighbor.' " 28The Levites did as Moses commanded. About 3,000 of the people died that day. 29Then Moses said to the Levites, "You have been set apart for the LORD today. You stood against your own sons and brothers. And he has blessed you this day."

30The next day Moses said to the people, "You have committed a terrible sin. But now I will go up to the LORD. Maybe if I pray to him, he will forgive your sin."

31So Moses went back to the LORD. He said, "These people have committed a terrible sin. They have made a god out of gold for themselves. 32Now please forgive their sin. But if you won't, then erase my name from the scroll you have written."

33The LORD replied to Moses, "I will erase from my scroll only the names of those who have sinned against me. 34Now go. Lead the people to the place I spoke about. My angel will go ahead of you. But when the time comes for me to punish, I will punish them for their sin."

35The LORD struck the people with a plague. That's because of what they did with the calf Aaron had made.

33 Then the LORD spoke to Moses. He said, "Leave this place. You and the people you brought up out of Egypt must leave it. Go up to the land I promised with an oath to give to Abraham, Isaac and Jacob. I said to them, 'I will give it to your children after you.' 2I will send an angel ahead of you. I will drive out the Canaanites, Amorites, Hittites, Perizzites, Hivites and Jebusites.

3"Go up to the land that has plenty of milk and honey. But I will not go with you. You are stubborn. I might destroy you on the way."

4When the people heard those painful words, they became sad and began to sob. No one put on any jewelry.

5The LORD had said to Moses, "Tell the people of Israel, 'You are stubborn. If I went with you even for a moment, I might destroy you. Now take off your jewelry. Then I will decide what to do with you.' " 6So the people took off their jewelry at Mount Horeb.

The Tent of Meeting

7Moses used to take a tent and set it up far outside the camp. He called it the "tent of meeting." Anyone who wanted to ask the LORD a question would go to the tent of meeting that was outside the camp. 8When Moses would go out to the tent, all of the people would get up and stand at the entrances to their tents. They would watch Moses until he entered the tent.

9As Moses would go into the tent, the pillar of cloud would come down. It would stay at the entrance while the LORD spoke with Moses. 10The people would see the pillar of cloud standing at the entrance to the tent. Then all of them would stand and worship at the entrances to their tents.

11The LORD would speak to Moses face to face. It was like a man speaking to his friend. Then Moses would return to the camp.

But Joshua, his young helper, didn't leave the tent. Joshua was the son of Nun.

The LORD Shows Moses His Glory

12Moses said to the LORD, "You have been telling me, 'Lead these people.' But you haven't let me know whom you will send with me. You have said, 'I know your name. I know all about you. And I am pleased with you.' 13If you are pleased with me, teach me more about yourself. Then I can know you. And I can continue to please you. Remember that this nation is your people."

14The LORD replied, "I will go with you. And I will give you rest."

15Then Moses said to him, "If you don't go with us, don't send us up from here. 16How will anyone know that you are pleased with me and your people? You must go with us. How else will we be different from all of the other people on the face of the earth?"

17The LORD said to Moses, "I will do exactly what you have asked. I am pleased with you. And I know your name. I know all about you."

18Then Moses said, "Now show me your glory."

19The LORD said, "I will make all of my goodness pass in front of you. And I will announce my name, The LORD, in front of you. I will have mercy on whom I have mercy. And I will show love to those I love. **20**But you can't see my face," he said. "No one can see me and stay alive."

21The LORD continued, "There is a place near me where you can stand on a rock. **22**When my glory passes by, I will put you in an opening in the rock. I will cover you with my hand until I have passed by. **23**Then I will remove my hand. You will see my back. But my face must not be seen."

The New Stone Tablets

34 The LORD said to Moses, "Cut out two stone tablets that are just like the first ones. I will write on them the words that were on the first tablets, which you broke.

2"Be ready in the morning. Then come up on Mount Sinai. Meet with me there on top of the mountain. **3**No one must come with you. No one must be seen anywhere on the mountain. Not even the flocks and herds must be allowed to eat grass in front of the mountain."

4So Moses carved out two stone tablets that were just like the first ones. Early in the morning he went up Mount Sinai. He carried the two tablets in his hands. He did as the LORD had commanded him to do.

5Then the LORD came down in the cloud. He stood there with Moses and announced his name, The LORD.

6As he passed in front of Moses, he called out. He said, "I am the LORD, the LORD. I am a God who is tender and kind. I am gracious. I am slow to get angry. I am faithful and full of love. **7**I continue to show my love to thousands of people. I forgive those who do evil. I forgive those who refuse to obey. And I forgive those who sin. But I do not let guilty people go without punishing them. I punish the children, grandchildren and great-grand-children for the sin of their parents."

8Moses bowed down to the ground at once and worshiped. **9**"Lord," he said, "if you are pleased with me, then go with us.

Even though these people are stubborn, forgive the evil things we have done. Forgive our sin. And accept us as your people."

10Then the LORD said, "I am making a covenant with you. I will do wonderful things in front of all of your people. I will do miracles that have never been done before in any nation in the whole world. The people you live among will see the things that I, the LORD, will do for you. And they will see how wonderful those things really are.

11"Obey what I command you today. I will drive out the Amorites, Canaanites, Hittites, Perizzites, Hivites and Jebusites to make room for you.

12"Be careful. Do not make a peace treaty with those who live in the land where you are going. They will be a trap to you. **13**Tear down their altars. Smash their sacred stones. Cut down the poles they use to worship the goddess Asherah. **14**Do not worship any other god. I am a jealous God. In fact, my name is Jealous.

15"Be careful not to make a peace treaty with those who live in the land. They commit sin by offering sacrifices to their gods. They will invite you to eat their sacrifices. **16**You will choose some of their daughters as wives for your sons. And those daughters will commit sin by worshiping their gods. Then they will lead your sons to do the same thing.

17"Do not make statues of gods.

18"Celebrate the Feast of Unleavened Bread. For seven days eat bread that is made without yeast, just as I commanded you. Do it at the appointed time in the month of Abib. You came out of Egypt in that month.

19"Every male animal that is born first to its mother belongs to me. That includes your livestock. It includes herds and flocks alike. **20**Sacrifice a lamb to buy back every male donkey that is born first to its mother. But if you do not buy the donkey back, break its neck. Buy back every oldest son.

"You must not come to worship me with your hands empty.

21"Do your work in six days. But you must rest on the seventh day. Even when you are plowing your land or gathering your crops, you must rest on the seventh day.

22"Celebrate the Feast of Weeks. Bring the first share of your wheat crop.

"Celebrate the Feast of Booths. Hold it in the fall.

23"Three times a year all of your men must come to worship me. I am your Lord and King, the God of Israel. 24I will drive out nations ahead of you. I will increase your territory. Go up three times a year to worship me. While you are doing that, I will keep others from wanting to take any of your land for themselves. I am the Lord your God.

25"Do not include anything that is made with yeast when you offer me the blood of a sacrifice. You must not keep any of the meat from the sacrifice of the Passover Feast until morning.

26"Bring the best of the first share of your crops to my house. I am the Lord your God.

"Do not cook a young goat in its mother's milk."

27Then the Lord said to Moses, "Write down the words I have spoken. I have made a covenant with you and with Israel in keeping with those words."

28Moses was there with the Lord for 40 days and 40 nights. He didn't eat any food or drink any water. The Lord wrote on the tablets the words of the covenant. Those words are the Ten Commandments.

The Face of Moses Shines

29Moses came down from Mount Sinai. He had the two tablets of the covenant in his hands. His face was shining because he had spoken with the Lord. But he didn't realize it. 30Aaron and all of the people of Israel saw Moses. His face was shining. So they were afraid to come near him.

31But Moses called out to them. So Aaron and all of the leaders of the community came to him. And Moses spoke to them. 32After that, all of the people came near him. And he gave them all of the commands the Lord had given him on Mount Sinai.

33Moses finished speaking to them. Then he put a veil over his face. 34But when he would go to speak with the Lord, he would remove the veil. He would keep it off until he came out. Then he would tell the people what the Lord had commanded. 35They would see that his face was shining. So Moses would put the veil back over his face. He would keep it on until he went in again to speak with the Lord.

Rules for the Sabbath Day

35 Moses gathered the whole community of Israel together. He said to them, "Here are the things the Lord has commanded you to do. 2You must do your work in six days. But the seventh day will be your holy day. It will be a Sabbath in the Lord's honor. You must rest on it. Anyone who does any work on it must be put to death. 3Do not even light a fire in any of your homes on the Sabbath day."

Supplies for the Holy Tent

4Moses spoke to the whole community of Israel. He said, "Here is what the Lord has commanded. 5Take an offering for the Lord from what you have. Those who want to can bring an offering to the Lord. Here is what they can bring.

"gold, silver and bronze
6 blue, purple and bright red yarn
    and fine linen
    goat hair
7 ram skins that are dyed red
    the hides of sea cows
    acacia wood
8 olive oil for the lights
    spices for the anointing oil and for
        the sweet-smelling incense
9 onyx stones and other jewels for
    the linen apron and the chest
    cloth

10"All of the skilled workers among you

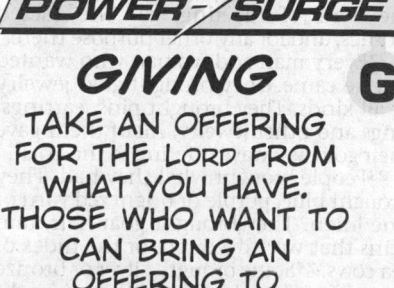

POWER-SURGE

GIVING G

TAKE AN OFFERING FOR THE Lord FROM WHAT YOU HAVE. THOSE WHO WANT TO CAN BRING AN OFFERING TO THE Lord.
— EXODUS 35:5 —

must come. They must make everything the LORD has commanded [11] for the holy tent and its covering. Here is what they must make.

"hooks
frames
crossbars
posts
bases
[12] the ark of the covenant
the poles and cover for the ark
the curtain that screens the ark
[13] the table for the holy bread
the poles and all of the articles for the table
the holy bread
[14] the lampstand for light and everything that is used with it
the lamps and the olive oil that gives light
[15] the altar for burning incense
the poles for the altar
the anointing oil
the sweet-smelling incense
the curtain for the entrance to the holy tent
[16] the altar for burnt offerings with its bronze grate
its poles and all of its tools
the large bronze bowl with its stand
[17] the curtains of the courtyard with their posts and bases
the curtain for the entrance to the courtyard
[18] the ropes and tent stakes for the holy tent and for the courtyard
[19] the sacred clothes for Aaron the priest
the clothes for his sons when they serve as priests"

[20] Then the whole community of Israel left Moses. [21] Everyone who wanted to give offerings to the LORD brought them to him. The offerings were for the work on the Tent of Meeting, for the sacred clothes, and for any other purpose there. [22] Every man and woman who wanted to give came. They brought gold jewelry of all kinds. They brought pins, earrings, rings and other jewelry. All of them gave their gold as a wave offering to the LORD. [23] People brought what they had. They brought blue, purple or bright red yarn or fine linen. They brought goat hair, ram skins that were dyed red, or the hides of sea cows. [24] Some brought silver or bronze as an offering to the LORD. Others brought acacia wood for any part of the work. [25] All of the skilled women spun yarn with their hands. They brought blue, purple or bright red yarn or fine linen. [26] All of the skilled women who wanted to spin the goat hair did so.

[27] The leaders brought onyx stones and other jewels for the linen apron and the chest cloth. [28] They also brought spices and olive oil. They brought them for the light, for the anointing oil, and for the sweet-smelling incense.

[29] All of the men and women of Israel who wanted to bring offerings to the LORD brought them to him. The offerings were for all of the work the LORD had commanded Moses to tell them to do.

Bezalel and Oholiab

[30] Then Moses spoke to the people of Israel. He said, "The LORD has chosen Bezalel, the son of Uri. Uri is the son of Hur. Bezalel is from the tribe of Judah. [31] The LORD has filled him with the Spirit of God. He has filled him with skill, ability and knowledge in all kinds of crafts. [32] He can make beautiful patterns in gold, silver and bronze. [33] He can cut and set stones. He can work with wood. In fact, he can work in all kinds of arts and crafts.

[34] "And the LORD has given both him and Oholiab the ability to teach others. Oholiab, the son of Ahisamach, is from the tribe of Dan.

[35] "The LORD has filled them with skill to do all kinds of work. They carve things and make patterns. They sew skillfully

GIVING G

EVERY MAN AND WOMAN WHO WANTED TO GIVE CAME. THEY BROUGHT GOLD JEWELRY OF ALL KINDS. THEY BROUGHT PINS, EARRINGS, RINGS AND OTHER JEWELRY. ALL OF THEM GAVE THEIR GOLD AS A WAVE OFFERING TO THE LORD.

— EXODUS 35:22 —

with blue, purple and bright red yarn and on fine linen. They use thread to make beautiful cloth. They have the skill to

36 work in all kinds of crafts. ¹Bezalel and Oholiab must do the work just as the LORD has commanded. So must every skilled worker to whom the LORD has given skill and ability. They must know how to do all of the work for every purpose connected with the sacred tent. And that includes setting it up."

²Then Moses sent for Bezalel and Oholiab. He sent for every skilled worker to whom the LORD had given ability and who wanted to come and do the work.

³They received from Moses all of the offerings the people of Israel had brought. They had brought the offerings for all of the work for every purpose connected with the holy tent. That included setting it up. The people kept bringing the offerings they chose to give. They brought them morning after morning.

⁴So all of the skilled workers who were working on the holy tent stopped what they were doing. ⁵They said to Moses, "The people are bringing more than enough for doing the work the LORD commanded us to do."

⁶Then Moses gave an order. A message was sent through the whole camp. It said, "No man or woman should make anything else and offer it for the holy tent." And so the people were kept from bringing more offerings. ⁷There was already more than enough to do all of the work.

The Holy Tent

⁸All of the skilled workers made the holy tent. They made ten curtains out of finely twisted linen. They made them with blue, purple and bright red yarn. A skilled worker sewed cherubim into the pattern. ⁹All of the curtains were the same size. They were 42 feet long and six feet wide.

¹⁰The workers joined five of the curtains together. They did the same thing with the other five. ¹¹Then they made loops out of blue strips of cloth along the edge of the end curtain in one set. They did the same thing with the end curtain in the other set. ¹²They also made 50 loops on the end curtain of the one set. They did the same thing on the end curtain of the other set. They put the loops across from each other. ¹³Then they made 50 gold hooks. They used them to join curtains together so that the holy tent was all one piece.

¹⁴The workers made a total of 11 cur-

POWER-SURGE

GIVING G

ALL OF THE SKILLED WORKERS WHO WERE WORKING ON THE HOLY TENT STOPPED WHAT THEY WERE DOING. THEY SAID TO MOSES, "THE PEOPLE ARE BRINGING MORE THAN ENOUGH FOR DOING THE WORK THE LORD COMMANDED US TO DO."

— EXODUS 36:4-5 —

tains out of goat hair to put over the holy tent. ¹⁵All 11 curtains were the same size. They were 45 feet long and six feet wide.

¹⁶The workers joined five of the curtains together into one set. They did the same thing with the other six. ¹⁷Then they made 50 loops along the edge of the end curtain in the one set. They did the same thing with the other set. ¹⁸They made 50 bronze hooks. They used them to join the tent together all in one piece.

¹⁹They made a covering for the tent. They made it out of ram skins that were dyed red. They put a covering of the hides of sea cows over that.

²⁰The workers made frames out of acacia wood for the holy tent. ²¹Each frame was 15 feet long and two feet three inches wide. ²²The workers added two small wooden pins to each frame. The pins stuck out so that they were even with each other. The workers made all of the frames of the holy tent in the same way.

²³They made 20 frames for the south side of the holy tent. ²⁴And they made 40 silver bases to go under them. They made two bases for each frame. They put one under each pin that stuck out.

²⁵For the north side of the holy tent they made 20 frames ²⁶and 40 silver bases. They put two bases under each frame.

²⁷The workers made six frames for the west end of the holy tent. ²⁸They made two frames for the corners of the holy tent at the far end. ²⁹At those two corners the frames were double from top to bottom.

They were fitted into a single ring. The workers made both of them the same. **30**So there were eight frames and 16 silver bases. There were two bases under each frame.

31The workers also made crossbars out of acacia wood. They made five for the frames on one side of the holy tent. **32**They made five for the frames on the other side. And they made five for the frames on the west, at the far end of the holy tent. **33**The center crossbar reached from end to end at the middle of the frames.

34They covered the frames with gold. They made gold rings to hold the crossbars. They also covered the crossbars with gold.

35They made the curtain out of blue, purple and bright red yarn and finely twisted linen. A skilled worker sewed cherubim into the pattern. **36**The workers made four posts out of acacia wood for the curtain. They covered the posts with gold. They made gold hooks and four silver bases for the posts.

37For the entrance to the tent the workers made a curtain out of blue, purple and bright red yarn and finely twisted linen. A person who sewed skillfully made it. **38**The workers made five posts with hooks for the curtains. They covered the tops of the posts and their bands with gold. And they made five bronze bases for them.

The Ark of the Covenant

37 Bezalel made the ark of the covenant out of acacia wood. It was three feet nine inches long and two feet three inches wide and high. **2**He covered it inside and outside with pure gold. He put a strip of gold around it.

3He made four gold rings for it. He joined them to its four bottom corners. He put two rings on one side and two rings on the other. **4**Then he made poles out of acacia wood. He covered them with gold. **5**He put the poles through the rings on the sides of the ark to carry it.

6He made its cover out of pure gold. It was three feet nine inches long and two feet three inches wide. The cover is the place where sin is paid for.

7He made two cherubim out of hammered gold at the ends of the cover. **8**He put one cherub on each end of it. **9**He made the cherubim as part of the cover itself. The cherubim's wings spread up over the cover. The cherubim faced each other and looked toward the cover.

The Table for the Holy Bread

10The workers made the table out of acacia wood. It was three feet long, one foot six inches wide and two feet three inches high. **11**They covered it with pure gold. They put a strip of gold around it. **12**They also made a rim three inches wide around it. They put a strip of gold around the rim.

13They made four gold rings for the table. They joined them to the four corners, where the four legs were. **14**The rings were close to the rim. They held the poles that were used to carry the table.

15The workers made the poles out of acacia wood. They covered them with gold. **16**They made plates, dishes and bowls out of pure gold for the table. They also made pure gold pitchers to pour out drink offerings.

The Gold Lampstand

17The workers made the lampstand out of pure gold. They hammered out its base and stem. Its buds, blooms and cups branched out from it.

18Six branches came out from the sides of the lampstand. There were three on one side and three on the other. **19**On one branch there were three cups that were shaped like almond flowers with buds and blooms. There were three on the next branch. There were three on all six branches that came out from the lampstand.

20On the lampstand there were four cups that were shaped like almond flowers with buds and blooms. **21**One bud was under the first pair of branches that came out from the lampstand. A second bud was under the second pair. And a third bud was under the third pair. There was a total of six branches. **22**The buds and branches came out from the lampstand.

The whole lampstand was one piece that was hammered out of pure gold.

23The workers made its seven lamps out of pure gold. They also made its trays and wick cutters out of pure gold. **24**They used 75 pounds of pure gold to make the lampstand and everything that was used with it.

The Altar for Burning Incense

25The workers made an altar for burning incense. They made it out of acacia wood. It was one foot six inches square and three feet high. A horn stuck out from each of its upper four corners. **26**The workers covered the top, sides and horns with pure gold. They put a strip of gold around it.

27They made two gold rings below the strip. They put the rings across from each other. The rings held the poles that were used to carry it. 28The workers made the poles out of acacia wood. They covered them with gold.

29They also made the sacred anointing oil and the pure, sweet-smelling incense. A person who makes perfume made them.

The Altar for Burnt Offerings

38 The workers made the altar for burnt offerings out of acacia wood. It was four feet six inches high and seven feet six inches square. 2They made a horn stick out from each of its four upper corners. They covered the altar with bronze.

3They made all of its tools out of bronze. They made its pots, shovels, sprinkling bowls, meat forks, and pans for carrying ashes.

4They made a bronze grate for the altar. They put the grate halfway up the altar on the inside. 5They made a bronze ring for each of the four corners of the grate.

6They made poles out of acacia wood. They covered them with bronze. 7They put the poles through the rings. The poles were on two sides of the altar for carrying it.

The workers made the altar out of boards. They made it hollow.

The Large Bowl for Washing

8The workers made the large bronze bowl and its bronze stand. They made them out of the bronze mirrors that belonged to the women who served at the entrance to the Tent of Meeting.

The Courtyard

9Next, the workers made the courtyard. The south side was 150 feet long. It had curtains that were made out of finely twisted linen. 10The curtains had 20 posts and 20 bronze bases. The posts had silver hooks and bands on them.

11The north side was also 150 feet long. Its curtains had 20 posts and 20 bronze bases. The posts had silver hooks and bands on them.

12The west end was 75 feet wide. It had curtains with ten posts and ten bases. The posts had silver hooks and bands on them.

13The east end, toward the sunrise, was also 75 feet wide. 14Curtains that were 22

feet six inches long were on one side of the entrance. They were hung on three posts. Each post had a base. 15Curtains that were 22 feet six inches long were also on the other side of the entrance to the courtyard. They were hung on three posts. Each post had a base.

16All of the curtains that were around the courtyard were made out of finely twisted linen. 17The bases for the posts were made out of bronze. The hooks and bands that were on the posts were made out of silver. Their tops were covered with silver. So all of the posts of the courtyard had silver bands.

18The curtain for the entrance to the courtyard was made out of blue, purple and bright red yarn and finely twisted linen. A person who sewed skillfully made it. It was 30 feet long. Like the curtains of the courtyard, it was seven feet six inches high. 19It had four posts and four bronze bases. Their hooks and bands were made out of silver. Their tops were covered with silver.

20All of the tent stakes of the holy tent were made out of bronze. So were all of the stakes of the courtyard that was around it.

The Amounts of the Metals Used

21Here are the amounts of the metals that were used for the holy tent, where the tablets of the covenant were kept. Moses commanded the Levites to record the amounts. The Levites did the work under the direction of Ithamar. Ithamar was the son of the priest Aaron.

22Bezalel, the son of Uri, made everything the LORD had commanded Moses. Uri was the son of Hur. Bezalel was from the tribe of Judah. 23Oholiab, the son of Ahisamach, helped Bezalel. Oholiab was from the tribe of Dan. He could carve things and make patterns. And he could sew skillfully with blue, purple and bright red yarn and on fine linen.

24The total weight of the gold from the wave offering was more than a ton. It was weighed out in keeping with the standard weights that are used in the sacred tent. The gold was used for all of the work that was done in connection with the sacred tent.

25The silver that was received from the men in the community who were listed and counted weighed four tons. It was weighed out in keeping with the weights used in the sacred tent. 26It amounted to a fifth of an ounce for each person. It was weighed out in keeping with the weights used in the sacred tent. The silver was received from the men who had been listed and counted. All of them were 20 years old or more. Their total number was 603,550.

27The four tons of silver were used to make the bases for the holy tent and for the curtain. The 100 bases were made from the four tons. Each base used more than 75 pounds of silver. 28The workers used 45 pounds to make the hooks for the posts, to cover the tops of the posts, and to make their bands.

29The bronze from the wave offering weighed two and a half tons. 30The workers used some of it to make the bases for the entrance to the Tent of Meeting. They used some for the bronze altar for burnt offerings and its bronze grate and all of its tools. 31They used some for the bases for the courtyard that was around the holy tent. They used some for the bases for the courtyard entrance. And they used the rest to make all of the tent stakes for the holy tent and the courtyard that was around it.

The Clothes for the Priests

39 The workers made clothes from the blue, purple and bright red yarn. The clothes were worn by those who served in the holy tent. The workers also made sacred clothes for Aaron. They made them just as the LORD had commanded Moses.

The Linen Apron

2The workers made the linen apron out of fine gold wire, and out of blue, purple and bright red yarn, and out of finely twisted linen. 3They hammered out thin sheets of gold. They cut it into fine wire. They sewed it into the blue, purple and bright red yarn and fine linen. A skilled worker made it. 4The workers made shoulder straps for the apron. The straps were joined to two of its corners.

5Its skillfully made waistband was made like it. The waistband was part of the apron itself. It was made out of fine gold wire, and out of blue, purple and bright red yarn, and out of finely twisted linen. The workers made it just as the LORD had commanded Moses.

6They put the onyx stones in fancy gold settings. They carved the names of the sons of Israel on them. They did it the way a person carves a seal. 7Then they connected them to the shoulder straps of the linen apron. The stones stood for the sons of Israel and were a reminder for

them. The workers did those things just as the LORD had commanded Moses.

The Chest Cloth

8Skilled workers made the chest cloth. They made it like the linen apron. They used fine gold wire, and blue, purple and bright red yarn, and finely twisted linen. 9The chest cloth was nine inches square. It was folded in half.

10They put four rows of valuable jewels on it. A ruby, a topaz and a beryl were in the first row. 11A turquoise, a sapphire and an emerald were in the second row. 12A jacinth, an agate and an amethyst were in the third row. 13And a chrysolite, an onyx and a jasper were in the fourth row. The workers put them in fancy gold settings. 14They used a total of 12 stones. There was one stone for each of the names of the sons of Israel. Each stone was carved like a seal with the name of one of the 12 tribes.

15The workers made braided chains out of pure gold for the chest cloth. They made them like ropes. 16They made two fancy gold settings and two gold rings. They connected them to two corners of the chest cloth. 17They joined the two gold chains to the rings at the corners of the chest cloth. 18They joined the other ends of the chains to the two settings. They joined them to the shoulder straps on the front of the linen apron.

19The workers made two gold rings. They connected them to the other two corners of the chest cloth. They put them on the inside edge next to the apron. 20They made two more gold rings. They connected them to the bottom of the shoulder straps on the front of the apron. They put them close to the seam right above the waistband of the apron. 21They tied the rings of the chest cloth to the rings of the apron with blue cord. That connected it to the waistband. Then the chest cloth would not swing out from the linen apron. The workers did those things just as the LORD had commanded Moses.

More Clothes for the Priests

22The workers made the outer robe of the linen apron completely from blue cloth. The cloth was made by a skillful person. 23The workers made an opening like a collar in the center of the robe. They made an edge around the opening. Then it couldn't tear.

24They made pomegranates out of blue, purple and bright red yarn and finely twisted linen. They sewed them around the hem of the robe.

²⁵They made bells out of pure gold. They sewed them around the hem between the pomegranates. ²⁶They sewed a bell between every two pomegranates all around the hem of the robe. Aaron had to wear the robe when he served as priest. That's what the LORD commanded Moses.

²⁷The workers made inner robes out of fine linen for Aaron and his sons. The linen cloth was made by a skillful person. ²⁸The workers also made the turban out of fine linen. And they made the headbands and the underwear out of finely twisted linen. ²⁹The belt was made out of finely twisted linen and blue, purple and bright red yarn. A person who sewed skillfully made it. The workers did those things just as the LORD had commanded Moses.

³⁰They made the plate out of pure gold. It was a sacred crown. They carved words on it as if it were a seal. They carved the words SET APART FOR THE LORD. ³¹Then they tied the plate to the turban with a blue cord. They did those things just as the LORD had commanded Moses.

The Holy Tent Is Completed

³²So all of the work on the holy tent, the Tent of Meeting, was completed. The people of Israel did everything just as the LORD had commanded Moses.

³³Then they brought the holy tent to Moses along with everything that belonged to it. Here are the things they brought.

hooks
frames
crossbars
posts
bases

³⁴the covering of ram skins that were dyed red
the covering of the hides of sea cows
the curtain that screens the ark

³⁵the ark where the tablets of the covenant are kept
the poles and cover for the ark

³⁶the table for the holy bread with all of its articles
the holy bread

³⁷the pure gold lampstand with its row of lamps and everything that is used with it
the olive oil that gives light

³⁸the gold altar for burning incense
the anointing oil
the sweet-smelling incense
the curtain for the entrance to the tent

³⁹the bronze altar for burnt offerings with its bronze grate
its poles and all of its tools
the large bowl with its stand

⁴⁰the curtains of the courtyard with their posts and bases
the curtain for the entrance to the courtyard
the ropes and tent stakes for the courtyard

⁴¹the sacred clothes for the priest Aaron
the clothes for his sons when they serve as priests

⁴²The people of Israel had done all of the work just as the LORD had commanded Moses. ⁴³Moses looked over the work carefully. He saw that the workers had done it just as the LORD had commanded. So Moses gave them his blessing.

Moses Sets Up the Holy Tent

40 Then the LORD said to Moses, ²"Set up the holy tent, the Tent of Meeting. Set it up on the first day of the first month.

³"Place in it the ark where the tablets of the covenant are kept. Screen the ark with the curtain. ⁴Bring in the table for the holy bread. Arrange the loaves of bread on it. Then bring in the lampstand. Set up its lamps. ⁵Place the gold altar for burning incense in front of the ark where the tablets of the covenant are kept. Put up the curtain at the entrance to the holy tent.

⁶"Place the altar for burnt offerings in front of the entrance to the holy tent, the Tent of Meeting. ⁷Place the large bowl between the Tent of Meeting and the altar. Put water in the bowl.

⁸"Set up the courtyard around the holy tent. Put the curtain at the entrance to the courtyard.

⁹"Get the anointing oil. Anoint the holy tent and everything that is in it. Set apart the holy tent and everything that belongs to it. Then it will be holy. ¹⁰Anoint the altar for burnt offerings and all of its tools. Set the altar apart. Then it will be a very holy place. ¹¹Anoint the large bowl and its stand. Set them apart.

¹²"Bring Aaron and his sons to the entrance to the Tent of Meeting. Wash them with water. ¹³Dress Aaron in the sacred clothes. Anoint him and set him apart. Then he will be able to serve me as priest.

¹⁴"Bring his sons and dress them in their inner robes. ¹⁵Anoint them just as

you anointed their father. Then they will be able to serve me as priests. They will be anointed to do the work of priests. That work will last for all time to come."

¹⁶Moses did everything just as the LORD had commanded him.

¹⁷So the holy tent was set up. It was the first day of the first month in the second year. ¹⁸Moses set up the holy tent. He put the bases in place. He put the frames in them. He put in the crossbars. He set up the posts. ¹⁹He spread the holy tent over the frames. Then he put the coverings over the tent. Moses did it as the LORD had commanded him.

²⁰He got the tablets of the covenant. He placed them in the ark. He put the poles through its rings. And he put the cover on it. The cover was the place where sin is paid for. ²¹Moses brought the ark into the holy tent. He hung the curtain to screen the ark where the tablets of the covenant are kept. Moses did it as the LORD had commanded him.

²²He placed the table for the holy bread in the Tent of Meeting. It was on the north side of the holy tent outside the curtain. ²³He arranged the loaves of bread on it in the sight of the LORD. Moses did it as the LORD had commanded him.

²⁴He placed the lampstand in the Tent of Meeting. It stood across from the table on the south side of the holy tent. ²⁵He set up the lamps in the sight of the LORD. Moses did it as the LORD had commanded him.

²⁶He placed the gold altar for burning incense in the Tent of Meeting. He placed it in front of the curtain. ²⁷He burned sweet-smelling incense on it. Moses did it as the LORD had commanded him.

²⁸Then he put up the curtain at the entrance to the holy tent.

²⁹He set the altar for burnt offerings near the entrance to the holy tent, the Tent of Meeting. He sacrificed burnt offerings and grain offerings on it. Moses did it as the LORD had commanded him.

³⁰He placed the large bowl between the Tent of Meeting and the altar. He put water in the bowl for washing. ³¹Moses and Aaron and his sons used it to wash their hands and feet. ³²They washed when they entered the Tent of Meeting or approached the altar. They did it as the LORD had commanded Moses.

³³Then Moses set up the courtyard around the holy tent and altar. He put up the curtain at the entrance to the courtyard. And so Moses completed the work.

The Glory of the LORD

³⁴Then the cloud covered the Tent of Meeting. The glory of the LORD filled the holy tent. ³⁵Moses couldn't enter the Tent of Meeting because the cloud had settled on it. The glory of the LORD filled the holy tent.

³⁶The people of Israel continued their travels. When the cloud lifted from above the holy tent, they started out. ³⁷But if the cloud didn't lift, they did not start out. They stayed until the day it lifted.

³⁸So the cloud of the LORD was above the holy tent during the day. Fire was in the cloud at night. The whole community of Israel could see the cloud during all of their travels.

LEVITICUS

The book of Leviticus records rules and laws for the people of Israel. God wants to be sure his people know exactly how he wants them to live. Hundreds of rules and laws are listed in Leviticus. The laws cover murder, stealing, skin diseases, worship, festivals and many other parts of day-to-day living. The laws are clear and make sense (at least for the people who lived back then). Read Leviticus to discover how a holy God wants a holy people to live.

CODE OF HONOR IN THIS BOOK . . .

GIVING
PAGES 138, 146

OBEYS
PAGES 126, 137, 140, 147

HONEST
PAGES 138, 139

LOVING
PAGE 139

HELPFUL
PAGE 146

KIND
PAGE 147

Rules for Burnt Offerings

1 The LORD called out to Moses. He spoke to him from the Tent of Meeting. He said, 2"Speak to the people of Israel. Tell them, 'Suppose any one of you brings an offering to the LORD. You must bring an animal from your herd or flock.

3" 'If a man brings a burnt offering from the herd, he must offer a male animal. It must not have any flaws. He must bring it to the entrance to the Tent of Meeting. Then the LORD will accept it.

4" 'The man must place his hand on the head of the burnt offering. Then the LORD will accept it in place of him. It will pay for his sin. 5The young bull must be killed there in the sight of the LORD.

" 'Then the priests who are in Aaron's family line must bring its blood to the altar. They must sprinkle it against every side of the altar. The altar stands at the entrance to the Tent of Meeting.

6" 'The skin must be removed from the animal that is brought for the burnt offering. Then the animal must be cut into pieces.

7" 'The priests who are in Aaron's family line must build a fire on the altar. They must place wood on the fire. 8Then they must place the pieces of the animal on the burning wood on the altar. The pieces include the head and the fat.

9" 'The inside parts of the animal must be washed with water. The legs must also be washed. The priest must burn all of it on the altar.

" 'It is a burnt offering. It is an offering that is made with fire. It gives a smell that is pleasant to the LORD.

10" 'If the offering is a burnt offering from the flock, it must be a male animal. It can be a sheep or a goat. It must not have any flaws.

11" 'It must be killed at the north side of the altar in the sight of the LORD. The priests who are in Aaron's family line must sprinkle its blood against every side of the altar.

12" 'The animal must be cut into pieces. The priest must place them on the burning wood on the altar. The pieces include the head and the fat.

13" 'The inside parts must be washed with water. The legs must also be washed. The priest must bring all of it to the altar. He must burn it there.

" 'It is a burnt offering. It is an offering that is made with fire. It gives a smell that is pleasant to the LORD.

14" 'If the offering to the LORD is a burnt offering of birds, it must be a dove or a young pigeon.

15" 'The priest must bring it to the altar. He must twist its head off. Then he must burn the rest of the bird on the altar. Its blood must be emptied out on the side of the altar.

16" 'The priest must remove the small bag inside the bird's throat. He must also remove what is in the bag. Then he must throw all of it to the east side of the altar. That is where the ashes are. 17He must take hold of the wings of the bird and tear it open. But he must not tear it in two. Then the priest will burn it on the wood that is on the fire on the altar.

" 'It is a burnt offering. It is an offering that is made with fire. It gives a smell that is pleasant to the LORD.

Rules for Grain Offerings

2 " 'Suppose someone brings a grain offering to the LORD. Then his offering must be made out of fine flour. He must pour olive oil on it. He must also put incense on it.

2" 'He must take it to the priests who are in Aaron's family line. A priest must take a handful of the fine flour and oil. He must mix it with all of the incense. Then he must burn that part on the altar. It will be a reminder that all good things come from the LORD. It is an offering that is made with fire. It gives a smell that is pleasant to the LORD.

3" 'The rest of the grain offering belongs to Aaron and to the priests who are in his family line. It is a very holy part of the offerings that are made to the LORD with fire.

4" 'If you bring a grain offering that is baked in an oven, make it out of fine flour. It can be flat cakes that are made without yeast. Mix them with olive oil. Or it can be wafers that are made without yeast. Spread oil on them. 5If your grain offering is grilled on a metal plate, make it out of fine flour. Mix it with oil. Make it without yeast. 6Break it into pieces. Pour oil on it. It is a grain offering. 7If your grain offering is cooked in a pan, make it out of fine flour and oil.

8" 'Bring to the LORD your grain offering that is made out of all of those things. Give it to the priest. He must take it to the altar. 9He must take out the part of the grain offering that reminds you that all good things come from the LORD. He must burn it on the altar. It is an offering that is made with fire. It gives a smell that is pleasant to the LORD.

NOAH

Noah did everything exactly as God commanded him.
(Genesis 6:22)

GO TO PAGE 9

ABRAHAM

[Abraham] believed the LORD.
The LORD accepted [Abraham] because he believed. So his
faith made him right with the LORD. (Genesis 15:6)

GO TO PAGE 18

JACOB

The man said, "Your name will not be Jacob anymore.
Instead, it will be Israel. You have struggled with God and with men.
And you have won." (Genesis 32:28)

GO TO PAGE 44

JOSEPH

Joseph said to [his brothers], "Don't be afraid... You planned to harm me. But God planned it for good. He planned to do what is now being done. He wanted to save many lives." (Genesis 50:19–20)

GO TO PAGE 64

10 " 'The rest of the grain offering belongs to Aaron and the priests who are in his family line. It is a very holy part of the offerings that are made to the LORD with fire.

11 " 'Every grain offering you bring to the LORD must be made without yeast. You must not burn any yeast or honey in an offering that is made to the LORD with fire.

12 " 'You can bring them to the LORD as an offering of the first share of the food you gather or produce. But they must not be offered on the altar as a pleasant smell.

13 " 'Put salt on all of your grain offerings. Salt stands for the lasting covenant between you and your God. So do not leave it out of your grain offerings. Add it to all of your offerings.

14 " 'Suppose you bring to the LORD a grain offering of the first share of your food. Then offer crushed heads of your first grain that have been cooked in fire. **15** Put olive oil and incense on it. It is a grain offering.

16 " 'The priest must burn part of the crushed grain and the oil. It will remind you that all good things come from the LORD. The priest must burn it together with all of the incense. It is an offering that is made to the LORD with fire.

Rules for Friendship Offerings

3 " 'Suppose someone brings a friendship offering. If he offers an animal from the herd, it can be either male or female. It must not have any flaws. He must offer it in the sight of the LORD.

2 " 'The man must place his hand on the animal's head. It must be killed at the entrance to the Tent of Meeting. Then the priests who are in Aaron's family line must sprinkle the blood against every side of the altar.

3 " 'Part of the friendship offering must be given to the LORD as an offering that is made with fire. It must include all of the fat that covers the inside parts or is connected to them. **4** It must include both kidneys with the fat on them next to the lower back muscles. It must also include the covering of the liver. All of it must be removed together with the kidneys.

5 " 'Then the priests who are in Aaron's family line must burn it on the altar. They must burn it on top of the burnt offering on the burning wood.

" 'It is an offering that is made with fire. It gives a smell that is pleasant to the LORD.

6 " 'If a man brings an animal from the flock as a friendship offering to the LORD,

it can be either male or female. It must not have any flaws. **7** If he brings a lamb, he must offer it in the sight of the LORD. **8** The man must place his hand on the lamb's head. It must be killed there in front of the Tent of Meeting. Then the priests who are in Aaron's family line must sprinkle its blood against every side of the altar. **9** Part of the offering must be brought as a sacrifice that is made to the LORD with fire. It must include the lamb's fat and the entire fat tail cut off close to the backbone. It must include all of the fat that covers the inside parts or is connected to them. **10** It must include both kidneys with the fat on them next to the lower back muscles. It must also include the covering of the liver. All of it must be removed together with the kidneys.

11 " 'Then the priest must burn it on the altar as food. It is an offering that is made to the LORD with fire.

12 " 'If a man brings a goat, he must offer it in the sight of the LORD. **13** The man must place his hand on its head. It must be killed there in front of the Tent of Meeting. Then the priests who are in Aaron's family line must sprinkle its blood against every side of the altar.

14 " 'Part of the offering must be brought as an offering that is made to the LORD with fire. It must include all of the fat that covers the inside parts or is connected to them. **15** It must include both kidneys with the fat on them next to the lower back muscles. It must also include the covering of the liver. All of it must be removed together with the kidneys.

16 " 'Then the priest must burn it on the altar as food. It is an offering that is made with fire. It has a pleasant smell. All of the fat belongs to the LORD.

17 " 'You must not eat any fat or any blood. That is a law that will last for all time to come. It applies no matter where you live.' "

Rules for Sin Offerings

4 The LORD spoke to Moses. He said, **2** "Speak to the people of Israel. Tell them, 'Suppose someone sins without meaning to. And that person does something the LORD commands us not to do.

3 " 'Suppose it is the anointed priest who sins. And suppose he brings guilt on the people. Then he must bring a young bull to the LORD. It must not have any flaws. He must bring it as a sin offering for the sin he has committed. **4** He must bring the bull to the entrance to the Tent of

Meeting in the sight of the LORD. He must place his hand on its head. He must kill it there in the sight of the LORD.

5 " 'Then the priest must take some of the bull's blood. He must carry it into the Tent of Meeting. 6He must dip his finger into the blood. He must sprinkle some of it seven times in the sight of the LORD. He must do it in front of the curtain of the Most Holy Room.

7 " 'Then the priest must put some of the blood on the horns that stick out from the upper four corners of the altar for burning incense. The incense has a sweet smell. The altar stands in front of the LORD in the Tent of Meeting. The priest must pour out the rest of the bull's blood at the bottom of the altar for burnt offerings. That altar stands at the entrance to the tent.

8 " 'He must remove all of the fat from the bull for the sin offering. It includes the fat that covers the inside parts or is connected to them. 9It includes both kidneys with the fat on them next to the lower back muscles. It also includes the covering of the liver. He must remove all of it together with the kidneys. 10He must remove it in the same way the fat is removed from an ox that is sacrificed as a friendship offering. Then the priest must burn all of it on the altar for burnt offerings.

11 " 'But the bull's hide must be taken away. So must all of its meat. So must its head and legs. And so must its inside parts and guts. 12In other words, all of the rest of the bull must be taken away. The priest must take it outside the camp. He must take it to a place that is "clean." He must take it to the place where the ashes are thrown. There he must burn it in a wood fire on a pile of ashes.

13 " 'Or suppose the whole community of Israel sins without meaning to. They do something the LORD commands us not to do. Even if they are not aware of what they have done, they are guilty.

14 " 'But suppose they become aware of the sin they have committed. Then they must bring a young bull as a sin offering. They must offer it in front of the Tent of Meeting. 15The elders of the community must place their hands on the bull's head in the sight of the LORD. The bull must be killed in the sight of the LORD.

16 " 'Then the anointed priest must take some of the bull's blood into the Tent of Meeting. 17He must dip his finger into the blood. He must sprinkle it seven times in

the sight of the LORD. He must do it in front of the curtain. 18He must put some of the blood on the horns that stick out from the upper four corners of the altar. The altar stands in front of the LORD in the Tent of Meeting. The priest must pour out the rest of the blood at the bottom of the altar for burnt offerings. That altar stands at the entrance to the tent.

19 " 'He must remove all of the fat from the bull. He must burn it on the altar. 20He must do the same thing with that bull as he did with the bull for the sin offering. When he does, he will pay for the sin of the people. And they will be forgiven.

21 " 'Then he must take the bull outside the camp. He must burn it just as he burned the first bull. It is the sin offering for the whole community.

22 " 'Or suppose a leader sins without meaning to. If he disobeys any of the commands of the LORD his God, he is guilty.

23 " 'But suppose he is made aware of the sin he has committed. Then he must bring an offering. It must be a male goat. It must not have any flaws. 24He must place his hand on the goat's head. He must kill it. He must do it at the place where the animals for burnt offerings are killed in the sight of the LORD. His offering is a sin offering.

25 " 'Then the priest must dip his finger into some of the blood of the sin offering. He must put it on the horns that stick out from the upper four corners of the altar for burnt offerings. He must pour out the rest of the blood at the bottom of the altar.

26 " 'He must burn all of the fat on the altar. He must burn it in the same way he burned the fat of the friendship offering. When he does, he will pay for the sin of the leader. And the leader will be forgiven.

27 " 'Or suppose someone in the community sins without meaning to. If he disobeys any of the LORD's commands, he is guilty.

28 " 'But suppose he is made aware of the sin he has committed. Then he must bring an offering for the sin he has committed. It must be a female goat. It must not have any flaws. 29He must place his hand on the head of the animal for the sin offering. It must be killed at the place where the animals for burnt offerings are killed.

30 " 'Then the priest must dip his finger into some of the blood. He must put it on

the horns that stick out from the upper four corners of the altar for burnt offerings. He must pour out the rest of the blood at the bottom of the altar.

31 " 'He must remove all of the fat in the same way the fat is removed from the friendship offering. He must burn it on the altar. It gives a smell that is pleasant to the LORD. When the priest burns the offering, he will pay for the sin of that person. And he will be forgiven.

32 " 'Suppose he brings a lamb as his sin offering. Then he must bring a female animal. It must not have any flaws. **33** He must place his hand on its head. He must kill it as a sin offering. He must do it at the place where the animals for burnt offerings are killed.

34 " 'Then the priest must dip his finger into some of the blood of the sin offering. He must put it on the horns that stick out from the upper four corners of the altar for burnt offerings. He must pour out the rest of the blood at the bottom of the altar.

35 " 'He must remove all of the fat in the same way the fat is removed from the lamb for the friendship offering. He must burn it on the altar on top of the offerings that are made to the LORD with fire. When he does, he will pay for the sin that person has committed. And he will be forgiven.

5 " 'Suppose a person has been called as a witness to something he has seen or learned about. Then if he does not tell what he knows, he has sinned. And he will be held accountable for it.

2 " 'Or suppose a person touches something that is not "clean." It could be the dead bodies of wild animals or of livestock. Or it could be the dead bodies of creatures that move along the ground. Even though he is not aware that he touched them, he has become "unclean." And he is guilty.

3 " 'Or suppose he touches something "unclean" that comes from a human being. It could be anything that would make him "unclean." Suppose he is not aware that he touched it. When he finds out about it, he will be guilty.

4 " 'Or suppose a person takes an oath and makes a promise to do something without thinking it through. It does not matter what he promised. It does not matter whether he took the oath without thinking about it carefully. And suppose he is not aware that he did not think it through. When he finds out about it, he will be guilty.

5 " 'When someone is guilty in any of those ways, he must admit he has sinned. **6** He must bring a sin offering to pay for the sin he has committed. He must bring to the LORD a female lamb or goat from the flock. The priest will sacrifice the animal. That will pay for the person's sin.

7 " 'Suppose he can't afford a lamb. Then he must get two doves or two young pigeons. He must bring them to the LORD to pay for his sin. One of them is for a sin offering. The other is for a burnt offering.

8 " 'He must bring them to the priest. The priest will offer the one for the sin offering first. He must twist its head. But he must not twist it off completely.

9 " 'Then he must sprinkle some of the blood of the sin offering against the side of the altar. He must empty out the rest of the blood at the bottom of the altar. It is a sin offering.

10 " 'Then the priest will offer the other bird as a burnt offering. He must do it in the way the law requires. That will pay for the sin the person has committed. And he will be forgiven.

11 " 'But suppose he can't afford two doves or two young pigeons. Then he must bring eight cups of fine flour as an offering for his sin. It is a sin offering. He must not put olive oil or incense on it. That is because it is a sin offering.

12 " 'He must bring it to the priest. The priest must take a handful of it. He must burn that part on the altar. It will be a reminder that all good things come from the LORD. The priest must burn it on top of the offerings that are made to the LORD with fire. It is a sin offering.

13 " 'In that way the priest will pay for any of the sins the person has committed. And he will be forgiven. The rest of the offering will belong to the priest. It is the same as in the case of the grain offering.' "

Rules for Guilt Offerings

14 The LORD spoke to Moses. He said, **15** "Suppose a person sins by breaking the law. And he does it without meaning to. He sins against me or my priests by refusing to give them one of the holy things that are set apart for them.

"Then he must bring me a ram from the flock. It must not have any flaws. It must be worth the required amount of silver. It must be weighed out in keeping with the standard weights that are used in the sacred tent. It is a guilt offering. It will pay for his sin.

16 "He must also pay for the holy thing he refused to give. He must add a fifth of its value to it. He must give all of it to the priest. The priest will pay for the person's sin with the ram. It is a guilt offering. And he will be forgiven.

17"Suppose a person sins by doing something I command him not to do. Even though he does not know it, he is guilty. He will be held accountable for it. **18**"He must bring to the priest a ram from the flock as a guilt offering. It must not have any flaws. And it must be worth the required amount of money.

"The priest will sacrifice the animal. That will pay for what the person has done wrong without meaning to. And he will be forgiven. **19**It is a guilt offering. He has been guilty of doing wrong against me."

6 The LORD spoke to Moses. He said, **2**"Suppose a person sins by not being faithful to me. He does it by tricking his neighbors. He tricks them in connection with something they have placed in his care. He steals from them. Or he cheats them. **3**Or he finds something they have lost and then tells a lie about it. Or he goes to court. He takes an oath and tells a lie when he witnesses about it. Or he commits any other sin like those sins.

4"When he sins in any of those ways, he becomes guilty. He must return what he stole. He must give back what he took by cheating his neighbors. He must return what they placed in his care. He must return the lost property he found. **5**He must return anything he told a lie about when he witnessed in court. He must pay back everything in full. He must add a fifth of its value to it. He must give all of it to the owner on the day he brings his guilt offering.

6"He must bring his guilt offering to the priest to pay for his sin. It is an offering to me. He must bring a ram from the flock. It must not have any flaws. It must be worth the required amount of money.

7"The priest will sacrifice the ram to pay for the person's sin. He will do it in my sight. And the person will be forgiven for any of the things he did that made him guilty."

More Rules for Burnt Offerings

8The LORD spoke to Moses. He said, **9**"Give Aaron and the priests who are in his family line a command. Tell them, 'Here are some more rules for burnt offerings. The burnt offering must remain on the altar through the whole night. The fire on the altar must be kept burning until morning.

10" 'The priest must put on his linen clothes. He must put on linen underwear next to his body. He must remove the ashes of the burnt offering that the fire has burned up on the altar. He must place them beside the altar. **11**Then he must take his clothes off and put others on. He must carry the ashes outside the camp to a place that is "clean."

12" 'The fire on the altar must be kept burning. It must not go out. Every morning the priest must add more wood to the fire. He must place the burnt offering on the fire. He must burn the fat of the friendship offerings on it. **13**The fire must be kept burning on the altar all the time. It must not go out.

More Rules for Grain Offerings

14" 'Here are some more rules for grain offerings. The priests who are in Aaron's family line must bring the grain offering to the LORD in front of the altar.

15" 'The priest must take a handful of fine flour and olive oil. He must add to it all of the incense that is on the grain offering. He must burn that part on the altar. It will remind him that all good things come from the LORD. It gives a smell that is pleasant to the LORD.

16" 'Aaron and the priests who are in his family line will eat the rest of it. But they must eat it without yeast in a holy place. They must eat it in the courtyard of the Tent of Meeting. **17**It must not be baked with yeast. The LORD has given it to the priests as their share of the offerings that are made to him with fire. It is very holy, just like the sin offering and the guilt offering.

18" 'Any priests who are in Aaron's family line can eat it. It is their regular share of the offerings that are made to the LORD with fire. It is their share for all time to come. Anyone who touches those offerings will become holy.' "

19The LORD spoke to Moses. He said, **20**"On the day each high priest who is in Aaron's family line is anointed, he must bring an offering to me. He must bring eight cups of fine flour as a regular grain offering. He must bring half of it in the morning. He must bring the other half in the evening. **21**Mix it with olive oil. Grill it on a metal plate. Break it in pieces. Bring it as a grain offering. It gives a smell that is pleasant to me.

22"The son of Aaron who will become the next high priest after him will prepare the grain offering. It is my regular share. It must be completely burned up. **23**Every grain offering a high priest offers must be completely burned up. It must not be eaten."

More Rules for Sin Offerings

24The LORD spoke to Moses. He said, **25**"Speak to Aaron and the priests who are in his family line. Tell them, 'Here are some more rules for sin offerings. You must kill the animal for the sin offering in the sight of the LORD. Kill it in the place where the burnt offering is killed. It is very holy. **26**The priest who offers it will eat it. He must eat it in a holy place. He must eat it in the courtyard of the Tent of Meeting. **27**" 'Anyone who touches any of its meat will become holy. Suppose some of the blood is spilled on someone's clothes. Then you must wash them in a holy place. **28**Break the clay pot the meat is cooked in. But suppose you cook it in a bronze pot. Then you must scrub the pot and rinse it with water.

29" 'Any male in a priest's family can eat the meat. It is very holy.

30" 'But suppose some of the blood of a sin offering is brought into the Tent of Meeting. And that blood is brought into the Holy Room to pay for sin. Then that sin offering must not be eaten. It must be burned.

More Rules for Guilt Offerings

7 " 'Here are some more rules for guilt offerings. The guilt offering is very holy. **2**You must kill the animal for the guilt offering in the same place where you kill the animal for the burnt offering. Sprinkle its blood against every side of the altar.

3" 'Offer all of its fat. It must include the fat tail and the fat that covers the inside parts. **4**It must include both kidneys with the fat on them next to the lower back muscles. It must also include the covering of the liver. Remove all of it together with the kidneys. **5**The priest must burn all of it on the altar. It is an offering that is made to the LORD with fire. It is a guilt offering.

6" 'Any male in a priest's family can eat it. But he must eat it in a holy place. It is very holy.

7" 'The same law applies to the sin offering and the guilt offering. Both of them belong to the priest who offers them to pay for sin. **8**The priest who offers a burnt offering for anyone can keep its hide for himself.

9" 'Every grain offering that is baked in an oven belongs to the priest who offers it. So does every grain offering that is cooked in a pan or grilled on a metal plate. **10**Every grain offering belongs equally to all of the priests who are in Aaron's family line. That is true whether it is mixed with olive oil or it is dry.

More Rules for Friendship Offerings

11" 'Here are some more rules for friendship offerings a person may bring to the LORD.

12" 'Suppose he offers a friendship offering to show he is thankful. Then together with the thank offering he must offer flat cakes of bread. He must make them without yeast. He must mix them with olive oil. Or he must offer wafers that are made without yeast. He must spread oil on them. Or he must offer flat cakes that are made out of fine flour. He must add oil to it. He must work the flour and mix it well.

13" 'He must bring another friendship offering along with his thank offering. It should be flat cakes of bread that are made with yeast. **14**He must bring one of each kind of bread as an offering. One kind is made with yeast. The other is not. Both of them are a gift to the LORD. They belong to the priest who sprinkles the blood of the friendship offerings.

15" 'The person must eat the meat from his thank offering on the day he offers it. He must not leave any of it until morning.

16" 'But suppose he brings a friendship offering to keep a promise he has made. Or suppose he brings an offering he chooses to give. Then he must eat the sacrifice on the day he offers it. But if anything is left over, he may eat it the next day.

17" 'He must burn up any meat from the sacrifice that is left over until the third day. **18**Suppose he eats any meat from the friendship offering on the third day. Then the LORD will not accept the offering. He will not accept it as a gift from that person. It is not pure. If the person eats any of it, he will be held accountable for it.

19" 'He must not eat meat that touches anything that is "unclean." He must burn it up. Anyone who is "clean" may eat any other meat.

20" 'But suppose a person is not "clean" and eats any meat from the friendship offering that belongs to the LORD. Then that person will be cut off from his people.

21" 'Suppose a person touches something that is not "clean." It does not matter whether it comes from a human being who is not "clean." It does not matter whether it comes from an animal that is not "clean." It does not matter whether it comes from something that is hated and is not "clean." And suppose the person eats any of the meat from the friendship offering that belongs to the LORD. Then that person will be cut off from his people.' "

Israel Must Not Eat Fat or Blood

22The LORD spoke to Moses. He said, 23"Speak to the people of Israel. Tell them, 'Do not eat any of the fat of cattle, sheep or goats. 24Do not eat the fat of any animal that is found dead. Do not eat the fat of an animal that wild animals have torn apart. But you can use the fat for any other purpose.

25" 'Suppose an animal has been sacrificed as an offering that is made to the LORD with fire. No one may eat its fat. If he does, he will be cut off from his people.

26" 'No matter where you live, do not eat the blood of any bird or animal. 27If anyone does, he will be cut off from his people.' "

The Share That Belongs to the Priests

28The LORD spoke to Moses. He said, 29"Speak to the people of Israel. Tell them, 'Suppose a person brings a friendship offering to the LORD. Then he must bring part of it as his special gift to the LORD. 30He must bring it with his own hands. It is an offering that is made to the LORD with fire. He must bring the fat together with the breast. He must lift the breast up and wave it in front of the LORD as a wave offering. 31The priest will burn the fat on the altar.

" 'But the breast belongs to Aaron and the priests who are in his family line. 32Give the right thigh from your friendship offerings to the priest as a gift. 33The priest who offers the blood and fat from the friendship offering must be given the right thigh. It is his share.

34" 'I, the LORD, have taken the breast that is waved and the thigh that is given. I have taken them from the friendship offerings of the people of Israel. And I have given them to the priest Aaron and the priests who are in his family line. The offerings are their regular share from the people of Israel.' "

35That is the part of the offerings that are made to the LORD with fire and given to Aaron and the priests who are in his family line. It was given to Aaron and his sons on the day they were set apart to serve the LORD as priests. 36On the day they were anointed, the LORD commanded the people of Israel to give that part to them. For all time to come, it will be the regular share of Aaron and the priests who are in his family line.

37Those are the rules for burnt offerings, grain offerings, sin offerings, guilt offerings and friendship offerings. They are also the rules for the offerings that are given when priests are being prepared to serve the LORD. 38They are the rules the LORD gave Moses on Mount Sinai. He gave them on the day he commanded the people of Israel to bring their offerings to the LORD. That took place in the Sinai Desert.

Preparing the Priests to Serve the LORD

8 The LORD spoke to Moses. He said, 2"Bring Aaron and his sons to the entrance to the Tent of Meeting. Bring their clothes and the anointing oil. Bring the bull for the sin offering. Also bring two rams. And bring the basket with the bread that is made without yeast. 3Then gather the whole community at the entrance to the Tent of Meeting."

4Moses did just as the LORD had commanded him. All of the people gathered together at the entrance to the Tent of Meeting.

5Moses said to the people, "Here is what the LORD has commanded us to do."

6Then Moses brought Aaron and his sons to the people. He washed Aaron and his sons with water. 7He put the inner robe on Aaron. He tied the belt around him. He dressed him in the outer robe. He put the linen apron on him. He took the skillfully made waistband and tied the apron on him with it. He wanted to make sure it was securely tied to him.

8Moses placed the chest cloth on Aaron. He put the Urim and Thummim in the chest cloth. 9Then he placed the turban on Aaron's head. On the front of the turban he put the gold plate. It was a sacred crown. Moses did everything just as the LORD had commanded him.

10Then Moses took the anointing oil and poured it on the holy tent. He also poured it on everything that was in it. That's how he set those things apart for the LORD. 11He sprinkled some of the oil on the altar seven times. He poured oil on the altar and all of its tools. He poured it on the large bowl and its stand. He did it to set them apart.

¹²He poured some of the anointing oil on Aaron's head. He anointed him to set him apart to serve the LORD. ¹³Then Moses brought Aaron's sons to the people. He put the inner robes on them. He tied belts around them. He put headbands on them. He did everything just as the LORD had commanded him.

¹⁴Then he brought the bull for the sin offering. Aaron and his sons placed their hands on its head. ¹⁵Moses killed the bull. He dipped his finger into some of the blood. He put it on all of the horns that stick out from the upper four corners of the altar. He did it to make the altar pure. He poured out the rest of the blood at the bottom of the altar. So he set it apart to make it pure.

¹⁶Moses also removed all of the fat that was around the inside parts of the bull. He removed the covering of the liver. He took both kidneys and their fat. Then he burned all of it on the altar.

¹⁷But he burned the rest of the bull outside the camp. He burned up its hide, its meat and its guts. He did it just as the LORD had commanded him.

¹⁸Then Moses brought the ram for the burnt offering. Aaron and his sons placed their hands on its head. ¹⁹Moses killed the ram. He sprinkled the blood against every side of the altar.

²⁰He cut the ram into pieces. He burned the head, the other pieces and the fat. ²¹He washed the inside parts and the legs with water. He burned the whole ram on the altar as a burnt offering. It had a pleasant smell. It was an offering that was made to the LORD with fire. Moses did everything just as the LORD had commanded him.

²²Then he brought the other ram. It was sacrificed to prepare the priests for serving the LORD. Aaron and his sons placed their hands on its head.

²³Moses killed the ram. He put some of its blood on Aaron's right ear lobe. He put some on the thumb of Aaron's right hand. He also put some on the big toe of Aaron's right foot. ²⁴Then Moses brought Aaron's sons to the people. He put some of the blood on their right ear lobes. He put some on the thumbs of their right hands. He also put some on the big toes of their right feet. Then he sprinkled the rest of the blood against every side of the altar.

²⁵He removed the fat, the fat tail and all of the fat around the inside parts. He removed the covering of the liver. He

removed both kidneys and their fat. And he removed the right thigh. ²⁶Then he took a flat cake of bread from the basket of bread that was made without yeast. The basket was in front of the LORD. Moses took a cake of bread that was made with olive oil. He also took a wafer. He put all of it on the fat parts of the ram and on its right thigh.

²⁷He put everything in the hands of Aaron and his sons. He told them to lift it up and wave it in front of the LORD as a wave offering.

²⁸Then Moses took it from their hands. He burned it on the altar on top of the burnt offering. It was the offering that was sacrificed to prepare the priests for serving the LORD. It had a pleasant smell. It was an offering that was made to the LORD with fire.

²⁹Moses also lifted the ram's breast up and waved it in front of the LORD as a wave offering. The breast was Moses' share of the ram that was sacrificed to prepare the priests for serving the LORD. Moses did everything just as the LORD had commanded him.

³⁰Then Moses took some of the anointing oil. He also took some of the blood from the altar. He sprinkled some of the oil and blood on Aaron and his clothes. He also sprinkled some on Aaron's sons and their clothes. That's how he set apart Aaron and his clothes. And that's how he set apart Aaron's sons and their clothes.

³¹Then Moses spoke to Aaron and his sons. He said, "Cook the meat at the entrance to the Tent of Meeting. Eat it there along with the bread from the basket of the offerings that are brought to prepare the priests for serving the LORD. Do it just as I commanded you. I said, 'Aaron and his sons must eat it.' ³²Then burn up the rest of the meat and the bread.

³³"Don't leave the entrance to the Tent of Meeting for seven days. Don't leave until the days that are required to prepare you for serving the LORD have been completed. Stay here for the full seven days. ³⁴The LORD commanded what has been done here today. It was done to pay for your sin. ³⁵Stay at the entrance to the Tent of Meeting for seven days. Stay here day and night. Do what the LORD requires. Then you won't die. That's the command the LORD gave me."

³⁶So Aaron and his sons did everything just as the LORD had commanded through Moses.

OBEYS ✔

AARON AND HIS SONS DID EVERYTHING JUST AS THE LORD HAD COMMANDED THROUGH MOSES.
—— LEVITICUS 8:36 ——

The Priests Offer Sacrifices

9 On the eighth day Moses sent for Aaron, his sons and the elders of Israel. ²He said to Aaron, "Bring a bull calf for your sin offering. Bring a ram for your burnt offering. They must not have any flaws. Offer them to the LORD.

³"Then speak to the people of Israel. Tell them, 'Bring a male goat for a sin offering. Bring a calf and a lamb for a burnt offering. Both of them must be a year old. They must not have any flaws. ⁴Bring an ox and a ram for a friendship offering. Sacrifice all of them to the LORD. Also bring a grain offering. Mix it with olive oil. Today the LORD will appear to you.' "

⁵The people got the things Moses commanded them to get. They took them to the front of the Tent of Meeting. The whole community came up close to the tent. They stood there in front of the LORD.

⁶Then Moses said, "You have done what the LORD has commanded. So the glory of the LORD will appear to you."

⁷Moses said to Aaron, "Come to the altar. Sacrifice your sin offering and your burnt offering. Pay for your sin and the sin of the people. Sacrifice the people's offering. Pay for their sin. Do just as the LORD has commanded."

⁸So Aaron came to the altar. He killed the calf as a sin offering for himself. ⁹His sons brought its blood to him. He dipped his finger into the blood. He put some on the horns that stick out from the upper four corners of the altar. He poured out the rest at the bottom of the altar.

¹⁰He burned the fat and the kidneys on the altar. He also burned the covering of the liver. All of those parts were from the sin offering. Aaron did just as the LORD had commanded Moses. ¹¹He burned up the meat and the hide outside the camp.

¹²Then he killed the animal for the burnt offering. His sons handed him its blood. He sprinkled it against every side of the altar. ¹³They handed him the burnt offering piece by piece. It included the animal's head. Aaron burned everything on the altar. ¹⁴He washed the inside parts and the legs. He burned them on top of the burnt offering on the altar.

¹⁵Then Aaron brought the people's offering. He took the goat for their sin offering and killed it. He offered it for a sin offering. He did just as he had done with his own sin offering.

¹⁶He brought the animal for the burnt offering. He offered it in the way the law requires. ¹⁷He also brought the grain offering. He took a handful of it and burned it on the altar. It was in addition to that morning's burnt offering.

¹⁸Aaron killed the ox and the ram as the friendship offering for the people. His sons handed him the blood. He sprinkled it against every side of the altar.

¹⁹His sons also brought the fat parts of the ox and the ram. They included the fat tail and the layer of fat. They also included the kidneys and the covering of the liver. ²⁰Aaron's sons placed everything on the breasts of the animals.

Aaron burned the fat on the altar. ²¹He lifted up the breasts and the right thigh and waved them in front of the LORD as a wave offering. He did it just as Moses had commanded.

²²Then Aaron lifted up his hands toward the people. He gave them a blessing. He had already sacrificed the sin offering, the burnt offering and the friendship offering. So he stepped down from the altar.

²³Moses and Aaron went into the Tent of Meeting. When they came out, they gave the people a blessing. The glory of the LORD appeared to all of the people. ²⁴The LORD sent fire on the altar. It burned up the burnt offering and the fat parts that were on it. All of the people saw it. Then they shouted for joy. They fell with their faces to the ground.

The LORD Kills Nadab and Abihu

10 Nadab and Abihu were two of Aaron's sons. They got their shallow cups for burning incense. They put fire in them. They added incense to it. They made an offering to the LORD by using fire that wasn't allowed. They did it against his command. ²So the LORD sent fire on them. It burned them up. They died in front of the LORD.

³Then Moses spoke to Aaron. He said,

"That's what the LORD was talking about when he said,

" 'Among those who approach me
    I will show that I am holy.
In the sight of all of the people
    I will be honored.' "

So Aaron remained silent.

4Moses sent for Mishael and Elzaphan. They were sons of Aaron's uncle Uzziel. Moses said to them, "Come here. Carry the bodies of your cousins outside the camp. Take them away from in front of the Holy Room." **5**So they came and carried them outside the camp. It was just as Moses had ordered. The bodies of Nadab and Abihu still had their inner robes on them.

6Moses spoke to Aaron and to Eleazar and Ithamar. They were Aaron's sons. Moses said, "Don't let your hair hang loose. Don't tear your clothes. If you do, you will die. And the LORD will be angry with the whole community.

"But all of the people of Israel are allowed to show they are sad. They are your relatives. They can sob over those the LORD has destroyed with fire.

7"Don't leave the entrance to the Tent of Meeting. If you do, you will die. That's because the LORD's anointing oil has made you holy." So they did what Moses told them to do.

8Then the LORD spoke to Aaron. He said, **9**"You and your sons must not drink any kind of wine when you go into the Tent of Meeting. If you do, you will die. That is a law that will last for all time to come.

10"You must be able to tell the difference between what is holy and what is not. You must be able to tell the difference between what is 'clean' and what is not. **11**You must teach the people of Israel all of the rules I have given them through Moses."

12Moses spoke to Aaron and to Eleazar and Ithamar. They were Aaron's two remaining sons. Moses said, "Take the grain offering that is left over from the offerings that are made to the LORD with fire. It is very holy. Make bread without yeast from it. Eat it beside the altar. **13**Eat it in a holy place. It's your share and your sons' share of the offerings that are made to the LORD with fire. Those rules are in keeping with the command the LORD gave me.

14"But you and your sons and your daughters can eat the breast that was waved. You can also eat the thigh that was offered. Eat them in a place that is 'clean.' They have been given to you and your children. They are your share of the friendship offerings the people of Israel bring.

15"The thigh that was offered must be brought together with the fat parts of the offerings that are made with fire. The breast that was waved must be brought in the same way. All of it must be lifted up and waved in front of the LORD as a wave offering. It will be the regular share for you and your children. That's what the LORD has commanded."

16Moses asked about the goat that was brought as the sin offering. He found out that it had been burned up. So he became angry with Eleazar and Ithamar. They were Aaron's two remaining sons.

Moses asked them, **17**"Why didn't you eat the sin offering in a place that is near the Holy Room? The offering is very holy. It was given to you to take the people's guilt away. It paid for their sin in the sight of the LORD. **18**The blood of the offering wasn't taken into the Holy Room. So you should have eaten the goat in a place that is near the Holy Room. That's what I commanded."

19Aaron replied to Moses, "Today the people sacrificed their sin offering to the LORD. They also sacrificed their burnt offerings to him. But a terrible thing has happened to me. Two of my sons have died. Would the LORD have been pleased if I had eaten the sin offering today?" **20**When Moses heard that, he was satisfied.

Food That Is "Clean" and Food That Is Not

11 The LORD spoke to Moses and Aaron. He said to them, **2**"Speak to the people of Israel. Tell them, 'Many animals live on land. Here are the only ones you can eat. **3**You can eat any animal that has hoofs that are separated completely in two. But it must also chew the cud.

4" 'Some animals only chew the cud. Some only have hoofs that are separated in two. You must not eat those animals.

" 'Camels chew the cud. But their hoofs are not separated in two. So they are not "clean" for you.

5" 'Rock badgers chew the cud. But their hoofs are not separated in two. So they are not "clean" for you.

6" 'Rabbits chew the cud. But their hoofs are not separated in two. So they are not "clean" for you.

7" 'Pigs have hoofs that are separated

completely in two. But they do not chew the cud. So they are not "clean" for you.

8" 'You must not eat the meat of those animals. You must not even touch their dead bodies. They are not "clean" for you.

9" 'Many creatures live in the water of the oceans and streams. You can eat all of those that have fins and scales.

10" 'But be sure to avoid all of the creatures in the oceans or streams that do not have fins and scales. That includes all of those that move together in groups and all of those that do not. **11**Be sure to avoid them. Do not eat their meat. Do not even touch their dead bodies. **12**Be sure to avoid everything that lives in the water that does not have fins and scales.

13" 'Here are the birds you must be sure to avoid. Do not eat them. Be sure to avoid them.

" 'They include eagles, vultures and black vultures. **14**They include red kites and all kinds of black kites. **15**They include all kinds of ravens. **16**They include horned owls, screech owls, gulls and all kinds of hawks.

17" 'They include little owls, cormorants and great owls. **18**They include white owls, desert owls and ospreys. **19**They also include storks, hoopoes, bats and all kinds of herons.

20" 'Be sure to avoid every flying insect that walks on all fours. **21**But you can eat some creatures that have wings and walk on all fours. Their legs have joints so they can hop on the ground.

22" 'Here are the insects you can eat. You can eat all kinds of locusts, katydids, crickets and grasshoppers. **23**But be sure to avoid every other creature that has wings and four legs.

24" 'You will make yourselves "unclean" if you eat those things. If you touch their dead bodies, you will be "unclean" until evening. **25**If a person picks up one of their dead bodies, he must wash his clothes. He will be "unclean" until evening.

26" 'Suppose an animal has hoofs that are not separated completely in two. Or suppose an animal does not chew the cud. Then those animals are not "clean" for you. If you touch the dead body of any of them, you will not be "clean."

27" 'Many animals walk on all fours. But those that walk on their paws are not "clean" for you. Anyone who touches their dead bodies will be "unclean" until evening. **28**If he picks up their dead bodies, he must wash his clothes. He will be

"unclean" until evening. They are not "clean" for him.

29" 'Many animals move around on the ground. Here are the ones that are not "clean" for you. They include weasels, rats and all kinds of large lizards. **30**They also include geckos, monitor lizards, wall lizards, skinks and chameleons. **31**Those are the animals that move around on the ground that are not "clean" for you. If you touch their dead bodies, you will be "unclean" until evening.

32" 'Suppose one of them dies and falls on something. Then that article will not be "clean." It does not matter what it is used for. It does not matter whether it is made out of wood, cloth, hide or black cloth. Put it in water. It will be "unclean" until evening. After that, it will be "clean."

33" 'Suppose one of those animals falls into a clay pot. Then everything that is in the pot will be "unclean." You must break the pot. **34**Any food that could be eaten but has water on it that came from that pot is not "clean." And any liquid that could be drunk from it is not "clean."

35" 'Anything that the dead body of one of those animals falls on becomes "unclean." If it is an oven or cooking pot, break it. It is "unclean." And you must consider it "unclean."

36" 'But a spring or a well for collecting water remains "clean." That is true even if the dead body of one of those animals falls into it. But anyone who touches the dead body is not "clean."

37" 'If the dead body falls on any seeds that have not been planted yet, the seeds remain "clean." **38**But suppose water has already been put on the seeds. And suppose the dead body falls on them. Then they are not "clean" for you.

39" 'Suppose an animal you are allowed to eat dies. If anyone touches its dead body, he will be "unclean" until evening. **40**If he eats part of the dead body, he must wash his clothes. He will be "unclean" until evening. If he picks up the dead body, he must wash his clothes. He will be "unclean" until evening.

41" 'Be sure to avoid every creature that moves around on the ground. Do not eat it. **42**Do not eat any of those creatures. It does not matter whether they move on their bellies. It does not matter whether they walk on all fours or on many feet. Be sure to avoid them. **43**Do not make yourselves "unclean" by eating any of those animals. Do not make yourselves "unclean" because of them. Do not let them make you "unclean."

44" 'I am the LORD your God. Set yourselves apart. Be holy, because I am holy. Do not make yourselves "unclean" by eating any creatures that move around on the ground. **45**I am the LORD. I brought you up out of Egypt to be your God. So be holy, because I am holy.

46" 'Those are the rules about animals and birds. Those are the rules about every living thing that moves in the water. And those are the rules about every creature that moves around on the ground. **47**You must be able to tell the difference between what is "clean" and what is not. You must also be able to tell the difference between the living creatures that can be eaten and those that can't.' "

Becoming "Clean" After Having a Baby

12 The LORD spoke to Moses. He said, **2**"Speak to the people of Israel. Tell them, 'Suppose a woman becomes pregnant and has a baby boy. Then she will be "unclean" for seven days. It is the same as when she is "unclean" during her monthly period. **3**On the eighth day the boy must be circumcised.

4" 'After that, the woman must wait for 33 days to be made pure from her bleeding. She must not touch anything that is sacred until the 33 days are over. During that time she must not go to the sacred tent.

5" 'But suppose she has a baby girl. Then she will be "unclean" for two weeks. It is the same as during her period. After the two weeks, she must wait for 66 days to be made pure from her bleeding.

6" 'After she has waited the required number of days to be made pure, she must bring two offerings. She must take them to the priest at the entrance to the Tent of Meeting. She must bring a lamb that is a year old for a burnt offering. She must also bring a young pigeon or a dove for a sin offering. **7**The priest must offer them to the LORD. They will pay for her sin. Then she will be "clean" from her bleeding.

" 'Those are the rules for a woman who has a baby boy or girl.

8" 'But suppose she can't afford a lamb. Then she must bring two doves or two young pigeons. One is for a burnt offering. The other is for a sin offering. The priest will sacrifice those offerings. That will pay for her sin. And she will be "clean." ' "

Rules About Skin Diseases

13 The LORD spoke to Moses and Aaron. He told them to say to the people, **2**"Suppose someone's skin has a swelling or a rash or a bright spot. And suppose it could become a skin disease. Then he must be brought to the priest Aaron. Or he must be brought to a priest who is in Aaron's family line.

3"The priest must look carefully at the sore on the person's skin. He must see whether the hair in the sore has turned white. He must also see whether the sore seems to be under the skin. If the sore is white and is under the skin, it is a skin disease. When the priest looks that person over carefully, he must announce that the person is 'unclean.'

4"Suppose the spot on the skin is white but does not seem to be under the skin. And suppose the hair in the spot has not turned white. Then the priest must make the person stay away from everyone else for seven days. **5**On the seventh day the priest must look carefully at the sore again. Suppose it has not changed and has not spread in the skin. Then the priest must make the person stay away from everyone else for another seven days. **6**On the seventh day the priest must look carefully at the sore again. If it has faded and has not spread, he must announce that the person is 'clean.' It is only a rash. He must wash his clothes. He will be 'clean.'

7"But suppose the rash spreads in the skin after he has shown himself to the priest a second time. Then he must appear in front of the priest again. **8**The priest must look carefully at the sore. If the rash has spread, he must announce that the person is 'unclean.' He has a skin disease.

9"When anyone has a skin disease, he must be brought to the priest. **10**The priest must look him over carefully. Suppose there is a white swelling in the skin. Suppose it has turned the hair white. And suppose there are open sores in the swelling. **11**Then the person has a skin disease that will never go away. The priest must announce that he is 'unclean.' The priest must not make the person stay away from everyone else. He is already 'unclean.'

12"Suppose the disease breaks out all over his skin. And suppose it covers him from head to foot, as far as the priest can tell. **13**Then the priest must look him over carefully. If the disease has covered his whole body, the priest must announce that he is 'clean.' All of his skin has turned white. So he is 'clean.'

14 "But when open sores appear on his skin, he will not be 'clean.' **15** When the priest sees the open sores, he must announce that he is 'unclean.' The open sores are not 'clean.' He has a skin disease.

16 "But if the open sores change and turn white, he must go to the priest. **17** The priest must look him over carefully. If the sores have turned white, the priest must announce that the person is 'clean.' Then he will be 'clean.'

18 "Suppose someone has a boil on his skin and it heals. **19** And suppose a white swelling or shiny pink spot appears where the boil was. Then he must show himself to the priest.

20 "The priest must look at the boil carefully. Suppose it seems to be under the skin. And suppose the hair in it has turned white. Then the priest must announce that the person is 'unclean.' A skin disease has broken out where the boil was.

21 "But suppose that when the priest looks at the boil carefully, there is no white hair in it. The boil is not under the skin. And it has faded. Then the priest must make the person stay away from everyone else for seven days. **22** If the boil is spreading in the skin, the priest must announce that the person is 'unclean.' He has a skin disease.

23 "But suppose the spot has not changed. And suppose it has not spread. Then it is only a scar from the boil. And the priest must announce that the person is 'clean.'

24 "Suppose someone has a burn on his skin. And suppose a white or shiny pink spot shows up in the open sores of the burn. **25** Then the priest must look at the spot carefully. Suppose the hair in it has turned white. And suppose the spot seems to be under the skin. Then the person has a skin disease. It has broken out where he was burned. The priest must announce that the person is 'unclean.' He has a skin disease.

26 "But suppose the priest looks at the spot carefully. Suppose there is no white hair in it. Suppose the spot is not under the skin. And suppose it has faded. Then the priest must make the person stay away from everyone else for seven days. **27** On the seventh day the priest must look him over carefully. If the spot is spreading in the skin, the priest must announce that the person is 'unclean.' He has a skin disease.

28 "But suppose the spot has not changed. It has not spread in the skin. And it has faded. Then the burn has caused it to swell. The priest must announce that the person is 'clean.' It is only a scar from the burn.

29 "Suppose a man or woman has a sore on the head or chin. **30** Then the priest must look at the sore carefully. Suppose it seems to be under the skin. And suppose the hair in the sore is yellow and thin. Then the priest must announce that the person is 'unclean.' The sore is an itch. It is a skin disease on the head or chin.

31 "But suppose the priest looks carefully at that kind of sore. It does not seem to be under the skin. And there is no black hair in it. Then the priest must make the person stay away from everyone else for seven days.

32 "On the seventh day the priest must look at the sore carefully. Suppose the itch has not spread in the skin. It does not have any yellow hair in it. And it does not seem to be under the skin. **33** Then the person must shave his head. But he must not shave the area where the disease is. And the priest must make him stay away from everyone else for another seven days.

34 "On the seventh day the priest must look at the itch carefully. Suppose it has not spread in the skin. And suppose it does not seem to be under the skin. Then the priest must announce that the person is 'clean.' He must wash his clothes. He will be 'clean.'

35 "But suppose the itch spreads in the skin after the priest announces that the person is 'clean.' **36** Then the priest must look him over carefully. Suppose the itch has spread. Then the priest does not have to look for yellow hair. The person is not 'clean.'

37 "But suppose the itch has been stopped and black hair has grown in it, as far as the priest can tell. Then the itch is healed. The person is 'clean.' The priest must announce that he is 'clean.'

38 "Suppose a man or woman has white spots on the skin. **39** Then the priest must look at them carefully. Suppose he sees that the spots are dull white. Then a harmless rash has broken out on the skin. That person is 'clean.'

40 "Suppose a man loses all of the hair on his head. Then he is 'clean.' **41** Suppose he loses only the hair on the front of his head. Then he is 'clean.'

42 "But suppose he has a shiny pink sore on his head where his hair was. Then he has a skin disease. It is breaking out on his whole head or on the front of his head.

43 "The priest must look him over carefully. Suppose the swollen sore on his head or on the front of it is pink and shiny. And suppose it looks like a skin disease. **44**Then he has a skin disease. He is not 'clean.' The priest must announce that the man is 'unclean.' That is because he has a sore on his head.

45"Suppose someone has a skin disease that makes him 'unclean.' Then he must wear torn clothes. He must let his hair hang loose. He must cover the lower part of his face. He must cry out, 'Unclean! Unclean!' **46**As long as he has the disease, he remains 'unclean.' He must live alone. He must live outside the camp.

Rules About Mold

47"Suppose some clothes have mold on them. The clothes could be made out of wool or linen. **48**Or there could be cloth that is woven or knitted out of linen or wool. There could be pieces of leather. Or there could be articles that are made out of leather. **49**And suppose the mold that is on the clothes or on the woven or knitted cloth looks green or red. Or suppose the green or red mold is on the pieces of leather or the leather articles. Then it is mold that spreads. It must be shown to the priest.

50"The priest must look at it carefully. He must keep the article with the mold on it away from everything else for seven days. **51**On the seventh day he must look at it carefully. Suppose the mold has spread in the clothes or in the woven or knitted cloth. Or suppose it has spread on the pieces of leather or on the leather articles. Then it is mold that destroys. The article is not 'clean.'

52"The priest must burn up everything that has the mold in it. He must burn up the clothes or the woven or knitted cloth that is made out of wool or linen. He must burn up the leather articles. The mold destroys. So everything must be burned up.

53"But suppose the priest looks at the article carefully. The mold has not spread in the clothes. And it has not spread in the woven or knitted cloth or in the leather articles. **54**Then he will order someone to wash the article that has the mold on it. After that, the priest must keep the articles away from everything else for another seven days.

55"After the article that has the mold on it has been washed, the priest must look at it carefully. Suppose the way the mold looks has not changed. Then even though the mold has not spread, it is not

'clean.' Burn it up. It does not matter which side of the article the mold is on.

56"But suppose the priest looks at it carefully. And suppose the mold has faded after the article has been washed. Then the priest must tear out the part that has mold on it. He must tear it out of the clothes or leather. He must tear it out of the woven or knitted cloth.

57"But suppose it shows up again in the clothes. Or suppose it shows up again in the woven or knitted cloth or in the leather articles. Then it is spreading. Everything that has the mold on it must be burned up.

58"The clothes that have been washed and do not have any more mold on them must be washed again. So must the woven or knitted cloth or the leather articles. Then they will be 'clean.' "

59Those are the rules about what to do with anything that has mold on it. They apply to clothes that are made out of wool or linen. They apply to woven and knitted cloth and to leather articles. They give a priest directions about when to announce whether something is "clean" or not.

Making People "Clean" From Skin Diseases

14 The LORD spoke to Moses. He told him to say to the people, **2**"Here are the rules for making someone 'clean' if he has had a skin disease. They apply when he is brought to the priest.

3"The priest must go outside the camp. He must look the person over carefully. Suppose he has been healed of his skin disease. **4**Then the priest will order someone to bring him two live 'clean' birds. He will also order someone to bring him some cedar wood, bright red yarn and branches of a hyssop plant. All of those things will be used to make the person 'clean.'

5"The priest will order someone to kill one of the birds. It must be killed over fresh water in a clay pot. **6**Then the priest must take the live bird. He must dip it into the blood of the bird that was killed over the fresh water. He must dip it into the blood together with the cedar wood, the bright red yarn and the hyssop plant.

7"The priest will sprinkle the blood on the person who had the skin disease. That will make him 'clean.' The priest must sprinkle him seven times. Then the priest must announce that he is 'clean.' After that, the priest must let the live bird go free in the open fields.

8"The person must also wash his

clothes to be made 'clean.' He must shave off all of his hair. He must take a bath. Then he will be 'clean.' After that, he may come into the camp. But he must stay outside his tent for seven days.

9 "On the seventh day he must shave off all of his hair. He must shave his head. He must shave off his beard. He must also shave off his eyebrows and the rest of his hair. He must wash his clothes. He must take a bath. Then he will be 'clean.'

10 "On the eighth day he must bring two male lambs and one female lamb as an offering. The female must be a year old. The lambs must not have any flaws. He must also bring 24 cups of fine flour as a grain offering. He must mix it with olive oil. He must also bring five ounces of oil. 11 The priest who announces that the person is 'clean' must bring him and his offerings to me. He must do it at the entrance to the Tent of Meeting.

12 "Then the priest must take one of the male lambs. He must offer it as a guilt offering. He must offer it along with five ounces of oil. He must lift all of it up and wave it in front of me as a wave offering. 13 "He must kill the lamb in the holy place where sin offerings and burnt offerings are killed. The guilt offering belongs to the priest, just as the sin offering does. The guilt offering is very holy.

14 "The priest must take some of the blood from the guilt offering and put it on the person's right ear lobe. He must put some on the thumb of his right hand. He must also put some on the big toe of his right foot.

15 "Then the priest must take some of the oil and pour it into his own left hand. 16 He must dip his right forefinger into the oil that is in his hand. He must use his finger to sprinkle some of the oil in front of me seven times.

17 "The priest must put some of the oil that is in his hand on the same places he put the blood of the guilt offering. He must put some on the person's right ear lobe. He must put some on the thumb of his right hand. He must put some on the big toe of his right foot. 18 He must put on his head the rest of the oil that is in his hand. It will pay for the person's sin in my sight.

19 "Then the priest must sacrifice the sin offering. It will pay for the person's sin. He will be made 'clean' after being 'unclean.' After that, the priest will kill the burnt offering. 20 He will offer it on the altar. He will offer it together with the grain offer-

ing. It will pay for the person's sin. Then he will be 'clean.'

21 "But suppose he is poor. Suppose he can't afford all of those offerings. Then he must bring one male lamb as a guilt offering. It must be lifted up and waved in front of me to pay for his sin. He must also bring eight cups of fine flour along with the lamb. He must mix the flour with olive oil. It is a grain offering. He must offer it along with five ounces of oil. 22 He must also bring two doves or two young pigeons that he can afford. One is for a sin offering. The other is for a burnt offering.

23 "On the eighth day he must bring them to the priest so he can be made 'clean.' He must bring them to the entrance to the Tent of Meeting. He must do it in my sight.

24 "The priest must take the lamb for the guilt offering. He must take it together with the five ounces of oil. He must lift all of it up and wave it in front of me as a wave offering. 25 He must kill the lamb for the guilt offering. He must take some of its blood and put it on the person's right ear lobe. He must put some on the thumb of his right hand. He must also put some on the big toe of his right foot.

26 "The priest must pour some of the oil into his own left hand. 27 He must dip his right forefinger into the oil that is in his hand. He must use his finger to sprinkle some of it seven times in front of me.

28 "He must put some of the oil that is in his hand on the same places he put the blood of the guilt offering. He must put some on the person's right ear lobe. He must put some on the thumb of his right hand. He must also put some on the big toe of his right foot. 29 He must put on his head the rest of the oil that is in his hand. It will pay for the person's sin in my sight.

30 "The priest will sacrifice the doves or the young pigeons that the person can afford. 31 One is for a sin offering. The other is for a burnt offering. The priest must offer them together with the grain offering. In that way he will pay for the person's sin in my sight. He will do it to make him 'clean.' "

32 Those are the rules for anyone who has a skin disease. They are for people who can't afford the regular offerings that are required to make them "clean."

Making Things "Clean" From Mold

33 The LORD spoke to Moses and Aaron. He told them to say to the people, 34 "You will enter the land of Canaan. I am giving

it to you as your own. When you enter it, suppose I put mold in one of your houses. And suppose the mold spreads. 35Then the owner of that house must go and speak to the priest. He must say, 'I've seen something that looks like mold in my house.'

36"The priest must order everything to be taken out of the house. It must be done before he goes in to look carefully at the mold. If it is not done, the priest must announce that everything in the house is 'unclean.'

"After the house is empty the priest must go in and check it. 37He must look carefully at the mold that is on the walls. Suppose it looks as if it has green or red dents in it. And suppose the dents look as if they are behind the surface of the wall. 38Then the priest must go out the door. He must close the house up for seven days.

39"On the seventh day the priest will return to check the house. Suppose the mold that is on the walls has spread. 40Then he must order someone to tear out the stones that have mold on them. He must have them thrown into an 'unclean' place outside the town. 41He must have all of the inside walls of the house scraped. Everything that is scraped off must be dumped into an 'unclean' place outside the town.

42"Then other stones must be put in the place of the stones that had mold on them. The inside walls of the house must be coated with new clay.

43"Suppose the stones have been torn out. The house has been scraped. And the walls have been coated with new clay. But the mold appears again.

44"Then the priest must go and look things over carefully. Suppose the mold has spread in the house. Then it is the kind of mold that destroys things. The house is not 'clean.'

45"It must be torn down. The stones, the wood and all of the clay coating must be torn out. All of it must be taken out of the town to an 'unclean' place.

46"Suppose someone goes into the house while it is closed up. Then he will be 'unclean' until evening. 47If he sleeps or eats in the house, he must wash his clothes.

48"But suppose the priest comes to look things over carefully. And suppose the mold has not spread after the walls had been coated with new clay. Then he will announce that the house is 'clean.' The mold is gone.

49"To make the house pure, the priest must get two birds. He must also get some cedar wood, bright red yarn and branches of a hyssop plant. 50He must kill one of the birds over fresh water in a clay pot.

51"Then he must take the cedar wood, the hyssop plant, the bright red yarn and the live bird. He must dip all of them into the blood of the dead bird. He must also dip them into the fresh water. He must sprinkle the house seven times.

52"The priest will use the blood and the water to make the house pure. He will use the live bird to make it pure. He will also use the cedar wood, the hyssop plant and the bright red yarn to make it pure.

53"Then he must let the live bird go free in the open fields outside the town. In that way he will make the house pure. It will be 'clean.'"

54Those are the rules for skin diseases. They apply to itches. 55They apply to mold in clothes or in houses. 56They also apply to swellings, rashes or bright red spots on the skin. 57Use those rules to decide whether something is "clean" or not.

Those are the rules for skin diseases and for mold.

Rules About Liquid Body Wastes

15 The LORD spoke to Moses and Aaron. He said, 2"Speak to the people of Israel. Tell them, 'Suppose liquid waste is flowing out of a man's body. That liquid is not "clean." 3It does not matter whether it continues to flow out of his body or is blocked. It will make him "unclean." Here is how his liquid body waste will make him "unclean."

4"'Any bed the man who has the flow of liquid body waste lies on will not be "clean." Anything he sits on will not be "clean."

5"'If any of you touches the man's bed, you must wash your clothes. You must take a bath. You will be "unclean" until evening. 6Suppose you sit on anything the man sat on. Then you must wash your clothes. You must take a bath. You will be "unclean" until evening.

7"'Suppose you touch the man who has the flow of liquid body waste. Then you must wash your clothes. You must take a bath. You will be "unclean" until evening.

8"'Suppose you are "clean." And suppose the man who has the flow of liquid waste spits on you. Then you must wash your clothes. You must take a bath. You will be "unclean" until evening.

⁹" 'Everything the man sits on when he is riding will be "unclean." ¹⁰Suppose you touch any of the things that were under him. Then you will be "unclean" until evening. Even if you pick up those things, you must wash your clothes. You must take a bath. You will be "unclean" until evening.

¹¹" 'Suppose the man who has the liquid flow touches you. And suppose he does it without rinsing his hands with water. Then you must wash your clothes. You must take a bath. You will be "unclean" until evening.

¹²" 'Suppose the man touches a clay pot. Then that pot must be broken. Any wooden article he touches must be rinsed with water.

¹³" 'Suppose the man has been healed from his liquid flow. Then he must wait seven days. He must wash his clothes. He must take a bath in fresh water. After that, he will be "clean."

¹⁴" 'On the eighth day he must get two doves or two young pigeons. He must come to the LORD at the entrance to the Tent of Meeting. There he must give the birds to the priest. ¹⁵The priest must sacrifice them. One is for a sin offering. The other is for a burnt offering. In that way the priest will pay for the man's sin in the sight of the LORD. He will do it because the man had a liquid flow.

¹⁶" 'Suppose semen flows from a man's body. Then he must wash his whole body with water. He will be "unclean" until evening.

¹⁷" 'Suppose clothes or leather have semen on them. Then they must be washed with water. They will be "unclean" until evening.

¹⁸" 'Suppose a man makes love to a woman. And suppose semen flows from his body and touches both of them. Then they must take a bath. They will be "unclean" until evening.

¹⁹" 'Suppose a woman is having her regular period. Then for seven days she will not be pure. Anyone who touches her will be "unclean" until evening.

²⁰" 'Anything she lies on during her period will be "unclean." Anything she sits on will be "unclean."

²¹" 'If anyone touches her bed, he must wash his clothes. He must take a bath. He will be "unclean" until evening. ²²If anyone touches anything she sits on, he must wash his clothes. He must take a bath. He will be "unclean" until evening.

²³" 'It does not matter whether it was her bed or anything she was sitting on. If anyone touches it, he will be "unclean" until evening.

²⁴" 'Suppose a man makes love to that woman. And suppose blood from her monthly period touches him. Then he will be "unclean" for seven days. Any bed he lies on will be "unclean."

²⁵" 'Suppose blood flows from a woman's body for many days. And it happens at a time other than her monthly period. Or blood keeps flowing after her period is over. Then she will be "unclean" as long as the blood continues to flow. She will be "unclean," just as she is during the days of her period.

²⁶" 'Any bed she lies on while her blood continues to flow will be "unclean." It is the same as it is when she is having her period. Anything she sits on will be "unclean." It is the same as it is when she is having her period.

²⁷" 'If anyone touches those things, he will not be "clean." He must wash his clothes. He must take a bath. He will be "unclean" until evening.

²⁸" 'Suppose the woman has been healed from her flow of blood. Then she must wait seven days. After that, she will be "clean." ²⁹On the eighth day she must get two doves or two young pigeons. She must bring them to the priest at the entrance to the Tent of Meeting.

³⁰" 'The priest must sacrifice them. One is for a sin offering. The other is for a burnt offering. In that way he will pay for her sin in the sight of the LORD. He will do it because her flow of blood made her "unclean."

³¹" 'You must keep the people of Israel away from things that make them "unclean." Then they will not die for being "unclean." And they will not die for making the place where the LORD lives "unclean." It is in the middle of the camp.' "

³²Those are the rules for a man who has liquid waste flowing out of his body. They apply to a man who is made "unclean" by semen that flows from his body. ³³They apply to a woman who is having her monthly period. They apply to a man or woman who has a liquid flow. And they apply to a man who makes love to a woman who is not "clean."

The Day When Sin Is Paid For

16 The LORD spoke to Moses after two of Aaron's sons had died. They were the sons who died when they came near the LORD. ²The LORD said to Moses, "Speak to your brother Aaron. Tell him not to come into the Most Holy Room just anytime he wants to. Tell him not to come behind the curtain that is in front of the cover of the ark. The cover is the place where sin is paid for. If he comes behind the curtain, he will die. That is because I appear in the cloud over the cover.

3 "Aaron must not enter the area of the sacred tent without bringing a sacrifice. He must bring a young bull for a sin offering. He must also bring a ram for a burnt offering.

4 "He must put on the sacred inner robe that is made out of linen. He must wear linen underwear next to his body. He must tie the linen belt around him. And he must put on the linen turban. Those are sacred clothes. So he must take a bath before he puts them on.

5 "The community of Israel must give him two male goats and a ram. The goats are for a sin offering. The ram is for a burnt offering.

6 "Aaron must offer the bull for his own sin offering. It will pay for his own sin and the sin of his whole family.

7 "Then he must take the two goats and bring them to me at the entrance to the Tent of Meeting. **8** He must cast lots for the two goats. One lot is for me. The other is for the goat that carries the people's sins away. **9** Aaron must bring the goat that is chosen for me by lot. He must sacrifice it for a sin offering.

10 "But the goat that is chosen by the other lot must remain alive. First it must be brought in to me to pay for the people's sin. Then it must be sent into the desert as a goat that carries the people's sins away.

11 "Aaron must bring the bull for his own sin offering. It will pay for his own sin and the sin of his whole family. He must kill the bull for his own sin offering.

12 "He must take a shallow cup full of burning coals from the altar in my sight. He must get two handfuls of incense that is completely ground up. The incense must smell sweet. He must take the cup and the incense behind the curtain. **13** He must put the incense on the fire in my sight. The smoke from the incense will hide the cover of the ark where the tablets of the covenant are kept. The cover is the place where sin is paid for. Aaron must burn the incense so that he will not die.

14 "He must dip his finger in the bull's blood. He must sprinkle it on the front of the cover of the ark. He must sprinkle some in front of the cover. He must do it seven times.

15 "Then Aaron must kill the goat for the sin offering for the people. He must take its blood behind the curtain. There he must do the same thing with it as he did with the bull's blood. He must sprinkle it on the cover of the ark. He must also sprinkle some in front of it.

16 "That is how he will make the Most Holy Room pure. He must do it because the people of Israel are not 'clean.' They have not obeyed me. They have also committed other sins. Aaron must do the same for the Tent of Meeting because it stands in the middle of the camp. And the camp is not 'clean.'

17 "No one can be in the Tent of Meeting when Aaron goes into the Most Holy Room to pay for the people's sin. No one can enter the tent until Aaron comes out. He will not come out until he has paid for his own sin and the sin of his whole family. He will not come out until he has also paid for the sin of the whole community of Israel.

18 "Then he will come out to the altar for burnt offerings. It is in front of the tent where the ark of the LORD is. He will make the altar pure and clean. He will take some of the bull's blood and some of the goat's blood. Then he will put the blood on all of the horns that stick out from the upper four corners of the altar. **19** He will sprinkle some of the blood on it with his finger seven times. He will do it to make the altar pure. He will do it to set it apart from the people of Israel. They are not 'clean.'

20 "Aaron will finish making the Most Holy Room pure and clean. He will finish making the Tent of Meeting and the altar pure.

"Then he will bring the live goat out. **21** He must place both of his hands on its head. While he does that, he must tell me about all of the sins the people of Israel have committed. He must tell me about all of their evil acts and the times they did not obey me. In that way he puts their sins on the goat's head.

"Then he will send the goat away into the desert. The goat will be led away by a man who was appointed to do it. **22** The goat will carry all of their sins on itself to a place where there are no people. And the man will set the goat free in the desert.

23 "Then Aaron must go into the Tent of Meeting. He must take off the linen clothes he put on before he entered the Most Holy Room. He must leave them there. **24** He must take a bath in a holy place. And he must put on his regular clothes.

"Then he will come out and sacrifice

the burnt offering for himself. He will also sacrifice the burnt offering for the people. That will pay for his own sin and the people's sin. 25 He will also burn the fat of the sin offering on the altar.

26 "The man who sets free the goat that carries the people's sins away must wash his clothes. He must take a bath. After that, he can come back into the camp. 27 "The bull and the goat for the sin offerings must be taken outside the camp. Their blood was brought into the Most Holy Room. It paid for sin. The hides, meat and guts must be burned up. 28 "The man who burns them must wash his clothes. He must take a bath. After that, he can come back into the camp.

29 "Here is a law for you that will last for all time to come. On the tenth day of the seventh month you must not eat anything. You must not do any work. It does not matter whether you are Israelites or outsiders.

30 "On that day your sin will be paid for. You will be made pure and clean. You will be clean from all of your sins in my sight. 31 That day is a sabbath for you. You must rest on it. You must not eat anything on that day. That is a law that will last for all time to come.

32 "The high priest must pay for sin. He must make everything pure and clean. He has been anointed and prepared to become the next high priest after his father. He must put on the sacred clothes that are made out of linen. 33 He must make the Most Holy Room, the Tent of Meeting and the altar pure. And he must pay for the sin of the priests and all of the people in the whole community.

34 "Here is a law for you that will last for all time to come. Once a year you must pay for all of the sin of the people of Israel."

So it was done, just as the LORD commanded Moses.

Do Not Eat Meat That Has Blood in It

17 The LORD spoke to Moses. He said, 2 "Speak to Aaron and his sons. Speak to all of the people of Israel. Tell them, 'Here is what the LORD has commanded. He has said, 3 "Suppose someone sacrifices an ox, a lamb or a goat. He sacrifices it in the camp or outside of it. 4 He does it instead of bringing the animal to the entrance to the Tent of Meeting. He sacrifices it instead of giving it as an offering to me in front of my holy tent. Then

he will be thought of as guilty of spilling blood. Because he has done that, he must be cut off from his people.

5 " ' "The people of Israel are now making sacrifices in the open fields. But they must bring their sacrifices to the priest. They must bring them to me at the entrance to the Tent of Meeting. There they must sacrifice them as friendship offerings. 6 The priest must sprinkle the blood against my altar. It is the altar at the entrance to the Tent of Meeting. He must burn the fat. It will give a pleasant smell to me.

7 " ' "Israel must stop offering any of their sacrifices to statues of gods that look like goats. When they offer sacrifices to those statues, they are not faithful to me. That is a law for them that will last for all time to come." '

8 "Tell them, 'Suppose someone offers a burnt offering or sacrifice. It does not matter whether he is an Israelite or an outsider. 9 And suppose he does not bring it to the entrance to the Tent of Meeting to sacrifice it to me. Then he must be cut off from his people.

10 " 'Suppose someone eats meat that still has blood in it. It does not matter whether he is an Israelite or an outsider. I will turn against him if he eats it. I will cut him off from his people.

11 " ' The life of each creature is in its blood. So I have given you the blood of animals to pay for your sin on the altar. Blood is life. That is why blood pays for your sin.

12 " 'So I say to the people of Israel, "You must not eat meat that still has blood in it. And an outsider who lives among you must not eat it either."

13 " 'Suppose any of you hunts any animal or bird that can be eaten. It does not matter whether you are an Israelite or an outsider. You must let the blood flow out of the animal or bird. You must cover the blood with dirt.

14 " 'That is because every creature's life is its blood. And that is why I have said to the people of Israel, "You must not eat any creature's meat that still has blood in it. Every creature's life is its blood. Anyone who eats that kind of meat must be cut off."

15 " 'Suppose someone eats anything that is found dead or is torn apart by wild animals. It does not matter whether he is an Israelite or an outsider. He must wash his clothes. He must take a bath. He will be "unclean" until evening. After that, he will be "clean."

16" 'But suppose he does not wash his clothes. And suppose he does not take a bath. Then he will be held accountable for what he has done.' "

Do Not Commit Sexual Sins

18 The LORD spoke to Moses. He said, **2**"Speak to the people of Israel. Tell them, 'I am the LORD your God. **3**You must not do what the people of Egypt do. You used to live there. And you must not do what the people of Canaan do. I am bringing you into their land. Do not follow their practices.

OBEYS ✔

YOU MUST OBEY MY LAWS. YOU MUST BE CAREFUL TO FOLLOW MY RULES. I AM THE LORD YOUR GOD.

— LEVITICUS 18:4 —

4" 'You must obey my laws. You must be careful to follow my rules. I am the LORD your God. **5**Keep my rules and laws. The one who obeys them will live by them. I am the LORD.

6" 'Do not have sex with any of your close relatives. I am the LORD.

7" 'Do not bring shame on your father by having sex with your mother. Do not have sex with her. She is your mother.

8" 'Do not have sex with any other wife of your father. That would bring shame on your father.

9" 'Do not have sex with your sister. It does not matter whether she is your father's daughter or your mother's daughter. It does not matter whether she was born in the same home as you were or somewhere else.

10" 'Do not have sex with your son's daughter or your daughter's daughter. That would bring shame on you.

11" 'Do not have sex with the daughter of your father's wife. She was born to your father. She is your sister.

12" 'Do not have sex with your father's sister. She is a close relative on your father's side.

13" 'Do not have sex with your mother's sister. She is a close relative on your mother's side.

14" 'Do not bring shame on your father's brother by having sex with his wife. She is your aunt.

15" 'Do not have sex with your daughter-in-law. She is your son's wife. Do not have sex with her.

16" 'Do not have sex with your brother's wife. That would bring shame on your brother.

17" 'Do not have sex with both a woman and her daughter. Do not have sex with either her son's daughter or her daughter's daughter. They are close relatives on her side. Having sex with them is an evil thing.

18" 'Do not take your wife's sister as another wife and have sex with her. Do not do it while your wife is still living.

19" 'Do not make love to a woman during her monthly period. She is not "clean" at that time.

20" 'Do not have sex with your neighbor's wife. That would make you "unclean."

21" 'Do not hand over any of your children to be sacrificed to the god Molech. That would be treating my name as if it were not holy. I am the LORD your God.

22" 'Do not have sex with a man as you would have sex with a woman. I hate that.

23" 'Do not have sex with an animal. Do not make yourself "unclean" by doing that. A woman must not offer herself to an animal to have sex with it. That is a twisted use of sex.

24" 'Do not make yourselves "unclean" in any of those ways. That is how other nations became "unclean." So I am going to drive those nations out of the land to make room for you. **25**Even their land was not "clean." So I punished it because of its sin. The land itself threw out the people who lived there.

26" 'But you must keep my rules and my laws. You must not do any of the things I hate. It does not matter whether you are Israelites or outsiders.

27" 'All of those things were done by the people who lived in the land before you. That is how the land became "unclean." **28**If you make the land "unclean," it will throw you out. It will get rid of you just as it got rid of the nations that were there before you.

29" 'Suppose you do any of the things I hate. Then you must be cut off from your people.

30" 'Do exactly what I require. When you arrive in Canaan, do not follow any of the practices of its people. I hate the things they do. Do not make yourselves "unclean" by doing them. I am the LORD your God.' "

Other Laws

19 The LORD spoke to Moses. He said, ²"Speak to the whole community of Israel. Tell them, 'Be holy, because I am holy. I am the LORD your God.

³" 'All of you must have respect for your mother and father. You must always keep my Sabbath days. I am the LORD your God.

⁴" 'Do not turn away from me to worship statues of gods. Do not make gods out of metal for yourselves. I am the LORD your God.

⁵" 'Suppose you sacrifice a friendship offering to me. Then do it in the right way. And I will accept it from you. ⁶You must eat it on the same day you sacrifice it or on the next day. Anything that is left over until the third day must be burned up.

⁷" 'If you eat any of it on the third day, it is not pure. I will not accept it. ⁸If you eat it, you will be held accountable. You have misused what is holy to me. You will be cut off from your people.

⁹" 'Suppose you are harvesting your crops. Then do not harvest all the way to the edges of your field. And do not pick up the grain you missed. ¹⁰Do not go over your vineyard a second time. Do not pick up the grapes that have fallen to the

POWER-SURGE
GIVING　G

DO NOT HARVEST ALL THE WAY TO THE EDGES OF YOUR FIELD. AND DO NOT PICK UP THE GRAIN YOU MISSED. DO NOT GO OVER YOUR VINEYARD A SECOND TIME. DO NOT PICK UP THE GRAPES THAT HAVE FALLEN TO THE GROUND. LEAVE THEM FOR POOR PEOPLE AND OUTSIDERS.
— LEVITICUS 19:9-10 —

POWER-SURGE
HONEST　H

DO NOT STEAL.
DO NOT TELL LIES.
DO NOT CHEAT ONE ANOTHER.
DO NOT CHEAT YOUR NEIGHBOR. DO NOT ROB HIM.
— LEVITICUS 19:11,13 —

ground. Leave them for poor people and outsiders. I am the LORD your God.

¹¹" 'Do not steal.

" 'Do not tell lies.

" 'Do not cheat one another.

¹²" 'Do not take an oath and give false witness in my name. That would be treating it as if it were not holy. I am the LORD your God.

¹³" 'Do not cheat your neighbor. Do not rob him.

" 'Do not hold back the pay of a hired worker until morning.

¹⁴" 'Do not call a curse down on deaf people. Do not put anything in front of blind people that will make them trip. Instead, have respect for me. I am the LORD your God.

¹⁵" 'Do not make something that is wrong appear to be right. Treat poor people and rich people in the same way. Do not favor one person over another. Instead, judge everyone fairly.

¹⁶" 'Do not go around spreading lies among your people.

" 'Do not do anything that puts your neighbor's life in danger. I am the LORD.

¹⁷" 'Do not hate your brother in your heart. Correct your neighbor boldly when he does something wrong. Then you will not share his guilt.

¹⁸" 'Do not try to get even. Do not hold anything against one of your people. Instead, love your neighbor as you love yourself. I am the LORD.

¹⁹" 'Obey my rules.

" 'Do not let different kinds of animals mate with each other.

" 'Do not mix two kinds of seeds and then plant them in your field.

" 'Do not wear clothes that are made out of two kinds of cloth.

20 " 'Suppose a man has sex with a female slave. But she and another man have promised to get married to each other. And her freedom has not yet been paid for or given to her. Then she and the man who had sex with her must be punished. But they must not be put to death, because she had not been set free.

21 " 'The man must bring a ram to the entrance to the Tent of Meeting. It is for a guilt offering to me. **22**The priest must take the ram for the guilt offering. He must sacrifice it to pay for the man's sin in my sight. Then his sin will be forgiven.

23 " 'When you enter the land, suppose you plant a fruit tree. Then do not eat its fruit for the first three years. The fruit is not "clean." **24**In the fourth year all of the fruit will be holy. Offer it as a way of showing praise to me. **25**But in the fifth year you can eat the fruit. Then you will gather more and more fruit. I am the LORD your God.

26 " 'Do not eat any meat that still has blood in it.

" 'Do not practice any kind of evil magic at all.

27 " 'Do not cut the hair on the sides of your head. Do not clip off the edges of your beard.

28 " 'Do not make cuts on your bodies when someone dies. Do not put marks on your skin. I am the LORD.

29 " 'Do not dishonor your daughter's body by making a prostitute out of her. If you do, the people of Israel will start using prostitutes. The land will be filled with evil.

30 " 'You must always keep my Sabbath days. Have respect for my sacred tent. I am the LORD.

31 " 'Do not look for advice from people who get messages from those who have

POWER-SURGE

LOVING ♥

DO NOT TRY TO GET
EVEN. DO NOT HOLD
ANYTHING AGAINST
ONE OF YOUR PEOPLE.
INSTEAD, LOVE YOUR
NEIGHBOR AS YOU
LOVE YOURSELF.
— LEVITICUS 19:18 —

POWER-SURGE

HONEST H

BE HONEST WHEN YOU
MEASURE LENGTHS,
WEIGHTS OR
AMOUNTS. USE
HONEST SCALES AND
HONEST WEIGHTS.
— LEVITICUS 19:35-36 —

died. Do not go to people who talk to the spirits of the dead. If you do, they will make you "unclean." I am the LORD your God.

32 " 'Stand up in order to show your respect for old people. Also have respect for me. I am the LORD your God.

33 " 'Suppose an outsider lives with you in your land. Then do not treat him badly. **34**Treat him as if he were one of your own people. Love him as you love yourself. Remember that all of you were outsiders in Egypt. I am the LORD your God.

35 " 'Be honest when you measure lengths, weights or amounts. **36**Use honest scales and honest weights. Use honest dry measures. And use honest liquid measures. I am the LORD your God, I brought you out of Egypt.

37 " 'Obey all of my rules and laws. Follow them. I am the LORD.' "

Israel Will Be Punished for Their Sins

20 The LORD spoke to Moses. He said, **2**"Say to the people of Israel, 'Suppose a person sacrifices one of his children to the god Molech. It does not matter whether that person is an Israelite or an outsider who lives in Israel. He must be put to death. The people of the community must kill him by throwing stones at him. **3**I will turn against that man. I will cut him off from his people. That is because he sacrificed his child to Molech. He has made my sacred tent "unclean." He has treated my name as if it were not holy.

4 " 'Suppose the people of the community close their eyes to the fact that the man sacrificed his child to Molech. And suppose they fail to put him to death. **5**Then I will turn against that man and his family. I will cut him off from his people. I will also cut off all those who follow him

POWER-SURGE

OBEYS ✔

**OBEY MY RULES.
FOLLOW THEM. I AM
THE LORD.**
— LEVITICUS 20:8 —

by joining themselves to Molech. They are not faithful to me.

6 " 'Suppose someone looks for advice from people who get messages from those who have died. Or he goes to people who talk to the spirits of the dead. And he follows their advice. Then he has not been faithful to me. So I will turn against him. I will cut him off from his people.

7 " 'Set yourselves apart for me. Be holy, because I am the LORD your God. **8**Obey my rules. Follow them. I am the LORD. I make you holy.

9 " 'If anyone calls down a curse on his father or mother, he will be put to death. He has cursed his father or mother. Anything that happens to him will be his own fault.

10 " 'Suppose a man commits adultery with his neighbor's wife. Then the man and the woman must be put to death.

11 " 'Suppose a man has sex with his father's wife. Then he has brought shame on his father. The man and the woman must be put to death. Anything that happens to them will be their own fault.

12 " 'Suppose a man has sex with his daughter-in-law. Then they must be put to death. They have used sex in a twisted way. Anything that happens to them will be their own fault.

13 " 'Suppose a man has sex with another man as he would have sex with a woman. I hate what they have done. They must be put to death. Anything that happens to them will be their own fault.

14 " 'Suppose a man gets married to both a woman and her mother. That is evil. All of them must be burned to death. Then there will not be any evil among you.

15 " 'Suppose a man has sex with an animal. Then he must be put to death. You must also kill the animal.

16 " 'Suppose a woman has sex with an animal. Then kill the woman and the animal. They must be put to death. Anything that happens to them will be their own fault.

17 " 'Suppose a man gets married to his sister and has sex with her. That is a shameful thing to do. It does not matter whether she is the daughter of his father or of his mother. They must be cut off right in front of their own people. That man has brought shame on his sister. He will be held accountable for what he has done.

18 " 'Suppose a man makes love to a woman during her monthly period. He has uncovered the place where her bleeding was coming from. And she has let him do it. So they must be cut off from their people.

19 " 'Do not have sex with the sister of either your mother or your father. That would bring shame on a close relative. Both of you would be held accountable for what you have done.

20 " 'Suppose a man has sex with his aunt. Then he has brought shame on his uncle. Both of them will be held accountable for what they have done. They will die without having any children.

21 " 'Suppose a man gets married to his brother's wife. That is something that should never be done. He has brought shame on his brother. Neither of them will have any children.

22 " 'Obey all of my rules and laws. Follow them. Then the land where I am bringing you to live will not throw you out. **23**To make room for you, I am going to drive out the nations that are in the land. You must not follow the practices of those nations. I hated those nations because they did all of those things.

24 " 'But I said to you, "You will take over their land as your own. I will give it to you. It will belong to you. It is a land that has plenty of milk and honey." I am the LORD your God. I have set you apart from the other nations.

25 " 'So you must be able to tell the difference between animals that are "clean" and those that are not. You must know which birds are "clean" and which are not. Do not make yourselves "unclean" by eating any animal or bird that is not "clean." Do not make yourselves "unclean" by eating anything that moves along the ground. I have set all of them apart. They are "unclean" for you.

26 " 'You must be holy. You must be set apart to me. I am the LORD. I am holy. I have set you apart from the other nations to be my own people.

27 " 'Suppose a man or woman gets messages from those who have died. Or suppose a man or woman talks to the spirits of the dead. Then you must put that man or woman to death. You must kill them by throwing stones at them. Anything that happens to them will be their own fault.' "

Rules for Priests

21 The LORD said to Moses, "Speak to the priests, the sons of Aaron. Tell them, 'A priest must not make himself "unclean" by going near the dead body of any of his people. ²But he can go near the body of a close relative. It could be his mother, father, son, daughter or brother. ³He can also go near a sister who is not married. She would have depended on him because she did not have a husband. The priest can make himself "unclean" by going near her body. ⁴But he must not make himself "unclean" by going near the bodies of people who were only related to him by marriage. Going near them would make him "unclean."

⁵" 'Priests must not shave any part of their heads. They must not shave off the edges of their beards. They must not make cuts on their bodies when someone dies.

⁶" 'Priests must be holy. They must be set apart for me. I am their God. They must not treat my name as if it were not holy. They must be holy because they bring offerings that are made to me with fire. That is my food.

⁷" 'They must not get married to women who are "unclean" because they are prostitutes. They must not marry women who are divorced from their husbands. That is because priests are holy. They are set apart for me. I am their God. ⁸Consider them as holy, because they offer up food to me. Consider them as holy, because I am holy. I am the LORD. I make you holy.

⁹" 'Suppose a priest's daughter makes herself "unclean" by becoming a prostitute. Then she brings shame on her father. She must be burned to death.

¹⁰" 'The high priest is the one among his brothers whose head has been anointed with olive oil. He has been appointed to wear the priest's clothes.

" 'When someone dies, the high priest must not let his hair hang loose. He must not tear his clothes to show how sad he is. ¹¹He must not enter a place where there is a dead body. He must not make himself "unclean," even if his father or mother dies. ¹²He must not leave my sacred tent to take part in burying a body. That would bring shame on the tent. My anointing oil has set the high priest apart. I am the LORD.

¹³" 'The woman the high priest gets married to must be a virgin. ¹⁴He must not marry a widow or a woman who is divorced. He must not marry a woman who is "unclean" because she is a prostitute. He must only get married to a virgin. She must come from his own people. ¹⁵If he marries a virgin, he makes the children he has by her "clean." I am the LORD. I make him holy.' "

¹⁶The LORD spoke to Moses. He said, ¹⁷"Speak to Aaron. Tell him, 'For all time to come, no man in your family line who has any flaws can come near to offer food to me.

¹⁸" 'No man who has any flaws can come near. No man who is blind or disabled can come. No man whose body is scarred or twisted can come. ¹⁹No man whose foot or hand is disabled can come. ²⁰No man whose back is bent can come. No man who is too short can come. No man who has anything wrong with his eyes can come. No man who has boils or running sores can come. No man whose sex glands are crushed can come.

²¹" 'No man in the family line of the priest Aaron who has any flaws can come near me. He can't come to bring the offerings that are made to me with fire. If he has any flaws, he must not come near to offer food to me. ²²He can eat the holy food. He can also eat my very holy food. ²³But because he has a flaw, he must not go near the curtain or approach the altar. If he does, he will make my sacred tent "unclean." I am the LORD. I make everything holy.' "

²⁴So Moses told all of those things to Aaron and his sons. He also told them to all of the people of Israel.

22 The LORD spoke to Moses. He said, ²"Here is what I want you to tell Aaron and his sons. Tell them to treat the sacred offerings with respect. They are the offerings the people of Israel set apart to honor me. So Aaron and his sons must never treat my name as if it were not holy. I am the LORD.

³"Say to them, 'Suppose a man in your family line is "unclean." And suppose he comes near the sacred offerings. They are the offerings the people of Israel set apart to honor me. That man must be cut off from serving me as a priest. That applies for all time to come. I am the LORD.

⁴" 'Suppose a man in Aaron's family line has a skin disease. Or suppose liquid waste is flowing out of his body. Then he

can't eat the sacred offerings until he is made pure and clean.

5 " 'Suppose he touches something that has been made "unclean" by coming near a dead body. Or suppose he touches someone who has semen flowing from his body. Then he will not be "clean." 5Or suppose he touches any crawling thing that makes him "unclean." Or suppose he touches any person who makes him "unclean." It does not matter what he touches that is "unclean." It will make him "unclean."

6 " 'The one who touches anything of that kind will be "unclean" until evening. He must not eat any of the sacred offerings unless he has taken a bath. 7When the sun goes down, he will be "clean." After that, he can eat the sacred offerings. They are his food.

8 " 'He must not eat anything that is found dead or torn apart by wild animals. If he does, it will make him "unclean." I am the LORD.

9 " 'The priests must do what I require. But suppose they make fun of what I require. Then they will become guilty and die. I am the LORD. I make them holy.

10 " 'Only a member of a priest's family can eat the sacred offering. The guest of a priest can't eat it. A priest's hired worker can't eat it either.

11 " 'But suppose a priest buys a slave with money. Or suppose a slave is born in his house. Then that slave can eat the sacred food.

12 " 'Suppose a priest's daughter gets married to someone who is not a priest. Then she can't eat any of the food that is brought as a sacred gift. 13But suppose the priest's daughter becomes a widow or is divorced. She does not have any children. And she returns to live in her father's house, where she lived when she was young. Then she can eat her father's food. But a person who does not belong to a priest's family can't eat any of it.

14 " 'Suppose someone eats a sacred offering by mistake. Then he must pay back the priest for the offering. He must also add a fifth of its value to it.

15 " 'The priests must not allow the sacred offerings to become "unclean." They are the offerings the people of Israel bring to me. 16The priests must not allow the offerings to become "unclean" by letting the people eat them. If they do, they will bring guilt on the people. They will have to pay for what they have done. I am the LORD. I make them holy.' "

Sacrifices the LORD Does Not Accept

17The LORD spoke to Moses. He said, 18"Speak to Aaron and his sons. Speak to all of the people of Israel. Tell them, 'Suppose any of you brings a gift for a burnt offering to the LORD. It does not matter whether you are an Israelite or an outsider who lives in Israel. It does not matter whether you bring the offering to keep a promise or because you choose to give it. 19You must bring a male animal that does not have any flaws if you want the LORD to accept it from you. It does not matter whether it is from your cattle, sheep or goats. 20Do not bring an animal that has any flaws. If you do, the LORD will not accept it from you.

21 " 'Suppose any of you brings an animal for a friendship offering to the LORD. Then it must not have any flaws at all. If it does, the LORD will not accept it. It does not matter whether the animal is from your herd or flock. It does not matter whether you bring it to keep a promise or because you choose to give it. 22Do not offer a blind animal to the LORD. Do not bring an animal that is hurt or wounded. And do not offer one that has warts or boils or running sores. Do not place any of them on the altar as an offering that is made to the LORD with fire.

23 " 'But suppose you bring an offering you choose to give. Then you can bring an ox or a sheep whose body is twisted or too small. But the LORD will not accept it if you offer it to keep a promise.

24 " 'You must not offer the LORD a male animal whose sex glands have been hurt. The glands also must not be crushed, torn or cut. You must not offer that kind of animal in your own land. 25And you must not accept that kind of animal from someone who comes from another land. You must not offer it as food for your God. He will not accept it from you. Its body is twisted and has flaws.' "

26The LORD spoke to Moses. He said, 27"When a calf, lamb or goat is born, it must remain with its mother for seven days. From the eighth day on, I will accept it as an offering that is made to me with fire. 28Do not kill a cow and its calf on the same day. Do not kill a female sheep and its lamb on the same day.

29"Sacrifice a thank offering to me in the right way. Then I will accept it from you. 30You must eat it that same day. Do not leave any of it until morning. I am the LORD.

31"Obey my commands. Follow them. I

am the LORD. ³²Do not treat my name as if it were not holy. The people of Israel must recognize me as the holy God. I am the LORD. I make you holy. ³³I brought you out of Egypt to be your God. I am the LORD."

23 The LORD spoke to Moses. He said, ²"Speak to the people of Israel. Tell them, 'Here are my appointed feast days. They are the appointed feast days of the LORD. Tell the people that they must come together for these sacred feasts.

The Sabbath Day

³" 'There are six days when you can work. But the seventh day is a Sabbath. You must rest on it. Come together on that sacred day. You must not do any work on it. No matter where you live, it is a Sabbath day in my honor.

Passover and Unleavened Bread

⁴" 'Here are my appointed feasts. Tell the people that they must come together for these sacred feasts at their appointed times. ⁵My Passover begins when the sun goes down on the 14th day of the first month.

⁶" 'My Feast of Unleavened Bread begins on the 15th day of that month. For seven days you must eat bread that is made without yeast. ⁷On the first day you must come together for a special service. Do not do any regular work on that day. ⁸On each of the seven days bring an offering that is made to me with fire. On the seventh day come together for a special service. Do not do any regular work on that day.' "

The First Share of Israel's Crops Belongs to the LORD

⁹The LORD spoke to Moses. He said, ¹⁰"Speak to the people of Israel. Tell them, 'When you enter the land I am going to give you, bring an offering to me. Gather your crops. Bring the first bundle of grain to the priest. ¹¹He must lift the grain up and wave it in front of me. Then I will accept it from you. The priest must wave it on the day after the Sabbath. ¹²" 'On the day he waves the grain for you, you must sacrifice a burnt offering to me. It must be a lamb that does not have any flaws. It must be a year old. ¹³You must bring it together with its grain offering. The grain offering must be 16 cups of fine flour. Mix it with olive oil. It is an offering that is made to me with fire. It has a pleasant smell. You must offer a drink offering along with the burnt offering. It must be a quart of wine.

¹⁴" 'You must not eat any bread until the very day you bring your offering to me. You must not eat any grain that has been cooked or any of your first grain until that time. That is a law that will last for all time to come. It applies no matter where you live.

The Feast of Weeks

¹⁵" 'The day you brought the grain for the wave offering was the day after the Sabbath. Count off seven full weeks from that day. ¹⁶Count off 50 days up to the day after the seventh Sabbath. On that day bring me an offering of your first grain. ¹⁷Bring two loaves of bread that are made with 16 cups of fine flour. They must be baked with yeast. Bring them to me as a wave offering from the first share of your crops. That applies no matter where you live.

¹⁸" 'Together with the bread, bring seven male lambs. Each lamb must be a year old. It must not have any flaws. Also bring one young bull and two rams. They will be a burnt offering to me. They will be offered together with their grain offerings and drink offerings. They are an offering that is made with fire. They give a pleasant smell to me.

¹⁹" 'Then sacrifice one male goat for a sin offering. Also sacrifice two lambs for a friendship offering. Each of the lambs must be a year old. ²⁰The priest must lift the two lambs up and wave them in front of me as a wave offering. He must offer them together with the bread that is made out of the first share of your crops. They are a sacred offering to me. They will be given to the priest.

²¹" 'On that same day tell the people that they must come together for a special service. They must not do any regular work. That is a law that will last for all time to come. It applies no matter where you live.

²²" 'Suppose you are gathering your crops. Then do not harvest all the way to the edges of your field. And do not pick up the grain you missed. Leave some for poor people and outsiders. I am the LORD your God.' "

The Feast of Trumpets

²³The LORD spoke to Moses. He said, ²⁴"Say to the people of Israel, 'On the first day of the seventh month you must have a day of rest. It must be a special service that is announced with trumpet blasts.

25Do not do any regular work on that day. Instead, bring an offering that is made to me with fire.' "

The Day When Sin Is Paid For

26The LORD spoke to Moses. He said, 27"The tenth day of the seventh month is the day when sin is paid for. Come together for a special service. Do not eat any food. Bring an offering that is made to me with fire. 28Do not do any work on that day. It is the day when sin is paid for. On that day your sin will be paid for in my sight. I am the LORD your God. 29"Suppose you do eat food on that day. Then you will be cut off from your people. 30I will destroy anyone among your people who does any work on that day. 31You must not do any work at all. That is a law that will last for all time to come. It applies no matter where you live.

32"That day is a sabbath for you. You must rest on it. You must not eat anything on that day. You must keep your sabbath from the evening of the ninth day of the month until the following evening."

The Feast of Booths

33The LORD spoke to Moses. He said, 34"Say to the people of Israel, 'On the 15th day of the seventh month my Feast of Booths begins. It lasts for seven days. 35" 'On the first day you must come together for a special service. Do not do any regular work on that day. 36On each of the seven days bring an offering that is made to me with fire. On the eighth day come together for a special service. Bring an offering that is made to me with fire. That special service is the closing feast. Do not do any regular work on that day.

37" 'Those are my appointed feasts. Tell the people that they must come together for those sacred feasts. During those times, the people must bring offerings that are made to me with fire. They are burnt offerings and grain offerings. They are sacrifices and drink offerings. Each offering must be brought at its required time. 38" 'The feasts are in addition to my Sabbath days. The offerings are in addition to your gifts and anything you have promised. They are also in addition to all of the offerings you choose to give me. 39" 'Begin with the 15th day of the seventh month. That is after you have gathered your crops. On that day celebrate my Feast of Booths for seven days. The first day is a day of rest. The eighth day is also a day of rest. 40On the first day you must get the best fruit from the trees. You must also get palm leaves, leafy branches and poplar branches. You must be filled with joy in my sight for seven days. I am the LORD your God.

41" 'Celebrate my Feast of Booths for seven days each year. That is a law that will last for all time to come. Celebrate the feast in the seventh month. 42Live in booths for seven days. All of the people of Israel must live in booths. 43Then your children after you will know that I made the people of Israel live in booths. I made them do it after I brought them out of Egypt. I am the LORD your God.' "

44So Moses announced to the people of Israel the appointed feasts of the LORD.

Olive Oil, Bread and Incense

24 The LORD spoke to Moses. He said, 2"Command the people of Israel to bring you clear oil that is made from pressed olives. Use it to keep the lamps burning and giving light all the time.

3"Aaron must take care of the lamps in my sight from evening until morning all the time. That is a law that will last for all time to come. The lamps are outside the curtain that is in front of the tablets of the covenant in the Tent of Meeting. 4The lamps are on the pure gold lampstand in front of me. They must be taken care of all the time.

5"Get fine flour and bake 12 loaves of bread. Use 16 cups of flour for each loaf. 6Place them in two rows. Put six loaves in each row on the table that is made out of pure gold. The table stands in front of me. 7"Along each row put some pure incense. It will remind you that all good things come from me. Burn the incense in place of the bread. The incense is an offering that is made to me with fire.

8"The bread must be set out in front of me regularly. Do it every Sabbath day. It will be Israel's duty to provide it for all time to come. 9"The bread belongs to Aaron and his sons. They must eat it in a holy place. It is a very holy part of their regular share of the offerings that are made to me with fire."

A Person Who Speaks Evil Is Put to Death

10There was a man who had an Israelite mother. His father was born in Egypt. The man went out among the people of Israel. A fight broke out in the camp between him and an Israelite. 11The son of the Israelite woman spoke evil things against the

LORD by using a curse. So the people brought him to Moses. The name of the man's mother was Shelomith. She was the daughter of Dibri. Dibri was from the tribe of Dan. **12**The people kept her son under guard until they could find out what the LORD wanted them to do.

13Then the LORD spoke to Moses. He said, **14**"Get the man who spoke evil things against me. Take him outside the camp. All those who heard him say those things must place their hands on his head. Then the whole community must kill him by throwing stones at him.

15"Say to the people of Israel, 'If anyone calls down a curse on me, he will be held accountable. **16**If anyone speaks evil things against my Name, he must be put to death. The whole community must kill him by throwing stones at him. It does not matter whether he is an outsider or an Israelite. When he speaks evil things against my Name, he must be put to death.

17" 'If anyone kills another human being, he must be put to death. **18**If anyone kills someone's animal, he must pay its owner. A life must be taken for a life.

19" 'Suppose someone hurts his neighbor. Then what he has done must be done to him. **20**A bone must be broken for a bone. An eye must be put out for an eye. A tooth must be knocked out for a tooth. He must be hurt in the same way he hurt someone else.

21" 'If anyone kills an animal, he must pay its owner. But if he kills a human being, he must be put to death. **22**The same law applies whether he is an outsider or an Israelite. I am the LORD your God.' "

23Then Moses spoke to the people of Israel. They got the man who had spoken evil things against the LORD. They took him outside the camp. There they killed him by throwing stones at him. The people of Israel did just as the LORD had commanded Moses.

The Sabbath Year

25 The LORD spoke to Moses on Mount Sinai. He said, **2**"Speak to the people of Israel. Tell them, 'You will enter the land I am going to give you. When you do, you must honor me every seventh year by not farming the land that year.

3" 'For six years plant your fields. Trim the branches in your vineyards and gather your crops.

4" 'But the seventh year must be a sab-

bath for the land. The land must rest during it. It is a sabbath year in my honor. Do not plant your fields. Do not trim the branches in your vineyards. **5**Do not gather what grows without being planted. And do not gather the grapes from the vines you have not taken care of. The land must have a year of rest.

6" 'Anything the land produces during the sabbath year will be food for you. It will be for you and your male and female servants. Your hired workers will eat it. So will people who live with you for a while. **7**And so will your livestock and the wild animals that are in your land. Anything the land produces can be eaten.

The Year of Jubilee

8" 'Count off seven sabbaths of years. Count off seven times seven years. The seven sabbaths of years add up to a total of 49 years. **9**The tenth day of the seventh month is the day when sin is paid for. On that day blow the trumpet all through your land.

10" 'Set the 50th year apart. Announce freedom all over the land to everyone who lives there. The 50th year will be a Year of Jubilee for you. Each of you must return to your own family property. And each of you must return to your own tribe.

11" 'The 50th year will be a Year of Jubilee for you. Do not plant anything. Do not gather what grows without being planted. And do not gather the grapes from the vines you have not taken care of. **12**It is a Year of Jubilee. It will be holy for you. Eat only what the fields produce.

13" 'In the Year of Jubilee all of you must return to your own property.

14" 'Suppose you sell land to one of your own people. Or you buy land from him. Then do not take advantage of each other. **15**The price you pay must be based on the number of years since the last Year of Jubilee. And the price you charge must be based on the number of years left for gathering crops before the next Year of Jubilee.

16" 'When there are many years left, you must raise the price. When there are only a few years left, you must lower the price. That is because what the man is really selling you is the number of crops the land will produce. **17**Do not take advantage of each other. Instead, have respect for me. I am the LORD your God.

18" 'Follow my rules. Be careful to obey my laws. Then you will live safely in the land. **19**The land will produce its fruit. You will eat as much as you want. And you will live there in safety.

20" 'Suppose you say, "In the seventh year we will not plant anything or gather our crops. So what will we eat?" 21I will send you a great blessing in the sixth year. The land will produce enough for three years. 22While you plant during the eighth year, you will eat food from the old crop. You will continue to eat food from it until the crops from the ninth year are gathered.

23" 'The land must not be sold without a way of getting it back. That is because it belongs to me. You are only outsiders who rent my land. 24You must make sure that you can buy the land back. That applies to all of the land that belongs to you.

25" 'Suppose one of your own people becomes poor. And suppose he has to sell some of his land. Then his nearest relative must come and buy back what he has sold.

26" 'But suppose he does not have anyone to buy it back for him. And suppose things go well for him and he earns enough money to buy it back himself. 27Then he must decide how much the crops have become worth since the time he sold the land. He must take that amount off the price the land was sold for. He must give the man who is selling it back to him the money that is left. Then he can go back to his own property.

28" 'But suppose he has not earned enough money to pay the man back. Then the buyer he sold the land to will keep it until the Year of Jubilee. At that time it will be returned to him. Then he can go back to his property.

29" 'Suppose a man sells a house in a city that has a wall around it. Then for a full year after he sells it he has the right to buy it back.

30" 'But suppose he does not buy it back before the full year has passed. Then the house in the walled city will continue to belong to the buyer and his children after him. It will not be returned to the seller in the Year of Jubilee.

31" 'But houses in villages that do not have walls around them must be treated like property outside walled cities. Those houses can be bought back at any time. And they must be returned in the Year of Jubilee.

32" 'The Levites always have the right to buy back their houses in the towns that belong to them. 33So their property among the people of Israel can be bought back. That applies to a house that is sold

POWER–SURGE

GIVING   **G**

SUPPOSE ONE OF YOUR OWN PEOPLE BECOMES POOR. AND SUPPOSE HE CAN'T TAKE CARE OF HIMSELF. THEN HELP HIM.
— LEVITICUS 25:35 —

HELPFUL

in any of their towns. Any house that is sold must be returned to its original owner in the Year of Jubilee. That is because the houses of the Levites will always belong to them.

34" 'But the grasslands around their towns must never be sold. They will belong to them for all time to come.

35" 'Suppose one of your own people becomes poor. And suppose he can't take care of himself. Then help him just as you would help an outsider or someone who is living among you for a while. In that way, the man who is poor can continue to live among you.

36" 'Do not charge him interest of any kind. Instead, have respect for me. Then the man who has become poor can continue to live among you. 37If you lend him money, you must not charge him interest. And you must not sell him food for more than it cost you.

38" 'I am the LORD your God. I brought you out of Egypt. I did it to give you the land of Canaan. I wanted to be your God.

39" 'Suppose one of your own people becomes poor. And suppose he sells himself to you. Then do not make him work as a slave. 40You must treat him like a hired worker. Or you must treat him like someone who is living among you for a while.

" 'He must work for you until the Year of Jubilee. 41Then he and his children must be set free. He will go back to his own tribe. He will go back to the property his people have always owned.

42" 'The people of Israel are my servants. I brought them out of Egypt. So they must not be sold as slaves. 43Show

KIND K

WHEN YOU RULE OVER YOUR OWN PEOPLE, YOU MUST BE KIND TO THEM.

— LEVITICUS 25:46 —

them pity when you rule over them. Have respect for me.

44 " 'You must get your male and female slaves from the nations that are around you. You can buy slaves from them. **45** You can buy as slaves some of the people who are living among you for a while. You can also buy members of their families who were born among you. They will become your property. **46** You can leave them to your children as their share of your property. You can make them slaves for life. But when you rule over your own people, you must be kind to them.

47 " 'Suppose an outsider or someone who is living among you for a while becomes rich. Then suppose one of your own people becomes poor. He sells himself to the outsider who is living among you. Or he sells himself to a member of the outsider's family. **48** Then he keeps the right to buy himself back after he has sold himself. One of his relatives can buy him back. **49** An uncle or a cousin can buy himself back after he has sold himself. In fact, any relative in his tribe can do it. Or suppose things go well for him. Then he can buy himself back.

50 " 'He and his buyer must count the number of years from the time of the sale up to the Year of Jubilee. The price for his freedom must be based on the amount that is paid to a hired man for that number of years.

51 " 'Suppose there are many years until the Year of Jubilee. Then for his freedom he must pay a larger share of the price that was paid for him. **52** But suppose there are only a few years left until the Year of Jubilee. Then he must count the number of years that are left. The payment for his freedom must be based on that number.

53 " 'He must be treated as if he had been hired from year to year. You must make sure that his owner is kind to him when he rules over him.

54 " 'Suppose he is not bought back in any of those ways. Then he and his chil-

dren must still be set free in the Year of Jubilee. **55** That is because the people of Israel belong to me. They are my servants. I brought them out of Egypt. I am the LORD their God.

Rewards for Obeying the LORD

26 " 'Do not make statues of gods for yourselves. Do not set up a likeness of a god or a sacred stone for yourselves. Do not place a carved stone in your land and bow down in front of it. I am the LORD your God.

2 " 'You must always keep my Sabbath days. Have respect for my sacred tent. I am the LORD.

3 " 'Follow my rules. Be careful to obey my commands. **4** Then I will send you rain at the right time. The ground will produce its crops. The trees of the field will bear their fruit. **5** You will continue to thresh your grain until you gather your grapes. You will continue to gather your grapes until you plant your crops. You will have all you want to eat. And you will live in safety in your land.

6 " 'I will give you peace in the land. You will sleep, and no one will make you afraid. I will remove wild animals from the land. There will not be any war in your country. **7** You will hunt down your enemies. You will kill them with your swords. **8** Five of you will chase 100. And 100 of you will chase 10,000. You will kill your enemies with your swords.

9 " 'I will look with favor on you. I will give you many children and increase your numbers. And I will keep my covenant with you. **10** You will still be eating last year's crops when you have to move them out to make room for new crops.

11 " 'I will live among you. I will not turn away from you. **12** I will walk among you. I will be your God. And you will be my people. **13** I am the LORD your God. I brought you out of Egypt. I did not want you to be slaves in Egypt anymore. I threw off your heavy load. I helped you walk with your heads held high.

OBEYS ✔

FOLLOW MY RULES. BE CAREFUL TO OBEY MY COMMANDS.

— LEVITICUS 26:3 —

Punishment for Not Obeying the Lord

14" 'But suppose you will not listen to me. You will not carry out all of my commands. **15**You will say no to my rules and turn away from my laws. And you will break my covenant by failing to carry out all of my commands. **16**Then here is what I will do to you. All at once I will bring terror on you. I will send sicknesses that will make you weak. I will send fever that will destroy your sight. It will slowly take your life away. When you plant seeds, it will not do you any good. Instead, your enemies will eat what you have planted. **17**I will turn against you. Then your enemies will win the battle over you. Those who hate you will rule over you. You will run away even when no one is chasing you.

18" 'After all of that, suppose you still will not listen to me. Then I will punish you for your sins seven times. **19**I will break down your stubborn pride. I will make the sky above you like iron, and it will not rain. I will make the ground under you like bronze, and you will not be able to farm it. **20**You will work with all of your strength, but it will not do you any good. That is because your soil will not produce any crops. The trees of the land will not bear any fruit.

21" 'Suppose you continue to be my enemy. And suppose you still refuse to listen to me. Then I will multiply your troubles many times because of your sins. **22**I will send wild animals against you. They will kill your children. They will destroy your cattle. There will be so few of you left that your roads will be deserted.

23" 'After all of those things, suppose you still do not accept my warnings. And suppose you continue to be my enemy. **24**Then I myself will be your enemy. I will make you suffer for your sins again and again. **25**I will send war against you to punish you for breaking my covenant. When you go back into your cities, I will send a plague among you. You will be handed over to your enemies. **26**I will cut off your supply of bread. Ten women will need only one oven to bake your bread. They will weigh out the bread piece by piece. Even when you eat all of it, it will not be enough to satisfy you.

27" 'After all of that, suppose you still do not listen to me. And suppose you continue to be my enemy. **28**Then I will be angry with you. I will be your enemy. I myself will again punish you for your sins over and over. **29**You will eat the dead bodies of your sons. You will also eat the dead bodies of your daughters.

30" 'I will destroy the high places where you worship other gods. I will pull down your incense altars. I will pile up your dead bodies on the lifeless statues of your gods. And I will turn away from you. **31**I will completely destroy your cities. I will destroy your places of worship. The pleasant smell of your offerings will not give me any delight.

32" 'I will destroy your land so completely that your enemies who live there will be shocked. **33**I will scatter you among the nations. I will pull out my sword and hunt you down. Your land and your cities will be completely destroyed. **34**" 'Then the deserted land will enjoy its sabbath years. It will rest. It will not be farmed. It will enjoy its sabbaths. But you will become prisoners in the country of your enemies. **35**The land will rest the whole time it is deserted. It was not able to rest during the sabbaths you lived in it.

36" 'Some of you will be left in the lands of your enemies. I will fill your hearts with fear. The sound of a leaf that is blown by the wind will scare you away. You will run as if you were escaping from swords. You will fall down, even though no one is chasing you. **37**You will trip over one another as if you were running away from the battle. You will run away, even though no one is chasing you. You will not be able to stand and fight against your enemies.

38" 'While you are still scattered among the nations, you will die. The lands of your enemies will destroy you. **39**You who are left in those lands will become weaker and weaker. You will die because of your sins and the sins of your parents.

40" 'But suppose you admit that you and your parents have sinned. You admit the evil and dishonest things you have done against me. And you admit you have become my enemy. **41**What you did made me become your enemy. I let your enemies take you into their land. But suppose you stop being stubborn. You stop being proud. And you pay for your sin. **42**Then I will remember my covenant with Jacob. I will remember my covenant with Isaac. I will remember my covenant with Abraham. I will remember what I said to them about the land.

43" 'You will leave the land. It will enjoy its sabbaths while it lies deserted because you are not there. You will pay for your sins because you said no to my laws. You turned away from my rules. **44**" 'But even after all of that, I will not say no to you or turn away from you. I will not destroy you completely in the land of your enemies. I will not break my covenant with you. I am the LORD your God. **45**Because of you, I will remember the covenant I made with the people of Israel who lived before you. I brought them out of Egypt to be their God. The nations saw me do it. I am the LORD.' "

46Those are the orders, the laws and the rules of the covenant the LORD made on Mount Sinai. He made it between himself and the people of Israel through Moses.

Keep Your Promises to the LORD

27 The LORD spoke to Moses. He said, **2**"Speak to the people of Israel. Tell them, 'Suppose someone makes a special promise to set a person apart to serve me. Here is how much it will cost to set that person free from the promise to serve.

3" 'The cost for a male between the ages of 20 and 60 is 20 ounces of silver. It must be weighed out in keeping with the standard weights that are used in the sacred tent. **4**The cost for a female of the same age is 12 ounces of silver.

5" 'The cost for a male between the ages of five and 20 is eight ounces of silver. The cost for a female of the same age is four ounces of silver.

6" 'The cost for a male between the ages of one month and five years is two ounces of silver. The cost for a female of the same age is one and a fourth ounces of silver.

7" 'The cost for a male who is 60 years old or more is six ounces of silver. The cost for a female of the same age is four ounces of silver.

8" 'But suppose the one who makes the special promise is too poor to pay the required amount. Then he must bring to the priest the person who will be set free. The priest will decide the right value for that person. It will be based on how much the one who makes the promise can afford.

9" 'Suppose what he promised is an animal that I will accept as an offering. Then the animal that is given to me becomes holy. **10**The one who makes the promise must not trade it. He must not trade a good animal for a bad one. And he must not trade a bad animal for a good one. Suppose he chooses one animal instead of another. Then both animals become holy.

11" 'Suppose the animal he promised is not "clean." Suppose I will not accept it as an offering. Then the animal must be brought to the priest. **12**He will decide whether it is good or bad. Its value will be what he decides it will be. **13**Suppose the owner wants to buy the animal back. Then he must add a fifth to its cost.

14" 'Suppose a man sets his house apart as something that is holy to me. Then the priest will decide whether it is good or bad. Its value will remain what he decides it will be. **15**Suppose the man sets his house apart. And suppose later he wants to buy it back. Then he must add a fifth to its value. The house will belong to him again.

16" 'Suppose a man sets apart a piece of his family's land to me. Then its value must be decided based on the number of seeds that are required to grow a full crop on it. That value will be 20 ounces of silver for every six bushels of barley seeds.

17" 'Suppose he sets his field apart during the Year of Jubilee. Then the value that has been decided will not be changed. **18**But suppose he sets his field apart after the Year of Jubilee. Then the priest will decide its value based on the number of years that are left until the next Year of Jubilee. The value that was decided will be reduced.

19" 'Suppose the man who sets his field apart wants to buy it back. Then he must add a fifth to its value. The field will belong to him again. **20**But suppose he does not buy the field back. Instead, suppose he sells it to someone else. Then he can never buy it back.

21" 'When the field is set free in the Year of Jubilee, it will become holy. It will be like a field that is set apart to me. It will become the property of the priests.

22" 'Suppose a man sets apart to me a field he has bought. And suppose it is not part of his family's land. **23**Then the priest will decide its value based on the number of years that are left until the Year of Jubilee. The man must pay that value on the day it is decided. The money is holy. It is set apart for me.

24" 'In the Year of Jubilee the field will go back to the person the man bought it from. That person is the one who had owned the land before.

25" 'Every amount of money must be weighed out in keeping with the standard weights that are used in the sacred tent.

26" 'But no one can set apart the first male animal that is born to its mother. That animal already belongs to me. It does not matter whether it is an ox or a sheep. It belongs to me.

27" 'Suppose it is an animal that is not "clean." Then the owner may buy it back at the value that has been decided. And he must add a fifth to its value. But suppose he does not buy it back. Then it must be sold at the value that has been decided.

28 " 'But nothing a man owns and sets apart to me can be sold or bought back. It does not matter whether it is a person or an animal or a family's land. Everything that is set apart to me is very holy to me.

29 " 'No one who is set apart in a special way to be destroyed can be bought back. He must be put to death.

30 " 'A tenth of everything the land produces belongs to me. That includes grain from the soil and fruit from the trees. It is holy. It is set apart for me. 31 Suppose a man buys back some of his tenth. Then he must add a fifth of the cost to it.

32 " 'The whole tenth of his herds and flocks will be holy. They will be set apart for me. That includes every tenth animal that its shepherd marks with his wooden staff. 33 The owner must not pick out the good animals from the bad. He must not choose one animal instead of another. But if he does, both animals become holy. They can't be bought back.' "

34 The Lord gave Moses all of those commands on Mount Sinai for the people of Israel.

NUMBERS

The book of Numbers is just what it says—numbers. This book records two times when God tells Moses and his leaders to count the people of Israel. The book also tells many stories of how the Israelites rebel, grumble and disobey while they wander in the desert. More than that, the book records God's faithful love for his people even though they are not faithful to him. Read Numbers to get a picture of a God who loves his people in spite of their sins, even today.

HEROES IN THIS BOOK . . .

CALEB
PAGE 170

BALAAM
(Sort of)
PAGE 184

FIVE SISTERS
PAGE 189

The Men of Israel Are Counted

1 The Lord spoke to Moses in the Tent of Meeting. It happened in the Desert of Sinai. The Lord spoke to him on the first day of the second month. It was the second year after the people of Israel came out of Egypt.

The Lord said, **2**"Count all of the men of Israel. Make a list of them by their tribes and families. List every man by name. List them one by one. **3**Count all of the men who are able to serve in the army. They must be 20 years old or more. I want you and Aaron to make a list of them company by company. **4**One man from each tribe must help you. Those who help must be the heads of their families.

5"Here are the names of the men who must help you.

"From the tribe of Reuben will come Elizur, the son of Shedeur.
6From the tribe of Simeon will come Shelumiel, the son of Zurishaddai.
7From the tribe of Judah will come Nahshon, the son of Amminadab.
8From the tribe of Issachar will come Nethanel, the son of Zuar.
9From the tribe of Zebulun will come Eliab, the son of Helon.
10From the tribe of Ephraim will come Elishama, the son of Ammihud.
From the tribe of Manasseh will come Gamaliel, the son of Pedahzur.
Ephraim and Manasseh were Joseph's two sons.
11From the tribe of Benjamin will come Abidan, the son of Gideoni.
12From the tribe of Dan will come Ahiezer, the son of Ammishaddai.
13From the tribe of Asher will come Pagiel, the son of Ocran.
14From the tribe of Gad will come Eliasaph, the son of Deuel.
15From the tribe of Naphtali will come Ahira, the son of Enan."

16Those were the men who were appointed from the community. They were the leaders of the tribes of their people. They were the heads of the major families in Israel.

17Moses and Aaron went and got the men whose names had been given to them. **18**Then Moses and Aaron gathered all of the men of Israel together. It was the first day of the second month. The men announced the tribe and family they belonged to. Those who were 20 years old or more were listed by name. They were listed one by one.

POWER-SURGE

OBEYS ✔

EVERYTHING WAS DONE JUST AS THE Lord HAD COMMANDED MOSES.
— NUMBERS 1:19 —

19Everything was done just as the Lord had commanded Moses. So Moses counted them in the Desert of Sinai.

20Here is the number of men from the tribe of Reuben, Israel's oldest son.
All of the men who were able to serve in the army were counted. They were 20 years old or more. They were listed by name. They were listed one by one. They were listed in keeping with the records of their tribes and families. **21**The number from the tribe of Reuben was 46,500.

22Here is the number of men from the tribe of Simeon.
All of the men who were able to serve in the army were counted. They were 20 years old or more. They were listed by name. They were listed one by one. They were listed in keeping with the records of their tribes and families. **23**The number from the tribe of Simeon was 59,300.

24Here is the number of men from the tribe of Gad.
All of the men who were able to serve in the army were counted. They were 20 years old or more. They were listed by name. They were listed in keeping with the records of their tribes and families. **25**The number from the tribe of Gad was 45,650.

26Here is the number of men from the tribe of Judah.
All of the men who were able to serve in the army were counted. They were 20 years old or more. They were listed by name. They were listed in keeping with the records of their tribes and families. **27**The number from the tribe of Judah was 74,600.

28Here is the number of men from the tribe of Issachar.

All of the men who were able to serve in the army were counted. They were 20 years old or more. They were listed by name. They were listed in keeping with the records of their tribes and families. **29**The number from the tribe of Issachar was 54,400.

30Here is the number of men from the tribe of Zebulun.

All of the men who were able to serve in the army were counted. They were 20 years old or more. They were listed by name. They were listed in keeping with the records of their tribes and families. **31**The number from the tribe of Zebulun was 57,400.

32Here is the number of men from the tribe of Ephraim, the son of Joseph.

All of the men who were able to serve in the army were counted. They were 20 years old or more. They were listed by name. They were listed in keeping with the records of their tribes and families. **33**The number from the tribe of Ephraim was 40,500.

34Here is the number of men from the tribe of Manasseh, the son of Joseph.

All of the men who were able to serve in the army were counted. They were 20 years old or more. They were listed by name. They were listed in keeping with the records of their tribes and families. **35**The number from the tribe of Manasseh was 32,200.

36Here is the number of men from the tribe of Benjamin.

All of the men who were able to serve in the army were counted. They were 20 years old or more. They were listed by name. They were listed in keeping with the records of their tribes and families. **37**The number from the tribe of Benjamin was 35,400.

38Here is the number of men from the tribe of Dan.

All of the men who were able to serve in the army were counted. They were 20 years old or more. They were listed by name. They were listed in keeping with the records of their tribes and families.

39The number from the tribe of Dan was 62,700.

40Here is the number of men from the tribe of Asher.

All of the men who were able to serve in the army were counted. They were 20 years old or more. They were listed by name. They were listed in keeping with the records of their tribes and families. **41**The number from the tribe of Asher was 41,500.

42Here is the number of men from the tribe of Naphtali.

All of the men who were able to serve in the army were counted. They were 20 years old or more. They were listed by name. They were listed in keeping with the records of their tribes and families. **43**The number from the tribe of Naphtali was 53,400.

44Those were the men Moses and Aaron counted. The 12 leaders of Israel helped them. There was one leader from each tribe. **45**The men who were counted were able to serve in Israel's army. All of them were 20 years old or more. They were counted family by family. **46**The total number was 603,550.

47But the families of the tribe of Levi were not counted along with the others. **48**The Lord had spoken to Moses. He had said, **49**"You must not count the men from the tribe of Levi. Do not include them when you list the other men of Israel.

50"Instead, put the Levites in charge of the holy tent. That is where the tablets of the covenant are kept. The Levites will be in charge of everything that belongs to the holy tent. They must carry the tent and everything that belongs to it. They must take care of it. They must set up camp around it.

51"When the holy tent must be moved, the Levites must take it down. And when the tent must be set up, the Levites must do it. Anyone else who goes near it will be put to death.

52"The people of Israel must set up their tents by companies. All of them must be in their own camps under their own flags.

53"But the Levites must set up their tents around the holy tent where the tablets of the covenant are kept. Then my anger will not fall on the community of Israel. The Levites will be held accountable for taking care of the tent."

54The people of Israel did everything just as the LORD had commanded Moses.

The Tribes Camp Around the Tent of Meeting

2 The LORD spoke to Moses and Aaron. He said, **2**"The people of Israel must camp around the Tent of Meeting. But they must not camp too close to it. All of them must camp under their flags and under the banners of their families."

3The companies of the camp of Judah must be on the east side. They must set up camp toward the sunrise. They must camp under their flag. The leader of the tribe of Judah is Nahshon, the son of Amminadab. **4**There are 74,600 men in his company.

5The tribe of Issachar will camp next to them. The leader of the tribe of Issachar is Nethanel, the son of Zuar. **6**There are 54,400 men in his company.

7The tribe of Zebulun will be next. The leader of the tribe of Zebulun is Eliab, the son of Helon. **8**There are 57,400 men in his company.

9So a total of 186,400 men will be set apart for the camp of Judah. They will be arranged company by company. They will start out first.

10The companies of the camp of Reuben will be on the south side. They will be under their flag. The leader of the tribe of Reuben is Elizur, the son of Shedeur. **11**There are 46,500 men in his company.

12The tribe of Simeon will camp next to them. The leader of the tribe of Simeon is Shelumiel, the son of Zurishaddai. **13**There are 59,300 men in his company.

14The tribe of Gad will be next. The leader of the tribe of Gad is Eliasaph, the son of Deuel. **15**There are 45,650 men in his company.

16So a total of 151,450 men will be set apart for the camp of Reuben. They will be arranged company by company. They will start out second.

17Then the camp of the Levites will start out. The Tent of Meeting will go with them. They will march in the middle of the other camps. They will start out in the same order as they do when they set up camp. Each one will be in his own place under his flag.

18The companies of the camp of Ephraim will be on the west side. They will be under their flag. The leader of the tribe of Ephraim is Elishama, the son of Ammihud. **19**There are 40,500 men in his company.

20The tribe of Manasseh will be next to them. The leader of the tribe of Manasseh is Gamaliel, the son of Pedahzur. **21**There are 32,200 men in his company.

22The tribe of Benjamin will be next. The leader of the tribe of Benjamin is Abidan, the son of Gideoni. **23**There are 35,400 men in his company.

24So a total of 108,100 men will be set apart for the camp of Ephraim. They will be arranged company by company. They will start out third.

25The companies of the camp of Dan will be on the north side. They will be under their flag. The leader of the tribe of Dan is Ahiezer, the son of Ammishaddai. **26**There are 62,700 men in his company.

27The tribe of Asher will camp next to them. The leader of the tribe of Asher is Pagiel, the son of Ocran. **28**There are 41,500 men in his company.

29The tribe of Naphtali will be next. The leader of the tribe of Naphtali is Ahira, the son of Enan. **30**There are 53,400 men in his company.

31So a total of 157,600 men will be set apart for the camp of Dan. They will start out last. They will march under their flags.

32Those are the men of Israel. They were counted in keeping with their families. The total number of all of the men who were in the camps is 603,550, company by company. **33**But the Levites weren't counted along with the other men of Israel. That's what the LORD had commanded Moses.

34So the people of Israel did everything the LORD had commanded Moses. That's the way they set up camp under their flags. And that's the way they started out. Each man marched out with his own tribe and family.

The Levites

3 Here is the story of the family of Aaron and Moses. It belongs to the time when the LORD talked with Moses on Mount Sinai.

²Aaron's oldest son was Nadab. His other sons were Abihu, Eleazar and Ithamar. ³Those were the names of Aaron's sons. They were the anointed priests. They were prepared to serve the LORD as priests. ⁴But Nadab and Abihu made an offering to the LORD by using fire that wasn't allowed. So they fell dead in front of him. That happened in the Desert of Sinai. They didn't have any sons. Only Eleazar and Ithamar served as priests while their father Aaron was living.

⁵The LORD spoke to Moses. He said, ⁶"Bring the men of the tribe of Levi to the priest Aaron. They will help him. ⁷They must work at the Tent of Meeting for Aaron and for the whole community. They must do what needs to be done at the holy tent. ⁸They must take care of everything that is connected with the Tent of Meeting. When they do, they are acting for all of the people of Israel. ⁹Give the Levites to Aaron and his sons. They are the men of Israel who must be given completely to him.

¹⁰"Appoint Aaron and his sons to serve as priests. Anyone else who approaches the sacred tent must be put to death."

¹¹The LORD also said to Moses, ¹²"I have taken the Levites from among the people of Israel. I have taken them in place of the oldest son who is born to each woman in Israel. The Levites belong to me. ¹³That is because every male that is born first to a mother is mine. In Egypt I struck down all of the males that were born first. I did it when I set apart for myself every male that is born first to a mother in Israel. That is true for men and animals alike. They belong to me. I am the LORD."

¹⁴The LORD spoke to Moses in the Desert of Sinai. He said, ¹⁵"Count the Levites by their family groups. Count every male who is a month old or more." ¹⁶So Moses counted them. He did just as the word of the LORD had commanded him.

¹⁷The sons of Levi were
Gershon, Kohath and Merari.
¹⁸The major families from Gershon were
Libni and Shimei.
¹⁹The major families from Kohath were
Amram, Izhar, Hebron and Uzziel.
²⁰The major families from Merari were
Mahli and Mushi.
Those were the major families of the Levites.

²¹The families of Libni and Shimei belonged to the family of Gershon. ²²All of the males who were a month old or more were counted. There were 7,500 of them. ²³The families of Gershon had to camp on the west side. They had to camp behind the holy tent. ²⁴The leader of the families of Gershon was Eliasaph, the son of Lael.

²⁵Here are the duties of the families of Gershon at the Tent of Meeting. They were held accountable for taking care of the holy tent and its coverings. They took care of the curtain at the entrance to the Tent of Meeting. ²⁶They took care of the curtains of the courtyard. They took care of the curtain at the entrance to the courtyard. The courtyard was all around the holy tent and altar. They also took care of the ropes. In fact, they had to take care of everything that was connected with the use of all of those things.

²⁷The families of Amram, Izhar, Hebron and Uzziel belonged to the family of Kohath. ²⁸All of the males who were a month old or more were counted. There were 8,600 of them. The families of Kohath were held accountable for taking care of the sacred tent. ²⁹They had to camp on the south side of the holy tent. ³⁰The leader of the families of Kohath was Elizaphan, the son of Uzziel.

³¹They were held accountable for taking care of the ark of the covenant. They took care of the table for the holy bread. They took care of the lampstand and the two altars. They took care of the articles that were used for serving in the sacred tent. They also took care of the inner curtain. In fact, they had to take care of everything that was connected with the use of all of those things.

³²The chief leader of the Levites was Eleazar. He was the son of the priest Aaron. Eleazar was appointed over those who were held accountable for taking care of the sacred tent.

³³The families of Mahli and Mushi belonged to the family of Merari. ³⁴All of the males who were a month old or more were counted. There were 6,200 of them. ³⁵The leader of the families of Merari was Zuriel, the son of Abihail. They had to camp on the north side of the holy tent.

³⁶They were appointed to take care of the frames of the tent. They took care of its crossbars, posts and bases. They took care of all of its supplies. In fact, they had to take care of everything that was connected with the use of all of those things.

37They also took care of the posts of the courtyard that was around the holy tent. And they took care of the bases, tent stakes and ropes.

38Moses, Aaron and Aaron's sons had to camp to the east of the holy tent. They had to camp toward the sunrise in front of the Tent of Meeting. They were held accountable for taking care of the sacred tent. They had to do it for the people of Israel. Anyone else who approached the tent would be put to death.

39The total number of the Levites was 22,000. They were counted family by family. Every male who was a month old or more was counted. Moses and Aaron counted them, just as the LORD had commanded.

40The LORD said to Moses, "Count the males among the people of Israel who were the oldest sons born in their families. Count all those who are a month old or more. Make a list of their names. **41**Take the Levites for me in their place. And take the livestock of the Levites in place of all of the male animals in Israel that were born first to their mothers. I am the LORD."

42So Moses counted all of the oldest sons in Israel. He did just as the LORD had commanded him. **43**There were 22,273 of those sons who were a month old or more. They were listed by name.

44The LORD also said to Moses, **45**"Take the Levites in place of all the males who were born first in Israel. Also take the livestock of the Levites in place of the livestock of Israel. The Levites belong to me. I am the LORD.

46"But there are 273 more males who were born first in Israel than there are male Levites. **47**Collect two ounces of silver for each of them. Weigh it out in keeping with the standard weights that are used in the sacred tent. **48**Give the silver to Aaron and his sons. It will buy the freedom of the additional sons in Israel."

49So Moses collected the silver from the additional sons in Israel to buy their freedom. The Levites took the place of all of the others. **50**Moses collected 35 pounds of silver. It was weighed out in keeping with the weights that are used in the sacred tent. Moses collected it from the oldest sons in Israel. **51**He gave the silver to Aaron and his sons. He did just as the LORD had commanded him.

The Kohath Families

4 The LORD spoke to Moses and Aaron. He said, **2**"Count the Kohath families of the Levites. Make a list of them family by family. **3**Count all of the men who are from 30 to 50 years old. Those are the men who must come and serve at the Tent of Meeting.

4"Here is the work the men of Kohath must do at the Tent of Meeting. They must take care of the things that are very holy.

5"When the camp is ready to move, Aaron and his sons must go into the tent. They must take down the curtain that screens the ark where the tablets of the covenant are kept. They must cover the ark with the curtain. **6**Then they must cover that with the hides of sea cows. They must spread a solid blue cloth over the hides. And they must put the poles in place.

7"They must spread a blue cloth over the table for the holy bread. They must put the plates, dishes and bowls on the cloth. They must also put the jars for drink offerings on it. The bread that is always kept there must remain on it. **8**They must spread a bright red cloth over everything. Then they must cover that with the hides of sea cows. And they must put the poles of the table in place.

9"They must get a blue cloth. With it they must cover the lampstand that gives light. They must also cover its lamps, trays and wick cutters. And they must cover all of its jars. The jars are for the olive oil that is used in the lampstand. **10**Then Aaron and his sons must wrap the lampstand and all of the things that are used with it. They must cover it with the hides of sea cows. And they must put it on a frame to carry it.

11"They must spread a blue cloth over the gold altar for burning incense. They must cover that with the hides of sea cows. And they must put the poles of the altar in place.

12"They must get all of the articles that are used for serving in the sacred tent. They must wrap them in a blue cloth. They must cover that with the hides of sea cows. Then they must put the articles on a frame to carry them.

13"They must remove the ashes from the bronze altar for burnt offerings. They must spread a purple cloth over it. **14**Then they must place all of the tools on it. The tools are used for serving at the altar. They include the pans for carrying ashes. They also include the meat forks, shovels and sprinkling bowls. Aaron and his sons must cover the altar with the hides of sea cows. And they must put its poles in place.

15 "Aaron and his sons must cover all of the holy articles that belong to the holy tent. Then the men of Kohath must get ready to carry everything. They must do it when the camp is ready to move. But they must not touch the holy things. If they do, they will die. The men of Kohath must carry everything that is in the Tent of Meeting.

16 "The priest Eleazar will be in charge of the olive oil for the light. He is the son of Aaron. Eleazar will be in charge of the sweet-smelling incense. He will be in charge of the regular grain offering and the anointing oil. He will be in charge of the entire holy tent. He will also be in charge of everything that is in it. That includes all of the articles that belong to the tent."

17 The LORD spoke to Moses and Aaron. He said, 18 "Make sure that the Kohath families are not cut off from the Levites. 19 I want them to live and not die when they come near the very holy things. So here is what you must do for them. Aaron and his sons must go into the sacred tent and tell each man what to do. They must tell each man what to carry. 20 But the men of Kohath must not go in and look at the holy things. They must not look at them even for a moment. If they do, they will die."

The Gershon Families

21 The LORD said to Moses, 22 "Count the Gershon families. Make a list of them family by family. 23 Count all of the men who are from 30 to 50 years old. Those are the men who must come and serve at the Tent of Meeting.

24 "Here is how the Gershon families must serve. They must carry things. 25 They must carry the curtains of the holy Tent of Meeting. They must carry its covering and the outside covering of the hides of sea cows. They must carry the curtains that cover the entrance to the Tent of Meeting. 26 They must carry the curtains of the courtyard. The courtyard is all around the holy tent and altar. They must carry the curtain for the entrance. They must carry the ropes. They must also carry all of the supplies that are used for any purpose in the tent. The men of Gershon must do everything that needs to be done with those things.

27 "All of their work must be done under the direction of Aaron and his sons. That

includes carrying and everything else they do. Aaron and his sons must tell them what to carry. And that will be their work. 28 It is what the Gershon families must do at the Tent of Meeting. They must work under the direction of the priest Ithamar. He is the son of Aaron.

The Merari Families

29 "Count the Merari families. Count them family by family. 30 Count all of the men who are from 30 to 50 years old. Those are the men who must come and serve at the Tent of Meeting.

31 "Here is the work they must do at the Tent of Meeting. They must carry the frames of the holy tent. They must carry its crossbars, posts and bases. 32 They must also carry the posts of the courtyard. The courtyard is all around the holy tent. And they must carry the bases for the posts as well as their tent stakes and ropes. They must also carry all of the supplies and everything that is connected with their use. Tell each man exactly what to carry. 33 That is the work the Merari families must do at the Tent of Meeting. They must work under the direction of the priest Ithamar. He is the son of Aaron."

Counting the Families of the Levites

34 Moses, Aaron and the leaders of the community counted the men of Kohath. They counted them family by family. 35 They counted all of the men who were from 30 to 50 years old. Those were the men who came and served at the Tent of Meeting. 36 There were 2,750 men. They were counted family by family. 37 That was the total of all of the men in the Kohath families who served at the Tent of Meeting. Moses and Aaron counted them. They did just as the LORD had commanded through Moses.

38 The men of Gershon were counted family by family. 39 All of the men who were from 30 to 50 years old were counted. They were the men who came and served at the Tent of Meeting. 40 There were 2,630 men. They were counted family by family. 41 That was the total of the men in the Gershon families who served at the Tent of Meeting. Moses and Aaron counted them. They did just as the LORD had commanded.

42 The men of Merari were counted family by family. 43 All of the men who were from 30 to 50 years old were counted. They were the men who came and served at the Tent of Meeting. 44 There

were 3,200 men. They were counted family by family. **45**That was the total of the men in the Merari families. Moses and Aaron counted them. They did just as the LORD had commanded through Moses.

46So Moses and Aaron counted all of the Levites. The leaders of Israel helped them. They counted the Levites family by family. **47**All of the men who were from 30 to 50 years old were counted. They were the men who came and served at the Tent of Meeting. They were also supposed to carry it. **48**The total number of men was 8,580. **49**Everything was done as the LORD had commanded through Moses. Each man was given his work. And each one was told what to carry.

So they were counted, just as the LORD had commanded Moses.

Making the Camp Pure

5 The LORD spoke to Moses. He said, **2**"Tell the Israelites that certain people must be sent away from the camp. Command them to send away anyone who has a skin disease. They must send away all those who have a liquid waste coming from their bodies. And they must send away those who are not 'clean' because they have touched a dead body. **3**That applies to men and women alike. Send them out of the camp. They must not make their camp 'unclean.' That is where I live among them."

4So the people of Israel did what the LORD commanded. They sent those who were not "clean" out of the camp. They did just as the LORD had directed Moses.

Sins Against Others Must Be Paid For

5The LORD said to Moses, **6**"Speak to the people of Israel. Say to them, 'Suppose a man or woman does something wrong to someone else. Then that person is not being faithful to the LORD. People like that are guilty.

7" 'They must admit they have committed a sin. They must pay in full for what they did wrong. And they must add a fifth to it. Then they must give all of it to the person they have sinned against.

8" 'But suppose the person has died. And suppose there is not a close relative who can be paid for the sin that was committed. Then what is paid belongs to the LORD. It must be given to the priest. A ram must be given along with it. The ram must be sacrificed to the LORD to pay for the sin.

9" 'All of the sacred gifts the people of Israel bring to a priest will belong to him.

10Sacred gifts belong to the man who gives them. But what he gives to a priest will belong to the priest.' "

The Test for a Wife Who Is Not Faithful

11Then the LORD spoke to Moses again. He said, **12**"Speak to the people of Israel. Say to them, 'Suppose a man's wife goes down the wrong path. And suppose she is not faithful to him. **13**She has sex with another man. And suppose what she has done is hidden from her husband. No one knows she is not "clean." So there is no witness against her. And she has not been caught in the act.

14" 'Suppose her husband becomes jealous. He does not trust his wife, and she is really not "clean." Or suppose he does not trust her even though she is "clean." **15**Then he must take his wife to the priest.

" 'He must also bring an offering. It must be eight cups of barley flour. The offering is for his wife. He must not pour olive oil on it. And he must not put incense on it. It is a grain offering for being jealous. It calls attention to a person's guilt.

16" 'The priest must have her stand in front of the LORD. **17**He must pour some holy water into a clay jar. He must get some dust from the floor of the holy tent. And he must put it into the water. **18**The priest must have the woman stand in front of the LORD. Then he must untie her hair. He must place in her hands the offering that calls attention to a person's guilt. It is the grain offering for being jealous. The priest must keep the bitter water with him. It is the water that brings a curse.

19" 'Then the priest must have the woman take an oath. He must say to her, "Suppose no other man has had sex with you. And suppose you haven't gone down the wrong path. You have kept yourself pure while you are married to your husband. Then may the bitter water that brings a curse not harm you. **20**But suppose you have gone down the wrong path while you are married to your husband. You have made yourself 'unclean.' You have had sex with a man who isn't your husband."

21" 'At that point the priest must put the woman under the curse of the oath. He must say, "May the LORD cause your people to call a curse down on you. May he cause them to speak against you. May they do it when the LORD makes your body unable to have children. **22**May this water that brings a curse enter your body.

May it make your body unable to have children."

" 'Then the woman must say, "Amen. Let it happen."

23" 'The priest must write the curses on a scroll. He must wash them off in the bitter water. **24**It is the water he will have the woman drink. It is bitter water that brings a curse. It will enter her body. And it will cause her to suffer bitterly.

25" 'The priest must take from her hands the grain offering for being jealous. He must lift it up and wave it in front of the Lord. He must bring it to the altar. **26**Then the priest must take a handful of the grain offering. It is the offering that calls attention to a person's guilt. He must burn it on the altar. After that, he must have the woman drink the water.

27" 'Suppose she has made herself "unclean." She has not been faithful to her husband. And she has drunk the water that brings a curse. Then it will go into her body. It will cause her to suffer bitterly. It will make her body unable to have children. Her people will call a curse down on her.

28" 'But suppose the woman has not made herself "unclean." And suppose she is free from anything that is not "clean." Then she will be free of guilt. And she will be able to have children.

29" 'That is the law about being jealous. It applies to a woman who has gone down the wrong path. She has made herself "unclean" while she is married to her husband. **30**And it applies to a man who becomes jealous. He has doubts about his wife. The priest must have her stand in front of the Lord. He must apply the entire law to her. **31**The husband will not be guilty of doing anything wrong. But the woman will be punished for her sin.' "

Becoming a Nazirite

6 The Lord said to Moses, **2**"Speak to the people of Israel. Say to them, 'Suppose a man or woman wants to make a special promise. They want to set themselves apart to the Lord for a certain period of time. They want to be Nazirites.

3" 'Then they must not drink any kind of wine. They must not drink vinegar that is made out of wine of any kind. They must not drink grape juice. They must not eat grapes or raisins. **4**As long as they are Nazirites, they must not eat anything grapevines produce. They must not even eat the seeds or skins of grapes.

5" 'They must not use razors on their heads. They must not cut their hair dur-ing the whole time they have set themselves apart to the Lord. They must be holy until that time is over. They must let the hair on their heads grow long. **6**And they must not go near a dead body during that whole time.

7" 'But what if their father or mother dies? Or what if their brother or sister dies? Then they must not make themselves "unclean" because of them. The hair on their heads shows they are set apart for God. **8**During the whole time they are set apart they are holy to the Lord.

9" 'Suppose someone dies suddenly in front of them. That makes the hair they have set apart to the Lord "unclean." So they must shave their heads on the day they will be made "clean." That is the seventh day.

10" 'Then on the eighth day they must bring two doves. Or they can bring two young pigeons. They must bring them to the priest. He will be at the entrance to the Tent of Meeting. **11**The priest must offer one of the birds as a sin offering. And he must offer the other as a burnt offering. The sacrifices will pay for the sin of the Nazirite man or woman. They sinned by being near a dead body. That same day they must set their heads apart as holy.

12" 'They must set themselves apart to the Lord again. They must do it for the same period of time they had agreed to at first. And they must bring a male lamb that is a year old as a guilt offering. The days before that day do not count. That is because they became "unclean" during the time they were set apart.

13" 'The time when the Nazirites are set apart will come to an end. Here is the law that applies to them at that time. They must be brought to the entrance to the Tent of Meeting.

14" 'There they must sacrifice their offerings to the Lord. They must bring a male lamb that is a year old. It must not have any flaws. It is for a burnt offering. Then they must bring a female lamb that is a year old. It must not have any flaws. It is for a sin offering. And they must bring a ram that does not have any flaws. It is for a friendship offering.

15" 'They must sacrifice the offerings together with their grain offerings and drink offerings. And they must also bring a basket of bread that is made without yeast. The offering must include flat cakes that are made out of fine flour mixed with olive oil. And it must include wafers that are spread with oil.

16 " 'The priest must bring all of those things to the LORD. He must sacrifice the sin offering and the burnt offering. 17 He must bring the basket of bread that is made without yeast. And he must sacrifice the ram. It will be a friendship offering to the LORD. The priest must bring it together with its grain offering and drink offering.

18 " 'Then the Nazirites must shave off the hair they had set apart to the Lord. They must do it at the entrance to the Tent of Meeting. And they must put the hair in the fire that burns the sacrifice of the friendship offering.

19 " 'After the Nazirites have shaved off their hair, the priest must take a boiled shoulder of the ram. He must remove a cake and a wafer from the basket. They must be made without yeast. And he must place the shoulder and the bread in the hands of the Nazirites.

20 " 'Then he must lift up the shoulder and bread and wave them in front of the LORD. They are a wave offering. They are holy. They belong to the priest. The breast that was waved belongs to him. The thigh that was offered belongs to him too. After the offering is waved, the Nazirites can drink wine.

21 " 'That is the law of the Nazirites. They promise to sacrifice offerings to the LORD. They do it when they set themselves apart. And they should bring anything else they can afford. They must carry out the promises they have made. They must do it in keeping with the law of the Nazirites.' "

How the Priests Bless the People

22 The LORD spoke to Moses. He said, 23 "Tell Aaron and his sons, 'Here is how I want you to bless the people of Israel. Say to them,

24 " ' "May the LORD bless you
and take good care of you.
25 May the LORD smile on you
and be gracious to you.
26 May the LORD look on you with favor
and give you his peace." '

27 "In that way they will put the blessing of my name on the people of Israel. And I will bless them."

Israel's Leaders Bring Offerings for the Holy Tent

7 Moses finished setting up the holy tent. Then he anointed it with olive oil. He set it apart to the LORD. He did the same thing with everything that

POWER-SURGE

GIVING   G

THE LEADERS OF ISRAEL BROUGHT THEIR OFFERINGS... THEY BROUGHT GIFTS TO THE LORD... THE LORD SPOKE TO MOSES. HE SAID, "ACCEPT THE GIFTS FROM THE LEADERS. I WANT THEIR GIFTS TO BE USED IN THE WORK AT THE TENT OF MEETING."
— NUMBERS 7:2-5 —

belonged to it. He also anointed the altar. And he set apart to the LORD the altar and all of its tools.

2 Then the leaders of Israel brought their offerings. The leaders were the heads of the families. They were the leaders of the tribes. They were in charge of the men who had been counted. 3 They brought gifts to the LORD. They brought six covered carts and 12 oxen. Each leader gave an ox. And every two leaders gave a cart. They put their gifts in front of the holy tent.

4 The LORD spoke to Moses. He said, 5 "Accept the gifts from the leaders. I want their gifts to be used in the work at the Tent of Meeting. Give them to the Levites. They need them to do their work."

6 So Moses gave the carts and the oxen to the Levites. 7 He gave two carts and four oxen to the men from the family of Gershon. They needed them to do their work. 8 He gave four carts and eight oxen to the men from the family of Merari. They needed them to do their work. All of those men were under the direction of the priest Ithamar, the son of Aaron.

9 But Moses didn't give any carts or oxen to the men from the family of Kohath. They had to carry the holy things on their shoulders. They were accountable for the holy things.

10 When the altar was anointed, the leaders brought their offerings. They placed them in front of the altar. They

brought their offerings to set the altar apart. ¹¹The LORD had spoken to Moses. He had said, "Each day one leader must bring his offering. He must bring it to set the altar apart."

¹²On the first day Nahshon, the son of Amminadab, brought his offering. Nahshon was from the tribe of Judah.

¹³He brought one silver plate and one silver sprinkling bowl. The plate weighed three pounds four ounces. The sprinkling bowl weighed one pound 12 ounces. They were weighed in keeping with the standard weights that are used in the sacred tent. Each plate and bowl was filled with fine flour that was mixed with olive oil. It was a grain offering. ¹⁴He brought one gold dish. It weighed four ounces. It was filled with incense.

¹⁵Nahshon brought one young bull, one ram, and one male lamb that was a year old. They would be sacrificed as a burnt offering. ¹⁶He brought one male goat to be sacrificed as a sin offering. ¹⁷He brought two oxen, five rams and five male goats. He also brought five male lambs that were a year old. All of them would be sacrificed as a friendship offering.

That was everything that Nahshon, the son of Amminadab, brought as his offering.

¹⁸On the second day Nethanel, the son of Zuar, brought his offering. Nethanel was the leader of the tribe of Issachar.

¹⁹He brought one silver plate and one silver sprinkling bowl. The silver plate weighed three pounds four ounces. The sprinkling bowl weighed one pound 12 ounces. Both were weighed in keeping with the standard weights that are used in the sacred tent. Each plate and bowl was filled with fine flour that was mixed with olive oil. It was a grain offering. ²⁰He brought one gold dish. It weighed four ounces. It was filled with incense.

²¹Nethanel brought one young bull, one ram, and one male lamb that was a year old. They would be sacrificed as a burnt offering. ²²He brought one male goat to be sacrificed as a sin offering. ²³He brought two oxen, five rams and five male goats. He also brought five male lambs that were a year old. All of

them would be sacrificed as a friendship offering.

That was everything that Nethanel, the son of Zuar, brought as his offering.

²⁴On the third day Eliab, the son of Helon, brought his offering. Eliab was the leader of the people of Zebulun.

²⁵He brought one silver plate and one silver sprinkling bowl. The plate weighed three pounds four ounces. The sprinkling bowl weighed one pound 12 ounces. They were weighed in keeping with the standard weights that are used in the sacred tent. Each plate and bowl was filled with fine flour that was mixed with olive oil. It was a grain offering. ²⁶He brought one gold dish. It weighed four ounces. It was filled with incense.

²⁷Eliab brought one young bull, one ram, and one male lamb that was a year old. They would be sacrificed as a burnt offering. ²⁸He brought one male goat to be sacrificed as a sin offering. ²⁹He brought two oxen, five rams and five male goats. He also brought five male lambs that were a year old. All of them would be sacrificed as a friendship offering.

That was everything that Eliab, the son of Helon, brought as his offering.

³⁰On the fourth day Elizur, the son of Shedeur, brought his offering. Elizur was the leader of the people of Reuben.

³¹He brought one silver plate and one silver sprinkling bowl. The plate weighed three pounds four ounces. The sprinkling bowl weighed one pound 12 ounces. They were weighed in keeping with the standard weights that are used in the sacred tent. Each plate and bowl was filled with fine flour that was mixed with olive oil. It was a grain offering. ³²He brought one gold dish. It weighed four ounces. It was filled with incense.

³³Elizur brought one young bull, one ram, and one male lamb that was a year old. They would be sacrificed as a burnt offering. ³⁴He brought one male goat to be sacrificed as a sin offering. ³⁵He brought two oxen, five rams and five male goats. He also brought five male lambs that were a year old. All of

them would be sacrificed as a friendship offering.

That was everything that Elizur, the son of Shedeur, brought as his offering.

36On the fifth day Shelumiel, the son of Zurishaddai, brought his offering. Shelumiel was the leader of the people of Simeon.

37He brought one silver plate and one silver sprinkling bowl. The plate weighed three pounds four ounces. The sprinkling bowl weighed one pound 12 ounces. They were weighed in keeping with the standard weights that are used in the sacred tent. Each plate and bowl were filled with fine flour that was mixed with olive oil. It was a grain offering. 38He brought one gold dish. It weighed four ounces. It was filled with incense.

39Shelumiel brought one young bull, one ram, and one male lamb that was a year old. They would be sacrificed as a burnt offering. 40He brought one male goat to be sacrificed as a sin offering. 41He brought two oxen, five rams and five male goats. He also brought five male lambs that were a year old. All of them would be sacrificed as a friendship offering.

That was everything that Shelumiel, the son of Zurishaddai, brought as his offering.

42On the sixth day Eliasaph, the son of Deuel, brought his offering. Eliasaph was the leader of the people of Gad.

43He brought one silver plate and one silver sprinkling bowl. The plate weighed three pounds four ounces. The sprinkling bowl weighed one pound 12 ounces. They were weighed in keeping with the standard weights that are used in the sacred tent. Each plate and bowl was filled with fine flour that was mixed with olive oil. It was a grain offering. 44He brought one gold dish. It weighed four ounces. It was filled with incense.

45Eliasaph brought one young bull, one ram, and one male lamb that was a year old. They would be sacrificed as a burnt offering. 46He brought one male goat to be sacrificed as a sin offering. 47He brought two oxen, five rams and five male goats. He also brought five male

lambs that were a year old. All of them would be sacrificed as a friendship offering.

That was everything that Eliasaph, the son of Deuel, brought as his offering.

48On the seventh day Elishama, the son of Ammihud, brought his offering. Elishama was the leader of the people of Ephraim.

49He brought one silver plate and one silver sprinkling bowl. The plate weighed three pounds four ounces. The sprinkling bowl weighed one pound 12 ounces. They were weighed in keeping with the standard weights that are used in the sacred tent. Each plate and bowl was filled with fine flour that was mixed with olive oil. It was a grain offering. 50He brought one gold dish. It weighed four ounces. It was filled with incense.

51Elishama brought one young bull, one ram, and one male lamb that was a year old. They would be sacrificed as a burnt offering. 52He brought one male goat to be sacrificed as a sin offering. 53He brought two oxen, five rams and five male goats. He also brought five male lambs that were a year old. All of them would be sacrificed as a friendship offering.

That was everything that Elishama, the son of Ammihud, brought as his offering.

54On the eighth day Gamaliel, the son of Pedahzur, brought his offering. Gamaliel was the leader of the people of Manasseh.

55He brought one silver plate and one silver sprinkling bowl. The plate weighed three pounds four ounces. The sprinkling bowl weighed one pound 12 ounces. They were weighed in keeping with the standard weights that are used in the sacred tent. Each plate and bowl was filled with fine flour that was mixed with olive oil. It was a grain offering. 56He also brought one gold dish. It weighed four ounces. It was filled with incense.

57Gamaliel brought one young bull, one ram, and one male lamb that was a year old. They would be sacrificed as a burnt offering. 58He brought one male goat to be sacrificed as a sin offering. 59He brought two oxen, five rams and five male goats. He also brought five male lambs that were a year old. All of them would be sacrificed as a friendship offering.

That was everything that Gamaliel, the son of Pedahzur, brought as his offering.

⁶⁰On the ninth day Abidan, the son of Gideoni, brought his offering. Abidan was the leader of the people of Benjamin. ⁶¹He brought one silver plate and one silver sprinkling bowl. The plate weighed three pounds four ounces. The sprinkling bowl weighed one pound 12 ounces. They were weighed in keeping with the standard weights that are used in the sacred tent. Each plate and bowl was filled with fine flour that was mixed with olive oil. It was a grain offering. ⁶²He brought one gold dish. It weighed four ounces. It was filled with incense.

⁶³Abidan brought one young bull, one ram, and one male lamb that was a year old. They would be sacrificed as a burnt offering. ⁶⁴He brought one male goat to be sacrificed as a sin offering. ⁶⁵He brought two oxen, five rams and five male goats. He also brought five male lambs that were a year old. All of them would be sacrificed as a friendship offering.

That was everything that Abidan, the son of Gideoni, brought as his offering.

⁶⁶On the tenth day Ahiezer, the son of Ammishaddai, brought his offering. Ahiezer was the leader of the people of Dan. ⁶⁷He brought one silver plate and one silver sprinkling bowl. The plate weighed three pounds four ounces. The sprinkling bowl weighed one pound 12 ounces. They were weighed in keeping with the standard weights that are used in the sacred tent. Each plate and bowl was filled with fine flour that was mixed with olive oil. It was a grain offering. ⁶⁸He brought one gold dish. It weighed four ounces. It was filled with incense.

⁶⁹Ahiezer brought one young bull, one ram, and one male lamb that was a year old. They would be sacrificed as a burnt offering. ⁷⁰He brought one male goat to be sacrificed as a sin offering. ⁷¹He brought two oxen, five rams and five male

goats. He also brought five male lambs that were a year old. All of them would be sacrificed as a friendship offering.

That was everything that Ahiezer, the son of Ammishaddai, brought as his offering.

⁷²On the eleventh day Pagiel, the son of Ocran, brought his offering. Pagiel was the leader of the people of Asher. ⁷³He brought one silver plate and one silver sprinkling bowl. The plate weighed three pounds four ounces. The sprinkling bowl weighed one pound 12 ounces. They were weighed in keeping with the standard weights that are used in the sacred tent. Each plate and bowl was filled with fine flour that was mixed with olive oil. It was a grain offering. ⁷⁴He brought one gold dish. It weighed four ounces. It was filled with incense.

⁷⁵Pagiel brought one young bull, one ram, and one male lamb that was a year old. They would be sacrificed as a burnt offering. ⁷⁶He brought one male goat to be sacrificed as a sin offering. ⁷⁷He brought two oxen, five rams and five male goats. He also brought five male lambs that were a year old. All of them would be sacrificed as a friendship offering.

That was everything that Pagiel, the son of Ocran, brought as his offering.

⁷⁸On the twelfth day Ahira, the son of Enan, brought his offering. Ahira was the leader of the people of Naphtali. ⁷⁹He brought one silver plate and one silver sprinkling bowl. The plate weighed three pounds four ounces. The sprinkling bowl weighed one pound 12 ounces. They were weighed in keeping with the standard weights that are used in the sacred tent. Each plate and bowl was filled with fine flour that was mixed with olive oil. It was a grain offering. ⁸⁰He brought one gold dish. It weighed four ounces. It was filled with incense.

⁸¹Ahira brought one young bull, one ram, and one male lamb that was a year old. They would be sacrificed as a burnt offering. ⁸²He brought one male goat to be sacrificed as a sin offering. ⁸³He brought two oxen, five rams and five male

goats. He also brought five male lambs that were a year old. All of them would be sacrificed as a friendship offering.

That was everything that Ahira, the son of Enan, brought as his offering.

84Those were the offerings the leaders of the people of Israel brought. They gave them to set the altar apart when it was anointed with olive oil. They gave 12 silver plates, 12 silver sprinkling bowls and 12 gold dishes. 85Each silver plate weighed three pounds four ounces. Each sprinkling bowl weighed one pound 12 ounces. The total weight of the silver dishes was 60 pounds. Everything was weighed in keeping with the standard weights that are used in the sacred tent. 86Each of the 12 gold dishes weighed four ounces. They were filled with incense. They were weighed in keeping with the weights used in the sacred tent. The total weight of the gold dishes was three pounds.

87The leaders brought 12 young bulls, 12 rams and 12 male lambs that were a year old. That was the total number of animals they gave for the burnt offering. They gave them together with the grain offering. They brought 12 male goats for the sin offering.

88The leaders brought 24 oxen, 60 rams, 60 male goats and 60 male lambs that were a year old. That was the total number of animals that were sacrificed as the friendship offering.

Those were the offerings they brought to set the altar apart. The leaders brought them after the altar was anointed with oil.

89Moses entered the Tent of Meeting. He wanted to speak with the LORD. There Moses heard the LORD talking to him. The LORD's voice was speaking to him from between the two cherubim. The cherubim were over the place where sin is paid for. It was the cover on the ark where the tablets of the covenant were kept. The LORD spoke with Moses there.

Aaron Sets Up the Lamps

8 The LORD said to Moses, 2"Speak to Aaron. Say to him, 'Set up the seven lamps. They will give light to the area that is in front of the lampstand.' "

3So Aaron did it. He set up the lamps so that they faced forward on the lampstand. He did just as the LORD had commanded Moses. 4The lampstand was made out of hammered gold. From its base to its blooms it was made out of hammered gold. The lampstand was made exactly like the pattern the LORD had shown Moses.

Moses Sets the Levites Apart

5The LORD spoke to Moses. He said, 6"Take the Levites from among the other men of Israel. Make them 'clean' in the usual way. 7Here is how to make them pure. Sprinkle the special water on them. Then have them shave their whole bodies. Also have them wash their clothes. That is how they will make themselves pure.

8"Have them get a young bull along with its grain offering. The offering must be made out of fine flour mixed with olive oil. Then you must get a second young bull. You must sacrifice it as a sin offering.

9"Bring the Levites to the front of the Tent of Meeting. Gather the whole community of Israel together. 10You must bring the Levites to me. The men of Israel must place their hands on them. 11Aaron must bring the Levites to me. They are a wave offering from the people of Israel. That is how they will be set apart to do my work.

12"I want the Levites to place their hands on the heads of the bulls. Then they must sacrifice one bull as a sin offering to me. And they must sacrifice the other as a burnt offering. The blood of the bulls will pay for the sin of the Levites.

13"Have the Levites stand in front of Aaron and his sons. Then give them as a wave offering to me. 14That is how I want you to set the Levites apart from the other men of Israel. The Levites will belong to me.

15"Make the Levites pure. Give them to me as a wave offering. Then they must come to do their work at the Tent of Meeting. 16They are the men of Israel who will be given to me completely. I have taken them to be my own. I have taken them in place of every son who is born first in his family in Israel.

17"Every male that is born first in Israel belongs to me. That is true whether it is a man or an animal. I struck down all of the males that were born first to a mother in Egypt. Then I set apart for myself all of the males that were born first in Israel. 18And I have taken the Levites in place of all of the sons who are born first in Israel.

19"I have given the Levites as gifts to Aaron and his sons. I have taken them from all of the men of Israel. I have appointed them to do the work at the

Tent of Meeting. They will do it in place of the men of Israel.

"That is how they will keep the men of Israel from being guilty when they go near the sacred tent. Then no plague will strike the people of Israel when they go near the tent."

20So Moses and Aaron and the whole community of Israel did with the Levites just as the LORD had commanded Moses. 21The Levites made themselves pure. They washed their clothes. Then Aaron gave them to the LORD as a wave offering. That's how he paid for their sin to make them pure.

22After that, the Levites came to do their work at the Tent of Meeting. They worked under the direction of Aaron and his sons. And so Moses and Aaron and the whole community of Israel did with the Levites just as the LORD had commanded Moses.

23The LORD spoke to Moses. He said, 24"Here is what the Levites must do. Men who are 25 years old or more must come and take part in the work at the Tent of Meeting.

25"But when they reach the age of 50, they must not work any longer. They must stop doing their regular work. 26They can help their brothers with their duties at the Tent of Meeting. But they themselves should not do the work. That is how you must direct the Levites to do their work."

Israel Celebrates the Passover Feast

9 The LORD spoke to Moses in the Desert of Sinai. It was the first month of the second year after the people came out of Egypt. He said, 2"Tell the people of Israel to celebrate the Passover Feast. Have them do it at the appointed time. 3Celebrate it when the sun goes down on the 14th day of this month. Obey all of its rules and laws."

4So Moses told the people of Israel to celebrate the Passover Feast. 5They did it in the Desert of Sinai. They celebrated it when the sun went down on the 14th day of the first month. The people of Israel did everything just as the LORD had commanded Moses.

6But some of them couldn't celebrate the Passover Feast on that day. That's because they weren't "clean." They had gone near a dead body. So they came to Moses and Aaron that same day. 7They said to Moses, "We went near a dead body. So we aren't 'clean.' But why should we be kept from bringing the LORD's offering at the appointed time? Why shouldn't we bring it along with the other people of Israel?"

8Moses answered them, "Wait until I find out what the LORD wants you to do."

9Then the LORD spoke to Moses. He said, 10"Tell the people of Israel, 'Suppose any of you or your children are not "clean" because you have gone near a dead body. Or suppose you are away on a journey. You can still celebrate the LORD's Passover.

11"'I want you to celebrate it on the 14th day of the second month. You have to do it when the sun goes down. You have to eat the lamb together with bread that is made without yeast. Eat it with bitter plants. 12Do not leave any of it until morning. Do not break any of its bones. When you celebrate the Passover Feast, follow all of the rules.

13"'But suppose a man is "clean." He is not on a journey. And he fails to celebrate the Passover Feast. Then he must be cut off from the community of Israel. He did not bring the LORD's offering at the appointed time. He will be punished for his sin.

14"'What if there is an outsider living among you? And what if he wants to celebrate the LORD's Passover? Then he must obey its rules and laws. You must have the same laws for outsiders as you do for the people of Israel.'"

The Cloud Covers the Holy Tent

15The holy tent was set up. It was the tent where the tablets of the covenant were kept. On the day it was set up, the cloud covered it. From evening until morning the cloud that was above the tent looked like fire. 16That's what continued to happen. The cloud covered the tent. At night the cloud looked like fire.

17When the cloud lifted from its place above the tent, the people of Israel started out. Where the cloud settled, the people of Israel camped. 18When the LORD gave the command, the people of Israel started out. And when he gave the command, they camped. As long as the cloud stayed above the holy tent, they remained in camp.

19Sometimes the cloud remained above the tent for a long time. Then the people of Israel obeyed the LORD's order. They didn't start out. 20Sometimes the cloud was above the tent for only a few days. When the LORD would give the command, they would camp. Then when he would give the command, they would start out. 21Sometimes the cloud stayed only from evening until morning. When it lifted in the morning, they started out. It didn't matter whether it was day or night. When the cloud lifted, the people started out. 22It didn't matter whether the cloud stayed above the holy tent for two days or a month or a year. The people of Israel would remain in camp. They wouldn't start out. But when the cloud lifted, they would start out.

23When the LORD gave the command, they camped. And when he gave the command, they started out. They obeyed the LORD's order. They obeyed him, just as he had commanded them through Moses.

The Silver Trumpets

10 The LORD spoke to Moses. He said, 2"Make two trumpets out of hammered silver. Blow them when you want the community to gather together. And blow them when you want the camps to start out. 3When both trumpets are blown, the whole community must gather in front of you. They must come to the entrance to the Tent of Meeting. 4Suppose only one trumpet is blown. Then the leaders must gather in front of you. They are the heads of the tribes of Israel. 5When a trumpet blast is blown, the tribes that are camped on the east side must start out. 6When the second blast is blown, the camps on the south side must start out. The blast will tell them when to start. 7Blow the trumpets to gather the people together. But do not use the same kind of blast.

8"The sons of Aaron, the priests, must blow the trumpets. That is a law for you and your children after you for all time to come. 9Suppose you go into battle in your own land. And suppose it is against an enemy who is beating you down. Then blow a blast on the trumpets. If you do, I will remember you. I will save you from your enemies. I am the LORD your God. 10You must also blow the trumpets when you are happy. Blow them at your appointed feasts. Blow them at your New Moon Feasts. Blow them when you sacrifice your burnt offerings. Blow them when you sacrifice your friendship offerings. They will remind me of you. I am the LORD your God."

The People of Israel Leave the Sinai Desert

11It was the 20th day of the second month of the second year. On that day the cloud began to move. It went up from above the holy tent where the tablets of the covenant were kept.

12Then the people of Israel started out from the Desert of Sinai. They traveled from place to place. They kept going until the cloud came to rest in the Desert of Paran. 13The first time they started out, the LORD commanded Moses to tell them to do it. And they did it.

14The companies of the camp of Judah went first. They went out under their flag. Nahshon was their commander. He was the son of Amminadab. 15Nethanel was over the company of the tribe of Issachar. Nethanel was the son of Zuar. 16Eliab was over the company of the tribe of Zebulun. Eliab was the son of Helon.

17The holy tent was taken down. The men of Gershon and Merari started out. They carried the tent.

18The companies of the camp of Reuben went next. They went out under their flag. Elizur was their commander. He was the son of Shedeur. 19Shelumiel was over the company of the tribe of Simeon. Shelumiel was the son of Zurishaddai. 20Eliasaph was over the company of the tribe of Gad. Eliasaph was the son of Deuel.

21The men of Kohath started out. They carried the holy things. The holy tent had to be set up before they arrived.

22The companies of the camp of Ephraim went next. They went out under their flag. Elishama was their commander. He was the son of Ammihud. 23Gamaliel was over the company of the tribe of Manasseh. Gamaliel was the son of Pedahzur. 24Abidan was over the company of the tribe of Benjamin. Abidan was the son of Gideoni.

25Finally, the companies of the camp of Dan started out. They marched out under their flag. They followed behind all of the other companies and guarded them. Ahiezer was their commander. He was the son of Ammishaddai. 26Pagiel was over the company of the tribe of Asher. Pagiel was the son of Ocran. 27Ahira was over the company of the tribe of Naphtali. Ahira was the son of Enan.

28As the companies of Israel started out, that was the order they marched in.

29Moses spoke to Hobab, the son of Reuel. Reuel was Moses' father-in-law. Reuel was from Midian. Moses said to Hobab, "We're starting out for the place the LORD promised to us. He said to us, 'I will give it to you.' So come with us. We'll treat you well. The LORD has promised to give good things to Israel."

³⁰Hobab answered, "No. I can't go. I'm going back to my own land. I'm returning to my own people."

³¹But Moses said, "Please don't leave us. You know where we should camp in the desert. You can be our guide. ³²So come with us. The LORD will give us good things. We'll share them with you."

³³So they started out from the mountain of the LORD. They traveled for three days. The ark of the covenant of the LORD went in front of them during those three days. It went ahead of them to find a place for them to rest. ³⁴They started out from the camp by day. And the cloud of the LORD was above them.

³⁵When the ark started out, Moses said,

"LORD, rise up!
Let your enemies be scattered.
Let them run away from you."

³⁶When the ark came to rest, Moses said,

"LORD, return.
Return to the many thousands of
    people in Israel."

The LORD Sends Fire Among the People

11 The people weren't happy about the hard times they were having. The LORD heard what they were saying. It made him burn with anger. Then the LORD sent fire on them. It blazed out among the people. It burned up some of the outer edges of the camp.

²The people cried out to Moses. Then he prayed to the LORD. And the fire died down.

³So that place was named Taberah. That's because fire from the LORD had blazed out among them there.

The LORD Sends Meat for the People

⁴Some people who were with them began to long for other food. Again the people of Israel began to cry out. They said, "We wish we had meat to eat. ⁵We remember the fish we ate in Egypt. It didn't cost us anything. We also remember the cucumbers, melons, leeks, onions and garlic. ⁶But now we've lost all interest in eating. We never see anything but this manna!"

⁷The manna was like coriander seeds. It looked like sap from a tree. ⁸The people went around gathering it. Then they

ground it in a small mill they held in their hands. Or they crushed it in a stone bowl. They cooked it in a pot. Or they made cakes out of it. It tasted like something made with olive oil. ⁹When the dew came down on the camp at night, the manna also came down.

¹⁰Moses heard people from every family crying. They were sobbing at the entrances to their tents.

The LORD burned with hot anger. So Moses became troubled. ¹¹He asked the LORD, "Why have you brought this trouble on me? Why aren't you pleased with me? Why have you loaded me down with the troubles of all of these people?

¹²"Am I like a mother to them? Are they my children? Why do you tell me to carry them in my arms? Do I have to carry them the way a nurse carries a baby? Do I have to carry them to the land you promised? You took an oath and promised the land to their people of long ago.

¹³"Where can I get meat for all of these people? They keep crying out to me. They say, 'Give us meat to eat!' ¹⁴I can't carry all of these people by myself. The load is too heavy for me.

¹⁵"Is this how you are going to treat me? If you are pleased with me, just put me to death right now. Don't let me live if I have to see myself destroyed anyway."

¹⁶The LORD said to Moses, "Bring me 70 of Israel's elders. Bring men that you know are leaders and officials among the people. Have them come to the Tent of Meeting. I want them to stand there with you. ¹⁷I will come down. I will speak with you there. I will take some of my Spirit that is on you. And I will put the Spirit on them. They will help you carry the people's load. Then you will not have to carry it alone.

¹⁸"Tell the people, 'Set yourselves apart for tomorrow. At that time you will eat meat. The LORD heard you when you cried out. You said, "We wish we had meat to eat. We were better off in Egypt."

" 'Now the LORD will give you meat. And you will eat it. ¹⁹You will not eat it for just one or two days. You will not eat it for just five, ten or 20 days. ²⁰Instead, you will eat it for a whole month. You will eat it until it comes out of your nose. You will eat it until you hate it.

" 'The LORD is among you. But you have turned your back on him. You have cried out while he was listening. You have said, "Why did we ever leave Egypt?" ' "

²¹But Moses said, "Here I am among 600,000 men on the march. And you say,

'I will give them meat to eat for a whole month'! **22**Would they have enough if flocks and herds were killed for them? Would they have enough even if all of the fish in the ocean were caught for them?"

23The LORD answered Moses, "Am I not strong enough? Now you will see whether what I say will come true for you."

24So Moses went out. He told the people what the LORD had said. He gathered 70 of their elders together. He had them stand around the Tent of Meeting.

25Then the LORD came down in the cloud. He spoke with Moses. He took some of his Spirit that was on Moses. And he put the Spirit on the 70 elders. When the Spirit came on them, they prophesied. But they didn't do it again.

26Two men had remained in the camp. Their names were Eldad and Medad. They were listed among the elders. But they didn't go out to the Tent of Meeting. In spite of that, the Spirit came on them too. So they prophesied in the camp.

27A young man ran up to Moses. He said, "Eldad and Medad are prophesying in the camp."

28Joshua spoke up. He was the son of Nun. Joshua had been Moses' helper from the time he was young. He said, "Moses! Please stop them!"

29But Moses replied, "Are you jealous for me? I wish that all of the LORD's people were prophets. And I wish that the LORD would put his Spirit on them." **30**Then Moses and the elders of Israel returned to the camp.

31The LORD sent out a wind. It drove quail in from the Red Sea. It brought them down all around the camp. They were about three feet above the ground. They could be seen in every direction as far as a person could walk in a day.

32The people went out all day and gathered quail. They gathered them all night and all the next day. No one gathered less than 60 bushels. Then they spread the quail out all around the camp.

33But while the meat was still in their mouths, the LORD acted. Before the people could swallow it, his anger burned against them. He struck them with a terrible plague.

34So the place was named Kibroth Hattaavah. That's where the bodies of the people who had longed for other food were buried.

35From Kibroth Hattaavah the people traveled to Hazeroth. And they stayed there.

Miriam and Aaron Speak Against Moses

12 Miriam and Aaron began to say bad things about Moses. That's because Moses had married a woman from Cush. **2**"Has the LORD spoken only through Moses?" they asked. "Hasn't he also spoken through us?" The LORD heard what they said.

3Moses wasn't very proud at all. In fact, he had less pride than anyone else on the face of the earth.

4The LORD spoke to Moses, Aaron and Miriam. He said, "All three of you, come out to the Tent of Meeting." So they did. **5**Then the LORD came down in a pillar of cloud. He stood at the entrance to the tent. And he told Aaron and Miriam to come to him. Both of them stepped forward. **6**Then the LORD said, "Listen to my words.

"Suppose one of my prophets is among
you.
I make myself known to him in
visions.
I speak to him in dreams.

FAITHFUL ()

[MOSES] IS FAITHFUL IN
EVERYTHING HE DOES.
— NUMBERS 12:7 —

7But that is not true of my servant
Moses.
He is faithful in everything he does
in my house.
8With Moses I speak face to face.
I speak with him clearly. I do not
speak in riddles.
I let him see something of what I
look like.
So why were you not afraid
to speak against my servant Moses?"

9The anger of the LORD burned against them. And he left them.

10When the cloud went up from above the tent, there stood Miriam. She had a disease that made her skin as white as snow.

Aaron turned toward her. He saw that she had a skin disease. **11**So he said to Moses, "We have committed a very foolish sin. Please don't hold it against us.

¹²Don't let Miriam be like a baby that was born dead. Don't let her look like a dead baby whose body is half eaten away."

¹³So Moses cried out to the LORD. He said, "God, please heal her!"

¹⁴The LORD answered Moses. He said, "Suppose her father had spit in her face. Then she would have been put to shame for seven days. So keep her outside the camp for seven days. After that, you can bring her back."

¹⁵So Miriam was kept outside the camp for seven days. The people didn't move on until she was brought back.

¹⁶After that, the people left Hazeroth. They camped in the Desert of Paran.

Some Men Check Out the Land of Canaan

13 The LORD spoke to Moses. He said, ²"Send some men to check out the land of Canaan. I am giving it to the people of Israel. Send one leader from each of Israel's tribes."

³So Moses sent them out from the Desert of Paran. He sent them as the LORD had commanded. All of them were leaders of the people of Israel.

⁴Here are their names.

There was Shammua from the tribe of Reuben. Shammua was the son of Zaccur.

⁵There was Shaphat from the tribe of Simeon. Shaphat was the son of Hori.

⁶There was Caleb from the tribe of Judah. Caleb was the son of Jephunneh.

⁷There was Igal from the tribe of Issachar. Igal was the son of Joseph.

⁸There was Hoshea from the tribe of Ephraim. Hoshea was the son of Nun.

⁹There was Palti from the tribe of Benjamin. Palti was the son of Raphu.

¹⁰There was Gaddiel from the tribe of Zebulun. Gaddiel was the son of Sodi.

¹¹There was Gaddi from the tribe of Manasseh. Gaddi was the son of Susi. Manasseh was a tribe of Joseph.

¹²There was Ammiel from the tribe of Dan. Ammiel was the son of Gemalli.

¹³There was Sethur from the tribe of Asher. Sethur was the son of Michael.

¹⁴There was Nahbi from the tribe of Naphtali. Nahbi was the son of Vophsi.

¹⁵There was Geuel from the tribe of Gad. Geuel was the son of Maki.

¹⁶Those are the men Moses sent to check out the land. He gave the name Joshua to Hoshea, the son of Nun.

¹⁷Moses sent them to check out Canaan. He said, "Go up through the Negev Desert. Go on into the central hill country. ¹⁸See what the land is like. See whether the people who live there are strong or weak. See whether they are few or many.

¹⁹"What kind of land do they live in? Is it good or bad? What kind of towns do they live in? Do the towns have high walls around them or not? ²⁰How is the soil? Is it rich land or poor land? Are there trees on it or not? Do your best to bring back some of the fruit of the land." It was the season for the first ripe grapes.

²¹So the men went up and checked out the land. They went from the Desert of Zin as far as Rehob. It was in the direction of Lebo Hamath. ²²They went up through the Negev Desert and came to Hebron. That's where Ahiman, Sheshai and Talmai lived. They belonged to the family line of Anak. Hebron had been built seven years before Zoan. Zoan was a city in Egypt.

²³The men came to the Valley of Eshcol. There they cut off a branch that had a single bunch of grapes on it. Two of them carried it on a pole between them. They carried some pomegranates and figs along with it. ²⁴That place was called the Valley of Eshcol. That's because the men of Israel cut off a bunch of grapes there.

²⁵At the end of 40 days, the men returned from checking out the land.

The Men Report on What They Found

²⁶The men came back to Moses, Aaron and the whole community of Israel. The people were at Kadesh in the Desert of Paran. There the men reported to Moses and Aaron and all of the people. They showed them the fruit of the land.

²⁷They gave Moses their report. They said, "We went into the land you sent us to. It really does have plenty of milk and honey! Here's some fruit from the land.

²⁸"But the people who live there are powerful. Their cities have high walls around them and are very large. We even saw members of the family line of Anak there. ²⁹The Amalekites live in the Negev Desert. The Hittites, Jebusites and Amo-

rites live in the central hill country. The Canaanites live near the Mediterranean Sea. They also live along the Jordan River."

30Then Caleb interrupted the men who were speaking to Moses. He said, "We should go up and take the land. We can certainly do it."

31But the men who had gone up with him spoke. They said, "We can't attack those people. They are stronger than we are." 32The men spread a bad report about

CALEB

NUMBERS 13:30

◆ **Then Caleb interrupted the men who were speaking to Moses. He said, "We should go up and take the land. We can certainly do it."**

B

ψ

*C*aleb stood before Moses with eleven other spies. They all felt tired and dirty. But before resting, they reported to Moses what they found in the land of Canaan. God had promised to give the Israelites this land.

One spy waved his arms as he told of the fresh rivers and green fields and lush crops. Another spy lifted his hand high above his head to show how tall some of the people were. "We can *never* fight these people and win," he exclaimed. "THEY'RE JUST TOO BIG AND STRONG!"

Caleb turned toward the other men in surprise when he heard them say the land was wonderful, but the people were too strong and big for them to conquer.

"You're wrong!" Caleb bravely disagreed. "With God's help, we can win the land." Joshua agreed with Caleb. But the ten other spies said they shouldn't try it.

God was angry when the people trusted the ten scared spies instead of trusting him. He told them that none of them would get to see this wonderful land. None of them except Caleb and Joshua, that is. Caleb and Joshua would be blessed for trusting God.

BE A CALEB

You may be afraid when something is hard for you to do. Caleb was probably afraid, too. But he knew that God would go with them. Be a Caleb! Instead of trusting in your own strength, trust in God's. He loves to help those who trust in him.

CALEB TRUSTED IN GOD AND BRAVELY DISAGREED WITH THE OTHER SPIES.

Go to page 184 for the next Super Hero

the land among the people of Israel. They said, "The land we checked out destroys those who live in it. All of the people we saw there are very big and tall. ³³We saw the Nephilim there. We seemed like grasshoppers in our own eyes. And that's also how we seemed to them." The children of Anak came from the Nephilim.

The People Refuse to Obey the LORD

14 That night all of the people in the community raised their voices. They sobbed out loud.

²The people of Israel spoke against Moses and Aaron. The whole community said to them, "We wish we had died in Egypt or even in this desert. ³Why is the LORD bringing us to this land? We're going to be killed with swords. Our enemies will capture our wives and children. Wouldn't it be better for us to go back to Egypt?"

⁴They said to one another, "We should choose another leader. We should go back to Egypt."

⁵Then Moses and Aaron fell with their faces to the ground. They did it in front of the whole community of Israel that was gathered there.

⁶Joshua, the son of Nun, tore his clothes. So did Caleb, the son of Jephunneh. Joshua and Caleb were two of the men who had checked out the land. ⁷They spoke to the whole community of Israel. They said, "We passed through the land and checked it out. It's very good. ⁸If the LORD is pleased with us, he'll lead us into that land. It's a land that has plenty of milk and honey. He'll give it to us.

⁹"But don't refuse to obey him. And don't be afraid of the people of the land. We will swallow them up. The LORD is with us. So nothing can save them. Don't be afraid of them."

¹⁰But all of the people talked about killing Joshua and Caleb by throwing stones at them.

Then the glory of the LORD appeared at the Tent of Meeting. All of the people of Israel saw it. ¹¹The LORD spoke to Moses. He said, "How long will these people make fun of me? How long will they refuse to believe in me? They refuse even though I have done many miraculous signs among them. ¹²So I will strike them down with a plague. I will destroy them. But I will make you into a greater and stronger nation than they are."

¹³Moses said to the LORD, "Then the Egyptians will hear about it. You used

your power to bring these people up from among them.

¹⁴"And the Egyptians will tell the people who live in Canaan about it. LORD, they have already heard a lot about you. They've heard that you are with these people. They've heard that you have been seen face to face. They've been told that your cloud stays over them. They've heard that you go in front of them in a pillar of cloud by day. They've been told that you go in front of them in a pillar of fire at night.

¹⁵"Suppose you put these people to death all at one time. Then the nations who have heard those things about you will talk. They'll say, ¹⁶'The LORD took an oath. He promised to give these people the land of Canaan. But he wasn't able to bring them into it. So he killed them in the desert.'

¹⁷"Now, Lord, show your strength. You have said, ¹⁸'I am the LORD. I am slow to get angry. I am full of love. I forgive those who sin. I forgive those who refuse to obey. But I do not let guilty people go without punishing them. I punish the children, grandchildren and great-grandchildren for the sin of their parents.'

¹⁹"LORD, your love is great. So forgive the sin of these people. Forgive them just as you have done from the time they left Egypt until now."

²⁰The LORD replied, "I have forgiven them, just as you asked. ²¹You can be sure that I live. You can be sure that my glory fills the whole earth.

²²"And you can be just as sure that these men will not see the land I promised to give them. They have seen my glory. They have seen the miraculous signs I did

POWER SURGE

FORGIVING F

I AM THE LORD. I AM SLOW TO GET ANGRY. I AM FULL OF LOVE. I FORGIVE THOSE WHO SIN. I FORGIVE THOSE WHO REFUSE TO OBEY.
— NUMBERS 14:18 —

LOVING

in Egypt. And they have seen what I did in the desert. But they did not obey me. And they have put me to the test ten times. 23So not even one of them will ever see the land I promised with an oath to give to their people of long ago. No one who has made fun of me will ever see it. 24"But my servant Caleb has a different spirit. He follows me with his whole heart. So I will bring him into the land he went to. And his children after him will receive land there.

25"The Amalekites and Canaanites are living in the valleys. So turn back tomorrow. Start out toward the desert. Go along the way that leads to the Red Sea."

26The LORD spoke to Moses and Aaron. He said, 27"How long will this evil community speak against me? I have heard these Israelites talk about how unhappy they are. 28So tell them, 'Here is what I, the LORD, am announcing. You can be sure that I live. And you can be just as sure that I will do to you the very things that I heard you say. 29" 'You will die in this desert. Every one of you who is 20 years old or more will die. Every one of you who was counted in the list of the people will die. Every one of you who has spoken out against me will be wiped out. 30I lifted up my hand and promised with an oath to make this land your home. But now not all of you will enter the land. Caleb, the son of Jephunneh, will enter it. So will Joshua, the son of Nun. They are the only ones who will enter the land.

31" 'You have said that your enemies would capture your children. But I will bring your children in to enjoy the land you have turned your backs on. 32As for you, you will die in the desert. 33Your children will be shepherds here for 40 years. They will suffer because you were not faithful. They will suffer until the last of your bodies lies here in the desert. 34For 40 years you will suffer for your sins. That is one year for each of the 40 days you checked out the land. You will know what it is like to have me against you.'

35"I, the LORD, have spoken. You can be sure that I will do those things to this whole evil community. They have joined together against me. They will meet their end in this desert. They will die here."

36So the LORD struck down the men Moses had sent to check out the land. They had returned and had spread a bad report about the land. And that had made the whole community speak out against Moses. 37Those men were to blame for spreading the bad report. So the LORD struck them down. They died of a plague.

38Only two of the men who went to check out the land remained alive. One of them was Joshua, the son of Nun. The other was Caleb, the son of Jephunneh.

39Moses reported to all of the people of Israel what the LORD had said. And they became very sad. 40Early the next morning they went up toward the high hill country. "We have sinned," they said. "We will go up to the place the LORD promised to give us."

41But Moses said, "Why aren't you obeying the LORD's command? You won't succeed. 42So don't go up. The LORD isn't with you. Your enemies will win the battle over you. 43The Amalekites and Canaanites will meet you on the field of battle. You have turned away from the LORD. So he won't be with you. And you will be killed with swords."

44But they wouldn't listen. They still went up toward the high hill country. They went up even though Moses didn't move from the camp. They went even though the ark of the LORD's covenant didn't move from the camp. 45Then the Amalekites and Canaanites who lived in that hill country came down. They attacked the people of Israel. They won the battle over them. They chased them all the way to Hormah.

Other Offerings

15 The LORD said to Moses, 2"Speak to the people of Israel. Say to them, 'You are going to enter the land I am giving you as a home. 3When you do, you will give offerings that are made to the LORD with fire. The animals must come from your herd or flock. The offerings will give a smell that is pleasant to the LORD. They can be either burnt offerings or sacrifices. They can be either for special promises or for feast offerings. Or they can be for offerings you choose to give.

4" 'With each of the offerings, the one who brings it must give the LORD a grain offering. It must be eight cups of fine flour. It must be mixed with a quart of olive oil. 5Also prepare a quart of wine as a drink offering. You must give it with each lamb that you bring for the burnt offering or the sacrifice.

6" 'With a ram prepare a grain offering. It must be 16 cups of fine flour. It must be mixed with two and a half pints of olive oil. 7You must bring two and a half pints of wine as a drink offering. Offer everything as a smell that is pleasant to the LORD.

8" 'Suppose you prepare a young bull as a burnt offering or sacrifice. You prepare it to keep a special promise to the LORD. Or you prepare it to give as a friendship offering. 9Then bring a grain offering with the bull. The grain offering must be 24 cups of fine flour. It must be mixed with two quarts of olive oil. 10Also bring two quarts of wine as a drink offering. It will be an offering that is made with fire. It will give a smell that is pleasant to the LORD.

11" 'Each bull or ram must be prepared in the same way. Each lamb or young goat must also be prepared in that way. 12Do it for each animal. Do it for as many animals as you prepare.

13" 'Everyone in Israel must do those things in that way. He must do them when he brings an offering that is made with fire. Offerings like that give a smell that is pleasant to the LORD.

14" 'Everyone must always do what the law requires. It does not matter whether he is an outsider or someone else who is living among you. He must do exactly as you do when he brings an offering that is made with fire. Offerings like that give a smell that is pleasant to the LORD.

15" 'The community must have the same rules for you and for the outsider who is living among you. That law will last for all time to come. In the sight of the LORD, the law applies to you and the outsider alike. 16The same laws and rules will apply to you and to the outsider who is living among you.' "

17The LORD said to Moses, 18"Speak to the people of Israel. Say to them, 'You are going to enter the land I am taking you to. 19You will eat its food. When you do, bring part of it as an offering to the LORD. 20Bring a loaf that is made from the first flour you grind. Give it as an offering from the threshing floor. 21You must bring the offering to the LORD. You must give it from the first grain you grind. You must do it for all time to come.

Offerings for Sins That Aren't Committed on Purpose

22" 'Suppose you fail to keep any of the commands the LORD gave Moses. And suppose you do it without meaning to. 23That applies to any of the commands the LORD told Moses to give you. And they are in effect from the day the LORD gave them and for all time to come. 24Suppose the community sins without meaning to. And suppose they do not know they have

sinned. Then the whole community must offer a young bull. They must offer it for a burnt offering. It will give a smell that is pleasant to the LORD. Along with it, they must offer its required grain offering and drink offering. They must also offer a male goat for a sin offering.

25" 'With it the priest will pay for the sin of the whole community of Israel. Then they will be forgiven. They did not mean to commit that sin. And they have brought to the LORD an offering that is made with fire for the wrong thing they did. They have brought a sin offering with it.

26" 'The LORD will forgive the whole community of Israel and the outsiders living among them. All of the people had a part in the sin, even though they did not mean to do it.

27" 'But suppose just one person sins without meaning to. Then he must bring a female goat for a sin offering. It must be a year old. 28With it the priest will pay for the person's sin in the sight of the LORD. He will do it for the one who did wrong by sinning without meaning to. When the sin is paid for, that person will be forgiven.

29" 'The same law applies to everyone who sins without meaning to. It does not

POWER - SURGE

GIVING Ⓖ

"MOSES, SPEAK TO THE PEOPLE OF ISRAEL... 'YOU ARE GOING TO ENTER THE LAND I AM TAKING YOU TO. YOU WILL EAT ITS FOOD. WHEN YOU DO, BRING PART OF IT AS AN OFFERING TO THE LORD. BRING A LOAF THAT IS MADE FROM THE FIRST FLOUR YOU GRIND. GIVE IT AS AN OFFERING FROM THE THRESHING FLOOR... YOU MUST DO IT FOR ALL TIME TO COME.' "
—— NUMBERS 15:17-21 ——

matter whether he is an Israelite or an outsider. 30 " 'But suppose someone sins on purpose. It does not matter whether he is an Israelite or an outsider. He speaks evil things against the LORD. He must be cut off from his people. 31 He has made fun of what the LORD has said. He has broken the LORD's commands. He must certainly be cut off. He is still guilty.' "

A Man Breaks the Sabbath Day

32 The people of Israel were in the desert. One Sabbath day, people saw a man gathering wood. 33 They brought him to Moses and Aaron and the whole community. 34 They kept him under guard. It wasn't clear what should be done to him. 35 Then the LORD said to Moses, "The man must die. The whole community must kill him by throwing stones at him. They must do it outside the camp." 36 So the people took the man outside the camp. There they killed him by throwing stones at him. They did just as the LORD had commanded Moses.

Tassels on Clothes

37 The LORD said to Moses, 38 "Speak to the people of Israel. Say to them, 'You must make tassels on the corners of your clothes. A blue cord must be on each tassel. You must do it for all time to come. 39 You will have the tassels to look at. They will remind you to obey all of the LORD's commands. Then you will be faithful to him. You will not go after what your own hearts and eyes long for. 40 " 'You will remember to obey all of my commands. And you will be set apart for your God. 41 I am the LORD your God. I brought you out of Egypt to be your God. I am the LORD your God.' "

Korah, Dathan and Abiram

16 Korah was the son of Izhar, the son of Kohath. Kohath was the son of Levi. Korah and certain men from the tribe of Reuben turned against Moses. The men from Reuben were Dathan, Abiram and On. Dathan and Abiram were the sons of Eliab. On was the son of Peleth. 2 All of those men rose up against Moses. And 250 men of Israel joined them. All of them were known as leaders in the community. They had been appointed as members of the ruling body.

3 They came as a group to oppose Moses and Aaron. They said to Moses and Aaron, "You have gone too far! The whole community is holy. Every one in it is holy. And the LORD is with them. So why do you put yourselves above the LORD's people?"

4 When Moses heard what they said, he fell with his face to the ground. 5 Then he spoke to Korah and all of his followers. He said, "In the morning the LORD will show who belongs to him. He will show who is holy. He'll bring that person near him. He'll bring the man he chooses near him. 6 "Korah, here's what you and all of your followers must do. Get some shallow cups for burning incense. 7 Tomorrow put fire and incense in them. Offer it to the LORD. The man the LORD chooses will be the one who is holy. You Levites have gone too far!"

8 Moses also said to Korah, "Listen, you Levites! 9 The God of Israel has separated you from the rest of the community of Israel. He has brought you near him to work at the LORD's holy tent. He has given you to the people so that you can serve them. Isn't all of that enough for you? 10 He has already brought you and all of the other Levites near him. But now you want to be priests too. 11 You and all of your followers have joined together against the LORD. Why are you telling Aaron you aren't happy with him?"

12 Then Moses sent for Dathan and Abiram, the sons of Eliab. But they said, "We won't come! 13 You have brought us up out of a land that has plenty of milk and honey. You have brought us here to kill us in this desert. Isn't that enough? Now do you also want to act as if you were ruling over us?

14 "Besides, you haven't brought us into a land that has plenty of milk and honey. You haven't given us fields and vineyards of our own. Are you going to poke out the eyes of these men? No! We won't come!"

15 Then Moses became very angry. He said to the LORD, "Don't accept their offering. I haven't taken even a donkey from them. In fact, I haven't done anything wrong to any of them."

16 Moses said to Korah, "You and all of your followers must stand in front of the LORD tomorrow. You must appear there along with Aaron. 17 Each man must get his shallow cup. He must put incense in it. There will be a total of 250 incense cups. Each man must bring his cup to the LORD. You and Aaron must also bring your cups."

18 So each man got his cup. He put fire and incense in it. All of the men came with Moses and Aaron. They stood at the entrance to the Tent of Meeting. 19 Korah

gathered all of his followers together at the entrance to the tent. They opposed Moses and Aaron.

Then the glory of the LORD appeared to the whole community. **20**The LORD spoke to Moses and Aaron. He said, **21**"Separate yourselves from these people. Then I can put an end to all of them at once."

22But Moses and Aaron fell with their faces to the ground. They cried out, "God, you are the God who creates the spirits of all people. Will you be angry with the whole community when only one man sins?"

23Then the LORD spoke to Moses. He said, **24**"Tell the community, 'Move away from the tents of Korah, Dathan and Abiram.' "

25Moses got up. He went to Dathan and Abiram. The elders of Israel followed him. **26**Moses warned the community. He said, "Move away from the tents of those evil men! Don't touch anything that belongs to them. If you do, the LORD will sweep you away because of all of their sins."

27So they moved away from the tents of Korah, Dathan and Abiram. Dathan and Abiram had already come out. They were standing at the entrances to their tents. Their wives, children and little ones were standing there with them.

28Then Moses said, "What is about to happen wasn't my idea. The LORD has sent me to do everything I'm doing. Here is how you will know I'm telling you the truth. **29**Those men won't die a natural death. Something will happen to them that doesn't usually happen to people. If what I'm telling you isn't true, then you will know that the LORD hasn't sent me.

30"But the LORD will make something totally new happen. The ground will open its mouth and swallow them up. It will swallow up everything that belongs to them. They will go down into the grave alive. When that happens, you will know that those men have made fun of the LORD."

31As soon as Moses finished speaking all of those words, what he had said came true. The ground under them broke open. **32**It opened its mouth. It swallowed up those men. In fact, it swallowed up everyone who lived in their houses. It swallowed all of Korah's men. And it swallowed up everything they owned. **33**They went down into the grave alive. Everything they owned went down with them. The ground closed over them. They died. And so they disappeared from the community.

34All of the people of Israel who were around them heard their cries. They ran away from them. They shouted, "The ground is going to swallow us up too!"

35Then the LORD sent down fire. It burned up the 250 men who were offering the incense.

36The LORD spoke to Moses. He said, **37**"Speak to the priest Eleazar. He is the son of Aaron. Remind him that the shallow cups are holy. He must take them out of the fire. He must scatter the burning coals away from there. **38**The men who sinned used those cups. And it cost them their lives. Hammer the cups into bronze sheets that will cover the altar. The cups were offered to the LORD. They have become holy. Let them serve as a warning to the people of Israel."

39So the priest Eleazar collected the bronze incense cups. They had been brought by the men who had been burned up. He had them hammered out to cover the altar. **40**He did just as the LORD had directed Moses to tell him to do. The covering would be a reminder to the people of Israel. It would remind them that no one except a son of Aaron should come and burn incense to the LORD. If people other than priests did that, they would become like Korah and his followers.

41The next day the whole community of Israel told Moses and Aaron they weren't happy with them. "You have killed the LORD's people," they said.

42The community gathered together to oppose Moses and Aaron. The people walked toward the Tent of Meeting. Suddenly the cloud covered it. The glory of the LORD appeared. **43**Then Moses and Aaron went to the front of the Tent of Meeting. **44**The LORD spoke to Moses. He said, **45**"Get away from these people. Then I can put an end to all of them at once." And Moses and Aaron fell with their faces to the ground.

46Moses said to Aaron, "Take your incense cup. Put incense in it. And put fire from the altar in it. Then hurry to the people and pay for their sin. The LORD has sent his anger. The plague has started."

47So Aaron did as Moses said. He ran in among the people. The plague had already started among them. But Aaron offered the incense and paid for their sin. **48**He stood between those who were alive and those who were dead. And the plague stopped. **49**But 14,700 people died from the plague. That doesn't include those who had died because of what Korah did.

50Then Aaron returned to Moses at the entrance to the Tent of Meeting. The plague had stopped.

Aaron's Wooden Staff Produces Buds

17 The LORD spoke to Moses. He said, **2**"Speak to the people of Israel. Get 12 wooden staffs from them. Get one from the leader of each of Israel's tribes. Write the name of each man on his staff. **3**Write Aaron's name on the staff of Levi. There must be one staff for the head of each of Israel's tribes.

4"Put the staffs in the Tent of Meeting. Place them in front of the ark where the tablets of the covenant are kept. That is where I meet with you. **5**The staff that belongs to the man I choose will begin to grow new shoots. The people of Israel are never happy with what you do. I will put an end to what they are saying."

6So Moses spoke to the people of Israel. Their leaders gave him 12 wooden staffs. They gave one for the leader of each of Israel's tribes. Aaron's staff was among them. **7**Moses put the staffs in front of the LORD in the tent where the tablets of the covenant were kept.

8The next day Moses entered the tent. He looked at Aaron's staff. It stood for the tribe of Levi. Moses saw that it had not only begun to grow new shoots. It had also produced buds and flowers and almonds. **9**Then Moses brought out all of the staffs from in front of the LORD. He brought them to all of the people of Israel. They looked at them. And each man took his own staff.

10The LORD said to Moses, "Put Aaron's staff back in front of the ark where the tablets of the covenant are kept. The staff will be kept there as a warning to those who refuse to obey. They are never happy with what I do. Aaron's staff will put an end to what they are saying. Then they will not die." **11**Moses did just as the LORD commanded him.

12The people of Israel said to Moses, "We'll die! We are lost! All of us are lost! **13**Anyone who even comes near the LORD's holy tent will die. Are all of us going to die?"

Duties of Priests and Levites

18 The LORD spoke to Aaron. He said, "You, your sons and your father's family are in charge of the sacred tent. You will be held accountable for sins that are committed against it. And you and your sons will be held accountable for sins that are committed against the office of priest.

2"Bring the Levites from your tribe to join you. They will help you when you and your sons serve at the tent where the tablets of the covenant are kept. **3**They will work for you. They must do everything that needs to be done at the tent. But they must not go near anything that belongs to the sacred tent. And they must not go near the altar. If they do, they and you will die. **4**They will help you take care of the Tent of Meeting. They will join you in all of the work at the tent. No one else can come near you there.

5"You will be held accountable for taking care of the sacred tent and the altar. Then my anger will not fall on the people of Israel again. **6**I myself have chosen the Levites. I have chosen them from among the people of Israel. They are a gift to you. I have set them apart to do the work at the Tent of Meeting.

7"But only you and your sons can serve as priests. Only you and your sons can work with everything at the altar and inside the curtain. I am letting you serve as priests. It is a gift from me. Anyone else who comes near the sacred tent must be put to death."

Offerings for Priests and Levites

8Then the LORD spoke to Aaron. He said, "I have put you in charge of the offerings that are brought to me. The people of Israel will give me holy offerings. I will give all of their offerings to you and your sons. They are the part that belongs to you. They are your regular share.

9"You will have a part of the very holy offerings. It is the part that is not burned in the fire. That part belongs to you and your sons. You will have a part of all of the gifts the people bring me as very holy offerings. It does not matter whether they are grain offerings or sin offerings or guilt offerings. **10**Eat your part as something that is very holy. Every male will eat it. You must consider it holy.

11"Part of the gifts the people of Israel bring as wave offerings will be set to one side. That part will also belong to you. I will give it to you and your sons and daughters. It is your regular share. Everyone in your home who is 'clean' can eat it.

12"I will give you all of the finest olive oil and grain the people give me. And I will give you all of the finest fresh wine they give me. They give all of those things as the first share of their harvest. **13**All of the first shares of the harvest they bring me will belong to you. Everyone in your home who is 'clean' can eat it.

14 "Everything in Israel that is set apart to me belongs to you. **15** Offer to me every male that is born first to its mother. It belongs to you. That is true for men and animals alike. But you must buy back every oldest son. Suppose certain animals are not 'clean.' Then you must buy back every male that is born first to its mother. **16** When they are a month old, you must buy them back. You must pay the price to buy them back. The price is set at two ounces of silver. It must be weighed out in keeping with the standard weights that are used in the sacred tent.

17 "But you must not buy back any male calf that is born first. And you must not buy back any male sheep or goat that is born first. They are holy. Sprinkle their blood on the altar. And burn their fat as an offering that is made with fire. It gives a smell that is pleasant to me.

18 "The meat will belong to you. It is just like the breast and the right thigh of the wave offering. Those parts belong to you. **19** Part of the holy offerings the people of Israel bring to me will be set to one side. No matter what it is, I will give it to you and your sons and daughters. It is your regular share. It is a covenant of salt from me. The salt means that the covenant will last for all time to come for you and your children."

20 The LORD spoke to Aaron. He said, "You will not receive any part of the land I am giving to Israel. You will not have any share among them. I am your share. I am what you will receive among the people of Israel.

21 "The people of Israel will give me a tenth of everything they produce. And I will give it to the Levites. They serve at the Tent of Meeting. I will give them the tenth for the work they do there. **22** From now on the people of Israel must not go near the Tent of Meeting. If they do, they will be punished for their sin. They will die. **23** "The Levites will do the work at the Tent of Meeting. They will be held accountable for sins that are committed against it. That is a law that will last for all time to come. The Levites will not receive any share among the people of Israel. **24** Instead, I will give the Levites the tenth as their share. It is the tenth that the people of Israel bring me as an offering. That is why I said the Levites would not have any share of land among the people of Israel."

25 The LORD said to Moses, **26** "Speak to the Levites. Say to them, 'You will receive the tenth from the people of Israel. I will give it to you as your share. When I do, you must give a tenth of that tenth as an offering to the LORD. **27** Your offering will be considered as if you gave grain from a threshing floor. It will be considered as juice from a winepress.

28 " 'In that way, you also will bring an offering to the LORD. You will bring it from the tenth you receive from the people of Israel. You must give the LORD's part to the priest Aaron. You must bring it from the tenth you receive. **29** You must bring to the LORD a part of everything that is given to you. It must be the best and holiest part.'

30 "Say to the Levites, 'You must bring the best part. Then it will be considered as if you gave grain from a threshing floor. It will be considered as juice from a winepress. **31** You and your families can eat the rest of it anywhere. It is your pay for your work at the Tent of Meeting. **32** Bring the best part of what you receive. Then you will not be guilty of holding anything back. You will not make the holy offerings of the people of Israel "unclean." You will not die.' "

The Special Water That Makes People "Clean"

19 The LORD spoke to Moses and Aaron. He said, **2** "Here is what the law I have commanded requires. Tell the people of Israel to bring you a young red cow. It must not have any flaws at all. It must never have pulled a load.

3 "Give it to the priest Eleazar. It must be taken outside the camp and killed in front of him. **4** Then the priest Eleazar must put some of its blood on his finger. He must sprinkle the blood toward the front of the Tent of Meeting. He must do it seven times.

5 "While he watches, the young cow must be burned. Its hide, meat, blood and guts must be burned. **6** The priest must get some cedar wood, branches of a hyssop plant, and bright red wool. He must throw them on the young cow as it burns. **7** "After that, the priest must wash his clothes. He must also take a bath. Then he can come into the camp. But he will be 'unclean' until evening.

8 "The man who burns the young cow must wash his clothes. He must also take a bath. He too will be 'unclean' until evening.

9 "A man who is 'clean' will gather up the ashes of the young cow. He must put them in a place that is 'clean.' The place must be outside the camp. The ashes will be kept by the community of Israel. They will be added to the special water. The water will be used to make people pure from their sin.

10"The man who gathers up the ashes of the young cow must wash his clothes. He too will be 'unclean' until evening. That law is for the people of Israel. It is also for the outsiders who are living among them. The law will last for all time to come.

11"Anyone who touches a dead person's body will be 'unclean' for seven days. **12**He must make himself pure and clean with the special water. He must do it on the third day. He must also do it on the seventh day. Then he will be 'clean.'

"But suppose he does not make himself pure and clean on the third and seventh days. Then he will not be 'clean.' **13**Anyone who touches a dead person's body and does not make himself pure and clean makes my holy tent 'unclean.' He must be cut off from Israel. The special water has not been sprinkled on him. So he is 'unclean.' And he remains 'unclean.'

14"Here is the law that applies when a person dies in a tent. Anyone who enters the tent will be 'unclean' for seven days. Anyone who is in the tent will also be 'unclean' for seven days. **15**And anything in it that is open and has no lid will be 'unclean.'

16"Suppose someone is out in the country. And suppose he touches someone who has been killed with a sword. Or he touches someone who has died a natural death. Or he touches a human bone or a grave. Then anyone who touches any of those things will be 'unclean' for seven days.

17"Here is what I want you to do for someone who is not 'clean.' Put some ashes from the burned young cow into a jar. Pour fresh water on the ashes. **18**Then a man who is 'clean' must dip branches of a hyssop plant in the water. He must sprinkle the tent with it. Everything that belongs to the tent must be sprinkled with it. The people who were in the tent must also be sprinkled. Anyone who has touched a human bone or a grave must be sprinkled. So must anyone who has touched someone who has been killed. So must anyone who has touched someone who has died a natural death.

19"The man who is 'clean' must sprinkle the person who is not. That must be done on the third and seventh days. On

the seventh day the person who is not 'clean' must be made pure and clean. The one who is being made 'clean' must wash his clothes. He must take a bath. Then that evening he will be 'clean.'

20"But what if a person who is 'unclean' does not make himself pure and clean? Then he must be cut off from the community. He has made my holy tent 'unclean.' The special water has not been sprinkled on him. He is not 'clean.' **21**That law will apply to all of those people for all time to come.

"The man who sprinkles the special water must also wash his clothes. Anyone who touches the water will be 'unclean' until evening. **22**Anything that an 'unclean' person touches becomes 'unclean.' And anyone who touches it becomes 'unclean' until evening."

The LORD Gives Israel Water Out of the Rock

20 In the first month the whole community of Israel arrived at the Desert of Zin. They stayed at Kadesh. Miriam died there. Her body was also buried there.

2The people didn't have any water. So they gathered together to oppose Moses and Aaron. **3**They argued with Moses. They said, "We wish we had died when our people fell dead in front of the LORD. **4**"Why did you bring the LORD's people into this desert? We and our livestock will die here. **5**Why did you bring us up out of Egypt? Why did you bring us to this terrible place? It doesn't have any grain or figs. It doesn't have any grapes or pomegranates. There isn't even any water for us to drink!"

6Moses and Aaron left the people. They went to the entrance to the Tent of Meeting. There they fell with their faces to the ground.

Then the glory of the LORD appeared to them. **7**The LORD spoke to Moses. He said, **8**"Get your wooden staff. You and your brother Aaron gather the people together. Then speak to that rock while everyone is watching. It will pour out its water. You will bring water out of the rock for the community. Then they and their livestock can drink it."

9So Moses took the wooden staff from the tent. He did just as the LORD had commanded him. **10**He and Aaron gathered the people together in front of the rock. Moses said to them, "Listen, you who refuse to obey! Do we have to bring water out of this rock for you?"

11Then Moses raised his arm. He hit the rock twice with his staff. Water poured out. And the people and their livestock drank it.

12But the LORD spoke to Moses and Aaron. He said, "You did not trust in me enough to honor me. You did not honor me as the holy God in front of the people of Israel. So you will not bring this community into the land I am giving them."

13Those were the waters of Meribah. That's where the people of Israel argued with the LORD. And that's where he showed them he is holy.

Edom Doesn't Let Israel Pass Through Its Territory

14Moses sent messengers from Kadesh to the king of Edom. The messengers said,

"The nation of Israel is your brother. They say, 'You know about all of the hard times we've had. **15**Long ago our people went down into Egypt. We lived there for many years. The Egyptians treated us and our people badly. **16**But we cried out to the LORD. He heard our cry. He sent an angel and brought us out of Egypt.

" 'Now here we are at the town of Kadesh. It's on the edge of your territory. **17**Please let us pass through your country. We won't go through any field or vineyard. We won't drink water from any well. We'll travel along the king's highway. We won't turn to the right or the left. We'll just go straight through your territory.' "

18But the people of Edom answered,

"You can't pass through here. If you try to, we'll march out against you. We'll attack you with our swords."

19The people of Israel replied,

"We'll go along the main road. We and our livestock won't drink any of your water. If we do, we'll pay for it. We only want to walk through your country. That's all we ask."

20Again the people of Edom answered,

"You can't pass through here."

Then the people of Edom came out against them. They came with a large and powerful army. **21**Edom refused to let Israel go through their territory. So Israel turned away from them.

Aaron Dies

22The whole community of Israel started out from Kadesh. They arrived at Mount Hor. **23**It was near the border of Edom. There the LORD spoke to Moses and Aaron. He said, **24**"Aaron will join the members of his family who have already died. He will not enter the land I am giving to the people of Israel. Both of you refused to obey my command. You did it at the waters of Meribah.

25"So get Aaron and his son Eleazar. Take them up Mount Hor. **26**Take Aaron's official robes off him. Put them on his son Eleazar. Aaron will die on Mount Hor. He will join the members of his family who have already died."

27Moses did just as the LORD had commanded. The three men went up Mount Hor while the whole community was watching. **28**Moses took Aaron's official robes off him. He put them on Aaron's son Eleazar. And Aaron died there on top of the mountain. Then Moses and Eleazar came down from the mountain.

29The whole community found out that Aaron had died. So the entire nation of Israel sobbed over him for 30 days.

Israel Destroys Arad

21 The Canaanite king of the city of Arad lived in the Negev Desert. He heard that Israel was coming along the road to Atharim. So he attacked the people of Israel. He captured some of them.

2Then Israel made a promise to the LORD. They said, "Hand these people over to us. If you do, we will set their cities apart to you in a special way to be destroyed."

3The LORD gave Israel what they asked for. He handed the Canaanites over to them. Israel completely destroyed them. They also destroyed their towns. So that place was named Hormah.

Moses Makes a Bronze Snake

4The people of Israel traveled from Mount Hor along the way to the Red Sea. They wanted to go around Edom. But they grew tired on the way. **5**So they spoke against God. They also spoke against Moses. They said to them, "Why have you brought us up out of Egypt? Do you want us to die here in the desert? We don't have any bread! We don't have any water! And we hate this awful food!"

6Then the LORD sent poisonous snakes among the people of Israel. The snakes bit them. Many of the people died. **7**The others came to Moses. They said, "We sinned when we spoke against the LORD and against you. Pray that the LORD will take the snakes away from us." So Moses prayed for the people.

⁸The LORD said to Moses, "Make a snake. Put it up on a pole. Then anyone who is bitten can look at it and remain alive." ⁹So Moses made a bronze snake. He put it up on a pole. Then anyone who was bitten by a snake and looked at the bronze snake remained alive.

The People Continue On to Moab

¹⁰The people of Israel moved on. They camped at Oboth. ¹¹Then they started out from Oboth. They camped in Iye Abarim. It's in the desert on the eastern border of Moab. ¹²From there they moved on. They camped in the Zered Valley. ¹³They started out from there and camped by the Arnon River. It's in the desert that spreads out into the territory of the Amorites. The Arnon is the border of Moab. It's between Moab and the Amorites.

¹⁴Here is what the Book of the Wars of the LORD says about it. It says,

"Sing about Waheb in Suphah and the valleys.
Sing about the Arnon ¹⁵and the slopes of the valleys.
They lead to the place called Ar.
They lie along the border of Moab."

¹⁶From there the people of Israel continued on to Beer. That was the well where the LORD spoke to Moses. He said, "Gather the people together. I will give them water to drink."

¹⁷Then Israel sang a song. They said,

"Spring up, you well!
Sing about it.
¹⁸ Sing about the well the princes dug.
Sing about the well the nobles of the people dug.
All of their rulers were holding their rods and staffs."

Then the people of Israel went from the desert to Mattanah. ¹⁹They went from Mattanah to Nahaliel. They went from Nahaliel to Bamoth. ²⁰And they went from Bamoth to a valley in Moab. It's the valley where the highest slopes of Pisgah look out over a dry and empty land.

Israel Wins the Battle Over Sihon and Og

²¹The people of Israel sent messengers to speak to Sihon. He was the king of the Amorites. The messengers said to him,

²²"Let us pass through your country. We won't go off the road into any field or vineyard. We won't drink water from any well. We'll travel along the king's highway. We'll just go straight through your territory."

²³But Sihon wouldn't let Israel pass through his territory. He gathered his whole army together. Then he marched out into the desert against Israel. When he reached Jahaz, he fought against Israel.

²⁴But Israel put him to death with their swords. They took over his land. They took everything from the Arnon River to the Jabbok River. But they didn't take over any of the land of the Ammonites. That's because the Ammonites had built strong forts along their border. ²⁵The people of Israel captured all of the cities of the Amorites. Then they settled down in them. They captured the city of Heshbon. They also captured all of the settlements that were around it.

²⁶Sihon, the king of the Amorites, ruled in Heshbon. He had fought against an earlier king of Moab. Sihon had taken from him all of his land all the way to the Arnon River.

²⁷That's why the poets say,

"Come to Heshbon. Let it be built again.
Let Sihon's city be made as good as new.

²⁸ "Fire went out from Heshbon.
A blaze went out from the city of Sihon.
It burned up Ar in Moab.
It burned up the citizens who lived on Arnon's hills.
²⁹ Moab, how terrible it is for you!
People of Chemosh, you are destroyed!
Chemosh has deserted his sons and daughters.
His sons have run away from the battle.
His daughters have become prisoners.
He has handed all of them over to Sihon,
the king of the Amorites.

³⁰ "But we have taken them over.
Heshbon is destroyed all the way to Dibon.
We have destroyed them as far as Nophah.
Nophah goes all the way to Medeba."

31So Israel settled in the land of the Amorites.

32Moses sent spies to the city of Jazer. The people of Israel captured the settlements that were around it. They drove out the Amorites who were there. **33**Then they turned and went up along the road toward Bashan. Og was the king of Bashan. He and his whole army marched out. They went to fight against Israel at Edrei.

34The LORD said to Moses, "Do not be afraid of Og. I have handed him over to you. I have given you his whole army. I have also given you his land. Do to him what you did to Sihon, the king of the Amorites. He ruled in Heshbon."

35So the people of Israel struck Og down. They struck his sons down. And they wiped out his whole army. They didn't leave anyone alive. They took over his land for themselves.

Balak Sends For Balaam

22 Then the people of Israel traveled to the flatlands of Moab. They camped along the Jordan River across from Jericho.

2Balak saw everything that Israel had done to the Amorites. Balak was the son of Zippor. **3**The people of Moab were terrified because there were so many Israelites. In fact, Moab was filled with panic because of the people of Israel.

4The Moabites spoke to the elders of Midian. They said, "This huge mob is going to lick up everything around us. They'll lick it up as an ox licks up all of the grass in the fields."

Balak, the son of Zippor, was the king of Moab at that time. **5**He sent messengers to get Balaam. Balaam was the son of Beor. Balaam was at the city of Pethor near the Euphrates River. Pethor was in the land where Balaam had been born. Balak told the messengers to say to Balaam,

"A nation has come out of Egypt. They are covering the face of the land. They've settled down next to me. **6**So come and put a curse on those people. They are too powerful for me. Maybe I'll be able to win the battle over them. Maybe I'll be able to drive them out of the country. I know that those you bless will be blessed. And I know that those you put a curse on will be cursed."

7The elders of Moab and Midian left. They took with them the money they knew Balaam would ask for. They wanted

him to use magic and figure things out for them. They came to where Balaam was. And they told him what Balak had said.

8"Spend the night here," Balaam said to them. "I'll bring you back the answer the LORD gives me." So the princes of Moab stayed with him.

9God came to Balaam. He asked, "Who are these men who are with you?"

10Balaam said to God, "Balak king of Moab, the son of Zippor, sent me a message. **11**He said, 'A nation has come out of Egypt. They are covering the whole surface of the land. So come. Put a curse on them for me. Maybe I'll be able to fight them. Maybe I'll be able to drive them away.' "

12But God said to Balaam, "Do not go with them. You must not put a curse on those people. I have blessed them."

13The next morning Balaam got up. He said to Balak's princes, "Go back to your own country. The LORD won't let me go with you."

14So the princes of Moab returned to Balak. They said, "Balaam wouldn't come with us."

15Then Balak sent other princes. They were more important than the first ones. And there were more of them. **16**They came to Balaam. They said,

"Balak, the son of Zippor, says, 'Don't let anything keep you from coming to me. **17**I'll make you very rich. I'll do anything you say. Come. Put a curse on those people for me.' "

18But Balaam gave them his answer. He said, "Balak could give me his palace filled with silver and gold. Even then, I still couldn't do anything at all that goes beyond what the LORD my God commands. **19**Stay here tonight, just as the others did. I'll find out what else the LORD will tell me."

20That night God came to Balaam. He said, "These men have come to get you. So go with them. But do only what I tell you to do."

Balaam's Donkey

21Balaam got up in the morning. He put a saddle on his donkey. Then he went with the princes of Moab.

22But God was very angry when Balaam went. So the angel of the LORD stood in the road to oppose him. Balaam was riding on his donkey. His two servants were with him. **23**The donkey saw the angel of the LORD standing in the road. The angel was holding a sword. He was ready for battle. So the donkey left the road and went into a field. Balaam hit the donkey. He wanted to get it back on the road.

24 Then the angel of the LORD stood in a narrow path. The path went between two vineyards. There were walls on both sides. 25 The donkey saw the angel of the LORD. So it moved close to the wall. It crushed Balaam's foot against the wall. He hit the donkey again.

26 Then the angel of the LORD moved on ahead. He stood in a narrow place. There was no room to turn, either right or left. 27 The donkey saw the angel of the LORD. So it lay down under Balaam. That made him angry. He hit the donkey with his walking stick.

28 Then the LORD opened the donkey's mouth. It said to Balaam, "What have I done to you? Why did you hit me those three times?"

29 Balaam answered the donkey. He said, "You have made me look foolish! I wish I had a sword in my hand. If I did, I'd kill you right now."

30 The donkey said to Balaam, "I'm your own donkey. I'm the one you have always ridden. Haven't you been riding me to this very day? Have I ever made you look foolish before?"

"No," he said.

31 Then the LORD opened Balaam's eyes. He saw the angel of the LORD standing in the road. He saw that the angel was holding a sword. The angel was ready for battle. So Balaam bowed down. He fell with his face to the ground.

32 The angel of the LORD spoke to him. He asked him, "Why have you hit your donkey three times? I have come here to oppose you. What you are doing is foolish. 33 The donkey saw me. It turned away from me three times. Suppose it had not turned away. Then I would certainly have killed you by now. But I would have spared the donkey."

34 Balaam spoke to the angel of the LORD. He said, "I have sinned. I didn't realize you were standing in the road to oppose me. Tell me whether you are pleased with me. If you aren't, I'll go back."

35 The angel of the LORD spoke to Balaam. He said, "Go with the men. But say only what I tell you to say." So Balaam went with the princes of Balak.

36 Balak heard that Balaam was coming. So he went out to meet him. They met at a Moabite town near the Arnon River. The town was on the border of Balak's territory. 37 Balak spoke to Balaam. He said, "Didn't I send messengers to you? I wanted you to come quickly. So why didn't you come? I can make you very rich."

38 "Well, I've come to you now," Balaam replied. "But I can't say just anything. I can only speak the words God puts in my mouth."

39 Then Balaam went with Balak to Kiriath Huzoth. 40 Balak sacrificed cattle and sheep. He gave some to Balaam. He also gave some to the princes who were with him.

41 The next morning Balak took Balaam up to Bamoth Baal. From there he saw part of the people of Israel.

Balaam's First Message From God

23 Balaam said to Balak, "Build me seven altars here. Prepare seven bulls and seven rams for me to sacrifice." 2 Balak did just as Balaam said. The two of them offered a bull and a ram on each altar.

3 Then Balaam said to Balak, "Stay here beside your offering. I'll go and try to find out what the LORD wants me to do. Maybe he'll come and meet with me. Then I'll tell you what he says to me." So Balaam went off to a bare hilltop.

4 God met with him there. Balaam said, "I've prepared seven altars. On each altar I've offered a bull and a ram."

5 The LORD put a message in Balaam's mouth. The LORD said, "Go back to Balak. Give him my message."

6 So Balaam went back to him. He found Balak standing beside his offering. All of the princes of Moab were with him.

7 Then Balaam spoke the message he had received from God. He said,

"Balak brought me from the land of
    Aram.
  The king of Moab sent for me from
      the mountains in the east.
  'Come,' he said. 'Put a curse on Jacob's
      people for me.
  Come. Speak against Israel.'
8 But how can I put a curse on
    people God hasn't cursed?
How can I speak against
    people the LORD hasn't spoken
        against?
9 I see them from the rocky peaks.
  I view them from the hills.
I see a group of people who live by
    themselves.
  They don't consider themselves to
      be one of the nations.

¹⁰Jacob's people are like the dust of the
    earth.
  Can dust be counted?
  Who can count even a fourth of the
    people of Israel?
  Let me die as godly people die.
  Let my death be like theirs!"

¹¹Balak said to Balaam, "What have you
done to me? I brought you here to put a
curse on my enemies! But all you have
done is give them a blessing!"

¹²He answered, "I have to speak only
the words the LORD puts in my mouth."

Balaam's Second Message From God

¹³Then Balak said to Balaam, "Come
with me to another place. You can see the
people of Israel from there. You will see
only some of them. You won't see all of
them. From there, put a curse on them
for me."

¹⁴So Balak took Balaam to the field of
Zophim. It was on the highest slopes of
Pisgah. There he built seven altars. He
offered a bull and a ram on each altar.

¹⁵Balaam said to Balak, "Stay here
beside your offering. I'll meet with the
LORD over there."

¹⁶The LORD met with Balaam. He put a
message in Balaam's mouth. The LORD
said, "Go back to Balak. Give him my message."

¹⁷So he went to him. He found him
standing beside his offering. The princes
of Moab were with him. Balak asked him,
"What did the LORD say?"

¹⁸Then Balaam spoke the message he
had received from God. He said,

  "Balak, rise up and listen.
    Son of Zippor, hear me.
¹⁹God isn't a mere man. He can't lie.
    He isn't a human being. He doesn't
      change his mind.
  He speaks, and then he acts.
    He makes a promise, and then he
      keeps it.
²⁰He has commanded me to bless Israel.
    He has given them his blessing. And
      I can't change it.

²¹ "I don't see any trouble coming on the
      people of Jacob.
  I don't see any suffering in Israel.
  The LORD their God is with them.
    The shout of the King is among
      them.
²²God brought them out of Egypt.
    They are as strong as a wild ox.

²³There isn't any magic that can hurt the
      people of Jacob.
  No one can use magic words to
      harm Israel.
  Here is what will be said about the
      people of Jacob.
    Here is what will be said about Israel.
    People will say, 'See what God has
      done!'
²⁴The people of Israel are going to wake
      up like a female lion.
  They are going to get up like a male
      lion.
  They are like a lion that won't rest
      until it eats what it has caught.
  They are like a lion that won't rest
      until it drinks the blood of what it
      has killed."

²⁵Then Balak said to Balaam, "Don't
put a curse on them at all! And don't give
them a blessing at all!"

²⁶Balaam answered, "Didn't I tell you
that I have to do only what the LORD
says?"

Balaam's Third Message From God

²⁷Then Balak said to Balaam, "Come.
Let me take you to another place. Perhaps
God will be pleased to let you put a curse
on them for me from there." ²⁸Balak took
Balaam to the top of Mount Peor. It looks
out over a dry and empty land.

²⁹Balaam said, "Build me seven altars
here. Prepare seven bulls and seven rams
for me to sacrifice." ³⁰Balak did just as
Balaam said. He offered a bull and a ram
on each altar.

24 Balaam saw that the LORD was
pleased to give his blessing to Israel. So he didn't try to use evil magic as he
had done at other times. Instead, he
turned and looked toward the desert. ²He
looked out and saw Israel. They had set up
their camps tribe by tribe. The Spirit of
God came on him.

³Balaam spoke the message he had
received from God. He said,

  "Here is the message God gave Balaam,
      the son of Beor.
  It's the message God gave to the one
      who sees clearly.
⁴It's the message God gave to the one
      who hears the words of God.
  He sees a vision from the Mighty
      One.
  He falls down flat with his face toward
      the ground.
  His eyes have been opened by the
      LORD.

5 "People of Jacob, your tents are very
   beautiful.
   Israel, the places where you live are
      very beautiful.
6 "They spread out like valleys.
   They are like gardens beside a river.
   They are like aloes the LORD has
      planted.
   They are like cedar trees beside a
      stream.
7 Their water buckets will run over.
   Their seeds will have plenty of water.

   "Their king will be greater than King
      Agag.

Their kingdom will be honored.
8 "God brought them out of Egypt.
   They are as strong as a wild ox.
   They eat up nations that are at war
      with them.
   They break their bones in pieces.
   They wound them with their
      arrows.
9 Like a male lion they lie down and
      sleep.
   They are like a female lion.
   Who dares to wake them up?

May those who bless you be blessed!

BALAAM

(Sort of)

NUMBERS 23:12

✔ *He answered, "I have to speak only the words
the LORD puts in my mouth."*

B alaam (BAY-lum) and his donkey trotted along in the hot
summer sun. Balaam rode this same donkey every day and
barely had to think about directing him. But today was different.
Today God was trying to get Balaam's attention. Balaam wasn't
watching. But the donkey was!

The donkey saw God's angel in the road and, first, left the road.
Next, he walked against a wall and crushed Balaam's foot.
When the angel appeared again, the donkey lay down in the
middle of the road. Each time, Balaam hit the donkey with his
stick, trying to get it to go. Finally, the donkey had had enough.
He talked!

**"WHY DO YOU KEEP HITTING ME?" THE DONKEY
ASKED A SHOCKED BALAAM.** While Balaam talked to his
donkey, his eyes were opened. He saw God's angel. Finally, God
had Balaam's attention. Finally, Balaam was ready to listen to
God and obey him.

BE A BALAAM

Balaam took a while to get around to it, but when God talked to
him, he listened and obeyed. Be sure you do the same. God is
speaking to you through the Bible, through people around you,
through his world—open your ears to hear him. Then obey.

BALAAM LISTENED TO GOD AND OBEYED HIM.

Go to page 189 for the next Super Heroes

May those who call down a curse on
you be cursed!"

10Then Balak's anger burned against
Balaam. He slapped his hands together.
He said to Balaam, "I sent for you to put a
curse on my enemies. But you have given
them a blessing three times. **11**Get out of
here right away! Go home! I said I'd make
you very rich. But the Lord has kept you
from getting rich."

12Balaam answered Balak, "Here is
what I told the messengers you sent me.
13I said, 'Balak could give me his palace
filled with silver and gold. Even if I wanted to, I still couldn't do anything at all
that goes beyond what the Lord commands. I have to say only what the Lord
tells me to say.'

14"Now I'm going back to my people.
But come. Let me warn you about what
these people will do to your people in
days to come."

Balaam's Fourth Message From God

15Then Balaam spoke the message he
had received from God. He said,

"Here is the message God gave Balaam,
the son of Beor.
It's the message God gave to the one
who sees clearly.
16It's the message God gave to the one
who hears the words of God.
The Most High God has given him
knowledge.
He sees a vision from the Mighty One.
He falls down flat with his face
toward the ground.
His eyes have been opened by the
Lord.

17"I see him, but I don't see him now.
I view him, but he isn't near.
A star will come from among the
people of Jacob.
A king will rise up out of Israel.
He'll crush the foreheads of the people
of Moab.
He'll crush the skulls of all of the
sons of Sheth.
18He'll win the battle over Edom.
He'll win the battle over his enemy
Seir.
But Israel will grow strong.
19A ruler will come from among the
people of Jacob.
He'll destroy those from the city
who are still alive."

Balaam's Fifth Message From God

20Then Balaam saw the people of Amalek. He spoke the message he had received
from God. He said,

"Amalek was the first nation to attack
Israel.
But they will finally be destroyed."

Balaam's Sixth Message From God

21Then he saw the Kenites. He spoke
the message he had received from God.
He said,

"The place where you live is safe.
Your nest is on a high cliff.
22But you Kenites will be destroyed.
Assyria will take you as prisoners."

Balaam's Seventh Message From God

23Then he spoke the message he had
received from God. He said,

"Who can live when God does this?
24   Ships will come from the shores of
Kittim.
They will bring Assyria and Eber under
their control.
But they themselves will also be
destroyed."

25Then Balaam got up and returned
home. And Balak went on his way.

Moab Leads Israel Down the Wrong Path

25 Israel was staying in Shittim. The
men of Israel began to commit
sexual sins with the women of Moab.
2The women invited the men to feasts
and sacrifices in honor of their gods. The
people ate and bowed down in front of
the statues of those gods.

3So Israel joined in worshiping the god
Baal that was worshiped at Peor. The
Lord's anger burned against Israel.
4The Lord said to Moses, "Take all of
the leaders of these people. Kill them.
Put their dead bodies out in the open. I
want to see you do it in the middle of the
day. Then my anger will not burn against
Israel."

5So Moses spoke to Israel's judges. He
said, "Some of your men have joined in
worshiping the god Baal that is worshiped
at Peor. Each of you must kill the men in
your tribe who have done that."

6Then a man of Israel brought a woman
of Midian to his family. He did it right in
front of the eyes of Moses and the whole
community of Israel. They were sobbing
at the entrance to the Tent of Meeting.

7Phinehas was a priest. He was the son of Eleazar, the son of Aaron. When Phinehas saw what had happened, he left the people. He took a spear in his hand. **8**He followed the man into a tent. Phinehas stuck the spear through both the man and the woman.

Then the Lord stopped the plague against the people of Israel. **9**But the plague had already killed 24,000 of them.

10The Lord spoke to Moses. He said, **11**"Phinehas is a priest. He is the son of Eleazar, the son of Aaron. Phinehas has turned my anger away from the people of Israel. I am committed to making sure I am honored among them. And he is as committed as I am. Even though I was angry with them, I did not put an end to them.

12"So tell Phinehas I am making my covenant with him. It promises to give him peace. **13**He and his sons after him will have a covenant to be priests forever. That is because he was committed to making sure that I, his God, was honored. In that way he paid for the sin of the people of Israel."

14The name of the man of Israel who was killed was Zimri. He was the son of Salu. Zimri was killed along with the woman of Midian. Salu was a family leader in the tribe of Simeon. **15**The name of the woman of Midian who was killed was Cozbi. She was the daughter of Zur. Zur was the chief of a family in Midian.

16The Lord spoke to Moses. He said, **17**"Treat the people of Midian just as you would treat enemies. Kill them. **18**After all, they treated you like enemies. They tricked you into worshiping the god Baal that is worshiped at Peor. They also tricked you because of what Cozbi did. She was the woman who was killed when the plague that was connected with Peor came. Cozbi was the daughter of a leader of Midian."

The Men of Israel Are Counted a Second Time

26 After the plague the Lord spoke to Moses and the priest Eleazar. Eleazar was the son of Aaron. The Lord said, **2**"Count all of the men of Israel. Make a list of them by their families. Count all of the men who are able to serve in Israel's army. They must be 20 years old or more."

3At that time the people of Israel were on the flatlands of Moab. They were by the Jordan River across from Jericho. Moses and the priest Eleazar spoke with them. They said, **4**"Count all of the men who are 20 years old or more. Do it just as the Lord commanded Moses."

Here are the men of Israel who came out of Egypt.

5Reuben was Israel's oldest son. Here are the names of his sons.

The Hanochite family came from Hanoch.

The Palluite family came from Pallu.

6The Hezronite family came from Hezron.

The Carmite family came from Carmi.

7Those were the families of Reuben. The number of men was 43,730.

8Eliab was the son of Pallu. **9**Eliab's sons were Nemuel, Dathan and Abiram. Dathan and Abiram were the same community officials who refused to obey Moses and Aaron. They were among the followers of Korah who refused to obey the Lord. **10**The ground opened its mouth. It swallowed them up along with Korah. The followers of Korah died when fire burned up 250 men. Their deaths were a warning to the rest of Israel. **11**But the family line of Korah didn't die out completely.

12Here are the names of Simeon's sons. They are listed by their families.

The Nemuelite family came from Nemuel.

The Jaminite family came from Jamin.

The Jakinite family came from Jakin.

13The Zerahite family came from Zerah.

The Shaulite family came from Shaul.

14Those were the families of Simeon. The number of the men was 22,200.

15Here are the names of Gad's sons. They are listed by their families.

The Zephonite family came from Zephon.

The Haggite family came from Haggi.

The Shunite family came from Shuni.

16The Oznite family came from Ozni.

The Erite family came from Eri.

17The Arodite family came from Arodi.

The Arelite family came from Areli.

18Those were the families of Gad. The number of the men was 40,500.

19Er and Onan were sons of Judah. But they died in Canaan.

²⁰Here are the names of Judah's sons. They are listed by their families.

The Shelanite family came from Shelah.

The Perezite family came from Perez.

The Zerahite family came from Zerah.

²¹Here are the names of the sons of Perez.

The Hezronite family came from Hezron.

The Hamulite family came from Hamul.

²²Those were the families of Judah. The number of the men was 76,500.

²³Here are the names of Issachar's sons. They are listed by their families.

The Tolaite family came from Tola.

The Puite family came from Puah.

²⁴The Jashubite family came from Jashub.

The Shimronite family came from Shimron.

²⁵Those were the families of Issachar. The number of the men was 64,300.

²⁶Here are the names of Zebulun's sons. They are listed by their families.

The Seredite family came from Sered.

The Elonite family came from Elon.

The Jahleelite family came from Jahleel.

²⁷Those were the families of Zebulun. The number of the men was 60,500.

²⁸Here are the names of Joseph's sons. They are listed by their families. The families came from Manasseh and Ephraim, the sons of Joseph.

²⁹Here are the names of Manasseh's sons.

The Makirite family came from Makir. Makir was the father of Gilead.

The Gileadite family came from Gilead.

³⁰Here are the names of Gilead's sons.

The Iezerite family came from Iezer.

The Helekite family came from Helek.

³¹The Asrielite family came from Asriel.

The Shechemite family came from Shechem.

³²The Shemidaite family came from Shemida.

The Hepherite family came from Hepher.

³³Zelophehad was the son of Hepher. Zelophehad didn't have any sons. All he had was daughters. Their names were Mahlah, Noah, Hoglah, Milcah and Tirzah.

³⁴Those were the families of Manasseh. The number of the men was 52,700.

³⁵Here are the names of Ephraim's sons. They are listed by their families.

The Shuthelahite family came from Shuthelah.

The Bekerite family came from Beker.

The Tahanite family came from Tahan.

³⁶The sons of Shuthelah were the Eranite family.

They came from Eran.

³⁷Those were the families of Ephraim. The number of the men was 32,500.

Those were the sons of Joseph. They are listed by their families.

³⁸Here are the names of Benjamin's sons. They are listed by their families.

The Belaite family came from Bela.

The Ashbelite family came from Ashbel.

The Ahiramite family came from Ahiram.

³⁹The Shuphamite family came from Shupham.

The Huphamite family came from Hupham.

⁴⁰Bela's sons came from Ard and Naaman.

The Ardite family came from Ard.

The Naamite family came from Naaman.

⁴¹Those were the families of Benjamin. The number of the men was 45,600.

⁴²Here is the name of Dan's son. He is listed by his family.

The Shuhamite family came from Shuham.

That was the family of Dan. ⁴³All of the men in Dan's family were Shuhamites. The number of the men was 64,400.

⁴⁴Here are the names of Asher's sons. They are listed by their families.

The Imnite family came from Imnah.

The Ishvite family came from Ishvi.

The Beriite family came from Beriah.

⁴⁵Here are the names of the families that came from Beriah's sons.

The Heberite family came from Heber.

The Malkielite family came from Malkiel.

⁴⁶Asher also had a daughter named Serah.

47Those were the families of Asher. The number of the men was 53,400.

48Here are the names of Naphtali's sons. They are listed by their families.
The Jahzeelite family came from Jahzeel.
The Gunite family came from Guni.
49The Jezerite family came from Jezer.
The Shillemite family came from Shillem.
50Those were the families of Naphtali. The number of the men was 45,400.

51The total number of the men of Israel was 601,730.

52The LORD spoke to Moses. He said, **53**"I will give the land to them. The amount of land each family receives will be based on the number of its men. **54**Give a larger share to a larger family. Give a smaller share to a smaller family. Each family will receive its share based on the number of men who are listed in it. **55**"Be sure that you use lots when you give out the land. What each family receives will be based on the number of men listed in its tribe. **56**Use lots when you give out each share. Use lots for the larger and smaller families alike."

57Here are the names of the Levites. They are listed by their families.
The Gershonite family came from Gershon.
The Kohathite family came from Kohath.
The Merarite family came from Merari.
58Here are the names of the other Levite families. They are
the Libnite family,
the Hebronite family,
the Mahlite family,
the Mushite family,
the Korahite family.
Amram came from the Kohathite family.

59The name of Amram's wife was Jochebed. She was from the family line of Levi. She was born to the Levites in Egypt. Aaron, Moses and their sister Miriam were born in the family line of Amram and Jochebed.

60Aaron was the father of Nadab and Abihu. He was also the father of Eleazar and Ithamar. **61**But Nadab and Abihu made an offering to the LORD by using fire that wasn't allowed. So they died.

62The number of male Levites who were a month old or more was 23,000. They weren't listed along with the other men of Israel. That's because they didn't receive a share among them.

63Those are the men who were counted by Moses and the priest Eleazar. At that time the people of Israel were on the flatlands of Moab. They were by the Jordan River across from Jericho.

64The men of Israel had been counted before in the Sinai Desert by Moses and the priest Aaron. But not one of them was among the men who were counted this time. **65**The LORD had told the people of Israel at Kadesh Barnea that they would certainly die in the desert. Not one of them was left alive except Caleb, the son of Jephunneh, and Joshua, the son of Nun.

Zelophehad's Daughters

27 The daughters of Zelophehad belonged to the family groups of Manasseh. Zelophehad was the son of Hepher. Hepher was the son of Gilead. Gilead was the son of Makir. Makir was the son of Manasseh. And Manasseh was the son of Joseph. The names of Zelophehad's daughters were Mahlah, Noah, Hoglah, Milcah and Tirzah. They approached **2**the entrance to the Tent of Meeting. There they stood in front of Moses and the priest Eleazar. The leaders and the whole community were there too.

Zelophehad's daughters said, **3**"Our father died in the Sinai Desert. But he wasn't one of the men who followed Korah. He wasn't one of those who joined together against the LORD. Our father died because of his own sin. He didn't leave any sons.

4"Why should our father's name disappear from his family just because he didn't have a son? Give us property among our father's relatives."

5So Moses brought their case to the LORD. **6**The LORD spoke to him. He said, **7**"What Zelophehad's daughters are saying is right. You must certainly give them property. Give them a share among their father's relatives. Turn their father's property over to them.

8"Say to the people of Israel, 'Suppose a man dies who doesn't have a son. Then turn his property over to his daughter. **9**Suppose the man doesn't have a daughter. Then give his property to his brothers. **10**Suppose the man doesn't have any brothers. Then give his property to his father's brothers. ¹¹Suppose his father doesn't have any brothers. Then give his property to the nearest male relative in his family group. It will belong to him. That is what the law will require of the people of Israel. It is just as the LORD commanded me.' "

Joshua Becomes Israel's New Leader

¹²Then the LORD spoke to Moses. He said, "Go up this mountain in the Abarim range. See the land I have given the people of Israel. ¹³After you have seen it, you too will join the members of your family who have already died. You will die, just as your brother Aaron did.

¹⁴"The community refused to obey me at the waters of Meribah Kadesh. At that time, you and Aaron did not obey my command. You did not honor me in front of them as the holy God." Meribah Kadesh is in the Desert of Zin.

¹⁵Moses spoke to the LORD. He said, ¹⁶"LORD, you are the God who creates the spirits of all people. Please appoint a man to lead this community. ¹⁷Put him in charge of them. Tell him to take care of

FIVE SISTERS

NUMBERS 27:4

B

T

✦

"Why should our father's name disappear from his family just because he didn't have a son? Give us property among our father's relatives."

Five sisters walked slowly and bravely together up to the front of the Tent of Meeting. They were the daughters of Zelophehad (zel OH fuh had). Moses and the high priest stood there waiting. These women were doing something new in Israel.

"OUR FATHER DIED IN THE DESERT AND LEFT ONLY US—five daughters and no sons. It wouldn't be right for his name to die out of our family just because he had only daughters. Please, give us land in Israel so his name can continue."

Up to this time, only men could have land. But Moses went to God and asked him what to do. God agreed with these women. Each of them was given a piece of land in Israel, all because they were brave enough to ask.

BE LIKE THE FIVE SISTERS

Doing something you've never done before can be scary. These women must have been afraid when they talked to Moses. But their bravery gained them what they wanted. Be like them! Be brave! Do something you've never done before and trust God to be with you.

ZELOPHEHAD'S DAUGHTERS BRAVELY DID SOMETHING NEW.

Go to page 244 for the next Super Hero

WISE

W

JOSHUA, THE SON OF NUN, HAS THE ABILITY TO BE A WISE LEADER.
— NUMBERS 27:18 —

them. Then your people won't be like sheep that don't have a shepherd."

18So the LORD said to Moses, "Joshua, the son of Nun, has the ability to be a wise leader. Get him and place your hand on him. **19**Have him stand in front of the priest Eleazar and the whole community. Put him in charge while everyone is watching. **20**Give him some of your authority. Then the whole community of Israel will obey him.

21"Joshua will stand in front of the priest Eleazar. Eleazar will help him make decisions. Eleazar will get help from me by using the Urim. Joshua and the whole community of Israel must not make any move at all unless I command them to."

22Moses did just as the LORD commanded him. He got Joshua and had him stand in front of the priest Eleazar and the whole community. **23**Then Moses placed his hands on Joshua. And he put him in charge of the people. He did just as the LORD had directed through Moses.

Offerings That Israel Must Bring Each Day

28 The LORD spoke to Moses. He said, **2**"Here is a command I want you to give the people of Israel. Tell them, 'Be sure to bring to the LORD the food for the offerings that are made to him with fire. Do it at the appointed time. It will give a smell that is pleasant to him.'

3"Tell them, 'Here is the offering you must bring to the LORD. It should be made with fire. Bring him two lambs that are a

POWER-SURGE

OBEYS

✔

MOSES DID JUST AS THE LORD COMMANDED HIM.
— NUMBERS 27:22 —

year old. They must not have any flaws. Bring them as a regular burnt offering each day.

4"'Prepare one lamb in the morning. Prepare the other when the sun goes down. **5**Bring a grain offering along with them. It must have eight cups of fine flour. Mix it with a quart of oil that is made from pressed olives. **6**It is the regular burnt offering. The LORD established it at Mount Sinai. It has a pleasant smell. It is an offering that is made to him with fire. **7**Along with that, offer a quart of wine as a drink offering. It must be given along with each lamb. Pour out the drink offering to the LORD at the sacred tent.

8"'Prepare the second lamb when the sun goes down. Sacrifice it along with the same kind of grain offering and drink offering that you prepare in the morning. It is an offering that is made with fire. It gives a smell that is pleasant to the LORD.

Offerings That Israel Must Bring on the Sabbath Day

9"'On the Sabbath day, bring an offering of two lambs. They must be a year old. They must not have any flaws. Offer them along with their drink offering. Offer them along with a grain offering of 16 cups of fine flour. Mix it with olive oil. **10**It is the burnt offering for every Sabbath day. It is in addition to the regular burnt offering and its drink offering.

Offerings That Israel Must Bring Every Month

11"'On the first day of every month, bring to the LORD a burnt offering. Bring two young bulls and one ram. Also bring seven male lambs that are a year old. They must not have any flaws.

12"'Bring a grain offering along with each bull. It must have 24 cups of fine flour. Mix it with olive oil. Bring a grain offering along with the ram. It must have 16 cups of fine flour. Mix it with oil. **13**Bring a grain offering along with each lamb. It must have eight cups of fine flour. Mix it with oil. It is for a burnt offering. It has a pleasant smell. It is an offering that is made to the LORD with fire.

14"'Bring a drink offering along with each bull. It must have two quarts of wine. Offer two and a half pints along with the ram. And offer one quart along with each lamb.

"'It is the burnt offering for each month. It must be made on the day of each New Moon Feast during the year.

15"'One male goat must be brought to

the LORD as a sin offering. It is in addition to the regular burnt offering and its drink offering.

The Passover Feast

16 " 'The LORD's Passover Feast must be held on the 14th day of the first month. **17**On the 15th day of the month there must be a feast. For seven days eat bread that is made without yeast. **18**On the first day come together for a special service. Do not do any regular work.

19 " 'Bring to the LORD an offering that is made with fire. Bring a burnt offering of two young bulls and one ram. Also bring seven male lambs that are a year old. They must not have any flaws.

20 " 'Prepare a grain offering along with each bull. The offering must have 24 cups of fine flour. Mix it with olive oil. Offer 16 cups along with the ram. **21**Offer eight cups along with each of the seven lambs.

22 " 'Include a male goat as a sin offering. It will pay for your sin.

23 "Prepare everything in addition to the regular morning burnt offering. **24**Prepare the food in that way for the offering that is made with fire. Do it every day for seven days. The offering will give a smell that is pleasant to the LORD. You must prepare the offering in addition to the regular burnt offering and its drink offering.

25 " 'On the seventh day come together for a special service. Do not do any regular work.

The Feast of Weeks

26 " 'On the day you gather the first share of your crops, bring to the LORD an offering of your first grain. Do it during the Feast of Weeks. Come together for a special service. Do not do any regular work.

27 " 'Bring a burnt offering of two young bulls and one ram. Also bring seven male lambs that are a year old. The offering will give a smell that is pleasant to the LORD.

28 " 'Bring a grain offering along with each bull. It must have 24 cups of fine flour. Mix it with olive oil. Offer 16 cups along with the ram. **29**Offer eight cups along with each of the seven lambs.

30 " 'Include a male goat to pay for your sin.

31 " 'Prepare everything along with the drink offerings. Do it in addition to the regular burnt offering and its grain offering. Be sure the animals do not have any flaws.

The Feast of Trumpets

29 " 'On the first day of the seventh month, come together for a special service. Do not do any regular work. Blow the trumpets on that day.

2 " 'Prepare a burnt offering. It will give a smell that is pleasant to the LORD. Prepare one young bull and one ram. Also prepare seven male lambs that are a year old. They must not have any flaws.

3 " 'Prepare a grain offering along with the bull. It must have 24 cups of fine flour. Mix it with olive oil. Offer 16 cups along with the ram. **4**Offer eight cups along with each of the seven lambs.

5 " 'Include a male goat as a sin offering. It will pay for your sin.

6 " 'Each month and each day you must bring burnt offerings. Bring them along with their grain offerings and drink offerings as they are required.

" 'The offerings for the Feast of Trumpets are in addition to them. They are offerings that are made to the LORD with fire. They have a pleasant smell.

The Day When Sin Is Paid For

7 " 'On the tenth day of the seventh month, come together for a special service. You must not eat anything on that day. You must not do any work on it.

8 " 'Bring a burnt offering. It will give a smell that is pleasant to the LORD. Bring one young bull and one ram. Also bring seven male lambs that are a year old. They must not have any flaws.

9 " 'Prepare a grain offering along with the bull. It must have 24 cups of fine flour. Mix it with olive oil. Offer 16 cups along with the ram. **10**Offer eight cups along with each of the seven lambs.

11 " 'Include a male goat as a sin offering. It is in addition to the offering that pays for sin. It is in addition to the regular burnt offering along with its grain offering. It is also in addition to their drink offerings.

The Feast of Booths

12 " 'On the 15th day of the seventh month, come together for a special service. Do not do any regular work. Celebrate the Feast of Booths in honor of the LORD for seven days.

13 " 'Bring an offering that is made with fire. It will give a smell that is pleasant to the LORD. Bring a burnt offering of 13 young bulls and two rams. Also bring 14 male lambs that are a year old. They must not have any flaws.

14 " 'Prepare a grain offering along with

each of the 13 bulls. It must have 24 cups of fine flour. Mix it with olive oil. Offer 16 cups along with each of the two rams. **15**Offer eight cups along with each of the 14 lambs.

16 'Include a male goat as a sin offering. It is in addition to the regular burnt offering. It is also in addition to its grain offering and drink offering.

17 'On the second day prepare 12 young bulls and two rams. Also prepare 14 male lambs that are a year old. They must not have any flaws.

18 'Prepare their grain offerings and drink offerings. Prepare them along with the bulls, rams and lambs. Prepare them in keeping with the required number.

19 'Include a male goat as a sin offering. It is in addition to the regular burnt offering along with its grain offering. It is also in addition to their drink offerings.

20 'On the third day prepare 11 bulls and two rams. Also prepare 14 male lambs that are a year old. They must not have any flaws.

21 'Prepare their grain offerings and drink offerings. Prepare them along with the bulls, rams and lambs. Prepare them in keeping with the required number.

22 'Include a male goat as a sin offering. It is in addition to the regular burnt offering. It is also in addition to its grain offering and drink offering.

23 'On the fourth day prepare ten bulls and two rams. Also prepare 14 male lambs that are a year old. They must not have any flaws.

24 'Prepare their grain offerings and drink offerings. Prepare them along with the bulls, rams and lambs. Prepare them in keeping with the required number.

25 'Include a male goat as a sin offering. It is in addition to the regular burnt offering. It is also in addition to its grain offering and drink offering.

26 'On the fifth day prepare nine bulls and two rams. Also prepare 14 male lambs that are a year old. They must not have any flaws.

27 'Prepare their grain offerings and drink offerings. Prepare them along with the bulls, rams and lambs. Prepare them in keeping with the required number.

28 'Include a male goat as a sin offering. It is in addition to the regular burnt offering. It is also in addition to its grain offering and drink offering.

29 'On the sixth day prepare eight bulls and two rams. Also prepare 14 male lambs that are a year old. They must not have any flaws.

30 'Prepare their grain offerings and drink offerings. Prepare them along with the bulls, rams and lambs. Prepare them in keeping with the required number.

31 'Include a male goat as a sin offering. It is in addition to the regular burnt offering. It is also in addition to its grain offering and drink offering.

32 'On the seventh day prepare seven bulls and two rams. Also prepare 14 male lambs that are a year old. They must not have any flaws.

33 'Prepare their grain offerings and drink offerings. Prepare them along with the bulls, rams and lambs. Prepare them in keeping with the required number.

34 'Include a male goat as a sin offering. It is in addition to the regular burnt offering. It is also in addition to its grain offering and drink offering.

35 'On the eighth day come together for a sacred service. Do not do any regular work.

36 'Bring an offering that is made with fire. It will give a smell that is pleasant to the LORD. Bring a burnt offering of one bull and one ram. Also bring seven male lambs that are a year old. They must not have any flaws.

37 'Prepare their grain offerings and drink offerings. Prepare them along with the bull, the ram and the lambs. Prepare them in keeping with the required number.

38 'Include a male goat as a sin offering. It is in addition to the regular burnt offering. It is also in addition to the grain offering and drink offering.

39 'Here are the offerings you must prepare for the LORD at your appointed feasts. They are burnt offerings, grain offerings, drink offerings and friendship offerings. They are in addition to the offerings you bring to keep a special promise you make to the LORD. They are also in addition to the offerings you choose to give.' "

40Moses told the people of Israel everything the LORD had commanded him.

Oaths and Special Promises

30 Moses spoke to the heads of the tribes of Israel. He said, "Here is what the LORD commands. **2**Suppose a man makes a special promise to the LORD. Or suppose he takes an oath and agrees to do something. Then he must keep his promise. He must do everything he said he would do.

3"Suppose a young woman is still living in her father's house. She makes a special promise to the LORD. Or she takes an oath and agrees to do something. ⁴"Suppose her father hears about her promise or oath. And he doesn't say anything to her about it. Then she must keep her promise. She must do what she agreed to do. ⁵"But suppose her father doesn't allow her to keep her promises when he hears about them. Then she doesn't have to do what she promised or agreed to do. The LORD will set her free. He'll do it because her father hasn't allowed her to keep her promises.

⁶"Suppose she gets married after she makes a special promise. Or she gets married after agreeing to do something without thinking it through. ⁷Suppose her husband hears about what she did. And he doesn't say anything to her about it. Then she must keep her promise. She must do what she agreed to do.

⁸"But suppose her husband doesn't allow her to keep her promises when he hears about them. Then she doesn't have to do what she promised. She doesn't have to do what she agreed to do without thinking it through. The LORD will set her free.

⁹"Suppose a widow makes a special promise. Or suppose she takes an oath and agrees to do something. Then she must keep her promise. She must do what she agreed to do. The same rules apply to a woman who has been divorced.

¹⁰"Suppose a woman who is living with her husband makes a special promise. Or she takes an oath and agrees to do something. ¹¹Suppose her husband hears about what she did. He doesn't say anything to her about it. And he doesn't try to stop her from keeping her promises. Then she must keep her promise. She must do what she agreed to do.

¹²"But suppose her husband doesn't allow her to keep her promises when he hears about them. Then she doesn't have to do what she agreed to do. Her husband has kept her from doing what she said she would do. The LORD will set her free.

¹³"Her husband can let her keep any special promise she makes. Or he can refuse to let her keep it.

"Suppose she takes an oath and agrees not to eat anything. Then her husband can let her keep her promise. Or he can refuse to let her keep it.

¹⁴"But suppose day after day her husband doesn't say anything to her about

what she did. Then he lets her keep all of her promises. He lets her do everything she agreed to do. That's because he didn't say anything to her when he heard about what she had done.

¹⁵"But suppose some time after he hears about her promises he doesn't let her keep them. Then she will be guilty. But he will be held accountable for it."

¹⁶Those are the rules the LORD gave Moses about a man and his wife. And those are the rules the LORD gave about a father and his young daughter who is still living in his house.

The LORD Punishes the People of Midian

31 The LORD spoke to Moses. He said, ²"Pay the people of Midian back for what they did to the Israelites. After that, you will join the members of your family who have already died."

³So Moses said to the people, "Prepare some of your men for battle. They must go to war against Midian. They will carry out the LORD's plan to punish Midian. ⁴Send 1,000 men from each of the tribes of Israel into battle." ⁵So Moses prepared 12,000 men for battle. There were 1,000 from each tribe. They came from the families of Israel.

⁶Moses sent them into battle. He sent 1,000 from each tribe. The priest Phinehas went along with them. Phinehas was the son of Eleazar. Phinehas took some articles from the sacred tent with him. He also took the trumpets. The trumpet blasts would tell the people what to do and when to do it.

⁷They fought against Midian, just as the LORD had commanded Moses. They killed every man. ⁸Evi, Rekem, Zur, Hur and Reba were among the men they killed. Those men were the five kings of Midian. The people of Israel also killed Balaam, the son of Beor, with a sword.

⁹They captured the women and children of Midian. They took for themselves all of the herds, flocks and goods.

¹⁰They burned up all of the towns where the people of Midian had settled. They also burned up all of their camps.

¹¹They carried off everything they had taken. That included the people and the animals. ¹²They brought back to Israel's camp the prisoners and everything else they had taken. They took them to Moses and to the priest Eleazar. They brought them to the whole community. Israel was camped on the flatlands of Moab. They

were by the Jordan River across from Jericho.

13Moses and the priest Eleazar went to meet them outside the camp. So did all of the leaders of the community. 14Moses was angry with the officers of the army who had returned from the battle. Some of them were the commanders of thousands of men. Others were the commanders of hundreds.

15"Have you let all of the women remain alive?" Moses asked them. 16"The women followed Balaam's advice. They caused the people of Israel to turn away from the LORD. The people worshiped the god Baal that was worshiped at Peor. So a plague struck them. 17Kill all of the boys. And kill every woman who has made love to a man. 18But save for yourselves every woman who has never made love to a man.

19"All of you who have killed anyone must stay outside the camp for seven days. And all of you who have touched anyone who was killed must do the same thing. On the third and seventh days you must make yourselves pure. You must also make your prisoners pure. 20Make all of your clothes pure and clean. Everything that is made out of leather, goat hair or wood must be made pure."

21Then the priest Eleazar spoke to the soldiers who had gone into battle. He said, "Here is what the law the LORD gave Moses requires. 22All of your gold, silver, bronze, iron, tin and lead 23must be put through fire. So must everything else that doesn't burn up. Then those things will be 'clean.' But they must also be made pure with the special water. In fact, everything that won't burn up must be put through that water. 24On the seventh day wash your clothes. And you will be 'clean.' Then you can come into the camp."

The People Divide Up What They Had Taken

25The LORD spoke to Moses. He said, 26"Here is what you and the priest Eleazar and the family heads of the community must do. You must count all of the people and animals you took. 27Divide up some of what you took with the soldiers who fought in the battle. Divide up the rest with the others in the community.

28"Set apart a gift for me. Take something from the soldiers who fought in the battle. Set apart one out of every 500 people, cattle, donkeys, sheep and goats.

29Take my gift from the soldiers' half. Give it to the priest Eleazar. It is my share.

30"Also take something from the half that belongs to the people of Israel. Choose one out of every 50 people, cattle, donkeys, sheep, goats or other animals. Give them to the Levites. They are accountable for taking care of my holy tent."

31So Moses and the priest Eleazar did just as the LORD had commanded Moses.

32What the soldiers took included 675,000 sheep. 33There were also 72,000 cattle 34and 61,000 donkeys. 35And there were 32,000 women who had never made love to a man.

36Here is the half that belonged to those who had fought in the battle.

There were 337,500 sheep. 37From among them, the LORD's gift was 675.

38There were 36,000 cattle. From among them, the LORD's gift was 72.

39There were 30,500 donkeys. From among them, the LORD's gift was 61.

40There were 16,000 women. From among them, the LORD's gift was 32.

41Moses gave the gift to the priest Eleazar. It was the LORD's share. Moses did just as the LORD had commanded him.

42The other half belonged to the people of Israel. Moses set it apart from what belonged to the fighting men. 43The community's half was 337,500 sheep, 4436,000 cattle, 4530,500 donkeys 46and 16,000 women. 47Moses chose one out of every 50 people and animals. He gave them to the Levites. They were accountable for taking care of the LORD's holy tent. Moses did just as the LORD had commanded him.

48Then the army officers went to Moses. Some of them were the commanders of thousands of men. Others were the commanders of hundreds. 49All of them said to Moses, "We have counted the soldiers under our command. Not a single one is missing.

50"So we've brought an offering to the LORD. We've brought the gold articles each of us took in the battle. We've also brought armbands, bracelets, rings, earrings and necklaces. We've brought them to pay for our sin in the sight of the LORD."

51Moses and the priest Eleazar accepted the beautiful gold articles from the army officers. 52The gold that was received from the commanders of thousands and commanders of hundreds weighed 420 pounds. Moses and Eleazar offered all of it as a gift to the LORD. 53Each soldier had taken things from the battle for himself. 54Moses and the priest Eleazar accepted the gold from all of the commanders. They brought it into the Tent of Meeting. It reminded the LORD of the people of Israel.

The Tribes on the East Side of the Jordan River

32 The tribes of Reuben and Gad had very large herds and flocks. They looked at the lands of Jazer and Gilead. They saw that those lands were just right for livestock.

2So they came to Moses and the priest Eleazar. They also came to the leaders of the community. They said, 3"We have seen the cities of Ataroth, Dibon, Jazer, Nimrah and Heshbon. We've seen Elealeh, Sebam, Nebo and Beon. 4All of them are in the land the LORD has brought under Israel's control. This land is just right for livestock. And we have livestock.

5"We hope you are pleased with us," they continued. "If you are, please give us this land. Then it will belong to us. But don't make us go across the Jordan River."

6Moses spoke to the people of Gad and Reuben. He said, "Should the rest of us go to war while you stay here? 7The LORD has given the land of Canaan to the people of Israel. So why would you want to keep them from going over into it?

8"That's what your fathers did. I sent them from Kadesh Barnea to check out the land. 9They went up to the Valley of Eshcol and looked at the land. Then they talked the people of Israel out of entering the land the LORD had given them.

10"The LORD's anger was stirred up that day. So he took an oath and made a promise. He said, 11'Not one of the men who is 20 years old or more who came up out of Egypt will see the land. They have not followed me with their whole heart. I took an oath and promised to give the land to Abraham, Isaac and Jacob.

12" 'But not one of these men will see it except Caleb and Joshua. Caleb is the son of Jephunneh, the Kenizzite. And Joshua is the son of Nun. They will see the land. They followed me with their whole heart.'

13"The LORD's anger burned against Israel. He made them wander around in the desert for 40 years. They wandered until all of the people who had done evil in his sight had died.

14"Now here you are, you bunch of sinners! You have taken the place of your fathers. And you are making the LORD even more angry with Israel. 15What if you turn away from following him? Then he'll leave all of these people in the desert again. And it will be your fault when they are destroyed."

16Then they came up to Moses. They said, "We would like to build pens here for our livestock. We would also like to build cities for our women and children.

17"But we're ready to prepare ourselves for battle. We're even ready to go ahead of the people of Israel. We'll go with them until we've brought them to their place. While we're gone, our women and children will live in cities that have high walls around them. That will keep them safe from the people who are living in this land.

18"We won't return to our homes until all of the people of Israel have received their share of the land.

19"We won't receive any share with them on the west side of the Jordan River. We've already received our share here on the east side."

20Then Moses said to them, "Do what you have promised to do. Prepare yourselves to fight for the LORD. 21Prepare yourselves and go across the Jordan River. Fight for the LORD until he has driven out his enemies in front of him.

22"When the land is under the LORD's control, you can come back here. Your duty to the LORD and Israel will be over. Then the LORD will give you this land as your own.

23"But what if you fail to do your duty? Then you will be sinning against the LORD. And you can be sure that your sin will be discovered. It will be brought out into the open.

24"So build up cities for your women and children. Make sheep pens for your flocks. But do what you have promised to do."

25The people of Gad and Reuben spoke to Moses. They said, "We will do just as you command. 26Our children and wives will remain here in the cities of Gilead. So will our flocks and herds. 27But we will prepare ourselves for battle. We'll go across the Jordan River and fight for the LORD. We will do just as you have said."

28Then Moses gave orders about them to the priest Eleazar. He gave the same orders to Joshua, the son of Nun. He also spoke to the family heads of the tribes of Israel.

29He said, "The men of Gad and Reuben must prepare themselves for battle. They must go across the Jordan River with you. They must help you fight for the LORD. They must stay with you until the land has been brought under your control. If they do, give them the land of Gilead as their own.

30"But what if they don't get ready for battle? What if they don't go across the Jordan with you? Then they must accept a share with you in Canaan."

31The people of Gad and Reuben gave their answer. They said, "We will do what the LORD has said. **32**We'll get ready for battle. We'll go across the Jordan into Canaan. We'll fight for the LORD there. But the property we receive will be on this side of the Jordan River."

33Then Moses gave their land to them. He gave it to the tribes of Gad and Reuben and half of the tribe of Manasseh. Manasseh was Joseph's son. One part of that land had belonged to the kingdom of Sihon, the king of the Amorites. The other part had belonged to the kingdom of Og, the king of Bashan. Moses gave that whole land to those two and a half tribes. It included its cities and the territory around them.

34The people of Gad built up the cities of Dibon, Ataroth and Aroer. **35**They built up Atroth Shophan, Jazer, Jogbehah, **36**Beth Nimrah and Beth Haran. They built a high wall around each of those cities. They also built sheep pens for their flocks.

37The people of Reuben built up Heshbon, Elealeh and Kiriathaim. **38**They also built up Nebo, Baal Meon and Sibmah. They gave new names to the cities they had built up.

39The people of Makir, the son of Manasseh, went to the land of Gilead. They captured it. They drove out the Amorites who were living there. **40**So Moses gave Gilead to the people of Makir, the son of Manasseh. And they settled there. **41**Jair was a man in the family line of Manasseh. Jair captured Gilead's settlements. He called them Havvoth Jair. **42**Nobah captured Kenath and the settlements that were around it. He named it after himself.

The Places Where Israel Stopped During Their Journey

33 Here are the places where the people of Israel stopped during their journey. When they came out of Egypt, they marched in companies like an army.

Moses and Aaron led them. **2**The LORD commanded Moses to record their journey. Here are the places where they stopped.

3The people of Israel started out from Rameses. It was the 15th day of the first month. It was the day after the Passover Feast. They marched out boldly in plain sight of all of the Egyptians. **4**The Egyptians were burying all of their oldest sons. The LORD had struck them down. He had done it when he punished their gods.

5The people of Israel left Rameses and camped at Succoth.

6They left Succoth and camped at Etham. Etham was on the edge of the desert.

7They left Etham and turned back to Pi Hahiroth. It was east of Baal Zephon. They camped near Migdol.

8They left Pi Hahiroth. Then they passed through the Red Sea into the desert. They traveled for three days in the Desert of Etham. Then they camped at Marah.

9They left Marah and went to Elim. Twelve springs and 70 palm trees were there. So they camped at Elim.

10They left Elim and camped by the Red Sea.

11They left the Red Sea and camped in the Desert of Sin.

12They left the Desert of Sin and camped at Dophkah.

13They left Dophkah and camped at Alush.

14They left Alush and camped at Rephidim. But there was no water there for the people to drink.

15They left Rephidim and camped in the Desert of Sinai.

16They left the Desert of Sinai and camped at Kibroth Hattaavah.

17They left Kibroth Hattaavah and camped at Hazeroth.

18They left Hazeroth and camped at Rithmah.

19They left Rithmah and camped at Rimmon Perez.

20They left Rimmon Perez and camped at Libnah.

21They left Libnah and camped at Rissah.

22They left Rissah and camped at Kehelathah.

23They left Kehelathah and camped at Mount Shepher.

24They left Mount Shepher and camped at Haradah.

25They left Haradah and camped at Makheloth.

26They left Makheloth and camped at Tahath.

27They left Tahath and camped at Terah.

28They left Terah and camped at Mithcah.

29They left Mithcah and camped at Hashmonah.

30They left Hashmonah and camped at Moseroth.

31They left Moseroth and camped at Bene Jaakan.

32They left Bene Jaakan and camped at Hor Haggidgad.

33They left Hor Haggidgad and camped at Jotbathah.

34They left Jotbathah and camped at Abronah.

35They left Abronah and camped at Ezion Geber.

36They left Ezion Geber and camped at Kadesh. Kadesh was in the Desert of Zin.

37They left Kadesh and camped at Mount Hor. It was on the border of Edom.

38The priest Aaron went up Mount Hor when the LORD commanded him to. That's where he died. It happened on the first day of the fifth month. It was the 40th year after the people of Israel came out of Egypt. **39**Aaron was 123 years old when he died on Mount Hor.

40The Canaanite king of Arad lived in the Negev Desert in Canaan. He heard that the people of Israel were coming.

41They left Mount Hor and camped at Zalmonah.

42They left Zalmonah and camped at Punon.

43They left Punon and camped at Oboth.

44They left Oboth and camped at Iye Abarim. It was on the border of Moab.

45They left Iyim and camped at Dibon Gad.

46They left Dibon Gad and camped at Almon Diblathaim.

47They left Almon Diblathaim and camped in the mountain range of Abarim near Nebo.

48They left the mountain range of Abarim and camped on the flatlands of Moab. They were by the Jordan River across from Jericho. **49**They camped there along the Jordan River from Beth Jeshimoth to Abel Shittim.

50On the flatlands of Moab the LORD spoke to Moses. He spoke to him by the Jordan River across from Jericho. The LORD said, **51**"Speak to the people of Israel. Tell them, 'Go across the Jordan River into Canaan. **52**Drive out all those who are living in the land. The statues of their gods are made out of stone and metal. Destroy all of those statues. And destroy all of the high places where they are worshiped.

53" 'Take the land as your own. Settle down in it. I have given it to you. **54**Use lots when you give out the land. Do it based on the number of men who are in each tribe and family. Give a larger share to a larger group. And give a smaller group a smaller share. The share they receive by using lots will belong to them. Give out the shares based on the number of men in Israel's tribes.

55" 'But suppose you do not drive out the people who are living in the land. Then those you allow to remain there will become like needles in your eyes. They will become like thorns in your sides. They will give you trouble in the land where you will live. **56**Then I will do to you what I plan to do to them.' "

Israel Arrives at the Borders of Canaan

34 The LORD spoke to Moses. He said, **2**"Give the people of Israel a command. Tell them, 'You are going to enter Canaan. The land will be given to you as your own. Here are the borders it will have.

3" 'Your southern border will include some of the Desert of Zin. It will be along the border of Edom. On the east, your southern border will start from the end of the Dead Sea. **4**It will cross south of Scorpion Pass. It will continue on to Zin. From there it will go south of Kadesh Barnea. Then it will go to Hazar Addar and over to Azmon. **5**There it will turn and join the Wadi of Egypt. It will come to an end at the Mediterranean Sea.

6" 'Your western border will be the coast of the Mediterranean Sea. That will be your border on the west.

7" 'For your northern border, run a line from the Mediterranean Sea to Mount Hor. **8**Continue it from Mount Hor to Lebo Hamath. Then the border will go to Zedad. **9**It will continue to Ziphron. It will come to an end at Hazar Enan. That will be your border on the north.

10 " 'For your eastern border, run a line from Hazar Enan to Shepham. **11** The border will go down from Shepham to Riblah. Riblah is on the east side of Ain. From there the border will continue along the slopes east of the Sea of Galilee. **12** Then the border will go down along the Jordan River. It will come to an end at the Dead Sea.

" 'That will be your land. And those will be its borders on every side.' "

13 Moses gave the people of Israel a command. He said, "Use lots when you give out the land. Each tribe will have its own share. The LORD has ordered it to be given to the nine and a half tribes.

14 "The families of the tribes of Reuben and Gad have already received their shares. The families of half of the tribe of Manasseh have also received their share. **15** Those two and a half tribes have received their shares east of the Jordan River. It flows near Jericho. Their land is toward the sunrise."

16 The LORD spoke to Moses. He said, **17** "Here are the names of the men who will give out the shares of the land to your people. They are the priest Eleazar and Joshua, the son of Nun. **18** Also appoint one leader from each tribe to help give out the land. **19** Here are their names.

"Caleb, the son of Jephunneh,
    is from the tribe of Judah.
20 Shemuel, the son of Ammihud,
    is from the tribe of Simeon.
21 Elidad, the son of Kislon,
    is from the tribe of Benjamin.
22 Bukki, the son of Jogli,
    is the leader from the tribe of Dan.
23 Hanniel, the son of Ephod,
    is the leader from the tribe of Manasseh. Manasseh was the son of Joseph.
24 Kemuel, the son of Shiphtan,
    is the leader from the tribe of Ephraim. Ephraim was the son of Joseph.
25 Elizaphan, the son of Parnach,
    is the leader from the tribe of Zebulun.
26 Paltiel, the son of Azzan,
    is the leader from the tribe of Issachar.
27 Ahihud, the son of Shelomi,
    is the leader from the tribe of Asher.
28 Pedahel, the son of Ammihud,

is the leader from the tribe of Naphtali."

29 Those are the men the LORD commanded to give out the shares of the land. They were commanded to give them to Israel in the land of Canaan.

The Levites Receive Their Towns

35 On the flatlands of Moab, the LORD spoke to Moses. It was by the Jordan River across from Jericho. The LORD said, **2** "Command the people of Israel to give the Levites towns to live in. The towns must come from the shares of land the people will have as their own. Also give the Levites the grasslands that are around the towns. **3** Then the Levites will have towns to live in. They will also have grasslands that are for their cattle, flocks and all of their other livestock.

4 "The grasslands that are around each town you give them will go out to 1,500 feet from the town wall. **5** Outside each town, the east side will measure 3,000 feet. The south side will measure 3,000 feet. The west side will measure 3,000 feet. And the north side will measure 3,000 feet. The town must be in the center. The Levites will have the area around it as grasslands.

Cities to Go to for Safety

6 "Six of the towns you give the Levites will be cities to go to for safety. A person who has killed someone can run to one of them. Also give the Levites 42 other towns. **7** You must give the Levites a total of 48 towns. Also give them the grasslands that are around the towns.

8 "The towns you give the Levites must come from the land the people of Israel have as their own. So the number you give from each tribe will depend on the size of that tribe's share. Take many towns from a tribe that has many. But take only a few towns from a tribe that has only a few."

9 Then the LORD spoke to Moses. He said, **10** "Speak to the people of Israel. Tell them, 'You will soon go across the Jordan River. You will enter Canaan. **11** When you do, choose the cities to go to for safety. People who have killed someone by accident can run to one of those cities. **12** They will be places of safety for them. People will be safe there from those who want to kill them. Then those who are charged with murder will not die before their case has been brought to the community court.

13 " 'Six towns will be the cities you can

go to for safety. **14**Three will be east of the Jordan River. The other three will be in Canaan.

15" 'Those six towns will be places where the people of Israel can go for safety. Outsiders and any other people living in Israel can also go to them for safety. So anyone who has killed another person by accident can run there.

16" 'Suppose a person uses an iron object to hit and kill someone. Then he is a murderer. He must be put to death. **17**Or suppose a person is holding a stone that could kill. And he uses it to hit and kill someone. Then he is a murderer. He must be put to death. **18**Or suppose a person is holding a wooden object that could kill. And he uses it to hit and kill someone. Then he is a murderer. He must be put to death.

19" 'The dead person's nearest male relative should kill the murderer. When he meets him, he should kill him.

20" 'What if a person makes evil plans against someone else? And what if that person pushes him so that he dies? Or what if that person throws something at him so that he dies? **21**Or what if that person hits the other person with a fist so that the other dies? Then the person who does any of those things must be put to death. He is a murderer.

" 'The dead person's nearest male relative should kill the murderer. When he meets him, he should kill him.

22" 'But what if a person suddenly pushes someone else without being angry? Or what if that person throws something at him without meaning to? **23**Or what if that person does not see him and drops a stone on him that kills him? He was not the dead person's enemy. He did not mean to harm him.

24" 'Then the court must decide between the person who did the act and the nearest male relative of the one who was killed. Here are the rules the court must follow.

25" 'The court must provide a safe place for the person who is charged with murder. It must keep him safe from those who want to kill him. The court must send him back to the city he ran to for safety. He must stay there until the high priest dies. The priest is the one who has been anointed with the holy oil.

26" 'But suppose the one who has been charged with murder goes outside that city. **27**And suppose the dead person's nearest male relative finds that one outside the city. Then the relative can kill the one who has been charged. The relative will not be guilty of murder.

28" 'The one who has been charged must stay in that city until the high priest dies. Only then can the one who has been charged return home.

29" 'That is what the law requires of you for all time to come. It will apply to you no matter where you live.

30" 'Suppose a person kills someone. That person must be put to death as a murderer. But do it only when there are witnesses who can tell what happened. Do not put anyone to death if only one witness tells what happened.

31" 'Do not accept payment for a murderer's life. He should die. He must certainly be put to death.

32" 'Do not accept payment for anyone who has run to a city for safety. Do not let him buy his freedom to return home. He must not go back and live on his own land before the high priest dies.

33" 'Do not pollute the land where you are. Murder pollutes the land. Only one thing can pay to remove the pollution in the land where murder has been committed. The blood of the one who spilled another's blood must be spilled. **34**So do not make the land where you live "unclean." I live there too. I live among the people of Israel. I am the LORD.' "

The Property Zelophehad's Daughters Will Receive

36 The heads of the families of Gilead came to Moses. Gilead was the son of Makir. The family heads were from the tribe of Manasseh. So they were in the family line of Joseph. They spoke to Moses in front of the leaders of the families of Israel.

2They said, "The LORD commanded you to give shares of the land to the people of Israel. He told you to use lots when you do it. At that time the LORD ordered you to give our brother Zelophehad's share to his daughters.

3"Suppose they get married to men who are from other tribes in Israel. Then their share will be taken away from our family's land. It will be added to the land of the tribe they marry into. So a part of the share that was given to us will be taken away. **4**The Year of Jubilee for the people of Israel will come. Then their share will be added to the land of the tribe they marry into. Their land will be taken away from the share that was given to our tribe."

5Then the LORD gave a command to Moses. He told Moses to give an order to the people of Israel. Moses said, "What the tribe in the family line of Joseph is saying is right.

6 "Here is what the LORD commands for Zelophehad's daughters. They can get married to anyone they want to. But they have to get married to someone in their own family's tribe.

7 "Property in Israel must not pass from one tribe to another. Everyone in Israel must keep his family's share of his tribe's land.

8 "Suppose a daughter in any tribe of Israel receives land from her parents. Then she must get married to someone in her father's family and tribe. In that way, every family's share will remain in its family line in Israel.

9 "Property can't pass from one tribe to another. Each tribe of Israel must keep the land it receives."

10 So Zelophehad's daughters did just as the LORD commanded Moses. 11 The names of the daughters were Mahlah, Tirzah, Hoglah, Milcah and Noah. All of them got married to their cousins on their father's side. 12 They married men who were in the family line of Manasseh, the son of Joseph. So the land they received remained in their father's family and tribe.

13 Those are the commands and rules the LORD gave through Moses. He gave them to the people of Israel on the flatlands of Moab. They were by the Jordan River across from Jericho.

DEUTERONOMY

The book of Deuteronomy records Moses' last speeches to the people of Israel before he dies. He recalls their years together since they left Egypt, helping everyone remember the exciting events of leaving Egypt and wandering in the desert. Moses reminds the people of God's faithfulness to them. He wants the people to try their hardest to follow God. Read Deuteronomy to understand how much God loves his people (including you) and wants them to love and follow him.

CODE OF HONOR IN THIS BOOK . . .

BRAVE
PAGES 207, 236

STRONG
PAGES 207, 236, 241

OBEYS
PAGES 209, 210, 211, 213, 222, 230

BELIEVES
PAGE 216

The LORD Commands Israel to Leave Mount Horeb

1 These are the words Moses spoke to all of the people of Israel. At that time, they were in the desert east of the Jordan River. It's in the Arabah Valley across from Suph. They were between Paran and Tophel, Laban, Hazeroth and Dizahab. 2It takes 11 days to go from Mount Horeb to Kadesh Barnea if you travel on the Mount Seir road.

3It was now the 40th year since the people of Israel had left Egypt. On the first day of the 11th month, Moses spoke to them. He told them everything the LORD had commanded him to tell them. 4They had already won the battle over Sihon. Sihon was the king of the Amorites. He had ruled in Heshbon. Israel had also won the battle over Og at Edrei. Og was the king of Bashan. He had ruled in Ashtaroth.

5The people were east of the Jordan River in the territory of Moab. There Moses began to explain the law. Here is what he said.

6The LORD our God spoke to us at Mount Horeb. He said, "You have stayed long enough at this mountain. 7Take your tents down. Go into the hill country of the Amorites. Go to all of the people who are their neighbors. Go to the people who live in the Arabah Valley. Travel to the mountains and the western hills. Go to the people in the Negev Desert and along the coast. Travel to the land of Canaan and to Lebanon. Go as far as the great Euphrates River.

8"I have given you all of that land. Go in and take it as your own. I took an oath. I promised I would give the land to your fathers. I promised it to Abraham, Isaac and Jacob. I also said I would give it to their children after them."

Some Officials Help Moses

9At that time I spoke to you. I said, "You are too heavy a load for me to carry alone. 10The LORD your God has increased your numbers. Today you are as many as the stars in the sky. 11The LORD is the God of your people. May he increase your numbers a thousand times. May he bless you, just as he promised he would. 12But I can't handle your problems and troubles all by myself. I can't settle your arguments.

13"So choose some wise men from each of your tribes. They must understand how to give good advice. The people must have

respect for them. I will appoint those men to have authority over you."

14You answered me, "Your suggestion is good."

15So I took the leading men of your tribes who were wise and respected. I appointed them to have authority over you. I made them commanders of thousands, hundreds, fifties and tens. I appointed them to be officials over the tribes.

16Here is what I commanded your judges at that time. I said, "Listen to your people's cases when they argue with one another. Judge them fairly. It doesn't matter whether the case is between fellow Israelites or between an Israelite and an outsider. 17When you judge them, treat everyone the same. Listen to those who are important and those who are not. Don't be afraid of any man. God is the highest judge. Bring me any case that is too hard for you. I'll listen to it." 18At that time I told you everything you should do.

Twelve Men Check Out the Land of Canaan

19The LORD our God commanded us to start out from Mount Horeb. So we did. We went toward the hill country of the Amorites. We traveled all through the huge and terrible desert you saw. Finally, we reached Kadesh Barnea.

20Then I said to you, "You have reached the hill country of the Amorites. The LORD our God is giving it to us. 21The LORD your God has given you the land. Go up and take it. Do what the LORD says. He's the God of your people. Don't be afraid. Don't lose hope."

22Then all of you came to me. You said, "Let's send some men ahead of us. They can check out the land for us and bring back a report. They can suggest to us which way to go. They can tell us about the towns we'll come to."

23That seemed like a good idea to me. So I chose 12 of you. I picked one man from each tribe. 24They left and went up into the hill country. There they came to the Valley of Eshcol. They checked it out. 25They got some of the fruit of that land. They brought it down to us and gave us their report. They said, "The LORD our God is giving us a good land."

Israel Refuses to Obey the LORD

26But you wouldn't go up. You refused to obey the command of the LORD your God. 27You spoke against him in your tents. You said, "The LORD hates us. That's why he brought us out of Egypt to hand us over to the Amorites. He wanted to destroy us. **28**Where can we go? The men who checked out the land have made us lose hope. They say, 'The people are stronger and taller than we are. The cities are large. They have walls that reach up to the sky. We even saw the Anakites there.' "

29Then I said to you, "Don't be terrified. Don't be afraid of them. **30**The LORD your God will go ahead of you. He will fight for you. With your own eyes you saw how he fought for you in Egypt.

31"You also saw how the LORD your God brought you through the desert. He carried you everywhere you went, just as a father carries his son. And now you have arrived here."

32In spite of that, you didn't trust in the LORD your God. **33**He went ahead of you on your journey. He was in the fire at night and in the cloud during the day. He found places for you to camp. He showed you the way you should go.

34The LORD heard what you said. So he became angry. He took an oath and made a promise. He said, **35**"I promised to give this good land to your people long ago. But not one of you evil men who are alive today will see it.

36"Only Caleb will see the land. He is the son of Jephunneh. I will give him and his children after him the land he walked on. He followed me with his whole heart."

37Because of you, the LORD became angry with me also. He said, "You will not enter the land either. **38**But Joshua, the son of Nun, is your helper. Joshua will enter the land. Help him to be brave. Give him hope. He will lead Israel to take the land as their own.

39"You said your little ones would be taken prisoner. But they will enter the land. They do not know right from wrong yet. But I will give them the land. They will take it as their own. **40**As for you, turn around. Start out toward the desert. Go along the road that leads to the Red Sea."

41Then you replied, "We have sinned against the LORD. We will go up and fight. We'll do just as the LORD our God has commanded us." So all of you got your swords and put them on. You thought it would be easy to go up into the hill country.

42But the LORD spoke to me. He said, "Tell them, 'Do not go up and fight. I will not be with you. Your enemies will win the battle over you.' "

43So I told you what the LORD said. But you wouldn't listen. You refused to obey his command. You were so filled with pride that you marched up into the hill country. **44**The Amorites who lived in those hills came out and attacked you. Like large numbers of bees they chased you. They beat you down from Seir all the way to Hormah.

45You came back and sobbed in front of the LORD. But he didn't pay any attention to your sobs. He wouldn't listen to you. **46**So you stayed in Kadesh for many years. You spent a long time in that area.

Israel Wanders in the Desert

2 We turned back and started out toward the desert. We went along the road that leads to the Red Sea. That's how the LORD had directed me. For a long time we made our way around the hill country of Seir.

2Then the LORD spoke to me. He said, **3**"You have made your way around this hill country long enough. So now turn north.

4"Here are the orders I want you to give the people. Tell them, 'You are about to pass through the territory of your relatives. They are from the family line of Esau. They live in Seir. They will be afraid of you. But be very careful. **5**Do not make them angry. If you do, they will go to war against you. I will not give you any of their land. You will not have even enough to put your foot on. I have given Esau the hill country of Seir as his own. **6**Pay them with silver for the food you eat and the water you drink.' "

7The LORD your God has blessed you in everything your hands have done. He watched over you when you traveled through that huge desert. For these 40 years the LORD your God has been with you. So you have had everything you need.

8We went on past our relatives. They are from the family line of Esau. They live in Seir. We turned away from the Arabah Valley road. It comes up from Elath and Ezion Geber. We traveled along the desert road of Moab.

9Then the LORD said to me, "Do not attack the Moabites. Do not even make them angry. If you do, they will go to war against you. I will not give you any part of their land. I have given Moab to the people in the family line of Lot. I have given it to them as their own."

10The Emites used to live there. They were strong people. There were large numbers of them. They were as tall as the Anakites. [11]Like the Anakites, they too were thought of as Rephaites. But the Moabites called them Emites.

[12]The Horites used to live in Seir. But the people of Esau drove them out. They destroyed the Horites to make room for themselves. Then they settled in their territory. They did just as Israel has done in the land the LORD gave them as their own.

[13]The LORD said, "Now get up. Go across the Zered Valley." So we went across it.

[14]Between the time we left Kadesh Barnea and the time we went across the Zered Valley, 38 years passed. By then, all of the fighting men who had been in our camp from the beginning had died. The LORD had warned them with an oath that it would happen. [15]He used his power against them until he had gotten rid of all of them. Not one was left in the camp.

[16]Finally, the last of the fighting men among the people died.

[17]Then the LORD spoke to me. He said, [18]"Today you must pass near the border of Moab. Moab is also called Ar.

[19]"When you come to the Ammonites, do not attack them. Do not make them angry. If you do, they will go to war against you. I will not give you any of their land as your own. I have given it to the people in the family line of Lot. I have given it to them as their own."

[20]That land was also thought of as a land of the Rephaites. They used to live there. But the Ammonites called them Zamzummites. [21]The Rephaites were strong people. There were large numbers of them. They were as tall as the Anakites. The LORD destroyed the Rephaites to make room for the Ammonites. So the Ammonites drove them out. Then they settled in the territory of the Rephaites.

[22]The LORD had done the same thing for the people of Esau. They lived in Seir. He destroyed the Horites to make room for them. They drove the Horites out. So the people of Esau have lived in Seir in the territory of the Horites to this very day.

[23]The Avvites lived in villages as far away as Gaza. But people came from Crete. They destroyed the Avvites. Then they settled in the territory of the Avvites.

Israel Wins the Battle Over Sihon

[24]The LORD said, "Start out and go across the valley of the Arnon River. I have handed Sihon over to you. He is the Amorite king of Heshbon. I have also given you

his country. Begin to take it as your own. Go to war against him.

[25]"This very day I will bring fear and terror on all of the nations because of you. They will hear about you. They will tremble with fear. Pain and suffering will take hold of them because of you."

[26]I sent messengers from the Desert of Kedemoth. I told them to go to Sihon, the king of Heshbon. They offered him peace. They said, [27]"Let us pass through your country. We'll stay on the main road. We won't turn off it to one side or the other. [28]We'll pay you the right amount of silver for food to eat and water to drink. Just let us walk through your country. [29]The people of Esau, who live in Seir, allowed us to do that. The people of Moab, who live in Ar, also allowed us to do it. So let us walk through until we go across the Jordan River. Then we'll be able to go into the land the LORD our God is giving us."

[30]But Sihon, the king of Heshbon, refused to let us walk through. The LORD your God had made his heart and spirit stubborn. The LORD wanted to hand him over to you. And that's exactly what he has done.

[31]The LORD said to me, "I have begun to hand Sihon and his country over to you. So begin the battle to take his land as your own."

[32]Sihon and his whole army came out to fight against us at Jahaz. [33]But the LORD our God handed him over to us. We struck him down together with his sons and his whole army. [34]At that time we took all of his towns. We completely destroyed them. We killed all of the men, women and children. We didn't leave any of them alive. [35]But we took for ourselves the livestock and everything else from the towns we had captured.

[36]Not a single town was too strong for us. That includes all of the towns from Aroer on the rim of the Arnon River valley all the way to Gilead. It also includes the town in the valley. The LORD our God gave us all of them.

[37]And you obeyed the LORD's command. You didn't go near any part of the land of the Ammonites. That includes the land along the Jabbok River. It also includes the land around the towns that are in the hills.

Israel Wins the Battle Over Og

3 Next, we turned and went up along the road toward Bashan. Og, the king of Bashan, marched out with his whole army. They fought against us at Edrei.

2The LORD said to me, "Do not be afraid of Og. I have handed him over to you. I have also handed over his whole army and his land. Do to him what you did to Sihon. Sihon was the Amorite king who ruled in Heshbon."

3So the LORD our God also handed Og, the king of Bashan, and his whole army over to us. We struck them down. We didn't leave any of them alive. 4At that time we took all of his cities. There were 60 of them. We took the whole area of Argob. That was Og's kingdom in Bashan. 5All of those cities had high walls around them. The city gates were made secure with heavy metal bars. There were also large numbers of villages that didn't have walls. 6We completely destroyed them. We did to them just as we had done to Sihon, the king of Heshbon. We destroyed all of their cities. We destroyed the men, women and children. 7But we kept for ourselves the livestock and everything else we took from their cities.

8So at that time we took the territory east of the Jordan River. We captured it from those two Amorite kings. The territory goes all the way from the Arnon River valley to Mount Hermon. 9Hermon is called Sirion by the people of Sidon. The Amorites call it Senir.

10We captured all of the towns on the high flatlands. We took the whole land of Gilead. And we captured the whole land of Bashan as far away as Salecah and Edrei. Those were towns that belonged to Og's kingdom in Bashan.

11Og, the king of Bashan, was the only Rephaite left. His bed was made out of iron. It was more than 13 feet long and six feet wide. It is still in the Ammonite city of Rabbah.

Moses Divides Up the Land

12I divided up the land we took over at that time. I gave the tribes of Reuben and Gad the territory north of Aroer by the Arnon River valley. It includes half of the hill country of Gilead together with its towns.

13I gave the rest of Gilead to half of the tribe of Manasseh. I also gave them the whole land of Bashan, the kingdom of Og. The whole area of Argob in Bashan used to be known as a land of the Rephaites.

14Jair took the whole area of Argob. He was from the family line of Manasseh. Argob goes all the way to the border of the people of Geshur and Maacah. It was named after Jair. So Bashan is called Hav-

voth Jair to this very day. 15I gave Gilead to Makir.

16But I gave to the tribes of Reuben and Gad the territory that reaches from Gilead down to the Arnon River valley. It reaches all the way to the Jabbok River. The Jabbok is the northern border of Ammon. The middle of the Arnon River valley is its southern border.

17The western border of Reuben and Gad is the Jordan River in the Arabah Valley. It reaches from the Sea of Galilee to the Dead Sea. It runs below the slopes of Pisgah.

18Here is the command I gave at that time to the tribes of Reuben and Gad and half of the tribe of Manasseh. I said, "The LORD your God has given you this land as your very own. But all of your strong men must be prepared for battle. They must cross over ahead of the rest of your fellow Israelites.

19"But your wives and children can stay in the towns I've given you. You can keep your livestock there too. I know you have a lot of livestock. 20Let your families and livestock stay in those towns until the LORD gives peace and rest to the other tribes, just as he has given you peace and rest. And let them stay until the other tribes have taken over the land the LORD your God is giving them. That land is across the Jordan River. After that, each of you may go back to the land I've given you as your very own."

The LORD Will Not Allow Moses to Cross the Jordan River

21At that time I gave Joshua a command. I said, "Your own eyes have seen everything the LORD your God has done to Sihon and Og. He will do the same thing to all of the kingdoms in the land where you are going. 22Don't be afraid of them. The LORD your God himself will fight for you."

23At that time I made my appeal to the LORD. I said, 24"LORD and King, you have begun to show me how great you are. You have shown me how strong your hand is. You do great works and mighty acts. There isn't any god in heaven or on earth that can do what you do. 25Let me go across the Jordan River. Let me see the good land that is beyond it. I want to see that fine hill country and Lebanon."

26But the LORD was angry with me because of what you did. He wouldn't listen to me. "That is enough!" the LORD said. "Do not speak to me anymore about this matter. 27Go up to the highest slopes

POWER-SURGE

BRAVE   B

SO APPOINT JOSHUA AS THE NEW LEADER. HELP HIM TO BE BRAVE. GIVE HIM HOPE AND STRENGTH.
— DEUTERONOMY 3:28 —

STRONG

of Pisgah. Look west and north and south and east. Look at the land with your own eyes. But you are not going to go across that Jordan River.

28 "So appoint Joshua as the new leader. Help him to be brave. Give him hope and strength. He will take these people across the Jordan. You will see the land. But he will lead them into it to take it as their own." 29 So we stayed in the valley near Beth Peor.

Obey the LORD

4 Israel, listen to the rules and laws I'm going to teach you. Follow them. Then you will live. You will go in and take over the land. The LORD was the God of your people long ago. He's giving you the land. 2 Don't add to what I'm commanding you. Don't subtract from it either. Instead, obey the commands of the LORD your God that I'm giving you.

3 Your own eyes saw what the LORD your God did at Baal Peor. He destroyed every one of your people who followed the Baal that was worshiped at Peor. 4 But all of you who remained true to the LORD your God are still alive today.

5 I have taught you rules and laws, just as the LORD my God commanded me. Follow them in the land you are entering to take as your very own. 6 Be careful to keep them. That will show the nations how wise and understanding you are. They will hear about all of those rules. They'll say, "That great nation certainly has wise and understanding people."

7 The LORD our God is near us every time we pray to him. What other nation is great enough to have its gods that close to them? 8 I'm giving you the laws of the LORD today. What other nation is great enough to have rules and laws that are as fair as these?

9 Don't be careless. Instead, be very careful. Don't forget the things your eyes have seen. As long as you live, don't let them slip from your mind. Teach them to your children and their children after them. 10 Remember the day you stood at Mount Horeb. The LORD your God was there. He said to me, "Bring the people to me to hear my words. I want them to learn to have respect for me as long as they live in the land. I want them to teach my words to their children."

11 You came near and stood at the foot of the mountain. It blazed with fire that reached as high as the very heavens. There were black clouds and deep darkness.

12 Then the LORD spoke to you out of the fire. You heard the sound of his words. But you didn't see any shape or form. You only heard a voice. 13 He announced his covenant to you. That covenant is the Ten Commandments. He commanded you to follow them. Then he wrote them down on two stone tablets.

14 At that time the LORD directed me to teach you his rules and laws. You must follow them in the land you are crossing the Jordan River to take as your own.

Don't Make or Worship Statues of Gods

15 The LORD spoke to you at Mount Horeb out of the fire. But you didn't see any shape or form that day. So be very careful.

16 Make sure you don't commit a horrible sin. Don't make for yourselves a statue of a god. Don't make a god that looks like a man or woman or anything else. 17 Don't make one that looks like any animal on earth or any bird that flies in the sky. 18 Don't make a statue that looks like any creature that moves along the ground or any fish that swims in the water.

19 When you look up at the heavens, you will see the sun and moon. And you will see huge numbers of stars. Don't let anyone tempt you to bow down to the sun, moon or stars. Don't worship things the LORD your God has provided for all of the nations on earth.

20 Egypt was like a furnace that melts iron down and makes it pure. But the LORD took you and brought you out of Egypt. He wanted you to be his very own people. And that's exactly what you are.

21 The LORD was angry with me because of what you did. He took an oath that he

would never let me go across the Jordan River. He promised that I would never enter that good land. It's the land the LORD your God is giving you as your own. 22I'll die here in this land. I won't go across the Jordan. But you are about to cross over it. And you are about to take that good land as your own.

23Be careful. Don't forget the covenant the LORD your God made with you. Don't make for yourselves a statue of any god at all. He has told you not to. So don't do it. 24The LORD your God is like a fire that burns everything up. He's a jealous God.

25You will have children and grandchildren. And you will live in the land a long time.

But don't commit a horrible sin. Don't make a statue of a god. If you do, that will be an evil thing in the sight of the LORD your God. You will make him angry. 26I'm calling out to heaven and earth to be witnesses against you this very day. If you do those things, you will quickly die in the land you are going across the Jordan River to take over. You won't live there very long. You will certainly be destroyed. 27The LORD will drive you out of your land. He will scatter you among the nations. Only a few of you will remain alive there. 28There you will worship gods that men have made out of wood and stone. Those gods can't see, hear, eat or smell.

29Perhaps while you are there, you will look to the LORD your God. You will find him if you look for him with all your heart and with all your soul.

30All of the things I've told you about might happen to you. And you will be in trouble. But later you will return to the LORD your God. You will obey him. 31The LORD your God is tender and loving. He won't leave you or destroy you. He won't forget the covenant he made with your people long ago. He took an oath when he made it.

The LORD Is God

32Ask now about the days of long ago. Learn what happened long before your time. Ask about what has happened since the time God created man on the earth. Ask from one end of the world to the other. Has anything as great as this ever happened? Has anything like it ever been heard of? 33You heard the voice of God speaking out of fire. And you lived! Has that happened to any other people?

34Has any god ever tried to take one nation out of another to be his own? Has any god done it by putting his people to the test? Has any god done it with miraculous signs and wonders or with a war? Has any god reached out his mighty hand and powerful arm? Or has any god shown his people his great and wonderful acts?

The LORD your God did all of those things for you in Egypt. With your very own eyes you saw him do them.

35The LORD showed you those things so that you might know he is God. There is no other God except him. 36From heaven he made you hear his voice. He wanted to teach you. On earth he showed you his great fire. You heard his words coming out of the fire.

37He loved your people long ago. He chose their children after them. So he brought you out of Egypt. He used his great strength to do it. 38He drove out nations to make room for you. They were greater and stronger than you are. He will bring you into their land. He wants to give it to you as your very own. The whole land is as good as yours right now.

39The LORD is God in heaven above and on the earth below. Today you must agree with that and take it to heart. There is no other God.

40I'm giving you his rules and commands today. Obey them. Then things will go well with you and your children after you. You will live a long time in the land. The LORD your God is giving you the land for all time to come.

Cities to Go to for Safety

41I set apart three cities east of the Jordan River. 42Anyone who killed a person he didn't hate and without meaning to do it could run to one of those cities. He could go there and stay alive.

43Here are the names of the cities. Bezer was for the people of Reuben. It was in the high flatlands in the desert. Ramoth was for the people of Gad. It was in Gilead. Golan was for the people of Manasseh. It was in Bashan.

Moses Gives the Law to Israel

44Here is the law I gave the people of Israel. 45Here are its terms, rules and laws. I gave them to the people when they came out of Egypt.

46They were now east of the Jordan River in the valley near Beth Peor. They were in the land of Sihon, the king of the Amorites. He ruled in Heshbon. But the people of Israel and I won the battle over him after we came out of Egypt. 47We captured his land and made it our own. We also took the land of Og, the king of Bashan. Sihon and Og were the two Amorite kings east of the Jordan River.

48Their land reached from Aroer on the rim of the Arnon River valley to Mount Hermon. **49**It included the whole Arabah Valley east of the Jordan. It included land all the way to the Dead Sea below the slopes of Pisgah.

The Ten Commandments

5 I sent for all of the people of Israel. Here is what I said to them.

Israel, listen to me. Here are the rules and laws I'm announcing to you today. Learn them well. Be sure to follow them.

2The Lord our God made a covenant with us at Mount Horeb. **3**He didn't make it only with our parents. He also made it with us. In fact, he made it with all of us who are alive here today. **4**The Lord spoke to you face to face. His voice came out of the fire on the mountain.

5At that time I stood between the Lord and you. I announced to you the Lord's message. I did it because you were afraid of the fire. You didn't go up the mountain.

The Lord said,

6 "I am the Lord your God. I brought you out of Egypt. That is the land where you were slaves.

7 "Do not put any other gods in place of me.

8 "Do not make statues of gods that look like anything in the sky or on the earth or in the waters. **9**Do not bow down to them or worship them. I am the Lord your God. I am a jealous God. I punish the children for the sin of their parents. I judge the grandchildren and great-grandchildren of those who hate me. **10**But for all time to come I show love to all those who love me and keep my commandments.

11 "Do not misuse the name of the Lord your God. The Lord will find guilty anyone who misuses his name.

12 "Observe the Sabbath day. Keep it holy, just as the Lord your God commanded you. **13**Do all of your work in six days. **14**But the seventh day is a Sabbath in honor of the Lord your God. Do not do any work on that day. The same command applies to your

sons and daughters, your male and female servants, your oxen, your donkeys and your other animals. It also applies to any outsiders who live in your cities. I want your male and female servants to rest, just as you do. **15**Remember that you were slaves in Egypt. The Lord your God reached out his mighty hand and powerful arm and brought you out of there. So he has commanded you to observe the Sabbath day.

16 "Honor your father and mother, just as the Lord your God commanded you. Then you will live a long time in the land he is giving you. And things will go well with you there.

POWER–SURGE

OBEYS ✔

HONOR YOUR FATHER AND MOTHER, JUST AS THE Lord YOUR GOD COMMANDED YOU.
— DEUTERONOMY 5:16 —

17 "Do not commit murder.

18 "Do not commit adultery.

19 "Do not steal.

20 "Do not give false witness against your neighbor.

21 "Do not long for your neighbor's wife. Do not long to have anything that belongs to your neighbor. Do not long to have your neighbor's house or land, male or female servant, ox or donkey."

22Those are the commandments the Lord announced in a loud voice to your whole community. He gave them to you there on the mountain. He spoke out of the fire, cloud and deep darkness. He didn't add anything else. Then he wrote the commandments on two stone tablets. And he gave them to me.

23The mountain was blazing with fire. You heard the voice coming out of the darkness. So your elders and all of the leaders of your tribes came to me.

24You said, "The Lord our God has shown us his glory and majesty. We have heard his voice coming out of the fire. Today we have seen that a man can still stay alive even if God speaks with him. 25But why should we die? This great fire will burn us up. We'll die if we hear the voice of the LORD our God again.

26"We have heard the voice of the living God. We've heard him speaking out of the fire. Has any other human being ever heard him speak like that and stayed alive? 27Go near and listen to everything the LORD our God says. Then tell us what he tells you. We will listen and obey."

28The LORD heard you when you spoke to me. He said to me, "I have heard what these people said to you. Everything they said was good. 29But I wish they would always have respect for me in their hearts. I wish they would always obey all of my commands. Then things would go well with them and their children forever.

30"Go and tell them to return to their tents. 31But you stay here with me. Then I will give you all of my commands, rules and laws. You must teach the people to follow them in the land I am giving them as their very own."

32So be careful to do what the LORD your God has commanded you. Don't turn away from his commands to the right or the left. 33Live exactly as the LORD

OBEYS ✔

BE CAREFUL TO DO WHAT THE LORD YOUR GOD HAS COMMANDED YOU. DON'T TURN AWAY FROM HIS COMMANDS TO THE RIGHT OR THE LEFT. LIVE EXACTLY AS THE LORD YOUR GOD HAS COMMANDED YOU TO LIVE. THEN YOU WILL ENJOY LIFE IN THE LAND YOU WILL SOON OWN. THINGS WILL GO WELL WITH YOU THERE.

— DEUTERONOMY 5:32-33 —

your God has commanded you to live. Then you will enjoy life in the land you will soon own. Things will go well with you there. You will live there for a long time.

Love the LORD Your God

6 The LORD your God has directed me to teach you his commands, rules and laws. Obey them in the land you will take over when you go across the Jordan River. 2Then you, your children and their children after them will have respect for the LORD your God as long as you live. Keep all of his rules and commands I'm giving you. If you do, you will enjoy long life.

3Israel, listen to me. Make sure you obey me. Then things will go well with you. Your numbers will increase greatly in a land that has plenty of milk and honey. That's what the LORD, the God of your parents, promised you.

4Israel, listen to me. The LORD is our God. The LORD is the one and only God. 5Love the LORD your God with all your heart and with all your soul. Love him with all your strength.

6The commandments I give you today must be in your hearts. 7Make sure your children learn them. Talk about them when you are at home. Talk about them when you walk along the road. Speak about them when you go to bed. And speak about them when you get up. 8Write them down and tie them on your hands as a reminder. Also tie them on your foreheads. 9Write them on the doorframes of your houses. Also write them on your gates.

10The LORD your God will bring you into the land of Canaan. He took an oath. He promised he would give the land to your fathers. He promised it to Abraham, Isaac and Jacob.

The land has large, wealthy cities you didn't build. 11It has houses that are filled with all kinds of good things you didn't provide. It has wells you didn't dig. And it has vineyards and groves of olive trees you didn't plant. You will have plenty to eat.

12But be careful that you don't forget the LORD. Remember that he brought you out of Egypt. That's the land where you were slaves.

13Worship the LORD your God. He is the only one you should serve. When you make promises, take your oaths in his name. 14Don't follow other gods. Don't worship the gods of the nations that are around you.

¹⁵The LORD your God is among you. He is a jealous God. If you worship other gods, his anger will burn against you. And he will destroy you from the face of the land. ¹⁶Don't put the LORD your God to the test as you did at Massah.

¹⁷Be sure to obey the LORD's commands. Follow the terms and rules he has given you. ¹⁸Do what is right and good in the LORD's eyes. Then things will go well with you. You will go in and take over the land. It's the good land the LORD promised with an oath to your people long ago. ¹⁹You will drive out all of your enemies to make room for you. That's what the LORD said would happen.

²⁰Later on, your son might ask you, "What is the meaning of the terms, rules and laws the LORD our God has commanded you to obey?"

²¹If he does, tell him, "We were Pharaoh's slaves in Egypt. But the LORD used his mighty hand to bring us out of Egypt. ²²With our own eyes we saw the LORD send miraculous signs and wonders. They were great and terrible. He sent them on Egypt and Pharaoh and everyone in his house.

²³"But the LORD brought us out of Egypt. He planned to bring us into the land of Canaan and give it to us. It's the land he promised with an oath to our people long ago.

²⁴"The LORD our God commanded us to obey all of his rules. He commanded us to have respect for him. If we do, we will always succeed and be kept alive. That's what is happening today. ²⁵We must make sure we obey the whole law in the sight of the LORD our God. That's what he has commanded us to do. If we obey his law, we'll be doing what he requires of us."

The LORD Will Drive Many Nations Out

7 The LORD your God will bring you into the land. You are going to enter it and take it as your own. He'll drive many nations out to make room for you. He'll drive out the Hittites, Girgashites, Amorites, Canaanites, Perizzites, Hivites and Jebusites. Those seven nations are larger and stronger than you are.

²The LORD your God will hand them over to you. You will win the battle over them. You must completely destroy them. Don't make a peace treaty with them. Don't show them any mercy. ³Don't get married to any of them. Don't give your daughters to their sons. And don't take their daughters for your sons. ⁴If you do,

POWER-SURGE

OBEYS ✔

THE LORD OUR GOD COMMANDED US TO OBEY ALL OF HIS RULES. HE COMMANDED US TO HAVE RESPECT FOR HIM. IF WE DO, WE WILL ALWAYS SUCCEED AND BE KEPT ALIVE. THAT'S WHAT IS HAPPENING TODAY. WE MUST MAKE SURE WE OBEY THE WHOLE LAW IN THE SIGHT OF THE LORD OUR GOD. THAT'S WHAT HE HAS COMMANDED US TO DO. IF WE OBEY HIS LAW, WE'LL BE DOING WHAT HE REQUIRES OF US.

— DEUTERONOMY 6:24-25 —

those people will turn your children away from following the LORD. Then your children will serve other gods. The LORD's anger will burn against you. It will quickly destroy you.

⁵So here is what you must do to those people. Break down their altars. Smash their sacred stones. Cut down the poles they use to worship the goddess Asherah. Burn the statues of their gods in the fire.

⁶You are a holy nation. The LORD your God has set you apart for himself. He has chosen you to be his special treasure. He chose you out of all of the nations on the face of the earth to be his people.

⁷The LORD chose you because he loved you very much. He didn't choose you because you had more people than other nations. In fact, you had the smallest number of all.

⁸The LORD chose you because he loved you. He wanted to keep the promise he had made with an oath to your people long ago. That's why he brought you out of Egypt with a mighty hand. He bought you back from the land where you were

slaves. He set you free from the power of Pharaoh, the king of Egypt.

⁹So I want you to realize that the LORD your God is God. He is the faithful God. He keeps his covenant for all time to come. He keeps it with those who love him and obey his commands. He shows them his love. ¹⁰But he will pay back those who hate him. He'll destroy them. He'll quickly pay back those who hate him. ¹¹So be careful to follow the commands, rules and laws I'm giving you today.

¹²Pay attention to the laws of the LORD your God. Be careful to obey them. Then he will keep his covenant of love with you. That's what he promised with an oath to your people long ago.

¹³The LORD will love you and bless you. He'll increase your numbers. He'll give you many children. He'll bless the crops of your land. He'll give you plenty of grain, olive oil and fresh wine. He'll bless your herds with many calves. He'll give your flocks many lambs. He'll do all of those things for you in the land of Canaan. It's the land he promised your people long ago that he would give you. ¹⁴He will bless you more than any other nation. All of your men and women will have children. All of your livestock will have little ones.

¹⁵The LORD will keep you from getting sick. He won't send on you any of the horrible sicknesses you saw all around you in Egypt. But he'll send them on everyone who hates you.

¹⁶You must destroy all of the nations the LORD your God hands over to you. Don't feel sorry for them. Don't serve their gods. If you do, they will be a trap for you.

¹⁷You might say to yourselves, "These nations are stronger than we are. How can we drive them out?" ¹⁸But don't be afraid of them.

Be sure to remember what the LORD your God did to Pharaoh and all of the Egyptians. ¹⁹With your own eyes you saw what the LORD did to them. You saw his miraculous signs and wonders. He reached out his mighty hand and powerful arm. The LORD your God used all of those things to bring you out. He will do the same things to all of the nations you are now afraid of.

²⁰The LORD your God will also send hornets among them. Some of the people who are left alive will hide from you. But even they will die. ²¹So don't be terrified by them. The LORD your God is with you. He is a great and wonderful God.

²²The LORD your God will drive out those nations to make room for you. But he will do it little by little. You won't be allowed to get rid of them all at once. If you did, wild animals would multiply all around you.

²³But the LORD your God will hand those nations over to you. He will throw them into a panic until they are destroyed. ²⁴He will hand their kings over to you. You will wipe out their names from the earth. No one will be able to stand up against you. You will destroy them.

²⁵Burn the statues of their gods in the fire. Don't long for the silver and gold that is on those statues. Don't take it for yourselves. If you do, it will be a trap for you. The LORD your God hates it. ²⁶Don't bring anything he hates into your house. If you do, you will be completely destroyed along with it. So hate it with all your heart. It is set apart to be destroyed.

Remember What the LORD Has Done

8 Make sure you follow every command I'm giving you today. Then you will live. You will increase your numbers. You will enter the land and take it as your own. It's the land the LORD promised with an oath to your people long ago.

²Remember how the LORD your God led you all the way. He guided you in the desert for these 40 years. He wanted to take your pride away. He wanted to put you to the test and know what was in your hearts. He wanted to see whether you would obey his commands.

³He took your pride away. He let you go hungry. Then he gave you manna to eat. You and your parents had never even known anything about manna before. He tested you to teach you that man doesn't live only on bread. He also lives on every word that comes from the mouth of the LORD. ⁴Your clothes didn't wear out during these 40 years. Your feet didn't swell.

⁵Here is what I want you to know in your hearts. The LORD your God trains you, just as parents train their children.

⁶Obey the commands of the LORD your God. Live as he wants you to live. Have respect for him.

⁷The LORD your God is bringing you into a good land. It has streams and pools of water. Springs flow in its valleys and hills. ⁸It has wheat, barley, vines, fig trees, pomegranates, olive oil and honey.

⁹There is plenty of food in that land. You will have everything you need. Its rocks have iron in them. And you can dig copper out of its hills.

¹⁰When you have eaten and are satisfied, praise the LORD your God. Praise him for the good land he has given you. ¹¹Make sure you don't forget the LORD your God. Don't fail to obey his commands, laws and rules. I'm giving them to you today.

¹²But suppose you don't obey his commands. And suppose you have plenty to eat. You build fine houses and settle down in them. ¹³Your herds and flocks increase their numbers. You also get more and more silver and gold. And everything you have multiplies. ¹⁴Then your hearts will become proud. And you will forget the LORD your God.

The LORD brought you out of Egypt. That's the land where you were slaves. ¹⁵He led you through that huge and terrible desert. It was a dry land. It didn't have any water. It had poisonous snakes and scorpions. The LORD gave you water out of solid rock. ¹⁶He gave you manna to eat in the desert. Your parents had never even known anything about manna before.

The LORD took your pride away. He put you to the test. He did it so that things would go well with you in the end. ¹⁷You might say to yourselves, "Our power and our strong hands have made us rich."

¹⁸But remember the LORD your God. He gives you the ability to produce wealth. That shows he stands by the terms of his covenant. He promised it with an oath to your people long ago. And he's still faithful to his covenant today.

¹⁹Don't forget the LORD your God. Don't follow other gods. Don't worship them and bow down to them. I give witness against you today that if you do, you will certainly be destroyed. ²⁰You will be destroyed just like the nations the LORD your God is destroying to make room for you. That's what will happen if you don't obey him.

Why the LORD Gave Canaan to Israel

9 Israel, listen to me. You are now about to go across the Jordan. You will take over the land of the nations that live there.

Those nations are greater and stronger than you are. Their large cities have walls that reach up to the sky. ²The people who live there are Anakites. They are strong and tall. You know all about them. You have heard people say, "Who can stand up against the Anakites?"

³But today you can be sure the LORD your God will go over there ahead of you. He is like a fire that will burn them up. He'll destroy them. He'll bring them under your control. You will drive them out. You will put an end to them quickly, just as the LORD has promised you.

⁴The LORD your God will drive them out to make room for you. When he does, don't say to yourselves, "The LORD has done it because we are godly. That's why he brought us here to take over this land." That isn't true. The LORD is going to drive out those nations to make room for you because they are very evil.

⁵You are not going in to take over their land because you have done what is right or honest. It's because those nations are so evil. That's why the LORD your God will drive them out ahead of you. He will do what he said he would do. He took an oath and made a promise to your fathers. He made it to Abraham, Isaac and Jacob.

⁶The LORD your God is giving you this good land to take as your own. But you must understand that it isn't because you are a godly nation. In fact, you are stubborn.

Israel Worshiped the Golden Calf

⁷Here is something you must remember. Never forget it. You made the LORD your God angry in the desert. You refused to obey him from the day you left Egypt until you arrived here.

⁸At Mount Horeb you made the LORD angry enough to destroy you. ⁹I went up the mountain. I went there to receive the tablets of the covenant. They were made out of stone. It was the covenant the LORD had made with you. I stayed on the mountain for 40 days and 40 nights. I didn't eat any food or drink any water.

POWER-SURGE

OBEYS ✔

OBEY THE COMMANDS OF THE LORD YOUR GOD. LIVE AS HE WANTS YOU TO LIVE. HAVE RESPECT FOR HIM.

— DEUTERONOMY 8:6 —

10The LORD gave me two stone tablets. The words on them were written by the finger of God. All of the commandments the LORD gave you were written on the tablets. He announced them to you out of the fire on the mountain. He wrote them on the day you gathered together there.

11The 40 days and 40 nights came to an end. Then the LORD gave me the two stone tablets. They were the tablets of the covenant. **12**The LORD told me, "Go down from here right away. The people you brought out of Egypt have become very sinful. They have quickly turned away from what I commanded them. They have made a metal statue of a god for themselves."

13The LORD said to me, "I have seen these people. They are so stubborn! **14**Do not try to stop me. I am going to destroy them. I will wipe them out from the earth. Then I will make you into a great nation. Your people will be stronger than they were. There will be more of you than there were of them."

15So I turned and went down the mountain. It was blazing with fire. I was carrying the two tablets of the covenant.

16When I looked, I saw that you had sinned against the LORD your God. You had made for yourselves a metal statue of a god. It looked like a calf. You had quickly turned away from the path the LORD had commanded you to follow.

17So I threw the two tablets out of my hands. You watched them break into pieces.

18Then once again I fell down flat in front of the LORD with my face toward the ground. I lay there for 40 days and 40 nights. I didn't eat any food or drink any water. You had committed a terrible sin. You had done an evil thing in the LORD's sight. You had made him angry.

19I was afraid of the LORD's burning anger. He was so angry with you he wanted to destroy you. But the LORD listened to me again. **20**And he was so angry with Aaron he wanted to destroy him too. But at that time I prayed for Aaron.

21I also got that sinful calf you had made. I burned it in the fire. I crushed it and ground it into fine powder. Then I threw the powder into a stream that was flowing down the mountain.

22You also made the LORD angry at Taberah, Massah and Kibroth Hattaavah.

23The LORD sent you out from Kadesh Barnea. He said, "Go up and take over the land I have given you." But you refused to do what the LORD your God had commanded you to do. You didn't trust him or obey him. **24**You have been refusing to obey the LORD as long as I've known you.

25I lay down in front of the LORD with my face toward the ground for 40 days and 40 nights. I did it because the LORD had said he would destroy you.

26I prayed to him. "LORD and King," I said, "don't destroy your people. They belong to you. You set them free by your great power. You used your mighty hand to bring them out of Egypt. **27**Remember your servants Abraham, Isaac and Jacob. Forgive the people of Israel for being so stubborn. Don't judge them for the evil and sinful things they've done.

28"If you do, the Egyptians will say, 'The LORD wasn't able to take them into the land he had promised to give them. He hated them. So he brought them out of Egypt to put them to death in the desert.' **29**But they are your people. They belong to you. You used your great power to bring them out of Egypt. You reached out your mighty arm and saved them."

The New Stone Tablets

10 At that time the LORD spoke to me. He said, "Carve out two stone tablets, just like the first ones. Then come up to me on the mountain. Also make a wooden chest. **2**I will write on the tablets the words that were on the first tablets, which you broke. Then you must put the tablets in the chest."

3So I made the ark out of acacia wood. I carved out two stone tablets that were just like the first ones. I went up the mountain. I carried the two tablets in my hands. **4**The LORD wrote on the tablets what he had written before. It was the Ten Commandments. He had announced them to you out of the fire on the mountain. It was on the day you had gathered together there. So the LORD gave the tablets to me.

5Then I came back down the mountain. I put the tablets in the ark I had made, just as the LORD had commanded me. And that's where they are now.

6Remember how the people of Israel traveled from the wells of Bene Jaakan to Moserah. That's where Aaron died. And his body was buried there. His son Eleazar became the next priest after him. **7**From Moserah the people traveled to Gudgodah. Then they went on to Jotbathah. That land has streams of water.

8At that time the LORD set the tribe of Levi apart. He appointed them to carry the ark of the covenant of the LORD. He wanted them to serve him. He told them to bless the people in his name. And they still do it today. **9**That's why the Levites don't have any part of the land the LORD gave the other tribes in Israel. They don't have any share among them. The LORD himself is their share. That's what the LORD your God told them.

10I had stayed on the mountain for 40 days and nights, just as I did the first time. The LORD listened to me that time also. He didn't want to destroy you.

11"Go," the LORD said to me. "Lead the people on their way. Then they can enter the land and take it over. I have taken an oath. I promised I would give the land to their fathers. I promised it to Abraham, Isaac and Jacob."

Have Respect for the LORD

12And now, Israel, what is the LORD your God asking you to do? Have respect for him. Live exactly as he wants you to live. Love him. Serve him with all your heart and with all your soul. **13**Obey the LORD's commands and rules. I'm giving them to you today for your own good.

14The heavens belong to the LORD your God. Even the highest heavens belong to him. He owns the earth and everything in it.

15But the LORD loved your people very much long ago. You are their children. And he chose you above all of the other nations. His love and his promise remain with you to this very day. **16**So don't let your hearts be stubborn anymore. Obey the LORD.

17The LORD your God is the greatest God of all. He is the greatest Lord of all. He is the great God. He is mighty and wonderful. He treats everyone the same. He doesn't accept any money from those who want special favors. **18**He stands up for widows and for children whose fathers have died. He loves outsiders. He gives them food and clothes. **19**So you also must love outsiders. Remember that you yourselves were outsiders in Egypt.

20Have respect for the LORD your God. Serve him. Remain true to him. When you make promises, take your oaths in his name. **21**He is the one you should praise. He's your God. With your own eyes you saw the great and wonderful miracles he did for you.

22Long ago, your people went down into Egypt. The total number of them was 70. And now the LORD your God has made you as many as the stars in the sky.

Love and Obey the LORD

11 Love the LORD your God. Do what he requires. Always obey his rules, laws and commands.

2Remember today that your children weren't the ones the LORD your God taught and trained. They didn't see his majesty. They weren't in Egypt when he reached out his mighty hand and powerful arm. **3**They didn't see the miraculous signs and the other things he did in Egypt. They didn't see what he did to Pharaoh, the king of Egypt, and to his whole country. **4**They weren't there when he destroyed the army of Egypt and its horses and chariots. The LORD swept the waters of the Red Sea over the Egyptians while they were chasing you. He wiped them out forever.

5Your children didn't see what he did for you in the desert before you arrived here. **6**They didn't see what he did to Dathan and Abiram, who were the sons of Eliab. Eliab was from the tribe of Reuben. The earth opened its mouth right in the middle of the Israelite camp. It swallowed up Dathan and Abiram. It swallowed them up together with their families, tents and every living thing that belonged to them.

7But with your own eyes you saw all of the great things the LORD has done.

8So obey all of the commands I'm giving you today. Then you will be strong enough to go in and take over the land. You will go across the Jordan River and take it as your own.

9You will live in the land for a long time. It's the land the LORD promised to give to Abraham, Isaac and Jacob and their children after them. He took an oath when he made that promise. It's a land that has plenty of milk and honey. **10**You will enter it and take it over.

It isn't like the land of Egypt. That's where you came from. You planted your seeds there. You had to water them, just as you have to water a vegetable garden.

11But you will soon go across the Jordan River. The land you are going to take over has mountains and valleys in it. It drinks rain from heaven. **12**It's a land the LORD your God takes care of. His eyes always look on it with favor. He watches over it from the beginning of the year to its end.

13So be faithful. Obey the commands the LORD your God is giving you today. Love him. Serve him with all your heart and with all your soul.

14Then the LORD will send rain on your land at the right time. He'll send rain in the fall and in the spring. You will be able to gather your grain. You will also be able to make olive oil and fresh wine. **15**He'll provide grass in the fields for your cattle. You will have plenty to eat.

16But be careful. Don't let anyone tempt you to do something wrong. Don't turn away and worship other gods. Don't bow down to them. **17**If you do, the LORD's anger will burn against you. He'll close up the sky. It won't rain. The ground won't produce its crops. Soon you will die. You won't live to enjoy the good land the LORD is giving you.

18So keep my words in your hearts and minds. Write them down and tie them on your hands as a reminder. Also tie them on your foreheads. **19**Teach them to your children. Talk about them when you are at home. Talk about them when you walk along the road. Speak about them when you go to bed. And speak about them when you get up. **20**Write them on the doorframes of your houses. Also write them on your gates.

21Then you and your children will live for a long time in the land. The LORD took an oath and promised to give the land to Abraham, Isaac and Jacob. Your family line will continue as long as the heavens remain above the earth.

22So be careful. Obey all of the commands I'm giving you to follow. Love the LORD your God. Live exactly as he wants you to live. Remain true to him. **23**Then the LORD will drive out all of the nations to make room for you. They are larger and stronger than you are. But you will take their land.

24Every place you walk on will belong to you. Your territory will go all the way from the desert to Lebanon. It will go from the Euphrates River to the Mediterranean Sea.

25No man will be able to stand up against you. The LORD your God will throw the whole land into a panic because of you. He'll do it everywhere you go, just as he promised you.

26Listen to me. I'm setting a blessing and a curse in front of you today. **27**I'm giving you the commands of the LORD your God today. You will be blessed if you obey them. **28**But you will be cursed if you don't obey them. So don't turn away from the path I'm now commanding you to take. Don't worship other gods. You haven't known anything about them before.

29The LORD your God will bring you into the land to take it over. When he does, you must announce the blessings from Mount Gerizim. You must announce the curses from Mount Ebal. **30**As you know, those mountains are across the Jordan River. They are beyond the road that runs along the west side of the Jordan. They are near the large trees of Moreh. The mountains are in the territory of the Canaanites, who live in the Arabah Valley near Gilgal.

31You are about to go across the Jordan River. You will enter the land and take it over. The LORD your God is giving it to you. You will take it over and live there. **32**When you do, make sure you obey all of the rules and laws I'm giving you today.

Worship Only Where the LORD Wants You To

12 Here are the rules and laws you must obey. Be careful to follow them in the land the LORD has given you

---

POWER / SURGE

BELIEVES ✝

SO KEEP MY WORDS IN YOUR HEARTS AND MINDS. WRITE THEM DOWN AND TIE THEM ON YOUR HANDS AS A REMINDER. ALSO TIE THEM ON YOUR FOREHEADS. TEACH THEM TO YOUR CHILDREN. TALK ABOUT THEM WHEN YOU ARE AT HOME. TALK ABOUT THEM WHEN YOU WALK ALONG THE ROAD. SPEAK ABOUT THEM WHEN YOU GO TO BED. AND SPEAK ABOUT THEM WHEN YOU GET UP.

— DEUTERONOMY 11:18–19 —

TELLS OTHERS

to take as your own. He's the God of your people who lived long ago. Obey these rules and laws as long as you live in the land.

²You will soon drive the nations out of it. Completely destroy all of the places where they worship their gods. Destroy them on the high mountains, on the hills, and under every green tree. ³Break down their altars. Smash their sacred stones. Burn up the poles they use to worship the goddess Asherah. Cut down the statues of their gods. Wipe out the names of their gods from those places.

⁴You must not worship the LORD your God the way those nations worship their gods. ⁵Instead, go to the special place he will choose from among all of your tribes. He will put his Name there. That's where you must go.

⁶Take your burnt offerings and sacrifices to that place. Bring your special gifts and a tenth of everything you produce. Take with you what you have promised to give. Bring any other offerings you choose to give. And bring the male animals among your livestock that were born first to their mothers.

⁷You and your families will eat at the place the LORD your God will choose. He will be with you there. You will find joy in everything you have done. That's because he has blessed you.

⁸You must not do as we're doing here today. All of us are doing only what we think is right. ⁹That's because you haven't yet reached the place the LORD is giving you. Your God will give you peace and rest there.

¹⁰But first you will go across the Jordan River. You will settle in the land he's giving you. It will belong to you as your share. He will give you peace and rest from all of your enemies around you. You will live in safety.

¹¹The LORD your God will choose a special place. He will put his Name there. That's where you must bring everything I command you to bring. That includes your burnt offerings and sacrifices. It includes your special gifts and a tenth of everything you produce. It also includes all of the things of value that you promised to give to the LORD.

¹²Be filled with joy there in the sight of the LORD your God. Your children should also be joyful. So should your male and female servants. And so should the Levites from your towns. The Levites won't receive any part of the land as their share.

¹³Be careful not to sacrifice your burnt offerings anywhere you want to. ¹⁴Offer them only at the place the LORD will choose in one of your tribes. There obey everything I command you.

¹⁵But you can kill your animals in any of your towns. You can eat as much of the meat as you want to. You can eat it as if it were antelope or deer meat. That's in keeping with the blessing the LORD your God is giving you. Those who are "clean" and those who are not can eat it.

¹⁶But you must not eat meat that still has blood in it. Pour the blood out on the ground like water.

¹⁷Here are the things you must not eat in your own towns. You must not eat the tenth part of your grain, olive oil and fresh wine. It belongs to the LORD. You must not eat the male animals among your livestock that were born first to their mothers. Don't eat anything you have promised to give. Don't eat any offerings you have chosen to give. And you must not eat any of your special gifts.

¹⁸Instead, you must eat all of those things in the sight of the LORD your God. Do it at the place he will choose. You, your children, your male and female servants and the Levites from your towns can eat them.

Be filled with joy in the sight of the LORD your God. Be joyful in everything you do.

POWER SURGE

CHEERFUL ✳

BE FILLED WITH JOY IN THE SIGHT OF THE LORD YOUR GOD. BE JOYFUL IN EVERYTHING YOU DO.
— DEUTERONOMY 12:18 —

¹⁹Don't forget to take care of the Levites as long as you live in your land.

²⁰The LORD your God will increase your territory, just as he has promised you. When he does, you might get hungry for meat. You might say, "I'd really like some meat." Then you can eat as much of it as you want to.

²¹The LORD your God will choose a special place. He will put his Name there. But suppose it's too far away for you to go to it.

Then you can kill animals from the herds and flocks the LORD has given you. Do it just as I have commanded you. In your own towns you can eat as much of the meat as you want to. 22Eat it as you would eat antelope or deer meat. Those who are "clean" and those who are not can eat it.

23But be sure you don't eat meat that still has blood in it. The blood is the animal's life. So you must not eat the life along with the meat. 24You must not eat the blood. Pour it out on the ground like water. 25Don't eat it. Then things will go well with you and your children after you. You will be doing what is right in the eyes of the LORD.

26But go to the place the LORD will choose. Take with you the things you have set apart for him. Bring what you have promised to give him. 27Sacrifice your burnt offerings on the altar of the LORD your God. Offer the meat and the blood there. The blood of your sacrifices must be poured out beside his altar. But you can eat the meat.

28Make sure you obey all of the rules I'm giving you. Then things will always go well with you and your children after you. That's because you will be doing what is good and right in the eyes of the LORD your God.

29You are about to attack the land and take it over as your own. When you do, the LORD your God will cut off the nations who live there. He will do it to make room for you. You will drive them out. You will settle in their land. 30They will be destroyed to make room for you. But when they are, be careful.

Don't be trapped. Don't ask questions about their gods. Don't say, "How do these nations serve their gods? We'll do it in the same way." 31You must not worship the LORD your God the way they worship their gods. When they worship, they do all kinds of evil things the LORD hates. They even burn up their children in the fire as sacrifices to their gods.

32Be sure you do everything I'm commanding you to do. Don't add anything to my commands. And don't take anything away from them.

Don't Worship Other Gods

13 Suppose a prophet appears among you. Or someone comes who uses dreams to tell what's going to happen. He tells you that a miraculous sign or wonder is going to take place. 2The sign or wonder he has spoken about might really take place. And he might say, "Let's follow oth-

er gods. Let's worship them." But you haven't known anything about those gods before. 3So you must not listen to what that prophet or dreamer has said.

The LORD your God is putting you to the test. He wants to know whether you love him with all your heart and with all your soul. 4You must follow him. You must have respect for him. Keep his commands. Obey him. Serve him. Remain true to him.

5That prophet or dreamer must be put to death. He told you not to obey the LORD your God. The LORD brought you out of Egypt. He set you free from the land where you were slaves. He commanded you to live the way he wants you to. But that prophet or dreamer has tried to make you turn away from it. Get rid of that evil person.

6Suppose your very own brother or sister secretly tempts you to do something wrong. Or your child or the wife you love tempts you. Or your closest friend does it. Suppose one of them says, "Let's go and worship other gods." But you and your people long ago hadn't known anything about those gods before. 7They are the gods of the nations that are around you. Those nations might be near or far away. In fact, they might reach from one end of the land to the other. 8Don't give in to those who are tempting you. Don't listen to them. Don't feel sorry for them. Don't spare them or save them.

POWER-SURGE

TRIES HARD T

DON'T GIVE IN TO THOSE WHO ARE TEMPTING YOU. DON'T LISTEN TO THEM.
— DEUTERONOMY 13:8 —

9You must certainly put them to death. You must be the first to throw stones at them. Then all of the people must do the same thing. 10Put them to death by throwing stones at them. They tried to turn you away from the LORD your God. He brought you out of Egypt. That's the land where you were slaves.

11After you kill those who tempted you, all of the people of Israel will hear about it. And they will be too scared to do an evil thing like that again.

12The LORD your God is giving you

towns to live in. But suppose you hear something bad about one of those towns. 13You hear that evil men have appeared among you. They've tried to get the people of their town to do something wrong. They've said, "Let's go and worship other gods." But you haven't known anything about those gods before. 14So you must question people. You must check the matter out carefully.

If it's true, an evil thing has really happened among you. It's something the LORD hates. 15Then you must certainly kill with your swords everyone who lives in that town. Destroy it completely. Wipe out its people and livestock. 16Gather all of the goods of that town into the middle of the main street. Burn the town completely. Burn up everything in it.

It's a whole burnt offering to the LORD your God. The town must remain a pile of stones forever. It must never be built again.

17Don't keep anything that should be destroyed. Then the LORD will turn away from his burning anger. He will show you mercy. He'll have deep concern for you. He'll increase your numbers. That's what he promised your people long ago. He took an oath when he made the promise. 18The LORD your God will do those things if you obey him. I'm giving you his commands today. And you must obey all of them. You must do what is right in his eyes.

Food That Is "Clean" and Food That Is Not

14 You are the children of the LORD your God. Don't cut yourselves to honor the dead. Don't shave the front of your heads to honor them.

2You are a holy nation. The LORD your God has set you apart for himself. He has chosen you to be his special treasure. He chose you out of all of the nations on the face of the earth.

3Don't eat anything the LORD hates. 4Here are the only animals you can eat. You can eat oxen, sheep, goats, 5deer, gazelles, roe deer, wild goats, ibexes, antelope and mountain sheep.

6You can eat any animal that has hoofs that are separated completely in two. But it must also chew the cud. 7Some animals only chew the cud. Others only have hoofs that are completely separated in two. The camel, rabbit and rock badger chew the cud, but they don't have hoofs that are completely separated. So you can't eat them. They are not "clean" for you.

8Pigs aren't "clean" for you either. They have hoofs that are completely separated, but they don't chew the cud. So don't eat their meat. And don't touch their dead bodies.

9Many creatures live in water. You can eat all of the ones that have fins and scales. 10But don't eat anything that doesn't have fins and scales. It isn't "clean" for you.

11You can eat any "clean" bird. 12But there are many birds you can't eat. They include eagles, vultures, and black vultures. 13They include red kites, black kites and all kinds of falcons. 14They include all kinds of ravens. 15They include horned owls, screech owls, gulls and all kinds of hawks. 16They include little owls, great owls, white owls 17and desert owls. They include ospreys and cormorants. 18They include storks and all kinds of herons. They also include hoopoes and bats.

19All insects that fly together in groups are "unclean" for you. So don't eat them. 20But you can eat any creature that has wings and is "clean."

21If you find something that's already dead, don't eat it. You can give it to an outsider who is living in any of your towns. He can eat it. Or you can sell it to someone who is from another country. But you are a holy nation. The LORD your God has set you apart for himself.

Don't cook a young goat in its mother's milk.

Give a Tenth of What You Produce

22Be sure to set apart a tenth of everything your fields produce each year. 23Here are the things you should eat in the sight of the LORD your God. You should eat a tenth part of your grain, olive oil and fresh wine. You should also eat the male animals among your livestock that were born first to their mothers. Eat all of those things at the special place the LORD your God will choose. He will put his Name there. You will learn to have respect for him always.

24But suppose the place the LORD will choose for his Name is too far away from you. And suppose your God has blessed you. And your tenth part is too heavy for you to carry. 25Then sell it for silver. Take the silver with you. Go to the place the LORD your God will choose. 26Use the silver to buy anything you like. It can be cattle or sheep. It can be any kind of wine. In fact, it can be anything else you wish. Then you and your family can eat there in the sight of the LORD your God. You can be filled with joy.

27 Don't forget to take care of the Levites who will live in your towns. They won't receive any part of the land as their share.

28 At the end of every three years, bring a tenth of everything you produce that year. Store it in your towns. 29 Then the Levites can come and eat. That's because they won't receive any part of the land as their share. The outsiders and widows who live in your towns can come. So can the children whose fathers have died. Everyone can have plenty to eat. Then the LORD your God will bless you in everything you do.

The Year for Forgiving People What They Owe

15 At the end of every seven years you must forgive people what they owe you. 2 Have you made a loan to one of your own people? Then forgive what is owed to you. You can't require that person to pay you back. The LORD's time to forgive what is owed has been announced. 3 You can require someone from another nation to pay you back. But you must forgive your own people what they owe you.

4 There shouldn't be any poor people among you. The LORD will greatly bless you in the land he is giving you. You will take it over as your own. 5 The LORD your God will bless you if you obey him completely. Be careful to follow all of the commands I'm giving you today.

6 The LORD your God will bless you, just as he has promised. You will lend money to many nations. But you won't have to borrow from any of them. You will rule over many nations. But none of them will rule over you.

7 Suppose there are poor people among you. And suppose they live in one of the towns in the land the LORD your God is giving you. Then don't be mean to them. They are poor. So don't hold back money from them. 8 Instead, open your hands and lend them what they need. Do it freely.

9 Be careful not to have an evil thought in your mind. Don't say to yourself, "The seventh year will soon be here. It's the year for forgiving people what they owe." If you think like that, you might treat your needy people badly. You might not give them anything. Then they might make their appeal to the LORD against you. And he will find you guilty of sin.

10 So give freely to those who are needy.

Open your hearts to them. Then the LORD your God will bless you in all of your work. He will bless you in everything you do. 11 There will always be poor people in the land. So I'm commanding you to give freely to those who are poor and needy in your land. Open your hands to them.

Set Your Hebrew Servants Free

12 Suppose Hebrew men or women sell themselves to you. If they do, they will serve you for six years. Then in the seventh year you must let them go free.

13 But when you set them free, don't send them away without anything to show for all of their work. 14 Freely give them some animals from your flock. Also give them some of your grain and wine. The LORD your God has blessed you richly. Give to them as he has given to you.

15 Remember that you were slaves in Egypt. The LORD your God set you free. That's why I'm giving you this command today.

16 But suppose your servant says to you, "I don't want to leave you." He loves you and your family. And you are taking good care of him. 17 Then take him to the door of your house. Poke a hole through his ear lobe into the doorpost. And he will become your servant for life. Do the same with your female servant.

18 Don't think you are being cheated when you set your servants free. After all, they have served you for six years. The service of each of them has been worth twice as much as the service of a hired worker. And the LORD your God will bless you in everything you do.

Male Animals That Are Born First to Their Mothers

19 Set apart to the LORD your God every male animal among your livestock that was born first to its mother. Don't put that kind of ox to work. Don't clip the wool from that kind of sheep. 20 Each year you and your family must eat them. Do it in the sight of the LORD your God at the place he will choose.

21 Suppose an animal has something wrong with it. It might not be able to see or walk. Or it might have a bad flaw. Then you must not sacrifice it to the LORD your God. 22 You must eat it in your own towns. Those who are "clean" and those who are not can eat it. Eat it as if it were antelope or deer meat.

23 But you must not eat meat that still has blood in it. Pour the blood out on the ground like water.

The Passover Feast

16 Celebrate the Passover Feast of the LORD your God in the month of Abib. In that month he brought you out of Egypt at night.

2Sacrifice an animal from your flock or herd. It is the Passover sacrifice in honor of the LORD your God. Sacrifice it at the special place the LORD will choose. He will put his Name there.

3Don't eat the animal along with bread that is made with yeast. Instead, for seven days eat bread that is made without yeast. It's the bread that reminds you of how much you suffered. Remember that you left Egypt in a hurry. Remember it all the days of your life. Don't forget the day you left Egypt. **4**Don't keep any yeast anywhere in your land for seven days.

Don't let any of the meat you sacrifice on the evening of the first day be left over until the next morning.

5You must not sacrifice the Passover animal in any town the LORD your God is giving you. **6**Sacrifice it only in the special place he will choose for his Name. Sacrifice it there in the evening when the sun goes down. Do it on the same day every year. Be sure it's the day you left Egypt. **7**Cook it and eat it. Do it at the place the LORD your God will choose. Then in the morning return to your tents.

8For six days eat bread that is made without yeast. On the seventh day come together for a service in honor of the LORD your God. Don't do any work.

The Feast of Weeks

9Count off seven weeks from the time you begin to cut your grain in the field. **10**Then celebrate the Feast of Weeks in honor of the LORD your God. Give anything you choose to give as an offering. Do it in keeping with the blessings the LORD has given you.

GIVING G

GIVE ANYTHING YOU CHOOSE TO GIVE AS AN OFFERING. DO IT IN KEEPING WITH THE BLESSINGS THE LORD HAS GIVEN YOU.
— DEUTERONOMY 16:10 —

11Be filled with joy in the sight of the LORD your God. Be joyful at the special place he will choose for his Name. You, your children, and your male and female servants should be joyful. So should the Levites who are living in your towns. So should the outsiders and widows who are living among you. And so should the children whose fathers have died. **12**Remember that you were slaves in Egypt. Be careful to obey the rules I'm giving you.

The Feast of Booths

13Gather the grain from your threshing floors. Take the fresh wine from your winepresses. Then celebrate the Feast of Booths for seven days. **14**Be filled with joy at your Feast. You, your children, and your male and female servants should be joyful. So should the Levites, the outsiders, and the widows who are living in your towns. And so should the children whose fathers have died.

15For seven days celebrate the Feast in honor of the LORD your God. Do it at the place he will choose. The LORD will bless you when you gather all of your crops. He'll bless you in everything you do. And you will be full of joy.

16All of your men must appear in front of the LORD your God at the holy tent. They must go to the place he will choose. They must do it three times a year. They must go there to celebrate the Feast of Unleavened Bread, the Feast of Weeks and the Feast of Booths.

No man should appear in front of the LORD without bringing something with him. **17**Each of you must bring a gift. Do it in keeping with the way the LORD your God has blessed you.

Appoint Judges and Officials

18Appoint judges and officials for each of your tribes. Do it in every town the LORD your God is giving you. They must judge the people fairly. **19**Do what is right. Treat everyone the same. Don't take money from people who want special favors. It makes those who are wise close their eyes to the truth. It twists the words of those who do what is right. **20**Follow only what is right. If you do, you will live. You will take over the land the LORD your God is giving you.

Don't Worship Other Gods

21Don't set up a wooden pole that is used to worship the goddess Asherah. Don't set it up beside the altar you build to worship the LORD your God. **22**Don't set

OBEYS ✔

FOLLOW ONLY WHAT IS RIGHT. IF YOU DO, YOU WILL LIVE.
— DEUTERONOMY 16:20 —

up a sacred stone to honor another god. The LORD your God hates Asherah poles and sacred stones.

17 Suppose an ox or sheep has anything at all wrong with it. Then don't sacrifice it to the LORD your God. He hates it.

²Someone who is living among you might do what is evil in the sight of the LORD your God. It might happen in one of the towns the LORD is giving you. That person is breaking the LORD's covenant. ³The person might have worshiped or bowed down to other gods. That person might have bowed down to the sun or moon or stars in the sky. I have commanded you not to do those things. ⁴When you hear that people have done something like that, check the matter out carefully. If it's true, an evil thing has been done in Israel. It's something the LORD hates.

⁵So take the person who has done that evil thing to your city gate. Put that person to death with stones. ⁶The witness of two or three people is required to put someone to death. No one can be put to death because of what only one witness says. It needs the witness of two or three people. ⁷The witnesses must throw the first stones. Then the rest of the people must also throw stones. Get rid of that evil person.

Law Courts

⁸People will bring their cases to your courts. But some cases will be too hard for you to judge. They might be about murders, attacks or other crimes. Then take those hard cases to the place the LORD your God will choose. ⁹Go to a priest, who is a Levite. And go to the judge who is in office at that time. Ask them for their decision. They will give it to you.

¹⁰They'll hand down their decisions at the place the LORD will choose. You must do what they decide. Be careful to do everything they direct you to do. ¹¹Act in keeping with the laws they teach you.

Accept the decisions they give you. Don't turn away from what they tell you. Don't turn to the right or the left.

¹²Someone might make fun of the judge. Or he might make fun of the priest who serves the LORD your God at the place he will choose. If the man does that, he must be put to death. Remove that evil person from Israel. ¹³All of the people of Israel will hear about it. And they will be afraid to make fun of a judge or priest again.

Appoint the King the LORD Chooses

¹⁴You will enter the land the LORD your God is giving you. You will take it as your own. You will settle down in it. When you do, you will say, "Let's appoint a king over us, just like all of the nations around us." ¹⁵When that happens, make sure you appoint over you the king the LORD your God chooses. He must be from among your own people. Don't appoint over you someone from another country. Don't choose anyone who isn't from one of the tribes of Israel.

¹⁶The king must not get large numbers of horses for himself. He must not make the people return to Egypt to get more horses. The LORD has told you, "You must not go back there again." ¹⁷The king must not have a lot of wives. If he does, he will be led down the wrong path. He must not store up large amounts of silver and gold.

¹⁸When he sits on the throne of his kingdom, he must make himself a copy of the law I'm teaching you. He must write it on a scroll. He must copy it from the scroll of a priest, who is a Levite. ¹⁹The king must keep the scroll close to him at all times. He must read it all the days of his life. Then he can learn to have respect for the LORD his God. He can carefully follow all of the words of that law and those rules. ²⁰He won't think of himself as being better than his people are. He won't turn away from the law. He won't turn to the right or the left. Then he and his sons after him will rule over his kingdom in Israel for a long time.

Offerings for Priests and Levites

18 The priests, who are Levites, won't receive any part of the land of Israel. That also applies to the whole tribe of Levi. They will eat the offerings that are made to the LORD with fire. That will be their share. ²They won't have any part of the land the LORD gave the other tribes in

Israel. The LORD himself is their share, just as he promised them.

³Anyone who sacrifices a bull or a sheep owes a share of it to the priests. Their share is the shoulder, jaws and inside parts. ⁴You must give the priests the first share of the harvest of your grain, olive oil and fresh wine. You must also give them the first wool you clip from your sheep. ⁵The LORD your God has chosen the Levites and their sons after them to serve him in his name always. He hasn't chosen priests from any of your other tribes.

⁶Sometimes a Levite will move from the town in Israel where he's living. And he will come to the place the LORD will choose. He'll do it because he really wants to. ⁷Then he can serve in the name of the LORD his God. He'll be like all of the other Levites who serve the LORD there. ⁸He must have an equal share of the good things they have. That applies even if he has already received money by selling things his family owned.

Practices the LORD Hates

⁹You will enter the land the LORD your God is giving you. When you do, don't copy the practices of the nations that are there. The LORD hates those practices. ¹⁰Here are things you must not do. Don't sacrifice your children in the fire to other gods. Don't practice any kind of evil magic at all. Don't use magic to try to explain the meaning of warnings in the sky or of any other signs. Don't take part in worshiping evil powers. ¹¹Don't put a spell on anyone. Don't get messages from those who have died. Don't talk to the spirits of the dead. Don't get advice from the dead.

¹²The LORD your God hates it when anyone does those things. The nations that are in the land he's giving you practice the things he hates. So he will drive out those nations to make room for you. ¹³You must be without blame in the sight of the LORD your God.

The Prophet of the LORD

¹⁴You will take over the nations that are in the land the LORD is giving you. They listen to those who practice all kinds of evil magic. But you belong to the LORD your God. He says you must not do those things.

¹⁵The LORD your God will raise up for you a prophet like me. He will be one of your own people. You must listen to him. ¹⁶At Mount Horeb you asked the LORD your God for a prophet. You asked him on the day you gathered together. You said, "We don't want to hear the voice of the LORD our God. We don't want to see this great fire anymore. If we do, we'll die."

¹⁷The LORD said to me, "What they are saying is good. ¹⁸I will raise up for them a prophet like you. He will be one of their own people. I will put my words in his mouth. He will tell them everything I command him to say.

¹⁹"The prophet will speak in my name. But someone might not listen to what I say through the prophet. Then that person will be accountable to me.

²⁰"But suppose a prophet dares to speak in my name something I have not commanded him to say. Or he speaks in the name of other gods. Then that prophet must be put to death."

²¹You will say to yourselves, "How can we know when a message hasn't been spoken by the LORD?" ²²Sometimes a prophet will announce something in the name of the LORD. And it won't take place or come true. Then that's a message the LORD hasn't told him to speak. That prophet has dared to speak on his own authority. So don't be afraid of him or what he says.

Cities to Go to for Safety

19 The LORD your God will destroy the nations whose land he is giving you. You will drive them out. And you will settle down in their towns and houses.

²When you do, set apart for yourselves three cities in the land. It's the land the LORD your God is giving you to take as your own. ³Build roads to those cities and separate the land into three parts. Then anyone who kills another person can run to one of the cities for safety. They are in the land the LORD your God is giving you as your own.

⁴Here is the rule about a person who kills someone. That person can run to one of those cities for safety. The rule applies to all those who kill a neighbor they didn't hate and didn't mean to kill.

⁵For example, suppose a man goes into a forest with his neighbor to cut wood. When he swings his ax to chop down a tree, the head of the ax flies off. And it hits his neighbor and kills him. Then that man can run to one of those cities and save his life.

⁶If he doesn't go to one of those cities, the dead man's nearest male relative might become very angry. He might

chase the man. If the city is too far away, he might catch him and kill him. But he isn't worthy of death, because he didn't hate his neighbor. **7**That's why I command you to set apart for yourselves three cities.

8The LORD your God will increase the size of your territory. He took an oath and promised your fathers he would do it. He will give you the whole land he promised them. **9**But he'll do it only if you are careful to obey all of the laws I'm commanding you today. I'm commanding you to love the LORD your God. I want you to live always as he wants you to live.

When he gives you additional land, you must set apart three more cities. **10**Do it so the blood of those who aren't guilty of murder won't be spilled in your land. It's the land the LORD your God is giving you as your own.

11But suppose a man hates his neighbor. So he hides and waits for him. Then he attacks him and kills him. And he runs to one of those cities for safety. **12**If he does, the elders of his own town must send for him. He must be brought back from the city and handed over to the dead man's nearest male relative. The relative will kill him.

13Don't feel sorry for him. He has killed someone who hadn't done anything wrong. Crimes like that must be punished in Israel. Then things will go well with you.

14Don't move your neighbor's boundary stone. It was set up by people who lived there before you. It marks the border of a field in the land you will receive as your own. The LORD your God is giving you that land. You will take it over.

Witnesses

15Suppose someone is charged with committing a crime of any kind. Then one witness won't be enough to prove he is guilty. Every matter must be proved by the words of two or three witnesses.

16Suppose a witness who tells lies goes to court and brings charges against someone. The witness says that person committed a crime. **17**Then the two people in the case must stand in front of the LORD. They must stand in front of the priests and the judges who are in office at that time. **18**The judges must check out the matter carefully. And suppose the witness is proved to be lying. Then he has given false witness against another Israelite.

19So do to the lying witness what he tried to do to the other person. Get rid of that evil person. **20**The rest of the people will hear about it. And they will be afraid. They won't allow such an evil thing to be done among them again.

21Don't feel sorry for that evil person. A life must be taken for a life. An eye must be put out for an eye. A tooth must be knocked out for a tooth. A hand must be cut off for a hand and a foot for a foot.

Going to War

20 When you go to war against your enemies, you might see that they have horses and chariots. They might even have an army that is stronger than yours. But don't be afraid of them. The LORD your God will be with you. After all, he brought you up out of Egypt.

2Just before you go into battle, the priest will come forward. He'll speak to the army. **3**He'll say, "Men of Israel, listen to me. Today you are going into battle against your enemies. Don't be scared. Don't be afraid. Don't panic. Don't be terrified by them. **4**The LORD your God is going with you. He'll fight for you. He'll help you win the battle over your enemies."

5The officers will speak to the army. They will say, "Has anyone built a new house and not started to live in it? Let him go home. If he doesn't, he might die in battle. Then someone else will live in his house. **6**Has anyone planted a vineyard and not started to enjoy it? Let him go home. If he doesn't, he might die in battle. Then someone else will enjoy his vineyard. **7**Has anyone promised to get married to a woman but hasn't done it yet? Let him go home. If he doesn't, he might die in battle. Then someone else will marry her." **8**The officers will continue, "Is any man afraid? Is anyone scared? Let him go home. Then the other men won't lose hope too."

9The officers will finish speaking to the army. When they do, they'll appoint commanders over it.

10Suppose you march up to attack a city. Before you attack it, offer peace to its people. **11**Suppose they accept your offer and open their gates. Then force all of the people in the city to be your slaves. They will have to work for you.

12But suppose they refuse your offer of peace and prepare for battle. Then surround that city. Get ready to attack it. **13**The LORD your God will hand it over to you. When he does, kill all of the men with your swords. **14**But you can take the women and children for yourselves. You can also take the livestock and everything else in the city. What you have captured from your enemies you can use for yourselves. The LORD your God has given it to you.

15That's how you must treat all of the cities that are far away from you. Those cities don't belong to the nations that are nearby.

16But what about the cities the LORD your God is giving you as your own? Kill everything in those cities that breathes. **17**Completely destroy them. Wipe out the Hittites, Amorites, Canaanites, Perizzites, Hivites and Jebusites. That's what the LORD your God commanded you to do.

18If you don't destroy them, they'll teach you to follow all of the things the LORD hates. He hates the way they worship their gods. If you do those things, you will sin against the LORD your God.

19Suppose you surround a city and get ready to attack it. And suppose you fight against it for a long time in order to capture it. Then don't chop its trees down and destroy them. You can eat their fruit. So don't cut them down. The trees of the field aren't people. So why should you attack them?

20But you can cut down trees that you know aren't fruit trees. You can build war machines out of their wood. You can use them until you capture the city you are fighting against.

What to Do When You Don't Know Who Killed Someone

21 Suppose you find someone who has been killed. The body is lying in a field in the land the LORD your God is giving you to take as your own. But no one knows who the killer was. **2**Then your elders and judges will go out and measure how far it is from the body to the nearby towns.

3The elders from the town that is nearest to the body will get a young cow. It must never have been used for work. It must never have pulled a load. **4**The elders must lead it down into a valley. The valley must not have been farmed. There must be a stream flowing through it. There in the valley the elders must break the cow's neck.

5The priests, who are sons of Levi, will step forward. The LORD your God has chosen them to serve him. He wants them to bless the people in his name. He wants them to decide all cases that have to do with people arguing and attacking others. **6**Then all of the elders from the town

that is nearest to the body will wash their hands. They will wash them over the young cow whose neck they broke in the valley. **7**They'll say to the LORD, "We didn't kill that person. We didn't see it happen. **8**Accept this payment for the sin of your people Israel. LORD, you have set your people free. Don't hold them guilty for spilling the blood of someone who hasn't done anything wrong." That will pay for the death of that person.

9So you will get rid of the guilt of killing someone who didn't do anything wrong. That's because you have done what is right in the LORD's eyes.

Getting Married to a Woman Who Is Your Prisoner

10Suppose you go to war against your enemies. And the LORD your God hands them over to you and you take them as prisoners. **11**Then you notice a beautiful woman among them. If you like her, you can get married to her.

12Bring her home. Have her shave her head. Have her cut her nails. **13**Have her throw away the clothes she was wearing when she was captured. Let her live in your house and sob over her parents for a full month. Then you can go to her and be her husband. And she will be your wife.

14But suppose you aren't pleased with her. Then let her go where she wants to. You must not sell her. You must not treat her as a slave. You have already brought shame on her.

The Rights of the Oldest Son

15Suppose a man has two wives. He loves one but not the other. And both of them have sons by him. But the oldest son is the son of the wife the man doesn't love. **16**Someday he'll leave his property to his sons. When he does, he must not give the rights of the oldest son to the son of the wife he loves. He must give those rights to his oldest son. He must do it even though his oldest son is the son of the wife he doesn't love.

17He must recognize the full rights of the oldest son, even though that son is the son of the wife he doesn't love. He must give that son a double share of everything he has. That son is the first sign of his father's strength. So the rights of the oldest son belong to him.

A Stubborn Son

18Suppose someone has a very stubborn son. He doesn't obey his father and mother. And he won't listen to them when they try to correct him. **19**Then his parents will take hold of him and bring him to the elders at the gate of his town. **20**They will say to the elders, "This son of ours is very stubborn. He won't obey us. He wastes his money. He's always getting drunk."

21Then all of the people in his town will put him to death by throwing stones at him. Get rid of that evil person. All of the people of Israel will hear about it. And they will be afraid to disobey their parents.

Several Other Laws

22Suppose a man is put to death for a crime that is worthy of death. And a pole is stuck through his body and set up where people can see it. **23**Then you must not leave the body on the pole all night. Make sure you bury it that same day.

Everyone who is hung on a pole is under God's curse. You must not make the land "unclean." The LORD your God is giving it to you as your own.

22 Suppose you see your neighbor's ox or sheep wandering away. Then don't act as if you didn't see it. Instead, make sure you take it back to him.

2Your neighbor might not live near you. Or you might not know who he is. Then take the animal home with you. Keep it until he comes looking for it. Then give it back.

3Do the same thing if you find his donkey, coat or anything he loses. Don't act as if you didn't see it.

4Suppose you see your neighbor's donkey or ox that has fallen down on the road. Then don't act as if you didn't see it. Help him get it up on its feet again.

5A woman must not wear men's clothes. And a man must not wear women's clothes. The LORD your God hates it when anyone does that.

6Suppose you happen to find a bird's nest beside the road. It might be in a tree or on the ground. And suppose the mother bird is sitting on her little birds or on the eggs. Then don't take the mother along with the little ones. **7**You can take the little ones. But make sure you let the mother go. Then things will go well with you. You will live for a long time.

8If you build a new house, put a low wall around the edge of your roof. Then you won't be held accountable if someone falls off your roof and dies.

9Don't plant two kinds of seeds in your vineyard. If you do, the crops you grow there will be polluted. Your grapes will also be polluted.

10Don't let an ox and a donkey pull the same plow together.

11Don't wear clothes made of wool and linen that are woven together.

12Make tassels on the four corners of the coat you wear.

Breaking Marriage Laws

13Suppose a man gets married to a woman and makes love to her. But then he doesn't like her. **14**So he tells lies about her and says she's a bad woman. He says, "I got married to this woman. But when I made love to her, I discovered she wasn't a virgin." **15**Then the woman's parents must bring proof that she was a virgin. They must give the proof to the elders at the gate of the town.

16The woman's father will speak to the elders. He'll say, "I gave my daughter to this man to be his wife. But he doesn't like her. **17**So now he has told lies about her. He has said, 'I discovered that your daughter wasn't a virgin.' But here's the proof that my daughter was a virgin." Then her parents will show the elders of the town the cloth that has her blood on it.

18The elders will punish the man. **19**They'll make him weigh out two and a half pounds of silver. They'll give it to the woman's father. That's because the man has said an Israelite virgin is a bad woman. She will continue to be his wife. He must not divorce her as long as he lives.

20But suppose the charge is true. And there isn't any proof that the woman was a virgin. **21**Then she must be brought to the door of her father's house. There the people of her town will put her to death by throwing stones at her. She has done a very terrible thing in Israel. She has had sex before she got married. Get rid of that evil person.

22Suppose a man is seen having sex with another man's wife. Then the man and the woman must both die. Get rid of those evil people.

23Suppose a man happens to see a virgin in a town. And she has promised to get married to another man. But the man who happens to see her has sex with her. **24**Then you must take both of them to the gate of that town. You must put them to death by throwing stones at them. You must kill the woman because she was in a town and didn't scream for help. And you must kill the man because he had sex with another man's wife. Get rid of those evil people.

25But suppose a man happens to see a woman out in the country. And she has promised to marry another man. But the man who happens to see her rapes her. Then only the man who has done that will die. 26Don't do anything to the woman. She hasn't committed a sin that is worthy of death. That case is like the case of someone who attacks and murders his neighbor. 27The man found the woman out in the country. And she screamed. But there wasn't anyone around who could save her.

28Suppose a man happens to see a virgin who hasn't promised to marry another man. And the man who happens to see her rapes her. But someone discovers them. 29Then the man must weigh out 20 ounces of silver. He must give it to the woman's father. The man must marry the woman, because he raped her. And he can never divorce her as long as he lives.

30A man must not get married to his stepmother. He must not bring shame on his father by having sex with her.

Who Can Worship With the LORD's People?

23 No man whose sex organs have been crushed or cut can join in worship with the LORD's people.

2No one who was born to a woman who wasn't married can join in worship with the LORD's people. That also applies to the person's children for all time to come.

3The people of Ammon and Moab can't join in worship with the LORD's people. That also applies to their children after them for all time to come. 4The Ammonites and Moabites didn't come to meet you with food and water on your way out of Egypt. They even hired Balaam from Pethor in Aram Naharaim to call down a curse on you. Balaam was the son of Beor. 5The LORD your God wouldn't listen to Balaam. Instead, he turned the curse into a blessing for you. He did it because he loves you. 6So don't make a peace treaty with the Ammonites and Moabites as long as you live.

7Don't hate the people of Edom. They are your relatives. Don't hate the people of Egypt. After all, you lived as outsiders in their country. 8The great-grandchildren of the Edomites and Egyptians can join in worship with the LORD's people.

Keep the Camp of the Soldiers Pure and Clean

9There will be times when you are at war with your enemies. And your soldiers will be in camp. Then keep away from anything that isn't pure and clean.

10Suppose semen flows from the body of one of your soldiers during the night. Then that will make him "unclean." He must go outside the camp and stay there. 11But as evening approaches, he must wash himself. When the sun goes down, he can return to the camp.

12Choose a place outside the camp where you can go to the toilet. 13Keep a shovel among your tools. When you go to the toilet, dig a hole. Then cover up your waste.

14The LORD your God walks around in your camp. He's there to keep you safe. He's also there to hand your enemies over to you. So your camp must be holy. Then he won't see anything among you that is shameful. He won't turn away from you.

Several Other Laws

15If a slave comes to you for safety, don't hand him over to his master. 16Let him live among you anywhere he wants to. Let him live in any town he chooses. Don't crush him.

17A man or woman in Israel must not become a temple prostitute. 18The LORD your God hates the money that men and women get for being prostitutes. So don't take that money into the house of the LORD to pay what you promised to give.

19Don't charge your own people any interest. Don't charge them when they borrow money, food or anything else. 20You can charge interest to people from another country. But don't charge your own people. Then the LORD your God will bless you in everything you do. He will bless you in the land you are entering to take as your own.

21Don't put off giving to the LORD your God everything you promise him. He will certainly require it from you. And you will be guilty of committing a sin. 22But if you don't make a promise, you won't be guilty. 23Make sure you do what you promised to do. With your own mouth you made the promise to the LORD your God. No one forced you to do it.

24When you enter your neighbor's vineyard, you can eat all of the grapes you want. But don't put any of them in your basket. 25When you enter your neighbor's field, you can pick heads of grain. But don't cut down his standing grain.

24 Suppose a man gets married to a woman. But later he decides he doesn't like her. He finds something

shameful about her. So he gives her a letter of divorce and sends her away from his house. **2**Then after she leaves his house she becomes another man's wife. **3**But her second husband doesn't like her either. So he gives her a letter of divorce and sends her away from his house. Or perhaps he dies. **4**Then her first husband isn't allowed to marry her again. The LORD would hate that. When her first husband divorced her, she became "unclean." Don't bring sin on the land the LORD your God is giving you as your own.

5Suppose a man has just gotten married. Then don't send him into battle. Don't give him any other duty either. He's free to stay home for one year. He needs time to make his new wife happy.

POWER-SURGE

CHEERFUL ✳

SUPPOSE A MAN HAS JUST GOTTEN MARRIED. THEN DON'T SEND HIM INTO BATTLE. DON'T GIVE HIM ANY OTHER DUTY EITHER. HE'S FREE TO STAY HOME FOR ONE YEAR. HE NEEDS TIME TO MAKE HIS NEW WIFE HAPPY.

— DEUTERONOMY 24:5 —

6Someone might borrow money from you and give you two millstones to keep until you are paid back. Don't keep them. Don't even keep the upper one. That person depends on the millstones to make a living.

7Suppose a man is caught kidnapping another Israelite. And he sells or treats that person as a slave. Then the kidnapper must die. Get rid of that evil person.

8What about skin diseases? Be very careful to do exactly what the priests, who are Levites, tell you to do. You must be careful to follow the commands I've given them. **9**Remember what the LORD your God did to Miriam on your way out of Egypt.

10Suppose your neighbor borrows something from you. And he offers you something to keep until you get paid back. Then don't go into his house to get it. **11**Stay outside. Let the man bring it out to you.

12He might be poor. You might be given his coat to keep until you get paid back. Don't go to sleep while you still have it. **13**Return it before the sun goes down. He needs it to sleep in and will thank you for returning it. The LORD your God will see it and know that you have done the right thing.

14Don't take advantage of any hired worker who is poor and needy. That applies to your own people. It also applies to outsiders who are living in one of your towns. **15**Give them their pay every day. They are poor and are counting on it. If you don't pay them, they might cry out to the LORD against you. Then you will be guilty of committing a sin.

16Parents must not be put to death because of what their children do. And children must not be put to death because of what their parents do. People must die because of their own sins.

17Do what is right and fair for outsiders and for children whose fathers have died. Suppose a widow borrows something from you. And she offers to give you her coat until she pays you back. Don't take it.

18Remember that you were slaves in Egypt. Remember that the LORD your God set you free from there. That's why I'm commanding you to do those things.

19When you are gathering crops in your field, you might leave some grain behind by mistake. Don't go back to get it. Leave it for outsiders and widows. Leave it for children whose fathers have died. Then the LORD your God will bless you in everything you do.

20When you knock olives off your trees, don't go back over the branches a second time. Leave what remains for outsiders and widows. Leave it for children whose fathers have died. **21**When you pick grapes in your vineyard, don't go back over the vines a second time. Leave what remains for outsiders and widows. Leave it for children whose fathers have died.

22Remember that you were slaves in Egypt. That's why I'm commanding you to do those things.

25 Suppose two men don't agree about something. Then they must take their case to court. The judges will decide the case. They will let the one who isn't guilty go free. And they will punish the one who is guilty.

2The guilty one might have done something that's worthy of a beating. Then the judge will make him lie down and be beaten with a whip right there in court. The number of strokes should fit the crime. **3**But the judge must not give the guilty man more than 40 strokes. If more than that are used, you will look down on your Israelite neighbor.

4Don't stop an ox from eating while you use it to separate grain from straw.

5Suppose two brothers are living near each other. And one of them dies without having a son. Then his widow must not get married to anyone outside the family. Her husband's brother should marry her. That's what a brother-in-law is supposed to do. **6**Her first baby boy will be named after her first husband. Then the dead man's name will not be wiped out in Israel.

7But suppose the man doesn't want to get married to his brother's wife. Then she will go to the elders at the gate of the town. She will say, "My husband's brother refuses to keep his brother's name alive in Israel. He won't do for me what a brother-in-law is supposed to do."

8Then the elders in his town will send for him. They will talk to him. But he still might say, "I don't want to marry her." **9**Then his brother's widow will go up to him in front of the elders. She'll pull one of his sandals off his foot. She'll spit in his face. And she'll say, "That's what we do to a man who won't build up his brother's family line." **10**That man's family line will be known in Israel as The Family of the Man Whose Sandal Was Pulled Off.

11Suppose two men are fighting. And the wife of one of them comes to save her husband from his attacker. So she reaches out and grabs hold of his sex organs. **12**Then you must cut off her hand. Don't feel sorry for her.

13Don't have two different scales. You must not have one that weighs things heavier than they really are and another that weighs them lighter than they are. **14**And don't have two different sets of measures. You must not have one set that measures things larger than they really are and another that measures them smaller than they are. **15**You must use weights and measures that are honest and exact. Then you will live a long time in the land the LORD your God is giving you. **16**He hates anyone who cheats.

17Remember what the Amalekites did to you on your way out of Egypt. **18**You were tired and worn out. They met you on your journey. They attacked everyone who was lagging behind. They didn't have any respect for God. **19**The LORD your God will give you peace and rest from all of the enemies who are around you. He'll do it in the land he's giving you to take over as your very own. Then you will wipe out the memory of the Amalekites from the earth. Don't forget to do it!

Give the LORD His Share

26 You will enter the land the LORD your God is giving you as your own. You will take it over. You will settle down in it. **2**When you do, get some of the first share of everything your soil produces. Put it in a basket. It's from the land the LORD your God is giving you. Take your gifts and go to the special place he will choose. He will put his Name there.

3Speak to the priest who is in office at that time. Tell him, "I announce today to the LORD your God that I have come to this land. It's the land he promised with an oath to our fathers to give us." **4**The priest will take the basket from you. He'll set it down in front of the altar of the LORD your God.

5Then you will speak while the LORD is listening. You will say, "My father Jacob was a wanderer from the land of Aram. He went down into Egypt with a few people. He lived there and became the father of a great nation. It had huge numbers of people. **6**"But the people of Egypt treated us badly. They made us suffer. They made us work very hard. **7**Then we cried out to the LORD. He is the God of our people who lived long ago. He heard our voice. He saw how much we were suffering. The Egyptians were crushing us. They were making us work very hard.

8"So the LORD reached out his mighty hand and powerful arm and brought us out of Egypt. He did great and wonderful things. He did miraculous signs and wonders. **9**He brought us to this place. He gave us this land. It's a land that has plenty of milk and honey.

10"Now, LORD, I'm bringing you the first share of crops from the soil. After all, you have given them to me." Place the basket in front of the LORD your God. Bow down to him.

11You and the Levites and the outsiders among you will be full of joy. You will enjoy all of the good things the LORD your God has given to you and your family.

12You will set apart a tenth of everything you produce in the third year. That's the year for giving the tenth to people who have special needs. You will give it to the Levites, outsiders and widows. You will also give it to children whose fathers have died. Then all of them will have plenty to eat in your towns.

13Speak to the LORD your God. Say to him, "I have taken your sacred share from my house. I have given it to the Levites, outsiders and widows. I have also given it to children whose fathers have died. I've done everything you commanded me to do. I haven't turned away from your commands. I haven't forgotten any of them. 14I haven't eaten any part of your sacred share while I was sobbing over someone who had died. I haven't taken any of it from my house while I was 'unclean.' And I haven't offered any of it to the dead. LORD my God, I've obeyed you. I've done everything you commanded me to do.

15"Look down from the holy place where you live in heaven. Bless your people Israel. Bless the land you have given us. It's the land you promised with an oath to give to our fathers. It's a land that has plenty of milk and honey."

Follow the LORD's Commands

16This very day the LORD your God commands you to follow all of those rules and laws. Be careful to obey them with all your heart and with all your soul.

17Today you have announced that the LORD is your God. You have said you would live exactly as he wants you to live. You have agreed to keep his rules, commands and laws. And you have said you would obey him.

18Today the LORD has announced that you are his people. He has said that you are his special treasure. He promised that

POWER-SURGE

OBEYS ✔

THIS VERY DAY THE LORD YOUR GOD COMMANDS YOU TO FOLLOW ALL OF THOSE RULES AND LAWS. BE CAREFUL TO OBEY THEM WITH ALL YOUR HEART AND WITH ALL YOUR SOUL.

— DEUTERONOMY 26:16 —

you would be. He has told you to keep all of his commands. 19He has announced that he will make you famous. He'll give you more praise and honor than all of the other nations he has made. And he has said that you will be a holy nation. The LORD your God has set you apart for himself. That's exactly what he promised to do.

The Altar on Mount Ebal

27 The elders of Israel and I gave commands to the people. We said, "Obey all of the commands we're giving you today.

2"You will go across the Jordan River. You will enter the land the LORD your God is giving you. When you do, set up some large stones. Put a coat of plaster on them. 3Write all of the words of this law on them. Do it when you have crossed over into the land the LORD your God is giving you. It's a land that has plenty of milk and honey. The LORD is the God of your fathers. He promised you that you would enter the land. 4After you have gone across the Jordan, set up those stones on Mount Ebal. Put a coat of plaster on them. We're commanding you today to do that.

5"Build an altar there to honor the LORD your God. Make it out of stones. Don't use any iron tool on them. 6Use stones you find in the fields to build his altar. Then offer burnt offerings on it to the LORD your God. 7Sacrifice friendship offerings there. Eat them and be filled with joy in the sight of the LORD your God.

8"You must write all of the words of this law on the stones you have set up. Write the words very clearly."

Curses for Not Obeying the LORD

9Then the priests, who are Levites, and I spoke to all of the people of Israel. We said, "Israel, be quiet! Listen! You have now become the people of the LORD your God. 10Obey him. Follow his commands and rules that we're giving you today."

11Here are the commands I gave the people that very day.

12You will go across the Jordan River. When you do, I want six tribes to stand on Mount Gerizim to bless the people. Those tribes are Simeon, Levi, Judah, Issachar, Joseph and Benjamin. 13I want the other six tribes to stand on Mount Ebal to announce some curses. Those tribes are Reuben, Gad, Asher, Zebulun, Dan and Naphtali.

14The Levites will speak to all of the

people of Israel in a loud voice. They will say,

15 "May any man who makes a wooden or metal statue of a god and sets it up in secret be under the LORD's curse. That statue is made by a skilled worker. And the LORD hates it."

Then all of the people will say, "Amen!"

16 "May anyone who brings shame on his father or mother be under the LORD's curse."

Then all of the people will say, "Amen!"

17 "May anyone who moves his neighbor's boundary stone be under the LORD's curse."

Then all of the people will say, "Amen!"

18 "May anyone who leads blind people down the wrong road be under the LORD's curse."

Then all of the people will say, "Amen!"

19 "May anyone who isn't fair in the way he treats outsiders, widows, and children whose fathers have died be under the LORD's curse."

Then all of the people will say, "Amen!"

20 "May any man who has sex with his stepmother be under the LORD's curse. That man brings shame on his father by doing that."

Then all of the people will say, "Amen!"

21 "May anyone who has sex with animals be under the LORD's curse."

Then all of the people will say, "Amen!"

22 "May any man who has sex with his sister be under the LORD's curse. It doesn't matter whether she is his full sister or his half sister."

Then all of the people will say, "Amen!"

23 "May any man who has sex with his mother-in-law be under the LORD's curse."

Then all of the people will say, "Amen!"

24 "May anyone who kills his neighbor secretly be under the LORD's curse."

Then all of the people will say, "Amen!"

25 "May anyone who accepts money to kill someone who isn't guilty of doing anything wrong be under the LORD's curse."

Then all of the people will say, "Amen!"

26 "May anyone who doesn't honor the words of this law by obeying them be under the LORD's curse."

Then all of the people will say, "Amen!"

Blessings for Obeying the LORD

28 Make sure you obey the LORD your God completely. Be careful to follow all of his commands. I'm giving them to you today. If you do those things, the LORD will honor you more than all of the other nations on earth. **2** If you obey the LORD your God, here are the blessings that will come to you and remain with you.

3 You will be blessed in the cities. You will be blessed out in the country.

4 Your children will be blessed. Your crops will be blessed. The young animals among your livestock will be blessed. That includes your calves and lambs.

5 Your baskets and bread pans will be blessed.

6 You will be blessed no matter where you go.

7 Enemies will rise up against you. But the LORD will help you win the battle over them. They will come at you from one direction. But they'll run away from you in seven directions.

8 The LORD your God will bless your barns with plenty of grain and other food. He will bless everything you do. He'll bless you in the land he's giving you.

9 The LORD your God will make you his holy people. He will set you apart for himself. He took an oath and promised to do that. He promised to do it if you would keep his commands and live exactly as he wants you to live. **10** All of the nations on earth will see that you belong to the LORD. And they will be afraid of you.

11 The LORD will give you more than you need. You will have many children. Your livestock will have many little ones. Your crops will do very well. All of that will happen in the land he promised with an oath to your fathers to give you.

12 The LORD will open up the heavens. That's where he stores his riches. He will send rain on your land at just the right time. He'll bless everything you do. You will lend money to many nations. But you won't have to borrow from any of them. **13** The LORD your God will make you leaders, not followers.

Pay attention to his commands that I'm giving you today. Be careful to follow them. Then you will always be on top. You will never be on the bottom.

14 Don't turn away from any of the commands I'm giving you today. Don't turn to the right or the left. Don't follow other gods. Don't worship them.

More Curses for Not Obeying the LORD

15 But suppose you don't obey the LORD your God. And you aren't careful to follow all of his commands and rules I'm giving you today. Then he will send curses on you. They'll catch up with you. Here are those curses.

16 You will be cursed in the cities. You will be cursed out in the country.

17 Your baskets and bread pans will be cursed.

18 Your children will be cursed. Your crops will be cursed. Your calves and lambs will be cursed.

19 You will be cursed no matter where you go.

20 The LORD will send curses on you. You won't know what's going on. In everything you do, he will be angry with you. You will be destroyed suddenly and completely. That will happen because you did an evil thing when you deserted the LORD.

21 He will send all kinds of sicknesses on you. He'll send them until he has destroyed you. He'll remove you from the land you are entering to take as your own. **22** The LORD will make you sick and very weak. He will strike you with fever and swelling. He'll send burning heat. There won't be any rain. The hot winds will completely dry up your crops. All of those things will happen until you die.

23 The sky above you will be like bronze. The ground beneath you will be like iron. **24** The LORD will turn the rain of your country into dust and powder. It will come down from the skies until you are destroyed.

25 The LORD will help your enemies win the battle over you. You will come at them from one direction. But you will run away from them in seven directions. You will look so bad that all of the kingdoms on earth will be completely shocked when they see you. **26** Birds and wild animals will eat up your dead bodies. There won't be anyone left to scare them away.

27 The LORD will send boils on you, just like the ones he sent on the Egyptians. You will have growths in your bodies and boils on your skin. You will itch all over. No one will be able to heal you.

28 The LORD will make you lose your mind. He will make you blind. You won't know what's going on. **29** Even at noon you will have to feel your way around like a blind person in the dark. You won't have success in anything you do. Day after day you will be robbed and beaten down. No one will be able to save you.

30 You and a woman will promise to get married to each other. But another man will take her and rape her. You will build a house. But you won't live in it. You will plant a vineyard. But you won't eat a single grape from it. **31** Your ox will be killed right in front of your eyes. But you won't eat any of it. Your donkey will be taken away from you by force. And you will never get it back. Your sheep will be given to your enemies. No one will be able to save them.

32 Your children will be given to another nation. Day after day you will watch for them to come back. But you will only wear out your eyes. You won't be able to help your children.

33 A nation you don't know anything about will eat what you work to produce on your land. You will be completely beaten down as long as you live. **34** The things you see will make you lose your mind. **35** The LORD will send painful boils on your knees and legs. No one will be able to heal them. They will cover you from head to toe.

36 The LORD will drive you out of the land. And he will drive out the king you place over you. All of you will go to a nation you and your people long ago didn't know anything about. There you will worship other gods. They will be made out of wood and stone. **37** You will look very bad to all of the nations where the LORD sends you. They will be completely shocked when they see you. They will laugh at you and make fun of you.

38 You will plant many seeds in your field. But you will gather very little food. Locusts will eat it up. **39** You will plant vineyards and take care of them. But you won't drink the wine. You won't gather the grapes. Worms will eat them up. **40** You will have olive trees through your whole country. But you won't use the oil. The olives will drop off the trees. **41** You will have children. But you won't be able to keep them. They'll be taken away as prisoners. **42** Large numbers of locusts will eat up the leaves on all of your trees. They will also eat up the crops on your land.

43 Outsiders who live among you will become your leaders. They will rise higher and higher. But you will sink lower and lower. **44**They will lend money to you. But you won't be able to lend money to them. They will be the leaders. But you will be the followers.

45The LORD your God will send all of those curses on you. They will follow you everywhere. They'll catch up with you. You will be under the LORD's curse until you are destroyed. That's because you didn't obey him. You didn't keep the commands and rules he gave you. **46**Those curses will remain as miraculous signs and wonders against you and your children after you forever.

47You didn't serve the LORD your God with joy and gladness when times were good. **48**So he will send enemies against you. You will have to serve them. You will be hungry and thirsty. You will be naked and poor. The LORD will put the iron chains of slavery around your necks until he has destroyed you.

49The LORD will bring a nation against you from far away. It will come from the ends of the earth. It will dive down on you like an eagle. You won't understand that nation's language. **50**Its people will look mean. They won't have any respect for old people. They won't show any kindness to young people.

51They will eat up the young animals among your livestock. They'll eat up the crops on your land. They'll destroy you. They won't leave you any grain, olive oil or fresh wine. They won't leave you any calves or lambs. They'll destroy you. **52**They'll surround all of the cities through your whole land. They'll get ready to attack them. They'll do those things until the high, strong walls you trust in fall down. That's what will happen to the cities in the land the LORD your God is giving you.

53Your enemies will surround you and get ready to attack you. They will make you suffer greatly. So you will eat your own children. You will eat the dead bodies of the sons and daughters the LORD your God has given you.

54There may be a gentle and caring man among you. But he will treat his own brother badly. He'll be just as mean to the wife he loves and to any of his children who are still alive. **55**He won't give to a single one of them any part of the dead bodies of his children that he's eating. It will be all he has left to eat. That's how much your enemies will make you suffer when they surround all of your cities to attack them.

56There may be a gentle and caring woman among you. She wouldn't even touch the ground with her feet without first putting her sandals on. But she will not share anything with the husband she loves. She won't share with her own children either. **57**She will eat what comes out of her body after she has a baby. Then she'll even eat her baby. She won't share it with anyone in her family. She'll plan to eat it in secret. There won't be anything else for her to eat because the city she lives in will be surrounded. That's an example of how much your enemies will make you suffer when they are getting ready to attack your cities.

58Be careful to follow all of the words of this law. They are written in this scroll. Have respect for the glorious and wonderful name of the LORD your God. If you don't, **59**he will send terrible plagues on you and your children after you. He'll send horrible and lasting troubles. He'll make you very sick for a long time. **60**He'll bring on you all of the sicknesses you were afraid of getting when you were in Egypt. You won't be able to get rid of them. **61**The LORD will also bring on you all of the other kinds of sickness and trouble I haven't written down in this Scroll of the Law. You will be destroyed.

62At one time you were as many as the stars in the sky. But there will only be a few of you left. That's because you didn't obey the LORD your God. **63**It pleased the LORD to give you success and to increase your numbers. But it will please him just as much to wipe you out and destroy you. You will be removed from the land you are entering to take as your own.

64Then the LORD will scatter you among all of the nations. He'll spread you around from one end of the earth to the other. There you will worship statues of gods that are made out of wood and stone. You and your people long ago hadn't known anything about those gods.

65Among those nations you won't find any peace. There won't be any place where you can settle down and rest your feet. There the LORD will give you minds that are filled with worry. He'll give you eyes that are worn out from sobbing. Your hearts won't have any hope.

66Your lives will always be in danger. You will be filled with fear night and day. You will never be sure you are safe. **67**In the morning you will say, "We wish it were evening!" In the evening you will say, "We wish it were morning!" Your hearts will be filled with fear. The things you see will terrify you.

68The Lord will send you back to Egypt in ships. He'll send you on a journey I said you should never have to make again. You will offer to sell yourselves to your enemies as slaves in Egypt. But no one will buy you.

Follow the Terms of the Covenant

29 These are the terms of the covenant the Lord commanded me to make with the people of Israel in Moab. The terms were added to the covenant he had made with them at Mount Horeb.

2I sent for all of the Israelites. Here is what I said to them.

With your own eyes you have seen everything the Lord did in Egypt to Pharaoh. You have seen what he did to all of Pharaoh's officials and to his whole land. **3**With your own eyes you saw how the Lord really made them suffer. You saw his miraculous signs and great wonders.

4But to this very day the Lord hasn't given you a mind that understands. He hasn't given you eyes that see. He hasn't given you ears that hear.

5He led you through the desert for 40 years. During that time your clothes didn't wear out. The sandals on your feet didn't wear out either. **6**You didn't eat any bread. You didn't drink any kind of wine. The Lord did all of those things because he wanted you to know that he is the Lord your God.

7When we got here, Sihon and Og came out to fight against us. Sihon was the king of Heshbon. And Og was the king of Bashan. But we won the battle over them. **8**We took their land. We gave it to the tribes of Reuben and Gad and half of the tribe of Manasseh as their share.

9Be careful to obey the terms of this covenant. Then you will have success in everything you do.

10Today all of you are standing here in the sight of the Lord your God. Your leaders and chief men are here. Your elders and officials are here. So are all of the other men of Israel. **11**Your children and wives are here with you too. So are the outsiders who are living in your camps. They chop your wood and carry your water. **12**All of you are standing here in order to enter into a covenant with the Lord your God. He is making the covenant with you today. He's sealing it with an oath. **13**Today he wants to show you that

you are his people and that he is your God. That's what he promised with an oath to your fathers. He promised it to Abraham, Isaac and Jacob.

14I'm making this covenant. I'm sealing it with an oath. I'm not making it only with you **15**who are standing here with us today in the sight of the Lord our God. I'm also making it with those who aren't here today.

16You yourselves know how we lived in Egypt. You also know how we passed through other countries on the way here. **17**You saw the statues of their gods that were made out of wood, stone, silver and gold. The Lord hates those statues.

18Make sure there isn't a man or woman among your families or tribes who turns away from the Lord our God. No one must worship the gods of those nations. Make sure that kind of worship doesn't spread like bitter poison through your whole community.

19Some people who worship those gods will hear the oath that seals the covenant I'm making. They think they can escape trouble by saying to themselves, "We'll be safe, even though we're stubborn and go our own way." But trouble will come on them everywhere in the land.

20The Lord will never be willing to forgive those people. His burning anger will blaze out against them. All of the curses I've written down in this scroll will fall on them. And the Lord will wipe out their names from the earth. **21**He will find those people in all of the tribes of Israel and give them nothing but trouble. That will be in keeping with all of the curses of the covenant. They are written down in this Scroll of the Law.

22Even your children's children will see the troubles that have fallen on the land. They'll see the sicknesses the Lord has brought on it. People who come from countries far away will also see those things.

23The whole land will be burned up. Nothing but salt and sulfur will be left. Nothing will be planted there. Nothing will grow there. In fact, nothing will even start to grow there. The land will be like Sodom, Gomorrah, Admah and Zeboiim after they were destroyed. The Lord wiped out those cities because he was very angry.

24All of the nations will ask, "Why has the Lord done this to the land? What could have made him so very angry?"

25And they will hear the answer, "It's because the people who are living there have broken the covenant of the Lord. He's the God of their parents. He made that covenant with them when he brought them out of Egypt. 26They went off and worshiped other gods. They bowed down to them. They hadn't known anything about those gods before. The Lord hadn't given those gods to them.

27"So the Lord's anger burned against the land. He brought on it all of the curses that are written down in this scroll. 28The Lord's anger blazed out against his people. So he pulled them up out of their land. He threw them into another land. And that's where they are now."

29The Lord our God keeps certain things hidden. But he makes other things known to us and our children forever. He does it so we can obey all of the words of this law.

The Lord Will Bless His People

30 I have told you about all of those blessings and curses. The Lord will bring them on you. Then you will think carefully about them everywhere the Lord your God scatters you among the nations. 2You and your children will return to the Lord your God. You will obey him with all your heart and with all your soul. That will be in keeping with everything I'm commanding you today.

3When all of that happens, the Lord your God will bless you with great success again. He will be very kind to you. He'll bring you back from all of the nations where he scattered you. 4Suppose you have been forced to go away to the farthest land on earth. The Lord your God will bring you back even from there.

5He will bring you to the land that belonged to your people long ago. You will take it over. He'll make you better off than your people were. He'll increase your numbers more than he increased theirs. 6The Lord your God will keep your hearts from being stubborn. He'll do the same thing for your children and their children. Then you will love him with all your heart and with all your soul. And you will live.

7The Lord your God will put all of those curses on your enemies. They hated you and hunted you down.

8You will obey the Lord again. You will follow all of his commands that I'm giving you today. 9Then the Lord your God will give you great success in everything you do. You will have many children. Your livestock will have many little ones.

Your crops will do very well. The Lord will take delight in you again. He'll give you success. That's what he did for your people long ago.

10But you must obey the Lord your God. You must keep his commands and rules. They are written in this Scroll of the Law. You must turn to the Lord your God with all your heart and with all your soul.

Choose Life

11What I'm commanding you today is not too hard for you. It isn't beyond your reach. 12It isn't up in heaven. So you don't have to ask, "Who will go up into heaven to get it? Who will announce it to us so we can obey it?" 13And it isn't beyond the ocean. So you don't have to ask, "Who will go across the ocean to get it? Who will announce it to us so we can obey it?"

14No, the message isn't far away at all. In fact, it's really near you. It's in your mouth and in your heart so that you can obey it.

15Today I'm giving you a choice. You can have life and success. Or you can have death and harm. 16I'm commanding you today to love the Lord your God. I'm commanding you to live exactly as he wants you to live. You must obey his commands, rules and laws. Then you will live. Your numbers will increase. The Lord your God will bless you in the land you are entering to take as your own.

17Don't let your hearts turn away from the Lord. Instead, obey him. Don't let yourselves be drawn away to other gods. And don't bow down to them and worship them. 18If you do, I announce to you this very day that you will certainly be destroyed. You are about to go across the Jordan River and take over the land. But you won't live there very long.

19I'm calling for heaven and earth to give witness against you this very day. I'm offering you the choice of life or death. You can choose either blessings or curses. But I want you to choose life. Then you and your children will live. 20And you will love the Lord your God. You will obey him. You will remain true to him. The Lord is your very life. He will give you many years in the land. He took an oath. He promised to give that land to your fathers. He promised it to Abraham, Isaac and Jacob.

Joshua Becomes the New Leader

31 Here are the words I spoke to all of the people of Israel. 2I said, "I am now 120 years old. I'm not able to lead

POWER-SURGE

BRAVE B

BE STRONG AND
BRAVE. DON'T BE
AFRAID OF THEM.
DON'T BE TERRIFIED
BECAUSE OF THEM.
THE LORD YOUR GOD
WILL GO WITH YOU. HE
WILL NEVER LEAVE
YOU. HE'LL NEVER
DESERT YOU."
— DEUTERONOMY 31:6 —

STRONG

you anymore. The LORD has said to me, 'You will not go across the Jordan River.'

3 "The LORD your God himself will go across ahead of you. He'll destroy the nations that are there in order to make room for you. You will take over their land. Joshua will also go across ahead of you, just as the LORD said he would.

4 "The LORD will do to those nations what he did to Sihon and Og. He destroyed those Amorite kings along with their land. 5 The LORD will hand those nations over to you. Then you must do to them everything I've commanded you to do.

6 "Be strong and brave. Don't be afraid of them. Don't be terrified because of them. The LORD your God will go with you. He will never leave you. He'll never desert you."

7 Then I sent for Joshua. I spoke to him in front of all of the people of Israel. I said, "Be strong and brave. You must go with these people. They are going into the land the LORD promised with an oath to give to their fathers. You must divide it up among them. They will each receive their share. 8 The LORD himself will go ahead of you. He will be with you. He will never leave you. He'll never desert you. So don't be afraid. Don't lose hope."

The Law Must Be Read

9 I wrote down that law. I gave it to the priests, who are sons of Levi. They carried the ark of the covenant of the LORD. I also gave the law to all of the elders of Israel.

10 Then I commanded them, "You must read this law at the end of every seven years. Do it in the year when you forgive people what they owe. Read it during the Feast of Booths. 11 That's when all of the people of Israel come to appear in front of the LORD your God at the holy tent. It will be at the place he will choose. You must read this law to them.

12 "Gather the people together. Gather the men, women and children. Also bring together the outsiders who are living in your towns. Then they can listen and learn to have respect for the LORD your God. And they'll be careful to obey all of the words of this law. 13 Their children must hear it read too. They don't know this law yet. They too must learn to have respect for the LORD your God. They must respect him as long as you live in the land. You are about to go across the Jordan River and take that land as your very own."

Israel Will Refuse to Obey the LORD

14 The LORD spoke to me. He said, "The day when you will die is near. Have Joshua go to the Tent of Meeting. Join him there. That is where I will appoint him as the new leader." So Joshua and I went to the Tent of Meeting.

15 Then the LORD appeared at the tent in a pillar of cloud. It stood over the entrance to the tent. 16 The LORD spoke to me. He said, "You are going to join the members of your family who have already died. The people will not be faithful to me. They will soon join themselves to the strange gods that are worshiped in the land they are entering. The people will desert me. They will break the covenant I made with them.

17 "On that day I will become angry with them. I will desert them. I will turn my face away from them. And they will be destroyed. Many horrible troubles and hard times will come on them. On that day they will say, 'Trouble has come on us. Our God isn't with us!'

18 "I will certainly turn away from them on that day. I will do it because they did a very evil thing when they turned to other gods.

19 "I want you to write down a song for yourselves. Teach it to the people of Israel. Have them sing it. It will be my witness against them.

20 "I will bring them into a land that has plenty of milk and honey. I promised the

land to their fathers. I took an oath when I promised it. In that land they will eat until they have had enough. They will get fat. When they do, they will turn to other gods and worship them. They will turn their backs on me. They will break my covenant.

21"Many horrible troubles and hard times will come on them. Then the song I am giving you will be a witness against them. That is because the song will not be forgotten by their children and their children's children. I know what they are likely to do. I know it even before I bring them into the land I promised them with an oath."

22So that day I wrote the song down. And I taught it to the people of Israel.

23The LORD gave a command to Joshua, the son of Nun. He said, "Be strong and brave. You will bring the Israelites into the land I promised them with an oath. I myself will be with you."

24I finished writing the words of that law in a scroll. I wrote them down from beginning to end. 25Then I gave a command to the Levites who carried the ark of the covenant of the LORD. I said, 26"Take this Scroll of the Law. Place it beside the ark of the covenant of the LORD your God. It will remain there as a witness against you. 27I know how you refuse to obey the LORD. I know how stubborn you are. You have refused to obey him while I've been living among you. So you will certainly refuse to obey him after I'm dead!

28Gather together all of the elders of your tribes and all of your officials. Bring them to me. Then I can speak these words to them. I can call for heaven and earth to give witness against them. 29I know that after I'm dead you will certainly become very sinful. You will turn away from the path I've commanded you to take. In days to come, trouble will fall on you. That's because you will do what is evil in the sight of the LORD. You will make him very angry because of the statues of gods your hands have made."

The Song of Moses

30I spoke the words of this song from beginning to end. The whole community of Israel heard them. Here is what I said.

32 Heavens, listen to me. Then I will speak.
    Earth, hear the words of my mouth.
  2 Let my teaching fall like rain.
    Let my words come down like dew.

Let them be like raindrops on new
    grass.
  Let them be like rain on tender
    plants.

3 I will make known the name of the
    LORD.
  Praise God! How great he is!
4 He is the Rock. His works are perfect.
  All of his ways are right.
  He is faithful. He doesn't do anything
    wrong.
  He is honest and fair.

5 Israel, you have sinned against him
    very much.
  It's too bad for you that you aren't
    his children anymore.
  You have become a twisted and evil
    nation.
6 Is that how you thank the LORD?
  You aren't wise. You are foolish.
  Remember, he's your Father. He's your
    Creator.
  He made you. He formed you.

7 Remember the days of old.
  Think about what the LORD did
    through those many years.
  Ask your father. He will tell you.
  Ask your elders. They'll explain it to
    you.
8 The Most High God gave the nations
    their lands.
  He divided up the human race.
  He set up borders for the nations.
  He did it based on the number of the
    sons of Israel.
9 The LORD's people are his share.
  Jacob is the nation he has received.

10 The LORD found Israel in a desert land.
  He found them in an empty and
    windy wasteland.
  He took care of them and kept them
    safe.
  He guarded them as he would guard
    his own eyes.
11 He was like an eagle that stirs up its
    nest.
  It hovers over its little ones.
  It spreads out its wings to catch them.
  It carries them on its feathers.
12 The LORD was the only one who led
    Israel.
  No other god was with them.

13 The LORD made them ride on the
    highest places in the land.
  He fed them what grew in the fields.
  He gave them the sweetest honey.
  He fed them olive oil from a rocky
    hillside.

14 He gave them butter and milk from the
   herds and flocks.
   He fed them the fattest lambs and
   goats.
He gave them the best of Bashan's
   rams.
   He fed them the finest wheat.
   They drank the bubbling red juice of
   grapes.
15 When Israel grew fat, they became
   stubborn.
   When they were filled with food,
   they became fat and heavy.
They left the God who made them.
   They turned away from the Rock
   who saved them.
16 They made him jealous by serving
   strange gods.
   They made him angry by
   worshiping statues of gods.
   He hated those gods.
17 The people sacrificed to demons, not
   to God.
   The demons were gods they hadn't
   known anything about.
Those gods were new to them.
   Their people long ago didn't
   worship them.
18 But then they deserted the Rock. He
   was their Father.
   They forgot the God who created
   them.
19 When the Lord saw that, he turned
   away from them.
   His sons and daughters made him
   angry.
20 "I will turn my face away from them,"
   he said.
   "I will see what will happen to them
   in the end.
They are sinful people.
   They are unfaithful children.
21 They made me jealous by serving what
   is not even a god.
   They made me angry by worshiping
   worthless statues of gods.
I will use people who are not a nation
   to make them jealous.
   I will use a nation that has no
   understanding to make them
   angry.
22 My anger has started a fire.
   It burns down to the kingdom of the
   dead.
It will eat up the earth and its crops.
   It will set the base of the mountains
   on fire.
23 "I will pile troubles on my people.
   I will shoot all of my arrows at them.

24 I will send them hunger. It will make
   them weak.
   I will send terrible sickness. I will
   send deadly plagues.
I will send wild animals that will tear
   them apart.
   Snakes that glide through the dust
   will bite them.
25 In the streets their children will be
   killed with swords.
   Their homes will be filled with
   terror.
Young men and women will die.
   Babies and old people will die.
26 I said I would scatter them.
   I said I would wipe them from
   human memory.
27 But I was afraid their enemies would
   make fun of that.
   I was afraid their attackers would not
   understand.
I was sure they would say, 'We're the
   ones who've beaten them!
   The Lord isn't the one who did it.' "
28 Israel is a nation that doesn't have any
   sense.
   They can't understand anything.
29 I wish they were wise. Then they
   would understand what's
   coming.
   They'd realize what would happen
   to them in the end.
30 How could one person chase a
   thousand?
   How could two make ten thousand
   run away?
It couldn't happen unless their Rock
   had deserted them.
   It couldn't take place unless the
   Lord had given them up.
31 Their rock is not like our Rock.
   Even our enemies know that.
32 Their vine comes from the vines of
   Sodom.
   It comes from the vineyards of
   Gomorrah.
Their grapes are filled with poison.
   Their bunches of grapes taste bitter.
33 Their wine is like the poison of snakes.
   It's like the deadly poison of cobras.

34 The Lord says, "I have kept all of those
   terrible things stored away.
   I have kept them sealed up in my
   strongbox.
35 I punish people. I will pay them back.
   The time will come when their feet
   will slip.
Their day of trouble is near.
   Very soon they will be destroyed."

36 The LORD will judge his people.
He'll show tender love to those who
serve him.
He will know when their strength is
gone.
He'll see that no one at all is left.
37 He'll say, "Where are their gods now?
Where is the rock they went to for
safety?
38 Where are the gods who ate the fat of
their sacrifices?
Where are the gods who drank the
wine of their drink offerings?
Let them rise up to help you!
Let them keep you safe!

39 "Look! I am the One!
There is no other God except me.
I put some people to death. I bring
others to life.
I have wounded, and I will heal.
No one can save you from my
powerful hand.
40 I raise my hand to heaven. Here is the
oath I take.
You can be sure that I live forever.
41 And you can be just as sure
that I will sharpen my flashing
sword.
My hand will hold it when I judge.
I will get even with my enemies.
I will pay back those who hate me.
42 I will make my arrows drip with blood.
My sword will destroy people.
It will kill some. It will even kill
prisoners.
It will cut off the heads of enemy
leaders."

43 You nations, be full of joy. Be joyful
together with God's people.
The LORD will get even with his
enemies.
He will pay them back for killing those
who serve him.
He will wipe away the sin of his land
and people.

44 I spoke all of the words of that song to
the people. Joshua, the son of Nun, was
with me. **45** I finished speaking all of those
words to all of the people of Israel.
46 Then I said to the people, "Think
carefully about all of the words I have
announced to you today. I want you to
command your children to be careful to
obey all of the words of this law. **47** They
aren't just useless words for you. They are
your very life. If you obey them, you will
live in the land for a long time. It's the
land you are going across the Jordan River
to take as your own."

Moses Will Die on Mount Nebo

48 On that same day the LORD spoke to
me. He said, **49** "Go up into the Abarim
Mountains. Go to Mount Nebo in Moab.
It is across from Jericho. From there look
out over Canaan. It is the land I am giving
the people of Israel to take as their own.
50 "You will die there on the mountain
you have climbed. You will join the members of your family who have already died.
In the same way, your brother Aaron died
on Mount Hor. He joined the members of
his family who had already died.
51 "You and Aaron disobeyed me in
front of the Israelites. It happened at the
waters of Meribah Kadesh in the Desert of
Zin. You did not honor me among the
Israelites as the holy God. **52** So you will
see the land. But you will see it only from
far away. You will not enter the land I am
giving to the people of Israel."

Moses Blesses the Tribes

33 Here is the blessing that Moses,
the man of God, gave to the peo-
ple of Israel before he died. **2** He said,

"The LORD came from Mount Sinai.
Like the rising sun, he shone on his
people from Mount Seir.
He shone on them from Mount
Paran.
He came with large numbers of angels.
He came from his mountain slopes
in the south.
3 LORD, I'm sure you love your people.
All of the Israelites are in your
hands.
At your feet all of them bow down.
And you teach them.
4 They learn the law I gave them.
It belongs to the community of the
people of Jacob.
5 The LORD was king over Israel
when the leaders of the people came
together.
The tribes of Israel were also there."

6 Here's what Moses said about Reuben.

"Let Reuben live. Don't let him die.
But let his people be few."

7 Here's what Moses said about Judah.

"LORD, listen to Judah cry out.
Bring him to his people.
By his own power he stands up for
himself.
LORD, help him fight against his
enemies!"

8 Here's what Moses said about Levi.

"Your Thummim and Urim belong to
the man you favored.
You put him to the test at Massah.
You argued with him at the waters
of Meribah.
9 Levi didn't show special favor to
anyone.
He did not spare his father and
mother.
He didn't excuse his relatives or his
children.
But he watched over your word.
He guarded your covenant.
10 He teaches your rules to the people of
Jacob.
He teaches your law to Israel.
He offers incense to you.
He sacrifices whole burnt offerings
on your altar.
11 LORD, bless all of his skills.
Be pleased with everything he does.
Destroy those who rise up against him.
Strike down his enemies until they
can't get up."

12 Here's what Moses said about Benjamin.

"Let the one the LORD loves rest safely
in him.
The LORD guards him all day long.
The one the LORD loves rests in his
arms."

13 Here's what Moses said about Joseph.

"May the LORD bless Joseph's land.
May he bless it with dew from the
highest heavens.
May he bless it with water from the
deepest oceans.
14 May he bless it with the best crops the
sun can produce.
May he bless it with the finest crops
the moon can give.
15 May he bless it with the best products
of the age-old mountains.
May he bless it with the many crops
of the ancient hills.
16 May he bless it with the best gifts that
fill the earth.
May he bless it with the favor of the
One who spoke out of the
burning bush.
Let all of those blessings rest on the
head of Joseph.
Let them rest on the head of the one
who is prince among his
brothers.
17 His glory is like the glory of a bull that
was born first to its mother.
His horns are like the horns of a wild
ox.

He will destroy the nations with them.
He'll wipe out the nations that are
very far away.
The ten thousands of men in
Ephraim's army are like the bull
and the ox.
So are the thousands in the army of
Manasseh."

18 Here's what Moses said about Zebulun and Issachar.

"Zebulun, be filled with joy when you
go out.
Issachar, be joyful in your tents.
19 You will call for all of the other
Israelites to go to the mountain.
There you will offer proper sacrifices.
You will enjoy the many good things
your ships bring you.
You will enjoy treasures that are
hidden in the sand."

20 Here's what Moses said about Gad.

"May the One who gives Gad more
land be praised!
Gad lives there like a lion
that tears off arms and heads.
21 He chose the best land for his livestock.
The leader's share was kept for him.
The leaders of the people came
together.
Then Gad carried out the LORD's
holy plan.
He carried out the LORD's decisions
for Israel."

22 Here's what Moses said about Dan.

"Dan is like a lion's cub
that charges out of the land of
Bashan."

23 Here's what Moses said about Naphtali.

"The LORD greatly favors Naphtali.
The LORD fills him with his blessing.
Naphtali's land will reach south to
the Sea of Galilee."

24 Here's what Moses said about Asher.

"Asher is the most blessed of sons.
Let his brothers show favor to him.
Let him wash his feet with olive oil.
25 The bars of his gates will be made out
of iron and bronze.
His strength will last as long as he
lives.

26 "There is no one like the God of Israel.
He rides in the heavens to help you.
He rides on the clouds in his glory.

POWER-SURGE

STRONG

MOSES WAS *120* YEARS OLD WHEN HE DIED. BUT HIS EYES WERE NOT WEAK. HE WAS STILL VERY STRONG.

— DEUTERONOMY 34:7 —

27 God lives forever! You can run to him
     for safety.
   His powerful arms are always there
     to carry you.
   He will drive out your enemies to make
     room for you.
   He'll say to you, 'Destroy them!'
28 So Israel will live alone in safety.
   Jacob's spring of water is safe
   in a land that has grain and fresh wine.
   There the heavens drop their dew.
29 Israel, how blessed you are!
   Who is like you?
   The LORD has saved you.
   He keeps you safe. He helps you.
   He's like a glorious sword to you.
   Your enemies will bow down to you in
     fear.
   You will bring them under your
     control."

Moses Dies

34 Moses climbed Mount Nebo. He went up from the flatlands of Moab to the highest slopes of Pisgah. It's across from Jericho.

At Pisgah the LORD showed him the whole land from Gilead all the way to Dan. 2 Moses saw the whole land of Naphtali. He saw the territory of Ephraim and Manasseh. The LORD showed him the whole land of Judah all the way to the Mediterranean Sea. 3 Moses saw the Negev Desert. He saw the whole area from the Valley of Jericho all the way to Zoar. Jericho was also known as The City of Palm Trees.

4 Then the LORD spoke to Moses. He said, "This is the land I promised with an oath to Abraham, Isaac and Jacob. I told them, 'I will give this land to your children and their children.' Moses, I have let you see it with your own eyes. But you will not go across the Jordan River to enter it."

5 Moses, the servant of the LORD, died there in Moab, just as the LORD had said. 6 The LORD buried the body of Moses in Moab. His grave is in the valley across from Beth Peor. But to this day no one knows where it is. 7 Moses was 120 years old when he died. But his eyes were not weak. He was still very strong.

8 The people of Israel sobbed over Moses on the flatlands of Moab for 30 days. They did it until their time for sobbing and crying was over.

9 Joshua, the son of Nun, was filled with wisdom. That's because Moses had placed his hands on him. So the Israelites listened to Joshua. They did what the LORD had commanded Moses.

10 Since then, Israel has never had a prophet like Moses. The LORD knew him face to face. 11 Moses did many miraculous signs and wonders. The LORD had sent him to do them in Egypt. Moses did them against Pharaoh, against all of his officials and against his whole land. 12 No one has ever had the mighty power Moses had. No one has ever done the wonderful acts he did in the sight of all of the people of Israel.

POWER-SURGE

STRONG

NO ONE HAS EVER HAD THE MIGHTY POWER MOSES HAD. NO ONE HAS EVER DONE THE WONDERFUL ACTS HE DID IN THE SIGHT OF ALL OF THE PEOPLE OF ISRAEL.

— DEUTERONOMY 34:12 —

JOSHUA

In the book of Joshua, the Israelites enter the promised land and begin to conquer it. They divide the land up between the twelve tribes, and each tribe settles into its new home. Moses has died. Joshua, the biggest hero in this book, now leads the people. God commands Joshua to be strong and brave. God also promises to be with Joshua as he leads, as long as Joshua obeys him. When you read Joshua, notice how God blesses the people when they obey him.

HEROES IN THIS BOOK . . .

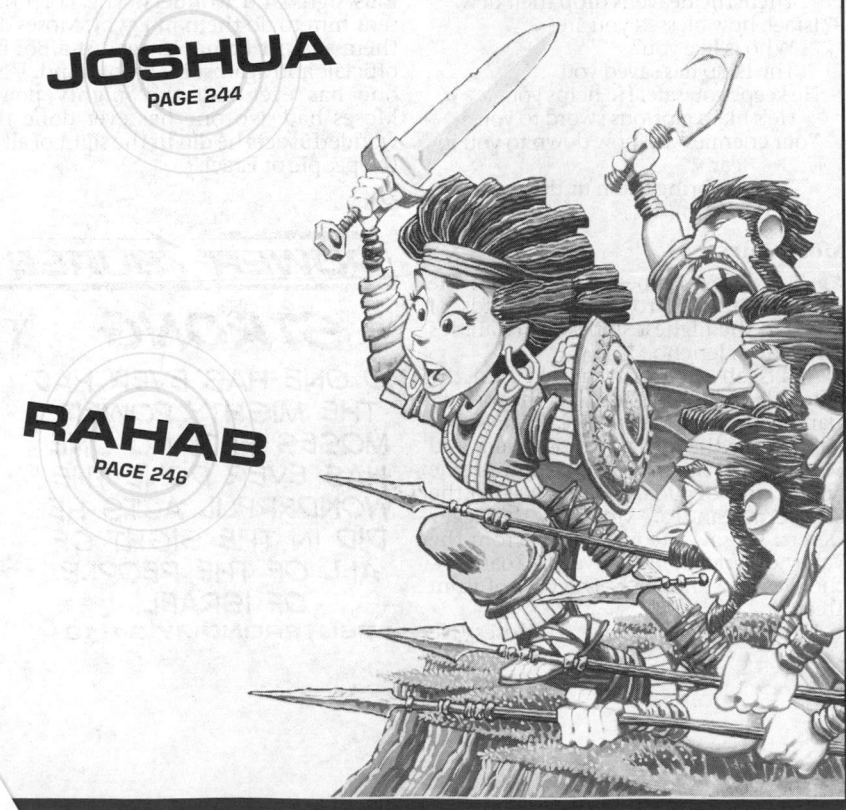

JOSHUA
PAGE 244

RAHAB
PAGE 246

The Lord Gives Commands to Joshua

1 Moses, the servant of the Lord, died. After that, the Lord spoke to Joshua, the son of Nun. Joshua was Moses' helper. The Lord said to Joshua, **2**"My servant Moses is dead. Now then, I want you and all of these people to get ready to go across the Jordan River. I want all of you to go into the land I am about to give to the people of Israel.

3"I will give all of you every place you walk on, just as I promised Moses. **4**Your territory will reach from the Negev Desert all the way to Lebanon. The great Euphrates River will be to the east. The Mediterranean Sea will be to the west. Your territory will include all of the Hittite country.

5"Joshua, no one will be able to stand up against you as long as you live. I will be with you, just as I was with Moses. I will never leave you. I will never desert you.

6"Be strong and brave. You will lead these people, and they will take the land as their very own. It is the land I promised with an oath to give their people long ago.

7"Be strong and very brave. Make sure you obey the whole law my servant Moses gave you. Do not turn away from it to the right or the left. Then you will have success everywhere you go. **8**Never stop reading this Scroll of the Law. Day and night you must think about what it says. Make sure you do everything that is written in it. Then things will go well with you. And you will have great success.

POWER-SURGE

STRONG

BE STRONG AND VERY BRAVE. MAKE SURE YOU OBEY THE WHOLE LAW MY SERVANT MOSES GAVE YOU. DO NOT TURN AWAY FROM IT TO THE RIGHT OR THE LEFT. THEN YOU WILL HAVE SUCCESS EVERYWHERE YOU GO.
— JOSHUA 1:7 —

B

BRAVE

9"Here is what I am commanding you to do. Be strong and brave. Do not be terrified. Do not lose hope. I am the Lord your God. I will be with you everywhere you go."

Joshua Gives Commands to the People

10So Joshua gave orders to the officers of the people. He said, **11**"Go through the camp. Tell the people, 'Get your supplies ready. Three days from now you will go across the Jordan River right here. You will go in and take over the land. The Lord your God is giving it to you as your very own.' "

12Joshua also spoke to the tribes of Reuben and Gad and half of the tribe of Manasseh. He said to them, **13**"Remember what Moses, the servant of the Lord, commanded you. He said, 'The Lord your God is giving you this land. It's a place where you can settle down and live in peace and rest.'

14"Your wives, children and livestock can stay here east of the Jordan River. Moses gave you this land. But all of your fighting men must get ready for battle. They must go across ahead of the other tribes. You must help them **15**until the Lord gives them rest. In the same way, he has already given you rest. You must help them until they also have taken over their land. It's the land the Lord your God is giving them. After that, you can come back here. Then you can live in your own land. It's the land that Moses, the servant of the Lord, gave you east of the Jordan River. It's toward the sunrise."

16Then the tribes of Reuben and Gad and half of the tribe of Manasseh answered Joshua. They said, "We'll do what you have commanded us to do. We'll go where you send us. **17**We obeyed Moses completely. And we'll obey you just as completely. But may the Lord your God be with you, just as he was with Moses.

18"Suppose people question your authority. And suppose they refuse to obey anything you command them to do. Then they will be put to death. Just be strong and brave!"

Rahab Helps the Spies

2 Joshua, the son of Nun, sent two spies from Shittim. He sent them in secret. He said to them, "Go. Look the land over. Most of all, check out Jericho."

So they went to Jericho. They stayed at the house of a prostitute. Her name was Rahab.

JOSHUA

JOSHUA 1:9

*Be strong and brave. Do not be terrified.
Do not lose hope. I am the Lord your God.
I will be with you everywhere you go.*

The bright sun glinted off Joshua's sword as he raised it and yelled at the top of his voice. Then the sun glinted off a *thousand* swords as the soldiers behind Joshua raised their weapons. The hills echoed with loud shouts and the blast of the priests' horns.

JOSHUA AND HIS MEN CONTINUED SHOUTING, RAISING THEIR VOICES LOUDER AND LOUDER. They watched and cheered as the walls of Jericho started to shake. One brick fell to the ground in front of the soldiers. Then another brick, and another. Soon the whole wall was rumbling and tumbling and falling down.

The ground shook beneath the feet of the soldiers. The dust and dirt flew into the faces of the soldiers. But each one held his sword and kept shouting. They waited for Joshua's signal. Slowly the rumbling quieted and the wind blew the dust and dirt away. Then Joshua shouted again for the men to follow him. They climbed over the rubble of the wall and went into Jericho and conquered it. They burned everything in it.

As the men began to rush into Jericho, Joshua gave special instructions to two of them. "Go to Rahab's house. She and those with her are the only ones we will save. We will protect her because she protected our spies. Go!" The two men rushed into Jericho and searched out Rahab's house and led Rahab and her family to safety. She and her family were the only ones who survived.

With God's help, Joshua and the people of Israel conquered mighty Jericho, the city no one else could defeat.

BE A JOSHUA

Wow! Can you imagine walking around that wall? It's huge! How will just marching ever knock it down? Because God is in control, it *does* fall down. Joshua knew he had to depend on God. God wants you to depend on him, too. He will be with you, just like he was with Joshua and his soldiers.

JOSHUA DEPENDED ON GOD.
THE WHOLE STORY: JOSHUA 5:13—6:27

Go to page 246 for the next Super Hero

2The king of Jericho was told, "Look! Some of the people of Israel have come here tonight. They've come to check out the land."

3So the king sent a message to Rahab. It said, "Bring out the men who came into your house. They've come to check out the whole land."

4But the woman had hidden the two men. She said, "It's true that the men came here. But I didn't know where they had come from. **5**They left at sunset, when it was time to close the city gate. I don't know which way they went. Go after them quickly. You might catch up with them."

6But in fact she had taken them up on the roof. There she had hidden them under some flax she had piled up.

7The king's men left to hunt down the spies. They took the road that leads to where the Jordan River can be crossed. As soon as they had gone out of the city, the gate was shut.

8Rahab went up on the roof before the spies settled down for the night. **9**She said to them, "I know that the LORD has given this land to you. We are very much afraid of you. Everyone who lives in this country is weak with fear because of you.

10"We've heard how the LORD dried up the Red Sea for you when you came out of Egypt. We've heard what you did to Sihon and Og, the two Amorite kings. They ruled east of the Jordan River. You completely destroyed them.

11"When we heard about it, our hearts melted away in fear. Because of you, we aren't brave anymore. The LORD your God is the God who rules over heaven above and earth below.

12"Now then, please take an oath. Promise me in the name of the LORD that you will be kind to my family. I've been kind to you. Promise me **13**that you will spare the lives of my father and mother. Spare my brothers and sisters. Also spare everyone in their families. Promise that you won't put any of us to death."

14So the men made a promise to her. "We'll give up our lives to save yours," they said. "But don't tell anyone what we're doing. Then we'll be kind and faithful to you when the LORD gives us the land."

15The house Rahab lived in was part of the city wall. So she let the spies down by a rope through the window. **16**She had said to them, "Go up into the hills. The men who are chasing you won't be able to find you. Hide yourselves there for three

days until they return. Then you can go on your way."

17The men said to her, "You made us take an oath and make a promise. But we won't keep it **18**unless you do what we say. When we enter the land, you must tie this bright red rope in the window. Tie it in the window you let us down through.

"Bring your father and mother into your house. Also bring your brothers and everyone else in your family into your house. **19**None of you must go out into the street. If you do, anything that happens to you will be your own fault. Don't hold us accountable.

"But if anyone hurts someone who is inside the house with you, it will be our fault. And you can hold us accountable.

20"Don't tell anyone what we're doing. If you do, we won't have to keep the promise you asked us to make."

21"I agree," Rahab replied. "I'll do as you say." So she sent them away, and they left. Then she tied the bright red rope in the window.

22When the spies left, they went up into the hills. They stayed there for three days. By that time the men who were chasing them had searched all along the road. They couldn't find them. So they returned.

23Then the two spies started back. They went down out of the hills. They went across the Jordan River. They came to Joshua, the son of Nun. They told him everything that had happened to them. **24**They said, "We're sure the LORD has given the whole land over to us. All of the people there are weak with fear because of us."

Israel Goes Across the Jordan River

3 Early one morning Joshua and all of the people of Israel started out from Shittim. They went down to the Jordan

POWER-SURGE

KIND **K**

PROMISE ME IN THE NAME OF THE LORD THAT YOU WILL BE KIND TO MY FAMILY. I'VE BEEN KIND TO YOU.

— JOSHUA 2:12 —

River. They camped there before they went across it.

2After three days the officers went all through the camp. 3They gave orders to the people. They said, "Watch for the ark of the covenant of the LORD your God. The priests, who are Levites, will be carrying it. When you see it, you must move out from where you are and follow it. 4Then you will know which way to go. You have never gone this way before. But don't go near the ark. Stay about 1,000 yards away from it."

5Joshua spoke to the people. He said, "Set yourselves apart to the LORD. Tomorrow he'll do amazing things among you."

6Joshua said to the priests, "Go and get the ark of the covenant. Walk on ahead of the people." So they went and got it. Then they walked on ahead of them.

7The LORD said to Joshua, "Today I will begin to honor you in the eyes of all of the people of Israel. Then they will know that I am with you, just as I was with Moses. 8Speak to the priests who carry the ark of the covenant. Tell them, 'When you reach

RAHAB

JOSHUA 2:11

The LORD your God is the God who rules over heaven above and earth below.

Rahab (RAY-hab) sat with all of her family members, squeezed into her little house in Jericho. They heard the awful noise of the city wall collapsing and the soldiers fighting. THE CLANGING OF SWORDS AND THE BANGING OF DOORS AND THE SCREAMING OF PEOPLE RANG IN THEIR EARS. But they sat quietly. Every now and then one of them would check to make sure the red cord was still hanging from the window. Every Israelite soldier who saw the red cord knew that house was protected.

Rahab believed the God of the Israelites was the most powerful God. So she helped the spies who came to Jericho. She bravely protected them by hiding them in her house. In exchange, they promised to protect her and her family when they conquered the city. The red cord was their signal.

Finally, a group of Israelite soldiers came to Rahab's house and took all of her family safely out of the city. Rahab lived with the Israelites from that day on.

BE LIKE RAHAB

Rahab believed God and bravely did what she knew was right. You can be like her! Bravery is something God will give you if you believe in him. He'll help you do what you know is right.

RAHAB BELIEVED IN GOD AND BRAVELY DID THE RIGHT THING.

Go to page 277 for the next Super Hero

GO TO PAGE 244

"Be strong and brave. Do not be terrified. Do not lose hope.
I am the LORD your God. I will be with you everywhere you go."
(Joshua 1:9)

JOSHUA

GO TO PAGE 277

Then Deborah said to Barak, "Go! Today the LORD will hand Sisera over to you. Hasn't the LORD gone ahead of you?"
(Judges 4:14)

DEBORAH

the edge of the Jordan River, go into the water and stand there.' "

⁹Joshua spoke to the people of Israel. He said, "Come here. Listen to what the LORD your God is saying. ¹⁰You will soon know that the living God is among you. You can be sure that he'll drive out the people who are now living in the land. He'll do it to make room for you. He'll drive out the Canaanites, Hittites, Hivites, Perizzites, Girgashites, Amorites and Jebusites.

¹¹"The ark will go into the Jordan River ahead of you. It's the ark of the covenant of the Lord of the whole earth.

¹²"Choose 12 men from the tribes of Israel. Choose one from each tribe.

¹³"The priests will carry the ark of the LORD. He's the Lord of the whole earth. As soon as the priests step into the Jordan, it will stop flowing. The water that's coming down the river will pile up in one place. That's how you will know that the living God is among you."

¹⁴So the people took their tents down. They prepared to go across the Jordan River. The priests who were carrying the ark of the covenant went ahead of them.

¹⁵The water of the Jordan was going over its banks. It always does that at the time the crops are being gathered. The priests came to the river. Their feet touched the water's edge. ¹⁶Right away the water that was coming down the river stopped flowing. It piled up far away at a town called Adam near Zarethan. The water that was flowing down to the Dead Sea was completely cut off. So the people went across the Jordan River opposite Jericho.

¹⁷The priests carried the ark of the covenant of the LORD. They stood firm on dry ground in the middle of the river. They stayed there until the whole nation of Israel had gone across on dry ground.

4 After the whole nation had gone across the Jordan River, the LORD spoke to Joshua. He said, ²"Choose 12 men from among the people. Choose one from each tribe. ³Tell them to get 12 stones from the middle of the river. They must pick them up from right where the priests stood. They must carry the stones over with all of you. And they must put them down at the place where you will stay tonight."

⁴So Joshua called together the 12 men he had appointed from among the people of Israel. There was one man from each tribe. ⁵He said to them, "Go back to the middle of the Jordan River. Go to where

the ark of the LORD your God is. Each one of you must pick up a stone. You must carry it on your shoulder. There will be as many stones as there are tribes in Israel.

⁶"The stones will serve as a reminder to you. In days to come, your children will ask you, 'What do these stones mean?' ⁷Tell them that the LORD cut off the flow of water in the Jordan River. Tell them its water stopped flowing when the ark of the covenant of the LORD went across. The stones will always remind the Israelites of what happened there."

⁸So the people of Israel did as Joshua commanded them. They took 12 stones from the middle of the Jordan River. There was one stone for each of the tribes of Israel. It was just as the LORD had told Joshua. The people carried the stones with them to their camp. There they put them down.

⁹Joshua piled up the 12 stones that had been in the middle of the river. They had been right where the priests who carried the ark of the covenant had stood. And they are still there to this very day.

¹⁰The priests who carried the ark remained standing in the middle of the Jordan River. They stayed there until the people had done everything the LORD had commanded Joshua. It was just as Moses had directed Joshua. All of the people went across quickly. ¹¹As soon as they did, the ark of the LORD and the priests also went across to the other side. The people were watching them.

¹²Among the people who went across the river were men from the tribes of Reuben and Gad and half of the tribe of Manasseh. The men were armed. They went across ahead of the rest of the people of Israel. It was just as Moses had directed them. ¹³There were about 40,000 of them. All of them were ready for battle. They went across in front of the ark of the LORD. They went to the flatlands around Jericho. They were prepared to go to war.

¹⁴That day the LORD honored Joshua in the eyes of all of the people of Israel. They had respect for Joshua as long as he lived. They respected him just as much as they had respected Moses.

¹⁵Then the LORD spoke to Joshua. He said, ¹⁶"Command the priests to come up out of the Jordan River. They are carrying the ark where the tablets of the covenant are kept."

¹⁷So Joshua gave a command to the priests. He said, "Come up out of the Jordan River."

¹⁸Then the priests came up out of the

river. They were carrying the ark of the covenant of the LORD. As soon as they stepped out on dry ground, the water of the Jordan began to flow again. It went over its banks, just as it had done before.

¹⁹On the tenth day of the first month the people went up out of the Jordan River. They camped at Gilgal on the eastern border of Jericho.

²⁰Joshua set up the 12 stones at Gilgal. They were the ones the people had taken out of the Jordan.

²¹Then he spoke to the people of Israel. He said, "In days to come, your children after you will ask their parents, 'What do these stones mean?' ²²Their parents must tell them, 'Israel went across the Jordan River on dry ground.' ²³The LORD your God dried up the Jordan for you until you had gone across it. He did to the Jordan River the same thing he had done to the Red Sea. He dried up the Red Sea ahead of us until we had gone across it. ²⁴He did it so that all of the nations on earth would know that he is powerful. He did it so that you would always have respect for the LORD your God."

Joshua Circumcises the Men of Israel

5 All of the Amorite and Canaanite kings heard how the LORD had dried up the Jordan River. They heard how he had dried it up for the people of Israel until they had gone across it. The Amorite kings lived west of the Jordan. The kings of Canaan lived along the Mediterranean Sea.

When all of those kings heard what the LORD had done, their hearts melted away in fear. They weren't brave enough to face the people of Israel anymore.

²At that time the LORD spoke to Joshua. He said, "Make knives out of hard stone. Circumcise the men of Israel."

³So Joshua made knives out of hard stone. Then he circumcised the men of Israel at Gibeath Haaraloth.

⁴Here is why Joshua circumcised them. All of the men who came out of Egypt had died. They died while they were going through the Sinai Desert after they had left Egypt. They were the men who were old enough to serve in the army. ⁵All of the men who came out had been circumcised. But all of the men who were born in the desert during the journey from Egypt hadn't been circumcised.

⁶The people of Israel had moved around in the desert for 40 years. By the end of that time all of the men who were

old enough to serve in the army when they left Egypt had died. That's because they hadn't obeyed the LORD. The LORD had taken an oath. He had told them they wouldn't see the land. It's the land he had promised with an oath to their people to give us. It's a land that has plenty of milk and honey.

⁷Because they hadn't obeyed him, he raised up their sons to take their place. They were the ones Joshua circumcised. They hadn't been circumcised yet. That's because no one had circumcised them during the journey. ⁸So Joshua circumcised all of those men. The whole nation remained in the camp until the men were healed.

⁹Then the LORD spoke to Joshua. He said, "Today I have taken away from you the shame of being laughed at by Egypt." That's why the place where the men were circumcised has been called Gilgal to this very day.

¹⁰The people of Israel celebrated the Passover Feast. They observed it on the evening of the 14th day of the month. They did it while they were camped at Gilgal on the flatlands around Jericho. ¹¹The day after the Passover, they ate some of the food that was grown in the land. On that very day they ate grain that had been cooked. They also ate bread that was made without yeast. ¹²The manna stopped coming down the day after they ate the food that was grown in the land. The people of Israel didn't have manna anymore. Instead, that year they ate food that was grown in Canaan.

Israel Captures Jericho

¹³When Joshua was near Jericho, he looked up and saw a man standing in front of him. The man was holding a sword. He was ready for battle. Joshua went up to him. He asked, "Are you on our side? Or are you on the side of our enemies?"

¹⁴"I am not on either side," he replied. "I have come as the commander of the LORD's army." Then Joshua fell with his face to the ground. He asked the man, "What message does my Lord have for me?"

¹⁵The commander of the LORD's army replied, "Take off your sandals. The place you are standing on is holy ground." So Joshua took them off.

6 The gates of Jericho were shut tight and guarded closely because of the people of Israel. No one went out. No one came in.

2Then the LORD spoke to Joshua. He said, "I have handed Jericho over to you. I have also handed its king and its fighting men over to you.

3"March around the city once with all of your fighting men. In fact, do it for six days. **4**Have seven priests get trumpets that are made out of rams' horns. They must carry them in front of the ark. On the seventh day, march around the city seven times. Have the priests blow the trumpets as you march.

5"You will hear them blow a long blast on the trumpets. When you do, have all of the men give a loud shout. The wall of the city will fall down. Then the whole army will go up to the city. Every man will go straight in."

6So Joshua, the son of Nun, called for the priests. He said to them, "Go and get the ark of the covenant of the LORD. I want seven of you to carry trumpets in front of it." **7**He gave an order to the men. He said, "Move out! March around the city. Some of the fighting men must march in front of the ark of the LORD."

8When Joshua had spoken to the men, the seven priests went forward. They were carrying the seven trumpets as they marched in front of the ark of the LORD. They were blowing the trumpets. The ark of the LORD's covenant was carried behind the priests. **9**Some of the fighting men marched ahead of the priests who were blowing the trumpets. The others followed behind the ark and guarded all of them. That whole time the priests were blowing the trumpets.

10But Joshua had given an order to the fighting men. He had said, "Don't give a war cry. Don't raise your voices. Don't say a word until the day I tell you to shout. Then shout!"

11So he had the ark of the LORD carried around the city once. Then the men returned to camp. They spent the night there.

12Joshua got up early the next morning. The priests went and got the ark of the LORD. **13**The seven priests who were carrying the seven trumpets started out. They marched in front of the ark of the LORD. They blew the trumpets. Some of the fighting men marched ahead of them. The others followed behind the ark and guarded all of them. The priests kept blowing the trumpets.

14On the second day they marched around the city once. Then the men returned to camp. They did all of those things for six days.

15On the seventh day, they got up at sunrise. They marched around the city, just as they had done before. But on that day they went around it seven times.

16On the seventh time around, the priests blew a long blast on the trumpets.

Then Joshua gave a command to the men. He said, "Shout! The LORD has given you the city! **17**The city and everything that is in it must be set apart to the LORD in a special way to be destroyed. But the prostitute Rahab and all those who are with her in her house must be spared. That's because she hid the spies we sent.

18"But keep away from the things that have been set apart to the LORD. If you take any of them, you will be destroyed. And you will bring trouble on the camp of Israel. You will cause it to be destroyed. **19**All of the silver and gold is holy. It is set apart to the LORD. So are all of the articles that are made out of bronze and iron. All of those things must be added to the treasures that are kept in the LORD's house."

20The priests blew the trumpets. As soon as the fighting men heard the sound, they gave a loud shout. Then the wall fell down. Every man charged straight in. So they took the city. **21**They set it apart to the LORD in a special way to be destroyed. They destroyed every living thing in it with their swords. They killed men and women. They wiped out young people and old people. They destroyed cattle, sheep and donkeys.

22Then Joshua spoke to the two men who had gone in to check out the land. He said, "Go into the prostitute's house. Bring her out. Also bring out everyone who is with her. That's what you promised her you would do when you took an oath."

23So the young men who had checked out the land went into Rahab's house. They brought her out along with her parents and brothers. They brought out everyone else who was there with her. They put them in a place that was outside the camp of Israel.

24Then they burned the whole city and everything that was in it. But they added the silver and gold to the treasures that were kept in the LORD's house. They also put there the articles that were made out of bronze and iron.

25But Joshua spared the prostitute Rahab. He spared her family. He also spared everyone else who was in the house with her. He did it because she hid the spies he had sent to Jericho. Rahab lives among the people of Israel to this very day.

26At that time Joshua took an oath and called down a curse. He said, "May the man who tries to rebuild this city of Jericho be under the LORD's curse.

"If he lays its foundations,
    it will cost the life of his oldest son.
If he sets up its gates,
    it will cost the life of his youngest
        son."

27So the LORD was with Joshua. And Joshua became famous everywhere in the land.

Achan Sins Against the LORD

7 But the people of Israel weren't faithful to the LORD. They didn't do what they were told to do with the things that had been set apart to him in a special way to be destroyed.

Achan had taken some of those things. So the LORD's anger burned against Israel. Achan was the son of Carmi. Carmi was the son of Zimri. And Zimri was the son of Zerah. They were from the tribe of Judah.

2Joshua sent men from Jericho to Ai. Ai is near Beth Aven east of Bethel. Joshua told the men, "Go up and check out the area around Ai." So the men went up and checked it out.

3Then they returned to Joshua. They said, "The whole army doesn't have to go up and attack Ai. Send only two or three thousand men. They can take the city. Don't make the whole army go up there. Ai only has a few men."

4So only about 3,000 men went up. But the men of Ai drove them away. 5They chased the men of Israel from the city gate all the way to Shebarim. They killed about 36 of them on the way down.

So the hearts of the people of Israel melted away in fear.

6Joshua and the elders of Israel became sad. Joshua tore his clothes. He fell in front of the ark of the LORD with his face to the ground. He remained there until evening. The elders did the same thing. They also sprinkled dust on their heads.

7Joshua said, "LORD and King, why did you ever bring these people across the Jordan River? Did you want to hand us over to the Amorites? Did you want them to destroy us? I wish we had been content to stay on the other side of the Jordan!

8"Lord, our enemies have driven us away. What can I say? 9The people of Canaan will hear about it. So will everyone else in the country. They will sur-

round us. They'll wipe our name from the face of the earth. Then what will you do when people don't honor your great name anymore?"

10The LORD said to Joshua, "Get up! What are you doing down there on your face?

11"Israel has sinned. I made a covenant with them. I commanded them to keep it. But they have broken it. They have taken some of the things that had been set apart to me in a special way to be destroyed. They have stolen. They have lied. They have taken the things they stole and have put them with their own things.

12"That is why the men of Israel can't stand up against their enemies. They turn their backs and run. It is because I have decided to let them be destroyed. You must destroy the things you took that had been set apart to me. If you do not, I will not be with you anymore.

13"Go. Set the people apart. Tell them, 'Make yourselves pure. Get ready for tomorrow. Here is what the LORD, the God of Israel, wants you to do. He says, "People of Israel, you have kept some of the things that had been set apart to me in a special way to be destroyed. You can't stand up against your enemies until you get rid of those things."

14" 'In the morning, come forward tribe by tribe. The tribe the LORD chooses will come forward group by group. The group the LORD chooses will come forward family by family. And the men in the family the LORD chooses will come forward one by one.

15" 'Anyone who is caught with the things that had been set apart to the LORD will be destroyed by fire. Everything that belongs to that person will also be destroyed. He has broken the LORD's covenant. He has done a very terrible thing in Israel!' "

16Early the next morning Joshua had Israel come forward by tribes. The tribe of Judah was picked. 17The groups of Judah came forward. Joshua picked the group of Zerah. He had the group of Zerah come forward by families. The family of Zimri was picked. 18He had their men come forward one by one. Achan was picked. Achan was the son of Carmi. Carmi was the son of Zimri. And Zimri was the son of Zerah. Zerah was from the tribe of Judah.

19Joshua spoke to Achan. He said, "My son, the LORD is the God of Israel. So give him glory by telling the truth! Give him praise by admitting you have sinned! Tell me what you have done. Don't hide it from me."

²⁰Achan replied, "It's true! I've sinned against the LORD, the God of Israel. Here is what I've done. ²¹I saw a beautiful robe from Babylonia among the things we had taken. I saw five pounds of silver. And I saw a gold bar that weighed 20 ounces. I wanted them, so I took them. I hid them in the ground inside my tent. The silver is on the bottom."

²²So Joshua sent some messengers. They ran to Achan's tent. And there was everything, hidden in his tent! The silver was on the bottom. ²³They brought the things out of the tent. They took them to Joshua and all of the people of Israel. And they spread them out in the sight of the LORD.

²⁴Then Joshua and all of the people grabbed hold of Achan, the son of Zerah. They took the silver, the robe and the gold bar. They took Achan's sons and daughters. They took his cattle, donkeys and sheep. They also took his tent and everything he had. They took all of it to the Valley of Achor.

²⁵Joshua said to Achan, "Why have you brought this trouble on us? The LORD will bring trouble on you today."

Then all of the people killed Achan by throwing stones at him. They also killed the rest of his family with stones. They burned all of them up. ²⁶They placed a large pile of rocks on top of Achan's body. The place has been called the Valley of Achor ever since. That pile is still there to this very day.

After the people killed Achan, the LORD turned his burning anger away from them.

Israel Destroys Ai

8 Then the LORD spoke to Joshua. He said, "Do not be afraid. Do not lose hope. Go up and attack Ai. Take the whole army with you. I have handed the king of Ai over to you. I have given you his people, his city and his land.

²"Remember what you did to Jericho and its king. You will do the same thing to Ai and its king. But this time you can keep for yourselves the livestock and everything else you take from them. Have some of your fighting men hide behind the city and take them by surprise."

³So Joshua and the whole army moved out to attack Ai. He chose 30,000 of his best fighting men. He sent them out at night. ⁴He gave them orders. He said, "Listen carefully to what I'm saying. You must

hide behind the city. Don't go very far away from it. All of you must be ready to attack it.

⁵"I and all of the men who are with me will go up to the city. The men of Ai will come out to fight against us, just as they did before. Then we'll run away from them. ⁶They'll chase us until we've drawn them away from the city. They'll say, 'They are running away from us, just as they did before.'

"When we run away from them, ⁷come out of your hiding place. Take over the city. The LORD your God will hand it over to you. ⁸When you have taken it, set it on fire. Do what the LORD has commanded. Make sure you obey my orders."

⁹Then Joshua sent them away. They went to the place where they had planned to hide. They hid in a place west of Ai. It was between Bethel and Ai. But Joshua spent that night with his men.

¹⁰Early the next morning Joshua brought his men together. He and the leaders of Israel marched in front of them to Ai. ¹¹The whole army that was with him marched up to the city. They stopped in front of it. They set up camp north of Ai. There was a valley between them and the city.

¹²Joshua had chosen about 5,000 soldiers. He had ordered them to hide in a place west of Ai. It was between Bethel and Ai.

¹³The men took up their battle positions. All of the men who were in the camp that was north of the city took up their positions. So did those who were supposed to hide west of the city. That night Joshua went into the valley.

¹⁴The king of Ai saw what the army of Israel was doing. So he and all of his men hurried out of the city early in the morning. They marched out to meet Israel in battle. They went to a place that looked out over the Arabah Valley. The king didn't know that some of Israel's fighting men were hiding behind the city.

¹⁵Joshua and all of his men let the men of Ai drive them back. The men of Israel ran away toward the desert.

¹⁶All of the men of Ai were called out to chase them. They chased Joshua. So they were drawn away from the city. ¹⁷Not even one man remained in Ai or Bethel. All of them went out to chase Israel. When they did, they left the city wide open.

¹⁸Then the LORD spoke to Joshua. He said, "Point the javelin that is in your

hand at Ai. I will hand the city over to you." So Joshua pointed his javelin at Ai.

19 As soon as he did, the men who were hiding behind the city got up quickly. They came out of their hiding places and rushed forward. They entered the city and captured it. They quickly set it on fire.

20 The men of Ai looked back. They saw smoke rising up from the city into the sky. But they couldn't escape in any direction. The men of Israel had been running away toward the desert. But now they turned around to face those who were chasing them. 21 Joshua and all of his men saw that the men who had been hiding behind the city had captured it. They also saw the smoke that was going up from it. So they turned around and attacked the men of Ai. 22 The men who had set Ai on fire came out of the city. They also fought against the men of Ai.

So the men of Ai were caught in the middle. The army of Israel was on both sides of them. Israel struck them down. They didn't let anyone remain alive or get away. 23 But they took the king of Ai alive. They brought him to Joshua.

24 Israel finished killing all of the men of Ai. They destroyed them in the fields and in the desert where they had chased them. They struck every one of them down with their swords. Then all of the men of Israel returned to Ai. And they killed those who were left in it.

25 The total number of men and women they killed that day was 12,000. They put to death all of the people of Ai.

26 Joshua kept the javelin that was in his hand pointed at Ai. He didn't lower his hand until he and his men had totally destroyed everyone who lived there.

27 But this time Israel kept for themselves the livestock and everything else they had taken from the city. The LORD had directed Joshua to let them do it.

28 So Joshua burned Ai down. He tore it down so it could never be built again. It has been deserted to this very day.

29 Joshua killed the king of Ai. He stuck a pole through the body. Then he set it up where people could see it. He left it there until evening. At sunset, Joshua ordered his men to remove the body from the pole. He told them to throw the body down at the entrance of the city gate. They put a large pile of rocks over the body. That pile is still there to this very day.

Joshua Reads the Scroll of the Law to the People

30 Joshua built an altar to honor the LORD, the God of Israel. He built it on Mount Ebal. 31 Moses, the servant of the LORD, had commanded the people of Israel to do that. Joshua built the altar in keeping with what is written in the Scroll of the Law of Moses. He built an altar out of stones that iron tools had never touched. Then the people offered on the altar burnt offerings to the LORD. They also sacrificed friendship offerings on it.

32 Joshua copied the written law of Moses on stones. He did it while all of the people of Israel were watching. 33 They were standing on both sides of the ark of the covenant of the LORD. All of the people of Israel, including outsiders and citizens, were there. Israel's elders, officials and judges were also there. All of them faced the priests, who were Levites. They were carrying the ark. Half of the people stood in front of Mount Gerizim. The other half stood in front of Mount Ebal. Moses, the servant of the LORD, had earlier told them to do it. It was when he had given directions to bless the people of Israel.

34 Then Joshua read all of the words of the law out loud. He read the blessings and the curses. He read them in keeping with what is written in the Scroll of the Law. 35 Joshua read every word Moses had commanded. He read them to the whole community of Israel. That included the women and children. It also included the outsiders who were living among them.

The People of Gibeon Trick Israel

9 All of the kings who ruled west of the Jordan River heard about the battles Israel had won. That included the kings who ruled in the central hill country and the western hills. It also included those who ruled along the entire coast of the Mediterranean Sea all the way to Lebanon. They were the kings of the Hittites, Amorites, Canaanites, Perizzites, Hivites and Jebusites. 2 They brought their armies together to fight against Joshua and Israel.

3 The people of Gibeon heard about what Joshua had done to Jericho and Ai. 4 So they decided to trick the people of Israel. They packed supplies as if they were going on a long trip. They loaded their donkeys with old sacks and old wineskins. The wineskins were cracked but had been mended. 5 The men put worn-out sandals on their feet. The sandals had been patched. The men also wore old

clothes. All of the bread they took along was dry and moldy.

6They went to Joshua in the camp at Gilgal. They spoke to him and the men of Israel. They said, "We've come from a country that's far away. Make a peace treaty with us."

7The men of Israel spoke to the Hivites. They said, "But suppose you live close to us. If you do, we can't make a peace treaty with you."

8"We'll serve you," they said to Joshua. But Joshua asked, "Who are you? Where do you come from?"

9They answered, "We've come from a country that's very far away. We've come because the LORD your God is famous. We've heard reports about him. We've heard about everything he did in Egypt.

10"We've heard about everything he did to Sihon and Og. They were the two kings of the Amorites. They ruled east of the Jordan River. Sihon was the king of Heshbon. Og was the king of Bashan. He ruled in Ashtaroth.

11"Our elders and all of the people who are living in our country spoke to us. They said, 'Take supplies for your trip. Go and meet the people of Israel. Say to them, "We'll serve you. Make a peace treaty with us." '

12"Look at our bread. It was warm when we packed it. We packed it at home on the day we left to come and see you. But look at how dry and moldy it is now. **13**When we filled these wineskins, they were new. But look at how cracked they are now. And our clothes and sandals are worn out because we've traveled so far."

14The men of Israel looked over the supplies those men had brought. But they didn't ask the LORD what they should do. **15**Joshua made a peace treaty with the men who had come. He agreed to let them live. The leaders of the community took an oath to show that they agreed with the treaty.

16The people of Israel made a peace treaty with the people of Gibeon. But three days later they heard that the people of Gibeon lived close to them. **17**So the people of Israel started out to go to the cities of those men. On the third day they came to Gibeon, Kephirah, Beeroth and Kiriath Jearim. **18**But they didn't attack those cities. That's because the leaders of the community had taken an oath and made a peace treaty with them. They had taken the oath in the name of the LORD, the God of Israel.

The whole community told the leaders they weren't happy with them.

19But all of the leaders answered, "We've made a peace treaty with them. We've taken an oath in the name of the LORD, the God of Israel. So we can't touch them now.

20"But here is what we'll do to them. We'll let them live. Then the LORD's anger won't fall on us because we didn't keep the oath we took." **21**They continued, "Let them live. But let them cut wood and carry water for the whole community." So the leaders kept their promise to them.

22Joshua sent for the people of Gibeon. He said, "Why did you trick us? You said, 'We live far away from you.' But in fact you live close to us. **23**So now you are under a curse. You will always serve us. You will always cut wood and carry water for the house of my God."

24They answered Joshua, "We were clearly told what the LORD your God had commanded his servant Moses to do. He commanded him to give you the whole land. He also ordered him to wipe out all of its people to make room for you. So we were afraid you would kill us. That's why we tricked you. **25**We are now in your hands. Do to us what you think is good and right."

26So Joshua saved the people of Gibeon. He didn't let the people of Israel kill them. **27**That day he made them cut wood and carry water. They had to serve the community of Israel. They also had to serve at the altar of the LORD at the place where he would choose to put it. And they still serve the people of Israel to this very day.

The Sun Stands Still

10 Adoni-Zedek was the king of Jerusalem. He heard that Joshua had taken Ai. He found out that the city had been set apart to the LORD in a special way to be destroyed. He heard that Joshua had done to Ai and its king the same thing he had done to Jericho and its king.

Adoni-Zedek heard that the people of Gibeon had made a peace treaty with Israel. He also found out that they were living among the people of Israel. **2**The things he heard alarmed him and his people very much. That's because Gibeon was an important city. It was like one of the royal cities. It was larger than Ai. All of its men were good soldiers.

3So Adoni-Zedek, the king of Jerusalem, made an appeal to Hoham, the king of Hebron. He appealed to Piram, the king of Jarmuth. He appealed to Japhia, the king of Lachish. He also made an appeal to Debir, the king of Eglon. **4**"Come up and help me attack Gibeon," he said. "Its people have made peace with Joshua and the people of Israel."

5The kings of Jerusalem, Hebron, Jarmuth, Lachish and Eglon gathered their armies together. Those five Amorite kings moved all of their troops into position to fight against Gibeon. Then they attacked it.

6Joshua was in the camp at Gilgal. The people of Gibeon sent a message to him there. It said, "Don't desert us. We serve you. Come up to us quickly! Save us! Help us! All of the Amorite kings from the central hill country have gathered their armies together to fight against us."

7So Joshua marched up from Gilgal with his whole army. The army included all of his best fighting men.

8The LORD said to Joshua, "Do not be afraid of them. I have handed them over to you. Not one of them will be able to fight against you and win."

9Joshua marched all night from Gilgal. He took the Amorite armies by surprise. **10**The LORD threw them into a panic as Israel marched toward them. Then Israel won a great battle over them at Gibeon. They chased them along the road that goes up to Beth Horon. They struck them down all the way to Azekah and Makkedah.

11The Amorites ran away as Israel marched toward them. They ran down the road from Beth Horon to Azekah. As they ran, the LORD threw large hailstones down on them from the sky. The hailstones killed more of them than the swords of the men of Israel did.

12So the LORD gave the Amorites over to Israel. On that day Joshua spoke to the LORD while the people of Israel were listening. He said,

"Sun, stand still over Gibeon.
Moon, stand still over the Valley of Aijalon."
13So the sun stood still.
The moon stopped.
They didn't move again until the nation won the battle over its enemies.

You can read about it in the Book of Jashar.
The sun stopped in the middle of the sky. It didn't go down for about a full day. **14**There has never been a day like it before or since. It was a day when the LORD lis-

tened to a mere man. You can be sure that the LORD was fighting for Israel!

15Joshua and his whole army returned to the camp at Gilgal.

Joshua Kills the Five Amorite Kings

16The five Amorite kings had run away. They had hidden in the cave at Makkedah.

17Joshua was told that the five kings had been found. He was also told that they were hiding in the cave at Makkedah. **18**He said, "Roll some large rocks up to the opening of the cave. Put some men there to guard it. **19**But keep on going! Chase your enemies. Attack them from behind. Don't let them get back to their cities. The LORD your God has handed them over to you."

20So Joshua and the men of Israel completely destroyed them. They killed almost every one of them. But a few escaped. They went back to their cities that had high walls around them.

21Then Israel's whole army returned safely to Joshua. He was in the camp at Makkedah. No one in the land dared to say anything against the people of Israel.

22Joshua said, "Open up the cave. Bring those five kings out to me." **23**So Joshua's men brought the five kings out of the cave. They were the kings of Jerusalem, Hebron, Jarmuth, Lachish and Eglon.

24The men brought them to Joshua. Then he sent for all of the men of Israel. He spoke to the army commanders who had come with him. He said, "Come here. Put your feet on the necks of these kings." So they came forward and placed their feet on the necks of the kings.

25Joshua said to them, "Don't be afraid. Don't lose hope. Be strong and brave. This

POWER-SURGE

BRAVE B

JOSHUA SAID TO THEM, "DON'T BE AFRAID. DON'T LOSE HOPE. BE STRONG AND BRAVE."
— JOSHUA 10:25 —

STRONG

is what the LORD will do to all of the enemies you are going to fight."

²⁶Joshua struck the five kings down and killed them. He stuck a pole through each of their bodies. Then he set the poles up where people could see the bodies. He left them there until evening.

²⁷At sunset Joshua ordered his men to take the bodies down. So they took them down and threw them into the cave where the kings had been hiding. They placed large rocks at the opening of the cave. And the rocks are still there to this very day.

²⁸That day Joshua took Makkedah. He killed its people and their king with the sword. He totally destroyed everyone in it. He didn't leave anyone alive. He did to the king of Makkedah the same thing he had done to the king of Jericho.

The Campaign Against the Cities in the South

²⁹Joshua moved on from Makkedah to Libnah. Israel's whole army went with him. They attacked Libnah. ³⁰The LORD also handed that city and its king over to Israel. Joshua destroyed the city. He and his men killed everyone in it with their swords. He didn't leave anyone alive there. He did to its king the same thing he had done to the king of Jericho.

³¹Joshua moved on from Libnah to Lachish. Israel's whole army went with him. The men took up their battle positions. Then Joshua attacked Lachish. ³²The LORD handed it over to Israel. Joshua took the city on the second day of the battle. He destroyed the city. He and his men killed everyone in it with their swords. He had done the same thing to Libnah.

³³While all of that was happening, Horam had come up to help Lachish. He was the king of Gezer. But Joshua won the battle over him and his army. No one was left alive.

³⁴Joshua moved on from Lachish to Eglon. Israel's whole army went with him. They took up their battle positions. Then they attacked Eglon. ³⁵They captured it that same day. They totally destroyed everyone in it with their swords. They had done the same thing to Lachish.

³⁶Joshua went up from Eglon to Hebron. Israel's whole army went with him. Then they attacked Hebron. ³⁷They took the city. They destroyed it and its villages. They killed all of its people and their king with their swords. They didn't leave anyone alive. They totally destroyed the city and everyone in it. They had done the same thing at Eglon.

³⁸Joshua turned back and attacked Debir. Israel's whole army went with him. ³⁹They took the city, its king and its villages. They totally destroyed everyone in Debir with their swords. They didn't leave anyone alive. They did to Debir and its king the same thing they had done to Libnah and its king. They had also done the same thing to Hebron.

⁴⁰So Joshua brought the whole area under his control. That included the central hill country and the Negev Desert. It included the western hills and the mountain slopes. It also included all of the kings in that whole area. Joshua didn't leave anyone alive. He totally destroyed everyone who breathed. He did just as the LORD, the God of Israel, had commanded.

⁴¹Joshua brought everyone from Kadesh Barnea to Gaza under his control. He also brought everyone from the whole area of Goshen to Gibeon under his control. ⁴²He won the battle over all of those kings and their lands. He did it in one campaign. That's because the LORD, the God of Israel, fought for Israel.

⁴³Then Joshua returned to the camp at Gilgal. Israel's whole army went with him.

The Campaign Against the Cities in the North

11 Jabin was the king of Hazor. He heard about the battles Israel had won. So he sent a message to Jobab. Jobab was the king of Madon. Jabin sent the same message to the kings of Shimron and Acshaph. ²He also sent it to a lot of other kings. Some ruled in the mountains in the north. Some ruled in the Arabah Valley south of Kinnereth. Others ruled in the western hills. Still others ruled in Naphoth Dor in the west. ³Jabin sent the same message to the people of east Canaan and west Canaan. He sent it to the Amorites, Hittites, Perizzites and Jebusites. They lived in the central hill country. He also sent it to the Hivites who lived below Mount Hermon in the area of Mizpah.

⁴Those kings marched out with all of their troops. They had a large number of horses and chariots. It was a huge army. The fighting men were as many as the grains of sand on the seashore. ⁵All of those kings gathered their armies together to fight against Israel. They set up camp together at the Waters of Merom.

⁶The LORD spoke to Joshua. He said,

"Do not be afraid of them. By this time tomorrow I will hand all of them over to Israel. All of them will be killed. You must cut the legs of their horses. You must burn up their chariots."

7So Joshua and his whole army attacked them suddenly. They fought against them at the Waters of Merom. **8**The LORD handed them over to Israel. Israel won the battle over them. They hunted them down all the way to Greater Sidon. They chased them to Misrephoth Maim. They chased them to the Valley of Mizpah in the east. Not one of them was left alive.

9Joshua did to them what the LORD had directed him to do. He cut the legs of their horses. He burned up their chariots.

10At that time Joshua turned back. He captured Hazor. He killed its king with his sword. Hazor was the most important city in all of those kingdoms. **11**The army of Israel killed everyone in Hazor with their swords. Its people had been set apart to the LORD in a special way to be destroyed. Israel's army didn't spare anything that breathed. Then Joshua burned up the city.

12Joshua took all of those royal cities and their kings. He and his men killed everyone in those cities with their swords. He totally destroyed them. He did just as Moses, the servant of the LORD, had commanded. **13**Many cities were built on top of earlier cities that had been destroyed. Israel didn't burn up any of those except Hazor. Joshua burned it up.

14The army of Israel kept for themselves the livestock and everything else they took from those cities. But they killed all of the people with their swords. They completely destroyed them. They didn't spare anyone who breathed.

15The LORD had commanded his servant Moses to do all of those things. Moses had passed that command on to Joshua. And Joshua carried it out. He did everything the LORD had commanded Moses.

16So Joshua took the whole land. He took the central hill country and the whole Negev Desert. He took the whole area of Goshen. He took the western hills. He took the Arabah Valley. He took the mountains of Israel and the hills around them. **17**He took the area that begins at Mount Halak, which rises toward Seir. The area ends at Baal Gad in the Valley of Lebanon below Mount Hermon. Joshua captured the kings who ruled over that whole land. He struck them

down and killed them. **18**He fought battles against all of those kings for a long time.

19Only the Hivites who lived in Gibeon made a peace treaty with the people of Israel. No other city made a treaty with them. So Israel captured all of those cities in battle. **20**The LORD himself made the hearts of their people stubborn. He made them go to war against Israel so he could totally destroy them. He wanted to wipe them out. He didn't show them any mercy. The LORD had commanded Moses to destroy the people of Canaan.

21At that time Joshua went and destroyed the Anakites. They lived all through the hill country of Judah and Israel. They lived in Hebron, Debir and Anab. Joshua totally destroyed the Anakites and their towns. **22**There weren't any Anakites left alive in Israel's territory. But a few were left alive in Gaza, Gath and Ashdod.

23So Joshua took the whole land, just as the LORD had directed Moses. Joshua gave the land to Israel as their very own. He divided it up and gave each tribe its share. Then the land had peace and rest.

Israel Wins the Battle Over the Kings in the Land

12 The people of Israel took over the territory east of the Jordan River. The land they took reached from the Arnon River valley to Mount Hermon. It included the whole east side of the Arabah Valley. Israel won the battle over the kings of that whole territory. Here are the lands Israel took from the kings they won the battle over.

2They took the land of Sihon. He was the king of the Amorites.

He ruled in Heshbon. The land he ruled over begins at Aroer. Aroer is on the rim of the Arnon River valley. He ruled from the middle of the valley to the Jabbok River. The Jabbok is the border of Ammon. Sihon's territory included half of Gilead. **3**He also ruled over the east side of the Arabah Valley. That land begins at the Sea of Galilee. It goes to the Dead Sea and over to Beth Jeshimoth. Then it goes south, below the slopes of Pisgah.

4Israel also took the territory of Og. He was the king of Bashan.

He was one of the last of the Rephaites. He ruled in Ashtaroth and Edrei. **5**He ruled over Mount Hermon, Salecah and the whole land of

Bashan. He ruled all the way to the border of Geshur and Maacah. He ruled over half of Gilead. His land reached the border of Sihon. Sihon was the king of Heshbon.

⁶Moses was the servant of the LORD. Moses and the people of Israel won the battle over those two kings. He gave their land to the tribes of Reuben and Gad and half of the tribe of Manasseh. He gave it to them as their share.

⁷Joshua and the people of Israel won the battle over the kings who ruled west of the Jordan River. The lands of the kings reached from Baal Gad in the Valley of Lebanon to Mount Halak, which rises toward Seir.

Joshua gave their lands to the tribes of Israel as their very own. He divided them up and gave each tribe its share. ⁸Those lands included the central hill country, the western hills and the Arabah Valley. They also included the mountain slopes, the Desert of Judah and the Negev Desert. Those lands belonged to the Hittites, Amorites, Canaanites, Perizzites, Hivites and Jebusites. Here are the kings Israel won the battle over.

⁹the king of Jericho	one
the king of Ai, which is near Bethel	one
¹⁰the king of Jerusalem	one
the king of Hebron	one
¹¹the king of Jarmuth	one
the king of Lachish	one
¹²the king of Eglon	one
the king of Gezer	one
¹³the king of Debir	one
the king of Geder	one
¹⁴the king of Hormah	one
the king of Arad	one
¹⁵the king of Libnah	one
the king of Adullam	one
¹⁶the king of Makkedah	one
the king of Bethel	one
¹⁷the king of Tappuah	one
the king of Hepher	one
¹⁸the king of Aphek	one
the king of Lasharon	one
¹⁹the king of Madon	one
the king of Hazor	one
²⁰the king of Shimron Meron	one
the king of Acshaph	one
²¹the king of Taanach	one
the king of Megiddo	one
²²the king of Kedesh	one
the king of Jokneam in Carmel	one
²³the king of Dor in Naphoth Dor	one
the king of Goyim in Gilgal	one
²⁴the king of Tirzah	one

The total number of kings was 31.

The Land That Remained to Be Taken Over

13 Joshua was now very old. The LORD said to him, "You are very old. And there are still very large areas of land that have not been taken over yet.

²"Here is the land that remains to be taken over. It includes all of the areas of Philistia and Geshur. ³Those areas begin at the Shihor River in the eastern part of Egypt. They go to the territory of Ekron in the north. All of that land is considered as belonging to the people of Canaan. The land that remains to be taken over includes the territory of the five rulers of Philistia. They rule over Gaza, Ashdod, Ashkelon, Gath and Ekron. The Avvites ⁴live south of them. The rest of the land of Canaan that remains to be taken over reaches from Arah all the way to Aphek. Arah belongs to the people of Sidon. The land that remains to be taken over includes the area where the Amorites live. ⁵It includes the area where the people of Byblos live. It also includes all of Lebanon to the east. It reaches from Baal Gad below Mount Hermon to Lebo Hamath.

⁶"I myself will drive out all of the people who live in the mountain areas. Those areas reach from Lebanon to Misrephoth Maim. They include the area where all of the people of Sidon live. I myself will drive those people out to make room for the people of Israel.

"Make sure you set that land apart for Israel. Give it to them as their share, just as I have directed you. ⁷Divide it up among the nine tribes and half of the tribe of Manasseh. Give each tribe its share."

Moses Had Given the Eastern Tribes Their Land

⁸The other half of Manasseh's tribe had already received the share of land Moses had given them. Their share was east of the Jordan River. The tribes of Reuben and Gad had already received their share too. Moses, the servant of the LORD, had given it to them.

⁹That land starts at Aroer on the rim of the Arnon River valley. It includes the town in the middle of the valley.

It includes the high flatlands of Medeba all the way to Dibon. **10**It also includes all of the towns of Sihon, the king of the Amorites. He had ruled in Heshbon. That area reaches to the border of Ammon. **11**It also includes Gilead. It includes the territory of Geshur and Maacah. It includes Mount Hermon and the whole land of Bashan all the way to Salecah.

12So it includes the entire kingdom of Og in Bashan. Og had ruled in Ashtaroth and Edrei. He was one of the last of the Rephaites. Moses had won the battle over Sihon and Og. He had taken over their land.

13But the people of Israel didn't drive out the people of Geshur and Maacah. So they continue to live among the people of Israel to this very day.

14Moses hadn't given any share of the land to the tribe of Levi. That's because the offerings that are made with fire are their share. Those offerings are made to the LORD, the God of Israel. Moses gave the Levites what he had promised them.

15Here is what Moses had given to the tribe of Reuben, family group by family group.

16Their territory starts at Aroer on the rim of the Arnon River valley. It includes the town in the middle of the valley. It includes all of the high flatlands that are near Medeba. **17**It includes Heshbon and all of its towns on those flatlands. Those towns include Dibon, Bamoth Baal, Beth Baal Meon, **18**Jahaz, Kedemoth and Mephaath. **19**They include Kiriathaim, Sibmah and Zereth Shahar on the hill in the valley. **20**They also include Beth Peor, Beth Jeshimoth and the slopes of Pisgah. **21**All of those towns are on the high flatlands.

The territory includes the whole kingdom of Sihon, the king of the Amorites. He had ruled in Heshbon. Moses had won the battle over him and over the chiefs of Midian. Those chiefs were Evi, Rekem, Zur, Hur and Reba. They were princes who helped Sihon fight against Israel. They lived in that country. **22**The people of Israel killed many of them in battle. They also killed Balaam with a sword. He was the son of Beor.

Balaam used magic to find out what was going to happen.

23The border of the tribe of Reuben was the bank of the Jordan River. All of those towns and their villages were given to the tribe of Reuben as their very own. Each family group received its share.

24Here is what Moses had given to the tribe of Gad, family group by family group.

25Their territory includes Jazer and all of the towns of Gilead. It includes half of the country of Ammon all the way to Aroer, which was near Rabbah. **26**Their territory reaches from Heshbon to Ramath Mizpah and Betonim. It reaches from Mahanaim to the territory of Debir. **27**In the valley their land includes Beth Haram, Beth Nimrah, Succoth and Zaphon. It also includes the rest of the kingdom of Sihon. He was the king of Heshbon. His kingdom included the east side of the Jordan River. It reached up to the south end of the Sea of Galilee. **28**All of those towns and their villages were given to the tribe of Gad as their very own. Each family group received its share.

29Here is what Moses had given to half of the tribe of Manasseh, family group by family group. It's what Moses had given to half of Manasseh's family line.

30Their territory starts at Mahanaim. It includes the whole land of Bashan. That was the entire kingdom of Og, the king of Bashan. Manasseh's territory includes all of the 60 towns of Jair in Bashan. **31**It includes half of the land of Gilead. It also includes Ashtaroth and Edrei. They were the royal cities of Og in Bashan. That land was given to half of the family line of Makir. He was the son of Manasseh. Each family group received its share.

32Those were the shares of land Moses had given the eastern tribes when he was in the flatlands of Moab. The flatlands are across the Jordan River east of Jericho. **33**But Moses hadn't given any share to the tribe of Levi. The LORD, the God of Israel, is their share. Moses gave the Levites what he had promised them.

The Western Tribes Are Given Their Land

14 The rest of the tribes of Israel received their shares of land in Canaan. The priest Eleazar and Joshua, the son of Nun, decided what each of the tribes should receive. The leaders of the tribes helped them make those decisions.

2 The shares of nine tribes and half of the tribe of Manasseh were decided by using lots. That's what the LORD had commanded through Moses.

3 Moses had given two tribes and the other half of the tribe of Manasseh their shares east of the Jordan River. But Moses had not given the Levites a share among the other tribes. 4 Manasseh and Ephraim were the sons of Joseph. They had become two tribes. The Levites didn't receive any share of the land. They only received towns to live in and grasslands for their flocks and herds.

5 So the people of Israel divided up the land, just as the LORD had commanded Moses.

Joshua Gives Hebron to Caleb

6 The men of Judah approached Joshua at Gilgal. Caleb, the son of Jephunneh the Kenizzite, spoke to Joshua. He said, "You know what the LORD said to Moses, the man of God. He spoke to him at Kadesh Barnea about you and me. 7 Moses, the servant of the LORD, sent me from Kadesh Barnea to check out the land. I was 40 years old at that time. I brought back an honest report to him. I told him exactly what I had seen. 8 Several other men of Israel went up with me. What they reported made the hearts of the people melt away in fear. But I followed the LORD my God with my whole heart.

9 "So on that day Moses took an oath and made a promise to me. He said, 'The land your feet have walked on will be your share. It will be the share of your children forever. That's because you have followed the LORD my God with your whole heart.' *(Deuteronomy 1:36)*

10 "The LORD has done just as he promised. He made the promise while Israel was wandering around in the desert. That was 45 years ago. He has kept me alive all of this time. So here I am today, 85 years old! 11 I'm still as strong today as I was the day Moses sent me out. I'm just as able to go out to battle now as I was then.

12 "So give me this hill country. The LORD promised it to me that day. At that time you yourself heard that the Anakites were living there. You also heard that

their cities were large and had high walls. But I'll drive them out, just as the LORD said I would. He will help me do it."

13 Then Joshua blessed Caleb, the son of Jephunneh. He gave him Hebron as his share.

14 So ever since that time Hebron has belonged to Caleb, the son of Jephunneh the Kenizzite. That's because he followed the LORD, the God of Israel, with his whole heart.

15 Hebron used to be called Kiriath Arba. It was named after Arba. He was the greatest man among the Anakites.

So the land had peace and rest.

Land Is Given to Judah

15 Land was given to the tribe of Judah, family group by family group. It reached down to the territory of Edom. It went as far south as the Desert of Zin.

2 Judah's border on the south started from the bay at the south end of

---

POWER–SURGE

BRAVE B

THE LORD HAS DONE JUST AS HE PROMISED. HE MADE THE PROMISE WHILE ISRAEL WAS WANDERING AROUND IN THE DESERT. THAT WAS 45 YEARS AGO. HE HAS KEPT ME [CALEB] ALIVE ALL OF THIS TIME. SO HERE I AM TODAY, 85 YEARS OLD! I'M STILL AS STRONG TODAY AS I WAS THE DAY MOSES SENT ME OUT. I'M JUST AS ABLE TO GO OUT TO BATTLE NOW AS I WAS THEN.

—— JOSHUA 14:10-11 ——

STRONG

the Dead Sea. 3It went across to the south of Scorpion Pass. It continued on to Zin. It went over to the south of Kadesh Barnea. Then it ran past Hezron up to Addar. It curved around to Karka. 4It then went along to Azmon. There it joined the Wadi of Egypt and ended at the Mediterranean Sea. That was the southern border of Judah.

5The border on the east was the Dead Sea. It went north all the way to where the Jordan River enters the sea.

The border on the north started at the bay of the Dead Sea. That's where the Jordan River enters the sea. 6From there it went up to Beth Hoglah. It continued north of Beth Arabah to the Stone of Bohan, the son of Reuben. 7Then it went from the Valley of Achor up to Debir. It turned north to Gilgal. Gilgal faces the Pass of Adummim south of the valley. The border continued along to the springs of En Shemesh. It came to an end at En Rogel. 8Then it ran up the Valley of Ben Hinnom. It went along the south slope of Jerusalem. From there it climbed to the top of the hill that is west of the Hinnom Valley. The hill is also at the north end of the Valley of Rephaim. 9From the top of the hill the border headed toward the springs of Nephtoah. It went to the towns near Mount Ephron. It went down toward Kiriath Jearim. 10Then it curved west from Kiriath Jearim to Mount Seir. It ran along the north slope of Mount Kesalon. It continued down to Beth Shemesh and crossed over to Timnah. 11It went to the north slope of Ekron. Then it turned toward Shikkeron. It passed along to Mount Baalah and reached Jabneel. The border came to an end at the Mediterranean Sea.

12The border on the west was the coastline of the Mediterranean Sea. Those were the borders of the family groups of the tribe of Judah.

13Joshua gave a part of Judah's share of land to Caleb, the son of Jephunneh. That was in keeping with the LORD's command to Joshua. The share Caleb received was the city of Hebron. It was also called Kiriath Arba. Anak came from the family line of Arba. 14Caleb drove three Anakites out of Hebron. Their names were Sheshai, Ahiman and Talmai. They were from the family line of Anak.

15From Hebron, Caleb marched out against the people who were living in Debir. It used to be called Kiriath Sepher. 16Caleb said, "I will give my daughter Acsah to be married. I'll give her to the man who attacks and captures Kiriath Sepher."

17Othniel captured it. So Caleb gave his daughter Acsah to him to be his wife. Othniel was the son of Kenaz. He was Caleb's brother.

18One day Acsah came to Othniel. She begged him to ask her father for a field. When she got off her donkey, Caleb spoke to her. He asked, "What can I do for you?"

19She replied, "Do me a special favor. You have given me some land in the Negev Desert. Give me springs of water also." So Caleb gave her the upper and lower springs.

20Here is the share of land that was given to the tribe of Judah, family group by family group.

21The towns farthest south that were given to Judah were in the Negev Desert. They were near the border of Edom. Here is a list of those towns.

Kabzeel, Eder, Jagur, 22Kinah, Dimonah, Adadah, 23Kedesh, Hazor, Ithnan, 24Ziph, Telem, Bealoth, 25Hazor Hadattah, Hazor, 26Amam, Shema, Moladah, 27Hazar Gaddah, Heshmon, Beth Pelet, 28Hazar Shual, Beersheba, Biziothiah, 29Baalah, Iim, Ezem, 30Eltolad, Kesil, Hormah, 31Ziklag, Madmannah, Sansannah, 32Lebaoth, Shilhim, Ain and Rimmon. The total number of towns was 29. Some of them had villages near them.

33Towns were also given to Judah in the western hills. Here is a list of those towns.

Eshtaol, Zorah, Ashnah, 34Zanoah, En Gannim, Tappuah, Enam, 35Jarmuth, Adullam, Socoh, Azekah, 36Shaaraim, Adithaim and Gederah. Gederah is also called Gederothaim. The total number of towns was 14. Some of them had villages near them.

37Here's another list of towns that were given to Judah in the western hills.

Zenan, Hadashah, Migdal Gad, 38Dilean, Mizpah, Joktheel, 39Lachish, Bozkath, Eglon, 40Cabbon, Lahmas, Kitlish, 41Gederoth, Beth Dagon, Naamah and Makkedah. The total number of towns was 16. Some of them had villages near them.

42Here's another list of towns that were given to Judah in the western hills.

Libnah, Ether, Ashan, **43**Iphtah, Ashnah, Nezib, **44**Keilah, Aczib and Mareshah. The total number of towns was nine. Some of them had villages near them.

45Judah was also given Ekron and the settlements and villages that were around it. **46**West of Ekron, Judah was given all of the settlements and villages that were near Ashdod. **47**Judah was given Ashdod and the settlements and villages that were around it. And Judah was given Gaza and its settlements and villages. Judah's territory went all the way to the Wadi of Egypt and the coast of the Mediterranean Sea.

48Towns were also given to Judah in the central hill country. Here is a list of those towns.

Shamir, Jattir, Socoh, **49**Dannah, Debir, **50**Anab, Eshtemoh, Anim, **51**Goshen, Holon and Giloh. The total number of towns was 11. Some of them had villages near them.

52Here's another list of towns that were given to Judah in the central hill country.

Arab, Dumah, Eshan, **53**Janim, Beth Tappuah, Aphekah, **54**Humtah, Hebron and Zior. The total number of towns was nine. Some of them had villages near them.

55Here's another list of towns that were given to Judah in the central hill country.

Maon, Carmel, Ziph, Juttah, **56**Jezreel, Jokdeam, Zanoah, **57**Kain, Gibeah and Timnah. The total number of towns was ten. Some of them had villages near them.

58Here's another list of towns that were given to Judah in the central hill country.

Halhul, Beth Zur, Gedor, **59**Maarath, Beth Anoth and Eltekon. The total number of towns was six. Some of them had villages near them.

60Here's another list of towns that were given to Judah in the central hill country.

Kiriath Jearim and Rabbah. The total number of towns was two. They had villages near them.

61Towns were also given to Judah in the desert. Here is a list of those towns.

Beth Arabah, Middin, Secacah, **62**Nibshan, the City of Salt and En Gedi. The total number of towns was six. Some of them had villages near them.

63Judah couldn't drive out the Jebusites who were living in Jerusalem. So they live there with the people of Judah to this very day.

Land Is Given to Ephraim and Manasseh

16 The land that was given to the two tribes in the family line of Joseph began at the Jordan River near Jericho. Their border started east of the springs of Jericho. It went up from there through the desert into the hill country of Bethel. **2**Bethel is also called Luz. From Bethel it crossed over to Ataroth. That's where the Arkites live. **3**Then it went west down to the territory of the Japhletites. It went all the way to the area of Lower Beth Horon. It went on to Gezer. It came to an end at the Mediterranean Sea.

4The tribes of Manasseh and Ephraim were from the family line of Joseph. So they received that land as their share.

5Here is the territory that was given to the tribe of Ephraim, family group by family group.

The border of their share of land started at Ataroth Addar in the east. It went to Upper Beth Horon. **6**It continued toward the Mediterranean Sea. From Micmethath on the north, it curved toward the east. It went to Taanath Shiloh. It passed by Taanath Shiloh to Janoah on the east. **7**Then it went down from Janoah to Ataroth and Naarah. It touched Jericho and came to an end at the Jordan River. **8**From Tappuah the border went west to the Kanah Valley. It came to an end at the Mediterranean Sea. That was the land that was given to the tribe of Ephraim. Each family group received its share.

9The tribe of Ephraim was also given other towns and villages that were set apart for them. Those towns and villages were in the share of land that was given to the tribe of Manasseh.

10The people of Ephraim didn't drive out the people of Canaan who were living in Gezer. The people of Canaan live among the people of Ephraim to this very day. But they are forced to work hard for the people of Ephraim.

17 Land was given to the tribe of Manasseh. It was given to Makir. Manasseh was Joseph's oldest son. Makir was Manasseh's oldest son. The people of Gilead came from the family line of Makir. The people of Gilead had received the lands of Gilead and Bashan. That's because the people of Makir were great soldiers. 2So land was given to the rest of the people of Manasseh. It was given to the family groups of Abiezer, Helek, Asriel, Shechem, Hepher and Shemida. They were the other men in the family line of Manasseh, the son of Joseph. Those were their names by their family groups.

3Makir was the son of Manasseh. Gilead was the son of Makir. Hepher was the son of Gilead. And Zelophehad was the son of Hepher. Zelophehad didn't have any sons. He only had daughters. Their names were Mahlah, Noah, Hoglah, Milcah and Tirzah.

4The daughters of Zelophehad went to the priest Eleazar and to Joshua, the son of Nun. They also went to the other leaders. They said, "The LORD commanded Moses to give us our share of land among our male relatives." So Joshua gave them land along with their male relatives. That was in keeping with what the LORD had commanded.

5Manasseh's share was made up of ten pieces of land. That land was in addition to Gilead and Bashan east of the Jordan River. 6So the five granddaughters of Hepher in the family line of Manasseh received land, just as the other five sons of Manasseh did. The land of Gilead belonged to the rest of the family line of Manasseh.

7The territory of Manasseh reached from Asher to Micmethath. Micmethath was east of Shechem. The border ran south from Micmethath. The people who were living at En Tappuah were inside the border. 8Manasseh had the land around Tappuah. But the town of Tappuah itself was on the border of Manasseh's land. It belonged to the people of Ephraim. 9The border continued south to the Kanah Valley. Some of the towns that belonged to Ephraim were located among the towns of Manasseh. But the border of Manasseh was the north side of the valley. The border came to an end at the Mediterranean Sea.

10The land on the south belonged to Ephraim. The land on the north belonged to Manasseh. The territory of Manasseh reached the Mediterranean Sea. The tribe of Asher was the border on the north. The tribe of Issachar was the border on the east.

11Inside the land that was given to Issachar and Asher, the towns of Beth Shan and Ibleam belonged to Manasseh. The towns of Dor, Endor, Taanach and Megiddo and their people also belonged to Manasseh. Manasseh was given all of those towns and the settlements that were around them. The third town in the list was also called Naphoth Dor.

12But the people of Manasseh weren't able to take over those towns. That's because the people of Canaan had made up their minds to live in that area. 13The people of Israel grew stronger. Then they forced the people of Canaan to work hard for them. But they didn't drive them out completely.

14The people in the family line of Joseph spoke to Joshua. They said, "Why have you given us only one share of the land to have as our own? There are large numbers of us. The LORD has blessed us greatly."

15"That's true," Joshua said. "There are large numbers of you. And the hill country of Ephraim is too small for you. So go up into the forest. Clear out some land for yourselves in the territory of the Perizzites and Rephaites."

16The people in Joseph's family line replied. They said, "The hill country isn't big enough for us. And all of the people of Canaan who live in the flatlands use chariots that have iron parts. They include the people of Beth Shan and its settlements. They also include the people who live in the Valley of Jezreel."

17Joshua spoke again to the people in Joseph's family line. He said to the people of Ephraim and Manasseh, "There are large numbers of you. And you are very powerful. You will have more than one piece of land. 18You will also have the central hill country. It's covered with trees. Cut them down and clear the land. That whole land from one end to the other will belong to you. The people of Canaan use chariots that have iron parts. And those people are strong. But you can drive them out."

The Rest of the Land Is Divided Up

18 The whole community of Israel gathered together at Shiloh. They set up the Tent of Meeting there. The country was brought under their control.

²But there were still seven tribes in Israel who had not yet received their shares of land.

³So Joshua spoke to the people of Israel. He said, "The LORD, the God of your people, has given you this land. How long will you wait before you begin to take it over? ⁴Appoint three men from each tribe. I'll send them to map out the land. Then they'll write a report about its features. The report will point out the share of land each tribe will receive. Then the men will return to me.

⁵"You must divide the land up into seven shares. Judah must remain in its territory in the south. The people in Joseph's family line must remain in their territory in the north. ⁶Write reports about the features of those seven shares of land. Bring them here to me. Then I'll cast lots for you in the sight of the LORD our God.

⁷"But the Levites don't get any share of your land. That's because their share is to serve the LORD as priests.

"The tribes of Gad and Reuben and half of the tribe of Manasseh have already received their shares. They are on the east side of the Jordan River. Moses, the servant of the LORD, gave their shares to them."

⁸The men started out on their way to map out the land. Joshua directed them, "Go and map out the land. Write a report about its features. Then return to me. I'll cast lots for you here at Shiloh in the sight of the LORD."

⁹So the men left and went through the land. They wrote a report about its features on a scroll. It showed how they divided up the land into seven shares. It listed the towns that were in each share. The men returned to Joshua in the camp at Shiloh.

¹⁰Then Joshua cast lots for them in Shiloh in the sight of the LORD. There he gave out a share of land to each of the remaining tribes in Israel.

Land Is Given to Benjamin

¹¹The first lot that was drawn out was for the tribe of Benjamin, family group by family group. The territory they were given was located between the tribes of the people of Judah and the people of Joseph. Here are the borders of Benjamin's territory.

¹²On the north side their border started at the Jordan River. It went past the north slope of Jericho. Then it headed west into the central hill country. It came to an end at the Desert of Beth Aven. ¹³From there it crossed to the south slope of Bethel. Then it went down to Ataroth Addar on the hill south of Lower Beth Horon.

¹⁴From the hill that faces Beth Horon on the south the border turned south along the west side of the hill. It came to an end at Kiriath Jearim. That town belongs to the people of Judah. That was the border on the west.

¹⁵The border on the south side started at the west edge of Kiriath Jearim. It came to an end at the springs of Nephtoah. ¹⁶It went down to the foot of the hill that faces the Valley of Ben Hinnom. The hill is north of the Valley of Rephaim. The border continued down the Hinnom Valley. It went along the south slope of Jerusalem, where the people of Jebus live. It continued on to En Rogel. ¹⁷Then it curved north. It went to En Shemesh. It continued on to Geliloth. Geliloth faces the Pass of Adummim. The border ran down to the Stone of Bohan, the son of Reuben. ¹⁸It continued to the north slope of Beth Arabah. It went on down into the Arabah Valley. ¹⁹From there it went to the north slope of Beth Hoglah. It came to an end at the north bay of the Dead Sea. That's where the Jordan River flows into the Dead Sea. That was the border on the south.

²⁰The Jordan River formed the border on the east side.

Those were the borders that marked out on all sides the land the family groups of Benjamin received as their share.

²¹Here is a list of towns that were given to the tribe of Benjamin, family group by family group.

Jericho, Beth Hoglah, Emek Keziz, ²²Beth Arabah, Zemaraim, Bethel, ²³Avvim, Parah, Ophrah, ²⁴Kephar Ammoni, Ophni and Geba. The total number of towns and their villages was 12.

²⁵Here is another list of towns that were given to Benjamin.

Gibeon, Ramah, Beeroth, ²⁶Mizpah, Kephirah, Mozah, ²⁷Rekem, Irpeel, Taralah, ²⁸Zelah, Haeleph, Jerusalem, Gibeah and Kiriath. The total number of towns and their villages was 14.

That was the share of land the family groups of Benjamin received.

Land Is Given to Simeon

19 The second lot that was drawn out was for the tribe of Simeon, family group by family group. The share of land they were given was in the territory of Judah. **2**Here is what Simeon's share included.

Beersheba, Moladah, **3**Hazar Shual, Balah, Ezem, **4**Eltolad, Bethul, Hormah, **5**Ziklag, Beth Marcaboth, Hazar Susah, **6**Beth Lebaoth and Sharuhen. The total number of towns was 13. Some of them had villages near them.

7Here's another list of towns that were given to Simeon.

Ain, Rimmon, Ether and Ashan. The total number of towns was four. Some of them had villages near them. **8**The towns and all of the villages that were around them reached all the way to Ramah in the Negev Desert.

That was the share of land the tribe of Simeon received, family group by family group. **9**Simeon's share of land was taken from Judah's share. That's because Judah had more land than they needed. So the people of Simeon received their share of land inside the territory of Judah.

Land Is Given to Zebulun

10The third lot that was drawn out was for the tribe of Zebulun, family group by family group. Here are the borders of Zebulun's territory.

The border of their share of land went as far as Sarid. **11**It ran west to Maralah and touched Dabbesheth. It reached to the valley near Jokneam. **12**It turned east from Sarid toward the sunrise. It went to the territory of Kisloth Tabor. It went on to Daberath and up to Japhia. **13**Then it continued east to Gath Hepher and Eth Kazin. It came to an end at Rimmon and turned toward Neah. **14**There the border went around on the north to Hannathon. It came to an end at the Valley of Iphtah El. **15**Zebulun's territory included Kattath, Nahalal, Shimron, Idalah and Bethlehem. The total number of towns was 12. Some of them had villages near them.

16Those towns and their villages were Zebulun's share, family group by family group.

Land Is Given to Issachar

17The fourth lot that was drawn out was for the tribe of Issachar, family group by family group. **18**Here is what Issachar's share included.

Jezreel, Kesulloth, Shunem, **19**Hapharaim, Shion, Anaharath, **20**Rabbith, Kishion, Ebez, **21**Remeth, En Gannim, En Haddah and Beth Pazzez. **22**The border touched Tabor, Shahazumah and Beth Shemesh. It came to an end at the Jordan River. The total number of towns was 16. Some of them had villages near them.

23Those towns and their villages were the share the tribe of Issachar received, family group by family group.

Land Is Given to Asher

24The fifth lot that was drawn out was for the tribe of Asher, family group by family group. **25**Here is what Asher's share included.

Helkath, Hali, Beten, Acshaph, **26**Allammelech, Amad and Mishal. On the west the border touched Carmel and Shihor Libnath. **27**Then it turned east toward Beth Dagon. It touched Zebulun and the Valley of Iphtah El. It went north to Beth Emek and Neiel. It went past Cabul on the left. **28**It went to Abdon, Rehob, Hammon and Kanah. It reached all the way to Greater Sidon. **29**The border then turned back toward Ramah. It went to Tyre, a city that had high walls around it. It turned toward Hosah. It came to an end at the Mediterranean Sea in the area of Aczib, **30**Ummah, Aphek and Rehob. The total number of towns was 22. Some of them had villages near them.

31Those towns and their villages were the share the tribe of Asher received, family group by family group.

Land Is Given to Naphtali

32The sixth lot that was drawn out was for Naphtali, family group by family group.

33Their border started at Heleph and the large tree in Zaanannim. It went past Adami Nekeb and Jabneel. It went to Lakkum and came to an end at the Jordan River. **34**The border ran west through Aznoth Tabor. It came to an end at Hukkok. It touched Zebulun on the south. It touched Asher on the west. It touched the Jordan on the east.

35The cities that had high walls around them were Ziddim, Zer, Ham-

math, Rakkath, Kinnereth, 36Ada-
mah, Ramah, Hazor, 37Kedesh, Edrei,
En Hazor, 38Iron, Migdal El, Horem,
Beth Anath and Beth Shemesh. The
total number of towns was 19. Some
of them had villages near them.
39Those towns and their villages were the
share the tribe of Naphtali received, family group by family group.

Land Is Given to Dan

40The seventh lot that was drawn out was
for the tribe of Dan, family group by family group. 41Here is what Dan's share of
land included.

Zorah, Eshtaol, Ir Shemesh, 42Sha-
alabbin, Aijalon, Ithlah, 43Elon, Timnah, Ekron, 44Eltekeh, Gibbethon,
Baalath, 45Jehud, Bene Berak, Gath
Rimmon, 46Me Jarkon and Rakkon.
Dan's share included the area that
faces Joppa.
47The people of Dan had trouble taking
over their territory. So they went up and
attacked Leshem. They took it. They
killed its people with their swords. Then
they moved into Leshem and settled
down there. They named it Dan. That's
because they traced their family line back
to him.
48All of those towns and their villages
were the share the tribe of Dan received,
family group by family group.

Land Is Given to Joshua

49The people of Israel finished dividing
up the shares of land the tribes received.
Then they gave a share to Joshua, the son
of Nun. 50They did what the LORD had
commanded them to do. They gave Joshua the town he asked for. It was Timnath
Serah in the hill country of Ephraim. He
built up the town and settled down there.
51All of those territories were given out
by using lots at Shiloh. The lots were
drawn out by the priest Eleazar and by
Joshua, the son of Nun. The leaders of the
tribes of Israel helped them. The lots were
drawn out in front of the LORD at the
entrance to the Tent of Meeting. So the
work of dividing up the land was finished.

Cities to Go to for Safety

20 Then the LORD spoke to Joshua.
He said, 2"Tell the people of Israel
to choose the cities to go to for safety, just
as I directed you through Moses. 3Anyone
who kills a person by accident can run
there for safety. So can anyone who kills a
person without meaning to. The one who
is charged with murder will be kept safe

from the nearest male relative of the person who was killed.
4"Suppose the one who is charged runs
for safety to one of those cities. Then he
must stand in the entrance of the city
gate. He must state his case in front of the
elders of that city. They must let him
come into their city. They must give him a
place to live there.
5"Suppose the nearest male relative of
the person who was killed comes after
him. Then the elders must not hand him
over to that relative. That's because he
didn't mean to kill his neighbor. He didn't
make evil plans to do it.
6"He must stay in that city until his case
has been brought to the community
court. He must stay there until the high
priest who is serving at that time dies.
Then he can go back to his own home. He
can return to the town he ran away from."
7So the people of Israel set apart Kedesh
in Galilee. It's in the hill country of Naphtali. They set apart Shechem. It's in the
hill country of Ephraim. They set apart
Kiriath Arba. It's in the hill country of
Judah. Kiriath Arba is also called Hebron.
8On the east side of the Jordan River
near Jericho they chose Bezer. It's in the
desert on the high flatlands. It's in the territory of the tribe of Reuben. They chose
Ramoth in Gilead. It's in the territory of
the tribe of Gad. They chose Golan in the
land of Bashan. It's in the territory of the
tribe of Manasseh.
9Suppose you kill someone by accident.
Or another Israelite does it. Or an outsider
who lives among you does it. Then any of
you can run for safety to one of those cities that have been chosen. There you
won't be killed by the nearest male relative of the person who was killed. First
your case must be brought to the community court.

Towns Are Given to the Levites

21 The leaders of the Levite family
groups approached the priest Eleazar and Joshua, the son of Nun. They
also approached the leaders of the family
groups of Israel's other tribes. 2They went
to all of them at Shiloh in Canaan. They
said to them, "Give us towns to live in.
Also give us grasslands for our livestock.
That's what the LORD commanded
through Moses."
3So the people of Israel gave the Levites
towns and grasslands out of their own
shares of land. They did what the LORD
had commanded. Here are the towns the
Levites were given.

⁴The first lot that was drawn out was for the people of Kohath, family group by family group. Some of the Levites came from the family line of the priest Aaron. They were given 13 towns from the tribes of Judah, Simeon and Benjamin. ⁵The rest of Kohath's family groups were given ten towns from the family groups of the tribes of Ephraim and Dan and half of the tribe of Manasseh.

⁶The family groups of Gershon were given 13 towns from the family groups of the tribes of Issachar, Asher and Naphtali and half of the tribe of Manasseh. That part of Manasseh was in the land of Bashan.

⁷The family groups of Merari received 12 towns from the tribes of Reuben, Gad and Zebulun. Each family group received its share.

⁸So the people of Israel gave those towns and their grasslands to the Levites. They did what the LORD had commanded through Moses.

⁹They gave some towns from the territories of the tribes of Judah and Simeon ¹⁰to the members of the family line of Aaron. The towns were given to the family groups of Kohath. They were Levites. The first lot that was drawn out was for them. Here are the towns the family groups of Kohath were given.

¹¹The people of Israel gave them Kiriath Arba and the grasslands that were around it. Kiriath Arba is also called Hebron. It's in the hill country of Judah. Anak came from the family line of Arba. ¹²But Israel had already given away the fields and villages around the city. They had given them to Caleb as his share. Caleb was the son of Jephunneh.

¹³So they gave Hebron to the members of the family line of the priest Aaron. Hebron was a city where anyone who was charged with murder could go for safety. They also gave them Libnah, ¹⁴Jattir, Eshtemoa, ¹⁵Holon, Debir, ¹⁶Ain, Juttah and Beth Shemesh. They gave those towns and their grasslands to the family groups of Kohath. The total number of towns from the tribes of Judah and Simeon was nine.

¹⁷The people of Israel gave some towns from the tribe of Benjamin to the family groups of Kohath. The towns were Gibeon, Geba, ¹⁸Anathoth and Almon. The total number of those towns and their grasslands was four.

¹⁹So the total number of towns and their grasslands that were given to the priests in the family line of Aaron was 13.

²⁰There were other family groups of Kohath among the Levites. They were given towns from the tribe of Ephraim. Here are the towns those other family groups of Kohath were given.

²¹In the hill country of Ephraim they were given Shechem. It was a city where anyone who was charged with murder could go for safety. They were also given Gezer, ²²Kibzaim and Beth Horon. The total number of those towns and their grasslands was four.

²³From the tribe of Dan they received Eltekeh, Gibbethon, ²⁴Aijalon and Gath Rimmon. The total number of those towns and their grasslands was four.

²⁵From half of the tribe of Manasseh they received Taanach and Gath Rimmon. The total number of those towns and their grasslands was two.

²⁶So all of those ten towns and their grasslands were given to the other family groups of Kohath.

²⁷Here are the towns the family groups of Gershon among the Levites were given.

From half of the tribe of Manasseh they received Golan in the land of Bashan. Golan was a city where anyone who was charged with murder could go for safety. They also received Be Eshtarah. The total number of those towns and their grasslands was two.

²⁸From the tribe of Issachar they received Kishion, Daberath, ²⁹Jarmuth and En Gannim. The total number of those towns and their grasslands was four.

³⁰From the tribe of Asher they received Mishal, Abdon, ³¹Helkath and Rehob. The total number of those towns and their grasslands was four.

³²From the tribe of Naphtali they received Kedesh in Galilee. Kedesh was a city where anyone who was charged with murder could go for safety. They also received Hammoth Dor and Kartan. The total number of those towns and their grasslands was three.

³³So the total number of towns and their

grasslands that were given to the family groups of Gershon was 13.

34The rest of the Levites were from the family groups of Merari. Here are the towns they were given.

From the tribe of Zebulun they received Jokneam, Kartah, **35**Dimnah and Nahalal. The total number of those towns and their grasslands was four.

36From the tribe of Reuben they received Bezer, Jahaz, **37**Kedemoth and Mephaath. The total number of those towns and their grasslands was four.

38From the tribe of Gad they received Ramoth in Gilead. Ramoth was a city where anyone who was charged with murder could go for safety. They also received Mahanaim, **39**Heshbon and Jazer. The total number of those towns and their grasslands was four.

40So the total number of towns that were given to the family groups of Merari was 12. That concludes the list of towns the rest of the Levites received.

41The total number of Levite towns and their grasslands in the territory that was given to Israel was 48. **42**Each of those towns had grasslands around it. That was true of all of them.

43So the LORD gave Israel all of the land he had promised with an oath to give to Abraham, Isaac and Jacob. And Israel took it over. Then they settled down there. **44**The LORD gave them peace and rest on every side. That's what he had promised their fathers he would do. Not one of their enemies was able to fight against Israel and win. The LORD handed all of their enemies over to them.

45The LORD kept all of the good promises he had made to the people of Israel. Every one of them came true.

The Eastern Tribes Return Home

22 Joshua sent for the tribes of Reuben and Gad and half of the tribe of Manasseh. **2**He said to them, "You have done everything that Moses, the servant of the LORD, commanded. You have also obeyed everything I commanded. **3**For a long time now you haven't deserted the other Israelites. Instead, you have done what the LORD your God sent you to do. You have obeyed him to this very day. **4**"Now the LORD your God has given the other tribes peace and rest. That's what he promised to do. So return to your homes. They are in the land that Moses, the servant of the LORD, gave you. It's on the east side of the Jordan River.

5"Be very careful to obey the law that Moses, the servant of the LORD, gave you. He commanded you to love the LORD your God. He told you to live exactly as the LORD wants you to. He told you to obey the LORD's commands. He told you to remain true to the LORD. And he told you to serve the LORD with all your heart and with all your soul."

6Joshua gave the eastern tribes his blessing. Then he sent them home. So they went.

7Moses had given land in Bashan to half of the tribe of Manasseh. Joshua had given land to the other half of the tribe along with the other tribes on the west side of the Jordan River.

When Joshua sent them home, he blessed them. **8**He said, "Return to your homes. Take your great wealth with you. Return with your large herds of livestock. Take your silver, gold, bronze and iron

---

POWER-SURGE

LOVING ♥

BE VERY CAREFUL TO OBEY THE LAW THAT MOSES, THE SERVANT OF THE LORD, GAVE YOU. HE COMMANDED YOU TO LOVE THE LORD YOUR GOD. HE TOLD YOU TO LIVE EXACTLY AS THE LORD WANTS YOU TO. HE TOLD YOU TO OBEY THE LORD'S COMMANDS. HE TOLD YOU TO REMAIN TRUE TO THE LORD. AND HE TOLD YOU TO SERVE THE LORD WITH ALL YOUR HEART AND WITH ALL YOUR SOUL.

— JOSHUA 22:5 —

✔ OBEYS

with you. Return with all of your clothes. Divide up the things you have taken from your enemies. Share them with your people."

9So the tribes of Reuben and Gad and half of the tribe of Manasseh went home. They left the other people of Israel at Shiloh in Canaan. They returned to Gilead. That was their own land. They had gotten it in keeping with the LORD's command through Moses.

10The tribes of Reuben and Gad and half of the tribe of Manasseh came to Geliloth. It was near the Jordan River in the land of Canaan. They built a large altar there by the Jordan.

11The rest of the people of Israel heard that they had built the altar. They heard that they had built it on the border of Canaan at Geliloth. It was near the Jordan River on the west side.

12So the whole community of Israel gathered together at Shiloh. They decided to go to war against the eastern tribes.

13The people of Israel sent the priest Phinehas to the land of Gilead. Phinehas was the son of Eleazar. They sent him to the tribes of Reuben and Gad and half of the tribe of Manasseh.

14They sent ten of their leaders with him. There was one for each of the tribes of Israel. Each man was the leader of a family group among the larger family groups of Israel.

15They went to the tribes of Reuben and Gad and half of the tribe of Manasseh in the land of Gilead. They said to them, **16**"We're speaking for the LORD's whole community. How could you disobey the God of Israel like this? How could you turn away from the LORD? How could you disobey him by building an altar for yourselves?

17"Don't you remember how we sinned at Peor? The LORD struck us with a plague because of what we did. Up to this very day we're still suffering because of that sin. **18**Are you turning away from the LORD now?

"Suppose you disobey the LORD today. If you do, he'll be angry with the whole community of Israel tomorrow.

19"If your own land isn't 'clean,' come over to the LORD's land. It's where his holy tent stands. Share our land with us. But don't disobey the LORD. Don't turn against us by building an altar for yourselves. Don't build any altar other than the altar of the LORD our God.

20"Remember Achan, the son of Zerah. Achan wasn't faithful to the LORD. He took the things that had been set apart to the LORD in a special way to be destroyed. Didn't the LORD's anger come on the whole community of Israel? And Achan wasn't the only one who died because of his sin."

21Then the tribes of Reuben and Gad and half of the tribe of Manasseh replied. They answered the leaders of the family groups of Israel. **22**They said, "The Mighty One, God, the LORD! The Mighty One, God, the LORD! He knows! And we want Israel to know! Have we opposed the LORD? Have we refused to obey him? If we have, don't spare us today.

23"Have we built our own altar so we can turn away from the LORD? Have we built it to offer burnt offerings and grain offerings on it? Have we built it to sacrifice friendship offerings on it? If we have, may the LORD himself hold us accountable.

24"No! We built it because we were afraid. Someday your children might speak to our children. We were afraid they might say, 'What do you have to do with the LORD? What do you have to do with the God of Israel? **25**The LORD has made the Jordan River a border between us and you. You people of Reuben! You people of Gad! You don't have anything to do with the LORD.' If your children say that, they might cause our children to stop worshiping the LORD.

26"That's why we said to ourselves, 'Let's get ready and build an altar. But let's not build it to offer burnt offerings or sacrifices on it.'

27"So just the opposite is true. The altar will be a witness between us and you. It will be a witness between our children and yours after us. It will also be a witness that we will worship the LORD at his sacred tent. We'll worship him there with our burnt offerings, sacrifices and friendship offerings. Then in days to come your children won't be able to say to ours, 'You don't have anything to do with the LORD.'

28"So we said to ourselves, 'Suppose they say that to us sometime. Or suppose they say it to our children after us. Then we'll answer, "Look at this altar. It's exactly like the LORD's altar. Our people built it. They didn't build it to offer burnt offerings and sacrifices on it. Instead, they built it to be a witness between us and you." '

29"We would never refuse to obey the LORD. We would never turn away from him now. We wouldn't build an altar to offer burnt offerings, grain offerings and sacrifices on it. We wouldn't use any altar other than the altar of the LORD our God. That altar stands in front of his holy tent."

30The priest Phinehas heard what the tribes of Reuben, Gad and Manasseh had to say. The leaders of the family groups of the community of Israel heard it too. All of them were pleased with what they heard.

31The priest Phinehas spoke to the tribes of Reuben, Gad and Manasseh. Phinehas was the son of Eleazar. He said, "Today we know that the LORD is with us. That's because you have been faithful to him in this matter. Now you have saved the people of Israel from the LORD's anger against them."

32Then the priest Phinehas, the son of Eleazar, returned to Canaan. So did the leaders. All of them went back from their meeting with the tribes of Reuben and Gad in Gilead. They brought a report back to the people of Israel. 33The people were glad to hear the report. They praised God. They didn't talk anymore about going to war against the eastern tribes. And they didn't talk anymore about destroying the country where the tribes of Reuben and Gad lived.

34The tribes of Reuben and Gad gave the altar a name. They called it A Witness Between Us That the LORD Is God.

Joshua Says Good-by to the Leaders

23 A long time had passed. The LORD had given Israel peace and rest from all of their enemies who were around them. By that time Joshua was very old. 2So he sent for all of the elders, leaders, judges and officials of Israel. He said to them, "I'm very old. 3You yourselves have seen everything the LORD your God has done. You have seen what he's done to all of those nations because of you. The LORD your God fought for you.

4"Remember how I've given you all of the land of the nations that remain here. I've given each of your tribes a share of it. It's the land of the nations I won the battle over. It's between the Jordan River and the Mediterranean Sea in the west. 5The LORD your God himself will drive those nations out of your way. He will push them out to make room for you. You will take over their land, just as the LORD your God promised you.

6"Be very strong. Be careful to obey everything that is written in the Scroll of the Law of Moses. Don't turn away from it to the right or the left.

7"Don't have anything to do with the nations that remain among you. Don't use the names of their gods for any reason at all. Don't take oaths and make promises in their names. You must not serve them. You must not bow down to them. 8You must remain true to the LORD your God, just as you have done until now.

9"The LORD has driven out great and powerful nations to make room for you. To this very day no one has been able to fight against you and win. 10One of you can chase a thousand away. That's because the LORD your God fights for you, just as he promised he would. 11So be very careful to love the LORD your God.

12"But suppose you turn away from him. You mix with the people who are left alive in the nations that remain among you. Later, you and they get married to each other. And you do other kinds of things with them. 13Then you can be sure of what the LORD your God will do. He won't drive out those nations to make room for you anymore. Instead, they will become traps and snares for you. They will be like whips on your backs. They will be like thorns in your eyes. All of that will continue until you are destroyed. It will continue until you are removed from this good land. It's the land the LORD your God has given you.

14"Now I'm about to die, just as everyone else on earth does. The LORD your God has kept all of the good promises he gave you. Every one of them has come true. Not one has failed to come true. And you know that with all your heart and soul.

POWER-SURGE

OBEYS ✔

BE VERY STRONG. BE CAREFUL TO OBEY EVERYTHING THAT IS WRITTEN IN THE SCROLL OF THE LAW OF MOSES. DON'T TURN AWAY FROM IT TO THE RIGHT OR THE LEFT.
— JOSHUA 23:6 —

STRONG

15 "Every good promise of the LORD your God has come true. So you know that the LORD will bring on you all of the evil things he has warned you about. He'll do it until he has destroyed you. He'll do it until he has removed you from this good land. It's the land he has given you.

16 "Suppose you break the covenant the LORD your God made with you. He commanded you to obey it. But suppose you go and serve other gods. And you bow down to them. Then the LORD's anger will burn against you. You will quickly be destroyed. You will be removed from the good land he has given you."

Joshua Tells Israel to Serve the LORD

24 Joshua gathered all of Israel's tribes together at Shechem. He sent for the elders, leaders, judges and officials of Israel. They came and stood there in the sight of God.

2 Joshua spoke to all of the people. He said, "The LORD is the God of Israel. He says, 'Long ago your people lived east of the Euphrates River. They worshiped other gods there. Your people included Terah. He was the father of Abraham and Nahor.

3 " 'I took your father Abraham from the land that is east of the Euphrates. I led him all through Canaan. I gave him many children and grandchildren. I gave him Isaac. **4** To Isaac I gave Jacob and Esau. I gave the hill country of Seir to Esau. But Jacob and his children went down to Egypt.

5 " 'Then I sent Moses and Aaron. I made the people of Egypt suffer because of the plagues I sent on them. But I brought you out of Egypt.

6 " 'When I brought your parents out, they came to the Red Sea. The people of Egypt chased them with chariots and with men on horses. They chased them all the way to the sea. **7** But your people cried out to me for help. So I put darkness between you and the people of Egypt. I swept them into the sea. It completely covered them. Your own eyes saw what I did to them. After that, you lived in the desert for a long time.

8 " 'I brought you to the land of the Amorites. They lived east of the Jordan River. They fought against you. But I handed them over to you. I destroyed them to make room for you. Then you took over their land.

9 " 'Balak, the son of Zippor, prepared to fight against Israel. Balak was king of Moab. He sent for Balaam. He wanted him to put a curse on you. Balaam was the son of Beor. **10** But I would not listen to Balaam's curses. So he blessed you again and again. And I saved you from his power.

11 " 'Then you went across the Jordan River. You came to Jericho. Its people fought against you. So did the Amorites, Perizzites, Canaanites, Hittites, Girgashites, Hivites and Jebusites. But I handed them over to you.

12 " 'I sent hornets ahead of you. They drove your enemies out to make room for you. That included the two Amorite kings. You did not do that with your own swords and bows. **13** So I gave you a land you had never farmed. I gave you cities you had not built. You are now living in them. And you are eating the fruit of vineyards and olive trees you did not plant.'

14 "So have respect for the LORD. Serve him. Be completely faithful to him. Throw away the gods your people worshiped east of the Euphrates River and in Egypt. Serve the LORD.

15 "But suppose you don't want to serve him. Then choose for yourselves right now whom you will serve. You can choose the gods your people served east of the Euphrates River. Or you can choose the gods the Amorites serve. After all, you are living in their land. But as for me and my family, we will serve the LORD."

16 Then the people answered Joshua. They said, "We would never desert the LORD! We would never serve other gods! **17** The LORD our God himself brought us and our parents up out of Egypt. He brought us out of that land where we were slaves. With our own eyes, we saw those great and miraculous signs he did. He kept

---

POWER-SURGE

FAITHFUL ()

SO HAVE RESPECT FOR THE LORD. SERVE HIM. BE COMPLETELY FAITHFUL TO HIM... CHOOSE FOR YOURSELVES RIGHT NOW WHOM YOU WILL SERVE...AS FOR ME AND MY FAMILY, WE WILL SERVE THE LORD.

— JOSHUA 24:14-15 —

us safe on our entire journey. He kept us safe as we traveled through all of the nations. **18**He drove them out to make room for us. That included the Amorites. They also lived in the land. We too will serve the LORD. That's because he is our God."

19Joshua spoke to the people. He said, "You aren't able to serve the LORD. He is a holy God. He is a jealous God. He won't forgive you when you disobey him. He won't forgive you when you sin against him.

20"Suppose you desert the LORD. Suppose you serve the gods that people in other lands serve. If you do, he will turn against you. He will bring trouble on you. He will destroy you, even though he has been good to you."

21But the people spoke to Joshua. They said, "No! We will serve the LORD."

22Then Joshua said, "You are witnesses against yourselves. You have said that you have chosen to serve the LORD."

"Yes. We are witnesses," they replied.

23"Now then," said Joshua, "throw away the gods that are among you. People from other lands serve those gods. Give yourselves completely to the LORD, the God of Israel."

24Then the people spoke to Joshua. They said, "We will serve the LORD our God. We will obey him."

25On that day Joshua made a covenant for the people. There at Shechem he wrote down rules and laws for them. **26**He recorded those things in the Scroll of the Law of God. Then he got a large stone. He set it up in Shechem under the oak tree. It was near the place that had been set apart for the LORD.

27"Look!" he said to all of the people. "This stone will be a witness against us. It has heard all of the words the LORD has spoken to us. Suppose you aren't true to your God. Then the stone will be a witness against you."

Joshua Dies

28Joshua sent the people away. He sent all of them to their own shares of land.

29Then Joshua, the servant of the LORD, died. He was the son of Nun. He was 110 years old when he died. **30**His people buried his body at Timnath Serah on his own property. It's north of Mount Gaash in the hill country of Ephraim.

31Israel served the LORD as long as Joshua lived. They also served him as long as the elders lived. Those were the elders who lived longer than Joshua did. They had seen for themselves everything the LORD had done for Israel.

32The people of Israel had brought Joseph's bones up from Egypt. They buried his bones at Shechem in the piece of land Jacob had bought. He had bought it from the sons of Hamor. He had paid 100 pieces of silver for it. Hamor was the father of Shechem. That piece of land became the share that belonged to Joseph's children after him.

33Aaron's son Eleazar died. His body was buried at Gibeah in the hill country of Ephraim. Gibeah had been given to Eleazar's son Phinehas.

JUDGES

The book of Judges records amazing stories of the Israelites as they disobey God, are punished, call on God to help them, obey God for a while, then begin to disobey again. The pattern is repeated over and over throughout the book. Each time the people call to God for help, he sends someone to deliver them. Those deliverers are the heroes of Judges—people like Gideon, Deborah and Samson. Read Judges to discover an awesome and forgiving God who gives his people a second (and third and fourth) chance to turn to him.

HEROES IN THIS BOOK . . .

Israel Fights Against the Canaanites Who Are Still Left

1 Joshua died. After that, the people of Israel spoke to the LORD. They asked him, "Who will go up first and fight for us against the people of Canaan?"

²The LORD answered, "The tribe of Judah will go. I have handed the land over to them."

³Then the men of Judah spoke to their fellow Israelites, the men of Simeon. They said, "Come up with us. Come into the territory Joshua gave us. Help us fight against the people of Canaan. Then we'll go with you into your territory." So the men of Simeon went with them.

⁴When the men of Judah attacked, the LORD helped them. He handed the Canaanites and Perizzites over to them. They struck down 10,000 men at Bezek.

⁵Judah found Adoni-Bezek there. They fought against him. They struck down the Canaanites and Perizzites. ⁶But Adoni-Bezek ran away. Judah chased him and caught him. Then they cut off his thumbs and big toes.

⁷Adoni-Bezek said, "I cut off the thumbs and big toes of 70 kings. I made them pick up scraps under my table. Now God has paid me back for what I did to them." The men of Judah brought Adoni-Bezek to Jerusalem. That's where he died.

⁸The men of Judah attacked Jerusalem and took it. They set the city on fire. They killed its people with their swords.

⁹After that, the men of Judah went down to fight against the people of Canaan who were living in the central hill country. They also fought against those who were living in the Negev Desert and the western hills.

¹⁰Then the men of Judah marched out against the Canaanites who were living in Hebron. The men of Judah won the battle over Sheshai, Ahiman and Talmai. Hebron used to be called Kiriath Arba.

¹¹From Hebron they marched out against the people who were living in Debir. It used to be called Kiriath Sepher.

¹²Caleb said, "I will give my daughter Acsah to be married. I'll give her to the man who attacks and captures Kiriath Sepher."

¹³Othniel captured it. So Caleb gave his daughter Acsah to him to be his wife. Othniel was the son of Kenaz. He was Caleb's younger brother.

¹⁴One day Acsah came to Othniel. She begged him to ask her father for a field. When she got off her donkey, Caleb spoke to her. He said, "What can I do for you?"

¹⁵She replied, "Do me a special favor. You have given me some land in the Negev Desert. Give me springs of water also." So Caleb gave her the upper and lower springs.

¹⁶Moses' father-in-law was a Kenite. His family went up from Jericho. They went up with the people of Judah to the Desert of Judah. They went there to live among its people. Those people were living in the Negev Desert near Arad. Jericho was also known as The City of Palm Trees.

¹⁷The men of Judah went with their fellow Israelites, the men of Simeon. They attacked the people of Canaan who were living in Zephath. They set the city apart to the LORD in a special way to be destroyed. That's why the city was called Hormah.

¹⁸The men of Judah took Gaza, Ashkelon and Ekron. They also took the territory that was around each of those cities.

¹⁹The LORD was with the men of Judah. They took over the central hill country. But they weren't able to drive the people out of the flatlands. That's because those people used chariots that had some iron parts.

²⁰Moses had promised to give Hebron to Caleb. So Hebron was given to Caleb. He drove the three sons of Anak out of it.

²¹But the people of Benjamin failed to drive out the Jebusites who were living in Jerusalem. So they live there with the people of Benjamin to this very day.

²²The men of Joseph attacked Bethel. The LORD was with them. ²³They sent men to Bethel to check it out. It used to be called Luz.

²⁴Those who were sent saw a man coming out of the city. They said to him, "Show us how to get into the city. If you do, we'll see that you are treated well." ²⁵So he showed them how to get in.

The men of Joseph killed the people in the city with their swords. But they spared the man from Bethel. They also spared his whole family. ²⁶Then he went to the land of the Hittites. He built a city there. He called it Luz. That's still its name to this very day.

²⁷But the tribe of Manasseh didn't drive out the people of Beth Shan. They didn't drive out the people of Taanach, Dor, Ibleam and Megiddo. And they didn't drive out the people of the settlements that are around those cities either. That's because the people of Canaan had made up their minds to continue living in that land.

²⁸Later, Israel became stronger. Then

they forced the people of Canaan to work hard for them. But Israel never drove them out completely.

²⁹The tribe of Ephraim didn't drive out the Canaanites who were living in Gezer. So they continued to live there among them.

³⁰The tribe of Zebulun didn't drive out the Canaanites who were living in Kitron and Nahalol. So they remained among them. But Zebulun forced the Canaanites to work hard for them.

³¹The tribe of Asher didn't drive out the people who were living in Acco and Sidon. They didn't drive out the people of Ahlab, Aczib, Helbah, Aphek and Rehob. ³²So the people of Asher lived among the Canaanites who were in the land.

³³The tribe of Naphtali didn't drive out the people who were living in Beth She-mesh and Beth Anath. So the people of Naphtali lived among the Canaanites who were in the land. The people of Beth Shemesh and Beth Anath were forced to work hard for them.

³⁴The Amorites made the people of Dan stay in the central hill country. They didn't let them come down into the flat-lands. ³⁵The Amorites made up their minds to stay in Mount Heres. They also stayed in Aijalon and Shaalbim.

But the power of the tribes of Joseph grew. Then the Amorites were forced to work hard for them.

³⁶The border of the Amorites started at Scorpion Pass. It went to Sela and even past it.

The Angel of the LORD Warns Israel

2 The angel of the LORD went up from Gilgal to Bokim. There he spoke to the people of Israel. "I brought you up out of Egypt," he said. "I led you into this land. It is the land I promised with an oath to give to Abraham, Isaac and Jacob. I said, 'I will never break the covenant I made with you. ²So you must not make a covenant with the people of this land. Instead, you must tear down their altars.'

"But you have disobeyed me. Why did you do it? ³I have something to tell you. I will not drive those people out to make room for you. They will be like thorns in your sides. Their gods will be a trap to you."

⁴The angel of the LORD spoke those things to all of the people of Israel. Then the people began to sob out loud. ⁵So that place was called Bokim. The people offered sacrifices to the LORD there.

The People Turn Away From the LORD

⁶Joshua sent the people of Israel away. Then they went to take over the land. All of them went to their own shares of land.

⁷The people served the LORD as long as Joshua lived. They also served him as long as the elders lived. Those were the elders who lived longer than Joshua did. They had seen all of the great things the LORD had done for Israel.

⁸Joshua, the servant of the LORD, died. He was the son of Nun. He was 110 years old when he died. ⁹His people buried his body on his own property at Timnath Heres. It's north of Mount Gaash in the hill country of Ephraim.

¹⁰All of the people of Joshua's time joined the members of their families who had already died. Then those who were born after them grew up. They didn't know the LORD. They didn't know what he had done for Israel.

¹¹The people of Israel did what was evil in the sight of the LORD. They served the gods that were named after Baal. ¹²They deserted the LORD, the God of their people. He had brought them out of Egypt. But now the people of Israel followed oth-er gods and worshiped them. They served the gods of the nations that were around them. They made the LORD angry ¹³because they deserted him. They served Baal. They also served the goddesses that were named after Ashtoreth.

¹⁴The LORD became angry with Israel. So he handed them over to robbers. The robbers stole everything from them. He gave them over to their enemies who were all around them. Israel wasn't able to fight against them anymore and win. ¹⁵When Israel went out to fight, the LORD's power was against them. He let their enemies win the battle over them. The LORD had warned them with an oath that it would happen. And now they were suffering ter-ribly.

¹⁶Then the LORD gave them leaders. The leaders saved them from the power of those robbers. ¹⁷But the people wouldn't listen to their leaders. They weren't faith-ful to the LORD. They joined themselves to other gods and worshiped them. They didn't obey the LORD's commands as their people before them had done. They quickly turned away from the path their people had taken.

¹⁸When the LORD gave them a leader, he was with that leader. He saved the peo-ple from the power of their enemies. He did it as long as the leader lived. He was

very sorry for the people. They groaned because of what their enemies did to them. The enemies beat them down. They treated them badly.

19But when the leader died, the people returned to their evil ways. The things they did were even more sinful than the things their people before them had done. They followed other gods. They served them. They worshiped them. They refused to give up their evil practices. They wouldn't change their stubborn ways.

20So the LORD's anger burned against the people of Israel. He said, "This nation has broken my covenant. I made it with their people of long ago. But this nation has not listened to me. **21**Joshua left some nations in the land when he died. I will not drive those nations out to make room for you anymore. **22**I will use them to put Israel to the test. I will see whether Israel will live the way I want them to. I will see whether they will follow my path, just as their people did long ago."

23The LORD had let those nations remain in the land. He didn't drive them out right away. He didn't hand them over to Joshua.

3 The LORD left some nations in the land. He left them there in order to put the people of Israel to the test. He did it for all those who hadn't lived through any of the wars in Canaan. **2**He wanted to teach the men in Israel who had never been in battle before. He wanted them to learn how to fight. **3**So he left the five rulers of the Philistines. He left the people of Canaan and the people of Sidon. He left the Hivites who were living in the Lebanon mountains. They lived in the area that was between Mount Baal Hermon and Lebo Hamath.

4The LORD left those nations where they were in order to put Israel to the test. He wanted to see whether they would obey his commands. He had given those commands through Moses to their people of long ago.

5So the people of Israel lived among the Canaanites, Hittites, Amorites, Perizzites, Hivites and Jebusites. **6**They got married to the daughters of those people. They gave their own daughters to the sons of those people. And they served the gods of those people.

Othniel

7The people of Israel did what was evil in the sight of the LORD. They forgot the LORD their God. They served the gods that

were named after Baal. They also served the goddesses that were named after Asherah.

8So the LORD's anger burned against Israel. He gave them over to the power of Cushan-Rishathaim. He was the king of Aram Naharaim. For eight years Israel was under his rule.

9They cried out to the LORD. Then he gave them a man to save them. His name was Othniel, the son of Kenaz. He was Caleb's younger brother. **10**The Spirit of the LORD came on Othniel. So he became Israel's leader. He went to war. The LORD handed Cushan-Rishathaim, the king of Aram, over to him. Othniel overpowered him.

11So the land was at peace for 40 years. Then Othniel, the son of Kenaz, died.

Ehud

12Once again the people of Israel did what was evil in the sight of the LORD. Because they did that, the LORD gave Eglon power over Israel. Eglon was the king of Moab. **13**He got the Ammonites and Amalekites to join him. All of them came and attacked Israel. They took over Jericho. Jericho was also known as The City of Palm Trees. **14**For 18 years the people of Israel were under the rule of Eglon, the king of Moab.

15Again the people of Israel cried out to the LORD. Then he gave them a man to save them. His name was Ehud, the son of Gera. Ehud was left-handed. He was from the tribe of Benjamin.

The people of Israel sent Ehud to Eglon, the king of Moab. They sent him to give the king what he required them to bring him. **16**Ehud had made a sword that had two edges. It was about a foot and a half long. He tied it to his right leg under his clothes. **17**Eglon, the king of Moab, was a very fat man. Ehud gave him the gift he had brought. **18**After that, he sent away those who had carried it.

19At the place where some statues of gods stood near Gilgal, Ehud turned back. He said, "King Eglon, I have a secret message for you."

The king said, "I want everyone to be quiet." And all of his attendants left him.

20Then Ehud approached him. King Eglon was sitting alone in the upstairs room of his summer palace. Ehud said, "I have a message from God for you." So the king got up from his seat.

21Then Ehud reached out his left hand. He pulled out the sword that was tied to his right leg. He stuck it into the king's stomach. ²²Even the handle sank in after the blade. The blade came right out the king's back. Ehud didn't pull the sword out. And the fat closed over it.

²³Ehud went out to the porch. He shut the doors of the upstairs room behind him. Then he locked them.

²⁴After he had gone, the servants came. They found the doors of the upstairs room locked. They said, "Eglon must be going to the toilet in the inside room of the house."

²⁵They waited for a long time. They waited so long they became worried. But the king still didn't open the doors of the room. So they took a key and unlocked them. There they saw their king. He had fallen to the floor. He was dead.

²⁶While Eglon's servants had been waiting, Ehud had gotten away. He passed by the statues of gods and escaped to Seirah. ²⁷There in the hill country of Ephraim he blew a trumpet. Then he led the people of Israel down from the hills.

²⁸"Follow me," Ehud ordered. "The LORD has handed your enemy Moab over to you."

So they followed him down. They took over the only places where people could go across the Jordan River to get to Moab. They didn't let anyone go across. ²⁹At that time they struck down about 10,000 men of Moab. All of those men were strong and powerful. But not even one escaped. ³⁰That day Moab was brought under the rule of Israel.

So the land was at peace for 80 years.

Shamgar

³¹After Ehud, Shamgar became the next leader. He was the son of Anath. He struck down 600 Philistines with a large, pointed stick that was used to drive oxen. He saved Israel too.

Deborah

4 After Ehud died, the people of Israel once again did what was evil in the sight of the LORD.

²So the LORD gave them over to the power of Jabin. He was a king in Canaan. He ruled in Hazor. The commander of his army was Sisera. Sisera lived in Harosheth Haggoyim. ³Jabin used 900 chariots that had some iron parts. He treated the people of Israel very badly for 20 years. So they cried out to the LORD for help.

⁴Deborah was a prophet. She was the wife of Lappidoth. She was leading Israel at that time. ⁵Under The Palm Tree of Deborah she served the people as their judge. That place was between Ramah and Bethel in the hill country of Ephraim. The people of Israel came to her there. They came to have her decide cases for them. She settled matters between them.

⁶Deborah sent for Barak. He was the son of Abinoam. Barak was from Kedesh in the land of Naphtali. Deborah said to Barak, "The LORD, the God of Israel, is giving you a command. He says, 'Go! Take 10,000 men from the tribes of Naphtali and Zebulun with you. Then lead the way to Mount Tabor. ⁷I will draw Sisera into a trap. He is the commander of Jabin's army. I will bring him, his chariots and his troops to the Kishon River. There I will hand him over to you.' "

⁸Barak said to her, "If you go with me, I'll go. But if you don't go with me, I won't go."

⁹"All right," Deborah said. "I'll go with you. But because of the way you are doing this, you won't receive any honor. The LORD will hand Sisera over to a woman." So Deborah went to Kedesh with Barak. ¹⁰There he sent for Zebulun and Naphtali. And 10,000 men followed him. Deborah also went with him.

¹¹Heber, the Kenite, had left the other Kenites. They came from the family line of Hobab. He was the brother-in-law of Moses. Heber set up his tent by the large tree in Zaanannim near Kedesh.

¹²Sisera was told that Barak, the son of Abinoam, had gone up to Mount Tabor. ¹³So Sisera gathered together his 900 chariots that had some iron parts. He also gathered all of his men together. He brought them from Harosheth Haggoyim to the Kishon River.

¹⁴Then Deborah said to Barak, "Go! Today the LORD will hand Sisera over to you. Hasn't the LORD gone ahead of you?" So Barak went down Mount Tabor. His 10,000 men followed him.

¹⁵As Barak's men marched out, the LORD drove Sisera away from the field of battle. He scattered all of Sisera's chariots. Barak's men struck down Sisera's army with their swords. Sisera left his chariot behind. He ran away on foot.

¹⁶But Barak chased Sisera's chariots and army. He chased them all the way to Harosheth Haggoyim. All of Sisera's men were killed with swords. Not even one was left.

¹⁷But Sisera ran away on foot. He ran to the tent of Jael. She was the wife of Heber, the Kenite. Sisera ran there because Heber's family was friendly toward Jabin, the king of Hazor.

DEBORAH

JUDGES 4:14

B

★

🏋

Then Deborah said to Barak, "Go! Today the LORD will hand Sisera over to you. Hasn't the LORD gone ahead of you?"

Deborah sat under a palm tree and talked to Barak. God wanted him to lead Israel's men in a battle against their enemies. But Barak said, "I won't go unless you go with me."

They set out early one morning. The sun was just peeking over the hills. They traveled north for several days. All along the way, they asked Israel's soldiers to join them. Barak and Deborah had a huge army of 10,000 when they reached Mount Tabor.

But their enemy had something Israel didn't have—*chariots*—huge wood and metal carts pulled by horses and armed with a driver and a soldier. Israel's foot soldiers were no match for these fast and dangerous chariots—especially 900 of them!

The morning of battle finally arrived. The 10,000 soldiers stood on the mountaintop and looked down on Sisera's army. There they saw the 900 chariots with horses lined up along the river. Behind the chariots were thousands and thousands of foot soldiers—possibly ten times as many as the Israelites.

Deborah saw Sisera's huge army, too. But she wasn't afraid. She knew God would give them victory. And she urged Israel's army to go into battle and trust God.

As Barak led his soldiers down the mountain, thunder began to crack. **LIGHTNING BOLTS TORE THROUGH THE SKY.** Heavy rain began to fall. The rain turned the ground to slippery mud. The rain turned the river to a rushing, roaring wall of water. Sisera's 900 chariots spun their wheels in the mud. They couldn't move forward or backward! Sisera's thousands of soldiers got caught up in the rushing river. Israel's soldiers went after them and won the battle!

BE A DEBORAH

When Deborah went into battle with Barak, most women were at home cooking and taking care of children. But Deborah obeyed God and went into battle. Do you ever think you're different from the other kids around you? So was Deborah. God will use your special gifts to do good things for him—maybe even win battles!

DEBORAH WAS A WOMAN WHO OBEYED GOD.
THE WHOLE STORY: JUDGES 4–5

Go to page 279 for the next Super Hero

18Jael went out to meet Sisera. "Come in, sir," she said. "Come right in. Don't be afraid." So he entered her tent. Then she covered him up.

19"I'm thirsty," he said. "Please give me some water." So Jael opened a bottle of milk. The bottle was made out of animal skin. She gave him a drink of milk. Then she covered him up again.

20"Stand in the doorway of the tent," he told her. "Someone might come by and ask you, 'Is anyone here?' If that happens, say 'No.' "

21But Heber's wife Jael picked up a tent stake and a hammer. She went quietly over to Sisera. He was lying there, fast asleep. He was very tired. She drove the stake through his head right into the ground. So he died.

22Barak came by because he was chasing Sisera. Jael went out to meet him. "Come right in," she said. "I'll show you the man you are looking for." So he went in with her. Sisera was lying there with the stake through his head. He was dead.

23On that day God brought Jabin under Israel's control. He was a king in Canaan. **24**Israel's power grew stronger and stronger against Jabin, a king in Canaan. They became so strong that they destroyed him.

The Song of Deborah

5 On that day Deborah and Barak sang a song. Barak was the son of Abinoam. Here is what Deborah and Barak sang.

2 "The princes in Israel lead the way.
  The people follow them just because
      they want to.
  Praise the LORD!

3 "Kings, hear this! Rulers, listen!
  I will sing to the LORD. I will sing.
  I will make music to the LORD. He is
      the God of Israel.

4 "LORD, you went out from Mount Seir.
  You marched out from the land of
      Edom.
The earth shook. The heavens poured.
  The clouds poured down their water.
5 The mountains shook because of the
      LORD. He was at Mount Sinai.
  They shook because of the LORD. He
      is the God of Israel.

6 "The roads were deserted. So travelers
      used the winding paths.
  That happened in the days of
      Shamgar, the son of Anath.
  It happened in the days of Jael.

7 Life in the villages of Israel stopped.
  It stopped until I, Deborah, came.
  I came as a mother in Israel.
8 The people chose new gods.
  Then war came to the city gates.
But no shields or spears were seen
      anywhere.
  There weren't any among 40,000
      men in Israel.
9 My heart is with the princes in Israel.
  It's with the people who follow
      them just because they want to.
  Praise the LORD!

10 "Some of you ride on white donkeys.
  Some of you sit on your saddle
      blankets.
  Some of you walk along the road.
  Think about **11**the voices of the singers
      at the watering places.
  They sing about the right things the
      LORD does.
  They sing about the right things his
      warriors in Israel do.

"The people of the LORD
  went down to the city gates.
12 'Wake up, Deborah! Wake up!' they
      said.
  'Wake up! Wake up! Begin to sing!
Barak, get up!
  Son of Abinoam, capture your
      prisoners!'

13 "Then the people who were left came
      down to the nobles.
  The people of the LORD
  came to me against the powerful
      enemy.
14 Some came from the part of Ephraim
      where some Amalekites lived.
  Benjamin was with the people who
      followed Ephraim.
Captains came down from Makir.
  Those who rule like commanders
      came down from Zebulun.
15 The princes of Issachar were with
      Deborah.
  The men of Issachar were with
      Barak.
  They rushed behind him into the
      valley.
  In the territories of Reuben,
  men looked deeply into their hearts.
16 Why did they stay among the
      campfires?
  Why did they stay to hear shepherds
      whistling for the flocks?
  In the territories of Reuben,
  men looked deeply into their hearts.
17 Gilead stayed east of the Jordan River.
  Why did Dan stay near the ships?

The men of Asher remained on the
coast of the Mediterranean Sea.
They stayed in their safe harbors.
18 The people of Zebulun put their very
lives in danger.
So did Naphtali on the hills in the
open country.

19 "Kings came and fought.
The kings of Canaan fought
at Taanach by the streams of
Megiddo.

But they didn't carry any silver away.
They didn't take anything at all.
20 From the heavens the stars fought.
From the sky they fought against
Sisera.
21 The Kishon River swept them away.
The Kishon is a very old river.
My spirit, march on! Be strong!
22 The hoofs of the horses pounded like
thunder.
The powerful horses of our enemies
galloped away.

JAEL

JUDGES 4:21

B

*Jael picked up a tent stake and a hammer.
She went quietly over to Sisera. He was lying
there, fast asleep. He was very tired. She
drove the stake through his head right into
the ground. So he died.*

Jael (JAY-ell) stood quietly in the doorway of her tent. She
watched as the soldier inside drank the milk she gave him,
then settled down to rest. This soldier was Sisera. He led the
armies of Israel's enemies. Now he was running away from the
Israelite soldiers. Jael invited him into her tent and promised to
watch for any soldiers while he slept.

STILL WATCHING, JAEL PICKED UP A TENT PEG AND
HAMMER. She quietly walked back into the tent where Sisera
slept. She knelt down next to him. Holding her breath and
squeezing her eyes shut tight, Jael quickly hammered the tent
peg through Sisera's head. Israel's enemy died, not in battle but
in the tent of a brave woman. Jael saw a way to protect the people of Israel, and, horrible as the deed was, she did it.

BE LIKE JAEL
No, you don't want to do anything as violent as Jael. She lived
in a very violent time, and there was a war on. She did what
needed to be done to protect innocent people. Innocent people
still need protection today. Babies, kids with disabilities, kids
who aren't well-liked. You can help them by being kind and by
protecting them when others are unkind.

*JAEL FEARLESSLY DID WHAT NEEDED TO BE DONE TO
PROTECT GOD'S PEOPLE.*

Go to page 282 for the next Super Hero

23 'Let Meroz be cursed,' said the angel of
     the LORD.
   'Let bitter curses fall on its people.
   They did not come to help the LORD.
   They did not come to help him
     against our powerful
     enemies.'

24 "May Jael be the most blessed woman
     of all.
   May the wife of the Kenite Heber be
     blessed.
   May she be the most blessed woman
     of all those who live in tents.
25 Sisera asked for water. She gave him
     milk.
   In a bowl that was fit for nobles she
     brought him buttermilk.
26 Her hand reached out for a tent
     stake.
   Her right hand reached for a
     hammer.
   She hit Sisera. She crushed his head.
   She drove the stake right through
     his head.
27 He sank down. He fell at her feet.
   He was lying there.
   At her feet he sank down. He fell.
   He fell where he sank down.
   That's where he died.

28 "Sisera's mother looked out through
     the window.
   From behind the wooden screen she
     cried out.
   'Why is his chariot taking so long to
     get here?' she said.
   'Why can't I hear the noise of his
     chariots yet?'
29 Her wisest ladies answer her.
   And here's what she keeps saying to
     herself.
30 She says, 'They must be finding riches
     to bring back.
   They must be dividing them up.
   Each man is getting a woman or two.
   They are giving colorful clothes to
     Sisera.
   The clothes are very beautiful.
   He will bring some for me to wear.
   The men must be finding many
     things to bring home.'

31 "LORD, may all of your enemies be
     destroyed.
   But may those who love you be like
     the morning sun.
   May they be like the sun when it
     shines the brightest."

So the land was at peace for 40 years.

Gideon

6 Once again the people of Israel did
what was evil in the sight of the
LORD. So for seven years he handed them
over to the people of Midian.

2 The Midianites treated the people of
Israel very badly. That's why they made
hiding places for themselves. They hid in
holes in the mountains. They also hid in
caves and in other safe places.

3 Each year the people planted their
crops. When they did, the Midianites
came into the country and attacked it. So
did the Amalekites and other tribes from
the east. **4** They camped on the land. They
destroyed the crops all the way to Gaza.
They didn't spare any living thing for Israel. They didn't spare sheep or cattle or
donkeys.

5 The Midianites came up with their
livestock and tents. They came like huge
numbers of locusts. It was impossible to
count all of those men and their camels.
They came into the land to destroy it.

6 Midian made the people of Israel very
poor. So they cried out to the LORD for
help.

7 They cried out to the LORD because of
what Midian had done. **8** So he sent a
prophet to them. The prophet said, "The
LORD is the God of Israel. He says, 'I
brought you up out of Egypt. That is the
land where you were slaves. **9** I saved you
from the power of Egypt. I saved you from
all those who were beating you down. I
drove the people of Canaan out to make
room for you. I gave you their land.

10 'I said to you, "I am the LORD your
God. You are now living in the land of the
Amorites. Do not worship their gods." But
you have not listened to me.' "

11 The angel of the LORD came. He sat
down under an oak tree in Ophrah. The
tree belonged to Joash. He was from the
family line of Abiezer.

Gideon was threshing wheat in a winepress at Ophrah. He was the son of Joash.
Gideon was threshing in a winepress to
hide the wheat from the Midianites.

12 The angel of the LORD appeared to
Gideon. He said, "Mighty warrior, the
LORD is with you."

13 "But sir," Gideon replied, "you say
the LORD is with us. Then why has all of
this happened to us? Where are all of the
wonderful things he has done? Our parents told us about them. They said,
'Didn't the LORD bring us up out of
Egypt?' But now the LORD has deserted us.
He has handed us over to Midian."

14 The LORD turned to Gideon. He said

to him, "You are strong. Go and save Israel from the power of Midian. I am sending you."

¹⁵"But Lord," Gideon asked, "how can I possibly save Israel? My family group is the weakest in the tribe of Manasseh. And I'm the least important member of my family."

¹⁶The LORD answered, "I will be with you. So you will strike down the men of Midian all at one time."

¹⁷Gideon replied, "If you are pleased with me, give me a special sign. Then I'll know that it's really you talking to me. ¹⁸Please don't go away until I come back. I'll bring my offering and set it down in front of you."

The LORD said, "I will wait until you return."

¹⁹Gideon went and prepared a young goat. From more than half a bushel of flour he made bread without using yeast. He put the meat in a basket. In a pot he put soup that was made from the meat. Then he brought all of it and offered it to the LORD under the oak tree.

²⁰The angel of God spoke to Gideon. He said, "Take the meat and the bread. Place them on this rock. Then pour out the soup." So Gideon did it.

²¹The angel of the LORD had a wooden staff in his hand. With the tip of his staff he touched the meat and the bread. Fire blazed out of the rock. It burned up the meat and the bread. Then the angel of the LORD disappeared.

²²Gideon realized it was the angel of the LORD. He cried out, "LORD and King, I have seen the angel of the LORD face to face!"

²³But the LORD said to him, "May peace be with you! Do not be afraid. You are not going to die."

²⁴So Gideon built an altar to honor the LORD there. He called it The LORD Is Peace. It still stands in Ophrah to this very day. Ophrah is in the territory that belongs to the family line of Abiezer.

²⁵That same night the LORD spoke to Gideon. He said, "Get the second bull from your father's herd. Get the one that is seven years old. Tear down the altar your father built in honor of Baal. Cut down the pole that is beside it. The pole is used to worship the goddess Asherah. ²⁶"Then build the right kind of altar. Build it in honor of the LORD your God. Build it on top of this hill. Then use the wood from the Asherah pole you cut down. Sacrifice the second bull as a burnt offering."

²⁷So Gideon went and got ten of his servants. He did just as the LORD had told him. But he was afraid of his family. He was also afraid of the men in the town. So he did everything at night instead of during the day.

²⁸In the morning the men in the town got up. They saw that Baal's altar had been torn down. The Asherah pole that was beside it had been cut down. And the second bull had been sacrificed on the new altar that had been built.

²⁹They asked each other, "Who did this?"

They looked into the matter carefully. Someone told them, "Gideon, the son of Joash, did it."

³⁰The men in the town spoke to Joash. They ordered him, "Bring your son out here. He must die. He has torn down Baal's altar. He has cut down the Asherah pole that was beside it."

³¹But Joash replied to the angry crowd that was around him. He said, "Are you going to stand up for Baal? Are you trying to save him? Those who stand up for him will be put to death by morning! Is Baal really a god? If he is, he can stand up for himself when someone tears down his altar."

³²That's why Gideon was called Jerub-Baal that day. He said, "Let Baal take his stand against him." Gideon had torn down Baal's altar.

³³All of the Midianites and Amalekites gathered their armies together. Other tribes from the east joined them. All of them went across the Jordan River. They camped in the Valley of Jezreel.

³⁴Then the Spirit of the LORD came on

POWER — SURGE

STRONG

THE ANGEL OF THE LORD APPEARED TO GIDEON. HE SAID, "MIGHTY WARRIOR, THE LORD IS WITH YOU...YOU ARE STRONG. GO AND SAVE ISRAEL FROM THE POWER OF MIDIAN. I AM SENDING YOU."

— JUDGES 6:12, 14 —

GIDEON

JUDGES 6:15-16

B

✓

✝

"Lord," Gideon asked, "how can I possibly save Israel? My family group is the weakest in the tribe of Manasseh. And I'm the least important member of my family." The Lord answered, "I will be with you."

Gideon (GID-ee-on) stood quietly on the dark hill overlooking the enemy camp. He could see hundreds of soldiers below. Firelight revealed their faces as they ate at the campfires dotting the valley. As far as Gideon could see, the enemies of Israel stretched out in front of him. Then Gideon turned to look at his army. Only 300 soldiers. Gideon, the weak man God had called "mighty warrior," couldn't believe he wasn't afraid. But he wasn't. He had something none of Midian's thousands of soldiers had—the might of the Lord God.

Gideon raised his right arm. He held a torch in his hand, covered by a jar. Each of his 300 soldiers raised their right arms with their torches and jars, too. Gideon raised his left arm. He held a trumpet in his left hand. Each of his 300 soldiers raised their left arms with their trumpets, too.

Stepping carefully and quietly in the dark, Gideon and his men approached the enemy camp. They moved into position around it. Then Gideon gave a signal. At once all 300 men broke the jars that covered their lighted torches. At once all 300 men blew their trumpets.

The soldiers of Midian jumped up. They ran around. They tried to find their swords. They ran into each other. In the darkness of their camp, they couldn't tell who was their friend and who was their enemy. **THEY SCREAMED. THEY SHOUTED. AND THEY RAN AWAY IN TERROR.** Gideon and his 300 men shouted at the top of their lungs, "A sword for the LORD and for Gideon!"

BE A GIDEON

Gideon and his little army did big things for God. With God size doesn't count. He can use you just like he used Gideon. Maybe you won't conquer an enemy army, but you can win battles for God, like making someone in your family happy or helping someone at school or being kind to a stranger.

GIDEON THOUGHT HE WAS WEAK, BUT WITH GOD HE WAS STRONG.

THE WHOLE STORY: JUDGES 7:1-25

Go to page 292 for the next Super Hero

Gideon. So Gideon blew the trumpet to send for the men of Abiezer. He told them to follow him. **35**He sent messengers all through Manasseh. He called for the men of Manasseh to fight. He also sent messengers to the men of Asher, Zebulun and Naphtali. So all of those men went up to join the others.

36Gideon said to God, "You promised you would use me to save Israel. **37**Please do something for me. I'll put a piece of wool on the threshing floor. Suppose dew is only on the wool tomorrow morning. And suppose the ground all around it is dry. Then I will know that you will use me to save Israel. I'll know that your promise will come true."

38And that's what happened. Gideon got up early the next day. He squeezed the dew out of the wool. The water filled a bowl.

39Then Gideon said to God, "Don't let your anger burn against me. Let me ask you for just one more thing. Let me use the wool for one more test. This time make the wool dry. And cover the ground with dew."

40So that night God did it. Only the wool was dry. The ground all around it was covered with dew.

Gideon Wins the Battle Over the Midianites

7 Early in the morning Jerub-Baal and all of his men camped at the spring of Harod. Jerub-Baal was another name for Gideon. The camp of Midian was north of Gideon's camp. It was in the valley near the hill of Moreh.

2The Lord spoke to Gideon. He said, "I want to hand Midian over to you. But you have too many men for me to do that. I do not want Israel to brag that their own strength has saved them. **3**So here is what I want you to announce to your men. Tell them, 'Those who tremble with fear can turn back. They can leave Mount Gilead.' " So 22,000 men left. But 10,000 remained.

4The Lord spoke to Gideon again. He said, "There are still too many men. So take them down to the water. I will sort them out for you there. If I say, 'This one will go with you,' he will go. But if I say, 'That one will not go with you,' he will not go."

5So Gideon took the men down to the water. There the Lord spoke to him. He said, "Some men will drink the way dogs do. They will lap up the water with their

tongues. Separate them from those who get down on their knees to drink."

6Three hundred men lapped up the water. They brought it up to their mouths with their hands. All of the rest got down on their knees to drink.

7The Lord spoke to Gideon. He said, "With the help of the 300 men who lapped up the water I will save you. I will hand the Midianites over to you. Let all of the other men go home."

8So Gideon sent the rest of the men of Israel to their tents. But he kept the 300 men. They took over the supplies and trumpets the others had left.

The Midianites had set up their camp in the valley below where Gideon was.

9During that night the Lord spoke to Gideon. He said, "Get up. Go down against the camp. I am going to hand it over to you. **10**But what if you are afraid to attack? Then go down to the camp with your servant Purah. **11**Listen to what they are saying. After that, you will not be afraid to attack the camp."

So Gideon and his servant Purah went down to the edge of the camp. **12**The Midianites had settled in the valley. So had the Amalekites and all of the other tribes from the east. There were so many of them that they looked like huge numbers of locusts. Like the grains of sand on the seashore, their camels couldn't be counted.

13Gideon arrived just as a man was telling a friend about his dream. "I had a dream," he was saying. "A round loaf of barley bread came rolling into the camp of Midian. It hit a tent with great force. The tent turned over and fell down flat."

14His friend replied, "That can only be the sword of Gideon, the son of Joash. Gideon is from Israel. God has handed the Midianites over to him. He has given him the whole camp."

15Gideon heard the man explain what the dream meant. Then Gideon worshiped God. He returned to the camp of Israel. He called out, "Get up! The Lord has handed the Midianites over to you."

16Gideon separated the 300 men into three companies. He put a trumpet and an empty jar into the hands of each man. And he put a torch inside each jar.

17"Watch me," he told them. "Do what I do. I'll go to the edge of the enemy camp. Then do exactly as I do. **18**I and everyone who is with me will blow our trumpets. Then blow your trumpets from your positions all around the camp. And shout the battle cry, 'For the Lord and for Gideon!' "

19Gideon and the 100 men who were with him reached the edge of the enemy camp. It was about ten o'clock at night. It was just after the guard had been changed. Gideon and his men blew their trumpets. They broke the jars that were in their hands.

20The three companies blew their trumpets. They smashed their jars. They held their torches in their left hands. They held in their right hands the trumpets they were going to blow. Then they shouted the battle cry, "A sword for the LORD and for Gideon!"

21Each man stayed in his position around the camp. But all of the Midianites ran away in fear. They were crying out as they ran.

22When the 300 trumpets were blown, the LORD caused all of the men in the enemy camp to start fighting each other. They attacked each other with their swords. The army ran away to Beth Shittah toward Zererah. They ran all the way to the border of Abel Meholah near Tabbath.

23The men of Israel from the tribes of Naphtali, Asher and all of Manasseh were called out. They chased the Midianites.

24Gideon sent messengers through the entire hill country of Ephraim. They said, "Come on down against the Midianites. Take control of the waters of the Jordan River before they get there. Do it all the way to Beth Barah."

So all of the men of Ephraim were called out. They took control of the waters of the Jordan all the way to Beth Barah.

25They also captured Oreb and Zeeb. Those men were two of the Midianite leaders. The men of Ephraim killed Oreb at the rock of Oreb. They killed Zeeb at the winepress of Zeeb. They chased the Midianites. And they brought the heads of Oreb and Zeeb to Gideon. He was by the Jordan River.

Gideon Destroys Midian's Whole Army

8 The men of Ephraim spoke to Gideon. They asked, "Why have you treated us like this? Why didn't you ask us to help you when you went out to fight against Midian?" They spoke very sharply against Gideon.

2But he answered them, "What I've done isn't anything compared to what you have done. After Ephraim's grapes have been gathered, isn't what is left over better than all of the grapes that have been gathered from Abiezer's vines? **3**God

handed Oreb and Zeeb over to you. They were Midianite leaders. So what was I able to do compared to what you did?"

After Gideon had said that, they didn't feel angry with him anymore.

4Gideon and his 300 men were very tired. But they kept on chasing their enemies. They came to the Jordan River and went across it. **5**Gideon spoke to the men of Succoth. He said, "Give my troops some bread. They are worn out. And I'm still chasing Zebah and Zalmunna. They are the kings of Midian."

6But the officials of Succoth objected. They said, "Have you already killed Zebah and Zalmunna? Have you cut their hands off and brought them back to prove it? If you haven't, why should we give bread to your troops?"

7Gideon replied, "The LORD will hand Zebah and Zalmunna over to me. When he does, I'll tear your skin with thorns from desert bushes."

8From there Gideon went up to Peniel. He asked its men for the same thing. But they answered as the men of Succoth had. **9**So he said to the men of Peniel, "I'll be back after I've won the battle. Then I'll tear down this tower."

10Zebah and Zalmunna were in Karkor. They had an army of about 15,000 men. That's all that was left of the armies of the tribes from the east. About 120,000 men who carried swords had died in battle.

11Gideon went up the trail the people of the desert had made. It ran east of Nobah and Jogbehah. He attacked the army by surprise. **12**Zebah and Zalmunna ran away. They were the two kings of Midian. Gideon chased them and captured them. He destroyed their whole army.

13Then Gideon, the son of Joash, returned from the battle. He came back through the Pass of Heres.

14He caught a young man from Succoth. He asked him about the elders of the town. The young man wrote down for him the names of Succoth's 77 officials.

15Then Gideon came and spoke to the men of Succoth. He said, "Here are Zebah and Zalmunna. You made fun of me because of them. You said, 'Have you already killed Zebah and Zalmunna? Have you cut their hands off and brought them back to prove it? If you haven't, why should we give bread to your tired men?' "

16Gideon went and got the elders of the town. Then he taught the men of Succoth a lesson. He tore their skin with thorns from desert bushes. **17**He also pulled down the tower at Peniel. He killed the men in the town.

¹⁸Then he spoke to Zebah and Zalmunna. He asked, "What were the men like that you killed at Tabor?"

"Men like you," they answered. "Each one walked as if he were a prince."

¹⁹Gideon replied, "Those were my brothers. They were the sons of my own mother. You can be sure that the LORD lives. And you can be just as sure that if you had spared their lives, I wouldn't kill you."

²⁰Then Gideon turned to his oldest son Jether. He said, "Kill them!" But Jether didn't pull out his sword. He was only a boy. So he was afraid.

²¹Zebah and Zalmunna said, "Come on. Do it yourself. 'The older the man, the stronger he is.' "

So Gideon stepped forward and killed them. Then he took the moon-shaped necklaces off the necks of their camels.

Gideon Refuses to Be Israel's Ruler

²²The people of Israel spoke to Gideon. They said, "Rule over us. We want you, your son and your grandson to be our rulers. You have saved us from the power of Midian."

²³But Gideon told them, "I will not rule over you. My son won't rule over you either. The LORD will rule over you."

²⁴He continued, "I do ask one thing. I want each of you to give me an earring. I'm talking about the earrings you took from your enemies." It was the practice of the people in the family line of Ishmael to wear gold earrings.

²⁵The people of Israel said, "We'll be glad to give them to you." So they spread out a piece of clothing. Each man threw a ring on it from what he had taken. ²⁶The weight of the gold rings Gideon asked for was 43 pounds. That didn't include the moon-shaped necklaces the kings of Midian had worn. It didn't include their other necklaces or their purple clothes. And it didn't include the gold chains that had been on the necks of their camels.

²⁷Gideon made an object out of all of the gold. It looked like the linen apron the high priest of Israel wore. He placed it in Ophrah. That was his hometown. All of the people of Israel worshiped it there. They weren't faithful to the LORD. So the gold object became a trap to Gideon and his family.

Gideon Dies

²⁸Israel brought Midian under their control. Midian wasn't able to attack Israel anymore. So the land was at peace for 40 years. The peace lasted as long as Gideon was living.

²⁹Jerub-Baal, the son of Joash, went back home to live. Jerub-Baal was another name for Gideon. ³⁰He had 70 sons of his own. That's because he had a lot of wives. ³¹And he had a concubine who lived in Shechem. She also had a son by him. Gideon named that son Abimelech.

³²Gideon, the son of Joash, died when he was very old. His body was buried in the tomb of his father Joash in Ophrah. Ophrah was in the territory that belonged to the family line of Abiezer.

³³As soon as Gideon had died, the people of Israel joined themselves to the gods that were named after Baal. Israel wasn't faithful to the LORD. They worshiped Baal-Berith as their god. ³⁴They forgot what the LORD their God had done for them. He had saved them from the power of their enemies who were all around them.

³⁵Jerub-Baal had done many good things for the people of Israel. But they weren't kind to his family. Jerub-Baal was another name for Gideon.

Abimelech Becomes King of Shechem

9 Abimelech was the son of Jerub-Baal. He went to his mother's brothers in Shechem. He spoke to them and to all of the members of his mother's family group. He said, ²"Speak to all of the citizens of Shechem. Tell them, 'You can have all 70 of Jerub-Baal's sons rule over you. Or you can have just one man rule over you. Which would you rather have?' Remember, I'm your own flesh and blood."

³The brothers told all of that to the citizens of Shechem. Then the people decided to follow Abimelech. They said, "He's related to us."

⁴They gave him 28 ounces of silver. They had taken it from the temple of the god Baal-Berith. Abimelech used it to hire some men. They were wild. They weren't good for anything. They became his followers.

⁵Abimelech went to his father's home in Ophrah. There on a big rock he murdered his 70 brothers. All of them were the sons of Jerub-Baal. But Jotham escaped by hiding. He was Jerub-Baal's youngest son.

⁶All of the citizens of Shechem and Beth Millo came together. They gathered at the stone pillar that was beside the large

tree in Shechem. They wanted to crown Abimelech as their king.

⁷Jotham was told about it. So he climbed up on top of Mount Gerizim. He shouted down to them, "Citizens of Shechem! Listen to me! Then God will listen to you. ⁸One day the trees went out to anoint a king for themselves. They said to an olive tree, 'Be our king.'

⁹"But the olive tree answered, 'Should I give up my olive oil? It's used to honor gods and people alike. Should I give that up just to rule over the trees?'

¹⁰"Next, the trees spoke to a fig tree. They said, 'Come and be our king.'

¹¹"But the fig tree replied, 'Should I give up my fruit? It's so good and sweet. Should I give that up just to rule over the trees?'

¹²"Then the trees spoke to a vine. They said, 'Come and be our king.'

¹³"But the vine answered, 'Should I give up my wine? It cheers up gods and people alike. Should I give that up just to rule over the trees?'

¹⁴"Finally, all of the trees spoke to a bush that had thorns. They said, 'Come and be our king.'

¹⁵"The bush spoke to the trees. It said, 'Do you really want to anoint me as king over you? If you do, come and rest in my shade. But if you don't, I will destroy you! Fire will come out of me and burn up the cedar trees of Lebanon!'

¹⁶"Did you act in an honest way when you made Abimelech your king? Did you really do the right thing? Have you been fair to Jerub-Baal and his family? Have you given him the honor he's worthy of?

¹⁷"Remember that my father fought for you. He put his life in danger for you. He saved you from the power of Midian. ¹⁸But today you have turned against my father's family. You have murdered his 70 sons on a big rock. Abimelech is only the son of my father's female slave. But you have made him king over the citizens of Shechem. You have done that because he's related to you.

¹⁹"Have you citizens of Shechem and Beth Millo acted in an honest way toward Jerub-Baal? Have you done the right thing to his family today? If you have, may you be happy with Abimelech! And may he be happy with you! ²⁰But if you haven't, let fire come out from Abimelech and burn you up! And let fire come out from you and burn Abimelech up!"

²¹Then Jotham ran away. He escaped to Beer. He lived there because he was afraid of his brother Abimelech.

²²Abimelech ruled over Israel for three years. ²³Then God sent an evil spirit to cause trouble between Abimelech and the citizens of Shechem. They turned against Abimelech. They decided not to follow him anymore.

²⁴God made that happen because of what Abimelech had done to Jerub-Baal's 70 sons. He had spilled their blood. God wanted to pay back their brother Abimelech for doing that. He also wanted to pay back the citizens of Shechem. They had helped Abimelech murder his brothers.

²⁵The citizens of Shechem opposed Abimelech. So they hid some men on top of the hills. They wanted them to attack and rob everyone who passed by. Abimelech was told about it.

²⁶Gaal and his relatives moved into Shechem. He was the son of Ebed. The citizens of Shechem put their trust in Gaal.

²⁷The people of Shechem went out into the fields. They gathered the grapes. They pressed the juice out of them by stomping on them. Then they held a feast in the temple of their god. While they were eating and drinking, they called down curses on Abimelech.

²⁸Then Gaal, the son of Ebed, spoke up. "Who is Abimelech?" he said. "And who is Shechem? Why should we be under Abimelech's rule? Isn't he Jerub-Baal's son? Isn't Zebul his helper? It would be better to serve the men of Hamor. He was the father of Shechem. So why should we serve Abimelech? ²⁹I wish these people were under my command. Then I would get rid of him. I would say to him, 'Call out your whole army!' "

³⁰Zebul was the governor of Shechem. He heard about what Gaal, the son of Ebed, had said. So he burned with anger. ³¹Zebul sent messengers to Abimelech secretly. They said, "Gaal, the son of Ebed, has come to Shechem. His relatives have come with him. They are stirring up the city against you. ³²So come with your men during the night. Hide in the fields and wait. ³³In the morning at sunrise, attack the city. Gaal and his men will come out against you. Then do what you can."

³⁴So Abimelech and all of his troops started out at night. They went into their hiding places near Shechem. Abimelech had separated them into four companies. ³⁵Gaal, the son of Ebed, had already gone out. He was standing at the entrance of the city gate. He had arrived there just

as Abimelech and his troops came out of their hiding places.

36Gaal saw them. He said to Zebul, "Look! People are coming down from the tops of the mountains!"

Zebul replied, "You are wrong. Those aren't people. They are just the shadows of the mountains."

37But Gaal spoke up again. He said, "Look! People are coming down from the center of the land. Another company is coming from the direction of the fortune tellers' tree."

38Then Zebul said to Gaal, "Where is your big talk now? You said, 'Who is Abimelech? Why should we be under his rule?' Aren't these the people you looked down on? Go out and fight against them!"

39So Gaal led the citizens out of Shechem. They fought against Abimelech. **40**He chased Gaal from the field of battle. Many men were wounded as they ran away. Abimelech chased them all the way to the entrance of the city gate. **41**He stayed in Arumah. Zebul drove Gaal and his relatives out of Shechem.

42The next day the people of Shechem went out to work in the fields. Abimelech was told about it. **43**So he gathered his men together. He separated them into three companies. Then he hid them in the fields and told them to wait. When he saw the people coming out of the city, he got up to attack them.

44Abimelech and the men who were with him ran forward. They placed themselves at the entrance of the city gate. Then the other two companies rushed over to the people who were in the fields. There they struck them down. **45**Abimelech kept up his attack against the city all day long. He didn't stop until he had captured it. Then he killed its people. He destroyed the city. He scattered salt on it to make sure that nothing would be able to grow there.

46The citizens who were in the tower of Shechem heard about what was happening. So they went to the safest place in the temple of the god El-Berith.

47Abimelech heard that they had gathered together there. **48**He and all of his men went up Mount Zalmon. He got an ax and cut off some branches. He carried them on his shoulders. He ordered the men who were with him to do the same thing. "Quick!" he said. "Do what you have seen me do!"

49So all of the men cut branches and followed Abimelech. They piled them against the place where the people had gone for safety. Then they set the place on fire with the people inside. There were about 1,000 men and women in the tower of Shechem. All of them died.

50Next, Abimelech went to Thebez. He surrounded it. Then he attacked it and captured it.

51But inside the city there was a strong tower. All of the people in the city ran to it for safety. All of the men and women went into it. They locked themselves in. They climbed up on the roof of the tower. **52**Abimelech went to the tower and attacked it. He approached the entrance to the tower to set it on fire. **53**But a woman dropped a large millstone on him. It broke his head open.

54He quickly called out to the man who was carrying his armor. He said, "Pull out your sword and kill me. Then people can't say, 'A woman killed him.'" So his servant stuck his sword through him. And Abimelech died. **55**When the people of Israel saw he was dead, they went home.

56That's how God paid Abimelech back for the evil thing he had done to his father. He had murdered his 70 brothers. **57**God also made the men of Shechem pay for all of the evil things they had done. The curse of Jotham came down on them. He was the son of Jerub-Baal.

Tola

10 Tola rose up to save Israel. That happened after the time of Abimelech. Tola was from the tribe of Issachar. He was the son of Puah, who was the son of Dodo. Tola lived in Shamir. It's in the hill country of Ephraim. **2**Tola led Israel for 23 years. After he died, his body was buried in Shamir.

Jair

3Jair became the leader after Tola. Jair was from the land of Gilead. He led Israel for 22 years. **4**He had 30 sons. They rode on 30 donkeys. They controlled 30 towns in Gilead. Those towns are called Havvoth Jair to this very day. **5**After Jair died, his body was buried in Kamon.

Jephthah

6Once again the people of Israel did what was evil in the sight of the LORD. They served the gods that were named after Baal. They served the goddesses that were named after Ashtoreth. They worshiped the gods of Aram and Sidon. They served the gods of Moab and Ammon. They also worshiped the gods of the Philistines. The people of Israel deserted the LORD. They didn't serve him anymore.

7So the LORD's anger burned against them. He handed them over to the Philistines and the Ammonites. **8**That year they broke Israel's power completely. They treated the people of Israel badly for 18 years. Those people lived east of the Jordan River. They lived in Gilead. That was the land of the Amorites.

9The Ammonites also went across the Jordan. They crossed over to fight against Judah, Benjamin and the people of Ephraim. Israel was suffering terribly.

10Then the people of Israel cried out to the LORD. They said, "We have sinned against you. We have deserted our God. We have served the gods that are named after Baal."

11The LORD replied, "The Egyptians and Amorites beat you down. So did the Ammonites and Philistines. **12**And so did the Amalekites and the people of Sidon and Maon. Each time you cried out to me for help. And I saved you from their power.

13"But you have deserted me. You have served other gods. So I will not save you anymore. **14**Go and cry out to the gods you have chosen. Let them save you when you get into trouble!"

15But the people of Israel replied to the LORD. They said, "We have sinned. Do to us what you think is best. But please save us now." **16**Then they got rid of the strange gods that were among them. They served the LORD. And he couldn't stand to see Israel suffer anymore.

17The Ammonites were called together to fight. They camped in the land of Gilead. Then the men of Israel gathered together. They camped at the city of Mizpah.

18The leaders of Gilead spoke to each other. They said, "Who will lead the attack against the Ammonites? That man will be the ruler of all of the people who live in Gilead."

11 Jephthah was a mighty warrior. He was from the land of Gilead. His father's name was Gilead. Jephthah's mother was a prostitute.

2Gilead's wife also had sons by him. When they had grown up, they drove Jephthah away. "You aren't going to get any share of our family's property," they said. "You are the son of another woman."

3So Jephthah ran away from his brothers. He settled in the land of Tob. A group of men who weren't good for anything gathered around him there. And they followed him.

4Some time later, the Ammonites went to war against Israel. **5**So the elders of Gilead went to get Jephthah from the land of Tob. **6**"Come with us," they said. "Be our commander. Then we can fight against the Ammonites."

7Jephthah said to them, "Didn't you hate me? Didn't you drive me away from my father's house? Why are you coming to me only when you are in trouble?"

8The elders of Gilead replied to him. "You are right," they said. "That's why we're turning to you now. Come with us and fight against the Ammonites. Then you will be our leader. You will rule over everyone who lives in Gilead."

9Jephthah said, "Suppose you take me back to fight against the Ammonites. And suppose the LORD gives them over to me. Then will I really be your leader?"

10The elders of Gilead replied, "The LORD is our witness. We'll certainly do as you say." **11**So Jephthah went with the elders of Gilead. And the people made him their leader and commander. He went to Mizpah. There he repeated to the LORD everything he had said.

12Then Jephthah sent messengers to the king of Ammon. They asked, "What do you have against us? Why have you attacked our country?"

13The king of Ammon answered Jephthah's messengers. He said, "Israel came up out of Egypt. At that time they took my land away. They took all of the land that was between the Arnon River and the Jabbok River. It reached all the way to the Jordan River. Now give it back. Then there will be peace."

14Jephthah sent messengers back to the king of Ammon. **15**They said,

"Here is what Jephthah says to you. Israel didn't take the land of Moab. They didn't take the land of Ammon. **16**When Israel came up out of Egypt, they went through the desert to the Red Sea. From there they went on to Kadesh.

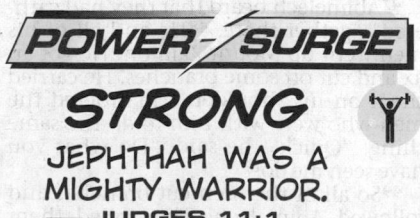

17"Then Israel sent messengers to the king of Edom. They said, 'Please let us go through your country.' But the king of Edom wouldn't listen to them.

"They sent the same message to the king of Moab. But he refused too. So Israel stayed at Kadesh.

18"Next, they traveled through the desert. They traveled along the borders of the lands of Edom and Moab. They passed along the east side of the country of Moab. They camped on the other side of the Arnon River. They didn't enter the territory of Moab. The Arnon River was Moab's border.

19"Then Israel sent messengers to Sihon. He was the king of the Amorites. He ruled in Heshbon. They said to him, 'Let us pass through your country to our own land.'

20"But Sihon didn't trust Israel to pass through his territory. Instead, he gathered all of his men together. They camped at Jahaz. And they fought against Israel.

21"Then the LORD, the God of Israel, handed Sihon and all of his men over to Israel. Israel won the battle over them. Amorites were living in the country at that time. And Israel took over all of their land. **22**They captured all of the land that was between the Arnon River and the Jabbok River. It reached from the desert all the way to the Jordan River.

23"The LORD, the God of Israel, has driven the Amorites out to make room for his people. So what right do you have to take it over? **24**You will take what your god Chemosh gives you, won't you? In the same way, we will take over what the LORD our God has given us. **25**Are you better than Balak, the son of Zippor? Balak was the king of Moab. Did he ever argue with Israel? Did he ever fight against them?

26"For 300 years Israel has been living in Heshbon and Aroer. They have been living in the settlements that are around those cities. They have also been living in all of the towns that are along the Arnon River. Why didn't you take those places back during that time?

27"I haven't done anything wrong to you. But you are doing something wrong to me. You have gone to war against me. The LORD is the Judge. So let him decide our case today. Let him settle matters between the people of Israel and the people of Ammon."

28But the king of Ammon didn't pay any attention to the message Jephthah sent him.

29Then the Spirit of the LORD came on Jephthah. He went across the territories of Gilead and Manasseh. He passed through Mizpah in the land of Gilead. From there he attacked the people of Ammon.

30Jephthah made a promise to the LORD. He said, "Hand the Ammonites over to me. **31**If you do, here's what I'll do when I come back from winning the battle. Anything that comes out the door of my house to meet me will belong to you. I will sacrifice it as a burnt offering."

32Then Jephthah went over to fight against the Ammonites. The LORD handed them over to him. **33**Jephthah destroyed 20 towns between Aroer and the area of Minnith. He destroyed them all the way to Abel Keramim. So Israel brought Ammon under their control.

34Jephthah returned to his home in Mizpah. And guess who came out to meet him. It was his daughter! She was dancing to the music of tambourines. She was his only child. He didn't have any other sons or daughters.

35When Jephthah saw her, he was so upset that he tore his clothes. He cried out, "My daughter! You have filled me with trouble and sorrow. I've made a promise to the LORD. And I can't break it."

36"My father," she replied, "you have given your word to the LORD. So do to me just what you promised to do. The Ammonites were your enemies. And the LORD has paid them back for what they did to you.

37"But please do one thing for me," she continued. "Give me two months to wander around in the hills. Let me sob there with my friends. I want to do that because I'll never get married."

38"You can go," he said. He let her go for two months. She and her friends went into the hills. They were filled with sadness because she would never get married.

39After the two months were over, she returned to her father. He did to her just what he had promised to do. And she was a virgin.

So that became a practice in Israel. **40**Each year the young women of Israel go away for four days. They do it in honor of the daughter of Jephthah. He was from the land of Gilead.

Jephthah Wins the Battle Over Ephraim

12 The men of Ephraim called out their troops. The troops went across the Jordan River to Zaphon. When they arrived, they said to Jephthah, "You went to fight against the Ammonites. Why didn't you ask us to go with you? We're going to burn down your house over your head."

2 Jephthah answered, "I and my people were taking part in a great struggle. We were at war with the Ammonites. I asked you for help. But you didn't come to save me from their power. 3 I saw that you wouldn't help. So I put my own life in danger. I went across the Jordan to fight against the Ammonites. The LORD helped me win the battle over them. So why have you come up today to fight against me?"

4 Then Jephthah called the men of Gilead together. They fought against Ephraim. The men of Gilead struck them down. The people of Ephraim had said, "You people of Gilead are nothing but deserters from Ephraim and Manasseh."

5 The men of Gilead captured the places where people go across the Jordan River to get to Ephraim. Some men of Ephraim weren't killed in the battle. When they arrived at the river, they would say, "Let us go across."

Then the men of Gilead would ask each one, "Are you from Ephraim?" Suppose he replied, "No." 6 Then they would say, "All right. Say 'Shibboleth.' " If he said "Sibboleth," the way he said the word would give him away. He couldn't say it correctly. So they would grab hold of him. Then they would kill him at one of the places where people go across the Jordan. At that time, 42,000 men of Ephraim were killed.

7 Jephthah led Israel for six years. Then he died. His body was buried in a town in Gilead. Jephthah was from the land of Gilead.

Ibzan, Elon and Abdon

8 After Jephthah, Ibzan from Bethlehem led Israel. 9 He had 30 sons and 30 daughters. He gave his daughters to be married to men who were outside his family group. He brought in 30 young women to be married to his sons. Those women also came from outside his family group. Ibzan led Israel for seven years. 10 Then he died. His body was buried in Bethlehem.

11 After Ibzan, Elon led Israel. He was from the tribe of Zebulun. Elon led Israel for ten years. 12 Then he died. His body was buried in Aijalon. It was in the land of Zebulun.

13 After Elon, Abdon led Israel. Abdon was the son of Hillel. Abdon was from Pirathon. 14 He had 40 sons and 30 grandsons. They rode on 70 donkeys. He led Israel for eight years. 15 Then he died. His body was buried at Pirathon in Ephraim. Pirathon was in the hill country of the Amalekites. Abdon was the son of Hillel.

Samson Is Born

13 Once again the people of Israel did what was evil in the sight of the LORD. So the LORD handed them over to the Philistines for 40 years.

2 A certain man from Zorah was named Manoah. He was from the tribe of Dan. Manoah had a wife who wasn't able to have children.

3 The angel of the LORD appeared to Manoah's wife. He said, "You are not able to have children. But you are going to become pregnant. You will have a baby boy. 4 Make sure you do not drink any kind of wine. Also make sure you do not eat anything that is 'unclean.'

5 "You will become pregnant. You will have a son. He must not use a razor on his head. He must not cut his hair. That is because the boy will be a Nazirite. He will be set apart to God from the day he is born. He will begin to save Israel from the power of the Philistines."

6 Then the woman went to her husband. She told him, "A man of God came to me. He looked like an angel of God. His appearance was so amazing that it filled me with great wonder. I didn't ask him where he came from. And he didn't tell me his name.

7 "But he said to me, 'You will become pregnant. You will have a son. So do not drink any kind of wine. Do not eat anything that is "unclean." That is because the boy will be a Nazirite. He will belong to God in a special way from the day he is born until the day he dies.' "

8 Then Manoah prayed to the LORD. He said, "Lord, I beg you to let the man of God you sent to us come again. He told us we would have a son. We want the man of God to teach us how to bring up the boy."

9 God heard Manoah. And the angel of God came again to the woman. He came while she was out in the field. But her husband Manoah wasn't with her. 10 The woman hurried to her husband. She told him, "He's here! The man who appeared to me the other day is here!"

¹¹Manoah got up and followed his wife. When he came to the man, he spoke to him. He said, "Are you the one who talked to my wife?"

"I am," he replied.

¹²So Manoah asked him, "What will happen when your words come true? What rules should we follow for the boy's life and work?"

¹³The angel of the LORD answered him. He said, "Your wife must do everything I have told her to do. ¹⁴She must not eat anything that comes from grapevines. She must not drink any kind of wine. She must not eat anything that is 'unclean.' She must do everything I have commanded her to do."

¹⁵Manoah spoke to the angel of the LORD. He said, "We would like you to stay and eat. We want to prepare a young goat for you."

¹⁶The angel of the LORD replied, "Even if I stay, I will not eat any of your food. But if you still want to prepare a burnt offering, you must offer it to the LORD." Manoah didn't realize it was the angel of the LORD.

¹⁷Then Manoah asked the angel of the LORD a question. "What is your name?" he said. "We want to honor you when your word comes true."

¹⁸The angel replied, "Why are you asking me what my name is? You would not be able to understand it."

¹⁹Manoah got a young goat. He brought it together with the grain offering. He sacrificed it on a rock to the LORD.

Then the LORD did an amazing thing. It happened while Manoah and his wife were watching. ²⁰A flame blazed up from the altar toward heaven. The angel of the LORD rose up in the flame. When Manoah and his wife saw it, they fell with their faces to the ground.

²¹The angel of the LORD didn't show himself again to Manoah and his wife. Then Manoah realized it was the angel of the LORD.

²²"We're going to die!" he said to his wife. "We've seen God!"

²³But his wife answered, "The LORD doesn't want to kill us. If he did, he wouldn't have accepted a burnt offering and a grain offering from us. He wouldn't have shown us all of those things. He wouldn't have told us we're going to have a son."

²⁴Later, the woman had a baby boy. She named him Samson. As he grew up, the LORD blessed him. ²⁵The Spirit of the LORD began to work in his life. It happened

while he was in Mahaneh Dan. It's between Zorah and Eshtaol.

Samson Gets Married

14 Samson went down to Timnah. There he saw a young Philistine woman. ²When he returned, he spoke to his father and mother. He said, "I've seen a Philistine woman in Timnah. Get her for me. I want her to be my wife."

³His father and mother replied, "Can't we find a wife for you among your relatives? Isn't there one among any of our people? Do you have to go to the Philistines to get a wife? They aren't God's people. They haven't even been circumcised."

But Samson said to his father, "Get her for me. She's the right one for me."

⁴Samson's parents didn't know that the LORD wanted things to happen that way. He was working out his plans against the Philistines. That's because the Philistines were ruling over Israel at that time.

⁵Samson went down to Timnah. His father and mother went with him. They approached the vineyards of Timnah. Suddenly a young lion came roaring toward Samson.

⁶Then the Spirit of the LORD came on Samson with power. He tore the lion apart with his bare hands. He did it as easily as he might have torn a young goat apart. But he didn't tell his father or mother what he had done.

⁷Then he went down and talked with the woman. He liked her.

⁸Some time later, he was going back to get married to her. But he turned off the road to look at the lion's dead body. Large numbers of bees and some honey were in

POWER-SURGE

STRONG

THEN THE SPIRIT OF THE LORD CAME ON SAMSON WITH POWER. HE TORE THE LION APART WITH HIS BARE HANDS. HE DID IT AS EASILY AS HE MIGHT HAVE TORN A YOUNG GOAT APART.

— JUDGES 14:6 —

SAMSON

JUDGES 13:24-25

The woman had a baby boy. She named him Samson. As he grew up, the Lᴏʀᴅ blessed him. The Spirit of the Lᴏʀᴅ began to work in his life.

Samson's strong legs carried him quickly along the path. He swung his muscled arms as he walked. A breeze blew through the seven long braids of his hair. Suddenly a lion sprang out at him from behind a rock. As it hurtled through the air toward Samson, it opened its huge mouth full of teeth and roared. **SAMSON PUT UP HIS MASSIVE ARMS AND CAUGHT THE LION.** Before it even had time to use its sharp teeth or claws, Samson ripped the lion apart with his bare hands. He didn't even need a weapon to kill a lion!

God had made Samson the strongest man who ever lived. But Samson didn't always do what was right. He was sometimes foolish. He fell in love with a wicked woman. He followed her instead of God. That wicked woman begged and bullied Samson until he told her the secret of his strength. And then she had his hair cut off. With his hair cut short, Samson's strength left him.

Samson's enemies captured him and poked out his eyes. He was weak. He could no longer see. He was a prisoner. Later, Samson stood in a temple and heard the people laughing him. And at his God.

So Samson prayed and asked God for one more blast of strength. Putting a hand on each of the huge pillars that held up the temple, Samson stiffened his legs. He gritted his teeth. And he bravely pushed. God's strength surged into Samson's weakened arms. The pillars started to move. With one last mighty push, the pillars of the temple gave way. The roof of the temple fell. Samson himself died that day. But he took many of God's enemies with him.

BE A SAMSON

Don't ever forget that Samson's real strength wasn't in his muscles. It was in God. He forgot that. But you don't have to. No matter what size your muscles—you are someone special and strong in God.

SAMSON WAS STRONG BUT FOOLISH, BUT GOD USED HIM.
THE WHOLE STORY: JUDGES 16:1-31

Go to page 296 for the next person

it. **9**He dug the honey out with his hands. He ate it as he walked along. Then he joined his parents again. He gave them some honey. They ate it too. But he didn't tell them he had taken it from the lion's dead body.

10Samson's father went down to see the woman. Samson had a big dinner prepared there. He was following the practice of men when they got married. **11**When the people saw Samson, they gave him 30 companions.

12"Let me tell you a riddle," Samson said to the companions. "The dinner will last for seven days. Give me the answer to the riddle before the dinner ends. If you do, I'll give you 30 linen shirts. I'll also give you 30 sets of clothes. **13**But suppose you can't give me the answer. Then you must give me 30 linen shirts. You must also give me 30 sets of clothes."

"Tell us your riddle," they said. "Let's hear it."

14Samson replied,

"Out of the eater came something to eat.
   Out of the strong came something sweet."

For three days they couldn't give him the answer.

15On the fourth day they spoke to Samson's wife. "Get your husband to explain the riddle for us," they said. "If you don't, we'll burn you to death. We'll burn up everyone in your family. Did you invite us here to rob us?"

16Then Samson's wife threw herself on him. She sobbed, "You hate me! You don't really love me. You have given my people a riddle. But you haven't told me the answer."

"I haven't even explained it to my father or mother," he replied. "So why should I explain it to you?"

17She cried during the whole seven days the dinner was going on. So on the seventh day he finally told her the answer to the riddle. That's because she kept on asking him to tell her. Then she explained the riddle to her people.

18Before sunset on the seventh day the men of the town spoke to Samson. They said,

"What is sweeter than honey?
   What is stronger than a lion?"

Samson said to them,

"You have plowed with my young cow.

If you hadn't, you wouldn't have
   known the answer to my
   riddle."

19Then the Spirit of the LORD came on Samson with power. He went down to Ashkelon. He struck down 30 of their men. He took everything they had with them. And he gave their clothes to those who had explained the riddle. Samson was burning with anger as he went up to his father's house.

20Samson's wife was given to someone else. She was given to a friend of Samson. The friend had helped him at his wedding.

Samson Gets Even With the Philistines

15 Later on, Samson went to visit his wife. He took a young goat with him. He went at the time the wheat was being gathered. He said, "I'm going to my wife's room." But her father wouldn't let him go in.

2Her father said, "I was sure you really hated her. So I gave her to your friend. Isn't her younger sister more beautiful? Take her instead."

3Samson said to them, "This time I have a right to get even with the Philistines. I'm going to hurt them badly."

4So he went out and caught 300 foxes. He tied them in pairs by their tails. Then he tied a torch to each pair of tails. **5**He lit the torches. He let the foxes loose in the fields of grain that belonged to the Philistines. He burned up the grain that had been cut and stacked. He burned up the grain that was still growing. He also burned up the vineyards and olive trees.

6The Philistines asked, "Who did this?" They were told, "Samson did. He's the son-in-law of the man from Timnah. Samson did it because his wife was given to his friend."

So the Philistines went up and burned the woman and her father to death.

7Samson said to them, "Is that how you act? Then I won't stop until I pay you back." **8**He struck them down with heavy blows. He killed many of them. Then he went down and stayed in a cave. It was in the rock of Etam.

9The Philistines went up and camped in Judah. They spread out near Lehi. **10**The men of Judah asked, "Why have you come to fight against us?"

"We've come to take Samson as our prisoner," they answered. "We want to do to him what he did to us."

11Then 3,000 men from Judah went to get Samson. They went down to the cave that was in the rock of Etam. They said to Samson, "Don't you realize the Philistines are ruling over us? What have you done to us?"

Samson answered, "I only did to them what they did to me."

12The men of Judah said to him, "We've come to tie you up. We're going to hand you over to the Philistines."

Samson said, "Take an oath and promise me you won't kill me yourselves."

13"We agree," they answered. "We'll only tie you up and hand you over to them. We won't kill you." So they tied him up with two new ropes. They led him up from the rock.

14Samson approached Lehi. The Philistines came toward him shouting. Then the Spirit of the LORD came on Samson with power. The ropes on his arms became like burned thread. They dropped off his hands. **15**He found a fresh jawbone of a donkey. He grabbed hold of it and struck down 1,000 men.

16Then Samson said,

"By using a donkey's jawbone
    I've made them look like donkeys.
By using a donkey's jawbone
    I've struck down 1,000 men."

17Samson finished speaking. Then he threw the jawbone away. That's why the place was called Ramath Lehi.

18Samson was very thirsty. So he cried out to the LORD. He said, "You have helped me win this great battle. Do I have to die of thirst now? Must I fall into the power of people who haven't even been circumcised? They aren't your people."

19Then God opened up the hollow place in Lehi. Water came out of it. When Samson drank the water, his strength returned. He felt as good as new. So the spring was called En Hakkore. It's still there in Lehi.

20Samson led Israel for 20 years. In those days the Philistines were in the land.

Samson and Delilah

16 One day Samson went to Gaza. There he saw a prostitute. He went in to spend the night with her.

2The people of Gaza were told, "Samson is here!" So they surrounded the place. They hid and waited for him at the city gate all night long. They didn't make any move against him during the night.

They said, "Let's wait until the sun comes up. Then we'll kill him."

3But Samson stayed there only until the middle of the night. Then he got up. He took hold of the doors of the city gate. He also took hold of the two doorposts. He tore them loose, together with their metal bar. He picked them up and put them on his shoulders. Then he carried them to the top of the hill that faces Hebron.

4Some time later, Samson fell in love again. The woman lived in the Valley of Sorek. Her name was Delilah.

5The rulers of the Philistines went to her. They said, "See if you can get him to tell you the secret of why he's so strong. Find out how we can overpower him. Then we can tie him up. We can bring him under our control. Each of us will give you 28 pounds of silver."

6So Delilah spoke to Samson. She said, "Tell me the secret of why you are so strong. Tell me how you can be tied up and controlled."

7Samson answered her, "Let someone tie me up with seven new leather straps. They must be straps that aren't completely dry. Then I'll become as weak as any other man."

8So the Philistine rulers brought seven new leather straps to her. They weren't completely dry. Delilah tied Samson up with them.

9Men were hiding in the room. She called out to him. She said, "Samson! The Philistines are attacking you!" But he snapped the leather straps easily. They were like pieces of string that had come too close to a flame. So the secret of why he was so strong wasn't discovered.

10Delilah spoke to Samson again. "You have made me look foolish," she said. "You told me a lie. Come on. Tell me how you can be tied up."

11Samson said, "Let someone tie me tightly with new ropes. They must be ropes that have never been used. Then I'll become as weak as any other man."

12So Delilah got some new ropes. She tied him up with them. Men were hiding in the room. She called out to him. She said, "Samson! The Philistines are attacking you!" But he snapped the ropes off his arms. They fell off just as if they were threads.

13Delilah spoke to Samson again. "Until now, you have been making me look foolish," she said. "You have been telling me lies. This time really tell me how you can be tied up."

He replied, "Weave the seven braids of my hair into the cloth on a loom. Then pin my hair to the loom. If you do, I'll become as weak as any other man."

So while Samson was sleeping, Delilah took hold of the seven braids of his hair. She wove them into the cloth on a loom. **14**Then she pinned his hair to the loom.

Again she called out to him. She said, "Samson! The Philistines are attacking you!" He woke up from his sleep. He pulled up the pin and the loom, together with the cloth.

15Then she said to him, "How can you say, 'I love you'? You won't even share your secret with me. This is the third time you have made me look foolish. And you still haven't told me the secret of why you are so strong."

16She continued to pester him day after day. She nagged him until he was sick and tired of it.

17So he told her everything. "I've never used a razor on my head," he said. "I've never cut my hair. That's because I've been a Nazirite since the day I was born. A Nazirite is set apart to God. If you shave my head, I won't be strong anymore. I'll become as weak as any other man."

18Delilah realized he had told her everything. So she sent a message to the Philistine rulers. She said, "Come back one more time. He has told me everything." So the rulers returned. They brought the silver with them.

19Delilah got Samson to go to sleep on her lap. Then she called for a man to shave off the seven braids of his hair. That's how she began to bring him under her control. And he wasn't strong anymore.

20She called out, "Samson! The Philistines are attacking you!"

He woke up from his sleep. He thought, "I'll go out just as I did before. I'll shake myself free." But he didn't know that the LORD had left him.

21Then the Philistines grabbed hold of him. They poked his eyes out. They took him down to Gaza. They put bronze chains around him. Then they made him grind grain in the prison. **22**His head had been shaved. But the hair on it began to grow again.

Samson Dies

23The rulers of the Philistines gathered together. They were going to offer a great sacrifice to their god Dagon. They were going to celebrate. They said, "Our god has handed our enemy Samson over to us."

24When the people saw Samson, they praised their god. They said,

"Our god has handed our enemy over to us.
Our enemy has destroyed our land.
He has killed large numbers of our people."

25After they had drunk a lot of wine, they shouted, "Bring Samson out. Let him put on a show for us." So they called Samson out of the prison. He put on a show for them.

They had him stand near the temple pillars. **26**Then he spoke to the servant who was holding his hand. He said, "Put me where I can feel the pillars. I'm talking about the ones that hold the temple up. I want to lean against them."

27The temple was crowded with men and women. All of the Philistine rulers were there. About 3,000 men and women were on the roof. They were watching Samson put on a show.

28Then he prayed to the LORD. He said, "LORD and King, show me that you still have concern for me. God, please make me strong just one more time. Let me pay the Philistines back for what they did to my two eyes. Let me do it with only one blow."

29Then Samson reached toward the two pillars that were in the middle of the temple. They held the temple up. He put his right hand on one of them. He put his left hand on the other. He leaned hard against them.

30Samson said, "Let me die together with the Philistines!" Then he pushed with all his might. The temple came down on the rulers. It fell on all of the people who were in it. So Samson killed many more Philistines when he died than he did while he lived.

31Then his brothers went down to get him. So did his father's whole family. All of them brought Samson's body back home. They buried his body in the tomb of his father Manoah. It's between Zorah and Eshtaol. Samson had led Israel for 20 years.

Micah Makes Some Statues of Gods

17 A man named Micah lived in the hill country of Ephraim. **2**He said to his mother, "Someone took 28 pounds of silver from you. I heard you call down a curse because of it. I have the silver with me. I'm the one who took it."

Then his mother said, "My son, may the LORD bless you!"

DELILAH

JUDGES 16:19

Delilah got Samson to go to sleep on her lap. Then she called for a man to shave off the seven braids of his hair. That's how she began to bring him under her control.

Delilah (duh-LIE-luh) swung her hips as she walked home from the market. *Tonight would be the night,* she thought. *Tonight!* Delilah had been pestering Samson for days. She desperately wanted to know the secret of his strength. Samson's enemies promised to give her lots of silver if she would trick him.

Delilah thought Samson was amazing. He was after all, the strongest man who had ever lived. But nothing was more amazing than money. Delilah wanted all she could get. And she would do anything to get it.

Later that night, Delilah sat with Samson. HE LAID HIS HEAD IN HER LAP AND WENT PEACEFULLY TO SLEEP, NEVER SEEING THE WICKED SMILE ON HER FACE. She had gotten his secret from him. She knew he wasn't lying this time. This was no trick of tying him up with leather straps or new ropes or weaving his hair into a loom. This time was for real. "Just cut off my hair," Samson admitted, "and my strength will be gone."

Samson's enemies stood outside the door, waiting for Delilah's signal. When she was sure Samson was asleep, she waved them in. One of them brought a razor blade and carefully began to cut off each of Samson's seven long braids. Delilah reached out her hand for the money they had promised. When the horrible haircut was finished, Delilah called to Samson to wake him, "Samson, quick! Get up! Your enemies are here!"

With his hair gone, Samson's strength was gone. His enemies grabbed him and put him into prison. They poked out his eyes and put him in chains.

DELILAH

You, of course, don't want to be anything like Delilah. She was a wicked woman. She betrayed Samson. But, when you talk about a friend behind his or her back, you're a bit like Delilah. When you lie to a friend, you're a bit like Delilah. So, watch out. Be as little like Delilah as you possibly can.

DELILAH BETRAYED SAMSON.
THE WHOLE STORY: JUDGES 16:4-22

Go to page 305 for the next Super Hero

3He gave the 28 pounds of silver back to his mother. She said to him, "I'm taking an oath and setting my silver apart to the LORD. My son, I want you to use part of it for a statue of a god that is made out of wood or stone and covered with silver. Use the rest of it to have another statue made out of silver. That's why I'll give the silver back to you."

4He gave the silver back to his mother. She gave five pounds of it to a skilled worker who made things out of silver. He used the silver for the two statues. They were put in Micah's house.

5That same Micah had a small temple. He made a sacred linen apron and some statues of gods. He prepared one of his sons to serve as his priest.

6In those days Israel didn't have a king. The people did anything they thought was right.

7A young Levite had been living in land that belonged to the tribe of Judah. He was from Bethlehem in Judah. **8**He left that town to look for some other place to stay. On his way he came to Micah's house. It was in the hill country of Ephraim.

9Micah asked him, "Where are you from?"

"I'm a Levite," he said. "I'm from Bethlehem in Judah. I'm looking for a place to stay."

10Then Micah said to him, "Live with me. Be my father and priest. I'll give you four ounces of silver a year. I'll also give you clothes and food."

11So the Levite agreed to live with him. The young man was just like a son to Micah.

12Then Micah prepared the Levite to serve as his priest. He lived in Micah's house. **13**Micah said, "Now I know that the LORD will be good to me. This Levite has become my priest."

The People of Dan Settle Down in Laish

18 In those days Israel didn't have a king.

And in those days the tribe of Dan was looking for a place where they could settle down. They hadn't been able to take over their own share of land among the tribes of Israel.

2So the people of Dan sent out five warriors from Zorah and Eshtaol. They told them to look the land over and check it out. Those men did it for all of their family groups. The people of Dan told the men, "Go. Check out the land."

So they entered the hill country of Ephraim. They went to the house of Micah. That's where they spent the night.

3When they came near Micah's house, they recognized a voice. It was the voice of the young Levite. So they turned off the road and stopped there. They asked him, "Who brought you here? What are you doing in this place? Why are you here?"

4The Levite told them what Micah had done for him. He said, "He has hired me. I'm his priest."

5Then they said to him, "Please ask God for advice. Try to find out whether we'll have success on our journey."

6The priest answered them, "Go in peace. The LORD is pleased with your journey."

7So the five men left. They came to Laish. There they saw that the people felt secure. They were living in safety. Like the people in Sidon, they weren't expecting anything bad to happen to them. Their land had everything they needed. Things were going very well for them. They lived a long way from the people of Sidon. And they didn't think they would ever need help from anyone else.

8The men returned to Zorah and Eshtaol. Their people asked them, "What did you find out?"

9They answered, "Come on! Let's attack them! We've seen that the land is very good. Aren't you going to do something? Don't wait any longer. Go there and take it over. **10**When you get there, you will find people who aren't expecting anything bad to happen to them. Their land has plenty of room. God has handed it over to you. It's a land that has everything you will ever need."

11So 600 men from the tribe of Dan started out from Zorah and Eshtaol. They were prepared for battle. **12**On their way they set up camp. Their camp was near Kiriath Jearim in Judah. That's why the place is called Mahaneh Dan to this very day. It's west of Kiriath Jearim. **13**From there they went to the hill country of Ephraim. They came to Micah's house.

14Then the five men who had looked over the land of Laish spoke to the other members of their tribe. They said, "Don't you know that one of these houses has a sacred linen apron in it? Some statues of family gods are there. It also has two statues of other gods in it. One of them is made out of wood or stone. The other is made out of silver. Now you know what to do."

15So they turned off the road and

stopped there. They went to the house of the young Levite. He was at Micah's place. They greeted the young man. ¹⁶The 600 men from Dan stood at the entrance of the gate. They were prepared for battle.

¹⁷The five men who had looked over the land went inside. They took the two statues. They also took the family gods and the linen apron.

During that time, the priest stood at the entrance of the gate. The 600 men stood there with him. They were prepared for battle.

¹⁸When those men went into Micah's house and took all of those things, the priest spoke to them. He asked, "What are you doing?"

¹⁹They answered him, "Be quiet! Don't say a word. Come with us. Be our father and priest. You can serve a whole tribe and family group in Israel as our priest. Isn't that better than serving just one man's family?"

²⁰The priest was glad. He took the linen apron and the family gods. He also took the statue of a god that was made out of wood or stone. Then he left with the people.

²¹They put their little children and their livestock in front of them. They also put everything else they owned in front of them. And they turned and went on their way.

²²The men who lived near Micah were called together. Then they left and caught up with the people of Dan. That's because Dan's people hadn't gone very far from Micah's house. ²³Those who lived near Micah shouted at them. The people of Dan turned around and spoke to Micah. "What's the matter with you?" they asked. "Why did you call your men out to fight against us?"

²⁴He replied, "You took away the gods I made. And you took my priest away. What do I have left? So how can you ask, 'What's the matter with you?' "

²⁵The people of Dan answered, "Don't argue with us. Some men get angry quickly. They might attack you. Then you and your family will lose your lives."

²⁶So the people of Dan went on their way. Micah saw that they were too strong for him. So he turned around and went back home.

²⁷The people of Dan took what Micah had made. They also took his priest. They continued on their way to Laish. They went there to fight against peaceful people who weren't expecting to be attacked. They struck them down with their swords. They burned their city down. ²⁸No one could save them. They lived a long way from Sidon. And they didn't think they would ever need help from anyone else. Their city was located in a valley near Beth Rehob.

The people of Dan rebuilt the city. Then they settled down there. ²⁹They named it Dan. That's because they traced their family line back to Dan. He was a son of Israel. The city used to be called Laish.

³⁰There the people of Dan set up the statues of gods for themselves. Jonathan and his sons were priests for the tribe of Dan. Jonathan was the son of Gershom, the son of Moses. Jonathan and his sons were priests until the time when the land was captured. ³¹They continued to use the statues Micah had made. They used them during the whole time the house of God was in Shiloh.

A Levite and His Concubine

19 In those days Israel didn't have a king.

There was a Levite who lived deep in the hill country of Ephraim. He got a concubine from Bethlehem in Judah. ²But she wasn't faithful to him. She left him. She went back to her father's house in Bethlehem in Judah. She stayed there for four months.

³Then her husband went to see her. He tried to talk her into coming back with him. He had his servant and two donkeys with him. She took her husband into her father's house. When her father saw him, he gladly welcomed him.

⁴His father-in-law, the woman's father, begged him to stay. So he remained with him for three days. He ate, drank and slept there.

⁵On the fourth day they got up early. The Levite prepared to leave. But the woman's father spoke to his son-in-law. He said, "Have something to eat. It will give you strength. Then you can go on your way."

⁶So the two of them sat down. They ate and drank together. After that, the woman's father said, "Please stay tonight. Enjoy yourself."

⁷The man got up to go. But his father-in-law talked him into staying. So he stayed there that night.

⁸On the morning of the fifth day, he got up to go. But the woman's father said, "Have something to eat. It will give you strength. Wait until this afternoon!" So the two of them ate together.

⁹Then the man got up to leave. His con-

cubine and his servant got up when he did. But his father-in-law, the woman's father, spoke to him again. "Look," he said. "It's almost evening. The day is nearly over. So spend another night here. Please stay. Enjoy yourself. Early tomorrow morning you can get up and go back home."

¹⁰But the man didn't want to stay another night. So he left. He went toward Jebus. He had his two donkeys and his concubine with him. The donkeys had saddles on them. Jebus is also called Jerusalem.

¹¹By the time the travelers came near Jebus, the day was almost over. So the servant said to his master, "Come. Let's stop at this Jebusite city. Let's spend the night here."

¹²His master replied, "No. We won't go into a city where strangers live. The people there aren't from Israel. We'll continue on to Gibeah." ¹³He added, "Come. Let's try to reach Gibeah or Ramah. We can spend the night in one of those places."

¹⁴So they continued on. As they came near Gibeah in Benjamin, the sun went down. ¹⁵They stopped there to spend the night. They went to the city's main street and sat down. But no one took them home for the night.

¹⁶That evening an old man came into the city. He had been working in the fields. He was from the hill country of Ephraim. But he was living in Gibeah. The people who lived there were from the tribe of Benjamin. ¹⁷The old man saw the traveler in the main street. He asked, "Where are you going? Where did you come from?"

¹⁸The Levite answered, "We've come from Bethlehem in Judah. We're on our way to Ephraim. I live deep in the hill country there. I've been to Bethlehem. Now I'm going to the house of the LORD. But no one has taken me home for the night. ¹⁹We have straw and feed for our donkeys. We have food and wine for ourselves. We have enough for me, my female servant and the young man who is with us. We don't need anything."

²⁰"You are welcome at my house," the old man said. "I'd be happy to supply anything you might need. But don't spend the night in the street."

²¹So the old man took him into his house and fed his donkeys. After the travelers had washed their feet, they had something to eat and drink.

²²They were inside enjoying themselves. But some of the evil men who lived in the city surrounded the house. They pounded on the door. They shouted to the old man who owned the house. They said, "Bring out the man who came to your house. We want to have sex with him."

²³The owner of the house went outside. He said to them, "No, my friends. Don't do such an evil thing. This man is my guest. So don't do this terrible thing. ²⁴"Look, here is my virgin daughter. And here's the Levite's concubine. I'll bring them out to you now. You can have them. Do to them what you want to. But don't do such a terrible thing to this man."

²⁵The men wouldn't listen to him. So the Levite sent his concubine out to them. They forced her to have sex with them. They raped her all night long. As the night was ending, they let her go. ²⁶At sunrise she went back to the house where her master was staying. She fell down at the door. She stayed there until daylight.

²⁷Later that morning her master got up. He opened the door of the house. He stepped out to continue on his way. But his concubine was lying there. She had fallen at the doorway of the house. Her hands were reaching out toward the door. ²⁸He said to her, "Get up. Let's go." But there wasn't any answer. Then he put her dead body on his donkey. And he started out for home.

²⁹When he reached home, he got a knife. He cut up his concubine. He cut her into 12 pieces. He sent them into all of the territories of Israel. ³⁰Everyone who saw it said, "Nothing like this has ever been seen or done before. Nothing like this has happened since the day the people of Israel came up out of Egypt. Think about it! Consider it! Tell us what to do!"

The Tribe of Benjamin Is Attacked by the Other Tribes

20 Then all of the people of Israel came out. They came from the whole land between Dan and Beersheba. They also came from the land of Gilead. All of them gathered together in the sight of the LORD at Mizpah. ²The leaders of all of the tribes of Israel came. They took their places among the people of God who were gathered together. There were 400,000 fighting men who were carrying swords. ³The tribe of Benjamin heard that the people of Israel had gone up to Mizpah. The people of Israel said, "Tell us how that awful thing happened."

4So the Levite spoke. He was the husband of the woman who had been murdered. He said, "I and my concubine went to Gibeah in Benjamin. We spent the night there. **5**During the night the men of Gibeah came after me. They surrounded the house. They were planning to kill me. They raped my concubine, and she died.

6"I took my concubine and cut her into pieces. I sent one piece to each part of Israel's territory. I did it because they had done a very terrible thing in Israel. **7**All of you men of Israel, speak up now. Give your decision."

8All of the men got up together. They said, "None of us will go home. Not one of us will return to his house. **9**Here is what we'll do to Gibeah. We'll use lots to tell us how to attack the city. **10**We'll take ten men out of every 100 from all of the tribes of Israel. We'll take 100 from every 1,000. We'll take 1,000 from every 10,000. The men we take will get supplies for the army. Then the army will go to Gibeah in Benjamin. They'll give Gibeah exactly what they should get because of the evil thing they did in Israel."

11So all of the men of Israel came together to fight against the city.

12The tribes of Israel sent men through the whole tribe of Benjamin. They said, "What about this awful crime that was committed among you? **13**Hand over those evil men of Gibeah. We'll put them to death. In that way we'll get rid of those evil people."

But the people of Benjamin wouldn't listen to the other people of Israel. **14**They came together at Gibeah from their towns. They came to fight against the other people of Israel.

15Right away the people of Benjamin gathered together 26,000 men from their towns. They were carrying swords. The men were added to the 700 who had been chosen from those who were living in Gibeah. **16**Among all of those men there were 700 who were left-handed. Each of them could sling a stone at a hair and not miss.

17Israel gathered 400,000 men together. They were carrying swords. All of them were fighting men. That number didn't include the tribe of Benjamin.

18The people of Israel went up to Bethel. There they spoke to God. They asked him, "Who will go up first and fight for us against the people of Benjamin?"

The LORD answered, "The tribe of Judah will go first."

19The next morning the people of Israel got up. They set up camp near Gibeah. **20**The men of Israel went out to fight against the men of Benjamin. They took up their battle positions against them at Gibeah. **21**The men of Benjamin came out of Gibeah. They killed 22,000 men of Israel on the field of battle that day. **22**But the men of Israel cheered each other on. They again took up their positions in the places where they had been the first day.

23The men of Israel went and sobbed in the sight of the LORD until evening. They spoke to the LORD. They asked, "Should we go up again to fight against the men of Benjamin? They are our fellow Israelites."

The LORD answered, "Go up and fight against them."

24The men of Israel came near the men of Benjamin on the second day. **25**The men of Benjamin came out from Gibeah to oppose them. That time they killed 18,000 more men of Israel. All of the men who died had been carrying swords.

26Then all of the people of Israel went up to Bethel. They sat there and sobbed in the sight of the LORD. They didn't eat anything that day until evening. Then they brought burnt offerings and friendship offerings to the LORD.

27Again the people of Israel spoke to the LORD. In those days the ark of the covenant of God was there. **28**Phinehas was serving as priest at the ark. He was the son of Eleazar. Eleazar was the son of Aaron. The people of Israel asked, "Should we go up again to fight against the men of Benjamin? They are our fellow Israelites."

The LORD answered, "Go. Tomorrow I will hand them over to you."

29Then Israel hid some men and had them wait all around Gibeah. **30**They went up to fight against the men of Benjamin on the third day. They took up their positions against Gibeah, just as they had done before.

31The men of Benjamin came out to fight against them. They were drawn away from the city. They began to wound and kill the men of Israel just as they had done before. About 30 men fell in battle. They fell in the open fields and on the roads. One of the roads led to Bethel. The other led to Gibeah.

32The men of Benjamin said, "We're winning the battle over them, just as we did before."

But the men of Israel said, "Let's pull

back. Let's draw them away from the city to the roads."

33 All of the men of Israel moved away from their places. They took up new battle positions at Baal Tamar. The men who had been hiding charged out. They came from west of Gibeah.

34 Then 10,000 of Israel's finest men attacked Gibeah. The men of Benjamin didn't realize they were about to be destroyed. The fighting was very heavy.

35 The LORD helped Israel win the battle over Benjamin. On that day the men of Israel struck down 25,100 men of Benjamin. All of the men who died had been carrying swords. **36** Then the men of Benjamin saw that they had lost the battle.

The men of Israel had moved away from their positions in front of Benjamin. They had depended on the men they had hidden near Gibeah. **37** Suddenly the men who had been hiding rushed into Gibeah. They spread out. Then they killed everyone in the city with their swords.

38 The men of Israel had made a plan with those who had been hiding. They had told them to send up a large cloud of smoke from the city. **39** Then the men of Israel would turn around and attack.

The men of Benjamin had begun to wound and kill the men of Israel. They had struck down about 30 of them. They had said, "We're winning the battle over them, just as we did the first time."

40 But a column of smoke began to go up from the city. The men of Benjamin turned around. They saw the smoke of the whole city going up into the sky.

41 Then the men of Israel turned around and attacked them.

The men of Benjamin were terrified. They realized they were going to be destroyed. **42** So they ran away from the men of Israel. They ran toward the desert. But they couldn't escape the battle. Other men of Israel came out of the towns. There they struck the men of Benjamin down. **43** They surrounded them. They chased them and easily caught up with them. That happened east of Gibeah.

44 So 18,000 men of Benjamin fell in battle. All of them were brave fighters.

45 Some men of Benjamin turned back. They ran toward the desert to the rock of Rimmon. As they did, the men of Israel struck down 5,000 of them along the roads. They kept chasing the men of Benjamin all the way to Gidom. Along the way they struck down 2,000 more.

46 On that day 25,000 men of Benjamin fell in battle. They had been carrying swords. All of them were brave fighters. **47** But 600 men turned back. They ran into the desert to the rock of Rimmon. They stayed there for four months.

48 The men of Israel went back to Benjamin. They killed the people in all of the towns with their swords. They even killed the animals. So they killed everything they found. They set on fire all of the towns they came to.

The Men of Benjamin Receive Wives

21 The men of Israel had taken an oath and made a promise at Mizpah. They had said, "Not one of us will give his daughter to be married to a man from Benjamin."

2 The people went to Bethel. They sat there until evening in the sight of God. They sobbed loudly and bitterly. **3** "LORD, you are the God of Israel," they cried. "Why has this happened to Israel? Why is one tribe missing from Israel today?"

4 Early the next day the people built an altar. They brought burnt offerings and friendship offerings.

5 Then the people of Israel asked, "Has anyone failed to come here in the sight of the LORD? Is anyone missing from all of the tribes of Israel?"

The people had made a promise with an oath. They had said that anyone who failed to come to Mizpah in the sight of the LORD should certainly be put to death.

6 The people of Israel were very sad because of what had happened to the tribe of Benjamin. After all, they were their fellow Israelites. "Today one tribe has been cut off from Israel," they said. **7** "How can we provide wives for the men who are left? We've made a promise with an oath in the sight of the LORD. We've promised not to give any of our daughters to be married to them."

8 Then they asked, "Has any tribe of Israel failed to come here to Mizpah in the sight of the LORD?"

They discovered that no one from Jabesh Gilead had come. No one from there had gathered together with the others in the camp. **9** They counted the people. They found that none of the people of Jabesh Gilead had come to Mizpah.

10 So the community sent 12,000 fighting men to Jabesh Gilead. They directed them to take their swords and kill those who were living there. That included the women and children.

11 "Here is what you must do," they

said. "Kill every male. Also kill every woman who is not a virgin."

12They found 400 young women in Jabesh Gilead who had never made love to a man. So they took them to the camp at Shiloh in Canaan.

13Then the whole community sent an offer of peace to the men of Benjamin. The men were at the rock of Rimmon. **14**So the men of Benjamin returned at that time. They were given the women of Jabesh Gilead who had been spared. But there weren't enough women for all of them.

15The people were very sad because of what had happened to the tribe of Benjamin. The LORD had left a gap in the tribes of Israel. They weren't complete without Benjamin.

16The elders of the community spoke up. They said, "All of the women of Benjamin have been wiped out. So how will we find wives for the men who are left? **17**The men of Benjamin who are still alive need to have children," they said. "If they don't, a tribe of Israel will be wiped out.

18"But we can't give them our daughters to be their wives. We Israelites have taken an oath and made a promise. We've said, 'May anyone who gives a wife to a man from Benjamin be under the LORD's curse.'

19"Look, a feast is celebrated every year in Shiloh in honor of the LORD. Shiloh is north of Bethel. It's east of the road that goes from Bethel to Shechem. It's south of Lebonah."

20So they told the men of Benjamin what to do. They said, "Go. Hide in the vineyards **21**and watch. The young women of Shiloh will come out. They'll join in the dancing. When they do, run out of the vineyards. Each of you grab hold of a young woman from Shiloh to be your wife. Then go to the land of Benjamin.

22"Their fathers or brothers might not be happy with what we're doing. If they aren't, we'll say to them, 'Do us a favor. Help the men of Benjamin. We didn't get wives for them during the battle. You aren't guilty of doing anything wrong. After all, you didn't give your daughters to them. They were stolen from you.' "

23So that's what the men of Benjamin did. While the young women were dancing, each man caught one. He carried her away to be his wife. Then the men returned to their own share of land. They built the towns again. They settled down in them.

24At that time the men of Israel also left. They went home to their tribes and family groups. Each one went to his own share of land.

25In those days Israel didn't have a king. The people did anything they thought was right.

RUTH

The book of Ruth tells a beautiful story of God's faithfulness to people who trust in him. Ruth, the main hero in this book, leaves her false gods behind in Moab to serve the one true God. She goes to Bethlehem with her mother-in-law Naomi. In Bethlehem Ruth experiences firsthand how faithful God is to those who trust him. She marries another hero, Boaz, and has a son. As you read the book of Ruth, remember that God is faithful to you today, too.

HEROES IN THIS BOOK . . .

RUTH
PAGE 305

BOAZ
PAGE 307

NAOMI
PAGE 309

Ruth Goes to Bethlehem With Naomi

1 There was a time when Israel didn't have kings to rule over them. But they had leaders to help them. This is a story about some things that happened during that time.

There wasn't enough food in the land of Judah. So a man went to live in the country of Moab for a while. He was from Bethlehem in Judah. His wife and two sons went with him.

2The man's name was Elimelech. His wife's name was Naomi. The names of his two sons were Mahlon and Kilion. They were Ephrathites from Bethlehem in Judah. They went to Moab and lived there.

3Naomi's husband Elimelech died. So she was left with her two sons. **4**They got married to women from Moab. One was named Orpah. The other was named Ruth. Naomi's family lived in Moab for about ten years. **5**Then Mahlon and Kilion also died. So Naomi was left without her two sons and her husband.

6While Naomi was in Moab, she heard that the Lord had helped his people. He had begun to provide food for them again. So Naomi and her daughters-in-law prepared to go from Moab back to her home. **7**She left the place where she had been living. Her two daughters-in-law went with her. They started out on the road that would take them back to the land of Judah.

8Naomi spoke to her two daughters-in-law. "Both of you go back," she said. "Each of you go to your own mother's home. You were kind to your husbands, who have died. You have also been kind to me. So may the Lord be just as kind to you. **9**May he help each of you find a secure place in the home of another husband. May he give you peace and rest."

Then she kissed them good-by. They broke down and sobbed loudly. **10**They said to her, "We'll go back to your people with you."

11But Naomi said, "Go home, my daughters. Why would you want to come with me? Am I going to have any more sons who could become your husbands?

12"Go home, my daughters. I'm too old to have another husband. Suppose I thought there was still some hope for me. Suppose I got married to a man tonight. And later I had sons by him. **13**Would you wait until they grew up? Would you stay single until you could get married to them? No, my daughters. My life is more bitter than yours. The Lord's powerful hand has been against me!"

14When they heard that, they broke down and sobbed again. Then Orpah kissed her mother-in-law good-by. But Ruth held on to her.

15"Look," said Naomi. "Your sister-in-law is going back to her people and her gods. Go back with her."

16But Ruth replied, "Don't try to make me leave you and go back. Where you go I'll go. Where you stay I'll stay. Your people will be my people. Your God will be my God. **17**Where you die I'll die. And there my body will be buried. I won't let anything except death separate you from me. If I do, may the Lord punish me greatly."

18Naomi realized that Ruth had made up her mind to go with her. So she stopped trying to make her go back.

19The two women continued on their way. At last they arrived in Bethlehem. The whole town was stirred up because of them. The women asked, "Can this possibly be Naomi?"

20"Don't call me Naomi," she told them. "Call me Mara. The Mighty One has made my life very bitter. **21**I was full when I went away. But the Lord has brought me back empty. So why are you calling me Naomi? The Lord has made me suffer. The Mighty One has brought trouble on me."

22So Naomi returned from Moab. Ruth, her daughter-in-law from Moab, came with her. They arrived in Bethlehem just when people were beginning to harvest the barley.

Ruth Meets Boaz

2 Naomi had a relative on her husband's side of the family. Her husband's name was Elimelech. The relative's

---

POWER-SURGE

KIND　　K

NAOMI SPOKE TO HER TWO DAUGHTERS-IN-LAW... "YOU HAVE ALSO BEEN KIND TO ME. SO MAY THE LORD BE JUST AS KIND TO YOU."

—— RUTH 1:8 ——

RUTH

RUTH 1:16

Ruth replied, "Don't try to make me leave you and go back. Where you go I'll go. Where you stay I'll stay. Your people will be my people. Your God will be my God."

Ruth was born and raised in Moab. So was Orpah. They both grew up worshiping idols. They each married one of Naomi's sons. And they each learned about God. God was not an idol made of wood or stone. God was alive and loving. Ruth knew it was true. She left her idols and chose to follow God.

Then terrible things started to happen. Naomi's husband died. Then Ruth's husband died. Then Orpah's husband died. Now all three women were left alone. When Naomi decided to leave Moab and return to Bethlehem, Orpah stayed in Moab. But Ruth told Naomi that she wanted to go with her. She wanted to follow the true God. **WITHOUT LOOKING BACK, RUTH WENT TO BETHLEHEM WITH NAOMI.**

Then Ruth worked in the fields of Boaz, a rich relative of Naomi. Ruth rubbed her rough and sore hands together. She stretched her aching back. She continued picking up stalks of grain and putting them into her sack. She was thankful for every piece. She and Naomi would use the grain to make bread. If Ruth didn't pick up the grain, they would have nothing to eat.

Boaz noticed Ruth as she worked in his fields. He knew she was a good woman, taking care of Naomi and following God faithfully. Soon Boaz married Ruth, and they had a son. When Naomi held little Obed for the first time, she cried tears of joy. God had given her a wonderful daughter-in-law and now a beautiful grandson. All the years of grief were passed. Ruth hugged Naomi and they smiled. They both looked down at baby Obed and thanked God for his blessings.

BE A RUTH

Most people today don't worship idols made of wood or stone. But they *do* worship idols. Perhaps their idol is money or music. Whatever gets between you and God is an idol. Ruth never looked back at the idols she worshiped as a child. She knew that she had met the one true God, and she followed only him.

RUTH SAW THE TRUTH AND FOLLOWED IT.
THE WHOLE STORY: RUTH 1–4

Go to page 307 for the next Super Hero

name was Boaz. He was a very important man.

²Ruth, who was from Moab, spoke to Naomi. She said, "Let me go out to the fields. I'll pick up the grain that has been left. I'll do it behind anyone who is pleased with me."

Naomi said to her, "My daughter, go ahead."

³So Ruth went out and began to pick up grain. She worked in the fields behind those who were cutting and gathering the grain. As it turned out, she was working in a field that belonged to Boaz. He was from the family of Elimelech.

⁴Just then Boaz arrived from Bethlehem. He greeted those who were cutting and gathering the grain. He said, "May the Lord be with you!"

"And may the Lord bless you!" they replied.

⁵Boaz spoke to the man who was in charge of his workers. He asked, "Who is that young woman?"

⁶The man replied, "She's from Moab. She came back from there with Naomi. ⁷She said, 'Please let me walk behind the workers. Let me pick up the grain that is left.' Then she went into the field. She has kept on working there from morning until now. She took only one short rest in the shade."

⁸So Boaz said to Ruth, "Dear woman, listen to me. Don't pick up grain in any other field. Don't go anywhere else. Stay here with my female servants. ⁹Keep your eye on the field where the men are cutting grain. Walk behind the women who are gathering it. Pick up the grain that is left. I've told the men not to touch you. When you are thirsty, go and get a drink. Take water from the jars the men have filled."

¹⁰When Ruth heard that, she bowed down with her face to the ground. She asked, "Why are you being so kind to me? In fact, why are you even noticing me? I'm from another country."

¹¹Boaz replied, "I've been told all about you. I've heard about everything you have done for your mother-in-law since your husband died. I know that you left your father and mother. I know that you left your country. You came to live with people you didn't know before. ¹²May the Lord reward you for what you have done. May the God of Israel bless you richly. You have come to him to find safety under his care."

¹³"Sir, I hope you will continue to be kind to me," Ruth said. "You have comforted me. You have spoken kindly to me.

And I'm not even as important as one of your female servants!"

¹⁴When it was time to eat, Boaz spoke to Ruth again. "Come over here," he said. "Have some bread. Dip it in the wine vinegar."

She sat down with the workers. Then Boaz offered her some grain that had been cooked. She ate all she wanted. She even had some left over.

¹⁵Ruth got up to pick up more grain. Then Boaz gave orders to his men. He said, "Suppose she takes some stalks from what the women have tied up. If she does, don't make her look bad. ¹⁶Instead, pull some stalks out for her. Leave them for her to pick up. Don't tell her she shouldn't do it."

¹⁷So Ruth picked up grain in the field until evening. Then she separated the barley from the straw. It amounted to more than half a bushel. ¹⁸She carried it back to town. Her mother-in-law saw how much she had gathered. Ruth also brought out the food that was left over from the lunch Boaz had given her. She gave it to Naomi.

¹⁹Her mother-in-law asked her, "Where did you pick up grain today? Where did you work? May the man who noticed you be blessed!"

Then Ruth told her about the man whose field she had worked in. "The name of the man I worked with today is Boaz," she said.

²⁰"May the Lord bless him!" Naomi said to her daughter-in-law. "The Lord is still being kind to those who are living and those who are dead."

She continued, "That man is a close relative of ours. He's one of our family protectors."

²¹Then Ruth, who was from Moab, said, "He told me more. He even said, 'Stay with my workers until they have finished bringing in all of my grain.'"

²²Naomi replied to her daughter-in-law Ruth. She said, "That will be good for you, my daughter. Go with his female servants. You might be harmed if you go to someone else's field."

²³So Ruth stayed close to the female servants of Boaz as she picked up grain. She worked until the time when all of the barley and wheat had been harvested. And she lived with her mother-in-law.

Ruth Goes to Boaz at the Threshing Floor

3 One day Ruth's mother-in-law Naomi spoke to her. She said, "My daughter, shouldn't I try to find a secure place for you? Shouldn't you have peace and rest? Shouldn't I find a home where things will go well with you? ²You have been with the female servants of Boaz. He's a relative of ours. Tonight he'll be separating the straw from his barley on the threshing floor.

³"So wash yourself. Put on some perfume. And put on your best clothes. Then go down to the threshing floor. But don't let Boaz know you are there. Wait until he has finished eating and drinking. ⁴Notice where he lies down. Then go over and uncover his feet. Lie down there. He'll tell you what to do."

⁵"I'll do everything you say," Ruth answered. ⁶So she went down to the threshing floor. She did everything her mother-in-law had told her to do.

⁷When Boaz had finished eating and

BOAZ

RUTH 2:11-12

Boaz replied, "I've been told all about you. I've heard about everything you have done for your mother-in-law since your husband died. I know that you left your father and mother. I know that you left your country. You came to live with people you didn't know before. May the LORD reward you for what you have done."

Boaz (BOW-az) looked over the field. The heads of ripe grain hung heavy in the afternoon sun. The workers busily cut the grain and stacked it. Behind the workers, several women followed and picked up what was dropped.

Boaz knew all but one of the women in the field. **"WHO IS THAT NEW YOUNG WOMAN WORKING OUT THERE?"** he asked his manager.

The manager answered, "A foreign woman named Ruth. She's worked hard all day, only taking one small rest in the shade."

Boaz had heard about Ruth. He knew what a good woman she was and that she was a relative by marriage. He told his manager to be extra kind to Ruth, to give her water to drink and extra grain to pick up.

BE A BOAZ

Boaz was kind to Ruth. She needed help and he gave it. He made sure she was safe in his fields and that she had enough eat. Then he went one step further. He married her and provided for her and for her mother-in-law Naomi. Be a Boaz! When someone needs your help, be kind and helpful.

BOAZ WAS KIND TO RUTH WHEN SHE NEEDED HELP.

Go to page 309 for the next Super Hero

drinking, he was in a good mood. He went over to lie down at the far end of the grain pile. Then Ruth approached quietly. She uncovered his feet and lay down there.

8In the middle of the night, something surprised Boaz and woke him up. He turned and found a woman lying there at his feet.

9"Who are you?" he asked.

"I'm Ruth," she said. "You are my family protector. So take good care of me by making me your wife."

10"Dear woman, may the LORD bless you," he replied. "You are showing even more kindness now than you did earlier. You didn't run after the younger men, whether they were rich or poor. **11**Dear woman, don't be afraid. I'll do for you everything you ask. All of the people of my town know that you are a noble woman.

12"It's true that I'm a relative of yours. But there's a family protector who is more closely related to you than I am. **13**So stay here for the night. In the morning if he wants to help you, good. Let him help you. But if he doesn't want to, then I'll do it. You can be sure that the LORD lives. And you can be just as sure that I'll help you. Lie down here until morning."

14So she stayed at his feet until morning. But she got up before anyone could be recognized. Boaz thought, "No one must know that a woman came to the threshing floor."

15He said to Ruth, "Bring me the coat you have around you. Hold it out." So she did. He poured more than fifty pounds of barley into it and helped her pick it up. Then he went back to town.

16Ruth came to her mother-in-law. Naomi asked, "How did it go, my daughter?"

Then Ruth told her everything Boaz had done for her. **17**She said, "He gave me all of this barley. He said, 'Don't go back to your mother-in-law with your hands empty.' "

18Naomi said, "My daughter, sit down until you find out what happens. The man won't rest until he settles the whole matter today."

Boaz Gets Married to Ruth

4 Boaz went up to the town gate and sat down there. The family protector he had talked about came by. Then Boaz said, "Come over here, my friend. Sit down." So the man went over and sat down.

2Boaz brought ten of the elders of the town together. He said, "Sit down here." So they did.

3Then he spoke to the family protector. He said, "Naomi has come back from Moab. She's selling the piece of land that belonged to our relative Elimelech. **4**I thought I should bring the matter to your attention. I suggest that you buy the land while those who are sitting here and the elders of my people are looking on as witnesses.

"If you are willing to buy it back, do it. But if you aren't, tell me. Then I'll know. No one has the right to buy it back except you. And I'm next in line."

"I'll buy it," he said.

5Then Boaz said, "When you buy the land from Naomi and Ruth, who is from Moab, you must get married to Ruth. She's the dead man's widow. So you must take her as your wife. His name must stay with his property."

6When the family protector heard that, he said, "Then I can't buy the land. If I did, I might put my own property in danger. So you buy it. I can't do it."

7In earlier times in Israel, there was a certain practice. It was used when family land was bought back and changed owners. The practice made the sale final. One person would take his sandal off and give it to the other. That was how people in Israel showed that a business matter had been settled.

8So the family protector said to Boaz, "Buy it yourself." And he took his sandal off.

9Then Boaz spoke to the elders and all of the people. He said, "Today you are witnesses. You have seen that I have bought land from Naomi. I have bought all of the property that had belonged to Elimelech, Kilion and Mahlon.

10"I've also taken Ruth, who is from Moab, to become my wife. She is Mahlon's widow. I've decided to get married to her so the dead man's name will stay with his property. Now his name won't disappear from his family line. It won't disappear from the town records. Today you are witnesses!"

11Then the elders and all who were at the gate spoke. They said, "We are witnesses. The woman is coming into your home. May the LORD make her to be like Rachel and Leah. Together they built up the nation of Israel. May you be an important person in Ephrathah. May you be famous in Bethlehem. **12**The LORD will give you children through this young woman. May your family be like the fami-

NAOMI

RUTH 4:14-15

We praise the LORD...May this child become famous all over Israel!...He's the son of your very own daughter-in-law. She loves you. She is better to you than seven sons."

For the first time Naomi held her baby grandson, Obed, in her arms. His face peaked out from his blankets. Such a sweet little face. Naomi looked around at the women of Bethlehem who had come to visit this new baby. Naomi smiled, then laughed with joy. Ruth watched and smiled, too, glad that baby Obed made Naomi happy.

After days and months and years of being sad, today Naomi's heart swelled with happiness. In Moab Naomi's husband and both of her sons had died. Now she was back home in Bethlehem with her daughter-in-law, Ruth. Ruth had married Naomi's relative, Boaz. And just a few days before, Ruth had had a son.

Naomi's friends continued laughing and talking together, until one of them began to sing. "Praise God for this little boy, Naomi. We hope he will be famous! God has blessed you after years of sadness. Your daughter-in-law, Ruth, is better than seven sons would be! She loves you. And she has given you a grandson."

Later that day, Naomi held little Obed again. Ruth had just fed him. He was satisfied and fell fast asleep. **NAOMI RAN THE BACK OF HER FINGER OVER HIS LITTLE LIPS, FEELING HIS SOFT BABY BREATH.** She smiled again. She felt like she had been smiling all day, that she wouldn't stop smiling for a long time. *My friends are right,* Naomi thought. *God has blessed me after years of being sad.* Little did she know that Obed would be the grandpa of famous King David and even in the family line of Jesus himself!

BE A NAOMI

Naomi knew that God had blessed her. God had promised to take care of her, and he was keeping that promise. God will take care of you, too. You may not always be happy. Naomi wasn't. But you can trust that even in hard times, God is with you. Be a Naomi. Thank God for being with you!

NAOMI PRAISED GOD FOR BLESSING HER.
THE WHOLE STORY: RUTH 1-4

Go to page 314 for the next Super Hero

ly of Perez. He was the son Tamar had by Judah."

The Family Line of David

¹³So Boaz got married to Ruth. She became his wife. Then he made love to her. The LORD blessed her so that she became pregnant. And she had a son.

¹⁴The women said to Naomi, "We praise the LORD. Today he has provided a family protector for you. May this child become famous all over Israel! ¹⁵He will make your life new again. He'll take care of you when you are old. He's the son of your very own daughter-in-law. She loves you. She is better to you than seven sons."

¹⁶Then Naomi put the child on her lap and took care of him. ¹⁷The women who were living there said, "Naomi has a son." They named him Obed. He was the father of Jesse. Jesse was the father of David.

¹⁸Here is the family line of Perez.

Perez was the father of Hezron.
¹⁹Hezron was the father of Ram.
Ram was the father of Amminadab.

POWER-SURGE

KIND   K

[OBED IS] THE SON OF YOUR VERY OWN DAUGHTER-IN-LAW. [RUTH] LOVES YOU. SHE IS BETTER TO YOU THAN SEVEN SONS.
— RUTH 4:15 —

LOVING

²⁰Amminadab was the father of Nahshon.
Nahshon was the father of Salmon.
²¹Salmon was the father of Boaz.
Boaz was the father of Obed.
²²Obed was the father of Jesse.
And Jesse was the father of David.

1 SAMUEL

The book of 1 Samuel tells the story of the last judge of Israel, Samuel, and the first king, Saul. When the people beg for a king, God tells Samuel to anoint Saul. Saul becomes king but quickly disobeys God. God rejects Saul as king and tells Samuel to anoint David, the young giant killer, as the next king of Israel. The heroes of 1 Samuel—Samuel, David, Jonathan and Abigail—live lives of high adventure. Read 1 Samuel and experience not only the adventure of its heroes but the involvement of God in their lives.

HEROES IN THIS BOOK . . .

HANNAH
PAGE 314

SAMUEL
PAGE 318

SAUL
(Not!)
PAGE 331

GOLIATH
(Not!)
PAGE 333

Samuel Is Born

1 A certain man from Ramathaim in the hill country of Ephraim was named Elkanah. He was the son of Jeroham. Jeroham was the son of Elihu. Elihu was the son of Tohu. Tohu was the son of Zuph. Elkanah belonged to the family line of Zuph. Elkanah lived in the territory of Ephraim. ²Elkanah had two wives. One was named Hannah. The other was named Peninnah. Peninnah had children, but Hannah didn't.

³Year after year Elkanah went up from his town to Shiloh. He went there to worship and sacrifice to the LORD who rules over all. Hophni and Phinehas served as priests of the LORD at Shiloh. They were the two sons of Eli.

⁴Every time the day came for Elkanah to offer a sacrifice, he would give a share of the meat to his wife Peninnah. He would also give a share to each of her sons and daughters. ⁵But he would give two shares of meat to Hannah. That's because he loved her. He also gave her two shares because the LORD had kept her from having children.

⁶Peninnah teased Hannah to make her angry. She did it because the LORD had kept Hannah from having children. ⁷Peninnah teased Hannah year after year. Every time Hannah would go up to the house of the LORD, Elkanah's other wife would tease her. She would keep doing it until Hannah cried and wouldn't eat.

⁸Her husband Elkanah would speak to her. He would say, "Hannah, why are you crying? Why don't you eat? Why are you so angry and unhappy? Don't I mean more to you than ten sons?"

⁹One time when they had finished eating and drinking in Shiloh, Hannah stood up. The priest Eli was sitting on a chair by the doorpost of the LORD's house. ¹⁰Hannah was very bitter. She sobbed and sobbed. She prayed to the LORD. ¹¹She made a promise to him. She said, "LORD, you rule over all. Please see how I'm suffering! Show concern for me! Don't forget about me! Please give me a son! If you do, I'll give him back to you. Then he will serve you all the days of his life. He'll never use a razor on his head. He'll never cut his hair."

¹²As Hannah kept on praying to the LORD, Eli watched her lips. ¹³She was praying in her heart. Her lips were moving. But she wasn't making a sound.

Eli thought Hannah was drunk. ¹⁴He said to her, "How long will you keep on getting drunk? Get rid of your wine."

¹⁵"That's not true, sir," Hannah replied. "I'm a woman who is deeply troubled. I haven't been drinking wine or beer. I was telling the LORD all of my troubles. ¹⁶Don't think of me as an evil woman. I've been praying here because I'm very sad. My pain is so great."

¹⁷Eli answered, "Go in peace. May the God of Israel give you what you have asked him for."

¹⁸She said, "May you be pleased with me." Then she left and had something to eat. Her face wasn't sad anymore.

¹⁹Early the next morning Elkanah and his family got up. They worshiped the LORD. Then they went back to their home in Ramah.

Elkanah made love to his wife Hannah. And the LORD showed concern for her. ²⁰After some time, Hannah became pregnant. She had a baby boy. She said, "I asked the LORD for him." So she named him Samuel.

Hannah Gives Samuel to the LORD

²¹Elkanah went up to Shiloh to offer the yearly sacrifice to the LORD. He also went there to keep a promise he had made. His whole family went with him. ²²But Hannah didn't go. She said to her husband, "When the boy doesn't need me to nurse him anymore, I'll take him to the LORD's house. I'll give him to the LORD there. He'll stay there for the rest of his life."

²³Her husband Elkanah told her, "Do what you think is best. Stay here at home until Samuel doesn't need you to nurse him anymore. May the LORD make his promise to you come true."

So Hannah stayed home. She nursed her son until he didn't need her milk anymore.

²⁴When the boy didn't need her to nurse him anymore, she took him with her to Shiloh. She took him there even though he was still very young. She brought him to the LORD's house. She brought along a bull that was three years old. She brought more than half a bushel of flour. She also brought a bottle of wine. The bottle was made out of animal skin.

²⁵After the bull was killed, Elkanah and Hannah brought the boy to Eli. ²⁶Hannah said to Eli, "Sir, I'm the woman who stood here beside you praying to the LORD. And that's just as sure as you are alive. ²⁷I prayed for this child. The LORD has given me what I asked him for. ²⁸So now I'm

HANNAH

1 SAMUEL 1:27-28

"I prayed for this child. The Lord has given me what I asked him for. So now I'm giving him to the Lord. As long as he lives he'll be given to the Lord."

Hannah prayed and prayed and prayed. Her shoulders shook with her sobs. Tears ran down her face. She prayed to God to have a baby. If God would do this, she would give her child back to God for his whole life.

Hannah didn't know it, but the priest Eli was watching her. He thought she was drunk, so he scolded her. But Hannah told him he was wrong and that she was just praying to God, telling him her troubles. Eli realized he had been wrong. He comforted her and told her that God had heard her prayer.

After only a little time had passed, God answered Hannah's prayer. She had a son. Precious Samuel. His name means "heard of God."

When Samuel was still very young, Hannah took him back to the house of God. She thought her heart would break all over again. But she was determined to keep her promise. She held him close for one last time. Then she gave little Samuel to Eli and said, "The Lord gave me a son. So now I'm giving him back to the Lord. As long as he lives he'll stay here with you and serve the Lord."

Each year Hannah made a new robe for Samuel. **SHE PRAYED FOR HIM WITH EACH STITCH OF HER NEEDLE AND THREAD.** Then she and her husband would go to God's house to see Samuel and give him his new clothes. Hannah looked forward all year to those visits with her son. Samuel stayed with Eli and served God as he grew up. And Hannah went home to her other children, for God had answered her prayer even beyond what she had asked. God had blessed her for keeping her promise.

BE A HANNAH

Promises aren't always easy to keep. Hannah's promise to God was very hard for her to keep. But she did it. She knew her promise was important. She knew God wanted her to keep it. God wants you to keep your promises, too. Even when it's hard.

HANNAH KEPT HER PROMISE TO GOD.
THE WHOLE STORY: 1 SAMUEL 1:1-28

Go to page 318 for the next Super Hero

CHEERFUL

HANNAH PRAYED.
SHE SAID,

"THE LORD HAS FILLED
MY HEART WITH JOY.

HE HAS MADE ME
STRONG."
— 1 SAMUEL 2:1 —

STRONG

giving him to the LORD. As long as he lives he'll be given to the LORD." And all of them worshiped the LORD there.

Hannah Gives Thanks to the LORD

2 Then Hannah prayed. She said,

"The LORD has filled my heart with joy.
He has made me strong.
I can laugh at my enemies.
I'm so glad he saved me.

2 "There isn't anyone holy like the LORD.
There isn't anyone except him.
There isn't any Rock like our God.

3 "Don't keep talking so proudly.
Don't let your mouth say such proud things.
The LORD is a God who knows everything.
He judges everything people do.

4 "The bows of great heroes are broken.
But those who trip and fall are made strong.

5 Those who used to be full have to work for food.
But those who used to be hungry aren't hungry anymore.
The woman who couldn't have children has seven of them now.
But the woman who has had many children is sad now because hers have died.

6 "The LORD causes people to die. He also gives people life.
He brings people down to the grave.
He also brings people up.

7 The LORD makes people poor. He also makes people rich.
He brings people down. He also lifts people up.

8 He raises poor people up from the trash pile.
He lifts needy people out of the ashes.
He lets them sit with princes.
He gives them places of honor.

"The foundations of the earth belong to the LORD.
On them he has set the world.

9 He guards the paths of those who are faithful to him.
But evil people will lie silent in their dark graves.

"People don't win just because they are strong.

10 Those who oppose the LORD will be totally destroyed.
He will thunder against them from heaven.
He will judge the earth from one end to the other.

"He will give power to his king.
He will give honor to his anointed one."

11 Then Elkanah went home to Ramah. But the boy Samuel served the LORD under the direction of the priest Eli.

Eli's Evil Sons

12 Eli's sons were evil men. They didn't know the LORD. 13 When anyone came to offer a sacrifice, here is what the priests would do. While the meat was being boiled, the servant of the priest would come with a large fork in his hand. 14 He would stick it into the pan or pot or small or large kettle. Then the priest would take for himself everything the fork brought up. That's how Eli's sons treated all of the people of Israel who came to Shiloh. 15 Even before the fat was burned, the servant of the priest would come over. He would speak to the man who was offering

FAITHFUL ◯

[GOD] GUARDS THE
PATHS OF THOSE WHO
ARE FAITHFUL TO HIM.
— 1 SAMUEL 2:9 —

the sacrifice. He would say, "Give the priest some meat to cook. He won't accept boiled meat from you. All he'll accept is raw meat."

16Sometimes the man would say to him, "Let the fat be burned up first. Then take what you want."

But the servant would answer, "No. Hand it over right now. If you don't, I'll take it away from you by force."

17That sin of Eli's sons was very great in the LORD's sight. That's because they were making fun of his offering.

18But the boy Samuel served the LORD. He wore a sacred linen apron. 19Each year his mother made him a little robe. She took it to him when she went up to Shiloh with her husband. She did it when her husband went to offer the yearly sacrifice.

20Eli would bless Elkanah and his wife. He would say, "May the LORD give you children by this woman. May they take the place of the boy she prayed for and gave to him." Then they would go home.

21The LORD was gracious to Hannah. She became pregnant. Over a period of years she had three more sons and two daughters. During that whole time the boy Samuel grew up serving the LORD.

22Eli was very old. He kept hearing about everything his sons were doing to all of the people of Israel. He also heard how they were sleeping with the women who served at the entrance to the Tent of Meeting.

23So Eli said to his sons, "Why are you doing those things? All of the people are telling me about the evil things you are doing. 24No, my sons. The report I hear isn't good. And it's spreading among the LORD's people. 25If a man sins against someone else, God can help that sinner. But if a man sins against the LORD, who can help him?"

In spite of what their father Eli said, his sons didn't pay any attention to his warning. That's because the LORD had already decided to put them to death.

26The boy Samuel continued to grow stronger. He also became more and more pleasing to the LORD and to people.

A Man of God Prophesies Against Eli's Family

27A man of God came to Eli. He told him, "The LORD says, 'I made myself clearly known to your relatives who lived long ago. I did it when they were in Egypt under Pharaoh. 28I chose your father Aaron to be my priest. I chose him out of all of the tribes of Israel. I told him to go up to my altar. I told him to burn incense. I chose him to wear a linen apron when he served me. I also gave his family all of the offerings that are made with fire by the people of Israel.

29" 'Why do all of you laugh at my sacrifices and offerings? I require them to be brought to the house where I live. Why do you honor your sons more than me? Why do you fatten yourselves on the best parts of every offering that is made by my people Israel?'

30"The LORD is the God of Israel. He announced, 'I promised that your family and the family of Aaron would serve me as priests forever.'

"But now the LORD announces, 'I will not let that happen! I will honor those who honor me. But I will turn away from those who look down on me. 31The time is coming when I will cut your life short. I will also cut short the lives of those in your family. No man in your family line will grow old.

32" 'You will see nothing but trouble in the house where I live. Good things will still happen to Israel. But no man in your family line will ever grow old. 33A member of your family will serve me at my altar. But what he does will bring tears to your eyes. Your heart will be sad. And the rest of the men in your family line will die while they are still young.

34" 'Something is going to happen to your two sons Hophni and Phinehas. When it does, it will show you that what I am saying is true. They will both die on the same day.

35" 'I will raise up for myself a faithful priest. He will do what my heart and mind want him to do. I will make his family line very secure. They will always serve as priests to my anointed king. 36Everyone who is left in your family line will come and bow down to him. They will beg him for a piece of silver and a crust of bread. They will say, "Please give me a place to serve among the priests. Then I can have food to eat." ' "

The LORD Calls Out to Samuel

3 The boy Samuel served the LORD under the direction of Eli. In those days the LORD didn't give many messages to his people. He didn't give them many visions.

2One night Eli was lying down in his usual place. His eyes were becoming so weak he couldn't see very well. 3Samuel was lying down in the LORD's house. That's where the ark of God was kept. The lamp of God was still burning. **4**The Lord called out to Samuel.

Samuel answered, "Here I am." **5**He ran over to Eli. He said, "Here I am. You called out to me."

But Eli said, "I didn't call you. Go back and lie down." So he went and lay down.

6Again the Lord called out, "Samuel!" Samuel got up and went to Eli. He said, "Here I am. You called out to me."

"My son," Eli said, "I didn't call you. Go back and lie down."

7Samuel didn't know the Lord yet. That's because the Lord still hadn't given him a message.

8The Lord called out to Samuel for the third time. Samuel got up and went to Eli. He said, "Here I am. You called out to me."

Then Eli realized that the Lord was calling the boy. **9**So Eli told Samuel, "Go and lie down. If someone calls out to you again, say, 'Speak, Lord. I'm listening.' " So Samuel went and lay down in his place.

10The Lord came and stood there. He called out, just as he had done the other times. He said, "Samuel! Samuel!"

Then Samuel replied, "Speak. I'm listening."

11The Lord said to Samuel, "Pay attention! I am about to do something terrible in Israel. It will make the ears of everyone who hears about it ring.

12"At that time I will do everything to Eli and his family that I said I would. I will finish what I have started. **13**I told Eli I would punish his family forever. He knew his sons were sinning. He knew they were making fun of me. In spite of that, he failed to stop them.

14"So I took an oath and made a promise to the family of Eli. I said, 'The sins of Eli's family will never be paid for by bringing sacrifices or offerings.' "

15Samuel lay down until morning. Then he opened the doors of the Lord's house. He was afraid to tell Eli about the vision he had received. **16**But Eli called out to him. He said, "Samuel, my son."

Samuel answered, "Here I am."

17"What did the Lord say to you?" Eli asked. "Don't hide from me anything he told you. If you do, may God punish you greatly."

18So Samuel told him everything. He didn't hide anything from him.

Then Eli said, "He is the Lord. Let him do what he thinks is best."

19As Samuel grew up, the Lord was with him. He made everything Samuel said come true. **20**So all of the people of Israel recognized that Samuel really was a prophet of the Lord. Everyone from Dan all the way to Beersheba knew it.

21The Lord continued to appear at Shiloh. There he made himself known to Samuel through the messages he gave him.

4 And Samuel gave those messages to all of the people of Israel.

The Philistines Capture the Ark

The people of Israel went out to fight against the Philistines. The Israelites camped at Ebenezer. The Philistines camped at Aphek. **2**The Philistines brought their forces together to fight against Israel. As the fighting spread, the men of Israel lost the battle to the Philistines. The Philistines killed about 4,000 of them on the field of battle.

3The rest of the Israelite soldiers returned to camp. Then the elders asked them, "Why did the Lord let the Philistines win the battle over us today? Let's bring the ark of the Lord's covenant from Shiloh. Let's take it with us. It will save us from the power of our enemies."

4So the people sent men to Shiloh. They brought back the ark of the covenant of the Lord. He sits there on his throne between the cherubim. He is the One who rules over all. Eli's two sons Hophni and Phinehas were with the ark of the covenant of God in Shiloh.

5The ark of the Lord's covenant was brought into the camp. Then all of the people of Israel shouted so loudly that the ground shook.

6The Philistines heard the noise. They asked, "What's all that shouting about in the Hebrew camp?"

Then the Philistines found out that the ark of the Lord had come into the camp. **7**So they were afraid. "A god has come into their camp," they said. "We're in trouble! Nothing like this has ever happened before. **8**How terrible it will be for us! Who will save us from the power of those mighty gods? They struck down the people of Egypt in the desert. They sent all kinds of plagues on them.

9"Philistines, be strong! Fight like men! If you don't, you will come under the control of the Hebrews. You will become their slaves, just as they have been your slaves. Fight like men!"

10So the Philistines fought. The people of Israel lost the battle. Every man ran back to his tent. A large number of them were killed. Israel lost 30,000 soldiers who were on foot.

SAMUEL

1 SAMUEL 3:19-20

As Samuel grew up, the LORD was with him. He made everything Samuel said come true. So all of the people of Israel recognized that Samuel really was a prophet of the LORD.

It was the middle of the night. Samuel sat up on his mat in God's house. He was sure he had heard someone call him. In the light of a lamp, he looked around the room. It was empty. Maybe Eli had called him. Samuel went to Eli's room. He peeked inside. Eli was sleeping, but Samuel woke him and said, "Here I am. You called me." But Eli said, "No, Samuel. I was sleeping. I didn't call you."

Three times Samuel thought he heard Eli calling. The third time, Eli finally realized what was happening. He told Samuel that if he heard the voice calling again, he was to say, "I hear you, Lord. I'm listening."

Samuel walked slowly back to his bed. *What would God want with me?* Samuel thought. *I'm just a boy.* But Samuel obeyed Eli. He went back to his mat. He lay down on his back, pulling his robe around him for warmth. **HE WATCHED THE DANCING SHADOWS MADE BY THE FLAME OF THE LANTERN.** He could still smell the incense that had been burned in God's house that day. He scratched a dry spot on his leg. And he waited. Would God call again?

Just as he started to feel sleepy, Samuel heard the voice. "Samuel. Samuel."

This time he knew how to answer. "I hear you, Lord. I'm listening." God gave Samuel a message. He had important work for Samuel to do.

That was the first message Samuel received from God. But it was not the last. Samuel lived in the house of God when he was a boy until he grew up to be a man. God spoke to the people through Samuel. Everything Samuel told the people came true.

BE A SAMUEL

Is listening hard for you? Would you rather talk or watch TV or run outside to play than listen to someone who's talking to you? Samuel was very young when he learned the importance of *listening*. Today God speaks to his people through the Bible. Are you like Samuel? Are you listening?

SAMUEL LISTENED TO GOD AND OBEYED HIM.
THE WHOLE STORY: 1 SAMUEL 3:1-21

Go to page 331 for the next person

¹¹The ark of God was captured. And Eli's two sons Hophni and Phinehas died.

Eli Dies

¹²That same day a man from the tribe of Benjamin ran from the front lines of the battle. He went to Shiloh. His clothes were torn. He had dust on his head. ¹³When he arrived, there was Eli sitting on his chair. He was by the side of the road. He was watching because his heart was really concerned about the ark of God. The man entered the town and told everyone what had happened. Then the whole town cried out.

¹⁴Eli heard the people crying out. He asked, "What's the meaning of all of this noise?"

The man hurried over to Eli. ¹⁵Eli was 98 years old. His eyes were so bad he couldn't see. ¹⁶The man told Eli, "I've just come from the front lines of the battle. I ran away from there this very day."

Eli asked, "What happened, son?"

¹⁷The man who brought the news replied, "Israel ran away from the Philistines. Large numbers of men in the army were wounded or killed. Your two sons Hophni and Phinehas are also dead. And the ark of God has been captured."

¹⁸When the man spoke about the ark of God, Eli fell backward off his chair. He had been sitting by the side of the gate. When he fell, he broke his neck and died. He was old and fat. He had led Israel for 40 years.

¹⁹The wife of Phinehas was pregnant. She was Eli's daughter-in-law. It was near the time for her baby to be born. She heard the news that the ark of God had been captured. She heard that her father-in-law and her husband were dead. So she went into labor and had her baby. Her pain was so great that her life was slipping away.

²⁰As she was dying, the women who were helping her spoke up. They said, "Don't be afraid. You have had a son." But she didn't reply. She didn't pay any attention.

²¹She named the boy Ichabod. She said, "The God of glory has left Israel." She said it because the ark of God had been captured. She also said it because her father-in-law and her husband had died. ²²She said, "The God of glory has left Israel." She said it because the ark of God had been captured.

The Ark Is Taken to Ashdod and Ekron

5 The Philistines had captured the ark of God. They took it from Ebenezer to Ashdod. ²They carried the ark into the temple of their god Dagon. They set it down beside the statue of Dagon.

³The people of Ashdod got up early the next day. They saw the statue of Dagon. There it was, lying on the ground! It had fallen on its face in front of the ark of the LORD. So they picked the statue of Dagon up. They put it back in its place.

⁴But the following morning when they got up, they saw the statue of Dagon. There it was, lying on the ground again! It had fallen on its face in front of the ark of the LORD. Its head and hands had been broken off. Only the body of the statue was left. Its head and hands were lying in the doorway of the temple. ⁵That's why to this very day no one steps on the bottom part of the doorway of Dagon's temple at Ashdod. Not even the priests of Dagon step there.

⁶The LORD's powerful hand punished the people of Ashdod and the settlements that were near it. He destroyed them. He made them suffer with growths in their bodies.

⁷The people of Ashdod saw what was happening. They said, "The ark of the god of Israel must not stay here with us. His powerful hand is punishing us and our god Dagon."

⁸So they called all of the rulers of the Philistines together. They asked them, "What should we do with the ark of the god of Israel?"

The rulers answered, "Have the ark moved to Gath." So they moved it.

⁹But after the people of Ashdod had moved the ark, the LORD's hand punished Gath. That threw its people into a great panic. The LORD made them break out with growths in their bodies. It happened to young people and old people alike. ¹⁰So the ark of God was sent to Ekron.

As the ark was entering Ekron, the people of the city cried out. They shouted, "They've brought the ark of the god of Israel to us. They want to kill us and our people."

¹¹So they called all of the rulers of the Philistines together. They said, "Send the ark of the god of Israel away. Let it go back to its own place. If you don't, it will kill us and our people." The death of so many people had filled the city with panic. God's powerful hand was punishing the city. ¹²Those who didn't die suffered with

growths in their bodies. The people of Ekron cried out to heaven for help.

The Philistines Return the Ark to Israel

6 The ark of the LORD had been in Philistine territory for seven months. 2The Philistines called for the priests and for those who practice evil magic. They wanted their advice. They said to them, "What should we do with the ark of the LORD? Tell us how we should send it back to its place."

3They answered, "If you return the ark of the god of Israel, don't send it away empty. Be sure you send a guilt offering to their god along with it. Then you will be healed. You will find out why his hand hasn't stopped punishing you."

4The Philistines asked, "What guilt offering should we send to him?"

Their advisers replied, "There are five Philistine rulers. So send five gold models of the growths that are in your bodies. Also send five gold models of rats. Do it because the same plague has struck you and your rulers alike. 5Make models of the growths and of the rats that are destroying the country. Pay honor to Israel's god. Perhaps his hand will stop punishing you. Maybe it will stop punishing your gods and your land.

6"Why are you stubborn, as Pharaoh and the people of Egypt were? God was very hard on them. Only then did they send the people of Israel out. Only then did they let them go on their way.

7"Now then, get a new cart ready. Get two cows that have just had calves. Be sure the cows have never pulled a cart before. Tie the cart to them. But take their calves away and put them in a pen.

8"Then put the ark of the LORD on the cart. Put the gold models in a chest beside the ark. Send them back to the LORD as a guilt offering. Send the cart on its way.

9"But keep an eye on the cart. See if it goes up toward Beth Shemesh to its own territory. If it does, then it's the LORD who has brought this horrible trouble on us. But if it doesn't, then we'll know it wasn't his hand that struck us. We'll know it happened to us by chance."

10So that's what they did. They took the two cows and tied the cart to them. They put the calves in a pen. 11They placed the ark of the LORD on the cart. They put the chest there along with it. The chest held the gold models of the rats and of the growths.

12Then the cows went straight up toward Beth Shemesh. They stayed on the road. They were mooing all the way. They didn't turn to the right or the left. The Philistine rulers followed them all the way to the border of Beth Shemesh.

13The people of Beth Shemesh were working in the valley. They were gathering their wheat crop. They looked up and saw the ark. When they saw it, they were filled with joy.

14The cart came to the field of Joshua of Beth Shemesh. It stopped there beside a large rock. The people chopped up the wood the cart was made out of. They sacrificed the cows as a burnt offering to the LORD.

15Some Levites had taken the ark of the LORD off the cart. They had also taken off the chest that held the gold models. They placed them on the large rock. On that day the people of Beth Shemesh offered burnt offerings to the LORD. They also made sacrifices to him.

16The five Philistine rulers saw everything that happened. On that same day they returned to Ekron.

17The Philistines sent gold models of growths as a guilt offering to the LORD. There was one each for Ashdod, Gaza, Ashkelon, Gath and Ekron. 18They also sent five gold models of rats. There was one for each of the Philistine towns that belonged to the five rulers. Each of those towns had high walls around it. The towns also had country villages around them.

The Levites set the ark of the LORD on a large rock. To this very day the rock gives witness to what happened there. It's in the field of Joshua of Beth Shemesh.

19But some of the people of Beth Shemesh looked into the ark of the LORD. So he struck them down. He put 70 of them to death. The rest of the people were filled with sorrow. That's because the LORD had killed so many of them.

20The people of Beth Shemesh said, "The LORD is a holy God. Who can stand in front of him? Where can the ark go up to from here?"

21Then messengers were sent to the people of Kiriath Jearim. They said, "The Philistines have returned the ark of the LORD. Come down and take it up to your place." 1So the men of Kiriath Jearim

7 came and got the ark of the LORD. They took it up to Abinadab's house on the hill. They set his son Eleazar apart to guard the ark.

Samuel Brings the Philistines Under Israel's Control

2The ark remained at Kiriath Jearim for a long time. It was there for a full 20 years. All of the people of Israel were filled with sorrow. They looked to the LORD for help.

3Samuel spoke to the whole community of Israel. He said, "Do you really want to return to the LORD with all your hearts? If you do, get rid of your strange gods. Get rid of your statues of goddesses that are named after Ashtoreth. Commit yourselves to the LORD. Serve him only. Then he will save you from the powerful hand of the Philistines."

4So the people of Israel put away their statues of gods that were named after Baal. They put away their statues of goddesses named after Ashtoreth. They served the LORD only.

5Then Samuel said, "Gather all of the people of Israel together at Mizpah. I will pray to the LORD for you."

6When the people had come together at Mizpah, they went to the well and got water. They poured it out in the sight of the LORD. On that day they didn't eat any food. They admitted they had sinned. They said, "We've sinned against the LORD." Samuel was the leader of Israel at Mizpah.

7The Philistines heard that Israel had gathered together at Mizpah. So the Philistine rulers came up to attack them. When the people of Israel heard about it, they were afraid. **8**They said to Samuel, "Don't stop crying out to the LORD our God to help us. Keep praying that he'll save us from the powerful hand of the Philistines."

9Then Samuel got a very young lamb. He sacrificed it as a whole burnt offering to the LORD. He cried out to the LORD to help Israel. And the LORD answered his prayer.

10The Philistines came near to attack Israel. At that time Samuel was sacrificing the burnt offering. But that day the LORD thundered loudly against the Philistines. He threw them into such a panic that the Israelites were able to chase them away. **11**The men of Israel rushed out of Mizpah. They chased the Philistines all the way to a point below Beth Car. They killed them all along the way.

12Then Samuel got a big stone. He set it up between Mizpah and Shen. He named it Ebenezer. He said, "The LORD has helped us every step of the way."

13So Samuel brought the Philistines under Israel's control. The Philistines didn't attack their territory again.

The LORD used his powerful hand against the Philistines as long as Samuel lived. **14**The Philistines had captured many towns between Ekron and Gath. But they had to give all of them back. Israel took back the territories near those towns from the powerful hand of the Philistines.

During that time Israel and the Amorites were friendly toward each other.

15Samuel continued to lead Israel all the days of his life. **16**From year to year he traveled from Bethel to Gilgal to Mizpah. He served Israel as judge in all of those places. **17**But he always went back to Ramah. That's where his home was. He served Israel as judge there too. And he built an altar there to honor the LORD.

Israel Asks Samuel for a King

8 When Samuel became old, he appointed his sons to serve as judges for Israel. **2**The name of his oldest son was Joel. The name of his second son was Abijah. They served as judges at Beersheba. **3**But his sons didn't live as he did. They were only interested in making money. They accepted money from people who wanted special favors. They made things that were wrong appear to be right.

4So all of the elders of Israel gathered together. They came to Samuel at Ramah. **5**They said to him, "You are old. Your sons don't live as you do. So appoint a king to lead us. We want a king just like the kings all of the other nations have."

6Samuel wasn't pleased when they said, "Give us a king to lead us." So he prayed to the LORD. **7**The LORD told him, "Listen to everything the people are saying to you. You are not the one they have turned their backs on. I am the one they do not want as their king. **8**They are doing just as they have always done. They have deserted me and served other gods. They have done that from the time I brought them up out of Egypt until this very day. Now they are deserting you too.

9"Let them have what they want. But give them a strong warning. Let them know what the king who rules over them will do."

10Samuel told the people who were asking him for a king everything the LORD had said. **11**Samuel told them, "Here's what the king who rules over you will do. He will take your sons. He'll make them serve with his chariots and horses. They will run in front of his chariots. 12He'll choose some of your sons to be commanders of thousands of men. Some will be commanders of fifties. Others will have to plow his fields and gather his crops. Still others will have to make weapons of war and parts for his chariots. 13"He'll also take your daughters. Some will have to make perfume. Others will be forced to cook and bake. 14"He will take away your best fields and vineyards and olive groves. He'll give them to his attendants. 15He will take a tenth of your grain and a tenth of your grapes. He'll give it to his officials and attendants. 16He will also take your male and female servants. He'll take your best cattle and donkeys. He'll use all of them any way he wants to. 17"He will take a tenth of your sheep and goats. You yourselves will become his slaves. 18"When that time comes, you will cry out for help because of the king you have chosen. But the LORD won't answer you at that time." 19In spite of what Samuel said, the people refused to listen to him. "No!" they said. "We want a king to rule over us. 20Then we'll be like all of the other nations. We'll have a king to lead us. He'll go out at the head of our armies and fight our battles." 21Samuel heard everything the people said. He told the LORD about it. 22The LORD answered, "Listen to them. Give them a king."

Then Samuel said to the men of Israel, "Each of you go back to your own town."

Samuel Anoints Saul to Be Israel's Leader

9 There was a man named Kish from the tribe of Benjamin. Kish was a very important person. He was the son of Abiel, the son of Zeror. Zeror was the son of Becorath, the son of Aphiah from the tribe of Benjamin. 2Kish had a son named Saul. Saul was a handsome young man. There wasn't anyone like him among the people of Israel. He was a head taller than any of them.

3The donkeys that belonged to Saul's father Kish were lost. So Kish spoke to his son Saul. He said, "Go and look for the donkeys. Take one of the servants with you." 4Saul and his servant went through the hill country of Ephraim. They also went through the area around Shalisha. But they didn't find the donkeys. So they went on into the area of Shaalim. But the donkeys weren't there either. Then Saul went through the territory of Benjamin. But they still didn't find the donkeys.

5When Saul and the servant who was with him reached the area of Zuph, Saul spoke to him. He said, "Come on. Let's go back. If we don't, my father will stop thinking about the donkeys and start worrying about us."

6But the servant replied, "There's a man of God here in Ramah. People have a lot of respect for him. Everything he says comes true. So let's go and see him now. Perhaps he'll tell us which way to go."

7Saul said to his servant, "If we go to see the man, what can we give him? There isn't any food in our sacks. We don't have a gift for the man of God. So what can we give him?"

8The servant answered Saul again. "Look," he said. "I've got a tenth of an ounce of silver. I'll give it to the man of God. Then maybe he'll tell us which way to go."

9In Israel, prophets used to be called seers. So if a man wanted to ask God for advice, he would say, "Come on. Let's go to the seer."

10Saul said to his servant, "That's a good idea. Come on. Let's go and ask the seer." So they started out for the town where the man of God lived.

11They were going up the hill toward the town. Along the way they met some young women who were coming out to get water from the well. Saul and his servant asked them, "Is the seer here?"

12"Yes, he is," they answered. "In fact, he's just up ahead of you. So hurry along. He has just come to our town today. The people are going to offer a sacrifice at the high place where they worship. 13As soon as you enter the town, you will find him. He'll be there until he goes up to the high place to eat. The people won't start eating until he gets there. He must bless the sacrifice first. After that, those who are invited will eat. So go on up. You should find him there just about now."

14They went up to the town. As they were entering it, they saw Samuel. He was coming toward them. He was on his way up to the high place.

15The LORD had spoken to Samuel the day before Saul came. He had said, 16"About this time tomorrow I will send you a man. He is from the land of Benjamin. Anoint him to be the leader of my people Israel. He will save them from the powerful hand of the Philistines. I have seen how much my people are suffering. Their cry for help has reached me."

17When Samuel saw a man coming toward him, the LORD spoke to Samuel again. He said, "He is the man I told you about. His name is Saul. He will govern my people."

18Saul approached Samuel at the gate of the town. He asked Samuel, "Can you please show me the house where the seer is staying?"

19"I'm the seer," Samuel replied. "Go on up to the high place ahead of me. I want you and your servant to eat with me today. Tomorrow morning I'll tell you what's on your mind. Then I'll let you go. **20**Don't worry about the donkeys you lost three days ago. They've already been found. But who are all of the people of Israel longing for? You and your father's whole family!"

21Saul answered, "But I'm from the tribe of Benjamin. It's the smallest tribe in Israel. And my family group is the least important in the whole tribe of Benjamin. So why are you saying that to me?"

22Then Samuel brought Saul and his servant into the room where they would be eating. He seated them at the head table. About 30 people had been invited. **23**Samuel said to the cook, "Bring the piece of meat I gave you. It's the one I told you to put to one side."

24So the cook went and got a choice piece of thigh. He set it in front of Saul. Samuel said, "Here is what has been kept for you. Eat it. It was put to one side for you for this special occasion. We've saved it for you ever since I invited the guests." And Saul ate with Samuel that day.

25They came down from the high place to the town. After that, Samuel talked with Saul on the roof of Samuel's house. **26**The next day they got up at about the time the sun was rising. Samuel called out to Saul on the roof. He said, "Get ready. Then I'll send you on your way." So Saul got ready. And he and Samuel went outside together.

27As they were on their way down to the edge of town, Samuel spoke to Saul. He said, "Tell the servant to go ahead of us." So the servant went on ahead. Then Samuel continued, "Stay here awhile. I'll give you a message from God."

10 Then Samuel took a bottle of olive oil. He poured it on Saul's head and kissed him. He said, "The LORD has anointed you to be the leader of his people. **2**When you leave me today, you will meet two men. They will be near Rachel's tomb at Zelzah on the border of Benjamin. They'll say to you, 'The donkeys you have been looking for have been found. Now your father has stopped thinking about them. Instead, he's worried about you. He's asking, "What can I do to find my son?" '

3"You will go on from Zelzah until you come to the large tree at Tabor. Three men will meet you there. They'll be on their way up to Bethel to worship God. One of them will be carrying three young goats. Another will be carrying three loaves of bread. A third will be carrying a bottle of wine. It will be a bottle that is made out of animal skin. **4**The men will greet you. They'll offer you two loaves of bread. You will accept the loaves from them.

5"After that, you will go to Gibeah of God. Some Philistine soldiers are stationed there. As you approach the town, you will meet a group of prophets. They'll be coming down from the high place where they worship. People will be playing lyres, tambourines, flutes and harps at the head of the group. The prophets will be prophesying. **6**The Spirit of the LORD will come on you with power. Then you will prophesy along with them. You will become a different person.

7"All of those things will happen. Then do what you want to do. God is with you.

8"Go down ahead of me to Gilgal. You can be sure that I'll come down to you there. I'll come and sacrifice burnt offerings and friendship offerings. But you must wait there for seven days until I come to you. Then I'll tell you what to do."

Saul Is Made King of Israel

9As Saul turned to leave Samuel, God changed Saul's heart. All of those things happened that day. **10**When Saul and his servant arrived at Gibeah, a group of prophets met Saul. Then the Spirit of God came on him with power. He prophesied along with them. **11**Those who had

POWER–SURGE

STRONG

THE SPIRIT OF GOD CAME ON [SAUL] WITH POWER. HE PROPHESIED.
—— **1 SAMUEL 10:10** ——

known Saul before saw him prophesying with the prophets. They asked one another, "What has happened to the son of Kish? Is Saul also one of the prophets?"

12A man who lived in Gibeah answered, "Yes, he is. In fact, he's their leader." That's why people say, "Is Saul also one of the prophets?"

13After Saul stopped prophesying, he went to the high place to worship.

14Later, Saul's uncle spoke to him and his servant. He asked, "Where have you been?"

"Looking for the donkeys," he said. "But we couldn't find them. So we went to Samuel."

15Saul's uncle said, "Tell me what Samuel said to you."

16Saul replied, "He told us the donkeys had been found." But Saul didn't tell his uncle that Samuel had said he would become king.

17Samuel sent a message to the people of Israel. He told them to meet with the LORD at Mizpah. 18He said to them, "The LORD is the God of Israel. He says, 'Israel, I brought you up out of Egypt. I saved you from their powerful hand. I also saved you from the powerful hand of all of the kingdoms that had beaten you down.'

19"But now you have turned your backs on your God. He saves you out of all of your trouble and suffering. In spite of that, you have said, 'We refuse to listen. Place a king over us.'

"So now gather together to meet with the LORD. Do it tribe by tribe and family group by family group."

20Then Samuel had each tribe of Israel come forward. The tribe of Benjamin was chosen. 21Next he had the tribe of Benjamin come forward, family group by family group. Matri's group was chosen. Finally Saul, the son of Kish, was chosen. But when people looked for him, they realized he wasn't there. 22They needed more help from the LORD. So they asked him, "Has the man come here yet?"

The LORD said, "Yes. He has hidden himself among the supplies."

23So they ran over there and brought him out. When he stood up, the people saw that he was a head taller than any of them.

24Samuel spoke to all of the people. He said, "Look at the man the LORD has chosen! There isn't anyone like him among all of the people."

Then the people shouted, "May the king live a long time!"

25Samuel explained to the people what the king who ruled over them should do. He wrote it down on a scroll. He placed it in front of the LORD in the holy tent. Then he sent the people away. He sent each of them to their own homes.

26Saul also went to his home in Gibeah. Some brave men whose hearts God had touched went with Saul.

27But some evil people who wanted to stir up trouble said, "How can this fellow save us?" They looked down on him. They didn't bring him any gifts. But Saul kept quiet about it.

Saul Saves the City of Jabesh Gilead

11 Nahash was the king of Ammon. He and his army went up to Jabesh Gilead. They surrounded it and got ready to attack it. All of the men of Jabesh spoke to Nahash. They said, "Make a peace treaty with us. Then we'll be under your control."

2Nahash, the king of Ammon, replied, "I will make a peace treaty with you. But I'll do it only on one condition. You must let me put out the right eye of every one of you. I want to bring shame on the whole nation of Israel."

3The elders of Jabesh said to him, "Give us seven days to report back to you. We'll send messengers all through Israel. If no one comes to save us, we'll hand ourselves over to you."

4The messengers came to Gibeah of Saul. They reported to the people the terms Nahash had required. Then all of the people sobbed out loud.

5Just then Saul was coming in from the fields. He was walking behind his oxen. He asked, "What's wrong with the people? Why are they sobbing?" He was told what the men of Jabesh had said.

6When Saul heard their words, the Spirit of God came on him with power. He burned with anger. 7He got a pair of oxen and cut them into pieces. He sent the pieces by messengers all through Israel. They announced, "You must follow Saul and Samuel. If you don't, this is what will happen to your oxen."

The terror of the LORD fell on the people. So all of them came together with one purpose in mind.

8Saul brought his army together at Bezek. There were 300,000 men from Israel and 30,000 from Judah.

9The messengers who had come were told, "Go back and report to the men of Jabesh Gilead. Tell them, 'By the hottest time of the day tomorrow, you will be saved.' "

The messengers went and reported it to the men of Jabesh. It made those men very happy. [10]They said to the people of Ammon, "Tomorrow we'll hand ourselves over to you. Then you can do to us what seems best to you."

[11]The next day Saul separated his men into three groups. While it was still dark, they broke into the camp of the Ammonite army. They kept killing the men of Ammon until the hottest time of the day. Those who got away alive were scattered. There weren't two of them left together anywhere.

The People Agree to Have Saul as King

[12]The people said to Samuel, "Who asked, 'Is Saul going to rule over us?' Bring those people to us. We'll put them to death."

[13]But Saul said, "We won't put anyone to death today! After all, this is the day the LORD has saved Israel."

[14]Then Samuel said to the people, "Come on. Let's go to Gilgal. There we'll agree to have Saul as our king."

[15]So all of the people went to Gilgal. There, with the LORD as witness, they agreed to have Saul as their king. There they sacrificed friendship offerings to the LORD. And there Saul and all of the people of Israel celebrated with great joy.

Samuel Tells Israel to Serve the LORD

12 Samuel spoke to all of the people of Israel. He said, "I've done everything you asked me to do. I've placed a king over you. [2]Now you have a king as your leader. But I'm old. My hair is gray. My sons are here with you. I've been your leader from the time I was young until this very day.

[3]"Here I stand. Bring charges against me if you can. The LORD is a witness. And so is his anointed king. Whose ox have I taken? Whose donkey have I taken? Have I cheated anyone? Have I beaten anyone down? Have I accepted money from anyone who wanted special favors? If I've done any of those things, I'll make it right."

[4]"You haven't cheated us," they replied. "You haven't beaten us down. You haven't taken anything from anyone."

[5]Samuel said to them, "The LORD is a witness against you this very day. And so is his anointed king. They are witnesses

that I haven't taken anything from any of you."

"The LORD is a witness," they said.

[6]Then Samuel said to the people, "The LORD appointed Moses and Aaron. He brought up out of Egypt your people who lived long ago. [7]Now then, stand here. I'm going to remind you of all of the good things the LORD has done for you and your people. He is a witness.

[8]"After Jacob's family entered Egypt, they cried out to the LORD for help. The LORD sent Moses and Aaron. They brought your people out of Egypt. They settled them in this land.

[9]"But the people forgot the LORD their God. So he gave them over to the powerful hand of Sisera. Sisera was the commander of the army of Hazor. The LORD also gave the people of Israel over to the powerful hand of the Philistines and the king of Moab. All of those nations fought against Israel.

[10]"So the people cried out to the LORD. They said, 'We have sinned. We've deserted the LORD. We've served the gods that are named after Baal. We've served the goddesses that are named after Ashtoreth. But save us now from the powerful hands of our enemies. Then we will serve you.'

[11]"The LORD sent Gideon, Barak, Jephthah and me. He saved you from the hands of your enemies, who were all around you. So you lived in safety.

[12]"But then you saw that Nahash, the king of Ammon, was about to attack you. So you said to me, 'No! We want a king to rule over us.' You said it even though the LORD your God was your king. [13]Now here is the king you have chosen. He's the one you asked for. The LORD has placed a king over you.

[14]"But you must have respect for the LORD. You must serve him and obey him.

POWER-SURGE

OBEYS ✔

YOU MUST HAVE RESPECT FOR THE LORD. YOU MUST SERVE HIM AND OBEY HIM. YOU MUST NOT SAY NO TO HIS COMMANDS.
— **1 SAMUEL 12:14** —

You must not say no to his commands. Both you and the king who rules over you must follow the LORD your God. If you do, that's good. **15**But you must not disobey him. You must not say no to his commands. If you do, his powerful hand will punish you. That's what happened to your people who lived before you.

16"So stand still. Watch the great thing the LORD is about to do right here in front of you! **17**It's time to gather in the wheat, isn't it? I'll call out to the LORD to send thunder and rain. Then you will realize what an evil thing you did in the sight of the LORD. You shouldn't have asked for a king."

18Samuel called out to the LORD. That same day the LORD sent thunder and rain. So all of the people had great respect for the LORD and for Samuel.

19They said to Samuel, "Pray to the LORD your God for us. Pray that we won't die because we asked for a king. That was an evil thing to do. We added it to all of our other sins."

20"Don't be afraid," Samuel replied. "It's true that you have done all of those evil things. But don't turn away from the LORD. Serve him with all your heart.

21"Don't turn away and worship statues of gods. They are useless. They can't do you any good. They can't save you either. They are completely useless.

22"But the LORD will be true to his great name. He won't turn his back on his people. That's because he was pleased to make you his own people.

23"I would never sin against the LORD by failing to pray for you. I'll teach you to live in a way that is good and right.

24"But be sure to have respect for the LORD. Serve him faithfully. Do it with all your heart. Think about the great things he has done for you. **25**But don't be stubborn. Don't continue to do what is evil. If you do, both you and your king will be swept away."

Saul Refuses to Obey the LORD's Command

13 Saul was 30 years old when he became king. He ruled over Israel for 42 years.

2He chose 3,000 of Israel's men. Two thousand of them were with him at Micmash and in the hill country of Bethel. One thousand were with Jonathan at Gibeah in the land of Benjamin. Saul sent the rest back to their homes.

3Some Philistine soldiers were sta-tioned at Geba. Jonathan attacked them. The other Philistines heard about it.

Saul announced, "Let the Hebrew peo-ple hear about what has happened!" He had trumpets blown all through the land. **4**So all of the people of Israel heard the news. They were told, "Saul has attacked the Philistine army camp at Geba. He has made Israel smell very bad to the Philis-tines." The people of Israel were called out to join Saul at Gilgal.

5The Philistines gathered together to fight against Israel. They had 3,000 chari-ots and 6,000 chariot drivers. Their sol-diers were as many as the grains of sand on the seashore. They went up and camped at Micmash. It was east of Beth Aven.

6The men of Israel saw that their army was in deep trouble. So they hid in caves and bushes. They hid among the rocks. They hid in pits and empty wells. **7**Some of them even went across the Jordan Riv-er. They went to the lands of Gad and Gil-ead.

Saul remained at Gilgal. All of the troops who were with him were shaking with fear. **8**He waited seven days, just as Samuel had told him to. But Samuel didn't come to Gilgal. And Saul's men began to scatter. **9**So he said, "Bring me the burnt offering and the friendship offerings." Then he offered up the burnt offering.

10Just as Saul finished offering the sacri-fice, Samuel arrived. Saul went out to greet him.

11"What have you done?" asked Sam-uel.

Saul replied, "I saw that the men were scattering. I saw that the Philistines were gathering together at Micmash. You didn't come when you said you would. **12**So I thought, 'Now the Philistines will come down to attack me at Gilgal. And I haven't asked the LORD to show us his favor.' So I felt I had to sacrifice the burnt offering."

13"You did a foolish thing," Samuel said. "You haven't obeyed the command the LORD your God gave you. If you had, he would have made your kingdom secure over Israel for all time to come. **14**But now your kingdom won't last. The LORD has already looked for a man who is dear to his heart. He has appointed him leader of his people. That's because you haven't obeyed the LORD's command."

15Then Samuel left Gilgal and went up to Gibeah in the land of Benjamin. Saul counted the men who stayed with him. The total number was about 600.

Israel Doesn't Have Swords or Spears

16Saul and his son Jonathan were staying in Gibeah in the land of Benjamin. What was left of the army was there with them. At the same time, the Philistines camped at Micmash.

17Three groups of soldiers went out from the Philistine camp to attack Israel. One group turned and went toward Ophrah in the area of Shual. **18**Another went toward Beth Horon. The third went toward the border that looked out over the Valley of Zeboim. That valley faces the desert.

19There weren't any blacksmiths in the whole land of Israel. That's because the Philistines had said, "The Hebrews might hire them to make swords or spears!" **20**So all of the people of Israel had to go down to the Philistines. They had to go to them to get their plows, hoes, axes and sickles sharpened. **21**It cost a fourth of an ounce of silver to sharpen a plow or a hoe. It cost an eighth of an ounce to sharpen a pitchfork or an axe. That's also what it cost to put new tips on large sticks that were used to drive oxen.

22So not one of Saul's or Jonathan's soldiers had a sword or spear in his hand when he went out to battle. Only Saul and his son Jonathan had those weapons.

Jonathan Attacks the Philistines

23A group of Philistine soldiers had gone out to the pass at Micmash. **14** **1**One day Jonathan, the son of Saul, spoke to the young man who was carrying his armor. "Come on," he said. "Let's go over to the Philistine army camp on the other side of the pass." But he didn't tell his father about it.

2Saul was staying just outside Gibeah. He was under a pomegranate tree in Migron. He had about 600 men with him. **3**Ahijah was one of them. He was wearing a sacred linen apron. He was a son of Ichabod's brother Ahitub. Ahitub was the son of Eli's son Phinehas. Eli had been the LORD's priest in Shiloh. No one was aware that Jonathan had left.

4Jonathan planned to go across the pass to reach the Philistine camp. But there was a cliff on each side of the pass. One cliff was called Bozez. The other was called Seneh. **5**One cliff stood on the north side of the pass toward Micmash. The other stood on the south side toward Geba.

6Jonathan spoke to the young man who was carrying his armor. He said, "Come on. Let's go over to the camp of those fellows who aren't circumcised. Perhaps the LORD will help us. If he does, it won't matter how many or how few of us there are. That won't keep the LORD from saving us."

7"Go ahead," the young man said. "Do everything you have in mind. I'm with you all the way."

8Jonathan said, "Come on, then. We'll go across the pass toward the Philistines and let them see us. **9**Suppose they say to us, 'Wait there until we come to you.' Then we'll stay where we are. We won't go up to them. **10**But suppose they say, 'Come up to us.' Then we'll climb up. That will show us that the LORD has handed them over to us."

11So Jonathan and the young man let the soldiers in the Philistine camp see them. "Look!" said the Philistines. "Some of the Hebrews are crawling out of the holes they were hiding in."

12The men in the Philistine camp shouted to Jonathan and the young man who was carrying his armor. They said, "Come on up here. We'll teach you a thing or two."

So Jonathan said to the young man, "Climb up after me. The LORD has handed them over to Israel."

13Using his hands and feet, Jonathan climbed up. The young man was right behind him. Jonathan struck the Philistines down. The young man followed him and killed those who were still alive. **14**In that first attack, Jonathan and the young man killed about 20 men. They did it in an area of about half an acre.

Israel Chases the Philistines Away

15Then panic struck the whole Philistine army. It struck those who were in the camp and the field. It struck those who were at the edge of the camp. It also struck those who were in the groups that had been sent out to attack Israel. The ground shook. It was a panic that God had sent.

16Saul's lookouts at Gibeah in the land of Benjamin saw what was happening. They saw the Philistine army melting away in all directions.

17Then Saul spoke to the men who were with him. He said, "Bring the troops together. See who has left our camp." When they did, they discovered that Jonathan and the young man who was carrying his armor weren't there.

¹⁸Saul said to the priest Ahijah, "Bring the ark of God." At that time it was with the people of Israel.

¹⁹While Saul was talking to the priest, the noise in the Philistine camp increased more and more. So Saul said to him, "Stop what you are doing."

²⁰Then Saul and all of his men gathered together. They went to the battle. They saw that the Philistines were in total disorder. They were striking each other with their swords.

²¹At an earlier time some of the Hebrews had been on the side of the Philistines. They had gone up with them to their camp. But now they changed sides. They joined the people of Israel who were with Saul and Jonathan.

²²Some of the people had hidden in the hill country of Ephraim. They heard that the Philistines were running away. They quickly joined the battle and chased after them.

²³So the LORD saved Israel that day. And the fighting continued on past Beth Aven.

Jonathan Eats Honey

²⁴The men of Israel became very hungry that day. That's because Saul had put the army under an oath. He had said, "None of you must eat any food before evening comes. You must not eat until I've paid my enemies back for what they did. If you do, may you be under a curse!" So none of the troops ate any food at all.

²⁵The whole army entered the woods. There was honey on the ground. ²⁶When they went into the woods, they saw the honey dripping out of a honeycomb. No one put any of the honey in his mouth. That's because they were afraid of the oath.

²⁷But Jonathan hadn't heard that his father had put the army under an oath. Jonathan had a long stick in his hand. He reached out and dipped the end of it into the honeycomb. He put some honey in his mouth. It gave him new life.

²⁸Then one of the soldiers told him, "Your father put the army under a strong oath. He said, 'None of you must eat any food today. If you do, may you be under a curse!' That's why the men are weak and ready to faint."

²⁹Jonathan said, "My father has made trouble for the country. See how I gained new life after I tasted a little of this honey. ³⁰Our soldiers took food from their enemies today. Suppose they had eaten some of it. How much better off they would have been! Even more Philistines would have been killed."

³¹That day the men of Israel struck the Philistines down. They killed them from Micmash to Aijalon. By that time they were tired and worn out. ³²They grabbed what they had taken from their enemies. They killed some of the sheep, cattle and calves right there on the ground. They ate the meat while the blood was still in it.

³³Then someone said to Saul, "Look! The men are sinning against the LORD. They're eating meat that still has blood in it."

Saul said to them, "You have broken your promise. Roll a large stone over here at once." ³⁴He continued, "Go out among the men. Tell them, 'Each of you bring me your cattle and sheep. Kill them here and eat them. Don't sin against the LORD by eating meat that still has blood in it.' "

So that night everyone brought the ox he had taken and killed it there.

³⁵Then Saul built an altar to honor the LORD. It was the first time he had done that.

³⁶Saul said, "Let's go down after the Philistines tonight. Let's not leave even one of them alive. Let's take everything they have before it gets light."

"Do what you think is best," they replied.

But the priest said, "Let's ask God for advice first."

³⁷So Saul asked God, "Should I go down after the Philistines? Will you hand them over to Israel?" But God didn't answer him that day.

³⁸Saul said to the leaders of the army, "Come here. Let's find out what sin has been committed today. ³⁹You can be sure that the LORD who saves Israel lives. And you can be just as sure that the sinner must die. He must die even if he's my son Jonathan." But no one said anything.

⁴⁰Then Saul spoke to all of Israel's men. He said, "You stand over there. I and my son Jonathan will stand over here."

"Do what you think is best," the men replied.

⁴¹Then Saul prayed to the LORD, the God of Israel. He said, "Give me an answer." Jonathan and Saul were chosen by using lots. The other men were cleared of blame.

⁴²Saul said, "Cast the lot to find out whether I or my son Jonathan is to blame." And Jonathan was chosen.

⁴³Then Saul said to Jonathan, "Tell me what you have done."

So Jonathan told him, "I only used the end of my stick to get a little honey and taste it. And now do I have to die?"

⁴⁴Saul said, "Jonathan, I must certainly put you to death. If I don't, may God punish me greatly."

⁴⁵But the men said to Saul, "Should Jonathan be put to death? Never! He has saved Israel in a wonderful way. He did it today with God's help. You can be sure that the LORD lives. And you can be just as sure that not even one hair on Jonathan's head will fall to the ground." So the men saved Jonathan. He wasn't put to death.

⁴⁶Then Saul stopped chasing the Philistines. They went back to their own land.

⁴⁷After Saul's kingdom was set firmly in place in Israel, he fought against their enemies who were all around them. He went to war against Moab, Ammon and Edom. He fought against the kings of Zobah and the Philistines. No matter where he went, he punished his enemies. ⁴⁸He fought bravely. He won the battle over the Amalekites. He saved Israel from the power of those who had carried off what belonged to Israel.

Saul's Family

⁴⁹Saul's sons were Jonathan, Ishvi and Malki-Shua. His older daughter was named Merab. His younger daughter was named Michal. ⁵⁰Saul's wife was named Ahinoam. She was the daughter of Ahimaaz.

The commander of Saul's army was named Abner. He was the son of Ner. Ner was Saul's uncle. ⁵¹Saul's father Kish and Abner's father Ner were sons of Abiel.

POWER-SURGE

BRAVE B

AS LONG AS SAUL WAS KING, HE HAD TO FIGHT HARD AGAINST THE PHILISTINES. SO EVERY TIME SAUL SAW A STRONG OR BRAVE MAN, HE TOOK HIM INTO HIS ARMY.
— 1 SAMUEL 14:52 —

STRONG

⁵²As long as Saul was king, he had to fight hard against the Philistines. So every time Saul saw a strong or brave man, he took him into his army.

The LORD Is Sorry He Has Made Saul King

15 Samuel said to Saul, "The LORD sent me to anoint you as king over his people Israel. So listen now to a message from him. ²The LORD who rules over all says, 'I will punish the Amalekites because of what they did to Israel. As the people of Israel came up from Egypt, the Amalekites attacked them.

³" 'Now go. Attack the Amalekites. Set everything apart that belongs to them. Set it apart to me in a special way to be destroyed. Do not spare the Amalekites. Put the men and women to death. Put the children and babies to death. Also kill the cattle, sheep, camels and donkeys.' "

⁴So Saul brought his men together at Telaim. The total number was 200,000 soldiers on foot from Israel and 10,000 men from Judah. ⁵He went to the city of Amalek. He had some of his men hide and wait in the valley.

⁶Then Saul said to the Kenites, "You were kind to all of the people of Israel when they came up out of Egypt. Get away from the Amalekites. Then I won't have to destroy you along with them." So the Kenites moved away from the Amalekites.

⁷Saul attacked the Amalekites. He struck them down all the way from Havilah to Shur. Shur was near the eastern border of Egypt. ⁸He took Agag, the king of the Amalekites, alive. He and his men totally destroyed all of Agag's people with swords.

⁹But Saul and the army spared Agag. They spared the best of the sheep and cattle. They spared the fat calves and lambs. They spared everything that was valuable. They weren't willing to completely destroy any of those things. But they totally destroyed everything that was worthless and weak.

¹⁰Then the LORD gave Samuel a message. He said, ¹¹"I am very sorry I have made Saul king. He has turned away from me. He has not done what I directed him to do."

When Samuel heard that, he was troubled. He cried out to the LORD during that whole night.

¹²Early the next morning Samuel got up. He went to see Saul. But Samuel was told, "Saul went to Carmel. There he set

up a monument in his own honor. Now he has gone on down to Gilgal."

13When Samuel got there, Saul said, "May the LORD bless you. I've done what he directed me to do."

14But Samuel said, "Then why do I hear the baaing of sheep? Why do I hear the mooing of cattle?"

15Saul answered, "The soldiers brought them from the Amalekites. They spared the best of the sheep and cattle. They did it to sacrifice them to the LORD your God. But we totally destroyed everything else."

16"Stop!" Samuel said to Saul. "Let me tell you what the LORD said to me last night."

"Tell me," Saul replied.

17Samuel said, "There was a time when you didn't think you were important. But you became the leader of the tribes of Israel. The LORD anointed you to be king over Israel. **18**He sent you to do something for him. He said, 'Go and set the Amalekites apart. Set those sinful people apart to me in a special way to be destroyed. Fight against them until you have wiped them out.'

19"Why didn't you obey the LORD? Why did you grab what you had taken from your enemies? Why did you do what is evil in the sight of the LORD?"

20"But I did obey the LORD," Saul said. "I went to do what he sent me to do. I totally destroyed the Amalekites. I brought back Agag, their king. **21**The soldiers took sheep and cattle from what had been taken from our enemies. They took the best of what had been set apart to God. They wanted to sacrifice them to the LORD your God at Gilgal."

22But Samuel replied,

"What pleases the LORD more?
　Burnt offerings and sacrifices, or
　　obeying him?
It is better to obey than to offer a
　sacrifice.
　It is better to do what he says than to
　　offer the fat of rams.
23Refusing to obey him is as sinful as
　using evil magic.
　Being proud is as evil as worshiping
　　statues of gods.
You have refused to do what the LORD
　told you to do.
　So he has refused to have you as
　　king."

24Then Saul said to Samuel, "I have sinned. I've broken the LORD's command. I haven't done what you directed me to do. I was afraid of the people. So I did

what they said I should do. **25**Now I beg you, forgive my sin. Come back into town with me so I can worship the LORD."

26But Samuel said to him, "I won't go back with you. You have refused to do what the LORD told you to do. So he has refused to have you as king over Israel!"

27Samuel turned to leave. But Saul grabbed hold of the hem of his robe, and it tore.

28Samuel said to Saul, "The LORD has torn the kingdom of Israel away from you today. He has given it to one of your neighbors. He has given it to someone who is better than you. **29**The One who is the Glory of Israel does not lie. He doesn't change his mind. That's because he isn't a mere man. If he were, he might change his mind."

30Saul replied, "I have sinned. But please honor me in front of the elders of my people and in front of Israel. Come back with me so I can worship the LORD your God."

31So Samuel went back with Saul. And Saul worshiped the LORD.

32Then Samuel said, "Bring me Agag, the king of the Amalekites."

Agag wasn't afraid when he came to Samuel. He thought, "The time for me to be put to death must have passed by now."

33But Samuel said,

"Your sword has killed the children of
　other women.
　So the child of your mother will be
　　killed."

Samuel put Agag to death at Gilgal in the sight of the LORD.

34Then Samuel left to go to Ramah. But Saul went up to his home in Gibeah of Saul. **35**Until the day Samuel died, he didn't go to see Saul again. Samuel was filled with sorrow because of Saul. And the LORD was very sorry he had made Saul king over Israel.

Samuel Anoints David to Be Israel's King

16 The LORD said to Samuel, "How long will you be filled with sorrow because of Saul? I have refused to have him as king over Israel. Fill your animal horn with olive oil and go on your way. I am sending you to Jesse in Bethlehem. I have chosen one of his sons to be king."

2But Samuel said, "How can I go? Saul will hear about it. Then he'll kill me."

The LORD said, "Take a young cow with

you. Tell the elders of Bethlehem, 'I've come to offer a sacrifice to the LORD.' ³Invite Jesse to the sacrifice. Then I will show you what to do. You must anoint for me the one I point out to you."

⁴Samuel did what the LORD said. He arrived at Bethlehem. The elders of the town met him. They were trembling with fear. They asked, "Have you come in peace?"

⁵Samuel replied, "Yes, I've come in peace. I've come to offer a sacrifice to the

SAUL

[Not!]

1 SAMUEL 15:22

What pleases the LORD more? Burnt offerings and sacrifices, or obeying him? It is better to obey than to offer a sacrifice.

Sheep and cows surrounded King Saul's soldiers. Dirt and sweat covered the soldiers. Their clothes were torn and bloody. But their eyes gleamed because they had won the battle. The soldiers took the animals from the Amalekites when they won the battle. They kept only the best animals to sacrifice to God. They killed all the rest.

King Saul stood tall and strong with his soldiers as the prophet Samuel walked toward him. "Welcome, Samuel," Saul greeted him proudly. **"WE WON THE BATTLE!** I did as God told me."

But Samuel didn't seem pleased. "If you've done as God commanded, what are all these animals? Didn't God tell you to destroy *everything?*"

"Oh, well," Saul said, "we saved the best of the animals to sacrifice to God to show how thankful we are for his help."

But that didn't satisfy the prophet Samuel. "Do you think God would rather have sacrifices than obedience? No! He wanted you to obey, and you didn't. Today your rule over Israel is taken away and given to someone else."

SAUL

Saul seemed to think it was OK to disobey God if what he was doing was something good, like sacrificing to him. You can learn an important lesson from Saul. Obey God above *everything,* even things you think are good or things that honor him. Obedience is more important than anything.

SAUL DISOBEYED GOD, EVEN THOUGH WHAT HE DID SEEMED GOOD TO HIM.

Go to page 333 for the next person

LORD. Set yourselves apart to him and come to the sacrifice with me."

Then he set Jesse and his sons apart to the LORD. He invited them to the sacrifice.

⁶When they arrived, Samuel saw Eliab. He thought, "This has to be the one the LORD wants me to anoint for him."

⁷But the LORD said to Samuel, "Do not consider how handsome or tall he is. I have not chosen him. I do not look at the things people look at. Man looks at how someone appears on the outside. But I look at what is in the heart."

⁸Then Jesse called for Abinadab. He had him walk in front of Samuel. But Samuel said, "The LORD hasn't chosen him either."

⁹Then Jesse had Shammah walk by. But Samuel said, "The LORD hasn't chosen him either."

¹⁰Jesse had seven of his sons walk in front of Samuel. But Samuel said to him, "The LORD hasn't chosen any of them." ¹¹So he asked Jesse, "Are these the only sons you have?"

"No," Jesse answered. "My youngest son is taking care of the sheep."

Samuel said, "Send for him. We won't sit down to eat until he arrives."

¹²So Jesse sent for his son and had him brought in. His skin was tanned. He had a fine appearance and handsome features.

Then the LORD said, "Get up and anoint him. He is the one."

¹³So Samuel got the animal horn that was filled with olive oil. He anointed David in front of his brothers. From that day on, the Spirit of the LORD came on David with power. Samuel went back to Ramah.

David Serves Saul

¹⁴The Spirit of the LORD had left Saul.

POWER-SURGE

STRONG

HE ANOINTED DAVID IN FRONT OF HIS BROTHERS. FROM THAT DAY ON, THE SPIRIT OF THE LORD CAME ON DAVID WITH POWER.
— 1 SAMUEL 16:13 —

POWER-SURGE

BRAVE B

I'VE SEEN SOMEONE WHO KNOWS HOW TO PLAY THE HARP. HE IS A SON OF JESSE FROM BETHLEHEM. HE'S A BRAVE MAN. HE WOULD MAKE A GOOD SOLDIER. HE'S A GOOD SPEAKER. HE'S VERY HANDSOME. AND THE LORD IS WITH HIM."
— 1 SAMUEL 16:18 —

And an evil spirit that was sent by the LORD terrified him.

¹⁵Saul's attendants said to him, "An evil spirit that was sent by God is terrifying you. ¹⁶Give us an order to look for someone who can play the harp. He will play it when the evil spirit that was sent by God comes on you. Then you will feel better."

¹⁷So Saul said to his attendants, "Find someone who plays the harp well. Bring him to me."

¹⁸One of the servants said, "I've seen someone who knows how to play the harp. He is a son of Jesse from Bethlehem. He's a brave man. He would make a good soldier. He's a good speaker. He's very handsome. And the LORD is with him."

¹⁹Then Saul sent messengers to Jesse. He said, "Send me your son David, the one who takes care of your sheep."

²⁰So Jesse got some bread and a bottle of wine. The bottle was made out of animal skin. He also got a young goat. He loaded everything on the back of a donkey. He sent all of it to Saul with his son David.

²¹David went to Saul and began to serve him. Saul liked him very much. David became one of the men who carried Saul's armor.

²²Saul sent a message to Jesse. It said, "Let David stay here. I want him to serve me. I'm pleased with him."

²³When the evil spirit that was sent by God would come on Saul, David would get his harp and play it. That would help Saul. He would feel better, and the evil spirit would leave him.

David Kills Goliath

17 The Philistines gathered their army together for war. They came to Socoh in Judah. They set up camp at Ephes Dammim. It was between Socoh and Azekah. ²Saul and the army of Israel gathered together. They camped in the Valley of Elah. They lined up their men to fight against the Philistines. ³The Philis-tine army was camped on one hill. Israel's army was on another. The valley was between them.

⁴A mighty hero named Goliath came out of the Philistine camp. He was from Gath. He was more than nine feet tall. ⁵He had a bronze helmet on his head. He wore a coat of bronze armor. It weighed 125 pounds. ⁶On his legs he wore bronze guards. He carried a bronze javelin on his

GOLIATH

(Not!)

1 SAMUEL 17:4, 8

A mighty hero named Goliath came out of the Philistine camp...Goliath stood and shouted to the soldiers of Israel.

Goliath's (go-LIE-uths) mammoth feet shook the ground as he stomped from the camp to the battlefield. He stood facing the Israelite camp. He roared, then threw his huge head back and laughed as the Israelite soldiers ran away in fright.

Then Goliath looked down. Who was this little boy? And why was he picking up stones from the stream? Did he think he could actually fight him?

"What?" Goliath boomed. "You fight with sticks and stones? I'll feed you to the birds, little boy!"

The boy's voice wasn't loud or deep when he answered, but it was firm and brave. "You are huge, and you fight me with a gigantic spear. But I fight you in the name of God, who owns you and the whole earth."

Goliath laughed as the boy put a stone into a sling and began to twirl it around his head. **HE SAW THE BOY'S WRIST FLICK** and, just before everything went black, he felt the sting of the stone hit his forehead.

GOLIATH

Goliath was a giant, powerful and brave. But he only fought with his own strength. He didn't know that God had more strength than he ever would. Don't ever be like Goliath. Don't trust in your own talents or abilities or strength to get you through. Trust in God.

GOLIATH THOUGHT HE COULD DO ANYTHING BECAUSE HE WAS SO STRONG.

Go to page 336 for the next Super Hero

back. **7**His spear was as big as a weaver's rod. Its iron point weighed 15 pounds. The man who carried his shield walked along in front of him.

8Goliath stood and shouted to the soldiers of Israel. He said, "Why do you come out and line up for battle? I'm a Philistine. You are servants of Saul. Choose one of your men. Have him come down and face me. **9**If he's able to fight and kill me, we'll become your slaves. But if I win and kill him, you will become our slaves and serve us." **10**Goliath continued, "This very day I dare the soldiers of Israel to send a man down to fight against me."

11Saul and the whole army of Israel heard what the Philistine said. They were terrified.

12David was the son of an Ephrathite. His name was Jesse. He was from Bethlehem in Judah. Jesse had eight sons. When Saul was king, Jesse was already very old. **13**Jesse's three oldest sons had followed Saul into battle. The oldest son was Eliab. The second was Abinadab. The third was Shammah. **14**David was the youngest. The three oldest sons followed Saul. **15**But David went back and forth from Saul's camp to Bethlehem. He went to Bethlehem to take care of his father's sheep.

16Every morning and evening Goliath came forward and stood there. He did it for 40 days.

17Jesse said to his son David, "Get at least half a bushel of grain that has been cooked. Also get ten loaves of bread. Take all of it to your brothers. Hurry to their camp. **18**Take along these ten chunks of cheese to the commander of their company. Find out how your brothers are doing. Bring me back some word about them. **19**They are with Saul and all of the men of Israel. They are in the Valley of Elah. They are fighting against the Philistines."

20Early in the morning David left his father's flock in the care of a shepherd. David loaded up the food and started out, just as Jesse had directed.

David reached the camp as the army was going out to its battle positions. The soldiers were shouting the war cry. **21**Israel and the Philistines were lining up their armies for battle. The armies were facing each other.

22David left what he had brought with the man who took care of the supplies. He ran to the battle lines and greeted his brothers. **23**As David was talking with them, Goliath stepped forward from his line. Goliath was a mighty Philistine hero from Gath. He again dared someone to fight him, and David heard it. **24**When Israel's army saw Goliath, all of them ran away from him. That's because they were filled with fear.

25The men of Israel had been saying, "Just look at how this man keeps stepping forward! Again and again he dares Israel to fight him. The king will make the man who kills him very wealthy. He will also give him his daughter to be his wife. He won't require anyone in his family to pay any taxes in Israel."

26David spoke to the men who were standing near him. He asked them, "What will be done for the man who kills this Philistine? Goliath is bringing shame on Israel. What will be done for the one who removes it? This Philistine isn't even circumcised. He dares the armies of the living God to fight him. Who does he think he is?"

27The men told David what Israel's soldiers had been saying. The men told him what would be done for the man who killed Goliath.

28David's oldest brother Eliab heard him speaking with the men. So he burned with anger at him. He asked him, "Why have you come down here? Who did you leave those few sheep in the desert with? I know how proud you are. I know how evil your heart is. The only reason you came down here was to watch the battle."

29"What have I done now?" said David. "Can't I even speak?"

30Then he turned away to speak to some other men. He asked them the same question he had asked before. And they gave him the same answer.

31Someone heard what David said and reported it to Saul. So Saul sent for him.

32David said to Saul, "Don't let anyone lose hope because of that Philistine. I'll go out and fight him."

33Saul replied, "You aren't able to go out there and fight that Philistine. You are too young. He's been a fighting man ever since he was a boy."

34But David said to Saul, "I've been taking care of my father's sheep. Sometimes a lion or a bear would come and carry off a sheep from the flock. **35**Then I would go after it and hit it. I would save the sheep it was carrying in its mouth. If it turned around to attack me, I would grab hold of its hair. I would strike it down and kill it. **36**In fact, I've killed both a lion and a bear. I'll do the same thing to this Philistine. He isn't even circumcised. He has dared the armies of the living God to fight him.

37 "The LORD saved me from the paw of the lion. He saved me from the paw of the bear. And he'll save me from the powerful hand of this Philistine too."

Saul said to David, "Go. And may the LORD be with you."

38 Then Saul dressed David in his own military clothes. He put a coat of armor on him. He put a bronze helmet on his head. **39** David put on Saul's sword over his clothes. He walked around for a while in all of that armor because he wasn't used to it.

"I can't go out there in all of this armor," he said to Saul. "I'm not used to it." So he took it off.

40 Then David picked up his wooden staff. He went down to a stream and chose five smooth stones. He put them in the pocket of his shepherd's bag. Then he took his sling in his hand and approached Goliath.

41 At that same time, the Philistine kept coming closer to David. The man who was carrying Goliath's shield walked along in front of him.

42 Goliath looked David over. He saw how young he was. He also saw how tanned and handsome he was. And he hated him. **43** He said to David, "Why are you coming at me with sticks? Do you think I'm only a dog?" The Philistine called down curses on David in the name of his god. **44** "Come over here," he said. "I'll feed your body to the birds of the air! I'll feed it to the wild animals!"

45 David said to Goliath, "You are coming to fight against me with a sword, a spear and a javelin. But I'm coming against you in the name of the LORD who rules over all. He is the God of the armies of Israel. He's the one you have dared to fight against.

46 "This very day the LORD will hand you over to me. I'll strike you down. I'll cut your head off. This very day I'll feed the bodies of the Philistine army to the birds of the air. I'll feed them to the wild animals. Then the whole world will know there is a God in Israel.

47 "The LORD doesn't save by using a sword or a spear. And everyone who is here will know it. The battle belongs to the LORD. He will hand all of you over to us."

48 As the Philistine moved closer to attack him, David ran quickly to the battle line to meet him. **49** He reached into his bag. He took out a stone. He put it in his sling. He slung it at Goliath. The stone hit him on the forehead and sank into it. He fell to the ground on his face.

50 So David won the fight against Goliath with a sling and a stone. He struck the Philistine down and killed him. He did it without even using a sword.

51 David ran and stood over him. He took hold of Goliath's sword and pulled it out. After he killed him, he cut off his head with the sword.

The Philistines saw that their hero was dead. So they turned around and ran away.

52 Then the men of Israel and Judah shouted and rushed forward. They chased the Philistines to the entrance of Gath. They chased them to the gates of Ekron. The dead bodies of the Philistines were scattered all along the road to Gath and Ekron. That's the road that leads to Shaaraim.

53 Israel's army returned from chasing the Philistines. They had taken everything from the Philistine camp.

54 David picked up Goliath's head. He brought it to Jerusalem. He put Goliath's weapons in his own tent.

55 Saul had been watching David as he went out to meet the Philistine. He spoke

---

POWER-SURGE

BRAVE B

DAVID SAID TO GOLIATH, "YOU ARE COMING TO FIGHT AGAINST ME WITH A SWORD, A SPEAR AND A JAVELIN. BUT I'M COMING AGAINST YOU IN THE NAME OF THE LORD WHO RULES OVER ALL. HE IS THE GOD OF THE ARMIES OF ISRAEL...THIS VERY DAY THE LORD WILL HAND YOU OVER TO ME."
— 1 SAMUEL 17:45-46 —

STRONG

DAVID

1 SAMUEL 17:47

The LORD doesn't save by using a sword or a spear. And everyone who is here will know it. The battle belongs to the LORD. He will hand all of you over to us.

David couldn't believe it. What was the matter with these soldiers? They were afraid of the giant, Goliath. Well, even though David wasn't a soldier, he wasn't afraid. He marched to King Saul's tent.

"King Saul," he said, "don't worry about that giant. I'll fight him! I've been watching my father's sheep all my life. When a bear or a lion attacked, I killed it. I'll do the same thing to Goliath. The Lord saved me from a bear and a lion. He'll save me from Goliath, too."

David walked down into the valley and bent over a small stream. He felt the bottom with his hands. Carefully, he chose five stones. Then he walked toward Goliath.

Goliath turned fierce eyes to David. His voice rumbled with anger. "Come here, you little twerp. I'll make hamburger of you and feed you to the birds and beasts!"

Goliath's words didn't frighten David. He boldly shouted back at Goliath, "You fight with a spear and sword. But I fight in the name of the mighty God!"

As he spoke David put one stone into his sling. He began to swing it round and round. With a strong twist of his wrist, David flicked the stone out of the sling. It shot straight at Goliath, sinking into his forehead. Goliath's eyes opened wide with surprise and then pain. HE WOBBLED ON HIS FEET. HE SHOOK. HE FELL FACEDOWN IN THE DIRT. Goliath was dead.

David defeated Goliath with a sling and a stone and the might of God. He proved to everyone that day—to the Israelite soldiers and to their enemies—that battles aren't won with spears and swords but with God.

BE A DAVID

David was a brave young man. But he wasn't brave because he was strong or smart. He was brave because he knew God was with him. That's where your courage comes from, too. Trust God to help you. He'll always be with you.

DAVID TRUSTED GOD TO WIN THE FIGHT.
THE WHOLE STORY: 1 SAMUEL 17

Go to page 338 for the next Super Hero

to Abner, the commander of the army. He said to him, "Abner, whose son is that young man?"

Abner replied, "King Saul, I don't know. And that's just as sure as you are alive."

⁵⁶The king said, "Find out whose son that young man is."

⁵⁷After David killed Goliath, he returned to the camp. Then Abner brought him to Saul. David was still carrying Goliath's head.

⁵⁸"Young man, whose son are you?" Saul asked him.

David said, "I'm the son of Jesse from Bethlehem."

Saul Becomes Jealous of David

18 David finished talking with Saul. After that, Jonathan and David became close friends. Jonathan loved David just as he loved himself.

²From that time on, Saul kept David

POWER-SURGE

GIVING G

JONATHAN TOOK OFF THE ROBE HE WAS WEARING AND GAVE IT TO DAVID. HE ALSO GAVE HIM HIS MILITARY CLOTHES. HE EVEN GAVE HIM HIS SWORD, HIS BOW AND HIS BELT.
—— 1 SAMUEL 18:4 ——

with him. He didn't let him return to his father's home.

³Jonathan made a covenant with David because he loved him just as he loved himself. ⁴Jonathan took off the robe he was wearing and gave it to David. He also gave him his military clothes. He even gave him his sword, his bow and his belt.

⁵David did everything Saul sent him to do. He did it so well that Saul gave him a high rank in the army. That pleased Saul's whole army, including his officers.

⁶After David had killed Goliath, the men of Israel returned home. The women came out of all of the towns of Israel to meet King Saul. They danced and sang

joyful songs. They played lutes and tambourines. ⁷As they danced, they sang,

"Saul has killed thousands of men.
    David has killed tens of thousands."

⁸That song made Saul very angry. It really upset him. He said to himself, "They are saying David has killed tens of thousands of men. But they are saying I've killed only thousands. The only thing left for him to get is the kingdom itself."
⁹From that time on, Saul became very jealous of David. So he watched him closely.

¹⁰The next day an evil spirit that was sent by God came on Saul with power. Saul began to prophesy in his house. At that same time David began to play the harp, just as he usually did. Saul was holding a spear. ¹¹He threw it at David. As he did, he said to himself, "I'll pin David to the wall." But David got away from him twice.

¹²The LORD had left Saul and was with David. So Saul was afraid of David. ¹³He sent David away. He put him in command of 1,000 men. David led the troops in battle. ¹⁴In everything he did, he was very successful. That's because the LORD was with him.

¹⁵When Saul saw how successful David was, he became afraid of him. ¹⁶But all of the troops of Israel and Judah loved David. That's because he led them in battle.

¹⁷Saul said to David, "Here is my older daughter Merab. I'll give her to you to be your wife. Just serve me bravely and fight the LORD's battles."

Saul said to himself, "I won't have to lift my hand to strike him down. The Philistines will do that!"

¹⁸But David said to Saul, "Who am I? Is anyone in my whole family that important in Israel? Am I worthy to become the king's son-in-law?"

¹⁹The time came for Saul to give his daughter Merab to David. Instead, Saul gave her to Adriel from Meholah to be his wife.

²⁰Saul's daughter Michal was in love with David. When they told Saul about it, he was pleased. ²¹"I'll give her to him to be his wife," he said to himself. "Then maybe she'll trap him. And maybe the powerful hand of the Philistines will strike him down." So Saul said to David, "Now you have a second chance to become my son-in-law."

²²Then Saul gave an order to his attendants. He said, "Speak to David in private.

JONATHAN

1 SAMUEL 18:1

Jonathan and David became close friends. Jonathan loved David just as he loved himself.

Jonathan and David had become great friends. Jonathan remembered watching as young David killed a giant with just a stone and a slingshot. Now Jonathan listened as David played his harp and calmed King Saul.

King Saul was Jonathan's father. David was just a poor shepherd. Yet they had become close friends. Prince Jonathan knew that when his father died, he would become king of all Israel. But Jonathan realized something no one else seemed to realize. Jonathan knew that God wanted David to be the next king.

Jonathan and David talked and laughed as they walked together. Jonathan stopped and put his hand on David's shoulder. He said, "I have never had a friend like you before. I love you as much as I love myself!"

Jonathan took off his beautiful prince's coat. He carefully put it on David's shoulders. **THEN HE TOOK OFF HIS SWORD AND HANDED IT TO DAVID.** Next he gave David his bow, then he took off his belt and put it around David's waist. David simply stood still and took what Jonathan gave him. When Jonathan finished, he said, "I'm giving all of this to you because I want you to know that I promise to always and forever be your friend. No matter what happens in the future, I will be there for you."

The friendship between Jonathan and David was amazing. Jonathan was supposed to be the next king. But he gave that up because he knew God wanted David to be king. And because he loved David more than he loved himself. That's *true* friendship.

BE A JONATHAN

Good friends always want what's best for each other. That's what made Jonathan such a good friend to David. He loved David enough to follow God's direction and not fight David to be king. Are you a Jonathan? Do you love anyone more than you love yourself? What would you be willing to give up for your friends?

JONATHAN LOVED DAVID MORE THAN HE LOVED HIMSELF AND WAS HIS FRIEND.
THE WHOLE STORY: 1 SAMUEL 18:1-4

Go to page 346 for the next Super Hero

Tell him, 'The king is pleased with you. All of his attendants like you. So become his son-in-law.' "

²³Saul's attendants spoke those very words to David. But David said, "Do you think it's a small thing to become the king's son-in-law? I'm only a poor man. I'm not very well known."

²⁴Saul's attendants told him what David had said. ²⁵Saul said, "Tell David, 'Here's the price the king wants for the bride. He wants you to kill 100 Philistines. Then bring back the skins you cut off when you circumcise them. That's how Saul will get even with his enemies.' " Saul hoped that the powerful hand of the Philistines would strike David down.

²⁶Saul's attendants also told David those things. Then David was pleased to become the king's son-in-law. So before the day that was set for the wedding, ²⁷David and his men went out and killed 200 Philistines. They circumcised them. Then David brought all of the skins and gave them to the king. By doing that, he could become the king's son-in-law. So Saul gave David his daughter Michal to be his wife.

²⁸Saul realized that the LORD was with David. He also realized that his daughter Michal loved David. ²⁹So Saul became even more afraid of him. He remained David's enemy as long as he was king.

³⁰The Philistine commanders kept on going out to battle. Every time they did, David had more success against them than the rest of Saul's officers. So his name became well known.

Michal Helps David Get Away

19 Saul told his son Jonathan and all of the attendants to kill David. But Jonathan liked David very much. ²So Jonathan warned him, "My father Saul is looking for a chance to kill you. Be very careful tomorrow morning. Find a place to hide and stay there. ³My father and I will come and stand in the field where you are hiding. I'll speak to him about you. Then I'll tell you what I find out."

⁴Jonathan told his father Saul some good things about David. He said to him, "Please don't do anything to harm David. He hasn't done anything to harm you. And what he's done has helped you a lot. ⁵He put his own life in danger when he killed Goliath. The LORD used him to win a great battle for the whole nation of Israel. When you saw it, you were glad. So why would you do anything to harm a man like David? He isn't guilty of doing

anything to harm you. Why would you want to kill him without any reason?"

⁶Saul paid attention to Jonathan. He took an oath and made a promise. He said, "You can be sure that the LORD lives. And you can be just as sure that David will not be put to death."

⁷So Jonathan sent for David and told him everything he and Saul had said. Then he brought David to Saul. David served Saul as he had done before.

⁸Once more war broke out. So David went out and fought against the Philistines. He struck them down with so much force that they ran away from him.

⁹But an evil spirit that was sent by the LORD came on Saul. It happened as he was sitting in his house and holding his spear. While David was playing the harp, ¹⁰Saul tried to pin him to the wall with his spear. But David got away from him just as Saul drove the spear into the wall. That night David escaped.

¹¹Saul sent some men to watch David's house. He told them to kill David the next morning.

But David's wife Michal warned him. She said, "You must run for your life tonight. If you don't, tomorrow you will be killed." ¹²So Michal helped David escape through a window. He ran and got away.

¹³Then Michal got a statue of a god. She laid it on David's bed. She covered it with clothes. And she put some goat hair at the place where David's head would have been.

¹⁴Saul sent the men to capture David. But Michal told them, "He's sick."

¹⁵Then Saul sent the men back to see David. He told them, "Bring him up here to me in his bed. Then I'll kill him."

¹⁶But when the men entered, they found nothing but the statue in the bed. Some goat hair was at the place where David's head would have been.

¹⁷Saul said to Michal, "Why did you trick me like this? Why did you help my enemy escape?"

Michal told him, "He said to me, 'Help me get away. If you don't, I'll kill you.' "

¹⁸After David had run away and escaped, he went to Samuel at Ramah. He told him everything Saul had done to him. Then David and Samuel went to Naioth and stayed there.

¹⁹Saul was told, "David is in Naioth at Ramah." ²⁰So Saul sent some men to capture him. When they got there, they saw a group of prophets who were prophesying. Samuel was standing there as their leader.

Then the Spirit of God came on Saul's men. So they also began to prophesy. [21]Saul was told about it. So he sent some more men. They began to prophesy too. Saul sent some men a third time. And they also began to prophesy.

[22]Finally, Saul decided to go to Ramah himself. He went to the large well at Secu. He asked some people, "Where are Samuel and David?"

"Over in Naioth at Ramah," they said.

[23]So Saul went to Naioth at Ramah. But the Spirit of God even came on him. He walked along and prophesied until he came to Naioth. [24]There he took off his royal robes. Then he prophesied in front of Samuel. He lay there without his robes on all that day and night. That's why people say, "Is Saul also one of the prophets?"

Jonathan Helps David Get Away

20 David was in Naioth at Ramah. He ran away from there to where Jonathan was. He asked him, "What have I done? What crime have I committed? I haven't done anything to harm your father. So why is he trying to kill me?"

[2]"That will never happen!" Jonathan replied. "You aren't going to die! My father doesn't do anything at all without telling me. So why would he hide that from me? He isn't going to kill you!"

[3]But David took an oath. Then he said, "Your father knows very well that you are pleased with me. He has said to himself, 'I don't want Jonathan to know I'm planning to kill David. If he finds out, he'll be very sad.' But I'm very close to being killed. And that's just as sure as the LORD and you are alive."

[4]Jonathan said to David, "I'll do anything you want me to do for you."

[5]So David said, "Tomorrow is the time for the New Moon Feast. I'm supposed to eat with the king. But let me go and hide in the field. I'll stay there until the evening of the day after tomorrow. [6]Your father might miss me. If he does, then tell him, 'David begged me to let him hurry home to Bethlehem. A yearly sacrifice is being offered there for his whole family group.' [7]Your father might say, 'That's all right.' If he does, it will mean I'm safe. But he might become very angry. If he does, you can be sure he's made up his mind to harm me.

[8]"Please be kind to me. You have made a covenant with me in the sight of the LORD. If I'm guilty, kill me yourself! Don't hand me over to your father!"

[9]"I would never do that!" Jonathan said. "Suppose I had even the smallest clue that my father had made up his mind to harm you. Then I would tell you."

[10]David asked, "Who will tell me if your father answers you in a mean way?"

[11]"Come on," Jonathan said. "Let's go out to the field." So they went there together.

[12]Then Jonathan spoke to David. He said, "I promise you that I'll find out what my father is planning to do. I'll find out by this time the day after tomorrow. The LORD, the God of Israel, is my witness. Suppose my father feels kind toward you. Then I'll send you a message and let you know. [13]But suppose he wants to harm you. And I don't let you know about it. I don't help you get away safely. Then may the LORD punish me greatly. May he be with you, just as he has been with my father.

[14]"But always be kind to me, just as the LORD is. Be kind to me as long as I live. Then I won't be killed. [15]And never stop being kind to my family. Don't stop even when the LORD has cut off every one of your enemies from the face of the earth."

[16]So Jonathan made a covenant with David and his family. He said, "May the LORD make David's enemies accountable for what they've done." [17]Jonathan had David take an oath again because he loved him. In fact, Jonathan loved David just as he loved himself.

[18]Then Jonathan said to David, "Tomorrow is the time for the New Moon Feast. You will be missed, because your seat at the table will be empty. [19]Go to the place where you hid when all of this trouble began. Go there the day after tomorrow, when evening is approaching. There's a stone out there called Ezel. [20]Wait by it.

"I'll shoot three arrows to one side of the stone. I'll pretend I'm practicing my shooting. [21]Then I'll send a boy out there. I'll tell him, 'Go and find the arrows.' Sup-

POWER-SURGE
KIND K

ALWAYS BE KIND TO ME, JUST AS THE LORD IS. BE KIND TO ME AS LONG AS I LIVE.
— 1 SAMUEL 20:14 —

pose I say to him, 'The arrows are on this side of you. Bring them here.' Then come. That will mean you are safe. You won't be in any danger. And that's just as sure as the LORD is alive. ²²But suppose I tell the boy, 'The arrows are far beyond you.' Then go. That will mean the LORD is sending you away.

²³"And remember what we talked about. Remember that the LORD is a witness between you and me forever."

²⁴So David hid in the field. When the time for the New Moon Feast came, the king sat down to eat. ²⁵He sat in his usual place by the wall. Jonathan sat across from him. Abner sat next to Saul. But David's place was empty.

²⁶Saul didn't say anything that day. He said to himself, "Something must have happened to David to make him 'unclean.' That must be why he isn't here."

²⁷But the next day, David's place was empty again. It was the second day of the month.

Finally, Saul spoke to his son Jonathan. He said, "Why hasn't the son of Jesse come to the meal? He hasn't been here yesterday or today."

²⁸Jonathan replied, "David begged me to let him go to Bethlehem. ²⁹He said, 'Let me go. Our family is offering a sacrifice in the town. My brother has ordered me to be there. Are you pleased with me? If you are, let me go and see my brothers.' That's why he hasn't come to eat at your table."

³⁰Saul burned with anger against Jonathan. He said to him, "You are an evil son. You have refused to obey me. I know that you are on the side of Jesse's son. You should be ashamed of that. And your mother should be ashamed of having a son like you. ³¹You will never be king as long as Jesse's son lives on this earth. And you will never have a kingdom either. So send for the son of Jesse. Bring him to me. He must die!"

³²"Why do you want to put him to death?" Jonathan asked his father. "What has he done?"

³³But Saul threw his spear at Jonathan to kill him. Then Jonathan knew that his father wanted to kill David.

³⁴So Jonathan got up from the table. He was burning with anger. On that second day of the month, he refused to eat. He was very sad that his father was treating David so badly.

³⁵The next morning Jonathan went out to the field to meet David. He took a young boy with him. ³⁶He said to the boy,

"Run and find the arrows I shoot." As the boy ran, Jonathan shot an arrow far beyond him. ³⁷The boy came to the place where Jonathan's arrow had fallen.

Then Jonathan shouted to him, "The arrow went far beyond you, didn't it?" ³⁸He continued, "Hurry up! Run fast! Don't stop!"

The boy picked up the arrow and returned to his master. ³⁹The boy didn't know what was going on. Only Jonathan and David knew. ⁴⁰Jonathan gave his weapons to the boy. He told him, "Go back to town. Take the weapons with you."

⁴¹After the boy had gone, David got up from the south side of the stone. He bowed down in front of Jonathan with his face to the ground. He did it three times. Then they kissed each other and cried. But David cried more than Jonathan did.

⁴²Jonathan said to David, "Go in peace. In the name of the LORD we have taken an oath. We've promised to be friends. We've said, 'The LORD is a witness between you and me. He's a witness between your children and my children forever.' "

Then David left, and Jonathan went back to the town.

Ahimelech Helps David

21 David went to the priest Ahimelech at Nob. Ahimelech trembled with fear when he met him. He asked David, "Why are you alone? Why isn't anyone with you?"

²David answered the priest Ahimelech, "The king gave me a special job to do. He said to me, 'I don't want anyone to know what I'm sending you to do. So don't say anything about it.' I've told my men to meet me at a certain place. ³Do you have anything for us to eat? Give me five loaves of bread, or anything else you can find."

⁴But the priest answered David, "I don't have any bread that isn't holy. I only have some holy bread here. But it's for men who haven't made love to women recently."

⁵David replied, "Well, we haven't made love to women recently. That's the way it is every time I lead my men out to battle. We keep ourselves holy even when we do jobs that aren't holy. And that's even more true today."

⁶So the priest gave him the holy bread. It was the only bread he had. It had been removed from the table that was in front of the LORD. On the same day, hot bread had been put in its place.

⁷One of Saul's servants was there that

day. He had been made to stay at the holy tent for a while. He was Doeg from Edom. He was Saul's chief shepherd.

⁸David asked Ahimelech, "Don't you have a spear or sword here? I haven't brought my sword or any other weapon. That's because the king's business had to be done right away."

⁹The priest replied, "The sword of Goliath, the Philistine, is here. You killed him in the Valley of Elah. His sword is wrapped in a cloth. It's behind the sacred linen apron. If you want it, take it. It's the only sword here."

David said, "There isn't any sword like it. Give it to me."

David Meets a Philistine King

¹⁰That day David ran away from Saul. He went to Achish, the king of Gath. ¹¹But the servants of Achish spoke to him. They said, "Isn't this David, the king of the land? Isn't he the one the Israelites sing about when they dance? They sing,

" 'Saul has killed thousands of men.
　David has killed tens of
　　thousands.' "

¹²David paid close attention to what the servants were saying. He became very much afraid of what Achish, the king of Gath, might do. ¹³So he pretended to be out of his mind when he was with them. As long as he was in Gath, he acted like someone who was crazy. He made marks on the doors of the city gate. He let spit run down his beard.

¹⁴Achish said to his servants, "Just look at the man! He's out of his mind! Why are you bringing him to me? ¹⁵Don't I have enough crazy people around me already? So why do you have to bring this fellow here? Just look at how he's carrying on in front of me! Why do you have to bring this man into my house?"

David Goes to Adullam and Mizpah

22 David left Gath and escaped to the cave of Adullam. His brothers and the other members of his family heard about it. So they went down to join him there. ²Everyone who was in trouble or owed money or was unhappy gathered around him. He became their leader. About 400 men were with him.

³From there David went to Mizpah in Moab. He spoke to the king of Moab. He said, "Please let my father and mother come and stay with you. Let them stay until I learn what God will do for me." ⁴So

David left his parents with the king of Moab. They stayed with him as long as David was in his usual place of safety.

⁵But the prophet Gad spoke to David. He said, "Don't stay in your usual place of safety. Go into the land of Judah." So David left and went to the forest of Hereth.

Saul Kills the Priests of Nob

⁶Saul heard that the place where David and his men were hiding had been discovered. Saul was sitting under a tamarisk tree on the hill at Gibeah. He was holding his spear. All of his officials were standing around him.

⁷Saul said to them, "Men of Benjamin, listen to me! Do you think Jesse's son will give all of you fields and vineyards? Do you think he'll make some of you commanders of thousands of men? Do you think he'll make the rest of you commanders of hundreds? ⁸Is that why all of you have joined together against me? No one tells me when my son makes a covenant with Jesse's son. None of you is concerned about me. No one tells me that my son has stirred up Jesse's son to hide and wait to attack me. But that's exactly what's happening now."

⁹Doeg was standing with Saul's officials. He was from Edom. He said, "I saw Jesse's son David come to Ahimelech at Nob. Ahimelech is the son of Ahitub. ¹⁰Ahimelech asked the LORD a question for David. He also gave him food and the sword of Goliath, the Philistine."

¹¹Then the king sent for the priest Ahimelech, the son of Ahitub. He sent for all of the men in his family. They were the priests at Nob. All of them came to the king.

¹²Saul said, "Son of Ahitub, listen to me."

"Yes, master," he answered.

¹³Saul said to him, "Why have you and Jesse's son joined together against me? Why did you give him bread and a sword? Why did you ask God a question for him? Now he has turned against me. He is hiding and waiting to attack me right now."

¹⁴Ahimelech answered the king, "David is true to you. In fact, he's more true to you than anyone else who serves you. He's your own son-in-law. He's the captain of your own personal guards. He's highly respected by everyone in your palace. ¹⁵Was that day the first time I asked God a question for him? Of course not!

"Please don't bring charges against me.

Please don't bring charges against anyone in my family. I don't know anything at all about this whole matter."

¹⁶But the king said, "Ahimelech, you will certainly be put to death. You and your whole family will be put to death."

¹⁷Then the king gave an order to the guards who were at his side. He said, "Go and kill the priests of the LORD. They are on David's side too. They knew he was running away from me. And they didn't even tell me."

But the king's officials wouldn't raise a hand to strike down the priests of the LORD.

¹⁸Then the king ordered Doeg, "You go and strike the priests down."

So Doeg, the Edomite, went and struck them down. That day he killed 85 men who wore linen aprons. ¹⁹He also killed the people of Nob with his sword. Nob was a town where priests lived. Doeg killed its men and women. He killed its children and babies. He also destroyed its cattle, donkeys and sheep.

²⁰But Abiathar, a son of Ahimelech, escaped. Ahimelech was the son of Ahitub. Abiathar ran away and joined David. ²¹He told David that Saul had killed the priests of the LORD. ²²Then David said to Abiathar, "One day I was at Nob. I saw Doeg, the Edomite, there. I knew he would be sure to tell Saul. Your whole family has been killed. And I'm accountable for it. ²³So stay with me. Don't be afraid. The man who wants to kill you wants to kill me too. You will be safe with me."

David Saves the People of Keilah

23 David was told, "The Philistines are fighting against the town of Keilah. They are stealing grain from the threshing floors." ²So he asked the LORD for advice. He said, "Should I go and attack those Philistines?"

The LORD answered him, "Go and attack them. Save Keilah."

³But David's men said to him, "We're afraid here in Judah. Suppose we go to Keilah and fight against the Philistine army. Then we'll be even more afraid."

⁴Once again David asked the LORD what he should do.

The LORD answered him, "Go down to Keilah. I am going to hand the Philistines over to you."

⁵So David and his men went to Keilah. They fought against the Philistines and carried off their livestock. David wounded

and killed large numbers of Philistines. And he saved the people of Keilah.

⁶Abiathar, the son of Ahimelech, had brought the linen apron down with him from Nob. He did it when he ran away to David at Keilah.

Saul Chases David

⁷Saul was told that David had gone to Keilah. He said, "God has handed him over to me. David has trapped himself by entering a town that has gates and heavy metal bars." ⁸So Saul brought together all of his soldiers to go to battle. He ordered them to go down to Keilah. He told them to surround David and his men. He told them to get ready to attack them.

⁹David learned that Saul was planning to attack him. So he said to the priest Abiathar, "Bring the linen apron." ¹⁰Then David said, "LORD, you are the God of Israel. I know for sure that Saul plans to come to Keilah. He plans to destroy the town because of me. ¹¹Will the citizens of Keilah hand me over to him? Will Saul come down here, as I've heard he would? LORD, you are the God of Israel. Please answer me."

The LORD said, "He will come down."

¹²Again David asked, "Will the citizens of Keilah hand me and my men over to Saul?"

And the LORD said, "They will."

¹³So David and his men left Keilah. The total number of them was about 600. They kept moving from place to place. Saul was told that David had escaped from Keilah. So he didn't go there.

¹⁴Sometimes David stayed in places of safety in the desert. At other times he stayed in the hills of the Desert of Ziph. Day after day Saul looked for him. But God didn't hand David over to him.

¹⁵David was at Horesh in the Desert of Ziph. There he learned that Saul had come out to kill him.

¹⁶Saul's son Jonathan went to David at Horesh. He told David that God would make him strong. ¹⁷"Don't be afraid," he said. "My father Saul won't lay a hand on you. You will be king over Israel. And I will be next in command. Even my father Saul knows this."

¹⁸The two of them made a covenant in the sight of the LORD. Then Jonathan went home. But David remained at Horesh.

¹⁹The people of Ziph went up to Saul at Gibeah. They said, "David is hiding among us. He's hiding in places of safety at Horesh. Horesh is south of Jeshimon on

the hill of Hakilah. ²⁰King Saul, come down when it pleases you to come. It will be our duty to hand David over to you."

²¹Saul replied, "May the LORD bless you because you were concerned about me. ²²Make sure you are right. Go and check things out again. Find out where David usually goes. Find out who has seen him there. People tell me he's very tricky. ²³Find out about all of the hiding places he uses. Come back to me with all of the facts. I'll go with you. Suppose he's in the area. Then I'll track him down among all of the family groups of Judah."

²⁴So they started out. They went to Ziph ahead of Saul. David and his men were in the Desert of Maon. Maon is south of Jeshimon in the Arabah Valley. ²⁵Saul and his men started out to look for David. David was told about it. So he went down to a rock in the Desert of Maon to hide. Saul heard he was there. So he went into the Desert of Maon to chase David.

²⁶Saul was going along one side of the mountain. David and his men were on the other side. They were hurrying to get away from Saul. Saul and his army were closing in on David and his men. They were about to capture them. ²⁷Just then a messenger came to Saul. He said, "Come quickly! The Philistines are attacking the land."

²⁸So Saul stopped chasing David. He went to fight against the Philistines. That's why they call that place Sela Hammahlekoth.

²⁹David left that place. He went and lived in places of safety near En Gedi.

David Spares Saul's Life

24 Saul returned from chasing the Philistines. Then he was told, "David is in the Desert of En Gedi." ²So Saul took 3,000 of the best soldiers from the whole nation of Israel. He started out to look for David and his men. He planned to look near the Rocky Cliffs of the Wild Goats.

³He came to some sheep pens along the way. A cave was there. Saul went in to go to the toilet. David and his men were far back in the cave.

⁴David's men said, "This is the day the LORD told you about. He said to you, 'I will hand your enemy over to you. Then you can deal with him as you want to.' "

So David came up close to Saul without being seen. He cut off a corner of Saul's robe.

⁵Later, David felt sorry that he had cut off a corner of Saul's robe. ⁶He said to his men, "May the LORD keep me from doing a thing like that to my master again. He is the LORD's anointed king. So I promise that I will never lift my hand to strike him down. The LORD has anointed him."

⁷David said that to warn his men. He didn't allow them to attack Saul. So Saul left the cave and went on his way.

⁸Then David went out of the cave. He called out to Saul, "King Saul! My master!" When Saul looked behind him, David bowed down. He lay down flat with his face toward the ground.

⁹He said to Saul, "Why do you listen when men say, 'David is trying to harm you'? ¹⁰This very day you have seen with your own eyes how the LORD handed you over to me in the cave. Some of my men begged me to kill you. But I spared you. I said, 'I will never lift my hand to strike my master down. He is the LORD's anointed king.'

¹¹"Look, my father! Look at this piece of your robe in my hand! I cut off the corner of your robe. But I didn't kill you. I want you to know and understand that I'm not guilty of doing anything wrong. I haven't turned against you. I haven't done anything to harm you. But you are hunting me down. You want to kill me.

¹²"May the LORD judge between you and me. And may the LORD pay you back because of the wrong things you have done to me. But I won't lay a hand on you. ¹³People say, 'Evil acts come from those who do evil.' So I won't lay a hand on you.

¹⁴"King Saul, who are you trying to catch? Who do you think you are chasing? I'm nothing but a dead dog or a flea! ¹⁵May the LORD be our judge. May he decide between us. May he consider my case and stand up for me. May he show that I'm not guilty of doing anything wrong. May he save me from your powerful hand."

¹⁶When David finished speaking, Saul asked him a question. He said, "My son David, is that your voice?" And Saul sobbed out loud. ¹⁷"You are a better person than I am," he said. "You have treated me well. But I've treated you badly. ¹⁸You have just now told me about the good things you did to me. The LORD handed me over to you. But you didn't kill me. ¹⁹Suppose a man finds his enemy. He doesn't let him get away without harming him. May the LORD reward you with many good things. May he do it because of the way you treated me today. ²⁰I know for sure that you will be king. I know that the kingdom of Israel will be made secure

under your control. 21Now take an oath in the name of the LORD. Promise me that you won't cut off my children from my family. Also promise me that you won't wipe out my name from my family line."

22So David took an oath and made that promise to Saul. Then Saul returned home. But David and his men went up to his usual place of safety.

David Gets Married to Abigail

25 Samuel died. The whole nation of Israel gathered together. They were filled with sorrow because he was dead. They buried his body at his home in Ramah.

Then David went down into the Desert of Maon. 2A certain man in Maon was very wealthy. He owned property there at Carmel. He had 1,000 goats and 3,000 sheep. He was clipping the wool off the sheep in Carmel. 3His name was Nabal. His wife's name was Abigail. She was a wise and beautiful woman. But her husband was rude and mean in the way he treated others. He was from the family of Caleb.

4David was staying in the Desert of Maon. While he was there, he heard that Nabal was clipping the wool off his sheep. 5So he sent for ten young men. He said to them, "Go up to Nabal at Carmel. Greet him for me. 6Say to him, 'May you live a long time! May everything go well with you and your family! And may things go well with everything that belongs to you!

7" 'I hear that you are clipping the wool off your sheep. When your shepherds were with us, we treated them well. The whole time they were at Carmel nothing that belonged to them was stolen. 8Ask your own servants. They'll tell you. We've come to you now at a happy time of the year. Please show favor to my young men. Please give me and my men anything you can find for us.' "

9When David's men arrived, they gave Nabal the message from David. Then they waited.

10Nabal answered David's servants, "Who is this David? Who is this son of Jesse? Many servants are running away from their masters these days. 11Why should I give away my bread and water? Why should I give away the meat I've prepared for those who clip the wool off my sheep? Why should I give food to men who come from who knows where?"

12So David's men turned around and went back. When they arrived, they reported to David every word Nabal had spoken. 13David said to his men, "Put on your swords!" So they put their swords on. David put his on too. About 400 men went up with David. Two hundred men stayed behind with the supplies.

14One of the servants warned Nabal's wife Abigail. He said, "David sent some messengers from the desert to give his greetings to our master. But Nabal shouted at them and made fun of them.

15"David's men had been very good to us. They treated us well. The whole time we were near them out in the fields, nothing was stolen. 16We were taking care of our sheep near them. During that time, they were like a wall around us night and day. They kept us safe.

17"Now think it over. See what you can do. Horrible trouble will soon come to our master and his whole family. He's such an evil man that no one can even talk to him."

18Abigail didn't waste any time. She got 200 loaves of bread and two bottles of wine. The bottles were made out of animal skins. She got five sheep that were ready to be cooked. She got a bushel of grain that had been cooked. She got 100 raisin cakes. And she got 200 cakes of pressed figs. She loaded all of it on the backs of donkeys. 19Then she told her servants, "Go on ahead. I'll follow you." But she didn't tell her husband Nabal about it.

20Abigail rode her donkey into a mountain valley. There she saw David and his men. They were coming down toward her. 21David had just said, "Everything we've done hasn't been worth a thing! I watched over that fellow's property in the desert. I made sure none of it was stolen. But he has paid me back evil for good. 22I won't leave even one of his men alive until morning. If I do, may God punish me greatly!"

23When Abigail saw David, she quickly got off her donkey. She bowed down in front of David with her face toward the ground. 24She fell at his feet. She said, "Please let me speak to you, sir. Listen to what I'm saying. Let me take the blame myself. 25Don't pay any attention to that evil man Nabal. His name means Foolish Person. And that's exactly what he is. He's always doing foolish things. I'm sorry I didn't get a chance to see the men you sent.

26"Sir, the LORD has kept you from killing Nabal and his men. He has kept you from using your own hands to get even. May what's about to happen to Nabal happen to all of your enemies. May

ABIGAIL

1 SAMUEL 25:3

B

K

W

[Nabal's] wife's name was Abigail. She was a wise and beautiful woman.

Abigail kicked the sides of her donkey. She was in a hurry. A line of donkeys clopped along after her. The donkeys were loaded with 200 loaves of bread, 2 skins of wine, a bushel of grain, 100 cakes of raisins, 200 cakes of fruity figs, and 5 sheep all ready to be cooked. What a feast!

Abigail scanned the hills. She wondered if she would make it in time. Months earlier, David and his men had saved Nabal's sheep from bandits and wild animals – all at no cost. But now, her husband Nabal had turned away David's men. David was angry and was coming to punish Nabal and his family.

Squaring her shoulders, Abigail continued toward David's camp. Would he even give her a chance to present her gifts? She had to try. **IN THE DISTANCE A CLOUD OF DUST GREW UNTIL SHE COULD SEE DAVID AND HIS POWERFUL MEN IN FRONT OF IT.** Abigail took a deep breath, jumped down off her donkey and went to David. She bowed low to the ground. "Please, sir, let me speak," she said. "I wish I had been there when your servants came. I would have given them plenty of food. In fact, I'm bringing it to you now. Please don't punish my family. That would be wrong. God wouldn't want you to act that way."

David looked down at Abigail. He was amazed at her courage. Did she have any idea how angry he was? But he realized that she was right. It *was* wrong for him to be so angry.

David reached down and helped Abigail up. He thanked her for coming and for keeping him from doing the wrong thing.

BE AN ABIGAIL

Abigail was a strong woman. When someone did something wrong—even when that someone was her husband—she stepped in and did the right thing. Sometimes doing the right thing is hard. Sometimes it's scary. Abigail knew all of that. But she still did it. So can you. Next time you have to do something hard, remember Abigail.

ABIGAIL WAS A BRAVE AND STRONG WOMAN WHO DID THE RIGHT THING.
THE WHOLE STORY: 1 SAMUEL 25:1-42

Go to page 366 for the next Super Hero

it also happen to everyone who wants to harm you. And may it happen just as surely as the LORD and you are alive.

27 "I've brought a gift for you. Give it to the men who follow you. 28 Please forgive me for what I've done wrong.

"The LORD will certainly give you and your family line a kingdom that will last. That's because you fight the LORD's battles. Don't do anything wrong as long as you live.

29 "Someone may chase you and try to kill you. But the LORD your God will keep your life safe like a treasure that is hidden in a bag. And he'll destroy your enemies. Their lives will be thrown away, just as a stone is thrown from a sling.

30 "The LORD will do for you every good thing he promised to do. He'll appoint you leader over Israel. 31 When that happens, you won't have this heavy load on your mind. You won't have to worry about how you killed people without any reason. You won't have to worry about how you got even. The LORD will give you success. When that happens, please remember me."

32 David said to Abigail, "Give praise to the LORD. He is the God of Israel. He has sent you today to find me. 33 May the LORD bless you for what you have done. You have shown a lot of good sense. You have kept me from killing Nabal and his men this very day. You have kept me from using my own hands to get even.

34 "It's a good thing you came quickly to meet me. If you hadn't come, not one of Nabal's men would have been left alive by sunrise. And that's just as sure as the LORD, the God of Israel, is alive. He has kept me from harming you."

35 Then David accepted from her what she had brought him. He said, "Go home in peace. I've heard your words. I'll do what you have asked."

36 Abigail went back to Nabal. He was having a dinner party in the house. It was the kind of dinner a king would have. He had been drinking too much wine. He was very drunk. So she didn't tell him anything at all until sunrise.

37 The next morning Nabal wasn't drunk anymore. Then his wife told him everything. When she did, his heart grew weak. He became like a stone. 38 About ten days later, the LORD struck Nabal down. And he died.

39 David heard that Nabal was dead. So he said, "Give praise to the LORD. Nabal made fun of me. But the LORD stood up for me. He has kept me from doing some-thing wrong. He has paid Nabal back for the wrong things he did."

Then David sent a message to Abigail. He asked her to become his wife. 40 His servants went to Carmel. They said to Abigail, "David has sent us to you. He wants you to come back with us and become his wife."

41 Abigail bowed down with her face toward the ground. She said, "Here I am. I'm ready to serve him. I'm ready to wash the feet of his servants."

42 Abigail quickly got on a donkey and went with David's messengers. Her five female servants went with her. She became David's wife.

43 David had also gotten married to Ahinoam from Jezreel. Both of them became his wives.

44 But Saul had given his daughter Michal, David's first wife, to Paltiel. Paltiel was from Gallim. He was the son of Laish.

David Spares Saul's Life Again

26 Some people from Ziph went to Saul at Gibeah. They said, "David is hiding on the hill of Hakilah. It faces Jeshimon."

2 So Saul went down to the Desert of Ziph. He took 3,000 of the best soldiers in Israel with him. They went to the desert to look for David. 3 Saul set up his camp beside the road. It was on the hill of Hakilah facing Jeshimon.

But David stayed in the desert. He saw that Saul had followed him there. 4 So he sent out scouts. From them he learned that Saul had arrived.

5 Then David started out. He went to the place where Saul had camped. He saw where Saul and Abner were lying down. Saul was lying inside the camp. The army was camped all around him. Abner was commander of the army. He was the son of Ner.

6 Then David spoke to Ahimelech, the Hittite. He also spoke to Joab's brother Abishai, the son of Zeruiah. He asked them, "Who will go down with me into the camp to Saul?"

"I'll go with you," said Abishai.

7 So that night David and Abishai went into the camp. They found Saul lying asleep inside the camp. His spear was stuck in the ground near his head. Abner and the soldiers were lying asleep around him.

8 Abishai said to David, "Today God has handed your enemy over to you. So let me pin him to the ground. I can do it with

one jab of my spear. I won't even have to strike him twice."

⁹But David said to Abishai, "Don't destroy him! No one can lay a hand on the LORD's anointed king and not be guilty. ¹⁰You can be sure that the LORD lives," he said. "And you can be just as sure that the LORD himself will strike Saul down. Perhaps he'll die a natural death. Or perhaps he'll go into battle and be killed. ¹¹May the LORD keep me from laying a hand on his anointed king. Now get the spear and water jug that are near his head. Then let's leave."

¹²So David took the spear and water jug that were near Saul's head. Then he and Abishai left. No one saw them. No one knew about what they had done. In fact, no one even woke up. Everyone was sleeping. That's because the LORD had put them into a deep sleep.

¹³David went across to the other side of the valley. He stood on top of a hill far away from Saul's camp. There was a wide space between them. ¹⁴He called out to the army and to Abner, the son of Ner. He said, "Abner! Aren't you going to answer me?"

Abner replied, "Who is calling out to the king?"

¹⁵David said, "You are a great soldier, aren't you? There isn't anyone else like you in Israel. So why didn't you guard the king? He's your master, isn't he? Someone came into the camp to destroy him. ¹⁶You didn't guard him. And that isn't good. You can be sure that the LORD lives. And you can be just as sure that you and your men are worthy of death. That's because you didn't guard your master. He's the LORD's anointed king. Look around you. Where are the king's spear and water jug that were near his head?"

¹⁷Saul recognized David's voice. He said, "My son David, is that your voice?"

David replied, "Yes it is, King Saul, my master." ¹⁸He continued, "Why are you chasing me? What evil thing have I done? What am I guilty of?

¹⁹"King Saul, please listen to what I'm saying. Was it the LORD who made you angry with me? If it was, may he accept my offering. Was it people who made you angry at me? If it was, may the LORD send down a curse on them. They have now driven me from my share of the LORD's land. By doing that, they might as well have said, 'Go and serve other gods.'

²⁰"Don't spill my blood on the ground far away from where the LORD lives. King Saul, you have come out to look for noth-

POWER–SURGE

FAITHFUL ⏻

THE LORD REWARDS EVERYONE FOR DOING WHAT IS RIGHT AND BEING FAITHFUL.
—— 1 SAMUEL 26:23 ——

ing but a flea. It's as if you were hunting a partridge in the mountains."

²¹Then Saul said, "I have sinned. My son David, come back. Today you thought my life was very special. So I won't try to harm you again. I've really acted like a foolish person. I've made a huge mistake."

²²"Here's your spear," David answered. "Send one of your young men over to get it. ²³The LORD rewards everyone for doing what is right and being faithful. He handed you over to me today. But I wouldn't lay a hand on you. You are the LORD's anointed king. ²⁴Today I thought your life had great value. In the same way, may the LORD think of my life as having great value. May he save me from all trouble."

²⁵Then Saul said to David, "My son David, may the LORD bless you. You will do great things. You will also have great success."

So David went on his way. And Saul returned home.

David Lives in Philistine Territory

27 David thought, "Some day the powerful hand of Saul will destroy me. So the best thing I can do is escape. I'll go to the land of the Philistines. Then Saul will stop looking for me everywhere in Israel. His hand won't be able to reach me."

²So David and his 600 men left Israel. They went to Achish, the king of Gath. He was the son of Maoch. ³David and his men settled down in Gath near Achish. Each of David's men had his family with him. David had his two wives with him. They were Ahinoam from Jezreel and Abigail from Carmel. Abigail was Nabal's widow.

⁴Saul was told that David had run away to Gath. So he didn't look for David anymore.

⁵David said to Achish, "If you are pleased with me, give me a place in one of your country towns. I can live there. I don't really need to live near you in the royal city."

⁶So on that day Achish gave David the town of Ziklag. It has belonged to the kings of Judah ever since that time. ⁷David lived in Philistine territory for a year and four months.

⁸Sometimes David and his men would go up and attack the Geshurites. At other times they would attack the Girzites or the Amalekites. All of those people had lived in the land that reached all the way to Shur and Egypt. They had been there for a long time.

⁹When David would attack an area, he wouldn't leave a man or woman alive. But he would take their sheep, cattle, donkeys, camels and clothes. Then he would return to Achish.

¹⁰Achish would ask, "Who did you attack today?" David would answer, "The people who live in the Negev Desert of Judah." Or he would answer, "The people in the Negev Desert of Jerahmeel." Or he would answer, "The people in the Negev Desert of the Kenites."

¹¹David wouldn't leave a man or woman alive to be brought back to Gath. He thought, "They might tell on us. They might tell Achish who we really attacked." That's what David did as long as he lived in Philistine territory.

¹²Achish trusted David. He thought, "David has made himself smell very bad to his people, the Israelites. So he'll serve me forever."

Saul Disobeys the LORD at Endor

28 While David was living in Ziklag, the Philistines gathered their army together. They planned to fight against Israel.

Achish said to David, "I want you to understand that you and your men must march out with me and my army."

²David said, "I understand. You will see for yourself what I can do."

Achish replied, "All right. I'll make you my own personal guard for life."

³Samuel had died. The whole nation of Israel was filled with sorrow because he was dead. They had buried his body in his own town of Ramah.

Saul had gotten rid of people who get messages from those who have died. He had also gotten rid of people who talk to the spirits of the dead. He had thrown all of them out of the land.

⁴The Philistines gathered together and set up camp at Shunem. At the same time, Saul gathered all of the fighting men of Israel together. They set up camp at Gilboa.

⁵When Saul saw the Philistine army, he was afraid. Terror filled his heart. ⁶He asked the LORD for advice. But the LORD didn't answer him through dreams or prophets. He didn't answer him when Saul had the priest use the Urim.

⁷Saul spoke to his attendants. He said, "Find me a woman who gets messages from those who have died. Then I can go and ask her some questions."

"There's a woman like that in Endor," they said.

⁸Saul put on different clothes so people wouldn't know who he was. At night he and two of his men went to see the woman. "I want you to talk to a spirit for me," he said. "Bring up the spirit of the dead person I choose."

⁹But the woman said to him, "By now you must know what Saul has done. He has cut off everyone who gets messages from those who have died. He has also cut off everyone who talks to the spirits of the dead. He has thrown all of them out of the land. Why are you trying to trap me? Why do you want to have me put to death?"

¹⁰Saul took an oath in the name of the LORD. He promised the woman, "You can be sure that the LORD lives. And you can be just as sure that you won't be punished for helping me."

¹¹Then the woman asked, "Whose spirit should I bring up for you?"

"Bring Samuel up," he said.

¹²When the woman saw Samuel, she let out a loud scream. She said to Saul, "Why have you tricked me? You are King Saul!"

¹³He said to her, "Don't be afraid. Tell me what you see."

The woman said, "I see a spirit. He's coming up out of the ground."

¹⁴"What does he look like?" Saul asked.

"An old man wearing a robe is coming up," she said.

Then Saul knew it was Samuel. He bowed down. He lay down flat with his face toward the ground.

¹⁵Samuel said to Saul, "Why have you troubled me by bringing me up from the dead?"

"I'm having big problems," Saul said. "The Philistines are fighting against me. God has turned away from me. He doesn't answer me anymore. He doesn't speak to me through prophets or dreams. So I've called on you to tell me what to do."

16Samuel said, "The LORD has turned away from you. He has become your enemy. So why are you asking me what you should do? **17**The LORD has spoken through me and has done what he said he would do. He has torn the kingdom out of your hands. He has given it to one of your neighbors. He has given it to David. **18**You didn't obey the LORD. You didn't carry out his burning anger against the Amalekites. So he's punishing you today.

19"He will hand both Israel and you over to the Philistines. Tomorrow you and your sons will be down here with me. The LORD will also hand Israel's army over to the Philistines."

20Immediately Saul fell flat on the ground. What Samuel had said filled Saul with fear. His strength was gone. He hadn't eaten anything all that day and night.

21The woman went over to Saul because she saw that he was very upset. She said, "Look, I've obeyed you. I put my own life in danger by doing what you told me to do. **22**So please listen to me. Let me give you some food. Eat it. Then you will have the strength to go on your way."

23But he refused. He said, "I don't want anything to eat."

Then his men joined the woman in begging him to eat. Finally, he paid attention to them. He got up from the ground and sat on a couch.

24The woman had a fat calf at her house. She killed it at once. She got some flour. She mixed it and baked some bread that didn't have any yeast in it. **25**Then she set the food in front of Saul and his men. They ate it. That same night they got up and left.

Achish Sends David Back to Ziklag

29 The Philistines gathered their whole army together at Aphek. Israel's army camped by the spring of water at Jezreel. **2**The Philistine rulers marched out in companies of hundreds and thousands. David and his men were marching with Achish behind the others.

3The commanders of the Philistines asked, "Why are these Hebrews here?"

Achish replied, "That's David, isn't it? Wasn't he an officer of Saul, the king of Israel? He has already been with me for more than a year. I haven't found any fault in him. That's been true from the day he left Saul until now."

4But the Philistine commanders were angry with Achish. They said, "Send David back. Let him return to the town you gave him. He must not go with us into battle. If he does, he'll turn against us during the fighting. In fact, he might even cut off the heads of our own men. What better way could he choose to win back his master's favor? **5**Isn't David the one the Israelites sang about when they danced? They sang,

" 'Saul has killed thousands of men.
    David has killed tens of
       thousands.' "

6So Achish called David over to him. He said, "You have been faithful to me. And that's just as sure as the LORD is alive. I would be pleased to have you serve with me in the army. I haven't found any fault in you. That's been true from the day you came to me until now. But the Philistine rulers aren't pleased to have you come along. **7**So go back home in peace. Don't do anything that wouldn't please the Philistine rulers."

8"But what have I done?" asked David. "What have you found against me from the day I came to you until now? Why can't I go and fight against your enemies? After all, you are my king and master."

9Achish answered, "You have been as pleasing to me as an angel of God. But the Philistine commanders have said, 'We don't want David to go up with us into battle.' **10**So get up early in the morning. Take with you the men who used to serve Saul. Leave as soon as the sun begins to come up."

11So David and his men got up early in the morning. They went back to the land of the Philistines. And the Philistines went up to Jezreel.

David Destroys the Amalekites

30 On the third day David and his men arrived in Ziklag. The Amalekites had attacked the people of the Negev Desert. They had also attacked Ziklag and burned it. **2**They had captured the women and everyone else who was in Ziklag. They had taken as prisoners young people and old people alike. But they didn't kill any of them. Instead, they carried them off as they went on their way.

3David and his men came to Ziklag. They saw that it had been destroyed by fire. They found out that their wives and sons and daughters had been captured. **4**So David and his men began to sob out loud. They sobbed until they couldn't sob anymore. **5**David's two wives had been

STRONG

DAVID WAS MADE STRONG BY THE LORD HIS GOD.
—— 1 SAMUEL 30:6 ——

captured. Their names were Ahinoam from Jezreel and Abigail from Carmel. Abigail was Nabal's widow.

⁶David was greatly troubled. His men were even talking about killing him by throwing stones at him. All of them were very bitter because their sons and daughters had been taken away. But David was made strong by the LORD his God.

⁷Then David spoke to the priest Abiathar, the son of Ahimelech. He said, "Bring me the linen apron." Abiathar brought it to him. ⁸David asked the LORD for advice. He said, "Should I chase after the men who attacked Ziklag? If I do, will I catch up with them?"

"Chase after them," the LORD answered. "You will certainly catch up with them. You will succeed in saving those who were captured."

⁹David and his 600 men came to the Besor Valley. Some of them stayed behind there. ¹⁰That's because 200 of them were too tired to go across the valley. But David and the other 400 continued the chase.

¹¹David's men found an Egyptian in a field. They brought him to David. They gave him water to drink and food to eat. ¹²They gave him part of a cake of pressed figs. They also gave him two raisin cakes. After he ate them, he felt as good as new. That's because he hadn't eaten any food for three days and three nights. He hadn't drunk any water during that time either.

¹³David asked him, "Who do you belong to? Where do you come from?"

The man said, "I'm from Egypt. I'm the slave of an Amalekite. My master deserted me when I became ill three days ago. ¹⁴We attacked the people in the Negev Desert of the Kerethites. We attacked the territory that belongs to Judah. We attacked the people in the Negev Desert of Caleb. And we burned Ziklag."

¹⁵David asked him, "Can you lead me down to the men who attacked Ziklag?"

He answered, "Take an oath in the name of God. Promise me that you won't kill me. Promise that you won't hand me over to my master. Then I'll take you down to them."

¹⁶He led David down to where the men were. They were scattered all over the countryside. They were eating and drinking and dancing wildly. That's because they had taken a large amount of goods from those they had attacked. They had taken it from the land of the Philistines and from the people of Judah.

¹⁷David fought against them from sunset until the evening of the next day. None of them escaped except 400 young men. They rode off on camels and got away.

¹⁸David got everything back that the Amalekites had taken. That included his two wives. ¹⁹Nothing was missing. Not one young person or old person or boy or girl was missing. None of the goods or anything else the Amalekites had taken was missing. David brought everything back. ²⁰He brought back all of the flocks and herds. His men drove them on ahead of the other livestock. They said, "Here's what David has captured."

²¹Then David came to the 200 men who had been too tired to follow him. They had been left behind in the Besor Valley. They came out to welcome David and the people who were with him. As David and his men approached, he greeted them. ²²But some of the men who had gone out with David were evil. They wanted to stir up trouble. They said, "The 200 men didn't go out into battle with us. So we won't share with them the goods we brought back. But each man can take his wife and children and go home."

²³David replied, "No, my friends. You must not hold back their share of what the LORD has given us. He has kept us safe. He has handed over to us the men who attacked Ziklag. ²⁴So no one will pay any attention to what you are saying. Each man who stayed with the supplies will receive the same share as each man who went down to the battle. Everyone's share will be the same." ²⁵David made that a law and a rule for Israel. It has been followed from that day until now.

²⁶David arrived in Ziklag. He sent some of the goods to the elders of Judah. They were his friends. He said, "Here's a present for you. It's part of the things we took from the LORD's enemies."

²⁷He sent some goods to the elders who were in Bethel, Ramoth Negev and Jattir. ²⁸He sent some to those who were in Aroer, Siphmoth, Eshtemoa ²⁹and Racal. He sent some to those who were in the towns

of the Jerahmeelites and Kenites. **30**He sent some to those who were in Hormah, Bor Ashan, Athach **31**and Hebron. He also sent some to those who were in all of the other places where he and his men had wandered around.

Saul Takes His Own Life

31 The Philistines fought against Israel. The men of Israel ran away from them. But many Israelites were killed on Mount Gilboa.

2The Philistines kept chasing Saul and his sons. They killed his sons Jonathan, Abinadab and Malki-Shua. **3**The fighting was heavy around Saul. Men who were armed with bows and arrows caught up with him. They shot their arrows at him and wounded him badly.

4Saul spoke to the man who was carrying his armor. He said, "Pull out your sword. Stick it through me. If you don't, those fellows who aren't circumcised will come. They'll stick their swords through me and hurt me badly."

But the man was terrified. He wouldn't do it. So Saul took his own sword and fell on it. **5**The man saw that Saul was dead. So he fell on his own sword and died with him.

6Saul and his three sons died together that same day. The man who carried his armor also died with them that day. So did all of Saul's men.

7The Israelites who lived along the valley saw that their army had run away. So did those who lived across the Jordan River. They saw that Saul and his sons were dead. So they left their towns and ran away. Then the Philistines came and settled down in them.

8The day after the Philistines had won the battle, they came to take what they wanted from the dead bodies. They found Saul and his three sons dead on Mount Gilboa. **9**So they cut off Saul's head. They took his armor from his body. Then they sent messengers through the whole land of the Philistines. They announced the news in the temple where they had set up statues of their gods. They also announced it among their people.

10They put Saul's armor in the temple where they had set up statues of goddesses that were named after Ashtoreth. They hung his body up on the wall of Beth Shan.

11The people of Jabesh Gilead heard about what the Philistines had done to Saul. **12**So all of their brave men traveled through the night to Beth Shan. They took down the bodies of Saul and his sons from the wall of Beth Shan. They brought them to Jabesh. There they burned them. **13**Then they got the bones of Saul and his sons and buried them under a tamarisk tree at Jabesh. They didn't eat anything for seven days.

2 SAMUEL

King David is the leading hero of the book of 2 Samuel. This book tells the story of David's forty-year reign over the people of Israel. While king, David wins great battles over Israel's enemies, moves the capital of Israel to Jerusalem, and helps Israel become a great nation. While king, David also commits a great sin. The beauty of the book is not in the hero David, however, but in God. God's love and forgiveness for David go far beyond what you would expect. Read the book of 2 Samuel to discover how great God's love is for David, and for you.

HEROES IN THIS BOOK . . .

NATHAN
PAGE 366

ABSALOM
(Not!)
PAGE 375

RIZPAH
PAGE 380

David Hears That Saul Has Died

1 After Saul died, David returned to Ziklag. He had won the battle over the Amalekites. He stayed in Ziklag for two days.

2 On the third day a man arrived from Saul's camp. His clothes were torn. He had dust on his head. When he came to David, he fell to the ground to show him respect.

3 "Where have you come from?" David asked him.

He answered, "I've escaped from Israel's camp."

4 "What happened?" David asked. "Tell me."

He said, "Israel's men ran away from the battle. Many of them were killed. Saul and his son Jonathan are dead."

5 David spoke to the young man who brought him the report. He asked him, "How do you know that Saul and his son Jonathan are dead?"

6 "I just happened to be there on Mount Gilboa," the young man said. "Saul was there too. He was leaning on his spear. The enemy chariots and chariot drivers had almost caught up with him. **7** Then he turned around and saw me. He called out to me. I said, 'What do you want me to do?'

8 "He asked me, 'Who are you?'

" 'An Amalekite,' I answered.

9 "Then he said to me, 'Stand over me and kill me! I'm close to death, but I'm still alive.'

10 "So I stood over him and killed him. I did it because I knew that after he had lost the battle he would be killed anyway. So I took the crown that was on his head. I also took his armband. I've brought them here to you. You are my master."

11 Then David took hold of his clothes and tore them. All of his men did the same thing. **12** All of them were filled with sadness. They sobbed over the whole nation of Israel. They didn't eat anything until evening. That's because Saul and Jonathan and the LORD's army had been killed with swords.

13 David spoke to the young man who had brought him the report. He asked, "Where are you from?"

"I'm the son of an outsider, an Amalekite," he answered.

14 David asked him, "Why weren't you afraid to lift your hand to kill the LORD's anointed king?"

15 Then David called for one of his men. He said, "Go! Strike him down!" So he struck the man down, and the man died. **16** That's because David had said to him,

"Anything that happens to you will be your own fault. What your own mouth has spoken is a witness against you. You said, 'I killed the LORD's anointed king.' "

David's Song of Sadness About Saul and Jonathan

17 David sang a song of sadness about Saul and his son Jonathan. **18** He ordered that it be taught to the people of Judah. It is called The Song of the Bow. It is written down in the Book of Jashar.

David sang,

19 "Israel, your glorious leaders lie dead
     on your hills.
   Your mighty men have fallen.

20 "Don't announce it in Gath.
   Don't tell it in the streets of
     Ashkelon.
If you do, the daughters of the
     Philistines will be glad.
   The daughters of men who haven't
     been circumcised will be joyful.

21 "Mountains of Gilboa,
   may no dew or rain fall on you.
   May your fields not produce any
     offerings of grain.
The shield of the mighty king lies
     polluted there.
   The shield of Saul lies there. It isn't
     rubbed with oil anymore.
22 The bow of Jonathan didn't turn back.
   The sword of Saul didn't return
     without being satisfied.
They spilled the blood of their
     enemies.
   They killed mighty men.

23 "In life Saul and Jonathan were loved
     and gracious.
   In death they were not parted.
They were faster than eagles.
   They were stronger than lions.

24 "Daughters of Israel, sob over Saul.
   He dressed you in the finest clothes.
     He decorated your clothes with
      ornaments of gold.

25 "Your mighty men have fallen in
     battle.
   Jonathan lies dead on your hills.
26 My brother Jonathan, I'm filled with
     sadness because of you.
   You were very special to me.
Your love for me was wonderful.
   It was more wonderful than the love
     of women.

27 "Israel's mighty men have fallen.
   Their weapons of war are broken."

David Is Anointed to Be King Over Judah

2 After Saul and Jonathan died, David asked the Lord for advice. "Should I go up to one of the towns of Judah?" he asked.

The Lord said, "Go up."

David asked, "Where should I go?"

"To Hebron," the Lord answered.

²So David went up there with his two wives. Their names were Ahinoam from Jezreel and Abigail from Carmel. Abigail was Nabal's widow. ³David also took his men and their families with him. They settled down in Hebron and its towns.

⁴Then the men of Judah came to Hebron. There they anointed David to be king over the people of Judah.

David was told that the men of Jabesh Gilead had buried Saul's body. ⁵So he sent messengers to them to speak for him.

The messengers said, "You were kind to bury the body of your master Saul. May the Lord bless you for that. ⁶And may he now be kind and faithful to you. David will treat you well for being kind to Saul's body. ⁷Now then, be strong and brave. Your master Saul is dead. And the people of Judah have anointed David to be king over them."

POWER-SURGE

BRAVE **B**

NOW THEN, BE STRONG AND BRAVE.
— 2 SAMUEL 2:7 —

STRONG

The Armies of David and Saul Fight Each Other

⁸Abner, the son of Ner, was commander of Saul's army. He had brought Saul's son Ish-Bosheth to Mahanaim. ⁹There he made him king over Gilead, Ashuri and Jezreel. He also made him king over Ephraim, Benjamin and other areas of Israel.

¹⁰Ish-Bosheth was 40 years old when he became king over Israel. He ruled for two years. But the people of Judah followed David. ¹¹David was king in Hebron over the people of Judah for seven and a half years.

¹²Abner, the son of Ner, left Mahanaim and went to Gibeon. The men of Ish-Bosheth, the son of Saul, went with him. ¹³Joab, the son of Zeruiah, and David's men also went out. All of them met at the pool in Gibeon. One group sat down on one side of the pool. The other group sat on the other side.

¹⁴Then Abner said to Joab, "Let's have some of the young men get up and fight. Let's tell them to fight hand to hand in front of us."

"All right. Let them do it," Joab said.

¹⁵So the young men stood up and were counted off. There were 12 on the side of Benjamin and Saul's son Ish-Bosheth. And there were 12 on David's side. ¹⁶Each man grabbed one of his enemies by the head. Each one stuck his dagger into the other man's side. And all of them fell down together and died. So that place in Gibeon was named Helkath Hazzurim.

¹⁷The fighting that day was very heavy. Abner and the men of Israel lost the battle to David's men.

¹⁸The three sons of Zeruiah were there. Their names were Joab, Abishai and Asahel. Asahel was as quick on his feet as a wild antelope. ¹⁹He chased Abner. He didn't turn to the right or the left as he chased him. ²⁰Abner looked behind him. He asked, "Asahel, is that you?"

"It is," he answered.

²¹Then Abner said to him, "Turn to the right or the left. Fight one of the young men. Take his weapons away from him." But Asahel wouldn't stop chasing him.

²²Again Abner warned Asahel, "Stop chasing me! If you don't, I'll strike you down. Then how could I look your brother Joab in the face?"

²³But Asahel refused to give up the chase. So Abner drove the dull end of his spear into Asahel's stomach. The spear came out of his back. He fell and died right there on the spot. Every man stopped when he came to the place where Asahel had fallen and died.

²⁴But Joab and Abishai chased Abner. As the sun was going down, they came to the hill of Ammah. It was near Giah on the way to the dry and empty land close to Gibeon. ²⁵The men of Benjamin gathered in a group around Abner. They took their stand on top of a hill.

²⁶Abner called out to Joab, "Do you want our swords to keep on killing us off? Don't you know that all of this fighting will end in bitter feelings? How long will it be before you order your men to stop chasing their fellow Israelites?"

27Joab answered, "It's a good thing you spoke up. If you hadn't, the men would have kept on chasing their fellow Israelites until morning. And that's just as sure as God is alive."

28So Joab blew a trumpet. All of the men stopped. They didn't chase Israel anymore. They didn't fight anymore either.

29All that night Abner and his men marched through the Arabah Valley. They went across the Jordan River. They kept on going through the whole Bithron. Finally, they came to Mahanaim.

30Then Joab returned from chasing Abner. He gathered all of his men together. Besides Asahel, only 19 of David's men were missing. 31But David's men had killed 360 men from Benjamin who were with Abner. 32They got Asahel's body and buried it in his father's tomb at Bethlehem. Then Joab and his men marched all night. They arrived at Hebron at sunrise.

3 The war between Saul's royal house and David's royal house lasted a long time. David grew stronger and stronger. But the royal house of Saul grew weaker and weaker.

2Sons were born to David in Hebron.

His first son was Amnon. Amnon's mother was Ahinoam from Jezreel.

3His second son was Kileab. Kileab's mother was Abigail. She was Nabal's widow from Carmel.

The third son was Absalom. His mother was Maacah. She was the daughter of Talmai, the king of Geshur.

4The fourth son was Adonijah. His mother was Haggith.

The fifth son was Shephatiah. His mother was Abital.

5The sixth son was Ithream. His mother was David's wife Eglah.

Those sons were born to David in Hebron.

Abner Goes Over to David's Side

6The fighting continued between David's royal house and Saul's royal house. Abner gained more and more power in the royal house of Saul.

7While Saul was still alive, he had a concubine named Rizpah. She was the daughter of Aiah. Ish-Bosheth said to Abner, "Why did you have sex with my father's concubine?"

8Abner burned with anger because of what Ish-Bosheth said. He answered, "Do you think I'm only a dog's head? Am I on Judah's side? To this very day I've been true to the royal house of your father Saul. I've been true to his family and friends. I haven't handed you over to David. But now you claim that I've sinned with this woman!

9"I will do for David what the Lord promised him with an oath. If I don't, may God punish me greatly. 10I'll take the kingdom away from Saul's royal house. I'll set up the throne of David's kingdom over Israel and Judah. He will rule from Dan all the way to Beersheba."

11Ish-Bosheth didn't dare to say another word to Abner. He was much too afraid of him.

12Then Abner sent messengers to David to speak for him. They said, "Who will rule over this land? Make a covenant with me. Then I'll help you bring all of the people of Israel over to your side."

13"Good," said David. "I will make a covenant with you. But there's one thing I want you to do. Bring Saul's daughter Michal to me. Don't come to see me unless she's with you."

14Then David sent messengers to Saul's son Ish-Bosheth. He ordered them to say, "Give me my wife Michal. She was promised to me. I paid for her with the skins I cut off when I circumcised 100 Philistines."

15So Ish-Bosheth gave the order. He sent men who took Michal away from her husband Paltiel. Paltiel was the son of Laish. 16But her husband followed her to Bahurim. He was crying all the way. Then Abner said to him, "Go back home!" So he did.

17Abner talked with the elders of Israel. He said, "For some time you have wanted to make David your king. 18Now do it! The Lord made a promise to David. He said, 'I will save my people Israel from the powerful hand of the Philistines. I will also save them from all of their enemies. I will save them through my servant David.' "

19Abner also spoke to the people of Benjamin in person. Then he went to Hebron to tell David everything. He told him what Israel and all of the people of Benjamin wanted to do. 20Abner had 20 men with him. They came to David at Hebron. So David prepared a big dinner for Abner and his men.

21Then Abner said to David, "Let me go right now. I'll gather together all of the people of Israel for you. After all, you are now my king and master. The people can make a covenant with you. Then you can rule over everyone you want to." So David sent Abner away. And he went in peace.

Joab Murders Abner

22Just then David's men and Joab came back from attacking their enemies. They brought with them the large amount of goods they had taken. But Abner wasn't with David in Hebron anymore. That's because David had sent him away, and he had gone in peace.

23Joab and all of the soldiers who were with him arrived. Then he was told that Abner, the son of Ner, had come to see the king. He was told that the king had sent Abner away. He was also told that Abner had gone in peace.

24So Joab went to the king. He said, "What have you done? Abner came to you. Why did you let him get away? Now he's gone! 25You know what Abner, the son of Ner, is like. He came to trick you. He wanted to watch your every move. He came to find out everything you are doing."

26Then Joab left David. He sent messengers to get Abner. They brought Abner back from the well of Sirah. But David didn't know about it.

27When Abner returned to Hebron, Joab took him to one side. He brought him to the entrance of the city gate. Joab acted as if he wanted to speak to him in private. But he really wanted to get even with him. That's because Abner had spilled the blood of Joab's brother Asahel. So Joab stabbed him in the stomach. And Abner died.

28Later on, David heard about it. He said, "I and the people of my kingdom aren't guilty of spilling the blood of Abner, the son of Ner. We are free of blame forever in the sight of the LORD.

29"May Joab and his whole family line be held accountable for spilling Abner's blood! May someone in Joab's family always have an open sore or skin disease. May someone in his family always have to use a crutch to walk. May someone in his family be killed with a sword. And may someone in his family never have enough food to eat."

30Joab and his brother Abishai murdered Abner. They did it because he had killed their brother Asahel in the battle at Gibeon.

31David spoke to Joab and all of the people who were with him. He said, "Tear your clothes. Put on black clothes. Sob when you walk in front of Abner's body." King David himself walked behind it.

32Abner's body was buried in Hebron. The king sobbed out loud at Abner's tomb. So did the rest of the people.

33King David sang a song of sadness over Abner. He said,

"Should Abner have died as sinful
        people do?
34   His hands were not tied.
      His feet were not chained.
He died as if he had been killed by evil
        people."

All of the people sobbed over Abner again.

35Then all of them came and begged David to eat something. They wanted him to eat while it was still day. But David took an oath. He said, "I won't taste bread or anything else before the sun goes down. If I do, may God punish me greatly!"

36All of the people heard it and were pleased. In fact, everything the king did pleased them. 37So on that day all of the people of Judah and Israel understood. They knew that the king didn't have anything to do with the murder of Abner, the son of Ner.

38The king spoke to his men. He said, "Don't you realize that a great commander has died in Israel today? 39I'm the anointed king. But today I'm weak. These sons of Zeruiah are too powerful for me. May the LORD pay back the one who killed Abner! May he pay him back for the evil thing he has done!"

Ish-Bosheth Is Murdered

4 Ish-Bosheth, the son of Saul, heard that Abner had died in Hebron. Then he wasn't so brave anymore. And all of the people of Israel became alarmed.

2Two men in Ish-Bosheth's army led small companies that attacked their enemies. The names of the men were Baanah and Recab. They were sons of Rimmon from the town of Beeroth. Rimmon was from the tribe of Benjamin. Beeroth is considered to be part of Benjamin. 3That's because the people who used to live in Beeroth had run away to Gittaim. They have lived there as outsiders to this very day.

4Jonathan, the son of Saul, had a son named Mephibosheth. Both of Mephibosheth's feet were hurt. He was five years old when the news that Saul and Jonathan had died came from Jezreel. His nurse picked him up and ran. But as she hurried to get away, he fell down. That's how his feet were hurt.

⁵Recab and Baanah started out for the house of Ish-Bosheth. They were the sons of Rimmon from Beeroth. They arrived there during the hottest time of the day. Ish-Bosheth was taking his early afternoon nap. ⁶Recab and his brother Baanah went into the inside part of the house. They acted as if they were going to get some wheat. Instead, they stabbed Ish-Bosheth in the stomach. Then they slipped away.

⁷They had gone into the house while Ish-Bosheth was lying on his bed in his bedroom. They stabbed him and killed him. Then they cut off his head and took it with them. They traveled all night through the Arabah Valley. ⁸They brought the head of Ish-Bosheth to King David at Hebron. They said to him, "Here's the head of Ish-Bosheth, the son of Saul. Saul was your enemy. He often tried to kill you. Today the Lord has paid Saul and his family back. He has let you get even with them. You are our king and master."

⁹David gave an answer to Recab and his brother Baanah. They were the sons of Rimmon of Beeroth. David said, "The Lord has saved me from all of my troubles. ¹⁰A man once told me, 'Saul is dead.' He thought he was bringing me good news. But I grabbed hold of him. I had him put to death in Ziklag. That's the reward I gave him for his news! And that's just as sure as the Lord is alive.

¹¹"Now you evil men have killed a man in his own house. He hadn't done anything wrong. You killed him while he was lying on his own bed. You spilled his blood. So shouldn't I spill your blood? Shouldn't I wipe you off the face of the earth?"

¹²Then David gave an order to his men. They killed Recab and Baanah. They cut off their hands and feet. They hung their bodies by the pool in Hebron. But they buried the head of Ish-Bosheth in Abner's tomb at Hebron.

David Becomes King Over Israel

5 All of the tribes of Israel came to see David at Hebron. They said, "We are your own flesh and blood. ²In the past, Saul was our king. But you led the men of Israel on their military campaigns. And the Lord said to you, 'You will be the shepherd over my people Israel. You will become their ruler.' "

³All of the elders of Israel came to see King David at Hebron. There the king made a covenant with them in the sight of the Lord. They anointed David as king over Israel.

⁴David was 30 years old when he became king. He ruled for 40 years. ⁵In Hebron he ruled over Judah for seven and a half years. In Jerusalem he ruled over all of Israel and Judah for 33 years.

David Captures Jerusalem

⁶The king and his men marched to Jerusalem. They went to attack the Jebusites who lived there.

The Jebusites said to David, "You won't get in here. Even blind people and those who are disabled can keep you from coming in." They thought, "David can't get in here."

⁷But David captured the fort of Zion. It became known as the City of David.

⁸On that day David said, "Anyone who wins the battle over the Jebusites will have to crawl through the water tunnel to get into the city. That's the only way he can reach those 'disabled and blind' enemies of mine." That's why people say, "Those who are 'blind and disabled' won't enter David's palace."

⁹David moved into the fort. He called it the City of David. He built up the area around the fort. He filled in the low places. He started at the bottom and worked his way up. ¹⁰David became more and more powerful. That's because the Lord God who rules over all was with him.

¹¹Hiram was king of Tyre. He sent messengers to David. He sent cedar logs along with them. He also sent skilled workers. They worked with wood and stone. They built a palace for David.

¹²David knew that the Lord had made his position as king secure. He knew that he had made him king over the whole nation of Israel. He knew that the Lord had greatly honored his kingdom. The

POWER-SURGE

STRONG

DAVID BECAME MORE AND MORE POWERFUL. THAT'S BECAUSE THE Lord GOD WHO RULES OVER ALL WAS WITH HIM.
— 2 SAMUEL 5:10 —

Lord had done it because the Israelites were his people.

13After David left Hebron, he got more concubines and wives in Jerusalem. More sons and daughters were born to him there. 14Here is a list of the children who were born to him in Jerusalem. Their names were Shammua, Shobab, Nathan, Solomon, 15Ibhar, Elishua, Nepheg, Japhia, 16Elishama, Eliada and Eliphelet.

David Wins the Battle Over the Philistines

17The Philistines heard that David had been anointed king over Israel. So their whole army went to look for him. But David heard about it. He went down to his usual place of safety. 18The Philistines had come and spread out in the Valley of Rephaim.

19So David asked the Lord for advice. He said, "Should I go and attack the Philistines? Will you hand them over to me?"

The Lord answered him, "Go. You can be sure that I will hand the Philistines over to you."

20So David went to Baal Perazim. There he won the battle over the Philistines. He said, "The Lord has broken through against my enemies when I've attacked them, just as water breaks through a dam." That's why the place was called Baal Perazim. 21The Philistines left the statues of their gods there. So David and his men carried the statues off.

22Once more the Philistines came up. They spread out in the Valley of Rephaim. 23So David asked the Lord for advice. The Lord answered, "Do not go straight up. Instead, circle around behind them. Attack them in front of the balsam trees. 24Listen for the sound of marching in the tops of the trees. Then move quickly. The sound will mean that I have gone out in front of you. I will strike down the Philistine army."

25So David did just as the Lord had commanded him. He struck down the Philistines. He struck them down from Gibeon all the way to Gezer.

David Brings the Ark to Jerusalem

6 Again David brought together the best soldiers in Israel. The total number was 30,000. 2He and all of his men started out from Baalah in Judah. They wanted to bring the ark of God up to Jerusalem from there. The ark is named after the Lord. He is the Lord who rules over all. He sits on his throne between the cherubim that are on the ark.

3The ark of God was placed on a new cart. Then it was brought from Abinadab's house, which was on a hill. Uzzah and Ahio were guiding the cart. They were the sons of Abinadab. 4The ark of God was on the cart. Ahio was walking in front of it.

5David was celebrating with all his might in the sight of the Lord. So was the whole community of Israel. All of them were singing songs. They were also playing harps, lyres, tambourines, rattles and cymbals.

6They came to the threshing floor of Nacon. The oxen nearly fell there. So Uzzah reached out and took hold of the ark of God. 7Then the Lord's anger burned against Uzzah. That's because what Uzzah did showed that he didn't have any respect for the Lord. So God struck him down. He died there beside the ark of God.

8David was angry because the Lord's burning anger had broken out against Uzzah. That's why the place is still called Perez Uzzah to this very day.

9David was afraid of the Lord that day. He asked, "How can the ark of the Lord ever be brought to me?" 10He didn't want to take the ark of the Lord to be with him in the City of David. Instead, he took it to the house of Obed-Edom. Obed-Edom was from Gath. 11The ark of the Lord remained in Obed-Edom's house for three months. And the Lord blessed him and his whole family.

12King David was told, "The Lord has blessed the family of Obed-Edom. He has also blessed everything that belongs to him. That's because the ark of God is in Obed-Edom's house."

So David went down there and brought up the ark. With great joy he brought it up from the house of Obed-Edom. He took it to the City of David. 13Those who were carrying the ark of the Lord took six steps forward. Then David sacrificed a bull and a fat calf. 14David was wearing a sacred linen apron. He danced in the sight of the Lord with all his might. 15He did it while he was bringing up the ark of the Lord. The whole community of Israel helped him bring it up. They shouted. They blew trumpets.

16The ark of the Lord was brought into the City of David. Saul's daughter Michal was watching from a window. She saw King David leaping and dancing in the sight of the Lord. That made her hate him in her heart.

17The ark of the Lord was brought into Jerusalem. It was put in its place in the

GIVING Ⓖ

[DAVID] BLESSED THE PEOPLE IN THE NAME OF THE LORD WHO RULES OVER ALL. HE GAVE TO EACH ISRAELITE MAN AND WOMAN A LOAF OF BREAD. HE ALSO GAVE EACH ONE A DATE CAKE AND A RAISIN CAKE.

—— 2 SAMUEL 6:18–19 ——

tent David had set up for it. David sacrificed burnt offerings and friendship offerings to the LORD.

18After he finished sacrificing those offerings, he blessed the people in the name of the LORD who rules over all. **19**He gave to each Israelite man and woman a loaf of bread. He also gave each one a date cake and a raisin cake. Then all of the people went home.

20David returned home to bless his family. Saul's daughter Michal came out to meet him. She said, "You are the king of Israel. You have really brought honor to yourself today, haven't you? You have taken off your royal robe right in front of the female slaves of your officials. You acted like someone who is very foolish!"

21David said to Michal, "I did it to honor the LORD. He chose me instead of your father or anyone else in Saul's family. He appointed me ruler over his people Israel. I will celebrate in honor of the LORD. **22**And that's not all. I will bring even less honor to myself. I will bring even more shame on myself. But those female slaves you spoke about will honor me."

23Saul's daughter Michal didn't have any children as long as she lived.

God Makes a Promise to David

7 The king settled down in his palace. The LORD had given him peace and rest from all of his enemies who were around him.

2Then the king spoke to the prophet Nathan. He said, "Here I am, living in a palace that has beautiful cedar walls. But the ark of God remains in a tent."

3Nathan replied to the king, "Go ahead and do what you want to. The LORD is with you."

4That night the word of the LORD came to Nathan. The LORD said,

5"Go and speak to my servant David. Tell him, 'The LORD says, "Are you the one to build me a house to live in? **6**I have not lived in a house from the day I brought the people of Israel up out of Egypt until now. I have been moving from place to place. I have been living in a tent. **7**I have moved from place to place with all of the people of Israel. I commanded their rulers to be shepherds over them. I never asked any of those rulers, 'Why haven't you built me a house that has beautiful cedar walls?' " '

8"So tell my servant David, 'The LORD who rules over all says, "I took you away from the grasslands. That's where you were taking care of your father's sheep and goats. I made you ruler over my people Israel. **9**I have been with you everywhere you have gone. I cut off all of your enemies when you were attacking them.

" ' "Now I will make you famous. Your name will be just as respected as the names of the most important people on earth. **10**I will provide a place where my people Israel can live. I will plant them in the land. Then they will have a home of their own. They will not be bothered anymore. Evil people will no longer crush them, as they did at first. **11**That is what your enemies have done ever since I appointed leaders over my people Israel. But I will give you peace and rest from all of them.

" ' "I tell you that I myself will set up a royal house for you. **12**Some day your life will come to an end. You will join the members of your family who have already died. Then I will make one of your own sons the next king after you. And I will make his kingdom secure. **13**He is the one who will build a house where I will put my Name.

" ' "I will set up the throne of his kingdom. It will last forever. **14**I will be his father. And he will be my son. When he does what is wrong, I will use other men to beat him with rods and whips. **15**I took my love away from Saul. I removed him from being king. You were there when I did it. But I will never take my love away from your son.

16" ' "Your royal house and your kingdom will last forever in my sight. Your throne will last forever." ' "

17Nathan reported to David all of the words that the LORD had spoken to him.

David Prays to the LORD

18Then King David went into the holy tent. He sat down in front of the LORD. He said,

"LORD and King, who am I? My family isn't important. So why have you brought me this far? **19**I would have thought that you had already done more than enough for me. But now, LORD and King, you have also spoken about what is going to happen to my royal house in days to come. LORD and King, is this your usual way of dealing with people? **20**"What more can I say to you? LORD and King, you know all about me. **21**You have done a wonderful thing. You have made it known to me. You have done it because that's what you said you would do. It's exactly what you wanted to do for me.

22"LORD and King, how great you are! There isn't anyone like you. There isn't any God but you. We have heard about it with our own ears.

23"Who is like your people Israel? God, we are the one nation on earth you have saved. You have set us free for yourself. Your name has become famous. You have done great and wonderful things. You have driven out nations and their gods to make room for your people. You saved us when you set us free from Egypt. **24**You made Israel your very own people forever. LORD, you have become our God.

25"And now, LORD God, keep forever the promise you have made to me and my royal house. Do exactly as you promised. **26**Then your name will be honored forever. People will say, 'The LORD rules over all. He is God over Israel.' My royal house will be made secure in your sight.

27"LORD who rules over all, you are the God of Israel. Here's what you

THANKFUL ♣

LORD AND KING, YOU ARE GOD! YOUR WORDS CAN BE TRUSTED.
— 2 SAMUEL 7:28 — ◆

TRUSTED

have shown me. You told me, 'I will build you a royal house.' So I can boldly offer this prayer to you. **28**LORD and King, you are God! Your words can be trusted. You have promised many good things to me.

29"Now please bless my royal house. Then it will continue forever in your sight. LORD and King, you have spoken. Because you have given my royal house your blessing, it will be blessed forever."

David Wins Many Battles

8 While David was king of Israel, he won many battles over the Philistines. He brought them under his control. He took Metheg Ammah away from them.

2David also won the battle over the people of Moab. He made them lie down on the ground. Then he measured them off with a piece of rope. He put two-thirds of them to death. He let the other third remain alive. So the Moabites were brought under David's rule. They gave him the gifts he required them to bring him.

3David fought against Hadadezer, the son of Rehob. Hadadezer was king of Zobah. He had gone to take back control of the land along the Euphrates River. **4**David captured 1,000 of Hadadezer's chariots, 7,000 chariot riders and 20,000 soldiers on foot. He cut the legs of all but 100 of the chariot horses.

5The Arameans of Damascus came to help Hadadezer, the king of Zobah. But David struck down 22,000 of them. **6**He stationed some soldiers in the Aramean kingdom of Damascus. The people of Aram were brought under his rule. They gave him the gifts he required them to bring him. The LORD helped David win his battles everywhere he went.

⁷David took the gold shields that belonged to the officers of Hadadezer. He brought the shields to Jerusalem. ⁸He took a huge amount of bronze from Tebah and Berothai. Those towns belonged to Hadadezer.

⁹Tou was king of Hamath. He heard that David had won the battle over the entire army of Hadadezer. ¹⁰So Tou sent his son Joram to King David. Joram greeted David. He praised him because he had won the battle over Hadadezer. Hadadezer had been at war with Tou. So Joram brought with him articles that were made out of silver, gold and bronze.

¹¹King David set those articles apart for the LORD. He had done the same thing with the silver and gold he had taken from the other nations he had brought under his control. ¹²Those nations were Edom, Moab, Ammon, Philistia and Amalek. He also set apart for the LORD what he had taken from Hadadezer, the son of Rehob. Hadadezer was king of Zobah.

¹³David returned after he had struck down 18,000 men of Edom in the Valley of Salt. He became famous for doing it.

¹⁴He stationed some soldiers all through Edom. The whole nation of Edom was brought under his rule. The LORD helped David win his battles everywhere he went.

David's Officials

¹⁵David ruled over the whole nation of Israel. He did what was fair and right for all of his people. ¹⁶Joab, the son of Zeruiah, was commander over the army. Jehoshaphat, the son of Ahilud, kept the records. ¹⁷Zadok, the son of Ahitub, was a priest. Ahimelech, the son of Abiathar, was also a priest. Seraiah was the secretary. ¹⁸Benaiah, the son of Jehoiada, was commander over the Kerethites and Pelethites. And David's sons were royal advisers.

David Is Kind to Mephibosheth

9 David asked, "Is anyone left from the royal house of Saul? If there is, I want to be kind to him because of Jonathan."

²Ziba was a servant in Saul's family. David sent for him to come and see him. The king said to him, "Are you Ziba?"

"I'm ready to serve you," he replied.

³The king asked, "Isn't anyone left from the royal house of Saul? God has been very kind to me. I would like to be kind to someone in the same way."

Ziba answered the king, "A son of Jonathan is still living. Both of his feet were hurt."

⁴"Where is he?" the king asked.

Ziba answered, "He's in the town of Lo Debar. He's staying at the house of Makir, the son of Ammiel."

⁵So King David had Mephibosheth brought from Makir's house in Lo Debar.

⁶Mephibosheth came to David. He was the son of Jonathan, the son of Saul. Mephibosheth bowed down to David to show him respect.

David said, "Mephibosheth!"

"I'm ready to serve you," he replied.

⁷"Don't be afraid," David told him. "You can be sure that I will be kind to you because of your father Jonathan. I'll give back to you all of the land that belonged to your grandfather Saul. And I'll always provide what you need."

⁸Mephibosheth bowed down to David. He said, "Who am I? Why should you pay attention to me? I'm nothing but a dead dog."

⁹Then the king sent for Saul's servant Ziba. He said to him, "I'm giving your master's grandson everything that belonged to Saul and his family. ¹⁰You and your sons and your servants must farm the land for him. You must bring in the crops. Then he'll be taken care of. I'll always provide what he needs." Ziba had 15 sons and 20 servants.

¹¹Then Ziba said to the king, "I'll do anything you command me to do. You are my king and master." So David provided what Mephibosheth needed. He treated him like one of the king's sons.

¹²Mephibosheth had a young son named Mica. All of the members of Ziba's family became servants of Mephibo-

POWER-SURGE

KIND   K

GOD HAS BEEN VERY KIND TO ME. I WOULD LIKE TO BE KIND TO SOMEONE IN THE SAME WAY.
— 2 SAMUEL 9:3 —

THANKFUL

sheth. ¹³Mephibosheth lived in Jerusalem. The king always provided what he needed. Both of his feet were hurt.

David Goes to War Against the People of Ammon

10 The king of Ammon died. His son Hanun became the next king after him. ²David thought, "I'm going to be kind to Hanun. His father Nahash was kind to me." So David sent messengers to Hanun. He wanted them to tell Hanun how sad he was that Hanun's father had died.

David's messengers went to the land of Ammon. ³The Ammonite nobles spoke to their master Hanun. They said, "David has sent messengers to tell you he is sad. They say he wants to honor your father. But the real reason they've come is to look the city over. They want to destroy it."

⁴So Hanun grabbed hold of David's men. He shaved off half of each man's beard. He cut their clothes off just below the waist and left them half naked. Then he sent them away.

⁵David was told about it. So he sent messengers to his men because they were filled with shame. King David said to them, "Stay at Jericho until your beards grow out again. Then come back here."

⁶The Ammonites realized that what they had done had made David very angry with them. So they hired 20,000 Aramean soldiers who were on foot. The soldiers came from Beth Rehob and Zobah. The Ammonites also hired the king of Maacah and 1,000 men. And they hired 12,000 men from Tob.

⁷David heard about it. So he sent Joab out with the entire army of Israel's fighting men.

⁸The Ammonites marched out. They took up their battle positions at the entrance of their city gate. The Arameans of Zobah and Rehob gathered their troops together in the open country. So did the men of Tob and Maacah.

⁹Joab saw that there were lines of soldiers in front of him and behind him. So he chose some of the best troops in Israel. He sent them to march out against the Arameans.

¹⁰He put the rest of the men under the command of his brother Abishai. Joab sent them to march out against the Ammonites. ¹¹He said, "Suppose the Arameans are too strong for me. Then you must come and help me. But suppose the Ammonites are too strong for you. Then I'll come and help you.

BRAVE

BE STRONG. LET'S BE BRAVE AS WE FIGHT FOR OUR PEOPLE AND THE CITIES OF OUR GOD. THE LORD WILL DO WHAT HE THINKS IS BEST.
—— **2 SAMUEL 10:12** ——

STRONG

¹²"Be strong. Let's be brave as we fight for our people and the cities of our God. The LORD will do what he thinks is best."

¹³Then Joab and the troops who were with him marched out to attack the Arameans. They ran away from him. ¹⁴The Ammonites saw that the Arameans were running away. So they ran away from Abishai. They went inside the city. After Joab had fought against the Ammonites, he went back to Jerusalem.

¹⁵The Arameans saw that they had been driven away by Israel. So they brought their troops together. ¹⁶Hadadezer had some Arameans brought from east of the Euphrates River. They went to Helam under the command of Shobach. He was the commander of Hadadezer's army.

¹⁷David was told about it. So he gathered the whole army of Israel together. They went across the Jordan River to Helam. The Arameans lined up their soldiers to go to war against David. They began to fight against him. ¹⁸But then they ran away from Israel. David killed 700 of their chariot riders. He killed 40,000 of their soldiers who were on foot. He also struck down Shobach, the commander of their army. Shobach died there.

¹⁹All of the kings who were under the rule of Hadadezer saw that Israel had won the battle over them. So they made a peace treaty with the Israelites. They were brought under Israel's rule.

After that, the Arameans were afraid to help the Ammonites anymore.

David and Bathsheba

11 It was spring. It was the time when kings go off to war. So David sent Joab out with the king's special troops and the whole army of Israel. They destroyed the Ammonites. They went to the city of Rabbah. They surrounded it and got ready to attack it. But David remained in Jerusalem.

2One evening David got up from his bed. He walked around on the roof of his palace. From the roof he saw a woman taking a bath. She was very beautiful.

3David sent a messenger to find out who she was. The messenger returned and said, "She is Bathsheba. She's the daughter of Eliam. She's the wife of Uriah. He's a Hittite."

4Then David sent messengers to get her. She came to him. And he slept with her. Then she went back home. All of that took place after she had already made herself "clean" from her monthly period.

5Later, Bathsheba found out she was pregnant. She sent a message to David. It said, "I'm pregnant."

6So David sent a message to Joab. It said, "Send me Uriah, the Hittite." Joab sent him to David.

7Uriah came to David. David asked him how Joab and the soldiers were doing. He also asked him how the war was going.

8David said to Uriah, "Go home and enjoy some time with your wife." So Uriah left the palace. Then the king sent him a gift.

9But Uriah didn't go home. Instead, he slept at the entrance to the palace. He stayed there with all of his master's servants.

10David was told, "Uriah didn't go home." So he sent for Uriah. He said to him, "You have been away for a long time. Why didn't you go home?"

11Uriah said to David, "The ark and the army of Israel and Judah are out there in tents. My master Joab and your special troops are camped in the open fields. How could I go to my house to eat and drink? How could I go there and make love to my wife? I could never do a thing like that. And that's just as sure as you are alive!"

12Then David said to him, "Stay here one more day. Tomorrow I'll send you back to the battle." So Uriah remained in Jerusalem that day and the next.

13David invited Uriah to eat and drink with him. David got him drunk. But Uriah still didn't go home. In the evening he went out and slept on his mat. He stayed there among his master's servants.

14The next morning David wrote a letter to Joab. He sent it along with Uriah. 15In it he wrote, "Put Uriah on the front lines. That's where the fighting is the heaviest. Then pull your men back from him. When you do, the Ammonites will strike him down and kill him."

16So Joab attacked the city. He put Uriah at a place where he knew the strongest enemy fighters were. 17The troops came out of the city. They fought against Joab. Some of the men in David's army were killed. Uriah, the Hittite, also died.

18Joab sent David a full report of the battle. 19He told the messenger, "Tell the king everything that happened in the battle. When you are finished, 20his anger might explode. He might ask you, 'Why did you go so close to the city to fight against it? Didn't you know that the enemy soldiers would shoot arrows down from the wall? 21Don't you remember how Abimelech, the son of Jerub-Besheth, was killed? A woman dropped a large millstone on him from the wall. That's how he died in Thebez. So why did you go so close to the wall?' If the king asks you that, tell him, 'Your servant Uriah, the Hittite, is also dead.' "

22The messenger started out for Jerusalem. When he arrived there, he told David everything Joab had sent him to say. 23The messenger said to David, "The men who were in the city were more powerful than we were. They came out to fight against us in the open. But we drove them back to the entrance of the city gate. 24Then those who were armed with bows shot arrows at us from the wall. Some of your special troops were killed. Your servant Uriah, the Hittite, is also dead."

25David told the messenger, "Tell Joab, 'Don't get upset over what happened. Swords kill one person as well as another. So keep on attacking the city. Destroy it.' Tell that to Joab. It will cheer him up."

26Uriah's wife heard that her husband was dead. She sobbed over him. 27When her time of sadness was over, David had her brought to his house. She became his wife. And she had a son by him. But the LORD wasn't pleased with what David had done.

David's Son Dies

12 The LORD sent the prophet Nathan to David. When Nathan came to him, he said, "Two men lived in the same town. One was rich. The other was poor. 2The rich man had a very large number of sheep and cattle. 3But all the poor man had was one little female lamb. He had bought it. He raised it. It grew up with him and his children. It shared his food. It drank from his cup. It even slept in his arms. It was just like a daughter to him.

4"One day a traveler came to the rich man. The rich man wanted to prepare a meal for him. But he didn't want to kill one of his own sheep or cattle. Instead, he took the little female lamb that belonged to the poor man. Then he cooked it for the traveler who had come to him."

5David burned with anger against the rich man. He said to Nathan, "The man who did that is worthy of death. And that's just as sure as the Lord is alive. **6**The man must pay back four times as much as that lamb was worth. How could he do such a thing? And he wasn't even sorry he had done it."

7Then Nathan said to David, "You are the man! The Lord, the God of Israel, says, 'I anointed you king over Israel. I saved you from Saul's powerful hand. **8**I gave you everything that belonged to your master Saul. I even put his wives into your arms. I made you king over the people of Israel and Judah. And if all of that had not been enough for you, I would have given you even more.

9" 'Why did you turn your back on what I told you to do? You did what is evil in my sight. You made sure that Uriah, the Hittite, would be killed in battle. You took his wife to be your own. You let the men of Ammon kill him with their swords.

10" 'So time after time members of your own royal house will be killed with swords. That's because you turned your back on me. You took the wife of Uriah, the Hittite, to be your own.'

11"The Lord also says, 'I am going to bring trouble on you. It will come from your own family. I will take your wives away. Your own eyes will see it. I will give your wives to a man who is close to you. He will lie with them in the middle of the day. **12**You committed your sins in secret. But I will make sure that the sin the man commits with your wives will take place in the middle of the day. Everyone in Israel will see it.' "

13Then David said to Nathan, "I have sinned against the Lord."

Nathan replied, "The Lord has taken away your sin. You aren't going to die. **14**But you have dared to make fun of the Lord. So the son who has been born to you will die."

15Nathan went home. Then the Lord made the child that had been born to Uriah's wife by David very sick.

16David begged God to heal the child. David didn't eat anything. He spent his nights lying on the ground. **17**His most trusted servants stood beside him. They wanted him to get up from the ground. But he refused to do it. And he wouldn't eat any food with them.

18On the seventh day the child died. David's servants were afraid to tell him the child was dead. They thought, "While the child was still alive, we spoke to David. But he wouldn't listen to us. So how can we tell him the child is dead? He might do something terrible to himself."

19David saw that his servants were whispering to each other. Then he realized the child was dead. "Has the child died?" he asked.

"Yes," they replied. "He's dead."

20Then David got up from the ground. After he washed himself, he put on lotions. He changed his clothes. He went into the house of the Lord and worshiped him. Then he went to his own house. He asked for some food. They served it to him. And he ate it.

21His servants asked him, "Why are you acting like this? While the child was still alive, you wouldn't eat anything. You cried a lot. But now that the child is dead, you get up and eat!"

22He answered, "While the child was still alive, I didn't eat anything. And I cried a lot. I thought, 'Who knows? The Lord might show favor to me. He might let the child live.' **23**But now he's dead. So why should I go without eating? Can I bring him back to life again? Someday I'll go to him. But he won't return to me."

24Then David comforted his wife Bathsheba. He went to her and made love to her. Some time later she had a son. He was given the name Solomon. The Lord loved him. **25**So the Lord sent a message through the prophet Nathan. It said, "Name the boy Jedidiah."

David Captures the City of Rabbah

26During that time, Joab fought against Rabbah. It was the royal city of the Ammonites. It had high walls around it. Joab was about to capture it. **27**He sent messengers to David. He told them to say, "I have fought against Rabbah. I've taken control of its water supply. **28**So bring the rest of the troops together. Surround the city and get ready to attack it. Then cap-

NATHAN

2 SAMUEL 12:25

The LORD sent a message [to David] through the prophet Nathan.

Nathan's heart pounded with fear as he walked into the throne room. He bent his shaky legs and bowed before King David. Nathan knew David well. He knew that David loved God and served him. But Nathan also knew that David had done some terrible things. He had taken another man's wife for his own. And he had had her husband killed. Nathan bravely obeyed God and gave God's message to King David.

Nathan began by telling David a story. A rich man owned many sheep. A poor man owned only one little lamb, which he loved very much. When the rich man had company, he killed the poor man's lamb for dinner instead of one of his own sheep. What did David think they should do to that rich man?

David was instantly angry with the rich man. He must be punished immediately!

Now the moment had come. Nathan stood firm and looked David straight in the eyes. **"YOU ARE THAT MAN," HE SAID.** "You took another man's only wife and had him killed. You deserve punishment as much as the rich man in the story."

Nathan waited for David's reaction. Would he signal his guards to have him kicked out? Or killed? David was king. He could do anything to Nathan. But Nathan had to give the message anyway. It was from *God*.

David sat quietly for several minutes. Then he looked sadly into Nathan's eyes. "I have sinned before God. I deserve to be punished." David truly did love the Lord. He knew he had sinned. And he knew he needed God's forgiveness.

Nathan breathed out a sigh of relief. He had given David the message from God. He had obeyed.

BE A NATHAN

Nathan knew that the most important thing was to obey God. So he did what he was afraid of doing. It isn't always easy to obey. What's most important to you? Being safe? Having fun? Or obeying God? Whenever you're having trouble deciding whether to obey or not, think of Nathan.

NATHAN BRAVELY OBEYED GOD AND GAVE HIS MESSAGE TO KING DAVID.
THE WHOLE STORY: 2 SAMUEL 12:1-25

Go to page 375 for the next person

ture it. If you don't, I'll capture it myself. Then it will be named after me."

²⁹So David brought the whole army together and went to Rabbah. He attacked it and captured it. ³⁰He took the gold crown off the head of the king of Ammon. The crown weighed 75 pounds. It had jewels in it. It was placed on David's head. He took a huge amount of goods from the city. ³¹He brought out the people who were there. He made them work with saws and iron picks and axes. He forced them to make bricks. He did that to all of the towns in Ammon. Then he and his entire army returned to Jerusalem.

Amnon Rapes Tamar

13 Some time later, David's son Amnon fell in love with Tamar. She was the beautiful sister of Absalom. He was another one of David's sons.

²Amnon's sister Tamar was a virgin. It seemed impossible for him to do what he wanted to do with her. But he wanted her so much it almost made him sick.

³Amnon had a friend named Jonadab. He was the son of David's brother Shimeah. Jonadab was a very clever man. ⁴He asked Amnon, "You are the king's son, aren't you? So why do you look so worn out every morning? Won't you tell me?"

Amnon answered, "I'm in love with Tamar. She's the sister of my brother Absalom."

⁵"Go to bed," Jonadab said. "Pretend to be sick. Your father will come to see you. When he does, tell him, 'I would like my sister Tamar to come and give me something to eat. Let her prepare the food right here in front of me where I can watch her. Then she can feed it to me.' "

⁶So Amnon went to bed. He pretended to be sick. The king came to see him. Amnon said to him, "I would like my sister Tamar to come here. I want to watch her make some special bread. Then she can feed it to me."

⁷David sent a message to Tamar at the palace. It said, "Go to your brother Amnon's house. Prepare some food for him."

⁸So Tamar went to the house of her brother Amnon. He was lying in bed. She got some dough and mixed it. She shaped the bread right there in front of him. And she baked it. ⁹Then she took the bread out of the pan and served it to him. But he refused to eat it.

"Send everyone out of here," Amnon said. So everyone left him.

¹⁰Then he said to Tamar, "Bring the food here into my bedroom. Please feed it to me."

So Tamar picked up the bread she had prepared. She brought it to her brother Amnon in his bedroom. ¹¹She took it to him so he could eat it.

But he grabbed hold of her. He said, "My sister, come and have sex with me."

¹²"Don't do this, my brother!" she said to him. "Don't force me to have sex with you. An evil thing like that should never be done in Israel! Don't do it! ¹³What about me? How could I ever get rid of my shame? And what about you? You would be as foolish as any evil person in Israel. Please speak to the king. He won't keep me from getting married to you."

¹⁴But Amnon refused to listen to her. He was stronger than she was. So he raped her.

¹⁵Then Amnon was filled with deep hatred for Tamar. In fact, he hated her now more than he had loved her before. He said to her, "Get up! Get out!"

¹⁶"No!" she said to him. "Don't send me away. That would be worse than what you have already done to me."

But he refused to listen to her. ¹⁷He sent for his personal servant. He said, "Get this woman out of here. Lock the door behind her."

¹⁸So his servant threw her out. Then he locked the door behind her.

Tamar was wearing a beautiful robe. It was the kind of robe the virgin daughters of the king wore. ¹⁹She put ashes on her head. She tore the beautiful robe she was wearing. She put her hands on her head and went away. She was sobbing out loud as she went.

²⁰When her brother Absalom saw her, he spoke to her. He said, "Has Amnon, that brother of yours, forced you to have sex with him? My sister, don't let it upset you. Don't let it bother you. He's your brother."

After that, Tamar lived in her brother Absalom's house. She was very lonely.

²¹King David heard about everything that had happened. So he became very angry.

²²Absalom never said a word of any kind to Amnon. He hated Amnon because he had brought shame on his sister Tamar.

Absalom Kills Amnon

²³Two years later, Absalom invited all of the king's sons to come to Baal Hazor. It was near the border of Ephraim. The

workers who clipped the wool off Absalom's sheep were there.

24Absalom went to the king. He said, "I've had my workers come to clip the wool. Will you and your officials please join me?"

25"No, my son," the king replied. "All of us shouldn't go. It would be too much trouble for you." Although Absalom begged him, the king still refused to go. But he gave Absalom his blessing.

26Then Absalom said, "If you won't come, please let my brother Amnon come with us."

The king asked him, "Why should he go with you?" 27But Absalom begged him. So the king sent Amnon with him. He also sent the rest of his sons.

28Absalom ordered his men, "Listen! When Amnon has had too much wine to drink, I'll say to you, 'Strike Amnon down.' When I do, kill him. Don't be afraid. I've given you an order, haven't I? Be strong and brave."

29So Absalom's men killed Amnon, just as Absalom had ordered. Then all of the king's sons got on their mules and rode away.

30While they were on their way, a report came to David. It said, "Absalom has struck down all of your sons. Not one of them is left alive."

31The king stood up and tore his clothes. Then he lay down on the ground. All of his servants stood near him. They had also torn their clothes.

32Jonadab, the son of David's brother Shimeah, spoke up. He said, "You shouldn't think that all of the princes have been killed. The only one who is dead is Amnon. Absalom had planned to kill him ever since the day Amnon raped his sister Tamar. 33You are my king and master. You shouldn't be concerned about this report. It's not true that all of your sons are dead. The only one who is dead is Amnon."

34While all of that was taking place, Absalom ran away.

The man on guard duty at Jerusalem looked up. He saw many people coming on the road west of him. They were coming down the side of the hill. He went and spoke to the king. He said, "I see men coming down the road from Horonaim. They are coming down the side of the hill."

35Jonadab said to the king, "See, your sons are coming. It has happened just as I said it would."

36As he finished speaking, the king's sons came in. They were sobbing out loud. The king and all of his servants were also sobbing very bitterly.

37When Absalom ran away, he went to Talmai, the son of Ammihud. Talmai was king of Geshur. King David sobbed over his son every day.

38So Absalom ran away and went to Geshur. He stayed there for three years.

39After some time the king got over his sorrow because of Amnon's death. Then he longed to go to Absalom.

Absalom Returns to Jerusalem

14 Joab, the son of Zeruiah, knew that the king longed to see Absalom. 2So Joab sent someone to Tekoa to have a wise woman brought back from there. Joab said to her, "Pretend you are filled with sadness. Put on black clothes. Don't use any makeup. Act like a woman who has spent many days sobbing over someone who has died. 3Then go to the king. Give him the message I'm about to give you." And Joab told her what to say.

4The woman from Tekoa went to the king. She bowed down with her face toward the ground. She did it to show him respect. She said, "King David, please help me!"

5The king asked her, "What's bothering you?"

She said, "I'm a widow. My husband is dead. 6I had two sons. They got into a fight with each other in the field. No one was there to separate them. One of my sons struck the other one down and killed him.

7"Now my whole family group has risen up against me. They say, 'Hand over the one who struck his brother down. Then we can put him to death for killing his brother. That will also get rid of the one who will receive the family property.' They want to kill the only living son I have left, just as someone would put out a burning coal. That would leave my husband without any son on the face of the earth to carry on his name."

8The king said to the woman, "Go home. I'll give an order to make sure you are taken care of."

9But the woman from Tekoa said to him, "You are my king and master. No matter what you do, I and my family will take the blame for it. You and your royal family won't be guilty of doing anything wrong."

10The king replied, "If people give you any trouble, bring them to me. They won't bother you again."

¹¹She said, "Please pray to the LORD your God. Pray that he will keep our nearest male relative from killing my other son. Then my son won't be destroyed."

"You can be sure that the LORD lives," the king said. "And you can be just as sure that not one hair of your son's head will fall to the ground."

¹²Then the woman said, "King David, please let me say something else to you."

"Go ahead," he replied.

¹³The woman said, "You are the king. So why have you done something that brings so much harm on God's people? When you do that, you hand down a sentence against yourself. You won't let the son you drove away come back. ¹⁴All of us must die. We are like water that is spilled on the ground. It can't be put back into the jar. But God doesn't take life away. Instead, he finds a way to bring back anyone who was driven away from him.

¹⁵"King David, I've come here to say this to you now. I've done it because people have made me afraid. I thought, 'I'll go and speak to the king. Perhaps he'll do what I'm asking. ¹⁶Perhaps he'll agree to save me from the man who is trying to cut off me and my son from the property God gave us.'

¹⁷"So now I'm saying, 'May what you have told me bring me peace and rest. You are like an angel of God. You know what is good and what is evil. May the LORD your God be with you.' "

¹⁸Then the king said to the woman, "I'm going to ask you a question. I want you to tell me the truth."

"Please ask me anything you want to," the woman said.

¹⁹The king asked, "Joab told you to say all of this, didn't he?"

The woman answered, "What you have told me is exactly right. And that's just as sure as you are alive. It's true that Joab directed me to do this. He told me everything he wanted me to say. ²⁰He did it to change the way things now are. You are as wise as an angel of God. You know everything that happens in the land."

²¹Later the king said to Joab, "All right. I'll do what you want. Go. Bring the young man Absalom back."

²²Joab bowed down with his face toward the ground. He did it to honor the king. And he asked God to bless the king. He said, "You are my king and master. Today I know that you are pleased with me. You have given me what I asked for."

²³Then Joab went to Geshur. He brought Absalom back to Jerusalem.

²⁴But the king said, "He must go to his own house. I don't want him to come and see me."

So Absalom went to his own house. He didn't go to see the king.

²⁵In the whole land of Israel there wasn't any man as handsome as Absalom was. That's why everyone praised him. From the top of his head to the bottom of his feet he didn't have any flaws. ²⁶He used to cut his hair when it became too heavy for him. Then he would weigh it. It weighed five pounds in keeping with the standard weights that were used in the palace.

²⁷Three sons and a daughter were born to Absalom. The daughter's name was Tamar. She became a beautiful woman.

²⁸Absalom lived in Jerusalem for two years without going to see the king. ²⁹Then Absalom sent for Joab. He wanted to send him to the king. But Joab refused to come to Absalom. So Absalom sent for him a second time. But Joab still refused to come.

³⁰Then Absalom said to his servants, "Joab's field is next to mine. He has barley growing there. Go and set it on fire." So Absalom's servants set the field on fire.

³¹Joab finally went to Absalom's house. He said to Absalom, "Why did your servants set my field on fire?"

³²Absalom said to Joab, "I sent a message to you. It said, 'Come here. I want to send you to the king. I want you to ask him for me, "Why did you bring me back from Geshur? I would be better off if I were still there!" ' Now then, I want to go and see the king. If I'm guilty of doing anything wrong, let him put me to death."

³³So Joab went to the king and told him that. Then the king sent for Absalom. He came in and bowed down to the king with his face toward the ground. And the king kissed Absalom.

Absalom Makes Secret Plans Against David

15 Some time later, Absalom got a chariot and horses for himself. He also got 50 men to run in front of him. ²He would get up early. He would stand by the side of the road that led to the city gate. Sometimes a person would come with a case for the king to decide.

Then Absalom would call out to him, "What town are you from?"

He would answer, "I'm from one of the tribes of Israel."

³Absalom would say, "Look, your claims

are based on the law. So you have every right to make them. But the king doesn't have anyone here who can listen to your case." [4]Absalom would continue, "I wish I were appointed judge in the land! Then anyone who has a case or a claim could come to me. I would make sure he is treated fairly."

[5]Sometimes people would approach Absalom and bow down to him. Then he would reach out his hand. He would take hold of them and kiss them.

[6]Absalom did that to all of the people of Israel who came to the king with their cases or claims. That's why the hearts of the people were turned toward him.

[7]After Absalom had lived in Jerusalem for four years, he went and spoke to the king. He said, "Let me go to Hebron. I want to keep a promise I made to the LORD. [8]When I was living at Geshur in Aram, I made a promise. I said, 'If the LORD takes me back to Jerusalem, I'll go to Hebron and worship him there.' "

[9]The king said to him, "Go in peace." So he went to Hebron.

[10]Then Absalom sent messengers secretly to all of the tribes of Israel. They said, "Listen for the sound of trumpets. As soon as you hear them, say, 'Absalom has become king in Hebron.' "

[11]Absalom had taken 200 men from Jerusalem with him to Hebron. He had invited them to be his guests. They went without having any idea what was going to happen. [12]While Absalom was offering sacrifices, he sent for Ahithophel. Ahithophel was David's adviser. He came to Absalom from Giloh, his hometown. The number of people who followed Absalom kept growing. So he became more and more able to carry out his plans against David.

David Runs Away From Absalom

[13]A messenger came and spoke to David. He told him, "The hearts of the people are turned toward Absalom."

[14]Then David spoke to all of his officials who were with him in Jerusalem. He said, "Come on! We have to leave right away! If we don't, none of us will escape from Absalom. He'll move quickly to catch up with us. He'll destroy us. His men will kill everyone in the city with their swords."

[15]The king's officials answered him, "You are our king and master. We're ready to do anything you want."

[16]The king started out. Everyone in his whole family went with him. But he left ten concubines behind to take care of the palace. [17]So the king and all those who were with him left. They stopped at a place that wasn't very far away.

[18]All of David's officials marched past him. All of the Kerethites and Pelethites marched along with them. And all of the 600 men who had come with him from Gath marched in front of him.

[19]The king spoke to Ittai. He was from Gath. The king said to him, "Why do you want to come along with us? Go back. Stay with King Absalom. You are a stranger. You left your own country. [20]You came to join me only a short time ago. So why should I make you wander around with us now? I don't even know where I'm going. So go on back. Take with you the others who are from your country. And may the LORD be kind and faithful to you."

[21]But Ittai replied to the king, "You are my king and master. I want to be where you are. It doesn't matter whether I live or die. And that's just as sure as the LORD and you are alive."

[22]David said to Ittai, "Go ahead then. Keep marching with my men."

So Ittai, the Gittite, kept marching. All of his men and their families marched with him.

[23]All of the people in the countryside sobbed out loud as David and all of his followers passed by. The king went across the Kidron Valley. He and all of the people who were with him moved on toward the desert.

[24]Zadok also went with them. Some of the Levites went with him. They were carrying the ark of the covenant of God. They set the ark down. Abiathar offered sacrifices until all of the people had left the city.

[25]Then the king said to Zadok, "Take the ark of God back into the city. If the LORD is pleased with me, he'll bring me back. He'll let me see the ark again. He'll also let me see Jerusalem again. That's the place where he lives. [26]But suppose he says, 'I am not pleased with you.' Then I accept that. Let him do to me what he thinks is best."

[27]The king spoke again to the priest Zadok. He said, "You are a prophet, aren't you? Go back to the city in peace. Take your son Ahimaaz with you. Also take Abiathar and his son Jonathan with you. [28]I'll wait at the place in the desert where we can go across the Jordan River. I'll wait there until you send word to let me know what's happening."

²⁹So Zadok and Abiathar took the ark of God back to Jerusalem. They stayed there. ³⁰But David went on up the Mount of Olives. He was sobbing as he went. His head was covered, and he was barefoot. All of the people who were with him covered their heads too. And they were sobbing as they went up. ³¹David had been told, "Ahithophel is one of those who are making secret plans with Absalom against you." So David prayed, "LORD, make Ahithophel's advice look foolish."

³²David arrived at the top of the Mount of Olives. That's where people used to worship God. Hushai, the Arkite, was there to meet him. His robe was torn. There was dust on his head. ³³David said to him, "If you go with me, you will be too much trouble for me. ³⁴So return to the city. Say to Absalom, 'King Absalom, I'll be your servant. In the past, I was your father's servant. But now I'll be your servant.' If you do that, you can help me by making sure Ahithophel's advice fails. ³⁵The priests Zadok and Abiathar will be there with you. Tell them everything you hear in the king's palace. ³⁶They have their sons Ahimaaz and Jonathan there with them. Send them to tell me everything you hear."

³⁷So David's friend Hushai went to Jerusalem. He arrived just as Absalom was entering the city.

Ziba Lies to David

16 David went just beyond the top of the Mount of Olives. Ziba was waiting there to meet him. He was Mephibosheth's manager. He had several donkeys with saddles on them. They were carrying 200 loaves of bread and 100 raisin cakes. They were also carrying 100 fig cakes and a bottle of wine. The bottle was made out of animal skin. ²The king asked Ziba, "Why have you brought all of these things?"

Ziba answered, "The donkeys are for the king's family to ride on. The bread and fruit are for the people to eat. The wine will make those who get tired in the desert feel like new again."

³Then the king asked, "Where is your master's grandson Mephibosheth?"

Ziba said to him, "He's staying in Jerusalem. He thinks, 'Today the people of Israel will give me back my grandfather Saul's kingdom.'"

⁴Then the king said to Ziba, "Everything that belonged to Mephibosheth belongs to you now."

"You are my king and master," Ziba said. "I make myself low in front of you. I bow down to you. May you be pleased with me."

Shimei Calls Down Curses on David

⁵King David approached Bahurim. As he did, a man came out toward him. The man was from the same family group that Saul was from. His name was Shimei. He was the son of Gera. As he came out of the town, he called down curses on David. ⁶He threw stones at David and all of his officials. He did it even though all of the troops and the special guard were there. They were to the right and left of David.

⁷As Shimei called down curses, he said, "Get out! Get out, you murderer! You are a worthless and evil man! ⁸You spilled the blood of a lot of people in Saul's family. You took over his kingdom. Now the LORD is paying you back. He has handed the kingdom over to your son Absalom. You have been destroyed because you are a murderer!"

⁹Then Abishai, the son of Zeruiah, spoke to the king. He said, "King David, why should we let this dead dog call down curses on you? Let me go over there. I'll cut off his head."

¹⁰But the king said, "You and Joab are sons of Zeruiah. What do you and I have in common? Maybe the LORD said to him, 'Call down curses on David.' If he did, who can ask him, 'Why are you doing this?'"

¹¹Then David spoke to Abishai and all of his officials. He said, "My very own son Absalom is trying to kill me. How much more should this man from Benjamin want to kill me! Leave him alone. Let him call down curses. The LORD has told him to do it. ¹²Maybe the LORD will see how much I'm suffering. Maybe he'll reward me with good things in place of the curses that are being called down on me today."

¹³So David and his men kept going along the road. At the same time, Shimei was going along the hillside across from him. He was calling down curses as he went. He was throwing stones at David. He was showering him with dirt. ¹⁴The king and all of the people who were with him came to the place they had planned to go to. They were very tired. So David rested there.

Hushai and Ahithophel Give Advice to Absalom

¹⁵During that time, Absalom and all of

the men of Israel came to Jerusalem. Ahithophel was with him.

¹⁶Then Hushai, the Arkite, went to Absalom. He said to him, "May the king live a long time! May the king live a long time!" Hushai was David's friend.

¹⁷Absalom asked Hushai, "Is this the way you show love to your friend? Why didn't you go with him?"

¹⁸Hushai said to Absalom, "Why should I? You are the one the LORD has chosen. These people and all of the men of Israel have also chosen you. I want to be on your side. I want to stay with you. ¹⁹After all, who else should I serve? Shouldn't I serve the king's son? I will serve you, just as I served your father."

²⁰Absalom said to Ahithophel, "Give us your advice. What should we do?"

²¹Ahithophel answered, "Your father left some concubines behind to take care of the palace. Go and have sex with them. Then all of the people of Israel will hear about it. They will hear that you have made yourself smell very bad to your father. Everyone who is with you will become braver."

²²So they set up a tent for Absalom on the roof of the palace. He went in and had sex with his father's concubines. Everyone in Israel saw it.

²³In those days the advice Ahithophel gave was good as advice from someone who asks God for guidance. That's what David and Absalom thought about all of Ahithopel's advice.

17 One day Ahithophel said to Absalom, "Here's what I suggest. Choose 12,000 men. Start out tonight and go after David. ²Attack him while he's tired and weak. Fill him with terror. Then all of the people who are with him will run away. Don't strike down anyone except the king. ³Bring all of the other people back. After the man you want to kill is dead, everyone else will return to you. And none of the people will be harmed."

⁴Ahithophel's plan seemed good to Absalom. It also seemed good to all of the elders of Israel.

⁵But Absalom said, "Send for Hushai, the Arkite. Then we can find out what he suggests."

⁶Hushai came to him. Absalom said, "Ahithophel has given us his advice. Should we do what he says? If we shouldn't, tell us what you would do."

⁷Hushai replied to Absalom, "The advice Ahithophel has given you isn't good this time. ⁸You know your father

POWER-SURGE

STRONG

YOU KNOW [DAVID] AND HIS MEN. THEY ARE FIGHTERS. THEY ARE AS STRONG AS A WILD BEAR WHOSE CUBS HAVE BEEN STOLEN FROM HER.
—— **2 SAMUEL 17:8** ——

and his men. They are fighters. They are as strong as a wild bear whose cubs have been stolen from her. Besides, your father really knows how to fight. He won't spend the night with his troops. ⁹In fact, he's probably hiding in a cave or some other place right now.

"Suppose he attacks your troops first. When people hear about it, they'll say, 'Many of the troops who followed Absalom have been killed.' ¹⁰Then the hearts of your soldiers will melt away in fear. Even those who are as brave as a lion will be terrified. That's because everyone in Israel knows that your father is a fighter. They know that those who are with him are brave.

¹¹"So here's what I suggest. Bring together all of the men of Israel from the town of Dan all the way to Beersheba. They are as many as the grains of sand on the seashore. You yourself should lead them into battle.

¹²"Then we'll attack David no matter where we find him. As dew completely covers the ground, we'll completely overpower his entire army. We won't leave him or any of his men alive. ¹³He might try to get away by going into a city. If he does, all of us will bring ropes to that city. We'll drag the whole city down into the valley. No one will be able to find even a piece of that city."

¹⁴Absalom and all of the men of Israel agreed. They said, "The advice of Hushai, the Arkite, is better than the advice of Ahithophel." The LORD had decided that Ahithophel's good advice would fail. The LORD wanted to bring horrible trouble on Absalom.

¹⁵Hushai spoke to the priests Zadok and Abiathar. He said, "Ahithophel has given advice to Absalom and the elders of

Israel. He suggested that they should do one thing. But I suggested something else.

¹⁶"Send a message right away. Tell David, 'Don't spend the night at the place in the desert where people can go across the Jordan River. Make sure you go on across. If you don't, you and all of the people who are with you will be swallowed up.' "

¹⁷Jonathan and Ahimaaz were staying at En Rogel just outside Jerusalem. They knew they would be in danger if anyone saw them entering the city. A female servant was supposed to go and tell them what had happened. Then they were supposed to go and tell King David. ¹⁸But a young man saw Jonathan and Ahimaaz and told Absalom about it. So the two men left quickly. They went to the house of a man in Bahurim. He had a well in his courtyard. They climbed down into it. ¹⁹The man's wife got a covering and spread it out over the opening of the well. Then she scattered grain on the covering. So no one knew that the men were hiding in the well.

²⁰Absalom's men came to the house. They asked the woman, "Where are Ahimaaz and Jonathan?"

She answered, "They went across the brook." When the men looked around, they didn't find anyone. So they returned to Jerusalem.

²¹After the men had gone, Jonathan and Ahimaaz climbed out of the well. They went to tell King David what they had found out. They said to him, "Go across the river right away. Ahithophel has told Absalom how to come after you and strike you down."

²²So David and all of the people who were with him started out. They went across the Jordan River. By sunrise, everyone had crossed over.

²³Ahithophel saw that his advice wasn't being followed. So he put a saddle on his donkey. He started out for his house in his hometown. When he got there, he put everything in order. He made out his will. Then he killed himself. So he died, and his body was buried in his father's tomb.

²⁴David went to Mahanaim. Absalom went across the Jordan River with all of the men of Israel.

²⁵Absalom had made Amasa commander of the army in place of Joab. Amasa was the son of a man named Jether. Jether belonged to the family line of Ishmael. He had gotten married to Abigail. She was the daughter of Nahash and the sister of Zeruiah. Zeruiah was the mother of Joab. ²⁶Absalom and the people of Israel camped in the land of Gilead.

²⁷David came to Mahanaim. Shobi, the son of Nahash, met him there. Shobi was from Rabbah in the land of Ammon. Makir, the son of Ammiel from Lo Debar, met him there too. So did Barzillai from Rogelim in the land of Gilead. ²⁸They brought beds, bowls and clay pots. They brought wheat, barley, flour, and grain that had been cooked. They brought beans and lentils. ²⁹They brought honey, butter, sheep and cheese that was made from cows' milk. They brought all of that food for David and his people to eat. They said, "These people have become hungry. They've become tired and thirsty in the desert."

Absalom Dies

18 David brought together the men who were with him. He appointed commanders of thousands over some of them. He appointed commanders of hundreds over the others.

²Then David sent the troops out in three companies. One company was under the command of Joab. Another was under Joab's brother Abishai, the son of Zeruiah. The last was under Ittai, the Gittite. The king told the troops, "You can be sure that I myself will march out with you."

³But the men said, "You must not march out. If we are forced to run away, our enemies won't care about us. Even if half of us die, they won't care. But you are worth 10,000 of us. So it would be better for you to stay here in the city. Then you can send us help if we need it."

⁴The king said, "I'll do what you think is best."

So the king stood beside the city gate. The whole army marched out in companies of hundreds and companies of thousands.

⁵The king gave an order to Joab, Abishai and Ittai. He commanded them, "Be gentle with the young man Absalom. Do it for me." All of the troops heard the king give the commanders that order about Absalom.

⁶David's army marched into the field to fight against Israel. The battle took place in the forest of Ephraim. ⁷There David's men won the battle over Israel's army. A huge number of men were wounded or killed that day. The total number was 20,000. ⁸The fighting spread out over the whole countryside. But more men were

killed in the forest that day than out in the open.

9Absalom happened to come across some of David's men. He was riding his mule. The mule went under the thick branches of a large oak tree. Absalom's head got caught in the tree. He was left hanging in the air. The mule he was riding kept on going.

10One of David's men saw what had happened. He told Joab, "I just saw Absalom hanging in an oak tree."

11Joab said to the man, "What! You saw him? Why didn't you strike him down right there? Then I would have had to give you four ounces of silver and a soldier's belt."

12But the man replied, "I wouldn't lift my hand to harm the king's son. I wouldn't do it even for 25 pounds of silver. We heard the king's command to you and Abishai and Ittai. He said, 'Be careful not to hurt the young man Absalom. Do it for me.' **13**Suppose I had put my life in danger by killing him. The king would have found out about it. Nothing is hidden from him. And you wouldn't have stood up for me."

14Joab said, "I'm not going to waste any more time on you." So he got three javelins. Then he went over and drove them into Absalom's heart. He did it while Absalom was still hanging there alive in the oak tree.

15Ten of the men who were carrying Joab's armor surrounded Absalom. They struck him down and killed him.

16Then Joab blew his trumpet. He ordered his troops to stop chasing Israel's army. **17**Joab's men threw Absalom's body into a big pit in the forest. They covered his body with a large pile of rocks. While all of that was going on, all of the Israelites ran back to their homes.

18Earlier in his life Absalom had set up a pillar in the King's Valley. He had put it up as a monument to himself. He thought, "I don't have a son to carry on the memory of my name." So he named the pillar after himself. It is still called Absalom's Monument to this very day.

David Sobs Over Absalom

19Ahimaaz said to Joab, "Let me run and take the news to the king. Let me tell him that the LORD has saved him from the power of his enemies." Ahimaaz was the son of Zadok.

20"I don't want you to take the news to the king today," Joab told him. "You can do it some other time. But you must not do it today, because the king's son is dead."

21Then Joab said to a man from Cush, "Go. Tell the king what you have seen." The man bowed down in front of Joab. Then he ran off.

22Ahimaaz, the son of Zadok, spoke again to Joab. He said, "I don't care what happens to me. Please let me run behind the man from Cush."

But Joab replied, "My son, why do you want to go? You don't have any news that will bring you a reward."

23He said, "I don't care what happens. I want to run."

So Joab said, "Run!" Then Ahimaaz ran across the flatlands of the Jordan River. As he ran, he passed the man from Cush.

24David was sitting in the area between the inner and outer gates of the city. The man on guard duty went up to the roof over the entrance of the gate by the wall. As he looked out, he saw someone running alone. **25**He called out to the king and reported it.

The king said, "If the runner is alone, he must be bringing good news." The man came closer and closer.

26Then the man on guard duty saw another man running. He called out to the man who was guarding the gate. He said, "Look! There's another man running alone!"

The king said, "He must be bringing good news too."

27The man on guard duty said, "I can see that the first one runs like Ahimaaz, the son of Zadok."

"He's a good man," the king said. "He's bringing good news."

28Then Ahimaaz called out to the king, "Everything's all right!" He bowed down in front of the king with his face toward the ground. He said, "You are my king and master. Give praise to the LORD your God! He has handed over to you the men who lifted their hands to kill you."

29The king asked, "Is the young man Absalom safe?"

Ahimaaz answered, "I saw total disorder. I saw it just as Joab was about to send the king's servant and me to you. But I don't know what it was all about."

30The king said, "Stand over there and wait." So he stepped over to one side and stood there.

31Then the man from Cush arrived. He said, "You are my king and master. I'm bringing you some good news. The LORD has saved you today from all those who were trying to kill you."

GIDEON

"Lord," Gideon asked, "how can I possibly save Israel? My family group is the weakest in the tribe of Manasseh. And I'm the least important member." The Lord answered, "I will be with you." (Judges 6:15–16)

GO TO PAGE 282

SAMSON

The woman had a baby boy. She named him Samson. As he grew up, the Lord blessed him. The Spirit of the Lord began to work in his life. (Judges 13:24–25)

GO TO PAGE 292

Ruth replied, "Don't try to make me leave you and go back. Where you go I'll go. Where you stay I'll stay. Your people will be my people. Your God will be my God." (Ruth 1:16)

GO TO PAGE 305

HANNAH

"I prayed for this child. The Lᴏʀᴅ has given me what I asked him for. So now I'm giving him to the Lᴏʀᴅ. As long as he lives he'll be given to the LORD." *(1 Samuel 1:27–28)*

GO TO PAGE 314

ABSALOM

(Not!)

2 SAMUEL 18:9

The mule went under the thick branches of a large oak tree. Absalom's head got caught in the tree. He was left hanging in the air. The mule he was riding kept on going.

Absalom (AB-suh-lum) smoothed his short battle robe over his strong, brown legs. He swung his heavy hair back from his face and pulled on his battle helmet. Then he buckled on his sword. Today a battle would be fought in Israel. Absalom had rebelled. He wanted to be king instead of his father, David. Today Absalom's soldiers would fight David's soldiers. The winner would be king.

The valley shimmered in the hot sun. The soldiers of Absalom and David fought each other from early morning until late afternoon. **THE GRASS OF THE VALLEY WAS STAINED WITH BLOOD FROM HURT AND DEAD SOLDIERS.** More dead and injured soldiers lay in the nearby forest.

Looking around, Absalom knew he had lost. He would never be king of Israel. He jumped on his mule. Kicking the mule and shouting, he rode through the battleground into the forest. There he saw some of David's men. Absalom tried to make his mule go faster. He turned to look behind him. David's men were following him. They were getting closer!

Absalom hit his head on the low branch of a huge oak tree. The branches twisted and turned together, and Absalom's long hair got caught in them. His frightened mule kept on running. But Absalom was going nowhere. His head was caught in the tree, his feet swinging above the ground.

David's men found Absalom. They knew how much David loved this son, even though he had rebelled. Should they take him down as a prisoner? Leave him there to die? Or kill him? Only one man could decide. Joab took a sword and killed Absalom.

ABSALOM

Absalom was brave, but he wasn't much of a hero. He rebelled against his father and got himself killed. He didn't care what God wanted for Israel. He just wanted what he wanted. A true hero is never that selfish. A true hero is honorable and obedient, not selfish and rebellious.

ABSALOM REBELLED AGAINST HIS FATHER.
THE WHOLE STORY: 2 SAMUEL 18:1-17

Go to page 380 for the next Super Hero

32The king asked the man from Cush, "Is the young man Absalom safe?"

The man replied, "King David, may your enemies be like that young man. May all those who rise up to harm you be like him."

33The king was very upset. He went up to the room over the entrance of the gate and sobbed. As he went, he said, "My son Absalom! My son, my son Absalom! I wish I had died instead of you. Absalom! My son, my son!"

19 Someone told Joab, "The king is sobbing over Absalom. He's filled with sadness because his son has died."

2The army had won a great battle that day. But their joy turned into sadness. That's because someone had told the troops, "The king is filled with sorrow because his son is dead." **3**The men came quietly into the city that day. They were like fighting men who are ashamed because they've run away from a battle.

4The king covered his face. He sobbed out loud, "My son Absalom! Absalom, my son, my son!"

5Then Joab went into the king's house. He said to him, "Today you have made all of your men feel ashamed. They have just saved your life. They have saved the lives of your sons and daughters. And they have saved the lives of your wives and concubines.

6"You love those who hate you. You hate those who love you. The commanders and their troops don't mean anything to you. You made that very clear today. I can see that you would be pleased if Absalom were alive today and all of us were dead.

7"Now go out there and cheer up your men. If you don't, you won't have any of them left with you by sunset. That will be worse for you than all of the troubles you have ever had in your whole life. That's what I promise you with an oath in the LORD's name."

8So the king got up and took his seat in the entrance of the city gate. His men were told, "The king is sitting in the entrance of the gate." Then all of them came and stood in front of him.

David Returns to Jerusalem

While all of that was going on, the Israelites had run back to their homes. **9**People from all of the tribes of Israel began to argue with one another. They were saying, "The king saved us from the power of our enemies. He saved us from the power of the Philistines. But now he has left the country because of Absalom. **10**We anointed Absalom to rule over us. But he has died in battle. So why aren't any of you talking about bringing the king back?"

11King David sent a message to the priests Zadok and Abiathar. It said, "Speak to the elders of Judah. Tell them I said, 'News has reached me where I'm staying. People all over Israel are talking about bringing me back to my palace. Why should you be the last to do something about it? **12**You are my relatives. You are my own flesh and blood. So why should you be the last to bring me back?'

13"Say to Amasa, 'Aren't you my own flesh and blood? From now on you will be the commander of my army in place of Joab. If that isn't true, may God punish me greatly.' "

14So the hearts of all of the men of Judah were turned toward David. All of them had the same purpose in mind. They sent a message to the king. It said, "We want you to come back. We want all of your men to come back too." **15**Then the king returned. He went as far as the Jordan River.

The men of Judah had come to Gilgal to welcome the king back. They had come to bring him across the Jordan. **16**Shimei, the son of Gera, was among them. Shimei was from Bahurim in the territory of Benjamin. He hurried down to welcome King David back. **17**There were 1,000 people from Benjamin with him. Ziba, the manager of Saul's house, was with him too. And so were Ziba's 15 sons and 20 servants. All of them rushed down to the Jordan River. That's where the king was. **18**They went across at the place where people usually cross it. Then they brought the king's family back over with them. They were ready to do anything he wanted them to do.

Shimei, the son of Gera, had also gone across the Jordan. When he did, he fell down flat with his face toward the ground in front of the king. **19**He said to him, "You are my king and master. Please don't hold me guilty. Please forgive me for the wrong things I did on the day you left Jerusalem. Please forget all about them. **20**I know I've sinned. But today I've come down here to welcome you. I'm the first member of Joseph's whole family to do it."

21Then Abishai, the son of Zeruiah, said, "Shouldn't Shimei be put to death for what he did? He called down curses on you. And you are the LORD's anointed king."

22But David replied, "You and Joab are sons of Zeruiah. What do you and I have in common? Abishai, you have now become my enemy! Should anyone be put to death in Israel today? Don't I know that today I am king over Israel again?"

23So the king took an oath and made a promise to Shimei. He said to him, "You aren't going to be put to death."

24Mephibosheth was Saul's grandson. He had also gone down to welcome the king back. He had not taken care of his feet. He hadn't trimmed his mustache or washed his clothes. He hadn't done any of those things from the day the king left Jerusalem until the day he returned safely. **25**He came from Jerusalem to welcome the king. The king asked him, "Mephibosheth, why didn't you go with me?"

26He said, "You are my king and master. I'm disabled. So I thought, 'I'll have a saddle put on my donkey. I'll ride on it. Then I can go with the king.' But my servant Ziba turned against me. **27**He has told you lies about me. King David, you are like an angel of God. So do what pleases you. **28**You should have put all of the members of my grandfather's family to death, including me. Instead, you always provided what I needed. So what right do I have to make any more appeals to you?"

29The king said to him, "You don't have to say anything else. I order you and Ziba to divide up Saul's fields between you."

30Mephibosheth said to the king, "I'm happy that you have arrived home safely. So just let Ziba have everything."

31Barzillai had also come down to go across the Jordan River with the king. He wanted to send the king on his way from there. Barzillai was from Rogelim in the land of Gilead. **32**He was a very old man. He was 80 years old. He had given the king everything he needed while the king was staying in Mahanaim. That's because Barzillai was very wealthy.

33The king said to Barzillai, "Come across the river with me. Stay with me in Jerusalem. I'll take good care of you."

34But Barzillai said to the king, "I won't live for many more years. So why should I go up to Jerusalem with you? **35**I'm already 80 years old. I can hardly tell the difference between what is good and what isn't. I can hardly taste what I eat and drink. I can't even hear the voices of male and female singers anymore. So why should I add my problems to yours? **36**"I'll go across the Jordan River with

you for a little way. Why should you reward me by taking care of me? **37**Let me go back home. Then I can die in my own town. I can be buried there in the tomb of my father and mother. But let Kimham take my place. Let him go across the river with you. Do for him what pleases you."

38The king said, "Kimham will go across with me. I'll do for him what pleases you. And I'll do for you anything you want me to do."

39So all of the people went across the Jordan River. Then the king crossed over. The king kissed Barzillai and gave him his blessing. And Barzillai went back home.

40After the king had gone across the river, he went to Gilgal. Kimham had gone across with him. All of the troops of Judah and half of the troops of Israel had taken the king across.

41Soon all of the men of Israel were coming to the king. They were saying to him, "Why did the men of Judah take you away from us? They are our relatives. What right did they have to bring you and your family across the Jordan River? What right did they have to bring all of your men over with you?"

42All of the men of Judah answered the men of Israel. They said, "We did that because the king is our close relative. So why should you be angry about what happened? Have we eaten any of the king's food? Have we taken anything for ourselves?"

43Then the men of Israel answered the men of Judah. They said, "We have ten of the 12 tribes in the kingdom. So we have a stronger claim on David than you have. Why then are you acting as if you hate us? Weren't we the first ones to talk about bringing back our king?"

But the men of Judah answered in an even meaner way than the men of Israel.

Sheba Tells Israel Not to Follow David

20 An evil man who always stirred up trouble happened to be in Gilgal. His name was Sheba, the son of Bicri. Sheba was from the tribe of Benjamin. He blew his trumpet. Then he shouted,

"We don't have any share in David's
    kingdom!
Jesse's son is not our king!
Men of Israel, every one of you go
    back home!"

2So all of the men of Israel deserted David. They followed Sheba, the son of Bicri. But the men of Judah stayed with their king. They remained with him from the Jordan River all the way to Jerusalem.

3David returned to his palace in Jerusalem. He had left ten concubines there to take care of the palace. He put them in a house and kept them under guard. He gave them what they needed. But he didn't make love to them. They were kept under guard until the day they died. They lived as if they were widows.

4The king said to Amasa, "Send for the men of Judah. Tell them to come to me within three days. And be here yourself." **5**So Amasa went to get the men of Judah. But he took longer than the time the king had set for him.

6David said to Abishai, "Sheba, the son of Bicri, will do more harm to us than Absalom ever did. Take my men and go after him. If you don't, he'll find cities that have high walls around them. He'll go into one of them and escape from us."

7So Joab's men marched out with the Kerethites and Pelethites. They went out with all of the mighty soldiers. All of them were under Abishai's command. They marched out from Jerusalem and went after Sheba, the son of Bicri.

8They arrived at the great rock in Gibeon. Amasa went there to welcome them. Joab was wearing his military clothes. Over them at his waist he strapped on a belt that held a dagger. As he stepped forward, the dagger fell out.

9Joab said to Amasa, "How are you, my friend?" Then Joab reached out his right hand. He took hold of Amasa's beard to kiss him.

10Amasa didn't pay any attention to the dagger that was in Joab's left hand. Joab stuck it into his stomach. His insides spilled out on the ground. Joab didn't have to stab him again. Amasa was already dead. Then Joab and his brother Abishai went after Sheba, the son of Bicri.

11One of Joab's men stood beside Amasa's body. He said to the other men, "Are you pleased with Joab? Are you on David's side? Then follow Joab!"

12Amasa's body lay covered with his blood in the middle of the road. The man saw that all of the troops stopped there. He realized that everyone was stopping to look at Amasa's body. So he dragged it from the road into a field. Then he threw some clothes on top of it. **13**After that happened, all of the men continued on with Joab. They went after Sheba, the son of Bicri.

14Sheba passed through all of the territory of the tribes of Israel. He arrived at the city of Abel Beth Maacah. He had gone through the entire area of the Berites. They had gathered together and followed him.

15Joab and all of his troops came to Abel Beth Maacah. They surrounded it because Sheba was there. They built a ramp up to the city. It stood against the outer wall. They pounded the wall with huge logs to bring it down.

16While that was going on, a wise woman called out from the city. She shouted, "Listen! Listen! Tell Joab to come here. I want to speak to him." **17**So Joab went toward her. She asked, "Are you Joab?"

"I am," he answered.

She said, "Listen to what I have to say."

"I'm listening," he said.

18She continued, "Long ago people used to say, 'Get your answer at Abel.' And that would settle the matter. **19**We are the most peaceful and faithful people in Israel. You are trying to destroy a city that is like a mother in Israel. Why do you want to swallow up what belongs to the LORD?"

20"I would never do anything like that!" Joab said. "I would never swallow up or destroy what belongs to the LORD! **21**That isn't what I have in mind at all. There's a man named Sheba, the son of Bicri, in your city. He's from the hill country of Ephraim. He's trying to kill King David. Hand that man over to me. Then I'll pull my men back from your city."

The woman said to Joab, "We'll throw his head down to you from the wall."

22Then the woman gave her wise advice to all of the people in the city. They cut off the head of Sheba, the son of Bicri. They threw it down to Joab. So he blew his trumpet. Then his men pulled back from the city. Each of them returned to his home. And Joab went back to the king in Jerusalem.

23Joab was commander over Israel's entire army. Benaiah, the son of Jehoiada, was commander over the Kerethites and Pelethites. **24**Adoniram was in charge of those who were forced to work hard. Jehoshaphat, the son of Ahilud, kept the records. **25**Sheva was the secretary. Zadok and Abiathar were priests. **26**Ira, the Jairite, was David's priest.

David Makes Things Right for the People of Gibeon

21 For three years in a row there wasn't enough food in the land. That was while David was king. So David asked the LORD why he wasn't showing his favor to his people. The LORD said, "It is because Saul and his family committed murder. He put the people of Gibeon to death."

2 The people of Gibeon weren't a part of Israel. Instead, they were some of the Amorites who were still left alive. The people of Israel had promised with an oath to spare them. But Saul had tried to put an end to them. That's because he wanted to make Israel and Judah strong.

So now King David sent for the people of Gibeon and spoke to them. 3 He asked them, "What would you like me to do for you? How can I make up for the wrong things that were done to you? I want you to be able to pray that the LORD will once again bless his land."

4 The people of Gibeon answered him. They said, "No amount of silver or gold can make up for what Saul and his family did to us. And we can't put anyone in Israel to death."

"What do you want me to do for you?" David asked.

5 They answered the king, "Saul nearly destroyed us. He made plans to wipe us out. We don't have anywhere to live in Israel. 6 So let seven of the males in his family line be given to us. We'll kill them. We'll put their dead bodies out in the open in the sight of the LORD. We'll do it at Gibeah of Saul. Saul was the LORD's chosen king."

So King David said, "I'll give seven males to you."

7 The king spared Mephibosheth. He was the son of Jonathan and the grandson of Saul. David had taken an oath in the sight of the LORD. He had promised to be kind to Jonathan and the family line of his father Saul.

8 But the king chose Armoni and another Mephibosheth. They were the two sons of Aiah's daughter Rizpah. Saul was their father. The king also chose the five sons of Saul's daughter Merab. Adriel, the son of Barzillai, was their father. Adriel was from Meholah.

9 King David handed them over to the people of Gibeon. They killed them. They put their dead bodies out in the open on a hill in the sight of the LORD. All seven of them died together. They were put to death during the first days of the harvest. It happened just when people were beginning to harvest the barley.

10 Aiah's daughter Rizpah got some black cloth. She spread it out for herself on a rock. She stayed there from the beginning of the harvest until it rained. The rain poured down from the sky on the dead bodies of the seven males. She didn't let the birds of the air touch them by day. She didn't let the wild animals touch them at night.

11 Someone told David what Rizpah had done. She was Aiah's daughter and Saul's concubine.

12 David got the bones of Saul and his son Jonathan. He got them from the citizens of Jabesh Gilead. They had taken them in secret from the main street in Beth Shan. That's where the Philistines had hung their bodies up on the city wall. They had done it after they struck Saul down on Mount Gilboa.

13 David brought the bones of Saul and his son Jonathan from Jabesh Gilead. The bones of the seven males who had been killed and put out in the open were also gathered up.

14 The bones of Saul and his son Jonathan were buried in the tomb of Saul's father Kish. The tomb was at Zela in the territory of Benjamin. Everything the king commanded was done. After that, God answered prayer and blessed the land.

Israel Goes to War Against the Philistines

15 Once again there was a battle between the Philistines and Israel. David went down with his men to fight against the Philistines. He became very tired.

16 Ishbi-Benob belonged to the family line of Rapha. The tip of his bronze spear weighed seven and a half pounds. He was also armed with a new sword. He said he would kill David.

17 But Abishai, the son of Zeruiah, came to save David. He struck the Philistine down and killed him.

Then David's men took an oath and made a promise. They said to David, "We never want you to go out with us to battle again. You are the lamp of Israel's kingdom. We want that lamp to keep on burning brightly."

18 There was another battle against the Philistines. It took place at Gob. At that time Sibbecai killed Saph. Sibbecai was a Hushathite. Saph was from the family line of Rapha.

19 In another battle against the Philistines at Gob, Elhanan killed Goliath's brother. Elhanan was the son of Jaare-Oregim from Bethlehem. Goliath was from the city of Gath. His spear was as big as a weaver's rod.

20There was still another battle. It took place at Gath. A huge man lived there. He had six fingers on each hand and six toes on each foot. So the total number of his toes and fingers was 24. He was also from the family of Rapha. **21**He made fun of Israel. So Jonathan killed him. Jonathan was the son of David's brother Shimeah.

22Those four Philistine men lived in Gath. They were from the family line of Rapha. David and his men killed them.

David Sings Praises to the LORD

22 David sang the words of this song to the LORD. He sang them when the LORD saved him from the powerful hand of all of his enemies and of Saul. **2**He said,

 "The LORD is my rock and my fort. He
  is the One who saves me.
3 My God is my rock. I go to him for
  safety.

RIZPAH

2 SAMUEL 21:10

P
T

Rizpah got some black cloth. She spread it out for herself on a rock...She didn't let the birds of the air touch [the dead bodies] by day. She didn't let the wild animals touch them at night.

Rizpah (RIZZ-puh) sat on a stone. During the day, she watched carefully to make sure no big black birds came nearby. She jumped up and waved her hands whenever one swooped down to pick at the flesh of the bodies that lay in front of her. During the night, Rizpah didn't sleep. **SHE MADE SURE NO WILD ANIMALS CAME AND DRAGGED ONE OF THE BODIES OFF.** Rizpah's sons had been killed in battle and no one would bury them.

For weeks Rizpah kept at her gruesome task. She didn't give up even though she was overcome with sadness. She patiently waited for someone to realize how terrible this was and take care of the bodies.

Finally, King David realized that something needed to be done. He sent men to pick up the bones of the dead and give them a proper burial. Finally Rizpah could rest.

BE A RIZPAH

Rizpah's job was dreadful. But instead of giving up, she patiently waited for the king to do the right thing for her sons. You can be like Rizpah. When you need to wait, be patient like she was. And when something is hard to do or seems impossible, don't give up. Remember Rizpah!

RIZPAH DIDN'T GIVE UP.

Go to page 395 for the next Super Hero

He is like a shield to me. He's the
power that saves me.
He's my place of safety. I go to him for
help. He's my Savior.
He saves me from those who want to
hurt me.
⁴ I call out to the LORD. He is worthy of
praise.
He saves me from my enemies.

⁵ "The waves of death were all around
me.
A destroying flood swept over me.
⁶ The ropes of the grave were tight
around me.
Death set its trap in front of me.
⁷ When I was in trouble I called out to
the LORD.
I called out to my God.
From his temple he heard my voice.
My cry for help reached his ears.

⁸ "The earth trembled and shook.
The pillars of the heavens rocked
back and forth.
They trembled because the LORD was
angry.
⁹ Smoke came out of his nose.
Flames of fire came out of his
mouth.
Burning coals blazed out of it.
¹⁰ He opened the heavens and came
down.
Dark clouds were under his feet.
¹¹ He got on the cherubim and flew.
The wings of the wind lifted him up.
¹² He covered himself with darkness.
The dark rain clouds of the sky were
like a tent around him.
¹³ From the brightness that was all
around him
flashes of lightning blazed out.
¹⁴ The LORD thundered from heaven.
The voice of the Most High God was
heard.
¹⁵ He shot his arrows and scattered our
enemies.
He sent flashes of lightning and
chased the enemies away.
¹⁶ The bottom of the sea could be seen.
The foundations of the earth were
uncovered.
It happened when the LORD's anger
blazed out.
It came like a blast of breath from his
nose.

¹⁷ "He reached down from heaven. He
took hold of me.
He lifted me out of deep waters.
¹⁸ He saved me from my powerful
enemies.

He set me free from those who were
too strong for me.
¹⁹ They stood up to me when I was in
trouble.
But the LORD helped me.
²⁰ He brought me out into a wide and
safe place.
He saved me because he was pleased
with me.

²¹ "The LORD has been good to me
because I do what is right.
He has rewarded me because I lead a
pure life.
²² I have lived the way the LORD wanted
me to.
I haven't done evil by turning away
from my God.
²³ I keep all of his laws in mind.
I haven't turned away from his
commands.
²⁴ He knows that I am without blame.
He knows I've kept myself from
sinning.
²⁵ The LORD has rewarded me for doing
what is right.
He has rewarded me because I
haven't done anything wrong.

²⁶ "LORD, to those who are faithful you
show that you are faithful.
To those who are without blame you
show that you are without
blame.
²⁷ To those who are pure you show that
you are pure.
But to those whose paths are crooked
you show that you are clever.
²⁸ You save those who aren't proud.
But you watch the proud to bring
them down.
²⁹ LORD, you are my lamp.
You bring light into my darkness.
³⁰ With your help I can attack a troop of
soldiers.
With the help of my God I can
climb over a wall.

³¹ "God's way is perfect.
The word of the LORD doesn't have
any flaws.
He is like a shield
to all who go to him for safety.
³² Who is God except the LORD?
Who is the Rock except our God?
³³ God gives me strength for the battle.
He makes my way perfect.
³⁴ He makes my feet like the feet of a deer.
He helps me stand on the highest
places.
³⁵ He trains my hands to fight every battle.
My arms can bend a bow of bronze.

36 LORD, you are like a shield that keeps
     me safe.
   You help me win the battle.
   You bend down to make me great.
37 You give me a wide path to walk in
   so that I don't twist my ankles.

38 "I chased my enemies and crushed
     them.
   I didn't turn back until they were
     destroyed.
39 I crushed them completely so that
     they couldn't get up.
   They fell under my feet.
40 LORD, you gave me strength to fight the
     battle.
   You made my enemies bow down at
     my feet.
41 You made them turn their backs and
     run away.
   So I destroyed my enemies.
42 They cried out for help. But there was
     no one to save them.
   They called out to you. But you
     didn't answer them.
43 I beat them as fine as the dust of the
     earth.
   I pounded them and walked on
     them like mud in the streets.

44 "You saved me when my own people
     attacked me.
   You have kept me as the ruler over
     nations.
   People I didn't know serve me now.
45   People from other lands bow down
     to me in fear.
   As soon as they hear me, they obey
     me.
46 All of them give up hope.
   They come trembling out of their
     hiding places.

47 "The LORD lives! Give praise to my
     Rock!
   Give honor to God, the Rock! He is
     my Savior!
48 He is the God who pays my enemies
     back.
   He brings the nations under my
     control.
49   He sets me free from my enemies.
   You have honored me more than
     them.
   You have saved me from men who
     want to hurt me.
50 LORD, I will praise you among the
     nations.
   I will sing praises to you.
51 You help me win great battles.
   You show your faithful love to your
     anointed king.

You show it to me and my family
     forever."

David's Last Words

23 Here are David's last words. He
said,

"I am David, the son of Jesse. God has
     given me a message.
   The Most High God has greatly
     honored me.
   The God of Jacob anointed me as king.
   I am Israel's singer of songs.

2 "The Spirit of the LORD spoke through
     me.
   I spoke his word with my tongue.
3 The God of Israel spoke.
   The Rock of Israel said to me,
'A king must rule over people in a way
     that is right.
   He must have respect for me when
     he rules.
4 Then he will be like the light of
     morning at sunrise
   when there aren't any clouds.
   He will be like the bright sun after rain
     that makes the grass grow on the
     earth.'

5 "Isn't my royal family right with God?
   Hasn't he made a covenant with me
     that will last forever?
   Every part of it was well prepared
     and made secure.
   Won't he save me completely?
   Won't he give me everything I long
     for?
6 But evil people are like thorns that are
     thrown away.
   You can't pick them up with your
     hands.
7 Even if you touch them,
   you must use an iron tool or a spear.
   Thorns are burned up right where
     they are."

David's Mighty Men

8 Here are the names of David's mighty
men.

Josheb-Basshebeth was chief of the
Three. He was a Tahkemonite. He used his
spear against 800 men. He killed all of
them at one time.

9 Next to him was Eleazar. He was one of
the three mighty men. He was the son of
Dodai, the Ahohite. Eleazar was with
David at Pas Dammim. That's where Israel's army made fun of the Philistines who
were gathered there for battle. Then the
men of Israel pulled back.

10 But Eleazar stayed right where he was.

He struck the Philistines down until his hand grew tired. But he still held on to his sword. The LORD helped him win a great battle that day. The troops returned to Eleazar. They came back to him only to take what they wanted from the dead bodies.

11 Next to him was Shammah, the son of Agee. Shammah was a Hararite. The Philistines gathered together at a place where there was a field full of lentils. Israel's troops ran away from them.

12 But Shammah took his stand in the middle of the field. He didn't let the Philistines capture it. He struck them down. The LORD helped him win a great battle.

13 David was at the cave of Adullam. During harvest time, three of the 30 chief men came down to him there. A group of Philistines was camped in the Valley of Rephaim. 14 At that time David was in his usual place of safety. Some Philistine troops were stationed at Bethlehem.

15 David longed for water. He said, "I wish someone would get me a drink of water from the well that is near the gate of Bethlehem."

16 So the three mighty men fought their way past the Philistine guards. They got some water from the well that was near the gate of Bethlehem. They took the water back to David.

But David refused to drink it. Instead, he poured it out as a drink offering to the LORD. 17 "LORD, I would never drink that water!" David said. "It stands for the blood of these men. They put their lives in danger by going to Bethlehem to get it." So David wouldn't drink it.

Those were some of the brave things the three mighty men did.

18 Abishai was chief over the Three. He was the brother of Joab, the son of Zeruiah. He used his spear against 300 men. He killed all of them. So he became as famous as the Three were. 19 In fact, he was even more honored than the Three. He became their commander. But he wasn't included among them.

20 Benaiah was a great hero from Kabzeel. He was the son of Jehoiada. Benaiah did many brave things. He struck down two of Moab's best fighting men. He also went down into a pit on a snowy day. He killed a lion there.

21 And he struck down a huge Egyptian. The Egyptian was holding a spear. Benaiah went out to fight against him with a club. He grabbed the spear out of the Egyptian's hand. Then he killed him with it.

22 Those were some of the brave things

Benaiah, the son of Jehoiada, did. He too was as famous as the three mighty men were. 23 He was honored more than any of the Thirty. But he wasn't included among the Three. David put him in charge of his own personal guards.

24 Here is a list of David's men who were among the Thirty.

> Asahel, the brother of Joab
> Elhanan, the son of Dodo, from Bethlehem
> 25 Shammah, the Harodite
> Elika, the Harodite
> 26 Helez, the Paltite
> Ira, the son of Ikkesh, from Tekoa
> 27 Abiezer from Anathoth
> Mebunnai, the Hushathite
> 28 Zalmon, the Ahohite
> Maharai from Netophah
> 29 Heled, the son of Baanah, from Netophah
> Ithai, the son of Ribai, from Gibeah in Benjamin
> 30 Benaiah from Pirathon
> Hiddai from the valleys of Gaash
> 31 Abi-Albon, the Arbathite
> Azmaveth, the Barhumite
> 32 Eliahba, the Shaalbonite
> the sons of Jashen
> Jonathan, 33 the son of Shammah, the Hararite
> Ahiam, the son of Sharar, the Hararite
> 34 Eliphelet, the son of Ahasbai, the Maacathite
> Eliam, the son of Ahithophel, from Giloh
> 35 Hezro from Carmel
> Paarai, the Arbite
> 36 Igal, the son of Nathan, from Zobah
> the son of Hagri
> 37 Zelek from Ammon
> Naharai from Beeroth, who carried the armor of Joab, the son of Zeruiah
> 38 Ira, the Ithrite
> Gareb, the Ithrite
> 39 Uriah, the Hittite

The total number of men was 37.

David Counts His Fighting Men

24 The LORD's anger burned against Israel. He stirred up David against them. He said, "Go! Count the men of Israel and Judah."

2 So the king spoke to Joab and the army commanders who were with him. He said, "Go all through the territories of the

tribes of Israel. Go from Dan all the way to Beersheba. Count the fighting men. Then I'll know how many there are."

3Joab replied to the king. He said, "King David, you are my master. May the LORD your God multiply the troops 100 times. And may you live to see it. But why would you want me to count the fighting men?"

4In spite of what Joab said, the king's word had more authority than the word of Joab and the army commanders did. So they left the king and went out to count the fighting men of Israel.

5They went across the Jordan River. They camped south of the town in the middle of the Arnon River valley near Aroer. Then they went through Gad and continued on to Jazer. **6**They went to Gilead and the area of Tahtim Hodshi. They continued to Dan Jaan and on around toward Sidon. **7**Then they went toward the fort of Tyre. They went to all of the towns of the Hivites and Canaanites. Finally, they went on to Beersheba. It was in the Negev Desert of Judah.

8They finished going through the entire land. Then they came back to Jerusalem. They had been gone for nine months and 20 days.

9Joab reported to the king how many fighting men he had counted. In Israel there were 800,000 men who were able to handle a sword. In Judah there were 500,000.

10David felt sorry that he had counted the fighting men. So he said to the LORD, "I committed a great sin when I counted Judah and Israel's men. LORD, I beg you to take away my guilt. I've done a very foolish thing."

11Before David got up the next morning, a message from the LORD came to the prophet Gad. He was David's seer. The message said, **12**"Go and tell David, 'The LORD says, "I could punish you in three different ways. Choose one of them for me to use against you." ' "

13So Gad went to David. He said to him, "Take your choice. Do you want three years when there won't be enough food in your land? Or do you want three months when you will run away from your enemies while they chase you? Or do you want three days when there will be a plague in your land? Think it over. Then take your pick. Tell me how to answer the One who sent me."

14David said to Gad, "I'm suffering terribly. Let us fall into the hands of the LORD. His mercy is great. But don't let me fall into the hands of men."

15So the LORD sent a plague on Israel. It lasted from that morning until he decided to end it. From Dan all the way to Beersheba 70,000 people died.

16The angel reached his hand out to destroy Jerusalem. But the LORD was very sad because of the plague. So he spoke to the angel who was making the people suffer. He said, "That is enough! Do not kill any more people." The angel of the LORD was at Araunah's threshing floor. Araunah was from the city of Jebus.

17David saw the angel who was striking the people down. David said to the LORD, "I'm the one who has sinned. I'm the one who has done what is wrong. These people are like sheep. What have they done? Let your powerful hand punish me and my family."

David Builds an Altar

18On that day Gad went to David. Gad said to him, "Go up to the threshing floor of Araunah, the Jebusite. Build an altar there to honor the LORD."

19So David went up and did it. He did what the LORD had commanded through Gad.

20Araunah looked and saw the king and his officials coming toward him. So he went out to welcome them. He bowed down to the king with his face toward the ground.

21Araunah said, "King David, you are my master. Why have you come to see me?"

"To buy your threshing floor," David answered. "I want to build an altar there to honor the LORD. When I do, the plague on the people will be stopped."

22Araunah said to David, "Take anything that pleases you. Offer it up. Here are oxen for the burnt offering. Here are threshing sleds. And here are wooden collars from the necks of the oxen. Use all of the wood to burn the offering. **23**King David, I'll give all of it to you." Araunah continued, "And may the LORD your God accept you."

24But the king replied to Araunah, "No. I want to pay you for it. I won't sacrifice to the LORD my God burnt offerings that haven't cost me anything."

So David bought the threshing floor and the oxen. He paid 20 ounces of silver for them. **25**David built an altar there to honor the LORD. He sacrificed burnt offerings and friendship offerings.

Then the LORD answered prayer and blessed the land. The plague on Israel was stopped.

1 KINGS

The book of 1 Kings begins with the reign of Solomon. Solomon begins great building projects, including a magnificent temple for worshiping God in Jerusalem. Solomon reigns for forty years. After he dies, Israel is divided into two nations, Israel and Judah. About half of the kings of Judah obey God and the other half disobey, while all of the kings of Israel disobey God. God sends his messengers to call the people back, but only a few listen. Read 1 Kings to learn the importance of obeying God all your life.

HEROES IN THIS BOOK . . .

KING SOLOMON
PAGE 395

QUEEN OF SHEBA
PAGE 404

REHOBOAM
(Not!)
PAGE 408

Adonijah Makes Himself King

1 King David was now very old. He couldn't keep warm even when blankets were spread over him. ²So his servants spoke to him. They said, "You are our king and master. Please let us try to find a young virgin to help you. She can take care of you. She can lie down beside you. Then you can keep warm."

³So David's servants looked all over Israel for a beautiful young woman. They found Abishag. She was from the town of Shunem. They brought her to the king. ⁴The woman was very beautiful. She took care of the king and served him. But the king didn't have sex with her.

⁵Adonijah was the son of David and his wife Haggith. He came forward and announced, "I'm going to be the next king." So he got chariots and horses ready. He also got 50 men to run in front of him.

⁶His father had never tried to stop him from doing what he wanted to. His father had never asked him, "Why are you acting the way you do?"

Adonijah was also very handsome. Now that Absalom was dead, Adonijah was David's oldest son.

⁷Adonijah talked things over with Joab, the son of Zeruiah. He also talked with the priest Abiathar. They agreed to help him.

⁸But the priest Zadok and Benaiah, the son of Jehoiada, didn't join Adonijah. The prophet Nathan didn't join him. Shimei and Rei didn't join him. And neither did David's special guard.

⁹Adonijah sacrificed sheep, cattle and fat calves. He sacrificed them at the Stone of Zoheleth near En Rogel. He invited all of his brothers, the king's sons, and all of the men of Judah who were royal officials. ¹⁰But he didn't invite Benaiah or the prophet Nathan. He didn't invite the special guard or his brother Solomon either.

¹¹Nathan spoke to Solomon's mother Bathsheba. He asked, "Haven't you heard? Adonijah, the son of Haggith, has made himself king. And King David doesn't even know about it. ¹²So let me tell you what to do to save your life. It will also save the life of your son Solomon. ¹³Go in and see King David. Say to him, 'You are my king and master. You took an oath. You promised me, "You can be sure that your son Solomon will be king after me. He will sit on my throne." If that's really true, why has Adonijah become king?' ¹⁴While you are still talking to the king, I'll come in. I'll tell him that what you have said is true."

¹⁵So Bathsheba went to see the old king in his room. Abishag, the Shunammite, was taking care of him there. ¹⁶Bathsheba bowed low. She got down on her knees in front of the king.

"What do you want?" the king asked.

¹⁷She said to him, "My master, you took an oath in the name of the LORD your God. You promised me, 'Your son Solomon will be king after me. He will sit on my throne.'

¹⁸"But now Adonijah has made himself king. And you don't even know about it. ¹⁹He has sacrificed large numbers of cattle, fat calves and sheep. He has invited all of the king's sons. He has also invited the priest Abiathar and Joab, the commander of the army. But he hasn't invited your son Solomon.

²⁰"You are my king and master. All of the people of Israel are watching to see what you will do. They want to find out from you who will sit on the throne after you. ²¹If you don't do something, I and my son Solomon will be treated like people who have committed crimes. That will happen as soon as you join the members of your family who have already died."

²²While she was still speaking with the king, the prophet Nathan arrived. ²³The king was told, "The prophet Nathan is here." So Nathan went to the king. He bowed down with his face toward the ground.

²⁴Nathan said, "You are my king and master. Have you announced that Adonijah will be king after you? Have you said he will sit on your throne? ²⁵Today he has gone down outside the city. He has sacrificed large numbers of cattle, fat calves and sheep. He has invited all of the king's sons. He has also invited the commanders of the army and the priest Abiathar. Even now they are eating and drinking with him. They are saying, 'May King Adonijah live a long time!'

²⁶"But he didn't invite me. He didn't invite the priest Zadok or Benaiah, the son of Jehoiada. He didn't invite your son Solomon either.

²⁷"King David, have you allowed all of that to happen? Did you do it without letting us know about it? Why didn't you tell us who is going to sit on your throne after you?"

David Makes Solomon King

²⁸King David said, "Tell Bathsheba to

come in." So she came and stood in front of the king.

29Then the king took an oath and made a promise. He said, "The LORD has saved me from all of my troubles. You can be sure that he lives. **30**And you can be just as sure that I will do today what I promised in the name of the LORD. He is the God of Israel. I promised you that your son Solomon would be king after me. He will sit on my throne in my place."

31Then Bathsheba bowed low with her face toward the ground. She got down on her knees in front of the king. She said, "King David, you are my master. May you live forever!"

32King David said, "Tell the priest Zadok and the prophet Nathan to come in. Also tell Benaiah, the son of Jehoiada, to come." So they came to the king.

33He said to them, "Take my officials with you. Put my son Solomon on my own mule. Take him down to the Gihon spring. **34**Have the priest Zadok and the prophet Nathan anoint him as king over Israel there. Blow a trumpet. Shout, 'May King Solomon live a long time!' **35**Then come back up to the city with him. Have him sit on my throne. He will rule in my place. I've appointed him ruler over Israel and Judah."

36Benaiah, the son of Jehoiada, answered the king. "Amen!" he said. "May the LORD your God make it come true. **37**You are my king and master. The LORD has been with you. May he also be with Solomon. King David, may the LORD make Solomon's kingdom even greater than yours!"

38So the priest Zadok and the prophet Nathan left the palace. Benaiah, the son of Jehoiada, went with them. So did the Kerethites and Pelethites. They put Solomon on King David's mule. And they brought him down to the Gihon spring.

39The priest Zadok had gotten an animal horn that was filled with olive oil. He had taken it from the sacred tent. He anointed Solomon with the oil. The trumpet was blown. All of the people shouted, "May King Solomon live a long time!"

40Then they went up toward the city. Solomon was leading the way. The people were playing flutes. They were filled with great joy. The ground shook because of all of the noise.

41Adonijah and all of his guests heard it. They were just finishing their meal. Joab heard the sound of the trumpet. So

he asked, "What does all of that noise in the city mean?"

42While Joab was still speaking, Jonathan arrived. Jonathan was the son of the priest Abiathar. Adonijah said, "Come in. I have respect for you. You must be bringing good news."

43"No! I'm not!" Jonathan answered. "Our master King David has made Solomon king. **44**David sent the priest Zadok and the prophet Nathan along with Solomon. He also sent Benaiah, the son of Jehoiada, with him. He sent the Kerethites and Pelethites with him too. They put him on the king's mule. **45**They took him down to the Gihon spring. There the priest Zadok and the prophet Nathan anointed him as king. Now they've gone back up to the city. They were cheering all the way. The city is filled with the sound of it. That's the noise you hear.

46"And that's not all. Solomon has taken his seat on the royal throne. **47**The royal officials came to give their blessing to our master King David. They said, 'May your God make Solomon's name more famous than yours! May he make Solomon's kingdom greater than yours!'

"While King David was sitting on his bed, he bowed in worship. **48**He said, 'I praise the LORD. He is the God of Israel. He has let me live to see my son sitting on my throne today as the next king.' "

49When all of Adonijah's guests heard that, they were terrified. So they got up and scattered.

50Adonijah was afraid of what Solomon might do to him. So he went and grabbed hold of the horns that stuck out

POWER-SURGE

CHEERFUL ✳

THEN [THE PEOPLE] WENT UP TOWARD THE CITY. SOLOMON WAS LEADING THE WAY. THE PEOPLE WERE PLAYING FLUTES. THEY WERE FILLED WITH GREAT JOY. THE GROUND SHOOK BECAUSE OF ALL OF THE NOISE.
— **1 KINGS 1:40** —

from the upper corners of the altar for burnt offerings.

⁵¹Then Solomon was told, "King Solomon, Adonijah is afraid of you. He's holding onto the horns of the altar. He says, 'I want King Solomon to take an oath today. I want him to promise that he won't kill me with his sword.' "

⁵²Solomon replied, "Let him show that he's a man people can respect. Then not even one hair on his head will fall to the ground. But if I find out he's done something evil, he will die."

⁵³King Solomon got some men to bring Adonijah down from the altar. He came and bowed down to King Solomon. Solomon said, "Go on home."

David Gives Orders to Solomon

2 The time came near for David to die. So he gave orders to his son Solomon. He said,

²"I'm about to die, just as everyone else on earth does. So be strong. Show how brave you are. ³Do everything the LORD your God requires. Live the way he wants you to. Obey his orders and commands. Keep his laws and rules. Do everything that is written in the Law of Moses. Then you will have success in everything you do. You will succeed everywhere you go.

⁴"The LORD will keep the promise he made to me. He said, 'Your sons must be careful about how they live. They must be faithful to me with all their heart and soul. Then you will always have a man sitting on the throne of Israel.'

BRAVE B

BE STRONG. SHOW HOW BRAVE YOU ARE. DO EVERYTHING THE LORD YOUR GOD REQUIRES. LIVE THE WAY HE WANTS YOU TO. OBEY HIS ORDERS AND COMMANDS. KEEP HIS LAWS AND RULES.
— 1 KINGS 2:2-3 —

STRONG

⁵"You yourself know what Joab, the son of Zeruiah, did to me. You know that he killed Abner, the son of Ner, and Amasa, the son of Jether. They were the two commanders of Israel's armies. He killed them in a time of peace. It wasn't a time of war. Joab spilled the blood of Abner and Amasa. It stained the belt that was around his waist. It also stained the sandals on his feet. ⁶You are wise. So I leave him in your hands. Just don't let him live to become an old man. Don't let him die peacefully.

⁷"But be kind to the sons of Barzillai from Gilead. Provide what they need. They were faithful to me when I had to run away from your brother Absalom.

⁸"Don't forget Shimei, the son of Gera. He's still around. He's from Bahurim in the territory of Benjamin. He called down bitter curses on me. He did it on the day I went to Mahanaim. Later, he came down to welcome me at the Jordan River. At that time I took an oath in the name of the LORD. I promised Shimei, 'I won't put you to death with my sword.' ⁹But now I want you to think of him as guilty. You are wise. You will know what to do to him. Don't let him live to become an old man. Put him to death."

¹⁰David joined the members of his family who had already died. His body was buried in the City of David. ¹¹He had ruled over Israel for 40 years. He ruled for seven years in Hebron. Then he ruled for 33 years in Jerusalem.

¹²So Solomon sat on the throne of his father David. His position as king was made secure.

Solomon's Kingdom Is Made Secure

¹³Adonijah was the son of David's wife Haggith. He went to Bathsheba. She was Solomon's mother. She asked Adonijah, "Have you come in peace?"

He answered, "Yes. I've come in peace." ¹⁴He continued, "I want to ask you something."

"Go ahead," she replied.

¹⁵He said, "As you know, the kingdom belonged to me. The whole nation of Israel thought of me as their king. But now things have changed. The kingdom belongs to my brother. The LORD has given it to him. ¹⁶But I have a favor to ask of you. Don't say no to me."

"Go ahead," she said.

¹⁷So he continued, "Please ask King Solomon for a favor. He won't say no to you. Ask him to give me Abishag from Shunem to be my wife."

18"All right," Bathsheba replied. "I'll speak to the king for you."

19So Bathsheba went to King Solomon. She went to him to speak for Adonijah. The king stood up to greet her. He bowed down to her. Then he sat down on his throne. He had a throne brought for his mother. She sat down at his right side.

20"I have one small favor to ask of you," she said. "Don't say no to me."

The king replied, "Mother, go ahead and ask. I won't say no to you."

21She said, "Let your brother Adonijah get married to Abishag, the Shunammite."

22King Solomon answered his mother, "Why are you asking for Abishag, the Shunammite, for Adonijah? You might as well ask me to give him the whole kingdom! After all, he's my older brother. And he doesn't want the kingdom only for himself. He also wants it for the priest Abiathar and for Joab, the son of Zeruiah."

23Then King Solomon took an oath and made a promise in the name of the LORD. He said, "Adonijah will pay with his life because of what he has asked for. If he doesn't, may God punish me greatly. **24**The LORD has made my position as king secure. I'm sitting on the throne of my father David. The LORD has built a royal house for me, just as he promised. You can be sure that the LORD lives. And you can be just as sure that Adonijah will be put to death today."

25So King Solomon gave the order to Benaiah, the son of Jehoiada. Benaiah struck Adonijah down. And Adonijah died.

26The king spoke to the priest Abiathar. He said, "Go back to your fields in Anathoth. You should really be put to death. But I won't have it done now. That's because you carried the ark of the LORD and King. You did it for my father David. You shared all of his hard times."

27So Solomon wouldn't let Abiathar serve as a priest of the LORD anymore. That's how the message the LORD had spoken at Shiloh came true. He had spoken it about the family of Eli.

28News of what Solomon had done reached Joab. Joab had never made evil plans along with Absalom. But he had joined Adonijah. So he ran to the tent of the LORD. He took hold of the horns that stuck out from the upper corners of the altar for burnt offerings.

29King Solomon was told that Joab had run to the tent. He was also told that Joab was by the altar.

Then Solomon gave the order to Benaiah, the son of Jehoiada. He told him, "Go! Strike him down!"

30So Benaiah entered the tent of the LORD. He said to Joab, "The king says, 'Come on out!' "

But Joab answered, "No. I'd rather die here."

Benaiah told the king what Joab had said to him.

31Then the king commanded Benaiah, "Do what he says. Strike him down. Bury his body. Then I and my family won't be held accountable for the blood Joab spilled. He killed people who weren't guilty of doing anything wrong. **32**The LORD will pay him back for the blood he spilled. Joab attacked two men. He killed them with his sword. And my father David didn't even know anything about it.

"Joab killed Abner, the son of Ner. Abner was the commander of Israel's army. Joab also killed Amasa, the son of Jether. Amasa was the commander of Judah's army. Abner and Amasa were better men than Joab is. They were more honest than he is. **33**May Joab and his children after him be held forever accountable for spilling the blood of Abner and Amasa.

"But may David and his children after him enjoy the LORD's peace and rest forever. May the LORD also give his peace to David's royal house and kingdom forever."

34So Benaiah, the son of Jehoiada, went up to the LORD's tent. There he struck Joab down. And he killed him. Joab's body was buried on his own land in the desert.

35The king put Benaiah in charge of the army. Benaiah took Joab's place. The king also put the priest Zadok in Abiathar's place.

36Then the king sent for Shimei. He said to him, "Build yourself a house in Jerusalem. Live there. Don't go anywhere else. **37**You must not leave the city and go across the Kidron Valley. If you do, you can be sure you will die. And it will be your own fault."

38Shimei replied to the king, "You are my king and master. What you say is good. I'll do it." Shimei stayed in Jerusalem for a long time.

39Three years after Solomon had talked with Shimei, two of Shimei's slaves ran off. They went to Achish, the king of Gath. He was the son of Maacah. Shimei was told, "Your slaves are in Gath." **40**When Shimei heard that, he put a sad-

HONEST   H

[DAVID'S] HEART WAS HONEST.
— 1 KINGS 3:6 —

dle on his donkey. Then he went to Achish at Gath to look for his slaves. Shimei found them and brought them back from Gath.

⁴¹Solomon was told that Shimei had left Jerusalem. He was told he had gone to Gath and had returned.

⁴²So the king sent for Shimei. He said to him, "Didn't I make you take an oath in the name of the LORD? Didn't I warn you? I said, 'You must not leave the city and go somewhere else. If you do, you can be sure you will die.' At that time you said to me, 'What you say is good. I'll obey your command.' ⁴³So why didn't you keep your oath to the LORD? Why didn't you obey the command I gave you?"

⁴⁴The king continued, "You know all of the wrong things you did to my father David. In your heart you know them. Now the LORD will pay you back for what you did. ⁴⁵But I will be blessed. The LORD will make David's kingdom secure forever."

⁴⁶Then the king gave the order to Benaiah, the son of Jehoiada. Benaiah left the palace and struck Shimei down. And he killed him.

So the kingdom was now made secure in Solomon's hands.

Solomon Asks God for Wisdom

3 Solomon and Pharaoh, the king of Egypt, agreed to help each other. So Solomon got married to Pharaoh's daughter. He brought her to the City of David. She stayed there until he finished building his palace, the LORD's temple, and the wall that was around Jerusalem.

²But the people continued to offer sacrifices at the high places where they worshiped. That's because a temple hadn't been built yet where the LORD would put his Name.

³Solomon showed his love for the LORD. He did it by obeying the laws his father David had taught him. But Solomon offered sacrifices at the high places. He also burned incense there.

⁴King Solomon went to the city of Gibeon to offer sacrifices. That's where the most important high place was. He offered 1,000 burnt offerings on the altar that was there.

⁵The LORD appeared to Solomon at Gibeon. He spoke to him in a dream during the night. God said, "Ask for anything you want me to give you."

⁶Solomon answered, "You have been very kind to my father David, your servant. That's because he was faithful to you. He did what was right. His heart was honest. And you have continued to be very kind to him. You have given him a son to sit on his throne this very day.

⁷"LORD my God, you have now made me king. You have put me in the place of my father David. But I'm only a little child. I don't know how to carry out my duties. ⁸I'm here among the people you have chosen. They are a great nation. They are more than anyone can count. ⁹So give me a heart that understands. Then I can rule over your people. I can tell the difference between what is right and what is wrong. Who can possibly rule over this great nation of yours?"

¹⁰The Lord was pleased that Solomon had asked for that. ¹¹So God said to him, "You have not asked to live for a long time. You have not asked to be wealthy. You have not even asked to have your enemies killed. Instead, you have asked for understanding. You want to do what is right and fair when you judge people. Because that is what you have asked for, ¹²I will give it to you. I will give you a wise

WISE   W

YOU HAVE PUT ME
IN THE PLACE OF
MY FATHER DAVID.
BUT... I DON'T KNOW
HOW TO CARRY OUT
MY DUTIES... SO GIVE
ME A HEART THAT
UNDERSTANDS... SO
GOD SAID TO HIM, "...I
WILL GIVE YOU A WISE
AND UNDERSTANDING
HEART."
— 1 KINGS 3:7,9,11-12 —

and understanding heart. So here is what will be true of you. There has never been anyone like you. And there never will be.

13 "And that is not all. I will give you what you have not asked for. I will give you riches and honor. As long as you live, no other king will be as great as you are. 14 Live the way I want you to. Obey my laws and commands, just as your father David did. Then I will let you live for a long time."

15 Solomon woke up. He realized he had been dreaming.

He returned to Jerusalem. He stood in front of the ark of the LORD's covenant. He sacrificed burnt offerings and friendship offerings. Then he gave a big dinner for all of his officials.

Solomon Judges Wisely

16 Two prostitutes came to the king. They stood in front of him. 17 One of them said, "My master, this woman and I live in the same house. I had a baby while she was there with me. 18 Three days after my child was born, this woman also had a baby. We were alone. There wasn't anyone in the house but the two of us.

19 "During the night this woman's baby died. It happened because she was lying on top of him. 20 So she got up in the middle of the night. She took my son from my side while I was asleep. She put him by her breast. Then she put her dead son by my breast. 21 The next morning, I got up to nurse my son. But he was dead! I looked at him closely in the morning light. And I saw that it wasn't my baby."

22 The other woman said, "No! The living baby is my son. The dead one belongs to you."

But the first woman said, "No! The dead baby is yours. The living one belongs to me." So they argued in front of the king.

23 The king said, "One of you says, 'My son is alive. Your son is dead.' The other one says, 'No! Your son is dead. Mine is alive.' "

24 He continued, "Bring me a sword." So a sword was brought to him. 25 Then he gave an order. He said, "Cut the living child in two. Give half to one woman and half to the other."

26 The woman whose son was alive was filled with deep concern for her son. She said to the king, "My master, please give her the living baby! Don't kill him!"

But the other woman said, "Neither one of us will have him. Cut him in two!"

27 Then the king made his decision. He said, "Give the living baby to the

POWER-SURGE

WISE   W

THEY SAW THAT GOD HAD GIVEN HIM WISDOM. THEY KNEW THAT SOLOMON WOULD DO WHAT WAS RIGHT AND FAIR WHEN HE JUDGED PEOPLE.
— 1 KINGS 3:28 —

first woman. Don't kill him. She's his mother."

28 All of the people of Israel heard about the decision the king had given. That gave them great respect for him. They saw that God had given him wisdom. They knew that Solomon would do what was right and fair when he judged people.

Solomon's Officials and Governors

4 So King Solomon ruled over the whole nation of Israel. 2 Here are the names of his chief officials.

Azariah was the priest. He was the son of Zadok.

3 Elihoreph and Ahijah were secretaries. They were the sons of Shisha.

Jehoshaphat kept the records. He was the son of Ahilud.

4 Benaiah was the commander in chief. He was the son of Jehoiada.

Zadok and Abiathar were priests.

5 Azariah was in charge of the local officials. He was the son of Nathan.

Zabud was a priest. He was the king's personal adviser. He was the son of Nathan.

6 Ahishar was in charge of the palace.

Adoniram was in charge of those who were forced to work for the king. He was the son of Abda.

7 Solomon also had 12 local governors over the whole land of Israel. They provided supplies for the king and the royal family. Each governor had to provide supplies for one month out of each year. 8 Here are their names and areas.

Ben-Hur's area was the hill country of Ephraim.

9 Ben-Deker's area was Makaz, Shaal-

bim, Beth Shemesh and Elon Beth-hanan.

10 Ben-Hesed's area was Arubboth. Socoh and the whole land of Hepher were included in his area.

11 Ben-Abinadab's area was Naphoth Dor. He got married to Solomon's daughter Taphath.

12 Baana's area was Taanach, Megiddo and the whole territory of Beth Shan. Beth Shan was next to Zarethan below Jezreel. Baana's area reached from Beth Shan all the way to Abel Meholah. It also went across to Jokmeam. Baana was the son of Ahilud.

13 Ben-Geber's area was Ramoth Gilead. The settlements of Jair, the son of Manasseh, were included in his area in Gilead. The area of Argob in Bashan was also included. That area had 60 large cities that had high walls around them. The city gates were made secure with heavy bronze bars.

14 Ahinadab's area was Mahanaim. He was the son of Iddo.

15 Ahimaaz's area was Naphtali. He had gotten married to Basemath. She was Solomon's daughter.

16 Baana's area was Asher and Aloth. He was the son of Hushai.

17 Jehoshaphat's area was Issachar. He was the son of Paruah.

18 Shimei's area was Benjamin. He was the son of Ela.

19 Geber's area was Gilead. He was the only governor over the area. He was the son of Uri. Gilead had been the country of Sihon and Og. Sihon had been king of the Amorites. Og had been king of Bashan.

Solomon's Daily Supplies

20 There were many people in Judah and Israel. In fact, they were as many as the grains of sand on the seashore. They ate, drank and were happy.

21 Solomon ruled over all of the kingdoms from the Euphrates River to the land of the Philistines. He ruled as far as the border of Egypt. All of those countries brought the gifts he required them to bring him. And Solomon ruled over those countries for his whole life.

22 Here are the supplies Solomon required every day.

> 185 bushels of fine flour
> 375 bushels of meal
> **23** ten head of cattle that had been fed by hand
> 20 head of cattle that had been fed on grasslands
> 100 sheep and goats
> deer, antelopes and roebucks
> the finest birds

24 Solomon ruled over all of the kingdoms that were west of the Euphrates River. He ruled from Tiphsah all the way to Gaza. And he had peace and rest on every side.

25 While Solomon was king, Judah and Israel lived in safety. They were secure from Dan all the way to Beersheba. Each man had his own vine and fig tree.

26 Solomon had 4,000 spaces where he kept his chariot horses. He had a total of 12,000 horses.

27 The local officials provided supplies for King Solomon. They provided them for all who ate at the king's table. Each official provided supplies for one month every year. The officials made sure the king had everything he needed. **28** They also brought barley and straw for the chariot horses and the other horses. Each of them brought the amounts that were required of them. They brought them to the proper places.

God Makes Solomon Very Wise

29 God made Solomon very wise. His understanding couldn't even be measured. It was like the sand on the seashore. People can't measure that either.

30 Solomon's wisdom was greater than the wisdom of all of the people of the east. It was greater than all of the wisdom of Egypt. **31** Solomon was wiser than any other man. He was wiser than Ethan, the Ezrahite. He was wiser than Heman, Calcol and Darda. They were the sons of

POWER-SURGE

WISE

GOD MADE SOLOMON
VERY WISE...
SOLOMON'S WISDOM
WAS GREATER THAN
THE WISDOM OF ALL
OF THE PEOPLE OF
THE EAST. IT WAS
GREATER THAN ALL OF
THE WISDOM OF
EGYPT.
— 1 KINGS 4:29-30 —

Mahol. Solomon became famous in all of the nations that were around him.

32He spoke 3,000 proverbs. He wrote 1,005 songs. **33**He explained all about plants. He knew everything about them, from the cedar trees in Lebanon to the hyssop plants that grow out of walls. He taught about animals and birds. He also taught about reptiles and fish.

34The kings of all of the world's nations heard about how wise Solomon was. So they sent their people to listen to him.

Solomon Asks Hiram to Help Build the Temple

5 Hiram was the king of Tyre. He heard that Solomon had been anointed as king. He heard that Solomon had become the next king after his father David. Hiram had always been David's friend. So Hiram sent his messengers to Solomon.

2Then Solomon sent a message back to Hiram. It said,

3"As you know, my father David had to fight many battles. His enemies attacked him from every side. So he couldn't build a temple where the LORD his God would put his Name. That wouldn't be possible until the LORD had put his enemies under his control.

4"But now the LORD my God has given me peace and rest on every side. We don't have any enemies. And we don't have any other major problems either. **5**So I'm planning to build a temple. I want to build it for the Name of the LORD my God. That's what he told my father David he

wanted me to do. He said, 'I will put your son on the throne in your place. He will build a temple. I will put my Name there.'

6"So give your men orders to cut down cedar trees in Lebanon for me. My men will work with yours. I'll pay you for your men's work. I'll pay any amount you decide on. As you know, we don't have anyone who is as skilled in cutting down trees as the men of Sidon are."

7When Hiram heard Solomon's message, he was very pleased. He said, "May the LORD be praised today. He has given David a wise son to rule over that great nation."

8So Hiram sent a message to Solomon. It said,

"I have received the message you sent me. I'll do everything you want me to. I'll provide the cedar and pine logs. **9**My men will bring them from Lebanon down to the Mediterranean Sea. I'll make them into rafts. I'll float them to the place you want me to. When the rafts arrive, I'll separate the logs from each other. Then you can take them away.

"And here's what I want in return. Provide food for all of the people in my palace."

10So Hiram supplied Solomon with all of the cedar and pine logs he wanted.

11Solomon gave Hiram 125,000 bushels of wheat as food for the people in his palace. He also gave him 115,000 gallons of oil that was made from pressed olives. He did that for Hiram year after year.

12The LORD made Solomon wise, just as he had promised him. There was peace between Hiram and Solomon. The two of them made a peace treaty.

13King Solomon forced men from all over Israel to work hard for him. There were 30,000 of them. **14**He sent them off

POWER-SURGE

WISE

THE LORD MADE
SOLOMON WISE,
JUST AS HE HAD
PROMISED HIM.
— 1 KINGS 5:12 —

SOLOMON

1 KINGS 4:31; 10:23

Solomon was wiser than any other man...King Solomon was richer than all of the other kings on earth. He was also wiser than they were.

Solomon stood with the morning sun warm on his back. His heart swelled with emotion as he looked at the new temple before him. Its pillars stood tall and straight. Its white stone glistened in the sunlight. Its golden doors gleamed bright. What a beautiful place now that it was all finished.

The people and priests were just beginning to gather for the dedication of the new temple. Solomon heard them, but only in the distance. He raised his hands high above his head, as if to reach to heaven. Thanking God for this special day, he remembered the night several years before when God had appeared to him in a dream. It seemed like only yesterday when he had asked God to give him wisdom to be a good king. God was pleased with Solomon's request, and he also promised to give Solomon more riches than any person who had ever lived.

The people and priests grew quiet behind him. Solomon knew they were waiting for him to begin the ceremonies. **WITH A DEEP BREATH AND A PRAYER IN HIS HEART, HE TURNED.** Keeping his hands high, Solomon began to pray a prayer of dedication. "Oh, Lord, you know we love you. We have built this beautiful temple just for you. Come and live in this temple, Lord. And we will worship you here."

Solomon knew he was wise only because God had given him wisdom. He knew he was rich only because God had given him riches. But he also knew that those gifts weren't the most important things in his life. The most important thing in his life was God himself.

BE A SOLOMON

What is most important to you? Do you wish you were smarter? Do you wish you had more things? A new house? A room of your own? A new bike or game? Next time you pray and ask God for something, remind yourself of what's most important. Not how smart you are. Not how many things you have. But the fact that God loves you and you love him.

SOLOMON ASKED GOD FOR WISDOM AND GOT RICHES AS WELL.
THE WHOLE STORY: 1 KINGS 5:1–6:38

Go to page 404 for the next Super Hero

to Lebanon in groups of 10,000 each month. They spent one month in Lebanon. Then they spent two months at home. Adoniram was in charge of the people who were forced to work. **15**Solomon had 70,000 people who carried things. He had 80,000 who cut stones in the hills. **16**He had 3,300 men who were in charge of the project. They also directed the workers.

17The people did what the king commanded. They removed large blocks of fine stone from a rock pit. They used them to provide a foundation for the temple. **18**The skilled workers of Solomon and Hiram cut and prepared the logs and stones. They would later be used in building the temple. The people of Byblos helped the workers.

Solomon Builds the Temple

6 Solomon began to build the temple of the LORD. It was 480 years after the people of Israel had come out of Egypt. It was in the fourth year of Solomon's rule over Israel. He started in the second month. That was the month of Ziv.

2The temple King Solomon built for the LORD was 90 feet long. It was 30 feet wide. And it was 45 feet high. **3**The temple had a porch in front of the main hall. The porch was as wide as the temple itself. It was 30 feet wide. It came out 15 feet from the front of the temple. **4**Solomon made narrow windows high up in the temple walls.

5He built side rooms around the temple. They were built against the walls of the main hall and the Most Holy Room. **6**On the first floor the side rooms were seven and a half feet wide. On the second floor they were nine feet wide. And on the third floor they were ten and a half feet wide. Solomon made the walls of the temple thinner as they went up floor by floor. The result was ledges along the walls. So the floor beams of the side rooms rested on the ledges. The beams didn't go into the temple walls.

7All of the stones that were used for building the temple were shaped where they were cut. So hammers, chisels and other iron tools couldn't be heard where the temple was being built.

8The entrance to the first floor was on the south side of the temple. A stairway led up to the second floor. From there it went on up to the third floor.

9So Solomon built the temple and finished it. He made its roof out of beams and cedar boards. **10**He built side rooms all along the temple. Each room was seven and a half feet high. They were joined to the temple by cedar beams.

11A message came to Solomon from the LORD. The LORD said, **12**"You are now building this temple. Follow my orders. Keep my rules. Obey all of my commands. Then I will make the promise I gave your father David come true. I will do it through you. **13**I will live among my people Israel. I will not desert them."

14So Solomon built the temple and finished it. **15**He put cedar boards on its inside walls. He covered them from floor to ceiling. He covered the temple floor with pine boards. **16**He put up a wall 30 feet from the back of the temple. He made it with cedar boards from floor to ceiling. That formed a room inside the temple. It was the Most Holy Room. **17**The main hall in front of the room was 60 feet long. **18**The inside of the temple was covered with cedar wood. Gourds and open flowers were carved on the wood. Everything was cedar. There wasn't any stone showing anywhere.

19Solomon prepared the Most Holy Room inside the temple. That's where the ark of the covenant of the LORD would be placed. **20**The Most Holy Room was 30 feet long. It was 30 feet wide. And it was 30 feet high. Solomon covered the inside of it with pure gold. He prepared the cedar altar for burning incense. He covered it with gold. **21**Solomon covered the inside of the main hall with pure gold. He placed gold chains across the front of the Most Holy Room. That room was covered with gold. **22**So Solomon covered the inside of the whole temple with gold. He also covered the altar for burning incense with gold. It was right in front of the Most Holy Room.

23For the Most Holy Room Solomon made a pair of cherubim. He made them out of olive wood. Each cherub was 15 feet high. **24**One wing of the first cherub was seven and a half feet long. The other wing was also seven and a half feet long. So the wings measured 15 feet from tip to tip. **25**The second cherub's wings also measured 15 feet from tip to tip. The two cherubim had the same size and shape. **26**Each cherub was 15 feet high.

27Solomon placed the cherubim inside the Most Holy Room in the temple. Their wings were spread out. The wing tip of one cherub touched one wall. The wing tip of the other touched the other wall. The tips of their wings touched each other in the middle of the room. **28**Solomon covered the cherubim with gold.

29On the walls that were all around the temple he carved cherubim, palm trees and open flowers. He carved them on the walls of the Most Holy Room and the main hall. **30**He also covered the floors of those two rooms with gold.

31For the entrance to the Most Holy Room he made two doors out of olive wood. Each doorpost had five sides. **32**On the two olive wood doors he carved cherubim, palm trees and open flowers. He covered the cherubim and palm trees with hammered gold.

33In the same way he made olive wood doorposts for the entrance to the main hall. Each doorpost had four sides. **34**He also made two pine doors. Each door had two parts. They turned in bases that were shaped like cups. **35**He carved cherubim, palm trees and open flowers on the doors. He covered the doors with gold. He hammered the gold evenly over the carvings.

36He used blocks of stone to build a wall around the inside courtyard. The first three layers of the wall were made out of stone. The top layer was made out of beautiful cedar wood.

37The foundation of the LORD's temple was laid in Solomon's fourth year. It was in the month of Ziv. **38**The temple was finished in his 11th year. It was in the month of Bul. That was the eighth month. Everything was finished just as the plans required. Solomon had spent seven years building the temple.

Solomon Builds His Palace

7 But it took Solomon 13 years to finish constructing his palace and the other buildings that were related to it.

2He built the Palace of the Forest of Lebanon. It was 150 feet long. It was 75 feet wide. And it was 45 feet high. It had four rows of cedar columns. They held up beautiful cedar beams. **3**Above the beams was a roof that was made out of cedar boards. It rested on the columns. There were three rows of beams with 15 in each row. The total number of beams was 45. **4**The windows of the palace were placed high up in the walls. They were in groups of three. And they faced each other. **5**All of the doorways had frames that were shaped like rectangles. They were in front. They were in groups of three. And they faced each other.

6Solomon made a covered area. It was 75 feet long. And it was 45 feet wide. Its roof was held up by columns. In front of it was a porch. In front of that were pillars and a roof that went out beyond them.

7Solomon built the throne hall. It was called the Hall of Justice. That's where he would serve as judge. He covered the hall with cedar boards from floor to ceiling.

8The palace where he would live was set farther back. Its plan was something like the plan for the hall. Solomon had gotten married to Pharaoh's daughter. He made a palace for her. It was like the hall.

9All of those buildings were made out of blocks of very fine stone. They were cut to the right size. They were shaped with a saw on the back and front sides. Those stones were used for the outside of each building and for the large courtyard. They were also used from the foundations up to the roofs. **10**Large blocks of very fine stone were used for the foundations. Some were 15 feet long. Others were 12 feet long. **11**The walls that were above them were made out of very fine stones. The stones were cut to the right size. On top of them was a layer of cedar beams.

12The large courtyard had a wall around it. The first three layers of the wall were made out of blocks of stone. The top layer was made out of beautiful cedar wood. The same thing was done with the inside courtyard of the LORD's temple and its porch.

More Facts About the Temple

13King Solomon sent messengers to Tyre. He wanted them to bring Huram back with them. **14**Huram's mother was a widow. She was from the tribe of Naphtali. Huram's father was from Tyre. He was skilled in working with bronze. Huram also was very skilled. He had done all kinds of work with bronze. He came to King Solomon and did all of the work he was asked to do.

15Huram made two bronze pillars. Each of them was 27 feet high. And each was 18 feet around. **16**Each pillar had a decorated top that was made out of bronze. Each top was seven and a half feet high.

17Chains that were linked together hung down from the tops of the pillars. There were seven chains for each top. **18**Huram made two rows of pomegranates. They circled the chains. The pomegranates decorated the tops of the pillars. Huram did the same thing for each pillar. **19**The tops on the pillars of the porch were shaped like lilies. The lilies were 6 feet high. **20**On the tops of both pillars were 200 pomegranates. They were in rows all around the tops. They were above the part that was shaped like a bowl. And they were next to the chains.

21Huram set the pillars up at the temple porch. The pillar on the south he named Jakin. The one on the north he named Boaz. 22The tops of the pillars were shaped like lilies. So the work on the pillars was finished.

23Huram made a huge metal bowl for washing. Its shape was round. It measured 15 feet from rim to rim. It was seven and a half feet high. And it was 45 feet around. 24Below the rim there was a circle of gourds around the bowl. In every 18 inches around the bowl there were ten gourds. The gourds were arranged in two rows. They were made as part of the bowl itself.

25The huge bowl stood on 12 bulls. Three of them faced north. Three faced west. Three faced south. And three faced east. The bowl rested on top of them. Their rear ends were toward the center. 26The bowl was three inches thick. Its rim was like the rim of a cup. The rim was shaped like the bloom of a lily. The bowl held 11,500 gallons of water.

27Huram also made ten stands out of bronze. They could be moved around. Each stand was six feet long. It was six feet wide. And it was four and a half feet high. 28Here is how the stands were made. They had sides that were joined to posts. 29On the sides between the posts were lions, bulls and cherubim. They were also on all of the posts. Above and below the lions and bulls were wreaths that were made out of hammered metal.

30Each stand had four bronze wheels with bronze axles. Each one had a bowl that rested on four supports. They had wreaths on each side.

31There was a round opening on the inside of each stand. The opening had a frame that was 18 inches deep. The sides were 27 inches high from the top of the opening to the bottom of the base. There was carving around the opening. The sides of the stands were square, not round.

32The four wheels were under the sides. The axles of the wheels were connected to the stand. Each wheel was 27 inches across. 33The wheels were made like chariot wheels. All of the axles, rims, spokes and hubs were made out of metal.

34Each stand had four handles on it. There was one on each corner. They came out from the stand. 35At the top of the stand there was a round band. It was nine inches deep. The sides and supports were connected to the top of the stand.

36Huram carved cherubim, lions and palm trees on the sides of the stands. He also carved them on the surfaces of the supports. His carving covered every open space. He had also carved wreaths all around.

37That's how he made the ten stands. All of them were made in the same molds. And they had the same size and shape.

38Then Huram made ten bronze bowls. Each one held 230 gallons. The bowls measured six feet across. There was one bowl for each of the ten stands. 39He placed five of the stands on the south side of the temple. He placed the other five on the north side. He put the huge bowl on the south side. It was at the southeast corner of the temple. 40He also made the bowls, shovels and sprinkling bowls.

So Huram finished all of the work he had started for King Solomon. Here's what he made for the LORD's temple.

41 He made the two pillars.
He made the two tops for the pillars. The tops were shaped like bowls.
He made the two sets of chains that were linked together. They decorated the two bowl-shaped tops of the pillars.

42 He made the 400 pomegranates for the two sets of chains. There were two rows of pomegranates for each chain. They decorated the bowl-shaped tops of the pillars.

43 He made the ten stands with their ten bowls.

44 He made the huge bowl. He made the 12 bulls that were under it.

45 He made the pots, shovels and sprinkling bowls.

Huram made all of those objects for King Solomon for the LORD's temple. He made them out of bronze. Then he shined them up. 46The king had made them in clay molds. It was done on the flatlands of the Jordan River between Succoth and Zarethan.

47Solomon didn't weigh any of those things. There were too many of them to weigh. No one even tried to weigh the bronze they were made out of.

48Solomon also made all of the articles that were in the LORD's temple.

He made the golden altar.
He made the golden table for the holy bread.

49 He made the pure gold lampstands. There were five on the right and five on the left. They were in front of the Most Holy Room.

He made the gold flowers. He made the gold lamps and tongs.
⁵⁰He made the bowls, wick cutters, sprinkling bowls, dishes, and shallow cups for burning incense. All of them were made out of pure gold.

He made the gold bases for the doors of the inside room. That's the Most Holy Room. He also made gold bases for the doors of the main hall of the temple.

⁵¹King Solomon finished all of the work for the LORD's temple. Then he brought in the things his father David had set apart for the LORD. They included the silver and gold and all of the articles for the LORD's temple. Solomon placed them with the other treasures that were there.

Solomon Brings the Ark to the Temple

8 Then King Solomon sent for the elders of Israel. He told them to come to him in Jerusalem. They included all of the leaders of the tribes. They also included the chiefs of the families of Israel. Solomon wanted them to bring up the ark of the LORD's covenant from Zion. Zion was the City of David. ²All of the men of Israel came together to where King Solomon was. It was at the time of the Feast of Booths. The feast was held in the month of Ethanim. That's the seventh month.

³All of the elders of Israel arrived. Then the priests picked up the ark and carried it. ⁴They brought up the ark of the LORD. They also brought up the Tent of Meeting and all of the sacred articles that were in the tent. The priests and Levites carried everything up.

⁵The entire community of Israel had gathered around King Solomon. All of them were in front of the ark. They sacrificed huge numbers of sheep and cattle. There were so many that they couldn't be recorded. In fact, they couldn't even be counted.

⁶The priests brought the ark of the LORD's covenant to its place in the Most Holy Room of the temple. They put it under the wings of the cherubim. ⁷The cherubim's wings were spread out over the place where the ark was. They covered the ark. They also covered the poles that were used to carry it. ⁸The poles were so long that their ends could be seen from the Holy Room in front of the Most Holy Room. But they couldn't be seen from

outside the Holy Room. They are still there to this very day.

⁹There wasn't anything in the ark except the two stone tablets. Moses had placed them in it at Mount Horeb. That's where the LORD had made a covenant with the Israelites. He made it after they came out of Egypt.

¹⁰The priests left the Holy Room. Then the cloud filled the temple of the LORD. ¹¹The priests couldn't do their work because of it. That's because the glory of the LORD filled his temple.

¹²Then Solomon said, "LORD, you have said you would live in a dark cloud. ¹³As you can see, I've built a beautiful temple for you. You can live in it forever."

¹⁴The whole community of Israel was standing there. The king turned around and gave them his blessing. ¹⁵Then he said,

"I praise the LORD. He is the God of Israel. With his own mouth he made a promise to my father David. With his own powerful hand he made it come true. He said, ¹⁶'I brought my people Israel out of Egypt. Ever since I did that, I have not chosen a city in any tribe of Israel where a temple could be built for my Name. But I have chosen David to rule over my people Israel.'

¹⁷"With all his heart my father David wanted to build a temple. He wanted to do it so the LORD could put his Name there. The LORD is the God of Israel.

¹⁸"But the LORD spoke to my father David. He said, 'With all your heart you wanted to build a temple for my Name. It is good that you wanted to do that. ¹⁹But you will not build the temple. Instead, your son will build the temple for my Name. He is your own flesh and blood.'

²⁰"The LORD has kept the promise he made. I've become the next king after my father David. Now I'm sitting on the throne of Israel. That's exactly what the LORD promised would happen. I've built the temple where the LORD will put his Name. He is the God of Israel. ²¹I've provided a place for the ark there. The tablets of the LORD's covenant are inside it. He made that covenant with our people of long ago. He made it when he brought them out of Egypt."

Solomon Prays to Set the Temple Apart to the LORD

22Then Solomon stood in front of the LORD's altar. He stood in front of the whole community of Israel. He spread out his hands toward heaven. **23**He said,

"LORD, you are the God of Israel. There is no God like you in heaven above or on earth below. You keep the covenant you made with us. You show us your love. You do that when we follow you with all our hearts. **24**You have kept your promise to my father David. He was your servant. With your mouth you made a promise. With your powerful hand you have made it come true. And today we can see it.

25"LORD, you are the God of Israel. Keep the promises you made to my father David. Do it for him. He was your servant. You said to him, 'You will always have a man to sit on the throne of Israel in my sight. That will be true only if your sons are careful in everything they do. They must live in my sight the way you have lived.' **26**God of Israel, let your promise to my father David come true.

27"But will you really live on earth? After all, the heavens can't hold you. In fact, even the highest heavens can't hold you. So this temple I've built certainly can't hold you!

28"But please pay attention to my prayer. LORD my God, show me your favor as I make my appeal to you. Listen to my cry for help. Hear the prayer I'm praying to you today. **29**Let your eyes look toward this temple night and day. You said, 'I will put my Name there.' So please listen to the prayer I'm praying toward this place.

30"Hear me when I ask you to show us your favor. Listen to your people Israel when they pray toward this place. Listen to us from heaven. It's the place where you live. When you hear us, forgive us.

31"Suppose a man does something wrong to his neighbor. And he is required to take an oath and make a promise. He must come and do it in front of your altar in this temple. **32**When he does, listen to him from heaven. Take action. Judge between those people. Punish the one who is guilty. Do to him what he has done to his neighbor. Tell everyone that the one who hasn't done anything wrong is free from blame. That will prove he isn't guilty.

33"Suppose your people Israel have lost the battle against their enemies. And suppose they've sinned against you. But they turn back to you and praise your name. They pray to you in this temple. And they ask you to show them your favor. **34**Then listen to them from heaven. Forgive the sin of your people Israel. Bring them back to the land you gave to their people who lived long ago.

35"Suppose your people have sinned against you. And because of that, the sky is closed up and there isn't any rain. But your people pray toward this place. They praise you by admitting they've sinned. And they turn away from their sin because you have made them suffer. **36**Then listen to them from heaven. Forgive the sin of your people Israel. Teach them the right way to live. Send rain on the land you gave them as their share.

37"Suppose there isn't enough food in the land. And a plague strikes the land. The hot winds completely dry up our crops. Or locusts or grasshoppers come and eat them up. Or an enemy surrounds one of our cities and gets ready to attack it. Or trouble or sickness comes. **38**But suppose one of your people prays to you. He asks you to show him your favor. He is aware of how much his own heart is suffering. And he spreads out

POWER-SURGE

FORGIVING F

HEAR ME WHEN I ASK YOU TO SHOW US YOUR FAVOR. LISTEN TO YOUR PEOPLE ISRAEL WHEN THEY PRAY TOWARD THIS PLACE. LISTEN TO US FROM HEAVEN. IT'S THE PLACE WHERE YOU LIVE. WHEN YOU HEAR US, FORGIVE US.

— 1 KINGS 8:30 —

his hands toward this temple to pray. **39**Then listen to him from heaven. It's the place where you live. Forgive him. Take action. Deal with him in keeping with everything he does. You know his heart. In fact, you are the only one who knows every human heart. **40**Your people will have respect for you. They will respect you as long as they are in the land you gave our people long ago.

41"Suppose there are strangers who don't belong to your people Israel. And they have come from a land far away. They've come because they've heard about your name. **42**When they get here, they will find out even more about your great name. They'll hear about how you reached out your mighty hand and powerful arm. So they'll come and pray toward this temple.

43"Then listen to them from heaven. It's the place where you live. Do what those strangers ask you to do. Then all of the nations on earth will know you. They will have respect for you. They'll respect you just as your own people Israel do. They'll know that your Name is in this house I've built.

44"Suppose your people go to war against their enemies. It doesn't matter where you send them. And suppose they pray to you toward the city you have chosen. They pray toward the temple I've built for your Name. **45**Then listen to them from heaven. Listen to their prayer. Listen to them when they ask you to show them your favor. Stand up for them.

46"Suppose your people sin against you. After all, there isn't anyone who doesn't sin. And suppose you get angry with them. You hand them over to their enemies. They take them as prisoners to their own land. It doesn't matter whether it's near or far away.

47"But suppose your people change their ways in the land where they are held as prisoners. They turn away from their sins. They beg you to help them in the land of those who won the battle over them. They say, 'We have sinned. We've done what is wrong. We've done what is evil.' **48**And they turn back to you with all their heart and soul. Suppose it happens in the land of their enemies who took them away as prisoners.

There they pray to you toward the land you gave their people long ago. They pray toward the city you have chosen. And they pray toward the temple I've built for your Name.

49"Then listen to them from heaven. It's the place where you live. Listen to their prayer. Listen to them when they ask you to show them your favor. Stand up for them.

50"Your people have sinned against you. Please forgive them. Forgive them for all of the wrong things they've done against you. And make those who won the battle over them show mercy to them. **51**After all, they are your people. They belong to you. You brought them out of Egypt. You brought them out of that furnace that melts iron down and makes it pure.

52"Let your eyes be open to me when I ask you to show us your favor. Let them be open to your people Israel when they ask you to show them your favor. Pay attention to them every time they cry out to you. **53**"After all, you chose them out of all of the nations in the world. You made them your very own people. You did it just as you had announced through your servant Moses. That's when you brought our people out of Egypt. You are our Lord and King."

54Solomon finished all of those prayers. He finished asking the Lord to show his favor to his people. Then he got up from in front of the Lord's altar. He had been down on his knees with his hands spread out toward heaven. **55**He stood in front of the whole community of Israel. He blessed them with a loud voice. He said,

56"I praise the Lord. He has given peace and rest to his people Israel. That's exactly what he promised to do. He gave his people good promises through his servant Moses. Every single word of those promises has come true.

57"May the Lord our God be with us, just as he was with our people who lived long ago. May he never leave us. May he never desert us. **58**May he turn our hearts to him. Then we will live the way he wants us to. We'll obey the commands, rules and directions he gave our people.

59"I've prayed these words to the Lord our God. May he keep them close to him day and night. May he

POWER-/SURGE

OBEYS ✔

MAY HE TURN OUR
HEARTS TO HIM. THEN
WE WILL LIVE THE WAY
HE WANTS US TO.
WE'LL OBEY THE
COMMANDS, RULES
AND DIRECTIONS.
—— 1 KINGS 8:58 ——

stand up for me. May he also stand up for his people Israel. May he give us what we need every day. **60**Then all of the nations on earth will know that the Lord is God. They'll know that there isn't any other god.

61 "But you must commit your lives completely to the Lord our God. You must live by his rules. You must obey his commands. You must always do as you are doing now."

Solomon Sets the Temple Apart to the Lord

62Then the king and the whole community of Israel offered sacrifices to the Lord. **63**Solomon sacrificed friendship offerings to the Lord. He sacrificed 22,000 head of cattle. He also sacrificed 120,000 sheep and goats. So the king and the whole community set the temple of the Lord apart to him.

64On that same day the king set the middle area of the courtyard apart to the Lord. It was in front of the Lord's temple. There Solomon sacrificed burnt offerings and grain offerings. He also sacrificed the fat of the friendship offerings there. He did it there because the bronze altar in front of the Lord was too small. It wasn't big enough to hold all of the burnt offerings, the grain offerings and the fat of the friendship offerings.

65At that time Solomon celebrated the Feast of Booths. The whole community of Israel was with him. It was a huge crowd. People came from as far away as Lebo Hamath and the Wadi of Egypt. For seven days they celebrated in front of the Lord our God. The feast continued for seven more days. That made a total of 14 days.

66On the following day Solomon sent the people away. They asked the Lord to bless the king. Then they went home. The people were glad. Their hearts were full of joy. That's because the Lord had done so many good things for his servant David and his people Israel.

The Lord Appears to Solomon

9 Solomon finished building the Lord's temple and the royal palace. He had accomplished everything he had planned to do. **2**The Lord appeared to him a second time. He had already appeared to him at Gibeon. **3**The Lord said to him,

"I have heard you pray to me. I have heard you ask me to show you my favor. You have built this temple. I have set it apart for myself. My Name will be there forever. My eyes and my heart will always be there.

4"But you must walk with me, just as your father David did. Your heart must be honest. It must be without blame. Do everything I command you to do. Obey my rules and laws. **5**Then I will set up your royal throne over Israel forever. I promised your father David I would do that. I said to him, 'You will always have a man on the throne of Israel.'

6"But suppose all of you turn away from me. Or your sons turn away from me. You refuse to obey the commands and rules I have given you. And you go off to serve other gods and worship them. **7**Then I will cut Israel off from the land. It is the land I gave them. I will turn my back on this temple. I will do it even though I have set it apart for my Name to be there. Then Israel will be hated by all of the nations. They will laugh and joke about Israel.

8"This temple is now grand and beautiful. But the time is coming when all those who pass by it will be shocked. They will make fun of it. And they will say, 'Why has the Lord done a thing like this to this land and temple?'

9"People will answer, 'Because they have deserted the Lord their God. He brought their people out of Egypt. But they have been holding on to other gods. They've been worshiping them. They've been serving them. That's why the Lord has brought all of this horrible trouble on them.' "

Other Things Solomon Did

10Solomon built the LORD's temple and the royal palace. It took him 20 years to construct those two buildings.

11King Solomon gave 20 towns in Galilee to Hiram. That's because Hiram had provided him with all of the cedar and pine logs he wanted. He had also provided him with all of the gold he wanted. Hiram was king of Tyre.

12Hiram went from Tyre to see the towns Solomon had given him. But he wasn't pleased with them. **13**"My friend," he asked, "what have you given me? What kind of towns are these?" So he called them the Land of Cabul. And that's what they are still called to this very day. **14**Hiram had sent four and a half tons of gold to Solomon.

15King Solomon forced people to work hard for him. Here is a record of what they did. They built the LORD's temple and Solomon's palace. They filled in the low places. They rebuilt the wall of Jerusalem. They built up Hazor, Megiddo and Gezer.

16Pharaoh, the king of Egypt, had attacked Gezer and captured it. He had set it on fire. He had killed the Canaanites who lived there. Then he had given Gezer as a wedding gift to his daughter. She was Solomon's wife.

17Solomon rebuilt Gezer. He built up Lower Beth Horon **18**and Baalath. He built up Tadmor in the desert. All of those towns were in his land. **19**He built up all of the cities where he could store things. He also built up the towns for his chariots and horses. He built anything he wanted to build in Jerusalem, Lebanon and all of the territory he ruled over.

20There were still many people left in the land who weren't Israelites. They included Amorites, Hittites, Perizzites, Hivites and Jebusites. **21**They were children of the people who had lived in the land before the Israelites came. Those people had been set apart to the LORD in a special way to be destroyed. But the Israelites hadn't been able to kill all of them. Solomon had forced them to work very hard as his slaves. And they still work for Israel to this very day.

22But Solomon didn't force any of the men of Israel to work as his slaves. Instead, some were his fighting men. Others were his government officials, his officers and his captains. Others were commanders of his chariots and chariot drivers. **23**Still others were the chief officials who were in charge of his projects. There were 550 officials in charge of those who did the work.

24Pharaoh's daughter moved from the City of David up to the palace Solomon had built for her. After that, he filled in the low places near the palace.

25Three times a year Solomon sacrificed burnt offerings and friendship offerings. He sacrificed them on the altar he had built to honor the LORD. Along with the offerings, he burned incense to the LORD. So he carried out his duties for the temple.

26King Solomon also built ships at Ezion Geber. It's near Elath in Edom. It's on the shore of the Red Sea.

27Hiram sent his men to serve on the ships together with Solomon's men. Hiram's sailors knew the sea. **28**All of them sailed to Ophir. They brought back 16 tons of gold. They gave it to King Solomon.

The Queen of Sheba Visits Solomon

10 The queen of Sheba heard about how famous Solomon was. She also heard about how he served and worshiped the LORD. So she came to test him with hard questions.

2She arrived in Jerusalem with a very large group of attendants. Her camels were carrying spices, huge amounts of gold, and valuable jewels. She came to Solomon and asked him about everything she wanted to know.

3Solomon answered all of her questions. There wasn't anything that was too hard for the king to explain to her.

4So the queen of Sheba saw how very wise Solomon was. She saw the palace he had built. **5**She saw the food that was on his table. She saw his officials sitting there. She saw the robes of the servants who waited on everyone. She saw his wine tasters. And she saw the burnt offerings Solomon sacrificed at the LORD's temple. She could hardly believe everything she had seen.

6She said to the king, "Back in my own country I heard a report about you. I heard about how much you had accomplished. I also heard about how wise you are. Everything I heard is true. **7**But I didn't believe those things. So I came to see for myself. And now I believe it! You are twice as wise and wealthy as people say you are. The report I heard doesn't even begin to tell the whole story about you.

8"How happy your men must be! How happy your officials must be! They always get to serve you and hear the wise things you say.

9"May the LORD your God be praised. He must take great delight in you. He placed you on the throne of Israel. The LORD will love Israel for all time to come. That's why he has made you king. He knows that you will do what is fair and right."

10She gave the king four and a half tons of gold. She also gave him huge amounts of spices and valuable jewels. No one would ever bring to King Solomon as many spices as the queen of Sheba gave him.

11Hiram's ships brought gold from Ophir. From there they also brought huge amounts of almugwood and valuable jew-

QUEEN OF SHEBA

1 KINGS 10:1

W

G

> The queen of Sheba heard about how famous Solomon was. She also heard about how he served and worshiped the LORD. So she came to test him with hard questions.

The Queen of Sheba looked around as she rode her camel into Jerusalem. Its beautiful buildings glittered white in the morning sun. The queen had heard all about the wise and rich king named Solomon who ruled Israel. She wanted to meet him. She had many gifts for him and many questions she wanted to ask.

The queen of Sheba was amazed at the beauty of the palace where Solomon and his wives lived. She ate at tables filled with wonderful food. The rich robes that even Solomon's servants wore surprised her. She herself was a queen. But **SHE HAD NEVER SEEN ANYONE SO RICH BEFORE, OR WISE.**

King Solomon answered all of her questions. Nothing was too hard for him. The Queen of Sheba knew that God blessed Solomon and gave him wisdom and riches.

BE LIKE THE QUEEN OF SHEBA

King Solomon could answer all of the Queen of Sheba's questions. She knew his wisdom came from God. You have somewhere to go too when you have questions. Perhaps your parents or a teacher can help you. But the wisest one of all is, of course, God. He loves you and will help you.

THE QUEEN OF SHEBA BELIEVED GOD GAVE SOLOMON HIS RICHES AND WISDOM.

Go to page 408 for the next person

GIVING G

SHE GAVE THE KING
FOUR AND A HALF
TONS OF GOLD. SHE
ALSO GAVE HIM HUGE
AMOUNTS OF SPICES
AND VALUABLE
JEWELS. NO ONE
WOULD EVER BRING
TO KING SOLOMON AS
MANY SPICES AS THE
QUEEN OF SHEBA
GAVE HIM.
— 1 KINGS 10:10 —

els. **12**The king used the almugwood to make supports for the LORD's temple and the royal palace. He also used it to make harps and lyres for those who played the music. That much almugwood has never been brought into Judah or seen there since that day.

13King Solomon gave the queen of Sheba everything she wanted and asked for. That was in addition to what he had given her out of his royal riches. Then she left. She returned to her own country with her attendants.

Solomon in All of His Glory

14Each year Solomon received 25 tons of gold. **15**That didn't include the money that was brought in by business and trade. It also didn't include the money from all of the kings of Arabia and the governors of Israel.

16King Solomon made 200 large shields out of hammered gold. Each one weighed seven and a half pounds. **17**He also made 300 small shields out of hammered gold. Each one weighed almost four pounds. The king put all of the shields in the Palace of the Forest of Lebanon.

18Then he made a large throne. It was decorated with ivory. It was covered with fine gold. **19**The throne had six steps. Its back had a rounded top. The throne had armrests on both sides of the seat. A statue of a lion stood on each side of the throne. **20**Twelve lions stood on the six steps. There was one at each end of each step.

Nothing like that throne had ever been made for any other kingdom.

21All of King Solomon's cups were made out of gold. All of the articles that were used in the Palace of the Forest of Lebanon were made out of pure gold. Nothing was made out of silver. When Solomon was king, silver wasn't considered to be worth very much.

22He had many ships that carried goods to be traded. His ships went to sea along with Hiram's ships. Once every three years the ships returned. They brought gold, silver, ivory, apes and baboons.

23King Solomon was richer than all of the other kings on earth. He was also wiser than they were. **24**People from the whole world wanted to meet Solomon in person. They wanted to see for themselves how wise God had made him. **25**Year after year, everyone who came to him brought a gift. They brought articles that were made out of silver and gold. They brought robes, weapons and spices. They also brought horses and mules.

26Solomon had 1,400 chariots and 12,000 horses. He kept some of his horses and chariots in the chariot cities. He kept the others with him in Jerusalem.

27The king made silver as common in Jerusalem as stones. He made cedar wood as common there as sycamore-fig trees in the western hills.

28Solomon got horses from Egypt and from Kue. The royal traders bought them from Kue. **29**They weighed out 15 pounds of silver for a chariot from Egypt. And they weighed out almost four pounds of silver for a horse. They also sold horses and chariots to all of the kings of the Hittites and the kings of the Arameans.

WISE W

PEOPLE FROM THE
WHOLE WORLD
WANTED TO MEET
SOLOMON IN PERSON.
THEY WANTED TO SEE
FOR THEMSELVES
HOW WISE GOD HAD
MADE HIM.
— 1 KINGS 10:24 —

Solomon's Wives Turn Him Away From the LORD

11 King Solomon loved many women besides Pharaoh's daughter. They were from other lands. They were Moabites, Ammonites, Edomites, Sidonians and Hittites.

2The LORD had warned Israel about women from other nations. He had said, "You must not get married to them. If you do, you can be sure they will turn your hearts toward their gods." But Solomon continued to love them anyway. He wouldn't give them up. **3**He had 700 wives who came from royal families. And he had 300 concubines. His wives led him down the wrong path.

4As Solomon grew older, his wives turned his heart toward other gods. He didn't follow the LORD his God with all his heart. So he wasn't like his father David. **5**Solomon worshiped Ashtoreth. Ashtoreth was the goddess of the people of Sidon. He also worshiped Molech. Molech was the god of the people of Ammon. The LORD hated that god.

6Solomon did what was evil in the sight of the LORD. He didn't follow the LORD completely. He didn't do what his father David had done.

7There is a hill east of Jerusalem. Solomon built a high place for worshiping Chemosh there. He built a high place for worshiping Molech there too. Chemosh was the god of Moab. Molech was the god of Ammon. The LORD hated both of those gods.

8Solomon also built high places so that all of his wives from other nations could worship their gods. Those women burned incense and offered sacrifices to their gods.

9The LORD became angry with Solomon. That's because his heart had turned away from the LORD. He is the God of Israel. He had appeared to Solomon twice. **10**He had commanded Solomon not to follow other gods. But Solomon didn't obey him.

11So the LORD said to Solomon, "You have chosen not to keep my covenant. You have decided not to obey my rules. I commanded you to do what I told you. But you did not do it. So you can be absolutely sure I will tear the kingdom away from you. I will give it to one of your officials. **12**But I will not do that while you are still living. Because of your father David I will wait. I will tear the kingdom out of your son's hand. **13**But I will not tear the whole kingdom away from him. I will give him one of the tribes because of my servant David. I will also do it because of Jerusalem. That is the city I have chosen."

The LORD Brings Enemies Against Solomon

14Then the LORD brought an enemy against Solomon. The enemy's name was Hadad. He was from Edom. In fact, he belonged to the royal family of Edom. **15**David had fought against Edom. Joab had been the commander of the army. He had gone up to bury the dead bodies of the Israelites who had been killed in battle. At that time he had struck down all of the men in Edom. **16**In fact, Joab and all of the men of Israel stayed there for six months. During that time they destroyed all of the men in Edom. **17**But when Hadad was only a boy, he ran away to Egypt. Some officials from Edom went with him. They had served Hadad's father. **18**They started out from Midian and went to Paran. They took some men from Paran with them. Then they went to Egypt. They went to Pharaoh, the king of Egypt. He gave Hadad a house and some land. He also supplied him with food.

19Pharaoh was very pleased with Hadad. Pharaoh's wife was Queen Tahpenes. He gave Hadad her sister to be his wife. **20**The sister of Tahpenes had a son by Hadad. The baby was named Genubath. Tahpenes brought him up in the royal palace. Genubath lived there with Pharaoh's own children.

21Hadad heard that David had joined the members of his family who had already died. He also heard that Joab, the commander of the army, was dead. Hadad heard those things while he was in Egypt. He said to Pharaoh, "Let me go. I want to return to my own country."

22"Why do you want to go back to your own country?" Pharaoh asked. "Don't you have everything you need right here?"

"Yes," Hadad replied. "But I want you to let me go anyway!"

23God brought another enemy against Solomon. The enemy's name was Rezon. He was the son of Eliada. Rezon had run away from his master Hadadezer, the king of Zobah. **24**He gathered some men together to follow him. He became the leader of a group of men who had refused to follow David. It happened when David destroyed the troops of Zobah. Then the group that was against David went to

Damascus. They settled down there and took control of it. **25**Rezon was Israel's enemy as long as Solomon was living. Rezon added to the trouble Hadad had caused. So Rezon ruled in Aram. He was Israel's enemy.

Jeroboam Refuses to Follow Solomon

26Jeroboam refused to follow King Solomon. He was one of Solomon's officials. He was from Zeredah in the territory of Ephraim. His father was Nebat. His mother was a widow named Zeruah.

27Here is the story of how Jeroboam refused to follow the king. Solomon had filled in the low places near the palace. He had also repaired the wall of the city of his father David. **28**Jeroboam was a very important young man. Solomon saw how well he did his work. So he put him in charge of all of the workers in northern Israel.

29About that time Jeroboam was going out of Jerusalem. The prophet Ahijah met him on the road. Ahijah was from Shiloh. He was wearing a new coat. The two of them were all alone out in the country. **30**Ahijah grabbed hold of the new coat he had on. He tore it up into 12 pieces. **31**Then he said to Jeroboam, "Take ten pieces for yourself. The LORD is the God of Israel. He says, 'I am going to tear the kingdom out of Solomon's hand. I will give you ten of its tribes. **32**Solomon will have one of its tribes. I will let him keep it because of my servant David and because of Jerusalem. I have chosen that city out of all of the cities in the tribes of Israel.

33" 'I will do those things because the tribes have deserted me. They have worshiped Ashtoreth, the goddess of the people of Sidon. They have worshiped Chemosh, the god of the people of Moab. And they have worshiped Molech, the god of the people of Ammon. They have not lived the way I wanted them to. They have not done what is right in my eyes. They have not obeyed my rules and laws as Solomon's father David did.

34" 'But I will not take the whole kingdom out of Solomon's hand. I have made him ruler all the days of his life. I have done it because of my servant David. I chose him. He obeyed my commands and rules.

35" 'I will take the kingdom out of his son's hands. And I will give you ten of the tribes.

36" 'I will give one of the tribes to David's son. Then my servant David will always have a son on his throne in Jerusalem. The lamp of David's kingdom will always burn brightly in my sight. Jerusalem is the city I chose for my Name.

37" 'But I will make you king over Israel. You will rule over everything your heart longs for. So you will be the king of Israel. **38**Do everything I command you to do. Live the way I want you to. Do what is right in my eyes. Obey my rules and commands. That is what my servant David did. If you do those things, I will be with you. I will build you a kingdom. It will last as long as the one I built for David. I will give Israel to you.

39" 'I will punish David's family because of what Solomon has done. But I will not punish them forever.' "

40Solomon tried to kill Jeroboam. But Jeroboam ran away to Egypt. He went to Shishak, the king of Egypt. He stayed there until Solomon died.

Solomon Dies

41The other events of Solomon's rule are written down. Everything he did and the wisdom he showed are written down. They are written in the official records of Solomon.

42Solomon ruled in Jerusalem over the whole nation of Israel for 40 years. **43**Then he joined the members of his family who had already died. His body was buried in the city of his father David. Solomon's son Rehoboam became the next king after him.

Israel Refuses to Follow Rehoboam

12 Rehoboam went to Shechem. All of the people of Israel had gone there to make him king. **2**Jeroboam heard about it. He was the son of Nebat. Jeroboam was still in Egypt at that time. He had gone there for safety. He wanted to get away from King Solomon. But now he returned from Egypt.

3So the people sent for Jeroboam. He and the whole community of Israel went to Rehoboam. They said to him, **4**"Your father put a heavy load on our shoulders. But now make our hard work easier. Make the heavy load on us lighter. Then we'll serve you."

5Rehoboam answered, "Go away for three days. Then come back to me." So the people went away.

6King Rehoboam asked the elders for advice. They had served his father Solomon while he was still living. Rehoboam asked them, "What advice can you give me? How should I answer these people?"

7They replied, "Serve them today. Give them what they are asking for. Then they'll always serve you."

8But Rehoboam didn't accept the advice the elders gave him. Instead, he asked for advice from the young men who had grown up with him and were now serving him. **9**He asked them, "What's your advice? How should I answer these people? They say to me, 'Make the load your father put on our shoulders lighter.' "

10The young men who had grown up with him gave their answer. They replied, "These people say to you, 'Your father put a heavy load on our shoulders. Make it lighter.' Tell them, 'My little finger is stronger than my father's legs. **11**My father put a heavy load on your shoulders.

REHOBOAM (Not!)

1 KINGS 12:13-14

[Rehoboam] answered the people in a mean way. He didn't accept the advice the elders had given him. Instead, he followed the advice of the young men. He said, "My father put a heavy load on your shoulders. But I'll make it even heavier. My father beat you with whips. But I'll beat you with bigger whips."

Rehoboam (ray-huh-BOW-um) stood up and shook out his royal robe. It hung heavy on his shoulders and made him hot and crabby. His father Solomon had been king for forty years and had built up the kingdom of Israel, making it one of the most important and richest in the world. Now it was Rehoboam's turn. HE WAS SCARED. AND FRUSTRATED.

He asked his friends how he should reign, and they gave one answer. Then he asked his father's officials how he should reign. And they gave a totally different answer. He didn't know which way to go. The way his young friends said to go would make him rich. The way his father's officials said to go would help the people he reigned over. Foolish Rehoboam. He chose to follow his friends' advice, and his kingdom divided and never got back together.

REHOBOAM

Rehoboam knew the right way to go. But he chose the selfish way that would be good for him alone instead of for his people. He asked for advice but took only what pleased him. Don't be like that. Do what you know in your heart is the right thing to do.

REHOBOAM SELFISHLY DID WHAT WAS GOOD FOR HIM INSTEAD OF WHAT WAS GOOD FOR HIS PEOPLE.

Go to page 416 for the next Super Hero

But I'll make it even heavier. My father beat you with whips. But I'll beat you with bigger whips.' "

12Three days later Jeroboam and all of the people returned to Rehoboam. That's because the king had said, "Come back to me in three days."

13The king answered the people in a mean way. He didn't accept the advice the elders had given him. **14**Instead, he followed the advice of the young men. He said, "My father put a heavy load on your shoulders. But I'll make it even heavier. My father beat you with whips. But I'll beat you with bigger whips."

15So the king didn't listen to the people. That's because the LORD had planned it that way. What he had said through Ahijah came true. Ahijah had spoken the LORD's message to Jeroboam, the son of Nebat. Ahijah was from Shiloh.

16All of the people of Israel saw that the king refused to listen to them. So they answered the king. They said,

"We don't have any share in David's
    royal family.
We don't have any share in Jesse's
    son.
People of Israel, let's go back to our
    homes.
David's royal family, take care of
    your own kingdom!"

So the people of Israel went home.

17But Rehoboam still ruled over the Israelites who were living in the towns of Judah.

18Adoniram was in charge of those who were forced to work hard for King Rehoboam. The king sent him out among all of the Israelites. But they killed him by throwing stones at him. King Rehoboam was able to get away in his chariot. He escaped to Jerusalem. **19**Israel has refused to follow the royal family of David to this very day.

20All of the people of Israel heard that Jeroboam had returned. They sent for him. They wanted him to meet with the whole community. Then they made him king over the entire nation of Israel. Only the tribe of Judah remained true to David's royal family.

21Rehoboam arrived in Jerusalem. He brought together 180,000 fighting men from the royal house of Judah and the tribe of Benjamin. He had decided to make war against the royal house of Israel. Solomon's son Rehoboam wanted his fighting men to get the kingdom of Israel back for him.

22But a message from God came to Shemaiah. He was a man of God. God said to him, **23**"Speak to Solomon's son Rehoboam, the king of Judah. Speak to the royal house of Judah and Benjamin. Also speak to the rest of the people. Tell all of them, **24**'The LORD says, "Do not go up to fight against the Israelites. They are your relatives. I want every one of you to go back home. Things have happened exactly the way I planned them." ' " So the fighting men obeyed the LORD's message. They went home again, just as he had ordered.

Jeroboam Sets Up Golden Calves at Bethel and Dan

25Jeroboam built up the walls of Shechem. It was in the hill country of Ephraim. Jeroboam made Shechem his home. From there he went out and built up Peniel.

26Jeroboam thought, "My kingdom still isn't secure. It could very easily go back to the royal family of David. **27**Suppose the people of Israel go up to Jerusalem to offer sacrifices at the LORD's temple. If they do, they will again decide to follow Rehoboam as their master. Then they'll kill me. They'll return to King Rehoboam. He is king of Judah."

28So King Jeroboam asked for advice. Then he made two golden statues that looked like calves. He said to the people, "It's too hard for you to go up to Jerusalem. Israel, here are your gods who brought you up out of Egypt." **29**He set up one statue in Bethel. He set up the other one in Dan.

30What Jeroboam did was sinful. And it caused Israel to sin. The people even went all the way to Dan to worship the statue that was there.

31Jeroboam built temples for worshiping gods on high places. He appointed all kinds of people as priests. They didn't even have to be Levites. **32**He established a feast. It was on the 15th day of the eighth month. He wanted to make it like the Feast of Booths that was held in Judah.

Jeroboam built an altar at Bethel. He offered sacrifices on it. He sacrificed to the calves he had made. He also put priests in Bethel. He did it at the high places he had made. **33**He offered sacrifices on the altar he had built at Bethel. It was on the 15th day of the eighth month. That's the month he had chosen for it. So he established the feast for the people of Israel. And he went up to the altar to sacrifice offerings.

A Man of God Goes to Bethel

13 A man of God went from Judah to Bethel. He had received a message from the LORD. He arrived in Bethel just as Jeroboam was standing by the altar to offer a sacrifice. **2**The man cried out. He shouted a message from the LORD against the altar. He said, "Altar! Altar! The LORD says, 'A son named Josiah will be born into the royal family of David. Altar, listen to me! Josiah will sacrifice the priests of the high places on you. They will be the children of the priests who are offering sacrifices here now. So human bones will be burned on you.' "

3That same day the man of God spoke about a miraculous sign. He said, "Here is the sign the LORD has announced. This altar will be broken to pieces. The ashes on it will be spilled out."

4The man of God announced that message against the altar at Bethel. When King Jeroboam heard it, he reached out his hand from the altar. He said, "Grab him!" But as he reached out his hand toward the man, it dried up. He couldn't even pull it back.

5Also, the altar broke into pieces. Its ashes spilled out. That happened in keeping with the miraculous sign the man of God had announced. He had received a message from the LORD.

6King Jeroboam spoke to the man of God. He said, "Pray to the LORD your God for me. Pray that my hand will be as good as new again."

So the man of God prayed to the LORD for the king. And the king's hand became as good as new. It was just as healthy as it had been before.

7The king said to the man of God, "Come home with me. Have something to eat. I'll give you a gift."

8But the man of God replied to the king. He said, "What if you were to give me half of what you own? Even then I wouldn't go with you. I wouldn't eat bread or drink water here. **9**The LORD gave me a command. He said, 'Do not eat bread or drink water there. Do not return the same way you came.' " **10**So he took another road. He didn't go back on the same road he had taken when he came to Bethel.

11An old prophet was living in Bethel. His sons came and spoke to him. They told him everything the man of God had done there that day. They also told their father what the man had said to the king. **12**Their father asked them, "Which way did he go?"

His sons showed him the road the man of God from Judah had taken. **13**So he said to his sons, "Put a saddle on the donkey for me."

When they had done it, he got on the donkey. **14**He traveled on the same road the man of God had taken. He found the man sitting under an oak tree. He asked him, "Are you the man of God who came from Judah?"

"I am," he replied.

15So the prophet said to him, "Come home with me. I'll give you something to eat."

16The man of God said, "I can't go back to Bethel with you. I can't eat bread or drink water with you there. **17**I've received a message from the LORD. He told me, 'Do not eat bread or drink water there. Do not return the same way you came.' "

18The old prophet answered, "I'm also a prophet, just like you. An angel gave me a message from the LORD. The message said, 'Bring the man of God back with you to your house. Then he can eat bread and drink water with you.' " But the old prophet was telling him a lie. **19**The man of God returned with him. He ate and drank in his house.

20They were sitting at the table. The LORD gave a message to the old prophet who had brought the man of God back. **21**He cried out to the man who had come from Judah. He told him, "The LORD says, 'You have not done what I told you to do. You have not obeyed the command I gave you. I am the LORD your God. **22**You came back here and ate bread and drank water. You did it in the place where I told you not to. So your body will not be buried in your family tomb.' "

23The man of God finished eating and drinking. Then the old prophet who had brought him back put a saddle on the man's donkey for him. **24**And the man went on his way. A lion attacked him on the road and killed him. His body was left lying on the road. The donkey and the lion were standing beside it.

25Some people passed by. They saw the body lying on the road. They saw the lion standing beside the body. Then they went and reported it in the city where the old prophet lived. **26**The prophet who had brought the man back from his journey heard about what had happened. He said, "It's the man of God. He didn't do what the LORD told him to do. So the LORD has given him over to the lion. The lion has attacked him and killed him. Everything has happened just as the LORD's message had warned him it would."

27The old prophet said to his sons, "Put a saddle on the donkey for me." So they did. 28Then he went out. He found the body of the man of God lying on the road. The donkey and the lion were standing beside it. The lion hadn't eaten the body. It hadn't attacked the donkey either.

29So the prophet picked up the man's body. He put it on the donkey. He brought it back to his own city. He wanted to sob over him and bury him. 30Then he placed the body in his own tomb. People sobbed over him. They said, "My friend! My dear friend!"

31After the old prophet had buried the body of the man of God, he spoke to his sons. He said, "When I die, bury my body in the grave where the man of God is buried. Put my bones next to his bones. 32I want you to do that because he announced a message from the LORD. He spoke against the altar in Bethel. He also spoke against all of the temples that were on the high places. They are in the towns of Samaria. What the man of God said will certainly come true."

33Even after all of that happened, Jeroboam still didn't change his evil ways. Once more he appointed priests for the high places. He made priests out of all kinds of people. In fact, he let anyone become a priest who wanted to. He set them apart to serve at the high places. 34All of that was the great sin the royal family of Jeroboam committed. It led to their fall from power. Because of it, they were destroyed from the face of the earth.

Ahijah Prophesies Against Jeroboam

14 At that time Abijah became sick. He was the son of Jeroboam. 2Jeroboam said to his wife, "Go. Put on some different clothes. Then no one will recognize you as my wife. Go to Shiloh. That's where the prophet Ahijah is. He told me I would be king over the people of Israel. 3Take ten loaves of bread with you. Take some cakes and a jar of honey. Go to him. He'll tell you what will happen to our son."

4So Jeroboam's wife did what he said. She went to Ahijah's house in Shiloh. Ahijah couldn't see. He was blind because he was so old. 5But the LORD had told Ahijah, "Jeroboam's wife is coming. Her son is sick. She'll ask you about him. Give her the answer I give you. When she arrives, she'll pretend to be someone else."

6Ahijah heard the sound of her footsteps at the door. He said, "Come in. I know that you are Jeroboam's wife. Why are you pretending to be someone else? I have some bad news for you.

7"Go. Tell Jeroboam that the LORD has a message for him. The LORD is the God of Israel. He says, 'I chose you from among the people. I made you the leader of my people Israel. 8I tore the kingdom away from the royal house of David. I gave it to you. But you have not been like my servant David. He obeyed my commands. He followed me with all his heart. He did only what was right in my eyes. 9You have done more evil things than all those who lived before you. You have made other gods for yourself. You have made statues of gods out of metal. You have made me very angry. You have turned your back on me.

10"'Because of that, I am going to bring horrible trouble on your royal house. I will cut off from you every male in Israel. It does not matter whether they are slaves or free. I will burn up your royal house, just as someone burns up trash. I will burn it until it is all gone. 11Some of the people who belong to you will die in the city. Dogs will eat them up. Others will die in the country. The birds of the air will eat them. I have spoken!'

12"Now go back home. When you enter your city, your son will die. 13All of the people of Israel will sob over him. Then his body will be buried. He is the only one who belongs to Jeroboam who will be buried. That is because he is the only one in Jeroboam's royal house in whom I have found anything good. I am the LORD, the God of Israel.

14"I will choose for myself a king over Israel. He will cut off the family of Jeroboam. This very day your son will die. Can that really be true? Yes. Even now, that is what I am telling you.

15"I will strike Israel down. Israel will be like tall grass swaying in the water. I will pull Israel up from this good land by the roots. I gave it to their people who lived long ago. I will scatter Israel to the east side of the Euphrates River. That is because they made me very angry. They made poles that were used to worship the goddess Asherah.

16"I will give Israel up because of the sins Jeroboam has committed. He has also caused Israel to commit those same sins."

17Then Jeroboam's wife got up and left.

She went to the city of Tirzah. As soon as she stepped through the doorway of the house, her son died. 18His body was buried. All of the people of Israel sobbed over him. That's what the LORD had said would happen. He had said it through his servant, the prophet Ahijah.

19The other events of Jeroboam's rule are written down. His wars and how he ruled are written down. They are written in the official records of the kings of Israel. 20Jeroboam ruled for 22 years. Then he joined the members of his family who had already died. Jeroboam's son Nadab became the next king after him.

Rehoboam, the King of Judah

21Rehoboam was king in Judah. He was the son of Solomon. Rehoboam was 41 years old when he became king. He ruled for 17 years in Jerusalem. It was the city the LORD had chosen out of all of the cities in the tribes of Israel. He wanted to put his Name there. Rehoboam's mother was Naamah from Ammon.

22The people of Judah did what was evil in the sight of the LORD. The sins they had committed stirred up his jealous anger. They did more to make him angry than their people who lived before them had done.

23Judah also set up for themselves high places for worship. They set up sacred stones. They set up poles that were used to worship the goddess Asherah. They did it on every high hill and under every green tree.

24There were even male prostitutes at the temples in the land. The people took part in all of the practices of other nations. The LORD hated those practices. He had driven those nations out to make room for the people of Israel.

25Shishak attacked Jerusalem. It was in the fifth year that Rehoboam was king. Shishak was king of Egypt. 26He carried away the treasures of the LORD's temple. He also carried the treasures of the royal palace away. He took everything. That included all of the gold shields Solomon had made.

27So King Rehoboam made bronze shields to take their place. He gave them to the commanders of the guards who were on duty at the entrance to the royal palace. 28Every time the king went to the LORD's temple, the guards carried the shields. Later, they took them back to the room where they were kept.

29The other events of Rehoboam's rule are written down. Everything he did is written down. All of those things are written down in the official records of the kings of Judah. 30Rehoboam and Jeroboam were always at war with each other. 31Rehoboam joined the members of his family who had already died. His body was buried in his family tomb in the City of David. His mother was Naamah from Ammon. His son Abijah became the next king after him.

Abijah Becomes King of Judah

15 Abijah became king of Judah. It was in the 18th year of Jeroboam's rule over Israel. Jeroboam was the son of Nebat. 2Abijah ruled in Jerusalem for three years. His mother's name was Maacah. She was Abishalom's daughter.

3Abijah committed all of the sins his father had committed before him. Abijah didn't follow the LORD his God with all his heart. He didn't do what King David had done.

4But the LORD still kept the lamp of Abijah's kingdom burning brightly in Jerusalem. He did it by giving him a son to be the next king after him. He also did it by making Jerusalem strong. The LORD did those things because of David. 5David had done what was right in the eyes of the LORD. He had kept all of the LORD's commands. He had obeyed them all the days of his life. But he hadn't obeyed the LORD in the case of Uriah, the Hittite.

6There was war between Jeroboam and Abijah's father Rehoboam. The war continued all through Abijah's life. 7The other events of Abijah's rule are written down. Everything he did is written down. All of those things are written in the official records of the kings of Judah. There was war between Abijah and Jeroboam.

8Abijah joined the members of his family who had already died. His body was buried in the City of David. His son Asa became the next king after him.

Asa Becomes King of Judah

9Asa became king of Judah. It was in the 20th year that Jeroboam was king of Israel. 10Asa ruled in Jerusalem for 41 years. His grandmother's name was Maacah. She was Abishalom's daughter.

11Asa did what was right in the eyes of the LORD. That's what King David had done.

12Asa threw out of the land the male prostitutes who were at the temples. He got rid of all of the statues of gods his people before him had made. 13He even removed his grandmother Maacah from her position as queen mother. That's because she had made a pole that was used to worship the goddess Asherah. The LORD hated it. So Asa cut it down. He burned it in the Kidron Valley.

14Asa didn't remove the high places from Israel. But he committed his whole life completely to the LORD. 15He and his father had set apart silver, gold and other articles to the LORD. He brought them into the LORD's temple.

16There was war between Asa and Baasha, the king of Israel. It lasted the whole time they were kings. 17Baasha was king of Israel. He marched out against Judah. He built up the walls of Ramah. He did it to keep people from leaving or entering the territory of Asa, the king of Judah.

18Asa took all of the silver and gold that was left among the treasures of the LORD's temple and his own palace. He put his officials in charge of it. He sent the officials to Ben-Hadad. Ben-Hadad was king of Aram. He was ruling in Damascus. He was the son of Tabrimmon and the grandson of Hezion.

19"Let's make a peace treaty between us," Asa said. "My father and your father had made a peace treaty between them. Now I'm sending you a gift of silver and gold. So break your treaty with Baasha, the king of Israel. Then he'll go back home."

20Ben-Hadad agreed with King Asa. He sent his army commanders against the towns of Israel. He attacked Ijon, Dan, Abel Beth Maacah and the whole area of Kinnereth in addition to Naphtali. 21Baasha heard about it. So he stopped building up Ramah. He went back home to Tirzah.

22Then King Asa gave an order to all of the men of Judah. Everyone was required to help. They carried away from Ramah the stones and wood Baasha had been using there. King Asa used them to build up Geba in the territory of Benjamin. He also used them to build up Mizpah.

23All of the other events of Asa's rule are written down. Everything he accomplished is written down. Everything he did and the cities he built are written down. They are written in the official records of the kings of Judah. But when Asa became old, his feet began to give him trouble. 24He joined the members of his family who had already died. His body was buried in his family tomb. It was in the city of King David. Asa's son Jehoshaphat became the next king after him.

Nadab Becomes King of Israel

25Nadab became king of Israel. It was in the second year that Asa was king of Judah. Nadab ruled over Israel for two years. He was the son of Jeroboam. 26Nadab did what was evil in the sight of the LORD. He lived the way his father had lived. He sinned as his father had sinned. Jeroboam had also caused Israel to commit the same sins.

27Baasha was from the tribe of Issachar. He was the son of Ahijah. Baasha made plans against Nadab and struck him down at Gibbethon. It was a Philistine town. Baasha struck him down while Nadab and all of the men of Israel were getting ready to attack Gibbethon. 28He killed Nadab in the third year that Asa was king of Judah. Baasha became the next king after Nadab.

29As soon as Baasha became king, he killed Jeroboam's whole family. He didn't leave any of them alive. He destroyed every one of them. He did what the LORD had said would happen. The LORD had spoken that message through his servant Ahijah from Shiloh.

30The LORD judged Jeroboam's family because of the sins Jeroboam had committed. He had also caused Israel to commit those same sins. He had made the LORD very angry. The LORD is the God of Israel.

31The other events of Nadab's rule are written down. Everything he did is written down. All of those things are written in the official records of the kings of Israel.

32There was war between Asa and Baasha, the king of Israel. It lasted the whole time they were kings.

Baasha Becomes King of Israel

33Baasha became king of Israel in Tirzah. It was in the third year that Asa was king of Judah. Baasha ruled for 24 years. He was the son of Ahijah. 34Baasha did what was evil in the sight of the LORD. He lived the way Jeroboam had lived. He sinned as Jeroboam had sinned. Jeroboam had also caused Israel to commit the same sins.

16 The LORD's message against Baasha came to Jehu. Jehu was the son of Hanani. The LORD said, 2"I lifted you up from the dust. I made you leader of my people Israel. But you lived the way Jeroboam had lived. You also caused my people Israel to sin. And their sins made me very angry.

3"So I am about to destroy you and your royal house. I will make your house like the royal house of Jeroboam, the son of

Nebat. **4**Some of the people who belong to you will die in the city. Dogs will eat them up. Others will die in the country. The birds of the air will eat them."

5The other events of Baasha's rule are written down. What he did and what he accomplished are written down. All of those things are written in the official records of the kings of Israel. **6**Baasha joined the members of his family who had already died. His body was buried in Tirzah. His son Elah became the next king after him.

7The Lord's message came through the prophet Jehu, the son of Hanani. It was against Baasha and his royal house. Baasha had done all kinds of evil things in the sight of the Lord. What he did had made the Lord very angry. So Baasha had become as sinful as the royal house of Jeroboam had been. He had also destroyed it.

Elah Becomes King of Israel

8Elah became king of Israel. It was in the 26th year that Asa was king of Judah. Elah ruled in Tirzah for two years. He was the son of Baasha.

9Zimri was one of Elah's officials. He commanded half of Elah's chariot drivers. He made plans against Elah. Elah was in Tirzah at the time. He was getting drunk in the home of Arza. Arza was in charge of the palace at Tirzah. **10**Zimri came in. He struck Elah down and killed him. It was in the 27th year of Asa, the king of Judah. Zimri became the next king after Elah.

11As soon as Zimri was seated on the throne as king, he killed off Baasha's whole family. He didn't even spare one male. It didn't matter whether it was a relative or a friend. **12**So Zimri destroyed the whole family of Baasha. That's what the Lord had said would happen. He had spoken against Baasha through the prophet Jehu.

13Baasha and his son Elah had committed all kinds of sin. They had also caused Israel to commit the same sins. So Israel made the Lord very angry. They did it by worshiping worthless statues of gods. The Lord is the God of Israel.

14The other events of Elah's rule are written down. Everything he did is written down. All of those things are written in the official records of the kings of Israel.

Zimri Becomes King of Israel

15Zimri ruled in Tirzah for seven days. It was in the 27th year that Asa was king of Judah. The army of Israel had set up camp near Gibbethon. It was a Philistine town.

16The people of Israel who were in the camp heard that Zimri had made plans against King Elah. They also heard that Zimri had murdered him. So they announced that Omri was king over Israel. He was the commander of the army. They made him king that very day in the camp. **17**Then Omri and all of his men pulled back from Gibbethon. They marched to Tirzah and surrounded it. They attacked it and captured it. **18**Zimri saw that they had taken over the city. So he went into the safest place in the royal palace. He set the palace on fire all around him. He died there **19**because of the sins he had committed. He had done what was evil in the sight of the Lord. He had lived the way Jeroboam had lived. He had sinned as Jeroboam had sinned. Jeroboam had also caused Israel to commit the same sins.

20The other events of Zimri's rule are written down. The way he turned against King Elah and killed him is written down. All of those things are written in the official records of the kings of Israel.

Omri Becomes King of Israel

21The people of Israel divided up into two groups. Half of them wanted Tibni to be king. He was the son of Ginath. The other half wanted Omri. **22**But Omri's followers were stronger than those of Tibni, the son of Ginath. So Tibni died. And Omri began to rule.

23Omri became king of Israel. It was in the 31st year that Asa was king of Judah. Omri ruled for 12 years. He ruled in Tirzah for six of those years. **24**He bought the hill of Samaria from Shemer. He weighed out 150 pounds of silver for it. Then he built a city on the hill. He called it Samaria. He named it after Shemer. Shemer had owned the hill before him.

25But Omri did what was evil in the sight of the Lord. He sinned more than all of the kings who had ruled before him. **26**He lived the way Jeroboam, the son of Nebat, had lived. He sinned as Jeroboam had sinned. Jeroboam had also caused Israel to commit the same sins. Israel made the Lord very angry. They did it by worshiping worthless statues of gods. The Lord is the God of Israel.

27The other events of Omri's rule are written down. Everything he did and the things he accomplished are written down. All of those things are written in the official records of the kings of Israel. **28**Omri joined the members of his family who had already died. His body was buried in Samaria. His son Ahab became the next king after him.

Ahab Becomes King of Israel

²⁹Ahab became king of Israel. It was in the 38th year that Asa was king of Judah. Ahab ruled over Israel in Samaria for 22 years. He was the son of Omri. ³⁰Ahab, the son of Omri, did what was evil in the sight of the LORD. He did more evil things than any of the kings who had ruled before him. ³¹He thought it was only a small thing to commit the sins Jeroboam, the son of Nebat, had committed.

Ahab also got married to Jezebel. She was Ethbaal's daughter. Ethbaal was king of the people of Sidon. Ahab began to serve the god Baal and worship him. ³²He set up an altar to honor Baal. He set it up in the temple of Baal that he built in Samaria. ³³Ahab also made a pole that was used to worship the goddess Asherah.

He made the LORD very angry. He did more to make him angry than all of the kings of Israel had done before him. The LORD is the God of Israel.

³⁴In Ahab's time, Hiel from Bethel rebuilt Jericho. When he laid its foundations, it cost him the life of his oldest son Abiram. When he set up its gates, it cost him the life of his youngest son Segub. That's what the LORD had said would happen. He had spoken it through Joshua, the son of Nun.

Elijah Is Fed by Ravens

17 Elijah was from Tishbe in the land of Gilead. He said to Ahab, "I serve the LORD. He is the God of Israel. You can be sure that he lives. And you can be just as sure that there won't be any dew or rain on the whole land. There won't be any during the next few years. It won't come until I say so."

²Then a message from the LORD came to Elijah. It said, ³"Leave this place. Go east and hide in the Kerith Valley. It is east of the Jordan River. ⁴You will drink water from the brook. I have ordered some ravens to feed you there."

⁵So Elijah did what the LORD had told him to do. He went to the Kerith Valley. It was east of the Jordan River. He stayed there. ⁶The ravens brought him bread and meat in the morning. They also brought him bread and meat in the evening. He drank water from the brook.

Elijah Visits a Widow at Zarephath

⁷Some time later the brook dried up. It hadn't rained in the land for quite a while. ⁸A message came to Elijah from the LORD. He said, ⁹"Go right away to Zarephath in the territory of Sidon. Stay there. I have commanded a widow in that place to supply you with food."

¹⁰So Elijah went to Zarephath. He came to the town gate. A widow was there gathering sticks. He called out to her. He asked, "Would you bring me a little water in a jar? I need a drink."

¹¹She went to get the water.

Then he called out to her, "Please bring me a piece of bread too."

¹²"I don't have any bread," she replied. "And that's just as sure as the LORD your God is alive. All I have is a small amount of flour in a jar and a little olive oil in a jug. I'm gathering a few sticks to take home. I'll make one last meal for myself and my son. We'll eat it. After that, we'll die."

¹³Elijah said to her, "Don't be afraid. Go home. Do what you have said. But first make a little bread for me. Make it out of what you have. Bring it to me. Then make some for yourself and your son.

¹⁴"The LORD is the God of Israel. He says, 'The jar of flour will not be used up. The jug will always have oil in it. You will have flour and oil until the day the LORD sends rain on the land.'"

¹⁵She went away and did what Elijah had told her to do. So Elijah had food every day. There was also food for the woman and her family. ¹⁶The jar of flour wasn't used up. The jug always had oil in it. That's what the LORD had said would happen. He had spoken that message through Elijah.

¹⁷Some time later the son of the woman who owned the house became sick. He got worse and worse. Finally he stopped breathing.

¹⁸The woman said to Elijah, "You are a man of God. What do you have against me? Did you come to bring my sin out into the open? Did you come to kill my son?"

¹⁹"Give me your son," Elijah replied. He took him from her arms. He carried him to the upstairs room where he was staying. He put him down on his bed.

²⁰Then Elijah cried out to the LORD. He said, "LORD my God, I'm staying with this widow. Have you brought pain and sorrow to her? Have you caused her son to die?"

²¹Then he lay down on the boy three times. He cried out to the LORD. He said, "LORD my God, give this boy's life back to him!"

²²The LORD answered Elijah's prayer. He gave the boy's life back to him. So the boy lived. ²³Elijah picked up the boy. He car-

ELIJAH

1 KINGS 17:1

Elijah was from Tishbe in the land of Gilead. He said to Ahab, "I serve the Lord. He is the God of Israel. You can be sure that he lives.

God's prophet Elijah had issued a challenge to the Israelites. Who would they follow? God or Baal? No one answered. They didn't *dare* to say they wanted to follow Baal. And they didn't *want* to say they would follow God.

So Elijah decided to prove to them who they should follow. The prophets of Baal built an altar and put a bull on it. They didn't light the fire. Instead they prayed to Baal to send fire from heaven on the altar. But no matter what they did, no fire came.

Elijah mocked them. "Maybe your god is sleeping," he joked. "Or maybe he's gone on a trip. Maybe you should shout louder!"

So they did. The prophets of Baal shouted and danced and even cut their skin to try to get their god's attention. But no fire came down on their altar.

Now it was Elijah's turn. He put his bull on the altar. He dug a ditch around the altar. Then he poured four large jugs of water over the bull and the wood and the altar. The water soaked the animal and the wood and ran down into the ditch. Surely no fire would burn here. *But then Elijah repeated the process two more times!* Everything on the altar and around it was drenched.

Elijah prayed, confident that God would answer. **AS SOON AS THE LAST WORDS WERE OUT OF HIS MOUTH, FIRE STREAKED DOWN FROM HEAVEN.** It burned up the bull and the wood and even the stones of the altar.

Now the people knew for certain what Elijah already knew. There was only one God. It wasn't Baal. It was God Almighty, the God of Israel.

BE AN ELIJAH

What is easier? To do what everyone else is doing? Or to do the right thing, no matter what others do? It is often easier to do what everyone else is doing. If you're ever in a situation where you want to do what others are doing and you know it isn't the right thing to do, think of Elijah. Remembering him will help you make the right choice.

ELIJAH WAS FAITHFUL TO GOD WHEN EVERYONE ELSE WAS FOLLOWING BAAL.
THE WHOLE STORY: 1 KINGS 18:16-39

Go to page 418 for the next Super Hero

ried him down from the upstairs room into the house. He gave him to his mother. He said, "Look! Your son is alive!"

24Then the woman said to Elijah, "Now I know that you are a man of God. I know that the message you have brought from the LORD is true."

Elijah Gives Obadiah a Message for Ahab

18 It was now three years since it had rained. A message came to Elijah from the LORD. He said, "Go. Speak to Ahab. Then I will send rain on the land."

2So Elijah went to speak to Ahab.

There wasn't enough food in Samaria. The people there were very hungry. 3Ahab had sent for Obadiah. He was in charge of Ahab's palace. Obadiah had great respect for the LORD.

4Ahab's wife Jezebel had been killing off the LORD's prophets. So Obadiah had hidden 100 prophets in two caves. He had put 50 in each cave. He had supplied them with food and water.

5Ahab had said to Obadiah, "Go through the land. Go to all of the springs of water and to the valleys. Maybe we can find some grass there. It will keep the horses and mules alive. Then we won't have to kill any of our animals." 6So they decided where each of them would look. Ahab went in one direction. Obadiah went in another.

7As Obadiah was walking along, Elijah met him. Obadiah recognized him. He bowed down to the ground. He said, "My master Elijah! Is it really you?"

8"Yes," he replied. "Go and tell your master Ahab, 'Elijah is here.' "

9"What have I done wrong?" asked Obadiah. "Why are you handing me over to Ahab to be put to death?

10"My master has sent people to look for you everywhere. There isn't a nation or kingdom where he hasn't sent someone to look for you. Suppose a nation or kingdom would claim you weren't there. Then Ahab would make them take an oath and say they couldn't find you. And that's just as sure as the LORD your God is alive.

11"But now you are telling me to go to my master. You want me to say, 'Elijah is here.' 12But the Spirit of the LORD might carry you away when I leave you. Then I won't know where you are. If I go and tell Ahab and he doesn't find you, he'll kill me.

"But I've worshiped the LORD ever since I was young. 13My master, haven't you heard what I did? Jezebel was killing the LORD's prophets. But I hid 100 of them in two caves. I put 50 in each cave. I supplied them with food and water. 14And now you are telling me to go to my master Ahab. You want me to say to him, 'Elijah is here.' He'll kill me!"

15Elijah said, "I serve the LORD who rules over all. You can be sure that he lives. And you can be just as sure that I will speak to Ahab today."

The LORD Answers Elijah's Prayer on Mount Carmel

16Obadiah went back to Ahab. He told Ahab that Elijah wanted to see him. So Ahab went to where Elijah was. 17When he saw Elijah, he said to him, "Is that you? You are always stirring up trouble in Israel."

18"I haven't made trouble for Israel," Elijah replied. "But you and your father's family have. You have turned away from the LORD's commands. You have followed the gods that are named after Baal.

19"Now send for people from all over Israel. Tell them to meet me on Mount Carmel. And bring the 450 prophets of the god Baal. Also bring the 400 prophets of the goddess Asherah. All of them eat at Jezebel's table."

20So Ahab sent that message all through Israel. He gathered the prophets together on Mount Carmel.

21Elijah went there and stood in front of the people. He said, "How long will it take you to make up your minds? If the LORD is the one and only God, follow him.

POWER / SURGE

BELIEVES †

ELIJAH WENT THERE AND STOOD IN FRONT OF THE PEOPLE. HE SAID, "HOW LONG WILL IT TAKE YOU TO MAKE UP YOUR MINDS? IF THE LORD IS THE ONE AND ONLY GOD, FOLLOW HIM."

— 1 KINGS 18:21 —

TELLS OTHERS

WIDOW OF ZAREPHATH

★ K G

1 KINGS 17:24

Then the woman said to Elijah, "Now I know that you are a man of God. I know that the message you have brought from the LORD is true."

The widow of Zarephath (ZAR-u-fath) reached out her skinny hand to pick up one more stick. Her stomach rumbled with hunger. No rain had fallen in a long time. Most people had no food to eat. The widow had only a little flour and oil left. She gathered sticks for a fire to bake one last loaf of bread. She and her son would eat it. And die.

As the widow passed through the town gate, a stranger called and asked her for a drink of water. She raised her head in surprise when the stranger also asked her to bring him a bit of bread. Didn't he realize that there was no food? Was she supposed to share what little she had left with a stranger?

The hungry widow didn't know it, but this stranger was Elijah, God's prophet. And she had been chosen to help him survive the famine. He seemed to understand her hesitation.

"Go and make a loaf of bread for me and for yourself and your son," he said. "The little bit of oil and flour you have will not run out. You will have enough until God sends rain."

The widow began to walk toward her house, a thousand questions racing through her head. *The oil and flour will not run out? But who would fill it? But why not share what little I have left? My son and I can eat the last loaf of bread and die. Or we can share the last loaf of bread and die.* EITHER WAY, WE DIE. UNLESS...

Reaching for her jar of flour and the jug of oil, the widow measured out the last little bit, then fearfully looked into each. There was as much flour and oil as before! She and her son would live! And they would share what they had with Elijah, God's messenger.

BE LIKE THE WIDOW OF ZAREPHATH

Sharing doesn't always come easy. Do you have things you would rather not share with anyone? This widow probably was afraid to share her last meal with Elijah. But she did it anyway. And God blessed her. God will bless you if you share, too.

SHE SHARED WHAT LITTLE SHE HAD, AND GOD PROVIDED.

THE WHOLE STORY: 1 KINGS 17:7-24

Go to page 424 for the next person

But if Baal is the one and only God, follow him."

The people didn't say anything.

22Then Elijah said to them, "I'm the only one of the LORD's prophets left. But Baal has 450 prophets. 23Get two bulls for us. Let Baal's prophets choose one for themselves. Let them cut it into pieces. Then let them put it on the wood. But don't let them set fire to it. I'll prepare the other bull. I'll put it on the wood. But I won't set fire to it. 24Then you pray to your god. And I'll pray to the LORD. The god who answers by sending fire down is the one and only God."

Then all of the people said, "What you are saying is good."

25Elijah spoke to the prophets of Baal. He said, "Choose one of the bulls. There are many of you. So prepare your bull first. Pray to your god. But don't light the fire."

26So they prepared the bull they had been given.

They prayed to Baal from morning until noon. "Baal! Answer us!" they shouted. But there wasn't any reply. No one answered. Then they danced around the altar they had made.

27At noon Elijah began to tease them. "Shout louder!" he said. "I'm sure Baal is a god! Perhaps he has too much to think about. Or maybe he has gone to the toilet. Or perhaps he's away on a trip. Maybe he's sleeping. You might have to wake him up."

28So they shouted louder. They cut themselves with swords and spears until their blood flowed. That's what they usually did when things really looked hopeless. 29It was now past noon. The prophets of Baal continued to prophesy with all their might. They did it until the time came to offer the evening sacrifice. But there wasn't any reply. No one answered. No one paid any attention.

30Then Elijah said to all of the people, "Come here to me." So they went to him. He rebuilt the altar of the LORD. It had been destroyed. 31Elijah got 12 stones. There was one for each tribe in the family line of Jacob. The LORD's message had come to Jacob. It had said, "Your name will be Israel." 32Elijah used the stones to build an altar in honor of the LORD. He dug a ditch around it. The ditch was large enough to hold 13 quarts of seeds. 33He arranged the wood for the fire. He cut the bull into pieces. He placed the pieces on the wood.

Then he said to some of the people,

"Fill four large jars with water. Pour it on the offering and the wood." So they did. 34"Do it again," he said. So they did it again.

"Do it a third time," he ordered. And they did it the third time. 35The water ran down around the altar. It even filled the ditch.

36When it was time to offer the evening sacrifice, the prophet Elijah stepped forward. He prayed, "LORD, you are the God of Abraham, Isaac and Israel. Today let everyone know that you are God in Israel. Let them know I'm your servant. Let them know I've done all of these things because you commanded me to. 37Answer me. LORD, answer me. Then these people will know that you are the one and only God. They'll know that you are turning their hearts back to you again."

38The fire of the LORD came down. It burned up the sacrifice. It burned up the wood and the stones and the soil. It even licked up the water in the ditch.

39All of the people saw it. Then they fell down flat with their faces toward the ground. They cried out, "The LORD is the one and only God! The LORD is the one and only God!"

40Then Elijah commanded them, "Grab hold of the prophets of Baal. Don't let a single one of them get away!"

So they grabbed them. Elijah had them brought down to the Kishon Valley. There he had them put to death.

41Elijah said to Ahab, "Go. Eat and drink. I can hear the sound of a heavy rain."

42So Ahab went off to eat and drink.

But Elijah climbed to the top of Mount Carmel. He bent down toward the ground. Then he put his face between his knees.

43"Go and look toward the sea," he told his servant. So he went up and looked.

"I don't see anything there," he said.

Seven times Elijah said, "Go back."

44The seventh time the servant said, "I see a cloud. It's as small as a man's hand. It's coming up over the sea."

Elijah said, "Go to Ahab. Tell him, 'Tie your chariot to your horse. Go down to Jezreel before the rain stops you.' "

45Black clouds filled the sky. The wind came up, and a heavy rain began to fall. Ahab rode off to Jezreel.

46The power of the LORD came on Elijah. He tucked his coat into his belt. And he ran ahead of Ahab all the way to Jezreel.

STRONG

THE POWER OF THE LORD CAME ON ELIJAH. HE TUCKED HIS COAT INTO HIS BELT. AND HE RAN AHEAD OF AHAB ALL THE WAY TO JEZREEL.
—— 1 KINGS 18:46 ——

Elijah Runs Away to Mount Horeb

19 Ahab told Jezebel everything Elijah had done. He told her how Elijah had killed all of the prophets with his sword.

2So Jezebel sent a message to Elijah. She said, "You can be sure that I will kill you, just as I killed the other prophets. I'll do it by this time tomorrow. If I don't, may the gods punish me greatly."

3Elijah was afraid. So he ran for his life. He came to Beersheba in Judah. He left his servant there.

4Then he traveled for one day into the desert. He came to a small tree. He sat down under it. He prayed that he would die. "LORD, I've had enough," he said. "Take my life. I'm no better than my people of long ago." **5**Then he lay down under the tree. And he fell asleep.

Suddenly an angel touched him. The angel said, "Get up and eat." **6**Elijah looked around. Near his head he saw a flat cake of bread. It had been baked over hot coals. A jar of water was also there. So Elijah ate and drank. Then he lay down again.

7The angel of the LORD came to him a second time. He touched him and said, "Get up and eat. Your journey will be long and hard."

8So he got up. He ate and drank. The food gave him new strength. He traveled for 40 days and 40 nights. He kept going until he arrived at Horeb. It was the mountain of God. **9**There he went into a cave and spent the night.

The LORD Appears to Elijah

A message came to Elijah from the LORD. He said, "Elijah, what are you doing here?"

10He replied, "LORD God who rules over all, I've been very committed to you. The people of Israel have turned their backs on your covenant. They have torn down your altars. They've put your prophets to death with their swords. I'm the only one left. And they are trying to kill me."

11The LORD said, "Go out. Stand on the mountain in front of me. I am going to pass by."

As the LORD approached, a very powerful wind tore the mountains apart. It broke up the rocks. But the LORD wasn't in the wind.

After the wind there was an earthquake. But the LORD wasn't in the earthquake.

12After the earthquake a fire came. But the LORD wasn't in the fire.

And after the fire there was only a gentle whisper. **13**When Elijah heard it, he pulled his coat over his face. He went out and stood at the entrance to the cave.

Then a voice said to him, "Elijah, what are you doing here?"

14He replied, "LORD God who rules over all, I've been very committed to you. The people of Israel have turned their backs on your covenant. They have torn down your altars. They've put your prophets to death with their swords. I'm the only one left. And they are trying to kill me."

15The LORD said to him, "Go back the way you came. Go to the Desert of Damascus. When you get there, anoint Hazael as king over Aram. **16**Also anoint Jehu as king over Israel. He is the son of Nimshi. And anoint Elisha from Abel Meholah as the next prophet after you. He is the son of Shaphat. **17**Jehu will put to death anyone who escapes Hazael's sword. And Elisha will put to death anyone who escapes Jehu's sword.

18"But I will keep 7,000 people in Israel for myself. They have not bowed down to Baal. And they have not kissed him."

The LORD Chooses Elisha

19Elijah left Mount Horeb. He saw Elisha, the son of Shaphat. Elisha was plowing in a field. He was driving the last of 12 pairs of oxen. Elijah went up to him. He threw his coat around him. **20**Then Elisha left his oxen. He ran after Elijah. "Let me kiss my father and mother good-by," he said. "Then I'll come with you."

"Go back," Elijah replied. "What have I done to you?"

21So Elisha left him and went back. He got his two oxen and killed them. He burned the plow to cook the meat. He gave it to the people, and they ate it.

Then he started to follow Elijah. He became Elijah's assistant.

Ben-Hadad Attacks Samaria

20 Ben-Hadad brought his whole army together. He was king of Aram. He went up to Samaria. He took 32 kings and their horses and chariots with him. All of them surrounded Samaria and attacked it.

2 Ben-Hadad sent messengers into the city. They spoke to Ahab, the king of Israel. They told him, "Ben-Hadad says, 3 'Your silver and gold belong to me. The best of your wives and children also belong to me.' "

4 The king of Israel replied, "What you say is true. You are my king and master. I belong to you. And everything I have belongs to you."

5 The messengers came again. They told Ahab, "Ben-Hadad says, 'I commanded you to give me your silver and gold. I also commanded you to give me your wives and children. 6 But now I'm going to send my officials to you. They will come about this time tomorrow. They'll search your palace. They'll search the houses of your officials. They'll take everything you value. And they'll carry all of it away.' "

7 The king of Israel sent for all of the elders of the land. He said to them, "This man is really looking for trouble! He sent for my wives and children. He sent for my silver and gold. And I agreed to give them to him."

8 All of the elders and people answered, "Don't listen to him. Don't agree to give him what he wants."

9 So Ahab replied to Ben-Hadad's messengers. He said, "Tell my king and master, 'I will do everything you commanded me to do the first time. But this time, I can't do what you want me to do.' " They took Ahab's answer back to Ben-Hadad.

10 Then Ben-Hadad sent another message to Ahab. It said, "There won't be enough dust left in Samaria to give each of my followers even a handful. If there is, may the gods punish me greatly."

11 The king of Israel replied. He said, "Tell him, 'Someone who puts his armor on shouldn't brag like someone who takes it off.' "

12 Ben-Hadad and the kings were in their tents drinking. That's when he heard the message. He ordered his men, "Get ready to attack." So they prepared to attack the city.

Ahab Wins the Battle Over Ben-Hadad

13 During that time a prophet came to Ahab, the king of Israel. He announced, "The LORD says, 'Do you see this huge army? I will hand it over to you today. Then you will know that I am the LORD.' "

14 "But who will do it?" Ahab asked. The prophet answered, "The LORD says, 'The young officers who are under the area commanders will do it.' "

"And who will start the battle?" he asked.

The prophet answered, "You will."

15 So Ahab sent for the young officers who were under the area commanders. The total number of officers was 232. Ahab gathered together the rest of the men of Israel. The total number of them was 7,000. 16 They started out at noon. At that time Ben-Hadad and the 32 kings who were helping him were in their tents. They were getting drunk. 17 The young officers who were under Ahab's area commanders marched out first.

Ben-Hadad had sent out scouts. They came back and reported, "Men are marching against us from Samaria."

18 Ben-Hadad said, "They might be coming to make peace. If they are, take them alive. Or they might be coming to make war. If they are, take them alive."

19 The young officers marched out of the city. The army was right behind them. 20 Each man struck down the one who was fighting against him. When that happened, the army of Aram ran away. The men of Israel chased them. But Ben-Hadad, the king of Aram, escaped on a horse. Some of his horsemen escaped with him.

21 The king of Israel attacked them. He overpowered the horses and chariots. Large numbers of the men of Aram were wounded or killed.

22 After that, the prophet came to the king of Israel again. He said, "Make your position stronger. Do what needs to be done. Next spring the king of Aram will attack you again."

23 During that time, the officials of the king of Aram gave him advice. They said, "The gods of Israel are gods of the hills. That's why they were too strong for us. But suppose we fight them on the flatlands. Then we'll certainly be stronger than they are.

24 "Here's what you should do. Don't let any of the kings continue as military leaders. Have other officers take their places. 25 You must also put another army togeth-

er. It should be just like the one you lost. It should have the same number of horses and chariots. Then we'll be able to fight against Israel on the flatlands. And we'll certainly be stronger than they are."

Ben-Hadad agreed with their advice. He did what they suggested.

26The next spring Ben-Hadad brought together the men of Aram. They went up to the city of Aphek to fight against Israel.

27The men of Israel were also brought together. They were given supplies. They marched out to fight against their enemies. Israel's army camped across from Aram's army. The men of Israel looked like two small flocks of goats that had become separated from the others. But the men of Aram covered the countryside.

28The man of God came up to the king of Israel again. He told him, "The LORD says, 'The men of Aram think I am a god of the hills. They do not think I am a god of the valleys. So I will hand their huge army over to you. Then you will know that I am the LORD.' "

29For seven days the two armies camped across from each other. On the seventh day the battle began. The men of Israel wounded or killed 100,000 Aramean soldiers on foot. That happened in a single day. 30The rest of the men of Aram escaped to the city of Aphek. Its wall fell down on 27,000 of them. Ben-Hadad ran to the city. He hid in a secret room.

31His officials said to him, "Look, we've heard that the kings of Israel's royal house often show mercy. So let's go to the king of Israel. Let's wear black clothes. Let's tie ropes around our heads. Perhaps Ahab will spare your life."

32So they wore black clothes. They tied ropes around their heads. Then they went to the king of Israel. They told him, "Your servant Ben-Hadad says, 'Please let me live.' "

The king answered, "Is he still alive? He used to be my friend."

33The men thought that was good news. So they quickly used the word Ahab had used. "Yes! Your friend Ben-Hadad!" they said.

"Go and get him," the king said.

Ben-Hadad came out of the secret room. Then Ahab had him get into his chariot.

34"I'll return the cities my father took from your father," Ben-Hadad offered. "You can set up your own market areas in Damascus. That's what my father did in Samaria."

Ahab said, "If we sign a peace treaty, I'll set you free."

So he made a treaty with him. Then Ahab let him go.

A Prophet Brings Charges Against Ahab

35There was a group that was called the company of the prophets. A message from the LORD came to one of their members. He said to his companion, "Strike me down with your weapon." But the man wouldn't do it.

36The prophet said, "You haven't obeyed the LORD. So as soon as you leave me, a lion will kill you."

The companion went away. And a lion found him and killed him.

37The prophet found another man. He said, "Please strike me down."

So the man struck him down and wounded him.

38Then the prophet went and stood by the road. He waited for the king to come by. He pulled his headband down over his eyes so no one would recognize him.

39The king passed by. Then the prophet called out to him. He said, "I went into the middle of the battle. Someone came to me with a prisoner. He said, 'Guard this man. Don't let him get away. If he does, you will pay for his life with yours. Or you can pay 75 pounds of silver.' 40While I was busy here and there, the man disappeared."

"That's your sentence," the king of Israel told him. "You have said so yourself."

41Then the prophet quickly removed the headband from his eyes. The king of Israel recognized him as one of the prophets. 42He told the king, "The LORD says, 'You have set a man free. But I had said he should be set apart to the LORD in a special way to be destroyed. So you must pay for his life with yours. You must pay for his people's lives with the lives of your people.' "

43The king of Israel was angry. He was in a bad mood. He went back to his palace in Samaria.

Ahab Takes Over Naboth's Vineyard

21 Some time later King Ahab wanted a certain vineyard. It belonged to Naboth from Jezreel. The vineyard was in Jezreel. It was close to the palace of Ahab, the king of Samaria.

2Ahab said to Naboth, "Let me have your vineyard. It's close to my palace. I want to use it for a vegetable garden. I'll trade you a better vineyard for it. Or, if you prefer, I'll pay you what it's worth."

3But Naboth replied, "May the LORD keep me from giving you the land my family handed down to me."

4So Ahab went home. He was angry. He was in a bad mood because of what Naboth from Jezreel had said. He had told him, "I won't give you the land my family handed down to me."

So Ahab lay on his bed. He was in a very bad mood. He wouldn't even eat anything.

5His wife Jezebel came in. She asked him, "Why are you in such a bad mood? Why won't you eat anything?"

6He answered her, "Because I spoke to Naboth from Jezreel. I said, 'Sell me your vineyard. Or, if you prefer, I'll give you another vineyard in its place.' But he said, 'I won't sell you my vineyard.' "

7His wife Jezebel said, "Is this how the king of Israel acts? Get up! Eat something! Cheer up. I'll get you the vineyard of Naboth from Jezreel."

8So she wrote some letters in Ahab's name. She stamped them with his seal. Then she sent them to the elders and nobles who lived in the city where Naboth lived. **9**In those letters she wrote,

"Announce a day when people are supposed to go without eating. Have Naboth sit in an important place among the people. **10**But put two worthless and evil men in seats across from him. Have them witness to the fact that he has called down curses on God and the king. Then take him out of the city. Kill him by throwing stones at him."

11So the elders and nobles who lived in that city did what Jezebel wanted. They did everything she directed in the letters she had written to them. **12**They announced a day of fasting. They had Naboth sit in an important place among the people.

13Then two worthless and evil men came and sat across from him. They brought charges against Naboth in front of the people. The two men said, "Naboth has called down curses on God and the king." So they took him outside the city. They killed him by throwing stones at him.

14Then they sent a message to Jezebel. They said, "Naboth is dead. We killed him by throwing stones at him."

15Jezebel heard that Naboth had been killed. As soon as she heard it, she said to Ahab, "Get up. Take over the vineyard of Naboth from Jezreel. It's the one he wouldn't sell to you. He isn't alive anymore. He's dead."

16Ahab heard that Naboth was dead. So he got up. He went down to take over Naboth's vineyard.

17Then a message from the LORD came to Elijah, who was from Tishbe. It said, **18**"Go down to see Ahab, the king of Israel. He rules in Samaria. You will find him in Naboth's vineyard. He has gone there to take it over. **19**Tell him, 'The LORD says, "Haven't you murdered a man? Haven't you taken over his property?" ' Then tell him, 'The LORD says, "Dogs licked up Naboth's blood. In that same place dogs will lick up your blood. Yes, I said your blood!" ' "

20Ahab said to Elijah, "My enemy! You have found me!"

"I have found you," he answered. "That's because you gave yourself over to do evil things. You did what was evil in the sight of the LORD. **21**So the LORD says, 'I am going to bring horrible trouble on you. I will destroy your children after you. I will cut off every male in Israel who is related to you. It does not matter whether they are slaves or free. **22**I will make your royal house like the house of Jeroboam, the son of Nebat. I will make it like the house of Baasha, the son of Ahijah. You have made me very angry. You have caused Israel to commit sin.'

23"The LORD also says, 'Dogs will eat up Jezebel near the wall of Jezreel.'

24"Some of the people who belong to Ahab will die in the city. Dogs will eat them up. Others will die in the country. The birds of the air will eat them."

25There was never anyone like Ahab. He gave himself over to do what was evil in the sight of the LORD. His wife Jezebel talked him into it. **26**He acted in the most evil way. He worshiped statues of gods. He was like the Amorites. The LORD drove them out to make room for Israel.

27When Ahab heard what Elijah had said, he tore his clothes. He put on black clothes. He went without eating. He even slept in his clothes. He went around looking sad.

28Then a message from the LORD came to Elijah, who was from Tishbe. It said, **29**"Have you seen how Ahab has made himself low in my sight? Because he has done that, I will not bring trouble on him while he lives. But I will bring it on his royal house when his son is king."

AHAB

1 KINGS 21:16

Ahab heard that Naboth was dead. So he got up. He went down to take over Naboth's vineyard.

K ing Ahab sat down on his bed and frowned. He threw off his rich royal robe. His servants looked at each other. What was the matter now? One servant tried to bring some tasty fruit to cheer up the king. But Ahab shouted at the servant to leave.

Queen Jezebel came into the room. She took one look at her husband and asked, **"WHAT ARE YOU SO MAD ABOUT?"**

King Ahab whined to her about his meeting that day with Naboth. Naboth owned a vineyard near Ahab's royal palace, and Ahab wanted it. But the vineyard had been in Naboth's family for many, many years. Naboth knew Ahab was the powerful king of Israel, but he refused to sell his land to him.

Jezebel cackled, then sneered at her husband, "Come on, Ahab! You're the king! You can have whatever you want! I'll get the vineyard for you."

So she did. She had two men accuse Naboth of cursing God and the king, something Naboth would never do. But Jezebel's men killed Naboth anyway. As soon as Jezebel got word that Naboth was dead, she went back to Ahab.

"OK," she said. "Naboth is dead. The vineyard is yours. See how easy it is?" Ahab's frown vanished. He didn't think about how unfair this was to Naboth or how sad Naboth's family now was. He was just glad to get what he wanted. Ahab took over the vineyard of Naboth.

Few people noticed what Ahab and Jezebel had done. But God noticed. And he wasn't pleased. Both Ahab and Jezebel would die for their wickedness.

AHAB

You don't want to be like foolish Ahab. But you can learn something from his story. After years of living with his wife, he became more and more wicked, just like she was. Be sure to choose your friends carefully. Choose those who will help you love and follow God.

AHAB WAS A WICKED MAN WHO DIDN'T FOLLOW GOD'S WAYS.
THE WHOLE STORY: 1 KINGS 21:1-19

Go to page 432 for the next Super Hero

Micaiah Prophesies Against Ahab

22 For three years there wasn't any war between Aram and Israel. **2**In the third year Jehoshaphat went down to see Ahab, the king of Israel. Jehoshaphat was king of Judah.

3The king of Israel had spoken to his officials. He had said, "Don't you know that Ramoth Gilead belongs to us? And we aren't even doing anything to take it back from the king of Aram."

4So Ahab asked Jehoshaphat, "Will you go with me to fight against Ramoth Gilead?"

Jehoshaphat replied to the king of Israel, "Yes. I'll go with you. My men will go with you. My horses will also go with you." **5**Jehoshaphat continued, "First ask the LORD for advice."

6So the king of Israel brought about 400 prophets together. He asked them, "Should I go to war against Ramoth Gilead? Or should I stay here?"

"Go," they answered. "The Lord will hand it over to you."

7But Jehoshaphat asked, "Isn't there a prophet of the LORD here? If there is, ask him what we should do."

8The king of Israel answered Jehoshaphat. He said, "There is still one other man we can go to. We can ask the LORD for advice through him. But I hate him. He never prophesies anything good about me. He only prophesies bad things. His name is Micaiah. He's the son of Imlah."

"You shouldn't say bad things about him," Jehoshaphat replied.

9So the king of Israel called for one of his officials. He told him, "Bring Micaiah, the son of Imlah, at once."

10The king of Israel and Jehoshaphat, the king of Judah, were wearing their royal robes. They were sitting on their thrones at the threshing floor. It was near the entrance of the gate of Samaria. All of the prophets were prophesying in front of them.

11Zedekiah was the son of Kenaanah. Zedekiah had made horns out of iron. They looked like animal horns. He announced, "The LORD says, 'With these horns you will drive back the men of Aram until they are destroyed.' "

12All of the other prophets were prophesying the same thing. "Attack Ramoth Gilead," they said. "Win the battle over it. The LORD will hand it over to you."

13A messenger went to get Micaiah. He said to him, "Look. The other prophets agree. All of them are saying the king will have success. So agree with them. Say the same thing they do."

14But Micaiah said, "You can be sure that the LORD lives. And you can be just as sure that I can only tell the king what the LORD tells me to say."

15When Micaiah arrived, the king spoke to him. He asked, "Should we go to war against Ramoth Gilead? Or should I stay here?"

"Attack," he answered. "You will win. The LORD will hand Ramoth Gilead over to you."

16The king said to him, "I've made you promise to tell the truth many times before. So don't tell me anything but the truth in the name of the LORD."

POWER–SURGE

HONEST H

I'VE MADE YOU PROMISE TO TELL THE TRUTH MANY TIMES BEFORE. SO DON'T TELL ME ANYTHING BUT THE TRUTH IN THE NAME OF THE LORD.
— 1 KINGS 22:16 —

17Then Micaiah answered, "I saw all of the people of Israel scattered on the hills. They were like sheep that didn't have a shepherd. The LORD said, 'These people do not have a master. Let each of them go home in peace.' "

18The king of Israel spoke to Jehoshaphat. He said, "Didn't I tell you he never prophesies anything good about me? He only prophesies bad things."

19Micaiah continued, "Listen to the LORD's message. I saw the LORD sitting on his throne. Some of the angels of heaven were standing at his right side. The others were standing at his left side. So all of them were standing around him. **20**The LORD said, 'Who will try to get Ahab to attack Ramoth Gilead? I want him to die there.'

"One angel suggested one thing. Another suggested something else. **21**Finally, a spirit came forward and stood in front of the LORD. The spirit said, 'I'll try to get Ahab to do it.'

22" 'How?' the LORD asked.

"The spirit said, 'I'll go out and put lies in the mouths of all of his prophets.'

" 'You will have success in getting Ahab to attack Ramoth Gilead,' said the LORD. 'Go and do it.'

23 "So the LORD has put lies in the mouths of all of your prophets. He has said that great harm will come to you."

24 Then Zedekiah, the son of Kenaanah, went up and slapped Micaiah in the face. "So you think the spirit that was sent by the LORD went away from me to speak to you, do you?" he asked. "Which way did he go?"

25 Micaiah replied, "You will find out on the day you go to hide in an inside room to save your life."

26 Then the king of Israel gave an order. He said, "Take Micaiah away. Send him back to Amon. Amon is the ruler of the city of Samaria. And send him back to Joash. Joash is a member of the royal court. 27 Tell him, 'The king says, "Put this fellow in prison. Don't give him anything but bread and water until I return safely." ' "

28 Micaiah announced, "Do you really think you will return safely? If you do, the LORD hasn't spoken through me." He continued, "All of you people, remember what I've said!"

Ahab Is Killed at Ramoth Gilead

29 So the king of Israel went up to Ramoth Gilead. Jehoshaphat, the king of Judah, went there too.

30 The king of Israel spoke to Jehoshaphat. He said, "I'll go into battle wearing different clothes. Then people won't recognize me. But you wear your royal robes."

So the king of Israel put on different clothes. Then he went into battle.

31 The king of Aram had given an order to his 32 chariot commanders. He had said, "Fight only against the king of Israel. Don't fight against anyone else."

32 The chariot commanders saw Jehoshaphat. They thought, "That has to be the king of Israel." So they turned to attack him. But Jehoshaphat cried out. 33 Then the commanders saw he wasn't the king of Israel after all. So they stopped chasing him.

34 But someone shot an arrow without taking aim. The arrow hit the king of Israel between the parts of his armor. The king told his chariot driver, "Turn the chariot around. Get me out of this battle. I've been wounded." 35 All day long the battle continued. The king kept himself standing up by leaning against the inside of his chariot. He kept his face toward the men of Aram. The blood from his wound ran down onto the floor of the chariot. That evening he died.

36 As the sun was setting, a cry spread through the army. "Every man must go to his own town!" they said. "Everyone must go to his own land!"

37 So the king died. He was brought to Samaria. They buried his body there. 38 They washed the chariot at a pool in Samaria. It was where the prostitutes took baths. The dogs licked up Ahab's blood. It happened exactly as the LORD had said it would.

39 The other events of Ahab's rule are written down. Everything he did is written down. That includes the palace he built and decorated with ivory. It also includes the cities he built up and put high walls around. All of those things are written in the official records of the kings of Israel. 40 Ahab joined the members of his family who had already died. His son Ahaziah became the next king after him.

Jehoshaphat's Rule Comes to an End

41 Jehoshaphat began to rule over Judah. It was in the fourth year that Ahab was king of Israel. Jehoshaphat was the son of Asa. 42 Jehoshaphat was 35 years old when he became king. He ruled in Jerusalem for 25 years. His mother's name was Azubah. She was the daughter of Shilhi.

43 Jehoshaphat followed all of the ways of his father Asa. He didn't wander away from them. He did what was right in the eyes of the LORD. But the high places weren't removed. The people continued to offer sacrifices and burn incense at them.

44 Jehoshaphat was also at peace with the king of Israel.

45 The other events of Jehoshaphat's rule are written down. The brave things he did in battle and everything else he accomplished are written down. All of those things are written in the official records of the kings of Judah.

46 Jehoshaphat got rid of the rest of the male prostitutes who were at the temples. They had remained in the land even after the rule of his father Asa.

47 At that time Edom didn't have a king. An appointed official was in charge.

48 Jehoshaphat built many ships that he used to carry goods to be traded. The ships were supposed to go to Ophir for gold. But

BRAVE B

THE BRAVE THINGS [JEHOSHAPHAT] DID IN BATTLE AND EVERYTHING ELSE HE ACCOMPLISHED ARE WRITTEN DOWN.
—— 1 KINGS 22:45 ——

they never had a chance to sail. They were wrecked at Ezion Geber. ⁴⁹At that time Ahaziah, the son of Ahab, spoke to Jehoshaphat. He said, "Let my men sail with yours." But Jehoshaphat refused.

⁵⁰Jehoshaphat joined the members of his family who had already died. His body was buried in the family tomb in the city of King David. His son Jehoram became the next king after him.

Ahaziah Becomes King of Israel

⁵¹Ahaziah became king of Israel in Samaria. It was in the 17th year that Jehoshaphat was king of Judah. Ahaziah ruled over Israel for two years. He was the son of Ahab.

⁵²Ahaziah did what was evil in the sight of the LORD. He lived the way his father and mother had lived. He lived the way Jeroboam, the son of Nebat, had lived. Jeroboam had caused Israel to commit sin. ⁵³Ahaziah served and worshiped the god Baal. He made the LORD, the God of Israel, very angry. That's exactly what his father had done.

2 KINGS

The book of 2 Kings continues the stories of the kings of Israel and Judah. Both the kings and the people continue to disobey God. Then God steps in. Foreign countries conquer both nations and take their people captive. But throughout the punishment, God promises that he won't forget his people. They will return to their homeland. You can read 2 Kings to understand God's judgment—sin must be punished—and also God's mercy—he will forgive those who are sorry for their sins.

HEROES IN THIS BOOK . . .

ELISHA
PAGE 432

A WIDOW
PAGE 434

WOMAN FROM SHUNEM
PAGE 436

NAAMAN'S SERVANT GIRL
PAGE 438

NAAMAN
PAGE 440

The LORD Judges Ahaziah

1 After Ahab died, Moab refused to remain under Israel's control.

2Ahaziah had fallen through the window of his upstairs room in Samaria. He had hurt himself. So he sent messengers to ask the god Baal-Zebub for advice. Baal-Zebub was the god of the city of Ekron. Ahaziah said to the messengers, "Go and ask Baal-Zebub whether I will get well again."

3But the angel of the LORD spoke to Elijah, who was from Tishbe. He said, "Go up to see the messengers of Ahaziah, the king of Samaria. Tell them, 'You are on your way to ask Baal-Zebub for advice. He is the god of Ekron. Are you going to that god because you think there is no God in Israel?' 4The LORD says to Ahaziah, 'You will never leave the bed you are lying on. You can be sure that you will die!' " So Elijah went to see the messengers.

5They returned to the king. He asked them, "Why have you come back?"

6"A man met us on our way there," they replied. "He said to us, 'Go back to the king who sent you. Tell him, "The LORD says, 'You are sending messengers to ask Baal-Zebub for advice. He is the god of Ekron. Are you going to that god because you think there is no God in Israel? You will never leave the bed you are lying on. You can be sure that you will die!' " ' "

7The king asked them, "What kind of man came to see you? Who told you those things?"

8They replied, "He was wearing clothes that were made out of hair. He had a leather belt around his waist."

The king said, "That was Elijah from Tishbe."

9Then Ahaziah sent a captain to Elijah. The captain had his company of 50 men with him. Elijah was sitting on top of a hill. The captain went up to him. He said to Elijah, "Man of God, the king says, 'Come down!' "

10Elijah answered the captain, "If I'm really a man of God, may fire come down from heaven! May it burn you and your 50 men up!"

Then fire came down from heaven. It burned up the captain and his men.

11After that happened, the king sent another captain to Elijah. The captain had his 50 men with him. He said to Elijah, "Man of God, the king says, 'Come down at once!' "

12Elijah replied, "If I'm really a man of God, may fire come down from heaven! May it burn you and your 50 men up!"

Then the fire of God came down from heaven. It burned up the captain and his 50 men.

13So the king sent a third captain with his 50 men. The captain went up to Elijah. He fell on his knees in front of him. "Man of God," he begged, "please have respect for my life! Please have respect for the lives of these 50 men! 14Fire has come down from heaven. It has burned up the first two captains and all of their men. But please have respect for my life!"

15The angel of the LORD spoke to Elijah. He said, "Go down with him. Don't be afraid of him."

So Elijah got up. He went down with the captain to the king.

16Elijah told the king, "The LORD says, 'You have sent messengers to ask Baal-Zebub for advice. He is the god of Ekron. Did you go to that god for advice because you think there is no God in Israel? You will never leave the bed you are lying on. You can be sure that you will die!' "

17So Ahaziah died. It happened just as the LORD had said it would. He had spoken that message through Elijah.

Ahaziah didn't have any sons. So Joram, his younger brother, became the next king after him. It was the second year of Jehoram, the king of Judah. Jehoram was the son of Jehoshaphat.

18All of the other events of Ahaziah's rule are written down. The things he did are written down. All of those things are written in the official records of the kings of Israel.

Elijah Is Taken Up to Heaven

2 Elijah and Elisha were on their way from Gilgal. The LORD was going to use a strong wind to take Elijah up to heaven. 2Elijah said to Elisha, "Stay here. The LORD has sent me to Bethel."

But Elisha said, "I won't leave you. And that's just as sure as the LORD and you are alive." So they went down to Bethel.

3There was a company of prophets at Bethel. They came out to where Elisha was. They asked him, "Do you know what the LORD is going to do? He's going to take your master away from you today."

"Yes, I know," Elisha replied. "But don't talk about it."

4Then Elijah said to him, "Stay here, Elisha. The LORD has sent me to Jericho."

Elisha replied, "I won't leave you. And that's just as sure as the LORD and you are alive." So they went to Jericho.

5There was a company of prophets at Jericho. They went up to where Elisha was. They asked him, "Do you know what the LORD is going to do? He's going to take your master away from you today."

"Yes, I know," Elisha replied. "But don't talk about it."

⁶Then Elijah said to him, "Stay here. The LORD has sent me to the Jordan River."

Elisha replied, "I won't leave you. And that's just as sure as the LORD and you are alive." So the two of them walked on.

⁷Fifty men from the company of the prophets followed them. The men stopped and stood not far away from them. They faced the place where Elijah and Elisha had stopped at the Jordan River. ⁸Elijah rolled his coat up. Then he struck the water with it. The water parted to the right and to the left. The two of them went across the river on dry ground.

⁹After they had gone across, Elijah spoke to Elisha. He said, "Tell me. What can I do for you before I'm taken away from you?"

"Please give me a double share of your spirit," Elisha replied.

¹⁰"You have asked me for something I can't give you," Elijah said. "Only the LORD can give it. But suppose you see me when I'm taken away from you. Then you will receive what you have asked for. If you don't see me, you won't receive it."

¹¹They kept walking along and talking together. Suddenly a chariot and horses appeared. Fire was all around them. The chariot and horses came between the two men. Then Elijah went up to heaven in a strong wind.

¹²Elisha saw it. He cried out to Elijah, "My father! You are like a father to me! You are the true chariots and horsemen of Israel!"

Elisha didn't see Elijah anymore. Then Elisha took hold of his own clothes and tore them apart.

¹³He picked up the coat that had fallen from Elijah. He went back and stood on the bank of the Jordan River. ¹⁴Then he struck the water with Elijah's coat. "Where is the power of the LORD?" he asked. "Where is the power of the God of Elijah?" When Elisha struck the water, it parted to the right and to the left. He went across the river.

¹⁵The company of the prophets from Jericho were watching. They said, "The spirit of Elijah has been given to Elisha." They went over to him. They bowed down to him with their faces toward the ground. ¹⁶"Look," they said. "We have 50 able men. Let them go and look for your master. Perhaps the Spirit of the LORD has lifted him up. Maybe he has put him down on a mountain or in a valley."

"No," Elisha replied. "Don't send them."

¹⁷But they kept asking until he felt he couldn't say no. So he said, "Send them." And they sent 50 men. They looked for Elijah for three days. But they didn't find him.

¹⁸So they returned to Elisha. He was staying in Jericho. Elisha said to them, "Didn't I tell you not to go?"

Elisha Makes Jericho's Water Pure

¹⁹The men of Jericho spoke to Elisha. "Look," they said. "This town has a good location. You can see that for yourself. But the spring of water here is bad. So the land doesn't produce anything."

²⁰"Bring me a new bowl," Elisha said. "Put some salt in it." So they brought it to him.

²¹Then he went out to the spring. He threw the salt into it. He told them, "The LORD says, 'I have made this water pure. It will never cause death again. It will never keep the land from producing crops again.' " ²²The water has stayed pure to this very day. That's what Elisha had said would happen.

Some Young Fellows Make Fun of Elisha

²³Elisha left Jericho and went up to Bethel. He was walking along the road. Some young fellows came out of the town. They made fun of him. "Go on up! You don't even have any hair on your head!" they said. "Go on up! You don't even have any hair on your head!"

²⁴He turned around and looked at them. And he called down a curse on them. He did it in the name of the LORD. Then two bears came out of the woods. They attacked 42 of the young fellows.

²⁵Elisha went on to Mount Carmel. From there he returned to Samaria.

Moab's King Refuses to Obey Israel's King

3 Joram became king of Israel in Samaria. It was in the 18th year that Jehoshaphat was king of Judah. Joram ruled for 12 years. He was the son of Ahab.

²Joram did what was evil in the sight of the LORD. But he wasn't as bad as his father and mother had been. His father had made a sacred stone that was used to worship the god Baal. Joram got rid of it. ³But he kept on committing the sins of

ELISHA

2 KINGS 2:11

B

[Elijah and Elisha] kept walking along and talking together. Suddenly a chariot and horses appeared. Fire was all around them. The chariot and horses came between the two men. Then Elijah went up to heaven in a strong wind.

T

✝

Elisha walked along the road with Elijah. Elisha had been working with him for a long time, and he knew Elijah was a true prophet from God. He also knew Elijah would be leaving him soon. Elijah's work was done. It was time for Elisha to take over.

Without a warning, Elisha felt himself fly through the air and then land on the side of the road with a thud! A burning heat rushed at him as a fiery horse pulling a fiery chariot raced toward them. Behind the chariot came a roaring wind, so strong **IT TORE AT ELISHA'S ROBES AND ROLLED HIM ALONG THE GROUND.** The wind picked up Elijah and carried him away. Elisha watched as the wind continued to blow and the form of Elijah grew smaller and smaller. Finally, he disappeared. His leader—Elijah—was gone.

Elisha tore his robes and began to cry. He now knew what an amazing man and prophet Elijah had been. He didn't die like ordinary people. God took him away.

Elisha picked up the coat that Elijah dropped when the wind took him away. It was the same coat that Elijah had thrown over him the first time they met. The coat was a sign of the power of Elijah that now belonged to Elisha. Elisha had a job to do. He was now God's voice in the land of Israel.

BE AN ELISHA

Without a doubt, Elisha knew the job ahead of him wasn't going to be easy. He had traveled with Elijah. He knew how much the king of Israel and many of the people hated Elijah. They didn't want to hear his messages from God. They wouldn't want to hear Elisha's either. But he would give them anyway. He was ready to do God's work. Be an Elisha! No matter what others think, do what God wants.

ELISHA WAS READY TO DO GOD'S WORK.
THE WHOLE STORY: 1 KINGS 19:19-21; 2 KINGS 2:1-18

Go to page 434 for the next Super Hero

Jeroboam, the son of Nebat. Jeroboam had also caused Israel to commit those same sins. Joram didn't turn away from them.

⁴Mesha raised sheep. He was king of Moab. He had to supply the king of Israel with 100,000 lambs a year. He also had to supply him with the wool of 100,000 rams a year.

⁵Ahab died. Moab's king refused to obey the next king of Israel. ⁶So at that time King Joram started out from Samaria. He gathered all of Israel's troops together.

⁷He also sent a message to Jehoshaphat, the king of Judah. It said, "The king of Moab is refusing to obey me. Will you go with me to fight against Moab?"

"Yes. I'll go with you," he replied. "My men will go with you. My horses will also go with you."

⁸"What road should we take to attack Moab?" Joram asked.

"The one that goes through the Desert of Edom," Jehoshaphat answered.

⁹So the king of Israel started out. The king of Judah and the king of Edom went with him. Their armies marched around the southern end of the Dead Sea. After seven days they ran out of water. There wasn't any water for the men or their animals.

¹⁰"What should we do now?" exclaimed the king of Israel. "The LORD has called us three kings together. Did he do it only to hand us over to Moab?"

¹¹But Jehoshaphat asked, "Isn't there a prophet of the LORD here? Can't we ask the LORD for advice through him?"

An officer of the king of Israel spoke up. He announced, "Elisha is here. He's the son of Shaphat. Elisha used to serve Elijah."

¹²Jehoshaphat said, "The LORD speaks through him." So the king of Israel went down to see Elisha. Jehoshaphat and the king of Edom also went there.

¹³Elisha spoke to the king of Israel. He said, "What do you and I have in common? Go to your father's prophets. Go to your mother's prophets."

"No," the king of Israel answered. "The LORD called us three kings together. He did it to hand us over to Moab."

¹⁴Elisha said, "I serve the LORD who rules over all. You can be sure that he lives. And you can be just as sure that I have respect for Jehoshaphat, the king of Judah. If I didn't, I wouldn't look at you or even notice you. ¹⁵But now bring me someone who plays the harp."

While that person was playing the harp, the LORD's powerful hand came on Elisha. ¹⁶Elisha announced, "The LORD says, 'Dig a lot of ditches in this valley.' ¹⁷Do it because the LORD says, 'You will not see wind or rain. But this valley will be filled with water. Then you, your cattle and your other animals will have water to drink.'

¹⁸"That's an easy thing for the LORD to do. He will also hand Moab over to you. ¹⁹You will destroy every city that has high walls around it. You will destroy every major town. You will cut down every good tree. You will stop up all of the springs of water. And you will cover every good field with stones."

²⁰The next day, the time came to offer the morning sacrifice. And then it happened! Water was flowing from the direction of Edom! In fact, the land was filled with water!

²¹Now all of the people of Moab had heard that the kings had come to fight against them. So Moab sent for all of its fighting men. It didn't matter whether they were young or old. They sent for everyone who could carry a weapon. All of them were stationed at the border.

²²They got up early in the morning. The sun was already shining on the water. Across the way, the water looked red to the men of Moab. It looked like blood. ²³"That's blood!" they said. "Those kings must have fought and killed each other. Let's go, Moab! Let's take everything that has any value."

²⁴So the men of Moab went to the camp of Israel. Just as they arrived there, the men of Israel got ready to fight. They fought against the men of Moab until they ran away. The men of Israel marched into the land and attacked it. They killed the people of Moab. ²⁵They destroyed the towns. Each man threw a large stone on every good field. They did that until the fields were covered. They stopped up all of the springs of water. And they cut down every good tree. The only town that was left with any stones in place was Kir Hareseth. But men who were armed with slings surrounded it. Then they attacked it.

²⁶The king of Moab saw that the battle had gone against him. So he took with him 700 men who had swords. They tried to break through the battle lines to the king of Edom. But they couldn't do it. ²⁷Then the king of Moab got his oldest son. He was the son who would become the next king after him. He offered his son as a sacrifice on the city wall. That

shocked and terrified the men of Israel. So they pulled back. And they returned to their own land.

Elisha Provides Olive Oil for a Widow

4 The wife of a man from the company of the prophets cried out to Elisha. She said, "My husband is dead. You know how much respect he had for the Lord. But he owed money to someone. And now that person is coming to take my two boys away. They will become his slaves."

²Elisha replied to her, "How can I help you? Tell me. What do you have in your house?"

"I don't have anything there at all," she said. "All I have is a little olive oil."

³Elisha said, "Go around to all of your neighbors. Ask them for empty jars. Get as many as you can. ⁴Then go inside your house. Shut the door behind you and your sons. Pour oil into all of the jars. As each jar is filled, put it over to one side."

⁵The woman left him. After that, she shut the door behind her and her sons. They brought the jars to her. And she kept pouring. ⁶When all of the jars were full,

A WIDOW

2 KINGS 4:7

Go and sell the oil. Pay what you owe. You and your sons can live on what is left.

The widow walked into the room and locked the door behind her. By the light of the lamp, she could see the jars her sons had collected. **BIG JARS. LITTLE JARS. FAT JARS. SKINNY JARS.** They covered the table, the chairs and the floor under the table.

The widow had gone to the prophet Elisha. Her husband was dead, and her sons were going into slavery to pay for his debts. She cried to Elisha for help. Now she was doing exactly as he had told her to do.

The widow took the small jar of oil. It was all she had left. Just as the prophet told her, she began pouring. The little jar of oil never ran out! How amazing! She filled jar after jar with oil— enough to pay her husband's debts and save her sons from slavery.

BE LIKE THE WIDOW

The widow obeyed Elisha's instructions, even though they didn't make sense. How could she possibly fill all those jars with oil from one little jar? But God blessed her because she obeyed, and all the jars were filled. Be like the widow. Obey God. He is waiting to bless you, too!

THE WIDOW OBEYED GOD, AND HE BLESSED HER AND TOOK CARE OF HER AND HER SONS.

Go to page 436 for the next Super Hero

she spoke to one of her sons. She said, "Bring me another jar."

But he replied, "There aren't any more left." Then the oil stopped flowing.

7She went and told the man of God about it. He said, "Go and sell the oil. Pay what you owe. You and your sons can live on what is left."

The Son of a Woman From Shunem Is Brought Back to Life

8One day Elisha went to the town of Shunem. A rich woman lived there. She begged him to stay and have a meal. So every time he came by, he stopped there to eat.

9The woman said to her husband, "That man often comes by here. I know that he is a holy man of God. **10**Let's make a small room for him on the roof. We'll put a bed and a table in it. We'll also put a chair and a lamp in it. Then he can stay there when he comes to visit us."

11One day Elisha came. He went up to his room. He lay down there. **12**He said to his servant Gehazi, "Go and get the Shunammite woman." So he did. She stood in front of Elisha.

13He said to Gehazi, "Tell her, 'You have gone to a lot of trouble for us. Now what can we do for you? Can we speak to the king for you? Or can we speak to the commander of the army for you?' "

She replied, "I live among my own people. I have everything I need here."

14After she left, Elisha asked Gehazi, "What can we do for her?"

Gehazi said, "Well, she doesn't have a son. And her husband is old."

15Then Elisha said, "Bring her here again." So he did. She stood in the doorway. **16**"You will hold a son in your arms," Elisha said. "It will be about this time next year."

"No, my master!" she objected. "You are a man of God. So don't lie to me!"

17But the woman became pregnant. She had a baby boy. It happened the next year about that same time. That's exactly what Elisha had told her would happen.

18The child grew. One day he went out to get his father. His father was with those who were gathering the crops.

19The boy said to his father, "My head hurts! It really hurts!"

His father told a servant, "Carry him to his mother." **20**The servant lifted the boy up. He carried him to his mother.

The boy sat on her lap until noon. Then he died. **21**She went up to the room on the roof. There she laid him on the bed of the man of God. Then she shut the door and went out.

22She sent for her husband. She said, "Please send me one of the servants and a donkey. Then I can go quickly to the man of God and return."

23"Why do you want to go to him today?" he asked. "It isn't the time for the New Moon Feast. It isn't the Sabbath day."

"Don't let that bother you," she said.

24She put a saddle on her donkey. She said to her servant, "Let's go. Don't slow down for me unless I tell you to." **25**So she started out. She came to Mount Carmel. That's where the man of God was.

When she was still a long way off, he saw her coming. He said to his servant Gehazi, "Look! There's the woman from Shunem! **26**Run out there to meet her. Ask her, 'Are you all right? Is your husband all right? Is your child all right?' "

"Everything is all right," she said.

27She came to the man of God at the mountain. Then she took hold of his feet. Gehazi came over to push her away. But the man of God said, "Leave her alone! She is suffering terribly. But the Lord hasn't told me the reason for it. He has hidden it from me."

28"My master, did I ask you for a son?" she said. "Didn't I tell you, 'Don't get my hopes up'?"

29Elisha said to Gehazi, "Tuck your coat into your belt. Take my wooden staff and run to Shunem. Don't say hello to anyone you see. If anyone says hello to you, don't answer. Lay my staff on the boy's face."

30But the child's mother said, "I won't leave you. And that's just as sure as the Lord and you are alive." So Elisha got up and followed her.

31Gehazi went on ahead. He laid Elisha's wooden staff on the boy's face. But there wasn't any sound. The boy didn't move at all.

So Gehazi went back to Elisha. He told him, "The boy hasn't awakened."

32Elisha arrived at the house. The boy was dead. He was lying on Elisha's bed.

33Elisha went into the room. He shut the door. He was alone with the boy. He prayed to the Lord.

34Then he got on the bed. He lay down on the boy. His mouth touched the boy's mouth. His eyes touched the boy's eyes. And his hands touched the boy's hands. As Elisha lay on the boy, the boy's body grew warm.

35Elisha turned away. He walked back and forth in the room. Then he got on the bed again. He lay down on the boy once

WOMAN FROM SHUNEM

K

T

2 KINGS 4:17

The woman...had a baby boy. It happened the next year about that same time. That's exactly what Elisha had told her would happen.

Every time Elisha came to Shunem he stayed with the same woman and her husband. They were always kind to him. They built a room on the roof of their house especially for him. Elisha wanted to do something kind for them. But the woman said she needed nothing. Elisha's servant, however, saw something. "They have no children," he said.

A year later, the woman had a baby boy. She held his little body close and smiled. She never thought she would have children. Now she had a son.

The little boy grew. One day he went to the fields with his father. Working in the hot fields one day, his head began to ache. It hurt until he began to cry. "Carry him home to his mother," his father told a servant.

The little boy felt better as soon as his mother held him. She rocked him. But, little by little, his breathing slowed, his movements stopped, and he died.

The boy's mother carried him up to Elisha's room and laid him on the prophet's bed. Then she rushed out the door to find the prophet. He could help her! SHE SADDLED HER DONKEY AND RODE AS FAST AS SHE COULD.

When the woman found Elisha, she cried, "I told you I needed nothing. But you gave me a son. Now he has died, and I'm worse off than I was before!"

Elisha went with her to her house. He shut the door of his room and covered the little boy's body with his own. Slowly, little by little, the boy began to get warm. His eyes fluttered open. He sneezed seven times. He was alive. Elijah called the woman. She came in and cried with joy when she saw her boy.

BE LIKE THE WOMAN FROM SHUNEM

She was a kind woman who did all she could to make life good for Elisha when he was in her town. She trusted that Elisha could help her when her son was in trouble. You can be like her. Be kind to those around you. Help those who need help. And be willing to trust others to help you when you need it.

SHE TRUSTED THAT GOD COULD HEAL HER SON
THE WHOLE STORY: 2 KINGS 4:8-37

Go to page 438 for the next Super Hero

more. The boy sneezed seven times. After that, he opened his eyes.

36Elisha sent for Gehazi. He said to him, "Go and get the Shunammite woman." So he did. When she came, Elisha said, "Take your son."

37She came in. She fell at Elisha's feet. She bowed down with her face toward the ground. Then she took her son and went out.

Deadly Food in a Pot

38Elisha returned to Gilgal. There wasn't enough food to eat in that area. The company of the prophets was meeting with Elisha. So he said to his servant, "Put the large pot over the fire. Cook some stew for these men."

39One of them went out into the fields to gather herbs. He found a wild vine. He gathered up some of its gourds. He brought them back with him in his coat. Then he cut them up into the pot of stew. But no one knew what they were.

40The stew was poured out for the men. They began to eat it. But then they cried out, "Man of God, the food in that pot will kill us!" They couldn't eat it.

41Elisha said, "Get some flour." He put it in the pot. He said, "Serve it to the men to eat." Then there wasn't anything in the pot that could harm them.

Elisha Feeds 100 People

42A man came from Baal Shalishah. He brought the man of God 20 loaves of barley bread. They had been baked from the first grain that had ripened. He also brought some heads of new grain. "Give this food to the people to eat," Elisha said.

43"How can I put this in front of 100 men?" his servant asked.

But Elisha answered, "Give it to the people to eat. Do it because the LORD says, 'They will eat and have some left over.' "

44Then the servant put the food in front of them. They ate it and had some left over. It happened just as the LORD had said it would.

Naaman Is Healed of a Skin Disease

5 Naaman was commander of the army of the king of Aram. He was a very important man in the eyes of his master. And he was highly respected. That's because the LORD had helped him win the battle over Aram's enemies. He was a brave soldier. But he had a skin disease.

2Companies of soldiers from Aram had marched out. They had captured a young girl from Israel. She became a servant of Naaman's wife. **3**She spoke to the woman she was serving. She said, "I wish my master would go and see the prophet who is in Samaria. He would heal my master of his skin disease."

4Naaman went to see his own master. He told him what the girl from Israel had said.

5"I think you should go," the king of Aram replied. "I'll give you a letter to take to the king of Israel."

So Naaman left. He took 750 pounds of silver with him. He also took 150 pounds of gold. And he took ten sets of clothes. **6**He carried the letter to the king of Israel. It said, "I'm sending my servant Naaman to you with this letter. I want you to heal him of his skin disease."

7The king of Israel read the letter. As soon as he did, he tore his royal robes. He said, "Am I God? Can I kill people and bring them back to life? Why does this fellow send someone to me to be healed of his skin disease? He must be trying to pick a fight with me!"

8Elisha, the man of God, heard that the king of Israel had torn his robes. So he sent the king a message. It said, "Why have you torn your robes? Tell the man to come to me. Then he will know there is a prophet in Israel."

9So Naaman went to see Elisha. He took his horses and chariots with him. He stopped at the door of Elisha's house. **10**Elisha sent a messenger out to him. The messenger said, "Go. Wash yourself in the Jordan River seven times. Then your skin will be healed. You will be pure and clean again."

11But Naaman went away angry. He said, "I was sure he would come out to me. I thought he would stand there and pray to the LORD his God. I thought he would wave his hand over my skin. Then I would be healed. **12**And what about the Abana and Pharpar rivers of Damascus? Aren't they better than any of the rivers of Israel? Couldn't I wash in them and be made pure and clean?" So he turned and went away. He was burning with anger.

13Naaman's servants went over to him. They said, "You are like a father to us. What if the prophet Elisha had told you to do some great thing? Wouldn't you have done it? But he only said, 'Wash yourself. Then you will be pure and clean.' You should be even more willing to do that!"

14So Naaman went down to the Jordan River. He dipped himself in it seven times.

B

★

K

2 KINGS 5:2-3

A young girl from Israel...said, "I wish my master would go and see the prophet who is in Samaria. He would heal my master of his skin disease."

The young Israelite slave girl watched as her master, Naaman, limped into his wife's room. His wife tried to keep the tears from forming in her eyes. But her husband, the strong and powerful commander of armies, was sick. Naaman had a skin disease.

The young Israelite girl had been captured in a war with the commander's army. He took her home and gave her to his wife as a slave. The young girl served the wife carefully and obediently.

When the young girl realized how much Naaman suffered, she knew what she had to do. Usually, she was told to keep quiet. She went about her duties and said little. BUT TODAY SHE WOULD SPEAK UP.

As soon as Naaman left the room, the servant girl went to her mistress. She stood quietly until her mistress gave her permission to speak. "I wish my master would go to Samaria in my country to see the prophet Elisha," the girl said to her mistress. "He would heal him."

Naaman learned about the servant girl's idea. He was willing to try anything to be healed, and so he did as she suggested. Many weeks later, he returned. As soon as he walked into the house, his wife and the Israelite slave girl could see he had been healed. He had many stories to tell of all that had happened to him in Samaria. But the most exciting one of all was how the God of Israel had healed him of his skin disease.

BE LIKE NAAMAN'S SERVANT GIRL

Sometimes being kind means stepping out and speaking up when you'd rather be quiet. Sometimes being kind means *doing* something, not just *waiting* for something to happen. Naaman's servant girl spoke up when she knew it would be the kind thing to do. Be like her. Speak up when you know it will help others.

SHE SPOKE UP WHEN IT WOULD HELP HER MASTER. THE WHOLE STORY: 2 KINGS 5:1-27

Go to page 440 for the next Super Hero

He did exactly what the man of God had told him to do. Then his skin was made pure again. It became clean like the skin of a young boy.

¹⁵Naaman and all of his attendants went back to the man of God. Naaman stood in front of Elisha. He said, "Now I know that there is no God anywhere in the whole world except in Israel. Please accept a gift from me."

¹⁶The prophet answered, "I serve the LORD. You can be sure that he lives. And you can be just as sure that I won't accept a gift from you." Even though Naaman begged him to take it, Elisha wouldn't.

¹⁷"I can see that you won't accept a gift from me," said Naaman. "But please let me have some soil from your land. Give me as much as a pair of mules can carry. Here's why I want it. I won't ever bring burnt offerings and sacrifices to any other god again. I'll bring them only to the LORD. I'll worship him on his own soil.

¹⁸"But there is one thing I hope the LORD will forgive me for. From time to time my master will enter the temple to bow down to his god Rimmon. When he does, he'll lean on my arm. Then I'll have to bow down there also. I hope the LORD will forgive me for that."

¹⁹"Go in peace," Elisha said.

Naaman started out on his way.

²⁰Gehazi was the servant of Elisha, the man of God. Gehazi said to himself, "My master was too easy on Naaman from Aram. He should have accepted the gift he brought. I'm going to run after Naaman. I'm going to get something from him. And that's just as sure as the LORD is alive."

²¹Gehazi hurried after Naaman. Naaman saw him running toward him. So he got down from the chariot to greet him. "Is everything all right?" he asked.

²²"Everything is all right," Gehazi answered. "My master sent me to say, 'Two young men from the company of the prophets have just come to me. They've come from the hill country of Ephraim. Please give them 75 pounds of silver and two sets of clothes.' "

²³"I wish you would take twice as much silver," said Naaman. He begged Gehazi to accept it. Then Naaman tied up 150 pounds of silver in two bags. He also gave Gehazi two sets of clothes. He gave all of it to two of his own servants. They carried it ahead of Gehazi.

²⁴Gehazi came to the hill where Elisha lived. Then the servants handed the things over to Gehazi. He put them away in Elisha's house. He sent the men away,

and they left. ²⁵Then he went back inside the house. He stood in front of his master Elisha.

"Gehazi, where have you been?" Elisha asked.

"I didn't go anywhere," Gehazi answered.

²⁶But Elisha said to him, "Didn't my spirit go with you? I know that the man got down from his chariot to greet you. Is this the time for you to accept money or clothes? Is it the time to take olive groves, vineyards, flocks or herds? Is it the time to accept male and female servants? ²⁷You and your children after you will have Naaman's skin disease forever."

Then Gehazi left Elisha. And he had Naaman's skin disease. His skin was as white as snow.

An Ax Blade Floats

6 The company of the prophets spoke to Elisha. They said, "Look. The place where we meet with you is too small for us. ²We would like to go to the Jordan River. Each of us can get some wood there. We want to build a place there for us to live in."

Elisha said, "Go."

³Then one of them said, "Won't you please come with us?"

"I will," Elisha replied. ⁴And he went with them.

They went to the Jordan. There they began to cut down trees. ⁵One of them was cutting a tree down. The iron blade of his ax fell into the water. "Master!" he cried out. "This ax was borrowed!"

⁶The man of God asked, "Where did the blade fall?" He showed him the place. Then Elisha cut a stick and threw it there. That made the iron blade float. ⁷"Take it out of the water," he said. So the man reached out and took it.

Elisha Makes the Soldiers of Aram Blind

⁸The king of Aram was at war with Israel. He talked things over with his officers. Then he said, "I'm going to set up my camp in a certain place."

⁹The man of God sent a message to the king of Israel. It said, "Try to stay away from that place. Aram's army is going to be down there." ¹⁰The king of Israel checked on the place the man of God had told him about. Time after time Elisha warned the king. So the king was on guard in those places.

¹¹All of that made the king of Aram very angry. He sent for his officers. He said

NAAMAN

2 KINGS 5:14

> **So Naaman went down to the Jordan River. He dipped himself in it seven times. He did exactly what the man of God had told him to do. Then his skin was made pure again. It became clean like the skin of a young boy.**

Naaman (NAY-mun) commanded the king's armies. He had an important position. But it could all be gone if he didn't find a cure for his skin disease.

One evening, Naaman's wife told him what their slave girl from Israel had suggested. Naaman's wife urged him to try seeing Elisha. Maybe Elisha could heal him.

In Samaria, Naaman found Elisha's house. Elisha himself didn't even come out to greet him. *Didn't this Elisha know what an important man he was?* Elisha just sent a servant who told Naaman to wash himself seven times in the Jordan River.

Now Naaman was furious. "I could just as easily have washed in the rivers of my own country!" he yelled. "Let's go home." But his servants didn't agree. What? His servants thought he should do it? Well, what did he have to lose?

Arriving at the Jordan River, Naaman got out of his chariot and walked quickly into the muddy water. **HE BENT HIS KNEES AND WENT UNDER.** He did it again and again, dipping himself seven times, just as Elisha had ordered.

Naaman came up out of the river, expecting to travel home in the same condition he had come. But he stopped when he saw his servant's faces. None of them said a word.

Almost scared to look, Naaman raised his hand up in front of his face. The skin looked clean and fresh, just like a baby's skin. He felt his nose. The skin felt smooth and soft. He had been healed! The God of Israel had healed him, just by doing such a little thing. Now he knew for sure! There was no God more powerful than the God of Israel!

BE A NAAMAN

The simplest, smallest things are important and significant if God is involved. Naaman discovered that. He was healed just by being obedient and doing a small thing. God may want you to do something simple for him. Be a Naaman. Be obedient and do what God wants, whether it's big or small.

NAAMAN DID AND SMALL THING AND WAS HEALED.
THE WHOLE STORY: 2 KINGS 5:1-27

Go to page 445 for the next person

to them, "Tell me. Which of us is on the side of the king of Israel?"

12"You are my king and master," said one of his officers. "None of us is on Israel's side. But Elisha is a prophet in Israel. He tells the king of Israel the very words you speak in your own bedroom."

13"Go and find out where he is," the king ordered. "Then I can send my men and capture him." The report came back. It said, "He's in Dothan."

14Then the king sent horses and chariots and a strong army there. They went at night and surrounded the city.

15The servant of the man of God got up the next morning. He went out early. He saw that an army with horses and chariots had surrounded the city. "My master!" the servant said. "What can we do?"

16"Don't be afraid," the prophet answered. "Those who are with us are more than those who are with them."

17Elisha prayed, "Lord, open my servant's eyes so he can see." Then the Lord opened his eyes. He looked up and saw the hills. He saw that Elisha was surrounded by horses and chariots. Fire was all around them.

18Aram's army came down toward Elisha. Then he prayed to the Lord. He said, "Make these soldiers blind." So the Lord made them blind, just as Elisha had prayed.

19Elisha told them, "This isn't the right road. This isn't the right city. Follow me. I'll lead you to the man you are looking for." He led them to Samaria.

20They entered the city. Then Elisha said, "Lord, open the eyes of these men. Help them see again." Then the Lord opened their eyes. They looked around. And there they were, inside Samaria!

21The king of Israel saw them. So he asked Elisha, "Should I kill them? I need your advice. You are like a father to me. Should I kill them?"

22"Don't kill them," he answered. "Would you kill men you have captured with your own sword or bow? Put some food and water in front of them. Then they can eat and drink. They can go back to their master."

23So he prepared a big dinner for them. After they had finished eating and drinking, he sent them away. They returned to their master. So the companies of soldiers from Aram stopped attacking Israel's territory.

Aram's Army Attacks Samaria

24Some time later, Ben-Hadad gathered his entire army together. Ben-Hadad was the king of Aram. His army marched up and surrounded Samaria. Then they attacked it.

25There wasn't enough food anywhere in the city. It was surrounded for so long that people had to weigh out two pounds of silver for a donkey's head. They had to weigh out two ounces of silver for half a pint of seed pods.

26One day the king of Israel was walking on top of the wall. A woman cried out to him, "You are my king and master. Please help me!"

27The king replied, "If the Lord doesn't help you, where can I get help for you? From the threshing floor? From the winepress?" 28He continued, "What's wrong?"

She answered, "A woman said to me, 'Give up your son. Then we can eat him today. Tomorrow we'll eat my son.' 29So we cooked my son. Then we ate him. The next day I said to her, 'Give up your son. Then we can eat him.' But she had hidden him."

30When the king heard the woman's words, he tore his royal robes. As he walked along the wall, the people looked up at him. They saw that he was wearing black clothes under his robes. 31He said, "I'll cut the head of Shaphat's son Elisha off his shoulders today. If I don't, may God punish me greatly!"

32Elisha was sitting in his house. The elders were sitting there with him. The king went to see Elisha. He sent a messenger on ahead of him. Before the messenger arrived, Elisha spoke to the elders. He said, "That murderer is sending someone here to cut my head off. Can't you see that? When the messenger comes, close the door. Hold it shut against him. Can't you hear his master's footsteps right behind him?"

33Elisha was still talking to the elders when the messenger came down to him. The king also arrived. He said, "The Lord has sent this horrible trouble on us. Why should I wait any longer for him to help us?"

7 Elisha said, "Listen to a message from the Lord. He says, 'About this time tomorrow, you will be able to buy seven quarts of flour for less than half of an ounce of silver. You will also be able to buy 13 quarts of barley for the same price. That's all you will have to pay for those things at the gate of Samaria.' "

2The king was leaning on an officer's arm. The officer spoke to the man of God. He said, "Suppose the Lord opens the windows of the skies. Suppose he pours food down on us. Even if he does, could what you are saying really happen?"

"You will see it with your own eyes," answered Elisha. "But you won't eat any of it!"

The Attack on Samaria Ends

3There were four men who had a skin disease. They were at the entrance of the gate of Samaria. They said to one another, "Why should we stay here until we die? 4Suppose we say, 'We'll go into the city.' There isn't any food there, and we'll die. But if we stay here, we'll die anyway. So let's go over to Aram's army camp. Let's give ourselves up. If they spare us, we'll live. If they kill us, we'll die."

5At sunset they got up. They went to Aram's army camp. They arrived at the edge of it. But no one was there. 6The Lord had caused the soldiers of Aram to hear a noise. It sounded like chariots and horses and a huge army. So the soldiers spoke to one another. They said, "Listen! The king of Israel has hired the Hittite and Egyptian kings. He has paid them to attack us!" 7So they had gotten up and had run away at sunset. They had left their tents and horses and donkeys behind. They had left the camp as it was. And they had run for their lives.

8The men who had a skin disease arrived at the edge of the camp. They entered one of the tents. They ate and drank. Then they carried away silver, gold and clothes. They went off and hid them. They returned and entered another tent. They took some things from it and hid them also.

9But then they said to one another, "What we're doing isn't right. This is a day of good news. And we're keeping it to ourselves. If we wait until sunrise, we'll be punished. Let's go at once. Let's report this to the royal palace."

10So they went. They called out to the people who were guarding the city gates. They told them, "We went into Aram's army camp. No one was there. We didn't hear anyone. The horses and donkeys were still tied up. The tents were left just as they were."

11The people who guarded the gates shouted the news. It was reported inside the palace.

12The king of Israel got up in the night. He spoke to his officers. He said, "I'll tell you what the men of Aram have done to us. They know we are very hungry. So they have left the camp to hide in the countryside. They are thinking, 'We are sure they'll come out. Then we'll take them alive. And we'll get into the city.'"

13One of the king's officers spoke up. He said, "A few horses are still left in the city. Have some men get five of them. They won't be any worse off than all of the other Israelites who are left here. In fact, all of us will soon be dead. So let's send the men to find out what happened."

14The men chose two chariots and their horses. The king sent them out to look for Aram's army. He commanded the drivers, "Go and find out what has happened."

15They followed the trail of Aram's soldiers all the way to the Jordan River. They found clothes and supplies all along the road. The soldiers had thrown them down when they ran away. So the men returned. They reported to the king what they had seen.

16Then the people went out of the city. They took everything of value from Aram's army camp. So seven quarts of flour sold for less than half of an ounce of silver. And 13 quarts of barley sold for the same price. That's exactly what the Lord had said would happen.

17The king had put an officer in charge of the city gate. He was the officer on whose arm the king leaned. On their way out of the city, the people knocked the officer down. In the entrance of the gate they walked all over him. And he died. That's exactly what the man of God had said would happen. He had said it when the king came down to his house.

18What the man of God had told the king came true. He had said, "About this time tomorrow, you will be able to buy seven quarts of flour for less than half of an ounce of silver. You will also be able to buy 13 quarts of barley for the same price. That's all you will have to pay for those things at the gate of Samaria."

19The officer had spoken to the man of God. He had said, "Suppose the Lord opens the windows of the skies. Suppose he pours food down on us. Even if he does, could what you are saying really happen?" The man of God had replied, "You will see it with your own eyes. But you won't eat any of it!"

20And that's exactly what happened to the officer. On their way out of the city, the people knocked him down. In the entrance of the gate they walked all over him. And he died.

The Woman from Shunem Gets Her Land Back

8 Elisha had brought a woman's son back to life. He had said to her, "Go away with your family. Stay for a while anywhere you can. The LORD has decided that there won't be enough food in the land. That will be true for seven years."

2 The woman did just as the man of God told her to. She and her family went away. They stayed in the land of the Philistines for seven years.

3 The seven years passed. Then she came back from the land of the Philistines. She went to the king of Israel. She wanted to beg him to get her house and land back.

4 The king was talking to Gehazi. Gehazi was the servant of the man of God. The king had said, "Tell me about all of the great things Elisha has done." 5 Gehazi was telling the king how Elisha had brought a dead boy back to life. Just then the woman came to beg the king to get her house and land back. She was the woman whose son Elisha had brought back to life.

Gehazi said, "King Joram, this is the woman I've been telling you about. And this is her son. He's the one Elisha brought back to life." 6 The king asked the woman about her house and land. And she told him.

Then he appointed an official to look into her case. The king told him, "Give her back everything that belonged to her. That includes all of the money that was earned from her land. It was earned from the day she left the country until now."

Hazael Murders Ben-Hadad

7 Elisha went to Damascus. Ben-Hadad was sick. He was king of Aram. The king was told, "The man of God has come all the way up here."

8 Then the king said to Hazael, "Take a gift with you. Go and see the man of God. Ask him for the LORD's advice. Ask him whether I will get well again."

9 Hazael went to see Elisha. He took 40 camels with him as a gift. The camels were loaded with all of the finest goods of Damascus. Hazael went into Elisha's house and stood in front of him. He said, "Ben-Hadad has sent me. He is the king of Aram. He asks, 'Will I get well again?'"

10 Elisha answered, "Go and speak to him. Tell him, 'Yes. You will get well again.' But the LORD has shown me that he will in fact die."

11 Elisha stared at him without looking away. He did it until Hazael felt ashamed. Then the man of God began to sob.

12 "Why are you sobbing?" asked Hazael.

"Because I know how much harm you will do to the people of Israel," he answered. "You will set fire to their cities that have high walls around them. You will kill their young men with your sword. You will smash their little children on the ground. You will rip open their pregnant women."

13 Hazael said, "How could I possibly do a thing like that? I'm nothing but a dog. I don't have that kind of power."

"You will become king of Aram," Elisha answered. "That's what the LORD has shown me."

14 Then Hazael left Elisha. He returned to his master. Ben-Hadad asked, "What did Elisha say to you?"

Hazael replied, "He told me you would get well again."

15 But the next day Hazael got a thick cloth. He soaked it in water. He spread it over the king's face. He held it there until the king died. Then Hazael became the next king after him.

Jehoram Becomes King of Judah

16 Jehoram began to rule as king over Judah. It was in the fifth year that Joram was king of Israel. Joram was the son of Ahab. Jehoram was the son of Jehoshaphat. 17 Jehoram was 32 years old when he became king. He ruled in Jerusalem for eight years.

18 He followed the ways of the kings of Israel, just as the royal family of Ahab had done. In fact, he got married to a daughter of Ahab. Jehoram did what was evil in the sight of the LORD.

19 But the LORD didn't want to destroy Judah. That's because the LORD had made a covenant with his servant David. He had promised to keep the lamp of David's kingdom burning brightly for him and his children after him forever.

20 When Jehoram was king over Judah, Edom refused to remain under Judah's control. They set up their own king. 21 So Jehoram went to Zair. He took all of his chariots with him. The men of Edom surrounded him and his chariot commanders. He got up at night and fought his way out. But his army ran back home.

22 To this very day Edom has refused to remain under Judah's control. At that same time, Libnah also refused to remain under the control of Judah.

23 The other events of Jehoram's rule are

written down. Everything he did is written down. All of those things are written in the official records of the kings of Judah.

24Jehoram joined the members of his family who had already died. His body was buried in the family tomb in the City of David. His son Ahaziah became the next king after him.

Ahaziah Becomes King of Judah

25Ahaziah began to rule as king over Judah. It was in the 12th year that Joram was king of Israel. Joram was the son of Ahab. Ahaziah was the son of Jehoram. 26Ahaziah was 22 years old when he became king. He ruled in Jerusalem for one year. His mother's name was Athaliah. She was a granddaughter of Omri. Omri had been the king of Israel.

27Ahaziah followed the ways of the royal family of Ahab. Ahaziah did what was evil in the sight of the LORD, just as the family of Ahab had done. That's because he had married into Ahab's family.

28Ahaziah joined forces with Joram. They went to war against Hazael at Ramoth Gilead. Joram was the son of Ahab. Hazael was king of Aram. The soldiers of Aram wounded King Joram. 29So he returned to Jezreel to give his wounds time to heal. The soldiers of Aram had wounded him at Ramoth in his battle against Hazael, the king of Aram.

Ahaziah, the son of Jehoram, went down to Jezreel. He went there to see Joram. That's because Joram had been wounded. Ahaziah was king of Judah. Joram was the son of Ahab.

Jehu Is Anointed as King of Israel

9 The prophet Elisha sent for a man from the company of the prophets. Elisha said to him, "Tuck your coat into your belt. Take this bottle of olive oil with you. Go to Ramoth Gilead.

2"When you get there, look for Jehu. He's the son of Jehoshaphat, the son of Nimshi. Go to him. Get him away from his companions. Take him into an inside room. 3Then get the bottle. Pour the oil on his head. Announce to him, 'The LORD says, "I anoint you as king over Israel." ' After that, open the door and run away. Do it quickly!"

4So the young prophet went to Ramoth Gilead. 5When he arrived, he found the army officers sitting together. "Commander, I have a message for you," he said.

"For which one of us?" asked Jehu.

"For you, commander," he replied.

6Jehu got up and went into the house. Then the prophet poured the oil on Jehu's head. He announced, "The LORD is the God of Israel. He says, 'I am anointing you as king over my people Israel. 7You must destroy the royal house of your master Ahab. I will pay them back for spilling the blood of my servants the prophets. I will also pay them back for the blood of all of my servants that Jezebel spilled. 8The whole house of Ahab will die out. I will cut off every male in Israel who is related to Ahab. It does not matter whether they are slaves or free.

9" 'I will make Ahab's royal house like the house of Jeroboam, the son of Nebat. I will make it like the house of Baasha, the son of Ahijah. 10Dogs will eat up Jezebel on a piece of land at Jezreel. No one will bury her.' " Then the prophet opened the door and ran away.

11Jehu went out to where the other officers were. One of them asked him, "Is everything all right? Why did that crazy man come to you?"

"You know the man. You know the kinds of things he says," Jehu replied.

12"That's not true!" they said. "Tell us."

Jehu said, "Here is what he told me. He announced, 'The LORD says, "I am anointing you as king over Israel." ' "

13The officers quickly grabbed their coats. They spread them out under Jehu on the bare steps of the house. Then they blew a trumpet. They shouted, "Jehu is king!"

Jehu Kills Joram and Ahaziah

14Jehu was the son of Jehoshaphat, the son of Nimshi. Jehu made plans against Joram. During that time Joram and Israel's whole army had been guarding Ramoth Gilead. They had been guarding it against Hazael, the king of Aram.

15But King Joram had returned to Jezreel. He had gone there to give his wounds time to heal. The soldiers of Aram had wounded him in his battle against Hazael, the king of Aram.

Jehu said to his men, "Are you really on my side? If you are, don't let anyone sneak out of the city. Don't let them go and tell the news in Jezreel." 16Then Jehu got into his chariot. He rode off to Jezreel. Joram was resting there. And Ahaziah, the king of Judah, had gone down to see him.

17A lookout was standing on the roof of the tower in Jezreel. He saw Jehu's troops approaching. So he called out, "I see some troops coming."

"Get a horseman," Joram ordered. "Send him to ride out to them. Have him ask, 'Are you coming in peace?' "

18The horseman rode out to where Jehu was. He said, "The king asks, 'Are you coming in peace?' "

"What do you know about peace?" Jehu answered. "Get in line behind me."

The lookout reported, "The messenger has reached them. But he isn't coming back."

19So the king sent out a second horseman. When he came to them, he told them, "The king asks, 'Are you coming in peace?' "

Jehu replied, "What do you know about peace? Get in line behind me."

20The lookout reported, "The second messenger has reached them. But he isn't coming back either. The one driving the chariot drives like Jehu, the son of Nimshi. He's driving like a crazy man."

21"Get my chariot ready," King Joram ordered. When it was ready, he rode out. Ahaziah, the king of Judah, rode out with him. Each of them was in his own chariot.

JEZEBEL

(Not!)

2 KINGS 9:7-8

I will also pay them back for the blood of all of my servants that Jezebel spilled. The whole house of Ahab will die out.

Queen Jezebel (JEZZ-uh-bell) sat in front of her mirror and put dark blue powder on her eyelids. She leaned forward to check her teeth, then held out a hand to check her long nails. Her black hair hung down to her waist until she screeched at a slave girl to come and put it up on her head. Her hair and face and nails finally done to her satisfaction, Jezebel stood up. She held out her arms for her richly sewn robe. She scrunched the belt tight around her bony waist. Then she went to sit in the window.

QUEEN JEZEBEL DIDN'T KNOW IT, BUT TODAY WAS HER LAST. She had gotten all dressed up only to die. She had spent her life fighting God and turning others away from him. She had killed God's prophets. She had had innocent people killed and had stolen from them. Now she would receive fair punishment for her sins.

JEZEBEL

Jezebel is probably known as one of the most wicked women of the Bible. She did everything she could to fight God. How senseless. If only she had believed God and turned toward him instead of away. He would have blessed her and preserved her life. Remember foolish Jezebel. God loves you and wants you to turn toward him, not away.

JEZEBEL CHOSE TO FIGHT GOD INSTEAD OF FOLLOW HIM.

Go to page 448 for the next Super Hero

They both went to meet Jehu. They met him at the piece of land that had belonged to Naboth from Jezreel.

22 When Joram saw Jehu he asked, "Have you come here in peace, Jehu?"

"Your mother Jezebel worships statues of gods," Jehu replied. "She also worships evil powers. The evil things she does have spread everywhere. As long as all of that goes on, how can there be peace?"

23 Joram turned around and tried to get away. He called out to Ahaziah. He said, "It's treason, Ahaziah!"

24 Then Jehu shot an arrow at Joram. It hit him between the shoulders. It went through his heart. He sank down slowly in his chariot.

25 Jehu spoke to Bidkar, his chariot officer. He said, "Pick him up. Throw him on the field that belonged to Naboth from Jezreel. Remember how you and I were riding together in chariots behind Joram's father Ahab? It was when the LORD made a prophecy about him. He announced, 26 'Yesterday I saw the blood of Naboth and the blood of his sons. You can be sure that I will make you pay for it on this piece of land.' So pick him up. Throw him on that piece of land. That's what the LORD said would happen."

27 Ahaziah, the king of Judah, saw what had happened. So he tried to get away. He went up the road toward Beth Haggan.

Jehu chased him. He shouted, "Kill him too!" Jehu's men wounded Ahaziah in his chariot. It happened on the way up to Gur near Ibleam. But he escaped to Megiddo. And that's where he died.

28 Ahaziah's servants took him to Jerusalem in his chariot. They buried his body in his family tomb in the City of David. 29 Ahaziah had become king of Judah. It was in the 11th year of Joram, the son of Ahab.

Jehu Kills Jezebel

30 Jehu went to Jezreel. Jezebel heard about it. So she put makeup on her eyes and fixed her hair. She looked out of a window. 31 Jehu entered the gate below. Then Jezebel said, "You are just like Zimri. You murdered your master. Have you come here in peace?"

32 He looked up at the window. "Who is on my side?" he called out. "Who?" Two or three officials looked down at him. 33 "Throw her down!" Jehu said. So they threw her down. Some of her blood splashed on the wall. Some of it splashed on Jehu's chariot horses as they ran over her.

34 Jehu went inside. He ate and drank. "The LORD put a curse on that woman," he said. "Take proper care of her body. Bury it. After all, she was a king's daughter."

35 So they went out to bury her body. But all they found was her skull, feet and hands.

36 They went back and reported it to Jehu. He told them, "That's what the LORD said would happen. He announced it through his servant Elijah, who was from Tishbe. He said, 'On a piece of land at Jezreel, dogs will eat up Jezebel's body. 37 Her body will be left to rot on that piece of land. So no one will be able to say, "Here's where Jezebel is buried." ' "

Jehu Wipes Out Ahab's Royal House

10 Ahab's royal family in the city of Samaria had a total of 70 sons. Jehu wrote some letters to the officials of the city. He also sent them to the elders there. And he sent them to those who took care of Ahab's children. He said, 2 "Your master's sons are with you. You also have chariots and horses and weapons. And you are living in a city that has high walls around it. As soon as you read this letter, here's what I want you to do. 3 Choose the best and most respected son of your master. Place him on his father Joram's throne. Then fight for your master's royal house."

4 The leaders of Samaria were terrified. They said, "King Joram and King Ahaziah couldn't stand up against Jehu. So how can we?"

5 The city governor and the person who was in charge of the palace sent a message to Jehu. The message was also from the elders and those who took care of Ahab's children. It said, "We will serve you. We'll do anything you say. We won't appoint anyone to be king. Do what you think is best."

6 Then Jehu wrote them a second letter. It said, "You say you are on my side. You say you will obey me. If you really mean it, bring me the heads of your master's sons. Meet me in Jezreel by this time tomorrow."

There were 70 royal princes. They were with the most important men of the city. Those men were in charge of raising them. 7 When Jehu's letter arrived, the men went and got the princes. They killed all 70 of them. They put their heads in baskets. Then they sent them to Jehu in Jezreel.

8 When the messenger arrived, he spoke

to Jehu. He told him, "The heads of the princes have been brought here."

Then Jehu ordered his men, "Put them in two piles. Stack them up at the entrance of the city gate until morning."

⁹The next morning Jehu went out. He stood in front of all of the people. He said, "You aren't guilty of doing anything wrong. I'm the one who made plans against my master Joram. I killed him. But who killed all of these? ¹⁰I want you to know that the LORD has spoken against Ahab's royal house. Not a word of what he has said will fail. The LORD has done exactly what he promised through his servant Elijah."

¹¹So Jehu killed everyone from Ahab's family who was in Jezreel. He also killed all of Ahab's chief men. And he killed Ahab's close friends and his priests. He didn't leave anyone in Ahab's family alive.

¹²Then Jehu started out for Samaria. At Beth Eked of the Shepherds, ¹³he saw some people. They were relatives of Ahaziah, the king of Judah. Jehu asked them, "Who are you?"

They said, "We are Ahaziah's relatives. We've come down to visit the families of the king and of his mother."

¹⁴"Take them alive!" Jehu ordered. So his men took them alive. Then they killed them by the well of Beth Eked. They killed a total of 42 men. Jehu didn't leave anyone alive.

¹⁵After Jehu left there, he came upon Jehonadab. He was the son of Recab. Jehonadab was on his way to see Jehu. Jehu greeted him. He asked, "Are you my friend? You know I'm your friend."

"I am," Jehonadab answered.

"If that's true," said Jehu, "hold out your hand." So he did. Then Jehu helped him up into the chariot. ¹⁶Jehu said, "Come along with me. See how committed I am to serve the LORD." He had him ride along in his chariot.

¹⁷Jehu came to Samaria. He killed everyone who was left there from Ahab's family. And so he wiped out Ahab's royal house. That's what the LORD had said would happen. He had spoken that message to Elijah.

Jehu Kills Those Who Serve Baal

¹⁸Then Jehu brought all of the people together. He said to them, "Ahab served the god Baal a little. I will serve him a lot. ¹⁹Send for all of Baal's prophets. Also send for all of his priests and the others who serve him. Make sure that not a single one is missing. I'm going to hold a great sacrifice to honor Baal. Anyone who doesn't come will be killed." But Jehu was lying to them. He was planning to destroy those who served Baal.

²⁰Jehu said, "Call everyone together to honor Baal." So they did. ²¹Then he sent a message all through Israel. All of those who served Baal came. Not a single one of them stayed away. They crowded into Baal's temple. It was full from one end to the other.

²²Jehu spoke to the one who took care of the sacred robes. He told him, "Bring robes for everyone who serves Baal." So he brought the robes out for them.

²³Then Jehu went into Baal's temple. Jehonadab, the son of Recab, went with him. Jehu spoke to those who served Baal. He said, "Look around. Make sure that no one who serves the LORD is here with you. Make sure only those who serve Baal are here." ²⁴So they went in to offer sacrifices and burnt offerings.

Jehu had stationed 80 men outside. He warned them, "I'm placing some men in your hands. Don't let a single one of them escape. If you do, you will pay for his life with yours."

²⁵Jehu finished sacrificing the burnt offering. As soon as he did, he gave an order to the guards and officers. He commanded them, "Go inside and kill everyone. Don't let a single one of them escape."

So they cut them down with their swords. The guards and officers threw the bodies outside. Then they entered the most sacred area inside Baal's temple. ²⁶They brought the sacred stone of Baal outside. They burned it up. ²⁷So they destroyed Baal's sacred stone. They also tore down Baal's temple. People have used it as a public toilet to this very day.

²⁸So Jehu destroyed the worship of the god Baal in Israel. ²⁹But he didn't turn away from the sins of Jeroboam, the son of Nebat. Jeroboam had caused Israel to commit those same sins. Jehu worshiped the golden calves at Bethel and Dan.

³⁰The LORD said to Jehu, "You have done well. You have accomplished what is right in my eyes. You have done to Ahab's royal house everything I wanted you to do. So your sons after you will sit on the throne of Israel. They will rule until the time of your children's grandchildren."

³¹But Jehu wasn't careful to obey the law of the LORD. He didn't obey the God of Israel with all his heart. He didn't turn away from the sins of Jeroboam. Jerobo-

JEHOSHEBA

2 KINGS 11:2

> **But Jehosheba...stole Joash away from among the royal princes. All of them were about to be murdered.**

B

★

♥

Jehosheba (jeh-HOE-shee-buh) ran through the palace until her side ached. Terrible things were happening. The king had died. His mother, Athaliah, wanted the throne for herself. So she was about to kill all the princes—all of her own sons and grandsons.

If Jehosheba hurried, maybe she could save some of the little ones. She ran down a wide, long hallway. Each room was empty. Jehosheba's sandals clattered on the marble floor as she ran. Then, above the noise of her sandals, she heard a cry, quick and short before it was cut off. Someone was hiding nearby.

Running boldly from one room to the next, Jehosheba found a nurse and a little prince. They crouched quietly together, hiding in the room until a group of soldiers passed. **THEN RUN-NING AND HIDING, RUNNING AND HIDING, THEY ESCAPED FROM THE PALACE.**

That day, Athaliah killed all the princes except this one little boy. Joash was only one year old, and he didn't understand what was happening. But he could tell something was not right. He clutched his nurse's neck, and she held him close and comforted him. Jehosheba brought them to the temple and found a place for them to stay there.

Joash and his nurse hid in the temple for the next six years. Athaliah ruled the land. No one even knew that a prince still lived, until the day Jehosheba's husband showed little Joash to the commanders of the armies. That day, when Joash was only seven years old, he became king of Judah.

BE A JEHOSHEBA

Jehosheba bravely took one of the princes and saved him from death. If she had been caught, she probably would have died herself. But she knew what was right, and she did it. Sometimes you might be afraid to do the right thing. When you are, remember Jehosheba—and do it!

JEHOSHEBA BRAVELY SAVED A PRINCE FROM DEATH.
*THE WHOLE STORY: 2 KINGS 11:1-21;
2 CHRONICLES 22:10-21*

Go to page 451 for the next Super Hero

am had caused Israel to commit those same sins.

32In those days the LORD began to make the kingdom of Israel smaller. Hazael gained control over many parts of Israel. He gained control over all of their territory **33**east of the Jordan River. It included the whole land of Gilead from Aroer by the Arnon River valley all the way to Bashan. That was the territory of Gad, Reuben and Manasseh.

34The other events of Jehu's rule are written down. Everything he did and accomplished is written down. All of those things are written in the official records of the kings of Israel.

35Jehu joined the members of his family who had already died. His body was buried in Samaria. His son Jehoahaz became the next king after him. **36**Jehu had ruled over Israel in Samaria for 28 years.

Athaliah and Joash

11 Athaliah was Ahaziah's mother. She saw that her son was dead. So she began to wipe out the whole royal house of Judah.

2But Jehosheba went and got Joash, the son of Ahaziah. She was the daughter of King Jehoram and the sister of Ahaziah. She stole Joash away from among the royal princes. All of them were about to be murdered. She put Joash and his nurse in a bedroom. That's how she hid him from Athaliah. And that's why Athaliah didn't kill him. **3**The child remained hidden with his nurse at the LORD's temple for six years. Athaliah ruled over the land during that time.

4In the seventh year the priest Jehoiada sent for the commanders of companies of 100 men. They were the commanders over the Carites and guards. He had them brought to him at the temple of the LORD. He made a covenant with them. He made them take an oath at the temple. Then he showed them the king's son.

5He gave them a command. He said, "Here's what you must do. There are five companies of you. Some of you are in the three companies that are going on duty on the Sabbath day. A third of you must guard the royal palace. **6**A third of you must guard the Sur Gate. And a third of you must guard the gate that is behind the guard. All of you must take turns guarding the temple.

7"The rest of you are in the other two companies. Normally you are not on duty on the Sabbath. But you also must guard

the temple for the king. **8**Station yourselves around the king. Each man must have his weapon in his hand. Anyone else who approaches your companies must be put to death. Stay close to the king no matter where he goes."

9The commanders of the companies did just as the priest Jehoiada ordered. Each commander got his men and came to Jehoiada. Some of the men were going on duty on the Sabbath day. Others were going off duty.

10Then Jehoiada gave weapons to the commanders. He gave them spears and shields. The weapons had belonged to King David. They had been in the LORD's temple.

11The guards stationed themselves around the new king. Each man had his weapon in his hand. They were near the altar and the temple. They stood from the south side of the temple to its north side. Their line formed half of a circle.

12Jehoiada brought Ahaziah's son out. He put the crown on him. He gave him a copy of the covenant. And he announced that Joash was king. Jehoiada and his sons anointed him. The people clapped their hands. Then they shouted, "May the king live a long time!"

13Athaliah heard the noise the guards and the people were making. So she went to the people at the LORD's temple. **14**She looked. And there was the king! He was standing next to the pillar. That was the usual practice. The officers and trumpet players were standing beside the king. All of the people of the land were filled with joy. They were blowing trumpets.

Then Athaliah tore her royal robes. She called out, "Treason! It's treason!"

15The priest Jehoiada gave an order to the commanders of the companies. They were in charge of the troops. He said to them, "Bring her away from the temple between the line of guards. Use your swords to kill anyone who follows her." The priest had said, "She must not be put to death at the LORD's temple."

16So they grabbed hold of her as she reached the place where the horses enter the palace grounds. There she was put to death.

17Then Jehoiada made a covenant between the LORD and the king and people. He had the king and people promise that they would be the LORD's people. Jehoiada also made a covenant between the king and the people.

18All of the people of the land went to Baal's temple. They tore it down. They smashed to pieces the altars and the statues of gods. They killed Mattan in front of the altars. He was the priest of Baal.

Then the priest Jehoiada stationed guards at the temple of the LORD. **19**He took with him the commanders of companies of 100 men. They were the commanders over the Carites and guards. He also took with him all of the people of the land. All of them brought the new king down from the LORD's temple. They went into the palace. They entered it by going through the gate of the guards. Then the king sat down on the royal throne. **20**All of the people of the land were filled with joy. And the city was quiet. That's because Athaliah had been killed with a sword at the palace. **21**Joash was seven years old when he became king.

Joash Repairs the Temple

12 Joash became king of Judah. It was in the seventh year of Jehu's rule. Joash ruled in Jerusalem for 40 years. His mother's name was Zibiah. She was from Beersheba.

2Joash did what was right in the eyes of the LORD. He lived that way as long as the priest Jehoiada was teaching him.

POWER-SURGE

OBEYS ✔

JOASH DID WHAT WAS RIGHT IN THE EYES OF THE LORD.
— 2 KINGS 12:2 —

3But the high places weren't removed. The people continued to offer sacrifices and burn incense there.

4Joash spoke to the priests. He said, "Collect all of the money the people bring as sacred offerings to the LORD's temple. That includes the money that is collected when the men who are able to serve in the army are counted. It includes the money that is received from people who make a special promise to the LORD. It also includes the money people bring to the temple just because they want to.

5"Let each priest receive the money from one of the people who are in charge of the temple's treasures. Let all of that money be used to repair the temple where it needs it."

6It was now the 23rd year of King Joash. And the priests still hadn't repaired the temple. **7**So the king sent for the priest Jehoiada and the other priests. He asked them, "Why aren't you repairing the temple where it needs it? Don't take any more money from the people who are in charge of the treasures. Instead, hand it over so the temple can be repaired."

8The priests agreed that they wouldn't collect any more money from the people. They also agreed that they wouldn't repair the temple themselves.

9The priest Jehoiada got a chest. He drilled a hole in its lid. He placed the chest beside the altar for burnt offerings. The chest was on the right side as people enter the LORD's temple. Some priests guarded the entrance. They put into the chest all of the money the people brought to the temple.

10From time to time there was a large amount of money in the chest. When that happened, the royal secretary and the high priest came. They counted the money the people had brought to the temple. Then they put it into bags. **11**After they added it all up, they used it to repair the temple. They gave it to the men who had been put in charge of the work. Those men used it to pay the workers. They paid the builders and those who worked with wood. **12**They paid those who cut stones and those who laid them. They bought lumber and blocks of stone. So they used the money to repair the LORD's temple. They also paid all of the other costs to make the temple like new again.

13The money the people brought to the LORD's temple wasn't used to make silver bowls. It wasn't used for wick cutters, sprinkling bowls or trumpets. And it wasn't used for any other articles made out of gold or silver. **14**Instead, it was paid to the workers. They used it to repair the temple. **15**The royal secretary and the high priest didn't require a report from those who were in charge of the work. That's because they were completely honest. They always paid the workers. **16**Money was received from those who brought guilt offerings and sin offerings. But it wasn't taken to the LORD's temple. It belonged to the priests.

17About that time Hazael, the king of Aram, went up and attacked Gath. Then he captured it. After that, he turned back to attack Jerusalem. **18**But Joash, the king of Judah, didn't want to go to war. So he got all of the

JOASH

2 KINGS 12:2

Joash did what was right in the eyes of the LORD. He lived that way as long as the priest Jehoiada was teaching him.

Joash stood as tall as he could. He was only seven. Standing on the porch of the temple, he looked seriously in front of him. Joash saw all the people gathered that day at the temple to worship God. He saw all the soldiers who stood on guard around the temple, at the gate and around him. He stood and waited.

Then Joash saw the priest, Jehoiada (Jeh-HOY-duh). Joash loved Jehoiada and his wife, Jehosheba (read more about her on page 448). They had saved him when his grandmother had killed all of his brothers and cousins. Joash had lived in the temple with Jehoiada for six years now. All that time, Joash's grandmother had been the cruel queen over Judah.

BUT TODAY HER REIGN WOULD END.

Joash watched as Jehoiada came toward him. He held his head very still as a crown was put on his head. His eyes opened wide with wonder as Jehoiada told the people, "This is the king's son, Joash. He is now the king of Judah!"

Joash looked from one face to another as the people began to clap their hands and shout. They seemed glad that he was their king, shouting, "Long live King Joash!"

Joash couldn't believe it. He was king! But he was only seven! How could he ever do the things a king must do? Joash knew he needed help.

For many years, Jehoiada helped Joash reign. When there was something Joash didn't understand, Jehoiada explained it. When there was something Joash couldn't do, Jehoiada did it. When Joash needed wisdom to make a good decision, Jehoiada helped him. For all the years that Jehoiada was alive, Joash was a good king.

BE A JOASH

Is it hard for you to ask for help? Everyone needs help now and then. Young Joash looked to Jehoiada for help. Is there someone who can help you learn the things you need to learn? Be a Joash. Don't be afraid to ask for help.

**JOASH WAS A YOUNG KING WHO ASKED FOR HELP.
THE WHOLE STORY: 2 KINGS 11:1–12:2**

Go to page 460 for the next Super Hero

sacred objects. They had been set apart to the LORD by the kings who had ruled over Judah before him. They were Jehoshaphat, Jehoram and Ahaziah. Joash got the gifts he himself had set apart. He got all of the gold that was among the temple treasures. He also got all of the gold from the royal palace. He sent all of those things to Hazael, the king of Aram. Then Hazael pulled his army back from Jerusalem.

¹⁹The other events of the rule of Joash are written down. Everything he did is written down. All of those things are written in the official records of the kings of Judah.

²⁰The officials of Joash made evil plans against him. They killed him at Beth Millo. It happened on the road that goes down to Silla. ²¹The officials who murdered him were Jozabad and Jehozabad. Jozabad was the son of Shimeath. Jehozabad was the son of Shomer.

After Joash died, his body was buried in the family tomb in the City of David. His son Amaziah became the next king after him.

Jehoahaz Becomes King of Israel

13 Jehoahaz became king of Israel in Samaria. It was in the 23rd year of Joash, the king of Judah. Jehoahaz ruled for 17 years. Joash was the son of Ahaziah. Jehoahaz was the son of Jehu.

²Jehoahaz did what was evil in the sight of the LORD. He committed the sins Jeroboam, the son of Nebat, had committed. Jeroboam had caused Israel to commit those same sins. Jehoahaz didn't turn away from them.

³So the LORD's anger burned against Israel. For a long time he kept them under the power of Hazael, the king of Aram. He also kept them under the power of his son Ben-Hadad.

⁴Then Jehoahaz asked the LORD to show him his favor. The LORD listened to him. The LORD saw how badly the king of Aram was treating Israel. ⁵The LORD provided someone to save Israel. And they escaped from the power of Aram. So the people of Israel lived in their own homes, just as they had before.

⁶But the people didn't turn away from the sins of the royal house of Jeroboam. He had caused Israel to commit those same sins. The people continued to commit them. And the pole that was used to worship the goddess Asherah remained standing in Samaria.

⁷The army of Jehoahaz had almost nothing left. All it had was 50 horsemen, 10 chariots and 10,000 soldiers on foot. The king of Aram had destroyed the rest of them. He had made them like dust at threshing time.

⁸The other events of the rule of Jehoahaz are written down. Everything he did and accomplished is written down. All of those things are written in the official records of the kings of Israel.

⁹Jehoahaz joined the members of his family who had already died. His body was buried in Samaria. His son Jehoash became the next king after him.

Jehoash Becomes King of Israel

¹⁰Jehoash became king of Israel in Samaria. It was in the 37th year that Joash was king of Judah. Jehoash ruled for 16 years. He was the son of Jehoahaz.

¹¹Jehoash did what was evil in the sight of the LORD. He didn't turn away from any of the sins of Jeroboam, the son of Nebat. Jeroboam had caused Israel to commit those same sins. And Jehoash continued to commit them.

¹²The other events of the rule of Jehoash are written down. Everything he did and accomplished is written down. That includes his war against Amaziah, the king of Judah. All of those things are written in the official records of the kings of Israel.

¹³Jehoash joined the members of his family who had already died. His body was buried in the royal tombs in Samaria. Jeroboam became the next king on Israel's throne after him.

¹⁴Elisha was suffering from a sickness. Later he would die from it. Jehoash, the king of Israel, went down to see him. He sobbed over him. "My father!" he cried. "You are like a father to me! You are the true chariots and horsemen of Israel!"

¹⁵Elisha said to Jehoash, "Get a bow and some arrows." So he did.

¹⁶"Hold the bow in your hands," Elisha said to the king of Israel. So Jehoash took hold of the bow. Then Elisha put his hands on the king's hands.

¹⁷"Open the east window," Elisha said. So he did. "Shoot!" Elisha said. So he shot. "That's the LORD's arrow!" Elisha announced. "It means you will win the battle over Aram! You will completely destroy the men of Aram at Aphek."

¹⁸He continued, "Get some arrows." So the king did. Elisha told him, "Strike the ground." He struck it three times. Then he stopped.

¹⁹The man of God was angry with him. He said, "You should have struck the

ground five or six times. Then you would have won the war over Aram. You would have completely destroyed them. But now you will win only three battles over them."

²⁰Elisha died. And his body was buried. Some robbers from Moab used to enter the country of Israel every spring. ²¹One day some people of Israel were burying a man's body. Suddenly they saw a group of robbers. So they threw the man's body into Elisha's tomb. The body touched Elisha's bones. When it did, the man came back to life again. He stood up on his feet.

²²Hazael, the king of Aram, treated Israel badly. He did it the whole time Jehoahaz was king.

²³But the LORD showed his favor to Israel. He was tender and kind to them. He showed concern for them. He did all of those things because of the covenant he had made with Abraham, Isaac and Jacob. To this very day he hasn't been willing to destroy them. And he hasn't driven them out of his land.

²⁴Hazael, the king of Aram, died. His son Ben-Hadad became the next king after him. ²⁵Then Jehoash took some towns back from Ben-Hadad, the son of Hazael. Ben-Hadad had captured them in battle from Jehoahaz, the father of Jehoash. Jehoash won three battles over Ben-Hadad. So Jehoash took back the Israelite towns.

Amaziah Becomes King of Judah

14 Amaziah began to rule as king over Judah. It was in the second year that Jehoash was king of Israel. He was the son of Jehoahaz. Amaziah was the son of Joash. ²Amaziah was 25 years old when he became king. He ruled in Jerusalem for 29 years. His mother's name was Jehoaddin. She was from Jerusalem.

³Amaziah did what was right in the eyes of the LORD. But he didn't do what King David had done. He always followed the example of his father Joash. ⁴The high places weren't removed. The people continued to offer sacrifices and burn incense there.

⁵The kingdom was firmly under his control. So he put to death the officials who had murdered his father, the king. ⁶But he didn't put their children to death. He obeyed what is written in the Scroll of the Law of Moses. There the LORD commanded, "Parents must not be put to death because of what their children do. And children must not be put to death because of what their parents do. People

must die because of their own sins." *(Deuteronomy 24:16)*

⁷Amaziah won the battle over 10,000 men of Edom. It happened in the Valley of Salt. During the battle he captured the town of Sela. He called it Joktheel. That's the name it still has to this very day.

⁸Then Amaziah sent messengers to Jehoash, the king of Israel. He was the son of Jehoahaz, the son of Jehu. The message said, "Come on. Meet me face to face in battle."

⁹But Jehoash, the king of Israel, answered Amaziah, the king of Judah. He said, "A thorn bush in Lebanon sent a message to a cedar tree there. It said, 'Give your daughter to be married to my son.' Then a wild animal in Lebanon came along. It walked all over the thorn bush. ¹⁰It's true that you have won the battle over Edom. So you are proud. Enjoy your success while you can. But stay home and enjoy it! Why ask for trouble? Why bring yourself crashing down? Why bring Judah down with you?"

¹¹But Amaziah wouldn't listen. So Jehoash, the king of Israel, attacked. He and Amaziah, the king of Judah, faced each other in battle. The battle took place at Beth Shemesh in Judah.

¹²Israel drove Judah away. Every man ran home. ¹³Jehoash king of Israel captured Amaziah king of Judah at Beth Shemesh. Amaziah was the son of Joash. Joash was the son of Ahaziah. Jehoash went to Jerusalem. He broke down part of its wall. It's the part that went from the Ephraim Gate to the Corner Gate. That part of the wall was 600 feet long.

¹⁴Jehoash took all of the gold, silver and articles that were in the LORD's temple. He also took all of those same kinds of things that were among the treasures of the royal palace. And he took the prisoners. Then he returned to Samaria.

¹⁵The other events of the rule of Jehoash are written down. Everything he did and accomplished is written down. That includes his war against Amaziah, the king of Judah. All of those things are written in the official records of the kings of Israel.

¹⁶Jehoash joined the members of his family who had already died. His body was buried in Samaria in the royal tombs of Israel. His son Jeroboam became the next king after him.

¹⁷Amaziah king of Judah lived for 15 years after Jehoash king of Israel died. Amaziah was the son of Joash. Jehoash was the son of Jehoahaz. ¹⁸The other

events of Amaziah's rule are written down. They are written in the official records of the kings of Judah.

19Some people made evil plans against Amaziah in Jerusalem. So he ran away to Lachish. But they sent men to Lachish after him. There they killed him. **20**His body was brought back on a horse. Then he was buried in the family tomb in Jerusalem, the City of David.

21All of the people of Judah made Uzziah king. He was 16 years old. They made him king in place of his father Amaziah. **22**Uzziah rebuilt Elath. He brought it under Judah's control again. He did it after Amaziah joined the members of his family who had already died.

Jeroboam II Becomes King of Israel

23Jeroboam became king of Israel in Samaria. It was in the 15th year that Amaziah was king of Judah. Jeroboam ruled for 41 years. Amaziah was the son of Joash. Jeroboam was the son of Jehoash.

24Jeroboam did what was evil in the sight of the LORD. He didn't turn away from any of the sins the earlier Jeroboam, the son of Nebat, had committed. That Jeroboam had caused Israel to commit those same sins.

25Jeroboam, the son of Jehoash, made the borders of Israel the same as they were before. They reached from Lebo Hamath all the way to the Dead Sea. That's what the LORD, the God of Israel, had said would happen. He had spoken that message through his servant Jonah. The prophet Jonah was the son of Amittai. Jonah was from Gath Hepher.

26The LORD had seen how much everyone in Israel was suffering. It didn't matter whether they were slaves or free. They didn't have anyone to help them. **27**The LORD hadn't said he would wipe out Israel's name from the earth. So he saved them by using the powerful hand of Jeroboam, the son of Jehoash.

28The other events of the rule of Jeroboam are written down. Everything he did is written down. What he and his army accomplished is written down. That includes how he brought Damascus and Hamath back under Israel's control. Damascus and Hamath had belonged to the territory of Yaudi. All of those things are written in the official records of the kings of Israel.

29Jeroboam joined the members of his family who had already died. His body was buried in the royal tombs of Israel. His son Zechariah became the next king after him.

Uzziah Becomes King of Judah

15 Uzziah began to rule as king over Judah. It was in the 27th year that Jeroboam was king of Israel. Uzziah was the son of Amaziah. **2**Uzziah was 16 years old when he became king. He ruled in Jerusalem for 52 years. His mother's name was Jecoliah. She was from Jerusalem.

3Uzziah did what was right in the eyes of the LORD, just as his father Amaziah had done.

4But the high places weren't removed. The people continued to offer sacrifices and burn incense there.

5The LORD caused King Uzziah to suffer from a skin disease until the day he died. He lived in a separate house. His son Jotham was in charge of the palace. Jotham ruled over the people of the land.

6The other events of the rule of Uzziah are written down. Everything he did is written down. All of those things are written in the official records of the kings of Judah.

7Uzziah joined the members of his family who had already died. His body was buried near them in the City of David. His son Jotham became the next king after him.

Zechariah Becomes King of Israel

8Zechariah became king of Israel in Samaria. It was in the 38th year that Uzziah was king of Judah. Zechariah ruled for six months. He was the son of Jeroboam, the son of Jehoash.

9Zechariah did what was evil in the sight of the LORD. He did what the kings of Israel before him had done. He didn't turn away from the sins Jeroboam, the son of Nebat, had committed. Jeroboam had caused Israel to commit those same sins.

10Shallum made evil plans against Zechariah. He attacked Zechariah in front of the people and killed him. Then he became the next king after him. Shallum was the son of Jabesh.

11The other events of the rule of Zechariah are written down. They are written in the official records of the kings of Israel. **12**That's what the LORD had said would happen. He had spoken that message to Jehu. It had said, "Your sons after you will sit on the throne of Israel. They will rule until the time of your children's grandchildren." *(2 Kings 10:30)*

Shallum Becomes King of Israel

13Shallum became king of Israel. It was in the 39th year that Uzziah was king of Judah. Shallum ruled in Samaria for one month. He was the son of Jabesh.

14Menahem went from Tirzah up to Samaria. There he attacked Shallum, the son of Jabesh. He killed him and became the next king after him. Menahem was the son of Gadi.

15The other events of Shallum's rule are written down. The evil things he planned are written down. All of those things are written in the official records of the kings of Israel.

16At that time Menahem started out from Tirzah and attacked Tiphsah. He attacked everyone in the city and the area around it. That's because they refused to open their gates for him. He destroyed Tiphsah. He ripped open all of their pregnant women.

Menahem Becomes King of Israel

17Menahem became king of Israel. It was in the 39th year that Uzziah was king of Judah. Menahem ruled in Samaria for ten years. He was the son of Gadi.

18Menahem did what was evil in the sight of the LORD. During his entire rule he didn't turn away from the sins Jeroboam, the son of Nebat, had committed. Jeroboam had caused Israel to commit those same sins.

19Then Tiglath-Pileser marched into the land of Israel. He was king of Assyria. Menahem gave him 37 tons of silver to get his help. He wanted to make his control over the kingdom stronger. 20Menahem forced Israel to give him that money. Every wealthy person had to give him 20 ounces of silver. All of it went to the king of Assyria. So he pulled his troops back. He didn't stay in the land anymore.

21The other events of the rule of Menahem are written down. Everything he did is written down. All of those things are written in the official records of the kings of Israel.

22Menahem joined the members of his family who had already died. His son Pekahiah became the next king after him.

Pekahiah Becomes King of Israel

23Pekahiah became king of Israel in Samaria. It was in the 50th year that Uzziah was king of Judah. Pekahiah ruled for two years. He was the son of Menahem.

24Pekahiah did what was evil in the sight of the LORD. He didn't turn away from the sins Jeroboam, the son of Nebat, had committed. Jeroboam had caused Israel to commit those same sins.

25One of Pekahiah's chief officers was Pekah. He was the son of Remaliah. Pekah made evil plans against Pekahiah. He took 50 men of Gilead with him and killed Pekahiah. He also killed Argob and Arieh. He killed all of them in the safest place in the royal palace at Samaria. So Pekah killed Pekahiah. He became the next king after him.

26The other events of the rule of Pekahiah are written down. Everything he did is written down. All of those things are written in the official records of the kings of Israel.

Pekah Becomes King of Israel

27Pekah became king of Israel in Samaria. It was in the 52nd year that Uzziah was king of Judah. Pekah ruled for 20 years. He was the son of Remaliah.

28Pekah did what was evil in the sight of the LORD. He didn't turn away from the sins Jeroboam, the son of Nebat, had committed. Jeroboam had caused Israel to commit those same sins.

29During the rule of Pekah, the king of Israel, Tiglath-Pileser marched into the land again. He was king of Assyria. He took the towns of Ijon, Abel Beth Maacah, Janoah, Kedesh and Hazor. He also took the lands of Gilead and Galilee. That included the whole territory of Naphtali. He took the people away from their own land. He sent them off to Assyria.

30Then Hoshea made evil plans against Pekah, the son of Remaliah. Hoshea was the son of Elah. Hoshea attacked Pekah and killed him. Then Hoshea became the next king after him. It was in the 20th year of the rule of Jotham, the son of Uzziah.

31The other events of the rule of Pekah are written down. Everything he did is written down. All of those things are written in the official records of the kings of Israel.

Jotham Becomes King of Judah

32Jotham began to rule as king over Judah. It was in the second year that Pekah was king of Israel. He was the son of Remaliah. Jotham was the son of Uzziah. 33Jotham was 25 years old when he became king. He ruled in Jerusalem for 16 years. His mother's name was Jerusha. She was the daughter of Zadok.

34Jotham did what was right in the eyes of the LORD, just as his father Uzziah had done.

35But the high places weren't removed. The people continued to offer sacrifices and burn incense there. Jotham rebuilt the Upper Gate of the LORD's temple.

36The other events of the rule of Jotham are written down. Everything he did is written down. All of those things are written in the official records of the kings of Judah.

37In those days the LORD began to send Rezin and Pekah against Judah. Rezin was king of Aram. Pekah was the son of Remaliah.

38Jotham joined the members of his family who had already died. His body was buried in the family tomb in the city of King David. His son Ahaz became the next king after him.

Ahaz Becomes King of Judah

16 Ahaz began to rule as king over Judah. It was in the 17th year of the rule of Pekah, the son of Remaliah. Ahaz was the son of Jotham. 2Ahaz was 20 years old when he became king. He ruled in Jerusalem for 16 years.

Ahaz didn't do what was right in the eyes of the LORD his God. He didn't do what King David had done. 3He followed the ways of the kings of Israel. He even sacrificed his son in the fire to another god. He followed the practices of the nations. The LORD hated those practices. He had driven out those nations to make room for the people of Israel. 4Ahaz offered sacrifices and burned incense at the high places. He also did it on the tops of hills and under every green tree.

5Rezin and Pekah marched up to Jerusalem and surrounded it. Rezin was king of Aram. Pekah, the son of Remaliah, was king of Israel. They attacked Ahaz. But they couldn't overpower him. 6At that time Rezin, the king of Aram, got back Elath for Aram. He drove out the people of Judah. Then the people of Edom moved into Elath. And they still live there to this very day.

7Ahaz sent messengers to Tiglath-Pileser. He was king of Assyria. The message of Ahaz said, "I am your servant. You are my master. Come up and save me from the powerful hands of the kings of Aram and Israel. They are attacking me."

8Ahaz took the silver and gold that were in the LORD's temple. He also took the silver and gold that were among the treasures in the royal palace. He sent all of it as a gift to the king of Assyria.

9So the king of Assyria did what Ahaz asked him to do. He attacked the city of Damascus and captured it. He sent its people away to Kir. And he put Rezin to death.

10Then King Ahaz went to Damascus. He went there to see Tiglath-Pileser, the king of Assyria. Ahaz saw an altar in Damascus. He sent a drawing of it to the priest Uriah. He also sent him plans for building it.

11So the priest Uriah built an altar. He followed all of the plans King Ahaz had sent from Damascus. He finished it before Ahaz returned.

12The king came back from Damascus. When he saw the altar, he approached it. Then he offered sacrifices on it. 13He offered up his burnt offering and grain offering. He poured out his drink offering. And he sprinkled blood from his friendship offerings on the altar.

14The bronze altar for burnt offerings stood in front of the LORD. It was between the new altar and the LORD's temple. Ahaz took it away from the front of the temple. He put it on the north side of the new altar.

15Then King Ahaz gave orders to the priest Uriah. He said, "Offer sacrifices on the large new altar. Offer the morning burnt offering and the evening grain offering. Offer my burnt offering and my grain offering. Offer the burnt offering of all of the people of the land. Offer their grain offering and their drink offering. Sprinkle on the altar all of the blood from the burnt offerings and sacrifices. But I will use the bronze altar to look for advice and direction."

16The priest Uriah did just as King Ahaz had ordered.

17Ahaz took away the sides of the bronze stands. He removed the bowls from the stands. He removed the huge bowl from the bronze bulls it stood on. He placed the bowl on a stone base. 18He took away the covered area that had been used on the Sabbath day. It had been built at the LORD's temple. He removed the royal entrance that was outside the temple. Ahaz did all of that to honor the king of Assyria.

19The other events of the rule of Ahaz are written down. Everything he did is written down. All of those things are written in the official records of the kings of Judah.

20Ahaz joined the members of his family who had already died. His body was buried in the family tomb in the City of David. His son Hezekiah became the next king after him.

Hoshea Becomes the Last King of Israel

17 Hoshea became king of Israel in Samaria. It was in the 12th year that Ahaz was king of Judah. Hoshea ruled for nine years. He was the son of Elah.

2Hoshea did what was evil in the sight of the LORD. But he wasn't as evil as the kings of Israel who ruled before him.

3Shalmaneser came up to attack Hoshea. Shalmaneser was king of Assyria. He had been Hoshea's master. He had forced Hoshea to bring him gifts. 4But the king of Assyria found out that Hoshea had turned against him. Hoshea had sent messengers to So, the king of Egypt. Hoshea didn't send gifts to the king of Assyria anymore. He had been sending them every year. So Shalmaneser grabbed hold of him and put him in prison.

5The king of Assyria marched into the whole land of Israel. He marched to Samaria and surrounded it for three years. From time to time he attacked it. 6Finally, the king of Assyria captured Samaria. It was in the ninth year of Hoshea. The king of Assyria took the people of Israel away from their own land. He sent them off to Assyria. He settled some of them in Halah. He settled others in Gozan on the Habor River. And he settled still others in the towns of the Medes.

Israel Is Forced to Go Away to Assyria

7All of that took place because the people of Israel had committed sins against the LORD their God. He had brought them up out of Egypt. He had brought them out from under the power of Pharaoh, the king of Egypt. But they worshiped other gods.

8The LORD had driven out other nations to make room for them. But they followed the evil practices of those nations. They also followed the practices that the kings of Israel had started. 9The people of Israel did things against the LORD their God in secret. What they did wasn't right. They built high places for worship in all of their towns. They built them at lookout towers. They also built them at cities that had high walls around them. 10They set up sacred stones. And they set up poles that were used to worship the goddess Asherah. They did that on every high hill and under every green tree.

11The LORD had driven out nations to make room for Israel. But the people of Israel burned incense at every high place,

just as those nations had done. The Israelites did evil things that made the LORD very angry. 12They worshiped statues of gods. They did it even though the LORD had said, "Do not do that."

13The LORD warned Israel and Judah through all of his prophets and seers. He said, "Turn from your evil ways. Keep my commands and rules. Obey every part of my Law. I commanded your people who lived long ago to obey it. And I gave it to you through my servants the prophets."

14But the people wouldn't listen. They were as stubborn as their people of long ago had been. Those people didn't trust in the LORD their God. 15They refused to obey his rules. They broke the covenant he had made with them. They didn't pay any attention to the warnings he had given them. They worshiped worthless statues of gods. Then they themselves became worthless. They followed the example of the nations that were around them. They did it even though the LORD had ordered them not to. He had said, "Do not do as they do." They did the very things the LORD had told them not to do.

16They turned away from all of the commands of the LORD their God. They made two statues of gods for themselves. The statues were shaped like calves. They made a pole that was used to worship the goddess Asherah. They bowed down to all of the stars. And they worshiped the god Baal.

17They sacrificed their sons and daughters in the fire. They practiced all kinds of evil magic. They gave themselves over to do what was evil in the sight of the LORD. All of those things made him very angry.

18So the LORD was filled with anger against Israel. He removed them from his land. Only the tribe of Judah was left. 19And even Judah didn't obey the commands of the LORD their God. They followed the practices Israel had started.

20So the LORD turned his back on all of the people of Israel. He made them suffer. He handed them over to people who stole everything they had. And finally he threw them out of his land.

21He tore Israel away from the royal house of David. The people of Israel made Jeroboam, the son of Nebat, their king. Jeroboam tried to get Israel to stop following the LORD. He caused them to commit a terrible sin. 22The people of Israel were stubborn. They continued to commit all of the sins Jeroboam had committed. They didn't turn away from them.

23So the LORD removed them from his

land. That's what he had warned them he would do. He had given that warning through all of his servants the prophets. So the people of Israel were taken away from their country. They were forced to go to Assyria. And that's where they still are.

Assyria Brings Other People to Samaria

24The king of Assyria brought people from Babylon. He also brought them from Cuthah, Avva, Hamath and Sepharvaim. He settled all of them in the towns of Samaria. They took the place of the people of Israel. They took over Samaria and lived in its towns.

25When they first lived there, they didn't worship the LORD. So he sent lions among them. And the lions killed some of the people.

26A report was given to the king of Assyria. He was told, "You forced people to leave their own homes. You settled them in the towns of Samaria. But they don't know what the god of that country requires. So he has sent lions among them. And the lions are killing the people off. That's because the people don't know what that god requires."

27Then the king of Assyria gave an order. He said, "Get one of the priests you captured from Samaria. Send him back to live there. Have him teach the people what the god of that land requires."

28So one of the priests went back to live in Bethel. He was one of those who had been forced to leave Samaria. He taught the people there how to worship the LORD.

29In spite of that, the people from each nation made statues of their own gods. They made them in all of the towns where they had settled. They set up those statues in small temples. The people of Samaria had built the temples at the high places. 30The people from Babylon made statues of the god Succoth Benoth. Those from Cuthah made statues of Nergal. Those from Hamath made statues of Ashima. 31The Avvites made statues of Nibhaz and Tartak. The Sepharvites sacrificed their children in the fire to Adrammelech and Anammelech. They were the gods of Sepharvaim.

32So the people of Samaria worshiped the LORD. But they also appointed all kinds of their own people to serve them as priests. The priests served in the small temples at the high places. 33The people worshiped the LORD. But they also served their own gods. They followed the evil practices of the nations from which they had been brought.

34They are still stubborn. They continue in their old practices to this very day. And now they don't even worship the LORD. They don't follow his directions and rules. They don't obey his laws and commands. The LORD had given all of those laws to the family of Jacob. He gave the name Israel to Jacob.

35The LORD made a covenant with the people of Israel. At that time he commanded them, "Do not worship any other gods. Do not bow down to them. Do not serve them or sacrifice to them. 36I am the one you must worship. I brought you up out of Egypt by my great power. I saved you by reaching out my mighty arm. You must bow down to me. You must offer sacrifices to me. 37You must always be careful to follow my directions and rules. You must obey the laws and commands I wrote for you. Do not worship other gods. 38Do not forget the covenant I made with you. And remember, you must not worship other gods. 39Instead, worship me. I will save you from the powerful hand of all of your enemies. I am the LORD your God."

40But the people wouldn't listen. Instead, they were stubborn. They continued in their old practices. 41They worshiped the LORD. But at the same time, they served the statues of their gods. And to this very day their children and grandchildren continue to do what their people before them did.

Hezekiah Becomes King of Judah

18 Hezekiah began to rule as king over Judah. It was in the third year that Hoshea was king of Israel. He was the son of Elah. Hezekiah was the son of Ahaz. 2Hezekiah was 25 years old when he became king. He ruled in Jerusalem for 29 years. His mother's name was Abijah. She was the daughter of Zechariah.

3Hezekiah did what was right in the eyes of the LORD, just as King David had done. 4Hezekiah removed the high places. He smashed the sacred stones. He cut down the poles that were used to worship the goddess Asherah. He broke into pieces the bronze snake Moses had made. Up to that time the people of Israel had been burning incense to it. They called it Nehushtan.

5Hezekiah trusted in the LORD, the God of Israel. There was no one like him among all of the kings of Judah. There was no king like him either before him or after

POWER-/SURGE

FAITHFUL ()

HEZEKIAH TRUSTED IN THE LORD, THE GOD OF ISRAEL. THERE WAS NO ONE LIKE HIM AMONG ALL OF THE KINGS OF JUDAH. THERE WAS NO KING LIKE HIM EITHER BEFORE HIM OR AFTER HIM. HEZEKIAH REMAINED TRUE TO THE LORD. HE DIDN'T STOP FOLLOWING HIM. HE OBEYED THE COMMANDS THE LORD HAD GIVEN MOSES.
— 2 KINGS 18:5-6 — ✔

OBEYS

him. **6**Hezekiah remained true to the LORD. He didn't stop following him. He obeyed the commands the LORD had given Moses.

7The LORD was with Hezekiah. He was successful in everything he did. He refused to remain under the control of the king of Assyria. He didn't serve him. **8**He won the war against the Philistines. He won battles at their lookout towers. He won battles at their cities that had high walls around them. He won battles against the Philistines all the way to Gaza and its territory.

9Shalmaneser marched to Samaria and surrounded it. It was in the fourth year of King Hezekiah. That was the seventh year of Hoshea, the king of Israel. He was the son of Elah. Shalmaneser was king of Assyria.

10At the end of three years the army of Assyria took Samaria. So it was captured in the sixth year of Hezekiah. That was the ninth year of Hoshea, the king of Israel. **11**The king of Assyria took the people of Israel away from their own land. He sent them off to Assyria. He settled some of

them in Halah. He settled others in Gozan on the Habor River. And he settled still others in the towns of the Medes.

12Those things happened because the Israelites hadn't obeyed the LORD their God. They had broken the covenant he had made with them. They had refused to do everything Moses, the servant of the LORD, had commanded. They hadn't paid any attention to those commands. They hadn't obeyed them.

13Sennacherib attacked and captured all of the cities of Judah that had high walls around them. It was in the 14th year of the rule of Hezekiah. Sennacherib was king of Assyria.

14Hezekiah, the king of Judah, sent a message to the king of Assyria at Lachish. It said, "I have done what is wrong. Pull your troops back from me. Then I'll pay you anything you ask me to."

The king of Assyria forced Hezekiah, the king of Judah, to give him 11 tons of silver. Hezekiah also had to give him a ton of gold. **15**So Hezekiah gave him all of the silver that was in the LORD's temple. He also gave him all of the silver that was among the treasures in the royal palace.

16Hezekiah, the king of Judah, had covered the doors and doorposts of the LORD's temple with gold. But now he had to strip it off. He had to give it to the king of Assyria.

Sennacherib Warns Jerusalem

17The king of Assyria sent his highest commander from Lachish to King Hezekiah at Jerusalem. He also sent his chief officer and his field commander along with a large army. All of them came up to Jerusalem. They stopped at the channel that brings water from the Upper Pool. It was on the road to the Washerman's Field. **18**They called for King Hezekiah. Eliakim, Shebna and Joah went out to them. Eliakim, the son of Hilkiah, was in charge of the palace. Shebna was the secretary. Joah, the son of Asaph, kept the records.

19The field commander said to them, "Give Hezekiah this message. Tell him,

" 'Sennacherib is the great king of Assyria. He says, "Why are you putting your faith in what your king says? **20**You say you have a military plan. You say you have a strong army. But your words don't mean anything. Who are you depending on? Why don't you want to stay under my control?

21" ' "You are depending on Egypt.

HEZEKIAH

2 KINGS 18:5-6

Hezekiah trusted in the Lord, the God of Israel...There was no king like him either before him or after him. Hezekiah remained true to the Lord. He didn't stop following him. He obeyed the commands the Lord had given Moses.

Young King Hezekiah's (hez-uh-KIE-uhz) robes flowed out behind him like a cape as he marched up to the top of the hill. He didn't notice the people who turned to stare or the smell of the incense in the air. He had only one thing on his mind.

Hezekiah had just been crowned king of Judah. He was only 25 years old. He didn't want to be like his father, Ahaz, who had worshiped idols. He wanted to follow God and obey him.

Hezekiah's first order of business as a new king was about to take place. He came to the top of the hill where the people had gathered to worship their idols. He raised a large club above his head. **HE SMASHED THE TOWERS OF STONE THEY WORSHIPED.** He cut down the wooden poles they worshiped. And he even broke into small pieces the bronze snake they worshiped.

The snake had been a holy thing of God, not an idol. About 700 years ago, the Israelites had disobeyed God when they were in the desert. God sent snakes to bite them, and they were dying. When they cried to God, he told Moses to build a large snake out of metal. If a live snake bit them, the Israelites just looked up to the bronze snake and they were healed!

But now the people used it to sin. They worshiped it instead of God. They burned incense in front of it as if it had special powers. But the snake had no power. Neither did the wooden idols or their piles of stone.

Hezekiah knew that. And he wanted the people to know it. The only one with power was God himself. The only one they should worship was God himself. So he began to show them.

BE A HEZEKIAH

Be a Hezekiah! Those who wrote about him said he trusted in God and followed him more than any other king before or after him. He obeyed God.

HEZEKIAH WAS FAITHFUL TO GOD ALL HIS LIFE.
THE WHOLE STORY: 2 KINGS 18:1—20:21

Go to page 468 for the next Super Hero

Why are you doing that? Egypt is nothing but a broken papyrus stem. Try leaning on it. It will only cut your hand. Pharaoh, the king of Egypt, is just like that to everyone who depends on him.

22" ' "Suppose you say to me, 'We are depending on the Lord our God.' Didn't Hezekiah remove your god's high places and altars? Didn't Hezekiah say to the people of Judah and Jerusalem, 'You must worship at the altar in Jerusalem'?

23" ' "Come on. Make a deal with my master, the king of Assyria. I'll give you 2,000 horses. But only if you can put riders on them! 24You are depending on Egypt for chariots and horsemen. You can't drive away even the least important officer among my master's officials.

25" ' "Besides, do you think I've come without receiving a message from the Lord? Have I come to attack and destroy this place without a message from him? The Lord himself told me to march out against your country. He told me to destroy it." ' "

26Then Shebna, Joah and Eliakim, the son of Hilkiah, spoke to the field commander. They said, "Please speak to us in the Aramaic language. We understand it. Don't speak to us in Hebrew. If you do, the people who are on the wall will be able to understand you."

27But the commander replied, "My master sent me to say these things. Are these words only for your master and you to hear? Aren't they also for the men who are sitting on the wall? They are going to suffer just like you. They'll have to eat their own waste. They'll have to drink their own urine."

28Then the commander stood up and spoke in the Hebrew language. He called out, "Pay attention to what the great king of Assyria is telling you. 29He says, 'Don't let Hezekiah trick you. He can't save you from my powerful hand. 30Don't let Hezekiah talk you into trusting in the Lord. Don't believe him when he says, "You can be sure that the Lord will save us. This city will not be handed over to the king of Assyria." '

31"Don't listen to Hezekiah. The king of Assyria says, 'Make a peace treaty with me. Come over to my side. Then every one of you will eat fruit from your own vine and fig tree. Every one of you will drink water from your own well. 32You

will do that until I come back. Then I'll take you to a land that is just like yours. It's a land that has a lot of grain and fresh wine. It has plenty of bread and vineyards. It has olive trees and honey. So choose life! Don't choose death!'

"Don't pay any attention to Hezekiah. He's telling you a lie when he says, 'The Lord will save us.'

33"Has the god of any nation ever saved his land from the powerful hand of the king of Assyria? 34Where are the gods of Hamath and Arpad? Where are the gods of Sepharvaim, Hena and Ivvah? Have they saved Samaria from my power?

35"Which one of all of the gods of those countries has been able to save his land from me? So how can the Lord save Jerusalem from my power?"

36But the people remained silent. They didn't say anything. That's because King Hezekiah had commanded, "Don't answer him."

37Then Eliakim, the son of Hilkiah, went to Hezekiah. Eliakim was in charge of the palace. The secretary Shebna went with him. So did Joah, the son of Asaph. Joah kept the records. All of them went to Hezekiah with their clothes torn. They told him what the field commander had said.

Isaiah Prophesies That Jerusalem Will Be Saved

19 When King Hezekiah heard what the field commander had said, he tore his clothes. He put on black clothes. Then he went into the Lord's temple.

2Hezekiah sent Eliakim, who was in charge of the palace, to the prophet Isaiah, the son of Amoz. He also sent the leading priests and the secretary Shebna to him. All of them were wearing black clothes.

3They told Isaiah, "Hezekiah says, 'Today we're in great trouble. The Lord is warning us. He's bringing shame on us. Sometimes babies come to the moment when they should be born. But their mothers aren't strong enough to allow them to be born. Today we are like those mothers. We aren't strong enough to save ourselves.

4" 'Perhaps the Lord your God will hear everything the field commander has said. His master, the king of Assyria, has sent him to make fun of the living God. Maybe the Lord your God will punish him for what he has heard him say. So pray for the remaining people who are still alive here.' "

5King Hezekiah's officials came to Isaiah. 6Then Isaiah said to them, "Tell your master, 'The LORD says, "Do not be afraid of what you have heard. The officers who are under the king of Assyria have spoken evil things against me. 7Listen! I will send him news from his own country. It will upset him so much that he will return home. There I will have him cut down with a sword." ' "

8The field commander heard that the king of Assyria had left Lachish. So the commander pulled his troops back from Jerusalem. He went to join the king. He found out that the king was fighting against Libnah.

9During that time Sennacherib received a report. He was told that Tirhakah was marching out to fight against him. Tirhakah was the king of Egypt. He was from the land of Cush.

Sennacherib sent messengers again to Hezekiah with a letter. It said, 10"Tell Hezekiah, the king of Judah, 'Don't let the god you depend on trick you. He says, "Jerusalem will not be handed over to the king of Assyria." But don't believe him.

11" 'I'm sure you have heard about what the kings of Assyria have done to all of the other countries. They have destroyed them completely. So do you think you will be saved? 12The kings who ruled before me destroyed many nations. Did the gods of those nations save them? Did the gods of Gozan, Haran or Rezeph save them? What about the gods of the people of Eden who were in Tel Assar? 13Where is the king of Hamath? Where is the king of Arpad? Where is the king of the city of Sepharvaim? Where are the kings of Hena or Ivvah?' "

Hezekiah Prays to the LORD

14When Hezekiah received the letter from the messengers, he read it. Then he went up to the LORD's temple. There he spread the letter out in front of the LORD.

15Hezekiah prayed to the LORD. He said, "LORD, you are the God of Israel. You sit on your throne between the cherubim. You alone are God over all of the kingdoms on earth. You have made heaven and earth. 16Listen, LORD. Hear us. Open your eyes, LORD. Look at the trouble we're in. Listen to what Sennacherib is saying. You are the living God. And he dares to make fun of you!

17"LORD, it's true that the kings of Assyria have completely destroyed many nations and their lands. 18They have thrown the statues of the gods of those nations into the fire. And they have destroyed them. That's because they weren't really gods at all. They were nothing but statues that were made out of wood and stone. They were made by the hands of men.

19"LORD our God, save us from the powerful hand of Sennacherib. Then all of the kingdoms on earth will know that you alone are God."

Isaiah Prophesies That Sennacherib Will Fall From Power

20Isaiah sent a message to Hezekiah. Isaiah was the son of Amoz. Isaiah said, "The LORD is the God of Israel. He says, 'I have heard your prayer about Sennacherib, the king of Assyria.'

21"Here is the message the LORD has spoken against him. The LORD says,

" 'You will not win the battle over Zion.
Its people hate you and make fun of you.
The people of Jerusalem lift up their heads proudly
as you run away.
22Who have you laughed at?
Who have you spoken evil things against?
Who have you raised your voice against?
Who have you looked at so proudly?
You have done it against me.
I am the Holy One of Israel!
23Through your messengers
you have laughed at me again and again.
And you have said,
"I have many chariots.
With them I have climbed to the tops of the mountains.
I've climbed the highest mountains in Lebanon.
I've cut down its tallest cedar trees.
I've cut down the best of its pine trees.
I've reached its farthest parts.
I've reached its finest forests.
24I've dug wells in strange lands.
I've drunk the water from them.
I've walked through all of Egypt's streams.
I've dried up every one of them."
25" 'But I, the LORD, say, "Haven't you heard what I have done?
Long ago I arranged for you to do all of that.
In days of old I planned it.
Now I have made it happen.

You have turned cities with high walls
    into piles of stone.
26 Their people do not have any power
        left.
    They are troubled and put to shame.
    They are like plants in the field.
    They are like new green plants.
    They are like grass that grows on a roof.
        It dries up before it is completely
            grown.
27 " ' "But I know where you live.
    I know when you come and go.
    I know how very angry you are with
        me.
28 You roar against me and brag.
    And I have heard your bragging.
    So I will put my hook in your nose.
    I will put my bit in your mouth.
    And I will make you go home
        by the same way you came." ' "

29 The LORD said, "Hezekiah, here is a
miraculous sign for you.

    "This year you will eat what grows by
        itself.
    In the second year you will eat what
        grows from that.
    But in the third year you will plant
        your crops and gather them in.
    You will plant your grapevines and
        eat their fruit.
30 The people of Judah who are still alive
        will be like plants.
    Once more they will put down roots
        and produce fruit.
31 Out of Jerusalem will come those who
        remain.
    Out of Mount Zion will come those
        who are still left alive.

    "My great love will make sure that
        happens.
    I rule over all.

32 "Here is a message from me about the
king of Assyria. It says,

    " 'He will not enter this city.
    He will not even shoot an arrow at it.
    He will not come near it with a shield.
    He will not build a ramp in order to
        climb over its walls.
33 By the same way he came he will go
        home.
    He will not enter this city,'
        announces the LORD.
34 " 'I will guard this city and save it.
    I will do it for myself. And I will do it
        for my servant David.' "

35 That night the angel of the LORD went
into the camp of the Assyrians. He put to

death 185,000 soldiers there. The people
of Jerusalem got up the next morning.
They looked out and saw all of the dead
bodies. 36 So Sennacherib, the king of
Assyria, took the army tents down. Then
he left. He returned to Nineveh and
stayed there.

37 One day Sennacherib was worshiping
in the temple of his god Nisroch. His sons
Adrammelech and Sharezer cut him
down with their swords. Then they
escaped to the land of Ararat. Esarhaddon
became the next king after his father Sennacherib.

Hezekiah Becomes Sick

20 In those days Hezekiah became
very sick. He knew he was about
to die.

The prophet Isaiah, the son of Amoz,
went to him. Isaiah told Hezekiah, "The
LORD says, 'Put everything in order. Make
out your will. You are going to die soon.
You will not get well again.' "

2 Hezekiah turned his face toward the
wall. He prayed to the LORD. He said,
3 "LORD, please remember how faithful
I've been to you. I've lived the way you
wanted me to. I've served you with all my
heart. I've done what is good in your
sight." And Hezekiah cried bitterly.

4 Isaiah was leaving the middle courtyard. Before he had left it, a message came
to him from the LORD. He said, 5 "Go back
and speak to Hezekiah. He is the leader of
my people. Tell him, 'The LORD, the God
of King David, says, "I have heard your
prayer. I have seen your tears. And I will
heal you. On the third day from now you
will go up to my temple. 6 I will add 15
years to your life. And I will save you and
this city from the powerful hand of the
king of Assyria. I will guard this city. I will
do it for myself. And I will do it for my servant David." ' "

7 Then Isaiah said, "Press some figs
together. Spread them on a piece of
cloth." So that's what they did. Then they
applied it to Hezekiah's boil. And he got
well again.

8 Hezekiah had said to Isaiah, "You say
the LORD will heal me. You say that I'll go
up to his temple on the third day from
now. What will the miraculous sign be to
prove he'll really do that?"

9 Isaiah answered, "The LORD will do
what he has promised. Here is his sign to
you. Do you want the shadow the sun
makes to go forward ten steps? Or do you
want it to go back ten steps?"

10 "It's easy for the shadow to go for-

ward ten steps," said Hezekiah. "So have it go back ten steps."

11Then the prophet Isaiah called out to the LORD. And the LORD made the shadow go back ten steps. It went back the ten steps it had gone down on the stairway Ahaz had made.

Messengers Come From Babylon to Hezekiah

12At that time Merodach-Baladan, the king of Babylonia, sent Hezekiah letters and a gift. He had heard that Hezekiah had been sick. Merodach-Baladan was the son of Baladan.

13Hezekiah received the messengers. He showed them everything that was in his storerooms. He showed them the silver and gold. He showed them the spices and the fine olive oil. He showed them where he kept his weapons. And he showed them all of his treasures. In fact, he showed them everything that was in his palace and in his whole kingdom.

14Then Isaiah the prophet went to King Hezekiah. He asked him, "What did those men say? Where did they come from?"

"They came from a land far away," Hezekiah said. "They came from Babylon."

15The prophet asked, "What did they see in your palace?"

"They saw everything in my palace," Hezekiah said. "I showed them all of my treasures."

16Then Isaiah said to Hezekiah, "Listen to the LORD's message. He says, **17**'You can be sure the time will come when everything in your palace will be carried off to Babylon. Everything the kings before you have stored up until this day will be taken away. There will not be anything left,' says the LORD. **18**'Some of the members of your family line will be taken away. They will be your own flesh and blood. They will include the children who will be born into your family line in years to come. And they will serve the king of Babylonia in his palace.' "

19"The message the LORD has spoken through you is good," Hezekiah replied. He thought, "There will be peace and safety while I'm still living."

20The other events of the rule of Hezekiah are written down. Everything he accomplished is written down. That includes how he made the pool and the tunnel. He used them to bring water into Jerusalem. All of those things are written in the official records of the kings of Judah.

21Hezekiah joined the members of his family who had already died. His son Manasseh became the next king after him.

Manasseh Becomes King of Judah

21 Manasseh was 12 years old when he became king. He ruled in Jerusalem for 55 years. His mother's name was Hephzibah.

2Manasseh did what was evil in the sight of the LORD. He followed the practices of the nations. The LORD hated those practices. He had driven those nations out to make room for the people of Israel.

3Manasseh rebuilt the high places. His father Hezekiah had destroyed them. Manasseh also set up altars to the god Baal. He made a pole that was used to worship the goddess Asherah. Ahab, the king of Israel, had done those same things. Manasseh even bowed down to all of the stars. And he worshiped them.

4He built altars in the LORD's temple. The LORD had said about his temple, "I will put my Name there in Jerusalem." **5**In both courtyards of the LORD's temple Manasseh built altars to honor all of the stars.

6He sacrificed his own son in the fire to another god. He practiced all kinds of evil magic. He got messages from those who had died. He talked to the spirits of the dead. He did many things that were evil in the sight of the LORD. He made him very angry.

7Manasseh had carved a pole for worshiping Asherah. He put it in the temple. The LORD had spoken to David and his son Solomon about the temple. He had said, "My Name will be in this temple and in Jerusalem forever. Out of all of the cities in the tribes of Israel I have chosen Jerusalem. **8**I gave this land to your people who lived long ago. I will not make the Israelites wander away from it again. But they must be careful to do everything I commanded them. They must obey the whole Law that my servant Moses gave them."

9But the people didn't pay any attention. Manasseh led them down the wrong path. They did more evil things than the nations the LORD had destroyed to make room for the people of Israel.

10The LORD spoke through his servants the prophets. He said, **11**"Manasseh, the king of Judah, has committed terrible sins. I hate them. Manasseh has done more evil things than the Amorites who were in the land before him. And he has led Judah to commit sin by worshiping his statues of gods.

¹²"I am the God of Israel. I tell you, 'I am going to bring trouble on Jerusalem and Judah. It will be so horrible that the ears of everyone who hears about it will ring. ¹³I will measure out punishment against Jerusalem, just as I did against Samaria. I used a plumb line against the royal family of Ahab to prove that they did not measure up to my standards. I will use the same plumb line against Jerusalem. I will wipe out Jerusalem, just as someone wipes a dish. I will wipe it and turn it upside down. ¹⁴I will desert those who remain among my people. I will hand them over to their enemies. All of their enemies will rob them.

¹⁵" 'That is because my people have done what is evil in my sight. They have made me very angry. They have done that from the day their own people came out of Egypt until this very day.' "

¹⁶Manasseh also spilled the blood of many people who weren't guilty of doing anything wrong. He spilled so much blood that he filled Jerusalem with it from one end of the city to the other. And he caused Judah to commit sin. So they also did what was evil in the sight of the LORD.

¹⁷The other events of the rule of Manasseh are written down. Everything he did is written down. That includes the sin he committed. All of those things are written in the official records of the kings of Judah.

¹⁸Manasseh joined the members of his family who had already died. His body was buried in his palace garden. It was called the garden of Uzza. Manasseh's son Amon became the next king after him.

Amon Becomes King of Judah

¹⁹Amon was 22 years old when he became king. He ruled in Jerusalem for two years. His mother's name was Meshullemeth. She was the daughter of Haruz. She was from Jotbah. ²⁰Amon did what was evil in the sight of the LORD, just as his father Manasseh had done. ²¹He lived the way his father had lived. He worshiped the statues of the gods his father had worshiped. He bowed down to them. ²²He deserted the LORD, the God of his people. He didn't live the way the LORD wanted him to.

²³Amon's officials made plans against him. They murdered the king in his palace. ²⁴Then the people of the land killed all those who had made plans against King Amon. They made his son Josiah king in his place.

²⁵The other events of the rule of Amon are written down. Everything he did is written down. All of those things are written in the official records of the kings of Judah. ²⁶Amon's body was buried in his grave in the garden of Uzza. His son Josiah became the next king after him.

Hilkiah Finds the Scroll of the Law

22 Josiah was eight years old when he became king. He ruled in Jerusalem for 31 years. His mother's name was Jedidah. She was the daughter of Adaiah. She was from Bozkath.

²Josiah did what was right in the eyes of the LORD. He lived the way King David had lived. He didn't turn away from it to the right or the left.

OBEYS ✔

JOSIAH DID WHAT WAS RIGHT IN THE EYES OF THE LORD. HE LIVED THE WAY KING DAVID HAD LIVED. HE DIDN'T TURN AWAY FROM IT TO THE RIGHT OR THE LEFT.
— 2 KINGS 22:2 —

³King Josiah sent his secretary Shaphan to the LORD's temple. It was in the 18th year of Josiah's rule. Shaphan was the son of Azaliah. Azaliah was the son of Meshullam. Josiah said, ⁴"Go up to the high priest Hilkiah. Have him add up the money that has been brought into the LORD's temple. Those who guard the doors have collected it from the people.

⁵"Have them put all of the money in the care of the men who have been put in charge of the work on the LORD's temple. Have them pay the workers who repair it. ⁶Have them pay the builders and those who work with wood. Have them pay those who lay the stones. Also have them buy lumber and blocks of stone to repair the temple.

⁷"But they don't have to report how they use the money that is given to them. That's because they are completely honest."

⁸The high priest Hilkiah spoke to the

secretary Shaphan. He said, "I've found the Scroll of the Law in the LORD's temple." He gave it to Shaphan, who read it.

⁹Then Shaphan went to King Josiah. He told him, "Your officials have paid out the money that was in the LORD's temple. They've put it in the care of the workers and directors there." ¹⁰Shaphan continued, "The priest Hilkiah has given me a scroll." Shaphan read some of it to the king.

¹¹The king heard the words of the Scroll of the Law. When he did, he tore his royal robes. ¹²He gave orders to the priest Hilkiah, Ahikam, Acbor, the secretary Shaphan and Asaiah. Ahikam was the son of Shaphan. Acbor was the son of Micaiah. And Asaiah was the king's attendant.

Josiah commanded them, ¹³"Go. Ask the LORD for advice. Ask him about what is written in this scroll that has been found. Do it for me. Also do it for the people and the whole nation of Judah. The LORD's anger is burning against us. That's because our people before us didn't obey the words of this scroll. They didn't do everything that is written there about us."

¹⁴The priest Hilkiah went to speak to the prophet Huldah. So did Ahikam, Acbor, Shaphan and Asaiah. Huldah was the wife of Shallum. Shallum was the son of Tikvah. Tikvah was the son of Harhas. Shallum took care of the sacred robes. Huldah lived in the New Quarter of Jerusalem.

¹⁵She said to them, "The LORD is the God of Israel. He says, 'Tell the man who sent you to me, ¹⁶"The LORD says, 'I am going to bring horrible trouble on this place and its people. Everything that is written in the scroll the king of Judah has read will take place.

¹⁷" ' " 'That is because the people have deserted me. They have burned incense to other gods. They have made me very angry because of the statues of gods their hands have made. So my anger will burn against this place. The fire of my anger will not be put out.' " '

¹⁸"The king of Judah sent you to ask the LORD for advice. Tell him, 'The LORD is the God of Israel. He has a message for you about the things you heard. He says, ¹⁹"Your heart was tender. You made yourself low in my sight. You heard what I spoke against this place and its people. I said they would be under a curse. I told them they would be destroyed. You tore your royal robes and sobbed. And I have heard you," announces the LORD.

²⁰" ' "You will join the members of your family who have already died. Your body will be buried in peace. Your eyes will not see all of the trouble I am going to bring on this place." ' "

Huldah's answer was taken back to the king.

Josiah Promises to Follow the Covenant

23 Then the king called together all of the elders of Judah and Jerusalem. ²He went up to the LORD's temple. The people of Judah and Jerusalem went with him. So did the priests and prophets. All of them went, from the least important of them to the most important.

The king had all of the words of the Scroll of the Covenant read to them. The scroll had been found in the LORD's temple.

³The king stood next to his pillar. He agreed to the terms of the covenant in front of the LORD. He promised to follow him and obey his commands, directions and rules. He promised to obey them with all his heart and with all his soul. So he agreed to the terms of the covenant that were written down in that scroll. Then all of the people committed themselves to the covenant.

⁴Certain articles that were in the LORD's temple had been made to honor the god Baal and the goddess Asherah and all of the stars in the sky. The king ordered the high priest Hilkiah to remove those articles. He ordered the priests who were under him and the men who guarded the doors to help Hilkiah. Josiah burned the articles outside Jerusalem. He burned them in the fields in the Kidron Valley. And he took the ashes to Bethel.

⁵He got rid of the priests who served other gods. The kings of Judah had appointed them to burn incense. They burned the incense on the high places of the towns of Judah. And they burned it on the high places around Jerusalem. They burned incense to honor Baal and the sun and moon. They burned it to honor all of the stars.

⁶Josiah removed the Asherah pole from the LORD's temple. It had been used to worship Asherah. He took it to the Kidron Valley outside Jerusalem. There he burned it. He ground it into powder. And he scattered it over the graves of the ordinary people.

⁷He also tore down the rooms where the male temple prostitutes stayed. Those rooms were in the LORD's temple. The

women had made cloth for Asherah in them.

8Josiah brought all of the priests from the towns of Judah and destroyed the high places. He destroyed them from Geba all the way to Beersheba. The priests had burned incense on them. Josiah broke down the high places at the gates. That included the high place at the entrance of the Gate of Joshua. It was on the left side of one of Jerusalem's gates. Joshua was the city governor.

9The priests of the high places didn't serve at the LORD's altar in Jerusalem. In spite of that, they ate with the other priests. All of them ate bread that was made without yeast.

10Josiah destroyed the high places at Topheth in the Valley of Ben Hinnom. He didn't want anyone to use them to sacrifice his son or daughter in the fire to the god Molech.

11He removed the statues of horses from the entrance to the LORD's temple. The kings of Judah had set them apart to honor the sun. The statues were in the courtyard. They were near the room of an official named Nathan-Melech. Josiah burned the chariots that had been set apart to honor the sun.

12He pulled down the altars the kings of Judah had set up. They had put them on the palace roof near the upstairs room of Ahaz. Josiah also pulled down the altars Manasseh had built. They were in the two courtyards of the LORD's temple. Josiah removed the altars from there. He smashed them to pieces. Then he threw the broken pieces into the Kidron Valley.

13The king also destroyed the high places that were east of Jerusalem. They were at the southern end of the Mount of Olives. They were the ones Solomon, the king of Israel, had built. He had built a high place for worshiping Ashtoreth. She was the evil goddess of the people of Sidon. Solomon had also built one for worshiping Chemosh. He was the evil god of Moab. And Solomon had built one for worshiping Molech. He was the god of the people of Ammon. The LORD hated that god.

14Josiah smashed the sacred stones. He cut down the poles that were used to worship the goddess Asherah. Then he covered all of those places with human bones.

15There was an altar at Bethel. It was at the high place that had been made by Jeroboam, the son of Nebat. Jeroboam had caused Israel to commit sin. Even that altar and high place were destroyed by Josiah. He burned the high place. He ground it into powder. He also burned the Asherah pole.

16Then Josiah looked around. He saw the tombs that were on the side of the hill. He had the bones removed from them. And he burned them on the altar to make it "unclean." That's what the LORD had said would happen. He had spoken that message through a man of God. The man had announced those things long before they took place.

17The king asked, "What's that stone on the grave over there?"

The men of the city said, "It marks the tomb where the body of a man of God is buried. He came from Judah. He spoke against the altar at Bethel. He announced the very things you have done to it."

18"Leave it alone," Josiah said. "Don't let anyone touch his bones."

So they spared his bones. They also spared the bones of the prophet who had come from the northern kingdom of Israel.

19Josiah did in the rest of the northern kingdom the same things he had done at Bethel. He removed all of the small temples at the high places. He made them "unclean." The kings of Israel had built them in the towns of the northern kingdom. The people in those towns had made the LORD very angry.

20Josiah killed all of the priests of those high places on the altars. He burned human bones on the altars. Then he went back to Jerusalem.

21The king gave an order to all of the people. He said, "Celebrate the Passover Feast to honor the LORD your God. Do what is written in this Scroll of the Covenant."

22A Passover Feast like that one had not been held for a long time. There hadn't been any like it since the days of the judges who led Israel. And there hadn't been any like it during the whole time the kings of Israel and Judah were ruling.

23King Josiah celebrated the Passover in Jerusalem to honor the LORD. It was in the 18th year of his rule.

24And that's not all. Josiah got rid of those who got messages from people who had died. He got rid of those who talked to the spirits of the dead. He got rid of the statues of family gods and the statues of other gods. He got rid of everything else the LORD hates that was in Judah and Jerusalem. He did it to carry out what the law required. That law was written in the scroll the priest Hilkiah had found in the LORD's temple.

²⁵There was no king like Josiah either before him or after him. None of them turned to the LORD as he did. He followed the LORD with all his heart and all his soul. He followed him with all his strength. He did everything the Law of Moses required.

²⁶In spite of that, the LORD didn't turn away from his burning anger. It blazed out against Judah. That's because of everything Manasseh had done to make him very angry.

²⁷So the LORD said, "I will remove Judah from my land. I will do to them what I did to Israel. I will turn my back on Jerusalem. It is the city I chose. I will also turn my back on this temple. I spoke about it. I said, 'I will put my Name here.' " *(1 Kings 8:29)*

JOSIAH

2 KINGS 23:25

There was no king like Josiah either before him or after him. None of them turned to the LORD as he did. He followed the LORD with all his heart and all his soul. He followed him with all his strength. He did everything the Law of Moses required.

Josiah (joe-SIE-uh) lay in his bed, but he couldn't sleep. He had been king of Judah since he was only eight years old. But he had never before had a day like today. He had sent his servant Shaphan to the temple. Shaphan returned to Josiah carrying a scroll that the priest had given him. He read parts of the scroll to Josiah. The scroll contained the words of God's law.

Josiah thought about how many of the laws he and his people were not obeying. More than anything, Josiah wanted to obey God and follow him completely.

Josiah decided right then to begin to obey all of God's laws.

He began by tearing down the idols and sending away all the priests who worshiped other gods. **HE TORE DOWN THE IDOL THAT WAS IN GOD'S TEMPLE AND GROUND IT TO DUST.** He showed the people how they should follow only the one true God.

BE A JOSIAH

Josiah was still young when he decided to follow God completely. He carefully read God's law and obeyed it. You can be just like him. No matter how old or young you are, you can decide today to follow God.

JOSIAH OBEYED GOD AND FOLLOWED HIM WITH HIS WHOLE HEART.

Go to page 564 for the next Super Hero

28The other events of the rule of Josiah are written down. Everything he did is written down. All of those things are written in the official records of the kings of Judah.

29Pharaoh Neco was king of Egypt. He marched up to the Euphrates River. He went there to help the king of Assyria. It happened while Josiah was king. Josiah marched out to meet Neco in battle. When Neco saw him at Megiddo, he killed him.

30Josiah's servants brought his body in a chariot from Megiddo to Jerusalem. They buried his body in his own tomb. Then the people of the land went and got Jehoahaz. They anointed him as king in place of his father Josiah.

Jehoahaz Becomes King of Judah

31Jehoahaz was 23 years old when he became king. He ruled in Jerusalem for three months. His mother's name was Hamutal. She was the daughter of Jeremiah. She was from Libnah.

32Jehoahaz did what was evil in the sight of the LORD. He did just as the kings who had ruled before him had done. 33Pharaoh Neco put him in chains at Riblah in the land of Hamath. That kept him from ruling in Jerusalem. Neco made the people of Judah pay him a tax of almost four tons of silver and 75 pounds of gold.

34Pharaoh Neco made Eliakim king in place of his father Josiah. He changed Eliakim's name to Jehoiakim. But he took Jehoahaz with him to Egypt. And that's where Jehoahaz died.

35Jehoiakim paid Pharaoh Neco the silver and gold he required. To get the money, Jehoiakim taxed the land. He forced the people to give him the silver and gold. He made each one pay him what he required.

Jehoiakim Becomes King of Judah

36Jehoiakim was 25 years old when he became king. He ruled in Jerusalem for 11 years. His mother's name was Zebidah. She was the daughter of Pedaiah. She was from Rumah.

37Jehoiakim did what was evil in the sight of the LORD. He did just as the kings who had ruled before him had done.

24 During Jehoiakim's rule, Nebuchadnezzar marched into the land and attacked it. He was king of Babylonia. He became Jehoiakim's master for three years. But then Jehoiakim decided he didn't want to remain under Nebuchadnezzar's control.

2The LORD sent robbers against Jehoiakim from Babylonia, Aram, Moab and Ammon. He sent them to destroy Judah. That's what the LORD had said would happen. He had spoken that message through his servants the prophets.

3Those things happened to Judah in keeping with what the LORD had commanded. He brought enemies against his people in order to remove them from his land. He removed them because of all of the sins Manasseh had committed. 4He had spilled the blood of many people who weren't guilty of doing anything wrong. In fact, he spilled so much of their blood that he filled Jerusalem with it. So the LORD refused to forgive him.

5The other events of the rule of Jehoiakim are written down. Everything he did is written down. All of those things are written in the official records of the kings of Judah.

6Jehoiakim joined the members of his family who had already died. His son Jehoiachin became the next king after him.

7The king of Egypt didn't march out from his own country again. That's because the king of Babylonia had taken so much of his territory. That territory reached from the Wadi of Egypt all the way to the Euphrates River.

Jehoiachin Becomes King of Judah

8Jehoiachin was 18 years old when he became king. He ruled in Jerusalem for three months. His mother's name was Nehushta. She was the daughter of Elnathan. She was from Jerusalem.

9Jehoiachin did what was evil in the sight of the LORD. He did just as his father Jehoiakim had done.

10At that time the officers of Nebuchadnezzar, the king of Babylonia, marched to Jerusalem. They surrounded it and got ready to attack it. 11Nebuchadnezzar himself came up to the city. He arrived while his officers were attacking it.

12Jehoiachin, the king of Judah, handed himself over to him. Jehoiachin's mother did the same thing. And so did all of his attendants, nobles and officials.

The king of Babylonia took Jehoiachin away as his prisoner. It was in the eighth year of Nebuchadnezzar's rule.

13He removed all of the treasures from the LORD's temple. He also removed all of the treasures from the royal palace. He took away all of the gold articles that Solomon, the king of Israel, had made for the temple. That's what the LORD had announced would happen.

¹⁴Nebuchadnezzar took all of the people of Jerusalem to Babylonia as prisoners. That included all of the officers and fighting men. It also included all of the skilled workers. The total number of prisoners was 10,000. Only the poorest people were left in the land.

¹⁵Nebuchadnezzar took Jehoiachin to Babylon as his prisoner. He also took the king's mother from Jerusalem to Babylon. And he took Jehoiachin's wives, his officials and the most important men in the land.

¹⁶The king also forced the whole army of 7,000 soldiers to go away to Babylonia. Those men were strong and able to go to war. And the king forced 1,000 skilled workers to go to Babylonia.

¹⁷Nebuchadnezzar made Jehoiachin's uncle Mattaniah king in his place. And he changed Mattaniah's name to Zedekiah.

Zedekiah Becomes King of Judah

¹⁸Zedekiah was 21 years old when he became king. He ruled in Jerusalem for 11 years. His mother's name was Hamutal. She was the daughter of Jeremiah. She was from Libnah.

¹⁹Zedekiah did what was evil in the sight of the LORD. He did just as Jehoiakim had done. ²⁰The enemies of Jerusalem and Judah attacked them because the LORD was angry. In the end he threw them out of his land.

Nebuchadnezzar Destroys Jerusalem

Zedekiah also refused to remain under the control of Nebuchadnezzar.

25 Nebuchadnezzar was king of Babylonia. He marched out against Jerusalem. All of his armies went with him. It was in the ninth year of the rule of Zedekiah. It was on the tenth day of the tenth month. Nebuchadnezzar set up camp outside the city. He brought in war machines all around it. ²It was surrounded until the 11th year of King Zedekiah's rule.

³By the ninth day of the fourth month, there wasn't any food left in the city. So the people didn't have anything to eat.

⁴Then the Babylonians broke through the city wall. Judah's whole army ran away at night. They went out through the gate between the two walls that were near the king's garden. They escaped even though the Babylonians surrounded the city. Judah's army ran toward the Arabah Valley.

⁵But the armies of Babylonia chased King Zedekiah. They caught up with him in the flatlands near Jericho. All of his soldiers were separated from him. They had scattered in every direction.

⁶The king was captured. He was taken to the king of Babylonia at Riblah. That's where Nebuchadnezzar decided how he would be punished. ⁷His men killed the sons of Zedekiah. They forced him to watch it with his own eyes. Then they poked out his eyes. They put him in bronze chains. And they took him to Babylon.

⁸Nebuzaradan was an official of the king of Babylonia. In fact, he was commander of the royal guard. He came to Jerusalem. It was in the 19th year that Nebuchadnezzar was king of Babylonia. It was on the seventh day of the fifth month.

⁹Nebuzaradan set the LORD's temple on fire. He also set fire to the royal palace and all of the houses in Jerusalem. He burned down every important building. ¹⁰The armies of Babylonia broke down the walls around Jerusalem. That's what the commander told them to do.

¹¹Some people still remained in the city. But the commander Nebuzaradan took them away as prisoners. He also took the rest of the people of the land. That included those who had joined the king of Babylonia.

¹²But the commander left some of the poorest people of the land behind. He told them to work in the vineyards and fields.

¹³The armies of Babylonia destroyed the LORD's temple. They broke the bronze pillars into pieces. They broke up the bronze stands that could be moved around. And they broke up the huge bronze bowl. Then they carried the bronze away to Babylon. ¹⁴They also took away the pots, shovels, wick cutters and dishes. They took away all of the bronze articles that were used for any purpose in the temple. ¹⁵The commander of the royal guard took away the shallow cups for burning incense. He took away the sprinkling bowls. So he took away everything that was made out of pure gold or silver.

¹⁶The bronze was more than anyone could weigh. It included the bronze from the two pillars. It also included the bronze from the huge bowl and the stands. Solomon had made all of those things for the LORD's temple. ¹⁷Each pillar was 27 feet high. The bronze top of one pillar was

four and a half feet high. It was decorated with a set of bronze chains and pomegranates all around it. The other pillar was just like it. It also had a set of chains.

18The commander of the guard took some prisoners. They included the chief priest Seraiah and the priest Zephaniah who was under him. They also included the three men who guarded the temple doors.

19Some people were still left in the city. The commander took as a prisoner the officer who was in charge of the fighting men. He took the five men who gave advice to the king. He also took the secretary who was the chief officer in charge of getting the people of the land to serve in the army. And he took 60 of the secretary's men who were still in the city.

20The commander Nebuzaradan took all of them away. He brought them to the king of Babylonia at Riblah. 21There the king had them put to death. Riblah was in the land of Hamath.

So the people of Judah were taken as prisoners. They were taken far away from their own land.

22Nebuchadnezzar, the king of Babylonia, appointed Gedaliah to be over the people he had left behind in Judah. Gedaliah was the son of Ahikam. Ahikam was the son of Shaphan.

23All of Judah's army officers and their men heard about what had happened. They heard that the king had appointed Gedaliah as governor. So they came to Gedaliah at Mizpah. Ishmael, the son of Nethaniah, came. So did Johanan, the son of Kareah. Seraiah, the son of Tanhumeth, also came. And so did Jaazaniah, the son of the Maacathite. All of their men came too. Seraiah was from Netophah.

24Gedaliah took an oath to give hope to all of those men. He spoke in a kind way to them. He said, "Don't be afraid of the officials from Babylonia. Settle down in the land of Judah. Serve the king of Babylonia. Then things will go well with you."

25But in the seventh month Ishmael, the son of Nethaniah, came with ten men. He killed Gedaliah. He also killed the people of Judah and Babylonia who were with Gedaliah at Mizpah. Nethaniah was the son of Elishama. Ishmael was a member of the royal family.

26After he had killed Gedaliah, all of the people ran away to Egypt. Everyone from the least important of them to the most important ran away. The army officers went with them. All of them went to Egypt because they were afraid of the Babylonians.

Jehoiachin Is Set Free

27Evil-Merodach set Jehoiachin, the king of Judah, free from prison. It was in the 37th year after Jehoiachin had been taken away to Babylon. It was also the year Evil-Merodach became king of Babylonia. It was on the 27th day of the 12th month. 28Evil-Merodach spoke kindly to Jehoiachin. He gave him a place of honor. Other kings were with Jehoiachin in Babylon. But his place was more important than theirs.

29So Jehoiachin put his prison clothes away. For the rest of Jehoiachin's life the king provided what he needed. 30The king did that for Jehoiachin day by day as long as he lived.

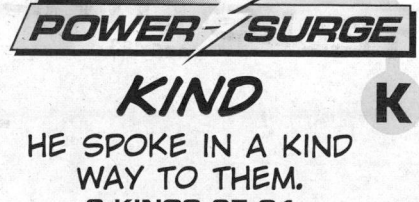

POWER-SURGE

KIND   K

HE SPOKE IN A KIND
WAY TO THEM.
— 2 KINGS 25:24 —

1 CHRONICLES

The book of 1 Chronicles begins with a long list of names that at first may seem boring. But the list forms the backbone of Israel's history and includes many heroes. The book continues with the story of King David's reign. David heroically conquers many of Israel's enemies. He also encourages the people to truly worship God by organizing the Levites into worship "teams," gatekeepers, treasurers, singers and instrument players. Reading 1 Chronicles will help you understand the importance of worshiping God.

CODE OF HONOR IN THIS BOOK . . .

STRONG
PAGES 474, 488, 497, 504, 507

BRAVE
PAGES 480, 490, 497, 500, 508

TELLS OTHERS
PAGE 493

THANKFUL
PAGES 493, 501

GIVING
PAGES 494, 508

OBEYS
PAGE 500

A List of Names From Adam to Abraham

A List of Names From Adam to the Sons of Noah

1 Adam, Seth, Enosh, ²Kenan, Maha- lalel, Jared, ³Enoch, Methuselah, Lamech, Noah.

⁴The sons of Noah were
Shem, Ham and Japheth.

The Sons of Japheth

⁵The sons of Japheth were
Gomer, Magog, Madai, Javan, Tubal, Meshech and Tiras.
⁶The sons of Gomer were
Ashkenaz, Riphath and Togarmah.
⁷The sons of Javan were
Elishah, Tarshish, the Kittim and the Rodanites.

The Sons of Ham

⁸The sons of Ham were
Cush, Egypt, Put and Canaan.
⁹The sons of Cush were
Seba, Havilah, Sabta, Raamah and Sabteca.
The sons of Raamah were
Sheba and Dedan.
¹⁰Cush was the father of
Nimrod. Nimrod grew up to be a mighty hero on the earth.

STRONG

NIMROD GREW UP TO BE A MIGHTY HERO ON THE EARTH.
— 1 CHRONICLES 1:10 —

¹¹Egypt was the father of
the Ludites, Anamites, Lehabites and Naphtuhites. ¹²He was also the father of the Pathrusites, Cas- luhites and Caphtorites. The Phi- listines came from the Casluhites.
¹³Canaan was the father of Sidon. Sidon was his oldest son.
Canaan was also the father of the Hittites, ¹⁴Jebusites, Amorites and Girgashites. ¹⁵And he was the father of the Hivites, Arkites, Sinites, ¹⁶Arvadites, Zemarites and Hamathites.

The Sons of Shem

¹⁷The sons of Shem were
Elam, Asshur, Arphaxad, Lud and Aram.
The sons of Aram were
Uz, Hul, Gether and Meshech.
¹⁸Arphaxad was the father of Shelah.
Shelah was the father of Eber.
¹⁹Eber was the father of two sons.
One was named Peleg. The earth was divided up in his time. His brother was named Joktan.
²⁰Joktan was the father of
Almodad, Sheleph, Hazarmaveth and Jerah. ²¹He was also the father of Hadoram, Uzal, Diklah, ²²Obal, Abimael, Sheba, ²³Ophir, Havilah and Jobab. All of them were sons of Joktan.

A List of Names From Shem to Abraham

²⁴Shem, Arphaxad, Shelah,
²⁵Eber, Peleg, Reu,
²⁶Serug, Nahor, Terah,
²⁷Abram. Abram was also called Abraham.

The Family Line of Abraham

²⁸The sons of Abraham were
Isaac and Ishmael.

The Family Line of Hagar

²⁹Here are the members of the family line of Hagar.
Nebaioth was Ishmael's oldest son. Then came Kedar, Adbeel, Mib- sam, ³⁰Mishma, Dumah, Massa, Hadad, Tema, ³¹Jetur, Naphish and Kedemah. All of them were Ishmael's sons.

The Family Line of Keturah

³²Here are the sons that were born to Abraham's concubine Keturah.
They were Zimran, Jokshan, Medan, Midian, Ishbak and Shu- ah.
The sons of Jokshan were
Sheba and Dedan.
³³The sons of Midian were
Ephah, Epher, Hanoch, Abida and Eldaah.
All of them came from Keturah.

The Family Line of Sarah

³⁴Abraham was the father of Isaac.
The sons of Isaac were
Esau and Israel.

The Family Line of Esau

35 The sons of Esau were
Eliphaz, Reuel, Jeush, Jalam and
Korah.
36 The sons of Eliphaz were
Teman, Omar, Zepho, Gatam and
Kenaz.
Timna had Amalek by Eliphaz.
37 The sons of Reuel were
Nahath, Zerah, Shammah and
Mizzah.

The People of Seir in Edom

38 The sons of Seir were
Lotan, Shobal, Zibeon, Anah,
Dishon, Ezer and Dishan.
39 The sons of Lotan were
Hori and Homam. Timna was
Lotan's sister.
40 The sons of Shobal were
Alvan, Manahath, Ebal, Shepho
and Onam.
The sons of Zibeon were
Aiah and Anah.
41 The son of Anah was
Dishon.
The sons of Dishon were
Hemdan, Eshban, Ithran and
Keran.
42 The sons of Ezer were
Bilhan, Zaavan and Akan.
The sons of Dishan were
Uz and Aran.

The Rulers of Edom

43 Before Israel had a king, there were
kings who ruled in Edom.
Bela was the son of Beor. Bela's city
was called Dinhabah.
44 When Bela died, Jobab became the
next king. Jobab was the son of
Zerah from Bozrah.
45 When Jobab died, Husham became
the next king. Husham was from
the land of the people of Teman.
46 When Husham died, Hadad became
the next king. Hadad was the son
of Bedad. Hadad had won the battle over Midian in the country of
Moab. Hadad's city was called
Avith.
47 When Hadad died, Samlah became
the next king. Samlah was from
Masrekah.
48 When Samlah died, Shaul became
the next king. Shaul was from
Rehoboth on the river.
49 When Shaul died, Baal-Hanan
became the next king. Baal-Hanan
was the son of Acbor.
50 When Baal-Hanan died, Hadad

became the next king. Hadad's
city was called Pau. His wife's
name was Mehetabel. She was the
daughter of Matred. Matred was
the daughter of Me-Zahab.
51 Hadad also died.

The chiefs of Edom were
Timna, Alvah, Jetheth, **52** Oholiba-
mah, Elah, Pinon, **53** Kenaz,
Teman, Mibzar, **54** Magdiel and
Iram. They were the chiefs of
Edom.

The Sons of Israel

2 Here are the names of the sons of
Israel.

Reuben, Simeon, Levi, Judah, Issachar, Zebulun, **2** Dan, Joseph, Benjamin, Naphtali, Gad, Asher.

The Family Line of Judah

The Family Line From Judah's Sons to Hezron's Sons

3 The sons of Judah were
Er, Onan and Shelah. A woman
from Canaan had those three sons
by him. She was the daughter of
Shua. Er was Judah's oldest son. He
was evil in the LORD's eyes. So the
LORD put him to death. **4** Tamar
was Judah's daughter-in-law. She
had Perez and Zerah by him. The
total number of Judah's sons was
five.

5 The sons of Perez were
Hezron and Hamul.
6 The sons of Zerah were
Zimri, Ethan, Heman, Calcol and
Darda. The total number of
Zerah's sons was five.
7 The son of Carmi was Achar.
He brought trouble on Israel. He
took some of the things that had
been set apart to the LORD in a special way to be destroyed. When he
did that, he disobeyed the LORD's
command.
8 The son of Ethan was
Azariah.
9 Hezron was the father of
Jerahmeel, Ram and Caleb.

The Family Line of Ram

10 Ram was the father of
Amminadab. Amminadab was the
father of Nahshon. Nahshon was
the leader of the people of Judah.
11 Nahshon was the father of Salmon. Salmon was the father of

Boaz. **12** Boaz was the father of Obed. And Obed was the father of Jesse.

13 Jesse's first son was

Eliab. His second son was Abinadab. The third was Shimea. **14** The fourth was Nethanel. The fifth was Raddai. **15** The sixth was Ozem. And the seventh was David. **16** Their sisters were Zeruiah and Abigail. Zeruiah's three sons were Abishai, Joab and Asahel. **17** Abigail was the mother of Amasa. Amasa's father was Jether. Jether belonged to the family line of Ishmael.

The Family Line of Caleb

18 Caleb was the son of Hezron. Caleb's wife Azubah had children by him. Jerioth also had children by him. Azubah's sons were Jesher, Shobab and Ardon. **19** When Azubah died, Caleb got married to Ephrath. She had Hur by him. **20** Hur was the father of Uri. And Uri was the father of Bezalel.

21 Later, Hezron made love to the daughter of Makir. He had gotten married to her when he was 60 years old. She had Segub by him. Makir was the father of Gilead. **22** Segub was the father of Jair. Jair controlled 23 towns in Gilead. **23** But Geshur and Aram captured Havvoth Jair. They also captured Kenath and the settlements that were around it. The total number of towns that were captured was 60. Hezron, Segub and Jair belonged to the family line of Makir. Makir was the father of Gilead.

24 Hezron died in Caleb Ephrathah. Abijah was Hezron's wife. She had Ashhur by him. Ashhur was born after Hezron died. Ashhur was the father of Tekoa.

The Family Line of Jerahmeel

25 Here are the sons of Jerahmeel. He was the oldest son of Hezron. Ram was Jerahmeel's oldest son. Then came Bunah, Oren, Ozem and Ahijah. **26** Jerahmeel had another wife. Her name was Atarah. She was the mother of Onam.

27 Here are the sons of Ram. He was the oldest son of Jerahmeel. The sons of Ram were

Maaz, Jamin and Eker.

28 The sons of Onam were

Shammai and Jada.

The sons of Shammai were

Nadab and Abishur.

29 Abishur's wife was named Abihail. She had Ahban and Molid by him.

30 The sons of Nadab were

Seled and Appaim. Seled died without having any children.

31 The son of Appaim was

Ishi. Ishi was the father of Sheshan.

Sheshan was the father of Ahlai.

32 The sons of Jada were

Jether and Jonathan. Jada was Shammai's brother. Jether died without having any children.

33 The sons of Jonathan were

Peleth and Zaza.

They belonged to the family line of Jerahmeel.

34 Sheshan didn't have any sons. All he had was daughters.

He had a servant from Egypt named Jarha. **35** Sheshan gave his daughter to be married to his servant Jarha. She had Attai by Jarha.

36 Attai was the father of Nathan.

Nathan was the father of Zabad.

37 Zabad was the father of Ephlal.

Ephlal was the father of Obed.

38 Obed was the father of Jehu.

Jehu was the father of Azariah.

39 Azariah was the father of Helez.

Helez was the father of Eleasah.

40 Eleasah was the father of Sismai.

Sismai was the father of Shallum.

41 Shallum was the father of Jekamiah.

And Jekamiah was the father of Elishama.

The Family Groups of Caleb

42 Caleb was the brother of Jerahmeel.

Caleb's oldest son was Mesha. Mesha was the father of Ziph. Caleb had another son named Mareshah. Mareshah was the father of Hebron.

43 The sons of Hebron were

Korah, Tappuah, Rekem and Shema. **44** Shema was the father of Raham. Raham was the father of Jorkeam. Rekem was the father of Shammai. **45** The son of Shammai was Maon. Maon was the father of Beth Zur.

46 Caleb had a concubine named Ephah. She was the mother of Haran, Moza and Gazez. Haran was the father of Gazez.

47 The sons of Jahdai were
Regem, Jotham, Geshan, Pelet,
Ephah and Shaaph.
48 Caleb had a concubine named Maacah. She was the mother of Sheber and Tirhanah. **49** She was also the mother of Shaaph and Sheva. Shaaph was the father of Madmannah. Sheva was the father of Macbenah and Gibea. Caleb's daughter was Acsah. **50** All of them belonged to the family line of Caleb.

Hur was the oldest son of Ephrathah. Hur was the brother of Shobal. Shobal was the father of Kiriath Jearim. **51** Hur was the father of Salma. Salma was the father of Bethlehem. Hur was also the father of Hareph. Hareph was the father of Beth Gader.
52 Here is the family line of Shobal, the father of Kiriath Jearim. It included
Haroeh and half of the people of Manahath. **53** It also included the family groups of Kiriath Jearim. They were the Ithrites, Puthites, Shumathites and Mishraites. The people of Zorah and Eshtaol belonged to those family groups.
54 Here is the family line of Salma. It included
Bethlehem, the people of Netophah, Atroth Beth Joab, half of the people of Manahath, and the Zorites. **55** It also included the family groups of secretaries who lived at Jabez. They were the Tirathites, Shimeathites and Sucathites. They were the Kenites who belonged to the family line of Hammath. Hammath was the father of the family line of Recab.

The Sons of David

3 Here are the sons of David who were born to him in Hebron.
His first son was Amnon. Amnon's mother was Ahinoam from Jezreel.
The second son was Daniel. His mother was Abigail from Carmel.
2 The third son was Absalom. His mother was Maacah. She was the daughter of Talmai, the king of Geshur.
The fourth son was Adonijah. His mother was Haggith.

3 The fifth son was Shephatiah. His mother was Abital.
The sixth son was Ithream. David's wife Eglah had Ithream by him.
4 Those six sons were born to David in Hebron. He ruled there for seven and a half years.
After that, he ruled in Jerusalem for 33 years. **5** Children were born to him there. They included Shammua, Shobab, Nathan and Solomon. The mother of those four sons was Bathsheba. She was the daughter of Ammiel.
6 David's children also included Ibhar, Elishua, Eliphelet, **7** Nogah, Nepheg, Japhia, **8** Elishama, Eliada and Eliphelet. There were nine of them. **9** David was the father of all of those sons. His concubines also had sons by him. David's sons had a sister named Tamar.

The Kings of Judah

10 Solomon's son was Rehoboam. Abijah was the son of Rehoboam. Asa was the son of Abijah. Jehoshaphat was the son of Asa.
11 Jehoram was the son of Jehoshaphat.
Ahaziah was the son of Jehoram. Joash was the son of Ahaziah.
12 Amaziah was the son of Joash. Azariah was the son of Amaziah. Jotham was the son of Azariah.
13 Ahaz was the son of Jotham. Hezekiah was the son of Ahaz. Manasseh was the son of Hezekiah.
14 Amon was the son of Manasseh. Josiah was the son of Amon.
15 Josiah's first son was Johanan. Jehoiakim was his second son. Zedekiah was the third son. Shallum was the fourth son.
16 The next king after Jehoiakim was his son Jehoiachin.
After that, Josiah's son Zedekiah became king.

The Royal Family Line After Jehoiachin

17 Here are the members of the family line of Jehoiachin. He was taken as a prisoner to Babylon.
His sons were Shealtiel, **18** Malkiram, Pedaiah, Shenazzar, Jekamiah, Hoshama and Nedabiah.
19 The sons of Pedaiah were Zerubbabel and Shimei.
The sons of Zerubbabel were Meshullam and Hananiah.

Shelomith was their sister.
²⁰ There were also five other sons.
They were Hashubah, Ohel, Berekiah, Hasadiah and Jushab-Hesed.
²¹ The family line of Hananiah included
Pelatiah and Jeshaiah. It also included the sons of Rephaiah,
Arnan, Obadiah and Shecaniah.
²² The family line of Shecaniah included
Shemaiah and his sons.
They were Hattush, Igal, Bariah,
Neariah and Shaphat. The total
number of men was six.
²³ The sons of Neariah were
Elioenai, Hizkiah and Azrikam.
The total number of sons was
three.
²⁴ The sons of Elioenai were
Hodaviah, Eliashib, Pelaiah, Akkub, Johanan, Delaiah and Anani.
The total number of sons was sev-
en.

Other Family Groups of Judah

4 The family line of Judah included
Perez, Hezron, Carmi, Hur and
Shobal.
² Reaiah was the son of Shobal and the
father of Jahath. Jahath was the
father of Ahumai and Lahad.
Those were the family groups of
the people of Zorah.
³ The sons of Etam were
Jezreel, Ishma and Idbash. Their
sister was named Hazzelelponi.
⁴ Penuel was the father of Gedor.
Ezer was the father of Hushah.
Those people belonged to the family
line of Hur. He was the oldest son
of Ephrathah and the father of
Bethlehem.
⁵ Ashhur was the father of Tekoa. Ashhur had two wives. Their names
were Helah and Naarah.
⁶ Naarah had Ahuzzam, Hepher, Tem-
eni and Haahashtari by Ashhur.
They belonged to the family line
of Naarah.
⁷ The sons of Helah were
Zereth, Zohar, Ethnan ⁸ and Koz.
Koz was the father of Anub and
Hazzobebah. He was also the
father of the family groups of
Aharhel. Aharhel was the son of
Harum.
⁹ Jabez was more respected than his
brothers. His mother had named him

Jabez. She had said, "I was in a lot of pain
when he was born."
¹⁰ Jabez cried out to the God of Israel.
He said, "I wish you would bless me. I
wish you would give me more territory.
Let your powerful hand be with me. Keep
me from harm. Then I won't have any
pain." God gave him what he asked for.

¹¹ Kelub was the brother of Shuhah and
the father of Mehir. Mehir was the
father of Eshton. ¹² Eshton was the
father of Beth Rapha, Paseah and
Tehinnah. Tehinnah was the
father of Ir Nahash. Those were
the men of Recah.

¹³ The sons of Kenaz were
Othniel and Seraiah.
The sons of Othniel were
Hathath and Meonothai. ¹⁴ Meon-
othai was the father of Ophrah.
Seraiah was the father of Joab.
Joab was
the father of Ge Harashim. Ge
Harashim was called by that name
because all of its people were
skilled workers.
¹⁵ The sons of Caleb were
Iru, Elah and Naam. Caleb was the
son of Jephunneh.
The son of Elah was
Kenaz.
¹⁶ The sons of Jehallelel were
Ziph, Ziphah, Tiria and Asarel.
¹⁷ The sons of Ezrah were
Jether, Mered, Epher and Jalon.
One of Mered's wives had Miriam,
Shammai and Ishbah by him. Ishbah was the father of Eshtemoa.
¹⁸ Those were the children of Pharaoh's daughter Bithiah. Mered had
gotten married to her. His wife
from Judah had Jered, Heber and
Jekuthiel by him. Jered was the
father of Gedor. Heber was the
father of Soco. Jekuthiel was the
father of Zanoah.
¹⁹ Hodiah's wife was the sister of
Naham. Her sons were
the father of Keilah the Garmite
and Eshtemoa the Maacathite.
²⁰ The sons of Shimon were
Amnon, Rinnah, Ben-Hanan and
Tilon.
The family line of Ishi included
Zoheth and Ben-Zoheth.
²¹ Shelah was the son of Judah.
The sons of Shelah were Er and
Laadah. Er was the father of Lecah.
Laadah was the father of Mareshah. He was also the father of the

family groups of the linen workers who lived in Beth Ashbea. 22Other sons of Shelah were Jokim, Joash, Saraph and the men of Cozeba. Moab and Jashubi Lehem were ruled by sons of Shelah. The records of all of those matters are very old. 23Some of Shelah's sons were potters who lived in Netaim and Gederah. They stayed there and worked for the king.

The Family Line of Simeon

24The family line of Simeon included Nemuel, Jamin, Jarib, Zerah and Shaul.
25Shallum was Shaul's son. Mibsam was Shallum's son. Mishma was Mibsam's son.
26The family line of Mishma included Hammuel. Hammuel was Mishma's son. Zaccur was Hammuel's son. Shimei was Zaccur's son.
27Shimei had 16 sons and six daughters. But his brothers didn't have many children. So their whole family group didn't have as many people as Judah had. 28Shimei's family group lived in Beersheba, Moladah, Hazar Shual, 29Bilhah, Ezem, Tolad, 30Bethuel, Hormah, Ziklag, 31Beth Marcaboth, Hazar Susim, Beth Biri and Shaaraim. Those were their towns until David became king. 32Five of the villages that were around those towns were Etam, Ain, Rimmon, Token and Ashan. 33The territory of all of the villages that were around those towns reached all the way to Baalath. Those were their settlements. The tribe of Simeon kept its own family history.

34Simeon's family line included Meshobab, Jamlech and Joshah. Joshah was the son of Amaziah. 35Simeon's family line also included Joel and Jehu. Jehu was the son of Joshibiah. Joshibiah was the son of Seraiah. Seraiah was the son of Asiel. 36And the family line included Elioenai, Jaakobah, Jeshohaiah, Asaiah, Adiel, Jesimiel, Benaiah 37and Ziza. Ziza was the son of Shiphi. Shiphi was the son of Allon. Allon was the son of Jedaiah. Jedaiah was the son of Shimri. And Shimri was the son of Shemaiah.

38The men whose names are listed above were leaders of their family groups. Their families greatly increased their numbers. 39They spread out all the way to the edge of Gedor east of the valley. They looked for grasslands for their flocks. 40They found grasslands that were rich and good. The land had plenty of room. It was peaceful and quiet. Some of the people of Ham had lived there before.

41The men whose names are listed lived at the time when Hezekiah was king of Judah. They came and attacked the Hamites in their homes. They also attacked the Meunites who were there. And they completely destroyed them. What happened to them is clear even to this very day. The men of Simeon settled down where the Meunites had lived. They had enough grasslands for their flocks.

42Five hundred of those men came into the hill country of Seir and attacked it. They were led by Pelatiah, Neariah, Rephaiah and Uzziel. Those four men were the sons of Ishi. 43They killed the rest of the Amalekites who had escaped. And they still live there to this very day.

The Family Line of Reuben

5 Here is a list of the sons of Reuben. First, here are a few things about him. Reuben was the oldest son of Israel. But he had sex with his father's concubine. He made his father's bed "unclean." That's why his rights as the oldest son were given to the sons of Joseph, the son of Israel. So Reuben isn't listed in the family history as the one who had the rights of the oldest son. 2Judah was the leader among his brothers. A ruler came from his family line. But the rights of the oldest son belonged to Joseph. 3Reuben was the oldest son of Israel. Reuben's sons were
Hanoch, Pallu, Hezron and Carmi.
4The family line of Joel includes
his son Shemaiah. Gog was the son of Shemaiah.
Shimei was the son of Gog.
5Micah was the son of Shimei.
Reaiah was the son of Micah. Baal was the son of Reaiah.
6And Beerah was the son of Baal. Beerah was a leader of the people of Reuben. Tiglath-Pileser took Beerah as a prisoner to another country. Tiglath-Pileser was the king of Assyria.
7Here are the relatives of the family groups of Reuben. They are listed in their family history.
They include Chief Jeiel, Zechariah 8and Bela. Bela was the son of Azaz. Azaz was the son of Shema. Shema was the son of Joel. All of them settled in the area from

Aroer to Nebo and Baal Meon. 9To the east they settled in the land up to the edge of the desert. That desert reaches all the way to the Euphrates River. They settled there because their livestock had increased their numbers in Gilead.

10While Saul was king, the people of Reuben went to war against the Hagrites. They won the battle over them. Then they settled down in their houses. They settled through the entire area east of Gilead.

The Family Line of Gad

11 The people of Gad lived next to the people of Reuben in Bashan. They spread out all the way to Salecah.

12 Joel was their chief. Shapham was next. Then came Janai and Shaphat in Bashan.

13 Here are their relatives family by family. They included
Michael, Meshullam, Sheba, Jorai, Jacan, Zia and Eber. The total number of them was seven.

14 Those were the sons of Abihail. Abihail was the son of Huri. Huri was the son of Jaroah. Jaroah was the son of Gilead. Gilead was the son of Michael. Michael was the son of Jeshishai. Jeshishai was the son of Jahdo. And Jahdo was the son of Buz.

15 Ahi was the leader of some of the families of Gad. Ahi was the son of Abdiel. Abdiel was the son of Guni.

16 The people of Gad lived in the land of Gilead. They lived in the villages of Bashan. They also lived on all of the grasslands of Sharon as far as they reached.

17 All of those names were written down in the family history. They were written during the time when Jotham was king of Judah and Jeroboam was king of Israel.

18 The tribes of Reuben and Gad and half of the tribe of Manasseh had 44,760 men who were able to serve in the army. They were able to handle a shield and sword. They were also able to use a bow. They were trained for battle. 19They went to war against the Hagrites, Jetur, Naphish and Nodab.

20 God helped his people fight against the Hagrites and all who were helping them. He handed all of those enemies over to his people. That's because they cried out to him during the battle. He answered their prayers, because they trusted in him.

21 They captured the livestock of the Hagrites. They captured 50,000 camels, 250,000 sheep and 2,000 donkeys. They also took 100,000 people as prisoners. 22Many others were killed, because God won the battle over them. His people lived in the land until they themselves were taken as prisoners to other countries.

The Family Line of Half of the Tribe of Manasseh

23 The people in half of the tribe of Manasseh greatly increased their numbers. They settled in the land from Bashan to Baal Hermon. Baal Hermon is also called Senir. Another name for it is Mount Hermon.

24 Here are the leaders of their families. They included Epher, Ishi, Eliel, Azriel, Jeremiah, Hodaviah and Jahdiel. They were brave fighting men. They were famous. They were the leaders of their families. 25But they weren't faithful to the

POWER-SURGE

BRAVE   B

HERE ARE THE LEADERS OF THEIR FAMILIES...THEY WERE BRAVE FIGHTING MEN. THEY WERE FAMOUS.
— 1 CHRONICLES 5:24 —

God of their people. They joined themselves to the gods of the nations of the land and worshiped them. God had destroyed those nations to make room for his people.

26So the God of Israel stirred up the spirit of Pul. He was king of Assyria. He was also called Tiglath-Pileser. He took the tribes of Reuben and Gad and half of the tribe of Manasseh to other countries as his prisoners. He took them to Halah, Habor, Hara and the river of Gozan. And that's where they still are to this very day.

The Family Line of Levi

6 The sons of Levi were
Gershon, Kohath and Merari.
2 The sons of Kohath were
Amram, Izhar, Hebron and Uzziel.
3 Aaron, Moses and Miriam

were born in the family line of
Amram.
The sons of Aaron were
    Nadab, Abihu, Eleazar and Itha-
    mar.
4 Eleazar was the father of Phinehas.
    Phinehas was the father of
    Abishua.
5 Abishua was the father of Bukki.
    Bukki was the father of Uzzi.
6 Uzzi was the father of Zerahiah.
    Zerahiah was the father of Mera-
    ioth.
7 Meraioth was the father of Ama-
    riah.
    Amariah was the father of Ahitub.
8 Ahitub was the father of Zadok.
    Zadok was the father of Ahimaaz.
9 Ahimaaz was the father of Aza-
    riah.
    Azariah was the father of Johanan.
10 Johanan was the father of Azariah.
    Azariah served as priest in the tem-
    ple Solomon built in Jerusalem.
11 Azariah was the father of Amariah.
    Amariah was the father of Ahitub.
12 Ahitub was the father of Zadok.
    Zadok was the father of Shallum.
13 Shallum was the father of Hilkiah.
    Hilkiah was the father of Azariah.
14 Azariah was the father of Seraiah.
    And Seraiah was the father of
    Jehozadak.
15 Jehozadak was taken away from his
own land. The LORD took the people
of Judah and Jerusalem to Babylonia.
He used Nebuchadnezzar to take
them there as prisoners.

16 The sons of Levi were
    Gershon, Kohath and Merari.
17 The names of the sons of Gershon
    were
    Libni and Shimei.
18 The sons of Kohath were
    Amram, Izhar, Hebron and Uzziel.
19 The sons of Merari were
    Mahli and Mushi.
Here are the members of the family
    groups of the Levites. They are list-
    ed under the names of their
    fathers.
20 Gershon was the father of Libni.
    Jahath was Libni's son.
    Zimmah was Jahath's son.
21 Joah was Zimmah's son.
    Iddo was Joah's son.
    Zerah was Iddo's son.
    And Jeatherai was Zerah's son.
22 The family line of Kohath included
    his son Amminadab.

Korah was Amminadab's son.
    Assir was Korah's son.
23 Elkanah was Assir's son.
    Ebiasaph was Elkanah's son.
    Assir was Ebiasaph's son.
24 Tahath was Assir's son.
    Uriel was Tahath's son.
    Uzziah was Uriel's son.
    And Shaul was Uzziah's son.
25 The family line of Elkanah included
    his son Amasai.
    Amasai was the father of Ahimoth.
26 Elkanah was Ahimoth's son.
    Zophai was Elkanah's son.
    Nahath was Zophai's son.
27 Eliab was Nahath's son.
    Jeroham was Eliab's son.
    Elkanah was Jeroham's son.
    And Samuel was Elkanah's son.
28 The sons of Samuel were
    his first son Joel
    and his second son Abijah.
29 The family line of Merari included
    his son Mahli.
    Libni was Mahli's son.
    Shimei was Libni's son.
    Uzzah was Shimei's son.
30 Shimea was Uzzah's son.
    Haggiah was Shimea's son.
    And Asaiah was Haggiah's son.

The Levites Who Were in Charge of the Music

31 Here are the Levites David put in
charge of the music in the house of the
LORD. He did it after the ark was placed
there. **32** The men used their music to
serve in front of the holy tent, the Tent of
Meeting. They served there until Solomon built the temple of the LORD in Jerusalem. They did their work based on the
rules they had been given.
    33 Here are the men who served. The list
also includes their sons.
    The family line of Kohath included
    Heman. He led the music.
    He was the son of Joel.
    Joel was the son of Samuel.
34 Samuel was the son of Elkanah.
    Elkanah was the son of Jeroham.
    Jeroham was the son of Eliel.
    Eliel was the son of Toah.
35 Toah was the son of Zuph.
    Zuph was the son of Elkanah.
    Elkanah was the son of Mahath.
    Mahath was the son of Amasai.
36 Amasai was the son of Elkanah.
    Elkanah was the son of Joel.
    Joel was the son of Azariah.
    Azariah was the son of Zephaniah.
37 Zephaniah was the son of Tahath.

Tahath was the son of Assir.
Assir was the son of Ebiasaph.
Ebiasaph was the son of Korah.
38 Korah was the son of Izhar.
Izhar was the son of Kohath.
Kohath was the son of Levi.
And Levi was the son of Israel.
39 Heman had a relative named Asaph.
Asaph served as Heman's helper at
his right side.
Asaph was the son of Berekiah.
Berekiah was the son of Shimea.
40 Shimea was the son of Michael.
Michael was the son of Baaseiah.
Baaseiah was the son of Malkijah.
41 Malkijah was the son of Ethni.
Ethni was the son of Zerah.
Zerah was the son of Adaiah.
42 Adaiah was the son of Ethan.
Ethan was the son of Zimmah.
Zimmah was the son of Shimei.
43 Shimei was the son of Jahath.
Jahath was the son of Gershon.
And Gershon was the son of Levi.
44 Here are the Levites in the family line
of Merari who served as Heman's
helpers at his left side. They were
relatives of the Kohathites.
Ethan was the son of Kishi.
Kishi was the son of Abdi.
Abdi was the son of Malluch.
45 Malluch was the son of Hasha-
biah.
Hashabiah was the son of Ama-
ziah.
Amaziah was the son of Hilkiah.
46 Hilkiah was the son of Amzi.
Amzi was the son of Bani.
Bani was the son of Shemer.
47 Shemer was the son of Mahli.
Mahli was the son of Mushi.
Mushi was the son of Merari.
And Merari was the son of Levi.

48 The rest of the Levites were appointed
to do all of the other work at the holy tent.
It was the house of God.
49 Aaron and his sons after him brought
the offerings. They sacrificed them on the
altar of burnt offering. They also burned
incense on the altar of incense. That was
part of what they did in the Most Holy
Room. That's how they paid for the sin of
Israel. They did everything just as Moses,
the servant of God, had commanded.

50 Here are the members of the family
line of Aaron.
Eleazar was Aaron's son.
Phinehas was Eleazar's son.
Abishua was Phinehas's son.
51 Bukki was Abishua's son.

Uzzi was Bukki's son.
Zerahiah was Uzzi's son.
52 Meraioth was Zerahiah's son.
Amariah was Meraioth's son.
Ahitub was Amariah's son.
53 Zadok was Ahitub's son.
And Ahimaaz was Zadok's son.

54 Here were the places where they settled. They were given to them as their territory. Some were given to the children of
Aaron who were from the family group of
Kohath. They were given out by using
lots. The first lot was for Kohath.
55 The Kohathites were given
Hebron in Judah. They also received
the grasslands that were around
Hebron. **56** But the fields and villages
that were around the city were given
to Caleb, the son of Jephunneh.
57 So the people in the family line
of Aaron received Hebron. It was a
city where people could go for safety.
Aaron's family line received Libnah,
Jattir, Eshtemoa, **58** Hilen and Debir.
59 They also received Ashan, Juttah
and Beth Shemesh. They were given
all of those towns together with
their grasslands. **60** From the tribe of
Benjamin they received Gibeon,
Geba, Alemeth and Anathoth. They
received those towns together with
their grasslands.
All of those towns were handed
out to the family groups of Kohath.
The total number of towns was 13.
61 The rest of the members of the family
line of Kohath were given ten towns. The
towns were from the family groups of half
of the tribe of Manasseh.
62 The members of the family line of
Gershon were given 13 towns. They
received them family group by family
group. Most of the towns were from the
tribes of Issachar, Asher and Naphtali. The
rest were from the other half of the tribe
of Manasseh. It's in Bashan.
63 The members of the family line of
Merari were given 12 towns. They
received them family group by family
group. The towns were from the tribes of
Reuben, Gad and Zebulun.
64 So the people of Israel gave the
Levites all of those towns and their grasslands. **65** They gave other towns to them
from the tribes of Judah, Simeon and Benjamin.
66 Some of the family groups of Kohath
were given towns from the tribe of Ephraim as their territory.
67 In the hill country of Ephraim

they received Shechem. Shechem was a city where people could go for safety. The Kohathites also received Gezer, **68**Jokmeam, Beth Horon, **69**Aijalon and Gath Rimmon. They were given all of those towns together with their grasslands.

70From half of the tribe of Manasseh the people of Israel gave the towns of Aner and Bileam. They gave them to the rest of the family groups of Kohath. They gave them together with their grasslands.

71Here is what the members of the family line of Gershon were given. They received Golan in Bashan and also Ashtaroth. They received them together with their grasslands.

They received them from half of the tribe of Manasseh.

72From the tribe of Issachar they received Kedesh, Daberath, **73**Ramoth and Anem. They received them together with their grasslands.

74From the tribe of Asher they received Mashal, Abdon, **75**Hukok and Rehob. They received them together with their grasslands.

76From the tribe of Naphtali they received Kedesh in Galilee. They also received Hammon and Kiriathaim. They were given all of those towns together with their grasslands.

77The members of the family line of Merari make up the rest of the Levites. Here is what they were given. From the tribe of Zebulun they received Jokneam, Kartah, Rimmono and Tabor. They received them together with their grasslands.

78The tribe of Reuben was across the Jordan River east of Jericho. From that tribe the Merarites received Bezer in the desert, Jahzah, **79**Kedemoth and Mephaath. They received them together with their grasslands.

80From the tribe of Gad they received Ramoth in Gilead. They also received Mahanaim, **81**Heshbon and Jazer. They received all of those towns together with their grasslands.

The Family Line of Issachar

7 The sons of Issachar were Tola, Puah, Jashub and Shimron. The total number of sons was four.

2The sons of Tola were Uzzi, Rephaiah, Jeriel, Jahmai, Ibsam and Samuel. They were the leaders of their families. The total number of fighting men who were listed in the history of the family line of Tola was 22,600. That was when David was king.

3The son of Uzzi was Izrahiah.

The sons of Izrahiah were Michael, Obadiah, Joel and Isshiah. All five of them were chiefs. **4**Based on their family history, 36,000 of their men were ready for battle. That's because they had many wives and children.

5The total number of fighting men who belonged to all of the family groups of Issachar was 87,000. The men were listed in their family history.

The Family Line of Benjamin

6The three sons of Benjamin were Bela, Beker and Jediael.

7The sons of Bela were Ezbon, Uzzi, Uzziel, Jerimoth and Iri. They were the leaders of their families. The total number of sons was five. Their family history listed 22,034 fighting men.

8The sons of Beker were Zemirah, Joash, Eliezer, Elioenai, Omri, Jeremoth, Abijah, Anathoth and Alemeth. All of them were the sons of Beker. **9**Their family history listed the leaders of their families. It also listed 20,200 fighting men.

10The son of Jediael was Bilhan.

The sons of Bilhan were Jeush, Benjamin, Ehud, Kenaanah, Zethan, Tarshish and Ahishahar. **11**All of those sons of Jediael were the leaders of their families. There were 17,200 fighting men who were ready to go to war.

12The Shuppites and Huppites belonged to the family line of Ir. The Hushites belonged to the family line of Aher.

The Family Line of Naphtali

13The sons of Naphtali were Jahziel, Guni, Jezer and Shillem.

They belonged to the family line of Bilhah.

The Family Line of Manasseh

14 Here is the family line of Manasseh.

He had a concubine who was from the land of Aram. She had Asriel and Makir by him. Makir was the father of Gilead. 15 Makir got married to a woman from among the Huppites and Shuppites. He had a sister named Maacah.

Another member of Manasseh's family line was Zelophehad. All he had was daughters.

16 Makir's wife Maacah had a son by him. She named the boy Peresh. He had a brother named Sheresh. The sons of Sheresh were Ulam and Rakem.

17 The son of Ulam was
Bedan.

Those were the members of the family line of Makir, the son of Manasseh. Gilead was the son of Makir. 18 Gilead's sister was Hammoleketh. She was the mother of Ishhod, Abiezer and Mahlah.

19 The sons of Shemida were
Ahian, Shechem, Likhi and Aniam.

The Family Line of Ephraim

20 Here are the members of the family line of Ephraim.

Shuthelah was Ephraim's son.
Bered was Shuthelah's son.
Tahath was Bered's son.
Eleadah was Tahath's son.
Tahath was Eleadah's son.

21 Zabad was Tahath's son.
And Shuthelah was Zabad's son.

Men from Gath killed Ezer and Elead when they went down to steal their livestock. 22 Their father Ephraim sobbed over them for many days. His relatives came to comfort him. 23 Then he made love to his wife. She became pregnant and had a baby boy. Ephraim named him Beriah. That's because something bad had happened in his family. 24 His daughter was Sheerah. She built Lower and Upper Beth Horon. She also built Uzzen Sheerah.

25 Rephah was Beriah's son.
Resheph was Rephah's son.
Telah was Resheph's son.
Tahan was Telah's son.

26 Ladan was Tahan's son.
Ammihud was Ladan's son.

Elishama was Ammihud's son.

27 Nun was Elishama's son.
And Joshua was the son of Nun.

28 The lands and settlements of the members of Ephraim's line included Bethel and the villages that were around it. Naaran was on the east. Gezer and its villages were on the west. The lands and settlements included Shechem. They also included the villages that were around Shechem all the way to Ayyah and its villages. 29 Along the borders of Manasseh were Beth Shan, Taanach, Megiddo and Dor, together with their villages. The members of the family line of Joseph lived in those towns. Joseph was the son of Israel.

The Family Line of Asher

30 The sons of Asher were
Imnah, Ishvah, Ishvi and Beriah.
They had a sister named Serah.

31 The sons of Beriah were
Heber and Malkiel. Malkiel was the father of Birzaith.

32 Heber was the father of Japhlet, Shomer, Hotham and their sister Shua.

33 The sons of Japhlet were
Pasach, Bimhal and Ashvath. They were Japhlet's sons.

34 The sons of Shomer were
Ahi, Rohgah, Hubbah and Aram.

35 The sons of Shomer's brother Helem were
Zophah, Imna, Shelesh and Amal.

36 The sons of Zophah were
Suah, Harnepher, Shual, Beri, Imrah, 37 Bezer, Hod, Shamma, Shilshah, Ithran and Beera.

38 The sons of Jether were
Jephunneh, Pispah and Ara.

39 The sons of Ulla were
Arah, Hanniel and Rizia.

40 All of them were members of the family line of Asher. They were the leaders of their families. They were fine men. They were brave fighting men. They were outstanding leaders. The total number of men who were ready for battle was 26,000. They were listed in their family history.

The Family History of Saul

8 Benjamin was the father of Bela. Bela was his first son.

Ashbel was his second son. Aharah was the third.

2 Nohah was the fourth. And Rapha was the fifth.

3 The sons of Bela were

Addar, Gera, Abihud, **4**Abishua, Naaman, Ahoah, **5**Gera, Shephuphan and Huram.

6Here are the members of the family line of Ehud. They were the leaders of the families who were living in Geba. Later, they were taken away from their own land. They were forced to go to Manahath. **7**The sons of Ehud were Naaman, Ahijah and Gera. Gera took them away from their land. He was the father of Uzza and Ahihud.

8Sons were born to Shaharaim in Moab. That happened after he had divorced his wives Hushim and Baara. **9**His wife Hodesh had sons by him. Their names were Jobab, Zibia, Mesha, Malcam, **10**Jeuz, Sakia and Mirmah. His sons were the leaders of their families. **11**His wife Hushim had Abitub and Elpaal by him.

12The sons of Elpaal were Eber, Misham and Shemed. Shemed built Ono and Lod and the villages that were around it. **13**Beriah and Shema were also sons of Elpaal. They were the leaders of the families who were living in Aijalon. Beriah and Shema drove out the people who were living in Gath.

14Ahio, Shashak, Jeremoth, **15**Zebadiah, Arad, Eder, **16**Michael, Ishpah and Joha were the sons of Beriah.

17Zebadiah, Meshullam, Hizki, Heber, **18**Ishmerai, Izliah and Jobab were other sons of Elpaal.

19Jakim, Zicri, Zabdi, **20**Elienai, Zillethai, Eliel, **21**Adaiah, Beraiah and Shimrath were the sons of Shimei.

22Ishpan, Eber, Eliel, **23**Abdon, Zicri, Hanan, **24**Hananiah, Elam, Anthothijah, **25**Iphdeiah and Penuel were the sons of Shashak.

26Shamsherai, Shehariah, Athaliah, **27**Jaareshiah, Elijah and Zicri were the sons of Jeroham.

28All of those men were the leaders of their families. They were listed as chiefs in their family history. They lived in Jerusalem.

29Jeiel lived in the city of Gibeon. He was the father of Gibeon.

Jeiel had a wife named Maacah. **30**His oldest son was Abdon. His other sons were Zur, Kish, Baal, Ner, Nadab, **31**Gedor, Ahio, Zeker

32and Mikloth. Mikloth was the father of Shimeah. Mikloth and Shimeah also lived in Jerusalem. They lived near their relatives.

33Ner was the father of Kish. Kish was the father of Saul. Saul was the father of Jonathan, Malki-Shua, Abinadab and Esh-Baal.

34The son of Jonathan was Merib-Baal. Merib-Baal was the father of Micah.

35The sons of Micah were Pithon, Melech, Tarea and Ahaz.

36Ahaz was the father of Jehoaddah. Jehoaddah was the father of Alemeth, Azmaveth and Zimri. Zimri was the father of Moza. **37**Moza was the father of Binea. Raphah was Binea's son. Eleasah was Raphah's son. And Azel was Eleasah's son.

38Azel had six sons. Their names were Azrikam, Bokeru, Ishmael, Sheariah, Obadiah and Hanan. All of them were the sons of Azel.

39Here are the sons of Azel's brother Eshek.

Ulam was his first son. Jeush was the second. Eliphelet was the third. **40**The sons of Ulam were brave fighting men. They could handle a bow. They had many sons and grandsons. The total number of sons and grandsons was 150.

All of those men belonged to the family line of Benjamin.

9 The whole community of Israel was listed in their family histories. They were written down in the records of the kings of Israel.

The People Who Lived in Jerusalem

The people of Judah were taken away from their own land. They were taken as prisoners to Babylonia. That's because they weren't faithful to the LORD. **2**The first ones who came back from there were some Israelites, priests, Levites and temple servants. They settled down again in their own towns on their own property.

3Some of them lived in Jerusalem. They included people from Judah, Benjamin, Ephraim and Manasseh.

4They included Uthai. He was the son of Ammihud. Ammihud was the son of Omri. Omri was the son of Imri. Imri was the son of Bani.

Bani belonged to the family line of Perez. Perez was the son of Judah.

5 The family line of Shelah included his oldest son Asaiah. It also included the sons of Asaiah.

6 The family line of Zerah included Jeuel.

The total number of the people of Judah was 690.

7 The family line of Benjamin included Sallu. He was the son of Meshullam. Meshullam was the son of Hodaviah. Hodaviah was the son of Hassenuah.

8 Ibneiah was the son of Jeroham. Elah was the son of Uzzi. Uzzi was the son of Micri. Meshullam was the son of Shephatiah. Shephatiah was the son of Reuel. Reuel was the son of Ibnijah.

9 The total number of the people of Benjamin was 956. They were listed in their family history. All of those men were the leaders of their families.

10 The family line of the priests included Jedaiah, Jehoiarib and Jakin.

11 It also included Azariah. He was the son of Hilkiah. Hilkiah was the son of Meshullam. Meshullam was the son of Zadok. Zadok was the son of Meraioth. Meraioth was the son of Ahitub. Azariah was the official who was in charge of the house of God.

12 Adaiah was the son of Jeroham. Jeroham was the son of Pashhur. Pashhur was the son of Malkijah. Maasai was the son of Adiel. Adiel was the son of Jahzerah. Jahzerah was the son of Meshullam. Meshullam was the son of Meshillemith. Meshillemith was the son of Immer.

13 The total number of priests was 1,760. They were the leaders of their families. They were able men. It was their duty to serve in the house of God.

14 The family line of the Levites included Shemaiah. He was the son of Hasshub. Hasshub was the son of Azrikam. Azrikam was the son of Hashabiah. Shemaiah belonged to the family line of Merari. 15 The family line of the Levites also included Bakbakkar, Heresh, Galal and Mattaniah. Mattaniah was the son of Mica. Mica was the son of Zicri. Zicri was the son of Asaph.

16 Obadiah was the son of Shema-iah. Shemaiah was the son of Galal. Galal was the son of Jeduthun. Berekiah was the son of Asa. Asa was the son of Elkanah. He lived in the villages of the people of Netophah.

17 The men who guarded the gates were Shallum, Akkub, Talmon, Ahiman and other Levites. Shallum was their chief. 18 He was stationed at the King's Gate on the east side of the temple. That duty has continued to this very day. Those guards belonged to the camp of the Levites.

19 Shallum was the son of Kore. Kore was the son of Ebiasaph. Ebiasaph was the son of Korah. Shallum and the other Levites in his family belonged to the family line of Korah. They had the duty of guarding the entrances to the temple.

Their fathers had also had the duty of guarding the entrance to the house of the LORD. 20 Long ago Phinehas, the son of Eleazar, was in charge of those who guarded the gate. And the LORD was with him.

21 Zechariah guarded the entrance to the Tent of Meeting. He was the son of Meshelemiah.

22 The total number of the men who were chosen to guard the entrances was 212. They were listed in their family history in their villages. David and the prophet Samuel had appointed them to their positions. They appointed them because they trusted them.

23 Those Levites and their children after them were in charge of guarding the gates of the house of the LORD. The house of the LORD was also called the temple. 24 The men who guarded the gates were on the four sides of the temple. They were on the east, west, north and south sides. 25 From time to time, their relatives in their villages had to come to the temple. They had to share their duties for a week at a time.

26 The four main men who guarded the gates were Levites. They were trusted with the duty of taking care of the storerooms and the other rooms in the house of God. 27 They spent the night in their positions around the house of God. That's because they had to guard it. They were in charge of the key that opened the temple each morning.

28 Some Levites were in charge of the articles that were used when they served

at the temple. They counted the articles when they were brought in. They also counted them when they were taken out. 29Other Levites were appointed to take care of all of the other articles that belonged to the temple. They also took care of the flour, wine, olive oil, incense and spices. 30Some of the priests took care of mixing the spices.

31There was a Levite named Mattithiah. He was the oldest son of Shallum. Shallum belonged to the family line of Korah. Mattithiah was trusted with the duty of baking the offering bread. 32The bread was placed on the table every Sabbath day. Some Levites in the family line of Kohath were in charge of preparing the bread.

33Those who led the music lived in rooms in the temple. They were the leaders of their Levite families. Their only duty was to lead the music. They had to do that work day and night.

34All of them were the leaders of their Levite families. They were listed as chiefs in their family history. They lived in Jerusalem.

The Family History of Saul

35Jeiel lived in the city of Gibeon. He was the father of Gibeon.
Jeiel had a wife named Maacah. 36His oldest son was Abdon. His other sons were Zur, Kish, Baal, Ner, Nadab, 37Gedor, Ahio, Zechariah and Mikloth. 38Mikloth was the father of Shimeam. Mikloth and Shimeam lived in Jerusalem. They lived near their relatives.
39Ner was the father of Kish. Kish was the father of Saul. Saul was the father of Jonathan, Malki-Shua, Abinadab and Esh-Baal.
40The son of Jonathan was Merib-Baal. Merib-Baal was the father of Micah.
41The sons of Micah were Pithon, Melech, Tahrea and Ahaz.
42Ahaz was the father of Jadah. Jadah was the father of Alemeth, Azmaveth and Zimri. Zimri was the father of Moza. 43Moza was the father of Binea. Rephaiah was Binea's son. Eleasah was Rephaiah's son. And Azel was Eleasah's son.
44Azel had six sons. Their names were Azrikam, Bokeru, Ishmael, Sheariah, Obadiah and Hanan. They were the sons of Azel.

Saul Takes His Own Life

10 The Philistines fought against Israel. The men of Israel ran away from them. But many Israelites were killed on Mount Gilboa. 2The Philistines kept chasing Saul and his sons. They killed his sons Jonathan, Abinadab and Malki-Shua. 3The fighting was heavy around Saul. Men who were armed with bows and arrows caught up with him. They shot their arrows at him and wounded him badly.

4Saul spoke to the man who was carrying his armor. He said, "Pull out your sword. Stick it through me. If you don't, those men who aren't circumcised will come and hurt me badly."

But the man was terrified. He wouldn't do it. So Saul took his own sword and fell on it. 5The man saw that Saul was dead. So he fell on his own sword and died. 6Saul and his three sons died. All of them died together.

7All of the Israelites who lived in the valley saw that their army had run away. They saw that Saul and his sons were dead. So they left their towns and ran away. Then the Philistines came and settled down in them.

8The day after the Philistines had won the battle, they came to take what they wanted from the dead bodies. They found Saul and his sons dead on Mount Gilboa. 9So they took what they wanted from Saul's body. They took his head and his armor. Then they sent messengers through the whole land of the Philistines. They announced the news to the statues of their gods. They also announced it among their people. 10They put Saul's armor in the temple of their gods. They hung his head up in the temple of their god Dagon.

11The people of Jabesh Gilead heard about everything the Philistines had done to Saul. 12So all of their brave men went and got the bodies of Saul and his sons. They brought them to Jabesh. Then they buried the bones of Saul and his sons under the great tree that was there. They didn't eat anything for seven days.

13Saul died because he wasn't faithful to the LORD. He didn't obey the word of the LORD. He even asked for advice from a person who gets messages from those who have died. 14He didn't ask the LORD for advice. So the LORD put him to death. He turned the kingdom over to David. David was the son of Jesse.

David Becomes King Over Israel

11 The whole community of Israel came together to see David at Hebron. They said, "We are your own flesh and blood. ²In the past, Saul was our king. But you led the men of Israel in battle. The LORD your God said to you, 'You will be the shepherd over my people Israel. You will become their ruler.' "

³All of the elders of Israel came to see King David at Hebron. There he made a covenant with them in the sight of the LORD. They anointed David as king over Israel. It happened just as the LORD had promised through Samuel.

David Captures Jerusalem

⁴David and all of the men of Israel marched to Jerusalem. Jerusalem was also called Jebus.

The Jebusites who lived there ⁵spoke to David. They said, "You won't get in here."

But David captured the fort of Zion. It became known as the City of David.

⁶David had said, "Anyone who leads the attack against the Jebusites will become the commander of Israel's army." Joab went up first. So he became the commander of the army. He was the son of Zeruiah.

⁷David moved into the fort. So it was called the City of David. ⁸He built up the city around the fort. He filled in the low places. He built a wall around it. During that time, Joab built up the rest of the city.

⁹David became more and more powerful. That's because the LORD who rules over all was with him.

David's Mighty Men

¹⁰The chiefs of David's mighty men and the whole community of Israel helped David greatly. They helped him become king over the entire land. That's

exactly what the LORD had promised him. ¹¹Here is a list of David's mighty men.

Jashobeam was chief of the officers. He was a Hacmonite. He used his spear against 300 men. He killed all of them at one time.

¹²Next to him was Eleazar. He was one of the three mighty men. He was the son of Dodai, the Ahohite. ¹³Jashobeam was with David at Pas Dammim. The Philistines had gathered there for battle. Israel's troops ran away from the Philistines. At the place where that happened, there was a field that was full of barley. ¹⁴The three mighty men took their stand in the middle of the field. They didn't let the Philistines capture it. They struck them down. The LORD helped them win a great battle.

¹⁵David was near the rock at the cave of Adullam. Three of the 30 chiefs came down to him there. A group of Philistines was camped in the Valley of Rephaim. ¹⁶At that time David was in his usual place of safety. Some Philistine troops were stationed at Bethlehem.

¹⁷David longed for water. He said, "I wish someone would get me a drink of water from the well that is near the gate of Bethlehem!"

¹⁸So the Three fought their way past the Philistine guards. They got some water from the well that was near the gate of Bethlehem. They took the water back to David.

But David refused to drink it. Instead, he poured it out as a drink offering to the LORD. ¹⁹"I would never drink that water!" David said. "It would be like drinking the blood of these men. They put their lives in danger by going to Bethlehem." The men had put their lives in danger by bringing the water back. So David wouldn't drink it.

Those were some of the brave things the three mighty men did.

²⁰Abishai was chief over the Three. He was the brother of Joab. He used his spear against 300 men. He killed all of them. So he became as famous as the Three were. ²¹He was honored twice as much as the Three. He became their commander. But he wasn't included among them.

²²Benaiah was a great hero from Kabzeel. He was the son of Jehoiada. Benaiah did many brave things. He struck down two of Moab's best fighting men. He also went down into a pit on a snowy day. He killed a lion there.

²³And Benaiah struck down an Egyptian who was seven and a half feet tall. The Egyptian was holding a spear as big as

POWER-SURGE

STRONG

DAVID BECAME MORE AND MORE POWERFUL. THAT'S BECAUSE THE LORD WHO RULES OVER ALL WAS WITH HIM.

— 1 CHRONICLES 11:9 —

a weaver's rod. Benaiah went out to fight against him with a club. He grabbed the spear out of the Egyptian's hand. Then he killed him with it.

24Those were some of the brave things Benaiah, the son of Jehoiada, did. He too was as famous as the three mighty men were. 25He was honored more than any of the Thirty. But he wasn't included among the Three. And David put him in charge of his own personal guards.

26Here is a list of David's mighty men.
Asahel, the brother of Joab
Elhanan, the son of Dodo, from Bethlehem
27Shammoth, the Harorite
Helez, the Pelonite
28Ira, the son of Ikkesh, from Tekoa
Abiezer from Anathoth
29Sibbecai, the Hushathite
Ilai, the Ahohite
30Maharai from Netophah
Heled, the son of Baanah, from Netophah
31Ithai, the son of Ribai, from Gibeah in Benjamin
Benaiah from Pirathon
32Hurai from the valleys of Gaash
Abiel, the Arbathite
33Azmaveth, the Baharumite
Eliahba, the Shaalbonite
34the sons of Hashem, the Gizonite
Jonathan, the son of Shagee, the Hararite
35Ahiam, the son of Sacar, the Hararite
Eliphal, the son of Ur
36Hepher, the Mekerathite
Ahijah, the Pelonite
37Hezro from Carmel
Naarai, the son of Ezbai
38Joel, the brother of Nathan
Mibhar, the son of Hagri
39Zelek from Ammon
Naharai, from Beeroth, who carried the armor of Joab, the son of Zeruiah
40Ira, the Ithrite
Gareb, the Ithrite
41Uriah, the Hittite
Zabad, the son of Ahlai
42Adina, the son of Shiza, the Reubenite, who was chief of the Reubenites and the 30 men with him
43Hanan, the son of Maacah
Joshaphat, the Mithnite
44Uzzia, the Ashterathite
Shama and Jeiel, the sons of Hotham from Aroer
45Jediael, the son of Shimri

his brother Joha, the Tizite
46Eliel, the Mahavite
Jeribai and Joshaviah, the sons of Elnaam
Ithmah from Moab
47Eliel
Obed
Jaasiel, the Mezobaite

Fighting Men Join David

12 Some fighting men came to David at Ziklag. They were among those who helped him in battle. David had been forced to hide from Saul, the son of Kish. 2The men were armed with bows. They were able to shoot arrows or throw stones from a sling with either hand. They were relatives of Saul from the tribe of Benjamin. Here is a list of them.

3Their chief Ahiezer and Joash, the sons of Shemaah the Gibeathite
Jeziel and Pelet, the sons of Azmaveth
Beracah
Jehu from Anathoth
4Ishmaiah, the Gibeonite, who was a mighty man among the Thirty and a leader of the Thirty
Jeremiah
Jahaziel
Johanan
Jozabad from Gederah
5Eluzai
Jerimoth
Bealiah
Shemariah
Shephatiah, the Haruphite
6the Korahites Elkanah, Isshiah, Azarel, Joezer and Jashobeam
7Joelah and Zebadiah, the sons of Jeroham from Gedor

8Some men of Gad went over to David's side at his usual place of safety in the desert. They were brave fighting men. They were ready for battle. They were able to use shields and spears. Their faces were like the faces of lions. They could run as fast as antelopes in the mountains.
9Ezer was their chief.
Obadiah was next in command. Eliab was third.
10Mishmannah was fourth. Jeremiah was fifth.
11Attai was sixth. Eliel was seventh.
12Johanan was eighth. Elzabad was ninth.
13Jeremiah was tenth. And Macbannai was eleventh.
14All of those men of Gad were army commanders. The least important of

them was equal to 100 men. The most important was equal to 1,000.

15They went across the Jordan River when it was flowing over its banks. That happened in the first month of spring. They chased away everyone who lived in the valleys. They chased them away from the east and west sides of the river.

16Some men from the territories of Benjamin and Judah also came to David at his usual place of safety.

17David went out to meet them. He said to them, "Have you come to me in peace? Have you come to help me? If you have, I'm ready to have you join me. But suppose you have come to hand me over to my enemies when I haven't even harmed anyone. Then may the God of our people see it and judge you."

18The Spirit of God came on Amasai. He was chief of the Thirty. He said,

"David, we belong to you!
Son of Jesse, we're on your side!
May you have great success.
    May those who help you also have
        success.
    Your God will help you."

So David welcomed them. He made them leaders in his army.

19Some men of Manasseh went over to David's side when he marched out with the Philistines to fight against Saul.

But David and his men didn't help the Philistines. That's because after all of the Philistine rulers had discussed the matter, they sent him away. They said, "Suppose he deserts to his master Saul. Then our heads will be cut off!"

20So David went to Ziklag. Here are the men of Manasseh who went over to his side. They were Adnah, Jozabad, Jediael, Michael, Jozabad, Elihu and Zillethai. They were leaders of companies of 1,000 men in Manasseh. **21**They helped David fight against enemy armies. All of the men of Manasseh were brave fighting men. They were commanders in David's army.

22Day after day men came to help him. Soon he had a large army. It was like the army of God.

Other Fighting Men Join David at Hebron

23Large numbers of men came to David at Hebron. They were prepared for battle. They came to hand Saul's kingdom over to him, just as the LORD had said. Here are the numbers of the men who came.

24The men from Judah carried shields and spears. They were prepared for battle. The total number of them was 6,800.

25The fighting men from Simeon were ready for battle. The total number of them was 7,100.

26The total number of men from Levi was 4,600. **27**They included Jehoiada. He was the leader of the family of Aaron. He came with 3,700 men. **28**They also included Zadok. He was a brave young fighter. He came with 22 officers from his family.

29The men from Benjamin were Saul's relatives. Most of them had remained faithful to Saul's family until that time. The total number of them was 3,000.

30The men from Ephraim were brave fighting men. They were famous in their own family groups. The total number of them was 20,800.

31The men from half of the tribe of Manasseh had been chosen by name to come and make David king. The total number of them was 18,000.

32The men from Issachar understood what was going on at that time. They knew what Israel should do. The total number of their chiefs was 200. They came with all of their relatives who were under their command.

33The men from Zebulun knew how to fight well. That's because they had done it many times before. They were prepared for battle. They had every kind of weapon. They came to help David with their whole heart. The total number of them was 50,000.

34The total number of officers from Naphtali was 1,000. They came

BRAVE B

ALL OF THE MEN OF MANASSEH WERE BRAVE FIGHTING MEN. THEY WERE COMMANDERS IN DAVID'S ARMY.

— 1 CHRONICLES 12:21 —

with 37,000 men who carried shields and spears.

35 The men from Dan were ready for battle. The total number of them was 28,600.

36 The men from Asher knew how to fight well. That's because they had done it many times before. They were prepared for battle. The total number of them was 40,000.

37 The men from the tribes of Reuben and Gad and half of the tribe of Manasseh were armed with every kind of weapon. The men came from the east side of the Jordan River. The total number of them was 120,000.

38 All of those fighting men offered to serve in the army. Before they came to Hebron, they had agreed completely to make David king over all of the people of Israel. All of the rest of the people also agreed to make David king.

39 The men spent three days there with David. They ate and drank what their families had given them. 40 Their neighbors also brought food. They brought it on donkeys, camels, mules and oxen. They came from as far away as the territories of Issachar, Zebulun and Naphtali. There was plenty of flour, fig cakes, raisin cakes, wine, olive oil, cattle and sheep. The people of Israel brought all of those things because they were so happy.

David Wants to Bring the Ark Back

13 David talked with each of his officers. He wanted to get their advice. Some of them were commanders of thousands of men. Others were commanders of hundreds.

2 David spoke to the whole community of Israel. He said, "Let's send word to the rest of our people no matter how far away they live. They live in all of the territories of Israel. Let's also send word to the priests and Levites who are with them in their towns and grasslands. Let's invite everyone to come and join us. Let's do it if it seems good to you and if that's what the LORD our God wants. 3 Let's bring the ark of our God back here to us. We didn't use it to ask God for advice during the whole time Saul was king."

4 So that's what the whole community agreed to do. It seemed right to them.

5 David gathered all of the people together. They came from the area between the Shihor River in Egypt and Lebo Hamath. They came to bring the ark

of God from Kiriath Jearim to Jerusalem. 6 David went to Baalah of Judah. The whole community of Israel went with him. Baalah is also called Kiriath Jearim. All of the people went there to get the ark of God the LORD. He sits on his throne between the cherubim. The ark is named after the LORD.

7 The ark of God was placed on a new cart. Then it was moved from Abinadab's house. Uzzah and Ahio were guiding it.

8 David was celebrating with all his might in the sight of God. So was the whole community of Israel. All of them were singing songs. They were also playing harps, lyres, tambourines, cymbals and trumpets.

9 They came to the threshing floor of Kidon. The oxen nearly fell there. So Uzzah reached out his hand to hold the ark steady.

10 Then the LORD's anger burned against Uzzah. He struck him down because he had put his hand on the ark. So Uzzah died there in front of God.

11 David was angry because the LORD's burning anger had broken out against Uzzah. That's why the place is still called Perez Uzzah to this very day.

12 David was afraid of God that day. He asked, "How can I ever bring the ark of God back here to me?"

13 So he didn't take the ark to be with him in the City of David. Instead, he took it to the house of Obed-Edom. Obed-Edom was from Gath. 14 The ark of God remained with the family of Obed-Edom. It stayed in his house for three months. And the LORD blessed his family. He also blessed everything that belonged to him.

David's Palace and Family

14 Hiram was king of Tyre. He sent messengers to David. He sent cedar logs along with them. He also sent skilled workers to build a palace for David. They worked with stone and wood.

2 David knew that the LORD had made his position as king secure. He knew that he had made him king over the whole nation of Israel. He knew that the LORD had greatly honored his kingdom. The LORD had done it because the Israelites were his people.

3 In Jerusalem David got married to more women. He also became the father of more sons and daughters. 4 Here is a list of the children who were born to him in Jerusalem. Their names were Shammua, Shobab, Nathan, Solomon, 5 Ibhar, Eli-

shua, Elpelet, 6Nogah, Nepheg, Japhia, 7Elishama, Beeliada and Eliphelet.

David Wins the Battle Over the Philistines

8The Philistines heard that David had been anointed king over the entire nation of Israel. So their whole army went to look for him. But David heard about it. He went out to where they were. 9The Philistines had come and attacked the people in the Valley of Rephaim.

10So David asked God for advice. He said, "Should I go and attack the Philistines? Will you hand them over to me?"

The LORD answered him, "Go. I will hand them over to you."

11So David and his men went up to Baal Perazim. There David won the battle over the Philistines. He said, "God has broken through against my enemies, just as water breaks through a dam." That's why the place was called Baal Perazim.

12The Philistines had left the statues of their gods there. So David gave orders to burn them up.

13Once more the Philistines attacked the people in the valley. 14So David asked God for advice again.

God answered him, "Do not go straight up. Instead, circle around them. Attack them in front of the balsam trees. 15Listen for the sound of marching in the tops of the trees. Then move out to fight. The sound will mean that I have gone out in front of you. I will strike down the Philistine army."

16So David did just as God had commanded him. He and his men struck down the Philistine army. They struck them down from Gibeon all the way to Gezer.

17So David became famous in every land. The LORD made all of the nations afraid of him.

David Brings the Ark to Jerusalem

15 David constructed buildings for himself in the City of David. Then he prepared a place for the ark of God. He set up a tent for it. 2He said, "Only Levites can carry the ark of God. That's because the LORD chose them to carry his ark. He chose them to serve him forever in front of the place where his throne is."

3David gathered the whole community of Israel together in Jerusalem. He wanted to bring the ark of the LORD up to the place he had prepared for it. 4He called together the members of the family line of Aaron. He also called the Levites together.

Here are the men who came from the families of the Levites.

5From the families of Kohath came the leader Uriel and 120 relatives.

6From the families of Merari came the leader Asaiah and 220 relatives.

7From the families of Gershon came the leader Joel and 130 relatives.

8From the families of Elizaphan came the leader Shemaiah and 200 relatives.

9From the families of Hebron came the leader Eliel and 80 relatives.

10From the families of Uzziel came the leader Amminadab and 112 relatives.

11David sent for the priests Zadok and Abiathar. He also sent for Uriel, Asaiah, Joel, Shemaiah, Eliel and Amminadab. They were Levites. 12He said to them, "You are the leaders of the families of Levi. You and the other Levites must set yourselves apart to serve the LORD and his people. You must bring up the ark of the LORD. He is the God of Israel. Put the ark in the place I've prepared for it.

13"Remember when the anger of the LORD our God broke out against us? It was because you Levites didn't bring the ark up the first time. We didn't ask the LORD how to do it in the way the law requires."

14So the priests and Levites set themselves apart. Then they brought up the ark of the LORD. He is the God of Israel. 15This time the Levites used the poles to carry the ark of God on their shoulders. That's what Moses had commanded in keeping with the word of the LORD.

16David told the Levite leaders to appoint their relatives as singers. He wanted them to sing joyful songs. He also wanted them to play lyres, harps and cymbals along with their singing.

17So the Levites appointed Heman, the son of Joel. From his relatives they chose Asaph, the son of Berekiah. Other relatives were from the family of Merari. From them they chose Ethan, the son of Kushaiah. 18Along with them they chose their relatives who were next in line. Their names were Zechariah, Jaaziel, Shemiramoth, Jehiel, Unni, Eliab, Benaiah, Maaseiah, Mattithiah, Eliphelehu, Mikneiah, Obed-Edom and Jeiel. They guarded the gates.

19Heman, Asaph and Ethan played the bronze cymbals. 20Zechariah, Aziel,

Shemiramoth, Jehiel, Unni, Eliab, Maaseiah and Benaiah played the high notes on the lyres. 21Mattithiah, Eliphelehu, Mikneiah, Obed-Edom, Jeiel and Azaziah played the low notes on the harps.

22Kenaniah was the leader of the Levites. He was in charge of the singing because he was good at it.

23Berekiah and Elkanah guarded the ark. 24Some of the priests blew trumpets in front of the ark of God. Their names were Shebaniah, Joshaphat, Nethanel, Amasai, Zechariah, Benaiah and Eliezer. Obed-Edom and Jehiah also helped guard the ark.

25David and the elders of Israel went to bring up the ark of the covenant of the LORD. So did the commanders of companies of 1,000 men. With great joy they brought the ark up from the house of Obed-Edom.

26God had helped the Levites who were carrying the ark of the covenant of the LORD. So seven bulls and seven rams were sacrificed.

27David was wearing a robe that was made out of fine linen. So were all of the Levites who were carrying the ark. And so were the singers and the choir director Kenaniah. David was also wearing a sacred linen apron.

28So the whole community of Israel brought up the ark of the covenant of the LORD. They shouted. They blew rams' horns and trumpets. They played cymbals, lyres and harps.

29The ark of the covenant of the LORD was brought into the City of David. Saul's daughter Michal was watching from a window. She saw King David dancing and celebrating. That made her hate him in her heart.

16 The ark of God was brought into Jerusalem. It was put in the tent David had set up for it. The priests brought burnt offerings and friendship offerings to God.

2After David finished sacrificing those offerings, he blessed the people in the name of the LORD. 3He gave to each Israelite man and woman a loaf of bread. He also gave each one a date cake and a raisin cake.

4He appointed some of the Levites to serve in front of the ark of the LORD. David wanted them to pray, give thanks and praise the LORD. He is the God of Israel. 5Asaph was the leader of those Levites. Zechariah was next. Then came Jeiel, Shemiramoth, Jehiel, Mattithiah, Eliab, Benaiah, Obed-Edom and Jeiel. They

played the lyres and harps. Asaph played the cymbals. 6The priests Benaiah and Jahaziel blew the trumpets. They blew them at regular times in front of the ark of the covenant of God.

David's Psalm of Thanks to the LORD

7That day was the first time David gave Asaph and his helpers this psalm of thanks to the LORD.

8 Give thanks to the LORD. Worship him.
   Tell the nations what he has done.
9 Sing to him. Sing praise to him.
   Tell about all of the wonderful
      things he has done.
10 Praise him, because his name is holy.
   Let the hearts of those who trust in
      the LORD be glad.
11 Look to the LORD and to his strength.
   Always look to him.
12 Remember the wonderful things he
      has done.
   Remember his miracles and how he
      judged our enemies.
13 Remember what he has done, you
      children of his servant Israel.
   Remember it, you people of Jacob.
   You are God's chosen ones.

14 He is the LORD our God.
   He judges the whole earth.
15 He will keep his covenant forever.
   He will keep his promise for all time
      to come.

TELLS OTHERS

GIVE THANKS TO THE LORD. WORSHIP HIM.

TELL THE NATIONS WHAT HE HAS DONE.

GIVE THANKS TO THE LORD, BECAUSE HE IS GOOD.

HIS FAITHFUL LOVE CONTINUES FOREVER.
— 1 CHRONICLES 16:8,34 —

THANKFUL

16 He will keep the covenant he made
with Abraham.
He will keep the oath he took when
he made his promise to Isaac.
17 He made it stand as a law for Jacob.
He made it stand as a covenant for
Israel. It will last forever.
18 He said, "I will give you the land of
Canaan.
It will belong to you."

19 At first there weren't very many of
God's people.
There were only a few. And they
were strangers in the land.
20 They wandered from nation to nation.
They wandered from one kingdom
to another.
21 But God didn't allow anyone to beat
them down.
To keep them safe, he gave a
command to kings.
22 He said to them, "Do not touch my
anointed ones.
Do not harm my prophets."

23 All you people of the earth, sing to the
LORD.
Day after day tell about how he saves
us.
24 Tell the nations about his glory.
Tell all people about the wonderful
things he has done.
25 The LORD is great. He is really worthy of
praise.
People should have respect for him
as the greatest God of all.
26 All of the gods of the nations are like
their statues.
They can't do anything.
But the LORD made the heavens.
27 Glory and majesty are all around him.
Strength and joy can be seen in the
place where he lives.
28 Praise the LORD, all you nations.
Praise the LORD for his glory and
strength.
29 Praise the LORD for the glory that
belongs to him.
Bring an offering and come to him.
Worship the LORD because of his
beauty and holiness.
30 All you people of the earth, tremble
when you are with him.
The world is firmly set in place. It
can't be moved.
31 Let the heavens be filled with joy. Let
the earth be glad.
Let them say among the nations,
"The LORD rules!"
32 Let the ocean and everything in it roar.

Let the fields and everything in
them be glad.
33 Then the trees in the forest will sing
with joy.
They will sing to the LORD.
He will judge the people of the
world.

34 Give thanks to the LORD, because he is
good.
His faithful love continues forever.
35 Cry out, "Save us, God our Savior.
Save us. Bring us back from among
the nations.
Then we will give thanks to you,
because your name is holy.
We will celebrate by praising you."
36 Give praise to the LORD, the God of
Israel,
for ever and ever.

Then all of the people said, "Amen!" They
also said, "Praise the LORD."

37 David left Asaph and his helpers to
serve in front of the ark of the covenant of
the LORD. They served there at regular
times. They did it as they were required to
do each day. **38** David also left Obed-Edom
and his 68 helpers to serve with them.
Obed-Edom and Hosah guarded the
gates. Obed-Edom was the son of Jeduthun.
39 David left the priest Zadok and some
other priests in front of the holy tent of
the LORD. It was at the high place in Gibeon. **40** David left them there to sacrifice
burnt offerings to the LORD on the altar
every morning and evening. They did it in
keeping with everything that is written in
the Law of the LORD. That's the Law he
had given to Israel.

POWER-SURGE

GIVING **G**

**PRAISE THE LORD FOR
THE GLORY THAT
BELONGS TO HIM.**

**BRING AN OFFERING
AND COME TO HIM.**

**WORSHIP THE LORD
BECAUSE OF HIS
BEAUTY AND
HOLINESS.**

— 1 CHRONICLES 16:29 —

⁴¹Heman and Jeduthun were with the priests. So were the rest of those who had been chosen by name and appointed to serve. They had been chosen to give thanks to the LORD, "because his faithful love continues forever." ⁴²It was the duty of Heman and Jeduthun to blow the trumpets. They also had the duty of playing the cymbals and other instruments for the sacred songs. The sons of Jeduthun were stationed at one of the gates.

⁴³All of the people left. Everyone went home. And David returned home to bless his family.

God Makes a Promise to David

17 David settled down in his palace. Then he spoke to the prophet Nathan. He said, "Here I am, living in a palace that has beautiful cedar walls. But the ark of the covenant of the LORD is under a tent."

²Nathan replied to David, "Do what you want to. God is with you."

³That night a message came to Nathan from God. He said,

⁴"Go and speak to my servant David. Tell him, 'The LORD says, "You are not the one who will build me a house to live in. ⁵I have not lived in a house from the day I brought Israel up out of Egypt until now. I have moved my tent from one place to another. I have moved my home from one place to another. ⁶I have moved from place to place with all of the people of Israel. I commanded their leaders to be shepherds over them. I never asked any of those leaders, 'Why haven't you built me a house that has beautiful cedar walls?' " '

⁷"So tell my servant David, 'The LORD who rules over all says, "I took you away from the grasslands. That is where you were taking care of your father's sheep and goats. I made you ruler over my people Israel. ⁸I have been with you everywhere you have gone. I cut off all of your enemies when you were attacking them. Now I will make you famous. Your name will be just as respected as the names of the most important people on earth.

⁹" ' "I will provide a place where my people Israel can live. I will plant them in the land. Then they will have a home of their own. They will not be bothered anymore. Sinful people will no longer crush them, as they did at first. ¹⁰That is what your enemies have done ever since I appointed leaders over my people Israel. But I will bring all of them under your control.

" ' "I tell you that I will build a royal house for your family. ¹¹Some day your life will come to an end. You will join the members of your family who have already died. Then I will give you one of your own sons to become the next king after you. I will make his kingdom secure.

¹²" ' "He is the one who will build me a house. I will set up his throne. It will last forever. ¹³I will be his father. And he will be my son. I took my love away from the man who ruled before you. But I will never take my love away from your son. ¹⁴I will place him over my house and my kingdom forever. His throne will last forever." ' "

¹⁵Nathan reported to David all of the words that the LORD had spoken to him.

David Prays to the LORD

¹⁶Then King David went into the holy tent. He sat down in front of the LORD. He said,

"LORD God, who am I? My family isn't important. So why have you brought me this far? ¹⁷I would have thought that you had already done more than enough for me. But now, God, you have spoken about what is going to happen to my royal house in days to come. LORD God, you have treated me as if I were the most honored man of all.

¹⁸"What more can I say to you for honoring me? You know all about me. ¹⁹LORD, you have done a wonderful thing. You have given me many great promises. All of them are for my good. They are exactly what you wanted to give me.

²⁰"LORD, there isn't anyone like you. There isn't any God but you. We have heard about it with our own ears.

²¹"Who is like your people Israel? God, we are the one nation on earth you have saved. You have set us free for yourself. Your name has become famous. You have done great and wonderful things. You have driven nations out to make room for your people. You saved us when you set us

free from Egypt. No other god has done any of those things for its people. 22You made Israel your very own people forever. LORD, you have become our God.

23"And now, LORD, let the promise you have made to me and my royal house stand forever. Do exactly as you promised. 24When your promise comes true, your name will be honored forever. People will say, 'The LORD rules over all. He is the God over Israel. He is Israel's God.' My royal house will be made secure in your sight.

25"My God, you have shown me that you will build me a royal house. So I can pray to you boldly. 26LORD, you are God! You have promised many good things to me. 27You have been pleased to bless my royal house. Now it will continue forever in your sight. LORD, you have blessed it. And it will be blessed forever."

David Wins Many Battles

18 While David was king of Israel, he won many battles over the Philistines. He brought them under his control. He took Gath away from the Philistines. He also captured the villages that were around Gath.

2David also won the battle over the people of Moab. They were brought under his rule. They gave him the gifts he required them to bring him.

3David fought against Hadadezer all the way to Hamath. Hadadezer was king of Zobah. He had gone to take complete control of the land along the Euphrates River. 4David captured 1,000 of Hadadezer's chariots, 7,000 chariot riders and 20,000 soldiers on foot. He cut the legs of all but 100 of the chariot horses.

5The Arameans of Damascus came to help Hadadezer, the king of Zobah. But David struck down 22,000 of them. 6He stationed some soldiers in the Aramean kingdom of Damascus. The people of Aram were brought under his rule. They gave him the gifts he required them to bring him. The LORD helped David win his battles everywhere he went.

7David took the gold shields that were carried by the officers of Hadadezer. He brought the shields to Jerusalem. 8He took a huge amount of bronze from Tebah and Cun. Those towns belonged to Hadadezer. Later, Solomon used the bronze to make the huge bronze bowl for washing. He also used it to make the pil-

lars and many other bronze articles for the temple.

9Tou was king of Hamath. He heard that David had won the battle over the entire army of Hadadezer, the king of Zobah. 10So Tou sent his son Hadoram to King David. Hadoram greeted David. He praised him because he had won the battle over Hadadezer. Hadadezer had been at war with Tou. So Hadoram brought David all kinds of articles that were made out of gold, silver and bronze.

11King David set those articles apart for the LORD. He had done the same thing with the silver and gold he had taken from other nations. The nations were Edom, Moab, Ammon, Philistia and Amalek.

12Abishai struck down 18,000 men of Edom in the Valley of Salt. Abishai was the son of Zeruiah. 13He stationed some soldiers in Edom. The whole nation of Edom was brought under his rule. The LORD helped David win his battles everywhere he went.

David's Officials

14David ruled over the whole nation of Israel. He did what was fair and right for all of his people. 15Joab, the son of Zeruiah, was commander over the army. Jehoshaphat, the son of Ahilud, kept the records. 16Zadok, the son of Ahitub, was a priest. Ahimelech, the son of Abiathar, was also a priest. Shavsha was the secretary. 17Benaiah, the son of Jehoiada, was commander over the Kerethites and Pelethites. And King David's sons were the chief officials who served at his side.

David Goes to War Against the People of Ammon

19 Nahash was king of Ammon. After he died, his son became the next king after him. 2David thought, "I'm going to be kind to Hanun. His father Nahash was kind to me." So David sent messengers to Hanun. He wanted them to tell Hanun how sad he was that Hanun's father had died.

David's messengers went to the land of Ammon. They told Hanun how sad David was.

3The Ammonite nobles spoke to Hanun. They said, "David has sent messengers to tell you he is sad. They say he wants to honor your father. But the real reason they've come is to look the land over. They want to destroy it."

4So Hanun grabbed hold of David's men. He shaved them. He cut their clothes off just below the waist and left them half naked. Then he sent them away.

⁵Someone came and told David what had happened to his men. So David sent messengers to them because they were filled with shame. King David said to them, "Stay at Jericho until your beards grow out again. Then come back here."

⁶The Ammonites realized that what they had done had made David very angry with them. So Hanun and the Ammonites got 37 tons of silver. They used it to hire chariots and chariot riders from Aram Naharaim, Aram Maacah and Zobah. ⁷They hired 32,000 chariots and riders. They also hired the king of Maacah and his troops. All of them came out and camped near Medeba. At the same time the Ammonites brought their troops together from their towns. Then they marched out to fight.

⁸David heard about it. So he sent Joab out with the entire army of Israel's fighting men. ⁹The Ammonites marched out. They took up their battle positions at the entrance to their city. The kings who came to help them gathered their troops together in the open country.

¹⁰Joab saw that there were lines of soldiers in front of him and behind him. So he chose some of the best troops in Israel. He sent them to march out against the Arameans. ¹¹He put the rest of the men under the command of his brother Abishai. They were sent to march out against the Ammonites.

¹²Joab said, "Suppose the Arameans are too strong for me. Then you must come and help me. But suppose the Ammonites are too strong for you. Then I'll come and help you. ¹³Be strong. Let's be brave as we fight for our people and the cities of our God. The LORD will do what he thinks is best."

¹⁴Then Joab and the troops who were with him marched out to attack the Arameans. They ran away from him. ¹⁵The Ammonites saw that the Arameans were running away. So they also ran away from Joab's brother Abishai. They went inside the city. Then Joab went back to Jerusalem.

¹⁶The Arameans saw that they had been driven away by Israel. So they sent messengers to get some Arameans from east of the Euphrates River. The Arameans were under the command of Shophach. He was the commander of Hadadezer's army.

¹⁷David was told about it. So he gathered the whole army of Israel together. They went across the Jordan River. David marched out against the Arameans. He lined up his soldiers opposite them. He lined them up to meet the Arameans in battle.

The Arameans began to fight against him. ¹⁸But then they ran away from Israel. David killed 7,000 of their chariot riders. He killed 40,000 of their soldiers who were on foot. He also killed Shophach, the commander of their army.

¹⁹The people who were under the rule of Hadadezer saw that Israel had won the battle over them. So they made a peace treaty with David. They were brought under his rule.

After that, the Arameans wouldn't help the Ammonites anymore.

Joab Captures the City of Rabbah

20 In the spring, Joab led Israel's army out. It was the time when kings go off to war. Joab destroyed the land of Ammon. He went to the city of Rabbah. He surrounded it and got ready to attack it. But David remained in Jerusalem. Later, Joab attacked Rabbah and completely destroyed it.

²David took the gold crown off the head of the king of Ammon. The crown weighed 75 pounds. It had jewels in it. It was placed on David's head. He took a huge amount of goods from the city. ³He brought out the people who were there. He made them work with saws and iron picks and axes. David did that to all of the towns in Ammon. Then he and his entire army returned to Jerusalem.

POWER-SURGE

BRAVE B

BE STRONG. LET'S BE BRAVE AS WE FIGHT FOR OUR PEOPLE AND THE CITIES OF OUR GOD. THE LORD WILL DO WHAT HE THINKS IS BEST.
— 1 CHRONICLES 19:13 —

STRONG

Israel Goes to War Against the Philistines

4War broke out at Gezer against the Philistines. At that time Sibbecai killed Sippai. So the Philistines were brought under Israel's control. Sibbecai was a Hushathite. Sippai was from the family line of Rapha.

5In another battle against the Philistines, Elhanan killed Lahmi. Elhanan was the son of Jair. Lahmi was the brother of Goliath. Goliath was from the city of Gath. Lahmi's spear was as big as a weaver's rod.

6There was still another battle. It took place at Gath. A huge man lived there. He had six fingers on each hand and six toes on each foot. So the total number of his toes and fingers was 24. He was also from the family line of Rapha. **7**He made fun of Israel. So Jonathan killed him. Jonathan was the son of David's brother Shimea.

8Those Philistine men lived in Gath. They were from the family line of Rapha. David and his men killed them.

David Counts His Fighting Men

21 Satan rose up against Israel. He stirred up David to count the men of Israel. **2**So David spoke to Joab and the commanders of the troops. He said, "Go! Count the men of Israel from Beersheba all the way to Dan. Report back to me. Then I'll know how many there are."

3Joab replied, "May the LORD multiply his troops 100 times. King David, you are my master. Aren't all of the men under your control? Why would you want me to count them? Do you want to make Israel guilty?"

4In spite of what Joab said, the king's word had more authority than Joab's word did. So Joab left and went all through Israel. Then he came back to Jerusalem. **5**Joab reported to David how many fighting men he had counted. In the whole land of Israel there were 1,100,000 men who could use a sword well. That included 470,000 men in Judah.

6But Joab didn't include the tribes of Levi and Benjamin in the total number. The king's command was sickening to Joab. **7**It was also evil in the sight of God. So he punished Israel.

8Then David said to God, "I committed a great sin when I counted Israel's men. I beg you to take away my guilt. I've done a very foolish thing."

9The LORD spoke to David's prophet Gad. He said, **10**"Go and tell David, 'The LORD says, "I could punish you in three

different ways. Choose one of them for me to use against you." ' "

11So Gad went to David. He said to him, "The LORD says, 'Take your choice. **12**You can have three years when there will not be enough food in the land. You can have three months when your enemies will sweep you away. They will catch up with you. They will cut you down with their swords. Or you can have three days when my sword will punish you. That means there would be three days of plague in the land. My angel would strike people down in every part of Israel.'

"So take your pick. Tell me how to answer the One who sent me."

13David said to Gad, "I'm suffering terribly. Let me fall into the hands of the LORD. His mercy is very great. But don't let me fall into the hands of men."

14So the LORD sent a plague on Israel. And 70,000 Israelites died. **15**God sent an angel to destroy Jerusalem. But as the angel was doing it, the LORD saw it. He was very sad because of the plague. So he spoke to the angel who was destroying the people. He said, "That is enough! Do not kill any more people!"

The angel of the LORD was standing at Araunah's threshing floor. Araunah was from the city of Jebus.

16David looked up. He saw the angel of the LORD standing between heaven and earth. The angel was holding out a sword over Jerusalem. David and the elders fell with their faces to the ground. They were wearing black clothes.

17David said to God, "I ordered the fighting men to be counted. I'm the one who has sinned. I'm the one who has done what is wrong. These people are like sheep. What have they done? LORD my God, let your powerful hand punish me and my family. But don't let this plague continue to strike your people."

David Builds an Altar

18Then the angel of the LORD ordered Gad to tell David to go up to the threshing floor of Araunah, the Jebusite. He wanted David to build an altar there to honor the LORD.

19So David went up and did it. He obeyed the message that Gad had spoken in the LORD's name.

20Araunah was threshing wheat. He turned and saw the angel. His four children were with him. They hid themselves. **21**David approached the threshing floor. Araunah looked up and saw him. So Araunah left the threshing floor. He bowed down to David with his face toward the ground. ²²David said to him, "Let me have the property your threshing floor is on. I want to build an altar there to honor the LORD. When I do, the plague on the people will be stopped. Sell the threshing floor to me for the full price."

²³Araunah said to David, "Take it! King David, you are my master. Do what you please. I'll even provide the oxen for the burnt offerings. Use boards from the threshing sleds for the wood. Use the wheat for the grain offering. I'll give all of it to you."

²⁴But King David replied to Araunah, "No! I want to pay the full price. I won't take what belongs to you and give it to the LORD. I won't sacrifice a burnt offering that hasn't cost me anything."

²⁵So David paid Araunah 15 pounds of gold for the property. ²⁶David built an altar there to honor the LORD. He sacrificed burnt offerings and friendship offerings. He called out to the LORD. The LORD answered him by sending fire from heaven on the altar for burnt offerings.

²⁷Then the LORD spoke to the angel. And the angel put his sword away. ²⁸When the angel did that, David was still at the threshing floor of Araunah, the Jebusite. David saw that the LORD had answered him. So he offered sacrifices there.

²⁹At that time, the LORD's holy tent was at the high place in Gibeon. The altar for burnt offerings was there too. Moses had made the holy tent in the desert. ³⁰David couldn't go to the tent to pray to God. That's because he was afraid of the sword of the angel of the LORD.

22 David announced, "The house of the LORD God will be built here. Israel's altar for burnt offerings will also be here."

David Makes Plans for Building the Temple

²David gave orders to bring together the outsiders who were living in Israel. He appointed some of them to cut stones. He wanted them to prepare blocks of stone for building the house of God.

³David provided a large amount of iron to make nails. They were for the doors of the gates and for the fittings. He provided more bronze than anyone could weigh. ⁴He also provided more cedar logs than anyone could count. The people of Sidon and Tyre brought large numbers of logs to David.

⁵David said, "My son Solomon is young. He's never done anything like this before. The house that will be built for the LORD should be very grand and wonderful. It should be famous and beautiful in the eyes of all of the nations. I'll get things ready for it." So David got many things ready before he died.

⁶Then he sent for his son Solomon. He told him to build a house for the LORD, the God of Israel.

⁷David said to Solomon, "My son, with all my heart I wanted to build a house for the LORD my God. That's where his Name will be. ⁸But a message from the LORD came to me. It said, 'You have spilled the blood of many people. You have fought many wars. You are not the one who will build a house for my Name. That is because I have seen you spill the blood of many people on the earth.

⁹" 'But you are going to have a son. He will be a man of peace. And I will give him peace and rest from all of his enemies on every side. His name will be Solomon. I will give Israel peace and quiet while he is king. ¹⁰He will build a house for my Name. He will be my son. And I will be his father. I will make his kingdom secure over Israel. It will last forever.'

¹¹"My son, may the LORD be with you. May you have success. May you build the house of the LORD your God, just as he said you would. ¹²May the LORD give you good sense. May he give you understanding when he makes you king over Israel. Then you will keep the law of the LORD your God.

¹³"Be careful to obey the rules and laws the LORD gave Moses for Israel. Then you will have success. Be strong and brave. Don't be afraid. Don't lose hope.

¹⁴"I've tried very hard to provide for the LORD's temple. I've provided 3,750 tons of gold and 37,500 tons of silver. I've provided more bronze and iron than anyone can weigh. I've also given plenty of wood and stone. You can add to it.

¹⁵"You have a lot of workers. You have people who can cut stones and people who can lay the stones. You have people who can work with wood. You also have people who are skilled in every other kind of work. ¹⁶Some of them can work with gold and silver. Others can work with bronze and iron. There are more workers than anyone can count. So begin the work. May the LORD be with you."

¹⁷Then David ordered all of Israel's leaders to help his son Solomon. ¹⁸He said to them, "The LORD your God is with you.

BRAVE B

BE CAREFUL TO OBEY
THE RULES AND LAWS
THE LORD GAVE
MOSES FOR ISRAEL.
THEN YOU WILL HAVE
SUCCESS. BE STRONG
AND BRAVE. DON'T
BE AFRAID. DON'T
LOSE HOPE.
— 1 CHRONICLES 22:13 — ✔

OBEYS

He's given you peace and rest on every side. He's handed the people who are living in the land over to me. The land has been brought under the control of the LORD and his people.

19 "So look to the LORD your God with all your heart and soul. Start building the temple of the LORD God. Then bring the ark of the covenant of the LORD into it. Also bring in the sacred articles that belong to God. The temple will be built for the Name of the LORD."

The Family Line of Levi

23 David had become very old. So he made his son Solomon king over Israel.

2 He gathered together all of the leaders of Israel. He also gathered the priests and the Levites together. 3 The Levites who were 30 years old or more were counted. The total number of men was 38,000.

4 David said, "From them, 24,000 will direct the work of the LORD's temple. And 6,000 will be officials and judges. 5 Another 4,000 will guard the gates. And 4,000 will praise the LORD with the instruments of music I've provided for that purpose."

6 David separated the Levites into groups. He did it based on the sons of Levi. The sons were Gershon, Kohath and Merari.

The Family of Gershon

7 Ladan and Shimei belonged to the family of Gershon.

8 The sons of Ladan were Jehiel, Zetham and Joel. Jehiel was the oldest son. The total number of sons was three.

9 The sons of Shimei were Shelomoth, Haziel and Haran. The total number of sons was three. They were the leaders of the families of Ladan.

10 The sons of Shimei were Jahath, Ziza, Jeush and Beriah. The total number of the sons of Shimei was four.

11 Jahath was the first son. Ziza was the second son. But Jeush and Beriah didn't have many sons. So they were counted as one family. They had only one task.

The Family of Kohath

12 The sons of Kohath were Amram, Izhar, Hebron and Uzziel. The total number of sons was four.

13 Aaron and Moses belonged to Amram's family line.

Aaron and his family line were set apart forever as the LORD's priests. They had the duty of setting the most holy things apart to the LORD. They offered sacrifices to the LORD. They served him. They gave blessings in his name forever.

14 The sons of Moses, the man of God, were counted as part of the tribe of Levi.

15 The sons of Moses were Gershom and Eliezer.

16 Shubael was the oldest son in the family line of Gershom.

17 Rehabiah was the oldest son in the family line of Eliezer.

Eliezer didn't have any other sons. But Rehabiah had a great many sons.

18 Shelomith was the oldest son of Izhar.

19 Jeriah was the first son of Hebron. Amariah was his second son. Jahaziel was the third. Jekameam was the fourth.

20 Micah was the first son of Uzziel. Isshiah was his second son.

The Family of Merari

21 The sons of Merari were Mahli and Mushi.

The sons of Mahli were Eleazar and Kish.

22 Eleazar died without having any sons. All he had was daughters. They got married to their cousins. The cousins were the sons of Kish.

23 The sons of Mushi were
   Mahli, Eder and Jerimoth. The
   total number of sons was three.

24 Those were the family lines of Levi. They were recorded under the names of the family leaders. Each worker who was 20 years old or more was counted. They served in the LORD's temple. **25** David had said, "The LORD is the God of Israel. He has given peace and rest to his people. He has come to Jerusalem to live there forever. **26** So the Levites don't need to carry the holy tent anymore. They don't need to carry any of its articles anymore. Those were the articles that were used to serve there."

27 The Levites who were 20 years old or more were counted. That was in keeping with David's final directions.

28 The Levites had the duty of helping the members of Aaron's family line. They helped them serve in the LORD's temple. They were in charge of the courtyards and the side rooms. They made all of the sacred things pure and clean.

They also had other duties at the house of God. **29** They were in charge of setting the holy bread out on the table. They prepared the flour for the grain offerings. They made the wafers without using any yeast. They did the baking and the mixing. They measured the amount and size of everything.

30 They stood every morning to thank and praise the LORD. They did the same thing every evening. **31** They also did it every time burnt offerings were brought to the LORD. Those offerings were brought every Sabbath day. They were also brought at every New Moon Feast and during the appointed yearly feasts.

The Levites served in front of the LORD at regular times. The proper number of Levites was always used when they served. They served in the way the law required of them.

32 So the Levites carried out their duties for the Tent of Meeting and for the Holy Room. They worked under their relatives who were in the family line of Aaron. They helped them serve at the LORD's temple.

The Groups of Priests

24 Here are the groups of priests the sons of Aaron were separated into.

The sons of Aaron were Nadab, Abihu, Eleazar and Ithamar. **2** But Nadab and Abihu died before their father did. They didn't have any sons. So Eleazar and Ithamar served as the priests.

3 With the help of Zadok and Ahimelech, David separated the priests into groups. Each group served in its appointed order and time. Zadok belonged to the family line of Eleazar. Ahimelech belonged to the family line of Ithamar. **4** More leaders were found among Eleazar's family line than among Ithamar's. So the priests were separated into their groups based on that fact. There were 16 family leaders from Eleazar's line. There were eight family leaders from Ithamar's line.

5 The priests were separated into their groups by using lots. That was the fair way to do it. The priests were officials of the temple and officials of God. They came from the family lines of Eleazar and Ithamar.

6 Shemaiah was a Levite. He was the son of Nethanel. He was the writer who recorded the names of the priests. He wrote them down in front of the king and the officials. The officials included the priest Zadok and Ahimelech. Ahimelech was the son of Abiathar. They also included the leaders of the families of the priests and the Levites. One family was chosen by lot from Eleazar. Then one was chosen from Ithamar.

7 The 1st lot that was drawn out was
   for Jehoiarib.
   The 2nd was for Jedaiah.
8 The 3rd was for Harim.
   The 4th was for Seorim.
9 The 5th was for Malkijah.
   The 6th was for Mijamin.
10 The 7th was for Hakkoz.
   The 8th was for Abijah.
11 The 9th was for Jeshua.

POWER-SURGE

FAITHFUL ()

[THE LEVITES] STOOD
EVERY MORNING TO
THANK AND PRAISE
THE LORD. THEY DID
THE SAME THING
EVERY EVENING.

— 1 CHRONICLES 23:30 — ♣

THANKFUL

The 10th was for Shecaniah.
12 The 11th was for Eliashib.
The 12th was for Jakim.
13 The 13th was for Huppah.
The 14th was for Jeshebeab.
14 The 15th was for Bilgah.
The 16th was for Immer.
15 The 17th was for Hezir.
The 18th was for Happizzez.
16 The 19th was for Pethahiah.
The 20th was for Jehezkel.
17 The 21st was for Jakin.
The 22nd was for Gamul.
18 The 23rd was for Delaiah.
The 24th was for Maaziah.

19 That was their appointed order for serving when they entered the LORD's temple. That order was based on the rules Aaron had given them long ago. Everything was done exactly as the LORD had commanded Aaron. The LORD is the God of Israel.

The Rest of the Levites

20 Here are the other members of the family line of Levi.
From the sons of Amram came Shubael.
From the sons of Shubael came Jehdeiah.
21 From the sons of Rehabiah came Isshiah.
Isshiah was the oldest.
22 From the people of Izhar came Shelomoth.
From the sons of Shelomoth came Jahath.
23 Jeriah was the first son of Hebron. Amariah was his second son. Jahaziel was the third. Jekameam was the fourth.
24 The son of Uzziel was Micah.
From the sons of Micah came Shamir.
25 The brother of Micah was Isshiah.
From the sons of Isshiah came Zechariah.
26 The sons of Merari were Mahli and Mushi.
The son of Jaaziah was Beno.
27 The sons of Merari
from Jaaziah were Beno, Shoham, Zaccur and Ibri.
28 From Mahli came Eleazar. Eleazar didn't have any sons.
29 From Kish came
Jerahmeel. Jerahmeel was the son of Kish.
30 The sons of Mushi were Mahli, Eder and Jerimoth.

Those were the Levites, family by family. 31 They cast lots, just as their relatives, the sons of Aaron, had done. They did it in front of King David, Zadok and Ahimelech. They did it in front of the family leaders of the priests. They also did it in front of the family leaders of the Levites. The families of the oldest brother were treated in the same way as the families of the youngest.

The Singers

25 David and the commanders of the army set apart some of the sons of Asaph, Heman and Jeduthun. They set them apart to serve the LORD by prophesying while harps, lyres and cymbals were being played. Here is the list of the men who served in that way.

2 From the sons of Asaph came
Zaccur, Joseph, Nethaniah and Asarelah. The sons of Asaph were under the direction of Asaph. He prophesied under the king's direction.
3 From the sons of Jeduthun came
Gedaliah, Zeri, Jeshaiah, Shimei, Hashabiah and Mattithiah. The total number was six. They were under the direction of their father Jeduthun. He prophesied while playing the harp. He used it to thank and praise the LORD.
4 From the sons of Heman came
Bukkiah, Mattaniah, Uzziel, Shubael, Jerimoth, Hananiah, Hanani, Eliathah, Giddalti, Romamti-Ezer, Joshbekashah, Mallothi, Hothir and Mahazioth. 5 All of them were sons of the king's prophet Heman. They were given to Heman to bring him honor. That's what God had promised. God gave him 14 sons and three daughters.

6 All of them were under the direction of their fathers. They played music for the LORD's temple. They served at the house of God by playing cymbals, lyres and harps. Asaph, Jeduthun and Heman were under the king's direction.
7 All of them were trained and skilled in playing music for the LORD. Their total number was 288. That included their relatives. 8 Young and old alike cast lots for their duties. That was true for students as well as teachers.

9 The 1st lot that was drawn out was
for Asaph. It was for Joseph
and his sons and relatives. The
total number was 12.

SAMUEL

As Samuel grew up, the LORD was with him. He made everything Samuel said come true. So all of the people of Israel recognized that Samuel really was a prophet of the LORD. (1 Samuel 3:19–20)

GO TO PAGE 318

DAVID

"The LORD doesn't save by using a sword or a spear. And everyone who is here will know it. The battle belongs to the LORD. He will hand all of you over to us." (1 Samuel 17:47)

GO TO PAGE 336

JONATHAN

*Jonathan and David became close friends.
Jonathan loved David just as he loved himself.
(1 Samuel 18:1)*

GO TO PAGE 338

*[Nabal's] wife's name was Abigail.
She was a wise and beautiful woman.*
(1 Samuel 25:3)

GO TO PAGE 346

The 2nd lot was for Gedaliah and his relatives and sons. The total number was 12. **10** The 3rd was for Zaccur and his sons and relatives. The total number was 12. **11** The 4th was for Izri and his sons and relatives. The total number was 12. **12** The 5th was for Nethaniah and his sons and relatives. The total number was 12. **13** The 6th was for Bukkiah and his sons and relatives. The total number was 12. **14** The 7th was for Jesarelah and his sons and relatives. The total number was 12. **15** The 8th was for Jeshaiah and his sons and relatives. The total number was 12. **16** The 9th was for Mattaniah and his sons and relatives. The total number was 12. **17** The 10th was for Shimei and his sons and relatives. The total number was 12. **18** The 11th was for Azarel and his sons and relatives. The total number was 12. **19** The 12th was for Hashabiah and his sons and relatives. The total number was 12. **20** The 13th was for Shubael and his sons and relatives. The total number was 12. **21** The 14th was for Mattithiah and his sons and relatives. The total number was 12. **22** The 15th was for Jerimoth and his sons and relatives. The total number was 12. **23** The 16th was for Hananiah and his sons and relatives. The total number was 12. **24** The 17th was for Joshbekashah and his sons and relatives. The total number was 12. **25** The 18th was for Hanani and his sons and relatives. The total number was 12. **26** The 19th was for Mallothi and his sons and relatives. The total number was 12. **27** The 20th was for Eliathah and his sons and relatives. The total number was 12. **28** The 21st was for Hothir and his sons and relatives. The total number was 12. **29** The 22nd was for Giddalti and his sons and relatives. The total number was 12. **30** The 23rd was for Mahazioth and his sons and relatives. The total number was 12. **31** The 24th was for Romamti-Ezer and his sons and relatives. The total number was 12.

The Men Who Guarded the Gates

26 Here are the groups of men who guarded the gates.

From the family of Korah came Meshelemiah, the son of Kore. Kore was one of the sons of Asaph. **2** Meshelemiah had sons. Zechariah was his first son. Jediael was his second son. Zebadiah was the third. Jathniel was the fourth. **3** Elam was the fifth. Jehohanan was the sixth. And Eliehoenai was the seventh. **4** Obed-Edom also had sons. Shemaiah was his first son. Jehozabad was his second son. Joah was the third. Sacar was the fourth. Nethanel was the fifth. **5** Ammiel was the sixth. Issachar was the seventh. And Peullethai was the eighth. God had blessed Obed-Edom.

6 His son Shemaiah also had sons. They were leaders in their family. That's because they were men of great ability. **7** The sons of Shemaiah were Othni, Rephael, Obed and Elzabad. Elzabad's brothers Elihu and Semakiah were also able men. **8** All of them belonged to the family line of Obed-Edom. They and their sons and relatives were men of ability. They were strong enough to do their work. The total number of men in the family line of Obed-Edom was 62. **9** Meshelemiah's sons and relatives were able men. Their total number was 18.

10 Hosah belonged to the family line of Merari. Hosah's first son was Shimri. But Shimri wasn't the oldest son. His father had made him the first. **11** Hilkiah was Hosah's second son. Tabaliah was the third. Zechariah was the fourth. The total number of Hosah's sons and relatives was 13.

POWER-SURGE

STRONG

[THEY] BELONGED TO
THE FAMILY LINE OF
OBED-EDOM. THEY
AND THEIR SONS AND
RELATIVES WERE MEN
OF ABILITY. THEY WERE
STRONG ENOUGH TO
DO THEIR WORK.
— 1 CHRONICLES 26:8 —

¹²Those groups of men guarded the gates. They worked under their chief men. They served at the LORD's temple, just as their relatives had served. ¹³Lots were cast for each gate, family by family. Young and old alike were chosen.

¹⁴The lot that was drawn out for the East Gate was for Shelemiah. Then lots were cast for his son Zechariah. He gave wise advice. The lot that was drawn out for the North Gate was for him. ¹⁵The lot for the South Gate was for Obed-Edom. The lot for the storeroom was for his sons. ¹⁶Lots were drawn out for the West Gate and the Shalleketh Gate on the upper road. Those lots were for Shuppim and Hosah.

One guard stood next to another. ¹⁷There were six Levites a day on the east. There were four a day on the north. There were four a day on the south. And there were two at a time at the storeroom. ¹⁸Two Levite guards were at the courtyard to the west. And four were at the road.

¹⁹Those were the groups of the men who guarded the gates. They belonged to the family lines of Korah and Merari.

Other Officials

²⁰The Levite relatives of the men who guarded the gates were in charge of the treasures in the house of God. They were also in charge of other treasures that had been set apart for God.

²¹Ladan was from the family line of Gershon. Some leaders of families belonged to Ladan's family line. One of them was Jehieli. ²²The sons of Jehieli were Zetham and his brother Joel. They were in charge of the treasures in the LORD's temple.

²³Here are the officials who were from the family lines of Amram, Izhar, Hebron and Uzziel.

²⁴Shubael was from the family line of Moses' son Gershom. Shubael was the officer in charge of the treasures. ²⁵His relatives through Eliezer included his son Rehabiah. Jeshaiah was Rehabiah's son. Joram was Jeshaiah's son. Zicri was Joram's son. And Shelomith was Zicri's son.

²⁶Shelomith and his relatives were in charge of all of the treasures that had been set apart for God. King David had set those treasures apart. Some family leaders had also set them apart. They were the commanders of thousands of men and commanders of hundreds. The treasures had also been set apart by other army commanders.

²⁷Some of the goods that had been taken in battle were set apart to repair the LORD's temple. ²⁸The prophet Samuel had set apart some things for God. Saul, the son of Kish, had set apart other things. So had Abner, the son of Ner. And so had Joab, the son of Zeruiah. All of those things and all of the others that had been set apart were taken care of by Shelomith and his relatives.

²⁹From the family line of Izhar came Kenaniah and his sons. They were given duties that were away from the temple. They were officials and judges over Israel.

³⁰From the family line of Hebron came Hashabiah and his relatives. They were able men. The total number was 1,700. It was their duty to serve the king in Israel west of the Jordan River. It was also their duty to do all of the LORD's work there.

³¹Jeriah was the chief of the family line of Hebron. That's based on their family history. In the 40th year of David's rule, a search was made in the records. That's how

POWER-SURGE

WISE

ZECHARIAH...GAVE
WISE ADVICE.
— 1 CHRONICLES 26:14 —

men of ability were found in the family line of Hebron at Jazer in Gilead. ³²Jeriah had 2,700 relatives. They were able men. They were family leaders. King David had put them in charge of the tribes of Reuben and Gad and half of the tribe of Manasseh. They were in charge of matters having to do with God and the king.

The Companies in the King's Army

27 Here is the list of the Israelites who served in the king's army. They included leaders of families. They included commanders of thousands of men and commanders of hundreds. They also included other officers. All of them served the king in everything concerning the army companies that were on duty month by month all through the year. The total number of men in each company was 24,000.

²Jashobeam was in charge of the first company for the first month. He was the son of Zabdiel. The total number of men in Jashobeam's company was 24,000. ³He belonged to the family line of Perez. He was chief of all of the army officers for the first month.

⁴Dodai was in charge of the second company for the second month. He belonged to the family line of Ahoah. Mikloth was the leader of Dodai's company. The total number of men in Dodai's company was 24,000.

⁵The third army commander for the third month was the priest Benaiah, the son of Jehoiada. Benaiah was the chief. The total number of men in Benaiah's company was 24,000. ⁶That same Benaiah was a mighty man among the Thirty. In fact, he was leader over the Thirty. His son Ammizabad was in charge of his company.

⁷The fourth commander for the fourth month was Joab's brother Asahel. Asahel's son Zebadiah was the next commander after him. The total number of men in Asahel's company was 24,000.

⁸The fifth commander for the fifth month was Shamhuth. He was an Izrahite. The total number of men in Shamhuth's company was 24,000.

⁹The sixth commander for the sixth month was Ira. He was the son of Ikkesh from Tekoa. The total number of men in Ira's company was 24,000.

¹⁰The seventh commander for the seventh month was Helez. He was a Pelonite from Ephraim. The total number of men in Helez's company was 24,000.

¹¹The eighth commander for the eighth month was Sibbecai. He was a Hushathite from Zerah. The total number of men in Sibbecai's company was 24,000.

¹²The ninth commander for the ninth month was Abiezer. He was from Anathoth in Benjamin. The total number of men in Abiezer's company was 24,000.

¹³The tenth commander for the tenth month was Maharai. He was a Netophathite from Zerah. The total number of men in Maharai's company was 24,000.

¹⁴The 11th commander for the 11th month was Benaiah. He was from Pirathon in Ephraim. The total number of men in Benaiah's company was 24,000.

¹⁵The 12th commander for the 12th month was Heldai. He was a Netophathite from the family line of Othniel. The total number of men in Heldai's company was 24,000.

The Officers Over the Tribes

¹⁶Here are the officers over the tribes of Israel.

Over the tribe of Reuben was Eliezer, the son of Zicri.

Over Simeon was Shephatiah, the son of Maacah.

¹⁷Over Levi was Hashabiah, the son of Kemuel.

Over Aaron was Zadok.

¹⁸Over Judah was Elihu. He was David's brother.

Over Issachar was Omri, the son of Michael.

¹⁹Over Zebulun was Ishmaiah, the son of Obadiah.

Over Naphtali was Jerimoth, the son of Azriel.

²⁰Over Ephraim was Hoshea, the son of Azaziah.

Over half of the tribe of Manasseh was Joel, the son of Pedaiah.

²¹Over the half of the tribe of Manasseh in Gilead was Iddo, the son of Zechariah.

Over Benjamin was Jaasiel, the son of Abner.

²²Over Dan was Azarel, the son of Jeroham.

Those were the officers over the tribes of Israel.

23David didn't count the men who were 20 years old or less. That's because the LORD had promised to make the people of Israel as many as the stars in the sky. 24Joab, the son of Zeruiah, began to count the men. But he didn't finish. The LORD was angry with Israel because David had begun to count the men. So the number wasn't written down in the official records of King David.

Other Officials of the King

25Azmaveth was in charge of the royal storerooms. He was the son of Adiel.

Jonathan was in charge of the storerooms in the fields, towns, villages and lookout towers. He was the son of Uzziah.

26Ezri was in charge of the workers who farmed the land. He was the son of Kelub.

27Shimei was in charge of the vineyards. He was from Ramah.

Zabdi was in charge of the grapes from the vineyards. He was also in charge of storing the wine. He was a Shiphmite.

28Baal-Hanan was in charge of the olive trees and sycamore-fig trees in the western hills. He was from Geder.

Joash was in charge of storing the olive oil.

29Shitrai was in charge of the herds that ate grass in Sharon. He was from Sharon.

Shaphat was in charge of the herds in the valleys. He was the son of Adlai.

30Obil was in charge of the camels. He was from the family line of Ishmael.

Jehdeiah was in charge of the donkeys. He was from Meronoth.

31Jaziz was in charge of the flocks. He was a Hagrite.

All of those men were the officials in charge of King David's property.

32Jonathan was David's uncle. He gave good advice. He was a man of understanding. He was also a secretary. Jehiel took care of the king's sons. He was the son of Hacmoni.

33Ahithophel was the king's adviser. Hushai was the king's friend. He was an Arkite. 34Jehoiada and Abiathar became the next advisers after Ahithophel. Jehoiada was the son of Benaiah.

Joab was the commander of the royal army.

David Talks About His Plans for the Temple

28 David asked all of the officials of Israel to come together at Jerusalem. He sent for the officers who were over the tribes. He sent for the commanders of the companies who served the king. He sent for the commanders of thousands of men and commanders of hundreds. He sent for the officials who were in charge of all of the royal property and livestock. They belonged to the king and his sons. He sent for the palace officials and the mighty men. He also sent for all of the brave fighting men.

2King David stood up. He said, "All of you, listen to me. With all my heart I wanted to build a house for the LORD. I wanted it to be a place of peace and rest for the ark of the covenant of the LORD. The ark is the stool for our God's feet. I made plans to build the LORD's house. 3But God said to me, 'You are not the one who will build a house for my Name. That is because you are a fighting man. You have spilled people's blood.'

4"But the LORD chose me. He is the God of Israel. He chose me from my whole family to be king over Israel forever. He chose Judah to lead the tribes. From the families of Judah he chose my family. From my father's sons he chose me. He was pleased to make me king over the whole nation of Israel.

5"The LORD has given me many sons. From all of them he has chosen my son Solomon. He wants Solomon to sit on the throne of the LORD's kingdom. He wants him to rule over Israel. 6He said to me, 'Your son Solomon is the one who will build my house and my courtyards. I have chosen him to be my son. And I will be his father. 7I will make his kingdom secure. It will last forever. That will happen if he does not turn away from my commands and laws. He must continue to obey them, just as he is doing now.'

8"So I'm giving you a command in the sight of all of the people of Israel. The LORD's community is watching. And our God is listening. I command you to be careful to follow all of the commands of the LORD your God. Then you will own this good land. You will pass it on to your children after you as their share forever.

9"My son Solomon, always remember the God of your father. Serve him with all your heart. Do it with a mind that wants to obey him. The LORD looks deep down inside every heart. He understands the real reasons for everything you think. If you look to him, you will find him. But if you desert him, he will turn his back on you forever. 10Think about it. The LORD has chosen you to build a temple as a holy place where he can live. So be strong. Get to work."

11 Then David gave his son Solomon the plans for the porch of the temple. He gave him the plans for its buildings and its storerooms. He gave him the plans for its upper parts and its inside rooms. He gave him the plans for the place where sin is paid for and forgiven. **12** He gave him the plans for everything the Spirit of the LORD had put in his mind. There were plans for the courtyards of the LORD's temple. There were plans for all of the rooms that were around it. There were plans for the places where the treasure of God's temple would be kept. There were plans for the places where the things that were set apart for God would be kept.

13 David told Solomon how to separate the priests and Levites into groups. He gave him directions for all of the work they should do when they served in the LORD's temple.

He also showed him how all of the articles should be used at the temple. **14** Different articles were used for different purposes.

David told Solomon how much gold should be used for each gold article. He also told him how much silver should be used for each silver article. **15** He told him how much gold should be used to make each gold lampstand and its lamps. He told him how much silver should be used to make each silver lampstand and its lamps. The amount depended on how each lampstand would be used.

16 David told Solomon how much gold should be used to make each table for holy bread. He told him how much silver should be used to make the silver tables.

17 He told him how much pure gold should be used to make the forks, sprinkling bowls and pitchers. He told him how much gold should be used to make each gold dish. He told him how much silver should be used to make each silver dish.

18 And he told him how much pure gold should be used to make the altar for burning incense. David also gave Solomon the plan for the chariot of the gold cherubim. They spread their wings over the ark of the covenant of the LORD.

19 David said, "I have written everything down. The LORD's powerful hand helped me. He helped me understand every part of the plan."

20 David also said to his son Solomon, "Be strong and brave. Get to work. Don't be afraid. Don't lose hope. The LORD God is my God. He is with you. He won't fail you. He won't desert you until all of the work for serving in the LORD's temple is finished. **21** The groups of the priests and Levites are ready to do all of the work on God's temple. Every worker who is willing and skilled can help you do all of the work. The officials and all of the people will obey every command you give them."

Gifts Are Brought for the Temple

29 Then King David spoke to the whole community. He said, "God has chosen my son Solomon. But Solomon is young. He's never done anything like this before. The task is huge. This grand and wonderful temple won't be built for human beings. It will be built for the LORD God.

2 "With all of my riches I've done everything I could for the temple of my God. I've provided gold for the gold work and silver for the silver work. I've provided

POWER SURGE

BRAVE

B

DAVID ALSO SAID TO HIS SON SOLOMON, "BE STRONG AND BRAVE. GET TO WORK. DON'T BE AFRAID. DON'T LOSE HOPE. THE LORD GOD IS MY GOD. HE IS WITH YOU. HE WON'T FAIL YOU. HE WON'T DESERT YOU."

— 1 CHRONICLES 28:20 —

TRIES HARD

T

bronze for the bronze work and iron for the iron work. I've given wood for the things that will be made out of wood. I've given onyx and turquoise for the settings. I've given stones of different colors and all kinds of fine stone and marble. I've provided everything in huge amounts.

³"With all my heart I want the temple of my God to be built. So I'm giving my personal treasures of gold and silver for it. I'm adding them to everything else I've provided for the holy temple. ⁴I'm giving 110 tons of gold and 260 tons of pure silver. Cover the walls of the buildings with it. ⁵Use it for the gold work and the silver work. Use it for everything the skilled workers will do. How many of you are willing to set yourselves apart to the LORD today?"

⁶Many people were willing to give. They included the leaders of families and the officers of the tribes of Israel. They included the commanders of thousands of men and commanders of hundreds. They also included the officials who were in charge of the king's work. ⁷All of them gave to the work on God's temple. They gave more than 190 tons of gold and 375 tons of silver. They also gave 675 tons of bronze and 3,750 tons of iron. ⁸Anyone who had valuable jewels added them to the treasure for the LORD's temple. Jehiel was in charge of the temple treasure. He was from the family line of Gershon.

⁹The people were happy when they saw what their leaders had been willing to give. The leaders had given freely. With their whole heart they had given everything to the LORD. King David was filled with joy.

David Praises the LORD

¹⁰David praised the LORD in front of the whole community. He said,

"LORD, we give you praise.
      You are the God of our father Israel.
      We give you praise for ever and ever.
¹¹ LORD, you are great and powerful.
      Glory, majesty and beauty belong to you.
      Everything in heaven and on earth belongs to you.
   LORD, the kingdom belongs to you.
      You are honored as the One who rules over all.
¹² Wealth and honor come from you.
      You are the ruler of all things.
   In your hands are strength and power.
      You can give honor and strength to everyone.
¹³ Our God, we give you thanks.
      We praise your glorious name.

¹⁴"But who am I? And who are my people? Without your help we wouldn't be

POWER SURGE

GIVING

G

MANY PEOPLE WERE WILLING TO GIVE...ALL OF THEM GAVE TO THE WORK ON GOD'S TEMPLE. THEY GAVE MORE THAN *190* TONS OF GOLD AND *375* TONS OF SILVER. THEY ALSO GAVE *675* TONS OF BRONZE AND *3,750* TONS OF IRON. ANYONE WHO HAD VALUABLE JEWELS ADDED THEM TO THE TREASURE FOR THE LORD'S TEMPLE.

— 1 CHRONICLES 29:6-8 —

POWER-SURGE

CHEERFUL *

THE PEOPLE WERE HAPPY WHEN THEY SAW WHAT THEIR LEADERS HAD BEEN WILLING TO GIVE. THE LEADERS HAD GIVEN FREELY. WITH THEIR WHOLE HEART THEY HAD GIVEN EVERYTHING TO THE LORD. KING DAVID WAS FILLED WITH JOY.

— 1 CHRONICLES 29:9 —

able to give this much. Everything comes from you. We've given back to you only what comes from you. 15We are outsiders and strangers in your sight. So were all of our people who lived long ago. Our days on this earth are like a shadow. We don't have any hope.

16"LORD our God, we've given more than enough. We've provided it to build you a temple where you will put your holy Name. But all of it comes from you. All of it belongs to you. 17My God, I know that you put our hearts to the test. And you are pleased when we are honest. I've given all of these things just because I wanted to. When I did it, I was completely honest with you. And I've been happy to see that your people who are here have also been willing to give to you.

18"LORD, you are the God of our fathers Abraham, Isaac and Israel. Keep this longing in the hearts of your people forever. Keep their hearts true to you. 19Help my son Solomon serve you with all his heart. Then he will keep your commands and rules. He will do what you require. He'll do everything to build the grand and wonderful temple I've provided for."

20Then David spoke to the whole community. He said, "Praise the LORD your God." So all of them praised the LORD. He's the God of their people who lived long ago. The whole community bowed low. They fell down flat with their faces toward the ground. They did it in front of the LORD and the king.

Solomon Becomes the Next King

21The next day they offered sacrifices to the LORD. They brought burnt offerings to him. They sacrificed 1,000 bulls, 1,000 rams and 1,000 male lambs. They also brought the required drink offerings. And they offered many other sacrifices for the whole community of Israel. 22They ate and drank with great joy that day. They did it in the sight of the LORD.

Then they announced a second time that Solomon was king. He was the son of David. They anointed Solomon to be ruler in the sight of the LORD. They also anointed Zadok to be priest.

23So Solomon sat on the throne of the LORD. He ruled as king in place of his father David. Things went well with him. All of the people of Israel obeyed him. 24All of the officers and mighty men promised to be completely faithful to King Solomon. So did all of King David's sons.

25The LORD greatly honored Solomon in the sight of all of the people. He gave him royal majesty. Solomon was given more glory than any king over Israel had ever had.

David Dies

26David was king over the whole nation of Israel. He was the son of Jesse. 27He ruled over Israel for 40 years. He ruled for seven years in Hebron and for 33 years in Jerusalem. 28He died when he was very old. He had enjoyed a long life. He had enjoyed wealth and honor. His son Solomon became the next king after him.

29The events of King David's rule from beginning to end are written down. They are written in the records of the prophets Samuel, Nathan and Gad. 30The records tell all about David's rule and power. They tell about what happened concerning him and Israel and the kingdoms of all of the other lands.

POWER-SURGE

HONEST H

MY GOD, I KNOW THAT YOU PUT OUR HEARTS TO THE TEST. AND YOU ARE PLEASED WHEN WE ARE HONEST.

— 1 CHRONICLES 29:17 —

2 CHRONICLES

The book of 2 Chronicles focuses on the nation of Judah. God's love for his people is clearly shown as the kings of Judah either follow or ignore him. The true heroes—kings like Jehoshaphat and Hezekiah and Josiah—honor God throughout their reigns. Eventually, however, the nation falls further into sin and ends up in captivity, far from Judah. Whether the people follow God or ignore him, he never stops loving them. You can read 2 Chronicles to discover God's love for Judah and for you in spite of your sin.

CODE OF HONOR IN THIS BOOK . . .

WISE
PAGES 512, 520

FORGIVING
PAGE 518

GIVING
PAGES 519, 521, 533, 538, 540, 542, 548

KIND
PAGE 521

CHEERFUL
PAGES 520, 540

BRAVE
PAGES 524, 528, 544

Solomon Asks God for Wisdom

1 Solomon was the son of David. Solomon made his position secure over his kingdom. The LORD his God was with him. He made Solomon very great.

²Solomon spoke to the whole community of Israel. He spoke to the commanders of thousands of men and commanders of hundreds. He spoke to the judges and all of the leaders in Israel. He spoke to the leaders of Israel's families. ³Solomon and the whole community went to the high place at Gibeon. That's because God's Tent of Meeting was there. The LORD's servant Moses had made the tent in the desert.

⁴David had brought the ark of God up from Kiriath Jearim. He had brought it to the place he had prepared for it. He had set up a tent for it in Jerusalem.

⁵But the bronze altar that Bezalel had made was in Gibeon. Bezalel was the son of Uri. Uri was the son of Hur. The altar was in front of the LORD's holy tent. So Solomon and the whole community asked the LORD for advice there.

⁶Solomon went up to the bronze altar in front of the LORD at the Tent of Meeting. Solomon sacrificed 1,000 burnt offerings on the altar.

⁷That night God appeared to Solomon. He said to him, "Ask for anything you want me to give you."

⁸Solomon answered God, "You were very kind to my father David. Now you have made me king in his place. ⁹LORD God, let the promise you gave to my father David come true. You have made me king. My people are like the dust of the earth. They can't be counted. ¹⁰Give me wisdom and knowledge. Then I'll be able to lead these people. Without your help, who would be able to rule this great nation of yours?"

¹¹God said to Solomon, "I am glad that those are the things you really want. You have not asked for wealth, riches or honor. You have not even asked to have your enemies killed. You have not asked to live for a long time. Instead, you have asked for wisdom and knowledge. You want to be able to rule my people wisely. I have made you king over them.

¹²"So wisdom and knowledge will be given to you. I will also give you wealth, riches and honor. You will have more than any king before you ever had. And no king after you will have as much."

¹³Then Solomon left the high place at Gibeon. He went from the Tent of Meeting there to Jerusalem. And he ruled over Israel.

¹⁴Solomon had 1,400 chariots and 12,000 horses. He kept some of them in the chariot cities. He kept others with him in Jerusalem.

¹⁵The king made silver and gold as common in Jerusalem as stones. He made cedar wood as common there as sycamore-fig trees in the western hills.

¹⁶Solomon got horses from Egypt and Kue. The king's buyers purchased them from Kue. ¹⁷They could get a chariot from Egypt for 15 pounds of silver. They could get a horse for less than four pounds of silver. They sold horses and chariots to all of the Hittite and Aramean kings.

Solomon Asks Hiram to Help Build the Temple

2 Solomon gave orders to build a temple. That's where the LORD would put his Name. Solomon also gave orders to build a royal palace for himself. ²He chose 70,000 men to carry things. He chose 80,000 to cut stones in the hills. He put 3,600 men in charge of them.

³Solomon sent a message to Hiram. Hiram was king of Tyre. The message said,

"Send me cedar logs, just as you did for my father David. You sent him cedar to build a palace to live in. ⁴Now I'm about to build a temple. The Name of the LORD my God will be there. I'll set the temple apart for him.

"Sweet-smelling incense will be burned in front of him there. The holy bread will be set out at regular times. Burnt offerings will be sacrificed there every morning and evening. They will be sacrificed every Sabbath day. They will be sacrificed at every New Moon Feast. And they will be sacrificed at every yearly appointed feast of the LORD our God.

WISE   W

GIVE ME [SOLOMON]
WISDOM AND
KNOWLEDGE. THEN
I'LL BE ABLE TO LEAD
THESE PEOPLE.
— 2 CHRONICLES 1:10 —

That's a law for Israel that will last for all time to come.

5 "The temple I'm going to build will be beautiful. That's because our God is greater than all other gods. 6 So who is able to build a temple for him? After all, the heavens can't hold him. In fact, not even the highest heavens can hold him. So who am I to build a temple for him? It will only be a place to burn sacrifices to him.

7 "Send me someone who is skilled at working with gold, silver, bronze and iron. He must also be able to work with purple, blue and bright red yarn. He must be skilled in the art of carving. Send him to work in Judah and Jerusalem with my skilled workers. My father David provided them to help me.

8 "Also send me cedar, pine and algum logs from Lebanon. I know that your men are skilled in cutting wood there. My men will work with yours. 9 They'll provide me with plenty of lumber. That's because the temple I'm building must be large and beautiful.

10 "I'll pay your servants. They will cut the wood. I'll pay them 125,000 bushels of wheat that has been ground up. I'll pay them 125,000 bushels of barley. I'll also pay them 115,000 gallons of wine and 115,000 gallons of olive oil."

11 King Hiram of Tyre replied to Solomon. He wrote a letter to him. It said,

"The LORD loves his people. That's why he has made you their king."

12 Hiram continued,

"I praise the LORD. He is the God of Israel. He made heaven and earth. He has given King David a wise son. You have good sense. You understand what is right. You will build a temple for the LORD. You will also build a palace for yourself.

13 "I'm sending Huram-Abi to you. He is very skillful. 14 His mother was from Dan. His father was from Tyre. He is trained to work with gold, silver, bronze and iron. He knows how to work with stone and wood. He can also work with purple, blue and bright red yarn and fine linen. He's skilled in all kinds of carving. He can follow any pattern you give him. He'll work with your skilled workers.

He'll also work with those of your father David. David was my master.

15 "Now please send us what you promised. Send us the wheat, barley, olive oil and wine. 16 And we'll cut all of the logs from Lebanon you need. We'll make rafts out of them. We'll float them by sea down to Joppa. Then you can take them up to Jerusalem."

17 Solomon counted all of the outsiders who were living in Israel. He did it after his father David had counted them. There were 153,600 of them. 18 He chose 70,000 to carry things. He chose 80,000 to cut stones in the hills. He put 3,600 men in charge of the people to keep them working.

Solomon Builds the Temple

3 Then Solomon began to build the temple of the LORD. He built it on Mount Moriah in Jerusalem. That's where the LORD had appeared to Solomon's father David. He had appeared at the threshing floor of Araunah. Araunah was from Jebus. David had provided the threshing floor. 2 Solomon began building the temple on the second day of the second month. It was in the fourth year of his rule.

3 Solomon laid the foundation for God's temple. It was 90 feet long and 30 feet wide. Solomon's men followed the standard measure that was used at that time. 4 The porch in front of the temple was 30 feet across and 30 feet high.

Solomon covered the inside of the temple with pure gold. 5 He covered the inside of the main hall with pine boards. Then he covered the boards with fine gold. He decorated the hall with palm tree patterns and chain patterns. 6 He decorated the temple with valuable jewels. The gold he used came from Parvaim. 7 He covered the ceiling beams, doorframes, walls and doors of the temple with gold. He carved cherubim on the walls.

8 He built the Most Holy Room. It was as long as the temple was wide. It was 30 feet long and 30 feet wide. He covered the inside of the Most Holy Room with 23 tons of fine gold. 9 He also covered the upper parts with gold. The gold on the nails weighed 20 ounces.

10 For the Most Holy Room, Solomon made a pair of carved cherubim. He covered them with gold. 11 The total length of the cherubim's wings from tip to tip was 30 feet. One wing of the first cherub was

seven and a half feet long. Its tip touched the temple wall. The other wing was also seven and a half feet long. Its tip touched the wing tip of the other cherub.

12In the same way one wing of the second cherub was seven and a half feet long. Its tip touched the other temple wall. The other wing was also seven and a half feet long. Its tip touched the wing tip of the first cherub. **13**So the total length of the wings of the two cherubim was 30 feet from tip to tip. The cherubim stood facing the main hall.

14Solomon made the curtain out of blue, purple and bright red yarn and fine linen. A skilled worker sewed cherubim into its pattern.

15In front of the temple, Solomon made two pillars. Each pillar was 26 feet tall. Each had a decorated top that was seven and a half feet high. **16**Solomon made chains that were linked together. He put them on top of the pillars. He also made 100 pomegranates. He fastened them to the chains.

17Solomon set the pillars up in front of the temple. One was on the south. The other was on the north. He named the one on the south Jakin. The one on the north he named Boaz.

More Facts About the Temple

4 Solomon made a bronze altar that was 30 feet long, 30 feet wide and 15 feet high. **2**He made a huge metal bowl for washing. Its shape was round. It measured 15 feet from rim to rim. It was seven and a half feet high. And it was 45 feet around. **3**Below the rim there was a circle of bull figures around the bowl. In every 18 inches around the bowl there were ten bulls. The bulls were arranged in two rows. They were made as part of the bowl itself.

4The bowl stood on 12 bulls. Three of them faced north. Three faced west. Three faced south. And three faced east. The bowl rested on top of them. Their rear ends were toward the center. **5**The bowl was three inches thick. Its rim was like the rim of a cup. The rim was shaped like the bloom of a lily. The bowl held 17,500 gallons of water.

6Solomon made ten smaller bowls for washing. He placed five of them on the south side of the huge bowl. He placed the other five on the north side.

The things that were used for the burnt offerings were rinsed in the smaller bowls. But the priests used the huge bowl for washing.

7Solomon made ten gold lampstands. He followed the pattern the Lord had given him. He placed the lampstands in the temple. He put five of them on the south side. He put the other five on the north side.

8He made ten tables. He placed them in the temple. He put five of them on the south side. He put the other five on the north side. He also made 100 gold sprinkling bowls.

9He made the courtyard of the priests. He also made the large courtyard. He made doors for it. He covered the doors with bronze.

10He placed the huge bowl on the south side of the courtyard. He put it at the southeast corner.

11He also made the pots, shovels and sprinkling bowls.

So Huram finished the work he had started for King Solomon. Here's what he made for God's temple.

12He made the two pillars.
   He made the two tops for the pillars. The tops were shaped like bowls.
   He made the two sets of chains that were linked together. They decorated the two bowl-shaped tops of the pillars.

13He made the 400 pomegranates for the two sets of chains. There were two rows of pomegranates for each chain. They decorated the bowl-shaped tops of the pillars.

14He made the stands and their bowls.

15He made the huge bowl. He made the 12 bulls that were under it.

16He made the pots, shovels and meat forks. He also made all of the articles that were connected with them.

Huram-Abi made all of those objects for King Solomon for the Lord's temple. He made them out of bronze. Then he shined them up. **17**The king had them made in clay molds. It was done on the flatlands of the Jordan River between Succoth and Zarethan.

18Solomon made huge numbers of those articles. There were too many of them to weigh. No one even tried to weigh the bronze they were made out of.

19Solomon also made all of the articles that were in God's temple.

He made the golden altar.
He made the tables for the holy bread.

20He made the pure gold lampstands

and their lamps. The lamps burned in front of the Most Holy Room, just as the law required.
21 He made the gold flowers. He made the gold lamps and tongs. They were made out of solid gold.
22 He made the wick cutters, sprinkling bowls, dishes, and shallow cups for burning incense. All of them were made out of pure gold. He made the gold doors of the temple. They were the inner doors to the Most Holy Room and the doors of the main hall.

5 Solomon finished all of the work for the Lord's temple. Then he brought in the things his father David had set apart for the Lord. They included the silver and gold and all of the articles for God's temple. Solomon placed them with the other treasures that were there.

Solomon Brings the Ark to the Temple

2 Then Solomon sent for the elders of Israel. He told them to come to Jerusalem. They included all of the leaders of the tribes. They also included the chiefs of the families of Israel. Solomon wanted them to bring up the ark of the Lord's covenant from Zion. Zion was the City of David.
3 All of the men of Israel came together to where the king was. It was at the time of the Feast of Booths. The feast was held in the seventh month.
4 All of the elders of Israel arrived. Then the Levites picked up the ark and carried it. 5 They brought up the ark. They also brought up the Tent of Meeting and all of the sacred articles that were in the tent. The priests, who were Levites, carried everything up.
6 The entire community of Israel had gathered around King Solomon. All of them were in front of the ark. They sacrificed huge numbers of sheep and cattle. There were so many that they couldn't be recorded. In fact, they couldn't even be counted.
7 The priests brought the ark of the Lord's covenant to its place in the Most Holy Room of the temple. They put it under the wings of the cherubim.
8 The cherubim's wings were spread out over the place where the ark was. They covered the ark. They also covered the poles that were used to carry it. 9 The poles reached out from the ark. They were so long that their ends could be seen from in front of the Most Holy Room. But they

couldn't be seen from outside the Holy Room. They are still there to this very day.
10 There wasn't anything in the ark except the two tablets. Moses had placed them in it at Mount Horeb. That's where the Lord had made a covenant with the Israelites. He made it after they came out of Egypt.
11 The priests left the Holy Room. All of the priests who were there had set themselves apart to the Lord. It didn't matter what group they were in.
12 All of the Levites who played music stood near the east side of the altar. They included Asaph, Heman, Jeduthun and their sons and relatives. They were dressed in fine linen. They were playing cymbals, harps and lyres. They were joined by 120 priests who were blowing trumpets.
13 The trumpet players and singers made music together as if they were only one voice. They praised the Lord. They gave thanks to him. Some of them played their trumpets, cymbals and other instruments. The others raised their voices to praise the Lord. They sang,

"He is good.
   His faithful love continues forever."

Then a cloud filled the temple of the Lord. 14 The priests couldn't do their work because of it. The glory of the Lord filled God's temple.

6 Then Solomon said, "Lord, you have said you would live in a dark cloud.
2 I've built a beautiful temple for you. You can live in it forever."
3 The whole community of Israel was standing there. The king turned around and gave them his blessing. 4 Then he said,

"I praise the Lord. He is the God of Israel. With his mouth he made a promise to my father David. With his powerful hands he made it come true. He said, 5 'I brought my people out of Egypt. Ever since I did that, I have not chosen a city in any tribe of Israel where a temple could be built for my Name. I have not chosen anyone to be the leader over my people Israel. 6 But now I have chosen Jerusalem. I will put my Name there. And I have chosen David to rule over my people Israel.'
7 "With all his heart my father David wanted to build a temple. He wanted to do it so the Name of the Lord could be there. The Lord is the God of Israel.

8"But the LORD spoke to my father David. He said, 'With all your heart you wanted to build a temple for my Name. It is good that you wanted to do that. 9But you will not build the temple. Instead, your son will build the temple for my Name. He is your own flesh and blood.'

10"The LORD has kept the promise he made. I've become the next king after my father David. Now I'm sitting on the throne of Israel. That's exactly what the LORD promised would happen. I've built the temple for the Name of the LORD. He is the God of Israel. 11I've placed the ark there. The tablets of the LORD's covenant are inside it. He made that covenant with the people of Israel."

Solomon Prays to Set the Temple Apart to the LORD

12Then Solomon stood in front of the LORD's altar. He stood in front of the whole community of Israel. He spread out his hands to pray. 13He had made a bronze stage. It was seven and a half feet long and seven and a half feet wide. It was four and a half feet high. He had placed it in the center of the outer courtyard. He stood on the stage. Then he got down on his knees in front of the whole community of Israel. He spread out his hands toward heaven. 14He said,

"LORD, you are the God of Israel. There is no God like you in heaven or on earth. You keep the covenant you made with us. You show us your love. You do that when we follow you with all our hearts. 15You have kept your promise to my father David. He was your servant. With your mouth you made a promise. With your powerful hand you have made it come true. And today we can see it.

16"LORD, you are the God of Israel. Keep the promises you made to my father David. Do it for him. He was your servant. You said to him, 'You will always have a son to sit on the throne of Israel in my sight. That will be true only if your sons are careful in everything they do. They must live the way my law tells them to. That is the way you have lived.' 17LORD, you are the God of Israel. So let your promise to your servant David come true.

18"But will you really live on earth with human beings? After all, the heavens can't hold you. In fact, even the highest heavens can't hold you. So this temple I've built certainly can't hold you!

19"But please pay attention to my prayer. LORD my God, show me your favor as I make my appeal to you. Listen to my cry for help. Hear the prayer I'm praying to you. 20Let your eyes look toward this temple day and night. You said you would put your Name here. Listen to the prayer I'm praying toward this place.

21"Hear me when I ask you to show us your favor. Listen to your people Israel when they pray toward this place. Listen to us from heaven. It's the place where you live. When you hear us, forgive us.

22"Suppose a man does something wrong to his neighbor. And he is required to take an oath and make a promise. He must come and do it in front of your altar in this temple. 23When he does, listen to him from heaven. Take action. Judge between the man and his neighbor. Pay back the one who is guilty. Do to him what he has done to the other person. Tell everyone that the person who hasn't done anything wrong is free of blame. That will prove he isn't guilty.

24"Suppose your people Israel have lost the battle against their enemies. And suppose they've sinned against you. But they turn back to you and praise your name. They pray to you in this temple. And they ask you to show them your favor. 25Then listen to them from heaven. Forgive the sin of your people Israel. Bring them back to the land you gave to them and their people who lived long ago.

26"Suppose your people have sinned against you. And because of that, the sky is closed up and there isn't any rain. But your people pray toward this place. They praise you by admitting they've sinned. And they turn away from their sin because you have made them suffer. 27Then listen to them from heaven. Forgive the sin of your people Israel. Teach them the right way to live. Send rain on the land you gave them as their share.

28"Suppose there isn't enough food in the land. And a plague strikes the land. The hot winds completely dry up our crops. Or locusts or grasshoppers come and eat them up. Or enemies surround one of our cities and get ready to attack it. Or trouble or sickness comes. **29**But suppose one of your people prays to you. He asks you to show him your favor. He is aware of how much he is suffering. And he spreads out his hands toward this temple to pray. **30**Then listen to him from heaven. It's the place where you live. Forgive him. Deal with him in keeping with everything he does. You know his heart. In fact, you are the only one who knows every human heart.

31"Your people will have respect for you. They will live the way you want them to. They'll live that way as long as they are in the land you gave our people long ago.

32"Suppose a stranger who doesn't belong to your people Israel has come from a land far away. He has come because he's heard about your great name. He has heard that you reached out your mighty hand and powerful arm. So he comes and prays toward this temple. **33**Then listen to him from heaven. It's the place where you live. Do what that stranger asks you to do.

"Then all of the nations on earth will know you. They will have respect for you. They'll respect you just as your own people Israel do. They'll know that your Name is in this house I've built.

34"Suppose your people go to war against their enemies. It doesn't matter where you send them. And suppose they pray to you toward this city you have chosen. They pray toward the temple I've built for your Name. **35**Then listen to them from heaven. Listen to their prayer. Listen to them when they ask you to show them your favor. Stand up for them.

36"Suppose they sin against you. After all, there isn't anyone who doesn't sin. And suppose you get angry with them. You hand them over to their enemies. They take them as prisoners to another land. It doesn't matter whether it's near or far away. **37**But suppose your people change their ways in the land where they are held as prisoners. They turn away from their sins. They beg you to help them in the land where they are prisoners. They say, 'We have sinned. We've done what is wrong. We've

done what is evil.' **38**And they turn back to you with all their heart and soul. Suppose it happens in the land where they were taken as prisoners. There they pray toward the land you gave their people long ago. They pray toward the city you have chosen. And they pray toward the temple I've built for your Name. **39**Then listen to them from heaven. It's the place where you live. Listen to their prayer. Listen to them when they ask you to show them your favor. Stand up for them. Your people have sinned against you. Please forgive them.

40"My God, let your eyes see us. Let your ears pay attention to the prayers that are offered in this place.

41 "LORD God, rise up and come to
        your resting place.
    Come in together with the ark.
        It's the sign of your power.
    LORD God, may your priests put
        on salvation as if it were
        their clothes.
    May your faithful people be
        glad because you are so
        good.
42 LORD God, don't turn your back
        on your anointed king.
    Remember the great love you
        promised to your servant
        David."

Solomon Sets the Temple Apart to the LORD

7 Solomon finished praying. Then fire came down from heaven. It burned up the burnt offering and the sacrifices. The glory of the LORD filled the temple. **2**The priests couldn't enter the temple of the LORD. His glory filled it.

3All of the people of Israel saw the fire coming down. They saw the glory of the LORD above the temple. So they got down on their knees in the courtyard with their faces toward the ground. They worshiped the LORD. They gave thanks to him. They said,

"He is good.
    His faithful love continues forever."

4Then the king and all of the people offered sacrifices to the LORD. **5**King Solomon sacrificed 22,000 head of cattle and 120,000 sheep and goats. So the king and all of the people set the temple of God apart.

6The priests and Levites took their positions. The Levites played the LORD's musical instruments. King David had made them for praising the LORD. They were used when he gave thanks to the LORD. He said, "His faithful love continues forever."

Across from where the Levites were, the priests blew their trumpets. All of the people of Israel were standing.

7Solomon set the middle area of the courtyard apart to the LORD. It was in front of the LORD's temple. There Solomon sacrificed burnt offerings. He also sacrificed the fat of the friendship offerings there. He did it there because the bronze altar he had made couldn't hold all of the burnt offerings, the grain offerings and the fat parts.

8At that time Solomon celebrated the Feast of Booths for seven days. The whole community of Israel was with him. It was a huge crowd. People came from as far away as Lebo Hamath and the Wadi of Egypt. 9On the eighth day they held a service. For seven days they had celebrated by setting the altar apart to honor God. The feast continued for seven more days.

10Then Solomon sent the people home. It was the 23rd day of the seventh month. The people were glad. Their hearts were full of joy. That's because the LORD had done good things for David and Solomon and his people Israel.

The LORD Appears to Solomon

11Solomon finished the LORD's temple and the royal palace. He had done everything he had planned to do in the LORD's temple and his own palace.

12The LORD appeared to him at night. He said,

"I have heard your prayer. I have chosen this place for myself. It is a temple where sacrifices will be offered.

13"Suppose I close up the sky and there isn't any rain. Suppose I command locusts to eat up the crops. And I send a plague among my people. 14But they make themselves low in my sight. They pray and look to me. And they turn from their evil ways. Then I will listen to them from heaven. I will forgive their sin. And I will heal their land. After all, they are my people.

15"Now my eyes will see them. My ears will pay attention to the prayers they offer in this place. 16I have chosen this temple. I have set it apart for myself. My Name will be there forever. My eyes and my heart will always be there.

17"But you must walk with me, just as your father David did. Do everything I command you to do. Obey my rules and laws. 18Then I will set up your royal throne. I made a covenant with your father David to do that. I said to him, 'You will always have a son to rule over Israel.'

19"But suppose all of you turn away from me. You refuse to obey the rules and commands I have given you. And you go off to serve other gods and worship them. 20Then I will remove Israel from my land. It is the land I gave them. I will turn my back on this temple. I will do it even though I have set it apart for my Name to be there. I will make all of the nations hate it. They will laugh and joke about it.

21"This temple is now so grand and beautiful. But the time is coming when all those who pass by it will be shocked. They will say, 'Why has the LORD done a thing like this to this land and temple?'

22"People will answer, 'Because they have deserted the LORD. He is the God of their people who lived long ago. He brought them out of Egypt. But they have been holding on to other gods. They've been worshiping them. They've been serving them. That's why he has brought all of this horrible trouble on them.' "

Other Things Solomon Did

8 Solomon built the LORD's temple and his own palace. It took him 20 years to build them. After that, 2Solomon rebuilt the villages Hiram had given him. He settled Israelites in them.

3Then Solomon went to Hamath Zobah. He captured it. 4He also built up Tadmor in the desert. He built up all of the cities in Hamath where he could store things. 5He rebuilt Lower Beth Horon and Upper Beth Horon. He put up high walls around them. He made their city gates secure with heavy metal bars. 6He rebuilt Baalath and all of the cities where he could store things. He also rebuilt all of the cities for his chariots and horses.

Solomon built anything he wanted to build in Jerusalem, Lebanon and all of the territory he ruled over.

⁷There were still many people left in the land who weren't Israelites. They included Hittites, Amorites, Perizzites, Hivites and Jebusites. ⁸They were children of the people who had lived in the land before the Israelites came. The people of Israel hadn't destroyed them. Solomon had forced them to work very hard as his slaves. And they still work for Israel to this very day.

⁹But Solomon didn't force the men of Israel to work as his slaves. Instead, some were his fighting men. Others were commanders of his captains, chariots and chariot drivers. ¹⁰Still others were King Solomon's chief officials. There were 250 officials in charge of the other men.

¹¹Solomon brought Pharaoh's daughter up from the City of David to the palace he had built for her. He said, "My wife must not live in the palace of David, who was the king of Israel. It's one of the places the ark of the LORD has entered. That makes it holy."

¹²Solomon had built the LORD's altar. It stood in front of the temple porch. On that altar Solomon sacrificed burnt offerings to the LORD. ¹³Each day he sacrificed what the Law of Moses required. He sacrificed the required offerings every Sabbath day. He also sacrificed them at each New Moon Feast and during the three yearly feasts. Those three were the Feast of Unleavened Bread, the Feast of Weeks and the Feast of Booths.

¹⁴Solomon followed the orders his father David had given him. He appointed the groups of priests for their duties. He appointed the Levites to lead the people in praising the LORD. They also helped the priests do their required tasks each day. Solomon appointed the groups of men who guarded all of the gates. That's what David, the man of God, had ordered. ¹⁵King David's commands were followed completely. They applied to the priests and Levites. They also applied to the temple treasure.

¹⁶All of Solomon's work was carried out. It started the day the foundation of the LORD's temple was laid. It ended when the LORD's temple was finished.

¹⁷Solomon went to Ezion Geber and Elath on the coast of Edom. ¹⁸Hiram sent him ships that his own officers commanded. They were men who knew the

POWER-SURGE

GIVING G

TOGETHER WITH SOLOMON'S MEN THEY SAILED TO OPHIR. THEY BROUGHT BACK 17 TONS OF GOLD. THEY GAVE IT TO KING SOLOMON.
— 2 CHRONICLES 8:18 —

sea. Together with Solomon's men they sailed to Ophir. They brought back 17 tons of gold. They gave it to King Solomon.

The Queen of Sheba Visits Solomon

9 The queen of Sheba heard about how famous Solomon was. So she came to Jerusalem to test him with hard questions. She arrived with a very large group of attendants. Her camels were carrying spices, huge amounts of gold, and valuable jewels. She came to Solomon and asked him about everything she wanted to know.

²He answered all of her questions. There wasn't anything that was too hard for him to explain to her.

³So the queen of Sheba saw how wise Solomon was. She saw the palace he had built. ⁴She saw the food that was on his table. She saw his officials sitting there. She saw the robes of the servants who waited on everyone. She saw the robes the wine tasters were wearing. And she saw the burnt offerings Solomon sacrificed at the LORD's temple. She could hardly believe everything she had seen.

⁵She said to the king, "Back in my own country I heard a report about you. I heard about how much you had accomplished. I also heard about how wise you are. Everything I heard is true. ⁶But I didn't believe what people were saying. So I came to see for myself. And now I believe it! You are twice as wise as people say you are. The report I heard doesn't even begin to tell the whole story about you.

⁷"How happy your men must be! How happy your officials must be! They always get to serve you and hear the wise things you say.

POWER-/SURGE

CHEERFUL ✳

HOW HAPPY YOUR MEN MUST BE! HOW HAPPY YOUR OFFICIALS MUST BE! THEY ALWAYS GET TO SERVE YOU AND HEAR THE WISE THINGS YOU SAY.
— 2 CHRONICLES 9:7 —

W

WISE

8"May the LORD your God be praised. He must take great delight in you. He placed you on his throne as king. He put you there to rule for him. Your God loves Israel very much. He longs to take good care of them forever. That's why he has made you king over them. He knows that you will do what is fair and right."

9She gave the king four and a half tons of gold. She also gave him huge amounts of spices and valuable jewels. There had never been as many spices as the queen of Sheba gave to King Solomon.

10The servants of Hiram and those of Solomon brought gold from Ophir. They also brought algumwood and valuable jewels. 11The king used the algumwood to make steps for the LORD's temple and the royal palace. He also used it to make harps and lyres for those who played the music. No one had ever seen that much algumwood in Judah before.

12King Solomon gave the queen of Sheba everything she wanted and asked for. In fact, he gave her more than she had brought to him. Then she left. She returned to her own country with her attendants.

Solomon in All of His Glory

13Each year Solomon received 25 tons of gold. 14That didn't include the money that was brought in by business and trade. All of the kings of Arabia also brought gold and silver to Solomon. So did the governors of Israel.

15King Solomon made 200 large shields out of hammered gold. Each one weighed seven and a half pounds. 16He also made 300 small shields out of hammered gold. Each one weighed almost four pounds. The king put all of the shields in the Palace of the Forest of Lebanon.

17Then he made a large throne. It was decorated with ivory. It was covered with pure gold. 18The throne had six steps. A gold stool for the king's feet was connected to it. The throne had armrests on both sides of the seat. A statue of a lion stood on each side of the throne. 19Twelve lions stood on the six steps. There was one at each end of each step. Nothing like that throne had ever been made for any other kingdom.

20All of King Solomon's cups were made out of gold. All of the articles that were used in the Palace of the Forest of Lebanon were made out of pure gold. Nothing was made out of silver. When Solomon was king, silver wasn't considered to be worth very much.

21He had many ships that carried goods to be traded. The crews of those ships were made up of Hiram's men. Once every three years the ships returned. They brought gold, silver, ivory, apes and baboons.

22King Solomon was richer than all of the other kings on earth. He was also wiser than they were.

23All of these kings wanted to meet Solomon in person. They wanted to see for themselves how wise God had made him. 24Year after year, everyone who came to him brought a gift. They brought articles that were made out of silver and gold. They brought robes, weapons and spices. They also brought horses and mules.

25Solomon had 4,000 spaces where he kept his horses and chariots. He had 12,000 horses. He kept some of his horses and chariots in the chariot cities. He kept the others with him in Jerusalem.

26Solomon ruled over all of the kings from the Euphrates River to the land of the Philistines. He ruled all the way to the border of Egypt.

27The king made silver as common in Jerusalem as stones. He made cedar wood as common there as sycamore-fig trees in the western hills.

28Solomon got horses from Egypt. He also got them from many other countries.

Solomon Dies

29The other events of Solomon's rule from beginning to end are written down. They are written in the records of the prophet Nathan. They are written in the prophecy of Ahijah. He was from Shiloh. They are also written in the records of the visions of the prophet Iddo about Jeroboam. Jeroboam was the son of Nebat.

30Solomon ruled in Jerusalem over the whole nation of Israel for 40 years. **31**Then he joined the members of his family who had already died. His body was buried in the city of his father David. Solomon's son Rehoboam became the next king after him.

Israel Refuses to Follow Rehoboam

10 Rehoboam went to Shechem. All of the people of Israel had gone there to make him king.

2Jeroboam heard about it. He was the son of Nebat. Jeroboam was in Egypt at that time. He had gone there for safety. He wanted to get away from King Solomon. But now he returned from Egypt.

3So the people sent for Jeroboam. He and all of the people went to Rehoboam. They said to him, **4**"Your father put a heavy load on our shoulders. But now make our hard work easier. Make the heavy load on us lighter. Then we'll serve you."

5Rehoboam answered, "Come back to me in three days." So the people went away.

6Then King Rehoboam asked the elders for advice. They had served his father Solomon while he was still living. Rehoboam asked them, "What advice can you give me? How should I answer these people?"

7They replied, "Be kind to them. Please them. Give them what they are asking for. Then they'll always serve you."

8But Rehoboam didn't accept the advice the elders gave him. He asked for advice from the young men who had grown up with him and were now serving him. **9**He asked them, "What's your advice? How should I answer these people? They said to me, 'Make the load your father put on our shoulders lighter.' "

10The young men who had grown up with him gave their answer. They replied, "The people have said to you, 'Your father put a heavy load on our shoulders. Make it lighter.' Tell them, 'My little finger is stronger than my father's legs. **11**My father put a heavy load on your shoulders. But I'll make it even heavier. My father beat you with whips. But I'll beat you with bigger whips.' "

12Three days later Jeroboam and all of the people returned to Rehoboam. That's because the king had said, "Come back to me in three days."

13The king answered them in a mean way. He didn't accept the advice of the elders. **14**Instead, he followed the advice of the young men. He said, "My father put a heavy load on your shoulders. But I'll make it even heavier. My father beat you with whips. But I'll beat you with bigger whips."

15So the king didn't listen to the people. That's because God had planned it that way. What the LORD had said through Ahijah came true. Ahijah had spoken the LORD's message to Jeroboam, the son of Nebat. Ahijah was from Shiloh.

16All of the people of Israel saw that the king refused to listen to them. So they answered the king. They said,

> "We don't have any share in David's
> royal family.
> We don't have any share in Jesse's
> son.
> People of Israel, let's go back to our
> homes.
> David's royal family, take care of
> your own kingdom!"

So all of the people of Israel went home. **17**But Rehoboam still ruled over the Israelites who were living in the towns of Judah.

18Adoniram was in charge of those who were forced to work hard for King Rehoboam. The king sent him out among the Israelites. But they killed him by throwing stones at him. Rehoboam was able to get away in his chariot. He escaped to Jerusalem. **19**Israel has refused to follow the royal family of David to this very day.

11 Rehoboam arrived in Jerusalem. He brought together 180,000 fighting men from the tribes of Judah and Benjamin. He had decided to make war

---

POWER-SURGE

GIVING **G**

BE KIND TO THEM. PLEASE THEM. GIVE THEM WHAT THEY ARE ASKING FOR. THEN THEY'LL ALWAYS SERVE YOU.

— 2 CHRONICLES 10:7 — **K**

KIND

against Israel. He wanted his fighting men to get the kingdom of Israel back for him. ²But a message came to Shemaiah from the LORD. He was a man of God. The LORD said to him, ³"Speak to Solomon's son Rehoboam, the king of Judah. Speak to all of the people of Israel in Judah and Benjamin. Tell them, ⁴'The LORD says, "Do not go up to fight against your relatives. I want every one of you to go back home. Things have happened exactly the way I planned them." ' "

So the fighting men obeyed the LORD's message. They turned back. They didn't march out against Jeroboam.

Rehoboam Builds Up Judah's Towns

⁵Rehoboam lived in Jerusalem. He made Judah more secure by building up their towns. ⁶He built up Bethlehem, Etam, Tekoa, ⁷Beth Zur, Soco and Adullam. ⁸He also built up Gath, Mareshah, Ziph, ⁹Adoraim, Lachish, Azekah, ¹⁰Zorah, Aijalon and Hebron. All of them were cities in Judah and Benjamin that had high walls around them.

¹¹Rehoboam made those cities even more secure. He put commanders in them. He gave them plenty of food, olive oil and wine. ¹²He put shields and spears in all of those cities. He made them very strong. So he ruled over Judah and Benjamin.

¹³The priests and Levites were on Rehoboam's side. They came from their territories all over Israel. ¹⁴The Levites even left their grasslands and other property behind. They came to Judah and Jerusalem. That's because Jeroboam and his sons had refused to accept them as priests of the LORD. ¹⁵Jeroboam appointed his own priests to serve at the high places. He had made statues of gods that looked like goats and calves. His priests served those gods.

¹⁶Some people from every tribe in Israel followed the Levites to Jerusalem. With all their hearts they wanted to worship the LORD. He is the God of Israel. They came to Jerusalem to offer sacrifices to him. He was the God of their people of long ago.

¹⁷All those who came to Jerusalem made the kingdom of Judah strong. They helped Solomon's son Rehoboam for three years. During that time they lived the way David and Solomon had lived.

Rehoboam's Family

¹⁸Rehoboam got married to Mahalath. She was the daughter of David's son Jerimoth. Her mother was Abihail. Abihail was the daughter of Jesse's son Eliab. ¹⁹Mahalath had sons by Rehoboam. Their names were Jeush, Shemariah and Zaham.

²⁰Then Rehoboam married Maacah. She was the daughter of Absalom. She had sons by Rehoboam. Their names were Abijah, Attai, Ziza and Shelomith. ²¹Rehoboam loved Absalom's daughter Maacah. In fact, he loved her more than any of his other wives and concubines. He had a total of 18 wives and 60 concubines. And he had a total of 28 sons and 60 daughters.

²²Rehoboam appointed Maacah's son Abijah to be the chief prince among his brothers. He did it to make him king. ²³He acted wisely. He scattered some of his sons through all of the territories of Judah and Benjamin. He put them in all of the cities that had high walls around them. He gave them plenty of food and everything else they needed. He also gave them many wives.

Shishak Attacks Jerusalem

12 Rehoboam had made his position as king secure. He had become very strong. Then he turned away from the law of the LORD. So did all of the people of Judah.

²They hadn't been faithful to the LORD. So Shishak attacked Jerusalem. It was in the fifth year that Rehoboam was king. Shishak was king of Egypt. ³He came with 1,200 chariots and 60,000 horsemen. Troops of Libyans, Sukkites and Cushites came with him from Egypt. There were so many of them they couldn't be counted. ⁴Shishak captured the cities of Judah that had high walls around them. He came all the way to Jerusalem.

⁵Then the prophet Shemaiah came to Rehoboam and the leaders of Judah. They had gathered together in Jerusalem. They were afraid of Shishak. Shemaiah said to them, "The LORD says, 'You have left me. So now I am leaving you to Shishak.' "

⁶The king and the leaders of Israel made themselves low in the LORD's sight. They said, "The LORD does what is right and fair."

⁷The LORD saw they had made themselves low. So he gave a message to Shemaiah. It said, "They have made themselves low in my sight. So I will not destroy them. Instead, I will soon save them. I will not pour out my burning anger on Jerusalem through Shishak. ⁸But its people will

be brought under his control. Then they will learn the difference between serving me and serving the kings of other lands."

9Shishak, the king of Egypt, attacked Jerusalem. He carried away the treasures of the LORD's temple. He also carried the treasures of the royal palace away. He took everything. That included the gold shields Solomon had made.

10So King Rehoboam made bronze shields to take their place. He gave them to the commanders of the guards who were on duty at the entrance to the royal palace. 11Every time the king went to the LORD's temple, the guards went with him. They carried the shields. Later, they took them back to the room where they were kept.

12Rehoboam had made himself low in the LORD's sight. So the LORD turned his anger away from him. Rehoboam wasn't totally destroyed. In fact, some good things happened in Judah.

13King Rehoboam had made his position secure in Jerusalem. He continued as king. He was 41 years old when he became king. He ruled for 17 years in Jerusalem. It was the city the LORD had chosen out of all of the cities in the tribes of Israel. He wanted to put his Name there. The name of Rehoboam's mother was Naamah from Ammon.

14Rehoboam did what was evil. That's because he hadn't worshiped the LORD with all his heart.

15The events of Rehoboam's rule from beginning to end are written down. They are written in the records of the prophets Shemaiah and Iddo. The records deal with family histories. Rehoboam and Jeroboam were always at war with each other.

16Rehoboam joined the members of his family who had already died. His body was buried in the City of David. His son Abijah became the next king after him.

Abijah Becomes King of Judah

13 Abijah became king of Judah. It was in the 18th year of Jeroboam's rule over Israel. 2Abijah ruled in Jerusalem for three years. His mother's name was Maacah. She was a daughter of Uriel. Uriel was from Gibeah.

There was war between Abijah and Jeroboam. 3Abijah went into battle with an army of 400,000 able fighting men. Jeroboam lined up his soldiers against them. He had 800,000 able troops.

4Abijah stood on Mount Zemaraim. It's in the hill country of Ephraim. Abijah said, "Jeroboam and all you men of Israel, listen to me! 5The LORD is the God of Israel. Don't you know that he has placed David and his sons after him on Israel's throne forever? The LORD made a covenant of salt with David. The salt means the covenant will last for all time to come.

6"Jeroboam, the son of Nebat, was an official of David's son Solomon. But he refused to obey his master. 7Some worthless and evil men gathered around him. They opposed Solomon's son Rehoboam. At that time Rehoboam was young. He couldn't make up his mind. He wasn't strong enough to stand up against those men.

8"Now you plan to stand up against the kingdom of the LORD. His kingdom is in the hands of men in David's family line. It's true that you have a huge army. You have the golden calves that Jeroboam made to be your gods.

9"But you drove out the priests of the LORD, the sons of Aaron. You also drove out the Levites. You appointed your own priests. That's what the people of other nations do. Anyone can come and set himself apart. All he has to do is sacrifice a young bull and seven rams. Then he becomes a priest of gods that aren't really gods at all!

10"But the LORD is our God. We haven't deserted him. The priests who serve the LORD belong to the family line of Aaron. The Levites help them. 11Every morning and evening the priests bring burnt offerings and sweet-smelling incense to the LORD. They set out the holy bread on the table. That table is 'clean.' They light the lamps on the gold lampstand every evening.

"We always do what the LORD our God requires in his law. But you have deserted him. 12God is with us. He's our leader. His priests will blow their trumpets. They will sound the battle cry against you. Men of Israel, don't fight against the LORD. He's the God of your people who lived long ago. You can't possibly succeed."

13Jeroboam had sent some troops behind Judah's battle lines. He told them to hide and wait there. He and his men stayed in front of Judah's lines.

14Judah turned and saw that they were being attacked from the front and from the back. Then they cried out to the LORD. The priests blew their trumpets. 15The men of Judah shouted the battle cry. When they did, God drove Jeroboam and all of Israel's men away from Abijah and Judah.

16The men of Israel ran away from

them. God handed Israel over to Judah. ¹⁷Abijah and his men wounded and killed large numbers of them. In fact, 500,000 of Israel's able men lay dead or wounded.

¹⁸So at that time the men of Israel were brought under Judah's control. The men of Judah won the battle over them. That's because they trusted in the LORD. He's the God of their people.

¹⁹Abijah chased Jeroboam. He took from him the towns of Bethel, Jeshanah and Ephron. He also took the villages that were around them. ²⁰Jeroboam didn't get his power back during the time of Abijah. In fact, the LORD struck him down. And he died.

²¹But Abijah grew stronger. He got married to 14 wives. He had 22 sons and 16 daughters.

²²The other events of Abijah's rule are written down. The things he did and said are written in the notes of the prophet Iddo.

14 Abijah joined the members of his family who had already died. His body was buried in the City of David. His son Asa became the next king after him. While Asa was king, the country had peace and rest for ten years.

Asa Becomes King of Judah

²Asa did what was good and right in the eyes of the LORD his God. ³He removed the altars where strange gods were worshiped. He took away the high places. He smashed the sacred stones. He cut down the poles that were used to worship the goddess Asherah. ⁴He commanded Judah to worship the LORD, the God of their people. He commanded them to obey the LORD's laws and commands.

⁵He removed the high places and incense altars from every town in Judah. The kingdom had peace and rest under him. ⁶He built up the cities of Judah that had high walls around them. The land was at peace. No one was at war with Asa during those years. That's because the LORD gave him peace and rest.

⁷"Let's build up our towns," Asa said to the people of Judah. "Let's put walls around them. Let's provide them with towers. Let's make them secure with gates that have heavy metal bars. The land still belongs to us. That's because we've trusted in the LORD our God. We trusted in him, and he has given us peace and rest on every side." So they built. And things went well for them.

⁸Asa had an army of 300,000 men from Judah. They carried spears and large

POWER-SURGE

BRAVE **B**

THEY WERE ARMED WITH BOWS AND SMALL SHIELDS. ALL OF THOSE MEN WERE BRAVE SOLDIERS.
— 2 CHRONICLES 14:8 —

shields. There were 280,000 men from Benjamin. They were armed with bows and small shields. All of those men were brave soldiers.

⁹Zerah marched out against them. He was from Cush. He had a huge army. He also had 300 chariots. They came all the way to Mareshah.

¹⁰Asa went out to meet Zerah in battle. They took up their positions in the Valley of Zephathah. It's near Mareshah. ¹¹Then Asa called out to the LORD his God. He said, "LORD, there isn't anyone like you. You help the weak against the strong. LORD our God, help us. We trust in you. In your name we have come out to fight against this huge army. LORD, you are our God. Don't let mere men win the battle over you."

¹²The LORD struck down the men of Cush for Asa and Judah. The Cushites ran away. ¹³Asa and his army chased them all the way to Gerar. A large number of Cushites fell down wounded or dead. So they couldn't fight back. The LORD and his army crushed them. The men of Judah carried off a large amount of goods.

¹⁴They attacked all of the villages around Gerar. The LORD had made the people in those villages afraid of him. The men of Judah took everything from all of the villages. ¹⁵They also attacked the camps of those who took care of the herds. They carried off large numbers of sheep, goats and camels. Then they returned to Jerusalem.

Asa Makes Judah a Better Nation

15 The Spirit of God came on Azariah. He was the son of Oded. ²Azariah went out to meet Asa. He said to him, "Asa and all you people of Judah and Benjamin, listen to me. The LORD is with you when you are with him. If you really look for him, you will find him. But if you desert him, he will desert you.

3"For a long time Israel didn't worship the true God. They didn't have a priest who taught them. So they didn't know God's law. 4But when they were in trouble, they turned to the LORD, the God of Israel. When they did, they found him.

5"In those days it wasn't safe to travel around. The people who lived in all of the areas of the land were having a lot of trouble. 6One nation was crushing another. One city was crushing another. That's because God was causing them to suffer terribly.

7"But be strong. Don't give up. God will reward you for your work."

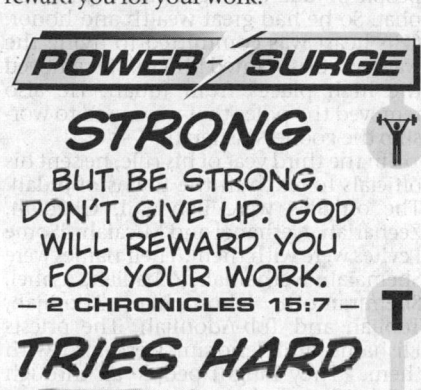

POWER–SURGE

STRONG

BUT BE STRONG. DON'T GIVE UP. GOD WILL REWARD YOU FOR YOUR WORK.
– 2 CHRONICLES 15:7 –

TRIES HARD

8Asa heard that prophecy. He paid attention to the words of the prophet Azariah, the son of Oded. So Asa became bolder than ever. He removed the statues of gods from the whole land of Judah and Benjamin. He also removed them from the towns he had captured in the hills of Ephraim. He did it because he hated those gods. He repaired the altar of the LORD. It was in front of the porch of the LORD's temple.

9Then he gathered all of the people of Judah and Benjamin together. He also gathered together the people from Ephraim, Manasseh and Simeon who had settled among them. Large numbers of people had come over to him from Israel. They came because they saw that the LORD his God was with him.

10They gathered in Jerusalem. It was the third month of the 15th year of Asa's rule. 11At that time they sacrificed to the LORD 700 head of cattle and 7,000 sheep and goats. The animals were among the things they had taken after the battle.

12They made a covenant to look to the LORD, the God of their people. They looked to him with all their heart and soul. 13All those who wouldn't look to the LORD, the God of Israel, would be killed. It wouldn't matter how important they were. It wouldn't matter whether they were men or women. 14They took an oath and made a promise to the LORD. They praised him out loud. They shouted. They blew trumpets and horns.

15All of the people of Judah were happy about the promise they had made. They turned to God with all their heart. When they did, they found him. So the LORD gave them peace and rest on every side.

16King Asa also removed his grandmother Maacah from her position as queen mother. That's because she had made a pole that was used to worship the goddess Asherah. The LORD hated it. So Asa cut it down. He broke it up. He burned it in the Kidron Valley.

17Asa didn't remove the high places from Israel. But he committed his whole life completely to the LORD. 18He and his father had set apart silver, gold and other articles to the LORD. He brought them into God's temple.

19There weren't any more wars until the 35th year of Asa's rule.

The Last Years of Asa's Rule

16 Baasha was king of Israel. He marched out against Judah. It was in the 36th year of Asa's rule over Judah. Baasha built up the walls of Ramah. He did it to keep people from leaving or entering the territory of Asa, the king of Judah.

2Asa took the silver and gold from among the treasures of the LORD's temple and his own palace. He sent it to Ben-Hadad. Ben-Hadad was king of Aram. He was ruling in Damascus. 3"Let's make a peace treaty between us," Asa said. "My father and your father had made a peace treaty between them. Now I'm sending you silver and gold. So break your treaty with Baasha, the king of Israel. Then he'll go back home."

4Ben-Hadad agreed with King Asa. He sent his army commanders against the towns of Israel. They attacked Ijon, Dan, Abel Maim and all of the cities in Naphtali where Baasha stored things.

5Baasha heard about it. So he stopped building up Ramah. He stopped working there. 6Then King Asa brought all of the men of Judah to Ramah. They carried away the stones and wood Baasha had been using. Asa used them to build up Geba and Mizpah.

7At that time the prophet Hanani came

to Asa, the king of Judah. He said to him, "You trusted the king of Aram. You didn't trust in the LORD your God. So the army of the king of Aram has escaped from you. ⁸The people of Cush and Libya had a strong army. They had large numbers of chariots and horsemen. But you trusted in the LORD. So he handed them over to you. ⁹The LORD looks out over the whole earth. He gives strength to those who commit their lives completely to him. You have done a foolish thing. From now on you will be at war."

POWER-SURGE

STRONG

THE LORD LOOKS OUT OVER THE WHOLE EARTH. HE GIVES STRENGTH TO THOSE WHO COMMIT THEIR LIVES COMPLETELY TO HIM.
— 2 CHRONICLES 16:9 —

¹⁰Asa was angry with the prophet because of what he had said. In fact, he was so angry he put him in prison. At the same time, Asa treated some of his own people very badly.

¹¹The events of Asa's rule from beginning to end are written down. They are written in the records of the kings of Judah and Israel.

¹²In the 39th year of Asa's rule his feet began to hurt. The pain was terrible. But even though he was suffering, he didn't look to the LORD for help. All he did was go to the doctors.

¹³In the 41st year of Asa's rule he joined the members of his family who had already died. ¹⁴His body was buried in a tomb. He had cut it out for himself in the City of David. His body was laid on a wooden frame. It was covered with spices and different mixes of perfume. A huge fire was made in his honor.

Jehoshaphat Becomes King of Judah

17 Jehoshaphat was the son of Asa. Jehoshaphat became the next king after him. He made his kingdom strong in case Israel would attack him. ²He placed troops in all of the cities of Judah that had high walls around them. He stationed some soldiers in Judah. He also put some in the towns of Ephraim that his father Asa had captured.

³The LORD was with Jehoshaphat. That's because in his early years he lived the way King David had lived. He didn't ask for advice from the gods that were named after Baal. ⁴Instead, he looked to the God of his father. He followed the LORD's commands instead of the practices of Israel.

⁵The LORD made the kingdom secure under Jehoshaphat's control. All of the people of Judah brought gifts to Jehoshaphat. So he had great wealth and honor. ⁶His heart was committed to living the way the LORD wanted him to. He removed the high places from Judah. He also removed the poles that were used to worship the goddess Asherah.

⁷In the third year of his rule, he sent his officials to teach in the towns of Judah. The officials were Ben-Hail, Obadiah, Zechariah, Nethanel and Micaiah. ⁸Some Levites were with them. Their names were Shemaiah, Nethaniah, Zebadiah, Asahel, Shemiramoth, Jehonathan, Adonijah, Tobijah and Tob-Adonijah. The priests Elishama and Jehoram were also with them. ⁹They taught people all through Judah. They took the Scroll of the Law of the LORD with them. They went around to all of the towns of Judah. And they taught the people.

¹⁰All of the kingdoms of the lands around Judah became afraid of the LORD. So they didn't go to war against Jehoshaphat. ¹¹Some Philistines brought to Jehoshaphat the gifts and silver he required of them. The Arabs brought him their flocks. They brought him 7,700 rams and 7,700 goats.

¹²Jehoshaphat became more and more powerful. He built forts in Judah. He also built cities in Judah where he could store things. ¹³He had large supplies in the towns of Judah. In Jerusalem he kept men who knew how to fight well. ¹⁴Here is a list of them, family by family.

From Judah there were commanders of companies of 1,000.
One of them was Adnah. He commanded 300,000 fighting men.
¹⁵Another was Jehohanan. He commanded 280,000.
¹⁶Another was Amasiah, the son of Zicri. Amasiah commanded 200,000. He had offered to serve the LORD.

17 From Benjamin there were also commanders.

One of them was Eliada. He was a brave soldier. He commanded 200,000 men. They were armed with bows and shields. **18** Another was Jehozabad. He commanded 180,000 men. They were prepared for battle.

19 Those were the men who served the king. He stationed some other men in the cities all through Judah. The cities had high walls around them.

Micaiah Prophesies Against Ahab

18 Jehoshaphat had great wealth and honor. He joined forces with Ahab by getting married to Ahab's daughter. **2** Some years later he went down to visit Ahab in Samaria. Ahab killed a lot of sheep and cattle for him and the people who were with him. Ahab tried to get Jehoshaphat to attack Ramoth Gilead. **3** Ahab was the king of Israel. He spoke to Jehoshaphat, the king of Judah. He asked, "Will you go with me to fight against Ramoth Gilead?"

Jehoshaphat replied, "Yes. I'll go with you. My men will also go with you. We'll join you in the war." **4** He continued, "First ask the LORD for advice."

5 So the king of Israel brought 400 prophets together. He asked them, "Should we go to war against Ramoth Gilead? Or should I stay here?"

"Go," they answered. "God will hand it over to you."

6 But Jehoshaphat asked, "Isn't there a prophet of the LORD here? If there is, ask him what we should do."

7 The king of Israel answered Jehoshaphat. He said, "There is still one other man we can go to. We can ask the LORD for advice through him. But I hate him. He never prophesies anything good about me. He only prophesies bad things. His name is Micaiah. He's the son of Imlah."

"You shouldn't say bad things about him," Jehoshaphat replied.

8 So the king of Israel called for one of his officials. He told him, "Bring Micaiah, the son of Imlah, at once."

9 The king of Israel and Jehoshaphat, the king of Judah, were wearing their royal robes. They were sitting on their thrones at the threshing floor. It was near the entrance of the gate of Samaria. All of the prophets were prophesying in front of them.

10 Zedekiah was the son of Kenaanah.

Zedekiah had made horns out of iron. They looked like animal horns. He announced, "The LORD says, 'With these horns you will drive back the men of Aram until they are destroyed.' "

11 All of the other prophets were prophesying the same thing. "Attack Ramoth Gilead," they said. "Win the battle over it. The LORD will hand it over to you."

12 A messenger went to get Micaiah. He said to him, "Look. The other prophets agree. All of them are saying the king will have success. So agree with them. Say the same thing they do."

13 But Micaiah said, "You can be sure that the LORD lives. And you can be just as sure that I can only tell the king what my God says."

14 When Micaiah arrived, the king spoke to him. He asked, "Should we go to war against Ramoth Gilead? Or should I stay here?"

"Attack," he answered. "You will win. The people of Ramoth Gilead will be handed over to you."

15 The king said to him, "I've made you promise to tell the truth many times before. So don't tell me anything but the truth in the name of the LORD."

16 Then Micaiah answered, "I saw all of the people of Israel scattered on the hills. They were like sheep that didn't have a shepherd. The LORD said, 'These people do not have a master. Let each of them go home in peace.' "

17 The king of Israel spoke to Jehoshaphat. He said, "Didn't I tell you he never prophesies anything good about me? He only prophesies bad things."

18 Micaiah continued, "Listen to the LORD's message. I saw the LORD sitting on his throne. Some of the angels of heaven were standing at his right side. The others were standing at his left side. **19** The LORD said, 'Who will try to get Ahab, the king of Israel, to attack Ramoth Gilead? I want him to die there.'

"One angel suggested one thing. Another suggested something else. **20** Finally, a spirit came forward and stood in front of the LORD. The spirit said, 'I'll try to get Ahab to do it.'

" 'How?' the LORD asked.

21 "The spirit said, 'I'll go and put lies in the mouths of all of his prophets.'

" 'You will have success in getting Ahab to attack Ramoth Gilead,' said the LORD. 'Go and do it.'

22 "So the LORD has put lies in the mouths of your prophets. He has said that great harm will come to you."

²³Then Zedekiah, the son of Kenaanah, went up and slapped Micaiah in the face. "So you think the spirit that was sent by the LORD went away from me to speak to you, do you?" he asked. "Which way did he go?"

²⁴Micaiah replied, "You will find out on the day you go to hide in an inside room to save your life."

²⁵Then the king of Israel gave an order. He said, "Take Micaiah away. Send him back to Amon. Amon is the ruler of the city of Samaria. And send him back to Joash. Joash is a member of the royal court. ²⁶Tell them, 'The king says, "Put this fellow in prison. Don't give him anything but bread and water until I return safely." ' "

²⁷Micaiah announced, "Do you really think you will return safely? If you do, the LORD hasn't spoken through me." He continued, "All of you people, remember what I've said!"

Ahab Is Killed at Ramoth Gilead

²⁸So the king of Israel went up to Ramoth Gilead. Jehoshaphat, the king of Judah, went there too.

²⁹The king of Israel spoke to Jehoshaphat. He said, "I'll go into battle wearing different clothes. Then people won't recognize me. But you wear your royal robes." So the king of Israel put on different clothes. Then he went into battle.

³⁰The king of Aram had given an order to his chariot commanders. He had said, "Fight only against the king of Israel. Don't fight against anyone else."

³¹The chariot commanders saw Jehoshaphat. They thought, "That's the king of Israel." So they turned to attack him. But Jehoshaphat cried out. And the LORD helped him. God drew the commanders away from him. ³²They saw he wasn't the king of Israel after all. So they stopped chasing him.

³³But someone shot an arrow without taking aim. The arrow hit the king of Israel between the parts of his armor. The king told the chariot driver, "Turn the chariot around. Get me out of this battle. I've been wounded."

³⁴All day long the battle continued. The king of Israel kept himself standing up by leaning against the inside of his chariot. He kept his face toward the men of Aram until evening. At sunset he died.

19 Jehoshaphat, the king of Judah, returned safely to his palace in Jerusalem. ²The prophet Jehu went out to meet him. He was the son of Hanani. Jehu said to the king, "You shouldn't help evil people. You shouldn't love those who hate the LORD. The LORD is angry with you. ³But there's some good in you. You have gotten rid of all of the poles in the land that are used to worship the goddess Asherah. And you have worshiped God with all your heart."

Jehoshaphat Appoints Judges

⁴Jehoshaphat lived in Jerusalem. He went out again among the people. He went from Beersheba to the hill country of Ephraim. He turned the people back to the LORD, the God of Israel.

⁵Jehoshaphat appointed judges in the land. He put them in all of the cities of Judah that had high walls around them. ⁶He told the judges, "Think carefully about what you do. After all, you aren't judging for mere men. You are judging for the LORD. He's with you every time you make a decision. ⁷Have respect for the LORD. Judge carefully. He is always right. He treats everyone the same. He doesn't want his judges to take money from people who want special favors."

⁸In Jerusalem, Jehoshaphat chose some Levites and priests. He also chose some leaders of Israelite families. He appointed all of them to apply the law of the LORD fairly. He wanted them to decide cases. He wanted them to settle matters between people. All of those judges lived in Jerusalem.

⁹Here are the orders Jehoshaphat gave them. He said, "Have respect for the LORD. Serve him faithfully. Do it with all your heart. ¹⁰Cases will come to you from your fellow judges who live in the other cities. The cases might be about murder or other matters that the law, commands, directions and rules deal with. Warn the judges not to sin against the LORD. If you don't warn them, he will be angry with you and your fellow judges. Do what I say. Then you won't sin.

¹¹"The chief priest Amariah will be over you in any matter that concerns the LORD. Zebadiah is the leader of the tribe of Judah. He is the son of Ishmael. Zebadiah will be over you in any matter that con-

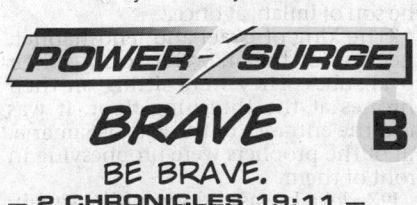

POWER-SURGE

BRAVE **B**

BE BRAVE.

— 2 CHRONICLES 19:11 —

cerns the king. The Levites will serve as your officials. Be brave. And may the LORD be with those of you who do well."

Jehoshaphat Wins the Battle Over Moab and Ammon

20 After that, the Moabites, Ammonites and some Meunites went to war against Jehoshaphat.

2Some people came and told him, "A huge army is coming from Edom to fight against you. They have come across the Dead Sea. They are already in Hazazon Tamar." Hazazon Tamar is also called En Gedi.

3Jehoshaphat was alarmed. So he decided to ask the LORD for advice. He told all of the people of Judah to go without eating. **4**The people came together to ask the LORD for help. In fact, they came from every town in Judah to pray to him.

5Then Jehoshaphat stood up among the people of Judah and Jerusalem. He was in front of the new courtyard at the LORD's temple. **6**He said,

"LORD, you are the God of our people. You are the God who is in heaven. You rule over all of the kingdoms of the nations. Your hands are strong and powerful. No one can fight against you and win.

7"Our God, you drove out the people who lived in this land. You drove them out to make room for your people Israel. You gave this land forever to those who belong to the family line of your friend Abraham.

8"They have lived in this land. They've built a temple here for your Name. They have said, **9**'Suppose trouble comes on us. It doesn't matter whether it's a punishing sword, plague or hunger. We'll serve you. We'll stand in front of this temple where your Name is. We'll cry out to you when we're in trouble. Then you will hear us. You will save us.'

10"But here are men from Ammon, Moab and Mount Seir. You wouldn't allow Israel to march in and attack their territory when the Israelites came from Egypt. So Israel turned away from them. They didn't destroy them. **11**See how they are paying us back. They are coming to drive us out. They want to take over the land you gave us as our share.

12"Our God, won't you please judge them? We don't have the power to face this huge army that's attacking us. We don't know what to do. But we're looking to you to help us."

13All of the men of Judah stood there in front of the LORD. Their wives, children and little ones were with them.

14Then the Spirit of the LORD came on Jahaziel. He was standing among the people of Israel. He was the son of Zechariah. Zechariah was the son of Benaiah. Benaiah was the son of Jeiel. Jeiel was the son of Mattaniah. Jahaziel was a Levite. He was from the family line of Asaph.

15Jahaziel said, "King Jehoshaphat, listen! All you who live in Judah and Jerusalem, listen! The LORD says to you, 'Do not be afraid. Do not lose hope because of this huge army. The battle is not yours. It is mine.

16" 'Tomorrow march down against them. They will be climbing up by the Pass of Ziz. You will find them at the end of the valley in the Desert of Jeruel. **17**You will not have to fight this battle. Take your positions. Stand firm. You will see how I will save you. Judah and Jerusalem, do not be afraid. Do not lose hope. Go out and face them tomorrow. I will be with you.' "

18Jehoshaphat bowed down with his face toward the ground. All of the people of Judah and Jerusalem also bowed down. They worshiped the LORD.

19Then some Levites from the families of Kohath and Korah stood up. They praised the LORD, the God of Israel. They praised him with very loud voices.

20Early in the morning all of the people left for the Desert of Tekoa. As they started out, Jehoshaphat stood up. He said, "Judah, listen to me! People of Jerusalem, listen to me! Have faith in the LORD your God. He'll take good care of you. Have faith in his prophets. Then you will have success."

21Jehoshaphat asked the people for advice. Then he appointed men to sing to the LORD. He wanted them to praise him

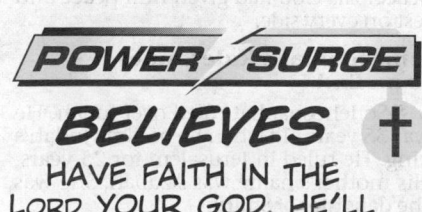

POWER-SURGE

BELIEVES ✝

HAVE FAITH IN THE LORD YOUR GOD. HE'LL TAKE GOOD CARE OF YOU.

— 2 CHRONICLES 20:20 —

because of his glory and holiness. They marched out in front of the army. They said,

"Give thanks to the LORD.
His faithful love continues forever."

²²They began to sing and praise him. Then the LORD hid some men and told them to wait. He wanted them to attack the people of Ammon, Moab and Mount Seir. They had gone into Judah and attacked it. But they lost the battle. ²³The men of Ammon and Moab rose up against the men from Mount Seir. They destroyed them. They put an end to them. When they finished killing the men from Seir, they destroyed each other.

²⁴The men of Judah came to the place that looks out over the desert. They turned to look down at the huge army. But all they saw was dead bodies lying there on the ground. No one had escaped.

²⁵So Jehoshaphat and his men went down there to carry off anything of value. Among the dead bodies they found a lot of supplies, clothes and articles of value. There was more than they could take away. There was so much it took three days to collect all of it.

²⁶On the fourth day they gathered together in the Valley of Beracah. There they praised the LORD. That's why it's called the Valley of Beracah to this very day.

²⁷Then all of the men of Judah and Jerusalem returned to Jerusalem. They were filled with joy. Jehoshaphat led them. The LORD had made them happy because all of their enemies were dead. ²⁸They entered Jerusalem and went to the LORD's temple. They were playing harps, lutes and trumpets.

²⁹All of the kingdoms of the surrounding countries began to have respect for God. They had heard how the LORD had fought against Israel's enemies. ³⁰The kingdom of Jehoshaphat was at peace. His God had given him peace and rest on every side.

Jehoshaphat's Rule Comes to an End

³¹So Jehoshaphat ruled over Judah. He was 35 years old when he became Judah's king. He ruled in Jerusalem for 25 years. His mother's name was Azubah. She was the daughter of Shilhi. ³²Jehoshaphat followed the ways of his father Asa. He didn't wander away from them. He did what was right in the eyes of the LORD.

³³But the high places weren't removed. The people still hadn't worshiped the God of Israel with all their hearts.

³⁴The other events of Jehoshaphat's rule from beginning to end are written down. They are written in the official records of Jehu, the son of Hanani. They are written in the records of the kings of Israel.

³⁵Jehoshaphat king of Judah and Ahaziah king of Israel agreed to be friends. Ahaziah was guilty of doing what was evil. ³⁶Jehoshaphat agreed with him to build a lot of ships. They were built at Ezion Geber. They carried goods that were traded for other goods. ³⁷Eliezer was the son of Dodavahu from Mareshah. Eliezer prophesied against Jehoshaphat. He said, "You have joined forces with Ahaziah. So the LORD will destroy what you have made." The ships were wrecked. They were never able to sail or trade goods.

21 Jehoshaphat joined the members of his family who had already died. His body was buried in the family tomb in the City of David. His son Jehoram became the next king after him.

²Jehoram's brothers, the sons of Jehoshaphat, were Azariah, Jehiel, Zechariah, Azariahu, Michael and Shephatiah. All of them were sons of Jehoshaphat, the king of Israel. ³Their father had given them many gifts. He had given them silver, gold and articles of value. He had also given them cities in Judah that had high walls around them. But he had made Jehoram king. That's because Jehoram was his oldest son.

Jehoram Becomes King of Judah

⁴Jehoram made his position secure over his father's kingdom. Then he killed all of his brothers with his sword. He also killed some of the princes of Israel.

⁵Jehoram was 32 years old when he became king. He ruled in Jerusalem for eight years. ⁶He followed the ways of the kings of Israel, just as the royal family of Ahab had done. In fact, he got married to a daughter of Ahab. Jehoram did what was evil in the sight of the LORD.

⁷But the LORD didn't want to destroy the royal family of David. That's because the LORD had made a covenant with him. He had promised to keep the lamp of David's kingdom burning brightly for him and his children after him forever.

⁸When Jehoram was king over Judah, Edom refused to remain under Judah's control. They set up their own king. ⁹So

Jehoram went to Edom. He took his officers and all of his chariots with him. The men of Edom surrounded him and his chariot commanders. But he got up at night and fought his way out. **10**To this very day Edom has refused to remain under Judah's control.

At that same time, Libnah also refused to remain under the control of Judah. That's because Jehoram had deserted the LORD, the God of his people. **11**He had also built high places on the hills of Judah. He had caused the people of Jerusalem to worship other gods. They weren't faithful to the LORD. Jehoram had led Judah down the wrong path.

12Jehoram received a letter from the prophet Elijah. It said,

"The LORD is the God of your father David. The LORD says, 'You have not followed the ways of your own father Jehoshaphat or of Asa, the king of Judah. **13**Instead, you have followed the ways of the kings of Israel. You have led Judah and the people of Jerusalem to worship other gods, just as the royal family of Ahab did. Also, you have murdered your own brothers. They were members of your own family. They were better men than you are.

14" 'So now I am about to strike your people down with a heavy blow. I will strike down your sons, your wives and everything that belongs to you. **15**And you yourself will be very sick for a long time. The sickness will finally cause your insides to come out.' "

16The LORD stirred up the anger of the Philistines against Jehoram. He also stirred up the anger of the Arabs. They lived near the people of Cush. **17**The Philistines and Arabs attacked Judah. They went in and carried off all of the goods they found in the king's palace. They also took his sons and wives. The only son he had left was Ahaziah. He was the youngest son.

18After all of that, the LORD made Jehoram very sick. He couldn't be healed. **19**After he had been sick for two years, the sickness caused his insides to come out. He died in great pain. His people didn't make a fire in his honor, as they had done for the kings who ruled before him.

20Jehoram was 32 years old when he became king. He ruled in Jerusalem for eight years. No one was sorry when he passed away. His body was buried in the City of David. But it wasn't placed in the tombs of the kings.

Ahaziah Becomes King of Judah

22 The people of Jerusalem made Ahaziah king in place of Jehoram. Ahaziah was Jehoram's youngest son. Robbers had come with the Arabs into Jehoram's camp. The robbers had killed all of his older sons. So Ahaziah, the king of Judah, began to rule. He was the son of Jehoram.

2Ahaziah was 22 years old when he became king. He ruled in Jerusalem for one year. His mother's name was Athaliah. She was a granddaughter of Omri.

3Ahaziah also followed the ways of the royal family of Ahab. That's because Ahaziah's mother gave him bad advice. She told him to do what was wrong. **4**So he did what was evil in the sight of the LORD, just as the family of Ahab had done.

After Ahaziah's father died, the members of Ahab's family became his advisers. That's what destroyed him. **5**He also followed their advice when he joined forces with Joram, the king of Israel. They went to war against Hazael at Ramoth Gilead. Joram was the son of Ahab. Hazael was king of Aram. The soldiers of Aram wounded Joram. **6**So he returned to Jezreel to give his wounds time to heal. His enemies had wounded him at Ramoth in his battle against Hazael, the king of Aram.

Ahaziah, the son of Jehoram, went down to Jezreel. He went there to see Joram. That's because Joram had been wounded. Ahaziah was king of Judah. Joram was the son of Ahab.

7Through Ahaziah's visit to Joram, God caused Ahaziah to fall from power. When Ahaziah arrived, he rode out with Joram to meet Jehu, the son of Nimshi. The LORD had anointed Jehu to destroy the royal family of Ahab. **8**So Jehu punished Ahab's family, just as the LORD had told him to. While he was doing it, he found the princes of Judah and the sons of Ahaziah's relatives. They had been serving Ahaziah. So Jehu killed them.

9Then he went to look for Ahaziah. Jehu's men captured him while he was hiding in Samaria. Ahaziah was brought to Jehu and put to death. People buried his body, because they said, "He was a grandson of Jehoshaphat, who followed the LORD with all his heart."

So no one in the royal family of Ahaziah was powerful enough to keep the kingdom.

Athaliah and Joash

10Athaliah was Ahaziah's mother. She saw that her son was dead. So she began to wipe out the whole royal house of Judah. **11**But Jehosheba went and got Joash, the son of Ahaziah. She was the daughter of King Jehoram. She stole Joash away from among the royal princes. All of them were about to be murdered. She put Joash and his nurse in a bedroom. Jehosheba, the daughter of King Jehoram, was the wife of the priest Jehoiada. She was also Ahaziah's sister.

So Jehosheba hid the child from Athaliah. That's why Athaliah couldn't kill him. **12**The child remained hidden with the priest and his wife at God's temple for six years. Athaliah ruled over the land during that time.

23 When Joash was seven years old, Jehoiada showed how strong he was. He made a covenant with the commanders of companies of 100 men. The commanders were Azariah son of Jeroham, Ishmael son of Jehohanan, Azariah son of Obed, Maaseiah son of Adaiah, and Elishaphat son of Zicri. **2**They went all through Judah. They gathered together the Levites and the leaders of Israelite families from all of the towns. They came to Jerusalem. **3**The whole community made a covenant with the new king at God's temple.

Jehoiada said to them, "Ahaziah's son will rule over Judah. That's what the LORD promised concerning the family line of David. **4**Here's what I want you to do. A third of you priests and Levites who are going on duty on the Sabbath day must guard the doors. **5**A third of you must guard the royal palace. And a third of you must guard the Foundation Gate. All of the other men must guard the courtyards of the LORD's temple.

6"Don't let anyone enter the temple except the priests and Levites who are on duty. They can enter because they are set apart to the LORD. But all of the other men must guard the places where the LORD has sent them.

7"The Levites must station themselves around the new king. Each man must have his weapons in his hand. Anyone else who enters the temple must be put to death. Stay close to the king no matter where he goes."

8The Levites did just as the priest Jehoiada ordered. So did all of the men of Judah. Each commander got his men. Some of the men were going on duty on the Sabbath day. Others were going off

duty. Jehoiada didn't let any of the groups go. **9**Then he gave weapons to the commanders of the companies. He gave them spears, large shields and small shields. The weapons had belonged to King David. They had been in God's temple.

10Jehoiada stationed all of the men around the new king. Each man had his weapon in his hand. They were standing near the altar and the temple. They stood from the south side of the temple to its north side. Their line formed half of a circle.

11Jehoiada and his sons brought Ahaziah's son out. They put the crown on him. They gave him a copy of the covenant. And they announced that he was king. They anointed him. Then they shouted, "May the king live a long time!"

12Athaliah heard the noise of the people running and cheering the new king. So she went to them at the LORD's temple. **13**She looked. And there was the king! He was standing next to his pillar at the entrance. The officers and trumpet players were standing beside the king. All of the people of the land were filled with joy. They were blowing trumpets. Singers with their musical instruments were leading the songs of praise.

Then Athaliah tore her royal robes. She shouted, "Treason! It's treason!"

14The priest Jehoiada sent out the commanders of the companies of 100 men. They were in charge of the troops. He said to them, "Bring her away from the temple between the line of guards. Use your swords to kill anyone who follows her." The priest had said, "Don't put her to death at the LORD's temple."

15So they grabbed hold of her as she reached the entrance of the Horse Gate on the palace grounds. There they put her to death.

16Then Jehoiada made a covenant. He promised that he, the people and the king would be the LORD's people.

17All of the people went to Baal's temple. They tore it down. They smashed the altars and the statues of gods. They killed Mattan in front of the altars. He was the priest of Baal.

18Then Jehoiada put the priests, who were Levites, in charge of the LORD's temple. David had given them their duties in the temple. He had appointed them to sacrifice burnt offerings to the LORD. He wanted them to do it in keeping with what was written in the Law of Moses. David wanted them to sing and be full of joy.

19Jehoiada stationed guards at the gates of the LORD's temple. No one who was "unclean" in any way could enter.
20Jehoiada took with him the commanders of hundreds, the nobles, the rulers of the people, and all of the people of the land. He brought the new king down from the LORD's temple. They went into the palace through the Upper Gate. Then they seated the king on the royal throne.
21All of the people of the land were filled with joy. And the city was quiet. That's because Athaliah had been killed with a sword.

Joash Repairs the Temple

24 Joash was seven years old when he became king. He ruled in Jerusalem for 40 years. His mother's name was Zibiah. She was from Beersheba.
2Joash did what was right in the eyes of the LORD. He lived that way as long as the priest Jehoiada was alive. 3Jehoiada chose two wives for Joash. They had sons and daughters by Joash.
4Some time later Joash decided to make the LORD's temple look like new again. 5He called together the priests and Levites. He said to them, "Go to the towns of Judah. Collect the money that the nation of Israel owes every year. Use it to repair the temple of your God. Do it now." But the Levites didn't do it right away.
6So the king sent for the chief priest Jehoiada. He said to him, "Why haven't you required the Levites to bring in the tax from Judah and Jerusalem? It was set up by the LORD's servant Moses and the whole community of Israel. It was used for the tent where the tablets of the covenant were kept."
7The children of that evil woman Athaliah had broken into God's temple. They had used even its sacred objects for the gods that were named after Baal.
8King Joash commanded that a wooden chest be made. It was placed outside near the gate of the LORD's temple. 9Then a message went out in Judah and Jerusalem. It said that the people should bring the tax to the LORD. God's servant Moses had required Israel to pay that tax when they were in the desert.
10All of the officials and people gladly brought their money. They dropped it into the chest until it was full.
11The chest was brought in by the Levites to the king's officials. Every time the officials saw there was a large amount of money in the chest, it was emptied out.

The royal secretary and the officer of the chief priest came and emptied it. Then they carried it back to its place. They did it regularly. They collected a great amount of money.
12The king and Jehoiada gave it to the men who were doing the work on the LORD's temple. They hired people who could lay the stones and people who could work with wood. They also hired people who could work with iron and bronze. They hired all of them to repair the temple.
13The men who were in charge of the work did their best. The repairs went very well under them. They rebuilt God's temple. They did it in keeping with its original plans. They made it stronger.
14So they finished the work. Then they brought the rest of the money to the king and Jehoiada. It was used to pay for the articles that were made for the LORD's temple. The articles were used for serving at the temple. They were also used for the burnt offerings. The articles included dishes and other objects that were made out of gold and silver. As long as Jehoiada lived, burnt offerings were sacrificed continually at the LORD's temple.
15Jehoiada had become very old. He died at the age of 130. 16His body was buried with the kings in the City of David. That's because he had done so many good things in Israel for God and his temple.

POWER-SURGE

GIVING G

ALL OF THE OFFICIALS AND PEOPLE GLADLY BROUGHT THEIR MONEY. THEY DROPPED IT INTO THE CHEST UNTIL IT WAS FULL... EVERY TIME THE OFFICIALS SAW THERE WAS A LARGE AMOUNT OF MONEY IN THE CHEST, IT WAS EMPTIED OUT...THEY COLLECTED A GREAT AMOUNT OF MONEY.
— 2 CHRONICLES 24:10-11 —

The Evil Things Joash Did

17 After Jehoiada died, the officials of Judah came to King Joash. They bowed down to him. He listened to them. **18** They turned their backs on the temple of the LORD, the God of their people. They worshiped poles that were made to honor the goddess Asherah. They also worshiped statues of other gods.

Because Judah and Jerusalem were guilty of sin, God became angry with them. **19** The LORD sent prophets to the people to bring them back to him. The prophets gave witness against the people. But they wouldn't listen.

20 Then the Spirit of God came on the priest Zechariah. He was the son of Jehoiada. Zechariah stood in front of the people. He told them, "God says, 'Why do you refuse to obey my commands? You will not have success. You have deserted me. So I have deserted you.' "

21 But the people made evil plans against Zechariah. The king ordered them to kill Zechariah by throwing stones at him. They did it in the courtyard of the LORD's temple. **22** King Joash didn't remember how kind Zechariah's father Jehoiada had been to him. So he killed Jehoiada's son.

As Zechariah was dying he said, "May the LORD see this. May he hold you accountable."

23 In the spring, the army of Aram marched into Judah and Jerusalem against Joash. They killed all of the leaders of the people. They took a large amount of goods from Judah. They sent it to their king in Damascus. **24** The army of Aram had come with only a few men. But the LORD allowed them to win the battle over a much larger army. Judah had deserted the LORD, the God of their people. That's why the LORD punished Joash.

25 The army of Aram pulled back. They left Joash badly wounded. His officials planned to do evil things to him. That's because he murdered the son of the priest Jehoiada. They killed Joash in his bed. So he died. His body was buried in the City of David. But it wasn't placed in the tombs of the kings.

26 Those who made the plans against Joash were Zabad and Jehozabad. Zabad was the son of Shimeath. She was from Ammon. Jehozabad was the son of Shimrith. She was from Moab.

27 The story of the sons of Joash is written in the notes on the records of the kings. The many prophecies about him are written there too. So is the record of how he made God's temple look like new again. His son Amaziah became the next king after him.

Amaziah Becomes King of Judah

25 Amaziah was 25 years old when he became king. He ruled in Jerusalem for 29 years. His mother's name was Jehoaddin. She was from Jerusalem. **2** Amaziah did what was right in the eyes of the LORD. But he didn't do it with all his heart. **3** The kingdom was firmly under his control. So he put to death the officials who had murdered his father, the king.

4 But he didn't put their children to death. He obeyed what is written in the Law, the Scroll of Moses. There the LORD commanded, "Parents must not be put to death because of what their children do. And children must not be put to death because of what their parents do. People must die because of their own sins." *(Deuteronomy 24:16)*

5 Amaziah called the people of Judah together. He arranged them by families under commanders of thousands and commanders of hundreds. He did it for all of the people of Judah and Benjamin. Then he brought together the men who were 20 years old or more. He found out there were 300,000 men who were able to serve in the army. They could handle spears and shields. **6** He also hired 100,000 fighting men from Israel. He had to pay them almost four tons of silver.

7 But a man of God came to him. He said, "King Amaziah, these troops from Israel must not march out with you. The LORD is not with Israel. He isn't with any of the people of Ephraim. **8** Go and fight bravely in battle if you want to. But God will destroy you right in front of your enemies. God has the power to help you or destroy you."

9 Amaziah asked the man of God, "But what about all of that silver I paid for these Israelite troops?"

The man of God replied, "The LORD can give you much more than that."

10 So Amaziah let the troops go who had come to him from Ephraim. He sent them home. They were very angry with Judah. In fact, they were burning with anger when they went home.

11 Then Amaziah showed how strong he was. He led his army to the Valley of Salt. There he killed 10,000 men of Seir. **12** The army of Judah also captured 10,000 men alive. They took them to the top of a cliff.

Then they threw them down. All of them were smashed to pieces.

13 The troops Amaziah had sent back attacked some towns in Judah. He hadn't allowed the troops to take part in the war. They attacked towns from Samaria to Beth Horon. They killed 3,000 people. They carried off huge amounts of goods.

14 Amaziah returned from killing the men of Edom. He brought back the statues of the gods of Seir. He set them up as his own gods. He bowed down to them. He burned sacrifices to them.

15 The LORD's anger burned against Amaziah. He sent a prophet to him. The prophet said, "Why do you ask the gods of those people for advice? They couldn't even save their own people from your power!"

16 While the prophet was still speaking, the king spoke to him. He said, "Did I ask you for advice? Stop! If you don't, you will be struck down."

So the prophet stopped. But then he said, "I know that God has decided to destroy you. That's because you have worshiped other gods. You haven't listened to my advice."

17 Amaziah, the king of Judah, spoke to his advisers. Then he sent a message to Jehoash, the king of Israel. Jehoash was the son of Jehoahaz. Jehoahaz was the son of Jehu. Amaziah dared Jehoash, "Come on. Meet me face to face in battle."

18 But Jehoash, the king of Israel, answered Amaziah, the king of Judah. He said, "A thorn bush in Lebanon sent a message to a cedar tree there. It said, 'Give your daughter to be married to my son.' Then a wild animal in Lebanon came along. It walked all over the thorn bush. **19** You brag that you have won the battle over Edom. You are very proud. But stay home! Why ask for trouble? Why bring yourself crashing down? Why bring Judah down with you?"

20 But Amaziah wouldn't listen. That's because God had planned to hand Judah over to Jehoash. After all, they had asked the gods of Edom for advice.

21 So Jehoash, the king of Israel, attacked. He and Amaziah, the king of Judah, faced each other in battle. The battle took place at Beth Shemesh in Judah. **22** Israel drove Judah away. Every man ran home.

23 Jehoash king of Israel captured Amaziah king of Judah at Beth Shemesh. Amaziah was the son of Joash. Joash was the son of Ahaziah. Jehoash brought Amaziah to Jerusalem. He broke down part of its

wall. It's the part that went from the Ephraim Gate to the Corner Gate. That part of the wall was 600 feet long.

24 Jehoash took all of the gold and silver. He took all of the articles he found in God's temple. Obed-Edom had been in charge of them. Jehoash also took the palace treasures and the prisoners. Then he returned to Samaria.

25 Amaziah king of Judah lived for 15 years after Jehoash king of Israel died. Amaziah was the son of Joash. Jehoash was the son of Jehoahaz.

26 The other events of Amaziah's rule from beginning to end are written down. They are written in the records of the kings of Judah and Israel.

27 Amaziah turned away from following the LORD. From that time on, some people made evil plans against him in Jerusalem. So he ran away to Lachish. But they sent men to Lachish after him. There they killed him. **28** His body was brought back on a horse. Then he was buried in the family tomb in Jerusalem, the City of Judah.

Uzziah Becomes King of Judah

26 All of the people of Judah made Uzziah king. He was 16 years old. They made him king in place of his father Amaziah.

2 Uzziah rebuilt Elath. He brought it under Judah's control again. He did it after Amaziah joined the members of his family who had already died.

3 Uzziah was 16 years old when he became king. He ruled in Jerusalem for 52 years. His mother's name was Jecoliah. She was from Jerusalem.

4 Uzziah did what was right in the eyes of the LORD, just as his father Amaziah had done. **5** He looked to God during the days of Zechariah. Zechariah taught him to have respect for God. As long as Uzziah looked to the LORD, God gave him success.

6 Uzziah went to war against the Philistines. He broke down the walls of Gath, Jabneh and Ashdod. Then he rebuilt some towns that were near Ashdod. He also rebuilt some other towns where Philistines lived. **7** God helped him fight against the Philistines. He also helped him fight against the Meunites and against the Arabs who lived in Gur Baal. **8** The Ammonites brought to Uzziah the gifts he required of them. He became famous all the way to the border of Egypt. That's because he had become very powerful.

9 Uzziah built towers in Jerusalem. They were at the Corner Gate, the Valley Gate and the angle of the wall. He made the towers very strong. [10]He also built towers in the desert.

He dug many wells, because he had a lot of livestock. The livestock were in the western hills and on the flatlands. Uzziah had people working in his fields and vineyards in the hills and in the rich lands. That's because he loved the soil.

[11]Uzziah's army was well trained. It was ready to march out by companies in keeping with their numbers. Jeiel and Maaseiah brought them together. Jeiel was the secretary. Maaseiah was the officer. They were under the direction of Hananiah. He was one of the royal officials. [12]The total number of family leaders who were over the fighting men was 2,600. [13]An army of 307,500 men was under their command. The men were trained for war. They were a powerful force. They helped the king against his enemies. [14]Uzziah provided the entire army with shields, spears, helmets, coats of armor, bows, and stones for their slings. [15]In Jerusalem he made machines that were based on patterns that skilled men had drawn up. The machines were used on the towers and on the corners of walls. They could shoot arrows. They could also throw large stones.

POWER-SURGE

HELPFUL ★

UZZIAH BECAME FAMOUS EVERYWHERE. GOD GREATLY HELPED HIM UNTIL HE BECAME POWERFUL.

—2 CHRONICLES 26:15—

STRONG

Uzziah became famous everywhere. God greatly helped him until he became powerful.

[16]But after Uzziah became powerful, his pride brought him down. He wasn't faithful to the LORD his God. He entered the LORD's temple to burn incense on the altar for burning incense.

[17]The priest Azariah followed him in. So did 80 other brave priests of the LORD. [18]They stood up to Uzziah. They said, "Uzziah, it isn't right for you to burn incense to the LORD. Only the priests are supposed to do that. They are members of the family line of Aaron. They have been set apart to burn incense. So get out of here. Leave the temple. You haven't been faithful. The LORD God won't honor you."

[19]Uzziah was holding a shallow cup. He was ready to burn incense. He became angry. He shouted at the priests in the LORD's temple. He did it near the altar for burning incense.

While he was shouting, a skin disease suddenly broke out on his forehead. [20]The chief priest Azariah looked at him. So did all of the other priests. They saw that Uzziah had a skin disease on his forehead. So they hurried him out of the temple. Actually, he himself really wanted to leave. He knew that the LORD was making him suffer.

[21]King Uzziah had the skin disease until the day he died. He lived in a separate house because he had the disease. And he wasn't allowed to enter the LORD's temple.

Uzziah's son Jotham was in charge of the palace. Jotham ruled over the people of the land.

[22]The other events of Uzziah's rule from beginning to end were written down by the prophet Isaiah. Isaiah was the son of Amoz.

[23]Uzziah joined the members of his family who had already died. His body was buried near theirs in a royal burial ground. People said, "He had a skin disease." His son Jotham became the next king after him.

Jotham Becomes King of Judah

27 Jotham was 25 years old when he became king. He ruled in Jerusalem for 16 years. His mother's name was Jerusha. She was the daughter of Zadok.

[2]Jotham did what was right in the eyes of the LORD, just as his father Uzziah had done. But Jotham didn't enter the LORD's temple as Uzziah had done. In spite of that, the people continued to do very sinful things.

[3]Jotham rebuilt the Upper Gate of the LORD's temple. He did a lot of work on the wall at the hill of Ophel. [4]He built towns in the hills of Judah. He also built forts and towers in areas that had a lot of trees in them.

[5]Jotham went to war against the king of Ammon. He won the battle over the people of Ammon. That year they paid Jotham almost four tons of silver. They

POWER-SURGE

STRONG

JOTHAM BECAME POWERFUL. THAT'S BECAUSE HE HAD WORSHIPED THE LORD HIS GOD WITH ALL HIS HEART.

— 2 CHRONICLES 27:6 —

paid him 62,000 bushels of wheat and 62,000 bushels of barley. They also brought him the same amount in the second and third years.

6Jotham became powerful. That's because he had worshiped the LORD his God with all his heart.

7The other events of Jotham's rule are written down. That includes all of his wars and the other things he did. All of those things are written in the records of the kings of Israel and Judah. 8Jotham was 25 years old when he became king. He ruled in Jerusalem for 16 years.

9Jotham joined the members of his family who had already died. His body was buried in the City of David. His son Ahaz became the next king after him.

Ahaz Becomes King of Judah

28 Ahaz was 20 years old when he became king. He ruled in Jerusalem for 16 years.

He didn't do what was right in the eyes of the LORD. He didn't do what King David had done. 2He followed the ways of the kings of Israel. He also made metal statues of gods that were named after Baal. 3He burned sacrifices in the Valley of Ben Hinnom. He sacrificed his children in the fire to other gods. He followed the practices of the nations. The LORD hated those practices. He had driven out those nations to make room for the people of Israel. 4Ahaz offered sacrifices and burned incense at the high places. He also did it on the tops of hills and under every green tree.

5So the LORD his God handed him over to the king of Aram. The men of Aram won the battle over him. They took many of his people as prisoners. They brought them to Damascus.

God also handed Ahaz over to Pekah. His army wounded or killed many of the troops of Ahaz. Pekah was king of Israel.

one day Pekah killed 120,000 soldiers Pekah. That's because Judah had deserted him. That's because Judah had deserted their people. 7Zicri, the God of their people. im. He killed son of Remaliah. nah. Maaseiah was hting man from Ephranah. Maaseiah was Azrikam and Elkakam was the officer writing's son. Azrithe palace. And Elkanah was in charge of mand after the king. 8The men of Israel captured 200,000 wives, sons and daughters from their relatives in Judah. They also took a large amount of goods. They carried all of it back to Samaria.

9But a prophet of the LORD was there. His name was Oded. When the army returned to Samaria, he went out to meet them. He said to them, "The LORD is the God of your people. He burned with anger against Judah. So he handed them over to you. But you have killed them. Your anger reached all the way to heaven.

10"Now you are planning to make the men and women of Judah and Jerusalem your slaves. But aren't you also guilty of sins against the LORD your God? 11Listen to me! You have taken your relatives from Judah as prisoners. The LORD's anger is burning against you. So send your relatives back."

12Then some of the leaders in Ephraim stood up to those who were returning from the war. The leaders were Azariah, Berekiah, Jehizkiah and Amasa. Azariah was the son of Jehohanan. Berekiah was the son of Meshillemoth. Jehizkiah was the son of Shallum. And Amasa was the son of Hadlai. 13"Don't bring those prisoners here," they said. "If you do, we'll be guilty in the sight of the LORD. Do you really want to add to our sin and guilt? We're already very guilty. The LORD's anger is burning against Israel."

14So the soldiers gave up the prisoners and the goods they had taken. They did it in front of the officials and the whole community. 15Azariah, Berekiah, Jehizkiah and Amasa received the prisoners. From the goods that had been taken they gave clothes to all those who were naked. They gave them clothes, sandals, food, drink and healing lotion. They put all of the weak people on donkeys. They took them back to their relatives at Jericho. Then they returned to Samaria. Jericho was also known as the City of Palm Trees.

16At that time King Ahaz sent men to the king of Assyria to get help. 17The men of Edom had come again and attacked Judah. They had carried prisoners away. 18At the same time the Philistines had

POWER-S

G

GIVI CLOTHES
THEY GALL THOSE
[PRISONERS] WHO
WERE NAKED. THEY
GAVE THEM CLOTHES,
SANDALS, FOOD,
DRINK AND HEALING
LOTION.
—2 CHRONICLES 28:15—

HELPFUL

attacked towns in the western hills and in the Negev Desert of Judah. They had captured Beth Shemesh, Aijalon and Gederoth. They had also captured Soco, Timnah and Gimzo and the villages that were around them. They had settled down in all of them.

19The LORD had brought Judah down because of Ahaz, their king. Ahaz had stirred up the people of Judah to do evil things. He hadn't been faithful to the LORD at all.

20Tiglath-Pileser came to Ahaz. But he gave Ahaz trouble instead of help. Tiglath-Pileser was king of Assyria. **21**Ahaz took some things from the LORD's temple. He also took some from the royal palace and from the princes. He gave all of them to the king of Assyria. But that didn't help him.

22When King Ahaz was in trouble, he became even more unfaithful to the LORD. **23**He offered sacrifices to the gods of Damascus. They had won the battle over him. He thought, "The gods of the kings of Aram have helped them. So I'll sacrifice to them. Then they'll help me." But they brought him down. In fact, they brought the whole nation of Israel down.

24Ahaz gathered together everything that belonged to God's temple. He took all of it away. He shut the doors of the LORD's temple. He set up altars at every street corner in Jerusalem. **25**In every town in Judah he built high places. Sacrifices were burned there to other gods. That made the LORD, the God of his people, very angry.

26The other events of the rule of Ahaz and all of his evil practices from beginning to end are written down. They are written in the records of the kings of Judah and Israel.

27Ahaz joined the members of his family who had already died. His body was buried in the city of Jerusalem. But it wasn't placed in the tombs of the kings of Israel. His son Hezekiah became the next king after him.

Hezekiah Purifies the Temple

29 Hezekiah was 25 years old when he became king. He ruled in Jerusalem for 29 years. His mother's name was Abijah. She was the daughter of Zechariah.

2Hezekiah did what was right in the eyes of the LORD, just as King David had done.

3In the first month of Hezekiah's first year as king, he opened the doors of the LORD's temple. He repaired them. **4**He brought the priests and Levites in. He gathered them together in the open area on the east side of the temple.

5He said, "Levites, listen to me! Set yourselves apart to the LORD. Set apart the temple of the LORD. He's the God of your people. Remove anything that is 'unclean' from the temple. **6**Our people weren't faithful. They did what was evil in the sight of the LORD our God. They deserted him. They turned their faces away from the place where he lives. They turned their backs on him. **7**They also shut the doors of the temple porch. They put the lamps out. They didn't burn incense at the temple. They didn't sacrifice burnt offerings to the God of Israel there.

8"So the LORD has become angry with Judah and Jerusalem. He has made them look so bad that everyone is shocked when they see them. They laugh at them. You can see it with your own eyes. **9**That's why our people have been killed with swords. That's why our sons and daughters and wives have become prisoners.

10"So I'm planning to make a covenant with the LORD, the God of Israel. Then he'll turn his burning anger away from us. **11**"My sons, don't fail to obey the LORD. He has chosen you to stand in front of him and work for him. He wants you to serve him and burn incense to him."

12Here are the Levites who went to work.

Mahath and Joel were from the family line of Kohath.

Mahath was the son of Ama... ...ICLES 29
Joel was the son of Azariah.
Kish and Azariah were from the family line of Merari.
Kish was the son of Abdi. Azariah was the son of Jehallelel.
Joah and Eden were from the family line of Gershon.
Joah was the son of Zimmah. Eden was the son of Joah.

13 Shimri and Jeiel were from the family line of Elizaphan.
Zechariah and Mattaniah were from the family line of Asaph.
14 Jehiel and Shimei were from the family line of Heman.
Shemaiah and Uzziel were from the family line of Jeduthun.

15 All of those Levites gathered the other Levites together. They set themselves apart to the LORD. Then they went in to purify the LORD's temple. That's what the king had ordered them to do. They did what the LORD told them to. 16 The priests went into the LORD's temple to make it pure. They brought out to the temple courtyard everything that was "unclean." They had found "unclean" things in the LORD's temple. The Levites took them and carried them out to the Kidron Valley.

17 On the first day of the first month they began to set everything in the temple apart to the LORD. By the eighth day of the month they reached the LORD's porch. For eight more days they set the LORD's temple itself apart to him. They finished on the 16th day of the first month.

18 Then they went to King Hezekiah. They reported, "We've purified the whole temple of the LORD. That includes the altar for burnt offerings and all of its tools. It also includes the table for the holy bread and all of its articles. 19 We've prepared all of the articles King Ahaz removed. We've set them apart to the LORD. Ahaz had removed them while he was king. He wasn't faithful to the LORD. The articles are now in front of the LORD's altar."

20 Early the next morning King Hezekiah gathered the city officials together. They went up to the LORD's temple. 21 They brought seven bulls, seven rams, seven male lambs and seven male goats with them. They sacrificed the animals as a sin offering for the kingdom, for the temple and for Judah. The king commanded the priests to offer them on the LORD's altar. The priests were from the family line of Aaron.

the...ey killed the bulls. Then they blood ...the blood on the altar. Next lambs and ...e rams and sprinkled the altar. ...r. Then they killed the ...the blood on the

23 The goats for the... brought to the king and the...ffering were munity. They placed their ha...le community on them. 24 Then the priests killed the goats. They put the blood on the altar as a sin offering. It paid for the sin of the whole nation of Israel. The king had ordered the burnt offering and the sin offering for the whole nation.

25 He stationed the Levites in the LORD's temple. They had cymbals, harps and lyres. They did everything in the way King David, his prophet Gad, and the prophet Nathan had required. The LORD had given commands about all of those things through his prophets. 26 So the Levites stood ready with David's musical instruments. And the priests had their trumpets ready.

27 Hezekiah gave the order to sacrifice the burnt offering on the altar. The offering began. Singing to the LORD also began. The singing was accompanied by the trumpets and by the instruments of David. He had been king of Israel. 28 The whole community bowed down. They worshiped the LORD. At the same time the singers sang. The priests blew their trumpets. All of that continued until the burnt offering had been sacrificed.

29 So the offerings were finished. King Hezekiah got down on his knees. He worshiped the LORD. So did everyone who was with him.

30 The king and his officials ordered the Levites to praise the LORD. They used the words of David and the prophet Asaph. They sang praises with joy. They bowed their heads and worshiped the LORD.

31 Then Hezekiah said, "You have set yourselves apart to the LORD. Come and bring sacrifices and thank offerings to his temple."

So the whole community brought sacrifices and thank offerings. Everyone who wanted to brought burnt offerings. 32 The whole community brought 70 bulls, 100 rams and 200 male lambs. They brought all of them as burnt offerings to the LORD. 33 The total number of animals that were set apart as sacrifices to the LORD was 600 bulls and 3,000 sheep and goats.

34 But there weren't enough priests to skin all of the burnt offerings. So their brother Levites helped them. They

POWER-S G

GIVING

HEZEKIAH SAID, "YOU HAVE SET YOURSELVES APART TO THE LORD. COME AND BRING SACRIFICES AND THANK OFFERINGS TO HIS TEMPLE."

— 2 CHRONICLES 29:31 —

worked until the task was finished. By that time other priests had been set apart to the LORD. The Levites had been more careful than the priests when they set themselves apart. ³⁵There were large numbers of burnt offerings, along with the drink offerings and the fat from the friendship offerings. They were offered along with the burnt offerings.

So the service of the LORD's temple was started up again. ³⁶Hezekiah and all of the people were filled with joy. That's because everything had been done so quickly. God had provided for his people in a wonderful way.

Hezekiah Celebrates the Passover Feast

30 Hezekiah sent a message to all of the people of Israel and Judah. He also wrote letters to the tribes of Ephraim and Manasseh. He invited everyone to come to the LORD's temple in Jerusalem. He wanted them to celebrate the Passover Feast in honor of the LORD. He is the God of Israel.

²The king, his officials and the whole community in Jerusalem decided to celebrate the Passover in the second month. ³They hadn't been able to celebrate it at the regular time. That's because there weren't enough priests who had set themselves apart to the LORD. Also, the people hadn't gathered together in Jerusalem.

⁴The plan seemed good to the king and the whole community. ⁵They decided to send a message all through Israel. It was sent out from Beersheba all the way to Dan. The message invited the people to come to Jerusalem. It invited them to celebrate the Passover in honor of the LORD, the God of Israel.

The Passover hadn't been celebrated by large numbers of people for a long time. It hadn't been done in keeping with what was written in the law.

⁶Messengers went all through Israel and Judah. They carried letters from the king and his officials. The king had ordered them to do that. The letters said,

"People of Israel, return to the LORD. He is the God of Abraham, Isaac and Israel. Return to him. Then he will return to you who are left in the land. You have escaped from the power of the kings of Assyria.

⁷"Don't be like the rest of your people and relatives. They weren't faithful to the LORD, the God of their people. That's why he punished them. He made them look so bad that everyone was shocked when they saw them. You can see it for yourselves.

⁸"Don't be stubborn. Don't be as your people were. Obey the LORD. Come to the temple. He has set it apart to himself forever. Serve the LORD your God. Then he'll turn his burning anger away from you.

⁹"Suppose you return to the LORD. Then those who captured your relatives and children will be kind to them. In fact, your relatives and children will come back to this land. The LORD your God is kind and tender. He won't turn away from you if you return to him."

¹⁰The messengers went from town to town in Ephraim and Manasseh. They went all the way to Zebulun. But the people made fun of them. They laughed at

POWER-SURGE

CHEERFUL ✳

HEZEKIAH AND ALL OF THE PEOPLE WERE FILLED WITH JOY...GOD HAD PROVIDED FOR HIS PEOPLE IN A WONDERFUL WAY.

—2 CHRONICLES 29:36— G

GIVING

them. **11** In spite of that, some ⌐ Asher, Manasseh and Zebulun humbled themselves low in the LORD's sight. They went to Jerusalem.

12 God's powerful hand helped the people of Judah. He helped them agree with one another. So they did what the king and his officials had ordered. They did what the LORD told them to do.

13 A very large crowd of people gathered together in Jerusalem. They went there to celebrate the Feast of Unleavened Bread. It took place in the second month. **14** They removed the altars in Jerusalem. They cleared away the altars for burning incense. They threw all of the altars into the Kidron Valley.

15 They killed the Passover lamb on the 14th day of the second month. The priests and Levites were filled with shame. They set themselves apart to the LORD. They brought burnt offerings to his temple. **16** Then they went to their regular positions. They did it just as the Law of Moses, the man of God, required. The Levites gave the blood of the animals to the priests. The priests sprinkled it on the altar.

17 Many people in the crowd hadn't set themselves apart to the LORD. They weren't "clean." They couldn't set their lambs apart to him. So the Levites had to kill the Passover lambs for all of them. **18** Many people came from Ephraim, Manasseh, Issachar and Zebulun. Most of them hadn't made themselves pure and clean. But they still ate the Passover meal. That was against what was written in the law. But Hezekiah prayed for them. He said, "The LORD is good. May he forgive everyone **19** who wants to worship God with all his heart. God is the LORD, the God of their people. May he forgive them even if they aren't 'clean' in keeping with the rules of the temple."

20 The LORD answered Hezekiah's prayer. He healed the people.

21 The people of Israel who were in Jerusalem celebrated the Feast of Unleavened Bread. They celebrated for seven days with great joy.

The Levites and priests sang to the LORD every day. Their singing was accompanied by musical instruments. The instruments were used to praise the LORD.

22 Hezekiah spoke words that gave hope to all of the Levites. They understood how to serve the LORD well. For the seven days of the Feast they ate the share that was given to them. They also sacrificed friendship offerings. They praised the LORD, the God of their people.

23 Then the whole community agreed to celebrate the Feast for seven more days. So for another seven days they celebrated with joy.

24 Hezekiah, the king of Judah, provided 1,000 bulls and 7,000 sheep and goats for the community. The officials provided 1,000 bulls and 10,000 sheep and goats for them. A large number of priests set themselves apart to the LORD.

25 The entire community of Judah was filled with joy. So were the priests and Levites. And so were all of the people who had gathered together from Israel. That included the outsiders who had come from Israel. It also included those who lived in Judah.

26 There was great joy in Jerusalem. There hadn't been anything like it in Israel since the days of Solomon, the son of David. Solomon had been king of Israel.

27 The priests and Levites gave their blessing to the people. God heard them. Their prayer reached all the way to heaven. It's the holy place where he lives.

31 The Feast came to an end. The people of Israel who were in Jerusalem went out to the towns of Judah. They smashed the sacred stones. They cut down the poles that were used to worship the goddess Asherah. They destroyed the high places and the altars. They did those things all through Judah and Benjamin. They also did them in Ephraim and Manasseh. They destroyed all of the objects that were used to worship other gods. Then the people returned to their own towns and property.

The People Bring Gifts to the LORD

2 Hezekiah put the priests and Levites in groups based on their duties. The priests sacrificed burnt offerings and friendship offerings. The Levites served the LORD by giving thanks and singing praises at the gates of his house.

POWER-S...

G

**GIV... ...AVE SOME
THE KI...HIS OWN
...SSESSIONS TO THE
TEMPLE... THE PEOPLE
OF ISRAEL BEGAN TO
GIVE FREELY. THEY
GAVE THE FIRST
SHARE OF THE
HARVEST OF THEIR
GRAIN, FRESH WINE,
OLIVE OIL AND HONEY.
THEY ALSO GAVE THE
FIRST SHARE OF
EVERYTHING ELSE
THEIR FIELDS
PRODUCED. THEY
BROUGHT A LARGE
AMOUNT.
— 2 CHRONICLES 31:3,5 —**

3 The king gave some of his own possessions to the temple. He gave them for the morning and evening burnt offerings. He gave them for the burnt offerings for every Sabbath day. He gave them for the burnt offerings for every New Moon feast. And he gave them for the burnt offerings for every yearly appointed feast. He did it in keeping with what is written in the Law of the LORD.

4 Hezekiah gave an order to the people who were living in Jerusalem. He commanded them to give to the priests and Levites the share they owed them. Then the priests and Levites could give their full attention to the Law of the LORD.

5 The order went out. Right away the people of Israel began to give freely. They gave the first share of the harvest of their grain, fresh wine, olive oil and honey. They also gave the first share of everything else their fields produced. They brought a large amount. It was a tenth of everything.

6 The people of Israel and Judah who lived in the towns of Judah brought a tenth of their herds and flocks. They also brought a tenth of the holy things they had set apart to the LORD their God. They

...ut them in piles. 7 They began doing it in the third month. They finished in the seventh month. 8 Hezekiah and his officials came and saw the piles. When they did, they praised the LORD. And they blessed his people Israel.

9 Hezekiah asked the priests and Levites about the piles. 10 The chief priest Azariah answered him. He said, "The people have been bringing their gifts to the LORD's temple. Ever since they began to bring them, we've had enough to eat. We have even had plenty to spare. That's because the LORD has blessed his people. So we have a large amount left over." Azariah was from the family line of Zadok.

11 Hezekiah gave orders to prepare storerooms in the LORD's temple. And it was done. 12 The people were faithful. They brought in their offerings, a tenth of everything they produced, and the gifts they had set apart to the LORD. The Levite Conaniah was in charge of those things. His brother Shimei was next in command after him. 13 Conaniah and his brother Shimei had directors who worked under them. Their names were Jehiel, Azaziah, Nahath, Asahel, Jerimoth, Jozabad, Eliel, Ismakiah, Mahath and Benaiah. King Hezekiah and Azariah had appointed them. Azariah was the official who was in charge of God's temple.

14 The Levite Kore guarded the East Gate. He was in charge of the offerings people chose to give to God. He handed out the offerings that were made to the LORD. He also handed out the gifts that had been set apart to the LORD. Kore was the son of Imnah. 15 Eden, Miniamin, Jeshua, Shemaiah, Amariah and Shecaniah helped Kore. They were faithful in helping him in the towns of the priests. They handed out gifts to their brother

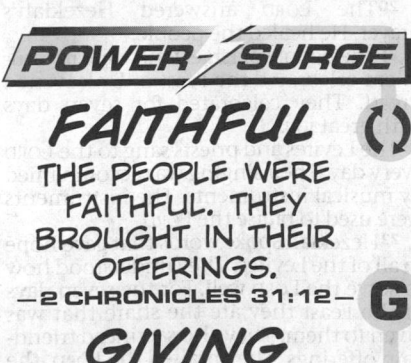

POWER-SURGE

FAITHFUL ()

**THE PEOPLE WERE
FAITHFUL. THEY
BROUGHT IN THEIR
OFFERINGS.**
—2 CHRONICLES 31:12— G

GIVING

POWER-SURGE

FAITHFUL ()

[THE LEVITES] WERE FAITHFUL IN SETTING THEMSELVES APART TO SERVE THE LORD.
— 2 CHRONICLES 31:18 —

priests, group by group. They gave the gifts to young men and old men alike.

16 In addition to that, they handed out gifts to the males who were three years old or more. The names of those males were listed in their family history. All of them would enter the LORD's temple. They would carry out their duties each day. Each group did all of the different things it was supposed to do.

17 Kore and his Levite companions also handed out gifts to the priests. The priests were listed by their families in their family history. Those Levites also handed out gifts to the Levites who were 20 years old or more. Each group did all of the different things it was supposed to do.

18 Those groups included all of the little ones, the wives, and the sons and daughters of the whole community. All of them were listed in their family history. They were faithful in setting themselves apart to serve the LORD.

19 Some of the priests, who were from the family line of Aaron, lived in other towns or on farms around their towns. Men were chosen by name to hand out shares to those priests. They gave a share to every male among them. They also gave a share to everyone whose name was written down in the family history of the Levites.

20 That's what Hezekiah did all through Judah. He did what was good and right. He was faithful to the LORD his God. **21** He looked to his God. He worked for him with all his heart. That's the way he worked in everything he did to serve God's temple. He obeyed the law. He followed the LORD's commands. So he had success.

Sennacherib's Army Surrounds Jerusalem

32 Hezekiah had been completely faithful to the LORD. But in spite of that, Sennacherib came and marched into Judah. He was the king of Assyria. He

...ruled the cities that had high walls over them. He got ready to attack them for might he could win the battle ...thought he could take

2 Hezekiah saw...

come to Jerusalem to Sennacherib had **3** So he asked his officials war against it. leaders for advice. He asked them military blocking off the water from the springs bout that were outside the city. They gave him the advice he asked for.

4 A large group of men gathered together. They blocked all of the springs. They also blocked the stream that flowed through the land. "Why should the kings of Assyria come and find plenty of water?" they asked.

5 Then Hezekiah worked hard repairing all of the broken parts of the wall. He built towers on it. He built another wall outside that one. He built up the areas that had been filled in around the City of David. He also made large numbers of weapons and shields.

6 He appointed military officers over the people. He gathered the officers together in front of him in the open area at the city gate. He gave them words of hope. He said, **7** "Be strong. Be brave. Don't be afraid. Don't lose hope. The king of Assyria has a huge army with him. But there's a greater power with us than there is with him. **8** The only thing he has is human strength. But the LORD our God is with us. He will help us. He'll fight our battles."

The people had great faith in what Hezekiah, the king of Judah, said.

9 Later Sennacherib, the king of Assyria, and all of his forces surrounded Lachish. They got ready to attack it. At that time, he sent his officers to Jerusalem. They went there with a message for Hezekiah, the king of Judah. The message was also for all of the people of Judah who were there. The message said,

10 "Sennacherib, the king of Assyria, says, 'Why are you putting your faith in what your king says? Why do you remain in Jerusalem when you are surrounded?

11 " 'Hezekiah says, "The LORD our God will save us from the powerful hand of the king of Assyria." But he isn't telling you the truth. If you listen to him, you will die of hunger and thirst.

12 " 'Didn't Hezekiah himself remove your god's high places and

POWER-STATEMENT

B

BE STRONG. BE BRAVE. DON'T BE AFRAID. DON'T LOSE HOPE. THE KING OF ASSYRIA HAS A HUGE ARMY WITH HIM. BUT THERE'S A GREATER POWER WITH US THAN THERE IS WITH HIM. THE ONLY THING HE HAS IS HUMAN STRENGTH. BUT THE LORD OUR GOD IS WITH US. HE WILL HELP US. HE'LL FIGHT OUR BATTLES.
—2 CHRONICLES 32:7-8—

STRONG

altars? Didn't Hezekiah say to the people of Judah and Jerusalem, "You must worship at one altar. You must burn sacrifices on it"?

13 " 'Don't you know what I and the kings who ruled before me have done? Don't you know what we've done to all of the peoples of the other lands? Were the gods of those nations ever able to save their lands from my power? 14The kings who ruled before me destroyed many nations. Which one of the gods of those nations has been able to save his people from me? So how can your god save you from my power?

15 " 'Don't let Hezekiah trick you. He's telling you lies. Don't believe him. No god of any nation or kingdom has been able to save his people from my power. No god has been able to save his people from the power of the kings who ruled before me. So your god won't save you from my power either!' "

16Sennacherib's officers spoke even more things against the LORD God and his servant Hezekiah. 17The king also wrote letters against the LORD. His letters made fun of the God of Israel. They said, "The peoples of other lands have their gods. But those gods didn't save their people from my powerful hand. So the god of Hezekiah won't save his people from my powerful hand either."

18Then the officers called out in the Hebrew language to the people of Jerusalem who were on the wall. They were trying to scare them and make them afraid. That's because they wanted to capture the city. 19They were comparing the God of Jerusalem to the gods of the other nations of the world. But those gods were only statues. They had been made by the hands of men.

20King Hezekiah cried out in prayer to God in heaven. He prayed about the problem Jerusalem was facing. So did the prophet Isaiah. He was the son of Amoz. 21The LORD sent an angel. The angel wiped out all of the enemy's fighting men, leaders and officers. He put an end to them right there in the camp of the Assyrian king.

So Sennacherib went back to his own land in shame. He went into the temple of his god. There some of his own sons cut him down with their swords.

22So the LORD saved Hezekiah and the people of Jerusalem. He saved them from the power of Sennacherib, the king of Assyria. He also saved them from all of their other enemies. He took care of them on every side.

23Many people brought offerings to Jerusalem for the LORD. They brought expensive gifts for Hezekiah, the king of Judah. From then on, all of the nations thought highly of him.

Hezekiah's Pride, Success and Death

24In those days Hezekiah became sick. He knew he was about to die. So he prayed to the LORD. And the LORD answered him. He gave him a miraculous sign. 25But Hezekiah's heart was proud. He didn't give thanks for the many kind things the LORD had done for him. So the LORD became angry with him. He also became angry with Judah and Jerusalem. 26Then Hezekiah had a change of heart. He was sorry he had been proud. The people of Jerusalem were also sorry they had sinned. So the LORD wasn't angry with them as long as Hezekiah was king. 27Hezekiah was very rich. He received great honor. He made storeroo... silver and gold. He also made them to... jewels, spices, shields and all kinds of expensive things. **28**He made buildings to store the harvest of grain, fresh wine and olive oil. He made barns for all kinds of cattle. He made sheep pens for his flocks. **29**He built villages. He gained large numbers of flocks and herds. God had made him very rich.

30Hezekiah blocked up the upper opening of the Gihon spring. He directed the water to flow down to the west side of the City of David. He had success in everything he did.

31The rulers of Babylon sent messengers to him. They asked him about the miraculous sign that had taken place in the land. Then God left him to put him to the test. He wanted to know everything that was in his heart.

32Hezekiah did many things that showed he was faithful to the LORD. Those things and the other events of his rule are written down. They are written in the record of the vision of the prophet Isaiah, the son of Amoz. That record is part of the records of the kings of Judah and Israel.

POWER-SURGE

FAITHFUL ()

HEZEKIAH DID MANY THINGS THAT SHOWED HE WAS FAITHFUL TO THE LORD.
— 2 CHRONICLES 32:32 —

33Hezekiah joined the members of his family who had already died. His body was buried on the hill where the tombs of David's family are. The whole nation of Judah honored him when he died. So did the people of Jerusalem. Hezekiah's son Manasseh became the next king after him.

Manasseh Becomes King of Judah

33 Manasseh was 12 years old when he became king. He ruled in Jerusalem for 55 years.

2Manasseh did what was evil in the sight of the LORD. He followed the practices of the nations. The LORD hated those practices. He had driven those nations out to make room for the people of Israel. **3**Manasseh rebuilt the high places. His

...ther Hezekiah had destroyed them. ...sseh also set up altars to the gods ...ess As... named after Baal. He made of the stars. ...e used to worship the god- ...even bowed down to all **4**He built altars ...orshiped them. The LORD had said about LORD's temple. Name will remain in Jerusa...emple, "My ...rever." **5**In both courtyards of the LORD's temple Manasseh built altars to honor all of the stars.

6He sacrificed his children in the fire to other gods. He did it in the Valley of Ben Hinnom. He practiced all kinds of evil magic. He took part in worshiping evil powers. He got messages from those who had died. He talked to the spirits of the dead. He did many things that were evil in the sight of the LORD. He made him very angry.

7Manasseh had carved a statue of a god. He put it in God's temple. God had spoken to David and his son Solomon about the temple. He had said, "My Name will be in this temple and in Jerusalem forever. Out of all of the cities in the tribes of Israel I have chosen Jerusalem. **8**I gave this land to your people who lived long ago. I will not make the Israelites leave it again. But they must be careful to do everything I commanded them. They must follow all of the laws, directions, and rules I gave them through Moses."

9But Manasseh led Judah and the people of Jerusalem down the wrong path. They did more evil things than the nations the LORD had destroyed to make room for the people of Israel.

10The LORD spoke to Manasseh and his people. But they didn't pay any attention to him. **11**So the LORD brought the army commanders of the king of Assyria against them. They took Manasseh as a prisoner. They put a hook in his nose. They put him in bronze chains. And they took him to Babylon.

12When Manasseh was in trouble, he asked the LORD his God to show favor to him. He made himself very low in the sight of the God of his people. **13**Manasseh prayed to him. When he did, the LORD felt sorry for him. He answered his prayer. He brought him back to Jerusalem and his kingdom. Then Manasseh knew that the LORD is God.

14After that, Manasseh rebuilt the outer wall of the City of David. It was west of the Gihon spring in the valley. It reached all the way to the entrance of the Fish Gate. It went around the entire hill of Ophel.

Manasseh also made the wall much high er. He stationed military com~~~~ all of the cities in Judah ~~the~~ walls around them. the strange

15Manasseh got ~~a~~ statue of one of gods. He remo~~ved~~ne LORD's temple. He those gods. all of the altars he had built also rem~~oved~~ temple hill and in Jerusalem. He on th~~e~~ threw them out of the city. **16**Then he made the LORD's altar look like new again. He sacrificed friendship offerings and thank offerings on it. He told the people of Judah to serve the LORD, the God of Israel. **17**The people continued to offer sacrifices at the high places. But they offered them only to the LORD their God.

18The other events of Manasseh's rule are written down in the official records of the kings of Israel. They include his prayer to his God. They also include the words the prophets spoke to him in the name of the LORD, the God of Israel. **19**Everything about Manasseh is written in the records of the prophets. That includes his prayer and the fact that God felt sorry for him. It includes everything he did before he made himself low in the LORD's sight. It includes all of his sins and the fact that he wasn't faithful to the LORD. It includes the locations where he built high places. It includes the places where he set up poles that were used to worship the goddess Asherah. And it includes the places where he set up statues of other gods.

20Manasseh joined the members of his family who had already died. His body was buried in his palace. His son Amon became the next king after him.

Amon Becomes King of Judah

21Amon was 22 years old when he became king. He ruled in Jerusalem for two years.

22Amon did what was evil in the sight of the LORD, just as his father Manasseh had done. Amon worshiped and offered sacrifices to all of the statues of gods that Manasseh had made. **23**He didn't make himself low in the LORD's sight as his father Manasseh had done. So Amon became even more guilty.

24Amon's officials made plans against him. They murdered him in his palace. **25**Then the people of the land killed all those who had made plans against King Amon. They made his son Josiah king in his place.

Josiah Makes Judah a Better Nation

34 Josiah was eight years old when he became king. He ruled in Jerusalem for 31 years.

2He did what was right in the eyes of the LORD. He lived the way King David had lived. He didn't turn away from it to the right or the left.

3While he was still young, he began to worship the God of King David. It was the eighth year of Josiah's rule.

In his 12th year he began to get rid of the high places in Judah and Jerusalem. He removed the poles that were used to worship the goddess Asherah. He also removed the wooden and metal statues of gods. **4**He ordered the altars of the gods that were named after Baal to be torn down. He cut to pieces the altars for burning incense that were above them. He smashed the Asherah poles. He also smashed the wooden and metal statues of gods. He broke all of them to pieces. He scattered the pieces over the graves of those who had offered sacrifices to those gods. **5**He burned the bones of the priests on their altars. That's the way he made Judah and Jerusalem pure and clean.

6He went to the towns of Manasseh, Ephraim and Simeon. He went all the way to Naphtali. He also went to the destroyed places around all of those towns. **7**Everywhere he went he tore down the altars and the Asherah poles. He crushed the statues of gods to powder. He cut to pieces all of the altars for burning incense. He destroyed all of those things everywhere in Israel. Then he went back to Jerusalem.

8In the 18th year of Josiah's rule, he decided to make the land and temple pure and clean. So he sent Shaphan, Maaseiah and Joah to repair the temple of the LORD his God. Shaphan was the son of Azaliah. Maaseiah was ruler of the city. And Joah, the son of Joahaz, kept the records.

9They went to the high priest Hilkiah. They gave him the money that had been brought into God's temple. The Levites who guarded the doors had collected it. They had received some of the money from the people of Manasseh, Ephraim and the others who remained in Israel. They had received the rest of it from the people of Judah and Benjamin and those who lived in Jerusalem.

10They put all of the money in the care of the men who had been appointed to direct the work on the LORD's temple. Those men paid the workers who repaired the temple and made it look like new again. **11**They also gave money to the builders and those who worked with wood. The workers used it to buy lumber and blocks of stone. The lumber was used for the supports and beams for the buildings. The kings of Judah had let the buildings fall down.

12The men were faithful in doing the work. Jahath and Obadiah directed them. They were Levites from the family line of Merari. Zechariah and Meshullam also directed them. They were from the family line of Kohath. The Levites were skilled in playing musical instruments. 13They were in charge of the laborers. They directed all of the workers from job to job. Some of the Levites were secretaries and writers. Others guarded the doors.

Hilkiah Finds the Scroll of the Law

14The money that had been taken into the Lord's temple was being brought out. At that time the priest Hilkiah found the Scroll of the Law of the Lord. It had been given through Moses. 15Hilkiah spoke to the secretary Shaphan. He said, "I've found the Scroll of the Law in the Lord's temple." He gave it to Shaphan.

16Then Shaphan took the scroll to King Josiah. He told him, "Your officials are doing everything they've been asked to do. 17They have paid out the money that was in the Lord's temple. They've put it in the care of the directors and workers." 18Shaphan continued, "The priest Hilkiah has given me a scroll." Shaphan read some of it to the king.

19The king heard the words of the Law. When he did, he tore his royal robes. 20He gave orders to Hilkiah, Ahikam, Abdon, the secretary Shaphan and Asaiah. Ahikam was the son of Shaphan. Abdon was the son of Micah. And Asaiah was the king's attendant. Josiah commanded them, 21"Go. Ask the Lord for advice. Ask him about what is written in this scroll that has been found. Do it for me. Also do it for those who remain in Israel and Judah. The Lord has poured out his burning anger on us. That's because our people before us didn't obey what the Lord had said. They didn't do everything that is written in this scroll."

22Hilkiah and those the king had sent with him went to speak to the prophet Huldah. She was the wife of Shallum. Shallum was the son of Tokhath. Tokhath was the son of Hasrah. Shallum took care of the sacred robes. Huldah lived in the New Quarter of Jerusalem.

23She said to them, "The Lord is the God of Israel. He says, 'Tell the man who sent you to me, 24"The Lord says, 'I am are to bring horrible trouble on this its people. All of the curses that been read down in the scroll that has place. 25That king of Judah will take deserted me. They the people have other gods. They have burned incense to angry because of everything their hands have made. So I will pour out my burning anger on this place. The fire of my anger will not be put out.' " '

26"The king of Judah sent you to ask for advice. Tell him, 'The Lord is the God of Israel. He has a message for you about the things you heard. 27He says, "Your heart was tender. You made yourself low in my sight. You heard what I spoke against this place and its people. So you made yourself low. You tore your royal robes and sobbed. And I have heard you," announces the Lord.

28" ' "You will join the members of your family who have already died. Your body will be buried in peace. Your eyes will not see all of the trouble I am going to bring on this place and those who live here." ' "

Huldah's answer was taken back to king.

29Then the king called together all of the elders of Judah and Jerusalem. 30He went up to the Lord's temple. The people of Judah and Jerusalem went with him. So did the priests and Levites. All of them went, from the least important of them to the most important. The king had all of the words of the Scroll of the Covenant read to them. The scroll had been found in the Lord's temple.

31The king stood next to his pillar. He agreed to the terms of the covenant in front of the Lord. He promised to follow him and obey his commands, directions and rules. He promised to obey them with all his heart and with all his soul. So he promised to obey the terms of the covenant that were written down in that scroll.

32Then he had everyone in Jerusalem and in Benjamin commit themselves to the covenant. The people of Jerusalem did it in keeping with the covenant of the God of Israel.

33Josiah removed all of the statues of gods from the whole territory that belonged to the people of Israel. The Lord hated those statues. Josiah had everyone in Israel serve the Lord their God. As long as he lived, they didn't fail to follow the Lord, the God of their people.

Josiah Celebrates the Passover Feast

35 Josiah celebrated ⟨the⟩ Passover Feast in Jerusalem. ⟨It was⟩ in honor of the LORD. The Passover ⟨lamb was⟩ killed on the 14th day of the ⟨first⟩ month. 2Josiah appointed the priests to their duties. He cheered them up as they served the LORD at his temple.

3The Levites taught all of the people of Israel. The Levites had been set apart to the LORD. Josiah said to them, "Put the sacred ark of the covenant in the temple Solomon built. He was the son of David and king of Israel. The ark must not be carried around on your shoulders. Serve the LORD your God. Serve his people Israel. 4Prepare yourselves by families in your groups. Do it based on the directions that were written by David, the king of Israel, and by his son Solomon.

5"Stand at the temple. Stand there with a group of Levites for each group of families among your people. 6Kill the Passover lambs. Set yourselves apart to the LORD. Prepare the lambs for your people. Do what the LORD commanded through Moses."

7Josiah provided animals for the Passover offerings. He gave them for all of the people who were there. He gave a total of 30,000 sheep and goats and 3,000 head of cattle. He gave all of them from his own possessions.

8His officials also gave freely. They gave to the people and the priests and Levites.

POWER-SURGE

GIVING G

[JOSIAH'S] OFFICIALS ALSO GAVE FREELY.
— 2 CHRONICLES 35:8 —

Hilkiah, Zechariah and Jehiel were in charge of God's temple. They gave the priests 2,600 Passover lambs and 300 head of cattle. 9Conaniah and his brothers Shemaiah and Nethanel also gave offerings. So did Hashabiah, Jeiel and Jozabad. All of them were the leaders of the Levites. They gave 5,000 Passover lambs and 500 head of cattle for the Levites.

10The Passover service was arranged. The priests stood in their places. The Levites were in their groups. That's what the king had ordered.

11The Passover lambs were killed. The priests sprinkled the blood that had been handed to them. The Levites skinned the animals.

12They set the burnt offerings to one side. Those offerings were for the smaller family groups of the people to offer to the LORD. That's what was written in the Scroll of Moses. The Levites did the same thing with the cattle.

13They cooked the Passover animals over the fire, just as the law required. They boiled the holy offerings in pots, large kettles and pans. They served the offerings quickly to all of the people.

14After that, they got things ready for themselves and the priests. That's because the priests, who were from the family line of Aaron, were busy until dark. They were sacrificing the burnt offerings and the fat parts. The Levites got things ready for themselves and for the priests, who belonged to Aaron's family line.

15Those who played music were from the family line of Asaph. They were in the places that had been set up by David, Asaph, Heman and Jeduthun. Jeduthun had been the king's prophet. The guards at each gate didn't have to leave their places. That's because their brother Levites got things ready for them.

16So at that time the entire service in honor of the LORD was carried out. The Passover Feast was celebrated. The burnt offerings were sacrificed on the LORD's altar. That's what King Josiah had ordered.

17The people of Israel who were there celebrated the Passover at that time. They observed the Feast of Unleavened Bread for seven days. 18The Passover hadn't been observed like that in Israel since the days of the prophet Samuel. None of the kings of Israel had ever celebrated a Passover like Josiah's. He celebrated it with the priests and Levites. All of the people of Judah and Israel were there along with the people of Jerusalem. 19That Passover Feast was celebrated in the 18th year of Josiah's rule.

Josiah Dies

20Josiah had put the temple in order. After all of that, Neco went up to fight at Carchemish. He was king of Egypt. Carchemish was on the Euphrates River. Josiah marched out to meet Neco in battle.

21But Neco sent messengers to him. They said, "King Josiah, there isn't any trouble between you and me. I'm not attacking you at this time. I'm at war with another country. God told me to hurry. He's with me. So stop opposing him. If you don't, he'll destroy you."

²²But Josiah wouldn't turn away from Neco. He wore different clothes so people wouldn't recognize him. He wanted to go to war against Neco. He wouldn't listen to what God had commanded Neco to say. Instead, he went out to fight him on the flatlands of Megiddo.

²³Men who had bows shot arrows at King Josiah. After he was hit, he told his officers, "Take me away. I'm badly wounded." ²⁴So they took him out of his chariot. They put him in his other chariot. They brought him to Jerusalem. There he died. His body was buried in the tombs of his family. All of the people of Judah and Jerusalem sobbed over him.

²⁵Jeremiah wrote songs of sadness about Josiah. To this very day all of the male and female singers remember Josiah by singing those songs. That became a practice in Israel. The songs are written down in the Book of the Songs of Sadness.

²⁶Josiah did many things that showed he was faithful to the LORD. Those things and the other events of Josiah's rule were in keeping with what is written in the Law of the LORD. ²⁷All of the events from beginning to end are written down. They are written in the records of the kings of **36** Israel and Judah. ¹The people of the land went and got Jehoahaz. He was the son of Josiah. The people made Jehoahaz king in Jerusalem in place of his father.

Jehoahaz Becomes King of Judah

²Jehoahaz was 23 years old when he became king. He ruled in Jerusalem for three months. ³The king of Egypt removed him from his throne in Jerusalem. The king of Egypt made the people of Judah pay him a tax of almost four tons of silver and 75 pounds of gold. ⁴Neco, the king of Egypt, made Eliakim king over Judah and Jerusalem. Eliakim was a brother of Jehoahaz. Neco changed Eliakim's name to Jehoiakim. But he took Eliakim's brother Jehoahaz with him to Egypt.

Jehoiakim Becomes King of Judah

⁵Jehoiakim was 25 years old when he became king. He ruled in Jerusalem for 11 years. He did what was evil in the sight of the LORD his God. ⁶Nebuchadnezzar attacked him. Nebuchadnezzar was king of Babylonia. He put Jehoiakim in bronze chains. And he took him to Babylon. ⁷Nebuchadnezzar also took articles from the LORD's temple. He took them to Babylon. He put them in his own temple there.

⁸The other events of Jehoiakim's rule are written in the records of the kings of Israel and Judah. He did things the LORD hated. Those things and everything that happened to him are also written in those records. His son Jehoiachin became the next king after him.

Jehoiachin Becomes King of Judah

⁹Jehoiachin was 18 years old when he became king. He ruled in Jerusalem for three months and ten days. He did what was evil in the sight of the LORD.

¹⁰In the spring, King Nebuchadnezzar sent for him. He brought him to Babylon. He also brought articles of value from the LORD's temple. He made Zedekiah king over Judah and Jerusalem. Zedekiah was Jehoiachin's uncle.

Zedekiah Becomes King of Judah

¹¹Zedekiah was 21 years old when he became king. He ruled in Jerusalem for 11 years.

¹²He did what was evil in the sight of the LORD his God. He didn't pay any attention to the message the LORD spoke through the prophet Jeremiah.

¹³Zedekiah also refused to remain under the control of King Nebuchadnezzar. The king had made him take an oath in God's name. But his heart became very stubborn. He wouldn't turn to the LORD, the God of Israel.

¹⁴And that's not all. The people and the leaders of the priests became more and more unfaithful. They followed all of the practices of the nations. The LORD hated those practices. The people and leaders made the LORD's temple "unclean." The LORD had set the temple in Jerusalem apart in a special way for himself.

Nebuchadnezzar Destroys Jerusalem

¹⁵The LORD, the God of Israel, sent word to his people through his messengers. He sent it to them again and again. He took pity on his people. He also took pity on the temple where he lived.

¹⁶But God's people made fun of his messengers. They hated his words. They laughed at his prophets. Finally the LORD's burning anger was stirred up against his people. Nothing could save them.

¹⁷The LORD brought the king of Babylonia against them. The Babylonian army

killed their young people with their swords at the temple. They didn't spare young men or women. They didn't spare the old people either. God handed all of them over to Nebuchadnezzar.

18Nebuchadnezzar carried off to Babylon all of the articles from God's temple. Some of the articles were large. Others were small. He carried off the treasures of the temple. He also carried off the treasures that belonged to the king and his officials.

19The Babylonians set God's temple on fire. They broke down the wall of Jerusalem. They burned all of the palaces. They destroyed everything of value there.

20Nebuchadnezzar took the rest of the people to Babylon as prisoners. They had escaped from being killed with swords. They served him and his sons. That lasted until the kingdom of Persia became stronger than Babylonia.

21The land of Israel enjoyed its sabbath years. It rested. That deserted land wasn't farmed for a full 70 years. What the LORD had spoken through Jeremiah came true.

22It was the first year of the rule of Cyrus. He was king of Persia. The LORD stirred him up to send a message all through his kingdom. It happened so that what the LORD had spoken through Jeremiah would come true. The message was written down. It said,

23Cyrus, the king of Persia, says,

" 'The LORD is the God of heaven. He has given me all of the kingdoms on earth. He has appointed me to build a temple for him at Jerusalem in Judah. Any one of his people among you can go up to Jerusalem. And may the LORD your God be with you.' "

EZRA

The book of Ezra records the fulfillment of God's promise to allow his people to return to Judah from captivity. They come in two groups, and Ezra leads the second group. They rebuild the temple and begin again to worship God there. The heroes of the book of Ezra are Ezra himself, an ordinary man God uses to lead his people, and the people, who work together to rebuild after they return to their homeland. Let the story of the book of Ezra help you remember that God always fulfills his promises.

HERO IN THIS BOOK . . .

EZRA
PAGE 564

Cyrus Helps the Jews Build the LORD's Temple

1 It was the first year of the rule of Cyrus. He was king of Persia. The LORD stirred him up to send a message all through his kingdom. It happened so that what the LORD had spoken through Jeremiah would come true. The message was written down. It said,

2 "Cyrus, the king of Persia, says,
  " 'The LORD is the God of heaven. He has given me all of the kingdoms on earth. He has appointed me to build a temple for him at Jerusalem in Judah.
  3 " 'Any one of his people among you can go up to Jerusalem. And may your God be with you. You can build the LORD's temple. He is the God of Israel. He is the God who is in Jerusalem.
  4 " 'The people who are still left alive in every place must bring him gifts. They must provide him with silver and gold. They must bring goods and livestock. They should also bring any offerings they choose to. All of those gifts will be for God's temple in Jerusalem.' "

5 Then everyone God had stirred up got ready to go. They wanted to go up to Jerusalem and build the LORD's temple there. They included the family leaders of Judah and Benjamin. They also included the priests and Levites. 6 All of their neighbors helped them. They gave them silver and gold articles. They gave them goods and livestock. And they gave them gifts of great value. All of those things were added to the other offerings the people chose to give. 7 King Cyrus also brought out the articles that belonged to the LORD's temple. Nebuchadnezzar had carried them off from Jerusalem. He had put them in the temple of his own god. 8 Cyrus, the king of Persia, told Mithredath to bring them out. Mithredath was in charge of the temple treasures. He counted the articles. Then he gave them to Sheshbazzar, the prince of Judah.

9 Here is a list of the articles.

There were 30 gold dishes.
There were 1,000 silver dishes.
There were 29 silver pans.
10 There were 30 gold bowls.
There were 410 matching silver bowls.
There were 1,000 other articles.

11 The total number of gold and silver articles was 5,400. Sheshbazzar took all of them with him to Jerusalem. He brought them along when the Jews who had been forced to leave Judah came back from Babylon.

A List of People Who Returned to Judah

2 Nebuchadnezzar had taken many Jews away from the land of Judah. He had forced them to go to Babylonia as prisoners. Now they returned to Jerusalem and Judah. All of them went back to their own towns. Nebuchadnezzar was king of Babylonia. 2 The leaders of the Jews included Zerubbabel, Jeshua, Nehemiah, Seraiah and Reelaiah. They also included Mordecai, Bilshan, Mispar, Bigvai, Rehum and Baanah.

Here is a list of the men of Israel who returned home.

3 There were 2,172 from the family line of Parosh.
4 There were 372 from Shephatiah.
5 There were 775 from Arah.

POWER-SURGE

GIVING   G

ALL OF THEIR NEIGHBORS HELPED [THOSE RETURNING TO JERUSALEM]. THEY GAVE THEM SILVER AND GOLD ARTICLES. THEY GAVE THEM GOODS AND LIVESTOCK. AND THEY GAVE THEM GIFTS OF GREAT VALUE. ALL OF THOSE THINGS WERE ADDED TO THE OTHER OFFERINGS THE PEOPLE CHOSE TO GIVE.
— EZRA 1:6 —

HELPFUL

⁶There were 2,812 from Pahath-Moab through the family line of Jeshua and Joab.
⁷There were 1,254 from Elam.
⁸There were 945 from Zattu.
⁹There were 760 from Zaccai.
¹⁰There were 642 from Bani.
¹¹There were 623 from Bebai.
¹²There were 1,222 from Azgad.
¹³There were 666 from Adonikam.
¹⁴There were 2,056 from Bigvai.
¹⁵There were 454 from Adin.
¹⁶There were 98 from Ater through the family line of Hezekiah.
¹⁷There were 323 from Bezai.
¹⁸There were 112 from Jorah.
¹⁹There were 223 from Hashum.
²⁰There were 95 from Gibbar.

²¹There were 123 from the men of Bethlehem.
²²There were 56 from Netophah.
²³There were 128 from Anathoth.
²⁴There were 42 from Azmaveth.
²⁵There were 743 from Kiriath Jearim, Kephirah and Beeroth.
²⁶There were 621 from Ramah and Geba.
²⁷There were 122 from Micmash.
²⁸There were 223 from Bethel and Ai.
²⁹There were 52 from Nebo.
³⁰There were 156 from Magbish.
³¹There were 1,254 from the other Elam.
³²There were 320 from Harim.
³³There were 725 from Lod, Hadid and Ono.
³⁴There were 345 from Jericho.
³⁵There were 3,630 from Senaah.

³⁶Here is a list of the priests.

There were 973 from the family line of Jedaiah through the line of Jeshua.
³⁷There were 1,052 from Immer.
³⁸There were 1,247 from Pashhur.
³⁹There were 1,017 from Harim.

⁴⁰Here is a list of the Levites.

There were 74 from the family lines of Jeshua and Kadmiel through the line of Hodaviah.

⁴¹Here is a list of the singers.

There were 128 from the family line of Asaph.

⁴²Here is a list of the men who guarded the temple gates.

There were 139 from the family lines of
Shallum, Ater, Talmon, Akkub, Hatita and Shobai.

⁴³Here is a list of the members of the family lines of the temple servants.

Ziha, Hasupha, Tabbaoth,
⁴⁴Keros, Siaha, Padon,
⁴⁵Lebanah, Hagabah, Akkub,
⁴⁶Hagab, Shalmai, Hanan,
⁴⁷Giddel, Gahar, Reaiah,
⁴⁸Rezin, Nekoda, Gazzam,
⁴⁹Uzza, Paseah, Besai,
⁵⁰Asnah, Meunim, Nephussim,
⁵¹Bakbuk, Hakupha, Harhur,
⁵²Bazluth, Mehida, Harsha,
⁵³Barkos, Sisera, Temah,
⁵⁴Neziah, Hatipha

⁵⁵Here is a list of the members of the family lines of the servants of Solomon.

Sotai, Hassophereth, Peruda,
⁵⁶Jaala, Darkon, Giddel,
⁵⁷Shephatiah, Hattil, Pokereth-Hazzebaim, Ami

⁵⁸The total number of the members of the family lines of the temple servants and the servants of Solomon was 392.

⁵⁹Many people came up to Judah from the towns of Tel Melah, Tel Harsha, Kerub, Addon and Immer. But they weren't able to prove that their families belonged to the people of Israel.

⁶⁰There were 652 of them from the family lines of
Delaiah, Tobiah and Nekoda.

⁶¹Here is a list of the members of the family lines of the priests.

They were Hobaiah, Hakkoz and Barzillai. Barzillai had married a daughter of Barzillai from Gilead. So he was also called Barzillai.
⁶²The priests looked for their family records. But they couldn't find them. So they weren't able to serve as priests. They weren't "clean."
⁶³The governor gave them an order. He told them not to eat any of the most sacred food. They had to wait until there was a priest who could use the Urim and Thummim to find out what the LORD wanted them to do.

POWER-SURGE

GIVING G

ALL OF THE PEOPLE ARRIVED AT THE LORD'S TEMPLE IN JERUSALEM. THEN SOME OF THE LEADERS OF THE FAMILIES BROUGHT OFFERINGS THEY CHOSE TO GIVE. THEY WOULD BE USED FOR REBUILDING THE HOUSE OF GOD...THE PEOPLE GAVE MONEY FOR THE WORK.

—— EZRA 2:68-69 ——

64The total number of the entire group that returned was 42,360. 65That didn't include their 7,337 male and female slaves. There were also 200 male and female singers. 66And there were 736 horses, 245 mules, 67435 camels and 6,720 donkeys.

68All of the people arrived at the LORD's temple in Jerusalem. Then some of the leaders of the families brought offerings they chose to give. They would be used for rebuilding the house of God. It would stand in the same place it had been before. 69The people gave money for the work. It was based on how much they had. They gave 1,100 pounds of gold. They also gave three tons of silver. And they gave 100 sets of clothes for the priests. All of that was added to the temple treasure.

70The priests and Levites settled in their own towns. So did the singers, the men who guarded the gates, and the temple servants. The rest of the people of Israel also settled in their own towns.

The People Rebuild the Altar

3 The people of Israel had settled down in their towns. In the seventh month all of them gathered together in Jerusalem. 2Then Jeshua began to build the altar for burnt offerings to honor the God of Israel. Jeshua was the son of Jehozadak. The other priests helped Jeshua. So did Zerubbabel and his men. They built the altar in keeping with what is written in the Law of Moses. Moses was a man of God. Zerubbabel was the son of Shealtiel.

3The people who built the altar were afraid of the nations that were around them. But they built it anyway. They set it up where it had stood before. They sacrificed burnt offerings on it to the LORD. They offered the morning and evening sacrifices on it.

4Then they celebrated the Feast of Booths. They did it in keeping with what is written in the Law. They sacrificed the number of burnt offerings that were required for each day.

5After they celebrated the Feast of Booths, they sacrificed the regular burnt offerings. They offered the New Moon sacrifices. They also offered the sacrifices for all of the appointed sacred feasts of the LORD. And they sacrificed the offerings the people chose to give him. 6On the first day of the seventh month they began to offer burnt offerings to the LORD. They did it even though the foundation of the LORD's temple hadn't been finished yet.

The People Begin to Rebuild the Temple

7The people gave money to those who worked with stone and those who worked with wood. They gave food and drink and olive oil to the people of Sidon and Tyre. Then those people brought cedar logs down from Lebanon to the Mediterranean Sea. They floated them down to Joppa. Cyrus, the king of Persia, authorized them to do it.

8It was the second month of the second year after they had arrived at the house of God in Jerusalem. Zerubbabel, the son of Shealtiel, began the work. Jeshua, the son of Jehozadak, helped him. So did everyone else. That included the priests and Levites. It also included the rest of those who had returned to Jerusalem. They had been prisoners in Babylonia. Levites who were 20 years old or more were appointed to be in charge of building the LORD's house.

9Those who joined together to direct the work included Jeshua and his sons and brothers. They also included Kadmiel and his sons. And they included the sons of Henadad and all of their sons and brothers. All of those men were Levites. Kadmiel and his sons were members of the family line of Hodaviah.

10The builders laid the foundation of

the LORD's temple. Then the priests came. They were wearing their special clothes. They brought their trumpets with them. The Levites who belonged to the family line of Asaph also came. They brought their cymbals with them. The priests and Levites took their places to praise the LORD. They did everything just as King David had required them to. **11**They sang to the LORD. They praised him. They gave thanks to him. They said,

"The LORD is good.
His faithful love to Israel continues
    forever."

FAITHFUL ()

THEY SANG TO THE LORD. THEY PRAISED HIM. THEY GAVE THANKS TO HIM. THEY SAID,

"THE LORD IS GOOD. HIS FAITHFUL LOVE TO ISRAEL CONTINUES FOREVER."

ALL OF THE PEOPLE GAVE A LOUD SHOUT. THEY PRAISED THE LORD.
—— EZRA 3:11 —— ♣

THANKFUL

All of the people gave a loud shout. They praised the LORD. They were glad because the foundation of the LORD's temple had been laid.

12But many of the older priests and Levites and family leaders sobbed out loud. They had seen the first temple. So when they saw the foundation of the second temple being laid, they sobbed. Others shouted with joy.

13No one could tell the difference between the shouts of joy and the sounds of sobbing. That's because the people made so much noise. The sound was heard far away.

Enemies Oppose the Rebuilding of the Temple

4 The enemies of Judah and Benjamin heard about what the people who had returned from Babylonia were doing. They heard that they were building a temple to honor the LORD. He is the God of Israel. **2**The enemies came to Zerubbabel. The family leaders of Israel were with him. The enemies said, "We want to help you build. We're just like you. We worship your God. We offer sacrifices to him. We've been doing that ever since the time of Esarhaddon. He was king of Assyria. He brought our people here."

3Zerubbabel and Jeshua answered them. So did the rest of the family leaders of Israel. They said, "You can't help us build a temple to honor our God. You aren't part of us. We'll build it ourselves. We'll do it to honor the LORD. He is the God of Israel. Cyrus, the king of Persia, commanded us to build it."

4Then the nations that were around Judah tried to make its people lose hope. They wanted to make them afraid to go on building. **5**So they hired advisers to work against them. They wanted their plans to fail. They did it during the whole time Cyrus was king of Persia. They kept doing it until Darius became king.

Later Enemies Also Oppose the Jews

6The enemies of the Jews brought charges against the people of Judah and Jerusalem. It happened when Xerxes began to rule over Persia.

7Then Artaxerxes became king of Persia. During his rule, Bishlam, Mithredath, Tabeel and their friends wrote a letter to him. It was written in the Aramaic language. And it used the Aramaic alphabet.

8Rehum and Shimshai also wrote a letter to King Artaxerxes. Rehum was the commanding officer. Shimshai was the secretary. Their letter was against the people of Jerusalem. It said,

9We, Rehum and Shimshai, are writing this letter. Rehum is the commanding officer. Shimshai is the secretary. Our friends join us in writing. They include the judges and officials who are in charge of the people from Tripolis, Persia, Erech and Babylon. They are also over the Elamites from Susa. **10**And they are over those who were forced to leave their countries. The great King Ashurbanipal, who is worthy of honor, forced them to leave. He settled them in the city of Samaria. He also settled them in other places west of the Euphrates River.

11 Here is a copy of the letter that was sent to Artaxerxes.

We are sending this letter to you, King Artaxerxes.

It is from your servants who live west of the Euphrates River.

12 We want you to know that the Jews who left you and came up to us have gone to Jerusalem. They are rebuilding that evil city. It has caused trouble for a long time. The Jews are making its walls like new again. They are repairing the foundations.

13 Here is something else we want you to know. Suppose this city is rebuilt. And suppose its walls are made like new again. Then no more taxes, gifts or fees will be collected. And there will be less money for you.

14 We owe a lot to you. We don't want to see dishonor brought on you. So we're sending this letter to tell you what is going on. **15** Then you can have a search made in the official records. Have someone check the records of the kings who ruled before you.

If you do, you will find out that Jerusalem is an evil city. It causes trouble for kings and countries. For a long time the city has refused to let anyone rule over it. That's why it was destroyed. **16** We want you to know that this city shouldn't be rebuilt. Its walls shouldn't be made like new again. If that happens, you won't have anything left west of the Euphrates River.

17 The king replied,

I am writing this letter to Rehum, the commanding officer. I am also writing it to Shimshai, the secretary. And I am writing it to your friends who are living in Samaria and in other places west of the Euphrates River.

I give you my greetings.

18 The letter you sent us has been read to me. It has been explained to me in my language. **19** I gave an order. I had a search made. We found out that Jerusalem has a long history of turning against the kings of the countries that have ruled over it. It

has refused to remain under their control. It is always stirring up trouble. **20** Jerusalem has had powerful kings. Some of them ruled over everything west of the Euphrates. Taxes, gifts and fees were paid to them.

21 So give an order to those men. Make them stop their work. Then the city won't be rebuilt until I give the order. **22** Pay careful attention to this matter. Why should we let this danger grow? That would not be in our best interests.

23 The copy of the letter of King Artaxerxes was read to Rehum and the secretary Shimshai. It was also read to their friends. Right away they went to the Jews in Jerusalem. They forced them to stop their work.

24 And so the work on the house of God in Jerusalem came to an end. Nothing more was done on it until the second year that Darius was king of Persia.

Tattenai Sends a Letter to King Darius

5 The prophets Haggai and Zechariah prophesied to the Jews in Judah and Jerusalem. They spoke to them in the name of the God of Israel. He had spoken to those prophets. Zechariah belonged to the family line of Iddo.

2 Zerubbabel, the son of Shealtiel, began to work. So did Jeshua, the son of Jehozadak. They began to rebuild the house of God in Jerusalem. The prophets of God were right there with them. They were helping them.

3 At that time Tattenai was governor of the land west of the Euphrates River. He and Shethar-Bozenai and their friends went to the Jews. They asked them, "Who authorized you to rebuild this temple? Who told you that you could make this building like new again?" **4** They also asked, "What are the names of the men who are putting up this building?"

5 But the God of the Jews was watching over their elders. So they didn't have to stop their work. First a report would have to be sent to Darius. Then they would have to receive his answer in writing.

6 Here is a copy of the letter that was sent to King Darius. It was from Tattenai, the governor of the land west of the Euphrates. Shethar-Bozenai joined him in writing it. So did their friends. They were officials of that land. **7** The report they sent to the king said,

We are sending this letter to you, King Darius.

We give you our most friendly greetings.

⁸We want you to know that we went to the land of Judah. We went to the temple of the great God. The people are building it with large stones. They are putting wooden beams in the walls. The people are working hard. The work is moving ahead very quickly under the direction of the people.

⁹We asked the elders some questions. We said to them, "Who authorized you to rebuild this temple? Who told you that you could make this building like new again?" ¹⁰We also asked them their names. We wanted to write down the names of their leaders for your information.

¹¹Here is the answer they gave us. They said,

"We serve the God of heaven and earth. We are rebuilding the temple that was built many years ago. The great King Solomon built it and finished it. ¹²But our people made the God of heaven angry. So he handed them over to Nebuchadnezzar from Chaldea. He was king of Babylonia. He destroyed this temple. He forced the Jews to leave their own country. He took them away to Babylonia.

¹³"But King Cyrus gave an order to rebuild this house of God. He gave it in the first year he was king of Babylonia. ¹⁴He even removed some gold and silver articles from the temple of Babylon. Nebuchadnezzar had brought them there from the house of God in Jerusalem. He had taken them to the temple in Babylon.

"Then King Cyrus brought them out. He gave them to a man named Sheshbazzar. Cyrus had appointed him as governor. ¹⁵He told him, 'Take these articles with you. Go and put them in the temple in Jerusalem. Rebuild the house of God in the same place where it stood before.'

¹⁶"So Sheshbazzar made the trip to Jerusalem. He laid the foundations of the house of God there. From that day until now the people have been working on it. But they haven't finished it yet."

¹⁷If it pleases you, King Darius, let a search be made in the official records of the kings of Babylonia. Find out whether King Cyrus really did give an order to rebuild this house of God in Jerusalem. Then tell us what you decide to do.

King Darius Sends a Reply to Tattenai

6 King Darius gave an order. He had a search made in the official records that were stored among the treasures at Babylon. ²A scroll was found in a safe storeroom at Ecbatana in the land of Media. Here is what was written on it.

This is my official reply to your letter.

³In the first year that Cyrus was king, he gave an order. It concerned God's temple in Jerusalem. It said,

Rebuild the temple. Then the Jews can offer sacrifices there. Lay its foundations. The temple must be 90 feet high and 90 feet wide. ⁴Its walls must have three layers of large stones. They must also have a layer of beautiful wood. Use money from the royal treasures to pay for everything.

⁵The gold and silver articles from the house of God must be returned. Nebuchadnezzar had taken them from the first temple in Jerusalem. And he had brought them to Babylon. Now they must be returned to their places in the temple at Jerusalem. They must be put in the house of God there.

⁶Tattenai, you are governor of the land west of the Euphrates River. I want you to stay away from the temple in Jerusalem. Shethar-Bozenai and the other officials of that area must also stay away from it. ⁷Don't try to stop the work on God's temple. Let the governor of the Jews and their elders rebuild the house of their God. Let them build it in the same place where it stood before.

⁸Here is what I want you to do for the elders of the Jews. Here is how you must help the men who build the house of their God.

Pay all of their expenses from the royal treasures. Use the money you collect from the people who live west of the Euphrates. Don't let the work on the temple stop. ⁹Don't fail to give the priests in Jerusalem what they ask for each day. Give them what they need. Give them young bulls, rams and male lambs. The priests can use them to sacrifice burnt offerings to the God of heaven. Also give them wheat, salt, wine and olive oil. **10**Give them those things so they can offer sacrifices that please the God of heaven. And I want them to pray that things will go well for me and my sons.

11Don't change this order. If a man tries to change it, he must be put to death. A pole must be pulled from his house. The pole must be stuck through his body. Then it must be set up where people can see it. Because the man tried to change my royal order, his house must be broken to pieces. **12**God has chosen to put his Name in the temple at Jerusalem. May he wipe out any king or nation that lifts a hand to change this order. May he also wipe out anyone who tries to destroy the temple in Jerusalem.

That's what I have ordered. I am King Darius. Make sure you carry out my order.

The Temple Is Completed and Set Apart to God

13The governor Tattenai carried out the order King Darius had sent. So did Shethar-Bozenai and their friends.

14The elders of the Jews continued to build the temple. They enjoyed great success because of the preaching of the prophets Haggai and Zechariah. Zechariah belonged to the family line of Iddo.

The people finished building the temple. That's what the God of Israel had commanded them to do. Cyrus and Darius had given orders allowing them to do it. Later, Artaxerxes supplied many things that were needed in the temple. Those three men were kings of Persia.

15So the temple was completed on the third day of the month of Adar. It was in the sixth year that Darius was king.

16When the house of God was set apart, the people of Israel celebrated with joy. The priests and Levites joined them. So did the rest of those who had returned from Babylonia. **17**When the house of God was set apart to him, the people sacrificed 100 bulls. They also sacrificed 200 rams and 400 male lambs. As a sin offering for the whole nation of Israel, the people sacrificed 12 male goats. One goat was sacrificed for each tribe in Israel.

18The priests were appointed to their companies. And the Levites were appointed to their groups. All of them served God at Jerusalem. They served him in keeping with what is written in the Scroll of Moses.

The People Celebrate the Passover Feast

19Those who had returned from Babylonia celebrated the Passover Feast. It was on the 14th day of the first month. **20**The priests and Levites had made themselves pure and clean. The Levites killed the Passover lamb for everyone who had returned from Babylonia. They also did it for themselves and their relatives, the priests.

21So the people of Israel who had returned ate the Passover lamb. They ate it together with all those who had separated themselves from the practices of their neighbors who weren't Jews. Those practices were "unclean." The people worshiped the LORD. He is the God of Israel.

22For seven days they celebrated the Feast of Unleavened Bread with joy. That's because the LORD had filled them with joy. They were glad because he had changed the mind of the king of Persia. So the king had helped them with the work on the house of the God of Israel.

Ezra Comes to Jerusalem

7 After all of those things had happened, Ezra came up to Jerusalem from Babylonia. It was during the rule of Artaxerxes. He was king of Persia. Ezra was the son of Seraiah. Seraiah was the son of Azariah. Azariah was the son of Hilkiah. **2**Hilkiah was the son of Shallum. Shallum was the son of Zadok. Zadok was the son of Ahitub. **3**Ahitub was the son of Amariah. Amariah was the son of Azariah. Azariah was the son of Meraioth. **4**Meraioth was the son of Zerahiah. Zerahiah was the son of Uzzi. Uzzi was the son of Bukki. **5**Bukki was the son of Abishua. Abishua was the son of Phinehas. Phinehas was the son of Eleazar. And Eleazar was the son of the chief priest Aaron.

6So Ezra came up from Babylonia. He was a teacher. He knew the Law of Moses very well. The LORD had given Israel that law. He is the God of Israel. The king had given Ezra everything he asked for. That's because the powerful hand of the LORD his God helped him.

7Some of the people of Israel came up to Jerusalem too. They included priests, Levites and singers. They also included the temple servants and those who guard-

POWER SURGE

OBEYS ✔

EZRA HAD COMMITTED
HIMSELF TO STUDY
AND OBEY THE LAW OF
THE LORD. HE ALSO
WANTED TO TEACH
THE LORD'S RULES
AND LAWS IN ISRAEL.
— EZRA 7:10 —

W

WISE

ed the temple gates. It was in the seventh year that Artaxerxes was king.

⁸Ezra arrived in Jerusalem in the fifth month of the seventh year of the king's rule. ⁹Ezra had begun his journey from Babylonia on the first day of the first month. He arrived in Jerusalem on the first day of the fifth month. That's because the gracious hand of his God helped him.

¹⁰Ezra had committed himself to study and obey the Law of the LORD. He also wanted to teach the LORD's rules and laws in Israel.

King Artaxerxes Gives Ezra a Letter

¹¹Ezra was a priest and teacher. He was an educated man. He knew the LORD's commands and rules for Israel very well. Here is a copy of a letter King Artaxerxes had given to Ezra. It said,

¹²I, Artaxerxes, am writing this letter. I am the greatest king of all.

I have given it to the priest Ezra. He is a teacher of the Law of the God of heaven.

I give you my greetings.

¹³Ezra, there are people from Israel in my kingdom. I am giving an order that any of them who want to go to Jerusalem with you can go. The order also allows priests and Levites to go with you.

¹⁴I and my seven advisers are sending you to see how things are going in Judah and Jerusalem. Find out whether the people there are obeying the Law of your God. You have a copy of that law with you.

¹⁵I and my advisers have freely given some silver and gold to the God of Israel. He lives in Jerusalem. Take the silver and gold with you. ¹⁶Also take any other silver and gold you can get from the land of Babylonia. And take the offerings the people and priests choose to give for the temple of their God in Jerusalem. ¹⁷Make sure you use the money to buy bulls, rams and male lambs. Also buy their grain offerings and drink offerings. Then sacrifice them on the altar of the temple of your God in Jerusalem.

¹⁸You and the other Jews can do what you think is best with the rest of the silver and gold. Do what your God wants you to do. ¹⁹Give to the God of Jerusalem all of the articles you are accountable for. Use them for worshiping your God in his temple. ²⁰You might need to supply some other things for the temple of your God. If you do, take them from among the royal treasures.

²¹I, King Artaxerxes, also give this order. It applies to all those who are in charge of the treasures west of the Euphrates River. Make sure you provide anything the priest Ezra might ask you to give. He is a teacher of the Law of the God of heaven. ²²Give Ezra up to three and three-fourths tons of silver. Give him up to 600 bushels of wheat. Give him up to 600 gallons of wine. Also give him up to 600 gallons of olive oil. And give him as much salt as he needs.

²³Work hard for the temple of the God of heaven. Do everything he has required. I don't want him to be angry with my kingdom and the kingdom of my sons.

²⁴I want you to know that you don't have any authority to collect taxes, gifts or fees from these people. You can't collect them from the priests, Levites, singers or those who guard the temple gates. And you can't collect them from the temple servants or other workers at the house of God in Jerusalem.

²⁵Ezra, appoint judges and other court officials. When you do it, use the wisdom your God gives you. Those you appoint should do what is right and fair when they judge people. They should do it for everyone who lives west of the Euphrates.

WISE

USE THE WISDOM YOUR GOD GIVES YOU.
— EZRA 7:25 —

They should do it for everyone who knows the laws of your God. And I want you to teach the people who don't know those laws.

26 Anyone who doesn't obey the law of your God must be punished. The same thing applies to anyone who doesn't obey my law. The people must be punished in keeping with the laws they have broken. Some of them must be put to death. Others must be forced to leave the places where they live. Others must have their property taken away from them. Still others must be put in prison.

Ezra Praises the LORD

27 People of Israel, give praise to the LORD. He is the God of our people who lived long ago. He has put it in the king's heart to bring honor to the LORD's temple in Jerusalem. The king has honored the LORD in his letter. 28 The LORD has shown his good favor to me. He has caused the king and his advisers to show me their favor. In fact, all of the king's powerful officials have shown favor to me. The strong hand of the LORD my God helped me. That gave me new strength. So I gathered together leaders from Israel to go up to Jerusalem with me.

The Family Leaders Who Returned to Jerusalem With Ezra

8 Many family leaders came up to Jerusalem with me from Babylonia. So did others who were listed with them. It was during the time when Artaxerxes was king. Here is a list of those who came.

2 Gershom came from the family line of Phinehas.

Daniel came from the family line of Ithamar.

Hattush came from the family line of David. 3 Hattush also belonged to the family of Shecaniah.

Zechariah came from the family line of Parosh. The total number of men who were listed with him was 150.

4 Eliehoenai came from the family line of Pahath-Moab. Eliehoenai was the son of Zerahiah. The total number of men with him was 200.

5 Shecaniah came from the family line of Zattu. Shecaniah was the son of Jahaziel. The total number of men with him was 300.

6 Ebed came from the family line of Adin. Ebed was the son of Jonathan. The total number of men with him was 50.

7 Jeshaiah came from the family line of Elam. Jeshaiah was the son of Athaliah. The total number of men with him was 70.

8 Zebadiah came from the family line of Shephatiah. Zebadiah was the son of Michael. The total number of men with him was 80.

9 Obadiah came from the family line of Joab. Obadiah was the son of Jehiel. The total number of men with him was 218.

10 Shelomith came from the family line of Bani. Shelomith was the son of Josiphiah. The total number of men with him was 160.

11 Zechariah came from the family line of Bebai. Zechariah was the son of Bebai. The total number of men with him was 28.

12 Johanan came from the family line of Azgad. Johanan was the son of Hakkatan. The total number of men with him was 110.

13 Eliphelet, Jeuel and Shemaiah came

KIND

K

ALL OF THE KING'S POWERFUL OFFICIALS HAVE SHOWN FAVOR TO ME. THE STRONG HAND OF THE LORD MY GOD HELPED ME. THAT GAVE ME NEW STRENGTH.
— EZRA 7:28 —

STRONG

from the family line of Adonikam. Some members of their family had gone up to Jerusalem before them. The total number of men with them was 60.

14 Uthai and Zaccur came from the family line of Bigvai. The total number of men with them was 70.

Ezra Leads Many Jews Back to Jerusalem

15 I gathered the people together at the waterway that flows toward Ahava. We camped there for three days. I looked for Levites among the people and priests. But I didn't find any. 16 So I sent for Eliezer, Ariel, Shemaiah, Elnathan and Jarib. I also sent for Elnathan, Nathan, Zechariah and Meshullam. All of them were leaders. And I sent for Joiarib and Elnathan. They were very well educated.

17 I sent all of those men to Iddo. He was the leader in Casiphia. He and his relatives were temple servants there. I told my men what to say to them. I wanted Iddo and his relatives to bring some attendants to us for the house of our God.

18 The gracious hand of our God helped us. So they brought us Sherebiah. He was a man of ability. He came from the family line of Mahli. Mahli was the son of Levi. Levi was a son of Israel. They also brought us Sherebiah's sons and brothers. The total number of men was 18. 19 And they brought Hashabiah and his brothers and nephews. They brought them together with Jeshaiah. He came from the family line of Merari. The total number of men was 20. 20 They also brought 220 of the temple servants. That was a special group David and his officials had established. They were supposed to help the Levites. All of them were listed by name.

21 I announced a fast by the waterway that flows toward Ahava. I told the people not to eat any food. In that way, we made ourselves low in the sight of God. We prayed that he would give us and our children a safe journey. We asked him to keep safe everything we owned.

22 I was ashamed to ask King Artaxerxes for soldiers and horsemen. They could have kept us safe from enemies on the road. But we had told the king that our God would keep us safe. We had said, "The gracious hand of our God helps everyone who looks to him. But he becomes very angry with anyone who deserts him."

23 So we didn't eat anything. We prayed to our God about all of those matters. And he answered our prayers.

24 Then I set 12 of the leading priests apart. I also set apart Sherebiah, Hashabiah and ten of their relatives.

25 I weighed out to them the offering of silver and gold and other articles. They had been given for the house of our God. The king, his advisers and officials, and all of the people of Israel who were there had given them. 26 I weighed out 25 tons of silver to those men. I weighed out almost four tons of silver articles. I weighed out almost four tons of gold. 27 I weighed out 20 gold bowls. They weighed 19 pounds. I also weighed out two fine articles. The bronze they were made out of was highly polished. They were as priceless as gold.

28 I said to those men, "You are set apart to the Lord. So are these articles. The silver and gold were offered to the Lord by those who chose to give them. He is the God of your people. 29 Guard all of those things carefully until you weigh them out. Weigh them in the special rooms of the Lord's temple in Jerusalem. Do it in front of the leading priests and the Levites. Make sure the family leaders of Israel are watching."

30 Then the priests and Levites received the silver and gold and sacred articles. All of them had been weighed out. They were going to take them to the house of our God in Jerusalem.

31 On the 12th day of the first month we started out. We left the waterway that flows toward Ahava. And we headed for Jerusalem. The powerful hand of our God helped us. He kept us safe from enemies and robbers along the way. 32 So we arrived in Jerusalem. There we rested for three days.

33 On the fourth day we weighed out the silver and gold. We also weighed out the sacred articles. We weighed everything in the house of our God. We handed all of it over to the priest Meremoth. He was the son of Uriah. Eleazar, Jozabad and Noadiah were with him. Eleazar was the son of Phinehas. Jozabad was the son of Jeshua. Noadiah was the son of Binnui. Jozabad and Noadiah were Levites. 34 Everything was listed by number and weight. And the total weight was recorded at that time.

35 Then the people sacrificed burnt offerings to the God of Israel. They had returned from Babylonia. They offered 12 bulls for the whole nation of Israel. They offered 96 rams and 77 male lambs. All of that was a burnt offering to the Lord.

They sacrificed 12 male goats as a sin offering. 36They also handed over the king's orders. They gave them to the royal officials and governors who ruled over the land west of the Euphrates River. Then those men helped the people. They also did many things for the house of God.

Ezra Prays for the People

9 After all of those things had been done, the leaders came to me. They said, "The people of Israel have committed sins. Even the priests and Levites have sinned. They haven't kept themselves separate from the nations that are around them. The LORD hates the practices of those nations. He hates what the Canaanites, Hittites, Perizzites and Jebusites do. He also hates what the Ammonites, Moabites, Egyptians and Amorites do. 2"The men of Israel have gotten married to the daughters of some of those people. They've also taken some of those women for their sons to marry. So they've mixed our holy nation with the nations around us. By getting married to women who don't worship the LORD, we leaders and officials have led the way in breaking our covenant with him. We haven't been faithful to him."

3When I heard that, I tore my inner robe and my coat. I pulled hair from my head and beard. I was so shocked I sat down. 4Then everyone who trembled with fear because of what the God of Israel had said gathered around me. They came because the people who had returned from Babylonia had not been faithful. So I sat there in shock until the time of the evening sacrifice.

5Then I got up. I had been very sad for quite a while. My inner robe and my coat were torn. I fell down on my knees. I spread my hands out to the LORD my God. 6I prayed,

"You are my God. I'm filled with shame and dishonor. I can hardly look to you and pray. That's because our sins are piled up above our heads. Our guilt reaches all the way to the heavens. 7We are filled with it. It has been like that ever since the days of our people who lived long ago.

"Kings of other countries have killed many of us and our kings and priests with their swords. They've forced others to leave their own land. They've taken them away as prisoners. They've robbed others. They've made still others feel ashamed and dishonored.

"All of those things have happened to us because we've committed so many sins. And that's how things still are to this very day. 8"But you are the LORD our God. Now you have shown us your favor for a short time. You have allowed a few of us to remain here. Your temple has given us new hope. So you have made things easier for us. You have given us a little rest from our slavery. 9We are still slaves. But you are our God. You haven't deserted us. You haven't left us in our slavery. You have been kind to us. The kings of Persia have seen it. You have given us new life to repair your temple and rebuild it. You have given us a place of safety in Judah and Jerusalem.

10"You are our God. What can we say after the way you have blessed us? We said no to what you commanded us to do.

11"You gave us your commands through your servants the prophets. You said, 'You are entering the land to take it as your own. The sinful practices of its people have polluted it. They have filled it with their unclean acts from one end to the other. The LORD hates all of their practices. 12So don't let your daughters get married to their sons. And don't let their daughters marry your sons. Don't make a peace treaty with them at any time. Then you will be strong. You will eat the good things the land produces. And you will leave all of it to your children as their share. They and their children after them will enjoy it forever.'

13"Our evil acts and our terrible sins have brought about the things that have happened to us. You are our God. Because we sinned so much, you should have punished us even more than you have. But you have left many of your people alive. 14Suppose we don't obey your commands again. And suppose we continue to get married to people who commit sins that you hate. If we do, you will be so angry with us that you will destroy us. You won't leave us even a few people. You won't leave anyone alive.

15"LORD, you are the God of Israel. You are holy. You always do what is right. Today you have left many of your people alive. Here we are with all of our guilt. You see the guilt of our sin. Because we have sinned, not one of us can stand in front of you."

The People Admit They Have Sinned

10 Ezra was praying and admitting to God that his people had sinned. He was sobbing and throwing himself down in front of the house of God. Then a large crowd gathered around him. Men, women and children were there. They too sobbed bitterly.

²Shecaniah spoke to Ezra. Shecaniah was the son of Jehiel. He belonged to the family line of Elam. Shecaniah said, "We haven't been faithful to our God. We've gotten married to women from the nations that are around us. In spite of that, there is still hope for Israel. ³So let's make a covenant in the sight of our God. Let's promise to send away all of those women and their children. That's what you have advised us to do. Those who respect our God's commands have given us the same advice. We want to do what the Law says.

⁴"Get up, Ezra. This matter is in your hands. Do what you need to. We will be behind you all the way. Be brave and do it."

POWER-SURGE

BRAVE   B

GET UP, EZRA. THIS MATTER IS IN YOUR HANDS. DO WHAT YOU NEED TO. WE WILL BE BEHIND YOU ALL THE WAY. BE BRAVE AND DO IT.
— EZRA 10:4 —

⁵So Ezra got up. He made the leading priests and Levites and all of the people of Israel take an oath. He made them promise they would do what Shecaniah had suggested. And they took the oath.

⁶Then Ezra left the house of God. He went to Jehohanan's room. Jehohanan was the son of Eliashib. While Ezra was there, he didn't eat any food. He didn't drink any water. That's because he was filled with sadness. He sobbed because the

people weren't faithful to the Lord's commands. Those people were the ones who had returned from Babylonia.

⁷Then an announcement was sent all through Judah and Jerusalem. All those who had returned were told to gather together in Jerusalem. ⁸They were supposed to come there before three days had passed. If they didn't, they would lose all of their property. They would also be removed from the community of those who had returned. That's what the officials and elders had decided.

⁹Before the three days were over, all of the men of Judah and Benjamin had gathered together in Jerusalem. It was the 20th day of the ninth month. They were sitting in the open area in front of the house of God. They were very upset by what they knew would happen. And they were upset because it was raining.

¹⁰Then the priest Ezra stood up. He said, "You haven't been faithful to the Lord. You have gotten married to women from other lands. So you have added to Israel's guilt. ¹¹Admit to the Lord that you have sinned. Tell the God of your people what you have done. Then do what he wants you to do. Separate yourselves from the nations that are around you. Send away your wives from other lands."

¹²The whole community answered with a loud voice. They said, "You are right! We must do as you say. ¹³But there are a lot of people here. And it's the rainy season. So we can't stand outside. Besides, this matter can't be taken care of in just a day or two. That's because we have sinned terribly by what we've done.

¹⁴"Our officials can act for the whole community. Have everyone in our towns who has married a woman from another land come at a certain time. Tell them to come together with the elders and judges of each town. Then our God will turn his burning anger away from us concerning this whole matter."

¹⁵Only a few men opposed that. They included Jonathan and Jahzeiah. Meshullam and the Levite Shabbethai joined them. Jonathan was the son of Asahel. Jahzeiah was the son of Tikvah.

¹⁶So those who had returned did what had been suggested. The priest Ezra chose some family leaders. There was one from each family group. All of them were chosen by name. They sat down to check out each case. They started on the first day of the tenth month. ¹⁷By the first day of the first month they were finished. They had

EZRA

EZRA 10:1

Ezra was praying and admitting to God that his people had sinned. He was sobbing and throwing himself down in front of the house of God. Then a large crowd gathered around him. Men, women and children were there. They too sobbed bitterly.

Ezra knelt in front of the rebuilt temple of God in Jerusalem and began to pray. He thanked God for bringing him and many other Israelites back. He praised God for his faithfulness.

Then, in an outburst of sadness, Ezra fell on his face and began to cry. He knew that in the past the people of Israel had sinned terribly. And they had ended up as slaves in a foreign country as a punishment. Now they were home in Judah. They had a wonderful future ahead of them. But Ezra knew the people were still sinning and had not asked God to forgive them.

Ezra had spent many years studying God's Word. He knew that when people sinned, God wanted them to come to him for forgiveness. God wanted to forgive the people and give them a chance to change, to quit sinning. But the people hadn't done that. They just continued to sin.

A group of people gathered around Ezra. Women and their children, men and priests—they all crowded around Ezra. **ON THE STEPS, IN THE STREET, NEAR THE GATES, THE PEOPLE CAME TOGETHER.** They knew why Ezra was crying. They knew they needed God's forgiveness. And they waited for Ezra to tell them what to do.

When Ezra finally got up and began to teach the people, they were ready to listen. They wanted to learn more about God. And they wanted to change. They wanted to be people who obeyed God.

BE AN EZRA

You may not be as wise or as smart as Ezra. You may not know the Bible as well as he did. But you can teach others, just like Ezra taught. You can teach by the way you talk, by what you laugh at (or don't laugh at), by the things you watch (or don't watch), by the way you treat other people. Don't think you have to wait until you're older or smarter. You can be an Ezra! Today! Just by how you live.

EZRA TAUGHT THE PEOPLE THAT THEY NEEDED GOD'S FORGIVENESS.
THE WHOLE STORY: EZRA 10:1-6

Go to page 568 for the next Super Hero

handled all of the cases of the men who had gotten married to women from other lands.

A List of Those Who Had Married Women From Other Lands

18 Among the family lines of the priests, here are the men who had married women from other lands.

Maaseiah, Eliezer, Jarib and Gedaliah came from the family line of Jeshua and his brothers. Jeshua was the son of Jehozadak. 19 All of them made a firm promise to send their wives away. Each of those men brought a ram from his flock as a guilt offering.

20 Hanani and Zebadiah came from the family line of Immer.

21 Maaseiah and Elijah came from the family line of Harim. So did Shemaiah, Jehiel and Uzziah.

22 Elioenai, Maaseiah and Ishmael came from the family line of Pashhur. So did Nethanel, Jozabad and Elasah.

23 Among the Levites, here are the men who had married women from other lands.

There were Jozabad, Shimei and Kelaiah. There were also Pethahiah, Judah and Eliezer. Kelaiah's other name was Kelita.

24 Eliashib came from the singers. Shallum, Telem and Uri came from the men who guarded the temple gates.

25 Among the other Israelites, here are the men who had married women from other lands.

Ramiah, Izziah, Malkijah and Mijamin came from the family line of Parosh. So did Eleazar, Malkijah and Benaiah.

26 Mattaniah, Zechariah and Jehiel came from the family line of Elam. So did Abdi, Jeremoth and Elijah.

27 Elioenai, Eliashib and Mattaniah came from the family line of Zattu. So did Jeremoth, Zabad and Aziza.

28 Jehohanan, Hananiah, Zabbai and Athlai came from the family line of Bebai.

29 Meshullam, Malluch and Adaiah came from the family line of Bani. So did Jashub, Sheal and Jeremoth.

30 Adna, Kelal, Benaiah and Maaseiah came from the family line of Pahath-Moab. So did Mattaniah, Bezalel, Binnui and Manasseh.

31 Eliezer, Ishijah, Malkijah, Shemaiah and Shimeon came from the family line of Harim. 32 So did Benjamin, Malluch and Shemariah.

33 Mattenai, Mattattah, Zabad and Eliphelet came from the family line of Hashum. So did Jeremai, Manasseh and Shimei.

34 Maadai, Amram and Uel came from the family line of Bani. 35 So did Benaiah, Bedciah, Keluhi, 36 Vaniah, Meremoth, Eliashib, 37 Mattaniah, Mattenai and Jaasu.

38 Shimei came from the family line of Binnui. 39 So did Shelemiah, Nathan, Adaiah, 40 Macnadebai, Shashai, Sharai, 41 Azarel, Shelemiah, Shemariah, 42 Shallum, Amariah and Joseph.

43 Jeiel, Mattithiah, Zabad and Zebina came from the family line of Nebo. So did Jaddai, Joel and Benaiah.

44 All of those men had married women from other lands. Some of them had even had children by those wives.

NEHEMIAH

While the book of Ezra records the return of the captives and rebuilding the temple, Nehemiah records the return and the rebuilding of the walls of Jerusalem. Nehemiah is the hero in this book not so much because of what he does as because he begins every project with prayer. He knows his ability comes only from God's strength, so he goes to God with every need. Read Nehemiah as a reminder that though you may be talented, you need God's help with everything you do, just like Nehemiah.

HERO IN THIS BOOK . . .

NEHEMIAH

PAGE 568

Nehemiah Prays to the LORD

1 These are the words of Nehemiah. He was the son of Hacaliah.

I was in the safest place in Susa. I was there in the 20th year that Artaxerxes was king. It was in the month of Kislev. **2**At that time Hanani came from Judah with some other men. He was one of my brothers. I asked him and the other men about the Jews who were left alive in Judah. They had returned from Babylonia. I also asked him about Jerusalem.

3He and the men who were with him said to me, "Some of the people who returned are still alive. They are back in the land of Judah. But they are having a hard time. People are making fun of them. The wall of Jerusalem is broken down. Its gates have been burned with fire."

4When I heard about those things, I sat down and sobbed. For several days I was very sad. I didn't eat any food. And I prayed to the God of heaven. **5**I said,

"LORD, you are the God of heaven. You are a great and wonderful God. You keep the covenant you made with those who love you and obey your commands. You show them your love.

6"Please pay careful attention to my prayer. See how your people are suffering. Please listen to me. I'm praying to you day and night. I'm praying for the people of Israel. We Israelites have committed sins against you. All of us admit it. I and my family have also sinned against you. **7**We've done some very evil things. We haven't obeyed the commands, rules and laws you gave your servant Moses.

8"Remember what you told him. You said, 'If you people are not faithful, I will scatter you among the nations. **9**But if you return to me, I will bring you back. If you obey my commands, I will gather you together again. I will bring you back from the farthest places on earth. I will bring you to the special place where I have chosen to put my Name.'

10"LORD, they are your people. They serve you. You used your great strength and mighty hand to set them free from Egypt. **11**Lord, please pay careful attention to my prayer. Listen to the prayers of all of us. We take delight in bringing honor to

your name. Give me success today. Help King Artaxerxes show me his favor."

I was the king's wine taster.

Artaxerxes Sends Nehemiah to Jerusalem

2 Wine was brought in for King Artaxerxes. It was the month of Nisan in the 20th year of his rule. I got the wine and gave it to him. I hadn't been sad in front of him before. But now I was. **2**So the king asked me, "Why are you looking so sad? You aren't sick. You must be feeling sad deep down inside."

I was really afraid. **3**But I said to the king, "May you live forever! Why shouldn't I look sad? The city where my people of long ago are buried has been destroyed. And fire has burned up its gates."

4The king said to me, "What do you want?"

I prayed to the God of heaven. **5**Then I answered the king, "Are you pleased with me, King Artaxerxes? If it pleases you, send me to Judah. Let me go to the city of Jerusalem. That's where my people are buried. I want to rebuild it."

6The queen was sitting beside the king. He turned and asked me, "How long will your journey take? When will you get back?" It pleased the king to send me. So I chose a certain time.

7I also said to him, "If it pleases you, may I take some letters with me? I want to give them to the governors of the land west of the Euphrates River. Then they'll help me travel safely through their territory until I arrive in Judah.

8"May I also have a letter to Asaph? He takes care of your forest. I want him to give me some logs so I can make beams out of them. I want to use them for the gates of the fort that is by the temple. Some of the logs will be used in the city wall. And I'll need some for the house I'm going to live in." The gracious hand of my God helped me. So the king gave me what I asked for.

9Then I went to the governors of the land west of the Euphrates. I gave them the king's letters. He had also sent army officers and horsemen along with me.

10Sanballat and Tobiah heard about what was happening. They were very upset that someone had come to work for the good of Israel's people. Sanballat was a Horonite. Tobiah was an official from Ammon.

NEHEMIAH

NEHEMIAH 2:4-5

B

★

W

I prayed to the God of heaven. Then I answered the king.

Nehemiah (Nee-huh-MY-uh) stood next to the king's table in Persia. He watched as a servant poured fresh wine into the king's cup. The cup was heavy, golden and covered with jewels. Nehemiah took a sip of the wine and waited. When nothing happened to him, he knew the wine was safe for the king.

Nehemiah handed the cup to the king, a frown on his face. He had never been sad in front of the king before. He hoped the king wouldn't notice.

But the king did notice. And he wondered what was wrong with Nehemiah. "Why are you so sad?" the king asked Nehemiah.

NEHEMIAH SHOOK WITH FEAR. No one was supposed to bother the king with personal problems. How should he answer? Nehemiah bravely looked at the king and answered straight from his heart. "Why shouldn't I be sad? My home in Judah is in ruins. The wall is broken down. The gates to the city have been burned. And my people there are suffering."

"What can I do?" the king asked.

Now Nehemiah shook with surprise instead of fear. In his heart he prayed to God for wisdom. Then he said, "Let me go to Jerusalem. I'll rebuild the wall there. Could you give me letters to the kings of the lands I'll have to cross to get there? Then they'll let me go through safely. I could also use a letter to the man who takes care of your forests. I'll need logs for rebuilding the wall and the gates."

The king gave Nehemiah all that he asked for. Soon after, Nehemiah left for Jerusalem. He inspected the wall and made plans. Then he led the people of Jerusalem in a great rebuilding project. The walls of Jerusalem and its gates were soon safe and strong again.

BE A NEHEMIAH

God gave Nehemiah the strength, the bravery and the wisdom to answer the king truthfully. The Bible says that before Nehemiah answered, he prayed. You can, too. God will help you just like he helped Nehemiah. You just have to ask.

NEHEMIAH ASKED FOR GOD'S HELP AND GOT IT.
THE WHOLE STORY: NEHEMIAH 2:1-8

Go to page 591 for the next Super Hero

Nehemiah Checks Out the Walls of Jerusalem

11I went to Jerusalem. I stayed there for three days. **12**Then at night I took a few men with me to check out the walls. I hadn't told anyone what my God wanted me to do for Jerusalem. There weren't any donkeys with me except the one I was riding on.

13That night I went out through the Valley Gate. I went toward the Jackal Well and the Dung Gate. I checked out the walls of Jerusalem. They had been broken down. I also checked the city gates. Fire had burned them up. **14**I moved on toward the Fountain Gate and the King's Pool. But there wasn't enough room for my donkey to get through. **15**It was still night. I went up the Kidron Valley. I kept checking the wall. Finally, I turned back. I went back in through the Valley Gate.

16The officials didn't know where I had gone. They didn't know what I had done either. That's because I hadn't said anything to anyone yet. I hadn't told the priests or nobles or officials. And I hadn't spoken to any others who would be rebuilding the wall.

17I said to them, "You can see the trouble we're in. Jerusalem has been destroyed. Fire has burned up its gates. Come on. Let's rebuild the wall of Jerusalem. Then people won't make fun of us anymore." **18**I also told them how the gracious hand of my God was helping me. And I told them what the king had said to me.

They replied, "Let's start rebuilding." So they began that good work.

19But Sanballat, the Horonite, heard about it. So did Tobiah, the official from Ammon. Geshem, the Arab, heard about it too. All of them laughed at us. They made fun of us. "What do you think you are doing?" they asked. "Are you turning against the king?"

20I answered, "The God of heaven will give us success. We serve him. So we'll start rebuilding the walls. But you don't have any share in Jerusalem. You don't have any claim to it. You don't have any right to worship here."

A List of the People Who Repaired the Wall

3 The high priest Eliashib and the other priests went to work. They rebuilt the Sheep Gate. They set it apart to God. They put its doors in place. They continued to rebuild the wall up to the Tower of the Hundred. They set the tower apart to God. Then they continued to rebuild the wall all the way to the Tower of Hananel. **2**Some men from Jericho rebuilt the next part of the wall. And Zaccur rebuilt the next part. He was the son of Imri.

3The sons of Hassenaah rebuilt the Fish Gate. They laid its beams. They put its doors and metal bolts and bars in place. **4**Meremoth repaired the next part of the wall. He was the son of Uriah. Uriah was the son of Hakkoz. Next to Meremoth, Meshullam made some repairs. He was the son of Berekiah. Berekiah was the son of Meshezabel. Next to Meshullam, Zadok also made some repairs. He was the son of Baana. **5**Some men from Tekoa repaired the next part of the wall. But their nobles refused to do any work at all. They didn't pay any attention to the people who were in charge of the work.

6Joiada and Meshullam repaired the Jeshanah Gate. Joiada was the son of Paseah. Meshullam was the son of Besodeiah. Joiada and Meshullam laid the beams of the gate. They put its doors and metal bolts and bars in place. **7**Next to them, some men from Gibeon and Mizpah made repairs. They included Melatiah from Gibeon and Jadon from Meronoth. Those places were under the authority of the governor of the land west of the Euphrates River.

8Uzziel repaired the next part of the wall. He made his living by working with gold. He was the son of Harhaiah. Hananiah made repairs on the next part. He made his living by making perfume. So the wall of Jerusalem was made like new again all the way to the Broad Wall. **9**Rephaiah repaired the next part. He was the son of Hur. Rephaiah ruled over half of the territory where Jerusalem was located.

10Jedaiah repaired the part of the wall that was across from his house. He was the son of Harumaph. Hattush made repairs next to Jedaiah. Hattush was the son of Hashabneiah. **11**Malkijah and Hasshub repaired another part of the wall. They also repaired the Tower of the Ovens. Malkijah was the son of Harim. Hasshub was the son of Pahath-Moab.

12Shallum repaired the next part. His daughters helped him. He was the son of Hallohesh. Shallum ruled over the other half of the territory where Jerusalem was located.

13Hanun repaired the Valley Gate. Some people who lived in Zanoah helped him. They rebuilt it. They put its doors and metal bolts and bars in place. They also repaired 500 yards of the wall. They repaired it all the way to the Dung Gate.

14Malkijah repaired the Dung Gate. He was the son of Recab. Malkijah ruled over the territory where Beth Hakkerem was located. He rebuilt the gate. He put its doors and metal bolts and bars in place.

15Shallun repaired the Fountain Gate. He was the son of Col-Hozeh. Shallun ruled over the territory where Mizpah was located. He rebuilt the gate. He put a roof over it. And he put the doors and metal bolts and bars of the gate in place. He also repaired the wall by the Pool of Siloam. It was near the King's Garden. Shallun repaired the wall as far as the steps that go down from the City of David.

16Next to Shallun, Nehemiah made some repairs. He was the son of Azbuk. Nehemiah ruled over half of the territory where Beth Zur was located. He repaired the wall up to the part that was across from the tombs of David. He repaired it all the way to the man-made pool and the House of Heroes.

17Next to Nehemiah, some Levites made repairs. They worked under the direction of Rehum. He was the son of Bani. Next to Rehum, Hashabiah made repairs for his territory. He ruled over half of the territory where Keilah was located. 18Next to him, other people from that territory made some repairs. They worked under the direction of Binnui. He was the son of Henadad. Binnui ruled over the other half of the territory where Keilah was located.

19Next to him, Ezer repaired another part of the wall. He was the son of Jeshua. Ezer ruled over the territory where Mizpah was located. He repaired the part that was across from the place that went up to the storeroom where the weapons were kept. He repaired the wall up to the angle. 20Next to him, Baruch worked hard to repair another part of the wall. He was the son of Zabbai. He repaired the part from the angle to the entrance to Eliashib's house. Eliashib was high priest. 21Next to Baruch, Meremoth repaired another part. He was the son of Uriah. Uriah was the son of Hakkoz. Meremoth repaired the part from the entrance to Eliashib's house to the end of the house.

22Next to Meremoth, some priests from the surrounding area made repairs. 23Next to them, Benjamin and Hasshub repaired the part of the wall that was in front of their house. Next to them, Azariah repaired the part that was beside his house. He was the son of Maaseiah. Maaseiah was the son of Ananiah.

24Next to Azariah, Binnui made repairs on another part. Binnui was the son of Henadad. Binnui repaired the wall from Azariah's house to the angle and the corner. 25Palal worked across from the angle. He was the son of Uzai. Palal also worked across from the tower that was part of the upper palace. It was near the courtyard of the guard. Next to him, Pedaiah made some repairs. He was the son of Parosh.

26The temple servants who lived on the hill of Ophel helped him. They repaired the wall up to the part that was across from the Water Gate. It was toward the east and the palace tower. 27Next to the temple servants, the men from Tekoa repaired another part. They made repairs from the large palace tower to the wall of Ophel.

28The priests made repairs above the Horse Gate. Each priest repaired the part of the wall that was in front of his own house. 29Next to them, Zadok made repairs across from his house. He was the son of Immer. Next to Zadok, Shemaiah made some repairs. He was the son of Shecaniah. Shemaiah guarded the East Gate.

30Next to him, Hananiah and Hanun repaired another part of the wall. Hananiah was the son of Shelemiah. Hanun was the sixth son of Zalaph. Next to Hananiah and Hanun, Meshullam made some repairs. He was the son of Berekiah. Meshullam repaired the part that was across from where he lived.

31Next to him, Malkijah made some repairs. He made his living by working with gold. He repaired the wall up to the house of the temple servants and the traders. It was across from the Inspection Gate. He also repaired the wall as far as the room that was above the corner. 32The traders and those who made their living by working with gold made some repairs. They repaired the wall from the room above the corner to the Sheep Gate.

Nehemiah's Enemies Oppose Him

4 Sanballat heard that we were rebuilding the wall. So he burned with anger. He became very upset. He made fun of the Jews. 2He spoke to his friends and the army of Samaria. He said, "What are those Jews trying to do? Can they make their city wall like new again? Will

they offer sacrifices? Can they finish everything in a single day? The stones from their city wall and buildings are piled up like trash. And everything has been badly burned. Can they use those stones to rebuild everything again?"

3Tobiah from Ammon was at Sanballat's side. He said, "What are they building? They're putting up a stone wall. But suppose a fox climbs on top of it. Even that will break it down!"

4I prayed to God. I said, "Our God, please listen to our prayer. Some people hate us. They're making fun of us. So let others make fun of them. Let them be carried off like stolen goods. Let them be taken to another country as prisoners. **5**Don't hide your eyes from their guilt. Don't forgive their sins. They have made fun of the builders."

6So we rebuilt the wall. We repaired it until all of it was half as high as we wanted it to be. The people worked with all their heart.

7But Sanballat and Tobiah heard that Jerusalem's walls continued to be repaired. The Arabs and some people from Ammon heard the same thing. Some men from Ashdod heard about it too. They heard that the gaps in the wall were being filled in. So they burned with anger. **8**All of them made evil plans to come and fight against Jerusalem. They wanted to stir up trouble against it.

9But we prayed to our God. We put guards on duty day and night to watch out for danger.

10During that time, the people in Judah spoke up. They said, "The workers are getting weaker and weaker all the time. Broken stones are piled up everywhere. They are in our way. So we can't rebuild the wall."

11And our enemies said, "We will be right there among them. We'll kill them. We'll put an end to their work. We'll do it before they even know it or see us."

12Then the Jews who lived near our enemies came to us. They told us ten times, "No matter where you are, they'll attack us."

13So I stationed some people behind the lowest parts of the wall. That's where our enemies could easily attack us. I stationed the people family by family. They had their swords, spears and bows with them.

14I looked things over. Then I stood up and spoke to the nobles, the officials and the rest of the people. I said, "Don't be afraid of your enemies. Remember the Lord. He is great and powerful. So fight for your brothers and sisters. Fight for your sons and daughters. Fight for your wives and homes."

15Our enemies heard that we knew what they were trying to do. They heard that God had blocked their evil plans. So all of us returned to the wall. Each of us did our own work.

16From that day on, half of my men did the work. The other half were given spears, shields, bows and armor. The officers stationed themselves behind all of the people of Judah. **17**The people continued to build the wall. Those who carried supplies did their work with one hand. They held a weapon in the other hand. **18**Each of the builders wore his sword at his side as he worked. But the man who blew the trumpet stayed with me.

19Then I spoke to the nobles, the officials and the rest of the people. I said, "This is a big job. It covers a lot of territory. We're separated too far from one another along the wall. **20**When you hear the sound of the trumpet, join us at that location. Our God will fight for us!"

21So we continued the work. Half of the men held spears. We worked from the first light of sunrise until the stars came out at night. **22**At that time I also spoke to the people. I told them, "Have every man and his helper stay inside Jerusalem at night. Then they can guard us at night. And they can work during the day."

23My relatives and I didn't take our clothes off. My men and the guards didn't take theirs off either. Each man kept his weapon with him, even when he went to get water.

Nehemiah Helps Some Poor People

5 Some men and their wives cried out against their Jewish brothers and sisters. **2**Some of them were saying, "We and our sons and daughters have increased our numbers. Now there are many of us. We have to get some grain so we can eat and stay alive."

3Others were saying, "We're being forced to sell our fields, vineyards and homes. We have to do it to buy grain. There isn't enough food for everyone."

4Still others were saying, "We've had to borrow money. We needed it to pay the king's tax on our fields and vineyards. **5**We belong to the same family lines as the rest of our people. Our sons and daughters are as good as theirs. But we've had to sell them off as slaves. Some of our daughters have already been made slaves. But we can't do anything about it. That's because our fields and vineyards now belong to others."

6I heard them when they cried out. And I burned with anger when I heard what they were saying. 7I thought it over for a while. Then I brought charges against the nobles and officials. I told them, "You are forcing your own people to pay too much interest!"

So I called together a large group of people to handle the matter. 8I said, "Our Jewish brothers and sisters were sold to other nations. We've done everything we could to buy them back and bring them home. But look at what you are doing! You are actually selling your own people! Now we'll have to buy them back too!"

The people kept quiet. They couldn't think of anything to say.

9So I continued, "What you are doing isn't right. Shouldn't you show respect for our God? Shouldn't you live in a way that will keep our enemies from making fun of us?

10"I'm lending the people money and grain. So are my relatives and my men. But you must stop charging too much interest!

11"Give the people's fields back to them. Give them back their vineyards, olive groves and houses. Do it right away. You have charged them too much. Give everything back to them. Give them back the one percent on the money, grain, fresh wine and olive oil you have charged them."

12"We'll give it back," they said. "And we won't require anything more from them. We'll do exactly as you say."

Then I sent for the priests. I made the nobles and officials take an oath to do what they had promised. 13I also shook out my pockets and emptied them. I said, "Some of you might decide not to keep the promise you have made. If that happens, may God shake you out of your house! May he empty you of everything you own! May you be left with nothing at all!"

The whole community said, "Amen." They praised the LORD. And the leaders did what they had promised to do.

14And that's not all. I was appointed as governor of Judah in the 20th year that Artaxerxes was king of Persia. I remained in that position until his 32nd year. During those 12 years, I and my relatives didn't eat the food that was provided for my table.

15But there had been governors before me. They had put a heavy load on the people. They had taken a pound of silver from each of them. They had also taken food and wine from them. Their officials had acted like high and mighty rulers over them.

But I have great respect for God. So I didn't act like that. 16Instead, I spent all of my time working on this wall. All of my men were gathered there to work on it too. We didn't receive any land for ourselves.

17Many people ate at my table. They included 150 Jews and officials. They also included leaders who came to us from the nations that were around us. 18Each day one ox, six of the best sheep and some birds were prepared for me. Every ten days plenty of wine of all kinds was brought in as well. In spite of all that, I never asked for the food that was provided for my table. That's because the people were already paying too many taxes.

19You are my God. Please remember me. Show me your favor. Keep in mind everything I've done for these people.

Nehemiah's Enemies Continue to Oppose Him

6 Sanballat, Tobiah and Geshem, the Arab, heard about what I had done. So did the rest of our enemies. All of them heard I had rebuilt the wall. In fact, they heard there weren't any gaps left in it. But up to that time I hadn't put up the gates at the main entrances to the city.

2Sanballat and Geshem sent me a message. They said, "Come. Let's talk with one another. Let's meet in one of the villages on the flatlands of Ono."

But they were planning to harm me. 3So I sent messengers to them with my answer. I replied, "I'm working on a huge project. So I can't get away. Why should the work stop while I leave it? Why should I go down and talk with you?"

4They sent me the same message four times. And I gave them the same answer each time.

5Sanballat sent his helper to me a fifth time. He brought the same message. He was carrying a letter that wasn't sealed. 6It said,

"A report is going around among the nations. Geshem says it's true. We hear that you and the other Jews are planning to turn against the Persian rulers. And that's why you are building the wall.

"It's also reported that you are about to become their king. 7People say that you have even appointed prophets to make an announcement about you. In Jerusalem they are going to say, 'Judah has a king!' That report will get back to the king of Persia. So come. Let's talk things over."

8I sent a reply to Sanballat. I said, "What you are saying isn't really happening. You are just making it up."

9All of them were trying to frighten us. They thought, "Their hands will get too weak to do the work. So it won't be completed."

But I prayed to God. I said, "Make my hands stronger."

10One day I went to Shemaiah's house. He was the son of Delaiah. Delaiah was the son of Mehetabel. Shemaiah had shut himself up in his home. He said, "Let's go to God's house. Let's meet inside the temple. Let's close the temple doors. Some people want to kill you. They will come at night."

11But I said, "Should a man like me run away? Should someone like me go into the temple just to save his life? No! I won't go!"

12I realized that God hadn't sent Shemaiah. Tobiah and Sanballat had hired him. That's why he had prophesied lies about me. 13They had hired him to scare me. They wanted me to commit a sin by doing what he said. That would give me a bad name in the community. People would find fault with me and my work.

14You are my God. Remember what Tobiah and Sanballat have done. Also remember the prophet Noadiah. She and the rest of the prophets have been trying to scare me.

The City Wall Is Completed

15So the city wall was completed on the 25th day of the month of Elul. It was finished in 52 days. 16All of our enemies heard about it. All of the nations that were around us became afraid. They weren't sure of themselves anymore. They realized that our God had helped us finish the work.

17In those days the nobles of Judah sent many letters to Tobiah. And replies from Tobiah came back to them. 18Many people in Judah had taken an oath that they would be faithful to him. That's because he was Shecaniah's son-in-law. Shecaniah was the son of Arah. Tobiah's son Jehohanan had married Meshullam's daughter. Meshullam was the son of Berekiah.

19Tobiah's friends kept reporting to me the good things he did. They also kept telling him what I said. And Tobiah himself sent letters to scare me.

7 The wall had been rebuilt. I had put up the gates at the main entrances to the city. Those who guarded the gates were appointed to their positions. So were the singers and Levites. 2I put my brother Hanani in charge of Jerusalem. Hananiah helped him. Hananiah was commander of the fort that was by the temple. Hanani was an honest man. He had more respect for God than most people do.

3I said to Hanani and Hananiah, "Don't open the gates of Jerusalem until the hottest time of the day. Tell the men who guard the gates to shut them before they go off duty. Make sure they lock them up tight. Also appoint as guards some people who live in Jerusalem. Station some of them at their appointed places. Station others near their own homes."

A List of People Who Returned to Judah

4Jerusalem was large. It had a lot of room. But only a few people lived there. The houses hadn't been rebuilt yet. 5So my God stirred me up to gather the people together. He also told me to gather the nobles and officials together with them. He wanted me to list them by families. I found the family history of those who had been the first to return. Here is what I found written in it.

6Nebuchadnezzar had taken many Jews away from the land of Judah. He had forced them to go to Babylonia as prisoners. Now they returned to Jerusalem and Judah. All of them went back to their own towns. Nebuchadnezzar was king of Babylonia. 7The leaders of the Jews included Zerubbabel, Jeshua, Nehemiah, Azariah, Raamiah and Nahamani. They also included Mordecai, Bilshan, Mispereth, Bigvai, Nehum and Baanah.

Here is a list of the men of Israel who returned home.

8There were 2,172 from the family line of Parosh.
9There were 372 from Shephatiah.
10There were 652 from Arah.
11There were 2,818 from Pahath-Moab through the family line of Jeshua and Joab.

12 There were 1,254 from Elam.

13 There were 845 from Zattu.

14 There were 760 from Zaccai.

15 There were 648 from Binnui.

16 There were 628 from Bebai.

17 There were 2,322 from Azgad.

18 There were 667 from Adonikam.

19 There were 2,067 from Bigvai.

20 There were 655 from Adin.

21 There were 98 from Ater through the family line of Hezekiah.

22 There were 328 from Hashum.

23 There were 324 from Bezai.

24 There were 112 from Hariph.

25 There were 95 from Gibeon.

26 There were 188 from the men of Bethlehem and Netophah.

27 There were 128 from Anathoth.

28 There were 42 from Beth Azmaveth.

29 There were 743 from Kiriath Jearim, Kephirah and Beeroth.

30 There were 621 from Ramah and Geba.

31 There were 122 from Micmash.

32 There were 123 from Bethel and Ai.

33 There were 52 from Nebo.

34 There were 1,254 from the other Elam.

35 There were 320 from Harim.

36 There were 345 from Jericho.

37 There were 721 from Lod, Hadid and Ono.

38 There were 3,930 from Senaah.

39 Here is a list of the priests.

There were 973 from the family line of Jedaiah through the line of Jeshua.

40 There were 1,052 from Immer.

41 There were 1,247 from Pashhur.

42 There were 1,017 from Harim.

43 The Levites belonged to the family line of Jeshua through Kadmiel through the line of Hodaviah. The total number of men was 74.

44 The singers belonged to the family line of Asaph. The total number of men was 148.

45 The men who guarded the temple gates belonged to the family lines of Shallum, Ater, Talmon, Akkub, Hatita and Shobai. The total number of men was 138.

46 Here is a list of the members of the family lines of the temple servants.

Ziha, Hasupha, Tabbaoth,

47 Keros, Sia, Padon,

48 Lebana, Hagaba, Shalmai,

49 Hanan, Giddel, Gahar,

50 Reaiah, Rezin, Nekoda,

51 Gazzam, Uzza, Paseah,

52 Besai, Meunim, Nephussim,

53 Bakbuk, Hakupha, Harhur,

54 Bazluth, Mehida, Harsha,

55 Barkos, Sisera, Temah,

56 Neziah, Hatipha

57 Here is a list of the members of the family lines of the servants of Solomon.

Sotai, Sophereth, Perida,

58 Jaala, Darkon, Giddel,

59 Shephatiah, Hattil, Pokereth-Hazzebaim, Amon

60 The total number of the members of the family lines of the temple servants and the servants of Solomon was 392.

61 Many people came up to Judah from the towns of Tel Melah, Tel Harsha, Kerub, Addon and Immer. But they weren't able to prove that their families belonged to the people of Israel.

62 There were 642 of them from the family lines of Delaiah, Tobiah and Nekoda.

63 Here is a list of the members of the family lines of the priests.

They were Hobaiah, Hakkoz and Barzillai. Barzillai had married a daughter of Barzillai from Gilead. So he was also called Barzillai.

64 The priests looked for their family records. But they couldn't find them. So they weren't able to serve as priests. They weren't "clean."

65 The governor gave them an order. He told them not to eat any of the most sacred food. They had to wait until there was a priest who could use the Urim and Thummim to get decisions from the LORD.

66 The total number of the entire group that returned was 42,360. **67** That didn't include their 7,337 male and female slaves. There were also 245 male and female singers. **68** And there were 736 horses, 245 mules, **69** 435 camels and 6,720 donkeys.

GIVING

G

THE FAMILY LEADERS
HELPED PAY FOR THE
WORK...ALL OF THAT
WAS ADDED TO THE
TEMPLE TREASURE.
THE REST OF THE
PEOPLE GAVE A TOTAL
OF 375 POUNDS OF
GOLD AND ONE AND
A FOURTH TONS
OF SILVER.
—NEHEMIAH 7:70-72—

HELPFUL

70Some of the family leaders helped pay for the work. The governor gave 19 pounds of gold to be added to the temple treasure. He also gave 50 bowls and 530 sets of clothes for the priests. **71**Some of the family leaders gave 375 pounds of gold for the work. They also gave one and a third tons of silver. All of that was added to the temple treasure. **72**The rest of the people gave a total of 375 pounds of gold and one and a fourth tons of silver. They also gave 67 sets of clothes for the priests.

73The priests and Levites settled down in their own towns. So did the singers, the temple servants and the men who guarded the gates. The rest of the people of Israel also settled in their own towns.

Ezra Reads the Law to the People

The people of Israel had settled down in their towns. In the seventh month,

8 **1**all of them gathered together. They went to the open area in front of the Water Gate. They told Ezra to bring out the Scroll of the Law of Moses. The LORD had given Israel that law so they would obey him. Ezra was a teacher of the law.

2The priest Ezra brought the Law out to the whole community. It was the first day of the seventh month. The group was made up of men and women and everyone who was old enough to understand what Ezra was going to read.

3He read the Law to them from sunrise until noon. He did it as he faced the open area in front of the Water Gate. He read it to the men, women and others who could understand. And all of the people paid careful attention as Ezra was reading the Scroll of the Law.

4Ezra, the teacher, stood on a high wooden stage. It had been built for the occasion. Mattithiah, Shema and Anaiah stood at his right side. So did Uriah, Hilkiah and Maaseiah. Pedaiah, Mishael and Malkijah stood at his left side. So did Hashum, Hashbaddanah, Zechariah and Meshullam.

5Ezra opened the scroll. All of the people could see him. That's because he was standing above them. As he opened the scroll, the people stood up. **6**Ezra praised the LORD. He is the great God. All of the people lifted up their hands. They said, "Amen! Amen!" Then they bowed down. They turned their faces toward the ground. And they worshiped the LORD.

7The Levites taught the Law to the people. They remained standing while the Levites taught them. The Levites who were there included Jeshua, Bani, Sherebiah, Jamin, Akkub, Shabbethai and Hodiah. They also included Maaseiah, Kelita, Azariah, Jozabad, Hanan and Pelaiah. **8**All of those Levites read parts of the Scroll of the Law of God to the people. They made it clear to them. They told them what it meant. So the people were able to understand what was being read.

9Then Nehemiah and Ezra spoke up. So did the Levites who were teaching the people. All of those men said to the people, "This day is set apart to honor the LORD your God. So don't sob. Don't be sad." All of the people had been sobbing as they listened to the words of the Law. Nehemiah was governor. Ezra was a priest and a teacher of the law.

10Nehemiah said, "Go and enjoy some good food and sweet drinks. Send some of it to those who don't have any. This day is set apart to honor our Lord. So don't be sad. The joy of the LORD makes you strong."

11The Levites calmed all of the people down. They said, "Be quiet. This is a sacred day. So don't be sad."

12Then all of the people went away to eat and drink. They shared their food with others. They celebrated with great joy. Now they understood the words they had heard. That's because everything had been explained to them.

13All of the family leaders gathered around Ezra, the teacher. So did the

POWER-SURGE

CHEERFUL ✳

THE JOY OF THE LORD MAKES YOU STRONG.
— NEHEMIAH 8:10 —

STRONG

priests and Levites. All of them paid attention to the words of the Law. It was the second day of the month.

¹⁴The LORD had given the Law through Moses. He wanted the people of Israel to obey it. It is written there that they were supposed to live in booths during the Feast of Booths. That Feast was celebrated in the seventh month. ¹⁵They were also supposed to spread the message all through their towns and in Jerusalem. They were supposed to announce, "Go out into the central hill country. Bring back some branches from olive and wild olive trees. Also bring some from myrtle, palm and shade trees. Use the branches to make booths."

¹⁶So the people went out and brought some branches back. They built themselves booths on their own roofs. They made them in their courtyards. They put them up in the courtyards of the house of God. They built them in the open area in front of the Water Gate. And they built them in the open area in front of the Gate of Ephraim.

¹⁷All those who had returned from Babylonia made booths. They lived in them during the Feast of Booths. They hadn't celebrated the Feast with so much joy for a long time. In fact, they had never celebrated it like that from the days of Joshua, the son of Nun, until that very day. So their joy was very great.

¹⁸Day after day, Ezra read parts of the Scroll of the Law of God to them. He read it out loud from the first day to the last. They celebrated the Feast of Booths for seven days. On the eighth day they gathered together. They followed the required rules for celebrating the Feast.

The People of Israel Pray to the LORD

9 It was the 24th day of the seventh month. The people of Israel gathered together again. They didn't eat any food. They wore black clothes. They put dust on their heads. ²The people of Israel separated themselves from everyone else. They stood and admitted they had sinned. They also admitted that their people before them had done evil things.

³They stood where they were. They listened while the Levites read parts of the Scroll of the Law of the LORD their God. They listened for a fourth of the day. They spent another fourth of the day admitting their sins. They also worshiped the LORD their God.

⁴The Levites stood on the stairs. They included Jeshua, Bani, Kadmiel and Shebaniah. They also included Bunni, Sherebiah, Bani and Kenani. With loud voices they called out to the LORD their God. ⁵Then some Levites spoke up. They included Jeshua, Kadmiel, Bani and Hashabneiah. They also included Sherebiah, Hodiah, Shebaniah and Pethahiah. They said to the people, "Stand up. Praise the LORD your God. He lives for ever and ever!"

So the people said, "LORD, may your glorious name be praised. May it be lifted high above every other name that is blessed and praised. ⁶You are the one and only LORD. You made the heavens. You made even the highest heavens. You created all of the stars in the sky. You created the earth and everything that is on it. And you made the oceans and everything that is in them. You give life to everything. Every living being in heaven worships you.

⁷"You are the LORD God. You chose Abram. You brought him out of Ur in Babylonia. You named him Abraham. ⁸You knew that his heart was faithful to you. And you made a covenant with him. You promised to give to his children after him a land of their own. It was the land of the Canaanites, Hittites and Amorites. The Perizzites, Jebusites and Girgashites also lived there. You have kept your promise. That's because you always do what is right and fair.

⁹"You saw how our people suffered long ago in Egypt. You heard them cry out to you at the Red Sea. ¹⁰You did miraculous signs and wonders against Pharaoh. You sent plagues on all of his officials. In fact, you sent them on all of the people of Egypt. You knew how they treated our people. They looked down on them. But

you made a name for yourself. That name remains to this very day.

11 "You parted the Red Sea for the people of Israel. They passed through it on dry ground. But you threw into the sea those who chased them. They sank down like a stone into the mighty waters. **12** By day you led them with a pillar of cloud. At night you led them with a pillar of fire. It gave them light to show them the way you wanted them to go.

13 "You came down on Mount Sinai. From heaven you spoke to our people. You gave them rules and laws. Those laws are right and fair. You gave them orders and commands that are good. **14** You taught them about your holy Sabbath day. You gave them commands, orders and laws. You did it through your servant Moses.

15 "When the people were hungry, you gave them bread from heaven. When they were thirsty, you brought them water out of a rock.

"You told them to go into the land of Canaan. You told them to take it as their own. It was the land you had promised to give them. You had even raised your hand and taken an oath to do it.

16 "But our people before us became proud and stubborn. They didn't obey your commands. **17** They refused to listen to you. They forgot the miracles you had done among them. So they became stubborn. When they refused to obey you, they appointed a leader for themselves. They wanted to go back to being slaves in Egypt. But you are a God who forgives. You are gracious. You are tender and kind. You are slow to get angry. You are full of love. So you didn't desert them.

18 "They made for themselves a metal statue of a god that looked like a calf. They said, 'Here is your god. He brought you up out of Egypt.' And they did evil things that dishonored you. But you still didn't desert them.

19 "Because you loved them so much, you didn't leave them in the desert. During the day the pillar of cloud didn't stop guiding them on their path. At night the pillar of fire didn't stop shining on the way you wanted them to go. **20** You gave them your good Spirit to teach them. You didn't hold back your manna from their mouths. And you gave them water when they were thirsty. **21** For 40 years you took good care of them in the desert. They had everything they needed. Their clothes didn't wear out. And their feet didn't swell up.

22 "You gave them kingdoms and nations. You even gave them lands far away. They took over the country of Sihon. He was king of Heshbon. They also took over the country of Og. He was king of Bashan. **23** You gave them as many children as there are stars in the sky. You told their parents to enter the land. You told them to take it over. And you brought their children into it. **24** Their children went into the land. They took it as their own. You brought the people of Canaan under Israel's control. The Canaanites lived in the land. But you handed them over to Israel. You also handed their kings and the other nations in the land over to Israel. You allowed Israel to deal with them just as they wanted to.

25 "Your people captured cities that had high walls around them. They also took over the rich land in Canaan. They took houses that were filled with all kinds of good things. They took over wells that had already been dug. They took many vineyards, olive groves and fruit trees. They ate until they were very full and satisfied. They were filled with joy because you were so good to them.

26 "But they didn't obey you. Instead, they turned against you. They turned their backs on your law. They killed your prophets. The prophets had warned them to turn back to you. But they did very evil things that dishonored you.

27 "So you handed them over to their enemies, who beat them down. Then they cried out to you. From heaven you heard them. You loved them very much. So you sent leaders

POWER–SURGE

FORGIVING **F**

YOU ARE A GOD WHO FORGIVES.
— NEHEMIAH 9:17 —

to help them. The leaders saved them from the powerful hand of their enemies.

28"But as soon as the people were enjoying peace and rest again, they did what was evil in your sight. Then you handed them over to their enemies. So their enemies ruled over them. When they cried out to you again, you heard them from heaven. You loved them very much. So you saved them time after time.

29"You warned them to obey your law again. But they became proud. They didn't obey your commands. They sinned against your rules. Anyone who obeys them will live by them. But the people didn't care about that. They turned their backs on you. They became very stubborn. They refused to listen to you.

30"For many years you put up with them. By your Spirit you warned them through your prophets. In spite of that, they didn't pay any attention. So you handed them over to the nations that were around them. 31But you loved them very much. So you didn't put an end to them. You didn't desert them. That's because you are a gracious God. You are tender and kind.

32"Our God, you are great, mighty and wonderful. You keep the covenant you made with us. You show us your love. So don't let all of our suffering seem like a small thing in your sight. We've suffered greatly. So have our kings and leaders. So have our priests and prophets. Our people who lived long ago also suffered. And all of your people are suffering right now. In fact, we've been suffering from the time of the kings of Assyria until today.

33"In spite of everything that has happened to us, you have been fair. You have been faithful in what you have done. But we did what was wrong. 34Our kings and leaders didn't follow your law. Our priests and our people before us didn't follow it either. They didn't pay any attention to your commands. They didn't listen to the warnings you gave them. 35They didn't serve you. They didn't turn from their evil ways. They didn't obey you even when they had a kingdom. You were very good to them. And they enjoyed it. You gave them a rich land. It had

plenty of room in it. But they still didn't serve you.

36"Now look at us. We are slaves today. We're slaves in the land you gave our people long ago. You gave it to them so they could eat its fruit and the other good things it produces. 37But we have sinned against you. So its great harvest goes to the kings of Persia. You have placed them over us. They rule over our bodies and cattle just as they please. And we are suffering terribly.

The People Agree to Obey God's Law

38"So we are making a firm agreement. We're writing it down. Our leaders are stamping it with their seals. And so are our Levites and priests."

10 Here are the names of those who stamped the agreement with their seals.

The governor Nehemiah, the son of Hacaliah

Zedekiah, 2Seraiah, Azariah, Jeremiah,
3Pashhur, Amariah, Malkijah,
4Hattush, Shebaniah, Malluch,
5Harim, Meremoth, Obadiah,
6Daniel, Ginnethon, Baruch,
7Meshullam, Abijah, Mijamin,
8Maaziah, Bilgai, Shemaiah

They were the priests.

9Here are the names of the Levites.

Jeshua, the son of Azaniah
Binnui, one of the sons of Henadad
Kadmiel

10Here are the names of those who helped them.

Shebaniah, Hodiah, Kelita, Pelaiah, Hanan,
11Mica, Rehob, Hashabiah,
12Zaccur, Sherebiah, Shebaniah,
13Hodiah, Bani, Beninu

14Here are the names of the leaders of the people.

Parosh, Pahath-Moab, Elam, Zattu, Bani,
15Bunni, Azgad, Bebai,
16Adonijah, Bigvai, Adin,
17Ater, Hezekiah, Azzur,
18Hodiah, Hashum, Bezai,
19Hariph, Anathoth, Nebai,
20Magpiash, Meshullam, Hezir,
21Meshezabel, Zadok, Jaddua,

22 Pelatiah, Hanan, Anaiah,
23 Hoshea, Hananiah, Hasshub,
24 Hallohesh, Pilha, Shobek,
25 Rehum, Hashabnah, Maaseiah,
26 Ahiah, Hanan, Anan,
27 Malluch, Harim, Baanah

28 The rest of the people gathered together. They included the priests, the Levites and the men who guarded the gates. They included the singers and temple servants. They also included all those who separated themselves from the surrounding nations to obey the Law of God. All of those men brought their wives with them. And they brought all of their sons and daughters who were old enough to understand what was being agreed to. 29 All of the men joined the nobles of their people. They made a firm agreement. They put themselves under a curse and took an oath. They promised to follow the Law of God. It had been given through Moses, the servant of God. They promised to obey carefully all of the commands, rules and laws of the LORD our Lord.

POWER SURGE

OBEYS ✔

ALL OF THE MEN JOINED THE NOBLES OF THEIR PEOPLE... THEY PROMISED TO OBEY CAREFULLY ALL OF THE COMMANDS, RULES AND LAWS OF THE LORD OUR LORD.
—— **NEHEMIAH 10:29** ——

---

30 The priests, Levites and people said, "We promise not to give our daughters to be married to men from the nations that are around us. And we promise not to let their daughters get married to our sons.

31 "The people around us will bring goods and grain to sell on the Sabbath day. But we won't buy anything from them on the Sabbath. In fact, we won't buy anything from them on any holy day. Every seventh year we won't farm the land. And we'll forgive people what they owe us.

32 "We will be accountable for carrying out the commands for serving in the house of our God. Each of us will give an eighth of an ounce of silver every year. 33 It will pay for the holy bread that is placed on the table in the temple. It will pay for the regular grain offerings and burnt offerings. It will pay for the offerings on the Sabbath days. It will pay for the offerings at the New Moon Feasts and appointed feasts. It will pay for the holy offerings. It will be used for sin offerings to pay for the sin of Israel. It will also pay for everything else that needs to be done at the house of our God.

34 "We are the priests, Levites and people. We have cast lots to decide when each of our families should bring a gift of wood to the house of our God. They will bring it at certain appointed times every year. The wood will be burned on the altar of the LORD our God. That's what the Law requires.

35 "We will also be accountable for bringing the first share of our crops each year. And we'll bring the first share of every fruit tree. We'll bring them to the LORD's house.

36 "Each of us will bring our oldest son to the priests who serve there. We'll also bring the male animals that were born first to their mothers among our cattle, herds and flocks. We'll bring them to the house of our God. That's what the Law requires.

37 "We will also bring the first part of the meal we grind. We'll bring the first of our grain offerings. We'll bring the first share of fruit from all of our trees. And we'll bring the first share of our olive oil and fresh wine. We'll give all of those things to the priests. They'll put them in the storerooms of the house of our God.

"And we'll give a tenth of our crops to the Levites. They collect the tenth shares. They do it in all of the towns where we work. 38 A priest from Aaron's family line must go with the Levites when they receive the tenth shares. And the Levites must bring a tenth of those shares up to the house of our God. They must put it in the rooms where the treasures are stored.

39 "The people of Israel, including

the Levites, must bring their gifts. They must bring grain, olive oil and fresh wine. They must put them in the storerooms where the articles for the temple are kept. That's where the priests stay when they are serving at the temple. The singers and the men who guard the gates also stay there.

"We won't forget to take care of the house of our God."

People Are Chosen to Live in Jerusalem

11 The leaders of the people settled down in Jerusalem. The rest of the people cast lots. They did it to choose one person out of every ten. That person was brought to live in the holy city of Jerusalem. The other nine had to stay in their own towns. **2** The people praised all those who agreed to live in Jerusalem.

3 Here are the leaders from different parts of the country who settled down in Jerusalem. Some Israelites, priests and Levites lived in the towns of Judah. So did some temple servants and some members of the family lines of Solomon's servants. All of them lived on their own property in the towns of Judah. **4** At the same time, other people from the tribes of Judah and Benjamin lived in Jerusalem.

Here are the leaders from the family line of Judah.

There was Athaiah. He was the son of Uzziah. Uzziah was the son of Zechariah. Zechariah was the son of Amariah. Amariah was the son of Shephatiah. Shephatiah was the son of Mahalalel. Mahalalel belonged to the family line of Perez. **5** There was also Maaseiah. He was the son of Baruch. Baruch was the son of Col-Hozeh. Col-Hozeh was the son of Hazaiah. Hazaiah was the son of Adaiah. Adaiah was the son of Joiarib. Joiarib was the son of Zechariah. Zechariah belonged to the family line of Shelah. **6** Many able men who belonged to the family line of Perez lived in Jerusalem. The total number of them was 468.

7 Here are the leaders from the family line of Benjamin.

There was Sallu. He was the son of Meshullam. Meshullam was the son of Joed. Joed was the son of Pedaiah. Pedaiah was the son of Kolaiah. Kolaiah was the son of Maaseiah. Maaseiah was the son of Ithiel. Ithiel was

the son of Jeshaiah. **8** There were also Gabbai and Sallai. They were Sallu's followers. The total number of men was 928. **9** Joel was their chief officer. He was the son of Zicri. A man named Judah was in charge of the New Quarter of Jerusalem. He was the son of Hassenuah.

10 Here are the leaders from among the priests.

There were Jedaiah, Jakin and the son of Joiarib. **11** There was also Seraiah. He was the son of Hilkiah. Hilkiah was the son of Meshullam. Meshullam was the son of Zadok. Zadok was the son of Meraioth. Meraioth was the son of Ahitub. Ahitub was a ruler in God's house. **12** There were also those who helped them. They carried out the work for the temple. The total number of men was 822.

There was also Adaiah. He was the son of Jeroham. Jeroham was the son of Pelaliah. Pelaliah was the son of Amzi. Amzi was the son of Zechariah. Zechariah was the son of Pashhur. Pashhur was the son of Malkijah. **13** There were also those who helped Adaiah. They were family leaders. The total number of men was 242.

There was also Amashsai. He was the son of Azarel. Azarel was the son of Ahzai. Ahzai was the son of Meshillemoth. Meshillemoth was the son of Immer. **14** There were also those who helped Amashsai. They were able men. The total number of them was 128. Their chief officer was Zabdiel. He was the son of Haggedolim.

15 Here are the leaders from among the Levites.

There was Shemaiah. He was the son of Hasshub. Hasshub was the son of Azrikam. Azrikam was the son of Hashabiah. Hashabiah was the son of Bunni. **16** There were also Shabbethai and Jozabad. They were two of the leaders of the Levites. They were in charge of the work that was done outside God's house.

17 There was also Mattaniah. He led in prayer and in giving thanks. He was the son of Mica. Mica was the son of Zabdi. Zabdi was the son of Asaph. There was also Bakbukiah. He was second among those who helped

Mattaniah. And there was Abda. He was the son of Shammua. Shammua was the son of Galal. Galal was the son of Jeduthun. **18**The total number of Levites in the holy city was 284.

19Here are the leaders from among the men who guarded the gates.

There were Akkub, Talmon and those who helped them. They stood guard at the gates. The total number of men was 172.

20The rest of the Israelites were in all of the towns of Judah. The priests and Levites were with them. All of them lived on their own family property.

21The temple servants lived on the hill of Ophel. Ziha and Gishpa were in charge of them.

22Uzzi was the chief officer of the Levites in Jerusalem. He was the son of Bani. Bani was the son of Hashabiah. Hashabiah was the son of Mattaniah. Mattaniah was the son of Mica. Uzzi was one of the members of Asaph's family line. They were singers. They were in charge of the worship services at God's house. **23**The singers received their orders from the Persian king. He told them what they should do every day.

24Pethahiah worked for the king in all matters that were connected with the people. He was the son of Meshezabel. Meshezabel belonged to the family line of Zerah. Zerah was the son of Judah.

25Many of the people of Judah lived in villages that had fields around them. Some of them lived in Kiriath Arba and the settlements that were around it. Others lived in Dibon and its settlements. Others lived in Jekabzeel and its villages. **26**Others lived in Jeshua, Moladah and Beth Pelet.

27Others lived in Hazar Shual and in Beersheba and its settlements. **28**Others lived in Ziklag and in Meconah and its settlements. **29**Others lived in En Rimmon and Zorah. Others lived in Jarmuth, **30**Zanoah and Adullam and their villages. Others lived in Lachish and its fields. Still others lived in Azekah and its settlements. So the people of Judah were living all the way from Beersheba to the Valley of Hinnom.

31Some of the members of the family line of Benjamin who were from Geba lived in Micmash. Others lived in Aija and in Bethel and its settlements. **32**Others lived in Anathoth, Nob and Ananiah. **33**Others lived in Hazor, Ramah and Git-

taim. **34**Others lived in Hadid, Zeboim and Neballat. **35**Others lived in Lod and Ono. Still others lived in the Valley of Skilled Workers.

36Some of the groups of the Levites from Judah settled in the territory of Benjamin.

The Priests and Levites Who Returned to Judah

12 Some priests and Levites returned to Judah with Zerubbabel and Jeshua. Zerubbabel was the son of Shealtiel. Here are the names of those priests and Levites.

Seraiah, Jeremiah, Ezra,
2Amariah, Malluch, Hattush,
3Shecaniah, Rehum, Meremoth,
4Iddo, Ginnethon, Abijah,
5Mijamin, Moadiah, Bilgah,
6Shemaiah, Joiarib, Jedaiah,
7Sallu, Amok, Hilkiah, Jedaiah

All of them were the leaders of the priests and those who helped them. They lived in the days of Jeshua.

8The Levites were Jeshua, Binnui, Kadmiel, Sherebiah and Judah. There were also Mattaniah and those who helped him. They were in charge of the songs for giving thanks. **9**Bakbukiah and Unni helped them. They stood and sang across from them during the services.

POWER-SURGE

THANKFUL ♣

[THE LEVITES]... WERE IN CHARGE OF THE SONGS FOR GIVING THANKS.
—— NEHEMIAH 12:8 ——

10Jeshua was the father of Joiakim. Joiakim was the father of Eliashib. Eliashib was the father of Joiada. **11**Joiada was the father of Jonathan. And Jonathan was the father of Jaddua.

12Here are the names of the family leaders of the priests. They were the leaders in the days of Joiakim.

Meraiah was from Seraiah's family.
Hananiah was from Jeremiah's family.
13Meshullam was from Ezra's family.
Jehohanan was from Amariah's family.

14 Jonathan was from Malluch's family. Joseph was from Shecaniah's family. 15 Adna was from Harim's family. Helkai was from Meremoth's family. 16 Zechariah was from Iddo's family. Meshullam was from Ginnethon's family. 17 Zicri was from Abijah's family. Piltai was from Miniamin's and Moadiah's family. 18 Shammua was from Bilgah's family. Jehonathan was from Shemaiah's family. 19 Mattenai was from Joiarib's family. Uzzi was from Jedaiah's family. 20 Kallai was from Sallu's family. Eber was from Amok's family. 21 Hashabiah was from Hilkiah's family. And Nethanel was from Jedaiah's family.

22 The names of the family leaders of the Levites in the days of Eliashib, Joiada, Johanan and Jaddua were written down. So were the names of the family leaders of the priests. That happened while Darius ruled over Persia. 23 The names of the leaders in Levi's family line up to the time of Johanan were written down. They were written in the official records. Johanan was the son of Eliashib. 24 The leaders of the Levites were Hashabiah, Sherebiah and Jeshua. Jeshua was the son of Kadmiel.

Those who helped them stood across from them to sing praises and give thanks. One group would sing back to the other. That's what David, the man of God, had ordered.

25 Mattaniah, Bakbukiah, Obadiah, Meshullam, Talmon and Akkub stood at the gates of the temple. They guarded the storerooms at the gates. 26 They served in the days of Joiakim. He was the son of Jeshua. Jeshua was the son of Jehozadak. They also served in the days of Nehemiah and Ezra. Nehemiah was governor. Ezra was a priest and a teacher of the law.

The Wall of Jerusalem Is Set Apart to God

27 The wall of Jerusalem was set apart to God. For that occasion, the Levites were gathered together from where they lived. They were brought to Jerusalem to celebrate that happy occasion. They celebrated the fact that the wall was being set apart to God. They did it by singing and giving their thanks to him. They celebrated by playing music on cymbals, harps and lyres.

28 The singers were also brought together. Some of them came in from the area around Jerusalem. Others came from the villages where the people of Netophah lived. 29 Others came from Beth Gilgal. Still others came from the area of Geba and Azmaveth. The singers had built villages for themselves around Jerusalem.

30 The priests and Levites made themselves pure. Then they made the people, the gates and the wall pure and clean.

31 I, Nehemiah, had the leaders of Judah go up on top of the wall. I also appointed two large choirs to sing and give thanks. I told one of them to walk south on top of the wall. That was toward the Dung Gate. 32 Hoshaiah and half of the leaders of Judah followed them. 33 Azariah, Ezra, Meshullam, 34 Judah, Benjamin, Shemaiah and Jeremiah also followed them.

35 Some priests who had trumpets followed them. So did Zechariah. He was the son of Jonathan. Jonathan was the son of Shemaiah. Shemaiah was the son of Mattaniah. Mattaniah was the son of Micaiah. Micaiah was the son of Zaccur. Zaccur was the son of Asaph. 36 Those who helped Zechariah also marched along. They were Shemaiah, Azarel, Milalai, Gilalai, Maai, Nethanel, Judah and Hanani. They brought instruments of music with them. That's what David, the man of God, had ordered. Ezra led the group that was marching south. He was a teacher of the law.

37 At the Fountain Gate they continued straight up the steps of the City of David that went up to the wall. Then the group passed above David's house. They continued on to the Water Gate on the east.

38 The second choir went north. I followed them on top of the wall. Half of the people went with me. They went past the Tower of the Ovens. They went to the Broad Wall. 39 They marched over the Gate of Ephraim. They went over the Jeshanah Gate and the Fish Gate. They went past the Tower of Hananel and the Tower of the Hundred. They continued on to the Sheep Gate. At the Gate of the Guard they stopped.

40 Then the two choirs that sang and gave thanks took their places in God's house. So did I. So did half of the officials. 41 And so did the priests. They were Eliakim, Maaseiah, Miniamin, Micaiah, Elioenai, Zechariah and Hananiah. They had their trumpets with them. 42 Maaseiah, Shemaiah, Eleazar, Uzzi, Jehohanan, Malkijah, Elam and Ezer were also there. The choirs sang under the direction of Jezrahiah.

POWER-SURGE

CHEERFUL ✳

THE PEOPLE WERE
GLAD BECAUSE GOD
HAD GIVEN THEM
GREAT JOY. THE
WOMEN AND CHILDREN
WERE ALSO VERY
HAPPY. THE JOYFUL
SOUND IN JERUSALEM
COULD BE HEARD
FAR AWAY.
—— NEHEMIAH 12:43 ——

43On that day large numbers of sacrifices were offered. The people were glad because God had given them great joy. The women and children were also very happy. The joyful sound in Jerusalem could be heard far away.

44At that time some men were put in charge of the storerooms. That's where all of the gifts the people brought were placed. They included the first shares of their crops. They also included a tenth of everything the Law required. From the fields that were around the towns the people had to bring the shares of their crops that were required by the Law. They gave them to the priests and Levites. That's because the people of Judah were pleased with the priests and Levites who were serving God.

45The priests and Levites did everything their God wanted them to do. They made things pure and clean. The singers and those who guarded the temple gates also served God. Everything was done just as David and his son Solomon had commanded. **46**A long time ago there had been directors for the singers. There had also been directors for the songs for giving thanks and praise to God. It was in the time of David and Asaph.

47So now in the days of Zerubbabel and Nehemiah, all of the people of Israel brought their gifts. They gave the singers and those who guarded the gates what they were supposed to give them every day. They also set apart the shares for the other Levites. And the Levites set apart the shares for the priests in the family line of Aaron.

Nehemiah Warns the People

13 On that same day the Scroll of Moses was read out loud. All of the people heard it. It was written there that no one from Ammon or Moab should ever be allowed to become a member of the community of God. **2**That's because they hadn't given the people of Israel food and water. Instead, they had hired Balaam to call a curse down on them. But our God turned the curse into a blessing.

3When that law was read, the people of Judah obeyed it. They put out of Israel everyone who was from another nation.

4The priest Eliashib had been put in charge of the storerooms in the house of our God. He had worked closely with Tobiah. **5**He had also provided a large room for Tobiah. It had been used to store the grain offerings. The incense and temple articles had been put there. And a tenth of the grain, olive oil and fresh wine had been kept there. That's what the Law required for the Levites. That's also what it required for the singers and those who guarded the temple gates. The gifts for the priests had been kept there too.

6But I wasn't in Jerusalem while all of that was going on. I had returned to the Persian King Artaxerxes, the king of Babylonia. I went to him in the 32nd year of his rule. Some time later I asked him to let me return to Jerusalem.

7When I got back, I learned about the evil thing Eliashib had done. He had provided a room for Tobiah. It was in the courtyards of God's house. **8**So I was very unhappy. I threw all of Tobiah's things out of the room.

9I gave orders to make the rooms pure and clean again. Then I put the supplies from God's house back into them. That included the grain offerings and the incense.

10I also learned that the shares the Levites were supposed to receive hadn't been given to them. So all of the Levites and singers had to leave their regular temple duties. They had to go back and farm their own fields.

11I gave a warning to the officials. I asked them, "Why aren't you taking care of God's house?" Then I brought them together. I stationed them in their proper places. I put them back to work.

12All of the people of Judah brought a tenth of the grain, olive oil and fresh wine. They took it to the storerooms.

13I put some men in charge of the storerooms. They were Shelemiah, Zadok and Pedaiah. Shelemiah was a priest. Zadok

POWER-SURGE

TRUSTED ✦

I KNEW THAT THOSE MEN COULD BE TRUSTED.
—— **NEHEMIAH 13:13** ——

was a teacher of the law. And Pedaiah was a Levite. I made Hanan their assistant. He was the son of Zaccur. Zaccur was the son of Mattaniah. I knew that those men could be trusted. They were put in charge of handing out the supplies to their people.

¹⁴You are my God. Remember me because of what I've done. I've worked faithfully for your temple and its services. So please don't forget the good things I've done.

¹⁵In those days I saw some men of Judah stomping on grapes in winepresses. They were doing it on the Sabbath day. Others were bringing in grain. They were loading it on donkeys. Still others were loading up wine, grapes, figs and other kinds of things. They were bringing all of it into Jerusalem on the Sabbath. So I warned them not to sell food on that day. ¹⁶People from Tyre who lived in Jerusalem were bringing in fish. In fact, they were bringing in all kinds of goods. They were selling them in Jerusalem on the Sabbath. The people of Judah were buying them.

¹⁷I gave a warning to the nobles of Judah. I said, "Why are you doing such an evil thing? You are misusing the Sabbath day! ¹⁸Your people before you did the very same things. That's why our God has brought all of this trouble on us. That's why he's making this city suffer so much. Now you are stirring up even more of his anger against Israel. You are misusing the Sabbath day."

¹⁹Evening shadows fell on the gates of Jerusalem before the Sabbath started. So I ordered the gates to be shut. They had to remain closed until the Sabbath was over. I stationed some of my own men at the gates. I told them not to let anything be brought in on the Sabbath day.

²⁰Once or twice some traders and sellers spent the night outside Jerusalem. They were hoping to sell all kinds of goods. ²¹But I gave them a warning. I said, "Why are you spending the night by the wall? If you do this again, I'll arrest you." So from that time on they didn't come on the Sabbath anymore.

²²I commanded the Levites to make themselves pure. Then I told them to go and guard the gates. I wanted the Sabbath day to be kept holy.

You are my God. Remember me because of the good things I've done. Be kind to me in keeping with your great love.

²³In those days I also saw that some men of Judah had gotten married to women from Ashdod. Others had married women from Ammon or Moab. ²⁴Half of their children spoke the language of Ashdod. Or they spoke the language of one of the other nations. They didn't even know how to speak the language of Judah.

²⁵So I gave them a warning. I called curses down on them. I beat some of them up. I pulled their hair out. I made them take an oath in God's name. I said, "You must promise not to give your daughters to be married to their sons. You must promise not to let their daughters marry your sons. And you must not marry their daughters either.

²⁶"That's how Solomon, the king of Israel, sinned. He married women from other nations. There wasn't a king like him anywhere. His God loved him. In fact, God made him king over the whole nation of Israel. But even he was led into sin by women from other lands. ²⁷Now I hear that you too are doing all of the same terrible and evil things. You aren't being faithful to our God. You are marrying women from other lands."

²⁸One of the sons of Joiada was the son-in-law of Sanballat. Joiada was the high priest. He was the son of Eliashib. I drove Joiada's son away from me. Sanballat was a Horonite.

POWER-SURGE

KIND   K

BE KIND TO ME IN KEEPING WITH YOUR GREAT LOVE.
—— **NEHEMIAH 13:22** —— ♥

LOVING

29You are my God. Remember what those priests have done. They have polluted their own work. They have also polluted the covenant that God made with the priests and Levites long ago.

30So I made the priests and Levites pure. I made them pure from every practice that had come from other countries and had polluted them. I gave them their duties. Each one had his own job to do. 31I also made plans for gifts of wood to be brought at certain appointed times. And I made plans for the first share of the crops to be brought.

You are my God. Please remember me. Show me your favor.

ESTHER

The book of Esther reveals a God who is completely aware of what his people are facing. In Esther, wicked Haman plots to kill all the Jews. God knows Haman's evil plans. He puts the young Jew, Esther, in a special place as queen of Persia. Because she is queen, she is able to help save her people. The heroes of Esther are the godly Mordecai, who raises Esther and urges her to use her high position to save her people, and Queen Esther, who risks death to save her people. Read Esther to discover how God knows and cares about all the details, big and small, of your life.

HEROES IN THIS BOOK . . .

MORDECAI
PAGE 591

ESTHER
PAGE 593

Vashti Is Removed From Her Position as Queen

1 King Xerxes ruled over the 127 territories in his kingdom. They reached from India all the way to Cush. Here is what happened during the time Xerxes ruled over the whole Persian kingdom. ²He was ruling from his royal throne in the safest place in Susa.

³In the third year of his rule King Xerxes gave a big dinner. It was for all of his nobles and officials. The military leaders of Persia and Media were there. So were the princes and the nobles of the territories he ruled over. ⁴Every day for 180 days he showed his guests the great wealth of his kingdom. He also showed them how glorious his kingdom was.

⁵When those days were over, the king gave another big dinner. It lasted for seven days. It was held in the garden of the king's courtyard. It was for all of the people who lived in the safest place in Susa. Everyone from the least important person to the most important was invited.

⁶The garden was decorated with white and blue linen banners. They hung from ropes that were made out of white linen and purple cloth. The ropes were connected to silver rings on marble pillars. There were gold and silver couches in the garden. They were placed on a floor that was made out of small stones. The floor had purple crystal, marble, mother-of-pearl and other stones of great value.

⁷Royal wine was served in gold cups. Each cup was different from all of the others. There was plenty of wine. The king always provided as much as his guests wanted. ⁸He commanded that they should be allowed to drink as much or as little as they wished. He directed all of his servants to give them what they asked for.

⁹Queen Vashti also gave a big dinner. Only women were invited. It was held in the royal palace of King Xerxes.

¹⁰On the seventh day Xerxes was in a good mood because he had drunk a lot of wine. So he gave a command to the seven officials who served him. They were Mehuman, Biztha, Harbona, Bigtha, Abagtha, Zethar and Carcas. ¹¹He told them to bring Queen Vashti to him. He wanted her to come wearing her royal crown. He wanted to show off her beauty to the people and nobles. She was lovely to look at.

¹²The attendants told Queen Vashti what the king had ordered her to do. But she refused to come. So the king became very angry. In fact, he burned with anger.

¹³It was the king's practice to ask advice from those who knew a lot about matters of law and fairness. So he spoke with the wise men who were supposed to understand what was going on at that time. ¹⁴They were the men who were closest to the king. They were Carshena, Shethar, Admatha, Tarshish, Meres, Marsena and Memucan. They were the seven nobles of Persia and Media. They were the king's special advisers. In fact, they were the most important men in the kingdom.

¹⁵"You know the law," the king said. "What should I do to Queen Vashti? She hasn't obeyed my command. The officials told her what I ordered her to do, didn't they?"

¹⁶Then Memucan gave a reply to the king and the nobles. He said, "Queen Vashti has done what is wrong. But she didn't do it only against you, King Xerxes. She did it also against all of the nobles. And she did it against the people in all of the territories you rule over.

¹⁷"All of the women will hear about what the queen has done. Then they will look down on their husbands. They'll say, 'King Xerxes commanded Queen Vashti to be brought to him. But she wouldn't come.' ¹⁸Starting today, the leading women in Persia and Media who have heard about the queen's actions will act in the same way. They'll disobey all of your nobles, just as she disobeyed you. They won't have any respect for their husbands. They won't honor them.

¹⁹"So if it pleases you, send out a royal order. Let it be written down in the laws of Persia and Media. They can never be changed. Let the royal order say that Vashti can never see you again. Also let her position as queen be given to someone who is better than she is.

²⁰"And let your order be announced all through your entire kingdom. Then all of the other women will have respect for their husbands from the least important to the most important."

²¹The king and his nobles were pleased with that advice. So he did what Memucan had suggested. ²²He sent messages out to every territory in the kingdom. He sent them to each territory in its own writing. He sent them to every nation in its own language. The messages announced in each nation's language that every man should rule over his own family.

Esther Becomes Queen of Persia

2 Later, the anger of King Xerxes calmed down. Then he remembered

Vashti and what she had done. He also remembered the royal order he had sent out concerning her.

²At that time the king's personal attendants made a suggestion. They said, "King Xerxes, let a search be made for some beautiful young virgins for you. ³Appoint some officials in every territory in your kingdom. Have them bring all of those beautiful virgins into the safest place in Susa. Put them in the special place where the virgins stay. Then put Hegai in charge of them. He's the eunuch who serves you. He's in charge of the virgins. Let beauty care be given to the new group of virgins. ⁴Then let the one who pleases you the most become queen in Vashti's place."

The king liked that advice. So he followed it.

⁵There was a Jew living in the safest place in Susa. He was from the tribe of Benjamin. His name was Mordecai. He was the son of Jair. Jair was the son of Shimei. Shimei was the son of Kish. ⁶Nebuchadnezzar had forced Mordecai to leave Jerusalem. He was among the prisoners who were carried off along with Jehoiachin. Jehoiachin had been king of Judah. Nebuchadnezzar was king of Babylonia.

⁷Mordecai had a cousin named Hadassah. He had brought her up in his own home. She didn't have a father or mother. Hadassah was also called Esther. She was very beautiful. Mordecai had adopted her as his own daughter. He had done it when her father and mother died.

⁸After the king's order and law were announced, many virgins were brought to the safest place in Susa. Hegai was put in charge of them. Esther was also taken to the king's palace. She was put under the control of Hegai. He was in charge of the place where the virgins stayed.

⁹Esther pleased him. He showed her his favor. Right away he provided her with her beauty care and special food. He appointed seven female attendants to help her. They were chosen from the king's palace. He moved her and her attendants into the best part of the place where the virgins stayed.

¹⁰Esther hadn't told anyone who her people were. She hadn't talked about her family. That's because Mordecai had told her not to.

¹¹Mordecai tried to find out how Esther was getting along. He wanted to know what was happening to her. So he walked back and forth near the courtyard by the place where the virgins stayed. He did it every day.

¹²Each virgin had to complete 12 months of beauty care. They used oil of myrrh for six months. And they used perfume and make-up for the other six months. A virgin's turn to go in to King Xerxes could come only after a full 12 months had passed.

¹³And here is how she would go to the king. She would be given anything she wanted from the place where the virgins stayed. She could take it with her to the king's palace. ¹⁴In the evening she would go there. In the morning she would leave. Then she would go to the special place where the king's concubines stayed. She would be put under the control of Shaashgaz. He was the king's eunuch who was in charge of the concubines. She would never return to the king unless he was pleased with her. He had to send for her by name before she could go to him again.

¹⁵Mordecai had adopted Esther. She had been the daughter of his uncle Abihail. Her turn came to go in to the king. She only asked for what Hegai suggested. He was the king's eunuch who was in charge of the place where the virgins stayed. Everyone who saw Esther was pleased with her. ¹⁶She was taken to King Xerxes in the royal house. It was now the tenth month. That was the month of Tebeth. It was the seventh year of the rule of Xerxes.

¹⁷The king liked Esther more than he liked any of the other women. She pleased him more than any of the other virgins. So he put a royal crown on her head. He made her queen in Vashti's place.

¹⁸Then the king gave a big dinner. It was in honor of Esther. All of his nobles and officials were invited. He announced a holiday all through the territories he ruled over. He freely gave many gifts in keeping with his royal wealth.

Mordecai Uncovers a Plan to Kill the King

¹⁹The virgins were gathered together a second time. At that time Mordecai was sitting at the palace gate. ²⁰Esther had kept her family history a secret. She hadn't told anyone who her people were. Mordecai had told her not to. She continued to follow his directions. That's what she had always done when he was bringing her up.

²¹Bigthana and Teresh were two of the king's officers. They guarded the door of

the royal palace. They became angry with King Xerxes. So they decided to kill him. They made their evil plans while Mordecai was sitting at the palace gate.

22So he found out about it. And he told Queen Esther. Then she reported it to the king. She told him that Mordecai had uncovered the plans against him. 23Some people checked Esther's report. And they found out it was true. So the two officials were put to death. Then poles were stuck through them. They were set up where people could see them. All of that was written in the official records. It was written down while the king was watching.

Haman Plans to Destroy the Jews

3 After those events, King Xerxes honored Haman. Haman was the son of Hammedatha. He was from the family line of Agag. The king gave Haman a higher position than he had before. He gave him a seat of honor. It was higher than the positions any of the other nobles had. 2All of the royal officials at the palace gate got down on their knees. They gave honor to Haman. That's because the king had commanded them to do it.

But Mordecai refused to get down on his knees. He wouldn't give Haman any honor at all.

3The royal officials at the palace gate asked Mordecai a question. They said, "Why don't you obey the king's command?" 4Day after day they spoke to him. But he still refused to obey. So they told Haman about it. They wanted to see whether he would let Mordecai get away with what he was doing. Mordecai had told them he was a Jew.

5Haman noticed that Mordecai wouldn't get down on his knees. He wouldn't give Haman any honor. So Haman burned with anger. 6But he had found out who Mordecai's people were. So he decided not to kill just Mordecai. He also looked for a way to destroy all of Mordecai's people. They were Jews. He wanted to kill all of them everywhere in the kingdom of Xerxes.

7The lot was cast in front of Haman. That was done to choose a day and a month. It was the 12th year that Xerxes was king. It was in the first month. That was the month of Nisan. The lot chose the 12th month. That was the month of Adar. The lot was also called *pur*.

8Then Haman said to King Xerxes, "Certain people are scattered among the nations. They live in all of the territories in your kingdom. Their practices are different from the practices of all other people. They don't obey your laws. It really isn't good for you to put up with them.

9"If it pleases you, give the order to destroy them. I'll even add 375 tons of silver to the royal treasures. You can use it to pay the men who take care of the matter."

10So the king took his ring off his finger. The ring had his royal seal on it. He gave the ring to Haman. Haman was the son of Hammedatha, the Agagite. He was the enemy of the Jews.

11"Keep the money," the king said to Haman. "Do what you want to with those people."

12The king sent for the royal secretaries. It was the 13th day of the first month. The secretaries wrote down all of Haman's orders. They wrote them down in the writing of each territory in the kingdom. They also wrote them in the language of each nation. The orders were sent to the royal officials. They were also sent to the governors of the territories. And they went out to the nobles of the nations. The orders were written in the name of King Xerxes himself. And they were stamped with his own royal seal. 13They were carried by messengers. They were sent to all of the king's territories.

The orders commanded people to destroy, kill and wipe out all of the Jews. That included young people and old people alike. It included women and little children. All of the Jews were supposed to be killed on a single day. That day was the 13th day of the 12th month. It was the month of Adar. The orders also commanded people to take the goods that belonged to the Jews.

14A copy of the order had to be sent out as law. It had to be sent to every territory

POWER-SURGE

OBEYS ✔

[ESTHER] CONTINUED TO FOLLOW [MORDECAI'S] DIRECTIONS. THAT'S WHAT SHE HAD ALWAYS DONE WHEN HE WAS BRINGING HER UP.

— ESTHER 2:20 —

in the kingdom. It had to be announced to the people of every nation. Then they would be ready for that day.

¹⁵The king commanded the messengers to go out. So they did. The order was sent out from the safest place in Susa. Then the king and Haman sat down to drink wine. But the people in the city were bewildered.

Mordecai Talks Esther Into Helping the Jews

4 Mordecai found out about everything that had been done. So he tore his clothes. He put on black clothes. He sat down in ashes. Then he went out into the city. He sobbed out loud. He cried bitter tears. ²But he only went as far as the palace gate. That's because no one who was dressed in black clothes was allowed to go through it.

³All of the Jews were very sad. They didn't eat anything. They sobbed and cried. Many of them put on black clothes. They were lying down in ashes. They did all of those things in every territory where the king's order and law had been sent.

⁴Esther's eunuchs and female attendants came to her. They told her about Mordecai. So she became very troubled. She wanted him to take his black clothes off. So she sent him other clothes to wear. But he wouldn't accept them. ⁵Then Esther sent for Hathach. He was one of the king's eunuchs. He had been appointed to take care of her. She ordered him to find out what was troubling Mordecai. She wanted to know why he was so upset.

⁶So Hathach went out to see Mordecai. He was in the open area in front of the palace gate. ⁷Mordecai told him everything that had happened to him. He told him about the exact amount of money Haman had promised to add to the royal treasures. He said Haman wanted it to be used to pay some men to destroy the Jews.

⁸Mordecai also gave Hathach a copy of the order. It commanded people to wipe out the Jews. The order had been sent from Susa.

Mordecai told Hathach to show the order to Esther. He wanted him to explain it to her. He told him to try and get her to go to the king. He wanted her to beg for mercy. He wanted her to make an appeal to the king for her people.

⁹Hathach went back. He reported to Esther what Mordecai had said. ¹⁰Then Esther directed him to give an answer to Mordecai. She told him to say, ¹¹"There is a certain law that everyone knows about.

All of the king's officials know about it. The people in the royal territories know about it. It applies to any man or woman who approaches the king in the inner courtyard without being sent for. It says they must be put to death. But there is a way out. Suppose the king reaches out his gold rod toward them. Then their lives will be spared. But 30 days have gone by since the king sent for me."

¹²Esther's words were reported to Mordecai. ¹³Then he sent back an answer. He said, "You live in the king's palace. But don't think that just because you are there you will be the only Jew who will escape. ¹⁴What if you don't say anything at this time? Then help for the Jews will come from another place. But you and your family will die. Who knows? It's possible that you became queen for a time just like this."

¹⁵Then Esther sent a reply to Mordecai. She said, ¹⁶"Go. Gather together all of the Jews who are in Susa. And fast for my benefit. Don't eat or drink anything for three days. Don't do it night or day. I and my attendants will fast just as you do. Then I'll go to the king. I'll do it even though it's against the law. And if I have to die, I'll die."

¹⁷So Mordecai went away. He carried out all of Esther's directions.

Esther Invites the King and Haman to a Big Dinner

5 On the third day Esther put her royal robes on. She stood in the inner courtyard of the palace. It was in front of the king's hall.

The king was sitting on his royal throne in the hall. He was facing the entrance. ²He saw Queen Esther standing in the courtyard. He was pleased with her. So he reached out toward her the gold rod that was in his hand. Then Esther approached him. She touched the tip of the rod.

³The king asked, "What is it, Queen Esther? What do you want? I'll give it to you. I'll even give you up to half of my kingdom."

⁴Esther replied, "King Xerxes, if it pleases you, come to a big dinner today. I've prepared it for you. Please have Haman come with you."

⁵"Bring Haman at once," the king said to his servants. "Then we'll do what Esther asks."

So the king and Haman went to the big dinner Esther had prepared. ⁶As they were drinking wine, the king asked Esther the same question again. He said, "What do

MORDECAI

ESTHER 4:13-14

[Mordecai] said, "You live in the king's palace. But don't think that just because you are there you will be the only Jew who will escape...Who knows? It's possible that you became queen for a time just like this."

Mordecai (MORE-duh-kai) tore his clothes. He sprinkled ashes over his head. Then he went into the city and cried so loud that all of those he met would know he was sad.

Mordecai was sad. But more than that, he was terrified. He had just found out that one of the nation's officials, Haman, had gotten the king to sign an order to kill all the Jews in Persia. Mordecai was a Jew. So was his cousin, Queen Esther.

Mordecai wept with his Jewish friends when they heard the news. They were going to die unless something was done, and done quickly. They, too, tore their clothes and cried out loud. When Queen Esther's maids saw Mordecai, they told her he was crying loudly in the streets. She sent one of them back to Mordecai. Mordecai sent Esther this message: "Haman has ordered all the Jews in the kingdom to be killed on a certain day. You must go to the king and ask for mercy!"

Now Esther was in a terrible fix. She could be killed if she went in to see the king without his permission. So she sent a message back to Mordecai saying she could do nothing. Mordecai shot a message back: "You think just because you live in the king's house you will escape? As soon as they find out you're a Jew, you will die, too. **MAYBE YOU HAVE BECOME QUEEN IN ORDER TO SAVE US!** Please, go to the king."

Esther had obeyed her cousin, Mordecai, all her life. This time was no different. She asked him to pray for her. She would go to the king. If she died, she died!

That day, Mordecai set in motion the events that would save the Jews. His knowledge of the law, his love for Esther, his trust in God—all saved the Jews from death in Persia.

BE A MORDECAI

When Mordecai got bad news, he didn't wait for someone else to act. Be a Mordecai! When something needs to be done—even if it's hard or scary—ask God for his help, then take action.

MORDECAI TOOK WHAT HE KNEW AND SAVED THE JEWS FROM DEATH.
THE WHOLE STORY: ESTHER 4:1–7:10

Go to page 593 for the next Super Hero

you want? I'll give it to you. What do you want me to do for you? I'll even give you up to half of my kingdom."

⁷Esther replied, "Here is what I want. Here is my appeal to you. ⁸I hope you will show me your favor. I hope you will be pleased to give me what I want. And I hope you will be pleased to listen to my appeal. If you are, I'd like you and Haman to come tomorrow to the big dinner I'll prepare for you. Then I'll answer your question."

Haman Brags About Being Invited to Esther's Dinner

⁹That day Haman was happy. So he left the palace in a good mood. But then he saw Mordecai at the palace gate. He noticed that Mordecai didn't stand up when he walked by. In fact, Mordecai didn't have any respect for him at all. So he burned with anger against him. ¹⁰But Haman was able to control himself. He went on home.

Haman called his friends and his wife Zeresh together. ¹¹He bragged to them about how rich he was. He talked about how many sons he had. He spoke about all of the ways the king had honored him. He bragged about how the king had given him a higher position than any of the other nobles and officials had. ¹²"And that's not all!" Haman added. "I'm the only person Queen Esther invited to come with the king to the big dinner she gave. Now she has invited me along with the king tomorrow.

¹³"But even all of that doesn't satisfy me. I won't be satisfied as long as I see that Jew Mordecai sitting at the palace gate."

¹⁴Haman's wife Zeresh and all of his friends spoke up. They said to him, "Get a pole. In the morning, ask the king to have Mordecai put to death. Have the pole stuck through his body. Set it up at a place where it will be 75 feet above the ground. Everyone will be able to see it there. Then go to the dinner with the king. Have a good time."

Haman was delighted with that suggestion. So he got the pole ready.

The King Honors Mordecai

6 That night the king couldn't sleep. So he ordered the official records of his rule to be brought in. He ordered someone to read them to him. ²It was written there that Mordecai had uncovered the plans of Bigthana and Teresh against the king. They had been two of the king's officers who guarded the door of the royal palace. They had decided to kill King Xerxes.

³"What great honor has Mordecai received for doing that?" the king asked.

"Nothing has been done for him," his attendants answered.

⁴The king asked, "Who is in the courtyard?"

Haman had just entered the outer courtyard of the palace. He had come to speak to the king about putting Mordecai to death. He wanted to talk about putting Mordecai's body up on the pole he had gotten ready for him.

⁵The king's attendants said to him, "Haman is standing in the courtyard."

"Bring him in," the king ordered.

⁶Haman entered. Then the king asked him, "What should be done for the man I want to honor?"

Haman said to himself, "Is there anyone the king would rather honor than me?" ⁷So he answered the king. He said, "Here is what you should do for the man you want to honor. ⁸Have your servants get a royal robe you have worn. Have them bring a horse you have ridden on. Have a royal crest placed on its head. ⁹Then give the robe and horse to one of your most noble princes. Let the robe be put on the man you want to honor. Let him be led on the horse through the city streets. Let people announce in front of him, 'This is what is done for the man the king wants to honor!' "

¹⁰"Go right away," the king commanded Haman. "Get the robe. Bring the horse. Do exactly what you have suggested. Do it for the Jew Mordecai. He's sitting out there at the palace gate. Make sure you do everything you have suggested."

¹¹So Haman got the robe and the horse. He put the robe on Mordecai. And he led him on horseback through the city streets. He walked along in front of him and announced, "This is what is done for the man the king wants to honor!"

¹²After that, Mordecai returned to the palace gate. But Haman rushed home. He covered his head because he was very sad. ¹³He told his wife Zeresh everything that had happened to him. He also told all of his friends.

His advisers and his wife Zeresh spoke to him. They said, "Your fall from power started with Mordecai. He's a Jew. So now you can't stand up against him. You are going to be destroyed!" ¹⁴They were still talking with him when the king's officials arrived. They hurried Haman away to the big dinner Esther had prepared.

ESTHER

B
K
W

ESTHER 4:16

*I and my attendants will fast just as you do.
Then I'll go to the king. I'll do it even though
it's against the law. And if I have to die,
I'll die.*

Queen Esther's maids helped her put on her royal robe. The robe's jewels and embroidery made it feel heavy on Esther's shoulders. Esther slipped her feet into her beautiful slippers. Her hair was carefully arranged. Her skin had been washed and oiled and perfumed. She was ready.

Esther was going to see the king. She was the queen, but it was against the law for her to go to see the king unless he asked for her. The king could have her killed!

But Esther had important business. Esther's cousin, Mordecai, had told her that someone was planning to kill all the Jews in Persia. Esther herself was a Jew, though no one in the royal household knew that. She had to protect her people. And the only way to do that was to go to the king. So Esther asked Mordecai and the other Jews in Persia to pray for her. Then she got herself ready—ready to save her people. Or die.

Raising her head high, Queen Esther walked into the throne room. **ALL EYES TURNED TO LOOK AT THIS WOMAN WHO DARED TO COME UNINVITED INTO THE KING'S PRESENCE.** All eyes then turned to the king to see what he would do. With a warm look, the king extended his golden rod toward Esther.

Breathing a sigh of relief, Esther touched the tip of the king's rod. He knew she had an important request or she would never have risked her life. "Tell me what I can do for you," he declared. "I'll give you anything, up to half of my kingdom."

That day, Esther's plans to save her people began. Now she knew why God had made her, a young Jewish girl, a queen.

BE AN ESTHER

Lots of things in life are scary to do. Be an Esther. Don't give up because you're scared. Take a deep breath, say a prayer and go forward to do what must be done.

ESTHER BRAVELY WENT TO SEE THE KING IN ORDER TO SAVE HER PEOPLE.
THE WHOLE STORY: ESTHER 3:1–8:8

Go to page 601 for the next Super Hero

Haman Is Put to Death

7 So the king and Haman went to dine with Queen Esther. **2**They were drinking wine on the second day. The king again asked, "What do you want, Queen Esther? I'll give it to you. What do you want me to do for you? I'll even give you up to half of my kingdom."

3Then Queen Esther answered, "King Xerxes, I hope you will show me your favor. I hope you will be pleased to let me live. That's what I want. Please spare my people. That's my appeal to you.

4"My people and I have been sold to be destroyed. We've been sold to be killed and wiped out. Suppose we had only been sold as male and female slaves. Then I wouldn't have said anything. That kind of suffering wouldn't be a good enough reason to bother you."

5King Xerxes asked Queen Esther, "Who is the man who has dared to do such a thing? And where is he?"

6Esther said, "The man hates us! He's our enemy! He's this evil Haman!"

Then Haman was terrified in front of the king and queen.

7The king got up. He was burning with anger. He left his wine and went out into the palace garden.

But Haman realized that the king had already decided what he was going to do to him. So he stayed behind to beg Queen Esther for his life.

8The king returned from the palace garden to the dinner hall. Just then he saw Haman falling on the couch where Esther was lying.

The king shouted, "Will he even molest the queen? Is he going to attack her while she's right here with me in the palace?"

As soon as the king finished speaking, his men covered Haman's face.

9Then Harbona said, "There's a pole standing near Haman's house. He has gotten it ready for Mordecai. Mordecai is the one who spoke up to help you. Haman had planned to have him put to death. He was going to have the pole stuck through his body. Then he was going to set it up at a place where it would be 75 feet above the ground." Harbona was one of the officials who attended the king.

The king said to his men, "Put Haman to death! Stick the pole through his body! Set it up where everyone can see it!" **10**So they did. And they used the pole Haman had gotten ready for Mordecai. Then the king's anger calmed down.

The King Allows the Jews to Fight for Their Lives

8 That same day King Xerxes gave Queen Esther everything Haman had owned. Haman had been the enemy of the Jews.

Esther had told the king that Mordecai was her cousin. So Mordecai came to see the king. **2**The king took his ring off. It had his royal seal on it. He had taken it back from Haman. Now he gave it to Mordecai. And Esther put Mordecai in charge of everything Haman had owned.

3Esther made another appeal to the king. She fell at his feet and sobbed. She begged him to put an end to the evil plan of Haman, the Agagite. He had decided to kill the Jews.

4The king reached out his gold rod toward Esther. She got up and stood in front of him.

5"King Xerxes, I hope you will show me your favor," she said. "I hope you will think that what I'm asking is the right thing to do. I hope you are pleased with me. If you are, and if it pleases you, let an order be written. Let it take the place of the messages Haman wrote. Haman was the son of Hammedatha, the Agagite. He planned to kill the Jews. He wrote orders to destroy us in all of your territories. **6**I couldn't stand by and see the horrible trouble that would fall on my people! I couldn't stand to see my family destroyed!"

7King Xerxes gave a reply to Queen Esther and the Jew Mordecai. He said, "Haman attacked the Jews. So I've given Esther everything he owned. My men have stuck a pole through his dead body. And they've set it up where everyone can see it.

8"Now write another order in my name. Do it for the benefit of the Jews. Do what seems best to you. Stamp the order with my royal seal. Nothing that is written in my name and stamped with my seal can ever be changed."

9Right away the king sent for the royal secretaries. It was the 23rd day of the third month. That was the month of Sivan. They wrote down all of Mordecai's orders to the Jews. They also wrote them to the royal officials, the governors and the nobles of the 127 territories in his kingdom. The territories reached from India all the way to Cush. The orders were written down in the writing of each territory. They were written in the language of each nation. They were also written to the Jews in their own writing and language.

¹⁰Mordecai wrote the orders in the name of King Xerxes. He stamped them with the king's royal seal. He sent them by messengers on horseback. They rode fast horses that were raised just for the king.

¹¹The Jews in every city could now gather together and fight for their lives. The king's order gave them that right. But what if soldiers from any nation or territory attacked them? What if they attacked their women and children? Then the Jews could destroy, kill and wipe out those soldiers. They could also take the goods that belonged to their enemies. ¹²A day was appointed for the Jews to do that in all of the king's territories. It was the 13th day of the 12th month. That was the month of Adar.

¹³A copy of the order was sent out as law in every territory. It was announced to the people of every nation. So the Jews would be ready on that day. They could pay their enemies back.

¹⁴The messengers rode on the royal horses. They raced along. That's what the king commanded them to do. The order was also sent out in the safest place in Susa.

¹⁵Mordecai left the king and went on his way. Mordecai was wearing royal clothes. They were blue and white. He was also wearing a large gold crown. And he was wearing a purple coat. It was made out of fine linen. The city of Susa celebrated with great joy.

¹⁶The Jews were filled with joy and happiness. They were very glad because now they were being honored. ¹⁷They celebrated and enjoyed good food. They were glad and full of joy. That was true everywhere the king's order went out. It was true in every territory and every city. Many people from other nations announced that they had become Jews. That's because they were so afraid of the Jews.

The Jews Win the Battle Over Their Enemies

9 The king's order had to be carried out on the 13th day of the 12th month. That was the month of Adar. On that day the enemies of the Jews had hoped to win the battle over them. But now everything had changed. The Jews had gained the advantage over those who hated them.

²The Jews gathered together in their cities. They gathered in all of the territories King Xerxes ruled over. They came together to attack those who were trying to destroy them. No one could stand up against them. The people from all of the other nations were afraid of them.

³All of the nobles in the territories helped the Jews. So did the royal officials, the governors and the king's officers. That's because they were so afraid of Mordecai. ⁴He was well known in the palace. His fame spread all through the territories. So he became more and more important.

⁵The Jews struck down all of their enemies with swords. They killed them and destroyed them. They did what they pleased to those who hated them. ⁶The Jews killed 500 men. They destroyed them in the safest place in Susa.

⁷They also killed Parshandatha, Dalphon, Aspatha, ⁸Poratha, Adalia, Aridatha, ⁹Parmashta, Arisai, Aridai and Vaizatha. ¹⁰They were the ten sons of Haman. He was the son of Hammedatha. Haman had been the enemy of the Jews. They didn't take anything that belonged to their enemies.

¹¹A report was brought to the king that same day. He was told how many men had been killed in the safest place in Susa. ¹²He said to Queen Esther, "The Jews have killed 500 men. They destroyed them in the safest place in Susa. They also killed the ten sons of Haman there. What have they done in the rest of my territories? Now what do you want? I'll give it to you. What do you want me to do for you? I'll do that too."

¹³"If it pleases you," Esther answered, "let the Jews in Susa carry out today's order tomorrow also. Stick poles through the dead bodies of Haman's ten sons. Set them up where everyone can see them."

14So the king commanded that it be done. An order was sent out in Susa. And the king's men did to the bodies of Haman's sons everything they were told to do. **15**The Jews in Susa came together on the 14th day of the month of Adar. They put 300 men to death in Susa. But they didn't take anything that belonged to those men.

16During that time, the rest of the Jews also gathered together. They lived in the king's territories. They came together to fight for their lives. They didn't want their enemies to bother them anymore. They wanted to get some peace and rest. So they killed 75,000 of their enemies. But they didn't take anything that belonged to them. **17**It happened on the 13th of Adar. On the 14th day they rested. They made it a day to celebrate with great joy. And they enjoyed good food.

Purim Is Celebrated

18But the Jews in Susa had gathered together on the 13th and 14th. Then on the 15th they rested. They made it a day to celebrate with great joy. And they enjoyed good food.

19That's why Jews who live out in the villages celebrate on the 14th of Adar. They celebrate that day with great joy. And they enjoy good food. They also give presents to each other on that day.

20Mordecai wrote down those events. He sent letters to all of the Jews all through the territories of King Xerxes. It didn't matter whether the Jews lived nearby or far away. **21**Mordecai told them to celebrate the 14th and 15th days of the month of Adar. He wanted them to do it every year.

22Mordecai told the Jews to celebrate the time when they got rest from their enemies. That was the month when their sadness was turned into joy. It was when their sobbing turned into a day for celebrating. He wrote the letters to celebrate those days as times of joy. He wanted the people to enjoy good food. He told them to give presents of food to one another. He also wanted them to give gifts to those who were poor.

23So the Jews agreed to continue the celebrating they had started. They kept doing what Mordecai had written to them.

24Haman was the son of Hammedatha, the Agagite. He had been the enemy of all of the Jews. He had planned to destroy them. He had cast the lot to destroy them completely. The lot was also called *pur*.

25But the king had found out about Haman's evil plan. So the king had sent out written orders. He had ordered that the evil plan Haman had made against the Jews should come back on his own head. He had also commanded that Haman and his sons should be put to death. Poles should be stuck through their dead bodies. Then they should be set up where everyone could see them.

26The days the Jews were celebrating were called Purim. Purim comes from the word *pur*. *Pur* means "lot." Now the Jews celebrate those two days every year. They do it because of everything that was written in Mordecai's letter. They also do it because of what they had seen and what had happened to them.

27So they established it as a regular practice. They decided they would always observe those two days of the year. They would celebrate in the required way. And they would celebrate at the appointed time. They and their children after them and everyone who joined them would always observe those days. **28**The days should be remembered and celebrated. They should be remembered by every family for all time to come. They should be celebrated in every territory and in every city. The Jews should never stop celebrating the days of Purim. Their children after them should always remember those days.

29So Queen Esther, the daughter of Abihail, wrote a second letter. She wrote it together with the Jew Mordecai. They wanted to give their full authority to this second letter about Purim. **30**Mordecai sent letters to all of the Jews in the 127 territories of the kingdom of Xerxes. The letters had messages of kindness and hope in them.

31The letters established the days of Purim at their appointed times. They spoke about what the Jew Mordecai and Queen Esther had ordered the people to do. Everything should be done in keeping

KIND

THE LETTERS HAD MESSAGES OF KINDNESS AND HOPE IN THEM.
—— ESTHER 9:30 ——

with the directions the Jews had set up for themselves and their children after them. The directions applied to their times of fasting and sadness. [32]Esther's order established the rules about Purim. It was written down in the records.

The Greatness of Mordecai

10 King Xerxes required people all through his kingdom to bring him gifts. He required gifts from its farthest shores. [2]All of his powerful and mighty acts are written down. That includes the whole story of how important Mordecai was. The king had given him a position of great honor. All of those things are written in the official records of the kings of Media and Persia.

[3]The Jew Mordecai's position was second only to the position of King Xerxes. Mordecai was the most important Jew. All of the other Jews had the highest respect for him. That's because he worked for the good of his people. And he spoke up for the benefit of all of the Jews.

JOB

The book of Job raises—but doesn't fully answer—many of life's most difficult questions: Why do good people suffer? What part does God have in their suffering? Job, the hero of the book, searches for answers to those questions. So do his friends. But they can't find any satisfying answers. God himself then responds, not with answers but with wonderful descriptions of his power and his love for his people. As you read Job, you'll discover how much Job suffered, how hurt he was by the words of his friends, and how God gave him comfort instead of answers.

HERO IN THIS BOOK . . .

JOB
PAGE 601

The Story Begins

1 There was a man who lived in the land of Uz. His name was Job. He was honest. He did what was right. He had respect for God and avoided evil.

2Job had seven sons and three daughters. **3**He owned 7,000 sheep and 3,000 camels. He owned 500 pairs of oxen and 500 donkeys. He also had a large number of servants. He was the most important man among all of the people in the east.

4His sons used to take turns giving big dinners in their homes. They would invite their three sisters to eat and drink with them.

5When the time for enjoying good food was over, Job would have his children made pure and clean. He would sacrifice a burnt offering for each of them. He would do it early in the morning. He would think, "Perhaps my children have sinned. Maybe they have spoken evil things against God in their hearts."

That's what Job always did for his children when he felt they had sinned.

Job Is Put to the Test

6One day angels came to the LORD. Satan also came with them. **7**The LORD said to Satan, "Where have you come from?"

Satan answered, "From traveling all around the earth. I've been going from one end of it to the other."

8Then the LORD said to Satan, "Have you thought about my servant Job? There isn't anyone on earth like him. He is honest. He does what is right. He has respect for me and avoids evil."

9"You always give Job everything he needs," Satan replied. "That's why he has respect for you. **10**Haven't you guarded him and his family? Haven't you taken care of everything he has? You have blessed everything he does. His flocks and herds are spread all through the land.

11"But reach out your hand and strike down everything he has. Then I'm sure he will speak evil things against you. In fact, he'll do it right in front of you."

12The LORD said to Satan, "All right. I am handing everything he has over to you. But do not touch the man himself."

Then Satan left the LORD and went on his way.

13One day Job's sons and daughters were at their oldest brother's house. They were enjoying good food and drinking wine. **14**During that time a messenger came to Job. He said, "The oxen were plowing.

The donkeys were eating grass near them. **15**Then the Sabeans attacked us and carried the animals off. They killed some of the servants with their swords. I'm the only one who has escaped to tell you!"

16While he was still speaking, a second messenger came. He said, "God sent lightning from the sky. It struck the sheep and killed them. It burned up some of the servants. I'm the only one who has escaped to tell you!"

17While he was still speaking, a third messenger came. He said, "The Chaldeans separated themselves into three groups. They attacked your camels and carried them off. They killed the rest of the servants with their swords. I'm the only one who has escaped to tell you!"

18While he was still speaking, a fourth messenger came. He said, "Your sons and daughters were at their oldest brother's house. They were enjoying good food and drinking wine. **19**Suddenly a strong wind blew in from the desert. It struck the four corners of the house. The house fell down on your children. Now all of them are dead. I'm the only one who has escaped to tell you!"

20After Job heard all of those reports, he got up and tore his robe. He shaved his head. Then he fell to the ground and worshiped the LORD. **21**He said,

"I was born naked.
    And I'll leave here naked.
You have given, and you have taken
        away.
    May your name be praised."

22In spite of everything, Job didn't sin by blaming God for doing anything wrong.

Job Is Put to the Test Again

2 On another day angels came to the LORD. Satan also came to him along with them. **2**The LORD said to Satan, "Where have you come from?"

Satan answered, "From traveling all around the earth. I've been going from one end of it to the other."

3Then the LORD said to Satan, "Have you thought about my servant Job? There isn't anyone on earth like him. He is honest. He does what is right. He has respect for me and avoids evil. You tried to turn me against him. You wanted me to destroy him without any reason. But he still continues to be faithful."

4Satan replied, "A man will give everything he has to save himself. So Job is willing to give up the lives of his family to save his own life.

5 "But reach out your hand and strike his flesh and bones. Then I'm sure he will speak evil things against you. In fact, he'll do it right in front of you."

6 The LORD said to Satan, "All right. I am handing him over to you. But you must spare his life."

7 Then Satan left the LORD and went on his way. He sent painful sores on Job. They covered him from the bottom of his feet to the top of his head. 8 He got part of a broken pot. He used it to scrape his skin. He did it while he was sitting in ashes.

9 His wife said to him, "Are you still continuing to be faithful to the LORD? Speak evil things against him and die!"

10 Job replied, "You are talking like a foolish woman. We accept good things from God. So we should also accept trouble when he sends it."

In spite of everything, Job didn't say anything that was sinful.

Job's Three Friends Come to Comfort Him

11 Job had three friends named Eliphaz the Temanite, Bildad the Shuhite, and Zophar the Naamathite. They heard about all of the troubles that had come to Job. So they started out from their homes. They had agreed to meet together. They wanted to go and show their concern for Job. They wanted to comfort him.

12 When they got closer to where he lived, they could see him. But they could hardly recognize him. They began to sob out loud. They tore their robes and sprinkled dust on their heads.

13 Then they sat down on the ground with him for seven days and seven nights. No one said a word to him. That's because they saw how much he was suffering.

Job Wishes He Had Never Been Born

3 After a while, Job opened his mouth to speak. He called down a curse on the day he had been born. 2 He said,

3 "May the day I was born be wiped out.
　　May the night be wiped away when people said, 'A boy is born!'
4 May that day turn into darkness.
　　May God in heaven not care about it.
　　May no light shine on it.
5 May darkness and deep shadow take it back.
　　May a cloud settle over it.
　　May blackness cover up its light.

6 May deep darkness take over the night I was born.
　　May it not be included among the days of the year.
　　May it never appear in any of the months.
7 May no children ever have been born on that night.
　　May no shout of joy be heard in it.
8 May people call down a curse on that day.
　　May those who are ready to wake up the sea monster Leviathan curse that day.
9 May its morning stars become dark.
　　May it lose all hope of ever seeing daylight.
　　May it not see the first light of the morning sun.
10 It didn't keep my mother from letting me be born.
　　It didn't keep my eyes from seeing trouble.

11 "Why didn't I die when I was born?
　　Why didn't I die as I came out of my mother's body?
12 Why was I placed on her knees?
　　Why did her breasts give me milk?
13 If all of that hadn't happened,
　　I would be lying down in peace.
　　I'd be asleep and at rest in the grave.
14 I'd be with the earth's kings and advisers.
　　They had built for themselves places that are now destroyed.
15 I'd be with rulers who used to have gold.
　　They had filled their houses with silver.
16 Why wasn't I buried like a baby who was born dead?
　　Why wasn't I buried like a child who never saw the light of day?
17 In the grave, sinful people don't cause trouble anymore.
　　And there those who are tired find rest.
18 Prisoners also enjoy peace there.
　　They don't hear a slave driver shouting at them anymore.
19 The least important and most important people are there.
　　And there the slaves are set free from their owners.

20 "Why is the light that leads to life given to those who suffer?
　　Why is it given to those whose spirits are bitter?
21 Why is life given to those who long for death that doesn't come?

JOB

JOB 2:10

( )

T

✝

"We accept good things from God. So we should also accept trouble when he sends it."
In spite of everything, Job didn't say anything that was sinful.

Job scratched a sore spot on his arm, then one on his leg. Sores covered Job's body, from his toes to the top of his shaved head. He used a piece of broken pottery to scratch. The sores bled, but Job hardly noticed. The pain in his heart was much worse than the pain from the sores.

Job had loved and worshiped God his whole life. He had been a rich man. But now he had lost everything. Enemies had stolen his oxen and donkeys and camels. Lightning had struck and killed his sheep. Then worst of all, a strong wind had come and blown over the house where his children were having a party. All of them died. Only Job and his wife were left.

And now Job himself was sick with these awful sores. *How was he supposed to go on living?* Job thought to himself. *Why had he even been born?* Job scratched another sore. His eyes blurred with tears. **EVERY BEAT OF HIS HEART BROUGHT PAIN.** Then he fell on his face and prayed.

"I was born a naked baby. I'll die naked, too. I know you gave me everything I had. And now you've taken it away. I'm sad, Lord. My pain is greater than I can stand. But I love you. You are still my God!"

With tears in her eyes, Job's wife told him, "Doesn't this make you angry with God? Why don't you say you hate him and die?" Job looked at his wife with amazement. "You don't know what you're saying. We can't accept only good things from God. Sometimes he sends trouble, too. I still love God, and I won't say I hate him!"

BE A JOB

Job was a good man. But terrible things happened to him. That's hard to understand. Today terrible things still happen to people who love God. Everyone finds that hard to understand. But you can still choose to follow God and love him, like Job, even when bad things happen.

JOB FOLLOWED GOD EVEN WHEN TROUBLE CAME.
THE WHOLE STORY: JOB 1:1–2:10

Go to page 790 for the next Super Hero

Why is it given to those who would
rather search for death
than for hidden treasure?
²² Why is life given to those who are
actually happy and glad
when they reach the grave?
²³ Why is life given to a man like me?
God hasn't told me what will
happen to me.
He has surrounded me with nothing
but trouble.
²⁴ I sigh instead of eating food.
Groans pour out of me like water.
²⁵ What I was afraid of has come on me.
What I worried about has happened
to me.
²⁶ I don't have any peace and quiet.
I can't find any rest. All I have is
trouble."

The First Speech of Eliphaz

4 Then Eliphaz the Temanite replied,

² "Job, suppose someone tries to talk to
you.
Will that make you uneasy?
I can't keep from speaking up.
³ Look, you taught many people.
You made weak hands strong.
⁴ Your words helped those who had
fallen down.
You made shaky knees strong.
⁵ Now trouble comes to you. And you
are unhappy about it.
It strikes you down. And you are
afraid.
⁶ Shouldn't you worship God and trust
in him?
Shouldn't your honest life give you
hope?

⁷ "Here's something to think about.
Have blameless people ever been
wiped out?
Have honest people ever been
completely destroyed?
⁸ Here's what I've observed.
People gather a crop from what they
plant.
If they plant evil and trouble, that's
what they will harvest.
⁹ The breath of God destroys them.
The blast of his anger wipes them
out.
¹⁰ Powerful lions might roar and growl.
But their teeth are broken.
¹¹ Lions die because they don't have any
food.
Then their cubs are scattered.

¹² "A message came to me in secret.
It was as quiet as a whisper.

¹³ I had a scary dream one night.
I was sound asleep.
¹⁴ Fear and trembling grabbed hold of me.
That made every bone in my body
shake.
¹⁵ A spirit glided past my face.
The hair on my body stood on end.
¹⁶ Then the spirit stopped.
But I couldn't tell what it was.
Something stood there in front of me.
I heard a soft voice.
¹⁷ It said, 'Can a human being be more
right than God?
Can a mere man be more pure than
the One who made him?
¹⁸ God doesn't trust those who serve
him.
He even brings charges against his
angels.
¹⁹ So he'll certainly find fault with
human beings.
After all, they are made out of dust.
They can be crushed more easily
than a moth.
²⁰ Between sunrise and sunset they are
broken to pieces.
Nobody even notices. They
disappear forever.
²¹ Like a tent that falls down, they get
weak.
They die because they didn't follow
God's wisdom.' "

5 Eliphaz continued,

"Call out if you want to, Job.
But who will answer you?
Which one of the holy angels will
you turn to?
² Anger kills foolish people.
Jealousy destroys those who are
childish.
³ I saw that foolish people were having
success.
But suddenly a curse came down on
their houses.
⁴ Their children aren't safe at all.
They lose their case in court.
No one speaks up for them.
⁵ Hungry people eat up the crops of
those who are foolish.
They even take the food that grows
among thorns.
Thirsty people long for the wealth of
the foolish.
⁶ Hard times don't just grow out of the
soil.
Trouble doesn't jump out of the
ground.
⁷ People are born to have trouble.
And that's just as sure as sparks fly up.

8 "If I were you, I'd make my appeal to
   God.
   I'd bring my case to be judged by
   him.
9 He does wonderful things that can't be
   understood.
   He does miracles that can't even be
   counted.
10 He sends rain on the earth.
   He sends water on the countryside.
11 He lifts up those who are lowly in
   spirit.
   He lifts up those who are sad.
   He keeps them safe.
12 He stops those who are tricky from
   doing what they plan to do.
   The work of their hands doesn't
   succeed.
13 Some people think they are so wise.
   But God catches them in their own
   tricks.
   He sweeps away the evil plans of
   sinful people.
14 Darkness covers them in the daytime.
   At noon they feel their way around
   as if it were night.
15 God saves needy people from the
   cutting words of their enemies.
   He saves them from their powerful
   hands.
16 So those who are poor have hope.
   And God shuts the mouths of
   people who don't treat others
   fairly.

17 "Blessed is the person God corrects.
   So don't hate the Mighty One's
   training.
18 He wounds. But he also bandages up
   those he wounds.
   He harms. But his hands also heal
   those he harms.
19 From six troubles he will save you.
   Even if you are in trouble seven
   times, no harm will come to
   you.
20 When there isn't enough food, God
   will keep you from dying.
   When you go into battle, he won't
   let a sword strike you down.
21 He will keep you safe from words that
   can hurt you.
   You won't need to be afraid
   when everything is being destroyed.
22 You will laugh when things are being
   destroyed.
   You will enjoy life even when there
   isn't enough food.
   You won't be afraid of wild animals.
23 You will make a covenant with the
   stones in the fields.

They won't keep your crops from
   growing.
   Even wild animals will be at peace
   with you.
24 You will know that the tent you live in
   is secure.
   You will check out your property.
   You will see that nothing is missing.
25 You can be sure you will have a lot of
   children.
   They will be as many as the blades of
   grass on the earth.
26 You will go down to the grave
   while you are still very strong.
   You will be like a crop that is
   gathered at the right time.

27 "We have carefully studied all of those
   things.
   And they are true.
   So pay attention to them.
   Apply them to yourself."

Job's Reply

6 Job replied,

2 "I wish my great pain could be
   weighed!
   I wish all of my suffering could be
   weighed on scales!
3 I'm sure they would weigh more than
   the grains of sand on the
   seashore.
   No wonder I've been so quick to
   speak!
4 The Mighty One has shot me with his
   arrows.
   I have to drink their poison.
   God's terrors are aimed at me.
5 Does a wild donkey cry out when it has
   enough grass?
   Does an ox call out when it has
   plenty of food?
6 Is food that doesn't have any taste
   eaten without salt?
   Is there any flavor in the white of an
   egg?
7 I refuse to touch that kind of food.
   It makes me sick.

8 "I wish I could have what I'm asking
   for!
   I wish God would give me what I'm
   hoping for!
9 I wish he would crush me!
   I wish his powerful hand would cut
   off my life!
10 Then I'd still have one thing to
   comfort me.
   It would be that I haven't said no to
   the Holy One's commands.

That would give me joy in spite of
my pain that never ends.
11 "I'm so weak that I no longer have any
hope.
Things have gotten so bad that I
can't wait for help anymore.
12 Am I as strong as stone?
Is my body made out of bronze?
13 I don't have the power to help myself.
All hope of success has been taken
away from me.

14 "A man's friends should love him
when his hope is gone.
They should be faithful to him
even if he stops showing respect for
the Mighty One.

KIND K

A MAN'S FRIENDS
SHOULD LOVE HIM
WHEN HIS HOPE
IS GONE.
— JOB 6:14 —

LOVING

15 But my friends aren't faithful to me.
They are like streams that only flow
for part of the year.
They are like rivers that flow over
their banks
16 when the ice begins to break up.
The streams rise when the snow
starts to melt.
17 But they stop flowing when the dry
season comes.
They disappear from their stream
beds when the weather warms
up.
18 Groups of traders turn away from their
usual paths.
They go up into the dry and empty
land.
And they die there.
19 Traders from Tema look for water.
Traveling merchants from Sheba
also hope to find it.
20 They become troubled because they
had expected to find some.
But when they arrive at the stream
beds,
they don't find any water at all.

21 And now, my friends, you haven't
helped me either.
You see the horrible condition I'm
in.
And that makes you afraid.
22 I've never said, 'Give me something to
help me.
Use your wealth to set me free.
23 Save me from the powerful hand of my
enemy.
Set me free from the power of mean
people.'

24 "Teach me. Then I'll be quiet.
Show me what I've done wrong.
25 Honest words are so painful!
But your reasoning doesn't prove
anything.
26 Are you trying to correct what I'm
saying?
You are treating the words of this
hopeless man
like nothing but wind.
27 You would even cast lots for those
whose fathers have died.
You would even trade away your
closest friend.

28 "But now please look at me.
Would I tell you a lie right here in
front of you?
29 Stop what you are saying. Don't be so
unfair.
Think it over again.
You are trying to take my honesty
away from me.
30 Has my mouth spoken anything that is
evil?
Do my lips say things that are
hateful?"

7 Job continued,

"Doesn't every man have to work hard
on this earth?
Aren't his days like the days of a
hired worker?
2 I've been like a slave
who longs for the evening shadows
to come.
I've been like a hired worker
who can hardly wait to get paid.
3 I've been given several months that
were useless to me.
My nights have been filled with
suffering.
4 When I lie down I think,
'How long will it be before I can get
up?'
The night drags on.
I toss and turn until sunrise.

5 My body is covered with worms and sores.
My skin is broken. It has boils all over it.

6 "My days pass by faster than a weaver can work.
They come to an end. I don't have any hope.

7 God, remember that my life is only a breath.
I'll never be happy again.

8 The eyes that see me now won't see me anymore.
You will look for me. But I'll be gone.

9 When a cloud disappears, it's gone forever.
And anyone who goes down to the grave never returns.

10 He never comes home again.
Even his own family doesn't remember him.

11 "So I won't keep quiet.
When I'm suffering greatly, I'll speak out.
When my spirit is bitter, I'll tell you how unhappy I am.

12 Am I the ocean? Am I the sea monster?
If I'm not, why do you guard me so closely?

13 Sometimes I think my bed will comfort me.
I think my couch will keep me from being unhappy.

14 But even then you send me dreams that frighten me.
You send me visions that terrify me.

15 So I would rather choke to death.
That would be better than living in this body of mine.

16 I hate my life. I don't want to live forever.
Leave me alone. My days don't mean anything to me.

17 "What are human beings that you think so much of them?
What are they that you pay so much attention to them?

18 You check up on them every morning.
You put them to the test every moment.

19 Won't you ever look away from me?
Won't you leave me alone even for one second?

20 If I've really sinned, tell me what I've done to you.
Why do you watch people so closely?
Why do you shoot your arrows at me?
Have I become a problem to you?

21 Why don't you forgive the wrong things I've done?
Why don't you forgive me for my sins?
I'll soon lie down in the dust of my grave.
You will search for me. But I'll be gone."

The First Speech of Bildad

8 Then Bildad the Shuhite replied,

2 "Job, how long will you talk like that?
Your words don't have any meaning.

3 Does God ever treat people unfairly?
Does the Mighty One make what is wrong
appear to be right?

4 Your children sinned against him.
So he punished them for their sin.

5 But look to God.
Make your appeal to the Mighty One.

6 Be pure and honest.
And he will rise up and help you now.
He'll return you to the place where you belong.

POWER-/SURGE

HONEST **H**

BE PURE AND HONEST.
— JOB 8:6 —

7 In the past, things went well with you.
But in days to come, things will get even better.

8 "Find out what your people who lived long ago taught.
Discover what those who lived before them learned.

9 After all, we were born only yesterday.
So we don't know anything.
Our days on this earth are like a shadow that disappears.

10 Won't your people of long ago teach you and tell you?
Won't the things they said help you understand?

11 Can grass grow tall where there isn't any swamp?
Can plants grow well where there isn't any water?

12 While they are still growing and haven't been cut,
they dry up faster than grass does.

13 The same thing happens to everyone
who forgets God.
The hope of ungodly people dies
out.
14 What they trust in is very weak.
What they depend on is like a
spider's web.
15 A person leans on it, but it falls apart.
He holds on to it, but it gives way.
16 He is like a plant in the sunshine
that receives plenty of water.
It spreads its new growth all over the
garden.
17 It wraps its roots around a pile of rocks.
It tries to find places to grow among
the stones.
18 But when a plant is pulled up from its
spot,
that place says, 'I never saw you.'
19 The life of that plant is sure to dry up.
But from the same soil other plants
will grow.

20 "I'm sure God doesn't turn his back on
anyone who is honest.
And he doesn't help those who do
what is evil.
21 He will fill your mouth with laughter.
Shouts of joy will come from your
lips.

POWER-SURGE

CHEERFUL ✳

[GOD] WILL FILL YOUR MOUTH WITH LAUGHTER.

SHOUTS OF JOY WILL COME FROM YOUR LIPS.

— JOB 8:21 —

22 Your enemies will put on shame as if it
were clothes.
The tents of sinful people will be
gone."

Job's Reply

9 Job replied,

2 "I'm sure that what you have said is
true.
But how can human beings be right
with God?
3 They might wish to argue with him.
But they couldn't answer him

even once in a thousand times.
4 His wisdom is deep. His power is great.
No one opposes him and comes
away unharmed.
5 He moves mountains, and they don't
even know it.
When he is angry, he turns them
upside down.
6 He shakes the earth loose from its
place.
He makes its pillars tremble.
7 When he tells the sun not to shine, it
doesn't.
He turns off the light of the stars.
8 He's the only one who can spread the
heavens out.
He alone can walk on the waves of
the ocean.
9 He made the Big Dipper and Orion.
He created the Pleiades and the
southern stars.
10 He does wonderful things that can't be
understood.
He does miracles that can't even be
counted.
11 When he passes by me, I can't see him.
When he goes past me, I can't
recognize him.
12 If he takes something, who can stop
him?
Who would dare to ask him, 'What
are you doing?'
13 God doesn't hold back his anger.
Even the helpers of the sea monster
Rahab
bowed in fear at his feet.

14 "So how can I disagree with God?
How can I possibly argue with him?
15 Even if I hadn't done anything wrong,
I couldn't answer him.
I could only beg my Judge to have
mercy on me.
16 Suppose I called out to him and he
answered.
I don't believe he'd listen to me.
17 He would send a storm to crush me.
He'd increase my wounds without
any reason.
18 He wouldn't let me catch my breath.
He'd make my life very bitter.
19 If it's a matter of strength, he is
mighty!
And if it's a matter of being fair,
who would dare to bring charges
against him?
20 Even if I hadn't sinned, what I said
would prove me guilty.
Even if I were honest, my words
would show that I'm wrong.

21 "Even though I'm honest,

I'm not concerned about myself.
I hate my own life.
22 It all amounts to the same thing.
That's why I say,
'God destroys honest people and
sinful people alike.'
23 Suppose a plague brings sudden death.
Then he laughs when those who
haven't sinned lose hope.
24 Suppose a nation falls into the power
of sinful people.
Then God makes its judges blind to
the truth.
If he isn't the one doing it, who is?

25 "God, my days race by like a runner.
They fly away without seeing any
joy.
26 They speed along like papyrus boats.
They are like eagles swooping down
on their food.
27 Suppose I say, 'I'll forget about all of
my problems.
I'll change my frown into a smile.'
28 Then I'd still be afraid I'd go on
suffering.
That's because I know you would say
I had done something wrong.
29 In fact, you have already said I'm
guilty.
So why should I struggle without
any reason?
30 Suppose I clean myself with soap.
Suppose I wash my hands with
cleanser.
31 Even then you would throw me into a
muddy pit.
And even my clothes would hate
me.

32 "God isn't a man like me. I can't
answer him.
We can't take each other to court.
33 I wish someone would settle matters
between us.
I wish someone would force us to
work things out.
34 I wish someone would keep God from
punishing me.
Then his terror wouldn't frighten
me anymore.
35 I would speak up without being afraid
of him.
But as things stand now, I can't do
that.

10 "I'm sick of living.
So I'll talk openly about my
problems.
I'll speak out because my spirit is
bitter.
2 I'll say to God, 'Don't find me guilty.

Instead, tell me what charges
you are bringing against me.
3 Does it make you happy when you
crush me?
Does it please you to turn your back
on what you have made?
While you do those things,
you smile on the plans of sinful
people!
4 You don't have human eyes.
You don't see as people see.
5 Your days aren't like the days of a
human being.
Your years aren't like the years of a
mere man.
6 So you search for my mistakes.
You look for my sin.
7 You already know I'm not guilty.
No one can save me from your
powerful hand.

8 " 'Your hands shaped me and made
me.
So are you going to destroy me now?
9 Remember, you molded me like clay.
So are you going to turn me back
into dust?
10 Didn't you pour me out like milk?
Didn't you form me like cheese?
11 Didn't you put skin and flesh on me?
Didn't you sew me together with
bones and muscles?
12 You gave me life. You were kind to me.
You took good care of me. You
watched over me.

13 " 'But here's what you hid in your
heart.
Here's what you had on your mind.
14 If I sinned, you would be watching me.
You wouldn't let me go without
punishing me.
15 If I were guilty, how terrible that would
be for me!
Even if I haven't sinned,
I can't be proud of what I've done.
That's because I'm so full of shame.
I'm drowning in my suffering.
16 If I become proud, you hunt me down
like a lion.
You show your mighty power
against me.
17 You bring new witnesses against me.
You become more and more angry
with me.
You use your power against me again
and again.
18 " 'Why did you bring me out of my
mother's body?
I wish I had died before anyone saw
me.

19 I wish I'd never been born!
    I wish I'd been carried straight from
      my mother's body to the grave!
20 Aren't my few days almost over?
    Leave me so I can have a moment of
      joy.
21 Turn away before I go to the place I
      can't return from.
    It's the land of darkness and deep
      shadow.
22 It's the land of darkest night
    and deep shadow and disorder.
    There even the light is like
      darkness.' "

The First Speech of Zophar

11 Then Zophar the Naamathite replied,

2 "Don't all of your words require an
      answer?
    I'm sure that what you are saying
      can't be right.
3 Your useless talk won't keep us quiet.
    Someone has to correct you when
      you make fun of truth.
4 You say to God, 'My beliefs are perfect.
    I'm pure in your sight.'
5 I wish God would speak.
    I wish he'd answer you.
6 I wish he'd show you the secrets of
      wisdom.
    After all, true wisdom has two sides.
Here's what I want you to know.
    God has forgotten some of your sins.

7 "Do you know how deep the mysteries
      of God are?
    Can you discover the limits of the
      Mighty One's knowledge?
8 They are higher than the heavens.
    What can you do?
They are deeper than the deepest
      grave.
    What can you know?
9 They are longer than the earth.
    They are wider than the ocean.

10 "Suppose God comes along and puts
      you in prison.
    Suppose he takes you to court.
    Then who can oppose him?
11 He certainly knows when people tell
      lies.
    When he sees evil, he pays careful
      attention to it.
12 A wild donkey's colt can't be born a
      human being.
    And a man who doesn't have any
      sense can't become wise.

13 "So commit yourself to God
      completely.
    Reach out your hands to him for
      help.
14 Get rid of all of the sin you have.
    Don't let anything that is evil stay in
      your tent.
15 Then you can face others without
      feeling any shame.
    You can stand firm without being
      afraid.
16 You can be sure you will forget your
      troubles.
    They will be like water that has
      flowed on by.
17 Life will be brighter than the sun at
      noon.
    And darkness will become like
      morning.
18 You will be secure, because there is
      hope.
    You will look around you and find a
      safe place to rest.
19 You will lie down, and no one will
      make you afraid.
    Many people will want you to show
      them your favor.
20 But sinful people won't find what they
      are looking for.
    They won't be able to escape.
    All they can hope for is to die."

Job's Reply

12 Job replied,
2 "You people think you know
      everything, don't you?
    You are sure that wisdom will die
      with you!
3 But I have a brain, just like you.
    I'm as clever as you are.
    In fact, everyone knows as much as
      you do.

4 "My friends laugh at me all the time,
      even though I called out to God and
      he answered.
My friends laugh at me,
      even though I'm honest and right.
5 People who have an easy life look
      down on those who have
      problems.
    They think trouble comes only to
      those whose feet are slipping.
6 Why doesn't anyone bother the tents
      of robbers?
    Why do those who make God angry
      remain secure?
    They carry the statues of their gods
      in their hands!

7 "But ask the animals what God does.

They will teach you.
Or ask the birds of the air.
They will tell you.
8 Or speak to the earth. It will teach you.
Or let the fish of the ocean educate
you.
9 Are there any of those creatures that
don't know
what the powerful hand of the LORD
has done?
10 He holds the life of every creature in
his hand.
He controls the breath of every
human being.
11 Our tongues tell us what tastes good
and what doesn't.
And our ears tell us what's true and
what isn't.
12 Old people are wise.
Those who live a long time have
understanding.

POWER-SURGE

WISE W

OLD PEOPLE ARE WISE.

THOSE WHO LIVE A LONG TIME HAVE UNDERSTANDING.
— JOB 12:12 —

---

13 "Wisdom and power belong to God.
Advice and understanding also
belong to him.
14 What he tears down can't be rebuilt.
Any man he puts in prison can't be
set free.
15 If he holds back the water, everything
dries up.
If he lets the water loose, it floods
the land.
16 Strength and success belong to him.
Those who tell lies and those who
believe them also belong to
him.
17 He removes the wisdom of advisers
and leads them away.
He makes judges look foolish.
18 He sets people free from the chains
that kings put on them.
Then he dresses the kings in the
clothes of slaves.
19 He removes the authority of priests
and leads them away.
He removes from their positions
those who have been in control for a
long time.

20 He shuts the mouths of trusted
advisers.
He takes away the understanding of
elders.
21 He looks down on proud leaders.
He takes away the strength of those
who are mighty.
22 He tells people the secrets of darkness.
He brings evil plans out into the
light.
23 He makes nations great, and then he
destroys them.
He makes nations grow, and then he
scatters them.
24 He takes away the understanding of
the leaders of the earth.
He makes them wander in a desert
where no one lives.
25 Without any light, they feel their way
along in darkness.
God makes them unsteady like
those who get drunk.

13 "My eyes have seen everything
God has done.
My ears have heard it and
understood it.
2 What you know, I also know.
I'm as clever as you are.
3 In fact, I long to speak to the Mighty
One.
I want to argue my case with God.
4 But you spread lies about me and take
away my good name.
If you are trying to heal me,
you aren't very good doctors!
5 I wish you would keep your mouths
shut!
Then people would think you were
wise.
6 Listen to my case.
Listen as I make my appeal.
7 Will you say evil things in order to
help God?
Will you tell lies for him?
8 Do you want to be on God's side?
Will you argue his case for him?
9 Would it turn out well if he looked you
over carefully?
Could you fool him as you fool
others?
10 He would certainly correct you
if you took his side in secret.
11 Wouldn't his glory terrify you?
Wouldn't the fear of him fall on
you?
12 Your sayings are as useless as ashes.
The answers you give are as weak as
clay.
13 "So be quiet and let me speak.

Then I won't care what happens to
      me.
14 Why do I put myself in danger?
      Why do I take my life in my hands?
15 Even if God kills me, I'll still put my
      hope in him.
      I'll argue my case in front of him.
16 No matter how things turn out,
      I'm sure I'll still be saved.
   After all, no ungodly person
      would dare to come into his court.
17 Listen carefully to what I'm saying.
      Pay close attention to my words.
18 I've prepared my case.
      And I know I'll be proved right.
19 Can others bring charges against me?
      If they can, I'll keep quiet and die.

20 "God, I won't hide from you.
      Here are the only two things I want.
21 Keep your powerful hand far away
      from me.
      And stop making me so afraid.
22 Then send for me, and I'll answer.
      Or let me speak, and you reply.
23 How many things have I done wrong?
      How many sins have I committed?
      Show me my crime. Show me my
      sin.
24 Why do you turn your face away from
      me?
      Why do you think of me as your
      enemy?
25 I'm already like a leaf that is blown by
      the wind.
      Are you going to terrify me even
      more?
   I'm already like dry straw.
      Are you going to keep on chasing
      me?
26 You write down bitter things against
      me.
      You make me suffer for the sins
      I committed when I was young.
27 You put my feet in chains.
      You watch every step I take.
      You do it by putting marks on the
      bottom of my feet.

28 "People waste away like something
      that is rotten.
      They are like clothes that are eaten
      by moths.

14 They have only a few days to live.
      Their lives are full of trouble.
2 They grow like flowers, and then they
      dry up.
      They are like shadows that quickly
      disappear.

3 "God, why do you keep looking at
      someone like me?

Are you planning to take me to
      court?
4 Who can bring what is pure from
      something that isn't pure?
   No one!
5 You decide how long anyone will live.
      You have established the number of
      his months.
      You have set a limit to the number
      of his days.
6 So look away from him. Leave him
      alone.
      Let him put in his time like a hired
      worker.

7 "At least there is hope for a tree.
      If it's cut down, it will begin to grow
      again.
      New branches will appear on it.
8 Its roots may grow old in the ground.
      Its stump may die in the soil.
9 But when it smells water, it will begin
      to grow.
      It will send out new growth like a
      plant.
10 No man is like that. When he dies, he
      is buried in a grave.
      He takes his last breath. Then he is
      gone.
11 Water disappears from lakes.
      Riverbeds become empty and dry.
12 In the same way, a man lies down and
      never gets up.
      He won't wake up or rise from his
      sleep
      until the heavens are gone.

13 "I wish you would hide me in a grave!
      I wish you would cover me up until
      your anger passes by!
   I wish you would set the time for me to
      spend in the grave
   and then bring me back up!
14 If a man dies, will he live again?
      All the days of my hard work
      I will wait for the time when you
      give me new life.
15 You will call out to me, and I will
      answer you.
      Your hands created me. So you will
      long for me.
16 Then you will count every step I take.
      But you won't keep track of my sin.
17 The wrong things I've done will be
      sealed up in a bag.
      You will wipe out my sins by
      forgiving them.

18 "A mountain wears away and
      crumbles.
      A rock is moved from its place.
19 Water wears stones away.

Storms wash soil away.
In the same way, you destroy our
    hope.
20 You overpower us completely, and
    then we're gone.
You change the way we look and
    send us to our graves.
21 If our children are honored, we don't
    even know it.
If they are dishonored, we don't
    even see it.
22 All we feel is the pain of our own
    bodies.
We are full of sadness only for
    ourselves."

The Second Speech of Eliphaz

15 Then Eliphaz the Temanite replied,

2 "Job, if you were wise,
    would you answer us with a lot of
        meaningless talk?
Would you fill your stomach with
    the hot east wind?
3 Would you argue with useless words?
Would you give worthless speeches?
4 But you even cause others to lose their
    respect for God.
You make it hard for them to be
    faithful to him.
5 Your sin makes you say evil things.
You talk like people who twist the
    truth.
6 Your own mouth judges you, not mine.
Your own lips witness against you.

7 "Are you the first man who was ever
    born?
Were you created before the hills?
8 Do you listen in when God speaks with
    his angels?
Do you think you are the only wise
    person?
9 What do you know that we don't
    know?
What understanding do you have
    that we don't have?
10 People who are old and gray are on our
    side.

And they are even older than your
    parents!
11 Aren't God's words of comfort enough
    for you?
He speaks them to you gently.
12 Why have you let your wild ideas carry
    you away?
Why do your eyes flash with anger?
13 Why do you get so angry with God?
Why do words like those pour out of
    your mouth?

14 "Can human beings really be pure?
Can mere men really be right with
    God?
15 God doesn't trust his holy angels.
Even the heavens aren't pure in his
    sight.
16 So he'll certainly find fault with
    human beings.
After all, they are evil and sinful.
They drink up evil as if it were water.

17 "Listen to me. I'll explain things to you.
Let me tell you what I've seen.
18 I'll tell you what those who are wise
    have said.
They don't hide anything they've
    received
from their people of long ago.
19 The land was given only to those
    people.
Their wisdom didn't come from
    outsiders.
And here's what those who are wise
    have said.
20 Sinful people always suffer pain.
Mean people suffer all their lives.
21 Terrifying sounds fill their ears.
When everything seems to be going
    well,
robbers attack them.
22 They lose all hope of escaping the
    darkness of death.
They will certainly be killed with
    swords.
23 They wander around. They are like
    food for vultures.
They know that the day they will die
    is near.
24 Suffering and pain terrify them.
Their troubles overpower them,
    like a king ready to attack his
        enemies.
25 They shake their fists at God.
They brag about themselves and
    oppose the Mighty One.
26 They boldly charge against him
    with their thick, strong shields.

27 "Their faces are very fat.
Their stomachs hang out.

POWER-SURGE

FORGIVING F

YOU WILL WIPE OUT
MY SINS BY
FORGIVING THEM.
— JOB 14:17 —

28 They'll live in towns that have been
　　destroyed.
　　They'll live in houses where no one
　　　else lives.
　　The houses will crumble to pieces.
29 They won't be rich anymore. Their
　　　wealth won't last.
　　Their property will no longer spread
　　　out over the land.
30 They won't escape the darkness of
　　　death.
　　A flame will dry up everything they
　　　have.
　　The breath of God will blow them
　　　away.
31 Don't let them fool themselves
　　by trusting in what is worthless.
　　They won't get anything out of it.
32 Even before they die, they'll be paid
　　　back in full.
　　No matter what they do, it won't
　　　succeed.
33 They'll be like vines
　　that are stripped of their unripe
　　　grapes.
　　They'll be like olive trees
　　that drop their flowers.
34 People who are ungodly won't have
　　　any children.
　　Fire will burn up the tents of people
　　　who accept money
　　from those who want special favors.
35 Instead of having children,
　　ungodly people create suffering.
　　All they produce is evil.
　　They are full of lies."

Job's Reply

16 Job replied,

2 "I've heard many of those things
　　before.
　　You are terrible at comforting me!
3 Your speeches go on forever.
　　Won't they ever end?
　　What's wrong with you?
　　Why do you keep on arguing?
4 If you and I changed places,
　　I could say the same things you are
　　　saying.
　　I could make fine speeches against you.
　　I could shake my head at you.
5 But what I might say would give you
　　　hope.
　　My words of comfort would help
　　　you.

6 "If I speak, it doesn't help me.
　　And if I keep quiet, my pain doesn't
　　　go away.
7 God has worn me out completely.

He has destroyed my whole family.
8 People can see the condition he has
　　　put me in.
　　My thin body stands as a witness
　　　against me.
9 God is angry with me.
　　He attacks me and tears me up.
　He grinds his teeth at me.
　　He stares at me as if he were my
　　　enemy.
10 People make fun of me.
　　They slap my face and laugh at me.
　　All of them join together against me.
11 God has turned me over to sinful
　　　people.
　　He has handed me over to them.
12 Everything was going well with me.
　　But he broke me into pieces like a
　　　clay pot.
　　He grabbed me by the neck and
　　　crushed me.
　He has taken aim at me.
13 　　He shoots his arrows at me from all
　　　sides.
　　Without pity, he stabs me in the
　　　kidneys.
　　He spills my insides on the ground.
14 He smashes through me as if I were a
　　　wall.
　　He rushes at me like a fighting man.

15 "I've sewed black cloth over my skin.
　　All I can do is sit here in the dust.
16 My face is red from crying.
　　I have deep circles under my eyes.
17 But I haven't harmed anyone.
　　My prayers to God are pure.

18 "Earth, please don't cover up my
　　　blood!
　　May God always hear my cry for
　　　help!
19 Even now my witness is in heaven.
　　The one who speaks up for me is
　　　there.
20 My go-between is my friend
　　as I pour out my tears to God.
21 He makes his appeal to God to help me
　　as a man begs someone to help his
　　　friend.

22 "Only a few years will pass by.
　　Then I'll go on a journey I won't
　　　return from.

17 ¹ My strength is almost gone.
　　I won't live much longer.
　　A grave is waiting for me.
2 People who make fun of me are all
　　　around me.
　　I'm forced to watch as they attack
　　　me with their words.

3 "God, please pay the price to have me
set free.
Who else would put up money for
me?
4 You have closed the minds of those
who are trying to comfort me.
They don't understand that I
haven't done anything wrong.
So don't let them win the argument.
5 Suppose a man tells lies about his
friends to get a reward.
Then his own children will suffer
for it.

6 "God has made everyone laugh at me.
People spit in my face.
7 My eyes have grown weak because I'm
so sad.
My body is so thin it hardly casts a
shadow.
8 Those who claim to be honest
are shocked when they see me.
Those who think they haven't sinned
are stirred up against me.
They think I'm ungodly.
9 But godly people will keep doing what
is right.
Those who have clean hands will
grow stronger.

10 "Come on, all of you! Try again!
I can't find a wise person among
you.
11 My life is almost over. My plans are
destroyed.
And so are the longings of my heart.
12 People like you turn night into day.
Even though it's dark you say,
'Light is nearby.'
13 Suppose the only home I can hope for
is a grave.
And suppose I make my bed in the
darkness of death.
14 Suppose I say to the grave,
'You are like a father to me.'
And suppose I say to its worms,
'You are like a mother or sister to
me.'
15 Then what hope do I have?
Who can give me any hope?
16 Will hope go down to the gates of
death with me?
Will we go down together into the
dust of the grave?"

The Second Speech of Bildad

18 Then Bildad the Shuhite replied,

2 "Job, when will you stop these
speeches of yours?
Be reasonable! Then we can talk.

3 Why do you look at us as if we were
cattle?
Why do you think of us as being
stupid?
4 Your anger is tearing you to pieces.
Does the earth have to be deserted
just to prove you are right?
Must all of the rocks be moved from
their places?

5 "The lamps of sinful people are blown
out.
Their flames will never burn again.
6 The lights in their tents become dark.
The lamps beside those who are evil
go out.
7 They walk more slowly than they
used to.
Their own evil plans make them fall.
8 Their feet take them into a net.
They wander right into it.
9 A trap grabs hold of their heels.
It refuses to let them go.
10 A trap lies in their path.
A rope to catch them is hidden on
the ground.
11 Terrors alarm them on every side.
They follow them every step of the
way.
12 Trouble would like to eat them up.
Danger waits for them when they
fall.
13 It eats away parts of their skin.
Death itself feeds on their arms and
legs.
14 They are torn away from the safety of
their tents.
They are marched off to the one
who rules over death.
15 Fire races through their tents.
Burning sulfur is scattered over their
homes.
16 Their roots dry up under them.
Their branches dry up above them.
17 No one on earth remembers them.
Their names are forgotten in the
land.
18 They are driven from light into
darkness.
They are thrown out of the world.
19 Their family dies out among their
people.
No one is left where they used to
live.
20 What has happened to them shocks
the people in the west.
It terrifies the people in the east.
21 Now you know what the homes of
sinners are like.
Those who don't know God live in
places like that."

Job's Reply

19
Job replied,

2 "How long will you people make me
suffer?
How long will you crush me with
your words?
3 You have already made fun of me
many times.
You have attacked me without
feeling any shame.
4 Suppose it's true that I've gone down
the wrong path.
Then it's my concern, not yours.
5 Suppose you want to place yourselves
above me.
Suppose you want to use my shame
to prove I'm wrong.
6 Then I want you to know that God
hasn't treated me right.
In fact, he has captured me in his
net.

7 "I cry out, 'Someone harmed me!'
But I don't get any reply.
I call out for help.
But I'm not treated fairly.
8 God has blocked my way, and I can't
get through.
He has made my paths so dark I
can't see where I'm going.
9 He has taken my wealth away from me.
He has stripped me of my honor.
10 He tears me down on every side until
I'm gone.
He pulls up the roots of my hope as
if I were a tree.
11 His anger burns against me.
He thinks I'm one of his enemies.
12 His troops march toward me in force.
They come at me from every
direction.
They camp around my tent.

13 "God has caused my brothers to desert
me.
The people I used to know are now
strangers to me.
14 My family has gone away.
My friends have forgotten me.
15 My guests and my female servants
think of me as a stranger.
They look at me as if I were an
outsider.
16 I send for my servant, but he doesn't
answer.
He doesn't come, even though I beg
him to.
17 My wife can't stand the way my breath
smells.
My own relatives won't have
anything to do with me.

18 Even little children laugh at me.
When I appear, they make fun of
me.
19 All of my close friends hate me.
Those I love have turned against me.
20 I'm nothing but skin and bones.
I've only escaped by the skin of my
teeth.

21 "Have pity on me, my friends! Please
have pity!
God has struck me down with his
powerful hand.
22 Why do you chase after me as he does?
Aren't you satisfied with what you
have done to me already?

23 "I wish my words were written down!
I wish they were written on a scroll!
24 I wish they were cut into lead with an
iron tool!
I wish they were carved in rock
forever!
25 I know that my Redeemer lives.
In the end he will stand on the
earth.
26 After my skin has been destroyed,
in my body I'll still see God.
27 I myself will see him with my own
eyes.
I'll see him, and he won't be a
stranger to me.
How my heart longs for that day!

28 "You might say, 'Let's keep bothering
Job.
After all, he's the cause of all of his
suffering.'
29 But you should be afraid when God
comes to judge you.
He'll be angry. He'll punish you with
his sword.
Then you will know that he is the
Judge."

The Second Speech of Zophar

20
Then Zophar the Naamathite
replied,

2 "My troubled thoughts force me to
answer you.
That's because I'm very upset.
3 What you have just said makes fun of
me.
So I really have to reply to you.

4 "I'm sure you must know how things
have always been.
They've been that way
ever since man was placed on this
earth.
5 Those who are evil are happy for only a
short time.

The joy of ungodly people lasts only
for a moment.
⁶ Their pride might reach all the way up
to the heavens.
Their heads might touch the clouds.
⁷ But they will disappear forever,
like the waste from their own
bodies.
Anyone who has seen them will say,
'Where did they go?'
⁸ Like a dream they will fly away.
They will never be seen again.
They will be driven away like visions
in the night.
⁹ The eyes that saw them won't see them
anymore.
Even their own families won't
remember them.
¹⁰ Their children must pay back what
they took from poor people.
Their own hands must give back the
wealth they stole.
¹¹ They might feel young and very strong.
But they will soon lie down in the
dust of their graves.

¹² "Anything that is evil tastes sweet to
them.
They keep it under their tongues for
a while.
¹³ They can't stand to let it go.
So they hold it in their mouths.
¹⁴ But their food will turn sour in their
stomachs.
It will become like the poison of a
serpent inside them.
¹⁵ They will spit out the rich food they
swallowed.
God will make their stomachs throw
it up.
¹⁶ They will suck the poison of a serpent.
The fangs of an adder will kill them.
¹⁷ They won't enjoy streams that flow
with honey.
They won't enjoy rivers that flow
with cream.
¹⁸ What they worked for they must give
back
before they can eat it.
They won't enjoy what they have
earned.
¹⁹ They've crushed poor people and left
them with nothing.
They've taken over houses they
didn't even build.

²⁰ "No matter how much they have,
they always long for more.
But their treasure can't save them.
²¹ There isn't anything left for them to
eat up.
Their success won't last.

²² While they are enjoying the good life,
trouble will catch up with them.
Terrible suffering will come on
them.
²³ When they've filled their stomachs,
God will pour out his burning anger
on them.
He'll strike them down with blow
after blow.
²⁴ They might run away from iron
weapons.
But arrows that have bronze tips will
wound them.
²⁵ They will pull the arrows out of their
backs.
They will remove the shining tips
from their livers.
They will be filled with terror.
²⁶ Total darkness hides and waits for
their treasures.
God will send a fire that will destroy
them.
It will burn up everything that's left
in their tents.
²⁷ Heaven will show their guilt to
everyone.
The earth will be a witness against
them.
²⁸ A flood will carry their houses away.
Rushing water will wash them away
on the day when God judges.
²⁹ Now you know what God will do to
sinful people.
Now you know what he has planned
for them."

Job's Reply

21 Job replied,

² "Listen carefully to what I'm saying.
Let that be the comfort you people
give me.
³ Put up with me while I speak.
After I've spoken, you can make fun
of me!

⁴ "I'm not arguing with mere human
beings.
So why shouldn't I be angry and
uneasy?
⁵ Look at me and be amazed.
Put your hand over your mouth and
stop talking!
⁶ When I think about these things, I'm
terrified.
My whole body trembles.
⁷ Why do sinful people keep on living?
The older they grow, the richer they
get.
⁸ They see their children grow up
around them.

They watch their family increase in
number.
9 Their homes are safe.
They don't have to be afraid.
God isn't punishing them.
10 Every time their bulls mate, their cows
become pregnant.
And the calves don't die before they
are born.
11 Sinful people send their children out
like a flock of lambs.
Their little ones dance around.
12 They sing to the music of tambourines
and harps.
They have a good time while flutes
are being played.
13 Those who are evil spend their years
living well.
They go down to their graves in
peace.
14 But they say to God, 'Leave us alone!
We don't want to know how you
want us to live.
15 Who is the Mighty One? Why should
we serve him?
What would we get if we prayed to
him?'
16 But they aren't in control of their own
success.
So I don't pay any attention to the
advice they give.

17 "How often are their lamps blown out?
How often does trouble come on
them?
How often does God punish them
when he's angry?
18 How often are they like dried-up seed
coverings blowing in the wind?
How often are they like straw swept
away by a storm?
19 People say, 'God punishes a man's
children for his sins.'
But let him punish the man himself.
Then he'll learn a lesson from it.
20 Let his own eyes see how he is
destroyed.
Let him drink the wine of the
Mighty One's anger.
21 What does he care about the family he
leaves behind?
What does he care about them
when his life comes to an end?

22 "Can anyone teach God anything?
After all, he judges even the angels
in heaven.
23 Some people die while they are still
very strong.
They are completely secure. They
have an easy life.
24 They are well fed.

Their bodies are healthy.
25 Others die while their spirits are bitter.
They've never enjoyed anything
good.
26 Side by side they lie in the dust of
death.
The worms in their graves cover all
of them.

27 "I know exactly what you people are
thinking.
I know you are planning to do bad
things to me.
28 You are saying to yourselves,
'Where is the great man's house
now?
Where are the tents where his evil
family lived?'
29 Haven't you ever asked questions of
those who travel?
Haven't you paid any attention to
their stories?
30 They'll tell you that sinful people
are spared from the day of trouble.
They'll say that those people
are saved from the day when God
will judge.
31 Who speaks against them for the way
they act?
Who pays them back for what
they've done?
32 Their bodies will be carried to their
graves.
Guards will watch over their tombs.
33 The soil in the valley will be pleasant
to those who have died.
Many people will walk along behind
their bodies.
Many others will walk in front of
them.

34 "So how can you comfort me with
your speeches?
They don't make any sense at all.
Your answers are nothing but lies!"

The Third Speech of Eliphaz

22 Then Eliphaz the Temanite replied,

2 "Can any man be of benefit to God?
Can even a wise man be of any help
to him?
3 Job, what pleasure would it give the
Mighty One if you were right?
What would he get if you were
completely honest?

4 "You say you have respect for him.
Is that why he corrects you?
Is that why he brings charges against
you?

5 Haven't you done many evil things?
Don't you sin again and again?
6 You took clothes away from your
relatives
just because they owed you some
money.
You left them naked for no reason at
all.
7 You didn't give any water to people
who were tired.
You held food back from those who
were hungry.
8 You did it even though you were
honored and powerful.
You owned land and lived on it.
9 But you sent widows away without
anything.
You mistreated children whose
fathers had died.
10 That's why traps have been set all
around you.
That's why sudden danger terrifies
you.
11 That's why it's so dark you can't even
see.
That's why a flood covers you up.

12 "Isn't God in the highest parts of
heaven?
See how high the highest stars are!
13 But you still say, 'What does God
know?
Can he see through the darkest
clouds to judge us?
14 He goes around in the highest
heavens.
Thick clouds keep him from seeing
us.'
15 Will you stay on the old path
that sinful people have walked on?
16 They were carried off even before they
died.
Their foundations were washed
away by a flood.
17 They said to God, 'Leave us alone!
What can you do to us, you Mighty
One?'
18 But he was the one who filled their
houses with good things.
So I don't pay any attention to the
advice they give.

19 "Those who do what is right are joyful
when they see sinners destroyed.
Those who haven't done anything
wrong make fun of them.
20 They say, 'Our enemies are completely
destroyed.
Fire has burned up their wealth.'

21 "Job, obey God and be at peace with
him.
Then he will help you succeed.
22 Do what he teaches you to do.
Keep his words in your heart.
23 If you return to the Mighty One,
you will have what you had before.
But first you must remove
everything that is evil far from your
tent.
24 You must throw your gold nuggets
away.
You must toss your gold from Ophir
into a valley.
25 Then the Mighty One himself will be
your gold.
He'll be like the finest silver to you.
26 You will find delight in the Mighty
One.
You will honor God and trust in him.
27 You will pray to him, and he will hear
you.
You will keep the promises you
made to him.
28 What you decide to do will be done.
Light will shine on the path you
take.
29 When people are brought low you will
say, 'Lift them up!'
Then God will help them.
30 He'll even save those who are guilty.
He'll save them because your hands
are clean."

Job's Reply

23 Job replied,

2 "Even today my problems are more
than I can handle.
In spite of my groans, God's hand is
heavy on me.
3 I wish I knew where I could find him!
I wish I could go to the place where
he lives!
4 I would state my case to him.
I'd give him all of my arguments.
5 I'd find out what his answers would be.
I'd think about what he would say.
6 Would he oppose me with his great
power?
No. He wouldn't bring charges
against me.
7 I'm an honest person. I could state my
case to him.
Then my Judge would tell me once
and for all that I'm not guilty.

8 "But if I go to the east, God isn't there.
If I go to the west, I don't find him.
9 When he's working in the north, I
don't see him there.
When he turns to the south, I don't
see him there either.

10 But he knows every step I take.
    When he has put me to the test,
    I'll come out as pure as gold.
11 My feet have closely followed his steps.
    I've stayed on his path without
    turning away.
12 I haven't disobeyed his commands.
    I've treasured his words more than
    my daily bread.

13 "But he's the only God. Who can
    oppose him?
    He does anything he wants to do.
14 He carries out his plans against me.
    And he still has many other plans
    just like them.
15 That's why I'm so terrified.
    When I think about all of this, I'm
    afraid of him.
16 God has made my heart weak.
    The Mighty One has filled me with
    terror.
17 But even the darkness of death won't
    make me silent.
    When the darkness of the grave
    covers my face, I won't be quiet.

24 "Why doesn't the Mighty One set
    a time for judging sinful
    people?
    Why do those who know him have
    to keep waiting for that day?
2 People move their neighbor's
    boundary stones.
    They steal their neighbor's flocks.
3 They take away the donkeys
    that belong to children whose
    fathers have died.
    They take a widow's ox until she has
    paid what she owes.
4 They push those who are needy out of
    their way.
    They force all of the poor people in
    the land to go into hiding.
5 The poor are like wild donkeys in the
    desert.
    They have to go around looking for
    food.
    The dry and empty land provides
    the only food for their children.
6 The poor go to the fields and get a little
    grain.
    They gather up what is left in the
    vineyards of sinners.
7 The poor don't have any clothes. So
    they spend the night naked.
    They don't have anything to cover
    themselves in the cold.
8 They are soaked by mountain rains.
    They hug the rocks because they
    don't have anything to keep
    them warm.

9 Children whose fathers have died
    are torn away from their mothers.
    A poor person's baby is taken away
    to pay back what is owed.
10 The poor don't have any clothes. They
    go around naked.
    They carry bundles of grain, but
    they still go hungry.
11 They work very hard as they crush
    olives.
    They stomp on grapes in
    winepresses,
    but they are still thirsty.
12 The groans of those who are dying are
    heard from the city.
    Those who are wounded cry out for
    help.
    But God doesn't charge anyone with
    doing what is wrong.

13 "Some people hate it when daylight
    comes.
    In the daytime they never walk
    outside.
14 When daylight is gone, murderers get
    up.
    They kill poor people and those who
    are in need.
    In the night they sneak around like
    robbers.
15 Those who commit adultery wait until
    the sun goes down.
    They think, 'No one will see us.'
    They keep their faces hidden.
16 In the dark, people break into houses.
    But by day they shut themselves in.
    They don't want anything to do
    with the light.
17 The deepest darkness is like morning
    to them.
    The terrors of darkness are their
    friends.

18 "But sinners are like bubbles on the
    surface of water.
    Their share of the land is under
    God's curse.
    So no one goes to their vineyards.
19 Melted snow disappears when the air is
    hot and dry.
    And sinners disappear when they go
    down into their graves.
20 Even their mothers forget them.
    The worms in their graves eat them
    up.
    No one remembers sinful people
    anymore.
    They are cut down like trees.
21 They mistreat women who aren't able
    to have children.
    They aren't kind to widows.
22 But God is powerful.

He even drags away people who are
strong.
When he rises up against them,
they can never be sure they are safe.
23 God might let them rest and feel
secure.
But his eyes see how they live.
24 For a little while they are honored.
Then they are gone.
They are brought low.
And they die like everyone else.
They are cut off like heads of grain.

25 "Who can prove that what I'm saying
is wrong?
Who can prove that my words aren't
true?"

The Third Speech of Bildad

25
Then Bildad the Shuhite replied,

2 "God is King. He should be feared.
He establishes peace in the highest
parts of heaven.
3 Can anyone count his troops?
Is there anyone his light doesn't
shine on?
4 How can human beings be right with
God?
How can mere people really be pure?
5 Even the moon isn't bright
and the stars aren't pure in God's
eyes.
6 So how about human beings? They are
like maggots.
How about mere people? They are
like worms."

Job's Reply

26
Job replied,

2 "Bildad, you haven't helped people
who aren't strong!
You haven't saved people who are
weak!
3 You haven't offered advice to those
who aren't wise!
In fact, you haven't understood
anything at all!
4 Who helped you say those things?
Whose spirit was speaking through
you?

5 "The spirits of the dead are suffering
greatly.
So are those that are under the
waters.
And so are all those that live in them.
6 Death is naked in the sight of God.
The Grave lies open in front of him.
7 He spreads out the northern skies over
empty space.

He hangs the earth over nothing.
8 He wraps up water in his clouds.
They are heavy, but they don't burst.
9 He covers the face of the full moon.
He spreads his clouds over it.
10 He marks out the place where the sky
meets the sea.
He marks out the boundary between
light and darkness.
11 The pillars of the heavens shake.
They are terrified when his anger
blazes out.
12 With his power he stirred up the
oceans.
In his wisdom he cut the sea
monster Rahab to pieces.
13 His breath made the skies bright and
clear.
His hand wounded the serpent that
glides through the sea.
14 Those are only on the edges of what he
does.
They are only the soft whispers that
we hear from him.
So who can understand how very
powerful he is?"

27
Job continued to speak. He said,

2 "God hasn't treated me fairly.
The Mighty One has made my spirit
bitter.
You can be sure that God lives.
And here's something else you can
be sure of.
3 As long as I have life
and God gives me breath,
4 my mouth won't say evil things.
My lips won't tell lies.
5 I'll never admit you people are right.
Until I die, I'll say I'm telling the
truth.
6 I'll continue to say I'm right.
I'll never let go of that.
I won't blame myself as long as I live.

7 "May my enemies suffer like sinful
people!
May my attackers be punished like
those who aren't fair!
8 What hope do ungodly people have
when their lives are cut off?
What hope do they have when God
takes away their lives?
9 God won't listen to their cry
when trouble comes on them.
10 They won't take delight in the Mighty
One.
They'll never call out to God.
11 "I'll teach all of you about God's
power.

I won't hide the things the Mighty
　　One does.
12 You have seen those things yourselves.
　　So why do you continue your useless
　　talk?

13 "Here's what God does to sinful
　　people.
　　Here's what those who are mean
　　　receive from the Mighty One.
14 All of their children will be killed with
　　swords.
　　They'll never have enough to eat.
15 A plague will kill those who are left
　　alive.
　　The widows of sinful men
　　won't even sob over their own
　　　children.
16 Sinners might store up silver like dust
　　and clothes like piles of clay.
17 But people who do what is right will
　　　wear those clothes.
　　People who haven't done anything
　　　wrong
　　will divide up that silver.
18 The house an evil person builds is like a
　　　moth's cocoon.
　　It's like a hut that's made by
　　　someone on guard duty.
19 Sinful people lie down wealthy, but
　　　their wealth is taken away.
　　When they open their eyes,
　　　everything is gone.
20 Terrors sweep over them like a flood.
　　A storm takes them away during the
　　　night.
21 The east wind carries them off, and
　　　they are gone.
　　It sweeps them out of their houses.
22 It blows against them without mercy.
　　They try to escape from its power.
23 It claps its hands and makes fun of
　　　them.
　　It hisses them out of their houses.

28 "There are mines where silver is
　　found.
　　There are places where gold is
　　　purified.
2 Iron is taken out of the earth.
　　Copper is melted down from ore.
3 A miner lights up the darkness.
　　He searches for ore in the deepest
　　　pits.
　　He looks for it in the blackest
　　　darkness.
4 Far from where people live he cuts a
　　　tunnel.
　　He does it in places where others
　　　don't go.
　　Far away from people he swings back
　　　and forth on ropes.

5 Food grows on the surface of the earth.
　　But far below, the earth is changed
　　　as if by fire.
6 Sapphires are taken from its rocks.
　　Its dust contains nuggets of gold.
7 No bird knows the miner's hidden
　　　path.
　　No falcon's eye has seen it.
8 Proud animals don't walk on it.
　　Lions don't prowl there.
9 The miner attacks the hardest rock.
　　His strong hands uncover the base of
　　　the mountains.
10 He tunnels through the rock.
　　His eyes see all of its treasures.
11 He searches the places where the rivers
　　　begin.
　　He brings hidden things out into the
　　　light.

12 "And where can wisdom be found?
　　Where does understanding live?
13 No one knows how much it's worth.
　　It can't be found anywhere in the
　　　world.
14 The ocean says, 'It's not in me.'
　　The sea says, 'It's not here either.'
15 It can't be bought with the finest gold.
　　Its price can't be weighed out in
　　　silver.
16 It can't be bought with gold from
　　　Ophir.
　　It can't be bought with priceless
　　　onyx or sapphires.
17 Gold or crystal can't compare with it.
　　It can't be bought with jewels made
　　　of gold.
18 Don't bother to talk about coral and
　　　jasper.
　　Wisdom is worth far more than
　　　rubies.
19 A topaz from Cush can't compare
　　　with it.
　　It can't be bought with the purest
　　　gold.

20 "So where does wisdom come from?
　　Where does understanding live?
21 It's hidden from the eyes of every
　　　living thing.
　　Even the birds of the air can't find it.

POWER-SURGE

WISE　Ⓦ

WISDOM IS WORTH FAR
MORE THAN RUBIES.
— JOB 28:18 —

²²Death and the Grave say,
'Only reports about it have reached
our ears.'
²³But God understands the way to it.
He's the only one who knows where
it lives.
²⁴He sees from one end of the earth to
the other.
He views everything in the world.
²⁵He made the mighty wind.
He measured out the waters.
²⁶He gave orders for the rain to fall.
He made paths for the
thunderstorms.
²⁷Then he looked at wisdom and set its
price.
He established it and put it to the
test.
²⁸He said to human beings,
'Have respect for me. That will prove
you are wise.
Avoid evil. That will show you have
understanding.' "

WISE W

[GOD] SAID TO HUMAN
BEINGS,

"HAVE RESPECT FOR
ME. THAT WILL PROVE
YOU ARE WISE.

AVOID EVIL. THAT WILL
SHOW YOU HAVE
UNDERSTANDING."
— JOB 28:28 —

29
Job continued to speak. He said,

²"How I long for the good old days!
That's when God watched over me.
³The light of his lamp shone on me.
I walked through darkness by his
light.
⁴Those were the best days of my life.
That's when God's friendship
blessed my house.
⁵The Mighty One was still with me.
My children were all around me.
⁶The path in front of me was like sweet
cream.
It was as if the rock poured out olive
oil for me.

⁷"In those days I went to the city gate.
I took my seat as a member of the
council.
⁸Young people who saw me stepped to
one side.
Old people stood up as I
approached.
⁹The leaders stopped speaking.
They covered their mouths with
their hands.
¹⁰The voices of the nobles became quiet.
Their tongues stuck to the roofs of
their mouths.
¹¹Everyone who heard me said good
things about me.
Those who saw me honored me.
¹²That's because I saved poor people who
cried out for help.
I saved helpless children whose
fathers had died.
¹³Those who were dying gave me their
blessing.
I made the hearts of widows sing.
¹⁴I put on a godly life as if it were my
clothes.
Fairness was my robe and my
turban.
¹⁵I was like eyes for those who were
blind.
I was like feet for those who couldn't
walk.
¹⁶I was like a father to needy people.
I stood up for strangers in court.
¹⁷Sinners are like animals that have
powerful teeth.
But I took from their mouths the
people they had caught.

¹⁸"I thought, 'I'll die in my own house.
The days of my life will be as many
as the grains of sand.
¹⁹My roots will reach down to the water.
The dew will lie all night on my
branches.
²⁰I will remain healthy and strong.
My bow will stay as good as new in
my hand.'

²¹"People wanted to hear what I had to
say.
They waited silently for the advice I
gave them.
²²After I had spoken, they didn't speak
anymore.
My words fell gently on their ears.
²³They waited for me just as they would
wait for showers.
They drank my words just as they
would drink the spring rain.
²⁴When I smiled at them, they could
hardly believe it.
The light of my face lifted their
spirits.

25 I chose the way they should go. I sat as
　　their chief.
　　I lived as a king lives among his
　　　troops.
　　I was like someone who comforts
　　　those who are sad.

30 "But now those who are younger
　　than I am make fun of me.
　　I wouldn't put even their parents
　　　with my sheep dogs!
2 Their strong hands couldn't give me
　　any help.
　　That's because their strength was
　　　gone.
3 They were weak because they were
　　needy and hungry.
　　They wandered through dry and
　　　empty deserts at night.
4 Among the bushes they gathered salty
　　plants.
　　They ate the roots of desert trees.
5 They were driven away from society.
　　They were shouted at as if they were
　　　robbers.
6 They were forced to live in dry stream
　　beds.
　　They had to stay among rocks
　　　and in holes in the ground.
7 Like donkeys they cried out among the
　　bushes.
　　There they crowded together and
　　　hid.
8 They were so foolish that no one
　　respected them.
　　They were driven out of the land.

9 "Now their children laugh at me.
　　They make fun of me with their
　　　songs.
10 They hate me. They stay away from me.
　　They even dare to spit in my face.
11 God has made my body weak.
　　It's like a tent that has fallen down.
　　So those children do what they want
　　　to in front of me.
12 Many people attack me on my right
　　side.
　　They lay traps for my feet.
　　They come at me from every
　　　direction.
13 They tear up the road I walk on.
　　They succeed in destroying me.
　　They do it without any help.
14 They attack me like troops smashing
　　through a wall.
　　Among the destroyed buildings they
　　　come rolling in.
15 Terrors sweep over me.
　　My honor is driven away as if by the
　　　wind.
　　My safety vanishes like a cloud.

16 "Now my life is slipping away.
　　Days of suffering grab hold of me.
17 At night my bones hurt.
　　My gnawing pains never stop.
18 God's great power becomes like clothes
　　to me.
　　He chokes me like the neck of my
　　　shirt.
19 He throws me down into the mud.
　　I'm nothing but dust and ashes.

20 "God, I cry out to you. But you don't
　　answer me.
　　I stand up. But all you do is look at
　　　me.
21 You do mean things to me.
　　Your mighty hand attacks me.
22 You pick me up and blow me away
　　with the wind.
　　You toss me around in the storm.
23 I know that you will bring me down to
　　death.
　　That's what you have appointed for
　　　everyone.

24 "No one would crush people
　　when they cry out for help in their
　　　trouble.
25 Haven't I sobbed over those who are in
　　trouble?
　　Haven't I felt sorry for poor people?
26 I hoped good things would happen,
　　but something evil came.
　　I looked for light, but all I saw was
　　　darkness.
27 My insides are always churning.
　　Nothing but days of suffering are
　　　ahead of me.
28 My skin has become dark, but the sun
　　didn't do it.
　　I stand up in the community and
　　　cry out for help.
29 I've become a brother to wild dogs.
　　Owls are my companions.
30 My skin grows black and peels.
　　My body burns with fever.
31 My harp is tuned to sadness.
　　My flute makes a sound like sobbing.

31 "I made an agreement with my
　　eyes.
　　I promised not to look at another
　　　woman with sexual longing.
2 What do human beings receive from
　　God above?
　　What do they get from the Mighty
　　　One in heaven?
3 Sinful people are destroyed.
　　Trouble comes to those who do
　　　what is wrong.
4 Doesn't God see how I live?
　　Doesn't he count every step I take?

5 "I haven't told any lies.
  My feet haven't hurried to cheat
    others.
6 So let God weigh me in honest scales.
  Then he'll know I haven't done
    anything wrong.
7 Suppose my steps have turned away
    from the right path.
  Suppose my heart has longed for
    what my eyes have seen.
  Or suppose my hands have become
    'unclean.'
8 Then may others eat what I've planted.
  May my crops be pulled up by the
    roots.

9 "Suppose my heart has been tempted
    by a woman.
  Or suppose I've prowled around my
    neighbor's door.
10 Then may my wife grind another
    man's grain.
  May other men have sex with her.
11 Wanting another woman would have
    been a shameful thing.
  It would have been a sin that should
    be judged.
12 It's like a fire that burns down to the
    grave.
  It would have caused my crops to be
    pulled up by the roots.

13 "Suppose I haven't treated my male
    and female servants fairly
  when they've brought charges
    against me.
14 Then what will I do when God opposes
    me?
  What answer will I give him
  when he asks me to explain myself?
15 Didn't he who made me make my
    servants also?
  Didn't the same God form us inside
    our mothers?

16 "I haven't said no to what poor people
    have wanted.
  I haven't let widows lose their hope.
17 I haven't kept my bread to myself.
  I've shared it with children whose
    fathers had died.
18 From the time I was young, I've helped
    those widows.
  I've raised those children as a father
    would.
19 Suppose I've seen people dying
    because they didn't have any
      clothes.
  I've seen needy people
    who had nothing to wear.
20 And they didn't give me their blessing

when I warmed them with wool
    from my sheep.
21 Suppose I've raised my hand
    against children whose fathers have
      died.
  And I did it because I knew
    I had power in the courts.
22 Then let my arm fall from my
    shoulder.
  Let it be broken off at the joint.
23 I was afraid God would destroy me.
  His glory terrifies me.
  So I'd never do things like that.

24 "Suppose I've put my trust in gold.
  I've said to pure gold, 'You make me
    feel secure.'
25 And I'm happy because I'm so wealthy.
  I'm glad because my hands have
    earned so much.
26 Suppose I've worshiped the sun in all
    of its glory.
  I've bowed down to the moon in all
    of its beauty.
27 My heart has been secretly tempted.
  My hand has thrown kisses to the
    sun and moon.
28 Then those things would have been
    sins that should be judged.
  And I wouldn't have been faithful to
    God in heaven.

29 "I wasn't happy when hard times came
    to my enemies.
  I didn't enjoy seeing the trouble
    they had.
30 I didn't allow my mouth to sin
    by calling down curses on them.
31 The workers in my house always said,
  'Job always gives plenty of food to
    everyone.'
32 No stranger ever had to spend the
    night in the street.
  My door was always open to
    travelers.
33 I didn't hide my sin as others do.
  I didn't hide my guilt in my heart.
34 I was never afraid of the crowd.
  I never worried that my relatives
    might hate me.
  I didn't have to keep quiet or stay
    inside.

35 "I wish someone would listen to me!
  I'm signing my name to everything
    I've said.
  I hope the Mighty One will give me his
    answer.
  I hope the one who brings charges
    against me will write them
      down.
36 I'll wear them on my shoulder.

I'll put them on my head like a
　　crown.
37 I'll give that person a report of every
　　step I take.
　　I'll approach him like a prince.

38 "Suppose my land cries out against me.
　　And all of its soil is wet with tears.
39 Suppose I've used up its crops without
　　paying for them.
　　Or I've broken the spirit of its
　　renters.
40 Then let thorns grow instead of wheat.
　　Let weeds come up instead of
　　barley."

The words of Job end here.

The Speech of Elihu

32 So the three men stopped answering Job, because he thought he was right.

2 But Elihu the Buzite burned with anger against Job. That's because he said he himself was right instead of God. Elihu was the son of Barakel. He was from the family of Ram.

3 Elihu's anger also burned against Job's three friends. They hadn't found any way to prove that Job was wrong. But they still said he was guilty.

4 Elihu had waited before he spoke to Job. That's because the others were older than he was. 5 But he saw that the three men didn't have anything more to say. So he burned with anger.

6 Elihu the Buzite, the son of Barakel, said,

"I'm young, and you are old.
　　So I was afraid to tell you what I
　　know.
7 I thought, 'Those who are older should
　　speak first.
　　Those who have lived for many
　　years
　　should teach people how to be wise.'
8 But the spirit in people gives them
　　understanding.
　　The breath of the Mighty One gives
　　them wisdom.
9 Older people aren't the only ones who
　　are wise.
　　They aren't the only ones who
　　understand what is right.

10 "So I'm saying you should listen to me.
　　I'll tell you what I know.
11 I waited while you men spoke.
　　I listened to your reasoning.
　　While you were searching for words,
12 　I paid careful attention to you.

But not one of you has proved that Job
　　is wrong.
　　None of you has answered his
　　arguments.
13 Don't claim, 'We have enough wisdom
　　to answer Job.'
　　Let God, not a mere man, prove that
　　he's wrong.
14 Job hasn't directed his words against
　　me.
　　I won't answer him with your
　　arguments.

15 "Job, those men are afraid.
　　They don't have anything else to say.
　　They've run out of words.
16 Do I have to keep on waiting, now that
　　they are silent?
　　They are just standing there with
　　nothing to say.
17 I too have something to say.
　　I too will tell what I know.
18 I'm full of words.
　　My spirit inside me forces me to
　　speak.
19 Inside I'm like wine that is bottled up.
　　I'm like new wineskins ready to
　　burst.
20 I must speak so I can feel better.
　　I must open my mouth and reply.
21 I'll treat everyone the same.
　　I won't praise anyone without
　　meaning it.
22 If I weren't honest when I praised
　　people,
　　my Maker would soon take me from
　　this life.

33 "Job, listen now to my words.
　　Pay attention to everything I say.
2 I'm about to open my mouth.
　　My words are on the tip of my
　　tongue.
3 What I say comes from an honest
　　heart.
　　My lips speak only what I know is
　　true.

POWER-SURGE

HONEST H

WHAT I SAY COMES
FROM AN HONEST
HEART.

MY LIPS SPEAK ONLY
WHAT I KNOW IS TRUE.
—— JOB 33:3 ——

⁴The Spirit of God has made me.
  The breath of the Mighty One gives
    me life.
⁵So answer me if you can.
  Prepare yourself to face me.
⁶In God's sight I'm just like you.
  I too have been made out of clay.
⁷You don't have to be afraid of me.
  My hand won't be too heavy on
    you.

⁸"But I heard what you said.
  And here are the exact words I
    heard.
⁹You said, 'I'm pure. I haven't sinned in
    the ways you have charged.
  I'm clean. I'm not guilty of doing
    anything wrong.
¹⁰But God has found fault with me.
  He thinks I'm his enemy.
¹¹He puts my feet in chains.
  He watches every step I take.'

¹²"But I'm telling you that you aren't
    right when you talk like that.
  After all, God is greater than a mere
    man.
¹³Why do you claim that God
  never answers any of our questions?
¹⁴He speaks in one way and then
    another.
  We might not even realize it.
¹⁵He might speak in a dream or in a
    vision at night.
  That's when people are sound asleep
    in their beds.
¹⁶He might speak in their ears.
  His warnings might terrify them.
¹⁷He warns men in order to turn them
    away from sinning.
  He wants to keep them from being
    proud.
¹⁸He wants to stop them from going
    down into the grave.
  He doesn't want them to be killed
    with swords.
¹⁹Someone might be punished by
    suffering in bed.
  The pain in his bones might never
    go away.
²⁰He might feel so bad he can't eat
    anything.
  He might even hate the finest food.
²¹His body might waste away to nothing.
  His bones might have been hidden.
  But now they stick out.
²²He might approach the very edge of
    the grave.
  The messengers of death might
    come for him.

²³"But suppose there is an angel who
    will speak up for him.
  The angel is very special. He's one
    out of a thousand.
  He will tell that person what is right
    for him.
²⁴He'll be gracious to him. He'll say to
    God,
  'Spare him from going down into
    the grave.
  I know a way that can set him free.'
²⁵Then his body is made like new again.
  He becomes as strong and healthy as
    when he was young.
²⁶He prays to God and finds favor with
    him.
  He sees God's face and shouts with
    joy.
  God makes him right with himself
    again.
²⁷Then the person comes to others and
    says,
  'I sinned. I made what was wrong
    appear to be right.
  But I wasn't punished as I should
    have been.
²⁸God set me free. He kept me from
    going down into the grave.
  So I'll live to enjoy the light that
    leads to life.'

²⁹"God does all of those things to
    people.
  In fact, he does them again and
    again.
³⁰He wants to stop people from going
    down into the grave.
  Then the light that leads to life will
    shine on them.

³¹"Pay attention, Job! Listen to me!
  Be quiet so I can speak.
³²If you have anything to say, answer
    me.
  Speak up. I want to help you be
    cleared of all charges.
³³But if you don't have anything to say,
    listen to me.
  Be quiet so I can teach you how to be
    wise."

34 Elihu continued,

²"Hear what I'm saying, you wise men.
  Listen to me, you who have learned
    so much.
³Our tongues tell us what tastes good
    and what doesn't.
  And our ears tell us what's true and
    what isn't.
⁴So let's choose for ourselves what is
    right.

Let's learn together what is good.

5 "Job says, 'I'm not guilty of doing
anything wrong.
But God doesn't treat me fairly.
6 Even though I'm right,
he thinks I'm a liar.
Even though I'm not guilty,
his arrows give me wounds that
can't be healed.'
7 Is there any other man like Job?
He laughs at God and makes fun of
him.
8 He's a companion of those who do
evil.
He spends his time with sinful
people.
9 He asks, 'What good is it
to try to please God?'

10 "So listen to me, you men who have
understanding.
God would never do what is evil.
The Mighty One would never do
what is wrong.
11 He pays a man back for what he's done.
He gives him exactly what he should
get.
12 It isn't possible for God to do wrong.
The Mighty One would never treat
people unfairly.
13 Who appointed him to rule over the
earth?
Who put him in charge of the whole
world?
14 If he really wanted to,
he could hold back his spirit and
breath.
15 Then everyone would die together.
They would return to the dust.

16 "Job, if you have understanding, listen
to me.
Pay attention to what I'm saying.
17 Can someone who hates to be fair
govern?
Will you bring charges against the
holy and mighty One?
18 He says to kings, 'You are worthless.'
He says to nobles, 'You are evil.'
19 He doesn't favor princes.
He treats rich people and poor
people the same.
His hands created all of them.
20 They die suddenly in the middle of the
night.
God strikes them down, and they
pass away.
Those who are mighty are removed,
but not by human hands.

21 "His eyes see how people live.
He watches every step they take.

22 There isn't a dark place or deep shadow
where those who do what is evil can
hide.
23 God doesn't need to bring charges
against men.
He knows they are guilty.
So he doesn't need to have them
appear in his court to be
judged.
24 He destroys the mighty without asking
them questions in court.
Then he sets others up in their
places.
25 He knows what they do.
So he crushes them during the
night.
26 He punishes them for the sins they
commit.
He does it where everyone can see
them.
27 That's because they turned away from
following him.
They didn't have respect for
anything he does.
28 They caused poor people to cry out to
him.
He heard the cries of those who were
in need.
29 But if he remains silent, who can judge
him?
If he turns his face away, who can
see him?
He rules over people and nations alike.
30   He keeps those who are ungodly
from ruling.
He keeps them from laying traps for
others.

31 "Someone might say to God,
'I'm guilty of sinning,
but I won't do it anymore.
32 Show me my sins that I'm not aware of.
If I've done what is wrong,
I won't do it again.'
33 But you refuse to turn away from your
sins.
So God won't treat you the way you
want to be treated.
You must decide, Job. I can't do it for
you.
So tell me what you know.

34 "You men who have understanding
have spoken.
You wise men who hear me have
said to me,
35 'Job doesn't know what he's talking
about.
The things he has said don't make
any sense.'
36 I wish Job would be put to the hardest
test!

He answered like someone who is
evil.
37 To his sin he adds even more sin.
He claps his hands and makes fun of
us.
He multiplies his words against
God."

35 Elihu continued,

2 "Job, do you think it's fair for you to
say,
'God will clear me of all charges'?
3 You ask him, 'What good is it for me
not to sin?
What do I get by not sinning?'
4 "I'd like to reply to you
and to your friends who are with
you.
5 Look up at the heavens.
Observe the clouds that are high
above you.
6 If you sin, what does that mean to
God?
If you sin many times, what does
that do to him?
7 If you do what is right, how does that
help him?
What does he get from you?
8 The evil things you do only hurt
someone like yourself.
The right things you do only help
other human beings.
9 "People cry out when they are beaten
down.
They beg to be set free from the
power of those who are over
them.
10 But no one says, 'Where is the God
who made me?
He gives us songs even during the
night.
11 He teaches more to us than to wild
animals.
He makes us wiser than the birds of
the air.'
12 He doesn't answer sinful people when
they cry out to him.
That's because they are so proud.
13 In fact, God doesn't listen to their
empty cries.
The Mighty One doesn't pay any
attention to them.
14 So he certainly won't listen to you.
When you say you don't see him, he
won't hear you.
He won't listen when you state your
case to him.
He won't pay attention even if you
wait for him.

15 When you say his anger never
punishes sin, he won't hear
you.
He won't listen when you say he
doesn't pay any attention to
evil.
16 So you say things that don't mean
anything.
You use a lot of words,
but you don't know what you are
talking about."

36 Elihu continued,

2 "Put up with me a little longer.
I'll show you I can speak up for God
even more.
3 I get my knowledge from far away.
I'll announce that the One who
made me is fair.
4 You can be sure that my words are true.
One who has perfect knowledge is
talking to you.
5 "God is mighty, but he doesn't hate
people.
He's mighty, and he knows exactly
what he's going to do.
6 He doesn't keep alive those who are
evil.
Instead, he gives suffering people
their rights.
7 He watches over those who do what is
right.
He puts them on thrones as if they
were kings.
He honors them forever.
8 But some people are held by chains.
They are tied up with painful ropes.
9 God tells them what they've done.
He tells them they've become proud
and sinned against him.
10 He makes them listen when he corrects
them.
He commands them to turn away
from the evil things they've done.
11 If they obey him and serve him,
they'll enjoy a long and happy life.
Things will go well with them.
12 But if they don't listen to him,
they'll be killed with swords.
They'll die because they didn't want
to know anything about him.
13 "Those whose hearts are ungodly are
always angry.
Even when God puts them in
chains,
they don't cry out for help.
14 They die while they are still young.
They die among the male prostitutes
at the temples.

POWER-SURGE

CHEERFUL ✳

**IF THEY OBEY [GOD]
AND SERVE HIM,
THEY'LL ENJOY A
LONG AND HAPPY LIFE.
THINGS WILL GO WELL
WITH THEM.**
— JOB 36:11 —

✔

OBEYS

15 But God saves suffering people while
they are suffering.
    He speaks to them while they are
hurting.
16 "Job, he wants to take you out of the
jaws of trouble.
    He wants to bring you to a wide and
safe place.
    He'd like to seat you at a table that is
loaded with the best food.
17 But now you are loaded down
    with the punishment sinners will
receive.
    You have been judged fairly.
18 Be careful that no one tempts you with
riches.
    Don't take money from people who
want special favors,
    no matter how much it is.
19 Can your wealth keep you out of
trouble?
    Can all of your mighty efforts keep
you going?
20 Don't long for the night to come
    so you can drag people away from
their homes.
21 Be careful not to do what is evil.
    You seem to like evil better than
suffering!
22 "God is honored because he is so
powerful.
    He has no equal as a teacher.
23 Who has told him what he can do?
    Who has said to him, 'You have
done what is wrong'?
24 Remember to thank him for what he's
done.
    People have praised him with their
songs.

25 Every human being has seen his work.
    People can see it from far away.
26 How great God is! We'll never
    completely understand him.
    We'll never find out how long he has
lived.
27 "He makes mist rise from the water.
    Then it falls as rain into the streams.
28 The clouds pour down their moisture.
    Rain showers fall on people
everywhere.
29 Who can understand how God spreads
out the clouds?
    Who can explain how he thunders
from his home in heaven?
30 See how he scatters his lightning
around him!
    He lights up the deepest parts of the
ocean.
31 The rain he sends makes things grow
for the nations.
    He provides them with plenty of
food.
32 He holds lightning bolts in his hands.
    He commands them to strike their
marks.
33 His thunder announces that a storm is
coming.
    Even the cattle let us know it's
approaching.

37   "When I hear the thunder, my
heart pounds.
    It beats faster inside me.
2 Listen! Listen to the roar of his voice!
    Listen to the thunder that comes
from him!
3 He sends his lightning across the sky.
    It reaches from one end of the earth
to the other.
4 Next comes the sound of his roaring
thunder.
    He thunders with his majestic voice.
    When his voice fills the air,
    he doesn't hold anything back.
5 God's voice thunders in wonderful
ways.
    We'll never understand the great
things he does.

POWER-SURGE

THANKFUL ♣

**REMEMBER TO THANK
[GOD] FOR WHAT
HE'S DONE.**
— JOB 36:24 —

⁶He says to the snow, 'Fall on the earth.'
  He tells the rain, 'Pour down your
    mighty waters.'
⁷He stops everyone from working.
  He wants them to see his work.
⁸The animals go inside.
  They remain in their dens.
⁹The storm comes out of its storeroom
    in the heavens.
  The cold comes from the driving
    winds.
¹⁰The breath of God produces ice.
  The shallow water freezes over.
¹¹He loads the clouds with moisture.
  He scatters his lightning through
    them.
¹²He directs the clouds to circle
    above the surface of the whole
    earth.
  They do everything he commands
    them to do.
¹³He tells the clouds to punish people.
  Or he brings them to water his earth
    and show his love.

¹⁴"Job, listen to me.
  Stop and think about the wonderful
    things God does.
¹⁵Do you know how he controls the
    clouds?
  Do you understand how he makes
    his lightning flash?
¹⁶Do you know how the clouds stay up
    in the sky?
  Do you understand the wonders of
    the One who has perfect
    knowledge?
¹⁷Even your clothes are too hot for you
    when the land lies quiet under the
    south wind.
¹⁸Can you help God spread out the
    skies?
  They are as hard as a mirror
    that's made out of bronze.

¹⁹"Job, tell us what we should say to
    God.
  We can't prepare our case
    because our minds are dark.
²⁰Should he be told that I want to speak?
  Would any man ask to be destroyed
    by him?
²¹No one can look at the sun.
  It's too bright after the wind has
    swept the skies clean.
²²Out of the north, God comes in his
    shining glory.
  He comes in all of his wonderful
    majesty.
²³We can't reach up to the Mighty One.
  He is lifted high because of his
    power.

Everything he does is fair and right.
  So he doesn't crush people.
²⁴That's why they have respect for him.
  He cares about all those who are
    wise."

The First Speech of the LORD

38 The LORD spoke to Job out of a
    storm. He said,

²"Who do you think you are to disagree
    with my plans?
  You do not know what you are
    talking about.
³Get ready to stand up for yourself.
  I will ask you some questions.
  Then I want you to answer me.

⁴"Where were you when I laid the
    earth's foundation?
  Tell me, if you know.
⁵Who measured it? I am sure you know!
  Who stretched a measuring line
    across it?
⁶What was it built on?
  Who laid its most important stone?
⁷When it happened, the morning stars
    sang together.
  All of the angels shouted with joy

⁸"Who created the ocean?
  Who caused it to be born?
⁹I put clouds over it as if they were its
    clothes.
  I wrapped it in thick darkness.
¹⁰I set limits for it.
  I put its doors and metal bars in
    place.
¹¹I said, 'You can come this far.
  But you can't come any farther.
  Here is where your proud waves have
    to stop.'

¹²"Job, have you ever commanded the
    morning to come?
  Have you ever shown the sun where
    to rise?
¹³The daylight takes the earth by its
    edges
  as if it were a blanket.
  Then it shakes sinful people out of it.
¹⁴The earth takes shape like clay under a
    seal.
  Its features stand out
  like the different parts of your
    clothes.
¹⁵Sinners would rather have darkness
    than light.
  When the light comes, their power
    is broken.

¹⁶"Have you traveled to the springs at
    the bottom of the ocean?

Have you walked in its deepest parts?
17 Have the gates of death been shown to
you?
Have you seen the gates of darkness?
18 Do you understand how big the earth
is?
Tell me, if you know all of those
things.

19 "Where does light come from?
And where does darkness live?
20 Can you take them to their places?
Do you know the paths to their
houses?
21 I am sure you know! After all, you were
already born!
You have lived so many years!

22 "Have you entered the places where
the snow is kept?
Have you seen the storerooms for
the hail?
23 I store up snow and hail for times of
trouble.
I keep them for days of war and
battle.
24 Where does lightning come from?
Where do the east winds that blow
across the earth live?
25 Who tells the rain where it should fall?
Who makes paths for the
thunderstorms?
26 They bring water to places where no
one lives.
They water deserts that do not have
anyone in them.
27 They satisfy the needs of dry and
empty lands.
They make grass start growing there.
28 Does the rain have a father?
Who is the father of the drops of
dew?
29 Does the ice have a mother?
Who is the mother of the frost from
the heavens?
30 The waters become as hard as stone.
The surface of the ocean freezes over.

31 "Can you tie up the beautiful Pleiades?
Can you untie the ropes that hold
Orion together?
32 Can you bring out all of the stars in
their seasons?
Can you lead out the Big Dipper and
the Little Dipper?
33 Do you know the laws that govern the
heavens?
Can you rule over the earth the way
I do?

34 "Can you give orders to the clouds?
Can you make them pour rain down
on you?

35 Do you send the lightning bolts on
their way?
Do they report to you, 'Here we are'?
36 Who put wisdom in people's hearts?
Who gave understanding to their
minds?
37 Who is wise enough to count the
clouds?
Who can tip over the water jars of
the heavens?
38 I tip them over when the ground
becomes hard.
I do it when the dirt sticks together.

39 "Do you hunt for food for mother
lions?
Do you satisfy the hunger of their
cubs?
40 Some of them lie low in their dens.
Others lie waiting in the bushes.
41 Who provides food for ravens
when their babies cry out to me?
They wander around because they
do not have anything to eat.

39 "Job, do you know when
mountain goats have their
babies?
Do you watch when female deer give
birth?
2 Do you count the months until the
animals have their babies?
Do you know the time when they
give birth?
3 They bend their back legs and have
their babies.
Then their labor pains stop.
4 Their little ones grow strong and
healthy in the wild.
They leave and do not come home
again.

5 "Who let the wild donkeys go free?
Who untied their ropes?
6 I gave them the dry and empty land as
their home.
I gave them salt flats to live in.
7 They laugh at all of the noise in town.
They do not hear the shouts of the
donkey drivers.
8 They wander over the hills to look for
grass.
They search for anything green to
eat.

9 "Job, will wild oxen agree to serve you?
Will they stay by your feed box at
night?
10 Can you keep them in straight rows
with harnesses?
Will they plow the valleys behind
you?

NATHAN

The LORD sent a message [to David]
through the prophet Nathan.
(2 Samuel 12:25)

GO TO PAGE 366

SOLOMON

Solomon was wiser than any other man...
[He] was richer than all of the other kings on earth. He was also
wiser than they were. (1 Kings 4:31; 10:23)

GO TO PAGE 395

ELIJAH

Elijah was from Tishbe in the land of Gilead.
He said to Ahab, "I serve the LORD. He is the God of Israel.
You can be sure that he lives." (1 Kings 17:1)

GO TO PAGE 416

A WIDOW

*"Go and sell the oil. Pay what you owe.
You and your sons can live on what is left."*
(2 Kings 4:7)

GO TO PAGE 434

11 Will you depend on them for their
  great strength?
  Will you let them do your heavy
  work?
12 Can you trust them to bring in your
  grain?
  Will they take it to your threshing
  floor?

13 "The wings of ostriches flap with joy.
  But they can't compare with the
  wings and feathers of storks.
14 Ostriches lay their eggs on the ground.
  They let them get warm in the sand.
15 They do not know that something
  might step on them.
  A wild animal might walk all over
  them.
16 Ostriches are mean to their little ones.
  They treat them as if they did not
  belong to them.
  They do not care that their work was
  useless.
17 I did not provide ostriches with
  wisdom.
  I did not give them good sense.
18 But when they spread their feathers to
  run,
  they laugh at a horse and its rider.

19 "Job, do you give horses their strength?
  Do you put flowing manes on their
  necks?
20 Do you make them jump like locusts?
  They terrify others with their proud
  snorting.
21 They paw the ground wildly.
  They are filled with joy.
  They charge at their enemies.
22 They laugh at fear. They are not afraid
  of anything.
  They do not run away from swords.
23 Many arrows rattle at their sides.
  Flashing spears and javelins are also
  there.
24 They are so stirred up that they eat up
  the ground.
  They can't stand still when trumpets
  are blown.
25 When they hear the trumpets they
  snort, 'Aha!'
  They catch the smells of battle far
  away.
  They hear the shouts of
  commanders and the battle
  cries.

26 "Job, are you wise enough to teach
  hawks where to fly?
  They spread their wings and fly
  toward the south.

27 Do you command eagles to fly so
  high?
  They build their nests as high as
  they can.
28 They live on cliffs and stay there at
  night.
  High up on the rocks they think
  they are safe.
29 From there they look for their food.
  They can see it from far away.
30 Their little ones like to eat blood.
  Eagles gather where they see dead
  bodies."

40 The Lord continued,

2 "I am the Mighty One.
  Will the man who argues with me
  correct me?
  Let him who brings charges against
  me answer me!"

Job's Reply

3 Job replied to the Lord,

4 "I'm not worthy. How can I reply to
  you?
  I'm putting my hand over my
  mouth. I'll stop talking.
5 I spoke once. But I really don't have
  any answer.
  I spoke twice. But I won't say
  anything else."

The Second Speech of the Lord

6 Then the Lord spoke to Job out of the
storm. He said,

7 "Get ready to stand up for yourself.
  I will ask you some more questions.
  Then I want you to answer me.

8 "Would you dare to claim that I am
  not being fair?
  Would you judge me in order to
  make yourself seem right?
9 Is your arm as powerful as mine is?
  Can your voice thunder as mine
  does?
10 Then put on glory and beauty as if
  they were your clothes.
  Also put honor and majesty on.
11 Let loose your great anger.
  Look at those who are proud and
  bring them low.
12 Look at proud people and bring them
  down.
  Crush those who are evil right
  where they are.
13 Bury their bodies in the dust together.
  Cover their faces in the grave.
14 Then I myself will admit to you

that your own right hand can save you.

15 "Look at the behemoth. It is a huge animal.
　I made both of you.
　It eats grass like an ox.
16 Look at the strength it has in its hips!
　What power it has in the muscles of its stomach!
17 Its tail sways back and forth like a cedar tree.
　The tendons of its thighs are close together.
18 Its bones are like tubes made out of bronze.
　Its legs are like rods made out of iron.
19 It ranks first among my works.
　I made it. I can approach it with my sword.
20 The hills produce food for it.
　All of the other wild animals play near it.
21 It lies under lotus plants.
　It hides in tall grass in the swamps.
22 The lotus plants hide it in their shade.
　Poplar trees near streams surround it.
23 It is not afraid when the river roars.
　It is secure even when the Jordan River rushes against its mouth.
24 Can anyone capture it by its eyes?
　Can anyone trap it and poke a hole through its nose?

41 "Job, can you pull the leviathan out of the sea with a fish hook?
　Can you tie down its tongue with a rope?
2 Can you put a rope through its nose?
　Can you stick a hook through its jaw?
3 Will it keep begging you for mercy?
　Will it speak gently to you?
4 Will it make an agreement with you?
　Can you make it your slave for life?
5 Can you make a pet out of it like a bird?
　Can you put it on a leash for your young women?
6 Will traders offer you something for it?
　Will they divide it up among the merchants?
7 Can you fill its body with harpoons?
　Can you throw fishing spears into its head?
8 If you touch it, it will fight you.
　Then you will remember never to touch it again!
9 No one can possibly control the leviathan.
　Just looking at it will terrify you.
10 No one dares to wake it up.

So who can possibly stand up to me?
11 Who has a claim against me that I must pay?
　Everything on earth belongs to me.

12 "Now I will speak about the leviathan's legs.
　I will talk about its strength and its graceful body.
13 Who can strip off its outer coat?
　Who would try to put a bridle on it?
14 Who dares to open its jaws?
　Its mouth is filled with terrifying teeth.
15 Its back has rows of shields that are close together.
16 Each one is so close to the next one that not even air can pass between them.
17 They are joined tightly to one another.
　They stick together and can't be forced apart.
18 The leviathan's snorting throws out flashes of light.
　Its eyes shine like the first light of day.
19 Fire seems to spray out of its mouth.
　Sparks of fire shoot out.
20 Smoke pours out of its nose.
　It is like smoke from a boiling pot over burning grass.
21 Its breath sets coals on fire.
　Flames fly out of its mouth.
22 Its neck is very strong.
　People run to get out of its way.
23 Its rolls of fat are close together.
　They are firm and can't be moved.
24 Its chest is as hard as rock.
　It is as hard as a lower millstone.
25 When the leviathan rises up, even mighty people are terrified.
　They run away when it moves around wildly.
26 A sword that strikes it has no effect.
　Neither does a spear or dart or javelin.
27 It treats iron as if it were straw.
　It crushes bronze as if it were rotten wood.
28 Arrows do not make it run away.
　Stones that are thrown from slings are like straw hitting it.
29 A club seems like a piece of straw to it.
　It laughs when it hears a javelin rattling.
30 Its undersides are like broken pieces of pottery.
　It leaves a trail in the mud like a threshing sled.
31 It makes the ocean churn like a boiling pot.

It stirs up the sea like perfume
someone is making.
32 It leaves a shiny trail behind it.
You would think the ocean had
white hair.
33 Nothing on earth is equal to the
leviathan.
That creature is not afraid of
anything.
34 It looks down on proud people.
It rules over all those who are
proud."

Job's Reply

42 Job replied to the Lord,

2 "I know that you can do anything.
No one can keep you from doing
what you plan to do.
3 You asked me, 'Who do you think you
are to disagree with my plans?
You do not know what you are
talking about.'
I spoke about things I didn't
completely understand.
I talked about things that were too
wonderful for me to know.

4 "You said, 'Listen now, and I will speak.
I will ask you some questions.
Then I want you to answer me.'
5 My ears had heard about you.
But now my own eyes have seen you.
6 So I hate myself.
I'm really sorry for what I said about
you.
That's why I'm sitting in dust and
ashes."

The Story Ends

7 After the Lord finished speaking to Job, he spoke to Eliphaz the Temanite. He said, "I am angry with you and your two friends. You have not said what is true about me, as my servant Job has.

8 "So now get seven bulls and seven rams. Go to my servant Job. Then sacrifice a burnt offering for yourselves. My servant Job will pray for you. And I will accept his prayer. I will not punish you for saying the foolish things you said. You have not said what is true about me, as my servant Job has."

9 So Eliphaz the Temanite, Bildad the Shuhite, and Zophar the Naamathite did what the Lord told them to do. And the Lord accepted Job's prayer.

10 After Job had prayed for his friends, the Lord made him successful again. He gave him twice as much as he had before. **11** All of his brothers and sisters and every-

---

POWER-SURGE

GIVING G

ALL OF HIS BROTHERS AND SISTERS AND EVERYONE WHO HAD KNOWN HIM BEFORE CAME TO SEE HIM. THEY ATE WITH HIM IN HIS HOUSE. THEY SHOWED THEIR CONCERN FOR HIM. THEY COMFORTED HIM BECAUSE OF ALL OF THE TROUBLES THE LORD HAD BROUGHT ON HIM. EACH ONE GAVE HIM A PIECE OF SILVER AND A GOLD RING.
— JOB 42:11 —

HELPFUL

---

one who had known him before came to see him. They ate with him in his house. They showed their concern for him. They comforted him because of all of the troubles the Lord had brought on him. Each one gave him a piece of silver and a gold ring.

12 The Lord blessed the last part of Job's life even more than the first part. He gave Job 14,000 sheep and 6,000 camels. He gave him 1,000 pairs of oxen and 1,000 donkeys.

13 Job also had seven sons and three daughters. **14** He named the first daughter Jemimah. He named the second Keziah. And he named the third Keren-Happuch. **15** Job's daughters were more beautiful than any other women in the whole land. Their father gave them a share of property along with their brothers.

16 After all of that happened, Job lived for 140 years. He saw his children, his grandchildren and his great-grandchildren. **17** And so he died. He had lived for a very long time.

PSALMS

The book of Psalms expresses directly to God almost every emotion that human beings experience. David, the hero of 1 and 2 Samuel, wrote most of these psalms. Many of the psalms express fear, some express anger, others joy, others praise to God. As you read the psalms, use them to be honest to God about your feelings. Whatever you're feeling, you'll find it expressed some place in the Psalms.

CODE OF HONOR IN THIS BOOK . . .

ALL OF THEM!

OBEYS ✔

BLESSED IS THE ONE WHO OBEYS THE LAW OF THE LORD.
— PSALM 1:1 —

BOOK I

Psalms 1–41

Psalm 1

1 Blessed is the one who obeys the law of
the LORD.
He doesn't follow the advice of evil
people.
He doesn't make a habit of doing what
sinners do.
He doesn't join those who make fun
of the LORD and his law.
2 Instead, he takes delight in the law of
the LORD.
He thinks about his law day and
night.
3 He is like a tree that is planted near a
stream of water.
It always bears its fruit at the right
time.
Its leaves don't dry up.
Everything godly people do turns
out well.

4 Sinful people are not like that at all.
They are like straw
that the wind blows away.
5 When the LORD judges them, their life
will come to an end.
Sinners won't have any place among
those who are godly.

6 The LORD watches over the lives of
those who are godly.
But the lives of sinful people will
lead to their death.

Psalm 2

1 Why do the nations plan evil together?
Why do they make useless plans?
2 The kings of the earth take their stand
against the LORD.
The rulers of the earth gather
together against his anointed
king.
3 "Let us break free from their chains,"
they say.
"Let us throw off their ropes."

4 The One who sits on his throne in
heaven laughs.
The Lord makes fun of those rulers
and their plans.
5 When he is angry, he warns them.
When his anger blazes out, he
terrifies them.
6 He says to them,
"I have placed my king on my holy
mountain of Zion."

7 I will announce what the LORD has
promised.

He said to me, "You are my son.
Today I have become your father.
8 Ask me, and I will give the nations to
you.
All nations on earth will belong to
you.
9 You will rule them with an iron rod.
You will break them to pieces like
clay pots."

10 Kings, be wise!
Rulers of the earth, be warned!
11 Serve the LORD and have respect for
him.
Serve him with joy and trembling.
12 Obey the son completely, or he will be
angry.
Your way of life will lead to your
death.
His anger can blaze out at any
moment.
Blessed are all those who go to him
for safety.

Psalm 3

A psalm of David when he ran away
from his son Absalom.
1 LORD, I have so many enemies!
So many people are rising up against
me!
2 Many are saying about me,
"God will not save him."   *Selah*

3 LORD, you are like a shield that keeps
me safe.
You honor me. You help me win the
battle.
4 I call out to the LORD.
He answers me from his holy hill.
                                     Selah

5 I lie down and sleep.
I wake up again, because the LORD
takes care of me.
6 I won't be afraid of the tens of
thousands
who are lined up against me on
every side.

7 Lord, rise up!
  My God, save me!
Strike all my enemies in the face.
  Break the teeth of sinful people.

8 Lord, you are the one who saves.
  May your blessing be on your
      people.   *Selah*

Psalm 4

*For the director of music. A psalm
of David to be played on stringed
instruments.*

1 My faithful God,
  answer me when I call out to you.
Give me rest from my trouble.
  Show me your favor. Hear my prayer.

2 How long will you people turn my
      glory into shame?
  How long will you love what will
      certainly fail you?
  How long will you pray to statues
      of gods?   *Selah*
3 Remember that the Lord has set his
      faithful people apart for
      himself.
  The Lord will hear me when I call
      out to him.

4 When you are angry, do not sin.
  When you are in bed,
  look deep down inside you and be
      silent.   *Selah*
5 Offer sacrifices to the Lord in the right
      way.
  Trust in him.

6 Many are asking, "Who can show us
      anything good?"
  Lord, let us see your face smiling on
      us with favor.
7 You have filled my heart with great joy.
  It is greater than the joy of people
      who have lots of grain and fresh
      wine.
8 I will lie down and sleep in peace.
  Lord, you alone keep me safe.

CHEERFUL ✳

YOU HAVE FILLED
MY HEART WITH
GREAT JOY.
— PSALM 4:7 —

Psalm 5

*For the director of music. A psalm
of David to be played on flutes.*

1 Lord, listen to my words.
  Pay attention when I sigh.
2 My King and my God,
  listen to me when I cry for help.
  I pray to you.
3 Lord, in the morning you hear my
      voice.
  In the morning I pray to you.
  I wait for you in hope.

4 God, you aren't happy with anything
      that is evil.
  Those who do what is wrong can't
      live where you are.
5 Those who are proud can't stand in
      front of you.
  You hate everyone who does what is
      evil.
6 You destroy those who tell lies.
  Lord, you hate murderers and those
      who cheat others.

7 Because of your great love
  I will come into your house.
With deep respect I will bow down
  toward your holy temple.
8 Lord, I have many enemies.
  Lead me in your right path.
  Make your way smooth and straight
      for me.

9 Not a word from their mouths can be
      trusted.
  Their hearts are filled with plans to
      destroy others.
Their throats are like open graves.
  With their tongues they tell lies.
10 God, show that they are guilty.
  Let their evil plans bring them
      down.
Send them away because of their many
      sins.
  They have refused to obey you.

11 But let all those who go to you for
      safety be glad.
  Let them always sing with joy.
Spread your cover over them and keep
      them safe.
  Then those who love you will be
      glad because of you.
12 Lord, you bless those who do what is
      right.
  Like a shield, your loving care keeps
      them safe.

Psalm 6

For the director of music. For *sheminith*.
A psalm of David to be played on stringed
instruments.

1 LORD, don't correct me when you are
    angry.
  Don't punish me when you are
    burning with anger.
2 LORD, have mercy on me. I'm so weak.
  LORD, heal me. My body is full of
    pain.
3 My soul is very troubled.
  LORD, how long will it be until you
    save me?

4 LORD, turn to me and help me.
  Save me. Your love never fails.
5 People can't remember you when they
    are dead.
  How can they praise you when they
    are in the grave?

6 My groaning has worn me out.
  All night long my tears flood my bed.
  My bed is wet because of my crying.
7 I'm so sad I can't see very well.
  My eyesight gets worse because of all
    of my enemies.

8 Get away from me, all of you who do
    evil.
  The LORD has heard my sobbing.
9 The LORD has heard my cry for his favor.
  The LORD accepts my prayer.
10 All of my enemies will be troubled and
    put to shame.
  They will turn back in dishonor. It
    will happen suddenly.

Psalm 7

A *shiggaion* of David. He sang it to the
LORD about Cush, who was from the tribe
of Benjamin.

1 LORD my God, I go to you for safety.
  Help me. Save me from all those
    who are chasing me.
2 If you don't, they will tear me apart as
    if they were lions.
  They will rip me to pieces so that no
    one can save me.

3 LORD my God, suppose I have done
    something wrong.
  Suppose I am guilty.
4 I have done evil to my friend.
  Or I have robbed my enemy without
    any reason.
5 If I have done any of those things, let
    my enemy chase me and
    catch me.
  Let him walk all over me.
  Let him bury me in the dust.   *Selah*

6 LORD, rise up in your anger.
  Rise up against the great anger of my
    enemies.
  My God, wake up. Command that
    the right thing be done.
7 Let all the people of the earth gather
    around you.
  Rule over them from your throne in
    heaven.
8   LORD, judge all people.
  LORD, judge me. But remember that I
    have done what is right.
  Most High God, remember that I am
    honest.
9 God, you always do what is right.
  You look deep down inside the
    hearts and minds of people.
  Bring to an end the terrible things
    sinful people do.
  Make godly people safe.

10 The Most High God is like a shield that
    keeps me safe.
  He saves those whose hearts are
    honest.

HONEST H

[GOD] SAVES THOSE WHOSE HEARTS ARE HONEST.
— PSALM 7:10 —

11 God judges fairly.
  He shows his anger every day.
12 If evil people don't change their ways,
    God will sharpen his sword.
  He will get his bow ready to use.
13 He has prepared his deadly weapons.
  He has made his flaming arrows
    ready.

14 Anyone who is full of evil
    plans trouble and ends up telling
    lies.
15 Anyone who digs a hole and shovels it
    out
  falls into the pit he has made.
16 The trouble he causes comes back on
    him.
  The terrible things he does come
    down on his own head.

17 I will give thanks to the LORD because
    he does what is right.
  I will sing praise to the LORD Most
    High.

Psalm 8

*For the director of music. For gittith.
A psalm of David.*

1 LORD, our Lord,
how majestic is your name in the
whole earth!

You have made your glory
higher than the heavens.
2 You have made sure that children
and infants praise you.
You have done it because of your
enemies.
You have done it to put a stop to
their talk.

3 I think about the heavens.
I think about what your fingers have
created.
I think about the moon and stars
that you have set in place.
4 What is a human being that you think
about him?
What is a son of man that you take
care of him?
5 You made him a little lower than the
heavenly beings.
You placed on him a crown of glory
and honor.

6 You made human beings the rulers
over all that your hands have
created.
You put everything under their
control.
7 They rule over all flocks and herds
and over the wild animals.
8 They rule over the birds of the air
and over the fish in the ocean.
They rule over everything that
swims in the oceans.

9 LORD, our Lord,
how majestic is your name in the
whole earth!

Psalm 9

*For the director of music. A psalm
of David to the tune of "The Death
of the Son."*

1 LORD, I will praise you with all my
heart.
I will tell about all of the miracles
you have done.
2 I will be glad and full of joy because of
you.
Most High God, I will sing praise to
you.

3 My enemies turn back.
They fall down and die right in front
of you.

4 You have proved that I haven't done
anything wrong.
You have sat on your throne and
judged fairly.
5 You have punished the nations. You
have destroyed evil people.
You have erased their names from
your book for ever and ever.
6 The enemy has been destroyed forever.
You have leveled their cities to the
ground.
Even the memory of them is gone.

7 The LORD rules forever.
He has set up his throne so that he
can judge people.
8 He will judge the world in keeping
with what is right.
He will rule over all of its people
fairly.
9 The LORD is a place of safety for those
who have been beaten down.
He keeps them safe in times of
trouble.
10 LORD, those who know you will trust in
you.
You have never deserted those who
look to you.

11 Sing praises to the LORD. He rules from
his throne in Zion.
Tell among the nations what he has
done.
12 The One who pays back murderers
remembers.
He doesn't forget the cries of those
who are hurting.

13 LORD, see how badly my enemies treat
me!
Show me your favor. Don't let me go
down to the gates of death.
14 Then I can give praise to you
at the gates of the city of Zion.
There I will be full of joy
because you have saved me.

15 The nations have fallen into the pit
they have dug.
Their feet are caught in the net they
have hidden.
16 The LORD is known to be fair.
Evil people are trapped by what they
have done.   *Higgaion. Selah*
17 Sinful people go down to the grave.
So do all the nations that forget
God.
18 But those who are in need will always
be remembered.
The hope of those who are hurting
will never die.

19 LORD, rise up. Don't let people win the
battle.

Let the nations come to you and be
judged.

²⁰ Lord, strike them with terror.
Let the nations know they are only
human. *Selah*

Psalm 10

¹ Lord, why are you so far away?
Why do you hide yourself in times
of trouble?

² An evil person is proud and hunts
down those who are weak.
He catches weak people by making
clever plans.

³ He brags about what his heart longs
for.
He speaks well of those who always
want more.
He attacks the Lord with his words.

⁴ Because he is proud, that evil person
doesn't turn to the Lord.
There is no room for God in any of
his thoughts.

⁵ Everything always goes well for him.
So he is proud.
He doesn't want to have anything to
do with God's laws.
He makes fun of all of his enemies.

⁶ He says to himself, "I will always be
secure.
I will always be happy. I'll never have
any trouble."

⁷ His mouth is full of curses and lies and
warnings.
With his tongue he speaks evil and
makes trouble.

⁸ Sinful people hide and wait near the
villages.
From their hiding places they
murder those who aren't guilty
of doing anything wrong.
They watch in secret for those they
want to attack.

⁹ They hide and wait like a lion in the
bushes.
From their hiding places they wait
to catch those who are helpless.
They catch them and drag them off
in their nets.

¹⁰ Those they have attacked are beaten
up. They fall to the ground.
They fall because their attackers are
too strong for them.

¹¹ Sinful people say to themselves, "God
doesn't pay any attention.
He covers his face. He never sees us."

¹² Lord, rise up! God, show your power!
Don't forget those who are helpless.

¹³ Why do sinful people attack you with
their words?
Why do they say to themselves,
"He won't hold us accountable"?

¹⁴ God, you see trouble and sadness.
You take note of it. You do
something about it.
So those who are attacked place
themselves in your care.
You help children whose fathers
have died.

¹⁵ Take away the power of bad and sinful
people.
Hold them accountable for the evil
things they do.
Uncover all the evil they have done.

¹⁶ The Lord is King for ever and ever.
The nations will disappear from his
land.

¹⁷ Lord, you hear the longings of those
who are hurting.
You cheer them up and give them
hope.
You listen to their cries.

POWER SURGE

CHEERFUL ✳

LORD, YOU HEAR THE
LONGINGS OF THOSE
WHO ARE HURTING.
YOU CHEER THEM UP
AND GIVE THEM HOPE.
YOU LISTEN TO THEIR
CRIES.
— **PSALM 10:17** —

K

KIND

¹⁸ You stand up for those whose fathers
have died
and for those who have been beaten
down.
You do it so that no one made of dust
may terrify others anymore.

Psalm 11

For the director of music.
A psalm of David.

¹ I run to the Lord for safety.
So how can you say to me,
"Fly away like a bird to your
mountain.

2 Look! Evil people are bending their
   bows.
   They are placing their arrows against
      the strings.
   They are planning to shoot from the
      shadows
   at those who have honest hearts.
3 When law and order are being
   destroyed,
   what can godly people do?"

4 The LORD is in his holy temple.
   The LORD is on his throne in heaven.
   He watches all people.
   His eyes study them.
5 The LORD watches over those who do
      what is right.
   But he hates sinful people and those
      who love to hurt others.
6 He will pour out flaming coals and
   burning sulfur
   on those who do what is wrong.
   A hot and dry wind will destroy
      them.

7 The LORD always does what is right.
   So he loves it when people do what
      is fair.
   Those who are honest will enjoy his
      blessing.

Psalm 12

For the director of music. For *sheminith*.
A psalm of David.
1 Help, LORD! Those who do what is right
   are gone.
   Those who are faithful have
      disappeared from the earth.
2 Everyone tells lies to his neighbors.
   With his lips he praises others, but
      he doesn't really mean it.

3 May the LORD cut off all lips that don't
   mean what they say.
   May he cut out every tongue that
      brags.
4 They say, "We will win the battle with
   our tongues.
   Our lips belong to us. No one else is
      in charge of us."

5 The LORD says, "The weak are beaten
   down.
   Those who are in need groan.
   So I will stand up to help them.
   I will keep them safe from those who
      tell lies about them."
6 The words of the LORD are perfect.
   They are like silver made pure in a
      clay furnace.
   They are like silver made pure seven
      times over.

7 LORD, you will keep us safe.
   You will always keep sinners from
      hurting us.
8 Proud and sinful people walk around
   openly
   when the evil they do is praised by
      others.

Psalm 13

For the director of music.
A psalm of David.
1 LORD, how long must I wait? Will you
   forget me forever?
   How long will you turn your face
      away from me?
2 How long must I struggle with my
   thoughts?
   How long must my heart be sad day
      after day?
   How long will my enemies keep
      winning the battle over me?

3 LORD my God, look at me and answer
   me.
   Give me new life, or I will die.
4 Then my enemies will say, "We have
   beaten him."
   They will be filled with joy when I
      die.

5 But I trust in your faithful love.
   My heart is filled with joy because
      you will save me.
6 I will sing to the LORD.
   He has been so good to me.

Psalm 14

For the director of music.
A psalm of David.
1 Foolish people say in their hearts,
   "There is no God."
   They do all kinds of horrible and evil
      things.
   No one does anything good.

2 The LORD looks down from heaven
   on all people.
   He wants to see if there are any who
      understand.
   He wants to see if there are any who
      trust in God.
3 All of them have turned away.
   They have all become evil.
   No one does anything good,
   no one at all.

4 Won't those who do evil ever learn?
   They eat up my people as if they
      were eating bread.
   They don't call out to the LORD for
      help.

5 Just look at them! They are filled with
      terror
   because God is among those who do
      right.
6 You who do evil make it hard for poor
      people to do what they plan
      to do.
   But the LORD is their place of safety.

7 How I pray that the One who saves
      Israel will come out of Zion!
   Then the LORD will bless his people
      with great success again.
   So let the people of Jacob be filled
      with joy! Let Israel be glad!

Psalm 15

A psalm of David.
1 LORD, who can live in your sacred tent?
   Who can stay on your holy hill?

2 Anyone who lives without blame
      and does what is right.
   He speaks the truth from his heart.
3   He doesn't tell lies about others.
   He doesn't do wrong to his neighbors.
   He doesn't say anything bad about
      them.
4 He hates sinful people.
   He honors those who have respect
      for the LORD.
   He keeps his promises
      even when it hurts.
5 He lends his money without charging
      too much interest.
   He doesn't accept money to harm
      those who aren't guilty.

Anyone who lives like that
   will always be secure.

POWER–SURGE

TRUSTED ◆

THE LORD LOOKS
DOWN FROM HEAVEN
ON ALL PEOPLE.
HE WANTS TO SEE IF
THERE ARE ANY WHO
UNDERSTAND.
HE WANTS TO SEE IF
THERE ARE ANY WHO
TRUST IN GOD.
— **PSALM 14:2** —

Psalm 16

A miktam of David.
1 God, keep me safe.
   I go to you for safety.

2 I said to the LORD, "You are my Lord.
   Without you, I don't have anything
      that is good."
3 God's people who live in our land are
      glorious.
   I take great delight in them.
4 Those who run after other gods
   will have nothing but trouble.
   I will not pour out offerings of blood to
      those gods.
   My lips will not speak their names.

5 LORD, everything you have given me is
      good.
   You have made my life secure.
6 I am very pleased with what you have
      given me.
   I am very happy with what I've
      received from you.

7 I will praise the LORD. He gives me
      good advice.
   Even at night my heart teaches me.
8 I know that the LORD is always with
      me.
   He is at my right hand.
   I will always be secure.

9 So my heart is glad. Joy is on my
      tongue.
   My body also will be secure.
10 You will not leave me in the grave.
   You will not let your faithful one rot
      away.
11 You always show me the path that
      leads to life.
   You will fill me with joy when I am
      with you.
   You will give me endless pleasures at
      your right hand.

Psalm 17

A prayer of David.
1 LORD, hear me when I ask you to treat
      me fairly.
   Listen to my cry for help.
   Hear my prayer.
   It doesn't come from lips that tell
      lies.
2 When you hand down your sentence,
      may it be in my favor.
   May your eyes see what is right.

3 Look deep down into my heart.
   Study me carefully at night.
   Put me to the test.
   You won't find anything wrong.

LOVING 🖤

**I LOVE YOU, LORD.
YOU GIVE ME
STRENGTH.**
—— PSALM 18:1 ——

STRONG

I have made up my mind
   that my mouth won't say sinful
     things.
⁴ I don't do the things other people do.
   By obeying your word
I have kept myself from acting
   like those who try to hurt others.
⁵ My steps have stayed on your paths.
   My feet have not slipped.

⁶ God, I call out to you because you will
   answer me.
   Listen to me. Hear my prayer.
⁷ Show the wonder of your great love.
   By using your powerful right hand,
     you save those who go to you for
     safety from their enemies.
⁸ Take good care of me, just as you would
   take care of your own eyes.
   Hide me in the shadow of your
     wings.
⁹ Save me from the sinful people who
   attack me.
   Save me from my deadly enemies
     who are all around me.

¹⁰ They make their hearts hard and
   stubborn.
   Their mouths speak with pride.
¹¹ They have tracked me down. They are
   all around me.
   Their eyes watch for a chance to
     throw me to the ground.
¹² They are like a hungry lion, waiting to
   attack.
   They are like a powerful lion, hiding
     in the bushes.

¹³ LORD, rise up. Oppose them and bring
   them down.
   With your sword, save me from
     those evil people.
¹⁴ LORD, by your power save me from
   people like that.
   They belong to this world. They get
     their reward in this life.

You satisfy the hunger of those you
   love.
   Their children have plenty.
   And those children store up wealth
     for their children.
¹⁵ Because I do what is right, I will enjoy
   your blessing.
   When I wake up, I will be satisfied
     because I will see you.

Psalm 18

For the director of music. A psalm of
David, the servant of the LORD. He sang
the words of this song to the LORD. He
sang them when the LORD saved him
from the powerful hand of all of his
   enemies and of Saul. He said,
¹ I love you, LORD.
   You give me strength.

² The LORD is my rock and my fort. He is
   the One who saves me.
   My God is my rock. I go to him for
     safety.
   He is like a shield to me. He's the
     power that saves me. He's my
     place of safety.
³ I call out to the LORD. He is worthy of
   praise.
   He saves me from my enemies.

⁴ The ropes of death were almost
   wrapped around me.
   A destroying flood swept over me.
⁵ The ropes of the grave were tight
   around me.
   Death set its trap in front of me.
⁶ When I was in trouble, I called out to
   the LORD.
   I cried to my God for help.
From his temple he heard my voice.
   My cry for help reached his ears.

⁷ The earth trembled and shook.
   The base of the mountains rocked
     back and forth.
   It trembled because the LORD was
     angry.
⁸ Smoke came out of his nose.
   Flames of fire came out of his
     mouth.
   Burning coals blazed out of it.
⁹ He opened the heavens and came
   down.
   Dark clouds were under his feet.
¹⁰ He got on the cherubim and flew.
   The wings of the wind lifted him up.
¹¹ He covered himself with darkness.
   The dark rain clouds of the sky were
     like a tent around him.
¹² Clouds came out of the brightness that
   was all around him.

POWER–SURGE

FAITHFUL

LORD, TO THOSE WHO ARE FAITHFUL YOU SHOW THAT YOU ARE FAITHFUL.
— **PSALM 18:25** —

They came with hailstones and
flashes of lightning.
¹³ The LORD thundered from heaven.
The voice of the Most High God was
heard.
¹⁴ He shot his arrows and scattered our
enemies.
He sent great flashes of lightning
and chased the enemies away.
¹⁵ The bottom of the sea could be seen.
The foundations of the earth were
uncovered.
LORD, it happened when your anger
blazed out.
It came like a blast of breath from
your nose.

¹⁶ He reached down from heaven. He
took hold of me.
He lifted me out of deep waters.
¹⁷ He saved me from my powerful
enemies.
He set me free from those who were
too strong for me.
¹⁸ They stood up to me when I was in
trouble.
But the LORD helped me.
¹⁹ He brought me out into a wide and
safe place.
He saved me because he was pleased
with me.
²⁰ The LORD has been good to me because
I do what is right.
He has rewarded me because I lead a
pure life.
²¹ I have lived the way the LORD wanted
me to.
I haven't done evil by turning away
from my God.
²² I keep all of his laws in mind.
I haven't turned away from his
commands.
²³ He knows that I am without blame.
He knows I've kept myself from
sinning.
²⁴ The LORD has rewarded me for doing
what is right.

He has rewarded me because I
haven't done anything wrong.
²⁵ LORD, to those who are faithful you
show that you are faithful.
To those who are without blame you
show that you are without
blame.
²⁶ To those who are pure you show that
you are pure.
But to those whose paths are crooked
you show that you are clever.
²⁷ You save those who aren't proud.
But you bring down those whose
eyes are proud.
²⁸ LORD, you keep the lamp of my life
burning brightly.
You are my God. You bring light
into my darkness.
²⁹ With your help I can attack a troop of
soldiers.
With the help of my God I can
climb over a wall.

³⁰ God's way is perfect.
The word of the LORD doesn't have
any flaws.
He is like a shield
to all who go to him for safety.
³¹ Who is God except the LORD?
Who is the Rock except our God?
³² God gives me strength for the battle.
He makes my way perfect.
³³ He makes my feet like the feet of a deer.
He helps me stand on the highest
places.
³⁴ He trains my hands to fight every
battle.
My arms can bend a bow of bronze.
³⁵ LORD, you are like a shield that keeps
me safe. You help me win the
battle.
Your strong right hand keeps me
going.
You bend down to make me great.
³⁶ You give me a wide path to walk on
so that I don't twist my ankles.

POWER–SURGE

STRONG

GOD GIVES ME STRENGTH FOR THE BATTLE.

HE MAKES MY WAY PERFECT.
— **PSALM 18:32** —

³⁷ I chased my enemies and caught them.
     I didn't turn back until they were
       destroyed.
³⁸ I crushed them so that they couldn't
       get up.
     They fell under my feet.
³⁹ Lord, you gave me strength to fight the
       battle.
     You made my enemies bow down at
       my feet.
⁴⁰ You made them turn their backs and
       run away.
     So I destroyed my enemies.
⁴¹ They cried out for help. But there was
       no one to save them.
     They called out to you. But you
       didn't answer them.
⁴² I beat them as fine as dust blown by
       the wind.
     I poured them out like mud in the
       streets.

⁴³ You saved me when my own people
       attacked me.
     You made me the ruler over nations.
     People I didn't know serve me now.
⁴⁴ As soon as they hear me, they obey me.
     People from other lands bow down
       to me in fear.
⁴⁵ All of them give up hope.
     They come trembling out of their
       hiding places.

⁴⁶ The Lord lives! Give praise to my Rock!
     Give honor to God my Savior!
⁴⁷ He is the God who pays my enemies
       back.
     He brings the nations under my
       control.
⁴⁸   He saves me from my enemies.
     You have honored me more than
       them.
     You have saved me from men who
       want to hurt me.
⁴⁹ Lord, I will praise you among the
       nations.
     I will sing praises to you.
⁵⁰ The Lord helps his king win great
       battles.
     He shows his faithful love to his
       anointed king.
     He shows it to me and my family
       forever.

Psalm 19

For the director of music.
A psalm of David.

¹ The heavens tell about the glory of
       God.
     The skies show that his hands
       created them.

² Day after day they speak about it.
     Night after night they make it
       known.
³ But they don't speak or use words.
     No sound is heard from them.
⁴ At the same time, their voice goes out
       into the whole earth.
     Their words go out from one end of
       the world to the other.

God has set up a tent in the heavens
     for the sun.
⁵   The sun is like a groom coming out
       of the room where he spent his
       wedding night.
     The sun is like a great runner who
       takes delight in running a race.
⁶ It rises at one end of the heavens.
     Then it moves across to the other
       end.
     Nothing can hide from its heat.

⁷ The law of the Lord is perfect.
     It gives us new strength.
     The laws of the Lord can be trusted.
     They make childish people wise.

POWER SURGE

STRONG

THE LAW OF THE LORD
IS PERFECT.

IT GIVES US NEW
STRENGTH.

THE LAWS OF THE LORD
CAN BE TRUSTED.

THEY MAKE CHILDISH
PEOPLE WISE.
— PSALM 19:7 —

W

WISE

⁸ The rules of the Lord are right.
     They give joy to our hearts.
     The commands of the Lord shine
       brightly.
     They give light to our minds.
⁹ The law that brings respect for the
       Lord is pure.
     It lasts forever.
     The directions the Lord gives are true.
     All of them are completely right.
¹⁰ They are more priceless than gold.

They have greater value than huge
amounts of pure gold.
They are sweeter than honey
that is taken from the honeycomb.
11 I am warned by them.
When I obey them, I am greatly
rewarded.

12 Can I know my mistakes?
Forgive my hidden faults.
13 Keep me also from the sins I want to
commit.
May they not be my master.
Then I will be without blame.
I will not be guilty of any great sin
against your law.

14 LORD, may the words of my mouth and
the thoughts of my heart
be pleasing in your eyes.
You are my Rock and my Redeemer.

Psalm 20

For the director of music.
A psalm of David.
1 May the LORD answer you when you
are in trouble.
May the God of Jacob keep you safe.
2 May he send you help from the sacred
tent.
May he give you aid from Zion.
3 May he remember all of your sacrifices.
May he accept your burnt offerings.
Selah
4 May he give you what your heart longs
for.
May he make all of your plans
succeed.
5 We will shout with joy when you win
the battle.
We will lift up our flags in the name
of our God.
May the LORD give you everything
you ask for.

6 Now I know that the LORD saves his
anointed king.
He answers him from his holy
heaven.
The power of God's right hand saves
the king.
7 Some trust in chariots. Some trust in
horses.
But we trust in the LORD our God.
8 They are brought to their knees and
fall down.
But we get up and stand firm.

9 LORD, save the king!
Answer us when we call out to you!

Psalm 21

For the director of music.
A psalm of David.
1 LORD, the king is filled with joy because
you are strong.
How great is his joy because you
help him win his battles!
2 You have given him what his heart
longed for.
You haven't kept back from him
what his lips asked for. *Selah*
3 You welcomed him with rich blessings.
You placed a crown of pure gold on
his head.
4 He asked you for life, and you gave it to
him.
You promised him days that would
never end.
5 His glory is great because you helped
him win his battles.
You have honored him with glory
and majesty.
6 You have given him blessings that will
last forever.
You have made him glad and joyful
because you are with him.

7 The king trusts in the LORD.
The faithful love of the Most High
God
will keep the king secure.

8 You, the king, will capture all of your
enemies.
Your right hand will take hold of
them.
9 When you appear,
you will be like a flaming furnace to
them.
The LORD will swallow them up in his
anger.
His fire will burn them up.
10 You will wipe their children from the
face of the earth.
You will remove them from the
human race.

TRUSTED ◆

SOME TRUST IN
CHARIOTS. SOME
TRUST IN HORSES.
BUT WE TRUST IN THE
LORD OUR GOD.
— **PSALM 20:7** —

11 Your enemies make evil plans against
  you.
  They think up evil things to do. But
    they can't succeed.
12 You will make them turn their backs
    and run away
  when you aim your arrows at them.

13 LORD, may you be honored because
    you are strong.
  We will sing and praise your might.

Psalm 22

For the director of music. A psalm
of David to the tune of "The Doe
of the Morning."

1 My God, my God, why have you
    deserted me?
  Why do you seem to be so far away
    when I need you to save me?
  Why do you seem to be so far away
    that you can't hear my groans?
2 My God, I cry out in the daytime. But
    you don't answer.
  I cry out at night. I can't keep quiet.

3 But you rule from your throne as the
    Holy One.
  You are the God Israel praises.
4 Our people of long ago put their trust
    in you.
  They trusted in you, and you saved
    them.
5 They cried out to you and were saved.
  They trusted in you, and you didn't
    let them down.

6 People treat me like a worm and not a
    man.
  They hate me and look down on me.
7 All those who see me laugh at me.
  They shout at me and make fun of
    me.
  They shake their heads at me.
8 They say, "He trusts in the LORD.
  Let the LORD help him.
  If the LORD is pleased with him,
    let him save him."

9 But you brought me out of my
    mother's body.
  You made me trust in you
  even when I was at my mother's
    breast.
10 From the time I was born, you took
    good care of me.
  Ever since I came out of my mother's
    body, you have been my God.
11 Don't be far away from me.
  Trouble is near,
  and there is no one to help me.

12 Many enemies are all around me.

They are like strong bulls from the
    land of Bashan.
13 They are like roaring lions that tear to
    pieces what they kill.
  They open their mouths wide to
    attack me.
14 My strength is like water that is poured
    out on the ground.
  I feel as if my bones aren't
    connected.
  My heart has turned to wax.
  It has melted away inside me.
15 My strength is dried up like a piece of
    broken pottery.
  My tongue sticks to the roof of my
    mouth.
  You bring me down to the edge of
    the grave.
16 A group of sinful people has closed in
    on me.
  They are all around me like a pack of
    dogs.
  They have pierced my hands and my
    feet.
17 I can see all of my bones right through
    my skin.
  People stare at me. They laugh when
    I suffer.
18 They divide up my clothes among
    them.
  They cast lots for what I am wearing.

19 LORD, don't be so far away.
  You give me strength. Come quickly
    to help me.
20 Save me from the sword.
  Save the only life I have. Save me
    from the power of those dogs.
21 Save me from the mouths of those
    lions.
  Save me from the horns of those
    wild oxen.

22 I will announce your name to my
    brothers and sisters.
  I will praise you among those who
    worship you.
23 You who have respect for the LORD,
    praise him!
  All you people of Jacob, honor him!
  All you people of Israel, worship
    him!
24 He has not forgotten the one who is
    hurting.
  He has not turned away from his
    suffering.
  He has not turned his face away from
    him.
  He has listened to his cry for help.

25 Because of what you have done,

I will praise you in the whole
community of those who
worship you.
In front of those who respect you,
I will keep my promises.
26 Those who are poor will eat and be
satisfied.
Those who look to the LORD will
praise him.
May their hearts be filled with new
hope!
27 People from one end of the earth to
the other
will remember and turn to the LORD.
The people of all the nations
will bow down before him.
28 The LORD is King.
He rules over the nations.

29 All the rich people of the earth will
worship God and take part in
his feasts.
All those who go down to the edge
of the grave will fall on their
knees in front of him.
I'm talking about those who can
hardly keep themselves alive.
30 Those who are not yet born will serve
him.
Those who are born later will be told
about the Lord.
31 And they will tell people who have not
yet been born
that he has done what is right.

Psalm 23

A psalm of David.
1 The LORD is my shepherd. He gives me
everything I need.
2   He lets me lie down in fields of green
grass.
He leads me beside quiet waters.
3   He gives me new strength.
He guides me in the right paths
for the honor of his name.
4 Even though I walk
through the darkest valley,
I will not be afraid.
You are with me.
Your shepherd's rod and staff
comfort me.

5 You prepare a feast for me
right in front of my enemies.
You pour oil on my head.
My cup runs over.
6 I am sure that your goodness and love
will follow me
all the days of my life.
And I will live in the house of the LORD
forever.

Psalm 24

A psalm of David.
1 The earth belongs to the LORD. And so
does everything in it.
The world belongs to him. And so
do all those who live in it.
2 He set it firmly on the oceans.
He made it secure on the waters.

3 Who can go up to the temple on the
hill of the LORD?
Who can stand in his holy place?
4 Anyone who has clean hands and a
pure heart.
He does not worship the statue of a
god.
He doesn't use the name of that god
when he makes a promise.
5 People like that will receive the LORD's
blessing.
When God their Savior hands down
his sentence, it will be in their
favor.
6 The people who look to God are like
that.
God of Jacob, they look to you. *Selah*

7 Open wide, you gates.
Open up, you age-old doors.
Then the King of glory will come in.
8 Who is the King of glory?
The LORD, who is strong and mighty.
The LORD, who is mighty in battle.
9 Open wide, you gates.
Open wide, you age-old doors.
Then the King of glory will come in.
10 Who is he, this King of glory?
The LORD who rules over all.
He is the King of glory.   *Selah*

Psalm 25

A psalm of David.
1 LORD, I worship you.
2   My God, I trust in you.
Don't let me be put to shame.
Don't let my enemies win the battle
over me.
3 Those who put their hope in you
will never be put to shame.
But those who can't be trusted
will be put to shame. They have no
excuse.

4 LORD, show me your ways.
Teach me how to follow you.
5 Guide me in your truth. Teach me.
You are God my Savior.
I put my hope in you all day long.
6 LORD, remember your great mercy and
love.

You have shown them to your
people for a long time.
7 Don't remember the sins I committed
when I was young.
Don't remember how often I refused
to obey you.
Remember me because you love me.
LORD, you are good.

8 The LORD is honest and good.
He teaches sinners to walk in his
ways.
9 He shows those who aren't proud how
to do what is right.
He teaches them his ways.
10 All of the LORD's ways are loving and
faithful
for those who obey what his
covenant commands.
11 LORD, be true to your name.
Forgive my sin, even though it is
great.

POWER-SURGE

FORGIVING F

LORD, BE TRUE TO YOUR NAME.

FORGIVE MY SIN, EVEN THOUGH IT IS GREAT.
— **PSALM 25:11** —

12 Who is the man who has respect for
the LORD?
God will teach him the way he has
chosen for him.
13 Things will always go well for him.
His children will be given the land.
14 The LORD shares his plans with those
who have respect for him.
He makes his covenant known to
them.
15 My eyes always look to the LORD.
He alone can set my feet free from
the trap.
16 Turn to me and show me your favor.
I am lonely and hurting.
17 The troubles of my heart have
increased.
Set me free from my great pain.
18 Look at how I'm hurting! See how
much I suffer!
Take away all of my sins.
19 Look at how many enemies I have!
See how terrible their hatred is
for me!

20 Guard my life. Save me.
Don't let me be put to shame.
I go to you for safety.
21 May my honest and good life keep me
safe.
I have put my hope in you.

22 God, set Israel free
from all of their troubles!

Psalm 26

A psalm of David.

1 LORD, when you hand down your
sentence, let it be in my favor.
I have lived without blame.
I have trusted in the LORD.
I have never doubted him.
2 LORD, test me. Try me out.
Look deep down into my heart and
mind.
3 Your love is always with me.
I have always lived by your truth.
4 I don't spend time with people who
tell lies.
I don't keep company with
pretenders.
5 I hate to be with a group of sinful
people.
I refuse to spend time with those
who are evil.
6 I wash my hands to show that I'm not
guilty.
LORD, I come near your altar.
7 I shout my praise to you.
I tell about all the wonderful things
you have done.
8 LORD, I love the house where you live.
I love the place where your glory is.

9 Don't destroy me together with
sinners.
Don't take my life away along with
murderers.
10 Their hands are always planning to do
evil.
Their right hands are full of money
that bought them off.
11 But I live without blame.
Set me free and show me your favor.

12 My feet stand on level ground.
In the whole community I will
praise the LORD.

Psalm 27

A psalm of David.

1 The LORD gives me light and saves me.
Why should I fear anyone?
The LORD is my place of safety.
Why should I be afraid?
2 My enemies are evil.

They will trip and fall
when they attack me
  and try to eat me alive.
³ Even if an army attacks me,
  my heart will not be afraid.
Even if war breaks out against me,
  I will still trust in God.

⁴ I'm asking the LORD for only one thing.
  Here is what I want.
I want to live in the house of the LORD
  all the days of my life.
I want to look at the beauty of the LORD.
  I want to worship him in his temple.
⁵ When I'm in trouble,
  he will keep me safe in his house.
He will hide me in the safety of his
    holy tent.
  He will put me on a rock that is very
    high.
⁶ Then I will win the battle
  over my enemies who are all around
    me.
At his holy tent I will offer my sacrifice
  with shouts of joy.
I will sing and make music to the
  LORD.

⁷ LORD, hear my voice when I call out to
    you.
  Show me your favor and answer me.
⁸ My heart says, "Look to him!"
  LORD, I will look to you.
⁹ Don't turn your face away from me.
  Don't turn me away because you are
    angry.
  You have helped me.
God my Savior, don't say no to me.
  Don't desert me.
¹⁰ My father and mother may desert me,
  but the LORD will accept me.
¹¹ LORD, teach me your ways.
  Lead me along a straight path.
  There are many people who beat me
    down.
¹² My enemies want to harm me. So
    don't turn me over to them.
  Witnesses who tell lies are rising up
    against me.
  They are trying to destroy me.

¹³ Here is something I am still sure of.
  I will see the LORD's goodness
  while I'm still alive.
¹⁴ Wait for the LORD.
  Be strong and don't lose hope.
  Wait for the LORD.

Psalm 28

A psalm of David.
¹ LORD, my Rock, I call out to you.
  Pay attention to me.

If you remain silent, I will die.
  I will be like those who have gone
    down into the grave.
² Hear my cry for your favor
  when I call out to you for help.
Hear me when I lift up my hands in
    prayer
  toward your Most Holy Room.

³ Don't drag me away with sinners.
  Don't drag me away with those who
    do evil.
They speak in a friendly way to their
    neighbors.
  But their hearts are full of hatred.
⁴ Pay them back for their evil actions.
  Pay them back for what their hands
    have done.
  Give them exactly what they should
    get.
⁵ They don't care about the LORD's
    mighty acts.
  They don't care about what his
    hands have done.
So he will tear them down.
  He will never build them up again.

⁶ Give praise to the LORD.
  He has heard my cry for his favor.
⁷ The LORD gives me strength. He is like a
    shield that keeps me safe.
  My heart trusts in him, and he helps
    me.
My heart jumps for joy.
  I will sing and give thanks to him.

⁸ The LORD gives strength to his people.
  He guards and saves his anointed
    king.
⁹ Save your people. Bless those who
    belong to you.
  Be their shepherd. Take care of them
    forever.

PATIENT P

WAIT FOR THE LORD.
BE STRONG AND
DON'T LOSE HOPE.
WAIT FOR THE LORD.
— **PSALM 27:14** —

STRONG

CHEERFUL

MY HEART TRUSTS IN [GOD], AND HE HELPS ME.

MY HEART JUMPS FOR JOY.

I WILL SING AND GIVE THANKS TO HIM.

— PSALM 28:7 —

THANKFUL

Psalm 29

A psalm of David.

1 Praise the LORD, you mighty angels.
Praise the LORD for his glory and
strength.
2 Praise the LORD for the glory that
belongs to him.
Worship the LORD because of his
beauty and holiness.

3 The voice of the LORD is heard over the
waters.
The God of glory thunders.
The LORD thunders over the mighty
waters.
4 The voice of the LORD is powerful.
The voice of the LORD is majestic.
5 The voice of the LORD breaks the cedar
trees.
The LORD breaks the cedars of
Lebanon into pieces.
6 He makes the mountains of Lebanon
skip like a calf.
He makes Mount Hermon jump like
a young wild ox.
7 The voice of the LORD strikes
with flashes of lightning.
8 The voice of the LORD shakes the
desert.
The LORD shakes the Desert of
Kadesh.
9 The voice of the LORD twists the oak
trees.
It strips the forests bare.
And in his temple everyone cries
out, "Glory!"

10 The LORD on his throne rules over the
flood.

The LORD rules from his throne as
King forever.
11 The LORD gives strength to his people.
The LORD blesses his people with
peace.

Psalm 30

*A psalm of David. A song for committing
the completed temple to God.*

1 LORD, I will give you honor.
You brought me out of deep trouble.
You didn't give my enemies the joy
of seeing me die.
2 LORD my God, I called out to you for
help.
And you healed me.
3 LORD, you brought me up from the
edge of the grave.
You kept me from going down into
the pit.

4 Sing to the LORD, you who are faithful
to him.
Praise him, because his name is holy.
5 His anger lasts for only a moment.
But his favor lasts for a person's
whole life.
Sobbing can remain through the
night.
But joy comes in the morning.

6 When I felt safe, I said,
"I will always be secure."
7 LORD, when you showed me your favor,
you made my mountain stand firm.
But when you turned your face away
from me,
I was terrified.

8 LORD, I called out to you.
I cried to you for your favor.
9 I said, "What good will come if I die?
What good will come if I go down
into the grave?
Can the dust of my dead body praise
you?
Can it tell how faithful you are?

STRONG

THE LORD GIVES STRENGTH TO HIS PEOPLE.

THE LORD BLESSES HIS PEOPLE WITH PEACE.

— PSALM 29:11 —

¹⁰ LORD, hear me. Show me your favor.
  LORD, help me."

¹¹ You turned my loud crying into
    dancing.
  You removed my black clothes and
    dressed me with joy.
¹² So my heart will sing to you. I can't
    keep silent.
  LORD, my God, I will give you thanks
    forever.

CHEERFUL ✳

MY HEART WILL SING
TO YOU. I CAN'T KEEP
SILENT.

LORD, MY GOD, I WILL
GIVE YOU THANKS
FOREVER.
— PSALM 30:12 —

THANKFUL

Psalm 31

For the director of music.
A psalm of David.

¹ LORD, I have gone to you for safety.
  Don't let me ever be put to shame.
  Save me, because you do what is
    right.
² Pay attention to me.
  Come quickly to help me.
  Be the rock I go to for safety.
  Be the strong fort that saves me.
³ You are my rock and my fort.
  Lead me and guide me for the honor
    of your name.
⁴ Free me from the trap that is set for me.
  You are my place of safety.
⁵ Into your hands I commit my very life.
  LORD, set me free. You are my
    faithful God.

⁶ I hate those who worship worthless
    statues of gods.
  I trust in the LORD.
⁷ I will be glad and full of joy because
    you love me.
  You saw that I was hurting.
  You took note of my great pain.
⁸ You have not handed me over to the
    enemy.

You have put me in a wide and safe
    place.

⁹ LORD, show me your favor. I'm in deep
    trouble.
  I'm so sad I can hardly see.
  My whole body grows weak with
    sadness.
¹⁰ Pain has taken over my life.
  My years are spent in groaning.
  I have no strength because I'm hurting
    so much.
  My body is getting weaker and
    weaker.
¹¹ My neighbors make fun of me
    because I have so many enemies.
  My friends are afraid of me.
  Those who see me on the street run
    away from me.
¹² They have forgotten me. I might as
    well be dead.
  I have become like broken pottery.
¹³ I hear the lies many people tell about
    me.
  There is terror all around me.
  Many have joined together against me.
  They plan to kill me.
¹⁴ But I trust in you, LORD.
  I say, "You are my God."
¹⁵ My whole life is in your hands.
  Save me from my enemies.
  Save me from those who are chasing
    me.
¹⁶ Let your face smile on me with favor.
  Save me because your love is faithful.
¹⁷ LORD, I have cried out to you.
  Don't let me be put to shame.
  But let sinners be put to shame.
  Let them lie silent in the grave.
¹⁸ Their lips tell lies. Let them be silenced.
  They speak with pride against those
    who do right.
  They make fun of them.

¹⁹ How great your goodness is!
  You have stored it up for those who
    have respect for you.
  While other people watch, you give it
    to those who run to you for
    safety.
²⁰ They are safe because you are with
    them.
  You hide them from the evil plans of
    their enemies.
  In your house you keep them safe
    from those who bring charges
    against them.

²¹ Give praise to the LORD.
  He showed me his wonderful love
    when my enemies attacked the city I
    was in.

22 I was afraid and said,
  "I've been cut off from you!"
But you heard my cry for your favor.
  You heard me when I called out to
    you for help.

23 Love the Lord, all of you who are
    faithful to him!
The Lord watches over the faithful.
  But he completely pays back those
    who are proud.
24 Be strong, all of you who put your
    hope in the Lord.
  Never give up.

POWER-SURGE

STRONG

BE STRONG, ALL OF
YOU WHO PUT YOUR
HOPE IN THE LORD.

NEVER GIVE UP.
— PSALM 31:24 —

TRIES HARD

Psalm 32

A *maskil* of David.
1 Blessed is the one whose lawless acts
    are forgiven.
  His sins have been taken away.
2 Blessed is the man whose sin the Lord
    never counts against him.
  He doesn't want to cheat anyone.

3 When I kept silent about my sin,
  my body became weak
    because I groaned all day long.
4 Day and night
  your heavy hand punished me.
I became weaker and weaker
  as I do in the heat of summer.   *Selah*
5 Then I admitted my sin to you.
  I didn't cover up the wrong I had
    done.
I said, "I will admit my lawless acts to
    the Lord."
  And you forgave the guilt of my sin.
                                  Selah

6 Let everyone who is godly pray to you
  while they can still look to you.
When troubles come like a flood,
  they certainly won't reach those
    who are godly.

7 You are my hiding place.
  You will keep me safe from trouble.
You will surround me with songs sung
    by those who praise you
  because you save your people.   *Selah*

8 I will guide you and teach you the way
    you should go.
  I will give you good advice and
    watch over you.
9 Don't be like the horse or the mule.
  They can't understand anything.
They have to be controlled by bits and
    bridles.
  If they aren't, they won't come to
    you.
10 Sinful people have all kinds of trouble.
  But the Lord's faithful love
    is all around those who trust in him.

11 Be glad because of what the Lord has
    done for you.
  Be joyful, you who do what is right!
Sing, all of you whose hearts are
    honest!

Psalm 33

1 You who are godly, sing with joy to the
    Lord.
  It is right for honest people to praise
    him.
2 Praise the Lord with the harp.
  Make music to him on the lyre that
    has ten strings.
3 Sing a new song to him.
  Play with skill, and shout with joy.

4 What the Lord says is right and true.
  He is faithful in everything he does.
5 The Lord loves what is right and fair.
  The earth is full of his faithful love.

6 The heavens were made when the
    Lord commanded it to happen.
  All of the stars were created by the
    breath of his mouth.
7 He gathers the waters of the sea
    together.
  He puts the oceans in their places.
8 Let the whole earth have respect for
    the Lord.
  Let all of the people in the world
    honor him.
9 He spoke, and the world came into
    being.
  He commanded, and it stood firm.
10 The Lord blocks the sinful plans of the
    nations.
  He keeps them from doing what
    they want to do.
11 But the plans of the Lord stand firm
    forever.

CHEERFUL ✳

OUR HEARTS ARE FULL OF JOY BECAUSE OF HIM.

WE TRUST IN HIM, BECAUSE HE IS HOLY.

— **PSALM 33:21** —

What he wants to do will last for all time.

12 Blessed is the nation whose God is the LORD.
Blessed are the people he chose to be his own.
13 From heaven the LORD looks down
and sees everyone.
14 From his throne he watches
all those who live on the earth.
15 He creates the hearts of all people.
He is aware of everything they do.
16 A king isn't saved just because his army is big.
A soldier doesn't escape just because he is very strong.
17 People can't trust a horse to save them either.
Though it is very strong, it can't save them.
18 But the LORD looks with favor on those who respect him.
He watches over those who put their hope in his faithful love.
19 He watches over them to save them from death.
He wants to keep them alive when there is no food in the land.

20 We wait in hope for the LORD.
He helps us. He is like a shield that keeps us safe.
21 Our hearts are full of joy because of him.
We trust in him, because he is holy.
22 LORD, may your faithful love rest on us.
We put our hope in you.

Psalm 34

A psalm of David when he was in front of Abimelech and pretended to be out of his mind. Abimelech drove him away, and he left.

1 I will thank the LORD at all times.
My lips will always praise him.
2 I will honor the LORD.

Let those who are hurting hear and be joyful.
3 Join me in giving glory to the LORD.
Let us honor him together.

4 I looked to the LORD, and he answered me.
He saved me from everything I was afraid of.
5 Those who look to him beam with joy.
They are never put to shame.
6 This poor man called out, and the LORD heard him.
He saved him out of all of his troubles.
7 The angel of the LORD stands guard around those who have respect for him.
And he saves them.

8 Taste and see that the LORD is good.
Blessed is the man who goes to him for safety.
9 You people of God, have respect for the LORD.
Those who respect him have everything they need.
10 The lions may grow weak and hungry.
But those who look to the LORD have every good thing they need.

11 My children, come. Listen to me.
I will teach you to have respect for the LORD.
12 Do you love life
and want to see many good days?
13 Then keep your tongues from speaking evil.
Keep your lips from telling lies.
14 Turn away from evil, and do good.
Look for peace, and go after it.

15 The LORD looks with favor on those who are godly.
His ears are open to their cry.

THANKFUL ♣

I WILL THANK THE LORD AT ALL TIMES.

MY LIPS WILL ALWAYS PRAISE HIM.

— **PSALM 34:1** —

TRUSTED

16 The LORD doesn't look with favor on
   those who do evil.
   He removes all memory of them
      from the earth.

17 Godly people cry out, and the LORD
   hears them.
   He saves them from all of their
      troubles.

18 The LORD is close to those whose hearts
   have been broken.
   He saves those whose spirits have
      been crushed.

19 Anyone who does what is right may
   have many troubles.
   But the LORD saves him from all of
      them.

20 The LORD watches over all of his bones.
   Not one of them will be broken.

21 Sinners will be killed by their own evil.
   The enemies of godly people will be
      judged.

22 The LORD sets those who serve him
   free.
   No one who goes to him for safety
      will be judged.

Psalm 35

A psalm of David.

1 LORD, stand up against those who
   stand up against me.
   Fight against those who fight against
      me.

2 Pick up your large shields and your
   small shields.
   Rise up and help me.

3 Get your spear and javelin ready to
   fight
   against those who are chasing me.
   Say to me, "I will save you."

4 Let those who are trying to kill me
   be brought down in dishonor.
   Let those who plan to destroy me
   be turned back in terror.

5 Let them be like straw blowing in the
   wind,
   while the angel of the LORD drives
      them away.

6 Let their path be dark and slippery,
   while the angel of the LORD chases
      them.

7 They set a trap for me without any
   reason.
   Without any reason they dug a pit
      to catch me.

8 So let them be destroyed without
   warning.
   Let the trap they set for me catch
      them.

Let them fall into the pit and be
   destroyed.

9 Then I will be full of joy because of
   what the LORD has done.
   I will be glad because he has saved
      me.

10 My whole being will cry out,
   "Who is like you, LORD?
   You save poor people from those who
      are too strong for them.
   You save poor and needy people
      from those who rob them."

11 Mean people come forward to give
   witness against me.
   They ask me things I don't know
      anything about.

12 They pay me back with evil, even
   though I was good to them.
   They leave me without hope.

13 But when they were sick, I put on black
   clothes.
   I made myself low by going without
      food.
   My prayers for them weren't always
      answered.

14   So I went around crying
      as if I were crying over my friend or
         relative.
   I bowed my head in sadness
      as if I were sobbing over my mother.

15 But when I tripped and fell, they were
   all very happy.
   Attackers gathered against me when
      I didn't even know it.
   They kept on telling lies about me.

16 They were like ungodly people. They
   made fun of me.
   They ground their teeth at me in
      hate.

17 Lord, how much longer will you just
   look on?
   Save me from their deadly attacks.
   Save the only life I have.
   Save me from those lions.

18 I will give you thanks in the whole
   community.
   Among all of your people I will
      praise you.

19 Don't let those who are my enemies
   without any reason
   laugh at me and make fun of me.
   Don't let those who hate me without
      any reason
   wink at me with an evil purpose.

20 They don't speak words of peace.
   They make up false charges
      against those who live quietly in the
         land.

21 They open their mouths wide at me.
   They make fun of me.

They say, "With our own eyes we
have seen what you did."
22 Lord, you have seen this. Don't be
silent.
Lord, don't be far away from me.
23 Wake up! Rise up to help me!
My God and Lord, stand up for me.
24 Lord my God, when you hand down
your sentence, let it be in my
favor.
You always do what is right.
Don't let my enemies have the joy of
seeing me fall.
25 Don't let them think, "That's exactly
what we wanted!"
Don't let them say, "We have
swallowed him up."

26 Let all those who laugh at me because
I'm in trouble
be ashamed and bewildered.
Let all who think they are better than
I am
put on shame and dishonor as if
they were clothes.
27 Let those who are happy when my
name is cleared
shout with joy and gladness.
Let them always say, "May the Lord be
honored.
He is pleased when everything goes
well with the one who serves
him."
28 You always do what is right. My
tongue will speak about it
and praise you all day long.

Psalm 36

For the director of music. A psalm
of David, the servant of the Lord.
1 Here are the words God has given me
to say
about the evil ways of anyone who
sins.
He doesn't have any respect for God.
2 He praises himself so much
that he can't see his sin or hate it.
3 His mouth speaks words that are evil
and false.
He has stopped being wise. He has
stopped doing good.
4 Even as he lies in bed he makes evil
plans.
He commits himself to a sinful way
of life.
He never says no to what is wrong.

5 Lord, your love is as high as the
heavens.
Your faithful love reaches up to the
skies.

6 You are as holy as the mountains are
high.
You are as honest as the oceans are
deep.
Lord, you keep people and animals
safe.
7 How priceless your faithful love is!
Important and ordinary people alike
find safety in the shadow of your
wings.
8 They eat well because there is more
than enough in your house.
You let them drink from your river
that flows with good things.
9 You have the fountain of life.
We are filled with light because you
give us light.

10 Keep on loving those who know you.
Keep on doing right to those whose
hearts are honest.
11 Don't let the feet of those who are
proud step on me.
Don't let the hands of those who are
evil drive me away.
12 See how those who do evil have fallen!
They are thrown down. They aren't
able to get up.

Psalm 37

A psalm of David.
1 Don't be upset because of sinful
people.
Don't be jealous of those who do
wrong.
2 Like grass, they will soon dry up.
Like green plants, they will soon die.

3 Trust in the Lord and do good.
Then you will live in the land and
enjoy its food.
4 Find your delight in the Lord.
Then he will give you everything
your heart really wants.

5 Commit your life to the Lord.
Here is what he will do if you trust in
him.
6 He will make your godly ways shine
like the dawn.
He will make your honest life shine
like the sun at noon.

7 Be still. Be patient. Wait for the Lord to
act.
Don't be upset when other people
succeed.
Don't be upset when they carry out
their evil plans.

8 Keep from being angry. Turn away
from anger.

POWER-SURGE

PATIENT (P)

BE STILL. BE PATIENT. WAIT FOR THE LORD TO ACT.
—— **PSALM 37:7** ——

Don't be upset. That only leads to evil.

9 Sinful people will be cut off from the land.
But it will be given to those who put their hope in the LORD.

10 In a little while, there won't be any more sinners.
Even if you look for them, you won't be able to find them.

11 But those who are free of pride will be given the land.
They will enjoy great peace.

12 Sinful people make plans to harm those who do what is right.
They grind their teeth at them.

13 But the Lord laughs at those who do evil.
He knows the day is coming when he will judge them.

14 Sinners pull out their swords.
They bend their bows.
They want to kill poor and needy people.
They plan to murder those who lead honest lives.

15 But they will be killed with their own swords.
Their own bows will be broken.

16 Those who do what is right may have very little.
But it's better than the wealth of many sinners.

17 The power of those who are evil will be broken.
But the LORD takes good care of those who do what is right.

18 Every day the LORD watches over those who are without blame.
What he has given them will last forever.

19 When trouble comes to them, they will have what they need.
When there is little food in the land, they still have plenty.

20 But sinful people will die.

The LORD's enemies will be like flowers in the field.
They will disappear like smoke.

21 Sinful people borrow and don't pay back.
But those who are godly give freely to others.

22 The LORD will give the land to those he blesses.
But he will cut off those he puts a curse on.

23 If the LORD is pleased with the way a man lives,
he makes his steps secure.

24 Even if the man trips, he won't fall.
The LORD's hand takes good care of him.

25 I once was young, and now I'm old.
But I've never seen godly people deserted.
I've never seen their children begging for bread.

26 The godly are always giving and lending freely.
Their children will be blessed.

27 Turn away from evil and do good.
Then you will live in the land forever.

28 The LORD loves those who are honest.
He will not desert those who are faithful to him.

They will be kept safe forever.
But the children of sinners will be cut off from the land.

29 Those who do what is right will be given the land.
They will live in it forever.

POWER-SURGE

FAITHFUL ( )

THE LORD LOVES THOSE WHO ARE HONEST.

HE WILL NOT DESERT THOSE WHO ARE FAITHFUL TO HIM.
—— **PSALM 37:28** ——

 (H)

HONEST

30 The mouths of those who do what is
     right speak words of wisdom.
     They say what is honest.
31 God's law is in their hearts.
     Their feet do not slip.

32 Those who are evil hide and wait for
     godly people.
     They are trying to kill them.
33 But the LORD will not leave the godly in
     their power.
     He will not let them be found guilty
     when they are brought into
     court.

34 Wait for the LORD to act.
     Live as he wants you to.
   He will honor you by giving you the
     land.
     When sinners are cut off from it, you
     will see it.

35 I saw a mean and sinful person.
     He was doing well, like a green tree
     in its own soil.
36 But he soon passed away and was
     gone.
     Even though I looked for him, I
     couldn't find him.

37 Think about those who are without
     blame. Look at those who are
     honest.
     A man who loves peace will have a
     tomorrow.
38 But all sinners will be destroyed.
     Those who are evil won't have a
     tomorrow.
     They will be cut off from the land.

39 The LORD saves those who do what is
     right.
     He is their place of safety when
     trouble comes.
40 The LORD helps them and saves them.
     He saves them from sinful people
     because they go to him for safety.

Psalm 38

A psalm of David. A prayer.
1 LORD, don't correct me when you are
     angry.
     Don't punish me when you are
     burning with anger.
2 You have wounded me with your
     arrows.
     You have struck me with your hand.
3 Because of your anger, my whole body
     is sick.
     Because of my sin, I'm not healthy.
4 My guilt has become too much for me.
     It is a load too heavy to carry.

5 My wounds are ugly. They stink.
     I've been foolish. I have sinned.
6 I am bent over. I've been brought very
     low.
     All day long I go around sobbing.
7 My back is filled with burning pain.
     My whole body is sick.
8 I am weak. I feel as if I've been broken
     in pieces.
     I groan because of the great pain in
     my heart.

9 Lord, everything I really want is clearly
     known to you.
     You always hear me when I sigh.
10 My heart pounds. My strength is gone.
     My eyes can hardly see.
11 My friends and companions avoid me
     because of my wounds.
     My neighbors stay far away from
     me.
12 Those who are trying to kill me set
     their traps.
     Those who want to harm me talk
     about destroying me.
     All day long they plan ways to trick
     me.
13 I'm like a deaf person. I can't hear.
     I'm like someone who can't speak,
     who can't say a word.
14 I'm like a man who doesn't hear.
     I'm like someone whose mouth
     can't make any reply.
15 LORD, I wait for you to help me.
     LORD my God, I know you will
     answer.
16 I said, "Don't let my enemies have the
     joy of seeing me fall.
     Don't let them brag when my foot
     slips."

17 I am about to fall.
     My pain never leaves me.
18 I admit that I have done wrong.
     I am troubled by my sin.
19 I have many powerful enemies. They
     are strong and healthy.
     They hate me without any reason.
20 They pay me back with evil, even
     though I was good to them.
     They tell lies about me because I try
     to do what is good.

21 LORD, don't desert me.
     My God, don't be far away from me.
22 Lord my Savior,
     come quickly to help me.

Psalm 39

For the director of music. For Jeduthun.
A psalm of David.

1 I said, "I will be careful about how I
live.
I will not sin by what I say.
I will keep my mouth closed
when sinful people are near me."
2 I was silent and kept quiet.
I didn't even say anything good.
But the pain inside me grew worse.
3 My heart was deeply troubled.
As I thought about what was
happening to me,
I became even more troubled.
Then I spoke out.

4 I said, "LORD, show me when my life
will end.
Show me how many days I have left.
Tell me how short my life will be.
5 You have given me only a few days to
live.
My whole life doesn't seem like
anything to you.
No man's life lasts any longer than
a breath.   *Selah*
6 People are only shadows as they go
here and there.
They rush around, but it doesn't
mean anything.
They pile up wealth, but they don't
know who will get it.

7 "Lord, what can I look forward to now?
You are the only hope I have.
8 Save me from all the wrong things I've
done.
Don't let foolish people make fun
of me.
9 I keep silent. I don't open my mouth.
You are the one who has caused all
of this to happen.
10 Please stop beating me.
I'm about to die from the blows of
your hand.
11 You correct and punish people for
their sin.
Just as a moth eats cloth, you destroy
their wealth.
No one's life lasts any longer than
a breath.   *Selah*

12 "LORD, hear my prayer.
Listen to my cry for help.
Pay attention to my sobbing.
I'm like a guest in your home.
I'm only a visitor, like all of my
family who lived before me.
13 Leave me alone.
Let me be full of joy again before I
die."

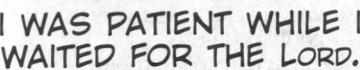

POWER-SURGE

HELPFUL ★

I WAS PATIENT WHILE I
WAITED FOR THE LORD.
HE TURNED TO ME
AND HEARD MY CRY
FOR HELP.
— PSALM 40:1 —

PATIENT

P

Psalm 40

For the director of music.
A psalm of David.

1 I was patient while I waited for the
LORD.
He turned to me and heard my cry
for help.
2 I was sliding down into the pit of
death, and he pulled me out.
He brought me up out of the mud
and dirt.
He set my feet on a rock.
He gave me a firm place to stand on.
3 He gave me a new song to sing.
It is a hymn of praise to our God.
Many people will see what he has done
and will worship him.
They will put their trust in the
LORD.

4 Blessed is the man
who trusts in the LORD.
He doesn't look to proud people for
help.
He doesn't turn away to worship
statues of gods.
5 LORD my God,
no one can compare with you.
You have done many miracles.
And you plan to do many more for
us.
There are too many of them
for me to talk about.

6 You didn't want sacrifices and
offerings.
You weren't pleased with burnt
offerings and sin offerings.
You gave me ears to hear you and
obey you.
7 Then I said, "Here I am.
It is written about me in the scroll.

8 My God, I have come to do what you
want.
Your law is in my heart."

9 I have told the whole community of
those who worship you
that what you do is right.
LORD, you know
that I haven't kept quiet.
10 I haven't kept to myself that what you
did for me was right.
I have spoken about how faithful
you were when you saved me.
I haven't hidden your love and truth
from the whole community.

11 LORD, don't hold back your mercy from
me.
May your love and truth always keep
me safe.
12 There are more troubles all around me
than I can count.
My sins have caught up with me,
and I can't see any longer.
My sins are more than the hairs of my
head.
I have lost all hope.

13 LORD, please save me.
LORD, come quickly to help me.
14 Let all those who are trying to kill me
be put to shame.
Let them not be honored.
Let all those who want to destroy me
be turned back in shame.
15 Some people make fun of me.
Let them be shocked when their
plans fail.
16 But let all those who look to you
be joyful and glad because of what
you have done.
Let those who love you because you
save them always say,
"May the LORD be honored!"

17 But I am poor and needy.
May the Lord be concerned about
me.
You are the One who helps me and
saves me.
My God, please don't wait any
longer.

Psalm 41

For the director of music.
A psalm of David.
1 Blessed is the one who cares about
weak people.
When he is in trouble, the LORD
saves him.
2 The LORD will guard him and keep him
alive.

He will bless him in the land.
He won't hand him over to the
wishes of his enemies.
3 The LORD will take care of him when he
is lying sick in bed.
He will make him well again.

4 I said, "LORD, show me your favor.
Heal me. I have sinned against you."
5 My enemies are saying bad things
about me.
They say, "When will he die and be
forgotten?"
6 When anyone comes to see me,
he says things he doesn't mean.
At the same time, he thinks up lies to
tell against me.
Then he goes out and spreads those
lies around.

7 All of my enemies whisper to each
other about me.
They want something terrible to
happen to me.
8 They say, "He is sick and will die very
soon.
He will never get up from his bed
again."
9 Even my close friend, whom I trusted,
has deserted me.
I even shared my bread with him.

10 But LORD, show me your favor.
Make me well, so I can pay them
back.
11 Then I will know that you are pleased
with me,
because my enemies haven't won
the battle over me.
12 You will take good care of me because
I've been honest.
You will let me be with you forever.

13 Give praise to the LORD, the God of
Israel,
for ever and ever.
Amen and Amen.

BOOK II

Psalms 42–72

Psalm 42

For the director of music. A *maskil* of the
Sons of Korah.
1 A deer longs for streams of water.
God, I long for you in the same way.
2 I am thirsty for God. I am thirsty for
the living God.
When can I go and meet with him?
3 My tears have been my food
day and night.

All day long people say to me,
"Where is your God?"
4 When I remember what has happened,
I tell God all of my troubles.
I remember how I used to walk along
with the crowd of worshipers.
I led them to the house of God.
We shouted with joy and gave thanks
as we went to the holy feast.

5 My spirit, why are you so sad?
Why are you so upset deep down
inside me?
Put your hope in God.
Once again I will have reason to
praise him.
He is my Savior and 6 my God.

My spirit is very sad deep down inside
me.
So I will remember you here where
the Jordan River begins.
I will remember you here on the
Hermon mountains
and on Mount Mizar.
7 You have sent wave upon wave of
trouble over me.
It roars down on me like a waterfall.
All of your waves and breakers have
rolled over me.

8 During the day the LORD sends his love
to me.
During the night I sing about him.
I say a prayer to the God who gives
me life.

9 I say to God my Rock,
"Why have you forgotten me?
Why must I go around in sorrow?
Why am I beaten down by my
enemies?"
10 My body suffers deadly pain
as my enemies make fun of me.
All day long they say to me,
"Where is your God?"

11 My spirit, why are you so sad?
Why are you so upset deep down
inside me?
Put your hope in God.
Once again I will have reason to
praise him.
He is my Savior and my God.

Psalm 43

1 God, when you hand down your
decision, let it be in my favor.
Stand up for me against an ungodly
nation.
Save me from those lying and sinful
people.
2 You are God, my place of safety.

Why have you turned your back on
me?
Why must I go around in sorrow?
Why am I beaten down by my
enemies?
3 Send out your light and your truth.
Let them guide me.
Let them bring me back to your holy
mountain,
to the place where you live.
4 Then I will go to the altar of God.
I will go to God. He is my joy and my
delight.
God, you are my God.
I will praise you by playing the harp.

5 My spirit, why are you so sad?
Why are you so upset deep down
inside me?
Put your hope in God.
Once again I will have reason to
praise him.
He is my Savior and my God.

Psalm 44

For the director of music. A *maskil* of the
Sons of Korah.
1 God, we have heard what you did.
Those who came before us have
told us
what you did in their days,
in days long ago.
2 With your powerful hand you drove
out the nations.
You settled our people in the land.
You crushed the people who were
there.
And you made our people do well.
3 They didn't win the land with their
swords.
They didn't gain success with their
powerful arms.
Your powerful right hand and your
mighty arm gave them success.
You looked on them with favor. You
loved them.

4 You are my King and my God.
You give success to the people of
Jacob.
5 With your help we push our enemies
back.
By your power we walk all over
them.
6 I don't trust in my bow.
My sword doesn't bring me success.
7 But you give us success over our
enemies.
You put them to shame.
8 All day long we talk about how great
God is.

We will praise your name forever.
Selah

9 But now you have turned your back on
us and made us low.
You don't march out with our
armies anymore.
10 You made us turn and run from our
enemies.
They have taken what belongs to us.
11 You handed us over to be eaten up like
sheep.
You have scattered us among the
nations.
12 You sold your people for very little.
You didn't gain anything when you
sold them.
13 You have made us something that our
neighbors laugh at.
Those who live around us make fun
of us and tease us.
14 The nations make jokes about us.
They shake their heads at us.
15 All day long I am reminded of my
shame.
My face is covered with it
16 because of those who laugh at me and
attack me with their words.
They want to get even with me.

17 All of this happened to us,
even though we had not forgotten
you.
We had been true to the covenant
you made with us.
18 Our hearts had not turned away from
you.
Our feet had not wandered from
your path.
19 But you crushed us and left us to the
wild dogs.
You covered us over with deep
darkness.

20 We didn't forget our God.
We didn't spread out our hands in
prayer to a strange god.
21 If we had, God would have discovered
it.
He knows the secrets of our hearts.
22 But because of you, we face death all
day long.
We are considered as sheep to be
killed.

23 Lord, wake up! Why are you sleeping?
Get up! Don't say no to us forever.
24 Why do you turn your face away from
us?
Why do you forget our pain and
troubles?

25 We are brought down to the dust.
Our bodies lie flat on the ground.
26 Rise up and help us.
Save us because of your faithful love.

Psalm 45

For the director of music. A *maskil* of the
Sons of Korah. A wedding song to the
tune of "Lilies."

1 My heart is full of beautiful words
as I say my poem for the king.
My tongue is like the pen of a skillful
writer.

2 You are the most excellent of men.
Your lips have been given the ability
to speak gracious words.
God has blessed you forever.
3 Mighty one, put your sword at your
side.
Put on glory and majesty as if they
were your clothes.
4 In your majesty ride out with power
in honor of what is true and right.
Do it in honor of all those who are not
proud.
Let your right hand do wonderful
things.
5 Shoot your sharp arrows into the
hearts of your enemies.
Let the nations come under your
control.
6 Your throne is the very throne of God.
Your kingdom will last for ever and
ever.
You will rule by treating everyone
fairly.
7 You love what is right and hate what is
evil.
So your God has placed you above
your companions.
He has filled you with joy by
pouring the sacred oil on your
head.
8 Myrrh and aloes and cassia make all of
your robes smell good.
In palaces decorated with ivory
the music played on stringed
instruments makes you glad.
9 Daughters of kings are among the
women you honor.
At your right hand is the royal bride
dressed in gold from Ophir.

10 Royal bride, listen. Think about this
and pay attention to it.
Forget about your people and the
home you came from.
11 The king is charmed by your beauty.
Honor him. He is now your master.
12 The people of Tyre will come with
gifts.

Wealthy people will try to gain your favor.

13 The princess comes into the palace in all her glory.
Her gown has gold threads running through it.

14 Dressed in beautiful clothes, she is led to the king.
Her virgin companions follow her and are brought to him.

15 They are led in with joy and gladness.
They enter the palace of the king.

16 Your sons will rule just as your father and grandfather did.
You will make them princes through the whole land.

17 I will make sure that people will always remember you.
The nations will praise you for ever and ever.

HELPFUL ★

GOD IS OUR PLACE OF SAFETY. HE GIVES US STRENGTH.

HE IS ALWAYS THERE TO HELP US IN TIMES OF TROUBLE.

— PSALM 46:1 —

STRONG

Psalm 46

For the director of music. A song of the Sons of Korah. For *alamoth*.

1 God is our place of safety. He gives us strength.
He is always there to help us in times of trouble.

2 The earth may fall apart.
The mountains may fall into the middle of the sea.
But we will not be afraid.

3 The waters of the sea may roar and foam.
The mountains may shake when the waters rise. *Selah*
But we will not be afraid.

4 God's blessings are like a river. They fill the city of God with joy.

That city is the holy place where the Most High God lives.

5 Because God is there, the city will not fall.
God will help it at the beginning of the day.

6 Nations are in disorder. Kingdoms fall.
God speaks, and the people of the earth melt in fear.

7 The LORD who rules over all is with us.
The God of Jacob is like a fort to us. *Selah*

8 Come and see what the LORD has done.
See the places he has destroyed on the earth.

9 He makes wars stop from one end of the earth to the other.
He breaks every bow. He snaps every spear.
He burns every shield with fire.

10 He says, "Be still, and know that I am God.
I will be honored among the nations.
I will be honored in the earth."

11 The LORD who rules over all is with us.
The God of Jacob is like a fort to us. *Selah*

Psalm 47

For the director of music. A psalm of the Sons of Korah.

1 Clap your hands, all you nations.
Shout to God with cries of joy.

2 How wonderful is the LORD Most High!
He is the great King over the whole earth.

3 He brought nations under our control.
He made them fall under us.

4 He chose our land for us.
The people of Jacob are proud of their land,
and God loves them. *Selah*

5 God went up to his throne while his people were shouting with joy.
The LORD went up while trumpets were playing.

6 Sing praises to God. Sing praises.
Sing praises to our King. Sing praises.

7 God is the King of the whole earth.
Sing a psalm of praise to him.

8 God rules over the nations.
He is seated on his holy throne.

9 The nobles of the nations come together.
They are now part of the people of the God of Abraham.
The kings of the earth belong to God.
He is greatly honored.

Psalm 48

A song. A psalm of the Sons of Korah.

1 The LORD is great. He is really worthy of
  praise.
  Praise him in the city of our God, his
    holy mountain.
2 Mount Zion is high and beautiful.
  It brings joy to everyone on earth.
  Mount Zion is like the highest parts of
    Mount Zaphon.
  It is the city of the Great King.
3 God is there to keep it safe.
  He has shown himself to be like a
    fort to the city.

4 Many kings joined forces.
  They entered Israel together.
5 But when they saw Mount Zion, they
    were amazed.
  They ran away in terror.
6 Trembling took hold of them.
  They felt pain like a woman giving
    birth to a baby.
7 LORD, you destroyed them like ships of
    Tarshish
  that were torn apart by an east wind.

8 What we heard we have also seen.
  We have seen it
  in the city of the LORD who rules over
    all.
  We have seen it in the city of our
    God.
  We have heard and seen that God
    makes her secure forever.   *Selah*

9 God, inside your temple
  we think about your faithful love.
10 God, your fame reaches from one end
    of the earth to the other.
  In the same way, people praise you
    from one end of the earth to
    the other.
  You use your power to do what is
    right.
11 Mount Zion is filled with joy.
  The villages of Judah are glad.
  That's because you judge fairly.

12 Walk around Zion. Go all around it.
  Count its towers.
13 Think carefully about its outer walls.
  Just look at how safe it is!
  Then you can tell its people that
    God keeps them safe.
14 This God is our God for ever and ever.
  He will be our guide to the very end.

Psalm 49

For the director of music. A psalm of the
  Sons of Korah.

1 Hear this, all you nations.
  Listen, all you who live in this world.
2 Listen, ordinary and important people
    alike.
  Listen, those of you who are rich or
    poor.
3 My mouth will speak wise words.
  What I say from my heart will give
    understanding.
4 I will pay attention to a proverb.
  I will explain my riddle as I play the
    harp.

5 Why should I be afraid when trouble
    comes?
  Why should I fear when sinners are
    all around me?
  They are the kind of people who
    want to take advantage of me.
6 They trust in their wealth.
  They brag about how rich they are.
7 No man can pay for the life of anyone
    else.
  No one can give God what that
    would cost.
8 The price for a life is very high.
  No payment is ever enough.
9 No one can pay enough to live forever
    and not rot in the grave.

10 Everyone can see that even wise people
    die.
  Foolish and dumb people also pass
    away.
  All of them leave their wealth to
    others.
11 Their graves will remain their houses
    forever.
  Their graves will be their homes for
    all time to come.
  Naming lands after themselves
    won't help either.
12 Even though people may be very rich,
    they don't live on and on.
  They are like the animals. They die.
13 That's what happens to those who
    trust in themselves.
  It also happens to their followers,
    who agree with what they say.
      Selah
14 Like sheep they will end up in the
    grave.
  Death will swallow them up.
  When honest people come to power, a
    new day will dawn.
  The bodies of sinners will waste
    away in the grave.
  They will end up far away from their
    princely houses.
15 But God will save me from the grave.
  He will certainly take me to himself.
      Selah

HONEST H

WHEN HONEST PEOPLE COME TO POWER, A NEW DAY WILL DAWN.
— **PSALM 49:14** —

16 Don't be upset when someone
became rich.
    Don't be troubled when he becomes
more and more wealthy.
17 He won't take anything with him
when he dies.
    His riches won't go down to the
grave with him.
18 While he lived, he believed he was
blessed.
    People praised him when things
were going well for him.
19 But he will die, like his people of long
ago.
    He will never again see the light that
leads to life.

20 People who have riches but don't
understand
    are like the animals. They die.

Psalm 50

A psalm of Asaph.
1 The Mighty One, God, the LORD,
speaks.
    He calls out to the earth
from the sunrise in the east
to the sunset in the west.
2 From Zion, perfect and beautiful,
    God's glory shines out.
3 Our God comes, and he won't be
silent.
    A burning fire goes ahead of him.
    A terrible storm is all around him.
4 He calls out to heaven and earth to be
his witnesses.
    Then he judges his people.
5 He says, "Gather my holy people
around me.
    They made a covenant with me by
offering a sacrifice."
6 The heavens announce that what God
decides is right.
    He himself is the Judge.   *Selah*

7 God says, "Listen, my people, and I
will speak.
    Listen, Israel, and I will give witness
against you.

I am God, your God.
8 I don't find fault with you because of
your sacrifices.
    I don't find fault with the burnt
offerings you always bring me.
9 I don't need a bull from your barn.
    I don't need goats from your pens.
10 Every animal in the forest already
belongs to me.
    And so do the cattle on a thousand
hills.
11 I own every bird in the mountains.
    The creatures of the field belong to
me.
12 If I were hungry, I wouldn't tell you.
    The world belongs to me. And so
does everything in it.
13 Do I eat the meat of bulls?
    Do I drink the blood of goats?
14 Bring me thank offerings, because I am
your God.
    Carry out the promises you made to
me, because I am the Most High
God.
15 Call out to me when trouble comes.
    I will save you. And you will honor
me."

16 But here is what God says to sinful
people.

"What right do you have to speak the
words of my laws?
    How dare you speak the words of my
covenant!
17 You hate my teaching.
    You turn your back on what I say.
18 When you see a thief, you join him.
    You make friends with those who
commit adultery.
19 You use your mouth to speak evil.
    You use your tongue to spread lies.
20 You always speak against your brother.
    You always tell lies about your own
mother's son.
21 You have done those things, and I kept
silent.
    So you thought I was just like you.
    But now I'm going to correct you.
    I will bring charges against you.

22 "You who forget God, think about this.
    If you don't, I will tear you to pieces.
    No one will be able to save you.
23 Anyone who sacrifices thank offerings
to me honors me.
    He makes it possible for me to show
him
    that I am the God who saves."

CHEERFUL ✳

LET ME HEAR YOU SAY, "YOUR SINS ARE FORGIVEN." THAT WILL BRING ME JOY AND GLADNESS.
— PSALM 51:8 —

F

Psalm 51

For the director of music. A psalm of David when the prophet Nathan came to him after David had committed adultery with Bathsheba.

1 God, show me your favor
in keeping with your faithful love.
Because your love is so tender and kind,
wipe out my lawless acts.
2 Wash away all of the evil things I've done.
Make me pure from my sin.

3 I know the lawless acts I've committed.
I can't forget my sin.
4 You are the one I've really sinned against.
I've done what is evil in your sight.
So you are right when you sentence me.
You are fair when you judge me.
5 I know I've been a sinner ever since I was born.
I've been a sinner ever since my mother became pregnant with me.
6 I know that you want truth to be in my heart.
You teach me wisdom deep down inside me.

7 Make me pure by sprinkling me with hyssop plant. Then I will be clean.
Wash me. Then I will be whiter than snow.
8 Let me hear you say, "Your sins are forgiven."
That will bring me joy and gladness.
Let the body you have broken be glad.

9 Take away all of my sins.
Wipe away all of the evil things I've done.

10 God, create a pure heart in me.
Give me a new spirit that is faithful to you.
11 Don't send me away from you.
Don't take your Holy Spirit away from me.
12 Give me back the joy that comes from being saved by you.
Give me a spirit that obeys you. That will keep me going.

13 Then I will teach your ways to those who commit lawless acts.
And sinners will turn back to you.
14 You are the God who saves me.
I have committed murder.
Take away my guilt.
Then my tongue will sing about how right you are
no matter what you do.
15 Lord, open my lips so that I can speak.
Then my mouth will praise you.
16 You don't take delight in sacrifice.
If you did, I would bring it.
You don't take pleasure in burnt offerings.
17 The greatest sacrifice you want is a broken spirit.
God, you will gladly accept a heart that is broken because of sadness over sin.

18 May you be pleased to give Zion success.
Build up the walls of Jerusalem.
19 Then holy sacrifices will be offered in the right way.
Whole burnt offerings will bring delight to you.
And bulls will be offered on your altar.

Psalm 52

For the director of music. A *maskil* of David when Doeg, who was from Edom, had gone to Saul. Doeg had told Saul, "David has gone to the house of Ahimelech."

1 You think you are such a big, strong man!
Why do you brag about the evil things you've done?
You are a dishonor to God all the time.
2 You plan ways to destroy others.
Your tongue is like a blade that has a sharp edge.
You are always telling lies.

³ You love evil instead of good.
You would rather lie than tell the
truth. *Selah*
⁴ You love to harm others with your
words, you liar!

⁵ So God will destroy you forever.
He will grab hold of you and throw
you out of your tent.
He will remove you from this life.
Selah

⁶ Those who do what is right will see it
and learn a lesson from it.
They will laugh at you and say,
⁷ "Just look at this fellow!
He didn't depend on God for his
safety.
He put his trust in all his wealth.
He grew strong by destroying
others!"

⁸ But I am like a healthy olive tree.
My roots are deep in the house of
God.
I trust in your faithful love
for ever and ever.
⁹ I will praise you forever for what you
have done.
I will put my hope in you because
you are good.
I will praise you when I'm with your
faithful people.

Psalm 53

For the director of music. For *mahalath.*
A *maskil* of David.
¹ Foolish people say in their hearts,
"There is no God."
They do all kinds of horrible and evil
things.
No one does anything good.

² God looks down from heaven
on all people.
He wants to see if there are any who
understand.
He wants to see if there are any who
trust in God.
³ All of them have turned away.
They have all become evil.
No one does anything good,
no one at all.

⁴ Won't those who do evil ever learn?
They eat up my people as if they
were eating bread.
They don't call out to God for help.
⁵ Just look at them! They are filled with
terror
even when there is nothing to be
afraid of!

People of Israel, God will scatter the
bones of those who attack you.
You will put them to shame, because
God hates them.

⁶ How I pray that the One who saves
Israel will come out of Zion!
God will bless his people with great
success again.
So let the people of Jacob be filled
with joy! Let Israel be glad!

Psalm 54

For the director of music. To be played on
stringed instruments. A *maskil* of David
when the men from Ziph had gone to
Saul. They had said, "Isn't David hiding
among us?"

¹ God, save me by your power.
Set me free by your might.
² God, hear my prayer.
Listen to what I'm saying.

³ Strangers are attacking me.
Mean people are trying to kill me.
They don't care about God. *Selah*

⁴ But I know that God helps me.
The Lord is the one who keeps me
going.
⁵ My enemies tell lies about me.
Do to them the evil things they
planned against me.
God, be faithful and destroy them.

⁶ I will sacrifice an offering to you
just because I choose to.
LORD, I will praise your name
because it is good.
⁷ You have saved me from all of my
troubles.
With my own eyes I have seen you
win the battle over my enemies.

Psalm 55

For the director of music.
A *maskil* of David to be played
on stringed instruments.
¹ God, listen to my prayer.
Pay attention to my cry for help.
² Hear me and answer me.
My thoughts upset me. I'm very
troubled.
³ I'm troubled by what my enemies
say about me.
I'm upset because sinful people stare
at me.
They cause me all kinds of suffering.
When they are angry, they attack
me with their words.

⁴ I feel great pain deep down inside me.

The terrors of death are crushing
me.
⁵ Fear and trembling have taken hold
of me.
Panic has overpowered me.
⁶ I said, "I wish I had wings like a dove!
Then I would fly away and be at rest.
⁷ I would escape to a place far away.
I would stay out in the desert. *Selah*
⁸ I would hurry to my place of safety.
It would be far away from the winds
and storms I'm facing."

⁹ Lord, destroy the plans of sinners. Keep
them from understanding one
another.
I see people destroying things and
fighting in the city.
¹⁰ Day and night they prowl around on
top of its walls.
The city is full of crime and trouble.
¹¹ Forces that destroy are at work inside it.
Its streets are full of people who
cheat others and take
advantage of them.

¹² If an enemy were making fun of me,
I could stand it.
If he were looking down on me,
I could hide from him.
¹³ But it's you, someone like myself.
It's my companion, my close friend.
¹⁴ We used to enjoy good friendship
as we walked with the crowds at the
house of God.

¹⁵ Let death take my enemies by surprise.
Let them be buried alive,
because their hearts and homes are
full of evil.

¹⁶ But I call out to God.
And the LORD saves me.
¹⁷ Evening, morning and noon
I groan and cry out.
And he hears my voice.
¹⁸ Even though many enemies are
fighting against me,
he brings me safely back from the
battle.
¹⁹ God sits on his throne forever.
He hears my prayers and makes my
enemies suffer. *Selah*
They never change their ways.
They don't have any respect for God.

²⁰ My companion attacks his friends.
He breaks his promise.
²¹ His talk is as smooth as butter.
But he has war in his heart.
His words flow like olive oil.
But they are like swords ready for
battle.

²² Turn your worries over to the LORD.
He will keep you going.
He will never let godly people fall.
²³ God, you will bring sinners
down to the grave.
Murderers and liars
won't live out even half of their
lives.

But I trust in you.

Psalm 56

For the director of music. A *miktam* of
David after the Philistines had captured
him in Gath. To the tune of "A Dove
on Distant Oak Trees."

¹ God, show me your favor. Men are
chasing me.
All day long they keep attacking me.
² Those who tell lies about me chase me
all day long.
Many proud people are attacking
me.

³ When I'm afraid,
I will trust in you.
⁴ I trust in God. I praise his word.
I trust in God. I will not be afraid.
What can people do to me?

⁵ All day long they twist my words.
They are always making plans to
harm me.
⁶ They get together and hide.
They watch my steps.
They hope to kill me.

⁷ Make sure you don't let them escape.
God, bring down the nations in
your anger.
⁸ Write down my poem of sadness.
List my tears on your scroll.
Aren't you making a record of them?

⁹ My enemies will turn back
when I call out to you for help.
Then I will know that God is on my
side.
¹⁰ I trust in God. I praise his word.
I trust in the LORD. I praise his word.
¹¹ I trust in God. I will not be afraid.
What can mere men do to me?

¹² God, I have made promises to you.
I will bring my thank offerings to
you.
¹³ You have saved me from death.
You have kept me from tripping and
falling.
Now I can live with you
in the light that leads to life.

Psalm 57

For the director of music. A *miktam* of
David when he had run away from Saul
into the cave. To the tune
of "Do Not Destroy."

1 Show me your favor, God. Show me
your favor.
I go to you for safety.
I will find safety in the shadow of your
wings.
There I will stay until the danger is
gone.

2 I cry out to God Most High.
I cry out to God, and he carries out
his plan for me.
3 He answers from heaven and saves me.
He puts to shame those who chase
me.   *Selah*
He shows me his love and his truth.

4 Men who are like lions are all around
me.
I am lying down among hungry
animals.
Their teeth are like spears and arrows.
Their tongues are like sharp swords.

5 God, may you be honored above the
heavens.
Let your glory be over the whole
earth.

6 My enemies spread a net to catch me
by the feet.
I felt helpless.
They dug a pit in my path.
But they fell into it themselves. *Selah*

7 God, my heart feels secure.
My heart feels secure.
I will sing and make music to you.
8 My spirit, wake up!
Harp and lyre, wake up!
I want to sing and make music
before the sun rises.

9 Lord, I will praise you among the
nations.
I will sing about you among the
people of the earth.
10 Great is your love. It reaches to the
heavens.
Your truth reaches to the skies.

11 God, may you be honored above the
heavens.
Let your glory be over the whole
earth.

Psalm 58

For the director of music. A *miktam*
of David to the tune of "Do Not Destroy."
1 Are you rulers really fair when you
speak?
Do you judge people honestly?
2 No, in your hearts you plan to be
unfair.
With your hands you do terrible
things on the earth.
3 Even from birth those who are evil go
down the wrong path.
From the day they are born they go
the wrong way and speak lies.
4 Their words are like the poison of a
snake.
They are like the poison of a cobra
that has covered up its ears.
5 It won't listen to any tune of a snake
charmer,
even if the charmer really plays well.

6 God, break the teeth in the mouths of
those sinners!
Lord, tear out the sharp teeth of
those lions!
7 Let those people disappear like water
that flows away.
When they draw their bows, let their
arrows be dull.
8 Let them be like a slug that melts away
as it moves along.
Let them be like a baby that is born
dead and never sees the sun.

9 Evil people will be swept away quicker
than a pot can feel the heat of
thorns burning under it.
And it doesn't matter if the thorns
are green or dry.
10 Godly people will be glad when those
who have hurt them are paid
back.
They will wash their feet in the
blood of those who do evil.
11 Then people will say,
"The godly will get their reward.
There really is a God who judges the
earth."

Psalm 59

For the director of music. A *miktam* of
David when Saul had sent men to watch
David's house in order to kill him. To the
tune of "Do Not Destroy."
1 God, save me from my enemies.
Keep me safe from those who rise up
against me.
2 Save me from those who do evil.
Save me from murderers.

³ See how they hide and wait for me!
  LORD, angry people plan to harm
    me,
  even though I haven't hurt them in
    any way or sinned against
    them.
⁴ I haven't done anything wrong to
    them. But they are ready to
    attack me.
  Rise up and help me! Look at what
    I'm up against!
⁵ LORD God who rules over all, rise up.
    God of Israel,
  punish all of the nations.
  Don't show any mercy to those sinful
    people
  who have turned against me.   *Selah*

⁶ My enemies are like a pack of barking
    dogs
  that come back to the city in the
    evening.
  They prowl around the city.
⁷ Listen to what pours out of their
    mouths.
  The words from their lips are like
    swords.
  They think, "Who can hear us?"
⁸ But you laugh at them, LORD.
  You make fun of all those nations.

⁹ You give me strength. I look to you.
  God, you are like a fort to me. ¹⁰ You
    are my loving God.

God will march out in front of me.
  He will let me look down on those
    who tell lies about me.
¹¹ Lord, you are like a shield that keeps us
    safe.
  Don't kill my enemies all at once.
  If you do, my people will forget
    about it.

LOVING ♥

YOU GIVE ME
STRENGTH. I LOOK
TO YOU.

GOD, YOU ARE LIKE A
FORT TO ME. YOU ARE
MY LOVING GOD.

— **PSALM 59:9-10** —

STRONG

Use your power to make my enemies
    wander around.
  Destroy them.
¹² They have sinned with their mouths.
  Their lips have spoken evil words.
  They have called down a curse on me
    and lied.
  Let them be caught in their pride.
¹³ Burn them up in your anger.
  Burn them up until there isn't
    anything left of them.
  Then everyone from one end of the
    earth to the other will know
  that God rules over the people of
    Jacob.   *Selah*

¹⁴ My enemies are like a pack of barking
    dogs
  that come back into the city in the
    evening.
  They prowl around the city.
¹⁵ They wander around looking for food.
  They groan if they don't find
    something that will satisfy
    them.
¹⁶ But I will sing about your strength.
  In the morning I will sing about
    your love.
You are like a fort to me.
  You keep me safe in times of trouble.

¹⁷ You give me strength. I sing praise to
    you.
  God, you are like a fort to me. You
    are my loving God.

Psalm 60

For the director of music. For teaching.
A *miktam* of David when he fought
against Aram Naharaim and Aram Zobah.
That was when Joab returned and struck
down 12,000 people from Edom in the
Valley of Salt. To the tune of "The Lily
of the Covenant."

¹ God, you have turned away from us.
  You have attacked us.
  You have been angry. Now turn back
    to us!
² You have shaken the land and torn it
    open.
  Fix its cracks, because it is falling
    apart.
³ You have shown your people hard
    times.
  You have made us drink the wine of
    your anger.
  Now we can't even walk straight.
⁴ But you lead into battle those who
    have respect for you.
  You give them a flag to wave against
    the enemy's weapons.   *Selah*

5 Save us. Help us with your powerful
　　right hand,
　so that those you love may be saved.
6 God has spoken from his temple.
　He has said, "I will win the battle.
　Then I will divide up the land around
　　Shechem.
　I will divide up the Valley of
　　Succoth.
7 Gilead belongs to me.
　So does the land of Manasseh.
　Ephraim is the strongest tribe.
　It is like a helmet for my head.
　Judah is the royal tribe.
　It is like a ruler's staff.
8 Moab serves me like one who washes
　　my feet.
　I toss my sandal on Edom to show
　　that I own it.
　I shout to Philistia that I have won
　　the battle."

9 Who will bring me to the city that has
　　high walls around it?
　Who will lead me to the land of
　　Edom?
10 God, isn't it you, even though you
　　have now turned away from us?
　Isn't it you, even though you don't
　　lead our armies into battle
　　anymore?
11 Help us against our enemies.
　The help people give doesn't
　　amount to anything.
12 With your help we will win the battle.
　You will walk all over our enemies.

Psalm 61

For the director of music.
A psalm of David to be played
on stringed instruments.
1 God, hear my cry for help.
　Listen to my prayer.

2 From a place far away I call out to you.
　I call out as my heart gets weaker.
　Lead me to the safety of a rock that
　　is high above me.
3 You have always kept me safe from my
　　enemies.
　You are like a strong tower to me.

4 I long to live in your holy tent forever.
　There I find safety in the shadow
　　of your wings.　　　　*Selah*
5 God, you have heard my promises.
　You have given me what belongs to
　　those who worship you.

6 Add many days to the king's life.
　Let him live on and on for many
　　years.

7 May he always enjoy your blessing as
　　he rules.
　Let your love and truth keep him
　　safe.

8 Then I will always sing praise to you.
　I will keep my promises day after
　　day.

Psalm 62

For the director of music. For Jeduthun.
A psalm of David.
1 I find my rest in God alone.
　He is the One who saves me.
2 He alone is my rock. He is the One
　　who saves me.
　He is like a fort to me. I will always
　　be secure.

3 How long will you enemies attack me?
　Will all of you throw me down?
　I'm like a leaning wall.
　I'm like a fence that is about to fall.
4 You only want to pull me down
　　from my place of honor.
　You take delight in telling lies.
　You bless me with what you say.
　But in your hearts you call down
　　curses on me.　　　　*Selah*

5 I will find my rest in God alone.
　He is the One who gives me hope.
6 He alone is my rock. He is the One
　　who saves me.
　He is like a fort to me. I will always
　　be secure.
7 I depend on God to save me and to
　　honor me.
　He is my mighty rock. He is my
　　place of safety.
8 Trust in him at all times, you people.
　Tell him all of your troubles.
　God is our place of safety.　　*Selah*

9 Ordinary people are only a breath.
　Important people are not what they
　　seem to be.
　If they were weighed on a scale, they
　　wouldn't amount to anything.
　Together they are only a breath.
10 Don't trust in money you have taken
　　from others.
　Don't be proud of things you have
　　stolen.
　Even if your riches grow,
　　don't put your trust in them.

11 God, I have heard you say two things.
　One is that you, God, are strong.
12 　The other is that you, Lord, are
　　loving.
　I'm sure you will reward each person
　　in keeping with what he has done.

Psalm 63

A psalm of David when he was in the
Desert of Judah.

¹ God, you are my God.
  I greatly long for you.
With all my heart I thirst for you
  in this dry desert
  where there isn't any water.

² I have seen you in the sacred tent.
  There I have seen your power and
    your glory.
³ Your love is better than life.
  I will bring glory to you with my
    lips.
⁴ I will praise you as long as I live.
  I will lift up my hands when I pray
    to you.
⁵ I will be as satisfied as if I had eaten the
    best food there is.
  I will sing praise to you with my
    mouth.

⁶ As I lie on my bed I remember you.
  I think of you all night long.
⁷ Because you have helped me,
  I sing in the shadow of your wings.
⁸ I hold on to you.
  Your powerful right hand takes good
    care of me.

⁹ Those who are trying to kill me will be
    destroyed.
  They will go down into the grave.
¹⁰ They will be killed with swords.
  They will become food for wild dogs.

¹¹ But the king will be filled with joy
    because of what God has done.
  All those who take an oath in God's
    name will praise him.
  But the mouths of liars will be shut.

Psalm 64

For the director of music.
A psalm of David.

¹ God, hear me as I tell you my problem.
  Don't let my enemies kill me.
² Hide me from those who make evil
    plans against me.
  Hide me from that crowd of people
    who are doing evil.

³ They make their tongues like sharp
    swords.
  They aim their words like deadly
    arrows.
⁴ They shoot from their hiding places at
    people who aren't guilty of
    doing anything wrong.
  They shoot quickly. They aren't
    afraid of being caught.

⁵ They help each other make evil plans.
  They talk about hiding their traps.
  They say, "Who can see what we are
    doing?"
⁶ They make plans to do what is evil.
  They say, "We have thought up a
    perfect plan!"
  The hearts and minds of people are
    so clever!

⁷ But God will shoot my enemies with
    his arrows.
  He will suddenly strike them down.
⁸ He will turn their own words against
    them.
  He will destroy them.
All those who see them will shake their
    heads
  and look down on them.

⁹ Everyone will respect God.
  They will tell about his works.
  They will think about what he has
    done.
¹⁰ Let godly people be full of joy because
    of what the LORD has done.
  Let them go to him for safety.
  Let all those whose hearts are honest
    praise him.

POWER-SURGE

HONEST H

LET ALL THOSE WHOSE HEARTS ARE HONEST PRAISE HIM.
—— **PSALM 64:10** ——

Psalm 65

For the director of music. A psalm
of David. A song.

¹ God, we look forward to praising you
    in Zion.
  We will keep our promises to you.
² All people will come to you,
    because you hear and answer prayer.
³ When our sins became too much
    for us,
  you forgave our lawless acts.
⁴ Blessed are those you choose
    and bring near to worship you.
You bring us into the courtyards of
    your holy temple.
  There in your house we are filled
    with all kinds of good things.

⁵ God our Savior, you answer us by
    doing wonderful things.

CHEERFUL ✳

WHAT YOU DO MAKES PEOPLE FROM ONE END OF THE EARTH TO THE OTHER SING FOR JOY.
— PSALM 65:8 —

You save us by your power.
People all over the world and beyond
    the farthest oceans
    put their hope in you.
6 You formed the mountains by your
    power.
    You showed how strong you are.
7 You calmed the oceans and their
    roaring waves.
    You calmed the angry words and
    actions of the nations.
8 Those who live far away are amazed at
    the miracles you have done.
    What you do makes people from
    one end of the earth to the
    other sing for joy.

9 You take care of the land and water it.
    You make it very rich.
    You fill your streams with water.
    You provide the people with grain.
    That's how you prepare the land.
10 You water its rows.
    You smooth out its bumps.
    You soften it with showers.
    And you bless its crops.
11 You bring the year to a close with huge
    crops.
    You provide more than enough
    food.
12 The grass grows thick even in the
    desert.
    The hills are dressed with gladness.
13 The meadows are covered with flocks
    and herds.
    The valleys are dressed with grain.
    They sing and shout with joy.

Psalm 66

For the director of music. A song.
A psalm.
1 Shout to God with joy, everyone on
    earth!
2   Sing about the glory of his name!
    Give him glorious praise!
3 Say to God, "What wonderful things
    you do!

Your power is so great
    that your enemies bow down to you
    in fear.
4 Everyone on earth bows down to you.
    They sing praise to you.
    They sing praise to your name." *Selah*

5 Come and see what God has done.
    See what wonderful things he has
    done for his people!
6 He turned the Red Sea into dry land.
    The people of Israel passed through
    the waters on foot.
    Come, let us be full of joy because of
    what he did.
7 He rules by his power forever.
    His eyes watch the nations.
    Let no one who refuses to obey him
    rise up against him.   *Selah*

8 Praise our God, you nations.
    Let the sound of the praise you give
    him be heard.
9 He has kept us alive.
    He has kept our feet from slipping.
10 God, you have put us to the test.
    You put us through fire to make us
    like silver.
11 You put us in prison.
    You placed heavy loads on our
    backs.
12 You let people run over our heads.
    We went through fire and water.
    But you brought us to a place
    where we have everything we need.

13 I will come to your temple with burnt
    offerings.
    I will keep my promises to you.
14 I made them with my lips.
    My mouth spoke them when I was
    in trouble.
15 I will sacrifice fat animals to you as
    burnt offerings.
    I will offer rams, bulls and goats
    to you.   *Selah*

16 Come and listen, all of you who have
    respect for God.
    Let me tell you what he has done
    for me.
17 I cried out to him with my mouth.
    I praised him with my tongue.
18 If I had enjoyed having sin in my
    heart,
    the Lord would not have listened.
19 But God has listened.
    He has heard my prayer.
20 Give praise to God.
    He has accepted my prayer.
    He has not held his love back from
    me.

Psalm 67

For the director of music. A psalm. A song
to be played on stringed instruments.

1 God, show us your favor. Bless us.
  May you smile on us with your
      favor.   *Selah*
2 Then your ways will be known on
      earth.
  All nations will see that you have the
      power to save.

3 God, may the nations praise you.
  May all of the people on earth praise
      you.
4 May the nations be glad and sing with
      joy.
  You rule the people of the earth
      fairly.
  You guide the nations of the earth.
                                Selah
5 God, may the nations praise you.
  May all of the people on earth praise
      you.

6 Then the land will produce its crops.
  God, our God, will bless us.
7 God will bless us.
  People from one end of the earth to
      the other
  will have respect for him.

Psalm 68

For the director of music. A psalm
of David. A song.

1 May God rise up and scatter his
      enemies.
  May they turn and run away from
      him.
2 As wind blows smoke away,
      so may God blow them away.
  As fire melts wax,
      so may he destroy sinful people.
3 But may those who do what is right be
      glad
  and filled with joy when they are
      with him.
  May they be happy and joyful.

4 Sing to God. Sing praise to his name.
  Lift up a song to the One who rides
      on the clouds.
  His name is the LORD.
  Be glad when you are with him.
5 God is in his holy temple.
  He is a father to those whose fathers
      have died.
  He takes care of women whose
      husbands have died.
6 God gives lonely people a family.
  He sets prisoners free, and they go
      out singing.

But those who refuse to obey him
  live in a land that is baked by the
      sun.

7 God, you led your people out.
  You marched through a dry and
      empty land.   *Selah*
8 The ground shook
  when you, the God of Sinai,
      appeared.
  The heavens poured down rain
  when you, the God of Israel,
      appeared.
9 God, you gave us plenty of rain.
  You renewed your worn-out land.
10 God, your people settled in it.
  From all of your riches, you provided
      for those who were poor.

11 The Lord gave a message.
  Many people made it widely known.
12 They said, "Kings and armies are
      running away.
  In the camps, Israel's soldiers are
      dividing up
  the things they have taken from
      their enemies.
13 Even while the soldiers sleep near the
      campfires,
  God wins the battle for them.
  He gives the enemy's silver and gold
  to Israel, his dove."
14 The Mighty One has scattered the
      kings around the land.
  It was like snow falling on Mount
      Zalmon.

15 The mountains of Bashan are majestic.
  The mountains of Bashan are very
      rocky.
16 You rocky mountains are jealous of
      Mount Zion, aren't you?
  That's where God chooses to rule.
  That's where the LORD himself will
      live forever.
17 God has come with tens of thousands
      of his chariots.
  He has come with thousands and
      thousands of them.
  The Lord has come from Mount Sinai.
  He has entered his holy place.
18 When he went up to his place on high,
  he led a line of prisoners.
  He received gifts from people,
      even from those who refused to
      obey him.
  The LORD God went up to live on
      Mount Zion.

19 Give praise to the Lord. Give praise to
      God our Savior.
  He carries our heavy loads day
      after day.   *Selah*

20 Our God is a God who saves.
He is the King and the Lord. He
saves us from death.
21 God will certainly smash the heads of
his enemies.
He will break the hairy heads of
those who keep on sinning.
22 The Lord says, "I will bring your
enemies from Bashan.
I will bring them up from the
bottom of the sea.
23 Then your feet can wade in their
blood.
The tongues of your dogs can lick up
all the blood they want."

24 God, those who worship you come
marching into view.
My God and King, those who follow
you have entered the sacred
tent.
25 The singers are walking in front.
Next come those who play the
music.
Young women playing tambourines
are with them.
26 The leaders sing, "Praise God among
all those who worship him.
Praise the Lord in the community of
Israel."
27 The little tribe of Benjamin leads the
worshipers.
Next comes the great crowd of
Judah's princes.
Then come the princes of Zebulun
and the princes of Naphtali.

28 God, show us your power.
Show us your strength.
God, do as you have done before.
29 Do it from your temple at Jerusalem,
where kings will bring you gifts.
30 Give a strong warning to Egypt, that
beast among the tall grass.
Warn the leaders of the nations,
who are like bulls among the
calves.
May they bow down before you with
gifts of silver.
Scatter the nations who like to make
war.
31 Messengers will come from Egypt.
The people of Cush will be quick to
bring gifts to you.

32 Sing to God, you kingdoms of the
earth.
Sing praise to the Lord.   *Selah*
33 He rides in the age-old skies above.
He thunders with his mighty voice.
34 Tell how powerful God is.
He rules as king over Israel.

POWER / SURGE

STRONG

HOW WONDERFUL IS GOD IN HIS HOLY PLACE!

THE GOD OF ISRAEL GIVES POWER AND STRENGTH TO HIS PEOPLE.

GIVE PRAISE TO GOD!
— **PSALM 68:35** —

The skies show how powerful he is.
35 How wonderful is God in his holy
place!
The God of Israel gives power and
strength to his people.

Give praise to God!

Psalm 69

For the director of music. A psalm
of David to the tune of "Lilies."
1 God, save me.
My troubles are like a flood.
I'm up to my neck in them.
2 I'm sinking in deep mud.
I have no firm place to stand.
I am out in deep water.
The waves roll over me.
3 I'm worn out from calling for help.
My throat is very dry.
My eyes grow tired
looking for my God.
4 Those who hate me without any reason
are more than the hairs on my head.
Many people who don't have any
reason to be my enemies
are trying to destroy me.
They force me to give back
what I didn't steal.

5 God, you know how foolish I've been.
My guilt is not hidden from you.

6 Lord, you are the Lord who rules over
all.
May those who put their hope in
you not be dishonored because
of me.
You are the God of Israel.
May those who worship you not be
put to shame because of me.
7 Because of you, people laugh at me.

My face is covered with shame.
⁸ I'm a stranger to my brothers.
I'm an outsider to my own mother's
sons.
⁹ My great love for your house destroys
me.
Those who make fun of you make
fun of me also.
¹⁰ When I sob and go without eating,
they laugh at me.
¹¹ When I put on black clothes to show
how sad I am,
people make jokes about me.
¹² Those who gather in public places
make fun of me.
Those who get drunk make up songs
about me.

¹³ But LORD, I pray to you.
May this be the time you show me
your favor.
God, answer me because you love me
so much.
Save me, as you always do.
¹⁴ Save me from the trouble I'm in.
It's like slippery mud. Don't let me
sink in it.
Save me from those who hate me.
Save me from the deep water I'm in.
¹⁵ Don't let the floods cover me.
Don't let the deep water swallow
me up.
Don't let the grave close its mouth
over me.
¹⁶ LORD, answer me because your love is
so good.
Turn to me because you are so kind.
¹⁷ Don't turn your face away from me.
Answer me quickly. I'm in trouble.
¹⁸ Come near and save me.
Set me free from my enemies.

¹⁹ You know how they make fun of me.
They dishonor me and put me to
shame.
You know all about my enemies.
²⁰ They have broken my heart by saying
evil things about me.
It has left me helpless.
I looked for pity, but I didn't find any.
I looked for someone to comfort me,
but I didn't find anyone.
²¹ They put bitter spices in my food.
They gave me vinegar when I was
thirsty.

²² Let their feast be a trap and a snare.
Let my enemies get what's coming
to them.
²³ Let their eyes grow weak so they can't
see.
Let their backs be bent forever.

²⁴ Pour out your anger on them.
Let them feel its burning heat.
²⁵ May their homes be deserted.
May no one live in their tents.
²⁶ They attack those you have wounded.
They talk about the pain of those
you have hurt.
²⁷ Charge them with one crime after
another.
Don't save them.
²⁸ May their names be erased from the
Book of Life.
Don't include them in the list of
those who do right.

²⁹ I'm in pain. I'm in deep trouble.
God, save me and keep me safe.
³⁰ I will praise God's name by singing to
him.
I will bring him glory by giving him
thanks.

POWER–SURGE

THANKFUL ♣

I WILL PRAISE GOD'S NAME BY SINGING TO HIM.

I WILL BRING HIM GLORY BY GIVING HIM THANKS.
— **PSALM 69:30** —

³¹ That will please the LORD more than
offering him an ox.
It will please him more than offering
him a bull with its horns and
hoofs.
³² Poor people will see it and be glad.
The hearts of those who worship
God will be strengthened.
³³ The LORD hears those who are in need.
He doesn't forget his people in
prison.
³⁴ Let heaven and earth praise him.
Let the oceans and everything that
moves in them praise him.
³⁵ God will save Zion.
He will build the cities of Judah
again.
Then people will live in them and own
the land.
³⁶ The children of those who serve
God will receive it.
Those who love him will live there.

Psalm 70

For the director of music. A prayer
of David.

1 God, hurry and save me.
Lord, come quickly and help me.
2 Let those who are trying to kill me be
put to shame.
Let them not be honored.
Let all those who want to destroy me
be turned back in shame.
3 Some people make fun of me.
Let them be turned back when their
plans fail.
4 But let all those who look to you
be joyful and glad because of what
you have done.
Let those who love you because you
save them always say,
"May God be honored!"

5 But I am poor and needy.
God, come quickly to me.
You are the One who helps me and
saves me.
Lord, please don't wait any longer.

Psalm 71

1 Lord, I have gone to you for safety.
Let me never be put to shame.
2 You do what is right. Save me and help
me.
Pay attention to me and save me.
3 Be my rock of safety
that I can always go to.
Give the command to save me.
You are my rock and my fort.
4 My God, save me from the power of
sinners.
Save me from the hands of those
who are mean and evil.

5 You are the King and the Lord. You
have always been my hope.
I have trusted in you ever since I was
young.
6 From the time I was born I have
depended on you.
You brought me out of my mother's
body.
I will praise you forever.
7 To many people I am an example of
how much you care.
You are strong. You are my place of
safety.
8 My mouth is filled with praise for you.
All day long I will talk about your
glory.
9 Don't push me away when I'm old.
Don't desert me when my strength
is gone.

10 My enemies speak against me.
Those who want to kill me get
together and make evil plans.
11 They say, "God has deserted him.
Go after him and grab him.
No one will save him."
12 God, don't stay so far away from me.
My God, come quickly and help me.
13 May those who bring charges against
me die in shame.
May those who want to harm me
be covered with shame and
dishonor.

14 But I will always have hope.
I will praise you more and more.
15 I will say that what you have done is
right.
All day long I will talk about how
you have saved your people.
It is more than I can understand.
16 Lord and King, I will come and
announce your mighty acts.
I will announce that you alone do
what is right.
17 God, ever since I was young you have
taught me about what you have
done.
To this very day I tell about your
wonderful acts.
18 God, don't leave me
even when I'm old and have gray
hair.
Let me live to tell my children about
your power.
Let me tell all of them about your
mighty acts.

19 God, your saving acts reach to the
skies.
You have done great things.
God, who is like you?
20 You have sent many bitter troubles my
way.
But you will give me new life.
Even if I'm almost in the grave,
you will bring me back.
21 You will honor me more and more.
You will comfort me once again.

22 My God, I will use the harp to praise
you
because you are always faithful.
Holy One of Israel,
I will use the lyre to sing praise to
you.
23 My lips will shout with joy
when I sing praise to you.
You have saved me.
24 All day long my tongue will say
that you have done what is right.

Those who wanted to harm me have
    been put to shame.
They have not been honored.

Psalm 72

A psalm of Solomon.
1 God, give the king the ability to judge
    fairly.
He is your royal son. Help him to do
    what is right.
2 Then he will rule your people in the
    right way.
He will be fair to those among your
    people who are hurting.
3 The mountains and the hills will
    produce rich crops,
because the people will do what is
    right.
4 The king will stand up for those who
    are hurting.
He will save the children of those
    who are in need.
He will crush those who beat others
    down.

5 He will rule as long as the sun shines
    and the moon gives its light.
He will rule for all time to come.
6 He will be like rain falling on the fields.
He will be like showers watering the
    earth.
7 Godly people will do well as long as he
    rules.
They will have more than they need
    as long as the moon lasts.

8 He will rule from ocean to ocean.
His kingdom will reach from the
    Euphrates River to the ends of
    the earth.
9 The desert tribes will bow down to
    him.
His enemies will lick the dust.
10 The kings of Tarshish and of places far
    away
will bring him gifts.
The kings of Sheba and Seba
will give him presents.
11 All kings will bow down to him.
All nations will serve him.

12 People who are in need will cry out,
    and he will save them.
He will save those who are hurting.
They don't have anyone else who
    can help them.
13 He will take pity on those who are
    weak and in need.
He will save them from death.
14 He will save them from people who
    beat others down.

He will save them from people who
    do mean things to them.
Their lives are very special to him.

15 May he live a long time!
May gold from Sheba be given to
    him.
May people always pray for him.
May they ask the Lord to bless him
    all day long.
16 Let there be plenty of grain everywhere
    in the land.
May it sway in the wind on the tops
    of the hills.
Let crops grow well, like those in
    Lebanon.
Let them grow like the grass of the
    field.
17 May the king's name be remembered
    forever.
May his fame last as long as the sun
    shines.

All nations will be blessed because of
    him.
They will call him blessed.

18 Give praise to the Lord God, the God
    of Israel.
Only he can do wonderful things.
19 Give praise to his glorious name
    forever.
May his glory fill the whole earth.
    Amen and Amen.

20 The prayers of David, the son of Jesse,
    end here.

BOOK III

Psalms 73–89

Psalm 73

A psalm of Asaph.
1 God is truly good to Israel.
He is good to those who have pure
    hearts.

2 But my feet had almost slipped.
I had almost tripped and fallen.
3 I saw that proud and sinful people
    were doing well.
And I began to long for what they
    had.

4 They don't have any troubles.
Their bodies are healthy and strong.
5 They don't have the problems others
    have.
They don't suffer as other people do.
6 Their pride is like a necklace.

They put on meanness as if it were
their clothes.
⁷ Many sins come out of their hard and
stubborn hearts.
There is no limit to their proud and
evil thoughts.
⁸ They laugh at others and speak words
of hatred.
They are proud. They warn others
about the harm they can do to
them.
⁹ They brag as if they owned heaven
itself.
They talk as if they controlled the
earth.
¹⁰ So people listen to them.
They lap up their words like water.
¹¹ They say, "How can God know what
we're doing?
Does the Most High God really
know that much?"

¹² Here is what sinful people are like.
They don't have a care in the world.
They keep getting richer and richer.

¹³ It seems as if I have kept my heart pure
without any reason.
It didn't do me any good to wash my
hands
to show that I wasn't guilty of doing
anything wrong.
¹⁴ Day after day I've been in pain.
God has punished me every
morning.

¹⁵ What if I had said, "I will speak as evil
people do"?
Then I wouldn't have been faithful
to God's children.
¹⁶ I tried to understand it all.
But it was more than I could handle.
¹⁷ It troubled me until I entered God's
temple.
Then I understood what will happen
to bad people in the end.

¹⁸ God, I'm sure you will make them slip
and fall.
You will throw them down and
destroy them.
¹⁹ It will happen very suddenly.
A terrible death will take them away
completely.
²⁰ A dream goes away when a person
wakes up.
Lord, it will be like that when you
rise up.
It will be as if those people were only
a dream.

²¹ At one time my heart was sad
and my spirit was bitter.

²² I didn't have any sense. I didn't know
anything.
I acted like a wild animal toward
you.

²³ But I am always with you.
You hold me by my right hand.
²⁴ You give me wise advice to guide me.
And when I die, you will take me
away
into the glory of heaven.
²⁵ I don't have anyone in heaven but you.
I don't want anything on earth
besides you.
²⁶ My body and my heart may grow
weak.
God, you give strength to my heart.
You are everything I will ever need.

STRONG

MY BODY AND MY HEART MAY GROW WEAK.
GOD, YOU GIVE STRENGTH TO MY HEART.
YOU ARE EVERYTHING I WILL EVER NEED.
— **PSALM 73:26** —

²⁷ Those who don't want anything to do
with you will die.
You destroy all those who aren't
faithful to you.
²⁸ But I am close to you. And that's good.
Lᴏʀᴅ and King, I have made you my
place of safety.
I will talk about everything you have
done.

Psalm 74

A *maskil* of Asaph.
¹ God, why have you turned your back
on us for so long?
Why does your anger burn against
us? We are your very own
sheep.
² Remember that you chose us to be
your own people a long time
ago.
Remember that you set us free from
slavery to be your very own
tribe.

Remember Mount Zion, where you
lived.
3 Walk through this place that has been
torn down beyond repair.
See how completely your enemies
have destroyed the temple!

4 In the place where you used to meet
with us,
your enemies have shouted, "We've
won the battle!"
They have set up their flags to show
they have beaten us.
5 They acted like people cutting down a
forest with axes.
6 They smashed all of the beautiful
wooden walls
with their axes and hatchets.
7 They burned your temple to the
ground.
They polluted the place where your
Name is.
8 They had said in their hearts, "We will
crush them completely!"
They burned every place where you
were worshiped in the land.
9 You don't give us miraculous signs
anymore.
There aren't any prophets left.
None of us knows how long that will
last.

10 God, how long will your enemies make
fun of you?
Will they attack you with their
words forever?
11 Why don't you help us? Why do you
hold back your powerful right
hand?
Use your strong arms to destroy your
enemies!

12 God, you have been my king for a long
time.
The whole earth has seen you save
us over and over again.
13 You parted the Red Sea by your power.
You broke the heads of that sea
monster in Egypt.
14 You crushed the heads of the sea
monster Leviathan.
You fed it to the creatures of the
desert.
15 You opened up streams and springs.
You dried up rivers that flow all year
long.
16 You rule over the day and the night.
You created the sun and the moon.
17 You decided where the borders of the
earth would be.
You made both summer and winter.

18 LORD, remember how your enemies
have made fun of you.
Remember how foolish people have
attacked you with their words.
19 Don't hand Israel, your dove, over to
those wild animals.
Don't forget your suffering people
forever.
20 Honor the covenant you made with us.
Horrible things are happening in
every dark corner of the land.
21 Don't let your suffering people be put
to shame.
May those who are poor and needy
praise you.

22 God, rise up. Stand up for your cause.
Remember how foolish people make
fun of you all day long.
23 Pay close attention to the shouts of
your enemies.
The trouble they cause never stops.

Psalm 75

For the director of music. A psalm
of Asaph. A song to the tune
of "Do Not Destroy."

1 God, we give thanks to you.
We give thanks because your Name
is near.
People talk about the wonderful
things you have done.

2 You say, "I choose the appointed time
to judge people.
And I judge them fairly.
3 When the earth and all of its people
tremble,
I keep everything from falling to
pieces.   Selah
4 To the proud I say, 'Don't brag
anymore.'
To sinners I say, 'Don't show off your
power.
5 Don't show it off against me.
Don't speak with your noses in the
air.' "

6 No one from east or west or north or
south
can act as judge.
7 God is the One who judges.
He says to one person, "You are
guilty."
To another he says, "You are not
guilty."
8 In the hand of the LORD is a cup.
It is full of wine mixed with spices.
It is the wine of his anger.
He pours it out. All of the evil people
on earth
drink it down to the very last drop.

BELIEVES

GOD WILL DESTROY
THE POWER OF ALL
SINFUL PEOPLE.

BUT HE WILL MAKE
GODLY PEOPLE MORE
POWERFUL.
— PSALM 75:10 —

STRONG

9 I will speak about this forever.
   I will sing praise to the God of Jacob.
10 God will destroy the power of all sinful
   people.
   But he will make godly people more
   powerful.

Psalm 76

For the director of music. A psalm of
Asaph. A song to be played on stringed
instruments.
1 In the land of Judah, God is known.
   His name is great in Israel.
2 His tent is in Jerusalem.
   The place where he lives is on
   Mount Zion.
3 There he broke the deadly arrows of his
   enemies.
   He broke their shields and swords.
   He broke their weapons of war. *Selah*

4 God, you shine like a very bright light.
   You are more majestic than
   mountains full of wild animals.
5 Brave soldiers have been robbed of
   everything they had.
   Now they lie there, sleeping in
   death.
   Not one of them can even lift his
   hands.
6 God of Jacob, at your command
   both horse and chariot lie still.
7 People should have respect for you
   alone.
   Who can stand in front of you when
   you are angry?
8 From heaven you handed down your
   sentence.
   The land was afraid and became
   quiet.

9 God, that happened when you rose up
   to judge.
   It happened when you came to save
   all of your suffering people in
   the land.   *Selah*
10 Your anger against sinners brings you
   praise.
   Those who live through your anger
   gather to worship you.
11 Make promises to the LORD your God
   and keep them.
   Let all of the neighboring nations
   bring gifts to the One who should be
   respected.
12 He breaks the proud spirit of rulers.
   The kings of the earth have respect
   for him.

Psalm 77

For the director of music. For Jeduthun.
A psalm of Asaph.
1 I cried out to God for help.
   I cried out to God to hear me.
2 When I was in trouble, I looked to the
   Lord.
   During the night I lifted up my
   hands in prayer.
   But I refused to be comforted.

3 God, I remembered you, and I
   groaned.
   I thought about you, and I became
   weak.   *Selah*
4 You kept me from going to sleep.
   I was so troubled I couldn't speak.
5 I thought about days gone by.
   I thought about the years of long
   ago.
6 I remembered how I used to sing praise
   to you in the night.
   I thought about it, and here is what I
   asked myself.

7 "Will the Lord turn away from us
   forever?
   Won't he ever show us his kindness
   again?
8 Has his faithful love disappeared
   forever?
   Has his promise failed for all time?
9 Has God forgotten to show us his
   favor?
   Has he held back his tender love
   because he was angry?"   *Selah*

10 Then I thought, "Here is what I will
   make my appeal to.
   For many years the Most High God
   showed how powerful his right
   hand is."
11 LORD, I will remember what you did.

Yes, I will remember your miracles of
       long ago.
12 I will spend time thinking about
       everything you have done.
    I will consider all of your mighty
       acts.

13 God, everything you do is holy.
    What god is so great as our God?
14 You are the God who does miracles.
    You show your power among the
       nations.
15 With your mighty arm you set your
       people free.
    You set the children of Jacob and
       Joseph free.   *Selah*

16 God, the water of the Red Sea saw you.
    It saw you and boiled up.
    The deepest waters were stirred up.
17 The clouds poured down rain.
    The skies rumbled with thunder.
    Lightning flashed back and forth
       like arrows.
18 Your thunder was heard in the
       windstorm.
    Your lightning lit up the world.
    The earth trembled and shook.
19 Your path led through the Red Sea
    You walked through the mighty
       waters.
    But your footprints were not seen.

20 You led your people like a flock.
    You led them by the hands of Moses
       and Aaron.

Psalm 78

A maskil of Asaph.
1 My people, listen to my teaching.
    Pay attention to what I say.
2 I will open my mouth and tell stories.
    I will speak about things that were
       hidden.
    They happened a long time ago.
3 We have heard about them and we
       know them.
    Our people who lived before us have
       told us about them.
4 We won't hide them from our
       children.
    We will tell them to those who live
       after us.
    We will tell them about what the LORD
       has done that is worthy of
       praise.
    We will talk about his power and the
       wonderful things he has done.
5 He gave laws to the people of Jacob.
    He gave Israel their law.
    He commanded our people who lived
       before us

to teach his laws to their children.
6 Then those born later would know his
       laws.
    Even their children yet to come
       would know them.
    And they in turn would tell their
       children.
7 Then they would put their trust in
       God.
    They would not forget what he had
       done.
    They would obey his commands.
8 They would not be like their people
       who lived before them.
    Those people were stubborn. They
       refused to obey God.
    Their hearts were not true to him.
    Their spirits were not faithful to
       him.

9 The soldiers of Ephraim were armed
       with bows.
    But they ran away on the day of
       battle.
10 They didn't keep the covenant God
       had made with them.
    They refused to live by his law.
11 They forgot what he had done.
    They didn't remember the wonders
       he had shown them.
12 He did miracles right in front of our
       people who lived long ago.
    At that time they were living in the
       land of Egypt, in the area of
       Zoan.
13 God parted the Red Sea and led them
       through it.
    He made the water stand up like a
       wall.
14 He guided them with the cloud during
       the day.
    He led them with the light of a fire
       all night long.
15 He broke the rocks open in the desert.
    He gave them as much water as
       there is in the oceans.
16 He brought streams out of a rocky cliff.
    He made water flow down like rivers.

17 But they continued to sin against him.
    In the desert they refused to obey
       the Most High God.
18 They were stubborn and put God to
       the test.
    They ordered him to give them the
       food they longed for.
19 They spoke against God. They said,
    "Can God put food on a table in the
       desert?
20 When he struck the rock, streams of
       water poured out.

Huge amounts of water flowed
  down.
But can he also give us food?
  Can he supply meat for his people?"
²¹ When the Lᴏʀᴅ heard what they said,
    he was very angry.
  His anger broke out like fire against
    the people of Jacob.
  He became very angry with Israel.
²² That was because they didn't believe in
    God.
  They didn't trust in his power to
    save them.
²³ But he gave a command to the skies
    above.
  He opened the doors of the heavens.
²⁴ He rained down manna for the people
    to eat.
  He gave them the grain of heaven.
²⁵ Mere men ate the bread of angels.
  He sent them all of the food they
    could eat.
²⁶ He made the east wind blow from the
    heavens.
  By his power he caused the south
    wind to blow.
²⁷ He rained meat down on them like
    dust.
  He sent them birds like sand on the
    seashore.
²⁸ He made the birds come down inside
    their camp.
  The birds fell all around their tents.
²⁹ People ate until they had more than
    enough.
  He gave them what they had longed
    for.
³⁰ But even before they had finished
    eating, God acted.
  He did it while the food was still in
    their mouths.
³¹ His anger rose up against them.
  He put to death the strongest among
    them.
  He struck down Israel's young men.

³² But even after all that, they kept on
    sinning.
  Even after they had seen the
    miracles he did, they still didn't
    believe.
³³ So he brought their days to an end like
    a puff of smoke.
  He ended their years with terror.
³⁴ Every time God killed some of them,
    the others would look to him.
  They gladly turned back to him
    again.
³⁵ They remembered that God was their
    Rock.

They remembered that God Most
  High had set them free.
³⁶ But they didn't mean it when they
    praised him.
  They lied to him when they spoke.
³⁷ Their hearts were not true to him.
  They weren't faithful to the
    covenant he had made with
    them.
³⁸ But he was full of tender love.
  He forgave their sins
  and didn't destroy his people.
Time after time he held back his anger.
  He didn't let all of his burning anger
    blaze out.

POWER-SURGE

FORGIVING F

[GOD] WAS FULL OF TENDER LOVE.

HE FORGAVE THEIR SINS.

— PSALM 78:38 —

LOVING

³⁹ He remembered that they were only
    human.
  He remembered they were only a
    breath of air
  that drifts by and doesn't return.
⁴⁰ How often they refused to obey him in
    the desert!
  How often they caused him sorrow
    in that dry and empty land!
⁴¹ Again and again they put God to the
    test.
  They made the Holy One of Israel
    sad and angry.
⁴² They didn't remember his power.
  They forgot the day he set them free
    from those who had beaten them
    down.
⁴³ They forgot how he had shown them
    his miraculous signs in Egypt.
  They forgot his miracles in the area
    of Zoan.
⁴⁴ He turned the rivers of Egypt into
    blood.
  The people of Egypt couldn't drink
    water from their streams.
⁴⁵ He sent large numbers of flies that bit
    them.

He sent frogs that destroyed their
land.
46 He gave their crops to the
grasshoppers.
He gave their food to the locusts.
47 He destroyed their vines with hail.
He destroyed their fig trees with
sleet.
48 He killed their cattle with hail.
Their livestock were struck by
lightning.
49 He brought great trouble on Egypt by
pouring out his blazing anger.
In his hot anger he sent destroying
angels against them.
50 God prepared a path for his anger.
He didn't spare their lives.
He gave them over to the plague.
51 He killed the oldest son of each family
in Egypt.
He struck down the oldest son in
every house in the land of Ham.
52 But he brought his people out like a
flock.
He led them like sheep through the
desert.
53 He guided them safely, and they
weren't afraid.
But the Red Sea swallowed up their
enemies.
54 He brought his people to the border of
his holy land.
He led them to the central hill
country he had taken by his
power.
55 He drove the nations out to make
room for his people.
He gave to each family a piece of
land to pass on to their
children.
He settled the tribes of Israel in their
homes.
56 But they put God to the test.
They refused to obey the Most High
God.
They didn't keep his laws.
57 Like their people who lived before
them,
they turned away from him and
were not faithful.
They were like a bow that doesn't
shoot straight.
They couldn't be trusted.
58 They made God angry by going to
their high places.
They made him jealous by
worshiping the statues of their
gods.
59 When God saw what the people were
doing, he was very angry.

He turned away from them
completely.
60 He deserted the holy tent at Shiloh.
He left the tent he had set up among
his people.
61 He allowed the ark to be captured.
Into the hands of his enemies he
sent the ark where his glory
rested.
62 He let his people be killed with swords.
He was very angry with them.
63 Fire destroyed their young men.
Their young women had no one to
get married to.
64 Their priests were killed with swords.
Their widows weren't able to cry.
65 Then the Lord woke up as if he had
been sleeping.
He was like a man waking up from
the deep sleep caused by wine.
66 He drove his enemies back.
He put them to shame that will last
forever.
67 He turned his back on the tents of the
people of Joseph.
He didn't choose to live in the tribe
of Ephraim.
68 Instead, he chose to live in the tribe of
Judah.
He chose Mount Zion, which he
loved.
69 There he built his holy place as secure
as the heavens.
He built it to last forever, like the
earth.
70 He chose his servant David.
He took him from the sheep pens.
71 He brought him from tending sheep
to be the shepherd of his people
Jacob.
He made him the shepherd of Israel,
his special people.
72 David cared for them with a faithful
and honest heart.
With skilled hands he led them.

Psalm 79

A psalm of Asaph.
1 God, an army from the nations has
attacked your land.
They have polluted your holy
temple.
They have completely destroyed
Jerusalem.
2 They have given the dead bodies of
your people
as food to the birds of the air.
They have given the bodies of your
faithful people
to the animals of the earth.

3 They have poured out the blood of
your people like water
all around Jerusalem.
No one is left to bury the dead.
4 We are something our neighbors joke
about.
The nations around us laugh at us
and make fun of us.

5 LORD, how long will you be angry with
us? Will it be forever?
How long will your jealousy burn
like fire?
6 Pour out your burning anger on the
nations
that don't pay any attention to you.
Pour it out on the kingdoms
that don't worship you.
7 They have swallowed up the people of
Jacob.
They have destroyed Israel's
homeland.
8 Don't hold against us the sins of our
people who lived before us.
May you be quick to show us your
tender love.
We are in great need.

9 God our Savior, help us.
Then glory will come to you.
Be true to your name.
Save us and forgive our sins.
10 Why should the nations say,
"Where is their God?"
Show the nations that you punish
those who kill your people.
We want to see it happen.
11 Listen to the groans of the prisoners.
Use your powerful arm
to save the lives of those who have
been sentenced to death.

12 Lord, our neighbors have laughed at
you.
Pay them back seven times for what
they have done.
13 We are your people. We are your very
own sheep.
We will praise you forever.
For all time to come
we will keep on praising you.

Psalm 80

For the director of music. A psalm
of Asaph to the tune of "The Lilies
of the Covenant."
1 Shepherd of Israel, hear us.
You lead the people of Joseph like a
flock.
You sit on your throne between the
cherubim.
Show your glory

2 to the people of Ephraim, Benjamin
and Manasseh.
Call your strength into action.
Come and save us.

3 God, make us new again.
Let your face smile on us with favor.
Then we will be saved.

4 LORD God who rules over all,
how long will your anger burn
against the prayers of your people?
5 You have given us tears as our food.
You have made us drink tears by the
bowlful.
6 You have let our neighbors fight
against us.
Our enemies laugh at us.

7 God who rules over all, make us new
again.
Let your face smile on us with favor.
Then we will be saved.

8 You brought Israel out of Egypt.
Israel was like a vine.
After you drove the nations out of
Canaan,
you planted the vine in their land.
9 You prepared the ground for it.
It took root and spread out over the
whole land.
10 The mountains were covered with its
shade.
The shade of its branches covered
the mighty cedar trees.
11 Your vine sent its branches out all the
way to the Mediterranean Sea.
They reached as far as the Euphrates
River.

12 Why have you broken down the walls
around your vine?
Now all who pass by it can pick its
grapes.
13 Wild pigs from the forest destroy it.
The creatures of the field feed on it.
14 God who rules over all, return to us!
Look down from heaven and see us!
Watch over your vine.
15 Guard the root you have planted
with your powerful right hand.
Take care of the branch you have
raised up for yourself.

16 Your vine has been cut down. Fire has
burned it up.
You have been angry with us, and
we are dying.
17 May you honor the people at your
right hand.
May you honor the nation you have
raised up for yourself.
18 Then we won't turn away from you.

Give us new life. We will worship
you.
19 LORD God who rules over all, make us
new again.
Let your face smile on us with favor.
Then we will be saved.

POWER-SURGE

CHEERFUL

SING JOYFULLY TO GOD! HE GIVES US STRENGTH.
— **PSALM 81:1** —

STRONG

Psalm 81

For the director of music. For *gittith*.
A psalm of Asaph.
1 Sing joyfully to God! He gives us
strength.
Give a loud shout to the God of
Jacob!
2 Let the music begin. Play the
tambourines.
Play sweet music on harps and lyres.
3 Blow the ram's horn on the day of the
New Moon Feast.
Blow it again when the moon is full
and the Feast of Booths begins.
4 This is an order given to Israel.
It is a law of the God of Jacob.
5 He gave it as a covenant law for the
people of Joseph
when God went out to punish
Egypt.
There we heard a language we didn't
understand.
6 God said, "I removed the load from
your shoulders.
I set your hands free from carrying
heavy baskets.
7 You called out when you were in
trouble, and I saved you.
I answered you out of a
thundercloud.
I put you to the test at the waters of
Meribah.   *Selah*
8 "My people, listen and I will warn you.
Israel, I wish you would listen to me!
9 Don't have anything to do with the
gods of other nations.

Don't bow down and worship
strange gods.
10 I am the LORD your God.
I brought you up out of Egypt.
Open your mouth wide, and I will
fill it with good things.
11 "But my people wouldn't listen to me.
Israel wouldn't obey me.
12 So I let them go their own stubborn
way.
I let them follow their own sinful
plans.
13 "I wish my people would listen to me!
I wish Israel would live as I want
them to live!
14 Then I would quickly bring their
enemies under control.
I would use my power against their
attackers.
15 Those who hate me would bow down
to me in fear.
They would be punished forever.
16 But you would be fed with the finest
wheat.
I would satisfy you with the sweetest
honey."

Psalm 82

A psalm of Asaph.
1 God takes his place at the head of a
large gathering of rulers and
judges.
He announces his decisions among
them.
2 He says, "How long will you stand up
for those who aren't fair to
others?
How long will you show favor to
sinful people?   *Selah*
3 Stand up for those who are weak and
for those whose fathers have
died.
See to it that those who are poor and
those who are beaten down are
treated fairly.
4 Save the weak and those who are in
need.
Save them from the power of sinful
people.
5 "You rulers and judges don't know
anything.
You don't understand anything.
You are in the dark about what is right.
Law and order have been destroyed
all over the world.
6 "I said, 'Rulers and judges, you are
"gods."

You are all children of the Most High
God.'
7 But you will die, just like everyone else.
You will die like every other ruler."

8 God, rise up. Judge the earth.
All of the nations belong to you.

Psalm 83

A song. A psalm of Asaph.
1 God, don't keep silent.
God, don't keep quiet. Don't be still.
2 See how your enemies are getting
ready for action.
See how they are rising up against
you.
3 They make clever plans against your
people.
They make evil plans against those
you love.
4 "Come," they say. "Let's destroy that
whole nation.
Then the name of Israel won't be
remembered anymore."

5 All of them agree on the evil plans
they have made.
They join forces against you.
6 Their forces include the people of
Edom,
Ishmael, Moab and Hagar.
7 They also include the people of Byblos,
Ammon, Amalek,
Philistia and Tyre.
8 Even Assyria has joined them
to give strength to the people of
Moab and Ammon.   *Selah*

9 Do to them what you did to the people
of Midian.
Do to them what you did to Sisera
and Jabin at the Kishon River.
10 Sisera and Jabin died near the town of
Endor.
Their bodies were left to rot on the
ground.
11 Do to the nobles of your enemies what
you did to Oreb and Zeeb.
Do to all of their princes what you
did to Zebah and Zalmunna.
12 They said, "Let's take over
the grasslands that belong to God."

13 My God, make them like straw that the
wind blows away.
Make them like tumbleweed.
14 Destroy them as fire burns up a forest.
Destroy them as a flame sets
mountains on fire.
15 Chase them with your mighty winds.
Terrify them with your storm.
16 LORD, put them to shame

so that people will worship you.
17 May they always be filled with terror
and shame.
May they die in dishonor.
18 Your name is the LORD. Let them know
that you alone are the Most High
God over the whole earth.

Psalm 84

For the director of music. For *gittith*.
A psalm of the Sons of Korah.
1 LORD who rules over all,
how lovely is the place where you
live!
2 I long to be in the courtyards of the
LORD's temple.
I deeply long to be there.
My whole being cries out
for the living God.

3 LORD who rules over all,
even the sparrow has found a home
near your altar.
My King and my God,
the swallow also has a nest there,
where she may have her young.
4 Blessed are those who live in your
house.
They are always praising you.   *Selah*

5 Blessed are those whose strength
comes from you.
They have decided to travel to your
temple.

POWER SURGE

STRONG

BLESSED ARE THOSE WHOSE STRENGTH COMES FROM YOU.
— **PSALM 84:5** —

6 As they pass through the dry Valley of
Baca,
they make it a place where water
flows.
The rain in the fall covers it with
pools.
7 Those people get stronger as they go
along,
until each of them appears in Zion,
where God lives.

8 LORD God who rules over all, hear my
prayer.
God of the people of Jacob, listen to
me.   *Selah*

POWER-SURGE

FORGIVES **F**

YOU FORGAVE THE EVIL THINGS YOUR PEOPLE DID.

YOU TOOK AWAY ALL OF THEIR SINS.

— **PSALM 85:2** —

⁹ God, look with favor on your anointed king.
    You appointed him to be like a
        shield that keeps us safe.
¹⁰ A single day in your courtyards is better
        than a thousand anywhere else.
    I would rather guard the door of the
        house of my God
    than live in the tents of sinful
        people.
¹¹ The LORD God is like the sun that gives
        us light.
    He is like a shield that keeps us safe.
    The LORD blesses us with favor and
        honor.
    He doesn't hold back anything good
        from those whose lives are without
        blame.
¹² LORD who rules over all,
    blessed is everyone who trusts in
        you.

Psalm 85

For the director of music. A psalm of the
    Sons of Korah.
¹ LORD, you showed favor to your land.
    You blessed the people of Jacob with
        great success again.
² You forgave the evil things your people
        did.
    You took away all of their sins. *Selah*
³ You stopped being angry with them.
    You turned your burning anger away
        from them.
⁴ God our Savior, make us new again.
    Stop being unhappy with us.
⁵ Will you be angry with us forever?
    Will you be angry for all time to
        come?
⁶ Won't you give us new life again?
    Then we'll be joyful because of what
        you have done.
⁷ LORD, show us your faithful love.
    Save us.

⁸ I will listen to what God the LORD will
        say.
    He promises peace to his faithful
        people.
    But they must not return to their
        foolish ways.
⁹ I know he's ready to save those who
        have respect for him.
    Then his glory can be seen in our
        land.
¹⁰ God's truth and faithful love join
        together.
    His peace and holiness kiss each
        other.
¹¹ His truth springs up from the earth.
    His holiness looks down from
        heaven.
¹² The LORD will certainly give what is
        good.
    Our land will produce its crops.
¹³ God's holiness leads the way in front
        of him.
    It prepares the way for his coming.

Psalm 86

A prayer of David.
¹ LORD, hear me and answer me.
    I am poor and needy.
² Keep my life safe. I am faithful to you.
    You are my God. Save me.
    I trust in you.
³ Lord, show me your favor.
    I call out to you all day long.
⁴ Bring joy to me.
    Lord, I worship you.
⁵ Lord, you are good. You are forgiving.
    You are full of love for all who call
        out to you.
⁶ LORD, hear my prayer.
    Listen to my cry for your favor.

POWER-SURGE

FAITHFUL ()

KEEP MY LIFE SAFE.
I AM FAITHFUL TO YOU.

YOU ARE MY GOD.
SAVE ME.

I TRUST IN YOU.
— **PSALM 86:2** —

TRUSTED

7 When I'm in trouble, I will call out to
you.
And you will answer me.

8 Lord, there's no one like you among
the gods.
No one can do what you do.
9 Lord, all of the nations you have made
will come and worship you.
They will bring glory to you.
10 You are great. You do wonderful
things.
You alone are God.

11 Lord, teach me how you want me to
live.
Then I will follow your truth.
Give me a heart that doesn't want
anything
more than to worship you.
12 Lord my God, I will praise you with all
my heart.
I will bring glory to you forever.
13 Great is your love for me.
You have kept me from going down
into the grave.

14 God, proud people are attacking me.
A gang of mean people is trying to
kill me.
They don't care about you.
15 But Lord, you are a God who is tender
and kind.
You are gracious.
You are slow to get angry.
You are faithful and full of love.
16 Turn to me and show me your favor.
Give me strength and save me.
17 Prove your goodness to me.
Then my enemies will see it and be
put to shame.
Lord, you have helped me and given
me comfort.

Psalm 87

A psalm of the Sons of Korah. A song.
1 The Lord has built his city
on the holy mountain.
2 He loves the city of Zion
more than all of the other places
where the people of Jacob live.
3 City of God,
the Lord says glorious things about
you.   *Selah*
4 He says, "I will include Egypt and
Babylon
in a list of those who recognize me
as king.
I will also include Philistia and Tyre,
along with Cush.
I will say about them, 'They were
born in Zion.' "

5 Certainly it will be said about Zion,
"This nation and that nation were
born in her.
The Most High God himself will
make her secure."
6 Here is what the Lord will write in his
list of the nations.
"Each of them was born in Zion."
Selah
7 As they make music they will sing,
"Zion, all of our blessings come from
you."

Psalm 88

For the director of music. For *mahalath
leannoth.* A song. A psalm of the Sons of
Korah. A *maskil* of Heman the Ezrahite.
1 Lord, you are the God who saves me.
Day and night I cry out to you.
2 Please hear my prayer.
Pay attention to my cry for help.

3 I have so many troubles
I'm about to die.
4 People think my life is over.
I'm like someone who doesn't have
any strength.
5 People treat me as if I were dead.
I'm like those who have been killed
and are now in the grave.
You don't even remember them
anymore.
They are cut off from your care.

6 It seems as if you have put me deep
down in the grave,
that deep and dark place.
7 Your burning anger lies heavy on me.
All the waves of your anger have
crashed over me.   *Selah*
8 You have taken my closest friends away
from me.
You have made me sickening to
them.
I feel trapped. I can't escape.
9   I'm crying so much I can't see very
well.

Lord, I call out to you every day.
I lift up my hands to you in prayer.
10 Do you work miracles for those who
are dead?
Do dead people rise up and praise
you?   *Selah*
11 Do those who are dead speak about
your love?
Do those who are in the grave tell
how faithful you are?
12 Are your miracles known in that dark
place?

Are your holy acts known in that
land where the dead are
forgotten?

13 LORD, I cry out to you for help.
In the morning I pray to you.
14 LORD, why do you say no to me?
Why do you turn your face away
from me?
15 I've been in pain ever since I was
young.
I've been close to death.
You have made me suffer terrible
things.
I have lost all hope.
16 Your burning anger has swept over me.
Your terrors have destroyed me.
17 All day long they surround me like a
flood.
They have closed in all around me.
18 You have taken my companions and
loved ones away from me.
The darkness is my closest friend.

Psalm 89

A *maskil* of Ethan the Ezrahite.

1 LORD, I will sing about your great love
forever.
For all time to come, I will tell how
faithful you are.
2 I will tell everyone that your love
stands firm forever.
I will tell them that you are always
faithful, even in heaven itself.

3 You said, "Here is the covenant I have
made with my chosen one.
Here is the promise I have made to
my servant David.
4 'I will make your family line continue
forever.
I will make your kingdom secure for
all time to come.' "   *Selah*

5 LORD, the heavens praise you for your
miracles.
When your holy angels gather
together,
they praise you for how faithful you
are.
6 Who in the skies above can compare
with the LORD?
Who among the angels is like the
LORD?
7 God is highly respected among his
holy angels.
He's more wonderful than all those
who are around him.
8 LORD God who rules over all, who is
like you?

LORD, you are mighty. You are
faithful in everything you do.
9 You rule over the stormy sea.
When its waves rise up, you calm
them down.
10 You crushed Egypt and killed her
people.
With your powerful arm you
scattered your enemies.
11 The heavens belong to you. The earth
is yours also.
You made the world and everything
that is in it.
12 You created everything from north to
south.
Mount Tabor and Mount Hermon
sing to you with joy.
13 Your arm is powerful.
Your hand is strong.
Your right hand is mighty.

14 Your kingdom is built on what is right
and fair.
Your truth and faithful love lead the
way in front of you.
15 Blessed are those who have learned to
shout praise to you.
LORD, they live in the light of your
favor.
16 All day long they are full of joy because
of who you are.
They praise you because you do
what is right.
17 You are their glory. You give them
strength.
You favor them by honoring our
king.
18 Our king is like a shield that keeps us
safe.
He belongs to the LORD.
He belongs to the Holy One of Israel.

19 You once spoke to your faithful people
in a vision.
You said, "I have given strength to a
soldier.
I have raised up a young man from
among the people.
20 I have found my servant David.
I have poured my sacred oil on his
head.
21 My powerful hand will keep him
going.
My mighty arm will give him
strength.
22 No enemies will require him to bring
gifts to them.
No evil person will beat him down.
23 I will crush the king's enemies.
I will completely destroy them.
24 I will love him and be faithful to him.

POWER-SURGE

STRONG

[GOD] SAID, "I HAVE GIVEN STRENGTH TO A SOLDIER.

I HAVE RAISED UP A YOUNG MAN FROM AMONG THE PEOPLE.

I HAVE FOUND MY SERVANT DAVID.

I HAVE POURED MY SACRED OIL ON HIS HEAD.

MY POWERFUL HAND WILL KEEP HIM GOING.

MY MIGHTY ARM WILL GIVE HIM STRENGTH.

— PSALM 89:19-21 —

Because of me his power will increase.

25 I will give him a great kingdom.
It will reach from the Mediterranean Sea to the Euphrates River.

26 He will call out to me, 'You are my Father.
You are my God. You are my Rock and Savior.'

27 I will also make him my oldest son.
Among all the kings of the earth, he will be the most important one.

28 I will continue to love him forever.
I will never break my covenant with him.

29 I will make his family line continue forever.
His kingdom will last as long as the heavens.

30 "What if his sons turn away from my laws
and do not follow them?

31 What if they disobey my orders
and fail to keep my commands?

32 Then I will punish them for their sins.
I will strike them with the rod.
I will whip them for their evil acts.

33 But I will not stop loving David.
I will always be faithful to him.

34 I will not break my covenant.

I will not go back on my word.

35 Once and for all, I have made a promise with an oath.
It is based on my holiness.
And I will not lie to David.

36 His family line will continue forever.
His kingdom will last as long as the sun.

37 It will last forever like the moon,
that faithful witness in the sky."

Selah

38 But you have turned your back on your anointed king.
You have been very angry with him.

39 You have broken the covenant you made with him.
You have thrown your servant's crown into the dirt.

40 You have broken through the walls around his city.
You have completely destroyed his secure places.

41 All those who pass by have carried off what belonged to him.
His neighbors make fun of him.

42 You have made his enemies strong.
You have made all of them happy.

43 You have made his sword useless.
You have not helped him in battle.

44 You have put an end to his glory.
You have knocked his throne to the ground.

45 You have cut short the days of his life.
You have covered him with shame.

Selah

46 Lord, how long will you hide yourself?
Will it be forever?
How long will your anger burn like fire?

47 Remember how short my life is.
You have created all people for such a useless purpose!

48 What man can live and not die?
Who can escape the power of the grave?   *Selah*

49 Lord, where is the great love you used to have?
You faithfully promised it to David.

50 Lord, remember how my enemies have made fun of me.
I've had to put up with mean words from all of the nations.

51 Lord, your enemies have said mean things.
They have laughed at everything your anointed king has done.

52 Give praise to the Lord forever!
Amen and Amen.

BOOK IV

Psalms 90–106

Psalm 90

A prayer of Moses, the man of God.

1 Lord, from the very beginning
you have been like a home to us.
2 Before you created the world and the
mountains were made,
from the beginning to the end you
are God.

3 You turn human beings back to dust.
You say to them, "Return to dust."
4 To you a thousand years
are like a day that has just gone by.
They are like a few hours of the
night.
5 You sweep people away, and they die.
They are like new grass that grows in
the morning.
6 In the morning it springs up new,
but by evening it's all dried up.

7 Your anger destroys us.
Your burning anger terrifies us.
8 You have put our sins right in front of
you.
You have placed our secret sins
where you can see them clearly.
9 You have been angry with us all of our
days.
We groan as we come to the end of
our lives.
10 We live to be about 70.
Or we may live to be 80, if we stay
healthy.
But all that time is filled with trouble
and sorrow.
The years quickly pass, and we are
gone.
11 Who knows how powerful your anger
is?
It's as great as the respect we should
have for you.
12 Teach us to realize how short our lives
are.
Then our hearts will become wise.

13 Lord, please stop punishing us!
How long will you keep it up?
Be kind to us.
14 Satisfy us with your faithful love every
morning.
Then we can sing with joy and be
glad all of our days.
15 Make us glad for as many days as you
have made us suffer.
Give us joy for as many years as
we've had trouble.

16 Show us your mighty acts.
Let our children see your glorious
power.
17 May the Lord our God show us his
favor.
Lord, make what we do succeed.
Please make what we do succeed.

Psalm 91

1 The person who rests in the shadow of
the Most High God
will be kept safe by the Mighty One.
2 I will say about the Lord,
"He is my place of safety.
He is like a fort to me.
He is my God. I trust in him."

3 He will certainly save you from hidden
traps
and from deadly sickness.
4 He will cover you with his wings.
Under the feathers of his wings you
will find safety.
He is faithful. He will keep you safe
like a shield or a tower.
5 You won't have to be afraid of the
terrors that come during the
night.
You won't have to fear the arrows
that come at you during the
day.
6 You won't have to be afraid of the
sickness that attacks in the
darkness.
You won't have to fear the plague
that destroys at noon.
7 A thousand may fall dead at your side.
Ten thousand may fall near your
right hand.
But no harm will come to you.
8 You will see with your own eyes
how God punishes sinful people.

9 The Lord is the one who keeps you safe.
So let the Most High God be like a
home to you.

WISE

TEACH US TO REALIZE
HOW SHORT OUR
LIVES ARE.

THEN OUR HEARTS
WILL BECOME WISE.
— PSALM 90:12 —

10 Then no harm will come to you.
No terrible plague will come near
your tent.
11 The LORD will command his angels
to take good care of you.
12 They will lift you up in their hands.
Then you won't trip over a stone.
13 You will walk all over lions and cobras.
You will crush mighty lions and
poisonous snakes.

14 The LORD says, "I will save the one who
loves me.
I will keep him safe, because he
trusts in me.
15 He will call out to me, and I will answer
him.
I will be with him in times of
trouble.
I will save him and honor him.
16 I will give him a long and full life.
I will save him."

Psalm 92

A psalm. A song for the Sabbath day.
1 LORD, it is good to praise you.
Most High God, it is good to make
music to honor you.
2 It is good to sing every morning about
your love.
It is good to sing every night about
how faithful you are.
3 I sing about it to the music of the lyre
that has ten strings.
I sing about it to the music of the
harp.

4 LORD, you make me glad by what you
have done.
I sing with joy about the works of
your hands.
5 LORD, how great are the things you do!
How wise your thoughts are!
6 Here is something a man who isn't
wise doesn't know.
Here is what a foolish person doesn't
understand.
7 Those who are evil spring up like grass.
Those who do wrong succeed.
But they will be destroyed forever.

8 But LORD, you are honored forever.

9 LORD, your enemies will certainly die.
All those who do evil will be
scattered.
10 You have made me as strong as a wild
ox.
You have poured the finest olive oil
on me.
11 I've seen my evil enemies destroyed.

I've heard that they have lost the
battle.
12 Those who do what is right will grow
like a palm tree.
They will grow strong like a cedar
tree in Lebanon.
13 Their roots will be firm in the house of
the LORD.
They will grow strong and healthy
in the courtyards of our God.
14 When they get old, they will still bear
fruit.
Like young trees they will stay fresh
and strong.
15 They will say to everyone, "The LORD is
honest.
He is my Rock. There is no evil in
him."

Psalm 93

1 The LORD rules.
He puts on majesty as if it were
clothes.
The LORD puts on majesty and
strength.
The world is firmly set in place.
It can't be moved.
2 LORD, you began to rule a long time
ago.
You have always existed.

3 LORD, the seas have lifted up their
voice.
They have lifted up their pounding
waves.
4 But LORD, you are more powerful than
the roar of the ocean.
You are stronger than the waves of
the sea.
LORD, you are powerful in heaven.

5 Your laws do not change.
LORD, your temple will be holy
for all time to come.

Psalm 94

1 LORD, you are the God who punishes.
Since you are the one who punishes,
come and show your anger.
2 Judge of the earth, rise up.
Pay back proud people for what they
have done.
3 LORD, how long will those who are evil
be glad?
How long will they be full of joy?

4 Proud words pour out of their mouths.
All those who do evil are always
bragging.
5 LORD, they crush your people.

They beat down those who belong
to you.
6 They kill outsiders. They kill widows.
They murder children whose fathers
have died.
7 They say, "The Lord doesn't see what's
happening.
The God of Jacob doesn't pay any
attention to it."

8 You who aren't wise, pay attention.
You foolish people, when will you
become wise?
9 Does he who made the ear not hear?
Does he who formed the eye not
see?
10 Does he who corrects nations not
punish?
Does he who teaches human beings
not know anything?
11 The Lord knows what people think.
He knows that their thoughts don't
amount to anything.

12 Lord, blessed is the man you correct.
Blessed is the person you teach from
your law.
13 You give him rest from times of
trouble,
until a pit is dug to trap sinners.
14 The Lord won't say no to his people.
He will never desert those who
belong to him.
15 He will again judge people in keeping
with what is right.
All those who have honest hearts
will follow the right way.

16 Who will rise up for me against sinful
people?
Who will stand up for me against
those who do evil?
17 Suppose the Lord had not helped me.
Then I would soon have been lying
quietly in the grave.
18 I said, "My foot is slipping."
But Lord, your love kept me from
falling.
19 I was very worried.

POWER-SURGE

HONEST ⓗ

ALL THOSE WHO
HAVE HONEST HEARTS
WILL FOLLOW THE
RIGHT WAY.
— PSALM 94:15 —

POWER-SURGE

CHEERFUL ✴

COME, LET US SING
WITH JOY TO THE LORD.

LET US GIVE A LOUD
SHOUT TO THE ROCK
WHO SAVES US.

LET US COME TO HIM
AND GIVE HIM THANKS.

LET US PRAISE HIM
WITH MUSIC AND
SONG.
— PSALM 95:1-2 —

THANKFUL

But your comfort brought joy to my
heart.
20 Can you have anything to do with
rulers who aren't fair?
Can those who make laws that cause
suffering be friends of yours?
21 They join together against those who
do what is right.
They sentence to death those who
aren't guilty of doing anything
wrong.
22 But the Lord has become like a fort to
me.
My God is my rock. I go to him for
safety.
23 He will pay them back for their sins.
He will destroy them for their evil
acts.
The Lord our God will destroy them.

Psalm 95

1 Come, let us sing with joy to the Lord.
Let us give a loud shout to the Rock
who saves us.
2 Let us come to him and give him
thanks.
Let us praise him with music and
song.

3 The Lord is the great God.
He is the greatest King.
He rules over all of the gods.
4 He owns the deepest parts of the earth.
The mountain peaks belong to him.

5 The ocean is his, because he made it.
  He formed the dry land with his
    hands.

6 Come, let us bow down and worship
    him.
  Let us fall on our knees in front of
    the Lord our Maker.
7 He is our God.
  We are the sheep belonging to his
    flock.
  We are the people he takes good
    care of.

Listen to his voice today.
8   If you hear it, don't be stubborn as
      you were at Meribah.
  Don't be stubborn as you were that
    day at Massah in the desert.
9 There your people of long ago really
    put me to the test.
  They did it even though they had
    seen what I had done for them.
10 For 40 years I was angry with them.
  I said, "Their hearts are always going
    down the wrong path.
  They do not know how I want them
    to live."
11 So when I was angry, I took an oath.
  I said, "They will never enjoy the rest
    I planned for them."

Psalm 96

1 Sing a new song to the Lord.
  All you people of the earth, sing to
    the Lord.
2 Sing to the Lord. Praise him.
  Day after day tell about how he saves
    us.
3 Tell the nations about his glory.
  Tell all people about the wonderful
    things he has done.

4 The Lord is great. He is really worthy of
    praise.
  People should have respect for him
    as the greatest God of all.
5 All of the gods of the nations are like
    their statues.
  They can't do anything.
  But the Lord made the heavens.
6 Glory and majesty are all around him.
  Strength and glory can be seen in his
    temple.

7 Praise the Lord, all you nations.
  Praise the Lord for his glory and
    strength.
8 Praise the Lord for the glory that
    belongs to him.
  Bring an offering and come into the
    courtyards of his temple.

9 Worship the Lord because of his
    beauty and holiness.
  All you people of the earth, tremble
    when you are with him.
10 Say to the nations, "The Lord rules."
  The world is firmly set in place. It
    can't be moved.
  The Lord will judge the people of
    the world fairly.
11 Let the heavens be full of joy. Let the
    earth be glad.
  Let the ocean and everything in it
    roar.
12   Let the fields and everything in
      them be glad.
  Then all of the trees in the forest will
    sing with joy.
13   They will sing to the Lord,
  because he is coming to judge the
    earth.
  He will judge the people of the world
    in keeping with what is right and
    true.

Psalm 97

1 The Lord rules. Let the earth be glad.
  Let countries that are far away be full
    of joy.
2 Clouds and thick darkness surround
    him.
  His rule is built on what is right and
    fair.
3 The Lord sends fire ahead of him.
  It burns up his enemies all around
    him.
4 His lightning lights up the world.
  The earth sees it and trembles.
5 The mountains melt like wax when
    the Lord is near.
  He is the Lord of the whole earth.
6 The heavens announce that what he
    does is right.
  All people everywhere see his glory.

7 All who worship statues of gods or brag
    about them are put to shame.
  All you gods, worship the Lord!

8 Zion hears about it and is filled with
    joy.
  Lord, the villages of Judah are glad
    because of how you judge.
9 Lord, you are the Most High God.
  You rule over the whole earth.
  You are honored much more than
    all gods.

10 Let those who love the Lord hate evil.
  He guards the lives of those who are
    faithful to him.

FAITHFUL ()

[GOD] GUARDS THE
LIVES OF THOSE
WHO ARE FAITHFUL
TO HIM ...

THE LIGHT OF HIS
FAVOR SHINES ON
THOSE WHO DO WHAT
IS RIGHT.

JOY COMES TO THOSE
WHOSE HEARTS ARE
HONEST.
— PSALM 97:10-11 —

HONEST

He saves them from the power of
sinful people.
11 The light of his favor shines on those
who do what is right.
Joy comes to those whose hearts are
honest.
12 You who are godly, be glad because of
what the LORD has done.
Praise him, because his name is
holy.

Psalm 98

A psalm.
1 Sing a new song to the LORD.
He has done wonderful things.
By the power of his right hand and his
holy arm
he has saved his people.
2 The LORD has made known his power
to save.
He has shown the nations that he
does what is right.
3 He has shown his faithful love
to the people of Israel.
People from one end of the earth to
the other
have seen that our God has saved us.
4 Shout to the LORD with joy, everyone
on earth.
Burst into joyful songs and make
music.
5 Make music to the LORD with the harp.

Sing and make music with the
harp.
6 Blow the trumpets. Give a blast on the
ram's horn.
Shout to the LORD with joy. He is the
King.

7 Let the ocean and everything in it
roar.
Let the world and all who live in it
shout.
8 Let the rivers clap their hands.
Let the mountains sing together
with joy.
9 Let them sing to the LORD,
because he is coming to judge the
earth.
He will judge the nations of the world
in keeping with what is right and
fair.

Psalm 99

1 The LORD rules.
Let the nations tremble.
He sits on his throne between the
cherubim.
Let the earth shake.
2 Great is the LORD in Zion.
He is honored over all of the
nations.
3 Let them praise his great and
wonderful name.
He is holy.

4 The King is mighty. He loves what is
fair.
He has set up the rules for fairness.
He has done what is right and fair
for the people of Jacob.
5 Honor the LORD our God.
Worship at his feet.
He is holy.

6 Moses and Aaron were two of his
priests.
Samuel was one of those who
worshiped him.
They called out to the LORD.
And he answered them.
7 He spoke to them from the pillar of
cloud.
They obeyed his laws and the orders
he gave them.

8 LORD our God, you answered them.
You showed Israel that you are a God
who forgives.
But when they did wrong, you
punished them.
9 Honor the LORD our God.
Worship at his holy mountain.
The LORD our God is holy.

Psalm 100

A psalm for giving thanks.

1 Shout to the LORD with joy, everyone
　　on earth.
2 　Worship the LORD with gladness.
　　Come to him with songs of joy.
3 I want you to realize that the LORD is
　　God.
　　He made us, and we belong to him.
　We are his people.
　　We are the sheep belonging to his
　　　flock.

4 Give thanks as you enter the gates of
　　his temple.
　　Give praise as you enter its
　　　courtyards.
　　Give thanks to him and praise his
　　　name.
5 The LORD is good. His faithful love
　　continues forever.
　　It will last for all time to come.

Psalm 101

A psalm of David.

1 I will sing about your love and fairness.
　　LORD, I will sing praise to you.
2 I will be careful to lead a life
　　that is without blame.
　　When will you come and help me?

　I will lead a life
　　that is without blame in my house.
3 　I won't look at anything that is evil.

　I hate the acts of people who aren't
　　faithful to you.
　　I don't even want people like that
　　　around me.
4 I will stay away from those whose
　　hearts are twisted.
　　I don't want to have anything to do
　　　with evil.

5 I will get rid of anyone
　　who tells lies about his neighbor in
　　　secret.
　I won't put up with anyone
　　whose eyes and heart are proud.

6 I will look with favor on the faithful
　　people in the land.
　　They will live with me.
　　Those whose lives are without blame
　　　will serve me.

7 No one who lies and cheats
　　will live in my house.
　No one who tells lies
　　will serve me.

8 Every morning I will get rid of
　　all the sinful people in the land.

I will remove from the city of the LORD
　　everyone who does what is evil.

Psalm 102

A prayer of a suffering man when he is
weak and pours out his problems
to the LORD.

1 LORD, hear my prayer.
　　Listen to my cry for help.
2 Don't turn your face away from me
　　when I'm in trouble.
　Pay attention to me.
　　When I call out for help, answer me
　　　quickly.

3 My days are disappearing like smoke.
　　My body burns like glowing coals.
4 My strength has dried up like grass.
　　I even forget to eat my food.
5 I groan out loud because of my
　　suffering.
　　I'm nothing but skin and bones.
6 I'm like a desert owl.
　　I'm like an owl among destroyed
　　　buildings.
7 I can't sleep. I've become
　　like a bird alone on a roof.
8 All day long my enemies laugh at me.
　　Those who make fun of me use my
　　　name as a curse.
9 I eat ashes as my food.
　　My tears fall into what I'm drinking.
10 You were very angry with me.
　　So you picked me up and threw me
　　　away.
11 The days of my life are like an evening
　　shadow.
　　I dry up like grass.

12 But LORD, you are seated on your
　　throne forever.
　　Your fame will continue for all time
　　　to come.
13 You will rise up and show deep
　　concern for Zion.
　　The time has come for you to show
　　　favor to it.
14 The stones of your destroyed city are
　　priceless to us.
　　Even its dust brings deep concern
　　　to us.
15 The nations will worship the LORD.
　　All of the kings on earth will respect
　　　his glorious power.
16 The LORD will build Zion again.
　　He will appear in his glory.
17 He will answer the prayer of those who
　　don't have anything.
　　He won't say no to their cry for help.

18 Let this be written down for those born
　　after us.

Then people who are not yet born
  can praise the LORD.
19 Here is what should be written.
  "The LORD looked down from his
    temple in heaven.
  From heaven he viewed the earth.
20 He heard the groans of the prisoners.
  He set free those who were
    sentenced to death."
21 So people will talk about him in Zion.
  They will praise him in Jerusalem.
22 Nations and kingdoms
  will gather there to worship the
    LORD.

23 When I was still young, he took away
    my strength.
  He wasn't going to let me live much
    longer.
24 So I said, "My God, don't let me die in
    the middle of my life.
  You will live for all time to come.
25 In the beginning you made the earth
    secure.
  You placed it on its foundations.
  Your hands created the heavens.
26 They will pass away. But you will
    remain.
  They will all wear out like a piece of
    clothing.
  You will make them like clothes
    that are taken off and thrown away.
27 But you remain the same.
  Your years will never end.
28 Our children will live with you.
  Their sons and daughters will be safe
    in your care."

Psalm 103

A psalm of David.
1 I will praise the LORD.
  Deep down inside me, I will praise
    him.
  I will praise him, because his name is
    holy.
2 I will praise the LORD.
  I won't forget anything he does for
    me.
3 He forgives all my sins.
  He heals all my sicknesses.
4 He saves my life from going down into
    the grave.
  His faithful and tender love makes
    me feel like a king.
5 He satisfies me with the good things I
    long for.
  Then I feel young and strong again,
    just like an eagle.

6 The LORD does what is right and fair
  for all who are beaten down.

7 He told Moses all about his plans.
  He let the people of Israel see his
    mighty acts.
8 The LORD is tender and kind. He is
    gracious.
  He is slow to get angry. He is full of
    love.
9 He won't keep bringing charges against
    us.
  He won't stay angry with us forever.
10 He doesn't punish us for our sins as
    much as we should be
    punished.
  He doesn't pay us back in keeping
    with the evil things we've done.
11 His love for those who have respect for
    him
  is as high as the heavens are above
    the earth.
12 He has removed our lawless acts from
    us
  as far as the east is from the west.
13 A father is tender and kind to his
    children.
  In the same way, the LORD is tender
    and kind
  to those who have respect for him.
14 He knows what we are made of.
  He remembers that we are dust.
15 People's lives are like grass.
  People grow like the flowers in the
    field.
16 When the wind blows on them, they
    are gone.
  No one can tell that they had ever
    been there.
17 But the LORD's love
  for those who have respect for him
    lasts for ever and ever.
  Their children's children will know
    that he always does what is right.
18 He always loves those who keep his
    covenant.

STRONG

HE SATISFIES ME WITH
THE GOOD THINGS I
LONG FOR.

THEN I FEEL YOUNG
AND STRONG AGAIN,
JUST LIKE AN EAGLE.
— PSALM 103:5 —

He always does what is right for
    those who remember to obey
    his commands.

19 The LORD has set up his throne in
    heaven.
    His kingdom rules over all.

20 Praise the LORD, you angels of his.
    Praise him, you mighty ones
    who carry out his orders and obey
    his word.
21 Praise the LORD, all you angels in
    heaven.
    Praise him, all you who serve him
    and do what he wants.
22 Let everything the LORD has made
    praise him
    everywhere in his kingdom.

I will praise the LORD.

Psalm 104

1 I will praise the LORD.

LORD my God, you are very great.
    You are dressed in glory and majesty.
2 You wrap yourself in light as if it were a
    robe.
    You spread the heavens out like a
    tent.
3   You build your palace high in the
    heavens.
    You make the clouds serve as your
    chariot.
    You ride on the wings of the wind.
4 You make the winds serve as your
    messengers.
    You make flashes of lightning serve
    you.
5 You placed the earth on its
    foundations.
    It can never be moved.
6 You covered it with the oceans like a
    blanket.
    The waters covered the mountains.
7 But you commanded the waters, and
    they ran away.
    At the sound of your thunder they
    rushed off.
8 They flowed down the mountains.
    They went into the valleys.
    They went to the place you
    appointed for them.
9 You drew a line they can't cross.
    They will never cover the earth
    again.

10 You make springs pour water into the
    valleys.
    It flows between the mountains.

11 The springs give water to all of the wild
    animals.
    The wild donkeys satisfy their thirst.
12 The birds of the air build nests by the
    waters.
    They sing among the branches.
13 You water the mountains from your
    palace high in the clouds.
    The earth is filled with the things
    you have made.
14 You make grass grow for the cattle
    and plants for people to take care of.
    That's how they get food from the
    earth.
15 There is wine to make people glad.
    There is olive oil to make them
    healthy.
    And there is bread to make them
    strong.
16 The cedar trees of Lebanon belong to
    the LORD.
    You planted them and gave them
    plenty of water.
17 There the birds make their nests.
    The stork has its home in the pine
    trees.
18 The high mountains belong to the
    wild goats.
    The cliffs are a safe place for the rock
    badgers.

19 The moon serves to mark off the
    seasons.
    The sun knows when to go down.
20 You bring darkness, and it becomes
    night.
    Then all the animals of the forest
    prowl around.
21 The lions roar while they hunt.
    All of their food comes from God.
22 The sun rises, and they slip away.
    They return to their dens and lie
    down.
23 Then a man gets up and goes to work.
    He keeps working until evening.

24 LORD, you have made so many things!
    How wise you were when you made
    all of them!
    The earth is full of your creatures.
25 Look at the ocean, so big and wide!
    It is filled with more creatures than
    people can count.
    It is filled with living things, from
    the largest to the smallest.
26 Ships sail back and forth on it.
    The leviathan, the sea monster you
    made, plays in it.

27 All of those creatures depend on you
    to give them their food when they
    need it.

28 When you give it to them,
they eat it.
When you open your hand,
they are satisfied with good things.
29 When you turn your face away from
them,
they are terrified.
When you take away their breath,
they die and turn back into dust.
30 When you send your Spirit,
you create them.
You give new life to the earth.

31 May the glory of the Lord continue
forever.
May the Lord be happy with what
he has made.
32 When he looks at the earth, it
trembles.
When he touches the mountains,
they pour out smoke.

33 I will sing to the Lord all my life.
I will sing praise to my God as long
as I live.
34 May these thoughts of mine please
him.
I find my joy in the Lord.

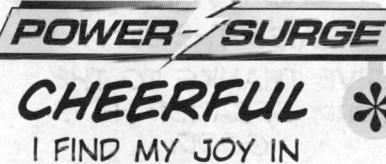

CHEERFUL ✳

I FIND MY JOY IN
THE LORD.
—— PSALM 104:34 ——

35 But may those who sin be gone from
the earth.
May evil people disappear.

I will praise the Lord.

Praise the Lord.

Psalm 105

1 Give thanks to the Lord. Worship him.
Tell the nations what he has done.
2 Sing to him. Sing praise to him.
Tell about all of the wonderful
things he has done.
3 Praise him, because his name is holy.
Let the hearts of those who trust in
the Lord be glad.
4 Look to the Lord and to his strength.
Always look to him.
5 Remember the wonderful things he
has done.
Remember his miracles and how he
judged our enemies.

6 Remember what he has done, you
children of his servant
Abraham.
Remember it, you people of Jacob,
God's chosen ones.
7 He is the Lord our God.
He judges the whole earth.

8 He will keep his covenant forever.
He will keep his promise for all time
to come.
9 He will keep the covenant he made
with Abraham.
He will keep the oath he took when
he made his promise to Isaac.
10 He made it stand as a law for Jacob.
He made it stand as a covenant for
Israel. It will last forever.
11 He said, "I will give you the land of
Canaan.
It will belong to you."

12 At first there weren't very many of
God's people.
There were only a few. And they
were strangers in the land.
13 They wandered from nation to nation.
They wandered from one kingdom
to another.
14 But God didn't allow anyone to beat
them down.
To keep them safe, he gave a
command to kings.
15 He said to them, "Do not touch my
anointed ones.
Do not harm my prophets."

16 He made the people in the land go
hungry.
He destroyed all their food supplies.
17 He sent a man ahead of them into
Egypt.
That man was Joseph. He had been
sold as a slave.
18 The Egyptians put his feet in chains.
They put an iron collar around his
neck.
19 He was in prison until what he said
would happen came true.
The word of the Lord proved that he
was right.
20 The king of Egypt sent for Joseph and
let him out of prison.
The ruler of many nations set him
free.
21 He put Joseph in charge of his palace.
He made him ruler over everything
he owned.
22 Joseph was in charge of teaching the
princes.
He taught the elders how to think
and live wisely.

²³ Then the rest of Jacob's family went to
Egypt.
The people of Israel lived as
outsiders in the land of Ham.
²⁴ The LORD gave his people so many
children
that there were too many of them
for their enemies.
²⁵ He made the Egyptians hate his
people.
The Egyptians made evil plans
against them.
²⁶ The LORD sent his servant Moses to the
king of Egypt.
He sent Aaron, his chosen one,
along with him.
²⁷ The LORD gave them the power to do
miraculous signs among the
Egyptians.
They did his wonders in the land of
Ham.
²⁸ He sent darkness over the land.
He did it because the Egyptians had
refused to obey his words.
²⁹ He turned their rivers and streams into
blood.
He caused the fish in them to die.
³⁰ Their land was covered with frogs.
Frogs even went into the bedrooms
of the rulers.
³¹ The LORD spoke, and large numbers of
flies came.
Gnats filled the whole country.
³² He turned their rain into hail.
Lightning flashed all through their
land.
³³ He destroyed their vines and fig trees.
He broke down the trees in Egypt.
³⁴ He spoke, and the locusts came.
There were so many of them they
couldn't be counted.
³⁵ They ate up every green thing in the
land.
They ate up what the land
produced.
³⁶ Then he killed the oldest son of every
family in Egypt.
He struck down the oldest of all of
their sons.
³⁷ He brought the people of Israel out of
Egypt.
The Egyptians loaded them down
with silver and gold.
From among the tribes of Israel no
one got tired or fell down.
³⁸ The Egyptians were glad when the
people of Israel left.
They were terrified because of Israel.
³⁹ The LORD spread out a cloud to cover
his people.

He gave them a fire to light up the
night.
⁴⁰ They asked for meat, and he brought
them quail.
He satisfied them with manna, the
bread of heaven.
⁴¹ He broke open a rock, and streams of
water poured out.
They flowed like a river in the desert.

⁴² He remembered the holy promise
he had made to his servant
Abraham.
⁴³ His chosen people shouted for joy
as he brought them out of Egypt.
⁴⁴ He gave them the lands of other
nations.
He let them take over what others
had worked for.
⁴⁵ He did it so they might obey his rules
and follow his laws.

Praise the LORD.

POWER-SURGE

LOVING ♥

PRAISE THE LORD.
GIVE THANKS TO THE
LORD, BECAUSE HE IS
GOOD.

HIS FAITHFUL LOVE
CONTINUES FOREVER.
— **PSALM 106:1** —

THANKFUL ♣

Psalm 106

¹ Praise the LORD.

Give thanks to the LORD, because he is
good.
His faithful love continues forever.
² Who can speak enough about the
mighty acts of the LORD?
Who can praise him as much as he
should be praised?
³ Blessed are those who always do what
is fair.
Blessed are those who keep doing
what is right.
⁴ LORD, remember me when you show
favor to your people.
Help me when you save them.

5 Then I will enjoy the good things you
   give your chosen ones.
   I will be joyful together with your
   people.
   I will join them when they praise
   you.

6 We have sinned, just as our people of
   long ago did.
   We too have done what is evil and
   wrong.
7 When our people were in Egypt,
   they forgot about the LORD's
   miracles.
   They didn't remember his many kind
   acts.
   At the Red Sea they refused to obey
   him.
8 But he saved them for the honor of his
   name.
   He did it to make his mighty power
   known.
9 He ordered the Red Sea to dry up, and
   it did.
   He led his people through it as if it
   were a desert.
10 He saved them from the power of their
   enemies.
   He set them free from their control.
11 The waters covered their enemies.
   Not one of them escaped alive.
12 Then his people believed his promises
   and sang praise to him.

13 But they soon forgot what he had
   done.
   They didn't wait for his advice.
14 In the desert they longed for food.
   In that dry and empty land they put
   God to the test.
15 So he gave them what they asked for.
   But he also sent a sickness that killed
   many of them.

16 In their camp some of them became
   jealous of Moses.
   They were also jealous of Aaron. He
   had been set apart to serve the
   LORD.
17 The ground opened up and swallowed
   Dathan.
   It buried Abiram and his followers.
18 Fire blazed among all of them.
   Flames destroyed those evil people.

19 At Mount Horeb they made a metal
   statue of a bull calf.
   They worshiped that statue of a god.
20 They traded their glorious God
   for a statue of a bull that eats grass.
21 They forgot the God who saved them.
   They forgot the One who had done
   great things in Egypt.

22 They forgot the miracles he did in the
   land of Ham.
   They forgot the wonderful things he
   did by the Red Sea.
23 So he said he would destroy them.
   But Moses, his chosen one,
   stood up for them.
   He kept God's anger from destroying
   them.

24 Later on, they refused to enter the
   pleasant land of Canaan.
   They didn't believe God's promise.
25 In their tents they told the LORD how
   unhappy they were.
   They didn't obey him.
26 So he lifted up his hand and promised
   with an oath
   that he would make them die in the
   desert.
27 He promised he would scatter their
   children's children among the
   nations.
   He would make them die in other
   lands.

28 They joined in worshiping the Baal
   that was worshiped at Peor.
   They ate food that had been offered
   to gods that aren't even alive.
29 Their evil ways made the LORD angry.
   So a plague broke out among them.
30 But Phinehas stood up and took
   action.
   Then the plague stopped.
31 What Phinehas did made him right
   with the LORD.
   It will be remembered for all time to
   come.

32 By the waters of Meribah the LORD's
   people made him angry.
   Moses got in trouble because of
   them.
33 They refused to obey the Spirit of God.
   So Moses spoke without thinking.

34 They didn't destroy the nations in
   Canaan
   as the LORD had commanded them.
35 Instead, they mixed with those nations
   and adopted their ways.
36 They worshiped statues of their gods.
   That became a trap for them.
37 They sacrificed their sons and
   daughters
   as offerings to demons.
38 They killed those who weren't guilty of
   doing anything wrong.
   They killed their own sons and
   daughters.
   They sacrificed them as offerings to
   statues of the gods of Canaan.

The land became "unclean" because
of the blood of their children.
39 The people polluted themselves by
what they had done.
They weren't faithful to the LORD.

40 So the LORD became angry with his
people.
He turned away from his own
children.
41 He handed them over to the nations.
Their enemies ruled over them.
42 They beat them down
and kept them under their power.
43 Many times the LORD saved them.
But they refused to obey him.
So he destroyed them because of
their sins.

44 But he heard them when they cried
out.
He paid special attention to their
suffering.
45 Because they were his people, he
remembered his covenant.
Because of his great love, he felt
sorry for them.
46 He made all those who held them as
prisoners
show concern for them.

47 LORD our God, save us.
Bring us back from among the
nations.
Then we will give thanks to you,
because your name is holy.
We will celebrate by praising you.

48 Give praise to the LORD, the God of
Israel,
for ever and ever.
Let all of the people say, "Amen!"

Praise the LORD.

BOOK V

Psalms 107–150

Psalm 107

1 Give thanks to the LORD, because he is
good.
His faithful love continues forever.
2 That's what those who have been set
free by the LORD should say.
He set them free from the power of
the enemy.
3 He brought them back from other
lands.
He brought them back from east and
west, from north and south.

4 Some of them wandered in deserts that
were dry and empty.
They couldn't find their way to a
city where they could settle
down.
5 They were hungry and thirsty.
Their lives were slipping away.
6 Then they cried out to the LORD
because of their problems.
And he saved them from their
troubles.
7 He led them straight
to a city where they could settle
down.
8 Let them give thanks to the LORD for
his faithful love.
Let them give thanks for the
miracles he does for his people.
9 He gives those who are thirsty all of
the water they want.
He gives those who are hungry all of
the good food they can eat.

10 Others lived in the deepest darkness.
They suffered as prisoners in iron
chains.
11 That's because they hadn't obeyed the
words of God.
They had refused to follow the
advice of the Most High God.
12 So he made them do work that was
hard and bitter.
They tripped and fell, and there was
no one to help them.
13 Then they cried out to the LORD
because of their problems.
And he saved them from their
troubles.
14 He brought them out of the deepest
darkness.
He broke their chains off.
15 Let them give thanks to the LORD for
his faithful love.

POWER-SURGE

FAITHFUL ( )

GIVE THANKS TO THE
LORD, BECAUSE HE IS
GOOD.

HIS FAITHFUL LOVE
CONTINUES FOREVER.
— PSALM 107:1 —

THANKFUL

Let them give thanks for the
miracles he does for his people.
16 He breaks down gates that are made of
bronze.
He cuts through bars that are made
of iron.
17 Others were foolish. They suffered
because of their sins.
They suffered because they wouldn't
obey the Lord.
18 They refused to eat anything.
They came close to passing through
the gates of death.
19 Then they cried out to the Lord
because of their problems.
And he saved them from their
troubles.
20 He gave his command and healed
them.
He saved them from the grave.
21 Let them give thanks to the Lord for
his faithful love.
Let them give thanks for the
miracles he does for his people.
22 Let them sacrifice thank offerings.
Let them talk about what he has
done as they sing with joy.
23 Others sailed out on the ocean in
ships.
They traded goods on the mighty
waters.
24 They saw the works of the Lord.
They saw the miracles he did on the
ocean.
25 He spoke and stirred up a storm.
It lifted the waves high.
26 They rose up to the heavens. Then
they went down deep into the
ocean.
In that kind of danger the people's
boldness melted away.
27 They were unsteady like those who get
drunk.
They didn't know what to do.
28 Then they cried out to the Lord
because of their problems.
And he brought them out of their
troubles.
29 He made the storm as quiet as a
whisper.
The waves of the ocean calmed
down.
30 The people were glad when the ocean
became calm.
Then he guided them to the harbor
they were looking for.
31 Let them give thanks to the Lord for
his faithful love.
Let them give thanks for the
miracles he does for his people.

32 Let them honor him among his people
who gather for worship.
Let them praise him in the meeting
of the elders.
33 He turned rivers into a desert.
He turned flowing springs into
thirsty ground.
34 He turned land that produced crops
into a salty land where nothing
could grow.
He did it because the people who
lived there were evil.
35 He turned the desert into pools of
water.
He turned the dry and cracked
ground into flowing springs.
36 He brought hungry people there to
live.
They built a city where they could
settle down.
37 They planted fields and vineyards
that produced large crops.
38 He blessed the people, and they greatly
increased their numbers.
He kept their herds from getting
smaller.
39 Then the number of God's people got
smaller.
They were brought low by trouble,
suffering and sorrow.
40 The One who looks down on proud
nobles
made them wander in a desert
where no one lives.
41 But he lifted needy people out of their
suffering.
He made their families increase like
flocks of sheep.
42 Honest people see it and are filled with
joy.
But no one who is evil has anything
to say.
43 Let those who are wise pay attention to
these things.
Let them think about the Lord's
great love.

Psalm 108

A song. A psalm of David.
1 God, my heart feels secure.
I will sing and make music to you
with all my heart.
2 Harp and lyre, wake up!
I want to sing and make music
before the sun rises.
3 Lord, I will praise you among the
nations.
I will sing about you among the
people of the earth.

4 Great is your love. It is higher than the
heavens.
Your truth reaches to the skies.
5 God, may you be honored above the
heavens.
Let your glory be over the whole
earth.

6 Save us. Help us with your powerful
right hand,
so that those you love may be saved.
7 God has spoken from his temple.
He has said, "I will win the battle.
Then I will divide up the land around
Shechem.
I will divide up the Valley of
Succoth.
8 Gilead belongs to me. So does the land
of Manasseh.
Ephraim is the strongest tribe. It is
like a helmet for my head.
Judah is the royal tribe. It is like a
ruler's staff.
9 Moab serves me like one who washes
my feet.
I toss my sandal on Edom to show
that I own it.
I shout to Philistia that I have won
the battle."

10 Who will bring me to the city that has
high walls around it?
Who will lead me to the land of
Edom?
11 God, isn't it you, even though you
have now turned away from us?
Isn't it you, even though you don't
lead our armies into battle
anymore?
12 Help us against our enemies.
The help people give doesn't
amount to anything.
13 With your help we will win the battle.
You will walk all over our enemies.

Psalm 109

For the director of music.
A psalm of David.

1 God, I praise you.
Don't remain silent.
2 Sinful people who lie and cheat have
spoken against me.
They have used their tongues to tell
lies about me.
3 They gather all around me with their
words of hatred.
They attack me without any reason.
4 They bring charges against me,
even though I love them
and pray for them.

5 They pay me back with evil for the
good things I do.
They pay back my love with hatred.

6 Appoint an evil person to take my
enemies to court.
Let him stand at their right hand
and bring charges against
them.
7 When they are tried, let them be found
guilty.
May even their prayers judge them.
8 May their days be few.
Let others take their places as
leaders.
9 May their children's fathers die.
May their wives become widows.
10 May their children be driven from
their destroyed homes.
May they wander around like
beggars.
11 May everything those people own be
taken away to pay for what they
owe.
May strangers rob them of
everything they've worked for.
12 May no one be kind to them
or take pity on the children they
leave behind.
13 May their family line come to an end.
May their names be forgotten by
those who live after them.
14 May the LORD remember the evil
things their fathers have done.
May he never erase the sins of their
mothers.
15 May the LORD never forget their sins.
Then he won't let people remember
those sinners anymore.

16 They never thought about doing
anything kind.
Instead, they drove those who were
poor and needy to their deaths.
They did the same thing to those
whose hearts were broken.
17 They loved to call down curses on
others.
May their curses come back on
them.
They didn't find any pleasure in giving
anyone their blessing.
May no blessing ever come to them.
18 They called down curses on others as
easily as they put on clothes.
Cursing was as natural to them as
getting a drink of water
or putting olive oil on their bodies.
19 May their curses cover them like coats.
May their curses be wrapped around
them like a belt forever.

20 May that be the LORD's way of paying
          back
      those who bring charges against me.
  May it happen to those who say
      evil things about me.

21 But LORD and King,
      be true to your name. Treat me well.
  Because your love is so good, save
          me.

22 I am poor and needy.
  My heart is wounded deep down
          inside me.

23 I fade away like an evening shadow.
  I'm like a locust that someone
          brushes off.

24 My knees are weak because I've gone
          without food.
  My body is very thin.

25 Those who bring charges against me
          laugh at me.
  When they see me, they shake their
          heads at me.

26 LORD my God, help me.
  Save me because you love me.

27 LORD, let my enemies know that you
          yourself have saved me.
  You have done it with your own
          hand.

28 They may call down a curse on me.
  But you will give me your blessing.
  When they attack me, they will be put
          to shame.
  But I will be filled with joy.

29 Those who bring charges against me
          will be clothed with dishonor.
  They will be wrapped in shame as if
          it were a coat.

30 With my mouth I will continually
          praise the LORD.
  I will praise him when all of his
          people gather for worship.

31 He stands ready to help those who
          need it.
  He saves them from those who have
          sentenced them to death.

Psalm 110

A psalm of David.
1 The LORD says to my Lord,
      "Sit at my right hand
  until I put your enemies
      under your control."

2 The LORD will make your royal
          authority spread out from Zion
          to other lands.
  You will rule over your enemies who
          are all around you.

3 Your troops will be willing to fight for
          you
      on the day of battle.
  You will be wrapped in holy majesty.
      Just as the dew falls fresh early in the
          morning,
      you will always be young and strong.

4 The LORD has taken an oath and made
          a promise.
  He will not change his mind.
  He has said, "You are a priest forever,
      just like Melchizedek."

5 The Lord is at your right hand.
  He will crush kings on the day when
          he is angry.

6 He will judge the nations. He will pile
          up dead bodies on the field of
          battle.
  He will crush the rulers of the whole
          earth.

7 He will drink from a brook along the
          way and receive new strength.
  And so he will win the battle.

Psalm 111

1 Praise the LORD.

  I will praise the LORD with all my heart.
  I will praise him where honest
          people gather for worship.

2 The LORD has done great things.
  All who take delight in what he has
          done will spend time thinking
          about it.

3 What he does shows his glory and
          majesty.
  He will always do what is right.

4 The LORD causes his miracles to be
          remembered.
  He is kind and tender.

5 He provides food for those who have
          respect for him.
  He remembers his covenant forever.

6 He has shown his people what his
          power can do.
  He has given them the lands of
          other nations.

7 He is faithful and right in everything
          he does.
  All his rules can be trusted.

8 They will stand firm for ever and ever.
  They were given by the LORD.
  He is faithful and honest.

9 He set his people free.
  He made a covenant with them that
          will last forever.
  His name is holy and wonderful.

10 If you really want to become wise,

OBEYS

IF YOU REALLY WANT TO BECOME WISE, YOU MUST BEGIN BY HAVING RESPECT FOR THE LORD.

ALL THOSE WHO FOLLOW HIS RULES HAVE GOOD UNDERSTANDING.

— **PSALM 111:10** —

WISE

you must begin by having respect for
   the LORD.
All those who follow his rules have
   good understanding.
   People should praise him forever.

Psalm 112

1 Praise the LORD.

Blessed is the one who has respect for
   the LORD.
   He finds great delight when he
     obeys God's commands.

2 His children will be powerful in the
   land.
   Because he is honest, his children
     will be blessed.
3 His family will have wealth and riches.
   He will always be blessed for doing
     what is right.
4 Even in the darkness light shines on
   honest people.
   It shines on those who are kind and
     tender and godly.
5 Good things will come to those who
   are willing to lend freely.
   Good things will come to those who
     are fair in everything they do.
6 They will always be secure.
   Those who do what is right will be
     remembered forever.
7 They aren't afraid when bad news
   comes.
   They stand firm because they trust
     in the LORD.

8 Their hearts are secure. They aren't
   afraid.
   In the end they will see their
     enemies destroyed.
9 They have spread their gifts around to
   poor people.
   Their good works continue forever.
   They will be powerful and honored.

10 Evil people will see it and be upset.
   They will grind their teeth and
     become weaker and weaker.
   What evil people long to do can't
     succeed.

Psalm 113

1 Praise the LORD.

Praise him, you who serve the LORD.
   Praise the name of the LORD.
2 Let us praise the name of the LORD,
   both now and forever.
3 From the sunrise in the east to the
   sunset in the west,
   may the name of the LORD be
     praised.

4 The LORD is honored over all of the
   nations.
   His glory reaches to the highest
     heavens.
5 Who is like the LORD our God?
   He sits on his throne in heaven.
6 He bends down to look
   at the heavens and the earth.

7 He raises poor people up from the
   trash pile.
   He lifts needy people out of the
     ashes.
8 He lets them sit with princes.

HONEST

EVEN IN THE DARKNESS LIGHT SHINES ON HONEST PEOPLE.

IT SHINES ON THOSE WHO ARE KIND AND TENDER AND GODLY.

— **PSALM 112:4** —

KIND

He lets them sit with the princes of
their own people.
9 He gives children to the woman who
doesn't have any children.
He makes her a happy mother in her
own home.

Praise the LORD.

Psalm 114

1 The people of Israel came out of Egypt.
The people of Jacob left a land where
a different language was
spoken.
2 Then Judah became the holy place
where God lived.
Israel became the land he ruled over.

3 The Red Sea saw him and parted.
The Jordan River stopped flowing.
4 The mountains leaped like rams.
The hills skipped like lambs.

5 Red Sea, why did you part?
Jordan River, why did you stop
flowing?
6 Why did you mountains leap like
rams?
Why did you hills skip like lambs?

7 Earth, tremble with fear when the Lord
comes.
Tremble when the God of Jacob is
near.
8 He turned the rock into a pool.
He turned the hard rock into springs
of water.

Psalm 115

1 LORD, may glory be given to you, not
to us.
You are loving and faithful.

2 Why do the nations ask,
"Where is their God?"
3 Our God is in heaven.
He does anything he wants to do.
4 But the statues of their gods are made
out of silver and gold.
They are made by the hands of men.
5 They have mouths, but they can't
speak.
They have eyes, but they can't see.
6 They have ears, but they can't hear.
They have noses, but they can't
smell.
7 They have hands, but they can't feel.
They have feet, but they can't walk.
They have throats, but they can't say
anything.
8 Those who make statues of gods will be
like them.

So will all those who trust in them.

9 People of Israel, trust in the LORD.
He helps you. He is like a shield that
keeps you safe.
10 Priests of Aaron, trust in the LORD.
He helps you. He is like a shield that
keeps you safe.
11 You who have respect for the LORD,
trust in him.
He helps you. He is like a shield that
keeps you safe.

12 The LORD remembers us and will bless
us.
He will bless the people of Israel.
He will bless the priests of Aaron.
13 The LORD will bless those who have
respect for him.
He will bless important and
unimportant people alike.

14 May the LORD give you many children.
May he give them to you and to your
children after you.
15 May the LORD bless you.
He is the Maker of heaven and earth.

16 The highest heavens belong to the
LORD.
But he has given the earth to human
beings.
17 Dead people don't praise the LORD.
Those who lie quietly in the grave
don't praise him.
18 But we who are alive praise the LORD,
both now and forever.

Praise the LORD.

Psalm 116

1 I love the LORD, because he heard my
voice.
He heard my cry for his favor.
2 Because he paid attention to me,
I will call out to him as long as I live.

3 The ropes of death were wrapped
around me.
The horrors of the grave came over
me.
I was overcome by trouble and
sorrow.
4 Then I called out to the LORD.
I cried out, "LORD, save me!"

5 The LORD is holy and kind.
Our God is full of tender love.
6 The LORD takes care of those who are as
helpless as children.
When I was in great need, he saved
me.

7 I said to myself, "Be calm.

The LORD has been good to me."

8 LORD, you have saved me from death.
   You have dried the tears from my
      eyes.
   You have kept me from tripping and
      falling.
9 So now I can enjoy life here with you
   while I'm still living.
10 I believed in you even when I said to
      myself,
   "I'm in great pain."
11 When I was terrified, I said to myself,
   "No one tells the truth."

12 The LORD has been so good to me!
   How can I ever pay him back?
13 I will bring an offering of wine to the
      LORD
   and thank him for saving me.
   I will worship him.
14 In front of all of the LORD's people,
   I will do what I promised him.

15 The LORD pays special attention
   when his faithful people die.
16 LORD, I serve you.
   I serve you just as my mother did.
   You have set me free from the chains
      of my suffering.

17 LORD, I will sacrifice a thank offering to
      you.
   I will worship you.
18 In front of all of the LORD's people,
   I will do what I promised him.
19 I will keep my promise in the
      courtyards of the LORD's temple.
   I will keep my promise in Jerusalem
      itself.

Praise the LORD.

Psalm 117

1 All you nations, praise the LORD.
   All you people on earth, praise him.
2 Great is his love for us.
   The LORD is faithful forever.

Praise the LORD.

Psalm 118

1 Give thanks to the LORD, because he is
      good.
   His faithful love continues forever.

2 Let the people of Israel say,
   "His faithful love continues forever."
3 Let the priests of Aaron say,
   "His faithful love continues forever."
4 Let those who have respect for the
      LORD say,
   "His faithful love continues forever."

5 When I was in great pain, I cried out to
      the LORD.
   He answered me and set me free.
6 The LORD is with me. I will not be
      afraid.
   What can mere men do to me?
7 The LORD is with me. He helps me.
   I will win the battle over my
      enemies.

8 It is better to go to the LORD for safety
   than to trust in mere men.
9 It is better to go to the LORD for safety
   than to trust in human leaders.

10 The nations were all around me.
   But by the LORD's power I destroyed
      them.
11 They were around me on every side.
   But by the LORD's power I destroyed
      them.
12 They attacked me like large numbers of
      bees.
   But they died out as quickly as
      burning thorns.
   By the LORD's power I destroyed
      them.

13 I was pushed back. I was about to be
      killed.
   But the LORD helped me.
14 The LORD gives me strength. I sing
      about him.
   He has saved me.

15 Shouts of joy ring out in the tents of
      godly people.
   They praise him for his help in
      battle.
   They shout, "The LORD's powerful right
      hand has done mighty things!
16   The LORD's powerful right hand has
      won the battle!
   The LORD's powerful right hand has
      done mighty things!"

17 I will not die. I will live.
   I will talk about what the LORD has
      done.
18 The LORD has really punished me.
   But he didn't let me die.

19 Open the gates of the temple for me.
   I will enter and give thanks to the
      LORD.
20 This is the gate of the LORD.
   Only those who do what is right can
      go through it.
21 LORD, I will give thanks to you, because
      you answered me.
   You have saved me.

22 The stone the builders didn't accept

has become the most important
stone of all.
23 The LORD has done it.
It is wonderful in our eyes.
24 The LORD has done it on this day.
Let us be joyful and glad in it.

25 LORD, save us.
LORD, give us success.
26 Blessed is the one who comes in the
name of the LORD.
From the temple of the LORD we
bless you.
27 The LORD is God.
He has made the light of his favor
shine on us.
Take branches in your hands. Join in
the march on the day of the
feast.
March up to the corners of the altar.

28 You are my God, and I will give thanks
to you.
You are my God, and I will honor
you.
29 Give thanks to the LORD, because he is
good.
His faithful love continues forever.

Psalm 119

א Aleph
1 Blessed are those who live without
blame.
They live in keeping with the law of
the LORD.
2 Blessed are those who obey his
covenant laws.
They trust in him with all their
hearts.
3 They don't do anything wrong.
They live as he wants them to live.
4 You have given me rules
that I must obey completely.
5 I hope I will always stand firm
in following your orders.
6 Then I won't be put to shame
when I think about all of your
commands.
7 I will praise you with an honest heart
as I learn about how fair your
decisions are.
8 I will obey your orders.
Please don't leave me all alone.

ב Beth
9 How can a young person keep his life
pure?
By living in keeping with your word.
10 I trust in you with all my heart.

Don't let me wander away from your
commands.
11 I have hidden your word in my heart
so that I won't sin against you.
12 LORD, I give praise to you.
Teach me your orders.
13 With my lips I talk about
all of the decisions you have made.
14 Following your covenant laws gives me
joy
just as great riches give joy to others.
15 I spend time thinking about your rules.
I consider how you want me to live.
16 I take delight in your orders.
I won't fail to obey your word.

ג Gimel
17 Be good to me, and I will live.
I will obey your word.

POWER-SURGE

FAITHFUL ()

I TAKE DELIGHT IN
YOUR ORDERS.

I WON'T FAIL TO OBEY
YOUR WORD.

BE GOOD TO ME, AND
I WILL LIVE.

I WILL OBEY YOUR
WORD.
— PSALM 119:16-17 — ✔

OBEYS

18 Open my eyes so that I can see
the wonderful truths in your law.
19 I'm a stranger on earth.
Don't hide your commands from me.
20 My heart is filled with longing
for your laws at all times.
21 You correct proud people. They are
under your curse.
They wander away from your
commands.
22 I obey your covenant laws.
So don't let evil people laugh at me
or hate me.
23 Even if rulers sit together and tell lies
about me,
I will spend time thinking about
your orders.

24 Your covenant laws are my delight.
They give me wise advice.

ד Daleth

25 I lie in the dust. I'm about to die.
Keep me alive as you have promised.
26 I told you how I've lived, and you gave
me your answer.
Teach me your orders.
27 Help me understand what your rules
can teach me.
Then I'll spend time thinking about
the miracles you have done.
28 My sadness has worn me out.
Give me strength as you have
promised.
29 Keep me from cheating and telling lies.
Be kind and teach me your law.
30 I have chosen to be faithful to you.
I put my trust in your laws.
31 LORD, I'm careful to obey your
covenant laws.
Don't let me be put to shame.
32 I am quick to follow your commands,
because you have set my heart free.

ה He

33 LORD, teach me to follow your orders.
Then I will obey them to the very
end.
34 Help me understand your law. Then I
will follow it
and obey it with all my heart.
35 Teach me to live as you command,
because that makes me very happy.
36 Make me want to follow your covenant
laws
instead of wanting to gain things
only for myself.
37 Turn my eyes away from things that
are worthless.
Keep me alive as you have promised.
38 Keep your promise to me.
Then other people will have respect
for you.
39 Please don't let me be put to shame.
Your laws are good.
40 I really want to follow your rules.
Keep me alive, because you do what
is right.

ו Waw

41 LORD, show me your faithful love.
Save me as you have promised.
42 Then I will answer those who make
fun of me,
because I trust in your word.
43 Help me always to tell the truth about
how faithful you are.
I have put my hope in your laws.
44 I will always obey your law,

POWER-SURGE

CHEERFUL *

I WILL LEAD A FULL
AND HAPPY LIFE,
BECAUSE I'VE TRIED TO
OBEY YOUR RULES.
— PSALM 119:45 — ✔

OBEYS

for ever and ever.
45 I will lead a full and happy life,
because I've tried to obey your rules.
46 I will talk about your covenant laws to
kings.
I will not be put to shame.
47 I take delight in obeying your
commands
because I love them.
48 I praise your commands, and I love
them.
I spend time thinking about your
orders.

ז Zayin

49 Remember what you have said to me.
You have given me hope.
50 Even when I suffer, I am comforted
because you promised to keep me
alive.
51 Proud people are always making fun of
me.
But I don't turn away from your law.
52 LORD, I remember the laws you gave
long ago.
I find comfort in them.
53 I am very angry
because evil people have turned
away from your law.
54 No matter where I live,
I sing about your orders.
55 LORD, during the night I remember
who you are.
That's why I keep your law.
56 I have really done my best
to obey your rules.

ח Heth

57 LORD, you are everything I need.
I have promised to obey your words.
58 I have looked to you with all my heart.
Be kind to me as you have promised.
59 I have thought about the way I live.

And I have decided to follow your
covenant laws.
60 I won't waste any time.
I will be quick to obey your
commands.
61 Evil people may tie me up with ropes.
But I won't forget to obey your law.
62 At midnight I get up to give you thanks
because your decisions are very fair.
63 I'm a friend to everyone who has
respect for you.
I'm a friend to everyone who follows
your rules.
64 LORD, the earth is filled with your love.
Teach me your orders.

ט Teth
65 LORD, be good to me
as you have promised.
66 Increase my knowledge and give me
good sense,
because I believe in your commands.
67 Before I went through suffering, I went
down the wrong path.
But now I obey your word.
68 You are good, and what you do is good.
Teach me your orders.
69 Proud people have spread lies about
me and have taken away my
good name.
But I follow your rules with all my
heart.
70 Their hearts are hard and stubborn.
They don't feel anything.
But I take delight in your law.
71 It was good for me to suffer.
That's what helped me to
understand your orders.
72 The law you gave is worth more to me
than thousands of pieces of silver
and gold.

י Yodh
73 You made me and formed me with
your own hands.
Give me understanding so that I can
learn your commands.
74 May those who have respect for you be
filled with joy when they see
me.
I have put my hope in your word.
75 LORD, I know that your laws are right.
You were faithful to your promise
when you made me suffer.
76 May your faithful love comfort me
as you have promised me.
77 Show me your tender love so that I can
live.
I take delight in your law.

78 Proud people have treated me badly
without any reason. May they
be put to shame.
I will spend time thinking about
your rules.
79 May those who have respect for you
come to me.
Then I can teach them your
covenant laws.
80 May my heart be without blame as I
follow your orders.
Then I won't be put to shame.

כ Kaph
81 I deeply long for you to save me.
I have put my hope in your word.
82 My eyes grow tired looking for what
you have promised.
I say, "When will you comfort me?"
83 I'm as useless as a wineskin that smoke
has dried up.
But I don't forget to follow your
orders.
84 How long do I have to wait?
When will you punish those who
attack me?
85 Proud people do what is against your
law.
They dig pits for me to fall into.
86 All of your commands can be trusted.
Help me, because people attack me
without any reason.
87 They almost wiped me off the face of
the earth.
But I have not turned away from
your rules.
88 Keep me alive, because you love me.
Then I will obey the covenant laws
you have given.

ל Lamedh
89 LORD, your word lasts forever.
It stands firm in the heavens.

POWER-SURGE

WISE
W

YOU MADE ME AND
FORMED ME WITH YOUR
OWN HANDS.

GIVE ME
UNDERSTANDING SO
THAT I CAN LEARN
YOUR COMMANDS.
— **PSALM 119:73** —

90 You will be faithful for all time to
come.
You made the earth, and it
continues to exist.
91 Your laws continue to this very day,
because all things serve you.
92 If I had not taken delight in your law,
I would have died because of my
suffering.
93 I will never forget your rules.
You have kept me alive, because I
obey them.
94 Save me, because I belong to you.
I've tried to obey your rules.
95 Sinful people are waiting to destroy
me.
But I will spend time thinking about
your covenant laws.
96 I've learned that everything has its
limits.
But your commands are perfect.
They are always there when I
need them.

ם Mem

97 LORD, I really love your law!
All day long I spend time thinking
about it.
98 Your commands make me wiser than
my enemies,
because your commands are always
in my heart.
99 I know more than all of my
teachers do,
because I spend time thinking about
your covenant laws.
100 I understand more than the elders do,
because I obey your rules.
101 I've kept my feet from every path that
sinners take
so that I might obey your word.
102 I haven't turned away from your laws,
because you yourself have taught
me.
103 Your words are very sweet to my taste!
They are sweeter than honey to me.
104 I gain understanding from your rules.
So I hate every path that sinners
take.

נ Nun

105 Your word is like a lamp that shows
me the way.
It is like a light that guides me.
106 I have taken an oath. I have promised
to follow your laws, because they are
right.
107 I have suffered very much.
LORD, keep me alive as you have
promised.

108 LORD, accept the praise I freely give
you.
Teach me your laws.
109 I keep putting my life in danger.
But I won't forget to obey your law.
110 Evil people have set a trap for me.
But I haven't wandered away from
your rules.
111 Your covenant laws are your gift to me
forever.
They fill my heart with joy.
112 I have decided to obey your orders
to the very end.

ס Samekh

113 I hate people who can't make up their
minds.
But I love your law.
114 You are my place of safety.
You are like a shield that keeps me
safe.
I have put my hope in your word.
115 Get away from me, you who do evil!
Then I can do what my God
commands me to do.
116 Keep me going as you have promised.
Then I will live.
Don't let me lose all hope.
117 Take good care of me, and I will be
saved.
I will always honor your orders.
118 You turn your back on all those who
wander away from your orders.
They lie and cheat, but it doesn't
amount to anything.
119 You throw away all of the sinners on
earth as if they were trash.
So I love your covenant laws.
120 My body trembles because I have
respect for you.
I have great respect for your laws.

ע Ayin

121 I have done what is right and fair.
So don't leave me to those who beat
me down.
122 Make sure that everything goes well
with me.
Don't let proud people beat me
down.
123 My eyes grow tired as I look to you to
save me.
Please save me as you have
promised.
124 Be good to me, because you love me.
Teach me your orders.
125 I serve you. Help me to understand
what is right.
Then I will understand your
covenant laws.
126 LORD, it's time for you to act.

People are breaking your law.
127 I love your commands more than
gold.
I love them more than pure gold.
128 I consider all of your rules to be right.
So I hate every path that sinners
take.

⅀ Pe

129 Your covenant laws are wonderful.
So I obey them.
130 When your words are made clear, they
bring light.
They bring understanding to
childish people.
131 I open my mouth and pant like a dog,
because I long to know your
commands.
132 Turn to me and show me your favor.
That's what you've always done for
those who love you.
133 Teach me how to live as you have
promised.
Don't let any sin be my master.
134 Set me free from men who beat me
down.
Then I will obey your rules.
135 Let your face smile on me with favor.
Teach me your orders.
136 Streams of tears flow from my eyes,
because people don't obey your law.

⅀ Tsadhe

137 LORD, you do what is fair.
And your laws are right.
138 The laws you have made are fair.
They can be completely trusted.
139 My anger is wearing me out,
because my enemies don't pay any
attention to your words.
140 Your promises have proved to be true.
I love them.
141 I'm not important. People look down
on me.
But I don't forget to obey your rules.
142 You always do what is right.
And your law is true.
143 I've had my share of trouble and
suffering.
But I take delight in your
commands.
144 Your covenant laws are always right.
Help me to understand them. Then I
will live.

ק Qoph

145 LORD, I call out to you with all my
heart.
Answer me, and I will obey your
orders.
146 I call out to you.

Save me, and I will keep your
covenant laws.
147 I get up before the sun rises. I cry out
for help.
I've put my hope in your word.
148 My eyes stay open all night long.
I spend my time thinking about
your promises.
149 Listen to me, because you love me.
LORD, keep me alive as you have
promised.
150 Those who think up evil plans are
near.
They have wandered far away from
your law.
151 But LORD, you are near.
All your commands are true.
152 Long ago I learned from your
covenant laws
that you made them to last forever.

ר Resh

153 Look at how I'm suffering!
Save me, because I haven't forgotten
to obey your law.
154 Stand up for me and set me free.
Keep me alive as you have promised.
155 Those who are evil are far from being
saved.
They don't want to obey your
orders.
156 LORD, you have deep concern for me.
Keep me alive as you have promised.
157 Many enemies attack me.
But I haven't turned away from your
covenant laws.
158 I get very angry when I see people
who aren't faithful to you.
They don't obey your word.
159 See how I love your rules!
LORD, keep me alive, because you
love me.
160 All your words are true.
All your laws are right. They last
forever.

ש Sin and Shin

161 Rulers attack me without any reason.
But my heart trembles because of
your word.
162 I'm filled with joy because of your
promise.
It's like finding a great fortune.
163 I hate lies with a deep hatred.
But I love your law.
164 Seven times a day I praise you
for your laws, because they are right.
165 Those who love your law enjoy great
peace.
Nothing can make them trip and
fall.

166 LORD, I wait for you to save me.
I follow your commands.
167 I obey your covenant laws,
because I love them greatly.
168 I obey your rules and your covenant
laws,
because you know all about how I
live.

ת Taw

169 LORD, may you hear my cry.
Give me understanding, just as you
said you would.
170 May you hear my prayer.
Save me, just as you promised.
171 May my lips pour out praise to you,
because you teach me your orders.
172 May my tongue sing about your word,
because all of your commands are
right.
173 May your hand be ready to help me,
because I have chosen to obey your
rules.
174 LORD, I long for you to save me.
I take delight in your law.
175 Let me live so that I can praise you.
May your laws keep me going.
176 Like a lost sheep, I've gone down the
wrong path.
Come and look for me,
because I haven't forgotten to obey
your commands.

Psalm 120

A song for those who go up to Jerusalem
to worship the LORD.

1 I call out to the LORD when I'm in
trouble,
and he answers me.
2 LORD, save me from people whose lips
tell lies.
Save me from people whose tongues
don't tell the truth.

3 What will the LORD do to you, you
lying tongue?
And what more will he do?
4 He will punish you with the sharp
arrows of a soldier.
He will punish you with burning
wood from a desert tree.

5 How terrible it is for me to live in the
tents of the people of Meshech!
How terrible to live in the tents of
the people of Kedar!
6 I have lived too long
among those who hate peace.
7 I want peace.
But when I speak, they want war.

Psalm 121

A song for those who go up to Jerusalem
to worship the LORD.

1 I look up to the hills.
Where does my help come from?
2 My help comes from the LORD.
He is the Maker of heaven and earth.

3 He won't let your foot slip.
He who watches over you won't get
tired.
4 In fact, he who watches over Israel
won't get tired or go to sleep.

5 The LORD watches over you.
The LORD is like a shade tree at your
right hand.
6 The sun won't harm you during the
day.
The moon won't harm you during
the night.

7 The LORD will keep you from every
kind of harm.
He will watch over your life.
8 The LORD will watch over your life no
matter where you go,
both now and forever.

Psalm 122

A song for those who go up to Jerusalem
to worship the LORD. A psalm of David.

1 I was very glad when they said to me,
"Let us go up to the house of the
LORD."
2 Jerusalem, our feet are standing
inside your gates.

3 Jerusalem is built like a city
where everything is close together.
4 The tribes of the LORD go there to
praise his name.
They do it in keeping with the law
he gave to Israel.
5 The thrones of the family line of David
are there.
That's where the people are judged.

6 Pray for the peace of Jerusalem. Say,
"May those who love you be secure.
7 May there be peace inside your walls.
May your people be kept safe."
8 I'm concerned for my family and
friends.
So I say to Jerusalem, "May you
enjoy peace."
9 I'm concerned about the house of the
LORD our God.
So I pray that things will go well
with Jerusalem.

Psalm 123

*A song for those who go up to Jerusalem
to worship the L*ORD.

1 I look up and pray to you.
Your throne is in heaven.
2 Slaves depend on their masters.
Maids depend on the women they
work for.
In the same way, we depend on the
LORD our God.
We wait for him to show us his favor.

3 LORD, show us your favor. Show us your
favor,
because people have made so much
fun of us.
4 We have had to put up with a lot from
those who are proud.
They were always laughing at us.

Psalm 124

*A song for those who go up to Jerusalem
to worship the L*ORD*. A psalm of David.*

1 Here is what Israel should say.
Suppose the LORD had not been on
our side.
2 Suppose the LORD had not been on our
side
when our enemies attacked us.
3 Suppose he had not been on our side
when their anger blazed out against
us.
Then they would have swallowed us
alive.
4 They would have been like a flood that
drowned us.
They would have swept over us like a
rushing river.
5 They would have washed us away
like a swollen stream.
6 Give praise to the LORD.
He has not let our enemies chew us
up.
7 We have escaped like a bird
from a hunter's trap.
The trap has been broken,
and we have escaped.
8 Our help comes from the LORD.
He is the Maker of heaven and earth.

Psalm 125

*A song for those who go up to Jerusalem
to worship the L*ORD.

1 Those who trust in the LORD are like
Mount Zion.
They will always be secure. They will
last forever.
2 Like the mountains around
Jerusalem,

the LORD is all around his people
both now and forever.
3 Evil people will not always rule
the land the LORD gave to those who
do right.
If they did, those who do right
might do what is evil.
4 LORD, do good to those who are good.
Do good to those whose hearts are
honest.
5 But what about those who have taken
paths that are crooked?
The LORD will drive them out, along
with those who do what is evil.

May Israel enjoy peace.

Psalm 126

*A song for those who go up to Jerusalem
to worship the L*ORD.

1 Our enemies took us away from Zion.
But when the LORD brought us
home,
it seemed like a dream to us.
2 Our mouths were filled with laughter.
Our tongues sang with joy.
Then the people of other nations said,
"The LORD has done great things for
them."
3 The LORD has done great things for us.
And we are filled with joy.

CHEERFUL ✳

THE LORD HAS DONE GREAT THINGS FOR US.
AND WE ARE FILLED WITH JOY.
— PSALM 126:3 —

4 LORD, bless us with great success
again,
as rain makes streams flow in the
Negev Desert.
5 Those who cry as they plant their
crops
will sing with joy when they gather
them in.
6 Those who go out sobbing
as they carry seeds to plant
will come back singing with joy.
They will bring the new crop back
with them.

Psalm 127

A song for those who go up to Jerusalem
to worship the LORD. A psalm
of Solomon.

1 If the LORD doesn't build a house,
the work of its builders is useless.
If the LORD doesn't watch over a city,
it's useless for those on guard duty to
stand watch over it.
2 It's useless for you to work from early
morning
until late at night
just to get food to eat.
God provides for those he loves even
while they sleep.

3 Children are a gift from the LORD.
They are a reward from him.
4 Children who are born to people when
they are young
are like arrows in the hands of a
soldier.
5 Blessed are those
who have many children.
They won't be put to shame
when they go up against their
enemies in court.

Psalm 128

A song for those who go up to Jerusalem
to worship the LORD.

1 Blessed are all those who have respect
for the LORD.
They live as he wants them to live.
2 Your work will give you what you need.
Blessings and good things will come
to you.
3 As a vine bears a lot of fruit,
so your wife will have many children
by you.
They will sit around your table
like young olive trees.
4 Only a man who has respect for the
LORD
will be blessed like that.

5 May the LORD bless you from Zion.
May you enjoy the good things that
come to Jerusalem
all the days of your life.
6 May you live to see your
grandchildren.

May Israel enjoy peace.

Psalm 129

A song for those who go up to Jerusalem
to worship the LORD.

1 Here is what Israel should say.

Many times my enemies have
beaten me down ever since I
was a young nation.
2 Many times my enemies have beaten
me down ever since I was a
young nation,
but they haven't won the battle.
3 They have made deep wounds in my
back.
It looks like a field a farmer has
plowed.
4 The LORD does what is right.
Sinners had tied me up with ropes.
But the LORD has set me free.

5 May all those who hate Zion
be driven back in shame.
6 May they be like grass that grows on
the roof of a house.
It dries up before it can grow.
7 There isn't enough of it to fill a
person's hand.
There isn't enough to tie up and
carry away.
8 May no one who passes by say to those
who hate Zion,
"May the blessing of the LORD be on
you.
We bless you in the name of the
LORD."

Psalm 130

A song for those who go up to Jerusalem
to worship the LORD.

1 LORD, I cry out to you
because I'm suffering so deeply.
2 Lord, listen to me.
Pay attention to my cry for your
favor.

3 LORD, suppose you kept a record of
sins.
Lord, who then wouldn't be found
guilty?
4 But you forgive.
So people have respect for you.

5 With all my heart I wait for the LORD to
help me.
I put my hope in his word.
6 I wait for the Lord to help me.
I wait with more longing than those
on guard duty wait for the
morning.
I'll say it again.
I wait with more longing than those
on guard duty wait for the
morning.

7 Israel, put your hope in the LORD,
because the LORD's love never fails.
He sets his people completely free.

8 He himself will set Israel
  free from all of their sins.

Psalm 131

A song for those who go up to Jerusalem
to worship the LORD. A psalm of David.
1 LORD, my heart isn't proud.
  My eyes aren't proud either.
  I don't concern myself with important
    matters.
  I don't concern myself with things
    that are too wonderful for me.
2 I have made myself calm and content
  like a young child in its mother's
    arms.
  Deep down inside me, I am as
    content as a young child.

3 Israel, put your hope in the LORD
  both now and forever.

Psalm 132

A song for those who go up to Jerusalem
to worship the LORD.
1 LORD, remember David
  and all of the hard times he went
    through.
2 LORD, he took an oath.
  Mighty One of Jacob, he made a
    promise to you.
3 He said, "I won't enter my house
  or go to bed.
4 I won't let my eyes sleep.
  I won't close my eyelids
5 until I find a place for the LORD.
  I want to build a house for the
    Mighty One of Jacob."

6 Here are the words we heard in
    Ephrathah.
  We heard them again in the fields of
    Kiriath Jearim.
7 "Let us go to the LORD's house.
  Let us worship at his feet.
8 LORD, rise up and come to your resting
    place.
  Come in together with the ark. It's
    the sign of your power.
9 May your priests put on godliness as if
    it were their clothes.
  May your faithful people sing with
    joy."

10 In honor of your servant David,
  don't turn your back on your
    anointed king.
11 The LORD took an oath and made a
    promise to David.
  It is a firm promise that he will never
    break.

He said, "After you die,
  I will place one of your own sons on
    your throne.
12 If your sons keep my covenant
  and the laws I teach them,
  then their sons will sit
    on your throne for ever and ever."

13 The LORD has chosen Zion.
  That's the place where he wants to
    live.
14 He has said, "This will be my resting
    place for ever and ever.
  Here I will sit on my throne, because
    that's what I want.
15 I will greatly bless Zion with
    everything it needs.
  I will give plenty of food to the poor
    people living there.
16 I will put salvation on its priests as if it
    were their clothes.
  God's faithful people will always
    sing with joy.

17 "Here in Jerusalem I will raise up a
    mighty king from the family of
    David.
  I will set up the lamp of David's
    kingdom for my anointed
    king.
  Its flame will burn brightly forever.
18 I will put shame on his enemies as if it
    were their clothes.
  But the royal crown he wears will
    shine with glory."

Psalm 133

A song for those who go up to Jerusalem
to worship the LORD. A psalm of David.
1 How good and pleasant it is
  when God's people live together in
    peace!
2 It's like the special olive oil
  that was poured on Aaron's head.
  It ran down on his beard
    and on the collar of his robe.
3 It's as if the dew of Mount Hermon
  were falling on Mount Zion.
  There the LORD gives his blessing.
  He gives life that never ends.

Psalm 134

A song for those who go up to Jerusalem
to worship the LORD.
1 All of you who serve the LORD, praise
    the LORD.
  All of you who serve at night in the
    house of the LORD, praise him.
2 Lift up your hands in the temple
  and praise the LORD.

3 May the LORD bless you from Zion.
He is the Maker of heaven and earth.

Psalm 135

1 Praise the LORD.

Praise the name of the LORD.
You who serve the LORD, praise him.
2 You who serve in the house of the
LORD, praise him.
You who serve in the courtyards of
the temple of our God, praise
him.

3 Praise the LORD, because he is good.
Sing praise to his name, because that
is pleasant.
4 The LORD has chosen the people of
Jacob to be his own.
He has chosen Israel to be his special
treasure.

5 I know that the LORD is great.
I know that our Lord is greater than
all gods.
6 The LORD does anything he wants
to do
in the heavens and on the earth.
He does it even in the deepest parts
of the oceans.
7 He makes clouds rise from one end of
the earth to the other.
He sends lightning with the rain.
He brings the wind out of his
storerooms.

8 He killed the oldest son of each family
in Egypt.
He struck down the oldest males
that were born to people and
animals.
9 He did miraculous signs in Egypt.
He did wonders against Pharaoh and
everyone who served him.
10 He destroyed many nations.
He killed mighty kings.
11 He killed Sihon, the king of the
Amorites,
and Og, the king of Bashan.
He killed all of the kings of Canaan.
12 He gave their land as a gift
to his people Israel.

13 LORD, your name continues forever.
LORD, your fame will last for all time
to come.
14 When the LORD hands down his
sentence, it will be in his
people's favor.
He will show deep concern for those
who serve him.

15 The statues of the gods of the nations
are made of silver and gold.
They are made by the hands of men.
16 They have mouths, but they can't
speak.
They have eyes, but they can't see.
17 They have ears, but they can't hear.
They have mouths, but they can't
breathe.
18 Those who make statues of gods will be
like them.
So will all those who trust in them.

19 People of Israel, praise the LORD.
Priests of Aaron, praise the LORD.
20 Tribe of Levi, praise the LORD.
You who have respect for the LORD,
praise him.
21 Give praise to the LORD in Zion.
Give praise to the One who lives in
Jerusalem.

Praise the LORD.

Psalm 136

1 Give thanks to the LORD, because he is
good.
His faithful love continues forever.
2 Give thanks to the greatest God of all.
His faithful love continues forever.
3 Give thanks to the most powerful Lord
of all.
His faithful love continues forever.

4 Give thanks to the only one who can
do great miracles.
His faithful love continues forever.
5 By his understanding he made the
heavens.
His faithful love continues forever.
6 He spread out the earth on the waters.
His faithful love continues forever.
7 He made the great lights in the sky.
His faithful love continues forever.
8 He made the sun to rule over the day.
His faithful love continues forever.
9 He made the moon and stars to rule
over the night.
His faithful love continues forever.

10 Give thanks to the One who killed the
oldest son of each family in
Egypt.
His faithful love continues forever.
11 He brought the people of Israel out of
Egypt.
His faithful love continues forever.
12 He did it by reaching out his mighty
hand and powerful arm.
His faithful love continues forever.

13 Give thanks to the One who parted the
Red Sea.

His faithful love continues forever.
¹⁴ He brought Israel through the middle
of it.
His faithful love continues forever.
¹⁵ But he swept Pharaoh and his army
into the Red Sea.
His faithful love continues forever.

¹⁶ Give thanks to the One who led his
people through the desert.
His faithful love continues forever.
¹⁷ He killed great kings.
His faithful love continues forever.
¹⁸ He struck down mighty kings.
His faithful love continues forever.
¹⁹ He killed Sihon, the king of the
Amorites.
His faithful love continues forever.
²⁰ He killed Og, the king of Bashan.
His faithful love continues forever.
²¹ He gave their land as a gift.
His faithful love continues forever.
²² He gave it as a gift to his servant Israel.
His faithful love continues forever.

²³ Give thanks to the One who
remembered us when things
were going badly for us.
His faithful love continues forever.
²⁴ He set us free from our enemies.
His faithful love continues forever.
²⁵ He gives food to every creature.
His faithful love continues forever.

²⁶ Give thanks to the God of heaven.
His faithful love continues forever.

Psalm 137

¹ We were sitting by the rivers of
Babylon.
We cried when we remembered
what had happened to Zion.
² On the nearby poplar trees
we hung up our harps.
³ Those who held us as prisoners asked
us to sing.
Those who enjoyed hurting us
ordered us to sing joyful songs.
They said, "Sing one of the songs of
Zion to us!"

⁴ How can we sing the songs of the Lord
while we are in another land?
⁵ Jerusalem, if I forget you,
may my right hand never be able to
play the harp again.
⁶ If I don't remember you,
may my tongue stick to the roof of
my mouth so I can't sing.
May it happen if I don't consider
Jerusalem
to be my greatest joy.

⁷ Lord, remember what the people of
Edom did
on the day Jerusalem fell.
"Tear it down!" they cried.
"Tear it down to the ground!"

⁸ People of Babylon, you are sentenced
to be destroyed.
Happy are those who pay you back
for what you have done to us.
⁹ Happy are those who grab your babies
and smash them against the rocks.

Psalm 138

A psalm of David.
¹ Lord, I will praise you with all my
heart.
In front of those who think they are
gods
I will sing praise to you.
² I will bow down facing your holy
temple.
I will praise your name,
because you are loving and faithful.
You have honored your name and your
word
more than anything else.
³ When I called out to you, you
answered me.
You made me strong and brave.

BRAVE ⒝

WHEN I CALLED OUT TO YOU, YOU ANSWERED ME.

YOU MADE ME STRONG AND BRAVE.

— PSALM 138:3 —

STRONG

⁴ Lord, may all of the kings on earth
praise you
when they hear about what you
have promised.
⁵ Lord, may they sing about what you
have done,
because your glory is great.
⁶ The Lord is in heaven. But he watches
over those who are free of pride.
He knows those who are proud and
stays far away from them.

7 Trouble is all around me,
   but you keep me alive.
You reach out your hand to put a stop
     to the anger of my enemies.
   With your powerful right hand you
     save me.
8 LORD, you will do everything you have
     planned for me.
   LORD, your faithful love continues
     forever.
   You have done so much for us.
   Don't stop now.

Psalm 139

For the director of music.
A psalm of David.

1 LORD, you have seen what is in my
     heart.
   You know all about me.
2 You know when I sit down and when I
     get up.
   You know what I'm thinking even
     though you are far away.
3 You know when I go out to work and
     when I come back home.
   You know exactly how I live.
4 LORD, even before I speak a word,
   you know all about it.

5 You are all around me. You are behind
     me and in front of me.
   You hold me in your power.
6 I'm amazed at how well you know me.
   It's more than I can understand.

7 How can I get away from your Spirit?
   Where can I go to escape from you?
8 If I go up to the heavens, you are there.
   If I lie down in the deepest parts of
     the earth, you are also there.
9 Suppose I were to rise with the sun in
     the east
   and then cross over to the west
     where it sinks into the ocean.
10 Your hand would always be there to
     guide me.
   Your right hand would still be
     holding me close.

11 Suppose I were to say, "I'm sure the
     darkness will hide me.
   The light around me will become as
     dark as night."
12 Even that darkness would not be dark
     to you.
   The night would shine like the day,
   because darkness is like light to you.

13 You created the deepest parts of my
     being.
   You put me together inside my
     mother's body.

14 How you made me is amazing and
     wonderful.
   I praise you for that.
   What you have done is wonderful.
   I know that very well.
15 None of my bones was hidden from
     you
   when you made me inside my
     mother's body.
   That place was as dark as the deepest
     parts of the earth.
   When you were putting me together
     there,
16   your eyes saw my body even before it
     was formed.
   You planned how many days I would
     live.
   You wrote down the number of
     them in your book
   before I had lived through even one
     of them.

17 God, your thoughts about me are
     priceless.
   No one can possibly add them all
     up.
18 If I could count them,
   they would be more than the grains
     of sand.
   If I were to fall asleep counting and
     then wake up,
   you would still be there with me.

19 God, I wish you would kill the people
     who are evil!
   I wish those murderers would get
     away from me!
20 They are your enemies. They misuse
     your name.
   They misuse it for their own evil
     purposes.
21 LORD, I really hate those who hate you!
   I really hate those who rise up
     against you!
22 I have nothing but hatred for them.
   I consider them to be my enemies.

23 God, see what is in my heart.
   Know what is there.
   Put me to the test.
   Know what I'm thinking.
24 See if there's anything in my life you
     don't like.
   Help me live in the way that is
     always right.

Psalm 140

For the director of music.
A psalm of David.

1 LORD, save me from sinful men.
   Keep me safe from those who want
     to hurt me.

2 They make evil plans in their hearts.
They are always starting fights.
3 Their tongues are as deadly as the
tongue of a serpent.
The words from their lips are like the
poison of a snake. *Selah*

4 LORD, keep me out of the hands of
sinful people.
Keep me safe from men who want to
hurt me.
They plan to trip me up and make
me fall.
5 Proud people have hidden their traps
to catch me.
They have spread out their nets.
They have set traps for me along my
path. *Selah*

6 LORD, I say to you, "You are my God."
LORD, hear my cry for your favor.
7 LORD and King, you save me because
you are strong.
You are like a shield that keeps me
safe in the day of battle.
8 LORD, don't give sinners what they
want.
Don't let their plans succeed.
If you do, they will become proud. *Selah*

9 Those who are all around me have
caused me trouble
by what their lips have said.
Let that trouble fall on their own
heads.
10 Let burning coals fall on people like
that.
May they be thrown into the fire.
May they be thrown into muddy
pits and never get out.
11 Don't let men who tell lies about me
settle down in the land.
May trouble hunt down those who
want to hurt me.

12 I know that the LORD makes sure that
poor people are treated fairly.
He stands up for those who are in
need.
13 I'm sure that those who do right will
praise your name.
Those who are honest will live with
you.

Psalm 141

A psalm of David.

1 LORD, I call out to you. Come quickly to
help me.
Listen to me when I call out to you.
2 May my prayer come to you like the
sweet smell of incense.

When I lift up my hands in prayer,
may it be like the evening
sacrifice.

3 LORD, guard my mouth.
Keep watch over the door of my lips.
4 Don't let my heart be drawn to what is
evil.
Don't let me join men who do evil.
They don't do what is right.
Don't let me join them and eat their
fancy food.

5 If a person who does what is right were
to strike me, it would be an act
of kindness.
If that person were to correct me, it
would be like pouring olive oil
on my head.
I wouldn't say no to it.

But I always pray against the things
that sinful people do.
6 When their rulers are thrown down
from the rocky cliffs,
those evil people will realize that my
words were true.
7 They will say, "As clumps of dirt are left
from plowing up the ground,
so our bones will be scattered near
an open grave."

8 But LORD and King, I keep looking to
you.
I go to you for safety. Don't let me
die.
9 Keep me from the traps of those who
do evil.
Save me from the traps they have set
for me.
10 Let evil people fall into their own nets.
But let me go safely on my way.

Psalm 142

A prayer of David when he was in the
cave. A *maskil.*

1 I call out to the LORD.
I pray to him for his favor.
2 I pour out my problem to him.
I tell him about my trouble.

3 When I grow weak,
you know what I'm going through.
In the path where I walk,
people have hidden a trap to catch
me.
4 Look around me, and you will see
that no one is concerned about me.
I have no place of safety.
No one cares whether I live or die.

5 LORD, I cry out to you.
I say, "You are my place of safety.

You are everything I need in this
life."
6 Listen to my cry.
   I am in great need.
Save me from those who are chasing
      me.
   They are too strong for me.
7 My troubles are like a prison.
   Set me free so I can praise your
      name.

Then those who do what is right will
      gather around me
   because you have been good to me.

Psalm 143

A psalm of David.
1 LORD, hear my prayer.
   Listen to my cry for your favor.
You are faithful and right.
   Come and help me.
2 Don't take me to court and judge me,
   because in your eyes no living
         person does what is right.

3 My enemies chase me.
   They crush me down to the ground.
They make me live in darkness
   like those who died long ago.
4 So I grow weak.
   Deep down inside me, I'm afraid.

5 I remember what happened long ago.
   I spend time thinking about all of
         your acts.
   I consider what your hands have
         done.
6 I spread out my hands to you in prayer.
   I'm thirsty for you, just as dry
         ground is thirsty for rain.   *Selah*

7 LORD, answer me quickly.
   I'm growing weak.
Don't turn your face away from me,
   or I will be like those who go down
         into the grave.
8 In the morning let me hear about your
         faithful love,
   because I've put my trust in you.
Show me the way I should live,
   because I pray to you.
9 LORD, save me from my enemies,
   because I go to you for safety.
10 Teach me to do what you want,
   because you are my God.
May your good Spirit
   lead me on a level path.

11 LORD, be true to your name. Keep me
         alive.
   Because you do what is right, get me
         out of trouble.

12 Because your love is faithful, put an
         end to my enemies.
   Destroy all of them, because I serve
         you.

Psalm 144

A psalm of David.
1 Give praise to the LORD. He is my rock.
   He trains my hands for war.
   He trains my fingers for battle.
2 He is my loving God. He is like a fort
         to me.
   He is my place of safety and the One
         who saves me.
He is like a shield that keeps me safe. I
         go to him for safety.
   He brings nations under my control.

3 LORD, what is a human being that you
         take care of him?
   What is a son of man that you think
         about him?
4 His life doesn't last any longer than a
         breath.
   His days are like a shadow that
         quickly disappears.

5 LORD, open up your heavens and come
         down.
   Touch the mountains, and they will
         pour out smoke.
6 Send flashes of lightning and scatter
         my enemies.
   Shoot your arrows and chase them
         away.
7 My enemies are like a mighty flood.
   Reach down from heaven and save
         me.
   Save me from strangers who attack
         me.
8 They tell all kinds of lies with their
         mouths.
   Even when they make a promise by
         raising their right hands, they
         don't mean it.

9 God, I will sing a new song to you.
   I will make music to you on a harp
         that has ten strings.
10 You are the One who helps kings win
         battles.
   You save your servant David from
         dying by the sword.

11 Save me. Set me free
   from strangers who attack me.
They tell all kinds of lies with their
         mouths.
   Even when they make a promise by
         raising their right hands, they
         don't mean it.

12 While our sons are young,

they will be like healthy plants.
Our daughters will be like pillars
    that have been made to decorate a
    palace.
13 Our storerooms will be filled
    with every kind of food.
The sheep in our fields will increase by
    thousands.
They will increase by tens of
    thousands.
14   Our oxen will pull heavy loads.
None of our city walls will be broken
    down.
No one will be carried off as a
    prisoner.
No cries of pain will be heard in our
    streets.

15 Blessed are the people about whom all
    of those things are true.
Blessed are the people whose God is
    the LORD.

Psalm 145

A psalm of praise. A psalm of David.
1 I will honor you, my God the King.
    I will praise your name for ever and
    ever.
2 Every day I will praise you.
    I will praise your name for ever and
    ever.

3 LORD, you are great. You are really
    worthy of praise.
No one can completely understand
    how great you are.
4 Parents will praise your works to their
    children.
They will tell about your mighty
    acts.
5 They will speak about your glorious
    majesty.
I will spend time thinking about
    your miracles.
6 They will speak about the powerful
    and wonderful things you do.
I will talk about the great things you
    have done.
7 They will celebrate your great
    goodness.
They will sing with joy about your
    holy acts.

8 The LORD is gracious. He is kind and
    tender.
He is slow to get angry. He is full of
    love.
9 The LORD is good to all.
He shows deep concern for
    everything he has made.
10 LORD, every living thing you have
    made will praise you.

Your faithful people will praise you.
11 They will tell about your glorious
    kingdom.
They will speak about your power.
12 Then all people will know about the
    mighty things you have done.
They will know about the glorious
    majesty of your kingdom.
13 Your kingdom is a kingdom that will
    last forever.
Your rule will continue for all time
    to come.

The LORD is faithful and will keep all of
    his promises.
He is loving toward everything he
    has made.
14 The LORD takes good care of all those
    who fall.
He lifts up all those who feel
    helpless.
15 Every living thing looks to you for food.
You give it to them exactly when
    they need it.
16 You open your hand
    and satisfy the needs of every living
    creature.

17 The LORD is right in everything he
    does.
He is loving toward everything he
    has made.
18 The LORD is ready to help all those who
    call out to him.
He helps those who really mean it
    when they call out to him.
19 He satisfies the needs of those who
    have respect for him.
He hears their cry and saves them.
20 The LORD watches over all those who
    love him.
But he will destroy all sinful people.

21 I will praise the LORD with my mouth.
Let every creature praise his holy
    name
for ever and ever.

Psalm 146

1 Praise the LORD.

I will praise the LORD.
2   I will praise the LORD all my life.
    I will sing praise to my God as long
    as I live.

3 Don't put your trust in human leaders.
Don't trust in people. They can't
    save you.
4 When they die, they return to the
    ground.
On that very day their plans are
    bound to fail.

5 Blessed are those who depend on the
God of Jacob for help.
Blessed are those who put their hope
in the LORD their God.
6 He is the Maker of heaven and earth
and the ocean.
He made everything in them.
The LORD remains faithful forever.
7 He stands up for those who are beaten
down.
He gives food to hungry people.
The LORD sets prisoners free.
8 The LORD gives sight to those who
are blind.
The LORD lifts up those who feel
helpless.
The LORD loves those who do what is
right.
9 The LORD watches over the outsiders
who live in our land.
He takes good care of children
whose fathers have died.
He also takes good care of widows.
But he causes evil people to fail
in everything they do.
10 The LORD rules forever.
The God of Zion will rule for all time
to come.

Praise the LORD.

Psalm 147

1 Praise the LORD.

How good it is to sing praises to our
God!
How pleasant and right it is to praise
him!

2 The LORD builds up Jerusalem.
He gathers the scattered people of
Israel.
3 He heals those who have broken
hearts.
He takes care of their wounds.
4 He decides how many stars there
should be.
He gives each one of them a name.
5 Great is our Lord. His power is mighty.
There is no limit to his
understanding.
6 The LORD gives strength to those who
aren't proud.
But he throws evil people down to
the ground.
7 Sing to the LORD and give thanks to
him.
Make music to our God on the harp.
8 He covers the sky with clouds.
He supplies the earth with rain.

POWER–SURGE

BELIEVES ✝

[THE LORD] DOESN'T TAKE PLEASURE IN THE STRENGTH OF HORSES.

HE DOESN'T TAKE DELIGHT IN THE STRONG LEGS OF MEN.

THE LORD TAKES DELIGHT IN THOSE WHO HAVE RESPECT FOR HIM.

THEY PUT THEIR HOPE IN HIS FAITHFUL LOVE.
— **PSALM 147:10-11** —

He makes grass grow on the hills.
9 He provides food for the cattle.
He provides for the young ravens
when they cry out.

10 He doesn't take pleasure in the
strength of horses.
He doesn't take delight in the strong
legs of men.
11 The LORD takes delight in those who
have respect for him.
They put their hope in his faithful
love.

12 Jerusalem, praise the LORD.
Zion, praise your God.
13 He makes the bars of your gates
stronger.
He blesses the people who live inside
you.
14 He keeps your borders safe and secure.
He satisfies you with the finest
wheat.

15 He sends his command to the earth.
His word arrives there quickly.
16 He spreads the snow like wool.
He scatters the frost like ashes.
17 He throws down his hail like small
stones.
No one can stand his icy blast.
18 He gives his command, and the ice
melts.
He stirs up his winds, and the waters
flow.

19 He has made his word known to the
        people of Jacob.
    He has made his laws and rules
        known to Israel.
20 He hasn't done that for any other
        nation.
    They don't know his laws.

Praise the LORD.

Psalm 148

1 Praise the LORD.

    Praise the LORD from the heavens.
        Praise him in the heavens above.
2 Praise him, all his angels.
        Praise him, all his angels in heaven.
3 Praise him, sun and moon.
        Praise him, all you shining stars.
4 Praise him, you highest heavens.
        Praise him, you waters above the
            skies.
5 Let all of them praise the name of the
        LORD,
    because he gave a command and
        they were created.
6 He set them in place for ever and ever.
    He gave them laws they will always
        have to obey.

7 Praise the LORD from the earth,
    you great sea creatures and all of the
        deepest parts of the ocean.
8 Praise him, lightning and hail, snow
        and clouds.
    Praise him, you stormy winds that
        obey him.
9 Praise him, all you mountains and hills.
    Praise him, all you fruit trees and
        cedar trees.
10 Praise him, all you wild animals and
        cattle.
    Praise him, you small creatures and
        flying birds.
11 Praise him, you kings of the earth and
        all nations.
    Praise him, all you princes and rulers
        on earth.
12 Praise him, young men and young
        women.
    Praise him, old people and children.

13 Let them praise the name of the LORD.
    His name alone is honored.
    His glory is higher than the earth
        and the heavens.
14 He has given his people a strong king.
    All of his faithful people praise him
        for that gift.
    All of the people of Israel are close to
        his heart.

Praise the LORD.

Psalm 149

1 Praise the LORD.

    Sing a new song to the LORD.
        Sing praise to him in the
            community of his faithful
            people.
2 Let Israel be filled with joy because
        God is their Maker.
    Let the people of Zion be glad
        because he is their King.
3 Let them praise his name with
        dancing.
    Let them make music to him with
        harps and tambourines.
4 The LORD takes delight in his people.
    He saves those who aren't proud. He
        makes them feel like kings.
5 Let his faithful people be filled with joy
        because of that honor.
    Let them sing with joy even when
        they are lying in bed.

6 May they praise God with their
        mouths.
    May they hold in their hands a
        sword that has two edges.
7 Let them pay the nations back.
    Let them punish the people of the
        earth.
8 Let them put the kings of those
        nations in chains.
    Let them put their nobles in iron
        chains.
9 Let them carry out God's sentence
        against the nations.
    That will bring glory to all of his
        faithful people.

Praise the LORD.

Psalm 150

1 Praise the LORD.

    Praise God in his holy temple.
        Praise him in his mighty heavens.
2 Praise him for his powerful acts.
        Praise him because he is greater than
            anything else.
3 Praise him by blowing trumpets.
        Praise him with harps and lyres.
4 Praise him with tambourines and
        dancing.
    Praise him with stringed
        instruments and flutes.
5 Praise him with clashing cymbals.
    Praise him with clanging cymbals.

6 Let everything that has breath praise
        the LORD.

Praise the LORD.

PROVERBS

The book of Proverbs is a collection of wise sayings, most of them by Solomon, the wisest king who ever lived. These proverbs are not only wise but also practical. The topics they cover range from seeking God to managing money, from knowing that wisdom is important to knowing that friends are important. As you ask God to help you make wise decisions, read the book of Proverbs. You'll find direction on just about every part of life.

CODE OF HONOR IN THIS BOOK . . .

ALL OF THEM!

Purpose

1 These are the proverbs of Solomon. He was the son of David and the king of Israel.

2 Proverbs teach you wisdom and train you.
They help you understand wise sayings.
3 They provide you with training and help you live wisely.
They lead to what is right and honest and fair.
4 They give understanding to childish people.
They give knowledge and good sense to those who are young.
5 Let wise people listen and add to what they have learned.
Let those who understand what is right get guidance.
6 What I'm teaching also helps you understand proverbs and stories.
It helps you understand the sayings and riddles of those who are wise.

Main Point

7 If you really want to gain knowledge, you must begin by having respect for the LORD.
But foolish people hate wisdom and training.

Think and Live Wisely

A Warning Against a Life of Crime

8 My son, listen to your father's advice.
Don't turn away from your mother's teaching.
9 What they teach you will be like a beautiful crown on your head.
It will be like a chain to decorate your neck.
10 My son, if sinners tempt you, don't give in to them.

POWER-SURGE

TRIES HARD T

MY SON, IF SINNERS TEMPT YOU,

DON'T GIVE IN TO THEM.

— PROVERBS 1:10 —

11 They might say, "Come along with us.
Let's hide and wait to spill someone's blood.
Let's catch some harmless people in our trap.
12 Let's swallow them alive, as the grave does.
Let's swallow them whole, like those who go down into the pit.
13 We'll get all kinds of valuable things.
We'll fill our houses with what we steal.
14 Come and join our gang.
We'll share everything we have."
15 My son, don't go along with them.
Don't even set your feet on their paths.
16 They are always in a hurry to sin.
They are quick to spill someone's blood.
17 How useless it is to spread a net while all the birds are watching!
18 Those who hide and wait will spill their own blood.
They will be caught in their own trap.
19 That's what happens to everyone who goes after money in the wrong way.
That kind of money takes away the lives of those who get it.

A Warning Against Turning Away From Wisdom

20 Wisdom calls out in the street.
She raises her voice in public places.
21 At the noisy street corners she cries out.
Here is what she says near the gates of the city.

22 "How long will you childish people love your childish ways?
How long will you rude people enjoy making fun of God and others?
How long will you foolish people hate knowledge?
23 Suppose you had paid attention to my warning.
Then I would have poured out my heart to you.
I would have told you what I was thinking.
24 But you turned away from me when I called out to you.
None of you paid attention when I reached out my hand.
25 You turned away from all my advice.
You wouldn't accept my warning.

POWER-SURGE

WISE   W

LET YOUR EARS
LISTEN TO WISDOM.

APPLY YOUR HEART TO
UNDERSTANDING.

THE LORD GIVES
WISDOM.

KNOWLEDGE AND
UNDERSTANDING
COME FROM HIS
MOUTH.

— PROVERBS 2:2, 6 —

26 So I will laugh at you when you are in
danger.
I will make fun of you when hard
times come.
27 I will laugh when hard times hit you
like a storm.
I will laugh when danger comes
your way like a windstorm.
I will make fun of you when
suffering and trouble come.
28 "Then you will call to me. But I won't
answer.
You will look for me. But you won't
find me.
29 You hated knowledge.
You didn't choose to have respect for
the LORD.
30 You wouldn't accept my advice.
You turned your backs on my
warnings.
31 So you will eat the fruit of the way you
have lived.
You will choke on the fruit of what
you have planned.
32 "Childish people go down the wrong
path. They will die.
Foolish people are satisfied with the
way they live. They will be
destroyed.
33 But those who listen to me will live in
safety.
They will not worry. They won't be
afraid of getting hurt."

Good Things Come From Wisdom

2 My son, accept my words.
Store up my commands inside you.

2 Let your ears listen to wisdom.
Apply your heart to understanding.
3 Call out for the ability to be wise.
Cry out for understanding.
4 Look for it as you would look for silver.
Search for it as you would search for
hidden treasure.
5 Then you will understand how to have
respect for the LORD.
You will find out how to know God.
6 The LORD gives wisdom.
Knowledge and understanding
come from his mouth.
7 He stores up success for honest people.
He is like a shield to those who live
without blame. He keeps them
safe.
8 He guards the path of those who are
honest.
He watches over the way of his
faithful ones.
9 You will understand what is right and
honest and fair.
You will understand the right way to
live.
10 Your heart will become wise.
Your mind will delight in
knowledge.
11 Good sense will keep you safe.
Understanding will guard you.
12 Wisdom will save you from the ways of
evil men.
It will save you from men who twist
their words.
13 Men like that leave the straight paths
to walk in dark ways.
14 They take delight in doing what is
wrong.
They take joy in twisting everything
around.

POWER-SURGE

FAITHFUL ()

[GOD] GUARDS THE
PATH OF THOSE WHO
ARE HONEST.

HE WATCHES OVER THE
WAY OF HIS FAITHFUL
ONES.

— PROVERBS 2:8 —   H

HONEST

15 Their paths are crooked.
Their ways are not straight.

16 Wisdom will save you from a woman
who commits adultery.
It will save you from a sinful wife
and her tempting words.
17 She leaves the man she married when
she was young.
She breaks the promise she made to
her God.
18 Her house leads down to death.
Her paths lead to the spirits of the
dead.
19 No one who goes to her comes back
or reaches the paths of life.
20 You will walk in the ways of good
people.
You will follow the paths of those
who do right.
21 Honest people will live in the land.
Those who are without blame will
remain in it.
22 But sinners will be cut off from the
land.
Those who aren't faithful will be
torn away from it.

More Good Things Come From Wisdom

3 My son, do not forget my teaching.
Keep my commands in your heart.
2 They will help you live for many years.
They will bring you success.

3 Don't let love and truth ever leave you.
Tie them around your neck.
Write them on the tablet of your
heart.
4 Then you will find favor and a good
name
in the eyes of God and people.

5 Trust in the LORD with all your heart.
Do not depend on your own
understanding.

HONEST

H

DON'T LET LOVE AND TRUTH EVER LEAVE YOU.
— PROVERBS 3:3 —

LOVING

WISE

W

BLESSED IS THE ONE WHO FINDS WISDOM.

BLESSED IS THE ONE WHO GAINS UNDERSTANDING.

WISDOM PAYS BETTER THAN SILVER DOES.

SHE EARNS MORE THAN GOLD DOES.
— PROVERBS 3:13-14 —

6 In all your ways remember him.
Then he will make your paths
smooth and straight.

7 Don't be wise in your own eyes.
Have respect for the LORD and avoid
evil.
8 That will bring health to your body.
It will make your bones strong.

9 Honor the LORD with your wealth.
Give him the first share of all your
crops.
10 Then your storerooms will be so full
they can't hold everything.
Your huge jars will spill over with
fresh wine.

11 My son, do not hate the LORD's
training.
Do not object when he corrects you.
12 The LORD trains those he loves.
He is like a father who trains the son
he is pleased with.

13 Blessed is the one who finds wisdom.
Blessed is the one who gains
understanding.
14 Wisdom pays better than silver does.
She earns more than gold does.
15 She is worth more than rubies.
Nothing you want can compare
with her.
16 Long life is in her right hand.
In her left hand are riches and
honor.
17 Her ways are pleasant ways.
All her paths lead to peace.
18 She is a tree of life to those who hold
her close.
Those who hold on to her will be
blessed.

19 By wisdom the Lord laid the earth's
foundations.
>Through understanding he set the
heavens in place.
20 By his knowledge the seas were
separated,
>and the clouds dropped their dew.

21 My son, hold on to good sense and the
understanding of what is right.
>Don't let them out of your sight.
22 They will be life for you.
>They will be like a gracious necklace
around your neck.
23 Then you will go on your way in safety.
>You will not trip and fall.
24 When you lie down, you won't be
afraid.
>When you lie down, you will sleep
soundly.
25 Don't be terrified by sudden trouble.
>Don't be afraid when sinners are
destroyed.
26 The Lord is the one you will trust in.
>He will keep your feet from being
caught in a trap.

27 Don't hold back good from those who
are worthy of it.
>Don't hold it back when you can
help.
28 Suppose you have something to give.
>Don't say to your neighbor,
"Come back later.
>I'll give it to you tomorrow."

29 Don't plan to harm your neighbor.
>He lives near you and trusts you.
30 Don't bring charges against a man
without any reason.
>He has not harmed you.

31 Don't be jealous of a man who hurts
others.
>Don't choose any of his ways.
32 The Lord really hates sinful people.
>But he makes honest people his
closest friends.

POWER-SURGE

TRUSTED ◆

**DON'T PLAN TO HARM
YOUR NEIGHBOR.**

**HE LIVES NEAR YOU
AND TRUSTS YOU.**

— **PROVERBS 3:29** —

POWER-SURGE

TRIES HARD **T**

**WISDOM IS BEST. SO
GET WISDOM.**

**NO MATTER WHAT IT
COSTS, GET
UNDERSTANDING.**

— **PROVERBS 4:7** —

WISE

---

33 The Lord puts a curse on the houses of
sinners.
>But he blesses the homes of those
who do what is right.
34 He laughs at proud people who make
fun of others.
>But he gives grace to those who are
not proud.
35 Wise people receive honor.
>But the Lord puts foolish people to
shame.

Wisdom Is Best

4 My children, listen to a father's
teaching.
>Pay attention and gain
understanding.
2 I give you good advice.
>So don't turn away from what I
teach you.
3 I was once a young boy in my father's
house.
>I was my mother's only child.
4 My father taught me.
>He said, "Hold on to my words with
all your heart.
>Keep my commands. Then you will
live.
5 Get wisdom. Get understanding.
>Don't forget my words. Don't turn
away from them.
6 Stay close to wisdom, and she will keep
you safe.
>Love her, and she will watch over
you.
7 Wisdom is best. So get wisdom.
>No matter what it costs, get
understanding.
8 Value wisdom, and she will lift you up.
>Hold her close, and she will honor
you.

9 She will set a beautiful crown on your
head.
She will give you a glorious crown."

10 My son, listen. Accept what I say.
Then you will live for many years.
11 I guide you in the way of wisdom.
I lead you along straight paths.
12 When you walk, nothing will slow you
down.
When you run, you won't trip and
fall.
13 Hold on to my teaching. Don't let it
go.
Guard it well. It is your life.
14 Don't take the path of evil people.
Don't live the way sinners do.
15 Stay away from their path. Don't travel
on it.
Turn away from it. Go on your way.
16 Sinners can't sleep until they do what
is evil.
They can't rest until they make
someone fall.
17 They do evil just as easily as they eat
food.
They hurt others as easily as they
drink wine.
18 The path of those who do what is right
is like the first gleam of dawn.
It shines brighter and brighter until
the full light of day.
19 But the way of those who do what is
wrong is like deep darkness.
They don't know what makes them
trip and fall.

20 My son, pay attention to what I say.
Listen closely to my words.
21 Don't let them out of your sight.
Keep them in your heart.
22 They are life to those who find them.
They are health to your whole body.
23 Above everything else, guard your
heart.
It is where your life comes from.
24 Don't speak with twisted words.
Keep evil talk away from your lips.
25 Let your eyes look straight ahead.
Keep looking right in front of you.
26 Make level paths for your feet to walk
on.
Only go on ways that are firm.
27 Don't turn to the right or left.
Keep your feet from the path of evil.

A Warning Against Committing Adultery

5 My son, pay attention to my
wisdom.
Listen carefully to my wise sayings.

2 Then you will continue to have good
sense.
Your lips will keep on speaking
words of knowledge.
3 A woman who commits adultery has
lips that drip honey.
What she says is smoother than oil.
4 But in the end she is like bitter poison.
She cuts like a sword that has two
edges.
5 Her feet go down to death.
Her steps lead straight to the grave.
6 She doesn't give any thought to her
way of life.
Her paths are crooked, but she
doesn't realize it.

7 My sons, listen to me.
Don't turn away from what I say.
8 Stay on a path far away from that evil
woman.
Don't even go near the door of her
house.
9 If you do, you will give your best
strength to others.
You will give the best years of your
life to someone who is mean.
10 Strangers will use up all of your wealth.
Your hard work will make someone
else rich.
11 At the end of your life you will groan.
Your skin and your body will be
worn out.
12 You will say, "How I hated to take
advice!
How my heart refused to be
corrected!
13 I would not obey my teachers.
I wouldn't listen to those who
taught me.
14 I was almost totally destroyed.
It happened right in front of the
whole community."

15 Drink water from your own well.
Drink running water from your own
spring.
16 Should your springs pour out into the
streets?
Should your streams of water pour
out in public places?
17 No! Let them belong to you alone.
Never share them with strangers.
18 May your fountain be blessed.
May the wife you married when you
were young make you happy.
19 She is like a loving doe, a graceful deer.
May her breasts always satisfy you.
May you always be captured by her
love.
20 My son, why be captured by a woman
who commits adultery?

Why hug the wife of another man?

21 The Lord watches a man's ways.
He studies all of his paths.
22 A sinner is trapped by his own evil acts.
He is held tight by the ropes of his
sins.
23 He will die because he refused to be
corrected.
His sins will capture him because he
was very foolish.

Warnings Against Foolish Acts

6 My son, don't put up money for
what your neighbor owes.
Don't agree to pay up for someone
else.
2 Don't be trapped by what you have
said.
Don't be caught by the words of
your mouth.
3 Instead, my son, do something to free
yourself.
Don't fall into your neighbor's
hands.
Don't be proud.
Hurry and make your appeal to your
neighbor.
4 Don't let your eyes go to sleep.
Don't let your eyelids close.
5 As a deer frees itself from a hunter, free
yourself.
As a bird frees itself from a trapper,
free yourself.

6 You people who don't want to work,
think about the ant!
Consider its ways and be wise!
7 It has no commander.
It has no leader or ruler.
8 But it stores up its food in summer.
It gathers its food at harvest time.

9 You lazy people, how long will you lie
there?
When will you get up from your
sleep?
10 You might sleep a little or take a little
nap.
You might even fold your hands and
rest.
11 Then you would be poor, as if someone
had robbed you.
You would have little, as if someone
had stolen from you.

12 A worthless and evil man
goes around saying twisted things
with his mouth.
13 He winks with his eyes.
He makes signals with his feet.
He motions with his fingers.

14 His plans are evil. He has lies in his
heart.
He is always stirring up fights.
15 Trouble will catch up with him in an
instant.
He will suddenly be destroyed.
Nothing can save him.

16 There are six things the Lord hates.
In fact, he hates seven things.
17 The Lord hates proud eyes,
a lying tongue,
and hands that kill those who
aren't guilty.
18 He also hates hearts that make
evil plans,
feet that are quick to do evil,
19 any witness who pours out lies,
and anyone who stirs up family
fights.

A Warning Against Committing Adultery

20 My son, keep your father's commands.
Don't turn away from your mother's
teaching.
21 Tie them to your heart forever.
Put them around your neck.
22 When you walk, they will guide you.
When you sleep, they will watch
over you.
When you wake up, they will speak
to you.
23 Your father's commands are like a
lamp.
Your mother's teaching is like a
light.
And the training that corrects you
leads to life.
24 It keeps you from a sinful woman.
It keeps you from the smooth
tongue of a woman who
commits adultery.
25 Don't hunger in your heart after her
beauty.
Don't let her eyes capture you.
26 A prostitute leaves you with only a loaf
of bread.
Another man's wife hunts your very
life.
27 You can't shovel fire into your lap
without burning your clothes.
28 You can't walk on hot coals
without burning your feet.
29 It's the same for anyone who has sex
with another man's wife.
Anyone who touches her will be
punished.

30 People don't hate a thief who steals
to fill his empty stomach.

³¹ But when he is caught, he must pay
seven times as much as he stole.
It may even cost him everything he
has.
³² A man who commits adultery has no
sense.
Anyone who does it destroys
himself.
³³ He will be beaten up and dishonored.
His shame will never be wiped away.
³⁴ Jealousy stirs up a husband's anger.
He will show no mercy when he gets
even.
³⁵ He won't accept any payment.
He won't take any money, no matter
how much he is offered.

A Warning Against a Woman Who Commits Adultery

7 My son, obey my words.
Store up my commands inside you.
² Obey my commands and you will live.
Guard my teachings as you would
your own eyes.
³ Tie them on your fingers.
Write them on the tablet of your
heart.
⁴ Say to wisdom, "You are my sister."
Call understanding a member of
your family.
⁵ They will keep you from a woman who
commits adultery.
They will keep you from the smooth
talk of a sinful wife.

⁶ I stood at the window of my house.
I looked out through it.
⁷ Among those who were childish
I saw a young man who had no
sense.
⁸ He went down the street near that
sinful woman's corner.
He walked toward her house.
⁹ The sun had gone down. Day was
fading.
The darkness of night was falling.

¹⁰ A woman came out to meet him.
She was dressed like a prostitute and
had a clever plan.
¹¹ She was a loud and pushy woman.
She never stayed at home.
¹² Sometimes in the streets, sometimes at
other places,
at every corner she would wait.
¹³ She took hold of the young man and
kissed him.
With a bold face she spoke to him.

¹⁴ She said, "At home I have meat left
over from my offerings.

Today I offered what I had promised
I would.
¹⁵ So I came out to meet you.
I looked for you. And I have found
you!
¹⁶ I have covered my bed
with colored sheets from Egypt.
¹⁷ I've perfumed my bed with spices.
I used myrrh, aloes and cinnamon.
¹⁸ Come, let's drink our fill of love until
morning.
Let's enjoy ourselves by having sex!
¹⁹ My husband isn't home.
He's gone on a long journey.
²⁰ He took his bag full of money.
He won't be home for several days."

²¹ She led him down the wrong path
with her clever words.
She charmed him with her smooth
talk.
²² All at once he followed her.
He was like an ox going to be killed.
He was like a deer stepping into a trap
²³ until an arrow struck its liver.
He was like a bird rushing into a trap.
Little did he know it would cost him
his life!

²⁴ My sons, listen to me.
Pay attention to what I say.
²⁵ Don't let your hearts turn to her ways.
Don't step onto her paths.
²⁶ She has brought down a lot of men.
She has killed a huge crowd.
²⁷ Her house is a road to the grave.
It leads down to the place of the
dead.

Wisdom Is Worth More Than Anything

8 Doesn't wisdom call out?
Doesn't understanding raise her
voice?
² On the high roads along the way,
she takes her place where the paths
meet.
³ Beside the gates leading into the city,
she cries out at the entrances.
⁴ She says, "Men, I call out to you.
I raise my voice to all human beings.
⁵ You who are childish, get some good
sense.
You who are foolish, gain
understanding.
⁶ Listen! I have worthy things to say.
I open my lips to speak what is right.
⁷ My mouth speaks what is true.
My lips hate evil.
⁸ All the words of my mouth are honest.
None of them is twisted or sinful.

HONEST

ALL THE WORDS OF
MY MOUTH ARE
HONEST.

NONE OF THEM IS
TWISTED OR SINFUL.
—— PROVERBS 8:8 ——

⁹ To those who have understanding, all
　　my words are right.
　　To those who have knowledge, they
　　　are true.
¹⁰ Choose my teaching instead of silver.
　　Choose knowledge rather than fine
　　　gold.
¹¹ Wisdom is worth more than rubies.
　　Nothing you want can compare
　　　with her.

¹² "I, wisdom, live together with
　　understanding.
　　I have knowledge and good sense.
¹³ To have respect for the Lord is to hate
　　　evil.
　　I hate pride and bragging.
　　I hate evil ways and twisted words.
¹⁴ I have good sense and give good advice.
　　I have understanding and power.
¹⁵ By me kings rule.
　　Leaders make laws that are fair.
¹⁶ By me princes govern.
　　By me all nobles rule on earth.
¹⁷ I love those who love me.
　　Those who look for me find me.
¹⁸ With me are riches and honor.
　　With me are lasting wealth and
　　　success.
¹⁹ My fruit is better than fine gold.
　　My gifts are better than the finest
　　　silver.
²⁰ I walk in ways that are honest.
　　I take paths that are right.
²¹ I leave riches to those who love me.
　　I give them more than they have
　　　room for.

²² "The Lord created me as the first of his
　　　works,
　　before his acts of long ago.
²³ I was formed at the very beginning.
　　I was formed before the world began.
²⁴ Before there were any oceans, I was
　　　born.
　　There weren't any springs of water at
　　　that time.

²⁵ Before the mountains were settled in
　　　place, I was born.
　　Before there were any hills, I was
　　　born.
²⁶ It happened before the Lord made the
　　　earth and its fields.
　　It was before he made the dust of the
　　　world.
²⁷ I was there when he set the heavens in
　　　place.
　　When he marked out the place
　　　where the sky meets the sea, I
　　　was there.
²⁸ That was when he put the clouds
　　　above.
　　It was when he fixed the ocean
　　　springs in place.
²⁹ It was when he set limits for the sea
　　so that the waters had to obey his
　　　command.
　　When he marked out the foundations
　　　of the earth, I was there.
³⁰ 　　I was the skilled worker at his side.
　　I was filled with delight day after day.
　　I was always happy to be with him.
³¹ His whole world filled me with joy.
　　I took delight in all human beings.

³² "My children, listen to me.
　　Blessed are those who keep my ways.
³³ Listen to my teaching and be wise.
　　Don't turn away from it.
³⁴ Blessed is the one who listens to me.
　　He watches every day at my doors.
　　He waits beside my doorway.
³⁵ Those who find me find life.
　　They receive favor from the Lord.
³⁶ But those who don't find me harm
　　　only themselves.
　　Everyone who hates me loves
　　　death."

Wisdom and Foolishness Call Out

9 Wisdom has built her house.
　　She has made its seven pillars.
² She has prepared her meat and mixed
　　her wine.

WISE

WISDOM IS WORTH
MORE THAN RUBIES.

NOTHING YOU WANT
CAN COMPARE...
—— PROVERBS 8:11 ——

BELIEVES ✝

TEACH A WISE MAN. HE WILL BECOME EVEN WISER.

TEACH A PERSON WHO DOES RIGHT. HE WILL LEARN EVEN MORE.

IF YOU REALLY WANT TO BECOME WISE, YOU MUST BEGIN BY HAVING RESPECT FOR THE LORD.

TO KNOW THE HOLY ONE IS TO GAIN UNDERSTANDING.
—PROVERBS 9:9-10—

WISE

She has also set her table.
3 She has sent out her female servants.
She calls out from the highest point of the city.
4 She says, "Let all who are childish come in here!"
She speaks to those who have no sense.
5 "Come and eat my food.
Drink the wine I have mixed.
6 Leave your childish ways and you will live.
Walk in the way that leads to understanding.
7 "When you correct someone who makes fun of others, you might be laughed at.
When you warn a sinner, you might get hurt.
8 Don't warn those who make fun of others. They will hate you.
Warn those who are wise. They will love you.
9 Teach a wise man. He will become even wiser.
Teach a person who does right. He will learn even more.

10 "If you really want to become wise, you must begin by having respect for the LORD.
To know the Holy One is to gain understanding.
11 Through me, you will live a long time.
Years will be added to your life.
12 If you are wise, your wisdom will reward you.
If you make fun of others, you alone will suffer."

13 The woman called Foolishness is loud.
She doesn't control herself. She doesn't know anything.
14 She sits at the door of her house.
She sits at the highest point of the city.
15 She calls out to those who pass by.
She calls out to those who go straight on their way.
16 She says, "Let all who are childish come in here!"
She speaks to those who have no sense.
17 She says, "Stolen water is sweet.
Food eaten in secret tastes good!"
18 But they don't know that dead people are there.
They don't know that her guests are in the deepest parts of the grave.

The Proverbs of Solomon

10 These are the proverbs of Solomon.

A wise son makes his father glad.
But a foolish son brings sorrow to his mother.

2 Riches that are gained by sinning aren't worth anything.
But doing what is right saves you from death.

3 The LORD gives those who do right the food they need.
But he lets those who do wrong go hungry.

4 Hands that don't want to work make you poor.
But hands that work hard bring wealth to you.

5 A child who gathers crops in summer is wise.
But a child who sleeps at harvest time brings shame.

6 Blessings are like crowns on the heads of those who do right.

POWER-SURGE

FORGIVING F

HATE STIRS UP FIGHTS.
BUT LOVE ERASES ALL SINS BY FORGIVING THEM.
— PROVERBS 10:12 —

LOVING

But the trouble caused by what
    sinners say destroys them.

7 To remember those who do right is a
    blessing.
But the names of those who do
    wrong will rot.

8 A wise heart accepts commands.
But foolish chattering destroys you.

9 Anyone who lives without blame
    walks safely.
But anyone who takes a crooked
    path will get caught.

10 An evil wink gets you into trouble.
And foolish chattering destroys you.

11 The mouths of those who do right are
    a fountain of life.
But the trouble caused by what
    sinners say destroys them.

12 Hate stirs up fights.
But love erases all sins by forgiving
    them.

13 Wisdom is found on the lips of those
    who understand what is right.
But those who have no sense are
    punished.

14 Wise people store up knowledge.
But the mouths of foolish people
    destroy them.

15 The wealth of rich people is like a city
    that makes them feel safe.
But having nothing destroys those
    who are poor.

16 People who do what is right earn life.
But what sinners earn causes them
    to be punished.

17 Anyone who pays attention to his
    training
is on his way to life.
But anyone who refuses to be corrected
    leads others down the wrong path.

18 Anyone who hides hatred has lying
    lips.
And anyone who spreads lies is
    foolish.

19 Those who talk a lot are likely to sin.
But those who control their tongues
    are wise.

20 The tongues of those who do right are
    like fine silver.
But the hearts of those who do
    wrong aren't worth very much.

21 The words of those who do right
    benefit many people.
But those who are foolish die
    because they have no sense.

22 The blessing of the LORD brings wealth.
Trouble doesn't come with it.

23 A foolish person finds pleasure in
    doing evil things.
But a man who has understanding
    takes delight in wisdom.

24 What sinners are afraid of will catch up
    with them.
But those who do right will get what
    they want.

25 When the storm is over, sinners are
    gone.
But those who do right stand firm
    forever.

26 Anyone who doesn't want to work
    hurts those who send him.
He is like vinegar on the teeth or
    smoke in the eyes.

27 Having respect for the LORD leads to a
    longer life.

POWER-SURGE

SELF-CONTROLLED N

THOSE WHO CONTROL THEIR TONGUES ARE WISE.
— PROVERBS 10:19 — W

WISE

But the years of evil people are cut
short.

28 Those who do right can expect joy.
But the hopes of sinners are bound
to fail.

29 The way of the LORD leads to a safe
place for those who do right.
But it destroys those who do evil.

30 Those who do right will never be
removed from the land.
But those who do wrong will not
remain in it.

31 The mouths of those who do right
produce wisdom.
But tongues that speak twisted
words will be cut out.

32 Those who do right know the proper
thing to say.
But those who do wrong speak only
twisted words.

11 The LORD hates it when people use
scales to cheat others.
But he is delighted when people use
honest weights.

2 When pride comes, shame follows.
But wisdom comes to those who are
not proud.

3 Those who do what is right are guided
by their honest lives.
But those who aren't faithful are
destroyed by their trickery.

4 Wealth isn't worth anything when
God judges you.
But doing what is right saves you
from death.

5 The ways of honest people are made
straight because they do what is
right.
But those who do what is wrong are
brought down by their own
sins.

6 Godly people are saved by doing what
is right.
But those who aren't faithful are
trapped by evil longings.

7 When an evil man dies, his hope dies
with him.
Everything he expected to gain from
his power will be lost.

8 Those who do right are saved from
trouble.
But trouble comes on those who do
wrong.

POWER-SURGE

SELF-CONTROLLED

THOSE WHO TALK
ABOUT OTHERS TELL
SECRETS.
BUT THOSE WHO CAN
BE TRUSTED KEEP
THINGS TO
THEMSELVES.
—PROVERBS 11:13—

TRUSTED

9 With their words ungodly people
destroy their neighbors.
But those who do what is right
escape because of their
knowledge.

10 When those who do right succeed,
their city is glad
When those who do wrong die,
people shout for joy.

11 The blessing of honest people builds
up a city.
But the words of sinners destroy it.

12 A person who has no sense makes fun
of his neighbor.
But a man who has understanding
controls his tongue.

13 Those who talk about others tell
secrets.
But those who can be trusted keep
things to themselves.

14 Without the guidance of good leaders
a nation falls.
But many good advisers can save it.

15 Anyone who puts up money for what
someone else owes will
certainly suffer.
But a person who doesn't agree to
pay up for someone else is safe.

16 A woman who has a kind heart gains
respect.
But men who are not kind gain only
wealth.

17 A kind man benefits himself.
But a mean person brings trouble on
himself.

KIND **K**

A WOMAN WHO HAS A KIND HEART GAINS RESPECT...

A KIND MAN BENEFITS HIMSELF.

BUT A MEAN PERSON BRINGS TROUBLE ON HIMSELF.

— PROVERBS 11:16-17 —

18 Those who do what is wrong really earn nothing.
But those who plant what is right will certainly be rewarded.

19 Right living leads to life.
But anyone who runs after evil will die.

20 The LORD hates those whose hearts are twisted.
But he is pleased with those who live without blame.

21 You can be sure that sinners will be punished.
And you can also be sure that godly people will go free.

22 A beautiful woman who has no sense is like a gold ring in a pig's nose.

23 What godly people long for ends only in what is good.
But what sinners hope for ends only in God's anger.

24 Some give freely but get even richer.
Others don't give what they should but get even poorer.

25 Anyone who gives a lot will succeed.
Anyone who renews others will be renewed.

26 People call down curses on those who store up grain for themselves.
But blessing makes those who are willing to sell feel like kings.

27 Anyone who looks for what is good finds favor.
But bad things happen to a person who plans to do evil.

28 Those who trust in their riches will fall.
But those who do right will be as healthy as a green leaf.

29 Those who bring trouble on their families will receive nothing but wind.
And foolish people will serve wise people.

30 The fruit that godly people bear is like a tree of life.
And those who lead others to do what is right are wise.

31 Godly people get what they should get on earth.
So ungodly people and sinners will certainly get what they should get!

12 Anyone who loves to be trained loves knowledge.
Anyone who hates to be corrected is stupid.

2 The LORD blesses anyone who does good.
But he judges any man who is tricky.

3 If a man does what is evil, he can't become strong and steady.
But if people do what is right, they can't be removed from the land.

4 A noble wife is her husband's crown.
But a wife who brings shame is like sickness in his bones.

5 The plans of godly people are right.
But the advice of sinners will lead you the wrong way.

6 The words of those who are evil hide and wait to spill people's blood.
But the speech of those who are honest saves them from traps like that.

7 Sinners are destroyed and taken away.
But the houses of godly people stand firm.

8 A man is praised for how wise he is.
But people hate those who have twisted minds.

9 Being nobody and having a servant is better than pretending to be somebody and having no food.

10 Those who do what is right take good care of their animals.
But the kindest acts of those who do wrong are mean.

11 Anyone who farms his land will have plenty of food.

WISE

A WISE PERSON LISTENS TO ADVICE.
— **PROVERBS 12:15** —

But a person who chases dreams has no sense.

12 Those who do what is wrong want to steal from others.
But those who do what is right bear good fruit because of their deep roots.

13 A sinner is trapped by his sinful talk.
But a godly person escapes trouble.

14 Many good things come from what a man says.
And the work of his hands rewards him.

15 The way of a foolish person seems right to him.
But a wise person listens to advice.

16 Foolish people are easily upset.
But wise people pay no attention to hurtful words.

17 An honest witness tells the truth.
But a dishonest witness tells lies.

18 Thoughtless words cut like a sword.
But the tongue of wise people brings healing.

19 Truthful words last forever.
But lies last for only a moment.

20 There are lies in the hearts of those who plan evil.
But there is joy for those who work to bring peace.

21 No harm comes to godly people.

HONEST H

TRUTHFUL WORDS LAST FOREVER.

BUT LIES LAST FOR ONLY A MOMENT.
— **PROVERBS 12:19** —

But sinners have all the trouble they can handle.

22 The LORD hates those whose lips tell lies.
But he is pleased with people who tell the truth.

23 Wise people keep their knowledge to themselves.
But the hearts of foolish people shout foolish things.

24 Hands that work hard will rule.
But people who don't want to work will become slaves.

25 Worry makes a man's heart heavy.
But a kind word cheers him up.

CHEERFUL ✳

WORRY MAKES A MAN'S HEART HEAVY.

BUT A KIND WORD CHEERS HIM UP.
— **PROVERBS 12:25** — K

KIND

26 Godly people are careful about the friends they choose.
But the way of sinners leads them down the wrong path.

27 Anyone who refuses to work doesn't even cook what he catches.
But a man who works hard values what he has.

28 There is life in doing what is right.
Along that path you will never die.

13 A wise child pays attention to what his father teaches him.
But anyone who makes fun of others doesn't listen to warnings.

2 The good things a man says benefit him.
But a liar loves to hurt others.

3 Anyone who guards what he says guards his life.
But anyone who speaks without thinking will be destroyed.

4 People who refuse to work want things and get nothing.

But the longings of people who
work hard are completely
satisfied.

5 Those who do right hate what is false.
But those who do wrong bring
shame and dishonor.

6 Doing right guards those who are
honest.
But evil destroys those who are
sinful.

7 Some people pretend to be rich but
have nothing.
Others pretend to be poor but have
great wealth.

8 A man who is rich might have to pay
to save his life.
But a poor person is not in danger of
that.

9 The lights of godly people shine
brightly.
But the lamps of sinners are blown
out.

10 Pride only leads to arguing.
But those who take advice are wise.

11 Money that is gained in the wrong way
disappears.
But money that is gathered little by
little grows.

12 Hope that is put off makes one sick at
heart.
But a longing that is met is like a tree
of life.

13 Anyone who hates what he is taught
will pay for it later.
But a person who respects a
command will be rewarded.

14 The teaching of wise people is like a
fountain that gives life.
It turns those who listen to it away
from the jaws of death.

15 Good understanding wins favor.
But the way of liars doesn't last.

16 Wise people act in keeping with the
knowledge they have.
But foolish people show how foolish
they are.

17 An evil messenger gets into trouble.
But a messenger who is trusted
brings healing.

18 Those who turn away from their
training become poor and
ashamed.
But those who accept warnings are
honored.

19 A longing that is met is like something
that tastes sweet.
But foolish people hate to turn away
from evil.

20 Anyone who walks with wise people
grows wise.
But a companion of foolish people
suffers harm.

21 Hard times chase those who are sinful.
But success is the reward of those
who do right.

22 A good person leaves what he owns to
his children and grandchildren.
But a sinner's wealth is stored up for
those who do right.

23 The fields of poor people might
produce a lot of food.
But those who beat them down
destroy it all.

24 Those who don't correct their children
hate them.
But those who love them are careful
to train them.

25 Those who do right eat until they are
full.
But the stomachs of those who do
wrong go hungry.

14 A wise woman builds her house.
But a foolish woman tears hers
down with her own hands.

2 An honest person has respect for the
LORD.
But a person whose paths are
crooked hates him.

3 Foolish people are punished for what
they say.
But the things wise people say keep
them safe.

HONEST

AN EVIL MESSENGER
GETS INTO TROUBLE.

BUT A MESSENGER
WHO IS TRUSTED
BRINGS HEALING.
—PROVERBS 13:17—

TRUSTED

⁴Where there are no oxen, the feed box
  is empty.
  But a strong ox brings in a great
    harvest.

⁵An honest witness does not lie.
  But a dishonest witness pours out
    lies.

⁶Those who make fun of others look for
    wisdom and don't find it.
  But knowledge comes easily to those
    who understand what is right.

⁷Stay away from a foolish man.
  You won't find knowledge in what
    he says.

⁸People are wise and understanding
    when they think about the way
    they live.
  But people are foolish when their
    foolish ways trick them.

⁹Foolish people laugh at making things
    right when they sin.
  But honest people try to do the right
    thing.

¹⁰Each heart knows its own sadness.
  And no one else can share its joy.

¹¹The houses of sinners will be
    destroyed.
  But the tents of honest people will
    stand firm.

¹²There is a way that may seem right to a
    man.
  But in the end it leads to death.

¹³Even when you laugh, your heart can
    be hurting.
  And your joy can end in sadness.

¹⁴Those who aren't faithful will be paid
    back
    for what they've done.
  And good men will receive rewards
    for how they've lived.

¹⁵A childish person believes anything.
  But a wise person thinks about how
    he lives.

¹⁶A wise person has respect for the LORD
    and avoids evil.
  But a foolish person gets mad and is
    thoughtless.

¹⁷Anyone who gets angry quickly does
    foolish things.
  And a man who is tricky is hated.

¹⁸Childish people act in keeping with
    their foolish ways.
  But knowledge makes wise people
    feel like kings.

KIND   K

BLESSED IS THE PERSON WHO IS KIND TO THOSE IN NEED.
— **PROVERBS 14:21** —

¹⁹Evil people will bow down in front of
    good people.
  And those who do wrong will bow
    down at the gates of those who
    do right.

²⁰Poor people are avoided even by their
    neighbors.
  But rich people have many friends.

²¹Anyone who hates his neighbor
    commits sin.
  But blessed is the person who is kind
    to those in need.

²²Those who plan evil go down the
    wrong path.
  But those who plan good find love
    and truth.

²³All hard work pays off.
  But if all you do is talk, you will be
    poor.

²⁴The wealth of wise people is their
    crown.
  But the foolish ways of foolish
    people lead to what is foolish.

²⁵An honest witness saves lives.
  But a dishonest witness tells lies.

²⁶Anyone who shows respect for the
    LORD has a strong tower.
  It will be a safe place for his children.

²⁷Respect for the LORD is like a fountain
    that gives life.
  It turns you away from the jaws of
    death.

²⁸A large population is a king's glory.
  But a prince without followers is
    destroyed.

²⁹Anyone who is patient has great
    understanding.
  But anyone who gets angry quickly
    shows how foolish he is.

³⁰A peaceful heart gives life to the body.
  But jealousy rots the bones.

³¹Anyone who crushes poor people
    makes fun of their Maker.

PATIENT P

ANYONE WHO IS PATIENT HAS GREAT UNDERSTANDING.

BUT ANYONE WHO GETS ANGRY QUICKLY SHOWS HOW FOOLISH HE IS.

— PROVERBS 14:29 —

WISE

But anyone who is kind to those in need honors God.

32 When trouble comes, sinners are brought down.
But godly people have a safe place even when they die.

33 Wisdom rests in the hearts of those who understand what is right.
And even among foolish people she makes herself known.

34 Doing what is right lifts people up.
But sin brings shame to any nation.

35 A king is pleased with a wise servant.
But a servant who is full of shame invites the king's anger.

15 A gentle answer turns anger away.
But mean words stir up anger.

2 The tongues of wise people use knowledge well.
But the mouths of foolish people pour out foolish words.

3 The eyes of the LORD are everywhere.
They watch those who are evil and those who are good.

KIND K

ANYONE WHO IS KIND TO THOSE IN NEED HONORS GOD.

— PROVERBS 14:31 —

4 A tongue that brings healing is like a tree of life.
But a tongue that tells lies produces a broken spirit.

5 A foolish person turns his back on how his father has trained him.
But anyone who accepts being corrected shows understanding.

6 The houses of those who do what is right hold great wealth.
But those who do what is wrong earn only trouble.

7 The lips of wise people spread knowledge.
But that's not true of the hearts of foolish people.

8 The LORD hates the sacrifice of sinful people.
But the prayers of honest people please him.

KIND

A GENTLE ANSWER TURNS ANGER AWAY.

BUT MEAN WORDS STIR UP ANGER.

— PROVERBS 15:1 —

SELF-CONTROLLED

9 The LORD hates how sinners live.
But he loves those who run after what is right.

10 Hard training is in store for anyone who leaves the right path.
A person who hates to be corrected will die.

11 Death and the Grave lie open in front of the LORD.
So the hearts of mere men certainly lie open to him!

12 Anyone who makes fun of others doesn't like to be corrected.
He won't ask wise people for advice.

13 A happy heart makes a face look cheerful.
But a sad heart produces a broken spirit.

PATIENT

A PERSON WHO IS PATIENT CALMS THINGS DOWN.
— **PROVERBS 15:18** —

14 A heart that understands what is right looks for knowledge.
But the mouths of foolish people feed on what is foolish.

15 All the days of those who are crushed are filled with pain and suffering.
But a cheerful heart enjoys a good time that never ends.

16 It is better to have respect for the LORD and have little
than to be rich and have trouble.

17 A meal of vegetables where there is love
is better than the finest meat where there is hatred.

18 A man who burns with anger stirs up fights.
But a person who is patient calms things down.

19 The way of people who don't want to work is blocked with thorns.
But the path of honest people is a wide road.

20 A wise son makes his father glad.
But a foolish son hates his mother.

21 A person who has no sense enjoys doing foolish things.
But a man who has understanding walks straight ahead.

22 Plans fail without good advice.
But they succeed when there are many advisers.

23 Joy is found in giving the right answer.
And how good is a word spoken at the right time!

24 The path of life leads up for those who are wise.
It keeps them from going down to the grave.

25 The LORD tears down the proud person's house.
But he keeps the widow's property safe.

26 The LORD hates the thoughts of sinful people.
But the thoughts of pure people are pleasing to him.

27 Anyone who always wants more brings trouble to his family.
But a person who refuses to be paid off will live.

28 The hearts of those who do right think about how they will answer.
But the mouths of those who do wrong pour out evil.

29 The LORD is far away from those who do wrong.
But he hears the prayers of those who do right.

30 A cheerful look brings joy to your heart.
And good news gives health to your body.

31 If you listen to a warning, you will live.
You will be at home among those who are wise.

32 Anyone who turns away from his training hates himself.
But anyone who accepts being corrected gains understanding.

33 Having respect for the LORD teaches you how to live wisely.
So don't be proud if you want to be honored.

16 People make plans in their hearts.
But the LORD controls what they say.

2 Everything a man does might seem right to him.

CHEERFUL ✳

A HAPPY HEART MAKES A FACE LOOK CHEERFUL.

A CHEERFUL LOOK BRINGS JOY TO YOUR HEART.

AND GOOD NEWS GIVES HEALTH TO YOUR BODY.
— **PROVERBS 15:13, 30** —

HONEST

KINGS ARE PLEASED
WHEN WHAT YOU SAY
IS HONEST.

THEY VALUE PEOPLE
WHO SPEAK THE
TRUTH.

— PROVERBS 16:13 —

TRUSTED

But the LORD knows what that man
is thinking.

3 Commit to the LORD everything you
do.
Then your plans will succeed.

4 The LORD works everything out for his
own purposes.
Even those who do wrong were
made for a day of trouble.

5 The LORD hates all those who have
proud hearts.
You can be sure that they will be
punished.

6 Through love and truth sin is paid for.
People avoid evil when they have
respect for the LORD.

7 When the way you live pleases the
LORD,
he makes even your enemies live at
peace with you.

8 It is better to have a little and do right
than to have a lot and be unfair.

9 In your heart you plan your life.
But the LORD decides where your
steps will take you.

10 A king might speak as if his words
come from God.
But what he says should not turn
right into wrong.

11 Honest scales and balances come from
the LORD.
He made all of the weights in the
bag.

12 A king hates it when his people do
what is wrong.

A ruler is made secure when they do
what is right.

13 Kings are pleased when what you say is
honest.
They value people who speak the
truth.

14 An angry king can order your death.
But a wise man will try to calm him
down.

15 When a king's face is happy, it means
life.
His favor is like rain in the spring.

16 It is much better to get wisdom than
gold.
It is much better to choose
understanding than silver.

17 The path of honest people takes them
away from evil.
Those who guard their ways guard
their lives.

18 If you are proud, you will be destroyed.
If you are proud, you will fall.

19 Suppose you are lowly in spirit and are
with those who are beaten
down.
That's better than sharing stolen
goods with those who are
proud.

20 If anyone pays attention to what he is
taught, he will succeed.
Blessed is the person who puts his
trust in the LORD.

21 Wise hearts are known for
understanding what is right.
Pleasant words make people want to
learn more.

POWER-SURGE

SELF-CONTROLLED

THE HEARTS OF WISE
PEOPLE GUIDE THEIR
MOUTHS.

THEIR WORDS MAKE
PEOPLE WANT TO
LEARN MORE.

—PROVERBS 16:23—

WISE

22 Understanding is like a fountain of life
   to those who have it.
   But foolish people are punished for
   the foolish things they do.

23 The hearts of wise people guide their
   mouths.
   Their words make people want to
   learn more.

24 Pleasant words are like honey.
   They are sweet to the spirit and
   bring healing to the body.

25 There is a way that may seem right to a
   man.
   But in the end it leads to death.

26 The hunger of a worker makes him
   work.
   His hunger drives him on.

27 A worthless man plans to do evil
   things.
   His words are like a burning fire.

28 A twisted person stirs up fights.
   Anyone who talks about others
   comes between close friends.

29 A man who wants to hurt others tries
   to get them to sin.
   He leads them down a path that
   isn't good.

30 When he winks with his eyes, he is
   planning to do wrong.
   When his lips are tightly closed, he
   is up to no good.

31 Gray hair is a glorious crown.
   You get it by living the right way.

32 It is better to be patient than to fight.
   It is better to control your temper
   than to take a city.

33 Lots are cast into the lap to make
   decisions.
   But everything they decide comes
   from the LORD.

17 It is better to eat a dry crust of
   bread in peace and quiet

POWER–SURGE

SELF-CONTROLLED N

**IT IS BETTER TO
CONTROL YOUR
TEMPER THAN TO TAKE
A CITY.**
— PROVERBS 16:32 —

POWER–SURGE

FORGIVING F

**THOSE WHO ERASE A
SIN BY FORGIVING IT
SHOW LOVE.**
— PROVERBS 17:9 — ♥

LOVING

than to eat a big dinner in a house
   that is full of fighting.

2 A wise servant will rule over a shameful
   child.
   He will be given part of the property
   as if he were a family member.

3 Fire tests silver. Heat tests gold.
   But the LORD tests our hearts.

4 An evil person listens to evil words.
   A liar pays attention to words that
   are harmful.

5 Anyone who laughs at those who are
   poor makes fun of their Maker.
   Anyone who is happy when others
   suffer will be punished.

6 Grandchildren are like a crown to older
   people.
   And children are proud of their
   parents.

7 It isn't proper for foolish people to
   brag.
   And it certainly isn't proper for
   rulers to tell lies!

8 Money buys favors for those who give
   it.
   No matter where they turn, they
   succeed.

9 Those who erase a sin by forgiving it
   show love.
   But those who talk about it come
   between close friends.

10 A person who understands what is
   right learns more from just a
   warning
   than a foolish person learns from
   100 strokes with a whip.

11 An evil person never wants to obey.
   An official who shows no mercy will
   be sent against him.

¹²It is better to meet a bear whose cubs
have been stolen
than to meet a foolish person who is
acting foolishly.

¹³Evil will never leave the house
of anyone who pays back evil for
good.

¹⁴Starting to argue is like making a crack
in a dam.
So drop the matter before a fight
breaks out.

¹⁵The LORD hates two things.
He hates it when the guilty are set
free.
He also hates it when those who
aren't guilty are punished.

¹⁶What good is money in the hands of a
foolish person?
He doesn't want to become wise.

¹⁷A friend loves at all times.
He is there to help when trouble
comes.

POWER-SURGE

HELPFUL ★

A FRIEND LOVES AT
ALL TIMES.
HE IS THERE TO HELP
WHEN TROUBLE
COMES.
— PROVERBS 17:17 — ♥

LOVING

¹⁸A man who has little sense agrees to
pay what other people owe.
It isn't wise to put up money for
others.

¹⁹The one who loves to argue loves to
sin.
The one who builds a high gate is
just asking to be destroyed.

²⁰If your heart is twisted, you won't
succeed.
If your tongue tells lies, you will get
into trouble.

²¹It is sad to have a foolish child.
The parents of a foolish person have
no joy.

²²A cheerful heart makes you healthy.
But a broken spirit dries you up.

²³Anyone who does wrong accepts favors
in secret.
Then he turns what is right into
wrong.

²⁴Anyone who understands what is right
keeps wisdom in view.
But the eyes of a foolish person look
everywhere else.

²⁵A foolish child makes his father sad
and his mother sorry.

²⁶It isn't good to punish those who
aren't guilty.
It isn't good to whip officials just
because they are honest.

²⁷Anyone who has knowledge controls
his words.
A man who has understanding is
not easily upset.

²⁸We think even a foolish person is wise
if he keeps silent.
We think he understands what is
right if he controls his tongue.

18 A person who isn't friendly looks
out only for himself.
He opposes all good sense.

²A foolish person doesn't want to
understand.
He takes delight in saying only what
he thinks.

³People hate it when evil comes.
And they refuse to honor those who
bring shame.

⁴The words of a person's mouth are like
deep water.
But the fountain of wisdom is like a
flowing stream.

⁵It isn't good to favor those who do
wrong.
And it isn't good to hold back what
is fair from those who aren't
guilty.

⁶What a foolish person says leads to
arguing.
He is just asking for a beating.

⁷The words of a foolish person drag him
down.
He is trapped by what he says.

⁸The words of anyone who talks about
others are like tasty bites of
food.
They go deep down inside you.

9 Anyone who doesn't want to work
is like someone who destroys.

10 The name of the LORD is like a strong
tower.
Godly people run to it and are safe.

11 The wealth of rich people is like a city
that makes them feel safe.
They think of it as a city with walls
that can't be climbed.

12 If a man's heart is proud, he will be
destroyed.
So don't be proud if you want to be
honored.

13 To answer before listening
is foolish and shameful.

14 A man's cheerful heart gives him
strength when he is sick.
You can't keep going if you have a
broken spirit.

POWER-SURGE

CHEERFUL ✳

A MAN'S CHEERFUL
HEART GIVES HIM
STRENGTH WHEN HE
IS SICK.
— PROVERBS 18:14 —

STRONG

15 Those whose hearts understand what
is right get knowledge.
The ears of those who are wise listen
for it.

16 A gift opens the way for the one who
gives it.
It helps him meet important people.

17 The first one to tell his case seems
right.
Then someone else comes forward
and questions him.

18 Casting lots will put a stop to arguing.
It will keep the strongest enemies
apart.

19 A broken friendship is harder to deal
with than a city that has high
walls around it.
And arguing is like the locked gates
of a mighty city.

20 A man can fill his stomach with what
he says.
The words from his lips can satisfy
him.

21 Your tongue has the power of life and
death.
Those who love to talk will eat the
fruit of their words.

22 The one who finds a wife finds what is
good.
He receives favor from the LORD.

23 Poor people beg for mercy.
But rich people answer in a mean
way.

24 Even a man who has many
companions can be destroyed.
But there is a friend who sticks closer
than a brother.

19 It is better to be poor and to live
without blame
than to be foolish and to twist words
around.

2 It isn't good to get all stirred up
without knowledge.
And it isn't good to be in a hurry
and miss the way.

3 A man's own foolish acts destroy his
life.
But his heart is angry with the LORD.

4 Wealth brings many friends.
But the friends of poor people leave
them alone.

5 A dishonest witness will be punished.
And those who pour out lies will not
go free.

6 Many try to win the favor of rulers.
And everyone is the friend of a man
who gives gifts.

7 A poor person is avoided by his whole
family.
His friends avoid him even more.
The poor person runs after them to
beg.
But he can't find them.

8 Anyone who gets wisdom loves
himself.
Anyone who values understanding
succeeds.

9 A dishonest witness will be punished.
And those who pour out lies will die.

10 It isn't proper for a foolish person to
live in great comfort.
And it is much worse when a slave
rules over princes!

POWER-SURGE

PATIENT P

A MAN'S WISDOM MAKES HIM PATIENT.
— PROVERBS 19:11 —

WISE W

¹¹ A man's wisdom makes him patient.
He will be honored if he forgives
someone who sins against him.

¹² A king's anger is like a lion's roar.
But his favor is like dew on the grass.

¹³ If a child is foolish, he destroys his
father.
A nagging wife is like dripping that
never stops.

¹⁴ You will receive houses and wealth
from your parents.
But a wise wife is given by the Lord.

¹⁵ Anyone who doesn't want to work
sleeps his life away.
And a person who refuses to work
goes hungry.

¹⁶ Those who obey what they are taught
guard their lives.
But those who don't care how they
live will die.

¹⁷ Anyone who is kind to poor people
lends to the Lord.
God will reward him for what he has
done.

¹⁸ Train your child. Then there is hope.
Don't do anything to bring about
his death.

¹⁹ Anyone who burns with anger must
pay for it.
If you save him, you will have to do
it again.

²⁰ Listen to advice and accept what you
are taught.
In the end you will be wise.

²¹ A man may have many plans in his
heart.
But the Lord's purpose wins out in
the end.

²² Every man longs for love that never
fails.

It is better to be poor than to be a
liar.

²³ Having respect for the Lord leads to
life.
Then you will be content and free
from trouble.

²⁴ A person who doesn't want to work
leaves his hand in the dish.
He won't even bring it back up to his
mouth!

²⁵ If you whip a person who makes fun of
others,
childish people will learn to be wise.
If you warn someone who already
understands what is right,
he will gain even more knowledge.

²⁶ A child who robs his father and drives
out his mother
brings shame and dishonor.

²⁷ My son, if you stop listening to what I
teach you,
you will wander away from the
words of knowledge.

²⁸ A dishonest witness makes fun of what
is right.
The mouths of those who do wrong
gulp down evil.

²⁹ Those who make fun of others will be
judged.
Foolish people will be punished.

20 Wine causes you to make fun of
others, and beer causes you to
start fights.
Anyone who is led down the wrong
path by them is not wise.

² A king's anger is like a lion's roar.
Anyone who makes him angry may
lose his life.

³ Avoiding a fight brings honor to a
man.

POWER-SURGE

KIND K

ANYONE WHO IS KIND TO POOR PEOPLE LENDS TO THE LORD.
GOD WILL REWARD HIM FOR WHAT HE HAS DONE.
— PROVERBS 19:17 —

But every foolish person is quick to
argue.

4 Anyone who refuses to work doesn't
plow in the right season.
When he looks for a crop at harvest
time, he doesn't find it.

5 The purposes of a man's heart are like
deep water.
But a man who has understanding
brings them out.

6 Many claim to have love that never
fails.
But who can find a faithful man?

7 Anyone who does what is right lives
without blame.
Blessed are his children after him.

8 A king sits on his throne to judge.
He gets rid of all evil when he sees it.

9 No one can say, "I have kept my heart
pure.
I'm clean. I haven't sinned."

10 The LORD hates two things.
He hates weights that weigh things
heavier or lighter than they
really are.
He also hates measures that measure
things larger or smaller than
they really are.

11 A child is known by his actions.
He is known by whether his conduct
is pure and right.

12 The LORD has made two things.
He has made ears that hear.
He has also made eyes that see.

13 Don't love sleep, or you will become
poor.
Stay awake, and you will have more
food than you need.

14 "It's no good. It's no good!" says a
buyer.
Then off he goes and brags about
what he bought.

15 There is gold. There are plenty of
rubies.
But lips that speak knowledge are a
priceless jewel.

16 Take the coat of one who puts up
money for what a stranger
owes.
Hold it until you get paid back if he
does it for a woman who
commits adultery.

17 Food gained by cheating tastes sweet to
a man.

But he will end up with a mouth full
of sand.

18 Make plans by asking for guidance.
If you go to war, get good advice.

19 A person who talks about others tells
secrets.
So avoid anyone who talks too
much.

20 If anyone calls down curses on his
father or mother,
his lamp will be blown out in total
darkness.

21 Property you gain quickly at the
beginning
will not be blessed in the end.

22 Don't say, "I'll get even with you for
the wrong you did to me!"
Wait for the LORD, and he will save
you.

23 The LORD hates weights that weigh
things heavier or lighter than
they really are.
Scales that are not honest don't
please him.

24 The LORD directs a man's steps.
So how can anyone understand his
own way?

25 A man is trapped if he makes a hasty
promise to God
and only later thinks about what he
said.

26 A wise king gets rid of evil people.
He runs the threshing wheel over
them.

27 The lamp of the LORD searches a man's
heart.
It searches deep down inside him.

28 Love and truth keep a king safe.
Faithful love makes his throne
secure.

29 Young men are proud of their strength.
Gray hair brings honor to old men.

30 Blows and wounds wash evil away.
And beatings make you pure deep
down inside.

21 The king's heart is in the hand of
the LORD.
He directs it like a stream of water
anywhere he pleases.

2 Everything a man does might seem
right to him.
But the LORD knows what he is
thinking.

3 Do what is right and fair.
   The LORD accepts that more than
      sacrifices.

4 Proud eyes and a proud heart are the
      lamp of sinful people.
   But those things are evil.

5 The plans of people who work hard
      succeed.
   You can be sure that those in a hurry
      will become poor.

6 A fortune made by people who tell lies
      amounts to nothing and leads to
      death.

7 The harmful things that evil people do
      will drag them away.
   They refuse to do what is right.

8 The path of those who are guilty is
      crooked.
   But the conduct of those who are
      not guilty is honest.

9 It is better to live on a corner of a roof
      than to share a house with a
      nagging wife.

10 A sinful person longs to do evil.
   He doesn't show his neighbor any
      mercy.

11 When you punish someone who
      makes fun of others, childish
      people get wise.
   If you teach a person who is already
      wise, he will get even more
      knowledge.

12 The Blameless One knows where
      sinners live.
   And he destroys them.

13 If you refuse to listen to the cries of
      poor people,
   you too will cry out and not be
      answered.

14 A secret gift calms anger down.
   A hidden favor softens great anger.

15 When you do what is fair, you make
      godly people glad.
   But you terrify those who do what is
      evil.

16 A man who leaves the path of
      understanding
   ends up with those who are dead.

17 Anyone who loves pleasure will
      become poor.
   Anyone who loves wine and oil will
      never be rich.

18 Those who do what is evil pay the
      price for setting godly people
      free.
   Those who aren't faithful pay the
      price for honest people.

19 It is better to live in a desert
   than to live with a nagging, angry
      wife.

20 The best food and olive oil are stored
      up in the houses of wise people.
   But a foolish man eats up everything
      he has.

21 Anyone who wants to be godly and
      loving
   finds life, success and honor.

22 Those who are wise can attack a strong
      city.
   They can pull down the place of
      safety its people trust in.

23 Anyone who is careful about what he
      says
   keeps himself out of trouble.

24 A proud person is called a "mocker."
   He thinks much too highly of
      himself.

25 Some people will die while they are
      still hungry.
   That's because their hands refuse to
      work.

26 All day long they hunger for more.
   But godly people give without
      holding back.

27 God hates sacrifices that are brought
      by evil people.
   He hates it even more when they
      bring them for the wrong
      reason.

28 Witnesses who aren't honest will die.
   And anyone who listens to them
      will be destroyed forever.

29 A sinful man tries to look as if he were
      bold.
   But an honest person thinks about
      how he lives.

30 No wisdom, wise saying or plan
   can succeed against the LORD.

31 You can prepare a horse for the day of
      battle.
   But the power to win comes from
      the LORD.

22 You should want a good name
      more than you want great
      riches.

STRONG

THE POWER TO WIN COMES FROM THE LORD.
—— PROVERBS 21:31 ——

To be highly respected is better than having silver or gold.

2 The LORD made rich people and poor people.
That's what they have in common.

3 Wise people see danger and go to a safe place.
But childish people keep going and suffer for it.

4 Have respect for the LORD and don't be proud.
That will bring you wealth and honor and life.

5 Thorns and traps lie in the paths of evil people.
But those who guard themselves stay far away from them.

6 Train a child in the way he should go.
When he is old, he will not turn away from it.

7 Rich people rule over those who are poor.
Borrowers are slaves to lenders.

8 Anyone who plants evil gathers a harvest of trouble.
His power to beat others down will be destroyed.

9 Anyone who gives freely will be blessed.
That's because he shares his food with those who are poor.

10 If you drive away those who make fun of others, fighting also goes away.
Arguing and unkind words will stop.

11 Have a pure and loving heart, and speak kindly.
Then you will be a friend of the king.

12 The eyes of the LORD keep watch over knowledge.
But he does away with the words of those who aren't faithful.

13 People who don't want to work say, "There's a lion outside!"
Or they say, "I'll be murdered if I go out into the streets!"

14 The mouth of a woman who commits adultery is like a deep pit.
Any man the LORD is angry with will fall into it.

15 A child is going to do foolish things.
But correcting him will drive his foolishness far away from him.

16 One person may beat poor people down in order to get rich.
Another person may give gifts to rich people. Both of them will become poor.

Sayings of Those Who Are Wise

17 Pay attention and listen to the sayings of those who are wise.
Apply your heart to the sayings I teach.

18 It is pleasing when you keep them in your heart.
Have all of them ready on your lips.

19 You are the one I am teaching today.
I want you to trust in the LORD.

20 I have written 30 sayings for you.
They will give you knowledge and good advice.

21 I am teaching you words that are completely true.
Then you can give the right answers to the one who sent you.

1.

22 Don't take advantage of poor people just because they are poor.
Don't beat down those who are in need by taking them to court.

23 The LORD will stand up for them in court.

KIND

HAVE A PURE AND LOVING HEART, AND SPEAK KINDLY.
—— PROVERBS 22:11 ——

LOVING

He will take back the stolen goods
from those who have robbed
them.

2.

²⁴ Don't be a friend with anyone who
burns with anger.
Don't go around with a person who
gets angry easily.
²⁵ You might learn his habits.
And then you will be trapped by
them.

3.

²⁶ Don't agree to pay for
what someone else owes.
²⁷ Don't put up money for him.
If you don't have the money to pay,
your bed will be taken right out from
under you!

4.

²⁸ Don't move old boundary stones
that your people set up long ago.

5.

²⁹ Do you see a man who does good
work?
He will serve kings.
He won't serve ordinary people.

6.

23 When you sit down to eat with a
ruler,
look carefully at what's in front of
you.
² Put a knife to your throat
if you like to eat too much.
³ Don't long for his fancy food.
It can fool you.

7.

⁴ Don't wear yourself out to get rich.
Be wise enough to say no.
⁵ When you take even a quick look at
riches, they are gone.
They grow wings and fly away into
the sky like an eagle.

8.

⁶ Don't eat the food of anyone who
won't share it.
Don't long for his fancy food.
⁷ He is the kind of person
who is always thinking about how
much it costs.
"Eat and drink," he says to you.
But he doesn't mean it.
⁸ You will throw up what little you have
eaten.

You will have wasted your words of
praise.

9.

⁹ Don't speak to a foolish person.
He will laugh at your wise words.

10.

¹⁰ Don't move old boundary stones.
Don't try to take over the fields of
children whose fathers have
died.
¹¹ The One who guards them is strong.
He will stand up for them in court
against you.

11.

¹² Apply your heart to what you are
taught.
Listen carefully to words of
knowledge.

12.

¹³ Don't hold back training from a child.
If you correct him, he won't die.
¹⁴ So correct him.
Then you will save him from death.

13.

¹⁵ My child, if your heart is wise,
my heart will be glad.
¹⁶ Deep down inside, I will be happy
when you say what is right.

14.

¹⁷ Do not long for what sinners have.
But always show great respect for the
LORD.
¹⁸ There really is hope for you tomorrow.
So your hope will not be cut off.

15.

¹⁹ My child, listen and be wise.
Keep your heart on the right path.

POWER – SURGE

OBEYS ✔

**MY CHILD, LISTEN AND
BE WISE.
KEEP YOUR HEART ON
THE RIGHT PATH.**
— **PROVERBS 23:19** —

W

WISE

20 Don't join those who drink too much wine.
Don't join those who stuff themselves with meat.
21 Those who drink or eat too much will become poor.
If they sleep too much, they'll have to wear rags.

16.

22 Listen to your father, who gave you life.
Don't hate your mother when she is old.
23 Buy the truth. Don't sell it.
Get wisdom, training and understanding.
24 The father of a godly child is very happy.
Anyone who has a wise child is glad.
25 May your father and mother be glad.
May the woman who gave birth to you be happy.

17.

26 My son, give me your heart.
Keep your eyes on the way I live.
27 A prostitute is like a deep pit.
A wife who commits adultery is like a narrow well.
28 She hides and waits like a thief.
She causes many men to sin.

18.

29 Who has trouble? Who has sorrow?
Who argues? Who has problems?
Who has wounds for no reason?
Who has red eyes?
30 Those who spend too much time with wine.
Or those who like to taste wine that is mixed with spices.
31 Don't look at wine when it is red.
Don't look at it when it bubbles in the cup.
And don't look at it when it goes down smoothly.
32 In the end it bites like a snake.
It bites like a poisonous serpent.
33 Your eyes will see strange sights.
Your mind will imagine weird things.
34 You will feel like someone sleeping on the ocean.
You will think you are lying among the ropes in a boat.
35 "They hit me," you will say. "But I'm not hurt!
They beat me. But I don't feel it!
When will I wake up
so I can find another drink?"

19.

24 Do not want what evil men have.
Don't long to be with them.
2 In their hearts they plan to hurt others.
With their lips they talk about making trouble.

20.

3 By wisdom a house is built.
Through understanding it is made secure.
4 Through knowledge its rooms are filled with priceless and beautiful things.

21.

5 A wise man has great power.
A man who has knowledge increases his strength.

POWER-SURGE

STRONG

A WISE MAN HAS GREAT POWER.

A MAN WHO HAS KNOWLEDGE INCREASES HIS STRENGTH.
— PROVERBS 24:5 —

WISE

6 If you go to war, you need guidance.
If you want to win, you need many good advisers.

22.

7 Wisdom is too high for anyone who is foolish.
He has nothing to say when people meet at the city gate to conduct business.

23.

8 Anyone who thinks up sinful things to do
will be known as one who plans evil.
9 Foolish plans are sinful.
People hate those who make fun of others.

24.

10 If you grow weak when trouble comes, your strength is very small!

25.

11 Save those who are being led away to death.
Hold back those who are about to be killed.
12 Don't say, "But we didn't know anything about this."
The One who knows what you are thinking sees it.
The One who guards your life knows it.
He will pay each person back for what he has done.

26.

13 Eat honey, my child. It is good.
Honey from a honeycomb has a sweet taste.
14 I want you to know that wisdom is sweet to you.
If you find it, there is hope for you tomorrow.
So your hope will not be cut off.

27.

15 Don't hide and wait like a burglar at a godly person's house.
Don't rob his home.
16 Even if godly people fall down seven times, they always get up.
But those who are evil are brought down by trouble.

28.

17 Don't be happy when your enemy falls.
When he trips, don't let your heart be glad.
18 The LORD will see it, but he won't be pleased.
He might turn his anger away from your enemy.

29.

19 Don't be upset because of evil people.
Don't long for what sinners have.
20 Tomorrow evil people won't have any hope.
The lamps of sinners will be blown out.

30.

21 My son, have respect for the LORD and the king.
Don't join those who disobey them.
22 The LORD and the king will suddenly destroy them.
Who knows what trouble those two can bring?

More Sayings of Those Who Are Wise

23 Here are more sayings of those who are wise.

Taking sides in court is not good.
24 A curse will fall on those who say the guilty are not guilty.
Nations will call down curses on them.
People will speak against them.
25 But it will go well with those who sentence guilty people.
Rich blessings will come to them.

26 An honest answer
is like a kiss on the lips.

POWER-SURGE

HONEST H

AN HONEST ANSWER IS LIKE A KISS ON THE LIPS.
— PROVERBS 24:26 —

27 Finish your outdoor work.
Get your fields ready.
After that, build your house.

28 Don't give witness against your neighbor without any reason.
Don't use your lips to tell lies.
29 Don't say, "I'll do to him what he did to me.
I'll get even with that man for what he did."

30 I went past the field of someone who didn't want to work.
I went past the vineyard of a man who didn't have any sense.
31 Thorns had grown up everywhere.
The ground was covered with weeds.
The stone wall had fallen down.
32 I applied my heart to what I observed.
I learned a lesson from what I saw.
33 You might sleep a little or take a little nap.
You might even fold your hands and rest.
34 Then you would be poor, as if someone had robbed you.
You would have little, as if someone had stolen from you.

More Proverbs of Solomon

25 These are more proverbs of Solomon. They were copied down by the men of Hezekiah, the king of Judah.

2 When God hides a matter, he gets
glory.
When kings figure out a matter, they
get glory.

3 The heavens are high and the earth is
deep.
In the same way, the minds of kings
are hard to figure out.

4 Remove the scum from the silver.
Then the master worker can make
something.

5 Remove sinful people from where the
king is.
When he does what is right, his
kingdom will be secure.

6 Don't brag in front of the king.
Don't claim a place among great
people.

7 Let the king say to you, "Come up
here."
That's better than for him to shame
you in front of nobles.

What you have seen with your own
eyes
8 don't bring too quickly to court.
What will you do in the end
if your neighbor puts you to shame?

9 If you talk about a matter with your
neighbor,
don't tell others what was said.

10 If you do, someone might hear it and
put you to shame.
Then no one will ever respect you
again.

11 The right word at the right time
is like golden apples in silver jewelry.

12 A wise person's warning to a listening
ear
is like a gold earring or jewelry made
of fine gold.

13 A messenger trusted by those who
send him
is like cool snow at harvest time.
He renews the spirit of his masters.

14 A man who brags about gifts he
doesn't give
is like wind and clouds that don't
produce rain.

15 If you are patient, you can win an
official over to your side.
And gentle words can break a bone.

16 If you find honey, eat just enough.
If you eat too much of it, you will
throw up.

17 Don't go to your neighbor's home very
often.
If he sees too much of you, he will
hate you.

18 A man who gives false witness against
his neighbor
is like a club, a sword or a sharp
arrow.

19 Trusting someone who is not faithful
when trouble comes
is like a bad tooth or a disabled
foot.

20 You may sing songs to a troubled
heart.
But that's like taking a coat away on
a cold day.
It's like pouring vinegar on baking
soda.

21 If your enemy is hungry, give him food
to eat.
If he is thirsty, give him water to
drink.

22 By doing those things, you will pile up
burning coals on his head.
And the LORD will reward you.

POWER-SURGE

GIVING G

**IF YOUR ENEMY IS
HUNGRY, GIVE HIM
FOOD TO EAT.**

**IF HE IS THIRSTY, GIVE
HIM WATER TO DRINK.**

**...AND THE LORD
WILL REWARD YOU.**
— PROVERBS 25:21-22 — **K**

KIND

23 The north wind brings rain.
And a crafty tongue brings angry
looks.

24 It is better to live on a corner of a roof
than to share a house with a
nagging wife.

25 Hearing good news from a land far
away
is like drinking cold water when you
are tired.

26 Sometimes a godly person gives in to
those who are evil.
Then he becomes like a muddy
spring of water or a polluted
well.

27 It isn't good for you to eat too much
honey.
And you shouldn't try to get others
to honor you.

28 A man who can't control himself
is like a city whose walls are broken
down.

26 It isn't proper to honor a foolish
person.
That's like having snow in summer
or rain at harvest time.

2 A curse given for no reason is like a
wandering bird or a flying
sparrow.
It doesn't go anywhere.

3 A whip is for a horse. A harness is for a
donkey.
And a beating is for the backs of
foolish people.

4 Don't answer a foolish person in
keeping with his foolish acts.
If you do, you will be like him
yourself.

5 Answer a foolish person in keeping
with his foolish acts.
If you do, he won't be wise in his
own eyes.

6 Sending a message in the hand of a
foolish person
is like cutting off your feet or
drinking something harmful.

7 A proverb in the mouth of a foolish
person
is like disabled legs that are useless.

8 Giving honor to a foolish person
is like tying a stone in a slingshot.

9 A proverb in the mouth of a foolish
person
is like a thorn in the hand of
someone who is drunk.

10 Anyone who hires a foolish person or
someone who is passing by
is like a person who shoots arrows at
just anybody.

11 A foolish person who does the same
foolish things again
is like a dog that returns to where it
has thrown up.

12 Do you see a man who is wise in his
own eyes?
There is more hope for a foolish
person than for him.

13 A person who doesn't want to work
says, "There's a lion in the road!
There's an angry lion wandering in
the streets!"

14 A person who doesn't want to work
turns over in bed
just like a door that swings back and
forth.

15 A person who doesn't want to work
leaves his hand in the dish.
He acts as if he is too tired to bring it
back up to his mouth.

16 A person who doesn't want to work is
wiser in his own eyes
than seven people who give careful
answers.

17 Don't get mixed up in someone else's
fight as you are passing by.
That's like picking a dog up by its
ears.

18 Suppose a crazy person shoots
flaming arrows that can kill.
19 A man who lies to his neighbor
and says, "I was only joking!" is just
like that person.

20 If you don't have wood, your fire goes
out.
If you don't talk about others,
arguing dies down.

21 Coal glows. Wood burns.
And a man who argues stirs up
fights.

22 The words of anyone who talks about
others are like tasty bites of
food.
They go deep down inside you.

23 Warm words that come from an evil
heart
are like shiny paint on a clay pot.

24 Someone who wants to hurt you uses
his words to hide his hatred.
But his heart is full of lies that cover
up his evil plans.

25 What a person says can be charming.
But don't believe him.
Seven things that God hates can fill
that person's heart.

26 Hatred can be hidden by lies.
But what is evil will be shown to
everyone.

27 If anyone digs a pit, he will fall into it.

If he rolls a big stone, it will roll back
on him.

28 A tongue that tells lies hates the people
it hurts.
And words that seem to praise you
destroy you.

27 Don't brag about tomorrow.
You don't know what a day will
bring.

2 Let another person praise you, and not
your own mouth.
Let someone else praise you, and not
your own lips.

3 Stones are heavy. Sand weighs a lot.
But letting a foolish person make
you angry is a heavier load than
both of them.

4 Anger is mean. Great anger overpowers
you.
But who can face jealousy?

5 Being warned openly is better
than being loved in secret.

6 Wounds from a friend can be trusted.
But an enemy kisses you many
times.

7 When you are full, you even hate
honey.
When you are hungry, even what is
bitter tastes sweet.

8 A man who wanders away from his
home
is like a bird that wanders from its
nest.

9 Perfume and incense bring joy to your
heart.
And a friend is sweeter when he
gives you honest advice.

10 Don't desert your friend or your
father's friend.
And don't go to your family when
trouble strikes you.
A neighbor nearby is better than a
family member far away.

11 My child, be wise and bring joy to my
heart.
Then I can answer anyone who
makes fun of me.

12 Wise people see danger and go to a safe
place.
But childish people keep on going
and suffer for it.

13 Take the coat of one who puts up
money for what a stranger
owes.
Hold it until you get paid back if he
does it for a woman who
commits adultery.

14 Suppose you loudly bless your
neighbor early in the morning.
Then you might as well be calling
down a curse on him.

15 A nagging wife is like
dripping that never stops on a rainy
day.

16 Stopping her is like trying to stop the
wind.
It's like trying to grab oil with your
hand.

17 As iron sharpens iron,
so one person sharpens another.

18 A person who takes good care of a fig
tree will eat its fruit.
And a person who looks after his
master will be honored.

19 When you look into water, you see a
likeness of your face.
When you look into your heart, you
see what you are really like.

20 Death and the Grave are never
satisfied.
A man's eyes are never satisfied
either.

21 Fire tests silver. Heat tests gold.
But a man is tested by the praise he
receives.

22 You can grind a foolish person in a
mill.
You can grind him as you would
grind grain with a tool.
But you can't remove his foolishness
from him.

23 Be sure you know how your flocks are
doing.
Pay careful attention to your herds.

24 Riches don't last forever.
And a crown is not secure for all time
to come.

POWER-SURGE

HONEST H

A FRIEND IS SWEETER
WHEN HE GIVES YOU
HONEST ADVICE.
— PROVERBS 27:9 —

²⁵The hay is removed, and new growth
    appears.
  The grass from the hills is gathered
    in.
²⁶Then your lambs will provide you with
    clothes.
  And the money from selling your
    goats will buy you a field.
²⁷You will have plenty of goats' milk.
  It will feed you and your family.
  It will also feed your female servants.

28 Sinners run away even when no
     one is chasing them.
  But those who do what is right are as
    bold as lions.

²A country has many rulers when its
    people don't obey.
  But an understanding king knows
    how to keep order.

³A ruler who beats poor people down
    is like a pounding rain that leaves no
    crops.

⁴Those who turn away from the law
    praise sinners.
  But those who obey the law oppose
    them.

⁵Sinful men don't understand what is
    fair.
  But those who worship the LORD
    understand it completely.

⁶It is better to be poor and live without
    blame
  than to be rich and follow a crooked
    path.

⁷A child who obeys the law understands
    what is right.
  But a child who likes to eat too
    much brings shame on his
    father.

⁸A person who increases his wealth by
    charging high interest
  piles it up for someone who will be
    kind to poor people.

⁹If you don't pay attention to the law,
  even your prayers are hated.

¹⁰Those who lead honest people down
    an evil path
  will fall into their own trap.
  But those who are without blame
  will receive good things.

¹¹Rich people may be wise in their own
    eyes.
  But a poor person who understands
    what is right knows what they
    are really like.

¹²When godly people win, everyone is
    very happy.
  But when sinners take charge,
    everyone hides.

¹³Anyone who hides his sins doesn't
    succeed.
  But anyone who admits his sins and
    gives them up finds mercy.

¹⁴Blessed is the one who always has
    respect for the LORD.
  But anyone who is stubborn will get
    into trouble.

¹⁵An evil person who rules over helpless
    people
  is like a roaring lion or an angry bear.

¹⁶A ruler who is mean to his people
    doesn't have any sense.
  But anyone who hates money
    gained in the wrong way will
    enjoy a long life.

¹⁷A man who is troubled because he is
    guilty of murder
  will be on the run until the day he
    dies.
  No one should give him any help.

¹⁸Anyone who lives without blame is
    kept safe.
  But anyone whose path is crooked
    will suddenly fall.

¹⁹Anyone who farms his land will have
    plenty of food.
  But anyone who chases dreams will
    be very poor.

²⁰A faithful man will be richly blessed.
  But anyone who wants to get rich
    will be punished.

²¹Favoring one person over another is
    not good.
  But some men will do wrong for a
    piece of bread.

²²A man who won't share what he has
    wants to get rich.

POWER-SURGE

OBEYS ✔

A CHILD WHO OBEYS
THE LAW
UNDERSTANDS WHAT
IS RIGHT.
— **PROVERBS 28:7** —

JOASH

Joash did what was right in the eyes of the LORD.
He lived that way as long as the priest Jehoiada was teaching him.
(2 Kings 12:2)

GO TO PAGE 451

NEHEMIAH

*I prayed to the God of heaven.
Then I answered the king.
(Nehemiah 2:4–5)*

GO TO PAGE 568

QUEEN ESTHER

"I and my attendants will fast just as you do. Then I'll go to the king. I'll do it even though it's against the law. And if I have to die, I'll die." (Esther 4:16)

GO TO PAGE 593

JOB

"We accept good things from God. So we should also accept trouble when he sends it." In spite of everything, Job didn't say anything that was sinful. (Job 2:10)

GO TO PAGE 601

But blessed are those who obey the
law.

19 A servant can't be corrected only by
words.
Even if he understands, he won't
obey.

20 Have you seen a man who speaks
without thinking?
There is more hope for foolish
people than for him.

21 If you spoil your servant while he is
young,
he will bring you sorrow later on.

22 An angry man stirs up fights.
And a person who burns with anger
commits many sins.

23 If a man is proud, he will be made low.
But if he isn't proud, he will be
honored.

24 Anyone who helps a thief is his own
enemy.
When he is put under oath, he
doesn't dare give witness.

25 If you are afraid of people, it will trap
you.
But if you trust in the LORD, he will
keep you safe.

26 Many people want to meet a ruler.
But only the LORD sees that people
are treated fairly.

27 Those who do what is right hate
dishonest people.
Those who do what is wrong hate
honest people.

The Sayings of Agur

30 These sayings are the words of
Agur, son of Jakeh. He spoke them
as if they came from God.

He spoke them to Ithiel
and to Ucal.

2 He said, "I know less than anyone.
I don't understand as other men do.
3 I haven't learned wisdom.
And I don't know the Holy One.
4 Who has gone up to heaven and come
down?
Who has gathered up the wind in
the palms of his hands?
Who has wrapped up the waters in his
coat?
Who has set all the boundaries of
the earth in place?
What is his name? What is his son's
name?
Tell me if you know!

5 "Every word of God is perfect.
He is like a shield to those who trust
in him.
He keeps them safe.
6 Don't add to his words.
If you do, he will correct you.
He will prove that you are a liar.

7 "LORD, I ask you for two things.
Don't refuse me before I die.
8 Keep lies far away from me.
Don't make me either poor or rich,
but give me only the bread I need
each day.
9 If you don't, I might have too much.
Then I might say I don't know you.
I might say, 'Who is the LORD?'
Or I might become poor and steal.
Then I would bring shame to the
name of my God.

10 "Don't tell lies about a servant when
you talk to his master.
If you do, he will call down curses on
you. And you will pay for it.

11 "Some people call down curses on
their fathers.
Others don't bless their mothers.
12 Some are pure in their own eyes.
But their dirty sins haven't been
washed away.
13 Some have eyes that are very proud.
They look down on others.
14 Some people have teeth like swords.
The teeth in their jaws are as sharp
as knives.
They are ready to eat up the poor
people of the earth.
They are ready to eat up those who
are the most needy.

15 "A bloodsucking worm has two
daughters.
They cry out, 'Give! Give!'

"Three things are never satisfied.
Four things never say, 'Enough!'
16 The first is the grave.
The second is a woman who can't
have a baby.
The third is land. It never gets enough
water.
And the fourth is fire. It never says,
'Enough!'

17 "Some make fun of their fathers.
Others laugh about obeying their
mothers.
The ravens of the valley will peck their
eyes out.
Then the vultures will eat them.

18 "Three things are too amazing for me.

He doesn't know he is going to be poor.

23 It is better to warn a man than to pretend to praise him.
In the end he will be more pleased with you.

24 Anyone who steals from his parents and says, "It's not wrong,"
is just like a man who destroys.

25 A person who always wants more stirs up fights.
But anyone who trusts in the LORD will succeed.

26 Anyone who trusts in himself is foolish.
But a person who lives wisely is kept safe.

27 Those who give to poor people will have everything they need.
But those who close their eyes to the poor
will be under many curses.

28 When those who are evil take charge, other people hide.
But when those who are evil die, godly people grow stronger.

29 A man who still won't obey after being warned many times
will suddenly be destroyed. Nothing can save him.

2 When those who do right grow stronger, the people are glad.
But when those who do wrong become rulers, the people groan.

3 A man who loves wisdom makes his father glad.
But a man who spends time with prostitutes wastes his father's wealth.

4 By doing what is fair, a king makes a country secure.
But the one who wants to be paid off tears it down.

5 A man who only pretends to praise his neighbor
is spreading a net to catch him by the feet.

6 A sinful man is trapped by his own sin.
But a godly person can sing and be glad.

7 Those who do what is right want to treat poor people fairly.

But those who do what is wrong don't care about the poor.

8 Those who make fun of others stir up a city.
But wise people turn anger away.

9 Suppose a wise man goes to court with a foolish person.
Then the foolish person gets mad and pokes fun. And there is no peace.

10 Murderers hate honest people.
They try to kill those who do what is right.

11 A foolish person lets his anger run wild.
But a wise person keeps himself under control.

POWER-SURGE

SELF-CONTROLLED

A WISE PERSON KEEPS HIMSELF UNDER CONTROL.
—PROVERBS 29:11—

WISE

12 If rulers listen to lies,
all their officials become evil.

13 The LORD gives sight to the eyes of poor people and those who beat others down.
That's what they both have in common.

14 If a king judges poor people fairly,
his throne will always be secure.

15 If a child is corrected, he becomes wise.
But a child left to himself brings shame to his mother.

16 When those who do wrong grow stronger, so does sin.
But those who do right will see them destroyed.

17 If you train your children, they will give you peace.
They will bring delight to you.

18 Where there is no message from God,
the people don't control themselves.

There are four things I don't
understand.
19 The first is the way of an eagle in the
sky.
The second is the way of a snake on
a rock.
The third is the way of a ship on the
ocean.
And the fourth is the way of a man
with a young woman.

20 "This is the way of a woman who
commits adultery.
She eats. She wipes her mouth.
Then she says, 'I haven't done
anything wrong.'

21 "Under three things the earth shakes.
Under four things it can't stand up.
22 The first is a servant who becomes a
king.
The second is a foolish person who
is full of food.
23 The third is a woman who is married
but not loved by her husband.
And the fourth is a woman servant
who takes the place of the
woman she works for.

24 "Four things on earth are small.
But they are very wise.
25 The first are ants. They aren't very
strong.
But they store up their food in the
summer.
26 The second are rock badgers. They
aren't very powerful.
But they make their home among
the rocks.
27 The third are locusts. They don't have
a king.
But they all march forward in ranks.
28 And the fourth are lizards. Your hand
can catch them.
But you will find them in kings'
palaces.

29 "Three things walk as if they were
kings.
Four things move as kings do.
30 The first is a lion. It is mighty among
the animals.
It doesn't back away from anything.
31 The second is a rooster that walks
proudly.
The third is a billy goat.
And the fourth is a king who has his
army around him.

32 "Have you been foolish?
Have you thought you were better
than others?
Have you planned evil?

If you have, put your hand over your
mouth and stop talking!
33 If you churn cream, you will produce
butter.
If you twist a nose, you will produce
blood.
And if you stir up anger, you will
produce a fight."

The Sayings of King Lemuel

31 These are the sayings of King Lemuel. His mother taught them to
him. She spoke them as if they came from
God.

2 She said, "My son! My very own son!
The son I prayed for!
3 Don't waste your strength on women.
Don't waste it on those who destroy
kings.

4 "Lemuel, it isn't good for kings to
drink wine.
It isn't good for rulers to long for
beer.
5 If they do, they might drink and forget
what the law commands.
They might take away the rights of
all those who are beaten down.
6 Give beer to those who are dying.
Give wine to those who are sad and
troubled.
7 Let them drink and forget how poor
they are.
Let them forget their suffering.

8 "Speak up for those who can't speak
for themselves.
Speak up for the rights of all those
who are poor.
9 Speak up and judge fairly.
Speak up for the rights of those who
are poor and needy."

The Noble Wife

10 Who can find a noble wife?
She is worth far more than rubies.
11 Her husband trusts her completely.
She gives him all the important
things he needs.
12 She brings him good, not harm,
all the days of her life.
13 She chooses wool and flax.
She loves to work with her hands.
14 She is like the ships of traders.
She brings her food from far away.
15 She gets up while it is still dark.
She provides food for her family.
She also gives some to her female
servants.
16 She considers a field and buys it.

TRUSTED

WHO CAN FIND A NOBLE WIFE?

SHE IS WORTH FAR MORE THAN RUBIES.

HER HUSBAND TRUSTS HER COMPLETELY.

— PROVERBS 31:10-11 —

She uses some of the money she earns to plant a vineyard.

17 She gets ready to work hard.
Her arms are strong.

18 She sees that her trading earns a lot of money.
Her lamp doesn't go out at night.

19 With one hand she holds the wool.
With the other she spins the thread.

20 She opens her arms to those who are poor.
She reaches out her hands to those who are needy.

21 When it snows, she's not afraid for her family.
All of them are dressed in the finest clothes.

22 She makes her own bed coverings.
She is dressed in fine linen and purple clothes.

23 Her husband is respected at the city gate.
There he takes his seat among the elders of the land.

24 She makes linen clothes and sells them.
She supplies belts to the traders.

25 She puts on strength and honor as if they were her clothes.
She can laugh at the days that are coming.

26 She speaks wisely.
She teaches faithfully.

27 She watches over family matters.
She is busy all the time.

28 Her children stand up and call her blessed.
Her husband also rises up, and he praises her.

29 He says, "Many women do noble things.
But you are better than all the others."

30 Charm can fool you. Beauty fades.
But a woman who has respect for the LORD should be praised.

31 Give her the reward she has earned.
Let everything she has done bring praise to her at the city gate.

ECCLESIASTES

Ecclesiastes is another book on wisdom, but it takes a different approach from the book of Proverbs. Here, the writer experiences all that life has to offer and discovers that nothing satisfies. He discovers that life means nothing without God in it. As you read Ecclesiastes, let it remind you that God is eager to be involved in every part of your life.

CODE OF HONOR IN THIS BOOK . . .

WISE
PAGES 765, 767, 768, 772

CHEERFUL
PAGES 765, 769, 770, 773

HELPFUL
PAGE 768

THANKFUL
PAGE 770

OBEYS
PAGES 772, 774

Nothing Has Any Meaning

1 These are the words of the Teacher. He was the son of David. He was also king in Jerusalem.

2 "Meaningless! Everything is
meaningless!"
says the Teacher.
"Everything is completely
meaningless!
Nothing has any meaning."

3 What does a man get for all of his
work?
Why does he work so hard on this
earth?
4 People come and people go.
But the earth remains forever.
5 The sun rises. Then it sets.
And then it hurries back to where it
rises.
6 The wind blows to the south.
Then it turns to the north.
Around and around it goes.
It always returns to where it started.
7 Every stream flows into the ocean.
But the ocean never gets full.
The streams return
to the place they came from.
8 All things are tiresome.
They are more tiresome than
anyone can say.
But our eyes never see enough of
anything.
Our ears never hear enough.
9 Everything that has ever been will
come back again.
Everything that has ever been done
will be done again.
Nothing is new on earth.
10 There isn't anything about which
someone can say,
"Look! Here's something new."
It was already here long ago.
It was here before we were.
11 No one remembers the men of long
ago.
Even those who haven't been born
yet
won't be remembered
by those who will be born after
them.

Wisdom Doesn't Have Any Meaning

12 I, the Teacher, was king over Israel in Jerusalem. 13 I spent all of my time studying. I used my wisdom to check everything out. I looked into everything that is done on earth. What a heavy load God has put on men!
14 I've seen what is done on this earth. It

doesn't have any meaning. It's like chasing the wind.

15 People can't straighten things that are
twisted.
They can't count things that don't
even exist.

16 I said to myself, "Look, my wisdom has really been growing. In fact, I'm now wiser than anyone who ruled over Jerusalem in the past. I have a lot of wisdom and knowledge."
17 Then I used my mind to understand what it really means to be wise. And I wanted to know what foolish pleasure is all about. But I found out that that's also like chasing the wind.

18 A lot of human wisdom leads to a lot of
sorrow.
More knowledge only brings more
sadness.

Pleasure Doesn't Have Any Meaning

2 I said to myself, "Come on. I'll put pleasure to the test. I want to find out what is good." But that also proved to be meaningless.
2 "Laughter is foolish," I said. "And what can pleasure do for me?" 3 I tried cheering myself up by drinking wine. I even tried living in a foolish way. But wisdom was still guiding my mind. I wanted to see what was really important for men to do on earth during the few days of their lives.
4 So I started some large projects. I built houses for myself. I planted vineyards. 5 I made gardens and parks. I planted all kinds of fruit trees in them. 6 I made lakes to water groves of healthy trees.
7 I bought male and female slaves. And I had other slaves who were born in my house. I also owned more herds and flocks than anyone in Jerusalem ever had before. 8 I stored up silver and gold for myself. I gathered up the treasures of kings and their kingdoms. I got some male and female singers. I also got many women for myself. Women delight the hearts of men.
9 I became far more important than anyone in Jerusalem had ever been before. And in spite of everything, I didn't lose my wisdom.

10 I gave myself everything my eyes
wanted.
There wasn't any pleasure that I
refused to give myself.
I took delight in everything I did.

POWER-SURGE

WISE W

WISDOM IS BETTER THAN FOOLISHNESS.
— ECCLESIASTES 2:13 —

And that was what I got for all of my
work.
11 But then I looked over everything my
hands had done.
I saw what I had worked so hard to
get.
And nothing had any meaning.
It was like chasing the wind.
Nothing was gained on this earth.

Wisdom and Foolish Pleasure Don't Have Any Meaning

12 I decided to think about wisdom.
I also thought about foolish
pleasure.
What more can a new king do?
Can he do anything more than
others have already done?
13 I saw that wisdom is better than
foolishness,
just as light is better than darkness.
14 The eyes of a wise man see things
clearly.
A person who is foolish lives in
darkness.
But I finally realized that death catches
up
with both of them.

15 Then I thought,

"What happens to a foolish person will
catch up with me too.
So what do I gain by being wise?"
I said to myself,
"That doesn't have any meaning
either."
16 Like a foolish person, a wise man won't
be remembered very long.
In days to come, both of them will
be forgotten.
Like a person who is foolish,
a wise man must die too!

Work Doesn't Have Any Meaning

17 So I hated life. That's because the
work that is done on this earth made me
sad. None of it has any meaning. It's like
chasing the wind.
18 I hated everything I had worked for
on earth. I'll have to leave all of it to someone who lives after me. 19 And who knows
whether he will be wise or foolish? Either
way, he'll take over everything on earth
I've worked so hard for. That doesn't have
any meaning either.
20 So I began to lose hope because of all
of my hard work on this earth. 21 A man
might use wisdom, knowledge and skill to
do his work. But then he has to leave
everything he owns to someone who
hasn't worked for it. That doesn't have
any meaning either. In fact, it isn't fair.
22 What does a man get for all of his
hard work on earth? What does he get for
all of his worries? 23 As long as he lives, his
work is nothing but pain and sorrow.
Even at night his mind can't rest. That
doesn't have any meaning either.
24 A man can't do anything better than
eat and drink and be satisfied with his
work. I'm finally seeing that those things
also come from the hand of God. 25 Without his help, who can eat or find pleasure?
26 God gives wisdom, knowledge and
happiness to a man who pleases him. But
to a sinner he gives the task of gathering
and storing up wealth. Then the sinner
must hand it over to the one who pleases
God. That doesn't have any meaning
either. It's like chasing the wind.

There Is a Time for Everything

3 There is a time for everything.
There's a time for everything that is
done on earth.

2 There is a time to be born.
And there's a time to die.
There is a time to plant.
And there's a time to pull up what is
planted.
3 There is a time to kill.
And there's a time to heal.
There is a time to tear down.
And there's a time to build up.

POWER-SURGE

CHEERFUL *

GOD GIVES WISDOM, KNOWLEDGE AND HAPPINESS TO A MAN WHO PLEASES HIM.
—ECCLESIASTES 2:26— W

WISE

4 There is a time to cry.
  And there's a time to laugh.
There is a time to be sad.
  And there's a time to dance.
5 There is a time to scatter stones.
  And there's a time to gather them.
There is a time to hug.
  And there's a time not to hug.
6 There is a time to search.
  And there's a time to stop searching.
There is a time to keep.
  And there's a time to throw away.
7 There is a time to tear.
  And there's a time to mend.
There is a time to be silent.
  And there's a time to speak.
8 There is a time to love.
  And there's a time to hate.
There is a time for war.
  And there's a time for peace.

9 What does the worker get for his hard work? **10** I've seen the heavy load God has put on men. **11** He has made everything beautiful in its time. He has also given men a sense of what he's been doing down through the ages. But they can't completely figure out what he's done from the beginning to the end.

12 They should be happy and do good while they live. I know there's nothing better for them to do than that. **13** Everyone should eat and drink. People should be satisfied with all of their hard work. That is God's gift to them.

14 I know that everything God does will last forever. Nothing can be added to it. And nothing can be taken from it. God does that so men will have respect for him.

15 Everything that now exists has already been.
  And what is coming has existed before.
God will judge those who treat others badly.

16 Here's something else I saw on earth.

Where people should be treated right, they are treated wrong.
Where people should be treated fairly, they are treated unfairly.

17 I said to myself,

"God will judge
godly and sinful people alike.
He has a time for every act.
  He has a time for everything that is done."

18 I also thought, "God puts human beings to the test. Then they can see they are just like animals. **19** What happens to animals happens to people too. Death waits for people and animals alike. People die, just as animals do. All of them have the same breath. People don't have any advantage over animals. Nothing has any meaning.

20 "People and animals go to the same place. All of them come from dust. And all of them return to dust. **21** Who can know whether the spirit of a man goes up? Who can tell whether the spirit of an animal goes down into the earth?"

22 So man should enjoy his work. That's what God made him for. I saw that there's nothing better for him to do than that. After all, who can show him what will happen after he is gone?

Suffering, Hard Work and Friendship

4 I looked and saw how much people were suffering on this earth.

I saw the tears of those who are suffering.
  They don't have anyone to comfort them.
Power is on the side of those who beat them down.
  Those who are suffering don't have anyone to comfort them.
2 Then I announced that those
  who have already died
are happier than those
  who are still alive.
3 But someone who hasn't been born yet
  is better off than the dead or the living.
That's because he hasn't seen the evil things
  that are done on earth.

4 I also saw that man works hard and accomplishes a lot. But he does it only because he wants what his neighbor has. That doesn't have any meaning either. It's like chasing the wind.

5 A foolish person folds his hands and doesn't work.
  And that destroys him.
6 One handful with peace and quiet
  is better than two handfuls with hard work.
  Working too hard is like chasing the wind.

7 Again I saw something on earth that didn't mean anything.

8 A man lived all by himself.

He didn't have any sons or brothers.
His hard work never ended.
But he wasn't happy with what he
had.
"Who am I working so hard for?" he
asked.
"Why don't I get the things I
enjoy?"
That doesn't have any meaning either.
In fact, it's a very bad deal!

9 Two people are better than one.
They can help each other in
everything they do.
10 Suppose someone falls down.
Then his friend can help him up.
But suppose the man who falls down
doesn't have anyone to help
him up.
Then feel sorry for him!
11 Or suppose two people lie down
together.
Then they'll keep warm.
But how can one person keep warm
alone?
12 One person could be overpowered.
But two people can stand up for
themselves.
And a rope made out of three cords
isn't easily broken.

Getting Ahead Doesn't Have Any Meaning

13 A poor but wise young man is better
off than an old but foolish king. That king
doesn't pay attention to a warning anymore. **14** The young man might have come
from prison to become king. Or he might
have been born poor within the kingdom
but still became king. **15** I saw that everyone was following the young man who
had become the new king.

16 At first, all of the people served him
when he became king. But those who
came later weren't pleased with the way
he was ruling. That doesn't have any
meaning either. It's like chasing the wind.

WISE

A POOR BUT WISE YOUNG MAN IS BETTER OFF THAN AN OLD BUT FOOLISH KING.
— ECCLESIASTES 4:13 —

Have Respect for God

5 Be careful what you say when you go
to God's house. Go there to listen.
Don't be like foolish people when you
offer your sacrifice. They do what is wrong
and don't even know it.

2 Don't be too quick to speak.
Don't be in a hurry to say anything
to God.
He is in heaven. You are on earth.
So use only a few words when you
speak.
3 Dreams come to people when they
worry a lot.
When foolish people talk, they use
too many words.

4 When you make a promise to God,
don't wait too long to carry it out. He isn't
pleased with foolish people. So do what
you have promised. **5** It is better to make
no promise at all than to make a promise
and not keep it.

6 Don't let your mouth cause you to sin.
Don't object to the temple messenger.
Don't say, "My promise was a mistake."
Why should God be angry with what you
say? Why should he destroy what you
have done? **7** Dreaming too much and
talking too much are meaningless. So
have respect for God.

Riches Don't Have Any Meaning

8 Suppose you see poor people being
mistreated somewhere. And what is being
done to them isn't right or fair. Don't be
surprised by that. One official is watched
by a higher one. Others who are even
higher are watching both of them. **9** All of
them take what the land produces. And
the king himself takes his share from the
fields.

10 Anyone who loves money never has
enough.
Anyone who loves wealth is never
satisfied with what he gets.
That doesn't have any meaning
either.

11 As more and more goods are made,
more and more people use them up.
So how can those goods benefit their
owner?
All he can do is look at them with
longing.

12 The sleep of a worker is sweet.
It doesn't matter whether he eats a
little or a lot.
But the wealth of a rich man
keeps him awake at night.

¹³I've seen something very evil on earth.

It's when wealth is stored up
    and then brings harm to its owner.
¹⁴It's also when wealth is lost
    because of an unwise business deal.
Then there won't be anything left
    for the owner's son.
¹⁵A man is born naked.
    He comes into the world with
        nothing.
And he goes out of it with nothing.
He doesn't get anything from his work
    that he can take with him.

¹⁶Here's something else that is very evil.

A man is born, and a man dies.
    And what does he get for his work?
Nothing. It's like working for the
        wind.
¹⁷All his life he eats in darkness.
    His life is full of trouble, suffering
        and anger.

¹⁸I realized that it's good and proper for a man to eat and drink. It's good for him to be satisfied with his hard work on this earth. That's what he should do during the few days of life God has given him. That's what God made him for.

¹⁹Sometimes God gives a man wealth and possessions. He makes it possible for

HELPFUL ★

SOMETIMES GOD GIVES A MAN WEALTH AND POSSESSIONS. HE MAKES IT POSSIBLE FOR HIM TO ENJOY THEM. HE HELPS HIM ACCEPT THE LIFE HE HAS GIVEN HIM. HE HELPS HIM TO BE HAPPY IN HIS WORK. ALL OF THOSE THINGS ARE GIFTS FROM GOD.

— ECCLESIASTES 5:19 —

WISE

him to enjoy them. He helps him accept the life he has given him. He helps him to be happy in his work. All of those things are gifts from God. ²⁰A man like that doesn't have to think about how his life is going. That's because God fills his heart with joy.

6 I've seen another evil thing on this earth. And it's a heavy load on men. ²God gives a man wealth, possessions and honor. He has everything his heart longs for. But God doesn't let him enjoy those things. Instead, strangers enjoy them. That doesn't have any meaning. It's a very evil thing.

³A man might have a hundred children. He might live a long time. But suppose he can't enjoy his wealth. And suppose he isn't buried in the proper way. Then it doesn't matter how long he lives. I'm telling you that a baby that is born dead is better off than he is. ⁴That kind of birth doesn't have any meaning. The baby dies in darkness and leaves this world. And in darkness it is forgotten. ⁵It didn't even see the sun. It didn't know anything at all. But it has more rest than that man does. ⁶And that's true even if he lives for 2,000 years but doesn't get to enjoy his wealth. All people die and go to the grave, don't they?

⁷Man eats up everything he works to
    get.
    But he is never satisfied.
⁸What advantage does a wise man have
    over someone who is foolish?
What does a poor man gain
    by knowing how to act toward
        others?
⁹Being satisfied with what you have
    is better than always wanting more.
That doesn't have any meaning either.
    It's like chasing the wind.

¹⁰God has already planned what now
    exists.
    He has already decided what man is.
A man can't argue with the One
    who is stronger than he is.
¹¹The more words people use,
    the less meaning there is.
    And that doesn't help anyone.

¹²Who knows what's good for a man? He lives for only a few meaningless days. He passes through life like a shadow. Who can tell him what will happen on earth after he is gone?

Good Advice About How to Live

7 A good name is better than fine
perfume.
People can learn more from sobbing
when someone dies
than from being happy when
someone is born.
² So it's better to go where people are
sobbing
than to go where people are having
a good time.
Everyone will die someday.
Those who are still living
should really think about that.
³ Sadness is good for the heart.
That's why sorrow is better than
laughter.
⁴ Those who are wise are found where
there is sorrow.
But foolish people are found where
there is pleasure.
⁵ Pay attention to a wise man's warning.
That's better than listening to the
songs of those who are foolish.
⁶ A foolish person's laughter
is like the crackling of thorns
burning under a pot.
That doesn't have any meaning
either.

⁷ When a wise man takes wealth by
force, he becomes foolish.
It is sinful to take money from
people who want special favors.

⁸ The end of a matter is better than its
beginning.
So it's better to be patient than
proud.
⁹ Don't become angry quickly.
Anger lives in the hearts of foolish
people.

¹⁰ Don't say, "Why were things better in
the good old days?"
It isn't wise to ask that kind of
question.

¹¹ Wisdom is a good thing.
It's like getting a share of the family
wealth.
It benefits those who live on this
earth.
¹² Wisdom provides safety,
just as money provides safety.
But here's the advantage of wisdom.
It guards the lives of those who
have it.

¹³ Think about what God has done.

Who can make straight
what he has made crooked?
¹⁴ When times are good, be happy.

POWER-SURGE

CHEERFUL ✳

**WHEN TIMES ARE
GOOD, BE HAPPY.**
— ECCLESIASTES 7:14 —

But when times are bad, here's
something to think about.
God has made bad times.
He has also made good times.
So a man can't find out anything
about what's ahead for him.

¹⁵ In my meaningless life here's what
I've seen.

I've seen a godly man dying
even though he is godly.
And I've seen a sinful man living a
long time
even though he is sinful.
¹⁶ Don't claim to be better than you are.
And don't claim to be wiser than
you are.
Why destroy yourself?
¹⁷ Don't be too sinful.
And don't be foolish.
Why die before your time comes?
¹⁸ It's good to hold on to both of those
things.
Don't let go of either one.
A man who has respect for God will
avoid
going too far in either direction.

¹⁹ Wisdom makes one wise man more
powerful
than ten rulers in a city.

²⁰ There isn't anyone on earth
who does only what is right and
never sins.

²¹ Don't pay attention to everything
people say.
If you do, you might hear your
servant calling down a curse on
you.
²² Many times you yourself have called
down curses on others.
Deep down inside, you know that's
true.

²³ I used wisdom to put all of those
things to the test. I said,

"I've made up my mind to be wise."
But it was more than I could
accomplish.
²⁴ No matter what else wisdom may be,

it's far away and very deep.
Who can find it?
25 So I tried to understand wisdom more
completely.
I wanted to study it and figure it out.
I tried to find out everything I could
about it.
I tried to understand why it's foolish to
be evil.
I wanted to see why choosing
foolishness is so unwise.

26 A woman who hunts a man down
is more painful than death.
Her heart is like a trap.
Her hands are like chains.
A man who pleases God will try to get
away from her.
But she will trap a sinner.

27 "Look," says the Teacher. "Here's
what I've discovered.

"I added one thing to another to find
out
everything I could about wisdom.
28 I searched and searched
but found very little.
I did find one honest man among a
thousand.
But I didn't find one honest woman
among a thousand.
29 Here's the only other thing I found.
God made men honest.
But they've made many evil plans."

8 Who is like a wise man?
Who knows how to explain things?
Wisdom makes a man's face bright.
It softens the look on his face.

Obey the King

2 I'm telling you to obey the king's command. You took an oath to serve him. You made a promise to God. 3 Don't be in a hurry to quit your job in the palace. Don't stand up for something the king doesn't like. He'll do anything he wants to. 4 He has the final word. So who can ask him, "What are you doing?"

5 No one who obeys his command will
be harmed.
Those who are wise will know the
proper time and way to
approach him.
6 There's a proper time and way for
people to do everything.
That's true even though a man
might be suffering greatly.

7 No one knows what lies ahead.
So who can tell a person what's
going to happen?

8 He can't stop the wind from blowing.
And he doesn't have the power to
decide when he will die.
No one is let out of the army in times
of war.
And evil won't let go of those who
practice it.

9 I understood all of those things. I used my mind to study everything that's done on earth. A man sometimes makes life hard for others. But he ends up hurting himself.

10 I also saw sinful people being buried. They used to come and go from the place of worship. And others praised them in the city where they worshiped. That doesn't have any meaning either.

11 Sometimes the sentence for a crime isn't carried out quickly. So people make plans to commit even more crimes.

12 An evil man may be guilty of a hundred crimes and still live a long time. But I know that things will go better with men who have great respect for God. 13 Sinful people don't respect God. So things won't go well with them. Like a shadow, they won't be around very long.

14 Here's something else on this earth that doesn't have any meaning. Sometimes godly men get what sinful people should receive. And sinful men get what godly people should receive. Here's what I'm telling you. That doesn't have any meaning either.

15 So I advise everyone to enjoy life. A man on this earth can't do anything better than eat and drink and be glad. Then

POWER-SURGE

CHEERFUL ✳

A MAN ON THIS EARTH
CAN'T DO ANYTHING
BETTER THAN EAT AND
DRINK AND BE GLAD.
THEN HE WILL ENJOY
HIS WORK. HE'LL BE
HAPPY ALL THE DAYS
OF THE LIFE GOD HAS
GIVEN HIM ON EARTH.
—ECCLESIASTES 8:15—

THANKFUL

he will enjoy his work. He'll be happy all the days of the life God has given him on earth.

16I used my mind to understand what it really means to be wise. I wanted to observe the hard work man does on earth. He doesn't close his eyes and go to sleep day or night.

17I saw everything God has done. No one can understand what happens on earth. Man might try very hard to figure it out. But he still can't discover what it all means. A wise man might claim he knows. But he can't really understand it either.

Everyone Dies

9 I thought about all of those things. I realized that those who are wise and do what is right are under God's control. What they do is also under his control.

But a man doesn't know whether God will show favor to him. **2**Everyone will die someday. Death comes to godly and sinful people alike. It comes to good and bad people alike. It comes to "clean" and "unclean" people alike. Those who offer sacrifices and those who don't offer them also die.

A good person dies,
      and so does a sinner.
Those who take oaths die.
      So do those who are afraid to take
         them.

3Here's what is so bad about everything that happens on this earth. Death catches up with all of us. Also, the hearts of people are full of evil. They live in foolish pleasure. After that, they join those who have already died.

4Anyone who is living still has hope. Even a live dog is better off than a dead lion!

5 People who are still alive know they'll
      die.
      But those who have died don't know
         anything.
They don't receive any more rewards.
      And they are soon forgotten.
6Their love, hate and jealousy
      disappear.
      They will never share again
   in anything that happens on earth.

7Go and enjoy your food. Be joyful as you drink your wine. Now is the time God favors what you do. **8**Always wear white clothes to show you are happy. Anoint your head with olive oil.

9You love your wife. So enjoy life with her. Do it all the days of this meaningless life God has given you on earth. That's what he made you for. That's what you get for all of your hard work on earth.

10No matter what you do, work at it with all your might. Remember, you are going to your grave. And there isn't any work or planning or knowledge or wisdom there.

11Here's something else I've seen on this earth.

Races aren't always won by those who
      run fast.
      Battles aren't always won by those
         who are strong.
Wise people don't always have plenty
      of food.
      Clever people aren't always wealthy.
      Those who have learned a lot aren't
         always favored.
God controls the timing of every
      event.
      He also controls how things turn
         out.

12A man doesn't know when trouble will come to him.

Fish are caught in nets.
      Birds are taken in traps.
And people are trapped by hard times
      that come when they don't expect
         them.

Being Wise Is Better Than Being Foolish

13Here's something else I saw on this earth. I saw an example of wisdom that touched me deeply. **14**There was once a small city. Only a few people lived there. A powerful king attacked it. He brought in war machines all around it.

15A certain man lived in that city. He was poor but wise. He used his wisdom to save the city. But no one remembered that poor man. **16**So I said, "It's better to be wise than to be powerful." But people looked down on the poor man's wisdom. No one paid any attention to what he said.

17 People should listen to the quiet words
      of those who are wise.
That's better than paying attention to
      the shouts
      of a ruler of foolish people.
18 Wisdom is better than weapons of war.
      But one sinner destroys a lot of good.

10 Dead flies give perfume a bad
         smell.
And a little foolishness can make a
      lot of wisdom useless.

OBEYS ✔

PEOPLE SHOULD LISTEN TO THE QUIET WORDS OF THOSE WHO ARE WISE.
— ECCLESIASTES 9:17 — **W**

WISE

2 The hearts of wise people lead them on the right path.
But the hearts of foolish people take them down the wrong path.
3 A foolish person doesn't have any sense at all.
He shows everyone he is foolish.
He does it even when he is walking along the road.
4 Suppose a ruler gets very angry with you.
If he does, don't quit your job in the palace.
Stay calm. That will overcome the effects of your big mistakes.

5 Here's something evil I've seen on this earth.
And it's the kind of mistake that rulers make.
6 Foolish people are given many important jobs.
Rich people are given unimportant ones.
7 I've seen slaves on horseback.
I've also seen princes who were forced to walk as if they were slaves.
8 Anyone who digs a pit might fall into it.
Anyone who breaks through a wall might be bitten by a snake.
9 Anyone who removes stones from rock pits might get hurt.
Anyone who cuts logs might get wounded.
10 Suppose the blade of an ax is dull.
And its edge hasn't been sharpened.
Then more effort is needed to use it.
But skill will bring success.

11 Suppose a snake bites before it is charmed.
Then there isn't any benefit in being a snake charmer.
12 A man who is wise says gracious things.
But a foolish person is destroyed by what his own lips speak.
13 At first what he says is foolish.
In the end his words are very evil.
14 He talks too much.

No one knows what lies ahead for him.
Who can tell him what will happen after he is gone?

15 The work a foolish person does makes him tired.
He doesn't even know the way to town.

16 How terrible it is for a land whose king used to be a servant!
How terrible if its princes get drunk in the morning!
17 How blessed is the land whose king was born into the royal family!
How blessed if its princes eat and drink at the proper time!
How blessed if they eat and drink to become strong and not to get drunk!

18 When a man won't work, the roof falls down.
When his hands aren't busy, the house leaks.

19 People laugh at a dinner party.
And wine makes life happy.
People think money can buy everything.

20 Don't call down curses on the king.
Don't even think about doing it.
Don't call down curses on rich people.

WISE **W**

A MAN WHO IS WISE SAYS GRACIOUS THINGS.

BUT A FOOLISH PERSON IS DESTROYED BY WHAT HIS OWN LIPS SPEAK.
— ECCLESIASTES 10:12 —

Don't even do it in your bedroom.
A bird might fly away and carry your
words.
It might report what you said.

Be Bold

11 Put your money into trade across
the ocean.
After a while you will earn
something from it.
2 Give shares of what you earn to a lot of
people.
After all, you don't know what great
trouble might come on the
land.
3 Clouds that are full of water
pour rain down on the earth.
A tree might fall to the south or the
north.
It will stay in the place where it falls.
4 Anyone who keeps on watching the
wind won't plant seeds.
Anyone who keeps looking at the
clouds won't gather crops.
5 You don't know the path the wind
takes.
You don't know how a baby is made
inside its mother.
So you can't understand how God
works either.
He made everything.

6 In the morning plant your seeds.
In the evening keep your hands
busy.
You don't know what will succeed.
It may be one or the other.
Or both might do equally well.

Remember the One Who Created You

7 Light is sweet.
People enjoy being out in the sun.
8 No matter how many years a man
might live,
let him enjoy all of them.
But let him remember the dark days.
There will be many of them.
Nothing that's going to happen will
have any meaning.

9 Young man, be happy while you are
still young.
Let your heart be joyful while you
are still strong.
Do what your heart tells you to do.
Go after what your eyes look at.
But I want you to know
that God will judge you for
everything you do.
10 So drive worry out of your heart.

Get rid of all of your troubles.
Being young and strong doesn't
have any meaning.

12 Remember the One who created
you.
Remember him while you are still
young.
Think about him before your times of
trouble come.
The years will come when you will
say,
"I don't find any pleasure in them."
2 That's when the sunlight will become
dark.
The moon and the stars will also
grow dark.
And the clouds will return after it
rains.
3 Remember your Creator before those
who guard the house tremble
with old age.
That's when strong men will be bent
over.
The women who grind grain will stop
because there are so few of
them left.
Those who look through the
windows won't be able to see
very well.
4 Remember your Creator before the
front doors are closed.
That's when the sound of grinding
will fade away.
Old men will rise up when they hear
birds singing.
But they will barely hear any of their
songs.
5 Remember your Creator before you
become afraid of places that are
too high.

CHEERFUL ✳

YOUNG MAN, BE HAPPY
WHILE YOU ARE STILL
YOUNG.

LET YOUR HEART BE
JOYFUL WHILE YOU
ARE STILL STRONG.
—ECCLESIASTES 11:9—

STRONG

You will also be terrified because of danger in the streets.
Remember your Creator before the almond trees have buds on them.
That's when grasshoppers will drag themselves along.
Old men will not want to make love anymore.
Man will go to his dark home in the grave.
And those who sob over the dead will walk around in the streets.

6 Remember your Creator before the silver cord is cut.
That's when the golden bowl will be broken.
The wheel will be broken at the well.
The pitcher will be smashed at the spring.
7 Remember your Creator before you return to the dust you came from.
That's when your spirit will go back to God who gave it.

8 "Meaningless! Everything is meaningless!"
says the Teacher.
"Nothing has any meaning."

Have Respect for God

9 The Teacher was wise. He gave knowledge to people. He put many proverbs to the test. He thought about them carefully. Then he wrote them down in order. 10 He did his best to find just the right words. And what he wrote was honest and true.
11 The sayings of those who are wise move people to take action. Their collected sayings really nail things down. They are given to us by one Shepherd. 12 My son, be careful not to pay attention to anything that is added to them.
Books will never stop being written. Too much studying makes people tired.

13 Everything has now been heard.
And here's the final thing I want to say.
Have respect for God and obey his commandments.
That's what everyone should do.
14 God will judge everything people do.
That includes everything they try to hide.
He'll judge everything, whether it's good or evil.

OBEYS ✔

HAVE RESPECT FOR GOD AND OBEY HIS COMMANDMENTS.

THAT'S WHAT EVERYONE SHOULD DO.
— ECCLESIASTES 12:13 —

SONG OF SONGS

The book of Song of Songs pictures a wonderful love story between a man and a woman. It can also be read as a picture of the love Jesus Christ has for those who follow him. The language of love in this book may at times seem too embarrassing. But it is a beautiful poem of deep love. When you read Song of Songs, think of the love Jesus has for you.

CODE OF HONOR IN THIS BOOK . . .

LOVING
PAGE 781

STRONG
PAGE 781

1 This is the greatest song Solomon ever wrote.

A Shulammite woman says to King Solomon,

2 "I long for your lips to kiss me!
  Your love makes me happier than
    wine does.
3 The lotion you have on pleases me.
  Your name is like perfume that is
    poured out.
  No wonder the young women love
    you!
4 Take me away with you. Let us hurry!
  King Solomon, bring me into your
    palace."

The other women say,

"King Solomon, you fill us with joy.
  You make us happy.
  We praise your love more than we
    praise wine."

The woman says to the king,

"It is right for them to love you!

5 "Women of Jerusalem,
  my skin is dark but lovely.
It is dark like the tents in Kedar.
  It's like the curtains of Solomon's
    tent.
6 Don't stare at me because I'm dark.
  The sun has made my skin look like
    this.
My brothers burned with anger against
  me.
  They made me take care of the
    vineyards.
  I haven't even taken care of my own
    vineyard.

7 "King Solomon, I love you.
  So tell me where you take care of
    your flock.
  Tell me where you rest your sheep at
    noon.
Why should I have to act like a
    prostitute
  near the flocks of your friends?"

The other women say,

8 "You are the most beautiful woman of
    all.
  Don't you know where to find the
    king?
  Follow the tracks the sheep make.
Take care of your young goats
  near the tents of the shepherds."

King Solomon says to the Shulammite
woman,

9 "You are my love.
  You are like a mare that pulls one of
    Pharaoh's chariots.
10 Your earrings make your cheeks even
    more beautiful.
  Your strings of jewels make your
    neck even more lovely."

The other women say to her,

11 "We will make gold earrings for you.
  We'll decorate them with silver."

The woman says,

12 "The king was at his table.
  My perfume gave off a sweet smell.
13 The one who loves me is like a small
    bag of myrrh
  resting between my breasts.
14 He is like henna flowers
  from the vineyards of En Gedi."

The king says,

15 "You are so beautiful, my love!
  So beautiful!
  Your eyes are like doves."

The woman says,

16 "You are so handsome, my love!
  So charming!
  The green field is our bed.
17 Cedar trees above us are the beams of
    our house.
  Fir trees overhead are its rafters.

2 "I am like a rose on the coast of
    Sharon.
  I'm like a lily in the valleys."

The king says,

2 "My love, among the young women
  you are like a lily among thorns."

The woman says,

3 "My love, among the young men
  you are like an apple tree among the
    trees of the forest.
I'm happy to sit in your shade.
  Your fruit tastes so sweet to me.
4 You have taken me to the dinner hall.
  Your banner of love is lifted high
    above me.
5 Give me some raisins to make me
    strong.
  Give me some apples to make me
    feel like new again.
  Our love has made me weak.
6 Your left arm is under my head.
  Your right arm is around me.
7 Women of Jerusalem, take an oath and
    make me a promise.

Let the antelopes and the does serve
as witnesses.
Don't stir up love.
Don't wake it up until it's ready.

8 "Listen! I hear my love!
Look! Here he comes!
He's leaping across the mountains.
He's coming over the hills.
9 The one who loves me is like an
antelope or a young deer.
Look! There he stands behind our
wall.
He's gazing through the window.
He's peering through the screen.
10 He said to me, 'Rise up, my love.
Come with me, my beautiful one.
11 Look! The winter is past.
The rains are over and gone.
12 Flowers are appearing on the earth.
The season for singing has come.
The cooing of doves
is heard in our land.
13 The fig trees are producing their early
fruit.
The flowers on the vines are giving
off their sweet smell.
Rise up and come, my love.
Come with me, my beautiful one.' "

The king says,

14 "You are like a dove in an opening in
the rocks.
You are like a dove in a hiding place
on a mountainside.
Show me your face.
Let me hear your voice.
Your voice is so sweet.
Your face is so lovely.
15 Catch the foxes for us.
Catch the little foxes.
They destroy our vineyards.
The vineyards are in bloom."

The woman says,

16 "My love belongs to me, and I belong
to him.
Like an antelope, he eats among the
lilies.
17 Until the day begins
and the shadows fade away,
turn to me, my love.
Be like an antelope
or like a young deer
on the rocky hills.

3 "All night long on my bed
I searched for the one my heart loves.
I looked for him but didn't find him.
2 I will get up. I'll go around in the city.
I'll look through all of its streets.
I'll search for the one my heart loves.

So I looked for him but didn't find
him.
3 Those on guard duty found me
as they were walking around in the
city.
'Have you seen the one my heart
loves?' I asked.
4 As soon as I had passed by them
I found the one my heart loves.
I threw my arms around him. I didn't
let him go
until I had brought him to my
mother's house.
I took him to my mother's room.
5 Women of Jerusalem, take an oath and
make me a promise.
Let the antelopes and the does serve
as witnesses.
Don't stir up love.
Don't wake it up until it's ready."

The other women say,

6 "Who is this man coming up from the
desert
like a column of smoke?
He smells like myrrh and incense
made from all of the spices of the
trader.
7 Look! There's Solomon's movable
throne.
Sixty soldiers accompany it.
They have been chosen from the
best warriors in Israel.
8 All of them are wearing swords.
They have fought many battles.
Each one has his sword at his side.
Each is prepared for the terrors of
the night.
9 King Solomon made the movable
throne for himself.
He made it out of wood from
Lebanon.
10 He formed its posts out of silver.
He made its base out of gold.
Its seat was covered with purple cloth.
It was decorated inside with loving
care
by the women of Jerusalem.
11 Women of Zion, come out.
Look at King Solomon wearing his
crown.
His mother placed it on him.
She did it on his wedding day.
His heart was full of joy."

4 The king says to the Shulammite
woman,

"You are so beautiful, my love!
So beautiful!
Your eyes behind your veil are like
doves.

Your hair flows like a flock of black
　　goats
　　coming down from Mount Gilead.
2 Your teeth are as clean as a flock of
　　sheep.
　　Their wool has just been clipped.
　　They have just come up from being
　　washed.
　Each of your teeth has its twin.
　　Not one of them is alone.
3 Your lips are like a bright red ribbon.
　　Your mouth is so lovely.
　Your cheeks behind your veil
　　are like the halves of a pomegranate.
4 Your neck is strong and beautiful like
　　the tower of David.
　　That tower is built with beautiful
　　　stones.
　A thousand shields are hanging on it.
　　All of them belong to mighty
　　　soldiers.
5 Your two breasts are lovely.
　　They are like two young antelopes
　　that eat among the lilies.
6 I will go to the mountain of myrrh.
　I'll go to the hill of incense.
　I'll stay there until the day begins
　　and the shadows fade away.
7 Every part of you is so beautiful, my
　　love.
　　There is no flaw in you.

8 "Come with me from Lebanon, my
　　bride.
　　Come with me from Lebanon.
　Come down from the top of Mount
　　Amana.
　　Come down from the top of Senir.
　　Come to me from the peak of
　　　Mount Hermon.
　Leave the dens where the lions live.
　　Leave the places in the mountains
　　where the leopards stay.
9 My bride, you have stolen my heart
　　with one glance of your eyes.
　My sister, you have stolen my heart
　　with one jewel in your necklace.
10 My bride, your love is so delightful.
　　My sister, your love makes me
　　　happier than wine does.
　　Your perfume smells better than any
　　　spice.
11 Your lips are as sweet as a honeycomb,
　　my bride.
　　Milk and honey are under your
　　　tongue.
　Your clothes smell like the cedar
　　trees in Lebanon.
12 My bride, you are like a garden that is
　　locked up.

My sister, you are like a spring of
　　water that has a fence around it.
　You are like a fountain that is sealed
　　up.
13 You are like trees whose branches are
　　loaded
　　with pomegranates, fine fruits,
　　　henna and nard,
14 　with saffron, cane and cinnamon.
　You are like every kind of incense tree.
　　You have myrrh, aloes
　　and all of the finest spices.
15 You are like a fountain in a garden.
　　You are like a well of flowing water
　　streaming down from Lebanon."

The woman says,

16 "Wake up, north wind!
　　Come, south wind!
　Blow on my garden.
　　Then its sweet smell will spread
　　　everywhere.
　Let my love come into his garden.
　　Let him taste its fine fruits."

5 The king says,

"My bride, I have come into my garden.
　　My sister, I've gathered my myrrh
　　　and my spice.
　I've eaten my honeycomb and my
　　honey.
　　I've drunk my wine and my milk."

The other women say to the Shulammite woman and to Solomon,

"Friends, eat and drink.
　　Lovers, drink all you want."

The woman says,

2 "I slept, but my heart was awake.
　　Listen! The one who loves me is
　　　knocking.
　He says, 'My sister, I love you.
　　Open up so I can come in.
　You are my dove.
　　You are perfect in every way.
　My head is soaked with dew.
　　The night air has made my hair wet.'

3 "But I've taken my robe off.
　　Must I put it on again?
　I've washed my feet.
　　Must I get them dirty again?
4 My love put his hand through the
　　opening.
　　My heart began to pound for him.
5 I got up to open the door for my love.
　　My hands dripped with myrrh.
　It flowed from my fingers
　　onto the handles of the lock.
6 I opened the door for my love.

But he had left. He was gone.
My heart sank because he had left.
I looked for him but didn't find him.
I called out to him, but he didn't
answer.
7 Those on guard duty found me
as they were walking around in the
city.
They beat me. They hurt me.
Those on guard duty at the walls
took my coat away from me.
8 Women of Jerusalem, take an oath and
make me a promise.
If you find the one who loves me,
tell him our love has made me
weak."

The other women say,

9 "You are the most beautiful woman
of all.
How is the one you love better than
others?
How is he better than anyone else?
Why do you ask us to make you a
promise?"

The woman says,

10 "The one who loves me is tanned and
handsome.
He's the finest man among 10,000.
11 His head is like the purest gold.
His hair is wavy and as black as a
raven.
12 His eyes are like doves
by streams of water.
They look as if they've been washed in
milk.
They are set like jewels in his head.
13 His cheeks are like beds of spice
that give off perfume.
His lips are like lilies
that drip with myrrh.
14 His arms are like gold
that are set with chrysolite.
His body is like polished ivory
that is decorated with sapphires.
15 His legs are like pillars of marble
that are set on bases of pure gold.
He looks like the finest cedar tree
in the mountains of Lebanon.
16 His mouth is very sweet.
Everything about him is delightful.
That's what the one who loves me is
like.
That's what my friend is like,
women of Jerusalem."

6 The other women say,

"You are the most beautiful woman
of all.

Where has the one who loves you
gone?
Which way did he turn?
We'll help you look for him."

The woman says,

2 "My love has gone down to his garden.
He's gone to the beds of spices.
He's eating in the gardens.
He's gathering lilies.
3 I belong to my love, and he belongs
to me.
He's eating among the lilies."

The king says,

4 "My love, you are as beautiful as the
city of Tirzah.
You are as lovely as Jerusalem.
You are as majestic as troops
carrying their banners.
5 Turn your eyes away from me.
They overpower me.
Your hair flows like a flock of black
goats
coming down from Mount Gilead.
6 Your teeth are as clean as a flock of
sheep
coming up from being washed.
Each of your teeth has its twin.
Not one of them is alone.
7 Your cheeks behind your veil
are like the halves of a pomegranate.
8 There might be 60 queens and 80
concubines.
There might be more virgins than
anyone can count.
9 But you are my perfect dove.
There isn't anyone like you.
You are your mother's favorite
daughter.
The young women see you and call
you blessed.
The queens and concubines praise
you."

The other women say,

10 "Who is this woman?
She is like the sunrise in all of its
glory.
She is as beautiful as the moon.
She is as bright as the sun.
She is as majestic as troops carrying
their banners."

The king says,

11 "I went down to a grove of nut trees.
I wanted to look at the new plants
growing in the valley.
I wanted to find out whether the vines
had budded.

I wanted to see if the pomegranate
    trees had bloomed.
12 Before I realized it,
    I was among the royal chariots of my
        people."

The other women say,

13 "Come back to us.
    Come back, Shulammite woman.
Come back to us.
    Come back. Then we can look at
        you."

The woman says,

"Why do you want to look at me
    as you would watch a dancer at
        Mahanaim?"

7 The king says to the Shulammite
    woman,

"You are like a prince's daughter.
    Your feet in sandals are so beautiful.
Your graceful legs are like jewels.
    The hands of a skilled worker must
        have shaped them.
2 Your navel is like a round bowl
    that always has mixed wine in it.
Your waist is like a mound of wheat
    that is surrounded by lilies.
3 Your two breasts are lovely.
    They are like two young antelopes.
4 Your neck is smooth and beautiful like
        an ivory tower.
Your eyes are like the pools of Heshbon
    by the gate of Bath Rabbim.
Your nose is like the towering
        mountains of Lebanon
    that face the city of Damascus.
5 Your head is like a crown on you.
    It is as beautiful as Mount Carmel.
Your hair is as smooth as purple silk.
    I am captured by your flowing curls.
6 You are so beautiful! You please me so
        much!
    You are so delightful, my love!
7 You are as graceful as a palm tree.
    Your breasts are as sweet as the
        freshest fruit.
8 I said, 'I will climb the palm tree.
    I'll take hold of its fruit.'
May your breasts be as sweet as the
        fruit on the vine.
May your breath smell like the
        tastiest apples.
9   May your lips be like the finest
        wine."

The woman says,

"May my wine go straight to you, my
    love.

May it flow gently over our lips as we
    sleep.
10 "I belong to you, my love.
    And you long for me.
11 Come, my love. Let's go to the country.
    Let's spend the night in the villages.
12 Let's go out to the vineyards early.
    Let's go and see if the vines have
        budded.
Let's find out whether their flowers
        have opened.
Let's see if the pomegranate trees are
        blooming.
I'll make love to you in the
        vineyards.
13 The mandrake flowers give off their
        strong smell.
All of the best things are waiting for
        us,
new and old alike.
    I've stored them up for you, my love.

8 "I wish you were like a brother to
    me.
    I wish my mother's breasts had
        nursed you.
Then if I found you outside,
    I could kiss you.
No one would look down on me.
2 I'd bring you to my mother's house.
    She taught me everything I know.
I'd give you spiced wine to drink.
    It's the juice of my pomegranates.
3 Your left arm is under my head.
    Your right arm is around me.
4 Women of Jerusalem, take an oath and
        make me a promise.
    Don't stir up love.
    Don't wake it up until it's ready."

The other women say,

5 "Who is this woman coming up from
        the desert?
    She's leaning on the one who loves
        her."

The woman says to the king,

"Under the apple tree I woke you up.
    That's where your mother became
        pregnant with you.
    She went into labor, and you were
        born there.
6 Hold me close to your heart like the
        seal around your neck.
    Keep me close to yourself like the
        ring on your finger.
My love for you is so strong it won't let
        you go.
Love is as powerful as death.
    Love's jealousy is as strong as the
        grave.

POWER—SURGE

LOVING

MY LOVE FOR YOU IS
SO STRONG IT WON'T
LET YOU GO.

LOVE IS AS POWERFUL
AS DEATH.

LOVE'S JEALOUSY IS
AS STRONG AS THE
GRAVE.

LOVE IS LIKE A
BLAZING FIRE.

IT BURNS LIKE A
MIGHTY FLAME.

—SONG OF SONGS 8:6—

STRONG

Love is like a blazing fire.
  It burns like a mighty flame.
⁷No amount of water can put it out.
  Rivers can't drown it.
Suppose someone offers
  all of his wealth to buy love.
  That won't even come close to being
    enough."

The woman's brothers say,

⁸"We have a little sister.
  Her breasts are still small.
What should we do for our sister
  when she gets engaged?
⁹If she were a wall,
  we'd build silver towers on her.
If she were a door,
  we'd cover her with cedar boards."

The woman says to the king,

¹⁰"I am a wall.
  My breasts are like well-built towers.
So in your eyes I've become
  like someone who makes you happy.
¹¹Solomon, you had a vineyard in Baal
    Hamon.
  You rented your vineyard to others.
They had to pay 25 pounds
  of silver for its fruit.
¹²But I can give my own vineyard to
    anyone I want to.
  So I give my 25 pounds of silver to
    you, Solomon.
  Give 5 pounds to those who take
    care of its fruit."

The king says,

¹³"My love, you live in the gardens.
  My friends listen for your voice.
  But let me hear it now."

The woman says,

¹⁴"Come away with me, my love.
  Be like an antelope
or like a young deer
  on mountains that are full of
    spices."

ISAIAH

The book of Isaiah is named after the prophet Isaiah. He came as a messenger from God and called the people of Israel to ask God to forgive their sins. He tells the people that if they don't repent, God will eventually punish them for their sins. Isaiah also writes some of the clearest prophecy about the coming Messiah, Jesus. The hero of Isaiah is, of course, Isaiah himself, who bravely relays God's messages to the people. Read Isaiah to become more aware of your sin and more thankful for the forgiveness Jesus offers.

HERO IN THIS BOOK . . .

ISAIAH
PAGE 790

1 Here is the vision about Judah and Jerusalem that Isaiah had. It came to him when Uzziah, Jotham, Ahaz and Hezekiah were ruling. They were kings of Judah. Isaiah was the son of Amoz.

Israel Refuses to Obey the Lord

2 Listen to me, heavens! Pay attention to
    me, earth!
  The Lord has said,
  "I raised children. I brought them up.
    But they have refused to obey me.
3 The ox knows its master.
    The donkey knows where its owner
      feeds it.
  But Israel does not know me.
    My people do not understand me."

4 They are a sinful nation.
    They are loaded down with guilt.
  They are people who do nothing but
    evil.
  They are children who are always
    sinning.
  They have deserted the Lord.
    They have turned against the Holy
      One of Israel.
    They have turned their backs on
      him.

5 Israel, why do you want to be beaten
    all the time?
  Why do you always refuse to obey
    the Lord?
  Your head is covered with wounds.
    Your whole heart is weak.
6 There isn't a healthy spot on your body
    from the bottom of your feet to the
      top of your head.
  There are only wounds, cuts
    and open sores.
  They haven't been cleaned up or
    bandaged
    or treated with olive oil.

7 Your country has been deserted.
    Your cities have been burned down.
  The food from your fields is being
    eaten up by outsiders.
    They are doing it right in front of
      you.
  Your land has been completely
    destroyed.
    It looks as if strangers have taken it
      over.
8 The city of Zion is left like a hut
    where someone stands guard in a
      vineyard.
  It is left like an empty cabin in a melon
    field.
    It's like a city that is being attacked.
9 The Lord who rules over all
    has let some people live through
      that time of trouble.
  If he hadn't, we would have become
    like Sodom.
    We would have been like Gomorrah.

10 Rulers of Sodom,
    hear the Lord's message.
  People of Gomorrah,
    listen to the law of our God.
11 "Do you think I need any more of your
      sacrifices?"
    asks the Lord.
  "I have more than enough of your
      burnt offerings.
    I have more than enough of rams
    and the fat of your fattest animals.
  I do not find any pleasure
    in the blood of your bulls, lambs and
      goats.
12 Who asked you to bring all of those
      animals
    when you come to worship me?
  Who asked you and your animals
    to walk all over my courtyards?
13 Stop bringing offerings that do not
      mean anything to me!
    I hate your incense.
  I can't stand your evil gatherings.
    I can't stand the way you celebrate
      your New Moon Feasts,
    Sabbath days and special services.
14 I hate your New Moon Feasts
    and your other appointed feasts.
  They have become a heavy load to me.
    I am tired of carrying it.
15 You might spread out your hands
    toward me when you pray.
    But I will not look at you.
  You might even offer many prayers.
    But I will not listen to them.
  Your hands are covered with the blood
    of the people you have
      murdered.
16   So wash your hands. Make
      yourselves clean.
  Get your evil actions out of my sight!
    Stop doing what is wrong!
17   Learn to do what is right!
  Treat people fairly.
    Give hope to those who are beaten
      down.
    Cheer them up.
  Stand up in court for children whose
    fathers have died.
    And do the same thing for widows.

18 "Come. Let us talk some more about
      this matter,"
    says the Lord.
  "Even though your sins are bright red,
    they will be as white as snow.

KIND K

**LEARN TO DO WHAT
IS RIGHT!**

TREAT PEOPLE FAIRLY.

**GIVE HOPE TO THOSE
WHO ARE BEATEN
DOWN.**

CHEER THEM UP.
—— ISAIAH 1:17 ——

LOVING

Even though they are deep red,
    they will be white like wool.
19 But you have to be willing to change
    and obey me.
    If you are, you will eat the best food
        that grows on the land.
20 You must follow me. You must obey
    me.
    If you do not, you will be killed with
        swords."
                    The LORD has spoken.

21 See how the faithful city of Jerusalem
    has become like a prostitute!
Once it was full of people who treated
    others fairly.
    Those who did what was right used
        to live in it.
But now murderers live there!
22 Jerusalem, your silver isn't pure
    anymore.
    Your best wine has been made weak
        with water.
23 Your rulers refuse to obey the LORD.
    They are companions of robbers.
All of them love to accept money from
        those who want special favors.
    They are always looking for gifts
        from other people.
They don't stand up in court for
        children whose fathers have
        died.
    They don't do it for widows either.
24 The Lord is the Mighty One of Israel.
    The LORD who rules over all
        announces,
    "Israel, you have become my enemies.
    I will pay you back for what you
        have done.

Then you will not trouble me
    anymore.
25 I will turn my powerful hand against
    you.
    I will make you completely clean.
    I will remove everything that is not
        pure.
26 I will give judges to you like the ones
    you had long ago.
    I will give you advisers like those you
        had at the beginning.
Then you will be called
    The City That Does What Is Right.
    You will also be called The Faithful
        City."

27 Zion will be saved when others are
    treated fairly.
    Those who are sorry for their sins
        will be saved
    when what is right is done.
28 But sinners and those who refuse to
    obey the LORD will be destroyed.
    And those who desert the LORD will
        die.

29 Israel, you take delight in worshiping
    among the sacred oak trees.
    You will be full of shame for doing
        that.
You have chosen to worship in the
    sacred gardens.
    You will be dishonored for doing
        that.
30 You will be like an oak tree whose
    leaves are dying.
    You will be like a garden that doesn't
        have any water.
31 Your strongest men will become like
    dry pieces of wood.
    Their worship of other gods will be
        the spark that lights the fire.
Everything will be burned up.
    No one will be there to put the fire
        out.

People From Many Nations Will Worship at Mount Zion

2 Here is a vision that Isaiah, the son of
Amoz, had about Judah and Jerusalem.

2 In the last days

the mountain where the LORD's temple
    is located will be famous.
    It will be the most important
        mountain of all.
It will stand out above the hills.
    All of the nations will go to it.

3 People from many nations will go
there. They will say,

"Come. Let us go up to the Lord's
mountain.
Let's go to the house of Jacob's God.
He will teach us how we should live.
Then we will live the way he wants
us to."
The law of the Lord will be taught at
Zion.
His message will go out from
Jerusalem.
4 He will judge between the nations.
He'll settle problems among many
of them.
They will hammer their swords into
plows.
They'll hammer their spears into
pruning tools.
Nations will not go to war against one
another.
They won't even train to fight
anymore.

5 People of Jacob, come.
Let us live the way the Lord has
taught us to.

The Day of the Lord Is Coming

6 Lord, you have deserted the people of
Jacob.
They are your people.
The land is full of false beliefs from the
east.
The people practice evil magic, just
as the Philistines do.
They make ungodly people their
friends.
7 Their land is full of silver and gold.
There is no end to their treasures.
Their land is full of horses.
There is no end to their chariots.
8 Their land is full of statues of gods.
They bow down to what their own
hands have made.
They bow down to what their
fingers have shaped.
9 So man will be brought low.
People will be put to shame.
Do not forgive them.

10 Go and hide in caves in the rocks, you
people!
Hide in holes in the ground.
Hide from the terror of the Lord!
Hide when he comes in glory and
majesty!
11 A man who brags will be brought low.
Men who are proud will be put to
shame.
The Lord alone will be honored at
that time.

12 The Lord who rules over all has set
apart a day when he will judge.
He has set it apart for all those who
are proud and think they are
important.
He has set it apart for all those who
brag about themselves.
All of them will be brought low.
13 The Lord has set that day apart for all
of the cedar trees in Lebanon.
They are very tall.
He has set it apart for all of the oak
trees in Bashan.
14 He has set it apart for all of the
towering mountains.
He has set it apart for all of the high
hills.
15 He has set it apart for every high tower
and every strong wall.
16 He has set it apart for every trading
ship
and every beautiful boat.
17 A man who brags will be brought low.
Men who are proud will be put to
shame.
The Lord alone will be honored at that
time.
18 And the statues of gods will totally
disappear.

19 People will run and hide in caves in
the rocks.
They will go into holes in the
ground.
They will run away from the terror of
the Lord.
They will run when he comes in
glory and majesty.
When he comes, he will shake the
earth.
20 Men had made some statues of gods
out of silver.
They had made others out of gold.
Then they worshiped them.
But when the Lord comes,
they will throw the statues away to
the rodents and bats.
21 They will run and hide in caves in the
rocks.
They will go into holes in the cliffs.
They will run away from the terror of
the Lord.
They will run when he comes in
glory and majesty.
When he comes, he will shake the
earth.
22 Stop trusting man. He can't help you.
He only lives for a little while.
What good is he?

The LORD Will Judge Jerusalem and Judah

3 Here is what
the LORD who rules over all is about
to do.
The Lord will take away from
Jerusalem and Judah
supplies and help alike.
He will take away all of the supplies of
food and water.
2 He'll take away heroes and soldiers.
He'll take away judges and prophets.
He'll take away fortune tellers and
elders.
3 He'll take away captains of companies
of 50 men.
He'll take away government leaders.
He'll take away advisers, skilled
workers
and those who are clever at doing
evil magic.

4 The LORD will make young boys rule
over all of them.
Mere children will govern them.
5 People will crush one another.
They will fight against each other.
They will fight against their
neighbors.
Young people will attack old people.
Ordinary people will attack those
who are more important.

6 A man will grab hold of one of his
brothers
at his father's home. He will say,
"You have a coat. So you be our leader.
Take charge of all of these broken-
down buildings!"
7 But at that time the brother will cry
out,
"I can't help you.
I don't have any food or clothing in
my house.
Don't make me the leader of these
people."

8 Jerusalem is about to fall.
And so is Judah.
They say and do things against the
LORD.
They dare to disobey him to his very
face.
9 The look on their faces is a witness
against them.
They show off their sin, just as the
people of Sodom did.
They don't even try to hide it.
How terrible it will be for them!
They have brought trouble on
themselves.

10 Tell those who do what is right that
things will go well with them.
They will enjoy the results of the
good things they've done.
11 But how terrible it will be for those
who do what is evil!
Trouble is about to fall on them.
They will be paid back for the evil
things they've done.

12 Those who are young crush my people.
Women rule over them.
My people, your leaders have taken
you down the wrong path.
They have turned you away from the
right path.

13 The LORD takes his place in court.
He stands up to judge the people.
14 He judges the elders and leaders of his
people.
He says to them,
"My people are like a vineyard.
You have destroyed them.
The things you have taken from
poor people are in your houses.
15 What do you mean by crushing my
people?
Why are you grinding the faces of
the poor into the dirt?"
announces the Lord.
He is the LORD who rules over all.

16 The LORD continues,
"The women in Zion are very proud.
They walk along with their noses in
the air.
They tease men with their eyes.
They walk with quick, short steps.
Little chains jingle on their ankles.
17 So I will put sores on the heads of
Zion's women.
And I will remove the hair from
their heads."

18 At that time the Lord will take away
the beautiful things they wear. He will
take away their decorations, headbands
and moon-shaped necklaces. 19 He'll take
away their earrings, bracelets and veils.
20 He'll remove their headdresses, ankle
chains and belts. He'll take away their perfume bottles and charms. 21 He'll remove
the rings they wear on their fingers and in
their noses. 22 He'll take away their fine
robes and their capes and coats. He'll take
away their purses 23 and mirrors. And he'll
take away their linen clothes, turbans and
shawls.

24 Instead of smelling sweet,
the women will smell bad.
Instead of wearing belts,

they will wear ropes.
Instead of having beautiful hair,
they won't have any hair at all.
Instead of wearing fine clothes,
they'll wear black clothes to show
how sad they are.
Instead of being beautiful,
they'll have the brands of slaves on
their bodies.
25 Jerusalem, your men will be killed with
swords.
Your soldiers will die in battle.
26 The city of Zion will be very sad.
Like a widow, she will lose
everything.
She will sit on the ground and sob.

4 At that time seven women
will grab hold of one man.
They'll say to him, "We will eat our
own food.
We'll provide our own clothes.
Just let us become your wives.
Take away our shame!"

The Branch of the LORD

2 At that time Israel's king will be beautiful and glorious. He will be called The Branch of the LORD. The fruit of the land will be the pride and glory of those who are still left alive in Israel.

3 Those who are left in Zion will be called holy. They will be recorded among those who are alive in Jerusalem. 4 The Lord will wash away the sin of the women in Zion. He will clean up the blood that was spilled there. He will judge those who spilled that blood. His burning anger will blaze out at them.

5 Then the LORD will create over Jerusalem a cloud of smoke by day. He will also create a glow of flaming fire at night. They will appear over all of Mount Zion and those who gather together there. The LORD's glory will be like a tent over them. 6 It will cover them and give them shade from the hot sun all day long. It will be a safe place where they can hide from storms and rain.

The Song of the Vineyard

5 I will sing a song for the LORD.
He is the one I love.
It's a song about his vineyard Israel.
The one I love had a vineyard.
It was on a hillside that had rich soil.
2 He dug up the soil and removed its
stones.
He planted the very best vines in it.
He built a lookout tower there.
He also cut out a winepress for it.

Then he kept looking for a crop of
good grapes.
But the vineyard produced only bad
fruit.

3 So the LORD said, "People of Jerusalem
and Judah,
you be the judge between me and
my vineyard.
4 What more could I have done for my
vineyard?
I did everything I could.
I kept looking for a crop of good
grapes.
So why did it produce only bad
ones?
5 Now I will tell you
what I am going to do to my
vineyard.
I will take away its fence.
And it will be destroyed.
I will break down its wall.
And people will walk all over it.
6 I will turn my vineyard into a dry and
empty desert.
It will not be pruned or taken care
of.
Thorns and bushes will grow there.
I will command the clouds
not to rain on it."

7 The vineyard of the LORD who rules
over all
is the nation of Israel.
The people of Judah
are the garden he takes delight in.
He kept looking for them to do what is
fair.
But all he saw was blood being
spilled.
He kept looking for them to do what is
right.
But all he heard were cries of
suffering.

The LORD Judges His Vineyard

8 How terrible it will be for you who get
too many houses!
How terrible for you who get too
many fields!
Finally there won't be any space left in
the land.
Then you will live all alone.

9 I heard the LORD who rules over all
announce a message. He said,

"You can be sure that the great houses
will become empty.
The fine homes will be left with no
one living in them.
10 A ten-acre vineyard will produce only
six gallons of wine.

Six bushels of seeds will produce less
than a bushel of grain."

11 How terrible it will be for those who
get up early in the morning
to start drinking!
How terrible for those who stay up late
at night
until they are drunk with wine!
12 They have harps and lyres at their big
dinners.
They have tambourines, flutes and
wine.
But they don't have any concern for
the mighty acts of the LORD.
They don't have any respect for
what his powerful hands have
done.
13 So my people will be taken away as
prisoners.
That's because they don't
understand what the LORD has
done.
Their government leaders will die of
hunger.
The rest of the people won't have
any water to drink.
14 So the grave is hungry to receive them.
Its mouth is open wide to swallow
them up.
Their nobles and the rest of the people
will go down into it.
They will go there together with all
those who have wild parties.
15 So man will be brought low.
People will be put to shame.
Those who brag will be brought
down.
16 But the LORD who rules over all will be
honored
because he judges fairly.
The holy God will show that he is holy
by doing what is right.
17 Then sheep will graze as if they were in
their own grasslands.
Lambs will eat grass among the
destroyed buildings
where rich people used to live.

18 How terrible it will be for those who
continue to sin
and lie about it!
How terrible for those who keep on
doing what is evil
as if they were tied to it!
19 How terrible for those who say,
"Let God hurry up and do what he
says he will.
We want to see it happen.
Let the Holy One of Israel carry out his
plan soon.
We want to know what it is."

20 How terrible it will be for those who
say
that what is evil is good!
How terrible for those who say
that what is good is evil!
How terrible for those who say
that darkness is light
and light is darkness!
How terrible for those who say
that what is bitter is sweet
and what is sweet is bitter!

21 How terrible it will be for those who
think they are wise!
How terrible for those who think
they are really clever!

22 How terrible it will be for those
who are heroes at drinking wine!
How terrible for those
who are heroes at mixing drinks!
23 How terrible for those
who take money to set guilty people
free!
How terrible for those
who don't treat good people fairly!
24 Flames of fire burn up straw.
Dry grass sinks down into those
flames.
Evil people will be like plants whose
roots rot away.
They will be like flowers that are
blown away like dust.
That's because they have said no to the
law of the LORD who rules over
all.
They have turned against the
message of the Holy One of
Israel.
25 So the LORD's anger burns against his
people.
He raises his hand against them. He
strikes them down.
The mountains shake.
The bodies of dead people lie in the
streets like trash.

Even then, the LORD is still angry.
His hand is still raised against them.

26 He lifts up a banner to gather the
nations that are far away.
He whistles for them to come
from the farthest places on earth.
Here they come.
They are moving very quickly.
27 None of them grows tired.
None of them falls down.
None of them sleeps or even takes a
nap.
All of them are ready for battle.
Every belt is pulled tight.
Not a single sandal strap is broken.

28 The enemies' arrows are sharp.
All of their bows are ready.
The hoofs of their horses are as hard as
rock.
Their chariot wheels turn like a
twister.
29 The sound of their army is like the roar
of lions.
It's like the roar of young lions.
They growl as they capture what they
were chasing.
They carry it off.
No one can take it away from them.
30 At that time the enemy army will roar
over Israel.
It will sound like the roaring of the
ocean.
If someone looks at the land of Israel,
he will see darkness and trouble.
The clouds will make even the light
become dark.

The Lord Appoints Isaiah to Speak for Him

6 In the year that King Uzziah died, I saw the Lord. He was seated on his throne. His long robe filled the temple. He was highly honored.

2 Above him were seraphs. Each of them had six wings. With two wings they covered their faces. With two wings they covered their feet. And with two wings they were flying. **3** They were calling out to one another. They were saying,

"Holy, holy, holy is the LORD who rules
over all.
The whole earth is full of his glory."

4 The sound of their voices caused the stone doorframe to shake. The temple was filled with smoke.

5 "How terrible it is for me!" I cried out. "I'm about to be destroyed! My mouth speaks sinful words. And I live among people who speak sinful words. Now I have seen the King with my own eyes. He is the LORD who rules over all."

6 A seraph flew over to me. He was holding a hot coal. He had used tongs to take it from the altar. **7** He touched my mouth with the coal. He said, "This has touched your lips. Your guilt has been taken away. Your sin has been paid for."

8 Then I heard the voice of the Lord. He said, "Who will I send? Who will go for us?"

I said, "Here I am. Send me!"

9 So he said, "Go and speak to these people. Tell them,

" 'You will hear but never understand.
You will see but never know what
you are seeing.'
10 Make the hearts of these people
stubborn.
Plug up their ears.
Close their eyes.
Otherwise they might see with their
eyes.
They might hear with their ears.
They might understand with their
hearts.
And they might turn to me and be
healed."

11 Then I said, "Lord, how long will it be like that?"

He answered,

"It will last until the cities of Israel are
destroyed
and no one is living in them.
It will last until the houses are
deserted.
The fields will be completely
destroyed.
12 It will last until I have sent everyone far
away.
The land will be totally deserted.
13 Even if a tenth of the people remain
there,
the land will be completely
destroyed again.
But when oak trees and terebinth trees
are cut down, stumps are left.
And my holy people will be like
stumps
that begin to grow again."

The Miraculous Sign of Immanuel

7 Ahaz was king of Judah. Rezin was king of Aram. And Pekah was king of Israel. Rezin and Pekah marched up to fight against Jerusalem. But they couldn't overpower it. Ahaz was the son of Jotham and the grandson of Uzziah. Pekah was the son of Remaliah.

2 The royal family of Ahaz was told, "The army of Aram has joined forces with Ephraim's army." So the hearts of Ahaz and his people trembled with fear. They shook just as trees in the forest shake when the wind blows through them.

3 The LORD said to me, "Go out and see Ahaz. Take your son Shear-Jashub with you. Meet Ahaz at the end of the channel that brings water from the Upper Pool. It is on the road to the Washerman's Field.

4 "Tell Ahaz, 'Be careful. Stay calm. Do not be afraid. Do not lose hope because of the burning anger of Rezin, Aram and the son of Remaliah. After all, they are nothing but a couple of pieces of smoking fire-

ISAIAH

ISAIAH 6:8

Then I heard the voice of the Lord. He said, "Who will I send? Who will go for us?" I said, "Here I am. Send me!"

The floors of the temple shook. Smoke filled the rooms. Seraphs, messengers from God, flapped their wings and called to each other. Their voices rose in a roar together as they praised God, calling him "*Holy!*"

Isaiah (i-ZAY-uh) cringed on the floor in terror. He had seen God! No one saw God and lived. Especially no one as sinful as Isaiah. He was sure he was going to die. Isaiah cried with his mouth open wide, "How terrible this is!"

One of the seraphs separated himself from the others and flew toward Isaiah. ISAIAH FELL BACK IN HORROR WHEN HE FELT THE AIR MOVE FROM THE BEAT OF THE SERAPH'S WINGS. He squeezed his eyes shut. Then he felt a burning on his mouth and cried out again.

Isaiah opened his eyes. The burning came from a hot coal. The seraph touched his mouth again with the coal and said, "You are no longer sinful. Your guilt has been taken away."

A cool rush of feeling coursed through Isaiah's body. He felt clean and pure, accepted by God. His body relaxed until another voice boomed around him. This time God himself was speaking. "My people are so stubborn. Who will I send to tell them my messages? Who will go and speak to them for me?"

Isaiah leaped to his feet. He was no longer afraid. He felt brave, and *ready.* He raised his hands and answered God, "Send me. I'm here. Send me."

BE AN ISAIAH

Are you willing for God to use you? Are you too scared? Isaiah was scared. And he thought he was too sinful to be used by God. But God wanted him to be his messenger. God wants to use you, too. Maybe he wants you to help a classmate who is struggling with math. Or to help a friend who is sad. Or to help your mom when she's tired. Or to tell your neighbors down the street that Jesus loves them and understands. No matter how sinful—or how scared—you are, God can use you, just like he used Isaiah. You just have to be willing.

ISAIAH WAS WILLING FOR GOD TO USE HIM.
THE WHOLE STORY: ISAIAH 6:1-8

Go to page 860 for the next Super Hero

wood. 5Aram, Ephraim and Remaliah's son have planned to destroy you. They said, 6"Let's march into Judah and attack it. Let's tear everything down. Then we can share the land among ourselves. And we can make Tabeel's son king over it."

7" 'But I am the Lord and King. I say,

" ' "That will not happen.
It will not take place.
8 The capital of Aram is Damascus.
And the ruler of Damascus is only
Rezin.
Do not worry about the people of
Ephraim.
They will be too crushed to be
considered a people.
That will happen before 65 years are
over.
9 The capital of Ephraim is Samaria.
And the ruler of Samaria is only
Remaliah's son.
If you do not stand firm in your faith,
you will not stand at all." ' "

10The Lord spoke to Ahaz through me again. He said, 11"I am the Lord your God. Ask me to give you a miraculous sign. It can be anything in the deepest grave or in the highest heaven."

12But Ahaz said, "I won't ask. I won't put the Lord to the test."

13Then I said, "Listen, you members of the royal family of Ahaz! Isn't it enough for you to test the patience of men? Are you also going to test the patience of my God? 14The Lord himself will give you a miraculous sign. The virgin is going to have a baby. She will give birth to a son. And he will be called Immanuel.

15"The time will come when he is old enough to decide between what is wrong and what is right. By that time he will have only butter and honey to eat. 16But even before that happens, the lands of the two kings you are afraid of will be completely destroyed.

17"The Lord will also bring the king of Assyria against you. And he will bring him against your people and the whole royal family. That will be a time of trouble unlike any since the people of Ephraim broke away from Judah."

18At that time the Lord will whistle for the Egyptians. They will come like flies from the streams of Egypt. He will also whistle for the Assyrians. They will come from their country like bees. 19All of them will come and camp in the deep valleys. They will camp in caves in the rocks. And they'll camp near bushes and water holes.

20At that time the Lord will use the Assyrians to punish you. Ahaz had hired them earlier from east of the Euphrates River. Now their king will be like a razor in the Lord's hand. He will shave the hair from your head and legs. He will also shave off your beards.

21At that time a man will only be able to keep one young cow and two goats alive. 22But they will give enough milk and butter to live on. Everyone who is left alive in the land will have nothing but butter and honey to eat.

23The land used to have vineyards with 1,000 vines worth 25 pounds of silver. But soon the whole land will be covered with thorns and bushes. 24Men will go there to hunt with bows and arrows. That's because it will be covered with bushes and thorns. 25All of the hills used to be plowed with hoes. But you won't go there anymore. That's because you will be afraid of the thorns and bushes. Cattle will be turned loose on those hills. And sheep will run there.

The Lord Uses Assyria to Judge Judah

8 The Lord said to me, "Get a large scroll. Write 'Maher-Shalal-Hash-Baz' on it with a pen. 2I will send for Zechariah and the priest Uriah. They can be trusted. They will be witnesses for me. Zechariah is the son of Jeberekiah."

3Then I went and made love to my wife, who was a prophet. She became pregnant and had a baby boy. The Lord said to me, "Name him Maher-Shalal-Hash-Baz.

4"The king of Assyria will carry off the wealth of Damascus. He will also carry away the goods that were taken from Samaria. That will happen before the boy knows how to say 'My father' or 'My mother.' "

5The Lord continued,

6 "I am like the gently flowing stream of
Siloam.
But the people of Judah have turned
their backs on me.

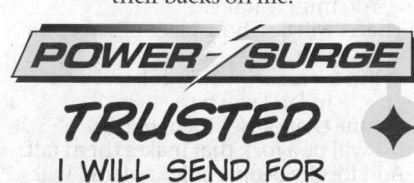

POWER-SURGE

TRUSTED ◆

I WILL SEND FOR
ZECHARIAH AND THE
PRIEST URIAH. THEY
CAN BE TRUSTED.
—— ISAIAH 8:2 ——

They are filled with joy because of the
    fall of Rezin
and the son of Remaliah.
⁷ So I am about to bring against these
    people
    the king of Assyria and his whole
        army.
The Assyrians will be like the mighty
    Euphrates River
    when it is flooding.
They will run over everything in
    their path.
⁸ They will sweep on into Judah like a
    flood.
They will pass through Judah and
    reach all the way to Jerusalem.
Immanuel, they will attack your land
    like an eagle.
Their wings will spread out and
    cover it."

⁹ Sound the battle cry, you nations!
    But you will be torn apart.
Listen, all of you lands far away!
Prepare for battle! But you will be torn
    apart.
    Prepare for battle! But you will be
        torn apart.
¹⁰ Make your battle plans! But you won't
    succeed.
    Give your orders! But they won't be
        carried out.
    That's because God is with us.

Have Respect for God

¹¹ The LORD put his powerful hand on
me and spoke to me. He warned me not to
live the way these people live. He said,

¹² "People of Judah, do not agree with
    those who say
    Isaiah is guilty of treason.
Do not fear what they fear.
    Do not be afraid.
¹³ I am the LORD who rules over all.
    You must think about me as holy.
You must have respect for me.
    You must fear me.
¹⁴ Then I will be a holy place of safety for
    you.
    But for many people in Israel and
        Judah I will be
a stone that causes them to trip.
    I will be a rock that makes them fall.
And for the people of Jerusalem I will
    be
    a trap and a snare.
¹⁵ Many of them will trip.
    They will fall and be broken.
    They will be trapped and captured."

¹⁶ Keep safe what the LORD said to you
    through me.
    Seal up among my followers what he
        taught you through me.
¹⁷ I will wait for the LORD.
    He is turning his face away from
        Jacob's people.
    I will put my trust in him.

¹⁸ Here I am. Here are the children the
LORD has given me. We are signs and
reminders to Israel from the LORD who
rules over all. He lives on Mount Zion.
¹⁹ Some will tell you to ask for advice
from people who get messages from those
who have died. Others will tell you to ask
for advice from people who talk to the
spirits of the dead. But those people only
whisper. Their words are barely heard. So
shouldn't you ask for advice from your
God? Why should you get advice from
dead people to help those who are alive?
²⁰ Follow what the LORD taught you and
said to you through me. People who don't
speak in keeping with those words won't
have any hope in the morning. ²¹ They
will suffer and be hungry. They'll wander
through the land. When they are very
hungry, they will become angry. They'll
look up toward heaven. They'll call down
curses on their king and their God.
²² Then they will look at the earth. They'll
see nothing but suffering and darkness.
They'll see terrible sadness. They'll be
driven into total darkness.

A Son Will Be Given to Us

9 But there won't be any more sadness
    for those who were suffering. In the
past the LORD brought shame on the land
of Zebulun. He also brought shame on
the land of Naphtali. But in days to come
he will honor Galilee, where people from
other nations live. He will honor the
land along the Mediterranean Sea. And
he will honor the territory east of the Jordan River.

² The people who are now living in
    darkness
    will see a great light.
They are now living in a very dark
    land.
    But a light will shine on them.
³ LORD, you will make our nation larger.
    You will increase their joy.
They will show you how glad they are.
    They will be as glad as people are at
        harvest time.
They will be as glad as soldiers are
    when they share the things they've
        taken after a battle.

4 You set Israel free from Midian long
       ago.
   In the same way, you will break
the heavy yoke that weighs Israel
       down.
   You will break the wooden beams
       that are on their shoulders.
   You will break the rods of those who
       strike them down.
5 Every fighting man's boot that is used
       in battle will be burned up.
   So will every piece of clothes
that is covered with blood.
   All of them will be thrown into the
       fire.
6 A child will be born to us.
   A son will be given to us.
   He will rule over us.
And he will be called
   Wonderful Adviser and Mighty God.
He will also be called Father Who Lives
       Forever
   and Prince Who Brings Peace.
7 The authority of his rule will continue
       to grow.
   The peace he brings will never end.
He will rule on David's throne
   and over his kingdom.
He will make the kingdom strong
   and secure.
His rule will be based on what is fair
   and right.
   It will last forever.
The Lord's great love will make sure
       that happens.
   He rules over all.

The Lord Is Angry With Israel

8 The Lord has sent a message against
       Jacob's people.
   He will punish Israel.
9 All of the people will know about it.
   Ephraim's people and those who
       live in Samaria will know
       about it.
   Their hearts are very proud.
   They say,
10 "The brick buildings have fallen down.
   But we will rebuild them with blocks
       of stone.
   The fig trees have been chopped down.
   But we'll plant cedar trees in place of
       them."
11 In spite of that, the Lord has made
       Rezin's enemies stronger.
   He has stirred up Assyria to fight
       against Israel.
12 Arameans from the east
   have opened their mouths and
       swallowed Israel up.
   So have Philistines from the west.

Even then, the Lord is still angry.
   His hand is still raised against them.

13 But his people have not returned
   to the One who struck them down.
   They haven't turned for help
   to the Lord who rules over all.
14 So he will cut off from Israel heads and
       tails alike.
   In a single day he will cut off palm
       branches and tall grass alike.
   The palm branches are the people who
       rule over others.
   The tall grass is the people who bow
       down to them.
15 The elders and important leaders are
       the heads.
   The prophets who teach lies are the
       tails.
16 Those who guide the people of Israel
       are leading them down the
       wrong path.
   So those who follow them aren't on
       the right road.
17 The Lord will not be pleased with the
       young men.
   He won't take pity on widows and
       on children whose fathers have
       died.
All of them are ungodly and evil.
   They say sinful things with their
       mouths.

Even then, the Lord is still angry.
   His hand is still raised against them.

18 What is evil burns like a fire.
   It burns up bushes and thorns.
   It sets the forest on fire.
   It sends up a huge column of smoke.
19 The Lord rules over all.
   When he gets angry, he will burn up
       the land.
   The people will die.
   Men will eat their brothers.
20 People will eat up everything they can
       find on their right.
   But they'll still be hungry.
   They will eat everything they can find
       on their left.
   But they won't be satisfied.
So they will eat the dead bodies of their
       children.
21   That's what Manasseh's people will
       do to Ephraim.
And that's what Ephraim's people will
       do to Manasseh.
   Together they will turn against
       Judah.

Even then, the Lord is still angry.
   His hand is still raised against them.

10 How terrible it will be for you
who make laws that aren't fair!
How terrible for you
    who write laws that make life hard
      for others!
² You take away the rights of poor
     people.
    You hold back what is fair from my
     people who are suffering.
    You take for yourselves what belongs to
     widows.
    You rob children whose fathers have
     died.
³ What will you do on the day when the
    Lᴏʀᴅ punishes you?
    On that day trouble will come from
     far away.
    Who will you run to for help?
    Who will you trust your riches with?
⁴ All you can do is bow down in fear
    among the prisoners.
    All you can do is fall among those
     who have died in battle.

Even then, the Lᴏʀᴅ is still angry.
    His hand is still raised against them.

The Lᴏʀᴅ Will Judge Assyria

⁵ The Lᴏʀᴅ says, "How terrible it will be
    for the people of Assyria!
    They are the war club that carries
     out my anger.
⁶ I will send them against the ungodly
    nation of Judah.
    I will order them to fight against my
     own people.
    They make me angry.
    I will order them to take their goods
     and carry them away.
    I will order them to walk on my
     people
    as if they were walking on mud.
⁷ But that is not what the king of Assyria
    plans.
    It is not what he has in mind.
    His purpose is to destroy many
     nations.
    His purpose is to put an end to
     them.
⁸ 'Aren't all of my commanders kings?'
    he says.
⁹   'I took over Calno just as I took
     Carchemish.
    I took over Hamath just as I did Arpad.
    I took Samaria just as I did
     Damascus.
¹⁰ My powerful hand grabbed hold of
    kingdoms
    whose people worship statues of
     gods.

They had more gods than Jerusalem
    and Samaria did.
¹¹ I took over Samaria and its statues of
    gods.
    In the same way, I will take
     Jerusalem and its gods.' "

¹² The Lord will finish everything he
has planned to do against Mount Zion
and Jerusalem. Then he'll say, "Now I will
punish the king of Assyria. I will punish
him because his heart and his eyes are so
proud.
¹³ "The king of Assyria says,

" 'I have used my powerful hand
    to take over all of those nations.
I am very wise.
    I have great understanding.
I have wiped out the borders between
    nations.
    I've taken their treasures.
    Like a great hero I've brought their
     kings under my control.
¹⁴ I've taken the wealth of the nations.
    It was as easy as reaching into a
     bird's nest.
I've gathered the riches of all of those
    countries.
    It was as easy as gathering eggs
     that have been left in a nest.
Not a single baby bird flapped its
    wings.
    Not one of them opened its mouth
     to chirp.' "

¹⁵ Does an ax claim to be more important
    than the one who swings it?
Does a saw brag that it is better
    than the one who uses it?
That would be like a stick
    swinging someone who picks it up!
It would be like a war club
    waving the one who carries it!
¹⁶ So the Lᴏʀᴅ who rules over all will send
    a sickness.
    The Lord will send it on the king of
     Assyria's strong fighting men.
    It will make them weaker and
     weaker.
The army he was so proud of will be
    completely destroyed.
    It will be as if it had been burned up
     in a fire.
¹⁷ The Lᴏʀᴅ is the light of Israel.
    He will become a fire.
    Israel's Holy One will become a
     flame.
In a single day he will burn up all of
    Assyria's bushes.
    He will destroy all of their thorns.
¹⁸ He will completely destroy the beauty

of their forests and rich farm lands.
The Assyrian army will be like a sick
man
who becomes weaker and weaker.
¹⁹ It will be like the trees of their forests.
So few of them will be left standing
that even a child could count them.

Israel Will Return to the LORD

²⁰ In days to come, some people will still
be left alive in Israel.
They will be from Jacob's family
line.
But they won't depend any longer on
the nation that struck them down.
Instead, they will truly depend on the
LORD.
He is the Holy One of Israel.
²¹ The people of Jacob who are still alive
will return to the Mighty God.
²² Israel, your people might be as many as
the grains of sand by the sea.
But only a few of them will return.
The LORD has handed down a death
sentence.
He will destroy his people.
What he does is right.
²³ The LORD who rules over all will carry
out his sentence.
The Lord will destroy the whole
land.

²⁴ The LORD rules over all. The Lord says,

"My people who live in Zion,
do not be afraid of the Assyrian
army.
They beat you with rods.
They lift up war clubs against you,
just as the Egyptians did.
²⁵ Very soon I will not be angry with you
anymore.
I will turn my anger against the
Assyrians.
I will destroy them."

²⁶ The LORD who rules over all will beat
them with a whip.
He will strike them down as he
struck Midian down at the rock
of Oreb.
And he will reach his wooden staff out
over the waters.
That's what he did in Egypt.
²⁷ People of Zion, in days to come he will
lift
the heavy load of the Assyrians from
your shoulders.
He will remove their yokes from
your necks.
They will be broken
because you have become so strong.

²⁸ The Assyrian army has entered the
town of Aiath.
They have passed through Migron.
They have stored up supplies at
Micmash.
²⁹ They have marched through the pass
there. They said,
"Let's camp for the night at Geba."
The people of Ramah tremble with
fear.
Those who live in Gibeah of Saul
run away.
³⁰ Town of Gallim, cry out!
Laishah, listen!
Poor Anathoth!
³¹ The people of Madmenah are running
away.
Those who live in Gebim are hiding.
³² Today the Assyrians have stopped at
Nob.
They are shaking their fists
at Mount Zion in the city of
Jerusalem.

³³ The Assyrian soldiers are like trees in a
forest.
The LORD who rules over all
will chop them down.
The Lord will cut off their branches
with his great power.
He will chop the tall trees down.
He will cut down even the highest
ones.
³⁴ The Mighty One will chop down the
forest with his ax.
He will cut down the cedar trees in
Lebanon.

A Branch Will Come From Jesse's Family Line

11 Jesse's family is like a tree that has
been cut down.
A new little tree will grow from its
stump.
From its roots a Branch will grow
and produce fruit.
² The Spirit of the LORD will rest on that
Branch.
He will help him to be wise and
understanding.
He will help him make wise plans and
carry them out.
He will help him know the LORD and
have respect for him.
³ The Branch will take delight
in respecting the LORD.

He will not judge things only by the
way they look.
He won't make decisions based
simply on what people say.
⁴ He will always do what is right

when he judges those who are in
  need.
He'll be completely fair
  when he makes decisions about
    poor people.
When he commands that people be
    punished,
  it will happen.
When he orders that evil people be put
    to death,
  it will take place.
5 He will put godliness on as if it were his
    belt.
  He'll wear faithfulness around his
    waist.

6 Wolves will live with lambs.
  Leopards will lie down with goats.
Calves and lions will eat together.
  And little children will lead them
    around.
7 Cows will eat with bears.
  Their little ones will lie down
    together.
  And lions will eat straw like oxen.
8 A baby will play near a hole where
    cobras live.
  A young child will put his hand into
    a nest
  where poisonous snakes live.
9 None of those animals will harm or
    destroy anything or anyone
  on my holy mountain of Zion.
The oceans are full of water.
  In the same way, the earth will be
    filled
  with the knowledge of the LORD.

10 At that time the man who is called
the Root from Jesse's family line will be
like a banner that brings nations together.
They will come to him. And the place
where he rules will be glorious.

11 At that time the Lord will reach out
his hand to gather his people a second
time. He will bring back those who are left
alive. He'll bring them back from Assyria,
Lower Egypt, Upper Egypt and Cush. He'll
bring them from Elam, Babylonia and
Hamath. He will also bring them from the
islands of the Mediterranean Sea.

12 He will lift up a banner.
  It will show the nations that he is
    gathering the people of Israel.
  He'll bring back those who had been
    taken away as prisoners.
  He'll gather together the scattered
    people of Judah.
  He'll bring them back from all four
    directions.

13 Ephraim's people won't be jealous
    anymore.
  Judah's attackers will be cut off.
  Ephraim won't be jealous of Judah.
  And Judah won't attack Ephraim.
14 Together they will rush down the
    slopes of Philistia to the west.
  They'll take what belongs to the
    people of the east.
  They'll take over Edom and Moab.
  The people of Ammon will be under
    their control.
15 The LORD will dry up
    the Red Sea in Egypt.
  With his powerful hand he'll send a
    burning wind
  to sweep over the Euphrates River.
  He will break it up into many
    streams.
  Then people will be able to go across
    it wearing sandals.
16 There was a road the people of Israel
    used
  when they came up from Egypt.
  In the same way, there will be a wide
    road coming out of Assyria.
  It will be used by the LORD's people
    who are left alive there.

Two Songs of Praise

12 In days to come, the people of
Israel will sing,

"LORD, we will praise you.
  You were angry with us.
But now your anger has turned away
    from us.
  And you have brought us comfort.
2 God, you are the one who saves us.
  We will trust in you.
  Then we won't be afraid.
LORD, you give us strength.
  We sing about you.
  LORD, you have saved us."
3 People of Israel, he will save you.

POWER–SURGE

STRONG

LORD, YOU GIVE US
STRENGTH.
WE SING ABOUT YOU.
LORD, YOU HAVE SAVED
US."
— ISAIAH 12:2 —

That will bring you joy like water
    that is brought up from wells.

4 In days to come, the people of Israel
will sing,

"Give thanks to the LORD. Worship
    him.
Tell the nations what he has done.
    Announce how honored he is.
5 Sing to the LORD. He has done glorious
    things.
Let it be known all over the world.
6 People of Zion, give a loud shout!
    Sing with joy!
The Holy One of Israel is among you.
    And he is great."

A Message About Babylonia

13 Here is the vision about Babylonia
that Isaiah, the son of Amoz, saw.

2 Lift up a banner on the top of a bare
    hill.
Shout to the enemy soldiers.
Wave for them to enter the gates
    that are used by the nobles of
    Babylon.
3 The LORD has set those soldiers apart to
    fight for him.
He has sent for them to carry out his
    anger against Babylon.
They will be happy when he wins
    the battle for them.

4 Listen! I hear a noise in the mountains.
    It sounds like a huge crowd.
Listen! I hear a loud noise among the
    kingdoms.
It sounds like nations gathering
    together.
The LORD who rules over all is bringing
    an army together for war.
5 They come from lands far away.
They come from the farthest places
    on earth.
The LORD and those weapons of his
    anger
are coming to destroy the whole
    country of Babylonia.

6 Cry out! The day of the LORD is near.
The Mighty One is coming to
    destroy them.
7 Their hands won't be able to help
    them.
Everyone's heart will melt away in
    fear.
8 The people will be filled with terror.
Pain and suffering will grab hold of
    them.
They will groan with pain like a
    woman having a baby.

They'll look at one another in terror.
    Their faces will burn with shame.

9 The day of the LORD is coming.
    It will be a terrible day.
The LORD's burning anger will blaze
    out.
He will make the land dry and empty.
    He'll destroy the sinners in it.
10 All of the stars in the sky
    will stop giving their light.
The sun will be darkened as soon as it
    rises.
The moon will not shine.
11 The LORD will punish the world
    because it is so evil.
He will punish evil people for their
    sins.
He'll put an end to the bragging of
    those who are proud.
He'll bring down the pride of those
    who don't show any pity.
12 He'll make men harder to find than
    pure gold.
They will be harder to find than gold
    from Ophir.
13 He will make the heavens tremble.
    He'll shake the earth out of its place.
The LORD who rules over all will show
    how angry he is.
At that time his burning anger will
    blaze out.

14 Outsiders who live in Babylonia will
    scatter
like antelope that are chased by a
    hunter.
They are like sheep that don't have a
    shepherd.
All of them will return to their own
    people.
They will run back to their own
    countries.
15 Those who are captured will have
    spears stuck through them.
Those who are caught will be killed
    with swords.
16 Their babies will be smashed to pieces
    right in front of their eyes.
Their houses will be robbed.
    Their wives will be raped.

17 The LORD will stir up the Medes to
    attack the Babylonians.
They aren't interested in getting
    silver.
They don't delight in gold.
18 Instead, they will use their bows and
    arrows
to strike the young men down.
They won't even show any mercy to
    babies.

They won't take pity on children.
19 The city of Babylon is the jewel of
kingdoms.
It is the glory and pride of the
Babylonians.
But God will destroy it
just as he did Sodom and Gomorrah.
20 No one will ever live in Babylon again.
No one will live there for all time to
come.
Arabs will never set up their tents
there.
Shepherds will never rest their flocks
there.
21 But desert creatures will lie down
there.
Wild dogs will fill its houses.
Owls will live there.
Wild goats will jump around in it.
22 Hyenas will cry out in its forts.
Wild dogs will bark in its beautiful
palaces.
The time for Babylon to be punished is
near.
Its days are numbered.

14 The LORD will show tender love
toward Jacob's people.
Once again he will choose Israel.
He'll settle them in their own land.
Outsiders will join them.
They and the people of Jacob will
become one people.
2 Nations will help Israel
return to their own land.
People from other nations will belong
to Israel.
They will serve them as male and
female servants in the LORD's
land.
The Israelites will make prisoners of
those who had held them as
prisoners.
They will rule over those who had
crushed them.

3 The LORD will put an end to Israel's suffering and trouble. They won't be slaves
anymore. **4** They will make fun of the king
of Babylonia. They will say,

"See how the one who crushed others
has fallen!
See how his anger has come to an
end!
5 The LORD has taken away the authority
of evil people.
He has broken the power of rulers.
6 When they became angry, they struck
nations down.
Their blows never stopped.

In their anger they brought nations
under their control.
They attacked them again and
again.
7 All of the lands now enjoy peace and
rest.
They break out into singing.
8 Even the pine trees are glad.
The cedar trees of Lebanon are
happy too.
They say, 'Babylon, you have fallen.
Now no one comes and cuts us
down.'

9 "King of Babylonia, many people in
the grave are really excited
about meeting you when you go
down there.
The spirits of the dead get up to
welcome you.
At one time all of them were leaders
in the world.
They were kings over the nations.
They get up from their thrones.
10 All of them call out to you.
They say,
'You have become weak, just as we are.
You have become like us.'
11 Your grand show of power has been
brought down to the grave.
The noise of your harps has come
down here along with your
power.
Maggots are spread out under you.
Worms cover you.

12 "King of Babylonia, you thought you
were the bright morning star.
But now you have fallen from
heaven!
You once brought nations down.
But now you have been thrown
down to the earth!
13 You said in your heart,
'I will go up to heaven.
I'll raise my throne
above the stars of God.
I'll sit as king on the mountain where
the gods meet.
I'll set up my throne on the highest
slopes of the sacred mountain.
14 I will rise above the tops of the clouds.
I'll make myself like the Most High
God.'
15 But now you have been brought down
to the grave.
You have been thrown into the
deepest part of the pit.

16 "Those who see you stare at you.
They think about what has
happened to you.

They say to themselves,
'Is this the man who shook the earth?
Is he the one who made kingdoms
tremble with fear?
17 Did he turn the world into a desert?
Did he destroy its cities?
Did he refuse to let his prisoners go
home?'

18 "All of the kings of the nations are
buried with honor.
Each of them lies in his own tomb.
19 But you have been thrown out of your
tomb.
You are like a branch that is cut off
and thrown away.
You are covered with the bodies
of those who have been killed with
swords.
You have been tossed into a stony
pit along with them.
You are like a dead body that people
have walked on.
20   You won't be buried like other kings.
That's because you have destroyed your
land.
You have killed your people.

"The children of that evil man will be
killed.
None of them will be left to carry on
the family name.
21 So prepare a place to kill his children.
Kill them because of the sins of the
rulers
who lived before them.
They must not rise to power.
They must not rule over the world.
They must not cover the earth with
their cities."

22 "I will rise up against them,"
announces the LORD who rules over
all.
"I will destroy Babylon.
It will not be remembered anymore.
No one will be left alive there.
I will destroy its people and their
children after them,"
announces the LORD.
23 "I will turn it into a place where
nothing but owls can live.
I will turn it into a swamp.
I will sweep through it like a broom
and destroy everything,"
announces the LORD who rules over
all.

A Message About Assyria

24 The LORD who rules over all has taken
an oath. He has said,

"You can be sure that what I have
planned will happen.
What I have decided will take place.
25 I will crush the Assyrians in my land.
On my mountains I will walk all
over them.
The yokes they put on my people will
be removed.
The heavy load they put on their
shoulders will be taken away."

26 That's how the LORD carries out his
plan all over the world.
That's how he reaches out his
powerful hand to punish all of
the nations.
27 The LORD who rules over all has
planned it.
Who can stop him?
He has reached out his powerful hand.
Who can keep him from using it?

A Message About the Philistines

28 A message came to me from the LORD
in the year King Ahaz died. The LORD said,

29 "The rod of Assyria has struck all of
you Philistines.
But do not be glad that it is broken.
That rod is like a snake that will
produce an even more
poisonous snake.
It will produce a darting, poisonous
serpent.
30 Even the poorest people in Israel will
have plenty to eat.
Those who are in need will lie down
in safety.
But I will destroy your families.
They will die of hunger.
I will kill any of them who are still
left alive.

31 "Cities of Philistia, cry out for help!
Scream in pain!
All of you Philistines, melt away in
fear!
An army is coming from the north in a
cloud of dust.
No one in its ranks is falling behind.
32 What answer should be given
to the messengers from that nation?
Tell them, 'The LORD has made Zion
secure.
His suffering people will find safety
there.' "

A Message About Moab

15 Here is a message the LORD gave
me about Moab.

The city of Ar in Moab is destroyed.

It happened in a single night.
Kir in Moab is also destroyed.
It happened in a single night.
2 The people of Dibon go up to their
     temple to worship.
They go to their high places to sob.
The people of Moab cry over the
     cities of Nebo and Medeba.
All of their heads are shaved.
All of their beards have been cut off.
3 In the streets they wear black clothes.
On their roofs and in the market
     places
all of them are crying.
They fall down flat with their faces
     toward the ground.
And they sob.
4 The people of Heshbon and Elealeh cry
     out.
Their voices are heard all the way to
     Jahaz.
So the fighting men of Moab cry out.
Their hearts are weak.

5 My heart cries out over Moab.
Some who run away get as far as
     Zoar.
Others run all the way to Eglath
     Shelishiyah.
Others go up the road to Luhith.
They are sobbing as they go.
Still others travel the road to
     Horonaim.
They sing a song of sadness because
     their town is being destroyed.
6 The waters at Nimrim are dried up.
And so is the grass.
The plants have died.
Nothing green is left.
7 The people are trying to escape
     through the Valley of the Poplar
     Trees.
They are carrying with them the
     wealth
they have collected and stored up.
8 Their loud cries echo along the border
     of Moab.
They reach as far as Eglaim.
Their songs of sadness reach all the
     way to Beer Elim.
9 The waters of the city of Dimon are full
     of blood.
But the Lord will bring even more
     trouble on Dimon.
He will bring lions against those who
     run away from Moab.
They will also attack those who
     remain in the land.

16 People of Moab, send lambs as a
     gift

to the ruler of Judah.
Send them from Sela.
Send them across the desert.
Send them to Mount Zion in the
     city of Jerusalem.
2 The women of Moab are at the places
     where people go across the Arnon
     River.
They are like birds that flap their wings
     when they are pushed from their
     nest.

3 The Moabites say to the rulers of
     Judah,
"Give us advice. Make a decision.
Cover us with your shadow.
Make it like night even at noon.
Hide those of us who are running
     away.
Don't turn them over to their
     enemies.
4 Let those who have run away from
     Moab stay with you.
Keep them safe from those who are
     trying to destroy them."

Those who crush others will be
     destroyed.
The killing will stop.
The attackers will disappear from
     the earth.
5 A man from the royal house of David
     will sit on Judah's throne.
He will rule with faithful love.
When he judges he will do what is fair.
He will be quick to do what is right.

6 We have heard all about Moab's pride.
We have heard how very proud they
     are.
They think they are so much better
     than others.
They brag about themselves.
But all of their bragging is nothing
     but empty words.

7 So the people of Moab cry out.
All of them cry over their country.
Sing a song of sadness.
Sob over the men of Kir Hareseth.
8 The vineyards of Heshbon dry up.
So do the vines of Sibmah.
The rulers of the nations
     have walked all over its finest vines.
Those vines once reached as far as
     Jazer.
They spread out toward the desert.
Their new growth went
     all the way to the Dead Sea.
9 Jazer sobs over the vines of Sibmah.
And so do I.
Heshbon and Elealeh,
I soak you with my tears!

There isn't any ripe fruit for people to
shout about.
There isn't any harvest to make
them happy.
10 Joy and gladness are taken away from
the orchards.
No one sings or shouts in the
vineyards.
No one stomps on grapes at the
winepresses.
That's because the LORD has put an
end to the shouting.
11 My heart sobs over Moab like a song of
sadness played on a harp.
Deep down inside me I sob over Kir
Hareseth.
12 Moab's people go to their high place to
pray.
But all they do is wear themselves
out.
Their god Chemosh can't help them
at all.

13 That's the message the LORD has
already spoken about Moab. 14 But now he
says, "In exactly three years, people will
look down on Moab's glory. Now Moab
has many people. But by that time only a
few of them will be left alive. And even
they will be weak."

Messages About Damascus and Israel

17 Here is a message the LORD gave
me about Damascus. He said,

"Damascus will not be a city anymore.
Instead, all of its buildings will be
knocked down.
2 The cities of Aroer will be deserted.
They will be left to the flocks that lie
down there.
No one will make them afraid.
3 Ephraim's people will no longer have
cities with high walls around
them.
Royal power will disappear from
Damascus.
Those who are left alive in Aram
will be like the glory of the people of
Israel,"
announces the LORD
who rules over all.

4 "In days to come, the glory of Jacob's
people will fade.
Their strength will get weaker and
weaker.
5 It will be as when a worker cuts and
gathers grain
in the Valley of Rephaim.
He gathers up stalks with his arms.

Only a few heads of grain are left.
6 In the same way, only a few people will
be left alive.
It will be as when workers knock
olives off the trees.
Only two or three olives are left on the
highest branches.
Four or five at most are left on the
limbs that produce fruit,"
announces the LORD,
the God of Israel.

7 In days to come, men will look to their
Maker for help.
They will turn their eyes to the Holy
One of Israel.
8 They won't trust in the altars
they made with their own hands.
They won't pay any attention to the
poles they used
to worship the goddess Asherah.
And they won't depend on the incense
altars
they made with their own fingers.

9 At that time the strong cities in Israel
will be deserted. They will be as they were
when the Israelites drove the Canaanites
out of them. They will be like places that
are taken over by bushes and weeds. The
whole land will become dry and empty.

10 Israel, you have forgotten God, who
saves you.
You have not remembered the Rock,
who keeps you safe.
You might set out the finest plants.
You might plant vines from other
lands.
11 The plants might start to grow on the
day you set them out.
The vines might begin to bud on the
morning you plant them.
But even if they do, there won't be any
harvest.
Instead, there will be sickness and
pain that won't go away.

12 How terrible it looks for us!
Many nations are marching against
us.
The noise of their armies is like the
sound of the ocean.
They are making a lot of noise.
It sounds like huge waves crashing
on the shore.
13 It sounds like the roar of rushing
waters.
But when the LORD speaks out
against them, they run far
away.
The wind blows them away like straw
on the hills.

A strong wind drives them along like
tumbleweeds.
14 In the evening, the nations terrify us.
But before morning comes, they are
gone.
That's what happens to those who
steal our goods.
That's what happens to those who
take what belongs to us.

A Message About Cush

18 How terrible it will be for the land
whose armies are like large
numbers of flying insects!
That land is along the rivers of Cush.
2 Its people send messengers on the Nile
River.
They travel over the water in
papyrus boats.

Messengers, hurry back home!
Go back to your people,
who are tall and have smooth skin.
Everyone is afraid of them.
They are warriors.
Their language is different from ours.
Their land is divided up by rivers.

3 Pay attention, all you people of the
world!
Listen, all you who live on earth!
Banners will be lifted up on the
mountains.
And you will see them.
Trumpets will be blown.
And you will hear them.
4 The Lord says to me,
"I will look down from heaven,
where I live.
I will be as quiet as summer heat in the
sunshine.
I will be as quiet as a cloud of dew in
the heat of harvest."
5 A farmer cuts off new growth with
pruning knives.
He cuts down spreading branches
and takes them away.
He does it before the grapes are
harvested.
That's when the blooms are gone
and the grapes are ripe.
In the same way, the Lord will cut off
the nations
that are gathered against his people.
6 Their dead bodies will be left for the
birds of the mountains to eat.
They will be left for the wild
animals.
The birds will eat the dead bodies all
summer long.
The wild animals will eat them all
through the winter.

7 At that time gifts will be brought to
the Lord who rules over all.

The people who are tall and have
smooth skin will bring them.
Everyone is afraid of those people.
They are warriors. Their language is
different from ours.
Their land is divided up by rivers.

They will bring their gifts to Mount Zion.
That's where the Lord who rules over all
has put his Name.

A Message About Egypt

19 Here is a message the Lord gave
me about Egypt.

The Lord is coming to Egypt.
He's riding on a cloud that moves
very fast.
The statues of the gods in Egypt
tremble with fear because of
him.
The hearts of the people there melt
away inside them.

2 The Lord says, "I will stir up one
Egyptian against another.
Relatives will fight against relatives.
Neighbors will fight against one
another.
Cities will fight against cities.
Kingdoms will fight against one
another.
3 The people of Egypt will lose hope.
I will keep them from doing what
they plan to do.
They will ask their gods for advice.
They will turn to the spirits of dead
people for help.
They will go to people who get
messages from those who have
died.
They will ask for advice from people
who talk to the spirits of the
dead.
4 I will hand the Egyptians over
to a mean and unkind master.
A powerful king will rule over them,"
announces the Lord.
He is the Lord who rules over all.

5 The waters of the Nile River will dry
up.
The bottom of it will be cracked and
dry.
6 Its waterways will stink.
And the streams of Egypt will get
smaller and smaller
until they dry up.
The tall grass that grows along the river
will dry up.

7 So will the plants along the banks of
  the Nile.
  Even the planted fields along the Nile
    will dry up.
  Everything that grows there will
    blow away and disappear.
8 The fishermen will moan.
  All those who drop hooks into the
    Nile will sob.
  Those who throw their nets on the
    water
  will become very sad.
9 Those who make clothes out of flax
    will lose hope.
  So will those who weave fine linen.
10 Those who work with cloth will be
    unhappy.
  And all those who work for money
    will be sick at heart.

11 The officials of the city of Zoan are
    very foolish.
  Pharaoh's wise men give advice that
    doesn't make any sense.
  How can they dare to say to Pharaoh,
    "We're among the wise men"?
  How can they say to him,
    "We're like the advisers to the kings
    of long ago"?
12 Pharaoh, where are your wise men
    now?
  Let them tell you
  what the LORD who rules over all
    has planned against Egypt.
13 The officials of Zoan have become
    foolish.
  The leaders of Memphis have been
    lied to.
  The most important leaders in Egypt
    have led its people down the wrong
    path.
14 The LORD has given them
    a spirit that makes them feel dizzy.
  They make Egypt unsteady in
    everything it does.
  Egypt is like a person who drinks too
    much.
  He throws up and then walks
    around in the mess he's made.
15 No one in Egypt can do anything to
    help them.
  Its elders and important leaders
    can't help them.
  Its prophets and priests can't do
    anything.
  Those who rule over others can't
    help.
  And those who bow down to them
    can't help either.

16 In days to come, the people of Egypt
will be as terrified as women. The LORD
who rules over all will raise his hand
against them. Then they will tremble
with fear. **17** The people of Judah will bring
terror to the Egyptians. Everyone in Egypt
who hears the name of Judah will be terrified. That's because of what the LORD who
rules over all is planning to do to them.

18 At that time the people of five cities
in Egypt will use the Hebrew language
when they worship the LORD who rules
over all. They will take an oath. And they
will promise to be faithful to him. One of
those cities is called The City of the Sun.

19 At that time there will be an altar to
the LORD in the middle of Egypt. There
will be a monument to him at its border.
20 They will remind people that the LORD
who rules over all is worshiped in Egypt.
The people there will cry out to the LORD
because of those who treat them badly. He
will send someone to stand up for them
and save them. And he will set them free.
21 So the LORD will make himself known
to the people of Egypt. At that time they
will recognize that he is the LORD. They
will worship him by bringing sacrifices
and grain offerings to him. They will
make promises to the LORD. And they will
keep them. **22** The LORD will strike Egypt
with a plague. But then he will heal them.
They will turn to the LORD. And he will
answer their prayers and heal them.

23 At that time there will be a wide road
from Egypt to Assyria. The people of
Assyria will go to Egypt. And the people of
Egypt will go to Assyria. The people of
Egypt and Assyria will worship the LORD
together.

24 At that time Egypt, Assyria and Israel
will be a blessing to the whole earth.
25 The LORD who rules over all will bless
those three nations. He will say, "Let the
Egyptians be blessed. They are my people.
Let the Assyrians be blessed. My hands
created them. And let the Israelites be
blessed. They are my very own people."

A Message About Egypt and Cush

20 Sargon sent his highest commander to the city of Ashdod. He
attacked it and captured it. Sargon was
king of Assyria. **2** Three years earlier the
LORD had spoken to me. He had said,
"Take off the black clothes you are wearing. And take your sandals off." So I did. I
went around barefoot. I didn't have anything on but my underwear.
3 After Ashdod was captured, the LORD
said, "My servant Isaiah has gone around
barefoot for three years. He has not worn

anything but his underwear. He is a sign and reminder to Egypt and Cush about what will happen to them.

4 "The king of Assyria will lead prisoners away from Egypt and Cush. Young people and old people alike will be taken away. Like Isaiah, they will be barefoot. They will not be wearing anything but their underwear. And their backsides will be bare. So the Egyptians will be put to shame.

5 "People trusted in Cush to help them. They bragged about what Egypt could do for them. But they will be afraid and put to shame. **6** At that time the people who live on the coast of Philistia will speak up. They will say, 'See what has happened to those we depended on! We ran to them for help. We wanted them to save us from the king of Assyria. Now how can we escape?' "

A Message About Babylonia

21 Here is a message the LORD gave me about Babylonia. It is known as the Desert by the Two Rivers.

An attack is coming through the desert.
  It is coming from a land of terror.
  It's sweeping along like a windstorm blowing across the Negev Desert.

2 I have seen a vision about something terrible that will happen.
  People are turning against Babylon.
  Robbers are taking its goods.
Elamites, attack the city! Medes, surround it!
  The LORD will put an end to all of the suffering Babylon has caused.

3 The vision fills my body with pain.
  Pains take hold of me.
They are like the pains of a woman having a baby.
I am shaken by what I hear.
  I'm terrified by what I see.
4 My heart grows weak.
  Fear makes me tremble.
I longed for evening to come.
  But it brought me horror instead of rest.

5 In my vision the Babylonians set the tables.
  They spread the rugs out.
  They eat. They drink.
Get up, you officers!
  Rub your shields with oil!

6 The Lord said to me,

"Go. Put a guard on duty on Jerusalem's walls.
  Have him report what he sees.
7 Tell him to watch for chariots
  that are pulled by teams of horses.
Tell him to watch for men riding on donkeys or camels.
  Make sure he stays awake.
  Make sure he stays wide awake."

8 "My master!" the guard shouts back.

"Day after day I stand here on the lookout tower.
  Every night I stay here on duty.
9 Look! Here comes a man in a chariot!
  It's being pulled by a team of horses.
He's calling out the news,
  'Babylon has fallen! It has fallen!
All of the statues of its gods
  lie broken in pieces on the ground!' "

10 My people, you have been crushed like grain on a threshing floor.
But now I'm telling you the good news I've heard.
  It comes from the LORD who rules over all.
  He is the God of Israel.

A Message About Edom

11 Here is a message the LORD gave me about Edom.

Someone is calling out to me from the land of Seir. He says,
  "Guard, when will the night be over?
  Guard, how soon will it end?"
12 The guard answers,
  "Morning is coming. But the night will return.
If you want to ask again,
  come back and ask."

A Message About Arabia

13 Here is a message the LORD gave me about Arabia.

He told me to give orders to traders from Dedan.
  They were camping in the bushes of Arabia.
14   I told them to bring water for those who are thirsty.
I also gave orders to those who live in Tema.
  I told them to bring food for those who are running away.
15 They are running away from where the fighting is heaviest.

That's where the swords are ready to
strike.
That's where the bows are ready to
shoot.

16The Lord says to me, "In exactly one
year, Kedar's grand show of power will
come to an end. 17Only a few of Kedar's
soldiers who shoot arrows will be left
alive." The LORD has spoken. He is the
God of Israel.

A Message About Jerusalem

22 Here is a message the LORD gave
me about the Valley of Vision.

People of Jerusalem, what's the matter
with you?
Why have all of you gone up on the
roofs of your houses?
2 Why is your town so full of noise?
Why is your city so full of the sound
of wild parties?
Those among you who died weren't
killed with swords.
They didn't die in battle.
3 All of your leaders have run away.
They've been captured without a
single arrow being shot.
All those who were caught were taken
away as prisoners.
They ran off while your enemies
were still far away.
4 So I said, "Leave me alone.
Let me sob bitter tears.
Don't try to comfort me.
My people have been destroyed."

5 The LORD who rules over all sent the
noise of battle against you.
The Lord brought disorder and
terror
to the Valley of Vision.
The walls of the city were knocked
down.
Cries for help were heard in the
mountains.
6 Soldiers from Elam came armed with
bows and arrows.
They came with their chariots and
horses.
Soldiers from Kir got their shields
ready.
7 Your rich valleys filled up with
chariots.
Horsemen took up their battle
positions at your city gates.
8 Judah wasn't a safe place to live in
anymore.

When all of that happened, you
depended

on the weapons in the Palace of the
Forest of Lebanon.
9 You saw that the City of David
had many holes in its walls.
They needed to be repaired.
You stored up water
in the Lower Pool.
10 You picked out the weaker buildings in
Jerusalem.
You tore them down and used their
stones
to strengthen the city walls against
attack.
11 You built a pool between the two walls.
You used it to save the water
that was running down from the
Old Pool.
But you didn't look to the One who
made it all possible.
You didn't pay any attention to the
One
who planned everything long ago.

12 The LORD who rules over all
called out to you at that time.
The Lord told you to sob and cry.
He told you to tear your hair out.
And he told you to put black clothes
on.
13 Instead, you are enjoying yourselves at
wild parties!
You are killing cattle and sheep.
You are eating their meat and
drinking wine.
You are saying, "Let's eat and drink,
because tomorrow we'll die."

14 I heard the LORD who rules over all
speaking. "Your sin can never be paid for
as long as you people live," says the Lord.

15 The LORD who rules over all speaks.
The Lord says,

"Go. Speak to the head servant
Shebna.
He is in charge of the palace. Tell
him,
16 'What are you doing here outside the
city?
Who allowed you to cut out a tomb
for yourself here?
Who said you could carve out your
grave on the hillside?
Who allowed you to cut out your
resting place in the rock?

17 " 'Watch out, you mighty man!
The LORD is about to grab hold of
you.
He is about to throw you away.
18 He will roll you up tightly like a ball.

He will throw you into a very large
country.
There you will die.
And there the chariots you are so
proud of will remain.
You bring shame on your master's
family!

19 The LORD will remove you from your
job.
You will be brought down from your
high position.

20 " 'At that time he will send for his servant Eliakim. He is the son of Hilkiah.
21 The LORD will put your robe on Eliakim.
He will tie your belt around him. He will
hand your authority over to him. Eliakim
will be like a father to the people of Jerusalem and Judah.
22 " 'The LORD will give Eliakim the key
of authority in David's royal house. No
one can shut what he opens. And no one
can open what he shuts. **23** The LORD will
set him firmly in place like a peg that is
driven into a wall. He will hold a position
of honor in his family. **24** The good name
of his whole family will depend on him.
They will be like bowls and jars hanging
on a peg.

25 " 'But a new day is coming,' " announces the LORD who rules over all. " 'At
that time the peg that was driven into the
wall will give way. It will break off and fall
down. And the heavy load hanging on it
will also fall.' " The LORD has spoken.

A Message About Tyre

23 Here is a message the LORD gave
me about Tyre.

Men in the ships of Tarshish, cry out!
The city of Tyre is destroyed.
Its houses and harbor are gone.
That's the message you have received
from the island of Cyprus.

2 People on the island of Tyre, be silent.
Traders from the city of Sidon, be
quiet.
Those who sail on the
Mediterranean Sea have made
you rich.
3 Grain from Egypt
came across the mighty waters.
The harvest of the Nile River brought
wealth to Tyre.
It became the market place of the
nations.
4 Sidon, be ashamed. Mighty Tyre out in
the sea, be ashamed.
The sea has spoken. It has said,

"It's as if I had never felt labor pains or
had children.
It's as if I had never brought up sons
or daughters.
It's as if the city of Tyre had never
existed."
5 The Egyptians will hear about what
has happened to Tyre.
They'll be very sad and troubled.

6 People of the island of Tyre, cry out!
Go across the sea to Tarshish.
7 Just look at Tyre.
It's no longer the old, old city that
was known for its wild parties.
It no longer sends its people out
to settle in lands far away.
8 Tyre was a city that produced kings.
Its traders were princes.
They were honored all over the earth.
So who planned to destroy such a
city?
9 The LORD who rules over all planned to
do it.
He wanted to bring down all of its
pride and glory.
He wanted to put to shame those
who were honored all over the
earth.

10 People of Tarshish, spread out over
your land
like the waters of the Nile.
There isn't anything to hold you
back anymore.
11 The LORD has reached his powerful
hand out over the sea.
He has made its kingdoms tremble
with fear.
He has given a command concerning
Phoenicia.
He has ordered that its forts be
destroyed.
12 He said, "No more wild parties for you!
People of Sidon, you are now
destroyed!

"Leave your city. Go across the sea to
Cyprus.
Even there you will not find any
rest."
13 Look at the land of the Babylonians.
No one lives there anymore.
The Assyrians have turned it
into a place for desert creatures.
They built their towers in order to
attack it.
They took everything out of its forts.
They knocked all of its buildings
down.

14 Men in the ships of Tarshish, cry out!
Mighty Tyre is destroyed!

15 A time is coming when people will forget about Tyre for 70 years. That's the length of a king's life. But at the end of those 70 years, Tyre will be like the prostitute that people sing about. They say,

16 "Forgotten prostitute, pick up a harp.
　　Walk through the city.
Play the harp well. Sing many songs.
　　Then you will be remembered."

17 At the end of the 70 years, the LORD will punish Tyre. He will let it return to its way of life as a prostitute. It will earn its living with all of the kingdoms on the face of the earth. **18** But the money it earns will be set apart for the LORD. The money won't be stored up or kept for Tyre. Instead, it will go to those who live the way the LORD wants them to. It will pay for plenty of food and fine clothes for them.

The LORD Will Destroy the Earth

24 The LORD is going to completely destroy everything on earth.
He will twist its surface.
He'll scatter those who live on it.
2 Priests and people alike will suffer.
　　So will masters and their servants.
　　And so will women and their female
　　　　servants.
Sellers and buyers alike will suffer.
　　So will those who borrow and those
　　　　who lend.
　　And so will those who owe money
　　　　and those who lend it.
3 The earth will be completely
　　　　destroyed.
　　Everything of value will be taken out
　　　　of it.
　　　　　That's what the LORD has said.

4 The earth will dry up completely.
　　The world will dry up and waste
　　　　away.
　　The most important people on earth
　　　　will fade away.
5 The earth is polluted by its people.
　　They haven't obeyed the laws of the
　　　　LORD.
　　They haven't done what he told them
　　　　to do.
　　They've broken the covenant that
　　　　will last forever.
6 So the LORD will send a curse on the
　　　　earth.
　　Its people will pay for what they've
　　　　done.
　　They will be burned up.
　　Very few of them will be left.

7 The vines and fresh wine will dry up
　　　　completely.
　　Those who used to have a good time
　　　　will groan.
8 The happy sounds of tambourines will
　　　　be gone.
　　The noise of those who enjoy wild
　　　　parties will stop.
　　The joyful music of harps will
　　　　become silent.
9 People will no longer sing as they
　　　　drink wine.
　　Beer will taste bitter to those who
　　　　drink it.
10 Destroyed cities will lie empty.
　　People will lock themselves inside
　　　　their houses.
11 In the streets people will cry out for
　　　　wine.
　　All joy will turn into sadness.
　　All happiness will be driven out of
　　　　the earth.
12 All of the buildings will be knocked
　　　　down.
　　Every city gate will be smashed to
　　　　pieces.
13 That's how it will be on the earth.
　　And that's how it will be among the
　　　　nations.
　　It will be as when workers knock all but
　　　　a few olives off the trees.
　　It will be like a vine that has only a
　　　　few grapes left after the harvest.

14 Those who are left alive will shout with
　　　　joy.
　　People from the west will praise the
　　　　LORD because he is the King.
15 So give glory to him, you who live in
　　　　the east.
　　Honor the name of the LORD, you
　　　　who are in the islands of the sea.
　　He is the God of Israel.
16 From one end of the earth to the other
　　　　we hear singing.
　　People are saying,
　　"Give glory to the One who always
　　　　does what is right."

But I said, "I feel very bad.
　　I'm getting weaker and weaker.
　　How terrible it is for me!
People turn against one another.
　　They can't be trusted.
　　So they turn against each other."
17 People of the earth,
　　terror, a pit and a trap are waiting for
　　　　you.
18 Anyone who runs away from the terror
　　　　will fall into the pit.
　　Anyone who climbs out of the pit
　　　　will be caught in the trap.

The LORD will open the windows of the
skies.
He will flood the land.
The foundations of the earth will
shake.
19 The earth will be broken up.
It will split open.
It will be shaken to pieces.
20 The earth will be unsteady like
someone who is drunk.
It will sway like a tent in the wind.
Its sin will weigh so heavily on it that it
will fall.
It will never get up again.
21 At that time the LORD will punish
the spiritual forces of evil in the
heavens above.
He will also punish the kings on the
earth below.
22 They will be brought together
like prisoners in chains.
They'll be locked up in prison.
After many days the LORD will
punish them.
23 The LORD who rules over all will rule
on Mount Zion in Jerusalem.
The elders of the city will be there.
They will see his glory.
His rule will be so glorious that the sun
and moon
will be too ashamed to shine.

A Song of Praise

25 LORD, you are my God.
I will honor you.
I will praise your name.
You have been perfectly faithful.
You have done wonderful things.
You had planned them long ago.
2 You have turned cities into piles of
trash.
You have pulled down the high
walls that were around them.
You have destroyed our enemies' forts.
They will never be rebuilt.
3 Powerful nations will honor you.
Even sinful people from their cities
will have respect for you.
4 Poor people have come to you for
safety.
You have kept needy people safe
when they were in trouble.
You have been a place to hide when
storms came.
You have been a shade from the heat
of the sun.
Evil people attack us.
They are like a storm beating against
a wall.
5 They are like the heat of the desert.

You stopped the noisy shouts of our
enemies.
You kept them from winning the
battle over us and singing
about it.
You are like the shadow of a cloud
that cools the earth.
6 On Mount Zion the LORD who rules
over all will prepare
a feast for all of the nations.
The best and richest foods
and the finest aged wines will be
served.
7 On that mountain the LORD will
destroy
the veil of sadness that covers all of
the nations.
He will destroy the gloom that is
spread over everyone.
8   He will swallow up death forever.
The LORD and King will wipe away the
tears
from everyone's face.
He will remove the shame of his
people
from the whole earth.
The LORD has spoken.

9 At that time they will say,

"He is our God.
We trusted in him, and he saved us.
He is the LORD. We trusted in him.
Let us be filled with joy because he
saved us."

10 The LORD's powerful hand will keep
Mount Zion safe.
But he will walk all over Moab.
Its people will be crushed,
just as straw is crushed in animal
waste.
11 They will try to swim their way out
of it.
They will spread their hands out
in it,
just as a swimmer spreads his hands
out to swim.
But God will bring down Moab's pride.
None of their skill will help them.
12 He will pull down their high, strong
walls.
He will bring them down to the
ground.
He'll bring them right down to the
dust.

Another Song of Praise

26 At that time a song will be sung in
the land of Judah. It will say,

"We have a strong city.

FAITHFUL

LORD, YOU WILL GIVE
PERFECT PEACE

TO ANYONE WHO
COMMITS HIMSELF TO
BE FAITHFUL TO YOU.

THAT'S BECAUSE HE
TRUSTS IN YOU.

— ISAIAH 26:3 —

TRUSTED

God's saving power surrounds it
like walls and towers.
2 Open its gates
so that those who do what is right
can enter.
They are the people who remain
faithful to God.
3 LORD, you will give perfect peace
to anyone who commits himself to
be faithful to you.
That's because he trusts in you.

4 "Trust in the LORD forever.
The LORD is the Rock.
The LORD will keep us safe forever.
5 He brings down those who are proud.
He pulls down cities that have high
walls.
They fall down flat on the ground.
He throws them down to the dust.
6 The feet of those who were crushed
stomp on them.
Those who were helpless walk all
over them."

7 LORD, you are honest and fair.
You guide those who do what is
right.
You lead them on a straight path.
You make their way smooth.
8 LORD, we are living the way your laws
command us to live.
We are waiting for you to act.
Our hearts long for you to be true to
your name.
That's what you are known for.
9 My heart longs for you at night.
My spirit longs for you in the
morning.
You will come and judge the earth.

Then the people of the world will
learn to do what is right.
10 Grace is shown to sinful people.
But they still don't learn to do what
is right.
They keep on doing evil even in a land
where others are honest and
fair.
They don't have any respect for the
majesty of the LORD.
11 LORD, you have raised your hand high
to punish them.
But they don't even see it.
Let them see how much you love your
people.
Then they will be put to shame.
Let the fire you are saving for your
enemies burn them up.

12 LORD, you give us peace.
You are the one who has done
everything we've
accomplished.
13 LORD, you are our God.
Other masters besides you have
ruled over us.
But your name is the only one we
honor.
14 Those other masters are now dead.
They will never live again.
Their spirits won't rise from the
dead.
You punished them and destroyed
them.
You wiped out all memory of them.
15 LORD, you have made our nation grow.
You have made it larger.
You have gained glory for yourself.
You have increased the size of our
land.

16 LORD, when your people were
suffering, they came to you.
When you punished them,
they could barely whisper a prayer.
17 LORD, you made us like a woman who
is having a baby.
She groans and cries out in pain.
18 We were pregnant. We groaned with
pain.
But nothing was born.
We didn't bring your saving power to
the earth.
We didn't give life to the people of
the world.

19 Israel, those among you who have died
will live again.
Their bodies will rise from the dead.
You who lie in the grave,
wake up and shout with joy.

The dew of the morning gives life to
the earth.
So the earth will give up its dead
people.

20 My people, go into your houses.
Shut the doors behind you.
Hide yourselves for a little while.
Do it until the LORD's anger is over.
21 He is coming from the place where he
lives.
He will punish the people of the
earth for their sins.
The blood that has been spilled on the
earth will be brought out into
the open.
The ground will no longer hide
those who have been killed.

Israel Will Be Saved

27 At that time

the LORD will punish Leviathan with
his sword.
His great, powerful and deadly
sword will punish
the serpent that glides through the sea.
He will kill that twisting sea
monster.

2 At that time the LORD will sing about
his fruitful vineyard. He will say,

3 "I am the LORD. I watch over my
vineyard.
I water it all the time.
I guard it day and night.
I do it so no one can harm it.
4 I am not angry with my vineyard.
I wish thorns and bushes would
come up in it.
Then I would march out against them
in battle.
I would set all of them on fire.
5 So the enemies of my people had
better come to me for safety.
They should make peace with me.
I will say it again.
They should make peace with me."

6 In days to come, Jacob's people will put
down roots like a vine.
Israel will bud and bloom.
They will fill the whole world with
fruit.

7 The LORD struck down those who
struck Israel down.
But he hasn't punished Israel as
much.
The LORD killed those who killed many
of his people.

But he hasn't punished his people as
much.
8 The LORD will use war to punish Israel.
He will make them leave their land.
With a strong blast of his anger he will
drive them out.
It will be as if the east wind were
blowing.
9 The people of Jacob will have to pay for
their sin.
That must happen in order for their
sin to be taken away.
They will make all of the altar stones
like chalk.
They will crush them to pieces.
No poles that had been used to
worship the goddess Asherah
will be left standing.
No incense altars will be left either.
10 Cities that have high walls around
them will become empty.
They will be deserted settlements.
They will be like a desert.
Calves will eat and lie down in them.
They will strip the branches of their
trees bare.
11 When their twigs are dry, they will be
broken off.
Then women will come and make
fires with them.
The people of Jacob don't understand
the LORD.
So the One who made them won't
be concerned about them.
Their Creator won't show them his
favor.

12 At that time the LORD will separate
Israel from other people. He will gather
the Israelites together. He will gather
them one by one from the Euphrates River all the way to the Wadi of Egypt. 13 At
that time a loud trumpet will be blown.
Those who were dying in Assyria will
come and worship the LORD. So will those
who were taken away to Egypt. All of
them will worship the LORD on his holy
mountain in Jerusalem.

The LORD Will Judge Israel

28 How terrible it will be for the city
of Samaria!
It sits on a hill like a crown of
flowers.
The leaders of Ephraim are drunk.
They take pride in their city.
It sits above a valley that has rich soil.
How terrible it will be for the
glorious beauty of that fading
flower!

2 The Lord will bring the strong and
    powerful king of Assyria against
    Samaria.
The Lord will throw that city down
    to the ground with great force.
It will be like a hailstorm.
It will be like a wind that destroys
    everything.
It will be like a driving rain and a
    flooding storm.
3 That city is like a crown.
The leaders of Ephraim are drunk.
They take pride in their city.
But its enemies will walk all over it.
4 It sits on a hill above a rich valley.
It's like a crown of flowers whose
    glorious beauty is fading away.
But it will become like a fig that is ripe
    before harvest.
As soon as someone sees it,
he picks it and swallows it.

5 At that time the LORD who rules over
    all
    will be like a glorious crown.
He will be like a beautiful wreath
    for those of his people who will be
    left alive.
6 He will help those
    who are fair when they judge.
He will give strength to those
    who turn back their enemies at the
    city gate.

7 Israel's leaders are drunk from wine.
They can't walk straight.
They are drunk from beer.
They are unsteady on their feet.
Priests and prophets drink beer.
They can't walk straight.
They are mixed up from drinking
    too much wine.
They drink too much beer.
They are unsteady on their feet.
The prophets see visions but don't
    really understand them.
The priests aren't able to make good
    decisions.
8 They throw up. All of the tables are
    covered
with the mess they've made.
There isn't one spot on the tables
    that isn't smelly and dirty.

9 My people are making fun of me. They
    say,
"Who does he think he's trying to
    teach?
Who does he think he's explaining
    his message to?
Is it to children who do not need their
    mother's milk anymore?

Is it to those who have just been
    taken from her breast?
10 Here is how he teaches.
Do this and do that.
Do that and do this.
Obey this rule and obey that rule.
    Obey that rule and obey this rule.
    Learn a little here and learn a little
    there."

11 All right then, these people won't
    listen to me.
    So God will speak to them.
He will speak by using people who
    speak unfamiliar languages.
He will speak by using the mouths
    of strangers.
12 He said to his people,
"I am offering you a resting place.
Let those who are tired rest."
He continued, "I am offering you a
    place of peace and quiet."
But they wouldn't listen.
13 So then, here is what the LORD's
    message will become to them.
Do this and do that.
Do that and do this.
Obey this rule and obey that rule.
    Obey that rule and obey this rule.
    Learn a little here and learn a little
    there.
So when they try to go forward,
    they'll fall back and be wounded.
They'll be trapped and captured.

14 Listen to the LORD's message,
    you who make fun of the truth.
Listen, you who rule over these
    people in Jerusalem.
15 You brag, "We have entered into a
    covenant with death.
We have made an agreement with
    the grave.
When a terrible plague comes to
    punish us,
    it can't touch us.
That's because we depend on lies to
    keep us safe.
We hide behind what isn't true."

16 So the LORD and King speaks. He says,

"Look! I am laying a stone in Zion.
It is a stone that has been tested.
It is the most important stone for a
    firm foundation.
The one who trusts in that stone will
    never be shaken.
17 I will use a measuring line to prove that
    you have not been fair.
I will use a plumb line to prove that
    you have not done what is
    right.

Hail will sweep away the lies you
    depend on to keep you safe.
    Water will flood your hiding place.
18 Your covenant with death will be
    called off.
    The agreement you made with the
    grave will not stand.
When the terrible plague comes to
    punish you,
    you will be beaten down by it.
19 As often as it comes, it will carry you
    away.
    Morning after morning, day and
    night,
    it will come to punish you."

If you understand this message,
    it will bring you absolute terror.
20 You will be like someone whose bed is
    too short to lie down on.
You will be like those whose
    blankets are too small to wrap
    themselves in.
21 The LORD will rise up to judge, just as
    he did at Mount Perazim.
    He will get up to act, just as he did in
    the Valley of Gibeon.
He'll do his work, but it will be strange
    work.
    He'll carry out his task, but it will be
    an unexpected one.
22 Now stop making fun of me.
    If you don't, your chains will
    become heavier.
The LORD who rules over all has spoken
    to me.
    The Lord has told me he has ordered
    that the whole land be
    destroyed.

23 Listen and hear my voice.
    Pay attention to what I'm saying.
24 When a farmer plows in order to plant,
    does he plow without
    stopping?
    Does he keep on breaking up the soil
    and making the field level?
25 When he's made the surface even,
    doesn't he plant caraway seeds?
    Doesn't he scatter cummin?
Doesn't he plant wheat in its proper
    place?
    Doesn't he plant barley where it
    belongs?
    Doesn't he plant spelt along the
    edge of the field?
26 His God directs him.
    He teaches him the right way to do
    his work.

27 Caraway seeds are beaten out with a
    rod.

They aren't separated out under a
    threshing sled.
Cummin seeds are beaten out with a
    stick.
    The wheel of a cart isn't rolled over
    them.
28 Grain must be ground up to make
    bread.
    A farmer separates it out.
    But he doesn't go on doing it
    forever.
He drives the wheels of a threshing
    cart over it.
    But he doesn't let the horses grind it
    to dust.
29 All of those insights come from the
    LORD who rules over all.
    His advice is wonderful. His wisdom
    is glorious.

The LORD Will Judge Jerusalem

29 Jerusalem, how terrible it will be
    for you!
    Ariel, you are the city where David
    settled.
The years will come and go.
    Keep on celebrating your regular
    feasts.
2 The LORD says, "Ariel, I will surround
    you.
    Jerusalem, I will get ready to attack
    you.
Your people will sob.
    They will sing songs of sadness.
I will make you like the front of an
    altar
    that is covered with blood.
3 I will be like an army that is camped
    against you on all sides.
    I will surround you with towers in
    order to attack you.
I will build my ramps all around you
    and set up my ladders.
4 You will be brought down to the grave.
    You will speak from deep down
    inside the ground.
    Your words will be barely heard out
    of the dust.
Your voice will sound like the voice of a
    ghost
    coming from under the ground.
    Your words will sound like a whisper
    out of the dust."

5 Jerusalem, all of your enemies will
    become like fine dust.
    Their terrifying armies will become
    like straw
    that the wind blows away.
All of a sudden, in an instant,

6 the LORD who rules over all will
  come.
He will come with thunder,
   earthquakes and a lot of noise.
He'll bring windstorms and
   rainstorms with him.
He'll send a blazing fire that will
   burn everything up.

7 Armies from all of the nations will
   fight against Ariel.
They will attack it and its fort.
They'll surround it completely.
But suddenly those armies will
   disappear like a dream.
They will vanish like a vision in the
   night.
8 They will be like a hungry person who
   dreams he is eating.
But when he wakes up, he's still
   hungry.
They will be like a thirsty person who
   dreams he is drinking.
But when he wakes up, he is weak.
His thirst hasn't been satisfied.
In the same way, the armies from all of
   the nations
   that fight against Mount Zion will
   disappear.

9 People of Jerusalem, be shocked and
   amazed.
Make yourselves blind so you can't
   see anything.
Get drunk, but not from wine.
Be unsteady on your feet, but not
   because of beer.
10 The LORD has made you fall into a deep
   sleep.
He has closed the eyes of your
   prophets.
He has covered the heads of your
   seers so they can't see.

11 For you, this whole vision is like
words that are sealed up in a scroll. Suppose you give it to someone who can read.
And suppose you say to him, "Please read
this for us." Then he'll answer, "I can't. It's
sealed up." **12** Or suppose you give the
scroll to someone who can't read. And
suppose you say, "Please read this for us."
Then he'll answer, "I don't know how to
read."

13 The Lord says,

"These people worship me only with
   their words.
They honor me by what they say.
But their hearts are far away from
   me.

Their worship doesn't mean anything
   to me.
They teach nothing but human
   rules.
14 So once more I will shock these people
   with many wonderful acts.
I will destroy the wisdom of those who
   think they are so wise.
I will do away with the cleverness of
   those who think they are so
   smart."

15 How terrible it will be for people who
   do everything they can
to hide their plans from the LORD!
They do their work in darkness.
They think, "Who sees us? Who will
   know?"
16 They turn everything upside down.
How silly they are to think that
   potters are like the clay they
   work with!
Can what is made say to the one who
   made it,
   "You didn't make me"?
Can the pot say to the potter,
   "You don't know anything"?

17 In a very short time, Lebanon will be
   turned into rich farm lands.
The rich farm lands will seem like a
   forest.
18 At that time those who can't hear will
   hear what is read from the
   scroll.
Those who are blind will come out
   of gloom and darkness.
They will be able to see.
19 Those who aren't proud will once
   again find their joy in the LORD.
And those who are in need will find
   their joy in the Holy One of
   Israel.

POWER-SURGE

CHEERFUL ✳

THOSE WHO AREN'T
PROUD WILL ONCE
AGAIN FIND THEIR JOY
IN THE LORD.

AND THOSE WHO ARE
IN NEED WILL FIND
THEIR JOY IN THE HOLY
ONE OF ISRAEL.
— ISAIAH 29:19 —

20 Those who don't show any pity will
vanish.
Those who make fun of others will
disappear.
All those who look for ways to do
what is evil will be cut off.
21 Without any proof, they claim that a
man is guilty.
In court they try to trap
the one who speaks up for others.
By using dishonest witnesses they keep
those who aren't guilty
from being treated fairly.

22 Long ago the LORD saved Abraham
from trouble. Now he says to Jacob's people,

"You will not be ashamed anymore.
Your faces will no longer grow pale
with fear.
23 You will see your children living
among you.
I myself will give you those children.
Then you will honor my name.
You will recognize how holy I am.
I am the Holy One of Jacob.
You will have great respect for me.
I am the God of Israel.
24 I will give understanding to you
who find yourselves going down the
wrong path.
You who are always speaking against
others
will accept what I teach you."

The LORD Will Judge His Stubborn People

30 "How terrible it will be for these
stubborn children of mine!"
announces the LORD.
"How terrible for those who carry out
plans that did not come
from me!
Their agreement with Egypt did not
come from my Spirit.
So they pile up one sin on top of
another.
2 They go down to Egypt
without asking me for advice.
They look to Pharaoh to help them.
They ask Egypt to keep them safe.
3 But looking to Pharaoh will only bring
them shame.
Asking Egypt for help will bring
them dishonor.
4 Their officials have gone to the city of
Zoan.
Their messengers have arrived in
Hanes.
5 But the people of Judah will be put to
shame

because they are trusting in a nation
that is useless to them.
Egypt will not bring them any help or
advantage.
Instead, it will bring them shame
and dishonor."

6 Here is a message the LORD gave me
about the animals in the Negev Desert.

Judah's messengers carry their riches
on the backs of donkeys.
They carry their treasures on the
humps of camels.
They travel through a land of danger
and suffering.
It's a land that is filled with lions.
Poisonous snakes are also there.
The messengers travel to a nation
that can't do them any good.
7 They travel to Egypt, whose help is
totally useless.
That's why I call it Rahab the
Do-Nothing.

8 The LORD said to me, "Go now.
Write on a tablet for the people of
Judah
what I am about to say.
Also write it on a scroll.
In days to come
it will be a witness that lasts forever.
9 The people of Judah refuse to obey me.
They are children who tell lies.
They will not listen to what I want to
teach them.
10 They say to the seers,
'Don't see any more visions!'
They say to the prophets,
'Don't give us any more visions of
what is right!
Tell us pleasant things.
Prophesy things we want to hear
even if they aren't true.
11 Get out of our way!
Get off our path!
Keep the Holy One of Israel away
from us!' "

12 So the Holy One of Israel speaks. He
says,

"You have turned your backs on what I
have said.
You have depended on telling
people lies.
You have crushed others.
13 Those sins are like cracks in a high
wall.
They get bigger and bigger.
Suddenly the wall breaks apart.
Then it quickly falls down.

14 It breaks into small pieces like a clay
pot.
It breaks up completely.
Not one piece is left big enough
for taking coals from a fireplace.
Not one piece is left for dipping
water out of a well."

15 The LORD and King is the Holy One of
Israel. He says,

"You will find peace and rest
when you turn away from your sins
and depend on me.
You will receive the strength you need
when you stay calm and trust in me.
But you do not want to do what I tell
you to.
16 You said, 'No. We'll escape on horses.'
So you will have to escape!
You said, 'We'll ride off on fast horses.'
So those who chase you will use
faster horses!
17 When one of them dares you to fight,
a thousand of you will run away.
When five of them dare you,
all of you will run away.
So few of you will be left that you will
be
like a flagpole on top of a mountain.
You will be like only one banner on
a hill."

18 But the LORD longs to show you his
favor.
He wants to give you his tender love.
The LORD is a God who is always fair.
Blessed are all those who wait for
him to act!

19 People of Zion, who live in Jerusalem,
you won't sob anymore. When you cry
out to the Lord for help, he will show you
his favor. As soon as he hears you, he'll
answer you. **20** He might treat you like prisoners. You might eat the bread of trouble.
You might drink the water of suffering.
But he will be your Teacher. He won't hide
himself anymore. You will see him with
your own eyes. **21** You will hear your
Teacher's voice behind you. You will hear
it whether you turn to the right or the left.
It will say, "Here is the path I want you to
take. So walk on it."

22 Then you will get rid of the silver statues of your gods. You won't have anything to do with the gold statues either.
All of them are "unclean." So you will
throw them away like dirty rags. You will
say to them, "Get away from us!"

23 The LORD will send rain on the seeds
you plant in the ground. The crops that

grow will be rich and plentiful. At that
time your cattle will eat grass in rolling
meadows. **24** The oxen and donkeys that
work the soil will eat the finest feed and
crushed grain. The farmers will use pitch-
forks and shovels to separate it from the
straw.

25 At that time the towers of your enemies will fall down. Their soldiers will die.
Streams of water will flow on every high
mountain and hill.

26 The moon will shine like the sun.
And the sunlight will be seven times
brighter than usual. It will be like the light
of seven full days. That will happen when
the LORD bandages and heals the wounds
and bruises he has brought on his people.

27 The LORD will come from far away
in all of his power and glory.
He will show his burning anger.
Thick clouds of smoke will be all
around him.
His mouth will speak angry words.
The words from his tongue will be
like a destroying fire.
28 His breath will be like a rushing flood
that rises up to the neck.
He'll separate out the nations he is
going to destroy.
He'll place a bit in their jaws.
It will lead them down the road to
death.
29 You will sing
as you do on the night you celebrate
a holy feast.
Your hearts will be filled with joy.
You will be as joyful as people
playing their flutes
as they go up to the mountain of the
LORD.
He is the Rock of Israel.
30 The LORD will cause people to hear his
powerful voice.
He will make them see his arm
coming down to punish them.
It will come down with burning anger
and destroying fire.
It will come down with rain,
thunderstorms and hail.
31 The voice of the LORD will tear the
Assyrians apart.
He will strike them down with his
mighty rod.
32 He will strike them
with his rod to punish them.
Each time he does, his people will
celebrate
with the music of harps and
tambourines.
He will use his powerful arm

to strike the Assyrians down in
    battle.
33 In the Valley of Ben Hinnom, Topheth
    has been prepared for a long
    time.
    It has been made ready for the king
      of Assyria.
Its fire pit has been made deep and
    wide.
It has plenty of wood for the fire.
The breath of the LORD
    will be like a stream of burning
      sulfur.
It will set the wood on fire.

The LORD Will Judge Those Who Depend on Egypt

31 How terrible it will be for those
    who go down to Egypt for help!
How terrible for those who depend
    on horses!
They trust in how many chariots they
    have.
    They trust in how strong their
      horsemen are.
But they don't look to the Holy One of
    Israel.
    They don't ask the LORD for his help.
2 He too is wise. He can bring horrible
    trouble.
    He does what he says he'll do.
He'll rise up against everyone who does
    what is evil.
    He'll fight against those who help
      them.
3 The men of Egypt are only human.
    They aren't God.
Their horses are only flesh and blood.
    They aren't spirits.
The LORD will reach out his powerful
    hand
    to punish everyone.
The Egyptians provide help.
    But they will be tripped up.
The people of Judah receive the help.
    But they will fall down.
All of them will be destroyed.

4 The LORD says to me,

"A powerful lion stands over its food
    and growls.
A lot of shepherds can be brought
    together to drive it away.
But the lion is not frightened by their
    shouts.
    It is not upset by the noise they
      make.
In the same way, I will come down
    from heaven.
I will fight on Mount Zion and on its
    hills.

Nothing will drive me away.
    I am the LORD who rules over all.
5 Like a bird hovering over its nest, I will
    guard Jerusalem.
I will keep it safe.
I will pass over it and save it.
    I am the LORD who rules over all."

6 People of Israel, return to the LORD.
He's the one you have so strongly
opposed. 7 The time will come when every
one of you will turn your backs on your
gods of silver and gold. You sinned when
you made them with your own hands.

8 The LORD says, "The Assyrians will be
    killed with swords.
    But it will not be men who use
      them.
The swords that kill them will not be
    used by human beings.
The Assyrians will run away from
    those swords.
But their young men will be caught
    and forced to work hard.
9 Their hiding places will be destroyed
    when terror strikes them.
When their commanders see their
      enemy's battle flags,
    they will be filled with panic,"
announces the LORD.
His fire blazes out from Mount Zion.
    His furnace burns in Jerusalem.

The King Who Will Do What Is Right

32 A king will come who will do
    what is right.
    His officials will govern fairly.
2 Each man will be like a place to get out
    of the wind.
He will be like a place to hide from
    storms.
He'll be like streams of water flowing in
    the desert.
He'll be like the shadow of a huge
    rock in a dry and thirsty land.

3 Then the eyes of those who see won't
    be closed anymore.
The ears of those who hear will
    listen to the truth.
4 The minds of thoughtless people will
    know and understand.
Tongues that stutter will speak
    clearly.
5 Foolish people won't be considered
    noble anymore.
Those who are worthless won't be
    highly respected.
6 A foolish person says foolish things.
    His mind is full of evil thoughts.

He doesn't do what is right.
  He tells lies about the LORD.
He doesn't give hungry people any
    food.
  He doesn't let thirsty people have
    any water.
7 The one who is worthless uses sinful
    methods.
  He makes evil plans against poor
    people.
He destroys them with his lies.
  He does it even when those people
    are right.
8 But the man who is noble makes noble
    plans.
  And by doing noble things he
    succeeds.

The Sinful Women in Jerusalem

9 You women who are so contented,
    pay attention to me.
You who feel so secure,
    listen to what I have to say.
10 You feel secure now.
  But in a little over a year you will
    tremble with fear.
The grape harvest will fail.
  There won't be any fruit.
11 So tremble, you contented women.
  Tremble with fear, you who feel so
    secure.
Take your fine clothes off.
  Put black clothes on.
12 Beat your chests to show how sad you
    are.
  The pleasant fields have been
    destroyed.
  The fruitful vines have dried up.
13 My people's land is overgrown with
    thorns and bushes.
  Sob over all of the houses that were
    once filled with joy.
  Cry over this city that used to be full
    of wild parties.
14 The royal palace will be left empty.
  The noisy city will be deserted.
The fort and lookout tower will
    become
  a dry and empty desert forever.
Donkeys will enjoy being there.
  Flocks will eat there.
15 That will continue until the Holy Spirit
    is poured out on us from heaven.
Then the desert will be turned into
    rich farm lands.
  The rich farm lands will seem like a
    forest.
16 In the desert and the rich farm lands
    people will do what is right.
  And they will treat one another
    fairly.

17 Doing what is right will bring peace
    and rest.
  When my people do that, they will
    stay calm
  and trust in the LORD forever.
18 They will live in a peaceful land.
  Their homes will be secure.
  They will enjoy peace and quiet.
19 Hail might strip the forests bare.
  Cities might be completely
    destroyed.
20 But how blessed you people will be!
  You will plant your seeds by every
    stream.
You will let your cattle and donkeys
  wander anywhere they want to.

The LORD Will Judge Assyria

33 How terrible it will be for you,
    you who destroy others!
  Assyria, you haven't been destroyed
    yet.
How terrible for you, you who turn
    against others!
  Others haven't turned against you
    yet.
When you stop destroying,
  you will be destroyed.
When you stop turning against others,
  others will turn against you.

2 LORD, show us your favor.
  We long for you to help us.
Make us strong every morning.
  Save us when we're in trouble.
3 When the nations hear you thunder,
    they run away.
  When you rise up against them,
    they scatter.
4 Nations, what you have taken in battle
    is destroyed.
  It's as if young locusts had eaten it
    up.
Like large numbers of locusts,
  people rush to get it.

5 The LORD is honored. He lives in
    heaven.
  He will fill Zion's people with what
    is fair and right.
6 He will be the firm foundation for their
    entire lives.
  He will give them all of the wisdom,
    knowledge and saving power
    they will ever need.
  Respect for the LORD is the key to
    that treasure.

7 Look! Judah's brave men cry out loud
    in the streets.
  The messengers who were sent to
    bring peace sob bitter tears.

WISE

[GOD] WILL GIVE THEM ALL OF THE WISDOM, KNOWLEDGE AND SAVING POWER THEY WILL EVER NEED.

RESPECT FOR THE LORD IS THE KEY TO THAT TREASURE.

— ISAIAH 33:6 —

8 The wide roads are deserted.
No one travels on them.
Our peace treaty with Assyria is broken.
Those who witnessed it are looked down on.
No one is respected.
9 The land is filled with sadness and wastes away.
Lebanon is full of shame and dries up.
The rich land of Sharon is like the Arabah Desert.
The trees of Bashan and Carmel drop their leaves.

10 "Now I will take action," says the LORD.
"Now I will be honored.
Now I will be respected.
11 Assyria, your plans and actions are like straw.
Your anger is a fire that will destroy you.
12 The nations will be burned to ashes.
They will be like bushes that are cut down and set on fire.

13 "You nations far away, listen to what I have done!
My people who are near, recognize how powerful I am!
14 The sinners in Zion are terrified.
They tremble with fear.
They say, 'Who of us can live through the LORD's destroying fire?
Who of us can live through the fire that burns forever?'
15 A person must do what is right.
He must be honest and tell the truth.
He must not get rich by cheating others.

His hands must not receive money from those who want special favors.
He must not let his ears listen to plans to commit murder.
He must close his eyes to even thinking about doing what is evil.
16 A person like that will be kept safe.
It will be as if he were living on high mountains.
It will be as if he were living in a mountain fort.
He will have all of the food he needs.
And he will never run out of water."

17 People of Judah, you will see the king in all of his glory and majesty.
You will view his kingdom spreading far and wide.
18 You will think about what used to terrify you.
You will say to yourself,
"Where is that chief officer of Assyria?
Where is the one who forced us to send gifts to his king?
Where is the officer in charge of the towers
that were used when we were attacked?"
19 You won't see those proud people anymore.
They spoke a strange language.
None of us could understand it.

20 Just look at Zion! It's the city where we celebrate our regular feasts.
Turn your eyes toward Jerusalem.
It will be a peaceful place to live in.
It will be like a tent that will never be moved.
Its stakes will never be pulled up.
None of its ropes will be broken.
21 There the LORD will be our Mighty One.
It will be like a place of wide rivers and streams.
No boat with oars will travel on them.
No mighty ship will sail on them.
22 That's because the LORD is our judge.
The LORD gives us our law.
The LORD is our king.
He will save us.

23 The ropes on your ship hang loose.
The mast isn't very secure.
The sail isn't spread out.
But the LORD will strike the Assyrians down.

Then a large amount of goods will
  be taken from them and
  divided up.
Even people who are disabled will
  carry off what was taken.
24 No one living in Zion will ever say
  again, "I'm sick."
And the sins of those who live there
  will be forgiven.

The LORD Will Judge the Nations

34 Nations, come near and listen to
  me!
Pay attention to what I'm about to
  say.
Let the earth and everything in it
  listen.
Let the world and everything that
  comes out of it pay attention.
2 The LORD is angry with all of the
  nations.
His anger burns against all of their
  armies.
He will totally destroy them.
He will have them killed.
3 Those who are killed won't be buried.
Their dead bodies will be thrown on
  the ground.
They will give off a very bad smell.
Their blood will cover the
  mountains.
4 All of the stars in the heavens will
  vanish.
The sky will be rolled up like a scroll.
All of the stars in the sky will fall like
  dried-up leaves from a vine.
They will drop like wrinkled figs
  from a fig tree.

5 The sword of the LORD will finish its
  deadly work in the sky.
Then it will come down to strike
  Edom.
He will totally destroy that nation.
6 His sword will be red with blood.
It will be covered with fat.
The blood will flow like the blood
  of lambs and goats being sacrificed.
The fat will be like the fat
  taken from the kidneys of rams.
That's because the LORD will offer a
  sacrifice
  in the city of Bozrah.
He will kill many people in Edom.
7 The people and their leaders will be
  killed
  like wild oxen and young bulls.
Their land will be wet with their blood.
The dust will be covered with their
  fat.

8 That's because the LORD has set aside a
  day to pay Edom back.
He has set aside a year to pay them
  back for what they did to the
  city of Zion.
9 The streams of Edom will be turned
  into tar.
Its dust will be turned into blazing
  sulfur.
Its land will become burning tar.
10 The fire will keep burning night and
  day.
It can't be put out.
Its smoke will go up forever.
Edom will lie empty for all time to
  come.
No one will ever travel through it
  again.
11 The desert owl and screech owl will
  make it their home.
The great owl and the raven will
  build their nests there.
God will use his measuring line
  to show how completely Edom will
  be destroyed.
He will use his plumb line
  to show how empty Edom will
  become.
12 Edom's nobles won't have anything
  left there
  that can be called a kingdom.
All of its princes will vanish.
13 Thorns will cover its forts.
Bushes and weeds will cover its safest
  places.
It will become a home for wild dogs.
It will become a place where owls
  live.
14 Desert creatures will meet with hyenas.
Wild goats will call out to each
  other.
Night creatures will also sleep there.
They will find places where they can
  rest.
15 Owls will make their nests and lay
  their eggs there.
And they will hatch them.
They will take care of their little ones
  under the shadow of their wings.
Male and female falcons will also
  gather there.

16 Look in the scroll of the LORD. There
you will read that

none of those animals will be missing.
Male and female alike will be there.
The LORD himself has commanded it.
And his Spirit will gather them
  together.
17 The LORD will decide what part of the
  land goes to each animal.

Then he will give each one its share.
It will belong to them forever.
And they will live there for all time
to come.

The LORD Will Set His People Free

35 The desert and the dry ground
will be glad.
The dry places will be full of joy.
Flowers will grow there.
Like the first crocus in the spring,
²   the desert will bloom with flowers.
It will be very glad and shout with
joy.
The glorious beauty of Lebanon will be
given to it.
It will be as beautiful as the rich
lands
of Carmel and Sharon.
Everyone will see the glory of the LORD.
They will see the beauty of our God.

³ Strengthen the hands of those who are
weak.
Help those whose knees give way.
⁴ Say to those whose hearts are afraid,
"Be strong. Do not fear.
Your God will come.
He will pay your enemies back.
He will come to save you."

POWER — SURGE

BRAVE   B

SAY TO THOSE WHOSE HEARTS ARE AFRAID,

"BE STRONG. DO NOT FEAR.

YOUR GOD WILL COME."

— ISAIAH 35:4 —

STRONG

⁵ Then the eyes of those who are blind
will be opened.
The ears of those who can't hear will
be unplugged.
⁶ Those who can't walk will leap like a
deer.
And those who can't speak will
shout with joy.
Water will pour out in dry places.
Streams will flow in the desert.

⁷ The burning sand will become a pool
of water.
The thirsty ground will become
bubbling springs.
In the places where wild dogs once lay
down,
tall grass and papyrus will grow.

⁸ A wide road will go through the land.
It will be called The Way of Holiness.
Only those who are pure and clean can
travel on it.
Only those who lead a holy life can
use it.
Evil and foolish people can't walk
on it.
⁹ No lions will use it.
No wild animals will be on it.
None of them will be there.
Only people who have been set free
will walk on it.
¹⁰   Those the LORD has saved will return
to their land.
They will sing as they enter the city of
Zion.
Joy that lasts forever will be
like beautiful crowns on their heads.
They will be filled with gladness and
joy.
Sorrow and sighing will be gone.

Sennacherib Warns Jerusalem

36 Sennacherib attacked and captured all of the cities of Judah that
had high walls around them. It was in the
14th year of the rule of Hezekiah. Sennacherib was king of Assyria. ² He sent his
field commander from Lachish to King
Hezekiah at Jerusalem. He sent him along
with a large army. The commander
stopped at the channel that brings water
from the Upper Pool. It was on the road to
the Washerman's Field.

³ Eliakim, Shebna and Joah went out to
him. Eliakim, the son of Hilkiah, was in
charge of the palace. Shebna was the secretary. Joah, the son of Asaph, kept the
records.

⁴ The field commander said to them,
"Give Hezekiah this message. Tell him,

" 'Sennacherib is the great king of
Assyria. He says, "Why are you putting your faith in what your king
says? ⁵ You say you have a military
plan. You say you have a strong army.
But your words don't mean anything. Who are you depending on?
Why don't you want to stay under
my control?

⁶ " ' "You are depending on Egypt.
Why are you doing that? Egypt is

nothing but a broken papyrus stem. Try leaning on it. It will only cut your hand. Pharaoh, the king of Egypt, is just like that to everyone who depends on him.

7" ' "Suppose you say to me, 'We are depending on the LORD our God.' Didn't Hezekiah remove your god's high places and altars? Didn't Hezekiah say to the people of Judah and Jerusalem, 'You must worship at the altar in Jerusalem'?

8" ' "Come on. Make a deal with my master, the king of Assyria. I'll give you 2,000 horses. But only if you can put riders on them! 9You are depending on Egypt for chariots and horsemen. You can't drive away even the least important officer among my master's officials.

10" ' "Besides, do you think I've come without being sent by the LORD? Have I come to attack and destroy this land without receiving a message from him? The LORD himself told me to march out against your country. He told me to destroy it." ' "

11Then Eliakim, Shebna and Joah spoke to the field commander. They said, "Please speak to us in the Aramaic language. We understand it. Don't speak to us in Hebrew. If you do, the people who are on the wall will be able to understand you."

12But the commander replied, "My master sent me to say these things. Are these words only for your master and you to hear? Aren't they also for the men who are sitting on the wall? They are going to suffer just like you. They'll have to eat their own waste. They'll have to drink their own urine."

13Then the commander stood up and spoke in the Hebrew language. He called out, "Pay attention to what the great king of Assyria is telling you. 14He says, 'Don't let Hezekiah trick you. He can't save you! 15Don't let Hezekiah talk you into trusting in the LORD. Don't believe him when he says, "You can be sure that the LORD will save us. This city will not be handed over to the king of Assyria." '

16"Don't listen to Hezekiah. The king of Assyria says, 'Make a peace treaty with me. Come over to my side. Then every one of you will eat fruit from your own vine and fig tree. Every one of you will drink water from your own well. 17You will do that until I come back. Then I'll take you to a land that is just like yours. It's

a land that has a lot of grain and fresh wine. It has plenty of bread and vineyards.

18" 'Don't let Hezekiah fool you. He's telling you a lie when he says, "The LORD will save us." Has the god of any nation ever saved his land from the powerful hand of the king of Assyria? 19Where are the gods of Hamath and Arpad? Where are the gods of Sepharvaim? Have they saved Samaria from my power? 20Which one of all of the gods of those countries has been able to save his land from me? So how can the LORD save Jerusalem from my power?' "

21But the people remained silent. They didn't say anything. That's because King Hezekiah had commanded, "Don't answer him."

22Then Eliakim, the son of Hilkiah, went to Hezekiah. Eliakim was in charge of the palace. The secretary Shebna went with him. So did Joah, the son of Asaph. Joah kept the records. All of them went to Hezekiah with their clothes torn. They told him what the field commander had said.

Isaiah Prophesies That Jerusalem Will Be Saved

37 When King Hezekiah heard what the field commander had said, he tore his clothes. He put on black clothes. Then he went into the LORD's temple. 2Hezekiah sent Eliakim, who was in charge of the palace, to me. He also sent the leading priests and the secretary Shebna to me. All of them were wearing black clothes.

3They told me, "Hezekiah says, 'Today we're in great trouble. The LORD is warning us. He's bringing shame on us. Sometimes babies come to the moment when they should be born. But their mothers aren't strong enough to allow them to be born. Today we are like those mothers. We aren't strong enough to save ourselves.

4" 'Perhaps the LORD your God will hear everything the field commander has said. His master, the king of Assyria, has sent him to make fun of the living God. Maybe the LORD your God will punish him for what he has heard him say. So pray for the remaining people who are still alive here.' "

5King Hezekiah's officials came to me. 6Then I said to them, "Tell your master, 'The LORD says, "Do not be afraid of what you have heard. The officers who are under the king of Assyria have spoken evil things against me. 7Listen! I will send him news from his own country. It will upset him so much that he will return home. There I will have him cut down with a sword." ' "

8The field commander heard that the king of Assyria had left Lachish. So the commander pulled his troops back from Jerusalem. He went to join the king. He found out that the king was fighting against Libnah.

9During that time Sennacherib received a report. He was told that Tirhakah was marching out to fight against him. Tirhakah was king of Egypt. He was from the land of Cush.

When Sennacherib heard the report, he sent messengers again to Hezekiah with a letter. It said, **10**"Tell Hezekiah, the king of Judah, 'Don't let the god you depend on trick you. He says, "Jerusalem will not be handed over to the king of Assyria." But don't believe him. **11**I'm sure you have heard about what the kings of Assyria have done to all of the other countries. They have destroyed them completely. So do you think you will be saved?

12" 'The kings who ruled before me destroyed many nations. Did the gods of those nations save them? Did the gods of Gozan, Haran or Rezeph save them? What about the gods of the people of Eden who were in Tel Assar? **13**Where is the king of Hamath? Where is the king of Arpad? Where is the king of the city of Sepharvaim? Where are the kings of Hena or Ivvah?' "

Hezekiah Prays to the LORD

14When Hezekiah received the letter from the messengers, he read it. Then he went up to the LORD's temple. There he spread the letter out in front of the LORD. **15**Hezekiah prayed to the LORD. He said, **16**"LORD who rules over all, you are the God of Israel. You sit on your throne between the cherubim. You alone are God over all of the kingdoms on earth. You have made heaven and earth. **17**Listen, LORD. Hear us. Open your eyes, LORD. Look at the trouble we're in. Listen to what Sennacherib is saying. You are the living God. And he dares to make fun of you!

18"LORD, it's true that the kings of Assyria have completely destroyed many nations and their lands. **19**They have thrown the statues of the gods of those nations into the fire. And they have destroyed them. That's because they weren't really gods at all. They were nothing but statues that were made out of wood and stone. They were made by human hands.

20"LORD our God, save us from the powerful hand of Sennacherib. Then all of the kingdoms on earth will know that you alone are God."

Sennacherib Falls From Power

21I sent a message to Hezekiah. I said, "The LORD is the God of Israel. He says, 'You have prayed to me about Sennacherib, the king of Assyria. **22**So here is the message I have spoken against him. I am telling him,

" ' "You will not win the battle over Zion.
　　Its people hate you and make fun of you.
The people of Jerusalem lift up their heads proudly
　　as you run away.
23Who have you laughed at?
　　Who have you spoken evil things against?
Who have you raised your voice against?
Who have you looked at so proudly?
　　You have done it against me.
　　I am the Holy One of Israel!
24Through your messengers
　　you have laughed at me again and again.
And you have said,
　　'I have many chariots.
With them I have climbed to the tops of the mountains.
　　I've climbed the highest mountains in Lebanon.
I've cut down its tallest cedar trees.
　　I've cut down the best of its pine trees.
I've reached its farthest mountains.
　　I've reached its finest forests.
25I've dug wells in strange lands.
　　I've drunk the water from them.
I've walked through all of Egypt's streams.
　　I've dried up every one of them.'
26" ' "But I, the LORD, say, 'Haven't you heard what I have done?
　　Long ago I arranged for you to do all of that.
In days of old I planned it.
　　Now I have made it happen.
You have turned cities with high walls into piles of stone.
27Their people do not have any power left.
　　They are troubled and put to shame.
　　They are like plants in the field.

They are like new green plants.
They are like grass that grows on a roof.
It dries up before it is completely
grown.

28 " ' " 'But I know where you live.
I know when you come and go.
I know how very angry you are with
me.
29 You roar against me and brag.
And I have heard your bragging.
So I will put my hook in your nose.
I will put my bit in your mouth.
And I will make you go home
by the same way you came.' " ' "

30 The LORD said, "Hezekiah, here is a
miraculous sign for you.

"This year you will eat what grows by
itself.
Next year you will eat what grows
from that.
But in the third year you will plant
your crops and gather them in.
You will plant your grapevines and
eat their fruit.
31 The people of Judah who are still alive
will be like plants.
Once more they will put down roots
and produce fruit.
32 Out of Jerusalem will come those who
remain.
Out of Mount Zion will come those
who are still left alive.
My great love will make sure that
happens.
I rule over all.

33 "Here is a message from me about the
king of Assyria. It says,

" 'He will not enter this city.
He will not even shoot an arrow at it.
He will not come near it with a shield.
He will not build a ramp in order to
climb over its walls.
34 By the way that he came he will go
home.
He will not enter this city,'
announces the LORD.
35 "I will guard this city and save it.
I will do it for myself.
And I will do it for my servant
David."

36 Then the angel of the LORD went into
the camp of the Assyrians. He put to
death 185,000 soldiers there. The people
of Jerusalem got up the next morning.
They looked out and saw all of the dead
bodies. 37 So Sennacherib, the king of
Assyria, took the army tents down. Then

he left. He returned to Nineveh and
stayed there.
38 One day Sennacherib was worshiping in the temple of his god Nisroch. His
sons Adrammelech and Sharezer cut him
down with their swords. Then they
escaped to the land of Ararat. Esarhaddon
became the next king after his father Sennacherib.

Hezekiah Praises the LORD for Healing Him

38 In those days Hezekiah became
very sick. He knew he was about
to die. I went to see him. I told him, "The
LORD says, 'Put everything in order. Make
out your will. You are going to die soon.
You will not get well again.' "
2 Hezekiah turned his face toward the
wall. He prayed to the LORD. He said,
3 "LORD, please remember how faithful
I've been to you. I've lived the way you
wanted me to. I've served you with all my
heart. I've done what is good in your
sight." And Hezekiah cried bitterly.
4 A message came to me from the LORD.
He said, 5 "Go and speak to Hezekiah. Tell
him, 'The LORD, the God of King David,
says, "I have heard your prayer. I have seen
your tears. I will add 15 years to your life.
6 And I will save you and this city from the
powerful hand of the king of Assyria. I will
guard this city.
7 " ' "Here is a miraculous sign from me.
It will show you that I will heal you, just as
I promised I would. 8 The shadow that was
made by the sun has gone down ten steps
on the stairway of Ahaz. I will make it go
back up those ten steps." ' " So the shadow went back up the ten steps it had gone
down.

9 Here is a song of praise that was written by Hezekiah, the king of Judah. He
wrote it after he was sick and had gotten
well again.

10 I said, "I'm enjoying the best years of
my life.
Must I now go through the gates of
death?
Will the rest of my years be taken
away from me?"
11 I said, "LORD, I'll never see you again
while I'm still alive.
I'll never see people anymore.
I'll never again be with those who
live in this world.
12 My body is like a shepherd's tent.
It has been pulled down and carried
off.

My life is like a piece of cloth that I've
　　rolled up.
You have cut it off from the loom.
In a short period of time you have
　　brought my life to an end.
13 I waited patiently until sunrise.
But like a lion you broke all of my
　　bones.
In a short period of time you have
　　brought my life to an end.
14 I cried softly like a weak little bird.
I groaned like a sad dove.
My eyes grew tired as I looked up
　　toward heaven.
Lord, I'm in trouble. Please come
　　and help me!

15 "But what can I say?
You have promised to heal me.
And you yourself have done it.
Once I was proud and bitter.
But now I will live the rest of my life
　　free of pride.
16 Lord, people find the will to live
　　because you keep your
　　promises.
And my spirit also finds life in your
　　promises.
You brought me back to health.
You let me live.
17 I'm sure it was for my benefit
　　that I suffered such great pain.
You love me. You kept me
　　from going down into the pit of
　　death.
You have put all of my sins
　　behind your back.
18 People in the grave can't praise you.
Dead people can't sing praise to you.
Those who go down to the grave
　　can't hope for you to be faithful to
　　them.
19 It is those who are alive who praise
　　you.
And that's what I'm doing today.
Fathers tell their children
　　about how faithful you are.

20 "You will save me.
So we will sing and play music on
　　stringed instruments.
We will sing all the days of our lives
　　in your temple."

21 When Hezekiah was sick, I had said,
"Press some figs together. Spread them on
a piece of cloth. Apply them to Hezekiah's
boil. Then he'll get well again."
22 At that time Hezekiah had asked me,
"What will the miraculous sign be to
prove I'll go up to the LORD's temple?"

That's when the LORD had made the shadow go back ten steps.

Messengers Come From Babylon to Hezekiah

39 At that time Merodach-Baladan,
the king of Babylonia, sent Hezekiah letters and a gift. He had heard that
Hezekiah had been sick but had gotten
well again. Merodach-Baladan was the
son of Baladan.

2 Hezekiah gladly received the messengers. He showed them what was in his
storerooms. He showed them the silver
and gold. He took them to where the
spices and the fine olive oil were kept. He
showed them where he kept all of his
weapons. And he showed them all of his
treasures. In fact, he showed them everything that was in his palace and in his
whole kingdom.

3 Then I went to King Hezekiah. I asked
him, "What did those men say? Where
did they come from?"

"They came from a land far away," Hezekiah said. "They came to me from Babylon."

4 I asked, "What did they see in your
palace?"

"They saw everything in my palace,"
Hezekiah said. "I showed them all of my
treasures."

5 Then I said to Hezekiah, "Listen to the
message of the LORD who rules over all. He
says, 6 'You can be sure the time will come
when everything in your palace will be
carried off to Babylon. Everything the
kings before you have stored up until this
day will be taken away. There will not be
anything left,' says the LORD.
7 " 'Some of the members of your family
line will be taken away. They will be your
own flesh and blood. They will include
the children who will be born into your
family line in years to come. And they will
serve the king of Babylonia in his
palace.' "

8 "The message the LORD has spoken
through you is good," Hezekiah replied.
He thought, "There will be peace and safety while I'm still living."

God Comforts His People

40 "Comfort my people," says your
God.
"Comfort them.
2 Speak tenderly to the people of
　　Jerusalem.
Announce to them
that their hard service has been
　　completed.

Tell them that their sin has been
paid for.
Tell them I have punished them
enough
for all of their sins."

3 A messenger is calling out,
"In the desert prepare
the way for the LORD.
Make a straight road through it
for our God.
4 Every valley will be filled in.
Every mountain and hill will be
made level.
The rough ground will be smoothed
out.
The rocky places will be made flat.
5 Then the glory of the LORD will appear.
And everyone will see it.
The LORD has spoken."

6 Another messenger says, "Cry out."
And I said, "What should I cry?"

"Cry out, 'All people are like grass.
They don't last any longer than
flowers in the field.
7 The grass dries up. The flowers fall to
the ground.
That happens when the LORD makes
his wind blow on them.
So people are just like grass.
8 The grass dries up. The flowers fall to
the ground.
But what our God says will stand
forever.' "

9 Zion, you are bringing good news to
your people.
Go up on a high mountain and
announce it.
Jerusalem, you are bringing good news
to them.
Shout the message loudly.
Shout it out loud. Don't be afraid.
Say to the towns of Judah,
"Your God is coming!"
10 The LORD and King is coming with
power.
His powerful arm will rule for him.
He has set his people free.
He is bringing them back as his
reward.
He has won the battle over their
enemies.
11 He takes care of his flock like a
shepherd.
He gathers the lambs in his arms.
He carries them close to his heart.
He gently leads those that have little
ones.

12 Who has measured the oceans by
using the palm of his hand?
Who has used the width of his hand
to mark off the sky?
Who has measured out the dust of the
earth in a basket?
Who has weighed the mountains on
scales?
Who has weighed the hills in a
balance?
13 Who can ever understand what is in
the LORD's mind?
Who can ever give him advice?
14 Did the LORD have to ask anyone to
help him understand?
Did he have to ask someone to teach
him the right way?
Who taught him what he knows?
Who showed him how to
understand?

15 The nations are only a drop in a bucket
to him.
He considers them as nothing but
dust on the scales.
He weighs the islands as if they were
only fine dust.
16 Lebanon doesn't have enough trees to
keep his altar fires burning.
It doesn't have enough animals to
sacrifice as burnt offerings to
him.
17 To him, all of the nations don't
amount to anything.
He considers them to be worthless.
In fact, they are less than nothing in
his sight.

18 So who will you compare God to?
Is there any other god like him?
19 Will you compare him to a statue of a
god?
Any skilled worker can make a
statue.
Then another worker covers it with
gold
and makes silver chains for it.
20 But someone who is too poor to bring
that kind of offering
will choose some wood that won't
rot.
Then he looks for a skilled worker.
He pays the worker to make a statue
of a god that won't fall over.
21 Don't you know who made
everything?
Haven't you heard about him?
Hasn't it been told to you from the
beginning?
Haven't you understood it ever since
the earth was made?

²² God sits on his throne high above the
earth.
　Its people look like grasshoppers to
　　him.
　He spreads the heavens out like a cover.
　He sets it up like a tent to live in.
²³ He takes the power of princes away
　　from them.
　He reduces the rulers of this world to
　　nothing.
²⁴ They are planted.
　They are scattered like seeds.
　They put down roots in the ground.
　But as soon as that happens, God
　　blows on them and they
　　dry up.
　Then a windstorm sweeps them
　　away like straw.

BELIEVES ✝

[GOD] GIVES
STRENGTH TO THOSE
WHO ARE TIRED.

HE GIVES POWER TO
THOSE WHO ARE
WEAK.

EVEN YOUNG PEOPLE
BECOME WORN OUT
AND GET TIRED.

EVEN THE BEST OF
THEM TRIP AND FALL.

BUT THOSE WHO
TRUST IN THE LORD

WILL RECEIVE NEW
STRENGTH.

THEY WILL FLY AS
HIGH AS EAGLES.

THEY WILL RUN AND
NOT GET TIRED.

THEY WILL WALK AND
NOT GROW WEAK.
—— ISAIAH 40:29-31 ——

STRONG

²⁵ "So who will you compare me to?
　Who is equal to me?" says the Holy
　　One.
²⁶ Look up toward the sky.
　Who created everything you see?
　The LORD causes the stars to come out
　　at night one by one.
　He gives each one of them a name.
　His power and strength are great.
　So none of the stars is missing.
²⁷ Family of Jacob, why do you say,
　"The LORD doesn't notice our
　　condition"?
　People of Israel, why do you say,
　"Our God doesn't pay any attention
　　to our rightful claims"?
²⁸ Don't you know who made
　　everything?
　Haven't you heard about him?
　The LORD is the God who lives forever.
　He created everything on earth.
　He won't become worn out or get tired.
　No one will ever know how great his
　　understanding is.
²⁹ He gives strength to those who are
　　tired.
　He gives power to those who are
　　weak.
³⁰ Even young people become worn out
　　and get tired.
　Even the best of them trip and fall.
³¹ But those who trust in the LORD
　　will receive new strength.
　They will fly as high as eagles.
　They will run and not get tired.
　They will walk and not grow weak.

The LORD Helps Israel

41 The LORD says, "People who live
on the islands,
　come and stand quietly in front of
　　me.
　Let the nations gain new strength
　　in order to state their case.
　Let them come forward and speak.
　Let us go to court and find out who
　　is right.

² "Who has stirred up a king from the
　　east?
　Who has helped him win his
　　battles?
　I hand nations over to him.
　I bring kings under his control.
　He turns them into dust with his
　　sword.
　With his bow he turns them into
　　straw blowing in the wind.
³ He hunts them down. Then he moves
　　on unharmed.
　He travels so fast that his feet

don't seem to touch the ground.
⁴ Who has made that happen? Who has
carried it out?
Who has created all of the people
who have ever lived?
I, the Lord, have done it.
I was with the first of them.
And I will be with the last of them."

⁵ The people on the islands have seen
that king coming.
And it has made them afraid.
People tremble with fear from one
end of the earth to the other.
They come and gather together.
⁶ They help each other.
They say to one another, "Be
strong!"
⁷ One skilled worker makes a statue of a
god.
Another covers it with gold.
The first worker says to the second,
"You have done a good job."
Another worker smooths out the metal
with a hammer.
Still another gives the statue its final
shape.
The third worker says to the last one,
"You have done a good job."
Then they nail the statue down so it
won't fall over.

⁸ The Lord says, "People of Israel, you
are my servants.
Family of Jacob, I have chosen you.
You are the children of my friend
Abraham.
⁹ I gathered you from one end of the
earth to the other.
From the farthest places on earth I
brought you together.
I said, 'You are my servants.'
I have chosen you.
I have not turned my back on you.
¹⁰ So do not be afraid. I am with you.
Do not be terrified. I am your God.
I will make you strong and help you.
My powerful right hand will take
good care of you.
I always do what is right.

¹¹ "All those who are angry with you will
be put to shame.
And they will be dishonored.
Those who oppose you will be
destroyed.
And they will vanish.
¹² You might search for your enemies.
But you will not find them.
Those who go to war against you
will completely disappear.
¹³ I am the Lord your God.

I take hold of your right hand.
I say to you, 'Do not be afraid.
I will help you.'
¹⁴ Family of Jacob, you are as weak as a
worm.
But do not be afraid.
People of Israel, there are only a few of
you.
But do not be afraid.
I myself will help you," announces the
Lord.
He is the one who sets his people
free.
He is the Holy One of Israel.
¹⁵ He says, "I will make you into a
threshing sled.
It will be new and sharp.
It will have many teeth.
You will grind the mountains down
and crush them.
You will turn the hills into nothing
but straw.
¹⁶ You will toss them in the air.
A strong wind will catch them and
blow them away.
You will be glad because I will make
that happen.
You will praise me.
I am the Holy One of Israel.

¹⁷ "Those who are poor and needy search
for water.
But there isn't any.
Their tongues are dry because they
are thirsty.
But I will help them. I am the Lord.
I will not desert them.
I am Israel's God.
¹⁸ I will make streams flow on the bare
hilltops.

POWER-SURGE

BRAVE B

**SO DO NOT BE AFRAID.
I AM WITH YOU.**

**DO NOT BE TERRIFIED.
I AM YOUR GOD.**

**I WILL MAKE YOU
STRONG AND HELP
YOU.**

— **ISAIAH 41:10** —

STRONG

I will make springs come up in the
valleys.
I will turn the desert into pools of
water.
I will turn the dry and cracked
ground into flowing springs.
19 I will make trees grow in the desert.
I will plant cedar and acacia trees
there.
I will plant myrtle and olive trees
there.
I will make pine trees grow in the dry
and empty desert.
I will plant fir and cypress trees
there.
20 Then people will see and know
that my powerful hand has done it.
They will consider and understand
that I have created it.
I am the Holy One of Israel."

21 The LORD says to the nations and their
gods,
"State your case."
Jacob's King says to them,
"Prove your case to me.
22 Show me your facts. Tell me and my
people
what is going to happen.
Tell us what happened in the past.
Then we can check it out
and see if it is really true.
Or announce to us the things that will
take place.
23   Tell us what will happen in the days
ahead.
Then we will know that you are
gods.
Do something. It does not matter
whether it is good or bad.
Then we will be terrified and filled
with fear.
24 But you are less than nothing.
Your actions are completely
worthless.
I hate it when people worship you.

25 "I have stirred up a king
who will come from the north.
He lives in the east.
He will bring honor to me.
He walks all over rulers as if they were
mud.
He steps on them just as a potter
stomps on clay.
26 Which one of you gods said those
things
would happen before they did?
Who told us about them
so we could know them?
Who told us ahead of time?
Who told us so we could say,

'You are right'?
None of you told us about them.
None of you told us ahead of time.
In fact, no one heard you say
anything at all.
27 I was the first to tell Zion.
I said, 'Look! The people of Israel are
coming back!'
I sent a prophet to Jerusalem with
the good news.
28 I look, but there is no one
among the gods that can give me
advice.
None of them can answer
when I ask them the simplest
question.
29 So they are not really gods at all.
What they do does not amount to
anything.
They are as useless as wind.

The LORD's Chosen Servant

42 "Here is my servant. I take good
care of him.
I have chosen him. I am very pleased
with him.
I will put my Spirit on him.
He will make everything right
among the nations.
2 He will not shout or cry out.
He will not raise his voice in the
streets.
3 He will not break a bent twig.
He will not put out a dimly burning
flame.
He will be faithful and make
everything right.
4   He will not grow weak or lose hope.
He will not give up until he makes
everything right on the earth.
The islands will put their hope in his
law."

5 God created the heavens and spread
them out.
The LORD made the earth and
everything that grows on it.
He gives breath to its people.
He gives life to those who walk on it.
He says to his servant,
6 "I, the LORD, have chosen you to do
what is right.
I will take hold of your hand.
I will keep you safe.
You will put my covenant with the
people of Israel into effect.
And you will be a light for the other
nations.
7 You will open eyes that can't see.
You will set prisoners free.

Those who sit in darkness will come
out of their cells.

8 "I am the LORD. That is my name!
I will not let any other god share my
glory.
I will not let statues of gods share my
praise.
9 What I said would happen has taken
place.
Now I announce new things to you.
Before they even begin to happen,
I announce them to you."

A Song of Praise to the LORD

10 Sing a new song to the LORD.
Sing praise to him from one end of
the earth to the other.
Sing, you who sail out on the ocean.
Sing, all of you creatures in it.
Sing, you islands.
Sing, all of you who live there.
11 Let the desert and its towns raise their
voices.
Let those who live in the settlements
of Kedar be glad.
Let the people of Sela sing with joy.
Let them shout from the tops of the
mountains.
12 Let them give glory to the LORD.
Let them praise him in the islands.
13 The LORD will march out like a mighty
warrior.
He will stir up his anger like a soldier
getting ready to fight.
He will shout the battle cry.
And he will win the battle over his
enemies.

14 The LORD says, "For a long time I have
kept silent.
I have been calm and quiet.
But now, like a woman having a baby,
I cry out. I am struggling to breathe.
15 I will completely destroy the
mountains and hills.
I will dry up everything that grows
there.
I will turn rivers into dry land.
I will dry up the pools.
16 Israel is blind.
So I will lead them along paths
they had not known before.
I will guide them on roads they are not
familiar with.
I will turn the darkness into light as
they travel.
I will make the rough places
smooth.
Those are the things I will do.
I will not desert my people.
17 Some people trust in statues of gods.

They say to them, 'You are our gods.'
But they will be dishonored.
They will be put to shame.

Israel Can't See or Hear

18 "Israel, listen to me! You can hear,
but you do not understand.
Look to me! You can see,
but you do not know what you are
seeing.
19 The people of Israel serve me. But who
is more blind than they are?
Who is more deaf than the
messengers I send?
Who is more blind than those who
have committed themselves to
be faithful to me?
Who is more blind than my
servants?
20 Israel, you have seen many things.
But you have not paid any attention
to me.
Your ears are open.
But you do not hear anything I say."
21 The LORD wanted his people to see
how great and glorious his law is.
He wanted to show them
that he always does what is right.
22 Enemies have carried off everything
they own.
All of my people are trapped in pits
or hidden away in prisons.
They themselves have become like
stolen goods.
No one can save them.
They have been carried off.
And there is no one who will say,
"Send them back."

23 Family of Jacob, who among you will
listen to what I'm saying?
People of Israel, which one of you
will pay close attention in days
to come?
24 Who allowed you to be carried off like
stolen goods?
Who handed you over to robbers?
The LORD did it!
We have sinned against him.
Israel, you wouldn't follow his ways.
You didn't obey his law.
25 So he poured his burning anger out on
you.
He had many of you killed off in
battle.
You were surrounded by flames.
But you didn't realize what was
happening.
Many of you were destroyed.
But you didn't learn anything
from it.

The LORD Saves Israel

43 Family of Jacob, the LORD created you.

People of Israel, he formed you.
He says, "Do not be afraid.
I will set you free.
I will send for you by name.
You belong to me.
2 You will pass through deep waters.
But I will be with you.
You will pass through the rivers.
But their waters will not sweep over you.
You will walk through fire.
But you will not be burned.
The flames will not harm you.
3 I am the LORD your God.
I am the Holy One of Israel.
I am the one who saves you.
I will give up Egypt to set you free.
I will give up Cush and Seba for you.
4 You are priceless to me.
I love you and honor you.
So I will trade other people for you.
I will give up other nations to save your lives.
5 Do not be afraid. I am with you.
I will bring your people back from the east.
I will gather you from the west.
6 I will say to the north, 'Let them go!'
And I will say to the south, 'Do not hold them back.'
Bring my sons from far away.
Bring my daughters from the farthest places on earth.
7 Bring back everyone who belongs to me.
I created them to bring glory to me.
I formed them and made them."

8 Lead my people into court.
They have eyes but can't see.
Bring those who have ears but can't hear.
9 All of the nations are gathering together.
All of them are coming.
Which one of their gods said ahead of time
that the people of Israel would return?
Which of them told us anything at all about the past?
Let them bring in their witnesses to prove they were right.
Then others will hear them. And they will say,
"What they said is true."

BELIEVES ✝

I WANTED YOU TO KNOW ME AND BELIEVE IN ME.

I WANTED YOU TO UNDERSTAND THAT I AM THE ONE AND ONLY GOD.

BEFORE ME, THERE WAS NO OTHER GOD AT ALL.

AND THERE WILL NOT BE ANY GOD AFTER ME.

I AM THE ONE AND ONLY LORD.

I AM THE ONLY ONE WHO CAN SAVE YOU.
— ISAIAH 43:10-11 —

10 "People of Israel, you are my witnesses," announces the LORD.
"I have chosen you to be my servants.
I wanted you to know me and believe in me.
I wanted you to understand that I am the one and only God.
Before me, there was no other god at all.
And there will not be any god after me.
11 I am the one and only LORD.
I am the only one who can save you.
12 I have made known what would happen.
I told you about it. And I saved you.
I did it. It was not some other god you worship.
You are my witnesses that I am God," announces the LORD.
13 "And that is not all! I have always been God,
and I always will be.
No one can save people from my powerful hand.

When I do something, who can
    undo it?"

The LORD Forgives Israel but Also Punishes Them

¹⁴ The LORD sets his people free.
    He is the Holy One of Israel. He says,
    "People of Israel, I will send an army to
        Babylon to save you.
    I will cause all of the Babylonians to
        run away.
    They will try to escape in the ships
        they were so proud of.
¹⁵ I am your LORD and King.
    I am your Holy One.
    I created you."

¹⁶ Long ago the LORD opened
    a way for his people to go through
        the Red Sea.
    He made a path through the mighty
        waters.
¹⁷ He caused Egypt to send out its
        chariots and horses.
    He sent its entire army to its death.
    Its soldiers lay down there.
    They never got up again.
    They were destroyed.
    They were blown out like a dimly
        burning flame.
    But the LORD says,
¹⁸ "Forget the things that happened in
        the past.
    Do not keep on thinking about
        them.
¹⁹ I am about to do something new.
    It is beginning to happen even now.
    Don't you see it coming?
    I am going to make a way for you to go
        through the desert.
    I will make streams of water in the
        dry and empty land.
²⁰ Even wild dogs and owls honor me.
    That is because I provide water in
        the desert
    for my people to drink.
    I cause streams to flow in the dry and
        empty land
    for my chosen ones.
²¹ I do it for the people I made for myself.
    I want them to sing praise to me.

²² "Family of Jacob, you have not prayed
        to me as you should.
    People of Israel, you have not even
        begun to get tired while doing
        it.
²³ You have not brought me sheep for
        burnt offerings.
    You have not honored me with your
        sacrifices.
    I have not loaded you down

by requiring grain offerings.
    I have not made you tired
    by requiring you to burn incense.
²⁴ But you have not bought any
        sweet-smelling cane for me.
    You have not given me the fattest
        parts
    of your animal sacrifices.
    Instead, you have loaded me down
        with your sins.
    You have made me tired with the
        wrong things you have done.

²⁵ "I am the one who wipes out your
        lawless acts.
    I do it because of who I am.
    I will not remember your sins
        anymore.
²⁶ But let us go to court together.
    Remind me of what you have done.
    State your case.
    Prove to me that you are not guilty.
²⁷ Your father Jacob sinned.
    Your priests and prophets refused to
        obey me.
²⁸ So I will put the high officials of your
        temple to shame.
    I will let Jacob's family be totally
        destroyed.
    And I will let people make fun of
        Israel.

The LORD Chooses Israel

44 "Family of Jacob, listen to me.
    You are my servants.
    People of Israel, I have chosen you.
² I made you. I formed you when you
        were born as a nation.
    I will help you.
    So listen to what I am saying.
    Family of Jacob, do not be afraid. You
        are my servants.
    People of Israel, I have chosen you.
³ I will pour water out on the thirsty
        land.
    I will make streams flow on the dry
        ground.
    I will pour out my Spirit on your
        children.
    I will pour out my blessing on their
        children after them.
⁴ They will spring up like grass in a
        meadow.
    They will grow like poplar trees near
        flowing streams.
⁵ Some will say, 'We belong to the LORD.'
    Others will call themselves by
        Jacob's name.
    Still others will write on their hands,
        'We belong to the Lord.'

And they will be called by the name
of Israel.

Worship the LORD, Not Other Gods

6 "I am Israel's King. I set them free.
I am the LORD who rules over all.
So listen to what I am saying.
I am the First and the Last.
I am the one and only God.
7 Who is like me? Let him come forward
and speak boldly.
Let him tell me everything that has
happened
since I created my people long ago.
And let him tell me what has not
happened yet.
Let him announce ahead of time
what is going to take place.
8 Do not tremble with fear. Do not be
afraid.
Didn't I announce everything that
has happened?
Didn't I tell you about it long ago?
You are my witnesses. Is there any
other God but me?
No! There is no other Rock. I do not
know even one."

9 Those who make statues of gods don't
amount to anything.
And the statues they think so much
of are worthless.
Those who would speak up for them
are blind.
They don't know anything.
So they will be put to shame.
10 People make statues of gods.
But those gods can't do them any
good.
11 People like that will be put to shame.
Those who make statues of gods are
mere men.
Let all of them come together and state
their case.
They will be terrified and put to
shame.

12 A blacksmith gets his tool.
He uses it to shape metal over the
burning coals.
He uses his hammers to make a statue
of a god.
He forms it with his powerful arm.
He gets hungry and loses his strength.
He doesn't drink any water.
He gets weaker and weaker.
13 A carpenter measures a piece of wood
with a line.
He draws a pattern on it with a
marker.
He cuts out a statue with sharp tools.
He marks it with compasses.

He shapes it into the form of a
handsome man.
He does all of that so he can put it in
a temple.
14 He cuts down a cedar tree.
Or perhaps he takes a cypress or an
oak tree.
It might be a tree that grew in the
forest.
Or it might be a pine tree he planted.
And the rain made it grow.
15 Man gets wood from trees for fuel.
He uses some of it to warm himself.
He starts a fire and bakes bread.
But he also uses some of it to make a
god and worship it.
He makes a statue of a god and bows
down to it.
16 He burns half of the wood in the fire.
He prepares a meal over it.
He cooks meat over it.
He eats until he is full.
He also warms himself. He says,
"Good! I'm getting warm.
The fire is nice and hot."
17 From the rest of the wood he makes a
statue.
It becomes his god.
He bows down and worships it.
He prays to it. He says,
"Save me. You are my god."
18 People like that don't even know what
they are doing.
Their eyes are shut so that they can't
see the truth.
Their minds are closed so that they
can't understand it.
19 No one even stops to think about this.
No one has any sense or
understanding.
If anyone did, he would say,
"I used half of the wood for fuel.
I even baked bread over the fire.
I cooked meat. Then I ate it.
Should I now make a statue of a god
out of the wood that's left over?
Should I bow down to a block of
wood?
The LORD would hate that."
20 That's as foolish as eating ashes!
The mind of someone like that
has led him down the wrong path.
He can't save himself.
He can't bring himself to say,
"This thing I'm holding in my right
hand
isn't really a god at all."

21 The LORD says, "Family of Jacob,
remember those things.
People of Israel, you are my servants.

I have made you. You are my servants.
Israel, I will not forget you.
²² I will sweep your sins away as if they
were a cloud.
I will blow them away as if they were
the morning mist.
Return to me.
Then I will set you free."

²³ Sing with joy, you heavens!
The LORD does wonderful things.
Shout out loud, you earth!
Burst into song, you mountains!
Sing, you forests and all of your
trees!
The LORD sets the family of Jacob free.
He shows his glory in Israel.

People Will Live in Jerusalem Again

²⁴ The LORD says,
"People of Israel, I set you free.
I formed you when you were born as
a nation.

"I am the LORD. I have made
everything.
I alone spread out the heavens.
I formed the earth by myself.

²⁵ "Some prophets are not really prophets
at all.
I show that their miraculous signs
are fake.
I make those who practice evil magic
look foolish.
I destroy the learning of those who
think they are wise.
Their knowledge does not make any
sense at all.
²⁶ I make the words of my servants the
prophets come true.
I carry out what my messengers say
will happen.

"I say about Jerusalem,
'My people will live there again.'
I say about the towns of Judah,
'They will be rebuilt.'
I say about their broken-down
buildings,
'I will make them like new again.'
²⁷ I say to the deep waters,
'Dry up. Let your streams become
dry.'
²⁸ I say about Cyrus,
'He is my shepherd.
He will accomplish everything I
want him to.
He will say about Jerusalem,
"Let it be rebuilt."
And he will say about the temple,
"Let its foundations be laid." '

45 "Cyrus is my anointed king.
I take hold of his right hand.
I give him the power
to bring nations under his control.
I help him strip kings of their power
to go to war against him.
I break city gates open so he can go
through them.
I say to him,
² 'I will march out ahead of you.
I will make the mountains level.
I will break down bronze gates.
I will cut through their heavy iron
bars.
³ I will give you treasures that are hidden
away in dark places.
I will give you riches that are stored
up in secret places.
Then you will know that I am the
LORD.
I am the God of Israel.
I am sending for you by name.
⁴ Cyrus, I am sending for you by name.
I am doing it for the good of the
family of Jacob.
They are my servants.
I am doing it for Israel.
They are my chosen people.
You do not know anything about me.
But I am giving you a title of honor.
⁵ I am the LORD. There is no other LORD.
I am the one and only God.
You do not know anything about me.
But I will make you strong.

POWER–SURGE

STRONG

I AM THE LORD. THERE
IS NO OTHER LORD.

I AM THE ONE AND
ONLY GOD...

I WILL MAKE YOU
STRONG.
—— ISAIAH 45:5 ——

⁶ Then people will know there is no God
but me.
Everyone from where the sun rises
in the east
to where it sets in the west will know
it.
I am the LORD.
There is no other LORD.
⁷ I cause light to shine. I also create
darkness.

I bring good times. I also create hard
    times.
I do all of those things. I am the
    Lord.

8 " 'Rain down godliness, you heavens
    above.
Let the clouds shower it down.
Let the earth open wide to receive it.
Let freedom spring to life.
Let godliness grow along with it.
I have created all of those things.
I am the Lord.' "

9 How terrible it will be for anyone who
    argues with his Maker!
He is like a broken piece of pottery
    lying on the ground.
Does clay say to a potter,
    "What are you making?"
Does a pot say,
    "You don't have any skill"?
10 How terrible it will be for anyone who
    says to his father,
    "Why did you give me life?"
How terrible for anyone who says to
    his mother,
    "Why have you brought me into the
    world?"

11 The Lord is the Holy One of Israel.
    He made them.
He says to them,
    "Are you asking me about what will
    happen to my children?
    Are you telling me what I should do
    with what my hands have
    made?
12 I made the earth.
    I created man to live there.
My own hands spread out the heavens.
    I put all of the stars in their places.
13 I will stir up Cyrus and help him win
    his battles.
I will make all of his roads straight.
He will rebuild Jerusalem.
    My people have been taken away
    from their country.
    But he will set them free.
I will not pay him to do it.
    He will not receive a reward for it,"
says the Lord who rules over all.

14 The Lord says to the people of Jerusalem,

    "You will get everything Egypt
    produces.
    You will receive everything the
    people of Cush
and the tall Sabeans get in trade.
    All of it will belong to you.

And all of those people will walk
    behind you as slaves.
They will be put in chains and come
    over to you.
They will bow down to you.
    They will admit,
'God is with you.
    There is no other God.' "

15 You are a God who hides yourself.
    You are the God of Israel. You save
    us.
16 All those who make statues of gods will
    be put to shame.
They will be dishonored.
They will be led away in shame
    together.
17 But the Lord will save Israel.
    He will save them forever.
They will never be put to shame or
    dishonored.
That will be true for all time to
    come.

18 The Lord created the heavens.
    He is God.
He formed the earth and made it.
    He set it firmly in place.
He didn't create it to be empty.
    Instead, he formed it for people to
    live on.
He says, "I am the Lord.
    There is no other Lord.
19 I have not spoken in secret.
    I have not spoken from a dark place.
I have not said to Jacob's people,
    'It is useless to look for me.'
I am the Lord. I always speak the truth.
    I always say what is right.

20 "Come together, you people of the
    nations
    who escaped from Babylonia.
    Gather together and come into
    court.
Only people who do not know
    anything
    would carry around gods that are
    made out of wood.
    They pray to gods that can't save
    them.
21 Tell me what will happen. State your
    case.
    Talk it over together.
Who spoke long ago about what would
    happen?
    Who said it a long time ago?
I did. I am the Lord.
    I am the one and only God.
I always do what is right.
    I am the one who saves.
    There is no God but me.

22 "All of you who live anywhere on
   earth,
      turn to me and be saved.
   I am God. There is no other God.
23 I have made a promise with an oath in
      my own name.
   I have spoken with complete
      honesty.
   I will not take back a single word. I
      said,
   'Everyone's knee will bow down to me.
   Everyone's mouth will take an oath
      in my name.'
24 They will say, 'The LORD always does
      what is right.
   Only he can make us strong.' "
   All those who have been angry with
      the LORD will come to him.
   And they will be put to shame.
25 But the LORD will help all of the people
      of Israel.
   He will make them right with
      himself.
   And they will praise him.

There Is No Other God

46 The gods Bel and Nebo are
   brought down in shame.
   The statues of them are being carried
      away on the backs of animals.
   They used to be carried around by the
      people who worshiped them.
   But now they've become a heavy
      load for tired animals.
2 Bel and Nebo are brought down in
      shame together.
   They aren't able to save their own
      statues.
   They themselves are carried off as
      prisoners.

3 The LORD says, "Family of Jacob, listen
      to me.
   Pay attention, you people of Israel
      who are left alive.
   I have taken good care of you since
      your life began.
   I have carried you since you were
      born as a nation.
4 I will continue to carry you even when
      you are old.
   I will take good care of you even
      when your hair is gray.
   I have made you. And I will carry
      you.
   I will take care of you. And I will save
      you.
   I am the LORD.

5 "Who will you compare me to?
   Who is equal to me?
   What am I like?

   Who can you compare me to?
6 Some people pour gold out of their
      bags.
   They weigh out silver on the scales.
   They hire someone who works with
      gold to make it into a god.
   They bow down to it and worship it.
7 They lift it up on their shoulders and
      carry it.
   They set it up in its place. And there
      it stands.
   It can't move from that spot.
   Someone might cry out to it.
   But it does not answer him.
   It can't save him from his troubles.
8 So remember that, you who refuse to
      obey me.
   Keep it in your minds and hearts.

9 "Remember what happened in the
      past.
   Think about what took place long
      ago.
   I am God. There is no other God.
   I am God. There is no one like me.
10 Before something even happens, I
      announce how it will end.
   In fact, from times long ago I
      announced what was still to
      come.
   I say, 'My plan will succeed.
   I will do anything I want to do.'
11 I will send for a man from the east to
      carry out my plan.
   From a land far away, he will come
      like a bird that eats dead bodies.
   I will bring about what I have said.
   I will do what I have planned.
12 Listen to me, you stubborn people.
   Pay attention, you who refuse to do
      what is right.
13 The time is almost here for me to make
      everything right.
   It is not far away.
   The time for me to save you will not
      be put off.
   I will save the city of Zion.
   I will bring honor to Israel.

Babylon Will Fall

47 "City of Babylon,
   go down and sit in the dust.
   Leave your throne and sit on the
      ground.
   City of the Babylonians,
      your life will not be comfortable
      and easy anymore.
2 Get millstones and grind some flour
      like a female slave.
   Take your veil off.
   Lift your skirts up. Make your legs bare.

Wade through the streams.
3 Everyone will see your naked body.
   Everyone will see your shame.
I will pay you back for what you did.
   I will not spare any of your people."

4 The one who sets us free is the Holy
   One of Israel.
   His name is The LORD Who Rules
   Over All.

5 The LORD says, "City of the
   Babylonians,
   go into a dark prison and sit there
   quietly.
You will not be called
   the queen of kingdoms anymore.
6 I was angry with my people.
   I treated them as if they did not
   belong to me.
I handed them over to you.
   And you did not show them any
   pity.
You even placed heavy loads on their
   old people.
7   You said, 'I will continue to be queen
   forever!'
But you did not think about what you
   were doing.
   You did not consider how things
   might turn out.

8 "So listen, you who love pleasure.
   You think you are safe and secure.
You say to yourself,
   'I am like a god.
   No one is greater than I am.'
I'll never be a widow.
   And my children will never be taken
   away from me.'
9 But both of those things will happen
   to you in a moment.
   They will take place on a single day.
You will lose your children.
   And you will become a widow.
That is what will happen to you.
   All of your evil magic
   and powerful spells will not save
   you.

10 You have felt secure in your evil ways.
   You have said, 'No one sees what I'm
   doing.'
Your wisdom and knowledge lead you
   down the wrong path.
You say to yourself,
   'I am like a god. No one is greater
   than I am.'
11 So horrible trouble will come on you.
   You will not know how to use your
   evil magic to make it go away.
Great trouble will fall on you.

No amount of money can keep it
   away.
Something terrible will happen to you
   all at once.
   You will not see it coming ahead of
   time.

12 "So keep on casting your magic spells.
   Keep on practicing your evil magic.
   You have been doing those things
   ever since you were a child.
Perhaps they will help you.
   Maybe they will scare your enemies
   away.
13 All of the advice you have received
   has only worn you out!
   Let those who study the heavens
   come forward.
They claim to know what is going to
   happen
   by watching the stars every month.
So let them save you from the trouble
   that is coming on you.
14 They are just like straw.
   Fire will burn them up.
They can't even save themselves
   from the powerful flames.
They are not like coals that can warm
   anyone.
   They are not like a fire to sit by.
15 They can't do you any good.
   You have done business with them
   ever since you were a child.
   You have always asked them for
   advice.
All of them are bewildered and
   continue in their own ways.
   None of them can save you."

Israel Is Stubborn

48 People of Jacob, listen to me.
   You are called by the name of
   Israel.
You come from the family line of
   Judah.
You take oaths in the name of the
   LORD.
   You pray to Israel's God.
But you aren't honest.
   You don't mean what you say.
2 You call yourselves citizens of the holy
   city of Jerusalem.
You say you depend on Israel's God.
   His name is The LORD Who Rules
   Over All. He says,
3 "Long ago I told you ahead of time
   what would happen.
   I announced it and made it known.
Then all of a sudden I acted.
   And those things took place.
4 I knew how stubborn you were.

Your neck was as unbending as iron.
Your forehead was as hard as bronze.
5 So I told you those things long ago.
Before they happened I announced
them to you.
I did it so you would not be able to say,
'My statues of gods did them.
My wooden and metal gods made
them happen.'
6 You have heard me tell you those
things.
Think about all of them.
Won't you admit they have taken
place?

"From now on I will tell you about new
things that will happen.
I have not made them known to you
before.
7 Those things are taking place right
now.
They did not happen long ago.
You have not heard of them before
today.
So you can't say,
'Oh, yes. I already knew about
them.'
8 You have not heard or understood
what I said.
Your ears have been plugged up for a
long time.
I knew very well that you would turn
against me.
From the day you were born, you
have refused to obey me.
9 For the honor of my own name I put
off showing my anger.
I hold it back from you so people
will continue to praise me.
I do not want to destroy you.
10 I have put you to the test in the
furnace of suffering.
I have tried to make you pure.
But I did not use as much heat as it
takes to make silver pure.
11 I tried to purify you for my own honor.
I did it for the honor of my name.
How can I let myself be dishonored?
I will not give up my glory to any
other god.

Israel Is Set Free

12 "Family of Jacob, listen to me.
People of Israel, pay attention.
I have chosen you.
I am the First and the Last.
I am the LORD.
13 With my own hand I laid the
foundations of the earth.
With my right hand I spread out the
heavens.

When I send for them,
they come and stand ready to obey
me.

14 "People of Israel, come together and
listen to me.
What other god has said ahead of
time that certain things would
happen?
I have chosen Cyrus.
He will carry out my plans against
Babylon.
He will use his powerful arm against
the Babylonians.
15 I myself have spoken.
I have chosen him to carry out my
purpose.
I will bring him to Babylon.
He will succeed in what I tell him
to do.

16 "Come close and listen to me.

"From the first time I said Cyrus was
coming,
I did not do it in secret.
When he comes, I will be there."

The LORD and King has filled me with
his Spirit.
People of Israel, he has sent me to
you.

17 The LORD is the Holy One of Israel.
He sets his people free. He says to
them,
"I am the LORD your God.
I teach you what is best for you.
I direct you in the way you should
go.
18 I wish you would pay attention to my
commands.
If you did, peace would flow over
you like a river.
Holiness would sweep over you like
the waves of the ocean.
19 Your family would be like the sand.
Your children after you would be as
many as the grains of sand by
the sea.
It would be impossible to count
them.
I would always accept the members of
your family line.
They would never be cut off or
destroyed."

20 People of Israel, leave Babylon!
Hurry up and get away from the
Babylonians!
Here is what I want you to announce.
Make it known with shouts of joy.
Send the news out from one end of the
earth to the other.

Say, "The Lord has set Jacob's people
free.
They are his servants."
21 They didn't get thirsty when he led
them through the deserts.
He made water flow out of the rock
for them.
He broke the rock open,
and water came out of it.

22 "There is no peace for those who are
evil," says the Lord.

The Servant of the Lord

49 People who live on the islands,
listen to me.
Pay attention, you nations far away.
Before I was born the Lord chose me to
serve him.
He appointed me by name.
2 He made my words like a sharp sword.
He hid me in the palm of his hand.
He made me into a sharpened arrow.
He took good care of me and kept
me safe.
3 He said to me, "You are my true
servant Israel.
I will show my glory through you."
4 But I said, "In spite of my hard work,
I feel as if I haven't accomplished
anything.
I've used up all of my strength.
It seems as if everything I've done is
worthless.
But the Lord will give me what I
should receive.
My God will reward me."

5 The Lord formed me in my mother's
body to be his servant.
He wanted me to bring the family of
Jacob back to him.
He wanted me to gather the people of
Israel to himself.
The Lord will honor me.
My God will give me strength.

6 The Lord says to me,

"It is not enough for you as my servant
to bring the tribes of Jacob back to
their land.
It is not enough for you to bring back
the people of Israel I have kept alive.
I will also make you a light for other
nations.
Then you will make it possible for
the whole world to be saved."

7 The Lord sets his people free.
He is the Holy One of Israel.

He speaks to his servant, who is looked
down on and hated by the
nations.
He speaks to the servant of rulers.
He says to him,
"Kings will see you and rise up to
honor you.
Princes will see you and bow down
to show you their respect.
I am the Lord. I am faithful.
I am the Holy One of Israel.
I have chosen you."

Israel Is Brought Back to Their Land

8 The Lord says to his servant,

"When it is time to show you my favor,
I will answer your prayers.
When it is time to save you, I will
help you.
I will keep you safe.
You will put my covenant with the
people of Israel into effect.
Then their land will be made like new
again.
Each tribe will be sent back to its
territory that was left empty.
9 I want you to say to the prisoners,
'Come out.'
Tell those who are in their dark cells,
'You are free!'

"On their way home they will eat
beside the roads.
They will find plenty to eat on every
bare hill.
10 They will not get hungry or thirsty.
The heat from the desert sun will
not beat down on them.
The One who shows his tender love to
them will guide them.
Like a shepherd, he will lead them
beside springs of water.
11 I will make roads across the
mountains.
I will build wide roads for my
people.
12 They will come from far away.
Some of them will come from the
north.
Others will come from the west.
Still others will come from Aswan in
the south."

13 Shout with joy, you heavens!
Be glad, you earth!
Burst into song, you mountains!
The Lord will comfort his people.
He will show his tender love to those
who are suffering.

14 But the city of Zion said, "The Lord has
deserted me.
The Lord has forgotten me."

15 The Lord answers, "Can a mother
forget the baby
who is nursing at her breast?
Can she stop showing her tender love
to the child who was born to her?
She might forget her child.
But I will not forget you.
16 I have written your name on the palms
of my hands.
Your walls are never out of my sight.
17 Your people will hurry back.
Those who destroyed you so
completely will leave you.
18 Look up. Look all around you.
All of your people are getting
together
to come back to you.
You can be sure that I live,"
announces the Lord.
"And you can be just as sure that your
people
will be like decorations you will
wear.
Like a bride, you will wear them
proudly.

19 "Zion, you were destroyed. Your land
was left empty.
It was turned into a dry and empty
desert.
But now you will be too small to hold
all of your people.
And those who destroyed you will be
far away.
20 The children who were born during
your time of sorrow
will speak to you. They will say,
'This city is too small for us.
Give us more space to live in.'
21 Then you will say to yourself,
'Whose children are these?
I lost my children.
And I couldn't have any more.
My children were taken far away from
me.
And no one wanted them.
Who brought these children up?
I was left all alone.
So where have these children come
from?' "

22 The Lord and King continues,

"I will call out to the nations.
I will give a signal to them.
They will bring back your sons in their
arms.

They will carry your daughters on
their shoulders.
23 Their kings will become like fathers to
you.
Their queens will be like mothers
who nurse you.
They will bow down to you with their
faces toward the ground.
They will kiss the dust at your feet to
show you their respect.
Then you will know that I am the
Lord.
Those who put their hope in me will
not be ashamed."

24 Can goods that were stolen by soldiers
be taken away from them?
Can prisoners be set free from the
powerful Babylonians?

25 "Yes, they can," the Lord answers.

"Prisoners will be taken away from
soldiers.
Stolen goods will be taken back from
the powerful Babylonians.
Zion, I will fight against those who
fight against you.
And I will save your people.
26 I will make those who beat you down
eat the flesh of others.
They will drink blood and get drunk
on it as if it were wine.
Then everyone on earth will know
that I am the one who saves you.
I am the Lord. I set you free.
I am the Mighty One of Jacob."

The Lord's Servant Obeys Him

50 The Lord says to the people in Jerusalem,

"Do you think I divorced your people
before you?
Is that why I sent them away?
If it is, show me the letter of divorce.
I did not sell you into slavery to pay
someone I owe.
You were sold because you sinned
against me.
Your people were sent away because
of their lawless acts.
2 When I came to save you, why didn't
anyone welcome me?
When I called out to you, why didn't
anyone answer me?
Wasn't my arm powerful enough to set
you free?
Wasn't I strong enough to save you?
I dry up the sea with a single
command.
I turn rivers into a desert.

Then fish rot because they do not have
    any water.
  They die because they are thirsty.
3 I make the sky turn dark.
  It looks as if it is dressed in black
    clothes."

4 The Lord and King has taught me
    what to say.
  He has taught me how to help those
    who are tired.
  He wakes me up every morning.
  He makes me want to listen like a
    good student.
5 The Lord and King has unplugged my
    ears.
  I've always obeyed him.
  I haven't turned away from him.
6 I let my enemies beat me on my bare
    back.
  I let them pull the hair out of my
    beard.
  I didn't turn my face away
    when they made fun of me and spit
      on me.
7 The Lord and King helps me.
  He won't let me be dishonored.
  So I've made up my mind to keep on
    serving him.
  I know he won't let me be put to
    shame.
8 He is near. He will prove I haven't done
    anything wrong.
  So who will bring charges against
    me?
  Let's face each other in court!
  Who can bring charges against me?
  Let him come and face me!
9 The Lord and King helps me.
  So who will judge me?
  My enemies will be like clothes that
    moths have eaten up.
  They will disappear.

10 Does anyone among you have respect
    for the Lord?
  Does anyone obey the message of
    the Lord's servant?
  Let the person who walks in the dark
    trust in the Lord.
  Let the one who doesn't have any light
    to guide him
    depend on his God.
11 But all of you sinners who light fires
    should go ahead and walk in their
      light.
  You who carry flaming torches
    should walk in their light.
  Here's what I'm going to do to you.
  I'll make you lie down in great pain.

Zion Will Be Saved

51 The Lord says, "Listen to me, you
    who want to do what is right.
  Pay attention, you who look to me.
  Consider the rock you were cut out of.
  Think about the rock pit you were
    dug from.
2 Consider Abraham. He is the father of
    your people.
  Think about Sarah. She is your
    mother.
  When I chose Abraham, he did not
    have any children.
  But I blessed him and gave him
    many of them.
3 You can be sure that I will comfort
    Zion's people.
  I will look with loving concern on
    all of their destroyed buildings.
  I will make their deserts like Eden.
  I will make their dry and empty land
    like my very own garden.
  Joy and gladness will be there.
  People will sing and give thanks
    to me.

4 "Listen to me, my people.
  Pay attention, my nation.
  My law will go out to the nations.
  I make everything right.
  That will be a guiding light for them.
5 The time for me to set you free is near.
  I will soon save you.
  My powerful arm will make
    everything right among the
      nations.
  The islands will put their hope in me.
  They will wait for my powerful arm
    to act.
6 Look up toward the heavens.
  Then look at the earth.
  The heavens will vanish like smoke.
  The earth will wear out like clothes.
  Those who live there will die like
    flies.
  But I will save you forever.
  My saving power will never end.

7 "Listen to me, you who know what is
    right.
  Pay attention, you who have my law
    in your hearts.
  Do not be afraid when mere people
    make fun of you.
  Do not be terrified when they laugh
    at you.
8 They will be like clothes that moths
    have eaten up.
  They will be like wool that worms
    have chewed up.
  But my saving power will last forever.
  I will save you for all time to come."

⁹ Wake up! Lord, wake up! Dress your
powerful arm with strength
as if it were your clothes.
Wake up, just as you did in the past.
Wake up, as you did long ago.
Didn't you cut Rahab to pieces?
Didn't you stab that sea monster to
death?
¹⁰ Didn't you dry up the Red Sea?
Didn't you dry up those deep
waters?
You made a road on the bottom of that
sea.
Then those who were set free went
across.
¹¹ Those the Lord has saved will return to
their land.
They will sing as they enter the city
of Zion.
Joy that lasts forever will be like
beautiful crowns on their
heads.
They will be filled with gladness and
joy.
Sorrow and sighing will be gone.

¹² The Lord says to his people,
"I comfort you because of who I am.
Why are you afraid of mere men?
They are only human beings.
They are like grass that dries up.
¹³ How can you forget me? I made you.
I spread out the heavens.
I laid the foundations of the earth.
Why are you terrified every day?
Is it because those who are angry
with you are crushing you?
Is it because they are trying to
destroy you?
Their anger can't harm you anymore.
¹⁴ You prisoners who are so afraid will
soon be set free.
You will not die in your prison cells.
You will not go without food.
¹⁵ I am the Lord your God.
I stir up the ocean. I make its waves
roar.
My name is The Lord Who Rules
Over All.
¹⁶ I have put my words in your mouth.
I have kept you safe in the palm of
my hand.
I set the heavens in place.
I laid the foundations of the earth.
I say to Zion, 'You are my people.' "

The Cup of the Lord's Burning Anger

¹⁷ Wake up, Jerusalem!
Wake up! Get up!

The Lord has handed you the cup of
his burning anger.
And you have drunk from it.
That cup makes men unsteady on their
feet.
And you have drunk from it to the
very last drop.
¹⁸ None of the children who were born to
you
are left to guide you.
None of the children you brought up
are left to lead you by the hand.
¹⁹ Nothing but trouble has come to you.
You have been wiped out and
destroyed.
And you have suffered hunger and
war.
No one feels sorry for you.
No one can comfort you.
²⁰ Your children have fainted.
They lie helpless at every street
corner.
They are like antelope that have
been caught in a net.
They have felt the full force of the
Lord's burning anger.
Jerusalem, your God had to warn
them strongly.

²¹ So listen to me, you suffering people of
Jerusalem.
You have been made drunk, but not
by drinking wine.
²² Your Lord and King speaks.
He is your God.
He stands up for his people. He says,
"I have taken from you the cup of
my burning anger.
It made you unsteady on your feet.
But you will never drink
from that cup again.
²³ Instead, I will give it to those who
made you suffer.
They said to you,
'Fall down flat on the ground.
Then we can walk all over you.'
And that is exactly what you did.
You made your back like a street to
be walked on."

52

Wake up! Zion, wake up!
Dress yourself with strength as if
it were your clothes.
Holy city of Jerusalem,
put on your clothes of glory.
Those who haven't been circumcised
will never enter you again.
Neither will those who are
"unclean."
² Get up, Jerusalem! Shake off your dust.
Take your place on your throne.

Captured people of Zion,
  remove the chains from your neck.

3 The LORD says,

"When you were sold as slaves, no one
    paid anything for you.
  Now no one will pay any money to
    set you free."

4 The LORD and King continues,

"Long ago my people went down to
    Egypt.
  They lived there for a while.
  Later, Assyria crushed them without
    any reason.

5 "Now look at what has happened to
them," announces the LORD.

"Once again my people have been
    taken away.
  And no one paid anything for them.
  Those who rule over them brag about
    it,"
                announces the LORD.
"All day long without stopping,
  people speak evil things against my
    name.
  6 So the day will come when my people
    will really know the meaning of
    my name.
  They will know what kind of God I
    am.
  They will know that I told them ahead
    of time they would return to
    their land.
  They will know that it was I."

7 What a beautiful sight it is
  to see messengers coming with good
    news!
How beautiful to see them coming
    down from the mountains
  with a message about peace!
How wonderful it is when they bring
    the good news
  that we are saved!
How wonderful when they say to Zion,
  "Your God rules!"

8 Listen! Those on guard duty are
    shouting out the message.
  With their own eyes
  they see the LORD returning to Zion.
  So they shout with joy.

9 Burst into songs of joy together,
  you broken-down buildings in
    Jerusalem.
  The LORD has comforted his people.
  He has set Jerusalem free.

10 The LORD will use the power of his holy
    arm to save his people.
  All of the nations will see him do it.

Everyone from one end of the earth
  to the other will see it.

11 You who carry the articles that belong
    to the LORD's temple, leave
    Babylon!
  Leave it! Get out of there!
  Don't touch anything that isn't pure
    and clean.
  Come out of Babylon and be pure.

12 But this time you won't have to leave
    in a hurry.
  You won't have to rush away.
  The LORD will go ahead of you and lead
    you.
  The God of Israel will follow behind
    you and guard you.

The Suffering and Glory
of the LORD's Servant

13 The LORD says, "My servant will act
    wisely and accomplish his task.
  He will be highly honored. He will
    be greatly respected.

14 Many people were shocked when they
    saw him.
  He was so scarred that he did not
    look like a man at all.
  His body was so twisted that he did
    not look like a human being
    anymore.

15 But many nations will be surprised
    when they see what he has
    done.
  Kings will be so amazed that they
    will not be able to say anything.
  They will understand things they were
    never told about.
  They will know the meaning of
    things they never heard about."

53 Who has believed what we've
    been saying?
  Who has seen the LORD's saving
    power?

2 His servant grew up like a tender
    young plant.
  He grew like a root coming up out of
    dry ground.
  He didn't have any beauty or majesty
    that made us notice him.
  There wasn't anything special about
    the way he looked that drew us
    to him.

3 Men looked down on him. They didn't
    accept him.
  He knew all about sorrow and
    suffering.
  He was like someone people turn their
    faces away from.
  We looked down on him. We didn't
    have any respect for him.

4 He suffered the things we should have
   suffered.
   He took on himself the pain that
      should have been ours.
But we thought God was punishing
   him.
   We thought God was wounding him
      and making him suffer.
5 But the servant was pierced because we
      had sinned.
   He was crushed because we had
      done what was evil.
He was punished to make us whole
   again.
   His wounds have healed us.
6 All of us are like sheep. We have
      wandered away from God.
   All of us have turned to our own
      way.
And the Lord has placed on his servant
   the sins of all of us.

7 He was beaten down and made to
      suffer.
   But he didn't open his mouth.
He was led away like a sheep to be
   killed.
   Lambs are silent while their wool is
      being cut off.
   In the same way, he didn't open his
      mouth.
8 He was arrested and sentenced to
      death.
   Then he was taken away.
   He was cut off from this life.
He was punished for the sins of my
   people.
   Who among those who were living
      at that time
   could have understood those
      things?
9 He was given a grave with those who
      were evil.
   But his body was buried in the tomb
      of a rich man.
He was killed even though he hadn't
   harmed anyone.
   And he had never lied to anyone.

10 The Lord says, "It was my plan to
      crush him
   and cause him to suffer.
   I made his life a guilt offering to pay
      for sin.
But he will see all of his children after
   him.
   In fact, he will continue to live.
   My plan will be brought about
      through him.
11 After he suffers, he will see the light
      that leads to life.
   And he will be satisfied.

My godly servant will make many
      people godly
   because of what he will accomplish.
   He will be punished for their sins.
12 So I will give him a place of honor
      among those who are great.
   He will be rewarded just like others
      who win the battle.
That is because he was willing to give
   his life as a sacrifice.
   He was counted among those who
      had committed crimes.
He took the sins of many people on
   himself.
   And he gave his life for those who
      had done what is wrong."

Jerusalem Will Be Glorious

54 "Jerusalem, sing!
   You are now like a woman who
      never had a child.
Burst into song! Shout with joy!
   You who have never had labor pains,
you are now all alone.
   But you will have more children
      than a woman who still has a
      husband,"
                        says the Lord.
2 "Make a large area for your tent.
   Spread out its curtains.
   Go ahead and make your tent wider.
Make its ropes longer.
   Drive the stakes down deeper.
3 You will spread out to the right and the
      left.
   Your children after you will drive
      out the nations that are now
      living in your land.
   They will settle down in the deserted
      cities of those nations.

4 "Do not be afraid. You will not be put
      to shame anymore.
   Do not be afraid of being
      dishonored.
   People will no longer make fun of
      you.
You will forget the time when you
      suffered as slaves in Egypt.
   You will no longer remember the
      shame
   of being a widow in Babylonia.
5 I made you. I am now your husband.
   My name is The Lord Who Rules
      Over All.
   I am the Holy One of Israel.
   I have set you free.
   I am the God of the whole earth.
6 You were like a wife who was deserted.
   And her heart was broken.

You were like a wife who married
young.
And her husband sent her away.
But now I am calling you to come
back," says your God.
7 "For a brief moment I left you.
But because I love you so much, I
will bring you back.
8 For a moment I turned my face away
from you.
I was very angry with you.
But I will show you my loving concern.
My faithful love will continue
forever,"
says the LORD. He is the one who set
you free.

9 "During Noah's time I took an oath
and made a promise.
I said I would never cover the earth
with water again.
In the same way, I have promised not
to be angry with you.
I will never punish you again.
10 The mountains might shake.
The hills might be removed.
But my faithful love for you will never
be shaken.
And my covenant that promises
peace to you will never be
broken,"
says the LORD. He shows you his
loving concern.

11 "Suffering city, you have been beaten
by storms.
You have not been comforted.
I will rebuild you with turquoise
stones.
I will rebuild your foundations with
sapphires.
12 I will line the top of your city wall with
rubies.
I will make your gates out of
gleaming jewels.
And I will make all of your walls out
of precious stones.
13 I will teach all of your children.
And they will enjoy great peace.
14 When you do what is right,
you will be made secure.
Your leaders will not be mean to you.
You will not have anything to be
afraid of.
You will not be terrified anymore.
Terror will not come near you.
15 People might attack you. But I will not
be the cause of it.
Those who attack you will give
themselves up to you.

16 "I created blacksmiths.

They fan the coals into flames of
fire.
They make weapons that are fit for
their work.
I also created those who destroy
others.
17 But no weapon that is used against
you will succeed.
People might bring charges against
you.
But you will prove that they are
wrong.
Those are the things I do for my
servants.
I make everything right for them,"
announces the LORD.

The LORD Invites His People to Come to Him

55 "Come, all of you who are thirsty.
Come and drink the water I offer
to you.
You who do not have any money,
come.
Buy and eat the grain I give you.
Come and buy wine and milk.
You will not have to pay anything
for it.
2 Why spend money on what is not
food?
Why work for what does not satisfy
you?
Listen carefully to me.
Then you will eat what is good.
You will enjoy the richest food there
is.
3 Listen and come to me.
Pay attention to me.
Then you will live.
I will make a covenant with you that
will last forever.
I will give you my faithful love.
I promised it to David.
4 I made him a witness to the nations.
He became a leader and commander
over them.
5 You too will send for nations you do
not know.
Even though they do not know you,
they will hurry and come to you.
That is what I will do. I am the LORD
your God.
I am the Holy One of Israel.
I have honored you."

6 Turn to the LORD before it's too late.
Call out to him while he's still ready
to help you.
7 Let the one who is evil stop doing evil
things.

POWER-SURGE

FORGIVING F

LET THE ONE WHO IS EVIL STOP DOING EVIL THINGS.

AND LET HIM QUIT THINKING EVIL THOUGHTS.

LET HIM TURN TO THE LORD.

THE LORD WILL SHOW HIM HIS TENDER LOVE.

LET HIM TURN TO OUR GOD.

HE IS ALWAYS READY TO FORGIVE.

— ISAIAH 55:7 —

LOVING

And let him quit thinking evil
    thoughts.
Let him turn to the LORD.
    The LORD will show him his tender
    love.
Let him turn to our God.
    He is always ready to forgive.

8 "My thoughts are not like your
        thoughts.
    And your ways are not like my
        ways,"
                announces the LORD.
9 "The heavens are higher than the
        earth.
    And my ways are higher than your
        ways.
    My thoughts are higher than your
        thoughts.
10 The rain and the snow
    come down from the sky.
They do not return to it
    without watering the earth.
They make plants come up and grow.
    The plants produce seeds for
        farmers.
    They also produce food for people
        to eat.

11 The words I speak are like that.
    They will not return to me without
        producing results.
    They will accomplish what I want
        them to.
    They will do exactly what I sent
        them to do.

12 "My people, you will leave Babylonia
        with joy.
    You will be led out of it in peace.
The mountains and hills
    will burst into song as you go.
And all of the trees in the fields
    will clap their hands.
13 Pine trees will grow where there used
        to be bushes that had thorns on
        them.
    And myrtle trees will grow where
        there used to be thorns.
That will bring me great fame.
    It will be a lasting reminder of what I
        can do.
    It will not be forgotten."

The LORD Will Save Those Who Come to Him

56 The LORD says,

"Do what is fair and right.
    I will soon come and save you.
    Soon everyone will know that what I
        do is right.
2 Blessed is the man who does what I
        want him to.
    He is faithful in keeping the Sabbath
        day.
    He does not misuse it.
    He does not do what is evil on that
        day."

3 Suppose an outsider wants to follow
        the LORD.
    Then he shouldn't say,
    "The LORD won't accept me as one of
        his people."
And a eunuch shouldn't say,
    "I'm like a dry tree
    that doesn't bear any fruit."

4 The LORD says,

"Suppose some eunuchs keep my
        Sabbath days.
    They choose to do what pleases me.
    And they are faithful in keeping my
        covenant.
5 Then I will set up a monument in the
        area of my temple.
    Their names will be written on it.
    That will be better for them than
        having sons and daughters.

The names of the eunuchs will be
    remembered forever.
  They will never be forgotten.

6 "Suppose outsiders want to follow me
    and serve me.
  They want to love me
    and worship me.
  They keep the Sabbath day and do not
    misuse it.
  And they are faithful in keeping my
    covenant.
7 Then I will bring them to my holy
    mountain of Zion.
  I will give them joy in my house.
  They can pray there.
    I will accept their burnt offerings
    and sacrifices on my altar.
  My house will be called
    a house where people from all
    nations can pray."
8 The LORD and King will gather
    those who were taken away from
    their homes in Israel.
  He announces, "I will gather them to
    myself.
  And I will gather others to join
    them."

The LORD Judges Israel's Evil Leaders

9 Come, all of you enemy nations! Come
    like wild animals.
  Come and destroy like animals in
    the forest.
10 Israel's prophets are blind.
    They don't know the LORD.
  All of them are like watchdogs that
    can't even bark.
  They just lie around and dream.
    They love to sleep.
11 They are like dogs that love to eat.
    They never get enough.
  They are like shepherds who don't
    have any understanding.
  All of them do as they please.
  They only look for what they can get
    for themselves.
12 "Come!" they shout. "Let's get some
    wine!
  Let's drink all the beer we can!
  Tomorrow we'll do the same thing.
    And that will be even better than
    today."

57 Those who are right with God
    die.
  And no one really cares about it.
  Men who are faithful to the LORD are
    swept away by trouble.

And no one understands why that
    happens
  to those who do what is right.
2 Those who lead honest lives
    will enjoy peace and rest when they
    die.

3 The LORD says, "Come here,
    you children of women who
    practice evil magic!
  You are children of prostitutes and
    those who commit adultery.
4 Who are you making fun of?
  Who are you laughing at?
  Who are you sticking your tongue
    out at?
  You are people who refuse to obey me.
  You are just a bunch of liars!
5 You burn with sinful longing among
    the oak trees.
  You worship your gods by having
    sex under every green tree.
  You sacrifice your children in the
    valleys.
  You also do it under the cliffs.
6 You have chosen some of the smooth
    stones in the valleys to be your
    gods.
  You have joined yourselves to them.
  You have even poured out drink
    offerings to them.
  You have given grain offerings to
    them.
  So why should I take pity on you?
7 You have made your bed to have sex
    on a very high hill.
  You went up there to offer your
    sacrifices.
8 You have set up statues to remind you
    of your gods.
  You have put them behind your
    doors and doorposts.
  You deserted me. You invited other
    lovers into your bed.
  You climbed into it and welcomed
    them.
  You made a deal with them.
  And you looked at their naked
    bodies.
9 You went to the god Molech with olive
    oil.
  You took a lot of perfume along with
    you.
  You sent your messengers to places far
    away.
  You even sent them down to the
    place of the dead.
10 All of your efforts wore you out.
  But you would not say, 'It's hopeless.'
  You received new strength.
  So you did not give up.

11 "Who are you so afraid of
      that you have not been true to me?
  You have not remembered me.
      You do not even care about me.
  I have not punished you for a long
      time.
      That is why you are not afraid of me.
12 You have not done what is right or
      good.
      I will let everyone know about it.
      And that will not be of any benefit
          to you.
13 Go ahead and cry out for help to all of
      the statues of your gods.
      See if they can save you!
  The wind will carry them off.
      Just a puff of air will blow them
          away.
  But anyone who comes to me for safety
      will receive the land.
      He will possess my holy mountain
          of Zion."

The LORD Comforts Those Who Aren't Proud

14 A messenger says,

  "Build up the road! Build it up! Get it
      ready!
      Remove anything that would keep
          my people from coming back."
15 The One who is highly honored lives
      forever.
      His name is holy. He says,
  "I live in a high and holy place.
      But I also live with anyone who
          turns away from his sins.
      I live with anyone who is not proud.

      I give new life to him.
      I give it to anyone who turns away
          from his sins.
16 I will not find fault with my people
      forever.
      I will not always be angry with
          them.
  If I were, I would cause their spirits to
      grow weak.
      The very breath of life would go out
          of the people I created.
17 I was very angry with them.
      They always longed for more and
          more of everything.
  So I punished them for that sin.
      I turned my face away from them
          because I was angry.
      But they kept on wanting their own
          way.
18 I have seen what they have done.
      But I will heal them.
  I will guide them.
      And I will comfort them just as I did
          before.
19   Then the people of Israel who are
          sorry for their sins will praise
          me.
  I will give perfect peace to those who
      are far away and those who are
      near.
      And I will heal them," says the LORD.
20 But those who are evil are like the
      rolling sea.
      It never rests.
      Its waves toss up mud and sand.

21 "There is no peace for those who are
evil," says my God.

What True Worship Is All About

58   The LORD told me,

  "Shout out loud. Do not hold back.
      Raise your voice like a trumpet.
  Tell my people that they have refused
      to obey me.
      Tell the family of Jacob how much
          they have sinned.
2 Day after day they worship me.
      They seem ready and willing to
          know how I want them to live.
  They act as if they were a nation that
      does what is right.
  They act as if they have not turned
      away from my commands.
  They claim to want me to give them
      fair decisions.
      They seem ready and willing to
          come near and worship me.
3 'We have gone without food,' they say.
      'Why haven't you noticed it?

We have made ourselves suffer.
  Why haven't you paid any attention
    to us?'

"On the day when you fast, you do as
    you please.
  You take advantage of all of your
    workers.
4 When you fast, it ends in arguing and
    fighting.
  You hit one another with your fists.
  That is an evil thing to do.
The way you are now fasting
  keeps your prayers from being heard
    in heaven.
5 Do you think that is the way I want
    you to fast?
  Is it only a time for a man to make
    himself suffer?
Is it only for people to bow their heads
    like tall grass that is bent by the
    wind?
  Is it only for people to lie down on
    black cloth and ashes?
Is that what you call a fast?
  Do you think I can accept that?

6 "Here is the way I want you to fast.

"Set free those who are held by chains
    without any reason.
  Untie the ropes that hold people as
    slaves.
Set free those who are crushed.
  Break every evil chain.
7 Share your food with hungry people.
  Provide homeless people with a
    place to stay.
Give naked people clothes to wear.
  Provide for the needs of your own
    family.
8 Then the light of my blessing will
    shine on you like the rising sun.
  I will heal you quickly.
I will march out ahead of you.
  And my glory will follow behind you
    and guard you.
  That is because I always do what is
    right.
9 You will call out to me for help.
  And I will answer you.
You will cry out.
  And I will say, 'Here I am.'

"Get rid of the chains you use to hold
    others down.
  Stop pointing your finger at others
    as if they had done something
    wrong.
  Stop saying harmful things about
    them.
10 Work hard to feed hungry people.

Satisfy the needs of those who are
    crushed.
Then my blessing will light up your
    darkness.
  And the night of your suffering will
    become as bright as the
    noonday sun.
11 I will always guide you.
  I will satisfy your needs in a land
    that is baked by the sun.
  I will make you stronger.
You will be like a garden that has
    plenty of water.
  You will be like a spring whose water
    never runs dry.
12 Your people will rebuild the cities that
    were destroyed long ago.
  And you will build again on the old
    foundations.
You will be called The One Who
    Repairs Broken Walls.
  You will be called The One Who
    Makes City Streets Like New
    Again.

13 "Do not work on the Sabbath day.
  Do not do just anything you want to
    on my holy day.
Make the Sabbath a day you can enjoy.
  Honor my holy day.
Do not work on it.
  Do not do just anything you want
    to.
  Do not talk about things that are
    worthless.
14 Then you will find your joy in me.
  I will give you control over the most
    important places in the land.
And you will enjoy all of the good
    things
  in the land I gave your father Jacob."
            The LORD has spoken.

The LORD Sets His People Free

59 People of Israel, the LORD's arm is
    not too weak to save you.
  His ears aren't too deaf to hear your
    cry for help.
2 But your sins have separated you from
    your God.
  They have caused him to turn his
    face away from you.
  So he won't listen to you.
3 Your hands and fingers are stained
    with blood.
  You are guilty of committing
    murder.
Your mouth has told lies.
  Your tongue says evil things.
4 People aren't fair when they present
    their cases in court.

They aren't honest when they state
their case.
They depend on weak arguments.
They tell lies.
They plan to make trouble.
Then they carry it out.
5 The plans they make are like the eggs
of poisonous snakes.
Anyone who eats those eggs will die.
When one of them is broken, a
snake comes out.
6 Those people weave their evil plans
together like a spider's web.
But the webs they make can't be
used as clothes.
They can't cover themselves with
what they make.
Their acts are evil.
They do things to harm others.
7 They are always in a hurry to sin.
They run quickly to murder those
who aren't guilty.
Their thoughts are evil.
They leave a trail of suffering and
pain.
8 They don't know how to live at peace
with others.
What they do isn't fair.
They lead twisted lives.
No one who lives like that will enjoy
peace and rest.

9 We aren't being treated fairly.
We haven't been set free yet.
The God who always does what is right
hasn't come to help us.
We look for light. But we see nothing
but darkness.
We look for brightness. But we walk
in deep shadows.
10 Like blind people we feel our way along
the wall.
We are like those who can't see.
At noon we trip and fall as if the sun
had already set.
Compared to those who are healthy,
we are like dead people.
11 All of us growl like hungry bears.
We cry like sad doves.
We want the LORD to do what is fair
and save us.
But he doesn't do it.
We long for him to set us free.
But the time for that seems far away.

12 That's because we've done so many
things he considers wrong.
Our sins prove that we are guilty.
The wrong things we've done are
always troubling us.
We admit that we have sinned.
13 We've refused to obey the LORD.

We've made evil plans against him.
We've turned our backs on our God.
We've stirred up trouble and refused to
follow him.
We've told lies that came from our
own minds.
14 So people stop others from doing what
is fair.
They keep them from doing what is
right.
No one tells the truth in court
anymore.
No one is honest there.
15 In fact, truth can't be found anywhere.
Those who refuse to do evil are
attacked.

The LORD sees that people aren't
treating others fairly.
That makes him unhappy.
16 He sees that there is no one who helps
his people.
He is shocked that no one stands up
for them.
So he will use his own powerful arm to
save them.
He has the strength to do it because
he is holy.
17 He will put the armor of holiness on
his chest.
He'll put the helmet of salvation on
his head.
He'll pay people back for the wrong
things they do.
He'll wrap himself in anger as if it
were a coat.
18 He will pay his enemies back for what
they have done.
He'll pour his anger out on them.
He'll punish those who attack him.
He'll give the people in the islands
what they have coming to
them.
19 People in the west will show respect for
the LORD's name.
People in the east will worship him
because of his glory.
The LORD will come like a rushing river
that was held back.
His breath will drive it along.

20 "I set my people free. I will come to
Mount Zion.
I will come to those in Jacob's family
who turn away from their sins,"
announces the LORD.

21 "Here is the covenant I will make
with them," says the LORD. "My Spirit is
on you. I have put my words in your
mouth. They will never leave your
mouth. And they will never leave the

mouths of your children or their children after them. That will be true for all time to come," says the LORD.

Zion Will Be Glorious

60 "People of Jerusalem, get up. Shine, because your light has come.
My glory will shine on you.
2 Darkness covers the earth.
Thick darkness spreads over the nations.
But I will rise and shine on you.
My glory will appear over you.
3 Nations will come to your light.
Kings will come to the brightness of your new day.

4 "Look up. Look all around you.
All of your people are getting together to come back to you.
Your sons will come from far away.
Your daughters will be carried like little children.
5 Then your face will glow with joy.
Your heart will beat fast because you are so happy.
Wealth from across the ocean will be brought to you.
The riches of the nations will come to you.
6 Herds of young camels will cover your land.
They will come from Midian and Ephah.
They will also come from Sheba.
They'll carry gold and incense.
And people will shout praises to me.
7 All of Kedar's flocks will be gathered to you.
The rams of Nebaioth will serve as your sacrifices.
I will accept them as offerings on my altar.
That is how I will bring honor to my glorious temple.

8 "Whose ships are these that sail along like clouds?
They fly like doves to their nests.
9 People from the islands are coming to me.
The ships of Tarshish are out in front.
They are bringing your children back from far away.
Your children are bringing their silver and gold with them.
They are coming to honor me.
I am the LORD your God.
I am the Holy One of Israel.
I have honored you.

10 "People from other lands will rebuild your walls.
Their kings will serve you.
When I was angry with you, I struck you.
But now I will show you my tender love.
11 Your gates will always stand open.
They will never be shut, day or night.
Then people can bring you the wealth of the nations.
Their kings will come along with them.
12 The nation or kingdom that will not serve you will be destroyed.
It will be completely wiped out.

13 "Lebanon's glorious trees will be brought to you.
Its pines, firs and cypress trees will be brought.
They will be used to make my temple beautiful.
And I will bring glory to the place where my throne is.
14 The children of those who crush you will come and bow down to you.
All those who hate you will kneel down at your feet.
Jerusalem, they will call you The City of the LORD.
They will name you Zion, the City of the Holy One of Israel.

15 "You have been deserted and hated.
No one even travels through you.
But I will make you into something to be proud of forever.
You will be a place of joy for all time to come.
16 You will get everything you need from kings and nations.
You will be like children who are nursing
at their mother's breasts.
Then you will know that I am the one who saves you.
I am the LORD. I set you free.
I am the Mighty One of Jacob.
17 Instead of bronze I will bring you gold.
In place of iron I will give you silver.
Instead of wood I will bring you bronze.
In place of stones I will give you iron.
I will make peace govern you.
I will make godliness rule over you.
18 People will no longer harm one another in your land.

They will not wipe out or destroy
  anything inside your borders.
You will call your walls Salvation.
  And you will name your gates Praise.
¹⁹ You will not need the light of the sun
  by day anymore.
  The bright light of the moon will no
    longer have to shine on you.
  I will be your light forever.
  My glory will shine on you.
  I am the LORD your God.
²⁰ Your sun will never set again.
  Your moon will never lose its light.
  I will be your light forever.
  Your days of sorrow will come to an
    end.
²¹ Then all of your people will do what is
    right.
  The land will belong to them
    forever.
  They will be like a young tree I have
    planted.
  My hands have created them.
  They will show how glorious I am.
²² The smallest family among you will
    become a tribe.
  The smallest tribe will become a
    mighty nation.
  I am the LORD.
  When it is the right time, I will act
    quickly."

The LORD's Servant Accomplishes His Work

61 The Spirit of the LORD and King is
  on me.
  The LORD has anointed me
  to tell the good news to poor people.
  He has sent me to comfort
    those whose hearts have been
    broken.
  He has sent me to announce freedom
    for those who have been captured.
  He wants me to set prisoners free
    from their dark prisons.
² He has sent me to announce the year
    when he will set his people free.
  He wants me to announce the day
    when he will pay his enemies back.
  Our God has sent me to comfort all
    those who are sad.
³ He wants me to help those in Zion
    who are filled with sorrow.
  I will put beautiful crowns on their
    heads
    in place of ashes.
  I will anoint them with oil to give
    them gladness
  instead of sorrow.
  I will give them a spirit of praise
    in place of a spirit of sadness.

They will be like oak trees that are
  strong and straight.
  The LORD himself will plant them in
    the land.
  That will show how glorious he is.

⁴ They will rebuild the places that were
    destroyed long ago.
  They will repair the buildings that
    have been broken down for
    many years.
  They will make the destroyed cities like
    new again.
  They have been broken down for a
    very long time.
⁵ Outsiders will serve you by taking care
    of your flocks.
  People from other lands will work in
    your fields and vineyards.
⁶ You will be called priests of the LORD.
  You will be named workers for our
    God.
  You will enjoy the wealth of nations.
  You will brag about getting their
    riches.

⁷ Instead of being put to shame
  my people will receive a double
    share of wealth.
  Instead of being dishonored
  they will be glad to be in their land.
  They will receive a double share of
    riches there.
  And they'll be filled with joy that
    will last forever.

⁸ The LORD says, "I love those who do
    what is right.
  I hate it when people steal and do
    other sinful things.

POWER-SURGE

CHEERFUL ✳

I WILL GIVE THEM A
SPIRIT OF PRAISE

IN PLACE OF A SPIRIT
OF SADNESS.

THEY WILL BE LIKE OAK
TREES THAT ARE
STRONG AND
STRAIGHT.
— ISAIAH 61:3 —

STRONG

So I will be faithful to those who do
what is right.
And I will bless them.
I will make a covenant with them
that will last forever.
9 Their children after them will be
famous among the nations.
Their families will be praised by
people everywhere.
All those who see them will agree
that I have blessed them."

10 The people of Jerusalem will say,
"We take great delight in the LORD.
We are joyful because we belong to
our God.
He has dressed us with salvation as if it
were our clothes.
He has put robes of godliness on us.
We are like a groom who is dressed up
for his wedding.
We are like a bride who decorates
herself with her jewels.
11 The soil makes the young plant come
up.
A garden causes seeds to grow.
In the same way, the LORD and King
will make godliness grow.
And all of the nations will praise
him."

The LORD Gives Zion a New Name

62 The LORD says, "For the good of
Zion I will not keep silent.
For Jerusalem's benefit I will not
remain quiet.
I will not keep silent until its people's
godliness
shines like the sunrise.
I will not remain quiet until they are
saved
and shine like a blazing torch.
2 Jerusalem, the nations will see
that I have made everything right
for you.
All of their kings will see your glory.
You will be called by a new name.
I myself will give it to you.
3 You will be like a glorious crown in my
strong hand.
You will be like a royal crown in my
powerful hand.
4 People will not call you Deserted
anymore.
They will no longer name your land
Empty.
Instead, you will be called The One the
LORD Delights In.
Your land will be named The
Married One.
I will take delight in you.

And your land will be like a bride.
5 As a young man gets married to a
young woman,
your people will marry you.
As a groom is happy with his bride,
I will be full of joy over you."

6 Jerusalem, I have stationed guards on
your walls.
They must never be silent day or
night.
You who call out to the LORD
must not give yourselves any rest.
7 And don't give him any rest
until he makes Jerusalem secure.
Don't give him any peace
until people all over the earth praise
that city.

8 The LORD has taken an oath and made
a promise.
He has lifted up his right hand and
mighty arm.
He has promised, "I will never give
your grain
to your enemies for food again.
Outsiders will never again drink the
fresh wine
you have worked so hard for.
9 Instead, those who gather the grain
will eat it themselves.
And they will praise me.
Those who gather grapes to make the
wine will enjoy it.
They will drink it in the courtyards
of my temple."

10 Go out through your gates, people of
Jerusalem! Go out!
Prepare the way for the rest of your
people to return.
Build up the road! Build it up!
Remove the stones.
Raise a banner over the city
for the nations to see.

11 The LORD has announced a message
from one end of the earth to the
other.
He has said, "Tell the people of Zion,
'Look! Your Savior is coming!
He is bringing his people back as his
reward.
He has won the battle over their
enemies.' "
12 They will be called The Holy People.
The LORD will set them free.
And Jerusalem will be named The City
the LORD Cares About.
It won't be deserted anymore.

God Will Save His People and Punish Their Enemies

63 Who is this man coming from
the city of Bozrah in Edom?
His clothes are stained bright red.
Who is he? He is dressed up in all of his
glory.
He is marching toward us with great
strength.

The LORD answers, "It is I.
I have won the battle.
I am mighty.
I have saved my people."

² Why are your clothes red?
They look as if you have been
stomping
on grapes in a winepress.

³ The LORD answers, "I have been
stomping on the nations
as if they were grapes.
No one was there to help me.
I walked all over the nations because I
was angry.
That is why I stomped on them.
Their blood splashed all over my
clothes.
So my clothes were stained bright
red.
⁴ I decided it was time to pay Israel's
enemies back.
The year for me to set my people free
had come.
⁵ I looked around, but no one was there
to help me.
I was shocked that no one gave me
any help.
So I used my own powerful arm to save
my people.
I had the strength to do it because I
was angry.
⁶ I walked all over the nations because I
was angry with them.
I made them drink from the cup of
my burning anger.
I poured their blood out on the
ground."

Isaiah Prays to the LORD

⁷ I will talk about the kind things the
LORD has done.
I'll praise him for everything he's
done for us.
He has done many good things
for the nation of Israel.
That's because he loves us and is
very kind to us.
⁸ In the past he said, "They are my
people.
They will not turn against me."

So he saved them.
⁹ When they suffered, he suffered with
them.
He sent his angel to save them.
He set them free because he is loving
and kind.
He lifted them up and carried them.
He did it again and again in days
long ago.
¹⁰ But they refused to obey him.
They made his Holy Spirit sad.
So he turned against them and became
their enemy.
He himself fought against them.

¹¹ Then his people remembered what he
did long ago.
They recalled the days of Moses and
his people.
They asked, "Where is the One who
brought
Israel through the Red Sea?
Moses led them as the shepherd of
his flock.
Where is the One who put
his Holy Spirit among them?
¹² He used his glorious and powerful arm
to help Moses.
He parted the waters of the sea in front
of them.
That mighty act made him famous
forever.
¹³   He led them through that deep sea.
Like a horse in open country,
they didn't trip and fall.
¹⁴ Like cattle that are taken down to the
flatlands,
they were given rest by the Spirit of
the LORD."
That's how he guided his people.
So he made a glorious name for
himself.

¹⁵ LORD, look down from heaven.
Look down from your holy and
glorious throne.

POWER-SURGE

KIND   **K**

I WILL TALK ABOUT THE
KIND THINGS THE LORD
HAS DONE.
— ISAIAH 63:7 —

TELLS OTHERS

Where is your great love for us?
Where is your power?
Why don't you show us
your tender love and concern?
16 You are our Father.
Abraham might not accept us as his
children.
Jacob might not recognize us as his
family.
But you are our Father, LORD.
Your name is The One Who Always
Sets Us Free.
17 LORD, why do you let us wander away
from you?
Why do you let us become so
stubborn
that we don't respect you?
Come back and help us.
We are the tribes that belong to you.
18 For a little while your holy people
possessed the land.
But now our enemies have torn your
temple down.
19 We are like people you never ruled
over.
We are like those who don't belong
to you.

64 I wish you would open up your
heavens
and come down to us!
I wish the mountains would tremble
when you show your power!
2 Be like a fire that causes twigs to burn.
It also makes water boil.
So come down and make yourself
known to your enemies.
Cause the nations to shake with fear
when they see your power!
3 Long ago you did some wonderful
things we didn't expect.
You came down, and the mountains
trembled
when you showed your power.
4 No one's ears have ever heard of a God
like you.
No one's eyes have ever seen a God
who is greater than you.
No God but you acts for the good
of those who trust in him.
5 You come to help those who enjoy
doing what is right.
You help those who thank you for
teaching them how to live.
But when we continued to disobey
you,
you became angry with us.
So how can we be saved?
6 All of us have become like someone
who is "unclean."

All of the good things we do are like
polluted rags to you.
All of us are like leaves that have dried
up.
Our sins sweep us away like the
wind.
7 No one prays to you.
No one asks you for help.
You have turned your face away from
us.
You have let us waste away
because we have sinned so much.

8 LORD, you are our Father.
We are the clay. You are the potter.
Your hands made all of us.
9 Don't be so angry with us, LORD.
Don't remember our sins anymore.
Please show us your favor.
All of us belong to you.
10 Your sacred cities have become a
desert.
Even Zion is a desert.
Jerusalem is a dry and empty place.
11 Our people used to praise you in our
holy and glorious temple.
But now it has been burned down.
Everything we treasured has been
destroyed.
12 LORD, won't you help us even after
everything that's happened?
Will you keep silent and punish us
more than we can stand?

The LORD Answers Isaiah's Prayer

65 The LORD says, "I made myself
known to those who were not
asking for me.
I was found by those who were not
trying to find me.

POWER – SURGE

HELPFUL ★

YOU COME TO HELP
THOSE WHO ENJOY
DOING WHAT IS RIGHT.

YOU HELP THOSE WHO
THANK YOU FOR
TEACHING THEM HOW
TO LIVE.

— ISAIAH 64:5 —

THANKFUL

I spoke to a nation that did not pray
    to me.
    'Here I am,' I said. 'Here I am.'
2 All day long I have held out my hands
    to welcome a stubborn nation.
They lead sinful lives.
    They go where their evil thoughts
    take them.
3 They are always making me very
    angry.
    They do it right in front of me.
They offer sacrifices in the gardens of
    other gods.
    They burn incense on altars that are
    made out of bricks.
4 They sit among the graves.
    They spend their nights talking to
    the spirits of the dead.
They eat the meat of pigs.
    Their cooking pots hold soup that
    has 'unclean' meat in it.
5 They say, 'Keep away! Don't come near
    us!
    We are too sacred for you!'
Those people are like smoke in my
    nose.
    They are like a fire that keeps
    burning all day.

6 "I will judge them. I have even written
    it down.
    I will not keep silent.
    Instead, I will pay them back for all
    of their sins.
7 I will punish them for their sins
    and the sins of their people before
    them,"
    says the LORD.
"They burned sacrifices on the
    mountains.
    They disobeyed me by worshiping
    other gods on the hills.
So I will really punish them
    for all of the sins they have
    committed."

8 The LORD says,

"Sometimes juice is still left in grapes
    that have been crushed.
    So people say, 'Don't destroy them.
    Some good juice is still left in them.'
That is what I will do for the good of
    those who serve me.
    I will not destroy all of my people.
9 I will give children
    to the families of Jacob and Judah.
    They will possess my entire land.
My chosen people will be given all
    of it.
    Those who serve me will live there.

10 Their flocks will eat in the rich
    grasslands of Sharon.
    Their herds will rest in the Valley of
    Achor.
That is what I will do for my people
    who follow me.

11 "But some of you have deserted me.
    You no longer worship on my holy
    mountain of Zion.
You spread a table for the god that is
    called Good Fortune.
    You offer bowls of mixed wine to the
    god named Fate.
12 So I will make it your fate to be killed
    with swords.
    Each of you will die a horrible death.
That is because I called out to you, but
    you did not answer me.
    I spoke to you, but you did not
    listen.
You did what is evil in my sight.
    You chose to do what does not
    please me."

13 So the LORD and King says,

"Those who serve me will have food to
    eat.
    But you will be hungry.
My servants will have plenty to drink.
    But you will be thirsty.
Those who serve me will be full of joy.
    But you will be put to shame.
14 My servants will sing
    with joy in their hearts.
But you will cry out
    because of the great pain in your
    hearts.
    You will cry because your spirits are
    sad.
15 My chosen ones will use your names
    when they call down curses on
    others.
I am your LORD and King.
    I will put you to death.
    But I will give new names to those
    who serve me.
16 They will ask me to bless their land.
    They will do it in my name.
    I am the God of truth.
They will take oaths and make
    promises in their land.
    They will do it in my name.
    I am the God of truth.
The troubles of the past will be
    forgotten.
    They will be hidden from my eyes.

The LORD Will Create New Heavens and a New Earth

17 "I will create new heavens and a new
earth.
The things that have happened
before will not be remembered.
They will not even enter your minds.
18 So be glad and full of joy forever
because of what I will create.
I will cause others to take delight in
Jerusalem.
They will be filled with joy
when they see its people.
19 And I will be full of joy because of
Jerusalem.
I will take delight in my people.
Sobbing and crying
will not be heard there anymore.

20 "Babies in Jerusalem will no longer
live only a few days.
Old people will not fail
to live for a very long time.
Those who live to the age of 100
will be thought of as still being
young when they die.
Those who die before they are 100
will be considered as having been
under God's curse.
21 My people will build houses and live in
them.
They will plant vineyards and eat
their fruit.
22 They will no longer build houses
only to have others live in them.
They will no longer plant crops
only to have others eat them.
My people will live to be as old as trees.
My chosen ones will enjoy for a long
time
the things they have worked for.
23 Their work will not be worthless
anymore.
They will not have children who are
sure to face sudden terror.
Instead, I will bless them.
I will also bless their children after
them.
24 Even before they call out to me, I will
answer them.
While they are still speaking, I will
hear them.
25 Wolves and lambs will eat together.
Lions will eat straw like oxen.
Serpents will not bite anyone.
They will eat nothing but dust.
None of those animals will harm or
destroy
anything or anyone on my holy
mountain of Zion,"
says the LORD.

The LORD Judges Some People and Blesses Others

66 The LORD says,

"Heaven is my throne.
The earth is under my control.
So how could you ever build a house
for me?
Where would my resting place be?
2 Didn't my powerful hand make
everything?
That is how all things were created,"
announces the LORD.

"The person I value is not proud.
He is sorry for the wrong things he
has done.
He has great respect for what I say.
3 But others are not like that.
They sacrifice bulls to me,
but at the same time they kill
people.
They offer lambs to me,
but they also sacrifice dogs to other
gods.
They bring grain offerings to me,
but they also offer pig's blood to
other gods.
They burn incense to me,
but they also worship statues of
gods.
They have chosen to go their own way.
They take delight in things I hate.
4 So I have also made a choice.
I will make them suffer greatly.
I will bring on them what they are
afraid of.
When I called out to them, no one
answered me.
When I spoke to them, no one
listened.
They did what is evil in my sight.
They chose to do what displeases
me."

5 Listen to the word of the LORD.
Listen, you who tremble with fear
when he speaks. He says,
"Some of your own people hate you.
They turn their backs on you
because you are faithful to me.
They make fun of you and say,
'Let the LORD show his glory by saving
you.
Then we can see how happy you
are.'
But they will be put to shame.
6 Hear the loud sounds coming from the
city!
Listen to the noise coming from the
temple!
I am the one who is causing it.

I am paying my enemies back for
everything they have done.

7 "Zion is like a woman who has a baby
before she goes into labor.
She has a son
even before her labor pains begin.
8 Who has ever heard of anything like
that?
Who has ever seen such a thing?
Can a country be born in a day?
Can a nation be created in a
moment?
But as soon as Zion goes into labor,
her people increase their numbers.
9 Zion, would I bring you to the
moment of birth
and not let it happen?" says the
LORD.
"Would I close up a mother's body
when it is time for her baby to be
born?" says your God.
10 "Be glad along with Jerusalem, all you
who love her.
Be filled with joy because of her.
Take great delight in her,
all you who sob over her.
11 You will nurse at her comforting
breasts.
And you will be satisfied.
You will drink until you are full.
And you will delight in her rich and
plentiful supply."

12 The LORD continues,

"I will cause peace to flow over her like
a river.
I will make the wealth of nations
sweep over her like a flooding
stream.
You will nurse and be carried in her
arms.
You will play on her lap.
13 As a mother comforts her child,
I will comfort you.
You will find comfort in Jerusalem."

14 When you see that happen, your
hearts will be filled with joy.
Just as grass grows quickly, you will
succeed.
The LORD will show his power to those
who serve him.
But he will pour out his anger on his
enemies.
15 The LORD will judge them with fire.
His chariots are coming like a
windstorm.
He will pour out his burning anger on
his enemies.

It will blaze out like flames of fire.
16 The LORD will bring everyone into
court.
He will use fire and his sword to
punish those he finds guilty.
He will put many people to death.

17 "Some people set themselves apart
and make themselves pure. They do it so
they can go into the gardens to worship
other gods. They do what the worship
leader tells them to do. They eat the meat
of pigs and rats. They also eat other
things I hate. All of those people will
come to a horrible end," announces the
LORD.

18 "They have done many evil things.
And they plan to do even more. So I will
come and gather the people of every
nation and language. They will see my
glory when I act.

19 "I will do a miracle among them. I
will send to the nations some of those
who are left alive. I will send some of
them to the people of Tarshish, Libya and
Lydia, who are famous for using bows. I
will send others to Tubal and Greece. And
I will send still others to islands far away.
The people who live there have not heard
about my fame. They have not seen my
glory. Those I send will tell the nations
about my glory when I act.

20 "And they will bring back all of the
people of Israel from all of those nations.
They will bring them to my holy mountain in Jerusalem. My people will ride on
horses, mules and camels. They will
come in chariots and wagons," says the
LORD. "Those messengers will bring my
people as an offering to me. They will
bring them to my temple, just as the Israelites bring their grain offerings in bowls
that are 'clean.' **21** And I will choose some
of them to be priests and Levites," says
the LORD.

22 "I will make new heavens and a new
earth. And they will last forever," announces the LORD. "In the same way, your
name and your children after you will
last. **23** Everyone will come and bow down
to me. They will do it at every New Moon
Feast and on every Sabbath day," says the
LORD.

24 "When they go out of Jerusalem,
they will see the dead bodies of those who
refused to obey me. The worms that eat
the bodies will not die. The fire that burns
them will not be put out. It will make
everyone sick just to look at them."

JEREMIAH

The book of Jeremiah tells the story of the prophet Jeremiah and his messages from God. God tells Jeremiah to perform several unusual acts. Jeremiah's acts portray, or picture, for the people the message God has for them. Even when the action will make him look foolish or will put him in danger, Jeremiah, the hero of the book, willingly obeys God. Because the people will not listen, God punishes them. They are conquered and sent away from their homes. Read the book of Jeremiah to discover the results of ignoring God and continuing in sin.

HEROES IN THIS BOOK . . .

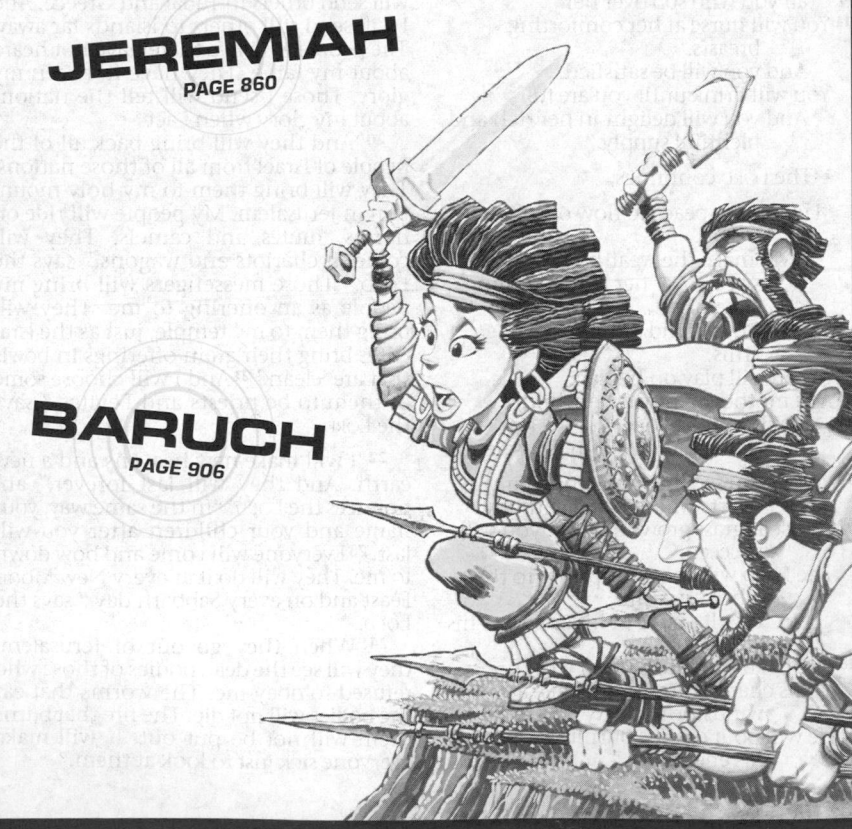

JEREMIAH
PAGE 860

BARUCH
PAGE 906

1 These are the words Jeremiah received from the LORD. He was the son of Hilkiah. Jeremiah was one of the priests at Anathoth. That's a town in the territory of Benjamin. ²A message came to Jeremiah from the LORD. It came in the 13th year that Josiah was king over Judah. Josiah was the son of Amon.

³The LORD's message also came to Jeremiah during the whole time Jehoiakim was king over Judah. Jehoiakim was the son of Josiah. The LORD continued to speak to Jeremiah until the fifth month of the 11th year that Zedekiah was king over Judah. That's when the people of Jerusalem were forced to leave their country. Zedekiah was the son of Josiah. Here is what Jeremiah said.

The LORD Chooses Jeremiah

⁴A message came to me from the LORD. He said,

⁵ "Before I formed you in your mother's
        body I chose you.
    Before you were born I set you apart
        to serve me.
    I appointed you to be a prophet to
        the nations."

⁶"You are my LORD and King," I said. "I don't know how to speak. I'm only a child."

⁷But the LORD said to me, "Do not say, 'I'm only a child.' You must go to everyone I send you to. You must say everything I command you to say. ⁸Do not be afraid of the people I send you to. I am with you. I will save you," announces the LORD.

⁹Then the LORD reached out his hand. He touched my mouth and spoke to me. He said, "I have put my words in your mouth. ¹⁰Today I am appointing you to speak to nations and kingdoms. I want you to pull them up by the roots and tear them down. I want you to destroy them and crush them. But I also want you to build them up and plant them."

¹¹A message came to me from the LORD. He asked me, "What do you see, Jeremiah?"

"The branch of an almond tree," I replied.

¹²The LORD said to me, "You have seen correctly. I am watching to see that my word comes true."

¹³Another message came to me from the LORD. He asked me, "What do you see?"

"A pot that has boiling water in it," I answered. "It's leaning toward us from the north."

¹⁴The LORD said to me, "Something very bad will be poured out on everyone who lives in this land. It will come from the north. ¹⁵I am about to send for all of the armies in the northern kingdoms," announces the LORD.

    "Their kings will come to Jerusalem.
        They will set up their thrones at the
            very gates of the city.
    They will attack all of the walls that
            surround the city.
    They will go to war against all of the
            towns of Judah.
¹⁶ I will judge my people.
        They have done many evil things.
        They have deserted me.
    They have burned incense to other
            gods.
        They have worshiped the gods
            their own hands have made.

¹⁷"So get ready! Stand up! Tell them everything I command you to. Do not let them terrify you. If you do, I will terrify you in front of them. ¹⁸Today I have made you like a city that has a high wall around it. I have made you like an iron pillar and a bronze wall. Now you can stand up against the whole land. You can stand against the kings and officials of Judah. You can stand against its priests and its people. ¹⁹They will fight against you. But they will not overcome you. I am with you. I will save you," announces the LORD.

Israel Deserts the LORD

2 A message came to me from the LORD. He said, ²"Go. Announce my message to the people in Jerusalem. I want everyone to hear it. Tell them,

    " 'I remember how faithful you were to
            me when you were young.
        You loved me as if you were my
            bride.
    You followed me through the desert.
        Nothing had been planted there.
³ Your people were holy to me.
        They were the first share of my
            harvest.
    All those who destroyed them were
            held guilty.
        And trouble came to their
            enemies,' "
                    announces the LORD.

⁴ People of Jacob, hear the LORD's
            message.
        Listen, all you tribes of Israel.

JEREMIAH

JEREMIAH 1:4-5; 15:11

B

( )

A message came to me from the LORD. He said, ..."Before you were born I set you apart to serve me. I appointed you to be a prophet to the nations...I will keep you safe for a good purpose."

Jeremiah (jer-uh-MY-uh) sat in the wet mud at the bottom of the empty well. He was covered with mud. Mud was even in his ears and under his fingernails and toenails. In the silence deep in the muddy well, the only thing he heard was the rumble of his stomach. Someone had let some bread down to him yesterday. But nothing today. *Will I die here at the bottom of a well?* he thought to himself. *Just because I gave the people a message from God?*

Jeremiah slumped back against the wall of the well. It was cold and wet, but he barely noticed. God's people just wouldn't listen. They were going to be conquered by Babylon's soldiers. Many of them would die. Others would be taken captive to Babylon. God was going to punish his people for worshiping idols.

The leaders of the people had especially hated Jeremiah's messages. So now Jeremiah had been dumped into a well. What better way to silence him? **THERE WAS NO ONE TO TALK TO HERE EXCEPT THE WALLS AND A FEW BUGS.**

Jeremiah heard a sound in the distance. Was someone coming? He looked up to see several men carrying ropes and some rags. "Put these rags under your arms to pad the ropes. Then we'll pull you up out of the well with the ropes."

Jeremiah did as they said. He hung on and was slowly lifted up out of the well. Wet mud dripped off his clothes and plopped down into the bottom of the well. When he got to the top, the bright sun hurt his eyes. But he was so glad to be out of the well that he didn't care. He knew God was going to protect him.

BE A JEREMIAH

Jeremiah told the people God's messages even when he knew it would get him in trouble. He did the right thing even when it was the hard thing to do. Be a Jeremiah! Even when your friends think you're weird, even when everyone else is doing the opposite, do what you know is right.

JEREMIAH GAVE THE PEOPLE GOD'S MESSAGES EVEN WHEN IT GOT HIM INTO TROUBLE.
THE WHOLE STORY: JEREMIAH 38:1-13

Go to page 906 for the next Super Hero

⁵The LORD says,

"What did your people find wrong
    with me?
  Why did they wander so far away
    from me?
They worshiped worthless statues of
    gods.
  Then they themselves became
    worthless.
⁶They did not ask, 'Where is the LORD?
  He brought us up out of Egypt.
He led us through a dry and empty
    land.
  He guided us through deserts and
    deep valleys.
It was a land of darkness where there
    wasn't any rain.
  No one lived or traveled there.'
⁷But I brought you into a land that has
    rich soil.
  I gave you its fruit and its finest food.
In spite of that, you polluted my land.
  You turned it into something I hate.
⁸The priests did not ask,
    'Where is the LORD?'
Those who taught my law did not
    know me.
  The leaders refused to obey me.
The prophets prophesied in the name
    of Baal.
  They worshiped worthless statues of
    gods.

⁹"So I am bringing charges against you
    again,"
                  announces the LORD.
  "And I will bring charges against
    your children's children.
¹⁰Go over to the coasts of the western
    nations and look.
  Send people to the land of Kedar
    and have them look closely.
See if there has ever been anything
    like this.
¹¹Has a nation ever changed its gods?
  Actually, they are not even gods at
    all.
But my people have traded away their
    glorious God.
  They have traded me for worthless
    statues of gods.
¹²Sky above, be shocked over that.
  Tremble with horror,"
                  announces the LORD.
¹³"My people have sinned twice.
  They have deserted me,
    even though I am the spring of
    water that gives life.
And they have dug their own wells.
  But those wells are broken.
  They can't hold any water.

¹⁴Are you people of Israel servants?
  You were not born as slaves, were
    you?
  Then why have you been carried off
    like stolen goods?
¹⁵Lions have roared.
  They have growled at you.
They have destroyed your land.
  Your towns are burned and deserted.
¹⁶The men of Memphis and Tahpanhes
  have shaved your heads to dishonor
    you.
¹⁷Haven't you brought that on
    yourselves?
  I am the LORD your God, but you
    deserted me.
  You left me even while I was leading
    you.
¹⁸Why do you go to Egypt
  to drink water from the Shihor
    River?
  Why do you go to Assyria
  to drink from the Euphrates River?
¹⁹You will be punished because you have
    sinned.
  You will be corrected for turning
    away from me.
I am the LORD your God.
  If you desert me, bad things will
    happen to you.
If you do not respect me, you will
    suffer bitterly.
  I want you to understand that,"
                  announces the LORD
                  who rules over all.

²⁰"Long ago you broke off the yoke I put
    on you.
  You tore off the ropes I tied you up
    with.
You said, 'I won't serve you!'
In fact, on every high hill
  you lay down like a prostitute.
  You worshiped other gods under
    every green tree.
²¹You were like a good vine when I
    planted you.
  You were a healthy plant.
Then how did you turn against me?
  How did you become a bad, wild
    vine?
²²You might wash yourself with baking
    soda.
  You might use plenty of soap.
But I can still see the stains your guilt
  covers you with,"
                announces the LORD and King.
²³"You say, 'I am "clean."
  I haven't followed the gods that are
    named after Baal.'
How can you say that?

Remember how you acted in the
valley.
Consider what you have done.
You are like a female camel running
quickly here and there.
24 You are like a wild donkey that lives in
the desert.
She smells the wind when she longs
for a mate.
Who can hold her back?
The males that run after her do not
need to wear themselves out.
At mating time they will easily find
her.
25 Do not run after other gods
until your sandals are worn out and
your throat is dry.
But you said, 'It's no use!
I love those gods.
I must go after them.'

26 "A thief is dishonored when he is
caught.
And you people of Israel are filled
with shame.
Your kings and officials are
dishonored.
So are your priests and your
prophets.
27 You say to a piece of wood, 'You are my
father.'
You say to a stone, 'You are my
mother.'
You have turned your backs to me.
You refuse to look at me.
But when you are in trouble, you say,
'Come and save us!'
28 So where are the gods you made for
yourselves?
Let them come when you are in
trouble!
Let them save you if they can!
Judah, you have as many gods
as you have towns.

29 "Why do you bring charges against
me?
All of you have refused to obey me,"
announces the LORD.
30 "I punished your people. But it did not
do them any good.
They did not pay attention when
they were corrected.
You have killed your prophets with
swords.
You have swallowed them up like a
hungry lion.

31 "You who are now living, consider
my message. I am saying,

"Have I been like a desert to Israel?

Have I been like a land of deep
darkness?
Why do my people say, 'We are free to
wander.
We won't come to you anymore'?
32 Does a young woman forget all about
her jewelry?
Does a bride forget her wedding
jewels?
But my people have forgotten me
more days than anyone can count.
33 You are very skilled at chasing after
love!
Even the worst of women can learn
from how you act.
34 The blood of those you have killed is
on your clothes.
You have destroyed poor people who
were not guilty.
You did not catch them in the act of
breaking in.
In spite of all of that,
35 you say, 'I'm not guilty of doing
anything wrong.
The LORD isn't angry with me.'
But I will judge you.
That is because you say, 'I haven't
sinned.'
36 Why do you keep on
changing your ways so much?
Assyria did not help you.
And Egypt will not help you either.
37 So you will also leave Egypt
with your hands tied together above
your heads.
I have turned my back on those you
trust.
They will not help you.

3 "Suppose a man divorces his wife.
What if she then gets married to
another man?
Should her first husband return to her
again?
If he does, won't the land become
completely 'unclean'?
People of Israel, you have lived like a
prostitute.
You have loved many other gods.
So do you think you can return to
me now?"
announces the LORD.
2 "Look up at the bare hilltops.
Is there any place where you have
not committed adultery with
other gods?
By the side of the road you sat waiting
for lovers.
You sat there like someone who
wanders in the desert.
You have polluted the land.

You are like a sinful prostitute.
³ So I have held the showers back.
I have kept the spring rains from
falling.
But you still have the bold face of a
prostitute.
You refuse to blush with shame.
⁴ You have just now called out to me.
You said,
'My Father, you have been my friend
ever since I was young.
⁵ Will you always be angry with me?
Will your anger continue forever?'
That is how you talk.
But you do all of the evil things you
can."

Israel Is Not Faithful to the LORD

⁶ During the time Josiah was king, the LORD spoke to me. He said, "Have you seen what the people of Israel have done? They have not been faithful to me. They have committed adultery with other gods. They worshiped them on every high hill and under every green tree. ⁷ "I thought that after they had done all of those things, they would return to me. But they did not. Their sister nation Judah saw it. And they were not faithful to me either.

⁸ "I gave Israel their letter of divorce. I sent them away because they were unfaithful to me so many times. But I saw that their sister nation Judah did not have any respect for me. They were not faithful to me either. They also went out and committed adultery with other gods. ⁹ "Israel was not faithful to me, but that did not bother them at all. They made the land 'unclean.' They worshiped gods that were made out of stone and wood. ¹⁰ In spite of all that, their sister Judah did not come back to me. They were not faithful to me either. They did not return with all their heart. They only pretended to," announces the LORD.

¹¹ The LORD said to me, "Israel and Judah have not been faithful to me. But Israel was not as bad as Judah was. ¹² "Go. Announce this message to the people in the north. Tell them,

" 'Israel, you have not been faithful,'
announces the LORD.
'Return to me. Then I will look on
you with favor again.
My love is faithful,' announces the
LORD.
'I will not be angry with you forever.
¹³ Admit that you are guilty of doing
what is wrong.

You have refused to obey me. I am
the LORD your God.
You have committed adultery with
other gods.
You worshiped them under every
green tree.
And you have not obeyed me,' "
announces the LORD.

¹⁴ "You people have not been faithful," announces the LORD. "Return to me. I am your husband. I will choose one of you from each town. I will choose two from each territory. And I will bring you to the city of Zion. ¹⁵ "Then I will give you shepherds who are dear to my heart. Their knowledge and understanding will help them lead you. ¹⁶ In those days your numbers will increase greatly in the land," announces the LORD.

"Then people will not talk about the ark of the covenant of the LORD anymore. It will never enter their minds. They will not remember it. The ark will not be missed. And another one will not be made. ¹⁷ "At that time they will call Jerusalem The Throne of the LORD. All of the nations will gather together there. They will go there to honor me. They will no longer do what their stubborn and evil hearts want them to do. ¹⁸ "In those days the people of Judah will join the people of Israel. Together they will come from a land in the north. They will come to the land I gave to your people long ago. I wanted them to have it as their very own.

¹⁹ "I myself said,

" 'I would gladly treat you like my
children.
I would give you a pleasant land.
It is the most beautiful land any
nation could have.'
I thought you would call me 'Father.'
I hoped you would always follow
me.
²⁰ But you people are like a woman who
is not faithful to her husband.
Israel, you have not been faithful to
me,"
announces the LORD.

²¹ A cry is heard on the bare hilltops.
The people of Israel are sobbing and
praying.
That's because their lives are so
twisted.
They've forgotten the LORD their
God.

²² "You have not been faithful,"
   says the LORD.
"Return to me. I will heal you.
   Then you will not turn away from
      me anymore."

"Yes," the people say. "We will come to
      you.
   You are the LORD our God.
²³ The gods we worship on the hills
      and mountains are useless.
   You are the LORD our God.
   You are the only one who can save
      us.
²⁴ From our earliest years shameful gods
      have eaten up
   everything our people worked for.
   They have eaten up our flocks and
      herds.
   They've destroyed our sons and
      daughters.
²⁵ Let us lie down in our shame.
   Let our dishonor cover us.
   You are the LORD our God. But we have
      sinned against you.
   We and our people before us have
      sinned.
   We haven't obeyed you
      from our earliest years until now."

4 "If you will return, Israel,
   return to me,"
                     announces the LORD.
   "Put the statues of your gods out of my
      sight.
   I hate them.
   Stop going down the wrong path.
² Take all of your oaths in my name.
   Say, 'You can be sure that the LORD is
      alive.'
   Let all of your promises be truthful,
      fair and honest.
   Then I will bless the nations.
   And they will take delight in me.' "

³ Here is what the LORD is telling the
people of Judah and Jerusalem. He says,

   "Your hearts are as hard as a field
      that has not been plowed.
   So change your ways and produce
      good crops.
   Do not plant seeds among thorns.
⁴ People of Judah and Jerusalem, obey
      me.
   Do not let your hearts be stubborn.
   If you do, my anger will blaze out
      against you.
   It will burn like fire because of the
      evil things you have done.
   No one will be able to put it out.

Trouble Will Come From the North

⁵ "Announce my message in Judah.
   Tell it in Jerusalem.
   Say, 'Blow trumpets all through the
      land!'
   Give a loud shout and say,
      'Gather together!
   Let's run to cities that have high
      walls around them!'
⁶ Warn everyone to go to Zion!
   Run for safety! Do not wait!
   I am bringing trouble from the north.
   Everything will be totally
      destroyed."

⁷ Lions have come out of their den.
   Those who destroy nations have
      begun to march out.
   They have left their place
      to destroy your land completely.
   Your towns will be broken to pieces.
   No one will live in them.
⁸ So put on black clothes.
   Sob and cry over what has
      happened.
   The LORD hasn't turned
      his burning anger away from us.

⁹ "A dark day is coming," announces the
      LORD.
   "The king and his officials will lose
      hope.
   The priests will be shocked.
   And the prophets will be terrified."

¹⁰ Then I said, "You are my LORD and
King. You have completely tricked the
people of Judah and Jerusalem. You have
told them, 'You will have peace and rest.'
But swords are pointed at our throats."

¹¹ At that time the people of Judah and
Jerusalem will be warned. They will be
told, "A hot and dry wind is coming, my
people. It is blowing toward you from the
bare hilltops in the desert. But it does not
separate straw from grain. ¹² It is much too
strong for that. The wind is coming from
me. I am making my decision against
you."

¹³ Look! Our enemies are approaching
      like the clouds.
   Their chariots are coming like a
      strong wind.
   Their horses are faster than eagles.
   How terrible it will be for us!
   We'll be destroyed!
¹⁴ People of Jerusalem, wash your sins
      from your hearts and be saved.
   How long will you hold on to your
      evil thoughts?

15 A voice is speaking all the way from
      the city of Dan.
    From the hills of Ephraim it
      announces
    that trouble is coming.
16 "Tell the nations.
    Warn Jerusalem.
Say, 'An army will attack you.
    It is coming from a land far away.
It will shout a war cry
    against the cities of Judah.
17 It will surround them like people who
      guard a field.
    Judah has refused to obey me,' "
               announces the LORD.
18 "The army will attack you
    because of your conduct and
      actions.
That is how you will be punished.
    It will be so bitter!
    It will cut deep down into your
      hearts!"

19 I'm suffering! I'm really suffering!
    I'm hurting badly.
My heart is suffering so much!
    It's pounding inside me.
    I can't keep silent.
I've heard the sound of trumpets.
    I've heard the battle cry.
20 One trouble follows another.
    The whole land is destroyed.
In an instant my tents are gone.
    My home disappears in a moment.
21 How long must I look at our enemy's
      battle flag?
    How long must I hear the sound of
      the trumpets?

22 The LORD says, "My people are foolish.
    They do not know me.
They are children who do not have any
      sense.
    They have no understanding at all.
They are skilled in doing what is evil.
    They do not know how to do what is
      good."

23 I looked at the earth.
    It didn't have any shape. And it was
      empty.
I looked at the sky.
    Its light was gone.
24 I looked at the mountains.
    They were shaking.
    All of the hills were swaying.
25 I looked. And there weren't any
      people.
    Every bird in the sky had flown
      away.
26 I looked. And the fruitful land had
    become a desert.

All of its towns were destroyed.
    The LORD had done all of that
      because of his burning anger.

27 The LORD says,

"The whole land will be destroyed.
    But I will not destroy it completely.
28 So the earth will be filled with sadness.
    The sky above will grow dark.
I have spoken, and I will not take pity
      on them.
I have made my decision, and I will
      not change my mind."

29 People can hear the sound of
      horsemen.
    Men who are armed with bows are
      coming.
The people in every town run away.
Some of them go into the bushes.
    Others climb up among the rocks.
All of the towns are deserted.
    No one is living in them.

30 What are you doing, you who are
      destroyed?
    Why do you dress yourself in bright
      red clothes?
    Why do you put on jewels of gold?
Why do you put makeup on your eyes?
    You make yourself beautiful for no
      reason at all.
Your lovers hate you.
    They are trying to kill you.

31 I hear a cry like the cry of a woman
      having a baby.
    I hear a groan like someone having
      her first child.
It's the cry of the people of Zion
      struggling to breathe.
    They reach out their hands and say,
"Help us! We're fainting!
    Murderers are about to kill us!"

No One Is Honest

5 The LORD says, "Go up and down the
    streets of Jerusalem.
    Look around.
    Think about what you see.
Search through the market places.
    See if you can find one honest
      person who tries to be truthful.
    If you can, I will forgive this city.
2 They take all of their oaths in my
      name.
    They say, 'You can be sure that the
      LORD is alive.'
But their oaths can't be trusted."

3 LORD, don't your eyes look for truth?
    You struck your people down.
    But they didn't feel any pain.

You crushed them.
But they refused to be corrected.
They made their faces harder than
stone.
They refused to turn away from their
sins.
4 I thought, "The people of
Jerusalem are foolish.
They don't know how the LORD wants
them to live.
They don't know what their God
requires of them.
5 So I will go to the leaders.
I'll speak to them.
They should know how the LORD
wants them to live.
They must know what their God
requires of them."
But all of them had broken off the yoke
the LORD had put on them.
They had torn off the ropes he had
tied them up with.
6 So a lion from the forest will attack
them.
A wolf from the desert will destroy
them.
A leopard will hide and wait near their
towns.
It will tear to pieces anyone who
dares to go out.
Again and again they have refused to
obey the LORD.
They have turned away from him
many times.

7 The LORD says, "Jerusalem, why should
I forgive you?
Your people have deserted me.
They have taken their oaths in the
names of gods
that are not really gods at all.
I supplied everything they needed.
But they committed adultery.
Large crowds went to the houses of
prostitutes.
8 Your people are like stallions that have
plenty to eat.
Their sinful longings are out of
control.
Each of them goes after another
man's wife.
9 Shouldn't I punish them for that?"
announces the LORD.
"Shouldn't I pay back the nation
that does those things?

10 "Armies of Babylonia, go through their
vineyards and destroy them.
But do not destroy them completely.
Strip off their branches.
Those people do not belong to me.
11 The people of Israel and Judah

have not been faithful to me at all,"
announces the LORD.

12 They have told lies about the LORD.
They said, "He won't do anything!
No harm will come to us.
We will never see war or be hungry.
13 The prophets are nothing but wind.
Their message doesn't come from
the LORD.
So let what they say will happen be
done to them."

14 The LORD God rules over all. He says
to me,

"The people have spoken those words.
So my words will be like fire in your
mouth.
I will make the people like wood.
And the fire will burn them up."

15 "People of Israel, listen to me,"
announces the LORD.
"I am bringing against you
a nation from far away.
It is an old nation. And it will last for a
long time.
Its people speak a language you do
not know.
You can't understand what they are
saying.
16 The bags they carry their arrows in are
like an open grave.
All of their soldiers are mighty.
17 They will eat up your crops and your
food.
They will strike down your sons and
daughters.
They will kill your sheep and cattle.
They will destroy your vines and fig
trees.
You trust in your cities that have high
walls around them.
But the people in them will be killed
with swords.

18 "In spite of that, even in those days I
will not destroy you completely," announces the LORD.
19 " 'Jeremiah,' the people will ask,
'Why has the LORD our God done all of
this to us?'
"Then you will tell them, 'You have deserted the LORD. You have served other
gods in your own land. So now you will
serve another nation in a land that is not
your own.'

20 "Here is what I want you to announce
to the people of Jacob.
Tell it in Judah.
Tell them I say,
21 'Listen to this, you foolish people,

who do not have any sense.
You have eyes, but you do not see.
   You have ears, but you do not hear.
22 Shouldn't you have respect for me?'
   announces the LORD.
'Shouldn't you tremble with fear in
   front of me?
I made the sand to hold the ocean
   back.
   It will do that forever.
   The ocean can't go past it.
The waves might roll, but they can't
   sweep over it.
They might roar, but they can't go
   across it.
23 But you people have stubborn hearts.
   You refuse to obey me.
You have turned away from me.
You have gone down the wrong
   path.
24 You do not say to yourselves,
   "Let us have respect for the LORD our
   God.
He sends rain in the fall and the
   spring
He promises us that the harvest will
   come
at the same time each year."
25 But the things you have done wrong
   have robbed you of those gifts.
Your sins have kept those good things
   far away from you.'

26 "Jeremiah, some of my people are evil.
They hide and wait just as people
   hide to catch birds.
   They set traps for men.
27 A hunter uses tricks to fill his cage with
   birds.
And my people have filled their
   houses with a lot of goods.
They have become rich and powerful.
28   They have grown fat and heavy.
There is no limit to the evil things
   they do.
In court they do not state the case
   of children whose fathers have died.
They do not stand up for poor
   people.
29 Shouldn't I punish them for that?"
   announces the LORD.
"Shouldn't I pay back the
   nation that does those things?

30 "Something horrible and shocking
   has happened in the land.
31 The prophets prophesy lies.
The priests rule by their own
   authority.
And my people love it that way.
   But what will they do in the end?"

Babylonia Will Attack Jerusalem

6 The LORD says, "People of Benjamin,
   run for safety!
Run away from Jerusalem!
Blow trumpets in Tekoa!
   Warn everyone in Beth Hakkerem!
Horrible trouble is coming from the
   north.
The Babylonians will destroy
   everything with awful power.
2 I will destroy the city of Zion,
   even though it is very beautiful.
3 Shepherds will come against it with
   their flocks.
They will set up their tents around
   it.
All of them will take care of their
   own sheep."

4 The Babylonians say, "Prepare for
   battle against Judah!
Get up! Let's attack them at noon!
But the daylight is fading.
The shadows of evening are getting
   longer.
5 So get up! Let's attack them at night!
   Let's destroy their strongest forts!"

6 The LORD who rules over all speaks to
the Babylonians. He says,

"Cut some trees down.
Use the wood to build ramps against
   Jerusalem's walls.
I must punish that city.
   It is filled with people who treat
   others badly.
7 Wells keep giving fresh water.
   And Jerusalem keeps on sinning.
Its people are always fighting and
   causing trouble.
When I look at them,
I see nothing but sickness and
   wounds.
8 Jerusalem, listen to my warning.
   If you do not, I will turn away from
   you.
Your land will become a desert.
   No one will be able to live there."

9 The LORD rules over all. He says to me,

"People gather the few grapes that are
   left on a vine.
So let Israel's enemies gather the few
   people
who are left alive in the land.
Look carefully at the branches again.
   Do it like someone who gathers the
   last few grapes."

10 Who can I speak to? Who can I warn?
   Who will even listen to me?
Their ears are closed

so they can't hear.
The LORD's message displeases them.
They don't take any delight in it.
11 But the LORD's anger burns inside me.
I can no longer hold it in.

The LORD says to me, "Pour out my
anger on the children in the
street.
Pour it out on the young people who
are gathered together.
Husband and wife alike will be caught
in it.
So will those who are very old.
12 I will reach out my hand
against those who live in the land,"
announces the LORD.
"Then their houses will be turned over
to others.
So will their fields and their wives.
13 Everyone wants to get richer and
richer,
from the least important of them to
the most important.
Prophets and priests alike
try to fool everyone they can.
14 They bandage the wounds of my
people
as if they were not very deep.
'Peace, peace,' they say.
But there isn't any peace.
15 Are they ashamed of their hateful
actions?
No. They do not feel any shame at
all.
They do not even know how to
blush.
So they will fall like others who have
already fallen.
They will be brought down when I
punish them,"
says the LORD.

16 The LORD tells the people of Judah,

"Stand where the roads cross, and look
around.
Ask where the old paths are.
Ask for the good path, and walk on it.
Then your hearts will find rest in
me.
But you said, 'We won't walk on it.'
17 I appointed prophets to warn you. I
said,
'Listen to the sound of the
trumpets!'
But you said, 'We won't listen.'
18 So pay attention, you nations.
Be witnesses for me.
Watch what will happen to my
people.
19 Earth, pay attention.

I am going to bring trouble on them.
I will punish them because of the
evil things they have done.
They have not listened to my words.
They have said no to my law.
20 What do I care about incense from the
land of Sheba?
Why should I bother with sweet-
smelling cane from a land far
away?
I do not accept your burnt offerings.
Your sacrifices do not please me."

21 So the LORD says,

"I will bring an army against the
people of Judah.
Parents and children alike will trip
and fall.
Neighbors and friends will die."

22 The LORD says to Jerusalem,

"Look! An army is coming
from the land of the north.
I am stirring up a great nation.
Its army is coming from a land that
is very far away.
23 Its soldiers are armed with bows and
spears.
They are mean. They do not show
any mercy at all.
They come riding in on their horses.
They sound like the roaring ocean.
They are lined up for battle.
They are marching out
to attack you, city of Zion."

24 We have heard reports about them.
And our hands can't help us.
We are suffering greatly.
It's like the pain of a woman having
a baby.
25 Don't go out to the fields.
Don't walk on the roads.
Our enemies have swords.
And there is terror on every side.
26 Put on black clothes, my people.
Roll among the ashes.
Cry with bitter sobbing
just as you would cry for an only
child.
The one who is going to destroy us
will come suddenly.

27 The LORD says to me, "I have made you
like one who tests metals.
My people are the ore.
I want you to watch them
and test the way they live.
28 All of them are used to disobeying me.
They go around telling lies about
others.
They are like bronze mixed with iron.

All of them do very sinful things.
²⁹The fire is made very hot
　so the lead will burn away.
But it is impossible to make those
　people pure.
The Those who are evil are not removed.
³⁰They are like silver that is thrown away.
　That is because I have not accepted
　them."

Worshiping Other Gods Is Worthless

7 A message came to me from the LORD. He said, ²"Stand at the gate of my house. Announce my message to the people there. Say,

" 'Listen to the LORD's message, all of you people of Judah. You always come through these gates to worship the LORD. ³The God of Israel is speaking to you. He is the LORD who rules over all. He says, "Change the way you live and act. Then I will let you live in this place.

⁴" ' "Do not trust in lies. Do not say, 'This is the temple of the LORD! This is the temple of the LORD! This is the temple of the LORD!'

⁵" ' "You must really change the way you live and act. Treat each other fairly. ⁶Do not treat outsiders or widows badly in this place. Do not take advantage of children whose fathers have died. Do not kill those who are not guilty of doing anything wrong. Do not worship other gods. That will only bring harm to you.

⁷" ' "If you obey me, I will let you live in this place. It is the land I gave your people who lived long ago. It was promised to them for ever and ever.

⁸" ' "But look! You are trusting in worthless lies.

⁹" ' "You continue to steal and commit murder. You commit adultery and tell lies. You burn incense to Baal. You worship other gods you have not known anything about before.

¹⁰" ' "Then you come and stand in front of me. You keep coming to this house where I have put my Name. You say, 'We are safe.' You think you are safe when you do so many things I hate. ¹¹My Name is in this house. But you have made it a den for robbers! I have been watching you!" announces the LORD.

¹²" ' "Go now to the town of Shiloh. Go to the place where I first made a home for my Name. See what I did to it because of the evil things my people Israel were doing.

¹³" ' "I spoke to you again and again," announces the LORD. "I warned you while you were doing all of those things. But you did not listen. I called out to you. But you did not answer. ¹⁴So what I did to Shiloh I will now do to the house where my Name is. It is the temple you trust in. It is the place I gave to you and your people of long ago.

¹⁵" ' "But I will throw you out of my land. That is exactly what I did to the people of Ephraim. And they are your relatives." '

¹⁶"Jeremiah, do not pray for those people. Do not make any appeal or request for them. Do not beg me. I will not listen to you.

¹⁷"Don't you see what they are doing? They are worshiping other gods in the towns of Judah. They are offering sacrifices to them in the streets of Jerusalem. ¹⁸The children go out and gather wood. The fathers light the fire. The women mix the dough. They make flat cakes of bread for the goddess who is called the Queen of Heaven. They pour out drink offerings to other gods. That makes me very angry.

¹⁹"But am I the one they are hurting?" announces the LORD. "Aren't they only harming themselves? They should be ashamed of it."

²⁰So the LORD and King says, "I will pour out my burning anger on this place. It will strike people and animals alike. It will destroy the trees and the crops in the fields. It will burn, and no one will be able to put it out."

²¹The LORD who rules over all is the God of Israel. He says, "Go ahead! Add your burnt offerings to your other sacrifices. Eat the meat yourselves! ²²When I brought your people out of Egypt, I spoke to them. But I did not just give them commands about burnt offerings and sacrifices. ²³I also gave them another command. I said, 'Obey me. Then I will be your God. And you will be my people. Live the way I command you to live. Then things will go well with you.'

²⁴"But they did not listen. They refused to pay any attention to me. Instead, they did what their stubborn and evil hearts wanted them to do. They went backward and not forward.

²⁵"Again and again I sent my servants the prophets to you. They came to you day after day. They prophesied from the time your people left Egypt until now.

²⁶"But the people did not listen. They refused to pay any attention to me. They were stubborn. They did more evil things than their people who lived before them.

²⁷"Jeremiah, when you tell them all of

OBEYS ✔

[GOD] SAID, "OBEY ME. THEN I WILL BE YOUR GOD. AND YOU WILL BE MY PEOPLE. LIVE THE WAY I COMMAND YOU TO LIVE. THEN THINGS WILL GO WELL WITH YOU."
—— JEREMIAH 7:23 ——

that, they will not listen to you. When you call out to them, they will not answer. **28**"So say to them, 'You are a nation that has not obeyed the LORD your God. You did not pay attention when you were corrected. Truth has died out. You do not tell the truth anymore.' "

29The LORD says to the people of Jerusalem, "Cut off your hair. Throw it away. Sing a song of sadness on the bare hilltops. I am very angry with you. I have turned my back on you. I have deserted you.

The Valley of Death

30"The people of Judah have done what is evil in my eyes," announces the LORD. "They have set up statues of their gods. They have worshiped them in the house where my Name is. They have made my house 'unclean.' I hate those statues. **31**The people have built the high places of Topheth in the Valley of Ben Hinnom. There they worship other gods. And there they sacrifice their children in the fire. That is something I did not command. It did not even enter my mind.

32"So watch out!" announces the LORD. "The days are coming when people will not call it Topheth anymore. And they will not call it the Valley of Ben Hinnom either. Instead, they will call it the Valley of Death. They will bury the dead bodies of some people in Topheth. But they will run out of room. **33**Then they will not be able to bury the bodies of other people there. So the bodies will become food for the birds of the air and the wild animals. And no one will scare them away.

34"I will put an end to the sounds of joy and gladness. The voices of brides and grooms will not be heard anymore. There will not be any sounds of joy in the towns of Judah and the streets of Jerusalem. The land will become a desert.

8 "At that time the tombs will be opened," announces the LORD. "The bones of the kings and officials of Judah will be brought out. The bones of the priests and prophets will be removed. So will the bones of the people of Jerusalem. **2**They will lie outside under the sun, moon and all of the stars.

"All of those people had loved and served those things. They had followed them and worshiped them. They had asked them for advice. So the bones of those people will not be gathered up or buried again. Instead, they will be like trash lying there on the ground.

3"Everyone who is left alive in this evil nation will want to die rather than live. That is what they will long for in the lands where I force them to go," announces the LORD who rules over all.

The LORD Punishes His Sinful People

4"Jeremiah, tell them, 'The LORD says,

" ' "When people fall down, don't they
        get up again?
    When someone turns away, doesn't
        he come back?
5Then why have the people of
        Jerusalem turned away from
        me?
    Why do they always turn away?
They keep on telling lies.
    They refuse to come back to me.
6I have listened carefully.
    But they do not say what is right.
They refuse to turn away from their
        sins.
    No one says, 'What have I done?'
All of them go their own way.
    They are like horses charging into
        battle.
7Storks know when to fly south.
    So do doves, swifts and thrushes.
But my people do not know
    what I require them to do.

8" ' "How can you people say, 'We are
        wise.
    We have the law of the LORD'?
Actually, the teachers of the law have
        told lies about it.
    Their pens have not written what is
        true.
9Those who think they are wise will be
        put to shame.

They will become terrified. They will
be trapped.
They have not accepted my message.
So what kind of wisdom do they
have?
10 I will give their wives to other men.
I will give their fields to new owners.
Everyone wants to get richer and
richer,
from the least important of them to
the most important.
Prophets and priests alike
try to fool everyone they can.
11 They bandage the wounds of my
people
as if they were not very deep.
'Peace, peace,' they say.
But there isn't any peace.
12 Are they ashamed of their hateful
actions?
No. They do not feel any shame at
all.
They do not even know how to
blush.
So they will fall like others who have
already fallen.
They will be brought down when I
punish them,"
says the LORD.

13 " ' "I will take away their harvest,"
announces the LORD.
"There will not be any grapes on the
vines.
The trees will not bear any figs.
The leaves on the trees will dry up.
What I have given them
will be taken away from them." ' "

14 Why are we sitting here?
Let's gather together!
Let's run to the cities that have high
walls around them!
Let's die there!
The LORD our God has sentenced us to
death.
He has given us poisoned water to
drink.
That's because we've sinned against
him.
15 We hoped peace would come.
But nothing good has happened to
us.
We hoped we would finally be healed.
But all we got was terror.
16 When our enemy's horses snort,
the noise is heard all the way from
Dan.
When their stallions neigh,
the whole land trembles with fear.
They have come to destroy
the land and everything in it.

The city and everyone who lives
there will be destroyed.

17 "People of Judah, I will send poisonous
snakes among you.
No one will be able to charm them.
And they will bite you,"
announces the LORD.

18 LORD, my heart is weak inside me.
You comfort me when I'm sad.
19 Listen to the cries of my people
from a land far away.
They cry out, "Isn't the LORD in Zion?
Isn't its King there anymore?"

The LORD says, "Why have they made
me so angry
by worshiping their wooden gods?
Why have they made me angry
with their worthless statues
of gods from other lands?"

20 The people say, "The harvest is over.
The summer has ended.
And we still haven't been saved."

21 My people are crushed, so I am
crushed.
I sob, and I am filled with horror.
22 Isn't there any healing lotion in
Gilead?
Isn't there a doctor there?
Then why doesn't someone heal
the wounds of my people?

9 **1** I wish my head were a spring of
water!
I wish my eyes were a fountain of
tears!
I would sob day and night
over my people who have been
killed.

2 I wish I had somewhere to go in the
desert
where a traveler could stay!
Then I could leave my people.
I could get away from them.
All of them commit adultery by
worshiping other gods.
They aren't faithful to the LORD.

3 "They get ready to use
their tongues like bows,"
announces the LORD.
"Their mouths shoot out lies like
arrows.
They tell lies to gain power in the
land.
They go from one sin to another.
They do not pay any attention to
me.
4 Be on guard against your friends.
Do not trust the members of your
own family.

Every one of them cheats.
Every friend tells lies.
5 One friend cheats another.
No one tells the truth.
They have taught their tongues how to
lie.
They wear themselves out sinning.
6 Jeremiah, you live among people who
tell lies.
When they lie, they refuse to pay
any attention to me,"
announces the LORD.

7 So the LORD who rules over all says,

"I will put them through the fire to test
them.
What else can I do?
My people are so sinful!
8 Their tongues are like deadly arrows.
They tell lies.
With their mouths all of them speak
kindly to their neighbors.
But in their hearts they set traps for
them.
9 Shouldn't I punish them for that?"
announces the LORD.
"Shouldn't I pay back the nation
that does those things?"

10 I will cry and sob over the fields in the
hills.
I will sing a song of sadness about
the desert grasslands.
They are dry and empty. No one travels
through them.
The mooing of cattle isn't heard
there.
The birds of the air have flown away.
All of the animals are gone.

11 The LORD says, "I will knock all of
Jerusalem's buildings down.
I will make it a home for wild dogs.
The towns of Judah will be completely
destroyed.
No one will be able to live in them."

12 Who is wise enough to understand
those things? Who has been taught by
the LORD? Who can explain them? Why
has the land been destroyed so completely? Why has it become like a desert that
no one can go across?

13 The LORD answered me, "Because my
people have turned away from my law. I
gave it to them. But they have not kept it.
They have not obeyed me. **14** Instead, they
have done what their stubborn hearts
wanted them to do. They have worshiped
the gods that are named after Baal. They
have done what their people have taught
them to do down through the years."

15 So now the LORD who rules over all
speaks. He is the God of Israel. He says, "I
will make these people eat bitter food.
I will make them drink poisoned water.
16 I will scatter them among the nations.
They and their people before them have
not had anything to do with those nations before. I will chase these people with
swords. I will hunt them down until I
have destroyed them."

17 The LORD rules over all. He says,

"Here is something I want you to think
about.
Send for the women who sob over
the dead.
Send for the most skilled among
them."

18 Let them come quickly
and sob over us.
Let them cry until tears flow from our
eyes.
Let them sob until water pours out
of our eyes.
19 People are heard sobbing in Zion.
They are saying, "We are destroyed!
We are filled with shame!
We must leave our land.
Our houses have been torn down."

20 Women, hear the LORD's message.
Listen to what he's saying.
Teach your daughters how to sob over
the dead.
Teach one another a song of sadness.
21 Death has climbed in through our
windows.
It has entered our forts.
It has removed the children from the
streets.
It has taken the young people out of
the market places.

22 Say, "The LORD announces,

" 'The dead bodies of men will be like
trash
lying in the open fields.
They will lie there like grain
that is cut down at harvest time.
No one will gather them up.' "

23 The LORD says,

"Do not let a wise man brag about how
wise he is.
Do not let a strong man boast about
how strong he is.
Do not let a rich person brag about
how rich he is.
24 But here is what the one who brags
should boast about.

He should brag that he has
    understanding and knows me.
I want him to know that I am the LORD.
No matter what I do on earth, I am
    always kind, fair and right.
And I take delight in that,"
            announces the LORD.

25 "The days are coming when I will
judge people," announces the LORD. "I
will punish all those who are circumcised
only in their bodies. 26 That includes the
people of Egypt, Judah, Edom, Ammon
and Moab. It also includes all those who
live in the desert in places far away. None
of the people in those nations is really circumcised. And not even the people of Israel are circumcised in their hearts."

The LORD Is the Only True God

10 People of Israel, listen to what the
LORD is telling you. 2 He says,

"Do not follow the practices of other
    nations.
Do not be terrified by warnings in
    the sky.
Do not be afraid, even though the
    nations are terrified by them.
3 The practices of those nations are
    worthless.
People cut a tree out of the forest.
A skilled worker shapes the wood
    with a sharp tool.
4 Others decorate it with silver and gold.
They use a hammer to nail it to the
    floor.
They want to keep it from falling
    down.
5 The statues of their gods can't speak.
They are like scarecrows in a field of
    melons.
They have to be carried around
    because they can't walk.
So do not worship them.
They can't do you any harm.
And they can't do you any good
    either."

6 LORD, no one is like you.
You are great.
You are mighty and powerful.
7 King of the nations,
everyone should have respect for
    you.
That's what people should give you.
Among all of the wise people in the
    nations
there is no one like you.
No one can compare with you in all
    of their kingdoms.

8 All of them are foolish. They don't
    have any sense.
They think they are taught by
    worthless wooden gods.
9 Hammered silver is brought from
    Tarshish.
Gold is brought from Uphaz.
People who are skilled in working with
    wood and gold make a statue.
Then they put blue and purple
    clothes on it.
The whole thing is made by skilled
    workers.
10 But you are the only true God.
You are the only living God.
You are the King who rules forever.
When you are angry, the earth
    trembles with fear.
The nations can't stand up under
    your anger.

11 The LORD says to the Jews who are living in Babylonia, "Tell the people of the
nations, 'Your gods did not make the
heavens and the earth. In fact, those gods
will disappear from the earth. They will
vanish from under the heavens.' "

12 But God used his power to make the
    earth.
His wisdom set the world in place.
His understanding spread the
    heavens out.
13 When he thunders, the waters in the
    heavens roar.
He makes clouds rise from one end
    of the earth to the other.
He sends lightning along with the
    rain.
He brings the wind out from his
    storerooms.

14 No one has any sense. No one knows
    anything at all.
Everyone who works with gold is
    put to shame by his wooden
    gods.
The metal gods he worships are fakes.
They can't even breathe.
15 They are worthless. People make fun of
    them.
When the LORD judges them, they
    will be destroyed.
16 The God of Jacob is not like them.
He gives his people everything they
    need.
He made everything that exists.
And that includes Israel.
It's the nation that belongs to him.
His name is The LORD Who Rules
    Over All.

The Land Will Be Destroyed

17 People of Jerusalem, your enemies
    have surrounded you.
  They are attacking you.
  So gather up what belongs to you.
    Then leave the land.
18 The LORD says,
  "I am about to throw out of this land
    everyone who lives in it.
  I will bring trouble on them.
    They will be captured."

19 How terrible it will be for me!
    I've been wounded!
  And my wound can't be healed!
  In spite of that, I said to myself,
    "I'm sick. But I'll have to put up
    with it."
20 Jerusalem is like a tent that has been
    destroyed.
  All of its ropes have snapped.
  My people have gone away from me.
    Now no one is left to set up my tent.
  I have no one to set it up for me.
21 The leaders of my people are like
    shepherds
    who don't have any sense.
  They don't ask the LORD for advice.
    That's why they don't succeed.
  And that's why their whole flock
    is scattered like sheep.
22 Listen! A message is coming!
  I hear the sound of a great army
    marching down from the north!
  It will turn Judah's towns into a desert.
  They will become a home for wild
    dogs.

Jeremiah Prays to the LORD

23 LORD, I know that a man doesn't
    control his own life.
  He doesn't direct his own steps.
24 Correct me, LORD. But please be fair.
  Don't correct me when you are
    angry.
  If you do, nothing will be left of me.
25 Pour out your burning anger on the
    nations.
  They don't pay any attention to you.
  They refuse to worship you.
  They have destroyed the people of
    Jacob.
  They've wiped them out completely.
  They've also destroyed the land they
    lived in.

The LORD's People Have Broken His Covenant

11 A message came to me from the
LORD. He said, **2** "Listen to the
terms of the covenant I made with my
people long ago. Tell Judah the terms still
apply to them. Tell those who live in Jerusalem that they must obey them too.

3 "I am the God of Israel. So let the people know what I want them to do. Tell
them I am saying, 'May the man who
does not obey the terms of the covenant
be under my curse. **4** I gave those terms to
your people long ago. That was when I
brought them out of Egypt. I saved them
out of that furnace that melts iron down
and makes it pure.' I said, 'Obey me. Do
everything I command you to do. Then
you will be my people. And I will be your
God.

5 " 'I raised my hand and made an oath
to your people long ago. I promised them
I would give them a land that had plenty
of milk and honey.' It is the land you own
today. I kept my promise."

I replied, "Amen, LORD."

6 The LORD said to me, "Here is what I
want you to announce in the towns of Judah. Say it also in the streets of Jerusalem.
Tell the people, 'Listen to the terms of
my covenant. Obey them. **7** Long ago I
brought your people up from Egypt. From
that time until today, I warned them
again and again. I said, "Obey me."

8 " 'But they did not listen. They did not
pay any attention to me. Instead, they did
what their stubborn and evil hearts wanted them to do. So I brought down on
them all of the curses of the covenant. I
commanded them to obey it. But they refused.' "

9 The LORD continued, "The people of
Judah have made some evil plans. So have
those who live in Jerusalem. **10** All of them
have returned to the sins their people
committed long ago. Those people refused to listen to what I told them. And
now the people of Israel and Judah alike
have worshiped other gods and served
them. They have broken the covenant I
made with their people who lived before
them.

11 "So I say, 'I will bring trouble on
them. They will not be able to escape it.
They will cry out to me. But I will not listen to them.

12 " 'The people of Jerusalem and of the
towns of Judah will cry out to the gods
they burn incense to. But those gods will
not help them at all when trouble strikes
them. **13** Judah, you have as many gods as
you have towns. And in Jerusalem you
have set up as many altars as there are
streets. You are burning incense to that
shameful god Baal.'

14 "Jeremiah, do not pray for those people. Do not make any appeal or request for them. They will call out to me when they are in trouble. But I will not listen to them.

15 "I love the people of Judah.
But they are working out their evil
plans along with many others.
So what are they doing in my
temple?
Can meat that is offered to me keep me
from punishing you?
When you do evil things, you get a
lot of pleasure from them."

16 People of Judah, the LORD once called
you a healthy olive tree.
He thought its fruit was beautiful.
But now he will come with the roar of
a mighty storm.
He will set the tree on fire.
And its branches will be broken.

17 The LORD who rules over all planted you. But now he has ordered your enemies to destroy you. The people of Israel and Judah have done what is evil. They have made the LORD very angry by burning incense to Baal.

Jeremiah's Enemies Make Evil Plans Against Him

18 The LORD told me about the evil plans of my enemies. That's how I knew about them. He showed me what they were doing. 19 I had been like a gentle lamb that was led off to be killed. I didn't realize they had made plans against me. They had said,

"Let's destroy the tree and its fruit.
Let's cut him off while he's still
living.
Then his name won't be
remembered anymore."
20 But LORD, you rule over all.
You always judge fairly.
You put people's hearts and minds
to the test.
So pay them back for what they've
done.
I've committed my cause to you.

21 The LORD says, "Jeremiah, here is what I am telling you about the men of Anathoth. They want to kill you. They are saying, 'Don't prophesy in the LORD's name. If you do, we will kill you with our own hands.'" 22 So the LORD who rules over all says, "I will punish them. Their young men will be killed with swords. Their sons and daughters will die of hunger. 23 Only a few

people will be left alive. I will judge the men of Anathoth. I will destroy them when the time to punish them comes."

Jeremiah Argues With the LORD

12 LORD, when I bring a matter to you,
you always do what is right.
But now I would like to speak with
you
about whether you are being fair.
Why are sinful people successful?
Why do those who can't be trusted
have an easy life?
2 You have planted them.
Their roots are deep in the ground.
They grow and produce fruit.
They honor you by what they say.
But their hearts are far away from
you.
3 LORD, you know me and see me.
You test my thoughts about you.
Drag those people off like sheep to be
killed!
Set them apart for the day of their
death!
4 How long will the land be thirsty for
water?
How long will the grass in every field
be dry?
The people who live in the land are
evil.
So the animals and birds have died.
And that's not all. The people are
saying,
"The LORD won't see what happens
to us."

The LORD Replies to Jeremiah

5 The LORD says, "Suppose you have run
in a race with other men.
And suppose they have worn you
out.
Then how would you be able to race
against horses?
Suppose you feel safe only in open
country.
Then how would you get along in
the bushes near the Jordan
River?
6 Even your own family has turned
against you.
They have shouted loudly at you.
They might say nice things about you.
But do not trust them.

7 "I will turn my back on my people.
I will desert my land.
I love the people of Judah.
In spite of that, I will hand them
over to their enemies.

8 My land has become to me
    like a lion in the forest.
It roars at me.
    So I hate it.
9 My own land has become like a spotted
    hawk.
And other hawks surround it and
    attack it.
Come, all of you wild animals!
    Gather together!
Come together to eat up my land.
10 Many shepherds will destroy my
    vineyard.
They will walk all over it.
They will turn my pleasant vineyard
    into a dry and empty land.
11 My vineyard will become a desert.
It will be dry and empty in my sight.
The whole land will be completely
    destroyed.
    And no one even cares.
12 Many will come to destroy it.
They will gather on the bare hilltops
    in the desert.
I will use them as my sword to destroy
    my people.
They will kill them from one end of
    the land to the other.
    No one will be safe.
13 People will plant wheat. But all they
    will gather is thorns.
They will wear themselves out. But
    they will not have anything to
    show for it.
My anger is burning against you.
    So you will be ashamed of the crop
    you gather."

14 The Lord continues, "All of my evil neighbors have taken over the land I gave my people Israel. So I will pull them up by their roots from the lands they live in. And I will pull up the roots of the people of Judah from among them. **15** "But after I pull those nations up, I will show my tender love to them again. I will bring all of them back to their own lands. I will take all of them back to their own countries. **16** "Suppose they learn to follow the practices of my people. And they take an oath and make a promise in my name. They say, 'You can be sure that the Lord is alive.' They do it just as they once taught my people to take oaths in Baal's name. Then I will give them a place among my people. **17** "But what if one of those nations does not listen? Then you can be sure I will pull it up by the roots and destroy it," announces the Lord.

A Linen Belt

13 The Lord said to me, "Go and buy a linen belt. Put it around your waist. But do not let it get wet."

2 So I bought a belt, just as the Lord had told me to do. And I put it around my waist.

3 Then another message came to me from the Lord. He said, **4** "Take off the belt you bought and are wearing around your waist. Go to Perath. Hide the belt there in a crack in the rocks."

5 So I went and hid it at Perath. I did just as the Lord had told me to do.

6 Many days later the Lord spoke to me again. He told me, "Go to Perath. Get the belt I told you to hide there."

7 So I went to Perath. I dug up the belt. I took it from the place where I had hidden it. But it had rotted. It was completely useless.

8 Then another message came to me from the Lord. He said, **9** "In the same way, I will destroy Judah's pride. And I will destroy the great pride of Jerusalem. **10** "Those people are evil. They refuse to listen to what I say. They do what their stubborn hearts want them to do. They chase after other gods. They serve them and worship them. So they will be like this belt. They will be completely useless. **11** A belt is tied around a man's waist. In the same way, I tied all of the people of Israel and Judah to me," announces the Lord. "I wanted them to be my people. They should have brought me fame and praise and honor. But they have not listened to me.

Wineskins

12 "Tell them, 'The Lord is the God of Israel. He says, "Every wineskin should be filled with wine." '

"The people might say to you, 'Don't we know that every wineskin should be filled with wine?'

13 "If they do, tell them, 'The Lord says, "I am going to fill with wine everyone who lives in this land. I will make the kings who sit on David's throne drunk. And I will fill with wine the priests, the prophets and everyone who lives in Jerusalem. **14** I will smash them against one another. I will punish parents and children alike," announces the Lord. "I will not feel sorry for them. I will not show them any kindness. My tender love for them will not keep me from destroying them." ' "

Judah Will Be Taken Away From Their Land

15 People of Judah, listen to me.
　　Pay attention. Don't be proud.
　　The LORD has spoken.
16 Give glory to the LORD your God.
　　Honor him before he sends
　　　darkness to cover the land.
　　Do it before you trip and fall
　　　on the darkened hills.
　　You hope that light will come.
　　But he will turn it into thick
　　　darkness.
　　He will change it to deep shadows.
17 If you don't listen,
　　I will sob in secret.
　　Because you are so proud,
　　I will sob bitterly.
　　Tears will flow from my eyes.
　　The LORD's flock will be taken away
　　　as prisoners.

18 Speak to the king and his mother. Tell
　　them,
　　"Come down from your thrones.
　　Your glorious crowns
　　　are about to fall from your heads."
19 The gates of the cities in the Negev
　　Desert will be shut tight.
　　There won't be anyone to open
　　　them.
　　You will be carried away as prisoners.
　　You will be taken away completely.

20 Jerusalem, look up!
　　Your enemies are coming from the
　　　north.
　　Where is the flock you were supposed
　　　to take care of?
　　Where are the sheep you were so
　　　proud of?
21 You have worked hard to make special
　　friends.
　　But the LORD will let them rule over
　　　you.
　　Then what will you say?
　　Suffering will take hold of you.
　　It will be like the pain of a woman
　　　having a baby.
22 Suppose you ask yourself,
　　"Why has this happened to me?"
　　It's because you have committed so
　　　many sins.
　　That's the reason your skirt has been
　　　torn off.
　　That's why your body has been
　　　treated so badly.
23 Can people from Ethiopia change their
　　skin?
　　Can leopards change their spots?
　　It's the same with you.
　　You have always done what is evil.

So how can you do what is good?
24 The LORD says, "I will scatter you like
　　straw
　　that the desert wind blows away.
25 That is what will happen to you.
　　I have appointed it for you,"
　　　　　　　　announces the LORD.
　　"You have forgotten me.
　　You have trusted in other gods.
26 So I will pull your skirt up over your
　　face.
　　Then people will see the shame of
　　　your naked body.
27 They will see that you have not been
　　faithful to me.
　　You have committed adultery with
　　　other gods.
　　And you have acted like a prostitute
　　　who does not have any shame.
　　I have seen what you did
　　　on the hills and in the fields.
　　And I hate it.
　　How terrible it will be for you,
　　　Jerusalem!
　　How long will you choose to be
　　　'unclean'?"

War and Hunger

14 A message came to me from the
LORD. He told me there wouldn't
be any rain in the land. He said,

2 "Judah is filled with sadness.
　　Its cities are wasting away.
　　The people sob over the land.
　　Crying is heard in Jerusalem.
3 The nobles send their servants to get
　　water.
　　They go to the wells.
　　But they do not find any water.
　　They return with empty jars.
　　They are terrified. They do not have
　　　any hope.
　　They cover their heads.
4 The ground is dry and cracked.
　　There isn't any rain in the land.
　　The farmers are terrified.
　　They cover their heads.
5 Even the does in the fields
　　desert their newborn fawns.
　　There isn't any grass to eat.
6 Wild donkeys stand on the bare
　　hilltops.
　　They long for water as wild dogs do.
　　Their eyesight fails
　　because they do not have any grass
　　　to eat."

7 Our sins are a witness against us.
　　LORD, do something for the honor of
　　　your name.

We have completely turned away from
    you.
We've sinned against you.
8 You are Israel's only hope.
    You save us when we're in trouble.
Why are you like a stranger to us?
    Why are you like a traveler who stays
        for only one night?
9 Why are you like a man who is taken
        by surprise?
Why are you like a soldier who can't
        save anyone?
Lord, you are among us.
    And we are your people.
    Please don't desert us!

10 The Lord has given me a message
about these people. He says,

"They really love to wander away from
    me.
Their feet go down the wrong path.
I do not accept these people.
I will remember the evil things they
    have done.
I will punish them for their sins."

11 The Lord continued, "Do not pray
that things will go well with them. **12** Even
if they go without food, I will not listen to
their cry for help. They might sacrifice
burnt offerings and grain offerings. But I
will not accept them. Instead, I will destroy them with war, hunger and plague."

13 But I said, "Lord and King, the prophets keep telling them something else.
They say, 'You won't have to suffer from
war or hunger. Instead, the Lord will give
you peace and rest in this place.' "

14 Then the Lord said to me, "The
prophets are prophesying lies in my
name. I have not sent them or appointed
them. I have not even spoken to them.
Everything they tell you about their visions or secret knowledge is a lie. They
pretend to bring you messages from other
gods. They try to get you to believe their
own mistaken ideas.

15 "So here is what I am saying about the
prophets who are prophesying in my
name. I did not send them. But they are
saying, 'No war or hunger will come to
this land.' Those same prophets will die
because of war and hunger. **16** And the
people they are prophesying to will be
thrown out into the streets of Jerusalem.
They will die because of hunger and war.
No one will bury their bodies. No one will
bury their wives or children. I will pour
trouble out on them. That is exactly what
they should get.

17 "Jeremiah, give them this message.
Tell them,

" 'Let tears flow from my eyes.
Let them pour out night and day.
Never let them stop.
The people of my own nation
    have suffered a terrible wound.
They have been crushed.
18 Suppose I go into the country.
    Then I see people who have been
        killed with swords.
Or suppose I go into the city.
    Then I see people who have died of
        hunger.
Prophet and priest alike have gone to a
    land
    they hadn't had anything to do with
        before.' "

19 Lord, have you turned your back on
    Judah completely?
Do you hate the city of Zion?
Why have you made us suffer?
    We can't be healed.
We hoped peace would come.
    But nothing good has happened to
        us.
We hoped we would finally be healed.
    But all we got was terror.
20 Lord, we admit we've done evil things.
    We also admit that our people of
        long ago were guilty.
It's true that we've sinned against
        you.
21 For the honor of your name, don't
    turn your back on us.
Don't bring shame on your glorious
    throne in the temple.
Remember the covenant you made
    with us.
Please don't break it.
22 Do any of the worthless gods of the
    nations bring rain?
Do the skies send down showers all
    by themselves?
No. Lord our God, you send the rain.
So we put our hope in you.
    You are the one who does all of
    those things.

15 Then the Lord said to me, "Suppose Moses and Samuel were
standing in front of me. Even then my
heart would not feel sorry for these people. Send them away from me! Let
them go!
2 "Suppose they ask you, 'Where should
we go?'
"Then tell them, 'The Lord says,

" ' "Those I have appointed to die will
    die.

Those I have appointed to be killed
with swords
will be killed with swords.
Those I have appointed to die of
hunger
will die of hunger.
Those I have appointed to be taken
away as prisoners
will be taken away." '

3 "I will send four kinds of destroyers against them," announces the LORD. "Swords will kill them. Dogs will drag them away. Birds of the air will eat them up. And wild animals will destroy them.

4 "I will make all of the kingdoms on earth hate them. That will happen because of what Manasseh did in Jerusalem. He was king of Judah and the son of Hezekiah.

5 "Jerusalem, who will have pity on you?
Who will sob over you?
Who will stop to ask how you are
doing?
6 You have said no to me," announces
the LORD.
"You keep on turning away from
me.
So I will destroy you with my own
hands.
I can't show you my tender love
anymore.
7 I will stand at the city gates of the land.
I will separate the straw from the
grain.
I will destroy my people. I will bring
great sorrow on them.
They have not changed their ways.
8 I will increase the number of their
widows.
They will be more than the grains of
sand on the seashore.
At noon I will bring a destroyer
against the mothers of the young
men among my people.
All at once I will bring down on them
great suffering and terror.
9 Mothers who have many children will
grow weak.
They will take their last breath.
The sun will set on them while it is still
day.
They will be dishonored and put to
shame.
All those who are left alive I will kill
with swords.
I will have their enemies do it,"
announces the LORD.

10 My mother, I wish I had never been
born!

The whole land opposes me.
They fight against me.
I haven't made loans to anyone.
And I haven't borrowed anything.
But everyone still calls down curses
on me.

11 The LORD said,

"Jeremiah, I will keep you safe for a
good purpose.
I will make your enemies ask you to
pray for them.
They will make their appeal to you
when they are in great trouble.

12 "People of Judah, the armies of
Babylonia
will come from the north.
They are as strong as iron and bronze.
Can anyone break their power?
13 I will give away your wealth and your
treasures.
Your enemies will carry off
everything.
And they will not pay anything
for it.
That will happen because you have
sinned so much.
You have done it all through your
country.
14 I will make you slaves to your enemies.
You will serve them in a land
you have not had anything to do
with before.
My anger will start a fire
that will burn you up."

15 LORD, you understand how much I'm
suffering.
Show concern for me. Take care of
me.
Pay back those who are trying to
harm me.
You are patient. Don't take my life
away from me.
Think about how much shame I
suffer because of you.
16 When I received your words, I ate
them.
They filled me with joy.
My heart took delight in them.
LORD God who rules over all,
I belong to you.
17 I never sat around with those who go
to wild parties.
I never had a good time with them.
I sat alone because you had put your
powerful hand on me.
Your anger against sin was burning
inside me.
18 Why does my pain never end?
Why is my wound so deep?

FORGIVING F

TURN AWAY FROM YOUR SINS. THEN I WILL HEAL YOU. AND THEN YOU WILL BE ABLE TO SERVE ME.

— JEREMIAH 15:19 —

Why can't I ever get well?
To me you are like a stream that runs
    dry.
You are like a spring that doesn't
    have any water.

¹⁹So the LORD says,

"Turn away from your sins. Then I will
    heal you.
And then you will be able to serve
    me.
Speak words that are worthy, not
    worthless.
Then you will be speaking for me.
Let these people turn to you.
But you must not turn to them.
²⁰ I will make you like a wall to them.
I will make you like a strong bronze
    wall.
The people will fight against you.
But they will not overcome you.
I am with you.
I will save you,"
                  announces the LORD.
²¹ "I will save you from the hands of evil
    people.
I will set you free from those who
    treat you badly."

Times of Trouble Are Coming

16 A message came to me from the
LORD. He said, ²"You must not get
married. You must not have any sons or
daughters in this land." ³Here is the LORD's message about the
children who are born in this place. He
says about them and their parents,
⁴"Some of them will die of deadly sicknesses. No one will sob over them. Their
bodies will not be buried. Instead, they
will be like trash lying there on the
ground. Others will die because of war
and hunger. Their bodies will not be
buried. Instead, they will become food for
the birds of the air and the wild animals."

⁵The LORD says, "Jeremiah, do not enter
a house where a meal is being served because someone has died. Do not go there
to sob or to comfort the family. I will not
bless these people anymore. I have taken
my love and pity away from them," announces the LORD.
⁶"Important and ordinary people alike
will die in this land. Their bodies will not
be buried. No one will sob over them. No
one will cut himself or shave his head because of them. ⁷No one will offer food or
drink to comfort those who sob over the
dead. No one will do it even if someone's
father or mother has died.
⁸"Do not enter a house where a big dinner party is being held. Do not sit down
there to eat and drink. ⁹I am the LORD
who rules over all. I am the God of Israel. I
am telling you, 'In your days I will judge
your people. You will see it with your own
eyes. I will put an end to the sounds of joy
and gladness here in Jerusalem. The
voices of brides and grooms will not be
heard anymore.'
¹⁰"Tell these people all of those things.
They will ask you, 'Why has the LORD decided to send so much trouble on us? We
haven't done anything wrong. We
haven't committed any sins against the
LORD our God.'
¹¹"When they say that, tell them, 'I did
it because your people of long ago deserted me,' announces the LORD. 'They followed other gods. They served them and
worshiped them. They deserted me. They
did not obey my law.
¹²" 'But you have done more evil things
than they did. All of you are doing what
your stubborn and evil hearts want you to
do. You are not obeying me.
¹³" 'So I will throw you out of this land.
I will send you away to a land that you and
your people have not had anything to do
with before. There you will serve other
gods day and night. And I will not show
you any favor.'
¹⁴"But a new day is coming," announces the LORD. "At that time people
will no longer say, 'The LORD brought the
people of Israel up out of Egypt. And
that's just as sure as he is alive.'
¹⁵"Instead, they will say, 'The LORD
brought the people of Israel up out of the
land of the north. He gathered them out
of all of the countries where he had forced
them to go. And that's just as sure as he is
alive.' I will bring them back to the land I
gave their people long ago.
¹⁶"But now I will send for many fishermen," announces the LORD. "They will

catch some of these people. After that, I will send for many hunters. They will hunt the others down on every mountain and hill. They will bring them out of the cracks in the rocks. **17**My eyes see everything these people do. What they do is not hidden from me. I always see their sin. **18**I will pay them back double for their sin and the evil things they have done. They have made my land 'unclean.' They have set up lifeless statues of their evil gods. They have filled my land with them. I hate those gods."

19Lord, you give me strength.
　　You are like a fort to me.
When I'm in trouble,
　　I go to you for safety.
The nations will come to you
　　from one end of the earth to the
　　　　other.
　　They will gather together and say,
"Our people of long ago didn't own
　　anything
except statues of gods.
The statues were worthless.
　　They didn't do them any good.

STRONG

LORD, YOU GIVE ME STRENGTH.

YOU ARE LIKE A FORT TO ME.

WHEN I'M IN TROUBLE,

I GO TO YOU FOR SAFETY.

—— JEREMIAH 16:19 ——

20Do men really make their own gods?
　　Yes. But they aren't really gods at
　　　　all!"

21The Lord says, "So I will teach them
　　about myself.
This time I will show them
　　how powerful and mighty I am.
Then they will know
　　that I am the Lord.

17 "Judah's sin is carved with an iron
　　tool.
It is written with a sharp stone.
It is carved on the tablets of their
　　hearts.

It is written on the horns that stick
　　out
　　from the corners of their altars.
2Even their children offer sacrifices
　　to other gods on those altars.
They use the poles that were made
　　to worship the goddess Asherah.
They worship strange gods beside the
　　green trees
　　and on the high hills.
3I will give away my holy Mount Zion to
　　the Babylonians.
Your enemies will carry off your
　　wealth
　　and all of your treasures.
I will give away your high places.
　　That will happen because you have
　　　　sinned.
You have done it all through your
　　country.
4You will lose the land I gave you.
　　And it will be your own fault.
I will make you slaves to your enemies.
　　You will serve them in a land you
　　　　have not had anything to do
　　　　with before.
You have set my anger on fire.
　　It will burn forever."

5The Lord says,

"Those who trust in man are under my
　　curse.
　　They depend on human strength.
　　Their hearts turn away from me.
6They will be like a bush in a dry and
　　empty land.
　　They will not enjoy success when it
　　　　comes.
They will live in dry places in the
　　desert.
　　It is a land of salt where no one else
　　　　lives.

7"But I will bless any man who trusts in
　　me.
　　I will show my favor to the one who
　　　　depends on me.
8He will be like a tree that is planted
　　near water.
　　It sends out its roots beside a stream.
It is not afraid when heat comes.
　　Its leaves are always green.
It does not worry when there is no
　　rain.
　　It always bears fruit."

9A human heart is more dishonest than
　　anything else.
　　It can't be healed.
　　Who can understand it?

10 The LORD says, "I look deep down
    inside human hearts.
I see what is in people's minds.
I reward a man in keeping with his
    conduct.
I bless him based on what he has
    done."

11 Some people get rich in the wrong
    way.
They are like a partridge that
    hatches eggs it didn't lay.
When their lives are half over, their
    riches will desert them.
In the end they will prove how
    foolish they have been.

12 Our temple is where the LORD's
    glorious throne is.
From the beginning it has been high
    and lifted up.
13 LORD, you are Israel's only hope.
Everyone who deserts you will be
    put to shame.
The names of those who turn away
    from you will be listed among
    the dead.
LORD, they have deserted you.
You are the spring of water that gives
    life.

14 LORD, heal me. Then I will be healed.
Save me from my enemies. Then I
    will be saved.
You are the one I praise.
15 They keep saying to me,
"What has happened to the message
    the LORD gave you?
Let it come true right now!"
16 I haven't run away from being the
    shepherd of your people.
You know I haven't wanted the day
    of Jerusalem's fall to come.
You are aware of every word that
    comes from my lips.
17 Don't be a terror to me.
When I'm in trouble, I go to you for
    safety.
18 Let those who attack me be put to
    shame.
But keep me from shame.
Let them be terrified.
But keep me from terror.
Bring the day of trouble on them.
Destroy them once and for all.

Keep the Sabbath Day Holy

19 The LORD said to me, "Go. Stand at
the city gate where the people gather together. That is where the kings of Judah
go in and out. Also go to all of the other
gates of Jerusalem. **20** Say, 'Listen to the
LORD's message, you kings of Judah and all
of you people of Judah and Jerusalem.
You always come through these gates.
21 " 'The LORD says, "Make sure you do
not carry a load on the Sabbath day. Do
not bring it through the gates of Jerusalem. **22** Do not bring a load out of your
houses on the Sabbath. Do not do any
work on that day. Instead, keep the Sabbath day holy. Do as I commanded your
people long ago. **23** But they did not listen.
They did not pay any attention to me.
They were stubborn. They would not listen or pay attention when I corrected
them.
24 " ' "Be careful to obey me," announces the LORD. "Do not bring a load
through the gates of this city on the Sabbath. Instead, keep the Sabbath day holy.
Do not do any work on it.
25 " ' "Then kings who sit on David's
throne will come through the gates of this
city. They and their officials will come riding in chariots and on horses. The people
of Judah and Jerusalem will come along
with them. And this city will always have
people living in it. **26** Some will come from
the towns of Judah. And some will come
in from the villages around Jerusalem.
Others will come from the territory of
Benjamin. And others will come in from
the western hills. Still others will come
from the central hill country and the Negev Desert. All of them will bring burnt offerings and sacrifices. They will come
bringing grain offerings, incense and
thank offerings. They will take all of those
offerings to my house.
27 " ' "But what if you do not obey me?
Suppose you do not keep the Sabbath day
holy. And suppose you carry a load
through the gates of Jerusalem on the
Sabbath. Then I will start a fire that can't
be put out. It will begin at the gates of Jerusalem. It will destroy its mighty towers." ' "

The LORD Sends Jeremiah
to the Potter's House

18 A message came to me from the
LORD. He said, **2** "Go down to the
potter's house. I will give you my message
there."
3 So I went down to the potter's house. I
saw him working at his wheel. **4** His hands
were shaping a pot out of clay. But he saw
that something was wrong with it. So he
formed it into another pot. He shaped it
in the way that seemed best to him.
5 Then the LORD's message came to me.
He said, **6** "People of Israel, I can do with

you just as this potter does," announces the LORD. "The clay is in the potter's hand. And you are in my hand, people of Israel.

7"Suppose at any time I announce that a nation or kingdom is going to be pulled up by the roots. And I tell it that it will be torn down and destroyed. **8**But suppose the nation I warned turns away from its sins. Then I will not do what I said I would. I will not bring trouble on it as I had planned.

9"Suppose at another time I announce that a nation or kingdom is going to be built up and planted. **10**But it does what is evil in my sight. It does not obey me. Then I will think again about the good things I had wanted to do for it.

11"So speak to the people of Judah and Jerusalem. Tell them, 'The LORD says, "Look! I am making plans against you. I am going to bring trouble on you. So each one of you must turn from your evil ways. Change the way you live and act." '

12"But they will reply, 'It's no use. We will continue to do what we've already planned. All of us will do what our stubborn and evil hearts want us to do.' "

13So the LORD says,

"Ask the nations a question. Say to them,
'Who has ever heard anything like this?
The people of Israel have done a very horrible thing.
14Does the snow ever disappear from Lebanon's rocky slopes?
Do its cool waters ever stop flowing from places far away?
15But my people have forgotten me. They burn incense to worthless gods.
Their gods made them trip and fall as they walked on the old paths.
They made them use side roads instead of roads that were built up.
16So their land will be completely destroyed.
People will make fun of it again and again.
All those who pass by it will be shocked.
They will shake their heads.
17I will sweep over my people like a wind from the east.
I will use the Babylonians to scatter them.
I will show them my back and not my face.
I will desert them when their day of trouble comes.' "

18They said, "Come on. Let's make plans against Jeremiah. We'll still have priests to teach us the law. We'll always have wise people to give us advice. We'll have prophets to bring us messages from the LORD. So come on. Let's speak out against Jeremiah. We shouldn't pay any attention to what he says."

19LORD, please listen to me!
Hear what my enemies are saying about me!
20Should the good things I've done be paid back with evil?
But my enemies have dug a pit for me.
Remember that I stood in front of you and spoke up for them.
I tried to turn your anger away from them.
21So let their children die of hunger.
Let my enemies be killed in war.
Let their wives lose their children and husbands.
Let their men be put to death.
Let their young men be killed in battle.
22Bring their enemies against them without warning.
Let cries be heard from their houses.
They have dug a pit to capture me.
They have hidden traps for my feet.
23But LORD, you know all about their plans to kill me.
Don't forgive their crimes.
Don't erase their sins from your sight.
Destroy my enemies.
Punish them when the time to show your anger comes.

19 The LORD said to me, "Go and buy a clay jar from a potter. Take along some of the elders of the people. Also tell some of the priests to go with you. **2**Go out to the Valley of Ben Hinnom. Stand near the entrance of the gate where broken pieces of pottery are thrown away.

"There announce the message I give you. **3**Tell the people, 'Listen to the LORD's message, you kings of Judah and people of Jerusalem. The LORD who rules over all is the God of Israel. He says, "Listen! I am going to bring trouble on Jerusalem. It will be so horrible that it will make the ears of everyone who hears about it ring.

4" ' "My people have deserted me. They have made this city a place where other gods are worshiped. They have burned sacrifices to them here. They and their people and the kings of Judah had never had anything to do with those gods before. My people have also filled this place with the blood of those who are not guilty of anything. 5They have built the high places where they worship Baal. There they sacrifice their children in the fire as offerings to Baal. That is something I did not command or talk about. It did not even enter my mind.

6" ' "So watch out!" announces the LORD. "The days are coming when people will not call this place Topheth anymore. And they will not call it the Valley of Ben Hinnom either. Instead, they will call it the Valley of Death.

7" ' "In this place I will make the plans of Judah and Jerusalem as useless as a broken jar. I will use their enemies to kill my people with swords. They will die at the hands of those who want to take their lives. I will give their dead bodies as food to the birds of the air and the wild animals.

8" ' "I will destroy this city completely. People will make fun of it. All those who pass by it will be shocked. They will laugh at its people because of all of their wounds. 9I will make the people of this city eat the dead bodies of their sons and daughters. And they will eat one another. They will do it because things will be so bad during the attack. The enemies who want to take their lives will bring all of that trouble on them." '

10"Jeremiah, break the jar while those who go with you are watching. 11Tell them, 'The LORD who rules over all says, "This potter's jar is smashed and can't be repaired. And I will smash this nation and this city. People will bury their dead in Topheth. But they will run out of room. 12Here is what I will do to Jerusalem and those who live here," announces the LORD. "I will make this city like Topheth. 13The houses in Jerusalem will be made 'unclean' like Topheth. So will the houses of the kings of Judah. All of those people burned incense on their roofs to all of the stars. They poured out drink offerings to other gods." ' "

14Then I returned from Topheth. That's where the LORD had sent me to prophesy. I stood in the courtyard of the LORD's temple. I spoke to all of the people. I said, 15"The LORD who rules over all is the God of Israel. He says, 'Listen! I am going to punish this city and the villages that are around it. I am going to bring against them all of the trouble I have announced. That is because my people were stubborn. They would not listen to what I said.' "

Jeremiah and Pashhur

20 The priest Pashhur was chief officer in the LORD's temple. He was the son of Immer. Pashhur heard me prophesying that Jerusalem would be destroyed. 2So he had me beaten. Then he put me in prison at the Upper Gate of Benjamin at the LORD's temple.

3The next day Pashhur set me free. I said to him, "The LORD's name for you isn't Pashhur. It's Magor-Missabib. That name means Terror on Every Side.

4"The LORD says to you, 'I will make you a terror to yourself. You will also be a terror to all of your friends. With your own eyes you will see them die. Their enemies will kill them with swords. I will hand all of the people of Judah over to the king of Babylonia. He will carry them away to Babylonia or kill them with swords.

5" 'I will hand all of the wealth of this city over to Judah's enemies. I will give them all of its products and everything of value. I will turn over to them all of the treasures that belonged to the kings of Judah. They will take those things and carry them off to Babylon.

6" 'Pashhur, you and everyone who lives in your house will also be forced to go there. You have prophesied lies to all of your friends. So all of you will die in Babylonia. And that's where your bodies will be buried.' "

Jeremiah Argues With the LORD

7LORD, you tricked me, and I was tricked.
    You overpowered me and won.
People make fun of me all day long.
    Everyone laughs at me.

8Every time I speak, I cry out.
    All you ever tell me to talk about
    is fighting and trouble.
Your message has brought me nothing
        but dishonor.
    It has made me suffer shame all day
        long.
9Sometimes I think, "I won't talk about
        him anymore.
    I'll never speak in his name again."
But then your message burns in my
        heart.
    It's like a fire inside my very bones.
I'm tired of holding it in.
    In fact, I can't.
10I hear many people whispering,
    "There is terror on every side!
    Report Jeremiah! Let's report him to
        the authorities!"
All of my friends
    are waiting for me to slip.

They are saying, "Perhaps he will be
tricked
into making a mistake.
Then we'll win out over him.
We'll get even with him."

11 But you are with me like a mighty
warrior.
So those who are trying to harm me
will trip and fall.
They won't win out over me.
They will fail. They'll be totally put to
shame.
Their dishonor will never be
forgotten.

12 LORD, you rule over all.
You test those who do what is right.
You see what is in people's hearts
and minds.
So pay them back for what they've
done.
I've committed my cause to you.

13 Sing to the LORD, you people!
Give praise to him!
He saves the lives of those who are in
need.
He saves them from the powerful
hands of sinful people.

14 May the day I was born be under a
curse!
May the day I was born to my
mother not be blessed!
15 May the man who brought my father
the news be under a curse!
He's the one who made my father
very glad.
He said, "You have had a baby! It's a
boy!"
16 May that man be like the towns
the LORD destroyed without pity.
May that man hear loud sobs in the
morning.
May he hear a battle cry at noon.
17 He should have killed me in my
mother's body.
He should have made my mother
my grave.
He should have let her body stay
large forever.
18 Why did I ever come out of my
mother's body?
I've seen nothing but trouble and
sorrow.
My days will end in shame.

The LORD Refuses Zedekiah's Appeal

21 A message came to me from the
LORD. It came when King Zedekiah
sent Pashhur to me. Pashhur was the son

of Malkijah. Zedekiah sent the priest
Zephaniah along with him. Zephaniah
was the son of Maaseiah. They said to me,
2 "Ask the LORD to help us. Nebuchadnezzar is attacking us. He is king of Babylonia.
In the past the LORD did wonderful things
for us. Maybe he'll do them again. Then
Nebuchadnezzar will pull his armies back
from us."

3 But I answered them, "Tell Zedekiah
and his people, 4 'The LORD is the God of
Israel. He says, "The king of Babylonia and
his armies are all around this city. They
are getting ready to attack you. You have
weapons of war in your hands to fight
against them. But I am about to turn your
weapons against you. And I will bring
your enemies inside this city.

5 " ' "I myself will fight against you. I
will reach out my powerful hand and
mighty arm. I will come against you with
all of my burning anger. 6 I will strike
down those who live in this city. I will kill
people and animals alike. They will die of
a terrible plague.

7 " ' "After that, I will hand you over to
your enemies who want to kill you," announces the LORD. "I will hand over Zedekiah, the king of Judah. I will hand over
his officials and the people in this city
who live through the plague, war and
hunger. All of them will be turned over to
Nebuchadnezzar, the king of Babylonia.
He will kill them with swords. He will not
show them any kindness. He will not feel
sorry for them. In fact, he will not have
any concern for them at all." '

8 "Tell the people, 'The LORD says, "I am
offering you a choice. You can choose the
way that leads to life. Or you can choose
the way that leads to death. 9 Those who
stay in this city will die of war, hunger or
plague. But those who go out and give
themselves up to the Babylonians who are
attacking you will live. They will escape
with their lives.

10 " ' "I have decided to do this city
harm and not good," announces the
LORD. "It will be handed over to the king
of Babylonia. And he will destroy it with
fire." '

11 "Also speak to Judah's royal family.
Tell them, 'Listen to the LORD's message.
12 The LORD says to you who belong to David's royal house,

" ' "Every morning do what is right
and fair.
Save those who have been robbed.
Set them free from the people who
have treated them badly.

If you do not, my anger will blaze out
against you.
It will burn like fire because of the
evil things you have done.
No one will be able to put it out.
¹³ Jerusalem, I am against you,"
announces the LORD.
"You live above this valley.
You are on a high, rocky flatland.
And you say, 'Who can come against
us?
Who can enter our place of safety?'
¹⁴ But I will punish you in keeping with
what you have done,"
announces the LORD.
"I will start a fire in your forests.
It will burn up everything around
you." ' "

The LORD Judges Evil Kings

22 The LORD said to me, "Jeremiah,
go down to the palace of the king
of Judah. Announce my message there.
Tell him, ² 'King of Judah, listen to the
LORD's message. You are sitting on David's
throne. You and your officials and your
people come through these gates. ³ The
LORD says, "Do what is fair and right. Save
those who have been robbed. Set them
free from the people who have treated
them badly. Do not do anything wrong to
outsiders or widows in this place. Do not
harm children whose fathers have died.
Do not kill those who are not guilty of doing anything wrong.
⁴ " ' "Be careful to obey those commands. Then kings who sit on David's
throne will come through the gates of this
palace. They will come riding in chariots
and on horses. Their officials and their
people will come along with them.
⁵ " ' "But suppose you do not obey
those commands," announces the LORD.
"Then I promise you that this palace will
be destroyed. I make that promise by taking an oath in my own name." ' "
⁶ The LORD speaks about the palace of
the king of Judah. He says,

"You are like the land of Gilead to me.
You are like the highest mountain in
Lebanon.
But I will make you like a desert.
You will become like towns that no
one lives in.
⁷ I will send destroyers against you.
All of them will come with their
weapons.
They will cut up your fine cedar beams.
They will throw them into the fire.

⁸ "People from many nations will pass

by this city. They will ask one another,
'Why has the LORD done such a thing to
this great city?'
⁹ "And the answer will be, 'Because its
people have turned away from the covenant the LORD their God made with
them. They have worshiped other gods.
And they have served them.' "

¹⁰ Don't sob over dead King Josiah.
Don't be sad because he's gone.
Instead, sob bitterly over King
Jehoahaz.
He was forced to leave his country.
He will never return.
He'll never see his own land again.

¹¹ Jehoahaz became king of Judah after his
father Josiah. But he has gone away from
this place. That's because the LORD says
about him, "He will never return. ¹² He
will die in Egypt. That is where he was tak-
en as a prisoner. He will not see this land
again."

¹³ The LORD says, "How terrible it will be
for King Jehoiakim!
He builds his palace
by mistreating his people.
He builds its upstairs rooms
with money that was gained by
sinning.
He makes his own people work for
nothing.
He does not pay them for what they
do.
¹⁴ He says, 'I will build myself a great
palace.
It will have large rooms upstairs.'
So he makes big windows in it.
He covers its walls with cedar
boards.
He decorates it with red paint.

¹⁵ "Jehoiakim, does having more and
more cedar boards
make you a king?
Your father Josiah had enough to eat
and drink.
He did what was right and fair.
So everything went well with him.
¹⁶ He stood up for those who were poor
or needy.
So everything went well with him.
That is what it means to know me,"
announces the LORD.
¹⁷ "Jehoiakim, the only thing on your
mind
is to get rich by cheating others.
You would even kill people who are
not guilty
of doing anything wrong.
You would mistreat them.

ISAIAH

Then I heard the voice of the Lord.
He said, "Who will I send? Who will go for us?"
I said, "Here I am. Send me!" (Isaiah 6:8)

GO TO PAGE 790

JEREMIAH

A message came to me from the LORD. He said,... "Before you were born I set you apart to serve me. I appointed you to be a prophet to the nations. I will keep you safe." (Jeremiah 1:4–5; 15:11)

GO TO PAGE 860

*Shadrach, Meshach and Abednego... said "King Nebuchadnezzar,...
Even if we knew that our God wouldn't save us, we still wouldn't...
worship the gold statue you set up." (Daniel 3:16,18)*

GO TO PAGE 995

"My God sent his angel. And [his angel] shut the mouths of the lions. They haven't hurt me at all. That's because I haven't done anything wrong in God's sight." (Daniel 6:22)

GO TO PAGE 1002

You would take everything they
own."

18So the LORD speaks about King Jehoiakim, the son of Josiah. He says,

"His people will not sob over him.
They will not say,
'My poor brother! My poor sister!'
They will not sob over him.
They will not say,
'My poor master! How sad that his
glory is gone!'
19In fact, he will be buried like a donkey.
His body will be dragged away and
thrown
outside the gates of Jerusalem."

20The LORD says, "People of Jerusalem, go
up to Lebanon.
Cry out for help.
Let your voice be heard in the land
of Bashan.
Cry out from the mountains of
Abarim.
All those who were going to help
you are crushed.
21When you felt secure, I warned you.
But you said, 'I won't listen!'
You have acted like that ever since you
were young.
You have not obeyed me.
22The wind will drive all of your
shepherds away.
All those who were going to help
you will be carried off as
prisoners.
Then you will be dishonored and put
to shame.
That will happen because you have
been so sinful.
23Some of you live in Jerusalem in the
Palace of the Forest of Lebanon.
You are comfortable in your cedar
buildings.
But you will groan when pain comes
on you.
It will be like the pain of a woman
having a baby.

24"King Jehoiachin, you are the son of
Jehoiakim," announces the LORD. "Suppose you were a ring on my right hand.
And suppose the ring even had my royal
seal on it. Then I would still pull you off
my finger. And that is just as sure as I am
alive. 25"I will hand you over to those who
are trying to kill you. I will turn you over
to people who you are afraid of. I will give you
to Nebuchadnezzar, the king of Babylonia. I will hand you over to his armies.
26"I will throw you out into another

country. I will throw your mother out.
Neither of you was born in that country.
But both of you will die there. 27You will
never come back to the land you long to
return to."

28This man Jehoiachin is like a broken
pot.
Everyone hates him. No one wants
him.
Why will he and his children be
thrown out of this land?
Why will they be sent to a land
they didn't have anything to do
with before?
29Land, land, land,
listen to the LORD's message!
30The LORD says,
"Let the record say that this man did
not have any children.
Let it report that he did not have any
success in life.
None of his children will have success
either.
None of them will sit on David's
throne.
None of them will ever rule over
Judah.

The True and Rightful Branch

23 "How terrible it will be for the
shepherds who lead my people
down the wrong path!" announces the
LORD. "They are destroying and scattering
the sheep that belong to my flock."

2So the LORD, the God of Israel, speaks
to the shepherds who take care of my people. He tells them, "You have scattered my
sheep. You have driven them away. You
have not taken good care of them. So I will
punish you for the evil things you have
done," announces the LORD.

3"I myself will gather together those
who are left alive in my flock. I will gather
them out of all of the countries where I
have driven them. And I will bring them
back to their own land. There my sheep
will have many lambs. Their numbers will
increase.

4"I will place shepherds over them who
will take good care of them. My sheep will
not be afraid or terrified anymore. And
none of them will be missing," announces the LORD.

5"A new day is coming," announces the
LORD.
"At that time I will raise up from
David's royal line
a true and rightful Branch.
He will be a King who will rule wisely.

He will do what is fair and right in
the land.
6 In his days Judah will be saved.
Israel will live in safety.
And the Branch will be called
The LORD Who Makes Us Right With
Himself.

7 "Other days are also coming," announces the LORD. "At that time people will no longer say, 'The LORD brought the people of Israel up out of Egypt. And that's just as sure as he is alive.'

8 "Instead, they will say, 'The LORD brought the people of Israel up out of the land of the north. He gathered them out of all of the countries where he had forced them to go. And that's just as sure as he is alive.' Then they will live in their own land."

Prophets Who Tell Lies

9 Here is my message about the prophets.

My heart is broken inside me.
All of my bones tremble with fear.
I am like a man who is drunk.
I am like someone who has had too
much wine.
That's what the LORD's holy words
have done to me.
10 The land is full of people
who aren't faithful to the LORD.
Now the land is under his curse.
And that's why it is thirsty for water.
That's why the grasslands in the
desert are dry.
The prophets are leading sinful lives.
They don't use their power in the
right way.

11 "Prophets and priests alike are
ungodly,"
announces the LORD.
"Even in my temple I find them
sinning.
12 So their path will become slippery.
They will be thrown out into
darkness.
There they will fall.
I will bring trouble on them
when the time to punish them
comes,"
announces the LORD.

13 "Among the prophets of Samaria
I saw something I can't stand.
They were prophesying in the name of
Baal.
They were leading my people Israel
down the wrong path.

14 I have also seen something horrible
among Jerusalem's prophets.
They are not faithful to me.
They are not living by the truth.
They strengthen the hands of those
who do evil.
So the people do not turn from their
sinful ways.
All of them are like the people of
Sodom to me.
They are just like the people of
Gomorrah."

15 So the LORD who rules over all speaks about the prophets. He says,

"I will make them eat bitter food.
I will make them drink poisoned
water.
The prophets of Jerusalem have spread
their ungodly ways all through the
land."

16 The LORD who rules over all says to the people of Judah,

"Do not listen to what the prophets are
saying to you.
They fill you with false hopes.
They talk about visions that come
from their own minds.
What they say does not come from
my mouth.
17 They keep speaking to those who hate
me. They say,
'The LORD says you will have peace.'
They speak to all those who do
what their stubborn hearts want
them to do.
They tell them, 'No harm will come
to you.'
18 But which of them has ever stood in
my courts?
Have they been there to see a vision
or hear my message?
Who has listened and heard my
message there?
19 A storm will burst out
because of my burning anger.
A windstorm will sweep down
on the heads of sinful people.
20 My anger will not turn back.
I will accomplish everything
I plan to do.
In days to come
you will understand it clearly.
21 I did not send those prophets.
But they have run to tell you their
message anyway.
I did not speak to them.
But they have still prophesied.
22 Suppose they had stood in my courts.

Then they would have announced
my message to my people.
They would have turned my people
from their evil ways.
They would have turned them away
from their sins.

23 "Am I only a God who is nearby?"
announces the LORD.
"Am I not a God who is also far
away?
24 Can anyone hide in secret places
so that I can't see him?"
announces the LORD.
"Don't I fill heaven and earth?"
announces the LORD.

25 "I have heard what the prophets are saying. They prophesy lies in my name. They say, 'I had a dream! The LORD has given me a dream!' 26 How long will that continue in the hearts of those prophets who tell lies? They try to get others to believe their own mistaken ideas. 27 They tell one another their dreams. They think that will make my people forget my name. In the same way, their people of long ago forgot my name when they worshiped Baal.

28 "Let the prophet who has a dream tell his dream. But let the one who has my message speak it faithfully. Your prophets have given you straw to eat instead of grain," announces the LORD.

29 "My message is like fire," announces the LORD. "It is like a hammer that breaks a rock in pieces.

30 "So I am against those prophets," announces the LORD. "I am against those who steal messages from one another. They claim that the messages come from me.

31 "Yes," announces the LORD. "I am against the prophets who wag their own tongues but still say, 'Here is what the LORD says.' 32 I am against prophets who talk about dreams that did not come from me," announces the LORD. "They tell foolish lies. Their lies lead my people down the wrong path.

"But I did not send those prophets. I did not appoint them. They do not help my people in the least," announces the LORD.

Prophets Who Give Messages That Are Not From the LORD

33 "Jeremiah, those people might ask you a question. Or a prophet or priest might do it. They might ask, 'What message have you received from the LORD?'

"Then tell them, 'You ask, "What message?" Here it is. "I will desert you," announces the LORD.'

34 "A prophet or priest might make a claim. Or someone else might do it. He might claim, 'I have received a message from the LORD.' Then I will punish him and his family.

35 "Here is what each of you people keeps on saying to your friend or relative. You ask, 'What is the LORD's answer?' Or you ask, 'What has the LORD spoken?' 36 But you must not talk about 'a message from the LORD' again. That is because your message becomes your own message. And so you twist my words. I am the living God. I am the LORD who rules over all. And I am your God.

37 "Here is what you keep saying to a prophet. You ask, 'What is the LORD's answer to you?' Or you ask, 'What has the LORD spoken?' 38 You claim, 'I have received a message from the LORD.' But I really say, 'You used the words, "I have received a message from the LORD." But I told you that you must not claim, "I have received a message from the LORD." '

39 "So you can be sure I will forget you. I will throw you out of my sight. I will also destroy the city I gave you and your people. 40 I will bring shame on you that will last forever. It will never be forgotten."

Judah Is Like Two Baskets of Figs

24 King Jehoiachin was forced to leave Jerusalem. He was the son of Jehoiakim. Jehoiachin was taken to Babylon by Nebuchadnezzar, the king of Babylonia. The officials and all of the skilled workers were forced to leave with him.

After they left, the LORD showed me two baskets of figs. They were in front of his temple. 2 One basket had very good figs in it. They were like figs that ripen early. The other basket had figs that weren't good at all. In fact, they were so bad they couldn't even be eaten.

3 Then the LORD asked me, "What do you see, Jeremiah?"

"Figs," I answered. "The good ones are very good. But the others are so bad they can't be eaten."

4 Then a message came to me from the LORD. He said, 5 "I am the LORD, the God of Israel. I say, 'I consider the people who were forced to leave Judah to be like those good figs. I sent them away from this place. I forced them to go to Babylonia. 6 My eyes will watch over them. I will be good to them. And I will bring them back to this land. I will build them up. I will not tear them down. I will plant them. I will not pull them up by the roots.

7" 'I will change their hearts. Then they will know that I am the LORD. They will be my people. And I will be their God. They will return to me with all their heart.

8" 'But there are also figs that are not very good. In fact, they are so bad they can't be eaten,' says the LORD. 'Zedekiah, the king of Judah, is like those bad figs. So are his officials and the people of Jerusalem who are still left alive. I will punish them whether they remain in this land or live in Egypt.

9" 'I will make all of the kingdoms on earth displeased with them. In fact, they will hate them a great deal. They will laugh and joke about them. They will call down curses on them. All of that will happen no matter where I force them to go. 10I will send war, hunger and plague against them. They will be destroyed from the land I gave them and their people of long ago.' "

Seventy Years in Babylonia

25 A message about all of the people of Judah came to me from the LORD. It came in the fourth year that Jehoiakim was king of Judah. It was the first year that Nebuchadnezzar was king of Babylonia. Jehoiakim was the son of Josiah.

2I, the LORD's prophet, spoke to all of the people of Judah and Jerusalem. I said, 3"For 23 years the LORD's messages have been coming to me. They began to come in the 13th year that Josiah was king of Judah. He was the son of Amon. The LORD's messages still come to me today. I've spoken to you people again and again. But you haven't listened to me.

4"The LORD has sent all of his servants the prophets to you. They've come to you again and again. But you haven't listened. You haven't paid any attention to them.

5"They said, 'Each of you must turn from your evil ways and practices. Then you can stay in the land forever. It's the land the LORD gave you and your people long ago. 6Don't follow other gods. Don't serve them or worship them. Don't make the LORD angry with the gods your own hands have made. Then he won't harm you.'

7" 'But you did not listen to me,' announces the LORD. 'You have made me very angry with the gods your hands have made. And you have brought harm on yourselves.'

8"The LORD who rules over all says, 'You have not listened to my words. 9So I will send for all of the nations in the north.

And I will send for my servant Nebuchadnezzar, the king of Babylonia,' announces the LORD.

" 'I will bring all of them against this land and against you who live here. They will march out against all of the nations that are around this land. I will set them apart in a special way to be destroyed. People will be shocked because of them. And they will make fun of them. Those nations will be destroyed forever.

10" 'I will put an end to the sounds of joy and gladness. I will put an end to the voices of brides and grooms. The sound of grinding millstones will not be heard anymore. And lamps will not be lit anymore. 11This whole country will become dry and empty. And those nations will serve the king of Babylonia for 70 years.

12" 'But I will punish that king and his nation because they are guilty. I will do it when the 70 years are over,' announces the LORD. 'I will make that land a desert forever.

13" 'I have spoken against that land. And I will make all of those things happen to it. Everything will happen that is written in this scroll. And I will make everything Jeremiah prophesied against all of the nations come true. 14The people of Babylonia will become slaves of many other nations and great kings. I will pay them back for what their hands have done.' "

The LORD Judges the Nations

15The LORD is the God of Israel. He said to me, "Take this cup from my hand. It is filled with the wine of my burning anger. Make all of the nations to which I send you drink it. 16When they drink it, they will not even be able to walk straight. It will drive them out of their minds. I am going to send war against them."

17So I took the cup from the LORD's hand. I made all of the nations to which he sent me drink from it. 18He sent me to Judah's kings and officials. He told me to go to Jerusalem and the towns of Judah. He wanted me to tell them they would be destroyed. Then people would be shocked because of them. They would make fun of them. They would call down curses on them. And that's how things still are today.

19Here is a list of the other kings and nations he sent me to.

Pharaoh, the king of Egypt
his attendants, his officials, all of his
   people

20 all of the people from other lands
who lived there
all of the kings of Uz
the Philistine kings of Ashkelon,
Gaza and Ekron
the Philistines who were still living
in Ashdod
21 Edom, Moab, Ammon
22 all of the kings of Tyre and Sidon
the kings of the islands and other
lands along the Mediterranean Sea
23 Dedan, Teman, Buz
all of the other places far away in the
east
24 all of the kings of Arabia
all of the other kings of people who
live in the desert
25 all of the kings of Zimri, Elam and
Media
26 all of the kings in the north, near and
far

So he sent me to all of the kingdoms on
the face of the earth, one after the other.
After all of them drink from the cup of the
LORD's anger, the king of Babylonia will
drink from it too.
27 The LORD says, "Tell them, 'The LORD
who rules over all is the God of Israel. He
says, "Drink from this cup. Get drunk and
throw up. Fall down and do not get up
again. I am going to send war against
you." '
28 "But they might refuse to take the
cup from your hand. They might not
want to drink from it. Then tell them,
'The LORD who rules over all says, "You
have to drink from it! 29 I am beginning to
bring trouble on the city where I have put
my Name. You might think you will not
be punished. But you will certainly be
punished. I am sending war against everyone who lives on earth," announces the
LORD who rules over all.'
30 "Jeremiah, prophesy against them.
Tell them,

" 'The LORD will roar from heaven like a
lion.
His voice will sound like thunder
from his holy temple there.
He will roar loudly against his land.
He will shout like those who stomp
on grapes in winepresses.
He will shout against everyone who
lives on earth.
31 The noise of battle will be heard
from one end of the earth to the
other.
That's because the LORD will bring
charges against the nations.
He will judge every human being.

He will kill sinful people with his
sword,' "
announces the LORD.

32 The LORD who rules over all says,

"Look! Horrible trouble is spreading
from one nation to another.
A mighty storm is rising.
It is coming from a place
that is very far away."

33 At that time those the LORD kills will be
lying around everywhere. They will be
found from one end of the earth to the
other. No one will sob over them. Their
dead bodies will not be gathered up or
buried. Instead, they will be like trash lying there on the ground.

34 Sob and cry, you shepherds.
Roll in the dust, you leaders of the
flock.
Your time to be killed has come.
You will fall and be broken to pieces
like fine clay pots.
35 The shepherds won't have any place to
run to.
The leaders of the flock won't be
able to escape.
36 Listen to the cries of the shepherds.
Hear the sobs of the leaders of the
flock.
The LORD is destroying their
grasslands.
37 Their peaceful meadows will be
completely destroyed
because of the LORD's burning anger.
38 Like a lion he will leave his den.
The land of those leaders will
become a desert.
That's because the sword of the LORD
brings great harm.
His anger will burn against them.

Jeremiah's Enemies Try to Have Him Killed

26 A message came to me from the
LORD. It was shortly after Jehoiakim became king of Judah. He was
the son of Josiah. 2 The LORD said, "Stand
in the courtyard of my house. Speak to
the people of the towns in Judah. Speak to
all those who come to worship in my
house. Tell them everything I command
you. Do not leave out a single word. 3 Perhaps they will listen. Maybe they will turn
from their evil ways. Then I will not do
what I said I would. I will not bring trouble on them. I had planned to punish
them because of the evil things they had
done.
4 "Tell them, 'The LORD says, "Listen to

me. Obey my law that I gave you. ⁵And listen to the words my servants the prophets are speaking. I have sent them to you again and again. But you have not listened to them. ⁶So I will make this house like Shiloh. All of the nations on earth will call down curses on this city." ' "

⁷I spoke those words in the LORD's house. The priests, the prophets and all of the people heard me. ⁸I finished telling all of the people everything the LORD had commanded me to say.

But as soon as I did, the priests, the prophets and all of the people grabbed hold of me. They said, "You must die! ⁹Why do you prophesy those things in the LORD's name? Why do you say that this house will become like Shiloh? Why do you say that this city will be empty and deserted?" And all of the people crowded around me in the LORD's house.

¹⁰The officials of Judah heard what had happened. So they went up from the royal palace to the LORD's house. There they took their places at the entrance of the New Gate. ¹¹Then the priests and prophets spoke to the officials and all of the people. They said, "This man should be sentenced to death. He has prophesied against this city. You have heard it with your own ears!"

¹²Then I spoke to all of the officials and people. I said, "The LORD sent me to prophesy against this house and this city. He told me to say everything you have heard. ¹³So change the way you live and act. Obey the LORD your God. Then he won't do what he said he would. He won't bring on you the trouble he said he would bring.

¹⁴"As for me, I'm in your hands. Do to me what you think is good and right. ¹⁵But you can be sure of one thing. If you put me to death, you will be held accountable for spilling my blood. And I haven't even done anything wrong. You will bring guilt on yourselves and this city and those who live in it. The LORD has sent me

to you. He wanted me to say all of those things so you could hear them. And that's the truth."

¹⁶Then the officials and all of the people spoke to the priests and prophets. They said, "This man shouldn't be sentenced to death! He has spoken to us in the name of the LORD our God."

¹⁷Some of the elders of the land stepped forward. They spoke to the whole community that was gathered there. They said, ¹⁸"Micah from Moresheth prophesied. It was during the time Hezekiah was king over Judah. Micah spoke to all of the people of Judah. He told them, 'The LORD who rules over all says,

" ' "Zion will be plowed up like a field.
　Jerusalem will be turned into a pile
　　of trash.
The temple hill will be covered with
　　bushes and weeds." ' *(Micah 3:12)*

¹⁹"Did King Hezekiah or anyone else in Judah put Micah to death? Hezekiah had respect for the LORD. He asked the LORD to show him his favor. And the LORD didn't judge Jerusalem as he said he would. He didn't bring on it the trouble he said he would bring. But we are about to bring horrible trouble on ourselves!"

²⁰Uriah was another man who prophesied in the name of the LORD. He was from Kiriath Jearim. He was the son of Shemaiah. Uriah prophesied against this city and this land. He said the same things I did.

²¹King Jehoiakim and all of his officers and officials heard Uriah's words. So the king tried to have him put to death.

But Uriah heard about it. He was afraid. And he ran away to Egypt.

²²So King Jehoiakim sent Elnathan to Egypt. He also sent some other men along with him. Elnathan was the son of Acbor. ²³Those men brought Uriah out of Egypt. They took him to King Jehoiakim. Then the king had Uriah struck down with a sword. He had Uriah's body thrown into one of the graves of the ordinary people.

²⁴In spite of that, Ahikam stood up for me. He was the son of Shaphan. Because of Ahikam, I wasn't handed over to the people to be put to death.

Judah Will Serve Nebuchadnezzar

27 A message came to me from the LORD. It was shortly after Zedekiah became king of Judah. He was the son of Josiah. ²The LORD said, "Make a yoke out of ropes and wooden boards. Put it on your neck.

POWER-SURGE

OBEYS ✔

SO CHANGE THE WAY YOU LIVE AND ACT. OBEY THE LORD YOUR GOD.
—— JEREMIAH 26:13 ——

3 "Then write down a message for the kings of Edom, Moab, Ammon, Tyre and Sidon. Give it to their messengers who have come to Jerusalem. They have come to see Zedekiah, the king of Judah. 4Give them a message for the kings who sent them. It should say, 'The LORD who rules over all is the God of Israel. He says, "Here is what I want you to tell your masters. 5I reached out my great and powerful arm. I made the earth. I made its people and animals. And I can give the earth to anyone I please.

6 " 'Now I will hand all of your countries over to my servant Nebuchadnezzar. He is king of Babylonia. I will put even the wild animals under his control. 7All of the nations will serve him and his son and grandson. After that, I will judge his land. Then many nations and great kings will make him serve them.

8 " "But suppose any nation or kingdom will not serve Nebuchadnezzar, the king of Babylonia. And suppose it refuses to put its neck under his yoke. Then I will punish that nation with war, hunger and plague," announces the LORD. "I will punish it until his powerful hand destroys it.

9 " "So do not listen to your prophets. Do not listen to those who claim to have secret knowledge. Do not listen to those who try to explain your dreams. Do not listen to those who get messages from people who have died. Do not listen to those who practice evil magic. All of them will tell you, 'You won't serve the king of Babylonia.'

10 " ' "But they prophesy lies to you. If you listen to them, you will be removed far away from your lands. I will drive you away from them. And you will die.

11 " ' "But suppose any nation will put its neck under the yoke of the king of Babylonia. And suppose it serves him. Then I will let that nation remain in its own land. I will let its people plow the land and live there," ' " announces the LORD.

12I gave the same message to Zedekiah, the king of Judah. I said, "Put your neck under the yoke of the king of Babylonia. Obey him. Serve his people. Then you will live. 13Why should you and your people die? Why should you die of war, hunger and plague? That's what the LORD said would happen to any nation that won't serve the king of Babylonia.

14"Don't listen to the words of the prophets who say to you, 'You won't serve the king of Babylonia.' They are prophesying lies to you. 15'I have not sent them,'

announces the LORD. 'They are prophesying lies in my name. So I will drive you away from your land. And you will die. So will the prophets who prophesy to you.' "

16Then I spoke to the priests and all of those people. I said, "The LORD says, 'Do not listen to the prophets who say, "Very soon the articles from the LORD's house will be brought back from Babylon." They are prophesying lies to you. 17Do not listen to them. Serve the king of Babylonia. Then you will live. Why should this city be destroyed?

18 " 'If they are prophets and have received a message from me, let them pray to me. I am the LORD who rules over all. Those prophets should pray that what is still in Jerusalem will remain here. They should pray that the articles in my house and the king's palace will not be taken to Babylon.

19 " 'I am the LORD who rules over all. Do you know what those articles are? They include the two pillars in front of the temple. They include the huge metal bowl. They include the bronze stands that can be moved around. And they include the other articles that are left in this city. 20Nebuchadnezzar, the king of Babylonia, did not take those things away at first. That was when he took King Jehoiachin from Jerusalem to Babylon. He also took all of the nobles of Judah and Jerusalem along with him. Jehoiachin is the son of Jehoiakim.

21 " 'I am the LORD who rules over all. I am the God of Israel. Here is what will happen to the things that are left in my house, the king's palace and Jerusalem. 22They will be taken to Babylon. They will remain there until the day I come for them,' announces the LORD. 'Then I will bring them back. I will return them to this place.' "

Hananiah Opposes Jeremiah

28 The prophet Hananiah spoke to me in the LORD's house. It was shortly after Zedekiah became king of Judah. It was in the fifth month of his fourth year. Hananiah was from Gibeon. He was the son of Azzur. In front of the priests and all of the people Hananiah said to me, 2"The LORD who rules over all is the God of Israel. He says, 'I will break the yoke of the king of Babylonia. 3Nebuchadnezzar, the king of Babylonia, removed all of the articles that belong to my house. He took them to Babylon. Before two years are over, I will bring them back to this place.

4 " 'I will also bring King Jehoiachin back. He is the son of Jehoiakim. And I will bring back all of the others who were taken from Judah to Babylon,' announces the LORD. 'I will break the yoke of the king of Babylonia.' "

5 Then I, the prophet Jeremiah, replied to the prophet Hananiah. I spoke to him in front of the priests and all of the people. They were standing in the LORD's house. **6** I said, "Amen, Hananiah! May the LORD do those things! May he make the words you have prophesied come true. May he bring back from Babylon the articles that belong to the LORD's house. May he bring back to this place all of the people who were taken away.

7 "But listen to what I have to say. I want you and all of the people to hear it. **8** There have been prophets long before you and I were ever born. They have prophesied against many countries and great kingdoms. They have spoken about war, trouble and plague. **9** But what if a prophet says peace will come? Only if it comes true will he be recognized as one who has been truly sent by the LORD."

10 The prophet Hananiah took the yoke off my neck. Then he broke it. **11** In front of all of the people he said, "The LORD says, 'In the same way, I will break the yoke of Nebuchadnezzar, the king of Babylonia. Before two years are over, I will remove it from the necks of all of the nations.' " When I heard that, I went on my way.

12 A message came to me from the LORD. It was shortly after the prophet Hananiah had broken the yoke off my neck. The message said, **13** "Go. Tell Hananiah, 'The LORD says, "You have broken a wooden yoke. But in its place you will get an iron yoke." **14** The LORD who rules over all is the God of Israel. He says, "I will put an iron yoke on the necks of all of those nations. I will make them serve Nebuchadnezzar, the king of Babylonia. So they will serve him. I will even give him control over the wild animals." ' "

15 Then I, the prophet Jeremiah, spoke to the prophet Hananiah. I said, "Listen, Hananiah! The LORD hasn't sent you. But you have tricked these people. Now they trust in lies. **16** So the LORD says, 'I am about to remove you from the face of the earth. Before this year is over, you will die. You have taught the people to turn against me.' "

17 In the seventh month of that very year, the prophet Hananiah died.

Jeremiah's Letter to the Jews in Babylonia

29 I, the prophet Jeremiah, sent a letter from Jerusalem to Babylonia. It was for the Jewish elders who were still alive there. It was also for the priests and prophets in Babylonia. And it was for all of the other people Nebuchadnezzar had taken from Jerusalem to Babylon. **2** It was sent to them after King Jehoiachin had been forced to leave Jerusalem. His mother and the court officials were taken with him. The leaders of Judah and Jerusalem and all of the skilled workers had also been forced to go to Babylon.

3 I gave the letter to Elasah and Gemariah. Zedekiah, the king of Judah, had sent them to King Nebuchadnezzar in Babylon. Elasah was the son of Shaphan. Gemariah was the son of Hilkiah. Here is what the letter said.

4 The LORD who rules over all is the God of Israel. He speaks to all those he forced to go from Jerusalem to Babylon. He says, **5** "Build houses and settle down. Plant gardens and eat what they produce. **6** Get married. Have sons and daughters. Find wives for your sons. Give your daughters to be married. Then they too can have sons and daughters. Increase your numbers there. Do not let the number of your people get smaller.

7 "Also work for the success of the city I have sent you to. Pray to the LORD for that city. If it succeeds, you too will enjoy success."

8 The LORD who rules over all is the God of Israel. He says, "Do not let the prophets trick you. Do not be fooled by those who claim to have secret knowledge. Do not listen to people who try to explain their dreams to you. **9** All of them are prophesying lies to you in my name. I have not sent them," announces the LORD.

10 The LORD says, "You will be forced to live in Babylonia for 70 years. After they are over, I will come to you. My gracious promise to you will come true. I will bring you back home.

11 "I know the plans I have for you," announces the LORD. "I want you to enjoy success. I do not plan to harm you. I will give you hope for the years to come. **12** Then you will call out to me. You will come and pray to me. And I will listen to you. **13** When you look for me with all your heart, you will find me.

14 "I will be found by you," announces the LORD. "And I will bring you back from where you were taken as prisoners. I will gather you from all of the nations. I will gather you from the places where I have forced you to go," announces the LORD. "I will bring you back to the place from which I sent you away."

15 You might say, "The LORD has given us prophets in Babylonia." **16** But here is what the LORD says about the king who now sits on David's throne. He also says it about all of the people who remain in this city. And he says it about all those who did not go with you to Babylon. **17** The LORD who rules over all says, "I will send war, hunger and plague against them. I will make them like bad figs. They are so bad they can't be eaten. **18** I will hunt them down with war, hunger and plague. I will make all of the kingdoms on earth dis-

pleased with them. They will call down curses on them. All of the nations where I drive them will be shocked at them. They will make fun of them. And they will bring shame on them.

19 "That is because they have not listened to my words," announces the LORD. "I sent messages to them again and again. I sent them through my servants the prophets. And you who were taken to Babylon have not listened either," announces the LORD.

20 So listen to the LORD's message. Listen, all of you whom he has sent away from Jerusalem to Babylon. **21** The LORD who rules over all is the God of Israel. He speaks about Ahab and Zedekiah. They are prophesying lies to you in my name. Ahab is the son of Kolaiah. Zedekiah is the son of Maaseiah. The LORD says about Ahab and Zedekiah, "I will hand them over to Nebuchadnezzar, the king of Babylonia. He will put them to death. You will see it with your own eyes.

22 "Because of what happens to them, people will use their names when they call down curses on someone. All those who have been taken from Judah to Babylon will use their names in that way. They will say, 'May the LORD treat you like Zedekiah and Ahab. The king of Babylonia burned them in the fire.'

23 "That will happen because they have done awful things in Israel. They have committed adultery with their neighbors' wives. They have spoken lies in my name. I did not tell them to do that. I know what they have done. And I am a witness to it," announces the LORD.

Shemaiah Opposes Jeremiah

24 Tell Shemaiah, the Nehelamite, **25** "The LORD who rules over all is the God of Israel. He says, 'You sent letters in your own name to all of the people in Jerusalem. You also sent them to the priest Zephaniah, the son of Maaseiah. And you sent them to all of the other priests.

" 'You said to Zephaniah, **26** "The LORD has appointed you priest in place of Jehoiada. He has put you in charge of the LORD's house. You are supposed to arrest any crazy person who claims to be a prophet. You should put him in prison.

POWER — SURGE

BELIEVES †

"I KNOW THE PLANS I HAVE FOR YOU," ANNOUNCES THE LORD. "I WANT YOU TO ENJOY SUCCESS. I DO NOT PLAN TO HARM YOU. I WILL GIVE YOU HOPE FOR THE YEARS TO COME. THEN YOU WILL CALL OUT TO ME. YOU WILL COME AND PRAY TO ME. AND I WILL LISTEN TO YOU. WHEN YOU LOOK FOR ME WITH ALL YOUR HEART, YOU WILL FIND ME."

— JEREMIAH 29:11-13 —

K

KIND

You should put iron bands around his neck.

27" ' "So why haven't you punished Jeremiah from Anathoth? He claims to be a prophet among you. 28He has sent a message to us in Babylon. It says, 'You will be there a long time. So build houses and settle down. Plant gardens and eat what they produce.' " ' "

29But the priest Zephaniah read the letter to me. 30Then a message came to me from the LORD. He said, 31"Send a message to all of the people who were taken away. Tell them, 'The LORD speaks about Shemaiah, the Nehelamite. He says, "Shemaiah has prophesied to you. But I did not send him. He has made you believe a lie.

32" ' "So I say, 'I will certainly punish Shemaiah, the Nehelamite. I will also punish his children after him. He will not have any children left among these people. I will do good things for my people. But he will not see them,' " ' " announces the LORD. " ' " "That is because he has taught people to turn against me.' " ' "

Israel Will Return to the LORD

30 A message came to me from the LORD. He said, 2"I am the LORD. I am the God of Israel. I say, 'Write on a scroll all of the words I have spoken to you. 3A new day is coming,' " announces the LORD. " 'At that time I will bring my people Israel and Judah back from where they have been taken as prisoners. I will bring them back to this land. Long ago I gave it to their people to have as their own,' " says the LORD.

4Here are the words the LORD spoke about Israel and Judah. He said, 5"I am the LORD. I say,

" 'Cries of fear are heard.
      There is terror. There isn't any peace.
6Ask and see.
      Can a man give birth to children?
Then why do I see every strong man
      with his hands on his stomach?
Each of them is acting like a woman
      having a baby.
Every face is as pale as death.
7How awful that day will be!
No other day will be like it.
It will be a time of trouble for the
      people of Jacob.
But they will be saved out of it.

8" ' 'At that time I will break the yoke off
      their necks,'
announces the LORD who rules over
      all.
'I will tear off the ropes that hold them.

People from other lands will not
      make them slaves anymore.
9Instead, they will serve me.
      And they will serve David their king.
I will raise him up for them.
      I am the LORD their God.

10" 'People of Jacob, do not be afraid.
      You are my servant.
Israel, do not be terrified,' "
                  announces the LORD.
" 'You can be sure that I will save you.
      I will bring you out of a place far
            away.
I will bring your children back
      from the land where they were
            taken.
Your people will have peace and
      security again.
      And no one will make them afraid.
11I am with you. I will save you,' "
      announces the LORD.
" 'I will completely destroy all of the
            nations
      among which I scatter you.
But I will not completely destroy
      you.
I will correct you. But I will be fair.
      I will punish you in a way that is fair
            and right.' "

12The LORD says,

"Your wound can't be cured.
      Your pain can't be healed.
13No one will stand up for you.
      There isn't any medicine for your
            sore.
      There isn't any healing for you.
14All those who were going to help you
      have forgotten you.
      They do not care about you.
I have struck you as if I were your
            enemy.
      I have punished you as if I were very
            mean.
That is because your guilt is so great.
      You have sinned so much.
15Why do you cry out about your
            wound?
      Your pain can't be healed.
Your guilt is very great.
      And you have committed many sins.
That is why I have done all of those
            things to you.

16"But everyone who destroys you will
      be destroyed.
All of your enemies will be forced
      to leave their countries.
Those who steal from you will be
      stolen from.
      I will take the belongings

of those who take things from you.
17 But I will make you healthy again.
I will heal your wounds,"
announces the LORD.
"That is because you have been thrown
out.
You are called Zion, the one no one
cares about."

18 The LORD says,

"I will bless Jacob's people with great
success again.
I will show tender love to Israel.
Jerusalem will be rebuilt where it was
destroyed.
The palace will stand in its proper
place.
19 From those places the songs of people
giving thanks will be heard.
The sound of great joy will come
from there.
I will increase the numbers of my
people.
Their numbers will not become
smaller.
I will bring them honor.
People will have respect for them.
20 Things will be as they used to be for
Jacob's people.
I will make their community firm
and secure.
I will punish everyone who treats
them badly.
21 Their leader will be one of their own
people.
Their ruler will rise up from among
them.
I will bring him near.
And he will come close to me.
He will commit himself to serve
me,"
announces the LORD.
22 "So you will be my people.
And I will be your God."

23 A storm will burst out
because of the LORD's burning anger.
A strong wind will sweep down
on the heads of evil people.
24 The LORD's burning anger won't turn
back.
He will accomplish everything
his heart plans to do.
In days to come
you will understand that.

31 "At that time I will be the God of
all of the tribes of Israel," announces the LORD. "And they will be my
people."
2 The LORD says,

"Some of my people will live through
everything their enemies do to
them.
They will find help in the desert.
I will come to give peace and rest to
Israel."

3 The LORD appeared to us in the past.
He said,

"I have loved you with a love that lasts
forever.
I have kept on loving you with
faithful love.
4 I will build you up again.
Nation of Israel, you will be rebuilt.
Once again you will use your
tambourines to celebrate.
You will go out and dance with joy.
5 Once again you will plant vineyards
on the hills of Samaria.
Farmers will plant them.
They will enjoy their fruit.
6 There will be a day when those on
guard duty will cry out.
They will stand on the hills of
Ephraim.
And they will shout,
'Come! Let's go up to Zion.
Let's go up to where the LORD our
God is.' "

7 The LORD says,

"Sing with joy because the people of
Jacob are blessed.
Shout because the LORD has made
them the greatest nation.
Make your praises heard.
Say, 'LORD, save your people.
Save the people who are left alive in
Israel.'
8 I will bring them from the land of the
north.
I will gather them from one end of
the earth to the other.
Even those who are blind and those
who can't walk
will be among them.
Pregnant women and women having
their babies
will be among them also.
A large number will return.
9 Their eyes will be filled with tears as
they come.
They will pray as I bring them back.
I will lead them beside streams of
water.
I will lead them on a level path
where they will not trip or fall.
I am Israel's father.
And Ephraim is my oldest son.

¹⁰ "Listen to my message, you nations.
  Announce it on shores far away.
Say, 'He who scattered Israel will gather
    them.
  He will watch over his flock like a
    shepherd.'
¹¹ I will set the people of Jacob free.
  I will save them from those who are
    stronger than they are.
¹² They will come and shout for joy on
    Mount Zion.
  They will be joyful because of
    everything I give them.
  I give them grain, olive oil and fresh
    wine.
  I give them the young animals in
    their flocks and herds.
Israel will be like a garden that has
    plenty of water.
  And they will not be sad anymore.
¹³ Then young women will dance and be
    glad.
  And so will the men, young and old
    alike.
  I will turn their sobbing into gladness.
  I will comfort them.
  And I will give them joy instead of
    sorrow.
¹⁴ I will satisfy the priests. I will give them
    more than enough.
  And my people will be filled with
    the good things I give them,"
              announces the LORD.

¹⁵ The LORD says,

"A voice is heard in Ramah.
  It is the sound of crying and deep
    sadness.
Rachel is crying over her children.
  She refuses to be comforted,
  because they are gone."

¹⁶ The LORD says,

"Do not sob anymore.
  Do not let tears fall from your eyes.
I will reward you for your work,"
              announces the LORD.
  "Your children will return from the
    land of the enemy.
¹⁷ So I am giving you hope for the years
    to come,"
              announces the LORD.
  "Your children will return to their
    own land.

¹⁸ "I have heard the groans of Ephraim's
    people. They say,
  'You corrected us like a calf you were
    training.
  And we have been trained.

Bring us back to you, and we will come
    back.
  You are the LORD our God.
¹⁹ After we wandered away from you,
  we turned away from our sins.
After we learned our lesson,
  we beat our chests in sorrow.
We were full of shame.
  What we did when we were young
    brought dishonor on us.'
²⁰ Aren't the people of Ephraim my dear
    children?
  Aren't they the children I take
    delight in?
I often speak against them.
  But I still remember them.
So my heart longs for them.
  I love them with a tender love,"
              announces the LORD.

²¹ The LORD says, "Put up road signs.
  Set up stones to show the way.
Look carefully for the highway.
  Look for the road you will take.
Return, people of Israel.
  Return to your towns.
²² How long will you wander,
  you people who are not faithful to
    me?
I will create a new thing on earth.
  A woman will guard a man."

²³ The LORD who rules over all is the
God of Israel. He says, "I will bring them
back from the place where they were tak-
en. The people in Judah and its towns will
say once again, 'Holy temple in Jerusalem,
may the LORD bless you. Sacred mountain,
may he bless you.'

²⁴ "People will live together in Judah
and all of its towns. Farmers and shepherds will live there. ²⁵ I will give rest to
those who are tired. I will satisfy those
who are weak."

²⁶ When I heard that, I woke up and
looked around. My sleep had been pleasant.

²⁷ The LORD announces, "The days are
coming when I will plant the nation of Israel and Judah again. I will plant it with
children and young animals.

²⁸ "I watched over Israel and Judah to
pull them up by the roots. I tore them
down. I crushed them. I destroyed them. I
brought horrible trouble on them. But
now I will watch over them to build them
up and plant them," announces the LORD.

²⁹ "In those days people will no longer
say,

'The fathers have eaten sour grapes.

But the children have a bitter taste in their mouths.'

30 Instead, everyone will die for his own sin. The one who eats sour grapes will taste how bitter they are.

31 "A new day is coming," announces the LORD.
"I will make a new covenant
with the people of Israel.
I will also make it with the people of Judah.
32 It will not be like the covenant
I made with their people long ago.
That was when I took them by the hand.
I led them out of Egypt.
But they broke my covenant.
They did it even though I was like a husband to them,"
announces the LORD.
33 "This is the covenant I will make with Israel
after that time," announces the LORD.
"I will put my law in their minds.
I will write it on their hearts.
I will be their God.
And they will be my people.
34 A man will not need to teach his neighbor anymore.
And he will not need to teach his friend anymore.
He will not say, 'Know the LORD.'
Everyone will know me.
From the least important of them to the most important,
all of them will know me,"
announces the LORD.
"I will forgive their evil ways.
I will not remember their sins anymore."

35 The LORD speaks.

He makes the sun
shine by day.
He orders the moon and stars
to shine at night.
He stirs up the ocean.
He makes its waves roar.
His name is The LORD Who Rules Over All.
36 "Suppose my orders for creation disappear from my sight,"
announces the LORD.
"Only then will the people of Israel stop being
a nation in my sight."

37 The LORD says,

"Suppose the sky above could be measured.
Suppose the foundations of the earth below could be completely discovered.
Only then would I turn the people of Israel away.
Even though they have committed many sins,
I will still accept them,"
announces the LORD.

38 "A new day is coming," announces the LORD. "At that time Jerusalem will be rebuilt for me. It will be rebuilt from the Tower of Hananel to the Corner Gate. 39 The measuring line will reach out from there. It will go straight to the hill of Gareb. Then it will turn and reach as far as Goah. 40 "There is a valley where dead bodies and ashes are thrown. That whole valley will be holy to me. The side of the Kidron Valley east of the city will be holy to me. It will be holy all the way to the corner of the Horse Gate. The city will never again be pulled up by the roots. It will never be destroyed."

Jeremiah Buys a Field

32 A message came to me from the LORD. It came in the 10th year that Zedekiah was king of Judah. It was in the 18th year of the rule of Nebuchadnezzar. 2 The armies of the king of Babylonia were getting ready to attack Jerusalem. I, the prophet Jeremiah, was being held as a prisoner. I was kept in the courtyard of the guard. It was part of Judah's royal palace.
3 Zedekiah, the king of Judah, had made me a prisoner there. He had said to me, "Why do you prophesy as you do? You say, 'The LORD says, "I am about to hand this city over to the king of Babylonia. He will capture it.
4 " ' "Zedekiah, the king of Judah, will not escape from the powerful hands of the armies of Babylonia. He will certainly

be handed over to the king of Babylonia. Zedekiah will speak with him face to face. He will see him with his own eyes. ⁵Nebuchadnezzar will take Zedekiah to Babylon. Zedekiah will remain there until I deal with him," announces the LORD. "Suppose you fight against the armies of Babylonia. If you do, you will not succeed." ' "

⁶I said, "A message came to me from the LORD. He said, ⁷'Hanamel is going to come to you. He is the son of your uncle Shallum. Hanamel will say, "Buy my field at Anathoth. You are my closest relative. So it's your right and duty to buy it." '

⁸"Then my cousin Hanamel came to me. I was in the courtyard of the guard. It happened just as the LORD had said it would. Hanamel said, 'Buy my field at Anathoth. It is in the territory of Benjamin. It is your right to buy it and own it. So buy it for yourself.'

"I knew that this was the LORD's message. ⁹So I bought the field at Anathoth from my cousin Hanamel. I weighed out seven ounces of silver for him. ¹⁰I signed and sealed the deed of purchase. I had some people witness everything. And I weighed out the silver on the scales.

¹¹"There were two copies of the deed. One was sealed and the other wasn't. The deed included the terms and conditions of the sale. ¹²I gave Baruch the copies of the deed. My cousin Hanamel saw me do it. The witnesses who had signed the deed were there too. So were all of the Jews who were sitting in the courtyard of the guard. Baruch was the son of Neriah. Neriah was the son of Mahseiah.

¹³"I gave Baruch directions in front of all of them. I said, ¹⁴'The LORD who rules over all is the God of Israel. He says, "Take this deed of purchase. Take the sealed and unsealed copies. Put them in a clay jar. Then they will last a long time." ¹⁵The LORD who rules over all is the God of Israel. He says, "Houses, fields and vineyards will again be bought in this land." '

¹⁶"I gave the deed of purchase to Baruch, the son of Neriah. Then I prayed to the LORD. I said,

¹⁷" 'LORD and King, you have reached out your great and powerful arm. You have made the heavens and the earth. Nothing is too hard for you. ¹⁸" 'You show your love to thousands of people. But you punish children for the sins of their fathers. Great and powerful God, your name is The LORD Who Rules Over All. ¹⁹Your purposes are great. Your acts are mighty. Your eyes see everything people do. You reward each one of them in keeping with his conduct. You do it based on what he has done.

²⁰" 'You performed miraculous signs and wonders in Egypt. And you have continued to do them to this very day. You have done them in Israel and among all people. You are still known for doing them. ²¹You brought your people Israel out of Egypt. You did it with miraculous signs and wonders. You reached out your mighty hand and powerful arm. You did great and wonderful things. ²²" 'You gave Israel this land. Long before that, you took an oath. You promised to give their people a land that had plenty of milk and honey. ²³They came in and took it over. But they did not obey you. They didn't follow your law. They didn't do what you commanded them to do. So you brought all of this trouble on them.

²⁴" 'See how ramps are built up against Jerusalem's walls to attack it. The city will be handed over to the armies of Babylonia. They are attacking it. It will fall because of war, hunger and plague. What you said would happen is now happening, as you can see. ²⁵LORD and King, the city will be handed over to the armies of Babylonia. In spite of that, you tell me to buy a field. You say, "Pay for it with silver. And have the sale witnessed." ' "

²⁶Then a message came to me from the LORD. He said, ²⁷"I am the LORD. I am the God of all people. Is anything too hard for me?"

²⁸So the LORD says, "I am about to hand this city over to the armies of Babylonia. I will give it to Nebuchadnezzar, the king of Babylonia. He will capture it. ²⁹The armies of Babylonia are now attacking this city. They will come in and set it on fire. They will burn it down. They will burn up the houses where the people made me very angry. They burned incense on their roofs to the god Baal. And they poured out drink offerings to other gods.

³⁰"The people of Israel and Judah have done nothing but evil in my sight. They have done it since the nation was young. In fact, they have done nothing but make me very angry. They have worshiped statues of gods their own hands have made," announces the LORD. ³¹"This city has always stirred up my burning anger. It has

done it since the day it was built. Now I must remove it from my sight.

32"The people of Israel and Judah have made me very angry. They have done many evil things. They, their kings and officials have sinned. So have their priests and prophets. And the people of Judah and Jerusalem have also sinned. 33They turned their backs to me. They would not face me. I taught them again and again. But they would not listen or pay attention when they were corrected.

34"They set up statues of their gods. They did it in the house where I have put my Name. They made my house 'unclean.' I hate those statues.

35"The people built high places for Baal in the Valley of Ben Hinnom. That is where they sacrifice their children to Molech in the fire. That is something I did not command. It did not even enter my mind. They did something I hate. They made Judah sin."

36You people of Judah are saying about this city, "By war, hunger and plague it will be handed over to the king of Babylonia."

But the LORD, the God of Israel, says, 37"You can be sure that I will gather my people again. I will bring them from all of the lands where I send them when my burning anger blazes out against them. I will bring them back to this place. And I will let them live in safety.

38"They will be my people. And I will be their God. 39I will give them a single purpose in life. Then, they will always have respect for me. I will do it for their own good. And it will be for the good of their children after them.

40"I will make a covenant with them that will last forever. I promise that I will never stop doing good to them. I will cause them to respect me. Then they will never turn away from me again. 41I will take pleasure in doing good things for them. I will certainly plant them in this land. I will do those things with all my heart and soul."

42The LORD says, "I have brought all of this horrible trouble on these people. But now I will give them all of the good things I have promised them.

43"Once more fields will be bought in this land. It is the land about which you now say, 'It is a dry and empty desert. It doesn't have any people or animals in it. It has been handed over to the armies of Babylonia.' 44Fields will be bought with silver. Deeds will be signed, sealed and witnessed. That will be done in the

territory of Benjamin. It will be done in the villages around Jerusalem and in the towns of Judah. It will also be done in the towns of the central hill country. And it will be done in the towns of the western hills and the Negev Desert. I will bless their people with great success again," announces the LORD.

The LORD Keeps His Promises

33 I was still being held as a prisoner. I was kept in the courtyard of the guard. Then another message came to me from the LORD. He said, 2"I made the earth. I formed it. And I set it in place. The LORD is my name. 3Call out to me. I will answer you. I will tell you great things you do not know. You will not be able to understand them."

4The LORD is the God of Israel. He speaks about the houses in Jerusalem. He talks about the royal palaces of Judah. The people had torn many of them down. They had used their stones to strengthen the city walls against attack. 5That was during their fight with the armies of Babylonia. The LORD says, "The houses will be filled with dead bodies. They will be the bodies of the men I will kill when my anger burns against them. I will hide my face from this city. That is because its people have committed so many sins.

6"But now I will bring health and healing to Jerusalem. I will heal my people. I will let them enjoy great peace and security. 7I will bring Judah and Israel back from the places where they have been taken. I will build up the nation again. It will be just as it was before.

8"I will wash from its people all of the sins they have committed against me. And I will forgive all of the sins they committed when they turned away from me.

9"Then this city will bring me fame, joy, praise and honor. All of the nations on earth will hear about the good things I do for this city. They will see the great success and peace I give it. Then they will be filled with wonder. And they will tremble with fear."

10The LORD says, "You say about this place, 'It's a dry and empty desert. It doesn't have any people or animals in it.' The towns of Judah and the streets of Jerusalem are now deserted. So they do not have any people or animals living in them. But happy sounds will be heard there once more. 11They will be the sounds of joy and gladness. The voices of brides and grooms will fill the streets.

"And the voices of those who bring

POWER-SURGE

LOVING ♥

GIVE THANKS TO THE LORD WHO RULES OVER ALL, BECAUSE HE IS GOOD. HIS FAITHFUL LOVE CONTINUES FOREVER.
— JEREMIAH 33:11 — ♣

THANKFUL

thank offerings to my house will be heard there. They will say,

'Give thanks to the LORD who rules
    over all,
    because he is good.
    His faithful love continues forever.'

That is because I will bless this land with great success again. It will be as it was before," says the LORD. **12**The LORD who rules over all says, "This place is a desert. It does not have any people or animals in it. But there will again be grasslands near all of its towns. Shepherds will rest their flocks there. **13**Flocks will again pass under the hands of shepherds as they count their sheep," says the LORD. "That will be done in the towns of the central hill country. It will be done in the western hills and the Negev Desert. It will be done in the territory of Benjamin. And it will be done in the villages around Jerusalem and in the towns of Judah.

14"A new day is coming," announces the LORD. "At that time my gracious promise to my people will come true. I made it to the people of Israel and the people of Judah.

15 "In those days and at that time
    I will make a true and rightful
        Branch grow from David's royal
        line.
    He will do what is fair and right in
        the land.
16 In those days Judah will be saved.
    Jerusalem will live in safety.
    And it will be called
        The LORD Who Makes Us Right With
        Himself."

17The LORD says, "David will always have a son to sit on the throne of the nation of Israel.

18"The priests, who are Levites, will always have a man to serve me. He will sacrifice burnt offerings. He will burn grain offerings. And he will offer sacrifices."

19A message came to me from the LORD. **20**He said, "Could you ever break my covenant with the day? Could you ever break my covenant with the night? Could you ever stop day and night from coming at their appointed times? **21**Only then could my covenant with my servant David be broken. Only then could my covenant with the Levites who serve me as priests be broken. Only then would David no longer have someone from his family line to rule on his throne.

22"Here is what I will do for my servant David. And here is what I will do for the Levites who serve me. I will make their children after them as many as the stars in the sky. And I will make them as many as the grains of sand on the seashore. It will be impossible to count them."

23A message came to me from the LORD. He said, **24**"Haven't you noticed what these people are saying? They say, 'The LORD once chose the two kingdoms of Israel and Judah. But now he has turned his back on them.' So they hate my people. They do not think of them as a nation anymore.

25"I say, 'What if I had not made my covenant with day and night? What if I had not established the laws of heaven and earth? **26**Only then would I turn my back on the children of Jacob and my servant David. Only then would I not choose one of David's sons to rule over the children of Abraham, Isaac and Jacob. But I will bless my people with great success again. I will love them with tender love.' "

Zedekiah Is Warned

34 Nebuchadnezzar, the king of Babylonia, and all of his armies were fighting against Jerusalem. They were also fighting against all of the towns that were around it. All of the kingdoms and nations Nebuchadnezzar ruled over were helping him.

At that time a message came to me from the LORD. He said, **2**"I am the LORD, the God of Israel. Go to Zedekiah, the king of Judah. Tell him, 'The LORD says, "I am about to hand this city over to the king of Babylonia. He will burn it down. **3**You will not escape from his powerful hand. You will certainly be captured. You will be handed over to him. You will see the king of Babylonia with your own eyes. He will speak with you face to face. And you will go to Babylon.

4 " ' "But listen to my promise, Zedekiah. Listen, king of Judah. I say that you will not be killed with a sword. 5You will die in a peaceful way. People made fires to honor the kings who died before you. In the same way, they will make a fire in your honor. They will sob over you. They will say, 'My poor master!' I myself make this promise," announces the LORD.' "

6Then I, the prophet Jeremiah, told all of that to King Zedekiah in Jerusalem. 7At that time Nebuchadnezzar's armies were fighting against Jerusalem. They were also fighting against Lachish and Azekah. Those two cities were still holding out. They were the only cities left in Judah that had high walls around them.

The People Set Their Slaves Free

8A message came to me from the LORD. King Zedekiah had made a covenant with all of the people in Jerusalem. He had told them to set their Hebrew slaves free. 9All of them had to do it. That applied to male and female slaves alike. No one was allowed to hold another Jew as a slave.

10So all of the officials and people entered into that covenant. They agreed to set their male and female slaves free. They agreed not to hold them as slaves anymore. Instead, they set them free. 11But later they changed their minds. They took back the people they had set free. They made them slaves again.

12Then a message came to me from the LORD. 13The LORD is the God of Israel. He says, "I made a covenant with your people long ago. I brought them out of Egypt. That is the land where they were slaves. I said, 14'Every seventh year you must set your people free. You must set free all of the Hebrews who have sold themselves to you. Let them serve you for six years. Then you must let them go free.' (Deuteronomy 15:12) But your people did not listen to me. They did not pay any attention to me.

15"Recently you turned away from your sins. You did what is right in my eyes. Each of you set your Hebrew slaves free. You even made a covenant in front of me. You did it in the house where I have put my Name. 16But now you have turned around. You have treated my name as if it were not holy. Each of you has taken back your male and female slaves. You had set them free to go where they wished. But

now you have forced them to become your slaves again."

17So the LORD says, "You have not obeyed me. You have not set your Hebrew slaves free. So now I will set you free," announces the LORD. "I will set you free to be destroyed by war, plague and hunger. I will make all of the kingdoms on earth displeased with you.

18"The men who have broken my covenant will be punished. They have not lived up to the terms of the covenant they made in front of me. When you made that covenant, you cut a calf in two. Then you walked between its pieces. Now I will cut you to pieces. 19That includes all of you who walked between the pieces of the calf. It includes the leaders of Judah and Jerusalem, the court officials and the priests. It also includes some of the people of the land.

20"So I will hand all of those people over to their enemies who are trying to kill them. Their dead bodies will become food for the birds of the air and the wild animals.

21"I will hand King Zedekiah and his officials over to their enemies. I will hand them over to those who want to kill them. I will give them over to the armies of the king of Babylonia. They have now pulled back from you. 22But I am going to give an order," announces the LORD. "I will bring them back to this city. They will fight against it. They will take it and burn it down. And I will completely destroy the towns of Judah. No one will be able to live there."

The Family of Recab

35 A message came to me from the LORD. It came during the time Jehoiakim was king over Judah. He was the son of Josiah. The message said, 2"Go to the members of the family line of Recab. Invite them to come to one of the side rooms in my house. Then give them wine to drink."

3So I went to get Jaazaniah. He was the son of Jeremiah. Jeremiah was the son of Habazziniah. I also went to get Jaazaniah's brothers and all of his sons. That included all of the members of the family line of Recab. 4I brought them into the LORD's house. I took them into the room of the sons of Hanan. He was the son of Igdaliah. He was also a man of God. His room was next to the room of the officials. Their room was above the room of Maaseiah. He was the son of Shallum. He also was one of those who guarded the temple doors. ⁵Then I got bowls full of wine and some cups. I set them down in front of the men from the family line of Recab. I said to them, "Drink some wine."

⁶But they replied, "We don't drink wine. That's because Jonadab gave us a command. He was the son of Recab. He was also one of our own people from long ago. He commanded, 'You and your children after you must never drink wine. ⁷Also you must never build houses. You must never plant crops or vineyards. You must never have any of those things. Instead, you must always live in tents. Then you will live a long time in the land where you are wandering around.'

⁸"We have done everything Jonadab, the son of Recab, commanded us to do. So we and our wives and our children have never drunk wine. ⁹We have never built houses to live in. We've never had vineyards, fields or crops. ¹⁰We've always lived in tents. We've completely obeyed everything Jonadab commanded our people of long ago.

¹¹"But Nebuchadnezzar, the king of Babylonia, marched into this land. Then we said, 'Come. We must go to Jerusalem. There we can escape the armies of Babylonia and Aram.' So we have remained in Jerusalem."

¹²Then a message came to me from the LORD. It said, ¹³"The LORD who rules over all is the God of Israel. He says, 'Go. Speak to the people of Judah and Jerusalem. Tell them, "Won't you ever learn a lesson? Won't you ever obey my words?" announces the LORD.

¹⁴" ' "Jonadab, the son of Recab, ordered his children not to drink wine. And they have kept his command. To this very day they do not drink wine. They obey the command Jonadab gave their people long ago. But I have spoken to you again and again. In spite of that, you have not obeyed me.

¹⁵" ' "Again and again I sent all of my servants the prophets to you. They said, 'Each of you must turn from your evil ways. You must change the way you act. Do not worship other gods. Do not serve them. Then you will live in the land. I gave it to you and your people long ago.' But you have not paid any attention. You have not listened to me.

¹⁶" ' "The children of Jonadab, the son of Recab, have obeyed the command Jonadab gave them long ago. But the people of Judah have not obeyed me." ' "

¹⁷So the LORD God who rules over all speaks. The God of Israel says, "Listen! I am going to bring horrible trouble on Judah. I will also bring it on everyone who lives in Jerusalem. I will bring on them every trouble I said I would. I spoke to them. But they did not listen. I called out to them. But they did not answer."

¹⁸Then I spoke to the members of the family line of Recab. I said, "The LORD who rules over all is the God of Israel. He says, 'You have obeyed the command Jonadab gave your people long ago. You have followed all of his directions. You have done everything he ordered.' ¹⁹So the LORD who rules over all speaks. The God of Israel says, 'Jonadab, the son of Recab, will always have a man from his family to serve me.' "

Jehoiakim Burns Up Jeremiah's Scroll

36 A message came to me from the LORD. It came in the fourth year that Jehoiakim was king of Judah. He was the son of Josiah. The message said, ²"Get a scroll. Write on it all of the words I have spoken to you. Write down what I have said about Israel, Judah and all of the other nations. Write what I have said to you from the time of King Josiah until now. ³The people of Judah will hear about all of the trouble I plan to bring on them. Maybe then all of them will turn from their evil ways. If they do, I will forgive their sins and the evil things they have done."

⁴So I sent for Baruch, the son of Neriah. I told him to write down all of the words the LORD had spoken to me. And Baruch wrote them on the scroll.

⁵Then I said to him, "I'm not allowed to go to the LORD's temple. ⁶So you go there. Go on a day when the people are fasting. Read to them from the scroll. Read the words of the LORD you wrote down as I gave them to you. Read them to all of the people of Judah who come in from their towns. ⁷They will hear what the LORD will do to them when his burning anger blazes out against them. Then perhaps they will pray to him. And maybe all of them will turn from their evil ways."

⁸Baruch, the son of Neriah, did everything I told him to do. He went to the LORD's temple. There he read the words of the LORD from the scroll. ⁹It was in the fifth year that Jehoiakim, the son of Josiah, was king of Judah. It was the ninth month of that year. A time of fasting at the LORD's temple had been ordered. All of the people in Jerusalem were told to take

part in it. So were those who had come in from the towns of Judah.

¹⁰Baruch read to all of the people who were at the LORD's temple. He read my words from the scroll. He was in the room of the secretary Gemariah. It was located in the upper courtyard at the entrance of the New Gate of the temple. Gemariah was the son of Shaphan.

¹¹Micaiah was the son of Gemariah, the son of Shaphan. Micaiah heard Baruch reading all of the LORD's words that were written on the scroll.

¹²Then he went down to the secretary's room in the royal palace. All of the officials were sitting there. They included the secretary Elishama and Delaiah, the son of Shemaiah. Elnathan, the son of Acbor, was also there. So was Gemariah, the son of Shaphan. Zedekiah, the son of Hananiah, was there too. And so were all of the other officials. ¹³Micaiah told all of them what he had heard. He told them everything Baruch had read to the people from the scroll.

¹⁴All of the officials sent Jehudi to speak to Baruch, the son of Neriah. Jehudi was the son of Nethaniah. Nethaniah was the son of Shelemiah. Shelemiah was the son of Cushi. Jehudi said to Baruch, "Come. Bring the scroll you have read to the people."

So Baruch went to them. He carried the scroll with him. ¹⁵The officials said to him, "Please sit down. Read the scroll to us."

So Baruch read it to them. ¹⁶They heard all of its words. Then they looked at each other in fear. They said to Baruch, "We must report all of these words to the king."

¹⁷They said to Baruch, "Tell us. How did you happen to write all of these things? Did Jeremiah tell you to do it?"

¹⁸"Yes," Baruch replied. "He told me to write down all of these words. So I wrote them in ink on the scroll."

¹⁹Then the officials spoke to Baruch. They said, "You and Jeremiah must go and hide. Don't let anyone know where you are."

²⁰The officials put the scroll in the room of the secretary Elishama. Then they went to the king in the courtyard. They reported everything to him.

²¹The king sent Jehudi to get the scroll. Jehudi brought it from the room of the secretary Elishama. He read it to the king. All of the officials were standing beside the king. So they heard it too. ²²It was the ninth month. The king was sitting in his winter apartment. A fire was burning in the fire pot in front of him. ²³Jehudi read three or four columns from the scroll. Then the king cut them off with a secretary's knife. He threw them into the fire pot. He did that until the entire scroll was burned up in the fire. ²⁴The king and some of his attendants heard all of those words. But they weren't afraid. They didn't tear their clothes.

²⁵Elnathan, Delaiah and Gemariah begged the king not to burn the scroll. But he wouldn't listen to them. ²⁶Instead, the king commanded three men to arrest the secretary Baruch and the prophet Jeremiah. But the LORD had hidden them. The three were Jerahmeel, Seraiah and Shelemiah. Jerahmeel was a member of the royal court. Seraiah was the son of Azriel. And Shelemiah was the son of Abdeel.

²⁷A message came to me from the LORD. It came after the king burned the scroll that had the words Baruch had written down. I had told him to write them. The message said, ²⁸"Get another scroll. Write on it all of the words that were on the first one. King Jehoiakim burned that one up.

²⁹"Also tell King Jehoiakim, 'The LORD says, "You burned that scroll. You said to Baruch, 'Why did you write that the king of Babylonia would certainly come? Why did you write that he would destroy this land? Why did you write that he would cut off people and animals alike from it?' "

³⁰" 'So now the LORD has something to say about Jehoiakim, the king of Judah. He says, "No one from Jehoiakim's family line will sit on David's throne. Jehoiakim's body will be thrown out. It will lie outside in the heat by day and in the frost at night. ³¹I will punish him and his children and his attendants. I will punish them for their sinful ways. I will bring on them all of the trouble I said I would. And I will bring it on the people of Jerusalem and Judah. They have not listened to me." ' "

³²So I got another scroll. I gave it to the secretary Baruch, the son of Neriah. I told him what to write on it. He wrote down all of the words that were on the scroll King Jehoiakim had burned up in the fire. And he added many more words the LORD had given to me. They were similar to those that had already been written.

Jeremiah Is Put in Prison

37 Nebuchadnezzar, the king of Babylonia, appointed Zedekiah to be king of Judah. He was the son of Josiah. Zedekiah ruled in place of Jehoiachin, the son of Jehoiakim. ²Zedekiah and his attendants didn't pay any attention to what the LORD had said through me. And the people of the land didn't pay any attention either.

³But King Zedekiah sent Jehucal to me. He sent the priest Zephaniah along with him. Jehucal was the son of Shelemiah. Zephaniah was the son of Maaseiah. Jehucal and Zephaniah brought the king's message to me. It said, "Please pray to the LORD our God for us."

⁴At that time I was free to come and go among the people. I had not yet been put in prison. ⁵The armies of Babylonia were attacking Jerusalem. They received a report that Pharaoh's army had marched out of Egypt to help Zedekiah. So they pulled back from Jerusalem.

⁶A message came to me from the LORD. ⁷The LORD is the God of Israel. He says, "The king of Judah has sent you to ask me for advice. Tell him, 'Pharaoh's army has marched out to help you. But it will go

BARUCH

JEREMIAH 36:32

[Jeremiah] told [Baruch] what to write on it. He wrote down all of the words that were on the scroll King Jehoiakim had burned up in the fire. And he added many more words the LORD had given to [Jeremiah].

Baruch (BAY-rook) put his pen down and rubbed his hand. He lifted his right arm and flexed his wrist and fingers. Hours of writing Jeremiah's words from God made Baruch's hand cramped and sore.

Baruch and Jeremiah had worked together before. God gave Jeremiah the message, and Baruch wrote it down in a scroll. The king had destroyed the last scroll. The message in the scroll was Jeremiah's prophecy that an enemy would come and conquer Judah and take its people away. **PIECE BY PIECE THE KING HAD CUT THE SCROLL UP AND BURNED IT IN THE FIRE.**

So now Baruch and Jeremiah began all over again. They wrote down the message of the original scroll plus some more words that God gave Jeremiah. Jeremiah and Baruch would not give up. No matter how many times they had to do it over again, they would rewrite the scroll and give the people God's message.

BE A BARUCH

Be a Baruch. Don't give up! When it's hard to keep going, when you have to try over and over again to do something right, when you have to do things you don't want to do—remember Baruch. Don't give up until you finish.

BARUCH DIDN'T GIVE UP.

Go to page 976 for the next Super Hero

back to its own land. It will return to Egypt. **8**Then the armies of Babylonia will come back here. They will attack this city. They will capture it. Then they will burn it down.'

9"The LORD says, 'Do not fool yourselves. You think, "The Babylonians will leave us alone." But they will not! **10**Suppose you destroy all of the armies of Babylonia that are attacking you. Suppose only wounded men are left in their tents. Even then they will come out and burn this city down.' "

11The armies of Babylonia had pulled back from Jerusalem because of Pharaoh's army. **12**So I started to leave the city. I was planning to go to the territory of Benjamin. I wanted to get my share of the property among the people there. **13**I got as far as the Benjamin Gate. But the captain of the guard arrested me. He said, "You are going over to the side of the Babylonians!" The captain's name was Irijah, the son of Shelemiah. Shelemiah was the son of Hananiah.

14I said to Irijah, "That isn't true! I'm not going to the side of the Babylonians."

But Irijah wouldn't listen to me. Instead, he arrested me. He brought me to the officials. **15**They were angry with me. So they had me beaten. Then they took me to the house of the secretary Jonathan. It had been made into a prison. That's where they put me.

16I was put into a prison cell that was below ground level. I remained there a long time. **17**Then King Zedekiah sent for me. He had me brought to the palace. There he spoke to me in private. He asked, "Do you have a message from the LORD for me?"

"Yes," I replied. "You will be handed over to the king of Babylonia."

18Then I continued, "Why have you put me in prison? What crime have I committed against you? What have I done to your officials or these people? **19**Where are your prophets who prophesied to you? They said, 'The king of Babylonia won't attack you. He won't march into this land.'

20"But now please listen, my king and master. Let me make my appeal to you. Please don't send me back to the house of the secretary Jonathan. If you do, I'll die there."

21Then King Zedekiah gave the order. His men put me in the courtyard of the guard. They gave me bread from the street of the bakers. They did it every day until all of the bread in the city was gone. So I remained in the courtyard of the guard.

Jeremiah Is Thrown Into an Empty Well

38 Shephatiah, Gedaliah, Jehucal and Pashhur heard what I was telling all of the people. Shephatiah was the son of Mattan. Gedaliah was the son of Pashhur. Jehucal was the son of Shelemiah. And Pashhur was the son of Malkijah. Those four men heard me say, **2**"The LORD says, 'Those who stay in this city will die of war, hunger or plague. But those who go over to the side of the Babylonians will live. They will escape with their lives. They will remain alive.' **3**The LORD also says, 'This city will certainly be handed over to the armies of the king of Babylonia. They will capture it.' "

4Then those officials said to the king, "That man should be put to death. What he says is making the soldiers who are left in this city lose hope. It's making all of the people lose hope too. He isn't interested in what is best for the people. In fact, he's trying to destroy them."

5"He's in your hands," King Zedekiah answered. "I can't do anything to oppose you."

6So they took me and put me into an empty well. It belonged to Malkijah. He was a member of the royal court. His well was in the courtyard of the guard. Zedekiah's men lowered me by ropes into the well. It didn't have any water in it. All it had was mud. And I sank down into the mud.

7Ebed-Melech was an official in the royal palace. He was from the land of Cush. He heard that I had been put into the well. The king was sitting by the Benjamin Gate at that time. **8**Ebed-Melech went out of the palace. He said to the king, **9**"My king and master, everything those men have done to the prophet Jeremiah is evil. They have thrown him into an empty well. Soon there won't be any more bread in the city. Then he'll starve to death."

10So the king gave an order to Ebed-Melech from Cush. He said, "Take 30 men from here with you. Lift the prophet Jeremiah out of the well before he dies."

11Then Ebed-Melech took the men with him. He went to a room under the place in the palace where the treasures were stored. He got some old rags and worn-out clothes from there. Then he let them down with ropes to me in the well.

12Ebed-Melech from Cush told me

what to do. He said, "Put these old rags and worn-out clothes under your arms. They'll pad the ropes." So I did. ¹³Then the men pulled me up with the ropes. They lifted me out of the well. And I remained in the courtyard of the guard.

Zedekiah Questions Jeremiah Again

¹⁴Then King Zedekiah sent for me. He had me brought to the third entrance to the LORD's temple. "I want to ask you something," the king said to me. "Don't hide anything from me."

¹⁵I said to Zedekiah, "Suppose I give you an answer. You will kill me, won't you? Suppose I give you good advice. You won't listen to me, will you?"

¹⁶But King Zedekiah took an oath. He promised me secretly, "I won't kill you. And I won't hand you over to those who want to take your life. That's just as sure as the LORD is alive. He's the one who has given us breath."

¹⁷So I said to Zedekiah, "The LORD God who rules over all is the God of Israel. He says, 'Give yourself up to the officers of the king of Babylonia. Then your life will be spared. And this city will not be burned down. You and your family will remain alive.

¹⁸" 'But what if you do not give yourself up to them? Then this city will be handed over to the Babylonians. They will burn it down. And you yourself will not escape from their powerful hands.' "

¹⁹King Zedekiah said to me, "I'm afraid of some of the Jews. They are the ones who have gone over to the side of the Babylonians. The Babylonians might hand me over to them. And those Jews will treat me badly."

²⁰"They won't hand you over to them," I replied. "Obey the LORD. Do what I tell you to do. Then things will go well with you. Your life will be spared.

²¹"Don't refuse to give yourself up. The LORD has shown me what will happen if you do. ²²All of the women who are left in your palace will be brought out. They'll be given to the officials of the king of Babylonia. Those women will say to you,

" 'Your trusted friends have tricked
         you.
    They have gotten the best of you.
    Your feet are sunk down in the mud.
    Your friends have deserted you.'

²³"All of your wives and children will be brought out to the Babylonians. You yourself won't escape from their powerful

hands. You will be captured by the king of Babylonia. And this city will be burned down."

²⁴Then Zedekiah said to me, "Don't let anyone know about the talk we've had. If you do, you might die. ²⁵Suppose the officials find out that I've talked with you. And suppose they come to you and say, 'Tell us what you said to the king. Tell us what the king said to you. Don't hide it from us. If you do, we'll kill you.' ²⁶Then tell them, 'I was begging the king not to send me back to Jonathan's house. I don't want to die there.' "

²⁷All of the officials came to me. And they questioned me. I told them everything the king had ordered me to say. None of them had heard what I told the king. So they didn't say anything else to me.

²⁸I remained in the courtyard of the guard. I stayed there until the day Jerusalem was captured.

Jerusalem Is Destroyed

39 Here is how Jerusalem was captured. ¹Nebuchadnezzar, the king of Babylonia, marched out against it. He came with all of his armies and attacked it. It was in the ninth year that Zedekiah was king of Judah. It was in the tenth month. ²The city wall was broken through. It happened on the ninth day of the fourth month. It was in the 11th year of Zedekiah's rule.

³All of the officials of the king of Babylonia came. They took seats near the Middle Gate. Nergal-Sharezer from Samgar was there. Nebo-Sarsekim, a chief officer, was also there. So was Nergal-Sharezer, a high official. And all of the other officials of the king of Babylonia were there too.

⁴King Zedekiah and all of the soldiers saw them. Then they ran away. They left the city at night. They went by way of the king's garden. They went out through the gate between the two walls. And they headed toward the Arabah Valley.

⁵But the armies of Babylonia chased them. They caught up with Zedekiah in the flatlands near Jericho. They captured him there. And they took him to Nebuchadnezzar, the king of Babylonia. He was at Riblah in the land of Hamath. That's where Nebuchadnezzar decided how he would be punished. ⁶The king of Babylonia killed the sons of Zedekiah at Riblah. He forced Zedekiah to watch it with his own eyes. He also killed all of the nobles of Judah. ⁷Then he poked out Zedekiah's

eyes. He put him in bronze chains. And he took him to Babylon.

⁸The Babylonians set the royal palace on fire. They also set fire to the houses of the people. And they broke down the walls of Jerusalem.

⁹Nebuzaradan was commander of the royal guard. Some people still remained in the city. But he took them away to Babylon as prisoners. He also took along those who had gone over to his side. And he took the rest of the people.

¹⁰Nebuzaradan, the commander of the guard, left some of the poor people of Judah behind. They didn't own anything. So at that time he gave them vineyards and fields.

¹¹Nebuchadnezzar, the king of Babylonia, had given orders about me. He had given them to Nebuzaradan, the commander of the royal guard. Nebuchadnezzar had said, ¹²"Take him. Look after him. Don't harm him. Do for him anything he asks."

¹³So that's what Nebuzaradan, the commander of the guard, did. Nebushazban and Nergal-Sharezer were with him. So were all of the other officers of the king of Babylonia. Nebushazban was a chief officer. Nergal-Sharezer was a high official. All of those men ¹⁴sent for me. They had me taken out of the courtyard of the guard. They turned me over to Gedaliah. They told him to take me back to my home. So I remained among my own people. Gedaliah was the son of Ahikam, the son of Shaphan.

¹⁵A message came to me from the LORD. It came while I was being kept in the courtyard of the guard. He said, ¹⁶"Go. Speak to Ebed-Melech from Cush. Tell him, 'The LORD who rules over all is the God of Israel. He says, "I am about to make the words I spoke against this city come true. I will not give success to it. Instead, I will bring horrible trouble on it. At that time my words will come true. You will see it with your own eyes.

¹⁷" ' "But I will save you on that day," announces the LORD. "You will not be handed over to those you are afraid of. ¹⁸I will save you. You will not be killed with a sword. Instead, you will escape with your life. That is because you trust in me," announces the LORD.' "

Jeremiah Is Set Free From His Chains

40 A message came to me from the LORD. It came after Nebuzaradan, the commander of the royal guard, had

set me free at Ramah. I was being held by chains when he found me. I was among all of the prisoners from Jerusalem and Judah. We were being taken to Babylon.

²But the commander of the guard found me. He said to me, "The LORD your God ordered that this place be destroyed. ³And now he has brought it about. He has done exactly what he said he would do. All of these things have happened because you people sinned against the LORD. You didn't obey him. ⁴But today I'm setting you free from the chains that are on your wrists. Come with me to Babylon if you want to. I'll take good care of you there. But if you don't want to come, then don't. The whole country lies in front of you. Go anywhere you want to."

⁵But before I turned to go, Nebuzaradan continued, "Go back to Gedaliah, the son of Ahikam. The king of Babylonia has appointed Gedaliah to be over the towns of Judah. Go and live with him among your people. Or go anywhere else you want to." Ahikam was the son of Shaphan.

The commander gave me food and water. He also gave me a gift. Then he let me go. ⁶So I went to Mizpah to see Gedaliah, the son of Ahikam. I stayed with him. I lived among the people who were left behind in the land.

Gedaliah Is Murdered

⁷Some of Judah's army officers and their men were still in the open country. They heard that the king of Babylonia had appointed Gedaliah, the son of Ahikam, as governor over Judah. He had put him in charge of the men, women and children who were still there. They were the poorest people in the land. They hadn't been taken to Babylon.

⁸When the army officers and their men heard those things, they came to Gedaliah at Mizpah. Ishmael, the son of Nethaniah, came. So did Johanan and Jonathan, the sons of Kareah. Seraiah, the son of Tanhumeth, also came. The sons of Ephai from Netophah came too. And so did Jaazaniah, the son of the Maacathite. All of their men came with them.

⁹Gedaliah son of Ahikam, the son of Shaphan, took an oath to give hope to all of those men. He spoke in a kind way to them. He said, "Don't be afraid to serve the Babylonians. Settle down in the land of Judah. Serve the king of Babylonia. Then things will go well with you. ¹⁰I myself will stay at Mizpah. I'll speak for you to the officials of Babylonia who come to

us. But you must harvest the wine, summer fruit and olive oil. Put them in your jars. Store them up. And live in the towns you have taken over."

11All of the Jews in Moab, Ammon and Edom heard what had happened. So did the Jews in all of the other countries. They heard that the king of Babylonia had left some people behind in Judah. They also heard that he had appointed Gedaliah, the son of Ahikam, as governor over them. Ahikam was the son of Shaphan.

12When they heard those things, all of them came back to the land of Judah. They went to Gedaliah at Mizpah. They came from all of the countries where they had been scattered. And they harvested a large amount of wine and summer fruit.

13Johanan and all of the other army officers who were still in the open country came to Gedaliah at Mizpah. Johanan was the son of Kareah. 14The officers said to Gedaliah, "Don't you know that Baalis, the king of Ammon, has sent someone to take your life? It's Ishmael, the son of Nethaniah." But Gedaliah, the son of Ahikam, didn't believe them.

15Then Johanan, the son of Kareah, spoke in private to Gedaliah in Mizpah. He said, "Let me go and kill Ishmael, the son of Nethaniah. No one will know about it. Why should he take your life? Why should he cause all of the Jews who are gathered around you to be scattered? Why should he cause the people who remain in Judah to die?"

16But Gedaliah, the son of Ahikam, spoke to Johanan, the son of Kareah. He said, "Don't do an awful thing like that! What you are saying about Ishmael isn't true."

41 In the seventh month Ishmael, the son of Nethaniah, came with ten men to Gedaliah, the son of Ahikam, at Mizpah. Nethaniah was the son of Elishama. Ishmael was a member of the royal family. He had been one of the king's officers. Ishmael and his ten men were eating together at Mizpah.

2They got up and struck down Gedaliah, the son of Ahikam, with their swords. They killed him even though the king of Babylonia had appointed him as governor over Judah. Ahikam was the son of Shaphan. 3Ishmael also killed all of the Jews who were with Gedaliah at Mizpah. And he killed the Babylonian soldiers who were there.

4On the next day, people still hadn't found out that Gedaliah had been murdered. 5On that day 80 men came from Shechem, Shiloh and Samaria. They had shaved off their beards. They had torn their clothes. And they had cut themselves. They brought grain offerings and incense with them. They took them to the LORD's house.

6Ishmael, the son of Nethaniah, went out from Mizpah to meet them. He was sobbing as he went. When he met them, he said, "Come to Gedaliah, the son of Ahikam."

7They went with him into the city. Then Ishmael, the son of Nethaniah, and the men who were with him killed them. And they threw them into an empty well.

8But ten of the men had spoken to Ishmael. They had said, "Don't kill us! We have some wheat and barley. We also have olive oil and honey. We've hidden all of it in a field." So he let them alone. He didn't kill them along with the others.

9But he had thrown all of the bodies of the men he had killed into the empty well. That included Gedaliah's body. The well was the one King Asa had made. He had made it when he strengthened Mizpah against attack by Baasha, the king of Israel. Ishmael, the son of Nethaniah, filled it with the bodies of those he had killed.

10Ishmael made prisoners of all the rest of the people who were in Mizpah. That included women who were members of the royal court. It also included all of the others who were left there. Nebuzaradan had appointed Gedaliah, the son of Ahikam, over them. Ishmael, the son of Nethaniah, took them as prisoners. Then he started out to go across the Jordan River to the land of Ammon. Nebuzaradan was the commander of the royal guard.

11Johanan, the son of Kareah, and all of the other army officers who were with him were told what had happened. They heard about all of the crimes Ishmael, the son of Nethaniah, had committed. 12So they brought all of their men together. Then they went to fight against Ishmael, the son of Nethaniah. They caught up with him near the large pool in Gibeon.

13Ishmael had many people with him. They saw Johanan, the son of Kareah. And they saw the other army officers who were with him. So the people who had been forced to go with Ishmael were glad. 14All those whom Ishmael had taken as prisoners at Mizpah turned and went over to the side of Johanan, the son of Kareah. 15But Ishmael, the son of Nethaniah, and eight of his men escaped from Johanan. They ran away to the land of Ammon.

Some Jews Take Jeremiah to Egypt

16Then Johanan, the son of Kareah, led away all of the people from Mizpah who were still alive. All of the other army officers who were with Johanan helped him do it. He had taken them away from Ishmael, the son of Nethaniah. That happened after Ishmael had murdered Gedaliah, the son of Ahikam. The people Johanan had taken away included the soldiers, women, children and court officials he had brought from Gibeon.

17They went on their way. They stopped at Geruth Kimham near Bethlehem. They were going to Egypt. **18**They wanted to get away from the Babylonians. They were afraid of them because Ishmael, the son of Nethaniah, had killed Gedaliah, the son of Ahikam. The king of Babylonia had appointed Gedaliah as governor over Judah.

42 Then all of the army officers approached me. They included Johanan, the son of Kareah, and Jezaniah, the son of Hoshaiah. All of the people from the least important of them to the most important also came. **2**All of them said to me, "Please listen to our appeal. Pray to the LORD your God. Pray for all of us who are left here. Once there were many of us. But as you can see, only a few of us are left now. **3**So pray to the LORD your God. Pray that he'll tell us where we should go. Pray that he'll tell us what we should do."

4"I've heard you," I replied. "I'll certainly pray to the LORD your God. I'll do what you have asked me to do. In fact, I'll tell you everything the LORD says. I won't keep anything back from you."

5Then they said to me, "We'll do everything the LORD your God sends us to tell us to do. If we don't, may he be a true and faithful witness against us. **6**It doesn't matter whether what you say is in our favor or not. We're asking you to pray to the LORD our God. And we'll obey him. Things will go well with us. That's because we will obey the LORD our God."

7Ten days later a message came to me from the LORD. **8**So I sent for Johanan, the son of Kareah, and all of the other army officers who were with him. I also gathered together all of the people from the least important of them to the most important.

9I said to all of them, "The LORD is the God of Israel. You asked me to present your appeal to him. **10**He told me, 'Stay in this land. Then I will build you up. I will not tear you down. I will plant you. I will not pull you up by the roots. I am very sad that I had to bring all of this trouble on you.

11" 'Do not be afraid of the king of Babylonia. You are afraid of him now. Do not be,' announces the LORD. 'I am with you. I will keep you safe. I will save you from his powerful hands. **12**I will show you my loving concern. Then he will have concern for you. And he will let you return to your land.'

13"But suppose you say, 'We won't stay in this land.' If you do, you will be disobeying the LORD your God. **14**And suppose you say, 'No! We'll go and live in Egypt. There we won't have to face war anymore. We won't hear the trumpets of war. And we won't get hungry.'

15"Then listen to what the LORD says to you who are left in Judah. He is the LORD who rules over all. He is the God of Israel. He says, 'Have you already made up your minds to go to Egypt? Are you going to settle down there?

16" 'Then the war you fear will catch up with you there. The hunger you are afraid of will follow you into Egypt. And you will die there. **17**In fact, that will happen to all those who go and settle in Egypt. All of them will die of war, hunger and plague. Not one of them will live. None of them will escape the trouble I will bring on them.'

18"He is the LORD who rules over all. He is the God of Israel. He says, 'My burning anger has been poured out on those who used to live in Jerusalem. In the same way, it will be poured out on you when you go

OBEYS ✔

WE'LL DO EVERYTHING THE LORD YOUR GOD SENDS YOU TO TELL US TO DO... IT DOESN'T MATTER WHETHER WHAT YOU SAY IS IN OUR FAVOR OR NOT. WE'RE ASKING YOU TO PRAY TO THE LORD OUR GOD. AND WE'LL OBEY HIM.

— JEREMIAH 42:5-6 —

to Egypt. People will call down curses on you. They will be shocked at you. They will say bad things about you. And they will bring shame on you. You will never see this place again.'

19 "The LORD has spoken to you who are left in Judah. He has said, 'Do not go to Egypt.' Here is something you can be sure of. I am warning you about it today. 20 You made a big mistake when you asked me to pray to the LORD your God. You said, 'Pray to the LORD our God for us. Tell us everything he says. We'll do it.'

21 "I have told you today what the LORD your God wants you to do. But you still haven't obeyed him. You haven't done anything he sent me to tell you to do. 22 So here is something else you can be sure of. You will die of war, hunger and plague. You want to go and settle down in Egypt. But you will die there."

43 I finished telling the people everything the LORD their God had said. I told them everything he had sent me to tell them. 2 After that, Azariah, the son of Hoshaiah, and Johanan, the son of Kareah, spoke to me. And all of the proud men joined them. They said, "You are lying! The LORD our God hasn't sent you to speak to us. He hasn't told you to say, 'You must not go to Egypt and settle down there.' 3 But Baruch, the son of Neriah, is turning you against us. He wants us to be handed over to the Babylonians. Then they can kill us. Or they can take us away to Babylon."

4 So Johanan, the son of Kareah, disobeyed the LORD's command. So did all of the other army officers and all of the people. They didn't stay in the land of Judah. 5 Instead Johanan, the son of Kareah, and all of the other army officers led away all of the people who were left in Judah. Those people had returned to Judah from all of the nations where they had been scattered. 6 Johanan and the other officers also led away many people Nebuzaradan had left in Mizpah. They included men, women and children. They also included women who were members of the royal court. Nebuzaradan had left them with Gedaliah, the son of Ahikam. He had also left them with the prophet Jeremiah and Baruch, the son of Neriah. Nebuzaradan was commander of the royal guard. Ahikam was the son of Shaphan.

7 So the Jewish leaders disobeyed the LORD. They took everyone to Egypt. They went all the way to Tahpanhes.

8 In Tahpanhes a message came to me from the LORD. He said, 9 "Make sure the Jews are watching you. Then get some large stones. Go to the entrance to Pharaoh's house in Tahpanhes. Bury the stones in the clay under the brick walkway there.

10 "Then tell the Jews, 'The LORD who rules over all is the God of Israel. He says, "I will send for my servant Nebuchadnezzar, the king of Babylonia. And I will set his throne over these stones that are buried here. He will set up his royal tent over them. 11 He will come and attack Egypt. He will bring death to those I have appointed to die. He will take away as prisoners those I have appointed to be taken away. And he will kill with swords those I have appointed to be killed.

12 " ' "He will set the temples of the gods of Egypt on fire. He will burn their temples down. He will take the statues of their gods away. Nebuchadnezzar will be like a shepherd who wraps his coat around himself. He will wrap Egypt around himself. And he will leave there unharmed. 13 At Heliopolis in Egypt he will smash the sacred pillars to pieces. And he will burn down the temples of the gods of Egypt." ' "

Don't Worship Other Gods

44 A message came to me from the LORD about all of the Jews who were living in Lower Egypt. They were living in Migdol, Tahpanhes and Memphis. It was also about all of the Jews who were living in Upper Egypt. 2 The LORD who rules over all is the God of Israel. He said, "You saw all of the trouble I brought on Jerusalem. I also brought it on all of the towns in Judah. Today they lie there deserted and destroyed. 3 That is because of the evil things their people did. They made me very angry. They burned incense to other gods. And they worshiped them. They and you and your people of long ago never had anything to do with those gods before.

4 "Again and again I sent my servants the prophets. They said, 'Don't worship other gods! The LORD hates it!'

5 "But the people didn't listen. They didn't pay any attention. They didn't turn from their sinful ways. They didn't stop burning incense to other gods.

6 "So my burning anger was poured out. It blazed out against the towns of Judah and the streets of Jerusalem. It made them the dry and empty places they are today."

7 The LORD God who rules over all is the God of Israel. He says, "Why do you want to bring all of this trouble on yourselves?

You are cutting off from Judah its men and women. You are cutting off the children and babies. Not one of you will be left. 8 Why do you want to make me angry with the gods your hands have made? Why do you burn incense to the gods of Egypt, where you have come to live? You will destroy yourselves. All of the nations on earth will call down curses on you. They will bring shame on you.

9 "Have you forgotten the evil things your people did long ago? The kings and queens of Judah did those same things. So did you and your wives. They were done in the land of Judah and the streets of Jerusalem.

10 "To this very day the people of Judah have not made themselves low in my sight. They have not shown any respect for me. They have not obeyed my law. They have not followed the rules I gave you and your people long ago."

11 The LORD who rules over all is the God of Israel. He says, "I have decided to bring horrible trouble on you. I will destroy the whole land of Judah. 12 I will destroy the people of Judah who are left. They had decided to go to Egypt and settle down there. But all of them will die in Egypt. They will die of war or hunger. All of them will die, from the least important of them to the most important. They will die of war or hunger. People will call down curses on them. They will be shocked at them. They will say bad things about them. And they will bring shame on them. 13 I will use war, hunger and plague to punish the Jews who live in Egypt. I punished Jerusalem in the same way.

14 "None of the people of Judah who have gone to live in Egypt will escape. Not one of them will live to return to Judah. They long to return and live there. But only a few will escape from Egypt and go back."

15 All of the Jews who were living in Lower and Upper Egypt gathered to give me their answer. A large crowd had come together. It included men who knew that their wives were burning incense to other gods. Their wives were there with them. All of them said to me, 16 "We won't listen to the message you have spoken to us in the LORD's name! 17 We will certainly do everything we said we would. We'll burn incense to the goddess who is called the Queen of Heaven. We'll pour out drink offerings to her. We'll do just as we and our people before us did. Our kings and our officials also did it. All of us did it in the towns of Judah and the streets of Jerusa-

lem. At that time we had plenty of food. We were well off. We didn't suffer any harm.

18 "But then we stopped burning incense to the Queen of Heaven. We stopped pouring out drink offerings to her. And ever since that time we haven't had anything. Instead, we've been dying of war and hunger."

19 The women added, "We burned incense to the Queen of Heaven. We poured out drink offerings to her. And our husbands knew we were making cakes that looked like her. They knew we were pouring out drink offerings to her."

20 Then I spoke to all of the people who were answering me. I spoke to men and women alike. I said, 21 "Didn't the LORD know you were burning incense in the towns of Judah? Didn't he care that you were also doing it in the streets of Jerusalem? You and your people before you were doing it. Your kings and officials were doing it too. So were the rest of the people in the land.

22 "The LORD couldn't put up with the evil things you were doing anymore. He hated the things you did. So people called down curses on your land. It became a dry and empty desert. No one lived there. And that's the way it still is today.

23 "You have burned incense to other gods. You have sinned against the LORD. You haven't obeyed him or his law. You haven't followed his rules. You haven't lived up to the terms of the covenant he made with you. That's why all of this trouble has come on you. You have seen it with your own eyes."

24 Then I spoke to all of the people. That included the women. I said, "All you people of Judah in Egypt, listen to the LORD's message. 25 The LORD who rules over all is the God of Israel. He says, 'You and your wives have done what you promised you would do. You said, "We will certainly keep the promises we made to the Queen of Heaven. We'll burn incense to her. We'll pour out drink offerings to her." '

"Go ahead then. Do what you said you would! Keep your promises! 26 But listen to the LORD's message. Listen, all you Jews living in Egypt. 'I take an oath in my own great name,' says the LORD. 'I promise that no one from Judah who lives anywhere in Egypt will ever again pray in my name. None of them will ever take an oath and say, "You can be sure that the LORD and King is alive."

27 " 'I am watching over them to do them harm and not good. The Jews in

Egypt will die of war and hunger until all of them are destroyed. [28]Some will not be killed. They will return to Judah from Egypt. But they will be very few. Then all of the people of Judah who came to live in Egypt will know the truth. They will know whether what I say or what they say will come true.

[29]" 'I will give you a miraculous sign that I will punish you in this place,' announces the Lord. 'Then you can be sure that my warnings of harm against you will come true.' [30]The Lord says, 'I am going to hand Pharaoh Hophra over to his enemies who want to take his life. In the same way, I handed King Zedekiah over to Nebuchadnezzar, the king of Babylonia. He was the enemy who wanted to take Zedekiah's life.' " Hophra was king of Egypt.

The Lord Speaks to Baruch

45 I, the prophet Jeremiah, talked to Baruch, the son of Neriah. It was in the fourth year that Jehoiakim, the son of Josiah, was king of Judah. But it was after Baruch had written down on a scroll the words I was telling him to write. I said, [2]"The Lord is the God of Israel. Baruch, he says to you, [3]'You have said, "How terrible it is for me! The Lord has added sorrow to my pain. I'm worn out from all of my groaning. I can't find any rest." ' "

[4]The Lord said, "Tell Baruch, 'I say, "I will destroy what I have built up. I will pull up by the roots what I have planted. I will do it all through the earth. [5]So should you long for great things for yourself? Do not long for them. I will bring trouble on everyone," announces the Lord. "But no matter where you go, I will let you escape with your life." ' "

The Lord's Message About the Nations

46 A message came to me from the Lord. It was about the nations.

A Message About Egypt

[2]Here is what the Lord says about Egypt.

Here is his message against the army of Pharaoh Neco. He was king of Egypt. Nebuchadnezzar, the king of Babylonia, won the battle over his army. That happened at Carchemish on the Euphrates River. It was in the fourth year that Jehoiakim was king of Judah. He was the son of Josiah.

The message says,

[3] "Egyptians, prepare your shields!
Prepare large and small shields alike!
March out for battle!
[4]Get the horses and chariots ready to
ride!
Take up your battle positions!
Put your helmets on!
Shine up your spears!
Put on your armor!
[5]What do I see?
The Egyptians are terrified.
They are pulling back.
Their soldiers are losing.
They run away as fast as they can.
They do not look back.
There is terror on every side,"
announces the Lord.
[6] "Those who run fast can't get away.
Those who are strong can't escape.
In the north by the Euphrates River
they trip and fall.

[7] "Who is this that rises like the Nile
River?
Who rises like rivers of rushing
waters?
[8]Egypt rises like the Nile River.
It rises like rivers of rushing waters.
Egypt says, 'I will rise and cover the
earth.
I'll destroy cities and their people.'
[9]Charge, you horses!
Drive fast, you chariot drivers!
March on, you soldiers!
March on, you men of Cush and Put
who carry shields.
March on, you men of Lydia who
draw bows.
[10]But that day belongs to me.
I am the Lord who rules over all.
It is a day for me to pay back my
enemies.
The sword will eat until it is satisfied.
It will drink until it has no more
thirst for blood.
I am the Lord. I am the Lord who rules
over all.
I will offer a sacrifice.
I will offer it in the land of the north
by the Euphrates River.

[11] "People of Egypt,
go up to Gilead and get some
healing lotion.
But no matter what you try, you will
not be healed.
There isn't any healing for you.
[12]The nations will hear about your
shame.
Your cries of pain will fill the earth.
One soldier will trip over another.
Both of them will fall down
together."

¹³Nebuchadnezzar, the king of Babylonia, was coming to attack Egypt. Here is the message the LORD spoke to me about it. He said,

¹⁴ "Egyptians, here is what I want you to announce in your land.
Announce it in Migdol.
Also announce it in Memphis and Tahpanhes.
Say, 'Take up your battle positions! Get ready!
The sword eats up those who are around you.'
¹⁵ Why are your soldiers lying on the ground?
They can't stand, because I bring them down.
¹⁶ They will trip again and again.
They will fall over one another.
They will say, 'Get up. Let's go back home.
Let's return to our own people and our own lands.
Let's get away from the swords that will bring us great harm.'
¹⁷ The Egyptian soldiers will cry out,
'Pharaoh is our king. But he's only a loud noise.
He has missed his chance to win the battle.'
¹⁸ "I am the King.
My name is The LORD Who Rules Over All.
Someone will come who is like Mount Tabor among the mountains.
He is like Mount Carmel by the Mediterranean Sea.
And that is just as sure as I am alive,"
announces the King.
¹⁹ "So pack your belongings, you who live in Egypt.
You will be taken away from your land.
Memphis will be completely destroyed.
Its buildings will be broken down.
No one will live there.
²⁰ "Egypt is like a beautiful young cow.
But Nebuchadnezzar is coming against her from the north.
He will bite her like a fly.
²¹ Hired soldiers are in Egypt's army.
They are like fat calves.
All of them will turn and run away.
They will not hold their positions.
The day of trouble is coming on them.
The time for them to be punished is near.
²² The Egyptians will hiss like a snake that is trying to get away.

A powerful army will advance against them.
Their enemies will come against them with axes.
They will be like those who cut down trees.
²³ Egypt is like a thick forest.
But they will chop it down,"
announces the LORD.
"There are more of them than there are locusts.
In fact, they can't even be counted.
²⁴ The nation of Egypt will be put to shame.
It will be handed over to the people of the north."

²⁵ The LORD who rules over all is the God of Israel. He says, "I am about to punish Amon, the god of Thebes. I will also punish Pharaoh. I will punish Egypt and its gods and kings. And I will punish those who depend on Pharaoh. ²⁶ I will hand them over to those who are trying to kill them. I will give them to Nebuchadnezzar, the king of Babylonia, and his officers. But later, many people will live in Egypt again as in times past," announces the LORD.

²⁷ "People of Jacob, do not be afraid.
You are my servant.
Israel, do not be terrified.
I will bring you safely out of a place far away.
I will bring your children back from the land where they were taken.
Your people will have peace and security again.
And no one will make them afraid.
²⁸ People of Jacob, do not be afraid.
You are my servant.
I am with you," announces the LORD.
"I will completely destroy all of the nations
among which I scatter you.
But I will not completely destroy you.
I will correct you. But I will be fair.
I will punish you in a way that is fair and right."

A Message About the Philistines

47 A message came to me from the LORD. It was about the Philistines before Pharaoh attacked Gaza.

²The LORD said,

"The armies of Babylonia are like waters rising in the north.

They will become a great flood.
They will flow over the land and
everything in it.
They will flow over the towns and
those who live in them.
The people will cry out.
All those who live in the land will
sob.
3 They will sob when they hear
galloping horses.
They will sob at the noise of enemy
chariots.
They will sob at the rumble of their
wheels.
Fathers will not even try to help their
children.
Their hands will not be able to help
them.
4 The day has come
to destroy all of the Philistines.
The time has come to cut off all those
who could help Tyre and Sidon.
I am about to destroy the Philistines.
I will not leave anyone alive
who came from the coasts of Crete.
5 The people of Gaza will be so sad
they will shave their heads.
And Ashkelon's people will be silent.
You who remain on the flatlands,
how long will you cut yourselves?

6 " 'Sword of the LORD!' you cry out.
'How long will it be until you rest?
Return to the place you came from.
Stop killing us! Be still!'
7 But how can my sword rest
when I have given it a command?
I have ordered it
to attack Ashkelon and the
Philistine coast."

A Message About Moab

48 Here is what the LORD says about
Moab.

The LORD who rules over all is the God
of Israel. He says,

"How terrible it will be for Nebo!
It will be destroyed.
Kiriathaim will be captured.
It will be put to shame.
Its fort will be broken down.
It will be put to shame.
2 Moab will not be praised anymore.
In Heshbon people will plan its fall
from power.
They will say, 'Come. Let's put an
end to that nation.'
City of Madmen, you too will be silent
because you are sad.
My sword will hunt you down.

3 Listen to the cries from Horonaim.
The town is being completely
destroyed.
4 Moab will be broken.
Her little ones will cry out.
5 The people go up the road to Luhith.
They are sobbing bitterly as they go.
Loud cries are heard on the road down
to Horonaim.
People cry out because the town is
being destroyed.
6 People of Moab run away! Run for your
lives!
Become like a lonely bush in the
desert.
7 You trust in the things you can do.
You trust in your riches.
So you too will be taken away as
prisoners.
Your god Chemosh will be carried
away.
So will its priests and officials.
8 The one who is going to destroy you
will come against every town.
Not even one of them will escape.
The valley and the high flatlands
will be destroyed.
I, the LORD, have spoken.
9 Sprinkle salt all over Moab.
It will be completely destroyed.
Its towns will be a dry and empty
desert.
No one will live in them.

10 "May a person who is lazy when he
does my work
be under my curse!
May anyone who keeps his sword from
killing
be under my curse!

11 "Moab has been at peace and rest from
its earliest days.
It is like wine that has not been
shaken up.
It has not been poured from one jar to
another.
Moab's people have not been taken
away from their land.
They are like wine that tastes as it
always did.
Its smell has not changed at all.
12 But other days are coming,"
announces the LORD.
"At that time I will send people who
pour wine from jars.
They will pour Moab out like wine.
They will empty its jars.
They will smash its jugs.
13 Then Moab's people will be ashamed
of their god Chemosh.

They will be ashamed just as the
  people of Israel were
when they trusted in their god at
  Bethel.
14 "How can you say, 'We are soldiers.
  We are men who are brave in battle'?
15 Moab will be destroyed.
  Its enemies will march into its
    towns.
  Her finest young men will die in
    battle,"
  announces the King.
  His name is The LORD Who Rules
    Over All.
16 "The fall of Moab is near.
  Its time of trouble will come quickly.
17 All you who live around it, sob over its
    people.
  Be sad, you who know how famous
    Moab is.
  Say, 'Its powerful ruler's rod is broken!
  His glorious staff is smashed.'
18 "Come down from your glorious city,
  you who live in Dibon.
  Come and sit on the thirsty ground.
  The one who destroys your country
    will come up and attack you
  Your enemies will destroy your cities
    that have high walls around them.
19 Stand by the road and watch,
  you who live in Aroer.
  Ask the men who are running away.
  Ask the women who are escaping.
  Ask them, 'What has happened?'
20 Moab has been put to shame.
  It has been destroyed.
  Sob and cry out!
  Tell everyone Moab has been
    destroyed.
  Announce it by the Arnon River.
21 The high flatlands have been judged.
  So have Holon, Jahzah and
    Mephaath.
22 Dibon, Nebo and Beth Diblathaim
  have been judged.
23   So have Kiriathaim, Beth Gamul and
    Beth Meon.
24 Kerioth and Bozrah have also been
    judged.
  And so have all of the towns of
    Moab, far and near alike.
25 Moab's power is gone.
  Its strength is broken,"
                announces the LORD.
26 "Moab's people think they are better
    than I am.
  So let their enemies make them
    drunk.
  Let the people get sick and throw up.

Let them roll around in the mess they
  have made.
  Let people laugh at them.
27 Moab, you laughed at Israel, didn't
    you?
  Were Israel's people caught among
    robbers?
  Is that why you shake your head at
    them?
  Is that why you make fun of them
    every time you talk about them?
28 Leave your towns,
  you who live in Moab.
  Go and live among the rocks.
  Be like a dove that makes its nest
    at the mouth of a cave.

29 "We have heard all about Moab's
    pride.
  We have heard how very proud they
    are.
  They think they are so much better
    than others.
  Their pride reaches deep down
    inside their hearts.
30 I know how rude they are.
  But it will not get them anywhere,"
                announces the LORD.
  "Their bragging does not
    accomplish anything.
31 So I cry out over Moab.
  I cry for all of Moab's people.
  I groan for the men of Kir Hareseth.
32 I sob over you as Jazer sobs,
  you vines of Sibmah.
  Your branches used to spread out.
  They went all the way down to the
    Dead Sea.
  They reached as far as the sea of
    Jazer.
  The one who destroys your country
    has taken away your grapes and ripe
    fruit.
33 Joy has left your orchards.
  Gladness is gone from your fields.
  I have stopped the flow of juice from
    your winepresses.
  No one stomps on your grapes with
    shouts of joy.
  There are shouts.
  But they are not shouts of joy.

34 "The sound of their cry rises from
    Heshbon.
  It rises as far as Elealeh and Jahaz.
  It rises from Zoar.
  It goes all the way to Horonaim and
    Eglath Shelishiyah.
  Even the waters at Nimrim are dried
    up.
35 In Moab people sacrifice offerings on
    the high places.

They burn incense to their gods.
But I will put an end to those
people,"
announces the LORD.
36 "Like a flute my heart sings a song of
sadness for Moab.
It sings like a flute for the men of Kir
Hareseth.
The wealth they had gotten is gone.
37 Every head is shaved.
Every beard is cut off.
Every hand is cut.
And every waist is covered with
black cloth.
38 Sobbing is the only sound in Moab.
It is heard on all of its roofs.
It is heard in the market places.
I have broken Moab
like a jar that no one wants,"
announces the LORD.
39 "How broken Moab is! How the people
sob!
They turn away from others
because they are so ashamed.
All those who are around them laugh
at them.
They are shocked at them."

40 The LORD says,

"Look! Nebuchadnezzar is like an eagle
diving down.
He is spreading his wings over Moab.
41 Kerioth will be captured.
Its forts will be taken.
At that time the hearts of Moab's
soldiers will tremble in fear.
They will be like the heart of a
woman having a baby.
42 Moab will be destroyed as a nation.
That is because its people thought
they were better than I am.
43 You people of Moab,"
announces the LORD,
"terror, a pit and a trap are waiting
for you.
44 Anyone who runs away from the terror
will fall into the pit.
Anyone who climbs out of the pit
will be caught in the trap.
The time is coming
when I will punish Moab,"
announces the LORD.

45 "In the shadow of Heshbon
those who are trying to escape stand
helpless.
A fire has blazed out from Heshbon.
Flames have come out from Sihon's
city.
It burns the foreheads of Moab's
people.

It burns the skulls of those who brag
loudly.
46 How terrible it will be for you, Moab!
Those who worship Chemosh are
destroyed.
Your sons are being taken to another
country.
Your daughters are taken away as
prisoners.

47 "But in days to come
I will bless Moab with great success
again,"
announces the LORD.

That's the report about how the LORD
said he would judge Moab.

A Message About Ammon

49 Here is what the LORD says about
the people of Ammon.

He says,

"Doesn't Israel have any sons?
Doesn't Israel have anyone
to take over the family property?
Then why has the god Molech taken
over Gad?
Why do those who worship him live
in its towns?
2 But a new day is coming,"
announces the LORD.
"At that time I will sound the battle cry.
I will sound it against Rabbah in the
land of Ammon.
It will become a pile of broken-down
buildings.
The villages that are around it will
be set on fire.
Then Israel will drive out
those who drove her out,"
says the LORD.
3 "Heshbon, sob over Ai! It is destroyed!
Cry out, you who live in Rabbah!
Put on black clothes and sob.
Run here and there inside the walls.
Your god Molech will be carried away.
So will its priests and officials.
4 Why do you brag about your valleys?
You brag that they produce so many
crops.
You are an unfaithful country.
You trust in your riches. You say,
'Who will attack me?'
5 I will bring terror on you.
It will come from all those who are
around you,"
announces the Lord.
He is the LORD
who rules over all.
"Every one of you will be driven away.

No one will bring back those who
escape.

6 "But after that, I will bless the people
of Ammon
with great success again,"
announces the LORD.

A Message About Edom

7 Here is what the LORD says about
Edom.

The LORD who rules over all says,

"Isn't there wisdom in the town of
Teman anymore?
Can't those who are wise give
advice?
Has their wisdom disappeared
completely?
8 Turn around and run away, you who
live in Dedan.
Hide in deep caves.
I will bring trouble on Esau's family
line.
I will do it at the time I punish them.
9 Edom, suppose grape pickers came to
harvest your vines.
They would still leave a few grapes.
Suppose robbers came at night.
They would steal only as much as
they wanted.
10 But I will strip everything away from
Esau's people.
I will uncover their hiding places.
They will not be able to hide
anywhere.
Their children, relatives and neighbors
will die.
Then Esau's people will be gone.
11 Leave your children whose fathers
have died.
I will watch over them.
Your widows can also trust in me."

12 The LORD says, "What if those who do
not have to drink the cup must drink it
anyway? Then shouldn't you be punished? You will certainly be punished.
You must drink the cup. **13** I make a promise with an oath in my own name. Bozrah
will be destroyed," announces the LORD.
"People will be shocked at it. They will
bring shame on it. They will call down
curses on it. And all of its towns will be destroyed forever."

14 I've heard a message from the LORD.
A messenger was sent to the nations.
The LORD told him to say,
"Gather yourselves together to attack
Edom!
Prepare for battle!"

15 The LORD says to Edom, "I will make
you weak among the nations.
They will look down on you.
16 You live in the safety of the rocks.
You live on top of the hills.
But the terror you stir up has now
turned against you.
Your proud heart has tricked you.
You build your nest as high as an eagle
does.
But I will bring you down from
there,"
announces the LORD.
17 "People of Edom,
all those who pass by you will be
shocked.
They will make fun of you
because of all of your wounds.
18 Sodom and Gomorrah were destroyed.
So were the towns that were near
them,"
says the LORD.
"You will be just like them.
No one will live in your land.
No one will stay there even for a
short time.

19 "I will be like a lion coming up
from the bushes by the Jordan River.
I will hunt in rich grasslands.
I will chase you from your land in an
instant.
What nation will I choose to do it?
Which one will I appoint?
Is anyone like me?
Who would dare to argue with me?
What leader can stand against me?"
20 So listen to what the LORD has planned
against the people of Edom.
Hear what he has planned against
those who live in Teman.
Edom's young people will be dragged
away.
The LORD will completely destroy
their grasslands because of them.
21 When the earth hears Edom fall, it will
shake.
The people's cries will be heard all
the way to the Red Sea.
22 Look! An enemy is coming.
It's like an eagle diving down.
It will spread its wings over Bozrah.
At that time the hearts of Edom's
soldiers
will tremble in fear.
They'll be like the heart of a woman
having a baby.

A Message About Damascus

23 Here is what the LORD says about Damascus. He says,

"The people of Hamath and Arpad are
    terrified.
They have heard bad news.
They have lost all hope.
    They are troubled like the rolling
        sea.
24 The people of Damascus have become
        weak.
They have turned to run away.
    Panic has taken hold of them.
Suffering and pain have taken hold of
        them.
    Their pain is like the pain of a
        woman having a baby.
25 Why hasn't the famous city been
        deserted?
    It is the town I take delight in.
26 You can be sure its young men will fall
        dead in the streets.
    All of its soldiers will be put to death
        at that time,"
                announces the LORD
                    who rules over all.
27 "I will set the walls of Damascus on
        fire.
    It will burn up the strong towers of
        King Ben-Hadad."

A Message About Kedar and Hazor

28 Here is what the LORD says about the
land of Kedar and the kingdoms of Hazor.
Nebuchadnezzar, the king of Babylonia,
was planning to attack them.

The LORD says to the armies of Babylonia,

"Prepare for battle. Attack Kedar.
    Destroy the people of the east.
29 Their tents and flocks will be taken
        away from them.
    Their tents will be carried off.
    All of their goods and camels will be
        stolen.
People will shout to them,
    'There is terror on every side!'
30 "Run away quickly!
    You who live in Hazor, stay in deep
        caves,"
                announces the LORD.
"Nebuchadnezzar, the king of
        Babylonia,
    has made plans against you.
    He has decided to attack you.
31 "Armies of Babylonia, prepare for
        battle.
    Attack a nation that feels secure.
    Its people do not have any worries,"
                announces the LORD.
"That nation does not have gates or
        heavy metal bars.

Its people live all alone.
32 Their camels will be stolen.
    Their large herds will be taken away.
I will scatter to the winds those who
        are in places far away.
I will bring trouble on them from
        every side,"
                announces the LORD.
33 "Hazor will become a home for wild
        dogs.
    It will be a dry and empty desert
        forever.
No one will live in that land.
    No one will stay there even for a
        short time."

A Message About Elam

34 A message came to me from the LORD.
It was about Elam. It came shortly after
Zedekiah became king of Judah.

35 The LORD who rules over all said,

"Elam's bow is the secret of its
        strength.
    But I will break it.
36 I will bring the four winds against
        Elam.
    I will bring them from all four
        directions.
I will scatter Elam's people to the four
        winds.
    They will be taken away
    to every nation on earth.
37 I will use Elam's enemies to smash
        them.
    Those who are trying to take their
        lives will kill them.
I will bring trouble on Elam's people.
    My anger will burn against them,"
                announces the LORD.
"I will chase them with swords.
    I will hunt them down
    until I have destroyed them.
38 I will set up my throne in Elam.
    I will destroy its king and officials,"
                announces the LORD.
39 "But in days to come I will bless Elam
    with great success again,"
                announces the LORD.

A Message About Babylonia

50 Here is the message the LORD
    spoke through me about the city
of Babylon and the land of Babylonia. He
said,

2 "Announce this message among the
        nations.
    Lift up a banner.
Let the nations hear the message.
    Do not keep anything back.

Say, 'Babylon will be captured.
　　The god Bel will be put to shame.
　　Marduk will be filled with terror.
Babylon's gods will be put to shame.
　　The gods its people made will be
　　　filled with terror.'
³ A nation from the north will attack it.
　　That nation will destroy Babylonia.
No one will live there.
　　People and animals alike will run
　　　away.

⁴ "A new day is coming,"
　　announces the LORD.
"At that time the people of Israel and
　　　Judah will gather together.
　　They will come in tears to me.
　　I am the LORD their God.
⁵ They will ask how to get to Zion.
　　Then they will turn their faces
　　　toward it.
They will come and join themselves to
　　　me.
　　They will enter into the covenant I
　　　make with them.
It will last forever.
　　It will never be forgotten.

⁶ "My people have been like lost sheep.
　　Their shepherds have led them
　　　down the wrong path.
　　They have caused them to wander in
　　　the mountains.
They have wandered over mountains
　　　and hills.
　　They have forgotten that I am their
　　　true resting place.
⁷ Everyone who found them destroyed
　　　them.
　　Their enemies said, 'We aren't guilty.
They sinned against the LORD.
　　He gave them everything they
　　　needed.
　　He has always been Israel's hope.'

⁸ "People of Judah, run away from
　　　Babylon.
　　Leave the land of Babylonia.
　　Be like the goats that lead the flock.
⁹ I will stir up great nations
　　that will join forces against Babylon.
I will bring them from the land of
　　　the north.
They will take up their battle positions
　　　against Babylon.
　　They will come from the north and
　　　capture it.
Their arrows will be like skilled
　　　soldiers.
　　They will not miss their mark.
¹⁰ So the riches of Babylonia will be taken
　　　away.

All those who steal from it will have
　　　more than enough,"
　　　　announces the LORD.

¹¹ "People of Babylonia, you have stolen
　　　what belongs to me.
　　That has made you glad and full of
　　　joy.
You dance around like a young cow on
　　　a threshing floor.
　　You neigh like stallions.
¹² Because of that, you will bring great
　　　shame on your land.
　　Your whole nation will be
　　　dishonored.
It will become the least important of
　　　the nations.
　　It will become a dry and empty
　　　desert.
¹³ Because I am angry with it, no one will
　　　live there.
　　It will be completely deserted.
All those who pass by it will be
　　　shocked.
　　They will make fun of it because of
　　　all of its wounds.

¹⁴ "All you who draw the bow,
　　take up your battle positions around
　　　Babylon.
Shoot at it! Do not spare any arrows!
　　Its people have sinned against me.
¹⁵ Shout against them on every side!
　　They are giving up.
The towers of the city are falling.
　　Its walls are being pulled down.
I am paying its people back.
　　So pay them back yourselves.
　　Do to them what they have done to
　　　others.
¹⁶ Do not leave anyone in Babylonia to
　　　plant the fields.
　　Do not leave anyone to harvest the
　　　grain.
Let each of them return to his own
　　　people.
　　Let him run away to his own land.
　　If he doesn't, his enemy's sword will
　　　bring him great harm.

¹⁷ "Israel is like a scattered flock
　　that lions have chased away.
The first lion that ate them up
　　was the king of Assyria.
The last one that broke their bones
　　was Nebuchadnezzar, the king of
　　　Babylonia."

¹⁸ The LORD who rules over all is the God
of Israel. He says,

"I punished the king of Assyria.
　　In the same way, I will punish

the king of Babylonia and his land.
¹⁹ But I will bring Israel back to their own
grasslands.
I will feed them on Mount Carmel
and in Bashan.
I will satisfy their hunger
on the hills of Ephraim and Gilead.
²⁰ A new day is coming,"
announces the LORD.
"At that time people will search for
Israel's guilt.
But they will not find any.
They will search for Judah's sins.
But they will not find any.
That is because I will forgive the
people I have spared.

²¹ "Enemies of Babylonia, attack their
land of Merathaim.
Make war against those who live in
Pekod.
Chase them and kill them. Destroy
them completely,"
announces the LORD.
"Do everything I have commanded
you to do.
²² The noise of battle is heard in the land.
It is the noise of a great city being
destroyed!
²³ It has been broken to pieces.
It was the hammer that broke the
whole earth.
How empty Babylonia is among the
nations!
²⁴ Babylonia, I set a trap for you.
And you were caught before you
knew it.
You were found and captured.
That is because you opposed me.
²⁵ I have opened up my storeroom.
I have brought out the weapons I use
when I am angry.
I am the LORD and King who rules over
all.
I have work to do in the land of the
Babylonians.
²⁶ So come against it from far away.
Open up its storerooms.
Stack everything up like piles of
grain.
Completely destroy that country.
Do not leave anyone alive there.
²⁷ Kill all of its people.
Let them die in battle.
How terrible it will be for them!
Their time to be judged has come.
Now they will be punished.
²⁸ Listen to those who have escaped.
Listen to those who have returned
from Babylonia.
They are announcing in Zion

how I have paid Babylonia back.
I have paid it back for destroying my
temple.

²⁹ "Send for men who are armed with
bows and arrows.
Send them against Babylon.
Set up camp all around it.
Do not let anyone escape.
Pay it back for what its people have
done.
Do to them what they have done to
others.
They have dared to disobey me.
I am the Holy One of Israel.
³⁰ You can be sure its young men will fall
dead in the streets.
All of its soldiers will be put to death
at that time,"
announces the LORD.
³¹ "Proud Babylonians, I am against you,"
announces the Lord.
The LORD who rules over all says,
"Your day to be judged has come.
It is time for you to be punished.
³² You proud people will trip and fall.
No one will help you up.
I will start a fire in your towns.
It will burn up everyone who is
around you."

³³ The LORD who rules over all says,

"The people of Israel are being treated
badly.
So are the people of Judah.
Those who have captured them are
holding them.
They refuse to let them go.
³⁴ But I am strong and will save them.
My name is The LORD Who Rules
Over All.
I will stand up for them.
I will bring peace and rest to their
land.
But I will bring trouble to those who
live in Babylonia.

³⁵ "A sword is coming against the
Babylonians!"
announces the LORD.
"It is coming against those who live in
Babylonia.
It is coming against their officials
and wise men.
³⁶ A sword is coming against their
prophets.
But they are not really prophets at
all!
So they will look foolish.
A sword is coming against their
soldiers!
They will be filled with terror.

37 A sword is coming against their horses
and chariots!
It is coming against all of the hired
soldiers in their armies.
They will become like weak women.
A sword is coming against their
treasures!
They will be stolen.
38 There will not be any rain for their
rivers.
So they will dry up.
Those things will happen because their
land is full of statues of gods.
Those gods will go crazy with terror.

39 "Desert creatures and hyenas will live
in Babylon.
And so will owls.
People will never live there again.
It will not be lived in for all time to
come.
40 I destroyed Sodom and Gomorrah.
I also destroyed the towns that were
near them,"
announces the LORD.
"Babylonia will be just like them.
No one will live there.
No one will stay there even for a
short time.

41 "Look! An army is coming from the
north.
I am stirring up a great nation and
many kings.
They are coming from a land that is
very far away.
42 Their soldiers are armed with bows and
spears.
They are mean.
They do not show any mercy at all.
They come riding in on their horses.
They sound like the roaring ocean.
They are lined up for battle.
They are coming to attack you, city
of Babylon.
43 The king of Babylonia has heard
reports about them.
His hands can't help him.
He is in great pain.
It is like the pain of a woman having
a baby.
44 I will be like a lion coming up from the
bushes by the Jordan River.
I will hunt in rich grasslands.
I will chase the people of Babylon from
their land in an instant.
What nation will I choose to do it?
Which one will I appoint?
Is anyone like me? Who would dare to
argue with me?
What leader can stand against me?"

45 So listen to what the LORD has planned
against Babylon.
Hear what he has planned against
the land of the Babylonians.
Their young people will be dragged
away.
The LORD will completely destroy
their grasslands because of
them.
46 When the earth hears that Babylonia
has been captured,
it will shake.
The people's cries will be heard
among the nations.

51 The LORD says,

"I will stir up the spirits of destroyers.
They will march out against
Babylonia and its people.
2 I will send other nations against it
to separate the straw from the grain.
I will send them to destroy
Babylonia completely.
They will oppose it on every side.
At that time it will be destroyed.
3 Do not let its soldiers get their bows
ready to use.
Do not let them put on their armor.
Do not spare their young men.
Destroy their armies completely.
4 They will fall down dead in Babylon.
They will receive deadly wounds in
its streets.
5 The land of Israel and Judah is full of
guilt.
Its people have sinned against me.
But I have not deserted them. I am
their God.
I am the LORD who rules over all.
I am the Holy One of Israel.

6 "People of Judah, run away from
Babylonia!
Run for your lives!
Do not be destroyed because of the
sins of its people.
It is time for me to pay them back.
I will punish them for what they
have done.
7 Babylon was like a gold cup in my
hand.
That city made the whole earth
drunk.
The nations drank its wine.
So now they have gone crazy.
8 Babylon will suddenly fall and be
broken.
Sob over it!
Get healing lotion for its pain.
Perhaps it can be healed.

9 "The nations say, 'We would have
　　healed Babylon.
But it can't be healed.
So let's leave it. Let's each go to our
　　own land.
Babylon's sins reach all the way to
　　the skies.
They rise up as high as the clouds.'

10 "The people of Judah say,
'The Lord has made things right for
　　us again.
So come. Let's tell in Zion
what the Lord our God has done.'

11 "I have stirred up you kings of the
　　Medes.
So sharpen your arrows!
Get your shields!
I plan to destroy Babylon.
I will pay the Babylonians back.
They have destroyed my temple.
12 Lift up a banner! Attack Babylon's
　　walls!
Put more guards on duty!
Station more of them to watch over
　　you!
Hide and wait to attack them!
I will do what I have planned.
I will do what I have decided to do
　　against the people of Babylon.
13 You who live by the rivers of Babylon,
　　your end has come.
You who are rich in treasures,
　　it is time for you to be destroyed.
14 I am the Lord who rules over all.
I have made a promise with an oath
　　in my own name.
I have said, 'I will certainly fill your
　　land with soldiers.
They will be as many as a huge
　　number of locusts.
They will win the battle over you.
They will shout for joy.'

15 "I used my power to make the earth.
I used my wisdom to set the world in
　　place.
I used my understanding to spread
　　the heavens out.
16 When I thunder, the waters in the
　　heavens roar.
I make clouds rise from one end of
　　the earth to the other.
I send lightning with the rain.
I bring out the wind from my
　　storerooms.

17 "No one has any sense.
No one knows anything.
Everyone who works with gold is put
　　to shame
　　by his wooden gods.

His metal gods are fakes.
They can't even breathe.
18 They are worthless. People make fun of
　　them.
When I judge them, they will be
　　destroyed.
19 I am not like them. I am the God of
　　Jacob.
I give my people everything they
　　need.
I can do it because I made
　　everything, including Israel.
It is the nation that belongs to me.
My name is The Lord Who Rules
　　Over All.

20 "Babylonia, you are my war club.
You are my weapon for battle.
I use you to destroy nations.
I use you to wipe out kingdoms.
21 I use you to destroy horses and their
　　riders.
I use you to destroy chariots and
　　their drivers.
22 I use you to destroy men and women.
I use you to destroy old people and
　　young people.
I use you to destroy young men and
　　young women.
23 I use you to destroy shepherds and
　　their flocks.
I use you to destroy farmers and
　　their oxen.
I use you to destroy governors and
　　officials.

24 "Judah, I will pay Babylon back. You
will see it with your own eyes. I will pay
back all those who live in Babylonia. I will
pay them back for all of the wrong things
they have done in Zion," announces the
Lord.

25 "Babylonia, I am against you.
Your kingdom is like a destroying
　　mountain.
You have destroyed the whole
　　earth,"
　　　　　　　　announces the Lord.
"I will reach out my hand against you.
I will roll you off the cliffs.
I will make you like a mountain that
　　has been burned up.
26 No rock will be taken from you to be
　　used
　　as the most important stone for a
　　building.
No stones will be taken from you
　　to be used for a foundation.
Your land will be empty forever,"
　　　　　　　　announces the Lord.

27 "Nations, lift up a banner in the land
of Babylonia!
Blow a trumpet among yourselves!
Prepare yourselves for battle against
Babylonia.
Send the kingdoms
of Ararat, Minni and Ashkenaz
against it.
Appoint a commander against it.
Send many horses against it.
Let them be as many as a huge
number of locusts.
28 Prepare yourselves for battle against
Babylonia.
Prepare the kings of the Medes.
Prepare their governors and all of their
officials.
Prepare all of the countries they rule
over.
29 The Babylonians tremble and shake
with fear.
My plans against them stand firm.
I plan to destroy their land completely.
Then no one will live there.
30 Babylon's soldiers have stopped
fighting.
They remain in their forts.
Their strength is all gone.
They have become like weak
women.
Their buildings are set on fire.
The heavy metal bars on their gates
are broken.
31 One messenger after another
comes to the king of Babylonia.
All of them announce that
his entire city is captured.
32 The places where people go across the
Euphrates River have been
captured.
The swamps have been set on fire.
And the soldiers are terrified."

33 The LORD who rules over all is the
God of Israel. He says,

"The city of Babylon is like a threshing
floor
when cattle are walking on it.
The time to destroy it will soon
come."

34 The people of Jerusalem say,
"Nebuchadnezzar, the king of
Babylonia, has destroyed us.
He has thrown us into a panic.
He has emptied us out like a jar.
Like a snake he has swallowed us up.
He has filled his stomach with our
rich food.
Then he has spit us out of his
mouth."

35 The people continue, "May the people
of Babylon
pay for the harmful things they have
done to us.
May those who live in Babylonia
pay for spilling the blood of our
people."
That's what the people who live in
Zion say.

36 So the LORD says,

"I will stand up for you.
I will pay the Babylonians back for
what they did to you.
I will dry up their water supply.
I will make their springs run dry.
37 Babylon will have all of its buildings
knocked down.
It will be a home for wild dogs.
No one will live there.
People will be shocked at it.
They will make fun of it.
38 All of its people roar like young lions.
They growl like lion cubs.
39 They are stirred up.
So I will set a big dinner in front of
them.
I will make them drunk.
And they will shout and laugh.
But then they will lie down and die.
They will never wake up,"
announces the LORD.
40 "I will lead them down like lambs to be
put to death.
They will be like rams and goats that
have been killed.

41 "Babylon will be captured!
The whole earth was very proud of
it.
But it will be taken over by others!
The nations will be shocked when it
falls.
42 Babylon's enemies will sweep over it
like an ocean.
Like roaring waves they will cover it.
43 The towns of Babylonia will be empty.
It will become a dry and desert land.
No one will live there.
No one will even travel through it.
44 I will punish the god Bel in Babylon.
I will make Bel spit out what it has
swallowed.
The nations will not come and
worship it anymore.
And Babylon's walls will fall down.

45 "Come out of there, my people!
Run for your lives!
Run away from my burning anger.
46 You will hear about terrible things
that are happening in Babylonia.

But do not lose hope. Do not be
afraid.
You will hear one thing this year.
And you will hear something else
next year.
You will hear about awful things in the
land.
You will hear about one ruler
fighting against another.
47 I will punish the gods of Babylon.
That time will certainly come.
Then the whole land will be full of
shame.
Its people will lie down and die
there.
48 So heaven and earth and everything in
them will shout for joy.
They will be glad because of what
will happen to Babylon.
Armies will attack it from the north.
And they will destroy it,"
announces the LORD.

49 "Babylon's people have killed my
people Israel.
They have also killed people all over
the earth.
So now Babylon itself must fall.
50 You who have not been killed in the
war against Babylon,
leave! Do not wait!
In a land far away remember me.
And think about Jerusalem."

51 The people of Judah reply, "No one
honors us anymore.
People make fun of us.
Our faces are covered with shame.
People from other lands have entered
the holy places of the LORD's house."

52 "But a new day is coming," announces
the LORD.
"At that time I will punish the gods
of Babylon.
And all through its land
wounded people will groan.
53 What if Babylon reached all the way to
the sky?
What if it made its high walls even
stronger?
I would still send destroyers against
it,"
announces the LORD.

54 "The noise of people screaming comes
from Babylon.
A terrible sound comes from its
land.
It is the sound of a mighty city being
destroyed.
55 I will destroy Babylon.
I will put an end to all of its noise.

Waves of enemies will sweep through
it like great waters.
The roar of their voices will fill the
air.
56 A destroying army will come against
Babylon.
The soldiers in the city will be
captured.
Their bows will be broken.
I am the LORD God who pays people
back.
I will pay them back in full.
57 I will make Babylon's officials and wise
men drunk.
I will do the same thing to its
governors, officers and soldiers.
They will lie down and die. They will
never wake up,"
announces the King. His name is
The LORD Who Rules Over All.

58 The LORD who rules over all says,

"Babylon's thick walls will fall down
flat.
Its high gates will be set on fire.
The nations wear themselves out for
no reason at all.
Their hard work will only be burned
up in the flames."

59 I gave a message to the staff officer Seraiah, the son of Neriah. I told him to take
it with him to Babylon. He went there
with Zedekiah, the king of Judah. He left
in the fourth year of Zedekiah's rule. Neriah was the son of Mahseiah. **60** I had written about all of the trouble that would
come on Babylon. I had written it down
on a scroll. It included everything that
had been recorded about Babylon.

61 I said to Seraiah, "When you get to
Babylon, here's what I want you to do.
Make sure that you read all of these words
out loud. **62** Then say, 'LORD, you have said
you will destroy this place. You have said
that no people or animals will live here. It
will be empty forever.'

63 "Finish reading the scroll. Tie a stone
to it. Throw it into the Euphrates River.
64 Then say, 'In the same way, Babylon will
sink down. It will never rise again. That is
because I will bring such horrible trouble
on it. And its people will fall along with
it.'"

The words of Jeremiah end here.

Nebuchadnezzar Destroys Jerusalem

52 Zedekiah was 21 years old when
he became king. He ruled in Jerusalem for 11 years. His mother's name was

Hamutal. She was the daughter of Jeremiah. She was from Libnah.

2Zedekiah did what was evil in the sight of the LORD. He did just as Jehoiakim had done. **3**The enemies of Jerusalem and Judah attacked them because the LORD was angry. In the end he threw them out of his land.

Zedekiah refused to obey the king of Babylonia.

4Nebuchadnezzar was king of Babylonia. He marched out against Jerusalem. All of his armies went with him. It was in the ninth year of the rule of Zedekiah. It was on the tenth day of the tenth month. The armies set up camp outside the city. They set up ladders and built ramps and towers all around it. **5**It was surrounded until the 11th year of King Zedekiah's rule.

6By the ninth day of the fourth month, there wasn't any food left in the city. So the people didn't have anything to eat. **7**Then the Babylonians broke through the city wall.

Judah's whole army ran away. They left the city at night. They went out through the gate between the two walls that were near the king's garden. They escaped even though the Babylonians surrounded the city. Judah's army ran toward the Arabah Valley.

8But the armies of Babylonia chased King Zedekiah. They caught up with him in the flatlands near Jericho. All of his soldiers were separated from him. They had scattered in every direction. **9**The king was captured.

He was taken to the king of Babylonia at Riblah. Riblah was in the land of Hamath. That's where Nebuchadnezzar decided how he would be punished. **10**At Riblah the king of Babylonia killed the sons of Zedekiah. He forced him to watch it with his own eyes. Nebuchadnezzar also killed all of the officials of Judah. **11**Then he poked out Zedekiah's eyes. He put him in bronze chains. And he took him to Babylon. There he put Zedekiah in prison until the day he died.

12Nebuzaradan served the king of Babylonia. In fact, he was commander of the royal guard. He came to Jerusalem. It was in the 19th year that Nebuchadnezzar was king of Babylonia. It was on the tenth day of the fifth month.

13Nebuzaradan set the LORD's temple on fire. He also set fire to the royal palace and all of the houses in Jerusalem. He burned down every important building. **14**The armies of Babylonia broke down all of the walls around Jerusalem. That's what the commander told them to do.

15Some of the poorest people still remained in the city along with the others. But the commander Nebuzaradan took them away as prisoners. He also took the rest of the skilled workers. That included the people who had joined the king of Babylonia. **16**But Nebuzaradan left the rest of the poorest people of the land behind. He told them to work in the vineyards and fields.

17The armies of Babylonia destroyed the LORD's temple. They broke the bronze pillars into pieces. They broke up the bronze stands that could be moved around. And they broke up the huge bronze bowl. Then they carried all of the bronze away to Babylon. **18**They also took away the pots, shovels, wick cutters, sprinkling bowls and dishes. They took away all of the bronze articles that were used for any purpose in the temple. **19**The commander of the royal guard took away the bowls and the shallow cups for burning incense. He took away the sprinkling bowls, the pots, the lampstands and the dishes. He took away the bowls that were used for drink offerings. So he took away everything that was made out of pure gold or silver.

20The bronze was more than anyone could weigh. It included the bronze from the two pillars. It included the bronze from the huge bowl and the 12 bronze bulls that were under it. It also included the stands. King Solomon had made all of those things for the LORD's temple. **21**Each of the pillars was 27 feet high and 18 feet around. The pillars were hollow. The metal in each of them was three inches thick. **22**The bronze top of one pillar was seven and a half feet high. It was decorated with a set of bronze chains and pomegranates all around it. The other pillar was just like it. It also had pomegranates. **23**There were 96 pomegranates on the sides of each of the two tops. The total number of pomegranates above the bronze chains around each top was 100.

24The commander of the guard took many prisoners. They included the chief priest Seraiah and the priest Zephaniah who was under him. They also included the three men who guarded the temple doors. **25**Some people were still left in the city. The commander took as a prisoner the officer who was in charge of the fighting men. He took the seven men who gave advice to the king. He also took the secretary who was the chief officer in charge of getting the people of the land to serve in the army. And he took 60 of the secretary's men who were still in the city.

26The commander Nebuzaradan took all of them away. He brought them to the king of Babylonia at Riblah. 27There the king had them put to death. Riblah was in the land of Hamath.

So the people of Judah were taken as prisoners. They were taken far away from their own land. 28Here is the number of the people Nebuchadnezzar took to Babylon as prisoners.

In the seventh year of his rule, he took 3,023 Jews.
29In his 18th year,
he took 832 people from Jerusalem.
30In Nebuchadnezzar's 23rd year, Nebuzaradan, the commander of the royal guard, took 745 Jews to Babylon.

The total number of people who were taken to Babylon was 4,600.

Jehoiachin Is Set Free

31Evil-Merodach set Jehoiachin, the king of Judah, free from prison. It was in the 37th year after Jehoiachin had been taken away to Babylon. It was also the year Evil-Merodach became king of Babylonia. It was on the 25th day of the 12th month. 32Evil-Merodach spoke kindly to Jehoiachin. He gave him a place of honor. Other kings were with Jehoiachin in Babylon. But his place was more important than theirs.

33So Jehoiachin put his prison clothes away. For the rest of Jehoiachin's life the king of Babylonia provided what he needed. 34The king did that for Jehoiachin day by day as long as he lived. He did it until the day Jehoiachin died.

LAMENTATIONS

The book of Lamentations is a book of "laments," or poems, that express deep sadness. The writer of Lamentations, probably Jeremiah, feels sad because of what is happening around him. The people of Judah are being punished because they refuse to obey God. The city of Jerusalem and the temple are being destroyed, and the writer feels depressed and hopeless. As you read Jeremiah, remember that God wants you to be sorry when you sin. He's waiting to forgive you, but only if you ask.

CODE OF HONOR IN THIS BOOK . . .

FAITHFUL
PAGE 933

LOVING
PAGE 933

1 The city of Jerusalem is so empty!
   It used to be full of people.
But now it's like a woman whose
   husband has died.
     She used to be great among the
      nations.
She was like a queen among the
   kingdoms.
     But now she is a slave.

2 Jerusalem sobs bitterly at night.
   Tears run down her cheeks.
   None of her friends comforts her.
All those who were going to help her
   have turned against her.
   They have become her enemies.

3 After Judah's people had suffered
   greatly,
   they were taken away as prisoners.
Now they live among the nations.
   They can't find any place to rest.
All those who were chasing them have
   caught up with them.
   And they can't get away.

4 The roads to Zion are empty.
   No one travels to its appointed
     feasts.
All of the public places near its gates
   are deserted.
   Its priests groan.
Its young women are sad.
   And Zion itself sobs bitterly.

5 Its enemies have become its masters.
   They have an easy life.
The LORD has brought suffering to
   Jerusalem
     because its people have committed
      so many sins.
Its children have been taken away as
   prisoners.
   Their enemies have forced them to
     leave their homes.

6 The city of Zion used to be full of glory.
   But now its glory has faded away.
Its princes are like deer.
   They can't find anything to eat.
They are almost too weak to get away
   from those who hunt them down.

7 Jerusalem's people are suffering and
   wandering.
   They remember all of the treasures
     they used to have.
But they fell into the hands of their
   enemies.
   And no one was there to help them.
Their enemies looked at them.
   They laughed because Jerusalem had
     been destroyed.

8 Its people have committed many sins.
   They have become polluted.
All those who honored Jerusalem now
   look down on it.
   They look at it as if it were a naked
     woman.
The city groans and turns away in
   shame.

9 Her skirts are dirty.
   She didn't think about how things
     might turn out.
Her fall from power amazed everyone.
   And no one was there to comfort
     her.
She said, "LORD, please pay attention to
   how much I'm suffering.
   My enemies have won the battle
     over me."

10 Jerusalem's enemies took away
   all of its treasures.
Its people saw strangers
   enter its temple.
The LORD had commanded them
   not to do that.

11 All of Jerusalem's people groan
   as they search for bread.
They trade their treasures for food
   just to stay alive.
They say, "LORD, look at us.
   Think about our condition.
   Everyone looks down on us."

12 They also say, "All of you who are
     passing by,
   don't you care about what has
     happened to us?
Just look at our condition.
Has anyone suffered the way we have?
   The LORD has brought all of this
     on us.
He has made us suffer.
   His anger has burned against us.

13 "He sent fire down from heaven.
   It went deep down into our very
     bones.
He spread a net to catch us by the feet.
   He stopped us right where we were.
He made our city empty.
   We are sick all the time.

14 "We must carry the heavy load of our
     sins.
   He tied it on us with his hands.
Our sins are heavy on our necks.
   The Lord has taken away our
     strength.
He has handed us over to our enemies.
   We can't win the battle over them.

15 "The Lord has refused to accept

any of our soldiers.
He has sent for an army
    to crush our young men.
We are like grapes in the Lord's
        winepress.
    He has stomped on us,
    even though we are his very own
        people.

16 "That's why we are sobbing.
    Tears are flowing from our eyes.
No one is near to comfort us.
    No one can heal our spirits.
Our children don't have anything.
    Our enemies are much too strong
        for us."

17 Zion reaches out its hands.
    But no one is there to comfort its
        people.
The LORD has ordered that
    the neighbors of Jacob's people
        would become their enemies.
Jerusalem has become polluted
    among them.

18 Its people say, "The LORD always does
        what is right.
    But we refused to obey his
        commands.
Listen, all of you nations.
    Pay attention to how much we're
        suffering.
Our young women and young men
    have been taken away as prisoners.

19 "We called out to those who were
        going to help us.
    But they turned against us.
Our priests and elders
    died in the city.
They were searching for food
    just to stay alive.

20 "LORD, see how upset we are!
    We are suffering deep down inside.
Our hearts are troubled.
    Again and again we have refused to
        obey you.
Outside the city, people are being
        killed with swords.
    Inside, there is nothing but death.

21 "People have heard us groan.
    But no one is here to comfort us.
Our enemies have heard about all of
        our troubles.
    What you have done makes them
        happy.
So please judge them, just as you said
        you would.
    Let them become like us.

22 "Please pay attention to all of their
        sinful ways.
    Punish them as you have punished
        us.
You judged us because we had
        committed so many sins.
We groan all the time.
    And our hearts are weak."

2 See how the Lord covered the city of
        Zion
    with the cloud of his anger!
He threw Israel's glory down
    from heaven to earth.
When he was angry, he turned his
        back
    on his own city.

2 Without pity the Lord swallowed up
    all of the homes of Jacob's people.
When he was angry, he tore down
    the forts of the people of Judah.
He brought their kingdom and its
        princes
    down to the ground in dishonor.

3 When he burned with anger,
    he took away Israel's power.
He pulled back his powerful right hand
    as the enemy approached.
His burning anger blazed out in Jacob's
        land.
    It burned up everything that was
        near it.

4 Like an enemy the Lord got his bow
        ready to use.
    He had a sword in his right hand.
Like an enemy he destroyed
    everything that used to be pleasing
        to him.
His anger blazed out like fire.
    It burned up the homes in the city
        of Zion.

5 The Lord was like an enemy.
    He swallowed up Israel.
He swallowed up all of its palaces.
    He destroyed its forts.
He filled the people of Judah
    with sorrow and sadness.

6 The LORD's temple was like a garden.
    But he completely destroyed it.
He destroyed the place
    where he used to meet with his
        people.
He made Zion's people forget
    their appointed feasts and Sabbath
        days.
When he was very angry, he turned his
        back on
    king and priest alike.

7 The Lord deserted his altar.
   He left his temple.
He handed the walls of Jerusalem's
      palaces
      over to its enemies.
They shouted loudly in the house of
      the LORD.
   You would have thought it was the
      day
   of an appointed feast.

8 The LORD decided to tear down
   the walls around the city of Zion.
He measured out what he wanted to
      destroy.
   Then he destroyed it with his
      powerful hand.
He made even its towers and walls sing
      songs of sadness.
   All of them fell down.

9 Its gates sank down into the ground.
   He broke their metal bars and
      destroyed them.
Its king and princes were taken away to
      other nations.
   There is no law anymore.
Jerusalem's prophets no longer receive
   visions from the LORD.

10 The elders of the city of Zion
   sit silently on the ground.
They have sprinkled dust on their
      heads.
   They've put on black clothes to
      show how sad they are.
The young women of Jerusalem
   have bowed their heads toward the
      ground.

11 I've cried so much I can't see very well.
   I'm suffering deep down inside.
My heart is broken
   because my people are destroyed.
Children and babies are fainting
   in the streets of the city.

12 They say to their mothers,
   "Where can we find something to
      eat and drink?"
They faint like wounded soldiers
   in the streets of the city.
Their lives are slipping away
   in their mothers' arms.

13 City of Jerusalem, what can I say about
   you?
   What can I compare you to?
People of Zion, what are you like?
   I want to comfort you.
Your wound is as deep as the ocean.
   Who can heal you?

14 The visions of your prophets were lies.
   They weren't worth anything.
They didn't show you the sins you had
      committed.
   So that's why you were captured.
The messages they gave you were lies.
   They led you down the wrong path.

15 All those who pass by
   clap their hands and make fun of
      you.
They laugh at you and shake their
      heads
   at the city of Jerusalem.
They say, "Could that be the city
   that was called perfect and
      beautiful?
Is that the city that brought joy to
   everyone on earth?"

16 All of your enemies open their mouths
   wide against you.
They laugh at you and grind their
      teeth.
   They say, "We have swallowed
      Jerusalem's people up.
This is the day we've waited for.
   And we've lived to see it."

17 The LORD has done what he planned
   to do.
He has made what he said come
   true.
He gave the command long ago.
   He has destroyed you without pity.
He has let your enemies laugh at
   you.
He has made them stronger than
   you are.

18 People in the city of Zion,
   cry out from your heart to the Lord.
Let your tears flow like a river
   day and night.
Don't stop at all.
   Don't give your eyes any rest.

19 Get up. Cry out as the night begins.
   Tell the Lord all of your troubles.
Lift up your hands to him.
   Pray that the lives of your children
      will be spared.
At every street corner they faint
   because they are so hungry.

20 Jerusalem says, "LORD, look at me.
   Think about my condition.
   Have you ever treated anyone else
      like this?
Should women have to eat their
      babies?
   Should they eat the children they've
      taken care of?
Should priests and prophets be killed
   in your own temple?

21 "Young people and old people alike
   lie dead in the dust of my streets.
My young women and young men
   have been killed with swords.
You killed them when you were angry.
   You put them to death without pity.

22 "You sent for terrors to come against
      me on every side.
   It was as if you were inviting people
      to enjoy a feast day.
Because you were angry, no one
      escaped.
   No one was left alive.
I took good care of my children and
      brought them up.
   But my enemies have destroyed
      them."

3 I am a man who has suffered greatly.
   The LORD has used the Babylonians
   to punish our people.
2 He has driven me away. He has made
      me walk
   in darkness instead of light.
3 He has turned his powerful hand
      against me.
   He has done it again and again, all
      day long.

4 He has worn my body out.
   He has broken my bones.
5 He has surrounded me and attacked
      me.
   He has made me suffer bitterly.
   He has made things hard for me.
6 He has made me live in darkness
   like those who are dead and gone.

7 He has built walls around me. I can't
      escape.
   He has put heavy chains on me.
8 I call out and cry for help.
   But he won't listen to me when I
      pray.
9 He has put up a stone wall to block my
      way.
   He has made my paths crooked.

10 He has been like a bear waiting to
      attack me.
   He has been like a lion hiding in the
      bushes.
11 He has dragged me off the path.
   He has torn me to pieces.
   And he has left me helpless.
12 He has gotten his bow ready to use.
   He has shot his arrows at me.

13 The arrows from his bag
   have gone through my heart.
14 My people laugh at me all the time.

They sing and make fun of me all
      day long.
15 The LORD has made my life bitter.
   He has made me suffer bitterly.

16 He made me chew stones that broke
      my teeth.
   He has walked all over me in the
      dust.
17 I have lost all hope of ever having any
      peace.
   I've forgotten what good times are
      like.
18 So I say, "My glory has faded away.
   My hope in the LORD is gone."

19 I remember how I suffered and
      wandered.
   I remember how bitter my life was.
20 I remember it very well.
   My spirit is very sad deep down
      inside me.
21 But here is something else I remember.
   And it gives me hope.

22 The LORD loves us very much.
   So we haven't been completely
      destroyed.
   His loving concern never fails.
23 His great love is new every morning.
   LORD, how faithful you are!
24 I say to myself, "The LORD is everything
      I will ever need.
   So I will put my hope in him."

25 The LORD is good to those who put
      their hope in him.
   He is good to those who look to
      him.

POWER-SURGE

FAITHFUL ()

THE LORD LOVES US
VERY MUCH...

HIS LOVING CONCERN
NEVER FAILS.

HIS GREAT LOVE IS
NEW EVERY MORNING.

LORD, HOW FAITHFUL
YOU ARE!

LAMENTATIONS 3:22-23

LOVING

26 It is good when people wait quietly
for the Lord to save them.
27 It is good for a man to carry a heavy
load of suffering
while he is young.

28 Let him sit alone and not say anything.
The Lord has placed that load on
him.
29 Let him bury his face in the dust.
There might still be hope for him.
30 Let him turn his cheek toward those
who would slap him.
Let him be filled with shame.

31 The Lord doesn't turn his back
on people forever.
32 He might bring suffering.
But he will also show loving
concern.
How great his faithful love is!
33 He doesn't want to bring pain
or suffering to people.

34 Every time people crush prisoners
under their feet,
the Lord knows all about it.
35 When people refuse to give a man his
rights,
the Most High God knows it.
36 When people don't treat a man fairly,
the Lord knows it.

37 Suppose people order something to
happen.
It won't happen unless the Lord has
planned it.
38 Troubles and good things alike come to
people
because the Most High God has
commanded them to come.
39 A man who is still alive shouldn't
blame God
when God punishes him for his sins.

40 Let's take a good look at the way we're
living.
Let's return to the Lord.
41 Let's lift up our hands to God in
heaven.
Let's pray to him with all our hearts.
42 Let's say, "We have sinned.
We've refused to obey you.
And you haven't forgiven us.

43 "You have covered yourself with the
cloud of your anger.
You have chased us.
You have killed our people without
pity.
44 You have covered yourself with the
cloud of your anger.
Our prayers can't get through to
you.

45 You have made us become like trash
and garbage
among the nations.
46 "All of our enemies have opened their
mouths wide
to swallow us up.
47 We are terrified and trapped.
We are broken and destroyed."
48 Streams of tears flow from my eyes.
That's because my people are
destroyed.

49 Tears will never stop flowing from my
eyes.
My eyes can't get any rest.
50 I'll sob until the Lord looks down from
heaven.
I'll cry until he notices my tears.
51 What I see brings pain to my spirit.
All of the people in my city are
suffering so much.

52 Those who were my enemies for no
reason at all
hunted me down as if I were a bird.
53 They tried to end my life
by throwing me into a deep pit.
They threw stones down at me.
54 The water rose and covered my head.
I thought I was going to die.

55 Lord, I called out to you.
I called out from the bottom of the
pit.
56 I prayed, "Please don't close your ears
to my cry for help."
And you heard my appeal.
57 You came near when I called out to
you.
You said, "Do not be afraid."

58 Lord, you stood up for me in court.
You saved my life and set me free.
59 Lord, you have seen the wrong things
people have done to me.
Stand up for me again!
60 You have seen how my enemies
have tried to get even with me.
You know all about their plans
against me.

61 Lord, you have heard them laugh at
me.
You know all about their plans
against me.
62 You have heard my enemies
whispering among themselves.
They speak against me all day long.
63 Just look at them sitting and standing
there!
They sing and make fun of me.

64 Lord, pay them back.

Punish them for what their hands
have done.
⁶⁵ Cover their minds with a veil.
Put a curse on them!
⁶⁶ LORD, get angry with them and hunt
them down.
Wipe them off the face of the earth.

4 Look at how the gold has lost its
brightness!
See how dull the fine gold has
become!
The sacred jewels are scattered
at every street corner.

² The priceless children of Zion
were worth their weight in gold.
But now they are thought of as clay
pots
made by the hands of a potter.

³ Even wild dogs
nurse their young pups.
But my people are as mean
as ostriches in the desert.

⁴ When our babies get thirsty,
their tongues stick to the roofs of
their mouths.
When our children beg for bread,
no one gives them any.

⁵ Those who once ate fine food
are dying in the streets.
Those who wore fancy clothes
are now lying on piles of trash.

⁶ My people have been punished
more than Sodom was.
It was destroyed in a moment.
No one offered it a helping hand.

⁷ Jerusalem's princes were brighter than
snow.
They were whiter than milk.
Their bodies were redder than rubies.
They looked like sapphires.

⁸ But now they are blacker than coal.
No one even recognizes them in the
streets.
Their skin is wrinkled on their bones.
It has become as dry as a stick.

⁹ Those who have been killed with
swords are better off
than those who have to die of
hunger.
Those who are hungry waste away to
nothing.
They don't have any food from the
fields.

¹⁰ With their own hands, loving mothers

have had to cook even their own
children.
They ate their children
when my people were destroyed.

¹¹ The LORD has become very angry.
He has poured out his burning
anger.
He started a fire in Zion.
It burned up the very foundations.

¹² The kings of the earth couldn't believe
what was happening.
Neither could any of the world's
people.
Enemies actually attacked and entered
the gates of Jerusalem.

¹³ It happened because Jerusalem's
prophets had sinned.
Its priests had done evil things.
All of them spilled the blood
of those who did what was right.

¹⁴ Now those prophets and priests
have to feel their way along the
streets
like people who are blind.
The blood of those they killed has
made them "unclean."
So no one dares even to touch their
clothes.

¹⁵ "Go away! You are 'unclean'!"
people cry out to them.
"Go away! Get out of here!
Don't touch us!"
So they run away and wander around.
Then people among the nations say,
"They can't stay here anymore."

¹⁶ The LORD himself has scattered them.
He doesn't watch over them
anymore.
No one shows the priests any respect.
No one honors the elders.

¹⁷ And that's not all. Our eyes grew tired.
We looked for help that never came.
We watched from our towers.
We kept looking for a nation that
couldn't save us.

¹⁸ People hunted us down no matter
where we went.
We couldn't even walk in our streets.
Our end was near. We only had a few
days to live.
Our end had come.

¹⁹ Those who were hunting us down were
faster
than eagles in the sky.
They chased us over the mountains.

They hid and waited for us in the
   desert.
20 Zedekiah, the LORD's anointed king,
   was our last hope.
But he was caught in their traps.
We thought he would keep us safe.
We expected to continue living
   among the nations.

21 People of Edom, be joyful.
   You who live in the land of Uz, be
      glad.
But the cup of the LORD's anger will
   also be passed to you.
Then you will become drunk.
Your clothes will be stripped off.

22 People of Zion, the time for you to be
   punished
will come to an end.
The LORD won't keep you away from
   your land any longer.
But he will punish your sin, people of
   Edom.
He will show you the evil things you
   have done.

5 LORD, think about what has
   happened to us.
Look at the shame our enemies have
   brought on us.
2 The land you gave us has been turned
   over to outsiders.
Our homes have been given to
   strangers.
3 Our fathers have been killed.
Our mothers don't have husbands.
4 We have to buy the water we drink.
We have to pay for the wood we use.
5 Those who chase us are right behind
   us.
We're tired. We can't get any rest.
6 We put ourselves under the control of
   Egypt and Assyria
just to get enough bread.
7 Our people before us sinned.
And they are now dead.
We are being punished because of
   their sins.

8 Slaves rule over us.
No one can set us free
   from their powerful hands.
9 We put our lives in danger just to get
   some bread to eat.
Robbers in the desert might kill us
   with their swords.
10 Our skin is as hot as an oven.
We are so hungry we're burning up
   with fever.
11 Our women have been raped in Zion.
Our virgins have been raped in the
   towns of Judah.
12 Our princes have been hung up by
   their hands.
No one shows our elders any
   respect.
13 Our young men are forced to grind
   grain at the mill.
Our boys almost fall down
as they carry heavy loads of wood.
14 Our elders don't go to the city gate
   anymore.
Our young men have stopped
   playing their music.
15 There isn't any joy in our hearts.
Our dancing has turned into
   sobbing.
16 All of our honor is gone.
How terrible it is for us! We have
   sinned.
17 So our hearts are weak.
Our eyes can't see very clearly.
18 Mount Zion has been deserted.
Wild dogs are prowling all around
   on it.

19 LORD, you rule forever.
Your throne will last for all time to
   come.
20 Why do you always forget us?
Why have you deserted us for so
   long?
21 LORD, please bring us back to you.
Then we can return.
Make our lives like new again.
22 Or have you completely turned away
   from us?
Are you really that angry with us?

EZEKIEL

The prophet Ezekiel is living far from home with the other people of Judah when God sends him these messages. Many of the messages come in strange and hard to understand visions. The point God is trying to make is that the people are being punished for rejecting God. But he still is eager to forgive them and to let them return home. As you read the book of Ezekiel, let it teach you that God speaks in many ways and that his main message is one of love and forgiveness.

HERO IN THIS BOOK . . .

EZEKIEL

PAGE 976

The LORD Gives Ezekiel Visions of His Glory

1 I was 30 years old. I was with my people who had been taken away from their country. We were by the Kebar River in the land of Babylonia. On the fifth day of the fourth month, the heavens were opened. I saw visions of God.

2 It was the fifth day of the month. Jehoiachin had been king of Judah. It was the fifth year since he had been brought to Babylon as a prisoner. 3 A message came to me from the LORD. I was by the Kebar River in Babylonia. The LORD put his strong hand on me there. I am Ezekiel, the son of Buzi. I'm a priest.

POWER-SURGE

STRONG

THE LORD PUT HIS STRONG HAND ON ME THERE. I AM EZEKIEL, THE SON OF BUZI. I'M A PRIEST.
— EZEKIEL 1:3 —

4 I looked up and saw a windstorm coming from the north. I saw a huge cloud. The fire of lightning was flashing out of it. Bright light surrounded it. The center of the fire looked like glowing metal.

5 I saw in the fire something that looked like four living creatures. They appeared to have the shape of a man. 6 But each of them had four faces and four wings. 7 Their legs were straight. Their feet looked like the feet of a calf. They were as bright as polished bronze.

8 The creatures had a man's hands under their wings on their four sides. All four of them had faces and wings. 9 Their wings touched one another. Each of the creatures went straight ahead. They didn't change their direction as they moved.

10 Here's what their faces looked like. Each of the four creatures had a man's face. On the right side each had the face of a lion. On the left each had the face of an ox. Each one also had an eagle's face. 11 That's what their faces looked like.

Two of their wings were spread out and lifted up. Each one touched the wing of another creature on either side. The other two wings covered their bodies. 12 All of the creatures went straight ahead. Any-

where their spirits would lead them to go, they would go. They didn't change their direction as they went.

13 The living creatures looked like burning coals of fire or like torches. Fire moved back and forth among the creatures. It was bright. Lightning flashed out of it. 14 The creatures raced back and forth like flashes of lightning.

15 As I looked at the living creatures, I saw wheels on the ground beside them. Each creature had four faces. 16 Here's how the wheels looked and worked. They gleamed like chrysolite. All four of them looked alike. Each one seemed to be made like a wheel inside another wheel at right angles.

17 The wheels could go in any one of the four directions the creatures faced. The wheels didn't change their direction as the creatures moved. 18 Their rims were high and terrifying. All four rims were full of eyes all the way around them.

19 When the creatures moved, the wheels beside them moved. When the living creatures rose from the ground, the wheels also rose. 20 Anywhere their spirits would lead them to go, they would go. And the wheels would rise along with them. That's because the spirits of the living creatures were in the wheels.

21 When the creatures moved, the wheels also moved. When the creatures stood still, they also stood still. When the creatures rose from the ground, the wheels rose along with them. That's because the spirits of the living creatures were in the wheels.

22 Something that looked like a huge space was spread out above the heads of the living creatures. It gleamed like ice. It was terrifying. 23 The wings of the creatures were spread out under the space. They reached out toward one another. Each creature had two wings covering its body.

24 When the creatures moved, I heard the sound of their wings. It was like the roar of rushing waters. It sounded like the thundering voice of the Mighty One. It was like the loud noise an army makes. When the creatures stood still, they lowered their wings.

25 Then a voice came from above the huge space over their heads. They stood with their wings lowered. 26 Above the space over their heads was something that looked like a throne made out of sapphire.

On the throne high above was a figure that appeared to be human. 27 From his waist up he looked like glowing metal that was full of fire. From his waist down he looked like fire. Bright light surrounded him. **28**The glow around him looked like a rainbow in the clouds on a rainy day.

That's what the glory of the LORD looked like. When I saw it, I fell with my face toward the ground. Then I heard the voice of someone speaking.

The LORD Chooses Ezekiel

2 He said to me, "Son of man, stand up on your feet. I will speak to you." **2**As he spoke, the Spirit of the LORD came into me. He raised me to my feet. I heard him speaking to me.

3He said, "Son of man, I am sending you to the people of Israel. That nation has refused to obey me. They have turned against me. They and their people before them have been against me to this very day. **4**The people I am sending you to are very stubborn. Tell them, 'Here is what the LORD and King says.'

5"They might listen, or they might not. After all, they refuse to obey me. But whether they listen or not, they will know that a prophet was among them.

6"Son of man, do not be afraid of them or of what they say. Do not be afraid, even if thorns and bushes are all around you and you live among scorpions. Do not be afraid of what they say. Do not be terrified by them. They always refuse to obey me.

7"You must give them my message. They might listen, or they might not. After all, they refuse to obey me. **8**Son of man, listen to what I tell you. Do not be like those who refuse to obey me. Open your mouth. Eat what I give you."

9Then I looked up. I saw a hand reach out to me. A scroll was in it. **10**He unrolled it in front of me. Both sides had words written on them. They spoke about sadness, sorrow and trouble.

3 He said to me, "Son of man, eat what is in front of you. Eat this scroll. Then go and speak to the people of Israel." **2**So I opened my mouth. And he gave me the scroll to eat.

3Then he said to me, "Son of man, eat this scroll I am giving you. Fill your stomach with it." So I ate it. And it tasted as sweet as honey in my mouth.

4Then he said to me, "Son of man, go to the people of Israel. Give them my message.

5"I am not sending you to people who speak another language that is hard to learn. Instead, I am sending you to the people of Israel. **6**You are not being sent to

POWER-SURGE

BRAVE

I WILL MAKE YOU VERY BRAVE. SO DO NOT BE AFRAID OF THEM. DO NOT LET THEM TERRIFY YOU, EVEN THOUGH THEY REFUSE TO OBEY ME.

— EZEKIEL 3:9 —

many nations whose people speak other languages that are hard to learn. You would not be able to understand them. Suppose I had sent you to them. Then they certainly would have listened to you. **7**But the people of Israel do not want to listen to you. That is because they do not want to listen to me.

"All of the people of Israel are very stubborn. **8**But I will make you just as stubborn as they are. **9**I will make you very brave. So do not be afraid of them. Do not let them terrify you, even though they refuse to obey me."

10He continued, "Son of man, listen carefully. Take to heart everything I tell you. **11**Go now to your own people who were brought here as prisoners. Speak to them. Tell them, 'Here is what the LORD and King says.' Speak to them whether they listen or not.'

12Then the Spirit of the LORD lifted me up. I heard a loud rumbling sound behind me. May the glory of the LORD be praised in the place where he lives! **13**The sound was made by the wings of the living creatures. They were brushing against one another. The sound was also made by the wheels beside them. It was a loud rumbling sound.

14Then the Spirit lifted me up and took me away. My spirit was bitter. I was burning with anger. The strong hand of the LORD was on me. **15**I came to my people who had been brought as prisoners to Tel Abib. It was near the Kebar River. I went to where they were living. There I sat among them for seven days. I was shocked by everything that had happened.

The LORD Warns Israel

16After seven days, a message came to me from the LORD. **17**He said, "Son of man, I have appointed you as a prophet to warn the people of Israel. So listen to my message. Give them a warning from me.

18 "Suppose I say to a sinful person, 'You can be sure you will die.' And you do not warn him. You do not try to get him to change his evil ways in order to save his life. Then he will die because he has sinned. And I will hold you accountable for his death.

19 "But suppose you do warn that sinful person. And he does not turn away from his sin or his evil ways. Then he will die because he has sinned. But you will have saved yourself.

20 "Or suppose a godly person turns away from his godliness and does what is evil. And suppose I put something in his way that will trip him up. Then he will die. Since you did not warn him, he will die for his sin. The godly things he did will not be remembered. And I will hold you accountable for his death.

21 "But suppose you do warn a godly person not to sin. And he does not sin. Then you can be sure that he will live because he listened to your warning. And you will have saved yourself."

22 The strong hand of the LORD was on me. He said, "Get up. Go out to the flatlands. I will speak to you there."

23 So I got up and went out to the flatlands. The glory of the LORD was standing there. It was just like the glory I had seen by the Kebar River. So I fell with my face toward the ground.

24 Then the Spirit of the LORD came into me. He raised me to my feet. He said to me, "Go, son of man. Shut yourself inside your house. 25 Some people will tie you up with ropes. So you will not be able to go out among your people. 26 I will make your tongue stick to the roof of your mouth. Then you will be silent. You will not be able to correct them. They always refuse to obey me.

27 "But later I will speak to you. I will open your mouth. Then you will tell them, 'Here is what the LORD and King says.' Those who listen will listen. And those who refuse to listen will refuse. They always refuse to obey me.

An Attack on Jerusalem Is Pictured

4 "Son of man, get a clay tablet. Put it in front of you. Draw the city of Jerusalem on it. 2 Then pretend to surround it and attack it. Make some little models of war machines. Build a ramp up to it. Set camps up around it. Surround it with models of logs to be used for knocking down its gates. 3 Then get an iron pan. Put it between you and the city. Pretend it is an iron wall. Turn your face toward the city. It will be under attack when you begin to attack it. That will show the people of Israel what is going to happen to Jerusalem.

4 "Next, lie down on your left side. Pretend that you are putting Israel's sin on yourself. Keep their sin on you for the number of days you lie on your side. 5 Let each day you lie there stand for one year of their sin. So you will keep Israel's sin on you for 390 days.

6 "After you have finished that, lie down again. This time lie on your right side. Pretend that you are putting Judah's sin on yourself. Lie there for 40 days. That is one day for each year of their sin.

7 "Next, turn your face toward the model of Jerusalem under attack. Uncover your arm as if you were a soldier ready to fight. Prophesy against the city.

8 "I will tie you up with ropes. Then you will not be able to turn from one side to the other. You will stay that way until you have finished attacking Jerusalem.

9 "Get some wheat and barley. Also get some beans and lentils. And get some millet and spelt. Put everything in a storage jar. Use it to make some bread for yourself. Eat it during the 390 days you are lying down on your side. 10 Weigh out eight ounces of food to eat each day. Eat it at your regular mealtimes. 11 Also measure out two thirds of a quart of water. Drink it at your regular mealtimes.

12 "Eat your food as you would eat a barley cake. Bake it over human waste in front of the people." 13 The LORD said, "That is how the people of Israel will eat 'unclean' food. They will eat it in the nations where I will drive them."

14 Then I said, "No, LORD and King! I won't do it! I've never eaten anything that was 'unclean.' From the time I was young until now, I've never eaten anything that was found dead. And I've never eaten anything that was torn apart by wild animals. 'Unclean' meat has never entered my mouth."

15 "All right," he said. "I will let you bake your bread over waste from cows. You can use that instead of human waste."

16 He continued, "Son of man, I will cut off the food supply in Jerusalem. The people will be worried as they eat their tiny share of food. They will not have any hope as they drink their tiny share of water. 17 There will be very little food and water. The people will be shocked as they

look at one another. They will become weaker and weaker because of their sin.

5 "Son of man, get a sharp sword. Use it as a barber's razor. Shave your head and beard with it. Then get a set of scales and weigh the hair. Separate it into three piles.

2 "Burn up a third of the hair inside the city. Do it when you stop attacking the model of Jerusalem. Next, get another third of the hair. Strike it with a sword all around the city. Then scatter the last third to the winds. That is because I will chase the people with a sword that is ready to strike them down. 3 But save a few of the hairs. Tuck them away in the clothes you are wearing.

4 "Next, get a few more hairs. Throw them into the fire. Burn them up. The fire will spread to all of the people of Israel."

5 The LORD and King says, "This little model stands for Jerusalem. I have placed that city in the center of the nations. Countries are all around it. 6 But its people are sinful. They have refused to obey my laws and rules. They have turned their backs on my laws. They have not followed my rules. Those people are worse than the nations and countries around them."

7 The LORD and King continues, "You people have been worse than the nations around you. You have not lived by my rules or kept my laws. You have not even lived up to the standards of the nations around you."

8 The LORD and King continues, "Jerusalem, I myself am against you. I will punish you in the sight of the nations. 9 I will do to you what I have never done before and will never do again. That is because you worship statues of gods. I hate them. 10 So parents will eat their own children inside the city. And children will eat their parents. I will punish you. And I will scatter to the winds anyone who is left alive.

11 "You have made my temple 'unclean.' You have set up statues of all of your evil gods. You have done other things I hate. So I will not show you my favor anymore. I will not spare you or feel sorry for you. And that is just as sure as I am alive," announces the LORD and King.

12 "A third of your people will die of the plague inside your walls. Or they will die of hunger there. Another third will be killed with swords outside your walls. And I will scatter the last third of your people to the winds. I will chase them with a sword that is ready to strike them down.

13 "Then I will not be angry anymore. My burning anger against them will die down. And I will be satisfied. Then they will know that I have spoken with strong feelings. And my burning anger toward them will come to an end. I am the LORD.

14 "I will destroy you. I will bring shame on you in the sight of the nations that are around you. All those who pass by will see it. 15 You will be put to shame. The nations will make fun of you. You will serve as a warning to others. They will be shocked when they see you. So I will punish you because my anger burns against you. You will feel the sting of my warning. I have spoken. I am the LORD.

16 "I will shoot at you with my deadly, destroying arrows of hunger. I will shoot to kill. I will bring more and more hunger on you. I will cut off your food supply. 17 I will send hunger and wild animals against you. They will destroy all of your children. Plague and murder will sweep over you. And I will send swords to kill you. I have spoken. I am the LORD."

Ezekiel Prophesies Against the Mountains of Israel

6 A message came to me from the LORD. He said, 2 "Son of man, turn your attention to the mountains of Israel. Prophesy against them. 3 Say, 'Mountains of Israel, listen to the message of the LORD and King. Here is what he says to the mountains and hills. And here is what he says to the canyons and valleys. He tells them, "I will send swords to kill your people. I will destroy the high places where you worship other gods.

4 " ' "Your altars will be torn down. Your incense altars will be smashed. And I will kill your people in front of the statues of your gods. 5 I will put the dead bodies of Israelites in front of those statues. I will scatter your bones around your altars.

6 " ' "No matter where you live, the towns will be destroyed. The high places will be torn down. So your altars will be completely destroyed. The statues of your gods will be smashed to pieces. Your incense altars will be broken down. And everything you have made will be wiped out. 7 Your people will fall down dead among you. Then you will know that I am the LORD.

8 " ' "But I will spare some of you. Some will escape from being killed with swords. You will be scattered among other lands and nations. 9 You will be taken away to those nations as prisoners. Those of you who escape will remember me. You will recall how much pain your unfaithful hearts gave me. You turned away from

me. Your eyes longed to see the statues of your gods. You will hate yourselves because of all of the evil things you have done. I hate those things too. ¹⁰You will know that I am the LORD. I said I would bring trouble on you. And my warning came true." ' "

¹¹The LORD and King said to me, "Clap your hands. Stamp your feet. Cry out, 'How sad!' Do it because the people of Israel have done so many evil things. I hate those things. Israel will be destroyed by war, hunger and plague. ¹²Those who are far away will die of the plague. Those who are near will be killed with swords. Those who are left alive and are spared will die of hunger. And my burning anger toward them will come to an end.

¹³"Then they will know that I am the LORD. Their people will lie dead among the statues of their gods around their altars. Their bodies will lie on every high hill and every mountaintop. They will lie under every green tree and leafy oak tree. They used to offer sweet-smelling incense to all of their gods at those places. ¹⁴I will reach out my powerful hand against them. The land will become dry and empty. Those people will live from the desert all the way to Diblah. They will know that I am the LORD."

The End Has Come

7 A message came to me from the LORD. He said, ²"Son of man, I am the LORD and King. I say to the land of Israel, 'The end has come! It has come on the four corners of the land. ³The end has now come for you. I will pour out my anger on you. I will judge you based on how you have lived. I will pay you back for all of your evil practices. I hate them.

⁴" 'I will not spare you or feel sorry for you. You can be sure that I will pay you back in keeping with how you have lived. I will judge you for your evil practices. I hate them. You will know that I am the LORD.'

⁵"I am the LORD and King. I say, 'Horrible trouble is coming! No one has ever heard of anything like it.

⁶" 'The end has come! The end has come! It has stirred itself up against you. It is here! ⁷Death has come on you who live in the land. The time for you to be destroyed has come. The day when it will happen is near. There is no joy on your mountains. There is nothing but panic.

⁸" 'I am about to pour out all of my burning anger on you. I will judge you based on how you have lived. I will pay

you back for all of your evil practices. I hate them.

⁹" 'I will not spare you or feel sorry for you. I will pay you back based on how you have lived. I will judge you for your evil practices. I hate them. You will know that I am the one who strikes you down. I am the LORD.

¹⁰" 'The day for me to punish you is here! It has come! Death has arrived. The time is ripe for you to be judged. Your pride has grown so much that you will be destroyed. ¹¹Your mean and harmful acts have become like a rod. I will use it to punish you for your sins. None of you will be left. No wealth or anything of value will remain.

¹²" 'The time has come! The day has arrived! I will soon pour out my burning anger on the whole crowd of you. Do not let the buyer be happy. Do not let the seller be sad. ¹³The seller will not get back the land that was sold as long as both of them are alive.

" 'Ezekiel, the vision I gave you about that whole crowd will come true. They have committed many sins. So none of them will remain alive. ¹⁴They might blow trumpets. They might get everything ready. But no one will go into battle. I will soon pour out my burning anger on the whole crowd.

¹⁵" 'There is trouble everywhere. War is outside the city. Plague and hunger are inside it. Those who are out in the country will die in battle. Those in the city will be destroyed by hunger and plague. ¹⁶All those who escape and are left alive will run to the mountains. They have committed many sins. So they will cry like sad doves in the valleys.

¹⁷" 'Their hands will be powerless to help them. Their knees will become as weak as water. ¹⁸They will put on black clothes. They will put on terror as if it were their clothes. Their faces will be covered with shame. Their heads will be shaved.

¹⁹" 'They will throw their silver into the streets. Their gold will be like an "unclean" thing. Their silver and gold will not be able to save them on the day I pour out my anger on them. They will not be able to satisfy their hunger. Their stomachs will not be full. Their silver and gold have tripped them up. They have made them fall into sin. ²⁰My people were so proud of their beautiful jewelry. They used it to make statues of their evil gods. I hate those gods. So I will turn their statues into an "unclean" thing for them.

²¹" 'I will hand everything over to

strangers. I will turn it over to sinful people in other countries. They will pollute it. 22I will turn my face away from my people. Their enemies will pollute my beautiful temple. Robbers will enter it and pollute it.

23" 'Ezekiel, get ready to put my people in chains. The land is full of murderers. They are harming one another all over Jerusalem. 24I will bring the most evil nations against them. They will take over the houses in the city. I will put an end to the pride of those who are mighty. Their holy places will be polluted.

25" 'When terror comes, they will look for peace. But there will not be any. 26Trouble after trouble will come. One report will follow another. But they will not be true. The people will try to get visions from the prophets. But there will not be any. The teaching of the law by the priests will be gone. So will advice from the elders.

27" 'The king will be filled with sadness. The princes will lose all hope. The hands of the people of the land will tremble. I will punish them based on how they have lived. I will judge them by their own standards. Then they will know that I am the LORD.' "

The People Worship Other Gods in the Temple

8 It was the sixth year since King Jehoiachin had been brought to Babylon as a prisoner. On the fifth day of the sixth month, I was sitting in my house. The elders of Judah were sitting there with me. The LORD and King put his powerful hand on me there.

2I looked up and saw a figure that appeared to be human. From his waist down he looked like fire. From his waist up he looked as bright as glowing metal. 3He reached out what appeared to be a hand. He took hold of me by the hair of my head. The Spirit of the LORD lifted me up between earth and heaven. In visions God gave me, the Spirit took me to Jerusalem. He brought me to the entrance of the north gate of the inner courtyard. The statue of a god was standing there. It made God very angry. 4There in front of me was the glory of the God of Israel. It looked just as it did in the vision I had seen on the flatlands.

5Then the LORD said to me, "Son of man, look toward the north." So I did. I saw a statue that made God angry. It was in the entrance of the gate north of the altar.

6He said to me, "Son of man, do you see what the people of Israel are doing here? They are doing things I hate very much. Those things will cause me to go far away from my temple. But you will see things I hate even more."

7Then he brought me to the entrance to the courtyard. I looked up and saw a hole in the wall. 8He said to me, "Son of man, dig into the wall." So I did. And I saw a door there.

9He continued, "Go through it. Look at the evil things they are doing here. I hate those things."

10So I went in and looked. All over the walls were pictures of all kinds of crawling things and other animals. The LORD hates it when people worship those things. There were also carvings of all of the gods of the people of Israel.

11In front of them stood 70 elders of Israel. Jaazaniah was standing there among them. He is the son of Shaphan. Each elder was holding a shallow cup. A sweet-smelling cloud of incense was rising from the cups.

12The LORD said to me, "Son of man, do you see what the elders of Israel are doing in the dark? Each of them is in his own room worshiping his own god. They say, 'The LORD doesn't see us. He has deserted the land.' " 13He continued, "You will see them doing things I hate even more."

14Then he brought me to the entrance of the north gate of the LORD's house. I saw women sitting there. They were sobbing over the god Tammuz. 15The LORD said to me, "Son of man, do you see what they are doing? You will see things I hate even more."

16Then he brought me into the inner courtyard of the LORD's house. About 25 men were there. They were at the entrance to the LORD's temple between the porch and the altar. Their backs were turned toward the temple. Their faces were turned toward the east. And they were bowing down to the sun.

17He said to me, "Son of man, have you seen all of that? The people of Judah are doing things here that I hate. This is a very serious matter. They are harming one another all through the land. They continue to make me very angry. Just look at them making fun of me! 18So I am angry with them. I will punish them. I will not spare them or feel sorry for them. They might even shout in my ears. But I will not listen to them."

The LORD Judges Those Who Worship Other Gods

9 Then I heard the LORD call out in a loud voice. He said, "Bring those who guard the city here. Make sure each of them has a weapon." ²I saw six men coming from the direction of the upper gate. It faces north. Each of them had a deadly weapon. A man who was wearing linen clothes came along with them. He was carrying a writing kit at his side. They came in and stood beside the bronze altar.

³The glory of the God of Israel had been above the cherubim. It moved from there to the doorway of the temple.

Then the LORD called to the man who was dressed in linen clothes. He had the writing kit. ⁴The LORD said to him, "Go all through Jerusalem. Look for those who are sad and sorry about all of the things that are being done there. I hate those things. Put a mark on the foreheads of those people."

⁵I heard him speak to the six men. He said, "Follow him through the city. Do not show any pity or concern. ⁶Kill old men and women, young men and women, and children. But do not touch anyone who has the mark. Start at my temple." So they began with the elders who were in front of the temple.

⁷Then he said to the men, "Make the temple 'unclean.' Fill the courtyards with dead bodies. Go!" So they went out and started killing people all through the city.

⁸While they were doing it, I was left alone. I fell with my face toward the ground. I cried out, "LORD and King, are you going to destroy all of the Israelites who are still left alive? Will you pour out your burning anger on all those who remain in Jerusalem?"

⁹He answered me, "The sin of Israel and Judah is very great. The land is full of murderers. They are not being fair to one another anywhere in Jerusalem. They say, 'The LORD has deserted the land. He doesn't see us.' ¹⁰So I will not spare them or feel sorry for them. Anything that happens to them will be their own fault."

¹¹Then the man who was wearing linen clothes returned. He had the writing kit. He reported, "I've done what you commanded."

The Glory of the LORD Moves Out of the Temple

10 I looked up and saw something that appeared to be a throne made out of sapphire. It was above the huge space that was spread out over the heads of the cherubim. ²The LORD spoke to the man who was wearing linen clothes. He said, "Go in among the wheels beneath the cherubim. Fill your hands with burning coals from the fire that is among the cherubim. Scatter the coals over the city." As I watched, he went in.

³The cherubim were standing on the south side of the temple when the man went in. A cloud filled the inner courtyard. ⁴Then the glory of the LORD rose from above the cherubim. It moved to the doorway of the temple. The cloud filled the temple. And the courtyard was full of the brightness of the glory of the LORD. ⁵The sound the wings of the cherubim made could be heard as far away as the outer courtyard. It was like the voice of the Mighty God when he speaks.

⁶The LORD gave a command to the man who was dressed in linen clothes. He said, "Get some coals of fire from among the wheels. Take them from among the cherubim." So the man went in and stood beside a wheel. ⁷Then one of the cherubim reached out his hand. He picked up some of the burning coals that were among the wheels. He handed them to the man who was wearing linen clothes. The man took them and left. ⁸I saw what looked like a man's hands. They were under the wings of the cherubim.

⁹I looked up and saw four wheels beside the cherubim. One wheel was beside each of them. The wheels gleamed like chrysolite. ¹⁰All four of them looked alike. Each wheel appeared to be inside another wheel at right angles. ¹¹The wheels could go in any one of the four directions the cherubim faced. The wheels didn't change their direction as the cherubim moved. The cherubim went in the direction their heads faced. They didn't change their direction as they moved.

¹²Their whole bodies were completely covered with eyes. That included their backs, hands and wings. Their four wheels were covered with eyes too. ¹³I heard someone tell the wheels to start spinning around. ¹⁴Each of the cherubim had four faces. One face was the face of a cherub. The second was a man's face. The third was the face of a lion. And the fourth was an eagle's face.

¹⁵The cherubim rose from the ground. They were the same living creatures I had seen by the Kebar River. ¹⁶When the cherubim moved, the wheels beside them moved. The cherubim spread their wings to rise from the ground. As they did, the wheels didn't leave their side. ¹⁷When the

cherubim stood still, the wheels also stood still. When the cherubim rose, the wheels rose along with them. That's because the spirits of the living creatures were in the wheels.

18 Then the glory of the LORD moved away from the doorway of the temple. It stopped above the cherubim. **19** While I watched, they spread their wings. They rose from the ground. As they went, the wheels went along with them. They stopped at the entrance of the east gate of the LORD's house. And the glory of the God of Israel was above them.

20 Those were the same living creatures I had seen by the Kebar River. I had seen them beneath the God of Israel. I realized that they were cherubim. **21** Each one had four faces and four wings. Under their wings was what looked like a man's hands. **22** Their faces looked the same as the ones I had seen by the Kebar River. Each of the cherubim went straight ahead.

The LORD Punishes Israel's Leaders

11 Then the Spirit of the LORD lifted me up. He brought me to the east gate of the LORD's house. There were 25 men at the entrance of the gate. I saw Jaazaniah and Pelatiah among them. They were leaders of the people. Jaazaniah is the son of Azzur. Pelatiah is the son of Benaiah.

2 The LORD said to me, "Son of man, these men are making evil plans. They are giving bad advice to the city. **3** They say, 'This is not the time to build houses. The city is like a cooking pot. And we are the meat.' **4** So prophesy against them. Prophesy, son of man."

5 Then the Spirit of the LORD came on me. He told me to tell them, "The LORD says, 'People of Israel, that is what you are saying. But I know what you are thinking. **6** You have killed many people in this city. In fact, you have filled its streets with dead bodies.'

7 "So the LORD and King says, 'The bodies you have thrown there are the meat. And the city is the cooking pot. But I will drive you out of it. **8** You are afraid of the swords of war. But I will bring them against you,' announces the LORD and King.

9 " 'I will drive you out of the city. I will hand you over to strangers. And I will punish you. **10** You will be killed with swords. I will judge you at the borders of Israel. Then you will know that I am the LORD.

11 " 'This city will not be a pot for you. And you will not be the meat in it. I will judge you at the borders of Israel. **12** Then you will know that I am the LORD. You have not followed my rules. You have not kept my laws. Instead, you have lived by the standards of the nations that are around you.' "

13 Pelatiah, the son of Benaiah, died as I was prophesying. Then I fell with my face toward the ground. I cried out in a loud voice. I said, "LORD and King, will you destroy all of the Israelites who are still left alive?"

14 A message came to me from the LORD. He said, **15** "Son of man, the people of Jerusalem have spoken about your relatives. They have also spoken about all of the other people of Israel. They have said, 'Stay far away from the LORD. This land was given to us. And it belongs to us.'

The LORD Will Bring His People Back Home

16 "So tell them, 'The LORD and King says, "I sent some of my people far away among the nations. I scattered them among the countries. But for a little while I have been their temple in the countries where they have gone." '

17 "Tell them, 'The LORD and King says, "I will gather you from the nations. I will bring you back from the countries where you have been scattered. I will give you back the land of Israel." '

18 "They will return to it. They will remove all of its statues of evil gods. I hate those gods. **19** I will give my people hearts that are completely committed to me. I will give them a new spirit that is faithful to me. I will remove their stubborn hearts from them. And I will give them hearts that obey me. **20** Then they will follow my rules. They will be careful to keep my laws. They will be my people. And I will be their God.

21 "But some people have hearts that are committed to worshiping the statues of their evil gods. I hate those gods. Anything that happens to those people will be their own fault," announces the LORD and King.

22 Then the cherubim spread their wings. The wheels were beside them. The glory of the God of Israel was above them. **23** The glory of the LORD went up from the city. It stopped above the Mount of Olives east of it.

24 The Spirit of God lifted me up. He took me to those who had been brought to Babylonia as prisoners. Those are the

POWER-SURGE

BELIEVES ✝

I WILL GIVE MY
PEOPLE HEARTS THAT
ARE COMPLETELY
COMMITTED TO ME. I
WILL GIVE THEM A
NEW SPIRIT THAT IS
FAITHFUL TO ME. I
WILL REMOVE THEIR
STUBBORN HEARTS
FROM THEM. AND I
WILL GIVE THEM
HEARTS THAT OBEY
ME. THEN THEY WILL
FOLLOW MY RULES.
THEY WILL BE
CAREFUL TO KEEP MY
LAWS. THEY WILL BE
MY PEOPLE. AND I
WILL BE THEIR GOD.

— EZEKIEL 11:19-20 — ✔

OBEYS

things that happened in the visions the Spirit gave me.

Then the visions I had seen were gone. **25**I told my people everything the LORD had shown me.

Many People Will Be Taken to Babylonia

12 A message came to me from the LORD. He said, **2**"Son of man, you are living among people who refuse to obey me. They have eyes that can see. But they do not really see. They have ears that can hear. But they do not really hear. They refuse to obey me.

3"Son of man, pack your belongings as if you were going on a long trip. Leave in the daytime. Let the people see you. Start out from where you are. Go to another place. Perhaps they will understand the meaning of what you are doing. But they will still refuse to obey me. **4**Bring out your belongings packed for a long trip. Do

it during the daytime. Let the people see you. Then in the evening, pretend you are being forced to leave home. Let the people see you.

5"While the people are watching, dig through the mud bricks of your house. Then take your belongings out through the hole in the wall. **6**Put them on your shoulder. Carry them out at sunset. Let the people see you. Cover your face so you can't see the land. All of that will show the people of Israel what is going to happen to them."

7So I did just as he commanded me. During the day I brought out my things as if I were going on a long trip. In the evening I dug through the wall of my house with my hands. At sunset I took my belongings out. I put them on my shoulders. The people watched what I was doing.

8In the morning a message came to me from the LORD. He said, **9**"Son of man, didn't the people of Israel ask you, 'What are you doing?' They always refuse to obey me.

10"Tell them, 'The LORD and King says, "This message is about Zedekiah, the prince in Jerusalem. It is also about all of the people of Israel who still live there."' **11**Tell them, 'The things I've done are a picture of what's going to happen to you. So what I've done will happen to you. You will be forced to leave home. You will be taken to Babylonia as prisoners.'

12"The prince among them will put his things on his shoulder and leave. He will do it at sunset. Someone will dig a hole in a wall for him to go through. He will cover his face so he can't see the land. **13**I will spread out my net to catch him. He will be caught in my trap. I will bring him to Babylonia. It is the land where the Chaldeans live. But he will not see it. He will die there. **14**I will scatter to the winds all those who are around him. I will scatter his officials and all of his troops. And I will chase them with a sword that is ready to strike them down.

15"They will know that I am the LORD when I scatter them among the nations. I will send them to other countries. **16**But I will spare a few of them. I will save them from war, hunger and plague. In those countries they will admit they have done all kinds of evil things. I hate those things. They will know that I am the LORD."

17A message came to me from the LORD. He said, **18**"Son of man, tremble with fear as you eat your food. Tremble as you drink your water. **19**Speak to the people of the land. Say to them, 'Here is what the LORD and King says about those who live in Jerusalem and Israel. He tells them, "They will be worried as they eat their food. They will not have any hope as they drink their water. Their land will be stripped of everything in it because all those who live there are harming one another. 20The towns where people live will be completely destroyed. The land will become a dry and empty desert. Then you will know that I am the LORD." ' "

21A message came to me from the LORD. He said, 22"Son of man, you have a proverb in the land of Israel. It says, 'The days go by, and not even one vision comes true.' 23Tell them, 'The LORD and King says, "I am going to put an end to that proverb. They will not use that saying in Israel anymore." ' Tell them, 'The days are coming soon when every vision will come true. 24There will be no more false visions. People will no longer use magic to find out whether good things are going to happen in Israel. 25I am the LORD. So I will say what I want to. And it will come true when I want it to. In your days I will do everything I say I will. But you people always refuse to obey me,' announces the LORD and King."

26A message came to me from the LORD. He said, 27"Son of man, the people of Israel are saying, 'The vision Ezekiel sees won't come true for many years. He is prophesying about a time that is a long way off.'

28"So tell them, 'The LORD and King says, "Everything I say will come true. It will happen when I want it to," announces the LORD and King.' "

The LORD Punishes Those Who Pretend to Be True Prophets

13 A message came to me from the LORD. He said, 2"Son of man, prophesy against those who are now prophesying in Israel. What they prophesy comes out of their own minds. Tell them, 'Listen to the LORD's message! 3The LORD and King says, "How terrible it will be for you foolish prophets! You say what your own minds tell you to. Your visions did not come from me.

4" ' "Israel, your prophets are like wild dogs that live among broken-down buildings. 5You have not repaired the cracks in the city wall for the people of Israel. So it will not stand firm in the battle on the day I judge you. 6The visions of those prophets are false. They use magic to try to find out what is going to happen. But their

magic tricks are lies. They say, 'The LORD announces.' But I have not sent them. In spite of that, they expect their words to come true.

7" ' "You prophets have seen false visions. You have used magic to try to find out what is going to happen. But your magic tricks are lies. So you lied when you said, 'The LORD announces.' I did not even speak to you at all."

8" 'The LORD and King says, "I am against you prophets. Your messages are false. Your visions do not come true," announces the LORD and King.

9" ' "Israel, my powerful hand will be against the prophets who see false visions. Their magic tricks are lies. They will not be among the leaders of my people. They will not be listed in the records of Israel. In fact, they will not even enter the land. Then you will know that I am the LORD and King.

10" ' "They lead my people away from me. They say, 'Peace.' But there isn't any peace. They are like people who build a weak wall. They try to cover up the weakness by painting the wall white. 11Tell those who do it that their wall is going to fall. Heavy rains will come. I will send hailstones crashing down. Powerful winds will blow. 12The wall will fall down. Then people will ask them, 'Now where is the paint you covered it with?' "

13" 'So the LORD and King speaks. He says, "When I am burning with anger, I will send a powerful wind. Hailstones and heavy rains will come. They will fall with great force. 14I will tear down the wall you prophets painted over. I will knock it down. The only thing left will be its foundation. When it falls, you will be destroyed along with it. Then you will know that I am the LORD.

15" ' "So I will pour out all of my burning anger on the wall. I will also send it against you prophets who painted it. I will say to you, 'The wall is gone. You who painted it will be gone too. 16You prophets of Israel prophesied to Jerusalem. You saw visions of peace for its people. But there wasn't any peace,' announces the LORD and King." '

17"Son of man, turn your attention to the daughters of your people. What they prophesy comes out of their own minds. So prophesy against them. 18Tell them, 'The LORD and King says, "How terrible it will be for you women who sew magic charms to put around your wrists! You make veils of different lengths to put on your heads. You do those things to trap people. You trap my people. But you will also be trapped. **19**You have treated me as if I were not holy. You did it among my very own people. You did it for a few handfuls of barley and scraps of bread. You told lies to my people. They like to listen to lies. You killed those who should have lived. And you spared those who should have died."

20" 'So the Lord and King says, "I am against your magic charms. You use them to trap people as if they were birds. I will tear them off your arms. I will set free the people you trap like birds. **21**I will tear your veils off your heads. I will save my people from your powerful hands. They will no longer be under your control. Then you will know that I am the Lord.

22" ' "I had not made godly people sad. But when you told them lies, you made them lose all hope. You advised sinful people not to turn from their evil ways. You did not want them to save their lives. **23**So you will never see false visions again. You will not use your magic tricks anymore. I will save my people from your powerful hands. Then you will know that I am the Lord." ' "

The Lord Judges Those Who Worship Other Gods

14 Some of the elders of Israel came to see me. They sat down with me. **2**Then a message came to me from the Lord. He said, **3**"Son of man, these men have thought about nothing but other gods. They have fallen into the evil trap of worshiping them. Should I let those men ask me for any advice?

4"Speak to them. Tell them, 'The Lord and King says, "Suppose an Israelite thinks about other gods. And he falls into the evil trap of worshiping them. Then he goes to a prophet to ask for advice. If he does, I myself will tell the prophet to answer him in keeping with his worship of many gods. **5**I will win back the hearts of the people of Israel. All of them have deserted me for their other gods." '

6"So speak to the people of Israel. Tell them, 'The Lord and King says, "Turn away from your sins! Also turn away from your gods. Give up all of the evil things you have done. I hate them.

7" ' "Suppose an Israelite or outsider who lives in Israel separates himself from me. And he thinks about other gods. He falls into the evil trap of worshiping them. Then he goes to a prophet to ask me for advice. If he does, I myself will tell the prophet to answer him. **8**I will turn

against him. I will make an example out of him. People will laugh at him. I will cut him off from you. Then you will know that I am the Lord.

9" ' "Suppose that prophet is stirred up to give a prophecy. Then I am the one who has stirred him up. And I will reach out my powerful hand against him. I will destroy him from among my people Israel. **10**The prophet will be as much to blame as the one who asks him for advice. Both of them will be guilty. **11**Then the people of Israel will no longer wander away from me. And they will not pollute themselves anymore with their many sins. They will be my people. And I will be their God," ' announces the Lord and King."

The Lord Punishes All Sinners

12A message came to me from the Lord. He said, **13**"Son of man, suppose the people in a certain country sin against me. And they are not faithful to me. So I reach out my powerful hand against them. I cut off their food supply. I make them very hungry. I kill them and their animals. **14**And suppose Noah, Daniel and Job were in that country. Then those three men could save only themselves by doing what is right," announces the Lord and King.

15"Or suppose I send wild animals through that country. And they kill all of its children. It becomes a dry and empty desert. No one can pass through it because of the animals. **16**And suppose those three men were in that country. Then they could not save their own sons or daughters. They alone would be saved. But the land would become a dry and empty desert. And that is just as sure as I am alive," announces the Lord and King.

17"Or suppose I send swords to kill the people in that country. And I say, 'Let swords sweep all through the land.' And I kill its people and their animals. **18**And suppose those three men were in that country. Then they could not save their own sons or daughters. They alone would be saved. And that is just as sure as I am alive," announces the Lord and King.

19"Or suppose I send a plague into that land. And I pour out my burning anger on it by spilling blood. I kill its people and their animals. **20**And suppose Noah, Daniel and Job were in that land. Then they could not save their own sons or daughters. They could save only themselves by doing what is right. And that is just as sure as I am alive," announces the Lord and King.

²¹The LORD and King says, "It will get much worse. I will punish Jerusalem in four horrible ways. There will be war, hunger, wild animals and plague. They will destroy the people and their animals.

²²"But some people will be left alive. Some children will be brought out of the city. They will come to you. You will see how they act and the way they live. And you will be comforted in spite of all of the trouble I brought on Jerusalem. ²³You will be comforted when you see how they act and the way they live. Then you will know that I did not do anything there without a reason," announces the LORD and King.

Jerusalem Is Like a Useless Vine

15 A message came to me from the LORD. He said, ²"Son of man, is the wood of a vine better than the wood of any of the trees in the forest? ³Can its wood ever be made into anything useful? Can pegs be made from it to hang things on?

⁴"Suppose it is thrown in the fire to be burned. And the fire burns both ends and blackens the middle. Then is it useful for anything? ⁵It was not useful when it was whole. So how can it be made into something useful now? The fire has burned it and blackened it."

⁶The LORD and King says, "Instead of the wood of any tree in the forest, I have given the vine to burn in the fire. I will treat the people who live in Jerusalem the same way. ⁷I will turn against them. They might have come out of the fire. But the fire will destroy them anyway. I will turn against them. Then they will know that I am the LORD. ⁸I will make the land a dry and empty desert. My people have not been faithful to me," announces the LORD and King.

A Story That Pictures Unfaithful Jerusalem

16 A message came to me from the LORD. He said, ²"Son of man, tell the people of Jerusalem the evil things they have done. I hate those things.

³"Tell them, 'The LORD and King speaks to Jerusalem. He says, "Your history in the land of Canaan goes back a long way. Your father was an Amorite. Your mother was a Hittite. ⁴On the day you were born your cord was not cut. You were not washed with water to clean you up. You were not rubbed with salt. And you were not wrapped in large strips of cloth. ⁵No one took pity on you. No one was concerned enough to do any of those things for you.

Instead, you were thrown out into an open field. You were hated on the day you were born.

⁶" ' "I was passing by. I saw you kicking around in your blood. As you were lying there, I said to you, 'Live!' ⁷I made you grow like a plant in a field. Soon you had grown up. You became the most beautiful jewel of all. Your breasts had formed. Your hair had grown. But you were naked and bare.

⁸" ' "Later, I was passing by again. I looked at you. I saw that you were old enough for love. So I got married to you and took good care of you. I covered your naked body. I took an oath and made a firm promise to you. I entered into a covenant with you. And you became mine," announces the LORD and King.

⁹" ' "I bathed you with water. I washed the blood off you. And I put lotions on you. ¹⁰I put a beautiful dress on you. I gave you leather sandals. I dressed you in fine linen. I covered you with expensive clothes. ¹¹I decorated you with jewelry. I put bracelets on your arms. I gave you a necklace for your neck. ¹²I put rings on your nose and ears. And I gave you a beautiful crown for your head.

¹³" ' "So you were decorated with gold and silver. Your clothes were made out of fine linen. They were made of expensive and beautiful cloth. Your food was made out of fine flour, honey and olive oil. You became very beautiful. You became a queen. ¹⁴You were so beautiful that your fame spread among the nations. The glory I had given you made your beauty perfect," announces the LORD and King.

¹⁵" ' "But you trusted in your beauty. You used your fame to become a prostitute. You offered your body freely to anyone who passed by. In fact, you gave yourself to anyone who wanted you. ¹⁶You used some of your clothes to make high places colorful. That is where people worshiped other gods. You were a prostitute there. Things like that should never happen. They should never take place.

¹⁷" ' "I had given you fine jewelry. It was made out of gold and silver. You used it to make for yourself statues of male gods. You worshiped those gods. You were not faithful to me. ¹⁸You put your beautiful clothes on them. You offered my oil and incense to them. ¹⁹You also offered them the food that was made out of fine flour, olive oil and honey. I had given it to you to eat. You offered it as sweet-smelling incense to them. That is what you did," announces the LORD and King.

20" ' "Then you got your sons and daughters who belonged to me. And you sacrificed them as food to other gods. Wasn't it enough for you to be a prostitute? **21**You killed my children. You sacrificed them to other gods.

22" ' "You did not remember the days when you were young. At that time you were naked and bare. You were kicking around in your blood. But now you have done evil things. I hate them. You have worshiped other gods. You have not been faithful to me.

23" ' "How terrible it will be for you!" announces the LORD and King. "How terrible for you! You continued to sin against me. **24**Your people built up mounds for themselves in every market place. They put little places of worship on them. **25**They set them up at every street corner. Jerusalem, you misused your beauty. You offered your body to anyone who passed by. You did it again and again.

26" ' "You committed shameful acts with the people of Egypt. They were your neighbors, and they were filled with longing for their lovers. You offered yourself to others again and again. That made me very angry. **27**So I reached out my powerful hand against you. I made your territory smaller. I handed you over to your Philistine enemies. The people in their towns were shocked by your impure conduct.

28" ' "You also committed shameful acts with the people of Assyria. Nothing ever seemed to satisfy you. You could never get enough. **29**Then you offered yourself to the people of Babylonia. But that did not satisfy you either. There are many traders in the land of Babylonia.

30" ' "You can't control yourself," announces the LORD and King. "Just look at all of the things you are doing! You are acting like a prostitute who has no shame at all. **31**Your people built up mounds at every street corner. You put little places of worship on them in every market place. But you did not really act like a prostitute. You refused to let your lovers pay you anything.

32" ' "You unfaithful wife! You would rather be with strangers than with your own husband! **33**Every prostitute gets paid. But you give gifts to all of your lovers. You offer them money to come to you from everywhere. You want them to make love to you. You are not faithful to me. **34**As a prostitute, you are the opposite of others. No one runs after you to make

love to you. You are exactly the opposite. You pay them. They do not pay you." ' "

35You prostitute, listen to the LORD's message. **36**The LORD and King says, "You poured out your wealth on your lovers. You took your clothes off and made love to them. You did it again and again. You worshiped other gods. I hate them. You even sacrificed your children to them.

37"So I am going to gather together all of the lovers you found pleasure with. They include those you loved and those you hated. I will gather them against you from everywhere. I will take your clothes off right in front of them. Then they will see you completely naked. **38**I will hand down my sentence against you. You will be punished like women who commit adultery and sacrifice their children to other gods. My anger burns against you so much that I will sentence you to death for everything you have done.

39"Then I will hand you over to your lovers. They will tear down those mounds you built. They will destroy the little places of worship you put on them. They will take your clothes off. They will remove your fine jewelry. And they will leave you naked and bare.

40"They will bring a crowd against you. The crowd will put you to death by throwing stones at you. And they will chop you to pieces with their swords. **41**They will burn your houses down and punish you. Many women will see it.

"I will not let you be a prostitute anymore. You will no longer pay your lovers. **42**Then my burning anger against you will die down. My jealous anger will turn away from you. I will be calm. I will not be angry anymore.

43"You did not remember the days when you were young. The things you did made me very angry. So anything that happens to you will be your own fault," announces the LORD and King. "You added impure conduct to all of the other evil things you did. I hate all of those things.

44"All those who use proverbs will use this one about you. They will say, 'Like mother, like daughter.' **45**You are a true daughter of your mother. She hated her husband and children. And you are a true sister of your sisters. They hated their husbands and children.

"Your mother was a Hittite. Your father was an Amorite. **46**Your older sister was Samaria. She lived north of you with her daughters. Your younger sister was Sodom. She lived south of you with her daughters. **47**You lived exactly the way they did. You copied their evil practices. I hate those practices. Everything you did was so sinful that you soon became even worse than they were.

48"Your sister Sodom and her daughters never did what you and your daughters have done. And that is just as sure as I am alive," announces the LORD and King.

49"Here is the sin your sister Sodom committed. She and her daughters were proud. They ate too much. They were not concerned about others. They did not help those who were poor and in need. **50**They were very proud. They did many things that were evil in my sight. I hated those things. So I got rid of Sodom and her daughters, just as you have seen.

51"Samaria did not commit half the sins you did. You sinned even more than they did. I hate those sins. Compared to what you did, you made your sisters seem godly. **52**So you will be dishonored. You have given your sisters an excuse for what they did. Your sins were far worse than theirs. In fact, your sisters appear to be more godly than you. So then, be ashamed. You will be dishonored. You have made them appear to be godly.

53"I will not only give you back what you had before. I will also do the same thing for Sodom and her daughters. And I will do the same for Samaria and her daughters. **54**That will make you feel dishonored. You will be ashamed of everything you have done. You have made them feel better because you sinned more and were punished more than they were. **55**Your sisters Sodom and Samaria and their daughters will return to what they were before. And you and your daughters will return to what you were before.

56"In the past you would not even mention your sister Sodom. You were proud at that time. **57**That was before your sin was uncovered. Now the daughters of Edom make fun of you. So do all of her neighbors and the daughters of the Philistines. Everyone who lives around you looks down on you. **58**You will be punished for your impure conduct. I will also punish you for the other evil things you have done. I hate all of those things," announces the LORD.

59The LORD and King says, "I will punish you in keeping with what you have done. I sealed with an oath the covenant I made with you. You hated that oath. And you broke my covenant.

60"But I will remember my covenant with you. I made it with you when you were young. Now I will make a new covenant with you. It will last forever. **61**Then you will remember how you have lived. You will be ashamed when I give you Samaria and Sodom. Samaria is your older sister. Sodom is your younger one. I will give them and their daughters to you as daughters. That can't happen based on my old covenant with you. **62**So I will make my new covenant with you. Then you will know that I am the LORD.

63"I will pay for all of the sins you have committed. Then you will remember what you have done. You will be ashamed of it. Because of your shame, you will never speak against me again," announces the LORD and King.

Two Eagles and a Vine

17 A message came to me from the LORD. He said, **2**"Son of man, tell the people of Israel a story about their kings. Let them know what will happen to them. **3**Tell them, 'The LORD and King says, "A great eagle came to the city of 'Lebanon.' It had powerful wings and a lot of long feathers. The feathers were colorful and beautiful. The eagle landed in the top of a cedar tree. **4**It broke off the highest twig. It carried it away to Babylonia. There are many traders in that land. The eagle planted the twig in the city of Babylon.

5" ' "Then it got a seed from your land. It put it in rich soil near plenty of water. It planted the seed like a willow tree. **6**The seed grew into a low, spreading vine. Its branches turned toward the eagle. And its roots remained under the eagle. So the seed became a vine. It produced branches and put out leaves.

7" ' "But there was another great eagle. It also had powerful wings and a lot of feathers. The vine now sent its roots out toward that eagle. It sent them out from the place where it was planted. And it reached out its branches to the eagle for water. **8**The seed had been planted in good soil near plenty of water. Then it could produce branches and bear fruit. It could become a beautiful vine." '

9"Ezekiel, tell the Israelites, 'The LORD and King asks, "Will the vine grow? Won't it be pulled up by its roots? Won't all of its fruit be stripped off? Won't it dry up? All of its new growth will dry up. It will not take a strong arm or many people to pull it up. **10**It will not grow even if it is pulled up and planted somewhere else. It will dry up completely when the east wind strikes it. It will dry up in the place where it grew." ' "

11 A message came to me from the LORD. He said, 12 "These people refuse to obey me. Ask them, 'Don't you know what these things mean?' Tell them, 'Nebuchadnezzar went to Jerusalem. He was king of Babylonia. He carried off King Jehoiachin and the nobles. He brought them back with him to the city of Babylon.

13 " 'Then Nebuchadnezzar made a peace treaty with Zedekiah. He was a member of Jerusalem's royal family. Nebuchadnezzar made him take an oath and promise he would keep the treaty. He also took the leading men of the land away as prisoners. 14 He did it to bring their kingdom down. It would not rise again. In fact, it would be able to last only by keeping his treaty.

15 " 'But Zedekiah turned against him. He sent messengers to Egypt. They went there to get horses and a large army. Will he succeed? Will he who does things like that escape? Can he break the peace treaty and still escape?

16 " 'Zedekiah will die in Babylon,' announces the LORD and King. 'And that is just as sure as I am alive. He will die in the land of King Nebuchadnezzar, who put him on the throne. He is the king whose oath Zedekiah hated. He also broke Nebuchadnezzar's treaty.

17 " 'So Nebuchadnezzar will build ramps against the walls of Jerusalem. He will set up war machines to destroy many lives. Pharaoh will not be able to help Zedekiah during the war. The huge and mighty army of Egypt will not be of any help.

18 " 'Zedekiah hated Nebuchadnezzar's oath and broke his treaty. He had made a firm promise to keep it. But he broke it anyway. So he will not escape.

19 " 'The LORD and King says, "Zedekiah hated the oath he took in my name. He broke the treaty. So I will pay him back. And that is just as sure as I am alive. 20 I will spread out my net to catch him. He will be caught in my trap. I will bring him to Babylon. I will judge him there because he was not faithful to me.

21 " ' "All of Zedekiah's troops will be killed with swords when they try to run away. Those who are left alive will be scattered to the winds. Then you will know that I have spoken. I am the LORD."

22 " 'The LORD and King says, "I myself will get a twig from the very top of a cedar tree and plant it. I will break off the high-

est twig. I will plant it on a very high mountain. 23 I will plant it on the high mountains of Israel. It will produce branches and bear fruit. It will become a beautiful cedar tree. All kinds of birds will make their nests in it. They will live in the shade of its branches. 24 All of the trees in the fields will know that I bring tall trees down. I make short trees grow tall. I dry up green trees. And I make dry trees green."

" 'I have spoken. I will do it. I am the LORD.' "

People Will Die Because of Their Own Sins

18 A message came to me from the LORD. He said, 2 "You people have a proverb about the land of Israel. What do you mean by it? It says,

" 'The parents eat sour grapes.
But the children have a bitter taste
in their mouths.'

3 "You will not use that proverb in Israel anymore," announces the LORD and King. "And that is just as sure as I am alive. 4 Everyone belongs to me. Father and son alike belong to me. People will die because of their own sins.

5 "Suppose a godly man
does what is fair and right.
6 And he does not eat at the mountain
temples.
He does not worship the statues of
Israel's gods.
He does not have sex with another
man's wife.
He does not make love to his own
wife
during her monthly period.
7 He does not treat anyone badly.
Instead, he always gives back
what he took as security for a loan.
He does not steal.
Instead, he gives his food to hungry
people.
He provides clothes for those who
are naked.
8 He does not lend money and charge
too much interest.
He keeps himself from doing what is
wrong.
He judges cases fairly.
9 He follows my rules.
He is faithful in keeping my laws.
He always does what is right.
You can be sure he will live,"
announces the LORD and King.

10 "But suppose he has a mean son who

harms other people. The son commits murder. Or he does some other things that are wrong. **11**Suppose he does those things even though his father never did.

"Suppose he eats at the mountain
   temples.
And he has sex with another man's
   wife.
12He treats poor and needy people badly.
   He steals.
He does not pay back what he owes.
   He worships statues of gods.
He does other things I hate.
13   He lends money and charges too
   much interest.

Will a man like that live? He will not! You can be sure he will be put to death. And what happens to him will be his own fault. He did many things I hate.

14"But suppose that son has a son of his own. And the son sees all of the sins his father commits. He sees them, but he does not do them.

15 "Suppose he does not eat at the
   mountain temples.
And he does not worship the statues
   of Israel's gods.
He does not have sex with another
   man's wife.
16He does not treat anyone badly.
He does not make people give him
   something
   to prove they will pay back what
   they owe him.
He does not steal.
   Instead, he gives his food to hungry
   people.
He provides clothes for those who
   are naked.
17He keeps himself from committing
   sins.
He does not lend money and charge
   too much interest.
He keeps my laws and follows my
   rules.

He will not die because of his father's sin. You can be sure he will live. **18**But his father will die because of his own sin. He got rich by cheating others. He robbed his relatives. He also did what was wrong among his people.

19"But you still ask, 'Is the son guilty along with his father?' No! The son did what was fair and right. He was careful to keep all of my rules. So you can be sure he will live. **20**People will die because of their own sins. The son will not be guilty because of what his father did. And the father will not be guilty because of what his

son did. The right things a godly person does will be added to his account. The wrong things a sinful person does will be charged against him.

21"But suppose a sinful person turns away from all of the sins he has committed. And he keeps all my rules. He does what is fair and right. Then you can be sure he will live. He will not die. **22**None of the sins he has committed will be held against him. Because of the godly things he has done, he will live.

23"When sinful people die, it does not give me any joy," announces the Lord and King. "But when they turn away from their sins and live, that makes me very happy.

24"Suppose a godly person stops doing what is right. And he commits sin. He does the same evil things a sinful person does. He does things I hate. Then he will not live. I will not remember any of the right things he has done. He has not been faithful to me. He has also committed many other sins. So he is guilty. He will die.

25"But you say, 'What the Lord does isn't fair.' Listen to me, people of Israel. What I do is always fair. What you do is not.

26"Suppose a godly person stops doing what is right. And he commits sin. Then he will die because of it. He will die because of the sin he has committed.

27"But suppose a sinful person turns away from the evil things he has done. And he does what is fair and right. Then he will save his life. **28**He thinks about all of the evil things he has done. And he turns away from them. So you can be sure he will live. He will not die.

29"But the people of Israel still say, 'What the Lord does isn't fair.' People of Israel, what I do is always fair. What you do is not.

30"So I will judge you people. I will judge each of you in keeping with what you have done," announces the Lord and King.

"Turn away from your sins! Turn away from all of the evil things you have done. Then sin will not bring you down. **31**Get rid of all of the evil things you have done. Let me give you a new heart and a new spirit. Then you will be faithful to me. Why should you die, people of Israel? **32**When anyone dies, it does not give me any joy," announces the Lord and King. "So turn away from your sins. Then you will live!

A Song of Sadness About Israel's Princes

19 "Sing a song of sadness about Israel's princes. ²Say to Israel,

" 'You were like a mother lion to your
    princes.
She lay down among the young
    lions.
She brought up her cubs.
³ One of them was Jehoahaz.
    He became a strong lion.
He learned to tear apart what he
    caught.
And he ate men up.
⁴ The nations heard about him.
    They trapped him in their pit.
They put hooks in his face.
And they led him away to Egypt.

⁵ " 'The mother lion looked and waited.
    But all of her hope was gone.
So she got another one of her cubs.
    She made him into a strong lion.
⁶ He prowled with the lions.
    He became very strong.
He learned to tear apart what he
    caught.
And he ate men up.
⁷ He broke down their forts.
    He completely destroyed their
    towns.
The land and all those who were in it
    were terrified when he roared.
⁸ Then nations came against him.
    They came from all around him.
They spread out their net to catch him.
    He was trapped in their pit.
⁹ They used hooks to pull him into a
    cage.
They brought him to the king of
    Babylonia.
They put him in prison.
So his roar was not heard anymore
    on the mountains of Israel.

¹⁰ " 'Israel, you were like a vine in a
    vineyard.
It was planted near water.
It had a lot of fruit and many branches.
    There was plenty of water.
¹¹ Its branches were strong.
    Each was good enough to be made
        into a ruler's rod.
The vine grew high
    above all of the leaves.
It stood out because it was so tall
    and had so many branches.
¹² But Nebuchadnezzar became angry.
    He pulled it up by its roots.
He threw it to the ground.
The east wind dried it up.
Its fruit was stripped off.
Its strong branches dried up.
    And fire destroyed them.
¹³ Now it is planted in the Babylonian
    desert.
It is in a dry and thirsty land.
¹⁴ One of its main branches was
    Zedekiah.
Fire spread from it and burned up its
    fruit.
None of its branches is good enough
    to be made into a ruler's rod.'

"That is a song of sadness. And that is how it should be used."

Israel Refuses to Obey the Lord

20 It was the seventh year since King Jehoiachin had been brought to Babylon as a prisoner. On the tenth day of the fifth month, some of the elders of Israel came to ask the Lord for advice. They sat down with me.

²Then a message came to me from the Lord. He said, ³"Son of man, speak to the elders of Israel. Tell them, 'The Lord and King says, "Have you come to ask me for advice? I will not let you do that," announces the Lord and King. "And that is just as sure as I am alive." '

⁴"Are you going to judge them, son of man? Will you judge them? Tell them the evil things their people did long ago. I hate those things. ⁵Tell them, 'The Lord and King says, "I chose Israel. On that day I raised my hand and took an oath. I made a promise to the members of Jacob's family line. I made myself known to them in Egypt. I raised my hand and told them, 'I am the Lord your God.'

⁶" ' "On that day I promised I would bring them out of Egypt. I told them I would take them to a land I had found for them. It had plenty of milk and honey. It was the most beautiful land of all. ⁷I said to them, 'Each of you must get rid of the statues of the evil gods you worship. Do not pollute yourselves by worshiping the gods of Egypt. I am the Lord your God.'

⁸" ' "But they refused to obey me. They would not listen to me. They did not get rid of the evil gods they worshiped. And they did not turn away from Egypt's gods. So I said I would pour out all of my burning anger on them in Egypt.

⁹" ' "But I wanted my name to be honored. I kept it from being treated as if it were not holy. I did not want that to happen in front of the nations my people lived among. I had made myself known to

Israel in the sight of those nations. I had brought my people out of Egypt.

10 " ' "So I led them out of Egypt. I brought them into the Desert of Sinai. 11 I gave them my rules. I made my laws known to them. The one who obeys them will live by them. 12 I also told them to observe my Sabbath days. That is the sign of the covenant I made with them. I wanted them to know that I made them holy. I am the LORD.

13 " ' "But the people of Israel refused to obey me in the desert. They did not follow my rules. They turned their backs on my laws. The one who obeys them will live by them. They totally misused my Sabbath days. So I said I would pour out my burning anger on them. I would destroy them in the desert.

14 " ' "But I wanted my name to be honored. I kept it from being treated as if it were not holy. I did not want that to happen in front of the nations. They had seen me bring Israel out of Egypt.

15 " ' "I also raised my hand and took an oath in the desert. I told my people I would not bring them into the land I had given them. It had plenty of milk and honey. It was the most beautiful land of all. 16 But they turned their backs on my laws. They did not follow my rules. They misused my Sabbaths. Their hearts were committed to worshiping the statues of their gods.

17 " ' "Then I felt sorry for them. So I did not destroy them. I did not put an end to them in the desert. 18 I spoke to their children there. I said, 'Do not follow the rules your parents gave you. Do not obey their laws. Do not pollute yourselves by worshiping their gods. 19 I am the LORD your God. So follow my rules. Be careful to obey my laws. 20 Keep my Sabbath days holy. That is the sign of the covenant I made with you. You will know that I am the LORD your God.'

21 " ' "But their children refused to obey me. They did not follow my rules. They were not careful to keep my laws. The one who obeys them will live by them. They misused my Sabbaths. So I said I would pour out all of my burning anger on them in the desert.

22 " ' "But I kept myself from punishing them at that time. I wanted my name to be honored. So I kept it from being treated as if it were not holy. I did not want that to happen in front of the nations. They had seen me bring Israel out of Egypt.

23 " ' "I also raised my hand and took an oath in the desert. I told my people I would scatter them among the nations. I would send them to other countries. 24 They had not obeyed my laws. They had turned their backs on my rules. They had misused my Sabbaths. Their eyes longed to see the statues of their parents' gods.

25 " ' "I even let them follow rules that were not good. I let them have laws they could not live by. 26 I let them become polluted by offering sacrifices to other gods. They even sacrificed the first male child who was born in each family. I wanted to fill them with horror. Then they would know that I am the LORD." '

27 "Son of man, speak to the people of Israel. Tell them, 'The LORD and King says, "Your people spoke evil things against me long ago. They deserted me. 28 But I brought them into the land. I had taken an oath and promised to give the land to them. Then they offered sacrifices that made me very angry. They did it on every high hill and under every green tree. There they brought their sweet-smelling incense. And there they poured out their drink offerings. 29 Then I said to them, 'What? You are going to a high place?' " ' " That high place is called Bamah to this very day.

The LORD Judges Israel and Blesses Them

30 The LORD said to me, "Speak to the people of Israel. Tell them, 'The LORD and King says, "Are you going to pollute yourselves the way your people did? Do you long to see the statues of their evil gods? 31 You pollute yourselves by offering sacrifices to other gods. You even sacrifice your children in the fire. You continue to do those things to this very day. People of Israel, should I let you ask me for advice? I will not let you do that," announces the LORD and King. "And that is just as sure as I am alive.

32 " ' "You say, 'We want to be like the other nations. We want to be like all of the other people in the world. They serve

gods that are made out of wood and stone.' But what you have in mind will never happen. 33I will rule over you by reaching out my mighty hand and powerful arm. I will pour my burning anger out on you," announces the Lord and King. "And that is just as sure as I am alive.

34" ' "I will bring you back from the nations. I will gather you together from the countries where you have been scattered. I will reach out my mighty hand and powerful arm. I will pour my burning anger out on you. 35I will send you among the nations. There I will judge you face to face. It will be as if I were judging you in the desert again. 36Long ago, I judged your people in the desert of Egypt. In the same way, I will judge you," announces the Lord and King.

37" ' "I will take note of you as you pass under my shepherd's rod. I will separate those who obey me from those who do not. And I will give the blessings of the new covenant to those of you who obey me. 38I will get rid of those among you who turn against me and refuse to obey me. I will bring them out of the land where they are living. But they will not enter the land of Israel. Then you will know that I am the Lord.

39" ' "People of Israel, the Lord and King says, 'Go, every one of you! Serve your gods. But later you will listen to me. You will no longer treat my name as if it were not holy. You will not offer sacrifices to other gods anymore.

40" ' " "People of Israel, you will serve me,' announces the Lord and King. 'You will serve me on my high and holy mountain in Jerusalem. There I will accept you. I will require your offerings and your finest gifts. I want you to bring them along with all of your other holy sacrifices. 41I will bring you back from the nations. I will gather you together from the countries where you have been scattered. Then I will accept you as if you were sweet-smelling incense. I will show that I am holy among you. The nations will see it.

42" ' " 'I will bring you into the land of Israel. Then you will know that I am the Lord. Long ago I raised my hand and took an oath. I promised to give that land to your people. 43There you will remember your conduct. You will think about everything you did that polluted you. And you will hate yourselves because of all of the evil things you have done.

44" ' " 'People of Israel, I will deal with you for the honor of my name. I will not deal with you based on your evil conduct

and sinful practices. Then you will know that I am the Lord,' announces the Lord and King." ' "

Ezekiel Prophesies Against the South

45A message came to me from the Lord. He said, 46"Son of man, turn your attention to Judah in the south. Preach against it. Prophesy against its forests. 47Tell them, 'Listen to the Lord's message. The Lord and King says, "I am about to set you on fire. The fire will destroy all of your trees. It will burn up green trees and dry trees alike. The blazing flame will not be put out. The faces of everyone from south to north will be burned by it. 48Everyone will see that I started the fire. It will not be put out. I am the Lord." ' "

49Then I said, "Lord and King, people are talking about me. They are saying, 'Isn't he just telling stories?' "

God Uses Babylonia to Judge Israel

21 A message came to me from the Lord. He said, 2"Son of man, turn your attention to Jerusalem. Preach against the temple. Prophesy against the land of Israel.

3"Tell them, 'The Lord says, "I am against you. I will pull out my sword. I will cut off from you godly people and sinful people alike. 4Because I am going to cut them off, my sword will be ready to use. I will strike everyone down from south to north. 5Then all people will know that I have pulled out my sword. I will not put it back. I am the Lord." '

6"Groan, son of man! Groan in front of your people with a broken heart and bit-

GIVING   G

"YOU WILL SERVE ME," ANNOUNCES THE LORD AND KING. "YOU WILL SERVE ME ON MY HIGH AND HOLY MOUNTAIN IN JERUSALEM. THERE I WILL ACCEPT YOU. I WILL REQUIRE YOUR OFFERINGS AND YOUR FINEST GIFTS."
— EZEKIEL 20:40 —

ter sorrow. **7**They will ask you, 'Why are you groaning?'

"Then you will say, 'Because of the news that is coming. The hearts of all of the people will melt away in fear. Their hands will not be able to help them. Their spirits will grow weak. And their knees will become as weak as water.'

"The news is coming! You can be sure those things will happen," announces the LORD and King.

8A message came to me from the LORD. He said, **9**"Son of man, prophesy. Say, 'The Lord says,

" ' "A sword! A sword!
A sharp and shiny sword is coming
from Babylonia!
10It is sharpened to kill people.
It flashes like lightning." ' "

The people say, "Should we take delight in the rod of the ruler of the LORD's son Judah? The sword looks down on every stick like that."

11The LORD says,

"I have told Nebuchadnezzar to shine
his sword.
It is in his hand.
It has been sharpened and shined.
It is ready for the killer's hand.
12Son of man, cry out and sob.
The sword is against my people.
It is against all of the princes of
Israel.
It will kill them
along with the rest of my people.
So beat your chest in sorrow.

13"You can be sure that testing will come. Why does the sword look down on the rod? Because the rod will not continue to rule," announces the LORD and King.

14"Son of man, prophesy.
Clap your hands.
Let the sword strike twice.
Let it strike even three times.
It is a sword to kill people.
It is a sword to kill many people.
It is closing in on them from every
side.
15People's hearts will melt away in fear.
Many will be wounded or killed.
I have prepared the sword to kill
people
at all of their city gates.
It flashes like lightning.
It is in the killer's hand.
16Sword, cut to the right.
Then cut to the left.

Strike people down everywhere your
blade is turned.
17I too will clap my hands.
My burning anger will calm down.
I have spoken. I am the LORD."

18A message came to me from the LORD. He said, **19**"Son of man, mark out on a map two roads for the sword to take. The sword belongs to the king of Babylonia. Both roads start from the same country. Put up a sign where the road turns off to the city of Rabbah. **20**Mark out one road for the sword to take against Rabbah in Ammon. Mark out another against Judah and the walls of Jerusalem.

21"The king of Babylonia will stop at the place where the two roads meet. He will ask his gods to tell him which way to go. He will cast lots by pulling arrows out of a bag. And he will look carefully at the liver of a sheep.

22"His right hand will pull out the arrow for Jerusalem. There he will get huge logs ready to knock down its gates. He will give the command to kill its people. He will sound the battle cry. He will build a ramp up to the city wall. He will bring in his war machines.

23"The decision to attack Jerusalem will seem like the wrong advice to those who made a treaty with Nebuchadnezzar. But he will remind them that they are guilty. And he will take them away as prisoners."

24So the LORD and King says, "You people have reminded everyone of how guilty you are. You have done it by refusing to obey me or any other authority. Everything you do clearly shows how sinful you are. So you will be taken away as prisoners."

25King Zedekiah, the day for you to be punished has finally come. You are an unholy and evil prince in Israel. Your time is up. **26**The LORD and King says, "Take off your turban. Remove your crown. Things will not be as they were in the past. Those who are not important will be honored. And those who are honored will be brought down. **27**Jerusalem will fall. I will destroy it. It will not be rebuilt until the true king comes. After all, the kingdom belongs to him. I will give it to him.

28"Son of man, prophesy. Say, 'The LORD and King speaks about the Ammonites. He also talks about the way they laugh because of Jerusalem's fall. He says,

" ' "A sword! A sword!
Nebuchadnezzar's sword is ready to
kill you.
It is shined to destroy you.

It flashes like lightning.
29 The visions of your prophets are false.
They use magic to try to find out
what is going to happen to you.
But their magic tricks are lies.
The sword will strike the necks of
you sinful people.
You will be killed.
The day for you to be punished has
finally come.
Your time is up.
30 Ammon, return your sword to its
place.
In the land where you were created, I
will judge you.
That is where you came from.
31 I will pour out my anger on you.
I will breathe out my burning anger
against you.
I will hand you over to mean people.
They are skilled at destroying others.
32 You will be burned in the fire.
Your blood will be spilled in your
land.
You will not be remembered anymore.
I have spoken. I am the Lord." ' "

Jerusalem Sins Against the Lord

22 A message came to me from the
Lord. He said, 2 "Son of man, are
you going to judge Jerusalem? Will you
judge this city that has so many murderers in it? Then tell its people they have
done many evil things. I hate those
things. 3 Tell them, 'The Lord and King
says, "Your city brings death on itself. You
spill blood inside its walls. You pollute
yourselves by making statues of gods.
4 You are guilty of spilling blood. The statues you have made have polluted you.

" ' "You have brought your days to a
close. The end of your years has come. So
the nations will make fun of you. All of
the countries will laugh at you. 5 Those
who are near you will tell jokes about you.
So will those who are far away. Trouble
fills the streets of your sinful city.

6 " ' "The princes of Israel are in your
city. All of them use their power to spill
blood. 7 They have made fun of fathers
and mothers alike. They have crushed
outsiders. They have treated badly the
children whose fathers have died. They
have done the same thing to widows.

8 " ' "You have looked down on the
holy things that were set apart to me. You
have misused my Sabbath days. 9 You
have spread lies about others so you can
spill someone's blood. You eat at the
mountain temples. You commit impure
acts.

10 " ' "You bring shame on your fathers
by having sex with their wives. You have
sex with women during their monthly
period. That is when they are 'unclean.'
11 One of you has sex with another man's
wife. I hate that sin. Another brings
shame on his daughter-in-law by having
sex with her. Still another has sex with his
sister, even though she is his own father's
daughter.

12 " ' "You accept money from people
who want special favors. You do it to spill
someone's blood. You charge too much
interest when you lend money. You get
rich by cheating your neighbors. And you
have forgotten me," announces the Lord
and King.

13 " ' "I will clap my hands because I am
so angry. You got rich by cheating others.
You spilled blood inside the walls of your
city. 14 Will you be brave on the day I deal
with you? Will you be strong at that time?
I have spoken. I will do it. I am the Lord.

15 " ' "I will scatter you among the nations. I will send you to other countries. I
will put an end to your 'uncleanness.'
16 You will be polluted in the sight of the
nations. Then you will know that I am the
Lord." ' "

17 A message came to me from the Lord.
He said, 18 "Son of man, the people of Israel have become like scum to me. All of
them are like the copper, tin, iron and
lead that are left inside a furnace. They are
only the scum that is removed from silver."

19 So the Lord and King says, "People of
Israel, all of you have become like scum.
So I will gather you together in Jerusalem.
20 Men put silver, copper, iron, lead and
tin into a furnace. They melt it with a
blazing fire. In the same way, I will gather
you. I will pour out my burning anger on
you. I will put you inside the city and melt
you. 21 I will gather you together. My
burning anger will blaze out at you. And
you will be melted inside Jerusalem. 22 Silver is melted in a furnace. And you will be
melted inside the city. Then you will
know that I have poured out my burning
anger on you. I am the Lord."

23 Another message came to me from
the Lord. He said, 24 "Son of man, speak to
the land. Tell it, 'You have not had any
rain or showers. That is because I am angry with you.'

25 "Ezekiel, the princes of the land are
like a roaring lion that tears its food apart.
They eat people up. They take treasures
and other valuable things. They cause

many women in the land to become widows.

26"Its priests break my law. They treat things that are set apart to me as if they were not holy. They treat holy and common things as if they were the same. They teach that there is no difference between things that are 'clean' and things that are not. They refuse to keep my Sabbath days. So they treat me as if I were not holy.

27"The officials in the land are like wolves that tear their food apart. They spill blood and kill people to get rich. 28The prophets cover up those acts for them. The visions of those prophets are false. They use magic to try to find out what is going to happen. But their magic tricks are lies. They say, 'The LORD and King says,' But I have not spoken to them. 29"The people of the land get rich by cheating others. They steal. They crush those who are poor and in need. They treat outsiders badly. They refuse to be fair to them.

30"I looked for a man among them who would stand up for Jerusalem. I tried to find someone who would pray to me for the land. Then I would not have to destroy it. But I could not find anyone who would pray for it. 31So I will pour out my anger on its people. I will destroy them because my anger burns against them. And anything that happens to them will be their own fault," announces the LORD and King.

Samaria and Jerusalem Are Like Two Impure Sisters

23 A message came to me from the LORD. He said, 2"Son of man, once there were two women. They had the same mother. 3They became prostitutes in Egypt. They have been unfaithful to me since they were young. In that land they allowed their breasts to be touched. They permitted their virgin breasts to be kissed.

4"The older sister was named Oholah. The younger one was Oholibah. They belonged to me. Sons and daughters were born to them. Oholah stands for Samaria. And Oholibah stands for Jerusalem.

5"Oholah was unfaithful to me even while she still belonged to me. She longed for her Assyrian lovers. 6They included soldiers who wore blue uniforms. They also included governors and commanders. All of them were young and handsome. They rode horses. 7She gave herself as a prostitute to all of Assyria's finest warriors. She polluted herself with the statues of the gods of everyone she longed for.

8"She started being a prostitute in Egypt. And she never stopped. When she was young, men had sex with her. They kissed her virgin breasts. They used up all of their sinful longings on her.

9"So I handed her over to her Assyrian lovers. She longed for them. 10They stripped her naked. They took her sons and daughters away. And they killed her with their swords. Other women laughed when that happened. I was the one who had punished her.

11"Her sister Oholibah saw it. But her evil longing for sexual sin was worse than her sister's. 12She too longed for the men of Assyria. They included governors and commanders. They included soldiers who wore uniforms. They also included men who rode horses. All of them were young and handsome. 13I saw that she too polluted herself. So both sisters did the same evil things.

14"But Oholibah went even further with her sexual sins. She saw pictures of men drawn on a wall. They were figures of Babylonians drawn in red. 15They had belts around their waists. They wore flowing turbans on their heads. All of them looked like Babylonian chariot officers. They were from the land of the Chaldeans.

16"As soon as she saw the pictures, she longed for the men. So she sent messengers to them in Babylonia. 17Then the Babylonians came to her. They went to bed with her. They made love to her. They polluted her when they had sex with her. After they did it, she became sick of them. So she turned away from them.

18"She acted like a prostitute who had no shame at all. She openly showed her naked body. I became sick of what she was doing. So I turned away from her. I had also turned away from her sister.

19"But Oholibah offered her body to her lovers again and again. She remembered the days when she was a young prostitute in Egypt. 20There she had longed for her lovers. Their private parts seemed as big as those of donkeys. And their flow of semen appeared to be as much as that of horses. 21So you wanted to return to the days when you were young. You longed for the time when you first became impure in Egypt. That was when you allowed your breasts to be kissed. And you permitted your young breasts to be touched."

22So the LORD and King says, "Oholibah, I will stir up your lovers against you. You became sick of them. You turned away from them. But I will bring them against you from every side. **23**They include the Babylonians and all of the Chaldeans. They include the men from Pekod, Shoa and Koa. They also include all of the Assyrians. They are young and handsome. Some of them are governors and commanders. Others are chariot officers. Still others are very high officials. All of them ride horses.

24"So a huge army will come against you with weapons, chariots and wagons. They will take up positions against you on every side. They will carry large and small shields. They will wear helmets. I will turn you over to them to be punished. They will punish you in their own way.

25"I will pour out my jealous anger on you. And the army's anger will burn against you. They will cut off your noses and ears. Some of you who are left will be killed with swords. They will take your sons and daughters away. Others of you who are left will be burned up. **26**The army will also strip your clothes off. They will take your fine jewelry away from you.

27"You became an impure prostitute in Egypt. But I will put a stop to all of that. You will no longer want to do any of it. You will not remember Egypt anymore."

28The LORD and King says, "I am about to hand you over to people you hate. You became sick of them. You turned away from them. **29**They will punish you because they hate you so much. They will take everything you have worked for away from you. They will leave you naked and bare. Then everyone will see that you are a prostitute who has no shame at all. You were impure. You offered your body to your lovers again and again.

30"That is why you will be punished. You longed for lovers in other nations. You polluted yourself by worshiping their gods. **31**You did the same things your sister Oholah did. So I will put her cup in your hand. It is filled with the wine of my anger."

32The LORD and King says to Oholibah,

"You will drink from your sister's cup.
    It is large and deep.
It is filled with the wine of my anger.
    So others will laugh at you.
    They will make fun of you.
33You will become drunk and sad.
    The cup of my anger will completely
      destroy you.
It is the same cup your sister Samaria
      drank from.
34You will drink from it until it is empty.

Then you will throw it down and
    break it in pieces.
And you will claw at your breasts.

I have spoken," announces the LORD and King.

35So the LORD and King says, "You have forgotten me. You have pushed me behind your back. You have been impure. You have acted like a prostitute. So I will punish you."

36The LORD said to me, "Son of man, are you going to judge Oholah and Oholibah? Then tell them they have done many evil things. I hate those things. **37**They have committed adultery. Their hands are covered with the blood of the people they have murdered. They have worshiped other gods. They have not been faithful to me. They have even sacrificed their children as food to other gods. Those children belonged to me.

38"Here are some other things the sisters have done to me. They have polluted my temple. They have misused my Sabbath days. **39**They have sacrificed their children to their gods. On that same day they entered my temple and polluted it. That is what they have done in my house.

40"They even sent messengers to bring men from far away. When the men arrived, Oholibah took a bath. She put makeup on her eyes. She put her jewelry on. **41**She sat down on a beautiful couch. A table was in front of it. There she put the incense and olive oil that belonged to me.

42"The noise of a carefree crowd was all around her. Sabeans were brought from the desert. Other men were brought along with them. They put bracelets on the arms of the two sisters. They put beautiful crowns on their heads.

43"Then I spoke about Oholibah. She was worn out by adultery. I said, 'Let them use her as a prostitute. After all, that is what she is.' **44**So they had sex with her. In fact, they had sex with both of those impure women, Oholah and Oholibah. It was just like having sex with prostitutes.

45"But men who are right with God will sentence the sisters to be punished. They will be punished in the same way as women who commit adultery and murder. After all, they have committed adultery. And their hands are covered with the blood of the people they have murdered."

46The LORD and King says, "Bring an angry crowd against the sisters. Hand them over to those who will terrify them and steal everything they have. **47**The crowd will kill them by throwing stones at them. They will cut them down with their swords. They will kill their sons and daughters. And they will burn their houses down.

48 "So I will put an end to impurity in the land. Then all of its women will be warned. They will not want to be like the sisters. **49** Those sisters will be punished because of the impure things they have done. They will be judged because they have worshiped other gods. Then they will know that I am the LORD and King."

Jerusalem Is Like a Cooking Pot

24 It was the ninth year since King Jehoiachin had been brought to Babylon as a prisoner. On the tenth day of the tenth month, a message came to me from the LORD. He said, **2** "Son of man, write down today's date. The king of Babylonia has surrounded Jerusalem and attacked it this very day.

3 "Your people refuse to obey me. So tell them a story. Say to them, 'The LORD and King told me,

" ' "Put a cooking pot on the fire.
Pour water into it.
4 Put pieces of meat in it.
Use all of the best pieces.
Use the leg and shoulder.
Fill it with the best bones.
5 Pick the finest animal in the flock.
Pile wood under the pot to cook the bones.
Bring the water to a boil.
Cook the bones in it." ' "

6 The LORD and King says,

"How terrible it will be for this city!
It has so many murderers in it.
How terrible for the pot that is coated with scum!
The scum on it will not go away.
Take the meat and bones out of the pot piece by piece.
Do not cast lots for them.

7 "The blood Jerusalem's people spilled is inside its walls.
They poured it out on a bare rock.
They did not pour it on the ground.
If they had, dust would have covered it up.
8 So I put their blood on the bare rock.
I did not want it to be covered up.
I poured my burning anger out on them.
I paid them back."

9 So the LORD and King said to me,

"How terrible it will be for this city!

It has so many murderers in it.
I too will pile the wood high.
10 So pile on the wood.
Light the fire.
Cook the meat well.
Mix in the spices.
Let the bones be blackened.
11 Then set the empty pot on the coals.
Let it get hot. Let its copper glow.
Then what is not pure in it will melt.
Its scum will be burned away.
12 But it can't be cleaned up.
Its thick scum has not been removed.
Even fire can't burn it off.

13 "Jerusalem, you are really impure. I tried to clean you up. But you would not let me make you pure. So you will not be clean again until my burning anger against you has calmed down.

14 "I have spoken. The time has come for me to act. I will not hold back. I will not feel sorry for you. I will do what I said I would do. You will be judged for your conduct and actions. I am the LORD," announces the LORD and King.

Ezekiel's Wife Dies

15 A message came to me from the LORD. He said, **16** "Son of man, I will take away from you the wife you delight in. It will happen very soon. But do not sing songs of sadness. Do not let any tears flow from your eyes. **17** Groan quietly. Do not sob out loud over your wife when she dies. Keep your turban on your head. Keep your sandals on your feet. Do not cover the lower part of your face. Do not eat the food people eat to comfort them when someone dies."

18 So I spoke to my people in the morning. And in the evening my wife died. The next morning I did what I had been commanded to do.

19 Then the people said to me, "Tell us what these things have to do with us."

20 So I told them. I said, "A message came to me from the LORD. He said, **21** 'Speak to the people of Israel. Tell them, "The LORD and King says, 'I am about to pollute my temple. I will let the Babylonians burn it down. It is the beautiful building you are so proud of. You take delight in it. You love it. The sons and daughters you left behind will be killed with swords.

22 " ' " 'So do what Ezekiel did. Do not cover the lower part of your face. Do not eat the food people eat to comfort them when someone dies. **23** Keep your turbans on your heads. Keep your sandals on your feet. Do not cry or sob. You will waste away because you have sinned so much. You will groan among yourselves.

24"'"'What Ezekiel has done will show you what is going to happen to you. You will do just as he has done. Then you will know that I am the LORD and King.'"'

25"Son of man, I will take away their beautiful temple. It is their joy and glory. They take delight in it. Their hearts long for it. I will also take away their sons and daughters. 26On the day I destroy everything, a man will escape. He will come and tell you the news. 27"At that time I will open your mouth. Then you will no longer be silent. You will speak with the man. That will show them what will happen to them. And they will know that I am the LORD."

A Message About Ammon

25 A message came to me from the LORD. He said, 2"Son of man, turn your attention to the Ammonites. Prophesy against them. 3Tell them, 'Listen to the message of the LORD and King. He says, "You laughed when my temple was polluted. You also laughed when the land of Israel was completely destroyed. You made fun of the people of Judah when they were taken away as prisoners. 4So I am going to hand you over to the people of the east. They will set up their tents in your land. They will camp among you. They will eat your fruit. They will drink your milk. 5I will turn the city of Rabbah into grasslands for camels. Ammon will become a resting place for sheep. Then you will know that I am the LORD."'"

6The LORD and King says, "You clapped your hands. You stamped your feet. You hated the land of Israel deep down inside you. You were glad because of what happened to it. 7So I will reach out my powerful hand against you. I will give you and everything you have to the nations. I will cut you off from them. I will wipe you out. I will destroy you. Then you will know that I am the LORD."

A Message About Moab

8The LORD and King says, "Moab and Edom said, 'Look! The people of Judah have become like all of the other nations.' 9So I will let Moab's enemies attack its lower hills. They will begin at the border towns. Those towns include Beth Jeshimoth, Baal Meon and Kiriathaim. They are the glory of that land. 10I will hand Moab over to the people of the east. I will

also give the Ammonites to them. And the Ammonites will no longer be remembered among the nations. 11I will punish Moab. Then they will know that I am the LORD."

A Message About Edom

12The LORD and King says, "Edom got even with the people of Judah. That made them very guilty." 13He continues, "I will reach out my hand against Edom. I will kill its people and their animals. I will completely destroy it. They will be killed with swords from Teman all the way to Dedan. 14I will use my people Israel to pay Edom back. They will punish Edom because my anger burns against it. They will know how I pay my enemies back," announces the LORD and King.

A Message About the Philistines

15The LORD and King says, "The Philistines hated Judah deep down inside them. So they tried to get even with them. They had been Judah's enemies for many years. So they tried to destroy them." 16He continues, "I am about to reach out my hand against the Philistines. I will cut off the Kerethites. I will destroy those who remain along the coast. 17You can be sure that I will pay them back. I will punish them because my anger burns against them. When I pay them back, they will know that I am the LORD."

A Message About Tyre

26 It was the first day of a month near the end of the 11th year since King Jehoiachin had been brought to Babylon as a prisoner. A message came to me from the LORD. He said, 2"Son of man, Tyre laughed because of what happened to Jerusalem. The people of Tyre said, 'Jerusalem is the gateway to the nations. But the gate is broken. Its doors have swung open to us. Jerusalem has been destroyed. So now we will succeed.'"

3The LORD and King says, "But I am against you, Tyre. I will bring many nations against you. They will come in like the waves of the sea. 4They will destroy your walls. They will pull your towers down. I will clear away the stones of your broken-down buildings. I will turn you into nothing but a bare rock.

5"Out in the Mediterranean Sea your island city will become a place to spread fishnets. I have spoken," announces the LORD and King. "The nations will take you and everything you have. 6Your settlements on the coast will be destroyed by war. Then you will know that I am the LORD."

7 The LORD and King says, "From the north I am going to bring Nebuchadnezzar against Tyre. He is king of Babylonia. He is the greatest king of all. He will come with horses and chariots. Horsemen and a great army will be brought along with him.

8 "He will go to war against you. He will destroy your settlements on the coast. He will bring in war machines to attack you. A ramp will be built up to your walls. He will use his shields against you. **9** He will use huge logs to knock your walls down. He will destroy your towers with his weapons.

10 "He will have so many horses that they will cover you with dust. Your walls will shake because of the noise of his war horses, wagons and chariots. He will enter your gates, just as men enter a city whose walls have been broken through. **11** The hoofs of his horses will pound in your streets. He will kill your people with swords. Your strong pillars will fall to the ground.

12 "His men will take away from you your wealth and anything else you have. They will pull your walls down. They will completely destroy your fine houses. They will throw the stones and lumber of your broken-down buildings into the sea.

13 "I will put an end to your noisy songs. No one will hear the music of your harps anymore. **14** I will turn you into nothing but a bare rock. You will become a place to spread fishnets. You will never be rebuilt. I have spoken. I am the LORD," announces the LORD and King.

15 The LORD and King speaks to Tyre. He says, "The lands along the coast will shake because of the sound of your fall. Wounded people will groan because so many are dying there.

16 "Then all of the princes along the coast will step down from their thrones. They will put their robes away. They will take off their beautiful clothes. They will sit on the ground. They will put on terror as if it were their clothes. They will tremble with fear all the time. They will be shocked because of what has happened to you.

17 "Then they will sing a song of sadness about you. They will say to you,

" 'Famous city, you have been
       completely destroyed!
   You were filled with sea traders.
   You and your citizens
       were a mighty power on the seas.

You terrified everyone
    who lived in you.
18 The lands along the coast trembled
       with fear
    when you fell.
The islands in the sea
    were terrified when you were
       destroyed.' "

19 The LORD and King says to Tyre, "I will turn you into an empty city. You will be like cities where no one lives anymore. I will cause the ocean to sweep over you. Its mighty waters will cover you. **20** So I will bring you down together with those who go down into the grave. The people who are there lived long ago. You will have to live in the earth below. It will be like living in buildings that were destroyed many years ago. You will go down into the grave along with others. And you will never come back. You will not take your place in this world again. **21** I will bring you to a horrible end. You will be gone forever. People will look for you. But they will never find you," announces the LORD and King.

A Song of Sadness About Tyre

27 A message came to me from the LORD. He said, **2** "Son of man, sing a song of sadness about Tyre. **3** It is located at the gateway to the Mediterranean Sea. It does business with nations on many coasts. Say to it, 'The LORD and King says,

" ' "Tyre, you say,
    'I am perfect and beautiful.'
4 You were like a ship that ruled over the
       high seas.
   Your builders made you perfect and
       beautiful.
5 They cut all of your lumber
    from pine trees on Mount Hermon.
   They used a cedar tree from Lebanon
    to make a mast for you.
6 They made your oars
    out of oak trees from Bashan.
   They made your deck out of cypress
       wood
    from the coasts of Cyprus.
   They decorated it with ivory.
7 Your sail was made out of beautiful,
       Egyptian linen.
    It served as your banner.
   Your shades were made out of blue and
       purple cloth.
   They were from the coasts of
       Elishah.
8 Men from Sidon and Arvad manned
       your oars.
   Tyre, your sailors were skillful.

⁹Very skilled workers from Byblos were
        on board.
They kept you waterproof.
All of the ships on the sea and their
        sailors
    came up beside you.
They brought their goods to trade
        for yours.

¹⁰ " ' "City of Tyre, men from Persia,
        Lydia and Put
    served as soldiers in your army.
They hung their shields and helmets
        on your walls.
That brought glory to you.
¹¹ Men from Arvad and Cilicia
    guarded your walls on every side.
Men from Gammad
    were in your towers.
They hung their shields around your
        walls.
They made you perfect and
        beautiful.

¹² " ' "Tarshish did business with you
because you had so much wealth. They
traded silver, iron, tin and lead for your
goods.
¹³ " ' "Greece, Tubal and Meshech did
business with you. They traded slaves and
bronze articles for your products.
¹⁴ " ' "Men from Beth Togarmah traded
work horses, war horses and mules for
your goods.
¹⁵ " ' "Men from Rhodes did business
with you. Many lands along the coast
bought goods from you. They paid you
with ivory tusks and ebony wood.
¹⁶ " ' "Aram did business with you because you had so many products for sale.
They traded turquoise, purple cloth and
needlework for your goods. They also
traded fine linen, coral and rubies for
them.
¹⁷ " ' "Judah and Israel did business
with you. They traded wheat from Minnith, sweets, honey, olive oil and lotion
for your products.
¹⁸ " ' "Damascus traded wine from Hel-
bon and wool from Zahar to you. They did
business with you because you had so
many products and so much wealth.
¹⁹ " ' "Danites and Greeks from Uzal
bought goods from you. They traded
wrought iron, cassia and cane for your
products.
²⁰ " ' "Dedan traded saddle blankets to
you.
²¹ " ' "Arabia and all of the princes of
Kedar bought goods from you. They traded you lambs, rams and goats for them.
²² " ' "Traders from Sheba and Raamah

did business with you. They traded the
finest spices, jewels and gold for your
goods.
²³ " ' "Haran, Canneh and Eden did
business with you. So did traders from
Sheba, Asshur and Kilmad. ²⁴In your market place they traded beautiful clothes,
blue cloth, and needlework to you. They
also traded colorful rugs that had twisted
cords and tight knots.

²⁵ " ' "The ships of Tarshish
    carry your products.
You are like a ship filled with a heavy
        load
    in the middle of the sea.
²⁶ The sailors who man your oars take you
        out to the high seas.
But the east wind will break you in
        pieces
    in the middle of the sea.
²⁷ You will be wrecked on that day.
    Your wealth, goods and products
        will sink deep into the sea.
So will all your sailors, officers, carpenters,
        traders and all of your soldiers.
    Anyone else on board will sink too.
²⁸ The lands along the coast will shake
    when your officers cry out.
²⁹ All those who man the oars
    will desert their ships.
The sailors and all of the officers
    will stand on the shore.
³⁰ They will raise their voices.
    They will cry bitterly over you.
They will sprinkle dust on their heads.
    They will roll in ashes.
³¹ They will shave their heads because of
        you.
    And they will put on black clothes.
They will sob over you.
    Their spirits will be greatly troubled.
    They will be very sad.
³² As they sob and cry over you,
    they will sing a song of sadness
        about you.
They will say, 'Who was ever like Tyre?
    It was destroyed in the sea.'
³³ Your goods went out on the seas.
    You supplied many nations with
        what they needed.
You had so much wealth and so many
        products.
    You made the kings of the earth
        rich.
³⁴ Now the sea has torn you apart.
    You have sunk deep down into it.
Your products and all of your people
    have gone down with you.
³⁵ All those who live in the lands along
        the coast

are shocked because of what has
  happened to you.
Their kings tremble with fear.
  Their faces are twisted in horror.
36 The traders among the nations hiss at
    you.
  You have come to a horrible end.
  And you will be gone forever." ' "

A Message About the King of Tyre

28 A message came to me from the
LORD. He said, 2 "Son of man,
speak to Ethbaal. He is the ruler of Tyre.
Tell him, 'The LORD and King says,

" ' "In your proud heart
  you say, 'I am a god.
I sit on the throne of a god
  in the Mediterranean Sea.'
But you are only a man. You are not a
    god.
  In spite of that, you think you are as
    wise as a god.
3 Are you wiser than Daniel?
  Isn't even one secret hidden from
    you?
4 You are wise and understanding.
  So you have become very wealthy.
You have piled up gold and silver
  among your treasures.
5 You have used your great skill in
    trading
  to increase your wealth.
You are very rich.
  So your heart has become proud." ' "

6 The LORD and King says,

"You think you are wise.
  In fact, you claim to be as wise as a
    god.
7 So I am going to bring strangers against
    you.
  They will not show you any pity at
    all.
They will use their swords against your
    beauty and wisdom.
  They will strike down your shining
    glory.
8 They will bring you down to the grave.
  You will die a horrible death
  in the middle of the sea.
9 Then will you say, 'I am a god'?
  Will you say that to those who kill
    you?
You will be only a man to those who
    kill you.
  You will not be a god to them.
10 You will die just like those who have
    not been circumcised.
  Strangers will kill you.

I have spoken," announces the LORD and
King.

11 A message came to me from the LORD.
He said, 12 "Son of man, sing a song of sad-
ness about the king of Tyre. Tell him, 'The
LORD and King says,

" ' "You were the model of perfection.
  You were full of wisdom.
  You were perfect and beautiful.
13 You were in Eden.
  It was my garden.
All kinds of jewels decorated you.
  Here is a list of them.

  ruby, topaz and emerald
  chrysolite, onyx and jasper
  sapphire, turquoise and beryl

Your settings and mountings were
    made out of gold.
  On the day you were created,
  they were prepared.
14 I appointed you to be like a guardian
    cherub.
  I anointed you for that purpose.
You were on my holy mountain.
  You walked among the gleaming
    jewels.
15 Your conduct was without blame
    from the day you were created.
  But soon you began to sin.
16 You traded with many nations.
  You harmed people everywhere.
  And you sinned.
So I sent you away from my mountain
    in shame.
  Guardian cherub, I drove you away
  from among the gleaming jewels.
17 You thought you were so handsome
    that it made your heart proud.
You thought you were so glorious
    that it spoiled your wisdom.
So I threw you down to the earth.
  I made an example out of you in
    front of kings.
18 Your many sins and dishonest trade
  polluted your temple.
So I made you go up in flames.
  I turned you into nothing but ashes
    on the ground.
  I let everyone see it.
19 All of the nations that knew you
  are shocked because of what
    happened to you.
You have come to a horrible end.
  And you will be gone forever." ' "

A Message About Sidon

20 A message came to me from the LORD.
He said, 21 "Son of man, turn your atten-

tion to the city of Sidon. Prophesy against it. 22Say, 'The LORD and King says,

" ' "Sidon, I am against your people.
I will gain glory for myself inside
your city walls.
I will punish your people.
I will show that I am holy among
them.
Then they will know that I am the
LORD.
23I will send a plague on them.
I will make blood flow in your
streets.
Those who are killed will fall inside
you.
Swords will strike your people on
every side.
Then they will know that I am the
LORD.

24" ' "The people of Israel will no longer have neighbors who hate them. Those neighbors will not be like sharp and painful thorns anymore. Then Israel will know that I am the LORD and King." ' "

25The LORD and King says, "I will gather the people of Israel together from the nations where they have been scattered. I will show that I am holy among them. I will let the nations see it. Then Israel will live in their own land. I gave it to my servant Jacob. 26My people will live there in safety. They will build houses. They will plant vineyards. They will live in safety. I will punish all of their neighbors who told lies about them. Then Israel will know that I am the LORD their God."

A Message About Egypt

29 It was the tenth year since King Jehoiachin had been brought to Babylon as a prisoner. On the 12th day of the tenth month, a message came to me from the LORD. He said, 2"Son of man, turn your attention to Pharaoh Hophra. He is king of Egypt. Prophesy against him and the whole land of Egypt. 3Tell him, 'The LORD and King says,

" ' "Pharaoh Hophra, I am against you.
King of Egypt, you are like a huge
monster
lying among your streams.
You say, 'The Nile River belongs to me.
I made it for myself.'
4But I will put hooks in your jaws.
I will make the fish in your streams
stick to your scales.
I will pull you out from among your
streams.

All of the fish will stick to your
scales.
5I will leave you out in the desert.
All of the fish in your streams
will be there with you.
You will fall down in an open field.
You will not be picked up.
I will feed you to the wild animals
and to the birds of the air.

6Then everyone who lives in Egypt will know that I am the LORD.

" ' "You have been like a walking stick made out of a papyrus stem. The people of Israel tried to lean on you. 7They took hold of you. But you broke under their weight. You tore their shoulders open. They leaned on you. But you snapped in two. And their backs were broken." ' "

8So the LORD and King says, "I will send Nebuchadnezzar's sword against you. He will kill your people and their animals. 9Egypt will become a dry and empty desert. Then your people will know that I am the LORD.

"You said, 'The Nile River belongs to me. I made it for myself.' 10So I am against you and your streams. I will destroy the land of Egypt. I will turn it into a dry and empty desert from Migdol all the way to Aswan. I will destroy everything as far as the border of Cush.

11"No people or animals will travel through Egypt. No one will even live there for 40 years. 12Egypt will be more empty than any other land. Its destroyed cities will lie empty for 40 years. I will scatter the people of Egypt among the nations. I will send them to other countries."

13But the LORD and King says, "At the end of 40 years I will gather the Egyptians together from the nations where they were scattered. 14I will bring them back from where they were taken as prisoners. I will return them to Upper Egypt. That is where they came from. There they will be an unimportant kingdom.

15"Egypt will be the least important kingdom of all. It will never place itself above the other nations again. I will make it very weak. Then it will never again rule over the nations. 16The people of Israel will no longer trust in Egypt. Instead, Egypt will remind them of how they sinned when they turned to it for help. Then they will know that I am the LORD and King."

17It was the 27th year since King Jehoiachin had been brought to Babylon as a prisoner. On the first day of the first month, a message came to me from the LORD. He said, **18**"Son of man, Nebuchadnezzar, the king of Babylonia, drove his army in a hard military campaign against Tyre. Their helmets rubbed their heads bare. The heavy loads they carried made their shoulders raw. But he and his army did not gain anything from the campaign he led against Tyre.

19"So I am going to give Egypt to Nebuchadnezzar, the king of Babylonia. He will carry off its wealth. He will take away anything else you have. He will give it to his army. **20**I have given Egypt to him as a reward for his efforts. After all, he and his army attacked Egypt because I told them to," announces the LORD and King.

21"When Nebuchadnezzar wins the battle over Egypt, I will make the people of Israel strong again. Ezekiel, I will open your mouth. And you will be able to speak to them. Then they will know that I am the LORD."

A Song of Sadness About Egypt

30 A message came to me from the LORD. He said, **2**"Son of man, prophesy. Say, 'The LORD and King says,

" ' "Cry out,
    'A terrible day is coming!'
3 The day is near.
    The day of the LORD is coming.
    It will be a cloudy day.
    The nations have been sentenced to
        die.
4 I will send Nebuchadnezzar's sword
        against Egypt.
    Cush will suffer terribly.
    Many will die in Egypt.
    Then its wealth will be carried away.
    Its foundations will be torn down.

5 The people of Cush, Put, Lydia, Libya and the whole land of Arabia will be killed with swords. So will the Jews who live in Egypt. They went there from the covenant land of Israel. And the Egyptians will die too." ' "

6 The LORD says,

"Those who were going to help Egypt
        will die.
    The strength Egypt was so proud of
        will fail.
    Its people will be killed with swords
        from Migdol all the way to Aswan,"
            announces the LORD and King.
7 "Egypt will be more empty than any
        other land.

    Its cities will be completely
        destroyed.
8 I will set Egypt on fire.
    All those who came to help it will be
        crushed.
    Then they will know that I am the
        LORD.

9 "At that time I will send messengers out in ships. They will terrify the people of Cush who are so contented. Cush will suffer greatly when Egypt falls. And you can be sure it will fall."

10 The LORD and King says,

"I will put an end to the huge armies of
        Egypt.
    I will use Nebuchadnezzar, the king
        of Babylonia, to do it.
11 He and his armies will attack the land
        and destroy it.
    They will not show its people any
        pity at all.
    They will use their swords against
        Egypt.
    They will fill the land with dead
        bodies.
12 I will dry up the streams of the Nile
        River.
    I will sell the land to evil men.
    I will use the powerful hands of
        strangers
    to destroy the land and everything
        in it.

"I have spoken. I am the LORD."

13 The LORD and King says,

"I will destroy the statues of Egypt's
        gods.
    I will put an end to the gods
    the people in Memphis worship.
    Egypt will not have princes anymore.
    I will spread fear all through the
        land.
14 I will completely destroy Upper Egypt.
    I will set Zoan on fire.
    I will punish Thebes.
15 I will pour out my burning anger on
        Pelusium.
    It is a fort in eastern Egypt.
    I will cut off the huge army of
        Thebes.
16 I will set Egypt on fire.
    Pelusium will groan with terrible
        pain.
    Thebes will be ripped apart.
    Memphis will suffer greatly
    because of everything that happens.
17 The young men of Heliopolis and
        Bubastis
    will be killed with swords.

Their people will be taken away as
prisoners.
18 I will break Egypt's power over other
lands.
That will be a dark day for
Tahpanhes.
There the strength Egypt was so proud
of
will come to an end.
Egypt will be covered with clouds.
The people in its villages
will be taken away as prisoners.
19 So I will punish Egypt.
Then they will know that I am the
LORD."

20 It was the 11th year since King Jehoiachin had been brought to Babylon as
a prisoner. On the seventh day of the first
month, a message came to me from the
LORD. He said, 21 "Son of man, I have broken the powerful arm of Pharaoh Hophra,
the king of Egypt. No bandages have been
put on his arm to heal it. It has not been
put in a cast. So his arm will not be strong
enough to use a sword. 22 I am against
Pharaoh, the king of Egypt. I will break
both of his arms. I will break his healthy
arm and his broken one. His sword will
fall from his hand. 23 I will scatter the people of Egypt among the nations. I will
send them to other countries.

24 "I will make the arms of the king of
Babylonia stronger. I will put my sword in
his hand. But I will break the arms of
Pharaoh. And he will groan in front of
Nebuchadnezzar. He will cry out like
someone dying from his wounds. 25 I will
make the arms of the king of Babylonia
stronger. But the arms of Pharaoh will not
be able to help Egypt. I will put my sword
in Nebuchadnezzar's hand. He will get
ready to use it against Egypt. Then they
will know that I am the LORD.

26 "I will scatter the Egyptians among
the nations. I will send them to other
countries. Then they will know that I am
the LORD."

A Cedar Tree in Lebanon

31 It was the 11th year since King Jehoiachin had been brought to
Babylon as a prisoner. On the first day of
the third month, a message came to me
from the LORD. He said, 2 "Son of man,
speak to Pharaoh Hophra, the king of
Egypt. Also speak to his huge army. Tell
him,

" 'Who can be compared with your
majesty?

3 Think about what happened to
Assyria.
Once it was like a cedar tree in
Lebanon.
It had beautiful branches
that provided shade for the forest.
It grew very high.
Its top was above all of the leaves.
4 The waters fed it.
Deep springs made it grow tall.
Their streams flowed
all around its base.
They made their way
to all of the trees in the fields.
5 So it grew higher
than any other tree in the fields.
It grew more limbs.
Its branches grew long.
They spread because they had
plenty of water.
6 All of the birds of the air
made their nests in its limbs.
All of the wild animals
had their babies under its branches.
All of the great nations
lived in its shade.
7 Its spreading branches
made it majestic and beautiful.
Its roots went down deep
to where there was plenty of water.
8 The cedar trees in my garden
were no match for it.
The pine trees
could not equal its limbs.
The plane trees
could not compare with its
branches.
No tree in my garden
could match its beauty.
9 I gave it many branches.
They made it beautiful.
All of the trees in my Garden of Eden
were jealous of it.' "

10 So the LORD and King says, "The cedar
tree grew very high. Its top was above all
of the leaves. It was proud of how tall it
was. 11 So I handed it over to the Babylonian ruler of the nations. I wanted him to
punish it because it was so evil. I decided
to get rid of it.

12 "The Babylonians cut it down and
left it there. They did not show it any pity
at all. Some of its branches fell on the
mountains. Others fell in all of the valleys. They lay broken in all of the stream
beds in the land. All of the nations on
earth came out from under its shade. And
they went on their way. 13 All of the birds
of the air settled on the fallen tree. All of

the wild animals moved among its branches.

14"So trees that receive plenty of water must never grow so high that it makes them proud. Their tops must never be above the rest of the leaves. No other trees that receive a lot of water must ever grow that high. They are appointed to die and go down into the earth below. They will join the other nations that go down into the grave."

15The LORD and King says, "Assyria was like a cedar tree. But I brought it down to the grave. On that day I dried up the deep springs of water and covered them. I held its streams back. I shut off its rich supply of water. Because of that, Lebanon was dressed in darkness as if it were clothes. All of the trees in the fields dried up.

16"I brought the cedar tree down to the grave. It joined the other nations that go down there. I made the nations on earth shake because of the sound of its fall. Then all of the trees of Eden were comforted in the earth below. That included the finest and best trees in Lebanon. And it included all the trees that received plenty of water **17**Others also went down into the grave along with it. That included those that lived in its shade. And it included those nations that were going to help it. They joined those who had been killed with swords.

18"Which one of the trees of Eden can be compared with you? What tree is as glorious and majestic as you are? But you too will be brought down to the earth below. There you will join the trees of Eden. You will lie down with those who have not been circumcised. You will be among those who were killed with swords.

"That is what will happen to Pharaoh and his huge armies," announces the LORD and King.

A Song of Sadness About Pharaoh

32 It was the 12th year since King Jehoiachin had been brought to Babylon as a prisoner. On the first day of the 12th month, a message came to me from the LORD. He said, **2**"Son of man, sing a song of sadness about Pharaoh Hophra, the king of Egypt. Tell him,

" 'You are like a lion among the
nations.
You are like a monster in the sea.
You move around wildly in your rivers.
You churn the water with your feet.
You make the streams muddy.' "

3The LORD and King says,

"I will use a large crowd of people
to throw my net over you.
They will pull you up in it.
4Then I will throw you on the land.
I will toss you into an open field.
I will let all of the birds of the air settle
on you.
I will let all of the wild animals eat
you up.
5I will scatter the parts of your body all
over the mountains.
I will fill the valleys with your
remains.
6I will soak the land with your blood.
It will flow all the way to the
mountains.
The valleys will be filled with the
parts of your body.
7When I wipe you out,
I will put a cover over the heavens.
I will darken the stars.
I will cover the sun with a cloud.
The moon will stop shining.
8I will darken all of the bright lights
in the sky above you.
I will bring darkness over your land,"
announces the LORD and King.
9"The hearts of many people will be
troubled.
That is because I will destroy you
among the nations.
You had never known anything
about those lands before.
10Many nations will be shocked
when they see what has happened
to you.
Their kings will tremble with fear
when they find out about it.
I will get ready to use Nebuchadnezzar
as my sword against them.
On the day you fall from power,
each of the kings will tremble with
fear.
Each will be afraid he is the next to
die."

11The LORD and King says,

"I will send against you
the sword of the king of Babylonia.
12I will destroy your huge army.
They will be killed with the swords
of Babylonia's mighty soldiers.
The soldiers will not show them any
pity.
They will bring Egypt down in all of
its pride.
Its huge armies will be thrown
down.
13I will destroy all of its cattle
from the places where they have
plenty of water.

Human feet will never stir the water up
again.
The hoofs of cattle will not make it
muddy anymore.
14 I will let the waters of Egypt settle.
I will make its streams flow like olive
oil,"
announces the LORD and King.
15 "I will turn Egypt into an empty land.
I will strip away everything in it.
I will strike down everyone who lives
there.
Then they will know that I am the
LORD.

16 "That is the song of sadness people
will sing about Egypt. Women from other
nations will sing it. They will sob over
Egypt and its huge armies," announces
the LORD and King.

17 It was the 15th day of a month near
the end of the 12th year since King Jehoiachin had been brought to Babylon as
a prisoner. A message came to me from
the LORD. He said, 18 "Son of man, sob over
the huge army of Egypt. Tell the Egyptians
they will go down into the earth below.
The women singers from the other
mighty nations will go down into the
grave along with them and others.

19 "Tell them, 'Are you any better than
others? Since you are not, go down there.
Lie down with those who have not been
circumcised.'

20 "They will fall dead among those
who were killed with swords. Nebuchadnezzar is ready to use his sword against
them. Let Egypt be dragged off together
with its huge armies.

21 "The mighty leaders who are already
in the grave will talk about Egypt. They
will also speak about the nations that
were going to help it. They will say, 'They
have come down here. They are lying
down with those who had not been circumcised. They are here with those who
were killed with swords.'

22 "Assyria is there with its whole army.
Its king is surrounded by the graves of all
of its people who were killed with swords.
23 Their graves are deep down in the pit.
Assyria's army lies around the grave of its
king. All those who spread terror while
they were alive are now dead. They were
killed with swords.

24 "Elam is also there. Its huge armies lie
around the grave of its king. All those who
spread terror while they were alive are
now dead. They were killed with swords.
They had not been circumcised. They
went down into the earth below. Their

shame is like the shame of others who go
down into the grave.

25 "A bed is made for Elam's king among
the dead. His huge armies lie around his
grave. They had not been circumcised.
They were killed with swords. They had
spread terror while they were alive. So
now their shame is like the shame of others who go down into the grave. They lie
down among the dead.

26 "Meshech and Tubal are also there.
Their huge armies lie around the graves of
their kings. They had not been circumcised. They had spread their terror while
they were alive. So they were killed with
swords.

27 "They lie down with the other dead
soldiers who had not been circumcised.
They and their weapons had gone down
into the grave. Their swords had been
placed under their heads. They had
spread their terror while they were alive.
But now the shame of their sin covers
their bones.

28 "Pharaoh Hophra, you too will be
broken. You will lie down among those
who had not been circumcised. You will
be there with those who were killed with
swords.

29 "Edom is also there. So are its kings
and all of its princes. In spite of their power, they lie down with those who were
killed with swords. They lie down with
those who had not been circumcised.
They are there with others who went
down into the grave.

30 "All of the princes of the north are
there too. So are all of the people of Sidon.
They went down into the grave in dishon-
or. While they were alive, they used their
power to spread terror. They had never
been circumcised. But now they lie down
there with those who were killed with
swords. Their shame is like the shame of
others who go down into the grave.

31 "Pharaoh and his whole army will see
all of them. That will comfort him in spite
of the fact that his huge armies were killed
with swords," announces the LORD and
King. 32 "I let Pharaoh spread terror while
he was alive. But now he and his huge armies will be buried with those who had
not been circumcised. They will lie down
there with those who were killed with
swords," announces the LORD and King.

The LORD Warns Israel

33 A message came to me from the
LORD. He said, 2 "Son of man,
speak to the people of your own country.
Tell them, 'Suppose I send enemies

against a land. And its people choose one of their men to stand guard. ³He sees the enemies coming against the land. He blows a trumpet to warn the people.

⁴" 'Someone hears the trumpet. But he does not pay any attention to the warning. The enemies come and kill him. Then what happens to him will be his own fault. ⁵He heard the sound of the trumpet. But he did not pay any attention to the warning. So what happened to him was his own fault. If he had paid attention, he would have saved himself.

⁶" 'But suppose the guard sees the enemies coming. And he does not blow the trumpet to warn the people. The enemies come and kill one of them. Then his life has been taken away from him because he sinned. But I will hold the guard accountable for his death.'

⁷"Son of man, I have appointed you as a prophet to warn the people of Israel. So listen to my message. Give them a warning from me.

⁸"Suppose I say to a sinful person, 'You can be sure that you will die.' And suppose you do not try to get him to change his ways. Then he will die because he has sinned. And I will hold you accountable for his death.

⁹"But suppose you do warn that sinful person. You tell him to change his ways. But he does not do it. Then he will die because he has sinned. But you will have saved yourself.

¹⁰"Son of man, speak to the people of Israel. Tell them, 'You are saying, "Our sins and the wrong things we have done weigh us down. We are wasting away because we have sinned so much. So how can we live?" '

¹¹"Tell them, 'When sinful people die, it does not give me any joy. But when they turn away from their sins and live, that makes me very happy. And that is just as sure as I am alive,' announces the LORD and King. 'So turn away from your sins! Change your evil ways! Why should you die, people of Israel?'

¹²"Son of man, speak to the people of your own country. Tell them, 'The right things a godly person does will not save him when he does not obey the LORD. The wrong things a sinful person does will not destroy him when he turns away from them. If a godly person sins, he will not be allowed to live just because he used to do what is right.'

¹³"Suppose I tell someone who is godly that he will live. And he trusts in the fact that he used to do what was right. But

now he does what is evil. Then I will not remember any of the right things he has done. He will die because he has done so many evil things.

¹⁴"Suppose I say to a sinful person, 'You can be sure you will die.' And then he turns away from his sin. He does what is fair and right. ¹⁵He gives back what he took as security for a loan. He returns what he has stolen. He follows my rules that give life. He does not do what is evil. Then you can be sure he will live. He will not die. ¹⁶None of the sins he has committed will be held against him. He has done what is fair and right. So you can be sure he will live.

¹⁷"In spite of that, your people say, 'What the Lord does isn't fair.' But it is what you do that is not fair.

¹⁸"Suppose someone who is godly stops doing what is right. And he does what is evil. Then he will die because of it. ¹⁹But suppose a sinful person turns away from the evil things he has done. And he does what is fair and right. Then he will live by doing that.

²⁰"In spite of that, you people of Israel say, 'What the Lord does isn't fair.' But I will judge each of you based on how you have lived."

The LORD Explains Why Jerusalem Fell

²¹It was the 12th year since we had been brought to Babylonia as prisoners. On the fifth day of the tenth month, a man who had escaped from Jerusalem came to bring me a report. He said, "The city has fallen!"

²²The evening before the man arrived, the LORD put his strong hand on me. He opened my mouth before the man came to me in the morning. So my mouth was opened. I was no longer silent.

²³Then a message came to me from the LORD. He said, ²⁴"Son of man, the people who live in those broken-down buildings in Israel are saying, 'Abraham was only one man. But he owned the land. We are many people. The land must certainly belong to us.'

²⁵"So tell them, 'The LORD and King says, "You eat meat that still has blood in it. You worship your gods. You commit murder. So should you still possess the land? ²⁶You depend on your swords. You do things I hate. Each one of you has sex with your neighbor's wife. So should you still possess the land?" '

²⁷"Tell them, 'The LORD and King says, "The people who are left in those broken-

down buildings will be killed with swords. Wild animals will eat up those who are out in the country. Those who are in caves and other safe places will die of a plague. And that is just as sure as I am alive.

28 " ' "I will turn the land into a dry and empty desert. The strength Jerusalem is so proud of will come to an end. The mountains of Israel will be deserted. No one will travel across them. 29So I will turn the land into a dry and empty desert. I will punish my people because of all of the evil things they have done. I hate those things. They will know that I am the LORD." '

30"Son of man, your people are talking about you. They are getting together by the walls of their houses and at their doors. They are saying to one another, 'Come. Listen to the LORD's message.'

31"My people come to you, just as they usually do. They sit in front of you. They listen to what you say. But they do not put it into practice. With their mouths they claim to be faithful to me. But in their hearts they want what belongs to others. They try to get rich by cheating them. 32You are nothing more to them than someone who sings love songs. They say you have a beautiful voice. They think you play an instrument well. They listen to what you say. But they do not put it into practice.

33"Everything I have told you will come true. You can be sure of it. Then the people will know that a prophet has been among them."

The LORD Is the Shepherd of His People

34 A message came to me from the LORD. He said, 2"Son of man, prophesy against the shepherds of Israel. Tell them, 'The LORD and King says, "How terrible it will be for you shepherds of Israel! You only take care of yourselves. You should take good care of your flocks. 3Instead, you eat the butter. You dress yourselves with the wool. You kill the finest animals. But you do not take care of your flocks. 4You have not made the weak ones in the flock stronger. You have not healed the sick. You have not bandaged those that are hurt. You have not brought back those that have wandered away. You have not searched for the lost. When you ruled over them, you were mean to them. You treated them badly.

5" ' "So they were scattered because they did not have a shepherd. They became food for all of the wild animals. 6My sheep wandered all over the mountains and high hills. They were scattered over the whole earth. No one searched for them. No one looked for them."

7" 'Shepherds, listen to the LORD's message. 8He says, "My flock does not have a shepherd. Many of my sheep have been stolen. They have become food for all of the wild animals. My shepherds did not care for my sheep. They did not even search for them. Instead, they only took care of themselves. And that is just as sure as I am alive," announces the LORD and King.

9" 'Shepherds, listen to the LORD's message. 10The LORD and King says, "I am against the shepherds. I will hold them accountable for my flock. I will stop them from taking care of the flock. Then they will not be able to feed themselves anymore. I will save my flock from their mouths. My sheep will no longer be food for them." ' "

11The LORD and King says, "I myself will search for my sheep. I will look after them. 12A shepherd looks after his scattered flock when he is with them. And I will look after my sheep. I will save them from all of the places where they were scattered on a dark and cloudy day.

13"I will bring them out from among the nations. I will gather them together from other countries. I will bring them into their own land. They will eat grass on the mountains of Israel. I will also let them eat in the valleys and in all of the places in the land where people live. 14I will take care of them in the best grasslands. They will eat grass on the high mountains of Israel. There they will lie down in the finest grasslands. They will eat grass in the best places on Israel's mountains.

15"I myself will take care of my sheep. I will let them lie down in safety," announces the LORD and King. 16"I will search for the lost. I will bring back those that have wandered away. I will bandage the ones that are hurt. I will make the weak ones stronger. But I will destroy those that are fat and strong. I will take good care of my sheep. I will treat them fairly."

17The LORD and King says, "You are my flock. I will judge between one sheep and another. I will judge between rams and goats. 18You already eat in the best grasslands. Must you also stomp all over the other fields? You already drink clear water. Must you also make the rest of the water muddy with your feet? 19Must my flock have to eat the grass you have stomped on? Must they drink the water you have made muddy?"

²⁰So the LORD and King speaks to them. He says, "I myself will judge between the fat sheep and the skinny sheep. ²¹You push the other sheep around with your hips and shoulders. You use your horns to butt all of the weak sheep. Finally, you drive them away. ²²But I will save my sheep. They will not be carried off anymore. I will judge between one sheep and another.

²³"I will place one shepherd over them. He will belong to the family line of my servant David. He will take good care of them. He will look after them. He will be their shepherd. ²⁴I am the LORD. I will be their God. And my servant from David's line will be prince among them. I have spoken. I am the LORD.

²⁵"I will make a covenant with them. It promises to give them peace. I will get rid of the wild animals in the land. Then my sheep can live safely in the desert. They can sleep in the forests.

²⁶"I will bless them. I will also bless the places surrounding my holy mountain of Zion. I will send down rain at the right time. There will be showers of blessing. ²⁷The trees in the fields will bear their fruit. And the ground will produce its crops. The people will be secure in their land. I will break the chains that hold them. I will save them from the powerful hands of those who made them slaves. Then they will know that I am the LORD.

²⁸"The nations will not carry them off anymore. Wild animals will no longer eat them up. They will live in safety. And no one will make them afraid. ²⁹I will give them a land that is famous for its crops. They will never be hungry there again. The nations will not make fun of them anymore.

³⁰"Then they will know that I am with them. I am the LORD their God. And they will know that they are my people Israel," announces the LORD and King.

³¹"You are the sheep belonging to my flock. You are my people. And I am your God," announces the LORD and King.

A Message About Edom

35 A message came to me from the LORD. He said, ²"Son of man, turn your attention to Mount Seir. Prophesy against it. ³Tell it, 'The LORD and King says, "Mount Seir, I am against you. I will reach out my powerful hand against you. I will turn you into a dry and empty desert.

⁴I will destroy your towns. Your land will become empty. Then you will know that I am the LORD.

⁵"'"People of Edom, you have been Israel's enemies for a long time. You let many Israelites be killed with swords when they were in great trouble. At that time I used Nebuchadnezzar to punish them and destroy them completely. ⁶Now I will hand you over to murderers. They will hunt you down. You murdered others. So murderers will chase you. And that is just as sure as I am alive," announces the LORD and King.

⁷"'"I will turn Mount Seir into a dry and empty desert. No one will be able to go anywhere or do anything there. ⁸I will fill your mountains with dead bodies. Some of those who are killed with swords will fall down dead on your hills. Others will die in your valleys and in all of your canyons. ⁹I will make your land empty forever. No one will live in your towns. Then you will know that I am the LORD.

¹⁰"'"You said, 'The nations of Israel and Judah will belong to us. We will take them over.' You said that, even though I was there. I am the LORD. ¹¹You were full of anger, jealousy and hatred toward my people. So I will punish you. When I judge you, they will know that I am the LORD. And that is just as sure as I am alive," announces the LORD and King.

¹²"'"You will know that I have heard all of the terrible things you said about those who live in the mountains of Israel. You made fun of them. You said, 'They have been destroyed. They've been handed over to us. Let's wipe them out.' ¹³You bragged that you were better than I am. You spoke against me. You did not hold anything back. But I heard it."'"

¹⁴The LORD and King says, "The whole earth will be glad. But I will make your land empty. ¹⁵You were happy when the land of Israel became empty. So I will treat you in the same way. Mount Seir, you will be empty. So will the whole land of Edom. Then you will know that I am the LORD."

A Message About Israel

36 "Son of man, prophesy to the mountains of Israel. Tell them, 'Mountains of Israel, listen to the LORD's message. ²The LORD and King says, "Your enemies made fun of you. They bragged, 'The hills you lived in for a long time belong to us now.'"'

³"Ezekiel, prophesy. Say, 'The LORD and King says, "Your enemies destroyed you. They hunted you down from every side.

So the rest of the nations took over your land. People talked about you. They told lies about you." ' "

4Mountains of Israel, listen to the message of the LORD and King. He speaks to you mountains, hills, canyons and valleys. He speaks to you destroyed cities and deserted towns. The rest of the nations around you took everything of value away from you. They made fun of you. **5**So the LORD and King says, "My anger burns against those nations. I have spoken against them and the whole land of Edom. They were very happy when they took over my land. Deep down inside them they hated Israel. They wanted to take its grasslands.

6"Ezekiel, prophesy about the land of Israel. Speak to the mountains, hills, canyons and valleys. Tell them, 'The LORD and King says, "My jealous anger burns against the nations. They have laughed at you." **7**So the LORD and King says, "I raise my hand and take an oath. I promise that the nations around you will also be laughed at.

8" ' "Mountains of Israel, you will produce branches and bear fruit for my people Israel. They will come home soon. **9**I am concerned about you. I will look on you with favor. Farmers will plow your ground. They will plant seeds in it.

10" ' "I will multiply the number of people who live in Israel. The towns will no longer be empty. Their broken-down houses will be rebuilt. **11**I will increase the number of your people and animals. They will have many babies. I will settle people in your towns, just as I did in the past. I will help you succeed more than ever before. Then you will know that I am the LORD.

12" ' "I will let my people Israel walk there again. They will possess you. They will receive you as their own. You will never take their children away from them again." ' "

13The LORD and King says, "People say to you mountains, 'You destroy people. You let your nation's children be taken away.' **14**But I will not let you destroy people anymore. I will no longer let your nation's children be taken away," announces the LORD and King.

15"You will not have to listen to the nations laughing at you anymore. People will no longer make fun of you. You will not let your nation fall," announces the LORD and King.

16Another message came to me from the LORD. He said, **17**"Son of man, the peo-

ple of Israel used to live in their own land. But they polluted it because of how they acted and the way they lived. To me they were 'unclean' like a woman who was having her monthly period.

18"They spilled people's blood in the land. They polluted the land by worshiping other gods. So I poured out my burning anger on them. **19**I scattered them among the nations. I sent them to other countries. I judged them based on how they acted and the way they lived.

20"They treated my name as if it were not holy. They did it everywhere they went among the nations. People said about them, 'They are the LORD's people. But they were forced to leave his land.' **21**I was concerned about my holy name. The people of Israel treated it as if it were not holy. They did it everywhere they went among the nations.

22"But tell the people of Israel, 'The LORD and King speaks. He says, "People of Israel, I will not take action for your benefit. Instead, I will act for the honor of my holy name. You have treated it as if it were not holy. You did it everywhere you went among the nations. **23**But I will show everyone how holy my great name is. You have treated it as if it were not holy. So I will use you to show the nations how holy I am. Then they will know that I am the LORD," announces the LORD and King.

24" ' "I will take you out of the nations. I will gather you together from all of the countries. I will bring you back into your own land.

25" ' "I will sprinkle pure water on you. Then you will be 'clean.' I will make you completely pure and clean. I will take all of the statues of your gods away from you. **26**I will give you new hearts. I will give you a new spirit that is faithful to me. I will remove your stubborn hearts from you. I will give you hearts that obey me.

27" ' "I will put my Spirit in you. I will move you to follow my rules. I want you to be careful to keep my laws. **28**You will live in the land I gave your people long ago. You will be my people. And I will be your God.

29" ' "I will save you from all of your 'uncleanness.' I will give you plenty of grain. You will have more than enough. So you will never be hungry again. **30**I will multiply the fruit on your trees. I will increase the crops in your fields. Then the nations will no longer make fun of you because you are hungry.

31" ' "You will remember your evil ways and the sinful things you have done. You will hate yourselves because you have sinned so much. I also hate your evil practices. **32**I want you to know that I am not doing those things for your benefit," announces the LORD and King. "People of Israel, you should be ashamed of yourselves! Your conduct has brought dishonor to you." ' "

33The LORD and King says, "I will make you pure from all of your sins. On that day I will settle you in your towns again. Your broken-down houses will be rebuilt. **34**The dry and empty land will be farmed again.

"Everyone who passes through it will see that it is no longer empty. **35**They will say, 'This land was completely destroyed. But now it's like the Garden of Eden. The cities were full of broken-down buildings. They were destroyed and empty. But now they have high walls around them. And people live in them.'

36"Then the nations that remain around you will know that I have rebuilt what was once destroyed. I have planted again the fields that were once empty. I have spoken. And I will do it. I am the LORD."

37The LORD and King says, "Once again I will answer the prayers of the people of Israel. Here is what I will do for them. I will multiply them as if they were sheep. **38**Large flocks of animals are sacrificed at Jerusalem during the appointed feasts there. In the same way, the destroyed cit-

ies will be filled with flocks of people. Then they will know that I am the LORD."

Israel's Dry Bones Will Come to Life Again

37 The LORD put his strong hand on me. His Spirit brought me away from my home. He put me down in the middle of a valley. It was full of bones. **2**He led me back and forth among them. I saw a huge number of bones in the valley. The bones were very dry.

3The LORD asked me, "Son of man, can these bones live?"

I said, "LORD and King, you are the only one who knows."

4Then he said to me, "Prophesy to these bones. Tell them, 'Dry bones, listen to the LORD's message. **5**The LORD and King speaks to you. He says, "I will put breath in you. Then you will come to life again. **6**I will attach tendons to you. I will put flesh on you. I will cover you with skin. So I will put breath in you. And you will come to life again. Then you will know that I am the LORD." ' "

7So I prophesied just as the LORD commanded me to. As I was prophesying, I heard a noise. It was a rattling sound. The bones came together. One bone connected itself to another. **8**I saw tendons and flesh appear on them. Skin covered them. But there was no breath in them.

9Then the LORD said to me, "Prophesy to the breath. Prophesy, son of man. Tell it, 'The LORD and King says, "Breath, come from all four directions. Go into these dead bodies. Then they can live." ' "

10So I prophesied just as he commanded me to. And the breath entered them. Then they came to life again. They stood up on their feet. They were like a huge army.

11Then the LORD said to me, "Son of man, these bones stand for all of the people of Israel. The people say, 'Our bones are dried up. We've lost all hope. We are cut off.'

12"So prophesy. Tell them, 'The LORD and King says, "My people, I am going to open up your graves. I am going to bring you out of them. I will take you back to the land of Israel. **13**So I will open up your graves and bring you out of them. Then you will know that I am the LORD. You are my people. **14**I will put my Spirit in you. And you will live again. I will settle you in your own land. Then you will know that I have spoken. I have done it," announces the LORD.' "

POWER-SURGE

FAITHFUL

I WILL GIVE YOU NEW HEARTS. I WILL GIVE YOU A NEW SPIRIT THAT IS FAITHFUL TO ME. I WILL REMOVE YOUR STUBBORN HEARTS FROM YOU. I WILL GIVE YOU HEARTS THAT OBEY ME.

— EZEKIEL 36:26 —

OBEYS

EZEKIEL

✝

✔

Ⓦ

> *The LORD put his strong hand on me. His Spirit brought me away from my home. He put me down in the middle of a valley. It was full of bones.*

Ezekiel (ee-ZEKE-yul) raised his head up from the dry grass. His mouth felt dry. His eyes seemed stuck shut. He knew God's Spirit had brought him to this valley, but he didn't remember how. Ezekiel blinked and tried to see what new vision God had for him.

Ezekiel stood up and began to look around. **EVERYWHERE HE LOOKED, HE SAW BONES.** Old bones. Human bones. The sight filled Ezekiel with dread and horror. What could a vision like this one mean?

God's voice boomed in Ezekiel's ears, "Ezekiel! Can these bones live?" *Well, now,* Ezekiel thought. *That's a strange question. These bones are old and dry and worthless. Of course, they can't live. Unless...*Ezekiel was wise enough to know that God could make something as dead as these bones alive again. So he answered, "Only you know these things, Lord."

Now God told Ezekiel to talk to the bones, to tell them God wanted them to live again. Ezekiel obeyed God and began to talk. As he talked, his ears were filled with unusual sounds—rattling, clinking and clattering. The bones began to connect with each other, and then muscles covered the bones and skin covered the muscles. Ezekiel kept talking, his eyes growing bigger and bigger at the sight before him.

When God spoke, Ezekiel began to understand what all this meant. The bones stood for the people of Israel. The people were now "dead" as a nation, in slavery in another country. But God would bring them back again and make a living, breathing nation of them again. Why? Because he loved them.

Over and over Ezekiel had visions that held messages from God for the people of Israel.

BE AN EZEKIEL

You'll probably never have visions from God of dry bones. But through the Bible and other believers, God can speak to you. Are you listening? Be like Ezekiel, listen to God's messages to you, and know that he loves you!

EZEKIEL LISTENED TO GOD.
THE WHOLE STORY: EZEKIEL 37:1-14

Go to page 995 for the next Super Hero

Israel Will Be One Nation Under One King

15A message came to me from the LORD. He said, **16**"Son of man, get a stick of wood. Write on it, 'Belonging to the tribe of Judah and the Israelites who are connected with it.' Then get another stick. Write on it, 'Ephraim's stick. Belonging to the tribes of Joseph and all of the Israelites connected with them.' **17**Join them together into one stick in your hand.

18"The people of your own country will ask you, 'What do you mean by this?' **19**Tell them, 'The LORD and King says, "I am going to get the stick of Joseph and the Israelites connected with it. That stick is in Ephraim's hand. I am going to join it to Judah's stick. They will become a single stick of wood in my hand."'

20"Show them the sticks you wrote on. **21**Tell them, 'The LORD and King says, "I will take the Israelites out of the nations where they have gone. I will gather them together from all around. I will bring them back to their own land. **22**There I will make them one nation. They will live on the mountains of Israel. All of them will have one king. They will never be two nations again. They will never again be separated into two kingdoms.

23"'"They will no longer pollute themselves by worshiping any of their evil gods. They will not do wrong things anymore. They always turn away from me. But I will save them from that sin. I will make them pure and clean. They will be my people. And I will be their God.

24"'"A man who belongs to the family line of my servant David will be their king. All of them will have one shepherd. They will follow my laws. And they will be careful to keep my rules. **25**They will live in the land I gave to my servant Jacob. That is where your people lived long ago. They, their children, their children's children, and their children after them will live there forever. And my servant from David's line will be their prince forever.

26"'"I will make a covenant with them. It promises to give them peace. The covenant will last forever. I will make them my people. And I will increase their numbers. I will put my temple among them forever. **27**I will live with them. I will be their God. And they will be my people. **28**My temple will be among them forever. Then the nations will know that I make Israel holy. I am the LORD."'"

A Message About Gog

38 A message came to me from the LORD. He said, **2**"Son of man, turn your attention to Gog. He is from the land of Magog. He is the chief prince of Meshech and Tubal. Prophesy against him.

3"Tell him, 'The LORD and King says, "Gog, I am against you. You are the chief prince of Meshech and Tubal. **4**But I will turn you around. I will put hooks in your jaws. I will bring you out of your land along with your whole army. Your horses will come with you. Your horsemen will be completely armed. Your huge army will carry large and small shields. All of them will be ready to use their swords.

5"'"The men of Persia, Cush and Put will march out with them. All of them will have shields and helmets. **6**Gomer and all of its troops will be there too. Beth Togarmah from the far north will also come with all of its troops. Many nations will help you.

7"'"Get ready. Be prepared. Take command of the huge armies that are gathered around you. **8**After many years you will be called together to fight. Later, you will march into a land that has not had war for a while. Its people were gathered together from many nations. They came to the mountains of Israel. No one had lived in those mountains for a long time. So the people had been brought back from other nations. Now all of the people live in safety. **9**You, all of your troops and the many nations with you will march up to attack them. All of you will advance like a storm. You will be like a cloud covering their land."

10"'The LORD and King says, "At that time some ideas will come to you. You will make evil plans. **11**You will say, 'I will march out against a land whose villages don't have walls around them. I'll attack those peaceful people. I'll do it when they aren't expecting it. None of their villages has walls or gates with heavy metal bars on them.

12"'"'I will rob those people. I'll steal everything they have. Then I'll turn my attention to the destroyed houses where people are living again. They have returned there from other nations. Now they are rich. They have plenty of livestock and all kinds of goods. They are living in Israel. It is the center of the earth.'

13"'"The people of Sheba and Dedan will speak to you. So will the traders of Tarshish and all of its villages. They will say, 'Have you come to rob us? Have you gathered your huge army together to steal our silver and gold? Are you going to take our livestock and goods away from us? Do you plan to carry off everything we have?' " '

¹⁴"Son of man, prophesy. Tell Gog, 'The LORD and King says, "A time is coming when my people Israel will be living in safety. You will see that it is a good time to attack them. ¹⁵So you will come from your place in the far north. Many nations will join you. All of their men will be riding on horses. You will have a huge and mighty army. ¹⁶They will advance against my people Israel. They will be like a cloud covering their land. Gog, in days to come I will bring you against my land. Then the nations will know me. I will use you to show them how holy I am."

¹⁷" 'The LORD and King says to Gog, "In the past I spoke about you through my servants, the prophets of Israel. At that time they prophesied for years that I would bring you against them. ¹⁸Here is what will happen in days to come. You will attack the land of Israel. That will stir up my hot anger," announces the LORD and King.

¹⁹" ' "At that time my burning anger will blaze out at you. There will be a great earthquake in the land of Israel. ²⁰The fish in the sea, the birds of the air and the wild animals will tremble with fear because of what I will do. So will every creature that moves along the ground. And so will all of the people on earth. The mountains will come crashing down. The cliffs will break into pieces. Every wall will fall to the ground.

²¹" ' "I will punish you on all of my mountains," announces the LORD and King. "Your men will use their swords against one another. ²²I will judge you. I will send a plague against you. A lot of blood will be spilled. I will send heavy rain, hailstones and burning sulfur down to the earth. They will fall on you and your troops. They will also come down on the many nations that are helping you. ²³That will show how great and holy I am. I will make myself known to many nations. Then they will know that I am the LORD." '

39 "Son of man, prophesy against Gog. Tell him, 'The LORD and King says, "Gog, I am against you. You are the chief prince of Meshech and Tubal. ²But I will turn you around. I will drag you along. I will bring you from the far north. I will send you against the mountains of Israel. ³Then I will knock your bow out of your left hand. I will make your arrows drop from your right hand.

⁴" ' "You will fall dead on the mountains of Israel. You and all of your troops will die there. So will the nations that join you. I will feed you to all kinds of birds that eat dead bodies. So they and the wild animals will eat you up. ⁵You will fall dead in the open fields. I have spoken," announces the LORD and King.

⁶" ' "I will send fire on the land of Magog. It will burn up the people who live in safety on the coast. So they will know that I am the LORD.

⁷" ' "I will make my holy name known among my people Israel. I will no longer let them treat my name as if it were not holy. Then the nations will know that I am the Holy One in Israel. I am the LORD. ⁸The day I will judge you is coming. You can be sure of it," announces the LORD and King. "It is the day I have spoken about.

⁹" ' "At that time those who live in the towns of Israel will go out and light a fire. They will use it to burn up the weapons. That includes small and large shields. It also includes bows and arrows, war clubs and spears. It will take seven years to burn all of them up. ¹⁰People will not gather wood from the fields. They will not cut the forests down. Instead, they will burn the weapons. And they will rob those who robbed them. They will steal from those who stole from them," announces the LORD and King.

¹¹" ' "Gog, at that time I will bury you in a grave in Israel. It will be in the valley where people travel east of the Dead Sea. It will block the path of travelers. That is because you and your huge armies will be buried there. So it will be called The Valley of Gog's Armies.

¹²" ' "It will take seven months for the people of Israel to bury the bodies. They will do it to make the land 'clean' again. ¹³All of the people in the land will bury them. That will bring glory to me. It will be a time to remember," announces the LORD and King.

¹⁴" ' "After the seven months are over, men will be hired to finish the job of making the land 'clean' again. Some will go all through it. They will look for any remaining human bones on the ground. Other people will bury the bones. ¹⁵So some will go through the land. When they see a bone, they will put a marker beside it. Then those who dig the graves will take it to The Valley of Gog's Armies. There they will bury it. ¹⁶That is how they will make the land 'clean' again." ' " Also a town called Gog's Armies will be located there.

17The LORD and King said to me, "Son of man, speak to every kind of bird. Call out to all of the wild animals. Tell them, 'Gather together. Come from everywhere. Gather around the sacrifice I am preparing for you. It is the great sacrifice on the mountains of Israel. There you will eat human bodies and drink human blood.

18" 'You will eat the bodies of mighty men. You will drink the blood of the princes of the earth. You will eat their bodies and drink their blood as if they were rams and lambs, goats and bulls. You will enjoy it as if you were eating the fattest animals from Bashan.

19" 'So I am preparing a sacrifice for you. You will eat fat until you are completely full. You will drink blood until you are drunk. **20**At my table you will eat horses, riders, mighty men and soldiers until you are full,' announces the LORD and King.

21" 'I will show all of the nations my glory. They will see how I punish them when I use my powerful hand against them. **22**From that time on, the people of Israel will know that I am the LORD their God.

23" 'The nations will know that the people of Israel were taken away as prisoners because they sinned against me. They were not faithful to me. So I turned my face away from them. I handed them over to their enemies. All of them were killed with swords. **24**I punished them because they were "unclean." They did many things that were wrong. So I turned my face away from them.' "

25The LORD and King says, "I will now bring the people of Jacob back home again. I will show my tender love for all of the people of Israel. I will make sure that my name is kept holy.

26"My people will forget the shameful things they have done. They will not remember all of the ways they were unfaithful to me. They used to live in safety in their land. At that time no one made them afraid.

27"So I will bring them back from the nations. I will gather them from the countries of their enemies. And I will use them to show many nations how holy I am. **28**Then they will know that I am the LORD their God. I let the nations take my people away as prisoners. But now I will bring them back to their own land. I will not leave anyone behind. **29**I will no longer turn my face away from the people of Israel. I will pour out my Spirit on them," announces the LORD and King.

The New Temple Area

40 It was the 14th year after Jerusalem had been captured. It was the tenth day of a month near the beginning of the 25th year since we had been brought to Babylonia as prisoners. On that very day the LORD put his strong hand on me. He took me back to my land. **2**In visions God gave me, he brought me to the land of Israel. He set me on a very high mountain. Some buildings were on the south side of it. They looked like a city.

3He took me there. I saw a man who appeared to be made out of bronze. He was standing at the gate of the outer courtyard. He was holding a linen measuring tape and a measuring rod. **4**The man said to me, "Son of man, look with your eyes. Listen with your ears. Pay attention to everything I show you. That is why the LORD brought you here. Tell the people of Israel everything you see."

The East Gate to the Outer Courtyard

5I saw a wall that completely surrounded the temple area. The measuring rod in the man's hand was ten and a half feet long. He measured the wall with it. The wall was as thick and as high as one measuring rod.

6Then the man went to the gate that faced east. He climbed its steps. He measured the gateway. It was one rod wide. **7**The rooms where the guards stood were one rod long and one rod wide. The walls between the rooms were almost nine feet thick. The gateway next to the porch was one rod wide. The porch faced the front of the temple.

8Then the man measured the porch of the gateway. **9**It was 14 feet wide. Each of its doorposts was three and a half feet thick. The porch of the gateway faced the front of the temple.

10Inside the east gate were three rooms on each side. All of the rooms were the same size. The walls on each side of the rooms had the same thickness.

11Then the man measured the entrance of the gateway. It was 17 and a half feet wide and almost 23 feet long. **12**In front of each room was a wall. It was 21 inches high. The rooms measured ten and a half feet on each side.

13Then he measured the gateway from the back wall of one room to the back wall of the room across from it. It was almost 44 feet from the top of one wall to the top of the other.

14He measured along the front of the

side walls that were all around the inside of the gateway. The total was 105 feet. That didn't include the porch that faced the courtyard. **15**It was 87 and a half feet from the entrance of the gateway to the far end of its porch.

16The rooms and their side walls inside the gateway had narrow openings on top of them. So did the porch. All of the openings faced the inside. The front of each side wall was decorated with a palm tree.

The Outer Courtyard

17Then the man brought me into the outer courtyard. There I saw some rooms and a sidewalk. They had been built all around the courtyard. Along the sidewalk were 30 rooms. **18**The sidewalk went all the way up to the sides of the gateways. It was as wide as they were long. That was the lower sidewalk.

19Then he measured from the inside of the lower gateway to the outside of the inner courtyard. The east side measured 175 feet. So did the north side.

The North Gate

20Then the man measured the gate that faced north. He wanted to show me how long and wide it was. The gate led into the outer courtyard. **21**It had three rooms on each side. Their side walls and porch measured the same as the ones at the first gateway. They measured 87 and a half feet long and almost 44 feet wide. **22**Its openings, porch and palm tree decorations measured the same as the ones at the east gate. Seven steps led up to the north gate. Its porch was across from them.

23The inner courtyard had a gate. It faced the gate on the north. It was just like the east gate. He measured from one gate to the one across from it. The total was 175 feet.

The South Gate

24Then the man led me to the south side of the courtyard. There I saw a gate that faced south. He measured its doorposts and porch. They measured the same as the others. **25**The gateway and its porch had narrow openings all around. The openings were the same as the others had. The side walls and porch measured 87 and a half feet long and almost 44 feet wide. **26**Seven steps led up to it. Its porch was across from them. The front of each side wall was decorated with a palm tree.

27The inner courtyard also had a gate that faced south. The man measured from that gate to the outer gate on the south side. The total was 175 feet.

The Gates to the Inner Courtyard

28Then the man brought me into the inner courtyard. We went through the south gate. He measured it. It was the same size as the others. **29**Its rooms, side walls and porch measured the same as the ones at the other gateways. The gateway and its porch had openings all around. The side walls and porch measured 87 and a half feet long and almost 44 feet wide. **30**The porches of the gateways around the inner courtyard were almost 44 feet wide and 9 feet long. **31**Its porch faced the outer courtyard. Palm trees decorated its doorposts. Eight steps led up to it.

32Then the man brought me to the east side of the inner courtyard. There he measured the gateway. It was the same size as the others. **33**Its rooms, side walls and porch measured the same as the ones at the other gateways. The gateway and its porch had openings all around. The side walls and porch measured 87 and a half feet long and almost 44 feet wide. **34**Its porch faced the outer courtyard. Each doorpost was decorated with a palm tree. Eight steps led up to the porch.

35Then the man brought me to the north gate. He measured it. It was the same size as the others. **36**Its rooms, side walls and porch measured the same as the ones at the other gateways. It had openings all around. The side walls and the porch measured 87 and a half feet long and almost 44 feet wide. **37**The porch faced the outer courtyard. Each doorpost was decorated with a palm tree. Eight steps led up to the porch.

The Rooms for Preparing Sacrifices

38A room with a doorway was by the porch of each inner gateway. The burnt offerings were washed there. **39**On each side of the porch of the gateway were two tables. The burnt offerings were killed on them. So were the sin offerings and guilt offerings.

40Two more tables were by the outer wall of the gateway porch. They were near the steps at the entrance of the north gateway. Two more tables were on the other side of the steps. **41**So there were four tables on each side of the gateway. The total number of tables was eight. Animals for sacrifice were killed on all of them.

42There were also four other tables for

the burnt offerings. They were made out of blocks of stone. Each table was two and a half feet long and two and a half feet wide. And each was almost two feet high. The tools for killing the burnt offerings and other sacrifices were placed on them. **43**Large hooks hung on the walls all around. Each was three inches long. The meat of the offerings was placed on the tables.

The Rooms for the Priests

44Near the inner gates were two rooms. They were in the inner courtyard. One room was next to the north gate. It faced south. The other one was next to the south gate. It faced north. **45**The man said to me, "The room that faces south is for the priests who are in charge of the temple. **46**The one that faces north is for the priests who are in charge of the altar. All of those priests are the sons of Zadok. They are the only Levites who can approach the Lord to serve him."

47Then the man measured the courtyard. It was square. It measured 175 feet long and 175 feet wide. And the altar was in front of the temple.

The Temple

48The man brought me to the porch of the temple. He measured the doorposts of the porch. Each of them was almost nine feet wide. The entrance was 24 and a half feet wide. Each of the side walls was a little over five feet wide. **49**The porch was 35 feet wide. It was 21 feet from front to back. It was reached by some stairs. Pillars were on each side of the doorposts.

41 Then the man brought me to the Holy Room in the temple. There he measured the doorposts. Each of them was ten and a half feet wide. **2**The entrance was 17 and a half feet wide. Each of its side walls was almost nine feet wide. He also measured the Holy Room. It was 70 feet long and 35 feet wide.

3Then he went into the Most Holy Room. There he measured the doorposts at the entrance. Each one of them was three and a half feet wide. The entrance itself was ten and a half feet wide. Each of its side walls was a little over 12 feet wide.

4He also measured the Most Holy Room. It was 35 feet long and 35 feet wide. He said to me, "This is the Most Holy Room." It was beyond the back wall of the Holy Room.

5Then the man measured the wall of the temple. It was ten and a half feet thick. Each side room around the temple was

seven feet wide. **6**The side rooms were on three floors. There were 30 rooms on each floor. Ledges had been built all around the wall of the temple. So the floor beams of the side rooms rested on the ledges. The beams didn't go into the temple wall. **7**The side rooms of the temple were wider as we went up floor by floor. A stairway went from the lowest floor all the way up to the top floor. It passed through the middle floor.

8I saw that the temple had a raised base all around it. The base formed the foundation of the side rooms. It was as long as one measuring rod. So it was ten and a half feet long. **9**The outer wall of each side room was almost nine feet thick. The open area between the side rooms of the temple **10**and the priests' rooms was 35 feet wide all around the temple. **11**The side rooms had entrances from the open area. One was on the north side. Another was on the south. The base next to the open area was almost nine feet wide all around.

12There was a large building right behind the temple. It was on the west side of the outer courtyard. It was 122 and a half feet wide. Its wall was almost nine feet thick all around. And it was 157 and a half feet long.

13Then the man measured the temple. It was 175 feet long. The open area and the large building behind the temple also measured 175 feet. **14**The east side of the inner courtyard was 175 feet wide. That included the front of the temple.

15Then the man measured the building that was on the west side of the outer courtyard. It was behind the temple. It was 175 feet long. That included the walkways of the building on each side.

The Holy Room, the Most Holy Room and the porch that faced the inner courtyard **16**were covered with wood. So were the gateways, narrow openings and walkways around those three places. The gateways and everything beyond them were covered with wood. The floor, the wall up to the openings, and the openings themselves were also covered.

17The area above the outside of the entrance to the Most Holy Room was decorated. There were also decorations all around the walls of the Most Holy Room. **18**Carved cherubim and palm trees were used in the decorations. Each cherub had a palm tree next to it. And each palm tree had a cherub next to it.

Each cherub had two faces. **19**One was a man's face. It looked toward the palm tree on one side. The other was the face of a lion. It looked toward the palm tree on the other side. The decorations were carved all around the whole temple.

20Cherubim and palm trees decorated the wall of the Holy Room. They were carved from the floor all the way up to the area above the entrance.

21The Holy Room had a doorframe that was shaped like a rectangle. So did the Most Holy Room. 22A wooden altar stood in the Holy Room. It was a little over five feet high. It was three and a half feet long and three and a half feet wide. Its corners, base and sides were made out of wood. The man said to me, "This is the table that stands in front of the LORD."

23The Holy Room had double doors. So did the Most Holy Room. 24Each door had two parts that could swing back and forth. 25Cherubim and palm trees were carved on the doors of the Holy Room. The decorations were like the ones on the walls. A wooden roof went out beyond the front of the porch. 26The side walls of the porch had narrow openings on top of them. Palm trees were carved on each side. A wooden roof went out beyond the entrance to each side room of the temple.

The Rooms for the Priests

42 Then the man led me north into the outer courtyard of the temple. He brought me to the rooms that were across from the inner courtyard. They were across from the outer wall of the temple on the north side. 2The rooms were in a building north of the temple. The building had a door that faced north. It was 175 feet long. It was 87 and a half feet wide.

3One row of rooms was next to the inner courtyard. The other row was across from the sidewalk of the outer courtyard. Each room was 35 feet long. Walkways in front of each row faced each other on all three floors. 4Between the two rows was an inner sidewalk. It was 17 and a half feet wide and 175 feet long. Each of the rooms had a door on the north side.

5The rooms on the top floor were narrower than the others. The walkways took up more space from them than they did from the rooms on the other two floors. 6The courtyards had pillars. But the rooms on the third floor didn't. So their floor space was smaller than the space in the rooms on the other floors.

7The building had an outer wall that was even with the outer row of rooms and with the outer courtyard. The wall continued east of the outer row for 87 and a

half feet. 8So there were two rows of rooms. The row next to the outer courtyard was 87 and a half feet long. The one closest to the temple was 175 feet long. 9The first floor of the building had an entrance on the east side. It led to the outer courtyard.

10There were also two rows of rooms in a building next to the south side of the inner courtyard. The building was across from the south wall of the outer courtyard. 11Between the two rows was an inner sidewalk. The rooms were like the ones in the north building. They were as long and wide as the rooms on the north. The doorways of the rooms on the south were like the ones on the north. 12People entered the south rooms through the doorway at the east end of the inner sidewalk. The south wall continued east of the outer row of rooms.

13The man said to me, "The north and south rooms face the inner courtyard. They are the priests' rooms. That is where the priests who approach the LORD will eat the very holy offerings. They will also store them there. That includes the grain offerings, sin offerings and guilt offerings. This place is holy.

14"The priests who enter these holy rooms must leave behind the clothes they served in. Then they can go into the outer courtyard. The clothes they served in are holy. So they must put other clothes on. They have to do that before they go near the places where other people go."

15The man finished measuring what was inside the temple area. Then he led me out through the east gate. He measured all around the area. 16He measured the east side with his measuring rod. It was 875 feet long. 17He measured the north side. It was 875 feet long. 18He measured the south side. It was 875 feet long. 19Finally, he turned and measured the west side. It was 875 feet long. 20So he measured the area on all four sides. It had a wall around it. The wall was 875 feet long and 875 feet wide. It separated what was holy from what was not.

The Glory of the LORD Returns to the Temple

43 Then the man brought me to the east gate. 2There I saw the glory of the God of Israel. He was coming from the east. His voice was like the roar of rushing waters. His glory made the land shine brightly.

3The vision I saw was like the one I had when he came to destroy the city. It was also like the visions I had seen by the Kebar River. I fell with my face toward the ground. ⁴The glory of the LORD entered the temple through the east gate. ⁵Then the Spirit lifted me up. He brought me into the inner courtyard. The glory of the LORD filled the temple.

⁶The man was standing beside me. I heard someone speaking to me from inside the temple. ⁷He said, "Son of man, this is the place where my throne is. The stool for my feet is also here. I will live here among the people of Israel forever. They will never again treat my name as if it were not holy. They and their kings will not serve other gods anymore. The people will no longer worship the lifeless gods of their kings at their high places.

⁸"The people of Israel placed their own doorway next to my holy doorway. They put their doorposts right beside mine. Nothing but a thin wall separated us. They treated my name as if it were not holy. I hated it when they did that. So I became angry with them and destroyed them. ⁹Now let them stop serving other gods. Let them quit worshiping the lifeless gods of their kings. If they obey me, I will live among them forever.

POWER-SURGE

OBEYS ✔

IF THEY OBEY ME, I WILL LIVE AMONG THEM FOREVER.
— EZEKIEL 43:9 —

¹⁰"Son of man, tell the people of Israel about the temple. Then they will be ashamed of their sins. Let them think carefully about the plan of the temple. ¹¹What if they are ashamed of everything they have done? Then show them all of the plans of the temple. Explain to them how it is laid out. Tell them about its exits and entrances. Show them exactly what it will look like. Give them all of its rules and laws. Write everything down so they can see it. Then they will be faithful to its plan. And they will obey all of its rules.

¹²"Here is the law of the temple. The whole area on top of Mount Zion will be very holy. That is the law of the temple."

The Altar

¹³The man said, "Here is the size of the altar. The standard measurement I am using is 21 inches. The base of the altar is 21 inches high. The base has a ledge that is 21 inches wide. It also has a rim that is nine inches wide around the edge. Here is how high the altar is. ¹⁴The lower part is three and a half feet high. It has a ledge that is 21 inches wide. The middle part is seven feet high. It has a ledge that is 21 inches wide.

¹⁵"The top part is where the sacrifices are burned. It is seven feet high. A horn sticks out from each of its upper four corners. ¹⁶The top part of the altar is square. It is 21 feet long and 21 feet wide. ¹⁷The middle part is also square. It is 24 and a half feet long. It is 24 and a half feet wide. Its rim is ten and a half inches wide. The base of the altar is 21 inches high all the way around. The steps leading up to the top of the altar face east."

¹⁸Then the man said to me, "Son of man, the LORD and King speaks. He says, 'Here are the rules for the altar when it is built. Follow them when you sacrifice burnt offerings and sprinkle blood on it. ¹⁹Give a young bull to the priests as a sin offering. They are Levites from the family of Zadok. They approach me to serve me,' announces the LORD and King. ²⁰'Get some of the bull's blood. Put it on the four horns. Also put it on the four corners of the middle part of the altar and all around the rim. That will make the altar pure and clean. ²¹Use the bull for the sin offering. Burn it in the proper place outside the temple.

²²" 'On the second day offer a male goat. It must not have any flaws. It is a sin offering to make the altar pure and clean. So do as you did with the bull. ²³When you finish making the altar pure, offer a young bull and a ram from the flock. They must not have any flaws. ²⁴Offer them to me. The priests must sprinkle salt on them. Then they must sacrifice them as a burnt offering to me.

²⁵" 'Provide a male goat each day for seven days. It is a sin offering. Also provide a young bull and a ram from the flock. They must not have any flaws. ²⁶For seven days the priests must make the altar pure and clean. That is how they will set it apart to me.

²⁷" 'From the eighth day on, the priests must bring your burnt offerings and friendship offerings. They must sacrifice them on the altar. Then I will accept you,' announces the LORD and King."

The Prince, the Levites and the Priests

44 Then the man brought me back to the outer gate of the temple. It was the one that faced east. It was shut. 2The LORD said to me, "This gate must remain shut. It must not be opened. No one can enter through it. It must remain shut because I have entered through it. I am the God of Israel. 3The prince is the only one who can sit in the gateway. There he can eat in front of me. He must enter through the porch of the gateway. And he must go out the same way."

4Then the man brought me through the north gate. He took me to the front of the temple. I looked up and saw the glory of the LORD. It filled his temple. I fell with my face toward the ground.

5The LORD said to me, "Son of man, pay attention. Look carefully. Listen closely to everything I tell you about all of the rules concerning my temple. Pay attention to the entrance to the temple and to all of its exits.

6"Speak to the people of Israel. They refuse to obey me. Tell them, 'The LORD and King says, "People of Israel, I have had enough of your evil practices. I hate them. 7You brought strangers into my temple. They were not circumcised. Their hearts were stubborn. You polluted my temple. But you offered me food, fat and blood anyway. When you did all of those things, you broke the covenant I made with you. I hated all of the evil things you did.

8" ' "You did not do what I told you to. You did not take care of my holy things. Instead, you put other people in charge of my temple." ' " 9The LORD and King says, "No stranger whose heart is stubborn can enter my temple. They have not been circumcised. Even if they live among the people of Israel they can't enter it.

10"Some Levites wandered far away from me when Israel went down the wrong path. They worshiped the statues of their gods. So they will be punished because they have sinned. 11They might serve in my temple. They might be in charge of its gates. They might kill the burnt offerings and sacrifices for the people. And they might stand in front of the people and serve them in other ways. 12"But they served the people of Israel while they were worshiping their gods. They made the people fall into sin. So I raised my hand and took an oath. I warned them that I would punish them because of their sin," announces the LORD and King. 13"They must not approach me

to serve me as priests. They must not come near any of my holy things. They must stay away from my very holy offerings. They did many things they should have been ashamed of. I hated those things.

14"But I will still put them in charge of the temple duties. They can do all of the work that has to be done there.

15"But the priests must approach me to serve me. They are Levites from Zadok's family line. They faithfully carried out their duties in my temple. They obeyed me when the people of Israel turned away from me. Those priests must serve me by offering sacrifices of fat and blood," announces the LORD and King. 16"They are the only ones who can enter my temple. Only they can come near to serve me and do my work.

17"They will enter the gates of the inner courtyard. When they do, they must wear linen clothes. They will serve at the gates of the inner courtyard or inside the temple. When they do, they must not wear any clothes that are made out of wool. 18They must have linen turbans on their heads. They must wear linen underwear around their waists. They must not put anything on that makes them sweat.

19"They will go into the outer courtyard where the people are. When they do, they must take off the clothes they have been serving in. They must leave them in the sacred rooms. And they must put other clothes on. Then they will not make the people holy if the people happen to touch their clothes.

20"The priests must not shave their heads. They must not let their hair grow long. They must keep it cut short. 21No priest can drink wine when he enters the inner courtyard. 22They must not get married to widows or divorced women. They can only marry Israelite virgins or the widows of priests.

23"The priests must teach my people the difference between what is holy and what is not. They must show them how to tell the difference between what is 'clean' and what is not.

24"When people do not agree, the priests must serve as judges between them. They must make their decisions based on my laws. They must obey my laws and rules for all of my appointed feasts. And they must keep my Sabbath days holy.

25"A priest must not make himself 'unclean' by going near a dead person. But suppose the dead person was his father or mother. Or suppose it was his son or daughter or brother or unmarried sister. Then the priest can make himself 'unclean.' 26After he is pure and clean again, he must wait seven days. 27Then he can go to the inner courtyard to serve in the temple. But when he does, he must sacrifice a sin offering for himself," announces the LORD and King.

28"The priests will not receive any part of the land of Israel. I myself will be their only share. 29They will eat the grain offerings, sin offerings and guilt offerings. Everything in Israel that is set apart to me in a special way will belong to them. 30The best of every first share of the people's crops will belong to the priests. So will all of their special gifts. The people must give the priests the first share of their ground meal. Then I will bless my people's families.

31"The priests must not eat any bird or animal that is found dead. They must not eat anything that wild animals have torn apart.

Dividing Up the Land

45 "People of Israel, you will divide up the land you will receive. When you do, give me my share of it. It will be a sacred area. It will be eight and a fourth miles long and six and a half miles wide. The entire area will be holy. 2The temple area in it will be 875 feet long and 875 feet wide. An 87-and-a-half-foot strip around it will be open land.

3"In the sacred area, measure off a large strip of land. It will be eight and a fourth miles long and three and a third miles wide. The temple will be in it. It will be the most holy place of all. 4The large strip will be the sacred share of land for the priests. There they will serve in the temple. And they will approach me to serve me there. Their houses will be built on that land. The holy temple will also be located there.

5"So the Levites will serve in the temple. They will have an area eight and a fourth miles long and three and a third miles wide. The towns they live in will be located there.

6"Give the city an area one and two thirds miles wide and eight and a fourth miles long. It will be right next to the sacred area. It will belong to all of the people of Israel.

7"The prince will have land on both sides of the sacred area and the city. Its border will run east and west along the land of one of the tribes. 8The prince will own that land in Israel. And my princes

will not crush my people anymore. Instead, they will allow the people of Israel to receive their own share of land. It will be divided up based on their tribes."

9The LORD and King says, "Princes of Israel, you have gone far enough! Stop hurting others. Do not crush them. Do what is fair and right. Stop taking my people's land away from them," announces the LORD and King.

10"Use weights and measures that are honest and exact. 11Use the same standard to measure dry and liquid products. Use a 6-bushel measure for dry products. And use a 60-gallon measure for liquids. 12Every amount of money must be weighed out in keeping with the standard weights.

Offerings and Holy Days

13"You must offer a special gift. It must be 13 and a third cups out of every six bushels of grain. 14Give two and a half quarts out of every 60 gallons of olive oil. 15Also give one sheep from every flock of 200 sheep. Get them from the grasslands of Israel that receive plenty of water. Use them for grain offerings, burnt offerings and friendship offerings. They will be used to pay for the sin of the people," announces the LORD and King.

16"All of the people in the land will take part in that special gift. The prince in Israel will use it. 17He must provide the burnt offerings, grain offerings and drink offerings. They will be for the yearly feasts, New Moon Feasts and Sabbath days. So they will be for all of the appointed feasts of the people of Israel. The prince will provide the sin offerings, grain offerings, burnt offerings and friendship offerings. They will be used to pay for the sin of the people."

18The LORD and King says, "Get a young bull. It must not have any flaws. Use it to make the temple pure and clean. Do it on the first day of the first month. 19The priest must get some of the blood from the sin offering. He must put some on the doorposts of the temple. He must apply some to the four corners of the middle part of the altar. He must put the rest on the gateposts of the inner courtyard.

20"Do the same thing on the seventh day of the month. Do it for those who sin without meaning to. And do it for those who sin without realizing what they are doing. So you will make the temple pure and clean.

21"Keep the Passover Feast on the 14th day of the first month. It will last for seven days. During that time you must eat bread that is made without yeast.

22 "The prince must provide a bull as a sin offering. It will be for him and all of the people of the land. 23 For each of the seven days of the Feast he must provide seven bulls and seven rams. They must not have any flaws. They will be a burnt offering to me. The prince must also provide a male goat for a sin offering. 24 He must bring a little over half a bushel for each bull or ram. He must also provide four quarts of olive oil for each of them.

25 "The seven days of the Feast begin on the 15th day of the seventh month. During those days the prince must provide the same sin offerings, burnt offerings, grain offerings and olive oil."

46 The LORD and King says, "On the six working days of each week you must keep the east gate of the inner courtyard of the temple shut. But open it on Sabbath days and during New Moon Feasts. 2 The prince must enter the temple area through the porch of the gateway. He must stand by the gatepost. The priests must sacrifice his burnt offering and friendship offerings. He must worship at the entrance of the gateway. Then he must leave. But the gate will not be shut until evening.

3 "On Sabbath days and during New Moon Feasts the people of the land must gather together at the entrance of the temple gateway. That is where they must worship me.

4 "The prince must bring a burnt offering to me on the Sabbath. It will be six male lambs and a ram. They must not have any flaws. 5 He must offer a little over half a bushel of grain along with the ram. The grain he offers along with the lambs can be as much as he wants to give. He must also offer four quarts of olive oil for every half bushel of grain.

6 "On the day of the New Moon Feast the prince must also offer a young bull, six lambs and a ram. They must not have any flaws. 7 He must offer a little over half a bushel of grain along with the bull or ram. The grain he offers along with the lambs can be as much as he wants to give. He must also offer four quarts of olive oil for every half bushel of grain.

8 "When the prince enters the temple area, he must go in through the porch of the gateway. He must leave the same way. 9 "The people of the land must worship me at the appointed feasts. Those who enter through the north gate must leave through the south gate. Those who enter

through the south gate must leave through the north gate. They must not leave through the same gate they entered. Each one must go out the opposite gate. 10 The prince must be among them. He must go in when they go in. And he must leave when they leave.

11 "At the yearly feasts and other appointed feasts there must be grain offerings. The prince must offer a little over half a bushel of grain along with a bull or ram. The grain he offers along with the lambs can be as much as he wants to give. He must also offer four quarts of olive oil for every half bushel of grain. 12 He can also bring another offering to me because he chooses to. It might be a burnt offering or friendship offering. When he brings it, the east gate must be opened for him. He will bring his offering just as he does on the Sabbath day. Then he will leave. After he has gone out, the gate must be shut.

13 "Every day you must provide a lamb that is a year old. It must not have any flaws. It is a burnt offering to me. You must provide it every morning. 14 You must also offer grain along with it every morning. Bring 13 and a third cups of grain. Also bring one and a third quarts of olive oil to make the flour a little wet. So you will give the grain offering to me. That will be a law that will last for all time to come. 15 Provide the lamb, grain offering and oil every morning. They will be used for a regular burnt offering."

16 The LORD and King says, "Suppose the prince makes a gift from his share of land. And he gives it to one of his sons. Then the property will also belong to his sons after him. It will be handed down to them.

17 "But suppose he makes a gift from his share of land to one of his servants. Then the servant can keep it until the Year of Jubilee. After that, it will be returned to the prince. His property can be handed down only to his sons. It belongs to them.

18 "The prince must not take any share of land that belongs to the people. He must not drive them off their property. He must give his sons their share out of his own property. Then my people will not be separated from their property."

19 The man brought me through the entrance at the side of the north building. That's where the priests' sacred rooms were located. He showed me a place west of the building. 20 He said to me, "This is where the priests will cook the guilt offerings and sin offerings. They will also bake the grain offerings here. Then they will

not have to bring the offerings into the outer courtyard. That will keep the people from touching the offerings and becoming holy."

²¹Then the man brought me to the outer courtyard. He led me around to its four corners. In each corner I saw another smaller courtyard. ²²So in the four corners of the outer courtyard were walled courtyards. Each one was 70 feet long and 52 and a half feet wide. All of them were the same size. ²³Around the inside of each of the four courtyards was a stone ledge. Places for fire were built all around under each ledge. ²⁴The man said to me, "These are the kitchens. Those who serve at the temple will cook the people's sacrifices here."

A River Will Flow From the Temple

47 The man brought me back to the entrance to the temple. I saw water flowing east from under a temple gateway. The temple faced east. The water was coming down from under the south side of the temple. It was flowing south of the altar.

²Then he brought me out through the north gate of the outer courtyard. He led me around the outside to the outer gate that faced east. The water was flowing from the south side of the east gate.

³Then the man went toward the east. He had a measuring line in his hand. He measured off 1,750 feet. He led me through water that was up to my ankles. ⁴Then he measured off another 1,750 feet. He led me through water that was up to my knees. Then he measured off another 1,750 feet. He led me through water that was up to my waist. ⁵Then he measured off another 1,750 feet. But now it was a river that I could not go across. The water had risen so high that it was deep enough to swim in. ⁶He asked me, "Son of man, do you see this?"

Then he led me back to the bank of the river. ⁷When I arrived there, I saw a large number of trees. They were on both sides of the river.

⁸The man said to me, "This water flows toward the eastern territory. It goes down into the Arabah Valley. There it enters the Dead Sea. When it empties into it, the water there becomes fresh. ⁹Large numbers of creatures will live where the river flows. It will have huge numbers of fish. This water flows there and makes the salt water fresh. So where the river flows everything will live.

¹⁰"People will stand along the shore to fish. From En Gedi all the way to En Eglaim there will be places for spreading fishnets. The Dead Sea will have many kinds of fish. They will be like the fish in the Mediterranean Sea.

¹¹"But none of the swamps will have fresh water in them. They will stay salty.

¹²"Fruit trees of all kinds will grow on both banks of the river. Their leaves will not dry up. The trees will always have fruit on them. Every month they will bear fruit. The water from the temple will flow to them. Their fruit will be used for food. And their leaves will be used for healing."

The Borders of the Land

¹³The LORD and King says, "People of Israel, here are the borders you will have after you divide up the land. Each of the 12 tribes will receive a share. But the family of Joseph will have two shares. ¹⁴Divide the land into equal parts. Long ago I raised my hand and took an oath. I promised to give the land to your people. So all of it will belong to you.

¹⁵"Here are the borders of the land.

"On the north side the border will start at the Mediterranean Sea. It will go by the Hethlon road past Lebo Hamath. Then it will continue on to Zedad, ¹⁶Berothah and Sibraim. Sibraim is between Damascus and Hamath. The border will reach all the way to Hazer Hatticon. It is right next to Hauran. ¹⁷The border will go from the sea to Hazar Enan. It will run north of Damascus and south of Hamath. That will be the north border.

¹⁸"On the east side the border will run between Hauran and Damascus. It will continue along the Jordan River between Gilead and the land of Israel. It will reach to the Dead Sea and all the way to Tamar. That will be the east border.

¹⁹"On the south side the border will start at Tamar. It will reach all the way to the waters of Meribah Kadesh. Then it will run along the Wadi of Egypt. It will end at the Mediterranean Sea. That will be the south border.

²⁰"On the west side, the Mediterranean Sea will be the border. It will go to a point across from Lebo Hamath. That will be the west border.

²¹"You must divide up this land among yourselves. Do it based on the number of

men in your tribes. ²²Each of the tribes must receive a share of the land.

"You must also give some land to the outsiders who have settled among you and who have children. Treat them as if they had been born in Israel. Let them have some land among your tribes. ²³Outsiders can settle in any tribe. There you must give them their share," announces the LORD and King.

The Land Will Be Divided Up

48 "Here are the tribes. They are listed by their names. Dan will receive one share of land. It will be at the northern border of Israel. The border will follow the Hethlon road to Lebo Hamath. Hazar Enan will be part of the border. So will the northern border of Damascus next to Hamath. Dan's northern border will run from east to west.

²"Asher will receive one share. It will border the territory of Dan from east to west.

³"Naphtali will receive one share. It will border the territory of Asher from east to west.

⁴"Manasseh will receive one share. It will border the territory of Naphtali from east to west.

⁵"Ephraim will receive one share. It will border the territory of Manasseh from east to west.

⁶"Reuben will receive one share. It will border the territory of Ephraim from east to west.

⁷"Judah will receive one share. It will border the territory of Reuben from east to west.

⁸"You must give one share as a special gift to me. It will border the territory of Judah from east to west. It will be eight and a fourth miles wide. It will be as long as the border of each of the territories of the tribes. Its border will run from east to west. The temple will be in the center of that strip of land.

⁹"Give that special share of land to me. It will be eight and a fourth miles long and three and a third miles wide. ¹⁰It will be the sacred share of land for the priests. It will be eight and a fourth miles long on the north side. It will be three and a third miles wide on the west side. It will be three and a third miles wide on the east side. And it will be eight and a fourth miles long on the south side. My temple will be in the center of it.

¹¹"This share of land will be for the priests who are set apart to me. They will come from the family line of Zadok. The members of that family served me faithfully. They did not go down the wrong path as the Levites and other Israelites did. ¹²Their share of land will be a special gift to them. It will be part of the sacred share of the land. It will be very holy. Its border will run along the territory of the Levites.

¹³"The Levites will receive a share. It will be next to the territory of the priests. The Levites' share will be eight and a fourth miles long and three and a third miles wide. ¹⁴They must not sell or trade any of it. It is the best part of the land. It must not be handed over to anyone else. It is set apart to me.

¹⁵"The area that remains is one and two thirds miles wide. It is eight and a fourth miles long. It will not be holy. The people in Jerusalem can build houses there. They can use some of it as grasslands. The city will be in the center of it. ¹⁶Each of the four sides of the city will be one and a half miles long. ¹⁷Each of the four sides of the city's grasslands will be 437 and a half feet long.

¹⁸"What remains of the area will be three and a third miles long on the east and west sides. Its border will run along the border of the sacred share. Its crops will supply food for the city workers. ¹⁹They will farm the area. They will come from all of the tribes of Israel. ²⁰The entire area will be a square. Each of its four sides will be eight and a fourth miles long. Set the sacred share apart as a special gift to me. Do the same thing with the property of the city.

²¹"The area that remains on both sides will belong to the prince. So his land does not include the sacred share and the city property. The eastern part of his land will reach from the sacred share all the way to the eastern border. The western part will reach from the sacred share to the western border. The sacred share itself is eight and a fourth miles long on its east and west sides. Both of those areas will be right next to the borders of the two tribes on the north and south sides. They will belong to the prince. The sacred share will be in the center of them. It will have the temple in it.

²²"The property of the Levites will lie in the center of the prince's share. So will the property of the city. The prince's land will lie between the borders of the tribes of Judah and Benjamin.

²³"Here is the land for the rest of the tribes. Benjamin will receive one share. It

will reach from the eastern border to the western border.

²⁴"Simeon will receive one share. It will border the territory of Benjamin from east to west.

²⁵"Issachar will receive one share. It will border the territory of Simeon from east to west.

²⁶"Zebulun will receive one share. It will border the territory of Issachar from east to west.

²⁷"Gad will receive one share. It will border the territory of Zebulun from east to west.

²⁸"The southern border of Gad will run south from Tamar to the waters of Meribah Kadesh. It will continue along the Wadi of Egypt. It will end at the Mediterranean Sea.

²⁹"That is the land you must divide among the tribes of Israel. And those will be the shares they will receive," announces the LORD and King.

The Gates of the City

³⁰"Here is a list of the gates of the city. Start with its north side. It will be a mile and a half long. ³¹The city gates will be named after the tribes of Israel. The north side will have three gates. They will be the gates of Reuben, Judah and Levi.

³²"The east side will be a mile and a half long. It will have three gates. They will be the gates of Joseph, Benjamin and Dan.

³³"The south side will be a mile and a half long. It will have three gates. They will be the gates of Simeon, Issachar and Zebulun.

³⁴"The west side will be a mile and a half long. It will have three gates. They will be the gates of Gad, Asher and Naphtali.

³⁵"The city will be six miles around.

"From that time on, its name will be

THE LORD IS THERE."

DANIEL

One of the true heroes of the Bible wrote the book of Daniel. And he's also the main character. Daniel is a captive in Babylon. He must do as the Babylonian kings order. But no matter what they command, Daniel's first obedience is to God. He and his three friends, Shadrach, Meshach, and Abednego, all obey God above anyone else, even when it means danger and possible death. Read the exciting book of Daniel to discover how God can work through those who are willing to obey him.

HEROES IN THIS BOOK . . .

SHADRACH, MESHACH AND ABEDNEGO
PAGE 995

DANIEL
PAGE 1002

BELSHAZZAR (Not!)
PAGE 1000

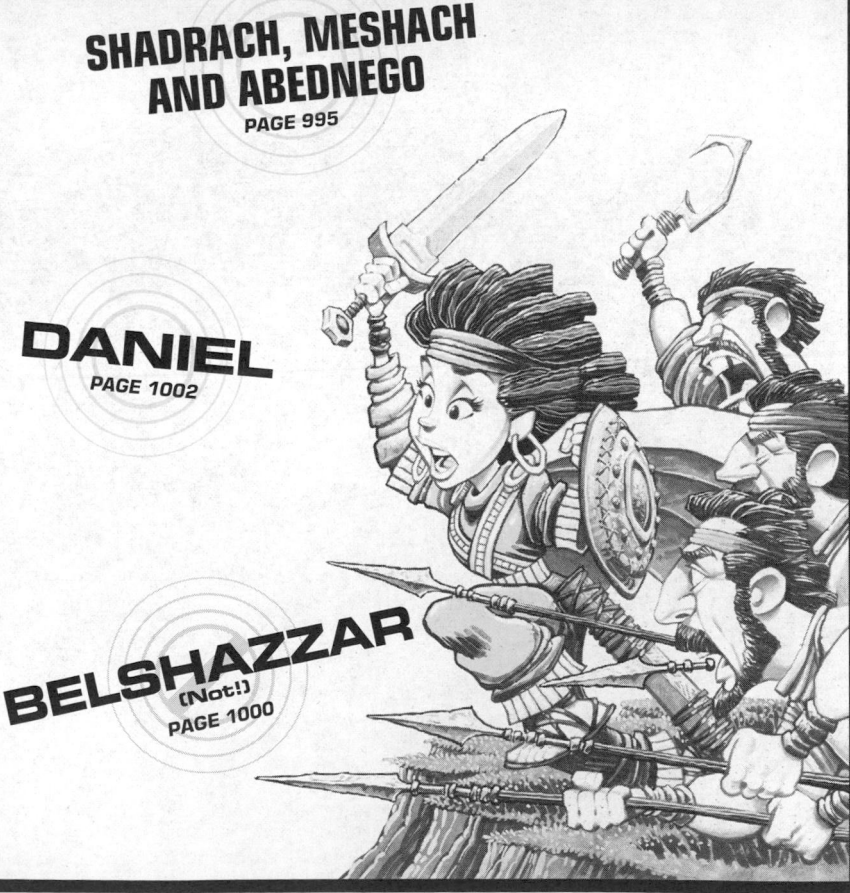

Daniel Is Trained in Babylon

1 It was the third year that Jehoiakim was king of Judah. Nebuchadnezzar came to Jerusalem. His armies surrounded the city and attacked it. Nebuchadnezzar was king of Babylonia.

²The LORD handed Jehoiakim, the king of Judah, over to him. Nebuchadnezzar also took some of the articles from God's temple. He carried them off to the temple of his god in Babylonia. He put them among the treasures of his god.

³The king gave Ashpenaz an order. Ashpenaz was the chief of Nebuchadnezzar's court officials. The king told him to bring in some of the Israelites. He wanted nobles and men from the royal family. ⁴He was looking for young men who were healthy and handsome. They had to be able to learn anything. They had to be well educated. They had to have the ability to understand new things quickly and easily. The king wanted men who could serve in his palace. Ashpenaz was supposed to teach them the Babylonian language and writings.

⁵The king had his servants give them food and wine from his own table. They received a certain amount every day. The young men had to be trained for three years. After that, they could begin to serve the king.

⁶Some of the men were from Judah. Their names were Daniel, Hananiah, Mishael and Azariah. ⁷The chief official gave them new names. He gave Daniel the name Belteshazzar. He gave Hananiah the name Shadrach. He gave Mishael the name Meshach. And he gave Azariah the name Abednego.

⁸Daniel decided not to make himself "unclean" by eating the king's food and drinking his wine. So he asked the chief official for a favor. He wanted permission not to make himself "unclean" with the king's food and wine.

⁹God had caused the official to be kind and friendly to Daniel. ¹⁰But the official refused to do what Daniel asked for. He said, "I'm afraid of the king. He is my master. He has decided what you and your three friends must eat and drink. Why should he see you looking worse than the other young men who are the same age you are? When he sees how you look, he might kill me."

¹¹So Daniel spoke to one of the guards. The chief official had appointed him over Daniel, Hananiah, Mishael and Azariah. ¹²Daniel said to him, "Please test us for ten days. Give us nothing but vegetables to eat. And give us only water to drink. ¹³Then compare us with the young men who eat the king's food. See how we look. After that, do what you want to."

¹⁴So the guard agreed. He tested them for ten days.

¹⁵After the ten days they looked healthy and well fed. In fact, they looked better than any of the young men who ate the king's food. ¹⁶So the guard didn't require Daniel and his friends to eat the special food or drink the wine. He gave them vegetables instead.

¹⁷God gave knowledge and understanding to those four young men. So they understood all kinds of writings and subjects. And Daniel could understand all kinds of visions and dreams.

¹⁸The three years the king had set for their training ended. So the chief official brought them to Nebuchadnezzar. ¹⁹The king talked with them. He didn't find anyone equal to Daniel, Hananiah, Mishael and Azariah. So they began to serve the king. ²⁰He asked them for advice in matters that required wisdom and understanding. He always found their answers to be the best. In fact, the men were ten times better than anyone in his kingdom who claimed to get knowledge by using magic.

²¹Daniel served in Babylon until the first year Cyrus ruled over Babylonia. Cyrus was king of Persia.

Nebuchadnezzar Dreams About a Large Statue

2 In the second year of Nebuchadnezzar's rule, he had a dream. His mind was troubled. He couldn't sleep.

²So the king sent for those who claimed to get knowledge by using magic. He also sent for those who practiced evil magic and those who studied the heavens. He wanted them to tell him what he had dreamed. They came in and stood in front of the king. ³He said to them, "I had a dream. It troubles me. So I want to know what it means."

⁴Then those who studied the heavens answered the king. They spoke in Aramaic. They said, "King Nebuchadnezzar, may you live forever! Tell us what you dreamed. Then we'll explain what it means."

⁵The king replied to them, "I have made up my mind. You must tell me what I dreamed. And you must tell me what it means. If you don't, I'll have you cut to pieces. And I'll have your houses turned into piles of trash.

⁶"So tell me what I dreamed. Explain it to me. Then I'll give you gifts. I'll reward you. I'll give you great honor. So tell me the dream. And tell me what it means."

⁷Once more they replied, "King Nebuchadnezzar, tell us what you dreamed. Then we'll tell you what it means."

⁸The king answered, "I know what you are doing. You are trying to gain more time. You realize that I've made up my mind. ⁹You must tell me the dream. If you don't, you will pay for it. You have gotten together and made evil plans. You hope things will change. So you are telling me lies. But I want you to tell me what I dreamed. Then I'll know that you can tell me what it means."

¹⁰They answered the king, "There isn't a man on earth who can do what you are asking! No king has ever asked for anything like that. Not even a king as great and mighty as you has asked for it. Those who get knowledge by using magic have never been asked to do what you are asking. And those who study the heavens haven't been asked to do it either. ¹¹What you are asking is much too hard. No one can tell you what you dreamed except the gods. And they don't live among human beings."

¹²That made the king very angry. He ordered that all of the wise men in Babylon be put to death. ¹³So the order was given to kill them. Men were sent out to look for Daniel and his friends. They were also supposed to be put to death.

¹⁴Arioch was the commander of the king's guard. He went out to put the wise men of Babylon to death. So Daniel spoke to him wisely and carefully. ¹⁵He asked the king's officer, "Why did Nebuchadnezzar give a terrible order like that?" Then Arioch explained to Daniel what was going on.

¹⁶When Daniel heard that, he went to the king. He told him he would explain the dream to him. But he needed more time.

¹⁷Then Daniel returned to his house. He explained everything to his friends Hananiah, Mishael and Azariah. ¹⁸He asked them to pray that the God of heaven would give him mercy. He wanted God to help him understand the mystery of the king's dream. Then he and his friends wouldn't be killed along with the other wise men in Babylon.

¹⁹During that night, God gave Daniel a vision. He showed him what the mystery was all about. Then Daniel praised the God of heaven. ²⁰He said,

"May God be praised for ever and ever!
    He is wise and powerful.
²¹He changes times and seasons.
    He sets up kings.
    He removes them from power.
The wisdom of those who are wise
        comes from him.
    He gives knowledge to those who
        have understanding.
²²He explains deep and hidden things.
    He knows what happens in the
        darkest places.
    And where he is, everything is light.
²³God of my people, I thank and praise
        you.
    You have given me wisdom and
        power.
You have made known to me what we
        asked you for.
    You have shown us the king's
        dream."

POWER-SURGE

THANKFUL ♣

GOD OF MY PEOPLE,
I THANK AND
PRAISE YOU.
YOU HAVE GIVEN ME
WISDOM AND POWER.
— DANIEL 2:23 —

WISE

Daniel Tells the King What His Dream Means

²⁴Then Daniel went to Arioch. The king had appointed him to put the wise men of Babylon to death. Daniel said to him, "Don't kill the wise men of Babylon. Take me to the king. I'll tell him what his dream means."

²⁵So Arioch took Daniel to the king at once. Arioch said, "I have found a man among those you brought here from Judah. He can tell you what your dream means."

²⁶Nebuchadnezzar spoke to Daniel, who was also called Belteshazzar. The king asked him, "Are you able to tell me what I saw in my dream? And can you tell me what it means?"

²⁷Daniel replied, "You have asked us to explain a mystery to you. But no wise man

can do that. And those who try to figure things out by using magic can't do it either.

28 "But there is a God in heaven who can explain mysteries. Nebuchadnezzar, he has shown you what is going to happen. Here is what you dreamed. And here are the visions that passed through your mind while you were lying on your bed.

29 "My king, while you were still in bed your mind thought about things that haven't happened yet. The One who explains mysteries showed those things to you.

30 "Now the mystery has been explained to me. But it isn't because I have greater wisdom than anyone else. It's because God wants you to know what the mystery means, my king. He wants you to understand what went through your mind.

31 "King Nebuchadnezzar, you looked up and saw a large statue standing in front of you. It was huge. It shone brightly. And it terrified you. 32 The head of the statue was made out of pure gold. Its chest and arms were made of silver. Its stomach and thighs were bronze. 33 Its legs were made out of iron. And its feet were partly iron and partly baked clay.

34 "While you were watching, a rock was cut out. But human hands didn't do it. It struck the statue on its feet of iron and clay. It smashed them. 35 Then the iron and clay were broken to pieces. So were the bronze, silver and gold. All of them were broken to pieces at the same time. They became like straw on a threshing floor at harvest time. The wind blew them away without leaving a trace. But the rock that struck the statue became a huge mountain. It filled the whole earth.

36 "That was your dream. Now I will tell you what it means. 37 Nebuchadnezzar, you are the greatest king of all. The God of heaven has given you authority and power. He has given you might and glory. 38 He has put everyone under your control. He has also given you authority over the wild animals and the birds of the air. It doesn't matter where they live. He has made you ruler over all of them. You are that head of gold.

39 "After you, another kingdom will take over. It won't be as powerful as yours. Next, a third kingdom will rule over the whole earth. The bronze part of the statue stands for that kingdom.

40 "Finally, there will be a fourth kingdom. It will be as strong as iron. Iron breaks and smashes everything to pieces. And the fourth kingdom will crush and break all of the others. 41 You saw that the feet and toes were made out of iron and baked clay. And the fourth kingdom will be divided up. But it will still be almost as strong as iron. That's why you saw iron mixed with clay. 42 The toes were partly iron and partly clay. And the fourth kingdom will be partly strong and partly weak. 43 You saw the iron mixed with baked clay. And the fourth kingdom will be made up of all kinds of people. They won't hold together any more than iron mixes with clay.

44 "In the time of those kings, the God of heaven will set up a kingdom. It will never be destroyed. And no other nation will ever take it over. It will crush all of those other kingdoms. It will bring them to an end. But it will last forever. 45 That's what the vision of the rock cut out of a mountain means. Human hands didn't cut the rock out. It broke the statue to pieces. It smashed the iron, bronze, clay, silver and gold.

"The great God has shown you what will take place in days to come. The dream is true. And you can trust the meaning I have given you for it."

46 Then King Nebuchadnezzar bowed low in front of Daniel. He wanted to honor him. So he ordered that an offering and incense be offered up to him.

47 The king said to Daniel, "I'm sure your God is the greatest God of all. He is the Lord of kings. He explains mysteries. That's why you were able to explain the mystery of my dream."

48 Then the king put Daniel in a position of authority. He gave him many gifts. He made him ruler over the city of Babylon and the towns around it. He put him in charge of all of its other wise men.

49 The king also did what Daniel asked him to. He appointed Shadrach, Meshach and Abednego to help Daniel govern Babylon and the towns around it. Daniel himself remained at the royal court.

Daniel's Friends Are Thrown Into a Blazing Furnace

3 King Nebuchadnezzar made a statue that was covered with gold. It was 90 feet tall and 9 feet wide. He set it up on the flatlands of Dura near the city of Babylon.

2 Then the king sent for the royal rulers, high officials and governors. He sent for the advisers, treasurers, judges and court officers. And he sent for all of the other officials of Babylon. He asked them to come

to a special gathering to honor the statue he had set up.

3So the royal rulers, high officials and governors came together. So did the advisers, treasurers, judges and court officers. All of the other officials joined them. They came to honor the statue that King Nebuchadnezzar had set up. They stood in front of it.

4Then a messenger called out loudly, "Listen, you people who come from every nation! Pay attention, you who speak other languages! Here is what the king commands you to do. 5You will soon hear the sound of horns and flutes. You will hear zithers, lyres, harps and pipes. In fact, you will hear all kinds of music. When you do, you must fall down and worship the gold statue that King Nebuchadnezzar has set up. 6If you don't, you will be thrown into a blazing furnace right away."

7All of the people heard the sound of the horns and flutes. They heard the zithers, lyres, harps and other musical instruments. As soon as they did, they fell down and worshiped Nebuchadnezzar's gold statue. They had come from every nation and language.

8At that time some people who studied the heavens came forward. They spoke against the Jews. 9They said, "King Nebuchadnezzar, may you live forever! 10You commanded everyone to fall down and worship the gold statue. You told them to do it when they heard the horns, flutes, zithers, lyres, harps, pipes and other musical instruments. 11If they didn't, they would be thrown into a blazing furnace. 12But you have appointed some Jews to help Daniel govern Babylon and the towns around it. Their names are Shadrach, Meshach and Abednego. They don't pay any attention to you, King Nebuchadnezzar. They don't serve your gods. And they refuse to worship the gold statue you have set up."

13Nebuchadnezzar burned with anger. He sent for Shadrach, Meshach and Abednego. So they were brought to him.

14The king said to them, "Shadrach, Meshach and Abednego, is what I heard about you true? Don't you serve my gods? Don't you worship the gold statue I set up? 15You will hear the horns, flutes, zithers, lyres, harps, pipes and other musical instruments. When you do, fall down and worship the statue I made. If you will, that's very good. But if you won't, you will be thrown at once into a blazing furnace. Then what god will be able to save you from my powerful hand?"

16Shadrach, Meshach and Abednego replied to the king. They said, "King Nebuchadnezzar, we don't need to talk about this anymore. 17We might be thrown into the blazing furnace. But the God we serve is able to bring us out of it alive. He will save us from your powerful hand.

18"But we want you to know this. Even if we knew that our God wouldn't save us, we still wouldn't serve your gods. We wouldn't worship the gold statue you set up."

19Then Nebuchadnezzar's anger burned against Shadrach, Meshach and Abednego. The look on his face changed. And he ordered that the furnace be heated seven times hotter than usual. 20He also gave some of the strongest soldiers in his army a command. He ordered them to tie up Shadrach, Meshach and Abednego. Then he told his men to throw them into the blazing furnace. 21So they were tied up. Then they were thrown into the furnace. They were wearing their robes, pants, turbans and other clothes.

22The king's command was carried out quickly. The furnace was so hot that its flames killed the soldiers who threw Shadrach, Meshach and Abednego into it. 23So the three men were firmly tied up. And they fell into the blazing furnace.

24Then King Nebuchadnezzar leaped to his feet. He was so amazed he asked his advisers, "Didn't we tie three men up? Didn't we throw three men into the fire?"

"Yes, we did," they replied.

25The king said, "Look! I see four men walking around in the fire. They aren't tied up. And the fire hasn't even harmed them. The fourth man looks like a son of the gods."

26Then the king approached the opening of the blazing furnace. He shouted, "Shadrach, Meshach and Abednego, come out! You who serve the Most High God, come here!"

So they came out of the fire. 27The royal rulers, high officials, governors and advisers crowded around them. They saw that the fire hadn't harmed their bodies. Not one hair on their heads was burned. Their robes weren't burned either. And they didn't even smell like smoke.

28Then Nebuchadnezzar said, "May the God of Shadrach, Meshach and Abednego be praised! He has sent his angel and saved his servants. They trusted in him. They refused to obey my command. They were willing to give up their lives. They would rather die than serve or worship any god except their own God.

SHADRACH, MESHACH AND ABEDNEGO

DANIEL 3:16, 18

> **Shadrach, Meshach and Abednego...said, "King Nebuchadnezzar,...Even if we knew that our God wouldn't save us, we still wouldn't... worship the gold statue you set up."**

Shadrach (SHAD-rack) and Meshach (MEE-shack) bumped into Abednego (uh-BED-nee-go). Abednego had stopped all of a sudden and looked up. A huge golden statue towered before them, taller than any building they had ever seen. Thousands of people stood around the three men, just as amazed.

Then they heard music—trumpets, drums, harps and flutes. Like thousands of puppets, all the people turned toward the statue and fell to the ground to worship it. Everyone, that is, except Shadrach, Meshach and Abednego.

No matter what the punishment, they refused to bow down to an idol. The king said that anyone who wouldn't worship his golden statue would be thrown into a blazing furnace. **THEY WOULD BE BURNED UP AND CHARRED IN SECONDS.**

Some officials dragged Shadrach, Meshach and Abednego before the king. He was so angry that he ordered the furnace to be heated seven times hotter than before. The three men were tied up with ropes, so tight they couldn't move their feet or hands. Then they were hurled into the furnace.

There! thought the king. *That takes care of them!* Then he jumped up. Looking into the furnace, he exclaimed, "Didn't we throw three men into the furnace to die? I see four men walking around inside. The fourth person looks like an angel! What's going on?" The king walked closer to the furnace to see better. The heat burned his face. He shouted to the men to come out.

Shadrach, Meshach and Abednego stepped out of the furnace. Their ropes had burned off. But their robes and their hair weren't even smoky! God had saved them!

BE LIKE SHADRACH, MESHACH AND ABEDNEGO

These men knew how important it was to follow God and obey him, no matter what. Even when obeying God meant disobeying the king—even when obeying God meant they would probably die—they obeyed God anyway.

SHADRACH, MESHACH AND ABEDNEGO OBEYED GOD EVEN WHEN IT WAS AGAINST THE LAW.
THE WHOLE STORY: DANIEL 3:1-30

Go to page **1000** for the next person

29 "No other god can save people that way. So I'm giving an order. No one from any nation or language can say anything against the God of Shadrach, Meshach and Abednego. If they do, they'll be cut to pieces. And their houses will be turned into piles of trash."

30 Then the king honored Shadrach, Meshach and Abednego. He gave them higher positions in the city of Babylon and the towns around it.

Nebuchadnezzar Dreams About a Tree

4 I, King Nebuchadnezzar, am writing this letter.

I am sending it to you people from every nation and language in the whole world.

May you have great success!

2 I am pleased to tell you what has happened. The Most High God has done miraculous signs and wonders for me.

3 His miraculous signs are great.
His wonders are mighty.
His kingdom will last forever.
His rule will never end.

4 I was at home in my palace. I was content and very successful. **5** But I had a dream that made me afraid. I was lying on my bed. Then dreams and visions passed through my mind. They terrified me.

6 So I commanded that all of the wise men in Babylon be brought to me. I wanted them to tell me what my dream meant. **7** Those who try to figure things out by using magic came. So did those who study the heavens. I told all of them what I had dreamed. But they couldn't tell me what it meant.

8 Finally, Daniel came to me. He is called Belteshazzar, after the name of my god. The spirit of the holy gods is in him. I told him my dream.

9 I said, "Belteshazzar, you are chief of the magicians. I know that the spirit of the holy gods is in you. No mystery is too hard for you to figure out. Here is my dream. Tell me what it means.

10 "Here are the visions I saw while I was lying on my bed. I looked up and saw a tree standing in the middle of the land. It was very tall. **11** It had grown to be large and

strong. Its top touched the sky. It could be seen anywhere on earth. **12** Its leaves were beautiful. It had a lot of fruit on it. It provided enough food for people and animals. Under the tree, the wild animals found shade. The birds of the air lived in its branches. Every creature was fed from that tree.

13 "While I was still lying on my bed, I looked up. In my visions, I saw a holy messenger. He was coming down from heaven. **14** He called out in a loud voice. He said, 'Cut the tree down. Break off its branches. Strip its leaves off. Scatter its fruit. Let the animals that are under it run away. Let the birds that are in its branches fly off. **15** But leave the stump with its roots in the ground. Let it stay in the field. Put a band of iron and bronze around it.

" 'Let King Nebuchadnezzar become wet with the dew of heaven. Let him live like the animals among the plants of the earth. **16** Let him no longer have the mind of a man. Instead, let him be given the mind of an animal. Let him stay that way until seven periods of time pass by.

17 " 'The decision is announced by holy messengers. So all who are alive will know that the Most High God is King. He rules over all of the kingdoms of men. He gives them to anyone he wants. Sometimes he puts the least important men in charge of them.'

18 "That's the dream I, King Nebuchadnezzar, had. Now tell me what it means, Belteshazzar. None of the wise men in my kingdom can explain it to me. But you can. After all, the spirit of the holy gods is in you."

Daniel Explains Nebuchadnezzar's Dream

19 Daniel, who was also called Belteshazzar, was very bewildered for a while. His thoughts terrified him. So the king said, "Belteshazzar, don't let the dream or its meaning make you afraid."

Belteshazzar answered, "My master, I wish the dream were about your enemies! I wish its meaning had to do with them! **20** You saw a tree. It grew to be large and strong. Its top touched the sky. It could be seen from anywhere on earth. **21** Its leaves were beautiful. It had a lot of fruit on it. It provided enough food for people and animals. Under the tree, the wild animals found shade. The birds of the air lived in its branches.

22"My king, you are that tree! You have become great and strong. Your greatness has grown until it reaches the sky. Your rule has spread to all parts of the earth.

23"My king, you saw a holy messenger. He came down from heaven. He said, 'Cut the tree down. Destroy it. But leave the stump with its roots in the ground. Let it stay in the field. Put a band of iron and bronze around it. Let King Nebuchadnezzar become wet with the dew of heaven. Let him live like the wild animals. Let him stay that way until seven periods of time pass by.'

24"My king and master, here is what your dream means. The Most High God has given an order against you. 25You will be driven away from people. You will live like the wild animals. You will eat grass just as cattle do. You will become wet with the dew of heaven. Seven periods of time will pass by for you. Then you will recognize that the Most High God rules over all of the kingdoms of men. He gives them to anyone he wants.

26"But he gave a command to leave the stump of the tree along with its roots. That means your kingdom will be given back to you. It will happen when you recognize that the God of heaven rules.

27"So, my king, I hope you will accept my advice. Stop being sinful. Do what is right. Give up your evil practices. Show kindness to those who are being treated badly. Then perhaps things will continue to go well with you."

KIND   K

SHOW KINDNESS TO THOSE WHO ARE BEING TREATED BADLY.
— DANIEL 4:27 —

Nebuchadnezzar's Dream Comes True

28All of that happened to me. 29It took place twelve months later. I was walking on the roof of my palace in Babylon. 30I said, "Isn't this the great Babylon I have built as a place for my royal palace? I used my mighty power to build it. It shows how glorious my majesty is."

31I was still speaking when a voice was heard from heaven. It said, "King Nebuchadnezzar, here is what has been ordered concerning you. Your royal authority has been taken from you. 32You will be driven away from people. You will live like the wild animals. You will eat grass just as cattle do. Seven periods of time will pass by for you. Then you will recognize that the Most High God rules over all of the kingdoms of men. He gives them to anyone he wants."

33What had been said about me came true at once. I was driven away from people. I ate grass just as cattle do. My body became wet with the dew of heaven. I stayed that way until my hair grew like the feathers of an eagle. My nails became like the claws of a bird.

34At the end of that time I, Nebuchadnezzar, looked up toward heaven. My mind became clear again. Then I praised the Most High God. I gave honor and glory to the One who lives forever.

His rule will last forever.
His kingdom will never end.
35 He considers all of the nations on earth
to be nothing.
He does as he pleases
with the powers of heaven.
He does what he wants
with the nations of the earth.
No one can hold his hand back.
No one can say to him,
"What have you done?"

36My honor and glory were returned to me when my mind became clear again. The glory of my kingdom was given back to me. My advisers and nobles came to me. And I was put back on my throne. I became even greater than I had been before.

37Now I, Nebuchadnezzar, give praise and honor and glory to the King of heaven. Everything he does is right. All of his ways are fair. He is able to bring down those who live proudly.

A Hand Writes on the Palace Wall

5 King Belshazzar gave a big dinner. He invited a thousand of his nobles to it. He drank wine with them.

2While Belshazzar was drinking his wine, he gave orders to his servants. He commanded them to bring in some gold and silver cups. They were the cups his father Nebuchadnezzar had taken from the temple in Jerusalem. Belshazzar had them brought in so everyone could drink from them. That included the king himself, his nobles, his wives and his concubines.

3So the servants brought in the gold cups that had been taken from God's temple in Jerusalem. The king and his nobles drank from them. So did his wives and concubines. 4As they drank the wine, they praised their gods. The statues of those gods were made out of gold, silver, bronze, iron, wood or stone.

5Suddenly the fingers of a human hand appeared. They wrote something on the plaster of the palace wall. It happened near the lampstand.

The king watched the hand as it wrote. 6His face turned pale. He became so afraid that his knees knocked together. His legs couldn't hold him up any longer.

7The king sent for those who try to figure things out by using magic. He also sent for those who study the heavens. All of them were wise men in Babylon. He ordered that they be brought to him. He said to them, "I want one of you to read this writing and tell me what it means. If you do, you will be dressed in purple clothes. A gold chain will be put around your neck. And you will be made the third highest ruler in the kingdom."

8Then all of the king's wise men came in. But they couldn't read the writing. They couldn't tell him what it meant. 9So King Belshazzar became even more terrified. His face grew more pale. And his nobles were bewildered.

10The queen heard the king and his nobles talking. So she came into the dining hall. "King Belshazzar, may you live forever!" she said. "Don't be afraid! Don't look so pale! 11I know a man in your kingdom who has the spirit of the holy gods in him. He has understanding and wisdom and good sense just like the gods. That was discovered when your father Nebuchadnezzar was king. Nebuchadnezzar appointed him chief of those who tried to figure things out by using magic. He also put him in charge of those who studied the heavens.

12"The man's name is Daniel. Your father called him Belteshazzar. He has a clever mind and knowledge and understanding. He is also able to tell what dreams mean. He can explain riddles and solve hard problems. Send for him. He'll tell you what the writing means."

13So Daniel was brought to the king. The king said to him, "Are you Daniel? Are you one of the prisoners my father the king brought here from Judah? 14I have heard that the spirit of the gods is in you. I've also heard that you have understanding and good sense and special wisdom. 15"The wise men and those who practice magic were brought to me. They were asked to read this writing and tell me what it means. But they couldn't.

16"I have heard that you are able to explain things and solve hard problems. I hope you can read this writing and tell me what it means. If you can, you will be dressed in purple clothes. A gold chain will be put around your neck. And you will be made the third highest ruler in the kingdom."

17Then Daniel answered the king. He said, "You can keep your gifts for yourself. You can give your rewards to someone else. But I will read the writing for you. I'll tell you what it means.

18"King Belshazzar, the Most High God was good to your father Nebuchadnezzar. He gave him authority and greatness and glory and honor. 19God gave him a high position. Then all of the people from every nation and language became afraid of the king. He put to death anyone he wanted to. He spared anyone he wanted to spare. He gave high positions to anyone he wanted to. And he brought down anyone he wanted to bring down.

20"But his heart became very stubborn and proud. So he was removed from his royal throne. His glory was stripped away from him. 21He was driven away from people. He was given the mind of an animal. He lived like the wild donkeys. He ate grass just as cattle do. His body became wet with the dew of heaven. He stayed that way until he recognized that the Most High God rules over all of the kingdoms of men. He puts anyone he wants to in charge of them.

22"But you knew all of that, Belshazzar. After all, you are Nebuchadnezzar's son. In spite of that, you are still proud. 23You have taken your stand against the Lord of heaven. You had your servants bring cups from his temple to you. You and your nobles drank wine from them. So did your wives and concubines. You praised your gods. The statues of those gods are made out of silver, gold, bronze, iron, wood or stone. They can't see or hear or understand anything. But you didn't honor the God who holds in his hand your very life and everything you do. **24**So he sent the hand that wrote on the wall.

25"Here is what was written.

MENE, MENE, TEKEL, PARSIN

26"And here is what those words mean.

> *Mene* means that God has limited the time of your rule. He has brought it to an end.
> **27** *Tekel* means that you have been weighed on scales. And you haven't measured up to God's standard.
> **28** *Peres* means that your authority over your kingdom will be taken away from you. It will be given to the Medes and Persians."

29Then Belshazzar commanded his servants to dress Daniel in purple clothes. So they did. They put a gold chain around his neck. And he was made the third highest ruler in the kingdom.

30That very night Belshazzar, the king of Babylonia, was killed. **31**His kingdom was given to Darius the Mede. Darius was 62 years old.

Daniel Is Thrown Into a Den of Lions

6 It pleased Darius to appoint 120 royal rulers over his entire kingdom. **2**He placed three leaders over them. One of the leaders was Daniel. The royal rulers were made accountable to the three leaders. Then the king wouldn't lose any of his wealth. **3**Daniel did a better job than the other two leaders or any of the royal rulers. He was an unusually good and able man. So the king planned to put him in charge of the whole kingdom.

4But the other two leaders and the royal rulers heard about it. So they looked for a reason to bring charges against Daniel. They tried to find something wrong with the way he ran the government. But they weren't able to. They couldn't find any fault with his work. He could always be trusted. He never did anything wrong. And he always did what he was supposed to.

5Finally those men said, "It's almost impossible for us to come up with a reason to bring charges against this man Daniel. If we do, it will have to be in connection with the law of his God."

6So the two leaders and the royal rulers went as a group to the king. They said, "King Darius, may you live forever! **7**All of the royal leaders, high officials, royal rulers, advisers and governors want to make a suggestion. We've agreed that you should give an order. And you should make sure it's obeyed. Here is the command you should give. King Darius, during the next 30 days don't let any of your people pray to any god or man except to you. If they do, throw them into the lions' den.

8"Now give the order. Write it down in the laws of the Medes and Persians. Then it can't be changed." **9**So King Darius put the order in writing.

10Daniel found out that the king had signed the order. In spite of that, he did just as he had always done before. He went home to his upstairs room. Its windows opened toward Jerusalem. He went to his room three times a day to pray. He got down on his knees and gave thanks to his God.

POWER SURGE

THANKFUL ♣

[DANIEL] GOT DOWN ON HIS KNEES AND GAVE THANKS TO HIS GOD.
— DANIEL 6:10 —

11Some of the other royal officials went to where Daniel was staying. They saw him praying and asking God for help. **12**So they went to the king. They spoke to him about his royal order. They said, "King Darius, didn't you sign an official order? It said that for the next 30 days none of your people could pray to any god or man except to you. If they did, they would be thrown into the lions' den."

The king answered, "The order must still be obeyed. It's one of the laws of the Medes and Persians. So it can't be changed."

13Then they spoke to the king again. They said, "Daniel is one of the prisoners from Judah. He doesn't pay any attention

BELSHAZZAR (Not!)

DANIEL 5:30-31

That very night Belshazzar, the king of Babylonia, was killed. His kingdom was given to Darius the Mede.

King Belshazzar (bell-SHAH-zar) held the beautiful golden cup as his slave filled it up. One refill, two refills, who was counting? When everyone had a full cup again, Belshazzar stood and lifted his cup up above his head. He didn't say praise to God. He said praise to his favorite idol. Everyone in the huge banquet hall lifted their cups and praised their favorite idols.

The cup Belshazzar raised was no ordinary cup. It came from the temple of God in Jerusalem, and it was a holy thing. God surely did not want the things from his holy temple to be used to praise idols! Foolish Belshazzar!

As Belshazzar stood at the table, laughing and drinking, the room grew quiet. He looked up to see what everyone was looking at. The fingers of a hand appeared on a wall near him. No body, no arm, only the fingers of a hand. And it began to write:

MENE, MENE, TEKEL, PARSIN

Belshazzar's own hand shook so hard he spilled his drink all over his robe. His knees knocked together until he couldn't stand. He fell back in his chair and wiped the sweat from his head. Whatever did this mean? This was no language he or the others at the party could understand. So they called for Daniel. Daniel was a young man from Israel, a captive in Babylon, but wise because he followed God (read more about Daniel on page 1002). Right away Daniel knew what the words meant. And this is what he bravely told Belshazzar:

Though he was king of a huge land, Belshazzar was a foolish man, one who didn't pay any attention to God. He even mocked God by drinking out of temple cups and praising idols. Now he would pay for his foolishness. His rule was almost over. Someone else would take over his kingdom. That very night!

BELSHAZZAR

Foolish King Belshazzar. Don't be like him. Make sure you include God in your life. Nothing—not more things, not a smarter brain, not more fun—*nothing* is more important than God.

BELSHAZZAR IGNORED GOD IN HIS LIFE.
THE WHOLE STORY: DANIEL 5:1-30

Go to page 1002 for the next Super Hero

to you, King Darius. He doesn't obey the order you put in writing. He still prays to his God three times a day."

¹⁴When the king heard that, he was very upset. He didn't want Daniel to be harmed in any way. Until sunset, he did everything he could to save him.

¹⁵Then the men went as a group to the king. They said to him, "King Darius, remember that no order or law you make can be changed. That's what the laws of the Medes and Persians require."

¹⁶So the king gave the order. Daniel was brought out and thrown into the lions' den. The king said to him, "You always serve your God faithfully. So may he save you!"

¹⁷A stone was brought and placed over the opening of the den. The king sealed it with his own special ring. He also sealed it with the rings of his nobles. Then nothing could be done to help Daniel.

¹⁸The king returned to his palace. He didn't eat anything that night. He didn't ask for anything to be brought to him for his enjoyment. And he couldn't sleep.

¹⁹As soon as the sun began to rise, the king got up. He hurried to the lions' den. ²⁰When he got near it, he called out to Daniel. His voice was filled with great concern. He said, "Daniel! You serve the living God. You always serve him faithfully. So has he been able to save you from the lions?"

²¹Daniel answered, "My king, may you live forever! ²²My God sent his angel. And his angel shut the mouths of the lions. They haven't hurt me at all. That's because I haven't done anything wrong in God's sight. I've never done anything wrong to you either, my king."

²³The king was filled with joy. He ordered his servants to lift Daniel out of the den. So they did. They didn't see any wounds on him. That's because he had trusted in his God.

²⁴Then the king gave another order. The men who had said bad things about Daniel were brought in. They were thrown into the lions' den. So were their wives and children. Before they hit the bottom of the den, the lions attacked them. And the lions crushed all of their bones.

²⁵Then King Darius wrote to the people from every nation and language in the whole world. He said,

"May you have great success!

²⁶"I order people in every part of my kingdom to respect and honor Daniel's God.

"He is the living God.
    He will live forever.
His kingdom will not be destroyed.
    His rule will never end.
²⁷He sets people free and saves them.
    He does miraculous signs and
        wonders.
    He does them in the heavens and on
        the earth.
He has saved Daniel
    from the power of the lions."

²⁸So Daniel had success while Darius was king. Things went well with him during the rule of Cyrus, the Persian.

Daniel Has a Vision About Four Animals

7 It was the first year that Belshazzar was king of Babylon. Daniel had a dream. He was lying on his bed. In his dream, visions passed through his mind. He wrote down what he saw.

²Daniel said, "I had a vision at night. I looked up and saw the four winds of heaven. They were stirring up the Mediterranean Sea. ³Four large animals came up out of the sea. Each one was different from the others.

⁴"The first animal was like a lion. It had the wings of an eagle. I watched until its wings were torn off. Then it was lifted up from the ground. It stood on two feet like a man. And a man's heart was given to it.

⁵"I saw a second animal. It looked like a bear. It was raised up on one of its sides. And it had three ribs between its teeth. It was told, 'Get up! Eat meat until you are full!'

⁶"After that, I saw another animal. It looked like a leopard. On its back were four wings like the wings of a bird. It had four heads. And it was given authority to rule.

⁷"After that, in my vision I looked up and saw a fourth animal. It was terrifying and very powerful. It had large iron teeth. It crushed those it attacked and ate them up. It stomped on anything that was left. It was different from the other animals. And it had ten horns.

⁸"I thought about the horns. Then I saw another horn. It was a little one. It grew up among the other horns. Three of the first horns were pulled up by their roots to make room for it. The little horn had eyes like the eyes of a man. Its mouth was always bragging.

⁹"As I watched,

DANIEL

DANIEL 6:21-22

B

()

H

> Daniel answered, "My king, may you live forever! My God sent his angel. And his angel shut the mouths of the lions. They haven't hurt me at all. That's because I haven't done anything wrong in God's sight."

Daniel knelt at the window of an upstairs room in Babylon. The window faced toward his home far away in Jerusalem. Looking off into the distance, Daniel prayed to God. His prayer was disturbed by sounds in the street below. He saw some officers of the kingdom hurrying away. Daniel knew he was in trouble. Serious trouble. The king had made a law that the people could pray only to him. Daniel had been caught breaking that law.

Sweat dripped down Daniel's forehead when he was called by the king later that morning. "Daniel!" the king cried. "Didn't you know what would happen if you prayed to your God?"

Of course Daniel knew what would happen. But he also knew that worshiping God was more important than any law the king could make against it.

The king didn't really want to throw Daniel into a lions' den. But a law was a law. Just before they closed the door, he said to Daniel, "I hope your God can save you!"

It was very dark. **DANIEL COULD SEE THE GLEAMING EYES OF THE LIONS ALL AROUND HIM.** Then, behind them, he saw something lighter. It was an angel! Now Daniel knew he would be safe. The angel had already shut the mouths of the lions. They would not hurt him.

A soft gray light filled the lions' den as morning came. Daniel heard the king's voice shouting from above, "Daniel! Did your God save you?" With a huge smile Daniel answered the king.

BE A DANIEL

Daniel knew it was dangerous to disobey the king's law. But he knew that following God was more important than anything else. Daniel was a person just like you are. God gave him courage to do the right thing. God will give you courage when you choose to do the right thing, too.

DANIEL CHOSE TO DO THE RIGHT THING EVEN WHEN IT WAS DANGEROUS.

THE WHOLE STORY: DANIEL 6:1-28

Go to page 1011 for the next Super Hero

"thrones were set in place.
The Eternal God took his seat.
His clothes were as white as snow.
The hair on his head was white like
wool.
His throne was blazing with fire.
And flames were all around its
wheels.
10 A river of fire was flowing.
It was coming out from in front of
God.
Thousands and thousands of angels
served him.
Millions of them stood in front of
him.
The court was seated.
And the books were opened.

11 "Then I continued to watch because of the way the horn was bragging. I kept looking until the fourth animal was killed. I watched until its body was destroyed. It was thrown into the blazing fire. **12** The authority of the other animals had been stripped away from them. But they were allowed to live for a period of time.

13 "In my vision I saw One who looked like a son of man. He was coming with the clouds of heaven. He approached the Eternal God. He was led right up to him. **14** And he was given authority, glory and a kingdom. People from every nation and language worshiped him. His authority will last forever. It will not pass away. His kingdom will never be destroyed.

An Angel Tells Daniel What His Dream Means

15 "My spirit was troubled. The visions that passed through my mind upset me. **16** I approached an angel who was standing there. I asked him what all of those things really meant.

"So he explained everything to me. He told me what it meant. He said, **17** 'The four large animals stand for four kingdoms. The kingdoms will appear on the earth. **18** But the holy people of the Most High God will receive the kingdom. They will possess it forever. It will belong to them for ever and ever.'

19 "Then I wanted to know what the fourth animal stood for. It was different from the others. It was the most terrifying of all. It had iron teeth and bronze claws. It crushed those it attacked and ate them up. It stomped on anything that was left. **20** "I also wanted to know about the ten horns on its head. And I wanted to know about the other horn that grew up later. It

caused three of the ten horns to fall out. It appeared to be stronger than the others. It had eyes. And its mouth was always bragging. **21** "I saw that the horn was at war with God's people. It was winning the battle over them. **22** But then the Eternal God came. He decided in favor of his holy people. So the time came when the kingdom was given to them.

23 "Here's how the angel explained it to me. He said, 'The fourth animal stands for a fourth kingdom. It will appear on earth. It will be different from the other kingdoms. It will eat up the whole earth. It will stomp on it and crush it. **24** The ten horns stand for ten kings. They will come from the fourth kingdom.

" 'After them another king will appear. He will be different from the earlier ones. He'll bring three kings under his control. **25** He'll speak against the Most High God. He'll treat God's people badly. He will try to change the times and laws that were given by God. God's people will be handed over to him for three and a half years.

26 " 'But the court will open. And the power of that king will be taken away from him. It will be completely destroyed forever. **27** Then the authority, power and greatness of all of the kingdoms on earth will be handed over to the people of the Most High God. His kingdom will last forever. Every ruler will worship and obey him.'

28 "That's all I saw. My thoughts deeply troubled me. My face turned pale. But I kept those things to myself."

Daniel Has a Vision About a Ram and a Goat

8 It was the third year of King Belshazzar's rule. After the vision that had already appeared to me, I had another one. **2** In my vision I saw myself in the city of Susa. It has high walls around it. It is in the land of Elam. In the vision I was beside the Ulai Waterway.

3 I looked up and saw a ram that had two horns. He was standing beside the waterway. His horns were long. One of them was longer than the other. But it grew up later. **4** I watched the ram as he charged toward the west. He also charged toward the north and the south. No animal could stand up against him. Not one of them could save anyone from his power. He did as he pleased. And he became great.

5 I was thinking about all of that. Then a goat suddenly came from the west. He had a large horn between his eyes. He raced across the whole earth without even touching the ground. **6**He came toward the ram that had the two horns. It was the ram I had seen standing beside the waterway. The goat was burning with anger. He charged at the ram. **7**I saw him attack the ram with mighty force. He struck the ram and broke his two horns. The ram didn't have the power to stand up against him. The goat knocked him to the ground and stomped on him. No one could save the ram from his power.

8The goat became very great. But when his power was at its greatest, his large horn was broken off. In its place four large horns grew up toward the four winds of heaven.

9Out of one of the four horns came another horn. It started small but became more and more powerful. It grew to the south and to the east and toward the beautiful land of Israel. **10**It grew until it reached the stars in the sky. It threw some of them down to the earth. And it stomped on them.

11It set itself up to be as great as God. He is the Prince of the heavenly army. It took the daily sacrifices away from him. And his temple in Jerusalem was brought low. **12**Because many of God's people refused to obey him, they were handed over to the horn. The daily sacrifices were also given over to it. It was successful no matter what it did. And the true worship of God was thrown down to the ground.

13Then I heard a holy angel speaking. Another holy angel spoke to him. He asked, "How long will it take for the vision to come true? The daily sacrifices will be stopped. Those who refuse to obey God will be destroyed. The temple will be handed over to an enemy. And some of the stars will be stomped on."

14One of the holy angels said to me, "It will take 2,300 evenings and mornings. Then the temple will be made holy again."

Gabriel Tells Daniel What His Vision Means

15I was watching the vision. And I was trying to understand it. Then I saw someone who looked like a man. **16**I heard a voice from the Ulai Waterway. It called out, "Gabriel, tell Daniel what his vision means."

17Gabriel came close to where I was standing. I was terrified and fell down flat with my face toward the ground. He said to me, "Son of man, I want you to understand that the vision tells about the time of the end."

18While he was speaking to me, I was sound asleep. I lay with my face toward the ground. Then he touched me. He raised me to my feet.

19He said, "I am going to tell you what will happen later. It will take place when God is angry. The vision tells about the appointed time of the end. **20**You saw a ram that had two horns. It stands for the kings of Media and Persia. **21**The goat stands for the king of Greece. The large horn between his eyes is the first king. **22**Four horns took its place when it was broken off. They stand for four kingdoms that will come from his nation. But those kingdoms will not be as powerful as his.

23"Toward the end of their rule, those who refuse to obey God will become completely evil. Then another king will appear. He will have a mean-looking face. He will be a master at making clever plans. **24**He will become very strong. But he will not get that way by his own power. People will be amazed at the way he destroys everything. He will be successful no matter what he does. He will destroy the mighty men and the holy people.

25"He will tell lies in order to succeed. He will think he is more important than anyone else. When people feel safe, he will destroy many of them. He will stand up against the greatest Prince of all. Then he will be destroyed. But he will not be killed by human beings.

26"The vision of the evenings and mornings that has been given to you is true. But seal up the vision. It tells about a time far off."

27I was worn out. I lay sick for several days. Then I got up and returned to my work for the king. The vision bewildered me. I couldn't understand it.

Daniel Prays to the LORD

9 It was the first year that Darius was king of Babylonia. He was from Media and was the son of Xerxes. **2**In that year I learned from the Scriptures that Jerusalem would remain destroyed for 70 years. That was what the LORD had told the prophet Jeremiah. **3**So I prayed to the Lord God. I begged him. I made many appeals to him. I didn't eat anything. I put on black clothes. And I sat down in ashes.

4I prayed to the LORD my God. I admitted that we had sinned. I said,

"Lord, you are a great and wonderful God. You keep the covenant you

POWER - SURGE

LOVING

LORD, YOU ARE A GREAT AND WONDERFUL GOD. YOU KEEP THE COVENANT YOU MADE WITH ALL THOSE WHO LOVE YOU AND OBEY YOUR COMMANDS. YOU SHOW THEM YOUR LOVE.
— DANIEL 9:4 —

OBEYS

made with all those who love you and obey your commands. You show them your love.

5 "We have sinned and done what is wrong. We have been evil. We have refused to obey you. We have turned away from your commands and laws. 6 We haven't listened to your servants the prophets. They spoke in your name to our kings and princes. They also brought your message to all of our people in the land.

7 "Lord, you always do what is right. But we are covered with shame today. We are the people of Judah and Jerusalem. All of us are Israelites, no matter where we live. We are now living in many countries. You scattered us among the nations because we weren't faithful to you. 8 LORD, we and our kings and princes and people are covered with shame. We have sinned against you.

9 "You are the Lord our God. You show us your tender love. You forgive us. But we have turned against you. 10 You are the LORD our God. But we haven't obeyed you. We haven't kept the laws you gave us through your servants the prophets. 11 All of the people of Israel have broken your law and turned away from it. They have refused to obey you.

"Curses and warnings are written down in the Law of Moses. He was your servant. Those curses have been poured out on us. That's because we have sinned against you. 12 The warnings you gave us and our rulers have come true. You have brought great trouble on us. Nothing like what has been done to Jerusalem has ever happened anywhere else on earth.

13 "The curses that are written in the Law of Moses have fallen on us. We have received nothing but trouble. You are the LORD our God. But we haven't asked for your favor. We haven't turned away from our sins. We've refused to pay attention to the laws you gave us. 14 LORD, you didn't hold back from bringing this trouble on us. You always do what is right. But we haven't obeyed you.

15 "Lord our God, you used your mighty hand to bring your people out of Egypt. You made a name for yourself. It is still great to this very day. But we have sinned. We've done what is wrong. 16 Lord, you saved your people before. So turn your burning anger away from Jerusalem again. After all, it is your city. It's your holy mountain. All those who live around us laugh at Jerusalem and your people. That's because we have sinned. Our people before us did evil things too.

17 "Our God, hear my prayers. Pay attention to the appeals I make to you. Look with favor on your temple that has been destroyed. Do it for your own honor. 18 Our God, please listen to us. The city that belongs to you has been destroyed. Open your eyes and see it. We aren't asking you to answer our prayers because we are

POWER - SURGE

FORGIVING F

YOU ARE THE LORD OUR GOD. YOU SHOW US YOUR TENDER LOVE. YOU FORGIVE US.
— DANIEL 9:9 —

LOVING

godly. Instead, we're asking you to do it because you love us so much.

19"Lord, please listen! Lord, please forgive us! Lord, hear our prayers! Take action for your own honor. Our God, please don't wait. Your city and your people belong to you."

Gabriel Tells Daniel About Seventy "Weeks"

20I was speaking and praying. I was admitting that I and my people Israel had sinned. I was making my appeal to the LORD my God concerning his holy mountain of Zion.

21While I was still praying, Gabriel came to me. I had seen him in my earlier vision. He flew over to me very quickly. It was about the time when the evening sacrifice is offered. **22**He helped me understand. He said, "Daniel, I have come now to give you a good knowledge and understanding of these things. **23**You are highly respected. So as soon as you began to pray, the LORD gave you an answer. I have come to tell you what it is. Here is how you must understand the vision.

24"The LORD has appointed 70 'weeks' for your people and your holy city. During that time, acts against God's law will be stopped. Sin will come to an end. And the evil things people do will be paid for. Then everyone will always do what is right. Everything that has been made known in visions and prophecies will come true. And the Most Holy Room in the temple will be anointed.

25"Here is what I want you to know and understand. There will be seven 'weeks.' Then there will be 62 'weeks.' The seven 'weeks' will begin when an order is given to rebuild Jerusalem and make it like new again.

"At the end of the 62 'weeks,' the Anointed King will come. Jerusalem will have streets and a water system when it is rebuilt. But that will be done in times of trouble. **26**After the 62 'weeks,' the Anointed King will be cut off. His followers will desert him. And everything he has will be taken away from him. The army of the ruler who will come will destroy the city and the temple. The end will come like a flood. War will continue until the end. The LORD has ordered that many places be destroyed.

27"A covenant will be put into effect with many people for one 'week.' In the middle of the 'week' sacrifices and offerings will come to an end. In one part of the temple a hated thing that destroys will be set up. It will remain until the LORD brings the end he has ordered."

Daniel Has a Vision About What Will Happen to Israel

10 It was the third year that Cyrus, the king of Persia, ruled over Babylonia. At that time I was living in Babylon. There the people called me Belteshazzar. A message came to me from God. It was true. It was about a great war. I had a vision that showed me what it meant.

2At that time I was very sad for three weeks. **3**I didn't eat any rich food. No meat or wine touched my lips. I didn't use any lotions at all until the three weeks were over.

4I was standing on the bank of the great Tigris River. It was the 24th day of the first month. **5**I looked up and saw a man who was dressed in linen clothes. A belt that was made out of the finest gold was around his waist. **6**His body gleamed like chrysolite. His face shone like lightning. His eyes were like flaming torches. His arms and legs were as bright as polished bronze. And his voice was like the sound of a large crowd.

7I was the only one who saw the vision. The men who were there with me didn't see it. But they were so terrified that they ran and hid. **8**So I was left alone as I was watching that great vision. I felt very weak. My face turned as pale as death. And I was helpless.

9Then I heard the man speak. As I listened to him, I fell sound asleep. My face was toward the ground.

10A hand touched me. It pulled me up on my hands and knees. I began to tremble with fear. **11**The man said, "Daniel, you are highly respected. Think carefully about what I am going to say to you. And stand up. God has sent me to you." When he said that, I trembled as I stood up.

12He continued, "Do not be afraid, Daniel. You decided to get more understanding. You went without food as you worshiped your God. Since the first day you did those things, your words were heard. I have come to give you an answer. **13**But the prince of Persia opposed me for 21 days. Then Michael came to help me. He is one of the leaders of the angels. He helped me win the battle over the king of Persia.

14"Now I have come to explain the vision to you. I will tell you what will happen to your people. The vision shows what will take place in days to come."

15While he was telling me those things,

I bowed with my face toward the ground. I wasn't able to speak. **16**Then someone who looked like a man touched my lips. I opened my mouth. I began to speak to the one who was standing in front of me. I said, "My master, I'm greatly troubled because of the vision I've seen. And I'm helpless. **17**How can I talk with you? I feel very weak. In fact, I can hardly breathe."

18The one who looked like a man touched me again. He gave me strength. **19**"Do not be afraid," he said. "You are highly respected. May peace be with you! Be strong now. Be strong."

When he spoke to me, I became stronger. I said, "Speak, my master. You have given me strength."

20So he said, "Do you know why I have come to you? Soon I will return to fight against the prince of Persia. When I go, the prince of Greece will come. **21**But first I will tell you what is written in the Book of Truth. No one gives me any help against those princes except Michael. He

11 is your leader. **1**I stepped forward to help him and keep him safe. It was the first year that Darius, the Mede, was king.

The Kings of Egypt and Syria

2"Now then, what I'm about to tell you is true. Three more kings will appear in Persia. Then a fourth one will rule. He will be much richer than all of the others. He will use his wealth to gain power. And he will stir up everyone against the kingdom of Greece.

3"After him, a mighty king will appear. He will rule with great power. He will do as he pleases. **4**Not long after his rule ends, his kingdom will be broken up. It will be divided up into four parts. His children will not receive it when he dies. And it will not be as strong as his kingdom. It will be pulled up by the roots. And it will be given to others.

5"The king of Egypt will become strong. But one of his commanders will become even stronger. He will rule over his own kingdom with great power. **6**After many years, the two kingdoms will join forces. The daughter of the next king of Egypt will go to the king of Syria. She will join forces with him. But she will not hold on to her power. And he and his power will not last either. In those days she and her attendants will be put to death. Her father will die. So will the one who helped her.

7"Someone from her family line will take her place. He will attack the army of the next king of Syria. Then he will enter his fort. He will fight against that army and win. **8**He will take the metal statues of their gods. He will also take away their priceless articles of silver and gold. He will carry everything off to Egypt. For many years he will leave the king of Syria alone.

9"That king will march into territory that was controlled by Egypt. Then he will return to his own country. **10**His sons will prepare for war. They will gather a huge army. It will sweep along like a mighty flood. It will fight its way as far as one of the Egyptian forts.

11"Another king of Egypt will march out with mighty force. He will fight against the next king of Syria. That king will gather a huge army. But it will lose the battle. **12**His soldiers will be carried off. Then the king of Egypt will be filled with pride. He will kill many thousands of soldiers. But his success will not last.

13"The king of Syria will bring another army together. It will be larger than the first one. After several years, he will march out with a huge army. It will have everything it needs for battle.

14"In those times many people will rise up against the next king of Egypt. Lawless men in your own nation will refuse to obey him. That is what you saw in your vision. But they will not succeed.

15"Then the king of Syria will go to a certain city that has high walls around it. He will build ramps against them. And he will capture that city. The forces of Egypt will not have the power to stop him. Even their best troops will not be strong enough to stand up against him. **16**He will do anything he wants to. No one will be able to stand up against him. He will take over the beautiful land of Israel. And he will have the power to destroy it.

17"He will decide to come with the might of his entire kingdom. He will join forces with the king of Egypt. And he will give him his daughter to become his wife. He will do it in order to take control of Egypt. But his plans will not succeed. They will not help him.

18"Then he will turn his attention to the lands along the Mediterranean coast. He will take over many of them. But a commander will put an end to his proud actions. He will turn his pride back on him.

19"After that, the king of Syria will return to the forts in his own country. But he will trip and fall. And he will never be seen again.

20"The next king after him will send

someone out to collect taxes. The taxes will help maintain the glory of his kingdom. But in a few years the king will be destroyed. It will not happen because someone becomes angry with him or kills him in battle.

21 "Another king will take his place. Many people will hate him. He will not be honored as a king should be. He will lead an army into the kingdom when its people feel secure. He will make clever plans to capture it. 22 Then he will sweep away a huge army. The army and a prince of the covenant will be destroyed.

23 "The king of Syria will make an agreement with that prince. But then he will not keep his word. He will rise to power with the help of only a few people. 24 When the people in the richest areas feel secure, he will attack them. He will do what the kings before him could not do. And he will reward his followers with the goods and wealth he takes. He will make clever plans to take over the forts. But that will last for only a short time.

25 "He will stir up his strength and courage. With a large army he will go to war against the next king of Egypt. That king will fight against him with a huge and very powerful army. But he will not be able to stand up against him. So the plans of the king of Syria will succeed. 26 The trusted advisers of the king of Egypt will try to destroy him. His army will be swept away. Many of his soldiers will be wounded or killed.

27 "The kings of Syria and Egypt will sit at the same table. But in their hearts they will plan to do what is evil. And they will tell lies to each other. But it will not do them any good. God will put an end to their plans at his appointed time.

28 "The king of Syria will return to his own country. He will go back there with great wealth. But he will make evil plans against the holy temple in Jerusalem. He will do a lot of harm to the temple and the people who worship there. Then he will return to his own country.

29 "At God's appointed time, the king of Syria will march south again. But this time things will turn out differently. 30 Roman ships will oppose him. He will lose hope. Then he will turn back. He will take out his anger against the holy temple. And he will show favor to the Jews who desert it.

31 "His army will come and make the temple area 'unclean.' They will put a stop to the daily sacrifices. Then they will set up a hated thing that destroys. 32 He will

pretend to praise those who have broken the covenant. He will lead them to do what is evil. But the people who know their God will firmly oppose him.

33 "Those who are wise will teach many others. But for a while, some of the wise will be killed with swords. Others will be burned to death. Still others will be made prisoners. Or they will be robbed of everything they have. 34 When that happens, they will receive a little help. Many who are not honest will join them.

35 "So some of the wise people will suffer. They will be made pure in the fire. They will be made spotless until the time of the end. It will still come at God's appointed time.

A King Will Honor Himself

36 "A certain king will do as he pleases. He will honor himself. He will put himself above every god. He will say things that have never been heard before against the greatest God of all. He will have success until God is not angry anymore. What God has decided to do must take place.

37 "The king will not show any respect for the gods his people have always worshiped. He will not respect the one women long for. He will not have respect for any god. Instead, he will put himself above all of them. 38 In place of them, he will worship a god of war. He will honor a god his people have not had anything to do with before. He will give gold and silver to that god. He will bring jewels and expensive gifts to it.

39 "He will attack the strongest forts. A new god will help him do it. He will greatly honor those who recognize him as their leader. He will make them rulers over many people. And he will give them land as a reward.

40 "A king in the south will go to war against him. It will happen at the time of the end. The king who will honor himself will rush out against him. He will come with chariots and horsemen. He will attack with a lot of ships. He will lead his army into many countries. He will sweep through them like a flood.

41 "He will also march into the beautiful land of Israel. Many countries will fall. But Edom, Moab and the leaders of Ammon will be saved from his mighty hand. 42 His power will reach out into many countries. Even Egypt will not escape. 43 He will gain control of all of Egypt's riches. He will take their gold and silver treasures. The people of Libya and Cush will be under his control.

44"But reports from the east and the north will terrify him. He will burn with anger and march out to destroy many people and wipe them out. 45He will set up his royal tents. He will put them between the Mediterranean Sea and the beautiful holy mountain of Zion. But his end will come. And no one will help him.

The Time of the End

12 "At that time Michael will appear. He is the great leader of the angels who guards your people. There will be a time of terrible suffering. Things will be worse than at any time since nations began. But at that time of suffering your people will be saved. Their names are written in the Book of Life.

2"Huge numbers of people who lie dead in their graves will wake up. Some will rise up to life that will never end. Others will rise up to shame that will never end. 3Those who are wise will shine like the brightness of the sky. Those who lead many others to do what is right will be like the stars for ever and ever.

4"But I want you to roll up the scroll, Daniel. Seal it until the time of the end. Many people will go here and there to increase their knowledge."

5Then I looked up and saw two other angels. One was on this side of the Tigris River. And one was on the other side. 6The man who was dressed in linen was above the waters of the river. One of the angels said to him, "How long will it be before these amazing things come true?" 7The man raised both hands toward heaven. I heard him take an oath in the name of the One who lives forever. He answered me, "Three and a half years. Then the power of the holy people will be broken at last. And all of those things will come true."

8I heard what he said. But I didn't understand it. So I asked, "My master, what will come of all of this?"

9He answered, "Go on your way, Daniel. The scroll is rolled up. It is sealed until the time of the end. 10Many people will be made pure in the fire. They will be made spotless. But sinful people will continue to be evil. Not one sinful person will understand. But those who are wise will.

11"The daily sacrifices will be stopped. And the hated thing that destroys will be set up. After that, there will be 1,290 days. 12Blessed are those who wait for the 1,335 days and reach the end of them.

13"Daniel, go on your way until the end. Your body will rest in the grave. Then at the end of the days you will rise from the dead. And you will receive what God has appointed for you."

POWER-SURGE

TELLS OTHERS

THOSE WHO ARE WISE WILL SHINE LIKE THE BRIGHTNESS OF THE SKY. THOSE WHO LEAD MANY OTHERS TO DO WHAT IS RIGHT WILL BE LIKE THE STARS FOR EVER AND EVER.
— DANIEL 12:3 —

W

WISE

HOSEA

The events of the book of Hosea happen just before the Israelites go into captivity because of their sins. Hosea's marriage to unfaithful Gomer is a picture of God and the unfaithful Israelites. Hosea's experiences show that God will punish his people if they do not repent but that he is willing to forgive them if they turn to him. As you read Hosea, remember that God is speaking to you, too, through these words. He will bless you when you ask him to forgive your sins.

HERO IN THIS BOOK . . .

HOSEA
PAGE 1011

1 A message came to Hosea from the LORD. He was the son of Beeri. The message came while Uzziah, Jotham, Ahaz and Hezekiah were kings of Judah. It also came while Jeroboam was king of Israel. He was the son of Jehoash. Here is what Hosea said.

Hosea's Wife and Children

2The LORD began to speak through me. He said to me, "Go. Get married to a woman who will commit adultery. Take as your own the children who will be born as a result of her adultery. Marry her because the people of the land are guilty of the worst kind of adultery. They have not been faithful to me." **3**So I married Gomer. She was the daughter of Diblaim. Gomer became pregnant. And she had a son by me.

4Then the LORD said to me, "Name him Jezreel. That is because I will soon punish Jehu's royal family. He killed many people at the city of Jezreel. So I will put an end to the kingdom of Israel. **5**At that time I will break their military power. It will happen in the Valley of Jezreel."

6Gomer became pregnant again. She had a daughter. Then the LORD said to me, "Name her Lo-Ruhamah. That is because I will no longer show love to the people of Israel. I will not forgive them anymore. **7**But I will show love to the people of Judah. And I will save them. I will not use

HOSEA

HOSEA 1:2

✓ **The LORD began to speak through me. He said to me, "Go. Get married to a woman who will commit adultery."**

✝ **H**osea (hoe-ZAY-uh) sat with his head in his hands. Did God really want him to do this thing? Marry a woman that he *knew* would be unkind and unfaithful to him? Why would Hosea want to marry someone who didn't love him and didn't want to stay with him?

Hosea sighed. He understood the message. Just as his wife would be unfaithful to him, so God's people were unfaithful to God. And just as Hosea would love her anyway and want her back, so God loves his people and wants them to return to him.

Getting to his feet, Hosea prepared to go to the house of Gomer. He would obey God. He would marry Gomer in spite of the pain she would bring him—just because God told him to do it.

BE A HOSEA

Hosea knew how important obedience was. So he obeyed God even when what God asked him to do was hard. Be a Hosea. Being obedient isn't always easy. But it is important, and you can do it!

HOSEA OBEYED GOD.

Go to page 1042 for the next Super Hero

bows or swords or other weapons of war to do it. I will not save them by using horses and horsemen either. Instead, I will use my own power to save them. I am the LORD their God."

8Later, Gomer stopped nursing Lo-Ruhamah. After that, she had another son. 9Then the LORD said, "Name him Lo-Ammi. That is because Israel is no longer my people. And I am no longer their God.

10"But the time will come when the people of Israel will be like the sand on the seashore. It can't be measured or counted. Now it is said about them, 'You are not my people.' But at that time they will be called 'children of the living God.' 11The people of Judah and Israel will be brought together again. They will appoint one leader. They will increase their numbers in the land. And Jezreel's day will be great. That is because I will plant Israel in the land again.

2 "People of Israel, call your brothers My People. And call your sisters My Loved Ones."

Israel Is Punished and Brought Back to the LORD

2I said to my children,

"Talk things over with your mother.
   Talk to her.
She isn't acting like a wife to me
   anymore.
   She no longer treats me as her
     husband.
Tell her to stop looking and acting like
   a prostitute.
   Tell her not to let her lovers
   lie on her breasts anymore.
3If she doesn't stop it, I will strip her
   naked.
   I'll make her as bare as she was on
     the day she was born.
I'll make her like a desert.
   She will become like dry land.
   And I'll let her die of thirst."

4I won't show my love to Gomer's
   children.
   They are the children of other men.
5Their mother hasn't been faithful to
   me.
   She who became pregnant with
     them
   has brought shame on herself.
She said, "I will chase after my lovers.
   They give me my food and water.
They provide me with wool and linen.
   They give me olive oil and wine."
6So I will block her path with bushes
   that have thorns.

I'll build a wall around her.
   Then she can't go to her lovers.
7She will still chase after her lovers.
   But she won't catch them.
She'll look for them.
   But she won't find them.
Then she'll say,
   "I'll go back to my husband.
That's where I was at first.
   I was better off then than I am now."
8She wouldn't admit that I was the one
   who gave her everything she had.
I provided her with grain, olive oil
   and fresh wine.
I gave her plenty of silver and gold.
   But she used it to make statues of
     Baal.

9So I will take away my grain when it
     gets ripe.
   I'll take my fresh wine when it's
     ready.
I'll take back my wool and my linen.
   I gave them to her to cover her
     naked body.
10So now I'll uncover her body.
   All of her lovers will see it.
   No one can stop me from punishing
     her.
11I will put a stop to the special times she
   celebrates.
   I'll bring an end to the feasts she
     celebrates each year.
I'll stop her New Moon Feasts and her
   Sabbath days.
   I'll bring all of her appointed feasts
     to an end.
12I will destroy her vines and her fig
   trees.
   She said they were her pay from her
     lovers.
I'll make them like clumps of bushes
   and weeds.
   Wild animals will eat them up.

13The LORD announces,

"Israel burned incense to the gods
   that were named after Baal.
I will punish her
   for all of the times she did that.
She decorated herself with rings and
   jewelry.
   Then she went after her lovers.
   But she forgot all about me.

14"So now I am going to draw her back to
   me.
I will lead her into the desert.
   There I will speak tenderly to her.
15I will give her back her vineyards.
   I will make the Valley of Achor a
     door of hope for her.

Then she will love me, as she did when
she was young.
She will love me just as she did
when she came up out of Egypt.

16 "A new day is coming," announces the
LORD.
"Israel will call me My Husband.
She will no longer call me My
Master.
17 She will no longer speak about the
gods
that are named after Baal.
She will not pray to them for help
anymore.
18 At that time I will make a covenant
for the good of my people.
I will make it with the wild animals
and the birds of the air.
It will also be made with the creatures
that move on the ground.
I will remove bows and swords
and other weapons of war from the
land.
Then my people can lie down in
safety.
19 I will make Israel my own.
She will belong to me forever.
I will do to her what is right and fair.
I will love her tenderly.
20 I will be faithful to her.
And she will recognize me as the
LORD.

21 "So at that time I will answer her,"
announces the LORD.
"I will command the skies
to send rain on the earth.
22 Then the earth will produce grain,
olive oil and fresh wine.
And Israel will be called Jezreel.
That is because I will answer her
prayers.
23 I will plant her in the land for myself.
I will show my love to the one I
called Not My Loved One.
I will say, 'You are my people'
to those who were called Not My
People.
And they will say, 'You are my
God.' "

Hosea Brings His Wife Back to Himself

3 The LORD said to me, "Go. Show your
love to your wife again. She is loved
by another man. And she has committed
adultery. But I want you to love her just as
I love the people of Israel. They turn to
other gods. And they love to offer raisin
cakes to Baal and eat them. In spite of
that, I love my people."

2 So I bought Gomer for six ounces of
silver and about ten bushels of barley.
3 Then I told her, "You must wait for me
for a long time. You must not be a prostitute. You must not have sex with any
man. And I will wait for you."

4 So the people of Israel will live for a
long time without a king or prince. They
won't have sacrifices or sacred stones.
They won't have sacred linen aprons or
statues of family gods. 5 After that, the
people of Israel will return to the LORD
their God. They will look to him and to a
king from the family line of David. In the
last days, they will tremble with fear as
they come to the LORD. And they will receive his full blessing.

The LORD Brings Charges Against Israel

4 People of Israel, listen to the LORD's
message.
He is bringing charges
against you who live in Israel.
He says, "There is no faithfulness
or love in the land.
No one recognizes me as God.
2 People call down curses on others.
They tell lies and commit murder.
They steal and commit adultery.
They break all of my laws.
They keep on spilling the blood of
others.
3 That is why the land is drying up.
All those who live in it
are getting weaker and weaker.
The wild animals and the birds of the
air are dying.
So are the fish in the ocean.

4 "But you priests should not blame the
people.
You should not find fault with one
another.
After all, your people
could also bring charges against you.
5 You trip and fall day and night.
And the prophets fall down along
with you.
So I will destroy your nation.
She is the one who gave birth to you.
6 My people are destroyed
because they do not know me.

"You priests have refused to obey me.
So I will refuse to accept you as my
priests.
You have not paid any attention to my
law.
So I will not let your children be my
priests.
7 The more priests there are,

the more they sin against me.
They have traded their glorious God
for that shameful god Baal.
8 They live off the sins of my people.
And they want them to keep on
sinning.
9 So here is what I will do.
I will punish people and priests
alike.
I will judge them because of their
sinful lives.
I will pay them back
for the evil things they have done.

10 "My people will eat.
But they will not have enough.
They will have sex with prostitutes.
But they will not have any children.
That is because they have deserted
me.
11 They have sex with prostitutes.
They drink old wine and fresh wine.
When they do those things,
it destroys their ability to
understand.
12 They ask a wooden statue of a god for
advice.
They expect to get answers from a
stick of wood.
They act like prostitutes.
That leads them down the wrong
path.
I am their God.
But they are not faithful to me.
13 They offer sacrifices on the
mountaintops.
They burn offerings on the hills.
They worship under oak, poplar and
terebinth trees.
The trees provide plenty of shade.
So your daughters become prostitutes.
And your daughters-in-law commit
adultery.

14 "I will not punish your daughters
when they become prostitutes.
I will not judge your daughters-in-law
when they commit adultery.
After all, the men themselves have sex
with sinful women.
They offer sacrifices where temple
prostitutes earn their living.
People who can't understand will be
destroyed!

15 "Israel, you are not faithful to me.
But I do not want Judah to become
guilty too.

"My people, do not go to Gilgal to offer
sacrifices.
Do not go up to Bethel to worship
other gods.

Do not take an oath and say,
'You can be sure that the LORD is
alive.'
16 The people of Israel are stubborn.
They are as stubborn as a young cow.
So how can I take care of them
like lambs in a meadow?
17 The people of Ephraim have joined
themselves to other gods.
And nothing can be done to help
them.
18 They continue to be unfaithful to me
even when their drinks are gone.
And their rulers love to do shameful
things.
19 A windstorm will blow all of them
away.
And their sacrifices will bring shame
on them.

The LORD Judges Israel

5 "Listen to me, you priests!
Pay attention, people of Israel!
Listen, you members of the royal
family!
Here is my decision against you.
You have been like a trap at Mizpah.
You have been like a net spread out
on Mount Tabor.
2 You refuse to obey me.
You offer sacrifices to other gods.
So I will punish all of you.
3 People of Ephraim, I know all about
you.
What you are doing is not hidden
from me.
Now you have joined yourselves to
other gods.
You have made yourselves 'unclean.'

4 "You can't return to me
because you have done so many evil
things.
In your hearts you long to act like
prostitutes.
You do not recognize me as the
LORD.
5 Israel, your pride witnesses that you are
guilty.
People of Ephraim, you trip and fall
because you have sinned.
Judah, you fall down along with
them.
6 Israel, you will come to worship me.
You will bring your animals to offer
as sacrifices.
But you will not find me.
I have turned away from you.
7 You are not faithful to me.
Your children do not belong to me.

JONAH

From inside the fish Jonah prayed... "When I was in trouble, I called out to you. And you answered me. When I had almost drowned, I called out for help, and you listened to my cry." (Jonah 2:1–2)

GO TO PAGE 1042

MARY

"I serve the Lord," Mary answered.
"May it happen to me just as you said it would."
Then the angel left her. (Luke 1:38)

JOHN THE BAPTIST

"I baptize you with water, calling you to turn away from your sins. But after me, one will come who is more powerful ... I'm not fit to carry his sandals. He will baptize you with the Holy Spirit ..." (Matthew 3:11)

GO TO PAGE 1096

ROMAN COMMANDER

When Jesus heard this, he was amazed. He said to those following him, "What I'm about to tell you is true. In Israel I have not found anyone else whose faith is so strong." (Matthew 8:10)

GO TO PAGE 1103

The way you act at your New Moon
Feasts
will destroy you and your fields.

8 "My people, blow trumpets in Gibeah!
Blow horns in Ramah!
Shout the battle cry in Bethel!
Say to Benjamin, 'The Assyrian army
is coming!'
9 People of Ephraim, you will be
completely destroyed
when it is time for me to punish
you.
You can be sure it will happen.
I am announcing it among your
tribes.
10 Judah, your leaders have stolen some
land.
They have moved their borders
farther north.
So I will pour out my anger on you
like a flood of water.
11 Ephraim, you will soon be crushed.
The Assyrians will stomp all over
you.
It will happen because you have made
up your minds
to chase after other gods.
12 Ephraim, I will be like a moth to you.
Judah, I will cause you to rot away.

13 "Ephraim, you saw how sick you were.
Judah, you saw that you were
wounded.
Ephraim, you turned to Assyria for
help.
You sent gifts to the great King
Tiglath-Pileser.
But he is not able to make you well.
He can't heal your wounds.
14 Ephraim, I will be like a lion to you.
Judah, I will attack you like a
powerful lion.
I will tear you to pieces.
I will drag you off.
Then I will leave you.
No one will be able to save you.
15 I will go back to my home in heaven.
I will stay there until you admit you
have sinned.
Then you will turn to me.
You will suffer so much
that you will really want me to help
you."

Israel Refuses to Turn Away From Their Sins

6 The people say, "Come.
Let us return to the LORD.
He has torn us to pieces.
But he will heal us.
He has wounded us.

POWER-SURGE

CHEERFUL ✳

[GOD WILL] MAKE US LIKE NEW AGAIN.

THEN WE WILL ENJOY HIS BLESSING.
— **HOSEA 6:2** —

But he'll bandage our wounds.
2 After two days he will give us new life.
On the third day he'll make us like
new again.
Then we will enjoy his blessing.
3 Let's recognize him as the LORD.
Let's keep trying to really know him.
You can be sure the sun will rise.
And you can be just as sure the LORD
will appear.
He will come to renew us like the
winter rains.
He will be like the spring rains that
water the earth."

4 The LORD says, "Ephraim, what can I
do with you?
And what can I do with you, Judah?
Your love for me vanishes like the
morning mist.
It soon disappears like the early dew.
5 So I used the words of my prophets to
cut you in pieces.
I used my words to put you to death.
When I judged you, I struck you like
lightning.
6 I want mercy and not sacrifice.
I want you to recognize me as God
instead of bringing me burnt
offerings.
7 Just as Adam disobeyed me,
you have broken the covenant I
made with you.
You were not faithful to me in the
land I gave you.
8 Ramoth Gilead is a city where sinful
people live.
It is stained with footprints of blood.
9 On the road to Shechem, groups of
priests act like robbers.
They hide and wait to attack people.
They murder them
and commit other shameful crimes.
10 People of Israel, I have seen
a horrible thing in your land.
People of Ephraim, you have joined
yourselves to other gods.
You have made yourselves 'unclean.'

11 "People of Judah, I have appointed a
time
for you to be destroyed.

"My people, I would like to bless you
with great success again."

7 The LORD says,

"I would like to heal Israel.
But when I try to, Ephraim's sins
are brought out into the open.
The crimes of Samaria
are made known to everyone.
The people tell lies.
They break into houses and steal.
They rob others in the streets.
2 But they do not realize
that I remember all of the evil things
they do.
Their sins pile up and cover them.
I am always aware of those sins.

3 "Their evil conduct even makes the
king glad.
Their lies make the princes happy.
4 But all of the people are unfaithful to
the king.
Their anger against him burns
like the coals in an oven.
The baker does not even need to stir up
the fire
until the dough is ready."

5 On special days to honor our king,
the princes get drunk with wine.
And the king enjoys the party.
He joins hands with those
who pretend to be faithful to him.
6 Their hearts are as hot as an oven.
They make evil plans to get rid of
him.
Their anger burns like a slow fire all
night.
In the morning it blazes out like a
flaming fire.
7 All of them are as hot as an oven.
They destroy their rulers.
All of their kings fall from power.
But none of them calls on the LORD
for help.

8 The people of Ephraim mix with the
nations.
They are like a flat cake
that is baked on only one side.
9 People from other lands make them
weaker and weaker.
But they don't realize it.
Their hair is becoming gray.
But they don't even notice it.
10 The pride of Israel witnesses that they
are guilty.
But in spite of everything,

they don't return to the LORD their
God.
They don't go to him for help.

11 The LORD says,

"The people of Ephraim are like a dove.
They are easily tricked.
They do not have any sense at all.
First they call out to Egypt for help.
Then they turn to Assyria.
12 When they send for help,
I will throw my net over them.
I will capture them like birds of the air.
I will punish them,
just as I warned them I would.
13 How terrible it will be for them!
They have wandered away from me.
So they will be destroyed.
They have refused to obey me.
I long to save them.
But they tell lies about me.
14 They do not cry out to me from their
hearts.
Instead, they just lie on their beds
and sob.
They cut themselves when they pray to
Baal
for grain and fresh wine.
So they turn away from me.
15 I brought them up and made them
strong.
But they make evil plans against me.
16 I am the Most High God. But they do
not turn to me.
They are like a bow that does not
shoot straight.
Their leaders will be killed with swords.
They will die because they have
spoken too proudly.
The people of Egypt
will make fun of them."

Israel Will Harvest a Windstorm

8 The LORD said to me,

"Put a trumpet to your lips!
Give a warning to my people!
Assyria is like an eagle.
It is ready to attack my land.
My people have broken the covenant I
made with them.
They have refused to obey my law.
2 Israel shouts to me,
'We recognize you as our God!'
3 But they have turned away from what
is good.
So an enemy will chase them.
4 My people appoint kings I do not
want.
They choose princes without my
permission.

They use their silver and gold
    to make statues of gods.
    That is how they destroy
        themselves."
⁵ The LORD says, "People of Samaria,
    throw out your god that looks like a
        calf!
    My anger burns against you.
How long will it be until you are able
    to remain faithful to me?
⁶ Your calf is not God.
    A skilled worker from Israel made it.
    But it will be broken to pieces."

⁷ The LORD says,

"Worshiping other gods is like
        worshiping the wind.
    It is like planting worthless seeds.
Assyria is like a windstorm.
    That is all my people will harvest.
There are no heads of grain
    on the stems that will come up.
    So they will not produce any flour.
Even if they did produce grain,
    the Assyrians would eat all of it up.
⁸ So the people of Israel are swallowed
        up.
    Now they are like a worthless pot to
        me
    among the nations.
⁹ They have gone up to Assyria for help.
    They are like a wild donkey
        that wanders around by itself.
Ephraim's people have sold themselves
    to their Assyrian lovers.
¹⁰ They have sold themselves to the
        nations
    to get their help.
    But now I will gather them together.
They will get weaker and weaker.
    The mighty kings of Assyria will
        crush them.

¹¹ "Ephraim built many altars where they
        sacrificed
    sin offerings to other gods.
So their altars have become
    places where they commit sin.
¹² I wrote down many things in my law
        for their good.
    But they considered my laws as
        something strange.
¹³ They offer sacrifices to me.
    They eat the meat of the animals
        they bring.
    But I am not pleased with any of
        that.
I will remember the evil things they
    have done.
    I will punish them for their sins.
    And they will return to Egypt.

¹⁴ Israel has forgotten the One who made
        them.
    They have built palaces for
        themselves.
    Judah has built forts in many towns.
But I will send fire down on their cities.
    It will burn up their forts."

Israel Will Be Punished

9 Israel, don't be joyful.
    Don't be glad as the other nations
        are.
You haven't been faithful to your God.
    You love to get paid for being a
        prostitute.
    Your pay is the grain at every
        threshing floor.
² But soon there won't be any grain or
        wine to feed you.
    There won't even be any fresh wine.
³ You won't remain in the LORD's land.
    Ephraim, you will return to Egypt.
    You will eat "unclean" food in
        Assyria.
⁴ You won't pour out wine offerings to
        the LORD.
    Your sacrifices won't please him.
They'll be like the bread people eat
        when someone dies.
    Everyone who eats those sacrifices
        will be "unclean."
They themselves will have to eat that
        kind of food.
    They can't bring it into the LORD's
        temple.

⁵ What will you do when your
        appointed feasts come?
    What will you do on the LORD's
        special days?
⁶ Some of you will escape without being
        destroyed.
    But you will die in Egypt.
    Your bodies will be buried at
        Memphis.
Weeds will cover your treasures of
        silver.
    Thorns will grow up in your tents.
⁷ The time when God will punish you is
        coming.
    The day when he will judge you is
        near.
    I want you to know that.
You have committed many sins.
    And you hate me very much.
That's why you think I'm foolish.
    You think I'm crazy.
    But the LORD speaks through me.
⁸ People of Ephraim, I'm a true prophet.
    My God is warning you through me.

But you set traps for me everywhere
    I go.
    You hate me so much
      you even wait for me in God's house.
⁹ You have sunk very deep into sin,
    just as our people did at Gibeah long
      ago.
God will remember the evil things you
    have done.
    He will punish you for your sins.

¹⁰The LORD says,

"When I first found Israel,
    it was like finding grapes in the
      desert.
When I saw your people long ago,
    it was like seeing the early fruit on a
      fig tree.
But then they went to Baal Peor.
    There they gave themselves to that
      shameful god Baal.
    They became as evil as the god they
      loved.
¹¹ Ephraim's greatness and glory will be
    gone.
    It will fly away like a bird.
Women will no longer have children.
    They will not be able to get
      pregnant.
¹² But suppose they do have children.
    Then I will kill every one of them.
How terrible it will be for them
    when I turn away from them!"

¹³ Tyre is planted in a pleasant place.
    And so is Ephraim.
But the Assyrians will kill
    Ephraim's children.
¹⁴ LORD, what should you do to Ephraim's
    people?
    Give them women whose babies die
      before they are born.
    Give them women whose breasts
      don't have any milk.

¹⁵The LORD says,

"My people did many evil things in
    Gilgal.
    That is why I hated them there.
They committed many sins.
    So I will drive them out of my land.
I will not love them anymore.
    All of their leaders refuse to obey me.
¹⁶ Ephraim is like a worthless plant.
    Its roots are dried up.
    It does not produce any fruit.
Suppose Ephraim's people have
    children.
    Then I will kill the children they
      love so much."

¹⁷ My God will turn his back on his
    people.
    They have not obeyed him.
    So they will wander among other
      nations.

10

Israel was like a spreading vine.
    They produced fruit for
    themselves.
As they grew more fruit,
    they built more altars.
As their land became richer,
    they made the sacred stones they
      worshiped more beautiful.
² Their hearts are dishonest.
    So now they must pay for their sins.
The LORD will tear their altars down.
    He'll destroy their sacred stones.

³ Then they'll say, "We don't have a
    king.
    That's because we didn't have
      any respect for the LORD.
But suppose we did have a king.
    What could he do for us?"
⁴ They make a lot of promises.
    They make agreements among
      themselves.
    They take oaths they don't mean to
      keep.
So court cases spring up
    like poisonous weeds in a plowed
      field.
⁵ The people who live in Samaria are
    filled with fear.
    They are afraid their god that looks
      like a calf
    will be carried off from Bethel.
They will sob over it.
    So will the priests who lead them to
      worship it.
The priests were full of joy
    because their statue was so glorious.
But it will be captured
    and taken far away from them.
⁶ It will be carried off to Assyria.
    The people of Ephraim will be forced
      to give it to the great king.
They will be dishonored.
    Israel will be ashamed
    that all they have left to worship is a
      wooden god.
⁷ Samaria's king will be carried off.
    He will be like a twig floating away
      in a river.
⁸ The high places where Israel worshiped
    other gods
    will be destroyed.
    That's where they sinned against the
      LORD.
Thorns and weeds will grow up there.
    They will cover the altars.

Then the people will say to the
mountains, "Cover us!"
They'll say to the hills, "Fall on us!"

⁹The LORD says,

"Israel, you have done evil things
ever since your people sinned at
Gibeah long ago.
And you are still doing what is evil.
War caught up
with those who sinned at Gibeah.
¹⁰So I will punish you when I want to.
Nations will gather together to fight
against you.
They will put you in chains
because you have committed so
many sins.
¹¹Ephraim, you were like a well-trained
young cow.
It loved to thresh grain.
I spared its pretty neck
from pulling heavy loads.
But now I will make you do hard work.
Judah also must plow.
So all of the people of Jacob
must break up the ground.
¹²Your hearts are as hard as a field
that has not been plowed.
If you change your ways,
you will produce good crops.
So plant the seeds of doing what is
right.
Then you will harvest the fruit of
your faithful love.
It is time to turn to me.
When you do, I will come
and shower my blessings on you.
¹³But you have planted the seeds of
doing what is wrong.
So you have harvested the fruit of
your evil conduct.
You have had to eat the fruit of your
lies.
You have trusted in your own strength.
You have depended on your many
soldiers.
¹⁴But the roar of battle will come against
you.
All of your forts will be completely
destroyed.
It will happen just as Shalman
destroyed Beth Arbel in a battle.
Mothers and their children
were smashed on the ground.
¹⁵People of Bethel, that will happen to
you.
You have committed far too many
sins.
When the time for me to punish you
comes,

your king will be completely
destroyed."

The LORD Loves Israel

11 The LORD continues,

"When Israel was a young nation, I
loved them.
I chose to bring my son out of Egypt.
²But the more I called out to Israel,
the further they went away from
me.
They brought sacrifices to the statues
of the gods
that were named after Baal.
And they burned incense to them.
³I taught Israel to walk.
I took them up in my arms.
But they did not realize
I was the one who took care of
them.
⁴I led them with kindness and love.
I did not lead them with ropes.
I lifted the heavy loads from their
shoulders.
I bent down and fed them.

⁵"But they refuse to turn away from
their sins.
So they will return to Egypt.
And Assyria will rule over them.
⁶Swords will flash in their cities.
The heavy metal bars on their gates
will be destroyed.
Their plans will come to an end.
⁷My people have made up their minds
to turn away from me.
Even if they call out to me,
I will certainly not honor them.
I am the Most High God."

⁸The LORD continues,

"People of Ephraim, how can I give
you up?
Israel, how can I hand you over to
your enemies?
Can I destroy you as I did the town of
Admah?
Can I treat you like Zeboiim?
My heart is stirred inside me.
It is filled with pity for you.
⁹My anger will not burn against you
anymore.
I will not completely destroy you.
After all, I am God.
I am not a mere man.
I am the Holy One among you.
My burning anger will not come
against you.
¹⁰I will roar like a lion against my
enemies.

You will follow me.
When I roar, my children will come
home trembling with fear.
You will return from the west.
11 You will come trembling like birds
from Egypt.
You will return like doves from
Assyria.
I will settle you again in your homes,"
announces the LORD.

Israel Has Sinned

12 The people of Ephraim tell nothing
but lies.
Israel has not been honest with me.
And Judah continues to wander away
from God.
They have deserted the faithful Holy
One.

12 1 The people of Ephraim look to
others for help.
It's like chasing the wind.
The wind they keep chasing
is hot and dry.
They tell more and more lies.
They are always hurting others.
They make a peace treaty with Assyria.
They send olive oil to Egypt to get
help.
2 The LORD is bringing charges against
Judah.
He will punish Jacob's people
because of how they act.
He'll pay them back
for the evil things they've done.
3 Even before Jacob was born,
he was holding on to his brother's
heel.
When he became a man,
he struggled with God.
4 At Peniel he struggled with the angel
and won.
He sobbed and begged for his
blessing.
God also met with him at Bethel.
He talked with him there.
5 He is the LORD God who rules over all.
He wants us to remember
that his name is The LORD.
6 People of Jacob, you must return to
your God.
You must hold on to love and do
what is fair.
You must trust in your God always.

7 You are like a trader who uses
dishonest scales.
You love to cheat others.
8 People of Ephraim, you brag,
"We are very rich.
We've become wealthy.

And no one can prove we sinned
to gain all of this wealth."

9 The LORD says,

"I am the LORD your God.
I brought you out of Egypt.
But I will make you live in tents again.
That is what you did when you
celebrated
the Feast of Booths in the desert.
10 I spoke to the prophets.
They saw many visions.
I gave you warnings through them."

11 The people of Gilead are evil!
They aren't worth anything!
Gilgal's people sacrifice bulls to other
gods.
Their altars will become like piles of
stones
on a plowed field.
12 Jacob ran away to the country of Aram.
There Israel served Laban to get a
wife.
He took care of sheep to pay for her.
13 The prophet Moses brought Israel up
from Egypt.
The LORD used him to take care of
them.
14 But Ephraim's people have made the
LORD very angry.
Their Lord will hold them
accountable for the blood
they've spilled.
He'll pay them back for the
shameful things they've done.

The LORD Is Angry With Israel

13 When the tribe of Ephraim spoke,
the other tribes trembled with
fear.
Ephraim was honored in Israel.
But its people sinned by worshiping
Baal.
So they were as good as dead.
2 Now they sin more and more.
They use their silver
to make statues of gods for
themselves.
The statues come from their own
clever ideas.
Skilled workers make all of them.
The people pray to those gods.
They offer human sacrifices to them.
They kiss the gods that look like
calves.
3 So those people will vanish like the
morning mist.
They will soon disappear like the
early dew.
They will be like straw

that the wind blows around on a
    threshing floor.
They will be like smoke
    that escapes through a window.

⁴The LORD says,

"People of Israel, I am the LORD your
    God.
    I brought you out of Egypt.
You must not recognize any God but
    me.
You must not have any Savior except
    me.
⁵I took care of you in the desert.
    It was a land of burning heat.
⁶I fed you until you were satisfied.
    Then you became proud.
    You forgot all about me.
⁷So I will leap on you like a lion.
    I will hide and wait
    beside the road like a leopard.
⁸I will attack you like a bear
    that is robbed of her cubs.
    I will rip you wide open.
Like a lion I will eat you up.
    Like a wild animal I will tear you
    apart.

⁹"Israel, you will be destroyed.
    I helped you. But you turned against
    me.
¹⁰Where is your king?
    Wasn't he supposed to save you?
Where are the rulers in all of your
    towns?
    You said, 'Give us a king and
    princes.'
¹¹So I became angry and gave you a king.
    Then I took him away from you.
¹²Ephraim, your guilt is piling up.
    I am keeping a record of all of your
    sins.
¹³You will suffer pain like a woman
    having a baby.
    You are like a foolish child.
It is time for you to be born.
    But you refuse to come out of your
    mother's body.

¹⁴"I will set you free from the power of
    the grave.
    I will save you from death.
Death, where are your plagues?
    Grave, where is your power to
    destroy?

"Ephraim, I will no longer pity you.
¹⁵   Even though you are doing well
        among the other tribes,
    trouble will come to you.
I will send a hot and dry wind from the
    east.

It will blow in from the desert.
Your springs will not have any water.
    Your wells will dry up.
All of your treasures
    will be taken out of your storerooms.
¹⁶People of Samaria, you must pay for
    your sins.
    You have refused to obey me.
You will be killed with swords.
    Your little children will be smashed
        on the ground.
    Your pregnant women will be ripped
        wide open."

The LORD Blesses Those Who Turn Away From Sin

14 Israel, return to the LORD your
    God.
    Your sins have destroyed you!
²Tell the LORD you are turning away
    from your sins.
    Return to him.
Say to him,
    "Forgive us for all of our sins.
Please be kind to us.
    Welcome us back to you.
    Then our lips will offer you our
        praise.
³Assyria can't save us.
    We won't trust in our war horses.
Our own hands have made statues of
    gods.
    But we will never call them our gods
        again.
We are like children whose fathers
    have died.
    But you show us your tender love."

⁴Then the LORD will answer,

"My people always wander away from
    me.
    But I will put an end to that.
My anger has turned away from them.
    Now I will love them freely.
⁵I will be like the dew to Israel.
    They will bloom like a lily.
They will send their roots down deep
    like a cedar tree in Lebanon.
⁶They will spread out like new
    branches.
    They will be as beautiful as an olive
        tree.
    They will smell as sweet as the cedar
        trees in Lebanon.
⁷Once again my people will live
    in the safety of my shade.
    They will grow like grain.
They will bloom like vines.
    And they will be as famous
        as wine from Lebanon.

HONEST

IF YOU ARE WISE, YOU
WILL REALIZE

THAT WHAT I'VE SAID
IS TRUE.
— HOSEA 14:9 —

WISE

8 Ephraim will have nothing more to do
with other gods.
I will answer the prayers of my
people.
I will take good care of them.
I will be like a green pine tree to them.
All of the fruit they bear will come
from me."

9 If you are wise, you will realize
that what I've said is true.
If you have understanding,
you will know what it means.
The ways of the LORD are right.
People who are right with God live
the way he wants them to.
But those who refuse to obey him
trip and fall.

JOEL

J oel uses a cloud of grasshoppers, which comes and destroys all the food in Judah, to picture the judgment that is coming if God's people don't turn away from their sins. The book of Joel beautifully ties the Old Testament with the New Testament when Joel tells about the coming of the Holy Spirit. As you read this book, consider how God will punish those who don't turn to him but will lovingly care for those who do.

CODE OF HONOR IN THIS BOOK . . .

CHEERFUL

PAGE 1026

1
A message came to Joel from the LORD. He was the son of Pethuel. Here is what Joel said.

Locusts Attack the Land

2 Elders, listen to me.
　Pay attention, all you who live in the land.
Has anything like this ever happened in your whole life?
　Did it ever happen to your people who lived long ago?
3 Tell your children about it.
　Let them tell their children.
And let their children tell it
　to those who live after them.
4 The giant locusts have eaten
　what the common locusts have left.
The young locusts have eaten
　what the giant locusts have left.
And other locusts have eaten
　what the young locusts have left.

5 Get up and sob, you people who drink too much!
　Cry, all you who drink wine!
Cry because the fresh wine
　has been taken away from you.
6 The locusts are like an army
　that has marched into our land.
There are so many of them
　they can't even be counted.
Their teeth are as sharp as a lion's teeth.
　They are like the fangs of a female lion.
7 The locusts have completely destroyed our vines.
　They have wiped out our fig trees.
They've stripped off the bark and thrown it away.
　They've left the branches bare.

8 My people, sob like a virgin
　who is dressed in black clothes.
She is sad because she has lost
　the young man she was going to marry.
9 No one brings grain offerings and drink offerings
　to the LORD's house anymore.
So the priests who serve the LORD
　are filled with sorrow.
10 Our fields are wiped out.
　The ground is dried up.
The grain is destroyed.
　The fresh wine is gone.
　And there isn't any more olive oil.
11 Farmers, be sad.
　Cry, you who grow vines.
Sob because the wheat and barley are gone.

The crops in the fields are destroyed.
12 The vines and fig trees are dried up.
　The pomegranate, palm and apple trees
　don't have any fruit on them.
In fact, all of the trees in the fields are dried up.
　And my people's joy has faded away.

Turn Away From Sin

13 Priests, put on black clothes and sob.
　Cry, you who serve at the altar.
Come, you who serve my God in the temple.
　Spend the night dressed in black clothes.
Sob because no one brings grain offerings and drink offerings
　to the house of your God anymore.
14 Announce a holy fast.
　Tell the people not to eat anything.
　Gather them together for a special service.
Send for all of the elders
　who live in the land.
Have them come to the house of the LORD your God.
　And pray to him.

15 The day of the LORD is near.
　How sad it will be on that day!
The Mighty One is coming to destroy you.

16 Our food has been taken away
　right in front of our eyes.
There isn't any joy or gladness
　in the house of our God.
17 The seeds have dried up in the ground.
　The grain is also gone.
The storerooms have been destroyed.
　The barns are broken down.
18 Listen to the cattle groan!
　The herds wander around.
They don't have any grass to eat.
　The flocks of sheep are also suffering.

19 LORD, I call out to you.
　Fire has burned up the grasslands.
　Flames have destroyed all of the trees in the fields.
20 Even the wild animals cry out to you for help.
　The streams of water have dried up.
　Fire has burned up the grasslands.

The LORD Sends an Army of Locusts

2
Priests, blow the trumpets in Zion.
　Give a warning on my holy mountain.

Let everyone who lives in the land
    tremble with fear.
  The day of the Lord is coming.
    It is very near.
2 That day will be dark and sad.
    It will be black and cloudy.
  A huge army of locusts is coming.
    They will spread across the
      mountains
    like the sun when it rises.
  There has never been an army like it.
    And there will never be another
    for all time to come.

3 Like fire they eat up everything in their
      path.
    Behind them it looks as if flames
      have burned the land.
  In front of them the land is like the
      Garden of Eden.
    Behind them it is a dry and empty
      desert.
    Nothing escapes them.
4 They look like horses.
    Like war horses they charge ahead.
5 They sound like chariots as they leap
      over the mountaintops.
    They crackle like fire burning up dry
      weeds.
  They are like a mighty army
    that is ready for battle.

6 When people see them, they tremble
      with fear.
    All of their faces turn pale.
7 The locusts charge ahead like warriors.
    They climb over walls like soldiers.
  All of them march in line.
    They don't turn to the right or the
      left.
8 They don't bump into one another.
    Each of them marches straight
      ahead.
  They charge through everything that
      tries to stop them.
    But they still stay in line.
9 They attack a city.
    They run along its wall.
  They climb into houses.
    They enter through windows like
      robbers.

10 As they march forward, the earth
      shakes.
    The sky trembles as they approach.
  The sun and moon grow dark.
    And the stars stop shining.
11 The Lord thunders with his mighty
      voice
    as he leads his army.
  He has so many forces they can't even
    be counted.

Those who obey his commands are
    great in number.
  The day of the Lord is great and
    terrifying.
  Who can live through it?

Let Your Hearts Be Broken

12 The Lord announces to his people,

"Return to me with all your heart.
    There is still time.
Do not eat any food.
    Sob and cry."

13 Don't just tear your clothes to show
      how sad you are.
    Let your hearts be broken.
  Return to the Lord your God.
    He is gracious.
    He is tender and kind.
  He is slow to get angry.
    He is full of love.
  He takes pity on you.
    He won't destroy you.
14 Who knows? He might turn toward
      you
    and have pity on you.
  He might even give you his blessing.
  Then you can bring grain offerings and
    drink offerings
    to the Lord your God.

15 Priests, blow the trumpets in Zion.
    Announce a holy fast.
  Tell the people not to eat anything.
    Gather them together for a special
      service.
16 Bring them together.
    Set all of them apart to me.
  Bring together the elders.
    Gather the children and the babies
    who are still nursing.
  Let the groom leave his bedroom.
    Let the bride leave their marriage
      bed.
17 Let the priests who serve the Lord sob.
    Let them cry between the temple
      porch and the altar.
  Let them say, "Lord, spare your people.
    Don't let others make fun of them.
    Don't let the nations laugh at them.
  Don't let them tease your people and
      say,
    'Where is their God?' "

The Lord Answers the Prayer of His People

18 Then the Lord will show concern for
      his land.
    He will take pity on his people.

19 He will reply,

"I will send you grain, olive oil and
fresh wine.
It will be enough to satisfy you
completely.
I will never allow other nations
to make fun of you again.

20 "I will drive far away from you
the army that comes from the
north.
I will send some of its forces
into a dry and empty land.
Those in front will be pushed into the
Dead Sea.
The ones in back will be driven into
the Mediterranean Sea.
Their dead bodies will give off a bad
smell."

The LORD has done great things.
21   Land, don't be afraid.
Be glad and full of joy.
The LORD has done great things.
22 Wild animals, don't be afraid.
The grasslands are turning green
again.
The trees are bearing their fruit.
The vines and fig trees are producing
rich crops.
23 People of Zion, be glad.
Be joyful because of what the LORD
your God has done.
He has given you the right amount of
rain in the fall.
He has sent you plenty of showers.
He has sent fall and spring rains alike,
just as he did before.

POWER-SURGE

CHEERFUL ✳

BE JOYFUL BECAUSE
OF WHAT THE LORD
YOUR GOD HAS DONE.
—— JOEL 2:23 ——

24 Your threshing floors will be covered
with grain.
Olive oil and fresh wine will spill
over
from the places where they are
stored.

25 The LORD says,

"I sent a great army of locusts to attack
you.
They included common locusts,
giant locusts,
young locusts and other locusts.

I will make up for the years
they ate your crops.
26 You will have plenty to eat.
It will satisfy you completely.
Then you will praise me.
I am the LORD your God.
I have done wonderful miracles for
you.
My people will never be put to
shame again.
27 You will know that I am with you in
Israel.
I am the LORD your God.
There is no other God.
So my people will never be put to
shame again.

The Day of the LORD Is Coming

28 "After that, I will pour out my Spirit on
all people.
Your sons and daughters will
prophesy.
Your old men will have dreams.
Your young men will have visions.
29 In those days I will pour out my Spirit
on those who serve me, men and
women alike.
30 I will show wonders in the heavens
and on the earth.
There will be blood and fire and
clouds of smoke.
31 The sun will become dark.
The moon will turn red like blood.
It will happen before the great and
terrible day of the LORD comes.
32 Everyone who calls out to me will be
saved.
On Mount Zion and in Jerusalem
some of my people will be left alive.
I have chosen them.
That is what I have promised.

The LORD Judges the Nations

3 "At that time I will bless Judah and
Jerusalem
with great success again.
2 I will gather all of the nations together.
I will bring them down to the Valley
of Jehoshaphat.
There I will judge them.
I will punish them for what they
have done
to my people Israel.
They scattered them among the
nations.
They divided up my land among
themselves.
3 They cast lots for my people.
They sold boys into slavery to get
prostitutes.

They sold girls to buy some wine to
drink.

4 "Tyre and Sidon, why are you doing
things like that to me? And why are you
doing them, all of you people in Philistia?
Are you trying to get even with me for
something I have done? If you are, I will
pay you back for it in a quick and speedy
way. **5** You took my silver and gold. You
carried off my finest treasures to your temples. **6** You sold the people of Judah and
Jerusalem to the Greeks. You wanted to
send them far away from their own country.

7 "But now I will stir them up into action. I will bring them back from the
places you sold them to. And I will do to
you what you did to them. **8** I will sell your
sons and daughters to the people of Judah. And they will sell them to the Sabeans far away." The LORD has spoken.

9 Announce this among the nations.
Tell them to prepare for battle.
Nations, get your soldiers ready!
Bring all of your fighting men
together
and march out to attack.
10 Hammer your plows into swords.
Hammer your pruning tools into
spears.
Let those who are weak say,
"We are soldiers!"
11 Come quickly, all of you surrounding
nations.
Gather together in the Valley of
Jehoshaphat.

LORD, send your soldiers
down from heaven!

12 The LORD says,

"Stir up the nations into action!
Let them march into the valley
where I will judge them.
I will take my seat in court.
I will judge all of the surrounding
nations.
13 My soldiers, swing your sickles.
The nations are ripe for harvest.
Come. Stomp on them as if they were
grapes.
Crush them until the winepress of
my anger is full.
Do it until the wine spills over
from the places where it is stored.

The nations have committed far too
many sins!"

14 Huge numbers of soldiers are gathered
in the valley
where the LORD will hand down his
sentence.
The day of the LORD is near in that
valley.
15 The sun and moon will become dark.
The stars won't shine anymore.
16 The LORD will roar like a lion from
Jerusalem.
His voice will sound like thunder
from Zion.
The earth and sky will tremble.
But the LORD will keep the people of
Israel safe.
He will be a place of safety for them.

The LORD Blesses His People

17 The LORD says,

"You will know that I am the LORD
your God.
I live in Zion.
It is my holy mountain.
Jerusalem will be my holy city.
People from other lands
will never attack it again.
18 "At that time fresh wine will drip from
the mountains.
Milk will flow down from the hills.
Water will run through all of Judah's
valleys.
A fountain will flow out of my temple.
It will water the places where acacia
trees grow.
19 But Egypt will be deserted.
Edom will become a dry and empty
desert.
They did terrible harm to the people of
Judah.
My people were not guilty of doing
anything wrong.
But Egypt and Edom spilled their
blood anyway.
20 My people will live in Judah and
Jerusalem forever.
The land will be their home for all
time to come.
21 Egypt and Edom have spilled my
people's blood.
I will punish them for it."

The LORD lives in Zion!

AMOS

The prophet Amos wrote this book when many of the people of Israel were very rich—and many were very poor. The rich people didn't care and didn't help the poor people. Amos tells the rich people not to ignore the needs of the poor people. He clearly shows that God hates this kind of injustice. As you read the book of Amos, be sure to look carefully at your own actions and attitudes toward those who don't have as much as you do.

CODE OF HONOR IN THIS BOOK . . .

TRIES HARD
x

PAGE 1032

1 These are the words of Amos. He was a shepherd from the town of Tekoa. Here is the vision he saw concerning Israel. It came to him two years before the earthquake. At that time Uzziah was king of Judah. Jeroboam was king of Israel. He was the son of Jehoash. Here are the words of Amos.

²I said,

"The LORD roars like a lion from
　Jerusalem.
　　His voice sounds like thunder from
　　Zion.
　The grasslands of the shepherds turn
　　brown.
　　The top of Mount Carmel dries up."

The LORD Punishes Israel's Neighbors

³The LORD says,

"The people of Damascus have sinned
　again and again.
　　So I will punish them.
They used threshing sleds with iron
　teeth
　　to crush Gilead's people.
⁴So I will send fire to destroy the palace
　of King Hazael.
　　It will burn up the forts of his son
　　Ben-Hadad.
⁵I will break down the city gate of
　Damascus.
　I will cut off the king
　　who lives in the Valley of Aven.
He holds the ruler's rod in Beth Eden.
　The people of Aram will be taken
　　away to Kir as prisoners,"
　　　　　　　　　　says the LORD.

⁶The LORD says,

"The people of Gaza have sinned again
　and again.
　　So I will punish them.
They captured whole communities.
　They sold them to Edom.
⁷So I will send fire to destroy the walls of
　Gaza.
　It will burn up its forts.
⁸I will cut off the king of Ashdod.
　He holds the ruler's rod in Ashkelon.
I will use my powerful hand against
　Ekron.
　Every single Philistine will die,"
　　　　　　says the LORD and King.

⁹The LORD says,

"The people of Tyre have sinned again
　and again.
　　So I will punish them.
They captured whole communities.

They sold them to Edom.
They did not honor the treaty
　of friendship they had made.
¹⁰So I will send fire to destroy the walls of
　Tyre.
　It will burn up its forts."

¹¹The LORD says,

"The people of Edom have sinned
　again and again.
　　So I will punish them.
They chased Israel with swords
　that were ready to strike them down.
　They did not show them any pity.
They were angry all the time.
　Their anger blazed out.
　　It could not be stopped.
¹²So I will send fire to destroy the city of
　Teman.
　It will burn up Bozrah's forts."

¹³The LORD says,

"The people of Ammon have sinned
　again and again.
　　So I will punish them.
They ripped open the pregnant
　women in Gilead.
　They wanted to add land to their
　　territory.
¹⁴So I will set fire to destroy the walls of
　Rabbah.
　It will burn up its forts.
War cries will be heard on that day of
　battle.
　Strong winds will blow on that
　　stormy day.
¹⁵Ammon's god Molech will be carried
　away.
　So will its officials,"
　　　　　　　　　　says the LORD.

2 The LORD says,

"The people of Moab have sinned
　again and again.
　　So I will punish them.
They burned the bones
　of Edom's king to ashes.
²So I will send fire to destroy Moab.
　It will burn up Kerioth's forts.
Moab will come crashing down with a
　loud noise.
　War cries will be heard.
　So will the blast of trumpets.
³I will cut off Moab's ruler.
　I will also kill all of its officials,"
　　　　　　　　　　says the LORD.

⁴The LORD says,

"The people of Judah have sinned
　again and again.
　　So I will punish them.

They have refused to obey my law.
They have not kept my rules.
Other gods have led them down the
wrong path.
Their people before them
worshiped those gods.
5 So I will send fire to destroy Judah.
It will burn up Jerusalem's forts."

The LORD Punishes Israel

6 The LORD says,

"The people of Israel have sinned again
and again.
So I will punish them.
They sell into slavery those who do
what is right.
They trade needy people
for a mere pair of sandals.
7 They grind the heads of the poor
into the dust of the ground.
They refuse to be fair to those who
are crushed.
A father and his son have sex with the
same girl.
They treat my name as if it were not
holy.
8 They lie down beside every altar
on clothes they had taken
until the owner paid back what was
owed.
In the house of their God
they drink wine that was taken as
fines.

9 "I destroyed the Amorites to make
room
for my people in the land.
The Amorites were as tall as cedar trees.
They were as strong as oak trees.
But I cut off their fruit above the
ground
and their roots below it.

10 "People of Israel, I brought you up out
of Egypt.
I led you in the desert for 40 years.
I gave you the land of the Amorites.
11 I raised up prophets from among your
children.
I also set some of your young people
apart to me as Nazirites.
Isn't that true, people of Israel?"
announces the LORD.
12 "But you made the Nazirites drink
wine.
You commanded the prophets not
to prophesy.

13 "A cart that is loaded with grain
crushes anything it runs over.
In the same way, I will crush you.
14 Your fastest runners will not escape.

The strongest people will not get
away.
Even soldiers will not be able
to save their own lives.
15 Men who are armed with bows will
lose the battle.
Soldiers who are quick on their feet
will not escape.
Horsemen will not be able
to save their own lives.
16 Even your bravest soldiers
will run away naked on that day,"
announces the LORD.

The LORD Judges His Chosen People

3 People of Israel, listen to the LORD's
message. It is against you. It is against
the whole family he brought up out of
Egypt. He says,

2 "Out of all of the families on earth
I have chosen only you.
So I will punish you
because you have committed so
many sins."

3 Do two people walk together
unless they've agreed to do so?
4 Does a lion roar in the bushes
when it doesn't have any food?
Does it growl in its den
when it hasn't caught anything?
5 Does a bird fall into a trap on the
ground
where no one has set a trap for it?
Does a net spring up from the earth
when there isn't anything for it to
catch?
6 When someone blows a trumpet in a
city,
don't the people tremble with fear?
When trouble comes to a city,
hasn't the LORD caused it?

7 The LORD and King never does
anything
without telling his servants the
prophets about it.

8 A lion has roared.
Who isn't afraid?
The LORD and King has spoken.
Who can do anything but
prophesy?

9 Speak to the people in the forts of
Ashdod and Egypt.
Tell them, "Gather together
on the mountains of Samaria.
Look at the great trouble in that city.
Its people are committing many
crimes."

10 "They do not know how to do what is
     right,"
  announces the LORD.
  "They pile up stolen goods in their
     forts."

11 So the LORD and King says,

"Enemies will take over your land.
  They will pull down your places of
     safety.
  They will rob your forts."

12 The LORD says,

"Suppose a shepherd saves only two
     leg bones
  from a lion's mouth.
Or he might save only a piece of an ear.
  That is how the Israelites will be
     saved.
They sit in Samaria
  on the edge of their beds.
They lie down in Damascus
  on their couches."

13 "Listen to me," announces the LORD.
"Witness against the people of Jacob,"
says the LORD God who rules over all.

14 "I will punish Israel for their sins.
  When I do, I will destroy their altars
     at Bethel.
The horns that stick out from the
     upper corners
  of their main altar will be cut off.
  They will fall to the ground.
15 I will tear their winter houses down.
  I will also pull down their summer
     houses.
The houses they have decorated with
     ivory will be destroyed.
  And their princely houses will be
     torn down,"
          announces the LORD.

Israel Has Not Returned to the LORD

4 Listen to the LORD's message,
  you women who live on the hill of
     Samaria.
You treat poor people badly.
  You crush those who are in need.
You say to your husbands,
  "Bring us some drinks!"
But you are already as fat
  as the cows in Bashan.
2 The LORD and King has taken an oath
  in his own holy name.
He says, "You can be sure
  that the time will come
when your enemies will put hooks in
     your faces.
  They will lead every one of you away
     with fishhooks.

3 Each of you will go straight out
  through a gap in the wall.
You will be thrown out of the city
  on the hill where you crush others,"
          announces the LORD.
4 "People of Samaria, go to Bethel and
     sin!
  Go to Gilgal! Sin there even more!
Bring your sacrifices every morning.
  Every third year, bring a tenth
  of everything you produce.
5 Bake some bread with yeast.
  Burn it as a thank offering.
Brag about the offerings you freely give.
  That is what you Israelites love to
     do,"
          announces the LORD and King.

6 "I made sure your stomachs were
     empty in every city.
  You did not have enough bread in
     any of your towns.
In spite of that, you still have not
     returned to me,"
          announces the LORD.

7 "I also held rain back from you.
  The time to harvest crops
  was still three months away.
I sent rain on one town
  But I held it back from another.
One field had rain.
  Another did not. So it dried up.
8 People wandered from town to town to
     look for water.
  But they did not get enough to
     drink.
In spite of that, you still have not
     returned to me,"
          announces the LORD.

9 "Many times I struck your gardens and
     vineyards.
  I sent hot winds to dry them up
     completely.
Locusts ate up your fig and olive trees.
  In spite of that, you still have not
     returned to me,"
          announces the LORD.

10 "I sent plagues on you,
  just as I did on Egypt.
I killed your young men with swords.
  I also let the horses you had
     captured be killed.
I filled your noses with the bad smell of
     your camps.
  In spite of that, you still have not
     returned to me,"
          announces the LORD.

11 "I destroyed some of you,
  just as I did Sodom and Gomorrah.

You were like a burning stick that was
pulled out of the fire.
In spite of that, you still have not
returned to me,"
announces the LORD.

12 "People of Israel, I will punish you.
Because I will do that to you,
prepare to meet your God!"

13 The LORD forms the mountains.
He creates the wind.
He makes his thoughts known to
human beings.
He turns sunrise into darkness.
He rules over the highest places on
earth.
His name is The LORD God Who
Rules Over All.

Look to the LORD and Live

5 People of Israel, listen to the LORD's
message. Hear my song of sadness
about you. I say,

2 "The people of Israel have fallen.
They will never get up again.
They are deserted in their own land.
No one can lift them up."

3 The LORD and King says,

"A thousand soldiers will march out
from a city in Israel.
But only a hundred will return.
A hundred soldiers will march out
from a town.
But only ten will come back."

4 The LORD speaks to the people of Israel. He says,

"Look to me and live.
5 Do not look to Bethel.
Do not go to Gilgal.
Do not travel to Beersheba.
The people of Gilgal will be taken away
as prisoners.
Nothing will be left of Bethel."

6 Israel, look to the LORD and live.
If you don't, he will sweep through
the people of Joseph like a fire.
It will burn everything up.
And Bethel won't have anyone to
put it out.

7 You turn what is fair into something
bitter.
What is right you throw down to the
ground.
8 The LORD made the Pleiades and
Orion.
He turns darkness into sunrise.
He makes the day fade into night.

He sends for the waters in the clouds.
Then he pours them out on the
surface of the land.
His name is The LORD.
9 He destroys places of safety.
He tears down cities
that have high walls around them.
10 Israel, you hate those who do what is
right in court.
You can't stand those who tell the
truth.

11 You walk all over poor people.
You make them give you grain.
You have built stone houses.
But you won't live in them.
You have planted fruitful vineyards.
But you won't drink the wine they
produce.
12 I know how many crimes you have
committed.
You have sinned far too much.

You crush those who do what is right.
You accept money from people who
want special favors.
You take away the rights of poor
people in the courts.
13 So those who are wise keep quiet in
times like these.
That's because the times are evil.

14 Look to what is good, not to what is
evil.
Then you will live.
And the LORD God who rules over all
will be with you,
just as you say he is.
15 Hate what is evil. Love what is good.
Do what is fair in the courts.
Perhaps the LORD God who rules over
all
will show you his favor.
After all, you are the only ones left
in the family line of Joseph.

16 The LORD God rules over all. The Lord
says,

"People will sob in all of the streets.
They will be very sad in every market
place.
Even farmers will be told to cry loudly.

POWER-SURGE

TRIES HARD T

HATE WHAT IS EVIL.
LOVE WHAT IS GOOD.
— AMOS 5:15 —

People will sob over the dead.
17 Workers will cry in all of the
vineyards.
That is because I will punish you,"
says the LORD.

The Day of the LORD Is Coming

18 How terrible it will be for you
who long for the day of the LORD!
Why do you want it to come?
That day will be dark, not light.
19 It will be like a man running away
from a lion
only to meet a bear.
He enters his house and rests his hand
on a wall
only to be bitten by a snake.
20 The day of the LORD will be dark, not
light.
It will be very black.
There won't be a ray of sunlight
anywhere.

21 The LORD says,

"I hate your holy feasts.
I can't stand them.
I hate it when you gather together.
22 You bring me burnt offerings and grain
offerings.
But I will not accept them.
You bring your best friendship
offerings.
But I will not even look at them.
23 Take the noise of your songs away!
I will not listen to the music of your
harps.
24 I want you to treat others fairly.
So let fair treatment roll on
just as a river does!
Always do what is right.
Let right living flow along
like a stream that never runs dry!

25 "People of Israel, did you bring me
sacrifices and offerings
for 40 years in the desert?
26 Yes. But you have honored the place
where your king worshiped other
gods.
You have carried the stands
the statues of your gods were on.
You have lifted up the banners
of the stars you worship as gods.
You made all of those things for
yourselves.
27 So I will send you away
as prisoners beyond Damascus,"
says the LORD.
His name is God Who Rules
Over All.

The LORD Judges Israel's Pride

6 How terrible it will be for you men
who are so contented on Mount
Zion!
How terrible it will be for you who feel secure
on the hill of Samaria!
You are famous men from the greatest
nation.
The people of Israel come to you
for help and advice.
2 Go to the city of Calneh. Look at it.
Go from there to the great city of
Hamath.
Then go down to Gath in Philistia.
Are those places better off than your
two kingdoms?
Is their land larger than yours?
3 You are trying to avoid the time
when trouble will come.
But you are only bringing closer
the Assyrian rule of terror.
4 You lie down on beds
that are decorated with ivory.
You rest on your couches.
You eat the best lambs
and the fattest calves.
5 You pluck away on your harps as David
did.
You play new songs on musical
instruments.
6 You drink wine by the bowlful.
You use the finest lotions.
But Joseph's people will soon be
destroyed.
And you aren't even sad about it.
7 So you will be among the first
to be taken away as prisoners.
You won't be able to enjoy good food.
You won't lie around on couches
anymore.

8 The LORD and King has taken an oath
in his own name. He is the LORD God who
rules over all. He announces,

"I hate the pride of Jacob's people.
I can't stand their forts.
I will hand the city of Samaria
and everything in it over to their
enemies."

9 Ten men might be left in one house. If
they are, they will die there. **10** Relatives
might come to burn the dead bodies. If
they do, they'll have to carry them out of
the house first. They might ask someone
still hiding there, "Is anyone here with
you?" If the answer is no, the relatives will
say, "Be quiet! We must not pray in the
LORD's name."

11 The LORD has already given an order.
He will smash large houses to pieces.

He will crush small houses to bits.

12 Horses don't run on rocky ground.
People don't plow there with oxen.
But you have turned fair treatment
into poison.
You have turned the fruit of right
living into bitterness.
13 You are happy because you captured
the town of Lo Debar.
You say, "We were strong enough to
take Karnaim too."

14 But the LORD God rules over all. He
announces, "People of Israel,
I will stir up a nation against you.
They will crush you from Lebo
Hamath
all the way down to the Arabah
Valley."

The LORD Gives Amos Three Visions

7 The LORD and King gave me a vision.
He was bringing large numbers of locusts on the land. The king's share of the
first crop had already been harvested.
Now the second crop was coming up.
2 The locusts stripped the land clean. Then
I cried out, "LORD and King, forgive Israel!
How can Jacob's people continue? They
are such a weak nation!"

3 So the LORD had pity on them.

"I will let them continue for now," he
said.

4 The LORD and King gave me a second
vision. He was using fire to punish his
people. It dried up the deep waters. It
burned the land up. 5 Then I cried out,
"LORD and King, please stop! How can Jacob's people continue? They are such a
weak nation!"

6 So the LORD had pity on them.

"I will let them continue for now," the
LORD and King said.

7 Then the Lord gave me a third vision.
He was standing by a wall. It had been
built very straight, all the way up and
down. He was holding a plumb line. 8 The
LORD asked me, "What do you see,
Amos?"

"A plumb line," I replied.

Then the Lord said, "Look at what I am
doing. I am hanging a plumb line next to
my people Israel. It will show how
crooked they are. I will no longer spare
them.

9 "The high places where Isaac's people
worship other gods will be
destroyed.

The other places of worship in Israel
will also be torn down.
I will use my sword
to attack Jeroboam's royal family."

Amaziah Tells Amos to Stop Prophesying

10 Amaziah was priest of Bethel. He sent
a message to Jeroboam, the king of Israel.
He said, "Amos is making evil plans
against you right here in Israel. The people in the land can't stand to listen to
what he's saying. 11 Amos is telling them,

" 'Jeroboam will be killed with a sword.
The people of Israel will be taken
away as prisoners.
They will be carried off from their
own land.' "

12 Then Amaziah said to Amos, "Get out
of Israel, you prophet! Go back to the land
of Judah. Earn your living there. Do your
prophesying there. 13 Don't prophesy
here at Bethel anymore. This is where the
king worships. The main temple in the
kingdom is located here."

14 Amos answered Amaziah, "I was not a
prophet. I wasn't even a prophet's son. I
was a shepherd. I also took care of sycamore-fig trees. 15 But the LORD took me
away from taking care of the flock. He said
to me, 'Go. Prophesy to my people Israel.'
16 Now then, listen to the LORD's message.
You say,

" 'Don't prophesy against Israel.
Stop preaching against the people of
Isaac.'

17 "But the LORD says,

" 'Your wife will become a prostitute
in the city of Bethel.
Your sons and daughters will be
killed with swords.
Your land will be measured and
divided up.
And you yourself will die in another
country.
The people of Israel will be taken away
as prisoners.
They will be carried off from their
own land.' "

The LORD Gives Amos Another Vision

8 The LORD and King gave me a vision.
He showed me a basket of ripe fruit.
2 "What do you see, Amos?" he asked.

"A basket of ripe fruit," I replied.

Then the LORD said to me, "The time is

ripe for my people Israel. I will no longer spare them.

³"The time is coming when the songs in the temple will turn to crying," announces the LORD and King. "Many, many bodies will be thrown everywhere! So be quiet!"

⁴Listen to me, you who walk all over
    needy people.
You crush those who are poor in the
    land.

⁵You say,

"When will the New Moon Feast be
    over?
Then we can sell our grain.
When will the Sabbath day come to an
    end?
Then people can buy our wheat."
But you don't measure out the right
    amount.
You raise your prices.
You cheat others by using dishonest
    scales.
⁶You buy poor people to make slaves
    out of them.
You buy those who are in need for a
    mere pair of sandals.
You even sell the worthless parts of
    your wheat.

⁷People of Jacob, you are proud that the LORD is your God. But he has taken an oath in his own name. He says, "I will never forget anything Israel has done.

⁸"The land will tremble because of what
    will happen.
Everyone who lives in it will sob.
So the whole land will rise like the Nile
    River.
It will be stirred up.
Then it will settle back down again
    like that river in Egypt."

⁹The LORD and King announces,

"At that time I will make the sun go
    down at noon.
The earth will become dark in the
    middle of the day.
¹⁰I will turn your holy feasts into times
    for sobbing.
I will turn all of your songs into
    crying.
You will have to wear black clothes.
You will shave your heads.
I will make you sob as if your only son
    had died.
The end of that time will be like a
    bitter day."

¹¹The LORD and King announces,

"The days are coming
    when I will send hunger through
      the land.
But people will not be hungry for food.
    They will not be thirsty for water.
Instead, they will be hungry
    to hear a message from me.
¹²People will wander from the Dead Sea
    to the Mediterranean.
They will travel from north to east.
They will look for a message from me.
    But they will not find it.

¹³"At that time

"the lovely young women and strong
    young men
will faint because they are so thirsty.
¹⁴Some people take oaths in the name
    of Samaria's shameful god.
Others say, 'People of Dan, you can be
    sure
that your god is alive.'
Still others say, 'You can be sure
    that Beersheba's god is alive.'
But all of those people will fall dead.
    They will never get up again."

The LORD Gives Amos a Final Vision

9 I saw the Lord standing next to the altar in the temple. He said to me,

"Strike the tops of the temple pillars.
    Then the heavy stones at the base of
      the entrance will shake.
Bring everything down on the heads of
    everyone there.
I will kill with my swords
    those who are left alive.
Not one of them will escape.
    None will get away.
²They might dig down to the deepest
    parts of the grave.
But my powerful hand will take
    them out of there.
They might climb up to the heavens.
    But I will bring them down from
      there.
³They might hide on top of Mount
    Carmel.
But I will hunt them down
    and grab hold of them.
They might hide from me at the
    bottom of the ocean.
But I will command the serpent to
    bite them.
⁴Their enemies might take them away
    as prisoners to another country.
But I will command their enemies
    to kill them with their swords.

I will turn my eyes toward them to
    harm them.
I will not help them."

5 The LORD rules over all.
    The Lord touches the earth, and it
       melts.
    Everyone who lives in it sobs.
The whole land rises like the Nile River.
    Then it settles back down again
    like that river in Egypt.
6 The LORD builds his palace high in the
      heavens.
He lays its foundation on the earth.
He sends for the waters in the clouds.
    Then he pours them out on the
      surface of the land.
    His name is The LORD.

7 "You Israelites are just like
    the people of Cush to me,"
                announces the LORD.
"I brought Israel up from Egypt.
    I also brought the Philistines from
      Crete
    and the Arameans from Kir.

8 "I am the LORD and King.
    My eyes are watching the sinful
      kingdom of Israel.
I will wipe it off the face of the earth.
    But I will not totally destroy the
      people of Jacob,"
                announces the LORD.
9 "I will give an order.
    I will shake the people of Israel
    among all of the nations.
They will be like grain that is shaken
      through a screen.
    Not a pebble will fall to the ground.
10 All of the sinners among my people
    will be killed with swords.
    They say, 'Nothing bad will ever
      happen to us.'

Israel Will Be Made Like New Again

11 "The time will come when I will
      rebuild
    David's fallen tent.
I will repair its broken places.
    I will rebuild what was destroyed.
    I will make it what it used to be.
12 Then my people will take control of
      those
    who are left alive in Edom.
They will also possess all of the nations
    that belong to me,"
                announces the LORD.
He will do all of those things.

13 "A new day is coming," announces
the LORD.

"At that time those who plow the land
    will catch up with those who
      harvest the crops.
Those who stomp on grapes
    will catch up with those who plant
      the vines.
Fresh wine will drip from the
      mountains.
    It will flow down from all of the
      hills.
14 I will bring my people Israel back
      home.
    I will bless them with great success
      again.
    They will rebuild the destroyed cities
      and live in them.
They will plant vineyards and drink
      the wine they produce.
    They will make gardens and eat their
      fruit.
15 I will plant Israel in their own land.
    They will never again be removed
    from the land I have given them,"
              says the LORD your God.

OBADIAH

The book of Obadiah tells how God will respond to those who hurt his people. When Babylon conquers Judah, the people of Edom cheer. They even steal from the poor people who are left behind. Through Obadiah, God shows his love for his people and how he will punish those who hurt them. Read the book to learn about God's love and protection for all of those who follow him.

THE PEOPLE OF EDOM WERE:

HELPFUL (Not!)

KIND (Not!)

LOVING (Not!)

1 This is the vision about Edom that Obadiah had. Here is what he said.

We've heard a message from the LORD
and King.
A messenger was sent to the nations.
The LORD told him to say,
"Get up! Let us go and make war
against Edom."

2 The LORD says to Edom,

"I will make you weak among the
nations.
They will look down on you.
3 You live in the safety of the rocks.
You make your home high up in the
mountains.
But your proud heart has tricked
you.
So you say to yourself,
'No one can bring me down to the
ground.'
4 You have built your home as high as an
eagle does.
You have made your nest among the
stars.
But I will bring you down from
there,"
announces the LORD.
5 "Edom, suppose robbers came to you
at night.
They would steal only as much as
they wanted.
Suppose grape pickers came to harvest
your vines.
They would still leave a few grapes.
But you are facing horrible trouble!
6 People of Esau, everything will be
taken away from you.
Your hidden treasures will be stolen.
7 All those who are helping you
will force you to leave your country.
Your friends will trick you and
overpower you.
Those who eat bread with you
will set a trap for you.
But you will not see it."

8 The LORD announces, "At that time
I will destroy the wise men of Edom.
I will wipe out the men of
understanding
in the mountains of Esau.
9 People of Teman, your soldiers will be
terrified.
Everyone in Esau's mountains
will be cut down with swords.
10 You did harmful things to your
brothers,
the people of Jacob.
So you will be covered with shame.

You will be destroyed forever.
11 Strangers entered the gates of
Jerusalem.
They cast lots to see what each one
would get.
They carried off its wealth.
When that happened, you just stood
there and did nothing.
You were like one of them.
12 That was a time of trouble for your
brothers.
So you should not have looked
down on them.
The people of Judah were destroyed.
So you should not have been happy
about it.
You should not have laughed at them
so much
when they were in trouble.
13 You should not have marched
through the gates of my people's
city
when they were having so much
trouble.
You should not have looked down on
them.
You should not have stolen their
wealth.
14 You waited where the roads cross.
You wanted to cut down those who
were running away.
You should not have done that.
You handed over to their enemies
those who were still left alive.
You should not have done that.
They were in trouble.

15 "The day of the LORD is near
for all of the nations.
Others will do to you
what you have done to them.
You will be paid back
for what you have done.
16 You Edomites polluted my holy
mountain of Zion
by drinking and celebrating there.
So all of the nations will drink
from the cup of my anger.
And they will keep on drinking
from it.
They will vanish.
It will be as if they had never existed.
17 But on Mount Zion some of my people
will be left alive.
I will save them.
Zion will be my holy mountain once
again.
And the people of Jacob
will again receive the land as their
own.
18 They will be like a fire.

Joseph's people will be like a flame.
The nation of Esau will be like straw.
Jacob's people will set Edom on fire
   and burn it up.
No one will be left alive
   among Esau's people."
                              The LORD has spoken.

19 Israelites from the Negev Desert
   will take over Esau's mountains.
Israelites from the western hills
   will possess Philistia.
They'll take over the territories
   of Ephraim and Samaria.
Israelites from the tribe of Benjamin
   will possess the land of Gilead.

20 Some Israelites were forced to leave
   their homes.
They'll come back to Canaan and
   possess
it all the way to the town of
   Zarephath.
Some people from Jerusalem were
   taken
to the city of Sepharad.
They'll return and possess
   the towns of the Negev Desert.
21 Leaders from Mount Zion will go
   and rule over the mountains of Esau.
And the kingdom will belong to the
   LORD.

JONAH

The book of Jonah is a book of second chances. Jonah runs from God's will and finds himself in a dangerous situation—first in a boat during a huge storm, then in the stomach of a great fish. But God hasn't forgotten Jonah. He gives him another chance to obey. As a hero, Jonah is far from perfect. But as you read his book, you'll discover that God doesn't wait for his people to be perfect so that he can use them. He is only waiting for them to be willing and obedient.

HERO IN THIS BOOK . . .

JONAH
(Sort of)
PAGE 1042

Jonah Runs Away From the LORD

1 A message from the LORD came to Jonah. He was the son of Amittai. The LORD said, **2**"Go to the great city of Nineveh. Preach against it. The sins of its people have come to my attention."

3But Jonah ran away from the LORD. He headed for Tarshish. So he went down to the port of Joppa. There he found a ship that was going to Tarshish. He paid the fare and went on board. Then he sailed for Tarshish. He was running away from the LORD.

4But the LORD sent a strong wind over the Mediterranean Sea. A wild storm came up. It was so wild that the ship was in danger of breaking apart. **5**All of the sailors were afraid. Each one cried out to his own god for help. They threw the ship's contents into the sea. They were trying to make the ship lighter.

But Jonah had gone below deck. There he lay down and fell into a deep sleep. **6**The captain went down to him and said, "How can you sleep? Get up and call out to your god for help! Maybe he'll pay attention to what's happening to us. Then we won't die."

7The sailors said to one another, "Come. Let's cast lots to find out who is to blame for getting us into all of this trouble." So they did. And Jonah was picked.

8They asked him, "What terrible thing have you done to bring all of this trouble on us? Tell us. What do you do for a living? Where do you come from? What is your country? What people do you belong to?"

9He answered, "I'm a Hebrew. I worship the LORD. He is the God of heaven. He made the sea and the land."

10They found out he was running away from the LORD. That's because he had told them. Then they became terrified. So they asked him, "How could you do a thing like that?"

11The sea was getting rougher and rougher. So they asked him, "What should we do to you to make the sea calm down?"

12"Pick me up and throw me into the sea," he replied. "Then it will become calm. I know it's my fault that this terrible storm has come on you."

13Instead of doing what he said, the men did their best to row back to land. But they couldn't. The sea got even rougher than before.

14Then they cried out to the LORD. They prayed, "LORD, please don't let us die for taking this man's life. After all, he might not be guilty of doing anything wrong. So don't hold us accountable for killing him. LORD, you always do what you want to." **15**Then they took Jonah and threw him overboard. And the stormy sea became calm.

16When the men saw what had happened, they began to have great respect for the LORD. They offered a sacrifice to him. And they made promises to him.

17But the LORD sent a huge fish to swallow Jonah. And Jonah was inside the fish for three days and three nights.

Jonah Prays to the LORD

2 From inside the fish Jonah prayed to the LORD his God. **2**He said,

"When I was in trouble, I called out to
    you.
  And you answered me.
When I had almost drowned,
  I called out for help.
  And you listened to my cry.
3You threw me into the Mediterranean
    Sea.
  I was in the middle of its waters.
  They were all around me.
All of your rolling waves
  were sweeping over me.
4I said, 'I have been driven away from
    you.
  But I will look again
  toward your holy temple in
    Jerusalem.'
5I had almost drowned in the waves.
  The deep waters were all around me.
  Seaweed was wrapped around my
    head.
6I sank down to the bottom of the
    mountains.
  I thought I had died
  and gone down into the grave
    forever.
But you brought my life up
  from the very edge of the pit.
  You are the LORD my God.

7"When my life was nearly over,
  I remembered you, LORD.
My prayer rose up to you.
  It reached you in your holy temple
    in heaven.

8"Some people worship the worthless
    statues of their gods.
  They turn away from the grace
  you want to give them.
9But I will sacrifice a thank offering to
    you.
  And I will sing a song of thanks.

JONAH

JONAH 2:1-2

B

> *From inside the fish Jonah prayed...* "When I was in trouble, I called out to you. And you answered me. When I had almost drowned, I called out for help. And you listened to my cry."

Jonah coughed in the dark. The stench made breathing almost impossible. He rubbed his eyes clear of water and seaweed. It was so dark he couldn't see anything. He felt like he was moving. He *was* moving. Then he remembered . . .

He had been on a ship during a terrible storm. He knew the storm had come because he had run away. God wanted him to preach to the sinful people of Nineveh. But Jonah didn't. He climbed aboard a ship going in the opposite direction.

Then a terrible storm came. The ship swayed back and forth, up and down. **HUGE WAVES SENT BONE-CHILLING WATER RUSHING INTO THE BOAT.** The men threw everything overboard to make the ship lighter. They prayed to their gods for help. But the storm just got worse. The sailors decided to cast lots (kind of like drawing straws) to find out who caused the storm. The lot fell on Jonah. All eyes turned to him. What had he done to make the gods so angry?

Jonah knew. He had run away from God. He hadn't done what God wanted him to do. "Throw me into the sea and the storm will stop," he told them. The sailors thought he was crazy, but they were desperate. The men first asked God to forgive them, then they dropped Jonah into the swirling, cold waters. Instantly, the waves and the wind calmed down.

Suddenly, an enormous fish appeared and swallowed Jonah. Jonah thanked God for saving him. And he asked God to forgive him for not going to Nineveh. God gave the fish a bellyache. Its stomach rumbled and roared, and it spit Jonah out on the shore. Now Jonah knew what he had to do—go to Nineveh. And he did!

BE BETTER THAN JONAH

Jonah knew all along he was supposed to go to Nineveh. But he didn't want to. He went through some terrifying events before God got his attention. Finally Jonah decided to obey God. Reading about Jonah will help you remember how important it is to obey God.

JONAH HAD TO BE TAUGHT A HARD LESSON BEFORE HE WAS WILLING TO OBEY GOD.
THE WHOLE STORY: JONAH 1–4

Go to page 1090 for the next Super Hero

THANKFUL ♣

I WILL SING A SONG OF THANKS.
—— JONAH 2:9 ——

I will do what I have promised.
  LORD, you are the one who saves."

10The LORD gave the fish a command. And it spit Jonah up onto dry land.

Jonah Goes to Nineveh

3 A message came to Jonah from the LORD a second time. He said, **2**"Go to the great city of Nineveh. Announce to its people the message I give you."

3Jonah obeyed the LORD. He went to Nineveh. It was a very important city. In fact, it took about three days to see all of it. **4**On the first day, Jonah started into the city. He announced, "In 40 days Nineveh will be destroyed."

5The people of Nineveh believed God's warning. They decided not to eat any food for a while. All of them put on black clothes. That's what everyone from the least important of them to the most important did.

6The news reached the king of Nineveh. He got up from his throne. He took his royal robes off and dressed himself in black clothes. He sat down in the dust. **7**Then he sent out a message to the people of Nineveh. He said,

"I and my nobles give this order.

"Don't let any person or animal taste anything. That includes your herds and flocks. People and animals must not eat or drink anything. **8**Let people and animals alike be covered with black cloth. All of you must call out to God with all your hearts. Stop doing what is evil. Don't harm others. **9**Who knows? God might take pity on us. He might turn away from his burning anger. Then we won't die."

10God saw what they did. They stopped doing what was evil. So he took pity on them. He didn't destroy them as he had said he would.

The LORD Shows Concern for Nineveh

4 But Jonah was very upset. He became angry. **2**He prayed to the LORD and said, "LORD, isn't this exactly what I thought would happen when I was still at home? That's why I was so quick to run away to Tarshish. I knew that you are gracious. You are tender and kind. You are slow to get angry. You are full of love. You are a God who takes pity on people. You don't want to destroy them. **3**LORD, take away my life. I'd rather die than live."

4But the LORD replied, "Do you have any right to be angry?"

5Jonah left the city. He sat down at a place east of it. There he put some branches over his head. He sat in their shade. He waited to see what would happen to the city.

6Then the LORD God sent a vine and made it grow up over Jonah. It gave him more shade for his head. It made him more comfortable. Jonah was very happy he had the vine. **7**But before sunrise the next day, God sent a worm. It chewed the vine so much that it dried up.

8When the sun rose, God sent a burning east wind. The sun beat down on Jonah's head. It made him very weak. He wanted to die. So he said, "I'd rather die than live."

9But God said to Jonah, "Do you have any right to be angry about what happened to the vine?"

"I do," he said. "In fact, I'm angry enough to die."

10But the LORD said, "You have been concerned about this vine. But you did not take care of it. You did not make it grow. It grew up in one night and died the next. **11**Nineveh has more than 120,000 people. They can't tell right from wrong. Nineveh also has a lot of cattle. So shouldn't I show concern for that great city?"

OBEYS ✔

JONAH OBEYED THE LORD.
—— JONAH 3:3 ——

MICAH

The prophet Micah writes God's words of judgment against the sinful people of Judah. They refuse to follow God and worship him, and their society is growing more and more corrupt. Micah bravely turns their attention toward God's coming judgment. He also includes a clear prophecy about the Savior who will be born in Bethlehem. As you read Micah, be thankful to God for fulfilling his prophecy to send a Savior.

CODE OF HONOR IN THIS BOOK . . .

BRAVE
PAGE 1047

STRONG
PAGE 1047

OBEYS
PAGES 1048, 1050

LOVING
PAGES 1050, 1051

FORGIVING
PAGE 1051

1 A message came to Micah from the LORD. He was from the town of Moresheth. The message came while Jotham, Ahaz and Hezekiah were kings of Judah. This is the vision Micah saw concerning Samaria and Jerusalem. Here is what he said.

² Listen to me, all of you nations!
Earth and everyone who lives in it,
pay attention!
The LORD and King will be a witness
against you.
The Lord will speak from his holy
temple in heaven.

The LORD Will Judge Samaria and Jerusalem

³ The LORD is about to come down
from his home in heaven.
He rules over the highest places on
earth.
⁴ The mountains will melt under him
like wax near a fire.
The valleys will be broken apart
by water rushing down a slope.
⁵ All of that will happen because
Jacob's people have done what is
wrong.
The people of Israel
have committed many sins.
Who is to blame
for the wrong things Jacob has
done?
Samaria!
Who is to blame for the high places
where Judah's people worship other
gods?
Jerusalem!

⁶ So the LORD says,

"I will turn Samaria into a pile of trash.
It will become a place for planting
vineyards.
I will dump its stones down into the
valley.
And I will destroy it
down to its very foundations.
⁷ All of the statues of Samaria's gods
will be broken to pieces.
All of the gifts its people gave to temple
prostitutes
will be burned with fire.
I will destroy all of the statues of its
gods.
Samaria collected gifts that were paid
to temple prostitutes.
So the Assyrians will use the gifts
to pay their own temple prostitutes."

Micah Sobs Over His People

⁸ I will sob and cry because Samaria will
be destroyed.
I'll walk around barefoot.
I won't have anything on but my
underwear.
I'll bark like a wild dog.
I'll hoot like an owl.
⁹ Samaria's wounds can't be healed.
The LORD will also judge Judah.
Enemies will march up to the very gate
of my people.
They will reach Jerusalem itself.
¹⁰ Don't tell the people of Gath about it.
Don't let them see you sob.
People in Beth Ophrah, roll in the
dust.
¹¹ You who live in the town of Shaphir,
leave in shame and without your
clothes.
Those who live in Zaanan
won't come out to help you.
The people in Beth Ezel will sob.
They won't be able to help keep you
safe.
¹² Those who live in Maroth will groan
with pain
as they wait for help.
That's because the LORD will bring
trouble on them.
It will reach the very gate of
Jerusalem.
¹³ You who live in Lachish,
get your horses ready to pull their
chariots.
You trust in military power.
That was the beginning of sin
for the people of Zion.
The wrong things Israel did
were also done by you.
¹⁴ People of Judah, you might as well say
good-by
to Moresheth near Gath.
The town of Aczib won't give any help
to the kings of Israel.
¹⁵ An enemy will attack
you who live in Mareshah.
Israel's glorious leaders will have to run
away
and hide in the cave of Adullam.
¹⁶ The children you enjoy so much
will be taken away as prisoners.
So shave your heads and sob.
Make them as bare as the head of a
vulture.

People's Plans and God's Plans

2 How terrible it will be for those
who plan to harm others!
How terrible for those who make evil
plans

before they even get out of bed!
As soon as daylight comes,
they carry them out.
That's because they have the power
to do it.
2 If they want fields or houses,
they take them.
They cheat men out of
their homes and property.

3 So the Lord says to them,

"I am planning to send trouble on you.
You will not be able to save
yourselves from it.
You will not live so proudly anymore.
It will be a time of trouble.
4 At that time people will make fun of
you.
They will tease you by singing a song
of sadness.
They will pretend to be you and say,
'We are totally destroyed.
Our enemies have divided up our
land.
The Lord has taken it away from us!
He has given our fields to those
who turned against us.' "

5 So you won't even have anyone left
in the Lord's community
who can divide up the land for you.

Some Prophets Aren't Really Prophets at All

6 "Don't prophesy," the people's
prophets say.
"Don't prophesy about bad things.
Nothing shameful is going to
happen to us."
7 People of Jacob, should others say,
"The Lord isn't angry with us.
He doesn't do things like that"?

The Lord replies, "What I promise
brings good things
to those who lead honest lives.
8 But lately my people have attacked one
another
as if they were enemies.
You strip the rich robes off
those who happen to pass by.
They thought they were as safe as men
returning from a battle they had
won.
9 You drive the women among my
people
out of their pleasant homes.
You take my blessing away
from their children forever.
10 Get up! Leave this land!
It is no longer your resting place.
You have made it 'unclean.'

You have completely destroyed it.
11 Suppose a prophet goes around telling
lies.
And he prophesies that you will
have
plenty of wine and beer.
Then that kind of prophet would be
just right for this nation!

The Lord Promises He Will Save His People

12 "People of Jacob, I will gather all of
you.
I will bring together
you who are still left alive in Israel.
I will gather you together like sheep in
a pen.
You will be like a flock in its
grasslands.
Your country will be filled with
people.
13 I will open the way for you to return.
I will march in front of you.
You will break through the city gates
and go free.
I am your King. I will pass through the
gates
in front of you.
I will lead the way."

The Lord Warns Israel's Leaders and Prophets

3 Then I said,

"Listen, you leaders of Jacob's people!
Pay attention, you rulers of Israel!
You should know how to judge others
fairly.
2   But you hate what is good.
And you love what is evil.
You are like someone
who tears the skin off my people.
You pull the meat off their bones.
3 You eat my people's bodies.
You strip their skin off.
You break their bones in pieces.
You chop them up like meat.
You put them in a cooking pot."

4 The time will come when Israel
will cry out to the Lord.
But he won't answer them.
In fact, he'll turn his face away from
them.
They have done what is evil.

5 The Lord says,

"You prophets are leading my people
down the wrong path.
If they feed you,
you promise them peace.

If they do not,
you prepare to go to war against
them.
⁶ So night will come on you.
But you will not have any visions.
Darkness will cover you.
But you will not be able
to figure out what is going to
happen.
The sun will set on you prophets.
The day will become dark for you.
⁷ You who see visions will be put to
shame.
You who try to figure out what is
going to happen
will be dishonored.
All of you will cover your faces.
I will not answer you."

⁸ The Spirit of the LORD
has filled me with power.
He helps me do what is fair.
He makes me brave.
Now I'm prepared to tell Jacob's people
what they've done wrong.

POWER-/SURGE

BRAVE B

THE SPIRIT OF
THE LORD
HAS FILLED ME
WITH POWER.
HE HELPS ME DO
WHAT IS FAIR.
HE MAKES ME BRAVE.
— MICAH 3:8 —

STRONG

I'm ready to tell Israel they've
sinned.
⁹ Listen to me, you leaders of Jacob's
people!
Pay attention, you rulers of Israel!
You hate to do what is fair.
You twist everything that is right.
¹⁰ You build up Zion by spilling the blood
of others.
You build Jerusalem by doing what
is evil.
¹¹ Your judges take money from people
who want special favors.

Your priests teach only if they get
paid for it.
Your prophets won't tell fortunes
unless they receive money.
But you still claim to depend on the
LORD.
You say, "The LORD is with us.
No trouble will come on us."
¹² So because of what you have done,
Zion will be plowed up like a field.
Jerusalem will be turned into a pile of
trash.
The temple hill will be covered with
bushes and weeds.

People From Many Nations Will Worship at Mount Zion

4 In the last days

the mountain where the LORD's temple
is located will be famous.
It will be the most important
mountain of all.
It will stand out above the hills.
And nations will go to it.

² People from many nations will go
there. They will say,

"Come, let us go up to the LORD's
mountain.
Let's go to the house of Jacob's God.
He will teach us how we should live.
Then we will live the way he wants
us to."
The law of the LORD will be taught at
Zion.
His message will go out from
Jerusalem.
³ He will judge between people from
many nations.
He'll settle problems among strong
nations everywhere.
They will hammer their swords into
plows.
They'll hammer their spears into
pruning tools.
Nations will not go to war against one
another.
They won't even train to fight
anymore.
⁴ Every man will have
his own vine and fig tree.
And no one will make them afraid.
That's what the LORD who rules over
all has promised.
⁵ Other nations worship and trust in
their gods.
But we will worship and obey the
LORD.
He will be our God for ever and ever.

OBEYS ✔

WE WILL WORSHIP
AND OBEY THE LORD.
HE WILL BE OUR GOD
FOR EVER AND EVER.
—— MICAH 4:5 ——

The Lord's Kingdom Will Come

6 "The time is coming
　　when I will gather those who are
　　　disabled,"
　　announces the LORD.
"I will bring together those
　　who were taken away as prisoners.
I will gather those I have allowed to
　　suffer.
7 I will make the disabled my faithful
　　people.
　　I will make those who were driven
　　　away from their homes a strong
　　　nation.
I will rule over them on Mount Zion.
　　I will be their King from that time
　　　on and forever.
8 Jerusalem, you used to be
　　like a guard tower for my flock.
City of Zion, you used to be
　　a place of safety for my people.
The glorious kingdom you had before
　　will be given back to you.
　　Once again a king will rule over your
　　　people."

9 Why are you crying out so loudly now?
　　Don't you have a king?
Have your advisers died?
　　Is that why pain comes on you
　　like the pain of a woman having a
　　　baby?
10 People of Zion, groan with pain.
　　Cry out like a woman having a baby.
Soon you must leave your city.
　　You must camp in the open fields.
You will have to go to Babylonia.
　　But that's where the LORD will save
　　　you.
There he will set you free
　　from the powerful hand of your
　　　enemies.

11 But now many nations
　　have gathered together to attack
　　　you.
They say, "Let Jerusalem be polluted.

We want to see others laugh when
　　Zion suffers!"
12 But those nations don't know
　　what the LORD has in mind.
They don't understand his plan.
　　He will gather them up like bundles
　　　of grain.
　　He will take them to his threshing
　　　floor.

13 The LORD says,

"People of Zion, get up
　　and crush your enemies.
I will make you like a threshing ox.
I will give you iron horns and bronze
　　hoofs.
　　So you will crush many nations."

They got their money in the wrong
　　way.
　　But you will set it apart to the LORD.
You will give their wealth
　　to the Lord of the whole earth.

A Ruler Will Come
From Bethlehem

5 Jerusalem, you are being attacked.
　　So bring your troops together.
Our enemies have surrounded us.
　　They want to slap the face of Israel's
　　　ruler.

2 The LORD says,

"Bethlehem, you might not be
　　an important town in the nation of
　　　Judah.
But out of you will come
　　a ruler over Israel for me.
His family line goes back
　　to the early years of your nation.
It goes all the way back
　　to days of long ago."
　　Bethlehem was also called
　　　Ephrathah.

3 The LORD will hand his people over to
　　their enemies.
　　That will last until the promised
　　　ruler is born.
Then his relatives in Judah
　　will return to their land.
The LORD will rule over them
　　and the people of Israel.

4 The promised ruler will stand firm
　　and take care of his flock.
The LORD will give him the strength to
　　do it.
　　The LORD his God will give him
　　　the authority to rule.
His people will live safely.
　　His greatness will reach

from one end of the earth to the other.
5 And he will bring them peace.

The Lord Will Save His People From Their Enemies

The Assyrians will attack our land.
    Enemies will march through our
        forts.
But we will raise up many shepherds
    against them.
    We'll send out against them
    as many leaders as we need to.
6 They will use their swords to rule over
        Assyria.
    They'll rule the land of Nimrod
    with swords that are ready to strike.
The Assyrians will march across our
        borders
    and attack our land.
    But the promised ruler will save us
        from them.

7 Jacob's people who are still left alive
    will be scattered among many
        nations.
They will be like dew the Lord has
        sent.
    It doesn't wait for a man's
        command.
They will be like rain that falls on the
        grass.
    Rain doesn't wait for someone to
        give it orders.
8 So Jacob's people will be scattered
    among many nations.
They will be like a lion
    among the animals in the forest.
They'll be like a young lion
    among flocks of sheep.
Lions attack and tear as they move
        along.
    No one can keep them
    from killing what they want.
9 Lord, your powerful hand will win the
        battle
    over your enemies.
    All of them will be destroyed.

10 "At that time I will destroy
    your war horses," announces the
        Lord.
    "I will smash your chariots.
11 I will destroy the cities in your land.
    I will tear down all of your forts.
12 I will destroy your worship of evil
        powers.
    You will no longer be able
    to put a spell on anyone.
13 I will destroy the statues of your gods.
    I will take your sacred stones away
        from you.
    You will no longer bow down

to the gods your hands have made.
14 I will pull down the poles you used
    to worship the goddess Asherah.
    And I will destroy your cities
        completely.
15 I will pay back the nations
    that have not obeyed me.
    My anger will burn against them."

The Lord Brings Charges Against Israel

6 Israel, listen to the Lord's message.
    He says to me,

"Stand up in court.
    Let the mountains serve as
        witnesses.
    Let the hills hear what you have to
        say."

2 Hear the Lord's case, you mountains.
    Listen, you age-old foundations of
        the earth.
The Lord has a case against his people
        Israel.
    He is bringing charges against them.

3 The Lord says,

"My people, what have I done to you?
    Have I made things too hard for
        you? Answer me.
4 I brought your people up out of Egypt.
    I set them free from the land
    where they were slaves.
I sent Moses to lead them.
    Aaron and Miriam helped him.
5 Remember how Balak, the king of
        Moab,
    planned to put a curse on your
        people.
But Balaam, the son of Beor,
    gave them a blessing instead.
Remember their journey from Shittim
        to Gilgal.
    I want you to know
    that I always do what is right."

6 The people of Israel say,

"What should we bring with us
    when we go to worship the Lord?
What should we offer the God of
        heaven
    when we bow down to him?
Should we take burnt offerings to him?
    Should we sacrifice calves
    that are a year old?
7 Will the Lord be pleased with
    thousands of rams?
    Will he take delight in 10,000 rivers
        of olive oil?
Should we offer our oldest sons

POWER-SURGE

OBEYS ✔

THE LORD HAS SHOWN
YOU WHAT IS GOOD.

HE HAS TOLD YOU
WHAT HE REQUIRES
OF YOU.

YOU MUST TREAT
PEOPLE FAIRLY.

YOU MUST LOVE
OTHERS FAITHFULLY.

AND YOU MUST BE
VERY CAREFUL TO LIVE

THE WAY YOUR GOD
WANTS YOU TO.
— MICAH 6:8 — ♥

LOVING

for the wrong things we've done?
Should we sacrifice our own children
to pay for our sins?"

8 The LORD has shown you what is good.
He has told you what he requires of
you.
You must treat people fairly.
You must love others faithfully.
And you must be very careful to live
the way your God wants you to.

The LORD Will Punish His People

9 The LORD is calling out to Jerusalem.
And it would be wise to pay
attention to him.
He says, "Listen, tribe of Judah
and you people who are gathered in
the city.
10 You sinful people, should I forget
that you got your treasures by
stealing them?
You use dishonest measures to cheat
others.
I have placed a curse on that
practice.
11 Should I forgive you who use dishonest
scales?
You use weights that weigh things
heavier

or lighter than they really are.
12 The rich people among you harm
others.
You are always telling lies.
You try to fool others by what you
say.
13 So I will strike you down.
I will destroy you
because you have sinned so much.
14 You will eat. But you will not be
satisfied.
Your stomachs will still be empty.
You will try to save what you can.
But you will not be able to.
If you do save something,
it will be destroyed in battle.
15 You will plant seeds.
But you will not harvest any crops.
You will press olives.
But you will not use the oil for
yourselves.
You will crush grapes.
But you will not drink the wine
that is made from them.
16 You have followed the evil practices
of King Omri of Israel.
You have done what the family
of King Ahab did.
You have followed their bad example.
So I will let you be destroyed.
Others will make fun of you.
The nations will laugh at you."

Micah Is Sad Because Israel Has Sinned

7 I'm suffering very much!
I'm like someone who gathers
summer fruit in a vineyard
after the good fruit has already been
picked.
No grapes are left to eat.
None of the early figs I long for
remain.
2 Faithful people have disappeared from
the land.
Those who are honest are gone.
All men hide and wait
to spill the blood of others.
They use nets to try and trap one
another.
3 They are very good at doing what is
evil.
Rulers require gifts.
Judges accept money from people
who want special favors.
Those who are powerful
always get what they want.
All of them make evil plans together.
4 The best of them are as harmful as
thorns.

The most honest of them are even
worse.
The time your prophets warned you
about has come.
God is about to punish you.
Panic has taken hold of you.
⁵ Don't trust your neighbors.
Don't put your faith in your friends.
Be careful of what you say
even to your own wife.
⁶ Sons don't honor their fathers.
Daughters refuse to obey their
mothers.
Daughters-in-law are against their
mothers-in-law.
A man's enemies are the members of
his own family.

⁷ So I will look to the LORD.
I'll put my trust in God my Savior.
He will hear me.

Jerusalem Will Be Rebuilt

⁸ The people of Jerusalem say,

"Don't laugh when we suffer,
you enemies of ours!
We have fallen.
But we'll get up.
Even though we sit in the dark,
the LORD will give us light.
⁹ We've sinned against the LORD.
So he is angry with us.
That will continue until he takes up
our case.
Then he'll do what is right for us.
He'll bring us out into the light.
Then we'll see him save us.
¹⁰ The people of Nineveh will see it too.
And they will be put to shame.
After all, they said to us,
'Where is the LORD your God?'
But we will see them destroyed.
Soon they will be stomped on
like mud in the streets."

¹¹ People of Jerusalem, the time will
come
when your walls will be rebuilt.
Land will be added to your territory.
¹² At that time your people will come
back to you.
They'll return from Assyria
and the cities of Egypt.
They'll come from the countries
between Egypt and the Euphrates
River.
They'll return from the lands
between the seas.
They'll come back from the countries
between the mountains.

¹³ But the rest of the earth will be
deserted.
The people who live in it
have done many evil things.

Prayer and Praise

¹⁴ LORD, be like a shepherd to your people.
Take good care of them.
They are your flock.
They live by themselves
in the safety of a forest.
Rich grasslands are all around them.
Let them eat grass in Bashan and
Gilead
just as they did long ago.

¹⁵ The LORD says to his people,

"I showed your people my wonders
when they came out of Egypt long
ago.
In the same way, I will show them to
you."

¹⁶ When the nations see those wonders,
they will be put to shame.
All of their power will be taken away
from them.
They will be so amazed
that they won't be able to speak or
hear.

POWER - SURGE

FORGIVING F

LORD, WHO IS A GOD
LIKE YOU?

YOU FORGIVE SIN.

YOU FORGIVE YOUR
PEOPLE

WHEN THEY DO WHAT
IS WRONG.

YOU DON'T STAY
ANGRY FOREVER.

INSTEAD, YOU TAKE
DELIGHT IN SHOWING

YOUR FAITHFUL LOVE
TO THEM.
— MICAH 7:18 —

LOVING

17 They'll be forced to eat dust like a
snake.
They'll be like creatures
that have to crawl on the ground.
They'll come out of their dens
trembling with fear.
They'll show respect for the LORD our
God.
They will also have respect for his
people.
18 LORD, who is a God like you?
You forgive sin.
You forgive your people
when they do what is wrong.
You don't stay angry forever.

Instead, you take delight in
showing
your faithful love to them.
19 Once again you will show loving
concern for us.
You will completely wipe out
the evil things we've done.
You will throw all of our sins
into the bottom of the sea.
20 You will be true to Jacob's people.
You will show your faithful love
to Abraham's children.
You will do what you promised to do
for our people
when you took an oath long ago.

NAHUM

The book of Nahum contains the words of the prophet Nahum. His message is one of judgment against Assyria, the nation that conquers Israel and has some power over Judah. Nahum assures the people that God is still in control of all that happens. As you read Nahum, you'll see both God's judgment—he punishes those who sin—and God's mercy—he's waiting to forgive those who are willing to turn to him.

CODE OF HONOR IN THIS BOOK . . .

KIND
PAGE 1054

TRUSTED
PAGE 1054

1 Here is a message the LORD gave Nahum in a vision about Nineveh. It is written on a scroll. Nahum was from the town of Elkosh. Here is what he said.

The LORD Is Angry With Nineveh

² The LORD is a jealous God who
punishes people.
He pays them back for the evil
things they do.
His anger burns against them.
The LORD punishes his enemies.
He holds his anger back
until the right time to use it.
³ The LORD is slow to get angry.
He is very powerful.
The LORD will not let guilty people go
without punishing them.
When he marches out, he stirs up
winds and storms.
Clouds are the dust kicked up by his
feet.
⁴ He controls the seas. He dries them up.
He makes all of the rivers run dry.
Bashan and Mount Carmel dry up.
The flowers in Lebanon fade.
⁵ He causes the mountains to shake.
The hills melt away.
The earth trembles because he is there.
So do the world and all those who
live in it.
⁶ Who can stand firm when his anger
burns?
Who can live when he is angry?
His anger blazes out like fire.
He smashes the rocks to pieces.

⁷ The LORD is good.
When people are in trouble,
they can go to him for safety.
He takes good care of those
who trust in him.
⁸ But he will destroy Nineveh
with a powerful flood.
He will chase his enemies
into the darkness of punishment.

⁹ The LORD will put an end
to anything they plan against him.
He won't allow Assyria to win the
battle
over his people a second time.
¹⁰ His enemies will be tangled up among
thorns.
Their wine will make them drunk.
They'll be burned up like dry straw.
¹¹ Nineveh, a king has marched out from
you.
He makes evil plans against the
LORD.
He gives harmful advice.

¹² The LORD says,

"His army has many soldiers.
Other nations are helping them.
But they will be cut off and pass
away.
Judah, I punished you.
But I will not do it anymore.
¹³ Now I will break Assyria's yoke off your
neck.
I will tear off the ropes that hold
you."

¹⁴ Nineveh, the LORD has given an order
concerning you.
He has said, "You will not have any
children
to carry on your name.
I will destroy the wooden and metal
statues
that are in the temple of your gods.
I will get your grave ready for you.
You are worthless."

¹⁵ Look at the mountains of Judah!
I see a messenger running to bring
good news!
He's telling us that peace has come!
People of Judah, celebrate your feasts.
Carry out your promises.
The evil Assyrians won't attack you
again.
They'll be completely destroyed.

The LORD Will Destroy Nineveh

2 Nineveh, armies are coming to
attack you.
Guard the forts!
Watch the roads!

KIND   **K**

THE LORD IS GOOD.
WHEN PEOPLE ARE IN
TROUBLE,
THEY CAN GO TO HIM
FOR SAFETY.
HE TAKES GOOD CARE
OF THOSE
WHO TRUST IN HIM.
— NAHUM 1:7 —

TRUSTED

Get ready!
Gather all of your strength!

2 Assyria once took everything of value
from God's people.
Its army destroyed all of their vines.
But the LORD will bring back
the glory of Jacob's people.
He'll make Israel glorious again.

3 The shields of the soldiers attacking
Nineveh are red.
The armies are dressed in bright red
uniforms.
The metal on their chariots flashes
when they are prepared for war.
Their spears are ready to use.
4 The chariots race through the main
streets.
They rush back and forth through
them.
They look like flaming torches.
They dart around like lightning.

5 The commander of the attackers
sends for his special troops.
But they trip and fall on their way.
They run toward the city wall.
They keep their shield in front of
them.
6 They open the gates that hold back
the waters of the river.
And the palace falls down.
7 The attackers order that the city's
people
be taken away as prisoners.
The female slaves cry like sad doves.
They beat their chests.
8 Nineveh is like a pool.
Its water is draining away.
"Stop running away!" someone cries
out.
But no one turns back.
9 "Steal the silver!" the attackers shout.
"Grab the gold!"
The supply is endless.
There is plenty of wealth
among all of the city's treasures.
10 Nineveh is destroyed, robbed and
stripped!
Hearts melt away in fear.
Knees give way.
Bodies tremble with fear.
Everyone's face turns pale.

11 Assyria is like a lion.
Where is the lions' den now?
Where did they feed their cubs?
Where did all of the lions go?
In their den they had nothing to
fear.
12 The lion killed enough for his cubs
to eat.

He choked what he caught for his
mate.
He filled his home with what he had
killed.
He brought to his dens what he had
caught.

13 "Nineveh, I am against you,"
announces the LORD who rules over
all.
"I will burn up your chariots with fire.
Your young lions will be killed with
swords.
I will leave you nothing on earth to
catch.
The voices of your messengers
will no longer be heard."

The LORD Will Judge Nineveh

3 How terrible it will be for Nineveh!
It is a city of murderers!
It is full of liars!
It's filled with stolen goods!
The killing never stops!
2 Whips crack!
Wheels clack!
Horses charge!
Chariots rumble!
3 Horsemen attack!
Swords flash!
Spears gleam!
Many people die.
Dead bodies pile up.
They can't even be counted.
People trip over them.
4 All of that was caused by the evil
longings
of the prostitute Nineveh.
That woman who practiced evil magic
was very beautiful.
She used her sinful charms
to make slaves out of the nations.
She worshiped evil powers
in order to trap others.

5 "Nineveh, I am against you,"
announces the LORD who rules over
all.
"I will pull your skirts up over your face.
I will show the nations your naked
body.
Kingdoms will make fun of your
shame.
6 I will throw garbage at you.
I will look down on you.
I will make an example out of you.
7 All those who see you will run away
from you.
They will say, 'Nineveh is destroyed.
Who will sob over it?'
Where can I find someone
to comfort your people?"

⁸ Nineveh, are you better than Thebes
     on the Nile River?
There was water all around that city.
     The river helped to keep it safe.
     The waters were like a wall
         around it.
⁹ Cush and Egypt gave it all of the
     strength it needed.
     Put and Libya also helped it.
¹⁰ But Thebes was captured anyway.
     Its people were taken away as
         prisoners.
Its babies were smashed to pieces
     at every street corner.
The Assyrian soldiers cast lots
     for all of its great leaders.
They put them in chains
     and made slaves out of them.
¹¹ People of Nineveh, you too will get
     drunk.
     You will try to hide from your
         enemies.
     You will look for a place of safety.

¹² All of your forts are like fig trees
     that have their first ripe fruit on
         them.
When the trees are shaken,
     the figs fall into the mouths
     of those who eat them.
¹³ Look at your troops.
     All of them are weak.
The gates of your forts
     are wide open to your enemies.
     Fire has destroyed their heavy metal
         bars.
¹⁴ Prepare for the attack by storing up
     water!

Make your walls as strong as you can!
Make some bricks out of clay!
     Mix the mud to hold them together!
     Use them to repair the walls!
¹⁵ In spite of all of your hard work,
     fire will burn you up inside your city.
Your enemies will cut you down with
     their swords.
     They will destroy you
     just as grasshoppers eat up crops.
Multiply like grasshoppers!
     Increase your numbers like locusts!
¹⁶ You have more traders
     than the number of stars in the sky.
But like locusts they strip the land.
     Then they fly away.
¹⁷ Your guards are like grasshoppers.
     Your officials are like large numbers
         of locusts.
     They settle in the walls on a cold
         day.
But when the sun appears, they fly
     away.
     And no one knows where they go.

¹⁸ King of Assyria, your leaders are asleep.
     Your nobles lie down to rest.
Your people are scattered on the
     mountains.
     No one is left to gather them
         together.
¹⁹ Nothing can heal your wounds.
     You will die of them.
All those who hear the news about you
     clap their hands
     because you have fallen from power.
All of them suffered
     because you never showed them any
         pity.

HABAKKUK

Habakkuk's book is full of questions. He wonders how a just God can let evil people get away with their sins. He wonders why God allows good people to suffer. As he tries to understand God and how God works, Habakkuk discovers that God can be trusted. His book ends with heroic words of trust in God—no matter what happens. As you read Habakkuk, remember that in the end God is in control and can be trusted.

CODE OF HONOR IN THIS BOOK . . .

BELIEVES
PAGE 1059

CHEERFUL
PAGE 1060

STRONG
PAGE 1060

1

This is a vision the prophet Habakkuk received from the LORD. Here is what Habakkuk said.

Habakkuk Asks the LORD a Question

2 LORD, how long do I have to call out for
　　help?
　　Why don't you listen to me?
How long must I keep telling you
　　that things are terrible?
　　Why don't you save us?
3 Why do you make me watch while
　　people treat others so unfairly?
Why do you put up with the wrong
　　things
　　they are doing?
I have to look at death.
　　People are harming others.
　　They are arguing and fighting all the
　　　time.
4 The law can't do what it's supposed to
　　do.
　　Fairness never comes out on top.
Sinful people surround those
　　who do what is right.
　　So people are never treated fairly.

The LORD Gives His Answer

5 The LORD replies,

"Look at the nations. Watch them.
　　Be totally amazed at what you see.
I am going to do something in your days
　　that you would never believe.
You would not believe it
　　even if someone told you about it.
6 I am going to send the armies of
　　Babylonia to attack you.
　　They are very mean. They move
　　　quickly.
They sweep across the whole earth.
　　They take over places
　　that do not belong to them.
7 They terrify others.
　　They do not recognize any laws but
　　　their own.
　　That is how proud they are.
8 Their horses are faster than leopards.
　　They are meaner than wolves in the
　　　dark.
Their horsemen charge straight into
　　battle.
　　They ride in from far away.
They come down like an eagle
　　diving for its food.
9 All of them are ready to destroy others.
　　Their huge armies advance like a
　　　wind out of the desert.
　　They gather prisoners like sand.
10 They laugh at kings

and make fun of rulers.
They laugh at all of the cities
　　that have high walls around them.
They build dirt ramps against the walls
　　and capture the cities.
11 They sweep past like the wind.
　　Then they go on their way.
They are guilty.
　　They worship their own strength."

Habakkuk Asks the LORD Another Question

12 LORD, haven't you existed forever?
　　You are my holy God.
　　So we won't die, will we?
LORD, you have appointed the
　　Babylonians
　　to punish your people.
My Rock, you have chosen them to
　　judge us.
13 Your eyes are too pure to look at what
　　is evil.
　　You can't put up with the wrong
　　　things people do.
So why do you put up
　　with those who can't be trusted?
The evil Babylonians swallow up
　　those who are more godly than
　　　themselves.
　　So why are you silent?
14 You have made men as if they were
　　only fish in the sea.
　　They are like sea creatures that don't
　　　have a ruler.
15 The evil Babylonians pull all of them
　　up with hooks.
　　They catch them in their nets.
They gather them up.
　　So they celebrate.
　　They are glad.
16 They offer sacrifices to their nets.
　　They burn incense to them.
Their nets allow them to live in great
　　comfort.
　　They enjoy the finest food.
17 Are you going to let them
　　keep on emptying their nets?
Will they go on destroying nations
　　without showing them any mercy?

2

I will go up to the lookout tower.
　　I'll station myself on the city wall.
I'll wait to see how the LORD will reply
　　to me.
　　Then I'll try to figure out how to
　　　answer him.

The LORD Gives His Answer

2 The LORD replies,

"Write down the message I am
　　showing you in a vision.

Write it clearly on the tablets you
use.
Then a messenger can read it
and run to announce it.
³ The message I give you
waits for the time I have appointed.
It speaks about what is going to
happen.
And all of it will come true.
It might take a while.
But wait for it.
You can be sure it will come.
It will happen when I want it to.

⁴ "The Babylonians are very proud.
What they want is not good.

"But the one who is right with God
will live by faith.

POWER-/SURGE

BELIEVES ✝

**THE ONE WHO IS
RIGHT WITH GOD
WILL LIVE BY FAITH.**
— **HABAKKUK 2:4** —

⁵ "Wine makes the Babylonians do
foolish things.
They are proud. They never rest.
Like the grave, they are always hungry
for more.
Like death, they are never satisfied.
They gather all of the nations to
themselves.
They take their people away as
prisoners.

⁶ "Won't those people laugh at the
Babylonians? Won't they make fun of
them? They will say to them,

" 'How terrible it will be for you
who pile up stolen goods!
You get rich by cheating others.
How long will that go on?
⁷ Those who owe you money will
suddenly rise up.
You charge them too much
interest.
So they will wake up
and make you tremble with fear.
Then they will take away
everything you have.
⁸ You have robbed many nations.
So the nations that are left will rob
you.
You have spilled man's blood.

You have destroyed lands and cities
and everyone in them.'

⁹ "How terrible it will be for the
Babylonians!
They build their kingdom with
money
they gained by cheating others.
They have tried to make the kingdom
as secure as possible.
After all, they did not want to be
destroyed.
¹⁰ They have planned to wipe out many
nations.
But they have brought shame on
their own kingdom.
So they must pay with their own
lives.
¹¹ The stones in the walls of their homes
will cry out.
And the wooden beams will echo
that cry.

¹² "How terrible it will be for the
Babylonians!
They build cities by spilling the
blood of others.
They establish towns by committing
crimes.
¹³ I am the Lᴏʀᴅ who rules over all.
Human effort is no better than wood
that feeds a fire.
So the nations wear themselves out
for nothing.
¹⁴ The oceans are full of water.
In the same way, the earth will be
filled
with the knowledge of my glory.

¹⁵ "How terrible it will be for the
Babylonians!
They give drinks to their
neighbors.
They pour the drinks from wineskins
until their neighbors are drunk.
They want to look at their naked
bodies.
¹⁶ But the Babylonians will be filled
with shame instead of glory.
So now it is their turn to drink
and be stripped of their clothes.
The cup of anger in my powerful right
hand
is going to punish them.
They will be covered with shame
instead of glory.
¹⁷ The harm they have done to Lebanon
will bring them down.
Because they have killed so many
animals,
animals will terrify them.
They have spilled man's blood.

They have destroyed lands and cities
and everyone in them.

18 "If someone carves a statue of a god,
what is it worth?
What value is there in a god
that teaches lies?
The one who trusts in another god
worships his own creation.
He makes statues of gods that can't
speak.
19 How terrible it will be for the
Babylonians!
They say to a wooden god, 'Come to
life!'
They say to a stone god, 'Wake up!'
Can those gods give advice?
They are covered with gold and silver.
They can't even breathe.
20 But I am in my holy temple.
Let the whole earth be silent in front
of me."

Habakkuk Prays to the LORD

3 This is a prayer of the prophet Habakkuk. It is on *shigionoth*. Here is what
he said.

2 LORD, I know how famous you are.
I have great respect for you
because of your mighty acts.
Do them again for us.
Make them known in our time.
When you are angry,
please show us your tender love.

3 God, you came from Teman.
You, the Holy One, came from
Mount Paran.   *Selah*
Your glory covered the heavens.
Your praise filled the earth.
4 Your glory was like the sunrise.
Rays of light flashed from your
mighty hand.
Your power was hidden there.
5 You sent plagues ahead of you.
Sickness followed behind you.
6 When you stood up, the earth shook.
When you looked at the nations,
they trembled with fear.
The age-old mountains crumbled.
The ancient hills fell down.
Your mighty acts will last forever.
7 I saw the tents of Cushan in trouble.
The people of Midian were suffering
greatly.

8 LORD, did your anger burn against the
rivers?
Were you angry with the streams?
Were you angry with the Red Sea?
You rode your horses and chariots
to overcome it.

POWER-SURGE

CHEERFUL ✴

I WILL STILL BE GLAD
BECAUSE OF WHAT THE
LORD HAS DONE.
GOD MY SAVIOR FILLS
ME WITH JOY.
THE LORD AND KING
GIVES ME STRENGTH.
HE MAKES MY FEET
LIKE THE FEET OF
A DEER.
HE HELPS ME WALK ON
THE HIGHEST PLACES.
— HABAKKUK 3:18-19 —

STRONG

9 You got your bow ready to use.
You asked for many arrows.   *Selah*
You broke up the surface
of the earth with rivers.
10 The mountains saw you and shook.
Floods of water swept by.
The sea roared.
It lifted its waves high.

11 The sun and moon stood still in the
sky.
They stopped because your flying
arrows flashed by.
Your gleaming spear shone like
lightning.
12 When you were angry, you marched
across the earth.
Because of your anger you destroyed
the nations.
13 You came out to set your people free.
You saved your chosen ones.
You crushed Pharaoh, the leader of
that evil land of Egypt.
You stripped him from head to foot.
Selah
14 His soldiers rushed out to scatter us.
They were laughing at us.
They thought they would easily
destroy us.
They saw us as weak people who were
trying to hide.

So you wounded Pharaoh's head
  with his own spear.
15 Your horses charged into the Red
    Sea.
  They stirred up the great waters.

16 I listened and my heart pounded.
  My lips trembled at the sound.
My bones seemed to rot.
  And my legs shook.
But I will be patient.
  I'll wait for the day of trouble to
    come on Babylonia.
  It's the nation that is attacking us.
17 The fig trees might not bud.
  The vines might not produce any
    grapes.
  The olive crop might fail.

The fields might not produce any
    food.
There might not be any sheep in the
    pens.
There might not be any cattle in the
    barns.
18 But I will still be glad
  because of what the LORD has done.
  God my Savior fills me with joy.

19 The LORD and King gives me strength.
  He makes my feet like the feet of a
    deer.
  He helps me walk on the highest
    places.

This prayer is for the director of music.
It should be sung while being accompanied by stringed instruments.

ZEPHANIAH

The prophet Zephaniah writes this book to warn the people that if they don't repent, God's judgment against them can't be avoided. They will be conquered and taken away from their homes. But he also writes to assure them that God will, in the end, restore them and bring them home. As you read the book of Zephaniah, remember that only turning to God for forgiveness can help you avoid punishment for what you have done wrong.

CODE OF HONOR IN THIS BOOK . . .

TRIES HARD
PAGE 1065

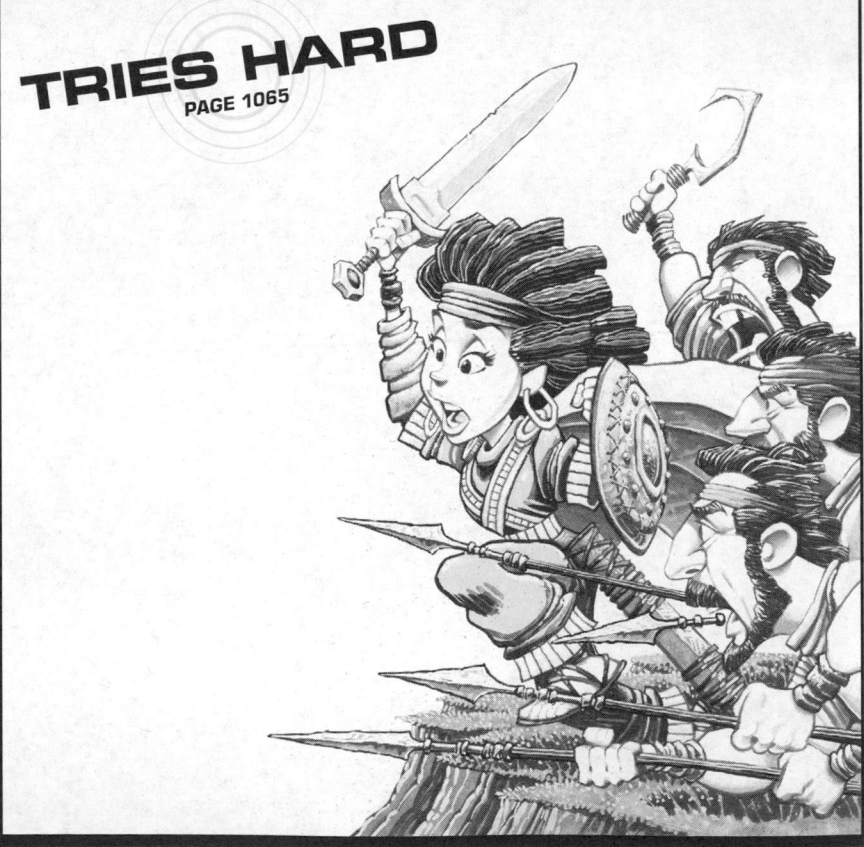

1

A message came to Zephaniah from the LORD. He was the son of Cushi. Cushi was the son of Gedaliah. Gedaliah was the son of Amariah. Amariah was the son of King Hezekiah. The LORD spoke to Zephaniah during the rule of Josiah. He was king of Judah and the son of Amon.

The LORD Will Judge the World

2 "I will sweep away everything
from the face of the earth,"
announces the LORD.
3 "I will destroy people and animals
alike.
I will wipe out the birds of the air
and the fish in the waters.
I will destroy sinful people along with
their gods.
I will wipe man off the face of the
earth,"
announces the LORD.

The LORD Warns Judah

4 "I will reach out my powerful hand
against Judah.
I will punish all those who live in
Jerusalem.
I will cut off from that place
what is left of Baal worship.
The officials and priests who serve
other gods
will be removed.
5 I will wipe out those who bow down
on their roofs
to worship all of the stars.
I will destroy those who take oaths
not only in my name but also in the
name of Molech.
6 I will cut off those who stop following
me.
They no longer look to me or ask me
for advice.
7 Be silent in front of me.
I am the LORD and King.
The day of the LORD is near.
I have prepared a sacrifice.
I have set apart for myself
the people I invited.
8 When my sacrifice is ready to be
offered,
I will punish the princes and the
king's sons.
I will also judge all those who follow
the practices of other nations.
9 At that time I will punish
all those who worship other gods.
They fill the temples of their gods
with lies and other harmful things.

10 "At that time people at the Fish Gate in
Jerusalem
will cry out," announces the LORD.

"So will those at the New Quarter.
The buildings on the hills will come
crashing down
with a loud noise.
11 Cry out, you who live in the market
places.
All of your merchants will be wiped
out.
Those who trade in silver will be
destroyed.
12 At that time I will search Jerusalem
with lamps.
I will punish those who are so
contented.
They are like wine that has not been
shaken up.
They think, 'The LORD won't do
anything.
It doesn't matter whether it's good
or bad.'
13 Their wealth will be stolen.
Their houses will be destroyed.
They will build houses.
But they will not live in them.
They will plant vineyards.
But they will not drink the wine
they produce.

The Day of the LORD Is Coming

14 "The great day of the LORD is near.
In fact, it is coming quickly.
Listen! The cries on that day will be
bitter.
Even soldiers will cry out in fear.
15 At that time I will pour out my anger.
There will be great suffering and
pain.
It will be a day of horrible trouble.
It will be a time of darkness and
gloom.
It will be filled with the blackest
clouds.
16 Trumpet blasts and battle cries will be
heard.
Soldiers will attack cities
that have forts and corner towers.
17 I will bring trouble on the people.
They will trip and fall as if they were
blind.
They have sinned against me.
Their blood will be poured out like
dust.
Their bodies will lie rotting on the
ground.
18 Their silver and gold
will not be able to save them
on the day I pour out my anger.
The whole world will be burned up
when my jealous anger blazes out.
Everyone who lives on earth
will come to a sudden end."

2 Gather your people together,
you shameful nation of Judah!
Gather them together!
2 Come together before the appointed
time arrives.
The day of the LORD will sweep in
like straw blown by the wind.
Soon the LORD's anger will burn against
you.
The day of his anger will come on
you.
3 So look to him, all of you people in the
land
who worship him faithfully.
You always do what he commands
you to do.
Continue to do what is right.
Don't be proud.
Then perhaps the LORD will keep you
safe
on the day he pours out his anger on
the world.

A Message About Philistia

4 Gaza will be deserted.
Ashkelon will be destroyed.
Ashdod will be emptied out at noon.
Ekron will be pulled up by its roots.
5 How terrible it will be for you
Kerethites
who live by the Mediterranean Sea!
Philistia, the LORD has spoken against
you.
What happened to Canaan will
happen to you.

The LORD says, "I will destroy you.
No one will be left."

6 The Kerethites live in the land by the
sea.
It will become a place for shepherds
and sheep pens.
7 It will belong to those who are still left
alive
among the people of Judah.
They will find grasslands there.
They will take over
the houses in Ashkelon and live in
them.
The LORD their God will take care of
them.
He will bless them with great success
again.

A Message About Moab and Ammon

8 The LORD says,

"I have heard Moab make fun of my
people.

The Ammonites also laughed at
them.
They told them that bad things
would happen to their land.
9 So Moab will become like Sodom,"
announces the LORD who rules over
all.
"Ammon will be like Gomorrah.
Weeds and salt pits will cover those
countries.
They will be dry and empty deserts
forever.
Those who are still left alive among my
people
will take all of their valuable things.
So they will receive those lands as
their own.
And that is just as sure as I am alive."
The LORD is the God of Israel.

10 Moab and Ammon will be judged
because they are so proud.
They made fun of the LORD's people.
They laughed at them.
11 The LORD who rules over all will terrify
Moab and Ammon.
He will destroy all of the gods on
earth.
Then the nations on every shore will
worship him.
All of them will serve him in their
own lands.

A Message About Cush

12 The LORD says, "People of Cush,
you too will be killed with my
sword."

A Message About Assyria

13 The LORD will reach out his powerful
hand against the north.
He will destroy Assyria.
He'll leave Nineveh totally empty.
It will be as dry as a desert.
14 Flocks and herds will lie down there.
So will creatures of every kind.
Desert owls and screech owls
will rest on its pillars.
Their cries will echo through the
windows.
The doorways will be full of trash.
The cedar beams will be showing.
15 Nineveh is a carefree city.
It lived in safety.
It said to itself,
"I am like a god.
No one is greater than I am."
But it has been destroyed.
Wild animals make their home
there.
All those who pass by laugh
and shake their fists at it.

The Lord Will Save Jerusalem

3 How terrible it will be for Jerusalem!
Its people crush others.
They refuse to obey the Lord.
They are "unclean."
² They don't obey anyone.
They don't accept the Lord's
warnings.
They don't trust in him.
They don't ask their God for his
help.
³ Their officials are like roaring lions.
Their rulers are like wolves that hunt
in the evening.
They don't leave anything to eat in
the morning.
⁴ Their prophets are proud.
They can't be trusted.
Their priests pollute the temple.
They break the law they teach others
to obey.
⁵ In spite of that, the Lord is good to
Jerusalem.
He never does anything that is
wrong.
Every morning he does what is fair.
Each new day he does the right
thing.
But those who do what is wrong
aren't even ashamed of it.

⁶ The Lord says to his people,

"I have cut off other nations.
I have wiped out their forts.
I have left their streets deserted.
No one walks along them.
Their cities are destroyed.
Not even one person is left.
⁷ I said to you people of Jerusalem,
'Because I cut off other nations,
you will have respect for me.
Now you will accept my warning.'
I wish you had returned to me.
Then your homes would not have
been torn down.
And I would not have had to punish
you so much.
But you still wanted to go on
sinning
in every way you could.
⁸ So wait for me to come as judge,"
announces the Lord.
"Wait for the day I will stand up
to witness against all sinners.
I have decided to gather the nations.
I will bring the kingdoms together.
And I will pour out all of my burning
anger on them.
The fire of my jealous anger
will burn the whole world up.

⁹ "But then I will purify what all of the
nations say.
And they will use their words to
worship me.
They will serve me together.
¹⁰ My scattered people, you will come to
me
from beyond the rivers of Cush.
You will worship me.
You will bring me offerings.
¹¹ You have done many wrong things to
me.
But at that time you will not be put
to shame anymore.
Then I will remove from this city
those who take delight in their
pride.
You will never be proud again
on my holy mountain of Zion.
¹² But inside your city I will leave
those who are not proud at all.
They trust in me.
¹³ Those who are still left alive in Israel
will not do anything wrong.
They will not tell any lies.
They will not say anything to fool
others.
They will eat and lie down in peace.
And no one will make them afraid."

¹⁴ People of Zion, sing!
Israel, shout loudly!
People of Jerusalem, be glad!
Let your hearts be full of joy.
¹⁵ The Lord has stopped punishing you.
He has made your enemies turn
away from you.
The Lord is the King of Israel.
He is with you.
You will never again be afraid
that others will harm you.
¹⁶ The time is coming when people will
say to Jerusalem,
"Zion, don't be afraid.
Don't give up.
¹⁷ The Lord your God is with you.
He is mighty enough to save you.
He will take great delight in you.
The quietness of his love will calm
you down.
He will sing with joy because of
you."

POWER–SURGE

TRIES HARD T

DON'T GIVE UP.
— ZEPHANIAH 3:16 —

18The LORD says to his people,

"You used to celebrate my appointed
feasts in Jerusalem.
You are sad because you can't do
that anymore.
So others make fun of those feasts.
That was a heavy load for you to carry.
But I will bring you back to your city.
19 At that time I will punish
all those who crushed you.
I will save those among you who are
disabled.

I will gather those who have been
scattered.
I will give you praise and honor
in every land where you were put to
shame.
20 At that time I will gather you together.
And I will bring you home.
I will give you honor and praise
among all of the nations on earth.
I will bless you with great success
again,"

says the LORD.

HAGGAI

The book of Haggai shows the people of Judah where they have gone wrong. They have been allowed to return to their homes. But they have concentrated on rebuilding their homes before rebuilding the temple. God must always come first, says Haggai. As you read this book, that same message will be clear to you. Whatever your life is like, whatever you are doing, make sure you put God before anyone or anything else.

CODE OF HONOR IN THIS BOOK . . .

BRAVE
PAGE 1068

STRONG
PAGE 1068

Haggai Tells His People to Rebuild the LORD's Temple

1 A message came to the prophet Haggai from the LORD. Haggai gave it to Zerubbabel and Jeshua. It came on the first day of the sixth month of the second year that Darius was king of Persia. Zerubbabel was governor of Judah and the son of Shealtiel. Jeshua was high priest and the son of Jehozadak. Here is what Haggai said.

2The LORD who rules over all says, "The people of Judah are saying, 'The time hasn't come yet for the LORD's temple to be rebuilt.'"

3So the message came to me from the LORD. He said, **4**"My temple is still destroyed. In spite of that, you are living in your houses that have beautiful wooden walls."

5The LORD who rules over all says, "Think carefully about how you are living. **6**You have planted many seeds. But the crops you have gathered are small. So you eat. But you never have enough. You drink. But you are never full. You put your clothes on. But you are not warm. You earn your pay. But it will not buy everything you need."

7He continues, "Think carefully about how you are living. **8**Go up into the mountains. Bring logs down. Use them to rebuild my house. Then I will enjoy it. And you will honor me," says the LORD.

9"You expected a lot. But you can see what a small amount it turned out to be," announces the LORD who rules over all. "I blew away what you brought home. Why? Because my temple is still destroyed. In spite of that, each one of you is busy with your own house.

10"So because of what you have done, the heavens have held back the dew. And the earth has not produced its crops. **11**I ordered the rain not to fall on the fields and mountains. Then the ground did not produce any grain. There were not enough grapes to make fresh wine. The trees did not bear enough olives to make oil. People and cattle suffered. All of your hard work failed."

12Then Zerubbabel, the son of Shealtiel, and the high priest Jeshua, the son of Jehozadak, obeyed the LORD their God. So did all of the LORD's people who were still left alive. He had given his message to them through me. He had sent me to speak to them. And the people had respect for him.

13I was the LORD's messenger. So I gave his message to the people. I told them, "The LORD announces, 'I am with you.'"

14So the LORD stirred up the spirits of Zerubbabel, the governor of Judah, and the high priest Jeshua. He also stirred up the rest of the people to help them. Then everyone began to work on the temple of the LORD who rules over all. He is their God. **15**It was the 24th day of the sixth month of the second year that Darius was king.

The New Temple Will Be Beautiful

2 A second message came to me from the LORD. It came on the 21st day of the seventh month. The LORD said, **2**"Speak to Zerubbabel, the governor of Judah and the son of Shealtiel. Also speak to the high priest Jeshua, the son of Jehozadak. And speak to all of my people who are still left alive. Ask them, **3**'Did any of you who are here see how beautiful this temple used to be? How does it look to you now? It doesn't look so good, does it?

4"'But be strong, Zerubbabel,' announces the LORD. 'Be strong, Jeshua. Be strong, all of you people in the land,' announces the LORD. 'Start rebuilding. I am with you,' announces the LORD who rules over all. **5**'That is what I promised you when you came out of Egypt. My Spirit continues to be with you. So do not be afraid.'"

POWER-SURGE

BRAVE B

"BE STRONG, ALL OF YOU PEOPLE IN THE LAND," ANNOUNCES THE LORD. "...I AM WITH YOU...THAT IS WHAT I PROMISED YOU WHEN YOU CAME OUT OF EGYPT. MY SPIRIT CONTINUES TO BE WITH YOU. SO DO NOT BE AFRAID."

— **HAGGAI 2:4-5** —

STRONG

6The LORD says, "In a little while I will shake the heavens and the earth once more. I will also shake the ocean and the dry land. **7**I will shake all of the nations. Then what they consider to be priceless will come to my temple. And I will fill the temple with glory," says the LORD who rules over all.

8"The silver belongs to me. So does the gold," announces the LORD. **9**"The new temple will be more beautiful than the first one was," says the LORD. "And in this place I will give peace to my people," announces the LORD who rules over all.

The LORD Will Make His People Pure and Clean

10A third message came to me from the LORD. It came on the 24th day of the ninth month of the second year that Darius was king. **11**The LORD who rules over all speaks. He says, "Ask the priests what the law says. **12**Suppose someone carries holy meat in the clothes he is wearing. And the clothes touch some bread or stew. Or they touch some wine, olive oil or other food. Then do those things also become holy?"

The priests answered, "No."

13So I said, "Suppose someone is made 'unclean' by touching a dead body. And then he touches one of those things. Does it become 'unclean' too?"

"Yes," the priests replied. "It does."

14Then I said, "The LORD announces, 'That is how I look at these people and this nation. Anything they do and anything they sacrifice on the altar is "unclean."

15" 'Now think carefully about the time before one stone was laid on top of another in my temple. **16**People went to get 20 measures of grain. But they could find only 10. They went to where the wine was stored to get 50 measures. But only 20 were there. **17**You worked very hard to produce all of those things. But I struck them with rot, mold and hail. And you still did not turn to me,' announces the LORD.

18" 'It is the 24th day of the ninth month. From this day on, think carefully about the day when the foundation of my temple was laid. Think about it carefully. **19**Are any seeds still left in your barns? Until now, your vines and fig trees have not produced any fruit. Your pomegranate and olive trees have not produced any either.

" 'But from this day on I will bless you.' "

The LORD Compares Zerubbabel to His Royal Ring

20A final message came to me from the LORD. It also came on the 24th day of the ninth month. He said, **21**"Speak to Zerubbabel, the governor of Judah. Tell him I will shake the heavens and the earth. **22**I will throw down royal thrones. I will smash the power of other kingdoms. I will destroy chariots and their drivers. Horses and their riders will fall. They will be killed with the swords of their relatives.

23" 'Zerubbabel, at that time I will pick you,' announces the LORD. 'You are my servant,' announces the LORD. 'You will be like a ring that has my royal seal on it. I have chosen you,' announces the LORD who rules over all."

ZECHARIAH

God allows the prophet Zechariah to see several visions, which Zechariah tells about in his book. Zechariah's visions show the people that God is still in control of the events of their lives. Though they have been having a hard time, Zechariah encourages them not to give up. When you're discouraged and think you can't go on, read Zechariah. You'll be encouraged to keep going and not to give up.

CODE OF HONOR IN THIS BOOK . . .

BRAVE
PAGE 1075

STRONG
PAGES 1075, 1077, 1078

HONEST
PAGE 1075

OBEYS
PAGE 1077

The LORD Wants His People to Return to Him

1 A message came to the prophet Zechariah from the LORD. It was the eighth month of the second year that Darius was king of Persia. Zechariah was the son of Berekiah. Berekiah was the son of Iddo. Here is what Zechariah said.

²The LORD who rules over all was very angry with our people years ago. ³And now he says to us, "Return to me. Then I will return to you," announces the LORD. ⁴"Do not be like your people years ago. The earlier prophets gave them my message. I said, 'Stop doing what is evil. Turn away from your sinful practices.' But they would not listen to me. They would not pay any attention," announces the LORD. ⁵"Where are those people now? And what about my prophets? Do they live forever? ⁶I commanded my servants the prophets what to say. I told them what I planned to do. But your people refused to obey me. So I had to punish them.

"Then they had a change of heart. They said, 'The LORD who rules over all has punished us because of how we have lived. He was fair and right to do that. He has done to us just what he decided to do.' "

A Vision of a Horseman Among Some Myrtle Trees

⁷During the second year that Darius was king, a message came to me from the LORD. It was the 24th day of the 11th month. That's the month of Shebat. ⁸I had a vision at night. I saw a man riding a red horse. He was standing among the myrtle trees in a valley. Behind him were red, brown and white horses.

⁹An angel was talking with me. I asked him, "Sir, what are these?"

He answered, "I will show you what they are."

¹⁰Then the man who was standing among the myrtle trees said, "They are the messengers the LORD has sent out. He told them to go all through the earth."

¹¹They brought a report to the angel of the LORD. He was standing among the myrtle trees. They said to him, "We have gone all through the earth. We've found the whole world enjoying peace and rest."

¹²Then the angel of the LORD spoke up. He said, "LORD, you rule over all. How long will you keep from showing your tender love to Jerusalem? How long will you keep it from the towns of Judah? You have been angry with them for 70 years."

¹³So the LORD replied with kind and comforting words. He spoke them to the angel who talked with me.

¹⁴Then the angel said, "Announce this message. Say, 'The LORD who rules over all says, "I am very jealous for my people in Jerusalem and Zion. ¹⁵But I am very angry with the nations that feel secure. I was only a little angry with my people. But the nations went too far and tried to wipe them out."

¹⁶" 'So the LORD says, "I will return to Jerusalem. I will show its people my tender love. My temple will be rebuilt there. Workers will use a measuring line when they rebuild Jerusalem," announces the LORD.

¹⁷" 'He says, "My towns will be filled with good things once more. I will comfort Zion. And I will choose Jerusalem again." ' "

A Vision of Four Horns and Four Skilled Workers

¹⁸Then I looked up and saw four animal horns. ¹⁹I spoke to the angel who was talking with me. "What are these horns?" I asked.

He said, "They are the powerful nations that scattered Judah, Israel and Jerusalem."

²⁰Then the LORD showed me four skilled workers. ²¹I asked, "What are they coming to do?"

He answered, "They are the powerful nations that scattered the people of Judah. That made them helpless. But the workers have come to terrify the horns. They will destroy the power of those nations. They had used their power to scatter Judah's people."

A Vision of a Man Holding a Measuring Line

2 Then I looked up and saw a man. He was holding a measuring line. ²"Where are you going?" I asked.

"To measure Jerusalem," he answered. "I want to find out how wide and how long it is."

³Then the angel who was talking with me left. Another angel came over to him. ⁴He said to him, "Run! Tell that young man Zechariah, 'Jerusalem will be like a city that does not have any walls around it. It will have huge numbers of people and animals in it. ⁵And I myself will be like a wall of fire around it,' announces the LORD. 'I will be the city's glory.' "

⁶"Israel, I have scattered you in all four directions," announces the LORD. "Come

quickly! Run away from the land of the north," announces the LORD.

7 "Come, people of Zion who are in Babylonia! Escape, you who live in the city of Babylon!" **8** The LORD rules over all. His angel says to Israel, "The LORD has sent me to honor him. He wants me to punish the nations that have robbed you of everything. After all, anyone who hurts you hurts those the LORD loves and guards. **9** So I will raise my powerful hand to strike your enemies down. Their own slaves will rob them of everything. Then you will know that the LORD who rules over all has sent me.

10 "'People of Zion, shout and be glad! I am coming to live among you,' announces the LORD. **11** 'At that time many nations will join themselves to me. And they will become my people. I will live among you.' says the LORD. Then you will know that the LORD who rules over all has sent me to you.

12 "He will receive Judah as his share in the holy land. And he will choose Jerusalem again.

13 "All you people of the world, be still because the LORD is coming. He is getting ready to come down from his holy temple in heaven."

A Vision of the High Priest Dressed in Fine Clothes

3 Then the LORD showed me the high priest Jeshua. He was standing in front of the angel of the LORD. Satan was standing to the right of Jeshua. He was there to bring charges against the high priest. **2** The LORD said to Satan, "May the LORD correct you! He has chosen Jerusalem. So may he correct you! Isn't this man Jeshua like a burning stick pulled out of the fire?"

3 Jeshua stood in front of the angel. He was wearing clothes that were very dirty. **4** The angel spoke to those who were standing near him. He said, "Take his dirty clothes off."

He said to Jeshua, "I have taken your sin away. I will put fine clothes on you."

5 I added, "Put a clean turban on his head." So they did. And they dressed him while the angel of the LORD stood by.

6 Then the angel spoke to Jeshua. He said, **7** "The LORD who rules over all says, 'You must live the way I want you to. And you must do what I want you to do. Then you will rule in my temple. You will be in charge of my courtyards. And I will give you a place among these who are standing here.

8 "'High priest Jeshua, pay attention! I want you other priests who are sitting with Jeshua to listen also. All of you men are signs of things to come. I am going to bring my servant the Branch. **9** Look at the stone I have put in front of Jeshua! There are seven eyes on that one stone. I will carve a message on it,' says the LORD who rules over all. 'And I will remove the sin of this land in one day.

10 "'At that time each of you will invite your neighbors to visit you. They will sit under your vines and fig trees,' announces the LORD."

A Vision of the Gold Lampstand and Two Olive Trees

4 Then the angel who was talking with me returned. He woke me up. It was as if I had been asleep. **2** "What do you see?" he asked me.

"I see a solid gold lampstand," I answered. "It has a bowl on top of it. There are seven lamps on it. Seven tubes lead to each of them. **3** There are two olive trees by the lampstand. One is on its right side. The other is on its left."

4 I asked the angel who was talking with me, "Sir, what are these?"

5 He answered, "Don't you know what they are?"

"No, sir," I replied.

6 So he said to me, "A message came to Zerubbabel from the LORD. He said, 'Your strength will not get my temple rebuilt. Your power will not do it either. Only the power of my Spirit will do it,' says the LORD who rules over all.

7 "So nothing can stop Zerubbabel from completing the temple. Even a mountain of problems will be smoothed out by him. When the temple is finished, he will put its most important stone in place. Then the people will shout, 'God bless it! God bless it!' "

8 A message came to me from the LORD. His angel said, **9** "The hands of Zerubbabel have laid the foundation of this temple. His hands will also complete it. Then you will know that the LORD who rules over all has sent me to you.

10 "Do not look down on the small amount of work done on the temple so far. People will be filled with joy when they see Zerubbabel holding the most important stone.

"The seven eyes on the stone are the eyes of the LORD himself. He looks out over the whole earth."

11 Then I said to the angel, "I see two olive trees. One is on the right side of the lampstand. The other is on the left. What are those trees?"

12I continued, "I also see two olive branches. They are next to the two gold pipes that pour out golden olive oil. What are those branches?"

13He answered, "Don't you know what they are?"

"No, sir," I said.

14So he told me, "They are Zerubbabel and Jeshua. The Lord of the whole earth has anointed them to serve him."

A Vision of a Flying Scroll

5 I looked up again and saw a flying scroll.

2"What do you see?" the angel asked me.

"A flying scroll," I replied. "It's 30 feet long and 15 feet wide."

3He said to me, "A curse sent by the LORD is written on it. It is going out over the whole land. Every thief will be driven out of the land. That is what it says on one side of the scroll. Everyone who lies when taking an oath to tell the truth will also be driven out. That is what it says on the other side. 4The LORD who rules over all announces, 'I will send the curse out. It will enter the house of the thief. It will also enter the house of anyone who lies when taking an oath in my name. It will remain in that house and destroy it. It will pull down its beams and stones.' "

A Vision of a Woman in a Basket

5Then the angel who was talking with me came forward. He said to me, "Look at what is coming."

6"What is it?" I asked.

"A measuring basket," he replied. "The sins of the people all through the land are in it."

7Then the basket's cover was lifted up. It was made out of lead. A woman was sitting in the basket! 8The angel said, "She stands for everything that is evil." Then he pushed her down into the basket. He put the lead cover back over its opening.

9I looked up and saw two other women. They had wings like the wings of a stork. A wind sent by the LORD carried them along. They lifted the basket up between heaven and earth.

10"Where are they taking the basket?" I asked the angel.

11He replied, "To the country of Babylonia. A temple will be built for it. When the temple is ready, the basket will be set there in its place."

A Vision of Four Chariots

6 I looked up again and saw four chariots. They were coming out from between two mountains. The mountains were made out of bronze.

2The first chariot was pulled by red horses. The second one had black horses. 3The third had white horses. And the fourth had spotted horses. All of the horses were powerful.

4I asked the angel who was talking with me, "Sir, what are these?"

5The angel answered, "The four spirits of heaven. They are going out to serve the Lord of the whole world. 6The chariot pulled by the black horses is going toward the north country. The one with the white horses is going toward the west. And the one with the spotted horses is going toward the south."

7The powerful horses went out. They were in a hurry to go all over the earth. The angel said, "Go all through the earth!" So they did.

8Then the LORD called out to me, "Look! The horses going toward the north have given my Spirit rest in the north country."

A Crown Is Given to Jeshua

9A message came to me from the LORD. His angel said, 10"Get some silver and gold from Heldai, Tobijah and Jedaiah. They have just come back from Babylonia. On that same day go to Josiah's house. He is the son of Zephaniah. 11Use the silver and gold to make a crown. Set it on the head of the high priest Jeshua. He is the son of Jehozadak.

12"Give Jeshua a message from the LORD who rules over all. He says, 'Here is the man whose name is The Branch. He will branch out and build my temple. 13That is what he will do. He will be dressed in majesty as if it were his royal robe. He will sit as king on his throne. He will also be a priest there. So he will combine the positions of king and priest in himself.'

14"The crown will be given to Heldai, Tobijah, Jedaiah and Zephaniah's son Hen. The crown will be kept in the LORD's temple. It will remind everyone that the LORD's promises will come true.

15"Those who are far away will come to Jerusalem. They will help build the LORD's temple. Then his people will know that the LORD who rules over all has sent me to them. It will happen if they are careful to obey the LORD their God."

Treat Everyone Fairly

7 During the fourth year that Darius was king, a message came to me from the LORD. It was the fourth day of the ninth month. That's the month of Kislev.

2The people of Bethel wanted to ask the LORD to show them his favor. So they sent Sharezer and Regem-Melech and their men. **3**They went to the prophets and priests at the LORD's temple. They asked them, "Should we sob and go without eating in the fifth month? That's what we've done for many years."

4Then the message came to me from the LORD who rules over all. He said, **5**"Ask the priests and all of the people in the land a question for me. Say to them, 'You sobbed and fasted in the fifth and seventh months. You did it for the past 70 years. But did you really do it for me? **6**And when you were eating and drinking, weren't you just enjoying good food for yourselves?

7" 'Didn't I tell you the same thing through the earlier prophets? That was when Jerusalem and the towns around it were at rest and enjoyed success. People lived in the Negev Desert and the western hills at that time.' "

8Another message came to me from the LORD. **9**He rules over all. He says to his people, "Treat everyone fairly. Show faithful love and tender concern to one another. **10**Do not take advantage of widows. Do not mistreat children whose fathers have died. Do not crush strangers or poor people. Do not make evil plans against one another."

11But they refused to pay attention to the LORD. They were stubborn. They turned their backs and covered up their ears. **12**They made their hearts as hard as the hardest stone. They wouldn't listen to the law. They wouldn't pay attention to the LORD's messages.

So the LORD who rules over all was very angry. After all, his Spirit had spoken to his people through the earlier prophets. **13**"When I called, they did not listen," says the LORD. "So when they called, I would not listen. **14**I used a windstorm to scatter them among all of the nations. They were strangers there. The land they left behind became dry and empty. No one could even travel through it. That is how they turned the pleasant land into a dry and empty desert."

The LORD Promises to Bless Jerusalem

8 Another message came to me from the LORD who rules over all. He said, **2**"I am very jealous for my people in Zion. In fact, I am burning with jealousy for them."

3He continued, "I will return to Zion. I will live among my people in Jerusalem. Then Jerusalem will be called The City of Truth. And my mountain will be called The Holy Mountain."

4He continued, "Once again old men and women will sit in the streets of Jerusalem. All of them will be using canes because they are old. **5**The city streets will be filled with boys and girls. They will be playing there."

6He continued, "All of that might seem wonderful to the people who are living at that time. But it will not seem wonderful to me."

7He continued, "I will save my people. I will gather them from the countries of the east and the west. **8**I will bring them back to live in Jerusalem. They will be my people. I will be their faithful God. I will keep my promises to them."

9The LORD who rules over all says to his people, "Listen to the words that were spoken by the prophets Haggai and Zechariah. They spoke to you when the work on my temple started up again. Let your hands be strong so that you can rebuild the temple.

10"Before the work was started again, there was no pay for the people or food for the animals. People could not go about their business safely because of their enemies. I had turned all of them against one another. **11**But now I will not punish you who are living at this time. I will not treat you as I treated your people before you," announces the LORD who rules over all.

12"Your seeds will grow well. Your vines will bear fruit. The ground will produce crops for you. And the heavens will drop their dew on your land. I will give all of those things to those who are still left alive here.

13"Judah and Israel, in the past the nations called down curses on you. But now I will save you. You will be a blessing to others. Do not be afraid. Let your hands be strong so that you can do my work."

14The LORD who rules over all says, "Years ago your people made me angry. So I decided to bring trouble on them. I did not show them any pity. **15**But now I plan to do good things to Jerusalem and Judah again. So do not be afraid.

¹⁶"Here is what you must do. Speak the truth to one another. Make true and wise decisions in your courts. ¹⁷Do not make evil plans against your neighbors. When you take an oath to tell the truth, do not lie. Many people love to do that. But I hate all of those things," announces the LORD.

¹⁸Another message came to me from the LORD who rules over all. He said, ¹⁹"You have established special times to go without eating. They are your fasts in the fourth, fifth, seventh and tenth months. They will become days of joy. They will be happy times for Judah. It will happen if you take delight in telling the truth and bringing about peace."

²⁰He continued, "Many nations will still come to you. And those who live in many cities will also come. ²¹The people who live in one city will go to another city. They will say, 'Let's go right away to ask the LORD to show us his favor. Let's look to him as our God. We ourselves are going.' ²²Large numbers of people and nations will come to Jerusalem. They will look to me. They will ask me to show them my favor."

²³He continued, "At that time many men from all nations and languages will take hold of one Jew. They will grab hold of the hem of his robe. And they will say, 'We want to go to Jerusalem with you. We've heard that God is with you.' "

The LORD Destroys Israel's Enemies

9 This is the LORD's message
against the land of Hadrach.
  He will judge Damascus.
That's because all of the tribes of Israel
    look to him.
    So do other people.

POWER-SURGE

BRAVE   **B**

YOU WILL BE A
BLESSING TO OTHERS.
DO NOT BE AFRAID.
LET YOUR HANDS BE
STRONG SO THAT YOU
CAN DO MY WORK.
— ZECHARIAH 8:13 —

STRONG

POWER-SURGE

HONEST   **H**

SPEAK THE TRUTH TO
ONE ANOTHER.
— ZECHARIAH 8:16 —

²The LORD will judge Hamath too.
  It's next to Damascus.
He will also punish Tyre and Sidon
  even though they are very clever.
³Tyre's people have built a fort for
    themselves.
  They've piled up silver like dust.
  They have as much gold as the dirt
    in the streets.
⁴But the Lord will take away everything
    they have.
  He'll destroy their power on the
    Mediterranean Sea.
  And Tyre will be completely burned
    up.
⁵Ashkelon will see it and become afraid.
  Gaza will groan with pain.
  So will Ekron. Its hope will vanish.
Gaza will no longer have a king.
  Ashkelon will be deserted.
⁶Strangers will take over Ashdod.
  The LORD says, "I will take away
    everything
  the Philistines are so proud of.
⁷They will no longer drink the blood of
    their animal sacrifices.
  I will remove the 'unclean' food
    from between their teeth.
The Philistines who are left will belong
    to our God.
  They will become leaders in Judah.
And Ekron will be like the Jebusites.
  So the Philistines will become part
    of Israel.
⁸But I will guard my temple
  against enemy armies.
No one will ever crush my people
  again.
  I will make sure it does not happen.

A King Comes to Zion

⁹"City of Zion, be full of joy!
  People of Jerusalem, shout!
See, your king comes to you.
  He always does what is right.
  He has the power to save.
He is gentle and riding on a donkey.
  He is sitting on a donkey's colt.
¹⁰I will take the chariots away from
    Ephraim.

I will remove the war horses from
Jerusalem.
I will break the bows that are used in
battle.
Your king will announce peace to the
nations.
He will rule from ocean to ocean.
His kingdom will reach from the
Euphrates River
to the ends of the earth.
11 I will set your prisoners free
from where their enemies are
keeping them.
I will do it because of the blood
that put my covenant with you into
effect.
12 Return to your place of safety,
you prisoners who still have hope.
Even now I announce that I will give
you back
much more than you had before.
13 I will bend Judah as I bend my bow.
I will make Ephraim's people my
arrows.
Zion, I will stir up your sons.
Greece, they will attack your sons.
My people, I will use you as my
sword."

The Lord Will Appear

14 Then the Lord will appear over his
people.
His arrows will flash like lightning.
The Lord and King will blow the
trumpet of his thunder.
He'll march out like a storm in the
south.
15 The Lord who rules over all
will be like a shield to his people.
They will destroy their enemies.
They'll use slings to throw stones at
them.
They'll drink the blood of their
enemies
as if it were wine.
They'll be full like the bowl that is used
for sprinkling the corners of the
altar.
16 The Lord their God will save his people
on that day.
They will be like sheep that belong
to his flock.
They will gleam in his land
like jewels in a crown.
17 How very beautiful they will be!
Grain and fresh wine
will make the young men and
women strong.

The Lord Will Take Care of Judah

10 People of Judah, ask the Lord
to send rain in the spring.
He is the one who makes the storm
clouds.
He sends down showers of rain on all
people.
He gives everyone the plants in the
fields.
2 Other gods tell lies.
Those who practice magic
see visions that aren't true.
They tell dreams that fool people.
They give comfort that doesn't do
any good.
So the people wander around like
sheep.
They are crushed because they don't
have a shepherd.

3 The Lord who rules over all says,

"My anger burns against the
shepherds.
I will punish the leaders.
I will take care of my flock.
They are the people of Judah.
I will make them like a proud horse
in battle.
4 The most important building stone
will come from the tribe of Judah.
The tent stake will also come from it.
And the bow that is used in battle will
come from it.
In fact, every ruler will come from it.
5 Together they will be like soldiers in
battle.
They will fight their way
through the muddy streets.
I will be with them.
So they will fight against the
horsemen
and destroy them.

6 "I will make the family of Judah strong.
I will save the people of Joseph.
I will bring them back
because I have tender love for them.
It will be as if
I had not sent them away.
I am the Lord their God.
I will help them.
7 The people of Ephraim will become
like mighty men.
Their hearts will be glad
as if they were drinking wine.
Their children will see it
and be filled with joy.
I will make their hearts glad.
8 I will whistle for my people
and gather them in.
I will set them free.

There will be as many of them as
　before.
9 I have scattered them among the
　nations.
But in lands far away they will
　remember me.
They and their children will be kept
　alive.
And they will return.
10 I will bring them back from Egypt.
I will gather them from Assyria.
I will bring them to Gilead and
　Lebanon.
There will not be enough room for
　them.
11 They will pass through a sea of trouble.
The stormy sea will calm down.
All of the deep places in the Nile
　River will dry up.
Assyria's pride will be brought down.
Egypt's right to rule will disappear.
12 I will make my people strong.
They will worship and obey me,"
　　　　　announces the LORD.

OBEYS ✔

"I WILL MAKE MY PEOPLE STRONG.

THEY WILL WORSHIP AND OBEY ME,"

ANNOUNCES THE LORD.
— ZECHARIAH 10:12 —

STRONG

11 Lebanon, open your doors!
　　Then fire can burn up your cedar
　　　trees.
2 Pine trees, cry out!
The cedar trees have fallen down.
The majestic trees are destroyed.
Cry out, you oak trees of Bashan!
The thick forest has been cut down.
3 Listen to the shepherds cry out!
Their rich grasslands are destroyed.
Listen to the lions roar!
The trees and bushes along the
　Jordan River are gone.

The Two Shepherds

4 The LORD my God says, "Take care of
the sheep that are set apart to be sacri-

ficed. 5 Those who buy them kill them.
And they are not punished for it. Those
who sell them say, 'Praise the LORD! We're
rich!' And their own shepherds do not
spare them.

6 "I will no longer have pity on the people in the land," announces the LORD. "I
will hand all of them over to their neighbors and their king. They will crush the
people in the land. And I will not save
them from their powerful hands."

7 So I took care of the sheep set apart to
be sacrificed. I took special care of those
that had been crushed. Then I got two
shepherd's staffs. I called one of them Favor. I called the other one Union. And I
took care of the flock. 8 In one month I got
rid of three worthless shepherds.

The sheep hated me. And I got tired of
them. 9 So I said, "I won't be your shepherd anymore. Let those of you who are
dying die. Let those who are passing away
pass away. Let those who are left eat one
another up."

10 Then I got my staff called Favor. I
broke it. That meant the covenant the
LORD had made with all of the nations was
broken. 11 It happened that very day. The
sheep that had been crushed were watching me. They knew it was the LORD's message.

12 I told them, "If you think it is best,
give me my pay. But if you don't think so,
you keep it." So they paid me 30 silver
coins.

13 The LORD said to me, "Throw the
coins to the potter." What a good price
they had set for me! So I threw the 30 silver coins to the potter in the LORD's temple.

14 Then I broke my second staff called
Union. That broke the union between Judah and Israel.

15 The LORD said to me, "Now pretend to
be a foolish shepherd. Get the things you
need. 16 I am going to raise up a shepherd
over the land. He will not take care of
those that are wounded. He will not look
for the young ones. He will not heal those
that are hurt. He will not feed the healthy
ones. Instead, he will eat the best sheep.
He will even tear their hoofs off.

17 "How terrible it will be for that
　　worthless shepherd!
He deserts the flock.
May a sword strike his arm and his
　　right eye!
May his powerful arm become weak!
May his right eye be totally
　　blinded!"

The LORD Will Destroy Jerusalem's Enemies

12 This is the LORD's message about Israel. The LORD spread out the heavens. He laid the foundation of the earth. He created the spirits of all men. He says, **2**"Jerusalem will be like a cup in my hand. It will make all of the surrounding nations drunk from the wine of my anger. Judah will be attacked by its enemies. So will Jerusalem.

3"At that time all of the nations on earth will gather together against Jerusalem. Then it will become like a rock that can't be moved. All of the nations that try to move it will only hurt themselves. **4**On that day I will fill every horse with panic. I will make every rider crazy," announces the LORD. "I will watch over the people of Judah. But I will make all of the horses of the nations blind.

5"Then the leaders of Judah will say in their hearts, 'The people of Jerusalem are strong. That's because the LORD who rules over all is their God.'

POWER / SURGE

STRONG

THE PEOPLE OF JERUSALEM ARE STRONG. THAT'S BECAUSE THE LORD WHO RULES OVER ALL IS THEIR GOD.
— ZECHARIAH 12:5 —

6"At that time Judah's leaders will be like a fire pot in a pile of wood. They will be like a burning torch among bundles of grain. They will destroy all of the surrounding nations on every side. But Jerusalem will remain unharmed in its place.

7"I will save the houses in Judah first. The honor of David's family line is great. So is the honor of those who live in Jerusalem. But their honor will not be greater than the honor of the rest of Judah.

8"At that time I will be like a shield to those who live in Jerusalem. Then even the weakest among them will be great warriors like David. And David's family line will be like the Angel of the LORD who leads them. **9**On that day I will begin to destroy all of the nations that attack Jerusalem.

Israel's People Will Sob Over the One They Pierced

10"I will pour out a spirit of grace and prayer on David's family line. I will also send it on those who live in Jerusalem. They will look to me. I am the one they have pierced. They will sob over me as someone sobs over an only child who has died. They will be full of sorrow over me, just like someone who is full of sorrow over an oldest son.

11"At that time there will be a lot of crying in Jerusalem. It will sound like the sobs of the people at Hadad Rimmon over Josiah's death in the Valley of Megiddo. **12**Everyone in the land will sob. Each family will cry by themselves and their wives by themselves. That will include the family lines of David, Nathan, **13**Levi, Shimei and **14**all of the others.

The LORD Makes Israel Pure and Clean

13 "At that time a fountain will be opened for the benefit of David's family line. It will also bless the others who live in Jerusalem. It will wash away their sins. It will make them pure and clean.

2"On that day I will remove the names of other gods from the land. They will not even be remembered anymore," announces the LORD who rules over all. "I will drive the evil prophets out of the land. I will get rid of the spirit that put lies in their mouths. **3**Some people might still prophesy. But their own fathers and mothers will speak to them. They will tell them, 'You must die. You have told lies in the LORD's name.' When they prophesy, their own parents will stab them.

4"At that time every prophet will be ashamed of his vision. He will no longer pretend to be a true prophet. He will not put on clothes that are made out of hair in order to trick people. **5**In fact, he will say, 'I'm not really a prophet. I'm a farmer. I've farmed the land since I was young.' **6**Suppose someone asks him, 'What are those wounds on your body?' Then he will answer, 'I was given these wounds at the house of my friends.'

The Good Shepherd Is Killed and the Sheep Are Scattered

7"My sword, wake up! Attack my
    shepherd!
  Attack the man who is close to me,"
    announces the LORD who rules over
    all.
"Strike the shepherd down.

Then the sheep will be scattered.
And I will turn my hand against
their little ones.
8 Here is what will happen in the whole
land,"
announces the LORD.
"Two-thirds of the people will be
struck down and die.
But one-third will be left.
9 I will put that third in the fire.
I will make them as pure as silver.
I will test them like gold.
They will call out to me.
And I will answer them.
I will say, 'They are my people.'
And they will say, 'The LORD is our
God.' "

The LORD Will Be King Over the Whole Earth

14 The day of the LORD is coming. At that time Jerusalem's enemies will steal everything its people have. They will divide it up right in front of them.

2 The LORD will gather all of the nations together. They will fight against Jerusalem. They'll capture the city. Its houses will be robbed. Its women will be raped. Half of the people will be taken away as prisoners. But the rest of them won't be taken.

3 Then the LORD will march out and fight against those nations. He will go to war against them.

4 On that day he will stand on the Mount of Olives. It's east of Jerusalem. It will be split in two from east to west. Half of the mountain will move north. The other half will move south. A large valley will be formed. **5** The people will run away through that mountain valley. It will reach all the way to Azel. They'll run away just as they ran from the earthquake when Uzziah was king of Judah. Then the LORD my God will come. All of the holy ones will come with him.

6 There won't be any light on that day. The sun, moon and stars will not shine. **7** It will be a day unlike any other. It won't be separated into day and night. It will be a day known only to the LORD. After that day is over, there will be light again.

8 At that time water that gives life will flow out from Jerusalem. Half of it will run into the Dead Sea. The other half will go to the Mediterranean Sea. The water will flow in summer and winter.

9 The LORD will be king over the whole earth. On that day there will be one LORD. His name will be the only name.

10 The whole land south of Jerusalem will be changed. From Geba to Rimmon it will become like the Arabah Valley. But Jerusalem will be raised up. It will remain in its place. From the Benjamin Gate to the First Gate to the Corner Gate nothing will be changed. From the Tower of Hananel to the royal winepress the city will remain the same. **11** People will live in it. Jerusalem will never be destroyed again. It will be secure.

12 The LORD will punish all of the nations that fought against Jerusalem. He'll strike them with a plague. It will make their bodies rot while they are still standing on their feet. Their eyes will rot in their heads. Their tongues will rot in their mouths. **13** On that day the LORD will fill people with great panic. They will grab one another by the hand. And they'll attack each other.

14 Judah will also fight at Jerusalem. The wealth of all of the surrounding nations will be collected. Huge amounts of gold, silver and clothes will be gathered up. **15** The same kind of plague will strike the horses, mules, camels and donkeys. In fact, it will strike all of the animals in the army camps.

16 But some people from all of the nations that have attacked Jerusalem will still be left alive. All of them will go up there to worship the King. He is the LORD who rules over all. Year after year they will celebrate the Feast of Booths.

17 Some nations might not go up to Jerusalem to worship the King. If they don't, they won't have any rain. **18** The people of Egypt might not go up there to take part. Then they won't have any rain either. That's the plague the LORD will send on the nations that don't go to celebrate the Feast of Booths. **19** Egypt will be punished. So will all of the other nations that don't celebrate the Feast.

20 On that day HOLY TO THE LORD will be carved on the bells of the horses. The cooking pots in the LORD's temple will be just like the sacred bowls in front of the altar for burnt offerings. **21** Every pot in Jerusalem and Judah will be set apart to the LORD. All those who come to offer sacrifices will get some of the pots and cook in them. At that time there won't be any Canaanites in the LORD's temple. He is the LORD who rules over all.

MALACHI

Malachi, the final book of the Old Testament, presents a sort of conversation between God and his people. God points out where they have gone wrong. The people respond by defending themselves. God answers and makes it clear that they have ignored him. Malachi wants the people to realize that they must never be bored or not care about their faith in God. God deserves their whole hearts, not just their outward motions of worship. As you read Malachi, ask yourself this question: Am I totally following God?

CODE OF HONOR IN THIS BOOK . . .

GIVING
PAGE 1083

1

This is the LORD's message to Israel through Malachi.

The LORD Chooses Jacob Instead of Esau

2"Israel, I have loved you," says the LORD.

"But you ask, 'How have you loved us?'

"Wasn't Esau Jacob's brother?" says the LORD. "But I chose Jacob 3instead of Esau. I turned Esau's mountains into a dry and empty land. I left that land of Edom to the wild dogs in the desert."

4Edom might say, "We have been crushed. But we'll rebuild our cities."

The LORD who rules over all says, "They might rebuild their cities. But I will destroy them. They will be called The Evil Land. My anger will always remain on them. 5You will see it with your own eyes. You will say, 'The LORD is great! He rules even beyond the borders of Israel!'

Give Your Best to the LORD

6"A son honors his father. A servant honors his master. If I am a father, where is the honor I should have? If I am a master, where is the respect you should give me?" says the LORD who rules over all. "You priests look down on me.

"But you ask, 'How have we looked down on you?'

7"You put 'unclean' food on my altar.

"But you ask, 'How have we made you "unclean?" '

"You do it by looking down on my altar. 8You sacrifice blind animals to me. Isn't that wrong? You sacrifice disabled or sick animals. Isn't that wrong? Try offering them to your governor! Would he be pleased with you? Would he accept you?" says the LORD who rules over all.

9"Now you dare to ask me to show you my favor! But as long as you give offerings like those, how can I accept you?" says the LORD.

10"You might as well shut the temple doors! Then you would not light useless fires on my altar. I am not pleased with you," says the LORD. "I will not accept any of the offerings you bring.

11"My name will be great among the nations. They will worship me from where the sun rises in the east to where it sets in the west. In every place, incense and pure offerings will be brought to me. That is because my name will be great among the nations," says the LORD.

12"But you treat my name as if it were not holy. You say my altar is 'unclean.' And you look down on its food. 13You say,

'What a heavy load our work is!' And you turn your nose up as if you hate working for me," says the LORD who rules over all.

"You bring animals that have been hurt. Or you bring disabled or sick animals. Then you dare to offer them to me as sacrifices! Should I accept them from you?" says the LORD.

14"Suppose you have a male sheep or goat that does not have any flaws. And you promise to offer it to me. But then you sacrifice an animal that has flaws. When you do that, you cheat me. And anyone who cheats me is under my curse. After all, I am a great king," says the LORD who rules over all. "The other nations have respect for my name. So why don't you respect it?

The LORD Warns the Priests

2

"Now I am giving a warning to you priests. 2Listen to it. Honor me with all your heart," says the LORD who rules over all. "If you do not, I will send a curse on you. I will turn your blessings into curses. In fact, I have already done that because you have not honored me with all your heart.

3"Because of what you have done, I will punish your children. I will smear the guts from your sacrifices on your faces. And you will be carried off to the dump along with them. 4You will know that I have given you a warning. I have warned you so that my covenant with Levi will continue," says the LORD who rules over all.

5"My covenant promised Levi life and peace. So I gave them to him. I required him to respect me. And he had great respect for my name. 6True teaching came from his mouth. Nothing but the truth came from his lips. He walked with me in peace. He did what was right. He turned many people away from their sins.

7"The lips of a priest should guard knowledge. People should look for true teaching from his mouth. After all, he is my messenger. 8But you have turned away from the right path. Your teaching has caused many people to trip and fall. You have broken my covenant with Levi," says the LORD who rules over all. 9"So I have caused all of the people to hate you. They have lost respect for you. You have not done what I told you to do. Instead, you have favored one person over another in matters of the law."

Judah Is Not Faithful to the LORD

10People of Judah, all of us have one Father. One God created us. So why do we break the covenant the LORD made with our people long ago? We don't even keep our promises to one another.

11You have broken your promises. A hateful thing has been done in Israel and Jerusalem. The LORD loves his temple. But you have polluted it. You men have married women who worship other gods.

12May the LORD punish you who do that. It doesn't matter who you are. May the LORD who rules over all cut you off from the tents of Jacob's people. May he remove you even if you bring offerings to him.

13Here's something else you do. You flood the LORD's altar with your tears. You sob and cry because he doesn't pay attention to your offerings anymore. He doesn't accept them from your hands with pleasure.

14You ask, "Why?" It's because the LORD is holding you accountable. He watches how you treat the wife you married when you were young. You have broken your promise to her. You did it even though she's your partner. You promised to stay married to her. And the LORD was a witness to it.

15Hasn't he made the two of you one? Both of you belong to him in body and spirit. And why has he made you one? Because he was looking for godly children. So guard yourself in your spirit. Don't break your promise to the wife you married when you were young.

16"I hate divorce," says the LORD God of Israel. "I hate it when people do anything that harms others," says the LORD who rules over all.

So guard yourself in your spirit. And don't break your promises.

The LORD Will Judge His People

17You have worn the LORD out by what you keep saying.

"How have we worn him out?" you ask.

You have done it by saying, "All those who do evil things are good in the LORD's sight. And he is pleased with them." Or you ask, "Is God really fair?"

3 The LORD who rules over all says, "I will send my messenger. He will prepare my way for me. Then suddenly the Lord you are looking for will come to his temple. The messenger of the covenant will come. He is the one you long for."

2But who can live through the day when he comes? Who will be left standing when he appears? He will be like a fire that makes things pure. He will be like soap that makes things clean. **3**He will act

like one who makes silver pure. And he will purify the Levites, just as gold and silver are purified with fire.

Then the LORD's people will bring proper offerings. **4**And the offerings of Judah and Jerusalem will be acceptable to him. It will be as it was in days and years gone by.

5"So I will come and judge you. I will be quick to bring charges against all of you," says the LORD who rules over all. "I will bring charges against you sinful people who do not have any respect for me. That includes those who practice evil magic. It includes those who commit adultery and those who tell lies in court. It includes those who cheat workers out of their pay. It includes those who crush widows. It also includes those who mistreat children whose fathers have died. And it includes those who take away the rights of outsiders in the courts.

Do Not Steal From God

6"I am the LORD. I do not change. That is why I have not destroyed you members of Jacob's family. **7**You have turned away from my rules. You have not obeyed them. You have lived that way ever since the days of your people long ago. Return to me. Then I will return to you," says the LORD who rules over all.

"But you ask, 'How can we return?'

8"Will a man dare to steal from me? But you rob me!

"You ask, 'How do we rob you?'

"By holding back your offerings. You also steal from me when you do not bring me a tenth of everything you produce. **9**So you are under my curse. In fact, your whole nation is under it. That is because you are robbing me.

10"Bring the entire tenth to the storerooms in my temple. Then there will be plenty of food. Put me to the test," says the LORD. "Then you will see that I will throw open the windows of heaven. I will pour out so many blessings that you will not have enough room for them. **11**I will keep bugs from eating up your crops. And your grapes will not drop from the vines before they are ripe," says the LORD.

12"Then all of the nations will call you blessed. Your land will be delightful," says the LORD who rules over all.

13"You have spoken bad things against me," says the LORD.

"But you ask, 'What have we spoken against you?'

14"You have said, 'It is useless to serve God. What did we gain by obeying his laws? And what did we get by pretending

POWER-SURGE

GIVING   G

"BRING THE ENTIRE
TENTH TO THE
STOREROOMS IN MY
TEMPLE. THEN THERE
WILL BE PLENTY OF
FOOD. PUT ME TO THE
TEST," SAYS THE LORD.
"THEN YOU WILL SEE
THAT I WILL THROW
OPEN THE WINDOWS
OF HEAVEN. I WILL
POUR OUT SO MANY
BLESSINGS THAT
YOU WILL NOT HAVE
ENOUGH ROOM
FOR THEM."
— MALACHI 3:10 —

to be sad in front of the LORD? **15**But now we call proud people blessed. Things go well with those who do what is evil. And God doesn't even punish those who argue with him.' "

16Those who had respect for the LORD talked with one another. They cheered each other up. And the LORD heard them. A list of people and what they did was written on a scroll in front of him. It included the names of those who respected the LORD and honored him.

17"They will belong to me," says the LORD who rules over all. "They will be my special treasure. I will spare them just as a loving father spares his son who serves him. **18**Then once again you will see the difference between godly people and sinful people. And you will see the difference between those who serve me and those who do not.

The Day of the LORD Is Coming

4 "You can be sure the day of the LORD is coming. My anger will burn like a furnace. All those who are proud will be like straw. So will all those who do what is evil. The day that is coming will set them on fire," says the LORD who rules over all. "Not even a root or a branch will be left to them.

2"But here is what will happen for you who have respect for me. The sun that brings life will rise. Its rays will bring healing to my people. You will go out and leap like calves that have just been let out of the barn.

3"Then you will stomp on sinful people. They will be like ashes under your feet. That will happen on the day I act," says the LORD.

4"Remember the law my servant Moses gave you. Remember the rules and laws I gave him at Mount Horeb. They were for the whole nation of Israel.

5"I will send you the prophet Elijah. He will come before the day of the LORD arrives. It will be a great and terrifying day. **6**Elijah will teach parents how to love their children. He will also teach children how to honor their parents. If that does not happen, I will come. And I will put a curse on the land."

the NEW
TESTAMENT

MATTHEW

The book of Matthew begins the New Testament and tells the story of Jesus—the greatest hero of all—and the start of the church. Jesus' disciple, Matthew, writes this book. He presents Jesus' teachings and ties them to the Old Testament and its teachings, forming a bridge between the Old and the New Testament. As you read this book, you'll get a better understanding of why Jesus came to earth and his power to save people—including you!

HEROES IN THIS BOOK . . .

JOSEPH
PAGE 1090

WISE MEN
PAGE 1092

HEROD (Not!)
PAGE 1094

JOHN THE BAPTIST
PAGE 1096

JESUS IS TEMPTED
PAGE 1098

JESUS TELLS ABOUT TWO BUILDERS
PAGE 1101

ROMAN COMMANDER
PAGE 1103

The Family Line of Jesus

1 This is a record of the family line of Jesus Christ. He is the son of David. He is also the son of Abraham.

2 Abraham was the father of Isaac.
Isaac was the father of Jacob.
Jacob was the father of Judah and his brothers.
3 Judah was the father of Perez and Zerah. Tamar was their mother.
Perez was the father of Hezron.
Hezron was the father of Ram.
4 Ram was the father of Amminadab.
Amminadab was the father of Nahshon.
Nahshon was the father of Salmon.
5 Salmon was the father of Boaz. Rahab was Boaz's mother.
Boaz was the father of Obed. Ruth was Obed's mother.
Obed was the father of Jesse.
6 And Jesse was the father of King David.

David was the father of Solomon. Solomon's mother had been Uriah's wife.
7 Solomon was the father of Rehoboam.
Rehoboam was the father of Abijah.
Abijah was the father of Asa.
8 Asa was the father of Jehoshaphat.
Jehoshaphat was the father of Jehoram.
Jehoram was the father of Uzziah.
9 Uzziah was the father of Jotham.
Jotham was the father of Ahaz.
Ahaz was the father of Hezekiah.
10 Hezekiah was the father of Manasseh.
Manasseh was the father of Amon.
Amon was the father of Josiah.
11 And Josiah was the father of Jeconiah and his brothers. At that time, the Jewish people were forced to go away to Babylon.

12 After this, the family line continued.
Jeconiah was the father of Shealtiel.
Shealtiel was the father of Zerubbabel.
13 Zerubbabel was the father of Abiud.
Abiud was the father of Eliakim.
Eliakim was the father of Azor.
14 Azor was the father of Zadok.
Zadok was the father of Akim.

Akim was the father of Eliud.
15 Eliud was the father of Eleazar.
Eleazar was the father of Matthan.
Matthan was the father of Jacob.
16 Jacob was the father of Joseph. Joseph was the husband of Mary. And Mary gave birth to Jesus, who is called Christ.

17 So there were 14 generations from Abraham to David. There were 14 from David until the Jewish people were forced to go away to Babylon. And there were 14 from that time to the Christ.

Jesus Christ Is Born

18 This is how the birth of Jesus Christ came about. His mother Mary and Joseph had promised to get married. But before they started to live together, it became clear that she was going to have a baby. She became pregnant by the power of the Holy Spirit. 19 Her husband Joseph was a godly man. He did not want to put her to shame in public. So he planned to divorce her quietly.
20 But as Joseph was thinking about this, an angel of the Lord appeared to him in a dream. The angel said, "Joseph, son of David, don't be afraid to take Mary home as your wife. The baby inside her is from the Holy Spirit. 21 She is going to have a son. You must give him the name Jesus. That is because he will save his people from their sins."
22 All of this took place to bring about what the Lord had said would happen. He had said through the prophet, 23 "The virgin is going to have a baby. She will give birth to a son. And he will be called Immanuel." *(Isaiah 7:14)* The name Immanuel means "God with us."
24 Joseph woke up. He did what the angel of the Lord commanded him to do. He took Mary home as his wife. 25 But he did not make love to her until after she gave birth to a son. And Joseph gave him the name Jesus.

The Wise Men Visit Jesus

2 Jesus was born in Bethlehem in Judea. This happened while Herod was king of Judea.
After Jesus' birth, Wise Men from the east came to Jerusalem. 2 They asked, "Where is the child who has been born to be king of the Jews? When we were in the east, we saw his star. Now we have come to worship him."
3 When King Herod heard about it, he was very upset. Everyone in Jerusalem was

JOSEPH

MATTHEW 1:24

Joseph woke up. He did what the angel of the Lord commanded him to do. He took Mary home as his wife.

Joseph stretched out on his mat for the night. He felt like someone had punched him in the stomach. He had just had bad news. The girl he was supposed to marry had told him she was pregnant. In his mind he could see her sweet face and the tears in her eyes. Joseph knew the baby wasn't his. He hadn't been with Mary that way.

Before he fell asleep, Joseph made a decision. Even though Mary had been unfaithful to him, he still cared about her. He couldn't marry her, of course. But he wouldn't embarrass or hurt her either. He would just call off the wedding.

GOD, HOWEVER, HAD OTHER THINGS IN MIND.

After tossing on his mat for several hours, Joseph finally fell asleep. In the middle of the night, he had a dream. An angel told Joseph something amazing! The baby Mary carried was Jesus, the Savior all Israel had been waiting for. So Joseph shouldn't be afraid to marry her.

When Joseph woke up, he knew what he had to do. Instead of going to work in his carpenter shop, Joseph went to see Mary. She was just leaving to get water for the day, so he walked along with her to the town well. Mary didn't dare look at Joseph. She knew something very special had happened to her. But she didn't know how to explain it to him. She had tried the night before . . . but without success.

Joseph put his hand on Mary's arm. She stopped walking. She was sure he was going to tell her he couldn't marry her. But one look at his face, and Mary knew. Joseph's warm smile told her more than any words could. Somehow, he understood.

BE A JOSEPH

Be a Joseph. Remember to be kind. Even when others are un-kind, even when others don't understand, even when it's hard, be a kind person like Joseph.

JOSEPH WAS KIND TO MARY.
THE WHOLE STORY: MATTHEW 1:18-25

Go to page 1092 for the next Super Heroes

troubled too. **4**So Herod called together all the chief priests of the people. He also called the teachers of the law. He asked them where the Christ was going to be born.

5"In Bethlehem in Judea," they replied. "This is what the prophet has written. He said,

6" 'But you, Bethlehem, in the land of Judah,
   are certainly not the least important
      among the towns of Judah.
A ruler will come out of you.
He will be the shepherd of my
      people Israel.' "   *(Micah 5:2)*

7Then Herod called for the Wise Men secretly. He found out from them exactly when the star had appeared. **8**He sent them to Bethlehem. He said, "Go! Make a careful search for the child. As soon as you find him, bring me a report. Then I can go and worship him too."

9After the Wise Men had listened to the king, they went on their way. The star they had seen when they were in the east went ahead of them. It finally stopped over the place where the child was. **10**When they saw the star, they were filled with joy.

11The Wise Men went to the house. There they saw the child with his mother Mary. They bowed down and worshiped him. Then they opened their treasures. They gave him gold, incense and myrrh.

12But God warned them in a dream not to go back to Herod. So they returned to their country on a different road.

POWER SURGE

GIVING G

THE WISE MEN WENT TO THE HOUSE. THERE THEY SAW [JESUS] WITH HIS MOTHER MARY. THEY BOWED DOWN AND WORSHIPED HIM. THEN THEY OPENED THEIR TREASURES. THEY GAVE HIM GOLD, INCENSE AND MYRRH.
— **MATTHEW 2:11** —

Jesus' Family Escapes to Egypt

13When the Wise Men had left, Joseph had a dream. In the dream an angel of the Lord appeared to him. "Get up!" the angel said. "Take the child and his mother and escape to Egypt. Stay there until I tell you to come back. Herod is going to search for the child. He wants to kill him."

14Joseph got up. During the night, he left for Egypt with the child and his mother Mary. **15**They stayed there until King Herod died. So the words the Lord had spoken through the prophet came true. He had said, "I chose to bring my son out of Egypt." *(Hosea 11:1)*

16Herod realized that the Wise Men had tricked him. So he became very angry. He gave orders concerning Bethlehem and the area around it. All the boys two years old and under were to be killed. This agreed with the time when the Wise Men had seen the star.

17In this way, the words the prophet Jeremiah spoke came true. He had said,

18"A voice is heard in Ramah.
   It's the sound of crying and deep
      sadness.
Rachel is crying over her children.
   She refuses to be comforted,
because they are gone."   *(Jeremiah 31:15)*

Jesus' Family Returns to Nazareth

19After Herod died, Joseph had a dream while he was still in Egypt. In the dream an angel of the Lord appeared to him. **20**The angel said, "Get up! Take the child and his mother. Go to the land of Israel. Those who were trying to kill the child are dead."

21So Joseph got up. He took the child and his mother Mary back to the land of Israel. **22**But then he heard that Archelaus was king of Judea. Archelaus was ruling in place of his father Herod. This made Joseph afraid to go there.

Warned in a dream, Joseph went back to the land of Galilee instead. **23**There he lived in a town called Nazareth. So what the prophets had said about Jesus came true. They had said, "He will be called a Nazarene."

John the Baptist Prepares the Way

3 In those days John the Baptist came and preached in the Desert of Judea. **2**He said, "Turn away from your sins! The kingdom of heaven is near."

3John is the one the prophet Isaiah had spoken about. He had said,

"A messenger is calling out in the
　　　desert,
'Prepare the way for the Lord.
　　Make straight paths for him.' "

(Isaiah 40:3)

4John's clothes were made out of camel's hair. He had a leather belt around his waist. His food was locusts and wild honey. **5**People went out to him from Jeru-salem and all of Judea. They also came from the whole area around the Jordan River. **6**When they admitted they had sinned, John baptized them in the Jordan. **7**John saw many Pharisees and Sad-ducees coming to where he was baptizing. He said to them, "You are like a nest of poisonous snakes! Who warned you to es-cape the coming of God's anger? **8**Pro-duce fruit that shows you have turned

WISE MEN

MATTHEW 2:9-11

The star they had seen when they were in the east went ahead of them. It finally stopped over the place where the child was. When they saw the star, they were filled with joy. The Wise Men went to the house. There they saw the child with his mother Mary. They bowed down and worshiped him.

The Wise Men stood up and left King Herod's palace. They had come from far away when they saw a star that told them a king had been born in Israel. They wanted to worship him. Her-od told them to go look for the child in Bethlehem. That's where the prophets said he would be born.

The Wise Men clumped along on their camels down dusty roads to the little town of Bethlehem. The star went ahead of them. When they arrived in Bethlehem, **THE BRIGHT STAR HUNG RIGHT OVER THE PLACE WHERE JESUS LIVED.**

The Wise Men bowed before little Jesus and worshiped him. They gave him expensive gifts, gold and spices and perfume.

That night one of the Wise Men had a dream. God told him that Herod planned to kill this new king. So instead of going back to Herod and reporting what they had seen, they went to their homes a different way.

BE LIKE THE WISE MEN

The Wise Men believed in Jesus and worshiped him. Be as wise as these men. The wisest thing you can do in life is to believe in Jesus and follow him.

THE WISE MEN BELIEVED IN JESUS AND WORSHIPED HIM.

Go to page 1094 for the next person

POWER-SURGE

STRONG

I BAPTIZE YOU WITH
WATER, CALLING YOU
TO TURN AWAY FROM
YOUR SINS. BUT
AFTER ME, ONE WILL
COME WHO IS MORE
POWERFUL THAN I AM.
—— MATTHEW 3:11 ——

away from your sins. **9**Don't think you can say to yourselves, 'Abraham is our father.' I tell you, God can raise up children for Abraham even from these stones. **10**The ax is already lying at the roots of the trees. All the trees that don't produce good fruit will be cut down. They will be thrown into the fire.

11"I baptize you with water, calling you to turn away from your sins. But after me, one will come who is more powerful than I am. And I'm not fit to carry his sandals. He will baptize you with the Holy Spirit and with fire. **12**His pitchfork is in his hand to clear the straw from his threshing floor. He will gather his wheat into the storeroom. But he will burn up the husks with fire that can't be put out."

Jesus Is Baptized

13Jesus came from Galilee to the Jordan River. He wanted to be baptized by John. **14**But John tried to stop him. He told Jesus, "I need to be baptized by you. So why do you come to me?"

15Jesus replied, "Let it be this way for now. It is right for us to do this. It carries out God's holy plan." Then John agreed.

16As soon as Jesus was baptized, he came up out of the water. At that moment heaven was opened. Jesus saw the Spirit of God coming down on him like a dove. **17**A voice from heaven said, "This is my Son, and I love him. I am very pleased with him."

Jesus Is Tempted

4 The Holy Spirit led Jesus into the desert. There the devil tempted him. **2**After 40 days and 40 nights of going without eating, Jesus was hungry.

3The tempter came to him. He said, "If you are the Son of God, tell these stones to become bread."

4Jesus answered, "It is written, 'Man doesn't live only on bread. He also lives on every word that comes from the mouth of God.' " *(Deuteronomy 8:3)*

5Then the devil took Jesus to the holy city. He had him stand on the highest point of the temple. **6**"If you are the Son of God," he said, "throw yourself down. It is written,

" 'The Lord will command his angels
    to take good care of you.
They will lift you up in their hands.
Then you won't trip over a stone.' "
                              (Psalm 91:11,12)

7Jesus answered him, "It is also written, 'Do not put the Lord your God to the test.' " *(Deuteronomy 6:16)*

8Finally, the devil took Jesus to a very high mountain. He showed him all the kingdoms of the world and their glory. **9**"If you bow down and worship me," he said, "I will give you all of this."

10Jesus said to him, "Get away from me, Satan! It is written, 'Worship the Lord your God. He is the only one you should serve.' " *(Deuteronomy 6:13)*

11Then the devil left Jesus. Angels came and took care of him.

Jesus Begins to Preach

12John had been put in prison. When Jesus heard about this, he returned to Galilee. **13**Jesus left Nazareth. He went to live in the city of Capernaum. It was by the lake in the area of Zebulun and Naphtali. **14**In that way, what the prophet Isaiah had said came true. He had said,

15 "Land of Zebulun! Land of Naphtali!
    Galilee, where non-Jewish people
        live!
    Land along the Mediterranean Sea!
    Territory east of the Jordan
        River!
16 The people who are now living in
        darkness
    will see a great light.
They are now living in a very dark land.
    But a light will shine on them."
                              (Isaiah 9:1,2)

17From that time on Jesus began to preach. "Turn away from your sins!" he said. "The kingdom of heaven is near."

Jesus Chooses the First Disciples

18One day Jesus was walking beside the Sea of Galilee. There he saw two brothers. They were Simon Peter and his brother Andrew. They were throwing a net into

MATTHEW 2:16

Herod realized that the Wise Men had tricked him. So he became very angry. He gave orders concerning Bethlehem and the area around it. All the boys two years old and under were to be killed.

King Herod (HARE-ud) paced up and down the thick rug in front of his throne. He stopped once in a while, thinking, then began pacing again. He began to pace faster and faster. And then he began to yell at anyone who got in his way or tried to talk to him. Some Wise Men had told him a new king had been born.

King Herod wanted to keep ruling the people of Israel himself. He rubbed his face, trying to think what he should do. He had sent the Wise Men to Bethlehem to visit. Then he asked them to return and tell him all about this new king. But the Wise Men hadn't returned.

So King Herod had to handle this on his own. He knew only two things about this new king. First, he had been born recently in Bethlehem. And second, Herod had to get rid of him. The more King Herod thought about it, the more worried he became. Then upset. Then *angry*! HE HAD TO DO SOMETHING TO PROTECT HIS THRONE. NOW!

So King Herod made a cruel decision. All the baby boys under two years old in Bethlehem would be killed. If he killed them all, he would be sure to kill the one who would become king. Herod sent his soldiers to Bethlehem to do his brutal work. But the very one King Herod wanted to kill survived! An angel warned Joseph about Herod's horrible plan. Joseph escaped from Bethlehem with Mary and Jesus.

HEROD

Herod's anger caused him to do something so terrible we can hardly imagine it. He ordered all the babies in Bethlehem to be killed. But Herod was a fool if he thought such an action could stop Jesus from growing up and becoming king of the world. God had his plan, and not even someone a wicked as Herod could stop it.

HEROD WAS A CRUEL KING.
THE WHOLE STORY: MATTHEW 2:1-16

Go to page 1096 for the next Super Hero

the lake. They were fishermen. **19**"Come. Follow me," Jesus said. "I will make you fishers of people."

20At once they left their nets and followed him.

21Going on from there, he saw two other brothers. They were James, son of Zebedee, and his brother John. They were in a boat with their father Zebedee. As they were preparing their nets, Jesus called out to them.

22Right away they left the boat and their father and followed Jesus.

Jesus Heals Sick People

23Jesus went all over Galilee. There he taught in the synagogues. He preached the good news of God's kingdom. He healed every illness and sickness the people had.

24News about him spread all over Syria. People brought to him all who were ill with different kinds of sicknesses. Some were suffering great pain. Others were controlled by demons. Some were shaking wildly. Others couldn't move at all. And Jesus healed all of them.

25Large crowds followed him. Some people came from Galilee, from the area known as the Ten Cities, and from Jerusalem and Judea. Others came from the area across the Jordan River.

Jesus Gives Blessings

5 Jesus saw the crowds. So he went up on a mountainside and sat down. His disciples came to him. **2**Then he began to teach them.

He said,

3 "Blessed are those who are spiritually needy.
The kingdom of heaven belongs to them.
4 Blessed are those who are sad.
They will be comforted.
5 Blessed are those who are free of pride.
They will be given the earth.
6 Blessed are those who are hungry and thirsty for what is right.
They will be filled.
7 Blessed are those who show mercy.
They will be shown mercy.
8 Blessed are those whose hearts are pure.
They will see God.
9 Blessed are those who make peace.
They will be called sons of God.
10 Blessed are those who suffer for doing what is right.
The kingdom of heaven belongs to them.

POWER-SURGE

CHEERFUL ✱

BE JOYFUL AND GLAD. YOUR REWARD IN HEAVEN IS GREAT.
— **MATTHEW 5:12** —

11"Blessed are you when people make fun of you and hurt you because of me. You are also blessed when they tell all kinds of evil lies about you because of me. **12**Be joyful and glad. Your reward in heaven is great. In the same way, people hurt the prophets who lived long ago.

Salt and Light

13"You are the salt of the earth. But suppose the salt loses its saltiness. How can it be made salty again? It is no longer good for anything. It will be thrown out. People will walk all over it.

14"You are the light of the world. A city on a hill can't be hidden. **15**Also, people do not light a lamp and put it under a bowl. Instead, they put it on its stand. Then it gives light to everyone in the house.

16"In the same way, let your light shine in front of others. Then they will see the good things you do. And they will praise your Father who is in heaven.

Jesus Gives Full Meaning to the Law

17"Do not think I have come to get rid of what is written in the Law or in the Prophets. I have not come to do that. Instead, I have come to give full meaning to what is written. **18**What I'm about to tell you is true. Heaven and earth will disappear before the smallest letter disappears from the Law. Not even the smallest stroke of a pen will disappear from the Law until everything is completed.

19"Do not break even one of the least important commandments. And do not teach others to break them. If you do, you will be called the least important person in the kingdom of heaven. Instead, practice and teach these commands. Then you will be called important in the kingdom of heaven.

20"Here is what I tell you. You must be more godly than the Pharisees and the teachers of the law. If you are not, you will certainly not enter the kingdom of heaven.

JOHN THE BAPTIST

MATTHEW 3:11

I baptize you with water, calling you to turn away from your sins. But after me, one will come who is more powerful than I am. And I'm not fit to carry his sandals. He will baptize you with the Holy Spirit.

The cool river water rippled around John's legs. A young man who was sorry for his sins went out to John in the water. John dunked him under the water. John called the people to turn away from their sins and to be baptized.

John looked up and saw the crowd of people part to let someone through. *Jesus.* John recognized him immediately. John had been telling the people for a long time about Jesus. Jesus would come and save people from their sins.

John knew what Jesus wanted. Jesus wanted John to baptize him. *No way,* John thought to himself. Then he said, "You are so much more powerful and righteous than I am, Jesus. I'm not good enough to even carry your sandals."

But Jesus insisted. "You must baptize me."

Still hesitating, John tipped Jesus until his head and body both went under water. He lifted Jesus' dripping body up from the water. Then John jumped back as something rustled in front of his face and landed on Jesus' head. It looked like a dove. John and all the people in the crowd grew silent as a voice boomed from the sky. **"THIS IS THE SON THAT I LOVE,"** THE VOICE THUNDERED. **"I AM PLEASED WITH HIM. I LOVE HIM."**

Jesus waded out of the water and through the crowd of people. John watched Jesus head out toward the desert. Then John turned to the people and said, "The man you just met is Jesus. He will save you from your sins. You need to follow him."

BE A JOHN

John the Baptist came before Jesus and prepared people for him. He knew Jesus was the Savior of the world. He told people they needed to follow Jesus. You can be like John, too, and tell your friends about Jesus.

JOHN FELT UNWORTHY OF BAPTIZING JESUS, BUT HE DID WHAT JESUS ASKED.
THE WHOLE STORY: MATTHEW 3:13-17

Go to page 1098 for the greatest Super Hero

Murder

21"You have heard what was said to people who lived long ago. They were told, 'Do not commit murder. *(Exodus 20:13)* Anyone who murders will be judged for it.' 22But here is what I tell you. Do not be angry with your brother. Anyone who is angry with his brother will be judged. Again, anyone who says to his brother, 'Raca,' must stand trial in the Sanhedrin. But anyone who says, 'You fool!' will be in danger of the fire in hell.

23"Suppose you are offering your gift at the altar. And you remember that your brother has something against you. 24Leave your gift in front of the altar. First go and make peace with your brother. Then come back and offer your gift.

25"Suppose someone has a claim against you and is taking you to court. Settle the matter quickly. Do it while you are still with him on your way. If you don't, he may hand you over to the judge. The judge may hand you over to the officer. And you may be thrown into prison. 26What I'm about to tell you is true. You will not get out until you have paid the very last penny!

Adultery

27"You have heard that it was said, 'Do not commit adultery.' *(Exodus 20:14)* 28But here is what I tell you. Do not even look at a woman in the wrong way. Anyone who does has already committed adultery with her in his heart.

29"If your right eye causes you to sin, poke it out and throw it away. Your eye is only one part of your body. It is better to lose it than for your whole body to be thrown into hell.

30"If your right hand causes you to sin, cut it off and throw it away. Your hand is only one part of your body. It is better to lose it than for your whole body to go into hell.

Divorce

31"It has been said, 'Suppose a man divorces his wife. If he does, he must give her a letter of divorce.' *(Deuteronomy 24:1)* 32But here is what I tell you. Anyone who divorces his wife causes her to commit adultery. And anyone who gets married to the divorced woman commits adultery. A man may divorce his wife only if she has not been faithful to him.

Oaths

33"Again, you have heard what was said to your people long ago. They were told,

'Do not break the promises you make to the Lord. Keep the oaths you have made to him.' 34But here is what I tell you. Do not make any promises like that at all. Do not make them in the name of heaven. That is God's throne. 35Do not make them in the name of the earth. That is the stool for God's feet. Do not make them in the name of Jerusalem. That is the city of the Great King. 36And do not take an oath in the name of your head. You can't make even one hair white or black.

37"Just let your 'Yes' mean 'Yes.' Let your 'No' mean 'No.' Anything more than this comes from the evil one.

Be Kind to Others

38"You have heard that it was said, 'An eye must be put out for an eye. A tooth must be knocked out for a tooth.' *(Exodus 21:24; Leviticus 24:20; Deuteronomy 19:21)* 39But here is what I tell you. Do not fight against an evil person.

"Suppose someone hits you on your right cheek. Turn your other cheek to him also. 40Suppose someone takes you to court to get your shirt. Let him have your coat also. 41Suppose someone forces you to go one mile. Go two miles with him.

42"Give to the one who asks you for something. Don't turn away from the one who wants to borrow something from you.

Love Your Enemies

43"You have heard that it was said, 'Love your neighbor. *(Leviticus 19:18)* Hate your enemy.' 44But here is what I tell you. Love your enemies. Pray for those who hurt you. 45Then you will be sons of your Father who is in heaven.

"He causes his sun to shine on evil people and good people. He sends rain on those who do right and those who don't.

46"If you love those who love you, what reward will you get? Even the tax collectors do that. 47If you greet only your own people, what more are you doing than others? Even people who are ungodly do that. 48So be perfect, just as your Father in heaven is perfect.

Giving to Needy People

6 "Be careful not to do 'good works' in front of others. Don't do them to be seen by others. If you do, your Father in heaven will not reward you.

2"When you give to needy people, do not announce it by having trumpets blown. Do not be like those who only pretend to be holy. They announce what

MATTHEW 4:11

> **Then the devil left Jesus. Angels came and took care of him.**

Jesus looked at the rock. His stomach rumbled and grumbled. He was so hungry. He had been in the desert for a long time praying and talking to God. Now the devil wanted him to turn the rock into a loaf of bread.

"If you are really God's Son, turn that rock into bread," the devil said. Warm, soft bread. Mmmm. But Jesus knew he should obey God, not the devil. He knew that talking to God was more important than eating. And he didn't have to prove to the devil that he was God's Son.

Next the devil took Jesus to the very top of the temple. Jesus looked down far below to where the people walked around. They looked so tiny, like little bugs crawling around on the ground.

"Jump!" the devil shouted. "If you're God's Son, he'll surely send his angels to save you!"

Jesus knew the devil was right. God *would* send angels to save him if he jumped. But he also knew God didn't want him to jump just to prove it to the devil.

The devil wasn't finished yet. He took Jesus to the highest peak of a mountain. Jesus stood and faced the wind and looked down at the rivers and valleys below.

"Bow down and worship me," the devil said, "and I'll give you everything you see below you."

Jesus glared at the devil and said, "Never! God's Word says we should only worship God. I WILL NEVER BOW DOWN TO YOU. NOW GET AWAY AND LEAVE ME ALONE!" Finally the devil gave up. He realized Jesus wasn't going to listen to him. So he left.

Jesus collapsed. He was so tired. God looked down from heaven and loved his obedient Son. He sent his angels to comfort and care for him.

BE LIKE JESUS

When Satan came and wanted Jesus to do something bad, Jesus refused. He didn't give in to temptation. When you're tempted to do something you know you shouldn't do, remember Jesus. Do what you know is right.

JESUS OBEYED GOD INSTEAD OF THE DEVIL.

Go to page 1101 for the greatest Super Hero

they do in the synagogues and on the streets. They want to be honored by others. What I'm about to tell you is true. They have received their complete reward.

3 "When you give to the needy, don't let your left hand know what your right hand is doing. **4** Then your giving will be done secretly. Your Father will reward you. He sees what you do secretly.

Prayer

5 "When you pray, do not be like those who only pretend to be holy. They love to stand and pray in the synagogues and on the street corners. They want to be seen by others. What I'm about to tell you is true. They have received their complete reward.

6 "When you pray, go into your room. Close the door and pray to your Father, who can't be seen. He will reward you. Your Father sees what is done secretly.

7 "When you pray, do not keep talking on and on the way ungodly people do. They think they will be heard because they talk a lot. **8** Do not be like them. Your Father knows what you need even before you ask him.

9 "This is how you should pray.

" 'Our Father in heaven,
    may your name be honored.
10 May your kingdom come.
    May what you want to happen be done
        on earth as it is done in heaven.
11 Give us today our daily bread.
12 Forgive us our sins,
    just as we also have forgiven those
        who sin against us.
13 Keep us from falling into sin when we
        are tempted.
    Save us from the evil one.'

14 "Forgive people when they sin against you. If you do, your Father who is in heaven will also forgive you. **15** But if you do not forgive people their sins, your Father will not forgive your sins.

Fasting

16 "When you go without eating, do not look gloomy like those who only pretend to be holy. They make their faces very sad. They want to show people they are fasting. What I'm about to tell you is true. They have received their complete reward.

17 "But when you go without eating, put olive oil on your head. Wash your face. **18** Then others will not know that you are fasting. Only your Father, who can't be

seen, will know it. He will reward you. Your Father sees what is done secretly.

Put Away Riches in Heaven

19 "Do not put away riches for yourselves on earth. Moths and rust can destroy them. Thieves can break in and steal them. **20** Instead, put away riches for yourselves in heaven. There, moths and rust do not destroy them. There, thieves do not break in and steal them. **21** Your heart will be where your riches are.

22 "The eye is like a lamp for the body. Suppose your eyes are good. Then your whole body will be full of light. **23** But suppose your eyes are bad. Then your whole body will be full of darkness. If the light inside you is darkness, then it is very dark!

24 "No one can serve two masters at the same time. He will hate one of them and love the other. Or he will be faithful to one and dislike the other. You can't serve God and Money at the same time.

Do Not Worry

25 "I tell you, do not worry. Don't worry about your life and what you will eat or drink. And don't worry about your body and what you will wear. Isn't there more to life than eating? Aren't there more important things for the body than clothes?

26 "Look at the birds of the air. They don't plant or gather crops. They don't put away crops in storerooms. But your Father who is in heaven feeds them. Aren't you worth much more than they are?

27 "Can you add even one hour to your life by worrying?

28 "And why do you worry about clothes? See how the wild flowers grow. They don't work or make clothing. **29** But here is what I tell you. Not even Solomon

POWER-SURGE

FORGIVING F

FORGIVE US OUR SINS,

JUST AS WE ALSO
HAVE FORGIVEN
THOSE WHO SIN
AGAINST US.

FORGIVE PEOPLE
WHEN THEY SIN
AGAINST YOU.
— MATTHEW 6:12, 14 —

in all of his glory was dressed like one of those flowers.

30 "If that is how God dresses the wild grass, won't he dress you even better? After all, the grass is here only today. Tomorrow it is thrown into the fire. Your faith is so small!

31 "So don't worry. Don't say, 'What will we eat?' Or, 'What will we drink?' Or, 'What will we wear?' **32** People who are ungodly run after all of those things. Your Father who is in heaven knows that you need them.

33 "But put God's kingdom first. Do what he wants you to do. Then all of those things will also be given to you.

34 "So don't worry about tomorrow. Tomorrow will worry about itself. Each day has enough trouble of its own.

Be Fair When You Judge Others

7 "Do not judge others. Then you will not be judged. **2** You will be judged in the same way you judge others. You will be measured in the same way you measure others.

3 "You look at the bit of sawdust in your friend's eye. But you pay no attention to the piece of wood in your own eye. **4** How can you say to your friend, 'Let me take the bit of sawdust out of your eye'? How can you say this while there is a piece of wood in your own eye?

5 "You pretender! First take the piece of wood out of your own eye. Then you will be able to see clearly to take the bit of sawdust out of your friend's eye.

6 "Do not give holy things to dogs. Do not throw your pearls to pigs. If you do, they might walk all over them. Then they might turn around and tear you to pieces.

Ask, Search, Knock

7 "Ask, and it will be given to you. Search, and you will find. Knock, and the door will be opened to you. **8** Everyone who asks will receive. He who searches will find. The door will be opened to the one who knocks.

9 "Suppose your son asks for bread. Which of you will give him a stone? **10** Or suppose he asks for a fish. Which of you will give him a snake? **11** Even though you are evil, you know how to give good gifts to your children. How much more will your Father who is in heaven give good gifts to those who ask him!

12 "In everything, do to others what you would want them to do to you. This is what is written in the Law and in the Prophets.

The Large and Small Gates

13 "Enter God's kingdom through the narrow gate. The gate is large and the road is wide that lead to death and hell. Many people go that way. **14** But the gate is small and the road is narrow that lead to life. Only a few people find it.

A Tree and Its Fruit

15 "Watch out for false prophets. They come to you pretending to be sheep. But on the inside they are hungry wolves. **16** You can tell what they really are by what they do.

"Do people pick grapes from bushes? Do they pick figs from thorns? **17** In the same way, every good tree bears good fruit. But a bad tree bears bad fruit. **18** A good tree can't bear bad fruit. And a bad tree can't bear good fruit. **19** Every tree that does not bear good fruit is cut down. It is thrown into the fire. **20** You can tell each tree by its fruit.

21 "Not everyone who says to me, 'Lord, Lord,' will enter the kingdom of heaven. Only those who do what my Father in heaven wants will enter.

22 "Many will say to me on that day, 'Lord! Lord! Didn't we prophesy in your name? Didn't we drive out demons in your name? Didn't we do many miracles in your name?' **23** Then I will tell them clearly, 'I never knew you. Get away from me, you who do evil!'

The Wise and Foolish Builders

24 "So then, everyone who hears my words and puts them into practice is like a wise man. He builds his house on the rock. **25** The rain comes down. The water rises. The winds blow and beat against that house. But it does not fall. It is built on the rock.

POWER-SURGE

OBEYS ✔

EVERYONE WHO HEARS MY WORDS AND PUTS THEM INTO PRACTICE IS LIKE A WISE MAN.
— MATTHEW 7:24 —

W

WISE

26"But everyone who hears my words and does not put them into practice is like a foolish man. He builds his house on sand. 27The rain comes down. The water rises. The winds blow and beat against that house. And it falls with a loud crash."

28Jesus finished saying all these things. The crowds were amazed at his teaching. 29He taught like one who had authority. He did not speak like their teachers of the law.

Jesus Heals a Man Who Had a Skin Disease

8 Jesus came down from the mountainside. Large crowds followed him. 2A man who had a skin disease came

and got down on his knees in front of Jesus. He said, "Lord, if you are willing to make me 'clean,' you can do it."

3Jesus reached out his hand and touched the man. "I am willing to do it," he said. "Be 'clean'!"

Right away the man was healed of his skin disease.

4Then Jesus said to him, "Don't tell anyone. Go and show yourself to the priest. Offer the gift Moses commanded. It will be a witness to them."

A Roman Commander Has Faith

5When Jesus entered Capernaum, a Roman commander came to him. He asked Jesus for help. 6"Lord," he said, "my ser-

JESUS TELLS A STORY

MATTHEW 7:24-25

So then, everyone who hears my words and puts them into practice is like a wise man. He builds his house on the rock...it does not fall.

Jesus told his followers this story about a wise and a foolish builder:

Two builders went to build houses for themselves. The first man built his house on a sandy beach. When a storm came, the house shook and shuddered in the wind. The waves beat at its foundation. **AND THE HOUSE FELL WITH A CRASH.** What a foolish builder!

The second man built his house on firm rock. The house stood tall and strong. A huge storm came up. The wind battered the house. The rain poured down and filled the rivers. The river water rushed against the house. But the house didn't even quiver. It stood firm because the wise builder had built it on rock.

BE LIKE JESUS

Following Jesus is like being a wise builder. Jesus wants his followers to be like that wise builder and build their houses firmly on his teachings. Follow Jesus faithfully and build the house of your life on a strong foundation.

JESUS WANTS HIS FOLLOWERS TO BUILD THEIR LIVES ON THE FIRM FOUNDATION OF HIS TEACHINGS.

Go to page 1103 for the next Super Hero

vant lies at home and can't move. He is suffering terribly."

⁷Jesus said, "I will go and heal him."

⁸The commander replied, "Lord, I am not good enough to have you come into my house. But just say the word, and my servant will be healed. ⁹I myself am a man under authority. And I have soldiers who obey my orders. I tell this one, 'Go,' and he goes. I tell that one, 'Come,' and he comes. I say to my servant, 'Do this,' and he does it."

¹⁰When Jesus heard this, he was amazed. He said to those following him, "What I'm about to tell you is true. In Israel I have not found anyone whose faith is so strong.

¹¹"I say to you that many will come from the east and the west. They will take their places at the feast in the kingdom of heaven. They will sit with Abraham, Isaac and Jacob. ¹²But those who think they belong to the kingdom will be thrown outside, into the darkness. There they will sob and grind their teeth."

¹³Then Jesus said to the Roman commander, "Go! It will be done just as you believed it would."

And his servant was healed at that very hour.

Jesus Heals Many People

¹⁴When Jesus came into Peter's house,

BELIEVES ✝

JESUS... WAS AMAZED. HE SAID TO THOSE FOLLOWING HIM, "WHAT I'M ABOUT TO TELL YOU IS TRUE. IN ISRAEL I HAVE NOT FOUND ANYONE WHOSE FAITH IS SO STRONG. THEN JESUS SAID TO THE ROMAN COMMANDER, "GO! IT WILL BE DONE JUST AS YOU BELIEVED IT WOULD."
— MATTHEW 8:10, 13 —

he saw Peter's mother-in-law. She was lying in bed. She had a fever. ¹⁵Jesus touched her hand, and the fever left her. She got up and began to wait on him.

¹⁶When evening came, many people controlled by demons were brought to Jesus. He drove out the spirits with a word. He healed all who were sick. ¹⁷He did it to make what the prophet Isaiah had said come true. He had said,

"He suffered the things we should have suffered.
He took on himself the sicknesses that should have been ours."
(Isaiah 53:4)

It Costs to Follow Jesus

¹⁸Jesus saw the crowd around him. So he gave his disciples orders to go to the other side of the Sea of Galilee.

¹⁹Then a teacher of the law came to him. He said, "Teacher, I will follow you no matter where you go."

²⁰Jesus replied, "Foxes have holes. Birds of the air have nests. But the Son of Man has no place to lay his head."

²¹Another follower said to him, "Lord, first let me go and bury my father."

²²But Jesus told him, "Follow me. Let the dead bury their own dead."

Jesus Calms the Storm

²³Jesus got into a boat. His disciples followed him. ²⁴Suddenly a terrible storm came up on the lake. The waves crashed over the boat. But Jesus was sleeping. ²⁵The disciples went and woke him up. They said, "Lord! Save us! We're going to drown!"

²⁶He replied, "Your faith is so small! Why are you so afraid?"

Then Jesus got up and ordered the winds and the waves to stop. It became completely calm.

²⁷The disciples were amazed. They asked, "What kind of man is this? Even the winds and the waves obey him!"

Jesus Heals Two Men Controlled by Demons

²⁸Jesus arrived at the other side of the lake in the area of the Gadarenes. Two men controlled by demons met him. They came from the tombs. The men were so wild that no one could pass that way.

²⁹"Son of God, what do you want with us?" they shouted. "Have you come here to punish us before the time for us to be judged?"

ROMAN COMMANDER

MATTHEW 8:10

When Jesus heard this, he was amazed. He said to those following him, "What I'm about to tell you is true. In Israel I have not found anyone whose faith is so strong."

The commander's strong muscles bulged under his robe. But the muscles of his sick servant were weak. The commander stood up straight and powerful. But the servant could only lie on his bed and barely keep his eyes open. The commander felt healthy. But the servant twisted in pain. The servant had worked for the commander for many years. They had grown up together, running and playing and fighting as young boys. They had traveled together wherever the commander's duties brought him.

The commander called in every doctor he could find. But his servant only grew weaker and more sick. So the commander decided to go to see Jesus, the healer who had just come to his town. The roads were dusty and hot, but the commander barely noticed. As he got near the town gate, he saw a crowd of people. They quickly stepped aside for the powerful commander, opening up a path for him that led directly to Jesus.

Kneeling before Jesus, he said, "My servant is sick and suffering." The commander knew how busy Jesus was. "I'm not a good enough person for you to come to my house, Jesus. Just say the word and my servant will be healed."

Jesus was surprised. Sometimes people didn't believe in him even when he did amazing things right before their eyes. But this man believed Jesus could heal the servant without even touching him.

Jesus looked up at the crowd and said, **"THIS MAN HAS MORE FAITH THAN ANYONE ELSE I'VE SEEN."** Looking at the commander, Jesus said, "You can go now. Your servant is healed." And at that very moment, the servant's body got strong and healthy again.

BE LIKE THE ROMAN COMMANDER

Do you believe in Jesus? Do you believe he can do anything? Is your faith strong like the Roman commander's? If it isn't, pray and ask Jesus to give you more faith. He will do it.

THE COMMANDER BELIEVED IN JESUS EVEN WHEN OTHERS DOUBTED.
THE WHOLE STORY: MATTHEW 8:5-13

Go to page 1105 for the next Super Hero

30Not very far away, a large herd of pigs was feeding. **31**The demons begged Jesus, "If you drive us out, send us into the herd of pigs."

32Jesus said to them, "Go!"

So the demons came out of the men and went into the pigs. The whole herd rushed down the steep bank. They ran into the lake and drowned in the water.

33Those who were tending the pigs ran off. They went into the town and reported all this. They told the people what had happened to the men who had been controlled by demons.

34Then the whole town went out to meet Jesus. When they saw him, they begged him to leave their area.

Jesus Heals a Man Who Could Not Walk

9 Jesus stepped into a boat. He went over to the other side of the lake and came to his own town. **2**Some men brought to him a man who could not walk. He was lying on a mat. Jesus saw that they had faith. So he said to the man, "Don't lose hope, son. Your sins are forgiven."

3Then some teachers of the law said to themselves, "This fellow is saying a very evil thing!"

4Jesus knew what they were thinking. So he said, "Why do you have evil thoughts in your hearts? **5**Is it easier to say, 'Your sins are forgiven'? Or to say, 'Get up and walk'? **6**I want you to know that the Son of Man has authority on earth to forgive sins."

Then he spoke to the man who could not walk. "Get up," he said. "Take your mat and go home." **7**The man got up and went home.

8When the crowd saw this, they were filled with wonder. They praised God for giving that kind of authority to men.

Jesus Chooses Matthew

9As Jesus went on from there, he saw a man named Matthew. He was sitting at the tax collector's booth.

"Follow me," Jesus told him. Matthew got up and followed him.

10Later Jesus was having dinner at Matthew's house. Many tax collectors and "sinners" came. They ate with Jesus and his disciples.

11The Pharisees saw this. So they asked the disciples, "Why does your teacher eat with tax collectors and 'sinners'?"

12Jesus heard that. So he said, "Those who are healthy don't need a doctor. Sick people do. **13**Go and learn what this means, 'I want mercy and not sacrifice.' *(Hosea 6:6)* I have not come to get those who think they are right with God to follow me. I have come to get sinners to follow me."

Jesus Is Asked About Fasting

14One day John's disciples came. They said to Jesus, "We and the Pharisees go without eating. Why don't your disciples go without eating?"

15Jesus answered, "How can the guests of the groom be sad while he is with them? The time will come when the groom will be taken away from them. Then they will fast.

16"People don't sew a patch of new cloth on old clothes. The new piece will pull away from the old. That will make the tear worse.

17"People don't pour new wine into old wineskins. If they do, the skins will burst. The wine will run out, and the wineskins will be destroyed. No, everyone pours new wine into new wineskins. Then both are saved."

A Dead Girl and a Suffering Woman

18While Jesus was saying this, a ruler came. He got down on his knees in front of Jesus. He said, "My daughter has just died. But come and place your hand on her. Then she will live again."

19Jesus got up and went with him. So did his disciples.

20Just then a woman came up behind Jesus. She had a sickness that made her bleed. It had lasted for 12 years. She touched the edge of his clothes. **21**She thought, "I only need to touch his clothes. Then I will be healed."

22Jesus turned and saw her. "Dear woman, don't give up hope," he said. "Your faith has healed you." The woman was healed at that very moment.

23When Jesus entered the ruler's house,

he saw the flute players there. And he saw the noisy crowd. ²⁴He said, "Go away. The girl is not dead. She is sleeping." But they laughed at him.

²⁵After the crowd had been sent outside, Jesus went in. He took the girl by the hand, and she got up. ²⁶News about what Jesus had done spread all over that area.

Jesus Heals Two Blind Men

²⁷As Jesus went on from there, two blind men followed him. They called out, "Have mercy on us, Son of David!"

²⁸When Jesus went indoors, the blind men came to him. He asked them, "Do you believe that I can do this?"

"Yes, Lord," they replied.

²⁹Then he touched their eyes. He said, "It will happen to you just as you believed." ³⁰They could now see again. Jesus strongly warned them, "Be sure that no one knows about this." ³¹But they went out and spread the news. They talked about him all over that area.

³²While they were going out, another man was brought to Jesus. A demon controlled him, and he could not speak.

MATTHEW

MATTHEW 9:9

✔ "Follow me," Jesus told him. Matthew got up and followed him.

✝ Matthew sat in his booth and looked at the long line of people waiting to pay their taxes. His fellow Israelites looked down on him because he worked for the Romans. But the job paid well. So he continued, taking money first from one person, then another.

Matthew looked up from adding a column of numbers together. Who was this man who thought he could go right to the front of the line? Jesus moved up to Matthew's booth as if he didn't even see the other people there. He saw only Matthew. When Matthew looked up, he saw only Jesus.

Jesus said two words to Matthew, **"FOLLOW ME."**

Matthew looked at the money lying on his table. He looked at the people waiting in line. He looked at the column of numbers he was in the middle of adding. And he stood up and followed Jesus, leaving it all behind.

BE A MATTHEW

Wow! Can you see it? Matthew just stood up and left everything behind to follow Jesus. No hesitation. No questions. Just following. Be like him! Follow Jesus quickly and with your whole heart, just like Matthew.

MATTHEW OBEYED JESUS, WILLINGLY AND QUICKLY FOLLOWING HIM.

Go to page 1107 for the next Super Heroes

33When the demon was driven out, the man spoke.

The crowd was amazed. They said, "Nothing like this has ever been seen in Israel." **34**But the Pharisees said, "He drives out demons by the power of the prince of demons."

There Are Only a Few Workers

35Jesus went through all the towns and villages. He taught in their synagogues. He preached the good news of the kingdom. And he healed every illness and sickness. **36**When he saw the crowds, he felt deep concern for them. They were beaten down and helpless, like sheep without a shepherd.

37Then Jesus said to his disciples, "The harvest is huge. But there are only a few workers. **38**So ask the Lord of the harvest to send workers out into his harvest field."

Jesus Sends Out the Twelve Disciples

10 Jesus called for his 12 disciples to come to him. He gave them authority to drive out evil spirits and to heal every illness and sickness.

2Here are the names of the 12 apostles. First are Simon Peter and his brother Andrew. Then come James, son of Zebedee, and his brother John. **3**Next are Philip and Bartholomew, and also Thomas and Matthew the tax collector. Two more are James, son of Alphaeus, and Thaddaeus. **4**The last are Simon the Zealot and Judas Iscariot. Judas is the one who was later going to hand Jesus over to his enemies.

5Jesus sent these 12 out with the following orders. "Do not go among those who aren't Jews," he said. "Do not enter any town of the Samaritans. **6**Instead, go to the people of Israel. They are like sheep that have become lost. **7**As you go, preach this message, 'The kingdom of heaven is near.' **8**Heal those who are sick. Bring those who are dead back to life. Make those who have skin diseases 'clean' again. Drive out demons. You have received freely, so give freely.

9"Do not take along any gold, silver or copper in your belts. **10**Do not take a bag for the journey. Do not take extra clothes or sandals or walking sticks. A worker should be given what he needs.

11"When you enter a town or village, look for someone who is willing to welcome you. Stay at that person's house until you leave. **12**As you enter the home, greet those who live there. **13**If that home

welcomes you, give it your blessing of peace. If it does not, don't bless it.

14"Some people may not welcome you or listen to your words. If they don't, shake the dust off your feet when you leave that home or town. **15**What I'm about to tell you is true. On judgment day it will be easier for Sodom and Gomorrah than for that town.

16"I am sending you out like sheep among wolves. So be as wise as snakes and as harmless as doves.

17"Watch out! Men will hand you over to the local courts. They will whip you in their synagogues. **18**You will be brought to governors and kings because of me. You will be witnesses to them and to those who aren't Jews.

19"But when they arrest you, don't worry about what you will say or how you will say it. At that time you will be given the right words to say. **20**It will not be you speaking. The Spirit of your Father will be speaking through you.

21"Brothers will hand over brothers to be killed. Fathers will hand over their children. Children will rise up against their parents and have them put to death. **22**Everyone will hate you because of me. But anyone who stands firm to the end will be saved.

23"When people attack you in one place, escape to another. What I'm about to tell you is true. You will not finish going through the cities of Israel before the Son of Man comes.

24"A student is not better than his teacher. A servant is not better than his master. **25**It is enough for the student to be like his teacher. And it is enough for the servant to be like his master. If the head of the house has been called Beelzebub, what can the others who live there expect?

26"So don't be afraid of your enemies. Everything that is secret will be brought out into the open. Everything that is hidden will be uncovered. **27**What I tell you in the dark, speak in the daylight. What is whispered in your ear, shout from the rooftops. **28**Do not be afraid of those who kill the body but can't kill the soul. Instead, be afraid of the One who can destroy both soul and body in hell.

29"Aren't two sparrows sold for only a penny? But not one of them falls to the ground without your Father knowing it. **30**He even counts every hair on your head! **31**So don't be afraid. You are worth more than many sparrows. **32**"What about someone who says in

MATTHEW 10:2-4

Here are the names of the 12 apostles. First are Simon Peter and his brother Andrew. Then come James, son of Zebedee, and his brother John. Next are Philip and Bartholomew, and also Thomas and Matthew the tax collector. Two more are James, son of Alphaeus, and Thaddaeus. The last are Simon the Zealot and Judas Iscariot. Judas is the one who was later going to hand Jesus over to his enemies.

A cool evening breeze whirled off the lake and made its way through the green hills of the countryside. The huge crowd of people with Jesus were getting hungry. Jesus asked Philip, "Where can we buy food for these people?" Philip answered quickly, "It would take almost a year's pay to feed this many people!" Andrew said eagerly, "I saw a little boy with some bread and fish." Jesus told Andrew to go find him.

Jesus took the boy's lunch and blessed it. The disciples handed the food out to the people. No matter how much they gave away, there was still more! A huge smile broke out on John's face, then on James' when they realized what was happening.

With a chuckle, Andrew picked up several baskets. He tossed one basket to Simon and another to Judas. Together the disciples picked up the leftovers. Imagine that! Andrew thought. **LEFTOVERS FROM SUCH A SMALL LUNCH!** Thaddaeus, James and Thomas hefted their overflowing baskets. Bartholomew, then Matthew set the twelve baskets of leftovers on the grass.

The amazed disciples sat in a circle around Jesus. It was a miracle! Jesus fed more than 5,000 people with only a little boy's lunch.

BE LIKE THE TWELVE DISCIPLES

Wherever Jesus went, his twelve disciples went with him. They were eager to learn from him. You can learn about Jesus, too, from the Bible and from other people. Are you like the disciples? Are you eager to learn about Jesus?

THE DISCIPLES LOVED JESUS AND WERE EAGER TO HELP HIM AND LEARN FROM HIM.

THE WHOLE STORY: MATTHEW 10:2-4; JOHN 6:1-15

Go to page 1114 for the next Super Hero

front of others that he knows me? I will also say in front of my Father who is in heaven that I know him. 33But what about someone who says in front of others that he doesn't know me? I will say in front of my Father who is in heaven that I don't know him.

34"Do not think that I came to bring peace to the earth. I didn't come to bring peace. I came to bring a sword. 35I have come to turn

" 'sons against their fathers.
    Daughters will refuse to obey their
        mothers.
Daughters-in-law will be against their
        mothers-in-law.
36   A man's enemies will be the
        members of his own family.'
(Micah 7:6)

37"Anyone who loves his father or mother more than me is not worthy of me. Anyone who loves his son or daughter more than me is not worthy of me. 38And anyone who does not pick up his cross and follow me is not worthy of me. 39If anyone finds his life, he will lose it. If anyone loses his life because of me, he will find it.

40"Anyone who welcomes you welcomes me. And anyone who welcomes me welcomes the One who sent me. 41Suppose someone welcomes a prophet as a prophet. That one will receive a prophet's reward. And suppose someone welcomes a godly person as a godly person. That one will receive a godly person's reward. 42Suppose someone gives even a cup of cold water to a little one who follows me. What I'm about to tell you is true. That one will certainly be rewarded."

Jesus and John the Baptist

11 Jesus finished teaching his 12 disciples. Then he went on to teach and preach in the towns of Galilee.

2John was in prison. When he heard what Christ was doing, he sent his disciples to him. 3They asked Jesus, "Are you the one who was supposed to come? Or should we look for someone else?"

4Jesus replied, "Go back to John. Report to him what you hear and see. 5Blind people receive sight. Disabled people walk. Those who have skin diseases are healed. Deaf people hear. Those who are dead are raised to life. And the good news is preached to those who are poor. 6Blessed are those who do not give up their faith because of me."

7As John's disciples were leaving, Jesus began to speak to the crowd about John. He said, "What did you go out into the desert to see? Tall grass waving in the wind? 8If not, what did you go out to see? A man dressed in fine clothes? No. People who wear fine clothes are in kings' palaces. 9Then what did you go out to see? A prophet? Yes, I tell you, and more than a prophet. 10He is the one written about in Scripture. It says,

" 'I will send my messenger ahead of
        you.
He will prepare your way for you.'
(Malachi 3:1)

11"What I'm about to tell you is true. No one more important than John the Baptist has ever been born. But the least important person in the kingdom of heaven is more important than he is. 12Since the days of John the Baptist, the kingdom of heaven has been advancing with force. And forceful people are taking hold of it. 13All the Prophets and the Law prophesied until John came. 14If you are willing to accept it, John is the Elijah who was supposed to come. 15Those who have ears should listen.

16"What can I compare today's people to? They are like children sitting in the market places and calling out to others. They say,

17" 'We played the flute for you.
    But you didn't dance.
We sang a funeral song.
    But you didn't become sad.'

18When John came, he didn't eat or drink as you do. And people say, 'He has a demon.' 19But when the Son of Man came, he ate and drank as you do. And people say, 'This fellow is always eating and drinking far too much. He's a friend of tax

POWER-SURGE

BELIEVES †

BLESSED ARE THOSE
WHO DO NOT GIVE UP
THEIR FAITH BECAUSE
OF ME.
— MATTHEW 11:6 —

TRIES HARD

collectors and "sinners." ' Those who act wisely prove that wisdom is right."

Cities That Do Not Turn Away From Sin

20Jesus began to speak against the cities where he had done most of his miracles. The people there had not turned away from their sins. So he said, **21**"How terrible it will be for you, Korazin! How terrible for you, Bethsaida! Suppose the miracles done in you had been done in Tyre and Sidon. They would have turned away from their sins long ago. They would have put on black clothes. They would have sat down in ashes. **22**But I tell you this. On judgment day it will be easier for Tyre and Sidon than for you.

23"And what about you, Capernaum? Will you be lifted up to heaven? No! You will go down to the place of the dead. Suppose the miracles done in you had been done in Sodom. It would still be here today. **24**But I tell you this. On judgment day it will be easier for Sodom than for you."

Rest for All Who Are Tired

25At that time Jesus said, "I praise you, Father. You are Lord of heaven and earth. You have hidden these things from the wise and educated. But you have shown them to little children. **26**Yes, Father. This is what you wanted.

27"My Father has given all things to me. The Father is the only one who knows the Son. And the only ones who know the Father are the Son and those to whom the Son chooses to make him known.

28"Come to me, all of you who are tired and are carrying heavy loads. I will give you rest. **29**Become my servants and learn from me. I am gentle and free of pride. You will find rest for your souls. **30**Serving me is easy, and my load is light."

Jesus Is Lord of the Sabbath Day

12 One Sabbath day Jesus walked through the grainfields. His disciples were hungry. So they began to break off some heads of grain and eat them. **2**The Pharisees saw this. They said to Jesus, "Look! It is against the Law to do this on the Sabbath. But your disciples are doing it anyway!"

3Jesus answered, "Haven't you read about what David did? He and his men were hungry. **4**So he entered the house of God. He and his men ate the holy bread. Only priests were allowed to eat it. **5**Haven't you read the Law? It tells how

every Sabbath day the priests in the temple have to do their work on that day. But they are not considered guilty.

6"I tell you that one who is more important than the temple is here. **7**Scripture says, 'I want mercy and not sacrifice.' *(Hosea 6:6)* You don't know what those words mean. If you did, you would not bring charges against those who are not guilty. **8**The Son of Man is Lord of the Sabbath day."

9Going on from that place, Jesus went into their synagogue. **10**A man with a weak and twisted hand was there. The Pharisees were trying to find fault with Jesus. So they asked him, "Does the Law allow us to heal on the Sabbath day?"

11He said to them, "What if one of your sheep falls into a pit on the Sabbath? Won't you take hold of it and lift it out? **12**A man is worth more than sheep! So the Law allows us to do good on the Sabbath day."

13Then Jesus said to the man, "Stretch out your hand." So he stretched it out. It was as good as new, just as good as the other hand. **14**But the Pharisees went out and planned how to kill Jesus.

God's Chosen Servant

15Jesus knew all about the Pharisees' plans. So he left that place. Many followed him, and he healed all their sick people. **16**But he warned them not to tell who he was. **17**This was to make what was spoken through the prophet Isaiah come true. It says,

18 "Here is my servant. I have chosen him.
He is the one I love. I am very
pleased with him.
I will put my Spirit on him.
He will announce to the nations that
everything will be made right.
19 He will not argue or cry out.
No one will hear his voice in the
streets.
20 He will not break a bent twig.
He will not put out a dimly burning
flame.
He will make everything right.
21 The nations will put their hope
in him."   *(Isaiah 42:1–4)*

Jesus and Beelzebub

22A man controlled by demons was brought to Jesus. The man was blind and could not speak. Jesus healed him. Then the man could speak and see. **23**All the people were amazed. They said, "Could this be the Son of David?"

24The Pharisees heard this. So they said, "This fellow drives out demons by the power of Beelzebub, the prince of demons."

25Jesus knew what they were thinking. So he said to them, "Every kingdom that fights against itself will be destroyed. Every city or family that is divided against itself will not stand. 26If Satan drives out Satan, he fights against himself. Then how can his kingdom stand? 27You say I drive out demons by the power of Beelzebub. Then by whose power do your people drive them out? So then, they will be your judges. 28But suppose I drive out demons by the Spirit of God. Then God's kingdom has come to you.

29"Or think about this. How can you enter a strong man's house and just take what the man owns? You must first tie him up. Then you can rob his house.

30"Anyone who is not with me is against me. Anyone who does not gather sheep with me scatters them. 31So here is what I tell you. Every sin and every evil word spoken against God will be forgiven. But speaking evil things against the Holy Spirit will not be forgiven. 32Anyone who speaks a word against the Son of Man will be forgiven. But anyone who speaks against the Holy Spirit will not be forgiven. A person like that won't be forgiven either now or in days to come.

33"If you make a tree good, its fruit will be good. If you make a tree bad, its fruit will be bad. You can tell a tree by its fruit.

34"You nest of poisonous snakes! How can you who are evil say anything good? Your mouths say everything that is in your hearts. 35A good man says good things. These come from the good that is put away inside him. An evil man says evil things. These come from the evil that is put away inside him. 36But here is what I tell you. On judgment day, people will have to account for every careless word they have spoken. 37By your words you will be found guilty or not guilty."

The Miraculous Sign of Jonah

38Some of the Pharisees and the teachers of the law came to Jesus. They said, "Teacher, we want to see a miraculous sign from you."

39He answered, "Evil and unfaithful people ask for a miraculous sign! But none will be given except the sign of the prophet Jonah. 40Jonah was in the stomach of a huge fish for three days and three nights. Something like that will happen to the Son of Man. He will spend three days and three nights in the grave.

41"The men of Nineveh will stand up on judgment day with the people now living. And the Ninevites will prove that those people are guilty. The men of Nineveh turned away from their sins when Jonah preached to them. And now one who is more important than Jonah is here.

42"The Queen of the South will stand up on judgment day with the people now living. And she will prove that they are guilty. She came from very far away to listen to Solomon's wisdom. And now one who is more important than Solomon is here.

43"What happens when an evil spirit comes out of a man? It goes through dry areas looking for a place to rest. But it doesn't find it. 44Then it says, 'I will return to the house I left.' When it arrives there, it finds the house empty. The house has been swept clean and put in order. 45Then the evil spirit goes and takes with it seven other spirits more evil than itself. They go in and live there. That man is worse off than before. That is how it will be with the evil people of today."

Jesus' Mother and Brothers

46While Jesus was still talking to the crowd, his mother and brothers stood outside. They wanted to speak to him. 47Someone told him, "Your mother and brothers are standing outside. They want to speak to you."

48Jesus replied to him, "Who is my mother? And who are my brothers?" 49Jesus pointed to his disciples. He said, "Here is my mother! Here are my brothers! 50Anyone who does what my Father in heaven wants is my brother or sister or mother."

The Story of the Farmer

13 That same day Jesus left the house and sat by the Sea of Galilee. 2Large crowds gathered around him. So he got into a boat. He sat down in it. All the people stood on the shore. 3Then he told them many things by using stories.

He said, "A farmer went out to plant his seed. 4He scattered the seed on the ground. Some fell on a path. Birds came and ate it up. 5Some seed fell on rocky places, where there wasn't much soil. The plants came up quickly, because the soil wasn't deep. 6When the sun came up, it burned the plants. They dried up because they had no roots. 7Other seed fell among thorns. The thorns grew up and crowded out the plants. **8**Still other seed fell on good soil. It produced a crop 100, 60 or 30 times more than what was planted. **9**Those who have ears should listen."

10The disciples came to him. They asked, "Why do you use stories when you speak to the people?"

11He replied, "You have been given the chance to understand the secrets of the kingdom of heaven. It has not been given to outsiders. **12**Everyone who has that kind of knowledge will be given more. In fact, they will have very much. If anyone doesn't have that kind of knowledge, even what little he has will be taken away from him. **13**Here is why I use stories when I speak to the people. I say,

"They look, but they don't really see.
They listen, but they don't really
hear or understand.

14"In them the words of the prophet Isaiah come true. He said,

" 'You will hear but never understand.
You will see but never know what
you are seeing.
15The hearts of these people have
become stubborn.
They can barely hear with their ears.
They have closed their eyes.
Otherwise they might see with their
eyes.
They might hear with their ears.
They might understand with their
hearts.
They might turn to the Lord, and then
he would heal them.'

(Isaiah 6:9,10)

16"But blessed are your eyes because they see. And blessed are your ears because they hear. **17**What I'm about to tell you is true. Many prophets and godly people wanted to see what you see. But they didn't see it. They wanted to hear what you hear. But they didn't hear it.

18"Listen! Here is the meaning of the story of the farmer. **19**People hear the message about the kingdom but do not understand it. Then the evil one comes. He steals what was planted in their hearts. Those people are like the seed planted on a path. **20**Others received the seed that fell on rocky places. They are those who hear the message and at once receive it with joy. **21**But they have no roots. So they last only a short time. They quickly fall away from the faith when trouble or suffering comes because of the message. **22**Others received the seed that fell among the thorns. They are those who hear the message. But then the worries of this life and the false promises of wealth crowd it out. They keep it from producing fruit. **23**But still others received the seed that fell on good soil. They are those who hear the message and understand it. They produce a crop 100, 60 or 30 times more than the farmer planted."

The Story of the Weeds

24Jesus told the crowd another story. "Here is what the kingdom of heaven is like," he said. "A man planted good seed in his field. **25**But while everyone was sleeping, his enemy came. The enemy planted weeds among the wheat and then went away. **26**The wheat began to grow and form grain. At the same time, weeds appeared.

27"The owner's servants came to him. They said, 'Sir, didn't you plant good seed in your field? Then where did the weeds come from?'

28" 'An enemy did this,' he replied.

"The servants asked him, 'Do you want us to go and pull the weeds up?'

29" 'No,' the owner answered. 'While you are pulling up the weeds, you might pull up the wheat with them. **30**Let both grow together until the harvest. At that time I will tell the workers what to do. Here is what I will say to them. First collect the weeds. Tie them in bundles to be burned. Then gather the wheat. Bring it into my storeroom.' "

The Stories of the Mustard Seed and the Yeast

31Jesus told the crowd another story. He said, "The kingdom of heaven is like a mustard seed. Someone took the seed and planted it in a field. **32**It is the smallest of all your seeds. But when it grows, it is the largest of all garden plants. It becomes a tree. Birds come and rest in its branches."

33Jesus told them still another story. "The kingdom of heaven is like yeast," he said. "A woman mixed it into a large amount of flour. The yeast worked its way all through the dough."

34Jesus spoke all these things to the crowd by using stories. He did not say anything to them without telling a story. **35**So the words spoken by the prophet came true. He had said,

"I will open my mouth and tell stories.
I will speak about things that were
hidden since the world was
made."

(Psalm 78:2)

Jesus Explains the Story of the Weeds

36Then Jesus left the crowd and went into the house. His disciples came to him. They said, "Explain to us the story of the weeds in the field."

37He answered, "The one who planted the good seed is the Son of Man. **38**The field is the world. The good seed stands for the people who belong to the kingdom. The weeds are the people who belong to the evil one. **39**The enemy who plants them is the devil. The harvest is judgment day. And the workers are angels.

40"The weeds are pulled up and burned in the fire. That is how it will be on judgment day. **41**The Son of Man will send out his angels. They will weed out of his kingdom everything that causes sin. They will also get rid of all who do evil. **42**They will throw them into the blazing furnace. There people will sob and grind their teeth. **43**Then God's people will shine like the sun in their Father's kingdom. Those who have ears should listen.

The Stories of the Hidden Treasure and the Pearl

44"The kingdom of heaven is like treasure that was hidden in a field. When a man found it, he hid it again. He was very happy. So he went and sold everything he had. And he bought that field.

45"Again, the kingdom of heaven is like a trader who was looking for fine pearls. **46**He found one that was very valuable. So he went away and sold everything he had. And he bought that pearl.

The Story of the Net

47"Again, the kingdom of heaven is like a net. It was let down into the lake. It caught all kinds of fish. **48**When it was full, the fishermen pulled it up on the shore. Then they sat down and gathered the good fish into baskets. But they threw the bad fish away. **49**This is how it will be on judgment day. The angels will come. They will separate the people who did what is wrong from those who did what is right. **50**They will throw the evil people into the blazing furnace. There the evil ones will sob and grind their teeth.

51"Do you understand all these things?" Jesus asked.

"Yes," they replied.

52He said to them, "Every teacher of the law who has been taught about the kingdom of heaven is like the owner of a house. He brings new treasures out of his storeroom as well as old ones."

A Prophet Without Honor

53Jesus finished telling these stories. Then he moved on from there. **54**He came to his hometown of Nazareth. There he began teaching the people in their synagogue. They were amazed.

"Where did this man get this wisdom? Where did he get this power to do miracles?" they asked. **55**"Isn't this the carpenter's son? Isn't his mother's name Mary? Aren't his brothers James, Joseph, Simon and Judas? **56**Aren't all his sisters with us? Then where did this man get all these things?" **57**They were not pleased with him at all.

But Jesus said to them, "A prophet is not honored in his hometown. He doesn't receive any honor in his own home."

58He did only a few miracles there because they had no faith.

John the Baptist's Head Is Cut Off

14 At that time Herod, the ruler of Galilee and Perea, heard reports about Jesus. **2**He said to his attendants, "This is John the Baptist. He has risen from the dead! That is why he has the power to do miracles."

3Herod had arrested John. He had tied him up and put him in prison because of Herodias. She was the wife of Herod's brother Philip. **4**John had been saying to Herod, "It is against the Law for you to have her." **5**Herod wanted to kill John. But he was afraid of the people, because they thought John was a prophet.

6On Herod's birthday the daughter of Herodias danced for Herod and his guests. She pleased Herod very much. **7**So he promised with an oath to give her anything she asked for. **8**Her mother told her what to say. So the girl said to Herod, "Give me the head of John the Baptist on a big plate."

9The king was very upset. But he thought of his promise and his dinner guests. So he told one of his men to give her what she asked for. **10**Herod had John's head cut off in the prison. **11**His head was brought in on a big plate and given to the girl. She then carried it to her mother. **12**John's disciples came and took his body and buried it. Then they went and told Jesus.

Jesus Feeds the Five Thousand

13Jesus heard what had happened to John. He wanted to be alone. So he went in a boat to a quiet place. The crowds heard about this. They followed him on foot from the towns. ¹⁴When Jesus came ashore, he saw a large crowd. He felt deep concern for them. He healed their sick people.

¹⁵When it was almost evening, the disciples came to him. "There is nothing here," they said. "It's already getting late. Send the crowds away. They can go and buy some food in the villages."

¹⁶Jesus replied, "They don't need to go away. You give them something to eat."

¹⁷"We have only five loaves of bread and two fish," they answered.

¹⁸"Bring them here to me," he said. ¹⁹Then Jesus directed the people to sit down on the grass. He took the five loaves and the two fish. He looked up to heaven and gave thanks. He broke the loaves into pieces. Then he gave them to the disciples. And the disciples gave them to the people.

²⁰All of them ate and were satisfied. The disciples picked up 12 baskets of leftover pieces. ²¹The number of men who ate was about 5,000. Women and children also ate.

Jesus Walks on the Water

²²Right away Jesus made the disciples get into the boat. He had them go on ahead of him to the other side of the Sea of Galilee. Then he sent the crowd away. ²³After he had sent them away, he went up on a mountainside by himself to pray. When evening came, he was there alone. ²⁴The boat was already a long way from land. It was being pounded by the waves because the wind was blowing against it.

²⁵Early in the morning, Jesus went out to the disciples. He walked on the lake. ²⁶They saw him walking on the lake and were terrified. "It's a ghost!" they said. And they cried out in fear.

²⁷Right away Jesus called out to them, "Be brave! It is I. Don't be afraid."

²⁸"Lord, is it you?" Peter asked. "If it is, tell me to come to you on the water."

²⁹"Come," Jesus said.

So Peter got out of the boat. He walked on the water toward Jesus. ³⁰But when Peter saw the wind, he was afraid. He began to sink. He cried out, "Lord! Save me!"

³¹Right away Jesus reached out his hand and caught him. "Your faith is so small!" he said. "Why did you doubt me?"

³²When they climbed into the boat, the wind died down. ³³Then those in the boat worshiped Jesus. They said, "You really are the Son of God!"

³⁴They crossed over the lake and landed at Gennesaret. ³⁵The men who lived there recognized Jesus. So they sent a message all over the nearby countryside. People brought all their sick to Jesus. ³⁶They begged him to let those who were sick just touch the edge of his clothes. And all who touched him were healed.

What Makes People "Unclean"?

15 Some Pharisees and some teachers of the law came from Jerusalem to see Jesus. They asked, ²"Why don't your disciples obey what the elders teach? Your disciples don't wash their hands before they eat!"

³Jesus replied, "And why don't you obey God's command? You would rather follow your own teachings! ⁴God said, 'Honor your father and mother.' *(Exodus 20:12; Deuteronomy 5:16)* He also said, 'If anyone calls down a curse on his father or mother, he will be put to death.' *(Exodus 21:17; Leviticus 20:9)* ⁵But you allow people to say to their parents, 'Any help you might have received from us is a gift set apart for God.' ⁶So they do not need to honor their parents with their gift. You make the word of God useless in order to follow your own teachings.

⁷"You pretenders! Isaiah was right when he prophesied about you. He said,

⁸" 'These people honor me by what
          they say.
     But their hearts are far away from
          me.
⁹Their worship doesn't mean anything
          to me.
     They teach nothing but human
          rules.' "   *(Isaiah 29:13)*

¹⁰Jesus called the crowd to him. He said, "Listen and understand. ¹¹What goes into your mouth does not make you 'unclean.' It's what comes out of your mouth that makes you 'unclean.' "

¹²Then the disciples came to him. They asked, "Do you know that the Pharisees were angry when they heard this?"

POWER-SURGE

BRAVE B

JESUS CALLED OUT
TO THEM, "BE BRAVE!
IT IS I. DON'T BE
AFRAID."
— MATTHEW 14:27 —

PETER

MATTHEW 14:28-29

"Lord, is it you?" Peter asked. "If it is, tell me to come to you on the water."

"Come," Jesus said. So Peter got out of the boat. He walked on the water toward Jesus.

The disciples' boat rocked wildly in the night wind. One wave after another crashed against its sides and splashed over the men inside. They rowed the oars hard, but they couldn't make much distance against such a wind.

One of the disciples peered into the darkness, trying to see if they were close to land yet. Instead of land, he spied a ghostly form walking toward them on the water. With eyes as big as quarters, he screamed and pointed. When the rest of the disciples looked up, they saw it, too. AND THEY YELLED IN FRIGHT, "IT'S A *GHOST!*"

Jesus heard them yelling. With a gentle voice, he called out to them, "Don't be afraid! It's only me!"

The disciples all breathed a sigh of relief that Jesus wasn't a ghost. Peter wondered at how Jesus could walk on water. He wanted to give it a try. "If it's you, Jesus, let me come out to you on the water!" Peter exclaimed. "OK, come," Jesus answered.

Peter didn't hesitate. Looking right at Jesus, he stepped out of the boat onto the water. It felt cool to his feet. And soft, but curiously hard. He didn't sink in. He was walking on water, just like Jesus!

Peter stepped over a small wave, then a larger one, then a huge one came toward him. He watched the wave, taking his eyes off Jesus. And he sank like a rock.

Peter swallowed a huge mouthful of water, then sputtered, "Jesus! Help!" Jesus reached out to Peter and helped him into the boat. "Why didn't you trust me, Peter? You should know I will take care of you."

BE BETTER THAN PETER

Be a Peter. Ask Jesus to save you from your troubles and then let him do all the worrying for you.

PETER TRUSTED JESUS.
THE WHOLE STORY: MATTHEW 14:22-33

Go to page 1129 for the greatest Super Hero

13Jesus replied, "There are plants that my Father in heaven has not planted. They will be pulled up by the roots. 14Leave them. The Pharisees are blind guides. If a blind person leads another who is blind, both of them will fall into a pit."

15Peter said, "Explain this to us."

16"Don't you understand yet?" Jesus asked them. 17"Don't you see? Everything that enters the mouth goes into the stomach. Then it goes out of the body. 18But the things that come out of the mouth come from the heart. Those are the things that make you 'unclean.' 19Evil thoughts come out of the heart. So do murder, adultery, and other sexual sins. And so do stealing, false witness, and telling lies about others. 20Those are the things that make you 'unclean.' But eating without washing your hands does not make you 'unclean.' "

The Faith of a Woman From Canaan

21Jesus left Galilee and went to the area of Tyre and Sidon. 22A woman from Canaan lived near Tyre and Sidon. She came to him and cried out, "Lord! Son of David! Have mercy on me! A demon controls my daughter. She is suffering terribly."

23Jesus did not say a word. So his disciples came to him. They begged him, "Send her away. She keeps crying out after us."

24Jesus answered, "I was sent only to the people of Israel. They are like lost sheep."

25Then the woman fell to her knees in front of him. "Lord! Help me!" she said.

26He replied, "It is not right to take the children's bread and throw it to their dogs."

27"Yes, Lord," she said. "But even the dogs eat the crumbs that fall from their owners' table."

28Then Jesus answered, "Woman, you have great faith! You will be given what you are asking for." And her daughter was healed at that very moment.

Jesus Feeds the Four Thousand

29Jesus left there. He walked along the Sea of Galilee. Then he went up on a mountainside and sat down. 30Large crowds came to him. They brought blind people and those who could not walk. They also brought disabled people, those who could not speak, and many others. They laid them at his feet, and he healed them.

31The people were amazed. Those who could not speak were speaking. The disabled were made well. Those not able to walk were walking. Those who were blind could see. So the people praised the God of Israel.

32Then Jesus called for his disciples to come to him. He said, "I feel deep concern for these people. They have already been with me three days. They don't have anything to eat. I don't want to send them away hungry. If I do, they will become too weak on their way home."

33His disciples answered him. "There is nothing here," they said. "Where could we get enough bread to feed this large crowd?"

34"How many loaves do you have?" Jesus asked.

"Seven," they replied, "and a few small fish."

35Jesus told the crowd to sit down on the ground. 36He took the seven loaves and the fish and gave thanks. Then he broke them and gave them to the disciples. And the disciples passed them out to the people. 37All of them ate and were satisfied. After that, the disciples picked up seven baskets of leftover pieces. 38The number of men who ate was 4,000. Women and children also ate.

39After Jesus had sent the crowd away, he got into the boat. He went to the area near Magadan.

Jesus Is Asked for a Miraculous Sign

16 The Pharisees and Sadducees came to put Jesus to the test. They asked him to show them a miraculous sign from heaven.

BELIEVES ✝

THEN JESUS ANSWERED, "WOMAN, YOU HAVE GREAT FAITH! YOU WILL BE GIVEN WHAT YOU ARE ASKING FOR." AND HER DAUGHTER WAS HEALED AT THAT VERY MOMENT.

— MATTHEW 15:28 —

2He replied, "In the evening you look at the sky. You say, 'It will be good weather. The sky is red.' 3And in the morning you say, 'Today it will be stormy. The sky is red and cloudy.' You know the meaning of what you see in the sky. But you can't understand the signs of what is happening right now. 4An evil and unfaithful people look for a miraculous sign. But none will be given to them except the sign of Jonah."

Then Jesus left them and went away.

The Yeast of the Pharisees and Sadducees

5The disciples crossed over to the other side of the lake. They had forgotten to take bread. 6"Be careful," Jesus said to them. "Watch out for the yeast of the Pharisees and Sadducees."

7The disciples talked about this among themselves. They said, "He must be saying this because we didn't bring any bread."

8Jesus knew what they were saying. So he said, "Your faith is so small! Why are you talking to each other about having no bread? 9Don't you understand yet? Don't you remember the five loaves for the 5,000? Don't you remember how many baskets of pieces you gathered? 10Don't you remember the seven loaves for the 4,000? Don't you remember how many baskets of pieces you gathered? 11How can you possibly not understand? I wasn't talking to you about bread. But watch out for the yeast of the Pharisees and Sadducees."

12Then the disciples understood that Jesus was not telling them to watch out for the yeast used in bread. He was warning them against what the Pharisees and Sadducees taught.

Peter Says That Jesus Is the Christ

13Jesus went to the area of Caesarea Philippi. There he asked his disciples, "Who do people say the Son of Man is?"

14They replied, "Some say John the Baptist. Others say Elijah. Still others say Jeremiah, or one of the prophets."

15"But what about you?" he asked. "Who do you say I am?"

16Simon Peter answered, "You are the Christ. You are the Son of the living God."

17Jesus replied, "Blessed are you, Simon, son of Jonah! No mere man showed this to you. My Father in heaven showed it to you. 18Here is what I tell you. You are Peter. On this rock I will build my church. The gates of hell will not be strong enough to destroy it. 19I will give you the

keys to the kingdom of heaven. What you lock on earth will be locked in heaven. What you unlock on earth will be unlocked in heaven."

20Then Jesus warned his disciples not to tell anyone that he was the Christ.

Jesus Tells About His Coming Death

21From that time on Jesus began to explain to his disciples what would happen to him. He told them he must go to Jerusalem. There he must suffer many things from the elders, the chief priests and the teachers of the law. He must be killed and on the third day rise to life again.

22Peter took Jesus to one side and began to scold him. "Never, Lord!" he said. "This will never happen to you!"

23Jesus turned and said to Peter, "Get behind me, Satan! You are standing in my way. You do not have in mind the things of God. Instead, you are thinking about human things."

24Then Jesus spoke to his disciples. He said, "If anyone wants to follow me, he must say no to himself. He must pick up his cross and follow me. 25If he wants to save his life, he will lose it. But if he loses his life for me, he will find it.

26"What good is it if someone gains the whole world but loses his soul? Or what can anyone trade for his soul? 27The Son of Man is going to come in his Father's glory. His angels will come with him. And he will reward everyone in keeping with what they have done.

28"What I'm about to tell you is true. Some who are standing here will not die before they see the Son of Man coming in his kingdom."

Jesus' Appearance Is Changed

17 After six days Jesus took Peter, James, and John the brother of James with him. He led them up a high mountain. They were all alone. 2There in front of them his appearance was changed. His face shone like the sun. His clothes became as white as the light. 3Just then Moses and Elijah appeared in front of them. Moses and Elijah were talking with Jesus.

4Peter said to Jesus, "Lord, it is good for us to be here. If you wish, I will put up three shelters. One will be for you, one for Moses, and one for Elijah."

5While Peter was still speaking, a bright cloud surrounded them. A voice from the cloud said, "This is my Son, and I love him. I am very pleased with him. Listen to him!"

6When the disciples heard this, they were terrified. They fell with their faces to the ground. **7**But Jesus came and touched them. "Get up," he said. "Don't be afraid." **8**When they looked up, they saw no one except Jesus.

9They came down the mountain. On the way down, Jesus told them what to do. "Don't tell anyone what you have seen," he said. "Wait until the Son of Man has been raised from the dead."

10The disciples asked him, "Why do the teachers of the law say that Elijah has to come first?"

11Jesus replied, "That's right. Elijah is supposed to come and make all things new again. **12**But I tell you, Elijah has already come. People didn't recognize him. They have done to him everything they wanted to do. In the same way, they are going to make the Son of Man suffer."

13Then the disciples understood that Jesus was talking to them about John the Baptist.

Jesus Heals a Boy Who Had a Demon

14When they came near the crowd, a man approached Jesus. He got on his knees in front of him. **15**"Lord," he said, "have mercy on my son. He shakes wildly and suffers a great deal. He often falls into the fire or into the water. **16**I brought him to your disciples. But they couldn't heal him."

17"You unbelieving and evil people!" Jesus replied. "How long do I have to stay with you? How long do I have to put up with you? Bring the boy here to me."

18Jesus ordered the demon to leave the boy, and it came out of him. He was healed at that very moment.

19Then the disciples came to Jesus in private. They asked, "Why couldn't we drive out the demon?"

20/21 He replied, "Because your faith is much too small. What I'm about to tell you is true. If you have faith as small as a mustard seed, it is enough. You can say to this mountain, 'Move from here to there.' And it will move. Nothing will be impossible for you."

22They came together in Galilee. Then Jesus said to them, "The Son of Man is going to be handed over to men. **23**They will kill him. On the third day he will rise from the dead."

Then the disciples were filled with deep sadness.

Jesus Pays the Temple Tax

24Jesus and his disciples arrived in Capernaum. There the tax collectors came to Peter. They asked him, "Doesn't your teacher pay the temple tax?"

25"Yes, he does," he replied.

When Peter came into the house, Jesus spoke first. "What do you think, Simon?" he asked. "Who do the kings of the earth collect taxes and fees from? Do they collect from their own sons or from others?"

26"From others," Peter answered.

"Then the sons don't have to pay," Jesus said to him. **27**"But we don't want to make them angry. So go to the lake and throw out your fishing line. Take the first fish you catch. Open its mouth. There you will find the exact coin you need. Take it and give it to them for my tax and yours."

Who Is the Most Important Person in the Kingdom?

18 At that time the disciples came to Jesus. They asked him, "Who is the most important person in the kingdom of heaven?"

2Jesus called a little child over to him. He had the child stand among them. **3**Jesus said, "What I'm about to tell you is true. You need to change and become like little children. If you don't, you will never enter the kingdom of heaven. **4**Anyone who becomes as free of pride as this child is the most important in the kingdom of heaven.

5"Anyone who welcomes a little child like this in my name welcomes me.

6"But what if someone leads one of these little ones who believe in me to sin? If he does, it would be better for him to have a large millstone hung around his neck and be drowned at the bottom of the sea.

7"How terrible it will be for the world because of the things that lead people to sin! Things like that must come. But how terrible for those who cause them!

8"If your hand or foot causes you to sin, cut it off and throw it away. It would be better for you to enter the kingdom of heaven with only one hand or one foot than to go into hell with two hands and two feet. In hell the fire burns forever. **9**If your eye causes you to sin, poke it out and throw it away. It would be better for you to enter the kingdom of heaven with one eye than to have two eyes and be thrown into the fire of hell.

The Story of the Lost Sheep

10/11"See that you don't look down on

POWER-SURGE

FORGIVING F

PETER CAME TO
JESUS. HE ASKED,
"LORD, HOW MANY
TIMES SHOULD I
FORGIVE MY BROTHER
WHEN HE SINS
AGAINST ME? UP TO
SEVEN TIMES?"

JESUS ANSWERED, "I
TELL YOU, NOT SEVEN
TIMES, BUT 77 TIMES."
— MATTHEW 18:21-22 —

one of these little ones. Here is what I tell you. Their angels in heaven can go at any time to see my Father who is in heaven.

12"What do you think? Suppose a man owns 100 sheep and one of them wanders away. Won't he leave the 99 sheep on the hills? Won't he go and look for the one that wandered off? **13**What I'm about to tell you is true. If he finds that sheep, he is happier about the one than about the 99 that didn't wander off. **14**It is the same with your Father in heaven. He does not want any of these little ones to be lost.

When Someone Sins Against You

15"If your brother sins against you, go to him. Tell him what he did wrong. Keep it between the two of you. If he listens to you, you have won him back.

16"But what if he won't listen to you? Then take one or two others with you. Scripture says, 'Every matter must be proved by the words of two or three witnesses.' *(Deuteronomy 19:15)* **17**But what if he also refuses to listen to the witnesses? Then tell it to the church. And what if he refuses to listen even to the church? Then don't treat him as your brother. Treat him as you would treat an ungodly person or a tax collector.

18"What I'm about to tell you is true. What you lock on earth will be locked in heaven. What you unlock on earth will be unlocked in heaven.

19"Again, here is what I tell you. Suppose two of you on earth agree about anything you ask for. My Father in heaven will do it for you. **20**Where two or three

people meet together in my name, I am there with them."

The Servant Who Had No Mercy

21Peter came to Jesus. He asked, "Lord, how many times should I forgive my brother when he sins against me? Up to seven times?"

22Jesus answered, "I tell you, not seven times, but 77 times.

23"The kingdom of heaven is like a king who wanted to collect all the money his servants owed him. **24**As the king began to do it, a man who owed him millions of dollars was brought to him. **25**The man was not able to pay. So his master gave an order. The man, his wife, his children, and all he owned had to be sold to pay back what he owed.

26"The servant fell on his knees in front of him. 'Give me time,' he begged. 'I'll pay everything back.'

27"His master felt sorry for him. He forgave him what he owed and let him go.

28"But then that servant went out and found one of the other servants who owed him a few dollars. He grabbed him and began to choke him. 'Pay back what you owe me!' he said.

29"The other servant fell on his knees. 'Give me time,' he begged him. 'I'll pay you back.'

30"But the first servant refused. Instead, he went and had the man thrown into prison. The man would be held there until he could pay back what he owed. **31**The other servants saw what had happened. It troubled them greatly. They went and told their master everything that had happened.

32"Then the master called the first servant in. 'You evil servant,' he said. 'I forgave all that you owed me because you begged me to. **33**Shouldn't you have had mercy on the other servant just as I had mercy on you?' **34**In anger his master turned him over to the jailers. He would be punished until he paid back everything he owed.

35"This is how my Father in heaven will treat each of you unless you forgive your brother from your heart."

Jesus Teaches About Divorce

19 When Jesus finished saying these things, he left Galilee. He went into the area of Judea on the other side of the Jordan River. **2**Large crowds followed him. He healed them there.

3Some Pharisees came to put him to the test. They asked, "Does the Law allow a man to divorce his wife for any reason at all?"

⁴Jesus replied, "Haven't you read that in the beginning the Creator 'made them male and female'? *(Genesis 1:27)* ⁵He said, 'That's why a man will leave his father and mother and be joined to his wife. The two will become one.' *(Genesis 2:24)* ⁶They are no longer two, but one. So a man must not separate what God has joined together."

⁷They asked, "Then why did Moses command that a man can give his wife a letter of divorce and send her away?"

⁸Jesus replied, "Moses let you divorce your wives because you were stubborn. But it was not this way from the beginning. ⁹Here is what I tell you. Anyone who divorces his wife and gets married to another woman commits adultery. A man may divorce his wife only if she has not been faithful to him."

¹⁰The disciples said to him, "If that's the way it is between a husband and wife, it is better not to get married."

¹¹Jesus replied, "Not everyone can accept the idea of staying single. Only those who have been helped to live without getting married can accept it. ¹²Some men are not able to have children because they were born that way. Some have been made that way by other people. Others have made themselves that way in order to serve the kingdom of heaven. The one who can accept living that way should do it."

Little Children Are Brought to Jesus

¹³Some people brought little children to Jesus. They wanted him to place his hands on the children and pray for them. But the disciples told the people to stop.

¹⁴Jesus said, "Let the little children come to me. Don't keep them away. The kingdom of heaven belongs to people like them." ¹⁵Jesus placed his hands on them. Then he went on from there.

POWER-SURGE

FORGIVING F

FORGIVE YOUR BROTHER FROM YOUR HEART.
— MATTHEW 18:35 —

Jesus and the Rich Young Man

¹⁶A man came up to Jesus. He asked, "Teacher, what good thing must I do to receive eternal life?"

¹⁷"Why do you ask me about what is good?" Jesus replied. "There is only One who is good. If you want to enter the kingdom, obey the commandments."

¹⁸"Which ones?" the man asked.

Jesus said, " 'Do not commit murder. Do not commit adultery. Do not steal. Do not give false witness. ¹⁹Honor your father and mother.' *(Exodus 20:12-16; Deuteronomy 5:16–20)* And 'love your neighbor as you love yourself.' " *(Leviticus 19:18)*

²⁰"I have obeyed all those commandments," the young man said. "What else do I need to do?"

²¹Jesus answered, "If you want to be perfect, go and sell everything you have. Give the money to those who are poor. You will have treasure in heaven. Then come and follow me."

²²When the young man heard this, he went away sad. He was very rich.

²³Then Jesus said to his disciples, "What I'm about to tell you is true. It is hard for rich people to enter the kingdom of heaven. ²⁴Again I tell you, it is hard for a camel to go through the eye of a needle. But it is even harder for the rich to enter God's kingdom."

²⁵When the disciples heard this, they were really amazed. They asked, "Then who can be saved?"

²⁶Jesus looked at them and said, "With man, that is impossible. But with God, all things are possible."

²⁷Peter answered him, "We have left everything to follow you! What reward will be given to us?"

²⁸"What I'm about to tell you is true," Jesus said to them. "When all things are made new, the Son of Man will sit on his glorious throne. Then you who have followed me will also sit on 12 thrones. You will judge the 12 tribes of Israel. ²⁹Everyone who has left houses or families or fields because of me will receive 100 times as much. They will also receive eternal life. ³⁰But many who are first will be last. And many who are last will be first.

The Story of the Workers in the Vineyard

20 "The kingdom of heaven is like a man who owned land. He went out early in the morning to hire people to work in his vineyard. ²He agreed to give them the usual pay for a day's work. Then he sent them into his vineyard.

3 "About nine o'clock in the morning he went out again. He saw others standing in the market place doing nothing. **4** He told them, 'You also go and work in my vineyard. I'll pay you what is right.' **5** So they went.

"He went out again about noon and at three o'clock and did the same thing. **6** About five o'clock he went out and found still others standing around. He asked them, 'Why have you been standing here all day long doing nothing?'

7 " 'Because no one has hired us,' they answered.

"He said to them, 'You also go and work in my vineyard.'

8 "When evening came, the owner of the vineyard spoke to the person who was in charge of the workers. He said, 'Call the workers and give them their pay. Begin with the last ones I hired. Then go on to the first ones.'

9 "The workers who were hired about five o'clock came. Each received the usual day's pay. **10** So when those who were hired first came, they expected to receive more. But each of them also received the usual day's pay.

11 "When they received it, they began to complain about the owner. **12** 'These people who were hired last worked only one hour,' they said. 'You have paid them the same as us. We have done most of the work and have been in the hot sun all day.'

13 "The owner answered one of them. 'Friend,' he said, 'I'm being fair to you. Didn't you agree to work for the usual day's pay? **14** Take your money and go. I want to give the ones I hired last the same pay I gave you. **15** Don't I have the right to do what I want with my own money? Do you feel cheated because I gave so freely to the others?'

16 "So those who are last will be first. And those who are first will be last."

Jesus Again Tells About His Coming Death

17 Jesus was going up to Jerusalem. On the way, he took the 12 disciples to one side to talk to them.

18 "We are going up to Jerusalem," he said. "The Son of Man will be handed over to the chief priests and the teachers of the law. They will sentence him to death. **19** Then they will turn him over to people who are not Jews. The people will make fun of him and whip him. They will nail him to a cross. On the third day, he will rise from the dead!"

A Mother Asks a Favor of Jesus

20 The mother of Zebedee's sons came to Jesus. Her sons came with her. Getting on her knees, she asked a favor of him.

21 "What do you want?" Jesus asked.

She said, "Promise me that one of my two sons may sit at your right hand in your kingdom. Promise that the other one may sit at your left hand."

22 "You don't know what you're asking for," Jesus said to them. "Can you drink the cup of suffering I am going to drink?"

"We can," they answered.

23 Jesus said to them, "You will certainly drink from my cup. But it is not for me to say who will sit at my right or left hand. These places belong to those my Father has prepared them for."

24 The other ten disciples heard about this. They became angry at the two brothers.

25 Jesus called them together. He said, "You know about the rulers of the nations. They hold power over their people. Their high officials order them around. **26** Don't be like that. Instead, anyone who wants to be important among you must be your servant. **27** And anyone who wants to be first must be your slave.

28 "Be like the Son of Man. He did not come to be served. Instead, he came to serve others. He came to give his life as the price for setting many people free."

Two Blind Men Receive Their Sight

29 Jesus and his disciples were leaving Jericho. A large crowd followed him. **30** Two blind men were sitting by the side of the road. They heard that Jesus was going by. So they shouted, "Lord! Son of David! Have mercy on us!"

31 The crowd commanded them to stop. They told them to be quiet. But the two men shouted even louder, "Lord! Son of David! Have mercy on us!"

32 Jesus stopped and called out to them. "What do you want me to do for you?" he asked.

33 "Lord," they answered, "we want to be able to see."

34 Jesus felt deep concern for them. He touched their eyes. Right away they could see. And they followed him.

Jesus Enters Jerusalem

21 As they all approached Jerusalem, they came to Bethphage. It was on the Mount of Olives. Jesus sent out two disciples. **2** He said to them, "Go to the village ahead of you. As soon as you get there, you will find a donkey tied up. Her colt will be with her. Untie them and bring them to me. 3If anyone says anything to you, say that the Lord needs them. The owner will send them right away."

4This took place so that what was spoken through the prophet would come true. It says,

5 "Say to the city of Zion,
  'See, your king comes to you.
He is gentle and riding on a donkey.
  He is riding on a donkey's colt.' "

(Zechariah 9:9)

6The disciples went and did what Jesus told them to do. 7They brought the donkey and the colt. They placed their coats on them. Then Jesus sat on the coats. 8A very large crowd spread their coats on the road. Others cut branches from the trees and spread them on the road. 9Some of the people went ahead of him, and some followed. They all shouted,

"Hosanna to the Son of David!"

"Blessed is the one who comes in the name of the Lord!"

(Psalm 118:26)

"Hosanna in the highest heaven!"

10When Jesus entered Jerusalem, the whole city was stirred up. The people asked, "Who is this?"

11The crowds answered, "This is Jesus. He is the prophet from Nazareth in Galilee."

Jesus Clears Out the Temple

12Jesus entered the temple area. He began chasing out all those who were buying and selling there. He turned over the tables of the people who were exchanging money. He also turned over the benches of those who were selling doves. 13He said to them, "It is written that the Lord said, 'My house will be called a house where people can pray.' *(Isaiah 56:7)* But you are making it a 'den for robbers.' " *(Jeremiah 7:11)*

14Blind people and those who were disabled came to Jesus at the temple. There he healed them. 15The chief priests and the teachers of the law saw the wonderful things he did. They also saw the children in the temple area shouting, "Hosanna to the Son of David!" But when they saw all of this, they became angry.

16"Do you hear what these children are saying?" they asked him.

"Yes," replied Jesus. "Haven't you ever read about it in Scripture? It says,

" 'You have made sure that children and infants
  praise you.' " *(Psalm 8:2)*

17Then Jesus left the people and went out of the city to Bethany. He spent the night there.

The Fig Tree Dries Up

18Early in the morning, Jesus was on his way back to Jerusalem. He was hungry. 19He saw a fig tree by the road. He went up to it but found nothing on it except leaves. Then he said to it, "May you never bear fruit again!" Right away the tree dried up.

20When the disciples saw this, they were amazed. "How did the fig tree dry up so quickly?" they asked.

21Jesus replied, "What I'm about to tell you is true. You must have faith and not doubt. Then you can do what was done to the fig tree. And you can say to this mountain, 'Go and throw yourself into the sea.' It will be done. 22If you believe, you will receive what you ask for when you pray."

POWER - SURGE

BELIEVES ✝

YOU MUST HAVE FAITH AND NOT DOUBT. THEN... YOU CAN SAY TO THIS MOUNTAIN, "GO AND THROW YOURSELF INTO THE SEA." IT WILL BE DONE. IF YOU BELIEVE, YOU WILL RECEIVE WHAT YOU ASK FOR WHEN YOU PRAY.
— MATTHEW 21:21-22 —

The Authority of Jesus Is Questioned

23Jesus entered the temple courtyard. While he was teaching there, the chief priests and the elders of the people came to him. "By what authority are you doing these things?" they asked. "Who gave you this authority?"

24Jesus replied, "I will also ask you one question. If you answer me, I will tell you by what authority I am doing these things. 25Where did John's baptism come from? Was it from heaven? Or did it come from men?"

They talked to each other about it. They said, "If we say, 'From heaven,' he will ask, 'Then why didn't you believe him?' 26But what if we say, 'From men'? We are afraid of the people. Everyone believes that John was a prophet."

27So they answered Jesus, "We don't know."

Jesus said, "Then I won't tell you by what authority I am doing these things either.

The Story of the Two Sons

28"What do you think about this? A man had two sons. He went to the first and said, 'Son, go and work today in the vineyard.'

29" 'I will not,' the son answered. But later he changed his mind and went.

30"Then the father went to the other son. He said the same thing. The son answered, 'I will, sir.' But he did not go.

31"Which of the two sons did what his father wanted?"

"The first," they answered.

Jesus said to them, "What I'm about to tell you is true. Tax collectors and prostitutes will enter the kingdom of God ahead of you. 32John came to show you the right way to live. And you did not believe him. But the tax collectors and the prostitutes did. You saw this. But even then you did not turn away from your sins and believe him.

POWER-SURGE

BELIEVES ✝

JOHN CAME TO SHOW YOU THE RIGHT WAY TO LIVE. AND YOU DID NOT BELIEVE HIM. BUT THE TAX COLLECTORS AND THE PROSTITUTES DID. YOU SAW THIS. BUT EVEN THEN YOU DID NOT TURN AWAY FROM YOUR SINS AND BELIEVE HIM.

— MATTHEW 21:32 —

The Story of the Renters

33"Listen to another story. A man who owned some land planted a vineyard. He put a wall around it. He dug a pit for a winepress in it. He also built a lookout tower. He rented the vineyard out to some farmers. Then he went away on a journey. 34When harvest time approached, he sent his servants to the renters. He told the servants to collect his share of the fruit.

35"But the renters grabbed his servants. They beat one of them. They killed another. They threw stones at the third to kill him. 36Then the man sent other servants to the renters. He sent more than he did the first time. The renters treated them the same way.

37"Last of all, he sent his son to them. 'They will respect my son,' he said.

38"But the renters saw the son coming. They said to each other, 'This is the one who will receive all the owner's property someday. Come, let's kill him. Then everything will be ours.' 39So they took him and threw him out of the vineyard. Then they killed him.

40"When the owner of the vineyard comes back, what will he do to those renters?"

41"He will destroy those evil people," they replied. "Then he will rent the vineyard out to other renters. They will give him his share of the crop at harvest time."

42Jesus said to them, "Haven't you ever read what the Scriptures say,

" 'The stone the builders didn't accept
has become the most important
stone of all.
The Lord has done it.
It is wonderful in our eyes'?
(Psalm 118:22,23)

43"So here is what I tell you. The kingdom of God will be taken away from you. It will be given to people who will produce its fruit. 44Everyone who falls on that stone will be broken to pieces. But the stone will crush anyone it falls on."

45The chief priests and the Pharisees heard Jesus' stories. They knew he was talking about them. 46So they looked for a way to arrest him. But they were afraid of the crowd. The people believed that Jesus was a prophet.

The Story of the Wedding Dinner

22 Jesus told them more stories. He said, 2"Here is what the kingdom of heaven is like. A king prepared a wedding dinner for his son. 3He sent his servants to those who had been invited to

the dinner. The servants told them to come. But they refused.

4"Then he sent some more servants. He said, 'Tell those who were invited that I have prepared my dinner. I have killed my oxen and my fattest cattle. Everything is ready. Come to the wedding dinner.'

5"But the people paid no attention. One went away to his field. Another went away to his business. 6The rest grabbed his servants. They treated them badly and then killed them.

7"The king became very angry. He sent his army to destroy them. They killed those murderers and burned their city.

8"Then the king said to his servants, 'The wedding dinner is ready. But those I invited were not fit to come. 9Go to the street corners. Invite to the dinner anyone you can find.' 10So the servants went out into the streets. They gathered all the people they could find, both good and bad. Soon the wedding hall was filled with guests.

11"The king came in to see the guests. He noticed a man there who was not wearing wedding clothes. 12'Friend,' he asked, 'how did you get in here without wedding clothes?' The man couldn't think of anything to say.

13"Then the king told his servants, 'Tie up his hands and feet. Throw him outside into the darkness. Out there people will sob and grind their teeth.'

14"Many are invited, but few are chosen."

Is It Right to Pay Taxes to Caesar?

15The Pharisees went out. They made plans to trap Jesus with his own words. 16They sent their followers to him. They sent the Herodians with them.

"Teacher," they said, "we know you are a man of honor. You teach the way of God truthfully. You don't let others tell you what to do or say. You don't care how important they are. 17Tell us then, what do you think? Is it right to pay taxes to Caesar or not?"

18But Jesus knew their evil plans. He said, "You pretenders! Why are you trying to trap me? 19Show me the coin people use for paying the tax."

They brought him a silver coin. 20He asked them, "Whose picture is this? And whose words?"

21"Caesar's," they replied.

Then he said to them, "Give to Caesar what belongs to Caesar. And give to God what belongs to God."

22When they heard this, they were amazed. So they left him and went away.

Marriage When the Dead Rise

23That same day the Sadducees came to Jesus with a question. They do not believe that people rise from the dead.

24"Teacher," they said, "here is what Moses told us. If a man dies without having children, his brother must get married to the widow. He must have children to carry on his brother's name. 25There were seven brothers among us. The first one got married and died. Since he had no children, he left his wife to his brother. 26The same thing happened to the second and third brothers. It happened right on down to the seventh brother. 27Finally, the woman died. 28Now then, when the dead rise, whose wife will she be? All seven of them were married to her."

29Jesus replied, "You are mistaken, because you do not know the Scriptures. And you do not know the power of God. 30When the dead rise, they won't get married. And their parents won't give them to be married. They will be like the angels in heaven.

31"What about the dead rising? Haven't you read what God said to you? 32He said, 'I am the God of Abraham. I am the God of Isaac. And I am the God of Jacob.' (Exodus 3:6) He is not the God of the dead. He is the God of the living."

33When the crowds heard this, they were amazed by what he taught.

The Most Important Commandment

34The Pharisees heard that the Sadducees weren't able to answer Jesus. So the Pharisees got together. 35One of them was an authority on the law. So he tested Jesus with a question. 36"Teacher," he asked, "which is the most important commandment in the Law?"

37Jesus replied, " 'Love the Lord your God with all your heart and with all your soul. Love him with all your mind.' (Deuteronomy 6:5) 38This is the first and most important commandment. 39And the second is like it. 'Love your neighbor as you love yourself.' (Leviticus 19:18) 40Everything that is written in the Law and the Prophets is based on these two commandments."

Whose Son Is the Christ?

41The Pharisees were gathered together. Jesus asked them, 42"What do you think about the Christ? Whose son is he?"

"The son of David," they replied.

43He said to them, "Then why does David call him 'Lord'? The Holy Spirit spoke through David himself. David said,

44 " 'The Lord said to my Lord,
"Sit at my right hand
until I put your enemies
under your control." ' *(Psalm 110:1)*

45So if David calls him 'Lord,' how can he be David's son?"

46No one could answer him with a single word. From that day on, no one dared to ask him any more questions.

Jesus Judges the Pharisees and the Teachers of the Law

23 Jesus spoke to the crowds and to his disciples. **2**"The teachers of the law and the Pharisees sit in Moses' seat," he said. **3**"So you must obey them. Do everything they tell you. But don't do what they do. They don't practice what they preach. **4**They tie up heavy loads and put them on other people's shoulders. But they themselves aren't willing to lift a finger to move them.

5 "Everything they do is done for others to see. On their foreheads and arms they wear little boxes that hold Scripture verses. They make the boxes very wide. And they make the tassels on their coats very long.

6"They love to sit down in the place of honor at dinners. They also love to have the most important seats in the synagogues. **7**They love to be greeted in the market places. They love it when people call them 'Rabbi.'

8"But you shouldn't be called 'Rabbi.' You have only one Master, and you are all brothers. **9**Do not call anyone on earth 'father.' You have one Father, and he is in heaven. **10**You shouldn't be called 'teacher.' You have one Teacher, and he is the Christ. **11**The most important person among you will be your servant. **12**Anyone who lifts himself up will be brought down. And anyone who is brought down will be lifted up.

13/14"How terrible it will be for you, teachers of the law and Pharisees! You pretenders! You shut the kingdom of heaven in people's faces. You yourselves do not enter. And you will not let those enter who are trying to.

15"How terrible for you, teachers of the law and Pharisees! You pretenders! You travel everywhere to win one person to your faith. Then you make him twice as much a son of hell as you are.

16"How terrible for you, blind guides! You say, 'If anyone takes an oath in the name of the temple, it means nothing. But anyone who takes an oath in the name of the gold of the temple must keep the oath.' **17**You are blind and foolish! Which is more important? Is it the gold? Or is it the temple that makes the gold holy?

18"You also say, 'If anyone takes an oath in the name of the altar, it means nothing. But anyone who takes an oath in the name of the gift on it must keep the oath.' **19**You blind men! Which is more important? Is it the gift? Or is it the altar that makes the gift holy?

20"So anyone who takes an oath in the name of the altar takes an oath in the name of it and of everything on it. **21**And anyone who takes an oath in the name of the temple takes an oath in the name of it and of the One who lives in it. **22**And anyone who takes an oath in the name of heaven takes an oath in the name of God's throne and of the One who sits on it.

23"How terrible for you, teachers of the law and Pharisees! You pretenders! You give God a tenth of your spices, like mint, dill and cummin. But you have not practiced the more important things of the law, like fairness, mercy and faithfulness. You should have practiced the last things without failing to do the first. **24**You blind guides! You remove the smallest insect from your food. But you swallow a whole camel!

25"How terrible for you, teachers of the law and Pharisees! You pretenders! You clean the outside of the cup and dish. But on the inside you are full of greed. You only want to satisfy yourselves. **26**Blind Pharisee! First clean the inside of the cup and dish. Then the outside will also be clean.

27"How terrible for you, teachers of the law and Pharisees! You pretenders! You are like tombs that are painted white. They look beautiful on the outside. But on the inside they are full of the bones of the dead. They are also full of other things that are not pure and clean. **28**It is the same with you. On the outside you seem to be doing what is right. But on the inside you are full of what is wrong. You pretend to be what you are not.

29"How terrible for you, teachers of the law and Pharisees! You pretenders! You build tombs for the prophets. You decorate the graves of the godly. **30**And you say, 'If we had lived in the days of those who lived before us, we wouldn't have done what they did. We wouldn't have helped to kill the prophets.' [31]So you give witness against yourselves. You admit that you are the children of those who murdered the prophets. [32]So finish the sins that those who lived before you started!

[33]"You nest of poisonous snakes! How will you escape from being sentenced to hell? [34]So I am sending you prophets, wise men, and teachers. You will kill some of them. You will nail some to a cross. Others you will whip in your synagogues. You will chase them from town to town.

[35]"So you will pay for all the godly people's blood spilled on earth. I mean from the blood of godly Abel to the blood of Zechariah, the son of Berekiah. Zechariah was the one you murdered between the temple and the altar. [36]What I'm about to tell you is true. All this will happen to those who are now living.

[37]"Jerusalem! Jerusalem! You kill the prophets and throw stones in order to kill those who are sent to you. Many times I have wanted to gather your people together. I have wanted to be like a hen who gathers her chicks under her wings. But you would not let me! [38]Look, your house is left empty. [39]I tell you, you will not see me again until you say, 'Blessed is the one who comes in the name of the Lord.' "
(Psalm 118:26)

Signs of the End

24 Jesus left the temple. He was walking away when his disciples came up to him. They wanted to call his attention to the temple buildings.

[2]"Do you see all these things?" Jesus asked. "What I'm about to tell you is true. Not one stone here will be left on top of another. Every stone will be thrown down."

[3]Jesus was sitting on the Mount of Olives. There the disciples came to him in private. "Tell us," they said. "When will this happen? And what will be the sign of your coming? What will be the sign of the end?"

[4]Jesus answered, "Keep watch! Be careful that no one fools you. [5]Many will come in my name. They will claim, 'I am the Christ!' They will fool many people.

[6]"You will hear about wars. You will also hear people talking about future wars. Don't be alarmed. Those things must happen. But the end still isn't here. [7]Nation will fight against nation. King-

dom will fight against kingdom. People will go hungry. There will be earthquakes in many places. [8]All these are the beginning of birth pains.

[9]"Then people will hand you over to be treated badly and killed. All nations will hate you because of me. [10]At that time, many will turn away from their faith. They will hate each other. They will hand each other over to their enemies. [11]Many false prophets will appear. They will fool many people. [12]Because evil will grow, most people's love will grow cold. [13]But the one who stands firm to the end will be saved. [14]This good news of the kingdom will be preached in the whole world. It will be a witness to all nations. Then the end will come.

[15]"The prophet Daniel spoke about 'the hated thing that destroys.' *(Daniel 9:27; 11:31; 12:11)* Someday you will see it standing in the holy place. The reader should understand this. [16]Then those who are in Judea should escape to the mountains. [17]No one on the roof should go down into his house to take anything out. [18]No one in the field should go back to get his coat. [19]How awful it will be in those days for pregnant women! How awful for nursing mothers! [20]Pray that you will not have to escape in winter or on the Sabbath day. [21]There will be terrible suffering in those days. It will be worse than any other from the beginning of the world until now. And there will never be anything like it again. [22]If the time had not been cut short, no one would live. But because of God's chosen people, it will be shortened.

[23]"At that time someone may say to you, 'Look! Here is the Christ!' Or, 'There he is!' Do not believe it. [24]False Christs and false prophets will appear. They will do great signs and miracles. They will try to fool God's chosen people if possible. [25]See, I have told you ahead of time.

[26]"So if anyone tells you, 'He is far out in the desert,' do not go out there. Or if anyone says, 'He is deep inside the house,' do not believe it. [27]Lightning that comes from the east can be seen in the west. It will be the same when the Son of Man comes. [28]The vultures will gather wherever there is a dead body.

[29]"Right after the terrible suffering of those days,

" 'The sun will be darkened.
    The moon will not shine.
The stars will fall from the sky.
    The heavenly bodies will be shaken.'
(Isaiah 13:10; 34:4)

30"At that time the sign of the Son of Man will appear in the sky. All the nations on earth will be sad. They will see the Son of Man coming on the clouds of the sky. He will come with power and great glory. **31**He will send his angels with a loud trumpet call. They will gather his chosen people from all four directions. They will bring them from one end of the heavens to the other.

32"Learn a lesson from the fig tree. As soon as its twigs get tender and its leaves come out, you know that summer is near. **33**In the same way, when you see all those things happening, you know that the end is near. It is right at the door. **34**What I'm about to tell you is true. The people living at that time will certainly not pass away until all those things have happened. **35**Heaven and earth will pass away. But my words will never pass away.

The Day and Hour Are Not Known

36"No one knows about that day or hour. Not even the angels in heaven know. The Son does not know. Only the Father knows.

37"Remember how it was in the days of Noah. It will be the same when the Son of Man comes.

38"In the days before the flood, people were eating and drinking. They were getting married. They were giving their daughters to be married. They did all those things right up to the day Noah entered the ark. **39**They knew nothing about what would happen until the flood came and took them all away. That is how it will be when the Son of Man comes.

40"Two men will be in the field. One will be taken and the other left. **41**Two women will be grinding with a hand mill. One will be taken and the other left.

42"So keep watch. You do not know on what day your Lord will come. **43**You must understand something. Suppose the owner of the house knew what time of night the robber was coming. Then he would have kept watch. He would not have let his house be broken into. **44**So you also must be ready. The Son of Man will come at an hour when you don't expect him.

45"Suppose a master puts one of his servants in charge of the other servants in his house. The servant's job is to give them their food at the right time. The master wants a faithful and wise servant for this. **46**It will be good for the servant if the master finds him doing his job when the master returns. **47**What I'm about to tell you is true. The master will put that servant in charge of everything he owns.

48"But suppose that servant is evil. Suppose he says to himself, 'My master is staying away a long time.' **49**Suppose he begins to beat the other servants. And suppose he eats and drinks with those who drink too much. **50**The master of that servant will come back on a day the servant doesn't expect him. He will return at an hour the servant does not know. **51**Then the master will cut him to pieces. He will send him to the place where pretenders go. There people will sob and grind their teeth.

The Story of Ten Bridesmaids

25 "Here is what the kingdom of heaven will be like at that time. Ten bridesmaids took their lamps and went out to meet the groom. **2**Five of them were foolish. Five were wise. **3**The foolish ones took their lamps but didn't take any olive oil with them. **4**The wise ones took oil in jars along with their lamps. **5**The groom did not come for a long time. So the bridesmaids all grew tired and fell asleep.

6"At midnight someone cried out, 'Here's the groom! Come out to meet him!'

7"Then all the bridesmaids woke up and got their lamps ready. **8**The foolish ones said to the wise ones, 'Give us some of your oil. Our lamps are going out.'

9" 'No,' they replied. 'There may not be enough for all of us. Instead, go to those who sell oil. Buy some for yourselves.'

10"So they went to buy the oil. But while they were on their way, the groom arrived. The bridesmaids who were ready went in with him to the wedding dinner. Then the door was shut.

11"Later, the other bridesmaids also came. 'Sir! Sir!' they said. 'Open the door for us!'

12"But he replied, 'What I'm about to tell you is true. I don't know you.'

13"So keep watch. You do not know the day or the hour that the groom will come.

The Story of Three Servants

14"Again, here is what the kingdom of heaven will be like. A man was going on a journey. He sent for his servants and put them in charge of his property. **15**He gave $10,000 to one. He gave $4,000 to another. And he gave $2,000 to the third. The man gave each servant the amount of money he knew the servant could take care of. Then he went on his journey.

16"The servant who had received the $10,000 went at once and put his money to work. He earned $10,000 more. **17**The one with the $4,000 earned $4,000 more. **18**But the man who had received $2,000 went and dug a hole in the ground. He hid his master's money in it.

19"After a long time the master of those servants returned. He wanted to collect all the money they had earned. **20**The man who had received $10,000 brought the other $10,000. 'Master,' he said, 'you trusted me with $10,000. See, I have earned $10,000 more.'

21"His master replied, 'You have done well, good and faithful servant! You have been faithful with a few things. I will put you in charge of many things. Come and share your master's happiness!'

22"The man with $4,000 also came. 'Master,' he said, 'you trusted me with $4,000. See, I have earned $4,000 more.'

23"His master replied, 'You have done well, good and faithful servant! You have been faithful with a few things. I will put you in charge of many things. Come and share your master's happiness!'

24"Then the man who had received $2,000 came. 'Master,' he said, 'I knew that you are a hard man. You harvest where you have not planted. You gather crops where you have not scattered seed. **25**So I was afraid. I went out and hid your $2,000 in the ground. See, here is what belongs to you.'

26"His master replied, 'You evil, lazy servant! So you knew that I harvest where I have not planted? You knew that I gather crops where I have not scattered seed? **27**Well then, you should have put my money in the bank. When I returned, I would have received it back with interest.'

28"Then his master commanded the other servants, 'Take the $2,000 from him. Give it to the one who has $20,000. **29**Everyone who has will be given more. He will have more than enough. And what about anyone who doesn't have? Even what he has will be taken away from him. **30**Throw that worthless servant outside. There in the darkness, people will sob and grind their teeth.'

The Sheep and the Goats

31"The Son of Man will come in all his glory. All the angels will come with him. Then he will sit on his throne in the glory of heaven. **32**All the nations will be gathered in front of him. He will separate the people into two groups. He will be like a shepherd who separates the sheep from the goats. **33**He will put the sheep to his right and the goats to his left.

34"Then the King will speak to those on his right. He will say, 'My Father has blessed you. Come and take what is yours. It is the kingdom prepared for you since the world was created. **35**I was hungry. And you gave me something to eat. I was thirsty. And you gave me something to drink. I was a stranger. And you invited me in. **36**I needed clothes. And you gave them to me. I was sick. And you took care of me. I was in prison. And you came to visit me.'

37"Then the people who have done what is right will answer him. 'Lord,' they will ask, 'when did we see you hungry and feed you? When did we see you thirsty and give you something to drink? **38**When did we see you as a stranger and invite you in? When did we see you needing clothes and give them to you? **39**When did we see you sick or in prison and go to visit you?'

40"The King will reply, 'What I'm about to tell you is true. Anything you did for one of the least important of these brothers of mine, you did for me.'

41"Then he will say to those on his left, 'You are cursed! Go away from me into the fire that burns forever. It has been prepared for the devil and his angels. **42**I was hungry. But you gave me nothing to eat. I was thirsty. But you gave me nothing to drink. **43**I was a stranger. But you did not invite me in. I needed clothes. But you did not give me any. I was sick and in prison. But you did not take care of me.'

44"They also will answer, 'Lord, when did we see you hungry or thirsty and not help you? When did we see you as a stranger or needing clothes or sick or in prison and not help you?'

45"He will reply, 'What I'm about to tell you is true. Anything you didn't do for one of the least important of these, you didn't do for me.'

46"Then they will go away to be punished forever. But those who have done what is right will receive eternal life."

The Plan to Kill Jesus

26 Jesus finished saying all these things. Then he said to his disciples, **2**"As you know, the Passover Feast is two days away. The Son of Man will be handed over to be nailed to a cross."

3Then the chief priests met with the elders of the people. They met in the palace of Caiaphas, the high priest. **4**They made plans to arrest Jesus in a clever way.

They wanted to kill him. 5"But not during the Feast," they said. "The people may stir up trouble."

A Woman Pours Perfume on Jesus

6Jesus was in Bethany. He was in the home of a man named Simon, who had a skin disease. 7A woman came to Jesus with a special sealed jar of very expensive perfume. She poured the perfume on his head while he was at the table.

8When the disciples saw this, they became angry. "Why this waste?" they asked. 9"The perfume could have been sold at a high price. The money could have been given to poor people."

10Jesus was aware of this. So he said to them, "Why are you bothering this woman? She has done a beautiful thing to me. 11You will always have poor people with you. But you will not always have me. 12She poured the perfume on my body to prepare me to be buried. 13What I'm about to tell you is true. What she has done will be told anywhere this good news is preached all over the world. It will be told in memory of her."

Judas Agrees to Hand Jesus Over

14One of the Twelve went to the chief priests. His name was Judas Iscariot. 15He asked, "What will you give me if I hand Jesus over to you?" So they counted out 30 silver coins for him. 16From then on, Judas watched for the right time to hand Jesus over to them.

The Lord's Supper

17It was the first day of the Feast of Unleavened Bread. The disciples came to Jesus. They asked, "Where do you want us to prepare for you to eat the Passover meal?"

18He replied, "Go into the city to a certain man. Tell him, 'The Teacher says, "My time is near. I am going to celebrate the Passover at your house with my disciples." ' "

19So the disciples did what Jesus had told them to do. They prepared the Passover meal.

20When evening came, Jesus was at the table with the Twelve. 21While they were eating, he said, "What I'm about to tell you is true. One of you will hand me over to my enemies."

22The disciples became very sad. One after the other, they began to say to him, "It's not I, Lord, is it?"

23Jesus replied, "The one who has dipped his hand into the bowl with me will hand me over. 24The Son of Man will go just as it is written about him. But how terrible it will be for the one who hands over the Son of Man! It would be better for him if he had not been born."

25Judas was the one who was going to hand him over. He said, "It's not I, Rabbi, is it?"

Jesus answered, "Yes. It is you."

26While they were eating, Jesus took bread. He gave thanks and broke it. He handed it to his disciples and said, "Take this and eat it. This is my body."

27Then he took the cup. He gave thanks and handed it to them. He said, "All of you drink from it. 28This is my blood of the new covenant. It is poured out to forgive the sins of many. 29Here is what I tell you. From now on, I won't drink wine with you again until the day I drink it with you in my Father's kingdom."

30Then they sang a hymn and went out to the Mount of Olives.

Jesus Says That Peter Will Fail

31Jesus told them, "This very night you will all turn away because of me. It is written that the Lord said,

" 'I will strike the shepherd down.
    Then the sheep of the flock will be
        scattered.'   *(Zechariah 13:7)*

32But after I rise from the dead, I will go ahead of you into Galilee."

33Peter replied, "All the others may turn away because of you. But I never will."

34"What I'm about to tell you is true," Jesus answered. "It will happen this very night. Before the rooster crows, you will say three times that you don't know me."

35But Peter said, "I may have to die with you. But I will never say I don't know you." And all the other disciples said the same thing.

Jesus Prays in Gethsemane

36Then Jesus went with his disciples to a place called Gethsemane. He said to them, "Sit here while I go over there and pray."

37He took Peter and the two sons of Zebedee along with him. He began to be sad and troubled. 38Then he said to them, "My soul is very sad. I feel close to death. Stay here. Keep watch with me."

39He went a little farther. Then he fell with his face to the ground. He prayed, "My Father, if it is possible, take this cup of suffering away from me. But let what you want be done, not what I want."

40Then he returned to his disciples and

found them sleeping. "Couldn't you men keep watch with me for one hour?" he asked Peter. **41**"Watch and pray. Then you won't fall into sin when you are tempted. The spirit is willing. But the body is weak."

42Jesus went away a second time. He prayed, "My Father, is it possible for this cup to be taken away? But if I must drink it, may what you want be done."

43Then he came back. Again he found them sleeping. They couldn't keep their eyes open. **44**So he left them and went away once more. For the third time he prayed the same thing.

45Then he returned to the disciples. He said to them, "Are you still sleeping and resting? Look! The hour is near. The Son of Man is about to be handed over to sinners. **46**Get up! Let us go! Here comes the one who is handing me over to them!"

Jesus Is Arrested

47While Jesus was still speaking, Judas arrived. He was one of the Twelve. A large

---

JESUS SUFFERS

MATTHEW 26:39

✔ **Then he fell with his face to the ground. He prayed, "My Father, if it is possible, take this cup of suffering away from me. But let what you want be done, not what I want."**

T he sky was dark with few stars. Jesus walked with three of his disciples in a garden. When they came to a clearing, the disciples sat on the ground to rest. Jesus sighed and said to them, "I'm so tired and sad. I know I'm going to die. I'm going to pray. Will you pray with me?"

Leaving the disciples, Jesus went just a little ways away. He fell on the ground and began to pray.

"Father, I know what you have planned for me. I'm scared. Are you sure this is the only way? Must I really die? **BUT I DON'T WANT MY WILL, FATHER. I WANT YOURS."**

When Jesus finished praying, he went back to his disciples. And he found them sleeping! They couldn't stay awake and pray with him. Jesus prayed and suffered all alone in the garden. Not even his friends were there to help him.

BE LIKE JESUS

No matter what the future would be like, no matter how hard or painful, Jesus wanted to do God's will. He was willing to suffer and die because that was the only way we could be saved. Doing God's will isn't always easy. But it *is* always best. So be like Jesus and be willing to do God's will.

JESUS WANTED TO DO GOD'S WILL EVEN THOUGH IT WAS HARD.

Go to page 1132 for the next person

crowd was with him. They were carrying swords and clubs. The chief priests and the elders of the people had sent them.

48Judas, who was going to hand Jesus over, had arranged a signal with them. "The one I kiss is the man," he said. "Arrest him."

49So Judas went to Jesus at once. He said, "Greetings, Rabbi!" And he kissed him.

50Jesus replied, "Friend, do what you came to do."

Then the men stepped forward. They grabbed Jesus and arrested him. **51**At that moment, one of Jesus' companions reached for his sword. He pulled it out and struck the servant of the high priest with it. He cut off the servant's ear.

52"Put your sword back in its place," Jesus said to him. "All who use the sword will die by the sword. **53**Do you think I can't ask my Father for help? He would send an army of more than 70,000 angels right away. **54**But then how would the Scriptures come true? They say it must happen in this way."

55At that time Jesus spoke to the crowd. "Am I leading a band of armed men against you?" he asked. "Do you have to come out with swords and clubs to capture me? Every day I sat in the temple courtyard teaching. And you didn't arrest me. **56**But all this has happened so that the words of the prophets would come true."

Then all the disciples left him and ran away.

Jesus Is Taken to the Sanhedrin

57Those who had arrested Jesus took him to Caiaphas, the high priest. The teachers of the law and the elders had come together there. **58**Not too far away, Peter followed Jesus. He went right up to the courtyard of the high priest. He entered and sat down with the guards to see what would happen.

59The chief priests and the whole Sanhedrin were looking for something to use against Jesus. They wanted to put him to death. **60**But they did not find any proof, even though many false witnesses came forward.

Finally, two other witnesses came forward. **61**They said, "This fellow claimed, 'I am able to destroy the temple of God. I can build it again in three days.' "

62Then the high priest stood up. He asked Jesus, "Aren't you going to answer? What are these charges that these men are bringing against you?"

63But Jesus remained silent.

The high priest said to him, "I command you under oath by the living God. Tell us if you are the Christ, the Son of God."

64"Yes. It is just as you say," Jesus replied. "But here is what I say to all of you. In days to come, you will see the Son of Man sitting at the right hand of the Mighty One. You will see the Son of Man coming on the clouds of heaven."

65Then the high priest tore his clothes. He said, "He has spoken a very evil thing against God! Why do we need any more witnesses? You have heard him say this evil thing. **66**What do you think?"

"He must die!" they answered.

67Then they spit in his face. They hit him with their fists. Others slapped him. **68**They said, "Prophesy to us, Christ! Who hit you?"

Peter Says He Does Not Know Jesus

69Peter was sitting out in the courtyard. A female servant came to him. "You also were with Jesus of Galilee," she said.

70But in front of all of them, Peter said he was not. "I don't know what you're talking about," he said.

71Then he went out to the gate leading into the courtyard. There another woman saw him. She said to the people, "This fellow was with Jesus of Nazareth."

72Again he said he was not. With an oath he said, "I don't know the man!"

73After a little while, those standing there went up to Peter. "You must be one of them," they said. "The way you talk gives you away."

74Then Peter began to call down curses on himself. He took an oath and said to them, "I don't know the man!"

Right away a rooster crowed. **75**Then Peter remembered what Jesus had said. "The rooster will crow," Jesus had told him. "Before it does, you will say three times that you don't know me." Peter went outside. He broke down and sobbed.

Judas Hangs Himself

27 It was early in the morning. All the chief priests and the elders of the people decided to put Jesus to death. **2**They tied him up and led him away. Then they handed him over to Pilate, who was the governor.

3Judas, who had handed him over, saw that Jesus had been sentenced to die. He felt deep shame and sadness for what he had done. So he returned the 30 silver coins to the chief priests and the elders.

4"I have sinned," he said. "I handed over a man who is not guilty."

"What do we care?" they replied. "That's your problem."

5So Judas threw the money into the temple and left. Then he went away and hanged himself.

6The chief priests picked up the coins. They said, "It's against the law to put this money into the temple fund. It is blood money. It has paid for a man's death." **7**So they decided to use the money to buy a potter's field. People from other countries would be buried there. **8**That is why it has been called The Field of Blood to this very day. **9**Then the words spoken by Jeremiah the prophet came true. He had said, "They took the 30 silver coins. That price was set for him by the people of Israel. **10**They used the coins to buy a potter's field, just as the Lord commanded me." *(Zechariah 11:12,13; Jeremiah 19:1–13; 32:6–9)*

Jesus Is Brought to Pilate

11Jesus was standing in front of the governor. The governor asked him, "Are you the king of the Jews?"

"Yes. It is just as you say," Jesus replied.

12But when the chief priests and the elders brought charges against him, he did not answer. **13**Then Pilate asked him, "Don't you hear the charges they are bringing against you?"

14But Jesus made no reply, not even to a single charge. The governor was really amazed.

15It was the governor's practice at the Passover Feast to let one prisoner go free. The people could choose the one they wanted. **16**At that time they had a well-known prisoner named Barabbas. **17**So when the crowd gathered, Pilate asked them, "Which one do you want me to set free? Barabbas? Or Jesus who is called Christ?" **18**Pilate knew that the leaders were jealous. He knew this was why they had handed Jesus over to him.

19While Pilate was sitting on the judge's seat, his wife sent him a message. It said, "Don't have anything to do with that man. He is not guilty. I have suffered a great deal in a dream today because of him."

20But the chief priests and the elders talked the crowd into asking for Barabbas and having Jesus put to death.

21"Which of the two do you want me to set free?" asked the governor.

"Barabbas," they answered.

22"Then what should I do with Jesus who is called Christ?" Pilate asked.

They all answered, "Crucify him!"

23"Why? What wrong has he done?" asked Pilate.

But they shouted even louder, "Crucify him!"

24Pilate saw that he wasn't getting anywhere. Instead, the crowd was starting to get angry. So he took water and washed his hands in front of them. "I am not guilty of this man's death," he said. "You are accountable for that!"

25All the people answered, "We and our children will accept the guilt for his death!"

26Pilate let Barabbas go free. But he had Jesus whipped. Then he handed him over to be nailed to a cross.

The Soldiers Make Fun of Jesus

27The governor's soldiers took Jesus into the palace, which was called the Praetorium. All the rest of the soldiers gathered around him. **28**They took off his clothes and put a purple robe on him. **29**Then they twisted thorns together to make a crown. They placed it on his head. They put a stick in his right hand. Then they fell on their knees in front of him and made fun of him. "We honor you, king of the Jews!" they said. **30**They spit on him. They hit him on the head with the stick again and again.

31After they had made fun of him, they took off the robe. They put his own clothes back on him. Then they led him away to nail him to a cross.

Jesus Is Nailed to a Cross

32On their way out of the city, they met a man from Cyrene. His name was Simon. They forced him to carry the cross. **33**They came to a place called Golgotha. The word Golgotha means The Place of the Skull. **34**There they mixed wine with bitter spices and gave it to Jesus to drink. After tasting it, he refused to drink it.

35When they had nailed him to the cross, they divided up his clothes by casting lots. **36**They sat down and kept watch over him there.

37Above his head they placed the written charge against him. It read, THIS IS JESUS, THE KING OF THE JEWS.

38Two robbers were crucified with him. One was on his right and one was on his left.

39Those who passed by shouted at Jesus and made fun of him. They shook their heads **40**and said, "So you are going to destroy the temple and build it again in

MATTHEW 27:24

Pilate saw that he wasn't getting anywhere. Instead, the crowd was starting to get angry. So he took water and washed his hands in front of them. "I am not guilty of this man's death," he said.

Pilate (PIE-lut) was in a dangerous situation. His people were counting on him to punish Jesus, to have him killed. But there was one problem. Pilate knew Jesus was innocent. How could he punish an innocent man? Pilate thought and he thought.

That's it! Pilate thought to himself, with a smile creeping across his face. *At this time every year, I usually let the people choose one prisoner to release. Perhaps if I give them a choice between Jesus and someone really dangerous, they'll agree to let Jesus go.* Pilate went out on the balcony to talk to the people.

"You know I usually let one prisoner go during Passover time. Who shall I release? Jesus? Or Barabbas?" Pilate shook his head and groaned when the crowd began to shout, "Barabbas!" "Well, then, what do you want me to do with Jesus?" he asked.

And the crowd screamed, "Kill him!"

Pilate groaned louder. He ran his hands through his hair in frustration. "He's done nothing wrong!" Pilate tried to shout over the crowd's noise. But they weren't listening. They just kept roaring that they wanted Jesus to die. **WHAT A MESS! PILATE THOUGHT. THIS IS GETTING OUT OF HAND.**

Pilate turned to a servant and asked him to bring a bowl of water. He put the bowl on the rail of the balcony and shouted to get the people's attention. While they watched, he dipped his hands in the water. He held them up, dripping wet, showing them what he was doing. Then he said, "I wash my hands of the whole business! This Jesus is yours to do with as you wish. I will not be responsible!"

So the people took Jesus out and crucified him.

PILATE

Don't ever be a Pilate! Be strong, be brave, and do what you know is right.

**PILATE WAS FOOLISH AND FEARFUL.
THE WHOLE STORY: MATTHEW 27:11-26**

Go to page 1134 for the greatest Super Hero

three days? Then save yourself! Come down from the cross, if you are the Son of God!"

⁴¹In the same way the chief priests, the teachers of the law and the elders made fun of him. ⁴²"He saved others," they said. "But he can't save himself! He's the King of Israel! Let him come down now from the cross! Then we will believe in him. ⁴³He trusts in God. Let God rescue him now if he wants him. He's the one who said, 'I am the Son of God.' "

⁴⁴In the same way the robbers who were being crucified with Jesus also made fun of him.

Jesus Dies

⁴⁵From noon until three o'clock, the whole land was covered with darkness. ⁴⁶About three o'clock, Jesus cried out in a loud voice. He said, *"Eloi, Eloi, lama sabachthani?"* This means "My God, my God, why have you deserted me?" *(Psalm 22:1)*

⁴⁷Some of those standing there heard Jesus cry out. They said, "He's calling for Elijah."

⁴⁸Right away one of them ran and got a sponge. He filled it with wine vinegar and put it on a stick. He offered it to Jesus to drink. ⁴⁹The rest said, "Leave him alone. Let's see if Elijah comes to save him."

⁵⁰After Jesus cried out again in a loud voice, he died.

⁵¹At that moment the temple curtain was torn in two from top to bottom. The earth shook. The rocks split. ⁵²Tombs broke open. The bodies of many holy people who had died were raised to life. ⁵³They came out of the tombs. After Jesus was raised to life, they went into the holy city. There they appeared to many people.

⁵⁴The Roman commander and those guarding Jesus saw the earthquake and all that had happened. They were terrified. They exclaimed, "He was surely the Son of God!"

⁵⁵Not very far away, many women were watching. They had followed Jesus from Galilee to take care of his needs. ⁵⁶Mary Magdalene was among them. Mary, the mother of James and Joses, was also there. So was the mother of Zebedee's sons.

Jesus Is Buried

⁵⁷As evening approached, a rich man came from the town of Arimathea. His name was Joseph. He had become a follower of Jesus. ⁵⁸He went to Pilate and asked for Jesus' body. Pilate ordered that it be given to him.

⁵⁹Joseph took the body and wrapped it in a clean linen cloth. ⁶⁰He placed it in his own new tomb that he had cut out of the rock. He rolled a big stone in front of the entrance to the tomb. Then he went away.

⁶¹Mary Magdalene and the other Mary were sitting there across from the tomb.

The Guards at the Tomb

⁶²The next day was the day after Preparation Day. The chief priests and the Pharisees went to Pilate. ⁶³"Sir," they said, "we remember something that liar said while he was still alive. He claimed, 'After three days I will rise again.' ⁶⁴So give the order to make the tomb secure until the third day. If you don't, his disciples might come and steal the body. Then they will tell the people that Jesus has been raised from the dead. This last lie will be worse than the first."

⁶⁵"Take some guards with you," Pilate answered. "Go. Make the tomb as secure as you can." ⁶⁶So they went and made the tomb secure. They put a seal on the stone and placed some guards on duty.

Jesus Rises From the Dead

28 The Sabbath day was now over. It was dawn on the first day of the week. Mary Magdalene and the other Mary went to look at the tomb.

²There was a powerful earthquake. An angel of the Lord came down from heaven. The angel went to the tomb. He rolled back the stone and sat on it. ³His body shone like lightning. His clothes were as white as snow. ⁴The guards were so afraid of him that they shook and became like dead men.

⁵The angel said to the women, "Don't be afraid. I know that you are looking for Jesus, who was crucified. ⁶He is not here! He has risen, just as he said he would! Come and see the place where he was lying. ⁷Go quickly! Tell his disciples, 'He has risen from the dead. He is going ahead of you into Galilee. There you will see him.' Now I have told you."

⁸So the women hurried away from the tomb. They were afraid, but they were filled with joy. They ran to tell the disciples.

⁹Suddenly Jesus met them. "Greetings!" he said.

They came to him, took hold of his feet and worshiped him.

¹⁰Then Jesus said to them, "Don't be afraid. Go and tell my brothers to go to Galilee. There they will see me."

JESUS LIVES AGAIN

MATTHEW 28:8-9

The women hurried away from the tomb. They were afraid, but they were filled with joy. They ran to tell the disciples. Suddenly Jesus met them. "Greetings!" he said. They came to him, took hold of his feet and worshiped him.

Jesus went immediately from lying dead on a slab of stone in his tomb to standing and living and breathing again. The cloth that had been over his face fell to the floor. He picked it up and folded it carefully. He had been dead since Friday. Today was Sunday, and now he lived again.

The earth rumbled and shook as if it understood the importance of what was happening. Jesus watched as an angel slowly moved the stone away from the entrance to the tomb. Morning light filled the tomb, and Jesus walked out.

Later that morning some of Jesus' women friends came to the tomb and found it empty. They saw the angel and heard his report that Jesus was no longer dead. They looked at each other in amazement. Jesus was alive! The horrors of Friday now became the joys of Sunday. The women ran from the tomb to find Jesus' disciples and give them the good news. Along the way, they saw someone up ahead. IT WAS JESUS!

Jesus stood in the road in front of them and simply said, "Hello!" He knew they were feeling happy and scared and mixed up all at once. So he stopped them to let them know he really and truly *was* alive.

Jesus stood quietly and looked down at the women who fell at his feet. He loved these women. "Don't be afraid," Jesus said to them. "Go to the disciples and tell them to meet me in Galilee."

Both women jumped to their feet as Jesus sent them on their way. A smile spread across his face at their obvious love for him. He watched as they ran toward Jerusalem, eager to tell the disciples what they had seen and heard.

BE LIKE JESUS
Even when earth-shaking events were taking place, Jesus took the time to be kind to those around him. So should we.

JESUS KINDLY REASSURED SOME WOMEN WHO HAD JUST HEARD HE WAS ALIVE.

Go to page 1139 for the next Super Hero

The Guards Report to the Chief Priests

[11] While the women were on their way, some of the guards went into the city. They reported to the chief priests all that had happened.

[12] When the chief priests met with the elders, they came up with a plan. They gave the soldiers a large amount of money. [13] They told the soldiers, "We want you to say, 'His disciples came during the night. They stole his body while we were sleeping.' [14] If the governor hears this report, we will pay him off. That will keep you out of trouble."

[15] So the soldiers took the money and did as they were told. This story has spread all around among the Jews to this very day.

Jesus' Final Orders to His Disciples

[16] Then the 11 disciples went to Galilee. They went to the mountain where Jesus had told them to go. [17] When they saw him, they worshiped him. But some still had their doubts.

[18] Then Jesus came to them. He said, "All authority in heaven and on earth has been given to me. [19] So you must go and make disciples of all nations. Baptize

OBEYS ✔

JESUS CAME TO THEM. HE SAID, "...TEACH [ALL NATIONS] TO OBEY EVERYTHING I HAVE COMMANDED YOU. AND YOU CAN BE SURE THAT I AM ALWAYS WITH YOU, TO THE VERY END."

—MATTHEW 28:18, 20—

TELLS OTHERS

them in the name of the Father and of the Son and of the Holy Spirit. [20] Teach them to obey everything I have commanded you. And you can be sure that I am always with you, to the very end."

MARK

Johhn Mark writes the book of Mark to tell the stories of Jesus. While Matthew writes about Jesus' teachings, Mark writes about Jesus healing sick people, telling stories, feeding great crowds and then dying on a cross. You can read the book of Mark almost like a storybook. It will give you a super picture of how Jesus and his disciples lived. More than that, it will tell you how Jesus died and rose again so you, and everyone else who believes, can be saved from sins.

HEROES IN THIS BOOK . . .

JAMES
PAGE 1139

A SICK WOMAN
PAGE 1144

JESUS HEALS A DEAD GIRL
PAGE 1146

JESUS LOVES KIDS
PAGE 1153

JUDAS ISCARIOT
(Not!)
PAGE 1160

JESUS SUFFERS
(in the book of Matthew)
PAGE 1129

JESUS DIES
(in the book of John)
PAGE 1246

JESUS LIVES AGAIN
(in the book of Matthew)
PAGE 1134

John the Baptist Prepares the Way

1 This is the beginning of the good news about Jesus Christ, the Son of God.

2 Long ago Isaiah the prophet wrote,

"I will send my messenger ahead of you.
  He will prepare your way."
(Malachi 3:1)
3 "A messenger is calling out in the
  desert,
'Prepare the way for the Lord.
  Make straight paths for him.' "
(Isaiah 40:3)

4 And so John came. He baptized people in the desert. He also preached that people should be baptized and turn away from their sins. Then God would forgive them. 5 All the people from the countryside of Judea went out to him. All the people from Jerusalem went too. When they admitted they had sinned, John baptized them in the Jordan River. 6 John wore clothes made out of camel's hair. He had a leather belt around his waist. And he ate locusts and wild honey. 7 Here is what John was preaching. "After me, one will come who is more powerful than I am. I'm not good enough to bend down and untie his sandals. 8 I baptize you with water. But he will baptize you with the Holy Spirit."

Jesus Is Baptized and Tempted

9 At that time Jesus came from Nazareth in Galilee. John baptized him in the Jordan River. 10 Jesus was coming up out of the water. Just then he saw heaven being torn open. He saw the Holy Spirit coming down on him like a dove. 11 A voice spoke to him from heaven. It said, "You are my Son, and I love you. I am very pleased with you."

12 At once the Holy Spirit sent Jesus out into the desert. 13 He was in the desert 40 days. There Satan tempted him. The wild animals didn't harm Jesus. Angels took care of him.

Jesus Chooses the First Disciples

14 After John was put in prison, Jesus went into Galilee. He preached God's good news. 15 "The time has come," he said. "The kingdom of God is near. Turn away from your sins and believe the good news!"

16 One day Jesus was walking beside the Sea of Galilee. There he saw Simon and his brother Andrew. They were throwing a net into the lake. They were fishermen.

17 "Come. Follow me," Jesus said. "I will make you fishers of people."

18 At once they left their nets and followed him.

19 Then Jesus walked a little farther. As he did, he saw James, son of Zebedee, and his brother John. They were in a boat preparing their nets. 20 Right away he called out to them. They left their father Zebedee in the boat with the hired men. Then they followed Jesus.

Jesus Drives Out an Evil Spirit

21 Jesus and those with him went to Capernaum. When the Sabbath day came, he went into the synagogue. There he began to teach. 22 The people were amazed at his teaching. He taught them like one who had authority. He did not talk like the teachers of the law.

23 Just then a man in their synagogue cried out. He was controlled by an evil spirit. He said, 24 "What do you want with us, Jesus of Nazareth? Have you come to destroy us? I know who you are. You are the Holy One of God!"

25 "Be quiet!" said Jesus firmly. "Come out of him!"

26 The evil spirit shook the man wildly. Then it came out of him with a scream.

27 All the people were amazed. So they asked each other, "What is this? A new teaching! And with so much authority! He even gives orders to evil spirits, and they obey him." 28 News about Jesus spread quickly all over Galilee.

Jesus Heals Many People

29 Jesus and those with him left the synagogue. Right away they went with James and John to the home of Simon and Andrew. 30 Simon's mother-in-law was lying in bed. She had a fever. They told Jesus about her. 31 So he went to her. He took her hand and helped her up. The fever left her. Then she began to serve them.

32That evening after sunset, the people brought to Jesus all who were sick. They also brought all who were controlled by demons. 33All the people in town gathered at the door. 34Jesus healed many of them. They had all kinds of sicknesses. He also drove out many demons. But he would not let the demons speak, because they knew who he was.

Jesus Prays in a Quiet Place

35It was very early in the morning and still dark. Jesus got up and left the house. He went to a place where he could be alone. There he prayed. 36Simon and his friends went to look for Jesus. 37When they found him, they called out, "Everyone is looking for you!"

38Jesus replied, "Let's go somewhere

JAMES

MARK 1:19-20

✔

✝

[Jesus] saw James, son of Zebedee, and his brother John. They were in a boat preparing their nets. Right away he called out to them. They left their father Zebedee in the boat with the hired men. Then they followed Jesus.

James and John sat in their boat with their father, Zebedee. They pulled on their nets, arranging them in the boat before going out to fish. Many days of working in the warm sun had tanned them a dark bronze. Small waves slapped the sides of the boat and made it rock and roll in the water. When a large wave splashed up and drenched them both, they laughed together.

A bit later James and John looked up to see Simon and Andrew with another man, the man named Jesus. They had heard about this Jesus, who was traveling around the countryside teaching.

Jesus stood on the shore near their boat and watched the brothers. His eyes held theirs, as if he looked not just at them, but *into* them. Then Jesus spoke, "COME AND FOLLOW ME!"

Without a second of hesitation, James and John stepped out of their boat and splashed to shore. From that day on they followed Jesus.

BE A JAMES

Don't wait another day to decide that you want to be a Jesus follower. Be like James! Believe in Jesus and obey him. James never regretted his decision. Neither will you.

JAMES FOLLOWED JESUS AS SOON AS JESUS CALLED HIM.

Go to page 1144 for the next Super Hero

else. I want to go to the nearby towns. I must preach there also. That is why I have come." **39**So he traveled all around Galilee. He preached in their synagogues. He also drove out demons.

Jesus Heals a Man Who Had a Skin Disease

40A man who had a skin disease came to Jesus. On his knees he begged Jesus. He said, "If you are willing to make me 'clean,' you can do it."

41Jesus was filled with deep concern. He reached out his hand and touched the man. "I am willing to do it," he said. "Be 'clean'!" **42**Right away the disease left him. He was healed.

43Jesus sent him away at once. He gave the man a strong warning. **44**"Don't tell this to anyone," he said. "Go and show yourself to the priest. Offer the sacrifices that Moses commanded. It will be a witness to the priest and the people that you are 'clean.' "

45But the man went out and started talking right away. He spread the news to everyone. So Jesus could no longer enter a town openly. He stayed outside in lonely places. But people still came to him from everywhere.

Jesus Heals a Man Who Could Not Walk

2 A few days later, Jesus entered Capernaum again. The people heard that he had come home. **2**So many people gathered that there was no room left. There was not even room outside the door. And Jesus preached the word to them.

3Four of those who came were carrying a man who could not walk. **4**But they could not get him close to Jesus because of the crowd. So they made a hole in the roof above Jesus. Then they lowered the man through it on a mat.

5Jesus saw their faith. So he said to the man, "Son, your sins are forgiven."

6Some teachers of the law were sitting there. They were thinking, **7**"Why is this fellow talking like that? He's saying a very evil thing! Only God can forgive sins!"

8Right away Jesus knew what they were thinking. So he said to them, "Why are you thinking these things? **9**Is it easier to say to this man, 'Your sins are forgiven'? Or to say, 'Get up, take your mat and walk'? **10**I want you to know that the Son of Man has authority on earth to forgive sins."

Then Jesus spoke to the man who could not walk. **11**"I tell you," he said, "get up. Take your mat and go home."

12The man got up and took his mat. Then he walked away while everyone watched. All the people were amazed. They praised God and said, "We have never seen anything like this!"

Jesus Chooses Levi

13Once again Jesus went out beside the Sea of Galilee. A large crowd came to him. He began to teach them. **14**As he walked along he saw Levi, son of Alphaeus. Levi was sitting at the tax collector's booth. "Follow me," Jesus told him. Levi got up and followed him.

15Later Jesus was having dinner at Levi's house. Many tax collectors and "sinners" were eating with him and his disciples. They were part of the large crowd following Jesus.

16Some teachers of the law who were Pharisees were there. They saw Jesus eating with "sinners" and tax collectors. So they asked his disciples, "Why does he eat with tax collectors and 'sinners'?"

17Jesus heard that. So he said to them, "Those who are healthy don't need a doctor. Sick people do. I have not come to get those who think they are right with God to follow me. I have come to get sinners to follow me."

Jesus Is Asked About Fasting

18John's disciples and the Pharisees were going without eating. Some people came to Jesus. They said to him, "John's disciples are fasting. The disciples of the Pharisees are also fasting. But your disciples are not. Why aren't they?"

19Jesus answered, "How can the guests of the groom go without eating while he is with them? They will not fast as long as he is with them. **20**But the time will come when the groom will be taken away from them. On that day they will go without eating.

21"People don't sew a patch of new cloth on old clothes. If they do, the new piece will pull away from the old. That will make the tear worse. **22**People don't pour new wine into old wineskins. If they do, the wine will burst the skins. Then the wine and the wineskins will both be destroyed. No, everyone pours new wine into new wineskins."

Jesus Is Lord of the Sabbath Day

23One Sabbath day Jesus was walking with his disciples through the grainfields. The disciples began to break off some heads of grain. **24**The Pharisees said to Jesus, "Look! It is against the Law to do this on the Sabbath. Why are your disciples doing it?"

25He answered, "Haven't you ever read about what David did? He and his men were hungry. They needed food. **26**It was when Abiathar was high priest. David entered the house of God and ate the holy bread. Only priests were allowed to eat it. David also gave some to his men."

27Then Jesus said to them, "The Sabbath day was made for man. Man was not made for the Sabbath day. **28**So the Son of Man is Lord even of the Sabbath day."

3 Another time Jesus went into the synagogue. A man with a weak and twisted hand was there. **2**Some Pharisees were trying to find fault with Jesus. They watched him closely. They wanted to see if he would heal the man on the Sabbath day.

3Jesus spoke to the man with the weak and twisted hand. "Stand up in front of everyone," he said.

4Then Jesus asked them, "What does the Law say we should do on the Sabbath day? Should we do good? Or should we do evil? Should we save life? Or should we kill?" But no one answered.

5Jesus looked around at them in anger. He was very upset because their hearts were stubborn. Then he said to the man, "Stretch out your hand." He stretched it out, and his hand was as good as new.

6Then the Pharisees went out and began to make plans with the Herodians. They wanted to kill Jesus.

Crowds Follow Jesus

7Jesus went off to the Sea of Galilee with his disciples. A large crowd from Galilee followed. **8**People heard about all that Jesus was doing. And many came to him. They came from Judea, Jerusalem, and Idumea. They came from the lands east of the Jordan River. And they came from the area around Tyre and Sidon.

9Because of the crowd, Jesus told his disciples to get a small boat ready for him. This would keep the people from crowding him. **10**Jesus had healed many people. So those who were sick were pushing forward to touch him.

11When people with evil spirits saw him, they fell down in front of him. The spirits shouted, "You are the Son of God!" **12**But Jesus ordered them not to tell who he was.

Jesus Appoints the Twelve Apostles

13Jesus went up on a mountainside. He called for certain people to come to him, and they came. **14**He appointed 12 of them and called them apostles. From that time on they would be with him. He would also send them out to preach. **15**They would have authority to drive out demons.

16So Jesus appointed the Twelve. Simon was one of them. Jesus gave him the name Peter. **17**There were James, son of Zebedee, and his brother John. Jesus gave them the name Boanerges. Boanerges means Sons of Thunder. **18**There were also Andrew, Philip, Bartholomew, Matthew, Thomas, and James, son of Alphaeus. And there were Thaddaeus and Simon the Zealot. **19**Judas Iscariot was one of them too. He was the one who was later going to hand Jesus over to his enemies.

Jesus and Beelzebub

20Jesus entered a house. Again a crowd gathered. It was so large that Jesus and his disciples were not even able to eat. **21**His family heard about this. So they went to take charge of him. They said, "He is out of his mind."

22Some teachers of the law were there. They had come down from Jerusalem. They said, "He is controlled by Beelzebub! He is driving out demons by the power of the prince of demons."

23So Jesus called them over and spoke to them by using stories. He said, "How can Satan drive out Satan? **24**If a kingdom fights against itself, it can't stand. **25**If a family is divided, it can't stand. **26**And if Satan fights against himself, and his helpers are divided, he can't stand. That is the end of him. **27**In fact, none of you can enter a strong man's house and just take what the man owns. You must first tie him up. Then you can rob his house.

28"What I'm about to tell you is true. Everyone's sins and evil words against God will be forgiven. **29**But anyone who speaks evil things against the Holy Spirit will never be forgiven. His guilt will last forever."

30Jesus said this because the teachers of the law were saying, "He has an evil spirit."

Jesus' Mother and Brothers

31Jesus' mother and brothers came and stood outside. They sent someone in to get him. **32**A crowd was sitting around Jesus. They told him, "Your mother and your brothers are outside. They are looking for you."

33 "Who is my mother? Who are my brothers?" he asked.

34 Then Jesus looked at the people sitting in a circle around him. He said, "Here is my mother! Here are my brothers! **35** Anyone who does what God wants is my brother or sister or mother."

The Story of the Farmer

4 Again Jesus began to teach by the Sea of Galilee. The crowd that gathered around him was very large. So he got into a boat. He sat down in it out on the lake. All the people were along the shore at the water's edge. **2** He taught them many things by using stories.

In his teaching he said, **3** "Listen! A farmer went out to plant his seed. **4** He scattered the seed on the ground. Some fell on a path. Birds came and ate it up. **5** Some seed fell on rocky places, where there wasn't much soil. The plants came up quickly, because the soil wasn't deep. **6** When the sun came up, it burned the plants. They dried up because they had no roots. **7** Other seed fell among thorns. The thorns grew up and crowded out the plants. So the plants did not bear grain. **8** Still other seed fell on good soil. It grew up and produced a crop 30, 60, or even 100 times more than the farmer planted."

9 Then Jesus said, "Those who have ears should listen."

10 Later Jesus was alone. The Twelve asked him about the stories. So did the others around him. **11** He told them, "The secret of God's kingdom has been given to you. But to outsiders everything is told by using stories. **12** In that way,

" 'They will see but never know what
     they are seeing.
  They will hear but never
     understand.
  Otherwise they might turn and be
     forgiven!' "   *(Isaiah 6:9,10)*

13 Then Jesus said to them, "Don't you understand this story? Then how will you understand any stories of this kind? **14** The seed the farmer plants is God's message. **15** What is seed scattered on a path like? The message is planted. The people hear the message. Then Satan comes. He takes away the message that was planted in them. **16** And what is seed scattered on rocky places like? The people hear the message. At once they receive it with joy. **17** But they have no roots. So they last only a short time. They quickly fall away from the faith when trouble or suffering comes because of the message. **18** And what is

seed scattered among thorns like? The people hear the message. **19** But then the worries of this life come to them. Wealth comes with its false promises. The people also long for other things. All of those are the kinds of things that crowd out the message. They keep it from producing fruit. **20** And what is seed scattered on good soil like? The people hear the message. They accept it. They produce a good crop 30, 60, or even 100 times more than the farmer planted."

A Lamp on a Stand

21 Jesus said to them, "Do you bring in a lamp to put it under a large bowl or a bed? Don't you put it on its stand? **22** What is hidden is meant to be seen. And what is put out of sight is meant to be brought out into the open. **23** Everyone who has ears should listen."

24 "Think carefully about what you hear," he said. "As you give, so you will receive. In fact, you will receive even more. **25** If you have something, you will be given more. If you have nothing, even what you have will be taken away from you."

The Story of the Growing Seed

26 Jesus also said, "Here is what God's kingdom is like. A farmer scatters seed on the ground. **27** Night and day the seed comes up and grows. It happens whether the farmer sleeps or gets up. He doesn't know how it happens. **28** All by itself the soil produces grain. First the stalk comes up. Then the head appears. Finally, the full grain appears in the head. **29** Before long the grain ripens. So the farmer cuts it down, because the harvest is ready."

The Story of the Mustard Seed

30 Again Jesus said, "What can we say God's kingdom is like? What story can we use to explain it? **31** It is like a mustard seed, which is the smallest seed planted in the ground. **32** But when you plant the seed, it grows. It becomes the largest of all garden plants. Its branches are so big that birds can rest in its shade."

33 Using many stories like those, Jesus spoke the word to them. He told them as much as they could understand. **34** He did not say anything to them without using a story. But when he was alone with his disciples, he explained everything.

Jesus Calms the Storm

35 When evening came, Jesus said to his disciples, "Let's go over to the other side of the lake." **36** They left the crowd behind.

And they took him along in a boat, just as he was. There were also other boats with him.

37A wild storm came up. Waves crashed over the boat. It was about to sink. **38**Jesus was in the back, sleeping on a cushion. The disciples woke him up. They said, "Teacher! Don't you care if we drown?"

39He got up and ordered the wind to stop. He said to the waves, "Quiet! Be still!" Then the wind died down. And it was completely calm.

40He said to his disciples, "Why are you so afraid? Don't you have any faith at all yet?"

41They were terrified. They asked each other, "Who is this? Even the wind and the waves obey him!"

Jesus Heals a Man Controlled by Demons

5 They went across the Sea of Galilee to the area of the Gerasenes. **2**Jesus got out of the boat. A man with an evil spirit came from the tombs to meet him. **3**The man lived in the tombs. No one could keep him tied up anymore. Not even a chain could hold him. **4**His hands and feet had often been chained. But he tore the chains apart. And he broke the iron cuffs on his ankles. No one was strong enough to control him. **5**Night and day he screamed among the tombs and in the hills. He cut himself with stones.

6When he saw Jesus a long way off, he ran to him. He fell on his knees in front of him. **7**He shouted at the top of his voice, "Jesus, Son of the Most High God, what do you want with me? Promise before God that you won't hurt me!" **8**This was because Jesus had said to him, "Come out of this man, you evil spirit!"

9Then Jesus asked the demon, "What is your name?"

"My name is Legion," he replied. "There are many of us." **10**And he begged Jesus again and again not to send them out of the area.

11A large herd of pigs was feeding on the nearby hillside. **12**The demons begged Jesus, "Send us among the pigs. Let us go into them." **13**Jesus allowed it. The evil spirits came out of the man and went into the pigs. There were about 2,000 pigs in the herd. The whole herd rushed down the steep bank. They ran into the lake and drowned.

14Those who were tending the pigs ran off. They told the people in the town and countryside what had happened. The people went out to see for themselves.

15Then they came to Jesus. They saw the man who had been controlled by many demons. He was sitting there. He was now dressed and thinking clearly. All this made the people afraid. **16**Those who had seen it told them what had happened to the man. They told about the pigs as well. **17**Then the people began to beg Jesus to leave their area.

18Jesus was getting into the boat. The man who had been controlled by demons begged to go with him. **19**Jesus did not let him. He said, "Go home to your family. Tell them how much the Lord has done for you. Tell them how kind he has been to you."

20So the man went away. In the area known as the Ten Cities, he began to tell how much Jesus had done for him. And all the people were amazed.

A Dying Girl and a Suffering Woman

21Jesus went across the Sea of Galilee in a boat. It landed at the other side. There a large crowd gathered around him. **22**Then a man named Jairus came. He was a synagogue ruler. Seeing Jesus, he fell at his feet. **23**He begged Jesus, "Please come. My little daughter is dying. Place your hands on her to heal her. Then she will live." **24**So Jesus went with him.

A large group of people followed. They crowded around him. **25**A woman was there who had a sickness that made her bleed. It had lasted for 12 years. **26**She had suffered a great deal, even though she had gone to many doctors. She had spent all the money she had. But she was getting worse, not better. **27**Then she heard about Jesus. She came up behind him in the crowd and touched his clothes. **28**She thought, "I just need to touch his clothes. Then I will be healed." **29**Right away her bleeding stopped. She felt in her body that her suffering was over.

30At once Jesus knew that power had gone out from him. He turned around in the crowd. He asked, "Who touched my clothes?"

31"You see the people," his disciples answered. "They are crowding against you. And you still ask, 'Who touched me?' "

32But Jesus kept looking around. He wanted to see who had touched him.

33Then the woman came and fell at his feet. She knew what had happened to her. She was shaking with fear. But she told him the whole truth.

34He said to her, "Dear woman, your

A SICK WOMAN

MARK 5:27, 29

Then she heard about Jesus. She came up behind him in the crowd and touched his clothes. Right away her bleeding stopped. She felt in her body that her suffering was over.

The woman's veil hung loosely around her pale face. The sharp bones of her elbows and knees pointed under the fabric of her robe. The woman had been bleeding for twelve years now. All of her money had gone to doctors. But nothing worked. She only got sicker and weaker. Jesus was her last—and best—hope for healing.

Without looking into the eyes of those in the crowd, the woman moved around one person after another. She needed to get closer to Jesus. *So many people*, she thought. Her breath came in gasps as the crowd closed in around her.

She didn't want to bother Jesus. She didn't need to talk to him. She just needed to touch him. Reaching a shaky hand between two men, she was just able to touch Jesus' robe.

THE WOMAN GASPED AT THE SURGE OF POWER THAT BOLTED INTO HER. A warm feeling rushed through her body. Her cheeks felt warm and went from pale to pink. Amazed by this miracle, she looked at Jesus. She didn't even need to say thank you. He knew what she was thinking.

"Who touched me?" Jesus asked. *Oh, no! Jesus felt my touch!* The woman stood for a moment, hoping Jesus would move on. But he insisted, "Who touched me?"

She moved through the crowd toward Jesus. Everyone turned to look at her. Terror gripped her throat. She couldn't think what to do except to bravely kneel before him. Gathering her robe around her, she fell in the dirt in front of Jesus.

Jesus touched her. Gently, kindly, he called her "Dear woman." And he told her to go home and enjoy her good health.

BE LIKE THE SICK WOMAN

When you need something from God, don't wait for him to act. Go to him and ask for his help. He loves you enough and will help you whenever you need him.

SHE WENT TO JESUS FOR HEALING.
THE WHOLE STORY: MARK 5:24-34

Go to page 1146 for the greatest Super Hero

POWER-SURGE

BELIEVES †

DON'T BE AFRAID.
JUST BELIEVE.
— MARK 5:36 —

faith has healed you. Go in peace. You are free from your suffering."

35While Jesus was still speaking, some people came from the house of Jairus. He was the synagogue ruler. "Your daughter is dead," they said. "Why bother the teacher anymore?"

36But Jesus didn't listen to them. He told the synagogue ruler, "Don't be afraid. Just believe."

37He let only Peter, James, and John, the brother of James, follow him. **38**They came to the home of the synagogue ruler. There Jesus saw a lot of confusion. People were crying and sobbing loudly. **39**He went inside. Then he said to them, "Why all this confusion and sobbing? The child is not dead. She is only sleeping." **40**But they laughed at him.

He made them all go outside. He took only the child's father and mother and the disciples who were with him. And he went in where the child was. **41**He took her by the hand. Then he said to her, *"Talitha koum!"* This means, "Little girl, I say to you, get up!" **42**The girl was 12 years old. Right away she stood up and walked around. They were totally amazed at this. **43**Jesus gave strict orders not to let anyone know what had happened. And he told them to give her something to eat.

A Prophet Without Honor

6 Jesus left there and went to his hometown of Nazareth. His disciples went with him. **2**When the Sabbath day came, he began to teach in the synagogue. Many who heard him were amazed.

"Where did this man get these things?" they asked. "What's this wisdom that has been given to him? He even does miracles! **3**Isn't this the carpenter? Isn't this Mary's son? Isn't this the brother of James, Joseph, Judas and Simon? Aren't his sisters here with us?" They were not pleased with him at all.

4Jesus said to them, "A prophet is not honored in his hometown. He doesn't receive any honor among his relatives. And he doesn't receive any in his own home."

5Jesus laid his hands on a few sick people and healed them. But he could not do any other miracles there. **6**He was amazed because they had no faith.

Jesus Sends Out the Twelve Disciples

Jesus went around teaching from village to village. **7**He called the Twelve to him. Then he sent them out two by two. He gave them authority to drive out evil spirits.

8Here were his orders. "Take only a walking stick for your trip. Do not take bread or a bag. Take no money in your belts. **9**Wear sandals. But do not take extra clothes. **10**When you are invited into a house, stay there until you leave town. **11**Some places may not welcome you or listen to you. If they don't, shake the dust off your feet when you leave. That will be a witness against the people living there."

12They went out. And they preached that people should turn away from their sins. **13**They drove out many demons. They poured olive oil on many sick people and healed them.

John the Baptist's Head Is Cut Off

14King Herod heard about this. Jesus' name had become well known. Some were saying, "John the Baptist has been raised from the dead! That is why he has the power to do miracles."

15Others said, "He is Elijah."

Still others claimed, "He is a prophet. He is like one of the prophets of long ago."

16But when Herod heard this, he said, "I had John's head cut off. And now he has been raised from the dead!"

17In fact, it was Herod himself who had given orders to arrest John. He had him tied up and put in prison. He did this because of Herodias. She was the wife of Herod's brother Philip. But now Herod was married to her. **18**John had been saying to Herod, "It is against the Law for you to have your brother's wife." **19**Herodias held that against John. She wanted to kill him. But she could not, **20**because Herod was afraid of John. So he kept John safe. Herod knew John was a holy man who did what was right. When Herod heard him, he was very puzzled. But he liked to listen to him.

21Finally the right time came. Herod gave a big dinner on his birthday. He invited his high officials and military leaders. He also invited the most important men in Galilee. **22**Then the daughter of Herodias came in and danced. She pleased Herod and his dinner guests.

The king said to the girl, "Ask me for

anything you want. I'll give it to you."
²³And he promised her with an oath, "Anything you ask for I will give you. I'll give you up to half of my kingdom."

²⁴She went out and said to her mother, "What should I ask for?"

"The head of John the Baptist," she answered.

²⁵At once the girl hurried to ask the king. She said, "I want you to give me the head of John the Baptist on a big plate right now."

²⁶The king was very upset. But he thought of his promise and his dinner guests. So he did not want to say no to the girl. ²⁷He sent a man right away to bring John's head. The man went to the prison and cut off John's head. ²⁸He brought it back on a big plate. He gave it to the girl, and she gave it to her mother.

²⁹John's disciples heard about this. So they came and took his body. Then they placed it in a tomb.

Jesus Feeds the Five Thousand

³⁰The apostles gathered around Jesus.

JESUS HEALS A DEAD GIRL

MARK 5:40-42

He went in where the child was. He took her by the hand. Then he said..., "Little girl, I say to you, get up!" The girl was 12 years old. Right away she stood up and walked around. They were totally amazed at this.

Jairus, a religious leader, worked his way through the people who crowded around Jesus. When he got right in front of Jesus, he fell to his knees.

"Please, Jesus," he begged. "My little girl is dying. If you touch her, she will get better."

Jesus felt sorry for Jairus and immediately left to go to his house. But as they went, someone came and told Jairus, "Your daughter is dead. You might as well not bother Jesus."

But Jesus ignored the person and told Jairus, **"DON'T WORRY. YOUR DAUGHTER WILL BE FINE."**

When they got closer to Jairus's house, they could hear the people sobbing. Jesus ignored them. He went into the little girl's room, took her hand and said to her, "Get up, little girl!" And she did. Jesus brought her back from death to life.

BE LIKE JESUS

Jesus knew Jairus was sad because his daughter was sick, and even sadder when she died. He kindly went to Jairus's house and brought the little girl back to life. Be just like Jesus. Help those who are sad or in trouble. Be kind to those around you.

JESUS BROUGHT A LITTLE GIRL BACK TO LIFE.

Go to page 1153 for the greatest Super Hero

They told him all they had done and taught. **31**But many people were coming and going. So they did not even have a chance to eat.

Then Jesus said to his apostles, "Come with me by yourselves to a quiet place. You need to get some rest." **32**So they went away by themselves in a boat to a quiet place.

33But many people who saw them leaving recognized them. They ran from all the towns and got there ahead of them. **34**When Jesus came ashore, he saw a large crowd. He felt deep concern for them. They were like sheep without a shepherd. So he began teaching them many things.

35By that time it was late in the day. His disciples came to him. "There is nothing here," they said. "It's already very late. **36**Send the people away. They can go and buy something to eat in the nearby countryside and villages."

37But Jesus answered, "You give them something to eat."

They said to him, "That would take eight months of a person's pay! Should we go and spend that much on bread? Are we supposed to feed them?"

38"How many loaves do you have?" Jesus asked. "Go and see."

When they found out, they said, "Five loaves and two fish."

39Then Jesus directed them to have all the people sit down in groups on the green grass. **40**So they sat down in groups of 100s and 50s.

41Jesus took the five loaves and the two fish. He looked up to heaven and gave thanks. He broke the loaves into pieces. Then he gave them to his disciples to set in front of the people. He also divided the two fish among them all.

42All of them ate and were satisfied. **43**The disciples picked up 12 baskets of broken pieces of bread and fish. **44**The number of men who had eaten was 5,000.

Jesus Walks on the Water

45Right away Jesus made his disciples get into the boat. He had them go on ahead of him to Bethsaida. Then he sent the crowd away. **46**After leaving them, he went up on a mountainside to pray.

47When evening came, the boat was in the middle of the Sea of Galilee. Jesus was alone on land. **48**He saw the disciples pulling hard on the oars. The wind was blowing against them.

Early in the morning, he went out to them. He walked on the lake. When he was about to pass by them, **49**they saw him walking on the lake. They thought he was a ghost. They cried out. **50**They all saw him and were terrified.

Right away he said to them, "Be brave! It is I. Don't be afraid."

51Then he climbed into the boat with them. The wind died down. And they were completely amazed. **52**They had not understood about the loaves. They were stubborn.

53They crossed over the lake and landed at Gennesaret. There they tied up the boat. **54**As soon as Jesus and his disciples got out, people recognized him. **55**They ran through that whole area to bring to him those who were sick. They carried them on mats to where they heard he was.

56He went into the villages, the towns and the countryside. Everywhere he went, the people brought the sick to the market places. Those who were sick begged him to let them touch just the edge of his clothes. And all who touched him were healed.

What Makes People "Unclean"?

7 The Pharisees gathered around Jesus. So did some of the teachers of the law. All of them had come from Jerusalem. **2**They saw some of his disciples eating food with "unclean" hands. That means they were not washed.

3The Pharisees and all the Jews do not

BRAVE B

EARLY IN THE MORNING, [JESUS] WENT OUT TO THEM. HE WALKED ON THE LAKE...[THE DISCIPLES] THOUGHT HE WAS A GHOST. THEY CRIED OUT. THEY ALL SAW HIM AND WERE TERRIFIED. RIGHT AWAY HE SAID TO THEM, "BE BRAVE! IT IS I. DON'T BE AFRAID."
—— MARK 6:48-50 ——

eat unless they wash their hands to make them pure. That's what the elders teach. ⁴When they come from the market place, they do not eat unless they wash. And they follow many other teachings. For example, they wash cups, pitchers, and kettles in a special way.

⁵So the Pharisees and the teachers of the law questioned Jesus. "Why don't your disciples live by what the elders teach?" they asked. "Why do they eat their food with 'unclean' hands?"

⁶He replied, "Isaiah was right. He prophesied about you people who pretend to be good. He said,

" 'These people honor me by what they say.
But their hearts are far away from me.
⁷Their worship doesn't mean anything to me.
They teach nothing but human rules.'   *(Isaiah 29:13)*

⁸You have let go of God's commands. And you are holding on to the teachings that men have made up."

⁹Jesus then said to them, "You have a fine way of setting aside God's commands! You do this so you can follow your own teachings. ¹⁰Moses said, 'Honor your father and mother.' *(Exodus 20:12; Deuteronomy 5:16)* He also said, 'If anyone calls down a curse on his father or mother, he will be put to death.' *(Exodus 21:17; Leviticus 20:9)* ¹¹But you allow people to say to their parents, 'Any help you might have received from us is Corban.' (Corban means 'a gift set apart for God.') ¹²So you no longer let them do anything for their parents. ¹³You make the word of God useless by putting your own teachings in its place. And you do many things like that."

¹⁴Again Jesus called the crowd to him. He said, "Listen to me, everyone. Understand this. ¹⁵/¹⁶Nothing outside of you can make you 'unclean' by going into you. It is what comes out of you that makes you 'unclean.' "

¹⁷Then he left the crowd and entered the house. His disciples asked him about this teaching.

¹⁸"Don't you understand?" Jesus asked. "Don't you see? Nothing that enters people from the outside can make them 'unclean.' ¹⁹It doesn't go into the heart. It goes into the stomach. Then it goes out of the body." In saying this, Jesus was calling all foods "clean."

²⁰He went on to say, "What comes out of people makes them 'unclean.' ²¹Evil thoughts come from the inside, from people's hearts. So do sexual sins, stealing and murder. Adultery, ²²greed, hate and cheating come from people's hearts too. So do desires that are not pure, and wanting what belongs to others. And so do telling lies about others and being proud and being foolish. ²³All those evil things come from inside a person. They make him 'unclean.' "

The Faith of a Greek Woman

²⁴Jesus went from there to a place near Tyre. He entered a house. He did not want anyone to know where he was. But he could not keep it a secret.

²⁵Soon a woman heard about him. An evil spirit controlled her little daughter. The woman came to Jesus and fell at his feet. ²⁶She was a Greek, born in Syrian Phoenicia. She begged Jesus to drive the demon out of her daughter.

²⁷"First let the children eat all they want," he told her. "It is not right to take the children's bread and throw it to their dogs."

²⁸"Yes, Lord," she replied. "But even the dogs under the table eat the children's crumbs."

²⁹Then he told her, "That was a good reply. You may go. The demon has left your daughter."

³⁰So she went home and found her child lying on the bed. And the demon was gone.

Jesus Heals a Man Who Could Not Hear or Speak

³¹Then Jesus left the area of Tyre and went through Sidon. He went down to the Sea of Galilee and into the area known as the Ten Cities.

³²There some people brought a man to him. The man was deaf and could hardly speak. They begged Jesus to place his hand on him.

³³Jesus took the man to one side, away from the crowd. He put his fingers into the man's ears. Then he spit and touched the man's tongue. ³⁴Jesus looked up to heaven. With a deep sigh, he said to the man, *"Ephphatha!"* That means "Be opened!" ³⁵The man's ears were opened. His tongue was freed up, and he began to speak clearly.

³⁶Jesus ordered the people not to tell anyone. But the more he did so, the more they kept talking about it.

³⁷People were really amazed. "He has done everything well," they said. "He even makes deaf people able to hear. And

he makes those who can't speak able to talk."

Jesus Feeds the Four Thousand

8 During those days another large crowd gathered. They had nothing to eat. So Jesus called for his disciples to come to him. He said, **2**"I feel deep concern for these people. They have already been with me three days. They don't have anything to eat. **3**If I send them away hungry, they will become too weak on their way home. Some of them have come from far away."

4His disciples answered him. "There is nothing here," they said. "Where can anyone get enough bread to feed them?"

5"How many loaves do you have?" Jesus asked.

"Seven," they replied.

6He told the crowd to sit down on the ground. He took the seven loaves and gave thanks to God. Then he broke them and gave them to his disciples. They set the loaves down in front of the people. **7**The disciples also had a few small fish. Jesus gave thanks for them too. He told the disciples to pass them around. **8**The people ate and were satisfied.

After that, the disciples picked up seven baskets of leftover pieces. **9**About 4,000 men were there. Jesus sent them away. **10**Then he got into a boat with his disciples. He went to the area of Dalmanutha.

11The Pharisees came and began to ask Jesus questions. They wanted to put him to the test. So they asked him for a miraculous sign from heaven. **12**He sighed deeply. He said, "Why do you people ask for a sign? What I'm about to tell you is true. No sign will be given to you."

13Then he left them. He got back into the boat and crossed to the other side of the lake.

The Yeast of the Pharisees and Herod

14The disciples had forgotten to bring bread. They had only one loaf with them in the boat.

15"Be careful," Jesus warned them. "Watch out for the yeast of the Pharisees. And watch out for the yeast of Herod."

16They talked about this with each other. They said, "He must be saying this because we don't have any bread."

17Jesus knew what they were saying. So he asked them, "Why are you talking about having no bread? Why can't you see or understand? Are you stubborn? **18**Do you have eyes and still don't see? Do

you have ears and still don't hear? And don't you remember? **19**Earlier I broke five loaves for the 5,000. How many baskets of pieces did you pick up?"

"Twelve," they replied.

20"Later I broke seven loaves for the 4,000. How many baskets of pieces did you pick up?"

"Seven," they answered.

21He said to them, "Can't you understand yet?"

Jesus Heals a Blind Man

22Jesus and his disciples came to Bethsaida. Some people brought a blind man. They begged Jesus to touch him. **23**He took the blind man by the hand. Then he led him outside the village. He spit on the man's eyes and put his hands on him.

"Do you see anything?" Jesus asked.

24The man looked up. He said, "I see people. They look like trees walking around."

25Once more Jesus put his hands on the man's eyes. Then his eyes were opened so that he could see again. He saw everything clearly. **26**Jesus sent him home. He told him, "Don't go into the village."

Peter Says That Jesus Is the Christ

27Jesus and his disciples went on to the villages around Caesarea Philippi. On the way he asked them, "Who do people say I am?"

28They replied, "Some say John the Baptist. Others say Elijah. Still others say one of the prophets."

29"But what about you?" he asked. "Who do you say I am?"

Peter answered, "You are the Christ."

30Jesus warned them not to tell anyone about him.

Jesus Tells About His Coming Death

31Jesus then began to teach his disciples. He taught them that the Son of Man must suffer many things. He taught them that the elders would not accept him. The chief priests and the teachers of the law would not accept him either. He must be killed and after three days rise again. **32**He spoke clearly about this.

Peter took Jesus to one side and began to scold him.

33Jesus turned and looked at his disciples. He scolded Peter. "Get behind me, Satan!" he said. "You are not thinking about the things of God. Instead, you are thinking about human things."

34Jesus called the crowd to him along with his disciples. He said, "If anyone wants to come after me, he must say no to himself. He must pick up his cross and follow me. **35**If he wants to save his life, he will lose it. But if he loses his life for me and for the good news, he will save it. **36**What good is it if someone gains the whole world but loses his soul? **37**Or what can anyone trade for his soul?

38"Suppose you are ashamed of me and my words among these adulterous and sinful people. Then the Son of Man will be ashamed of you when he comes in his Father's glory with the holy angels."

9 Jesus said to them, "What I'm about to tell you is true. Some who are standing here will not die before they see God's kingdom coming with power."

Jesus' Appearance Is Changed

2After six days Jesus took Peter, James and John with him. He led them up a high mountain. They were all alone. There in front of them his appearance was changed. **3**His clothes became so white they shone. They were whiter than anyone in the world could bleach them. **4**Elijah and Moses appeared in front of Jesus and his disciples. The two of them were talking with Jesus.

5Peter said to Jesus, "Rabbi, it is good for us to be here. Let us put up three shelters. One will be for you, one for Moses, and one for Elijah." **6**Peter didn't really know what to say, because they were so afraid.

7Then a cloud appeared and surrounded them. A voice came from the cloud. It said, "This is my Son, and I love him. Listen to him!"

8They looked around. Suddenly they no longer saw anyone with them except Jesus.

9They came down the mountain. On the way down, Jesus ordered them not to tell anyone what they had seen. He told them to wait until the Son of Man had risen from the dead. **10**So they kept the matter to themselves. But they asked each other what "rising from the dead" meant.

11Then they asked Jesus, "Why do the teachers of the law say that Elijah has to come first?"

12Jesus replied, "That's right. Elijah does come first. He makes all things new again. So why is it written that the Son of Man must suffer much and not be accepted? **13**I tell you, Elijah has come. They have done to him everything they wanted

to do. They did it just as it is written about him."

Jesus Heals a Boy Who Had an Evil Spirit

14When Jesus and those who were with him came to the other disciples, they saw a large crowd around them. The teachers of the law were arguing with them. **15**When all the people saw Jesus, they were filled with wonder. And they ran to greet him.

16"What are you arguing with them about?" Jesus asked.

17A man in the crowd answered. "Teacher," he said, "I brought you my son. He is controlled by a spirit. Because of this, my son can't speak anymore. **18**When the spirit takes hold of him, it throws him to the ground. He foams at the mouth. He grinds his teeth. And his body becomes stiff. I asked your disciples to drive out the spirit. But they couldn't do it."

19"You unbelieving people!" Jesus replied. "How long do I have to stay with you? How long do I have to put up with you? Bring the boy to me."

20So they brought him. As soon as the spirit saw Jesus, it threw the boy into a fit. He fell to the ground. He rolled around and foamed at the mouth.

21Jesus asked the boy's father, "How long has he been like this?"

"Since he was a child," he answered. **22**"The spirit has often thrown him into fire or water to kill him. But if you can do anything, take pity on us. Please help us."

23" 'If you can'?" said Jesus. "Everything is possible for the one who believes."

24Right away the boy's father cried out, "I do believe! Help me overcome my unbelief!"

25Jesus saw that a crowd was running over to see what was happening. Then he ordered the evil spirit to leave the boy. "You spirit that makes him unable to hear

POWER-SURGE
BELIEVES ✝
[JESUS SAID,]
"EVERYTHING IS POSSIBLE FOR THE ONE WHO BELIEVES."
— MARK 9:23 —

and speak!" he said. "I command you, come out of him. Never enter him again."

²⁶The spirit screamed. It shook the boy wildly. Then it came out of him. The boy looked so lifeless that many people said, "He's dead." ²⁷But Jesus took him by the hand. He lifted the boy to his feet, and the boy stood up.

²⁸Jesus went indoors. Then his disciples asked him in private, "Why couldn't we drive out the evil spirit?"

²⁹He replied, "This kind can come out only by prayer."

³⁰They left that place and passed through Galilee. Jesus did not want anyone to know where they were. ³¹That was because he was teaching his disciples.

He said to them, "The Son of Man is going to be handed over to men. They will kill him. After three days he will rise from the dead." ³²But they didn't understand what he meant. And they were afraid to ask him about it.

Who Is the Most Important Person?

³³Jesus and his disciples came to a house in Capernaum. There he asked them, "What were you arguing about on the road?" ³⁴But they kept quiet. On the way, they had argued about which one of them was the most important person.

³⁵Jesus sat down and called for the Twelve to come to him. Then he said, "If you want to be first, you must be the very last. You must be the servant of everyone."

³⁶Jesus took a little child and had the child stand among them. Then he took the child in his arms. He said to them, ³⁷"Anyone who welcomes one of these little children in my name welcomes me. And anyone who welcomes me doesn't welcome only me but also the One who sent me."

Anyone Who Is Not Against Us Is for Us

³⁸"Teacher," said John, "we saw a man driving out demons in your name. We told him to stop, because he was not one of us."

³⁹"Do not stop him," Jesus said. "No one who does a miracle in my name can in the next moment say anything bad about me. ⁴⁰Anyone who is not against us is for us.

⁴¹"What I'm about to tell you is true. Suppose someone gives you a cup of water in my name because you belong to me. That one will certainly not go without a reward.

Leading People to Sin

⁴²"What if someone leads one of these little ones who believe in me to sin? If he does, it would be better for him to be thrown into the sea with a large millstone tied around his neck.

⁴³/⁴⁴"If your hand causes you to sin, cut it off. It would be better for you to enter God's kingdom with only one hand than to go into hell with two hands. In hell the fire never goes out.

⁴⁵/⁴⁶"If your foot causes you to sin, cut it off. It would be better for you to enter God's kingdom with only one foot than to have two feet and be thrown into hell.

⁴⁷"If your eye causes you to sin, poke it out. It would be better for you to enter God's kingdom with only one eye than to have two eyes and be thrown into hell. ⁴⁸In hell,

" 'The worms do not die.
    The fire is not put out.'   *(Isaiah 66:24)*

⁴⁹Everyone will be salted with fire.

⁵⁰"Salt is good. But suppose it loses its saltiness. How can you make it salty again? Have salt in yourselves. And be at peace with each other."

Jesus Teaches About Divorce

10 Jesus left that place and went into the area of Judea and across the Jordan River. Again crowds of people came to him. As usual, he taught them.

²Some Pharisees came to put him to the test. They asked, "Does the Law allow a man to divorce his wife?"

³"What did Moses command you?" he replied.

⁴They said, "Moses allowed a man to write a letter of divorce and send her away."

⁵"You were stubborn. That's why Moses wrote you this law," Jesus replied. ⁶"But at the beginning of creation, God 'made them male and female.' *(Genesis 1:27)* ⁷'That's why a man will leave his father and mother and be joined to his wife. ⁸The two of them will become one.' *(Genesis 2:24)* They are no longer two, but one. ⁹So a man must not separate what God has joined together."

¹⁰When they were in the house again, the disciples asked Jesus about this.

¹¹He answered, "What if a man divorces his wife and gets married to another woman? He commits adultery against her. ¹²And what if she divorces her husband and gets married to another man? She commits adultery."

Little Children Are Brought to Jesus

13People were bringing little children to Jesus. They wanted him to touch them. But the disciples told the people to stop.

14When Jesus saw this, he was angry. He said to his disciples, "Let the little children come to me. Don't keep them away. God's kingdom belongs to people like them. **15**What I'm about to tell you is true. Anyone who will not receive God's kingdom like a little child will never enter it."

16Then he took the children in his arms. He put his hands on them and blessed them.

Jesus and the Rich Young Man

17As Jesus started on his way, a man ran up to him. He fell on his knees before Jesus. "Good teacher," he said, "what must I do to receive eternal life?"

18"Why do you call me good?" Jesus answered. "No one is good except God. **19**You know what the commandments say. 'Do not commit murder. Do not commit adultery. Do not steal. Do not give false witness. Do not cheat. Honor your father and mother.'" (Exodus 20:12–16; Deuteronomy 5:16–20)

20"Teacher," he said, "I have obeyed all those commandments since I was a boy."

21Jesus looked at him and loved him. "You are missing one thing," he said. "Go and sell everything you have. Give the money to those who are poor. You will have treasure in heaven. Then come and follow me."

22The man's face fell. He went away sad, because he was very rich.

23Jesus looked around. He said to his disciples, "How hard it is for rich people to enter God's kingdom!"

24The disciples were amazed at his words. But Jesus said again, "Children, how hard it is to enter God's kingdom! **25**Is it hard for a camel to go through the eye of a needle? It is even harder for the rich to enter God's kingdom!"

26The disciples were even more amazed. They said to each other, "Then who can be saved?"

27Jesus looked at them and said, "With man, that is impossible. But not with God. All things are possible with God."

28Peter said to him, "We have left everything to follow you!"

29"What I'm about to tell you is true," Jesus replied. "Has anyone left home or family or fields for me and the good news? **30**They will receive 100 times as much in this world. They will have homes and families and fields. But they will also be treated badly by others. In the world to come they will live forever. **31**But many who are first will be last. And the last will be first."

Jesus Again Tells About His Coming Death

32They were on their way up to Jerusalem. Jesus was leading the way. The disciples were amazed. Those who followed were afraid.

Again Jesus took the Twelve to one side. He told them what was going to happen to him. **33**"We are going up to Jerusalem," he said. "The Son of Man will be handed over to the chief priests and the teachers of the law. They will sentence him to death. Then they will hand him over to people who are not Jews. **34**The people will make fun of him and spit on him. They will whip him and kill him. Three days later he will rise from the dead!"

James and John Ask a Favor of Jesus

35James and John came to Jesus. They were the sons of Zebedee. "Teacher," they said, "we would like to ask a favor of you."

36"What do you want me to do for you?" he asked.

37They replied, "Let one of us sit at your right hand in your glorious kingdom. Let the other one sit at your left hand."

38"You don't know what you're asking for," Jesus said. "Can you drink the cup of suffering I drink? Or can you go through the baptism of suffering I must go through?"

39"We can," they answered.

Jesus said to them, "You will drink the cup I drink. And you will go through the baptism I go through. **40**But it is not for me to say who will sit at my right or left hand. These places belong to those they are prepared for."

41The other ten disciples heard about it. They became angry at James and John.

42Jesus called them together. He said, "You know about those who are rulers of the nations. They hold power over their people. Their high officials order them around. **43**Don't be like that. Instead, anyone who wants to be important among you must be your servant. **44**And anyone who wants to be first must be the slave of everyone. **45**Even the Son of Man did not come to be served. Instead, he came to serve others. He came to give his life as the price for setting many people free."

JESUS LOVES KIDS

MARK 10:14

Let the little children come to me. Don't keep them away. God's kingdom belongs to people like them.

Jesus threw his head back and laughed with the children. Some were just sitting near him. But others raced around in front and behind him. Others couldn't get close enough to him. One hung on his leg. Another swung from his arm. What fun children were!

More and more children came to Jesus. Their parents were eager for Jesus to bless their children. The children took turns sitting on his lap. They took turns giving him hugs. He smiled at them and talked and laughed with them . . . until he heard grumbling in the background. And until he noticed that the children were being pulled away. Jesus' disciples were telling the parents to take their children and go home.

"Jesus doesn't have time for this!" they said. "He has more important things to do!"

The smile left Jesus' face as he turned to the disciples and said, **"DON'T YOU DARE SEND THESE LITTLE CHILDREN AWAY!** They are important to me. You should know that! Everyone should be like these little children. See how loving they are? See how they trust me? You should be just like them!"

One by one parents turned around and walked back toward Jesus. As soon as the children saw Jesus, they left their parents and ran toward him again. So many came to him at once that he just sat down in the grass and let them climb all over him. Reaching out his hand, he pulled a shy little girl on to his lap. He smiled at her. He looked over her head and smiled at her parents. He turned and smiled at all the children and their parents.

BE LIKE JESUS

Every person is important. Jesus took time to pay attention to children. He knew that just because they were little didn't mean they weren't important. Just because someone is small or weak or poor doesn't mean he or she isn't important. You can treat them with love and kindness, just like Jesus did.

JESUS LOVED LITTLE CHILDREN.
THE WHOLE STORY: MARK 10:13-16

Go to page 1160 for the next person

Blind Bartimaeus Receives His Sight

46Jesus and his disciples came to Jericho. They were leaving the city. A large crowd was with them.

A blind man was sitting by the side of the road begging. His name was Bartimaeus. Bartimaeus means Son of Timaeus. 47He heard that Jesus of Nazareth was passing by. So he began to shout, "Jesus! Son of David! Have mercy on me!"

48Many people commanded him to stop. They told him to be quiet. But he shouted even louder, "Son of David! Have mercy on me!"

49Jesus stopped and said, "Call for him."

So they called out to the blind man, "Cheer up! Get up on your feet! Jesus is calling for you."

50He threw his coat to one side. Then he jumped to his feet and came to Jesus.

51"What do you want me to do for you?" Jesus asked him.

The blind man said, "Rabbi, I want to be able to see."

52"Go," said Jesus. "Your faith has healed you."

Right away he could see. And he followed Jesus along the road.

Jesus Enters Jerusalem

11 As they all approached Jerusalem, they came to Bethphage and Bethany at the Mount of Olives. Jesus sent out two of his disciples. 2He said to them, "Go to the village ahead of you. Just as you enter it, you will find a donkey's colt tied there. No one has ever ridden it. Untie it and bring it here. 3Someone may ask you, 'Why are you doing this?' If so, say, 'The Lord needs it. But he will send it back here soon.' "

4So they left. They found a colt out in the street. It was tied at a doorway. They untied it. 5Some people standing there asked, "What are you doing? Why are you untying that colt?" 6They answered as Jesus had told them to. So the people let them go.

7They brought the colt to Jesus. They threw their coats over it. Then he sat on it. 8Many people spread their coats on the road. Others spread branches they had cut in the fields. 9Those in front and those in back shouted,

"Hosanna!"

"Blessed is the one who comes in the name of the Lord!"
(Psalm 118:25,26)

10"Blessed is the coming kingdom of our father David!"

"Hosanna in the highest heaven!"

11Jesus entered Jerusalem and went to the temple. He looked around at everything. But it was already late. So he went out to Bethany with the Twelve.

Jesus Clears the Temple

12The next day as Jesus and his disciples were leaving Bethany, they were hungry. 13Not too far away, he saw a fig tree. It was covered with leaves. He went to find out if it had any fruit. When he reached it, he found nothing but leaves. It was not the season for figs.

14Then Jesus said to the tree, "May no one ever eat fruit from you again!" And his disciples heard him say it.

15When Jesus reached Jerusalem, he entered the temple area. He began chasing out those who were buying and selling there. He turned over the tables of the people who were exchanging money. He also turned over the benches of those who were selling doves. 16He would not allow anyone to carry items for sale through the temple courtyards.

17Then he taught them. He told them, "It is written that the Lord said,

" 'My house will be called
  a house where people from all
    nations can pray.'   *(Isaiah 56:7)*

But you have made it a 'den for robbers.' "
(Jeremiah 7:11)

18The chief priests and the teachers of the law heard about this. They began looking for a way to kill Jesus. They were afraid of him, because the whole crowd was amazed at his teaching.

19When evening came, Jesus and his disciples left the city.

The Dried-up Fig Tree

20In the morning as Jesus and his disciples walked along, they saw the fig tree. It was dried up all the way down to the roots.

21Peter remembered. He said to Jesus, "Rabbi, look! The fig tree you put a curse on has dried up!"

22"Have faith in God," Jesus said. 23"What I'm about to tell you is true. Suppose one of you says to this mountain, 'Go and throw yourself into the sea.' You must not doubt in your heart. You must believe that what you say will happen. Then it will be done for you.

24"So I tell you, when you pray for

POWER-SURGE

OBEYS ✔

SO I TELL YOU, WHEN
YOU PRAY FOR
SOMETHING, BELIEVE
THAT YOU HAVE
ALREADY RECEIVED
IT. THEN IT WILL
BE YOURS.
— MARK 11:24 —

BELIEVES ✝

something, believe that you have already received it. Then it will be yours. 25/26And when you stand praying, forgive anyone you have anything against. Then your Father in heaven will forgive your sins."

The Authority of Jesus Is Questioned

27Jesus and his disciples arrived again in Jerusalem. He was walking in the temple courtyards. Then the chief priests came to him. The teachers of the law and the elders came too.

28"By what authority are you doing these things?" they asked. "Who gave you authority to do this?"

29Jesus replied, "I will ask you one question. Answer me, and I will tell you by what authority I am doing these things. 30Was John's baptism from heaven? Or did it come from men? Tell me!"

31They talked to each other about it. They said, "If we say, 'From heaven,' he will ask, 'Then why didn't you believe him?' 32But what if we say, 'From men'?" They were afraid of the people. Everyone believed that John really was a prophet.

33So they answered Jesus, "We don't know."

Jesus said, "Then I won't tell you by what authority I am doing these things either."

The Story of the Renters

12 Jesus began to speak to the people by using stories. He said, "A man planted a vineyard. He put a wall around it. He dug a pit for a winepress. He also built a lookout tower. He rented the vine-yard out to some farmers. Then he went away on a journey.

2"At harvest time he sent a servant to the renters. He told the servant to collect from them some of the fruit of the vineyard. 3But they grabbed the servant and beat him up. Then they sent him away with nothing. 4So the man sent another servant to the renters. They hit this one on the head and treated him badly. 5The man sent still another servant. The renters killed him. The man sent many others. The renters beat up some of them. They killed the others.

6"The man had one person left to send. It was his son, and he loved him. He sent him last of all. He said, 'They will respect my son.'

7"But the renters said to each other, 'This is the one who will receive all the owner's property someday. Come, let's kill him. Then everything will be ours.' 8So they took him and killed him. They threw him out of the vineyard.

9"What will the owner of the vineyard do then? He will come and kill those renters. He will give the vineyard to others. 10"Haven't you read what Scripture says,

" 'The stone the builders didn't accept
has become the most important
stone of all.
11 The Lord has done it.
It is wonderful in our eyes'?"
(Psalm 118:22,23)

12Then the religious leaders looked for a way to arrest Jesus. They knew he had told the story against them. But they were afraid of the crowd. So they left him and went away.

Is It Right to Pay Taxes to Caesar?

13Later the religious leaders sent some of the Pharisees and Herodians to Jesus. They wanted to trap him with his own words.

14They came to him and said, "Teacher, we know you are a man of honor. You don't let others tell you what to do or say. You don't care how important they are. But you teach the way of God truthfully. Is it right to pay taxes to Caesar or not? 15Should we pay or shouldn't we?"

But Jesus knew what they were trying to do. So he asked, "Why are you trying to trap me? Bring me a silver coin. Let me look at it."

16They brought the coin.

He asked them, "Whose picture is this? And whose words?"

"Caesar's," they replied.

17Then Jesus said to them, "Give to Caesar what belongs to Caesar. And give to God what belongs to God."

They were amazed at him.

Marriage When the Dead Rise

18The Sadducees came to Jesus with a question. They do not believe that people rise from the dead. **19**"Teacher," they said, "Moses wrote for us about a man who died and didn't have any children. But he did leave a wife behind. That man's brother must get married to the widow. He must have children to carry on his dead brother's name. **20**"There were seven brothers. The first one got married. He died without leaving any children. **21**The second one got married to the widow. He also died and left no child. It was the same with the third one. **22**In fact, none of the seven left any children. Last of all, the woman died too. **23**When the dead rise, whose wife will she be? All seven of them were married to her."

24Jesus replied, "You are mistaken because you do not know the Scriptures. And you do not know the power of God. **25**When the dead rise, they won't get married. And their parents won't give them to be married. They will be like the angels in heaven. **26**"What about the dead rising? Haven't you read in the scroll of Moses the story of the bush? God said to Moses, 'I am the God of Abraham. I am the God of Isaac. And I am the God of Jacob.' *(Exodus 3:6)* **27**He is not the God of the dead. He is the God of the living. You have made a big mistake!"

The Most Important Commandment

28One of the teachers of the law came and heard the Sadducees arguing. He noticed that Jesus had given the Sadducees a good answer. So he asked him, "Which is the most important of all the commandments?"

29Jesus answered, "Here is the most important one. Moses said, 'Israel, listen to me. The Lord is our God. The Lord is one. **30**Love the Lord your God with all your heart and with all your soul. Love him with all your mind and with all your strength.' *(Deuteronomy 6:4,5)* **31**And here is the second one. 'Love your neighbor as you love yourself.' *(Leviticus 19:18)* There is no commandment more important than these."

LOVING

TO LOVE GOD WITH ALL YOUR HEART AND MIND AND STRENGTH IS VERY IMPORTANT. SO IS LOVING YOUR NEIGHBOR AS YOU LOVE YOURSELF.
— MARK 12:33 —

TRIES HARD

32"You have spoken well, teacher," the man replied. "You are right in saying that God is one. There is no other God but him. **33**To love God with all your heart and mind and strength is very important. So is loving your neighbor as you love yourself. These things are more important than all burnt offerings and sacrifices."

34Jesus saw that the man had answered wisely. He said to him, "You are not far from God's kingdom."

From then on, no one dared to ask Jesus any more questions.

Whose Son Is the Christ?

35Jesus was teaching in the temple courtyard. He asked, "Why do the teachers of the law say that the Christ is the son of David? **36**The Holy Spirit spoke through David himself. David said,

" 'The Lord said to my Lord,
　"Sit at my right hand
until I put your enemies
　under your control." '　*(Psalm 110:1)*

37David himself calls him 'Lord.' So how can he be David's son?"

The large crowd listened to Jesus with delight.

38As he taught, he said, "Watch out for the teachers of the law. They like to walk around in long robes. They like to be greeted in the market places. **39**They love to have the most important seats in the synagogues. They also love to have the places of honor at dinners. **40**They take over the houses of widows. They say long prayers to show off. God will punish those men very much."

The Widow's Offering

41Jesus sat down across from the place where people put their temple offerings. He watched the crowd putting their money into the offering boxes. Many rich people threw large amounts into them.

42But a poor widow came and put in two very small copper coins. They were worth much less than a penny.

43Jesus asked his disciples to come to him. He said, "What I'm about to tell you is true. That poor widow has put more into the offering box than all the others. **44**They all gave a lot because they are rich. But she gave even though she is poor. She put in everything she had. She gave all she had to live on."

Signs of the End

13 Jesus was leaving the temple. One of his disciples said to him, "Look, Teacher! What huge stones! What wonderful buildings!"

2"Do you see these huge buildings?" Jesus asked. "Not one stone here will be left on top of another. Every stone will be thrown down."

3Jesus was sitting on the Mount of Olives, across from the temple. Peter, James, John and Andrew asked him a question in private. **4**"Tell us," they said. "When will these things happen? And what will be the sign that they are all about to come true?"

5Jesus said to them, "Keep watch! Be careful that no one fools you. **6**Many will come in my name. They will claim, 'I am he.' They will fool many people.

7"You will hear about wars. You will also hear people talking about future wars. Don't be alarmed. Those things must happen. But the end still isn't here. **8**Nation will fight against nation. Kingdom will fight against kingdom. There will be earthquakes in many places. People will go hungry. All of those things are the beginning of birth pains.

9"Watch out! You will be handed over to the local courts. You will be whipped in the synagogues. You will stand in front of governors and kings because of me. In that way you will be witnesses to them. **10**The good news has to be preached to all nations before the end comes. **11**You will be arrested and brought to trial. But don't worry ahead of time about what you will say. Just say what God brings to your mind at the time. It is not you speaking, but the Holy Spirit.

12"Brothers will hand over brothers to be killed. Fathers will hand over their children. Children will rise up against their parents and have them put to death. **13**Everyone will hate you because of me. But the one who stands firm to the end will be saved.

14"You will see 'the hated thing that destroys.' *(Daniel 9:27; 11:31; 12:11)* It will stand where it does not belong. The reader should understand this. Then those who are in Judea should escape to the mountains. **15**No one on the roof should go down into his house to take anything out. **16**No one in the field should go back to get his coat. **17**How awful it will be in those days for pregnant women! How awful for nursing mothers! **18**Pray that this will not happen in winter.

19"Those days will be worse than any others from the time God created the world until now. And there will never be any like them again. **20**If the Lord had not cut the time short, no one would live. But because of God's chosen people, he has shortened it.

21"At that time someone may say to you, 'Look! Here is the Christ!' Or, 'Look! There he is!' Do not believe it. **22**False Christs and false prophets will appear. They will do signs and miracles. They will try to fool God's chosen people if possible. **23**Keep watch! I have told you everything ahead of time.

24"So in those days there will be terrible suffering. After that, Scripture says,

" 'The sun will be darkened.
The moon will not shine.
25The stars will fall from the sky.
The heavenly bodies will be shaken.'
(Isaiah 13:10; 34:4)

26"At that time people will see the Son of Man coming in clouds. He will come with great power and glory. **27**He will send his angels. He will gather his chosen people from all four directions. He will bring them from the ends of the earth to the ends of the heavens.

28"Learn a lesson from the fig tree. As soon as its twigs get tender and its leaves come out, you know that summer is near. **29**In the same way, when you see those things happening, you know that the end is near. It is right at the door. **30**What I'm about to tell you is true. The people living at that time will certainly not pass away until all those things have happened. **31**Heaven and earth will pass away. But my words will never pass away.

The Day and Hour Are Not Known

32"No one knows about that day or hour. Not even the angels in heaven know. The Son does not know. Only the Father knows.

33"Keep watch! Stay awake! You do not know when that time will come. **34**It's like a man going away. He leaves his house and puts his servants in charge. Each one is given a task to do. He tells the one at the door to keep watch.

35"So keep watch! You do not know when the owner of the house will come back. It may be in the evening or at midnight. It may be when the rooster crows or at dawn. **36**He may come suddenly. So do not let him find you sleeping. **37**"What I say to you, I say to everyone. 'Watch!' "

A Woman Pours Perfume on Jesus

14 The Passover and the Feast of Unleavened Bread were only two days away. The chief priests and the teachers of the law were looking for a clever way to arrest Jesus. They wanted to kill him. **2**"But not during the Feast," they said. "The people may stir up trouble."

3Jesus was in Bethany. He was at the table in the home of a man named Simon, who had a skin disease. A woman came with a special sealed jar of very expensive perfume. It was made out of pure nard. She broke the jar open and poured the perfume on Jesus' head.

4Some of the people there became angry. They said to one another, "Why waste this perfume? **5**It could have been sold for more than a year's pay. The money could have been given to poor people." So they found fault with the woman.

6"Leave her alone," Jesus said. "Why are you bothering her? She has done a beautiful thing to me. **7**You will always have poor people with you. You can help them any time you want to. But you will not always have me. **8**She did what she could. She poured perfume on my body to prepare me to be buried. **9**What I'm about to tell you is true. What she has done will be told anywhere the good news is preached all over the world. It will be told in memory of her."

10Judas Iscariot was one of the Twelve. He went to the chief priests to hand Jesus over to them. **11**They were delighted to hear that he would do this. They promised to give Judas money. So he watched for the right time to hand Jesus over to them.

The Lord's Supper

12It was the first day of the Feast of Unleavened Bread. That was the time to sacrifice the Passover lamb.

Jesus' disciples asked him, "Where do you want us to go and prepare for you to eat the Passover meal?"

13So he sent out two of his disciples. He told them, "Go into the city. A man carrying a jar of water will meet you. Follow him. **14**He will enter a house. Say to its owner, 'The Teacher asks, "Where is my guest room? Where can I eat the Passover meal with my disciples?" ' **15**He will show you a large upstairs room. It will have furniture and will be ready. Prepare for us to eat there."

16The disciples left and went into the city. They found things just as Jesus had told them. So they prepared the Passover meal.

17When evening came, Jesus arrived with the Twelve. **18**While they were at the table eating, Jesus said, "What I'm about to tell you is true. One of you who is eating with me will hand me over to my enemies."

19The disciples became sad. One by one they said to him, "It's not I, is it?"

20"It is one of the Twelve," Jesus replied. "It is the one who dips bread into the bowl with me. **21**The Son of Man will go just as it is written about him. But how terrible it will be for the one who hands over the Son of Man! It would be better for him if he had not been born."

22While they were eating, Jesus took bread. He gave thanks and broke it. He handed it to his disciples and said, "Take it. This is my body."

23Then he took the cup. He gave thanks and handed it to them. All of them drank from it.

24"This is my blood of the new covenant," he said to them. "It is poured out for many. **25**What I'm about to tell you is true. I won't drink wine with you again until the day I drink it in God's kingdom."

26Then they sang a hymn and went out to the Mount of Olives.

Jesus Says That Peter Will Fail

27"You will all turn away," Jesus told the disciples. "It is written,

" 'I will strike the shepherd down.
　　Then the sheep will be scattered.'
　　　　　　　　　　(Zechariah 13:7)

28But after I rise from the dead, I will go ahead of you into Galilee."

29Peter said, "All the others may turn away. But I will not."

30"What I'm about to tell you is true," Jesus answered. "It will happen today, this very night. Before the rooster crows twice, you yourself will say three times that you don't know me."

31But Peter would not give in. He said, "I may have to die with you. But I will never say I don't know you." And all the others said the same thing.

Jesus Prays in Gethsemane

32Jesus and his disciples went to a place called Gethsemane. Jesus said to them, "Sit here while I pray."

33He took Peter, James and John along with him. He began to be very upset and troubled. **34**"My soul is very sad. I feel close to death," he said to them. "Stay here. Keep watch."

35He went a little farther. Then he fell to the ground. He prayed that, if possible, the hour might pass by him. **36**"*Abba*," he said, "everything is possible for you. Take this cup of suffering away from me. But let what you want be done, not what I want." *Abba* means Father.

37Then he returned to his disciples and found them sleeping. "Simon," he said to Peter, "are you asleep? Couldn't you keep watch for one hour? **38**Watch and pray. Then you won't fall into sin when you are tempted. The spirit is willing. But the body is weak."

39Once more Jesus went away and prayed the same thing. **40**Then he came back. Again he found them sleeping. They couldn't keep their eyes open. They did not know what to say to him.

41Jesus returned the third time. He said to them, "Are you still sleeping and resting? Enough! The hour has come. Look! The Son of Man is about to be handed over to sinners. **42**Get up! Let us go! Here comes the one who is handing me over to them!"

Jesus Is Arrested

43Just as Jesus was speaking, Judas appeared. He was one of the Twelve. A crowd was with him. They were carrying swords and clubs. The chief priests, the teachers of the law, and the elders had sent them.

44Judas, who was going to hand Jesus over, had arranged a signal with them. "The one I kiss is the man," he said. "Arrest him and have the guards lead him away."

45So Judas went to Jesus at once. He said, "Rabbi!" And he kissed him.

46The men grabbed Jesus and arrested him.

47Then one of those standing nearby pulled his sword out. He struck the servant of the high priest and cut off his ear.

48"Am I leading a band of armed men against you?" asked Jesus. "Do you have to come out with swords and clubs to capture me? **49**Every day I was with you. I taught in the temple courtyard, and you didn't arrest me. But the Scriptures must come true."

50Then everyone left him and ran away.

51A young man was following Jesus. The man was wearing nothing but a piece of linen cloth. When the crowd grabbed him, **52**he ran away naked. He left his clothing behind.

Jesus Is Taken to the Sanhedrin

53The crowd took Jesus to the high priest. All of the chief priests, the elders, and the teachers of the law came together.

54Not too far away, Peter followed Jesus. He went right into the courtyard of the high priest. There he sat with the guards. He warmed himself at the fire.

55The chief priests and the whole Sanhedrin were looking for something to use against Jesus. They wanted to put him to death. But they did not find any proof. **56**Many witnesses lied about him. But their stories did not agree.

57Then some stood up. They gave false witness about him. **58**"We heard him say, 'I will destroy this temple made by human hands. In three days I will build another temple, not made by human hands.' " **59**But what they said did not agree.

60Then the high priest stood up in front of them. He asked Jesus, "Aren't you going to answer? What are these charges these men are bringing against you?"

61But Jesus remained silent. He gave no answer.

Again the high priest asked him, "Are you the Christ? Are you the Son of the Blessed One?"

62"I am," said Jesus. "And you will see the Son of Man sitting at the right hand of the Mighty One. You will see the Son of Man coming on the clouds of heaven."

63The high priest tore his clothes. "Why do we need any more witnesses?" he asked. **64**"You have heard him say a very evil thing against God. What do you think?"

They all found him guilty and said he must die.

65Then some began to spit at him. They blindfolded him. They hit him with their fists. They said, "Prophesy!" And the guards took him and beat him.

Peter Says He Does Not Know Jesus

66Peter was below in the courtyard. One of the high priest's female servants came by. **67**When she saw Peter warming himself, she looked closely at him.

"You also were with Jesus, that Nazarene," she said.

68But Peter said he had not been with him. "I don't know or understand what you're talking about," he said. He went out to the entrance to the courtyard.

69The servant saw him there. She said again to those standing around, "This fellow is one of them."

70Again he said he was not.

After a little while, those standing nearby said to Peter, "You must be one of them. You are from Galilee."

71He began to call down curses on him-

JUDAS ISCARIOT (Not!)

MARK 14:44-45

Judas, who was going to hand Jesus over, had arranged a signal with them. "The one I kiss is the man," he said. "Arrest him and have the guards lead him away." So Judas went to Jesus at once. He said, "Rabbi!" And he kissed him.

Judas swaggered into the garden. He knew Jesus would be there. He looked for him by the light of the torches carried by the soldiers and officials who followed him. The money clinked in the bag tied around his waist. Thirty pieces of silver. Such a lot of money just for telling some men who hated Jesus where to find him.

Coming around a bend in the path, Judas spotted Jesus up ahead. "There he is," he whispered to the official next to him. "Remember what I said. The one I kiss is the one you want."

WALKING BOLDLY UP TO JESUS, JUDAS ISCARIOT GREETED HIM. "Teacher!" he said. Then he took hold of Jesus' arms and kissed him.

Immediately the soldiers pushed Judas Iscariot out of the way and grabbed Jesus. Because Judas Iscariot betrayed him, Jesus was now on his way to die.

JUDAS ISCARIOT (iss-CARE-ee-ut)

No one is really sure why Judas betrayed Jesus. Did he need the money? Or did he really hate Jesus? We only know he did it. Be sure you guard yourself against being like Judas. Don't ever let anything be more important to you than believing in Jesus and being faithful to him.

JUDAS BETRAYED JESUS BY KISSING HIM.

Go to page 1167 for the next person

self. He took an oath and said to them, "I don't know this man you're talking about!"

72Right away the rooster crowed the second time. Then Peter remembered what Jesus had spoken to him. "The rooster will crow twice," he had said. "Before it does, you will say three times that you don't know me." Peter broke down and sobbed.

Jesus Is Brought to Pilate

15 It was very early in the morning. The chief priests, with the elders, the teachers of the law, and the whole Sanhedrin, made a decision. They tied Jesus up and led him away. Then they handed him over to Pilate.

2"Are you the king of the Jews?" asked Pilate.

"Yes. It is just as you say," Jesus replied.

3The chief priests brought many charges against him. 4So Pilate asked him again, "Aren't you going to answer? See how many things they charge you with."

5But Jesus still did not reply. Pilate was amazed.

6It was the usual practice at the Passover Feast to let one prisoner go free. The people could choose the one they wanted. 7A man named Barabbas was in prison. He was there with some other people who had fought against the country's rulers. They had committed murder while they were fighting against the rulers. 8The crowd came up and asked Pilate to do for them what he usually did.

9"Do you want me to let the king of the Jews go free?" asked Pilate. 10He knew that the chief priests had handed Jesus over to him because they were jealous. 11But the chief priests stirred up the crowd. So the crowd asked Pilate to let Barabbas go free instead.

12"Then what should I do with the one you call the king of the Jews?" Pilate asked them.

13"Crucify him!" the crowd shouted.

14"Why? What wrong has he done?" asked Pilate.

But they shouted even louder, "Crucify him!"

15Pilate wanted to satisfy the crowd. So he let Barabbas go free. He ordered that Jesus be whipped. Then he handed him over to be nailed to a cross.

The Soldiers Make Fun of Jesus

16The soldiers led Jesus away into the palace. It was called the Praetorium. They called together the whole company of soldiers.

17The soldiers put a purple robe on Jesus. Then they twisted thorns together to make a crown. They placed it on his head. 18They began to call out to him, "We honor you, king of the Jews!" 19Again and again they hit him on the head with a stick. They spit on him. They fell on their knees and pretended to honor him.

20After they had made fun of him, they took off the purple robe. They put his own clothes back on him. Then they led him out to nail him to a cross.

Jesus Is Nailed to a Cross

21A man named Simon from Cyrene was passing by. He was the father of Alexander and Rufus. Simon was on his way in from the country. The soldiers forced him to carry the cross.

22They brought Jesus to the place called Golgotha. The word Golgotha means The Place of the Skull. 23Then they gave him wine mixed with spices. But he did not take it.

24They nailed him to the cross. Then they divided up his clothes. They cast lots to see what each of them would get.

25It was nine o'clock in the morning when they crucified him. 26They wrote out the charge against him. It read, THE KING OF THE JEWS.

27/28They crucified two robbers with him. One was on his right and one was on his left.

29Those who passed by shouted at Jesus and made fun of him. They shook their heads and said, "So you are going to destroy the temple and build it again in three days? 30Then come down from the cross! Save yourself!"

31In the same way the chief priests and the teachers of the law made fun of him among themselves. "He saved others," they said. "But he can't save himself! 32Let this Christ, this King of Israel, come down now from the cross! When we see that, we will believe."

Those who were being crucified with Jesus also made fun of him.

Jesus Dies

33At noon, darkness covered the whole land. It lasted three hours. 34At three o'clock Jesus cried out in a loud voice, *"Eloi, Eloi, lama sabachthani?"* This means "My God, my God, why have you deserted me?" *(Psalm 22:1)*

35Some of those standing nearby heard

Jesus cry out. They said, "Listen! He's calling for Elijah."

36One of them ran and filled a sponge with wine vinegar. He put it on a stick. He offered it to Jesus to drink. "Leave him alone," he said. "Let's see if Elijah comes to take him down."

37With a loud cry, Jesus took his last breath.

38The temple curtain was torn in two from top to bottom.

39A Roman commander was standing there in front of Jesus. He heard his cry and saw how Jesus died. Then he said, "This man was surely the Son of God!"

40Not very far away, some women were watching. Mary Magdalene was among them. Mary, the mother of the younger James and of Joses, was also there. So was Salome. **41**In Galilee those women had followed Jesus. They had taken care of his needs.

Many other women were also there. They had come up with him to Jerusalem.

Jesus Is Buried

42It was the day before the Sabbath. That day was called Preparation Day. As evening approached, **43**Joseph went boldly to Pilate and asked for Jesus' body. Joseph was from the town of Arimathea. He was a leading member of the Jewish Council. He was waiting for God's kingdom.

44Pilate was surprised to hear that Jesus was already dead. So he called for the Roman commander. He asked him if Jesus had already died. **45**The commander said it was true. So Pilate gave the body to Joseph.

46Then Joseph bought some linen cloth. He took the body down and wrapped it in the linen. He put it in a tomb cut out of rock. Then he rolled a stone against the entrance to the tomb.

47Mary Magdalene and Mary the mother of Joses saw where Jesus' body had been placed.

Jesus Rises From the Dead

16 The Sabbath day ended. Mary Magdalene, Mary the mother of James, and Salome bought spices. They were going to apply them to Jesus' body.

2Very early on the first day of the week, they were on their way to the tomb. It was just after sunrise. **3**They asked each other, "Who will roll the stone away from the entrance to the tomb?"

4Then they looked up and saw that the

POWER-SURGE

BELIEVES ✝

[JESUS] SAID TO THEM, "GO INTO ALL THE WORLD. PREACH THE GOOD NEWS TO EVERYONE. ANYONE WHO BELIEVES AND IS BAPTIZED WILL BE SAVED.
— **MARK 16:15-16** —

TELLS OTHERS

stone had been rolled away. The stone was very large.

5They entered the tomb. As they did, they saw a young man dressed in a white robe. He was sitting on the right side. They were alarmed.

6"Don't be alarmed," he said. "You are looking for Jesus the Nazarene, who was crucified. But he has risen! He is not here! See the place where they had put him. **7**Go! Tell his disciples and Peter, 'He is going ahead of you into Galilee. There you will see him. It will be just as he told you.' "

8The women were shaking and confused. They went out and ran away from the tomb. They said nothing to anyone, because they were afraid.

9Jesus rose from the dead early on the first day of the week. He appeared first to Mary Magdalene. He had driven seven demons out of her. **10**She went and told those who had been with him. She found them crying. They were very sad. **11**They heard that Jesus was alive and that she had seen him. But they did not believe it.

12After that, Jesus appeared in a different form to two of them. This happened while they were walking out in the country. **13**The two returned and told the others about it. But the others did not believe them either.

14Later Jesus appeared to the Eleven as they were eating. He spoke firmly to them because they had no faith. They would not believe those who had seen him after he rose from the dead.

15He said to them, "Go into all the world. Preach the good news to everyone. **16**Anyone who believes and is baptized will be saved. But anyone who does not believe will be punished. **17**Here are the miraculous signs that those who believe will do. In my name they will drive out demons. They will speak in languages they had not known before. **18**They will pick up snakes with their hands. And when they drink deadly poison, it will not hurt them at all. They will place their hands on sick people. And the people will get well."

19When the Lord Jesus finished speaking to them, he was taken up into heaven. He sat down at the right hand of God.

20Then the disciples went out and preached everywhere. The Lord worked with them. And he backed up his word by the signs that went with it.

LUKE

Luke, a medical doctor, writes this book (and the book of Acts, too). The book of Luke presents for the third time Jesus' teachings and the stories of his life and death. Luke often writes in more detail than the other writers. The heroes in the book of Luke are the shepherds, who are the first people to visit baby Jesus; Simeon and Anna, who see Jesus on his first visit to the temple; John the Baptist, who prepares the way for Jesus; the centurion, who had more faith than many others; and Jesus' disciples. When you read the book of Luke, you'll discover more about Jesus' teachings and about how he lived and died and rose again.

HEROES IN THIS BOOK . . .

Luke Writes an Orderly Report

1 Many people have attempted to write about the things that have taken place among us. **2**Reports of these things were handed down to us. There were people who saw these things for themselves from the beginning and then passed the word on.

3I myself have carefully looked into everything from the beginning. So it seemed good also to me to write down an orderly report of exactly what happened. I am doing this for you, most excellent Theophilus. **4**I want you to know that the things you have been taught are true.

The Coming Birth of John the Baptist

5Herod was king of Judea. During the time he was ruling, there was a priest named Zechariah. He belonged to a group of priests named after Abijah. His wife Elizabeth also came from the family line of Aaron. **6**Both of them did what was right in God's eyes. They obeyed all the Lord's commandments and rules faithfully. **7**But they had no children, because Elizabeth was not able to have any. And they were both very old.

POWER-SURGE

FAITHFUL ()

[ZECHARIAH AND ELIZABETH] OBEYED ALL THE LORD'S COMMANDMENTS AND RULES FAITHFULLY.
— LUKE 1:6 —

✔

OBEYS

8One day Zechariah's group was on duty. He was serving as a priest in God's temple. **9**He happened to be chosen, in the usual way, to go into the temple of the Lord. There he was supposed to burn incense. **10**The time came for this to be done. All who had gathered to worship were praying outside.

11Then an angel of the Lord appeared to Zechariah. The angel was standing at the right side of the incense altar. **12**When Zechariah saw him, he was amazed and terrified.

13But the angel said to him, "Do not be afraid, Zechariah. Your prayer has been heard. Your wife Elizabeth will have a child. It will be a boy, and you must name him John. **14**He will be a joy and delight to you. His birth will make many people very glad. **15**He will be important in the Lord's eyes.

"He must never use wine or other such drinks. He will be filled with the Holy Spirit from the time he is born. **16**He will bring many of Israel's people back to the Lord their God. **17**And he will prepare the way for the Lord. He will have the same spirit and power that Elijah had. He will teach parents how to love their children. He will also teach people who don't obey to be wise and do what is right. In this way, he will prepare a people who are ready for the Lord."

18Zechariah asked the angel, "How can I be sure of this? I am an old man, and my wife is old too."

19The angel answered, "I am Gabriel. I serve God. I have been sent to speak to you and to tell you this good news. **20**And now you will have to be silent. You will not be able to speak until after John is born. That's because you did not believe my words. They will come true when the time is right."

21During that time, the people were waiting for Zechariah to come out. They wondered why he stayed in the temple so long. **22**When he came out, he could not speak to them. They realized he had seen a vision in the temple. They knew this because he kept motioning to them. He still could not speak.

23When his time of service was over, he returned home. **24**After that, his wife Elizabeth became pregnant. She stayed at home for five months. **25**"The Lord has done this for me," she said. "In these days, he has been kind to me. He has taken away my shame among the people."

The Coming Birth of Jesus

26In the sixth month after Elizabeth had become pregnant, God sent the angel Gabriel to Nazareth, a town in Galilee. **27**He was sent to a virgin. The girl was engaged to a man named Joseph. He came from the family line of David. The virgin's name was Mary. **28**The angel greeted her and said, "The Lord has given you special favor. He is with you."

29Mary was very upset because of his words. She wondered what kind of greeting this could be. **30**But the angel said to her, "Do not be afraid, Mary. God is very pleased with you. 31You will become pregnant and give birth to a son. You must name him Jesus. 32He will be great and will be called the Son of the Most High God. The Lord God will make him a king like his father David of long ago. 33He will rule forever over his people, who came from Jacob's family. His kingdom will never end."

34"How can this happen?" Mary asked the angel. "I am a virgin."

35The angel answered, "The Holy Spirit will come to you. The power of the Most High God will cover you. So the holy one that is born will be called the Son of God. 36Your relative Elizabeth is old. And even she is going to have a child. People thought she could not have children. But

ZECHARIAH (Sort of)

LUKE 1:19-20

The angel answered, "I am Gabriel. I serve God. I have been sent to speak to you and to tell you this good news. And now you will have to be silent. You will not be able to speak until after John is born. That's because you did not believe my words. They will come true when the time is right."

Zechariah (zek-uh-RIE-uh) squinted in the bright sunshine of the temple courtyard. An angel had just come to him inside the temple and brought him an amazing message. He opened his mouth to tell the people gathered there what had happened. But no words came out, not one sound. HIS VOICE WAS TOTALLY GONE.

The angel told Zechariah this would happen. Zechariah at first didn't believe the angel's amazing message. Therefore, the angel said Zechariah would not be able to speak until all the angel told him happened.

The angel said Zechariah's wife Elizabeth would have a baby. He would grow up to be a preacher. He would prepare people's hearts to hear about Jesus.

Zechariah may not have believed the angel at first. But as soon as he opened his mouth and couldn't speak, he knew that all the angel had said would come true.

BE A BETTER ZECHARIAH

All of God's words are true. Zechariah had trouble at first believing the words of God's angel. But that didn't last long. His son John the Baptist was born and prepared the people for Jesus. You can be like Zechariah. Believe God's message.

ZECHARIAH BELIEVED THE ANGEL'S MESSAGE.

Go to page 1169 for the next Super Hero

she has been pregnant for six months now. **37**Nothing is impossible with God."

38"I serve the Lord," Mary answered. "May it happen to me just as you said it would." Then the angel left her.

Mary Visits Elizabeth

39At that time Mary got ready and hurried to a town in Judea's hill country. **40**There she entered Zechariah's home and greeted Elizabeth. **41**When Elizabeth heard Mary's greeting, the baby inside her jumped. And Elizabeth was filled with the Holy Spirit. **42**In a loud voice she called out, "God has blessed you more than other women. And blessed is the child you will have! **43**But why is God so kind to me? Why has the mother of my Lord come to me? **44**As soon as I heard the sound of your voice, the baby inside me jumped for joy. **45**You are a woman God has blessed. You have believed that what the Lord has said to you will be done!"

POWER-SURGE

BELIEVES ✝

YOU ARE A WOMAN
GOD HAS BLESSED.
YOU HAVE BELIEVED
THAT WHAT THE LORD
HAS SAID TO YOU
WILL BE DONE!
— LUKE 1:45 —

Mary's Song

46Mary said,

"My soul gives glory to the Lord.
47 My spirit delights in God my Savior.
48 He has taken note of me
    even though I am not important.
From now on all people will call me
    blessed.
49 The Mighty One has done great
    things for me.
His name is holy.
50 He shows his mercy to those who have
    respect for him,
from parent to child down through
    the years.
51 He has done mighty things with his
    arm.
He has scattered those who are
    proud in their deepest thoughts.
52 He has brought down rulers from their
    thrones.

But he has lifted up people who are
    not important.
53 He has filled those who are hungry
    with good things.
But he has sent those who are rich
    away empty.
54 He has helped the people of Israel, who
    serve him.
He has always remembered to be
    kind
55 to Abraham and his children down
    through the years.
He has done it just as he said to our
    people of long ago."

56Mary stayed with Elizabeth about three months. Then she returned home.

John the Baptist Is Born

57The time came for Elizabeth to have her baby. She gave birth to a son. **58**Her neighbors and relatives heard that the Lord had been very kind to her. They shared her joy.

59On the eighth day, they came to have the child circumcised. They were going to name him Zechariah, like his father. **60**But his mother spoke up. "No!" she said. "He must be called John."

61They said to her, "No one among your relatives has that name."

62Then they motioned to his father. They wanted to find out what he would like to name the child. **63**He asked for something to write on. Then he wrote, "His name is John." Everyone was amazed.

64Right away Zechariah could speak again. His first words gave praise to God. **65**The neighbors were all filled with fear and wonder. All through Judea's hill country, people were talking about all these things. **66**Everyone who heard this wondered about it. And because the Lord was with John, they asked, "What is this child going to be?"

Zechariah's Song

67His father Zechariah was filled with the Holy Spirit. He prophesied,

68"Give praise to the Lord, the God of
    Israel!
He has come and set his people free.
69 He has acted with great power and has
    saved us.
He did it for those who are from the
    family line of his servant David.
70 Long ago holy prophets said he would
    do it.
71 He has saved us from our enemies.
    We are rescued from all who hate us.
72 He has been kind to our people.

MARY

LUKE 1:38

"I serve the Lord," Mary answered. "May it happen to me just as you said it would." Then the angel left her.

Mary's stomach growled. She needed some breakfast. A piece of bread, maybe some cheese. Her feet moved more quickly just thinking about it. She adjusted the water jar she carried so that she could walk faster.

Hurrying around the corner of a neighbor's house, Mary came to a quick stop. An angel stood in front of her on the path. The angel's eyes glittered. He spoke in a whisper that was as light and as soft as a breeze but as booming as thunder: "Mary, you are a special young woman. God is with you."

MARY JUMPED BACK WITH FRIGHT AS SOON AS SHE HEARD THE ANGEL SPEAK.

The angel watched her kindly, then spoke again. "Don't be afraid, Mary. You will have a very special baby. God has chosen you to be the mother of his son, Jesus. He will save people from their sins."

Now Mary was really afraid. *A baby?* she thought. *But I'm not even married yet. How can I have a baby?*

The angel watched. He knew Mary didn't know what to think. He knew she didn't really understand. Gently the angel told Mary that God's power would cover Mary and cause her to have a baby. The baby would be God's Son.

Mary only understood one thing. The angel was from God, and what he told her was the truth. She knew it would happen. Although she didn't completely understand, she wanted to do what God wanted. Mary turned to the angel and looked straight into his glittering eyes. "I'm God's servant," she said. "May God do to me everything you have said."

BE A MARY

Mary was frightened and confused by the angel's message. But that didn't matter to her. What mattered was doing what God wanted. She was willing. Be a Mary! When you know God wants you to do something, *do it*—just because God wants you to.

MARY WAS AFRAID BUT WILLING TO BE USED BY GOD.

THE WHOLE STORY: LUKE 1:26-38

Go to page 1171 for the next Super Hero

He has remembered his holy
covenant.
73 He made an oath to our father
Abraham.
74 He promised to save us from our
enemies,
so that we could serve him without
fear.
75 He wants us to be holy and godly as
long as we live.

76 "And you, my child, will be called a
prophet of the Most High God.
You will go ahead of the Lord to
prepare the way for him.
77 You will tell his people how they can
be saved.
You will tell them that their sins can
be forgiven.
78 All of that will happen because our
God is tender and caring.
His kindness will bring the rising
sun to us from heaven.
79 It will shine on those living in darkness
and in the shadow of death.
It will guide our feet on the path of
peace."

80 The child grew up, and his spirit became strong. He lived in the desert until
he appeared openly to Israel.

POWER-SURGE

STRONG

THE CHILD [JOHN]
GREW UP, AND HIS
SPIRIT BECAME
STRONG.
—— LUKE 1:80 ——

Jesus Is Born

2 In those days, Caesar Augustus made
a law. It required that a list be made of
everyone in the whole Roman world. 2 It
was the first time a list was made of the
people while Quirinius was governor of
Syria. 3 All went to their own towns to be
listed.

4 So Joseph went also. He went from the
town of Nazareth in Galilee to Judea. That
is where Bethlehem, the town of David,
was. Joseph went there because he belonged to the family line of David. 5 He
went there with Mary to be listed. Mary
was engaged to him. She was expecting a
baby.

6 While Joseph and Mary were there,
the time came for the child to be born.
7 She gave birth to her first baby. It was a
boy. She wrapped him in large strips of
cloth. Then she placed him in a manger.
There was no room for them in the inn.

Angels Appear to the Shepherds

8 There were shepherds living out in the
fields nearby. It was night, and they were
looking after their sheep. 9 An angel of the
Lord appeared to them. And the glory of
the Lord shone around them. They were
terrified.

10 But the angel said to them, "Do not
be afraid. I bring you good news of great
joy. It is for all the people. 11 Today in the
town of David a Savior has been born to
you. He is Christ the Lord. 12 Here is how
you will know I am telling you the truth.
You will find a baby wrapped in strips of
cloth and lying in a manger."

13 Suddenly a large group of angels from
heaven also appeared. They were praising
God. They said,

14 "May glory be given to God in the
highest heaven!
And may peace be given to those he
is pleased with on earth!"

15 The angels left and went into heaven.
Then the shepherds said to one another,
"Let's go to Bethlehem. Let's see this thing
that has happened, which the Lord has
told us about."

16 So they hurried off and found Mary
and Joseph and the baby. The baby was lying in the manger. 17 After the shepherds
had seen him, they told everyone. They
reported what the angel had said about
this child. 18 All who heard it were amazed
at what the shepherds said to them.

19 But Mary kept all these things like a
secret treasure in her heart. She thought
about them over and over.

20 The shepherds returned. They gave
glory and praise to God. Everything they
had seen and heard was just as they had
been told.

Joseph and Mary Take Jesus
to the Temple

21 When the child was eight days old,
he was circumcised. At the same time he
was named Jesus. This was the name the
angel had given him before his mother
became pregnant.

22 The time for making them pure came
as it is written in the Law of Moses. So Joseph and Mary took Jesus to Jerusalem.
There they presented him to the Lord.

23In the Law of the Lord it says, "The first boy born in every family must be set apart for the Lord." *(Exodus 13:2,12)* 24They also offered a sacrifice. They did it in keeping with the Law, which says, "a pair of doves or two young pigeons." *(Leviticus 12:8)*

25In Jerusalem there was a man named Simeon. He was a good and godly man. He was waiting for God's promise to Israel to happen. The Holy Spirit was with him. 26The Spirit had told Simeon that he would not die before he had seen the Lord's Christ. 27The Spirit led him into the temple courtyard.

Then Jesus' parents brought the child in. They came to do for him what the Law required.

28Simeon took Jesus in his arms and praised God. He said,

29 "Lord, you are the King over all.
>   Now let me, your servant, go in
>   peace.
>   That is what you promised.

ELIZABETH

LUKE 1:42-44

God has blessed you more than other women. And blessed is the child you will have! But why is God so kind to me? Why has the mother of my Lord come to me? As soon as I heard the sound of your voice, the baby inside me jumped for joy.

Elizabeth stood in the doorway of her home, her hands resting on her large belly. After many years of having no children, Elizabeth was going to have a baby. She watched as a young girl came up the path. It was her cousin, Mary! Mary smiled and called, **"HELLO!"** to Elizabeth.

As soon as Elizabeth heard Mary's voice, the baby she carried in her belly jumped. Elizabeth's hands pressed her belly, feeling the baby continue to move. She raised eyes filled with wonder to Mary.

"As soon as I heard your voice, my baby jumped for joy inside me!" Elizabeth shouted. "God will bless you, and the baby you're going to have!"

BE AN ELIZABETH

As soon as Elizabeth heard Mary's voice, God showed to her that Mary was also going to have a baby. That baby would be Jesus. Not for one second did Elizabeth doubt or wonder. She just believed. Be an Elizabeth! Believe in God and in his message of love to you through his Son, Jesus.

ELIZABETH BELIEVED MARY WAS GOING TO HAVE THE BABY JESUS.

Go to page 1173 for the greatest Super Hero

POWER-SURGE

STRONG

[JESUS] GREW AND BECAME STRONG. HE WAS VERY WISE. HE WAS BLESSED BY GOD'S GRACE.
— LUKE 2:40 —

W

WISE

30 My eyes have seen your salvation.
31   You have prepared it in the sight of all people.
32 It is a light to be given to those who aren't Jews.
   It will bring glory to your people Israel."

33 The child's father and mother were amazed at what was said about him. 34 Then Simeon blessed them. He said to Mary, Jesus' mother, "This child is going to cause many people in Israel to fall and to rise. God has sent him. But many will speak against him. 35 The thoughts of many hearts will be known. A sword will wound your own soul too."

36 There was also a prophet named Anna. She was the daughter of Penuel from the tribe of Asher. Anna was very old. After getting married, she lived with her husband seven years. 37 Then she was a widow until she was 84. She never left the temple. She worshiped night and day, praying and going without eating. 38 Anna came up to Jesus' family at that very moment. She gave thanks to God. And she spoke about the child to all who were looking forward to the time when Jerusalem would be set free.

39 Joseph and Mary did everything the Law of the Lord required. Then they returned to Galilee. They went to their own town of Nazareth. 40 And the child grew and became strong. He was very wise. He was blessed by God's grace.

The Boy Jesus at the Temple

41 Every year Jesus' parents went to Jerusalem for the Passover Feast. 42 When he was 12 years old, they went up to the Feast as usual.
43 After the Feast was over, his parents left to go back home. The boy Jesus stayed behind in Jerusalem. But they were not aware of it. 44 They thought he was somewhere in their group. So they traveled on for a day.

Then they began to look for him among their relatives and friends. 45 They did not find him. So they went back to Jerusalem to look for him. 46 After three days they found him in the temple courtyard. He was sitting with the teachers. He was listening to them and asking them questions. 47 Everyone who heard him was amazed at how much he understood. They also were amazed at his answers.

48 When his parents saw him, they were amazed. His mother said to him, "Son, why have you treated us like this? Your father and I have been worried about you. We have been looking for you everywhere."

49 "Why were you looking for me?" he asked. "Didn't you know I had to be in my Father's house?" 50 But they did not understand what he meant by that.

51 Then he went back to Nazareth with them, and he obeyed them. But his mother kept all these things like a secret treasure in her heart. 52 Jesus became wiser and stronger. He also became more and more pleasing to God and to people.

John the Baptist Prepares the Way

3 Tiberius Caesar had been ruling for 15 years. Pontius Pilate was governor of Judea. Herod was the ruler of Galilee.

POWER-SURGE

OBEYS ✔

THEN [JESUS] WENT BACK TO NAZARETH WITH [HIS PARENTS], AND HE OBEYED THEM... JESUS BECAME WISER AND STRONGER. HE ALSO BECAME MORE AND MORE PLEASING TO GOD AND TO PEOPLE.
— LUKE 2:51-52 —

WISE

JESUS IS BORN

LUKE 2:6-7

While Joseph and Mary were there, the time came for the child to be born. She gave birth to her first baby. It was a boy. She wrapped him in large strips of cloth. Then she placed him in a manger. There was no room for them in the inn.

The tiny baby wiggled and squirmed. His mouth puckered up in a little round bud, and a tiny pink tongue peaked out between his lips. Soft white cloths were wrapped around and around his small body and made him feel safe and warm.

His mother held him against her shoulder. She patted him gently on the back until he was sleeping. Then she laid him down in a bed made of soft hay. A cow mooed quietly. Sheep baa-ed. A nearby baby goat jumped around as if it had springs on its legs. Several mice skittered passed the open door.

Mary and Joseph and baby Jesus all fell asleep in a stable that night. Mary and Joseph were on a trip to Bethlehem. When they arrived, they could find no room to stay in for the night. So they stayed in a stable instead. They felt tired and cold, and the stable was warm and safe. During the night, Jesus was born in that stable.

Jesus was no ordinary baby. He was very special. An angel had come to tell Mary he would be born. And an angel had visited Joseph in a dream to tell him the same thing. The angel said they should name this little baby "Jesus." **HE WOULD GROW UP AND BECOME THE SAVIOR OF THE WORLD.**

Mary and Joseph didn't know what the future held. They didn't know that their little baby would grow up and teach. They didn't know he would heal sick people. They didn't know he would travel all over their country. They didn't know he would die like a criminal. And they didn't know he would rise again to life.

That night, in a stable in Bethlehem, they only knew their little baby had been born. And they loved him.

JESUS WAS BORN IN A STABLE.

Go to page 1175 for the next Super Hero

His brother Philip was the ruler of Iturea and Traconitis. Lysanias was ruler of Abilene. [2]Annas and Caiaphas were high priests. At that time God's word came to John, son of Zechariah, in the desert. [3]He went into all the countryside around the Jordan River. There he preached that people should be baptized and turn away from their sins. Then God would forgive them.

[4]Here is what is written in the scroll of the prophet Isaiah. It says,

"A messenger is calling out in the
    desert,
'Prepare the way for the Lord.
    Make straight paths for him.
[5] Every valley will be filled in.
    Every mountain and hill will be
        made level.
The crooked roads will become
    straight.
The rough ways will become
    smooth.
[6] And everyone will see God's
    salvation.' "   *(Isaiah 40:3–5)*

[7]John spoke to the crowds coming to be baptized by him. He said, "You are like a nest of poisonous snakes! Who warned you to escape the coming of God's anger? [8]Produce fruit that shows you have turned away from your sins. And don't start saying to yourselves, 'Abraham is our father.' I tell you, God can raise up children for Abraham even from these stones. [9]The ax is already lying at the roots of the trees. All the trees that don't produce good fruit will be cut down. They will be thrown into the fire."

[10]"Then what should we do?" the crowd asked.

[11]John answered, "If you have extra clothes, you should share with those who have none. And if you have extra food, you should do the same."

[12]Tax collectors also came to be baptized. "Teacher," they asked, "what should we do?"

[13]"Don't collect any more than you are required to," John told them.

[14]Then some soldiers asked him, "And what should we do?"

John replied, "Don't force people to give you money. Don't bring false charges against people. Be happy with your pay."

[15]The people were waiting. They were expecting something. They were all wondering in their hearts if John might be the Christ.

[16]John answered them all, "I baptize you with water. But One who is more powerful than I am will come. I'm not good enough to untie the straps of his sandals. He will baptize you with the Holy Spirit and with fire. [17]His pitchfork is in his hand to toss the straw away from his threshing floor. He will gather the wheat into his storeroom. But he will burn up the husks with fire that can't be put out."

[18]John said many other things to warn the people. He also preached the good news to them.

[19]But John found fault with Herod, the ruler of Galilee, because of Herodias. She was the wife of Herod's brother. John also spoke strongly to Herod about all the other evil things he had done. [20]So Herod locked him up in prison. He added this sin to all his others.

The Baptism and Family Line of Jesus

[21]When all the people were being baptized, Jesus was baptized too. And as he was praying, heaven was opened. [22]The Holy Spirit came down on him in the form of a dove. A voice came from heaven. It said, "You are my Son, and I love you. I am very pleased with you."

[23]Jesus was about 30 years old when he began his special work for God and others. It was thought that he was the son of Joseph.

Joseph was the son of Heli.
[24] Heli was the son of Matthat.
Matthat was the son of Levi.
Levi was the son of Melki.
Melki was the son of Jannai.
Jannai was the son of Joseph.
[25] Joseph was the son of Mattathias.
Mattathias was the son of Amos.
Amos was the son of Nahum.
Nahum was the son of Esli.
Esli was the son of Naggai.
[26] Naggai was the son of Maath.
Maath was the son of Mattathias.
Mattathias was the son of Semein.
Semein was the son of Josech.
Josech was the son of Joda.
[27] Joda was the son of Joanan.
Joanan was the son of Rhesa.
Rhesa was the son of Zerubbabel.
Zerubbabel was the son of Shealtiel.
Shealtiel was the son of Neri.
[28] Neri was the son of Melki.
Melki was the son of Addi.
Addi was the son of Cosam.
Cosam was the son of Elmadam.
Elmadam was the son of Er.
[29] Er was the son of Joshua.
Joshua was the son of Eliezer.

Eliezer was the son of Jorim.
Jorim was the son of Matthat.
Matthat was the son of Levi.
30 Levi was the son of Simeon.
Simeon was the son of Judah.
Judah was the son of Joseph.
Joseph was the son of Jonam.
Jonam was the son of Eliakim.
31 Eliakim was the son of Melea.
Melea was the son of Menna.
Menna was the son of Mattatha.
Mattatha was the son of Nathan.
Nathan was the son of David.

32 David was the son of Jesse.
Jesse was the son of Obed.
Obed was the son of Boaz.
Boaz was the son of Salmon.
Salmon was the son of Nahshon.
33 Nahshon was the son of Amminadab.
Amminadab was the son of Ram.
Ram was the son of Hezron.
Hezron was the son of Perez.
Perez was the son of Judah.
34 Judah was the son of Jacob.
Jacob was the son of Isaac.
Isaac was the son of Abraham.

SHEPHERDS

LUKE 2:15

> The angels left and went into heaven. Then the shepherds said to one another, "Let's go to Bethlehem. Let's see this thing that has happened, which the Lord has told us about."

All the shepherds fell to their faces on the ground. The grass was wet with dew, but none of them even noticed. They felt and saw the brightness of the angel. Then they heard his voice.

"Don't be afraid! I have good news for you. A baby has been born in Bethlehem. He will be your Savior."

Still trembling on the ground, the shepherds heard the sound of singing. THEY FINALLY DARED TO LOOK UP AND SAW HUNDREDS—NO THOUSANDS!—OF ANGELS IN THE SKY. They made the most amazing, heavenly sound as they sang, "Give all the glory to God!"

Then, as quickly as they came, they were gone. The silence rang in the shepherds' ears, until one of them said, "Come on! Let's go to Bethlehem and see this baby!"

BE LIKE THE SHEPHERDS

At first the shepherds were afraid. You probably would be, too, if you saw an angel in the sky. But when they heard the angel's message, they believed it. They went and saw Jesus, then they told others what they had seen and heard. You can be like them. Believe in Jesus and tell others about him.

THE SHEPHERDS BELIEVED WHAT THE ANGELS TOLD THEM ABOUT JESUS' BIRTH.

Go to page 1177 for the next Super Hero

Abraham was the son of Terah.
Terah was the son of Nahor.
35 Nahor was the son of Serug.
Serug was the son of Reu.
Reu was the son of Peleg.
Peleg was the son of Eber.
Eber was the son of Shelah.
36 Shelah was the son of Cainan.
Cainan was the son of Arphaxad.
Arphaxad was the son of Shem.
Shem was the son of Noah.
Noah was the son of Lamech.
37 Lamech was the son of Methuselah.
Methuselah was the son of Enoch.
Enoch was the son of Jared.
Jared was the son of Mahalalel.
Mahalalel was the son of Kenan.
38 Kenan was the son of Enosh.
Enosh was the son of Seth.
Seth was the son of Adam.
Adam was the son of God.

Jesus Is Tempted

4 Jesus, full of the Holy Spirit, returned from the Jordan River. The Spirit led him into the desert. **2** There the devil tempted him for 40 days.

Jesus ate nothing during that time. At the end of the 40 days, he was hungry.

3 The devil said to him, "If you are the Son of God, tell this stone to become bread."

4 Jesus answered, "It is written, 'Man doesn't live only on bread.' " *(Deuteronomy 8:3)*

5 Then the devil led Jesus up to a high place. In an instant, he showed Jesus all the kingdoms of the world. **6** He said to him, "I will give you all their authority and glory. It has been given to me, and I can give it to anyone I want to. **7** So if you worship me, it will all be yours."

8 Jesus answered, "It is written, 'Worship the Lord your God. He is the only one you should serve.' " *(Deuteronomy 6:13)*

9 Then the devil led Jesus to Jerusalem. He had him stand on the highest point of the temple. "If you are the Son of God," he said, "throw yourself down from here. **10** It is written,

" 'The Lord will command his angels
to take good care of you.
11 They will lift you up in their hands.
Then you won't trip over a stone.' "
(Psalm 91:11,12)

12 Jesus answered, "Scripture says, 'Do not put the Lord your God to the test.' " *(Deuteronomy 6:16)*

13 When the devil finished all this tempting, he left Jesus until a better time.

Jesus Is Not Accepted in Nazareth

14 Jesus returned to Galilee in the power of the Holy Spirit. News about him spread through the whole countryside. **15** He taught in their synagogues, and everyone praised him.

16 Jesus went to Nazareth, where he had been brought up. On the Sabbath day he went into the synagogue as he usually did. And he stood up to read.

17 The scroll of the prophet Isaiah was handed to him. He unrolled it and found the right place. There it is written,

18 "The Spirit of the Lord is on me.
He has anointed me
to tell the good news to poor people.
He has sent me to announce freedom
for prisoners.
He has sent me so that the blind will
see again.
He wants me to free those who are
beaten down.
19 And he has sent me to announce the
year when he will set his people
free."
(Isaiah 61:1,2)

20 Then Jesus rolled up the scroll. He gave it back to the attendant and sat down. The eyes of everyone in the synagogue were staring at him. **21** He began by saying to them, "Today this passage of Scripture is coming true as you listen."

22 Everyone said good things about him. They were amazed at the gracious words they heard from his lips. "Isn't this Joseph's son?" they asked.

23 Jesus said, "Here is a saying you will certainly apply to me. 'Doctor, heal yourself! Do the things here in your hometown that we heard you did in Capernaum.' "

24 "What I'm about to tell you is true," he continued. "A prophet is not accepted in his hometown. **25** I tell you for sure that there were many widows in Israel in the days of Elijah. And there had been no rain for three and a half years. There wasn't enough food to eat anywhere in the land. **26** But Elijah was not sent to any of those widows. Instead, he was sent to a widow in Zarephath near Sidon. **27** And there were many in Israel who had skin diseases in the days of Elisha the prophet. But not one of them was healed except Naaman the Syrian."

28 All the people in the synagogue were very angry when they heard that. **29** They got up and ran Jesus out of town. They took him to the edge of the hill on which the town was built. They planned to

SIMEON

LUKE 2:25-26

In Jerusalem there was a man named Simeon. He was a good and godly man...The Spirit had told Simeon that he would not die before he had seen the Lord's Christ.

Simeon (SIM-ee-un) walked slowly into the temple courtyard. His old legs didn't move so quickly anymore. He had to lean on a stick to keep steady on his feet. His beard puffed in and out as he sucked in air, trying to catch his breath after climbing the stairs. Simeon came to the temple almost every day. He was waiting for something to happen . . . for a promise to come true.

Years ago, when Simeon was already old (but not as old as he was now), God had promised he would see Jesus before he died. Simeon was waiting for that promise to come true. Each day he got up from his bed and shuffled to the temple. Simeon may have looked old and weak, but inside he felt young and happy. His wrinkled face cracked a smile as he thought of who, perhaps today, he would see in the temple.

Standing near the entrance, Simeon looked around. The feet of people and animals stirred up the dirt of the courtyard. Simeon rubbed his eyes, then looked from one group of worshipers to another.

Mary and Joseph entered with baby Jesus. **SUDDENLY SIMEON KNEW—THIS WAS THE ONE HE HAD BEEN WAITING FOR.** He was sure of it!

Hobbling over to the young couple, Simeon reached out trembling hands to the baby. As he took the baby into his arms, his eyes filled with tears and his heart swelled with joy. This was the promised one! This little baby would grow up to be the Savior. A smile stretched across the old man's face. He held little Jesus close to his heart and praised God for keeping his promise.

BE A SIMEON

Be a Simeon. Trust God. He will do what he says he will do. This is his promise. And he always keeps his promise.

SIMEON TRUSTED GOD TO KEEP HIS PROMISES.
THE WHOLE STORY: LUKE 2:25-35

Go to page 1179 for the next Super Hero

throw him down the cliff. [30]But Jesus walked right through the crowd and went on his way.

Jesus Drives Out an Evil Spirit

[31]Then Jesus went to Capernaum, a town in Galilee. On the Sabbath day he began to teach the people. [32]They were amazed at his teaching, because his message had authority.

[33]In the synagogue there was a man controlled by a demon, an evil spirit. He cried out at the top of his voice. [34]"Ha!" he said. "What do you want with us, Jesus of Nazareth? Have you come to destroy us? I know who you are. You are the Holy One of God!"

[35]"Be quiet!" Jesus said firmly. "Come out of him!"

Then the demon threw the man down in front of everybody. And it came out without hurting him.

[36]All the people were amazed. They said to each other, "What is this teaching? With authority and power he gives orders to evil spirits. And they come out!"

[37]The news about Jesus spread throughout the whole area.

Jesus Heals Many People

[38]Jesus left the synagogue and went to the home of Simon. At that time, Simon's mother-in-law was suffering from a high fever. So they asked Jesus to help her. [39]He bent over her and commanded the fever to leave, and it left her. She got up at once and began to serve them.

[40]At sunset, people brought to Jesus all who were sick. He placed his hands on each one and healed them. [41]Also, demons came out of many people. The demons shouted, "You are the Son of God!" But he commanded them to be quiet. He would not allow them to speak, because they knew he was the Christ.

[42]At dawn, Jesus went out to a place where he could be by himself. The people went to look for him. When they found him, they tried to keep him from leaving them. [43]But he said, "I must announce the good news of God's kingdom to the other towns also. That is why I was sent." [44]And he kept on preaching in the synagogues of Judea.

Jesus Chooses the First Disciples

5 One day Jesus was standing by the Sea of Galilee. The people crowded around him and listened to the word of God. [2]Jesus saw two boats at the edge of the water. They had been left there by the fishermen, who were washing their nets. [3]He got into the boat that belonged to Simon. Jesus asked him to go out a little way from shore. Then he sat down in the boat and taught the people.

[4]When he finished speaking, he turned to Simon. He said, "Go out into deep water. Let the nets down so you can catch some fish."

[5]Simon answered, "Master, we've worked hard all night and haven't caught anything. But because you say so, I will let down the nets."

[6]When they had done so, they caught a large number of fish. There were so many that their nets began to break. [7]So they motioned to their partners in the other boat to come and help them. They came and filled both boats so full that they began to sink.

[8]When Simon Peter saw this, he fell at Jesus' knees. "Go away from me, Lord!" he said. "I am a sinful man!"

[9]He and everyone with him were amazed at the number of fish they had caught. [10]So were James and John, the sons of Zebedee, who worked with Simon.

Then Jesus said to Simon, "Don't be afraid. From now on you will catch people."

[11]So they pulled their boats up on shore. Then they left everything and followed him.

Jesus Heals a Man With a Skin Disease

[12]While Jesus was in one of the towns, a man came along. He had a skin disease all over his body. When he saw Jesus, he fell with his face to the ground. He begged him, "Lord, if you are willing to make me 'clean,' you can do it."

[13]Jesus reached out his hand and touched the man. "I am willing to do it," he said. "Be 'clean'!" Right away the disease left him.

[14]Then Jesus ordered him, "Don't tell anyone. Go and show yourself to the priest. Offer the sacrifices that Moses commanded. It will be a witness to the priest and the people that you are 'clean.'"

[15]But the news about Jesus spread even more. So crowds of people came to hear him. They also came to be healed of their sicknesses. [16]But Jesus often went away to be by himself and pray.

Jesus Heals a Man Who Could Not Walk

[17]One day Jesus was teaching. Pharisees

and teachers of the law were sitting there. They had come from every village of Galilee and from Judea and Jerusalem. They heard that the Lord had given Jesus the power to heal the sick.

18Some men came carrying a man who could not walk. He was lying on a mat. They tried to take him into the house to place him in front of Jesus. **19**They could not find a way to do this because of the crowd. So they went up on the roof. Then they lowered the man on his mat through the opening in the roof tiles. They lowered him into the middle of the crowd, right in front of Jesus.

20When Jesus saw that they had faith, he said, "Friend, your sins are forgiven."

21The Pharisees and the teachers of the law began to think, "Who is this fellow who says such an evil thing? Who can forgive sins but God alone?"

22Jesus knew what they were thinking. So he asked, "Why are you thinking these things in your hearts? **23**Is it easier to say, 'Your sins are forgiven'? Or to say, 'Get up and walk'? **24**I want you to know that the Son of Man has authority on earth to forgive sins." So he spoke to the man who could not walk. "I tell you," he said, "get up. Take your mat and go home."

ANNA

LUKE 2:38

Anna came up to Jesus' family at that very moment. She gave thanks to God.

Anna had been married when she was young, but her husband had died after only seven years. For a long time, life had been hard and lonely. Now Anna was 84, and she spent her days praying in the temple.

Looking around at other worshipers, Anna saw Simeon. He came to the temple every day, too. Anna could tell by the look on Simeon's face that something exciting was happening.

Anna walked toward Simeon on wobbly old legs. Simeon held a baby boy while the child's parents looked on. The tears in his eyes told Anna the truth before she ever heard his words. **THE SAVIOR HAD BEEN BORN!**

Raising her arms, Anna began to praise God. She was an old woman, but she had lived long enough to see the Savior. What a wonderful day!

BE AN ANNA

Anna's life as a widow probably had been hard. But with God's help, she lived a joyful life. And before she died, she got to see Jesus. You sometimes have hard times, too. And it's not easy to be cheerful then. When you're having a hard time, think of Anna. Trust God to help you.

ANNA WAS HAPPY AND FULFILLED EVEN THOUGH SHE HAD A HARD LIFE.

Go to page 1181 for the greatest Super Hero

25Right away, the man stood up in front of them. He took his mat and went home praising God. 26Everyone was amazed and gave praise to God. They were filled with wonder. They said, "We have seen unusual things today."

Jesus Chooses Levi

27After this, Jesus left the house. He saw a tax collector sitting at the tax booth. The man's name was Levi.

"Follow me," Jesus said to him.

28Levi got up, left everything and followed him.

29Then Levi gave a huge dinner for Jesus at his house. A large crowd of tax collectors and others were eating with them. 30But the Pharisees and their teachers of the law complained to Jesus' disciples. They said, "Why do you eat and drink with tax collectors and 'sinners'?"

31Jesus answered them, "Those who are healthy don't need a doctor. Sick people do. 32I have not come to get those who think they are right with God to follow me. I have come to get sinners to turn away from their sins."

Jesus Is Asked About Fasting

33Some of the people who were there said to Jesus, "John's disciples often pray and go without eating. So do the disciples of the Pharisees. But yours go on eating and drinking."

34Jesus answered, "Can you make the guests of the groom go without eating while he is with them? 35But the time will come when the groom will be taken away from them. In those days they will fast."

36Then Jesus gave them an example. He said, "People don't tear a patch from new clothes and sew it on old clothes. If they do, they will tear the new clothes. Also, the patch from the new clothes will not match the old clothes. 37People don't pour new wine into old wineskins. If they do, the new wine will burst the skins. The wine will run out, and the wineskins will be destroyed. 38No, new wine must be poured into new wineskins. 39After people drink old wine, they don't want the new. They say, 'The old wine is better.' "

Jesus Is Lord of the Sabbath Day

6 One Sabbath day Jesus was walking through the grainfields. His disciples began to break off some heads of grain. They rubbed them in their hands and ate them.

2Some of the Pharisees said, "It is against the Law to do this on the Sabbath. Why are you doing it?"

3Jesus answered them, "Haven't you ever read about what David did? He and his men were hungry. 4He entered the house of God and took the holy bread. He ate the bread that only priests were allowed to eat. David also gave some to his men."

5Then Jesus said to them, "The Son of Man is Lord of the Sabbath day."

6On another Sabbath day, Jesus went into the synagogue and was teaching. A man whose right hand was weak and twisted was there. 7The Pharisees and the teachers of the law were trying to find fault with Jesus. So they watched him closely. They wanted to see if he would heal on the Sabbath.

8But Jesus knew what they were thinking. He spoke to the man who had the weak and twisted hand. "Get up and stand in front of everyone," he said. So the man got up and stood there.

9Then Jesus said to them, "What does the Law say we should do on the Sabbath day? Should we do good? Or should we do evil? Should we save life? Or should we destroy it?"

10He looked around at all of them.

Then he said to the man, "Stretch out your hand."

He did, and his hand was as good as new.

11But the Pharisees and the teachers of the law were very angry. They began to talk to each other about what they might do to Jesus.

Jesus Chooses the Twelve Apostles

12On one of those days, Jesus went out to a mountainside to pray. He spent the night praying to God. 13When morning came, he called for his disciples to come to him. He chose 12 of them and made them apostles.

14Simon was one of them. Jesus gave him the name Peter. There were also Simon's brother Andrew, James, John, Philip and Bartholomew. 15And there were Matthew, Thomas, and James, son of Alphaeus. There were also Simon who was called the Zealot 16and Judas, son of James. Judas Iscariot was one of them too. He was the one who would later hand Jesus over to his enemies.

Jesus Gives Blessings and Warnings

17Jesus went down the mountain with them and stood on a level place. A large crowd of his disciples was there. A large

JESUS AT THE TEMPLE

LUKE 2:46-47

[Jesus] was sitting with the teachers. He was listening to them and asking them questions. Everyone who heard him was amazed at how much he understood. They also were amazed at his answers.

The hot sun beat down on Jesus' head as he walked along toward Jerusalem. He and his family and others from his town were going to Jerusalem to celebrate a special feast called Passover.

After several days in Jerusalem, the time came to leave. Jesus' mother and father started walking toward home with friends and family. They walked all day. They didn't see Jesus, but they weren't worried about him. They thought he was with one of the other families. But night came, and they couldn't find Jesus. They searched and searched. But Jesus just wasn't there.

Mary and Joseph went back to Jerusalem. They walked quickly through the night. Perhaps Jesus had fallen and hurt himself along the way. Or perhaps he had wandered away from the group and was now trying to catch up. All along the road back to Jerusalem they saw lots of people. But they didn't see Jesus.

One day, two days, three days– they looked everywhere in Jerusalem for Jesus. Finally, they found him. Jesus sat in the temple courtyard talking to the teachers there.

Jesus amazed the teachers. He was only twelve years old. And he could talk with them and answer their questions with amazing wisdom. They couldn't believe someone so young could know so much.

Jesus' mother hugged him. With tears in her eyes, she asked him why he hadn't come along with them when they left Jerusalem. Jesus knew she didn't understand. He *had* to talk to the teachers in the temple. He had to prepare and learn so that he could grow up and do what God had planned.

Jesus hugged his mother. He had more growing up to do. He went home with her and Joseph to Nazareth. And he obeyed them.

BE LIKE JESUS

Jesus grew up and obeyed his parents. He wants you to do the same thing. Your parents love you and want what is best for you. Be like Jesus. Obey them!

JESUS TALKED TO THE TEACHERS IN THE TEMPLE AND OBEYED HIS PARENTS.

Go to page 1190 for the next Super Hero

number of other people were there too. They came from all over Judea, including Jerusalem. They also came from the coast of Tyre and Sidon.

18They had all come to hear Jesus and to be healed of their sicknesses. People who were troubled by evil spirits were made well. **19**Everyone tried to touch Jesus. Power was coming from him and healing them all.

20Jesus looked at his disciples. He said to them,

"Blessed are you who are needy.
    God's kingdom belongs to you.
21 Blessed are you who are hungry now.
    You will be satisfied.
Blessed are you who are sad now.
    You will laugh.
22 Blessed are you when people hate you,
    when they have nothing to do with
      you
    and say bad things about you,
    and when they treat your name as
      something evil.
      They do all this because you are
        followers of the Son of Man.

23"Their people treated the prophets the same way long ago. When these things happen to you, be glad and jump for joy. You will receive many blessings in heaven.

24 "But how terrible it will be for you who
      are rich!
    You have already had your easy life.
25 How terrible for you who are well fed
      now!
    You will go hungry.
How terrible for you who laugh now!
    You will cry and be sad.
26 How terrible for you when everyone
      says good things about you!
    Their people treated the false
      prophets the same way long
      ago.

Love Your Enemies

27"But here is what I tell you who hear me. Love your enemies. Do good to those who hate you. **28**Bless those who call down curses on you. And pray for those who treat you badly.

29"Suppose someone hits you on one cheek. Turn your other cheek to him also. Suppose someone takes your coat. Don't stop him from taking your shirt.

30"Give to everyone who asks you. And if anyone takes what belongs to you, don't ask to get it back. **31**Do to others as you want them to do to you.

32"Suppose you love those who love you. Should anyone praise you for that? Even 'sinners' love those who love them. **33**And suppose you do good to those who are good to you. Should anyone praise you for that? Even 'sinners' do that. **34**And suppose you lend money to those who can pay you back. Should anyone praise you for that? Even a 'sinner' lends to 'sinners,' expecting them to pay everything back.

35"But love your enemies. Do good to them. Lend to them without expecting to get anything back. Then you will receive a lot in return. And you will be sons of the Most High God. He is kind to people who are evil and are not thankful. **36**So have mercy, just as your Father has mercy.

Be Fair When You Judge Others

37"If you do not judge others, then you will not be judged. If you do not find others guilty, then you will not be found guilty. Forgive, and you will be forgiven. **38**Give, and it will be given to you. A good amount will be poured into your lap. It will be pressed down, shaken together, and running over. The same amount you give will be measured out to you."

POWER-SURGE

FORGIVING F

FORGIVE, AND YOU WILL BE FORGIVEN.
— LUKE 6:37 —

39Jesus also gave them another example. He asked, "Can a blind person lead another blind person? Won't they both fall into a pit? **40**Students are not better than their teachers. But everyone who is completely trained will be like his teacher. **41**"You look at the bit of sawdust in your friend's eye. But you pay no attention to the piece of wood in your own eye. **42**How can you say to your friend, 'Let me take the bit of sawdust out of your eye'? How can you say this while there is a piece of wood in your own eye? You pretender! First take the piece of wood out of your own eye. Then you will be able to see clearly to take the bit of sawdust out of your friend's eye.

A Tree and Its Fruit

43"A good tree doesn't bear bad fruit. And a bad tree doesn't bear good fruit.

[44]You can tell each tree by the kind of fruit it bears. People do not pick figs from thorns. And they don't pick grapes from bushes.

[45]"A good man says good things. These come from the good that is put away in his heart. An evil man says evil things. These come from the evil that is put away in his heart. Their mouths say everything that is in their hearts.

The Wise and Foolish Builders

[46]"Why do you call me, 'Lord, Lord,' and still don't do what I say? [47]Some people come to me and listen to me and do what I say. I will show you what they are like. [48]They are like someone who builds a house. He digs down deep and sets it on solid rock. When a flood comes, the river rushes against the house. But the water can't shake it. The house is well built.

[49]"But here is what happens when people listen to my words and do not obey them. They are like someone who builds a house on soft ground instead of solid rock. The moment the river rushes against that house, it falls down. It is completely destroyed."

A Roman Commander Has Faith

7 Jesus finished saying all those things to the people. Then he entered Capernaum.

[2]There the servant of a Roman commander was sick and about to die. His master thought highly of him. [3]The commander heard about Jesus. So he sent some elders of the Jews to him. He told them to ask Jesus to come and heal his servant.

[4]They came to Jesus and begged him, "This man deserves to have you do this. [5]He loves our nation and has built our synagogue." [6]So Jesus went with them.

When Jesus came near the house, the Roman commander sent friends to him. He told them to say, "Lord, don't trouble yourself. I am not good enough to have you come into my house. [7]That is why I did not even think I was fit to come to you. But just say the word, and my servant will be healed. [8]I myself am a man who is under authority. And I have soldiers who obey my orders. I tell this one, 'Go,' and he goes. I tell that one, 'Come,' and he comes. I say to my servant, 'Do this,' and he does it."

[9]When Jesus heard this, he was amazed at him. He turned to the crowd that was following him. He said, "I tell you, even in Israel I have not found anyone whose faith is so strong."

[10]Then the men who had been sent to Jesus returned to the house. They found that the servant was healed.

Jesus Raises a Widow's Son From the Dead

[11]Some time later, Jesus went to a town called Nain. His disciples and a large crowd went along with him. [12]He approached the town gate. Just then, a dead person was being carried out. He was the only son of his mother. She was a widow. A large crowd from the town was with her.

[13]When the Lord saw her, he felt sorry for her. So he said, "Don't cry."

[14]Then he went up and touched the coffin. Those carrying it stood still.

Jesus said, "Young man, I say to you, get up!"

[15]The dead man sat up and began to talk. Then Jesus gave him back to his mother.

[16]The people were all filled with wonder and praised God. "A great prophet has appeared among us," they said. "God has come to help his people." [17]This news about Jesus spread all through Judea and the whole country.

Jesus and John the Baptist

[18]John's disciples told him about all these things. So he chose two of them. [19]He sent them to the Lord. They were to ask Jesus, "Are you the one who was supposed to come? Or should we look for someone else?"

[20]The men came to Jesus. They said, "John the Baptist sent us to ask you, 'Are you the one who was supposed to come? Or should we look for someone else?' "

[21]At that very time Jesus healed many people. They had illnesses, sicknesses and evil spirits. He also gave sight to many who were blind. [22]So Jesus replied to the messengers, "Go back to John. Tell him what you have seen and heard. Blind people receive sight. Disabled people walk. Those who have skin diseases are healed. Deaf people hear. Those who are dead are raised to life. And the good news is preached to those who are poor. [23]Blessed are those who do not give up their faith because of me."

[24]So John's messengers left. Then Jesus began to speak to the crowd about John. He said, "What did you go out into the desert to see? Tall grass waving in the wind? [25]If not, what did you go out to

POWER-SURGE

FAITHFUL ( )

BLESSED ARE THOSE WHO DO NOT GIVE UP THEIR FAITH BECAUSE OF ME.
— LUKE 7:23 —

TRIES HARD

see? A man dressed in fine clothes? No. Those who wear fine clothes and have many expensive things are in palaces. 26Then what did you go out to see? A prophet? Yes, I tell you, and more than a prophet.

27"He is the one written about in Scripture. It says,

" 'I will send my messenger ahead of
    you.
He will prepare your way for you.'
                              (Malachi 3:1)

28I tell you, no one more important than John has ever been born. But the least important person in God's kingdom is more important than he is."

29All the people who heard Jesus' words agreed that God's way was right. Even the tax collectors agreed. These people had all been baptized by John. 30But the Pharisees and the authorities on the law did not accept God's purpose for themselves. They had not been baptized by John.

31"What can I compare today's people to?" Jesus asked. "What are they like? 32They are like children sitting in the market place and calling out to each other. They say,

" 'We played a flute for you.
But you didn't dance.
We sang a funeral song.
But you didn't cry.'

33"That is how it has been with John the Baptist. When he came to you, he didn't eat bread or drink wine. And you say, 'He has a demon.' 34But when the Son of Man came, he ate and drank as you do. And you say, 'This fellow is always eating and drinking far too much. He's a friend of tax collectors and "sinners." ' 35All who follow wisdom prove that wisdom is right."

A Sinful Woman Pours Perfume on Jesus

36One of the Pharisees invited Jesus to have dinner with him. So he went to the Pharisee's house. He took his place at the table.

37There was a woman in that town who had lived a sinful life. She learned that Jesus was eating at the Pharisee's house. So she came with a special sealed jar of perfume. 38She stood behind Jesus and cried at his feet. She began to wet his feet with her tears. Then she wiped them with her hair. She kissed them and poured perfume on them.

39The Pharisee who had invited Jesus saw this. He said to himself, "If this man were a prophet, he would know who is touching him. He would know what kind of woman she is. She is a sinner!"

40Jesus answered him, "Simon, I have something to tell you."

"Tell me, teacher," he said.

41"Two people owed money to a certain lender. One owed him 500 silver coins. The other owed him 50 silver coins. 42Neither of them had the money to pay him back. So he let them go without paying. Which of them will love him more?"

43Simon replied, "I suppose the one who owed the most money."

"You are right," Jesus said.

44Then he turned toward the woman. He said to Simon, "Do you see this woman? I came into your house. You did not give me any water to wash my feet. But she wet my feet with her tears and wiped them with her hair. 45You did not give me a kiss. But this woman has not stopped kissing my feet since I came in. 46You did not put any olive oil on my head. But she has poured perfume on my feet. 47So I tell you this. Her many sins have been forgiven. She has loved a lot. But the one who has been forgiven little loves only a little."

48Then Jesus said to her, "Your sins are forgiven."

49The other guests began to talk about this among themselves. They said, "Who is this who even forgives sins?"

50Jesus said to the woman, "Your faith has saved you. Go in peace."

The Story of the Farmer

8 After this, Jesus traveled around from one town and village to another. He announced the good news of God's kingdom. The Twelve were with him. 2So were some women who had been healed of evil spirits and sicknesses. One was Mary Mag-

dalene. Seven demons had come out of her. **3**Another was Joanna, the wife of Cuza. He was the manager of Herod's household. Susanna and many others were there also. These women were helping to support Jesus and the Twelve with their own money.

4A large crowd gathered together. People came to Jesus from town after town. As they did, he told a story. He said, **5**"A farmer went out to plant his seed. He scattered the seed on the ground. Some fell on a path. People walked on it, and the birds of the air ate it up. **6**Some seed fell on rocky places. When it grew, the plants dried up because they had no water. **7**Other seed fell among thorns. The thorns grew up with it and crowded out the plants. **8**Still other seed fell on good soil. It grew up and produced a crop 100 times more than the farmer planted."

When Jesus said this, he called out, "Those who have ears should listen."

9His disciples asked him what the story meant.

10He said, "You have been given the chance to understand the secrets of God's kingdom. But to outsiders I speak by using stories. In that way,

> " 'They see, but they will not know
>   what they are seeing.
> They hear, but they will not
>   understand what they are
>   hearing.'   (Isaiah 6:9)

11"Here is what the story means. The seed is God's message. **12**People on the path are those who hear. But then the devil comes. He takes away the message from their hearts. He does it so they won't believe. Then they can't be saved. **13**Those on the rock are the ones who hear the message and receive it with joy. But they have no roots. They believe for a while. But when they are put to the test, they fall away from the faith. **14**The seed that fell among thorns stands for those who hear the message. But as they go on their way, they are choked by life's worries, riches and pleasures. So they do not reach full growth.

15"But the seed on good soil stands for those with an honest and good heart. They hear the message. They keep it in their hearts. They remain faithful and produce a good crop.

A Lamp on a Stand

16"People do not light a lamp and then hide it in a jar or put it under a bed. Instead, they put it on a stand. Then those who come in can see its light. **17**What is hidden will be seen. And what is out of sight will be brought into the open and made known.

18"So be careful how you listen. If you have something, you will be given more. If you have nothing, even what you think you have will be taken away from you."

Jesus' Mother and Brothers

19Jesus' mother and brothers came to see him. But they could not get near him because of the crowd. **20**Someone told him, "Your mother and brothers are standing outside. They want to see you."

21He replied, "My mother and brothers are those who hear God's word and do what it says."

Jesus Calms the Storm

22One day Jesus said to his disciples, "Let's go over to the other side of the lake." So they got into a boat and left. **23**As they sailed, Jesus fell asleep. A storm came down on the lake. It was so bad that the boat was about to sink. They were in great danger.

24The disciples went and woke Jesus up. They said, "Master! Master! We're going to drown!"

He got up and ordered the wind and the huge waves to stop. The storm quieted down. It was completely calm. **25**"Where is your faith?" he asked his disciples.

They were amazed and full of fear. They asked one another, "Who is this? He commands even the winds and the waves, and they obey him."

Jesus Heals a Man Controlled by Demons

26Jesus and his disciples sailed to the area of the Gerasenes across the lake from Galilee. **27**When Jesus stepped on shore, he was met by a man from the town. The man was controlled by demons. For a long time he had not worn clothes or lived in a house. He lived in the tombs. **28**When he saw Jesus, he cried out and fell at his feet. He shouted at the top of his voice, "Jesus, Son of the Most High God, what do you want with me? I beg you, don't hurt me!" **29**This was because Jesus had commanded the evil spirit to come out of the man. Many times the spirit had taken hold of him. His hands and feet were chained, and he was kept under guard. But he had broken his chains. And then the demon had forced him to go out into lonely places in the countryside.

³⁰Jesus asked him, "What is your name?"

"Legion," he replied, because many demons had gone into him. ³¹And they begged Jesus again and again not to order them to go into the Abyss.

³²A large herd of pigs was feeding there on the hillside. The demons begged Jesus to let them go into the pigs. And he allowed it.

³³When the demons came out of the man, they went into the pigs. Then the herd rushed down the steep bank. They ran into the lake and drowned.

³⁴Those who were tending the pigs saw what had happened. They ran off and reported it in the town and countryside. ³⁵The people went out to see what had happened.

Then they came to Jesus. They found the man who was now free of the demons. He was sitting at Jesus' feet. He was dressed and thinking clearly. All this made the people afraid.

³⁶Those who had seen it told the others how the man who had been controlled by demons was now healed. ³⁷Then all the people who lived in the area of the Gerasenes asked Jesus to leave them. They were filled with fear. So he got into the boat and left.

³⁸The man who was now free of the demons begged to go with him. But Jesus sent him away. He said to him, ³⁹"Return home and tell how much God has done for you."

So the man went away. He told people all over town how much Jesus had done for him.

A Dying Girl and a Suffering Woman

⁴⁰When Jesus returned, a crowd welcomed him. They were all expecting him. ⁴¹Then a man named Jairus came. He was a synagogue ruler. He fell at Jesus' feet. He begged Jesus to come to his house. ⁴²His only daughter was dying. She was about 12 years old.

As Jesus was on his way, the crowds almost crushed him.

⁴³A woman was there who had a sickness that made her bleed. Her sickness had lasted for 12 years. No one could heal her. ⁴⁴She came up behind Jesus and touched the edge of his clothes. Right away her bleeding stopped.

⁴⁵"Who touched me?" Jesus asked.

They all said they didn't do it. Then Peter said, "Master, the people are crowding and pushing against you."

⁴⁶But Jesus said, "Someone touched me. I know that power has gone out from me."

⁴⁷The woman realized that people would notice her. Shaking with fear, she came and fell at his feet. In front of everyone, she told why she had touched him. She also told how she had been healed in an instant.

⁴⁸Then he said to her, "Dear woman, your faith has healed you. Go in peace."

⁴⁹While Jesus was still speaking, someone came from the house of Jairus. Jairus was the synagogue ruler. "Your daughter is dead," the messenger said. "Don't bother the teacher anymore."

⁵⁰Hearing this, Jesus said to Jairus, "Don't be afraid. Just believe. She will be healed."

⁵¹When he arrived at the house of Jairus, he did not let everyone go in with him. He took only Peter, John and James, and the child's father and mother.

⁵²During this time, all the people were crying and sobbing loudly over the child. "Stop crying!" Jesus said. "She is not dead. She is sleeping."

⁵³They laughed at him. They knew she was dead.

⁵⁴But he took her by the hand and said, "My child, get up!"

⁵⁵Her spirit returned, and right away she stood up. Then Jesus told them to give her something to eat. ⁵⁶Her parents were amazed. But Jesus ordered them not to tell anyone what had happened.

Jesus Sends Out the Twelve Disciples

9 Jesus called the Twelve together. He gave them power and authority to drive out all demons and to heal sicknesses. ²Then he sent them out to preach about God's kingdom and to heal those who were sick.

³He told them, "Don't take anything for the journey. Do not take a walking stick or a bag. Do not take any bread, money or extra clothes. ⁴When you are invited into a house, stay there until you leave town. ⁵Some people may not welcome you. If they don't, shake the dust off your feet when you leave their town. This will be a witness against the people living there."

⁶So the Twelve left. They went from village to village. They preached the good news and healed people everywhere.

⁷Now Herod, the ruler of Galilee, heard

about everything that was going on. He was bewildered, because some were saying that John the Baptist had been raised from the dead. **8**Others were saying that Elijah had appeared. Still others were saying that a prophet of long ago had come back to life. **9**But Herod said, "I had John's head cut off. So who is it that I hear such things about?" And he tried to see Jesus.

Jesus Feeds the Five Thousand

10The apostles returned. They told Jesus what they had done. Then he took them with him. They went off by themselves to a town called Bethsaida. **11**But the crowds learned about it and followed Jesus. He welcomed them and spoke to them about God's kingdom. He also healed those who needed to be healed.

12Late in the afternoon the Twelve came to him. They said, "Send the crowd away. They can go to the nearby villages and countryside. There they can find food and a place to stay. There is nothing here."

13Jesus replied, "You give them something to eat."

The disciples answered, "We have only five loaves of bread and two fish. We would have to go and buy food for all this crowd." **14**About 5,000 men were there.

But Jesus said to his disciples, "Have them sit down in groups of about 50 each." **15**The disciples did so, and everyone sat down.

16Jesus took the five loaves and the two fish. He looked up to heaven and gave thanks. He broke them into pieces. Then he gave them to the disciples to set in front of the people. **17**All of them ate and were satisfied. The disciples picked up 12 baskets of leftover pieces.

Peter Says That Jesus Is the Christ

18One day Jesus was praying alone. Only his disciples were with him. He asked them, "Who do the crowds say I am?"

19They replied, "Some say John the Baptist. Others say Elijah. Still others say that one of the prophets of long ago has come back to life."

20"But what about you?" he asked. "Who do you say I am?"

Peter answered, "The Christ of God."

21Jesus strongly warned them not to tell this to anyone. **22**He said, "The Son of Man must suffer many things. The elders will not accept him. The chief priests and teachers of the law will not accept him either. He must be killed and on the third day rise from the dead."

23Then he said to all of them, "If anyone wants to follow me, he must say no to himself. He must pick up his cross every day and follow me. **24**If he wants to save his life, he will lose it. But if he loses his life for me, he will save it. **25**What good is it if someone gains the whole world but loses or gives up his very self?

26"Suppose you are ashamed of me and my words. The Son of Man will come in his glory and in the glory of the Father and the holy angels. Then he will be ashamed of you.

27"What I'm about to tell you is true. Some who are standing here will not die before they see God's kingdom."

Jesus' Appearance Is Changed

28About eight days after Jesus said this, he went up on a mountain to pray. He took Peter, John and James with him.

29As he was praying, the appearance of his face changed. His clothes became as bright as a flash of lightning. **30**Two men, Moses and Elijah, **31**appeared in shining glory. Jesus and the two of them talked together. They spoke about his coming death. He was going to die soon in Jerusalem.

32Peter and his companions had been very sleepy. But then they became completely awake. They saw Jesus' glory and the two men standing with him.

33As the men were leaving Jesus, Peter spoke up. "Master," he said to him, "it is good for us to be here. Let us put up three shelters. One will be for you, one for Moses, and one for Elijah." He didn't really know what he was saying.

34While Jesus was speaking, a cloud appeared. It surrounded them. The disciples were afraid as they entered the cloud. **35**A voice came from the cloud. It said, "This is my Son, and I have chosen him. Listen to him." **36**When the voice had spoken, they found that Jesus was alone.

The disciples kept quiet about this. They didn't tell anyone at that time what they had seen.

Jesus Heals a Boy Who Had an Evil Spirit

37The next day Jesus and those who were with him came down from the mountain. A large crowd met Jesus.

38A man in the crowd called out. "Teacher," he said, "I beg you to look at my son. He is my only child. **39**A spirit takes hold of him, and he suddenly screams. It throws him into fits so that he foams at the mouth. It hardly ever leaves him. It is destroying him. **40**I begged your disciples to drive it out. But they couldn't do it."

41"You unbelieving and evil people!" Jesus replied. "How long do I have to stay with you? How long do I have to put up with you?"

Then he said to the man, "Bring your son here."

42Even while the boy was coming, the demon threw him into a fit. The boy fell to the ground. But Jesus ordered the evil spirit to leave the boy. Then Jesus healed him and gave him back to his father. **43**They were all amazed at God's greatness.

Everyone was wondering about all that Jesus did. Then Jesus said to his disciples, **44**"Listen carefully to what I am about to tell you. The Son of Man is going to be handed over to men." **45**But they didn't understand what this meant. That was because it was hidden from them. And they were afraid to ask Jesus about it.

Who Is the Most Important Person?

46The disciples began to argue about which one of them would be the most important person. **47**Jesus knew what they were thinking. So he took a little child and had the child stand beside him.

48Then he spoke to them. "Anyone who welcomes this little child in my name welcomes me," he said. "And anyone who welcomes me welcomes the One who sent me. The least important person among all of you is the most important."

49"Master," said John, "we saw a man driving out demons in your name. We tried to stop him, because he is not one of us."

50"Do not stop him," Jesus said. "Anyone who is not against you is for you."

The Samaritans Do Not Welcome Jesus

51The time grew near for Jesus to be taken up to heaven. So he made up his mind to go to Jerusalem. **52**He sent messengers on ahead. They went into a Samaritan village to get things ready for him. **53**But the people there did not welcome Jesus. That was because he was heading for Jerusalem.

54The disciples James and John saw this. They asked, "Lord, do you want us to call down fire from heaven to destroy them?"

55But Jesus turned and commanded

them not to do it. **56**They went on to another village.

It Costs to Follow Jesus

57Once Jesus and those who were with him were walking along the road. A man said to Jesus, "I will follow you no matter where you go."

58Jesus replied, "Foxes have holes. Birds of the air have nests. But the Son of Man has no place to lay his head."

59He said to another man, "Follow me." But the man replied, "Lord, first let me go and bury my father."

60Jesus said to him, "Let dead people bury their own dead. You go and tell others about God's kingdom."

61Still another man said, "I will follow you, Lord. But first let me go back and say good-by to my family."

62Jesus replied, "Suppose you start to plow and then look back. If you do, you are not fit for service in God's kingdom."

Jesus Sends Out the Seventy-two

10 After this the Lord appointed 72 others. He sent them out two by two ahead of him. They went to every town and place where he was about to go.

2He told them, "The harvest is huge, but the workers are few. So ask the Lord of the harvest to send out workers into his harvest field.

3"Go! I am sending you out like lambs among wolves. **4**Do not take a purse or bag or sandals. And don't greet anyone on the road.

5"When you enter a house, first say, 'May this house be blessed with peace.' **6**If someone there loves peace, your blessing of peace will rest on him. If not, it will return to you. **7**Stay in that house. Eat and drink anything they give you. Workers are worthy of their pay. Do not move around from house to house.

8"When you enter a town and are welcomed, eat what is set down in front of you. **9**Heal the sick people who are there. Tell them, 'God's kingdom is near you.'

10"But what if you enter a town and are not welcomed? Then go into its streets and say, **11**'We wipe off even the dust of your town that sticks to our feet. We do it to show that God isn't pleased with you. But here is what you can be sure of. God's kingdom is near.'

12"I tell you this. On judgment day it will be easier for Sodom than for that town.

13"How terrible it will be for you, Korazin! How terrible for you, Bethsaida! Suppose the miracles done in you had been done in Tyre and Sidon. They would have turned away from their sins long ago. They would have put on black clothes. They would have sat down in ashes. **14**On judgment day it will be easier for Tyre and Sidon than for you.

15"And what about you, Capernaum? Will you be lifted up to heaven? No! You will go down to the place of the dead.

16"Anyone who listens to you listens to me. Anyone who does not accept you does not accept me. And anyone who does not accept me does not accept the One who sent me."

17The 72 returned with joy. They said, "Lord, even the demons obey us when we speak in your name."

18Jesus replied, "I saw Satan fall like lightning from heaven. **19**I have given you authority to walk all over snakes and scorpions. You will be able to destroy all the power of the enemy. Nothing will harm you. **20**But do not be glad when the evil spirits obey you. Instead, be glad that your names are written in heaven."

21At that time Jesus was full of joy through the Holy Spirit. He said, "I praise you, Father. You are Lord of heaven and earth. You have hidden these things from the wise and educated. But you have shown them to little children. Yes, Father. This is what you wanted.

22"My Father has given all things to me. The Father is the only one who knows who the Son is. And the only ones who know the Father are the Son and those to whom the Son chooses to make the Father known."

23Then Jesus turned to his disciples. He said to them in private, "Blessed are the eyes that see what you see. **24**I tell you, many prophets and kings wanted to see what you see. But they didn't see it. They wanted to hear what you hear. But they didn't hear it."

The Story of the Good Samaritan

25One day an authority on the law stood up to put Jesus to the test. "Teacher," he asked, "what must I do to receive eternal life?"

26"What is written in the Law?" Jesus replied. "How do you understand it?"

27He answered, " 'Love the Lord your God with all your heart and with all your soul. Love him with all your strength and with all your mind.' *(Deuteronomy 6:5)* And, 'Love your neighbor as you love yourself.' " *(Leviticus 19:18)*

28"You have answered correctly," Jesus replied. "Do that, and you will live."

29But the man wanted to make himself look good. So he asked Jesus, "And who is my neighbor?"

30Jesus replied, "A man was going down from Jerusalem to Jericho. Robbers attacked him. They stripped off his clothes and beat him. Then they went away, leaving him almost dead. **31**A priest happened to be going down that same road. When he saw the man, he passed by on the other side. **32**A Levite also came by. When he saw the man, he passed by on the other side too.

33But a Samaritan came to the place where the man was. When he saw the man, he felt sorry for him. **34**He went to him, poured olive oil and wine on his wounds and bandaged them. Then he put the man on his own donkey. He took him to an inn and took care of him. **35**The next day he took out two silver coins. He gave them to the owner of the inn. 'Take care of him,' he said. 'When I return, I will pay you back for any extra expense you may have.'

36"Which of the three do you think was a neighbor to the man who was attacked by robbers?"

37The authority on the law replied, "The one who felt sorry for him."

Jesus told him, "Go and do as he did."

Jesus at the Home of Martha and Mary

38Jesus and his disciples went on their way. Jesus came to a village where a woman named Martha lived. She welcomed him into her home. **39**She had a sister named Mary.

Mary sat at the Lord's feet listening to what he said. **40**But Martha was busy with all the things that had to be done. She came to Jesus and said, "Lord, my sister has left me to do the work by myself. Don't you care? Tell her to help me!"

41"Martha, Martha," the Lord answered. "You are worried and upset about many things. **42**But only one thing is needed. Mary has chosen what is better. And it will not be taken away from her."

Jesus Teaches About Prayer

11 One day Jesus was praying in a certain place. When he finished, one of his disciples spoke to him. "Lord," he said, "teach us to pray, just as John taught his disciples."

2Jesus said to them, "When you pray, this is what you should say.

MARTHA

1 PETER 4:9

G

Welcome others into your homes without complaining.

✔

T

Martha stomped around the kitchen. Her feet hurt and her back ached. She felt grumpy as she prepared the meal for Jesus and his disciples. She thought, *Mary should be helping me!* But Mary instead sat at Jesus' feet, listening to him talk.

Martha grabbed a spoon and stirred the bubbling soup. The heat from the fire made her hot and sweaty. How she wished *she* could be sitting at Jesus' feet—like Mary—instead of slaving away alone in the kitchen. But *somebody* had to get dinner ready. Martha really didn't mind doing the work. What she *did* mind was doing it alone.

OK, I've had it, Martha muttered. She tossed the spoon on the table, and it clattered to the floor. Ignoring it, she headed toward Jesus and the others. "Lord, didn't you notice that Mary's just sitting here while I do all the work? **TELL HER TO HELP ME!"**

Jesus saw the frown on Martha's face. He smiled at her and answered gently, "Martha, Martha. Why are you so worried about dinner? I'm not. I know we'll get fed eventually. Mary wants to sit here and listen. That's a good thing, and I don't want her to leave just yet."

Martha sighed again, but this time with relief instead of anger. She had snapped at Jesus. *Jesus!* And he had answered her quietly, with a loving smile. Martha went back into the kitchen. She picked up her spoon to stir the soup again, this time with a smile on her face and an ear to hear what Jesus was saying to those around him.

BE A MARTHA

Martha *did* have a lot of work to do. But she needed to have Jesus adjust her attitude so that she was doing her work lovingly instead of with complaining and grumbling. Do you complain and grumble sometimes? Well, be like Martha! Stop complaining and grumbling and do your work lovingly and willingly.

MARTHA WELCOMED JESUS IN HER HOME.
THE WHOLE STORY: LUKE 10:38-42

Go to page 1198 for the next Super Hero

POWER-SURGE

FORGIVING F

FORGIVE US OUR SINS, AS WE ALSO FORGIVE EVERYONE WHO SINS AGAINST US.
— LUKE 11:4 —

" 'Father,
may your name be honored.
May your kingdom come.
³Give us each day our daily bread.
⁴Forgive us our sins,
  as we also forgive everyone who sins
    against us.
Keep us from falling into sin when we
  are tempted.' "

⁵Then Jesus said to them, "Suppose someone has a friend. He goes to him at midnight. He says, 'Friend, lend me three loaves of bread. ⁶A friend of mine on a journey has come to stay with me. I have nothing for him to eat.'

⁷"Then the one inside answers, 'Don't bother me. The door is already locked. My children are with me in bed. I can't get up and give you anything.'

⁸"I tell you, that person will not get up. And he won't give the man bread just because he is his friend. But because the man keeps on asking, he will get up. He will give him as much as he needs.

⁹"So here is what I say to you. Ask, and it will be given to you. Search, and you will find. Knock, and the door will be opened to you. ¹⁰Everyone who asks will receive. He who searches will find. And the door will be opened to the one who knocks.

¹¹"Fathers, suppose your son asks for a fish. Which of you will give him a snake instead? ¹²Or suppose he asks for an egg. Which of you will give him a scorpion? ¹³Even though you are evil, you know how to give good gifts to your children. How much more will your Father who is in heaven give the Holy Spirit to those who ask him!"

Jesus and Beelzebub

¹⁴Jesus was driving out a demon. The man who had the demon could not speak. When the demon left, the man began to speak. The crowd was amazed. ¹⁵But some of them said, "Jesus is driving out demons by the power of Beelzebub, the prince of demons." ¹⁶Others put Jesus to the test by asking for a miraculous sign from heaven.

¹⁷Jesus knew what they were thinking. So he said to them, "Any kingdom that fights against itself will be destroyed. A family that is divided against itself will fall. ¹⁸If Satan fights against himself, how can his kingdom stand?

"I say this because of what you claim. You say I drive out demons by the power of Beelzebub. ¹⁹Suppose I do drive out demons with Beelzebub's help. With whose help do your followers drive them out? So then, they will be your judges. ²⁰But suppose I drive out demons with the help of God's powerful finger. Then God's kingdom has come to you.

²¹"When a strong man is completely armed and guards his house, what he owns is safe. ²²But when someone stronger attacks, he is overpowered. The attacker takes away the armor the man had trusted in. Then he divides up what he has stolen.

²³"Anyone who is not with me is against me. Anyone who does not gather sheep with me scatters them.

²⁴"What happens when an evil spirit comes out of a man? It goes through dry areas looking for a place to rest. But it doesn't find it. Then it says, 'I will return to the house I left.' ²⁵When it arrives there, it finds the house swept clean and put in order. ²⁶Then the evil spirit goes and takes seven other spirits more evil than itself. They go in and live there. That man is worse off than before."

²⁷As Jesus was saying these things, a woman in the crowd called out. She shouted, "Blessed is the mother who gave you birth and nursed you."

²⁸He replied, "Instead, blessed are those who hear God's word and obey it."

The Miraculous Sign of Jonah

²⁹As the crowds grew larger, Jesus spoke to them. "The people of today are evil," he

POWER-SURGE

OBEYS ✔

BLESSED ARE THOSE WHO HEAR GOD'S WORD AND OBEY IT.
— LUKE 11:28 —

said. "They ask for a miraculous sign from God. But none will be given except the sign of Jonah. ³⁰He was a sign from God to the people of Nineveh. In the same way, the Son of Man will be a sign from God to the people of today.

³¹"The Queen of the South will stand up on judgment day with the men now living. And she will prove that they are guilty. She came from very far away to listen to Solomon's wisdom. And now one who is more important than Solomon is here.

³²"The men of Nineveh will stand up on judgment day with the people now living. And the Ninevites will prove that those people are guilty. The men of Nineveh turned away from their sins when Jonah preached to them. And now one who is more important than Jonah is here.

The Eye Is the Lamp of the Body

³³"No one lights a lamp and hides it. No one puts it under a bowl. Instead, people put a lamp on its stand. Then those who come in can see the light.

³⁴"Your eye is like a lamp for your body. Suppose your eyes are good. Then your whole body also is full of light. But suppose your eyes are bad. Then your body also is full of darkness. ³⁵So make sure that the light inside you is not darkness.

³⁶"Suppose your whole body is full of light. And suppose no part of it is dark. Then your body will be completely lit up. It will be as when the light of a lamp shines on you."

Six Warnings

³⁷Jesus finished speaking. Then a Pharisee invited him to eat with him. So Jesus went in and took his place at the table. ³⁸But the Pharisee noticed that Jesus did not wash before the meal. He was surprised.

³⁹Then the Lord spoke to him. "You Pharisees clean the outside of the cup and dish," he said. "But inside you are full of greed and evil. ⁴⁰You foolish people! Didn't the one who made the outside make the inside also? ⁴¹Give to poor people what is inside the dish. Then everything will be clean for you.

⁴²"How terrible it will be for you Pharisees! You give God a tenth of your garden plants, such as mint and rue. But you have forgotten to be fair and to love God. You should have practiced the last things without failing to do the first.

⁴³"How terrible for you Pharisees! You love the most important seats in the synagogues. You love having people greet you in the market places.

⁴⁴"How terrible for you! You are like graves that are not marked. People walk over them without knowing it."

⁴⁵An authority on the law spoke to Jesus. He said, "Teacher, when you say things like that, you say bad things about us too."

⁴⁶Jesus replied, "How terrible for you authorities on the law! You put such heavy loads on people that they can hardly carry them. But you yourselves will not lift one finger to help them.

⁴⁷"How terrible for you! You build tombs for the prophets. It was your people of long ago who killed them. ⁴⁸So you give witness that you agree with what your people did long ago. They killed the prophets, and now you build the prophets' tombs.

⁴⁹"So God in his wisdom said, 'I will send prophets and apostles to them. They will kill some. And they will try to hurt others.' ⁵⁰So the people of today will be punished. They will pay for all the prophets' blood spilled since the world began. ⁵¹I mean from the blood of Abel to the blood of Zechariah, who was killed between the altar and the temple. Yes, I tell you, the people of today will be punished for all these things.

⁵²"How terrible for you authorities on the law! You have taken away the key to the door of knowledge. You yourselves have not entered. And you have stood in the way of those who were entering."

⁵³When Jesus left there, the Pharisees and the teachers of the law strongly opposed him. They threw a lot of questions at him. ⁵⁴They set traps for him. They wanted to catch him in something he might say.

Jesus Gives Words of Warning and Hope

12 During that time a crowd of many thousands had gathered. There were so many people that they were stepping on one another.

Jesus spoke first to his disciples. "Be on your guard against the yeast of the Pharisees," he said. "They just pretend to be godly. ²Everything that is secret will be brought out into the open. Everything that is hidden will be uncovered. ³What you have said in the dark will be heard in the daylight. What you have whispered to someone behind closed doors will be shouted from the rooftops.

⁴"My friends, listen to me. Don't be

afraid of those who kill the body but can't do any more than that. **5**I will show you whom you should be afraid of. Be afraid of the One who can kill the body and also has the power to throw you into hell. Yes, I tell you, be afraid of him.

6"Aren't five sparrows sold for two pennies? But God does not forget even one of them. **7**In fact, he even counts every hair on your head! So don't be afraid. You are worth more than many sparrows.

8"What about someone who says in front of others that he knows me? I tell you, the Son of Man will say that he knows that person in front of God's angels. **9**But what about someone who says in front of others that he doesn't know me? I, the Son of Man, will say that I don't know him in front of God's angels.

10"Everyone who speaks a word against the Son of Man will be forgiven. But anyone who speaks evil things against the Holy Spirit will not be forgiven.

11"You will be brought before synagogues, rulers and authorities. But do not worry about how to stand up for yourselves or what to say. **12**The Holy Spirit will teach you at that time what you should say."

The Story of the Rich Man

13Someone in the crowd spoke to Jesus. "Teacher," he said, "tell my brother to divide the family property with me."

14Jesus replied, "Friend, who made me a judge or umpire between you?"

15Then he said to them, "Watch out! Be on your guard against wanting to have more and more things. Life is not made up of how much a person has."

16Then Jesus told them a story. He said, "A certain rich man's land produced a good crop. **17**He thought to himself, 'What should I do? I don't have any place to store my crops.'

18"Then he said, 'This is what I'll do. I will tear down my storerooms and build bigger ones. I will store all my grain and my other things in them. **19**I'll say to myself, "You have plenty of good things stored away for many years. Take life easy. Eat, drink and have a good time." '

20"But God said to him, 'You foolish man! This very night I will take your life away from you. Then who will get what you have prepared for yourself?'

21"That is how it will be for anyone who stores things away for himself but is not rich in God's eyes."

Do Not Worry

22Then Jesus spoke to his disciples. He said, "I tell you, do not worry. Don't worry about your life and what you will eat. And don't worry about your body and what you will wear. **23**There is more to life than eating. There are more important things for the body than clothes.

24"Think about the ravens. They don't plant or gather crops. They don't have any storerooms at all. But God feeds them. You are worth much more than birds!

25"Can you add even one hour to your life by worrying? **26**You can't do that very little thing. So why worry about the rest?

27"Think about how the lilies grow. They don't work or make clothing. But here is what I tell you. Not even Solomon in all of his glory was dressed like one of those flowers. **28**If that is how God dresses the wild grass, how much better will he dress you! After all, the grass is here only today. Tomorrow it is thrown into the fire. Your faith is so small!

29"Don't spend time thinking about what you will eat or drink. Don't worry about it. **30**People who are ungodly run after all of those things. Your Father knows that you need them.

31"But put God's kingdom first. Then those other things will also be given to you.

32"Little flock, do not be afraid. Your Father has been pleased to give you the kingdom. **33**Sell what you own. Give to those who are poor. Provide purses for yourselves that will not wear out. Put away riches in heaven that will not be used up. There, no thief can come near it. There, no moth can destroy it. **34**Your heart will be where your riches are.

Be Ready

35"Be dressed and ready to serve. Keep your lamps burning. **36**Be like servants waiting for their master to return from a wedding dinner. When he comes and knocks, they can open the door for him at once.

37"It will be good for those servants whose master finds them ready when he comes. What I'm about to tell you is true. The master will then dress himself so he can serve them. He will have them take their places at the table. And he will come and wait on them. **38**It will be good for those servants whose master finds them ready. It will even be good if he comes very late at night.

39"But here is what you must understand. Suppose the owner of the house knew at what hour the robber was coming. He would not have let his house be broken into. **40**You also must be ready. The Son of Man will come at an hour when you don't expect him."

41Peter asked, "Lord, are you telling this story to us, or to everyone?"

42The Lord answered, "Suppose a master puts one of his servants in charge of his other servants. The servant's job is to give them the food they are to receive at the right time. The master wants a faithful and wise manager for this. **43**It will be good for the servant if the master finds him doing his job when the master returns. **44**What I'm about to tell you is true. The master will put that servant in charge of everything he owns.

45"But suppose the servant says to himself, 'My master is taking a long time to come back.' Suppose he begins to beat the other servants. Suppose he feeds himself. And suppose he drinks until he gets drunk. **46**The master of that servant will come back on a day the servant doesn't expect him. He will return at an hour the servant doesn't know. Then the master will cut him to pieces. He will send him to the place where unbelievers go.

47"Suppose a servant knows his master's wishes. But he doesn't get ready. And he doesn't do what his master wants. That servant will be beaten with many blows. **48**But suppose the servant does not know his master's wishes. And suppose he does things for which he should be punished. He will be beaten with only a few blows.

"Much will be required of everyone who has been given much. Even more will be asked of the person who is supposed to take care of much.

Jesus Will Separate People From One Another

49"I have come to bring fire on the earth. How I wish the fire had already started! **50**But I have a baptism of suffering to go through. And I will be very troubled until it is completed.

51"Do you think I came to bring peace on earth? No, I tell you. I have come to separate people. **52**From now on there will be five members in a family, each one against the other. There will be three against two and two against three. **53**They will be separated. Father will turn against son and son against father. Mother will turn against daughter and daughter against mother. Mother-in-law will turn against daughter-in-law and daughter-in-law against mother-in-law."

Understanding What Is Happening

54Jesus spoke to the crowd. He said, "You see a cloud rising in the west. Right away you say, 'It's going to rain.' And it does. **55**The south wind blows. So you say, 'It's going to be hot.' And it is. **56**You pretenders! You know how to understand the appearance of the earth and the sky. Why can't you understand the meaning of what is happening right now?

57"Why don't you judge for yourselves what is right? **58**Suppose someone has a claim against you, and you are on your way to court. Try hard to settle the matter on the way. If you don't, that person may drag you off to the judge. The judge may turn you over to the officer. And the officer may throw you into prison. **59**I tell you, you will not get out until you have paid the very last penny!"

Jesus Gives a Warning

13 Some people who were there at that time told Jesus about certain Galileans. Pilate had mixed their blood with their sacrifices.

2Jesus said, "These people from Galilee suffered greatly. Do you think they were worse sinners than all the other Galileans? **3**I tell you, no! But unless you turn away from your sins, you will all die too. **4**Or what about the 18 people in Siloam? They died when the tower fell on them. Do you think they were more guilty than all the others living in Jerusalem? **5**I tell you, no! But unless you turn away from your sins, you will all die too."

6Then Jesus told a story. "A man had a fig tree," he said. "It had been planted in his vineyard. When he went to look for fruit on it, he didn't find any. **7**So he went to the man who took care of the vineyard. He said, 'For three years now I've been coming to look for fruit on this fig tree. But I haven't found any. Cut it down! Why should it use up the soil?'

8" 'Sir,' the man replied, 'leave it alone for one more year. I'll dig around it and feed it. **9**If it bears fruit next year, fine! If not, then cut it down.' "

Jesus Heals a Disabled Woman on the Sabbath Day

10Jesus was teaching in one of the synagogues on a Sabbath day. **11**A woman there had been disabled by an evil spirit for 18 years. She was bent over and could not stand up straight.

12Jesus saw her. He asked her to come to him. He said to her, "Woman, you will no longer be disabled. I am about to set you free." 13Then he put his hands on her.

Right away she stood up straight and praised God.

14Jesus had healed the woman on the Sabbath day. This made the synagogue ruler angry. He told the people, "There are six days for work. So come and be healed on those days. But do not come on the Sabbath."

15The Lord answered him, "You pretenders! Doesn't each of you go to the barn and untie his ox or donkey on the Sabbath day? Then don't you lead it out to give it water? 16This woman is a member of Abraham's family line. But Satan has kept her disabled for 18 long years. Shouldn't she be set free on the Sabbath day from what was keeping her disabled?"

17When Jesus said this, all those who opposed him were put to shame. But the people were delighted. They loved all the wonderful things he was doing.

The Stories of the Mustard Seed and the Yeast

18Then Jesus asked, "What is God's kingdom like? What can I compare it to? 19It is like a mustard seed. Someone took the seed and planted it in a garden. It grew and became a tree. The birds sat in its branches."

20Again he asked, "What can I compare God's kingdom to? 21It is like yeast that a woman used. She mixed it into a large amount of flour. The yeast worked its way all through the dough."

The Narrow Door

22Then Jesus went through the towns and villages, teaching the people. He was on his way to Jerusalem. 23Someone asked him, "Lord, are only a few people going to be saved?"

He said to them, 24"Try very hard to enter through the narrow door. I tell you, many will try to enter and will not be able to. 25The owner of the house will get up and close the door. Then you will stand outside knocking and begging. You will say, 'Sir, open the door for us.'

"But he will answer, 'I don't know you. And I don't know where you come from.'

26"Then you will say, 'We ate and drank with you. You taught in our streets.'

27"But he will reply, 'I don't know you. And I don't know where you come from. Get away from me, all you who do evil!'

28"You will sob and grind your teeth when you see those who are in God's kingdom. You will see Abraham, Isaac and Jacob and all the prophets there. But you yourselves will be thrown out. 29People will come from east and west and north and south. They will take their places at the feast in God's kingdom. 30Then the last will be first. And the first will be last."

Jesus' Sadness Over Jerusalem

31At that time some Pharisees came to Jesus. They said to him, "Leave this place. Go somewhere else. Herod wants to kill you."

32He replied, "Go and tell that fox, 'I will drive out demons. I will heal people today and tomorrow. And on the third day I will reach my goal.' 33In any case, I must keep going today and tomorrow and the next day. Certainly no prophet can die outside Jerusalem!

34"Jerusalem! Jerusalem! You kill the prophets and throw stones in order to kill those who are sent to you. Many times I have wanted to gather your people together. I have wanted to be like a hen who gathers her chicks under her wings. But you would not let me!

35"Look, your house is left empty. I tell you, you will not see me again until you say, 'Blessed is the one who comes in the name of the Lord.' " *(Psalm 118:26)*

Jesus Eats at a Pharisee's House

14 One Sabbath day, Jesus went to eat in the house of a well-known Pharisee. While he was there, he was being carefully watched. 2In front of him was a man whose body was badly swollen. 3Jesus turned to the Pharisees and the authorities on the law. He asked them, "Is it breaking the Law to heal on the Sabbath?"

4But they remained silent.

So Jesus took hold of the man and healed him. Then he sent him away.

5He asked them another question. He said, "Suppose one of you has a son or an ox that falls into a well on the Sabbath day. Wouldn't you pull him out right away?" 6And they had nothing to say.

7Jesus noticed how the guests picked the places of honor at the table. So he told them a story. 8He said, "Suppose someone invites you to a wedding feast. Do not take the place of honor. A person more important than you may have been invited. 9If so, the host who invited both of you will come to you. He will say, 'Give this person your seat.' Then you will be filled with shame. You will have to take the least important place.

10 "But when you are invited, take the lowest place. Then your host will come over to you. He will say, 'Friend, move up to a better place.' Then you will be honored in front of all the other guests. 11 Anyone who lifts himself up will be brought down. And anyone who is brought down will be lifted up."

12 Then Jesus spoke to his host. "Suppose you give a lunch or a dinner," he said. "Do not invite your friends, your brothers or sisters, or your relatives, or your rich neighbors. If you do, they may invite you to eat with them. So you will be paid back.

13 "But when you give a big dinner, invite those who are poor. Also invite those who can't walk, the disabled and the blind. 14 Then you will be blessed. Your guests can't pay you back. But you will be paid back when those who are right with God rise from the dead."

The Story of the Big Dinner

15 One of the people at the table with Jesus heard him say those things. So he said to Jesus, "Blessed is the one who will eat at the feast in God's kingdom."

16 Jesus replied, "A certain man was preparing a big dinner. He invited many guests. 17 Then the day of the dinner arrived. He sent his servant to those who had been invited. The servant told them, 'Come. Everything is ready now.'

18 "But they all had the same idea. They began to make excuses. The first one said, 'I have just bought a field. I have to go and see it. Please excuse me.'

19 "Another said, 'I have just bought five pairs of oxen. I'm on my way to try them out. Please excuse me.'

20 "Still another said, 'I just got married, so I can't come.'

21 "The servant came back and reported this to his master.

"Then the owner of the house became angry. He ordered his servant, 'Go out quickly into the streets and lanes of the town. Bring in those who are poor. Also bring those who can't walk, the blind and the disabled.'

22 " 'Sir,' the servant said, 'what you ordered has been done. But there is still room.'

23 "Then the master told his servant, 'Go out to the roads. Go out to the country lanes. Make the people come in. I want my house to be full. 24 I tell you, not one of those men who were invited will get a taste of my dinner.' "

It Costs to Be a Disciple

25 Large crowds were traveling with Jesus. He turned and spoke to them. He said, 26 "Anyone who comes to me must hate his father and mother. He must hate his wife and children. He must hate his brothers and sisters. And he must hate even his own life. Unless he does, he can't be my disciple. 27 Anyone who doesn't carry his cross and follow me can't be my disciple.

28 "Suppose someone wants to build a tower. Won't he sit down first and figure out how much it will cost? Then he will see whether he has enough money to finish it. 29 Suppose he starts building and is not able to finish. Then everyone who sees what he has done will laugh at him. 30 They will say, 'This fellow started to build. But he wasn't able to finish.'

31 "Or suppose a king is about to go to war against another king. And suppose he has 10,000 men, while the other has 20,000 coming against him. Won't he first sit down and think about whether he can win?

32 "And suppose he decides he can't win. Then he will send some men to ask how peace can be made. He will do this while the other king is still far away.

33 "In the same way, you must give up everything you have. If you don't, you can't be my disciple.

34 "Salt is good. But suppose it loses its saltiness. How can it be made salty again? 35 It is not good for the soil. And it is not good for the trash pile. It will be thrown out.

"Those who have ears should listen."

The Story of the Lost Sheep

15 The tax collectors and "sinners" were all gathering around to hear Jesus. 2 But the Pharisees and the teachers of the law were whispering among themselves. They said, "This man welcomes sinners and eats with them."

3 Then Jesus told them a story. 4 He said, "Suppose one of you has 100 sheep and loses one of them. Won't he leave the 99 in the open country? Won't he go and look for the one lost sheep until he finds it? 5 When he finds it, he will joyfully put it on his shoulders 6 and go home. Then he will call his friends and neighbors together. He will say, 'Be joyful with me. I have found my lost sheep.'

7 "I tell you, it will be the same in heav-

en. There will be great joy when one sinner turns away from sin. Yes, there will be more joy than for 99 godly people who do not need to turn away from their sins.

The Story of the Lost Coin

8"Or suppose a woman has ten silver coins and loses one. She will light a lamp and sweep the house. She will search carefully until she finds the coin. 9And when she finds it, she will call her friends and neighbors together. She will say, 'Be joyful with me. I have found my lost coin.'

10"I tell you, it is the same in heaven. There is joy in heaven over one sinner who turns away from sin."

The Story of the Lost Son

11Jesus continued, "There was a man who had two sons. 12The younger son spoke to his father. He said, 'Father, give me my share of the family property.' So the father divided his property between his two sons.

13"Not long after that, the younger son packed up all he had. Then he left for a country far away. There he wasted his money on wild living. 14He spent everything he had.

"Then the whole country ran low on food. So the son didn't have what he needed. 15He went to work for someone who lived in that country, who sent him to the fields to feed the pigs. 16The son wanted to fill his stomach with the food the pigs were eating. But no one gave him anything.

17"Then he began to think clearly again. He said, 'How many of my father's hired workers have more than enough food! But here I am dying from hunger! 18I will get up and go back to my father. I will say to him, "Father, I have sinned against heaven. And I have sinned against you. 19I am no longer fit to be called your son. Make me like one of your hired workers." ' 20So he got up and went to his father.

"While the son was still a long way off, his father saw him. He was filled with tender love for his son. He ran to him. He threw his arms around him and kissed him.

21"The son said to him, 'Father, I have sinned against heaven and against you. I am no longer fit to be called your son.'

22"But the father said to his servants, 'Quick! Bring the best robe and put it on him. Put a ring on his finger and sandals on his feet. 23Bring the fattest calf and kill it. Let's have a big dinner and celebrate. 24This son of mine was dead. And now he is alive again. He was lost. And now he is found.'

"So they began to celebrate.

25"The older son was in the field. When he came near the house, he heard music and dancing. 26So he called one of the servants. He asked him what was going on.

27" 'Your brother has come home,' the servant replied. 'Your father has killed the fattest calf. He has done this because your brother is back safe and sound.'

28"The older brother became angry. He refused to go in. So his father went out and begged him.

29"But he answered his father, 'Look! All these years I've worked like a slave for you. I have always obeyed your orders. You never gave me even a young goat so I could celebrate with my friends. 30But this son of yours wasted your money with some prostitutes. Now he comes home. And for him you kill the fattest calf!'

31" 'My son,' the father said, 'you are always with me. Everything I have is yours. 32But we had to celebrate and be glad. This brother of yours was dead. And now he is alive again. He was lost. And now he is found.' "

The Story of the Clever Manager

16 Jesus told his disciples another story. He said, "There was a rich man who had a manager. Some said that the manager was wasting what the rich man owned. 2So the rich man told him to come in. He asked him, 'What is this I hear about you? Tell me exactly how you have handled what I own. You can't be my manager any longer.'

3"The manager said to himself, 'What will I do now? My master is taking away my job. I'm not strong enough to dig. And I'm too ashamed to beg. 4I know what I'm going to do. I'll do something so that when I lose my job here, people will welcome me into their houses.'

5"So he called in each person who owed his master something. He asked the first one, 'How much do you owe my master?'

6" 'I owe 800 gallons of olive oil,' he replied.

"The manager told him, 'Take your bill. Sit down quickly and change it to 400 gallons.'

7"Then he asked the second one, 'And how much do you owe?'

" 'I owe 1,000 bushels of wheat,' he replied.

"The manager told him, 'Take your bill and change it to 800 bushels.'

8"The manager had not been honest. But the master praised him for being clever. The people of this world are clever in dealing with those who are like themselves. They are more clever than God's people.

9"I tell you, use the riches of this world to help others. In that way, you will make friends for yourselves. Then when your riches are gone, you will be welcomed into your eternal home in heaven.

10"Suppose you can be trusted with very little. Then you can be trusted with a lot. But suppose you are not honest with

JESUS TELLS A STORY

LUKE 15:18-20

F

🗣

♥

I will get up and go back to my father. I will say to him, "Father, I have sinned against heaven. And I have sinned against you. I am no longer fit to be called your son. Make me like one of your hired workers." So he got up and went to his father.

Jesus sat with his disciples and many other followers and told this story:

A father had two sons. One of them wanted to get his share of the family's money and leave home. So the father gave him his money and the son went far away.

The son quickly spent all of his money and had nothing to eat. So he decided to go home again. He knew he didn't deserve to be forgiven for wasting all that money. But he thought perhaps his father would take him back as a servant instead of as a son.

SO THE SON BEGAN TO WALK HOME.

The son didn't know it, but each day his father stood in the road and watched for his son to come home. One day the father's waiting ended. He saw his son coming and ran to meet him. Instantly he forgave his son for taking the money and going away. He didn't care about the money. He only knew that he loved his son and had him back again.

BE LIKE JESUS

Jesus told this story to make sure his followers knew how much he loved them and would forgive them for their sin. He loves you, too, you know. And he wants to forgive you whenever you do something wrong. He's waiting for you to come to him, just as the son went to the father.

THE FATHER FORGAVE HIS SON, AND JESUS FORGIVES US.

Go to page 1201 for the next Super Hero

POWER-SURGE

HONEST

SUPPOSE YOU CAN BE
TRUSTED WITH VERY
LITTLE. THEN YOU CAN
BE TRUSTED WITH A
LOT. BUT SUPPOSE
YOU ARE NOT HONEST
WITH VERY LITTLE.
THEN YOU WILL NOT
BE HONEST WITH
A LOT.
— LUKE 16:10 —

TRUSTED

very little. Then you will not be honest with a lot.

11 "Suppose you have not been worthy of trust in handling worldly wealth. Then who will trust you with true riches? 12 Suppose you have not been worthy of trust in handling someone else's property. Then who will give you property of your own?

13 "No servant can serve two masters at the same time. He will hate one of them and love the other. Or he will be faithful to one and dislike the other. You can't serve God and Money at the same time."

14 The Pharisees loved money. They heard all that Jesus said and made fun of him. 15 Jesus said to them, "You try to make yourselves look good in the eyes of other people. But God knows your hearts. What is worth a great deal among people is hated by God.

More Teachings

16 "The teachings of the Law and the Prophets were preached until John came. Since then, the good news of God's kingdom is being preached. And everyone is trying very hard to enter it. 17 It is easier for heaven and earth to disappear than for the smallest part of a letter to drop out of the Law.

18 "Anyone who divorces his wife and gets married to another woman commits adultery. Also, the man who gets married to a divorced woman commits adultery.

The Rich Man and Lazarus

19 "Once there was a rich man. He was dressed in purple cloth and fine linen. He lived an easy life every day. 20 A man named Lazarus was placed at his gate. Lazarus was a beggar. His body was covered with sores. 21 Even dogs came and licked his sores. All he wanted was to eat what fell from the rich man's table.

22 "The time came when the beggar died. The angels carried him to Abraham's side. The rich man also died and was buried. 23 In hell, the rich man was suffering terribly. He looked up and saw Abraham far away. Lazarus was by his side. 24 So the rich man called out, 'Father Abraham! Have pity on me! Send Lazarus to dip the tip of his finger in water. Then he can cool my tongue with it. I am in terrible pain in this fire.'

25 "But Abraham replied, 'Son, remember what happened in your lifetime. You received your good things. Lazarus received bad things. Now he is comforted here, and you are in terrible pain. 26 Besides, a wide space has been placed between us and you. So those who want to go from here to you can't go. And no one can cross over from there to us.'

27 "The rich man answered, 'Then I beg you, father. Send Lazarus to my family. 28 I have five brothers. Let Lazarus warn them. Then they will not come to this place of terrible suffering.'

29 "Abraham replied, 'They have the teachings of Moses and the Prophets. Let your brothers listen to them.'

30 " 'No, father Abraham,' he said. 'But if someone from the dead goes to them, they will turn away from their sins.'

31 "Abraham said to him, 'They do not listen to Moses and the Prophets. So they will not be convinced even if someone rises from the dead.' "

Sin, Faith and Duty

17 Jesus spoke to his disciples. "Things that make people sin are sure to come," he said. "But how terrible it will be for the person who brings them! 2 Suppose people lead one of these little ones to sin. It would be better for those people to be thrown into the sea with a millstone tied around their neck. 3 So watch what you do.

"If your brother sins, tell him he is wrong. Then if he turns away from his sins, forgive him. 4 Suppose he sins against you seven times in one day. And suppose he comes back to you each time and says, 'I'm sorry.' Forgive him."

POWER-SURGE

FORGIVING F

IF YOUR BROTHER SINS, TELL HIM HE IS WRONG. THEN IF HE TURNS AWAY FROM HIS SINS, FORGIVE HIM.
— LUKE 17:3 —

HONEST H

5The apostles said to the Lord, "Give us more faith!"

6He replied, "Suppose you have faith as small as a mustard seed. Then you can say to this mulberry tree, 'Be pulled up. Be planted in the sea.' And it will obey you.

7"Suppose one of you had a servant plowing or looking after the sheep. And suppose the servant came in from the field. Would you say to him, 'Come along now and sit down to eat'? **8**No. Instead, you would say, 'Prepare my supper. Get yourself ready. Wait on me while I eat and drink. Then after that you can eat and drink.' **9**Would you thank the servant because he did what he was told to do?

10"It's the same with you. Suppose you have done everything you were told to do. Then you should say, 'We are not worthy to serve you. We have only done our duty.' "

Jesus Heals Ten Men

11Jesus was on his way to Jerusalem. He traveled along the border between Samaria and Galilee. **12**As he was going into a village, ten men met him. They had a skin disease. They were standing close by. **13**And they called out in a loud voice, "Jesus! Master! Have pity on us!"

14Jesus saw them and said, "Go. Show yourselves to the priests." While they were on the way, they were healed.

15When one of them saw that he was healed, he came back. He praised God in a loud voice. **16**He threw himself at Jesus' feet and thanked him. The man was a Samaritan.

17Jesus asked, "Weren't all ten healed? Where are the other nine? **18**Didn't any-one else return and give praise to God except this outsider?"

19Then Jesus said to him, "Get up and go. Your faith has healed you."

The Coming of God's Kingdom

20Once the Pharisees asked Jesus when God's kingdom would come. He replied, "The coming of God's kingdom is not something you can see just by watching for it carefully. **21**People will not say, 'Here it is.' Or, 'There it is.' God's kingdom is among you."

22Then Jesus spoke to his disciples. "The time is coming," he said, "when you will long to see one of the days of the Son of Man. But you won't see it. **23**People will tell you, 'There he is!' Or, 'Here he is!' Don't go running off after them.

24"When the Son of Man comes, he will be like the lightning. It flashes and lights up the sky from one end to the other. **25**But first the Son of Man must suffer many things. He will not be accepted by the people of today.

26"Remember how it was in the days of Noah. It will be the same when the Son of Man comes. **27**People were eating and drinking. They were getting married. They were giving their daughters to be married. They did all those things right up to the day Noah entered the ark. Then the flood came and destroyed them all.

28"It was the same in the days of Lot. People were eating and drinking. They were buying and selling. They were planting and building. **29**But on the day Lot left Sodom, fire and sulfur rained down from heaven. And all the people were destroyed.

30"It will be just like that on the day the Son of Man is shown to the world. **31**Suppose someone is on the roof of his house on that day. And suppose his goods are inside the house. He should not go down to get them. No one in the field should go back for anything either. **32**Remember Lot's wife! **33**Anyone who tries to keep his life will lose it. Anyone who loses his life will keep it.

34"I tell you, on that night two people will be in one bed. One person will be taken and the other left. **35/36**Two women will be grinding grain together. One will be taken and the other left."

37"Where, Lord?" his disciples asked.

He replied, "The vultures will gather where there is a dead body."

The Story of the Widow Who Would Not Give Up

18 Jesus told his disciples a story. He wanted to show them that they should always pray and not give up. ²He said, "In a certain town there was a judge. He didn't have any respect for God or care about people. ³A widow lived in that town. She came to the judge again and again. She kept begging him, 'Make things right for me. Someone is doing me wrong.'

⁴"For some time the judge refused. But finally he said to himself, 'I don't have any respect for God. I don't care about people. ⁵But this widow keeps bothering me. So I will see that things are made right for her. If I don't, she will wear me out by coming again and again!' "

⁶The Lord said, "Listen to what the unfair judge says.

⁷"God's chosen people cry out to him day and night. Won't he make things right for them? Will he keep putting them off? ⁸I tell you, God will see that things are made right for them. He will make sure it happens quickly.

"But when the Son of Man comes, will he find people on earth who have faith?"

10ᵀᴴ LEPER

LUKE 17:15-16

When one [leper] saw that he was healed, he came back. He praised God in a loud voice. He threw himself at Jesus' feet and thanked him.

Ten men tripped and stumbled over the rocks in the road and over each other as they ran toward the healer. He was coming their way! They had heard how Jesus could heal any sickness. He could even raise dead people back to life! Certainly he could heal their skin disease, leprosy.

The ten lepers stopped before they got to Jesus. Because of their sickness, they weren't allowed to go near healthy people. But they shouted together at Jesus: "Jesus! Master! **WE'RE SO SICK! PLEASE, HEAL US!**"

Jesus healed all ten lepers. Their skin became soft and clean and new again. They looked at each other in amazement. Unbelievable! They were healed!

All ten lepers ran to tell the priests and their families that they were healed. But before getting very far, one stopped. He looked at his healed skin. And he looked at the backs of the other lepers who were now far down the road. And he turned around.

That one leper went back to Jesus to thank him for the healing. Ten men were healed, but only one was thankful.

JESUS HEALED TEN LEPERS, BUT ONLY ONE CAME BACK TO THANK HIM.

Go to page 1204 for the next Super Hero

TRIES HARD T

JESUS TOLD HIS
DISCIPLES A STORY.
HE WANTED TO SHOW
THEM THAT THEY
SHOULD ALWAYS PRAY
AND NOT GIVE UP.
— LUKE 18:1 —

The Story of the Pharisee and the Tax Collector

9Jesus told a story to some people who were sure they were right with God. They looked down on everybody else. **10**He said to them, "Two men went up to the temple to pray. One was a Pharisee. The other was a tax collector.

11"The Pharisee stood up and prayed about himself. 'God, I thank you that I am not like other people,' he said. 'I am not like robbers or those who do other evil things. I am not like those who commit adultery. I am not even like this tax collector. **12**I fast twice a week. And I give a tenth of all I get.'

13"But the tax collector stood not very far away. He would not even look up to heaven. He beat his chest and said, 'God, have mercy on me. I am a sinner.'

14"I tell you, the tax collector went home accepted by God. But not the Pharisee. Everyone who lifts himself up will be brought down. And anyone who is brought down will be lifted up."

Little Children Are Brought to Jesus

15People were also bringing babies to Jesus. They wanted him to touch them. When the disciples saw this, they told the people to stop.

16But Jesus asked the children to come to him. "Let the little children come to me," he said. "Don't keep them away. God's kingdom belongs to people like them. **17**What I'm about to tell you is true. Anyone who will not receive God's kingdom like a little child will never enter it."

Jesus and the Rich Ruler

18A certain ruler asked Jesus a question. "Good teacher," he said, "what must I do to receive eternal life?"

19"Why do you call me good?" Jesus an- swered. "No one is good except God. **20**You know what the commandments say. 'Do not commit adultery. Do not commit murder. Do not steal. Do not give false witness. Honor your father and mother.' " *(Exodus 20:12–16; Deuteronomy 5:16–20)*

21"I have obeyed all those command- ments since I was a boy," the ruler said.

22When Jesus heard this, he said to him, "You are still missing one thing. Sell everything you have. Give the money to those who are poor. You will have treasure in heaven. Then come and follow me."

23When the ruler heard this, he be- came very sad. He was very rich.

24Jesus looked at him. Then he said, "How hard it is for rich people to enter God's kingdom! **25**Is it hard for a camel to go through the eye of a needle? It is even harder for the rich to enter God's king- dom!"

26Those who heard this asked, "Then who can be saved?"

27Jesus replied, "Things that are impos- sible with people are possible with God."

28Peter said to him, "We have left everything we had in order to follow you!"

29"What I'm about to tell you is true," Jesus said to them. "Has anyone left home or family for God's kingdom? **30**They will receive many times as much in this world. In the world to come they will live forev- er."

Jesus Again Tells About His Coming Death

31Jesus took the Twelve to one side. He told them, "We are going up to Jerusalem. Everything that the prophets wrote about the Son of Man will come true. **32**He will be handed over to people who are not Jews. They will make fun of him. They will laugh at him and spit on him. They will whip him and kill him. **33**On the third day, he will rise from the dead!"

34The disciples did not understand any of this. Its meaning was hidden from them. So they didn't know what Jesus was talking about.

A Blind Beggar Receives His Sight

35Jesus was approaching Jericho. A blind man was sitting by the side of the road begging. **36**The blind man heard the crowd going by. He asked what was hap- pening. **37**They told him, "Jesus of Naza- reth is passing by."

38So the blind man called out, "Jesus! Son of David! Have mercy on me!"

39Those who led the way commanded him to stop. They told him to be quiet. But he shouted even louder, "Son of David! Have mercy on me!"

40Jesus stopped and ordered the man to be brought to him. When the man came near, Jesus spoke to him. **41**"What do you want me to do for you?" Jesus asked.

"Lord, I want to be able to see," the blind man replied.

42Jesus said to him, "Receive your sight. Your faith has healed you."

43Right away he could see. He followed Jesus, praising God. When all the people saw it, they also praised God.

Zacchaeus the Tax Collector

19 Jesus entered Jericho and was passing through. **2**A man named Zacchaeus lived there. He was a chief tax collector and was very rich.

3Zacchaeus wanted to see who Jesus was. But he was a short man. He could not see Jesus because of the crowd. **4**So he ran ahead and climbed a sycamore-fig tree. He wanted to see Jesus, who was coming that way.

5Jesus reached the spot where Zacchaeus was. He looked up and said, "Zacchaeus, come down at once. I must stay at your house today." **6**So Zacchaeus came down at once and welcomed him gladly.

7All the people saw this. They began to whisper among themselves. They said, "Jesus has gone to be the guest of a 'sinner.' "

8But Zacchaeus stood up. He said, "Look, Lord! Here and now I give half of what I own to those who are poor. And if I have cheated anybody out of anything, I will pay it back. I will pay back four times the amount I took."

9Jesus said to Zacchaeus, "Today salvation has come to your house. You are a member of Abraham's family line. **10**The Son of Man came to look for the lost and save them."

The Story of Three Servants

11While the people were listening to these things, Jesus told them a story. He was near Jerusalem. The people thought that God's kingdom was going to appear right away.

12Jesus said, "A man from an important family went to a country far away. He went there to be made king and then return home. **13**So he sent for ten of his servants. He gave them each about three months' pay. 'Put this money to work until I come back,' he said.

14"But those he ruled over hated him. They sent some messengers after him. They were sent to say, 'We don't want this man to be our king.'

15"But he was made king and returned home. Then he sent for the servants he had given the money to. He wanted to find out what they had earned with it.

16"The first one came to him. He said, 'Sir, your money has earned ten times as much.'

17" 'You have done well, my good servant!' his master replied. 'You have been faithful in a very small matter. So I will put you in charge of ten towns.'

18"The second servant came to his master. He said, 'Sir, your money has earned five times as much.'

19"His master answered, 'I will put you in charge of five towns.'

20"Then another servant came. He said, 'Sir, here is your money. I have kept it hidden in a piece of cloth. **21**I was afraid of you. You are a hard man. You take out what you did not put in. You harvest what you did not plant.'

22"His master replied, 'I will judge you by your own words, you evil servant! So you knew that I am a hard man? You knew that I take out what I did not put in? You knew that I harvest what I did not plant? **23**Then why didn't you put my money in the bank? When I came back, I could have collected it with interest.'

24"Then he said to those standing by, 'Take his money away from him. Give it to the one who has ten times as much.'

25" 'Sir,' they said, 'he already has ten times as much!'

26"He replied, 'I tell you that everyone who has will be given more. But here is what will happen to anyone who has nothing. Even what he has will be taken away from him. **27**And what about my enemies who did not want me to be king over them? Bring them here! Kill them in front of me!' "

Jesus Enters Jerusalem

28After Jesus had said this, he went on ahead. He was going up to Jerusalem.

29He approached Bethphage and Bethany. The hill there was called the Mount of Olives. Jesus sent out two of his disciples. He said to them, **30**"Go to the village ahead of you. As soon as you get there, you will find a donkey's colt tied up. No one has ever ridden it. Untie it and bring it here. **31**Someone may ask you, 'Why are you untying it?' If so, say, 'The Lord needs it.' "

ZACCHAEUS

LUKE 19:3-4

Zacchaeus wanted to see who Jesus was. But he was a short man. He could not see Jesus because of the crowd. So he ran ahead and climbed a sycamore-fig tree.

Zacchaeus (zack-EE-us) stood on the step of his house, trying to decide what to do. He had heard so much about this Jesus. He was coming to Jericho today, and Zacchaeus wanted to see him. But he had one problem.

He was short—so short that he knew he wouldn't be able to see over the people gathered around Jesus. Maybe he could go on the roof of a house where Jesus was walking. No, he didn't know anyone on that road. Maybe he could sit on someone's shoulders. But that would look silly. But then Zacchaeus decided, I DON'T CARE HOW SILLY I LOOK. I NEED TO SEE JESUS.

Running ahead of the crowd, Zacchaeus came to a tree. The tree's branches reached close to the ground—close enough that short Zacchaeus could swing himself up. Zacchaeus climbed up the tree and stood on a big branch. *That's more like it,* he thought. His eager eyes searched for Jesus.

He could hear the crowd before he saw anything. But then, there Jesus was, right under the tree. Jesus looked up into the tree, as if he knew someone was there.

"Zacchaeus, come down out of that tree," Jesus said. "I want to go with you to your house."

Me? Zacchaeus thought, looking around. *Well, of course, he means me. There's no one else way up here!*

Zacchaeus scrambled down out of the tree. He was so excited he didn't even notice that he tore his robe on a branch or that he had scraped his knee. Jesus wanted to go to his house! Not only would he get to see Jesus, he would get to know Jesus—in his own home! Before he even heard them, Zacchaeus decided he would do whatever Jesus wanted him to do.

ZACCHAEUS

Be a Zacchaeus. Don't be afraid of what others might think. Be sure you search for Jesus and follow his truths. Even if it makes you look a little foolish, or even if others think you're crazy, follow Jesus with all your heart, just like Zacchaeus.

ZACCHAEUS DID WHAT HE HAD TO DO IN ORDER TO GET TO KNOW JESUS.
THE WHOLE STORY: LUKE 19:1-10

Go to page 1207 for the next Super Hero

³²Those who were sent ahead went and found the young donkey. It was there just as Jesus had told them. ³³They were untying the colt when its owners came. The owners asked them, "Why are you untying the colt?"

³⁴They replied, "The Lord needs it."

³⁵Then the disciples brought the colt to Jesus. They threw their coats on the young donkey and put Jesus on it. ³⁶As he went along, people spread their coats on the road.

³⁷Jesus came near the place where the road goes down the Mount of Olives. There the whole crowd of disciples began to praise God with joy. In loud voices they praised him for all the miracles they had seen. They shouted,

³⁸ "Blessed is the king who comes in the
        name of the Lord!"

(Psalm 118:26)

    "May there be peace and glory in the
        highest heaven!"

³⁹Some of the Pharisees in the crowd spoke to Jesus. "Teacher," they said, "tell your disciples to stop!"

⁴⁰"I tell you," he replied, "if they keep quiet, the stones will cry out."

⁴¹He approached Jerusalem. When he saw the city, he began to sob. ⁴²He said, "I wish you had known today what would bring you peace! But now it is hidden from your eyes.

⁴³"The days will come when your enemies will arrive. They will build a wall of dirt up against your city. They will surround you and close you in on every side. ⁴⁴You didn't recognize the time when God came to you. So your enemies will smash you to the ground. They will destroy you and all the people inside your walls. They will not leave one stone on top of another."

Jesus Clears Out the Temple

⁴⁵Then Jesus entered the temple area. He began chasing out those who were selling there. ⁴⁶He told them, "It is written that the Lord said, 'My house will be a house where people can pray.' *(Isaiah 56:7)* But you have made it a 'den for robbers.' " *(Jeremiah 7:11)*

⁴⁷Every day Jesus was teaching at the temple. But the chief priests and the teachers of the law were trying to kill him. So were the leaders among the people. ⁴⁸But they couldn't find any way to do it. All the people were paying close attention to his words.

The Authority of Jesus Is Questioned

20 One day Jesus was teaching the people in the temple courtyard. He was preaching the good news to them.

The chief priests and the teachers of the law came up to him. The elders came with them. ²"Tell us by what authority you are doing these things," they all said. "Who gave you this authority?"

³Jesus replied, "I will also ask you a question. Tell me, ⁴was John's baptism from heaven? Or did it come from men?"

⁵They talked to each other about it. They said, "If we say, 'From heaven,' he will ask, 'Why didn't you believe him?' ⁶But if we say, 'From men,' all the people will throw stones at us and kill us. They believe that John was a prophet."

⁷So they answered Jesus, "We don't know where John's baptism came from."

⁸Jesus said, "Then I won't tell you by what authority I am doing these things either."

The Story of the Renters

⁹Jesus went on to tell the people a story. "A man planted a vineyard," he said. "He rented it out to some farmers. Then he went away for a long time.

¹⁰"At harvest time he sent a servant to the renters. They were supposed to give him some of the fruit of the vineyard. But the renters beat the servant. Then they sent him away with nothing. ¹¹So the man sent another servant. They beat that one and treated him badly. They also sent him away with nothing. ¹²The man sent a third servant. The renters wounded him and threw him out.

¹³"Then the owner of the vineyard said, 'What should I do? I have a son, and I love him. I will send him. Maybe they will respect him.'

¹⁴"But when the renters saw the son, they talked the matter over. 'This is the one who will receive all the owner's property someday,' they said. 'Let's kill him. Then everything will be ours.' ¹⁵So they threw him out of the vineyard. And they killed him.

"What will the owner of the vineyard do to the renters? ¹⁶He will come and kill them. He will give the vineyard to others."

When the people heard this, they said, "We hope this never happens!"

¹⁷Jesus looked right at them and said, "Here is something I want you to explain the meaning of. It is written,

" 'The stone the builders didn't accept
has become the most important
stone of all.' *(Psalm 118:22)*

18Everyone who falls on that stone will be
broken to pieces. But the stone will crush
anyone it falls on."

19The teachers of the law and the chief
priests looked for a way to arrest Jesus at
once. They knew he had told that story
against them. But they were afraid of the
people.

Is It Right to Pay Taxes to Caesar?

20The religious leaders sent spies to
keep a close watch on Jesus. The spies pretended to be honest. They hoped they
could trap Jesus with something he would
say. Then they could hand him over to the
power and authority of the governor.
21So the spies questioned Jesus.
"Teacher," they said, "we know that you
speak and teach what is right. We know
you don't favor one person over another.
You teach the way of God truthfully. 22Is
it right for us to pay taxes to Caesar or
not?"

23Jesus saw they were trying to trick
him. So he said to them, 24"Show me a silver coin. Whose picture and words are
on it?"

25"Caesar's," they replied.

He said to them, "Then give to Caesar
what belongs to Caesar. And give to God
what belongs to God."

26They were not able to trap him with
what he had said there in front of all the
people. Amazed by his answer, they became silent.

Marriage When the Dead Rise

27The Sadducees do not believe that
people rise from the dead. Some of them
came to Jesus with a question. 28"Teacher," they said, "Moses wrote for us about a
man's brother who dies. Suppose the
brother leaves a wife but has no children.
Then the man must get married to the
widow. He must have children to carry on
his dead brother's name.

29"There were seven brothers. The first
one got married to a woman. He died
without leaving any children. 30The second one got married to her. 31And then
the third one got married to her. One after
another, the seven brothers got married
to her. They all died. None left any children. 32Finally, the woman died too.
33Now then, when the dead rise, whose
wife will she be? All seven brothers were
married to her."

34Jesus replied, "People in this world
get married. And their parents give them
to get married. 35But it will not be like that
when the dead rise. Those who are considered worthy to take part in what happens at that time won't get married. And
their parents won't give them to be married. 36They can't die anymore. They are
like the angels. They are God's children.
They will be given a new form of life when
the dead rise.

37"Remember the story of Moses and
the bush. Even Moses showed that the
dead rise. The Lord said to him, 'I am the
God of Abraham. I am the God of Isaac.
And I am the God of Jacob.' *(Exodus 3:6)*
38He is not the God of the dead. He is the
God of the living. In his eyes, everyone is
alive."

39Some of the teachers of the law
replied, "You have spoken well, teacher!"
40And no one dared to ask him any more
questions.

Whose Son Is the Christ?

41Jesus said to them, "Why do people
say that the Christ is the Son of David?
42David himself says in the Book of
Psalms,

" 'The Lord said to my Lord,
    "Sit at my right hand
43until I put your enemies
    under your control." ' *(Psalm 110:1)*

44David calls him 'Lord.' So how can he be
David's son?"

45All the people were listening. Jesus
said to his disciples, 46"Watch out for the
teachers of the law. They like to walk
around in long robes. They love to be
greeted in the market places. They love to
have the most important seats in the synagogues. They also love to have the places
of honor at dinners. 47They take over the
houses of widows. They say long prayers
to show off. God will punish those men
very much."

The Widow's Offering

21 As Jesus looked up, he saw rich
people putting their gifts into the
temple offering boxes. 2He also saw a poor
widow put in two very small copper coins.

3"What I'm about to tell you is true,"
Jesus said. "That poor widow has put in
more than all the others. 4All of those
other people gave a lot because they are
rich. But even though she is poor, she put
in everything. She had nothing left to
live on."

[Jesus said to his disciples,] "anyone who welcomes you welcomes me. And anyone who welcomes me welcomes the One who sent me." (Matthew 10:40)

GO TO PAGE 1107

MARTHA

Welcome others into your homes without complaining.
(1 Peter 4:9)

GO TO PAGE 1190

JESUS LOVES KIDS

*"Let the little children come to me. Don't keep them away.
God's kingdom belongs to people like them."*
(Mark 10:14)

GO TO PAGE 1153

WIDOW WITH TWO COINS

Jesus said, "That poor widow has put in more than all the others. All of those other people gave a lot because they are rich. But even though she is poor, she put in everything." (Luke 21:3–4)

GO TO PAGE 1207

WIDOW WITH TWO COINS

LUKE 21:3-4

"What I'm about to tell you is true," Jesus said. "That poor widow has put in more than all the others. All of those other people gave a lot because they are rich. But even though she is poor, she put in everything. She had nothing left to live on."

The old widow's clothes looked more like rags than clothing, bunching up on a back bent from years of hard work. She limped slowly from her house to the temple.

When she arrived at the temple, her knees creaked and clicked as she walked up the stairs, one difficult step at a time. She shuffled across the stone floor of the courtyard as she made her way toward the offering boxes.

The widow found her place at the end of a line of people waiting to give. She stood next to a tall man who was dressed in rich, colorful clothing. He held a large bag of coins in his hand. The widow opened her hand to look at the two small coins she held. Then she looked at the bag in the man's hand again. Her offering was so small, probably almost not worth giving.

The man in line next to the widow finally had his turn. He opened his bag of coins. With a flourish, he poured the money into the offering box. **HIS COINS BOUNCED AND CLANGED INTO THE METAL BOX.** He was happy to see that many people turned their heads and watched.

Now it was the widow's turn. She waited a while. She had no desire for others to see—or hear—her gift. Carefully and quietly she laid her two small coins in the offering box. She walked away with a contented smile on her face. She had no money left to live on. She had given it all away. But she trusted God to take care of her.

BE LIKE THE WIDOW

What do you have to give to God? You can have a little money or a lot. You can have many gifts or only a few. What matters to God is that you give it, trusting him to take care of you. Be like this widow! Give your gifts to God because you love him, not because others will be impressed with your gift.

SHE GAVE EVEN THE LITTLE SHE HAD TO GOD.
THE WHOLE STORY: LUKE 21:1-4

Go to page 1212 for the next Super Hero

gns of the End

5Some of Jesus' disciples were talking bout the temple. They spoke about how .t was decorated with beautiful stones and with gifts that honored God. But Jesus asked, 6"Do you see all this? The time will come when not one stone will be left on top of another. Every stone will be thrown down."

7"Teacher," they asked, "when will these things happen? And what will be the sign that they are about to take place?"

8Jesus replied, "Keep watch! Be careful that you are not fooled. Many will come in my name. They will claim, 'I am he!' And they will say, 'The time is near!' Do not follow them. 9Do not be afraid when you hear about wars and about fighting against rulers. Those things must happen first. But the end will not come right away."

10Then Jesus said to them, "Nation will fight against nation. Kingdom will fight against kingdom. 11In many places there will be powerful earthquakes. People will go hungry. There will be terrible sicknesses. Things will happen that will make people afraid. There will be great and miraculous signs from heaven.

12"But before all this, people will arrest you and treat you badly. They will hand you over to synagogues and prisons. You will be brought to kings and governors. All this will happen to you because of my name. 13In that way you will be witnesses to them. 14But make up your mind not to worry ahead of time about how to stand up for yourselves. 15I will give you words of wisdom. None of your enemies will be able to withstand them or oppose them.

16"Even your parents, brothers, sisters, relatives and friends will hand you over to the authorities. They will put some of you to death. 17Everyone will hate you because of me. 18But not a hair on your head will be harmed. 19If you stand firm, you will gain life.

20"A time is coming when you will see armies surround Jerusalem. Then you will know that it will soon be destroyed. 21Those who are in Judea should then escape to the mountains. Those in the city should get out. Those in the country should not enter the city. 22This is the time when God will punish Jerusalem. Everything will come true, just as it has been written.

23"How awful it will be in those days for pregnant women! How awful for nursing mothers! There will be terrible suffering in the land. There will be great anger against those people. 24Some will be killed by the sword. Others will be taken as prisoners to all the nations. Jerusalem will be overrun by those who aren't Jews until the times of the non-Jews come to an end.

25"There will be miraculous signs in the sun, moon and stars. The nations of the earth will be in terrible pain. They will be puzzled by the roaring and tossing of the sea. 26Terror will make people faint. They will be worried about what is happening in the world. The sun, moon and stars will be shaken from their places.

27"At that time people will see the Son of Man coming in a cloud. He will come with power and great glory. 28When these things begin to take place, stand up. Hold your head up with joy and hope. The time when you will be set free will be very close."

29Jesus told them a story. "Look at the fig tree and all the trees," he said. 30"When you see leaves appear on the branches, you know that summer is near. 31In the same way, when you see these things happening, you will know that God's kingdom is near.

32"What I'm about to tell you is true. The people living at that time will certainly not pass away until all these things have happened. 33Heaven and earth will pass away. But my words will never pass away.

34"Be careful. If you aren't, your hearts will be loaded down with wasteful living, drunkenness and the worries of life. Then the day the Son of Man returns will close on you like a trap. You will not be expecting it. 35That day will come upon every person who lives on the whole earth. 36"Always keep watching. Pray that you will be able to escape all that is about to happen. Also, pray that you will not be judged guilty when the Son of Man comes."

37Each day Jesus taught at the temple. And each evening he went to spend the night on the hill called the Mount of Olives. 38All the people came to the temple early in the morning. They wanted to hear Jesus speak.

Judas Agrees to Hand Jesus Over

22 The Feast of Unleavened Bread, called the Passover, was near. 2The chief priests and the teachers of the law were looking for a way to get rid of Jesus. They were afraid of the people.

3Then Satan entered Judas, who was

called Iscariot. Judas was one of the Twelve. ⁴He went to the chief priests and the officers of the temple guard. He talked with them about how he could hand Jesus over to them. ⁵They were delighted and agreed to give him money

⁶Judas accepted their offer. He watched for the right time to hand Jesus over to them. He wanted to do it when no crowd was around.

The Last Supper

⁷Then the day of Unleavened Bread came. That was the time the Passover lamb had to be sacrificed. ⁸Jesus sent Peter and John on ahead. "Go," he told them. "Prepare for us to eat the Passover meal."

⁹"Where do you want us to prepare for it?" they asked.

¹⁰Jesus replied, "When you enter the city, a man carrying a jar of water will meet you. Follow him to the house he enters. ¹¹Then say to the owner of the house, 'The Teacher asks, "Where is the guest room? Where can I eat the Passover meal with my disciples?" ' ¹²He will show you a large upstairs room with furniture in it. Prepare for us to eat there."

¹³Peter and John left. They found things just as Jesus had told them. So they prepared the Passover meal.

¹⁴When the hour came, Jesus and his apostles took their places at the table. ¹⁵He said to them, "I have really looked forward to eating this Passover meal with you. I wanted to do this before I suffer. ¹⁶I tell you, I will not eat the Passover meal again until it is celebrated in God's kingdom."

¹⁷After Jesus took the cup, he gave thanks. He said, "Take this cup and share it among yourselves. ¹⁸I tell you, I will not drink wine with you again until God's kingdom comes."

¹⁹Then Jesus took bread. He gave thanks and broke it. He handed it to them and said, "This is my body. It is given for you. Every time you eat it, do it in memory of me."

²⁰In the same way, after the supper he took the cup. He said, "This cup is the new covenant in my blood. It is poured out for you. ²¹But someone here is going to hand me over to my enemies. His hand is with mine on the table. ²²The Son of Man will go to his death, just as God has already decided. But how terrible it will be for the one who hands him over!"

²³The apostles began to ask each other about this. They wondered which one of them would do it.

²⁴They also started to argue. They disagreed about which of them was thought to be the most important person.

²⁵Jesus said to them, "The kings of the nations hold power over their people. And those who order them around call themselves Protectors. ²⁶But you must not be like that. Instead, the most important among you should be like the youngest. The one who rules should be like the one who serves.

²⁷"Who is more important? Is it the one at the table, or the one who serves? Isn't it the one who is at the table? But I am among you as one who serves. ²⁸You have stood by me during my troubles. ²⁹And I give you a kingdom, just as my Father gave me a kingdom. ³⁰Then you will eat and drink at my table in my kingdom. And you will sit on thrones, judging the 12 tribes of Israel.

³¹"Simon, Simon! Satan has asked to sift you disciples like wheat. ³²But I have prayed for you, Simon. I have prayed that your faith will not fail. When you have turned back, help your brothers to be strong."

³³But Simon replied, "Lord, I am ready to go with you to prison and to death."

³⁴Jesus answered, "I tell you, Peter, you will say three times that you don't know me. And you will do it before the rooster crows today."

³⁵Then Jesus asked the disciples, "Did you need anything when I sent you without a purse, bag or sandals?"

"Nothing," they answered.

³⁶He said to them, "But now if you have a purse, take it. And also take a bag. If you don't have a sword, sell your coat and buy one. ³⁷It is written, 'He was counted among those who had committed crimes.' (Isaiah 53:12) I tell you that what is written about me must come true. Yes, it is already coming true."

³⁸The disciples said, "See, Lord, here are two swords."

"That is enough," he replied.

Jesus Prays on the Mount of Olives

³⁹Jesus went out as usual to the Mount of Olives. His disciples followed him. ⁴⁰When they reached the place, Jesus spoke. "Pray that you won't fall into sin when you are tempted," he said to them. ⁴¹Then he went a short distance away from them. There he got down on his knees and prayed. ⁴²He said, "Father, if you are willing, take this cup of suffering away from me. But do what you want, not what I want."

43An angel from heaven appeared to Jesus and gave him strength. 44Because he was very sad and troubled, he prayed even harder. His sweat was like drops of blood falling to the ground.

45After that, he got up from prayer and went back to the disciples. He found them sleeping. They were worn out because they were very sad.

46"Why are you sleeping?" he asked them. "Get up! Pray that you won't fall into sin when you are tempted."

Jesus Is Arrested

47While Jesus was still speaking, a crowd came up. The man named Judas was leading them. He was one of the Twelve. Judas approached Jesus to kiss him.

48But Jesus asked him, "Judas, are you handing over the Son of Man with a kiss?"

49Jesus' followers saw what was going to happen. So they said, "Lord, should we use our swords against them?" 50One of them struck the servant of the high priest and cut off his right ear.

51But Jesus answered, "Stop this!" And he touched the man's ear and healed him.

52Then Jesus spoke to the chief priests, the officers of the temple guard, and the elders. They had all come for him. "Am I leading a band of armed men against you?" he asked. "Do you have to come with swords and clubs? 53Every day I was with you in the temple courtyard. And you didn't lay a hand on me. But this is your hour. This is when darkness rules."

Peter Says He Does Not Know Jesus

54Then the men arrested Jesus and led him away. They took him into the high priest's house. Peter followed from far away. 55They started a fire in the middle of the courtyard. Then they sat down together. Peter sat down with them.

56A female servant saw him sitting there in the firelight. She looked closely at him. Then she said, "This man was with Jesus."

57But Peter said he had not been with him. "Woman, I don't know him," he said.

58A little later someone else saw Peter. "You also are one of them," he said.

"No," Peter replied. "I'm not!"

59About an hour later, another person spoke up. "This fellow must have been with Jesus," he said. "He is from Galilee."

60Peter replied, "Man, I don't know what you're talking about!"

Just as he was speaking, the rooster

crowed. 61The Lord turned and looked right at Peter. Then Peter remembered what the Lord had spoken to him. "The rooster will crow today," Jesus had said. "Before it does, you will say three times that you don't know me." 62Peter went outside. He broke down and sobbed.

The Guards Make Fun of Jesus

63There were men guarding Jesus. They began laughing at him and beating him. 64They blindfolded him. They said, "Prophesy! Who hit you?" 65They also said many other things to make fun of him.

Jesus Is Brought to Pilate and Herod

66At dawn the elders of the people met together. These included the chief priests and the teachers of the law. Jesus was led to them. 67"If you are the Christ," they said, "tell us."

Jesus answered, "If I tell you, you will not believe me. 68And if I asked you, you would not answer. 69But from now on, the Son of Man will be seated at the right hand of the mighty God."

70They all asked, "Are you the Son of God then?"

He replied, "You are right in saying that I am."

71Then they said, "Why do we need any more witnesses? We have heard it from his own lips."

23 Then the whole group got up and led Jesus off to Pilate. 2They began to bring charges against Jesus. They said, "We have found this man misleading our people. He is against paying taxes to Caesar. And he claims to be Christ, a king."

3So Pilate asked Jesus, "Are you the king of the Jews?"

"Yes. It is just as you say," Jesus replied.

4Then Pilate spoke to the chief priests and the crowd. He announced, "I find no basis for a charge against this man."

5But they kept it up. They said, "His teaching stirs up the people all over Judea. He started in Galilee and has come all the way here."

6When Pilate heard this, he asked if the man was from Galilee. 7He learned that Jesus was from Herod's area of authority. So Pilate sent Jesus to Herod. At that time Herod was also in Jerusalem.

8When Herod saw Jesus, he was very pleased. He had been wanting to see Jesus for a long time. He had heard much about him. He hoped to see Jesus do a miracle.

9Herod asked him many questions, but

Jesus gave him no answer. **10**The chief priests and the teachers of the law were standing there. With loud shouts they brought charges against him.

11Herod and his soldiers laughed at him and made fun of him. They dressed him in a beautiful robe. Then they sent him back to Pilate. **12**That day Herod and Pilate became friends. Before this time they had been enemies.

13Pilate called together the chief priests, the rulers and the people. **14**He said to them, "You brought me this man. You said he was turning the people against the authorities. I have questioned him in front of you. I have found no basis for your charges against him. **15**Herod hasn't either. So he sent Jesus back to us. As you can see, Jesus has done nothing that is worthy of death. **16/17**So I will just have him whipped and let him go."

18With one voice the crowd cried out, "Kill this man! Give Barabbas to us!" **19**Barabbas had been thrown into prison. He had taken part in a struggle in the city against the authorities. He had also committed murder.

20Pilate wanted to let Jesus go. So he made an appeal to the crowd again. **21**But they kept shouting, "Crucify him! Crucify him!"

22Pilate spoke to them for the third time. "Why?" he asked. "What wrong has this man done? I have found no reason to have him put to death. So I will just have him whipped and let him go."

23But with loud shouts they kept calling for Jesus to be crucified. The people's shouts won out.

24So Pilate decided to give them what they wanted. **25**He set free the man they asked for. The man had been thrown in prison for murder and for fighting against the authorities. Pilate gave Jesus over to them so they could carry out their plans.

Jesus Is Nailed to a Cross

26As they led Jesus away, they took hold of Simon. Simon was from Cyrene. He was on his way in from the country. They put a wooden cross on his shoulders. Then they made him carry it behind Jesus.

27A large number of people followed Jesus. Some were women whose hearts were filled with sorrow. They cried loudly because of him.

28Jesus turned and said to them, "Daughters of Jerusalem, do not cry for me. Cry for yourselves and for your children. **29**The time will come when you will say, 'Blessed are the women who can't have children! Blessed are those who never gave birth or nursed babies!' **30**It is written,

" 'The people will say to the
    mountains, "Fall on us!"
They'll say to the hills, "Cover us!" '
(Hosea 10:8)

31People do these things when trees are green. So what will happen when trees are dry?"

32Two other men were also led out with Jesus to be killed. Both of them had broken the law. **33**The soldiers brought them to the place called The Skull. There they nailed Jesus to the cross. He hung between the two criminals. One was on his right and one was on his left.

34Jesus said, "Father, forgive them. They don't know what they are doing." The soldiers divided up his clothes by casting lots.

35The people stood there watching. The rulers even made fun of Jesus. They said, "He saved others. Let him save himself if he is the Christ of God, the Chosen One."

36The soldiers also came up and poked fun at him. They offered him wine vinegar. **37**They said, "If you are the king of the Jews, save yourself."

38A written sign had been placed above him. It read, THIS IS THE KING OF THE JEWS.

39One of the criminals hanging there made fun of Jesus. He said, "Aren't you the Christ? Save yourself! Save us!"

40But the other criminal scolded him. "Don't you have any respect for God?" he said. "Remember, you are under the same sentence of death. **41**We are being punished fairly. We are getting just what our actions call for. But this man hasn't done anything wrong."

42Then he said, "Jesus, remember me when you come into your kingdom."

43Jesus answered him, "What I'm about to tell you is true. Today you will be with me in paradise."

Jesus Dies

44It was now about noon. The whole land was covered with darkness until three o'clock. **45**The sun had stopped shining. The temple curtain was torn in two. **46**Jesus called out in a loud voice, "Father, into your hands I commit my very life." After he said this, he took his last breath.

47The Roman commander saw what had happened. He praised God and said,

THE ROBBER

LUKE 23:42-43

"Jesus, remember me when you come into your kingdom." Jesus answered him, "What I'm about to tell you is true. Today you will be with me in paradise."

Tears ran from the robber's eyes into his hair and ears as he lay on top of the wooden cross. Soldiers were pounding nails into his hands. The sound of the hammer was almost as painful as the agony of the nails going through his flesh. A cry rose from deep in his lungs and echoed through the hills around him as the soldiers stood the cross up and pounded it into the ground.

The robber knew the other criminal who was being crucified. But the one in the middle . . . His name was Jesus. And he was no criminal. That was certain. He had heard about this Jesus—how he healed the sick and taught the people and even raised some from the dead.

WHAT WAS THAT HE SAID? The robber was certain he had just heard Jesus forgive those who were killing him. This man was truly amazing.

The robber looked at those who stood around the three crosses. The soldiers acted as if this were a party, laughing and gambling over the belongings of those being crucified. They mocked Jesus. "If you're really the Christ, save yourself," they jeered.

The criminal on the other side of Jesus spoke up, joining in the insults. "Yeah, Jesus, save yourself. And me, too!"

"What?!" the robber couldn't believe this. "We deserved to be punished," he yelled to the other criminal. "But this Jesus has done nothing wrong." Gritting his teeth with the pain, the robber asked, "Jesus, will you remember me when you come into your kingdom? Please?"

"Today," Jesus assured him, "you will be with me in heaven." The robber died a horrible death, but he was at peace because of what Jesus said to him.

THE ROBBER

You don't want to be a robber, of course. But you can learn something from him. He trusted Jesus as soon as he realized who he was. You know Jesus loves you and will forgive you for the things you do wrong. So be like the robber. Don't wait! Trust him today.

THE ROBBER TRUSTED JESUS.
THE WHOLE STORY: LUKE 23:32-43

Go to page 1214 for the next Super Hero

"Jesus was surely a man who did what was right."

48The people had gathered to watch that sight. When they saw what happened, they beat their chests and went away. **49**But all those who knew Jesus stood not very far away, watching those things. They included the women who had followed him from Galilee.

Jesus Is Buried

50A man named Joseph was a member of the Jewish Council. He was a good and honest man. **51**He had not agreed with what the leaders had decided and done. He was from Arimathea, a town in Judea. He was waiting for God's kingdom.

52Joseph went to Pilate and asked for Jesus' body. **53**He took it down and wrapped it in linen cloth. Then he put it in a tomb cut in the rock. No one had ever been buried there. **54**It was Preparation Day. The Sabbath was about to begin.

55The women who had come with Jesus from Galilee followed Joseph. They saw the tomb and how Jesus' body was placed in it. **56**Then they went home. There they prepared spices and perfumes. But they rested on the Sabbath day in order to obey the Law.

Jesus Rises From the Dead

24 It was very early in the morning on the first day of the week. The women took the spices they had prepared. Then they went to the tomb. **2**They found the stone rolled away from it. **3**When they entered the tomb, they did not find the body of the Lord Jesus. **4**They were wondering about this.

Suddenly two men in clothes as bright as lightning stood beside them. **5**The women were terrified. They bowed down with their faces to the ground.

Then the men said to them, "Why do you look for the living among the dead? **6**Jesus is not here! He has risen! Remember how he told you he would rise. It was while he was still with you in Galilee. **7**He said, 'The Son of Man must be handed over to sinful people. He must be nailed to a cross. On the third day he will rise from the dead.'"

8Then the women remembered Jesus' words.

9They came back from the tomb. They told all these things to the Eleven and to all the others. **10**Mary Magdalene, Joanna, Mary the mother of James, and the others with them were the ones who told the apostles. **11**But the apostles did not believe

the women. Their words didn't make any sense to them.

12But Peter got up and ran to the tomb. He bent over and saw the strips of linen lying by themselves. Then he went away, wondering what had happened.

On the Road to Emmaus

13That same day two of Jesus' followers were going to a village called Emmaus. It was about seven miles from Jerusalem. **14**They were talking with each other about everything that had happened.

15As they talked about those things, Jesus himself came up and walked along with them. **16**But God kept them from recognizing him.

17Jesus asked them, "What are you talking about as you walk along?"

They stood still, and their faces were sad. **18**One of them was named Cleopas. He said to Jesus, "You must be a visitor to Jerusalem. If you lived there, you would know the things that have happened there in the last few days."

19"What things?" Jesus asked.

"About Jesus of Nazareth," they replied. "He was a prophet. He was powerful in what he said and did in the eyes of God and all of the people. **20**The chief priests and our rulers handed Jesus over to be sentenced to death. They nailed him to a cross. **21**But we had hoped that he was the one who was going to set Israel free. Also, it is the third day since all this happened.

22"Some of our women amazed us too. Early this morning they went to the tomb. **23**But they didn't find his body. So they came and told us what they had seen. They saw angels, who said Jesus was alive. **24**Then some of our friends went to the tomb. They saw it was empty, just as the women had said. They didn't see Jesus' body there."

25Jesus said to them, "How foolish you are! How long it takes you to believe all that the prophets said! **26**Didn't the Christ have to suffer these things and then receive his glory?"

27Jesus explained to them what was said about himself in all the Scriptures. He began with Moses and all the Prophets.

28The two men approached the village where they were going. Jesus acted as if he were going farther. **29**But they tried hard to keep him from leaving. They said, "Stay with us. It is nearly evening. The day is almost over." So he went in to stay with them.

30He joined them at the table. Then he

took bread and gave thanks. He broke it and began to give it to them. **31**Their eyes were opened, and they recognized him. But then he disappeared from their sight.

32They said to each other, "He talked with us on the road. He opened the Scriptures to us. Weren't our hearts burning inside us during that time?"

33They got up and returned at once to Jerusalem. There they found the Eleven and those with them. They were all gathered together. **34**They were saying, "It's true! The Lord has risen! He has appeared to Simon!"

35Then the two of them told what had happened to them on the way. They told how they had recognized Jesus when he broke the bread.

Jesus Appears to the Disciples

36The disciples were still talking about this when Jesus himself suddenly stood among them. He said, "May peace be with you!"

JOSEPH OF ARIMATHEA

LUKE 23:52-53

★

K

T

Joseph went to Pilate and asked for Jesus' body. He took it down and wrapped it in linen cloth. Then he put it in a tomb cut in the rock. No one had ever been buried there.

Joseph of Arimathea (air-ih-muh-THEE-uh) walked quickly down the street in Jerusalem. Pilate had just given him permission to take Jesus' body and bury it. Joseph's mind worked as fast as his feet. How could this have happened? Jesus was dead! This Jesus was supposed to save them, not die himself.

Some friends helped Joseph take Jesus' body down from the cross. Joseph wrapped Jesus' body with fine, soft cloth, putting spices inside the wrappings. Then he tenderly put Jesus' body in a brand new tomb.

Using all of his strength, Joseph rolled a huge rock in front of the tomb. He stood looking at the tomb, **HIS SHOULDERS SLUMPED WITH GRIEF.** He just didn't understand. But he also didn't know how quickly his sadness would turn to amazement and then joy.

BE A JOSEPH OF ARIMATHEA

Joseph was a follower, a believer, in Jesus. He was very sad, but he was also a kind man. He carefully and tenderly prepared Jesus' body to be buried. Then he buried Jesus in his own tomb. His kindness is a good example. Even when you're sad or upset or angry, remember Joseph and remember to be kind.

JOSEPH KINDLY TOOK CARE OF JESUS' BODY AFTER HE DIED.

Go to page 1219 for the next Super Hero

37They were surprised and terrified. They thought they were seeing a ghost. **38**Jesus said to them, "Why are you troubled? Why do you have doubts in your minds? **39**Look at my hands and my feet. It is really I! Touch me and see. A ghost does not have a body or bones. But you can see that I do."

40After he said that, he showed them his hands and feet. **41**But they still did not believe it. They were amazed and filled with joy.

So Jesus asked them, "Do you have anything here to eat?"

42They gave him a piece of cooked fish. **43**He took it and ate it in front of them.

44Jesus said to them, "This is what I told you while I was still with you. Everything written about me must happen. Everything written about me in the Law of Moses, the Prophets and the Psalms must come true."

45Then he opened their minds so they could understand the Scriptures. **46**He told them, "This is what is written. The Christ will suffer. He will rise from the dead on the third day. **47**His followers will preach in his name. They will tell others to turn away from their sins and be forgiven. People from every nation will hear it, beginning at Jerusalem. **48**You have seen these things with your own eyes.

49"I am going to send you what my Father has promised. But for now, stay in the city. Stay there until you have received power from heaven."

Jesus Is Taken Up Into Heaven

50Jesus led his disciples out to the area near Bethany. Then he lifted up his hands and blessed them. **51**While he was blessing them, he left them. He was taken up into heaven.

52Then they worshiped him. With great joy, they returned to Jerusalem. **53**Every day they went to the temple, praising God.

JOHN

The book of John tells again many of the stories and teachings of Jesus. John, one of Jesus' disciples, writes this book to tell people about the amazing love Jesus has for them. John's purpose in writing is not just to let people know about Jesus, but to help them believe in him. As you read this book, remember why John wrote it and let it help you believe in Jesus—that he really lived and died so that you could live forever.

HEROES IN THIS BOOK . . .

ANDREW
PAGE 1219

NICODEMUS
(Sort of)
PAGE 1222

WOMAN FROM SAMARIA
PAGE 1224

BOY WITH LUNCH
PAGE 1227

The Word Became Human

1 In the beginning, the Word was already there. The Word was with God, and the Word was God. **2**He was with God in the beginning.

3All things were made through him. Nothing that has been made was made without him. **4**Life was in him, and that life was the light for all people. **5**The light shines in the darkness. But the darkness has not understood it.

6A man came who was sent from God. His name was John. **7**He came to give witness about that light. He gave witness so that all people could believe.

8John himself was not the light. He came only as a witness to the light. **9**The true light that gives light to every man was coming into the world.

10The Word was in the world that was made through him. But the world did not recognize him. **11**He came to what was his own. But his own people did not accept him.

12Some people did accept him. They believed in his name. He gave them the right to become children of God. **13**To be a child of God has nothing to do with human parents. Children of God are not born because of human choice or because a husband wants them to be born. They are born because of what God does.

14The Word became a human being. He made his home with us. We have seen his glory. It is the glory of the one and only Son.

He came from the Father. And he was full of grace and truth.

15John gives witness about him. He cries out and says, "This was the one I was talking about. I said, 'He who comes after me is more important than I am. He is more important because he existed before I was born.' "

16We have all received one blessing after another. God's grace is not limited. **17**Moses gave us the law. Jesus Christ has given us grace and truth.

18No one has ever seen God. But God, the one and only Son, is at the Father's side. He has shown us what God is like.

John the Baptist Is Not the Christ

19The Jews of Jerusalem sent priests and Levites to ask John who he was. John gave witness to them. **20**He did not try to hide the truth. He spoke to them openly. He said, "I am not the Christ."

21They asked him, "Then who are you? Are you Elijah?"

He said, "I am not."

"Are you the Prophet we've been expecting?" they asked.

"No," he answered.

22They asked one last time, "Who are you? Give us an answer to take back to those who sent us. What do you say about yourself?"

23John replied, using the words of Isaiah the prophet. John said, "I'm the messenger who is calling out in the desert, 'Make the way for the Lord straight.' " *(Isaiah 40:3)*

24Some Pharisees who had been sent **25**asked him, "If you are not the Christ, why are you baptizing people? Why are you doing that if you aren't Elijah or the Prophet we've been expecting?"

26"I baptize people with water," John replied. "But One is standing among you whom you do not know. **27**He is the One who comes after me. I am not good enough to untie his sandals."

28This all happened at Bethany on the other side of the Jordan River. That was where John was baptizing.

Jesus Is the Lamb of God

29The next day John saw Jesus coming toward him. John said, "Look! The Lamb of God! He takes away the sin of the world! **30**This is the One I was talking about. I said, 'A man who comes after me is more important than I am. That's because he existed before I was born.' **31**I did not know him. But God wants to make it clear to Israel who this person is. That's the reason I came baptizing with water."

32Then John told them, "I saw the Holy Spirit come down from heaven like a dove. The Spirit remained on Jesus. **33**I would not have known him. But the One who sent me to baptize with water told me, 'You will see the Spirit come down and remain on someone. He is the One who will baptize with the Holy Spirit.' **34**I have seen it happen. I give witness that this is the Son of God."

Jesus Chooses the First Disciples

³⁵The next day John was again with two of his disciples. ³⁶He saw Jesus walking by. John said, "Look! The Lamb of God!"

³⁷The two disciples heard him say this. So they followed Jesus.

³⁸Then Jesus turned around and saw them following. He asked, "What do you want?"

They said, "Rabbi, where are you staying?" *Rabbi* means Teacher.

³⁹"Come," he replied. "You will see."

So they went and saw where he was staying. They spent the rest of the day with him. It was about four o'clock in the afternoon.

⁴⁰Andrew was Simon Peter's brother. Andrew was one of the two disciples who heard what John had said. He had also followed Jesus. ⁴¹The first thing Andrew did was to find his brother Simon. He told

ANDREW

JOHN 1:41

The first thing Andrew did was to find his brother Simon. He told him, "We have found the Messiah."

Andrew kicked a stone along the road as he listened to John the Baptist teach. Then John stopped and pointed to a man who was walking by.

"Look!" John said. "The Lamb of God!"

Andrew turned and saw Jesus. Without looking back, Andrew left John and followed Jesus.

Andrew spent the whole day with Jesus, talking with him and listening to his teachings. Before the day was over, he knew that Jesus was the Messiah.

Late in the day, Andrew left Jesus. He didn't go home though. He went to find his brother Simon. Coming to Simon's house, Andrew couldn't contain his excitement for one more minute. "Simon!" he shouted. **"HURRY! COME WITH ME!** I've found the Messiah!"

Andrew grabbed Simon's arm and pulled him along. They went to where Jesus was staying, and Andrew introduced Simon to Jesus.

BE AN ANDREW

As soon as Andrew realized Jesus was the Messiah, he went to find his brother Simon. He needed to tell his brother the exciting news. You, too, have exciting news to share. Jesus is the Savior. Tell all your friends!

ANDREW TOLD HIS BROTHER SIMON ABOUT JESUS.

Go to page 1222 for the next person

him, "We have found the Messiah." Messiah means Christ. 42And he brought Simon to Jesus.

Jesus looked at him and said, "You are Simon, son of John. You will be called Cephas." Cephas means Peter (or rock).

Jesus Chooses Philip and Nathanael

43The next day Jesus decided to leave for Galilee. He found Philip and said to him, "Follow me."

44Philip was from the town of Bethsaida. So were Andrew and Peter. 45Philip found Nathanael and told him, "We have found the One that Moses wrote about in the Law. The prophets also wrote about him. He is Jesus of Nazareth, the son of Joseph."

46"Nazareth! Can anything good come from there?" Nathanael asked.

"Come and see," said Philip.

47Jesus saw Nathanael approaching. Here is what Jesus said about him. "He is a true Israelite. There is nothing false in him."

48"How do you know me?" Nathanael asked.

Jesus answered, "I saw you while you were still under the fig tree. I saw you there before Philip called you."

49Nathanael replied, "Rabbi, you are the Son of God. You are the King of Israel."

50Jesus said, "You believe because I told you I saw you under the fig tree. You will see greater things than that."

51Then he said to the disciples, "What I'm about to tell you is true. You will see heaven open. You will see the angels of God going up and coming down on the Son of Man."

Jesus Changes Water Into Wine

2 On the third day there was a wedding. It took place at Cana in Galilee. Jesus' mother was there. 2Jesus and his disciples had also been invited to the wedding. 3When the wine was gone, Jesus' mother said to him, "They have no more wine."

4"Dear woman, why do you bring me into this?" Jesus replied. "My time has not yet come."

5His mother said to the servants, "Do what he tells you."

6Six stone water jars stood nearby. The Jews used water from that kind of jar for special washings to make themselves pure. Each jar could hold 20 to 30 gallons.

7Jesus said to the servants, "Fill the jars with water." So they filled them to the top.

8Then he told them, "Now dip some out. Take it to the person in charge of the dinner."

They did what he said. 9The person in charge tasted the water that had been turned into wine. He didn't realize where it had come from. But the servants who had brought the water knew.

Then the person in charge called the groom to one side. 10He said to him, "Everyone brings out the best wine first. They bring out the cheaper wine after the guests have had too much to drink. But you have saved the best until now."

11That was the first of Jesus' miraculous signs. He did it at Cana in Galilee. Jesus showed his glory by doing it. And his disciples put their faith in him.

Jesus Clears Out the Temple

12After this, Jesus went down to Capernaum. His mother and brothers and disciples went with him. They all stayed there for a few days.

13It was almost time for the Jewish Passover Feast. So Jesus went up to Jerusalem. 14In the temple courtyard he found people who were selling cattle, sheep and doves. Others were sitting at tables exchanging money.

15So Jesus made a whip out of ropes. He chased all the sheep and cattle from the temple area. He scattered the coins of the people exchanging money. And he turned over their tables. 16He told those who were selling doves, "Get these out of here! How dare you turn my Father's house into a market!"

17His disciples remembered what had been written. It says, "My great love for your house will destroy me." *(Psalm 69:9)*

18Then the Jews asked him, "What miraculous sign can you show us? Can you prove your authority to do all of this?"

19Jesus answered them, "Destroy this temple. I will raise it up again in three days."

20The Jews replied, "It has taken 46 years to build this temple. Are you going to raise it up in three days?"

21But the temple Jesus had spoken about was his body.

22His disciples later remembered what he had said. That was after he had been raised from the dead. Then they believed the Scriptures. They also believed the words that Jesus had spoken.

23Meanwhile, he was in Jerusalem at the Passover Feast. Many people saw the miraculous signs he was doing. And they believed in his name. 24But Jesus did not fully trust them. He knew what people are like. 25He didn't need others to tell him what people are like. He already knew what was in the human heart.

Jesus Teaches Nicodemus

3 There was a Pharisee named Nicodemus. He was one of the Jewish rulers. 2He came to Jesus at night and said, "Rabbi, we know you are a teacher who has come from God. We know that God is with you. If he weren't, you couldn't do the miraculous signs you are doing."

3Jesus replied, "What I'm about to tell you is true. No one can see God's kingdom without being born again."

4"How can I be born when I am old?" Nicodemus asked. "I can't go back inside my mother! I can't be born a second time!"

5Jesus answered, "What I'm about to tell you is true. No one can enter God's kingdom without being born through water and the Holy Spirit. 6People give birth to people. But the Spirit gives birth to spirit. 7You should not be surprised when I say, 'You must all be born again.'

8"The wind blows where it wants to. You hear the sound it makes. But you can't tell where it comes from or where it is going. It is the same with everyone who is born through the Spirit."

9"How can this be?" Nicodemus asked.

10"You are Israel's teacher," said Jesus. "Don't you understand these things? 11"What I'm about to tell you is true. We speak about what we know. We give witness to what we have seen. But still you people do not accept our witness. 12I have spoken to you about earthly things, and you do not believe. So how will you believe if I speak about heavenly things?

13"No one has ever gone into heaven except the One who came from heaven. He is the Son of Man. 14Moses lifted up the snake in the desert. The Son of Man

POWER-SURGE

BELIEVES ✝

THEY BELIEVED THE SCRIPTURES. THEY ALSO BELIEVED THE WORDS THAT JESUS HAD SPOKEN.
— JOHN 2:22 —

POWER-SURGE

BELIEVES ✝

THEN EVERYONE WHO BELIEVES IN [JESUS] CAN LIVE WITH GOD FOREVER. GOD LOVED THE WORLD SO MUCH THAT HE GAVE HIS ONE AND ONLY SON. ANYONE WHO BELIEVES IN HIM WILL NOT DIE BUT WILL HAVE ETERNAL LIFE.
— JOHN 3:15-16 —

must be lifted up also. 15Then everyone who believes in him can live with God forever.

16"God loved the world so much that he gave his one and only Son. Anyone who believes in him will not die but will have eternal life.

17"God did not send his Son into the world to judge the world. He sent his Son to save the world through him. 18Anyone who believes in him is not judged. But anyone who does not believe is judged already. He has not believed in the name of God's one and only Son.

19"Here is the judgment. Light has come into the world, but people loved darkness instead of light. They loved darkness because what they did was evil. 20"Everyone who does evil things hates the light. They will not come into the light. They are afraid that what they do will be seen. 21But anyone who lives by the truth comes into the light. He does this so that it will be easy to see that what he has done is with God's help."

John the Baptist Gives Witness About Jesus

22After this, Jesus and his disciples went out into the countryside of Judea. There he spent some time with them. And he baptized people there.

23John was also baptizing. He was at Aenon near Salim, where there was plenty of water. People were coming all the time to be baptized. 24That was before John was put in prison.

25Some of John's disciples and a certain

Jew began to argue. They argued about special washings to make people "clean." **26**They came to John and said to him, "Rabbi, that man who was with you on the other side of the Jordan River is baptizing people. He is the one you gave witness about. Everyone is going to him."

27John replied, "A person can receive only what God gives him from heaven. **28**You yourselves are witnesses that I said, 'I am not the Christ. I was sent ahead of him.' **29**The bride belongs to the groom. The friend who helps the groom waits and listens for him. He is full of joy when he hears the groom's voice. That joy is mine, and it is now complete. **30**He must become more important. I must become less important.

31"The One who comes from above is above everything. The one who is from the earth belongs to the earth and speaks like someone from the earth. The One who comes from heaven is above everything. **32**He gives witness to what he has

NICODEMUS (Sort of)

JOHN 3:1-2

✝

There was a Pharisee named Nicodemus. He was one of the Jewish rulers. He came to Jesus at night.

The Jewish ruler peered around the corner of the building, trying to see Jesus in the darkness. He wanted to talk to Jesus, but he didn't want anyone to see. So he came at night, when the crowds around Jesus had gone home.

When Nicodemus (nick-oh-DEE-muss) finally got Jesus alone, Jesus said something amazing to him. "You must be born again," Jesus said to him.

"WHAT SORT OF CRAZINESS IS THIS?" Nicodemus asked. "Can a person go back into his mother's belly and be born all over again?

But Jesus meant another kind of being born. He meant a person had to be born first of a mother then of God. Only those born of God go to heaven.

Nicodemus had a hard time understanding Jesus. And because he was a Jewish ruler, he didn't tell anyone that he now believed in Jesus. Nicodemus had been born of his mother, then of God.

BE A NICODEMUS

Be a Nicodemus! And don't be a Nicodemus! Sounds silly, doesn't it? Try to be like Nicodemus and believe in Jesus. Be born of your mother, then born of God. But don't be like him and keep it to yourself. Let everyone know you're a Jesus follower!

NICODEMUS BELIEVED IN JESUS BUT KEPT IT A SECRET.

Go to page 1224 for the next Super Hero

seen and heard. But no one accepts what he says. 33Anyone who accepted it has said, 'Yes. God is truthful.' 34The One whom God has sent speaks God's words. God gives the Holy Spirit without limit.

35"The Father loves the Son and has put everything into his hands. 36Anyone who believes in the Son has eternal life. Anyone who says no to the Son will not have life. God's anger remains on him."

Jesus Talks With a Woman From Samaria

4 The Pharisees heard that Jesus was winning and baptizing more disciples than John. 2But in fact Jesus was not baptizing. His disciples were. 3When the Lord found out about all this, he left Judea. He went back to Galilee again.

4Jesus had to go through Samaria. 5He came to a town in Samaria called Sychar. It was near the piece of land Jacob had given his son Joseph. 6Jacob's well was there. Jesus was tired from the journey. So he sat down by the well. It was about noon.

7A woman from Samaria came to get some water. Jesus said to her, "Will you give me a drink?" 8His disciples had gone into the town to buy food.

9The Samaritan woman said to him, "You are a Jew. I am a Samaritan woman. How can you ask me for a drink?" She said this because Jews don't have anything to do with Samaritans.

10Jesus answered her, "You do not know what God's gift is. And you do not know who is asking you for a drink. If you did, you would have asked him. He would have given you living water."

11"Sir," the woman said, "you don't have anything to get water with. The well is deep. Where can you get this living water?

12"Our father Jacob gave us the well. He drank from it himself. So did his sons and his flocks and herds. Are you more important than he is?"

13Jesus answered, "All who drink this water will be thirsty again. 14But anyone who drinks the water I give him will never be thirsty. In fact, the water I give him will become a spring of water in him. It will flow up into eternal life."

15The woman said to him, "Sir, give me this water. Then I will never be thirsty. And I won't have to keep coming here to get water."

16He told her, "Go. Get your husband and come back."

17"I have no husband," she replied. Jesus said to her, "You are right when

you say you have no husband. 18The fact is, you have had five husbands. And the man you have now is not your husband. What you have just said is very true."

19"Sir," the woman said, "I can see that you are a prophet. 20Our people have worshiped on this mountain for a long time. But you Jews claim that the place where we must worship is in Jerusalem."

21Jesus said, "Believe me, woman. A time is coming when you will not worship the Father on this mountain or in Jerusalem. 22You Samaritans worship what you do not know. We worship what we do know. Salvation comes from the Jews.

23"But a new time is coming. In fact, it is already here. True worshipers will worship the Father in spirit and in truth. They are the kind of worshipers the Father is looking for.

24"God is spirit. His worshipers must worship him in spirit and in truth."

25The woman said, "I know that Messiah is coming." (He is called Christ.) "When he comes, he will explain everything to us."

26Then Jesus said, "I, the one speaking to you, am he."

The Disciples Join Jesus Again

27Just then Jesus' disciples returned. They were surprised to find him talking with a woman. But no one asked, "What do you want from her?" No one asked, "Why are you talking with her?"

28The woman left her water jar and went back to the town. She said to the people, 29"Come. See a man who told me everything I've ever done. Could this be the Christ?"

30The people came out of the town and made their way toward Jesus.

31His disciples were saying to him, "Rabbi, eat something!"

32But he said to them, "I have food to eat that you know nothing about."

33Then his disciples asked each other, "Did someone bring him food?"

34Jesus said, "My food is to do what my Father sent me to do. My food is to finish his work.

35"You say, 'Four months more, and then it will be harvest time.' But I tell you, open your eyes! Look at the fields! They are ripe for harvest right now. 36Those who gather the crop are already getting paid. They are already harvesting the crop for eternal life. So those who plant and those who gather can now be glad together.

37"Here is a true saying. 'One plants

and another gathers.' **38**I sent you to gather what you have not worked for. Others have done the hard work. You have gathered the benefits of their work."

Many Samaritans Believe in Jesus

39Many of the Samaritans from the town of Sychar believed in Jesus. They believed because of the woman's witness.

WOMAN FROM SAMARIA

JOHN 4:39

Many of the Samaritans...believed in Jesus. They believed because of the woman's witness. She said, "He told me everything I've ever done."

Around noontime the woman walked up to the well and put her jug down next to it. No other women were there, just one lone man. That was good. She went to the well at noon to avoid the other women from Samaria (suh-MARE-ee-uh). Most of the women went to the well in the morning or in the evening. They tended to either ignore the woman or preach at her when she met them at the well. She had had enough of that.

"COULD YOU GIVE ME A DRINK?"

The woman turned. *Jews usually have nothing to do with us Samaritans*, she thought to herself. But this one was obviously different. "You're asking me, a Samaritan and a woman, for a drink?"

"I know you're surprised," Jesus replied. "But if you knew who was asking, you would have asked *me* for a drink, and I would have given you living water. You would never be thirsty again."

It took some time for the woman to understand what Jesus meant. He continued to talk to her until she believed he was the Christ. She drank in all he said to her, then left her water jug sit and went back to town to tell all her friends about her wonderful discovery.

BE LIKE THE WOMAN FROM SAMARIA

The Samaritan woman didn't expect to find Jesus at the well. But she stopped what she was doing to listen to him. Then she believed in him. Then she went and told others about him. Be just like her! Take time from your everyday life to get to know Jesus better. Then tell your friends all about him.

THE SAMARITAN WOMAN LISTENED TO JESUS AND BELIEVED WHAT HE TOLD HER.

Go to page 1227 for the next Super Hero

She said, "He told me everything I've ever done."

⁴⁰Then the Samaritans came to him and tried to get him to stay with them. So he stayed two days. ⁴¹Because of his words, many more people became believers.

⁴²They said to the woman, "We no longer believe just because of what you said. We have now heard for ourselves. We know that this man really is the Savior of the world."

Jesus Heals the Official's Son

⁴³After the two days, Jesus left for Galilee. ⁴⁴He himself had pointed out that a prophet is not respected in his own country. ⁴⁵When he arrived in Galilee, the people living there welcomed him. They had seen everything he had done in Jerusalem at the Passover Feast. That was because they had also been there.

⁴⁶Once more, Jesus visited Cana in Galilee. Cana is where he had turned the water into wine. A royal official was there. His son was sick in bed at Capernaum. ⁴⁷The official heard that Jesus had arrived in Galilee from Judea. So he went to Jesus and begged him to come and heal his son. The boy was close to death.

⁴⁸Jesus told him, "You people will never believe unless you see miraculous signs and wonders."

⁴⁹The royal official said, "Sir, come down before my child dies."

⁵⁰Jesus replied, "You may go. Your son will live."

The man believed what Jesus said, and so he left. ⁵¹While he was still on his way home, his servants met him. They gave him the news that his boy was living. ⁵²He asked what time his son got better. They said to him, "The fever left him yesterday afternoon at one o'clock."

⁵³Then the father realized what had happened. That was the exact time Jesus had said to him, "Your son will live." So he and all his family became believers.

⁵⁴This was the second miraculous sign that Jesus did after coming from Judea to Galilee.

Jesus Heals a Disabled Man

5 Some time later, Jesus went up to Jerusalem for a Jewish feast. ²In Jerusalem near the Sheep Gate is a pool. In the Aramaic language it is called Bethesda. It is surrounded by five rows of columns with a roof over them. ³/⁴Here a great number of disabled people used to lie down. Among them were those who were blind, those who could not walk, and those who could hardly move.

⁵One person who was there had been disabled for 38 years. ⁶Jesus saw him lying there. He knew that the man had been in that condition for a long time. So he asked him, "Do you want to get well?"

⁷"Sir," the disabled man replied, "I have no one to help me into the pool when an angel stirs the water up. I try to get in, but someone else always goes down ahead of me."

⁸Then Jesus said to him, "Get up! Pick up your mat and walk."

⁹At once the man was healed. He picked up his mat and walked.

The day this happened was a Sabbath. ¹⁰So the Jews said to the man who had been healed, "It is the Sabbath. The law does not allow you to carry your mat."

¹¹But he replied, "The one who made me well said to me, 'Pick up your mat and walk.'"

¹²They asked him, "Who is this fellow? Who told you to pick it up and walk?"

¹³The one who was healed had no idea who it was. Jesus had slipped away into the crowd that was there.

¹⁴Later Jesus found him at the temple. Jesus said to him, "See, you are well again. Stop sinning, or something worse may happen to you." ¹⁵The man went away. He told the Jews it was Jesus who had made him well.

Life Because of the Son

¹⁶Jesus was doing these things on the Sabbath day. So the Jews began to oppose him.

¹⁷Jesus said to them, "My Father is always doing his work. He is working right up to this very day. I am working too."

¹⁸For this reason the Jews tried even harder to kill him. Jesus was not only breaking the Sabbath. He was even calling God his own Father. He was making himself equal with God.

¹⁹Jesus answered, "What I'm about to tell you is true. The Son can do nothing by himself. He can do only what he sees his Father doing. What the Father does, the Son also does. ²⁰This is because the Father loves the Son. He shows him everything he does. Yes, you will be amazed! The Father will show him even greater things than these.

²¹"The Father raises the dead and gives them life. In the same way, the Son gives life to anyone he wants to.

²²"Also, the Father does not judge anyone. He has given the Son the task of judg-

POWER SURGE

BELIEVES †

ANYONE WHO HEARS MY WORD AND BELIEVES HIM WHO SENT ME HAS ETERNAL LIFE. HE WILL NOT BE FOUND GUILTY. HE HAS CROSSED OVER FROM DEATH TO LIFE.

— JOHN 5:24 —

ing. 23Then all people will honor the Son just as they honor the Father. Those who do not honor the Son do not honor the Father, who sent him.

24"What I'm about to tell you is true. Anyone who hears my word and believes him who sent me has eternal life. He will not be found guilty. He has crossed over from death to life.

25"What I'm about to tell you is true. A time is coming for me to give life. In fact, it has already begun. The dead will hear the voice of the Son of God. Those who hear it will live.

26"The Father has life in himself. He has also allowed the Son to have life in himself. 27And the Father has given him the authority to judge. This is because he is the Son of Man.

28"Do not be amazed at this. A time is coming when all who are in the grave will hear his voice. 29They will all come out of their graves. Those who have done good will rise and live again. Those who have done evil will rise and be found guilty.

30"I can do nothing by myself. I judge only as I hear. And my judging is fair. I do not try to please myself. I try only to please the One who sent me.

Giving Witness About Jesus

31"If I give witness about myself, it doesn't count. 32There is someone else who gives witness in my favor. And I know that his witness about me counts.

33"You have sent people to John. He has given witness to the truth. 34I do not accept human witness. I only talk about it so you can be saved. 35John was like a lamp that burned and gave light. For a while you chose to enjoy his light.

36"The witness I have is more important than John's. I am doing the very work the Father gave me to finish. It gives witness that the Father has sent me.

37"The Father who sent me has himself given witness about me. You have never heard his voice. You have never seen what he really looks like. 38And his word does not live in you. This is because you do not believe the One he sent.

39"You study the Scriptures carefully. You study them because you think they will give you eternal life. The Scriptures you study give witness about me. 40But you refuse to come to me and receive life.

41"I do not accept praise from people. 42But I know you. I know that you do not have love for God in your hearts. 43I have come in my Father's name, and you do not accept me. But if someone else comes in his own name, you will accept him.

44"You accept praise from one another. But you make no effort to receive the praise that comes from the only God. So how can you believe?

45"Do not think I will bring charges against you in front of the Father. Moses is the one who does that. And he is the one you build your hopes on.

46"Do you believe Moses? Then you should believe me. He wrote about me. 47But you do not believe what he wrote. So how are you going to believe what I say?"

Jesus Feeds the Five Thousand

6 Some time after this, Jesus crossed over to the other side of the Sea of Galilee. It is also called the Sea of Tiberias. 2A large crowd of people followed him. They had seen the miraculous signs he had done on those who were sick.

3Then Jesus went up on a mountainside. There he sat down with his disciples. 4The Jewish Passover Feast was near.

5Jesus looked up and saw a large crowd coming toward him. So he said to Philip, "Where can we buy bread for these people to eat?" 6He asked this only to put Philip to the test. He already knew what he was going to do.

7Philip answered him, "Eight months' pay would not buy enough bread for each one to have a bite!"

8Another of his disciples spoke up. It was Andrew, Simon Peter's brother. 9He said, "Here is a boy with five small loaves of barley bread. He also has two small fish. But how far will that go in such a large crowd?"

10Jesus said, "Have the people sit

BOY WITH LUNCH

JOHN 6:9

[Andrew] said, "Here is a boy with five small loaves of barley bread. He also has two small fish. But how far will that go in such a large crowd?"

The little boy first jumped one way, then another, laughing as his shadow jumped along with him. His mother had put fish and bread in a sack for his lunch. He was off exploring for the day.

Climbing over rocks and running around the hills, he came to a huge crowd of thousands of people. He stopped to listen to the teacher, who was speaking to them. The little boy worked his way right to the front row. He tossed his lunch on the ground and plopped down next to it. Lying back on his arms, he listened to Jesus. He sat up in amazement when Jesus healed some sick people. *WOW! IF JESUS COULD MAKE SICK PEOPLE WELL, HE COULD DO ANYTHING!*

Later that day, Jesus started to talk to his disciples about feeding the people. The boy looked around. How could Jesus feed this many people? He had an idea. He got up and tugged on the robe of a nearby disciple named Andrew. Andrew tried to ignore him. But finally he gave in and bent down to listen.

"Five small loaves of bread and two fish? And you want me to give them to Jesus to feed the crowd?" Andrew looked at the little boy in surprise. But he gave the small lunch to Jesus.

Jesus took the little boy's lunch and fed not 5 people, not 500 people, but over 5,000 people! The boy watched as the disciples began to hand out the fish and bread. No matter how many people they handed food to, there was still more left.

Jesus smiled at the boy, and he smiled back at Jesus. The boy knew Jesus could do anything!

BE LIKE THE LITTLE BOY
Be like the boy. You may think you don't have much to give. But the amount isn't what matters. It's what you know Jesus can do with what you give—whether it's big or small.

THE LITTLE BOY KNEW JESUS COULD DO BIG THINGS WITH HIS SMALL GIFT.
THE WHOLE STORY: JOHN 6:1-13

Go to page 1246 for the greatest Super Hero

down." There was plenty of grass in that place, and they sat down. The number of men among them was about 5,000.

¹¹Then Jesus took the loaves and gave thanks. He handed out the bread to those who were seated. He gave them as much as they wanted. And he did the same with the fish.

¹²When all of them had enough to eat, Jesus spoke to his disciples. "Gather the leftover pieces," he said. "Don't waste anything."

¹³So they gathered what was left over from the five barley loaves. They filled 12 baskets with the pieces left by those who had eaten.

¹⁴The people saw the miraculous sign that Jesus did. Then they began to say, "This must be the Prophet who is supposed to come into the world." ¹⁵But Jesus knew that they planned to come and force him to be their king. So he went away again to a mountain by himself.

Jesus Walks on the Water

¹⁶When evening came, Jesus' disciples went down to the Sea of Galilee. ¹⁷There they got into a boat and headed across the lake toward Capernaum. By now it was dark. Jesus had not yet joined them.

¹⁸A strong wind was blowing, and the water became rough. ¹⁹They rowed three or three and a half miles. Then they saw Jesus coming toward the boat. He was walking on the water. They were terrified. ²⁰But he said to them, "It is I. Don't be afraid."

²¹Then they agreed to take him into the boat. Right away the boat reached the shore where they were heading.

²²The next day the crowd that had stayed on the other side of the lake realized something. They saw that only one boat had been there. They knew that Jesus had not gotten into it with his disciples. And they knew that the disciples had gone away alone. ²³Then some boats from Tiberias landed. It was near the place where the people had eaten the bread after the Lord gave thanks. ²⁴The crowd realized that Jesus and his disciples were not there. So they got into boats and went to Capernaum to look for Jesus.

Jesus Is the Bread of Life

²⁵They found him on the other side of the lake. They asked him, "Rabbi, when did you get here?"

²⁶Jesus answered, "What I'm about to tell you is true. You are not looking for me because you saw miraculous signs. You are looking for me because you ate the loaves until you were full. ²⁷Do not work for food that spoils. Work for food that lasts forever. That is the food the Son of Man will give you. God the Father has put his seal of approval on him."

²⁸Then they asked him, "What does God want from us? What works does he want us to do?"

²⁹Jesus answered, "God's work is to believe in the One he has sent."

³⁰So they asked him, "What miraculous sign will you give us? What will you do so we can see it and believe you? ³¹Long ago our people ate the manna in the desert. It is written in Scripture, 'The Lord gave them bread from heaven to eat.' " *(Exodus 16:4; Nehemiah 9:15; Psalm 78:24,25)*

³²Jesus said to them, "What I'm about to tell you is true. It is not Moses who has given you the bread from heaven. It is my Father who gives you the true bread from heaven. ³³The bread of God is the One who comes down from heaven. He gives life to the world."

³⁴"Sir," they said, "give us this bread from now on."

³⁵Then Jesus said, "I am the bread of life. No one who comes to me will ever go hungry. And no one who believes in me will ever be thirsty. ³⁶But it is just as I told you. You have seen me, and you still do not believe. ³⁷Everyone the Father gives me will come to me. I will never send away anyone who comes to me. ³⁸I have not come down from heaven to do what I want to do. I have come to do what the One who sent me wants me to do. ³⁹The One who sent me doesn't want me to lose anyone he has given me. He wants me to raise them up on the last day. ⁴⁰My Father wants all who look to the Son and believe in him to have eternal life. I will raise them up on the last day."

41Then the Jews began to complain about Jesus. That was because he said, "I am the bread that came down from heaven." **42**They said, "Isn't this Jesus, the son of Joseph? Don't we know his father and mother? How can he now say, 'I came down from heaven'?"

43"Stop complaining among yourselves," Jesus answered. **44**"No one can come to me unless the Father who sent me brings him. Then I will raise him up on the last day.

45"It is written in the Prophets, 'God will teach all of them.' *(Isaiah 54:13)* Everyone who listens to the Father and learns from him comes to me.

46"No one has seen the Father except the One who has come from God. Only he has seen the Father. **47**What I'm about to tell you is true. Everyone who believes has life forever.

48"I am the bread of life. **49**Long ago your people ate the manna in the desert, and they still died. **50**But here is the bread that comes down from heaven. A person can eat it and not die. **51**I am the living bread that came down from heaven. Everyone who eats some of this bread will live forever. The bread is my body. I will give it for the life of the world."

52Then the Jews began to argue sharply among themselves. They said, "How can this man give us his body to eat?"

53Jesus said to them, "What I'm about to tell you is true. You must eat the Son of Man's body and drink his blood. If you don't, you have no life in you. **54**Anyone who eats my body and drinks my blood has eternal life. I will raise him up on the last day.

55"My body is real food. My blood is real drink. **56**Anyone who eats my body and drinks my blood remains in me. And I remain in him.

57"The living Father sent me, and I live because of him. In the same way, those who feed on me will live because of me. **58**This is the bread that came down from heaven. Long ago your people ate manna and died. But those who feed on this bread will live forever."

59He said this while he was teaching in the synagogue in Capernaum.

Many Disciples Leave Jesus

60Jesus' disciples heard this. Many of them said, "This is a hard teaching. Who can accept it?"

61Jesus was aware that his disciples were complaining about his teaching. So he said to them, "Does this upset you? **62**What if you see the Son of Man go up to where he was before? **63**The Holy Spirit gives life. The body means nothing at all. The words I have spoken to you are from the Spirit. They give life. **64**But there are some of you who do not believe."

Jesus had known from the beginning which of them did not believe. And he had known who was going to hand him over to his enemies. **65**So he continued speaking. He said, "This is why I told you that no one can come to me unless the Father helps him."

66From this time on, many of his disciples turned back. They no longer followed him.

67"You don't want to leave also, do you?" Jesus asked the Twelve.

68Simon Peter answered him, "Lord, who can we go to? You have the words of eternal life. **69**We believe and know that you are the Holy One of God."

70Then Jesus replied, "Didn't I choose you, the 12 disciples? But one of you is a devil!" **71**He meant Judas, the son of Simon Iscariot. Judas was one of the Twelve. But later he was going to hand Jesus over to his enemies.

Jesus Goes to the Feast of Booths

7 After this, Jesus went around in Galilee. He stayed away from Judea on purpose. He knew that the Jews there were waiting to kill him.

2The Jewish Feast of Booths was near. **3**Jesus' brothers said to him, "You should leave here and go to Judea. Then your disciples will see the kinds of things you do. **4**No one who wants to be well known does things in secret. Since you are doing these things, show yourself to the world." **5**Even Jesus' own brothers did not believe in him.

6So Jesus told them, "The right time has not yet come for me. For you, any time is right. **7**The people of the world can't hate you. But they hate me. This is because I give witness that what they do is evil.

8"You go to the Feast. I am not yet going up to this Feast. For me, the right time has not yet come."

9After he said this, he stayed in Galilee.

10When his brothers had left for the Feast, he went also. But he went secretly, not openly. **11**At the Feast the Jews were watching for him. They were asking, "Where is he?"

12Many people in the crowd were whispering about him. Some said, "He is a good man."

Others replied, "No. He fools the people."

13But no one would say anything about him openly. They were afraid of the Jews.

Jesus Teaches at the Feast

14Jesus did nothing until halfway through the Feast. Then he went up to the temple courtyard and began to teach. **15**The Jews were amazed. They asked, "How did this man learn so much without studying?"

16Jesus answered, "What I teach is not my own. It comes from the One who sent me. **17**Anyone who chooses to do what God wants him to do will find out whether my teaching comes from God or from me. **18**Someone who speaks on his own does it to get honor for himself. But someone who works for the honor of the One who sent him is truthful. There is nothing false about him.

19"Didn't Moses give you the law? But not one of you keeps the law. Why are you trying to kill me?"

20"You are controlled by demons," the crowd answered. "Who is trying to kill you?"

21Jesus said to them, "I did one miracle, and you are all amazed. **22**Moses gave you circumcision, and so you circumcise a child on the Sabbath day. But circumcision did not really come from Moses. It came from Abraham. **23**You circumcise a child on the Sabbath day. You think that if you do, you won't break the law of Moses. Then why are you angry with me? I healed a whole man on the Sabbath! **24**"Stop judging only by what you see. Judge correctly."

Is Jesus the Christ?

25Then some of the people of Jerusalem began asking questions. They said, "Isn't this the man some people are trying to kill? **26**Here he is! He is speaking openly. They aren't saying a word to him. Have the authorities really decided that he is the Christ? **27**But we know where this man is from. When the Christ comes, no one will know where he is from."

28Jesus was still teaching in the temple courtyard. He cried out, "Yes, you know me. And you know where I am from. I am not here on my own. The One who sent me is true. You do not know him. **29**But I know him. I am from him, and he sent me."

30When he said this, they tried to arrest him. But no one laid a hand on him. His time had not yet come.

31Still, many people in the crowd put their faith in him. They said, "How will it be when the Christ comes? Will he do more miraculous signs than this man?"

32The Pharisees heard the crowd whispering things like this about him. Then the chief priests and the Pharisees sent temple guards to arrest him.

33Jesus said, "I am with you for only a short time. Then I will go to the One who sent me. **34**You will look for me, but you won't find me. You can't come where I am going."

35The Jews said to one another, "Where does this man plan to go? Does he think we can't find him? Will he go where our people live scattered among the Greeks? Will he go there to teach the Greeks? **36**What did he mean when he said, 'You will look for me, but you won't find me'? And, 'You can't come where I am going'?"

37It was the last and most important day of the Feast. Jesus stood up and spoke in a loud voice. He said, "Let anyone who is thirsty come to me and drink. **38**Does anyone believe in me? Then, just as Scripture says, streams of living water will flow from inside him."

39When he said this, he meant the Holy Spirit. Those who believed in Jesus would receive the Spirit later. Up to that time, the Spirit had not been given. This was because Jesus had not yet received glory.

40When some of the people heard his words, they said, "This man must be the Prophet we've been expecting."

41Others said, "He is the Christ."

Still others asked, "How can the Christ come from Galilee? **42**Doesn't Scripture say that the Christ will come from David's family? Doesn't it say that he will come from Bethlehem, the town where David lived?"

43So the people did not agree about who Jesus was. **44**Some wanted to arrest him. But no one laid a hand on him.

The Jewish Leaders Do Not Believe

45Finally the temple guards went back to the chief priests and the Pharisees. They asked the guards, "Why didn't you bring him in?"

46"No one ever spoke the way this man does," the guards replied.

47"You mean he has fooled you also?" the Pharisees asked. **48**"Have any of the rulers or Pharisees believed in him? **49**No! But this mob knows nothing about the law. There is a curse on them."

50Then Nicodemus, a Pharisee, spoke.

He was the one who had gone to Jesus earlier. He asked, [51]"Does our law find someone guilty without hearing him first? Doesn't it want to find out what he is doing?"

[52]They replied, "Are you from Galilee too? Look into it. You will find that a prophet does not come out of Galilee."

---

[53]Then each of them went home.

8 But Jesus went to the Mount of Olives. [2]At sunrise he arrived in the temple courtyard again. All the people gathered around him there. He sat down to teach them.

[3]The teachers of the law and the Pharisees brought in a woman. She had been caught in adultery. They made her stand in front of the group. [4]They said to Jesus, "Teacher, this woman was caught in the act of adultery. [5]In the Law, Moses commanded us to kill such women by throwing stones at them. Now what do you say?" [6]They were trying to trap Jesus with that question. They wanted to have a reason to bring charges against him.

But Jesus bent down and started to write on the ground with his finger. [7]They kept asking him questions. So he stood up and said to them, "Has any one of you not sinned? Then you be the first to throw a stone at her."

[8]He bent down again and wrote on the ground. [9]Those who heard what he had said began to go away. They left one at a time, the older ones first. Soon only Jesus was left. The woman was still standing there.

[10]Jesus stood up and asked her, "Woman, where are they? Hasn't anyone found you guilty?"

[11]"No one, sir," she said.

"Then I don't find you guilty either," Jesus said. "Go now and leave your life of sin."

Jesus' Witness Is True

[12]Jesus spoke to the people again. He said, "I am the light of the world. Those who follow me will never walk in darkness. They will have the light that leads to life."

[13]The Pharisees argued with him. "Here you are," they said, "appearing as your own witness. But your witness does not count."

[14]Jesus answered, "Even if I give witness about myself, my witness does count. I know where I came from. And I know where I am going. But you have no idea where I come from or where I am going. [15]You judge by human standards. I don't judge anyone.

[16]"But if I do judge, what I decide is right. This is because I am not alone. I stand with the Father, who sent me. [17]Your own Law says that the witness of two is what counts. [18]I give witness about myself. My other witness is the Father, who sent me."

[19]Then they asked him, "Where is your father?"

"You do not know me or my Father," Jesus replied. "If you knew me, you would know my Father also."

[20]He spoke these words while he was teaching in the temple area. He was near the place where the offerings were put. But no one arrested him. His time had not yet come.

[21]Once more Jesus spoke to them. "I am going away," he said. "You will look for me, and you will die in your sin. You can't come where I am going."

[22]This made the Jews ask, "Will he kill himself? Is that why he says, 'You can't come where I am going'?"

[23]But Jesus said, "You are from below. I am from heaven. You are from this world. I am not from this world. [24]I told you that you would die in your sins. Do you believe that I am the one I claim to be? If you don't, you will certainly die in your sins."

[25]"Who are you?" they asked.

"Just what I have been claiming all along," Jesus replied. [26]"I have a lot to say that will judge you. But the One who sent me can be trusted. And I tell the world what I have heard from him."

[27]They did not understand that Jesus was telling them about his Father. [28]So Jesus said, "You will lift up the Son of Man. Then you will know that I am the one I claim to be. You will also know that I do nothing on my own. I speak just what the Father has taught me. [29]The One who sent me is with me. He has not left me alone, because I always do what pleases him."

[30]Even while Jesus was speaking, many people put their faith in him.

The Children of Abraham

[31]Jesus spoke to the Jews who had believed him. "If you obey my teaching," he said, "you are really my disciples. [32]Then you will know the truth. And the truth will set you free."

[33]They answered him, "We are Abra-

ham's children. We have never been slaves of anyone. So how can you say that we will be set free?"

34Jesus replied, "What I'm about to tell you is true. Everyone who sins is a slave of sin. **35**A slave has no lasting place in the family. But a son belongs to the family forever. **36**So if the Son of Man sets you free, you will really be free.

37"I know you are Abraham's children. But you are ready to kill me. You have no room for my word. **38**I am telling you what I saw when I was with my Father. You do what you have heard from your father."

39"Abraham is our father," they answered.

Jesus said, "Are you really Abraham's children? If you are, you will do the things Abraham did. **40**But you have decided to kill me. I am a man who has told you the truth I heard from God. Abraham didn't do the things you want to do. **41**You are doing the things your own father does."

"We are not children of people who weren't married to each other," they objected. "The only Father we have is God himself."

The Children of the Devil

42Jesus said to them, "If God were your Father, you would love me. I came from God, and now I am here. I have not come on my own. He sent me.

43"Why aren't my words clear to you? Because you can't really hear what I say. **44**You belong to your father, the devil. You want to obey your father's wishes.

"From the beginning, the devil was a murderer. He has never obeyed the truth. There is no truth in him. When he lies, he speaks his natural language. He does this because he is a liar. He is the father of lies. **45**But because I tell the truth, you

don't believe me! **46**Can any of you prove I am guilty of sinning? Am I not telling the truth? Then why don't you believe me?

47"Everyone who belongs to God hears what God says. The reason you don't hear is that you don't belong to God."

Jesus Makes Claims About Himself

48The Jews answered Jesus, "Aren't we right when we say you are a Samaritan? Aren't you controlled by a demon?"

49"I am not controlled by a demon," said Jesus. "I honor my Father. You do not honor me. **50**I am not seeking glory for myself. But there is One who brings glory to me. He is the judge. **51**What I'm about to tell you is true. Anyone who obeys my word will never die."

52Then the Jews cried out, "Now we know you are controlled by a demon! Abraham died. So did the prophets. But you say that anyone who obeys your word will never die. **53**Are you greater than our father Abraham? He died. So did the prophets. Who do you think you are?"

54Jesus replied, "If I bring glory to myself, my glory means nothing. You claim that my Father is your God. He is the one who brings glory to me. **55**You do not know him. But I know him. If I said I did not, I would be a liar like you. But I do know him. And I obey his word.

56"Your father Abraham was filled with joy at the thought of seeing my day. He saw it and was glad."

57"You are not even 50 years old," the Jews said to Jesus. "And you have seen Abraham?"

58"What I'm about to tell you is true," Jesus answered. "Before Abraham was born, I am!"

59When he said this, they picked up stones to kill him. But Jesus hid himself. He slipped away from the temple area.

Jesus Heals a Man Born Blind

9 As Jesus went along, he saw a man who was blind. He had been blind since he was born. **2**Jesus' disciples asked him, "Rabbi, who sinned? Was this man born blind because he sinned? Or did his parents sin?"

3"It isn't because this man sinned," said Jesus. "It isn't because his parents sinned. This happened so that God's work could be shown in his life. **4**While it is still day, we must do the work of the One who sent me. Night is coming. Then no one can work. **5**While I am in the world, I am the light of the world."

⁶After he said this, he spit on the ground. He made some mud with the spit. Then he put the mud on the man's eyes.

⁷"Go," he told him. "Wash in the Pool of Siloam." Siloam means Sent.

So the man went and washed. And he came home able to see.

⁸His neighbors and those who had earlier seen him begging asked questions. "Isn't this the same man who used to sit and beg?" they asked.

⁹Some claimed that he was.

Others said, "No. He only looks like him."

But the man who had been blind kept saying, "I am the man."

¹⁰"Then how were your eyes opened?" they asked.

¹¹He replied, "The man they call Jesus made some mud and put it on my eyes. He told me to go to Siloam and wash. So I went and washed. Then I could see."

¹²"Where is this man?" they asked him. "I don't know," he said.

The Pharisees Want to Know What Happened

¹³They brought to the Pharisees the man who had been blind. ¹⁴The day Jesus made the mud and opened the man's eyes was a Sabbath. ¹⁵So the Pharisees also asked him how he was able to see.

"He put mud on my eyes," the man replied. "Then I washed. And now I can see."

¹⁶Some of the Pharisees said, "Jesus has not come from God. He does not keep the Sabbath day."

But others asked, "How can a sinner do such miraculous signs?"

So the Pharisees did not agree with each other.

¹⁷Finally they turned again to the blind man. "What do you have to say about him?" they asked. "It was your eyes he opened."

The man replied, "He is a prophet."

¹⁸The Jews still did not believe that the man had been blind and now could see. So they sent for his parents. ¹⁹"Is this your son?" they asked. "Is this the one you say was born blind? How is it that now he can see?"

²⁰"We know he is our son," the parents answered. "And we know he was born blind. ²¹But we don't know how he can now see. And we don't know who opened his eyes. Ask him. He is an adult. He can speak for himself."

²²His parents said this because they

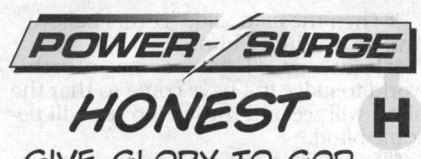

POWER-SURGE

HONEST H

GIVE GLORY TO GOD BY TELLING THE TRUTH!
— JOHN 9:24 —

were afraid of the Jews. The Jews had already decided that anyone who said Jesus was the Christ would be put out of the synagogue. ²³That was why the man's parents said, "He is an adult. Ask him."

²⁴Again they called the man who had been blind to come to them. "Give glory to God by telling the truth!" they said. "We know that the man who healed you is a sinner."

²⁵He replied, "I don't know if he is a sinner or not. I do know one thing. I was blind, but now I can see!"

²⁶Then they asked him, "What did he do to you? How did he open your eyes?"

²⁷He answered, "I have already told you. But you didn't listen. Why do you want to hear it again? Do you want to become his disciples too?"

²⁸Then they began to attack him with their words. "You are this fellow's disciple!" they said. "We are disciples of Moses! ²⁹We know that God spoke to Moses. But we don't even know where this fellow comes from."

³⁰The man answered, "That is really surprising! You don't know where he comes from, and yet he opened my eyes. ³¹We know that God does not listen to sinners. He listens to godly people who do what he wants them to do. ³²Nobody has ever heard of anyone opening the eyes of a person born blind. ³³If this man had not come from God, he could do nothing."

³⁴Then the Pharisees replied, "When you were born, you were already deep in sin. How dare you talk like that to us!" And they threw him out of the synagogue.

The Blind Will See

³⁵Jesus heard that the Pharisees had thrown the man out. When he found him, he said, "Do you believe in the Son of Man?"

³⁶"Who is he, sir?" the man asked. "Tell me, so I can believe in him."

³⁷Jesus said, "You have now seen him. In fact, he is the one speaking with you."

38Then the man said, "Lord, I believe." And he worshiped him.

39Jesus said, "I have come into this world to judge it. I have come so that the blind will see and those who see will become blind."

40Some Pharisees who were with him heard him say this. They asked, "What? Are we blind too?"

41Jesus said, "If you were blind, you would not be guilty of sin. But since you claim you can see, you remain guilty.

The Shepherd and the Flock

10 "What I'm about to tell you is true. What if someone does not enter the sheep pen through the gate but climbs in another way? That person is a thief and a robber. **2**The one who enters through the gate is the shepherd of the sheep. **3**The gatekeeper opens the gate for him. The sheep listen to his voice. He calls his own sheep by name and leads them out. **4**When he has brought all of his own sheep out, he goes on ahead of them. His sheep follow him because they know his voice. **5**But they will never follow a stranger. In fact, they will run away from him. They don't recognize a stranger's voice."

6Jesus used this story. But the Jews who were there didn't understand what he was telling them.

7So Jesus said again, "What I'm about to tell you is true. I am like a gate for the sheep. **8**All those who ever came before me were thieves and robbers. But the sheep did not listen to them. **9**I'm like a gate. Anyone who enters through me will be saved. He will come in and go out. And he will find plenty of food. **10**The thief comes only to steal and kill and destroy. I have come so they can have life. I want them to have it in the fullest possible way.

11"I am the good shepherd. The good shepherd gives his life for the sheep. **12**The hired man is not the shepherd who owns the sheep. So when the hired man sees the wolf coming, he leaves the sheep and runs away. Then the wolf attacks the flock and scatters it. **13**The man runs away because he is a hired man. He does not care about the sheep.

14"I am the good shepherd. I know my sheep, and my sheep know me. **15**They know me just as the Father knows me and I know the Father. And I give my life for the sheep.

16"I have other sheep that do not belong to this sheep pen. I must bring them in too. They also will listen to my voice.

Then there will be one flock and one shepherd.

17"The reason my Father loves me is that I give up my life. But I will take it back again. **18**No one takes it from me. I give it up myself. I have the authority to give it up. And I have the authority to take it back again. I received this command from my Father."

19After Jesus spoke these words, the Jews again could not agree with each other. **20**Many of them said, "He is controlled by a demon. He has gone crazy! Why should we listen to him?"

21But others said, "A person controlled by a demon does not say things like this. Can a demon open the eyes of someone who is blind?"

The Jews Do Not Believe

22Then came the Feast of Hanukkah at Jerusalem. It was winter. **23**Jesus was in the temple area walking in Solomon's Porch. **24**The Jews gathered around him. They said, "How long will you keep us waiting? If you are the Christ, tell us plainly."

25Jesus answered, "I did tell you. But you do not believe. The kinds of things I do in my Father's name speak for me. **26**But you do not believe, because you are not my sheep.

27"My sheep listen to my voice. I know them, and they follow me. **28**I give them eternal life, and they will never die. No one can steal them out of my hand. **29**My Father, who has given them to me, is greater than anyone. No one can steal them out of my Father's hand. **30**I and the Father are one."

31Again the Jews picked up stones to kill him.

32But Jesus said to them, "I have shown you many miracles from the Father. Which one of these are you throwing stones at me for?"

33"We are not throwing stones at you for any of these," replied the Jews. "We are stoning you for saying a very evil thing. You are only a man. But you claim to be God."

34Jesus answered them, "Didn't God say in your Law, 'I have said you are gods'? *(Psalm 82:6)* **35**We know that Scripture is always true. God spoke to some people and called them 'gods.' **36**If that is true, what about the One the Father set apart as his very own and sent into the world? Why do you charge me with saying a very evil thing? Is it because I said, 'I am God's Son'?

37"Don't believe me unless I do what my Father does. 38But what if I do it? Even if you don't believe me, believe the miracles. Then you will know and understand that the Father is in me and I am in the Father."

39Again they tried to arrest him. But he escaped from them.

40Then Jesus went back across the Jordan River. He went to the place where John had been baptizing in the early days. There he stayed. 41Many people came to him. They said, "John never did a miraculous sign. But everything he said about this man was true." 42And in that place many believed in Jesus.

Lazarus Dies

11 A man named Lazarus was sick. He was from Bethany, the village where Mary and her sister Martha lived. 2Mary would later pour perfume on the Lord. She would also wipe his feet with her hair. Her brother Lazarus was sick in bed. 3So the sisters sent a message to Jesus. "Lord," they told him, "the one you love is sick."

4When Jesus heard this, he said, "This sickness will not end in death. No, it is for God's glory. God's Son will receive glory because of it."

5Jesus loved Martha and her sister and Lazarus. 6But after he heard Lazarus was sick, he stayed where he was for two more days.

7Then he said to his disciples, "Let us go back to Judea."

8"But Rabbi," they said, "a short time ago the Jews tried to kill you with stones. Are you still going back there?"

9Jesus answered, "Aren't there 12 hours of daylight? A person who walks during the day won't trip and fall. He can see because of this world's light. 10But when he walks at night, he'll trip and fall. He has no light."

11After he said this, Jesus went on speaking to them. "Our friend Lazarus has fallen asleep," he said. "But I am going there to wake him up."

12His disciples replied, "Lord, if he's sleeping, he will get better."

13Jesus had been speaking about the death of Lazarus. But his disciples thought he meant natural sleep.

14So then he told them plainly, "Lazarus is dead. 15For your benefit, I am glad I was not there. Now you will believe. But let us go to him."

16Then Thomas, who was called Didymus, spoke to the rest of the disciples. "Let

us go also," he said. "Then we can die with Jesus."

Jesus Comforts the Sisters

17When Jesus arrived, he found out that Lazarus had already been in the tomb for four days. 18Bethany was less than two miles from Jerusalem. 19Many Jews had come to Martha and Mary. They had come to comfort them because their brother was dead.

20When Martha heard that Jesus was coming, she went out to meet him. But Mary stayed at home.

21"Lord," Martha said to Jesus, "I wish you had been here! Then my brother would not have died. 22But I know that even now God will give you anything you ask for."

23Jesus said to her, "Your brother will rise again."

24Martha answered, "I know he will rise again. This will happen when people are raised from the dead on the last day."

25Jesus said to her, "I am the resurrection and the life. Anyone who believes in me will live, even if he dies. 26And those who live and believe in me will never die. Do you believe this?"

POWER / SURGE

BELIEVES ✝

JESUS SAID TO [MARTHA], "I AM THE RESURRECTION AND THE LIFE. ANYONE WHO BELIEVES IN ME WILL LIVE, EVEN IF HE DIES. AND THOSE WHO LIVE AND BELIEVE IN ME WILL NEVER DIE.
— JOHN 11:25-26 —

27"Yes, Lord," she told him. "I believe that you are the Christ, the Son of God. I believe that you are the One who was supposed to come into the world."

28After she said this, she went back home. She called her sister Mary to one side to talk to her. "The Teacher is here," Martha said. "He is asking for you."

29When Mary heard this, she got up quickly and went to him. 30Jesus had not yet entered the village. He was still at the place where Martha had met him. **31**Some Jews had been comforting Mary in the house. They noticed how quickly she got up and went out. So they followed her. They thought she was going to the tomb to cry there.

32Mary reached the place where Jesus was. When she saw him, she fell at his feet. She said, "Lord, I wish you had been here! Then my brother would not have died."

33Jesus saw her crying. He saw that the Jews who had come along with her were crying also. His spirit became very sad, and he was troubled.

34"Where have you put him?" he asked. "Come and see, Lord," they replied.

35Jesus sobbed.

36Then the Jews said, "See how much he loved him!"

37But some of them said, "He opened the eyes of the blind man. Couldn't he have kept this man from dying?"

Jesus Raises Lazarus From the Dead

38Once more Jesus felt very sad. He came to the tomb. It was a cave with a stone in front of the entrance.

39"Take away the stone," he said.

"But, Lord," said Martha, the sister of the dead man, "by this time there is a bad smell. Lazarus has been in the tomb for four days."

40Then Jesus said, "Didn't I tell you that if you believed, you would see God's glory?"

41So they took away the stone.

Then Jesus looked up. He said, "Father, I thank you for hearing me. **42**I know that you always hear me. But I said this for the benefit of the people standing here. I said it so they will believe that you sent me."

43Then Jesus called in a loud voice. He said, "Lazarus, come out!"

44The dead man came out. His hands and feet were wrapped with strips of linen. A cloth was around his face.

Jesus said to them, "Take off the clothes he was buried in and let him go."

The Plan to Kill Jesus

45Many of the Jews who had come to visit Mary saw what Jesus did. So they put their faith in him.

46But some of them went to the Pharisees. They told the Pharisees what Jesus had done. **47**Then the chief priests and the Pharisees called a meeting of the Sanhedrin.

"What can we do?" they asked. "This man is doing many miraculous signs. **48**If we let him keep on doing this, everyone will believe in him. Then the Romans will come. They will take away our temple and our nation."

49One of them spoke up. His name was Caiaphas. He was high priest at that time. He said, "You don't know anything at all! **50**You don't realize what is good for you. It is better if one man dies for the people than if the whole nation is destroyed."

51He did not say this on his own. But he was high priest at that time. So he told ahead of time that Jesus would die for the Jewish nation. **52**He also prophesied that Jesus would die for God's children scattered everywhere. He would die to bring them together and make them one.

53So from that day on, the Jewish rulers planned to kill Jesus.

54Jesus no longer moved around openly among the Jews. Instead, he went away to an area near the desert. He went to a village called Ephraim. There he stayed with his disciples.

55It was almost time for the Jewish Passover Feast. Many people went up from the country to Jerusalem. They went there for the special washing that would make them pure before the Passover Feast. **56**They kept looking for Jesus as they stood in the temple area. They asked one another, "What do you think? Isn't he coming to the Feast at all?"

57But the chief priests and the Pharisees had given orders. They had commanded anyone who found out where Jesus was staying to report it. Then they could arrest him.

Mary Pours Perfume on Jesus

12 It was six days before the Passover Feast. Jesus arrived at Bethany, where Lazarus lived. Lazarus was the one Jesus had raised from the dead. **2**A dinner was given at Bethany to honor Jesus. Martha served the food. Lazarus was among those at the table with Jesus.

3Then Mary took about a pint of pure nard. It was an expensive perfume. She poured it on Jesus' feet and wiped them with her hair. The house was filled with the sweet smell of the perfume.

4But Judas Iscariot didn't like what Mary did. He was one of Jesus' disciples. Later he was going to hand Jesus over to his enemies. Judas said, **5**"Why wasn't this perfume sold? Why wasn't the money given to poor people? It was worth a year's pay."

6He didn't say this because he cared

about the poor. He said it because he was a thief. Judas was in charge of the money bag. He used to help himself to what was in it.

7"Leave her alone," Jesus replied. "The perfume was meant for the day I am buried. 8You will always have the poor among you. But you won't always have me."

9Meanwhile a large crowd of Jews found out that Jesus was there, so they came. But they did not come only because of Jesus. They also came to see Lazarus. After all, Jesus had raised him from the dead.

10So the chief priests made plans to kill Lazarus too. 11Because of Lazarus, many of the Jews were starting to follow Jesus. They were putting their faith in him.

POWER-SURGE

BELIEVES ✝

BECAUSE OF LAZARUS, MANY OF THE JEWS WERE STARTING TO FOLLOW JESUS. THEY WERE PUTTING THEIR FAITH IN HIM.
— JOHN 12:11 —

TELLS OTHERS

Jesus Enters Jerusalem

12The next day the large crowd that had come for the Feast heard that Jesus was on his way to Jerusalem. 13So they took branches from palm trees and went out to meet him. They shouted,

"Hosanna!"

"Blessed is the one who comes in the name of the Lord!"

(Psalm 118:25,26)

"Blessed is the King of Israel!"

14Jesus found a young donkey and sat on it. This is just as it is written in Scripture. It says,

15 "City of Zion, do not be afraid.
  See, your king is coming.
  He is sitting on a donkey's colt."

(Zechariah 9:9)

16At first, Jesus' disciples did not understand all this. They realized it only after he had received glory. Then they realized that these things had been written about him. They realized that the people had done these things to him.

17A crowd had been with Jesus when he called Lazarus from the tomb and raised him from the dead. So they continued to tell everyone about what had happened. 18Many people went out to meet him. They had heard that he had done this miraculous sign.

19So the Pharisees said to one another, "This isn't getting us anywhere. Look how the whole world is following him!"

Jesus Tells About His Coming Death

20There were some Greeks among the people who went up to worship during the Feast. 21They came to ask Philip for a favor. Philip was from Bethsaida in Galilee.

"Sir," they said, "we would like to see Jesus."

22Philip went to tell Andrew. Then Andrew and Philip told Jesus.

23Jesus replied, "The hour has come for the Son of Man to receive glory. 24What I'm about to tell you is true. Unless a grain of wheat falls to the ground and dies, it remains only one seed. But if it dies, it produces many seeds.

25"Anyone who loves his life will lose it. But anyone who hates his life in this world will keep it and have eternal life. 26Anyone who serves me must follow me. And where I am, my servant will also be. My Father will honor the one who serves me.

27"My heart is troubled. What should I say? 'Father, save me from this hour'? No. This is the very reason I came to this hour. 28Father, bring glory to your name!"

Then a voice came from heaven. It said, "I have brought glory to my name. I will bring glory to it again."

29The crowd there heard the voice. Some said it was thunder. Others said an angel had spoken to Jesus.

30Jesus said, "This voice was for your benefit, not mine. 31Now it is time for the world to be judged. Now the prince of this world will be thrown out. 32But I am going to be lifted up from the earth. When I am, I will bring all people to myself." 33He said this to show them how he was going to die.

34The crowd spoke up. "The Law tells us that the Christ will remain forever," they said. "So how can you say, 'The Son of

Man must be lifted up'? Who is this 'Son of Man'?"

35Then Jesus told them, "You are going to have the light just a little while longer. Walk while you have the light. Do this before darkness catches up with you. Anyone who walks in the dark does not know where he is going. **36**While you have the light, put your trust in it. Then you can become sons of light."

When Jesus had finished speaking, he left and hid from them.

The Jews Still Do Not Believe

37Jesus had done all these miraculous signs in front of them. But they still would not believe in him. **38**This happened as Isaiah the prophet had said it would. He had said,

"Lord, who has believed what we've
        been saying?
Who has seen the Lord's saving
        power?"   *(Isaiah 53:1)*

39For this reason, they could not believe. As Isaiah says in another place,

40"The Lord has blinded their eyes.
    He has closed their minds.
So they can't see with their eyes.
    They can't understand with their
        minds.
They can't turn to the Lord. If they
        could, he would heal them."
                        (Isaiah 6:10)

41Isaiah said this because he saw Jesus' glory and spoke about him.

42At the same time that Jesus did those miracles, many of the leaders believed in him. But because of the Pharisees, they would not admit they believed. They were afraid they would be thrown out of the synagogue. **43**They loved praise from people more than praise from God.

44Then Jesus cried out, "Anyone who believes in me does not believe in me only. He also believes in the One who sent me. **45**When he looks at me, he sees the One who sent me.

46"I have come into the world to be a light. No one who believes in me will stay in darkness.

47"I don't judge a person who hears my words but does not obey them. I didn't come to judge the world. I came to save it. **48**But there is a judge for anyone who does not accept me and my words. The very words I have spoken will judge him on the last day.

49"I did not speak on my own. The Father who sent me commanded me what to say. He also told me how to say it. **50**I know that his command leads to eternal life. So everything I say is just what the Father has told me to say."

Jesus Washes His Disciples' Feet

13 It was just before the Passover Feast. Jesus knew that the time had come for him to leave this world. It was time for him to go to the Father. Jesus loved his disciples who were in the world. So he now showed them how much he really loved them.

2The evening meal was being served. The devil had already tempted Judas Iscariot, son of Simon. He had told Judas to hand Jesus over to his enemies. **3**Jesus knew that the Father had put everything under his power. He also knew he had come from God and was returning to God.

4So he got up from the meal and took off his outer clothes. He wrapped a towel around his waist. **5**After that, he poured water into a large bowl. Then he began to wash his disciples' feet. He dried them with the towel that was wrapped around him.

6He came to Simon Peter.

"Lord," Peter said to him, "are you going to wash my feet?"

7Jesus replied, "You don't realize now what I am doing. But later you will understand."

8"No," said Peter. "You will never wash my feet."

Jesus answered, "Unless I wash you, you can't share life with me."

9"Lord," Simon Peter replied, "not just my feet! Wash my hands and my head too!"

10Jesus answered, "A person who has had a bath needs to wash only his feet. The rest of his body is clean. And you are clean. But not all of you are."

11Jesus knew who was going to hand him over to his enemies. That was why he said not every one was clean.

12When Jesus finished washing their feet, he put on his clothes. Then he returned to his place.

"Do you understand what I have done for you?" he asked them. **13**"You call me 'Teacher' and 'Lord.' You are right. That is what I am. **14**I, your Lord and Teacher, have washed your feet. So you also should wash one another's feet. **15**I have given you an example. You should do as I have done for you.

16"What I'm about to tell you is true. A servant is not more important than his master. And a messenger is not more important than the one who sends him. [17]Now you know these things. So you will be blessed if you do them

Jesus Tells What Judas Will Do

[18]"I am not talking about all of you. I know those I have chosen. But this will happen so that Scripture will come true. It says, 'The one who shares my bread has deserted me.' *(Psalm 41:9)*

[19]"I am telling you now, before it happens. When it does happen, you will believe that I am he. [20]What I'm about to tell you is true. Anyone who accepts someone I send accepts me. And anyone who accepts me accepts the One who sent me."

[21]After he had said this, Jesus' spirit was troubled. Here is the witness he gave. "What I'm about to tell you is true," he said. "One of you is going to hand me over to my enemies."

[22]His disciples stared at one another. They had no idea which one of them he meant. [23]The disciple Jesus loved was next to him at the table. [24]Simon Peter motioned to that disciple. He said, "Ask Jesus which one he means."

[25]The disciple was leaning back against Jesus. He asked him, "Lord, who is it?"

[26]Jesus answered, "It is the one I will give this piece of bread to. I will give it to him after I have dipped it in the dish."

He dipped the piece of bread. Then he gave it to Judas Iscariot, son of Simon. [27]As soon as Judas took the bread, Satan entered into him.

"Do quickly what you are going to do," Jesus told him.

[28]But no one at the meal understood why Jesus said this to him. [29]Judas was in charge of the money. So some of the disciples thought Jesus was telling him to buy what was needed for the Feast. Others thought Jesus was talking about giving something to poor people.

[30]As soon as Judas had taken the bread, he went out. And it was night.

Jesus Says That Peter Will Fail

[31]After Judas was gone, Jesus spoke. He said, "Now the Son of Man receives glory. And he brings glory to God. [32]If the Son brings glory to God, God himself will bring glory to the Son. God will do it at once.

[33]"My children, I will be with you only a little longer. You will look for me. Just as I told the Jews, so I am telling you now. You can't come where I am going.

[34]"I give you a new command. Love one another. You must love one another, just as I have loved you. [35]If you love one another, everyone will know you are my disciples."

[36]Simon Peter asked him, "Lord, where are you going?"

Jesus replied, "Where I am going you can't follow now. But you will follow me later."

[37]"Lord," Peter asked, "why can't I follow you now? I will give my life for you."

[38]Then Jesus answered, "Will you really give your life for me? What I'm about to tell you is true. Before the rooster crows, you will say three times that you don't know me!

Jesus Comforts His Disciples

14 "Do not let your hearts be troubled. Trust in God. Trust in me also.

[2]"There are many rooms in my Father's house. If this were not true, I would have told you. I am going there to prepare a place for you. [3]If I go and do that, I will come back. And I will take you to be with me. Then you will also be where I am. [4]"You know the way to the place where I am going."

Jesus Is the Way to the Father

[5]Thomas said to him, "Lord, we don't know where you are going. So how can we know the way?"

[6]Jesus answered, "I am the way and the truth and the life. No one comes to the Father except through me. [7]If you really knew me, you would know my Father also. From now on, you do know him. And you have seen him."

[8]Philip said, "Lord, show us the Father. That will be enough for us."

[9]Jesus answered, "Don't you know me, Philip? I have been among you such a long time! Anyone who has seen me has seen the Father. So how can you say, 'Show us the Father'?

[10]"Don't you believe that I am in the Father? Don't you believe that the Father is in me? The words I say to you are not just my own. The Father lives in me. He is the One who is doing his work. [11]Believe me when I say I am in the Father. Also believe that the Father is in me. Or at least believe what the miracles show about me.

[12]"What I'm about to tell you is true. Anyone who has faith in me will do what I have been doing. In fact, he will do even greater things. That is because I am going to the Father.

POWER SURGE

LOVING ♥

IF YOU LOVE ME,
YOU WILL OBEY WHAT
I COMMAND.
— JOHN 14:15 —

OBEYS ✔

13 "And I will do anything you ask in my name. Then the Son will bring glory to the Father. 14 You may ask me for anything in my name. I will do it.

The Father Will Send the Holy Spirit

15 "If you love me, you will obey what I command. 16 I will ask the Father. And he will give you another Friend to help you and to be with you forever. 17 The Friend is the Spirit of truth. The world can't accept him. That is because the world does not see him or know him. But you know him. He lives with you, and he will be in you. 18 I will not leave you like children who don't have parents. I will come to you.

19 "Before long, the world will not see me anymore. But you will see me. Because I live, you will live also. 20 On that day you will realize that I am in my Father. You will know that you are in me, and I am in you. 21 "Anyone who has my commands and obeys them loves me. My Father will love the one who loves me. I too will love him. And I will show myself to him."

22 Then Judas spoke. "Lord," he said, "why do you plan to show yourself only to us? Why not also to the world?" The Judas who spoke those words was not Judas Iscariot.

23 Jesus replied, "Anyone who loves me will obey my teaching. My Father will love him. We will come to him and make our home with him. 24 Anyone who does not love me will not obey my teaching. The words you hear me say are not my own. They belong to the Father who sent me.

25 "I have spoken all these things while I am still with you. 26 But the Father will send the Friend in my name to help you. The Friend is the Holy Spirit. He will teach you all things. He will remind you of everything I have said to you.

27 "I leave my peace with you. I give my peace to you. I do not give it to you as the world does. Do not let your hearts be troubled. And do not be afraid.

28 "You heard me say, 'I am going away. And I am coming back to you.' If you loved me, you would be glad I am going to the Father. The Father is greater than I am. 29 I have told you now before it happens. Then when it does happen, you will believe.

30 "I will not speak with you much longer. The prince of this world is coming. He has no power over me. 31 But the world must learn that I love the Father. They must also learn that I do exactly what my Father has commanded me to do.

"Come now. Let us leave.

The Vine and the Branches

15 "I am the true vine. My Father is the gardener. 2 He cuts off every branch joined to me that does not bear fruit. He trims every branch that does bear fruit. Then it will bear even more fruit.

3 "You are already clean because of the word I have spoken to you. 4 Remain joined to me, and I will remain joined to you. No branch can bear fruit by itself. It must remain joined to the vine. In the same way, you can't bear fruit unless you remain joined to me.

5 "I am the vine. You are the branches. If anyone remains joined to me, and I to him, he will bear a lot of fruit. You can't do anything without me. 6 If anyone does not remain joined to me, he is like a branch that is thrown away and dries up. Branches like those are picked up. They are thrown into the fire and burned.

7 "If you remain joined to me and my words remain in you, ask for anything you wish. And it will be given to you. 8 When you bear a lot of fruit, it brings glory to my Father. It shows that you are my disciples. 9 "Just as the Father has loved me, I have loved you. Now remain in my love. 10 If you obey my commands, you will remain in my love. In the same way, I have obeyed my Father's commands and remain in his love. 11 I have told you this so that my joy will be in you. I also want your joy to be complete.

12 "Here is my command. Love each other, just as I have loved you. 13 No one has greater love than the one who gives his life for his friends. 14 You are my friends if you do what I command.

15 "I do not call you servants anymore. Servants do not know their master's business. Instead, I have called you friends. I

have told you everything I learned from my Father.

¹⁶"You did not choose me. Instead, I chose you. I appointed you to go and bear fruit. It is fruit that will last. Then the Father will give you anything you ask for in my name.

¹⁷"Here is my command. Love each other.

The World Hates the Disciples

¹⁸"Does the world hate you? Remember that it hated me first. ¹⁹If you belonged to the world, it would love you like one of its own. But you do not belong to the world. I have chosen you out of the world. That is why the world hates you.

²⁰"Remember the words I spoke to you. I said, 'A servant is not more important than his master.' *(John 13:16)* If people hated me and tried to hurt me, they will do the same to you. If they obeyed my teaching, they will obey yours also. ²¹They will treat you like that because of my name. They do not know the One who sent me. ²²"If I had not come and spoken to them, they would not be guilty of sin. But now they have no excuse for their sin. ²³Those who hate me hate my Father also. ²⁴"I did miracles among them that no one else did. If I hadn't, they would not be guilty of sin. But now they have seen those miracles. And still they have hated both me and my Father. ²⁵This has happened so that what is written in their Law would come true. It says, 'They hated me without any reason.' *(Psalms 35:19; 69:4)*

²⁶"I will send the Friend to you from the Father. He is the Spirit of truth, who comes out from the Father. When the Friend comes to help you, he will give witness about me.

²⁷"You also must give witness. This is because you have been with me from the beginning.

16 "I have told you all of this so that you will not go down the wrong path. ²You will be thrown out of the synagogue. In fact, a time is coming when those who kill you will think they are doing God a favor. ³They will do things like that because they do not know the Father or me.

⁴"Why have I told you this? So that when the time comes, you will remember that I warned you. I didn't tell you this at first because I was with you.

What the Holy Spirit Will Do

⁵"Now I am going to the One who sent me. But none of you asks me, 'Where are you going?' ⁶Because I have said these things, you are filled with sadness.

⁷"But what I'm about to tell you is true. It is for your good that I am going away. Unless I go away, the Friend will not come to help you. But if I go, I will send him to you. ⁸When he comes, he will prove that the world's people are guilty. He will prove their guilt concerning sin and godliness and judgment.

⁹"The world is guilty as far as sin is concerned. That is because people do not believe in me. ¹⁰The world is guilty as far as godliness is concerned. That is because I am going to the Father, where you can't see me anymore. ¹¹The world is guilty as far as judgment is concerned. That is because the devil, the prince of this world, has already been judged.

¹²"I have much more to say to you. It is more than you can handle right now. ¹³But when the Spirit of truth comes, he will guide you into all truth. He will not speak on his own. He will speak only what he hears. And he will tell you what is still going to happen.

¹⁴"He will bring me glory by receiving something from me and showing it to you. ¹⁵Everything that belongs to the Father is mine. That is why I said the Holy Spirit will receive something from me and show it to you.

¹⁶"In a little while, you will no longer see me. Then after a little while, you will see me."

The Disciples' Sadness Will Turn Into Joy

¹⁷Some of his disciples spoke to one another. They said, "What does he mean by

POWER-SURGE

LOVING ♥

IF YOU OBEY MY COMMANDS, YOU WILL REMAIN IN MY LOVE. IN THE SAME WAY, I HAVE OBEYED MY FATHER'S COMMANDS AND REMAIN IN HIS LOVE.
— JOHN 15:10 —

✔

OBEYS

saying, 'In a little while, you will no longer see me. Then after a little while, you will see me'? And what does he mean by saying, 'I am going to the Father'?" **18**They kept asking, "What does he mean by 'a little while'? We don't understand what he is saying."

19Jesus saw that they wanted to ask him about those things. So he said to them, "Are you asking one another what I meant? Didn't you understand when I said, 'In a little while, you will no longer see me. Then after a little while, you will see me'? **20**What I'm about to tell you is true. You will cry and be full of sorrow while the world is full of joy. You will be sad, but your sadness will turn into joy.

21"A woman giving birth to a baby has pain. This is because her time to give birth has come. But when her baby is born, she forgets the pain. She forgets because she is so happy that a baby has been born into the world.

22"That's the way it is with you. Now it's your time to be sad. But I will see you again. Then you will be full of joy. And no one will take your joy away.

23"When that day comes, you will no longer ask me for anything. What I'm about to tell you is true. My Father will give you anything you ask for in my name. **24**Until now you have not asked for anything in my name. Ask, and you will receive what you ask for. Then your joy will be complete.

25"I have not been speaking to you plainly. But a time is coming when I will speak clearly. Then I will tell you plainly about my Father. **26**When that day comes, you will ask for things in my name. I am not saying I will ask the Father instead of you asking him. **27**No, the Father himself loves you because you have loved me. He also loves you because you have believed that I came from God.

28"I came from the Father and entered the world. Now I am leaving the world and going back to the Father."

29Then Jesus' disciples said, "Now you are speaking plainly. You are using examples that are clear. **30**Now we can see that you know everything. You don't even need anyone to ask you questions. This makes us believe that you came from God."

31"At last you believe!" Jesus said. **32**"But a time is coming when you will be scattered and go to your own homes. In fact, that time is already here. You will leave me all alone. But I am not really alone. My Father is with me.

POWER-SURGE

BELIEVES †

THE FATHER HIMSELF LOVES YOU BECAUSE YOU HAVE LOVED ME. HE ALSO LOVES YOU BECAUSE YOU HAVE BELIEVED THAT I CAME FROM GOD...IN THIS WORLD YOU WILL HAVE TROUBLE. BUT CHEER UP! I HAVE WON THE BATTLE OVER THE WORLD.
— JOHN 16:27, 33 —

LOVING

33"I have told you these things, so that you can have peace because of me. In this world you will have trouble. But cheer up! I have won the battle over the world."

Jesus Prays for Himself

17 After Jesus said this, he looked toward heaven and prayed. He said,

"Father, the time has come. Bring glory to your Son. Then your Son will bring glory to you. **2**You gave him authority over all people. He gives eternal life to all those you have given him.

3"And what is eternal life? It is knowing you, the only true God, and Jesus Christ, whom you have sent. **4**I have brought you glory on earth. I have finished the work you gave me to do. **5**So now, Father, give glory to me in heaven where your throne is. Give me the glory I had with you before the world began.

Jesus Prays for His Disciples

6"I have shown you to the disciples you gave me out of the world. They were yours. You gave them to me. And they have obeyed your word. **7**Now they know that everything you have given me comes from you. **8**I gave them the words you gave me. And they accepted them. They knew for certain that I came from you. They believed that you sent me.

9 "I pray for them. I am not praying for the world. I am praying for those you have given me, because they are yours. **10** All I have is yours, and all you have is mine. Glory has come to me because of my disciples.

11 "I will not remain in the world any longer. But they are still in the world, and I am coming to you. Holy Father, keep them safe by the power of your name. It is the name you gave me. Keep them safe so they can be one, just as you and I are one.

12 "While I was with them, I guarded them. I kept them safe through the name you gave me. None of them has been lost, except the one who was sentenced to be destroyed. It happened so that Scripture would come true.

13 "I am coming to you now. But I say these things while I am still in the world. I say them so that those you gave me can have all my joy inside them. **14** I have given them your word. The world has hated them. This is because they are not part of the world any more than I am. **15** I do not pray that you will take them out of the world. I pray that you will keep them safe from the evil one.

16 "They do not belong to the world, just as I do not belong to it. **17** Use the truth to make them holy. Your word is truth. **18** You sent me into the world. In the same way, I have sent them into the world. **19** I make myself holy for them so that they too can be made holy in a true sense.

Jesus Prays for All Believers

20 "I do not pray only for them. I pray also for those who will believe in me because of their message. **21** Father, I pray that all of them will be one, just as you are in me and I am in you. I want them also to be in us. Then the world will believe that you have sent me.

22 "I have given them the glory you gave me. I did this so they would be one, just as we are one. **23** I will be in them, just as you are in me. I want them to be brought together perfectly as one. This will let the world know that you sent me. It will also show the world that you have loved those

you gave me, just as you have loved me.

24 "Father, I want those you have given me to be with me where I am. I want them to see my glory, the glory you have given me. You gave it to me because you loved me before the world was created.

25 "Father, you are holy. The world does not know you, but I know you. Those you have given me know you have sent me. **26** I have shown you to them. And I will continue to show you to them. Then the love you have for me will be in them. I myself will be in them."

Jesus Is Arrested

18 When Jesus had finished praying, he left with his disciples. They crossed the Kidron Valley. On the other side there was a grove of olive trees. Jesus and his disciples went into it.

2 Judas knew the place. He was going to hand Jesus over to his enemies. Jesus had often met in that place with his disciples. **3** So Judas came to the grove. He was guiding a group of soldiers and some officials. The chief priests and the Pharisees had sent them. They were carrying torches, lanterns and weapons.

4 Jesus knew everything that was going to happen to him. So he went out and asked them, "Who is it that you want?"

5 "Jesus of Nazareth," they replied.

"I am he," Jesus said.

Judas, who was going to hand Jesus over, was standing there with them. **6** When Jesus said, "I am he," they moved back. Then they fell to the ground.

7 He asked them again, "Who is it that you want?"

They said, "Jesus of Nazareth."

8 "I told you I am he," Jesus answered. "If you are looking for me, then let these men go." **9** This happened so that the words Jesus had spoken would come true. He had said, "I have not lost anyone God has given me." *(John 6:39)*

10 Simon Peter had a sword and pulled it out. He struck the high priest's servant and cut off his right ear. The servant's name was Malchus.

11 Jesus commanded Peter, "Put your sword away! Shouldn't I drink the cup of suffering the Father has given me?"

Jesus Is Taken to Annas

12 Then the group of soldiers, their leader and the Jewish officials arrested Jesus. They tied him up **13** and brought him first to Annas. He was the father-in-law of Caiaphas, the high priest at that time. **14**Caiaphas had advised the Jews that it would be good if one man died for the people.

Peter Says He Is Not Jesus' Disciple

15Simon Peter and another disciple were following Jesus. The high priest knew the other disciple. So that disciple went with Jesus into the high priest's courtyard. **16**But Peter had to wait outside by the door.

The other disciple came back. He was the one the high priest knew. He spoke to the woman who was on duty there. Then he brought Peter in.

17The woman at the door spoke to Peter. "You are not one of Jesus' disciples, are you?" she asked him.

"I am not," he replied.

18It was cold. The servants and officials stood around a fire. They had made it to keep warm. Peter was also standing with them. He was warming himself.

The High Priest Questions Jesus

19Meanwhile, the high priest questioned Jesus. He asked him about his disciples and his teaching.

20"I have spoken openly to the world," Jesus replied. "I always taught in synagogues or at the temple, where all the Jews come together. I didn't say anything in secret. **21**Why question me? Ask the people who heard me. They certainly know what I said."

22When Jesus said that, one of the officials nearby hit him in the face. "Is this any way to answer the high priest?" he asked.

23"Have I said something wrong?" Jesus replied. "If I have, give witness to it. But if I spoke the truth, why did you hit me?"

24While Jesus was still tied up, Annas sent him to Caiaphas, the high priest.

Peter Again Says He Is Not Jesus' Disciple

25Simon Peter stood there. He was warming himself. Then someone asked him, "You aren't one of Jesus' disciples, are you?"

He said, "I am not."

26One of the high priest's servants was a relative of the man whose ear Peter had cut off. He said to Peter, "Didn't I see you with Jesus in the olive grove?"

27Again Peter said no.

At that very moment a rooster began to crow.

Jesus Is Brought to Pilate

28Then the Jews led Jesus from Caiaphas to the palace of the Roman governor. By now it was early morning. The Jews did not want to be made "unclean." They wanted to be able to eat the Passover meal. So they did not enter the palace.

29Pilate came out to them. He asked, "What charges are you bringing against this man?"

30"He has committed crimes," they replied. "If he hadn't, we would not have handed him over to you."

31Pilate said, "Take him yourselves. Judge him by your own law."

"But we don't have the right to put anyone to death," the Jews complained. **32**This happened so that the words Jesus had spoken about how he was going to die would come true.

33Then Pilate went back inside the palace. He ordered Jesus to be brought to him. Pilate asked him, "Are you the king of the Jews?"

34"Is that your own idea?" Jesus asked. "Or did others talk to you about me?"

35"Am I a Jew?" Pilate replied. "It was your people and your chief priests who handed you over to me. What have you done?"

36Jesus said, "My kingdom is not part of this world. If it were, those who serve me would fight. They would try to keep the Jews from arresting me. My kingdom is from another place."

37"So you are a king, then!" said Pilate.

Jesus answered, "You are right to say I am a king. In fact, that's the reason I was born. I came into the world to give witness to the truth. Everyone who is on the side of truth listens to me."

38"What is truth?" Pilate asked.

Then Pilate went out again to the Jews. He said, "I find no basis for any charge against him. **39**But it is your practice for me to set one prisoner free for you at Passover time. Do you want me to set 'the king of the Jews' free?"

40They shouted back, "No! Not him! Give us Barabbas!" Barabbas had taken part in an armed struggle against the country's rulers.

Jesus Is Sentenced to Be Crucified

19 Then Pilate took Jesus and had him whipped. **2**The soldiers twisted thorns together to make a crown. They put it on Jesus' head. Then they put a purple robe on him. **3**They went up to him again and again. They kept saying, "We honor you, king of the Jews!" And they hit him in the face.

4Once more Pilate came out. He said to the Jews, "Look, I am bringing Jesus out to you. I want to let you know that I find no basis for a charge against him."

5Jesus came out wearing the crown of thorns and the purple robe. Then Pilate said to them, "Here is the man!"

6As soon as the chief priests and their officials saw him, they shouted, "Crucify him! Crucify him!"

But Pilate answered, "You take him and crucify him. I myself find no basis for a charge against him."

7The Jews replied, "We have a law. That law says he must die. He claimed to be the Son of God."

8When Pilate heard that, he was even more afraid. **9**He went back inside the palace. "Where do you come from?" he asked Jesus.

But Jesus did not answer him.

10"Do you refuse to speak to me?" Pilate said. "Don't you understand? I have the power to set you free or to nail you to a cross."

11Jesus answered, "You were given power from heaven. If you weren't, you would have no power over me. So the one who handed me over to you is guilty of a greater sin."

12From then on, Pilate tried to set Jesus free. But the Jews kept shouting, "If you let this man go, you are not Caesar's friend! Anyone who claims to be a king is against Caesar!"

13When Pilate heard that, he brought Jesus out. Pilate sat down on the judge's seat. It was at a place called The Stone Walkway. In the Aramaic language it was called Gabbatha. **14**It was about noon on Preparation Day in Passover Week.

"Here is your king," Pilate said to the Jews.

15But they shouted, "Kill him! Kill him! Crucify him!"

"Should I crucify your king?" Pilate asked.

"We have no king but Caesar," the chief priests answered.

16Finally, Pilate handed Jesus over to them to be nailed to a cross.

Jesus Is Nailed to a Cross

So the soldiers took charge of Jesus. **17**He had to carry his own cross. He went out to a place called The Skull. In the Aramaic language it was called Golgotha.

18There they nailed Jesus to the cross. Two other men were crucified with him. One was on each side of him. Jesus was in the middle.

19Pilate had a notice prepared. It was fastened to the cross. It read, JESUS OF NAZARETH, THE KING OF THE JEWS. **20**Many of the Jews read the sign. The place where Jesus was crucified was near the city. The sign was written in the Aramaic, Latin and Greek languages.

21The chief priests of the Jews argued with Pilate. They said, "Do not write 'The King of the Jews.' Write that this man claimed to be king of the Jews."

22Pilate answered, "I have written what I have written."

23When the soldiers crucified Jesus, they took his clothes. They divided them into four parts. Each soldier got one part. Jesus' long, inner robe was left. It did not have any seams. It was made out of one piece of cloth from top to bottom.

24"Let's not tear it," they said to one another. "Let's cast lots to see who will get it."

This happened so that Scripture would come true. It says,

"They divided up my clothes among them.
They cast lots for what I was wearing." *(Psalm 22:18)*

So that is what the soldiers did.

25Jesus' mother stood near his cross. So did his mother's sister, Mary the wife of Clopas, and Mary Magdalene.

26Jesus saw his mother there. He also saw the disciple he loved standing nearby. Jesus said to his mother, "Dear woman, here is your son." **27**He said to the disciple, "Here is your mother." From that time on, the disciple took her into his home.

Jesus Dies

28Later Jesus said, "I am thirsty." He knew that everything was now finished. He knew that what Scripture said must come true. **29**A jar of wine vinegar was there. So they soaked a sponge in it. They put the sponge on a stem of the hyssop plant. Then they lifted it up to Jesus' lips.

30After Jesus drank he said, "It is finished." Then he bowed his head and died.

31It was Preparation Day. The next day would be a special Sabbath. The Jews did not want the bodies left on the crosses during the Sabbath. So they asked Pilate to have the legs broken and the bodies taken down. **32**The soldiers came and broke the legs of the first man who had been crucified with Jesus. Then they broke the legs of the other man.

33But when they came to Jesus, they saw that he was already dead. So they did not break his legs. **34**Instead, one of the soldiers stuck his spear into Jesus' side. Right away, blood and water flowed out. **35**The man who saw it has given witness. And his witness is true. He knows that he tells the truth. He gives witness so that you also can believe.

36These things happened in order that Scripture would come true. It says, "Not one of his bones will be broken." *(Exodus 12:46; Numbers 9:12; Psalm 34:20)* **37**Scripture also says, "They will look to the one they have pierced." *(Zechariah 12:10)*

Jesus Is Buried

38Later Joseph asked Pilate for Jesus' body. Joseph was from the town of Arimathea. He was a follower of Jesus. But he followed Jesus secretly because he was afraid of the Jews. After Pilate gave him permission, Joseph came and took the body away.

39Nicodemus went with Joseph. He was the man who had earlier visited Jesus at night. Nicodemus brought some mixed spices, about 75 pounds. **40**The two men took Jesus' body. They wrapped it in strips of linen cloth, along with the spices. That was the way the Jews buried people's bodies.

41At the place where Jesus was crucified, there was a garden. A new tomb was there. No one had ever been put in it before. **42**That day was the Jewish Preparation Day, and the tomb was nearby. So they placed Jesus there.

JESUS DIES

JOHN 19:30

F

♥

B

After Jesus drank he said, "It is finished." Then he bowed his head and died.

Jesus gritted his teeth and shook and tried not to cry out as they pounded spikes through his hands and into the cross. But when they lifted the cross up and stuck it into its hole in the ground, the pain became unbearable. He groaned loudly.

Opening his eyes, Jesus looked down at all those gathered around his cross. He saw some of his disciples. He saw his mother and other women who had been with him during his ministry. He saw the soldiers who had pounded the nails. And he loved each one. He remembered that all of the pain, all of the terrible suffering, was for them. Each of those who would turn to him and ask forgiveness for their sins would be forgiven. Jesus' death on the cross meant they wouldn't have to die for their sins.

Jesus hung on that cross in agony all day. Late in the afternoon he yelled out in pain, then said in a loud voice, "It is finished." And he died.

JESUS WILLINGLY DIED A TERRIBLE DEATH SO WE COULD BE SAVED FROM OUR SINS.

Go to page 1248 for the next Super Hero

The Tomb Is Empty

20 Early on the first day of the week, Mary Magdalene went to the tomb. It was still dark. She saw that the stone had been moved away from the entrance. **2**So she ran to Simon Peter and another disciple, the one Jesus loved. She said, "They have taken the Lord out of the tomb! We don't know where they have put him!"

3So Peter and the other disciple started out for the tomb. **4**Both of them were running. The other disciple ran faster than Peter. He reached the tomb first. **5**He bent over and looked in at the strips of linen lying there. But he did not go in.

6Then Simon Peter, who was behind him, arrived. He went into the tomb. He saw the strips of linen lying there. **7**He also saw the burial cloth that had been around Jesus' head. The cloth was folded up by itself. It was separate from the linen.

8The disciple who had reached the tomb first also went inside. He saw and believed. **9**They still did not understand from Scripture that Jesus had to rise from the dead.

Jesus Appears to Mary Magdalene

10Then the disciples went back to their homes. **11**But Mary stood outside the tomb crying. As she cried, she bent over to look into the tomb. **12**She saw two angels dressed in white. They were seated where Jesus' body had been. One of them was where Jesus' head had been laid. The other sat where his feet had been placed.

13They asked her, "Woman, why are you crying?"

"They have taken my Lord away," she said. "I don't know where they have put him."

14Then she turned around and saw Jesus standing there. But she didn't realize that it was Jesus.

15"Woman," he said, "why are you crying? Who are you looking for?"

She thought he was the gardener. So she said, "Sir, did you carry him away? Tell me where you put him. Then I will go and get him."

16Jesus said to her, "Mary."

She turned toward him. Then she cried out in the Aramaic language, "Rabboni!" Rabboni means Teacher.

17Jesus said, "Do not hold on to me. I have not yet returned to the Father. Instead, go to those who believe in me. Tell them, 'I am returning to my Father and your Father, to my God and your God.' "

18Mary Magdalene went to the disciples with the news. She said, "I have seen the Lord!" And she told them that he had said these things to her.

Jesus Appears to His Disciples

19On the evening of that first day of the week, the disciples were together. They had locked the doors because they were afraid of the Jews.

Jesus came in and stood among them. He said, "May peace be with you!" **20**Then he showed them his hands and his side. The disciples were very happy when they saw the Lord.

21Again Jesus said, "May peace be with you! The Father has sent me. So now I am sending you." **22**He then breathed on them. He said, "Receive the Holy Spirit. **23**If you forgive anyone's sins, they are forgiven. If you do not forgive them, they are not forgiven."

Jesus Appears to Thomas

24Thomas was one of the Twelve. He was called Didymus. He was not with the other disciples when Jesus came. **25**So they told him, "We have seen the Lord!"

But he said to them, "First I must see the nail marks in his hands. I must put my finger where the nails were. I must put my hand into his side. Only then will I believe what you say."

26A week later, Jesus' disciples were in the house again. Thomas was with them. Even though the doors were locked, Jesus came in and stood among them.

He said, "May peace be with you!" **27**Then he said to Thomas, "Put your finger here. See my hands. Reach out your hand and put it into my side. Stop doubting and believe."

POWER–SURGE

BELIEVES †

THESE [WORDS] ARE WRITTEN DOWN SO THAT YOU MAY BELIEVE THAT JESUS IS THE CHRIST, THE SON OF GOD. IF YOU BELIEVE THIS, YOU WILL HAVE LIFE BECAUSE YOU BELONG TO HIM.
— JOHN 20:31 —

MARY MAGDALENE

JOHN 20:18

Mary Magdalene went to the disciples with the news. She said, "I have seen the Lord!"

Mary Magdalene (MAG-duh-leen) walked slowly along the garden path. The sunrise turned the sky from blue to pink. Mary carried a bag of spices and ointment. She wanted to be sure Jesus' body was properly anointed for burial.

Pushing back her veil, Mary looked at the grave up ahead. The stone had been moved away from the entrance! She dropped her spices and ran to tell the disciples. Scarcely able to catch her breath, SHE WAILED, "JESUS IS GONE!"

Mary tried to keep up with Peter and John as they ran back to the grave. Pressing her fingers into her aching side, she arrived just as they came out of the empty grave. They looked sadly at her.

Peter and John left, but Mary stood crying outside the grave. After a time she bent her teary face and looked inside. She was shocked to see two angels sitting right where Jesus' body had been. She shivered as they asked her, "Why are you crying?"

How could they not know? Mary thought to herself. "They've taken Jesus' body away, and I don't know where it is," she answered.

Turning at a sound behind her, Mary thought she saw the gardener. Maybe he knew something. "Sir, did you carry Jesus' body away? Tell me where you have put him!" Instead of answering her, the man gazed into Mary's eyes. Then he gently said just one word. "Mary!"

Instantly Mary realized this was no gardener. This was Jesus himself! He wasn't dead. He was alive. She ran as fast as she could to tell the good news to Peter and John.

BE A MARY MAGDALENE

Mary's love for Jesus made her eager to do whatever she could to help him. How can you be like Mary? Could you help someone in need? Could you tell someone about Jesus' love? There are many ways you can be like Mary. Be on the lookout. You'll find a way!

MARY DID WHATEVER SHE COULD TO SHOW JESUS HER LOVE FOR HIM.
THE WHOLE STORY: JOHN 20:1-18

Go to page **1249** for the next Super Hero

28Thomas said to him, "My Lord and my God!"

29Then Jesus told him, "Because you have seen me, you have believed. Blessed are those who have not seen me but still have believed."

30Jesus did many other miraculous signs in front of his disciples. They are not written down in this book. **31**But these are written down so that you may believe that Jesus is the Christ, the Son of God. If you believe this, you will have life because you belong to him.

Jesus Does a Miracle at the Sea

21 After this, Jesus appeared to his disciples again. It was by the Sea of Galilee. Here is what happened.

2Simon Peter and Thomas, who was called Didymus, were there together. Nathanael from Cana in Galilee and the sons of Zebedee were with them. So were two other disciples.

THOMAS

JOHN 20:27-28

Then he said to Thomas, "Put your finger here. See my hands. Reach out your hand and put it into my side. Stop doubting and believe." Thomas said to him, "My Lord and my God!"

Thomas stood silently in the room with the other disciples. He had not been there the first time Jesus appeared to them. But he was with them now. And so was Jesus.

The first time Jesus appeared, the disciples came and told Thomas about it. But he didn't believe them. He told them he wouldn't believe. "Unless I put my finger in the holes in his hands and in his side, I WILL NEVER BELIEVE THIS!" he vowed.

Jesus turned to look at Thomas and said, "Stop doubting, Thomas, and believe."

That's all it took. Thomas shook with the realization that Jesus was truly alive. He had no need to touch his scars. He simply fell at Jesus feet and said, "Jesus! You're my Lord and you're my God!"

BE A THOMAS

The important thing to remember about Thomas is not that he first doubted, but that he *did* believe. Most people doubt at one time or another. If you do, remember Thomas. Believe in Jesus and follow him.

THOMAS DOUBTED AT FIRST BUT THEN BELIEVED IN JESUS.

Go to page 1250 for the greatest Super Hero

³"I'm going out to fish," Simon Peter told them. They said, "We'll go with you." So they went out and got into the boat. That night they didn't catch anything.

⁴Early in the morning, Jesus stood on the shore. But the disciples did not realize that it was Jesus.

⁵He called out to them, "Friends, don't you have any fish?"

"No," they answered.

⁶He said, "Throw your net on the right side of the boat. There you will find some fish."

When they did, they could not pull the net into the boat. There were too many fish in it.

⁷Then the disciple Jesus loved said to Simon Peter, "It is the Lord!"

As soon as Peter heard that, he put his

JESUS DOES A MIRACLE

JOHN 21:6

[Jesus] said, "Throw your net on the right side of the boat. There you will find some fish." When they did, they could not pull the net into the boat. There were too many fish in it.

The sun was just peeking over the horizon when the disciples in their boat heard someone calling them from shore. The man's voice carried clearly over the water. "Have you caught any fish yet?"

"Not one," they called back.

The disciples had been fishing all night. They rowed to different parts of the lake and put down their nets. But they caught no fish.

"Put your net down on the other side of the boat," the man shouted.

The disciples looked at each other in surprise. What good would that do? But they swung the net from the left side of the boat and lowered it down into the water on the right side. The net was so full of fish they couldn't pull it into the boat. Only then did they realize that the stranger on shore was Jesus.

BE LIKE JESUS

Jesus' miracles always helped people. Sick people were made well. Blind people could see. And fishermen found fish. Be like Jesus. You might not perform miracles, but you can be helpful. In big ways and small ways, help those around you.

JESUS TOLD THE DISCIPLES HOW TO CATCH LOTS OF FISH.

Go to page 1255 for the next Super Hero

coat on. He had taken it off earlier. Then he jumped into the water.

⁸The other disciples followed in the boat. They were towing the net full of fish. The shore was only about 100 yards away. ⁹When they landed, they saw a fire of burning coals. There were fish on it. There was also some bread.

¹⁰Jesus said to them, "Bring some of the fish you have just caught."

¹¹Simon Peter climbed into the boat. He dragged the net to shore. It was full of large fish. There were 153 of them. But even with that many fish the net was not torn.

¹²Jesus said to them, "Come and have breakfast."

None of the disciples dared to ask him, "Who are you?" They knew it was the Lord.

¹³Jesus came, took the bread and gave it to them. He did the same thing with the fish. ¹⁴This was the third time Jesus appeared to his disciples after he was raised from the dead.

Jesus Takes Peter Back

¹⁵When Jesus and the disciples had finished eating, Jesus spoke to Simon Peter. He asked, "Simon, son of John, do you really love me more than these others do?"

"Yes, Lord," he answered. "You know that I love you."

Jesus said, "Feed my lambs."

¹⁶Again Jesus asked, "Simon, son of John, do you really love me?"

He answered, "Yes, Lord. You know that I love you."

Jesus said, "Take care of my sheep."

¹⁷Jesus spoke to him a third time. He asked, "Simon, son of John, do you love me?"

Peter felt bad because Jesus asked him the third time, "Do you love me?" He answered, "Lord, you know all things. You know that I love you."

Jesus said, "Feed my sheep. ¹⁸What I'm about to tell you is true. When you were younger, you dressed yourself. You went wherever you wanted to go. But when you are old, you will stretch out your hands. Someone else will dress you. Someone else will lead you where you do not want to go."

¹⁹Jesus said this to point out how Peter would die. His death would bring glory to God.

Then Jesus said to him, "Follow me!"

²⁰Peter turned around. He saw that the disciple Jesus loved was following them. He was the one who had leaned back against Jesus at the supper. He had said, "Lord, who is going to hand you over to your enemies?" ²¹When Peter saw that disciple, he asked, "Lord, what will happen to him?"

²²Jesus answered, "Suppose I want him to remain alive until I return. What does that matter to you? You must follow me."

²³Because of what Jesus said, a false report spread among the believers. The story was told that the disciple Jesus loved wouldn't die. But Jesus did not say he would not die. He only said, "Suppose I want him to remain alive until I return. What does that matter to you?"

²⁴This is the disciple who gives witness to these things. He also wrote them down. We know that his witness is true.

²⁵Jesus also did many other things. What if every one of them were written down? I suppose that even the whole world would not have room for the books that would be written.

ACTS

L uke writes of the beginnings of the church in the book of Acts.
He begins with how the truth of Jesus' life and death spreads
from Jerusalem to Israel and then around the world. He tells of
miracles and how the early believers live and die for their faith.
Read the book of Acts to see how the people of the early church
lived and how you can follow their example in bravely telling
others about Jesus.

HEROES IN THIS BOOK . . .

JESUS GOES TO HEAVEN
PAGE 1255

JOHN
PAGE 1259

BARNABAS
PAGE 1261

STEPHEN
PAGE 1263

PHILIP
PAGE 1268

SAUL/PAUL
PAGE 1270

TABITHA
PAGE 1272

CORNELIUS
PAGE 1274

Jesus Is Taken Up Into Heaven

1 Theophilus, I wrote about Jesus in my earlier book. I wrote about all he did and taught ²until the day he was taken up to heaven. Before Jesus left, he gave orders to the apostles he had chosen. He did this through the Holy Spirit. ³After his suffering and death, he appeared to them. In many ways he proved that he was alive. He appeared to them over a period of 40 days. During that time he spoke about God's kingdom.

⁴One day Jesus was eating with them. He gave them a command. "Do not leave Jerusalem," he said. "Wait for the gift my Father promised. You have heard me talk about it. ⁵John baptized with water. But in a few days you will be baptized with the Holy Spirit."

⁶When the apostles met together, they asked Jesus a question. "Lord," they said, "are you going to give the kingdom back to Israel now?"

⁷He said to them, "You should not be concerned about times or dates. The Father has set them by his own authority. ⁸But you will receive power when the Holy Spirit comes on you. Then you will be my witnesses in Jerusalem. You will be my witnesses in all Judea and Samaria. And you will be my witnesses from one end of the earth to the other."

⁹After Jesus said this, he was taken up to heaven. They watched until a cloud hid him from their sight.

¹⁰While he was going up, they kept on looking at the sky. Suddenly two men dressed in white clothing stood beside them. ¹¹"Men of Galilee," they said, "why do you stand here looking at the sky? Jesus has been taken away from you into heaven. But he will come back in the same way you saw him go."

Matthias Is Chosen to Take the Place of Judas

¹²The apostles returned to Jerusalem from the Mount of Olives. It is almost a mile from the city. ¹³When they arrived, they went upstairs to the room where they were staying. Peter, John, James and Andrew were there. Philip, Thomas, Bartholomew and Matthew were there too. So were James, son of Alphaeus, Simon the Zealot, and Judas, son of James. ¹⁴They all came together regularly to pray. The women joined them too. So did Jesus' mother Mary and his brothers.

¹⁵In those days Peter stood up among the believers. About 120 of them were there. ¹⁶Peter said, "Brothers, a long time ago the Holy Spirit spoke through David's mouth about Judas. What he said in Scripture had to come true. Judas was the guide for the men who arrested Jesus. ¹⁷But Judas was one of us. He shared with us in our work for God."

¹⁸Judas bought a field with the reward he got for the evil thing he had done. He fell down headfirst in the field. His body burst open. All his insides spilled out. ¹⁹Everyone in Jerusalem heard about this. So they called that field Akeldama. In their language, Akeldama means The Field of Blood.

²⁰Peter said, "Here is what is written in the book of Psalms. It says,

" 'May his home be deserted.
　　May no one live in it.'　　*(Psalm 69:25)*

The Psalms also say,

" 'Let someone else take his place as
　　leader.'　　*(Psalm 109:8)*

²¹So we need to choose someone to take his place. It will have to be a man who was with us the whole time the Lord Jesus lived among us. ²²That time began when John was baptizing. It ended when Jesus was taken up from us. The one we choose must join us in giving witness that Jesus rose from the dead."

²³So they suggested two men. One was Joseph, who was called Barsabbas. He was also called Justus. The other man was Matthias. ²⁴Then they prayed. "Lord," they said, "you know everyone's heart. Show us which of these two you have chosen. ²⁵Show us who should take the place of Judas as an apostle. He gave up being an apostle to go where he belongs." ²⁶Then they cast lots. Matthias was chosen. So he was added to the 11 apostles.

The Holy Spirit Comes at Pentecost

2 The day of Pentecost came. The believers all gathered in one place. ²Suddenly a sound came from heaven. It was like a strong wind blowing. It filled the whole house where they were sitting. ³They saw something that looked like tongues of fire. The flames separated and settled on each of them. ⁴All of them were filled with the Holy Spirit. They began to speak in languages they had not known before. The Spirit gave them the ability to do this.

⁵Godly Jews from every country in the world were staying in Jerusalem. ⁶A crowd came together when they heard the sound. They were bewildered because they each heard the believers speaking in

their own language. ⁷The crowd was really amazed. They asked, "Aren't all these people from Galilee? ⁸Why, then, do we each hear them speaking in our own native language? ⁹We are Parthians, Medes and Elamites. We live in Mesopotamia, Judea and Cappadocia. We are from Pontus, Asia, ¹⁰Phrygia and Pamphylia. Others of us are from Egypt and the parts of Libya near Cyrene. Still others are visitors from Rome. ¹¹Some of the visitors are Jews. Others have accepted the Jewish faith. Also, Cretans and Arabs are here. We hear all these people speaking about God's wonders in our own languages!" ¹²They were amazed and bewildered. They asked one another, "What does this mean?"

¹³But some people in the crowd made fun of the believers. "They've had too much wine!" they said.

Peter Speaks to the Crowd

¹⁴Then Peter stood up with the Eleven. In a loud voice he spoke to the crowd. "My Jewish friends," he said, "let me explain this to you. All of you who live in Jerusalem, listen carefully to what I say. ¹⁵You think these people are drunk. But

JESUS GOES TO HEAVEN

ACTS 1:8-9

"You will receive power when the Holy Spirit comes on you. Then you will be my witnesses...from one end of the earth to the other." After Jesus said this, he was taken up to heaven. They watched until a cloud hid him from their sight.

Forty days had passed since Jesus had died on Friday and come back to life on Sunday. He took the eleven disciples with him out into the country. They talked and laughed and listened to Jesus as they walked.

Jesus told them that he was leaving them, but that he would send the Holy Spirit in his place. He told them that they should spend the rest of their lives telling others about the good news they had discovered in Jesus' death and life. Then he raised his hands up and gave them a blessing.

With his hands in the air, Jesus began to rise toward the sky. The disciples watched as Jesus went up into heaven. They were sad to see him go. But Jesus' work on earth was finished.

BE LIKE JESUS

Jesus willingly did all that God asked him to do. Then, when his work was finished, he went back to heaven. He asks you to be willing also. Be like him and do whatever you think God is asking you to do.

JESUS WENT BACK TO HEAVEN WHEN HE FINISHED HIS WORK ON EARTH.

Go to page 1259 for the next Super Hero

they aren't. It's only nine o'clock in the morning! 16No, here is what the prophet Joel meant. 17He said,

" 'In the last days, God says,
 I will pour out my Holy Spirit on all
  people.
 Your sons and daughters will prophesy.
 Your young men will see visions.
 Your old men will have dreams.
18 In those days I will pour out my Spirit
  even on those who serve me, both
   men and women.
 When I do, they will prophesy.
19 I will show wonders in the heavens
  above.
 I will show miraculous signs on the
  earth below.
 There will be blood and fire and
  clouds of smoke.
20 The sun will become dark.
 The moon will turn red like blood.
 This will happen before the coming
  of the great and glorious day of
  the Lord.
21 Everyone who calls
 on the name of the Lord will be
  saved.'   *(Joel 2:28–32)*

22 "Men of Israel, listen to this! Jesus of Nazareth was a man who had God's approval. God did miracles, wonders and signs among you through Jesus. You yourselves know this. 23Long ago God planned that Jesus would be handed over to you. With the help of evil people, you put Jesus to death. You nailed him to the cross. 24But God raised him from the dead. He set him free from the suffering of death. It wasn't possible for death to keep its hold on Jesus. 25David spoke about him. He said,

" 'I know that the Lord is always with
  me.
 He is at my right hand.
 I will always be secure.
26 So my heart is glad. Joy is on my
  tongue.
 My body also will be full of hope.
27 You will not leave me in the grave.
 You will not let your Holy One rot
  away.
28 You always show me the path that
  leads to life.
 You will fill me with joy when I am
  with you.'   *(Psalm 16:8–11)*

29 "Brothers, you can be sure that King David died. He was buried. His tomb is still here today. 30But David was a prophet. He knew that God had made a promise to him. He had taken an oath that some-

one in David's family line would be king after him. 31David saw what was ahead. So he spoke about the Christ rising from the dead. He said that the Christ would not be left in the grave. His body wouldn't rot in the ground. 32God has raised this same Jesus back to life. We are all witnesses of this. 33Jesus has been given a place of honor at the right hand of God. He has received the Holy Spirit from the Father. This is what God had promised. It is Jesus who has poured out what you now see and hear. 34David did not go up to heaven. But he said,

" 'The Lord said to my Lord,
 "Sit at my right hand.
35 I will put your enemies
  under your control." '   *(Psalm 110:1)*

36 "So be sure of this, all you people of Israel. You nailed Jesus to the cross. But God has made him both Lord and Christ."

37 When the people heard this, their hearts were filled with shame. They said to Peter and the other apostles, "Brothers, what should we do?"

38 Peter replied, "All of you must turn away from your sins and be baptized in the name of Jesus Christ. Then your sins will be forgiven. You will receive the gift of the Holy Spirit. 39The promise is for you and your children. It is also for all who are far away. It is for all whom the Lord our God will choose."

40 Peter said many other things to warn them. He begged them, "Save yourselves from these evil people." 41Those who accepted his message were baptized. About 3,000 people joined the believers that day.

The Believers Share Life Together

42 The believers studied what the apostles taught. They shared life together. They broke bread and ate together. And they prayed. 43Everyone felt that God was near. The apostles did many wonders and miraculous signs. 44All the believers were together. They shared everything they had. 45They sold what they owned. They gave each other everything they needed. 46Every day they met together in the temple courtyard. In their homes they broke bread and ate together. Their hearts were glad and honest and true. 47They praised God. They were respected by all the people. Every day the Lord added to their group those who were being saved.

Peter Heals the Disabled Beggar

3 One day Peter and John were going up to the temple. It was three o'clock in the afternoon. It was the time for prayer. ²A man unable to walk was being carried to the temple gate called Beautiful. He had been that way since he was born. Every day someone put him near the gate. There he would beg from people going into the temple courtyards.

³He saw that Peter and John were about to enter. So he asked them for money. ⁴Peter looked straight at him, and so did John. Then Peter said, "Look at us!" ⁵So the man watched them closely. He expected to get something from them.

⁶Peter said, "I don't have any silver or gold. But I'll give you what I have. In the name of Jesus Christ of Nazareth, get up and walk." ⁷Then Peter took him by the right hand and helped him up. At once the man's feet and ankles became strong. ⁸He jumped to his feet and began to walk. He went with Peter and John into the temple courtyards. He walked and jumped and praised God. ⁹All the people saw him walking and praising God. ¹⁰They recognized him as the same man who used to sit and beg at the temple gate called Beautiful. They were filled with wonder. They were amazed at what had happened to him.

Peter Speaks to the Jews

¹¹The beggar was holding on to Peter and John. All the people were amazed.

POWER-SURGE

GIVING　**G**

ALL THE BELIEVERS WERE TOGETHER. THEY SHARED EVERYTHING THEY HAD...THEY GAVE EACH OTHER EVERYTHING THEY NEEDED...THEIR HEARTS WERE GLAD AND HONEST AND TRUE.
— ACTS 2:44-46 —

KIND　**K**

POWER-SURGE

BELIEVES　†

THIS MAN WHOM YOU SEE AND KNOW WAS MADE STRONG BECAUSE OF FAITH IN JESUS' NAME. FAITH IN JESUS HAS HEALED HIM COMPLETELY. YOU CAN SEE IT WITH YOUR OWN EYES.
— ACTS 3:16 —

STRONG

They came running to them at Solomon's Porch. ¹²When Peter saw this, he said, "Men of Israel, why does this surprise you? Why do you stare at us? We haven't made this man walk by our own power or godliness. ¹³The God of our fathers, Abraham, Isaac and Jacob, has done this. He has brought glory to Jesus, who serves him. But you handed Jesus over to be killed. Pilate had decided to let him go. But you spoke against Jesus when he was in Pilate's court. ¹⁴You spoke against the Holy and Blameless One. You asked for a murderer to be set free instead. ¹⁵You killed the one who gives life. But God raised him from the dead. We are witnesses of this. ¹⁶This man whom you see and know was made strong because of faith in Jesus' name. Faith in Jesus has healed him completely. You can see it with your own eyes.

¹⁷"My friends, I know you didn't realize what you were doing. Neither did your leaders. ¹⁸But God had given a promise through all the prophets. And this is how he has made his promise come true. He said that his Christ would suffer. ¹⁹So turn away from your sins. Turn to God. Then your sins will be wiped away. The time will come when the Lord will make everything new. ²⁰He will send the Christ. Jesus has been appointed as the Christ for you. ²¹He must remain in heaven until the time when God makes everything new. He promised this long ago through his holy prophets. ²²Moses said, 'The Lord your God will raise up for you a prophet

like me. He will be one of your own people. You must listen to everything he tells you. 23Those who do not listen to him will be completely cut off from their people.' *(Deuteronomy 18:15,18,19)*

24"Samuel and all the prophets after him spoke about this. They said these days would come. 25What the prophets said was meant for you. The covenant God made with your people long ago is yours also. He said to Abraham, 'All nations on earth will be blessed through your children.' *(Genesis 22:18; 26:4)* 26God raised up Jesus, who serves him. God sent him first to you. He did it to bless you. He wanted to turn each of you from your evil ways."

Peter and John Are Taken to the Sanhedrin

4 Peter and John were speaking to the people. The priests, the captain of the temple guard, and the Sadducees came up to the apostles. 2They were very upset by what the apostles were teaching the people. The apostles were saying that because Jesus rose from the dead, people can be raised from the dead. 3So the temple authorities arrested Peter and John. It was already evening, so they put them in prison until the next day. 4But many who heard the message believed. The number of men who believed grew to about 5,000.

5The next day the rulers, the elders and the teachers of the law met in Jerusalem. 6Annas, the high priest, was there. So were Caiaphas, John, Alexander and others in the high priest's family. 7They had Peter and John brought to them. They wanted to question them. "By what power did you do this?" they asked. "And through whose name?"

8Peter was filled with the Holy Spirit. He said to them, "Rulers and elders of the people! 9Are you asking us to explain our actions today? Do you want to know why we were kind to a disabled man? Are you asking how he was healed? 10Then listen to this, you and all the people of Israel! You nailed Jesus Christ of Nazareth to the cross. But God raised him from the dead. It is through Jesus' name that this man stands healed in front of you. 11Scripture says that Jesus is

" 'the stone you builders did not
        accept.
    But it has become the most
        important stone of all.'
                              (Psalm 118:22)

12You can't be saved by believing in anyone else. God has given us no other name under heaven that will save us."

13The leaders saw how bold Peter and John were. They also realized that Peter and John were ordinary men with no training. This surprised the leaders. They realized that these men had been with Jesus. 14The leaders could see the man who had been healed standing there with them. So there was nothing they could say. 15They ordered Peter and John to leave the Sanhedrin. Then they talked things over. 16"What can we do with these men?" they asked. "Everybody in Jerusalem knows they have done an outstanding miracle. We can't say it didn't happen. 17We have to stop this thing. It must not spread any further among the people. We have to warn these men. They must never speak to anyone in Jesus' name again."

18Once again the leaders called in Peter and John. They commanded them not to speak or teach at all in Jesus' name. 19But Peter and John replied, "Judge for yourselves. Which is right from God's point of view? Should we obey you? Or God? 20There's nothing else we can do. We have to speak about the things we've seen and heard."

21The leaders warned them again. Then they let them go. They couldn't decide how to punish Peter and John. They knew that all the people were praising God for what had happened. 22The man who had been healed by the miracle was over 40 years old.

The Believers Pray

23Peter and John were allowed to leave. They went back to their own people. They reported everything the chief priests and

POWER-SURGE

BELIEVES ✝

MANY WHO HEARD THE MESSAGE BELIEVED. THE NUMBER OF MEN WHO BELIEVED GREW TO ABOUT 5,000.
— ACTS 4:4 —

TELLS OTHERS

the elders had said to them. 24When the
believers heard this, they raised their
voices together in prayer to God. "Lord
and King," they said, "you made the heavens, the earth and the sea. You made
everything in them. 25Long ago you
spoke by the Holy Spirit through the
mouth of our father David, who served
you. You said,

" 'Why are the nations angry?
    Why do the people make useless
        plans?
26 The kings of the earth take their stand
        against the Lord.
    The rulers of the earth gather
        together
    against his Anointed King.'

(Psalm 2:1,2)

JOHN

ACTS 4:13

B

*The leaders saw how bold Peter and John
were. They also realized that Peter and John
were ordinary men with no training. This
surprised the leaders. They realized that
these men had been with Jesus.*

†

John and Peter stood before some important Jewish officials.
The officials were angry because John and Peter had healed
a disabled man. And because they were teaching the people to
follow Jesus.

"WHERE ARE YOU GETTING THE POWER TO DO THIS?"
they asked.

John and Peter looked at each other and then answered the
questions bravely and clearly. They knew Jesus was with them,
so they weren't afraid. John and Peter told the officials about
Jesus, how he had died because these very officials hated him
and how he had come back to life.

The officials knew that John and Peter were only fishermen.
They were surprised at how brave and well-educated they acted.
And they could only think of one reason for this: John and Peter had been with Jesus. Jesus gave them courage and the right
words to speak.

BE A JOHN

John was in a dangerous situation. These officials had the right
to punish him. But he only knew one thing: He *had* to speak
clearly and freely about Jesus. Be like John. You may think you
don't have the courage, but you do. Your courage comes from
the same place John got his—from Jesus.

**JOHN BRAVELY TALKED ABOUT JESUS EVEN WHEN
HE WAS IN DANGER.**

Go to page 1261 for the next Super Hero

27"In fact, Herod and Pontius Pilate met together in this city with those who weren't Jews. They also met with the people of Israel. All of them made plans against your holy servant Jesus. He is the one you anointed. **28**They did what your power and purpose had already decided should happen. **29**Now, Lord, consider the bad things they say they are going to do. Help us to be very bold when we speak your word. **30**Stretch out your hand to heal. Do miraculous signs and wonders through the name of your holy servant Jesus."

31After they prayed, the place where they were meeting was shaken. They were all filled with the Holy Spirit. They were bold when they spoke God's word.

The Believers Share What They Own

32All the believers were agreed in heart and mind. They didn't claim that anything they had was their own. They shared everything they owned. **33**With great power the apostles continued their teaching. They gave witness that the Lord Jesus had risen from the dead. And they were greatly blessed by God.

34There were no needy persons among them. From time to time, those who owned land or houses sold them. They brought the money from the sales. **35**They put it down at the apostles' feet. It was then given out to anyone who needed it.

36Joseph was a Levite from Cyprus. The apostles called him Barnabas. The name Barnabas means Son of Help. **37**Barnabas sold a field he owned. He brought the money from the sale. He put it down at the apostles' feet.

Ananias and Sapphira

5 A man named Ananias and his wife, Sapphira, also sold some land. **2**He kept part of the money for himself. Sapphira knew he had kept it. He brought the rest of it and put it down at the apostles' feet.

3Then Peter said, "Ananias, why did you let Satan fill your heart? He made you lie to the Holy Spirit. You have kept some of the money you received for the land. **4**Didn't the land belong to you before it was sold? After it was sold, you could have used the money as you wished. What made you think of doing such a thing? You haven't lied to just anyone. You've lied to God."

5When Ananias heard this, he fell down and died. All who heard what had hap-pened were filled with fear. **6**Some young men came and wrapped up his body. They carried him out and buried him.

7About three hours later, the wife of Ananias came in. She didn't know what had happened. **8**Peter asked her, "Tell me. Is this the price you and Ananias sold the land for?"

"Yes," she said. "That's the price."

9Peter asked her, "How could you agree to test the Spirit of the Lord? Listen! You can hear the steps of the men who buried your husband. They are at the door. They will carry you out also."

10At that very moment she fell down at his feet and died. Then the young men came in. They saw that Sapphira was dead. So they carried her out and buried her beside her husband. **11**The whole church and all who heard about these things were filled with fear.

The Apostles Heal Many People

12The apostles did many miraculous signs and wonders among the people. All the believers used to meet together at Solomon's Porch. **13**No outsider dared to join them. But the people thought highly of them. **14**More and more men and women believed in the Lord. They joined the other believers. **15**So people brought those who were sick into the streets. They placed them on beds and mats. They hoped that at least Peter's shadow might fall on some of them as he walked by. **16**Crowds even gathered from the towns around Jerusalem. They brought their sick. They also brought those who were suffering because of evil spirits. All of them were healed.

An Angel Opens the Prison Doors

17The high priest and all his companions were Sadducees. They were very jealous of the apostles. **18**So they arrested them and put them in the public prison. **19**But during the night an angel of the Lord came. He opened the prison doors and brought the apostles out. **20**"Go! Stand in the temple courtyard," the angel said. "Tell the people all about this new life."

21Early the next day they did as they had been told. They entered the temple courtyard. There they began to teach the people.

The high priest and his companions arrived. They called the Sanhedrin together. The Sanhedrin was a gathering of all the elders of Israel. They sent for the apostles who were in prison. **22**The officers arrived at the prison. But they didn't find the apostles there. So they went back and reported it. **23**"We found the prison locked up tight," they said. "The guards were standing at the doors. But when we opened the doors, we didn't find anyone

BARNABAS

ACTS 4:37

G ★ K

Barnabas sold a field he owned. He brought the money from the sale. He put it down at the apostles' feet.

Barnabas (BAR-nuh-bus) walked up to the crowd of people around the disciples. Wherever Jesus' former disciples went, a crowd followed, eager to hear their teaching. Today was no different.

The bag of money Barnabas carried came from a field he had owned for several years. Barnabas had just sold the field. Barnabas loved to help others, sometimes by giving them jobs or by giving them money or food or whatever else they needed. This time would be no different.

Coming to the apostles, **BARNABAS LAID THE BAG OF MONEY AT THEIR FEET.**

"I've sold my field," he told them. "Here is the money to use however you think it should be used."

BE A BARNABAS

This is just the first time the Bible tells us about Barnabas and his love for giving. He went on to be a missionary with Paul, going from one country to the next to tell others about Jesus. Be a Barnabas, and be a giver. You don't have any money to give? That's OK. Give of yourself. Give your time. Give a kind word. There are many ways to give if you just look around to discover what others need.

BARNABAS WAS A GIVER.

Go to page 1263 for the next Super Hero

inside." 24When the captain of the temple guard and the chief priests heard this report, they were bewildered. They wondered what would happen next.

25Then someone came and said, "Look! The men you put in prison are standing in the temple courtyard. They are teaching the people." 26So the captain went with his officers and brought the apostles back. But they didn't use force. They were afraid the people would kill them by throwing stones at them.

27They brought the apostles to be judged by the Sanhedrin. The high priest questioned them. 28"We gave you clear orders not to teach in Jesus' name," he said. "But you have filled Jerusalem with your teaching. You want to make us guilty of this man's death."

29Peter and the other apostles replied, "We must obey God instead of people! 30You had Jesus killed by nailing him to a cross. But the God of our people raised Jesus from the dead. 31Now Jesus is Prince and Savior. God has proved this by giving him a place of honor at his own right hand. He did it so that he could turn Israel away from their sins and forgive them. 32We are witnesses of these things. And so is the Holy Spirit. God has given the Spirit to those who obey him."

33When the leaders heard this, they became very angry. They wanted to put the apostles to death. 34But a Pharisee named Gamaliel stood up in the Sanhedrin. He was a teacher of the law. He was honored by all the people. He ordered the men to be taken outside for a little while. 35Then he spoke to the Sanhedrin. "Men of Israel," he said, "think carefully about what you plan to do to these men. 36Some time ago Theudas appeared. He claimed he was really somebody. About 400 people followed him. But he was killed. All his followers were scattered. So they accomplished nothing. 37After this, Judas from Galilee came along. This was in the days when the Romans made a list of all the people. Judas led a gang of men against the Romans. He too was killed. All his followers were scattered. 38So let me give you some advice. Leave these men alone! Let them go! If their plans and actions are only human, they will fail. 39But if their plans come from God, you won't be able to stop these men. You will only find yourselves fighting against God."

40His speech won the leaders over. They called the apostles in and had them whipped. The leaders ordered them not to speak in Jesus' name. Then they let the apostles go.

41The apostles were full of joy as they left the Sanhedrin. They considered it an honor to suffer shame for the name of Jesus. 42Day after day, they kept teaching in the temple courtyards and from house to house. They never stopped telling the good news that Jesus is the Christ.

Seven Leaders Are Chosen

6 In those days the number of believers was growing. The Jews who followed Greek practices complained against the Jews who followed only Jewish practices. They said that the widows of men who followed Greek practices were not being taken care of. They weren't getting their fair share of food each day. 2So the Twelve gathered all the believers together. They said, "It wouldn't be right for us to give up teaching God's word in order to wait on tables. 3Brothers, choose seven of your men. They must be known as men who are wise and full of the Holy Spirit. We will turn this important work over to them. 4Then we can give our attention to prayer and to teaching the word."

5This plan pleased the whole group. They chose Stephen. He was full of faith and of the Holy Spirit. Philip, Procorus, Nicanor, Timon and Parmenas were chosen too. The group also chose Nicolas from Antioch. He had accepted the Jewish faith. 6The group brought them to the apostles. Then the apostles prayed and placed their hands on them.

7So God's word spread. The number of believers in Jerusalem grew quickly. Also, a large number of priests began to obey Jesus' teachings.

Stephen Is Arrested

8Stephen was full of God's grace and power. He did great wonders and miraculous signs among the people. 9But members of the group called the Synagogue of the Freedmen began to oppose him. Some of them were Jews from Cyrene and Alexandria. Others were Jews from Cilicia and Asia Minor. They all began to argue with Stephen. 10But he was too wise for them. They couldn't stand up against the Holy Spirit who spoke through him.

11Then in secret they talked some men into lying about Stephen. They said, "We heard Stephen speak evil things against Moses. He also spoke evil things against God."

12So the people were stirred up. The elders and the teachers of the law were

STEPHEN

ACTS 6:8

B

Stephen was full of God's grace and power.

Stephen stood still in the hot sun and looked at the angry faces that surrounded him on all sides. He took a shaky breath. He watched as the men around him picked up rocks. Small rocks. Big rocks. One man used his foot to dig out a huge rock from the dirt. He tossed it up in the air several times, to make sure his aim would be on target.

The target—Stephen—watched as some other men took their coats off and tossed them at the feet of a man named Saul. SWEAT DRIPPED DOWN STEPHEN'S FACE.

They planned to throw their rocks at Stephen and kill him.

Stephen knew what they were planning. But he bravely stood his ground. Instead of looking at all the faces around him, Stephen raised his eyes to the sky. What he saw there amazed him. The sky split open and gave Stephen a view straight into heaven. What a sight! The glory of God was shining right down from heaven onto Stephen. He saw Jesus standing next to God. Stephen burst out, "Look! I see heaven open. The Son of Man is standing at God's right hand."

Now the men around Stephen became even more angry. How dare he claim to see God! A man shouted at Stephen, then threw the first rock. Once it hurdled through the air, hundreds more followed, hitting Stephen like torpedoes . . . The stones hit his arms, his chest, his head. Some barely hurt. Others hurt a lot, bumping and bruising him.

One by one the stones wore down Stephen. He sank to his knees. Stephen was dying. He knew it. He prayed one last prayer before he breathed his last breath. "Jesus, take me to be with you. And forgive these men for what they're doing." Then, Stephen died.

BE A STEPHEN

You will probably never be killed for following Jesus. But you may be mocked or laughed at. Be a Stephen. Be strong and brave in the face of those who make fun of you. When others want you to do things you know you shouldn't do, be a Stephen. Like he did with Stephen, Jesus will give you strength to stand your ground, to stand up for what you believe in. You just have to ask and trust him.

STEPHEN BRAVELY FOLLOWED JESUS, EVEN WHEN IT MEANT HE HAD TO DIE.

THE WHOLE STORY: ACTS 6:8—8:3

Go to page 1268 for the next Super Hero

stirred up too. They arrested Stephen and brought him to the Sanhedrin. **13**They found people who were willing to tell lies. The false witnesses said, "This fellow never stops speaking against this holy place. He also speaks against the law. **14**We have heard him say that this Jesus of Nazareth will destroy this place. He says Jesus will change the practices that Moses handed down to us."

15All who were sitting in the Sanhedrin looked right at Stephen. They saw that his face was like the face of an angel.

Stephen Speaks to the Sanhedrin

7 Then the high priest questioned Stephen. "Is what these people are saying true?" he asked.

2"Brothers and fathers, listen to me!" Stephen replied. "The God of glory appeared to our father Abraham. At that time Abraham was still in Mesopotamia. He had not yet begun living in Haran. **3**'Leave your country and your people,' God said. 'Go to the land I will show you.' *(Genesis 12:1)*

4"So Abraham left the land of Babylonia. He settled in Haran. After his father died, God sent Abraham to this land where you are now living. **5**God didn't give him any property here. He didn't give him even a foot of land. But God made a promise to him and to all his family after him. He said they would possess the land. The promise was made even though at that time Abraham had no child.

6"Here is what God said to him. 'Your family after you will be strangers in a country that is not their own. They will be slaves and will be treated badly for 400 years. **7**But I will punish the nation that makes them slaves,' God said. 'After that, they will leave that country and worship me here.' *(Genesis 15:13,14)*

8"Then God made a covenant with Abraham. God told him that circumcision would show who the members of the covenant were. Abraham became Isaac's father. He circumcised Isaac eight days after he was born. Later, Isaac became Jacob's father. Jacob had 12 sons. They became the founders of the 12 tribes of Israel.

9"Jacob's sons were jealous of their brother Joseph. So they sold him as a slave. He was taken to Egypt. But God was with him. **10**He saved Joseph from all his troubles. God made Joseph wise. He helped him to become the friend of Pharaoh, the king of Egypt. So Pharaoh made Joseph ruler over Egypt and his whole palace.

11"There was not enough food for all Egypt and Canaan. This brought great suffering. Jacob and his sons couldn't find food. **12**But Jacob heard that there was grain in Egypt. So he sent his sons on their first visit. **13**On their second visit, Joseph told his brothers who he was. Pharaoh learned about Joseph's family.

14"After this, Joseph sent for his father Jacob and his whole family. The total number of people was 75. **15**Then Jacob went down to Egypt. There he and his family died. **16**Some of their bodies were brought back to Shechem. They were placed in a tomb Abraham had bought. He had purchased it from Hamor's sons at Shechem for a certain amount of money.

17"In Egypt the number of our people grew and grew. It was nearly time for God to make his promise to Abraham come true. **18**Another king became ruler of Egypt. He knew nothing about Joseph. **19**He was very evil and dishonest with our people. He beat them down. He forced them to throw out their newborn babies to die.

20"At that time Moses was born. He was not an ordinary child. For three months he was taken care of by his family. **21**Then he was placed outside. But Pharaoh's daughter took him home. She brought him up as her own son. **22**Moses was taught all the knowledge of the people of Egypt. He became a powerful speaker and a man of action.

23"When Moses was 40 years old, he decided to visit the people of Israel. They were his own people. **24**He saw one of them being treated badly by a man of

POWER-SURGE

STRONG

MOSES WAS TAUGHT ALL THE KNOWLEDGE OF THE PEOPLE OF EGYPT. HE BECAME A POWERFUL SPEAKER AND A MAN OF ACTION.
— ACTS 7:22 —

TRIES HARD

Egypt. So he went to help him. He got even by killing the man. **25**Moses thought his own people would realize that God was using him to save them. But they didn't.

26"The next day Moses saw two men of Israel fighting. He tried to make peace between them. 'Men, you are both of Israel,' he said. 'Why do you want to hurt each other?'

27"But the man who was treating the other one badly pushed Moses to one side. He said, 'Who made you ruler and judge over us? **28**Do you want to kill me as you killed the Egyptian yesterday?' *(Exodus 2:14)* **29**When Moses heard this, he escaped to Midian. He lived there as a stranger. He became the father of two sons there.

30"Forty years passed. Then an angel appeared to Moses in the flames of a burning bush. This happened in the desert near Mount Sinai. **31**When Moses saw the bush, he was amazed. He went over for a closer look. There he heard the Lord's voice. **32**'I am the God of your fathers,' the Lord said. 'I am the God of Abraham, Isaac and Jacob.' *(Exodus 3:6)* Moses shook with fear. He didn't dare to look.

33"Then the Lord said to him, 'Take off your sandals. The place you are standing on is holy ground. **34**I have seen my people beaten down in Egypt. I have heard their groans. I have come down to set them free. Now come. I will send you back to Egypt.' *(Exodus 3:5,7,8,10)*

35"This is the same Moses the two men of Israel would not accept. They had said, 'Who made you ruler and judge?' But God himself sent Moses to rule the people of Israel and set them free. He spoke to Moses through the angel who had appeared to him in the bush. **36**So Moses led them out of Egypt. He did wonders and miraculous signs in Egypt, at the Red Sea, and for 40 years in the desert.

37"This is the same Moses who spoke to the people of Israel. 'God will send you a prophet,' he said. 'He will be like me. He will come from your own people.' *(Deuteronomy 18:15)* **38**Moses was with the Israelites in the desert. He was with the angel who spoke to him on Mount Sinai. Moses was with our people of long ago. He received living words to pass on to us.

39"But our people refused to obey Moses. They would not accept him. In their hearts, they wished they were back in Egypt. **40**They told Aaron, 'Make us a god who will lead us. This fellow Moses led us out of Egypt. But we don't know what has

happened to him!' *(Exodus 32:1)* **41**That was the time they made a statue to be their god. It looked like a calf. They brought sacrifices to it. They were glad because of what they had made with their own hands. **42**But God turned away from them. He left them to worship the sun, moon and stars. This agrees with what is written in the book of the prophets. There it says,

" 'People of Israel, did you bring me
    sacrifices and offerings
for 40 years in the desert?
43You lifted up the place where Molech
    was worshiped.
You lifted up the star of your god
    Rephan.
You made statues of them to
    worship.
So I will send you away from your
    country.'   *(Amos 5:25–27)*
God sent them to Babylon and even
    farther.

44"Long ago our people had with them in the desert the holy tent where the tablets of the covenant were kept. Moses had made the holy tent as God had commanded him. It was made like the pattern he had seen. **45**Our people received the tent from God. They brought it with them when they took the land of Canaan. God drove out the nations that were in their way. At that time Joshua was Israel's leader.

"The tent remained in the land until David's time. **46**David was blessed by God. So David asked if he could build a house for the God of Jacob. **47**Instead, it was Solomon who built it for him.

48"But the Most High God does not live in houses made by human hands. As God says through the prophet,

49" 'Heaven is my throne.
The earth is under my control.
What kind of house will you build for
    me?
                says the Lord.
Where will my resting place be?
50Didn't my hand make all these
    things?'   *(Isaiah 66:1,2)*

51"You people! You won't obey! You are stubborn! You won't listen! You are just like your people of long ago! You always oppose the Holy Spirit! **52**Was there ever a prophet your people didn't try to hurt? They even killed those who told about the coming of the Blameless One. And now you have handed him over to his enemies. You have murdered him. **53**The law you received was brought by angels. But you haven't obeyed it."

Stephen Is Killed

54When the Sanhedrin heard this, they became very angry. They ground their teeth at Stephen. 55But he was full of the Holy Spirit. He looked up to heaven and saw God's glory. He saw Jesus standing at God's right hand. 56"Look!" he said. "I see heaven open. The Son of Man is standing at God's right hand."

57When the Sanhedrin heard this, they covered their ears. They yelled at the top of their voices. They all rushed at him. 58They dragged him out of the city. They began to throw stones at him to kill him. The witnesses took off their coats. They placed them at the feet of a young man named Saul.

59While the members of the Sanhedrin were throwing stones at Stephen, he prayed. "Lord Jesus, receive my spirit," he said. 60Then he fell on his knees. He cried out, "Lord! Don't hold this sin against them!" When he had said this, he died.

8 Saul was there. He had agreed that Stephen should die.

The Church Is Scattered

On that day the church in Jerusalem began to be attacked and treated badly. All except the apostles were scattered throughout Judea and Samaria.

2Godly Jews buried Stephen. They sobbed and sobbed over him.

3But Saul began to destroy the church. He went from house to house. He dragged men and women away and put them in prison.

Philip Goes to Samaria

4The believers who had been scattered preached the word everywhere they went. 5Philip went down to a city in Samaria. There he preached about the Christ. 6The crowds listened to Philip. They saw the miraculous signs he did. They all paid close attention to what he said. 7Evil spirits screamed and came out of many people. Many who were disabled or who couldn't walk were healed. 8So there was great joy in that city.

Simon the Evil Magician

9A man named Simon lived in the city. For quite a while he had practiced evil magic there. He amazed all the people of Samaria. He claimed to be someone great. 10All of the people listened to him, from the least important of them to the most

POWER–SURGE

BELIEVES ✝

PHILIP PREACHED THE GOOD NEWS OF GOD'S KINGDOM. HE PREACHED THE NAME OF JESUS CHRIST. SO MEN AND WOMEN BELIEVED AND WERE BAPTIZED.
— ACTS 8:12 —

TELLS OTHERS

important. They exclaimed, "This man is known as the Great Power of God!" 11He had amazed them for a long time with his magic. So they followed him.

12But Philip preached the good news of God's kingdom. He preached the name of Jesus Christ. So men and women believed and were baptized. 13Simon himself believed and was baptized. He followed Philip everywhere. He was amazed by the great signs and miracles he saw.

14The apostles in Jerusalem heard that people in Samaria had accepted God's word. So they sent Peter and John to them. 15When they arrived there, they prayed that the believers would receive the Holy Spirit. 16The Holy Spirit had not yet come on any of them. They had only been baptized in the name of the Lord Jesus. 17Then Peter and John placed their hands on them. And they received the Holy Spirit.

18Simon watched as the apostles placed their hands on them. He saw that the Spirit was given to them. So he offered money to Peter and John. 19He said, "Give me this power too. Then everyone I place my hands on will receive the Holy Spirit."

20Peter answered, "May your money be destroyed with you! Do you think you can buy God's gift with money? 21You have no part or share in this holy work. Your heart is not right with God. 22Turn away from this evil sin of yours. Pray to the Lord. Perhaps he will forgive you for having such a thought in your heart. 23I see that you are very bitter. You are a prisoner of sin."

24Then Simon answered, "Pray to the Lord for me. Pray that nothing you have said will happen to me."

25Peter and John gave witness and preached the Lord's word. Then they returned to Jerusalem. On the way they preached the good news in many villages in Samaria.

Philip and the Man From Ethiopia

26An angel of the Lord spoke to Philip. "Go south to the desert road," he said. "It's the road that goes down from Jerusalem to Gaza." **27**So Philip started out. On his way he met an Ethiopian official. The man had an important position. He was in charge of all the wealth of Candace. She was the queen of Ethiopia. He had gone to Jerusalem to worship. **28**On his way home he was sitting in his chariot. He was reading the book of Isaiah the prophet. **29**The Holy Spirit told Philip, "Go to that chariot. Stay near it."

30So Philip ran up to the chariot. He heard the man reading Isaiah the prophet. "Do you understand what you're reading?" Philip asked.

31"How can I?" he said. "I need someone to explain it to me." So he invited Philip to come up and sit with him.

32Here is the part of Scripture the official was reading. It says,

"He was led like a sheep to be killed.
   Just as lambs are silent while their
      wool is being cut off,
   he did not open his mouth.
33 When he was treated badly, he was
      refused a fair trial.
   Who can say anything about his
      children?
   His life was cut off from the earth."
      (Isaiah 53:7,8)

34The official said to Philip, "Tell me, please. Who is the prophet talking about? Himself, or someone else?" **35**Then Philip began with that same part of Scripture. He told him the good news about Jesus.

36/37 As they traveled along the road, they came to some water. The official said, "Look! Here is water! Why shouldn't I be baptized?" **38**He gave orders to stop the chariot. Then both Philip and the official went down into the water. Philip baptized him. **39**When they came up out of the water, the Spirit of the Lord suddenly took Philip away. The official did not see him again. He went on his way full of joy. **40**Philip was seen next at Azotus. From there he traveled all around. He preached the good news in all the towns. Finally he arrived in Caesarea.

Saul Becomes a Believer

9 Meanwhile, Saul continued to oppose the Lord's followers. He said they would be put to death. He went to the high priest. **2**He asked the priest for letters to the synagogues in Damascus. He wanted to find men and women who belonged to the Way of Jesus. The letters would allow him to take them as prisoners to Jerusalem.

3On his journey, Saul approached Damascus. Suddenly a light from heaven flashed around him. **4**He fell to the ground. He heard a voice speak to him. "Saul! Saul!" the voice said. "Why are you opposing me?"

5"Who are you, Lord?" Saul asked.

"I am Jesus," he replied. "I am the one you are opposing. **6**Now get up and go into the city. There you will be told what you must do."

7The men traveling with Saul stood there. They weren't able to speak. They had heard the sound. But they didn't see anyone. **8**Saul got up from the ground. He opened his eyes, but he couldn't see. So they led him by the hand into Damascus. **9**For three days he was blind. He didn't eat or drink anything.

10In Damascus there was a believer named Ananias. The Lord called out to him in a vision. "Ananias!" he said.

"Yes, Lord," he answered.

11The Lord told him, "Go to the house of Judas on Straight Street. Ask for a man from Tarsus named Saul. He is praying. **12**In a vision he has seen a man named Ananias. The man has come and placed his hands on him. Now he will be able to see again."

13"Lord," Ananias answered, "I've heard many reports about this man. They say he has done great harm to God's people in Jerusalem. **14**Now he has come here to arrest all those who worship you. The chief priests have given him authority to do this."

15But the Lord said to Ananias, "Go! I have chosen this man to work for me. He will carry my name to those who aren't Jews and to their kings. He will bring my name to the people of Israel. **16**I will show him how much he must suffer for me."

17Then Ananias went to the house and entered it. He placed his hands on Saul. "Brother Saul," he said, "you saw the Lord Jesus. He appeared to you on the road as you were coming here. He has sent me so

PHILIP

ACTS 8:35

Then Philip began with that same part of Scripture. He told him the good news about Jesus.

Dark clouds rolled in as Philip started walking south on the road out of Jerusalem. But he had been told by an angel to walk down that road, and a little rain, or even a lot of it, wasn't going to stop him.

Philip passed others on the road—a large family, a lonely old man, some soldiers. Then Philip saw a chariot. As he got closer Philip heard an inner voice telling him to go to the chariot.

Eager now that he knew why he had been sent down this road, Philip began to run. The chariot was slowly working its way down the dusty road. A rich man from Ethiopia sat inside. His robe flowed over the back of the chariot. **THE HUGE JEWEL ON HIS HEADDRESS SPARKLED WHEN THE SUN BROKE THROUGH THE CLOUDS.** Philip could hear the man reading out loud. He recognized the words. They were from the Bible, from the book of Isaiah.

"Do you understand what you are reading?" Philip asked the man. The man looked up. "I've read these words a hundred times, and I still don't understand. I need someone who can explain them."

Philip climbed into the chariot and explained what the words of Isaiah meant. He told the Ethiopian all about Jesus and the good news of salvation. The Ethiopian believed everything Philip told him. "Look," he said. "There's some water. I want to be baptized."

Getting out of the chariot together, Philip and the Ethiopian walked down into the water. There Philip baptized him as a new believer in Jesus. The cold water dripped off the Ethiopian's wet robe and beard, but he didn't even notice. He praised God for bringing Philip to him so that he could hear the good news.

BE A PHILIP

Philip didn't keep the good news about Jesus to himself. He told others so that they could believe, too. Be a Philip. Tell others about Jesus and his love. When you're at school, when you play in your neighborhood, when you're with your friends or family.

PHILIP TOLD OTHERS ABOUT JESUS' LOVE.
THE WHOLE STORY: ACTS 8:26-40

Go to page 1270 for the next Super Hero

that you will be able to see again. You will be filled with the Holy Spirit."

[18]Right away something like scales fell from Saul's eyes. And he could see again. He got up and was baptized. [19]After eating some food, he got his strength back.

Saul in Damascus and Jerusalem

Saul spent several days with the believers in Damascus. [20]At once he began to preach in the synagogues. He taught that Jesus is the Son of God. [21]All who heard him were amazed. They asked, "Isn't he the man who caused great trouble in Jerusalem for those who worship Jesus? Hasn't he come here to take them as prisoners to the chief priests?" [22]But Saul grew more and more powerful. The Jews living in Damascus couldn't believe what was happening. Saul proved to them that Jesus is the Christ.

[23]After many days, the Jews had a meeting. They planned to kill Saul. [24]But he learned about their plan. Day and night they watched the city gates closely in order to kill him. [25]But his followers helped him escape by night. They lowered him in a basket through an opening in the wall.

[26]When Saul came to Jerusalem, he tried to join the believers. But they were all afraid of him. They didn't believe he was really one of Jesus' followers. [27]But Barnabas took him to the apostles. He told them about Saul's journey. He said that Saul had seen the Lord. He told how the Lord had spoken to Saul. Barnabas also said that Saul had preached without fear in Jesus' name in Damascus.

[28]So Saul stayed with the believers. He moved about freely in Jerusalem. He spoke boldly in the Lord's name. [29]He talked and argued with Jews who followed Greek practices. But they tried to kill him. [30]The other believers heard about this. They took Saul down to Caesarea. From there they sent him off to Tarsus.

[31]Then the church throughout Judea, Galilee and Samaria enjoyed a time of peace. The Holy Spirit gave the church strength and boldness. So they grew in numbers. And they worshiped the Lord.

Peter Goes to Lydda and Joppa

[32]As Peter traveled around the country, he went to visit God's people in Lydda. [33]There he found a disabled man named Aeneas. For eight years the man had spent most of his time in bed. [34]"Aeneas," Peter said to him, "Jesus Christ heals you. Get up! Take care of your mat!" So Aeneas got up right away. [35]Everyone who lived in Lydda and Sharon saw him. They turned to the Lord.

[36]In Joppa there was a believer named Tabitha. Her name in the Greek language was Dorcas. She was always doing good and helping poor people. [37]About that time she became sick and died. Her body was washed and placed in a room upstairs. [38]Lydda was near Joppa. The believers heard that Peter was in Lydda. So they sent two men to him. They begged him, "Please come at once!"

[39]Peter went with them. When he arrived, he was taken upstairs to the room. All the widows stood around him crying. They showed him the robes and other clothes Dorcas had made while she was still alive.

[40]Peter sent them all out of the room. Then he got down on his knees and prayed. He turned toward the dead woman. He said, "Tabitha, get up." She opened her eyes. When she saw Peter, she sat up. [41]He took her by the hand and helped her to her feet. Then he called the believers and the widows. He brought her to them. They saw that she was alive. [42]This became known all over Joppa. Many people believed in the Lord. [43]Peter stayed in Joppa for some time. He stayed with Simon, a man who worked with leather.

POWER—SURGE

BELIEVES †

MANY PEOPLE BELIEVED IN THE LORD.
— ACTS 9:42 —

Cornelius Calls for Peter

10 A man named Cornelius lived in Caesarea. He was a Roman commander in the Italian Regiment. [2]Cornelius and all his family were faithful and worshiped God. He gave freely to people who were in need. He prayed to God regularly. [3]One day about three o'clock in the afternoon he had a vision. He saw an angel of God clearly. The angel came to him and said, "Cornelius!"

[4]Cornelius was afraid. He stared at the angel. "What is it, Lord?" he asked.

The angel answered, "Your prayers and gifts to poor people have come up like an offering to God. So he has remembered

SAUL/PAUL

ACTS 9:15

Go! I have chosen this man [Saul] to work for me. He will carry my name to those who aren't Jews and to their kings. He will bring my name to the people of Israel.

Saul hurried down the road. He was on his way to Damascus to put some Christians in jail. Saul hated the Christians. They turned everything he knew about God upside-down. *They are wrong, wrong, wrong!* Saul thought to himself.

Suddenly a blinding light flashed around Saul. He fell down with his face in the dirt road. He quickly covered his ears with his hands as a voice from above thundered, "Saul, Saul, what are you doing? Why are you trying to hurt those who follow me?" *Who is calling my name?* Saul wondered with terror. He managed to whisper this question out loud. The roar of the voice pressed down again on Saul. "I am Jesus. Get up and go into the city. Someone there will tell you what to do."

When the voice stopped, the silence seemed almost as loud. Saul lay in the road, his ears ringing, unable to move for several minutes. Then slowly he got to his feet and opened his eyes to find the others traveling with him. But he couldn't see them. It had been so bright when the voice was booming. Now it was so dark—**HE WAS BLIND!**

Saul's frightened friends led him into the city. They too had heard the voice and knew what Saul was supposed to do. After three days, God sent a man named Ananias to Saul. Ananias believed in Jesus. Saul had a bad reputation for hurting and killing Christians. But Ananias trusted that God would keep him safe.

"Saul," he said, "you have seen Jesus! He has work for you to do. Get up and begin!" Saul began to blink. His eyes itched and soon something like scales fell from each one. He could see again! And he knew what he had to do. Immediately he was baptized. He no longer hated Christians. He became one himself.

BE A SAUL

Saul hated Christians. You don't want to be like that. But Saul immediately followed Jesus when he discovered the truth. Whenever you learn something new, something exciting about God, be like Saul. Follow God and obey him wherever you are.

SAUL IMMEDIATELY FOLLOWED JESUS WHEN HE LEARNED THE TRUTH.
THE WHOLE STORY: ACTS 9:1-31

Go to page 1272 for the next Super Hero

POWER-SURGE

GIVING G

[CORNELIUS] GAVE
FREELY TO PEOPLE
WHO WERE IN NEED.
— ACTS 10:2 —

you. 5Now send men to Joppa. Have them bring back a man named Simon. He is also called Peter. 6He is staying with another Simon, a man who works with leather. His house is by the sea."

7The angel who spoke to him left. Then Cornelius called two of his servants. He also called a godly soldier who was one of his attendants. 8He told them everything that had happened. Then he sent them to Joppa.

Peter Has a Vision

9It was about noon the next day. The men were on their journey and were approaching the city. Peter went up on the roof to pray. 10He became hungry. He wanted something to eat. While the meal was being prepared, Peter had a vision. 11He saw heaven open up. There he saw something that looked like a large sheet. It was being let down to earth by its four corners. 12It had all kinds of four-footed animals in it. It also had reptiles of the earth and birds of the air. 13Then a voice told him, "Get up, Peter. Kill and eat."

14"No, Lord! I will not!" Peter replied. "I have never eaten anything that is not pure and 'clean.' "

15The voice spoke to him a second time. "Do not say anything is not pure that God has made 'clean,' " it said.

16This happened three times. Right away the sheet was taken back up to heaven.

17Peter was wondering what the vision meant. At that very moment the men sent by Cornelius found Simon's house. They stopped at the gate 18and called out. They asked if Simon Peter was staying there.

19Peter was still thinking about the vision. The Holy Spirit spoke to him. "Simon," he said, "three men are looking for you. 20Get up and go downstairs. Don't let anything keep you from going with them. I have sent them."

21Peter went down and spoke to the men. "I'm the one you're looking for," he said. "Why have you come?"

22The men replied, "We have come from Cornelius, the Roman commander. He is a good man who worships God. All the Jewish people respect him. A holy angel told him to invite you to his house. Cornelius wants to hear what you have to say." 23Then Peter invited the men into the house to be his guests.

Peter Goes to the House of Cornelius

The next day Peter went with the three men. Some of the believers from Joppa went along. 24The following day he arrived in Caesarea. Cornelius was expecting them. He had called together his relatives and close friends.

25When Peter entered the house, Cornelius met him. As a sign of respect, he fell at Peter's feet. 26But Peter made him get up. "Stand up," he said. "I am only a man myself."

27Talking with Cornelius, Peter went inside. There he found a large group of people. 28He said to them, "You know that it is against our law for a Jew to have anything to do with those who aren't Jews. But God has shown me that I should not say anyone is not pure and 'clean.' 29So when you sent for me, I came without asking any questions. May I ask why you sent for me?"

30Cornelius answered, "Four days ago at this very hour I was in my house praying. It was three o'clock in the afternoon. Suddenly a man in shining clothes stood in front of me. 31He said, 'Cornelius, God has heard your prayer. He has remembered your gifts to poor people. 32Send someone to Joppa to get Simon Peter. He is a guest in the home of another Simon, who works with leather. He lives by the sea.' 33So I sent for you right away. It was good of you to come. Now we are all here. And God is here with us. We are ready to listen to everything the Lord has commanded you to tell us."

34Then Peter began to speak. "I now realize how true it is that God treats everyone the same," he said. 35"He accepts people from every nation. He accepts all who have respect for him and do what is right.

36"You know the message God sent to the people of Israel. It is the good news of peace through Jesus Christ. He is Lord of all. 37You know what has happened all through Judea. It started in Galilee after John preached about baptism. 38You know how God anointed Jesus of Nazareth with the Holy Spirit and with power. Jesus went around doing good. He healed

TABITHA

In Joppa there was a believer named Tabitha...She was always doing good and helping poor people.

The tingling started in her fingers and toes and spread slowly up her arms and legs. She felt a shiver slide up the back of her neck. Her scalp prickled. Gradually her whole body began to feel warm. She heard a man's voice but only faintly, softly, like from a long distance away. It sounded like he was calling her name, but she wasn't sure. HER EYES FLUTTERED OPEN AND THEN SHUT AGAIN. Finally they stayed open. Tabitha knew she had been very sick. Had she died? Then who was this man? And why was she back in her old room in Joppa?

The man took her hand and helped her stand. He smiled, knowing from the look on Tabitha's face that she had questions about what had happened. "My name is Peter, Tabitha. You were sick, and you died. Your friends sent for me. They showed me all the clothes you made for them. They told me how you helped them. God's power brought you back to life!"

Peter led Tabitha into the room where her friends were waiting. Until Tabitha stepped into the room and heard their cries, she didn't realize that they had gathered to mourn her death. So many people! But the frowns and tears quickly turned to smiles and laughter when they saw Tabitha.

They all went to Tabitha, hugging and smiling. Then they praised God for bringing her back to life. Most of them were poor and couldn't afford clothes for themselves. Tabitha had spent lots of time sewing and giving away the clothes she made.

Later that day Tabitha stood on her rooftop with Peter and a few others. Together they praised God for bringing Tabitha back to life.

BE A TABITHA

You can be a helper just like Tabitha. Look around you. Did a classmate forget his or her lunch? You can share yours. Is a friend sad because her parents are fighting? You can invite her over to your house for some fun. No matter what your age or what you're good at, you can be a helper just like Tabitha.

TABITHA LOVINGLY HELPED OTHER PEOPLE.
THE WHOLE STORY: ACTS 9:36-43

Go to page 1274 for the next Super Hero

all who were under the devil's power. God was with him.

39"We are witnesses of everything he did in the land of the Jews and in Jerusalem. They killed him by nailing him to a cross. **40**But on the third day God raised him from the dead. God allowed Jesus to be seen. **41**But he wasn't seen by all the people. He was seen only by us. We are witnesses whom God had already chosen. We ate and drank with him after he rose from the dead.

42"He commanded us to preach to the people. He told us to give witness that he is the one appointed by God to judge the living and the dead. **43**All the prophets give witness about him. They say that all who believe in him have their sins forgiven through his name."

POWER—SURGE

BELIEVES †

ALL WHO BELIEVE IN HIM HAVE THEIR SINS FORGIVEN THROUGH HIS NAME.
— ACTS 10:43 —

FORGIVING

44While Peter was still saying these things, the Holy Spirit came on all who heard the message. **45**Some Jewish believers had come with Peter. They were amazed because the gift of the Holy Spirit had been poured out even on those who weren't Jews. **46**They heard them speaking in languages they had not known before. They also heard them praising God.

Then Peter said, **47**"Can anyone keep these people from being baptized with water? They have received the Holy Spirit just as we have." **48**So he ordered that they be baptized in the name of Jesus Christ. Then they asked Peter to stay with them for a few days.

Peter Explains His Actions

11 The apostles and the believers all through Judea heard that people who were not Jews had also received God's word. **2**Peter went up to Jerusalem. There the Jewish believers found fault with him. **3**They said, "You went into the

house of those who aren't Jews. You ate with them."

4Peter explained everything to them. He told them exactly what had happened. **5**"I was in the city of Joppa praying," he said. "There I had a vision. I saw something that looked like a large sheet. It was being let down from heaven by its four corners. It came down to where I was. **6**I looked into it and saw four-footed animals of the earth. There were also wild animals, reptiles and birds. **7**Then I heard a voice speaking to me. 'Get up, Peter,' the voice said. 'Kill and eat.'

8"I replied, 'No, Lord! I will not! Nothing that is not pure and "clean" has ever entered my mouth.'

9"A second time the voice spoke from heaven. 'Do not say anything is not pure that God has made "clean," ' the voice said. **10**This happened three times. Then the sheet was pulled up into heaven.

11"Just then three men stopped at the house where I was staying. They had been sent to me from Caesarea. **12**The Holy Spirit told me not to let anything keep me from going with them. These six brothers here went with me. We entered the man's house. **13**He told us how he had seen an angel appear in his house. The angel said, 'Send to Joppa for Simon Peter. **14**He has a message to bring to you. You and your whole family will be saved through it.'

15"As I began to speak, the Holy Spirit came on them. He came just as he had come on us at the beginning. **16**Then I remembered the Lord's words. 'John baptized with water,' he had said. 'But you will be baptized with the Holy Spirit.' **17**God gave them the same gift he gave those of us who believed in the Lord Jesus Christ. So who was I to think that I could oppose God?"

18When they heard this, they didn't object anymore. They praised God. They said, "So then, God has allowed even those who aren't Jews to turn away from their sins and live."

Believers Are Called Christians for the First Time

19Some believers had been scattered by the suffering that came to them after Stephen's death. They traveled as far as Phoenicia, Cyprus and Antioch. But they told the message only to Jews. **20**Some believers from Cyprus and Cyrene went to Antioch. There they began to speak to Greeks also. They told them the good news about the Lord Jesus. **21**The

Lord's power was with them. Large numbers of people believed and turned to the Lord.

22The church in Jerusalem heard about this. So they sent Barnabas to Antioch. 23When he arrived and saw what the grace of God had done, he was glad. He told them all to remain true to the Lord with all their hearts. 24Barnabas was a good man. He was full of the Holy Spirit and of faith. Large numbers of people came to know the Lord.

25Then Barnabas went to Tarsus to look for Saul. 26He found him there. Then he brought him to Antioch. For a whole year Barnabas and Saul met with the church. They taught large numbers of people. At Antioch the believers were called Christians for the first time.

27In those days some prophets came

CORNELIUS

ACTS 10:33

G K T

I [Cornelius] sent for you right away. It was good of you to come. Now we are all here. And God is here with us. We are ready to listen to everything the Lord has commanded you to tell us.

*C*ornelius (core-NEEL-ee-us) prayed on the roof of his house in the late afternoon. It had rained earlier in the day, and the air smelled fresh and sweet. Cornelius wasn't Jewish, but he believed in God. However, he had never heard about Jesus.

Without a warning, an angel stood right in front of him. Cornelius's voice shook with surprise as he asked, "What do you want?"

The angel told Cornelius, "God has been watching you. He sees how faithful you are to him. He sees how kind you are to the poor. **HE HAS A MESSAGE FOR YOU.** Send some men to Joppa to get Peter."

Right away Cornelius did as the angel told him. God had been preparing Peter to tell the good news of Jesus to someone who wasn't Jewish. When Peter came to his house several days later, he told Cornelius all about Jesus. And Cornelius and his whole family believed.

BE A CORNELIUS

Cornelius believed in God and was open to whatever teaching God had for him. He could have said, "No, I like things the way they are." But he didn't. Be like him! When you learn something new about God (or anything for that matter), get excited about it!

CORNELIUS BELIEVED IN GOD AND THEN IN JESUS.

Go to page 1276 for the next Super Hero

POWER-SURGE

BELIEVES †

SOME BELIEVERS...
TOLD THEM THE GOOD
NEWS ABOUT THE
LORD JESUS. THE
LORD'S POWER WAS
WITH THEM. LARGE
NUMBERS OF PEOPLE
BELIEVED AND TURNED
TO THE LORD.
— **ACTS 11:20-21** —

TELLS OTHERS

down from Jerusalem to Antioch. **28**One of them was named Agabus. He stood up and spoke through the Spirit. He said there would not be nearly enough food anywhere in the Roman world. This happened while Claudius was the emperor. **29**The believers decided to provide help for the brothers and sisters living in Judea. All of them helped as much as they could. **30**They sent their gift to the elders through Barnabas and Saul.

An Angel Helps Peter Escape From Prison

12 About this time, King Herod arrested some people who belonged to the church. He planned to make them suffer greatly. **2**He had James killed with a sword. James was John's brother. **3**Herod saw that the death of James pleased the Jews. So he arrested Peter also. This happened during the Feast of Unleavened Bread. **4**After Herod arrested Peter, he put him in prison. Peter was placed under guard. He was watched by four groups of four soldiers each. Herod planned to put Peter on public trial. It would take place after the Passover Feast.

5So Peter was kept in prison. But the church prayed hard to God for him.

6It was the night before Herod was going to bring him to trial. Peter was sleeping between two soldiers. Two chains held him there. Lookouts stood guard at the entrance. **7**Suddenly an angel of the Lord appeared. A light shone in the prison cell. The angel struck Peter on his

side. Peter woke up. "Quick!" the angel said. "Get up!" The chains fell off Peter's wrists.

8Then the angel said to him, "Put on your clothes and sandals." Peter did so. "Put on your coat," the angel told him. "Follow me." **9**Peter followed him out of the prison. But he had no idea that what the angel was doing was really happening. He thought he was seeing a vision. **10**They passed the first and second guards. Then they came to the iron gate leading to the city. It opened for them by itself. They went through it. They walked the length of one street. Suddenly the angel left Peter.

11Then Peter realized what had happened. He said, "Now I know for sure that the Lord sent his angel. He set me free from Herod's power. He saved me from everything the Jewish people were hoping for."

12When Peter understood what had happened, he went to Mary's house. Mary was the mother of John Mark. Many people had gathered in her home. They were praying there. **13**Peter knocked at the outer entrance. A servant named Rhoda came to answer the door. **14**She recognized Peter's voice. She was so excited that she ran back without opening the door. "Peter is at the door!" she exclaimed.

15"You're out of your mind," they said to her. But she kept telling them it was true. So they said, "It must be his angel."

16Peter kept on knocking. When they opened the door and saw him, they were amazed. **17**Peter motioned with his hand for them to be quiet. He explained how the Lord had brought him out of prison. "Tell James and the others about this," he said. Then he went to another place.

18In the morning the soldiers were bewildered. They couldn't figure out what had happened to Peter. **19**So Herod had them look everywhere for Peter. But they didn't find him. Then Herod questioned the guards closely. He ordered that they be put to death.

Herod Dies

Herod went from Judea to Caesarea. He stayed there awhile. **20**He had been quarreling with the people of Tyre and Sidon. So they got together and asked for a meeting with him. This was because they depended on the king's country to supply them with food. They gained the support of Blastus and asked for peace. Blastus was a trusted personal servant of the king.

21The appointed day came. Herod was seated on his throne. He was wearing his royal robes. He made a speech to the people. 22Then they shouted, "This is the voice of a god. It's not the voice of a man." 23Right away an angel of the Lord struck Herod down. Herod had not given praise to God. So he was eaten by worms and died.

24But God's word continued to increase and spread.

25Barnabas and Saul finished their task.

RHODA

ACTS 12:13-14

✝

🗣

A servant named Rhoda came to answer the door. She recognized Peter's voice. She was so excited that she ran back without opening the door. "Peter is at the door!" she exclaimed.

Who could be banging on the door this late at night? Rhoda (ROE-duh) shook with fear. Someone was probably coming to arrest all of the believers in their house. Peter was already chained up in prison. Now it was time to get the rest of them.

She tiptoed to the door so she could see who it was. Rhoda couldn't believe her eyes! It was Peter!

She ran through the house and burst into the prayer meeting. They looked at her like she was crazy. But Rhoda kept insisting that Peter was at the door. Finally they all heard it—BANG, BANG, BANG! She ran as fast as she could back to the door to let Peter in. Everyone shouted with excitement. They had seen a miracle!

BE A RHODA

Something exciting happened here. By a miracle Peter escaped from prison. And the very people who were praying for his release didn't believe it. But Rhoda did. Be just like her. God is doing exciting things today, too. You can be like Rhoda and believe!

RHODA BELIEVED WHEN GOD DID SOMETHING EXCITING.

Go to page 1282 for the next Super Hero

Then they returned from Jerusalem. They took John Mark with them.

Barnabas and Saul Are Sent Off

13 In the church at Antioch there were prophets and teachers. Among them were Barnabas, Simeon, and Lucius from Cyrene. Simeon was also called Niger. Another was Manaen. He had been brought up with Herod, the ruler of Galilee. Saul was among them too. 2While they were worshiping the Lord and fasting, the Holy Spirit spoke. "Set apart Barnabas and Saul for me," he said. "I have appointed them to do special work." 3The prophets and teachers fasted and prayed. They placed their hands on Barnabas and Saul. Then they sent them off.

Events on Cyprus

4Barnabas and Saul were sent on their way by the Holy Spirit. They went down to Seleucia. From there they sailed to Cyprus. 5They arrived at Salamis. There they preached God's word in the Jewish synagogues. John was with them as their helper.

6They traveled all across the island until they came to Paphos. There they met a Jew named Bar-Jesus. He was an evil magician and a false prophet. 7He was an attendant of Sergius Paulus, the governor. Paulus was a man of understanding. He sent for Barnabas and Saul. He wanted to hear God's word.

8But Elymas, the evil magician, opposed them. The name Elymas means "magician." He tried to keep the governor from becoming a believer. 9Saul was also known as Paul. He was filled with the Holy Spirit. He looked straight at Elymas. He said to him, 10"You are a child of the devil! You are an enemy of everything that is right! You cheat people. You use all kinds of tricks. Won't you ever stop twisting the right ways of the Lord? 11Now the Lord's hand is against you. You are going to go blind. You won't be able to see the light of the sun for a while."

Right away mist and darkness came over him. He tried to feel his way around. He wanted to find someone to lead him by the hand. 12When the governor saw what had happened, he believed. He was amazed at what Paul was teaching about the Lord.

Paul Preaches in Pisidian Antioch

13From Paphos, Paul and his companions sailed to Perga in Pamphylia. There John left them and returned to Jerusalem. 14From Perga they went on to Pisidian Antioch. On the Sabbath day they entered the synagogue and sat down. 15The Law and the Prophets were read aloud. Then the synagogue rulers sent word to Paul and his companions. They said, "Brothers, do you have a message of hope for the people? If you do, please speak."

16Paul stood up and motioned with his hand. Then he said, "Men of Israel, and you non-Jews who worship God, listen to me! 17The God of Israel chose our people who lived long ago. He blessed them greatly while they were in Egypt. With his mighty power he led them out of that country. 18He put up with them for about 40 years in the desert. 19He destroyed seven nations in Canaan. Then he gave the land to his people as their rightful share. 20All of this took about 450 years.

"After this, God gave them judges until the time of Samuel the prophet. 21Then the people asked for a king. He gave them Saul, son of Kish. Saul was from the tribe of Benjamin. He ruled for 40 years. 22God removed him and made David their king. Here is God's witness about him. 'David, son of Jesse, is a man dear to my heart,' he said. 'He will do everything I want him to do.'

23"From this man's family line God has brought to Israel the Savior Jesus. This is what he had promised. 24Before Jesus came, John preached that we should turn away from our sins and be baptized. He preached this to all Israel. 25John was coming to the end of his work. 'Who do you think I am?' he said. 'I am not the one you are looking for. No, he is coming after me. I am not good enough to untie his sandals.'

26"Listen, brothers, you children of Abraham! Listen, you non-Jews who worship God! This message of salvation has been sent to us. 27The people of Jerusalem and their rulers did not recognize Jesus. By finding him guilty, they made the prophets' words come true. These are read every Sabbath day. 28The people and their rulers had no reason at all for sentencing Jesus to death. But they asked Pilate to have him killed. 29They did everything that had been written about Jesus. Then they took him down from the cross. They laid him in a tomb. 30But God raised him from the dead. 31For many days he was seen by those who had traveled with him from Galilee to Jerusalem. Now they are his witnesses to our people.

32"We are telling you the good news.

What God promised our people long ago
³³he has done for us, their children. He
has raised up Jesus. This is what is written
in the second Psalm. It says,

" 'You are my Son.
Today I have become your Father.'
(Psalm 2:7)

³⁴God raised Jesus from the dead. He will
never rot in the grave. This is what is written
in Scripture. It says,

" 'Holy and sure blessings were
promised to David.
I will give them to you.'   *(Isaiah 55:3)*

³⁵In another place it says,

" 'You will not let your Holy One rot
away.'   *(Psalm 16:10)*

³⁶"David carried out God's purpose
while he lived. Then he died. He was
buried with his people. His body rotted
away. ³⁷But the One whom God raised
from the dead did not rot away.

³⁸"My brothers, here is what I want you
to know. I announce to you that your sins
can be forgiven because of what Jesus has
done. ³⁹Through him everyone who believes
is made right with God. Moses' law
could not make you right in God's eyes.
⁴⁰Be careful! Don't let what the prophets
spoke about happen to you. They said,

⁴¹" 'Look, you who make fun of the
truth!
Wonder and die!
I am going to do something in your
days
that you would never believe.
You wouldn't believe it even if
someone told you.' "
(Habakkuk 1:5)

⁴²Paul and Barnabas started to leave the
synagogue. The people invited them to
say more about these things on the next
Sabbath day. ⁴³The people were told they
could leave the service. Many Jews followed
Paul and Barnabas. Many non-Jews
who faithfully worshiped the God of the
Jews did the same. Paul and Barnabas
talked with them. They tried to get them
to keep living in God's grace.

⁴⁴On the next Sabbath day, almost the
whole city gathered to hear the word of
the Lord. ⁴⁵When the Jews saw the
crowds, they became very jealous. They
said evil things against what Paul was saying.

⁴⁶Then Paul and Barnabas answered
them boldly. "We had to speak God's
word to you first," they said. "But you

CHEERFUL ✳

**THE BELIEVERS WERE
FILLED WITH JOY AND
WITH THE HOLY SPIRIT.**
— ACTS 13:52 —

don't accept it. You don't think you are
good enough for eternal life. So now we
are turning to those who aren't Jews.
⁴⁷This is what the Lord has commanded
us to do. He said,

" 'I have made you a light for those
who aren't Jews.
You will bring salvation to the
whole earth.' "   *(Isaiah 49:6)*

⁴⁸When the non-Jews heard this, they
were glad. They honored the word of the
Lord. All who were appointed for eternal
life believed.

⁴⁹The word of the Lord spread through
the whole area. ⁵⁰But the Jews stirred up
the important women who worshiped
God. They also stirred up the men who
were leaders in the city. They tried to get
them to attack Paul and Barnabas. They
threw them out of that area. ⁵¹Paul and
Barnabas didn't like this. So they shook
the dust from their feet. They went on to
Iconium. ⁵²The believers were filled with
joy and with the Holy Spirit.

Paul and Barnabas Preach
in Iconium

14 At Iconium, Paul and Barnabas
went into the Jewish synagogue as
usual. They spoke there with great power.
Large numbers of Jews and non-Jews became
believers. ²But the Jews who refused

STRONG 🏋

**PAUL AND BARNABAS
WENT INTO THE
JEWISH SYNAGOGUE
AS USUAL. THEY
SPOKE THERE WITH
GREAT POWER.**
— ACTS 14:1 —

to believe stirred up those who weren't Jews. They poisoned their minds against the two men and the new believers. 3So Paul and Barnabas spent a lot of time there. They spoke boldly for the Lord. He gave them the ability to do miraculous signs and wonders. In this way the Lord showed that they were telling the truth about his grace.

4The people of the city did not agree with each other. Some were on the side of the Jews. Others were on the side of the apostles. 5Jews and non-Jews alike planned to treat Paul and Barnabas badly. Their leaders agreed. They planned to kill them by throwing stones at them. 6But Paul and Barnabas found out about the plan. They escaped to the Lycaonian cities of Lystra and Derbe and to the surrounding area. 7There they continued to preach the good news.

Paul Preaches in Lystra

8In Lystra there sat a man who couldn't walk. He hadn't been able to use his feet since the day he was born. 9He listened as Paul spoke. Paul looked right at him. He saw that the man had faith to be healed. 10So he called out, "Stand up on your feet!" Then the man jumped up and began to walk.

11The crowd saw what Paul had done. They shouted in the Lycaonian language. "The gods have come down to us in human form!" they exclaimed. 12They called Barnabas Zeus. Paul was the main speaker. So they called him Hermes. 13Just outside the city was the temple of the god Zeus. The priest of Zeus brought bulls and wreaths to the city gates. He and the crowd wanted to offer sacrifices to Paul and Barnabas.

14But the apostles Barnabas and Paul heard about this. So they tore their clothes. They rushed out into the crowd. They shouted, 15"Why are you men doing this? We are only human, just like you. We are bringing you good news. Turn away from these worthless things. Turn to the living God. He is the one who made the heavens and the earth and the sea. He made everything in them. 16In the past, he let all nations go their own way. 17But he has given proof of what he is like. He has shown kindness by giving you rain from heaven. He gives you crops in their seasons. He provides you with plenty of food. He fills your hearts with joy." 18Paul and Barnabas told them all these things. But they had trouble keeping the crowd from offering sacrifices to them.

19Then some Jews came from Antioch and Iconium. They won the crowd over to their side. They threw stones at Paul. They thought he was dead, so they dragged him out of the city. 20The believers gathered around Paul. Then he got up and went back into the city. The next day he and Barnabas left for Derbe.

Paul and Barnabas Return to Antioch

21Paul and Barnabas preached the good news in the city of Derbe. They won large numbers of followers. Then they returned to Lystra, Iconium and Antioch. 22There they helped the believers gain strength. They told them to remain true to what they had been taught. "We must go through many hard times to enter God's kingdom," they said. 23Paul and Barnabas appointed elders for them in each church. The elders had trusted in the Lord. Paul and Barnabas prayed and fasted. They placed the elders in the Lord's care.

24After going through Pisidia, Paul and Barnabas came into Pamphylia. 25They preached the word in Perga. Then they went down to Attalia.

26From Attalia they sailed back to Antioch. That was where they had been committed to God's grace. They had now completed the work God had given them to do. 27When they arrived at Antioch, they gathered the church together. They reported all that God had done through them. They told how he had opened the way for non-Jews to believe. 28And they stayed there a long time with the believers.

Church Leaders Meet in Jerusalem

15 Certain people came down from Judea to Antioch. Here is what they were teaching the believers. "Moses commanded you to be circumcised," they said. "If you aren't, you can't be saved." 2But Paul and Barnabas didn't agree with this. They argued strongly with them. So Paul and Barnabas were appointed to go up to Jerusalem. Some other believers were chosen to go with them. They were supposed to see the apostles and elders about this question.

3The church sent them on their way. As they traveled through Phoenicia and Samaria, they told how those who weren't Jews had turned to God. This news made all the believers very glad.

4When they arrived in Jerusalem, the church welcomed them. The apostles and elders welcomed them too. Then Paul and

Barnabas reported everything God had done through them.

⁵Some of the believers were Pharisees. They stood up and said, "Those who aren't Jews must be circumcised. They must obey the law of Moses."

⁶The apostles and elders met to consider this question. ⁷After they had talked it over, Peter got up and spoke to them.

"Brothers," he said, "you know that some time ago God chose me to take the good news to those who aren't Jews. He wanted them to hear the good news and believe. ⁸God knows the human heart. By giving the Holy Spirit to non-Jews, he showed that he accepted them. He did the same for them as he had done for us. ⁹He showed that there is no difference between us and them. He made their hearts pure because of their faith.

¹⁰"Now then, why are you trying to test God? You test him when you put a heavy load on the believers' shoulders. Our people of long ago couldn't carry that load. We can't either. ¹¹No! We believe we are saved through the grace of our Lord Jesus. Those who aren't Jews are saved in the same way."

¹²Everyone became quiet as they listened to Barnabas and Paul. They were telling about the miraculous signs and wonders God had done through them among non-Jews.

¹³When they finished, James spoke up. "Brothers," he said, "listen to me. ¹⁴Simon Peter has explained to us how God first showed his concern for those who aren't Jews. He chose some of them to be his very own people.

¹⁵The prophets' words agree with that. They say,

¹⁶ " 'After this I will return
    and rebuild David's fallen tent.
I will rebuild what was destroyed.
    I will make it what it used to be.
¹⁷Then the rest of the people can look to
        the Lord.
    This means all the non-Jews who
        belong to me.
The Lord says this. He is the one who
        does these things.' *(Amos 9:11,12)*
¹⁸   The Lord does things that have been
        known for a long time.

¹⁹"Now here is my opinion. We should not make it hard for the non-Jews who are turning to God. ²⁰Here is what we should write to them. They must not eat food polluted by being offered to statues of gods. They must not commit sexual sins. They must not eat the meat of ani-

mals that have been choked to death. And they must not drink blood. ²¹These laws of Moses have been preached in every city from the earliest times. They are read out loud in the synagogues every Sabbath day."

A Letter Is Written to Non-Jewish Believers

²²Then the apostles, the elders and the whole church decided what to do. They would choose some of their own men. They would send them to Antioch with Paul and Barnabas. So they chose two leaders among the believers. Their names were Judas Barsabbas and Silas. ²³Here is the letter they sent with them.

The apostles and elders, your brothers, are writing this letter.

We are sending it to the non-Jewish believers in Antioch, Syria and Cilicia.

Greetings.

²⁴We have heard that some of our people came to you and caused trouble. You were upset by what they said. But we had given them no authority to go. ²⁵So we all agreed to send our dear friends Barnabas and Paul to you. We chose some others to go with them. ²⁶Barnabas and Paul have put their lives in danger for the name of our Lord Jesus Christ. ²⁷So we are sending Judas and Silas with them. What they say will agree with this letter.

²⁸It seemed good to the Holy Spirit and to us not to give you a load that is too heavy. So here are a few basic rules. ²⁹Don't eat food that has been offered to statues of gods. Don't drink blood. Don't eat the meat of animals that have been choked to death. And don't commit sexual sins. You will do well to keep away from these things.

Farewell.

³⁰The men were sent down to Antioch. There they gathered the church together. They gave the letter to them. ³¹The people read it. They were glad for its message of hope. ³²Judas and Silas were prophets. They said many things to give strength and hope to the believers. ³³/³⁴Judas and Silas stayed there for some time. Then the believers sent them away with the bless-

ing of peace. They sent them back to those who had sent them out.

35Paul and Barnabas remained in Antioch. There they and many others taught and preached the word of the Lord.

Paul and Barnabas Do Not Agree

36Some time later Paul spoke to Barnabas. "Let's go back to all the towns where we preached the word of the Lord," he said. "Let's visit the believers and see how they are doing." **37**Barnabas wanted to take John Mark with them. **38**But Paul didn't think it was wise to take him. Mark had deserted them in Pamphylia. He hadn't continued with them in their work. **39**Barnabas and Paul strongly disagreed with each other. So they went their separate ways. Barnabas took Mark and sailed for Cyprus. **40**But Paul chose Silas. The believers asked the Lord to give his grace to Paul and Silas as they went. **41**Paul traveled through Syria and Cilicia. He gave strength to the churches there.

Timothy Joins Paul and Silas

16 Paul came to Derbe. Then he went on to Lystra. A believer named Timothy lived there. His mother was Jewish and a believer. His father was a Greek. **2**The believers at Lystra and Iconium said good things about Timothy. **3**Paul wanted to take him along on the journey. So he circumcised Timothy because of the Jews who lived in that area. They all knew that Timothy's father was a Greek. **4**Paul and his companions traveled from town to town. They reported what the apostles and elders in Jerusalem had decided. The people were supposed to obey what was in the report. **5**So the churches were made strong in the faith. The number of believers grew every day.

POWER-SURGE

HELPFUL ★

THEY SAID MANY THINGS TO GIVE STRENGTH AND HOPE TO THE BELIEVERS.
— ACTS 15:32 —

TELLS OTHERS

Paul's Vision of the Man From Macedonia

6Paul and his companions traveled all through the area of Phrygia and Galatia. The Holy Spirit had kept them from preaching the word in Asia Minor. **7**They came to the border of Mysia. From there they tried to enter Bithynia. But the Spirit of Jesus would not let them. **8**So they passed by Mysia. Then they went down to Troas.

9During the night Paul had a vision. He saw a man from Macedonia standing and begging him. "Come over to Macedonia!" the man said. "Help us!" **10**After Paul had seen the vision, we got ready at once to leave for Macedonia. We decided that God had called us to preach the good news there.

Lydia Becomes a Believer

11At Troas we got into a boat. We sailed straight for Samothrace. The next day we went on to Neapolis. **12**From there we traveled to Philippi, a Roman colony. It is an important city in that part of Macedonia. We stayed there several days.

13On the Sabbath day we went outside the city gate. We walked down to the river. There we expected to find a place of prayer. We sat down and began to speak to the women who had gathered together. **14**One of those listening was a woman named Lydia. She was from the city of Thyatira. Her business was selling purple cloth. She was a worshiper of God. The Lord opened her heart to accept Paul's message. **15**She and her family were baptized. Then she invited us to her home. "Do you consider me a believer in the Lord?" she asked. "If you do, come and stay at my house." She succeeded in getting us to go home with her.

Paul and Silas Are Thrown Into Prison

16One day we were going to the place of prayer. On the way we were met by a female slave. She had a spirit that helped her to tell ahead of time what was going to happen. She earned a lot of money for her owners by telling fortunes. **17**The woman followed Paul and the rest of us around. She shouted, "These men serve the Most High God. They are telling you how to be saved." **18**She kept this up for many days. Finally Paul became upset. Turning around, he spoke to the spirit. "In the name of Jesus Christ," he said, "I command you to come out of her!" At that very moment the spirit left her.

¹⁹The female slave's owners realized that their hope of making money was gone. So they grabbed Paul and Silas. They dragged them into the market place to face the authorities. ²⁰They brought them to the judges. "These men are Jews," her owners said. "They are making trouble in our city. ²¹They are suggesting prac-

LYDIA

ACTS 16:14-15

The Lord opened [Lydia's] heart to accept Paul's message. She and her family were baptized.

Lydia's (LID-ee-uhz) business was going great. It seemed as if everyone wanted her purple cloth for something. She was grateful for the business, but it was tiring her out.

Never mind that, Lydia thought to herself. *Today was the Sabbath. Time for worship.* Lydia knew she'd feel better after going to the service down by the river.

Many other women had already gathered to worship by the river when Lydia arrived. The group was made up of mostly women. Several gave her a warm welcome and hugged her. Lydia had served the God of Israel for many years now, and these other followers were important to her. Just as they began, several men joined the group. Strangers. But they were welcome. The men sat down and began to speak. They taught the group of women about Jesus. One of them, Paul, spoke with a fiery passion. His story of meeting Jesus amazed the women. This Jesus was the Son of the God they worshiped.

Lydia listened to the men. **TIME SEEMED TO STOP.** She could have listened to them forever. She wanted to know as much as possible about Jesus. That day Paul baptized Lydia in the river. She was a brand new believer in Jesus!

On her way back home, Lydia's walking turned into skipping because she was so happy. Had she been tired when she got up? She could barely remember. She certainly wasn't tired now. She was full of energy. And full of thanks to God for what he had done that morning.

BE A LYDIA
Be a Lydia. Decide to follow Jesus. Today!

LYDIA DECIDED TO FOLLOW JESUS AS SOON AS SHE HEARD ABOUT HIM.
THE WHOLE STORY: ACTS 16:13-15

Go to page 1284 for the next Super Hero

tices that are against Roman law. These are practices we can't accept or take part in."

22The crowd joined the attack against Paul and Silas. The judges ordered that Paul and Silas be stripped and beaten. **23**They were whipped without mercy. Then they were thrown into prison. The jailer was commanded to guard them carefully. **24**When he received his orders, he put Paul and Silas deep inside the prison. He fastened their feet so they couldn't get away.

25About midnight Paul and Silas were praying. They were also singing hymns to God. The other prisoners were listening to them. **26**Suddenly there was a powerful earthquake. It shook the prison from top to bottom. All at once the prison doors flew open. Everybody's chains came loose.

27The jailer woke up. He saw that the prison doors were open. He pulled out his sword and was going to kill himself. He thought the prisoners had escaped. **28**"Don't harm yourself!" Paul shouted. "We are all here!"

29The jailer called out for some lights. He rushed in, shaking with fear. He fell down in front of Paul and Silas. **30**Then he brought them out. He asked, "Sirs, what must I do to be saved?"

31They replied, "Believe in the Lord Jesus. Then you and your family will be saved." **32**They spoke the word of the Lord to him. They also spoke to all the others in his house.

33At that hour of the night, the jailer took Paul and Silas and washed their wounds. Right away he and his whole family were baptized. **34**The jailer brought them into his house. He set a meal in front of them. He and his whole family

BELIEVES †

THE JAILER...AND HIS WHOLE FAMILY WERE FILLED WITH JOY. THEY HAD BECOME BELIEVERS IN GOD.
— ACTS 16:34 —

CHEERFUL

BRAVE B

AFTER PAUL AND SILAS CAME OUT OF THE PRISON, THEY WENT TO LYDIA'S HOUSE. THERE THEY MET WITH THE BELIEVERS. THEY TOLD THEM TO BE BRAVE.
— ACTS 16:40 —

were filled with joy. They had become believers in God.

35Early in the morning the judges sent their officers to the jailer. They ordered him, "Let those men go." **36**The jailer told Paul, "The judges have ordered me to set you and Silas free. You can leave now. Go in peace."

37But Paul replied to the officers. "They beat us in public," he said. "We weren't given a trial. And we are Roman citizens! They threw us into prison. And now do they want to get rid of us quietly? No! Let them come themselves and personally lead us out."

38The officers reported this to the judges. When the judges heard that Paul and Silas were Roman citizens, they became afraid. **39**So they came and said they were sorry. They led them out of the prison. Then they asked them to leave the city. **40**After Paul and Silas came out of the prison, they went to Lydia's house. There they met with the believers. They told them to be brave. Then they left.

Paul and Silas Arrive in Thessalonica

17 Paul and Silas passed through Amphipolis and Apollonia. They came to Thessalonica. A Jewish synagogue was there. **2**Paul went into the synagogue as he usually did. For three Sabbath days in a row he talked about the Scriptures with the Jews. **3**He explained and proved that the Christ had to suffer and rise from the dead. "This Jesus I am telling you about is the Christ!" he said. **4**His words won some of the Jews over. They joined Paul and Silas. A large number of Greeks who worshiped God joined them too. So did quite a few important women.

THE JAILER

ACTS 16:29-30

> **[The jailer] rushed in, shaking with fear. He fell down in front of Paul and Silas...He asked, "Sirs, what must I do to be saved?"**

The jailer sat up in bed. Something had jolted him awake. Then it happened again. His bed bumped and rolled and tossed; in fact, the whole room was moving. The noise of wood cracking and chains rattling roared through the room.

Slowly the shaking stopped. The jailer's heart raced. Then he frowned and lifted his head to listen. He heard nothing. *That* was a problem. The jailer was in charge of a prison full of criminals—including Paul and Silas. They had been beaten and thrown into the prison for telling people about Jesus.

The jailer knew the punishment for those who let their prisoners escape. The punishment was death. THE SILENCE IN THE PRISON COULD ONLY MEAN ONE THING. THE PRISONERS WERE GONE!

A quick look outside his door confirmed his greatest fears. Rather than wait for his death sentence, the jailer decided to take his own life. He reached for his sword, then heard someone outside shouting. "No! Don't hurt yourself! We're all here!"

Grabbing a lantern, the jailer hurried through a door that hung crooked on only one hinge. He stepped over rocks and iron bars and chains. Everywhere he looked he saw prisoners who could have escaped but had stayed in their cells.

Paul and Silas hadn't escaped either! These two men, who didn't even deserve punishment, didn't run away! The jailer fell on his knees in front of them. He knew they had an important message. "Please, tell me about Jesus. What should I do to be saved?" That night, the jailer and his whole family believed in Jesus.

BE LIKE THE JAILER

As soon as the jailer understood what had happened, he asked Paul and Silas what he needed to do to be saved. He didn't want to waste one minute. You can be like the jailer, too. Don't waste your time. Decide today that you will follow Jesus. Then be like the jailer, and do it!

THE JAILER KNEW PAUL AND SILAS WERE PREACHING THE TRUTH AND HE BELIEVED. THE WHOLE STORY: ACTS 16:22-40

Go to page 1288 for the next Super Hero

5But the Jews were jealous. So they rounded up some evil fellows from the market place. Forming a crowd, they started all kinds of trouble in the city. The Jews rushed to Jason's house. They were looking for Paul and Silas. They wanted to bring them out to the crowd. 6But they couldn't find them. So they dragged Jason and some other believers to the city officials. "These men have caused trouble all over the world," they shouted. "Now they have come here. 7Jason has welcomed them into his house. They are all disobeying Caesar's commands. They say there is another king. He is called Jesus."

8When the crowd and the city officials heard this, they became very upset. 9They made Jason and the others give them money. They wanted to make sure they would return to the court. Then they let them go.

Paul and Silas Are Sent to Berea

10As soon as it was night, the believers sent Paul and Silas away to Berea. When they arrived, they went to the Jewish synagogue. 11The Bereans were very glad to receive Paul's message. They studied the Scriptures carefully every day. They wanted to see if what Paul said was true. So they were more noble than the Thessalonians. 12Many of the Jews believed. A number of important Greek women also became believers. And so did many Greek men.

13The Jews in Thessalonica found out that Paul was preaching God's word in Berea. So they went there too. They stirred up the crowds and got them all worked up. 14Right away the believers sent Paul to the coast. But Silas and Timothy stayed in Berea. 15The men who went with Paul took him to Athens. Then they returned with orders that Silas and Timothy were supposed to join him as soon as they could.

Paul Preaches in Athens

16Paul was waiting for Silas and Timothy in Athens. He was very upset to see that the city was full of statues of gods. 17So he went to the synagogue. There he talked with Jews and with Greeks who worshiped God. Each day he spoke with anyone who happened to be in the market place.

18A group of Epicurean and Stoic thinkers began to argue with him. Some of them asked, "What is this fellow chattering about?" Others said, "He seems to be telling us about gods we've never heard of." They said this because Paul was preaching the good news about Jesus. He was telling them that Jesus had risen from the dead.

19They took him to a meeting of the Areopagus. There they said to him, "What is this new teaching you're giving us? 20You have some strange ideas. We've never heard them before. We want to know what they mean."

21All the people of Athens spent their time talking about and listening to the latest ideas. People from other lands who lived there did the same.

22Then Paul stood up in the meeting of the Areopagus. He said, "Men of Athens! I see that you are very religious in every way. 23As I walked around, I looked carefully at the things you worship. I even found an altar with TO AN UNKNOWN GOD written on it. Now I am going to tell you about this 'unknown god' that you worship.

24"He is the God who made the world. He also made everything in it. He is the Lord of heaven and earth. He doesn't live in temples built by hands. 25He is not served by human hands. He doesn't need anything. He himself gives life and breath to all people. He also gives them everything else they have. 26From one man he made all the people of the world. Now they live all over the earth. He decided exactly when they should live. And he decided exactly where they should live. 27God did this so that people would seek him. Then perhaps they would reach out for him and find him. They would find him even though he is not far from any of us. 28'In him we live and move and exist.' As some of your own poets have also said, 'We are his children.'

29"Yes, we are God's children. So we shouldn't think that God is made out of

POWER-SURGE

BELIEVES ✝

MANY OF THE JEWS BELIEVED. A NUMBER OF IMPORTANT GREEK WOMEN ALSO BECAME BELIEVERS. AND SO DID MANY GREEK MEN.
— ACTS 17:12 —

gold or silver or stone. He isn't a statue planned and made by clever people. **30**In the past, God didn't judge people for what they didn't know. But now he commands all people everywhere to turn away from their sins. **31**He has set a day when he will judge the world fairly. He has appointed a man to be its judge. God has proved this to all people by raising that man from the dead."

32When they heard Paul talk about the dead rising, some of them made fun of it. But others said, "We want to hear you speak about this again." **33**So Paul left the meeting of the Areopagus. **34**A few men became followers of Paul and believed in Jesus. Dionysius was one of them. He was a member of the Areopagus. A woman named Damaris also became a believer. And so did some others.

Paul Goes to Corinth

18 After this, Paul left Athens and went to Corinth. **2**There he met a Jew named Aquila, who was a native of Pontus. Aquila had recently come from Italy with his wife Priscilla. The emperor Claudius had ordered all the Jews to leave Rome. Paul went to see Aquila and Priscilla. **3**They were tentmakers, just as he was. So he stayed and worked with them. **4**Every Sabbath day he went to the synagogue. He was trying to get both Jews and Greeks to believe in the Lord.

5Silas and Timothy came from Macedonia. Then Paul spent all his time preaching. He gave witness to the Jews that Jesus was the Christ. **6**But the Jews opposed Paul. They treated him badly. He didn't like this. So he shook out his clothes. Then he said to them, "Anything that happens to you will be your own fault! Don't blame me for it! From now on I will go to people who are not Jews."

7Then Paul left the synagogue. He went next door to the house of Titius Justus, a man who worshiped God. **8**Crispus was the synagogue ruler. He and his whole family came to believe in the Lord. Many others who lived in Corinth heard Paul. They too believed and were baptized.

9One night the Lord spoke to Paul in a vision. "Don't be afraid," he said. "Keep on speaking. Don't be silent. **10**I am with you. No one will attack you and harm you. I have many people in this city." **11**So Paul stayed there for a year and a half. He taught them God's word.

12At that time Gallio was governor of Achaia. The Jews got together and attacked Paul. They brought him into court.

13"This man," they charged, "is trying to talk people into worshiping God in ways that are against the law."

14Paul was about to speak up for himself. But just then Gallio spoke to the Jews. "You Jews are not claiming that Paul has committed a crime, whether large or small," he said. "If you were, it would make sense for me to listen to you. **15**But this is about your own law. It is a question of words and names. Settle the matter yourselves. I will not be a judge of such things." **16**So he had them thrown out of the court. **17**Then all the Jews turned against Sosthenes. He was the synagogue ruler. They beat him up in front of the court. But Gallio didn't care at all.

Priscilla and Aquila Teach Apollos

18Paul stayed in Corinth for some time. Then he left the believers and sailed for Syria. Priscilla and Aquila went with him. Before he sailed, he had his hair cut off at Cenchrea. He did this because he had made a promise to God. **19**They arrived at Ephesus. There Paul said good-by to Priscilla and Aquila. He himself went into the synagogue and talked with the Jews. **20**The Jews asked him to spend more time with them. But he said no. **21**As he left, he made them a promise. "If God wants me to," he said, "I will come back." Then he sailed from Ephesus. **22**When he landed at Caesarea, he went up to Jerusalem. There he greeted the church. He then went down to Antioch.

23Paul spent some time in Antioch. Then he left and traveled all over Galatia and Phrygia. He gave strength to all the believers there.

24At that time a Jew named Apollos came to Ephesus. He was an educated

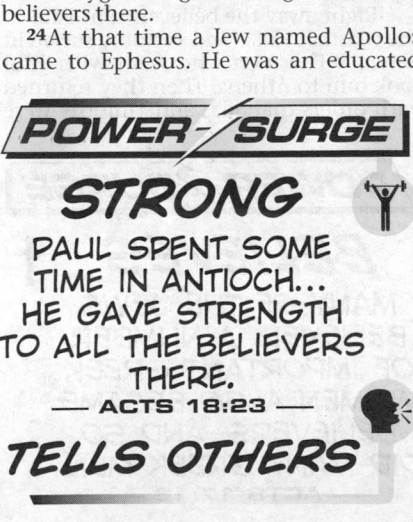

POWER-SURGE

STRONG

PAUL SPENT SOME TIME IN ANTIOCH... HE GAVE STRENGTH TO ALL THE BELIEVERS THERE.
— ACTS 18:23 —

TELLS OTHERS

man from Alexandria. He knew the Scriptures very well. 25Apollos had been taught the way of the Lord. He spoke with great power. He taught the truth about Jesus. But he only knew about John's baptism. 26He began to speak boldly in the synagogue. Priscilla and Aquila heard him. So they invited him to their home. There they gave him a better understanding of the way of God.

27Apollos wanted to go to Achaia. The brothers agreed with him. They wrote to the believers there. They asked them to welcome him. When he arrived, he was a great help to those who had become believers by God's grace. 28He argued strongly against the Jews in public meetings. He proved from the Scriptures that Jesus was the Christ.

Paul Goes to Ephesus

19 While Apollos was at Corinth, Paul took the road to Ephesus. When he arrived, he found some believers there. 2He asked them, "Did you receive the Holy Spirit when you became believers?"

"No," they answered. "We haven't even heard that there is a Holy Spirit."

3So Paul asked, "Then what baptism did you receive?"

"John's baptism," they replied.

4Paul said, "John baptized people, calling them to turn away from their sins. He told them to believe in the one who was coming after him. Jesus is that one." 5After hearing this, they were baptized in the name of the Lord Jesus. 6Paul placed his hands on them. Then the Holy Spirit came on them. They spoke in languages they had not known before. They also prophesied. 7There were about 12 of them in all.

8Paul entered the synagogue. There he spoke boldly for three months. He tried to talk the people into accepting his teaching about God's kingdom. 9But some of them wouldn't listen. They refused to believe. In public they said evil things about the Way of Jesus. So Paul left them. He took the believers with him. Each day he talked with people in the lecture hall of Tyrannus. 10This went on for two years. So all the Jews and Greeks who lived in Asia Minor heard the word of the Lord.

11God did amazing miracles through Paul. 12Even handkerchiefs and aprons that had touched him were taken to those who were sick. When this happened, their sicknesses were healed and evil spirits left them.

13Some Jews went around driving out evil spirits. They tried to use the name of the Lord Jesus to set free those who were controlled by demons. They said, "In Jesus' name I command you to come out. He is the Jesus that Paul is preaching about." 14Seven sons of Sceva were doing this. Sceva was a Jewish chief priest. 15One day the evil spirit answered them, "I know Jesus. And I know about Paul. But who are you?" 16Then the man who had the evil spirit jumped on Sceva's sons. He overpowered them all. He gave them a terrible beating. They ran out of the house naked and bleeding.

17The Jews and Greeks living in Ephesus heard about this. They were all overcome with fear. They held the name of the Lord Jesus in high honor. 18Many who believed now came and openly admitted the evil they had done. 19A number of those who had practiced evil magic brought their scrolls together. They set them on fire out in the open. They added up the value of the scrolls. They found that it would take more than two lifetimes to earn what the scrolls were worth.

20The word of the Lord spread everywhere. It became more and more powerful.

21After all this had happened, Paul decided to go to Jerusalem. He went through Macedonia and Achaia. "After I have been to Jerusalem," he said, "I must visit Rome also." 22He sent Timothy and Erastus, two of his helpers, to Macedonia. But he stayed a little longer in Asia Minor.

Trouble in Ephesus

23At that time many people became very upset about the Way of Jesus. 24There was a man named Demetrius who made things out of silver. He made silver models of the temple of the goddess Artemis. He brought in a lot of business for the other skilled workers. 25One day he called them together. He also called others who were in the same kind of business. "Men," he said, "you know that we make good money from our work. 26You have seen and heard what this fellow Paul is doing. He has talked to large numbers of people here in Ephesus. Almost everywhere in Asia Minor he has led people away from our gods. He says that the gods we make are not gods at all. 27Our work is in danger of losing its good name. People's faith in the temple of the great goddess Artemis will be weakened. Now she is worshiped through all of Asia Minor and the whole world. But soon she will be robbed of her greatness."

28When they heard this, they became

PRISCILLA AND AQUILA

ACTS 18:26

Priscilla and Aquila heard [Apollos]. So they invited him to their home. There they gave him a better understanding of the way of God.

Priscilla (pri-SILL-uh) gently washed and then wrapped up the gash on Aquila's (uh-KWILL-uhz) hand. He knew she was thinking he needed to be more careful. But making tents was a business where getting hurt happened a lot. Sometimes Aquila stabbed himself with a needle while sewing. OTHER TIMES HE SLICED A FINGER WITH THE SHARP KNIFE HE USED FOR CUTTING ROUGH AND STURDY CLOTH.

Aquila and Priscilla had just moved to the city of Corinth. They had lived and worked for many years in Rome. But recently all the Jews—including them—had been ordered to leave Rome.

At first life had been hard in Corinth. They knew so few people there. They had missed all their friends and family. But the Christians in Corinth had welcomed them, and they were making new friends every day.

One of their new friends now worked with them. His name was Paul. He also made tents. But more than that, Paul was a missionary and a teacher. Every chance he had, he taught the people in Corinth about Jesus.

Aquila left Priscilla in the kitchen and walked to the doorway of the shop, where Paul was already at work. This would be their last day in Corinth. Tomorrow they would all be leaving for Ephesus . . .

Aquila and Priscilla set up their tentmaking business as soon as they arrived in Ephesus. They met with the other believers in the city to worship and study. Some months later, Aquila and Priscilla met another teacher and missionary, Apollos. Apollos had studied the Bible. He spoke with power about God and Jesus. But he didn't know about Jesus' death on the cross and his resurrection. So they invited him to their house and began to teach Apollos what they knew.

BE AN AQUILA AND PRISCILLA

Aquila and Priscilla were not only faithful followers of Christ, they were good teachers. They passed on what they had learned to Apollos. Be an Aquila and Priscilla. Share what you have learned about Jesus!

AQUILA AND PRISCILLA SHARED WHAT THEY LEARNED.
THE WHOLE STORY: ACTS 18:1-4, 24-26

Go to page 1289 for the next Super Hero

very angry. They began shouting, "Great is Artemis of the Ephesians!" **29**Soon people were making trouble in the whole city. They all rushed into the theater. They dragged Gaius and Aristarchus along with them. These two men had come with Paul from Macedonia. **30**Paul wanted to appear in front of the crowd. But the believers wouldn't let him. **31**Some of the officials in Asia Minor were friends of Paul. They sent him a message, begging him not to go into the theater.

32The crowd didn't know what was going on. Some were shouting one thing

APOLLOS

ACTS 18:25-26

B

Y

T

Apollos had been taught the way of the Lord. He spoke with great power. He taught the truth about Jesus. But he only knew about John's baptism. He began to speak boldly in the synagogue. Priscilla and Aquila heard him. So they invited him to their home. There they gave him a better understanding of the way of God.

Apollos (ah-PALL-us) stood up in front of the Jews in Ephesus. There was so much he wanted to tell them. HE OPENED HIS MOUTH AND SPOKE FORCEFULLY AND WITH GREAT PASSION. He wanted these people to understand how important it was for them to know God and follow him. He wanted them to know they needed forgiveness from God for their sins, just as John the Baptist had preached. But he didn't know that Jesus had come.

When Apollos finished speaking he sat down. Many people came up to him and talked to him. Finally, when almost everyone was gone, two more people came. Aquila and Priscilla knew about Jesus and how he had lived and died and come back to life. And they wanted Apollos to know, too.

Aquila and Priscilla invited Apollos to their home. There they told Apollos all about Jesus so that he would understand and believe.

BE AN APOLLOS

Apollos spoke bravely to the people about God. And when he discovered he had more to learn, he listened and accepted the truths about Jesus. Be an Apollos: brave and strong and sure, but still willing to learn more.

APOLLOS WAS BRAVE AND CERTAIN AND WILLING TO LEARN.

Go to page 1291 for the next Super Hero

and some another. Most of the people didn't even know why they were there. 33The Jews pushed Alexander to the front. Some of the crowd tried to tell him what to say. But he motioned for them to be quiet. He wanted to speak up for himself in front of the people. 34But then they realized that he was a Jew. So they all shouted the same thing for about two hours. "Great is Artemis of the Ephesians!" they yelled.

35The city clerk quieted the crowd down. "Men of Ephesus!" he said. "The whole world knows that the city of Ephesus guards the temple of the great Artemis. They know that Ephesus guards her statue, which fell from heaven. 36These facts can't be questioned. So calm down. Don't do anything foolish.

37"These men haven't robbed any temples. They haven't said evil things against our goddess. But you have brought them here anyhow. 38Demetrius and the other skilled workers may feel they have been wronged by someone. Let them bring charges. The courts are open. We have our governors. 39Is there anything else you want to bring up? Settle it in a court of law. 40As it is, today we are in danger of being charged with causing all this trouble. But there is no reason for it. We wouldn't be able to explain what has happened." 41After he said this, he sent the people away.

Paul Travels Through Macedonia and Greece

20 All the trouble came to an end. Then Paul sent for the believers. After cheering them up, he said good-by. He then left for Macedonia. 2He traveled through that area, speaking many words of hope to the people. Finally he arrived in Greece. 3There he stayed for three months. He was just about to sail for Syria. But the Jews were making plans against him. So he decided to go back through Macedonia. 4Sopater, son of Pyrrhus, from Berea went with him. Aristarchus and Secundus from Thessalonica, Gaius from Derbe, and Timothy went too. Tychicus and Trophimus from Asia Minor also went with him. 5These men went on ahead. They waited for us at Troas. 6But we sailed from Philippi after the Feast of Unleavened Bread. Five days later we joined the others at Troas. We stayed there for seven days.

Eutychus Is Raised From the Dead

7On the first day of the week we met to break bread and eat together. Paul spoke to the people. He kept on talking until midnight because he planned to leave the next day. 8There were many lamps in the room upstairs where we were meeting. 9A young man named Eutychus was sitting in a window. He sank into a deep sleep as Paul talked on and on. Sound asleep, Eutychus fell from the third floor. When they picked him up from the ground, he was dead.

10Paul went down and threw himself on the young man. He put his arms around him. "Don't be alarmed," he told them. "He's alive!" 11Then Paul went upstairs again. He broke bread and ate with them. He kept on talking until daylight. Then he left. 12The people took the young man home. They were greatly comforted because he was alive.

Paul Says Good-by to the Ephesian Elders

13We went on ahead to the ship. We sailed for Assos. There we were going to take Paul on board. He had planned it this way because he wanted to go there by land. 14So he met us at Assos. We took him on board and went on to Mitylene. 15The next day we sailed from there. We arrived near Kios. The day after that we crossed over to Samos. We arrived at Miletus the next day. 16Paul had decided to sail past Ephesus. He didn't want to spend time in Asia Minor. He was in a hurry to get to Jerusalem. If he could, he wanted to be there by the day of Pentecost.

17From Miletus, Paul sent for the elders of the church at Ephesus. 18When they arrived, he spoke to them. "You know how I lived the whole time I was with you," he said. "From the first day I came into Asia Minor, 19I was free of pride. I served the Lord with tears. I served him even though I was greatly tested by the evil plans of the Jews. 20You know I haven't let anyone keep me from preaching anything that would be helpful to you. I have taught you in public and from house to house. 21I have told both Jews and Greeks that they must turn away from their sins to God. They must have faith in our Lord Jesus.

22"Now I am going to Jerusalem. The Holy Spirit compels me. I don't know what will happen to me there. 23I only know that in every city the Spirit warns me. He tells me that I will face prison and suffering. 24But my life means nothing to me. I only want to finish the race. I want to complete the work the Lord Jesus has given me. He wants me to give witness to

EUTYCHUS

ACTS 20:10-12

Paul went down and threw himself on the young man. He put his arms around him. "Don't be alarmed," he told them. "He's alive!" Then Paul went upstairs again. He broke bread and ate with them. He kept on talking until daylight. Then he left. The people took the young man home. They were greatly comforted because he was alive.

Young Eutychus (YOU-ti-kuss) walked up three sets of stairs and into the room where Paul was speaking. The room was crammed with people. A number of lamps were burning to give light. Eutychus stood in the doorway of the room and felt the heat from the people and the lamps. He worked his way through the people to a window. Maybe there he could hear Paul but also catch a cool night breeze.

Eutychus listened carefully to Paul teach. After a while, he began to feel tired. He tried to keep his eyes open, but they just kept falling shut. **HIS HEAD FELL BACK AGAINST THE WINDOW FRAME, THEN JERKED UP AGAIN.** Paul kept talking on and on, and Eutychus wanted to listen, but . . .

He just couldn't stay awake. Soon he was sleeping soundly in the window. So soundly that he slumped over, then fell out of the window to the ground floor. Several people saw him fall and screamed.

Paul rushed down the stairs. Some men had already picked up Eutychus, and he was dead. Paul threw himself on the young man and put his arms around him. Then he raised his head to look at the crowd that had gathered.

"Don't worry," he told them. "He's alive!"

Paul and Eutychus and the rest all went back up the stairs. They had something to eat and continued to talk together until it was almost morning. Eutychus and his friends couldn't stop smiling. What had looked like a terrible tragedy had turned into a night of smiles and happiness.

BE A EUTYCHUS

Eutychus was a serious follower of Jesus. He listened to Paul preach for a long time. Be just like him! Be a serious believer in Jesus and learn all you can about him. But don't sit in any windows when you're tired!

EUTYCHUS WAS BROUGHT BACK TO LIFE AND FOLLOWED JESUS.

Go to page 1299 for the next person

BELIEVES ✝

THEY MUST TURN AWAY FROM THEIR SINS TO GOD. THEY MUST HAVE FAITH IN OUR LORD JESUS.
— ACTS 20:21 —

others about the good news of God's grace.

25"I have spent time with you preaching about the kingdom. I know that none of you will ever see me again. 26So I tell you today that I am not guilty if anyone has not believed. 27I haven't let anyone keep me from telling you everything God wants you to do.

28"Keep watch over yourselves. Keep watch over all the believers. The Holy Spirit has made you leaders over them. Be shepherds of God's church. He bought it with his own blood.

29"I know that after I leave, wild wolves will come in among you. They won't spare any of the sheep. 30Even men from your own people will rise up and twist the truth. They want to get the believers to follow them. 31So be on your guard! Remember that for three years I never stopped warning you. Night and day I warned each of you with tears.

32"Now I commit you to God's care. I commit you to the word of his grace. It can build you up. Then you will share in what God plans to give all his people. 33I haven't longed for anyone's silver or gold or clothing. 34You yourselves know that I have used my own hands to meet my needs. I have also met the needs of my companions. 35In everything I did, I showed you that we must work hard and help the weak. We must remember the words of the Lord Jesus. He said, 'It is more blessed to give than to receive.' "

36When Paul had said this, he got down on his knees with all of them and prayed. 37They all cried as they hugged and kissed him. 38What hurt them the most was that he had said they would never see his face again. Then they went with him to the ship.

Paul Continues His Journey

21 After we had torn ourselves away from the Ephesian elders, we headed out to sea. We sailed straight to Cos. The next day we went to Rhodes. From there we continued on to Patara. 2We found a ship crossing over to Phoenicia. So we went on board and headed out to sea. 3We came near Cyprus and passed to the south of it. Then we sailed on to Syria. We landed at Tyre. There our ship was supposed to unload. 4We found the believers there and stayed with them for seven days. Led by the Holy Spirit, they tried to get Paul not to go on to Jerusalem. 5But when it was time to leave, we continued on our way. All the believers and their families went with us out of the city. There on the beach we got down on our knees to pray. 6We said good-by to each other. Then we went on board the ship. And they returned home.

7Continuing on from Tyre, we landed at Ptolemais. There we greeted the brothers and sisters. We stayed with them for a day. 8The next day we left and arrived at Caesarea. We stayed at the house of Philip the evangelist. He was one of the seven deacons. 9He had four unmarried daughters who prophesied.

10We stayed there several days. Then a prophet named Agabus came down from Judea. 11He came over to us. Then he took Paul's belt and tied his own hands and feet with it. He said, "The Holy Spirit says, 'This is how the Jews of Jerusalem will tie up the owner of this belt. They will hand him over to people who are not Jews.' "

12When we heard this, we all begged Paul not to go up to Jerusalem. 13He asked, "Why are you crying? Why are you breaking my heart? I'm ready to be put in prison. In fact, I'm ready to die in Jerusalem for the Lord Jesus." 14We couldn't change his mind. So we gave up. We said, "May what the Lord wants to happen be done."

15After this, we got ready and went up to Jerusalem. 16Some of the believers from Caesarea went with us. They brought us to Mnason's home. We were supposed to stay there. Mnason was from Cyprus. He was one of the first believers.

Paul Arrives in Jerusalem

17When we arrived in Jerusalem, the brothers and sisters gave us a warm welcome. 18The next day Paul and the rest of us went to see James. All the elders were there. 19Paul greeted them. Then he reported everything God had done among the non-Jews through his work.

20When they heard this, they praised God. Then they spoke to Paul. "Brother," they said, "you see that thousands of Jews have become believers. All of them try very hard to obey the law. 21They have been told that you teach all the Jews who live among the non-Jews to turn away from Moses. They think that you teach them not to circumcise their children. They think that you teach them to give up our Jewish ways.

22"What should we do? They will certainly hear that you have come. 23So do what we tell you. There are four men with us who have made a promise to God. 24Take them with you. Join them in the Jewish practice that makes people pure and clean. Pay their expenses so they can have their heads shaved. Then everybody will know that these reports about you are not true in any way. They will know that you yourself obey the law.

25"We have already given written directions to the believers who are not Jews. They must not eat food that has been offered to statues of gods. They must not drink blood. They must not eat the meat of animals that have been choked to death. And they must not commit sexual sins."

26The next day Paul took the men with him. They all made themselves pure and clean in the usual way. Then Paul went to the temple. There he reported the date when the days of cleansing would end. At that time the proper offering would be made for each of them.

Paul Is Arrested

27The seven days of cleansing were almost over. Some Jews from Asia Minor saw Paul at the temple. They stirred up the whole crowd. They arrested Paul, 28"Men of Israel, help us!" they shouted. "This is the man who teaches everyone in all places against our people. He speaks against our law and against this holy place. Besides, he has brought Greeks into the temple area. He has made this holy place unclean." 29They said this because they had seen Trophimus the Ephesian in the city with Paul. They thought Paul had brought him into the temple area.

30The whole city was stirred up. People came running from all directions. They grabbed Paul and dragged him out of the temple. Right away the temple gates were shut. 31The people were trying to kill Paul. But news reached the commander of the Roman troops. He heard that people were making trouble in the whole city of Jerusalem. 32At once he took some officers and soldiers with him. They ran down to

the crowd. The people causing the trouble saw the commander and his soldiers. So they stopped beating Paul.

33The commander came up and arrested Paul. He ordered him to be held with two chains. Then he asked who Paul was and what he had done. 34Some in the crowd shouted one thing, some another. But the commander couldn't get the facts because of all the noise. So he ordered that Paul be taken into the fort. 35Paul reached the steps. But then the mob became so wild that he had to be carried by the soldiers. 36The crowd that followed kept shouting, "Kill him!"

Paul Speaks to the Crowd

37The soldiers were about to take Paul into the fort. Then he asked the commander, "May I say something to you?"

"Do you speak Greek?" he replied. 38"Aren't you the Egyptian who turned some of our people against their leaders? Didn't you lead 4,000 terrorists out into the desert some time ago?"

39Paul answered, "I am a Jew from Tarsus in Cilicia. I am a citizen of an important city. Please let me speak to the people."

40The commander told him he could. So Paul stood on the steps and motioned to the crowd. When all of them were quiet, he spoke to them in the Aramaic language.

22 1"Brothers and fathers," Paul began, "listen to me now. I want to speak up for myself."

2When they heard that he was speaking to them in Aramaic, they became very quiet.

Then Paul said, 3"I am a Jew. I was born in Tarsus in Cilicia. But I grew up here in Jerusalem. I was well trained by Gamaliel in the law of our people. I wanted to serve God as much as any of you do today. 4I hurt the followers of the Way of Jesus. I sent many of them to their death. I arrested men and women. I threw them into prison. 5The high priest and the whole Council can give witness to this. I even had some official letters they had written to their friends in Damascus. So I went there to bring these people as prisoners to Jerusalem to be punished.

6"I had almost reached Damascus. About noon a bright light from heaven suddenly flashed around me. 7I fell to the ground and heard a voice speak to me. 'Saul! Saul!' it said. 'Why are you opposing me?'

8" 'Who are you, Lord?' I asked.

" 'I am Jesus of Nazareth,' he replied. 'I am the one you are opposing.'

9"The light was seen by my companions. But they didn't understand the voice of the one speaking to me.

10" 'What should I do, Lord?' I asked.

" 'Get up,' the Lord said. 'Go into Damascus. There you will be told everything you have been given to do.' **11**The brightness of the light had blinded me. So my companions led me by the hand into Damascus.

12"A man named Ananias came to see me. He was a godly Jew who obeyed the law. All the Jews living there respected him very much. **13**He stood beside me and said, 'Brother Saul, receive your sight!' At that very moment I was able to see him.

14"Then he said, 'The God of our people has chosen you. He wanted to tell you his plans for you. You have seen the Blameless One. You have heard words from his mouth. **15**Now you will give witness to all people about what you have seen and heard. **16**So what are you waiting for? Get up and call on his name. Be baptized. Have your sins washed away.'

17"I returned to Jerusalem and was praying at the temple. Then it seemed to me that I was dreaming. **18**I saw the Lord speaking to me. 'Quick!' he said. 'Leave Jerusalem at once. These people will not accept your witness about me.'

19" 'Lord,' I replied, 'these people know what I used to do. I went from one synagogue to another and put believers in prison. I also beat them. **20**Stephen was a man who also gave witness to others about you. I stood there when he was killed. I had agreed that he should die. I even guarded the coats of those who were killing him.'

21"Then the Lord said to me, 'Go. I will send you far away to people who are not Jews.' "

Paul the Roman Citizen

22The crowd listened to Paul until he said this. Then they shouted, "Kill him! He isn't fit to live!"

23They shouted and threw off their coats. They threw dust into the air. **24**So the commanding officer ordered Paul to be taken into the fort. He gave orders for Paul to be whipped and questioned. He wanted to find out why the people were shouting at him like this.

25A commander was standing there as they stretched Paul out to be whipped. Paul said to him, "Does the law allow you to whip a Roman citizen who hasn't even been found guilty?"

26When the commander heard this, he went to the commanding officer and reported it. "What are you going to do?" the commander asked. "This man is a Roman citizen."

27So the commanding officer went to Paul. "Tell me," he asked. "Are you a Roman citizen?"

"Yes, I am," Paul answered.

28Then the officer said, "I had to pay a lot of money to become a citizen."

"But I was born a citizen," Paul replied.

29Right away those who were about to question him left. Even the officer was alarmed. He realized that he had put Paul, a Roman citizen, in chains.

Paul Is Taken to the Sanhedrin

30The commanding officer wanted to find out exactly what the Jews had against Paul. So the next day he let Paul out of prison. He ordered a meeting of the chief priests and all the Sanhedrin. Then he brought Paul and had him stand in front of them.

23 Paul looked straight at the Sanhedrin. "My brothers," he said, "I have always done my duty to God. To this very day I feel that I have done nothing wrong."

2Ananias the high priest heard this. So he ordered the men standing near Paul to hit him on the mouth.

3Then Paul said to him, "You pretender! God will hit you! You sit there and judge me by the law. But you yourself broke the law when you commanded them to hit me!"

4Those who were standing near Paul said, "How dare you talk like that to God's high priest!"

5Paul replied, "Brothers, I didn't realize he was the high priest. It is written, 'Do not speak evil about the ruler of your people.' " *(Exodus 22:28)*

6Paul knew that some of them were Sadducees and the others Pharisees. So he called out in the Sanhedrin. "My brothers," he said, "I am a Pharisee. I am the son of a Pharisee. I believe that people will rise from the dead. That's why I am on trial."

7When he said this, the Pharisees and the Sadducees started to argue. They began to take sides. **8**The Sadducees say that people will not rise from the dead. They don't believe there are angels or spirits either. But the Pharisees believe all these things.

⁹People were causing trouble and making a lot of noise. Some of the teachers of the law who were Pharisees stood up. They argued strongly. "We find nothing wrong with this man," they said. "What if a spirit or an angel has spoken to him?" ¹⁰The arguing got out of hand. The commanding officer was afraid that Paul would be torn to pieces by those who were arguing. So he ordered the soldiers to go down and take him away from them by force. They were supposed to bring him into the fort.

¹¹The next night the Lord stood near Paul. He said, "Be brave! You have given witness about me in Jerusalem. You must do the same in Rome."

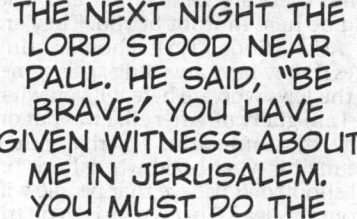

POWER-SURGE

BRAVE B

THE NEXT NIGHT THE LORD STOOD NEAR PAUL. HE SAID, "BE BRAVE! YOU HAVE GIVEN WITNESS ABOUT ME IN JERUSALEM. YOU MUST DO THE SAME IN ROME."
— ACTS 23:11 —

TELLS OTHERS

The Plan to Kill Paul

¹²The next morning the Jews gathered secretly to make plans against Paul. They took an oath that they would not eat or drink anything until they had killed him. ¹³More than 40 men took part in this plan. ¹⁴They went to the chief priests and the elders. They said, "We have taken a strong oath. We have made a special promise to God. We will not eat anything until we have killed Paul. ¹⁵Now then, you and the Sanhedrin must make an appeal to the commanding officer. Ask him to bring Paul to you. Pretend you want more facts about his case. We are ready to kill him before he gets here."

¹⁶But Paul's nephew heard about this plan. So he went into the fort and told Paul.

¹⁷Then Paul called one of the commanders. He said to him, "Take this young man to the commanding officer. He has something to tell him." ¹⁸So the commander took Paul's nephew to the officer.

The commander said, "Paul, the prisoner, sent for me. He asked me to bring this young man to you. The young man has something to tell you."

¹⁹The commanding officer took the young man by the hand. He spoke to him in private. "What do you want to tell me?" the officer asked.

²⁰He said, "The Jews have agreed to ask you to bring Paul to the Sanhedrin tomorrow. They will pretend they want more facts about him. ²¹Don't give in to them. More than 40 of them are waiting in hiding to attack him. They have taken an oath that they will not eat or drink anything until they have killed him. They are ready now. All they need is for you to bring Paul to the Sanhedrin."

²²The commanding officer let the young man go. But he gave him a warning. "Don't tell anyone you have reported this to me," he said.

Paul Is Taken to Caesarea

²³Then the commanding officer called for two of his commanders. He ordered them, "Gather a company of 200 soldiers, 70 horsemen and 200 men armed with spears. Get them ready to go to Caesarea at nine o'clock tonight. ²⁴Provide horses for Paul so that he may be taken safely to Governor Felix."

²⁵Here is the letter the officer wrote.

²⁶I, Claudius Lysias, am writing this letter.

I am sending it to His Excellency, Governor Felix.

Greetings.

²⁷The Jews grabbed Paul. They were about to kill him. But I came with my soldiers and saved him. I had learned that he is a Roman citizen. ²⁸I wanted to know why they were bringing charges against him. So I brought him to their Sanhedrin. ²⁹I found out that the charge against him was based on questions about their law. But there was no charge against him worthy of death or prison. ³⁰Then I was told about a plan against the man. So I sent him to you at once. I also ordered those bringing charges against him to tell you their case.

31The soldiers followed their orders. During the night they took Paul with them. They brought him as far as Antipatris. **32**The next day they let the horsemen go on with him. The soldiers returned to the fort. **33**The horsemen arrived in Caesarea. They gave the letter to the governor. Then they handed Paul over to him. **34**The governor read the letter. He asked Paul where he was from. He learned that Paul was from Cilicia. **35**So he said, "I will hear your case when those bringing charges against you get here." Then he ordered that Paul be kept under guard in Herod's palace.

Paul's Trial in Front of Felix

24 Five days later Ananias the high priest went down to Caesarea. Some elders and a lawyer named Tertullus went with him. They brought their charges against Paul to the governor. **2**So Paul was called in. Tertullus began to bring the charges against Paul. He said to Felix, "We have enjoyed a long time of peace while you have been ruling. You are a wise leader. You have made this a better nation. **3**Most excellent Felix, we gladly admit this everywhere and in every way. And we are very thankful. **4**I don't want to bother you. But would you be kind enough to listen to us for a short time?

POWER-SURGE

THANKFUL ♣
WE ARE VERY THANKFUL.
— ACTS 24:3 —

5"We have found that Paul is a troublemaker. He stirs up trouble among Jews all over the world. He is a leader of those who follow Jesus of Nazareth. **6/7**He even tried to pollute our temple. So we arrested him. **8**Question him yourself. Then you will learn the truth about all these charges we are bringing against him."

9The Jews said the same thing. They agreed that the charges were true.

10The governor motioned for Paul to speak. Paul said, "I know that you have been a judge over this nation for quite a few years. So I am glad to stand up for myself. **11**About 12 days ago I went up to Jerusalem to worship. You can easily check on this. **12**Those bringing charges against me did not find me arguing with anyone at the temple. I wasn't stirring up a crowd in the synagogues or anywhere else in the city. **13**They can't prove to you any of the charges they are making against me.

14"It is true that I worship the God of our people. I am a follower of the Way of Jesus. Those bringing charges against me call it a cult. I believe everything that agrees with the Law. I believe everything written in the Prophets. **15**I have the same hope in God that these men have. I believe that both the godly and the ungodly will rise from the dead. **16**So I always try not to do anything wrong in the eyes of God and man.

17"I was away for several years. Then I came to Jerusalem to bring my people gifts for those who were poor. I also came to offer sacrifices. **18**They found me doing this in the temple courtyard. I had already been made pure and clean in the usual way. There was no crowd with me. I didn't stir up any trouble.

19"But there are some other Jews who should be here in front of you. They are from Asia Minor. They should bring charges if they have anything against me. **20**Let the Jews who are here tell you what crime I am guilty of. After all, I was put on trial by the Sanhedrin. **21**Perhaps they blame me for what I said when I was on trial. I shouted, 'I believe that people will rise from the dead. That is why I am on trial here today.' "

22Felix knew all about the Way of Jesus. So he put off the trial for the time being. "Lysias the commanding officer will come," he said. "Then I will decide your case." **23**He ordered the commander to keep Paul under guard. He told him to give Paul some freedom. He also told him to allow Paul's friends to take care of his needs.

24Several days later Felix came with his wife Drusilla. She was a Jew. Felix sent for Paul and listened to him speak about faith in Christ Jesus. **25**Paul talked about how to live right. He talked about how people should control themselves. He also talked about the time when God will judge everyone. Then Felix became afraid. "That's enough for now!" he said. "You may leave. When I find the time, I will send for you." **26**He was hoping that Paul would offer him some money to let him go. So he often sent for Paul and talked with him.

27Two years passed. Porcius Festus took the place of Felix. But Felix wanted to do the Jews a favor. So he left Paul in prison.

Paul's Trial in Front of Festus

25 Three days after Festus arrived, he went up from Caesarea to Jerusalem. **2**There the chief priests and Jewish leaders came to him and brought their charges against Paul. **3**They tried to get Festus to have Paul taken to Jerusalem. They asked for this as a favor. They were planning to hide and attack Paul along the way. They wanted to kill him. **4**Festus answered, "Paul is being held at Caesarea. Soon I'll be going there myself. **5**Let some of your leaders come with me. If the man has done anything wrong, they can bring charges against him there."

6Festus spent eight or ten days in Jerusalem with them. Then he went down to Caesarea. The next day he called the court together. He ordered Paul to be brought to him. **7**When Paul arrived, the Jews who had come down from Jerusalem stood around him. They brought many strong charges against him. But they couldn't prove them.

8Then Paul spoke up for himself. He said, "I've done nothing wrong against the law of the Jews or against the temple. I've done nothing wrong against Caesar."

9But Festus wanted to do the Jews a favor. So he said to Paul, "Are you willing to go up to Jerusalem? Are you willing to go on trial there? Are you willing to face these charges in my court?"

10Paul answered, "I'm already standing in Caesar's court. This is where I should go on trial. I haven't done anything wrong to the Jews. You yourself know that very well. **11**If I am guilty of anything worthy of death, I'm willing to die. But the charges brought against me by these Jews are not true. No one has the right to hand me over to them. I make my appeal to Caesar!"

12Festus talked it over with the members of his court. Then he said, "You have made an appeal to Caesar. To Caesar you will go!"

Festus Talks With King Agrippa

13A few days later King Agrippa and Bernice arrived in Caesarea. They came to pay a visit to Festus. **14**They were spending many days there. So Festus talked with the king about Paul's case. He said, "There's a man here that Felix left as a prisoner. **15**When I went to Jerusalem, the Jewish chief priests and the elders brought charges against the man. They wanted him to be found guilty.

16"I told them that this is not the way Romans do things. We don't judge people before they have faced those bringing charges against them. They must have a chance to speak up for themselves. **17**When the Jews came back with me, I didn't waste any time. I called the court together the next day. I ordered the man to be brought in. **18**Those bringing charges against him got up to speak. But they didn't charge him with any of the crimes I had expected. **19**Instead, they argued with him about their own beliefs. They didn't agree about a dead man named Jesus. Paul claimed Jesus was alive.

20"I had no idea how to look into such matters. So I asked Paul if he would be willing to go to Jerusalem. There he could be tried on these charges. **21**But Paul made an appeal to have the Emperor decide his case. So I ordered him to be held until I could send him to Caesar."

22Then Agrippa said to Festus, "I would like to hear this man myself."

Festus replied, "Tomorrow you will hear him."

Paul Speaks to Agrippa

23The next day Agrippa and Bernice arrived. They acted like very important people. They entered the courtroom. The most important officers and the leading men of the city came with them. When Festus gave the command, Paul was brought in. **24**Festus said, "King Agrippa, and all who are here with us, take a good look at this man! Both in Jerusalem and here in Caesarea a large number of Jews have come to me about him. They keep shouting that he shouldn't live any longer. **25**I have found that he hasn't done anything worthy of death. But he made his appeal to the Emperor. So I decided to send him to Rome.

26"I don't have anything certain to write about him to His Majesty. So I have brought him here today. Now all of you

POWER-SURGE

SELF-CONTROLLED

PAUL TALKED ABOUT HOW TO LIVE RIGHT. HE TALKED ABOUT HOW PEOPLE SHOULD CONTROL THEMSELVES.
— ACTS 24:25 —

will be able to hear him. King Agrippa, it will also be very good for you to hear him. As a result of this hearing, I will have something to write. ²⁷It doesn't make sense to send a prisoner to Rome without listing the charges against him."

26

Agrippa said to Paul, "You may now speak for yourself."

So Paul motioned with his hand. Then he began to stand up for himself. ²"King Agrippa," he said, "I am happy to be able to stand here today. I will speak up for myself against all the charges brought by the Jews. ³I am very pleased that you are familiar with Jewish ways. You know the kinds of things they argue about. So I beg you to be patient as you listen to me.

⁴"The Jews all know how I have lived ever since I was a child. They know all about me from the beginning of my life. They know how I lived in my own country and in Jerusalem. ⁵They have known me for a long time. So if they wanted to, they could give witness that I lived by the rules of the Pharisees. Those rules are harder to obey than the rules of any other group in the Jewish faith.

⁶"Today I am on trial because of the hope I have. I believe in what God promised our people long ago. ⁷It is the promise that our 12 tribes are hoping to see come true. Because of this hope they serve God with a true and honest heart day and night. King Agrippa, it is also because of this hope that the Jews are bringing charges against me. ⁸Why should any of you think it is impossible for God to raise the dead?

⁹"I myself believed that I should do everything I could to oppose the name of Jesus of Nazareth. ¹⁰That's just what I was doing in Jerusalem. On the authority of the chief priests, I put many of God's people in prison. I agreed that they should die. ¹¹I often went from one synagogue to another to have them punished. I tried to force them to speak evil things against Jesus. I hated them so much that I even went to cities in other lands to hurt them.

¹²"On one of these journeys I was on my way to Damascus. I had the authority and commission of the chief priests. ¹³About noon, King Agrippa, I was on the road. I saw a light coming from heaven. It was brighter than the sun. It was shining around me and my companions. ¹⁴We all fell to the ground. I heard a voice speak to me in the Aramaic language. 'Saul! Saul!' it said. 'Why are you opposing me? It is hard for you to go against what you know is right.'

¹⁵"Then I asked, 'Who are you, Lord?'

" 'I am Jesus,' the Lord replied. 'I am the one you are opposing. ¹⁶Now get up. Stand on your feet. I have appeared to you to appoint you to serve me and be my witness. You will tell others that you have seen me today. You will also tell them that I will show myself to you again.

¹⁷" 'I will save you from your own people and from those who aren't Jews. I am sending you to them ¹⁸to open their eyes. I want you to turn them from darkness to light. I want you to turn them from Satan's power to God. I want their sins to be forgiven. They will be forgiven when they believe in me. They will have their place among God's people.'

¹⁹"So then, King Agrippa, I obeyed the vision that appeared from heaven. ²⁰First I preached to people in Damascus. Then I preached in Jerusalem and in all Judea. I preached also to people who are not Jews. I told them to turn away from their sins to God. The way they live must prove that they have turned away from their sins. ²¹That's why the Jews grabbed me in the temple courtyard and tried to kill me.

²²"But God has helped me to this very day. So I stand here and give witness to both small and great. I have been saying nothing different from what the prophets and Moses said would happen. ²³They said the Christ would suffer. He would be the first to rise from the dead. He would announce the light of life to his own people and to those who aren't Jews."

²⁴While Paul was still speaking up for himself, Festus interrupted. "You are out of your mind, Paul!" he shouted. "Your great learning is driving you crazy!"

²⁵"I am not crazy, most excellent Festus," Paul replied. "What I am saying is true and reasonable. ²⁶The king is familiar with these things. So I can speak openly to him. I am certain he knows everything that has been going on. After all, it was not done in secret. ²⁷King Agrippa, do you believe the prophets? I know you do."

²⁸Then Agrippa spoke to Paul. "Are you trying to talk me into becoming a Christian?" he said. "Do you think you can do that in such a short time?"

²⁹Paul replied, "I don't care if it takes a short time or a long time. I pray to God for you and all who are listening to me today. I pray that you may become like me, except for these chains."

³⁰The king stood up. The governor and Bernice and those sitting with them stood up too. ³¹They left the room and began to

talk with one another. "Why should this man die or be put in prison?" they said. "He has done nothing worthy of that!"

³²Agrippa said to Festus, "This man could have been set free. But he has made an appeal to Caesar."

Paul Sails for Rome

27 It was decided that we would sail for Italy. Paul and some other prisoners were handed over to a Roman commander named Julius. He belonged to the Imperial Guard. ²We boarded a ship from Adramyttium. It was about to sail for ports along the coast of Asia Minor. We headed out to sea. Aristarchus was with us. He was a Macedonian from Thessalonica.

³The next day we landed at Sidon. There Julius was kind to Paul. He let Paul visit his friends so they could give him what he needed. ⁴From there we headed out to sea again. We passed the calmer

AGRIPPA (Not!)

ACTS 26:28

Then Agrippa spoke to Paul. "Are you trying to talk me into becoming a Christian?" he said. "Do you think you can do that in such a short time?"

King Agrippa's (uh-GRIP-uhz) royal robes swung heavily as he walked into the room. He held his head high and proud. Soon Paul was brought into the room. Agrippa knew Paul was in prison because he believed in Jesus. Agrippa looked Paul up and down, then said, **"YOU HAVE PERMISSION TO SPEAK."**

Paul told Agrippa all about Jesus, starting with the prophecies in the Old Testament. Agrippa leaned forward in his chair to listen more closely. He understood the beliefs of the Jews, so he knew much of what Paul was talking about.

Paul looked at Agrippa and said, "You believe in the prophets, don't you? I know you do!"

Agrippa sat back in his chair and shook his head. "Come on, Paul! Do you really think you can convince me to believe in this Jesus in such a short time?" Agrippa stood and walked out of the room. He ignored the stories of Jesus and probably never believed.

AGRIPPA

What a sad story. Agrippa almost seemed to be convinced by Paul to follow Jesus. Then he decided to ignore what Paul taught. Don't ever be like that! You have many years ahead of you to learn more and more about Jesus. Learn all you can and follow him faithfully.

AGRIPPA DIDN'T BELIEVE IN JESUS.

Go to page 1311 for the next Super Hero Trait

side of Cyprus because the winds were against us. ⁵We sailed across the open sea off the coast of Cilicia and Pamphylia. Then we landed at Myra in Lycia. ⁶There the commander found a ship from Alexandria sailing for Italy. He put us on board. ⁷We moved along slowly for many days. We had trouble getting to Cnidus. The wind did not let us stay on course. So we passed the calmer side of Crete, opposite Salmone. ⁸It was not easy to sail along the coast. Then we came to a place called Fair Havens. It was near the town of Lasea.

⁹A lot of time had passed. Sailing had already become dangerous. By now it was after the Day of Atonement, a day of fasting. So Paul gave them a warning. ¹⁰"Men," he said, "I can see that our trip is going to be dangerous. The ship and everything in it will be lost. Our own lives will be in danger also."

¹¹But the commander didn't listen to what Paul said. Instead, he followed the advice of the pilot and the ship's owner. ¹²The harbor wasn't a good place for ships to stay during winter. So most of the people decided we should sail on. They hoped we would reach Phoenix. They wanted to spend the winter there. Phoenix was a harbor in Crete. It faced both southwest and northwest.

The Storm

¹³A gentle south wind began to blow. They thought that this was what they had been waiting for. So they pulled up the anchor and sailed along the shore of Crete. ¹⁴Before very long, a wind blew down from the island. It had the force of a hurricane. It was called a "northeaster." ¹⁵The ship was caught by the storm. We could not keep it sailing into the wind. So we gave up and were driven along. ¹⁶We passed the calmer side of a small island called Cauda. We almost lost the lifeboat. ¹⁷So the men lifted it on board. Then they tied ropes under the ship itself to hold it together. They were afraid it would get stuck on the sandbars of Syrtis. They lowered the sea anchor and let the ship be driven along.

¹⁸We took a very bad beating from the storm. The next day the crew began to throw the ship's contents overboard. ¹⁹On the third day, they even threw the ship's gear overboard with their own hands. ²⁰The sun and stars didn't appear for many days. The storm was terrible. So we gave up all hope of being saved.

²¹The men had not eaten for a long time. Paul stood up in front of them. "Men," he said, "you should have taken my advice not to sail from Crete. Then you would have avoided this harm and loss.

²²"Now I beg you to be brave. Not one of you will die. Only the ship will be destroyed. ²³I belong to God and serve him. Last night his angel stood beside me. ²⁴The angel said, 'Do not be afraid, Paul. You must go on trial in front of Caesar. God has shown his grace by sparing the lives of all those sailing with you.'

²⁵"Men, continue to be brave. I have faith in God. It will happen just as he told me. ²⁶But we must run the ship onto the beach of some island."

POWER SURGE

BELIEVES ✝

MEN, CONTINUE TO BE BRAVE. I HAVE FAITH IN GOD.
— ACTS 27:25 —

BRAVE **B**

The Ship Is Destroyed

²⁷On the 14th night we were still being driven across the Sea of Adria. About midnight the sailors had a feeling that they were approaching land. ²⁸They measured how deep the water was. They found that it was 120 feet deep. A short time later they measured the water again. This time it was 90 feet deep. ²⁹They were afraid we would crash against the rocks. So they dropped four anchors from the back of the ship. They prayed that daylight would come.

³⁰The sailors wanted to escape from the ship. So they let the lifeboat down into the sea. They pretended they were going to lower some anchors from the front of the ship. ³¹But Paul spoke to the commander and the soldiers. "These men must stay with the ship," he said. "If they don't, you can't be saved." ³²So the soldiers cut the ropes that held the lifeboat. They let it drift away.

³³Just before dawn Paul tried to get them all to eat. "For the last 14 days," he said, "you have wondered what would happen. You have gone without food.

You haven't eaten anything. **34**Now I am asking you to eat some food. You need it to live. Not one of you will lose a single hair from your head."

35After Paul said this, he took some bread and gave thanks to God. He did this where they all could see him. Then he broke it and began to eat. **36**All of them were filled with hope. So they ate some food. **37**There were 276 of us on board. **38**They ate as much as they wanted. They needed to make the ship lighter. So they threw the rest of the grain into the sea.

39When daylight came, they saw a bay with a sandy beach. They didn't recognize the place. But they decided to run the ship onto the beach if they could. **40**So they cut the anchors loose and left them in the sea. At the same time, they untied the ropes that held the rudders. They lifted the sail at the front of the ship to the wind. Then they headed for the beach. **41**But the ship hit a sandbar. So the front of it got stuck and wouldn't move. The back of the ship was broken to pieces by the pounding of the waves.

42The soldiers planned to kill the prisoners. They wanted to keep them from swimming away and escaping. **43**But the commander wanted to save Paul's life. So he kept the soldiers from carrying out their plan. He ordered those who could swim to jump overboard first and swim to land. **44**The rest were supposed to get there on boards or other pieces of the ship. That is how everyone reached land safely.

On Shore at Malta

28 When we were safe on shore, we found out that the island was called Malta. **2**The people of the island were unusually kind. It was raining and cold. So they built a fire and welcomed all of us.

3Paul gathered some sticks and put them on the fire. A poisonous snake was driven out by the heat. It fastened itself on Paul's hand. **4**The people of the island saw the snake hanging from his hand. They said to each other, "This man must be a murderer. He escaped from the sea. But Justice won't let him live." Justice was the name of a goddess.

5Paul shook the snake off into the fire. He was not harmed. **6**The people expected him to swell up. They thought he would suddenly fall dead. They waited for a long time. But they didn't see anything unusual happen to him. So they changed their minds. They said he was a god.

7Publius owned property nearby. He was the chief official on the island. He welcomed us to his home. For three days he took care of us. He treated us with kindness. **8**His father was sick in bed. The man suffered from fever and dysentery. So Paul went in to see him. Paul prayed for him. He placed his hands on him and healed him.

9Then the rest of the sick people on the island came. They too were healed. **10**The people of the island honored us in many ways. When we were ready to sail, they gave us the supplies we needed.

POWER—SURGE

GIVING G

THE PEOPLE OF THE ISLAND HONORED US IN MANY WAYS. WHEN WE WERE READY TO SAIL, THEY GAVE US THE SUPPLIES WE NEEDED.
— ACTS 28:10 —

Paul Arrives in Rome

11After three months we headed out to sea. We sailed in a ship that had stayed at the island during the winter. It was a ship from Alexandria. On the front of it the figures of twin gods were carved. Their names were Castor and Pollux. **12**We landed at Syracuse and stayed there for three days.

13From there we sailed to Rhegium. The next day the south wind came up. The day after that, we reached Puteoli. **14**There we found some believers. They invited us to spend a week with them.

At last we came to Rome. **15**The brothers and sisters there had heard we were coming. They traveled as far as the Forum of Appius and the Three Taverns to meet us. When Paul saw these people, he thanked God and was cheered up. **16**When we got to Rome, Paul was allowed to live by himself. But a soldier guarded him.

Paul Preaches in Rome

17Three days later Paul called a meeting of the Jewish leaders. So they came. Paul said to them, "My brothers, I have done nothing against our people. I have also done nothing against what our people of long ago practiced. But I was arrested in Jerusalem. I was handed over to the Romans.

18"They questioned me. And they wanted to let me go. They saw I wasn't guilty of any crime worthy of death. 19But the Jews objected. So I had to make an appeal to Caesar.

"It wasn't that I had anything against my own people. 20I share Israel's hope. That is why I am held with this chain. So I have asked to see you and talk with you."

21They replied, "We have not received any letters from Judea about you. None of our companions who came from there has reported or said anything bad about you. 22But we want to hear what your ideas are. We know that people everywhere are talking against those who believe as you do."

23They decided to meet Paul on a certain day. At that time even more people came to the place where he was staying. From morning until evening, he told them about God's kingdom and explained it to them. Using the Law of Moses and the Prophets, he tried to get them to believe in Jesus.

24Some believed what he said. Others did not. 25They didn't agree with each other. They began to leave after Paul had made a final statement. He said, "The Holy Spirit was right when he spoke to your people long ago. Through Isaiah the prophet the Spirit said,

26 " 'Go to your people. Say to them,
    "You will hear but never understand.
    You will see but never know what
        you are seeing."
27 These people's hearts have become
        stubborn.
    They can barely hear with their
        ears.
    They have closed their eyes.

POWER-SURGE

BELIEVES ✝

FROM MORNING UNTIL EVENING, [PAUL] TOLD THEM ABOUT GOD'S KINGDOM AND EXPLAINED IT TO THEM. USING THE LAW OF MOSES AND THE PROPHETS, HE TRIED TO GET THEM TO BELIEVE IN JESUS. SOME BELIEVED WHAT HE SAID. OTHERS DID NOT.
— ACTS 28:23-24 —

TELLS OTHERS

Otherwise they might see with their
        eyes.
    They might hear with their ears.
    They might understand with their
        hearts.
    They might turn, and then I would
        heal them.'   (Isaiah 6:9,10)

28/29"Here is what I want you to know. God has sent his salvation to people who are not Jews. And they will listen!"

30For two whole years Paul stayed there in a house he rented. He welcomed all who came to see him. 31He preached boldly about God's kingdom. No one could keep him from teaching people about the Lord Jesus Christ.

ROMANS

Paul writes the book of Romans to introduce himself to the believers in the city of Rome. He presents to them the basic teachings of the Christian faith—everyone is sinful, Jesus came because of God's love, and the only way to be saved from sin is through Jesus. Read the book of Romans to find out just how much God loves you—enough to send his Son Jesus to live and die to save you from your sins.

CHECK OUT THESE TRAITS OF A HERO . . .

SELF-CONTROLLED
PAGE 1311

BELIEVES
PAGE 1315

HELPFUL
PAGE 1318

1 I, Paul, am writing this letter. I serve Christ Jesus. I have been appointed to be an apostle. God set me apart to tell others his good news. **2**He promised the good news long ago. He announced it through his prophets in the Holy Scriptures.

3The good news is about God's Son. As a human being, the Son of God belonged to King David's family line. **4**By the power of the Holy Spirit, he was appointed to be the mighty Son of God because he rose from the dead. He is Jesus Christ our Lord.

5I received God's grace because of what Jesus did so that I could bring glory to him. He made me an apostle to all those who aren't Jews. I must invite them to have faith in God and obey him. **6**You also are among those who are appointed to belong to Jesus Christ.

7I am sending this letter to all of you in Rome who are loved by God and appointed to be his people.

May God our Father and the Lord Jesus Christ give you grace and peace.

Paul Longs to Visit Rome

8First, I thank my God through Jesus Christ for all of you. People all over the world are talking about your faith. **9**I serve God with my whole heart. I preach the good news about his Son. God knows that I always remember you **10**in my prayers. I pray that now at last it may be God's plan to open the way for me to visit you.

11I long to see you. I want to make you strong by giving you a gift from the Holy Spirit. **12**I want us to cheer each other up by sharing our faith.

POWER-SURGE

CHEERFUL ✳

I THANK MY GOD THROUGH JESUS CHRIST FOR ALL OF YOU. I WANT US TO CHEER EACH OTHER UP BY SHARING OUR FAITH.
— ROMANS 1:8, 12 —

THANKFUL

POWER-SURGE

BELIEVES †

I AM NOT ASHAMED OF THE GOOD NEWS. IT IS GOD'S POWER. AND IT WILL SAVE EVERYONE WHO BELIEVES.
— ROMANS 1:16 —

B

BRAVE

13Brothers and sisters, I want you to know that I planned many times to visit you. But until now I have been kept from coming. My work has produced results among others who are not Jews. In the same way, I want to see results among you.

14I have a duty both to Greeks and to non-Greeks. I have a duty both to wise people and to foolish people. **15**So I really want to preach the good news also to you who live in Rome.

16I am not ashamed of the good news. It is God's power. And it will save everyone who believes. It is meant first for the Jews. It is meant also for those who aren't Jews.

17The good news shows how God makes people right with himself. From beginning to end, becoming right with God depends on a person's faith. It is written, "Those who are right with God will live by faith." *(Habakkuk 2:4)*

God's Anger Against Sinners

18God shows his anger from heaven. It is against all the godless and evil things people do. They are so evil that they say no to the truth. **19**The truth about God is plain to them. God has made it plain.

20Ever since the world was created it has been possible to see the qualities of God that are not seen. I'm talking about his eternal power and about the fact that he is God. Those things can be seen in what he has made. So people have no excuse for what they do.

21They knew God. But they didn't honor him as God. They didn't thank him. Their thinking became worthless. Their foolish hearts became dark. **22**They claimed to be wise. But they made fools of themselves. **23**They would rather have statues of gods than the glorious God who lives forever. Their statues of gods are made to look like people, birds, animals and reptiles.

24So God let them go. He allowed them to do what their sinful hearts wanted to. He let them commit sexual sins. They polluted one another's bodies by what they did.

25They chose a lie instead of God's truth. They worshiped and served created things. They didn't worship the Creator. But he must be praised forever. Amen.

26So God let them go. They were filled with shameful longings. Their women committed sexual acts that were not natural. 27In the same way, the men turned away from their natural love for women. They burned with sexual longing for each other. Men did shameful things with other men. They suffered in their bodies for all the twisted things they did.

28They didn't think it was important to know God. So God let them go. He allowed them to have dirty minds. They did things they shouldn't do.

29They are full of every kind of sin, evil and ungodliness. They want more than they need. They commit murder. They want what belongs to other people. They fight and cheat. They hate others. They say mean things about other people. 30They tell lies about them. They hate God. They are rude and proud. They brag. They think of new ways to do evil. They don't obey their parents. 31They are foolish. They can't be trusted. They are not loving and kind.

32They know that God's commands are right. They know that those who do evil things should die. But they continue to do those very things. They also approve of others who do them.

God Judges Fairly

2 If you judge someone else, you have no excuse for it. When you judge another person, you are judging yourself. You do the same things you blame others for doing.

2We know that when God judges those who do evil things, he judges fairly. 3Though you are only a human being, you judge others. But you yourself do the same things. So how do you think you will escape when God judges you?

4Do you make fun of God's great kindness and favor? Do you make fun of God when he is patient with you? Don't you realize that God's kindness is meant to turn you away from your sins?

5But you are stubborn. In your heart you are not sorry for your sins. You are storing up anger against yourself. The day of God's anger is coming. Then his way of judging fairly will be shown. 6God "will give to each person in keeping with what he has done." *(Psalm 62:12; Proverbs 24:12)*

7God will give eternal life to those who keep on doing good. They want glory, honor, and life that never ends. 8But there are others who only look out for themselves. They don't accept the truth. They go down an evil path. God will pour out his burning anger on them. 9There will be trouble and suffering for everyone who does evil. That is meant first for the Jews. It is also meant for the non-Jews. 10But there will be glory, honor and peace for everyone who does good. That is meant first for the Jews. It is also meant for the non-Jews. 11God treats everyone the same.

12Some people do not know God's law when they sin. They will not be judged by the law when they die. Others do know God's law when they sin. They will be judged by the law. 13Hearing the law does not make a person right with God. People are considered to be right with God only when they obey the law.

14Those who aren't Jews do not have the law. Sometimes they just naturally do what the law requires. They are a law for themselves. This is true even though they don't have the law. 15They show that what the law requires is written on their hearts. The way their minds judge them gives witness to that fact. Sometimes their thoughts find them guilty. At other times their thoughts find them not guilty.

16People will be judged on the day God appoints Jesus Christ to judge their secret thoughts. That's part of my good news.

The Jews and the Law

17Suppose you call yourself a Jew. You trust in the law. You brag that you are close to God. 18You know what God wants. You agree with what is best because the law teaches you. 19You are sure you can lead people who are blind. You are sure you are a light for those who are in the dark. 20You claim to be able to teach foolish people. You can even teach babies. You think that in the law you have all knowledge and truth.

21You teach others. But you don't teach yourself! You preach against stealing. But you steal! 22You say that people should not commit adultery. But you commit adultery! You hate statues of gods. But you rob temples! 23You brag about the law. But when you break it, you rob God of his honor! 24It is written, "Those who aren't Jews say evil things against God's name because of you." *(Isaiah 52:5; Ezekiel 36:22)*

25Circumcision has value if you obey the law. But if you break the law, it is just as if you hadn't been circumcised.

26Sometimes those who aren't circumcised do what the law requires. Won't God accept them as if they had been circumcised? 27Many are not circumcised physically, but they obey the law. They will prove that you are guilty. You are breaking the law, even though you have the written law and are circumcised.

28A man is not a Jew if he is a Jew only on the outside. And circumcision is more than just something done to the outside of a man's body.

29No, a man is a Jew only if he is a Jew on the inside. And true circumcision means that the heart has been circumcised. It is done by the Holy Spirit. It is more than just obeying the written Law. Then a man's praise will not come from others. It will come from God.

God Is Faithful

3 Is there any advantage in being a Jew? Is there any value in being circumcised?

2There is great value in every way! First of all, the Jews have been given the very words of God.

3What if some Jews did not believe? Will the fact that they don't have faith keep God from being faithful? 4Not at all! God is true, even though every human being is a liar. It is written,

"You are right when you sentence me. You are fair when you judge me."
(Psalm 51:4)

5Doesn't the fact that we are wrong prove more clearly that God is right? Then what can we say? Can we say that God is not fair when he brings his anger down on us? As you can tell, I am just using human ways of thinking. 6God is certainly fair! If he weren't, how could he judge the world?

7Someone might argue, "When I lie, it becomes clearer that God is truthful. It makes his glory shine more brightly. Why then does he find me guilty of sin?" 8Why not say, "Let's do evil things so that good things will happen"? Some people actually lie by reporting that this is what we say. They are the ones who should be found guilty.

No One Is Right With God

9What should we say then? Are we Jews any better? Not at all! We have already claimed that Jews are sinners. The same is true of those who aren't Jews. 10It is written,

"No one is right with God, no one at all.
11 No one understands.
No one trusts in God.
12All of them have turned away.
They have all become worthless.
No one does anything good,
no one at all." *(Psalms 14:1–3; 53:1–3; Ecclesiastes 7:20)*
13"Their throats are like open graves.
With their tongues they tell lies."
(Psalm 5:9)
"The words from their lips are like the poison of a snake." *(Psalm 140:3)*
14 "Their mouths are full of curses and bitterness." *(Psalm 10:7)*
15"They run quickly to commit murder.
16 They leave a trail of failure and pain.
17They do not know the way of peace."
(Isaiah 59:7,8)
18 "They don't have any respect for God." *(Psalm 36:1)*

19What the law says, it says to those who are ruled by the law. Its purpose is to shut every mouth and make the whole world accountable to God. 20So it can't be said that anyone will be made right with God by obeying the law. Not at all! The law makes us more aware of our sin.

Becoming Right With God

21But now God has shown us how to become right with him. The Law and the Prophets give witness to this. It has nothing to do with obeying the law. 22We are made right with God by putting our faith in Jesus Christ. That happens to all who believe.

It is no different for the Jews than for anyone else. 23Everyone has sinned. No one measures up to God's glory. 24The free gift of God's grace makes all of us right with him. Christ Jesus paid the price to set us free. 25God gave him as a sacrifice to pay for sins. So he forgives the sins of those who have faith in his blood.

God did all of that to prove that he is fair. Because of his mercy he did not punish people for the sins they had committed before Jesus died for them. 26God did that to prove in our own time that he is fair. He proved that he is right. He also made right with himself those who believe in Jesus.

27So who can brag? No one! Are people

saved by obeying the law? Not at all! They are saved because of their faith. **28**We firmly believe that people are made right with God because of their faith. They are not saved by obeying the law.

29Is God the God of Jews only? Isn't he also the God of those who aren't Jews? Yes, he is their God too. **30**There is only one God. When those who are circumcised believe in him, he makes them right with himself. When those who are not circumcised believe in him, he also makes them right with himself. **31**Does faith make the law useless? Not at all! We agree with the law.

Abraham's Faith Made Him Right With God

4 What should we say about those things? What did our father Abraham discover about being right with God? **2**Did he become right with God because of something he did? If so, he could brag about it. But he couldn't brag to God. **3**What do we find in Scripture? It says, "Abraham believed God. God accepted Abraham's faith, and so his faith made him right with God." *(Genesis 15:6)*

4When a man works, his pay is not considered a gift. It is owed to him. **5**But things are different with God. He makes evil people right with himself. If people trust in him, their faith is accepted even though they do not work. Their faith makes them right with God.

POWER-SURGE

BELIEVES ✝

BUT NOW GOD HAS SHOWN US HOW TO BECOME RIGHT WITH HIM...BY PUTTING OUR FAITH IN JESUS CHRIST. THAT HAPPENS TO ALL WHO BELIEVE...HE FORGIVES THE SINS OF THOSE WHO HAVE FAITH IN HIS BLOOD.
— ROMANS 3:21-22, 25 —

FORGIVING **F**

6King David says the same thing. He tells us how blessed some people are. God makes those people right with himself. But they don't have to do anything in return. David says,

7 "Blessed are those
     whose lawless acts are forgiven.
Blessed are those
     whose sins are taken away.
8 Blessed is the man
     whose sin the Lord never counts
          against him." *(Psalm 32:1,2)*

9Is that blessing only for those who are circumcised? Or is it also for those who are not circumcised? We have been saying that God accepted Abraham's faith, and so his faith made him right with God. **10**When did it happen? Was it after Abraham was circumcised, or before? It was before he was circumcised, not after! **11**He was circumcised as a sign of the covenant God had made with him. It showed that his faith had made him right with God before he was circumcised.

So Abraham is the father of all believers who have not been circumcised. God accepts their faith. So their faith makes them right with him. **12**Abraham is also the father of the circumcised who believe. So just being circumcised is not enough. Those who are circumcised must also follow the steps of our father Abraham. He had faith before he was circumcised.

13Abraham and his family received a promise. God promised that Abraham would receive the world. It would not come to him because he obeyed the law. It would come because of his faith, which made him right with God.

14Do those who obey the law receive the promise? If they do, faith would have no value. God's promise would be worthless. **15**The law brings God's anger. Where there is no law, the law can't be broken.

16The promise is based on God's grace. The promise comes by faith. All of Abraham's children will certainly receive the promise. And it is not only for those who are ruled by the law. Those who have the same faith that Abraham had are also included. He is the father of us all. **17**It is written, "I have made you a father of many nations." *(Genesis 17:5)* God considers Abraham to be our father. The God that Abraham believed in gives life to the dead. Abraham's God also speaks of things that do not exist as if they do exist.

18When there was no reason for hope, Abraham believed because he had hope. He became the father of many nations,

POWER–SURGE

BELIEVES ✝

GOD ACCEPTED ABRAHAM BECAUSE HE BELIEVED. SO HIS FAITH MADE HIM RIGHT WITH GOD.
— ROMANS 4:22 —

exactly as God had promised. God said, "That is how many children you will have." *(Genesis 15:5)*

19Without becoming weak in his faith, Abraham accepted the fact that he was past the time when he could have children. At that time he was about 100 years old. He also realized that Sarah was too old to have children. **20**But he kept believing in God's promise. He became strong in his faith. He gave glory to God. **21**He was absolutely sure that God had the power to do what he had promised. **22**That's why "God accepted Abraham because he believed. So his faith made him right with God."

23The words "God accepted Abraham's faith" were written not only for Abraham. **24**They were written also for us. We believe in the God who raised Jesus our Lord from the dead. So God will accept our faith and make us right with himself. **25**Jesus was handed over to die for our sins. He was raised to life in order to make us right with God.

Peace and Joy

5 We have been made right with God because of our faith. Now we have peace with him because of our Lord Jesus Christ. **2**Through faith in Jesus we have received God's grace. In that grace we stand. We are full of joy because we expect to share in God's glory.

3And that's not all. We are full of joy even when we suffer. We know that our suffering gives us the strength to go on. **4**The strength to go on produces character. Character produces hope. **5**And hope will never let us down. God has poured his love into our hearts. He did it through the Holy Spirit, whom he has given to us.

6At just the right time Christ died for ungodly people. He died for us when we had no power of our own. **7**It is unusual for anyone to die for a godly person. Maybe someone would be willing to die for a good person. **8**But here is how God has shown his love for us. While we were still sinners, Christ died for us.

9The blood of Christ has made us right with God. So we are even more sure that Jesus will save us from God's anger. **10**Once we were God's enemies. But we have been brought back to him because his Son has died for us. Now that God has brought us back, we are even more secure. We know that we will be saved because Christ lives.

11And that is not all. We are full of joy in God because of our Lord Jesus Christ. Because of him, God has brought us back to himself.

Death Through Adam, Life Through Christ

12Sin entered the world because one man sinned. And death came because of sin. Everyone sinned, so death came to all people.

13Before the law was given, sin was in the world. But sin is not judged when there is no law. **14**Death ruled from the time of Adam to the time of Moses. Death ruled even over those who did not sin as Adam did. He broke God's command. But he also became a pattern of the One who was going to come.

15God's gift is different from Adam's sin. Many people died because of the sin of that one man. But it was even more sure that God's grace would also come through one man. That man is Jesus Christ. God's gift of grace was more than enough for the whole world.

16The result of God's gift is different from the result of Adam's sin. God judged one sin. That brought guilt. But after

POWER–SURGE

CHEERFUL ✳

WE ARE FULL OF JOY EVEN WHEN WE SUFFER. WE KNOW THAT OUR SUFFERING GIVES US THE STRENGTH TO GO ON.
— ROMANS 5:3 —

STRONG

many sins, God's gift made people right with him.

17One man sinned, and death ruled because of his sin. But we are even more sure of what will happen because of what the one man, Jesus Christ, has done. Those who receive the rich supply of God's grace will rule with Christ in his kingdom. They have received God's gift and have been made right with him.

18One man's sin brought guilt to all people. So also one right act made all people right with God. And all who are right with God will live. 19Many people were made sinners because one man did not obey. But one man did obey. That is why many people will be made right with God.

20The law was given so that sin would increase. But where sin increased, God's grace increased even more. 21Sin ruled because of death. So also grace rules in the lives of those who are right with God. The grace of God brings eternal life because of what Jesus Christ our Lord has done.

Living a New Life

6 What should we say then? Should we keep on sinning so that God's grace can increase? 2Not at all! As far as sin is concerned, we are dead. So how can we keep on sinning? 3All of us were baptized into Christ Jesus. Don't you know that we were baptized into his death? 4By being baptized, we were buried with Christ into his death. Christ has been raised from the dead by the Father's glory. And like Christ we also can live a new life.

5By being baptized, we have been joined with him in his death. We will certainly also be joined with him in his resurrection. 6We know that what we used to be was nailed to the cross with him. That happened so our sinful bodies would lose their power. We are no longer slaves of sin. 7Those who have died have been set free from sin.

8We died with Christ. So we believe that we will also live with him. 9We know that Christ was raised from the dead and will never die again. Death doesn't control him anymore. 10When he died, he died once and for all time as far as sin is concerned. Now that he lives, he lives as far as God is concerned.

11In the same way, consider yourselves to be dead as far as sin is concerned. Now that you believe in Christ Jesus, consider yourselves to be alive as far as God is concerned.

12So don't let sin rule your body, which is going to die. Don't obey its evil longings. 13Don't give the parts of your body to serve sin. Don't let them be used to do evil. Instead, give yourselves to God. You have been brought from death to life. Give the parts of your body to him to do what is right. 14Sin will not be your master. Law does not rule you. God's grace has set you free.

Slaves to Right Living

15What should we say then? Should we sin because we are not ruled by law but by God's grace? Not at all! 16Don't you know that when you give yourselves to obey someone you become that person's slave? You can be slaves of sin. Then you will die. Or you can be slaves who obey God. Then you will live a godly life. 17You used to be slaves of sin. But thank God that with your whole heart you obeyed the teachings you were given! 18You have been set free from sin. You have become slaves to right living.

POWER-SURGE

OBEYS ✓

THANK GOD THAT WITH YOUR WHOLE HEART YOU OBEYED THE TEACHINGS YOU WERE GIVEN!
— ROMANS 6:17 —

19Because you are human, you find this hard to understand. So I have said it in a way that will help you understand it. You used to give the parts of your body to be slaves to unclean living. You were becoming more and more evil. Now give your bodies to be slaves to right living. Then you will become holy.

20Once you were slaves of sin. At that time right living did not control you. 21What benefit did you gain from doing the things you are now ashamed of? Those things lead to death! 22You have been set free from sin. God has made you his slaves. The benefit you gain leads to holy living. And the end result is eternal life. 23When you sin, the pay you get is death. But God gives you the gift of eternal life because of what Christ Jesus our Lord has done.

An Example From Marriage

7 Brothers and sisters, I am speaking to you who know the law. Don't you know that the law has authority over us only as long as we are alive? 2For example, by law a married woman is joined to her husband as long as he is living. But suppose her husband dies. Then the marriage law no longer applies to her. 3But suppose that married woman gets married again while her husband is still alive. Then she is called a woman who commits adultery. But suppose her husband dies. Then she is free from that law. She is not guilty of adultery even if she marries another man.

4My brothers and sisters, when Christ died you also died as far as the law is concerned. Then it became possible for you to belong to him. He was raised from the dead. Now our lives can be useful to God. 5Our sinful nature used to control us. The law stirred up sinful longings in our bodies. So the things we did resulted in death.

6But now we have died to what used to control us. We have been set free from the law. Now we serve in the new way of the Holy Spirit. We no longer serve in the old way of the written law.

Struggling With Sin

7What should we say then? That the law is sin? Not at all! I wouldn't have known what sin was unless the law had told me. The law said, "Do not want what belongs to other people." *(Exodus 20:17; Deuteronomy 5:21)* If the law hadn't said that, I would not have known what it was like to want what belonged to others. 8But the commandment gave sin an opportunity. Sin caused me to want all kinds of things that belonged to others. No one can break a law that doesn't exist.

9Before I knew about the law, I was alive. But then the commandment came. Sin came to life, and I died. 10I found that the commandment that was supposed to bring life actually brought death. 11When the commandment gave sin the opportunity, sin tricked me. It used the commandment to put me to death. 12So the law is holy. The commandment also is holy and right and good.

13Did what is good cause me to die? Not at all! Sin had to be recognized for what it really is. So it produced death in me through what was good. Because of the commandment, sin became totally sinful.

14We know that the law is holy. But I am not. I have been sold to be a slave of sin. 15I don't understand what I do. I don't do what I want to do. Instead, I do what I hate to do. 16I do what I don't want to do. So I agree that the law is good. 17As it is, I am no longer the one who does these things. It is sin living in me that does them.

18I know there is nothing good in my sinful nature. I want to do what is good, but I can't. 19I don't do the good things I want to do. I keep on doing the evil things I don't want to do. 20I do what I don't want to do. But I am not really the one who is doing it. It is sin living in me.

21Here is the law I find working in me. When I want to do good, evil is right there with me. 22Deep inside me I find joy in God's law. 23But I see another law working in the parts of my body. It fights against the law of my mind. It makes me a prisoner of the law of sin. That law controls the parts of my body.

24What a terrible failure I am! Who will save me from this sin that brings death to my body? 25I give thanks to God. He will do it through Jesus Christ our Lord.

So in my mind I am a slave to God's law. But in my sinful nature I am a slave to the law of sin.

POWER-SURGE

THANKFUL
I GIVE THANKS TO GOD.
— ROMANS 7:25 —

The Holy Spirit Gives Life

8 Those who belong to Christ Jesus are no longer under God's sentence. 2I am now controlled by the law of the Holy Spirit. That law gives me life because of what Christ Jesus has done. It has set me free from the law of sin that brings death.

3The written law was made weak by our sinful nature. But God did what the written law could not do. He made his Son to be like those who have a sinful nature. He sent him to be an offering for sin. In that way, he judged sin in his Son's human body. 4Now we can do everything the law requires. Our sinful nature no longer controls the way we live. The Holy Spirit now controls the way we live.

5Don't live under the control of your sinful nature. If you do, you will think about what your sinful nature wants. Live under the control of the Holy Spirit. If you do, you will think about what the Spirit wants.

⁶The way a sinful person thinks leads to death. But the mind controlled by the Spirit brings life and peace. ⁷The sinful mind is at war with God. It does not obey God's law. It can't. ⁸Those who are controlled by their sinful nature can't please God.

⁹But your sinful nature does not control you. The Holy Spirit controls you. The Spirit of God lives in you. Anyone who does not have the Spirit of Christ does not belong to Christ.

¹⁰Christ lives in you. So your body is dead because of sin. But your spirit is alive because you have been made right with God. ¹¹The Spirit of the One who raised Jesus from the dead is living in you. So the God who raised Christ from the dead will also give life to your bodies, which are going to die. He will do this by the power of his Spirit, who lives in you.

¹²Brothers and sisters, we have a duty. Our duty is not to live under the control of our sinful nature. ¹³If you live under the control of your sinful nature, you will die. But by the power of the Holy Spirit you can put to death the sins your body commits. Then you will live.

¹⁴Those who are led by the Spirit of God are children of God. ¹⁵You didn't receive a spirit that makes you a slave to fear once again. Instead you received the Holy Spirit, who makes you God's child. By the Spirit's power we call God "Abba." Abba means Father. ¹⁶The Spirit himself joins

SELF-CONTROLLED

ROMANS 8:5

Don't live under the control of your sinful nature...Live under the control of the Holy Spirit.

Have you ever watched a show or read a book where someone just totally loses control? They go completely whacko. They throw things and break things and hit things and whip things and wave their arms and throw their bodies and yell at the top of their voices. Utterly and absolutely *out of control.*

That's just how God *doesn't* want you to be. God's love and direction in your life can make you a self-controlled person, able to control your speech and your actions. Look at young Isaac about to be dead meat on the altar (page 27) or Stephen when his enemies are flinging rocks at him (page 1263). Both of these people were self-controlled because they belonged to God.

BE SELF-CONTROLLED

You will probably never be in Isaac's or Stephen's shoes. But you'll still have times when you will need to be self-controlled. Maybe your brother or sister is driving you crazy; maybe you'll have a day once in awhile when everything goes wrong. Whatever the situation, remember that God can help you to be in control of yourself.

Go to page 1315 for the next Super Hero Trait

with our spirits. Together they give witness that we are God's children. ¹⁷As his children, we will receive all that he has for us. We will share what Christ receives. But we must share in his sufferings if we want to share in his glory.

The Hope of Future Glory

¹⁸What we are suffering now is nothing compared with the glory that will be shown in us. ¹⁹Everything God created looks forward to the time when his children will appear in their full and final glory. ²⁰The created world was bound to fail. But that was not the result of its own choice. It was planned that way by the One who made it. God planned ²¹to set the created world free. He didn't want it to rot away completely. Instead, he wanted it to have the same glorious freedom that his children have.

²²We know that all that God created has been groaning. It is in pain as if it were giving birth to a child. The created world continues to groan even now. ²³And that's not all. We have the Holy Spirit as the promise of future blessing. But we also groan inside ourselves as we look forward to the time when God will adopt us as full members of his family. Then he will give us everything he has for us. He will raise our bodies and give glory to them. ²⁴That's the hope we had when we were saved. But hope that can be seen is no hope at all. Who hopes for what he already has? ²⁵We hope for what we don't have yet. So we are patient as we wait for it.

²⁶In the same way, the Holy Spirit helps us when we are weak. We don't know what we should pray for. But the Spirit himself prays for us. He prays with groans too deep for words. ²⁷God, who looks into our hearts, knows the mind of the Spirit. And the Spirit prays for God's people just as God wants him to pray.

We Will Win

²⁸We know that in all things God works

for the good of those who love him. He appointed them to be saved in keeping with his purpose.

²⁹God planned that those he had chosen would become like his Son. In that way, Christ will be the first and most honored among many brothers. ³⁰And those God has planned for, he has also appointed to be saved. Those he has appointed, he has made right with himself. To those he has made right with himself, he has given his glory.

³¹What should we say then? Since God is on our side, who can be against us? ³²God did not spare his own Son. He gave him up for us all. Then won't he also freely give us everything else?

³³Who can bring any charge against God's chosen ones? God makes us right with himself. ³⁴Who can sentence us to death? Christ Jesus is at the right hand of God and is also praying for us. He died. More than that, he was raised to life.

³⁵Who can separate us from Christ's love? Can trouble or hard times or harm or hunger? Can nakedness or danger or war? ³⁶It is written,

> "Because of you, we face death all day
>   long.
>   We are considered as sheep to be
>   killed."　　*(Psalm 44:22)*

³⁷No! In all these things we will do even more than win! We owe it all to Christ, who has loved us.

³⁸I am absolutely sure that not even death or life can separate us from God's love. Not even angels or demons, the present or the future, or any powers can do that. ³⁹Not even the highest places or the lowest, or anything else in all creation can do that. Nothing at all can ever separate us from God's love because of what Christ Jesus our Lord has done.

God's Free Choice

9 I speak the truth in Christ. I am not lying. My mind tells me that what I say is true. It is guided by the Holy Spirit. ²My heart is full of sorrow. My sadness never ends. ³I am so concerned about my people, who are members of my own race. I am ready to be cursed, if that would help them. I am even willing to be separated from Christ.

⁴They are the people of Israel. They have been adopted as God's children. God's glory belongs to them. So do the covenants. They received the law. They were taught to worship in the temple. They were given the promises. ⁵The

founders of our nation belong to them. Christ comes from their family line. He is God over all. May he always be praised! Amen.

6Their condition does not mean that God's word has failed. Not everyone in the family line of Israel really belongs to Israel. **7**Not everyone in Abraham's family line is really his child. Not at all! Scripture says, "Your family line will continue through Isaac." *(Genesis 21:12)*

8In other words, God's children are not just Abraham's natural children. Instead, they are the children God promised to him. They are the ones considered to be Abraham's children. **9**God promised, "I will return at the appointed time. Sarah will have a son." *(Genesis 18:10,14)*

10And that's not all. Rebekah's children had the same father. He was our father Isaac.

11Here is what happened. Rebekah's twins had not even been born. They hadn't done anything good or bad yet. So they show that God's purpose is based firmly on his free choice. **12**It was not because of anything they did but because of God's choice. So Rebekah was told, "The older son will serve the younger one." *(Genesis 25:23)* **13**It is written, "I chose Jacob instead of Esau." *(Malachi 1:2,3)*

14What should we say then? Is God unfair? Not at all! **15**He said to Moses,

"I will have mercy on whom I have
　　mercy.
　I will show love to those I love."
　　　　　　　　　　(Exodus 33:19)

16So it doesn't depend on what we want or do. It depends on God's mercy.

17In Scripture, God says to Pharaoh, "I had a special reason for making you king. I decided to use you to show my power. I wanted my name to become known everywhere on earth." *(Exodus 9:16)* **18**So God does what he wants to do. He shows mercy to one person and makes another stubborn.

19One of you will say to me, "Then why

does God still blame us? Who can oppose what he wants to do?" **20**But you are a mere man. So who are you to talk back to God? Scripture says, "Can what is made say to the one who made it, 'Why did you make me like this?' " *(Isaiah 29:16; 45:9)* **21**Isn't the potter free to make different kinds of pots out of the same lump of clay? Some are for special purposes. Others are for ordinary use.

22What if God chose to show his great anger? What if he chose to make his power known? That is why he put up with people he was angry with. They had been made to be destroyed. **23**What if he did that to show the riches of his glory to others? Those are the people he shows his mercy to. He had prepared them to receive his glory. **24**We are those people. He has chosen us. We do not come only from the Jewish race. Many of us are not Jews. **25**God says in Hosea,

"I will call those who are not my
　　people 'my people.'
　I will call the one who is not my
　　loved one 'my loved one.' "
　　　　　　　　　　(Hosea 2:23)

26He also says,

"Once it was said to them,
　'You are not my people.'
In that very place they will be called
　'children of the living God.' "
　　　　　　　　　　(Hosea 1:10)

27Isaiah cries out concerning Israel. He says,

"The number of people from Israel
　may be like the sand by the sea.
But only a few of them will be saved.
28The Lord will carry out his sentence.
　He will be quick to carry it out on
　　earth, once and for all."
　　　　　　　　　　(Isaiah 10:22,23)

29Earlier Isaiah had said,

"The Lord who rules over all
　left us children and grandchildren.
If he hadn't, we would have become
　　like Sodom.
　We would have been like
　　Gomorrah."　　*(Isaiah 1:9)*

Israel Does Not Believe

30What should we say then? Those who aren't Jews did not look for a way to be right with God. But they found it by having faith. **31**Israel did look for a law that could make them right with God. But they didn't find it.

POWER SURGE

HONEST Ⓗ

I SPEAK THE TRUTH IN CHRIST. I AM NOT LYING.

— ROMANS 9:1 —

32Why not? Because they didn't look for it by faith. They tried to get it by working for it. They tripped over the stone that causes people to trip and fall. **33**It is written,

"Look! In Zion I am laying a stone that
    causes people to trip.
It is a rock that makes them fall.
The one who trusts in him will never
    be put to shame."

(Isaiah 8:14; 28:16)

10 Brothers and sisters, with all my heart I long for the people of Israel to be saved. I pray to God for them. **2**I can give witness about them that they really want to serve God. But how they are trying to do it is not based on what they know.

3They didn't know how God makes people right with himself. They tried to get right with God in their own way. They didn't do it in God's way.

4Christ has completed the law. So now everyone who believes can be right with God.

5Moses explained how the law could help a person do what God requires. He said, "The one who does those things will live by them." *(Leviticus 18:5)*

6But the way to do what God requires must begin by having faith in him. Scripture says, "Do not say in your heart, 'Who will go up into heaven?' " *(Deuteronomy 30:12)* That means to go up into heaven and bring Christ down. **7**"And do not say, 'Who will go down into the grave?' " *(Deuteronomy 30:13)* That means to bring Christ up from the dead.

8But what does it say? "The word is near you. It's in your mouth and in your heart." *(Deuteronomy 30:14)* That means the word we are preaching. You must put your faith in it.

9Say with your mouth, "Jesus is Lord." Believe in your heart that God raised him from the dead. Then you will be saved. **10**With your heart you believe and are made right with God. With your mouth you say that Jesus is Lord. And so you are saved. **11**Scripture says, "The one who trusts in him will never be put to shame." *(Isaiah 28:16)*

12There is no difference between those who are Jews and those who are not. The same Lord is Lord of all. He richly blesses everyone who calls on him. **13**Scripture says, "Everyone who calls on the name of the Lord will be saved." *(Joel 2:32)*

14How can they call on him unless they believe in him? How can they believe in him unless they hear about him? How can they hear about him unless someone preaches to them? **15**And how can anyone preach without being sent? It is written, "How beautiful are the feet of those who bring good news!" *(Isaiah 52:7)*

16But not all the people of Israel accepted the good news. Isaiah says, "Lord, who has believed our message?" *(Isaiah 53:1)* **17**So faith comes from hearing the message. And the message that is heard is the word of Christ.

18But I ask, "Didn't the people of Israel hear?" Of course they did. It is written,

"Their voice has gone out into the
    whole earth.
Their words have gone out from one
    end of the world to the other."

(Psalm 19:4)

19Again I ask, "Didn't Israel understand?" First, Moses says,

"I will use people who are not a nation
    to make you jealous.
I will use a nation that has no
    understanding to make you
    angry."   *(Deuteronomy 32:21)*

20Then Isaiah boldly speaks about what God says. God said,

"I was found by those who were not
    trying to find me.
I made myself known to those who
    were not asking for me."

(Isaiah 65:1)

21But Isaiah also speaks about what God says concerning Israel. God said,

"All day long I have held out my hands.
I have held them out to a stubborn
    people who do not obey me."

(Isaiah 65:2)

God's Faithful People in Israel

11 So here is what I ask. Did God turn his back on his people? Not at all! I myself belong to Israel. I am one of Abraham's children. I am from the tribe of Benjamin. **2**God didn't turn his back on his people. After all, he chose them.

Don't you know what Scripture says about Elijah? He complained to God about Israel. **3**He said, "Lord, they have killed your prophets. They have torn down your altars. I'm the only one left. And they are trying to kill me." *(1 Kings 19:10,14)*

4How did God answer him? God said, "I have kept 7,000 people for myself. They have not bowed down to Baal." *(1 Kings 19:18)*

⁵Some are also faithful today. They have been chosen by God's grace. ⁶And if they are chosen by grace, it is no longer a matter of working for it. If it were, grace wouldn't be grace anymore.

⁷What should we say then? Israel did not receive what they wanted so badly. But those who were chosen did. God made the rest of them stubborn.

⁸It is written,

"God made it hard for them to understand.

He gave them eyes that could not see.
He gave them ears that could not hear.
And they are still like that today."
(Deuteronomy 29:4; Isaiah 29:10)

⁹David says,

"Let their feast be a trap and a snare.
Let it make Israel trip and fall. Let Israel get what's coming to them.

BELIEVES

ROMANS 10:4, 9

Everyone who believes can be right with God. Say with your mouth, "Jesus is Lord." Believe in your heart that God raised him from the dead. Then you will be saved.

What do you believe in? Do you believe everything you see on television? Do you believe your friends will always be your friends? Do you believe you could climb Mount Everest? Do you believe the sun will come up tomorrow morning? Do you believe you could learn to speak Japanese or some other language? Do you believe the earth is round? Do you believe Jesus actually lived here on earth and died and rose again for your sins?

The New Testament section of this Bible has many great stories about men and women who *believed*. Elizabeth (page 1171) believed immediately that her cousin Mary was going to have a baby who would grow up to be the Savior of the world. Mary (page 1169), Jesus' mother, believed that what the angel told her was true. The shepherds (page 1175) believed the angels, and the Wise Men (page 1092) believed in the sign of the star. All of these people believed in the truth that Jesus was coming to be the Savior.

BE A BELIEVER

Everyone believes in something. You believe the bridge will hold you as your car goes across. You believe an apple will fall to the ground if you drop it. But the most important things to believe in aren't that obvious. The Bible is true—believe it! Jesus did live and die for you—believe it!

Go to page 1318 for the next Super Hero Trait

10 Let their eyes grow dark so they can't
see.
Let their backs be bent forever."
(Psalm 69:22,23)

Two Kinds of Olive Branches

11 Again, here is what I ask. They didn't
trip and fall once and for all time, did
they? Not at all! Because Israel sinned,
those who aren't Jews can be saved. That
will make Israel jealous of them. **12** Israel's
sin brought riches to the world. Their loss
brought riches to the non-Jews. What
greater riches will come when all Israel
turns to God!

13 I am talking to you who are not Jews.
I am the apostle to the non-Jews. So I
think the work I do for God and others is
very important.

14 I hope somehow to stir up my own
people to want what you have. Perhaps I
can save some of them. **15** When they were
not accepted, it became possible for the
whole world to be brought back to God.
So what will happen when they are accepted? It will be like life from the dead.

16 The first handful of dough that is offered is holy. This makes all of the dough
holy.

If the root is holy, so are the branches.

17 Some of the natural branches have
been broken off. You are a wild olive
branch. But you have been joined to the
tree with the other branches. Now you enjoy the life-giving sap of the olive tree root.
18 So don't think you are better than the
other branches. Remember, you don't give
life to the root. The root gives life to you.

19 You will say, "Some branches were
broken off so that I could be joined to the
tree." **20** That's true. But they were broken
off because they didn't believe. You stand
only because you do believe. So don't be
proud. Be afraid. **21** God didn't spare the
natural branches. He won't spare you either.

22 Think about how kind God is! Also
think about how firm he is! He was hard
on those who stopped following him. But
he is kind to you. So you must continue to
live in his kindness. If you don't, you also
will be cut off.

23 If the people of Israel do not continue
in their unbelief, they will again be joined
to the tree. God is able to join them to the
tree again.

24 After all, weren't you cut from a wild
olive tree? Weren't you joined to an olive
tree that was taken care of? And wasn't
that the opposite of how things should be
done? How much more easily will the

natural branches be joined to their own
olive tree!

All Israel Will Be Saved

25 Brothers and sisters, here is a mystery
I want you to understand. It will keep you
from being proud. Part of Israel has refused to obey God. That will continue until the full number of non-Jews has entered God's kingdom. **26** And so all Israel
will be saved. It is written,

"The One who saves will come from
Mount Zion.
He will remove sin from Jacob.
27 Here is my covenant with them.
I will take away their sins."
*(Isaiah 59:20,21; 27:9;
Jeremiah 31:33,34)*

28 As far as the good news is concerned,
the people of Israel are enemies. That is for
your good. But as far as God's choice is
concerned, the people of Israel are loved.
That is because of God's promises to the
founders of our nation. **29** God does not
take back his gifts. He does not change his
mind about those he has chosen.

30 At one time you did not obey God.
But now you have received mercy because
Israel did not obey. **31** In the same way, Israel has not been obeying God. But now
they receive mercy because of God's mercy to you. **32** God has found everyone
guilty of not obeying him. So now he can
have mercy on everyone.

Praise to God

33 How very rich are God's wisdom and
knowledge!
How he judges is more than we can
understand!
The way he deals with people is
more than we can know!
34 "Who can ever know what is in the
Lord's mind?
Or who can ever give him advice?"
(Isaiah 40:13)
35 "Has anyone ever given anything to
God,
so that God has to pay him back?"
(Job 41:11)
36 All things come from him.
All things are directed by him.
All things are for his good.
May God be given the glory forever!
Amen.

Living for God

12 Brothers and sisters, God has
shown you his mercy. So I am asking you to offer up your bodies to him

while you are still alive. Your bodies are a holy sacrifice that is pleasing to God. When you offer your bodies to God, you are worshiping him. **2**Don't live any longer the way this world lives. Let your way of thinking be completely changed. Then you will be able to test what God wants for you. And you will agree that what he wants is right. His plan is good and pleasing and perfect.

3God's grace has been given to me. So here is what I say to every one of you. Don't think of yourself more highly than you should. Be reasonable when you think about yourself. Keep in mind the amount of faith God has given you.

4Each of us has one body with many parts. And the parts do not all have the same purpose. **5**So also we are many persons. But in Christ we are one body. And each part of the body belongs to all the other parts.

6We all have gifts. They differ in keeping with the grace that God has given each of us. Do you have the gift of prophecy? Then use it in keeping with the faith you have. **7**Is it your gift to serve? Then serve. Is it teaching? Then teach. **8**Is it telling others how they should live? Then tell them. Is it giving to those who are in need? Then give freely. Is it being a leader? Then work hard at it. Is it showing mercy? Then do it cheerfully.

Love

9Love must be honest and true. Hate what is evil. Hold on to what is good. **10**Love each other deeply. Honor others more than yourselves. **11**Never let the fire in your heart go out. Keep it alive. Serve the Lord.

12When you hope, be joyful. When you suffer, be patient. When you pray, be faithful. **13**Share with God's people who are in need. Welcome others into your homes.

14Bless those who hurt you. Bless them, and do not call down curses on them. **15**Be joyful with those who are joyful. Be sad with those who are sad. **16**Agree with each other. Don't be proud. Be willing to be a friend of people who aren't considered important. Don't think that you are better than others.

17Don't pay back evil with evil. Be careful to do what everyone thinks is right. **18**If possible, live in peace with everyone. Do that as much as you can.

19My friends, don't try to get even. Leave room for God to show his anger. It is written, "I am the One who judges people. I will pay them back," *(Deuteronomy 32:35)* says the Lord. **20**Do just the opposite. Scripture says,

"If your enemies are hungry, give them food to eat.
If they are thirsty, give them something to drink.
By doing those things, you will pile up burning coals on their heads."
(Proverbs 25:21,22)

21Don't let evil overcome you. Overcome evil by doing good.

POWER-SURGE

OBEYS ✔

ALL OF YOU MUST BE WILLING TO OBEY COMPLETELY THOSE WHO RULE OVER YOU ...THOSE WHO NOW RULE HAVE BEEN CHOSEN BY GOD.
— ROMANS 13:1 —

Obey Those in Authority

13 All of you must be willing to obey completely those who rule over you. There are no authorities except the ones God has chosen. Those who now rule have been chosen by God. **2**So when you oppose the authorities, you are opposing those whom God has appointed. Those who do that will be judged.

3If you do what is right, you won't need to be afraid of your rulers. But watch out if you do what is wrong! You don't want to be afraid of those in authority, do you? Then do what is right. The one in authority will praise you. **4**He serves God and will do you good. But if you do wrong, watch out! The ruler doesn't carry a sword for no reason at all. He serves God. And God is carrying out his anger through him. The ruler punishes anyone who does wrong.

5You must obey the authorities. Then you will not be punished. You must also obey them because you know it is right.

6That's also why you pay taxes. The authorities serve God. Ruling takes up all their time. **7**Give to everyone what you owe. Do you owe taxes? Then pay them. Do you owe anything else to the government? Then pay it. Do you owe respect? Then give it. Do you owe honor? Then show it.

Love, Because the Day Is Near

8Pay everything you owe. But you can never pay back all the love you owe each other. Those who love others have done everything the law requires. 9Here are some commandments to think about. "Do not commit adultery." "Do not commit murder." "Do not steal." "Do not want what belongs to others." *(Exodus 20:13–15,17; Deuteronomy 5:17–19,21)* These and other commandments are all included in one rule. Here's what it is. "Love your neighbor as you love yourself." *(Leviticus 19:18)* 10Love does not harm its neighbor. So love does everything the law requires.

11When you do those things, keep in mind the times we are living in. The hour has come for you to wake up from your sleep. Our full salvation is closer now than it was when we first believed in Christ. 12The dark night of evil is nearly over. The day of Christ's return is almost here. So let us get rid of the works of darkness. Let us put on the armor of light.

13Let us act as we should, like people living in the daytime. Have nothing to do with wild parties. Don't get drunk. Don't take part in sexual sins or evil conduct. Don't fight with each other. Don't be jealous of anyone.

HELPFUL

ROMANS 12:13

Share with God's people who are in need.

Helping others can be tricky. It can be an easy or a hard thing to do. When someone needs help sweeping the sidewalk or getting up after they've fallen down, you can help him or her easily. But what about when someone needs help with his or her math homework? Or what if someone is shouting for help out in the middle of a lake because he or she can't swim? Then helping isn't quite so easy. In fact, it might be pretty hard.

When God called Moses to help free the Israelites from slavery in Egypt, he didn't think he could do it. "Too hard!" he told God. But God told Moses that together they could get it done (see page 74). Joseph of Arimathea was probably afraid to help after Jesus had been killed on the cross. He knew that the leaders hated Jesus and would probably hate him if he helped. But he did it anyway (see page 1214).

BE HELPFUL

What can you do to help others? If you just look around, you'll find many ways. Maybe you could help your mother by playing games with your brothers and sisters. Maybe you could help someone on your street by raking leaves or shoveling snow. Maybe you could be kind to the girl or boy in your class that no one seems to like. Lots of people in this world have lots of needs. You can help them!

Go to page 1334 for the next Super Hero Trait

14Instead, put on the Lord Jesus Christ as your clothing. Don't think about how to satisfy what your sinful nature wants.

The Weak and the Strong

14 Accept those whose faith is weak. Don't judge them where you have differences of opinion.

2The faith of some people allows them to eat anything. But others eat only vegetables because their faith is weak. **3**People who eat everything must not look down on those who do not. And people who don't eat everything must not judge those who do. God has accepted them.

4Who are you to judge someone else's servants? Whether they are faithful or not is their own master's concern. They will be faithful, because the Lord has the power to make them faithful.

5Some people consider one day to be more holy than another. Others think all days are the same. Each person should be absolutely sure in his own mind. **6**Those who think one day is special do it to honor the Lord. Those who eat meat do it to honor the Lord. They give thanks to God. Those who don't eat meat do it to honor the Lord. They also give thanks to God.

7We don't live for ourselves alone. And we don't die all by ourselves. **8**If we live, we live to honor the Lord. If we die, we die to honor the Lord. So whether we live or die, we belong to the Lord.

9Christ died and came back to life. He did this to become the Lord of both the dead and the living.

10Now then, who are you to judge your brother or sister? Why do you look down on them? We will all stand in God's court room to be judged. **11**It is written,

" 'You can be sure that I live,' says the Lord.
'And you can be just as sure that every knee will bow down in front of me.
Every tongue will tell the truth to God.' " *(Isaiah 45:23)*

12So we will all have to explain to God the things we have done.

13Let us stop judging one another. Instead, make up your mind not to put anything in your brother's way that would make him trip and fall.

14I am absolutely sure that no food is "unclean" in itself. I say this as one who belongs to the Lord Jesus. But some people may consider a thing to be "unclean." If they do, it is "unclean" for them. **15**Your brothers and sisters may be upset by what

you eat. If they are, you are no longer acting as though you love them. So don't destroy them by what you eat. Christ died for them. **16**Don't let something you consider good be spoken of as if it were evil.

17God's kingdom has nothing to do with eating or drinking. It is a matter of being right with God. It brings the peace and joy the Holy Spirit gives.

18Those who serve Christ in this way are pleasing to God. They are pleasing to people too.

19So let us do all we can to live in peace. And let us work hard to build each other up.

20Don't destroy the work of God because of food. All food is "clean." But it is wrong for you to eat anything that causes someone else to trip and fall. **21**Don't eat meat if it will cause your brothers and sisters to fall. Don't drink wine or do anything else that will make them fall.

22No matter what you think about those things, keep it between yourself and God. Blessed are those who do not have to feel guilty for what they allow.

23But those who have doubts are guilty if they eat. Their eating is not based on faith. Everything that is not based on faith is sin.

15 We who have strong faith should help the weak with their problems. We should not please only ourselves. **2**We should all please our neighbors. Let us do what is good for them. Let us build them up.

3Even Christ did not please himself. It is written, "Those who make fun of you have made fun of me also." *(Psalm 69:9)* **4**Everything that was written in the past was written to teach us. The Scriptures give us strength to go on. They cheer us up and give us hope.

5Our God is a God who strengthens you and cheers you up. May he help you agree with each other as you follow Christ Jesus. **6**Then you can give glory to God with one heart and voice. He is the God and Father of our Lord Jesus Christ.

7Christ has accepted you. So accept one another in order to bring praise to God.

8I tell you that Christ has become a servant of the Jews. He teaches us that God is true. He shows us that God will keep the promises he made to the founders of our nation. **9**Jesus became a servant of the Jews so that people who are not Jews could give glory to God for his mercy. It is written,

POWER-SURGE

CHEERFUL ✳

THE SCRIPTURES GIVE US STRENGTH TO GO ON. THEY CHEER US UP AND GIVE US HOPE. OUR GOD IS A GOD WHO STRENGTHENS YOU AND CHEERS YOU UP.
— ROMANS 15:4-5 —

STRONG

"I will praise you among those who aren't Jews.
I will sing praises to you."
(2 Samuel 22:50; Psalm 18:49)

10 Again it says,

"You non-Jews, be full of joy.
Be joyful together with God's people." *(Deuteronomy 32:43)*

11 And again it says,

"All you non-Jews, praise the Lord.
All you nations, sing praises to him."
(Psalm 117:1)

12 And Isaiah says,

"The Root of Jesse will grow up quickly.
He will rule over the nations.
Those who aren't Jews will put their hope in him." *(Isaiah 11:10)*

13 May the God who gives hope fill you with great joy. May you have perfect peace as you trust in him. May the power of the Holy Spirit fill you with hope.

Paul Serves the Non-Jews

14 My brothers and sisters, I am sure that you are full of goodness. What you know is complete. You are able to teach one another.

15 I have written to you very boldly about some things. I wanted you to think about them again. The grace of God has allowed me **16** to serve Christ Jesus among those who aren't Jews. My duty as a priest is to preach God's good news. Then the non-Jews will become an offering that pleases God. The Holy Spirit will make the offering holy.

17 Because I belong to Christ Jesus, I can take pride in my work for God. **18** I will not try to speak of anything except what Christ has done through me. He has been leading those who aren't Jews to obey God. He has been doing this by what I have said and done.

19 He has given me power to do signs and miracles. He has given me the power of the Holy Spirit.

From Jerusalem all the way around to Illyricum I have finished preaching the good news about Christ. **20** I have always wanted to preach the good news where Christ was not known. I don't want to build on what someone else has started. **21** It is written,

"Those who were not told about him
will understand.
Those who have not heard will
know what it all means."
(Isaiah 52:15)

22 That's why I have often been kept from coming to you.

Paul Plans to Visit Rome

23 Now there is no more place for me to work in those areas. For many years I have been longing to see you. **24** So I plan to see you when I go to Spain. I hope to visit you while I am passing through. And I hope you will help me on my journey there. But first I want to enjoy being with you for a while.

25 Now I am on my way to Jerusalem to serve God's people there. **26** The believers in Macedonia and Achaia were pleased to take an offering for those who were poor among God's people in Jerusalem. **27** They were happy to do it. And of course they owe it to them. Those who aren't Jews have shared from the Jews' spiritual blessings. So the non-Jews should share their earthly blessings with the Jews.

28 I want to finish my task. I want to make sure that the poor in Jerusalem have received the offering. Then I will go to Spain. On my way I will visit you. **29** I know that when I come to you, I will come with the full blessing of Christ.

30 Brothers and sisters, I am asking you through the authority of our Lord Jesus Christ to join me in my struggle by praying to God for me. Pray for me with the love the Holy Spirit provides. **31** Pray that I will be saved from those in Judea who do not believe. Pray that my work in Jerusalem will be accepted by God's people there. **32**Then, as God has planned, I will come to you with joy. Together we will be renewed.

33May the God who gives peace be with you all. Amen.

Personal Greetings

16 I would like you to welcome our sister Phoebe. She serves the church in Cenchrea. **2**I ask you to receive her as one who belongs to the Lord. Receive her in the way God's people should. Give her any help she may need from you. She has been a great help to many people, including me.

3Greet Priscilla and Aquila. They work together with me in serving Christ Jesus. **4**They have put their lives in danger for me. I am thankful for them. So are all the non-Jewish churches. **5**Greet also the church that meets in the house of Priscilla and Aquila.

Greet my dear friend Epenetus. He was the first person in Asia Minor to become a believer in Christ. **6**Greet Mary. She worked very hard for you. **7**Greet Andronicus and Junias, my relatives. They have been in prison with me. They are leaders among the apostles. They became believers in Christ before I did. **8**Greet Ampliatus. I love him as a brother in the Lord.

POWER–SURGE

CHEERFUL ✳

THE BELIEVERS IN MACEDONIA AND ACHAIA WERE PLEASED TO TAKE AN OFFERING FOR THOSE WHO WERE POOR AMONG GOD'S PEOPLE IN JERUSALEM. THEY WERE HAPPY TO DO IT.

— ROMANS 15:26-27 — **G**

GIVING

POWER–SURGE

CHEERFUL ✳

EVERYONE HAS HEARD THAT YOU OBEY GOD. SO YOU HAVE FILLED ME WITH JOY.

— ROMANS 16:19 — ✔

OBEYS

9Greet Urbanus. He works together with me in serving Christ. And greet my dear friend Stachys. **10**Greet Apelles. Even though he was put to the test, he remained faithful as one who belonged to Christ.

Greet those who live in the house of Aristobulus. **11**Greet Herodion, my relative.

Greet the believers who live in the house of Narcissus. **12**Greet Tryphena and Tryphosa. Those women work hard for the Lord.

Greet my dear friend Persis. She is another woman who has worked very hard for the Lord. **13**Greet Rufus. He is a choice believer in the Lord. And greet his mother. She has been like a mother to me too. **14**Greet Asyncritus, Phlegon and Hermes. Greet Patrobas, Hermas and the believers with them. **15**Greet Philologus, Julia, Nereus and his sister. Greet Olympas and all of God's people with them. **16**Greet one another with a holy kiss.

All the churches of Christ send their greetings.

17I am warning you, brothers and sisters, to watch out for those who try to keep you from staying together. They want to trip you up. They teach you things opposite to what you have learned. Stay away from them. **18**People like that are not serving Christ our Lord. They are serving only themselves. With smooth talk and with words they don't mean they fool people who don't know any better.

19Everyone has heard that you obey God. So you have filled me with joy. I want you to be wise about what is good. And I want you to have nothing to do with what is evil.

20The God who gives peace will soon crush Satan under your feet.

May the grace of our Lord Jesus be with you.

21Timothy works together with me. He sends his greetings to you. So do Lucius, Jason and Sosipater, my relatives.

22I, Tertius, wrote down this letter. I greet you as a believer in the Lord.

23/24 Gaius sends you his greetings. He has welcomed me and the whole church here into his house.

Erastus is the director of public works here in the city. He sends you his greet-ings. Our brother Quartus also greets you.

25May God receive glory. He is able to strengthen your faith because of the good news I preach. It is the message about Jesus Christ. It is in keeping with the mystery that was hidden for a very long time. **26**The mystery has now been made known through the writings of the prophets. The eternal God commanded that it be made known. He wanted all nations to believe and obey him. **27**May the only wise God receive glory forever through Jesus Christ. Amen.

1 CORINTHIANS

While Paul is preaching in Ephesus, he writes this first letter to the church in Corinth. He wants to be sure they know what he thinks about some problems they are having. He emphasizes that being a Christian should affect every part of a believer's life and that love is the most important thing of all. As you read this letter to the Corinthians, remember that everything in your life is affected by what you believe about Jesus and that love is more important than anything else.

CHECK OUT THIS TRAIT OF A HERO . . .

LOVING
PAGE 1334

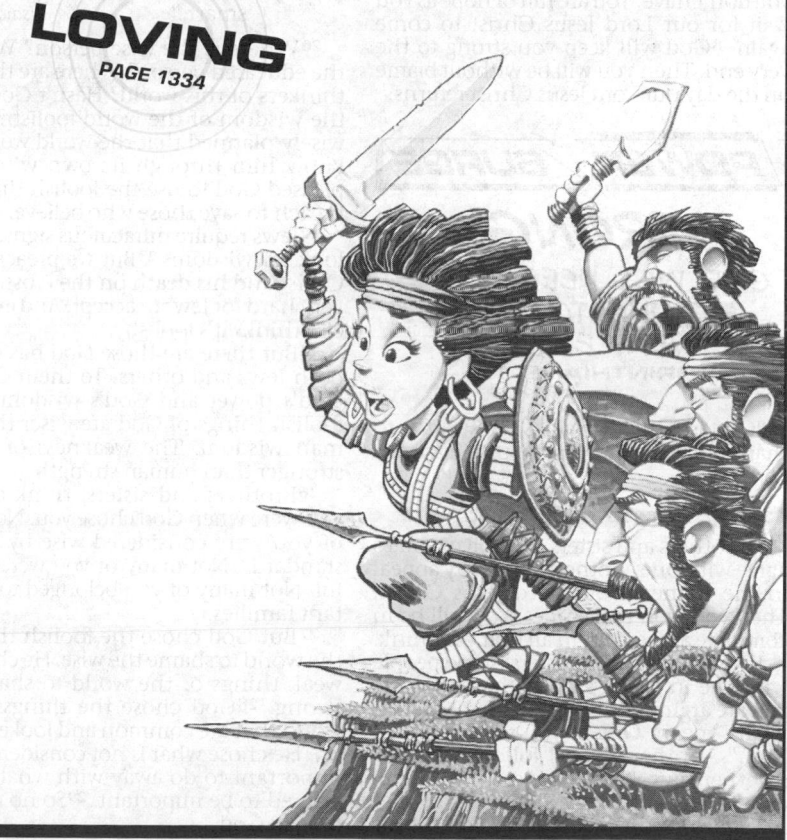

1 I, Paul, am writing this letter. I have been chosen to be an apostle of Christ Jesus just as God planned. Our brother Sosthenes joins me in writing.

2We are sending this letter to you, the members of God's church in Corinth. You have been made holy because you belong to Christ Jesus. God has chosen you to be his holy people. He has done the same for all those everywhere who pray to our Lord Jesus Christ. Jesus is their Lord and ours.

3May God our Father and the Lord Jesus Christ give you grace and peace.

Paul Gives Thanks

4I always thank God for you. I thank him because of the grace he has given to you who belong to Christ Jesus. 5You have been blessed in every way because of him. All your teaching of the truth is better. Your understanding of it is more complete. 6Our witness about Christ has been proved to be true in you.

7There is no gift of the Holy Spirit that you don't have. You are full of hope as you wait for our Lord Jesus Christ to come again. 8God will keep you strong to the very end. Then you will be without blame on the day our Lord Jesus Christ returns.

POWER-SURGE

STRONG

GOD WILL KEEP YOU STRONG TO THE VERY END.

— 1 CORINTHIANS 1:8 —

9God is faithful. He has chosen you to share life with his Son, Jesus Christ our Lord.

Taking Sides in the Church

10Brothers and sisters, I ask all of you to agree with one another. I make my appeal in the name of our Lord Jesus Christ. Then you won't take sides. You will be in complete agreement in all that you think.

11My brothers and sisters, some people who live in Chloe's house have told me you are arguing with each other. 12Here is what I mean. One of you says, "I follow Paul." Another says, "I follow Apollos." Another says, "I follow Peter." And still another says, "I follow Christ."

13Does Christ take sides? Did Paul die on the cross for you? Were you baptized in the name of Paul? 14I'm thankful that I didn't baptize any of you except Crispus and Gaius. 15No one can say that you were baptized in my name.

16It's true that I also baptized those who live in the house of Stephanas. Besides that, I don't remember if I baptized anyone else.

17Christ did not send me to baptize. He sent me to preach the good news. He commanded me not to use the kind of wisdom that people commonly use. That would take all the power away from the cross of Christ.

Christ Is God's Power and Wisdom

18The message of the cross seems foolish to those who are lost and dying. But it is God's power to us who are being saved. 19It is written,

"I will destroy the wisdom of those
    who are wise.
I will do away with the cleverness of
    those who think they are so
    smart." *(Isaiah 29:14)*

20Where is the wise person? Where is the educated person? Where are the great thinkers of this world? Hasn't God made the wisdom of the world foolish? 21God wisely planned that the world would not know him through its own wisdom. It pleased God to use the foolish things we preach to save those who believe.

22Jews require miraculous signs. Greeks look for wisdom. 23But we preach about Christ and his death on the cross. That is very hard for Jews to accept. And everyone else thinks it's foolish.

24But there are those God has chosen, both Jews and others. To them Christ is God's power and God's wisdom. 25The foolish things of God are wiser than human wisdom. The weakness of God is stronger than human strength.

26Brothers and sisters, think of what you were when God chose you. Not many of you were considered wise by human standards. Not many of you were powerful. Not many of you belonged to important families.

27But God chose the foolish things of the world to shame the wise. He chose the weak things of the world to shame the strong. 28God chose the things of this world that are common and looked down on. He chose what is not considered to be important to do away with what is considered to be important. 29So no one can brag to God.

30Because of what God has done, you belong to Christ Jesus. He has become God's wisdom for us. He makes us right with God. He makes us holy and sets us free. **31**It is written, "The one who brags should brag about what the Lord has done." *(Jeremiah 9:24)*

2 Brothers and sisters, when I came to you I didn't come with fancy words or great wisdom. I preached to you the truth about God's love. **2**I made up my mind to pay attention to only one thing while I was with you. That one thing was Jesus Christ and his death on the cross. **3**When I came to you, I was weak and afraid and trembling all over. **4**I didn't preach my message with clever and compelling words. As I preached, the Holy Spirit showed his power. **5**That was so you would believe not because of human wisdom but because of God's power.

Wisdom From the Holy Spirit

6The words we speak to those who have grown in the faith are wise. Our words are different from the words of the wise people or rulers of this world. People like that aren't going anywhere. **7**No, we speak about God's secret wisdom. His wisdom has been hidden. But before time began, God planned that his wisdom would bring us heavenly glory.

8None of the rulers of this world understood God's wisdom. If they had, they would not have nailed the Lord of glory to the cross. **9**It is written,

"No eye has seen,
 no ear has heard,
no mind has known
 what God has prepared for those
 who love him." *(Isaiah 64:4)*

10But God has shown it to us through his Spirit.

The Spirit understands all things. He understands even the deep things of God. **11**Who can know the thoughts of another person? Only a person's own spirit can know them. In the same way, only the Spirit of God knows God's thoughts. **12**We have not received the spirit of the world. We have received the Spirit who is from God. The Spirit helps us understand what God has freely given us. **13**That is what we speak about. We don't use words taught to us by people. We use words taught to us by the Holy Spirit. We use the words of the Spirit to teach the truths of the Spirit. **14**Some people don't have the Holy Spirit. They don't accept the things that come from the Spirit of God. Things like that are foolish to them. They can't understand them. In fact, such things can't be understood without the Spirit's help.

15Everyone who has the Spirit can judge all things. But no one can judge those who have the Spirit. It is written,

16 "Who can ever know what is in the
 Lord's mind?
 Can anyone ever teach him?"
 (Isaiah 40:13)

But we have the mind of Christ.

Taking Sides in the Church

3 Brothers and sisters, I couldn't speak to you as if you were guided by the Holy Spirit. I had to speak to you as if you were following the ways of the world. You aren't growing as Christ wants you to. You are still like babies. **2**The words I spoke to you were like milk, not like solid food. You weren't ready for solid food yet. And you still aren't ready for it.

3You are still following the ways of the world. Some of you are jealous. Some of you argue. So aren't you following the ways of the world? Aren't you acting like ordinary human beings? **4**One of you says, "I follow Paul." Another says, "I follow Apollos." Aren't you acting like ordinary human beings?

5After all, what is Apollos? And what is Paul? We are only people who serve. We helped you to believe. The Lord has given each of us our own work to do. **6**I planted the seed. Apollos watered it. But God made it grow.

7So the one who plants is not important. The one who waters is not important. It is God who makes things grow. He is the One who is important. **8**The one who plants and the one who waters have the same purpose. The Lord will give each of us a reward for our work. **9**We work together with God. You are like God's field. You are like his building.

10God has given me the grace to lay a foundation as a master builder. Now someone else is building on it. But each one should build carefully. **11**No one can lay any other foundation than the one that has already been laid. That foundation is Jesus Christ.

12A person may build on it using gold, silver, jewels, wood, hay or straw. **13**But each person's work will be shown for what it is. On judgment day it will be brought to light. It will be put through fire. The fire will test how good everyone's work is. **14**If the building doesn't burn up, God will give the builder a reward for his work. **15**If the building burns up, the builder will lose everything. The builder will be saved, but only like one escaping through the flames.

16Don't you know that you yourselves are God's temple? God's Spirit lives in you. **17**If anyone destroys God's temple, God will destroy him. God's temple is holy. And you are that temple.

18Don't fool yourselves. Suppose some of you think you are wise by the standards of the world. Then you should become a "fool" so that you can become wise.

19The wisdom of this world is foolish in God's eyes. It is written, "God catches wise people in their own tricks." *(Job 5:13)* **20**It is also written, "The Lord knows that the thoughts of the wise don't amount to anything." *(Psalm 94:11)*

21So no more bragging about human beings! All things are yours. **22**That means Paul or Apollos or Peter or the world or life or death or the present or the future. All are yours. **23**You are joined to Christ and belong to him. And Christ is joined to God.

Apostles of Christ

4 Here is how you should think of us. We serve Christ. We are trusted with God's secret truth. **2**Those who have been given a trust must prove that they are faithful.

3I care very little if I am judged by you or by any human court. I don't even judge myself. **4**I don't feel I have done anything wrong. But that doesn't mean I'm not guilty. The Lord judges me.

5So don't judge anything before the ap-pointed time. Wait until the Lord returns. He will bring to light what is hidden in the dark. He will show the real reasons why people do what they do. At that time each person will receive praise from God.

6Brothers and sisters, I have used myself and Apollos as examples to help you. You can learn from us the meaning of the saying, "Don't go beyond what is written." Then you won't be proud that you follow one person instead of another.

7Who makes you different from anyone else? What do you have that you did not receive? And if you did receive it, why do you brag as though you did not?

8You already have everything you want, don't you? Have you already become rich? Have you begun to rule as kings? And did you do that without us? I wish that you really had begun to rule. Then we could rule with you!

9It seems to me that God has put us apostles on display at the end of a parade. We are like men sentenced to die in front of a crowd. We have been made a show for the whole creation to see. Angels and people are staring at us.

10We are fools for Christ. But you are so wise in Christ! We are weak. But you are so strong! You are honored. But we are looked down on! **11**Up to this very hour we are hungry and thirsty. We are dressed in rags. We are being treated badly. We have no homes. **12**We work hard with our own hands. When others call down a curse on us, we bless them. When we are attacked, we put up with it. **13**When others say bad things about us, we answer kindly. Up to this moment we have become the world's garbage. We are everybody's trash.

14I am not writing this to shame you. You are my dear children, and I want to warn you. **15**You may have 10,000 believers in Christ watching over you. But you don't have many fathers. I became your father by serving Christ Jesus and telling you the good news. **16**So I'm asking you to follow my example.

17That's the reason I'm sending Timothy to you. He is like a son to me, and I love him. He is faithful in serving the Lord. He will remind you of my way of life in serving Christ Jesus. And that agrees with what I teach everywhere in every church.

18Some of you have become proud. You act as if I weren't coming to you. **19**But I will come very soon, if that's what the Lord wants. Then I will find out how those proud people are talking. I will also

POWER-SURGE

FAITHFUL

WE SERVE CHRIST. WE ARE TRUSTED WITH GOD'S SECRET TRUTH. THOSE WHO HAVE BEEN GIVEN A TRUST MUST PROVE THAT THEY ARE FAITHFUL.

— 1 CORINTHIANS 4:1-2 —

TRUSTED

find out what power they have. **20**The kingdom of God is not a matter of talk. It is a matter of power.

21Which do you want? Should I come to you with a whip? Or should I come in love and with a gentle spirit?

Throw the Evil Person Out!

5 It is actually reported that there is sexual sin among you. I'm told that a man is living with his father's wife and is having sex with her. Even people who do not know God don't commit that sin. **2**And you are proud! Shouldn't you be filled with sadness instead? Shouldn't you have put the man who did that out of your church?

3Even though I am not right there with you, I am with you in spirit. And I have already judged the one who did that, just as if I were there.

4When you come together in the name of our Lord Jesus, I will be with you in spirit. The power of our Lord Jesus will also be with you. **5**When you come together like that, hand that man over to Satan. Then his sinful nature will be destroyed. His spirit will be saved on the day the Lord returns.

6Your bragging is not good. It is like yeast. Don't you know that just a little yeast works its way through the whole batch of dough? **7**Get rid of the old yeast. Be like a new batch of dough without yeast. That is what you really are, because Christ has been offered up for us. He is our Passover lamb.

8So let us keep the Feast, but not with the old yeast. I'm talking about yeast that is full of hatred and evil. Let us keep the Feast with bread made without yeast. Let us do it with bread that is honest and true.

9I wrote a letter to you to tell you to stay away from people who commit sexual sins. **10**I didn't mean the people of this world who sin that way or who always want more and more. I didn't mean those who cheat or who worship statues of gods. In that case you would have to leave this world!

11But here is what I am writing to you. You must stay away from anyone who claims to be a believer but who does those things. Stay away from anyone who commits sexual sins or who always wants more and more things. Stay away from a person who worships statues of gods or who tells lies about others. Stay away from anyone who gets drunk or who cheats. Don't even eat with a person like that.

12Is it my business to judge those outside the church? Aren't you supposed to judge those inside the church? **13**God will judge those outside. Scripture says, "Get rid of that evil person!" *(Deuteronomy 17:7, 19:19; 21:21; 22:21,24, 24:7)*

Do Not Take Believers to Court

6 Suppose one of you wants to bring a charge against another believer. Should you take it to the ungodly to be judged? Why not take it to God's people?

2Don't you know that God's people will judge the world? And if you are going to judge the world, aren't you able to judge small cases? **3**Don't you know that we will judge angels? Then we should be able to judge the things of this life even more!

4So if you want to press charges in matters like that, appoint as judges members of the church who aren't very important! **5**I say this to shame you. Is it possible that no one among you is wise enough to judge matters between believers? **6**Instead, one believer goes to court against another. And this happens in front of unbelievers!

7The very fact that you take another believer to court means you have lost the battle already. Why not be treated wrongly? Why not be cheated? **8**Instead, you yourselves cheat and do wrong. And you do it to your brothers and sisters.

9Don't you know that evil people will not receive God's kingdom? Don't be fooled. Those who commit sexual sins will not receive the kingdom. Neither will those who worship statues of gods or commit adultery. Neither will men who are prostitutes or who commit homosexual acts. **10**Neither will thieves or those who always want more and more. Neither will those who are often drunk or tell lies or cheat. People who live like that will not receive God's kingdom.

11Some of you used to do those things. But your sins were washed away. You were made holy. You were made right with God. All of that was done in the name of the Lord Jesus Christ and by the Spirit of our God.

Sexual Sins

12Some of you say, "Everything is permitted for me." But not everything is good for me. Again some of you say, "Everything is permitted for me." But I will not be controlled by anything. **13**Some of you say, "Food is for the stomach. And the stomach is for food." But God will destroy both of them.

The body is not meant for sexual sins. The body is meant for the Lord. And the Lord is meant for the body. ¹⁴By his power God raised the Lord from the dead. He will also raise us up.

¹⁵Don't you know that your bodies belong to the body of Christ? Should I take what belongs to Christ and join it to a prostitute? Never! ¹⁶Don't you know that when you join yourself to a prostitute, you become one with her in body? Scripture says, "The two will become one." *(Genesis 2:24)* ¹⁷But anyone who is joined to the Lord becomes one with him in spirit.

¹⁸Keep far away from sexual sins. All the other sins a person commits are outside his body. But sexual sins are sins against one's own body.

¹⁹Don't you know that your bodies are temples of the Holy Spirit? The Spirit is in you. You have received him from God. You do not belong to yourselves. ²⁰Christ has paid the price for you. So use your bodies in a way that honors God.

Marriage

7 Now I want to deal with the things you wrote me about.

Some of you say, "It is good for a man not to have sex with a woman." ²But since there is so much sexual sin, each man should have his own wife. And each woman should have her own husband. ³A husband should satisfy his wife's sexual needs. And a wife should satisfy her husband's sexual needs.

⁴The wife's body does not belong only to her. It also belongs to her husband. In the same way, the husband's body does not belong only to him. It also belongs to his wife. ⁵You shouldn't stop giving yourselves to each other except when you both agree to do so. And that should be only to give yourselves time to pray for a while. Then you should come together again. In that way, Satan will not tempt you when you can't control yourselves.

⁶I say those things to you as my advice, not as a command. ⁷I wish all of you were like me. But you each have your own gift from God. One has this gift. Another has that.

⁸I speak to those who are not married. I also speak to widows. It is good for you to stay single like me. ⁹But if you can't control yourselves, you should get married. It is better to get married than to burn with sexual longing.

¹⁰I give a command to those who are married. It is a direct command from the Lord, not from me. A wife must not leave her husband. ¹¹But if she does, she must not get married again. Or she can go back to her husband. And a husband must not divorce his wife.

¹²I also have something to say to everyone else. It is from me, not a direct command from the Lord. Suppose a brother has a wife who is not a believer. If she is willing to live with him, he must not divorce her. ¹³And suppose a woman has a husband who is not a believer. If he is willing to live with her, she must not divorce him. ¹⁴The unbelieving husband has been made holy through his wife. The unbelieving wife has been made holy through her believing husband. If that were not the case, your children would not be pure and clean. But as it is, they are holy.

¹⁵If the unbeliever leaves, let that person go. In that case, a believing man or woman does not have to stay married. God wants us to live in peace. ¹⁶Wife, how do you know if you can save your husband? Husband, how do you know if you can save your?

¹⁷But each of you should remain in the place in life that the Lord has given you. Stay as you were when God chose you. That's the rule all the churches must follow.

¹⁸Was a man already circumcised when God chose him? Then he should not become uncircumcised. Was he uncircumcised when God chose him? Then he should not be circumcised. ¹⁹Being circumcised means nothing. Being uncircumcised means nothing. Doing what God commands is what counts. ²⁰Each of you should stay as you were when God chose you.

²¹Were you a slave when God chose you? Don't let it trouble you. But if you can get your master to set you free, do it. ²²Those who were slaves when the Lord chose them are now the Lord's free people. Those who were free when God chose them are now slaves of Christ. ²³Christ has paid the price for you. Don't become slaves of human beings.

²⁴Brothers and sisters, you are accountable to God. So all of you should stay as you were when God chose you.

²⁵Now I want to say something about virgins. I have no direct command from the Lord. But I give my opinion. Because of the Lord's mercy, I give it as one who can be trusted.

²⁶Times are hard for you right now. So I think it's good for you to stay as you are.

²⁷Are you married? Then don't get a divorce. Are you single? Then don't look for a wife. ²⁸But if you get married, you have not sinned. And if a virgin gets married, she has not sinned. But those who get married will have many troubles in this life. I want to save you from that.

²⁹Brothers and sisters, what I mean is that the time is short. From now on, those who have a husband or wife should live as if they did not. ³⁰Those who are sad should live as if they were not. Those who are happy should live as if they were not. Those who buy something should live as if it were not theirs to keep. ³¹Those who use the things of the world should not become all wrapped up in them. The world as it now exists is passing away.

³²I don't want you to have anything to worry about. A single man is concerned about the Lord's matters. He wants to know how he can please the Lord. ³³But a married man is concerned about the matters of this world. He wants to know how he can please his wife. ³⁴His concerns pull him in two directions.

A single woman or a virgin is concerned about the Lord's matters. She wants to serve the Lord with both body and spirit. But a married woman is concerned about the matters of this world. She wants to know how she can please her husband.

³⁵I'm saying those things for your own good. I'm not trying to hold you back. I want you to be free to live in a way that is right. I want you to give yourselves completely to the Lord.

³⁶Suppose a man thinks he is not acting properly toward the virgin he has promised to marry. Suppose she is getting old, and he feels that he should marry her. He should do as he wants. He is not sinning. They should get married.

³⁷But suppose the man has decided not to marry the virgin. And suppose he has no compelling need to get married and can control himself. If he has made up his mind not to get married, he also does the right thing.

³⁸So then, the man who marries the virgin does the right thing. But the man who doesn't marry her does an even better thing.

³⁹A woman has to stay married to her husband as long as he lives. If he dies, she is free to marry anyone she wants to. But the one she marries must belong to the Lord. ⁴⁰In my opinion, she is happier if she stays single. And I also think that I am led by the Spirit of God in saying that.

Food Offered to Statues of Gods

8 Now I want to deal with food offered to statues of gods.

We know that we all have knowledge. Knowledge makes people proud. But love builds them up. ²Those who think they know something still don't know as they should. ³But those who love God are known by God.

⁴So then, here is what I say about eating food that is offered to statues of gods. We know that a god made by human hands is really nothing at all in the world. We know there is only one God. ⁵There may be so-called gods either in heaven or on earth. In fact, there are many "gods" and many "lords." ⁶But for us there is only one God. He is the Father. All things came from him, and we live for him. And there is only one Lord. He is Jesus Christ. All things came because of him, and we live because of him.

⁷But not everyone knows that. Some people still think that statues of gods are real gods. When they eat food that was offered to statues of gods, they think of it as food that was offered to real gods. And because they have a weak sense of what is right and wrong, they feel guilty. ⁸But food doesn't bring us close to God. We are no worse if we don't eat. We are no better if we do eat.

⁹But be careful how you use your freedom. Be sure it doesn't trip up someone who is weaker than you.

¹⁰Suppose you who have that knowledge are eating in a temple of one of those gods. And suppose someone who has a weak sense of what is right and wrong sees you. Won't that person become bold and eat what has been offered to statues of gods? ¹¹If so, then your knowledge destroys that weak brother or sister for whom Christ died.

¹²When you sin against other believers in that way, you harm their weak sense of what is right and wrong. By doing that you sin against Christ.

¹³So what should I do if what I eat causes my brother or sister to fall into sin? I will never eat meat again. In that way, I will not cause them to fall.

The Rights of an Apostle

9 Am I not free? Am I not an apostle? Haven't I seen Jesus our Lord? Aren't you the result of my work for the Lord? ²Even though others may not think of me as an apostle, I am certainly one to you! You are the proof that I am the Lord's apostle. **3**That is what I say to stand up for myself when people judge me.

4Don't we have the right to eat and drink? **5**Don't we have the right to take a believing wife with us when we travel? The other apostles do. The Lord's brothers do. Peter does. **6**Or are Barnabas and I the only ones who have to work for a living?

7Who serves as a soldier but doesn't get paid? Who plants a vineyard but doesn't eat any of its grapes? Who takes care of a flock but doesn't drink any of the milk? **8**Do I say that from only a human point of view? The Law says the same thing.

9Here is what is written in the Law of Moses. "Do not stop an ox from eating while it helps separate the grain from the straw." *(Deuteronomy 25:4)* Is it oxen that God is concerned about? **10**Doesn't he say that for us? Yes, it was written for us. When a farmer plows and separates the grain, he does it because he hopes to share in the crop.

11We have planted spiritual seed among you. Is it too much to ask that we receive from you some of the things we need? **12**Others have the right to receive help from you. Don't we have even more right to do so?

But we didn't use that right. No, we have put up with everything. We didn't want to keep the good news of Christ from spreading.

13Don't you know that those who work in the temple get their food from the temple? Don't you know that those who serve at the altar eat from what is offered on the altar? **14**In the same way, those who preach the good news should receive their living from their work. That is what the Lord has commanded.

15But I haven't used any of those rights. And I'm not writing because I hope you will do things like that for me. I would rather die than have anyone take away my pride in my work. **16**But when I preach the good news, I can't brag. I have to preach it. How terrible it will be for me if I do not preach the good news!

17If I preach because I want to, I get a reward. If I preach because I have to, I'm only doing my duty. **18**Then what reward do I get? Here is what it is. I am able to preach the good news free of charge. And I can do it without making use of my rights when I preach it.

19I am free. I don't belong to anyone. But I make myself a slave to everyone. I do it to win as many as I can to Christ.

20To the Jews I became like a Jew. That was to win the Jews. To those under the law I became like one who was under the law, even though I myself am not under the law. That was to win those under the law. **21**To those who don't have the law I became like one who doesn't have the law. I am not free from God's law. I am under Christ's law. Now I can win those who don't have the law. **22**To those who are weak I became weak. That was to win the weak.

I have become all things to all people so that in all possible ways I might save some. **23**I do all of that because of the good news. And I want to share in its blessings.

24In a race all the runners run. But only one gets the prize. You know that, don't you? So run in a way that will get you the prize. **25**All who take part in the games train hard. They do it to get a crown that will not last. But we do it to get a crown that will last forever.

26So I do not run like someone who doesn't run toward the finish line. I do not fight like a boxer who hits nothing but air. **27**No, I train my body and bring it under control. Then after I have preached to others, I myself will not break the rules and fail to win the prize.

POWER-/SURGE

SELF-CONTROLLED

I TRAIN MY BODY AND BRING IT UNDER CONTROL.
— 1 CORINTHIANS 9:27 —

TRIES HARD

Warnings From Israel's History

10 Brothers and sisters, here is what I want you to know about our people who lived long ago. They were all led by the cloud. They all walked through the Red Sea. **2**They were all baptized into Moses in the cloud and in the sea. **3**They all ate the same supernatural food. **4**They all drank the same supernatural water. They drank from the supernatural rock that went with them. That rock was Christ.

5But God was not pleased with most of them. Their bodies were scattered all over the desert.

6Now those things happened as examples for us. They are supposed to keep us from longing for evil things, as the people of Israel did.

7So don't worship statues of gods, as some of them did. It is written, "The people sat down to eat and drink. Then they got up to dance wildly in front of their god." *(Exodus 32:6)* **8**We should not commit sexual sins, as some of them did. In one day 23,000 of them died. **9**We should not put the Lord to the test, as some of them did. They were killed by snakes. **10**Don't tell your leaders how unhappy you are with them. That's what some of the people of Israel did. And they were killed by the destroying angel.

11Those things happened to them as examples for us. They were written down to warn us who are living at the time when God's work is being completed. **12**So be careful. When you think you are standing firm, you might fall.

13You are tempted in the same way all other human beings are. God is faithful. He will not let you be tempted any more than you can take. But when you are tempted, God will give you a way out so that you can stand up under it.

Sharing in the Body and Blood of Christ

14My dear friends, run away from statues of gods. Don't worship them. **15**I'm talking to people who are reasonable. Judge for yourselves what I say.

16When we give thanks for the cup at the Lord's Supper, aren't we sharing in the blood of Christ? When we break the bread, aren't we sharing in the body of Christ? **17**Just as there is one loaf, so we who are many are one body. We all eat from the one loaf.

18Think about the people of Israel. Don't those who eat the offerings share in the altar? **19**Do I mean that what is offered to a statue of a god is anything? Do I mean that a statue of a god is anything? **20**No! But what is offered by those who worship statues of gods is really offered to demons. It is not offered to God. I don't want you to be sharing with demons.

21You can't drink the cup of the Lord and the cup of demons too. You can't have a part in both the Lord's table and the table of demons. **22**Are we trying to make the Lord jealous? Are we stronger than he is?

The Believer's Freedom

23You say, "Everything is permitted." But not everything is good for us. Again

you say, "Everything is permitted." But not everything builds us up. **24**We should not look out for our own interests. Instead, we should look out for the interests of others.

25Eat anything that is sold in the meat market. Don't ask if it's right or wrong. **26**Scripture says, "The earth belongs to the Lord. And so does everything in it." *(Psalm 24:1)* **27**Suppose an unbeliever invites you to a meal and you want to go. Then eat anything that is put in front of you. Don't ask if it's right or wrong.

28But suppose someone says to you, "This food has been offered to a statue of a god." Then don't eat it. Keep in mind the good of the one who told you. And don't eat because of a sense of what is right and wrong. **29**I'm talking about the other person's sense of what is right and wrong, not yours.

Why should my freedom be judged by what someone else thinks? **30**Suppose I give thanks when I eat. Then why should I be blamed for eating food I thank God for?

31So eat and drink and do everything else for the glory of God. **32**Don't do anything that causes another person to trip and fall. It doesn't matter if that person is a Jew or a Greek or a member of God's church.

33Follow my example. I try to please everyone in every way. I'm not looking out for what is good for me. I'm looking out for the interests of others. I do it so that they might be saved.

11 Follow my example, just as I follow the example of Christ.

Proper Worship

2I praise you for being faithful in remembering me. I also praise you for staying true to all my teachings, just as I gave them to you.

3Now I want you to know that the head of every man is Christ. The head of the woman is the man. And the head of Christ is God. **4**Every man who prays or prophesies with his head covered brings shame on his head. **5**And every woman who prays or prophesies with her head uncovered brings shame on her head. It is just as if her head were shaved.

6What if a woman does not cover her head? She should have her hair cut off. But it is shameful for her to cut her hair or shave it off. So she should cover her head.

7A man should not cover his head. He is the likeness and glory of God. But the woman is the glory of the man. **8**The man did not come from the woman. The woman came from the man.

9Also, the man was not created for the woman. The woman was created for the man. **10**That's why a woman should have her head covered. It shows that she is under authority. She should also cover her head because of the angels.

11But here is how things are for those who belong to the Lord. The woman is not independent of the man. And the man is not independent of the woman. **12**The woman came from the man, and the man is born from the woman. But everything comes from God.

13You be the judge. Is it proper for a woman to pray to God without covering her head? **14**Suppose a man has long hair. Doesn't the very nature of things teach you that it is shameful? **15**And suppose a woman has long hair. Doesn't the very nature of things teach you that it is her glory? Long hair is given to her as a covering.

16If anyone wants to argue about that, we don't have any other practice. And God's churches don't either.

The Lord's Supper

17In the following matters, I don't praise you. Your meetings do more harm than good.

18First, here is what people are telling me. When you come together as a church, you take sides. And in some ways I believe it. **19**No doubt you need to take sides in order to show which of you God agrees with!

20When you come together, it is not the Lord's Supper you eat. **21**As you eat, each of you goes ahead without waiting for anyone else. One remains hungry and another gets drunk. **22**Don't you have homes to eat and drink in? Or do you think so little of God's church that you shame those in it who have nothing? What should I say to you? Should I praise you for that? Certainly not!

23I passed on to you what I received from the Lord. On the night the Lord Jesus was handed over to his enemies, he took bread. **24**When he had given thanks, he broke it. He said, "This is my body. It is given for you. Every time you eat it, do it in memory of me." **25**In the same way, after supper he took the cup. He said, "This cup is the new covenant in my blood. Every time you drink it, do it in memory of me."

26When you eat the bread and drink the cup, you are announcing the Lord's death until he comes again.

27So do not eat the bread or drink the cup of the Lord in a way that isn't worthy of him. If you do, you will be guilty of sinning against the body and blood of the Lord. **28**A person should take a careful look at himself before he eats the bread and drinks from the cup. **29**Anyone who eats and drinks must recognize the body of the Lord. If he doesn't, God will judge him for it. **30**That is why many of you are weak and sick. That is why a number of you have died.

31We should judge ourselves. Then we would not be found guilty. **32**When the Lord judges us, he corrects us. Then we will not be judged along with the rest of the world.

33My brothers and sisters, when you come together to eat, wait for each other. **34**Those who are hungry should eat at home. Then when you come together, you will not be judged.

When I come, I will give you more directions.

Gifts of the Holy Spirit

12 Brothers and sisters, I want you to know about the gifts of the Holy Spirit.

2You know that at one time you were unbelievers. You were somehow drawn away to worship statues of gods that couldn't even speak. **3**So I tell you that no one who is speaking with the help of God's Spirit says, "May Jesus be cursed." And without the help of the Holy Spirit no one can say, "Jesus is Lord."

4There are different kinds of gifts. But they are all given by the same Spirit. **5**There are different ways to serve. But they all come from the same Lord. **6**There are different ways to work. But the same God makes it possible for all of us to have all those different things.

7The Holy Spirit is given to each of us in a special way. That is for the good of all. **8**To some people the Spirit gives the message of wisdom. To others the same Spirit gives the message of knowledge. **9**To others the same Spirit gives faith. To others that one Spirit gives gifts of healing. **10**To others he gives the power to do miracles. To others he gives the ability to prophesy. To others he gives the ability to tell the spirits apart. To others he gives the ability to speak in different kinds of languages they had not known before. And to still others he gives the ability to explain what was said in those languages.

11All of the gifts are produced by one and the same Spirit. He gives them to each person, just as he decides.

One Body but Many Parts

12There is one body. But it has many parts. Even though it has many parts, they make up one body. It is the same with Christ. 13We were all baptized by one Holy Spirit into one body. It didn't matter whether we were Jews or Greeks, slaves or free people. We were all given the same Spirit to drink.

14The body is not made up of just one part. It has many parts. 15Suppose the foot says, "I am not a hand. So I don't belong to the body." It is still part of the body. 16And suppose the ear says, "I am not an eye. So I don't belong to the body." It is still part of the body.

17If the whole body were an eye, how could it hear? If the whole body were an ear, how could it smell? 18God has placed each part in the body just as he wanted it to be. 19If all the parts were the same, how could there be a body? 20As it is, there are many parts. But there is only one body.

21The eye can't say to the hand, "I don't need you!" The head can't say to the feet, "I don't need you!" 22In fact, it is just the opposite. The parts of the body that seem to be weaker are the ones we can't do without. 23The parts that we think are less important we treat with special honor. The private parts aren't shown. But they are treated with special care. 24The parts that can be shown don't need special care. But God has joined together all the parts of the body. And he has given more honor to the parts that didn't have any. 25In that way, the parts of the body will not take sides. All of them will take care of each other. 26If one part suffers, every part suffers with it. If one part is honored, every part shares in its joy.

27You are the body of Christ. Each one of you is a part of it. 28First, God has ap-

pointed apostles in the church. Second, he has appointed prophets. Third, he has appointed teachers. Then he has appointed people who do miracles and those who have gifts of healing. He also appointed those able to help others, those able to direct things, and those who can speak in different kinds of languages they had not known before.

29Is everyone an apostle? Is everyone a prophet? Is everyone a teacher? Do all work miracles? 30Do all have gifts of healing? Do all speak in languages they had not known before? Do all explain what is said in those languages? 31But above all, you should want the more important gifts.

POWER-SURGE

KIND   K

LOVE IS PATIENT.
LOVE IS KIND.
— 1 CORINTHIANS 13:4 —

PATIENT   P

Love

And now I will show you the best way of all.

13 Suppose I speak in the languages of human beings and of angels. If I don't have love, I am only a loud gong or a noisy cymbal. 2Suppose I have the gift of prophecy. Suppose I can understand all the secret things of God and know everything about him. And suppose I have enough faith to move mountains. If I don't have love, I am nothing at all. 3Suppose I give everything I have to poor people. And suppose I give my body to be burned. If I don't have love, I get nothing at all.

4Love is patient. Love is kind. It does not want what belongs to others. It does not brag. It is not proud. 5It is not rude. It does not look out for its own interests. It does not easily become angry. It does not keep track of other people's wrongs.

6Love is not happy with evil. But it is full of joy when the truth is spoken. 7It always protects. It always trusts. It always hopes. It never gives up.

8Love never fails. But prophecy will pass away. Speaking in languages that had

POWER-SURGE

WISE   W

TO SOME PEOPLE THE
SPIRIT GIVES THE
MESSAGE OF WISDOM.
— 1 CORINTHIANS 12:8 —

not been known before will end. And knowledge will pass away.

⁹What we know now is not complete. What we prophesy now is not perfect. ¹⁰But when what is perfect comes, the things that are not perfect will pass away.

¹¹When I was a child, I talked like a child. I thought like a child. I had the understanding of a child. When I became a man, I put childish ways behind me.

¹²Now we see only a dim likeness of things. It is as if we were seeing them in a mirror. But someday we will see clearly. We will see face to face. What I know now

LOVING

1 CORINTHIANS 13:4-6

Love is patient. Love is kind. It does not want what belongs to others. It does not brag. It is not proud. It is not rude. It does not look out for its own interests. It does not easily become angry. It does not keep track of other people's wrongs. Love is not happy with evil. But it is full of joy when the truth is spoken.

What is love? Is it how you *feel* about someone or something? Or is it more than that? The Bible teaches that love is much more than a feeling. It is *action*. Real love is showing love by your actions even when you don't *feel* loving.

What does that mean? Well, maybe you'll have to do something kind for someone when you're angry with him or her. Maybe it means saying something kind when you feel like saying something mean. Maybe being loving means doing something nice for someone who hasn't been nice to you. And then, thank goodness, sometimes it will mean *feeling* like you love someone and *doing* something loving for them.

The Bible is full of great stories of love. Ruth (see page 305) loved Naomi so much that she left her home and family to stay with her. Then there was the amazing Jehosheba. She dashed through the palace when the wicked queen was killing all of the king's children. Jehosheba grabbed one little boy, the king's son, and hid. She showed her love for God and for right and for that little boy when she bravely hid from the queen. Her story is on page 448.

BE LOVING

Read the verse above to find out ways that you can be a loving person. You show God that you love him by how you love others. Is that amazing, or what? God knows you love him when you are loving to other people.

Go to page 1347 for the next Super Hero Trait

*Mary Magdalene went to the disciples with the news.
She said, "I have seen the Lord!"
(John 20:18)*

GO TO PAGE 1248

PHILIP

Then Philip began with that same part of Scripture. He told him the good news about Jesus.
(Acts 8:35)

GO TO PAGE 1268

SAUL/PAUL

GO TO PAGE 1270

"Go! I have chosen this man [Saul] to work for me. He will carry my name to those who aren't Jews and to their kings. He will bring my name to the people of Israel." (Acts 9:15)

THE JAILER

[The jailer] rushed in, shaking with fear. He fell down in front of Paul and Silas… He asked, "Sirs, what must I do to be saved?" (Acts 16:29–30)

GO TO PAGE 1284

someone must explain what was said. 28If there is no one to explain, the speakers should keep quiet in the church. They can speak to themselves and to God.

29Only two or three prophets are supposed to speak. Others should decide if what is being said is true. 30What if a message from God comes to someone else who is sitting there? Then the one who is speaking should stop.

31Those who prophesy can all take turns. In that way, everyone can be taught and be given hope. 32Those who prophesy should control their speaking. 33God is not a God of disorder. He is a God of peace.

As in all the churches of God's people, 34women should remain silent in the meetings. They are not allowed to speak. They must follow the lead of those who are in authority, as the Law says. 35If they have a question about something, they should ask their own husbands at home. It is shameful for women to speak in church meetings.

36Did the word of God begin with you? Or are you the only people it has reached? 37Suppose some think they are prophets or have gifts of the Holy Spirit. They should agree that what I am writing to you is the Lord's command. 38Anyone who does not recognize that will not be recognized.

39Brothers and sisters, you should want to prophesy. And don't stop people from speaking in languages they had not known before. 40But everything should be done in a proper and orderly way.

Paul Explains the Good News

15 Brothers and sisters, I want to remind you of the good news I preached to you. You received it and have put your faith in it. 2Because you believed the good news, you are saved. But you must hold firmly to the message I preached to you. If you don't, you have believed it for nothing.

POWER-SURGE

BELIEVES †

BECAUSE YOU
BELIEVED THE GOOD
NEWS, YOU ARE
SAVED.
— 1 CORINTHIANS 15:2 —

3What I received I passed on to you. And it is the most important of all. Here is what it is. Christ died for our sins, just as Scripture said he would. 4He was buried. He was raised from the dead on the third day, just as Scripture said he would be. 5He appeared to Peter.

Then he appeared to the Twelve. 6After that, he appeared to more than 500 believers at the same time. Most of them are still living. But some have died. 7He appeared to James. Then he appeared to all the apostles. 8Last of all, he also appeared to me. I was like someone who wasn't born at the right time or in a normal way.

9I am the least important of the apostles. I'm not even fit to be called an apostle. I tried to destroy God's church. 10But because of God's grace I am what I am. And his grace was not wasted on me. No, I have worked harder than all the other apostles. But I didn't do the work. God's grace was with me.

11So whether it was I or the other apostles who preached to you, that is what we preach. And that is what you believed.

Believers Will Rise From the Dead

12We have preached that Christ has been raised from the dead. So how can some of you say that no one rises from the dead? 13If no one rises from the dead, then not even Christ has been raised. 14And if Christ has not been raised, what we preach doesn't mean anything. Your faith doesn't mean anything either. 15More than that, we would be lying about God. We have given witness that God raised Christ from the dead. But he did not raise him if the dead are not raised.

16If the dead are not raised, then Christ has not been raised either. 17And if Christ has not been raised, your faith doesn't mean anything. Your sins have not been forgiven. 18Those who have died believing in Christ are also lost.

19Do we have hope in Christ only for this life? Then people should pity us more than anyone else.

20But Christ really has been raised from the dead. He is the first of all those who will rise.

21Death came because of what a man did. Rising from the dead also comes because of what a man did. 22Because of Adam, all people die. So because of Christ, all will be made alive.

23But here is the order of events. Christ is the first of those who rise from the dead. When he comes back, those who is not complete. But someday I will know completely, just as God knows me completely.

13The three most important things to have are faith, hope and love. But the greatest of them is love.

The Gifts the Holy Spirit Gives

14 Follow the way of love. You should also want the gifts the Holy Spirit gives. Most of all, you should want the gift of prophecy.

2Anyone who speaks in a language he had not known before doesn't speak to people. He speaks only to God. In fact, no one understands that person. What he says with his spirit remains a mystery. 3But anyone who prophesies speaks to people. He says things to make them stronger, to give them hope and to comfort them. 4Those who speak in other languages build themselves up. But those who prophesy build up the church.

5I would like all of you to speak in other languages. But I would rather have you prophesy. Those who prophesy are more helpful than those who speak in other languages. But that is not the case if those who speak in other languages explain what they have said. Then the whole church can be built up.

6Brothers and sisters, suppose I were to come to you and speak in other languages. What good would I be to you? None! I would need to come with new truth or knowledge, or a prophecy or a teaching.

7Here are some examples. Certain objects make sounds. Take a flute or a harp. No one will know what the tune is unless different notes are played. 8Also, if the trumpet call isn't clear, who will get ready for battle?

9It's the same with you. You must speak words that people understand. If you don't, no one will know what you are saying. You will just be speaking into the air. 10It is true that there are all kinds of languages in the world. And they all have meaning. 11But if I don't understand what someone is saying, I am a stranger to that person. And that person is a stranger to me.

12It's the same with you. You want to have gifts of the Spirit. So try to do your best in using gifts that build up the church.

13For that reason, those who speak in languages they had not known before should pray that they can explain what they say. 14If I pray in another language,

my spirit prays. But my mind does not pray. 15So what should I do? I will pray with my spirit. But I will also pray with my mind. I will sing with my spirit. But I will also sing with my mind.

16Suppose you are praising God with your spirit. And suppose there are visitors among you who don't understand what's going on. How can they say "Amen" when you give thanks? They don't know what you are saying. 17You might be giving thanks well enough. But the others are not being built up.

18I thank God that I speak in other languages more than all of you do. 19But in the church I would rather speak five words that people can understand than 10,000 words in another language. Then I would be teaching others.

20Brothers and sisters, stop thinking like children. Be like babies as far as evil is concerned. But be grown up in your thinking. 21In the Law it is written,

"Through people who speak
    unfamiliar languages
and through the lips of strangers
I will speak to these people.
But even then they will not listen
    to me."   (Isaiah 28:11,12)

That is what the Lord says.

22So speaking in other languages is a sign for those who don't believe. It is not a sign for those who do believe. But prophecy is for believers. It is not for those who don't believe.

23Suppose the whole church comes together and everyone speaks in other languages. And suppose visitors or unbelievers come in. Won't they say you are out of your minds? 24But suppose unbelievers or visitors come in while everyone is prophesying. Then they will be shown by all who speak that they are sinners. They will be judged by all. 25The secrets of their hearts will be brought out into the open. They will fall down and worship God. They will exclaim, "God is really here among you!"

Proper Worship

26Brothers and sisters, what should we say then? When you come together, every one of you brings something. You bring a hymn or a teaching or a word from God. You bring a message in another language or explain what was said. All of those things must be done to make the church strong.

27No more than two or three people should speak in another language. And they should speak one at a time. Then belong to him will be raised. ²⁴Then the end will come. Christ will destroy all rule, authority and power. He will hand over the kingdom to God the Father.

²⁵Christ must rule until he has put all his enemies under his control. ²⁶The last enemy that will be destroyed is death. ²⁷Scripture says that God "has put everything under his control." *(Psalm 8:6)* It says that "everything" has been put under him. But it is clear that this does not include God himself, who puts everything under Christ. ²⁸When he has done that, the Son also will be under God's rule. God puts everything under the Son. In that way, God will be all in all.

²⁹Suppose no one rises from the dead. Then what will people do who are baptized for the dead? Suppose the dead are not raised at all. Then why are people baptized for them? ³⁰And why would we put ourselves in danger every hour? ³¹I die every day. I really mean that, brothers and sisters. Here is something you can be sure of. I take pride in what Christ Jesus our Lord has done for you through my work. ³²Did I fight wild animals in Ephesus for only human reasons? Then what have I gotten for it? If the dead are not raised,

"Let us eat and drink,
  because tomorrow we will die."
  (Isaiah 22:13)

³³Don't let anyone fool you. "Bad companions make a good person bad." ³⁴You should come back to your senses and stop sinning. Some of you don't know anything about God. I say this to make you ashamed.

The Body That Rises From the Dead

³⁵But someone might ask, "How are the dead raised? What kind of body will they have?" ³⁶How foolish! What you plant doesn't come to life unless it dies. ³⁷When you plant something, it isn't a completely grown plant that you put in the ground. You only plant a seed. Maybe it's wheat or something else. ³⁸But God gives the seed a body just as he has planned. And to each kind of seed he gives its own body.

³⁹All earthly creatures are not the same. People have one kind of body. Animals have another. Birds have another kind. Fish have still another. ⁴⁰There are also heavenly bodies as well as earthly bodies. Heavenly bodies have one kind of glory. Earthly bodies have another. ⁴¹The sun has one kind of glory. The moon has another kind. The stars have still another. And one star's glory is different from that of another star.

⁴²It will be like that with bodies that are raised from the dead. The body that is planted does not last forever. The body that is raised from the dead lasts forever. ⁴³It is planted without honor. But it is raised in glory. It is planted in weakness. But it is raised in power. ⁴⁴It is planted as an earthly body. But it is raised as a spiritual body.

Just as there is an earthly body, there is also a spiritual body. ⁴⁵It is written, "The first man Adam became a living person." *(Genesis 2:7)* The last Adam became a spirit that gives life. ⁴⁶What is spiritual did not come first. What is earthly came first. What is spiritual came after that. ⁴⁷The first man came from the dust of the earth. The second man came from heaven.

⁴⁸Those who belong to the earth are like the one who came from the earth. And those who are spiritual are like the one who came from heaven. ⁴⁹We are like the earthly man. And we will be like the man from heaven.

⁵⁰Brothers and sisters, here is what I'm telling you. Bodies made of flesh and blood can't share in the kingdom of God. And what dies can't share in what never dies.

⁵¹Listen! I am telling you a mystery. We will not all die. But we will all be changed. ⁵²That will happen in a flash, as quickly as you can wink an eye. It will happen when the last trumpet sounds. The trumpet will sound, and the dead will be raised to live forever. And we will be changed.

⁵³Our natural bodies don't last forever. They must be dressed with what does last forever. What dies must be dressed with what does not die. ⁵⁴In fact, that is going to happen. What does not last will be dressed with what lasts forever. What dies will be dressed with what does not die. Then what is written will come true. It says, "Death has been swallowed up. It has lost the battle." *(Isaiah 25:8)*

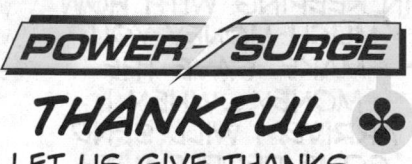

POWER–SURGE

THANKFUL ❖

LET US GIVE THANKS TO GOD! HE WINS THE BATTLE FOR US.
— 1 CORINTHIANS 15:57 —

55 "Death, where is the battle you
      thought you were winning?
Death, where is your sting?"

(Hosea 13:14)

56 The sting of death is sin. And the power of sin is the law. **57** But let us give thanks to God! He wins the battle for us because of what our Lord Jesus Christ has done.

58 My dear brothers and sisters, stand firm. Don't let anything move you. Always give yourselves completely to the work of the Lord. Because you belong to the Lord, you know that your work is not worthless.

The Offering for God's People

16 Now I want to deal with the offering of money for God's people. Do what I told the churches in Galatia to do. **2** On the first day of every week, each of you should put some money away. The amount should be in keeping with how much money you make. Save the money so that you won't have to take up an offering when I come. **3** When I arrive, I will send some people with your gift to Jerusalem. They will be people you consider to be good. And I will give them letters that explain who they are. **4** If it seems

POWER-/SURGE

GIVING   **G**

I WANT TO DEAL WITH
THE OFFERING OF
MONEY FOR GOD'S
PEOPLE...ON THE
FIRST DAY OF EVERY
WEEK, EACH OF YOU
SHOULD PUT SOME
MONEY AWAY. THE
AMOUNT SHOULD BE
IN KEEPING WITH HOW
MUCH MONEY YOU
MAKE. SAVE THE
MONEY...WHEN I
ARRIVE, I WILL SEND
SOME PEOPLE WITH
YOUR GIFT TO
JERUSALEM.
— 1 CORINTHIANS 16:1-3 —

POWER-/SURGE

BRAVE   **B**

BE ON YOUR GUARD.
STAND FIRM IN THE
FAITH. BE BRAVE.
BE STRONG.
— 1 CORINTHIANS 16:13 —

STRONG

good for me to go also, they will go with me.

What Paul Asks for Himself

5 After I go through Macedonia, I will come to you. I will only be passing through Macedonia. **6** But I might stay with you for a while. I might even spend the winter. Then you can help me on my journey everywhere I go.

7 I don't want to see you now while I am just passing through. I hope to spend some time with you, if the Lord allows it. **8** But I will stay at Ephesus until the day of Pentecost. **9** A door has opened wide for me to do some good work here. There are many people who oppose me.

10 Timothy might come to you. Make sure he has nothing to worry about while he is with you. He is doing the work of the Lord, just as I am. **11** No one should refuse to accept him. Send him safely on his way so he can return to me. I'm expecting him to come back along with the others.

12 I want to say something about our brother Apollos. I tried my best to get him to go to you with the others. But he didn't want to go right now. He will go when he can.

13 Be on your guard. Stand firm in the faith. Be brave. Be strong. **14** Be loving in everything you do.

15 You know that the first believers in Achaia were from the family of Stephanas. They have spent all their time serving God's people. Brothers and sisters, I am asking you **16** to follow the lead of people like them. Follow everyone who joins in the task and works hard at it.

17 I was glad when Stephanas, Fortunatus and Achaicus arrived. They have supplied me with what you couldn't give me. **18** They renewed my spirit, and yours also. People like that are worthy of honor.

Final Greetings

19The churches in Asia Minor send you greetings. Aquila and Priscilla greet you warmly because of the Lord's love. So does the church that meets in their house. **20**All the brothers and sisters here send you greetings. Greet one another with a holy kiss.

21I, Paul, am writing this greeting with my own hand.

22If anyone does not love the Lord, let a curse be on that person! Come, Lord!

23May the grace of the Lord Jesus be with you.

24I give my love to all of you who belong to Christ Jesus. Amen.

2 CORINTHIANS

The real Paul comes through clearly in this second letter he writes to the church in Corinth. His emotions, the pain he has experienced as a missionary, his disappointments and frustrations, as well as his joy—he honestly tells the reader everything. As you read 2 Corinthians, remember that expressing your true feelings to others and to God is important. God will help to build your relationship with him, not break it down. He is a big God, and he wants you to be honest and real with him, just as Paul was in this letter.

CHECK OUT THIS TRAIT OF A HERO . . .

GIVING
PAGE 1347

1 I, Paul, am writing this letter. I am an apostle of Christ Jesus just as God planned. Timothy our brother joins me in writing.

We are sending this letter to you, the members of God's church in Corinth. It is also for all of God's people everywhere in Achaia.

2 May God our Father and the Lord Jesus Christ give you grace and peace.

God Gives Comfort

3 Give praise to the God and Father of our Lord Jesus Christ! He is the Father who gives tender love. All comfort comes from him. 4 He comforts us in all our troubles. Now we can comfort others when they are in trouble. We ourselves have received comfort from God. 5 We share the sufferings of Christ. We also share his comfort.

6 If we are having trouble, it is so that you will be comforted and renewed. If we are comforted, it is so that you will be comforted. Then you will be able to put up with the same suffering we have gone through. 7 Our hope for you remains firm. We know that you suffer just as we do. In the same way, God comforts you just as he comforts us.

8 Brothers and sisters, we want you to know about the hard times we suffered in Asia Minor. We were having a lot of trouble. It was far more than we could stand. We even thought we were going to die. 9 In fact, in our hearts we felt as if we were under the sentence of death.

But that happened so that we would not depend on ourselves but on God. He raises the dead to life. 10 God has saved us from deadly dangers. And he will continue to do it. We have put our hope in him. He will continue to save us.

11 You must help us by praying for us. Then many people will give thanks because of what will happen to us. They will thank God for his kindness to us in answer to the prayers of many.

Paul Changes His Plans

12 Here is what we take pride in. Our sense of what is right and wrong gives witness that we have acted in God's holy and honest ways. That is how we live in the world. We live that way most of all when we are dealing with you. Our way of living is not wise in the eyes of the world. But it is in keeping with God's grace.

13 We are writing only what you can read and understand. And here is what I hope. 14 Up to this point you have understood some of the things we have said. But now I hope that someday you will be able to take pride in us, just as we will take pride in you on the day the Lord Jesus returns. When you are able to do that, you will understand us completely.

15 I was sure of those things. So I planned to visit you first. Here is how I thought you would be helped twice. 16 I planned to visit you on my way to Macedonia. I would have come back to you from there. Then you would have sent me on my way to Judea.

17 When I planned all of that, did I do it without much thought? No. I don't make my plans the way the world makes theirs. In the same breath the world says, "Yes! Yes!" and "No! No!"

18 But just as sure as God is faithful, our message to you is not "Yes" and "No." 19 Silas, Timothy and I preached to you about the Son of God, Jesus Christ. Our message did not say "Yes" and "No" at the same time. The message of Christ has always been "Yes."

20 God has made a great many promises. They are all "Yes" because of what Christ has done. So through Christ we say "Amen." We want God to receive glory.

21 He makes both us and you stand firm because we belong to Christ. He anointed us. 22 He put his Spirit in our hearts and marked us as his own. We can now be sure that he will give us everything he promised us.

23 I call God as my witness. I wanted to spare you. So I didn't return to Corinth. 24 Your faith is not under our control. You stand firm in your own faith. But we work together with you for your joy.

2 So I made up my mind that I would not make another painful visit to you. 2 If I make you sad, who is going to make me glad? Only you, the one I made sad.

3 I wrote what I did for a special reason. When I came, I didn't want to be troubled by those who should make me glad. I was sure that all of you would share my joy. 4 I was very troubled when I wrote to you. My heart was sad. My eyes were full of tears. I didn't want to make you sad. I wanted to let you know that I love you very deeply.

Forgive Those Who Make You Sad

5 Suppose someone has made us sad. In some ways, he hasn't made me sad so much as he has made all of you sad. But I don't want to put this too strongly. 6 He

has been punished because most of you decided he should be. That is enough for him. ⁷Now you should forgive him and comfort him. Then he won't be sad more than he can stand. ⁸So I'm asking you to tell him again that you still love him.

⁹I wrote to you for a special reason. I wanted to see if you could stand the test. I wanted to see if you could obey everything that was asked of you.

¹⁰Anyone you forgive I also forgive. Was there anything to forgive? If so, I have forgiven it for your benefit, knowing that Christ is watching. ¹¹We don't want Satan to outsmart us. We know how he does his evil work.

Serving Under the New Covenant

¹²I went to Troas to preach the good news about Christ. There I found that the Lord had opened a door of opportunity for me. ¹³But I still had no peace of mind. I couldn't find my brother Titus there. So I said good-by to the believers at Troas and went on to Macedonia.

POWER-SURGE

THANKFUL ✦

GIVE THANKS TO GOD!
HE ALWAYS LEADS US
IN THE WINNERS'
PARADE BECAUSE WE
BELONG TO CHRIST.
— 2 CORINTHIANS 2:14 —

¹⁴Give thanks to God! He always leads us in the winners' parade because we belong to Christ. Through us, God spreads the knowledge of Christ everywhere like perfume. ¹⁵God considers us to be the sweet smell that Christ is spreading among people who are being saved and people who are dying. ¹⁶To the one, we are the smell of death. To the other, we are the perfume of life. Who is able to do that work?

¹⁷Unlike many people, we aren't selling God's word to make money. In fact, it is just the opposite. Because of Christ we speak honestly before God. We speak like people God has sent.

3 Are we beginning to praise ourselves again? Some people need letters that speak well of them. Do we need those kinds of letters, either to you or from you?

²You yourselves are our letter. You are written on our hearts. Everyone knows you and reads you. ³You make it clear that you are a letter from Christ. You are the result of our work for God. You are a letter written not with ink but with the Spirit of the living God. You are a letter written not on tablets made out of stone but on human hearts.

⁴Through Christ, we can be sure of this because of our faith in God's power. ⁵In ourselves we are not able to claim anything for ourselves. The power to do what we do comes from God. ⁶He has given us the power to serve under a new covenant. The covenant is not based on the written Law of Moses. It comes from the Holy Spirit. The written Law kills, but the Spirit gives life.

The Glory of the New Covenant

⁷The Law was written in letters on stone. Even though it was a way of serving God, it led to death. But even that way of serving God came with glory. And even though the glory was fading, the people of Israel couldn't look at Moses' face very long. ⁸Since all of that is true, won't the work of the Holy Spirit be even more glorious? ⁹The Law that sentences people to death is glorious. How much more glorious is the work of the Spirit! His work makes people right with God.

¹⁰The glory of the old covenant is nothing compared with the far greater glory of the new. ¹¹The glory of the old is fading away. How much greater is the glory of the new! It will last forever.

¹²Since we have that kind of hope, we are very bold. ¹³We are not like Moses. He used to cover his face with a veil. That was to keep the people of Israel from looking at his face while the brightness was fading away.

¹⁴But their minds were made stubborn. To this very day, the same veil remains when the old covenant is read. The veil has not been removed. Only faith in Christ can take it away. ¹⁵To this very day, when the Law of Moses is read, a veil covers the minds of those who hear it.

¹⁶But when anyone turns to the Lord, the veil is taken away. ¹⁷Now the Lord is the Holy Spirit. And where the Spirit of the Lord is, freedom is also there.

¹⁸Our faces are not covered with a veil. We all display the Lord's glory. We are being changed to become more like him so that we have more and more glory. And the glory comes from the Lord, who is the Holy Spirit.

POWER-SURGE

TRIES HARD

SO BECAUSE OF
GOD'S MERCY, WE
HAVE WORK TO DO.
HE HAS GIVEN IT TO
US. AND WE DON'T
GIVE UP.
— 2 CORINTHIANS 4:1 —

A Treasure in Clay Jars

4 So because of God's mercy, we have work to do. He has given it to us. And we don't give up. **2**Instead, we have given up doing secret and shameful things. We don't twist God's word. In fact, we do just the opposite. We present the truth plainly. In the sight of God, we make our appeal to everyone's sense of what is right and wrong.

3Suppose our good news is covered with a veil. Then it is veiled to those who are dying. **4**The god of this world has blinded the minds of those who don't believe. They can't see the light of the good news of Christ's glory. He is the likeness of God.

5We do not preach about ourselves. We preach about Jesus Christ. We say that he is Lord. And we serve you because of him.

6God said, "Let light shine out of darkness." *(Genesis 1:3)* He made his light shine in our hearts. It shows us the light of God's glory in the face of Christ.

7Treasure is kept in clay jars. In the same way, we have the treasure of the good news in these earthly bodies of ours. That shows that the mighty power of the good news comes from God. It doesn't come from us.

8We are pushed hard from all sides. But we are not beaten down. We are bewildered. But that doesn't make us lose hope. **9**Others make us suffer. But God does not desert us. We are knocked down. But we are not knocked out. **10**We always carry around the death of Jesus in our bodies. In that way, the life of Jesus can be shown in our bodies.

11We who are alive are always in danger of death because we are serving Jesus. So his life can be shown in our earthly bodies. **12**Death is at work in us. But life is at work in you.

13It is written, "I believed, and so I have spoken." *(Psalm 116:10)* With that same spirit of faith we also believe. And we also speak.

14We know that God raised the Lord Jesus from the dead. And he will also raise us up with Jesus. He will bring us with you to God in heaven. **15**All of that is for your benefit. God's grace is reaching more and more people. So they will become more and more thankful. They will give glory to God.

16We don't give up. Our bodies are becoming weaker and weaker. But our spirits are being renewed day by day. **17**Our troubles are small. They last only for a short time. But they are earning for us a glory that will last forever. It is greater than all our troubles.

18So we don't spend all our time looking at what we can see. Instead, we look at what we can't see. What can be seen lasts only a short time. But what can't be seen will last forever.

Our Home in Heaven

5 We know that the earthly tent we live in will be destroyed. But we have a building made by God. It is a house in heaven that lasts forever. Human hands did not build it.

2During our time on earth we groan. We long to put on our house in heaven as if it were clothing. **3**Then we will not be naked.

4While we live in this tent of ours, we groan under our heavy load. We don't want to be naked. We want to be dressed with our house in heaven. What must die will be swallowed up by life.

5God has made us for that very purpose. He has given us the Holy Spirit as a down payment. The Spirit makes us sure of what is still to come.

6So here is what we can always be certain about. As long as we are at home in our bodies, we are away from the Lord. **7**We live by believing, not by seeing. **8**We are certain about that. We would rather be away from our bodies and at home with the Lord. **9**So we try our best to please him. We want to please him whether we are at home in our bodies or away from them.

10We must all stand in front of Christ to be judged. Each one of us will be judged for the good things and the bad things we do while we are in our bodies. Then each of us will receive what we are supposed to get.

POWER—SURGE

BELIEVES †

ANYONE WHO BELIEVES IN CHRIST IS A NEW CREATION. THE OLD IS GONE! THE NEW HAS COME!

— 2 CORINTHIANS 5:17 —

Christ Brings Us Back to God

11 We know what it means to have respect for the Lord. So we try to help other people to understand it.

What we are is plain to God. I hope it is also plain to your way of thinking. **12** We are not trying to make an appeal to you again. But we are giving you a chance to take pride in us. Then you can answer those who take pride in how people look rather than in what is really in their hearts.

13 Are we out of our minds? That is because we want to serve God. Does what we say make sense? That is because we want to serve you.

14 Christ's love controls us. We are sure that one person died for everyone. And so everyone died.

15 Christ died for everyone. He died so that those who live should not live for themselves anymore. They should live for Christ. He died for them and was raised again.

16 So from now on we don't look at anyone the way the world does. At one time we looked at Christ in that way. But we don't anymore.

17 Anyone who believes in Christ is a new creation. The old is gone! The new has come! **18** It is all from God. He brought us back to himself through Christ's death on the cross. And he has given us the task of bringing others back to him through Christ.

19 God was bringing the world back to himself through Christ. He did not hold people's sins against them. God has trusted us with the message that people may be brought back to him. **20** So we are Christ's official messengers. It is as if God were making his appeal through us. Here is what Christ wants us to beg you to do. Come back to God!

21 Christ didn't have any sin. But God made him become sin for us. So we can be made right with God because of what Christ has done for us.

6 We work together with God. So we are asking you not to receive God's grace and then do nothing with it. **2** He says,

> "When I showed you my favor, I heard
>   you.
> On the day I saved you, I helped
>   you." *(Isaiah 49:8)*

I tell you, now is the time God shows his favor. Now is the day he saves.

Paul's Sufferings

3 We don't put anything in anyone's way. So no one can find fault with our work for God. **4** Instead, we make it clear that we serve God in every way. We serve him by holding steady. We stand firm in all kinds of trouble, hard times and suffering.

5 We don't give up when we are beaten or put in prison. When people stir up trouble in the streets, we continue to serve God. We work hard for him. We go without sleep and food. **6** We remain pure. We understand completely what it means to serve God. We are patient and kind. We serve him in the power of the Holy Spirit. We serve him with true love. **7** We speak

POWER—SURGE

KIND K

WE DON'T GIVE UP...WE CONTINUE TO SERVE GOD. WE WORK HARD FOR HIM... WE UNDERSTAND COMPLETELY WHAT IT MEANS TO SERVE GOD. WE ARE PATIENT AND KIND. WE SERVE HIM IN THE POWER OF THE HOLY SPIRIT. WE SERVE HIM WITH TRUE LOVE. WE SPEAK THE TRUTH.

—2 CORINTHIANS 6:5-7— T

TRIES HARD

the truth. We serve in the power of God. We hold the weapons of godliness in the right hand and in the left. **8**We serve God in times of glory and shame. We serve him whether the news about us is bad or good. We are true to our calling.

But people treat us as if we were pretenders. **9**We are known, but people treat us as if we were unknown. We are dying, but we continue to live. We are beaten, but we are not killed. **10**We are sad, but we are always full of joy. We are poor, but we make many people rich. We have nothing, but we own everything.

11Believers at Corinth, we have spoken freely to you. We have opened our hearts wide to you. **12**We are not holding back our love from you. But you are holding back your love from us. **13**I speak to you as if you were my children. It is only fair that you open your hearts wide to us also.

Do Not Be Joined to Unbelievers

14Do not be joined to unbelievers. What do right and wrong have in common? Can light and darkness be friends? **15**How can Christ and Satan agree? What does a believer have in common with an unbeliever? **16**How can the temple of the true God and the statues of other gods agree?

We are the temple of the living God. God has said, "I will live with them. I will walk among them. I will be their God. And they will be my people." *(Leviticus 26:12; Jeremiah 32:38; Ezekiel 37:27)*

17 "So come out from among them
　　and be separate,
　　　　　　　　says the Lord.
Do not touch anything that is not pure
　　and clean.
Then I will receive you."
　　　　　(Isaiah 52:11; Ezekiel 20:34,41)
18 "I will be your Father.
You will be my sons and daughters,
　　　　　　　　says the Lord
　　　　who rules over all."
　　　　　　　(2 Samuel 7:14; 7:8)

7 Dear friends, we have these promises from God. So let us make ourselves pure from everything that pollutes our bodies and spirits. Let us be completely holy. We want to honor God.

Paul's Joy

2Make room for us in your hearts. We haven't done anything wrong to anyone. We haven't caused anyone to sin. We haven't taken advantage of anyone.

3I don't say this to judge you. I have

POWER-SURGE

CHEERFUL ✳

I AM VERY HAPPY. EVEN WITH ALL OUR TROUBLES, MY JOY HAS NO LIMIT.
— 2 CORINTHIANS 7:4 —

told you before that you have an important place in our hearts. We would live or die with you. **4**I have great faith in you. I am very proud of you. I am very happy. Even with all our troubles, my joy has no limit.

5When I came to Macedonia, my body wasn't able to rest. I was attacked no matter where I went. I had battles on the outside and fears on the inside.

6But God comforts those who are sad. He comforted me when Titus came. **7**I was comforted not only when he came but also by the comfort you had given him. He told me how much you longed for me. He told me about your deep sadness and concern for me. That made my joy greater than ever.

8Even if my letter made you sad, I'm not sorry I sent it. At first I was sorry. I see that my letter hurt you, but only for a little while. **9**Now I am happy. I'm not happy because you were made sad. I'm happy because your sadness led you to turn away from your sins. You became sad just as God wanted you to. So you were not hurt in any way by us.

10Godly sadness causes us to turn away from our sins and be saved. And we are certainly not sorry about that! But worldly sadness brings death.

11Look at what that godly sadness has produced in you. You are working hard to clear yourselves. You are angry and alarmed. You are longing to see me. You are concerned. You are ready to make sure that the right thing is done. In every way you have proved that you are not guilty in that matter.

12So even though I wrote to you, it wasn't because of the one who did the wrong. It wasn't because of the one who was hurt. Instead, I wrote you so that in the sight of God you could see for yourselves how faithful you are to us. **13**All of that cheers us up.

We were also very glad to see how happy Titus was. You have all renewed his spirit. **14**I had bragged about you to him. And you have not let me down. Everything we said to you was true. In the same way, our bragging about you to Titus has also turned out to be true. **15**His love for you is even greater when he remembers that you all obeyed his teaching. You received him with fear and trembling. **16**I am glad I can have complete faith in you.

Giving Freely to Others

8 Brothers and sisters, we want you to know about the grace that God has given to the churches in Macedonia. **2**They have suffered a great deal. But their joy was more than full. Even though they were very poor, they gave very freely. **3**I give witness that they gave as much as they could. In fact, they gave even more than they could. Completely on their own, **4**they begged us for the chance to share in serving God's people in that way. **5**They did more than we expected. First they gave themselves to the Lord. Then they gave themselves to us in keeping with what God wanted.

6Titus had already started collecting money from you. So we asked him to get you to finish making your kind gift. **7**You do well in everything else. You do well in faith and in speaking. You do well in knowledge and in complete commitment. And you do well in your love for us.

POWER-SURGE

GIVING   G

EVEN THOUGH THEY WERE VERY POOR, THEY GAVE VERY FREELY...THEY GAVE AS MUCH AS THEY COULD. IN FACT, THEY GAVE EVEN MORE THAN THEY COULD. COMPLETELY ON THEIR OWN, THEY BEGGED US FOR THE CHANCE TO SHARE IN SERVING GOD'S PEOPLE IN THAT WAY.

— 2 CORINTHIANS 8:2-4 —

So make sure that you also do well in the grace of giving to others.

8I am not commanding you to do it. But I want to put you to the test. I want to find out if you really love God. I want to compare your love with that of others.

9You know the grace shown by our Lord Jesus Christ. Even though he was rich, he became poor to help you. Because he became poor, you can become rich.

10Here is my advice about what is best for you in that matter. Last year you were the first to give. You were also the first to want to give. **11**So finish the work. Then your longing to do it will be matched by your finishing it. Give on the basis of what you have.

12Do you really want to give? Then the gift is received in keeping with what you have, not with what you don't have.

13We don't want others to have it easy at your expense. We want things to be equal. **14**Right now you have plenty in order to take care of what they need. Then they will have plenty to take care of what you need. That will make things equal. **15**It is written, "Those who gathered a lot didn't have too much. And those who gathered a little had enough." *(Exodus 16:18)*

Paul Sends Titus to Corinth

16God put into the heart of Titus the same concern I have for you. I am thankful to God for this. **17**Titus welcomed our appeal. He is also excited about coming to you. It was his own idea.

18Along with Titus, we are sending another brother. All the churches praise him for his service in telling the good news. **19**He was also chosen by the churches to go with us as we bring the offering. We are in charge of it. We want to honor the Lord himself. We want to show how ready we are to help.

20We want to keep anyone from blaming us for how we take care of that large gift. **21**We are trying hard to do what is right in the Lord's eyes and in the eyes of people.

22We are also sending another one of our brothers with them. He has often proved to us in many ways that he is very committed. He is now even more committed because he has great faith in you.

23Titus is my helper. He and I work together among you. Our brothers are messengers from the churches. They honor Christ. **24**So show them that you really love them. Show them why we are proud of you. Then the churches can see it.

9 I don't need to write to you about giving to God's people. ²I know how much you want to help. I have been bragging about it to the people in Macedonia. I have been telling them that since last year you who live in Achaia were ready to give. You are so excited that it has stirred up most of them to take action.

³But I am sending the brothers. Then our bragging about you in this matter will have a good reason. You will be ready, just as I said you would be.

⁴Suppose people from Macedonia come with me and find out that you are not prepared. Then we, as well as you, would be ashamed of being so certain.

⁵So I thought I should try to get the brothers to visit you ahead of time. They will finish the plans for the large gift you had promised. Then it will be ready as a gift that is freely given. It will not be given by force.

Planting Many Seeds

⁶Here is something to remember. The one who plants only a little will gather only a little. And the one who plants a lot will gather a lot. ⁷You should each give

GIVING

2 CORINTHIANS 9:7

G

G

G

You should each give what you have decided in your heart to give. You shouldn't give if you don't want to. You shouldn't give because you are forced to. God loves a cheerful giver.

Picture this: You're in church and the offering plate is being passed. Every time someone puts money into the plate, they start to laugh. Some giggle. Others let out a great big belly laugh. They're all cheerfully giving to God.

That's how God wants you to give, whether you're giving your money or your time or talents. He doesn't want you to give and be grumpy about it. He wants you to give and be cheerful while you do it.

You can read in the Bible about a man who loved to give. His name was Barnabas (see page 1261). He sold some land and gave all the money to God. Picture that: Do you think he was smiling or frowning when he gave the money? Then there was Tabitha (you'll find her story on page 1272). She spent all her time making clothes for people who were too poor to buy their own. What a wonderful way to give!

BE A GIVER

Now, of course, the laughing and giggling when the offering plate goes by in church may be a bit silly to think about. Then again, maybe it isn't. You laugh easily when you're cheerful, don't you? So next time you're giving to God, remember this verse and be cheerful. Smile and giggle and laugh as you give.

Go to page 1363 for the next Super Hero Trait

what you have decided in your heart to give. You shouldn't give if you don't want to. You shouldn't give because you are forced to. God loves a cheerful giver.

8And God is able to shower all kinds of blessings on you. In all things and at all times you will have everything you need. You will do more and more good works. **9**It is written,

"They have spread their gifts around to poor people.
Their good works continue forever."
(Psalm 112:9)

10God supplies seed to the planter. He supplies bread for food. God will also supply and increase the amount of your seed. He will increase the results of your good works. **11**You will be made rich in every way. Then you can always give freely. We will take your many gifts to the people who need them. And they will give thanks to God.

12Your gifts meet the needs of God's people. And that's not all. Your gifts also cause many people to thank God.

POWER–SURGE

OBEYS ✔

PEOPLE WILL PRAISE GOD BECAUSE YOU OBEY HIM.
— 2 CORINTHIANS 9:13 —

13You have shown yourselves to be worthy by what you have given. So people will praise God because you obey him. That proves that you really believe the good news about Christ. They will also praise God because you share freely with them and with everyone else. **14**Their hearts will be filled with longing for you when they pray for you. God has given you grace that is better than anything.

15Let us give thanks to God for his gift. It is so great that no one can tell how wonderful it really is!

Paul Speaks Up for Himself

10 Christ is gentle and free of pride. So I make my appeal to you. I, Paul, am the one you call shy when I am face to face with you. But when I am away from you, you call me bold. **2**I beg you that when I come I won't have to be as bold as I expect to be toward some people.

They think that I live the way the people of this world live. **3**I do live in the world. But I don't fight my battles the way the people of the world do. **4**The weapons I fight with are not the weapons the world uses. In fact, it is just the opposite. My weapons have the power of God to destroy the camps of the enemy.

5I destroy every claim and every reason that keeps people from knowing God. I keep every thought under control in order to make it obey Christ. **6**Until you have obeyed completely, I will be ready to punish you every time you don't obey.

7You are looking only at what appears on the surface of things. Suppose you are sure you belong to Christ. Then you should consider again that I belong to Christ just as much as you do.

8Do I brag too much about the authority the Lord gave me? If I do, it's because I want to build you up, not pull you down. And I'm not ashamed of that kind of bragging.

9Don't think that I'm trying to scare you with my letters. **10**Some say, "His letters sound important. They are powerful. But in person he doesn't seem like much. And what he says doesn't amount to anything." **11**People like that have a lot to learn. What I say in my letters when I'm away from you, I will do in my actions when I'm with you.

12I don't dare to compare myself with those who praise themselves. I'm not that kind of person. They measure themselves by themselves. They compare themselves with themselves. When they do that, they are not wise.

13But I won't brag more than I should. Instead, I will brag only about what I have done in the area God has given me. It is an area that reaches all the way to you. **14**I am not going too far in my bragging. I would be going too far if I hadn't come to where you live. But I did get there with the good news about Christ.

15And I won't brag about work done by others. If I did, I would be bragging more than I should. As your faith continues to grow, I hope that my work among you will greatly increase. **16**Then I will be able to preach the good news in the areas beyond you. I don't want to brag about work already done in someone else's territory.

17But, "The one who brags should brag about what the Lord has done." *(Jeremiah 9:24)* **18**Those who praise themselves are not accepted. Those the Lord praises are accepted.

Paul and Those Who Pretend to Be Apostles

11 I hope you will put up with a little of my foolish bragging. But you are already doing that.

²My jealousy for you comes from God himself. I promised to give you to only one husband. That husband is Christ. I wanted to be able to give you to him as if you were a pure virgin. ³But Eve was tricked by the snake's clever lies. And I'm afraid that in the same way your minds will somehow be led down the wrong path. They will be led away from your true and pure love for Christ.

⁴Suppose someone comes to you and preaches about a Jesus different from the Jesus we preached about. Or suppose you receive a spirit different from the one you received before. Or suppose you receive a message of good news different from the one you accepted earlier. You put up with those kinds of things easily enough.

⁵But I don't think I'm in any way less important than those "super-apostles." ⁶I may not be a trained speaker. But I do have knowledge. I've made that very clear to you in every way.

⁷When I preached God's good news to you free of charge, I put myself down in order to lift you up. Was that a sin? ⁸Did I rob other churches when I received help from them so that I could serve you? ⁹When I was with you and needed something, I didn't cause you any expense. The believers who came from Macedonia gave me what I needed. I haven't caused you any expense at all. And I won't ever do it. ¹⁰I'm sure that the truth of Christ is in me. And I'm just as sure that nobody in Achaia will keep me from bragging. ¹¹Why? Because I don't love you? No! God knows I do! ¹²And I will keep on doing what I'm doing. That will stop those who claim they have things to brag about. They think they have a chance to be considered equal with us.

¹³People like that are false apostles. They work hard to trick others. They only pretend to be apostles of Christ. ¹⁴That comes as no surprise. Even Satan himself pretends to be an angel of light. ¹⁵So it doesn't surprise us that those who serve Satan pretend to be serving God. They will finally get exactly what they should.

Paul Brags About His Sufferings

¹⁶I will say it again. Don't let anyone think I'm a fool. But if you do, receive me just as you would receive a fool. Then I can do a little bragging.

¹⁷When I brag about myself like this, I'm not talking the way the Lord would. I'm talking like a fool. ¹⁸Many are bragging the way the people of the world do. So I will brag like that too.

¹⁹You are so wise! You gladly put up with fools! ²⁰In fact, you even put up with anyone who makes you a slave or uses you. You put up with those who take advantage of you. You put up with those who claim to be better than you. You put up with those who slap you in the face.

²¹I'm ashamed to have to say that I was too weak for that!

What anyone else dares to brag about, I also dare to brag about. I'm speaking like a fool! ²²Are they Hebrews? So am I. Do they belong to the people of Israel? So do I. Are they Abraham's children? So am I. ²³Are they serving Christ? I am serving him even more. I'm out of my mind to talk like this!

I have worked much harder. I have been in prison more often. I have suffered terrible beatings. Again and again I almost died. ²⁴Five times the Jews gave me 39 strokes with a whip. ²⁵Three times I was beaten with sticks. Once they tried to kill me by throwing stones at me. Three times I was shipwrecked. I spent a night and a day in the open sea.

²⁶I have had to keep on the move. I have been in danger from rivers. I have been in danger from robbers. I have been in danger from people from my own country. I have been in danger from those who aren't Jews. I have been in danger in the city, in the country, and at sea. I have been in danger from people who pretended they were believers.

²⁷I have worked very hard. Often I have gone without sleep. I have been hungry and thirsty. Often I have gone without food. I have been cold and naked.

²⁸Besides everything else, every day I am concerned about all the churches. It is a very heavy load. ²⁹If anyone is weak, I feel weak. If anyone is led into sin, I burn on the inside.

³⁰If I have to brag, I will brag about the things that show how weak I am. ³¹I am not lying. The God and Father of the Lord Jesus knows this. May God be praised forever. ³²In Damascus the governor who served under King Aretas had their city guarded. He wanted to arrest me. ³³But I was lowered in a basket from a window in the wall. So I slipped through the governor's hands.

Paul's Vision and His Painful Problem

12 We can't gain anything by bragging. But I have to do it anyway. I am going to tell you what I've seen. I want to talk about what the Lord has shown me.

2 I know a believer in Christ who was taken up to the third heaven 14 years ago. I don't know if his body was taken up or not. Only God knows. 3 I don't know if that man was in his body or out of it. Only God knows. But I do know that 4 he was taken up to paradise. He heard things that couldn't be put into words. They were things that people aren't allowed to talk about.

5 I will brag about a man like that. But I won't brag about myself. I will brag only about how weak I am.

6 Suppose I decide to brag. That would not make me a fool, because I would be telling the truth. But I don't do it. Then no one will think more of me than he should because of what I do or say.

7 I could have become proud of myself because of the amazing and wonderful things God has shown me. So I was given a problem that caused pain in my body. It is a messenger from Satan to make me suffer. 8 Three times I begged the Lord to take it away from me. 9 But he said to me, "My grace is all you need. My power is strongest when you are weak."

So I am very happy to brag about how weak I am. Then Christ's power can rest on me. 10 Because of how I suffered for Christ, I'm glad that I am weak. I am glad in hard times. I am glad when people say mean things about me. I am glad when things are difficult. And I am glad when people make me suffer. When I am weak, I am strong.

Paul's Concern for the People of Corinth

11 I have made a fool of myself. But you made me do it. You should have praised me. Even though I am nothing, I am in no way less important than the "super-apos-

tles." 12 You can recognize apostles by the signs, wonders and miracles they do. Those things were faithfully done among you no matter what happened.

13 How were you less important than the other churches? The only difference was that I didn't cause you any expense. Forgive me for that wrong!

14 Now I am ready to visit you for the third time. I won't cause you any expense. I don't want what you have. What I really want is you. After all, children shouldn't have to save up for their parents. Parents should save up for their children. 15 So I will be very happy to spend everything I have for you. I will even spend myself. If I love you more, will you love me less?

16 In any case, I haven't caused you any expense. But I'm such a tricky fellow! I have caught you by tricking you!

17 Did I take advantage of you through any of the men I sent to you? 18 I asked Titus to go to you. And I sent our brother with him. Titus didn't take advantage of you, did he? Didn't I act in the same spirit? Didn't I follow the same path?

19 All this time, have you been thinking that I've been speaking up for myself? No, I've been speaking with God as my witness. I've been speaking like a believer in Christ. Dear friends, everything I do is to help you become stronger.

20 I'm afraid that when I come I won't find you as I want you to be. I'm afraid that you won't find me as you want me to be. I'm afraid there will be arguing, jealousy and fits of anger. I'm afraid you will separate into your own little groups. Then you will tell lies about each other. You will talk about each other. I'm afraid you will be proud and cause trouble.

21 I'm afraid that when I come again my God will put me to shame in front of you. Then I will be sad about many who sinned earlier and have not turned away from it. They have not turned away from uncleanness, sexual sins and wild living. They have done all those things.

Final Warnings

13 This will be my third visit to you. Scripture says, "Every matter must be proved by the words of two or three witnesses." *(Deuteronomy 19:15)* 2 I already warned you during my second visit. I now say it again while I'm away. When I return, I won't spare those who sinned earlier. I won't spare any of the others either.

3 You are asking me to prove that Christ is speaking through me. He is not weak in dealing with you. He is powerful among

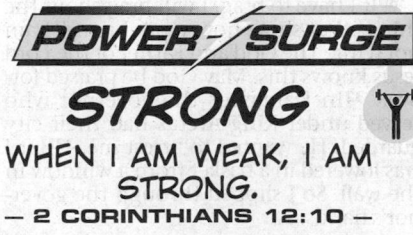

POWER—SURGE

STRONG

WHEN I AM WEAK, I AM STRONG.

— 2 CORINTHIANS 12:10 —

you. **4**It is true that Christ was nailed to the cross because he was weak. But he lives by God's power. In the same way, I share his weakness. But by God's power I will live with him to serve you.

5Take a good look at yourselves to see if you are really believers. Test yourselves. Don't you realize that Christ Jesus is in you? Unless, of course, you fail the test! **6**I hope you will discover that I haven't failed the test.

7I pray to God that you won't do anything wrong. I don't pray so that people will see that I have passed the test. Instead, I pray so that you will do what is right, even if it seems I have failed. **8**I can't do anything to stop the truth. I can only work for the truth.

9I'm glad when I am weak but you are strong. I pray that you will become per-fect. **10**That's why I write these things before I come to you. Then when I do come, I won't have to be hard on you when I use my authority.

The Lord gave me the authority to build you up. He didn't give it to me to tear you down.

Final Greetings

11Finally, brothers and sisters, good-by. Try to be perfect. Pay attention to what I'm saying. Agree with one another. Live in peace. And the God who gives love and peace will be with you.

12Greet one another with a holy kiss. **13**All of God's people send their greetings.

14May the grace shown by the Lord Jesus Christ, and the love that God has given us, and the sharing of life brought about by the Holy Spirit be with you all.

GALATIANS

The church in Galatia is having some problems. Paul writes this letter to help straighten them out. Some false teachers have made the people there think that they need to follow all the old laws in order to be saved. Paul makes it clear that salvation only comes through Jesus, not through following some laws. As you read this book, thank God that you are saved because of his grace, through Jesus. And be glad that you don't have to be perfect for God to love you and use you.

CODE OF HONOR IN THIS BOOK . . .

BELIEVES
PAGE 1356

PATIENT
PAGE 1357

SELF-CONTROLLED
PAGE 1357

FAITHFUL
PAGE 1357

TRIES HARD
PAGE 1357

1 I, Paul, am writing this letter. I am an apostle. People have not sent me. No human authority has sent me. I have been sent by Jesus Christ and by God the Father. God raised Jesus from the dead. 2All the brothers who are with me join me in writing.

We are sending this letter to you, the members of the churches in Galatia.

3May God our Father and the Lord Jesus Christ give you grace and peace. 4Jesus gave his life for our sins. He set us free from this evil world. That was what our God and Father wanted. 5Give glory to God for ever and ever. Amen.

There Is No Other Good News

6I am amazed. You are so quickly deserting the One who chose you because of the grace that Christ has provided. You are turning to a different "good news." 7What you are accepting is really not the good news at all.

It seems that some people have gotten you all mixed up. They are trying to twist the good news about Christ.

8But suppose even we should preach a different "good news." Suppose even an angel from heaven should preach it. I'm talking about a different one than the good news we gave you. Let anyone who does that be judged by God forever. 9I have already said it. Now I will say it again. Anyone who preaches a "good news" that is different from the one you accepted should be judged by God forever.

10Am I now trying to get people to think well of me? Or do I want God to think well of me? Am I trying to please people? If I were, I would not be serving Christ.

Paul Was Appointed by God

11Brothers and sisters, here is what I want you to know. The good news I preached is not something a human being made up. 12No one gave it to me. No one taught it to me. Instead, I received it from Jesus Christ. He showed it to me.

13You have heard of my earlier way of life as a Jew. With all my strength I attacked the church of God. I tried to destroy it. 14I was moving ahead in my Jewish way of life. I went beyond many Jews who were my own age. I held firmly to the teachings passed down by my people.

15But God set me apart from the time I was born. He showed me his grace by appointing me. He was pleased 16to show his Son in my life. He wanted me to preach about Jesus among those who aren't Jews.

When God appointed me, I didn't talk to anyone. 17I didn't go up to Jerusalem to see those who were apostles before I was. Instead, I went at once into Arabia. Later I returned to Damascus.

18Then after three years I went up to Jerusalem. I went there to get to know Peter. I stayed with him for 15 days. 19I didn't see any of the other apostles. I only saw James, the Lord's brother. 20Here is what you can be sure of. And God gives witness to it. What I am writing you is not a lie.

21Later I went to Syria and Cilicia. 22The members of Christ's churches in Judea did not know me in a personal way. 23They only heard others say, "The man who used to attack us has changed. He is now preaching the faith he once tried to destroy." 24And they praised God because of me.

Paul Is Accepted by the Apostles

2 Fourteen years later I went up again to Jerusalem. This time I went with Barnabas. I took Titus along also. 2I went because God showed me what he wanted me to do. I told the people there the good news that I preach among those who aren't Jews. But I spoke in private to those who seemed to be leaders. I was afraid that I was running or had run my race for nothing.

3Titus was with me. He was a Greek. But even he was not forced to be circumcised. 4That matter came up because some who pretended to be believers had slipped in among us. They wanted to find out about the freedom we have because we belong to Christ Jesus. They wanted to make us slaves again.

5We didn't give in to them for a moment. We wanted the truth of the good news to remain with you.

6Some people in Jerusalem seemed to be important. It makes no difference to me what they were. God does not judge by what he sees on the outside. Those people added nothing to my message.

7In fact, it was just the opposite. They saw that I had been trusted with the task of preaching the good news just as Peter had been. My task was to preach to the non-Jews. Peter's task was to preach to the Jews. 8God was working through Peter as an apostle to the Jews. He was also working through me as an apostle to the non-Jews.

9James, Peter and John are considered to be pillars in the church. They recognized the special grace that was given to me. So they shook my hand and the hand of Barnabas. They wanted to show they accepted us. They agreed that we should go to the non-Jews. They would go to the Jews. 10They asked only one thing. They wanted us to continue to remember poor people. That was what I really wanted to do anyway.

Paul Opposes Peter

11When Peter came to Antioch, I told him to his face that I was against what he was doing. He was clearly wrong. 12He used to eat with those who weren't Jews. But certain men came from the group that was led by James. When they arrived, Peter began to draw back. He separated himself from the non-Jews. He was afraid of the circumcision group.

13Peter's actions were not honest. The other Jews joined him. Even Barnabas was led down the wrong path.

14I saw what they were doing. It was not in line with the truth of the good news. So I spoke to Peter in front of them all. "You are a Jew," I said. "But you live like one who is not. So why do you force non-Jews to follow Jewish ways?"

God's Grace and Our Faith

15We are Jews by birth. We are not "non-Jewish sinners." 16We know that no one is made right with God by obeying the law. It is by believing in Jesus Christ. So we too have put our faith in Christ Jesus. That is so we can be made right with God by believing in Christ, not by obeying the law. No one can be made right with God by obeying the law.

17We are trying to be made right with God through Christ. But it is clear that we are sinners. So does that mean that Christ causes us to sin? Certainly not! 18Suppose I build again what I had destroyed. Then I prove that I break the Law.

19Because of the law, I died as far as the law is concerned. I died so that I might live for God. 20I have been crucified with Christ. I don't live any longer. Christ lives in me. My faith in the Son of God helps me to live my life in my body. He loved me. He gave himself for me.

21I do not get rid of the grace of God. What if a person could become right with God by obeying the law? Then Christ died for nothing!

Faith or Obeying the Law

3 You foolish people of Galatia! Who has put you under an evil spell? When I preached, I clearly showed you that Jesus Christ had been nailed to the cross.

2I would like to learn just one thing from you. Did you receive the Holy Spirit by obeying the law? Or did you receive the Spirit by believing what you heard? 3Are you so foolish? You began with the Holy Spirit. Are you now trying to complete God's work in you by your own strength?

4Have you suffered so much for nothing? And was it really for nothing? 5Why does God give you his Spirit? Why does he work miracles among you? Is it because you do what the law says? Or is it because you believe what you have heard?

6Think about Abraham. Scripture says, "Abraham believed God. God accepted Abraham because he believed. So his faith made him right with God." (Genesis 15:6) 7So you see, those who have faith are children of Abraham.

8Long ago, Scripture knew that God would make non-Jews right with himself by believing in him. He announced the good news ahead of time to Abraham. He said, "All nations will be blessed because of you." (Genesis 12:3; 18:18; 22:18) 9So those who have faith are blessed along with Abraham. He was the man of faith.

10All who depend on obeying the law are under a curse. It is written, "May everyone who doesn't continue to do everything that is written in the Book of the Law be under God's curse." (Deuteronomy 27:26) 11We know that no one is made right with God by keeping the law. Scripture says, "Those who are right with God will live by faith." (Habakkuk 2:4)

12The law is not based on faith. In fact, it is just the opposite. It teaches that "the one who does those things will live by them." (Leviticus 18:5)

13Christ set us free from the curse of the law. He did it by becoming a curse for us. It is written, "Everyone who is hung on a pole is under God's curse." (Deuteronomy 21:23) 14Christ Jesus set us free so that the blessing given to Abraham would come to non-Jews through Christ. He did it so that we might receive the promise of the Holy Spirit by believing in Christ.

The Law and the Promise

15Brothers and sisters, let me give you an example from everyday life. No one can get rid of an official agreement between people. No one can add to it. It can't be changed after it has been made. It is the same with God's covenant. 16The promises were given to Abraham. They were also given to his seed. Scripture does not say, "and to seeds." That means many people. It says, "and to your seed." *(Genesis 12:7; 13:15; 24:7)* That means one person. And that one person is Christ.

17Here is what I mean. The law came 430 years after the promise. But the law does not get rid of God's covenant and promise. The covenant had already been made by God. So the law does not do away with the promise.

18The great gift that God has for us does not depend on the law. If it did, it would no longer depend on a promise. But God gave it to Abraham as a free gift through a promise.

19Then what was the purpose of the law? It was added because of human sin. And it was supposed to control us until the promised Seed had come. The law was put into effect through angels by a go-between. 20A go-between does not take sides. God didn't use a go-between when he made his promise to Abraham. But the same God was at work in both the law and the promise.

21So is the law opposed to God's promises? Certainly not! What if a law had been given that could give life? Then people could become right with God by obeying the law. 22But Scripture announces that the whole world is a prisoner because of sin. It does so in order that what was promised might be given to those who believe. The promise comes through faith in Jesus Christ.

23Before faith in Christ came, we were held prisoners by the law. We were locked up until faith was made known. 24So the law was put in charge until Christ came. He came so that we might be made right with God by believing in Christ.

25But now faith in Christ has come. So we are no longer under the control of the law.

Children of God

26You are all children of God by believing in Christ Jesus. 27All of you who were baptized into Christ have put on Christ as if he were your clothes. 28There is no Jew or Greek. There is no slave or free person. There is no male or female. Because you belong to Christ Jesus, you are all one. 29You who belong to Christ are Abraham's seed. You will receive what God has promised.

4 Here is what I have been saying. As long as your own children are young, they are no different from slaves in your house. They are no different, even though

they own all of the property. 2They are under the care of guardians and those who manage the property. They are under their care until the time when their fathers give them the property. 3It is the same with us. When we were children, we were slaves to the basic things the people of the world believe.

4But then the right time came. God sent his Son. A woman gave birth to him. He was born under the authority of the law. 5He came to set free those who were under the law. He wanted us to be adopted as children with all the rights children have.

6Because you are his children, God sent the Spirit of his Son into our hearts. He is the Holy Spirit. By his power we call God *"Abba." Abba* means Father.

7So you aren't slaves any longer. You are God's children. Because you are his children, he gives you what he promised to give his people.

Paul's Concern for the Believers in Galatia

8At one time you didn't know God. You were slaves to gods that are really not gods at all. 9But now you know God. Even better, God knows you. So why are you turning back to those weak and worthless beliefs? Do you want to be slaves to them all over again?

10You are observing special days and months and seasons and years! 11I am afraid for you. I am afraid that somehow I have wasted my efforts on you.

Paul's Appeal to the Believers

12I make my appeal to you, brothers and sisters. I'm asking you to become like me. After all, I became like you. You didn't do anything wrong to me.

13As you know, it was because I was sick that I first preached the good news to you. 14My sickness was hard on you. But you didn't put me off. You didn't make fun of me. Instead, you welcomed me as if I were an angel of God. You welcomed me as if I were Christ Jesus himself.

15What has happened to all of your joy? If you could have torn out your own eyes and given them to me, you would have. I can give witness to that. 16Have I become your enemy now by telling you the truth?

17Those people are trying hard to win you over. But it is not for your good. They want to take you away from us. They want you to commit yourselves to them. 18It is fine to be committed to something, if the purpose is good. And you shouldn't be committed only when I am with you. You should always be committed.

19My dear children, I am in pain for you. Once again I have pain like a woman giving birth. And my pain will continue until Christ makes you like himself.

20I wish I could be with you now. I wish I could change my tone of voice. As it is, you bewilder me.

Hagar and Sarah

21You who want to be under the authority of the law, tell me something. Don't you know what the law says? **22**It is written that Abraham had two sons. The slave woman gave birth to one of them. The free woman gave birth to the other one. **23**Abraham's son by the slave woman was born in the usual way. But his son by the free woman was born because of God's promise.

24Those things can be taken as examples. The two women stand for two covenants. One covenant comes from Mount Sinai. It gives birth to children who are going to be slaves. It is Hagar. **25**Hagar stands for Mount Sinai in Arabia. She stands for the present city of Jerusalem. That's because she and her children are slaves. **26**But the Jerusalem that is above is free. She is our mother. **27**It is written,

"Be glad, woman,
　　you who have no children.
Start shouting,
　　you who have no labor pains.
The woman who is all alone has more
　　children
　　than the woman who has a
　　　　husband."　　　*(Isaiah 54:1)*

28Brothers and sisters, you are children because of God's promise just as Isaac was. **29**At that time, the son born in the usual way tried to hurt the son born by the power of the Holy Spirit. It is the same now. **30**But what does Scripture say? "Get rid of the slave woman. Get rid of her son. The slave woman's son will never have a share of the family's property with the free woman's son." *(Genesis 21:10)* **31**Brothers and sisters, we are not the slave woman's children. We are the free woman's children.

Christ Sets Us Free

5 Christ has set us free. He wants us to enjoy freedom. So stand firm. Don't let the chains of slavery hold you again.

2Here is what I, Paul, say to you. Don't

POWER-SURGE

BELIEVES ✝

WE EXPECT TO BE MADE COMPLETELY HOLY BECAUSE OF OUR FAITH IN CHRIST.
— GALATIANS 5:5 —

let yourselves be circumcised. If you do, Christ won't be of any value to you. **3**I say it again. Every man who lets himself be circumcised must obey the whole law.

4Some of you are trying to be made right with God by obeying the law. You have been separated from Christ. You have fallen away from God's grace.

5But we expect to be made completely holy because of our faith in Christ. Through the Holy Spirit we wait in hope. **6**Circumcision and uncircumcision aren't worth anything to those who believe in Christ Jesus. The only thing that really counts is faith that shows itself through love.

7You were running a good race. Who cut in on you and kept you from obeying the truth? **8**The One who chooses you does not keep you from obeying the truth. **9**You should know that "just a little yeast works its way through the whole batch of dough."

10The Lord makes me certain that you will not think in any other way. The one who has gotten you all mixed up will pay the price. It doesn't matter who that may be.

11Brothers and sisters, I am not still preaching that people must be circumcised. If I were, why am I still being opposed? If that were what I preach, then the cross wouldn't upset anyone.

12So then, what about troublemakers who try to get others to be circumcised? I wish they would go the whole way! I wish they would cut off everything that marks them as men!

Chosen to Be Free

13My brothers and sisters, you were chosen to be free. But don't use your freedom as an excuse to live in sin. Instead, serve one another in love. **14**The whole law can be found in a single command. "Love your neighbor as you love yourself." *(Leviticus 19:18)*

15You must not keep on biting each other. You must not keep eating each other up. Watch out! You might destroy each other.

Living by the Holy Spirit's Power

16So I say, live by the Holy Spirit's power. Then you will not do what your sinful nature wants you to do.

17The sinful nature does not want what the Spirit delights in. And the Spirit does not want what the sinful nature delights in. The two are at war with each other. That's what makes you do what you don't want to do. **18**But if you are led by the Spirit, you are not under the authority of the law.

19What the sinful nature does is clear. It enjoys sexual sins, impure acts and wild living. **20**It worships statues of gods. It also worships evil powers. It is full of hatred and fighting. It is full of jealousy and fits of anger. It is interested only in getting ahead. It stirs up trouble. It separates people into their own little groups. **21**It wants what others have. It gets drunk and takes part in wild parties. It does many things of that kind. I warn you now as I did before. People who live like that will not receive God's kingdom.

22But the fruit the Holy Spirit produces is love, joy and peace. It is being patient, kind and good. It is being faithful **23**and gentle and having control of oneself. There is no law against things of that kind.

24Those who belong to Christ Jesus have nailed their sinful nature to his cross. They don't want what their sinful nature loves and longs for.

POWER-SURGE

PATIENT P

THE FRUIT THE HOLY SPIRIT PRODUCES IS LOVE, JOY AND PEACE. IT IS BEING PATIENT, KIND AND GOOD. IT IS BEING FAITHFUL AND GENTLE AND HAVING CONTROL OF ONESELF.
— GALATIANS 5:22-23 —

SELF-CONTROLLED

POWER-SURGE

FAITHFUL ( )

LET US NOT BECOME TIRED OF DOING GOOD. AT THE RIGHT TIME WE WILL GATHER A CROP IF WE DON'T GIVE UP.
— GALATIANS 6:9 — T

TRIES HARD

25Since we live by the Spirit, let us march in step with the Spirit. **26**Let us not become proud. Let us not make each other angry. Let us not want what belongs to others.

Do Good to Everyone

6 Brothers and sisters, what if someone is caught in a sin? Then you who are guided by the Spirit should correct that person. Do it in a gentle way. But be careful. You could be tempted too. **2**Carry each other's heavy loads. If you do, you will give the law of Christ its full meaning.

3If you think you are somebody when you are nobody, you are fooling yourselves. **4**Each of you should put your own actions to the test. Then you can take pride in yourself. You won't be comparing yourself to somebody else. **5**Each of you should carry your own load.

6Those who are taught the word must share all good things with their teacher.

7Don't be fooled. You can't outsmart God. A man gathers a crop from what he plants. **8**Some people plant to please their sinful nature. From that nature they will harvest death. Others plant to please the Holy Spirit. From the Spirit they will harvest eternal life.

9Let us not become tired of doing good. At the right time we will gather a crop if we don't give up. **10**So when we can do good to everyone, let us do it. Let us make a special point of doing good to those who belong to the family of believers.

The Creation of a New Nature

11Look at the big letters I'm using as I write to you with my own hand!

12Some people want others to think well of them. They are trying to force you to be circumcised. They do it for only one reason. They don't want to suffer by being connected with the cross of Christ. [13]Even those who are circumcised don't obey the law. But they want you to be circumcised. Then they can brag about what has been done to your body.

[14]I never want to brag about anything except the cross of our Lord Jesus Christ. Through that cross the ways of the world have been crucified as far as I am concerned. And I have been crucified as far as the ways of the world are concerned.

[15]Circumcision and uncircumcision don't mean anything. What really counts is the creation of a new nature.

[16]May peace and mercy be given to all who follow this rule. May peace and mercy be given to the Israel that belongs to God.

[17]Finally, let no one cause trouble for me. My body has marks that show I belong to Jesus.

[18]Brothers and sisters, may the grace of our Lord Jesus Christ be with your spirit. Amen.

EPHESIANS

Paul writes this letter to the church in Ephesus while he is in prison. He wants the people in the church there to understand who they now are as believers. They are no longer tied to their old religions, they are new people in Jesus. Paul offers them practical suggestions on how to live as true believers. As you read Ephesians, think about how Paul's teachings might apply to your own life and how you can live as a new person in Jesus.

CHECK OUT THIS TRAIT OF A HERO . . .

HONEST
PAGE 1363

1

I, Paul, am writing this letter. I am an apostle of Christ Jesus just as God planned.

I am sending this letter to you, God's people in Ephesus. Because you belong to Christ Jesus, you are faithful.

2May God our Father and the Lord Jesus Christ give you grace and peace.

God Gives Spiritual Blessings

3Give praise to the God and Father of our Lord Jesus Christ. He has blessed us with every spiritual blessing. Those blessings come from the heavenly world. They belong to us because we belong to Christ.

4God chose us to belong to Christ before the world was created. He chose us to be holy and without blame in his eyes. He loved us. **5**So he decided long ago to adopt us as his children. He did it because of what Jesus Christ has done. It pleased God to do it. **6**All those things bring praise to his glorious grace. God freely gave us his grace because of the One he loves.

7We have been set free because of what Christ has done. Through his blood our sins have been forgiven. We have been set free because God's grace is so rich. **8**He poured his grace on us by giving us great wisdom and understanding.

9He showed us the mystery of his plan. It was in keeping with what he wanted to do. It was what he had planned through Christ. **10**It will all come about when history has been completed. God will then bring together all things in heaven and on earth under one ruler. The ruler is Christ.

11We were also chosen to belong to him. God decided to choose us long ago in keeping with his plan. He works out everything to fit his plan and purpose. **12**We were the first to put our hope in Christ. We were chosen to bring praise to his glory.

13You also became believers in Christ. That happened when you heard the message of truth. It was the good news about how you could be saved. When you believed, he marked you with a seal. The seal is the Holy Spirit that he promised.

14The Spirit marks us as God's own. We can now be sure that someday we will receive all that God has promised. That will happen after God sets all of his people completely free. All of those things will bring praise to his glory.

Paul Prays and Gives Thanks

15I have heard about your faith in the Lord Jesus. I have also heard about your love for all of God's people. That is why **16**I have not stopped thanking God for you. I always remember you in my prayers.

17I pray to the God of our Lord Jesus Christ. God is the glorious Father. I keep asking him to give you the wisdom and understanding that come from the Holy Spirit. I want you to know God better. **18**I also pray that your mind might see more clearly. Then you will know the hope God has chosen you to receive. You will know that the things God's people will receive are rich and glorious. **19**And you will know his great power. It can't be compared with anything else. It is at work for us who believe. It is like the mighty strength **20**God showed when he raised Christ from the dead.

He seated him at his right hand in his heavenly kingdom. **21**There Christ sits far above all who rule and have authority. He also sits far above all powers and kings. He is above every title that can be given in this world and in the world to come.

22God placed all things under Christ's rule. He appointed him to be ruler over everything for the church. **23**The church is Christ's body. It is filled by Christ. He fills everything in every way.

God Has Given Us New Life Through Christ

2

You were living in your sins and lawless ways. But in fact you were dead. **2**You used to live as sinners when you followed the ways of this world. You served the one who rules over the spiritual forces of evil. He is the spirit who is now at work in those who don't obey God.

3At one time we all lived among them. We tried to satisfy what our sinful nature wanted to do. We followed its longings and thoughts. God was angry with us and everyone else because of the kind of people we were.

4But God loves us deeply. He is full of mercy. **5**So he gave us new life because of what Christ has done. He gave us life even when we were dead in sin. God's grace has saved you.

6God raised us up with Christ. He has seated us with him in his heavenly kingdom because we belong to Christ Jesus. **7**He has done it to show the riches of his grace for all time to come. His grace can't be compared with anything else. He has shown it by being kind to us because of what Christ Jesus has done.

8God's grace has saved you because of your faith in Christ. Your salvation doesn't come from anything you do. It is

God's gift. ⁹It is not based on anything you have done. No one can brag about earning it.

¹⁰God made us. He created us to belong to Christ Jesus. Now we can do good things. Long ago God prepared them for us to do.

God's New Family

¹¹You who are not Jews by birth, here is what I want you to remember. You are called "uncircumcised" by those who call themselves "circumcised." But they have only been circumcised in their bodies by human hands.

¹²Before you believed in Christ, you were separated from him. You were not considered to be citizens of Israel. You were not included in what the covenants promised. You were without hope and without God in the world. ¹³At one time you were far away from God. But now you belong to Christ Jesus. He spilled his blood for you. That has brought you near to God.

¹⁴Christ himself is our peace. He has made Jews and non-Jews into one group of people. He has destroyed the hatred that was like a wall between us. ¹⁵Through his body on the cross, Christ put an end to the law with all its commands and rules. He wanted to create one new group of people out of the two. He wanted to make peace between them.

¹⁶He planned to bring both of them as one body back to God because of the cross. Christ put their hatred to death on that cross.

¹⁷He came and preached peace to you who were far away. He also preached peace to those who were near. ¹⁸Through Christ we both come to the Father by the power of one Holy Spirit.

POWER-SURGE

BELIEVES ✝

GOD'S GRACE HAS SAVED YOU BECAUSE OF YOUR FAITH IN CHRIST. YOUR SALVATION DOESN'T COME FROM ANYTHING YOU DO. IT IS GOD'S GIFT.
— EPHESIANS 2:8 —

¹⁹So you are no longer strangers and outsiders. You are citizens together with God's people. You are members of God's family.

²⁰You are a building that is built on the apostles and prophets. They are the foundation. Christ Jesus himself is the most important stone in the building. ²¹The whole building is held together by him. It rises to become a holy temple because it belongs to the Lord.

²²And because you belong to him, you too are being built together. You are being made into a house where God lives through his Spirit.

Paul Is the Messenger to Non-Jews

3 I, Paul, am a prisoner because of Christ Jesus. I am in prison because of my work among you who are not Jews.

²I am sure you have heard that God appointed me to share his grace with you. ³I'm talking about the mystery God showed me. I have already written a little about it. ⁴By reading it you will be able to understand what I know about the mystery of Christ.

⁵The mystery was not made known to people of other times. But now the Holy Spirit has made it known to God's holy apostles and prophets.

⁶Here is the mystery. Because of the good news, God's promises are for non-Jews as well as for Jews. Both groups are parts of one body. They share in the promise. It belongs to them because they belong to Christ Jesus.

⁷I now serve the good news because God gave me his grace. His power is at work in me. ⁸I am by far the least important of all of God's people. But he gave me the grace to preach to the non-Jews about the wonderful riches that Christ gives.

⁹God told me to make clear to everyone how the mystery came about. In times past it was kept hidden in the mind of God, who created all things. ¹⁰He wanted the rulers and authorities in the heavenly world to come to know his great wisdom. The church would make it known to them.

¹¹That was God's plan from the beginning. He has worked it out through Christ Jesus our Lord. ¹²Through him and through faith in him we can approach God. We can come to him freely. We can come without fear.

¹³So here is what I'm asking you to do. Don't lose hope because I am suffering for you. It will lead to the time when God will give you his glory.

POWER-SURGE

BELIEVES ✝

I PRAY THAT [GOD]
WILL USE HIS
GLORIOUS RICHES TO
MAKE YOU STRONG...
CHRIST WILL LIVE IN
YOUR HEARTS
BECAUSE YOU BELIEVE
IN HIM.
— EPHESIANS 3:16-17 —

STRONG

Paul Prays for God's People

14I bow in prayer to the Father because of my work among you. **15**From the Father his whole family in heaven and on earth gets its name.

16I pray that he will use his glorious riches to make you strong. May his Holy Spirit give you his power deep down inside you. **17**Then Christ will live in your hearts because you believe in him.

And I pray that your love will have deep roots. I pray that it will have a strong foundation. **18**May you have power with all God's people to understand Christ's love. May you know how wide and long and high and deep it is. **19**And may you know his love, even though it can't be known completely. Then you will be filled with everything God has for you.

20God is able to do far more than we could ever ask for or imagine. He does everything by his power that is working in us. **21**Give him glory in the church and in Christ Jesus. Give him glory through all time and for ever and ever. Amen.

The Body of Christ Is One

4 I am a prisoner because of the Lord. So I am asking you to live a life worthy of what God chose you for.

2Don't be proud at all. Be completely gentle. Be patient. Put up with one another in love. **3**The Holy Spirit makes you one in every way. So try your best to remain as one. Let peace keep you together.

4There is one body. There is one Spirit. You were appointed to one hope when you were chosen. **5**There is one Lord. There is one faith and one baptism. **6**There is one God and Father of all. He is over everything. He is through everything. He is in everything.

7But each one of us has received a gift of grace, just as Christ wanted us to have it. **8**That is why Scripture says,

"When he went up to his place on
　　high,
he led a line of prisoners.
He gave gifts to people." *(Psalm 68:18)*

9What does "he went up" mean? It can only mean that he also came down to the lower, earthly places. **10**The One who came down is the same as the One who went up higher than all the heavens. He did it in order to fill all of creation. **11**He is the One who gave some the gift to be apostles. He gave some the gift to be prophets. He gave some the gift of preaching the good news. And he gave some the gift to be pastors and teachers. **12**He did it so that they might prepare God's people to serve. If they do, the body of Christ will be built up.

13That will continue until we all become one in the faith and in the knowledge of God's Son. Then we will be grown up in the faith. We will receive everything that Christ has for us.

14We will no longer be babies in the faith. We won't be like ships tossed around by the waves. We won't be blown here and there by every new teaching. We won't be blown around by the cleverness and tricks of people who try to hide their evil plans. **15**Instead, we will speak the truth in love. We will grow up into Christ in every way.

He is the Head. **16**He makes the whole body grow and build itself up in love. Under the control of Christ, each part of the

LOVING ♥

DON'T BE PROUD AT
ALL. BE COMPLETELY
GENTLE. BE PATIENT.
PUT UP WITH ONE
ANOTHER IN LOVE.
— EPHESIANS 4:2 —

PATIENT

body does its work. It supports the other parts. In that way, the body is joined and held together.

Living as Children of Light

¹⁷Here is what I'm telling you. I am speaking for the Lord as I warn you. You must no longer live like those who aren't Jews. Their thoughts don't have any purpose. ¹⁸They can't understand the truth. They are separated from the life of God. That is because they don't know him. And they don't know him because their hearts are stubborn.

¹⁹They have lost all feeling for what is right. They have given themselves over to the evil pleasures of their bodies. They take part in every kind of unclean act. And they always long for more.

²⁰But that is not what you have learned about Christ. ²¹I'm sure you heard of him. I'm sure you were taught by him. What you learned was the truth about Jesus.

²²You were taught not to live the way

HONEST

EPHESIANS 4:15, 25

H

H

H

We will speak the truth in love. So each of you must get rid of your lying. Speak the truth to your neighbor.

Have you ever been tempted to lie about something? Maybe tell your dad you didn't do something when you really did? Or make up an exciting story to impress your friends? Or cheat on a test? Most people are tempted to lie now and then. But being honest is always better than lying.

Nathan, one of God's prophets, had to be honest even when it was dangerous. God had told him to tell something that Nathan knew King David wouldn't want to hear. Nathan was completely honest with David. Do you think he was tempted to tell just part of the truth? Do you think he was probably scared to be honest with David? He probably was. But he did it anyway. You'll find the story of Nathan's honesty and bravery on page 366. Another story about being honest can be found on page 1144. This sick woman was terrified to tell Jesus that she had touched him. But she did it anyway. And Jesus blessed her for being honest.

BE HONEST

When people aren't honest, they usually end up hurting each other. Your dad finds out the truth and has to punish you for lying. Your friends discover your story is all imagination, and they think you're crazy. You cheat on a test and when your teacher finds out he or she fails you...Not only are the other people involved hurt when you lie, you hurt yourself. So, being honest is always the best thing.

Go to page 1371 for the next Super Hero Trait

you used to. You must get rid of your old way of life. That's because it is polluted by longing for things that lead you down the wrong path.

23You were taught to be made new in your thinking. 24You were taught to start living a new life. It is created to be truly good and holy, just as God is.

25So each of you must get rid of your lying. Speak the truth to your neighbor. We are all parts of one body.

26Scripture says, "When you are angry, do not sin." *(Psalm 4:4)* Do not let the sun go down while you are still angry. 27Don't give the devil a chance.

28Those who have been stealing must never steal again. Instead, they must work. They must do something useful with their own hands. Then they will have something to give to people in need.

29Don't let any evil talk come out of your mouths. Say only what will help to build others up and meet their needs. Then what you say will help those who listen.

30Do not make God's Holy Spirit sad. He marked you with a seal for the day when God will set you completely free.

31Get rid of all hard feelings, anger and rage. Stop all fighting and lying. Put away every form of hatred. 32Be kind and tender to one another. Forgive each other, just as God forgave you because of what Christ has done.

5 You are the children that God dearly loves. So be just like him. 2Lead a life of love, just as Christ did. He loved us. He gave himself up for us. He was a sweet-smelling offering and sacrifice to God.

3There should not be even a hint of sexual sin among you. Don't do anything unclean. And do not always want more and more. Things like that are not what God's holy people should do.

4There must not be any unclean speech or foolish talk or dirty jokes. All of them are out of place. Instead, you should give thanks.

5Here is what you can be sure of. Those who give themselves over to sexual sins are lost. So are people whose lives are not pure. The same is true of those who always want more and more. People who do those things might as well worship statues of gods. No one who does them will receive a share in the kingdom of Christ and of God.

6Don't let anyone fool you with words that don't mean anything. Because of things like that, God is angry with those

who don't obey. 7So don't go along with people like that.

8At one time you were in the dark. But now you are in the light because of what the Lord has done. Live like children of the light. 9The light produces what is completely good, right and true. 10Find out what pleases the Lord.

11Have nothing to do with the acts of darkness. They don't produce anything good. Show what they are really like. 12It is shameful even to talk about what people who don't obey do in secret.

13But everything the light shines on can be seen. 14Light makes everything clear. That is why it is said,

"Wake up, sleeper.
   Rise from the dead.
Then Christ will shine on you."

15So be very careful how you live. Do not live like people who aren't wise. Live like people who are wise. 16Make the most of every opportunity. The days are evil. 17So don't be foolish. Instead, understand what the Lord wants.

18Don't fill yourself up with wine. Getting drunk will lead to wild living. Instead, be filled with the Holy Spirit.

19Speak to each other with psalms, hymns and spiritual songs. Sing and make music in your heart to the Lord. 20Always give thanks to God the Father for everything. Give thanks to him in the name of our Lord Jesus Christ.

21Follow the lead of one another because of your respect for Christ.

Wives and Husbands

22Wives, follow the lead of your husbands as you follow the Lord. 23The husband is the head of the wife, just as Christ is the head of the church. The church is Christ's body. He is its Savior. 24The church follows the lead of Christ. In the

POWER-SURGE

THANKFUL ♣

ALWAYS GIVE THANKS TO GOD THE FATHER FOR EVERYTHING. GIVE THANKS TO HIM IN THE NAME OF OUR LORD JESUS CHRIST.
— **EPHESIANS 5:20** —

same way, wives should follow the lead of their husbands in everything.

²⁵Husbands, love your wives. Love them just as Christ loved the church. He gave himself up for her. ²⁶He did it to make her holy. He made her clean by washing her with water and the word. ²⁷He did it to bring her to himself as a brightly shining church. He wants a church that has no stain or wrinkle or any other flaw. He wants a church that is holy and without blame.

²⁸In the same way, husbands should love their wives. They should love them as they love their own bodies. Any man who loves his wife loves himself. ²⁹After all, people have never hated their own bodies. Instead, they feed and care for their bodies. And that is what Christ does for the church. ³⁰We are parts of his body. ³¹Scripture says, "That's why a man will leave his father and mother and be joined to his wife. The two will become one." *(Genesis 2:24)* ³²That is a deep mystery. But I'm talking about Christ and the church. ³³A husband also must love his wife. He must love her just as he loves himself. And a wife must respect her husband.

Children and Parents

6 Children, obey your parents as believers in the Lord. Obey them because it's the right thing to do. ²Scripture says, "Honor your father and mother." That is the first commandment that has a promise. ³"Then things will go well with you. You will live a long time on the earth." *(Deuteronomy 5:16)*

⁴Fathers, don't make your children angry. Instead, train them and teach them the ways of the Lord as you raise them.

Slaves and Masters

⁵Slaves, obey your masters here on earth. Respect them and honor them

POWER-SURGE

OBEYS ✔

CHILDREN, OBEY YOUR PARENTS AS BELIEVERS IN THE LORD. OBEY THEM BECAUSE IT'S THE RIGHT THING TO DO.
— EPHESIANS 6:1 —

POWER-SURGE

STRONG

FINALLY, LET THE LORD MAKE YOU STRONG. DEPEND ON HIS MIGHTY POWER.
— EPHESIANS 6:10 —

TRUSTED

with a heart that is true. Obey them just as you would obey Christ. ⁶Don't obey them only to please them when they are watching. Do it because you are slaves of Christ. Be sure your heart does what God wants.

⁷Serve your masters with all your heart. Work as if you were not serving people but the Lord. ⁸You know that the Lord will give you a reward. He will give to each of you in keeping with the good you do. It doesn't matter whether you are slaves or free.

⁹Masters, treat your slaves in the same way. When you warn them, don't be too hard on them. You know that the One who is their Master and yours is in heaven. And he treats everyone the same.

God's Armor

¹⁰Finally, let the Lord make you strong. Depend on his mighty power. ¹¹Put on all of God's armor. Then you can stand firm against the devil's evil plans. ¹²Our fight is not against human beings. It is against the rulers, the authorities and the powers of this dark world. It is against the spiritual forces of evil in the heavenly world.

¹³So put on all of God's armor. Evil days will come. But you will be able to stand up to anything. And after you have done everything you can, you will still be standing.

¹⁴So stand firm. Put the belt of truth around your waist. Put the armor of godliness on your chest. ¹⁵Wear on your feet what will prepare you to tell the good news of peace. ¹⁶Also, pick up the shield of faith. With it you can put out all of the flaming arrows of the evil one. ¹⁷Put on the helmet of salvation. And take the sword of the Holy Spirit. The sword is God's word.

¹⁸At all times, pray by the power of the Spirit. Pray all kinds of prayers. Be watch-

ful, so that you can pray. Always keep on praying for all of God's people.

19 Pray also for me. Pray that when I open my mouth, the right words will be given to me. Then I can be bold as I tell the mystery of the good news. **20** Because of the good news, I am being held by chains as the Lord's messenger. So pray that I will be bold as I preach the good news. That's what I should do.

Final Greetings

21 Tychicus is a dear brother. He is faith-ful in serving the Lord. He will tell you everything about me. Then you will know how I am and what I am doing. **22** That's why I am sending him to you. I want you to know how we are. And I want him to cheer you up.

23 May God the Father and the Lord Jesus Christ give peace to the brothers and sisters. May they also give them love and faith.

24 May grace be given to everyone who loves our Lord Jesus Christ with a love that will never die.

PHILIPPIANS

Philippians is another letter that Paul writes while in prison. He writes to the church he started in the city of Philippi. Paul teaches the believers there how they can live joyful lives as Christians even if they are in trouble. He tells them that keeping their eyes on Jesus will help them to be strong and brave. You can read the short book of Philippians in only a few minutes. But it is packed with important messages for you. Read it to learn how to be content and how to keep your mind clean and pure.

CHECK OUT THIS TRAIT OF A HERO . . .

STRONG
PAGE 1371

1 We, Paul and Timothy, are writing this letter. We serve Christ Jesus.

We are sending this letter to you, all of God's people in Philippi. You belong to Christ Jesus. We are also sending this letter to your leaders and deacons.

²May God our Father and the Lord Jesus Christ give you grace and peace.

Paul Prays and Gives Thanks

³I thank my God every time I remember you. ⁴In all my prayers for all of you, I always pray with joy. ⁵I am happy because you have joined me in spreading the good news. You have done so from the first day until now.

POWER-SURGE

THANKFUL ❖

I THANK MY GOD EVERY TIME I REMEMBER YOU.
—— **PHILIPPIANS 1:3** ——

⁶I am sure that the One who began a good work in you will carry it on until it is completed. That will be on the day Christ Jesus returns.

⁷It is right for me to feel this way about all of you. I love you with all my heart. I may be held by chains, or I may be standing up for the truth of the good news. Either way, all of you share in God's grace together with me. ⁸God can give witness that I long for all of you. I love you with the love that Christ Jesus gives.

⁹I pray that your love will grow more and more. And let it be based on knowledge and understanding. ¹⁰Then you will be able to know what is best. You will be pure and without blame until the day Christ returns. ¹¹You will be filled with the fruit of right living produced by Jesus Christ. All of those things bring glory and praise to God.

Paul Honors Christ in Prison

¹²Brothers and sisters, here is what I want you to know. What has happened to me has really helped to spread the good news. ¹³One thing has become clear. I am being held by chains because of my stand for Christ. All of the palace guards and everyone else know it.

¹⁴Because I am being held by chains, most of the believers in the Lord have be-

come bolder. They now speak God's word more boldly and without fear.

¹⁵It's true that some preach about Christ because they are jealous. But others preach about Christ to help me in my work. ¹⁶The last group acts out of love. They know I have been put here to stand up for the good news. ¹⁷But the others preach about Christ only to get ahead. They are not honest and true. They think they can stir up trouble for me while I am being held by chains.

¹⁸But what does it matter? Here is the important thing. Whether for reasons that are right or wrong, Christ is being preached about. That makes me very glad.

And I will continue to be glad. ¹⁹I know that you are praying for me. I also know that the Spirit of Jesus Christ will help me. So no matter what happens, I'm sure I will still be saved.

²⁰I completely expect and hope that I won't be ashamed in any way. I'm sure I will be brave enough. Now as always Christ will be lifted high through my body. He will be lifted up whether I live or die.

²¹For me, life finds all of its meaning in Christ. Death also has its benefits.

²²Suppose I go on living in my body. Then I will be able to carry on my work. It will bear a lot of fruit. But what should I choose? I don't know. ²³I can't decide between the two. I long to leave this world and be with Christ. That is better by far.

²⁴But it is more important for you that I stay alive. ²⁵I'm sure of that. So I know I will remain with you. And I will continue with all of you to help you grow and be joyful in what you have been taught. ²⁶I'm sure I will be with you again. Then your joy in Christ Jesus will be greater than ever because of me.

²⁷No matter what happens, live in a way that brings honor to the good news about Christ. Then I will know that you stand firm with one purpose. I may come and see you or only hear about you. But I will know that you work together as one person. And I will know that you work to spread the teachings of the good news.

²⁸So don't be afraid in any way of those who oppose you. That will show them that they will be destroyed and that you will be saved. That's what God will do.

²⁹Here is what he has given you to do for Christ. You must not only believe in him. You must also suffer for him. ³⁰You are going through the same struggle you saw me go through. As you have heard, I am still struggling.

POWER–SURGE

CHEERFUL ✳

ARE YOU CHEERFUL
BECAUSE YOU BELONG
TO CHRIST? DOES HIS
LOVE COMFORT YOU?
IS THE HOLY SPIRIT
YOUR COMPANION?
HAS CHRIST BEEN
GENTLE AND LOVING
TOWARD YOU? THEN
MAKE MY JOY
COMPLETE BY
AGREEING WITH EACH
OTHER. HAVE THE
SAME LOVE. BE ONE
IN SPIRIT AND
PURPOSE.
— PHILIPPIANS 2:1-2 — ♥

LOVING

Thinking Like Christ

2 Are you cheerful because you belong to Christ? Does his love comfort you? Is the Holy Spirit your companion? Has Christ been gentle and loving toward you? ²Then make my joy complete by agreeing with each other. Have the same love. Be one in spirit and purpose.

³Don't do anything only to get ahead. Don't do it because you are proud. Instead, be free of pride. Think of others as better than yourselves.

⁴None of you should look out just for your own good. You should also look out for the good of others.

⁵You should think in the same way Christ Jesus does.

⁶ In his very nature he was God.
But he did not think that being
    equal with God was something
    he should hold on to.
⁷ Instead, he made himself nothing.
He took on the very nature of a
    servant.
He was made in human form.
⁸ He appeared as a man.

He came down to the lowest level.
He obeyed God completely, even
    though it led to his death.
In fact, he died on a cross.
⁹ So God lifted him up to the highest
    place.
He gave him the name that is above
    every name.
¹⁰ When the name of Jesus is spoken,
    everyone's knee will bow to
    worship him.
Every knee in heaven and on earth
    and under the earth will bow to
    worship him.
¹¹ Everyone's mouth will say that Jesus
    Christ is Lord.
And God the Father will receive the
    glory.

Living Like Christ

¹²My dear friends, you have always obeyed God. You obeyed while I was with you. And you have obeyed even more while I am not with you. So continue to work out your own salvation. Do it with fear and trembling. ¹³God is working in you. He wants your plans and your acts to be in keeping with his good purpose.

¹⁴Do everything without finding fault or arguing. ¹⁵Then you will be pure and without blame. You will be children of God without fault in a sinful and evil world. Among the people of the world you shine like stars in the heavens. ¹⁶You shine as you hold out to them the word of life. So I can brag about you on the day Christ returns. I can be happy that I didn't run or work for nothing.

¹⁷But my life might even be poured out like a drink offering on your sacrifices. I'm talking about the way you serve because you believe. Even so, I am glad. I am joyful with all of you. ¹⁸So you too should be glad and joyful with me.

Timothy and Epaphroditus

¹⁹I hope to send Timothy to you soon if the Lord Jesus allows it. Then I will be cheered up when I receive news about you. ²⁰I have no one else like Timothy. He truly cares about how you are doing.

²¹All the others are looking out for their own interests. They are not looking out for the interests of Jesus Christ. ²²But you know that Timothy has proved himself. He has served with me like a son with his father in spreading the good news.

²³So I hope to send him as soon as I see how things go with me. ²⁴And I'm sure I myself will come soon if the Lord allows it.

25But I think it's necessary to send Epaphroditus back to you. He is my brother in the Lord. He is a worker and a soldier of Christ together with me. He is also your messenger. You sent him to take care of my needs. 26He longs for all of you. He is troubled because you heard he was sick.

27He was very sick. In fact, he almost died. But God had mercy on him. He also had mercy on me. God spared me sadness after sadness. 28So I want even more to send him to you. Then when you see him again, you will be glad. And I won't worry so much.

29Welcome him as a brother in the Lord with great joy. Honor people like him. 30He almost died for the work of Christ. He put his life in danger to make up for the help you couldn't give me.

Do Not Trust Human Nature

3 Finally, my brothers and sisters, be joyful because you belong to the Lord. It is no trouble for me to write about some important matters to you again. If you know about them, you will have a safe path to follow.

POWER-SURGE

CHEERFUL ✱

BE JOYFUL BECAUSE YOU BELONG TO THE LORD.
—— PHILIPPIANS 3:1 ——

2Watch out for those dogs. They do evil things. When they circumcise, it is nothing more than a useless cutting of the body. 3But we have been truly circumcised. We worship God by the power of his Spirit. We brag about what Christ Jesus has done. We don't put our trust in our weak human nature.

4I have many reasons to trust in my human nature. Others may think they have reasons to trust in theirs. But I have even more. 5I was circumcised on the eighth day. I am part of the people of Israel. I am from the tribe of Benjamin. I am a pure Hebrew. As far as the law is concerned, I am a Pharisee. 6As far as being committed is concerned, I opposed and attacked the church. As far as keeping the Law is concerned, I kept it perfectly.

7I thought things like that were for my benefit. But now I consider them to be nothing because of Christ. 8Even more, I consider everything to be nothing compared to knowing Christ Jesus my Lord. To know him is the best thing of all. Because of him I have lost everything. But I consider all of it to be garbage so I can get to know Christ. 9I want to be joined to him.

For me, being right with God does not come from the law. It comes because I believe in Christ. It comes from God. It is received by faith.

10I want to know Christ better. I want to know the power that raised him from the dead. I want to share in his sufferings. I want to become like him by sharing in his death. 11Then by God's grace I will rise from the dead.

Moving on Toward the Goal

12I have not yet received all of those things. I have not yet been made perfect. But I move on to take hold of what Christ Jesus took hold of me for.

13Brothers and sisters, I don't consider that I have taken hold of it yet. But here is the one thing I do. I forget what is behind me. I push hard toward what is ahead of me. 14I move on toward the goal to win the prize. God has appointed me to win it. The heavenly prize is Christ Jesus himself.

15All of us who are grown up in the faith should see things that way. Maybe you think differently about something. But God will make it clear to you. 16Only let us live up to what we have already reached.

17Brothers and sisters, join with others in following my example. Pay close attention to those who live in keeping with the pattern we gave you.

18I have told you those things many times before. Now I say it again with tears in my eyes. Many people live like enemies of the cross of Christ. 19The only thing they have coming to them is death. Their stomach is their god. They brag about what they should be ashamed of. They think only about earthly things.

20But we are citizens of heaven. And we can hardly wait for a Savior from there. He is the Lord Jesus Christ. 21He has the power to bring everything under his control. By his power he will change our earthly bodies. They will become like his glorious body.

4 My brothers and sisters, that is how you should stand firm in the Lord's strength. I love you and long for you. Dear friends, you are my joy and my crown.

Do What Is Best

2Here is what I'm asking Euodia and Syntyche to do. I want them to agree with each other because they belong to the Lord.

3My true companion, here is what I ask you to do. Help those women. They have served at my side. They have helped me spread the good news. So have Clement and the rest of those who have worked together with me. Their names are all written in the Book of Life.

4Always be joyful because you belong to the Lord. I will say it again. Be joyful. **5**Let everyone know how gentle you are. The Lord is coming soon.

6Don't worry about anything. Instead, tell God about everything. Ask and pray. Give thanks to him. **7**Then God's peace will watch over your hearts and your minds because you belong to Christ Jesus. God's peace can never be completely understood.

8Finally, my brothers and sisters, always think about what is true. Think about what is noble, right and pure. Think about what is lovely and worthy of respect. If anything is excellent or worthy of praise, think about those kinds of things. **9**Do what you have learned or received or heard from me. Follow my example.

The God who gives peace will be with you.

STRONG

PHILIPPIANS 4:13

I can do everything by the power of Christ. He gives me strength.

How strong are you? Do you have big muscles? Are you strong enough to lift heavy weights? That's one kind of strength. But other kinds of strength are more important. God wants you to be "strong" in him. When someone you love gets sick or dies, God will help you be strong to get through the hard times. When you want to do things you know you shouldn't do, God will give you strength.

Caleb went with eleven other men to spy out the promised land (you'll find his story on page 170). He and Joshua were the only two who thought the Israelites were strong enough with God's help to win the land. The other ten spies were too afraid. When all the others were weak, Caleb and Joshua stood strong. When a Roman commander (see page 1103) went to see Jesus, he asked if Jesus would heal his servant. He had faith in Jesus that was so strong that he said he knew Jesus could heal his servant without even going to his house. Now that's a strong man!

BE STRONG

God wants you to know that he will always be with you, no matter what hard things you may face. And he wants you to know that he will make you strong. You may feel weak and scared, but with God on your side, you're a super hero of strength!

Go to page 1378 for the next Super Hero Trait

HONEST H

FINALLY, MY BROTHERS AND SISTERS, ALWAYS THINK ABOUT WHAT IS TRUE.

— PHILIPPIANS 4:8 —

Paul Gives Thanks for Help Received

10 At last you are concerned about me again. That makes me very happy. We belong to the Lord. I know that you have been concerned. But you had no chance to show it.

11 I'm not saying that because I need anything. I have learned to be content no matter what happens to me. 12 I know what it's like not to have what I need. I also know what it's like to have more than I need. I have learned the secret of being content no matter what happens. I am content whether I am well fed or hungry. I am content whether I have more than enough or not enough. 13 I can do everything by the power of Christ. He gives me strength.

14 But it was good of you to share in my troubles. 15 And you believers at Philippi know what happened when I left Macedonia. Not one church helped me in the matter of giving and receiving. You were the only one that did. That was in the early days when you first heard the good news. 16 Even when I was in Thessalonica, you sent me help when I needed it. You did it again and again.

17 I'm not looking for a gift. I'm looking for what is best for you. 18 I have received my full pay, and even more than that. I have everything I need. That's because Epaphroditus brought me the gifts you sent. They are a sweet-smelling offering. They are a gift that God accepts. He is pleased with it.

19 My God will meet all your needs. He will meet them in keeping with his wonderful riches that come to you because you belong to Christ Jesus.

20 Give glory to our God and Father for ever and ever. Amen.

Final Greetings

21 Greet all of God's people. They belong to Christ Jesus. The brothers who are with me send greetings. 22 All of God's people here send you greetings. Most of all, those who live in the palace of Caesar send you greetings.

23 May the grace of the Lord Jesus Christ be with your spirit. Amen.

COLOSSIANS

The missionary Paul writes this short letter to the church in Colosse. He is concerned because some teachers there are telling the believers things that aren't true. He wants to be sure the church in Colosse understands the simple, but deep, truths about Jesus and salvation. He wants to be sure they know the true way, not the wrong way taught by these teachers. As you read the book of Colossians, you will learn how important it is to know what you believe in and to stand firmly in your belief.

CHECK OUT THIS TRAIT OF A HERO . . .

FORGIVING
PAGE 1378

CODE OF HONOR IN THIS BOOK . . .

PATIENT
PAGE 1375

TRIES HARD
PAGE 1375

CHEERFUL
PAGE 1376

STRONG
PAGE 1376

BELIEVES
PAGE 1376

OBEYS
PAGES 1377, 1379

SELF-CONTROLLED
PAGE 1377

THANKFUL
PAGE 1379

1 I, Paul, am writing this letter. I am an apostle of Christ Jesus just as God planned. Our brother Timothy joins me in writing.

²We are sending this letter to you, our brothers and sisters in Colosse. You belong to Christ. You are holy and faithful.

May God our Father give you grace and peace.

Paul Prays and Gives Thanks

³We always thank God, the Father of our Lord Jesus Christ, when we pray for you. ⁴We thank him because we have heard about your faith in Christ Jesus. We have also heard that you love all of God's people.

⁵Your faith and love are based on the hope you have. What you hope for is stored up for you in heaven. You have already heard about it. You were told about it when the message of truth was given to you. I'm talking about the good news ⁶that has come to you.

All over the world the good news is bearing fruit and growing. It has been doing that among you since the day you heard it. That is when you understood God's grace in all its truth.

⁷You learned the good news from Epaphras. He is dear to us. He serves Christ together with us. He faithfully works for Christ and for us among you. ⁸He also told us about your love that comes from the Holy Spirit.

⁹That's why we have not stopped praying for you. We have been praying for you since the day we heard about you. We have been asking God to fill you with the knowledge of what he wants. We pray that he will give you spiritual wisdom and understanding.

¹⁰We pray that you will lead a life that is worthy of the Lord. We pray that you will please him in every way. So we want you to bear fruit in every good thing you do. We want you to grow to know God better. ¹¹We want you to be very strong, in keeping with his glorious power. We want you to be patient. Never give up. Be joyful ¹²as you give thanks to the Father.

He has made you fit to share with all his people. You will all receive a share in the kingdom of light.

¹³He has saved us from the kingdom of darkness. He has brought us into the kingdom of the Son he loves. ¹⁴Because of what the Son has done, we have been set free. Because of him, all of our sins have been forgiven.

Christ Is Far Above Everything

¹⁵Christ is the exact likeness of God, who can't be seen. He is first, and he is over all of creation. ¹⁶All things were created by him. He created everything in heaven and on earth. He created everything that can be seen and everything that can't be seen. He created kings, powers, rulers and authorities. Everything was created by him and for him. ¹⁷Before anything was created, he was already there. He holds everything together.

¹⁸And he is the head of the body, which is the church. He is the beginning. He is the first to be raised from the dead. That happened so that he would be far above everything. ¹⁹God was pleased to have his whole nature living in Christ. ²⁰God was pleased to bring all things back to himself because of what Christ has done. That includes all things on earth and in heaven. God made peace through Christ's blood, through his death on the cross.

²¹At one time you were separated from God. You were enemies in your minds because of your evil ways. ²²But because Christ died, God has brought you back to himself. Christ's death has made you holy in God's sight. So now you don't have any flaw. You are free from blame.

²³But you must keep your faith steady and firm. Don't move away from the hope that the good news holds out to you. It is the good news that you heard. It has been

PATIENT P

WE WANT YOU TO
GROW TO KNOW GOD
BETTER. WE WANT YOU
TO BE VERY STRONG,
IN KEEPING WITH HIS
GLORIOUS POWER.
WE WANT YOU TO BE
PATIENT. NEVER GIVE
UP. BE JOYFUL AS
YOU GIVE THANKS TO
THE FATHER.
—COLOSSIANS 1:10-12— T

TRIES HARD

preached to every creature under heaven. I, Paul, now serve the good news.

Paul's Work for the Church

24I am happy because of what was suffered for you. And in my body I fill up my share in Christ's sufferings. I do it for his body, which is the church. **25**I serve the church. God appointed me to bring all of his word to you.

26That word contains the mystery that has been hidden for many ages. But now it has been made known to God's people. **27**God has chosen to make known to them the glorious riches of that mystery. He has made it known among those who aren't Jews. And here is what it is. Christ is in you. He is your hope of glory.

28We preach about him. With all the wisdom we have, we warn and teach everyone. When we bring them to God, we want them to be perfect as people who belong to Christ.

29That's what I'm working for. I work hard with all of Christ's strength. His strength works powerfully in me.

2 I want you to know how hard I am working for you. I'm concerned for those who are in Laodicea. I'm also concerned for everyone who has not met me in person. **2**I want their hearts to be made cheerful and strong. I want them to be joined together in love. Then their understanding will be rich and complete. They will know the mystery of God. That mystery is Christ.

3All the treasures of wisdom and knowledge are hidden in him.

4But I don't want anyone to fool you with fast talk that only sounds good. **5**So

POWER-SURGE

CHEERFUL ✳

I WANT THEIR HEARTS TO BE MADE CHEERFUL AND STRONG...I AM HAPPY THAT YOUR FAITH IN CHRIST IS SO STRONG.
— COLOSSIANS 2:2, 5 —

STRONG

POWER-SURGE

BELIEVES †

YOU RECEIVED CHRIST JESUS AS LORD. SO KEEP ON LIVING IN HIM. HAVE YOUR ROOTS IN HIM. BUILD YOURSELVES UP IN HIM. GROW STRONG IN WHAT YOU BELIEVE, JUST AS YOU WERE TAUGHT.
— COLOSSIANS 2:6-7 —

STRONG

even though I am away from you in body, I am with you in spirit. I am glad to see that you are doing everything in good order. And I am happy that your faith in Christ is so strong.

Freedom From Human Rules

6You received Christ Jesus as Lord. So keep on living in him. **7**Have your roots in him. Build yourselves up in him. Grow strong in what you believe, just as you were taught. Be more thankful than ever before.

8Make sure no one captures you. They will try to capture you by using false reasoning that has no meaning. Their ideas depend on human teachings. They also depend on the basic things the people of this world believe. They don't depend on Christ.

9God's whole nature is living in Christ in human form. **10**Because you belong to Christ, you have everything you need. He is the ruler over every power and authority.

11When you received Christ, you were also circumcised by putting away your sinful nature. Human hands didn't circumcise you. Christ did.

12When you were baptized, you were buried together with him. You were raised to life together with him by believing in God's power. God raised Jesus from the dead.

13At one time you were dead in your sins. Your sinful nature was not circumcised. But God gave you new life together with Christ. He forgave us all of our sins.

14He wiped out the written Law with its rules. The Law was against us. It opposed us. He took it away and nailed it to the cross **15**He took away the weapons of the powers and authorities. He made a public show of them. He won the battle over them by dying on the cross.

16So don't let anyone judge you because of what you eat or drink. Don't let anyone judge you about holy days. I'm talking about special feasts and New Moons and Sabbath days. **17**They are only a shadow of the things that were going to come. But what is real is found in Christ.

18Some people enjoy pretending they aren't proud. They worship angels. But don't let people like that hold you back from winning the prize. They tell you every little thing about what they have seen. Their minds are not guided by the Holy Spirit. So they are proud of their useless ideas.

19They aren't connected to the Head. But the whole body grows from the Head. The muscles and tendons hold the body together. And God causes it to grow.

20The people of the world believe certain basic things. You died with Christ as far as things like that are concerned. So why do you act as if you still belong to the world? Here are the rules you follow. **21**"Do not handle! Do not taste! Do not touch!" **22**Rules like that are all going to die out as time goes by. They are only based on human rules and teachings.

23It is true that those rules seem wise. Because of them, people give themselves over to their own kind of worship. They pretend they aren't proud. They treat their bodies very badly. But rules like that don't help. They don't stop people from chasing after sinful pleasures.

Rules for Holy Living

3 You have been raised up with Christ. So think about things that are in heaven. That is where Christ is. He is sitting at God's right hand. **2**Think about things that are in heaven. Don't think about things that are on earth.

3You died. Now your life is hidden with Christ in God. **4**Christ is your life. When he appears again, you also will appear with him in heaven's glory.

5So put to death anything that belongs to your earthly nature. Get rid of your sexual sins and unclean acts. Don't let your feelings get out of control. Remove from your life all evil longings. Stop always

wanting more and more. You might as well be worshiping statues of gods. **6**God's anger is going to come because of those things. **7**That's the way you lived at one time in your life.

8But now here are the kinds of things you must get rid of. You must put away anger, rage, hate and lies. Let no dirty words come out of your mouths. **9**Don't lie to each other.

You have gotten rid of your old way of life and its habits. **10**You have started living a new life. It is being made new so that what you know has the Creator's likeness.

11Here there is no Greek or Jew. There is no difference between those who are circumcised and those who are not. There is no rude outsider, or even a Scythian. There is no slave or free person. But Christ is everything. And he is in everything.

12You are God's chosen people. You are holy and dearly loved. So put on tender mercy and kindness as if they were your clothes. Don't be proud. Be gentle and patient. **13**Put up with each other. Forgive the things you are holding against one another. Forgive, just as the Lord forgave you.

14And over all of those good things put on love. Love holds them all together perfectly as if they were one.

15Let the peace that Christ gives rule in your hearts. As parts of one body, you were appointed to live in peace. And be thankful.

16Let Christ's word live in you like a rich treasure. Teach and correct each other wisely. Sing psalms, hymns and spiritual songs. Sing with thanks in your hearts to God. **17**Do everything you say

POWER-SURGE

OBEYS ✔

SO PUT TO DEATH ANYTHING THAT BELONGS TO YOUR EARTHLY NATURE... DON'T LET YOUR FEELINGS GET OUT OF CONTROL.
— COLOSSIANS 3:5 —

SELF-CONTROLLED

or do in the name of the Lord Jesus. Always give thanks to God the Father through Christ.

Rules for Christian Families

18Wives, follow the lead of your husbands. That's what the Lord wants you to do.

19Husbands, love your wives. Don't be mean to them.

20Children, obey your parents in everything. That pleases the Lord.

21Fathers, don't make your children bitter. If you do, they will lose hope.

22Slaves, obey your earthly masters in everything. Don't do it just to please them when they are watching you. Obey them with an honest heart. Do it out of respect for the Lord.

23Work at everything you do with all your heart. Work as if you were working for the Lord, not for human masters. 24Work because you know that you will finally receive as a reward what the Lord wants you to have. You are serving the Lord Christ.

25Anyone who does wrong will be paid back for what he does. God treats everyone the same.

FORGIVING

COLOSSIANS 3:13

F **Put up with each other. Forgive the things you are holding against one another. Forgive, just as the Lord forgave you.**

F

F How do you feel if someone says something mean to you? Or does something mean to you? Do you want to find a way to get back at them? To make them hurt just like you hurt? That's a common reaction. But the Bible says instead that you should forgive others.

Many stories in the Bible teach about forgiveness. Jacob stole his brother, Esau's, blessing from their father. Esau threatened to kill Jacob, so Jacob went on an extended trip—like for twenty years. Over the years, Esau must have learned that by hating his brother he was only hurting himself. So he forgave him. The story of their reunion can be found on page 44. Joseph had the same problem. His brothers hated him and sold him into slavery. Years later, Joseph chose to forgive them instead of hurting them. Even when he had the chance to make their lives miserable, he chose instead to forgive. His story is found on page 64.

BE FORGIVING

Wow! Forgiving someone who has hurt you can be one of the hardest things you'll ever do. Certainly it had to be hard for Esau and Joseph to forgive their brothers. But they did. Forgiving someone is one of the greatest acts of love you can do, for yourself and for them.

Go to page **1382** for the next Super Hero Trait

THANKFUL

SING WITH THANKS IN YOUR HEARTS TO GOD...ALWAYS GIVE THANKS TO GOD THE FATHER THROUGH CHRIST.
— COLOSSIANS 3:16-17 —

4 Masters, give your slaves what is right and fair. Do it because you know that you also have a Master in heaven.

More Directions

²Spend a lot of time in prayer. Always be watchful and thankful.

³Pray for us too. Pray that God will open a door for our message. Then we can preach the mystery of Christ. Because I preached it, I am being held by chains. ⁴Pray that I will preach it clearly, as I should.

⁵Be wise in the way you act toward outsiders. Make the most of every opportunity. ⁶Let the words you speak always be full of grace. Season them with salt. Then you will know how to answer everyone.

Final Greetings

⁷Tychicus will tell you all the news about me. He is a dear brother. He is a faithful worker. He serves the Lord together with us. ⁸I am sending him to you for one reason. I want you to know what is happening here. I want him to cheer you up and make your hearts strong.

⁹He is coming with Onesimus, our faithful and dear brother. He is one of you. They will tell you everything that is happening here.

¹⁰Aristarchus is in prison with me. He sends you his greetings. So does Mark, the cousin of Barnabas. You have been given directions about him. If he comes to you, welcome him. ¹¹Jesus, who is called Justus, also sends greetings. They are the only Jews who work together with me for God's kingdom. They have been a comfort to me.

¹²Epaphras sends greetings. He is one of you. He serves Christ Jesus. He is always praying hard for you. He prays that you will stand firm in holding to all that God has in mind for us. He prays that you will continue to grow in your knowledge of what God wants you to do. He also prays that you will be completely sure about it. ¹³I am happy to tell you that he is working very hard for you. He is also working hard for everyone in Laodicea and Hierapolis.

¹⁴Our dear friend Luke, the doctor, sends greetings. So does Demas.

¹⁵Give my greetings to the brothers and sisters in Laodicea. Also give my greetings to Nympha and the church that meets in her house.

¹⁶After this letter has been read to you, send it on. Be sure that it is also read to the church in Laodicea. And be sure that you read the letter from Laodicea.

¹⁷Tell Archippus, "Be sure that you complete the work the Lord gave you to do."

¹⁸I, Paul, am writing this greeting with my own hand. Remember that I am being held by chains. May grace be with you.

OBEYS

CHILDREN, OBEY YOUR PARENTS IN EVERYTHING. THAT PLEASES THE LORD.
— COLOSSIANS 3:20 —

1 THESSALONIANS

The book of 1 Thessalonians is the first letter Paul writes to the church in Thessalonica. Paul started the church there and had to leave the city sooner than he had planned. He now writes to encourage them. He says he is thankful to God because he has heard they are growing strong as Christians. He tells them that he loves them. And he teaches them about what death means for believers. As you read this little letter, remember that as a Christian you are important to God and you will go to be with him when life is over.

CHECK OUT THESE TRAITS OF A HERO . . .

TELLS OTHERS
PAGE 1382

KIND
PAGE 1385

THANKFUL
PAGE 1386

1 I, Paul, am writing this letter. Silas and Timothy join me in writing.

We are sending this letter to you, the members of the church in Thessalonica. You belong to God the Father and the Lord Jesus Christ.

May grace and peace be given to you.

Paul Gives Thanks

2 We always thank God for all of you. We pray for you. 3 We never forget you when we pray to our God and Father. Your work is produced by your faith. Your service is the result of your love. Your strength to continue comes from your hope in our Lord Jesus Christ.

4 Brothers and sisters, you are loved by God. We know that he has chosen you. 5 Our good news didn't come to you only in words. It came with power. It came with the Holy Spirit's help. He gave us complete faith in what we were preaching. You know how we lived among you for your good.

6 We and the Lord were your examples. You followed us. You suffered terribly. Even so, you welcomed our message with the joy the Holy Spirit gives. 7 So you became a model to all the believers in the lands of Macedonia and Achaia.

8 The Lord's message rang out from you. That was true not only in Macedonia and Achaia. Your faith in God has also become known everywhere. So we don't have to say anything about it. 9 The believers themselves report the kind of welcome you gave us. They tell about how you turned away from statues of gods to serve the living and true God. 10 They tell about how you are waiting for his Son to come from heaven.

God raised him from the dead. He is Jesus. He saves us from God's anger, and his anger is sure to come.

POWER-SURGE

STRONG

YOUR STRENGTH TO CONTINUE COMES FROM YOUR HOPE IN OUR LORD JESUS CHRIST.
— 1 THESSALONIANS 1:3 —

POWER-SURGE

BELIEVES ✝

YOUR FAITH IN GOD HAS ALSO BECOME KNOWN EVERYWHERE.
1 THESSALONIANS 1:8

TELLS OTHERS

Paul's Work for God in Thessalonica

2 Brothers and sisters, you know that our visit to you was not a failure. 2 You know what happened earlier in the city of Philippi. We suffered, and people treated us badly there. But God gave us the boldness to tell you his good news. We preached to you even though people opposed us strongly.

3 The appeal we make is based on truth. It comes from a pure heart. We are not trying to trick you. 4 In fact, it is just the opposite. God has accepted us to preach. He has trusted us with the good news. We aren't trying to please people. We want to please God. He puts our hearts to the test.

5 As you know, we never praised you if we didn't mean it. We didn't put on a mask to cover up any sinful longing. God is our witness that this is true. 6 We were not expecting people to praise us. We were not looking for praise from you or anyone else.

As Christ's apostles, we could have caused you some expense. 7 But we were gentle among you. We were like a mother caring for her little children. 8 We loved you so much that we were happy to share with you God's good news. We were also happy to share our lives with you. You had become very special to us.

9 Brothers and sisters, I am sure you remember how hard we worked. We labored night and day while we preached to you God's good news. We didn't want to cause you any expense.

10 You are witnesses of how we lived among you believers. God is also a witness that we were holy and godly and without blame. 11 You know that we treated each of you as a father treats his own children. 12 We gave you hope and strength. We comforted you. We really wanted you to

live in a way that is worthy of God. He chooses you to enter his glorious kingdom.

13We never stop thanking God for the way you received his word. You heard it from us. But you didn't accept it as a human word. You accepted it for what it really is. It is God's word. It is at work in you who believe.

14Brothers and sisters, you became like the members of God's churches in Judea. They are believers in Christ Jesus, just as you are. People in your own country made you suffer. You went through the same things the church members in Judea suffered from the Jews.

15The Jews who killed the Lord Jesus and the prophets also forced us to leave. They do not please God. They are enemies of everyone. 16They try to keep us from speaking to those who aren't Jews. The Jews don't want them to be saved. In that way, the Jews always increase their sins to the limit. God's anger has come on them at last.

Paul Longs to See the Believers in Thessalonica

17Brothers and sisters, we were torn away from you for a short time. We were no longer with you in person, but we kept you in our thoughts. We really longed to see you. So we tried very hard to do so. 18We wanted to come to you. Again and again I, Paul, wanted to come. But Satan stopped us.

19What is our hope? What is our joy? When our Lord Jesus returns, what is the crown we will delight in? Isn't it you? 20Yes, you are our glory and our joy.

TELLS OTHERS

1 THESSALONIANS 2:4

God has accepted us to preach. He has trusted us with the good news. We aren't trying to please people. We want to please God.

When something exciting happens to you, what's the first thing you want to do? You want to tell someone! Exciting things are meant to be shared with others. Well, you have some "good news." That's what the Bible says the story of Jesus is. It's good news! So tell others about it!

When Andrew met Jesus, he was so excited he couldn't wait to tell his brother Simon, "I've found the Messiah!" You'll find his story on page 1219. Or how about the woman Jesus talked to at the well? She had lived a sinful life and was thirsty for the good news that Jesus had to give her. Did she keep that good news to herself? Of course not! She went right away and told all of her friends. You'll find this woman's story on page 1224.

TELL OTHERS

Did you know you're just like Andrew and Simon? You are! You know all about the good news of Jesus. Aren't you excited? Go and tell others!

Go to page **1385** for the next Super Hero Trait

CHEERFUL

WE LOVED YOU SO
MUCH THAT WE WERE
HAPPY TO SHARE WITH
YOU GOD'S GOOD
NEWS. WE WERE ALSO
HAPPY TO SHARE OUR
LIVES WITH YOU. YOU
HAD BECOME VERY
SPECIAL TO US.

— 1 THESSALONIANS 2:8 —

LOVING

3 We couldn't wait any longer. So we thought it was best to be left by ourselves in Athens. ²We sent our brother Timothy to give you strength and hope in your faith. He works together with God in spreading the good news about Christ. ³We sent him so that no one would be upset by times of testing.

You know very well that we have to go through them. ⁴In fact, when we were with you, we kept telling you that our enemies would make us suffer. As you know very well, it has turned out that way.

⁵That's the reason I sent someone to find out about your faith. I couldn't wait any longer. I was afraid that Satan might have tempted you in some way. Then our efforts would have been useless.

Timothy Brings a Good Report

⁶But Timothy has come to us from you just now. He has brought good news about your faith and love. He has told us that you always have happy memories of us. He has also said that you long to see us, just as we long to see you.

⁷Brothers and sisters, in all our trouble and suffering your faith cheered us up. ⁸Now we really live, because you are standing firm in the Lord. ⁹How can we thank God enough for you because of all the joy that comes only from our God? ¹⁰Night and day we pray very hard that we will see you again. We want to give you what is missing in your faith.

¹¹Now may our God and Father himself and our Lord Jesus open up a way for us to come to you. ¹²May the Lord make your love grow. May it be like a rising flood. May your love for one another increase. May it also increase for everyone else. May it be just like our love for you. ¹³May the Lord give you strength in your hearts. Then you will be holy and without blame in the sight of our God and Father. May that be true when our Lord Jesus comes with all his holy ones.

STRONG

MAY THE LORD GIVE
YOU STRENGTH IN
YOUR HEARTS.

— 1 THESSALONIANS 3:13 —

Living in a Way That Pleases God

4 Finally, brothers and sisters, we taught you how to live in a way that pleases God. In fact, that is how you are living. In the name of the Lord Jesus we ask and beg you to do it more and more.

²You know the directions we gave you. They were given by the authority of the Lord Jesus.

³God wants you to be made holy. He wants you to stay away from sexual sins. ⁴He wants all of you to learn to control your own bodies. You must live in a way that is holy. You must live with honor. ⁵Don't long to commit sexual sins like those who don't know God. ⁶None of you should sin against your brother by doing that. You should not take advantage of him. The Lord will punish everyone who commits those kinds of sins. We have already told you and warned you about

SELF-CONTROLLED

HE WANTS ALL OF YOU
TO LEARN TO CONTROL
YOUR OWN BODIES.
YOU MUST LIVE IN A
WAY THAT IS HOLY.
YOU MUST LIVE
WITH HONOR.

— 1 THESSALONIANS 4:4 —

that. ⁷God chose us to live pure lives. He wants us to be holy.

⁸So if you refuse to accept my teaching, you turn your back on God, not on people. God gives you his Holy Spirit.

⁹We don't need to write to you about love among believers. God himself has taught you to love each other. ¹⁰In fact, you do love all the brothers and sisters all around Macedonia. But we are asking you to love each other more and more.

¹¹Do everything you can to live a quiet life. Mind your own business. Work with your hands, just as we told you to. ¹²Then unbelievers will have respect for your everyday life. And you won't have to depend on anyone.

The Lord Is Coming

¹³Brothers and sisters, we want you to know what happens to those who die. We don't want you to be sad, as other people are. They don't have any hope.

¹⁴We believe that Jesus died and rose again. When he returns, many who believe in him will have died already. We believe that God will bring them back with Jesus.

¹⁵That agrees with what the Lord has said. When the Lord comes, many of us will still be alive. We tell you that we will certainly not go up before those who have died.

¹⁶The Lord himself will come down from heaven. We will hear a loud command. We will hear the voice of the leader of the angels. We will hear a blast from God's trumpet. Many who believe in

POWER-SURGE

CHEERFUL ✳

WE BELIEVE THAT
JESUS DIED AND
ROSE AGAIN. WHEN HE
RETURNS, MANY WHO
BELIEVE IN HIM WILL
HAVE DIED ALREADY.
WE BELIEVE THAT GOD
WILL BRING THEM
BACK WITH JESUS.

— 1 THESSALONIANS 4:14—

✝

BELIEVES

POWER-SURGE

SELF-CONTROLLED ⚡

SO LET US NOT BE
LIKE THE OTHERS.
THEY ARE ASLEEP.
INSTEAD, LET US BE
WIDE AWAKE AND IN
FULL CONTROL OF
OURSELVES...SO
LET US CONTROL
OURSELVES.

— 1 THESSALONIANS 5:6, 8 —

Christ will have died already. They will rise first. ¹⁷After that, we who are still alive and are left will be caught up together with them. We will be taken up in the clouds. We will meet the Lord in the air. And we will be with him forever.

¹⁸So cheer each other up with these words of comfort.

5 Brothers and sisters, we don't have to write to you about times and dates. ²You know very well that the day of the Lord will come like a thief in the night. ³People will be saying that everything is peaceful and safe. Then suddenly they will be destroyed. It will happen like birth pains coming on a pregnant woman. None of the people will escape.

⁴Brothers and sisters, you are not in darkness. So that day should not surprise you as a thief would. ⁵All of you are children of the light. You are children of the day. We don't belong to the night. We don't belong to the darkness.

⁶So let us not be like the others. They are asleep. Instead, let us be wide awake and in full control of ourselves.

⁷Those who sleep, sleep at night. Those who get drunk, get drunk at night. ⁸But we belong to the day. So let us control ourselves. Let us put the armor of faith and love on our chest. Let us put on the hope of salvation like a helmet.

⁹God didn't choose us to receive his anger. He chose us to receive salvation because of what our Lord Jesus Christ has done.

¹⁰Jesus died for us. Some will be alive when he comes. Others will be dead. Either way, we will live together with him. ¹¹So cheer each other up with the hope you have. Build each other up. In fact, that's what you are doing.

Final Directions

12Brothers and sisters, we ask you to have respect for the godly leaders who work hard among you. They have authority over you. They correct you. 13Have a lot of respect for them. Love them because of what they do. Live in peace with each other.

14Brothers and sisters, we are asking you to warn those who don't want to work. Cheer up those who are shy. Help those who are weak. Put up with everyone. 15Make sure that nobody pays back one wrong act with another. Always try to be kind to each other and to everyone else.

KIND

1 THESSALONIANS 5:14-15

K

K

K

Cheer up those who are shy. Help those who are weak. Put up with everyone. Make sure that nobody pays back one wrong act with another. Always try to be kind to each other and to everyone else.

*D*o you know anyone who is hurting? Maybe they're sad or just unhappy. Maybe you know others who are having a hard time, perhaps with schoolwork or getting along with their parents. When you help them, you are being kind.

Like love, kindness isn't just a feeling. If you *feel* kind, but don't do anything, you aren't really being kind. Kindness is *doing* something for someone else. Even if it's as small as getting your little brother or sister a drink of water (without complaining or being grouchy about it), you're being kind.

Shiphrah and Puah were two kind women in Egypt (their story is on page 70). When the Israelite women were about to have babies, Shiphrah and Puah would help. When Pharaoh told them to kill all the boy babies that were born, Shiphrah and Puah bravely and kindly saved those babies. When Joseph (he's on page 1090) found out his girlfriend, Mary, was pregnant, he could have been very angry and mean and made everyone laugh at her. Instead he was kind and he handled the situation quietly. He was kind to Mary.

BE KIND

Tomorrow morning when you get dressed, remember that God wants you to be kind to others. When you put on your shirt, put on kindness as well. When you put on your socks, remember that those who are having a hard time need your help. When you put on your shoes, put on a promise to be kind to those in trouble. God will be pleased with you. And you'll be happier yourself for having helped others.

Go to page 1386 for the next Super Hero Trait

¹⁶Always be joyful. ¹⁷Never stop praying. ¹⁸Give thanks no matter what happens. God wants you to thank him because you believe in Christ Jesus.

¹⁹Don't put out the Holy Spirit's fire. ²⁰Don't treat prophecies as if they amount to nothing. ²¹Put everything to the test. Hold on to what is good. ²²Stay away from every kind of evil.

²³God is the God who gives peace. May he make you holy through and through. May your whole spirit, soul and body be kept free from blame. May you be without blame from now until our Lord Jesus Christ comes. ²⁴The One who has chosen you is faithful. He will do all these things.

²⁵Brothers and sisters, pray for us. ²⁶Greet all the believers with a holy kiss. ²⁷While the Lord is watching, here is what I command you. Have this letter read to all the believers.

²⁸May the grace of our Lord Jesus Christ be with you.

THANKFUL

1 THESSALONIANS 5:18

> *Give thanks no matter what happens. God wants you to thank him because you believe in Christ Jesus.*

What does thankful look like? Do you have any ideas? Does it involve smiling? Or maybe sometimes a tear? What sorts of words go with being thankful? Can you think of any? How about "appreciate," or "pleased," or "grateful"? What does a thankful person's face look like? What sorts of actions go with being thankful? So many questions, huh? Let's look at how thankful appears in the Bible.

After the Israelites walked through the Red Sea on dry ground, and the waters came crashing back in and drowned the Egyptian soldiers, watch Miriam (see page 89). Her legs flew in a dance of thanksgiving. God had saved them from the Egyptians! Then picture Jonah, dirty and smelly after a big fish vomited him out on the beach (see page 1042). It's a different picture from Miriam, but it's still a thankful one. (You'd be thankful, too. wouldn't you, to find yourself on dry land after three days in a fish's stomach?) Then turn to page 1284 to see how thankful looked when the jailer discovered his prisoners were still there after an earthquake. All of these people were thankful, but each one showed it in a different way.

BE THANKFUL

What are you thankful for? Don't just think about them in your head, get out a piece of paper and a pencil and make a list. It's a great way to remember all that you have that makes life good. You'll be surprised at how long the list will get! Then run to the mirror. How does thankful look on your face?

Go to page 1392 for the next Super Hero Trait

2 THESSALONIANS

Paul writes his second letter to the Thessalonians only a short time after the first. He writes it to enlarge on the teachings of his first letter. He tells the believers in Thessalonica about the evil in the world and how they can still live faithful lives as they wait for Jesus to return. He wants them to be sure they are sure of what they believe as Christians. As you read 2 Thessalonians, you can learn from Paul's words how to live a Christian life in a sinful world.

CODE OF HONOR IN THIS BOOK . . .

TRIES HARD
PAGES 1388, 1389

STRONG
PAGE 1389

1

I, Paul, am writing this letter. Silas and Timothy join me in writing.

We are sending this letter to you, the members of the church in Thessalonica. You belong to God our Father and the Lord Jesus Christ.

²May God the Father and the Lord Jesus Christ give you grace and peace.

Paul Prays and Gives Thanks

³Brothers and sisters, we should always thank God for you. That is only right, because your faith is growing more and more. The love you all have for each other is increasing. ⁴So among God's churches we brag about the fact that you don't give up easily. We brag about your faith in all the suffering and testing you are going through.

⁵All of this proves that when God judges, he is fair. So you will be considered worthy to enter God's kingdom. You are suffering for his kingdom.

⁶God is fair. He will pay back trouble to those who give you trouble. ⁷He will help you who are troubled. And he will also help us.

All of those things will happen when the Lord Jesus appears from heaven. He will come in blazing fire. He will come with the angels who are given the power to do what God wants. ⁸He will punish those who don't know God. He will punish those who don't obey the good news about our Lord Jesus. ⁹They will be destroyed forever. They will be shut out of heaven. They will never see the glory of the Lord's power.

¹⁰All of those things will happen when he comes. On that day his glory will be seen in his holy people. Everyone who has believed will be amazed when they see him. That includes you, because you believed the witness we gave you.

¹¹Keeping this in mind, we never stop praying for you. Our God has chosen you. We pray that he will consider you worthy of his choice. We pray that by his power

he will make every good thing you have planned come true. We pray that he will make perfect all that you have done by faith. ¹²We pray this so that the name of our Lord Jesus will receive glory through what you have done. We also pray that you will receive glory through what he has done. We pray all these things in keeping with the grace of our God and the Lord Jesus Christ.

The Man of Sin

2

Brothers and sisters, we want to ask you something. It has to do with the coming of our Lord Jesus Christ. It concerns the time when we will go to be with him.

²What if you receive a prophecy, report or letter that is supposed to have come from us? What if it says that the day of the Lord has already come? If it does, we ask you not to become easily upset or alarmed.

³Don't let anyone trick you in any way. That day will not come until people rise up against God. It will not come until the man of sin appears. He is a marked man. He is sentenced to be destroyed. ⁴He will oppose everything that is called God. He will oppose everything that is worshiped. He will give himself power over everything. He will set himself up in God's temple. He will announce that he himself is God.

⁵Don't you remember? When I was with you, I used to tell you those things.

⁶Now you know what is holding the man of sin back. He is held back so that he can make his appearance at the right time. ⁷The secret power of sin is already at work. But the one who now holds that power back will keep doing it until he is taken out of the way.

⁸Then the man of sin will appear. The Lord Jesus will overthrow him with the breath of his mouth. The glorious brightness of Jesus' coming will destroy the man of sin.

⁹The coming of the man of sin will be Satan's work. His work will be seen in all kinds of fake miracles, signs and wonders. ¹⁰It will be seen in every kind of evil that fools people who are dying. They are dying because they refuse to love the truth. The truth would save them. ¹¹So God will fool them completely. Then they will believe the lie. ¹²Many will not believe the truth. They will take pleasure in evil. They will be judged.

Stand Firm

¹³Brothers and sisters, we should al-

ways thank God for you. The Lord loves you. God chose you from the beginning. He wanted you to be saved. Salvation comes through the Holy Spirit's work. He makes people holy. It also comes through believing the truth. **14**He chose you to be saved by accepting the good news that we preach. And you will share in the glory of our Lord Jesus Christ.

15Brothers and sisters, stand firm. Hold on to what we taught you. We passed our teachings on to you by what we preached and wrote.

16Our Lord Jesus Christ and God our Father loved us. By his grace God gave us comfort that will last forever. The hope he gave us is good.

May our Lord Jesus Christ and God our Father **17**comfort your hearts. May they make you strong in every good thing you do and say.

Paul Asks for Prayer

3 Finally, brothers and sisters, pray for us. Pray that the Lord's message will spread quickly. Pray that others will honor it just as you did. **2**And pray that we will be saved from sinful and evil people. Not everyone is a believer.

3But the Lord is faithful. He will strengthen you. He will guard you from the evil one.

4We trust in the Lord. So we are sure that you are doing the things we tell you to do. And we are sure that you will keep on doing them.

5May the Lord fill your hearts with God's love. May Christ give you the strength to go on.

Paul Warns Those Who Do Not Want to Work

6Brothers and sisters, here is a command we give you in the name of the Lord Jesus Christ. Keep away from every believer who doesn't want to work. Keep away from anyone who doesn't live up to the teaching you received from us.

7You know how you should follow our example. We worked when we were with you. **8**We didn't eat anyone's food without paying for it. In fact, it was just the opposite. We worked night and day. We worked very hard so that we wouldn't cause any expense to any of you.

9We worked, even though we have the right to receive help from you. We did it in order to be a model for you to follow. **10**Even when we were with you, we gave you a rule. We said, "Anyone who will not work will not eat."

11We hear that some people among you don't want to work. They aren't really busy. Instead, they are bothering others. **12**We belong to the Lord Jesus Christ. So we strongly command people like that to settle down. They have to earn the food they eat.

13Brothers and sisters, don't ever get tired of doing the right thing.

14Keep an eye on anyone who doesn't obey the directions in our letter. Watch that person closely. Have nothing to do with him. Then he will feel ashamed. **15**But don't think of him as an enemy. Instead, warn him as a brother or sister.

Final Greetings

16May the Lord who gives peace give you peace at all times and in every way. May the Lord be with all of you.

17I, Paul, write this greeting in my own handwriting. That's how I prove that I am the author of all my letters. I always do it that way.

18May the grace of our Lord Jesus Christ be with you all.

1 TIMOTHY

Paul writes this short letter to his friend, Timothy. Timothy is the young pastor at the church in Ephesus. Paul gives him instructions on how to organize the church and how to better lead the church. You can read 1 Timothy to find encouragement. You may be young, like Timothy, but you are important to God and he has work for you to do.

HERO IN THIS BOOK . . .

TIMOTHY
PAGE 1394

CHECK OUT THESE TRAITS OF A HERO . . .

TRUSTED
PAGE 1392

TRIES HARD
PAGE 1396

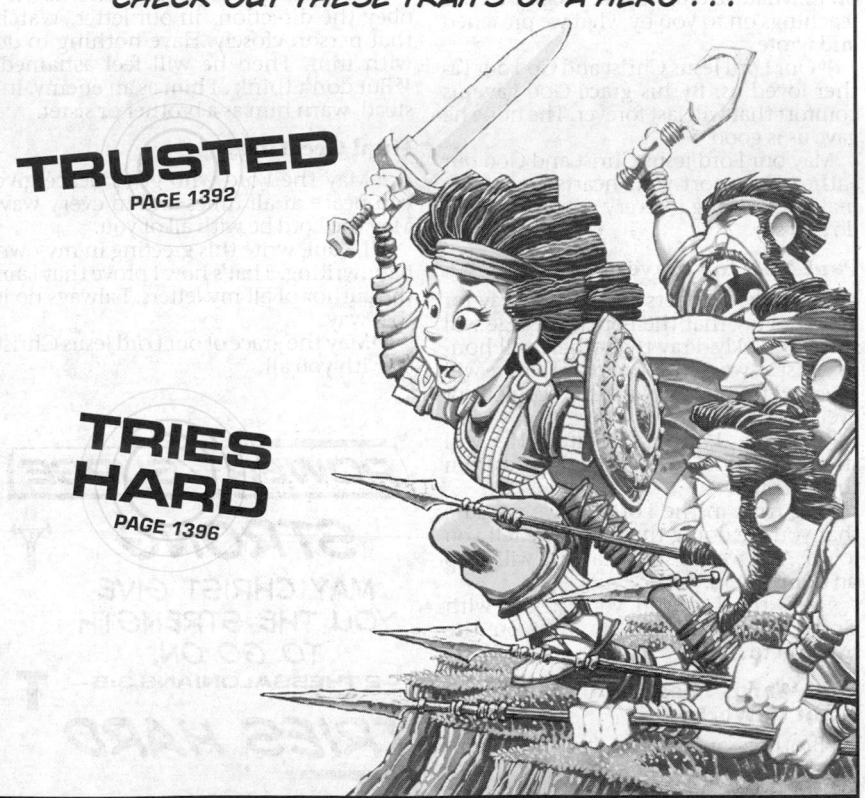

1 I, Paul, am writing this letter. I am an apostle of Christ Jesus, just as God our Savior commanded it. Christ Jesus also commanded it. We have put our hope in him.

2Timothy, I am sending you this letter. You are my true son in the faith.

May God the Father and Christ Jesus our Lord give you grace, mercy and peace.

Paul Warns Against Certain Teachers of the Law

3Stay there in Ephesus. That is what I told you to do when I went into Macedonia. I want you to command certain people not to teach things that aren't true. 4Command them not to spend their time on stories that aren't completely true. They must not waste time on family histories that never end. Things like that cause people to argue instead of doing God's work. His work is done by faith.

5Love is the purpose of my command. Love comes from a pure heart. It comes from a good sense of what is right and wrong. It comes from faith that is honest and true.

6Some have wandered away from those teachings. They would rather talk about things that have no meaning. 7They want to be teachers of the law. And they are very sure about that law. But they don't know what they are talking about.

8We know that the law is good if it is used properly. 9We also know that the law isn't made for godly people. It is made for those who break the law. It is for those who refuse to obey. It is for ungodly and sinful people. It is for those who aren't holy and who don't believe. It is for those who kill their fathers or mothers. It is for murderers.

10It is for those who commit adultery. It is for those who have a twisted view of sex. It is for people who buy and sell slaves. It is for liars. It is for those who give witness to things that aren't true. And it is for anything else that is the opposite of true teaching.

11True teaching agrees with the glorious good news of the blessed God. He trusted me with that good news.

The Lord Pours Out His Grace on Paul

12I am thankful to Christ Jesus our Lord. He has given me strength. I thank him that he considered me faithful. And I thank him for appointing me to serve him.

13I used to speak evil things against Jesus. I tried to hurt his followers. I really pushed them around. But God showed me mercy anyway. I did those things without knowing any better. I wasn't a believer. 14Our Lord poured out more and more of his grace on me. Along with it came faith and love from Christ Jesus.

15Here is a saying that you can trust. It should be accepted completely. Christ Jesus came into the world to save sinners. And I am the worst sinner of all. 16But for that very reason, God showed me mercy. And I am the worst of sinners. He showed me mercy so that Christ Jesus could show that he is very patient. I was an example for those who would come to believe in him. Then they would receive eternal life.

17The eternal King will never die. He can't be seen. He is the only God. Give him honor and glory for ever and ever. Amen.

18My son Timothy, I give you these teachings. They are in keeping with the prophecies that were once made about you. By following them, you can fight the good fight. 19Then you will hold on to faith. You will hold on to a good sense of what is right and wrong.

Some have not accepted these teachings. By doing that, they have destroyed their faith. They are like a ship that has sunk. 20Hymenaeus and Alexander are among them. I have handed them over to Satan. That will teach them not to speak evil things against God.

POWER SURGE

FAITHFUL ()

I AM THANKFUL TO CHRIST JESUS OUR LORD. HE HAS GIVEN ME STRENGTH. I THANK HIM THAT HE CONSIDERED ME FAITHFUL. AND I THANK HIM FOR APPOINTING ME TO SERVE HIM.

— 1 TIMOTHY 1:12 —

THANKFUL

Directions for Worship

2 First, I want all of you to pray for everyone. Ask God to bless them. Give thanks for them.

2 Pray for kings. Pray for all who are in authority. Pray that we will live peaceful and quiet lives. And pray that we will be godly and holy.

3 That is good. It pleases God our Savior. **4** He wants everyone to be saved. He wants them to come to know the truth.

5 There is only one God. And there is only one go-between for God and human beings. He is the man Christ Jesus. **6** He gave himself to pay for the sins of every-one. That was a witness given by God at just the right time.

7 I was appointed to be a messenger and an apostle to preach the good news. I am telling the truth. I'm not lying. God appointed me to be a teacher of the true faith to those who aren't Jews.

8 I want men everywhere to pray. I want them to lift up holy hands. I don't want them to be angry when they pray. I don't want them to argue.

9 I also want women to dress simply. They should wear clothes that are right and proper. They shouldn't braid their hair. They shouldn't wear gold or pearls.

TRUSTED

1 TIMOTHY 3:11

They must be worthy of trust in everything.

A little two-year-old girl jumps from a counter into her daddy's arms. She trusted her daddy to catch her. A climber pulls on a rope held by a friend. He trusts his friend not to let go of the rope. You ride in your car down one side of the street. You trust the people coming from the other direction to stay on their side of the street. You trust God to bring the sun up every morning, to bring spring after winter, to take care of you every day.

Abraham knew he could trust God. God had promised to give him a son. Even when Abraham was an old man and his wife, Sarah, was an old woman—too old to have children—Abraham trusted God. His story is on page 18. A poor widow trusted God, too. She gave an offering, only two little coins, but it was all she had. She walked out of the temple with no money to live on. But she trusted God to take care of her. You can read this amazing woman's story on page 1207.

TRUSTED

God wants his people to be trustworthy, which means they can be trusted by others. When you tell someone you'll do something, you can be trusted to do it. The most trustworthy person of all is God himself. You can trust him no matter what. He'll always be who he says he is, and he will always do what he says he will do.

Go to page 1394 for the next Super Hero

They shouldn't spend too much on clothes. ¹⁰Instead, they should put on good works as if they were their clothes. That is proper for women who claim to worship God.

¹¹When a woman is learning, she should be quiet. She should follow the leaders in every way. ¹²I do not let women teach. I do not let them have authority over men. They must be quiet.

¹³Adam was made first. Then Eve was made. ¹⁴Adam was not the one who was tricked. The woman was tricked and became a sinner. ¹⁵Will women be saved by having children? Only if they keep on believing, loving, and leading a holy life in a proper way.

Leaders and Deacons

3 Here is a saying you can trust. If anyone wants to be a leader in the church, he wants to do a good work for God and people.

²A leader must be free from blame. He must be faithful to his wife. In anything he does, he must not go too far. He must control himself. He must be worthy of respect. He must welcome people into his home. He must be able to teach. ³He must not get drunk. He must not push people around. He must be gentle. He must not be a person who likes to argue. He must not love money.

POWER-SURGE

SELF-CONTROLLED

A LEADER MUST BE FREE FROM BLAME... IN ANYTHING HE DOES, HE MUST NOT GO TOO FAR. HE MUST CONTROL HIMSELF.
— 1 TIMOTHY 3:2 —

⁴He must manage his own family well. He must make sure that his children obey him and show him proper respect. ⁵Suppose someone doesn't know how to manage his own family. Then how can he take care of God's church?

⁶The leader must not be a new believer. If he is, he might become proud. Then he would be judged just like the devil.

⁷The leader must also be respected by those who are outside the church. Then he will not be put to shame. He will not fall into the devil's trap.

⁸Deacons also must be worthy of respect. They must be honest and true. They must not drink too much wine. They must not try to get money by cheating people. ⁹They must hold on to the deep truths of the faith. Even their own minds tell them to do that. ¹⁰First they must be tested. Then let them serve as deacons if there is nothing against them.

¹¹In the same way, their wives must be worthy of respect. They must not say things that harm others. In anything they do, they must not go too far. They must be worthy of trust in everything.

¹²A deacon must be faithful to his wife. He must manage his children and family well. ¹³Those who have served well earn the full respect of others. They also become more sure of their faith in Christ Jesus.

¹⁴I hope I can come to you soon. But now I am writing these directions to you. ¹⁵Then if I have to put off my visit, you will know how you should act in God's family. The family of God is the church of the living God. It is the pillar and foundation of the truth.

¹⁶There is no doubt that godliness is a great mystery.

Jesus appeared in a body.
The Holy Spirit proved that he was the Son of God.
He was seen by angels.
He was preached among the nations.
People in the world believed in him.
He was taken up to heaven in glory.

Directions for Timothy

4 The Holy Spirit clearly says that in the last days some people will leave the faith. They will follow spirits that will fool them. They will believe things that demons will teach them.

²Teachings like those come from liars who pretend to be what they are not. Their sense of what is right and wrong has been burned as if with a hot iron. ³They do not allow people to get married. They order them not to eat certain foods. But God created those foods. So people who believe and know the truth should receive them and give thanks for them.

⁴Everything God created is good. You shouldn't turn anything down. Instead, you should thank God for it. ⁵The word of God and prayer make it holy.

⁶Point these things out to the brothers

and sisters. Then you will serve Christ Jesus well. You were brought up in the truths of the faith. You received good teaching. You followed it.

7 Don't have anything to do with godless stories and silly tales. Instead, train yourself to be godly. 8 Training the body has some value. But being godly has value in every way. It promises help for the life you are now living and the life to come.

9 Here is a saying you can trust. You can accept it completely. 10 We work hard for it. Here is the saying. We have put our hope in the living God. He is the Savior of all people. Most of all he is the Savior of those who believe.

11 Command those things. Teach them. 12 Don't let anyone look down on you because you are young. Set an example for the believers in what you say and in how you live. Also set an example in how you love and in what you believe. Show the believers how to be pure.

13 Until I come, spend your time reading Scripture out loud to one another. Spend your time preaching and teaching.

TIMOTHY

1 TIMOTHY 4:12

Don't let anyone look down on you because you are young. Set an example for the believers in what you say and in how you live.

Timothy stood in the doorway of his house in Ephesus. He held a letter from Paul in his hands. Paul, the missionary Timothy worked with, had sent him to Ephesus to help the church. Timothy was the leader of the church in Ephesus even though he was younger than many of the people who went to that church.

TIMOTHY TOOK A BIG BREATH AND HELD IT. He loved Jesus and wanted to serve him. And he loved Paul and didn't want to disappoint him. But the work at the church was almost more than he could handle at times.

Opening the letter from Paul, Timothy began to read: "Don't let anyone look down on you because you are young." With a smile, Timothy raised his head. How like Paul that was. He knew Timothy and understood just how he felt. Paul's words encouraged Timothy to continue to work hard.

BE A TIMOTHY

Do you ever feel like Timothy? Like people don't take you seriously just because you're young? Being young has nothing to do with how much God loves you or wants to use you. He can use the very old *and* the very young. Including Timothy and including you!

TIMOTHY WAS YOUNG, BUT HE LOVED GOD AND SERVED HIM.

Go to page 1396 for the next Super Hero Trait

¹⁴Don't fail to use the gift the Holy Spirit gave you. He gave it to you through a message from God. It was given when the elders placed their hands on you.

¹⁵Keep on doing those things. Give them your complete attention. Then everyone will see how you are coming along. ¹⁶Be careful of how you live and what you believe. Never give up. Then you will save yourself and those who hear you.

POWER SURGE

BELIEVES ✝

BE CAREFUL OF HOW YOU LIVE AND WHAT YOU BELIEVE. NEVER GIVE UP.
— 1 TIMOTHY 4:16 —

TRIES HARD

Advice About Widows, Elders and Slaves

5 Don't tell an older man off. Make an appeal to him as if he were your father. Treat younger men as if they were your brothers. ²Treat older women as if they were your mothers. Treat younger women as if they were your sisters. Be completely pure in the way you treat them.

³Take care of the widows who really need help. ⁴But suppose a widow has children or grandchildren. They should first learn to put their faith into practice. They should care for their own family. In that way they will pay back their parents and grandparents. That pleases God.

⁵The widow who really needs help and is left all alone puts her hope in God. Night and day she keeps on praying. Night and day she asks God for help. ⁶But the widow who lives for pleasure is dead even while she is still living.

⁷Give those directions to the people also. Then no one can be blamed. ⁸Everyone should provide for his own relatives. Most of all, everyone should take care of his own family. If he doesn't, he has left the faith. He is worse than someone who doesn't believe.

⁹No widow should be put on the list of widows unless she is more than 60 years old. She must also have been faithful to her husband. ¹⁰She must be well known for the good things she does. That includes bringing up children. It includes inviting guests into her home. It includes washing the feet of God's people. It includes helping those who are in trouble. A widow should spend her time doing all kinds of good things.

¹¹Don't put younger widows on that kind of list. They might want pleasure more than they want Christ. Then they would want to get married again. ¹²If they do that, they will be judged. They have broken their first promise.

¹³Besides, they get into the habit of having nothing to do. They go around from house to house. They waste time. They talk about others. They bother people. They say things they shouldn't say.

¹⁴So here is the advice I give to younger widows. Get married. Have children. Take care of your own homes. Don't give the enemy the chance to tell lies about you. ¹⁵In fact, some have already turned away to follow Satan.

¹⁶Suppose a woman is a believer and has widows in her family. She should help them. She shouldn't let the church pay the expenses. Then the church can help the widows who really need it.

¹⁷The elders who do the church's work well are worth twice as much honor. That is true in a special ¹⁸way of elders who preach and teach. Scripture says, "Do not stop the ox from eating while it helps separate the grain from the straw." *(Deuteronomy 25:4)* Scripture also says, "Workers are worthy of their pay." *(Luke 10:7)*

¹⁹Don't believe a charge against an elder unless two or three witnesses bring it. ²⁰Elders who sin should be corrected in front of the other believers. That will be a warning to the others.

²¹I command you to follow those directions. I command you in the sight of God and Christ Jesus and the chosen angels. Treat everyone the same. Don't favor one person over another.

²²Don't be too quick to place your hands on others to set them apart to serve God. Don't take part in the sins of others. Keep yourself pure.

²³Stop drinking only water. If your stomach is upset, drink a little wine. It can also help the other sicknesses you often have.

²⁴The sins of some people are easy to see. They are already being judged. Others will be judged later. ²⁵In the same way, good works are easy to see. But even

good works that are hard to see can't stay hidden.

6 All who are forced to serve as slaves should consider their masters worthy of full respect. Then people will not speak evil things against God's name and against what we teach. ²Some slaves have masters who are believers. They shouldn't show less respect for their masters just because they are believers. Instead, they should serve them even better. That's because those who benefit from their service are believers. They are loved by them.

Teach the slaves those things. Try hard to get them to do them.

Love for Money

³Suppose someone teaches ideas that are false. He doesn't agree with the true teaching of our Lord Jesus Christ. He doesn't agree with godly teaching. ⁴People like that are proud. They don't understand anything. They like to argue more than they should. They can't agree about what words mean.

All of that results in wanting what others have. It causes fighting, harmful talk, and evil distrust. ⁵It stirs up trouble all the time among people whose minds are twisted by sin. The truth they once had has been taken away from them.

TRIES HARD

1 TIMOTHY 6:11

T

Try hard to do what is right and godly...Hold on to what you believe.

T

T

*G*od wants us all to do what is right. But that's not always easy, is it? Sometimes it's hard work to choose to do the right thing. That's why the Bible tells us to "try hard."

A little boy who was following Jesus one day did that (page 1227). When the people around him were hungry, he offered his lunch. Now, his little lunch was pretty puny for feeding over 5,000 people. He only had 5 loaves and 2 little fish. But his effort to help really paid off! Jesus took that little bitsy lunch and fed all those people with it. Trying hard is all the little boy had to do. Jesus did the rest. Then there's Timothy (page 1394). It seemed like no matter how hard he tried to do the right thing, people just thought he was too young and too inexperienced. In the verse you see above, Paul told him to just keep trying.

TRY HARD

Does it ever seem like no matter how hard you try to do something, you just can't get it right? You work all night on a school project and still get a poor grade. You try to please your mother and she still yells at you. Sometimes the only reward for trying hard is the very fact that you did try hard and you did do your best. And that's reason enough to keep on trying!

Go to page 1405 for the next Super Hero Trait

POWER-SURGE

CHEERFUL ✳

BE HAPPY WITH WHAT YOU HAVE.
— 1 TIMOTHY 6:6 —

They think they can get rich by being godly.

⁶You gain a lot when you live a godly life. But you must be happy with what you have. ⁷We didn't bring anything into the world. We can't take anything out of it. ⁸If we have food and clothing, we will be happy with that.

⁹People who want to get rich are tempted. They fall into a trap. They are tripped up by wanting many foolish and harmful things. Those who live like that are dragged down by what they do. They are destroyed and die.

¹⁰Love for money causes all kinds of evil. Some people want to get rich. They have wandered away from the faith. They have wounded themselves with many sorrows.

Paul Gives a Command to Timothy

¹¹But you are a man of God. Run away from all of those things. Try hard to do what is right and godly. Have faith, love and gentleness. Hold on to what you believe. ¹²Fight the good fight along with all other believers. Take hold of eternal life. You were chosen for it when you openly told others what you believe. Many witnesses heard you.

¹³God gives life to everything. Christ Jesus told the truth when he gave witness to Pontius Pilate. In the sight of God and Christ, I give you a command. ¹⁴Obey it until our Lord Jesus Christ appears. Obey it completely. Then no one can find fault with it or you.

¹⁵God will bring Jesus back at a time that pleases him. God is the blessed and only Ruler. He is the greatest King of all. He is the most powerful Lord of all. ¹⁶God is the only one who can't die. He lives in light that no one can get close to. No one has seen him. No one can see him.

Give honor and power to him forever. Amen.

¹⁷Command people who are rich in this world not to be proud. Tell them not to put their hope in riches. Wealth is so uncertain. Command those who are rich to put their hope in God. He richly provides us with everything to enjoy.

¹⁸Command the rich to do what is good. Tell them to be rich in doing good things. They must give freely. They must be willing to share. ¹⁹In that way they will put riches away for themselves. It will provide a firm basis for the next life. Then they will take hold of the life that really is life.

²⁰Timothy, guard what God has trusted you with. Turn away from godless chatter. Stay away from opposing ideas that are falsely called knowledge. ²¹Some people believe them. By doing that they have wandered away from the faith.

May God's grace be with you.

2 TIMOTHY

The book of 2 Timothy is a very personal letter from Paul to Timothy. Paul writes from prison in Rome. He knows his time on earth is almost over. He has important things to tell Timothy before he dies. He wants Timothy to continue to be strong in the faith. He gives Timothy practical advice about living as a Christian. As you read 2 Timothy, look for short, quick statements from Paul that will give you clear advice on how you should live.

CODE OF HONOR IN THIS BOOK . . .

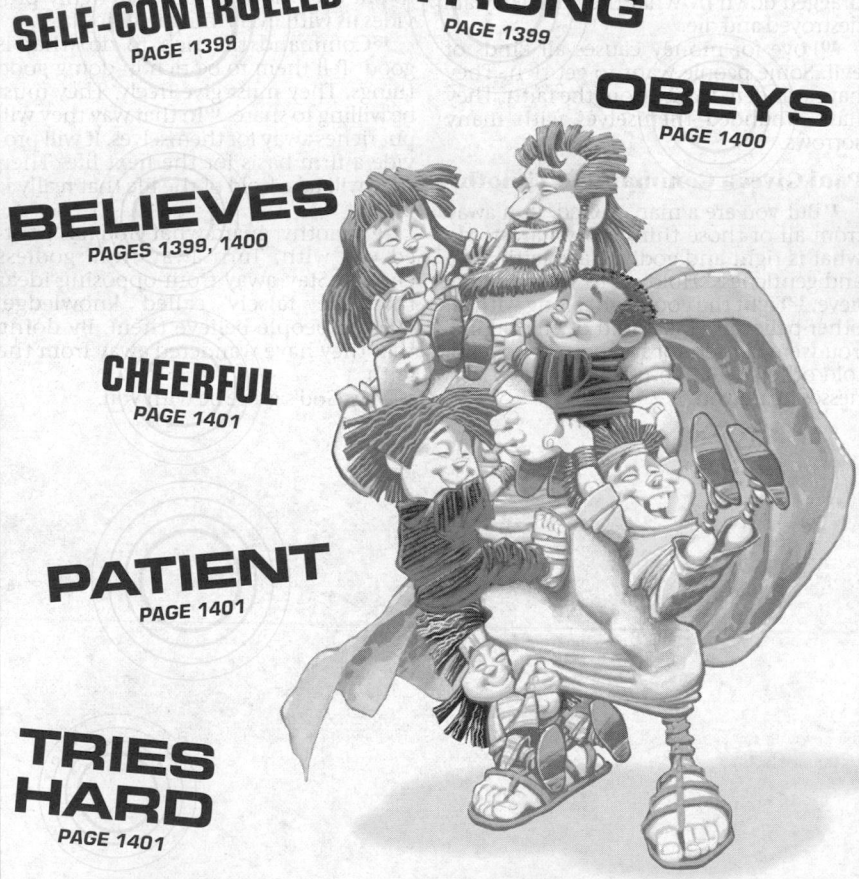

SELF-CONTROLLED
PAGE 1399

STRONG
PAGE 1399

OBEYS
PAGE 1400

BELIEVES
PAGES 1399, 1400

CHEERFUL
PAGE 1401

PATIENT
PAGE 1401

TRIES HARD
PAGE 1401

1 I, Paul, am writing this letter. I am an apostle of Christ Jesus just as God planned. He sent me to tell about the promise of life that is found in Christ Jesus.

²Timothy, I am sending you this letter. You are my dear son.

May God the Father and Christ Jesus our Lord give you grace, mercy and peace.

Paul Tells Timothy to Be Faithful

³I serve God, knowing that what I have done is right. That is how our people served him long ago. Night and day I thank God for you. Night and day I always remember you in my prayers.

⁴I remember your tears. I long to see you so that I can be filled with joy. ⁵I remember your honest and true faith. It was alive first in your grandmother Lois and in your mother Eunice. And I am certain that it is now alive in you also.

⁶That is why I remind you to help God's gift grow, just as a small spark grows into a fire. God put his gift in you when I placed my hands on you.

⁷God didn't give us a spirit that makes us weak and fearful. He gave us a spirit that gives us power and love. It helps us control ourselves.

⁸So don't be ashamed to give witness about our Lord. And don't be ashamed of me, his prisoner. Instead, join with me as I suffer for the good news. God's power will help us do that.

⁹God has saved us. He has chosen us to live a holy life. It wasn't because of anything we have done. It was because of his

POWER-SURGE

SELF-CONTROLLED

GOD DIDN'T GIVE US A SPIRIT THAT MAKES US WEAK AND FEARFUL. HE GAVE US A SPIRIT THAT GIVES US POWER AND LOVE. IT HELPS US CONTROL OURSELVES.
— 2 TIMOTHY 1:7 —

STRONG

POWER-SURGE

BELIEVES †

I KNOW THE ONE I HAVE BELIEVED IN.
— 2 TIMOTHY 1:12 —

own purpose and grace. Through Christ Jesus, God gave us that grace even before time began. ¹⁰It has now been made known through the coming of our Savior, Christ Jesus. He has destroyed death. Because of the good news, he has brought life out into the light. That life never dies.

¹¹I was appointed to announce the good news. I was appointed to be an apostle and a teacher. ¹²That's why I'm suffering the way I am. But I'm not ashamed. I know the One I have believed in. I am sure he is able to take care of what I have given him. I can trust him with it until the day he returns as judge.

¹³Follow what you heard from me as the pattern of true teaching. Follow it with faith and love because you belong to Christ Jesus. ¹⁴Guard the truth of the good news that you were trusted with. Guard it with the help of the Holy Spirit who lives in us.

¹⁵You know that all the believers in Asia Minor have deserted me. They include Phygelus and Hermogenes.

¹⁶May the Lord show mercy to all who live in the house of Onesiphorus. He often cheered me up. He was not ashamed that I was being held by chains. ¹⁷In fact, it was just the opposite. When he was in Rome, he looked everywhere for me. At last he found me.

¹⁸May Onesiphorus find mercy from the Lord on the day Jesus returns as judge. You know very well how many ways Onesiphorus helped me in Ephesus.

2 My son, be strong in the grace that is found in Christ Jesus. ²You have heard me teach in front of many witnesses. Pass on to men you can trust the things you've heard me say. Then they will be able to teach others also. ³Like a good soldier of Christ Jesus, share in the hard times with us.

⁴A soldier does not take part in things that don't have anything to do with the army. He wants to please his commanding officer. ⁵In the same way, anyone who takes part in a sport doesn't receive the winner's crown unless he plays by the

rules. **6**The farmer who works hard should be the first to receive a share of the crops. **7**Think about what I'm saying. The Lord will help you understand what all of it means.

8Remember Jesus Christ. He came from David's family line. He was raised from the dead. That is my good news. **9**I am suffering for it. I have even been put in chains like someone who has committed a crime. But God's word is not held back by chains.

10So I put up with everything for the good of God's chosen people. Then they also can be saved. Christ Jesus saves them. He gives them glory that will last forever. **11**Here is a saying you can trust.

If we died with him,
we will also live with him.
12If we don't give up,
we will also rule with him.
If we say we don't know him,
he will also say he doesn't know us.
13Even if we are not faithful,
he will remain faithful.
He must be true to himself.

A Worker Who Pleases God

14Keep reminding the believers of those things. While God is watching, warn them not to argue about words. That doesn't have any value. It only destroys those who listen.

15Do your best to please God. Be a worker who doesn't need to be ashamed. Teach the message of truth correctly.

16Stay away from godless chatter. Those who take part in it will become more and more ungodly. **17**Their teaching will spread like a deadly sickness.

Hymenaeus and Philetus are two of those teachers. **18**They have wandered away from the truth. They say that the time when people will rise from the dead has already come. They destroy the faith of some people.

19But God's solid foundation stands firm. Here is the message written on it. "The Lord knows who his own people are." *(Numbers 16:5)* Also, "All who say they believe in the Lord must turn away from evil."

20In a large house there are things made out of gold and silver. But there are also things made out of wood and clay. Some have honorable purposes. Others do not. **21**Suppose someone stays away from what is not honorable. Then the Master will be able to use him for honor-able purposes. He will be made holy. He will be ready to do any good work.

22Run away from the evil things that young people long for. Try hard to do what is right. Have faith, love and peace. Do these things together with those who call on the Lord from a pure heart. **23**Don't have anything to do with arguing. It is dumb and foolish. You know it only leads to fights.

24Anyone who serves the Lord must not fight. Instead, he must be kind to everyone. He must be able to teach. He must not hold anything against anyone. **25**He must gently teach those who oppose him.

Maybe God will give a change of heart to those who are against you. That will lead them to know the truth. **26**Maybe they will come to their senses. Maybe they will escape the devil's trap. He has taken them prisoner to do what he wanted.

Terrible Times in the Last Days

3 Here is what I want you to know. There will be terrible times in the last days. **2**People will love themselves. They will love money. They will brag and be proud. They will tear others down. They will not obey their parents. They won't be thankful or holy. **3**They won't love others. They won't forgive others. They will tell lies about people. They will be out of control. They will be wild. They will hate what is good.

4They will turn against their friends. They will act without thinking. They will think they are better than others. They will love what pleases them instead of loving God. **5**They will act as if they were serving God. But what they do will show that they have turned their backs on God's power. Have nothing to do with those people.

POWER-SURGE

BELIEVES ✝

ALL WHO SAY THEY BELIEVE IN THE LORD MUST TURN AWAY FROM EVIL.
— 2 TIMOTHY 2:19 — ✔

OBEYS

POWER—SURGE

CHEERFUL ✳

CHEER [PEOPLE] UP
WITH WORDS OF HOPE.
BE VERY PATIENT.
— 2 TIMOTHY 4:2 — P

PATIENT

6They are the kind who worm their way into the homes of silly women. They get control over them. Women like that are loaded down with sins. They give in to all kinds of evil longings. **7**They are always learning. But they never come to know the truth.

8Jannes and Jambres opposed Moses. In the same way, the teachers I'm talking about oppose the truth. Their minds are twisted. As far as the faith is concerned, God doesn't accept them. **9**They won't get very far. Just like Jannes and Jambres, their foolish ways will be clear to everyone.

Paul Gives a Command to Timothy

10But you know all about my teaching. You know how I live and what I live for. You know about my faith and love. You know how patient I am. You know I haven't given up. **11**You know that I was treated badly. You know that I suffered greatly. You know what kinds of things happened to me in Antioch, Iconium and Lystra. You know how badly I have been treated. But the Lord saved me from all of my troubles.

12In fact, everyone who wants to live a godly life in Christ Jesus will be treated badly. **13**Evil people and pretenders will go from bad to worse. They will fool others, and others will fool them.

14But I want you to continue to follow what you have learned. Don't give up what you are sure of. You know the people you learned it from. **15**You have known the Holy Scriptures ever since you were a little child. They are able to teach you how to be saved by believing in Christ Jesus.

16God has breathed life into all of Scripture. It is useful for teaching us what is true. It is useful for correcting our mistakes. It is useful for making our lives whole again. It is useful for training us to

do what is right. **17**By using Scripture, a man of God can be completely prepared to do every good thing.

4 I give you a command in the sight of God and Christ Jesus. Christ will judge the living and the dead. Because he and his kingdom are coming, here is the command I give you. **2**Preach the word. Be ready to serve God in good times and bad. Correct people's mistakes. Warn them. Cheer them up with words of hope. Be very patient as you do these things. Teach them carefully.

3The time will come when people won't put up with true teaching. Instead, they will try to satisfy their own longings. They will gather a large number of teachers around them. The teachers will say what the people want to hear. **4**The people will turn their ears away from the truth. They will turn to stories that aren't completely true.

5But I want you to keep your head no matter what happens. Don't give up when times are hard. Work to spread the good news. Do everything God has given you to do.

6I am already being poured out like a drink offering. The time has come for me to leave.

7I have fought the good fight. I have finished the race. I have kept the faith. **8**Now there is a crown waiting for me. It is given to those who are right with God. The Lord, who judges fairly, will give it to me on the day he returns. He will not give it only to me. He will also give it to all those who are longing for him to return.

Personal Words

9Do your best to come to me quickly.

10Demas has deserted me. He has gone to Thessalonica. He left me because he loved this world. Crescens has gone to Galatia. Titus has gone to Dalmatia. **11**Only Luke is with me. Get Mark and bring him with you. He helps me in my work for the Lord. **12**I sent Tychicus to Ephesus.

13When you come, bring my coat. I left it with Carpus at Troas. Also bring my

POWER—SURGE

TRIES HARD T

DON'T GIVE UP WHEN
TIMES ARE HARD.
— 2 TIMOTHY 4:5 —

scrolls. Most of all, bring the ones made out of animal skins.

¹⁴Remember Alexander, the one who works with metal? He did me a great deal of harm. The Lord will pay him back for what he has done. ¹⁵You too should watch out for him. He strongly opposed our message.

¹⁶The first time I was put on trial, no one came to help me. Everyone deserted me. I hope they will be forgiven for it.

¹⁷The Lord stood at my side. He gave me the strength to preach the whole message. Then all those who weren't Jews heard it. I was saved from the lion's mouth. ¹⁸The Lord will save me from every evil attack. He will bring me safely to his heavenly kingdom.

Give him glory for ever and ever. Amen.

Final Greetings

¹⁹Greet Priscilla and Aquila. Greet those who live in the house of Onesiphorus.

²⁰Erastus stayed in Corinth. I left Trophimus sick in Miletus.

²¹Do your best to get here before winter.

Eubulus greets you. So do Pudens, Linus, Claudia and all the brothers.

²²May the Lord be with your spirit. May God's grace be with you.

TITUS

Titus is the pastor of a church on the island of Crete. The church has problems. False teachers and arguments are dividing the church. Paul writes this letter to Titus to help him deal with these problems. As you read Titus, you'll discover what kind of life church leaders should live. You'll also find valuable insight on how the faith of believers should correct arguments and fights in the church.

CHECK OUT THIS TRAIT OF A HERO . . .

CHEERFUL
PAGE 1405

1 I, Paul, am writing this letter. I serve God. I am an apostle of Jesus Christ. God sent me to help his chosen people believe in Christ. I have been sent to help them understand the truth that leads to godly living. **2** Faith and understanding rest on the hope of eternal life. Before time began, God promised to give that life. And he does not lie. **3** At just the right time he made his word plain. He did it through the preaching that he trusted me with. God our Savior has commanded all those things.

4 Titus, I am sending you this letter. You are my true son in the faith we share.

May God the Father and Christ Jesus our Savior give you grace and peace.

The Work of Titus on Crete

5 I left you on the island of Crete. There were some things that hadn't been finished. You needed to sort them out. You also had to appoint elders in every town. I told you how to do it.

6 An elder must be without blame. He must be faithful to his wife. His children must be believers. They must not give anyone a reason to say that they are wild and don't obey.

7 A church leader is trusted with God's work. That's why he must be without blame. He must not look after only his own interests. He must not get angry easily. He must not get drunk. He must not push people around. He must not try to get money by cheating people.

8 Instead, he must welcome people into his home. He must love what is good. He must control his mind and feelings. He must do what is right. He must be holy. He must control what his body longs for. **9** The message as it has been taught can be trusted. He must hold firmly to it. Then he will be able to use true teaching to comfort others and build them up. He will be able to prove that people who oppose it are wrong.

10 Many people refuse to obey God. All they do is talk a lot. They try to fool others. No one does these things more than the circumcision group. **11** They must be stopped. They are destroying entire families. They are teaching things they shouldn't. They do it to get money by cheating people.

12 Even one of their own prophets has said, "People from Crete are always liars. They are evil beasts. They don't want to work. They live only to eat." **13** What I have just said is true. So give them a strong

warning. Then they will understand the faith correctly. **14** They will pay no attention to Jewish stories that aren't completely true. They won't listen to the commands of those who turn away from the truth.

15 To people who are pure, all things are pure. But to those who have twisted minds and don't believe, nothing is pure. In fact, their minds and their sense of what is right and wrong are twisted. **16** They claim to know God. But their actions show they don't know him. They are hated by God. They refuse to obey him. They aren't fit to do anything good.

Teaching God's People

2 What you teach must agree with true teaching. **2** Tell the older men that in anything they do, they must not go too far. They must be worthy of respect. They must control themselves. They must have true faith. They must love others. They must not give up.

3 In the same way, teach the older women to lead a holy life. They must not tell lies about others. They must not let wine control them. Instead, they must teach what is good. **4** Then they can train

SELF-CONTROLLED

A CHURCH LEADER IS TRUSTED WITH GOD'S WORK. THAT'S WHY HE MUST BE WITHOUT BLAME...

[A LEADER] MUST LOVE WHAT IS GOOD. HE MUST CONTROL HIS MIND AND FEELINGS. HE MUST DO WHAT IS RIGHT. HE MUST BE HOLY. HE MUST CONTROL WHAT HIS BODY LONGS FOR.

— TITUS 1:7-8 —

TRUSTED

the younger women to love their husbands and children.

5The younger women must control themselves. They must be pure. They must take good care of their homes. They must be kind. They must follow the lead of their husbands. Then no one will be able to speak evil things against God's word.

6In the same way, help the young men to control themselves. **7**Do what is good. Set an example for them in everything. When you teach, be honest and serious. **8**No one can question the truth. So teach what is true. Then those who oppose you will be ashamed. That's because they will have nothing bad to say about us.

9Teach slaves to obey their masters in everything they do. Tell them to try to please their masters. They must not talk back to them. **10**They must not steal from them. Instead, they must show that they can be trusted completely. Then they will make the teaching about God our Savior appealing in every way.

11God's saving grace has appeared to all people. **12**It teaches us to say no to godless ways and sinful longings. We must control ourselves. We must do what is right. We must lead godly lives in today's world. **13**That's how we should live as we wait for the blessed hope God has given us.

We are waiting for Jesus Christ to appear in all his glory. He is our great God and Savior. **14**He gave himself for us. By doing that, he set us free from all evil. He wanted to make us pure. He wanted us to

CHEERFUL

TITUS 2:15

Cheer people up and give them hope.

*D*o you ever wake up in the morning feeling kind of crabby? Grouchy? Just not happy? Your mom says, "Good morning!" And you frown at her. Your little sister smiles and laughs while she's eating breakfast. And you wish she'd just be quiet.

There are always reasons to be grouchy. But there are always reasons to be cheerful, too. Two old people, Simeon and Anna, found a good reason to be cheerful. You'll find their stories on pages 1177 and 1179. Both Simeon and Anna went to the temple every day. They hoped to some day see Jesus. Well, they did see him . . . when he was still a little baby! They both laughed and praised God. Anna and Simeon were happy and cheerful.

BE CHEERFUL

What do you do when you wake up feeling grouchy? You can *do* something to make yourself feel better, you know. Instead of waiting for your feelings to change, you can change your feelings. When you're feeling out of sorts, instead of thinking about bad things, think about good things. Even on grouchy days, you can think of good things God has done. Then maybe you won't feel so grouchy anymore!

Go to page 1414 for the next Super Hero Trait

be his very own people. He wanted us to long to do what is good.

15Those are the things you should teach. Cheer people up and give them hope. Correct them with full authority. Don't let anyone look down on you.

Do What Is Good

3 Remind God's people to obey rulers and authorities. Remind them to be ready to do what is good. 2Tell them not to speak evil things against anyone. Remind them to live in peace. They must consider the needs of others. They must be kind and gentle toward all people.

3At one time we too acted like fools. We didn't obey God. We were tricked. We were controlled by all kinds of longings and pleasures. We were full of evil. We wanted what belongs to others. People hated us, and we hated one another.

4But the kindness and love of God our Savior appeared. 5He saved us. It wasn't because of the good things we had done. It was because of his mercy. He saved us by washing away our sins. We were born again. The Holy Spirit gave us new life.

6God poured out the Spirit on us freely because of what Jesus Christ our Savior has done. 7His grace made us right with God. So now we have received the hope of eternal life as God's children.

8You can trust that saying. Those things are important. Treat them that way. Then those who have trusted in God will be careful to commit themselves to doing what is good. Those things are excellent. They are for the good of everyone.

9But keep away from foolish disagreements. Don't argue about family histories. Don't make trouble. Don't fight about what the law teaches. Don't argue about things like that. It doesn't do any good. It doesn't help anyone.

10Warn anyone who tries to get believers to take sides and separate into their own little groups. Warn him more than once. After that, have nothing to do with him. 11You can be sure that someone like that is twisted and sinful. His own actions judge him.

Final Words

12I will send Artemas or Tychicus to you. Then do your best to come to me at Nicopolis. I've decided to spend the winter there.

13Do everything you can to help Zenas the lawyer and Apollos. Send them on their way. See that they have everything they need.

14Our people must learn to commit themselves to doing what is good. Then they will be able to provide for the daily needs of others. If they do that, their lives won't turn out to be useless.

15Everyone who is with me sends you greetings. Greet those who love us in the faith.

May God's grace be with you all.

PHILEMON

Philemon is a beautiful little book about forgiveness. Paul writes to Philemon to ask him to forgive his slave for running away. Paul met Philemon's runaway slave and led him to Christ. Now Paul is sending the slave back to his master and asking the master to forgive. When you read this little book, remember how important it is for you to forgive others and, when you've done something wrong, to ask for forgiveness.

CODE OF HONOR IN THIS BOOK . . .

THANKFUL
PAGE 1408

CHEERFUL
PAGE 1408

LOVING
PAGE 1408

¹I, Paul, am writing this letter. I am a prisoner because of Christ Jesus. Our brother Timothy joins me in writing.

Philemon, we are sending you this letter. You are our dear friend. You work together with us. ²We are also sending it to our sister Apphia and to Archippus. He is a soldier of Christ together with us. And we are sending it to the church that meets in your home.

³May God our Father and the Lord Jesus Christ give you grace and peace.

Paul Prays and Gives Thanks

⁴I always thank my God when I remember you in my prayers. ⁵That's because I hear about your faith in the Lord Jesus. I hear about your love for all of God's people. ⁶I pray that you will be active in sharing what you believe. Then you will completely understand every good thing we have in Christ.

⁷Your love has given me great joy. It has cheered me up. My brother, you have renewed the hearts of God's people.

Paul Makes an Appeal for Onesimus

⁸Because of the authority Christ has given me, I could be bold. I could order you to do what you should do anyway. ⁹But I make my appeal to you on the basis of our love for each other.

I, Paul, am an old man. I am now also a prisoner because of Christ Jesus. ¹⁰I make an appeal to you for my son Onesimus. He became a son to me while I was being held by chains. ¹¹Before that, he was useless to you. But now he has become useful to you and to me.

¹²I'm sending Onesimus back to you. My very heart goes with him. ¹³I would have liked to keep him with me. Then he could have taken your place in helping me while I'm being held by chains because of the good news. ¹⁴But I didn't want to do anything unless you agreed. Any favor you do must be done because you want to do it, not because you have to.

¹⁵Onesimus was separated from you for a little while. Maybe that was so you could have him back for good. ¹⁶You could have him back not as a slave. Instead, he would be better than a slave. He would be a dear brother. He is very dear to me. But he is even more dear to you, both as a man and as a brother in the Lord.

¹⁷Do you think of me as a believer who works together with you? Then welcome Onesimus as you would welcome me. ¹⁸Has he done anything wrong to you? Does he owe you anything? Then charge it to me. ¹⁹I'll pay it back. I, Paul, am writing this with my own hand. I won't even mention that you owe me your very life.

²⁰My brother, I wish I could receive some benefit from you because we both belong to the Lord. Renew my heart. We know that Christ is the one who really renews it. ²¹I'm sure you will obey. So I'm writing to you. I know you will do even more than I ask.

²²There is one more thing. Have a guest room ready for me. I hope I can return to all of you in answer to your prayers.

²³Epaphras sends you greetings. Together with me, he is a prisoner because of Christ Jesus. ²⁴Mark, Aristarchus, Demas and Luke work together with me. They also send you greetings. ²⁵May the grace of the Lord Jesus Christ be with your spirit.

POWER-SURGE

CHEERFUL ✳

YOUR LOVE HAS GIVEN ME GREAT JOY.
— PHILEMON 7 — ♥

LOVING

POWER-SURGE

THANKFUL ♣

I ALWAYS THANK MY GOD WHEN I REMEMBER YOU IN MY PRAYERS.
— PHILEMON 4 —

HEBREWS

The book of Hebrews is written to encourage the Hebrew Christians not to give up. They are being persecuted and are tempted to go back to the Old Testament religion. The writer of Hebrews wants them to remember that only Christ can save them. Read Hebrews to find out how the Old Testament men and women and children of faith didn't quit, even when they suffered. You'll be encouraged to keep on growing in your faith in God and his Son Jesus.

CHECK OUT THIS TRAIT OF A HERO . . .

FAITHFUL

PAGE 1414

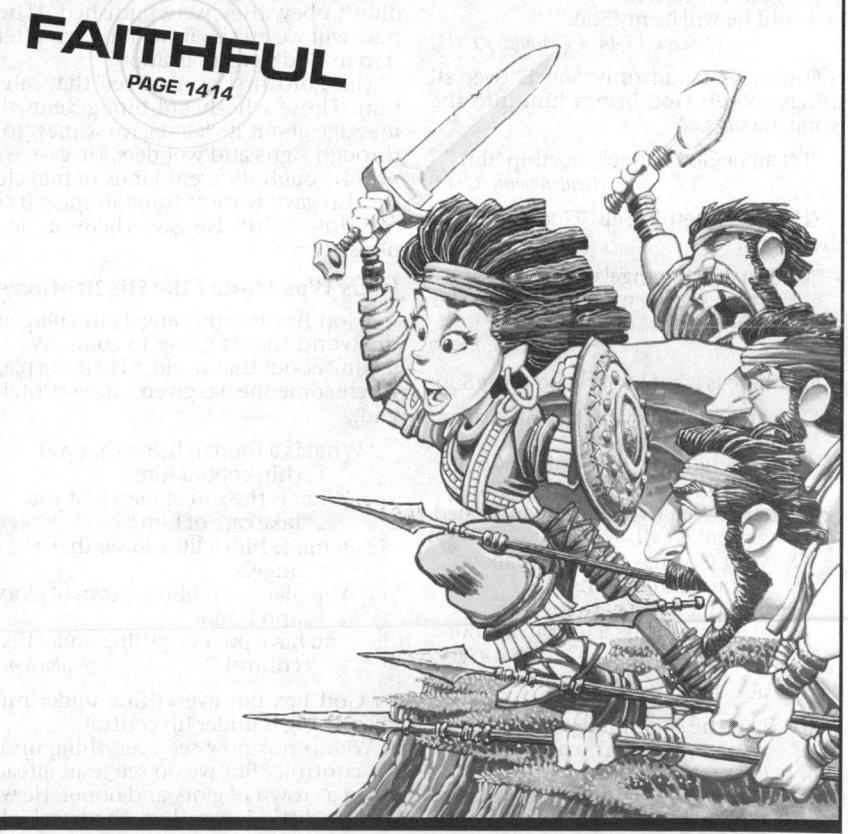

The Son Is Greater Than the Angels

1 In the past, God spoke to our people through the prophets. He spoke at many times. He spoke in different ways. ²But in these last days, he has spoken to us through his Son. He is the one whom God appointed to receive all things. God made everything through him. ³The Son is the gleaming brightness of God's glory. He is the exact likeness of God's being. He uses his powerful word to hold all things together. He provided the way for people to be made pure from sin. Then he sat down at the right hand of the King, the Majesty in heaven. ⁴So he became higher than the angels. The name he received is more excellent than theirs.

⁵God never said to any of the angels,

"You are my Son.
Today I have become your Father."
　　　　　　　　　　(Psalm 2:7)

Or,

"I will be his Father.
And he will be my Son."
　(2 Samuel 7:14; 1 Chronicles 17:13)

⁶God's first and only Son is over all things. When God brings him into the world, he says,

"Let all of God's angels worship him."
　　　　　　　(Deuteronomy 32:43)

⁷Here is something else God says about the angels.

"God makes his angels to be like winds.
He makes those who serve him to be like flashes of lightning."
　　　　　　　　　(Psalm 104:4)

⁸But here is what he says about the Son.

"You are God. Your throne will last for ever and ever.
Your kingdom will be ruled by what is right.
⁹ You have loved what is right and hated what is evil.
So your God has placed you above your companions.
He has filled you with joy by pouring the sacred oil on your head."　　　*(Psalm 45:6,7)*

¹⁰He also says,

"Lord, in the beginning you made the earth secure. You placed it on its foundations.
The heavens are the work of your hands.

¹¹They will pass away. But you remain.
They will all wear out like a piece of clothing.
¹²You will roll them up like a robe.
They will be changed as a person changes clothes.
But you remain the same.
Your years will never end."
　　　　　　　　(Psalm 102:25–27)

¹³God never said to an angel,

"Sit at my right hand
until I put your enemies
under your control."　　*(Psalm 110:1)*

¹⁴All angels are spirits who serve. God sends them to serve those who will receive salvation.

A Warning to Pay Attention

2 So we must pay more careful attention to what we have heard. Then we will not drift away from it. ²Even the message God spoke through angels had to be obeyed. Every time people broke the Law, they were punished. Every time they didn't obey, they were punished. ³Then how will we escape if we don't pay attention to God's great salvation?

The Lord first announced that salvation. Those who heard him gave us the message about it. ⁴God gave witness to it through signs and wonders. He gave witness through different kinds of miracles. He also gave witness through the gifts of the Holy Spirit. He gave them out as it pleased him.

Jesus Was Made Like His Brothers

⁵God has not put angels in charge of the world that is going to come. We are talking about that world. ⁶There is a place where someone has given witness to it. He said,

"What is a human being that you think about him?
What is the son of man that you take care of him?
⁷ You made him a little lower than the angels.
You placed on him a crown of glory and honor.
⁸ You have put everything under his control."　　　　*(Psalm 8:4–6)*

So God has put everything under him. Everything is under his control.

We do not now see everything under his control. ⁹But we do see Jesus already given a crown of glory and honor. He was made a little lower than the angels. He suffered death. By the grace of God, he tasted death for everyone. That is why he was given his crown.

¹⁰God has made everything. He has acted in exactly the right way. He is bringing his many sons and daughters to share in his glory. To do so, he has made the One who saved them perfect because of his sufferings.

¹¹The One who makes people holy and the people he makes holy belong to the same family. So Jesus is not ashamed to call them his brothers and sisters. ¹²He says,

"I will announce your name to my
    brothers and sisters.
I will sing your praises among those
    who worship you." *(Psalm 22:22)*

¹³Again he says,

"I will put my trust in him." *(Isaiah 8:17)*

And again he says,

"Here I am. Here are the children God
    has given me." *(Isaiah 8:18)*

¹⁴Those children have bodies made out of flesh and blood. So Jesus became human like them in order to die for them. By doing that, he could destroy the one who rules over the kingdom of death. I'm talking about the devil. ¹⁵Jesus could set people free who were afraid of death. All their lives they were held as slaves by that fear. ¹⁶It is certainly Abraham's children that he helps. He doesn't help angels. ¹⁷So he had to be made like his brothers in every way. Then he could serve God as a kind and faithful high priest. And then he could pay for the sins of the people by dying for them. ¹⁸He himself suffered when he was tempted. Now he is able to help others who are being tempted.

Jesus Is Greater Than Moses

3 Holy brothers and sisters, God chose you to be his people. So keep thinking about Jesus. He is our apostle. He is our high priest. We believe in him.

²Moses was faithful in everything he did in the house of God. In the same way, Jesus was faithful to the One who appointed him.

³The person who builds a house has greater honor than the house itself. In the same way, Jesus has been found worthy of greater honor than Moses. ⁴Every house is built by someone. But God is the builder of everything.

⁵Moses was faithful as one who serves in the house of God. He gave witness to what God would say in days to come. ⁶But Christ is faithful as a son over God's house. We are his house if we continue to come boldly to God. We must also hold on to the hope we take pride in.

A Warning Against Unbelief

⁷The Holy Spirit says,

"Listen to his voice today.
⁸   If you hear it, don't be stubborn.
You were stubborn when you opposed
    me.
    You did that when you were put to
        the test in the desert.
⁹There your people of long ago put me
        to the test.
    For 40 years they saw what I did.
¹⁰That is why I was angry with them.
    I said, 'Their hearts are always going
        down the wrong path.
    They have not known my ways.'
¹¹So in my anger I took an oath.
    I said, 'They will never enjoy the rest
        I planned for them.' "
                            (Psalm 95:7–11)

¹²Brothers and sisters, make sure that none of you has a sinful heart. Do not let an unbelieving heart turn you away from the living God. ¹³But build one another up every day. Do it as long as there is still time. Then none of you will become stubborn. You won't be fooled by sin's tricks. ¹⁴We belong to Christ if we hold firmly to the faith we had at first. But we must hold to it until the end. ¹⁵It has just been said,

"Listen to his voice today.
    If you hear it, don't be stubborn.
You were stubborn when you opposed
    me." *(Psalm 95:7,8)*

¹⁶Who were those who heard and refused to obey? Weren't they all the people Moses led out of Egypt? ¹⁷Who was God angry with for 40 years? Wasn't it with those who sinned? They died in the desert. ¹⁸What people did God promise with an oath that they would never enjoy the rest he planned for them? Wasn't it those who didn't obey? ¹⁹So we see that they weren't able to enter. That's because they didn't believe.

God's People Enter His Sabbath Rest

4 God's promise of enjoying his rest still stands. So be careful that none of you fails to receive it.

²The good news was preached to our

people long ago. It has also been preached to us. The message they heard didn't have any value for them. They didn't combine it with faith. 3Now we who have believed enjoy that rest. God said,

"When I was angry I took an oath.
    I said, 'They will never enjoy the rest
        I planned for them.' "
(Psalm 95:11)

Ever since God created the world, his work has been finished. 4Somewhere he spoke about the seventh day. He said, "On the seventh day God rested from all his work." *(Genesis 2:2)* 5In the part of Scripture I talked about earlier God said, "They will never enjoy the rest I planned for them." *(Psalm 95:11)* 6It is still true that some will enjoy that rest. But those who had the good news preached to them earlier didn't go in. That was because they didn't obey. 7So God again chose a certain day. He named it Today. He did that when he spoke through David a long time later. As it was said earlier,

"Listen to his voice today.
    If you hear it, don't be stubborn."
(Psalm 95:7,8)

8Suppose Joshua had given them rest. If he had, God would not have spoken later about another day. 9So there is still a Sabbath rest for God's people. 10God rested from his work. Those who enjoy God's rest also rest from their work. 11So let us make every effort to enjoy that rest. Then no one will fall into sin by following the example of those who didn't obey God.

12The word of God is living and active. It is sharper than any sword that has two edges. It cuts deep enough to separate soul from spirit. It can separate joints from bones. It judges the thoughts and purposes of the heart. 13Nothing God created is hidden from him. His eyes see everything. He will hold us accountable for everything we do.

Jesus Is the Great High Priest

14We have a great high priest. He has gone up into the heavens. He is Jesus the Son of God. So let us hold firmly to what we say we believe.

15We have a high priest who can feel it when we are weak and hurting. We have a high priest who has been tempted in every way, just as we are. But he did not sin. 16So let us boldly approach the throne of grace. Then we will receive mercy. We will find grace to help us when we need it.

5 Every high priest is chosen from among men. He is appointed to act for them in everything that has to do with God. He offers gifts and sacrifices for their sins. 2He is able to deal gently with those who have gone down the wrong path without knowing it. He can do that because he himself is weak. 3That's why he has to offer sacrifices for his own sins. He must also do it for the sins of the people.

4No one can take that honor for himself. He must be appointed by God, just as Aaron was. 5Even Christ did not take the glory of becoming a high priest for himself. God said to him,

"You are my Son.
    Today I have become your Father."
(Psalm 2:7)

6In another place he said,

"You are a priest forever,
    just like Melchizedek." *(Psalm 110:4)*

7Jesus prayed while he lived on earth. He made his appeal with loud cries and tears. He prayed to the One who could save him from death. God heard him because he truly honored God. 8Jesus was God's Son. But by suffering he learned what it means to obey. 9In that way he was made perfect. Eternal salvation comes from him. He saves all those who obey him. 10God appointed him to be the high priest, just like Melchizedek.

A Warning Against Falling Away

11We have a lot to say about that. But it is hard to explain it to you. You learn too slowly. **12**By this time you should be teachers. But in fact, you need someone to teach you all over again. You need even the simple truths of God's word. You need milk, not solid food.

13Anyone who lives on milk is still a baby. That person does not want to learn about living a godly life. **14**Solid food is for those who are grown up. They have trained themselves with a lot of practice. They can tell the difference between good and evil.

6 So let us leave the simple teachings about Christ. Let us grow up as believers. Let us not start all over again with the basic teachings. They taught us that we need to turn away from doing things that lead to death. They taught us that we must have faith in God. **2**They taught us about different kinds of baptism. They taught us about placing hands on people. They taught us that people will rise from the dead. They taught us that God will judge everyone. And they taught us that what he decides will last forever.

3If God permits, we will go beyond those teachings and grow up.

4What if some people fall away from the faith? It won't be possible to bring them back. It is true that they have seen the light. They have tasted the heavenly gift. They have shared in the Holy Spirit. **5**They have tasted the good things of God's word. They have tasted the powers of the age to come. **6**But they have fallen away from the faith. So it won't be possible to bring them back. They won't be able to turn away from their sins. They are losing everything. That's because they are nailing the Son of God to the cross all over again. They are bringing shame on him in front of everyone.

7Some land drinks the rain that falls on it. It produces a crop that is useful to those who farm the land. That land receives God's blessing. **8**But other land produces only thorns and weeds. That land isn't worth anything. It is in danger of coming under God's curse. In the end, it will be burned.

9Dear friends, we have to say these things. But we are sure of better things in your case. We are talking about the things that go along with being saved.

10God is fair. He will not forget what you have done. He will remember the love you have shown him. You showed it when you helped his people. And you show it when you keep on helping them.

11We want each of you to be faithful to the very end. We want you to be sure of what you hope for. **12**We don't want you to slow down. Instead, be like those who have faith and are patient. They will receive what God promised.

God Keeps His Promise

13When God made his promise to Abraham, he took an oath to keep it. But there was no one greater than himself to take an oath by. So he took his oath by making an appeal to himself.

14He said, "I will certainly bless you. I will give you many children." *(Genesis 22:17)* **15**Abraham was patient while he waited. Then he received what God promised him.

16People take oaths by someone greater than themselves. An oath makes a promise certain. It puts an end to all arguing. **17**So God took an oath when he made his promise. He wanted to make it very clear that his purpose does not change. He wanted those who would receive what was promised to know that.

18God took an oath so we would have good reason not to give up. We have run away from everything else to take hold of the hope offered to us in God's promise. So God gave his promise and his oath. Those two things can't change. He couldn't lie about them.

19Our hope is certain. It is something for the soul to hold on to. It is strong and secure. It goes all the way into the Most Holy Room behind the curtain. **20**That is where Jesus has gone. He went there to open the way ahead of us. He has become a high priest forever, just like Melchizedek.

Melchizedek the Priest

7 Melchizedek was the king of Salem. He was the priest of God Most High. He met Abraham, who was returning from winning a battle over some kings. Melchizedek blessed him. **2**Abraham gave him a tenth of everything.

First, the name Melchizedek means "king of what is right." Also, "king of Salem" means "king of peace." **3**Melchizedek has no father or mother. He has no family line. His days have no beginning. His life has no end. He remains a priest forever, just like the Son of God.

4Think how great Melchizedek was. Even our father Abraham gave him a tenth of what he had captured. **5**Now the law lays down a rule for the sons of Levi who become priests. They must collect a tenth from the people. They must collect it even from those who belong to the family line of Abraham.

⁶Melchizedek did not trace his family line from Levi. But he collected a tenth from Abraham. Melchizedek blessed the one who had received the promises. ⁷Without a doubt, the more important person blesses the less important one. ⁸In the one case, the tenth is collected by men who die. But in the other case, it is collected by the one who is said to be living.

⁹Levi collects the tenth. But we might say that Levi paid the tenth through Abraham. ¹⁰That's because when Melchizedek met Abraham, Levi was still in Abraham's body.

Jesus Is Like Melchizedek

¹¹Suppose the Levites who were priests could have made people perfect. The law was given to the people so they could become perfect through the priests. Then why was there still a need for another priest to come? And why did he need to be like Melchizedek? Why wasn't he from Aaron's family line?

FAITHFUL

HEBREWS 6:11-12

() () ()

We want each of you to be faithful to the very end. We want you to be sure of what you hope for. We don't want you to slow down. Instead, be like those who have faith and are patient. They will receive what God promised.

Do you know what it means to be *faithful*? To be faithful, to a friend or to God, means to always be loyal and always true. It means that person is at the top of your list. If you are a faithful friend, you won't say bad things about your friends behind their backs. If you are a faithful son or daughter, you'll listen to what your parents have to say.

In the Bible, Leah was a faithful wife (see her story on page 39). Her father tricked Jacob into marrying her. Jacob really wanted to marry Leah's sister, Rachel. Not a great beginning to a marriage. In spite of the fact that her husband always loved her sister better, Leah was faithful to Jacob all her life. And Elijah (his story is on page 416). Talk about being faithful to God! When everyone else was worshiping Baal, Elijah worshiped only God. He even dared to challenge the Baal worshipers to a contest. He put his faith in God on the *line*. And God didn't fail him.

BE FAITHFUL

If you are faithful to God, you'll put him at the top of your list. You will never love anyone or anything more than you love God. You will never worship anyone or anything other than God. He's the best thing in your life, and you're *faithful* to him.

Go to page 1426 for the next Super Hero Trait

POWER-SURGE

GIVING G

MELCHIZEDEK WAS
THE KING OF SALEM.
HE WAS THE PRIEST
OF GOD MOST HIGH.
HE MET ABRAHAM,
WHO WAS RETURNING
FROM WINNING A
BATTLE OVER SOME
KINGS. MELCHIZEDEK
BLESSED HIM.
ABRAHAM GAVE HIM A
TENTH OF EVERYTHING.
— HEBREWS 7:1-2 —

12 A change of priests requires a change of law. **13** Those things are said about one who is from a different tribe. No one from that tribe has ever served at the altar. **14** It is clear that our Lord came from the family line of Judah. Moses said nothing about priests who were from that tribe.

15 But suppose another priest like Melchizedek appears. Then what we have said is even more clear. **16** He has not become a priest because of a rule about his family line. He has become a priest because of his powerful life. His life can never be destroyed. **17** Scripture says,

"You are a priest forever,
    just like Melchizedek." *(Psalm 110:4)*

18 The old rule is done away with. It was weak and useless. **19** The law didn't make anything perfect. Now a better hope has been given to us. That hope brings us near to God.

20 The change of priests was made with an oath. Others became priests without any oath. **21** But Jesus became a priest with an oath. God said to him,

"The Lord has taken an oath and made
    a promise.
He will not change his mind. He has
    said,
'You are a priest forever.' " *(Psalm 110:4)*

22 Because of that oath, Jesus makes the promise of a better covenant certain.

23 There were many priests in Levi's family line. Death kept them from continuing in office. **24** But Jesus lives forever.

So he always holds the office of priest. **25** People now come to God through him. And he is able to save them completely and for all time. Jesus lives forever. He prays for them.

26 A high priest like that meets our need. He is holy, pure and without blame. He isn't like other people. He does not sin. He is lifted high above the heavens.

27 He isn't like the other high priests. They need to offer sacrifices day after day. First they bring offerings for their own sins. Then they do it for the sins of the people. But Jesus gave one sacrifice for the sins of the people. He gave it once and for all time. He did it by offering himself.

28 The law appoints men who are weak to be high priests. But God's oath came after the law. The oath appointed the Son. He has been made perfect forever.

The High Priest of a New Covenant

8 Here is the point of what we are saying. We have a high priest like that. He sat down at the right hand of the throne of the King, the Majesty in heaven. **2** He serves in the sacred tent. The Lord set up the true holy tent. A mere man did not set it up.

3 Every high priest is appointed to offer gifts and sacrifices. So that priest also had to have something to offer. **4** What if he were on earth? Then he would not be a priest. There are already priests who offer the gifts required by the law. **5** They serve at a sacred tent. But it is only a copy and shadow of what is in heaven. That's why God warned Moses when he was about to build the holy tent. God said, "Be sure to make everything just like the pattern I showed you on the mountain." *(Exodus 25:40)*

6 Jesus has been given a greater work to do for God. He is the go-between for the new covenant. That covenant is better than the old one. It is based on better promises.

7 Suppose nothing had been wrong with that first covenant. Then no one would have looked for another covenant. **8** But God found fault with the people. He said,

"A new day is coming, says the Lord.
    I will make a new covenant
with the people of Israel.
    I will also make it with the people of
        Judah.
9 It will not be like the covenant
    I made with their people of long
        ago.

That was when I took them by the
  hand.
I led them out of Egypt.
My new covenant will be different
  because they didn't remain
  faithful to my old covenant.
So I turned away from them,
                          says the Lord.
10 This is the covenant I will make with
    Israel
  after that time, says the Lord.
I will put my laws in their minds.
  I will write them on their hearts.
I will be their God.
  And they will be my people.
11 A man will not teach his neighbor
    anymore.
  And he will not teach his friend
    anymore.
He will not say, 'Know the Lord.'
Everyone will know me.
  From the least important of them to
    the most important,
  all of them will know me.
12 I will forgive their evil ways.
  I will not remember their sins
    anymore." *(Jeremiah 31:31–34)*

13 God called that covenant "new." So
he has made the first one out of date. And
what is out of date and getting older will
soon disappear.

Worship in the Holy Tent on Earth

9 The first covenant had rules for worship. It also had a sacred tent on
earth. 2 A holy tent was set up. The lampstand
was in the first room. So were the table
and the holy bread. That was called the
Holy Room. 3 Behind the second curtain
was a room called the Most Holy Room.
4 It had the golden altar for incense. It also
had the wooden chest called the ark of the
covenant. The ark was covered with gold.
It held the gold jar of manna. It held Aaron's wooden staff that had budded. It also
held the stone tablets. The words of the
covenant were written on them. 5 The cherubim were above the ark. God
showed his glory there. The cherubim
spread their wings over the place where
sin was paid for. But we can't deal with
those things more completely now.

6 That's how everything was arranged
in the holy tent. The priests entered it at
regular times. They went into the outer
room to do their work for God and others.
7 But only the high priest went into the inner room. He went in only once a year. He
never entered without taking blood with

him. He offered the blood for himself. He
also offered it for the sins the people had
committed because they didn't know any
better.

8 Here is what the Holy Spirit was showing us. He was telling us that God had not
yet clearly shown the way into the Most
Holy Room. It would not be clearly shown
as long as the first holy tent was still
standing.

9 That's an example for the present
time. It shows us that the gifts and sacrifices they offered were not enough. They
were not able to remove the worshiper's
feelings of guilt. 10 They deal only with
food and drink and different kinds of special washings. They are rules that deal
with things outside our bodies. People
had to obey them only until the new covenant came.

The Blood of Christ

11 Christ came to be the high priest of
the good things that are already here.
When he came, he went through the
greater and more perfect holy tent. The
tent was not made by people. In other
words, it is not a part of this creation.
12 He did not enter by spilling the blood
of goats and calves. He entered the Most
Holy Room by spilling his own blood. He
did it once and for all time. He paid the
price to set us free from sin forever.
13 The blood of goats and bulls is sprinkled on people. So are the ashes of a
young cow. They are sprinkled on people
the Law called unclean. The people are
sprinkled to make them holy. That makes
them clean on the outside.

14 But Christ offered himself to God
without any flaw. He did this through the
power of the eternal Holy Spirit. So how
much more will his blood wash from our
minds our feelings of guilt for committing
sin! Sin always leads to death. But now we
can serve the living God.

15 That's why Christ is the go-between
of a new covenant. Now those God calls to
himself will receive the eternal gift he
promised. They will receive it now that
Christ has died to save them. He died to
set them free from the sins they committed under the first covenant.

16 What happens in the case of a will? It
is necessary to prove that the person who
made the will has died. 17 A will is in effect
only when somebody has died. It never
takes effect while the one who made it is
still living. 18 That's why even the first covenant was not put into effect without the
spilling of blood.

¹⁹Moses first announced every commandment of the law to all the people. Then he took the blood of calves. He also took water, bright red wool and branches of a hyssop plant. He sprinkled the scroll. He also sprinkled all of the people. ²⁰He said, "This is the blood of the covenant God has commanded you to keep." *(Exodus 24:8)* ²¹In the same way, he sprinkled the holy tent with blood. He also sprinkled everything that was used in worship there.

²²In fact, the law requires that nearly everything be made clean with blood. Without the spilling of blood, no one can be forgiven.

²³So the copies of the heavenly things had to be made pure with those sacrifices. But the heavenly things themselves had to be made pure with better sacrifices.

²⁴Christ did not enter a sacred tent made by people. That tent was only a copy of the true one. He entered heaven itself. He did it to stand in front of God for us. He is there right now.

²⁵The high priest enters the Most Holy Room every year. He enters with blood that is not his own. But Christ did not enter heaven to offer himself again and again. ²⁶If he had, he would have had to suffer many times since the world was created. But now he has appeared once and for all time. He has come at the end of the ages to do away with sin. He has done that by offering himself.

²⁷People have to die once. After that, God will judge them. ²⁸In the same way, Christ was offered up once. He took away the sins of many people.

He will also come a second time. At that time he will not suffer for sin. Instead, he will come to bring salvation to those who are waiting for him.

Christ's Sacrifice Is Once and for All Time

10 The law is only a shadow of the good things that are coming. It is not the real things themselves. The same sacrifices have to be offered over and over again. They must be offered year after year. That's why the law can never make perfect those who come near to worship. ²If it could, wouldn't the sacrifices have stopped being offered? The worshipers would have been made clean once and for all time. They would not have felt guilty for their sins anymore.

³But those offerings remind people of their sins every year. ⁴It isn't possible for the blood of bulls and goats to take away sins.

⁵So when Christ came into the world, he said,

"You didn't want sacrifices and
offerings.
Instead, you prepared a body for me.
⁶You weren't pleased
with burnt offerings and sin
offerings.
⁷Then I said, 'Here I am. It is written
about me in the scroll.
God, I have come to do what you
want.' "   *(Psalm 40:6–8)*

⁸First Christ said, "You didn't want sacrifices and offerings. You didn't want burnt offerings and sin offerings. You weren't pleased with them." He said that even though the law required people to bring them. ⁹Then he said, "Here I am. I have come to do what you want." He did away with the first. He did it to put the second in place.

¹⁰We have been made holy by what God wanted. We have been made holy because Jesus Christ offered his body once and for all time.

¹¹Day after day every priest stands and does his special duties. He offers the same sacrifices again and again. But they can never take away sins.

¹²Jesus our priest offered one sacrifice for sins for all time. Then he sat down at the right hand of God. ¹³Since that time, he waits for his enemies to be put under his control. ¹⁴By that one sacrifice he has made perfect forever those who are being made holy.

¹⁵The Holy Spirit also gives witness to us about this. First he says,

¹⁶ "This is the covenant I will make with
them
after that time, says the Lord.
I will put my laws in their hearts.
I will write my laws on their minds."
        (Jeremiah 31:33)

¹⁷Then he adds,

"I will not remember their sins
anymore.
I will not remember the evil things
they have done." *(Jeremiah 31:34)*

¹⁸Where those have been forgiven, there is no longer any offering for sin.

A Warning to Remain Faithful

¹⁹Brothers and sisters, we are not afraid to enter the Most Holy Room. We enter boldly because of the blood of Jesus. ²⁰His

CHEERFUL ✳

LET US NOT GIVE UP
MEETING TOGETHER...
LET US CHEER EACH
OTHER UP WITH
WORDS OF HOPE.
— HEBREWS 10:25 —

TRIES HARD

way is new because he lives. It has been opened for us through the curtain. I'm talking about his body.

21We also have a great priest over the house of God. 22So let us come near to God with an honest and true heart. Let us come near with a faith that is sure and strong. Our hearts have been sprinkled. Our minds have been cleansed from a sense of guilt. Our bodies have been washed with pure water.

23Let us hold firmly to the hope we claim to have. The One who promised is faithful.

24Let us consider how we can stir up one another to love. Let us help one another to do good works. 25Let us not give up meeting together. Some are in the habit of doing this. Instead, let us cheer each other up with words of hope. Let us do it all the more as you see the day coming when Christ will return.

26What if we keep sinning on purpose? What if we do it even after we know the truth? Then there is no offering for our sins. 27All we can do is to wait in fear for God to judge. His blazing fire will burn up his enemies.

28Anyone who did not obey the law of Moses died without mercy if there were two or three witnesses. 29What should be done to anyone who has hated the Son of God or has said no to him? What should be done to a person who treated as an unholy thing the blood of the covenant that makes him holy? What should be done to someone who has made fun of the Holy Spirit who brings God's grace? Don't you think people like that should be punished more than anyone else?

30We know the One who said, "I am the One who judges people. I will pay

them back." *(Deuteronomy 32:35)* Scripture also says, "The Lord will judge his people." *(Deuteronomy 32:36; Psalm 135:14)*

31It is a terrible thing to fall into the hands of the living God.

32Remember those earlier days after you received the light. At that time you stood firm in a great struggle. You did it even in the face of suffering.

33Sometimes you were made fun of in front of others. You were treated badly. At other times you stood side by side with people who were being treated like that. 34You suffered together with people in prison. When your property was taken from you, you accepted it with joy. You knew that God had given you better and more lasting things.

35So don't throw away your bold faith. It will bring you rich rewards. 36You need to be faithful. Then you will do what God wants. You will receive what he has promised. 37In just a very little while,

"The one who is coming will come. He
    will not wait.
38   The one who is in the right will live
      by faith.
If he pulls back,
    I will not be pleased with him."
               (Habakkuk 2:3,4)

39But we aren't people who pull back and are destroyed. We are people who believe and are saved.

BELIEVES †

WE ARE PEOPLE WHO
BELIEVE AND ARE
SAVED.
— HEBREWS 10:39 —

Living by Faith

11 Faith is being sure of what we hope for. It is being certain of what we do not see. 2That is what the people of long ago were praised for.

3We have faith. So we understand that everything was made when God commanded it. That's why we believe that what we see was not made out of what could be seen.

4Abel had faith. So he offered to God a better sacrifice than Cain did. Because of his faith Abel was praised as a godly man. God said good things about his offerings.

POWER-SURGE

BELIEVES †

FAITH IS BEING SURE OF WHAT WE HOPE FOR. IT IS BEING CERTAIN OF WHAT WE DO NOT SEE. WITHOUT FAITH IT ISN'T POSSIBLE TO PLEASE GOD.

— **HEBREWS 11:1, 6** —

Because of his faith Abel still speaks. He speaks even though he is dead.

5Enoch had faith. So he was taken from this life. He didn't die. He just couldn't be found. God had taken him away. Before God took him, Enoch was praised as one who pleased God.

6Without faith it isn't possible to please God. Those who come to God must believe that he exists. And they must believe that he rewards those who look to him.

7Noah had faith. So he built an ark to save his family. He built it because of his great respect for God. God had warned him about things that could not yet be seen. Because of his faith he showed the world that it was guilty. Because of his faith he was considered right with God.

8Abraham had faith. So he obeyed God. God called him to go to a place he would later receive as his own. So he went. He did it even though he didn't know where he was going. **9**Because of his faith he made his home in the land God had promised him. He was like an outsider in a strange country. He lived there in tents. So did Isaac and Jacob. They received the same promise he did. **10**Abraham was looking forward to the city that has foundations. He was waiting for the city that God planned and built.

11Abraham had faith. So God made it possible for him to become a father. He became a father even though he was too old. Sarah also was too old to have children. But Abraham believed that the One who made the promise was faithful. **12**Abraham was past the time when he could have children. But many children came from that one man. They were as many as the stars in the sky. They were as many as the sand on the seashore. No one could count them.

13All those people were still living by faith when they died. They didn't receive the things God had promised. They only saw them and welcomed them from a long way off. They openly said that they were outsiders and strangers on earth.

14People who say things like that show that they are looking for a country of their own. **15**What if they had been thinking of the country they had left? Then they could have returned to it. **16**Instead, they longed for a better country. They wanted one in heaven.

So God is pleased when they call him their God. In fact, he has prepared a city for them.

17Abraham had faith. So he offered Isaac as a sacrifice. That happened when God put him to the test. Abraham had received the promises. But he was about to offer his one and only son. **18**God had said to him, "Your family line will continue through Isaac." *(Genesis 21:12)* Even so, Abraham was going to offer him up. **19**Abraham believed that God could raise the dead. In a way, he did receive Isaac back from death.

20Isaac had faith. So he blessed Jacob and Esau. He told them what was ahead for them.

21Jacob had faith. So he blessed each of Joseph's sons. He blessed them when he was dying. Because of his faith he worshiped God as he leaned on the top of his wooden staff.

22Joseph had faith. So he spoke to the people of Israel about their leaving Egypt. He gave directions about his bones. He did that toward the end of his life.

23Moses' parents had faith. So they hid him for three months after he was born. They saw he was a special child. They were not afraid of the king's command.

24Moses had faith. So he refused to be called the son of Pharaoh's daughter. That happened after he had grown up. **25**He chose to be treated badly together with the people of God. He chose that instead of enjoying sin's pleasures for a short time. **26**He suffered shame because of Christ. He thought it had great value. He considered it better than the riches of Egypt. He was looking ahead to God's reward.

27Because of his faith he left Egypt. It wasn't because he was afraid of the king's anger. He didn't let anything stop him. He saw the One who can't be seen. **28**Because of his faith he was the first to keep the Passover Feast. He commanded the people of Israel to sprinkle blood on their doorways. He did it so that the destroying angel would not touch their oldest sons. **29**The people had faith. So they passed through the Red Sea. They went through it as if it were dry land. The Egyptians tried to do it also. But they drowned. **30**The people had faith. So the walls of Jericho fell down. It happened after they had marched around the city for seven days. **31**Rahab, the prostitute, had faith. So she welcomed the spies. That's why she wasn't killed with those who didn't obey God.

32What more can I say? I don't have time to tell about all the others. I don't have time to talk about Gideon, Barak, Samson and Jephthah. I don't have time to tell about David, Samuel and the prophets. **33**Because of their faith they took over kingdoms. They ruled fairly. They received the blessings God had promised. They shut the mouths of lions. **34**They put out great fires. They escaped being killed by the sword. Their weakness was turned to strength. They became powerful in battle. They beat back armies from other countries. **35**Women received their dead back. The dead were raised to life again. Others were made to suffer greatly. But they refused to be set free. They did that so that after death they would be raised to a better life. **36**Some were laughed at. Some were whipped. Still others were held by chains. They were put in prison. **37**Some were killed with stones. They were sawed in two. They were put to death by the sword. They went around wearing the skins of sheep and goats. They were poor. They were attacked. They were treated badly. **38**The world was not worthy of them. They wandered in deserts and mountains. They lived in caves. They lived in holes in the ground.

39All of those people were praised because they had faith. But none of them received what God had promised. **40**God had planned something better for us. So they would only be made perfect together with us.

12 A huge cloud of witnesses is all around us. So let us throw off everything that stands in our way. Let us throw off any sin that holds on to us so tightly. Let us keep on running the race marked out for us.

2Let us keep looking to Jesus. He is the author of faith. He also makes it perfect. He paid no attention to the shame of the cross. He suffered there because of the joy he was looking forward to. Then he sat down at the right hand of the throne of God.

3He put up with attacks from sinners. So think about him. Then you won't get tired. You won't lose hope.

God Trains His Children

4You struggle against sin. But you have not yet fought to the point of spilling your blood. **5**You have forgotten that word of hope. It speaks to you as children. It says,

"My son, think of the Lord's training
     as important.
   Do not lose hope when he corrects
     you.
6 The Lord trains those he loves.
   He punishes everyone he accepts as
     a son."   *(Proverbs 3:11,12)*

7Put up with hard times. God uses them to train you. He is treating you as children. What children are not trained by their parents? **8**God trains all of his children. But what if he doesn't train you? Then you are like children of people who weren't married to each other. You are not truly God's children.

9Besides, we have all had human parents who trained us. We respected them for it. How much more should we be trained by the Father of our spirits and live! **10**Our parents trained us for a little while. They did what they thought was best. But God trains us for our good. He wants us to share in his holiness. **11**No training seems pleasant at the time. In fact, it seems painful. But later on it produces a harvest of godliness and peace. It does that for those who have been trained by it.

12So lift your sagging arms. Strengthen your weak knees. **13**"Make level paths for your feet to walk on." *(Proverbs 4:26)* Then those who have trouble walking won't be disabled. Instead, they will be healed.

A Warning Against Saying No to God

14Try your best to live in peace with everyone. Try to be holy. Without holiness no one will see the Lord. **15**Be sure that no one misses God's grace. See to it that a bitter plant doesn't grow up. If it does, it will cause trouble.

And it will pollute many people. ¹⁶See to it that no one commits sexual sins.

See to it that no one is godless like Esau. He sold the rights to what he would receive as the oldest son. He sold them for a single meal. ¹⁷As you know, after that he wanted to receive his father's blessing. But he was turned away. With tears he tried to get the blessing. But he couldn't get his father to change his mind.

¹⁸You haven't come to a mountain that can be touched. You haven't come to a mountain that is burning with fire. You haven't come to darkness, gloom and storm. ¹⁹You haven't come to a blast from God's trumpet. You haven't come to a voice speaking to you. When people heard that voice long ago, they begged it not to say anything more to them. ²⁰What God commanded was too much for them. He said, "If even an animal touches the mountain, it must be killed with stones." *(Exodus 19:12,13)* ²¹The sight was terrifying. Moses said, "I am trembling with fear." *(Deuteronomy 9:19)*

²²But you have come to Mount Zion. You have come to the Jerusalem in heaven. It is the city of the living God. You have come to a joyful gathering of angels. There are thousands and thousands of them. ²³You have come to the church of God's people. God's first and only Son is over all things. God's people share in what belongs to his Son. Their names are written in heaven. You have come to God. He is the judge of all people.

You have come to the spirits of godly people who have been made perfect. ²⁴You have come to Jesus. He is the go-between of a new covenant. You have come to the sprinkled blood. It promises better things than the blood of Abel.

²⁵Be sure that you don't say no to the One who speaks. People did not escape when they said no to the One who warned them on earth. And what if we turn away from the One who warns us from heaven? How much less will we escape!

²⁶At that time his voice shook the earth. But now he has promised, "Once more I will shake the earth. I will also shake the heavens." *(Haggai 2:6)* ²⁷The words "once more" point out that what can be shaken can be taken away. I'm talking about created things. Then what can't be shaken will remain.

²⁸We are receiving a kingdom that can't be shaken. So let us be thankful. Then we can worship God in a way that pleases him. We will worship him with deep respect and wonder. ²⁹Our "God is like a fire that burns everything up." *(Deuteronomy 4:24)*

Final Words

13 Keep on loving each other as brothers and sisters. ²Don't forget to welcome strangers. By doing that, some people have welcomed angels without knowing it.

³Remember those in prison as if you were in prison with them. And remember those who are treated badly as if you yourselves were suffering.

⁴All of you should honor marriage. You should keep the marriage bed pure. God will judge the person who commits adultery. He will judge everyone who commits sexual sins.

⁵Don't be controlled by love for money. Be happy with what you have. God has said,

> "I will never leave you.
> I will never desert you."
> *(Deuteronomy 31:6)*

⁶So we can say boldly,

> "The Lord helps me. I will not be
> afraid.
> What can a mere man do to me?"
> *(Psalm 118:6,7)*

⁷Remember your leaders. They spoke God's word to you. Think about the results of their way of life. Copy their faith.

⁸Jesus Christ is the same yesterday and today and forever.

⁹Don't be carried away by all kinds of strange teachings. It is good that God's grace makes our hearts strong. Don't depend on foods the Law requires. They have no value for the people who eat them. ¹⁰Some worship at the holy tent. But we have an altar that they have no right to eat from.

¹¹The high priest carries the blood of animals into the Most Holy Room. He brings their blood as a sin offering. But the bodies are burned outside the camp. ¹²Jesus also suffered outside the city gate.

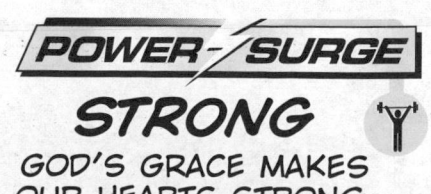

POWER SURGE

STRONG

GOD'S GRACE MAKES
OUR HEARTS STRONG.
— HEBREWS 13:9 —

He suffered to make the people holy by spilling his own blood.

¹³So let us go to him outside the camp. Let us be willing to suffer the shame he suffered. ¹⁴Here we do not have a city that lasts. But we are looking for the city that is going to come.

¹⁵So let us never stop offering to God our praise through Jesus. Let us offer it as the fruit of lips that say they believe in him.

¹⁶Don't forget to do good. Don't forget to share with others. God is pleased with those kinds of offerings.

¹⁷Obey your leaders. Put yourselves under their authority. They keep watch over you. They know they are accountable to God for everything they do. Obey them so that their work will be a joy. If you make

OBEY YOUR LEADERS.
— HEBREWS 13:17 —

their work a heavy load, it won't do you any good.

¹⁸Pray for us. We feel sure we have done what is right. We long to live as we should in every way.

¹⁹I beg you to pray that I may return to you soon.

²⁰Our Lord Jesus is the great Shepherd of the sheep. The God who gives peace brought him back from the dead. He did it because of the blood of the eternal covenant. May God ²¹supply you with everything good. Then you can do what he wants. May he do in us what is pleasing to him. We can do it only with the help of Jesus Christ. Give him glory for ever and ever. Amen.

²²Brothers and sisters, I beg you to accept my word. It tells you to be faithful. I have written you only a short letter.

²³I want you to know that our brother Timothy has been set free. If he arrives soon, I will come with him to see you.

²⁴Greet all of your leaders. Greet all of God's people. The believers from Italy send you their greetings.

²⁵May grace be with you all.

JAMES

Jesus' brother James writes this letter to tell early Christians to make sure their faith is shown by how they live. He points out several bad habits they have gotten into and how they should change. James's letter is packed with practical advice on a Christian lifestyle. You can read this little letter in just a few minutes. As you read it, you'll find clear teaching on how to live as a Christian day to day.

CHECK OUT THIS TRAIT OF A HERO . . .

WISE
PAGE 1426

1

I, James, am writing this letter. I serve God and the Lord Jesus Christ.

I am sending this letter to you, the 12 tribes that are scattered among the nations.

Greetings.

Facing All Kinds of Trouble

2My brothers and sisters, you will face all kinds of trouble. When you do, think of it as pure joy. **3**Your faith will be put to the test. You know that when that happens it will produce in you the strength to continue. **4**The strength to keep going must be allowed to finish its work. Then you will be all you should be. You will have everything you need.

5If any of you need wisdom, ask God for it. He will give it to you. God gives freely to everyone. He doesn't find fault.

6But when you ask, you must believe. You must not doubt. People who doubt are like waves of the sea. The wind blows and tosses them around. **7**A man like that shouldn't expect to receive anything from the Lord. **8**He can't make up his mind. He can never decide what to do.

9A believer who finds himself in a low position in life should be proud that God has given him a high position. **10**But someone who is rich should take pride in his low position. That's because he will fade away like a wild flower. **11**The sun rises. Its burning heat dries up the plants. Their blossoms fall. Their beauty is destroyed. In the same way, a rich person will fade away even as he goes about his business.

12Blessed is the man who keeps on going when times are hard. After he has come through them, he will receive a crown. The crown is life itself. God has promised it to those who love him.

POWER-SURGE

STRONG

YOUR FAITH WILL BE PUT TO THE TEST. YOU KNOW THAT WHEN THAT HAPPENS IT WILL PRODUCE IN YOU THE STRENGTH TO CONTINUE.
— JAMES 1:3 —

POWER-SURGE

GIVING   G

IF ANY OF YOU NEED WISDOM, ASK GOD FOR IT. HE WILL GIVE IT TO YOU. GOD GIVES FREELY TO EVERYONE.
— JAMES 1:5 —

WISE   W

13When you are tempted, you shouldn't say, "God is tempting me." God can't be tempted by evil. And he doesn't tempt anyone. **14**But your own evil longings tempt you. They lead you on and drag you away. **15**When they are allowed to grow, they give birth to sin. When sin has grown up, it gives birth to death.

16My dear brothers and sisters, don't let anyone fool you. **17**Every good and perfect gift is from God. It comes down from the Father. He created the heavenly lights. He does not change like shadows that move. **18**God chose to give us new birth through the message of truth. He wanted us to be the first and best of everything he created.

Listen to the Word and Do What It Says

19My dear brothers and sisters, pay attention to what I say. Everyone should be quick to listen. But they should be slow to speak. They should be slow to get angry. **20**A man's anger doesn't produce the kind of life God wants.

21So get rid of everything that is dirty and sinful. Get rid of the evil that is all around us. Don't be too proud to accept the word that is planted in you. It can save you.

22Don't just listen to the word. You fool yourselves if you do that. You must do what it says.

23Suppose you listen to the word but don't do what it says. Then you are like a man who looks at his face in a mirror. **24**After looking at himself, he leaves. Right away he forgets what he looks like. **25**But suppose you take a good look at the perfect law that gives freedom. You keep looking at it. You don't forget what you've heard, but you do what the law says. Then you will be blessed in what you do.

²⁶Suppose you think your beliefs are right because of how you live. But you don't control what you say. Then you are fooling yourselves. Your beliefs are not worth anything at all.

²⁷Here are the kinds of beliefs that God our Father accepts as pure and without fault. When widows and children who have no parents are in trouble, take care of them. And keep yourselves from being polluted by the world.

Treat Everyone the Same

2 My brothers and sisters, you are believers in our glorious Lord Jesus Christ. So treat everyone the same.

²Suppose a man comes into your meeting wearing a gold ring and fine clothes. And suppose a poor man in worn-out clothes also comes in. ³Would you show special attention to the one who is wearing fine clothes? Would you say, "Here's a good seat for you"? Would you say to the poor person, "You stand there"? Or "Sit on the floor by my feet"? ⁴If you would, aren't you treating some people better than others? Aren't you like judges who have evil thoughts?

⁵My dear brothers and sisters, listen to me. Hasn't God chosen those who are poor in the world's eyes to be rich in faith? Hasn't he chosen them to receive the kingdom? Hasn't he promised it to those who love him?

⁶But you have put poor people down. Aren't rich people taking advantage of you? Aren't they dragging you into court? ⁷Aren't they speaking evil things against the worthy name of Jesus? Remember, you belong to him.

⁸The royal law is found in Scripture. It says, "Love your neighbor as you love yourself." *(Leviticus 19:18)* If you really keep that law, you are doing what is right. ⁹But you sin if you don't treat everyone the same. The law judges you because you have broken it.

¹⁰Suppose you keep the whole law but trip over just one part of it. Then you are guilty of breaking all of it. ¹¹God said, "Do not commit adultery." *(Exodus 20:14; Deuteronomy 5:18)* He also said, "Do not commit murder." *(Exodus 20:13; Deuteronomy 5:17)* Suppose you don't commit adultery but do commit murder. Then you have broken the Law.

¹²Speak and act like people who are go-ing to be judged by the law that gives freedom. ¹³Those who have not shown mercy will not receive mercy when they are judged. To show mercy is better than to judge.

Show Your Faith by What You Do

¹⁴My brothers and sisters, what good is it if people claim they have faith but don't act like it? Can that kind of faith save them?

¹⁵Suppose a brother or sister has no clothes or food. ¹⁶Suppose one of you says to them, "Go. I hope everything turns out fine for you. Keep warm. Eat well." And you do nothing about what they really need. Then what good have you done?

¹⁷It is the same with faith. If it doesn't cause us to do something, it's dead.

¹⁸But someone will say, "You have faith. I do good works."

Show me your faith that doesn't do good works. And I will show you my faith by what I do. ¹⁹You believe there is one God. Good! Even the demons believe that. And they tremble!

²⁰You foolish man! Do you want proof that faith without good works is useless? ²¹Our father Abraham offered his son Isaac on the altar. Wasn't he considered to be right with God because of what he did? ²²So you see that what he believed and what he did were working together. What he did made his faith complete.

²³That is what Scripture means where it says, "Abraham believed God. God accepted Abraham because he believed. So his faith made him right with God." *(Genesis 15:6)* And that's not all. God called Abraham his friend. ²⁴So you see that a person is made right with God by what he does. It doesn't happen only because of what he believes.

²⁵Didn't God make even Rahab the prostitute right with him? That's because of what she did. She gave the spies a place to stay. Then she sent them off in a different direction.

²⁶The body without the spirit is dead. In the same way, faith without good works is dead.

Control What You Say

3 My brothers and sisters, most of you shouldn't want to be teachers. You know that those of us who teach will be held more accountable.

²All of us get tripped up in many ways. Suppose someone is never wrong in what he says. Then he is a perfect man. He is able to keep his whole body under control.

³We put a bit in the mouth of a horse to make it obey us. We can control the whole animal with it. ⁴And how about ships? They are very big. They are driven along by strong winds. But they are steered by a very small rudder. It makes them go where the captain wants to go.

⁵In the same way, the tongue is a small part of the body. But it brags a lot. Think about how a small spark can set a big forest on fire.

⁶The tongue also is a fire. The tongue is the most evil part of the body. It pollutes the whole person. It sets a person's whole way of life on fire. And the tongue is set on fire by hell.

⁷People have controlled all kinds of animals, birds, reptiles and creatures of the sea. They still control them. ⁸But no one can control the tongue. It is an evil thing that never rests. It is full of deadly poison.

⁹With our tongues we praise our Lord and Father. With our tongues we call down curses on people. We do it even

WISE

W
W
W

JAMES 3:17

But the wisdom that comes from heaven is pure. That's the most important thing about it. And that's not all. It also loves peace. It thinks about others. It obeys. It is full of mercy and good fruit. It is fair. It doesn't pretend to be what it is not.

How wise are you? Very? Sort of? A little? Not very? It may be hard to tell. Wisdom can't be measured as easily as how smart you are. You can't take a test to see how wise you are. Wisdom is something that you get only very slowly. It comes from studying God's Word and from making good choices in life. The older you grow, the more (or maybe less) wise you become.

King Solomon is known as the wisest person who ever lived (see page 395 for his story). When God promised to give him anything he asked for, Solomon didn't choose riches or a long life. He chose wisdom. He must have already been wise to make such a wise choice, don't you think? Of course, the Wise Men in the New Testament were wise also. (Why else would we call them the *Wise* Men?) When God sent them a sign that Jesus had been born, they wisely followed the sign instead of ignoring it. You'll find the story of their journey on page 1092.

BE WISE

You can grow and live wisely starting today. Look at the verse above. It gives you some very specific ways that you can be wise. Look at each sentence and then look at yourself. How are you doing? You're young yet, but you can be wise right now if you follow the lessons of this verse.

Go to page 1433 for the next Super Hero Trait

though they have been created to be like God. **10**Praise and cursing come out of the same mouth. My brothers and sisters, it shouldn't be that way.

11Can fresh water and salt water flow out of the same spring? **12**My brothers and sisters, can a fig tree bear olives? Can a grapevine bear figs? Of course not. And a saltwater spring can't produce fresh water either.

Two Kinds of Wisdom

13Are any of you wise and understanding? You should show it by living a good life. Wise people aren't proud when they do good works.

14But suppose your hearts are jealous and bitter. Suppose you are concerned only about getting ahead. Don't brag about it. Don't say no to the truth. **15**Wisdom like that doesn't come down from heaven. It belongs to the earth. It doesn't come from the Holy Spirit. It comes from the devil.

16Are you jealous? Are you concerned only about getting ahead? Then your life will be a mess. You will be doing all kinds of evil things.

17But the wisdom that comes from heaven is pure. That's the most important thing about it. And that's not all. It also loves peace. It thinks about others. It obeys. It is full of mercy and good fruit. It is fair. It doesn't pretend to be what it is not.

18Those who make peace should plant peace like a seed. If they do, it will produce a crop of right living.

Obey God

4 Why do you fight and argue among yourselves? Isn't it because of your sinful longings? They fight inside you.

2You want something, but you can't get it. You kill and want what others have. But you can't have what you want. You argue and fight. You don't have what you want, because you don't ask God. **3**When you do ask for something, you don't receive it. Why? Because you ask for the wrong reason. You want to spend your money on your sinful pleasures.

4You are not faithful to God. Don't you know that to be a friend of the world is to hate God? Anyone who chooses to be a friend of the world becomes an enemy of God. **5**Don't you know what Scripture says? The spirit that God caused to live in us wants us to belong only to God. Don't you think Scripture has a reason for say-

POWER - SURGE

OBEYS ✔

SO OBEY GOD. STAND UP TO THE DEVIL. HE WILL RUN AWAY FROM YOU. COME NEAR TO GOD, AND HE WILL COME NEAR TO YOU.
— JAMES 4:7-8 —

ing that? **6**God continues to give us more grace. That's why Scripture says,

"God opposes those who are proud.
But he gives grace to those who are
     not."   *(Proverbs 3:34)*

7So obey God. Stand up to the devil. He will run away from you. **8**Come near to God, and he will come near to you. Wash your hands, you sinners. Make your hearts pure, you who can't make up your minds.

9Be full of sorrow. Cry and sob. Change your laughter to crying. Change your joy to sadness. **10**Bow down to the Lord. He will lift you up.

11My brothers and sisters, don't speak against one another. Anyone who speaks against another believer speaks against the law. And anyone who judges another believer judges the law. When you judge the law, you are not keeping it. Instead, you are acting as if you were its judge.

12There is only one Lawgiver and Judge. He is the One who is able to save life or destroy it. But who are you to judge your neighbor?

Bragging About Tomorrow

13Now listen, you who say, "Today or tomorrow we will go to this or that city. We will spend a year there. We will buy and sell and make money." **14**You don't even know what will happen tomorrow. What is your life? It is a mist that appears for a little while. Then it disappears. **15**Instead, you should say, "If it pleases the Lord, we will live and do this or that."

16As it is, you are proud. You brag about it. That kind of bragging is evil. **17**So when you know the good things you should do and don't do them, you sin.

A Warning to Rich People

5 You rich people, listen to me. Cry and sob, because you will soon be suffering.

²Your riches have rotted. Moths have eaten your clothes. ³Your gold and silver have lost their brightness. Their dullness will give witness against you. Your wanting more and more will eat your body like fire. You have stored up riches in these last days.

⁴You have even failed to pay the workers who mowed your fields. Their pay is crying out against you. The cries of those who gathered the harvest have reached the ears of the Lord who rules over all.

⁵You have lived an easy life on earth. You have given yourselves everything you wanted. You have made yourselves fat like cattle that will soon be butchered. ⁶You have judged and murdered people who aren't guilty. And they weren't even opposing you.

Be Patient When You Suffer

⁷Brothers and sisters, be patient until the Lord comes. See how the farmer waits for the land to produce its rich crop. See how patient he is for the fall and spring rains. ⁸You too must be patient. You must stand firm. The Lord will soon come back.

⁹Brothers and sisters, don't find fault with one another. If you do, you will be judged. And the Judge is standing at the door!

¹⁰Brothers and sisters, think about the prophets who spoke in the name of the Lord. They are an example of how to be patient when you suffer. ¹¹As you know, we think that people who don't give up are blessed. You have heard that Job was patient. And you have seen what the Lord finally did for him. The Lord is full of tender mercy and loving concern.

POWER-SURGE

PATIENT P

BE PATIENT UNTIL THE LORD COMES.
— JAMES 5:7 —

POWER-SURGE

CHEERFUL *

PEOPLE WHO DON'T GIVE UP ARE BLESSED ...ARE ANY OF YOU HAPPY? THEN SING SONGS OF PRAISE.
— JAMES 5:11, 13 —

TRIES HARD T

¹²My brothers and sisters, don't take an oath when you make a promise. Don't call on heaven or earth or anything else to back up what you say. Let your "Yes" be yes. And let your "No" be no. If you don't, you will be judged.

The Prayer of Faith

¹³Are any of you in trouble? Then you should pray. Are any of you happy? Then sing songs of praise.

¹⁴Are any of you sick? Then send for the elders of the church to pray over you. Ask them to anoint you with oil in the name of the Lord. ¹⁵The prayer offered by those who have faith will make you well. The Lord will heal you. If you have sinned, you will be forgiven.

¹⁶So admit to one another that you have sinned. Pray for one another so that you might be healed. The prayer of a godly person is powerful. It makes things happen.

¹⁷Elijah was just like us. He prayed hard that it wouldn't rain. And it didn't rain on the land for three and a half years. ¹⁸Then he prayed again. That time it rained. And the earth produced its crops.

¹⁹My brothers and sisters, suppose one of you wanders away from the truth and someone brings you back. ²⁰Then here is what I want everyone to remember. Anyone who turns a sinner from going down the wrong path will save him from death. God will erase many sins by forgiving him.

1 PETER

Peter, one of the original twelve disciples, writes this book to Christians who are suffering for their faith. He wants them to know that their suffering can help them grow stronger. He wants them to know that although they suffer they can have hope because Jesus promises eternal life in heaven which no one can steal from them. He goes on to give them instructions on how to live their lives as Christians even while they are being persecuted. The book of 1 Peter will help you realize that nothing in your life happens without a purpose. God uses the good and the bad to help you grow in your faith.

CHECK OUT THIS TRAIT OF A HERO . . .

BRAVE
PAGE 1433

1 I, Peter, am writing this letter. I am an apostle of Jesus Christ.

I am sending this letter to you, God's chosen people. You are strangers in the world. You are scattered all over Pontus, Galatia, Cappadocia, Asia and Bithynia. ²You have been chosen in keeping with what God the Father had planned. That happened through the Spirit's work to make you pure and holy. God chose you so that you might obey Jesus Christ. He wanted you to be made clean by the blood of Christ.

May more and more grace and peace be given to you.

Peter Praises God for a Hope That Is Alive

³Give praise to the God and Father of our Lord Jesus Christ. In his great mercy he has given us a new birth and a hope that is alive. It is alive because Jesus Christ rose from the dead. ⁴He has given us new birth so that we might share in what belongs to him. It is a gift that can never be destroyed. It can never spoil or even fade away. It is kept in heaven for you. ⁵Through faith you are kept safe by God's power. Your salvation is going to be completed. It is ready to be shown to you in the last days.

⁶Because you know this, you have great joy. You have joy even though you may have had to suffer for a little while. You may have had to suffer sadness in all kinds of trouble.

⁷Your troubles have come in order to prove that your faith is real. It is worth more than gold. Gold can pass away even though fire has made it pure. Your faith is meant to bring praise, honor and glory to God. That will happen when Jesus Christ returns.

⁸Even though you have not seen him,

POWER–SURGE

OBEYS ✔

GOD CHOSE YOU SO THAT YOU MIGHT OBEY JESUS CHRIST. HE WANTED YOU TO BE MADE CLEAN BY THE BLOOD OF CHRIST.
— **1 PETER 1:2** —

POWER–SURGE

OBEYS ✔

SO PREPARE YOUR MINDS FOR ACTION. CONTROL YOURSELVES... YOU SHOULD OBEY.
— **1 PETER 1:13–14** —

SELF-CONTROLLED

you love him. Though you do not see him now, you believe in him. You are filled with a glorious joy that can't be put into words. ⁹You are receiving the salvation of your souls. It is the result of your faith.

¹⁰The prophets searched very hard and with great care to find out about that salvation. They spoke about the grace that was going to come to you. ¹¹They wanted to find out when that salvation would come. The Spirit of Christ in them was telling them about the sufferings of Christ that were going to come. He was also telling them about the glory that would follow.

¹²It was made known to the prophets that they were not serving themselves. Instead, they were serving you when they spoke about the things that you have now heard. Those who have preached the good news to you have told you those things. They have done it with the help of the Holy Spirit sent from heaven. Even angels long to look into those things.

Be Holy

¹³So prepare your minds for action. Control yourselves. Put your hope completely in the grace that will be given to you when Jesus Christ returns.

¹⁴You should obey. You shouldn't give in to evil longings. They controlled your life when you didn't know any better. ¹⁵The one who chose you is holy. So you should be holy in all that you do. ¹⁶It is written, "Be holy, because I am holy." *(Leviticus 11:44,45; 19:2)*

¹⁷You call on a Father who judges each person's work without favoring one over another. So live your lives as strangers here. Have the highest respect for God. ¹⁸The blood of Christ set you free from

an empty way of life. That way of life was handed down to you by your own people long ago. You know that you were not bought with things that can pass away, like silver or gold. ¹⁹Instead, you were bought by the priceless blood of Christ. He is a perfect lamb. He doesn't have any flaws at all. ²⁰He was chosen before God created the world. But he came into the world in these last days for you.

²¹Because of what Christ has done, you believe in God. It was God who raised him from the dead. And it was God who gave him glory. So your faith and hope are in God.

²²You have made yourselves pure by obeying the truth. So you have an honest and true love for your brothers and sisters. Love each other deeply, from the heart.

²³You have been born again by means of the living word of God. His word lasts forever. You were not born again from a seed that will die. You were born from a seed that can't die. ²⁴It is written,

"All people are like grass.
　All of their glory is like the flowers in
　　the field.
The grass dries up. The flowers fall to
　　the ground.
²⁵ But the word of the Lord stands
　　forever."　　　*(Isaiah 40:6–8)*

And that word was preached to you.

2 So get rid of every kind of evil. Stop telling lies. Don't pretend to be something you are not. Stop wanting what others have. Don't speak against each other.

²Like babies that were just born, you should long for the pure milk of God's word. It will help you grow up as believers. ³You can do it now that you have tasted how good the Lord is.

The Living Stone and a Chosen People

⁴Christ is the living Stone. People did not accept him. But God chose him. God places the highest value on him.

⁵You also are like living stones. As you come to him you are being built into a house for worship. There you will be holy priests. You will offer spiritual sacrifices. God will accept them because of what Jesus Christ has done.

⁶In Scripture it says,

"Look! I am placing a stone in Zion.
　It is a chosen and very valuable
　　stone.

It is the most important stone in the
　　building.
The one who trusts in him
　will never be put to shame."
　　　　　　　　(Isaiah 28:16)

⁷The stone is very valuable to you who believe. But to people who do not believe,

"The stone the builders did not accept
　has become the most important
　　stone of all."　　*(Psalm 118:22)*

⁸And,

"It is a stone that causes people to trip.
　It is a rock that makes them fall."
　　　　　　　　(Isaiah 8:14)

They trip and fall because they do not obey the message. That is also what God planned for them.

⁹But God chose you to be his people. You are royal priests. You are a holy nation. You are a people who belong to God. All of this is so that you can sing his praises. He brought you out of darkness into his wonderful light. ¹⁰Once you were not a people. But now you are the people of God. Once you had not received mercy. But now you have received mercy.

¹¹Dear friends, you are outsiders and strangers in this world. So I'm asking you not to give in to your sinful longings. They fight against your soul. ¹²People who don't believe might say you are doing wrong. But lead good lives among them. Then they will see your good works. And they will give glory to God on the day he comes to judge.

Obey Your Rulers and Masters

¹³Follow the lead of every human authority. Do it because the Lord wants you to. Obey the king. He is the highest authority. ¹⁴Obey the governors. The king sends them to punish those who do wrong. He also sends them to praise those who do right. ¹⁵By doing good you will put a stop to the talk of foolish people. They don't know what they are saying. God wants you to stop them.

¹⁶Live like free people. But don't use your freedom to cover up evil. Live like people who serve God. ¹⁷Show proper respect to everyone. Love the community of believers. Have respect for God. Honor the king.

¹⁸Slaves, obey your masters with all the respect you should give them. Obey not only those who are good and kind. Obey also those who are not kind. ¹⁹Suppose a person suffers pain unfairly because he

OBEYS ✔

SUPPOSE A PERSON SUFFERS PAIN UNFAIRLY BECAUSE HE WANTS TO OBEY GOD. THAT IS WORTHY OF PRAISE.
—— 1 PETER 2:19 ——

wants to obey God. That is worthy of praise. 20But suppose you receive a beating for doing wrong, and you put up with it. Will anyone honor you for that? Of course not. But suppose you suffer for doing good, and you put up with it. God will praise you for that.

21Christ suffered for you. He left you an example. He expects you to follow in his steps. You too were chosen to suffer. 22Scripture says,

"He didn't commit any sin.
No lies ever came out of his mouth."
(Isaiah 53:9)

23People shouted at him and made fun of him. But he didn't do the same back to them. He suffered. But he didn't say that bad things would happen to them. Instead, he trusted in the One who judges fairly. 24He himself carried our sins in his body on the cross. He did it so that we would die as far as sins are concerned. Then we would lead godly lives. His wounds have made you whole. 25You were like sheep who were wandering away. But now you have returned to the Shepherd. He is the Leader of your souls.

Wives and Husbands

3 Wives, follow the lead of your husbands. Suppose some of them don't believe God's word. Then let them be won to Christ without words by seeing how their wives behave. 2Let them see how pure you are. Let them see that your lives are full of respect for God. 3Braiding your hair doesn't make you beautiful. Wearing gold jewelry or fine clothes doesn't make you beautiful. 4Instead, your beauty comes from inside you. It is the beauty of a gentle and quiet spirit.

Beauty like that doesn't fade away. God places great value on it. 5This is how the holy women of the past used to make themselves beautiful. They put their hope in God. And they followed the lead of their own husbands. 6Sarah was like that. She obeyed Abraham. She called him her master. Do you want to be like her? Then do what is right. And don't give in to fear.

7Husbands, take good care of your wives. They are weaker than you. So treat them with respect. Honor them as those who will share with you the gracious gift of life. Then nothing will stand in the way of your prayers.

Suffering for Doing Good

8Finally, I want all of you to live together in peace. Be understanding. Love one another like members of the same family. Be kind and tender. Don't be proud. 9Don't pay back evil with evil. Don't pay back unkind words with unkind words. Instead, pay them back with kind words. That's what you have been chosen to do. You can receive a blessing by doing it. 10Scripture says,

"Do you want to love life
and see good days?
Then keep your tongues from speaking evil.
Keep your lips from telling lies.
11 Turn away from evil, and do good.
Look for peace, and go after it.
12 The Lord's eyes look with favor on those who are godly.
His ears are open to their prayers.
But the Lord doesn't look with favor on those who do evil."
(Psalm 34:12–16)

13Who is going to hurt you if you really want to do good? 14But suppose you suffer for doing what is right. Then you will be blessed. Scripture also says, "Don't fear what others fear. Don't be afraid." *(Isaiah 8:12)* 15But make sure in your hearts that Christ is Lord. Always be ready to give an answer to anyone who asks you about the hope you have. Be ready to give the reason for it. But do it gently and with respect. 16Live so that you don't have to feel you've done anything wrong. Some people may say evil things about your good conduct as believers in Christ. If they do, they will be put to shame for speaking like that about you. 17It is better to suffer for doing good than for doing evil if that's what God wants.

18Christ died for sins once and for all time. The One who did what is right died for those who don't do right. He died to bring you to God. His body was put to death. But the Holy Spirit brought him back to life.

19By means of the Spirit, Christ went and preached to the spirits in prison. 20Long ago they did not obey. God was patient while Noah was building the ark. He waited, but only a few people went into the ark. A total of eight were saved by means of water.

21The water of the flood is a picture of the baptism that now saves you also. The baptism I'm talking about has nothing to do with removing dirt from your body. Instead, it promises God that you will keep a clear sense of what is right and wrong. Jesus Christ has saved you by rising from the dead. 22He has gone into heav-en. He is at God's right hand. Angels, authorities and powers are under his control.

Living for God

4 Christ suffered in his body. So get ready as a soldier does. Prepare yourselves to think in the same way Christ did. Do it because those who have suffered in their bodies are finished with sin. 2As a result, they don't live the rest of their lives on earth controlled by evil human longings. Instead, they live to do what God wants.

3You have spent enough time in the past doing what ungodly people choose to do. You lived a wild life. You longed for evil things. You got drunk. You went to wild parties. You worshiped statues of gods. The Lord hates that.

4Ungodly people think that it's strange

BRAVE

1 PETER 3:6

Don't give in to fear.

B
B
B

A re you ever scared? Of course, you are. *Everyone* is scared at times.

What makes you afraid? The dark? Strangers? A new school? Mean people? Accidents? Fires? The list can go on and on. Most people are afraid of *something*.

Over and over again in the Bible God tells his people not to be afraid. He gives them a good reason to be brave: he will be with them. Take David, for instance. Do you think he was afraid when he stood in front of gigantic Goliath? You can be sure he was. But he knew God was with him, so he bravely fought and won. His amazing story is found on page 336. Then there's John and Peter. They knew that standing up for Jesus could mean death for them. But they bravely did it anyway. Their incredible story is found on page 1259.

BE BRAVE

God has promised you the same things he promised the people in the Bible. Whatever the scary situation, God is with you. He will never make you face the frightening alone.

Go to page 1442 for the next Super Hero Trait

POWER SURGE

SELF-CONTROLLED
KEEP A CLEAR MIND.
CONTROL
YOURSELVES.
—— 1 PETER 4:7 ——

when you no longer join them in what they do. They want you to rush into the same flood of wasteful living. So they say bad things about you.

5 But they will have to explain their actions to God. He is ready to judge the living and the dead. 6 That's why the good news was preached even to people who are now dead. Human judges said they were guilty as far as their bodies were concerned. But God set their spirits free to live as he wanted them to.

7 The end of all things is near. So keep a clear mind. Control yourselves. Then you can pray. 8 Most of all, love one another deeply. Love erases many sins by forgiving them. 9 Welcome others into your homes without complaining.

10 God's gifts of grace come in many forms. Each of you has received a gift in order to serve others. You should use it faithfully. 11 If you speak, you should do it like one speaking God's very words. If you serve, you should do it with the strength God provides. Then in all things God will be praised through Jesus Christ.

Give him the glory and the power for ever and ever. Amen.

Suffering for Being a Christian

12 Dear friends, don't be surprised by the painful suffering you are going through. Don't feel as if something strange were happening to you. 13 Be joyful that you are taking part in Christ's sufferings. Then you will be filled with joy when Christ returns in glory.

14 Suppose people make fun of you because you believe in Christ. Then you are blessed, because God's Spirit rests on you. He is the Spirit of glory. 15 Suppose you suffer. Then it shouldn't be because you are a murderer or a thief. It shouldn't be because you do evil things. It shouldn't be because you poke your nose into other people's business. 16 But suppose you suffer for being a Christian. Then don't be ashamed. Instead, praise God because you are known by that name.

17 It is time for people to be judged. It will begin with the family of God. And since it begins with us, what will happen to people who don't obey God's good news? 18 Scripture says,

"Suppose it is hard for godly people to
    be saved.
Then what will happen to ungodly
    people and sinners?"
(Proverbs 11:31)

19 Some people will suffer because God has planned it that way. They should commit themselves to their faithful Creator. And they should continue to do good.

To Elders and Young Men

5 I'm speaking to the elders among you. I was a witness of Christ's sufferings. And I will also share in the glory that is going to come. I'm making my appeal to you as one who is an elder together with you. 2 Be shepherds of God's flock, the believers who are under your care. Serve as their leaders. Don't serve them because you have to. Instead, do it because you want to. That's what God wants you to do. Don't do it because you want to get more and more money. Do it because you really want to serve.

3 Don't act as if you were a ruler over those who are under your care. Instead, be examples to the flock. 4 The Chief Shepherd will come again. Then you will receive the crown of glory. It is a crown that will never fade away.

5 Young men, follow the lead of those who are older. All of you, put on a spirit that is free of pride toward each other as if it were your clothes. Scripture says,

"God opposes those who are proud.
    But he gives grace to those who are
    not."   *(Proverbs 3:34)*

6 So don't be proud. Put yourselves under God's mighty hand. Then he will honor you at the right time. 7 Turn all your worries over to him. He cares about you.

8 Control yourselves. Be on your guard. Your enemy the devil is like a roaring lion. He prowls around looking for someone to chew up and swallow. 9 Stand up to him. Stand firm in what you believe. All over the world you know that your brothers and sisters are going through the same kind of suffering.

10 God always gives you all the grace you need. So you will only have to suffer for a little while. Then God himself will

SELF-CONTROLLED

CONTROL
YOURSELVES. BE ON
YOUR GUARD...STAND
FIRM IN WHAT YOU
BELIEVE...GOD
HIMSELF WILL...MAKE
YOU STRONG AND
STEADY.
— 1 PETER 5:8-10 —

STRONG

build you up again. He will make you strong and steady. And he has chosen you to share in his eternal glory because you belong to Christ.

[11]Give him the power for ever and ever. Amen.

Final Greetings

[12]I consider Silas to be a faithful brother. With his help I have written you this short letter. I have written it to cheer you up. And I have written to give witness about the true grace of God. Stand firm in it.

[13]The members of the church in Babylon send you their greetings. They were chosen together with you. Mark, my son in the faith, also sends you his greetings. [14]Greet each other with a friendly kiss.

May God give peace to all of you who believe in Christ.

2 PETER

The disciple Peter writes this second book to early believers who are being taken in by false teachers. These Christians are not sure what is true anymore, and Peter wants to set them straight. He tells them that their best defense is to know Jesus and the truths of God's Word. Reading 2 Peter will help you see the importance of knowing God's Word so that you won't be tricked by false teachers.

CODE OF HONOR IN THIS BOOK . . .

KIND
PAGE 1437

SELF-CONTROLLED
PAGE 1437

1 I, Simon Peter, am writing this letter. I serve Jesus Christ. I am his apostle.

I am sending this letter to you who have received a faith as valuable as ours. You received it because our God and Savior Jesus Christ does what is right and fair for everyone.

2 May more and more grace and peace be given to you. May they come to you as you learn more about God and about Jesus our Lord.

Be Sure That God Has Chosen You

3 God's power has given us everything we need to lead a godly life. All of that has come to us because we know the One who chose us. He chose us because of his own glory and goodness. 4 He has also given us his very great and valuable promises. He did it so you could share in his nature. He also did it so you could escape from the evil in the world. That evil is caused by sinful longings. 5 So you should try very hard to add goodness to your faith. To goodness, add knowledge. 6 To knowledge, add the ability to control yourselves. To the ability to control yourselves, add the strength to keep going. To the strength to keep going, add godliness. 7 To godliness, add kindness to believers. And to kindness to believers, add love.

8 You should possess more and more of those good points. They will make you useful and fruitful as you get to know our Lord Jesus Christ better. 9 But what if some of you do not have those good points? Then you can't see very well. You are blind. You have forgotten that your past sins have been washed away.

10 My brothers and sisters, be very sure that God has appointed you to be saved. Be sure that he has chosen you. If you do everything I have just said, you will never trip and fall. 11 You will receive a rich welcome into the kingdom that lasts forever. It is the kingdom of our Lord and Savior Jesus Christ.

Prophecy Comes From God

12 So I will always remind you of these things. I'll do it even though you know them. I'll do it even though you now have deep roots in the truth. 13 I think it is right for me to remind you. It is right as long as I live in this tent. I'm talking about my body. 14 I know my tent will soon be removed. Our Lord Jesus Christ has made that clear to me. 15 I hope that you will always be able to remember these things after I'm gone. I will try very hard to see that you do.

16 We told you about the time our Lord Jesus Christ came with power. But we didn't make up stories when we told you about it. With our own eyes we saw him in all his majesty. 17 God the Father gave him honor and glory. The voice of the Majestic Glory came to him. It said, "This is my Son, and I love him. I am very pleased with him." *(Matthew 17:5; Mark 9:7; Luke 9:35)* 18 We ourselves heard the voice that came from heaven. We were with him on the sacred mountain.

19 The word of the prophets is made more certain. We have that word. You must pay attention to it. It is like a light shining in a dark place. It will shine until the day Jesus comes. Then the Morning Star will rise in your hearts. 20 Above all, here is what you must understand. No prophecy in Scripture ever came from a prophet's own understanding. 21 It never came simply because a prophet wanted it to. Instead, the Holy Spirit guided the prophets as they spoke. So prophecy comes from God.

POWER–SURGE

KIND   K

TO KNOWLEDGE, ADD THE ABILITY TO CONTROL YOURSELVES. TO THE ABILITY TO CONTROL YOURSELVES, ADD THE STRENGTH TO KEEP GOING. TO THE STRENGTH TO KEEP GOING, ADD GODLINESS. TO GODLINESS, ADD KINDNESS TO BELIEVERS. AND TO KINDNESS TO BELIEVERS, ADD LOVE.

—— 2 PETER 1:6-7 ——

SELF-CONTROLLED

False Teachers Will Be Destroyed

2 But there were also false prophets among the people. In the same way there will be false teachers among you. In secret they will bring in teachings that will destroy you. They will even turn against the Lord and Master who died to save them. His death paid for their sins. They will quickly destroy themselves. 2Many people will follow their shameful ways. They will give the way of truth a bad name.

3Those teachers are never satisfied. They want to get something out of you. So they make up stories to take advantage of you. They have been under a sentence of death for a long time. The One who will destroy them has not been sleeping.

4God did not spare angels when they sinned. Instead, he sent them to hell. He put them in dark prisons. He will keep them there until he judges them. 5God did not spare the world's ungodly people long ago. He brought the flood on them. But Noah preached about the right way to live. God kept him safe. He also saved seven others. 6God judged the cities of Sodom and Gomorrah. He burned them to ashes. He made them an example of what is going to happen to ungodly people.

7God saved Lot. He was a man who did what was right. He was shocked by the dirty, sinful lives of people who didn't obey God's laws. 8That good man lived among them day after day. He saw and heard the evil things they were doing. They were breaking God's laws. And his godly spirit was deeply troubled.

9So the Lord knows how to keep godly people safe in times of testing. He also knows how to keep ungodly people under guard until the day they will be judged. In the meantime, he continues to punish them. 10Most of all, this is true of people who follow the evil longings of their sinful natures. They hate to be under authority.

Those false prophets are bold and proud. They aren't afraid to speak evil things against heavenly beings. 11Angels are stronger and more powerful than those people. But even angels don't bring to the Lord evil charges against heavenly beings.

12Those people speak evil about things they don't understand. They are like wild animals. They do what comes naturally to them. They are born only to be caught and destroyed. Just like animals, they too will die.

13They will be paid back with harm for the harm they have done. Their idea of pleasure is to have wild parties in the middle of the day. They are like spots and stains. They enjoy their sinful pleasures while they eat with you. 14They stare at women who are not their wives. They want to have sex with them. They never stop sinning. They trap those who are not firm in their faith. They have mastered the art of getting what they want. God has placed them under his curse.

15They have left God's way. They have wandered off. They follow the way of Balaam, son of Beor. He loved to get paid for doing his evil work. 16But a donkey corrected him for the wrong he did. Animals don't speak. But the donkey spoke with a human voice. It tried to stop the prophet from doing a very dumb thing.

17Those false prophets are like springs without water. They are like mists driven by a storm. The blackest darkness is reserved for them.

18They speak empty, bragging words. They make their appeal to the earthly longings of people's sinful nature. They tempt new believers who are just escaping from the company of sinful people. 19They promise to give freedom to the new believers. But they themselves are slaves to sinful living. A person is a slave to anything that controls him.

20They may have escaped the sin of the world. They may have come to know our Lord and Savior Jesus Christ. But what if they are once again caught up in sin? And what if it has become their master? Then they are worse off at the end than they were at the beginning.

21What if they had not known the way of godliness? That would have been better than to have known it and then to have turned their backs on it. The way of godliness is the sacred command that was passed on to them.

22What the proverbs say about them is true. "A dog returns to where it has thrown up." *(Proverbs 26:11)* And, "A pig that is washed goes back to rolling in the mud."

The Day of the Lord

3 Dear friends, this is now my second letter to you. I have written both of them as reminders. I want to stir you up to think in a way that is pure. 2I want you to remember the words the holy prophets spoke in the past. Remember the command our Lord and Savior gave through your apostles.

3First of all, here is what you must understand. In the last days people will make fun of the truth. They will laugh at it. They will follow their own evil longings. ⁴They will say, "Where is this 'return' he promised? Everything goes on in the same way it has since our people of long ago died. In fact, it has continued that way since God first created everything."

⁵Long ago, God's word brought the heavens into being. His word separated the earth from the waters. And the waters surrounded it. But those people forget things like that on purpose. ⁶The waters also flooded the world of that time. It was destroyed.

⁷By God's word the heavens and earth of today are being reserved for fire. They are being kept for the day when God will judge. Then ungodly people will be destroyed.

⁸Dear friends, here is one thing you must not forget. With the Lord a day is like a thousand years. And a thousand years are like a day. ⁹The Lord is not slow to keep his promise. He is not slow in the way some people understand it. He is patient with you. He doesn't want anyone to be destroyed. Instead, he wants all people to turn away from their sins.

¹⁰But the day of the Lord will come like a thief. The heavens will disappear with a roar. Fire will destroy everything in them. God will judge the earth and everything in it.

¹¹So everything will be destroyed. And what kind of people should you be? You should lead holy and godly lives. ¹²Live like that as you look forward to the day of God. It will make the day come more quickly. On that day fire will destroy the heavens. Its heat will melt everything in them.

¹³But we are looking forward to a new heaven and a new earth. Godliness will make its home there. All of this is in keeping with God's promise.

¹⁴Dear friends, I know you are looking forward to that. So try your best to be found pure and without blame. Be at peace with God. ¹⁵Remember that while our Lord is waiting patiently to return, people are being saved.

Our dear brother Paul also wrote to you about that. God made him wise to write as he did. ¹⁶He writes the same way in all his letters. He speaks about what I have just told you. His letters include some things that are hard to understand. People who don't know better and aren't firm in the faith twist what he says. They twist the other Scriptures too. So they will be destroyed.

¹⁷Dear friends, you already know that. So be on your guard. Then you won't be led down the wrong path by the mistakes of people who don't obey the law. You won't fall from your safe position.

¹⁸Grow in the grace of our Lord and Savior Jesus Christ. Get to know him better.

Give him glory both now and forever. Amen.

1 JOHN

John the disciple, who also wrote the book of John, writes this letter to tell early Christians about God's love. He wants them to realize first, that God loves them and second, that God wants them to love each other. False teachers are trying to draw people away from godly living. John teaches the truth so that Christians will have a defense against such false teachings. As you read 1 John, look at your life. Are you loving others as God loves you?

CHECK OUT THIS TRAIT OF A HERO . . .

OBEYS
PAGE 1442

The Word of Life

1 Here is what we announce to every-one about the Word of life. He was already here from the beginning. We have heard him. We have seen him with our eyes. We have looked at him. Our hands have touched him. **2**That life has appeared. We have seen him. We give witness about him. And we announce to you that same eternal life. He was already with the Father. He has appeared to us.

3We announce to you what we have seen and heard. We do it so you can share life together with us. And we share life with the Father and with his Son, Jesus Christ. **4**We are writing this to make our joy complete.

Walking in the Light

5Here is the message we have heard from him and announce to you. God is light. There is no darkness in him at all. **6**Suppose we say that we share life with God but still walk in the darkness. Then we are lying. We are not living by the truth. **7**But suppose we walk in the light, just as he is in the light. Then we share life with one another. And the blood of Jesus, his Son, makes us pure from all sin.

8Suppose we claim we are without sin. Then we are fooling ourselves. The truth is not in us. **9**But God is faithful and fair. If we admit that we have sinned, he will forgive us our sins. He will forgive every wrong thing we have done. He will make us pure. **10**If we say we have not sinned, we are calling God a liar. His word has no place in our lives.

2 My dear children, I'm writing this to you so that you will not sin. But suppose someone does sin. Then we have one who speaks to the Father for us. He stands up for us. He is Jesus Christ, the Blameless One. **2**He gave his life to pay for our sins. But he not only paid for our sins. He also paid for the sins of the whole world.

3We know that we have come to know God if we obey his commands. **4**Suppose someone says, "I know him." But suppose that person does not do what God commands. Then that person is a liar and is not telling the truth. **5**But if anyone obeys God's word, then God's love is truly made complete in that person. Here is how we know we belong to him. **6**Those who claim to belong to him must live just as Jesus did.

7Dear friends, I'm not writing you a new command. Instead, I'm writing one you have heard before. You have had it since the beginning.

8But I am writing what amounts to a new command. Its truth was shown in how Jesus lived. It is also shown in how you live. The darkness is passing away. The true light is already shining.

9Suppose someone claims to be in the light but hates his brother or sister. Then he is still in the darkness. **10**Those who love their brothers and sisters are living in the light. There is nothing in them to make them fall into sin. **11**But those who hate a brother or sister are in the darkness. They walk around in the darkness. They don't know where they are going. The darkness has made them blind.

12Dear children, I'm writing to you
  because your sins have been
    forgiven.
  They have been forgiven because of
    what Jesus has done.
13Fathers, I'm writing to you
  because you have known the One
    who is from the beginning.
Young people, I'm writing to you
  because you have won the battle
    over the evil one.

Dear children, I'm writing to you
  because you have known the Father.
14Fathers, I'm writing to you
  because you have known the One
    who is from the beginning.
Young people, I'm writing to you
  because you are strong.
  God's word lives in you.
  You have won the battle over the
    evil one.

Do Not Love the World

15Do not love the world or anything in it. If you love the world, love for the Father is not in you.

16Here is what people who belong to this world do. They try to satisfy what their sinful natures want to do. They long for what their sinful eyes look at. They brag about what they have and what they do. All of this comes from the world. It doesn't come from the Father.

17The world and its evil longings are passing away. But those who do what God wants them to do live forever.

A Warning About the Enemies of Christ

18Dear children, we are living in the last days. You have heard that the great enemy of Christ is coming. But even now many enemies of Christ have already come. That's how we know that these are the last days.

19The enemies left our group. They didn't really belong to us. If they had belonged to us, they would have remained with us. But by leaving they showed that none of them belonged to us.

20You have received the Spirit from the Holy One. And all of you know the truth. 21I'm not writing to you because you don't know the truth but because you do know it. I'm writing to you because no lie comes from the truth.

22Who is the liar? The person who says that Jesus is not the Christ. People who say that are the enemies of Christ. They say no to the Father and the Son. 23Those who say no to the Son don't belong to the Father. But anyone who says yes to the Son belongs to the Father also.

24Make sure that you don't forget what you have heard from the beginning. Then you will remain joined to the Son and to the Father. 25That's what God has promised us. We have eternal life.

26I'm writing these things to warn you about those who are trying to lead you down the wrong path.

OBEYS

1 JOHN 2:3, 5

✔
✔
✔

We know that we have come to know God if we obey his commands...if anyone obeys God's word, then God's love is truly made complete in that person.

Obey your mom and dad. Obey your teachers. Obey the police. Obey the Bible. Obey God. Does it seem like every time you turn around, someone is telling you to obey? Well, maybe that should tell you something about obeying. Like that it's very important!

Elisha the prophet told a widow to get a bunch of jars, then start pouring the oil from a tiny jar into lots and lots of big jars. Now that didn't make much sense. The little jar would run out before the first big jar was filled. But the widow obeyed. Because she obeyed, even when it didn't make sense, the little jar didn't run out until all the big jars were filled. God protected and provided for the widow because she obeyed (see her story on page 434). Matthew was one of the first disciples that Jesus called to follow him. Jesus said only two words, "Follow me." And Matthew obeyed. His obedience that day changed his life forever (see his story on page 1105).

OBEY

Did you know that just obeying isn't enough? If you obey just because you're a nice person, that's, well, *nice.* But it's not all that God wants. He wants you to obey because you love him. True obedience comes from a heart that loves God and wants to please him.

Go to page 1464 for the next Super Hero Trait

27But you have received the Holy Spirit from God. He continues to live in you. So you don't need anyone to teach you. God's Spirit teaches you about everything. What he says is true. He doesn't lie. Remain joined to Christ, just as you have been taught by the Spirit.

Children of God

28Dear children, remain joined to Christ. Then when he comes, we can be bold. We will not be ashamed to meet him when he comes.

29You know that God is right and always does what is right. And you know that everyone who does what is right has been born again because of what God has done.

3 How great is the love the Father has given us so freely! Now we can be called children of God. And that's what we really are! The world doesn't know us because it didn't know him.

2Dear friends, now we are children of God. He still hasn't let us know what we will be. But we know that when Christ appears, we will be like him. We will see him as he really is. **3**He is pure. All who hope to be like him make themselves pure.

4Everyone who sins breaks the law. In fact, breaking the law is sin. **5**But you know that Christ came to take our sins away. And there is no sin in him. **6**No one who remains joined to him keeps on sinning. No one who keeps on sinning has seen him or known him.

7Dear children, don't let anyone lead you down the wrong path. Those who do what is right are holy, just as Christ is holy. **8**Those who do what is sinful belong to the devil. They are just like him. He has been sinning from the beginning. But the Son of God came to destroy the devil's work.

9Those who are born again because of what God has done will not keep on sinning. God's very nature remains in them. They can't go on sinning. They have been born again because of what God has done.

10Here is how you can tell the difference between the children of God and the children of the devil. Those who don't do what is right do not belong to God. Those who don't love their brothers and sisters do not belong to him either.

Love One Another

11From the beginning we have heard that we should love one another. **12**Don't be like Cain. He belonged to the evil one.

He murdered his brother. And why did he murder him? Because the things Cain had done were wrong. But the things his brother had done were right.

13My brothers and sisters, don't be surprised if the world hates you. **14**We know that we have left our old dead condition and entered into new life. We know it because we love one another. Those who do not are still living in their old condition.

15Those who hate their brothers and sisters are murderers. And you know that murderers do not have eternal life in their hearts.

16We know what love is because Jesus Christ gave his life for us. So we should give our lives for our brothers and sisters.

17Suppose someone sees a brother or sister in need and is able to help them. If he doesn't take pity on them, how can the love of God be in him?

18Dear children, don't just talk about love. Put your love into action. Then it will truly be love. **19**That's how we know that we hold to the truth. And that's how we put our hearts at rest, knowing that God is watching. **20**Our hearts may judge us. But God is greater than our hearts. He knows everything.

21Dear friends, if our hearts do not judge us, we can be bold with God. **22**And he will give us anything we ask. That's because we obey his commands. We do what pleases him.

23God has commanded us to believe in the name of his Son, Jesus Christ. He has also commanded us to love one another. **24**Those who obey his commands remain joined to him. And he remains joined to them.

How do we know that God lives in us? We know it because of the Holy Spirit he gave us.

Put the Spirits to the Test

4 Dear friends, do not believe every spirit. Put the spirits to the test to see

POWER-SURGE

BELIEVES ✝

GOD HAS COMMANDED US TO BELIEVE IN THE NAME OF HIS SON, JESUS CHRIST.
— 1 JOHN 3:23 —

if they belong to God. Many false prophets have gone out into the world.

²How can you recognize the Spirit of God? Every spirit that agrees that Jesus Christ came in a human body belongs to God. ³But every spirit that doesn't agree with this does not belong to God. It is the spirit of the great enemy of Christ. You have heard that the enemy is coming. Even now he is already in the world.

⁴Dear children, you belong to God. You have not accepted the teachings of the false prophets. That's because the One who is in you is more powerful than the one who is in the world.

⁵False prophets belong to the world. So they speak from the world's point of view. The world listens to them. ⁶We belong to God. And those who know God listen to us. But those who don't belong to God don't listen to us. That's how we can tell the difference between the Spirit of truth and the spirit of lies.

We Love Because God Loved Us

⁷Dear friends, let us love one another, because love comes from God. Everyone who loves has been born again because of what God has done. That person knows God. ⁸Anyone who does not love does not know God, because God is love.

⁹How did God show his love for us? He sent his one and only Son into the world. He sent him so we could receive life through him.

¹⁰What is love? It is not that we loved God. It is that he loved us and sent his Son to give his life to pay for our sins.

¹¹Dear friends, since God loved us that much, we should also love one another. ¹²No one has ever seen God. But if we love one another, God lives in us. His love is made complete in us.

¹³We know that we belong to him and he belongs to us. He has given us his Holy Spirit.

¹⁴The Father has sent his Son to be the Savior of the world. We have seen it. We give witness to it. ¹⁵God lives in anyone who agrees that Jesus is the Son of God. That kind of person remains joined to God. ¹⁶So we know that God loves us. We depend on it.

God is love. Anyone who leads a life of love shows that he is joined to God. And God is joined to him.

¹⁷So love is made complete among us. We will be bold on the day God judges us. That's because in this world we love as Jesus did.

¹⁸There is no fear in love. Instead, perfect love drives fear away. Fear has to do with being punished. The one who fears does not have perfect love.

¹⁹We love because he loved us first. ²⁰Anyone who says he loves God but in fact hates his brother or sister is a liar. He doesn't love his brother or sister, whom he has seen. So he can't love God, whom he has not seen.

²¹Here is the command God has given us. Anyone who loves God must also love his brothers and sisters.

Faith in the Son of God

5 Everyone who believes that Jesus is the Christ is born again because of what God has done. And everyone who loves the Father loves his children as well.

²How do we know that we love God's children? We know it when we love God and obey his commands. ³Here is what it means to love God. It means that we obey his commands. And his commands are not hard to obey. ⁴That's because everyone who is a child of God has won the battle over the world. Our faith has won the battle for us.

POWER-SURGE

LOVING ♥

HERE IS WHAT IT MEANS TO LOVE GOD. IT MEANS THAT WE OBEY HIS COMMANDS.
— 1 JOHN 5:3 —

✔

OBEYS

⁵Who is it that has won the battle over the world? Only the person who believes that Jesus is the Son of God.

⁶Jesus Christ is the one who was baptized in water and died on the cross. He wasn't just baptized in water. He also died on the cross. The Holy Spirit has given a truthful witness about him. That's because the Spirit is the truth.

⁷There are three that give witness about Jesus. ⁸They are the Holy Spirit, the baptism of Jesus and his death. And the three of them agree.

⁹We accept the witness of people. But the witness of God is more important be-

BELIEVES ✝

WHO IS IT THAT HAS WON THE BATTLE OVER THE WORLD? ONLY THE PERSON WHO BELIEVES THAT JESUS IS THE SON OF GOD.

—— 1 JOHN 5:5 ——

cause it is God who gives it. He has given witness about his Son.

¹⁰Those who believe in the Son of God have accepted that witness in their hearts. Those who do not believe God's witness are calling him a liar. That's because they have not believed his witness about his Son. ¹¹Here is God's witness. He has given us eternal life. That life is found in his Son. ¹²Those who belong to the Son have life. Those who do not belong to the Son of God do not have life.

Final Words

¹³I'm writing these things to you who believe in the name of the Son of God. I'm doing it so you will know that you have eternal life.

¹⁴There is one thing we can be sure of when we come to God in prayer. If we ask anything in keeping with what he wants, he hears us. ¹⁵If we know that God hears what we ask for, we know that we have it.

¹⁶Suppose you see your brother or sister commit a sin. But that sin is not the kind that leads to death. Then you should pray for them. And God will give life to them. I'm talking about someone whose sin does not lead to death. But there is a sin that does lead to death. I'm not saying that you should pray about that. ¹⁷Every wrong thing we do is sin. But there are sins that do not lead to death.

¹⁸We know that those who are children of God do not keep on sinning. The Son of God keeps them safe. The evil one can't harm them. ¹⁹We know that we are children of God. We know that the whole world is under the control of the evil one.

²⁰We also know that the Son of God has come. He has given us understanding. Now we can know the One who is true. And we belong to the One who is true. We also belong to his Son, Jesus Christ. He is the true God. He is eternal life.

²¹Dear children, keep away from statues of gods.

2 JOHN

John writes this second letter to warn believers to watch out and to be sure of what they believe. False teachers can quickly lead the unsure away from the truth, and John wants to be sure believers are prepared. Read this little letter—it will help you understand how important it is to be sure of what you believe.

CODE OF HONOR IN THIS BOOK . . .

LOVING
PAGE 1447

OBEYS
PAGE 1447

¹I, the elder, am writing this letter.

I am sending it to the chosen lady and her children. I love all of you because of the truth. I'm not the only one who loves you. So does everyone who knows the truth. ²I love you because of the truth that is alive in us. That truth will be with us forever.

³God the Father and Jesus Christ his Son will give you grace, mercy and peace. Those blessings will be with us because we love the truth.

⁴It has given me great joy to find some of your children living by the truth. That's just what the Father commanded us to do.

⁵Dear lady, I'm not writing you a new command. I'm writing a command we've

POWER-SURGE

LOVING ♥

I'M WRITING A COMMAND WE'VE HAD FROM THE BEGINNING. I'M ASKING THAT WE LOVE ONE ANOTHER. THE WAY WE SHOW OUR LOVE IS TO OBEY GOD'S COMMANDS. HE COMMANDS YOU TO LEAD A LIFE OF LOVE.
— 2 JOHN 5-6 —   ✔

OBEYS

POWER-SURGE

OBEYS ✔

THOSE WHO FOLLOW THE TEACHING OF CHRIST BELONG TO THE FATHER AND THE SON.
— 2 JOHN 9 —

had from the beginning. I'm asking that we love one another. ⁶The way we show our love is to obey God's commands. He commands you to lead a life of love. That's what you have heard from the beginning.

⁷Many people who try to fool others have gone out into the world. They don't agree that Jesus Christ came in a human body. People like that try to trick others. They are enemies of Christ. ⁸Watch out that you don't lose what you have worked for. Make sure that you get your complete reward.

⁹Some people run ahead of others. They don't follow the teaching of Christ. People like that don't belong to God. But those who follow the teaching of Christ belong to the Father and the Son.

¹⁰Suppose someone comes to you and doesn't teach these truths. Then don't take him into your house. Don't welcome him. ¹¹Anyone who welcomes him shares in his evil work.

¹²I have a lot to write to you. But I don't want to use paper and ink. Instead, I hope I can visit you. Then I can talk with you face to face. That will make our joy complete.

¹³The children of your chosen sister send their greetings.

3 JOHN

The apostle John, one of the original twelve disciples, writes this third letter to his friend, Gaius. He tells Gaius that he is glad that Gaius welcomes other believers in his home. He also warns him about another church leader who might cause problems. You can read 3 John quickly to find that being a friend to other Christians is important.

CODE OF HONOR IN THIS BOOK . . .

HONEST
PAGE 1449

FAITHFUL
PAGE 1449

¹I, the elder, am writing this letter.

I am sending it to you, my dear friend Gaius. I love you because of the truth.

²Dear friend, I know that your spiritual life is going well. I pray that you also may enjoy good health. And I pray that everything else may go well with you.

³Some believers came to me and told me that you are faithful to the truth. They told me that you continue to live by it. That gave me great joy. ⁴I have no greater joy than to hear that my children are living by the truth.

⁵Dear friend, you are faithful in what you are doing for the believers. You are faithful even though they are strangers to you. ⁶They have told the church about your love. Please help them by sending them on their way in a manner that honors God.

⁷They started on their journey to serve Jesus Christ. They didn't receive any help from those who aren't believers. ⁸So we should welcome people like them. We should work together with them for the truth.

⁹I wrote to the church. But Diotrephes won't have anything to do with us. He loves to be the first in everything. ¹⁰So if I come, I will point out what he is doing. He is saying evil things about us to others. Even that doesn't satisfy him. He refuses to welcome other believers. He also keeps others from welcoming them. In fact, he throws them out of the church.

¹¹Dear friend, don't be like those who do evil. Be like those who do good. Anyone who does what is good belongs to God. Anyone who does what is evil hasn't really seen or known God.

POWER-SURGE

FAITHFUL ( )

SOME BELIEVERS CAME TO ME AND TOLD ME THAT YOU ARE FAITHFUL TO THE TRUTH. THEY TOLD ME THAT YOU CONTINUE TO LIVE BY IT. THAT GAVE ME GREAT JOY. I HAVE NO GREATER JOY THAN TO HEAR THAT MY CHILDREN ARE LIVING BY THE TRUTH.
— 3 JOHN 3-4 —

HONEST

¹²Everyone says good things about Demetrius. He lives in keeping with the truth. We also say good things about him. And you know that our witness is true.

¹³I have a lot to write to you. But I don't want to write with pen and ink. ¹⁴I hope I can see you soon. Then we can talk face to face.

May you have peace. The friends here send their greetings. Greet the friends there by name.

JUDE

Jude, another brother of Jesus (along with James), writes this short book to tell believers not to give up when defending the truths about Jesus. False teachers are trying to get believers to turn away from the true faith. Jude warns them to stand firm. Read this little book to get support and teaching on how to be strong in your faith.

CHARACTER TRAIT OF A HERO . . .

BELIEVES

PAGE 1451

¹I, Jude, am writing this letter. I serve Jesus Christ. I am a brother of James.

I am sending this letter to you who have been chosen by God. You are loved by God the Father. You are kept safe by Jesus Christ.

²May more and more mercy, peace, and love be given to you.

A Warning Against Ungodly Teachers

³Dear friends, I really wanted to write to you about the salvation we share. But now I feel I should write and ask you to stand up for the faith. God's people were trusted with it once and for all time.

⁴Certain people have slipped in among you in secret. Long ago it was written that they would be judged. They are godless people. They use the grace of our God as an excuse for sexual sins. They say no to Jesus Christ. He is our only Lord and King.

⁵I want to remind you about some things you already know. The Lord saved his people. He brought them out of Egypt. But later he destroyed those who did not believe. ⁶Some of the angels didn't stay where they belonged. They didn't keep their positions of authority. The Lord has kept those angels in darkness. They are held by chains that last forever. On judgment day, God will judge them.

⁷The people of Sodom and Gomorrah and the towns around them also did evil things. They gave themselves over to sexual sins. They committed sins of the worst possible kind. They are an example of those who are punished with fire. The fire never goes out.

⁸In the very same way, those dreamers pollute their own bodies. They don't accept authority. They speak evil things against heavenly beings. ⁹But not even Michael did that. He was the leader of the angels. He argued with the devil about the body of Moses. But he didn't dare to speak evil things against the devil. Instead, he said, "May the Lord stop you!"

¹⁰But those people speak evil things against what they don't understand. They are like wild animals. They can't think for themselves. They do what comes naturally to them. Those are the very things that destroy them.

¹¹How terrible it will be for them! They followed the way of Cain. They rushed ahead and made the same mistake as Balaam did. They did it because they loved money. They are like Korah. He turned against his leaders. Those people will certainly be destroyed, just as Korah was.

¹²They are like stains at the meals you share. They eat too much. They have no shame. They are shepherds who feed only themselves. They are like clouds without rain. They are blown along by the wind. They are like trees in the fall. Since they have no fruit, they are pulled up. So they die twice.

¹³They are like wild waves of the sea. Their shame rises up like foam. They are like falling stars. God has reserved a place of very black darkness for them. He will keep them there forever.

¹⁴Enoch was the seventh man in the family line of Adam. He gave a prophecy about those people. He said, "Look! The Lord is coming with thousands and thousands of his holy ones. ¹⁵He is coming to judge everyone. He is coming to sentence all ungodly people. He will judge them for all the ungodly acts they have done. They have done them in ungodly ways. He will sentence ungodly sinners for all the bad things they have said about him."

¹⁶Those people complain. They find fault with others. They follow their own evil longings. They brag about themselves. They praise others to help themselves.

Remain in God's Love

¹⁷Dear friends, remember what the apostles of our Lord Jesus Christ said was going to happen. ¹⁸They told you, "In the last days, some people will make fun of the truth. They will follow their own ungodly longings." ¹⁹They are the people who separate you from one another. They do only what comes naturally. They are not led by the Holy Spirit.

²⁰Dear friends, build yourselves up in your most holy faith. Let the Holy Spirit guide and help you when you pray. ²¹The mercy of our Lord Jesus Christ will bring you eternal life. As you wait for his mercy, remain in God's love.

POWER-SURGE

BELIEVES ✝

DEAR FRIENDS, BUILD YOURSELVES UP IN YOUR MOST HOLY FAITH.

—— JUDE 20 ——

²²Show mercy to those who doubt. ²³Pull others out of the fire. Save them. To others, show mercy mixed with fear. Hate even the clothes that are stained by the sins of those who wear them.

Praise to God

²⁴Give praise to the One who is able to keep you from falling into sin. He will bring you into his heavenly glory without any fault. He will bring you there with great joy. ²⁵Give praise to the only God. He is our Savior. Glory, majesty, power and authority belong to him. Give praise to him through Jesus Christ our Lord. Give praise to the One who was before all time, who now is, and who will be forever. Amen.

REVELATION

Does it ever seem to you like the bad guys are winning? John, one of the original twelve disciples, writes this book to make sure you know that now and in the future, Jesus wins! John writes of the visions and dreams he has that picture what will happen in the end times. Although this book may be hard to understand, you'll get the big picture if you read it—God and those who follow him are the final winners!

CHECK OUT THIS CHARACTER TRAIT AND HERO . . .

PATIENT
PAGE 1464

YOU!
PAGE 1472

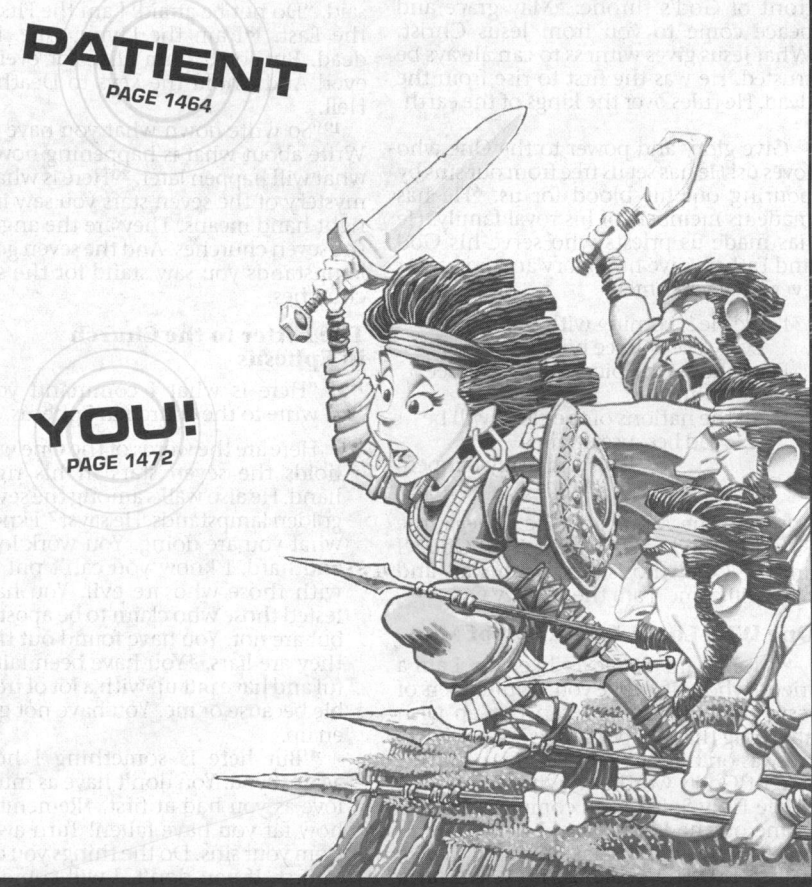

1 This is the revelation that God gave to Jesus Christ. Jesus shows those who serve God what will happen soon. God made it known by sending his angel to his servant John. [2]John gives witness to everything he saw. The things he gives witness to are God's word and what Jesus Christ has said.

[3]Blessed is the one who reads the words of this prophecy. Blessed are those who hear it and think everything it says is important. The time when these things will come true is near.

Greetings

[4]I, John, am writing this letter.

I am sending it to the seven churches in Asia Minor.

May grace and peace come to you from the One who is, and who was, and who will come. May grace and peace come to you from the seven spirits who are in front of God's throne. [5]May grace and peace come to you from Jesus Christ. What Jesus gives witness to can always be trusted. He was the first to rise from the dead. He rules over the kings of the earth.

Give glory and power to the One who loves us! He has set us free from our sins by pouring out his blood for us. [6]He has made us members of his royal family. He has made us priests who serve his God and Father. Give him glory and power for ever and ever! Amen.

[7]Look! He is coming with the clouds!
Every eye will see him.
Even those who pierced him will see
him.
All the nations of the earth will be
sad because of him.
This will really happen!
Amen.

[8]"I am the Alpha and the Omega, the First and the Last," says the Lord God. "I am the One who is, and who was, and who will come. I am the Mighty One."

One Who Looks Like a Son of Man

[9]I, John, am a believer like you. I am a friend who suffers like you. As members of Jesus' royal family, we can put up with anything that happens to us.

I was on the island of Patmos because I taught God's word and what Jesus said. [10]The Holy Spirit took complete control of me on the Lord's Day. I heard a loud voice behind me that sounded like a trumpet. [11]The voice said, "Write on a scroll what you see. Send it to the seven churches in Asia Minor. They are Ephesus, Smyrna, Pergamum, Thyatira, Sardis, Philadelphia and Laodicea."

[12]I turned around to see who was speaking to me. When I turned, I saw seven golden lampstands. [13]In the middle of them was someone who looked "like a son of man." *(Daniel 7:13)*

He was dressed in a long robe with a gold strip of cloth around his chest. [14]The hair on his head was white like wool, as white as snow. His eyes were like a blazing fire. [15]His feet were like bronze metal glowing in a furnace. His voice sounded like rushing waters. [16]He held seven stars in his right hand. Out of his mouth came a sharp sword that had two edges. His face was like the sun shining in all of its brightness.

[17]When I saw him, I fell at his feet as if I were dead.

Then he put his right hand on me and said, "Do not be afraid. I am the First and the Last. [18]I am the Living One. I was dead. But look! I am alive for ever and ever! And I hold the keys to Death and Hell.

[19]"So write down what you have seen. Write about what is happening now and what will happen later. [20]Here is what the mystery of the seven stars you saw in my right hand means. They are the angels of the seven churches. And the seven golden lampstands you saw stand for the seven churches.

The Letter to the Church in Ephesus

2 "Here is what I command you to write to the church in Ephesus.

Here are the words of the One who holds the seven stars in his right hand. He also walks among the seven golden lampstands. He says, [2]'I know what you are doing. You work long and hard. I know you can't put up with those who are evil. You have tested those who claim to be apostles but are not. You have found out that they are liars. [3]You have been faithful and have put up with a lot of trouble because of me. You have not given up.

[4]'But here is something I hold against you. You don't have as much love as you had at first. [5]Remember how far you have fallen! Turn away from your sins. Do the things you did at first. If you don't, I will come to

you and remove your lampstand from its place.

6'But you do have this in your favor. You hate the way the Nicolaitans act. I hate it too.

7'Those who have ears should listen to what the Holy Spirit says to the churches. I will allow those who overcome to eat from the tree of life in God's paradise.'

The Letter to the Church in Smyrna

8"Here is what I command you to write to the church in Smyrna.

Here are the words of the One who is the First and the Last. He is the One who died and came to life again. He says, 9'I know that you suffer and are poor. But you are rich! Some people say they are Jews but are not. I know that their words are evil. Their worship is satanic.

10'Don't be afraid of what you are going to suffer. I tell you, the devil will put some of you in prison to test you. You will be treated badly for ten days. Be faithful, even if it means you must die. Then I will give you a crown. The crown is life itself.

11'Those who have ears should listen to what the Holy Spirit says to the churches. Those who overcome will not be hurt at all by the second death.'

The Letter to the Church in Pergamum

12"Here is what I command you to write to the church in Pergamum.

Here are the words of the One with the sharp sword that has two edges. He says, 13'I know that you live where Satan has his throne. But you remain true to me. You did not give up your faith in me, even in the days of Antipas, my faithful witness. He was put to death in your city, where Satan lives.

14'But I have a few things against you. You have people there who follow the teaching of Balaam. He taught Balak to lead the people of Israel into sin. So they ate food that had been offered to statues of gods. And they committed sexual sins. 15You also have people who follow the teaching of the Nicolaitans.

16'So turn away from your sins! If you don't, I will come to you soon. I will fight against those people with the sword that comes out of my mouth.

17'Those who have ears should listen to what the Holy Spirit says to the churches. I will give hidden manna to those who overcome. I will also give each of them a white stone with a new name written on it. Only the one who receives that name will know what it is.'

The Letter to the Church in Thyatira

18"Here is what I command you to write to the church in Thyatira.

Here are the words of the Son of God. He is the One whose eyes are like blazing fire. His feet are like polished bronze. He says, 19'I know what you are doing. I know your love and your faith. I know how well you have served. I know you don't give up easily. In fact, you are doing more now than you did at first.

20'But here is what I have against you. You put up with that woman Jezebel. She calls herself a prophet. With her teaching, she has led my servants into sexual sin. She has tricked them into eating food offered to statues of gods.

21'I've given her time to turn away from her sinful ways. But she doesn't want to. 22She sinned on a bed. So I will make her suffer on a bed. And those who commit adultery with her will suffer greatly. Their only way out is to turn away from what she taught them to do. 23I will strike her children dead. Then all the churches will

POWER SURGE

BELIEVES ✝

I KNOW YOUR LOVE AND YOUR FAITH. I KNOW HOW WELL YOU HAVE SERVED. I KNOW YOU DON'T GIVE UP EASILY.
— REVELATION 2:19 —

TRIES HARD

know that I am the One who searches hearts and minds. I will pay each of you back for what you have done.

24'I won't bother the rest of you in Thyatira. You don't follow the teaching of Jezebel. You haven't learned what some people call Satan's deep secrets. 25Just hold on to what you have until I come.

26'I'll give authority over the nations to all who overcome and who carry out my plans to the end. 27It is written,

  ' "He will rule them with an iron
      rod.
  He will break them to pieces
      like clay pots."   *(Psalm 2:9)*

I have received this authority from my Father. 28I will also give the morning star to all who overcome.

29'Those who have ears should listen to what the Holy Spirit says to the churches.'

The Letter to the Church in Sardis

3 "Here is what I command you to write to the church in Sardis.

Here are the words of the One who holds the seven spirits of God. He has the seven stars in his hand. He says, 'I know what you are doing. People think you are alive, but you are dead. 2Wake up! Strengthen what is left, or it will die. You have not done all that my God wants you to do.

3'So remember what you have been taught and have heard. Obey it. Turn away from your sins. If you don't wake up, I will come like a thief. You won't know when I will come to you.

4'But you have a few people in Sardis who have kept their clothes clean. They will walk with me, dressed in white, because they are worthy. 5Those who overcome will also be dressed in white. I will never erase their names from the Book of Life. I will speak of them by name to my Father and his angels.

6'Those who have ears should listen to what the Holy Spirit says to the churches.'

The Letter to the Church in Philadelphia

7"Here is what I command you to write to the church in Philadelphia.

Here are the words of the One who is holy and true. He holds the key of David. No one can shut what he opens. And no one can open what he shuts. He says, 8'I know what you are doing. Look! I have put an open door in front of you. No one can shut it. I know that you don't have much strength. But you have obeyed my word. You have not said no to me.

9'Some people claim they are Jews but are not. They are liars. Their worship is from Satan. I will make them come and fall down at your feet. I will make them say in public that I love you.

10'You have kept my command to put up with anything that happens. So I will keep you from the time of suffering that is going to come to the whole world. It will test those who live on the earth.

11'I am coming soon. Hold on to what you have. Then no one will take away your crown.

12'I'll see to it that those who overcome will be pillars in the temple of my God. They will never leave it again. I will write the name of my God on them. I will write the name of the city of my God on them. This is the new Jerusalem, which is coming down out of heaven from my God. I will also write my new name on them.

13'Those who have ears should listen to what the Holy Spirit says to the churches.'

The Letter to the Church in Laodicea

14"Here is what I command you to write to the church in Laodicea.

Here are the words of the One who is the Amen. What he gives witness to is faithful and true. He rules over what God has created. He says, 15'I

POWER-SURGE

OBEYS ✔

REMEMBER WHAT YOU
HAVE BEEN TAUGHT
AND HAVE HEARD.
OBEY IT.
— REVELATION 3:3 —

know what you are doing. I know you aren't cold or hot. I wish you were either one or the other! **16**But you are lukewarm. You aren't hot or cold. So I am going to spit you out of my mouth.

17'You say, "I am rich. I've become wealthy and don't need anything." But you don't realize how pitiful and miserable you have become. You are poor, blind and naked.

18'So here's my advice. Buy from me gold made pure by fire. Then you will become rich. Buy from me white clothes to wear. Then you will be able to cover your shameful nakedness. And buy from me healing lotion to put on your eyes. Then you will be able to see.

19'I correct and train those I love. So be sincere, and turn away from your sins.

POWER SURGE

LOVING ♥

I CORRECT AND TRAIN THOSE I LOVE.
—— REVELATION 3:19 ——

20'Here I am! I stand at the door and knock. If any of you hears my voice and opens the door, I will come in and eat with you. And you will eat with me.

21'I'll give those who overcome the right to sit with me on my throne. In the same way, I overcame. Then I sat down with my Father on his throne.

22'Those who have ears should listen to what the Holy Spirit says to the churches.' "

The Throne in Heaven

4 After this I looked, and there in front of me was a door standing open in heaven. I heard the voice I had heard before. It sounded like a trumpet. The voice said, "Come up here. I will show you what must happen after this."

2At once the Holy Spirit took complete control of me. There in front of me was a throne in heaven with someone sitting on it. **3**The One who sat there shone like jewels. Around the throne was a rainbow that looked like an emerald.

4Twenty-four other thrones surround-

ed that throne. Twenty-four elders were sitting on them. The elders were dressed in white. They had gold crowns on their heads.

5From the throne came flashes of lightning, rumblings and thunder. Seven lamps were blazing in front of the throne. These stand for the seven spirits of God. **6**There was something that looked like a sea of glass in front of the throne. It was as clear as crystal.

In the inner circle, around the throne, were four living creatures. They were covered with eyes, in front and in back. **7**The first creature looked like a lion. The second looked like an ox. The third had a man's face. The fourth looked like a flying eagle. **8**Each of the four living creatures had six wings. Each creature was covered all over with eyes, even under the wings. Day and night, they never stop saying,

> "Holy, holy, holy
> is the Lord God who rules over all.
> He was, and he is, and he will come."

9The living creatures give glory, honor and thanks to the One who sits on the throne and who lives for ever and ever. **10**At the same time, the 24 elders fall down and worship the One who sits on the throne and who lives for ever and ever. They lay their crowns in front of the throne. They say,

11 "You are worthy, our Lord and God!
> You are worthy to receive glory and
> honor and power.
> You are worthy because you created all
> things.
> They were created and they exist.
> That is the way you planned it."

The Scroll and the Lamb

5 Then I saw a scroll in the right hand of the One sitting on the throne. The scroll had writing on both sides. It was sealed with seven seals.

2I saw a mighty angel calling out in a loud voice, "Who is worthy to break the seals and open the scroll?" **3**But no one in heaven or on earth or under the earth could open the scroll. No one could even look inside it.

4I cried and cried because no one was found who was worthy to open the scroll or look inside.

5Then one of the elders said to me, "Do not cry! The Lion of the tribe of Judah has won the battle. He is the Root of David. He is able to break the seven seals and open the scroll."

6Then I saw a Lamb that looked as if he had been put to death. He stood in the center of the area around the throne. The Lamb was surrounded by the four living creatures and the elders. He had seven horns and seven eyes. The eyes stand for the seven spirits of God, which are sent out into all the earth.

7The Lamb came and took the scroll from the right hand of the One sitting on the throne. **8**Then the four living creatures and the 24 elders fell down in front of the Lamb. Each one had a harp. They were holding golden bowls full of incense, which stand for the prayers of God's people.

9Here is the new song they sang.

"You are worthy to take the scroll
    and break open its seals.
You are worthy because you were put
    to death.
    With your blood you bought people
        for God.
    They come from every tribe,
        language, people and nation.
10You have made them members of a
        royal family.
    You have made them priests to serve
        our God.
    They will rule on the earth."

11Then I looked and heard the voice of millions and millions of angels. They surrounded the throne. They surrounded the living creatures and the elders. **12**In a loud voice they sang,

"The Lamb, who was put to death, is
    worthy!
He is worthy to receive power and
    wealth and wisdom and
    strength!
He is worthy to receive honor and
    glory and praise!"

13All creatures in heaven, on earth, under the earth, and on the sea, and all that is in them, were singing. I heard them say,

"May praise and honor for ever and
    ever
    be given to the One who sits on the
        throne and to the Lamb!
Give them glory and power
        for ever and ever!"

14The four living creatures said, "Amen." And the elders fell down and worshiped.

The Seals

6 I watched as the Lamb broke open the first of the seven seals. Then I heard one of the four living creatures say in a voice that sounded like thunder, "Come!" **2**I looked, and there in front of me was a white horse! Its rider held a bow in his hands. He was given a crown. He rode out like a hero on his way to victory.

3The Lamb broke open the second seal. Then I heard the second living creature say, "Come!" **4**Another horse came out. It was flaming red. Its rider was given power to take peace from the earth and to make people kill each other. He was given a large sword.

5The Lamb broke open the third seal. Then I heard the third living creature say, "Come!" I looked, and there in front of me was a black horse! Its rider was holding a pair of scales in his hand. **6**Next, I heard what sounded like a voice coming from among the four living creatures. It said, "A quart of wheat for a day's pay. And three quarts of barley for a day's pay. But don't spoil the olive oil and the wine!"

7The Lamb broke open the fourth seal. Then I heard the voice of the fourth living creature say, "Come!" **8**I looked, and there in front of me was a pale horse! Its rider's name was Death. Following close behind him was Hell. They were given power over a fourth of the earth. They were given power to kill people with the sword, hunger and sickness. They could also use the earth's wild animals to kill.

9He broke open the fifth seal. I saw souls under the altar. They were the souls of people who were killed because of God's word and their faithful witness. **10**They called out in a loud voice. "How long, Lord and King, holy and true?" they asked. "How long will you wait to judge those who live on the earth? How long will it be until you pay them back for killing us?"

11Then each of them was given a white robe. "Wait a little longer," they were told. "There are still more of your believing brothers and sisters who must be killed."

12I watched as he broke open the sixth seal. There was a powerful earthquake. The sun turned black like black clothes that were made from the hair of a goat. The whole moon turned as red as blood. **13**The stars in the sky fell to earth. They dropped like ripe figs from a tree shaken by a strong wind. **14**The sky rolled back like a scroll. Every mountain and island was moved out of its place.

15Everyone hid in caves and among the

rocks of the mountains. This included the kings of the earth, the princes and the generals, rich people and powerful people. It also included every slave and everyone who was free. ¹⁶They called out to the mountains and rocks, "Fall on us! Hide us from the face of the One who sits on the throne! Hide us from the anger of the Lamb! ¹⁷The great day of their anger has come. Who can live through it?"

144,000 Are Sealed

7 After this I saw four angels. They were standing at the four corners of the earth. They were holding back the four winds of the earth. This kept the winds from blowing on the land or on the sea or on any tree.

²Then I saw another angel coming up from the east. He had the seal of the living God. He called out in a loud voice to the four angels who had been allowed to harm the land and the sea. ³"Do not harm the land or the sea or the trees," he said. "Wait until we mark with a seal the foreheads of those who serve our God."

⁴Then I heard how many people were sealed. There were 144,000 from all the tribes of Israel.

⁵ From the tribe of Judah, 12,000 were
     sealed.
  From the tribe of Reuben, 12,000.
  From the tribe of Gad, 12,000.
⁶ From the tribe of Asher, 12,000.
  From the tribe of Naphtali, 12,000.
  From the tribe of Manasseh, 12,000.
⁷ From the tribe of Simeon, 12,000.
  From the tribe of Levi, 12,000.
  From the tribe of Issachar, 12,000.
⁸ From the tribe of Zebulun, 12,000.
  From the tribe of Joseph, 12,000.
  From the tribe of Benjamin, 12,000.

The Huge Crowd Wearing White Robes

⁹After this I looked, and there in front of me was a huge crowd of people. They stood in front of the throne and in front of the Lamb. There were so many that no one could count them. They came from every nation, tribe, people and language. They were wearing white robes. In their hands they were holding palm branches. ¹⁰They cried out in a loud voice,

"Salvation belongs to our God,
who sits on the throne.
Salvation also belongs to the Lamb."

¹¹All the angels were standing around the throne. They were standing around

POWER-SURGE

THANKFUL ✿

**MAY PRAISE AND GLORY AND WISDOM BE GIVEN TO OUR GOD FOR EVER AND EVER.
GIVE HIM THANKS AND HONOR AND POWER AND STRENGTH.**
—— REVELATION 7:12 ——

the elders and the four living creatures. They fell down on their faces in front of the throne and worshiped God. ¹²They said,

"Amen!
May praise and glory
and wisdom be given to our God for
     ever and ever.
Give him thanks and honor and power
     and strength.
Amen!"

¹³Then one of the elders spoke to me. "Who are these people dressed in white robes?" he asked. "Where did they come from?"

¹⁴I answered, "Sir, you know."

He said, "They are the ones who have come out of the time of terrible suffering. They have washed their robes and made them white in the blood of the Lamb.
¹⁵So

"they are in front of the throne of God.
  They serve him day and night in his
       temple.
The One who sits on the throne will
     spread his tent over them.
¹⁶Never again will they be hungry.
  Never again will they be thirsty.
The sun will not beat down on them.
  The heat of the desert will not harm
       them.
¹⁷The Lamb, who is at the center of the
     area around the throne, will be
     their shepherd.
  He will lead them to springs of living
       water.
And God will wipe away every tear
     from their eyes."

The Seventh Seal and the Gold Cup

8 The Lamb opened the seventh seal. Then there was silence in heaven for about half an hour.

²I saw the seven angels who stand in front of God. Seven trumpets were given to them.

³Another angel came and stood at the altar. He had a shallow gold cup for burning incense. He was given a lot of incense to offer on the golden altar in front of the throne. With the incense he offered the prayers of all God's people. ⁴The smoke of the incense together with the prayers of God's people rose up from the angel's hand. It went up in front of God.

⁵Then the angel took the cup and filled it with fire from the altar. He threw it down on the earth. There were rumblings and thunder, flashes of lightning, and an earthquake.

The Trumpets

⁶Then the seven angels who had the seven trumpets got ready to blow them.

⁷The first angel blew his trumpet. Hail and fire mixed with blood were thrown down on the earth. A third of the earth was burned up. A third of the trees were burned up. All the green grass was burned up.

⁸The second angel blew his trumpet. Something that looked like a huge mountain on fire was thrown into the sea. A third of the sea turned into blood. ⁹A third of the living creatures in the sea died. A third of the ships were destroyed.

¹⁰The third angel blew his trumpet. Then a great star fell from the sky. It looked like a blazing torch. It fell on a third of the rivers and on the springs of water. ¹¹The name of the star is Wormwood. A third of the water turned bitter. Many people died from it.

¹²The fourth angel blew his trumpet. Then a third of the sun was struck. A third of the moon was struck. A third of the stars were struck. So a third of each of them turned dark. Then a third of the day had no light. The same thing happened to a third of the night.

¹³As I watched, I heard an eagle that was flying high in the air. It called out in a loud voice, "How terrible! How terrible it will be for those living on the earth! How terrible! They will suffer as soon as the next three angels blow their trumpets!"

9 The fifth angel blew his trumpet. Then I saw a star that had fallen from the sky to the earth. The star was given the key to the tunnel leading down into the Abyss. ²When the star opened the Abyss, smoke rose up from it like the smoke from a huge furnace. The sun and sky were darkened by the smoke from the Abyss.

³Out of the smoke came locusts. They settled down on the earth. They were given power like the power of scorpions of the earth. ⁴They were told not to harm the grass of the earth or any plant or tree. They were supposed to harm only the people who didn't have God's seal on their foreheads. ⁵They were not allowed to kill them. But they could hurt them over and over for five months. The pain the people suffered was like the sting of a scorpion when it strikes a man.

⁶In those days, people will look for a way to die but won't find it. They will want to die, but death will escape them.

⁷The locusts looked like horses ready for battle. On their heads they wore something like crowns of gold. Their faces looked like human faces. ⁸Their hair was like women's hair. Their teeth were like lions' teeth. ⁹Their chests were covered with something that looked like armor made out of iron. The sound of their wings was like the thundering of many horses and chariots rushing into battle. ¹⁰They had tails and stings like scorpions. And in their tails they had power to hurt people over and over for five months. ¹¹Their king was the angel of the Abyss. In the Hebrew language his name is Abaddon. In Greek it is Apollyon. ¹²The first terrible judgment is past. Two others are still coming.

¹³The sixth angel blew his trumpet. Then I heard a voice coming from the corners of the golden altar that stands in front of God. ¹⁴The voice spoke to the sixth angel who had the trumpet. It said, "Set the four angels free who are held at the great river Euphrates."

¹⁵The four angels had been ready for this very hour and day and month and year. They were set free to kill a third of all people. ¹⁶The number of troops on horseback was 200,000,000. I heard how many there were.

¹⁷The horses and riders I saw in my vision had armor on their chests. It was flaming red, dark blue, and yellow like sulfur. The heads of the horses looked like lions' heads. Out of their mouths came fire, smoke and sulfur. ¹⁸A third of all people were killed by the three plagues of fire, smoke and sulfur that came out of the horses' mouths. ¹⁹The power of the

horses was in their mouths and in their tails. The tails were like snakes whose heads could bite.

20The people who were not killed by these plagues still did not turn away from what they had been doing. They did not stop worshiping demons. They kept worshiping statues of gods made out of gold, silver, bronze, stone and wood, which can't see or hear or walk. 21The people also did not turn away from their murders, witchcraft, sexual sins and stealing.

The Angel and the Little Scroll

10 Then I saw another mighty angel coming down from heaven. He was wearing a cloud like a robe. There was a rainbow above his head. His face was like the sun. His legs were like pillars of fire.

2He was holding a little scroll. It was lying open in his hand. The angel put his right foot on the sea and his left foot on the land. 3Then he gave a loud shout like the roar of a lion. When he shouted, the voices of the seven thunders spoke.

4When they had spoken, I was getting ready to write. But I heard a voice from heaven say, "Seal up what the seven thunders have said. Do not write it down."

5Then the angel I had seen standing on the sea and on the land raised his right hand to heaven. 6He made a promise in the name of the One who lives for ever and ever. He took an oath in the name of the One who created the sky, earth and sea and all that is in them. He said, "There will be no more waiting! 7But in the days when the seventh angel is ready to blow his trumpet, the last part of God's plan will be carried out. God told all this to the prophets who served him long ago."

8Then the voice I had heard from heaven spoke to me again. It said, "Go and take the scroll from the angel standing on the sea and on the land. It is lying open in his hand."

9So I went to the angel and asked him to give me the little scroll. He said to me, "Take it and eat it. It will become sour in your stomach. But in your mouth it will taste as sweet as honey." 10I took the little scroll from the angel's hand and ate it. In my mouth it tasted as sweet as honey. But when I had eaten it, it became sour in my stomach. 11Then I was told, "You must prophesy again about many peoples, nations, languages and kings."

The Two Witnesses

11 I was given a long stick that looked like a measuring rod. I was told,

"Go and measure the temple of God and the altar. Count the worshipers who are there. 2But do not measure the outer courtyard. It has been given to those who aren't Jews. They will overrun the holy city for 42 months.

3"I will give power to my two witnesses. They will prophesy for 1,260 days. They will be dressed in black clothes to show how sad they are."

4The witnesses are the two olive trees and the two lampstands that stand in front of the Lord of the earth. 5If anyone tries to harm them, fire comes from their mouths and eats up their enemies. This is how anyone who wants to harm them must die.

6These witnesses have power to close up the sky. Then it will not rain while they are prophesying. They also have power to turn the waters into blood. And they can strike the earth with every kind of plague as often as they want to.

7When they have finished giving their witness, the beast that comes up from the Abyss will attack them. He will overpower them and kill them. 8Their bodies will lie in the street of the great city where their Lord was nailed to the cross. The city is sometimes pictured as Sodom, or as Egypt.

9For three and a half days, people from every tribe, language and nation will stare at their bodies. They will refuse to bury them. 10Those who live on the earth will be happy about this and will celebrate. They will send each other gifts, because these two prophets had made them suffer.

11But after the three and a half days, a breath of life from God entered the two witnesses. They stood up. Terror struck those who saw them.

12Then the two witnesses heard a loud voice from heaven. It said to them, "Come up here." They went up to heaven in a cloud. Their enemies watched it happen.

13At that very hour there was a powerful earthquake. A tenth of the city crumbled and fell. In the earthquake, 7,000 people were killed. Those who lived through it were terrified. They gave glory to the God of heaven.

14The second terrible judgment has passed. The third is coming soon.

The Seventh Trumpet

15The seventh angel blew his trumpet. There were loud voices in heaven. They said,

"The kingdom of the world has
  become the kingdom of our
  Lord and of his Christ.
  He will rule for ever and ever."

16The 24 elders were sitting on their thrones in front of God. They fell on their faces and worshiped God. **17**They said,

"Lord God who rules over all, we give
  thanks to you.
  You are the One who is and who
  was.
We give you thanks because you have
  taken your great power
  and have begun to rule.

POWER — SURGE

THANKFUL ✢

LORD GOD WHO RULES OVER ALL, WE GIVE THANKS TO YOU.
— REVELATION 11:17 —

18The nations were angry,
  and the time for your anger has
  come.
  The time has come to judge the
  dead.
It is time to reward your servants the
  prophets
  and your own people and those who
  honor you.
There is a reward for all your people,
  both great and small.
It is time to destroy
  those who destroy the earth."

19Then God's temple in heaven was opened. Inside it the wooden chest called the ark of his covenant could be seen. There were flashes of lightning, rumblings and thunder, an earthquake and a great hailstorm.

The Woman and the Dragon

12 A great and miraculous sign appeared in heaven. It was a woman wearing the sun like clothes. The moon was under her feet. On her head she wore a crown of 12 stars. **2**She was pregnant. She cried out in pain because she was about to have a baby.

3Then another sign appeared in heaven. It was a huge red dragon. He had seven heads and ten horns. On his seven heads he wore seven crowns. **4**His tail swept a third of the stars out of the sky. It threw them down to earth.

The dragon stood in front of the woman who was about to have a baby. He wanted to eat her child the moment it was born.

5She gave birth to a son. He will rule all the nations with an iron rod. Her child was taken up to God and to his throne.

6The woman escaped into the desert where God had a place prepared for her. There she would be taken care of for 1,260 days.

7There was war in heaven. Michael and his angels fought against the dragon. And the dragon and his angels fought back. **8**But the dragon wasn't strong enough. He and his angels lost their place in heaven.

9The great dragon was thrown down to the earth, and his angels with him. The dragon is that old serpent called the devil, or Satan. He leads the whole world down the wrong path.

10Then I heard a loud voice in heaven. It said,

"Now the salvation and the power and
  the kingdom of our God have
  come.
  The authority of his Christ has
  come.
Satan, who brings charges against our
  brothers and sisters,
  has been thrown down.
  He brings charges against them
  before our God day and night.
11They overcame him
  because the Lamb gave his life's
  blood for them.
They overcame him
  by giving witness about Jesus to
  others.
They were willing to risk their lives,
  even if it led to death.
12So be joyful, you heavens!
  Be glad, all you who live there!
But how terrible it will be for the earth
  and the sea!
  The devil has come down to you.
  He is very angry.
  He knows his time is short."

13The dragon saw that he had been thrown down to the earth. So he chased the woman who had given birth to the boy. **14**The woman was given the two wings of a great eagle so that she could fly away. She could fly to the place prepared for her in the desert. There she would be taken care of for three and a half years. She would be out of the serpent's reach.

15Then the serpent spit water like a river out of his mouth. He wanted to catch her and sweep her away in the flood. **16**But the earth helped the woman. It opened its mouth and swallowed the river that the dragon had spit out.

17The dragon was very angry with the woman. He went off to make war against the rest of her children. They obey God's commands and hold firmly to what Jesus **13** has said. **1**The dragon stood on the seashore.

The Beast out of the Sea

I saw a beast coming out of the sea. He had ten horns and seven heads. There were ten crowns on his horns. On each head was an evil name that was displeasing to God.

2The beast I saw looked like a leopard. But he had feet like a bear and a mouth like a lion. The dragon gave the beast his power, his throne, and great authority. **3**One of the beast's heads seemed to have had a deadly wound. But the wound had been healed. The whole world was amazed and followed the beast.

4People worshiped the dragon, because he had given authority to the beast. They also worshiped the beast. They asked, "Who is like the beast? Who can make war against him?"

5The beast was given a mouth to brag and speak evil things against God. The beast was allowed to use his authority for 42 months. **6**He opened his mouth to speak evil things against God. He told lies about God's character and about the place where God lives and about those who live in heaven with him. **7**He was allowed to make war against God's people and to overcome them. He was given authority over every tribe, people, language and nation.

8All who live on earth whose names have not been written in the Book of Life will worship the beast. The Book of Life belongs to the Lamb whose death was planned before the world was created.

9Everyone who has ears should listen.

10Everyone who is supposed to be
    captured
    will be captured.
Everyone who is supposed to be killed
    with a sword
    will be killed with a sword.

So God's people must be patient and faithful.

The Beast out of the Earth

11Then I saw another beast. This one came out of the earth. He had two horns like a lamb. But he spoke like a dragon. **12**He had all the authority of the first beast. He did what that beast wanted. He made the earth and all who live on it worship the first beast. The first beast was the one whose deadly wound had been healed.

13The second beast did great and miraculous signs. He even made fire come from heaven. It came down to earth where everyone could see it. **14**He did the signs the first beast wanted him to do. In that way the second beast tricked those who live on the earth. He ordered them to set up a statue to honor the first beast.

The first beast was the one who had been wounded by the sword and still lived.

15The second beast was allowed to give breath to the statue so it could speak. He was allowed to kill all who refused to worship the statue. **16**He also forced everyone to receive a mark on the right hand or on the forehead. People great or small, rich or poor, free or slave had to receive the mark. **17**They could not buy or sell anything unless they had the mark. The mark is the name of the beast or the number of his name.

18Here is a problem that you have to be wise to figure out. If you can, figure out what the beast's number means. It is man's number. His number is 666.

The Lamb and the 144,000

14 I looked, and there in front of me was the Lamb. He was standing on Mount Zion. With him were 144,000 people. Written on their foreheads were his name and his Father's name.

2I heard a sound from heaven. It was like the roar of rushing waters and loud thunder. The sound I heard was like the music of harps being played.

3Then everyone sang a new song in front of the throne. They sang it in front of the four living creatures and the elders. No one could learn the song except the 144,000. They had been set free from the evil of the earth.

4They had not committed sexual sins with women. They had kept themselves pure. They follow the Lamb wherever he goes. They were purchased from among people as a first offering to God and the Lamb. **5**Their mouths told no lies. They are without blame.

The Three Angels

6I saw another angel. He was flying high in the air. He came to tell everyone on earth the good news that will always be true. He told it to every nation, tribe, language and people. **7**In a loud voice he said, "Have respect for God. Give him glory. The hour has come for God to judge. Worship him who made the heavens and the earth. Worship him who made the sea and the springs of water."

8A second angel followed him. He said, "Fallen! Babylon the Great has fallen! The city of Babylon made all the nations drink the strong wine of her terrible sins."

9A third angel followed them. He said in a loud voice, "Watch out, all you who worship the beast and his statue! Watch out, all you who have his mark on your forehead or your hand! **10**You, too, will drink the wine of God's great anger. His wine has been poured full strength into

---

PATIENT

P
P
P

REVELATION 14:12

God's people need to be very patient.

What's the opposite of patient? Yes, that's right, it's *impatient.* Most of us know more about being impatient than being patient. It's easy to feel impatient when you have to wait your turn for something. Being patient can be a hard lesson to learn. And the only way to learn it is by waiting!

Poor Rizpah. She had one of the most awful waiting jobs in the Bible (see page 380). She patiently waited and protected the dead bodies of her sons until King David decided to give them a proper burial. Martha, however, wasn't quite as good at patience. Martha got impatient while she was cooking and waiting for her sister Mary to help her. Jesus and his disciples needed to be fed *right now*, Martha thought. But Jesus had a different idea. He told Martha to settle down and let Mary listen to Jesus talk. Martha needed to be patient (see page 1190).

BE PATIENT

When do you find yourself feeling impatient? Think of times when you're waiting and you get upset that you have to wait. That's being impatient. Those times are good times to remember this verse!

Go to page 1472 for the next Super Hero

the cup of his anger. You will be burned with flaming sulfur. The holy angels and the Lamb will see it happen. **11**The smoke of your terrible suffering will rise for ever and ever. Day and night, there is no rest for you who worship the beast and his statue. There is no rest for you who receive the mark of his name."

12God's people need to be very patient. They are the ones who obey God's commands. They remain faithful to Jesus.

13Then I heard a voice from heaven. "Write this," it said. "Blessed are the dead who die as believers in the Lord from now on."

"Yes," says the Holy Spirit. "They will rest from their labor. What they have done will not be forgotten."

The Harvest of the Earth

14I looked, and there in front of me was a white cloud. Sitting on the cloud was One who looked "like a son of man." *(Daniel 7:13)* He wore a gold crown on his head. In his hand was a sharp, curved blade for cutting grain.

15Then another angel came out of the temple. He called in a loud voice to the one sitting on the cloud. "Take your blade," he said. "Cut the grain. The time has come. The earth is ready to be harvested."

16So the one sitting on the cloud swung his blade over the earth. And the earth was harvested.

17Another angel came out of the temple in heaven. He too had a sharp, curved blade. **18**Still another angel came from the altar. He was in charge of the fire on the altar. He called out in a loud voice to the angel who had the sharp blade. "Take your blade," he said, "and gather the bunches of grapes from the earth's vine. Its grapes are ripe."

19So the angel swung his blade over the earth. He gathered its grapes. Then he threw them into a huge winepress. The winepress stands for God's anger. **20**In the winepress outside the city, the grapes were stomped on. Blood flowed out of the pit. It spread over the land for about 180 miles. It rose as high as the horses' heads.

Seven Angels With Seven Plagues

15 I saw in heaven another great and miraculous sign. Seven angels were about to bring the seven last plagues. The plagues would complete God's anger.

2Then I saw something that looked like a sea of glass mixed with fire. Standing beside the sea were those who had won the battle over the beast. They had also overcome his statue and the number of his name. They held harps given to them by God.

3They sang the song of Moses, who served God, and the song of the Lamb. They sang,

"Lord God who rules over all,
    everything you do is great and
        wonderful.
King of the ages,
    your ways are true and fair.
4Lord, who will not have respect for
        you?
    Who will not bring glory to your
        name?
You alone are holy.
All nations will come
    and worship you.
They see that the things you do are
        right."

5After this I looked, and the temple was opened in heaven. The temple is the holy tent where the tablets of the covenant were kept. **6**Out of the temple came the seven angels who were bringing the seven plagues. They were dressed in clean, shining linen. They wore gold strips of cloth around their chests. **7**Then one of the four living creatures gave seven golden bowls to the seven angels. The bowls were filled with the anger of God, who lives for ever and ever. **8**The temple was filled with smoke that came from the glory and power of God. No one could enter the temple until the seven plagues of the seven angels were completed.

The Seven Bowls of God's Anger

16 Then I heard a loud voice from the temple speaking to the seven angels. "Go," it said. "Pour out the seven bowls of God's anger on the earth."

2The first angel went and poured out his bowl on the land. Ugly and painful sores broke out on the people who had the mark of the beast and worshiped his statue.

3The second angel poured out his bowl on the sea. It turned into blood like the blood of a dead person. Every living thing in the sea died.

4The third angel poured out his bowl on the rivers and on the springs of water. They became blood. **5**Then I heard the angel who was in charge of the waters. He said,

"The way you judge is fair.
You are the Holy One.
You are the One who is and who was.

6 The beast's worshipers have poured out the life's blood of your people and your prophets.
So you have given those worshipers blood to drink.
That's exactly what they should get."

7 Then I heard the altar reply,

"Lord God who rules over all,
the way you judge is true and fair."

8 The fourth angel poured out his bowl on the sun. The sun was allowed to burn people with fire. **9** They were burned by the blazing heat. So they spoke evil things against the name of God, who controlled these plagues. But they refused to turn away from their sins. They did not give glory to God.

10 The fifth angel poured out his bowl on the throne of the beast. The kingdom of the beast became very dark. People bit their tongues because they were suffering so much. **11** They spoke evil things against the God of heaven because of their pains and their sores. But they refused to turn away from the sins they had committed.

12 The sixth angel poured out his bowl on the great river Euphrates. Its water dried up to prepare the way for the kings from the East.

13 Then I saw three evil spirits that looked like frogs. They came out of the mouths of the dragon, the beast and the false prophet. **14** They are spirits of demons performing miraculous signs. They go out to gather the kings of the whole world for battle. That battle will take place on the great day of the God who rules over all.

15 "Look! I am coming like a thief! Blessed are those who stay awake and keep their clothes with them. They will not be caught naked. They will not be put to shame."

16 Then the evil spirits gathered the kings together. The place where the kings met is called Armageddon in the Hebrew language.

17 The seventh angel poured out his bowl into the air. Out of the temple came a loud voice from the throne. It said, "It is done!"

18 Then there came flashes of lightning, rumblings, thunder and a powerful earthquake. There has never been an earthquake as terrible as this since man has lived on earth. **19** The great city split into three parts. The cities of the nations crumbled and fell. God remembered Babylon the Great. He gave her the cup filled with the wine of his terrible anger.

20 Every island ran away. The mountains could not be found. **21** Huge hailstones of about 100 pounds each fell from the sky. The hail crushed people. They spoke evil things against God because the plague of hail was so terrible.

The Woman and the Beast

17 One of the seven angels who had the seven bowls came to me. He said, "Come. I will show you how the great prostitute will be punished. She is the one who sits on many waters. **2** The kings of the earth took part in her evil ways. The people living on earth were drunk with the wine of her terrible sins."

3 Then the angel carried me away in a vision. The Holy Spirit took me into a desert. There I saw a woman sitting on a bright red beast. It was covered with names that say evil things that are displeasing to God. It had seven heads and ten horns.

4 The woman was dressed in purple and bright red. She was gleaming with gold, jewels and pearls. In her hand she held a golden cup filled with things that God hates. It was filled with her terrible, dirty sins. **5** Here is the name that was written on her forehead.

MYSTERY
THE GREAT CITY OF BABYLON
THE MOTHER OF PROSTITUTES
THE MOTHER OF EVERYTHING ON EARTH
THAT GOD HATES

6 I saw that the woman was drunk with the blood of God's people. They are the ones who gave witness to Jesus.

When I saw her, I was very amazed.

7 Then the angel said to me, "Why are you amazed? I will explain to you the mystery of the woman and of the beast she rides on. The beast is the one who has the seven heads and ten horns. **8** The beast that you saw used to exist. But now he does not. He will come up out of the Abyss. He will be destroyed. Some of the people who live on the earth will be amazed when they see the beast. Their names have not been written in the Book of Life from the time the world was created. They will be amazed because even though the beast used to exist and now does not, he will come again.

9 "Here is a problem that you have to be wise to understand. The seven heads are seven hills that the woman sits on. 10 They are also seven kings. Five have fallen, one is ruling, and the other has still not come. When he does come, he must remain for a little while.

11 "The beast who used to exist, and now does not, is an eighth king. He belongs to the other seven. He will be destroyed.

12 "The ten horns you saw are ten kings. They have not yet received a kingdom. But for one hour they will receive authority to rule together with the beast. 13 They have only one purpose. So they give their power and authority to the beast. 14 They will make war against the Lamb. But the Lamb will overcome them because he is the most powerful Lord of all and the greatest King of all. His appointed, chosen and faithful followers will be with him."

15 Then the angel spoke to me. "You saw the waters the prostitute sits on," he said. "They stand for all the nations of the world, no matter what their race or language is. 16 The beast and the ten horns you saw will hate the prostitute. They will destroy her and leave her naked. They will eat her flesh and burn her with fire. 17 God has put it into their hearts to carry out his purpose. So they agreed to give the beast their power to rule. They will give him that power until God's words come true. 18 "The woman you saw stands for the great city that rules over the kings of the earth."

Babylon Falls

18 After these things I saw another angel coming down from heaven. He had great authority. His glory filled the earth with light. 2 With a mighty voice he shouted,

"Fallen! Babylon the Great has fallen!
    She has become a place where
        demons live.
She has become a den for every evil
    spirit.
She has become a nest for every
    'unclean' and hated bird.
3 All the nations have drunk
    the strong wine of her terrible sins.
The kings of the earth took part in her
    evil ways.
    The traders of the world grew rich
        from her great wealth."

4 Then I heard another voice from heaven. It said,

"Come out of her, my people.
    Then you will not take part in her
        sins.
    You will not suffer from any of her
        plagues.
5 Her sins are piled up to heaven.
    God has remembered her crimes.
6 Do to her as she has done to others.
    Pay her back double for what she has
        done.
    Mix her a double dose of what she
        has mixed for others.
7 Give her as much pain and suffering
    as the glory and wealth she gave
        herself.
She brags to herself,
    'I rule like a queen. I am not a
        widow.
    I will never be sad.'
8 But she will be plagued by death,
        sadness and hunger.
    In a single day they will all catch up
        with her.
She will be burned up by fire.
    The Lord God who judges her is
        mighty.

9 "The kings of the earth who committed terrible sins with her will sob. They will be sad because they used to share her riches. They will see the smoke rising as she burns. 10 They will be terrified by her suffering. Standing far away, they will exclaim,

" 'How terrible! How terrible it is for
        you, great city!
    How terrible for you, Babylon, city
        of power!
In just one hour you have been
        destroyed!'

11 "The traders of the world will cry and be sad over her. No one buys what they sell anymore. 12 Here is what they had for sale.

Gold, silver, jewels, pearls.
Fine linen, purple, silk, bright red
    cloth.
Every kind of expensive wood.
All sorts of articles made out of
    ivory, valuable wood, bronze,
    iron and marble.
13 Cinnamon, spice, incense, myrrh,
    frankincense.
Wine, olive oil, fine flour, wheat.
Cattle, sheep, horses, carriages,
    human slaves.

14 "The merchants will say, 'The pleasure you longed for has left you. All your riches and glory have disappeared forever.' 15 The traders who sold these things

and became rich because of her will stand far away. Her suffering will terrify them. They will cry and be sad. **16**They will cry out,

> " 'How terrible! How terrible it is for you, great city,
>   dressed in fine linen, purple and bright red!
> How terrible for you, great city,
>   gleaming with gold, jewels and pearls!
> **17** In just one hour your great wealth has been destroyed!'

"Every sea captain and all who travel by ship will stand far away. So will the sailors and all who earn their living from the sea. **18**They will see the smoke rising as Babylon burns. They will ask, 'Was there ever a city like this great city?' **19**They will throw dust on their heads. They will cry and be sad. They will cry out,

> " 'How terrible! How terrible it is for you, great city!
> All who had ships on the sea
>   became rich because of her wealth!
> In just one hour she has been destroyed!
> **20** Heaven, be glad for this!
>   God's people, be glad! Apostles and prophets, be glad!
> God has judged her for the way she treated you.' "

21Then a mighty angel picked up a huge rock. It was the size of a large millstone. He threw it into the sea. Then he said,

> "That is how
>   the great city of Babylon will be thrown down.
>   Never again will it be found.
> **22** The songs of musicians will never be heard in you again.
>   Gone will be the music of harp, flute and trumpet.
> No worker of any kind
>   will ever be found in you again.
> The sound of a millstone
>   will never be heard in you again.
> **23** The light of a lamp
>   will never shine in you again.
> The voices of brides and grooms
>   will never be heard in you again.
> Your traders were among the world's most important people.
> By your magic spell all the nations were led down the wrong path.
> **24** You were guilty of the murder of prophets and God's people.

You were guilty of the blood of all who have been killed on the earth."

Hallelujah!

19 After these things I heard a roar in heaven. It sounded like a huge crowd shouting,

> "Hallelujah!
> Salvation and glory and power belong to our God.
> **2**   The way he judges is true and fair.
> He has judged the great prostitute.
>   She polluted the earth with her terrible sins.
> God has paid her back for killing those who served him."

3Again they shouted,

> "Hallelujah!
> The smoke from her fire goes up for ever and ever."

4The 24 elders and the four living creatures bowed down. They worshiped God, who was sitting on the throne. They cried out,

> "Amen! Hallelujah!"

5Then a voice came from the throne. It said,

> "Praise our God,
>   all you who serve him!
> Praise God, all you who have respect for him,
>   both great and small!"

6Then I heard the noise of a huge crowd. It sounded like the roar of rushing waters and like loud thunder. The people were shouting,

> "Hallelujah!
>   Our Lord God is the King who rules over all.
> **7** Let us be joyful and glad!
>   Let us give him glory!
> It is time for the Lamb's wedding.
>   His bride has made herself ready.
> **8** Fine linen, bright and clean,
>   was given to her to wear."

POWER-SURGE

CHEERFUL ✳

LET US BE JOYFUL AND GLAD!

— REVELATION 19:7 —

Fine linen stands for the right things that God's people do.

9Here is what the angel told me to write. "Blessed are those who are invited to the wedding supper of the Lamb!" Then he added, "These are the true words of God."

10When I heard this, I fell at his feet to worship him.

But he said to me, "Don't do that! I serve God, just as you do. I am God's servant, just like other believers who hold firmly to what Jesus has taught. Worship God! What Jesus taught is the very heart of prophecy."

The Rider on the White Horse

11I saw heaven standing open. There in front of me was a white horse. Its rider is called Faithful and True. When he judges or makes war, he is always fair. 12His eyes are like blazing fire. On his head are many crowns. A name is written on him that only he knows. 13He is dressed in a robe dipped in blood. His name is The Word of God.

14The armies of heaven were following him, riding on white horses. They were dressed in fine linen, white and clean.

15Out of the rider's mouth comes a sharp sword. He will strike down the nations with it. Scripture says, "He will rule them with an iron rod." *(Psalm 2:9)* He stomps on the grapes of God's winepress. The winepress stands for the terrible anger of the God who rules over all.

16Here is the name that is written on the rider's robe and on his thigh.

THE GREATEST KING OF ALL AND THE MOST
POWERFUL LORD OF ALL

17I saw an angel standing in the sun. He cried in a loud voice to all the birds flying high in the air, "Come! Gather together for the great supper of God. 18Come and eat the dead bodies of kings, generals, and other mighty people. Eat the bodies of horses and their riders. Eat the bodies of all people, free and slave, great and small."

19Then I saw the beast and the kings of the earth with their armies. They had gathered together to make war against the rider on the horse and his army.

20But the beast and the false prophet were captured. The false prophet had done miraculous signs for the beast. In this way the false prophet had tricked those who had received the mark of the beast and had worshiped his statue. The beast and the false prophet were thrown

alive into the lake of fire that burns with sulfur. 21The rest of them were killed with the sword that came out of the rider's mouth. All the birds stuffed themselves with the dead bodies.

The Thousand Years

20 I saw an angel coming down out of heaven. He had the key to the Abyss. In his hand he held a heavy chain. 2He grabbed the dragon, that old serpent. The serpent is also called the devil, or Satan. The angel put him in chains for 1,000 years. 3Then he threw him into the Abyss. He locked it and sealed him in. This was to keep Satan from fooling the nations anymore until the 1,000 years were ended. After that, he must be set free for a short time.

4I saw thrones. Those who had been given authority to judge were sitting on them. I also saw the souls of those whose heads had been cut off because they had given witness for Jesus and because of God's word. They had not worshiped the beast or his statue. They had not received his mark on their foreheads or hands. They came to life and ruled with Christ for 1,000 years.

5This is the first resurrection. The rest of the dead did not come to life until the 1,000 years were ended.

6Blessed and holy are those who take part in the first resurrection. The second death has no power over them. They will be priests of God and of Christ. They will rule with him for 1,000 years.

Satan Is Judged

7When the 1,000 years are over, Satan will be set free from his prison. 8He will go out to fool the nations. He will gather them from the four corners of the earth. He will bring Gog and Magog together for battle.

Their troops are as many as the grains of sand on the seashore. 9They marched across the whole earth. They surrounded the place where God's people were camped. It was the city he loves. But fire came down from heaven and burned them up.

10The devil, who fooled them, was thrown into the lake of burning sulfur. That is where the beast and the false prophet had been thrown. They will all suffer day and night for ever and ever.

The Dead Are Judged

11I saw a great white throne and the One who was sitting on it. When the earth and sky saw his face, they ran away. There was no place for them.

¹²I saw the dead, great and small, standing in front of the throne. Books were opened. Then another book was opened. It was the Book of Life. The dead were judged by what they had done. The things they had done were written in the books. ¹³The sea gave up the dead that were in it. And Death and Hell gave up their dead. Each of the dead was judged by what he had done.

¹⁴Then Death and Hell were thrown into the lake of fire. The lake of fire is the second death. ¹⁵Anyone whose name was not written in the Book of Life was thrown into the lake of fire.

The New Jerusalem

21 I saw a new heaven and a new earth. The first heaven and the first earth were completely gone. There was no longer any sea.

²I saw the Holy City, the new Jerusalem. It was coming down out of heaven from God. It was prepared like a bride beautifully dressed for her husband.

³I heard a loud voice from the throne. It said, "Now God makes his home with people. He will live with them. They will be his people. And God himself will be with them and be their God. ⁴He will wipe away every tear from their eyes. There will be no more death or sadness. There will be no more crying or pain. Things are no longer the way they used to be."

⁵He who was sitting on the throne said, "I am making everything new!" Then he said, "Write this down. You can trust these words. They are true."

⁶He said to me, "It is done. I am the Alpha and the Omega, the First and the Last. I am the Beginning and the End. Anyone who is thirsty may drink from the spring of the water of life. It doesn't cost anything! ⁷Anyone who overcomes will receive all this from me. I will be his God, and he will be my child.

⁸"But others will have their place in the lake of fire that burns with sulfur. Those who are afraid and those who do not believe will be there. Murderers and those who pollute themselves will join them. Those who commit sexual sins and those who practice witchcraft will go there. Those who worship statues of gods and all who tell lies will be there too. It is the second death."

⁹One of the seven angels who had the seven bowls came and spoke to me. The bowls were filled with the seven last plagues. The angel said, "Come. I will show you the bride, the wife of the Lamb."

¹⁰Then he carried me away in a vision. The Spirit took me to a huge, high mountain. He showed me Jerusalem, the Holy City. It was coming down out of heaven from God. ¹¹It shone with the glory of God. It gleamed like a very valuable jewel. It was like a jasper, as clear as crystal.

¹²The city had a huge, high wall with 12 gates. Twelve angels were at the gates, one at each of them. On the gates were written the names of the 12 tribes of Israel. ¹³There were three gates on the east and three on the north. There were three gates on the south and three on the west. ¹⁴The wall of the city had 12 foundations. Written on them were the names of the 12 apostles of the Lamb.

¹⁵The angel who talked with me had a gold measuring rod. He used it to measure the city, its gates and its walls. ¹⁶The city was laid out like a square. It was as long as it was wide. The angel measured the city with the rod. It was 1,400 miles long. It was as wide and high as it was long.

¹⁷He measured the wall of the city. It was 200 feet thick. The angel did the measuring as a man would. ¹⁸The wall was made out of jasper. The city was made out of pure gold, as pure as glass.

¹⁹The foundations of the city walls were decorated with every kind of jewel. The first foundation was made out of jasper. The second was made out of sapphire. The third was made out of chalcedony. The fourth was made out of emerald. ²⁰The fifth was made out of sardonyx. The sixth was made out of carnelian. The seventh was made out of chrysolite. The eighth was made out of beryl. The ninth was made out of topaz. The tenth was made out of chrysoprase. The eleventh was made out of jacinth. The twelfth was made out of amethyst.

²¹The 12 gates were made from 12 pearls. Each gate was made out of a single pearl. The main street of the city was made out of pure gold, as clear as glass.

²²I didn't see a temple in the city. This was because the Lamb and the Lord God who rules over all are its temple. ²³The city does not need the sun or moon to shine on it. God's glory is its light, and the Lamb is its lamp.

²⁴The nations will walk by the light of the city. The kings of the world will bring their glory into it. ²⁵Its gates will never be

shut, because there will be no night there. **26**The glory and honor of the nations will be brought into it.

27Only what is pure will enter it. No one who fools others or does shameful things will enter it. Only those whose names are written in the Lamb's Book of Life will enter the city.

The River of Life

22 Then the angel showed me the river of the water of life. It was as clear as crystal. It flowed from the throne of God and of the Lamb. **2**It flowed down the middle of the city's main street.

On each side of the river stood the tree of life, bearing 12 crops of fruit. Its fruit was ripe every month. The leaves of the tree bring healing to the nations.

3There will no longer be any curse. The throne of God and of the Lamb will be in the city. God's servants will serve him. **4**They will see his face. His name will be on their foreheads.

5There will be no more night. They will not need the light of a lamp or the light of the sun. The Lord God will give them light. They will rule for ever and ever.

6The angel said to me, "You can trust these words. They are true. The Lord is the God of the spirits of the prophets. He sent his angel to show those who serve him the things that must soon take place."

Jesus Is Coming

7"Look! I am coming soon! Blessed are those who obey the words of the prophecy in this book."

8I, John, am the one who heard and saw these things.

After I had heard and seen them, I fell

POWER-SURGE

OBEYS ✔

BLESSED ARE THOSE WHO OBEY THE WORDS OF THE PROPHECY IN THIS BOOK.

—— **REVELATION 22:7** ——

down to worship at the feet of the angel. He is the one who had been showing me these things.

9But he said to me, "Don't do that! I serve God, just as you do. I am God's servant, just like the other prophets and all who obey the words of this book. Worship God!"

10Then he told me, "Do not seal up the words of the prophecy in this book. These things are about to happen. **11**Let those who do wrong keep on doing wrong. Let those who are evil continue to be evil. Let those who do what is right keep on doing what is right. And let those who are holy continue to be holy."

12"Look! I am coming soon! I bring my rewards with me. I will reward each person for what he has done. **13**I am the Alpha and the Omega. I am the First and the Last. I am the Beginning and the End.

14"Blessed are those who wash their robes. They will have the right to come to the tree of life. They will be allowed to go through the gates into the city.

15"Outside the city are the dogs and those who practice witchcraft. Outside are also those who commit sexual sins and murder. Those who worship statues of gods, and everyone who loves and does what is false, are outside too.

16"I, Jesus, have sent my angel to give you this witness for the churches. I am the Root and the Son of David. I am the bright Morning Star."

17The Holy Spirit and the bride say, "Come!" Let those who hear say, "Come!" Anyone who is thirsty should come. Anyone who wants to take the free gift of the water of life should do so.

18I am warning everyone who hears the words of the prophecy of this book. If you add anything to them, God will add to you the plagues told about in this book. **19**If you take any words away from this book of prophecy, God will take away from you your share in the tree of life. He will also take away your place in the Holy City. This book tells about these things.

20He who gives witness to these things says, "Yes. I am coming soon."

Amen. Come, Lord Jesus!

21May the grace of the Lord Jesus be with God's people. Amen.

YOU

PHILIPPIANS 4:13

I can do everything by the power of Christ. He gives me strength.

All the heroes of the Bible are examples of what you can be for Jesus.

Joshua was scared, but God helped him to be brave.

Deborah was a woman, but she led an army.

David was little, but God used him to fight a huge giant.

Isaiah felt full of sin, but God told him he would use him anyway.

Timothy was young, but God told him that didn't matter.

God doesn't want you to think that you have to be just like these people. He just wants you to be *you.*

The heroes of the Bible were plain, ordinary people. Many of them were not as obedient as they should have been. Many of them were scared. Many of them were weak. Maybe you are all those things, too.

But one thing all of the heroes had in common is that they were willing to let God use them.

That's all Jesus asks of you, too. Just be willing.

Don't ever start to think you're too young.

Or not smart enough.

Or not strong enough.

Or not brave enough.

Jesus only asks you to be willing.

He'll give you the smarts and the strength and the bravery to do as he asks.

TO BE CONTINUED

This is the end of the Bible, God's Word. But don't let it be the end of the super heroes. In this Bible you've read other heroes' codes of honor. What is *your* code of honor? Fill in the circles on this page, and be a super hero for Jesus today.

GOD WILL HELP YOU TO BE A SUPER HERO FOR HIM.

Go to page 9 for the next Super Hero

SUPER HEROES
BIBLE QUIZ

1

I did everything exactly as God told me to do it.
I built a great big boat when I didn't even live near water.
I saw the world's first rainbow.

My name is _____.

Genesis 6:22 (8) • *Genesisis 6:14 (8)* • *Genesis 9:13 (12)*

I believed God's promise that he would create a huge nation of people through me.
I was one hundred years old when my son was born.
My son's name meant "laughter."

My name is _____.

Genesis 15:15 (19) • *Genesis 21:5 (24)* • *Genesis 21:3 (24)*

3

I bought my brother's inheritance for a bowl of stew.
I had a dream about a stairway to heaven.
I fought with my brother and with God.

My name is _____.

Genesis 25:29–34 (31–32) • *Genesis 28:11–12 (36)* •
Genesis 27:41; 32:24–28 (35; 43)

My beautiful, colorful coat made my brothers jealous.
I told a king the meaning of his dream.
I was a slave, a prisoner, and a ruler in Egypt.

My name is _____.

Genesis 37:3 (49) • *Genesis 41:14–16 (53)* • *Genesis 37:36;
39:20; 41:41 (50; 52; 54)*

5

I set my baby boy afloat in a basket in the river.
My young daughter watched over her little brother in the basket.
I let a king's daughter raise my son.

My name is _____.

Exodus 2:3 (69) • *Exodus 2:4 (69)* • *Exodus 2:10 (70)*

I saw a bush that was on fire but didn't burn up.
My face was shining after I spent time alone with God.
I dropped and broke the two stone tablets that God gave to me.

My name is _____.

Exodus 3:2 (71) • Exodus 34:29–30 (109) • Exodus 32:15, 19 (106)

6

I knew God would help us conquer the Promised Land even when others didn't.
I led the people of Israel after Moses died.
When the people and I marched around Jericho, its walls came crashing down.

My name is _____.

Numbers 14:6–10 (171) • Joshua 1:1–2 (243) • Joshua 6:1–20 (248–249)

7

I served as a judge and leader of Israel at a place called The Palm Tree of Deborah.
I was a woman who led the soldiers of Israel into battle.
God helped us whip General Sisera and his army of chariots.

My name is _____.

Judges 4:4–5 (276) • Judges 4:9–10 (276) • Judges 4:14–16 (276)

8

I thought I was weak, but God called me a "mighty warrior."
I used the skin of a lamb to discover God's will.
God used me and my army of only 300 men to defeat the whole army of Midian.

My name is _____.

Judges 6:12, 15–16 (280–281) • Judges 6:36–40 (283) • Judges 7 (283–284)

9

I wore my hair in seven braids.
I played with fire and foxes.
I could carry huge city gates with my super strong arms.

My name is _____.

Judges 16:13 (294) • Judges 15:3–5 (293)• Judges 16:13 (294)

10

I left my home in Moab to follow God and my mother–in–law to Israel.
I picked up leftover grain in the fields so we had food to eat.
I married an Israelite man named Boaz, and we had a son named Obed.

My name is _____.

Ruth 1:16 (304) • Ruth 2:2–3 (306) • Ruth 4:13 (310)

11

A priest thought I was drunk when I prayed in the temple.
For many years I begged God for children, and he finally gave me Samuel.
I gave my son Samuel back to God to live and work in the temple.

My name is _____.

1 Samuel 1:10–14 (313) • 1 Samuel 1:2, 20 (313) • 1 Samuel 1:24 (313)

12

I was just a little boy when I went to live with the priest Eli in the temple.
I heard God calling my name.
I used oil to anoint the first two kings of Israel.

13

My name is _____.

1 Samuel 2:11 (315) • 1 Samuel 3:1–10 (316–317) • 1 Samuel 10:1; 16:12–13 (323, 332)

I played my harp to praise God and to calm King Saul.
I was just a little guy next to the giant Goliath, but I killed him with a stone.
I wanted to build a great temple for God, but God said my son should do it.

My name is _____.

1 Samuel 16:23 (332) • 1 Samuel 17:4, 40–50 (333, 335) • 2 Samuel 7:12–13 (360)

14

I got in trouble for eating honey in a battle.
I loved David, but my father hated him.
David took care of my son Mephibosheth after I died.

15

My name is _____.

1 Samuel 14:24–27 (328) • 1 Samuel 18:1, 9 (337) • 2 Samuel 4:4; 9:3–13 (357, 362–363)

My foolish husband made David angry by refusing to feed his men.
Instead, I hurried to bring food and wine to David's men.
When my husband died, David asked me to marry him.

My name is _____.

16

1 Samuel 25:9–11 (345) • 1 Samuel 25:18–19 (345) • 1 Samuel 25:39 (347)

As a prophet, I brought God's Word to David while he was king.
I told David that God was angry at him for having Bathsheba's husband killed.
I had the terrible job of telling David that his little son would die, and he did.

17

My name is _____.

2 Samuel 7:1–17 (360) • 2 Samuel 12:7–9 (365) • 2 Samuel 12:14–18 (365)

18

God would have given me riches or honor, but I asked him for wisdom.

God gave me wisdom, then heaped riches and honor on me as well.

I was so rich that silver was as common as stones in my city.

My name is _____.

1 Kings 3:5–9 (391) • 1 Kings 3:10–14 (391–392) • 1 Kings 10:27 (405)

19

I called down fire from heaven to prove God was God, not Baal.

I looked for God in the wind, an earthquake, and fire then found in him a whisper.

I took a ride to heaven in a whirlwind.

My name is _____.

1 Kings 18:30–38 (419) • 1 Kings 19:11–12 (420) • 2 Kings 2:11 (431)

20

When my husband died, a man came to take my sons to pay our debt.

I went around my neighborhood and gathered as many empty jars as I could find.

I took my little jar of olive oil, and it never ran empty until all those jars were filled.

My name is _____.

2 Kings 4:1 (434) • 2 Kings 4:3 (434) • 2 Kings 4:5–7 (434–435)

21

I was only seven when I became king of Judah.

The priest Jehoiada helped me be a good king.

God's temple in Jerusalem was a mess, and I repaired it.

My name is _____.

2 Kings 11:21 (450) • 2 Kings 12:2 (450) • 2 Kings 12:5 (450)

22

My job was to taste the king's wine to be sure no one tried to poison him.

News of the trouble my people were having in Jerusalem made me sad.

With the people's help, I rebuilt the wall around Jerusalem.

My name is _____.

Nehemiah 1:11 (567) • Nehemiah 1:3–4 (567) • Nehemiah 6:15–16 (573)

23

I became queen of Persia even though I was a Hebrew orphan.

I was afraid to go to the king but I did it anyway.

I helped to save my people from those who were planning to kill them.

My name is _____.

Esther 2:7, 17 (588) • Esther 4:15–16 (590) • Esther 7:4; 9:1 (594, 595)

24

I still trusted God even though I lost all my children and my wealth and my health.
I wanted God to help me understand why all this had happened.
God gave me back all that I had lost, and more!

My name is _____.

Job 1:1–2:10 (599–600) • Job 3 (600–602) • Job 42:12–17 (633)

I saw God's glory in the temple, and it scared me silly.
When God asked for help, I said, "Send me!"
God sent me to King Hezekiah with the bad news that he would die soon.

My name is _____.

25

Isaiah 6:1–5 (789) • Isaiah 6:8 (789) • 2 Kings 20:1 (463)

26

I told the Israelites that God was going to send them to Babylon for their sins.
I also told them that after a while he would bring them back to Israel.
I got myself thrown into a deep well for what I said.

My name is _____.

Jeremiah 4:5–6; 5:18–19 (864, 866) • Jeremiah 29:10–14 (894–895) • Jeremiah 38:6 (907)

We refused to bow down to King Nebuchadnezzar's idol.
The king threw us into a pit of fire to kill us.
The fire didn't burn us even one little bit.

Our names are _____.

27

Daniel 3:8–12 (994) • Daniel 3:19–21 (994) • Daniel 3:24–27 (994)

28

When a hand wrote a message on the palace wall, I told the king what it meant.
When the king said people could only pray to him, I prayed to God anyway.
The king threw me into a pit of lions, but God saved me.

My name is _____.

Daniel 5:5, 8, 17 (998) • Daniel 6:7–10 (999) • Daniel 6:21 (1001)

When God told me to go to Nineveh to preach, I ran the other way.
I ended up taking a ride in a fish's stomach.
When the fish spit me out on land, I took off for Nineveh.

My name is _____.

29

Jonah 1:2–3 (1041) • Jonah 1:10–17 (1041) • Jonah 2:10–3:3 (1043)

An angel came to tell me I was going to have a baby.
I had my baby in a barn in Bethlehem.
My baby's name was Jesus.

My name is _____.

Luke 1:26–35 (1166–1167) • Luke 2:4–7 (1170) • Luke 1:31 (1167)

30

My clothes were made of fur, and I ate bugs with honey for lunch.
I baptized Jesus in the Jordan River.
A young girl and her mother tricked the king into killing me.

My name is _____.

Matthew 3:4 (1092) • Matthew 3:13–17 (1093) • Matthew 14:6–12 (1112)

31

I commanded soldiers in the Roman army.
I didn't think I was good enough for Jesus to come to
    my home.
Jesus healed my servant and told me I had amazing
    faith.

My name is _____.

*Matthew 8:5 (1101) • Matthew 8:8 (1102) • Matthew
    8:9–10, 13 (1102)*

32

There were twelve of us.
When Jesus said, "Follow me," we did.
All but one of us remained faithful to the end.

Our name is _____.

*Matthew 10:1–4 (1106) • Matthew 4:19; 9:9 (1095, 1104) •
    Matthew 26:14–16 (1128)*

33

I lived in Bethany with my sister Mary and my brother Lazarus.
I thought my sister Mary should help me in the kitchen.
When Jesus said the word, my dead brother Lazarus walked out
    of his grave.

My name is _____.

John 11:1 (1235) • Luke 10:40–42 (1189) • John 11:38–44 (1236)

34

I loved to go from town to town doing good things.
I took little children on my lap and loved them.
I love you more than anyone else.

35 **My name is** _____.

Acts 10:38 (1271) • Mark 10:13–16 (1152) • John 3:16 (1221)

My husband had died, and I was very poor.
I had only two small coins left, but I gave them both to God.
Jesus said I gave more than all the rich people who gave many coins.

My name is _____.

Luke 21:2 (1206) • Luke 21:4 (1206) • Luke 21:3 (1206)

36

Jesus drove seven demons out of me.
I watched Jesus die on the cross.
I was the first person to see Jesus after he rose from the dead.

37

My name is _____.

Mark 16:9 (1162) • Matthew 27:56 (1133) • John 20:10–18 (1247)

I preached about Jesus and performed many miracles in Samaria.
I rode in a chariot with a man from Ethiopia and told him about Jesus.
When we came to some water, I baptized the man.

38

My name is _____.

Acts 8:4–8 (1266) • Acts 8:26–35 (1267) • Acts 8:36–38 (1267)

I hated those who followed Jesus and wanted to kill them.
A vision of Jesus shocked me on the road to Damascus, and I became a follower.
I survived a shipwreck, being stoned, and being beaten with sticks and whips.

39

My name is _____.

Acts 7:59–8:1, 3 (1266) • Acts 9:3–6 (1267) • 2 Corinthians 11:23–27 (1349)

Paul and Silas sang hymns in my prison.
An earthquake broke all the chains and opened all the doors, but no one escaped.
Instead of killing myself, I believed in the God of Paul and Silas.

40

My name is _____.

Acts 16:25 (1283) • Acts 16:26–28 (1283) • Acts 16:30–32 (1283)

Index To Color Pictures

Traits of a Hero Index

NIrV
DICTIONARY

A

Abyss – A deep pit where evil spirits live. Satan will be held there in chains.

adultery – Having a sexual relationship with someone who is not your husband or wife.

altar – A table or raised place on which a gift, or sacrifice, was offered to God.

Amen – A word that means "it is true" or "let it be true."

angel – A spirit who is God's helper. A spirit who tells people God's words. See also cherubim.

anoint – 1. To pour olive oil on people or things. This sets them apart for God. 2. To pour oil on people as part of praying for their healing.

anointed – To be set apart as God's special servant.

apostle – One of the twelve men who spent about three years with Jesus. They taught others about Jesus, too. See also disciple.

Aramaic – A language spoken by many people during Bible times. The Jews in Jesus' time most often spoke this language.

ark of the covenant – A large gold box that held the stone tablets of the Ten Commandments. The ark was God's throne on earth.

armor – A special outer covering like clothes made of metal. People wore it to help keep them safe in battle.

Asherah – A false god. People thought she was the Canaanite mother goddess and goddess of the sea.

B

Baal – The name of the most popular false god of Canaan.

Babel – A city where people tried to build a tower up to the sky.

Babylon – 1. The capital city of the empire of Babylonia. 2. Any powerful, sinful city

baptize – To sprinkle, pour on or cover a person with water. It is a sign that the person belongs to Jesus.

Beelzebub – Another name for the devil. Satan.

believe – To accept as true. To trust. See also faith.

blessed – 1. Made joyful. 2. Helped by God.

C

cast lots – Something done to find out what God wants. It is like drawing straws to see who will go first.

chariot – A cart with two wheels pulled by horses. People, especially soldiers, rode in them.

cherubim – 1. Spirits like angels who have large wings. They were and are a sign that God is sitting on his throne. 2. Spirits who serve God.

chief priest – See high priest.

Christ – A Greek word that means "the Anointed One". It is one of the names given to Jesus. It means the same thing as the Hebrew word Messiah. See also Jesus.

circumcision – Cutting off a male's foreskin (a piece of skin at the end of a penis). It was a sign that the person belonged to God.

clean – 1. Something that God accepts. 2. Something that doesn't have sin.

clean animals – Animals that God said were acceptable to eat or to give as offerings.

commandment – A law or rule that God gives. See also law.

concubine – A woman who belonged to a man but was not his legal wife.

Council – See Sanhedrin.

covenant – 1. A treaty, or promise, between two persons or groups. In the Bible it is a promise made between God and the people. 2. Promises from God for salvation.

cross – A wooden post with a bar near the top that extends to the right and left. A cross looks like the letter "T." The Romans killed people by nailing them to crosses.

crucify – To kill people by nailing them to crosses.

cud – Food that is chewed again. An animal such as a cow brings its food back from its stomach to its mouth. This food, or cud, can be chewed again. God told the people of Israel they could eat any animal that chews the cud and has hoofs that are separated.

curse – 1. A call for God to punish someone. 2. A command of God that punishment will come on someone or something.

D

deacon – A church leader who helps people in Jesus' name.

dedicate – To set apart for a special purpose, often for God's use.

demon – An evil spirit.

devil – The one who tempts people to sin. See also Satan.

disciple – A person who follows a teacher. This person does what their teacher says to do. See also apostle. See also Twelve, the.

divorce – The end of a husband and wife's marriage. God rarely approves of this.

doubt – A lack of faith or trust in something or someone. To not be sure.

Eden – The place where God made a garden for Adam and Eve.

elder – The leader of a church, town or nation. This person makes important decisions.

eternal – Forever. Without beginning or end.

evangelist – A person who tells others the Good News of Jesus.

evil – Bad. Wicked. Doing things that do not please God.

evil spirit – A demon. One of the devil's helpers.

faith – Trust and belief in God. Knowing that God is real, even though one can't see him. See also believe.

faithful – Able to be trusted or counted on.

famine – A time when there is not enough food to eat.

fast – Going without food and/or drink for a special reason.

Feast of Booths – A celebration or festival when the Israelites thanked God for the harvest of their crops. During the feast they lived in little tents for seven days to help remember when they traveled to Canaan.

Feast of Hanukkah – A celebration praising God that the Israelites and Jews today have to remember the cleaning and rededication of the temple. The temple had been made "unclean" by an enemy.

Feast of Weeks – A festival or celebration day at the beginning of the wheat harvest when the Israelites gave thanks to God. See also Pentecost.

Feast of Passover – See Passover.

Feast of Unleavened Bread – A week for remembering when God set the Israelites free from Egypt. It began the day after the Feast of Passover. During this time the people ate bread made without yeast, like they did when they left Egypt in a hurry.

fig – A sweet fruit that grows on trees in warm countries like Israel.

glory – 1. God's greatness. 2. Praise and honor.

God – The maker and ruler of the world and all people.

grace – The kindness and forgiveness God gives to people. This is a gift. It cannot be earned.

hallelujah – A Hebrew word that means "praise the LORD."

Hanukkah – See Feast of Hanukkah.

harvest – Picking a crop when it is ripe.

heaven – 1. God's home. 2. The sky. 3. Where Christians go after they die.

Hebrew – 1. Another name for an Israelite. 2. The language spoken by the Israelites. The Old Testament is written in this language.

hell – A place of punishment for people who don't follow Jesus. God sends them there after they die.

Herod – The first name of five rulers from the same family. They ruled over Israel during the time of the New Testament.

high places – Places where people worshiped false gods. These places were found on top of hills.

high priest – A person from the family line of Aaron. He was in charge of everything in the holy tent or in the temple. He was in charge of everyone who came there to work and worship, too.

holy – Set apart for God. Belonging to God. Pure.

holy bread – Twelve loaves of bread placed in the Holy Room of the holy tent each week. They were a gift to God.

Holy Spirit – God's Spirit who creates life. He helps people do God's work. He helps people to believe in Jesus, to love him and to live like him.

holy tent – Also called the Tent of Meeting. A place where the Israelites worshiped God. They used this tent after they left Egypt and while they were in the desert for forty years. Years later

Solomon built the first temple. Then the people worshiped God there and not in the tent.

Honor – To show respect to. To give credit to.

hosanna – A Hebrew word used to praise God.

hymn – A song of praise to God.

hyssop – A plant that smelled like mint. Its branches were used to shake water or blood on something to make it pure.

I

Immanuel – A name for Jesus that means "God with us."

incense – Spices that give a pleasing smell when they are burned. It was placed on the altar in the holy tent.

Israel – 1. The new name God gave to Abraham's grandson Jacob. 2. The nation that came from the family line of Jacob. 3. The northern tribes that broke away from Judah to serve their own king.

Israelites – People from the nation of Israel. God's chosen people.

J

jealous – 1. How God feels when people worship other things. 2. How we feel when someone else has something we want.

Jesus – The Greek form of the Hebrew name Joshua. It means "the LORD saves." See also Christ. See also Immanuel. See also Savior.

Jews – Another name for the people of Israel. This name was used after 600 B.C.

Jubilee – See Year of Jubilee.

judge – 1. To decide if something is right or wrong. 2. A person who decides what is right or wrong in legal matters.

K

kingdom – An area or group of people ruled by a king.

L

law – Rules about what is right and wrong that God gave the people of Israel. See also law, the.

Law, the – The first five books of the Bible.

Levites – Men from the tribe of Levi. They took care of the holy tent and the temple.

locust – A type of insect similar to a grasshopper. A huge number of them sometimes eats and destroys crops.

Lord – A personal name for God or Christ. It shows respect to him as our master and ruler.

lots – See cast lots.

M

manger – A food box for animals.

manna – Special food sent from heaven. It tasted like wafers, or crackers, sweetened with honey. God gave it to the Israelites in the desert, after they left Egypt.

mercy – More kindness and forgiveness than people deserve to get.

Messiah – A Hebrew word that means, "The Anointed One." It means the same thing as the Greek word Christ. See also Jesus.

millstone – A heavy rock used to crush grain to make flour.

miracle – An amazing thing that happens that only God can do. This includes such things as calming a storm or bringing someone back to life.

miraculous signs – Amazing things that God does to point us to him. These things cannot be explained by the laws of nature.

myrrh – A spice with a sweet smell. It came from plants and was made into perfume, incense and medicine.

N

nard – A costly oil made from a plant grown in India. It was used as a perfume to make skin smell good.

Nazarene – A person who came from the town of Nazareth. Jesus was called a Nazarene.

Nazirite – A person who was set apart to God in a special way. Or, a person who promised to do something special for God. They were not allowed to cut their hair, drink any wine or grape juice, eat grapes or raisins, or touch a dead body.

O

oath – A promise made before God.

obey – To do what you are told to do. To carry out God's commands.

offering – Something people give to God. It was and is a part of their worship. See also sacrifice.

oxen – Large cattle that are very strong. They were used to pull carts or plows.

P

papyrus – A tall, grassy plant that grows in water that is not deep. People made boats with these plants and paper from their stems.

Passover – A feast that happened every year. It reminded the people of the time when God "passed over" their homes in Egypt. Since the people put blood on the doorways, God did not hurt them.

paradise – A perfect place. Another name used for heaven.

pasture – A field of grassy land where cows or sheep may eat.

Pentecost – 1. A celebration that was and is held 50 days after Passover. 2. The day the Holy Spirit came in a special way to live in Christians.

Pharaoh – The title of the ruler of Egypt in Bible times.

Pharisees – A group of Jews who carefully followed God's laws and their own rules about God's laws. Some Pharisees were also known as "teachers of the law."

Philistines – Strong enemies of Israel, especially during Saul and David's time.

pierce – To poke through with a sharp instrument.

pillar – 1. A tall, upright post that helped to hold up a building. 2. A pillar could also mark a special place.

pillar of cloud – A cloud God used to lead the people of Israel. They could see it all day long when they were in the desert.

pillar of fire – A column of fire God used to lead the people of Israel. They could see it all night long when they were in the desert.

plague – 1. A sickness that kills many people. 2. Anything that brings a lot of suffering or loss.

plumb line – A string that has a weight tied to the end of it. It is used to tell whether a wall is straight or not.

pomegranate – A round fruit with a tough skin, many seeds and a juicy red center.

praise – To give glory or honor to someone. To say good things about someone or something.

pregnant – Carrying a baby inside a woman's body until the baby is born.

Preparation Day – The day before the Sabbath day. A day to get all work done so that a person could rest on the Sabbath.

priest – A person who worked in the holy tent or the temple. He was responsible to give his own as well as other people's gifts and prayers to God.

prophecy – Important words or messages that God gives to his people. God gives these words through a special person called a prophet.

prophesy – 1. To give a message from God. 2. To tell what the future will be.

prophet – A person who hears messages from God and tells them to others.

prostitutes – People who get paid to let other people have sexual relationships with them.

proverb – A wise saying.

psalm – A poem of praise, prayer or teaching. The book of Psalms is full of these poems.

Purim – A feast in which the Israelites remembered when God helped Queen Esther save the Jews.

R

Rabbi – The title of a teacher of Jewish law.

Raca – A word that made someone feel bad. It meant that they were foolish or stupid.

resurrection – Coming back to life in a whole new way and never dying again.

right hand – A place of honor and power. Jesus is at the right hand of God.

Rome – 1. The empire that controlled a lot of the world when Jesus lived here on the earth. 2. The capital city of that empire. It is in Italy.

S

Sabbath – The seventh day of the week. On that day the Israelites rested from their work and turned their thoughts toward God.

sacred – Set apart for God. Holy.

sacrifice – 1. To give something to God as a gift. 2. Something that is given to God as a gift of worship. See also offering.

Sadducees – A group of Jewish leaders. They followed only the first five books of the Bible. They did not believe that people rise from the dead.

salvation – Free from the guilt of sin. Jesus died for our sins and rose up from the dead. With this sacrifice, he paid for our sin. He has saved us if we believe in him.

Sanhedrin – A group of 71 Jewish leaders. They were led by the high priest. They were the most important Jewish court of law in Jesus' time.

Satan – God's most powerful enemy in the spirit world. Also called the devil.

saved – Set free from danger or sin.

Savior – The One who sets us free from our sins. A name belonging to Jesus Christ. See also Jesus.

Scripture – God's written Word to us. We also call this the Bible.

scroll – A long strip of paper or animal skin to write on. It was rolled up on two sticks to make it easy to use and store.

seal – 1. A tool or a ring with a drawing or pattern cut into it 2. A mark made by pressing this tool into clay, wax or paper.

seer – A person who can tell the future with God's help. See also prophet.

shepherd – A person who takes care of sheep or goats.

sin – To disobey or displease God.

Sodom and Gomorrah – Two cities that God destroyed. The people who lived there were very evil.

Son of Man – A name Jesus gave to himself. It shows he is the Messiah. See also Messiah.

soul – A person's true inner self.

spiritual – Having to do with the things of God or the Bible.

staff – A stick a shepherd uses to take care of sheep or goats.

synagogue – A Jewish place of worship and teaching.

T

tambourine – A hand-held drum with metal pieces around the edge. It rattles when it is shaken or tapped.

tassels – Hanging groups of thread that are tied together at one end. God told the Israelites to sew tassels onto their clothing to remind them of God's commands.

temple – 1. Any place of worship. 2. The building where the people of Israel worshiped God and brought their sacrifices. God was present there in a special way.

tempt – To try to get someone to do bad things.

Tent of Meeting – See holy tent.

threshing floor – A place where heads, or tops, of grain are beaten or stepped on. This is done to knock the seeds of grain from the stems.

tomb – A place to put dead bodies. It was often a cave with a big, stone door.

treaty – An agreement between two people or groups or nations.

Twelve, the – The men who Jesus chose to be his special followers. See also disciples.

U

unclean – Something that God does not accept. Not pure. Not pleasing to God.

Urim and Thummim – Objects that were worn on the high priest's vest. They were used by the high priest to get a message from God.

V

vineyard – A place where grapes grow and are picked.

virgin – A woman who has never had a sexual relationship with a man.

vision – A dream from God. The person who saw it was usually awake. God gave these kinds of dreams to people to show them what he was going to do.

W

wafer – A thin, crisp cracker. Wafers were one kind of offering the Israelites brought to the Lord.

widow – A woman whose husband has died.

winepress – A place where juice is pressed out of grapes to make wine.

wisdom – Understanding that comes from God. Wise thinking.

worship – To give praise, honor and glory to God.

Year of Jubilee – A special year that was to happen every 50 years in Israel. No crops could be planted. Any money that was owed was forgiven. Slaves were set free. Property was given back to its first owner.

yeast – Something added to bread dough to make the bread rise.

yoke – 1. A strong piece of wood. It fit on the necks of two oxen so that they could pull carts or plows. 2. A piece of wood put on the neck of a slave or a prisoner.

Zealot – A Jew who was willing to fight to get rid of the Roman rulers. Simon may have been part of this group before becoming one of Jesus' twelve disciples.

Zion – 1. The city of Jerusalem. 2. The hill on which King David's house and the temple once stood. 3. Another name sometimes used for heaven.

A Word About the

NEW INTERNATIONAL READER'S VERSION

Have You Ever Heard of the New International Version?

We call it the NIV. A lot of people read the NIV. In fact, more people read the NIV than any other English Bible. They like it because it's easy to read.

And now we are happy to give you another Bible that's easy to read and understand. It's the New International Reader's Version. We call it the NIrV.

Who Will Enjoy Reading the New International Reader's Version?

We made sure that people who are just starting to read could understand and enjoy the NIrV. Children will be able to read it and understand it. So will older people who are learning how to read or those who are reading the Bible for the first time. So will people who have a hard time understanding what they read. And so will people who use English as their second language. We hope this Bible will be just right for you.

How Is the NIrV Different From the NIV?

The NIrV is based on the NIV. The NIV Committee on Bible Translation (CBT) didn't produce the NIrV. But several members of CBT worked hard to make the NIrV possible. We used the words of the NIV when we could. When the NIV words were long, we used words that were shorter. We wanted to use words that are easy to understand. We explained words that might be hard to understand in a dictionary at the back of the Bible. We also made the NIV sentences much shorter.

Why did we do all of those things?

Because we wanted to make the NIrV really easy to read and understand.

What Other Helps Does the NIrV Have?

We decided to give you a lot of other help too. For example, sometimes a verse is quoted from another place in the Bible. When it is, we put the Bible book's name, chapter and verse right after the verse that quotes another place.

We separated each chapter into shorter sections. We gave a title to almost every chapter. Sometimes we even gave a title to a section. We did it to help you understand what the chapter or section is all about.

Sometimes the writers of the Bible used more than one name for the same person or place. For example, in the New Testament the Sea of Galilee is also called the Sea of Gennesaret and the Sea of Tiberias. But in the NIrV we decided to call it the Sea of Galilee everywhere it appears in the New Testament. We did it because that is its most familiar name.

We also wanted to help our readers learn the names of people and places even in verses where those names don't actually appear. For example, when we knew that "the River" meant "the Euphrates River," we used those words even in verses where only the words "the River" are found. When we knew that the name of "Pharaoh" in a certain verse was "Hophra," we wrote his name in that verse. We did all of those things because we wanted to make the NIrV as clear as possible.

Does the NIrV Say What the First Writers of the Bible Said?

We wanted the NIrV to say just what the first writers of the Bible said. So we kept checking the Greek New Testament as we did our work. That's because the New Testament's first writers used Greek.

We used the best and oldest copies of the Greek New Testament. Earlier English Bibles couldn't use those copies because they had not yet been found. The oldest Greek New Testaments are best because they are closer in time to the ones the first Bible writers wrote. That's why we kept checking the older copies instead of newer ones.

Later copies of the Greek New Testament added several verses that the earlier ones don't have. Sometimes it's several verses in a row. When that's the case, we included them in the NIrV. But we set those verses off with a long line. That tells you that the first writers didn't write them. The verses were added later on. You will find the long lines at Mark 16:9–20 and John 7:53 – 8:11. Sometimes it's a single verse. An example is Mark 9:44. That verse is not in the oldest Greek New Testaments. So we put the number 43/44 right before Mark 9:43. Then you can look on the list below for Mark 9:44 and locate the verse that was added.

Verses That Were Not Found in Earliest Greek New Testaments

Matthew 17:21 But that kind does not go out except by prayer and fasting.

Matthew 18:11 The Son of Man came to save what was lost.

Matthew 23:14 How terrible for you, teachers of the law and Pharisees! You pretenders! You take over the houses of widows. You say long prayers to show off. So God will punish you much more.

Mark 7:16 Everyone who has ears to hear should listen.

Mark 9:44 In hell, " 'the worms don't die, and the fire doesn't go out.'

Mark 9:46 In hell, " 'the worms don't die, and the fire doesn't go out.'

Mark 11:26 But if you do not forgive, your Father who is in heaven will not forgive your sins either.

Mark 15:28 Scripture came true. It says, "And he was counted among those who disobey the law."

Luke 17:36 Two men will be in the field. One will be taken and the other left.

Luke 23:17 It was Pilate's duty to let one prisoner go free for them at the Feast.

John 5:4 From time to time an angel of the Lord would come down. The angel would stir up the waters. The first disabled person to go into the pool after it was stirred would be healed.

Acts 8:37 Philip said, "If you believe with all your heart, you can." The official answered, "I believe that Jesus Christ is the Son of God."

Acts 15:34 But Silas decided to remain there.

Acts 24:7 But Lysias, the commander, came. By using a lot of force, he took Paul from our hands.

Acts 28:29 After he said that, the Jews left. They were arguing strongly among themselves.

Romans 16:24 May the grace of our Lord Jesus Christ be with all of you. Amen.

What Is Our Prayer for You?

The Lord has blessed the New International Version in a wonderful way. He has used it to help millions of Bible readers. Many people have put their faith in Jesus after reading it. Many others have become stronger believers because they have read it.

We hope and pray that the New International Reader's Version will help you in the same way. If that happens, we will give God all of the glory.

A Word About This Edition

This edition of the New International Reader's Version has been revised so that the gender language more closely matches that of the New International Version. When we prepared this new edition, we had help from people who were not part of the first team. We want to thank them for their help. They are Ben Aker from the Assemblies of God Theological Seminary, Paul House from the Southern Baptist Seminary, and Scott Munger from International Bible Society.

The NIrV Super Heroes Bible

Project Management and Editorial
Catherine DeVries

Theological Review
Michael J. Klassen, M.Div., Fuller Theological Seminary

Interior Proofreading
Peachtree Editorial and Proofreading Service, Peachtree City, GA

Interior Typesetting
Blue Heron Bookcraft, Battle Ground, WA

Art Direction
Jody Langley

Production Management
Mark Luce

Printing and Binding
R.R. Donnelley and Sons, Inc., Crawfordsville, IN

Published in association with the literary agency of
Ann Spangler and Company, 1420 Pontiac Rd S.E., Grand Rapids, MI 49506

The NIrV Super Heroes Bible was produced in partnership
with Brother Jones ArtWorks (brotherjones.com).

Cover Design
Donald Jones, Laura M. Maitner, Lisa Workman

Interior Design
Donald Jones

Cover Illustration and Interior Illustrations
Dennis Jones

GUARANTEE

Zondervan's manufacturer's warranty provides coverage for defective bindings on hardcover, softcover, Leather-Look™ and Italian Duo-Tone™ Bibles for four years, and on bonded and top-grain leather Bibles for six years. This warranty does not apply to normal wear. A lifetime warranty applies to defects within the Bible—for example: missing or misplaced pages, chapters or books. Please return defective Bibles to the original place of purchase for replacement or refund. If this is not possible, please go to www.zondervan.com and click on "Contact Us."

CARE

We suggest loosening the binding of your new Bible by gently pressing on a small section of pages at a time from the center. To ensure against breakage of the spine, it is best not to bend the cover backward around the spine or to carry study notes, church bulletins, pens, etc., inside the cover. Because a felt-tipped marker will "bleed" through the pages, we recommend use of a ball-point pen or pencil to underline favorite passages. Your Bible should not be exposed to excessive heat, cold or humidity. Protecting the gold or silver edges of the paper from moisture will avoid spotting, streaking or fading.